1006014755

Canadian Business Corporations Law

CANADIAN BUSINESS CORPORATIONS LAW

SECOND EDITION

Kevin Patrick McGuinness

LL.B., LL.M., S.J.D.
Barrister, Solicitor and Notary Public (Ontario)
Solicitor (England and Wales)

Counsel
Crown Law Office—Civil
Ministry of the Attorney General of Ontario

LIBRARY
GRANT MacEWAN
UNIVERSITY

Canadian Business Corporations Law
© LexisNexis Canada Inc. 2007
August 2007

All rights reserved. No part of this publication may be reproduced, stored in any material form (including photocopying or storing it in any medium by electronic means and whether or not transiently or incidentally to some other use of this publication) without the written permission of the copyright holder except in accordance with the provisions of the Copyright Act. Applications for the copyright holder's written permission to reproduce any part of this publication should be addressed to the publisher.

Warning: The doing of an unauthorized act in relation to a copyrighted work may result in both a civil claim for damages and criminal prosecution.

Members of the LexisNexis Group worldwide

Canada	LexisNexis Canada Inc, 123 Commerce Valley Dr. E. Suite 700, MARKHAM, Ontario
Argentina	Abeledo Perrot, Jurisprudencia Argentina and Depalma, BUENOS AIRES
Australia	Butterworths, a Division of Reed International Books Australia Pty Ltd, CHATSWOOD, New South Wales
Austria	ARD Betriebsdienst and Verlag Orac, VIENNA
Chile	Publitecsa and Conosur Ltda, SANTIAGO DE CHILE
Czech Republic	Orac, sro, PRAGUE
France	Éditions du Juris-Classeur SA, PARIS
Hong Kong	Butterworths Asia (Hong Kong), HONG KONG
Hungary	Hvg Orac, BUDAPEST
India	Butterworths India, NEW DELHI
Ireland	Butterworths (Ireland) Ltd, DUBLIN
Italy	Giuffré, MILAN
Malaysia	Malayan Law Journal Sdn Bhd, KUALA LUMPUR
New Zealand	Butterworths of New Zealand, WELLINGTON
Poland	Wydawnictwa Prawnicze PWN, WARSAW
Singapore	Butterworths Asia, SINGAPORE
South Africa	Butterworth Publishers (Pty) Ltd, DURBAN
Switzerland	Stämpfli Verlag AG, BERNE
United Kingdom	Butterworths Tolley, a Division of Reed Elsevier (UK), LONDON, WC2A
USA	LexisNexis, DAYTON, Ohio

Library and Archives Canada Cataloguing in Publication

McGuinness, Kevin Patrick
    Canadian business corporations law / Kevin McGuinness. — 2nd ed.

Originally publ. under title: The law and practice of Canadian business corporations.
Includes index.
ISBN 978-0-433-44302-5

    1. Corporation law—Canada. I. Title.

KE1389.M33 2007   346.71'066   C2007-903881-6
KF1415.ZA2M33 2007

Printed and bound in Canada.

PREFACE

The First Edition of this work was written in 1998, and revised in 1999 as it wound its way through the editorial and publication process. As work on the Second Edition progressed, I found it hard to believe that the First Edition could become so dated in such a short period of time. Among the key changes that have taken place over the past seven years are the following:

- Since 1999, there have been several hundred cases decided in Canada (plus many times that number decided in England, the Commonwealth and the United States) that are likely to influence the future trend in the law and practice relating to Canadian business corporations.
- A series of major corporate scandals in Canada and elsewhere led to a significant strengthening of corporate governance requirements, particularly in the case of publicly traded corporations. Similarly, the bursting of the "dot-com" bubble led to significant re-thinking with respect to the disclosure of forward looking information. A discussion of these new requirements has been included in this text to the extent that doing so is consistent with a text on corporate law (as opposed to securities law).
- In 2001, the CBCA was significantly amended; a number of wide ranging amendments are now pending for the OBCA. These have been incorporated into the text.
- In 2004, the new *British Columbia Business Corporations Act* was enacted in place of the *Company Act* of that province. With the passing of the *Company Act,* there is little purpose to be served in discussing the rules applicable to memorandum companies, and therefore the lengthy discussions of the old BC legislation have been deleted.
- Alberta has followed Nova Scotia in providing for unlimited liability companies. Ontario has also indicated some interest in following suit. The Second Edition contains a discussion of the utility of this vehicle, as well as a commentary on the limitations of the existing regimes that govern such entities.
- Ontario enacted the new *Securities Transfer Act, 2006,* based upon the draft *Uniform Securities Transfer Act* that was prepared by the Canadian Securities Administrators. The CSA draft was based on Article 8 of the Uniform Commercial Code. The STA replaces Part VI of the OBCA, which was discussed in some considerable detail in Chapter 7 of the First Edition. Similar legislation has now been enacted in Alberta, Manitoba, Quebec, and Newfoundland and Labrador. The government of British Columbia introduced Bill 9 in March, which will update the law of that province. These new statutes recognize the use of electronic record-keeping in respect of securities transactions and investments, and facilitate the use of investment securities as loan collateral. They were necessitated by the fact that modern securities holdings and settlements involve substantial quantities of securities held and traded through a complex system of intermediaries that often involve multiple jurisdictions. The text of the Second Edition reflects the major changes

effected by the STA. Unfortunately, due to the length and detail of the new legislation, it is not practical to attempt to cover it adequately in a general text on corporate law. For this reason the material formerly included in Chapter 7 has been deleted.
- Growing concerns with respect to corporate governance issues have prompted increase focus on securities law requirements. Numerous rules of securities law that are of general relevance in the corporate law area have been completely revised since the First Edition was published. So far as practical, a discussion of these rules has been incorporated into the revised text.

For obvious reasons, readers of legal texts are primarily concerned with the currency and scope of coverage that a law book provides. The bulk of the research for the Second Edition was completed in 2005, with the process of consolidating the old and new material taking up all of 2006. Comprehensive coverage of Canadian case law initially ended with 8 B.L.R. (4th), but editorial revision allowed cases to be included up to 23 B.L.R. (4th). Leading English and Australian cases up to April, 2006, are included together with some subsequent additional material. Canadian statute references are current to the end of 2006. Unfortunately, it was not practical to revise the text to accommodate changes made to the law of England, by the *Companies Act 2006*. The text also covers a number of recent proposals made during the first quarter of 2007 by the Canadian Securities Administrators for changes in a number of multilateral and national instruments and policies. In terms of the authorities drawn upon, however, the most notable change from the First Edition is the significant expansion of coverage of leading U.S. case law. As American securities law and the *Model Business Corporations Act* far more closely resemble the *Securities Act*, the CBCA and OBCA than does the corresponding U.K. or Australian legislation, the growing importance of American authority is self-evident. Fortunately, with the advent of the Internet, for the first time in more than a century, American legal materials are now becoming readily available to all Canadian practitioners.

This text does not include any discussion of income trusts, which for a brief while appeared to be emerging as an alternative to the business corporation as an investment vehicle. While income trusts are not subject to corporate law as such, it is worthwhile making brief mention of them — if only for the purpose of recording their coming and going. The term "income trust" describes a capital market investment that is structured as a trust, and which holds income-producing assets in trust for investors who have purchased trust units rather than shares. These assets are generally used by an underlying operating entity (often a corporation) to carry on business.

Typically, a corporation would securitize its income-producing assets by selling them to a trust. The trust would sell trust units to investors, which would be listed for subsequent trade on a stock exchange (primarily the TSX in Canada). Normally, the trust would be structured so that an unlimited number of units might be issued by the trust. Each such unit would be transferable, voting and represent an equal undivided beneficial interest in any distributions from the trust, whether made from net income, net realized capital gains or other amounts. Units also evidenced a participatory interest in the net assets of the trust, in the event of its termination or winding-up.

Income trusts emerged an alternative to an equity investment in a corporation, due to the favourable tax treatment that they enjoyed. Income trusts in the form of real estate investment trusts (or "REITs") have been around for many years. From real estate, they spread into the oil and gas sectors. The depression of the equity security market following the burst of the high-tech bubble, stimulated demand for such instruments across the full range of Canadian industry and commerce. A sudden growth in popularity began in 2001. During the first half of 2002, income trust offerings composed approximately 94 per cent of all initial public offerings in Canada. Their popularity continued to grow after that date.

The tax treatment of such investments may be summarized briefly: The income paid to an income trust by the operating entity may take the form of interest, or a royalty or lease payment. These payments are normally deductible in computing the operating entity's income for tax purposes. Maintaining payments at a high level can be used to reduce the operating entity's taxable income to zero, or close to it. The trust in turn, distributes all of its income received from the operating entity to its unit-holders. Historically, distributions paid by a trust reduce the trust's own taxable income, so it too will pay little to no income tax. The net effect is that the interest, royalty or lease payments are taxed at the individual unit-holder level. Aside from the tax advantage, there appeared to be little benefit derived from the trust structure[1] — although from the operating corporation's perspective (and more importantly that of its control group), an added benefit of the income trust structure was that it insulated the corporation from the risk of a take-over bid.

The tax benefit was not to last. On October 31, 2006, changes to the *Income Tax Act* were announced, to introduce a new trust distribution tax to be applied at the rate of 31.5 per cent. This tax would eliminate the tax advantage attached to income trusts by 2011. The prior tax treatment will continue only for trusts that were actually trading on October 31, 2006; for income trusts that began trading after that day, the new tax will apply beginning with their 2007 taxation year. Noting that no other country allowed the preferential tax treatment accorded to income trusts by Canada, Federal Finance Minister, Jim Flaherty justified the new tax, by stating that income trusts were:

> ... creating an economic distortion that is threatening Canada's long-term economic growth and shifting any future tax burden onto hardworking individuals and families. If left unchecked, these corporate decisions would result in billions of dollars in less revenue for the federal government to invest in the priorities of Canadians, including more personal income tax relief. These decisions would also mean less revenue for the provinces and territories.

Within days of this announcement, the Standard & Poor's TSX Income Trust Index had declined by 11.3 per cent. Since the value of an investment is closely related to the net present value of the income stream that it is expected to pro-

---

[1] Limited liability for income and other widely held investment trusts was conferred under the *Trust Beneficiaries' Liability Act, 2004*. Until this change was made, pension funds were reluctant to investment in trust units.

duce, the eventual effect of the new tax likely will be to lower the value of income trust investments by approximately the same percentage as the rate of the new tax. Legislation to give effect to the proposals was tabled in the House of Commons on March 29, 2007 as Bill C-52. Since this October surprise, there has been little interest in the further employment of income trusts as an investment vehicle. Indeed, even existing income trusts are being re-thought.

Readers familiar with the First Edition will find that a number of major changes have been made to the text. Several of the chapters grew so long, as a result of the steady expansion of case law, that it has proven necessary to split them into two — and in one case, three — different chapters. The section on the oppression and derivative action remedies has been completely revisited. The chapter on winding-up has been expanded from a quick summary of the key provisions, to something more in keeping with the approach adopted in other chapters of the text.

The result of all these changes is a text of 15 chapters, in contrast to the previous 11. The primary focus of the text remains on the OBCA and CBCA, under which most of the corporations in Canada currently operate. However, for the benefit of readers in other provinces, the publisher has included a table of concordance to the other business corporation's statutes in force across Canada.

Editing a work of this length is an enormous exercise for the staff of the publisher. I would be remiss if I did not expressly thank Janet Kim, Myrsini Rovos and Tina Eng at LexisNexis for their tremendous support in the production of this work — particularly Tina and her staff for bearing with a number of late changes. Their work was complicated by numerous significant changes in the law during the 18 months that it took to complete editorial work on the manuscript. However, if the book contains any errors or other deficiencies, they are mine rather than those of others.

Before concluding the preface, it is only fair to set out the usual public service disclaimers that:

(a) all material in this text is taken from published sources, and it contains no confidential or other proprietary information belonging to the Government of Ontario or any agency thereof (other than extracts from or summaries of statutes, regulations, case reports, notices, policies and rules of the Ontario Securities Commission, Hansard, published government reports, studies and discussion papers and other material expressly placed on the public record by the government of Ontario); and
(b) all views expressed in this text are my own, and they do not represent, and have not been reviewed or approved by, the Government of Ontario or any officer or agency thereof, or any other person.

Kevin McGuinness
Stoney Creek
May, 2007

ACKNOWLEDGMENT

Preparation of the first edition of this book was assisted by William C.V. Johnson of Borden Ladner Gervals LLP, Ottawa.

TABLE OF CONTENTS

Preface v
Acknowledgment ix
Table of Cases xxxi
Table of Concordance cxxxiii

Chapter 1: The Corporate Concept 1
    A.   Overview of Corporate Law 1
    B.   The Nature of a Corporation 3
        (i)   The Different Classes of Corporation 4
        (ii)   Corporations Sole 4
        (iii) Corporations Aggregate 6
        (iv) The Evolution of Incorporation in Ontario 8
    C.   Business Corporations 11
        (i)   The Corporate Legislative Realm 12
        (ii)   Special Legislation Governing Business Corporations 15
        (iii) Business Corporations as a Species of Business Enterprise .. 18
        (iv) The Distinguishing Feature of a Corporate Entity 19
    D.   Corporate Theory 22
    E.   Jurisprudential Conceptions of a Corporation 24
    F.   Creation a Sovereign Act 27
    G.   Conclusion 32

Chapter 2: Personality and Its Implications 33
    A.   Introduction 33
    B.   The Salomon Case 34
    C.   The Implications of Separate Personality 36
    D.   Limited Liability 42
        (i)   The Evolution of Limited Liability 43
        (ii)   The Limits of Limited Liability 44
        (iii) Piercing (Lifting) the Corporate Veil 47
              (1) Where Provided by Statute 50
              (2) Fraud 51
              (3) The Corporation as Agent 52
              (4) The Corporation as Facade or Alter Ego 53
              (5) Miscellaneous Cases Involving Lifting the Veil 58
              (6) Principal Appearing in Court 60
              (7) Contract vs. Tort 60
              (8) Where the Shareholder Will Benefit from Lifting
                   the Veil 64
        (iv) The Corporate Group Concept 67
        (v)   The Veil Cases Are Exceptions 73
    E.   Unlimited Companies 75
        (i)   Overview of the Nova Scotia Regime 75

		(ii)	The Alberta Regime 79

        (ii)   The Alberta Regime 79
        (iii)   A Possible Ontario Regime 80
            (1) Identification of Unlimited Status 81
            (2) General Liability Regime 82
            (3) Limitation on the Term of Shareholder Liability 85
            (4) Director Liability 87
            (5) Issue of Shares for a Debt Instrument, Repayment of Capital, etc. 87
            (6) Continuation and Fundamental Changes 88
    F.   Separation of the Ownership of the Corporation and Its Assets 92
    G.   Separation of Management From Ownership 93
    H.   Perpetual Existence 94
    I.   Lesser Duty of Loyalty 95
    J.   Conclusion 95

Chapter 3: Corporate Liability 97
    A.   Introduction 97
    B.   Liability of a Corporation for the Acts of Its Insiders 97
    C.   Separate Taxation 108
    D.   Criminal Liability of a Corporation 109
        (i)   Corporate Criminal Liability at Common Law 110
        (ii)   Approaches to Liability 114
            (1) The Aggregation Principle 114
            (2) The Identification Theory 115
            (3) Impact of Bill C-45 117
            (4) The Innocent Corporate Operative 120
        (iii)   The Logic of Corporate Criminal Liability 121
        (iv)   Sentencing 125
        (v)   Conspiracy 126
    E.   Liability of Directors, Officers and Others 128
    F.   Related Persons, Affiliated Corporations and Associates 133

Chapter 4: Constitutional Considerations 139
    A.   Introduction 139
    B.   Paramountcy 139
    C.   Jurisdiction to Incorporate 145
        (i)   The Territorial Limits of Corporate Law 148
            (1) The Canadian Approach to Extraterritoriality 149
            (2) Conduct of Business Outside the Province ... 152
            (3) Regulation of Extraprovincial Corporations 154
        (ii)   Limitation on Federal Incorporation Power 160
    D.   Regulatory Jurisdiction 161
        (i)   Federal Regulation of Provincially Incorporated Corporations 162
        (ii)   Provincial Regulation of Federal Companies 162
        (iii)   The Vital Part Doctrine 166
        (iv)   Regulation of Securities 168

		(v)	Nationalization of Federal Corporation by Provincial Government 172

| | | (v) | Nationalization of Federal Corporation by Provincial Government .... 172 |

        (v)   Nationalization of Federal Corporation by Provincial Government 172
        (vi)   Applying for Provincial/Federal Powers 174
   E.   Conclusion Re Division of Jurisdiction.. 174
   F.   Corporations and the Canadian Charter of Rights and Freedoms 175
        (i)   Corporate Investigations and Charter Rights..................... 177
        (ii)   Laws of Special Application 178
   G.   Public and Quasi-Public Corporations 179
        (i)   Corporations Charged with a Statutory Mandate 179
        (ii)   Government Owned Corporations...................................... 181

Chapter 5: Incorporation 183
   A.   Introduction 183
        (i)   Types of Corporate Enterprise.. 184
        (ii)   Terminology 187
   B.   Restrictions on Incorporation 190
        (i)   Legality of Purpose 190
        (ii)   Incorporation of Professional Practices.............................. 191
        (iii) "Three-Two" Corporations... 198
        (iv) The Procedure for Incorporation 199
        (v)   The Role of Incorporators 203
   C.   The Corporate Constitution 204
        (i)   The Articles of a Corporation 204
        (ii)   By-laws 209
             (1)   Enactment of By-laws 211
             (2)   Judicial Review of By-laws...................................... 214
             (3)   Record of By-laws 216
   D.   Corporate Names 217
        (i)   General Requirements and Restrictions 219
        (ii)   Use of a Name Other Than the Legal Name 223
        (iii) Each Name Must Be Unique 225
             (1)   NUANS Search 229
             (2)   Use of Personal Names 230
             (3)   Permitted Similar Names 231
             (4)   Passing-off and Trade-marks 235
             (5)   Use of Names Under Executive and Legislative Sanction 235
             (6)   Geographic and Descriptive Names 236
             (7)   Objections to Names 238
             (8)   Other General Prohibitions and Restrictions 244
             (9)   Language of Name 248
             (10) Number Names 250
             (11) Identifying the Status of a Corporate Entity 250
             (12) Alternate Name 254
             (13) Change of Name 254
   E.   Corporate Seal 255

F. Minimum Capitalization 257
G. Certificate of Incorporation 257
H. Ontario Corporation Number 260
I. Effect of Incorporation 260
J. Organization of the Corporation 263
K. Promoters 264
    (i) Identification of Promoters 265
    (ii) The Duties of Promoters 266
    (iii) Protecting Promoters 272
    (iv) Liability of Promoters Among Themselves 272
    (v) Promotion Expenses 273
    (vi) Pre-incorporation Contracts 273
        (1) Overview 273
        (2) Common Law and Pre-incorporation Contracts 274
        (3) The Statutory Regime 276
            (a) Adoption of a Pre-incorporation Contract 278
            (b) Excluding Liability of the Promoter 279
            (c) Old Style Contracts 281
            (d) Power of the Court to Make Orders 281
        (4) Mistake Made as to Corporate Status 282
        (5) Where Pre-incorporation Rules Not Applicable 284
        (6) Corporate Status Must Be Disclosed 284

Chapter 6: The Capacity and Powers of Corporations and the Manner of Their Exercise 287

A. Introduction 287
    (i) The Doctrine of *Ultra Vires* 291
    (ii) Restrictions Set out in the Articles 298
    (iii) Excluded Rights 299
    (iv) Special Legislative Grants of Power 300
    (v) Financial Assistance by Corporation 301
    (vi) Statutory and Contractual References to "Persons" 303
B. Contracts and Corporate Undertakings 304
    (i) The Authority of Corporate Agents 305
    (ii) Actual, Implied and Ostensible Authority 306
    (iii) The Indoor Management Rule 314
        (1) Codification of the Indoor Management Rule 317
        (2) The Authority of Corporate Officers 323
        (3) Exceptional Cases Where Outsiders Are Not Protected 330
    (iv) Ratification 332
    (v) Evidentiary Issues 333
        (1) Plenipotentiary Authority 333
        (2) Director Resolutions 334
        (3) Execution by Same Person in Two Capacities 334
        (4) Corporate Seal 334
C. Fraud by an Agent or Forgery of a Corporate Document 335

D.	Corporate Domicile			339
E.	Registered Office of a Corporation			344
F.	Records of a Corporation			345
	(i)	OBCA and CBCA Requirements		346
	(ii)	Canada Revenue Agency Requirements		348
	(iii)	Business Records Protection		350
	(iv)	Electronic Provision of Information		351

Chapter 7: Equity Finance 355

A.	Introduction			355
	(i)	Equity and Debt		356
	(ii)	Working Capital Distinguished		363
	(iii)	Fixed and Circulating Capital		364
B.	Shares			364
	(i)	Location (*Situs*) of Shares		371
	(ii)	Classification of Shares		372
		(1)	Common and Preference Defined	373
		(2)	Popular Share Designations Within the Securities Industry	376
	(iii)	The Presumption of Equality and the Creation of Preferences		378
	(iv)	Interpretation of Share Terms, etc.		381
	(v)	Key Concepts		382
		(1)	Authorized and Issued Capital	382
		(2)	Alteration of Share Capital	383
		(3)	Creation and Issue of Shares	384
		(4)	Classes and Series of Shares	388
		(5)	Coattail Provisions	391
	(vi)	Abolition of Par Value		392
	(vii)	Subscription		396
		(1)	Offer and Acceptance	399
		(2)	Conditional Subscriptions	403
C.	Misrepresentation and Share Subscriptions			405
	(i)	The Common Law		406
	(ii)	Liability for Misrepresentation Under the Securities Act and Securities Act Regulation		416
		(1)	Disclosure of Material Facts	417
	(iii)	Liability for in the Secondary Market		428
	(iv)	Securities Disclosure Obligations		432
	(v)	Wash Trading, etc.		432
D.	Price			436
	(i)	Payment of the Price		441
		(1)	Payment by Cheque	443
		(2)	Payment by Transfer of Property	444
		(3)	Payment for Shares by the Issue of a Promissory Note	449
		(4)	Payment for Shares in Services to the Corporation	450

		(5)	Shares in an Unlimited Liability Corporation	454
	(ii)		Commission on the Sale of Shares	455
	(iii)		Share Splits and Exchanges	455
E.	Special Shareholder Considerations			457
	(i)		Shares Held in Trust	457
	(ii)		Shares Held by an Intermediary (CBCA)	458
	(iii)		Shares Held by Aliens	459
	(iv)		Shares Held by a Minor	459
	(v)		Restrictions on the Issue and Transfer of Shares	461
F.	Transfer of Shares			464
	(i)		Restrictions on Transfer	468
	(ii)		Presumption Against Restriction	472
	(iii)		Transmission of Shares	475
G.	Accounting for Share Capital — The Stated Capital Account			477
H.	Special Rights			480
	(i)		Shares Non-Assessable	480
	(ii)		Securities Convertible to Shares	481
		(1)	Conversion Rights and Options	482
		(2)	Warrants and Options	483
		(3)	Back-Dating Stock Options	484
	(iii)		Sinking Funds	486
	(iv)		Pre-emptive Rights	488
I.	Trafficking, Reduction in Capital, and Related Questions			490
	(i)		Redemption and Retraction	493
	(ii)		Purchase by a Corporation of Its Shares	497
		(1)	Repurchase	498
		(2)	Effect of the Purchase by a Corporation of Its Shares	500
	(iii)		Reduction in Share Capital	501
	(iv)		Contract Re the Purchase of Shares	504
	(v)		Gifts of Shares	505
	(vi)		Entitlement to Repayment of Share Capital	505
J.	Share Certificates			506
K.	Dividends			510
	(i)		Nature of Dividend Entitlement — Are Dividends Gifts?	512
	(ii)		Director Discretion over Dividend Declaration	512
	(iii)		Form of Declaration	515
	(iv)		Restrictions on the Declaration and Payment of Dividends	517
	(v)		Preferential Dividends	523
		(1)	Cumulative Dividends	524
		(2)	Proportionate Abatement	526
		(3)	"Guaranteed" Dividend Payments	527
	(vi)		Entitlement to Dividends	528
	(vii)		Dividends to Controlling Shareholder/Directors	530
	(viii)		Stock Dividends	531
	(ix)		Corporations With Wasting Assets	533
	(x)		Liability for Dividends Improperly Paid	534
	(xi)		Unclaimed Dividends	534

| | | L. | Lien on Shares and Related Considerations .... 535 |

Chapter 8: Debt Financing 537
    A.   Introduction 537
           (i)   The Nature of Debt 537
                  (1)   Importance of the Distinction Between Debt
                            and Equity 540
                  (2)   The Nature of the Obligation Arising Under an
                            Exercise of Redemption or Retraction Rights 542
                  (3)   Debt and Trust 546
           (ii)   Secured and Unsecured Debt 546
           (iii)   Book Value 549
           (iv)   Authority to Borrow 549
           (v)   Identifying Contracts of the Corporation 551
           (vi)   Interest 552
                  (1)   The Effect of Default and Judgment on Interest
                            Entitlement 555
                  (2)   Usury 557
                  (3)   Interest After Default 562
                  (4)   Interest and Bankruptcy 563
    B.   Common Types of Debt 564
           (i)   Foreign Currency Debt 567
           (ii)   Participatory Loans and Similar Interests 569
    C.   Types of Security Interest 570
    D.   Types of Security Agreement 573
           (i)   Real Property Charges and Mortgages 574
                  (1)   The Nature of a Mortgage and a Charge and the
                            Distinction Between Them 574
                  (2)   Property Subject to the Charge 578
                  (3)   Personal Covenant to Pay 579
                  (4)   Right to Remain in Possession 579
                  (5)   Foreclosure and Powers of Sale 580
                  (6)   Charge Terms 581
                          (a)   Warranties 586
                          (b)   Covenants 590
                  (7)   Defeasance 599
                  (8)   Waiver 600
           (ii)   Chattel Mortgage 600
           (iii)   Debentures and Bonds 601
                  (1)   Fixed and Floating Charges 603
                          (a)   The Rule in *Lister v. Dunlop* 612
                          (b)   Waiver of Default 614
                          (c)   Action by Some Third Parties 615
                          (d)   "Automatic" Crystallization Under the
                                Terms of the Security Agreement 615
                          (e)   Floating Charges Under the *Personal Property*
                                Security Property Act 616
                  (2)   Pledging of Debentures 618

		(3)	Trust Deeds 619
			(a) Standard of Care 625
			(b) Conflict of Interest.. 625
			(c) No Action Clauses 630
			(d) Fees and Expenses of the Trustee 633
		(4)	Debenture Stock.. 634
		(5)	Income Bonds 635
	(iv)	Assignment of Debts (or Accounts) 637
		(1)	General Assignment of Book Debts (General Assignment of Accounts)............................. 637
		(2)	Assignment of Specific Debts and Accounts 639
	(v)	General Security Agreement 640
	(vi)	Conditional Sale Agreement... 640
	(vii)	Leases 640
	(viii)	Equipment Trust Certificates... 641
	(ix)	Pledge 641
	(x)	Hypothecation Agreement.. 642
	(xi)	Assignment of Specific Securities.................................... 643
	(xii)	*Bank Act* Security 643
		(1)	Section 427 Security 644
			(a) Nature of Section 427 Security.......................... 645
			(b) Procedure for Taking the Security — Overview 648
			(c) Loans and Advances 650
			(d) Conditions Precedent... 650
			(e) Permitted Borrowers and Security..................... 651
		(2)	Section 426 Security 657
			(a) Procedure for Taking and Perfecting Section 426 Security... 660
			(b) Priority of Section 426 Security 660
	(xiii)	Receivers and Receiver-Managers 661
E.	Registered Debt Securities 666
F.	Negotiable Debt Securities.. 667
G.	The *Depository Bills and Notes Act* 672
H.	Perpetual Debt Securities 674
I.	Other Critical Concerns.. 675
	(i)	Priority of Future Advances 675
	(ii)	Securing Revolving Debt 677
	(iii)	Subordination Agreements 677
	(iv)	Proof of Claim 686
	(v)	Bond and Other Credit Rating 688
	(vi)	Project Financing... 693
J.	Challenging the Validity of a Security Agreement 695
K.	Fraudulent Preferences, Conveyances and Related Issues 697

Chapter 9: Directors, Officers and the Notion of Corporate Governance 709
| A. | Control of the Corporation .... 709 |
| B. | The General Process of Corporate Control .... 711 |

C.	Nature of Directorship		715
	(i)	Theories of Directorship	718
	(ii)	The Term "Director" Defined	722
	(iii)	Promoters and Directors Distinguished	723
	(iv)	The Requirement for a Board of Directors	723
D.	The Growing Role of the Board		726
	(i)	Creation of a Suitable Governance Regime	733
	(ii)	Strategic Role	735
	(iii)	The Role of the Board of Directors in Corporate Governance	738
	(iv)	Board Composition	739
	(v)	Executive and Board Compensation	740
	(vi)	The Board and the CEO	747
E.	Appointment or Election to Office		748
	(i)	Qualification of Directors	751
		(1) Resident Canadians	757
		(2) Qualifying Shareholding	759
	(ii)	Number of Directors	761
	(iii)	Selecting Among Candidates	762
		(1) Independent Directors	762
		(2) Board Evaluation	764
		(3) Close Personal Relationships and Director Independence	766
	(iv)	Director Election	767
		(1) General	767
		(2) Appointment	769
		(3) Invalid Appointment or Election	770
	(v)	Cumulative Voting	771
	(vi)	*De Facto* Directors	775
	(vii)	Assumption of Office	779
	(viii)	Resignation and Removal of Directors	780
F.	Officers		785
	(i)	The Meaning of "Officer"	785
	(ii)	Appointment of Officers	786
G.	Director Disclosure, Audit and Related Obligations		788
	(i)	Overview	788
	(ii)	OBCA and CBCA Disclosure Requirements	791
		(1) OBCA Requirements	792
		(2) CBCA Requirements	793
		(3) The Audit Process and Requirement	795
		(a) The Place of the Audit in the Governance Process	795
		(b) The Nature of an Audit	795
		(c) Independence	797
		(d) Status of the Auditor	799
		(e) The Duties of an Auditor	800
		(f) Reasonable Reliance Upon Management	804
		(g) Upon Detection of Error	806

		(h)	Standard of Care	808
		(i)	Dispensing with the Audit Requirement	812
		(j)	Change of Auditor	812
		(k)	Audit Committees	812
		(l)	Auditor Liability	813
	(iii)	Securities Law Disclosure Obligations		818
		(1)	Financial Information	818
		(2)	Management Discussion and Analysis	821
		(3)	Annual Information Form	822
		(4)	Information Circular Requirements	823
		(5)	Timely Disclosure Requirements (Material Changes)	823

Chapter 10: Corporate Management 827

A. The Board Decision-Making Process 827
    (i) Director Meetings 827
    (ii) Telephone and Similar Meetings 832
    (iii) Resolutions in Lieu of Meetings 833
    (iv) Minutes of Director Meetings 834
    (v) Board Confidentiality 835

B. General Managerial Rights of Directors 836
    (i) Sterilized Board of Directors 836
    (ii) Overview of Managerial Powers 838
    (iii) Residual Powers after Receivership, etc. 842
    (iv) Specific Rights Enabling Directors to Carry out Duties 844
    (v) Power and Duty to Manage 846
    (vi) Control over Litigation 847
    (vii) Statutory Requirements for Disclosure of Conflict of Interest 849
        (1) Generally 849
            (a) Full and Fair Disclosure 850
            (b) General Disclosure Statements 852
            (c) Single Director Corporations 852
        (2) Material Contracts and Material Interests 853
        (3) Disclosure Procedure 853
            (a) Attendance at Meetings 856
            (b) Effect of Non-Compliance 857
        (4) The Fairness Requirements 858
            (a) Fair Dealing 858
            (b) Fair Terms 859
        (5) Specific Areas of Concern 862
            (a) Director Remuneration 862
            (b) Payments to Directors 865
            (c) Vote Renting 866
        (6) Shareholder Ratification 866
        (7) Shareholder Access to Disclosure Information 868

C. Delegation of Managerial Powers 868
    (i) Board Committee Structure 871
        (1) Audit Committee 872
        (2) Nominating and Corporate Governance Committees . 875

		(3) Compensation Committee	875
		(4) Legal Restrictions on Committee Authority	876
	(ii)	Corporate Responsibility of Management	880
	(iii)	Reliance on Officers of the Corporation	881
		(1) Honesty	885
		(2) Verification of Reports, Advice of Outside Experts, etc.	886
		(3) The Due Diligence Defence	888
		(4) Blind Reliance	892
		(5) Corporations in Financial Distress	896
D.	The Impact of Foreign Law on Corporate Management		897
	(i)	The *Sarbanes-Oxley Act* of 2002	897
		(1) Reporting Obligations	897
		(2) Overview of SOX	898
		(3) Oversight of Accounting Practice	900
		(4) Integrity of Financial Statements	901
		(5) Integrity of Internal Controls	902
		(6) Integrity of the Disclosure Process	903
		(7) Integrity of the Audit Process	904
		(8) Integrity of Financial Records	904
		(9) Conflict of Interest	905
		(10) Audit Committees	906
		(11) Special Remedies	907
	(ii)	Conflicting International Corporate Behaviour Requirements	907
E.	Routine Disclosure and Certification of Accuracy of Investor Information		911
	(i)	Continuous Disclosure and Certification Requirements	912
	(ii)	Distribution of Financial Statements, etc.	916
	(iii)	The Audit Process	918
	(iv)	Verification of Financial Disclosure	920
F.	Conclusion		924

Chapter 11: Duties and Liabilities of Directors and Officers 925

A.	Introduction		925
B.	Specific Director Liability		925
C.	General Principles		928
	(i)	Relationship Between Liability and Duty	930
	(ii)	The Director's Duty of Care	931
		(1) The Business Judgment Rule	935
		(2) Informed and Independent Decision Making	941
		(3) Knowledge, Skill and Experience	942
		(4) Extent of Care	943
		(5) Degree of Care	946
		(6) Directors' Duty to Create Safeguards	951
		(7) Director's Duty of Disclosure	953
	(iii)	Duty to Act Honestly and in Good Faith	957

		(iv)	Director's Duty of Good Faith 958

- (iv) Director's Duty of Good Faith 958
- (v) Best Interests of the Corporation 959
    - (1) Poison Pills and the Best Interests of the Corporation 962
    - (2) Best Interests and Stakeholder Theory 971
    - (3) Excessive Generosity, or Giving Away the Farm 980
    - (4) The Cakes and Ale Case Law 983
    - (5) The Proper Purpose Rule 988
    - (6) Altruism is Not the Required Standard 989
- D. The Fiduciary Duties of Directors 994
    - (i) Overview 994
    - (ii) Extension of the Fiduciary Concept to Officers of a Corporation 996
    - (iii) General Principles 998
    - (iv) Conflict of Interest 1001
    - (v) Conflicting Duties 1003
    - (vi) Remoteness and Related Defences 1005
    - (vii) Nominee Directors 1006
        - (1) The Orthodox Position 1007
        - (2) Are the Courts Moving to a More Moderate Stance? 1009
        - (3) Material Contracts Involving the Nominating Shareholder 1012
        - (4) Responsibilities of the Nominating Shareholder 1013
    - (viii) Going into Competition with the Director's Former Corporation 1014
        - (1) Non-competing Businesses 1016
        - (2) Self-dealing 1017
    - (ix) Misappropriation of Corporate Property 1021
        - (1) The Corporate Opportunity Doctrine 1021
        - (2) Exceptions to the Corporate Opportunity Doctrine .. 1025
        - (3) Use of Knowledge Gained During Employment 1026
        - (4) Liability to Account for Profit 1028
        - (5) The Rule in *Keech v. Sandford* 1032
    - (x) Director Fiduciary Duty and the Individual Shareholder .. 1036
    - (xi) Duty to Inform 1040
    - (xii) Restraining Freedom of Action (Fettering Discretion) 1041
    - (xiii) Maintaining an Even Hand 1043
    - (xiv) Termination of Fiduciary Duty 1044
- E. Liability for Civil Wrongs of the Corporation 1045
    - (i) General Principles 1045
    - (ii) Torts 1048
        - (1) Personal Involvement in Wrongdoing 1050
        - (2) Separate Duty of Care 1051
        - (3) Misrepresentation 1052
        - (4) Intentional Torts 1054
        - (5) Claims Against Multiple Directors or Officers 1054
        - (6) Sole Shareholder Corporation 1055

Table of Contents   **xxiii**

		(iii)	Breach of Trust	1058
		(iv)	Liability in Contract	1059
		(v)	Procuring Breach of Contract	1060
		(vi)	Conspiracy	1064
		(vii)	Directors Acting Beyond Their Power and Authority	1064
		(viii)	Corporation Must Exist and Carry on Business	1069
	F.	Other Critical Liability Concerns		1070
		(i)	Liability for Wages	1070
			(1) The Arguments in Favour of Wage Earner Protection	1072
			(2) The Counter-arguments	1072
			(3) Review of the Current Schemes	1073
			(a) OBCA and CBCA Wage Protection	1073
			(b) Employment Standards	1079
			(c) Bankruptcy and Insolvency	1081
			(d) Bill C-55	1082
		(ii)	Liability for Income Taxes	1085
		(iii)	Liability for Oppression	1087
	G.	The Special Position of Outside Directors		1088
	H.	Indemnification of Directors and Officers		1090
	I.	OBCA Director and Officer Insurance		1097
		(i)	Claims Made vs. Occurrence Policies	1098
		(ii)	Caps and Policy Limits	1099
		(iii)	Scope of Coverage	1099
	J.	Director Disqualification		1101

Chapter 12: Shareholders and Their Rights 1103

	A.	Introduction		1103
	B.	On Becoming a Shareholder		1105
		(i)	Status of a Shareholder	1108
		(ii)	Trustee Shareholders	1109
		(iii)	Shareholder by Estoppel (*de facto* Shareholders)	1111
		(iv)	Subsidiaries	1113
		(v)	Inspection of Lists	1114
	C.	Pre-emptive Rights		1116
	D.	Limited Liability		1117
	E.	Shareholders and Corporate Management		1118
		(i)	Disclosure of Information	1121
		(ii)	Shareholders' Meetings	1123
			(1) When Meetings Required	1127
			(2) Quorum for Meeting	1131
			(3) Place of Meeting	1134
			(4) Manner of Calling	1135
			(5) Business of Meeting	1137
			(6) Notice of Meeting	1137
			(7) Form of Notice	1138
			(8) Record Date	1139

		(9)	Sufficiency (Duration) and Content of Notice 1142

       (9) Sufficiency (Duration) and Content of Notice 1142
      (10) Special Rights of Attendance in the Case of Reporting Issuers 1149
      (11) Presiding Officer 1150
      (12) Adjournments 1154
  (iii) Voting and the Right to Vote 1155
      (1) General Considerations 1159
      (2) Voting Trusts and Similar Arrangements 1160
      (3) The Role of By-laws as a Governance Device 1162
      (4) Voting Procedure 1162
      (5) Fiduciary Obligations of Shareholders 1169
          (a) Generally 1169
          (b) Voting for the Benefit of the Class 1173
      (6) Vote by Attorney 1176
  (iv) Proxy Solicitation 1176
      (1) Proxies Under the OBCA and the CBCA 1179
      (2) Proxy Solicitation Under the *Securities Act* 1181
          (a) Securities Law Requirements 1183
          (b) Information Circular Requirements 1184
          (c) Case Law Regarding Proxy Solicitation 1189
      (3) Exemptions From the *Securities Act* Proxy Requirements 1191
      (4) Proxy Fights 1193
      (5) Fiduciary Obligations of Proxy Holder 1194
  (v)   Vote Withholding 1194
  (vi) Minutes of Shareholders' Meetings 1195
      (1) Generally 1195
      (2) Deficiencies in the Corporate Records and the Practice of Cooperizing 1195
  (vii) Right to Inspect Shareholder Register 1197
  (viii) Application to Court to Restrain or Set Aside Meeting 1199

F. Resolutions 1200
  (i)   As an Alternative to Meetings 1200
  (ii) Discretionary Authority Conferred 1203

G. Right to Receive an Accounting 1203

H. Constraining Director Power 1204
  (i)   Articles or By-laws 1206
  (ii) Shareholder Proposal 1206
      (1) Generally 1206
      (2) Proposals Under the CBCA 1210
  (iii) Unanimous Shareholder Agreement 1212
      (1) Generally 1212
      (2) Status 1214
      (3) Interpretation 1215
      (4) Subject Matter 1215
          (a) Core (Managerial) Terms 1217
          (b) Collateral Matters 1217
      (5) Formation 1218

		(a)	Evidence of Approval 1218

            (a)   Evidence of Approval 1218
            (b)   Non-Shareholder Parties 1219
            (c)   Successor Rights and Obligations 1219
        (6)   Amendment and Termination 1222
        (7)   OBCA Proposed Reforms 1222
  I.   The STA Book Entry System 1223

Chapter 13: Shareholder Remedies 1229

  A.   Introduction 1229
  B.   The Oppression Remedy 1230
      (i)   Need for the Remedy 1233
      (ii)   Meaning of Oppression, etc. 1236
            (1)   The Distinction Among the Grounds of Relief 1238
            (2)   Oppression and Majority Rule 1242
            (3)   Specific Cases 1245
            (4)   Must Be More Than a Dispute 1248
            (5)   When Available 1250
                 (a)   Both Unfairness and Prejudice Required 1250
                 (b)   Misconduct by Party in Control 1251
                 (c)   Application of General Principles of Equity 1252
      (iii)   Reasonable Expectations of the Complainant 1254
            (1)   Determination of Reasonable Expectations 1256
            (2)   Quasi-Partnership Cases 1258
            (3)   Contracting Out of Oppression Protection 1261
            (4)   Summary Regarding Reasonable Expectations 1262
      (iv)   Reasonable Conduct On the Part of the Control Group 1265
      (v)   Standing 1266
            (1)   Generally 1266
                 (a)   Difficulties of Interpretation 1268
                 (b)   Discretionary Claimants 1270
                 (c)   Timing of a Claim (Buying into an Action) 1271
            (2)   Creditors as Complainants 1272
            (3)   Relief Not Limited to Those with a Minority
                    Interest 1275
            (4)   Claims by Former Directors and Officers 1276
                 (a)   Generally 1276
                 (b)   Oppression and Wrongful Dismissal 1276
      (vi)   Special Cases 1277
            (1)   Claims with Respect to Affiliates 1277
            (2)   Widely Held Corporations 1278
            (3)   Oppression and the Family Business 1279
      (vii)   Oppression Not a Remedy of Last Resort 1282
      (viii) Procedural Considerations 1282
            (1)   Limitation Issues 1285
            (2)   Onus of Proof and the Nature of Proof Required 1285
            (3)   Bars to Action 1287
      (ix)   Forms of Relief 1288
            (1)   The Statutory Regime 1288

		(2)	Interim Relief	1291
		(3)	Final Relief	1294
			(a) General Principles Governing Relief	1294
			(b) Buying Out of Interest	1300
			(c) Valuation	1302
			(c.1) Solicitor and Client Costs	1304
			(d) Minority Discount	1305
			(e) Premiums	1306
			(f) Removal of a Director	1306
			(g) Unwinding of Transactions, etc.	1307
			(h) Damages and Similar Compensation	1307
			(i) Discontinuance and Settlement	1310
		(4)	Relief Against Third Parties	1311
	(x)	Is the Oppression Remedy a Cure Worse Than the Disease?		1311
C.	Insolvency and Related Concerns			1320
	(i)	General Rules Regarding Claims by a Shareholder		1320
	(ii)	Equity Claims Should Not be Treated as Debt Claims		1324
	(iii)	Is Equitable Subordination Part of Canadian Law		1325
		(1)	Origin of Equitable Subordination	1327
		(2)	Oppressive Conduct and U.S. Equitable Subordination	1327
		(3)	Relating Equitable Subordination to Oppression	1329
		(4)	When is the Remedy Appropriate?	1330
	(iv)	Insolvent Trading and Oppression		1331
D.	Derivative Actions			1332
	(i)	Common Law Position		1335
	(ii)	The Statutory Regime		1340
		(1)	Discretionary Nature of the Remedy	1343
		(2)	Conditions Precedent to Relief	1347
			(a) Generally	1347
			(b) Good Faith	1348
			(c) Notice of Claim	1349
		(3)	Derivative Relief Distinguished from Oppression and Other Personal Claims	1358
		(4)	Procedural Considerations	1360
			(a) Bankruptcy and Derivative Claims	1362
			(b) Double Derivative Actions	1363
			(c) Buying-in to a Derivative Proceeding	1366
			(d) Jurisdiction of the Court in Derivative Proceedings	1367
			(e) Interim Relief	1368
			(f) Conflict of Laws	1370
	(iii)	Ratification of Director Misconduct, etc.		1370
E.	Orders for Compliance			1374
F.	Curative Powers of the Courts			1375
G.	Investigation (Inspection) Orders			1375
H.	Conclusion			1381

Chapter 14: Fundamental Changes 1383
- A. Introduction 1383
- B. Amending the Articles of a Corporation 1383
  - (i) Special Voting Rights 1387
  - (ii) Extent of Approval Required 1395
  - (iii) Procedure Following Approval of Special Resolution 1397
  - (iv) Amendments Changing the Name of a Corporation 1398
  - (v) Restated Articles 1399
  - (vi) Delegation to Directors 1401
  - (vii) Special Powers of Directors to Amend Certain Aspects of the Articles 1402
- C. Sale, Lease or Exchange of Corporate Property 1403
- D. Rights of Dissent (the "Appraisal" Remedy) 1405
  - (i) Dissent Rights Limited to Registered Holders 1407
  - (ii) Overview of the Dissent Procedure 1407
  - (iii) Nature of the Dissent Right 1409
  - (iv) Opposition Not the Same as Dissent 1411
  - (v) Procedure for Sole Benefit of Dissidents 1413
  - (vi) Court Valuation 1416
    - (1) General Procedure 1416
    - (2) American Case Law Concerning Valuation 1424
  - (vii) Costs 1430
  - (viii) Effect of Insolvency on the Dissent and Appraisal Procedure 1431
- E. Amalgamation 1432
  - (i) Amalgamating Corporations Must be Governed by Same Law 1433
  - (ii) Long-Form Amalgamation 1435
    - (1) Amalgamation Agreement 1436
    - (2) Shareholder Approval 1440
    - (3) Shareholder Dissent Rights 1442
    - (4) Private Company Exemption 1443
    - (5) Procedure Following Approval of Special Resolution 1443
  - (iii) Vertical Short-form Amalgamation 1448
  - (iv) Horizontal Short-form Amalgamation 1450
  - (v) Two-stream Amalgamation, CBCA Restrictions on 1452
  - (vi) Discretion to Refuse to Approve an Amalgamation 1452
  - (vii) Court Approval of Amalgamation 1453
  - (viii) Effect of Amalgamation 1454
  - (ix) Takeover Bids 1458
  - (x) Poison Pills 1464
- F. Going Private Transactions 1465
  - (i) Overview 1465
  - (ii) The OBCA Regime 1466
  - (iii) CBCA Going Private Provisions 1471
  - (iv) OSC Rule 61-501 and Going Private Transactions 1472

		(1)	Subject Transactions	1473
		(2)	Disclosure Requirements	1475
		(3)	Information to be Provided in the Valuation	1481
		(4)	Independent Committee	1485
		(5)	Minority Approval	1488
		(6)	Exemptions	1494
		(7)	Proposed National Instrument 62-104	1494
G.	Related Party Transactions			1496
H.	Private Company Squeeze-outs			1498
I.	Continuation			1499
	(i)	Importation of Companies		1501
	(ii)	Export of Corporations		1504
J.	Arrangements and Reorganizations			1507
	(i)	Arrangements with Shareholders		1507
	(ii)	Shareholder Arrangement Procedure		1510
	(iii)	Rights of Dissent in a Shareholder Arrangement		1517
	(iv)	Other Procedural Considerations		1519
	(v)	Arrangement as an Alternative to Amendment		1520
	(vi)	Arrangements with Creditors — the *Companies' Creditors Arrangement Act*		1521
	(vii)	Reorganization		1525
K.	Conclusion			1527

Chapter 15: Winding-up & Dissolution 1529

A.	Introduction			1529
B.	General Principles			1530
	(i)	Internal Affairs Doctrine		1533
	(ii)	The Process of Liquidation and Dissolution		1535
C.	Voluntary Wind-up Procedures Under the OBCA			1536
	(i)	Commencement of Voluntary Winding-up		1539
	(ii)	Effect of Voluntary Winding-up		1539
	(iii)	Repayment of Debt of the Corporation		1542
	(iv)	Arrangements		1542
	(v)	Sale of Assets for Shares		1543
	(vi)	Account of Voluntary Wind-up		1543
D.	Court Ordered Winding-Up			1545
	(i)	Voluntary Wind-up Under Court Order		1545
	(ii)	Involuntary Winding-up Under Court Order		1546
		(1)	Oppressive or Prejudicial Conduct	1548
		(2)	Satisfaction of the Corporate Purpose	1550
		(3)	Frustration of the Corporate Purpose	1551
		(4)	Just and Equitable	1554
			(a) The Deadlock Cases	1556
			(b) Loss of Confidence	1559
			(c) Application of the Majority Rule Concept	1560
			(d) So-called "Incorporated Partnerships"	1561
	(iii)	Procedure		1563

		(1)	Generally 1563
		(2)	Conflicts of Law Issues 1565
		(3)	Appointment and Responsibilities of the Liquidator 1567
			(a) Generally 1567
			(b) Replacement Appointment 1568
			(c) Duty to Report and Approving a Liquidator's Accounts 1568
			(d) Shareholder Meetings 1572
		(4)	Effect of Wind-up Order 1572
			(a) Participation in Distributions 1574
			(b) Suing a Liquidator 1577
E.	Provisions of General Application Relating to Liquidation 1579		
	(i)	Administration of the Corporate Estate 1579	
	(ii)	Effect of the Liquidation Upon the Directors of the Corporation 1583	
	(iii)	Absence of a Liquidator 1584	
	(iv)	Costs of a Liquidator 1585	
	(v)	Duties and Powers of the Liquidator 1585	
	(vi)	Discharge of the Liquidator 1595	
	(vii)	Rights of Shareholders 1597	
F.	Contributories 1599		
G.	Dissolution 1603		
	(i)	Generally 1603	
	(ii)	Cancellation for Cause 1605	
	(iii)	Effect of Dissolution 1608	
	(iv)	Revival and Surviving Rights 1609	
	(v)	Dissolution of a Sole Shareholder Corporation (Proposed Reform) 1612	
	(vi)	Property Forfeit to the Crown 1612	
H.	Liquidation and Dissolution Under the CBCA 1619		
	(i)	Voluntary Liquidation and Dissolution of a Corporation .. 1619	
	(ii)	Liquidator 1621	
	(iii)	Involuntary Dissolution 1624	
	(iv)	Revival Procedure Under the CBCA 1626	
I.	Interplay Between Insolvency Legislation and Winding-up Provisions 1627		
J.	Conclusion 1630		

Index 1633

TABLE OF CASES

References are to paragraph numbers. Cases are listed under the name of the accused whenever the usual method of citation would cause them to be preceded by the abbreviation "R. v." signifying that the prosecution was undertaken by the Crown.

"A" Company, Re 15.42, 15.45
"Rhone" (The) v. "Peter A.B. Widener" (The) 3.29
1080409 Ontario Ltd. v. Hunter 5.200
1127905 Ontario Inc. v. Misir 11.236
1394918 Ontario Ltd. v. 1310210 Ontario Inc. 5.194
218125 Investments Ltd. v. Patel 13.29, 13.137, 13.157
2671914 Manitoba Ltd. v. Suncorp Pacific Ltd. 6.63, 6.82
3026709 Nova Scotia Ltd., Re 13.41, 13.62
3253791 Canada Inc. v. Armstrong 5.206
3464920 Canada Inc. v. Strother 2.21
347883 Alberta Ltd. v. Producers Pipelines Ltd. 13.73
3834761 Manitoba Ltd. v. Optimum Frontier Ins. Co. 15.162
390346 Ontario Ltd. v. Malidav Holdings Ltd. 2.9
400280 Alberta Ltd. v. Franko's Heating & Air Conditioning
 (1992) Ltd. 13.29, 13.157
460354 Ontario Ltd. v. Canada 15.160
484887 Alberta Inc. v. Faraci 11.124
512760 Ontario Inc., Re 13.88
57134 Manitoba Ltd. v. Palmer 11.118
599291 Alberta Ltd. v. Luff 5.26
602533 Ontario Inc. v. Shell Canada Ltd. 15.162
618469 Ontario Ltd. v. Szanto 8.43
671122 Ontario Ltd. v. Sagaz Industries Canada Inc. 3.4
677950 Ontario Ltd. v. Artell Developments Ltd. 8.40, 8.66
6784733 Alberta Ltd. v. Money's Mushrooms Ltd. 13.31
689531 B.C. Ltd. v. Anthem Works Ltd. 14.51, 14.72
692331 Ontario Ltd. v. Garay 11.177
741290 Ontario Inc., R. v. 4.64, 4.68
781952 Alberta Ltd. v. 781944 Alberta Ltd. 13.106, 15.57
816682 Ontario Inc., Re 12.167
820099 Ontario Inc. v. Harold E. Ballard
 Ltd. 11.65, 11.73, 11.138, 11.202, 13.18, 13.22, 13.43, 13.105
827365 Alberta Ltd. v. Alco Gas & Oil Production Equipment Ltd. 13.106
85956 Holdings Ltd. v. Fayerman Brothers Ltd. 14.41, 14.42, 14.43, 14.67
87118 Canada Ltd. v. Canada 5.74
8th Street Theatre Co. v. Besenski 13.213
923087 NWT Ltd. v. Anderson Mills Ltd. 3.57

A

A Company (No. 002470 of 1988), ex p. Nicholas, Re 2.10
A Company (No. 00314 of 1989), Re 13.108
A Company (No. 00370 of 1987), Re 11.61
A Company (No. 005136 of 1986), Re 13.231
A Company (No. 007623 of 1984), Re 13.157
A Company (No. 007828 of 1985), Re 12.5
A Company (No. 00836 of 1995), Re 13.101
A Company (No. 04377 of 1986), Re 13.133
A Company (No. 06834 of 1988), Re 13.133
A Company, ex p. Glossop, Re 13.157
A Company, Re 2.29, 6.69
A. MacDonald Co. v. Western Grocers Ltd. 5.71
A.G. British Columbia v. Smith 4.5
A.G. British Columbia v. Vancouver, Victoria & Eastern Rlwy.
  Navigation Co. 6.109
A.G. Canada (Attorney General) v. Hellenic Colonization Association 15.155
A.G. Canada v. A.G. Alberta 4.42
A.G. Canada v. A.G. Ontario 4.4
A.G. Canada v. C.P.R. and C.N.R. 4.5
A.G. Canada v. Standard Trust Co. of New York 5.181
A.G. Manitoba v. A.G. Canada 4.43, 4.52
A.G. Manitoba v. Rosenbaum 4.53
A.G. Nova Scotia v. A.G. Canada 4.4
A.G. Ontario v. A.G. Canada 4.6, 4.48
A.G. Ontario v. Reciprocal Insurers 4.42
A.G. v. Equiticorp Industries Group Ltd. 5.163
A.G. v. Great Eastern Rlwy. Co. 6.5
A.G. v. Mersey Rlwy. 6.5
A.G.'s Reference (No. 2 of 1982), Re 2.12
A.L. Campbell & Co. Pty. Ltd. v. FCT 7.228
A.L. Underwood v. Bank of Liverpool and Martins 11.164
A.N.Z. Executors & Trustee Co. v. Quintex Australia Ltd. 11.80
A.R. Williams Machinery Co. v. Crawford Tug Co. 6.79
A.U.P.E. v. University Hospital Board 12.116
AACR Enterprises Ltd. v. Grimwood 3.2
Aaron's Reefs Ltd. v. Twiss 7.99, 7.107
Abana Mines Ltd. v. Wall 6.63
Abbey Glen Property Corp. (Genstar Corp.) v. Stumborg 11.180
Abbey Glen Property Corp. v. Stumborg (1975) 11.180
Abbey Glen Property Corp. v. Stumborg (1976) 11.168
Abbey Malvern Wells Ltd. v. Ministry of Local Government & Planning 2.29
Abdool v. Anaheim Management Ltd. 5.172
Abercrombie v. Davies 10.20
Aberdeen Rlwy. Co. v. Blaikie Brothers 11.127, 11.135, 11.158, 11.169
ABI Biotechnology Inc. v. Apotex Inc. 10.26
Abitibi Power & Paper Co. v. Montreal Trust Co. 4.46

Abraham v. Inter Wide Investments Ltd. 14.68
Abraham v. Inter Wide Investments Ltd. (No. 1) 13.123, 13.148
Abraham v. Prosoccer Ltd. 13.215
Abrams v. Koether 13.230
Abrey v. Victoria Printing Co. 7.114
ACA Cooperative Association Ltd. v. Associated Freezers of Canada Inc. 3.5
Acapulco Holdings Ltd. v. Jegen 13.109, 13.236
Access Advertising Management Inc. v. Servex Computers Inc. 8.150, 8.155
Accles Ltd., Re; Hodgson v. Accles 8.194
Acer v. Percy 3.12
Acme Products Ltd., Re 12.19
Acqualane Shores Inv. v. Commissioner 7.13
Action Plumbing Ltd. v. Alberta (Registrar of Companies) 5.117, 5.118
Adair v. Old Bushmills Distillery Co. 7.322
Adam Eyton Ltd., Re 15.133
Adams and Burns v. Bank of Montreal 8.23
Adams v. Cape Industries plc 2.69, 2.70, 5.164
Adams v. Morgan & Co. 11.297
Adams v. National Electric Tramway & Lighting Co. 3.7
Adams v. Newbigging 7.114
Addlestone Linoleum Co., Re 7.222
Adelaide Capital Corp. v. Integrated Transportation Finance Inc. 8.207
ADGA Systems International Ltd. v. Valcom Ltd. 2.50, 3.55, 11.211, 11.227
ADI Ltd. v. 052987 NB Inc. 13.30
Advance Bank of Australia Ltd. v. FAI Insurance Australia Ltd. 11.108, 12.161
Advanta Corp. Sec. Litig., Re 11.35
Advocate Mines Ltd., Re 15.95
AE Realisations (1985) Ltd. v. Time Air Inc. 13.68
Aerators Ltd. v. Tollitt 5.110
Aeroguard v. A.G. British Columbia 4.10
AEVO Co. v. D & A Macleod Co. 13.178
Agranoff v. Miller 11.121
Agricultural Wholesale Society Ltd. v. Biddulph & District Agricultural
  Society 7.76, 7.77
Agrium Inc. v. Hamilton 12.123
Ah Toy, Re 15.123
Ainley & Associates Ltd. v. Tatham 11.133
Air Canada v. M & L Travel Ltd. 11.218, 11.220, 11.233
Air Canada v. Ontario (Liquor Control Board) 4.50
Air Canada, Re 8.300
Air India Flight 182 Disaster Claimants v. Air India 13.93
Airline Industry Revitalization Co. v. Air Canada 12.41
Akiba Investment Ltd., Re 3.24
Albert Cheese Co. v. Leeming 6.99
Alberta (Provincial Treasurer) v. Long 4.14
Alberta (Treasury Branches) v. Seven Way Capital Corp. 14.50
Alberta Gas Ethylene Co. v. R. 5.164
Alberta Government Telephones v. CRTC 5.162

Alberta Improvement Co. v. Everett 7.76, 7.77
Alberta Paper Co. v. Metropolitan Graphics Ltd. 8.146
Alberta Rolling Mills Co. v. Christie 7.87, 7.275
Alberta Treasury Branches v. Ghermezian 3.9
Alberts v. Mountjoy 11.119, 11.132, 11.152, 11.175, 11.206
Albion Motor-Car Co. Ltd. v. Albion Carriage & Motor Body Works Ltd. 5.113
Alder v. Dobie 12.205
Alers-Hankey v. Solomon 2.25
Alexander v. Automatic Telephone Co. 10.34
Alexander v. Bar SP Ranches Ltd. 5.51
Alexander v. Simpson 12.118, 12.144
Alexander v. Westeel-Rosco Ltd. 13.118, 14.158
Alexander Ward & Co. v. Samyang Navigation Co. 10.7, 10.35, 12.32
Alexandra Oil & Development Co. v. Cook 5.176, 5.180
Aleyn v. Belchier 7.56
Alf's Roofing & Contracting Ltd., Re 15.60
Alfano v. KPMG Inc. 13.195
Algonquin Mercantile Corp. v. Enfield Corp. 13.116
Ali Baba Steakhouse Ltd. v. 257593 Restaurant Ltd. 15.127, 15.128
Allam & Co. v. Europa Poster Services Ltd. 10.81
Allan v. The Manitoba and Northwestern Railway Co. 4.76
Allaun v. Consolidated. Oil Co. 11.25
Alldrew Holdings Ltd. v. Nibro Holdings Ltd. 13.138
Allebart Pty Ltd. and the Companies Act, Re 15.232
Allen v. Gold Reefs of West Africa Ltd. 6.24, 11.105, 12.211, 14.45
Allen v. Hamilton 15.27
Allen v. Hyatt 11.120, 11.194, 13.257
Allen v. Ontario & Rainy River Rlwy. 6.99
Allen, Craig & Co. (London) Ltd., Re 9.160
Alles v. Maurice 13.114
Alliance Securities Ltd. v. Posnikoff 5.149
Allied Cellular Systems Ltd. v. Bullock 12.85
Allish v. Allied Engineering of B.C. Ltd. 9.128, 10.5
Alliston Creamery v. Grosdanoff 5.206
Allsco Building Supplies Ltd. v. McAllister 14.121
Allsco Building Supplies Ltd. v. New Brunswick (Director, Business
    Corporations Act) 14.121
Almon v. Law 6.77
Alper Development Inc. v. Harrowston Corp. 3.55
Aluminium Industrie Vaassen BV v. Romalpa Aluminium Ltd. 8.68
Aluminum Co. of Canada v. Toronto (City) 2.36
Alvi v. Misir 2.50, 11.69
Amalgamated Investment & Property Co. Ltd., Re 8.50
Amalgamated Society of Rlwy. Servants v. Osborne 1.58, 6.5
Amalgamated Syndicates Ltd., Re 15.23
Amaranth L.L.C. v. Counsel Corp. 8.169, 8.171
Amerco, U-Haul International Inc. v. Shoen 11.52, 11.124, 11.126
American Express Financial Advisors, Inc. v. County of Carver 14.67

Table of Cases

American Reserve Energy Corp. v. McDorman 13.43
American Seamless Tube Corp. v. Goward 7.79
American Union Financial Corp. v. University National Bank of Peoria 6.85
American Wholesale Corp. v. Mauldin 2.35
American Wollastonite Mining Corp. v. Scott 7.170
Ammonia Soda Co. v. Chamberlain 7.15, 7.310, 7.311
Amneet Holdings Ltd. v. 79548 Manitoba Ltd. 12.209, 13.31
Amrose Lake & Tin Copper Co., Re 7.49
Amway of Canada Ltd., R. v. 4.68
Anderson Lumber Co. v. Canadian Conifer Ltd. 8.24
Anderson v. Atlantic Enterprises Ltd. 14.63
Anderson v. Envoy Realty Ltd. 9.135
Anderson v. McNair Lumber & Shingle Co. 8.162
Anderson v. Wittich 13.211
Anderson, Smyth & Kelly Customs Brokers Ltd. v. World Wide Customs
  Brokers Ltd. 11.152, 11.176
Andrews v. Gas Meter Co. 12.12
Andrews v. Law Society of British Columbia 9.76
Andrews v. Mockford 7.98
Anglesey (Marquis); Wilmot v. Gardner, Re 8.29
Anglo-American Insurance Co., Re 7.158
Anglo-American Lumber Co. v. McLellan 7.54
Anglo-Continental Corp. of Western Australia, Re 12.12
Anglo-French Exploration Co., Re 7.8
Angus v. R. Angus Alberta Ltd. 11.48, 11.104
Antle v. Stratos Global Corp. 6.52
Antoniades v. Wong 13.128
ANZ Banking Group (N.Z.) Ltd. v. Gibson 8.149
ANZ Executors & Trustee Co. v. Qintex Australia Ltd. 7.334
Apotex Fermentation Inc. v. Novopharm Ltd. 11.227
Apple Computer Inc. v. Mackintosh Computers Ltd. 11.242
Appleby v. Minister of National Revenue 2.31
Appley Brothers v. United States 9.164
Appotive v. Computrex Centres Ltd. 13.234
Aquino v. First Choice Capital Fund Ltd. 13.131, 13.141
Arab Monetary Fund v. Hashim (No. 3) 5.162
Arbuthnott v. Feltrim Underwriting Agencies Ltd. 2.94
Arbutus Garden Homes Ltd. v. Arbutus Apartments Corp. 5.192
Arcadia Coal Co., R. v. 4.47, 4.49
Argo Protective Coatings Inc., Re 13.59
Argyll's Ltd. v. Coxeter 15.35
Arizona Dept. of Rev. v. Asarco Inc. 14.189
Arizona Western Insurance Co. v. L.L. Constantin Co. 7.42, 7.302
Armagas Ltd. v. Mundogas S.A. (The Ocean Frost) 6.43, 6.50
Armitage v. Nurse 8.176
Armitage, Re 7.303
Armour v. Thyssen Edelstahlwerke AG 8.68
Armstrong v. Frostie 13.196

Armstrong v. Gardner 13.211
Armstrong v. McGibbon 12.76
Armstrong v. Shaw 14.133
Armstrong World Industries Inc. v. Arcand 13.27
Arnaud, R. v. 7.194
Arnold v. Fleming 8.331
Arnold v. Society for Savs. Bancorp, Inc. 11.199
Arnot v. United African Lands 12.113
Aronson v. Lewis 10.22, 10.114, 11.5, 11.17, 11.21, 11.25,
                                                         11.35, 11.45, 13.209, 13.218, 14.8
Arrotta v. Avva Light Corp. 12.3, 13.29, 13.157
Arsenault v. Arsenault 2.28
Art Reproduction Co., Re 15.115
Arthur Andersen Inc. v. Toronto Dominion Bank 2.10
Arthur v. Signum Communications Ltd. 13.100
Artisan's Land & Mortgage Corp., Re 7.321, 7.327
Arton Lumber Co., Re 10.69
Ascot Investments Pty. Ltd. v. Harper 2.35
Ash v. I.B.M. 13.196
Ashburton Oil N.L. v. Alpha Minerals N.L. 10.21, 11.108, 11.252, 12.31
Ashbury Railway Carriage & Iron Co. v. Riche 5.50, 6.12, 6.13
Ashbury v. Watson 5.51, 5.62
Ashby v. Prince Albert (City) 5.59
Ashland Co. v. Armstrong 6.113
Ashley v. Brown 8.332
Ashrae Controls Inc., Re 5.120
Ash-Temple Co., R. v. 3.29
ASI Holdings Inc., Re 11.65
ASIC v. Burke 15.64
Askew v. Manning 1.52
Asphalt Products (B.C.) Ltd., Re 5.142
Aspiotis v. Coffee Time Donuts Inc. 11.211
Associated Asbestos Services Ltd. v. Canadian Occidental Petroleum Ltd. . 15.162
Associated Color Laboratories Ltd., Re 10.3, 10.9, 12.181
Associated Growers of B.C. Ltd. v. B.C. Fruit Land Ltd. 6.46
Associated Investors of Canada Ltd., Re 13.271, 13.274, 15.5, 15.95
Associated Securities and the Companies Act, Re 8.17
Associated Stevedoring Co. v. Callanan 7.54
Associates Finance Co. v. Webber 3.2, 7.24
Association of Certified Public Accountants of Britain v. Secretary of
    State for Trade & Industry 5.77
Astec (BSR) plc., Re 13.45, 13.51
Athenaeum Life Assurance Society, Re 6.56
Atkinson & Yates Boatbuilders Ltd. v. Hanlon 15.158
Atlantic Acceptance Corp. v. Burns & Dutton Construction (1962), Ltd. .. 8.185
Atlantic Ova Pro Ltd., Re 8.329
Atlantic States Construction Inc. v. Beavers 14.80
Atlas Development Co. v. Calof 10.20, 11.253

Atlas Loan Co., Re 7.315, 8.23
Attorney General of Canada v. Roger M. Bourbonnais Professional Corp. ... 5.29
Attree v. Hawe 8.195
Atwool v. Merryweather 13.232
Auditorium Ltd. v. Lumsden 7.180
Auerbach v. Wallenstein 9.9
Aujla v. Yellow Cab Co. 11.15
Aukland Gas Co. v. Point Chevalier Road Board 10.14, 12.169
Austin Mining Co. v. Gemmel 12.39
Austin v. Habitat Development Ltd. 11.233
Austral Brick & Co. Pty. Ltd. v. Falgat Constructions Pty. Ltd. 15.188
Australia, etc. Building Society v. Wells 12.23.1
Australian Conference Association Ltd. v. Mainline Constructions Pty. Ltd.
  (in liq.) 8.17
Australian Metropolitan Life Assurance Co. v. Ure 7.222, 11.56
Australian Pacific Technology Ltd. 7.150
Automatic Bottle Makers Ltd., Re 8.114
Automatic Phone Recorder Co., Re 13.268
Automatic Self-Cleansing Filter Syndicate Co. v.
  Cuninghame 9.17, 10.20, 10.21, 11.252, 12.33, 12.191
Aveling Barford Ltd. v. Per Ion Ltd. 2.32
Avon Downs Pty. Ltd. v. F.C.T. 7.211
AWA Ltd. v. Daniels 9.67
Ayerst (Inspector of Taxes) v. C & K (Construction) Ltd. 15.113, 15.115
Aylwards (1975) Ltd., Re 5.159
Ayr Harbour Trustees v. Oswald 6.24
Azoff-Don Commercial Bank, Re 15.169

B

B & A Log Homes Ltd. v. Evans 2.23
B. Liggett (Liverpool) Ltd. v. Barclays Bank Ltd. 6.82
B. Love Ltd. v. Bulk Steel & Salvage
  Ltd. 11.124, 12.50, 15.62, 15.63, 15.67, 15.68
B.C. Brick & Tile Co., R. v. 2.11
B.C. Portland Cement Co., Re 14.264
B.C. Timber Industry Journal Ltd. v. Black 11.48, 11.127, 11.185
B.G. Preeco I (Pacific Coast) Ltd. v. Bon Street Holdings Ltd. 2.29, 11.245
B.J. Kennedy Agency (1984) Ltd. v. Kilgour-Bell Insurance Agencies Ltd. 13.30
Babic v. Milinkovic 12.76, 12.105
Bacal Contracting Ltd. v. Modern Engineering (Bristol) Ltd. 15.28
Baden Pacific Ltd. v. Portreeve Pty. Ltd. 7.211
Bagby v. Gustavson International Drilling Co. 2.3
Baglan Hall Colliery Co., Re 7.161
Bagnall v. Carlton 5.181
Bagot Pneumatic Tyre Co. v. Clipper Pneumatic Tyre Co. 5.186
Bagshaw v. Eastern Union Railway Co. 13.255
Bagshaw v. Eastern Union Rlwy. Co. 6.13

Baillie v. Oriental Telephone & Electric Co. 12.76, 12.77
Baird v. Lees 15.66
Baird v. Red Bluff Inns Ltd. 7.210
Baker v. Guaranty Savings & Loan Association...................... 7.78, 7.107, 7.114
Baker v. Paddock Inn Peterborough Ltd. 13.262
Balaban v. Bryndon Ventures Inc. 10.78
Balaton Hungarian Dancers Inc. v. Saskatchewan
 (Director of Corporations)... 5.117
Baldwin Iron & Steel Works Ltd. v. Dominion Carbide Co. 5.160, 6.63
Balkwill v. Burrard Saw Mills Ltd. 8.184
Ballman v. 600560 Saskatchewan Ltd. 11.222
Bally's Grand Derivative Litigation, Re 10.114
Balsamides v. Protameen Chemicals, Inc. 14.82
Balston Ltd. v. Headline Filters Ltd. 11.154, 11.189
Bamford v. Bamford 13.254
Banco de Vizcaya v. Don Alfonso de Borbon y Austria............................ 15.169
Bancorp. Financial Ltd. v. Thomas N. Mather Professional Corp. 5.27
Bangor & North Wales Mutual Marine Protection Association, Re 7.196, 7.236
Baniuk v. Carpenter 11.48, 13.30, 13.123, 13.263
Bank of Africa v. Salisbury Gold Mining Co. 7.260, 7.345, 7.346
Bank of America National Trust & Savings Association v. West End
 Chemical Co. 7.42
Bank of Credit and Commerce International S.A. (No. 8), Re 2.61, 8.75
Bank of Ireland v. Cogry Spinning Co. 9.72
Bank of Montreal v. Bethune................................... 1.3, 1.52, 1.58, 5.4, 6.2
Bank of Montreal v. Bole... 1.57
Bank of Montreal v. Bray 8.326
Bank of Montreal v. Canadian Westgrowth Ltd. 2.11
Bank of Montreal v. Century Ltd. (Trustee) 8.201
Bank of Montreal v. Dome Petroleum Ltd. 13.30, 13.66
Bank of Montreal v. Dynex Petroleum Ltd. 8.285
Bank of Montreal v. Elgin Co-operative Services 8.228
Bank of Montreal v. Ewing... 8.328
Bank of Montreal v. Guaranty Silk Dyeing & Finishing Co. 8.216
Bank of Montreal v. Hall 4.10, 8.215, 8.217, 8.219
Bank of Montreal v. Nican Trading Co. 15.90
Bank of Montreal v. Perry.. 6.113
Bank of Montreal v. Stephen 15.160
Bank of Montreal v. Sweeny... 12.16
Bank of Montreal v. Union Gas Co. 8.146
Bank of Montreal v. Vandine.. 8.330
Bank of Montreal v. Woodtown Development Ltd. 8.146
Bank of N.T. Butterfield & Son Ltd. v. Golinksy 7.21
Bank of Nova Scotia v. Dunphy Leasing Enterprises Ltd. 8.46
Bank of Nova Scotia v. International Harvester Credit Corp. 8.219
Bank of Nova Scotia v. LeBlanc... 6.59
Bank of Ottawa v. Newton... 15.125
Bank of Syria, Re 8.321, 9.16

Bank of Tokyo v. Karoon 2.70
Bank of Toronto v. Cobourg, Peterborough & Marmora Rlwy. 8.35, 8.130
Bank of Toronto v. Lambe 4.47
Bank of Toronto v. Pickering 6.110, 6.113
Bank of Virginia v. Craig 7.192
Bank Voor Handel en Scheepvaart N.V. v. Slatford 1.31, 2.28, 2.30
Banker's Trust, Re 6.14, 7.40, 7.80
Banks, Re 9.123, 11.36
Banque Financiere de la Cite v. Parc (Battersea) Ltd. 13.189
Banque Indosuez v. Ferromet Resources 15.77
Banque Internationale de Commerce de Petrograd v. Goukassow 15.13
Banque Nationale du Canada v. Houle 8.149
Barakot Ltd. v. Epiette Ltd. 2.3, 2.45
Barclay Construction Corp. v. Bank of Montreal 8.149
Barclays Bank Ltd. v. Quistclose Investments Ltd. 8.17
Barclays Bank plc v. British & Commonwealth Holdings plc 7.8
Barclays Bank plc v. Willowbrook International Ltd. 8.201
Bargain Tire Centre Ltd. v. Registrar of Business Corporations Act and
    Pro-Western Tire Corp. 5.116
Barkan v. Amsted Indus. 14.146, 14.148
Barle v. Home Owners Cooperative 2.29
Barnabe v. Touhey 11.175
Barnard v. Duplessis Independent Shoe Machinery Co. 12.202
Barned's Banking Co. (Peel's Case), Re 5.159
Barnes v. Addy 11.232
Barnes v. Andres 11.35
Baron v. Allied Artists Pictures Corp. 7.310
Baroness Wenlock v. River Dee Co. 12.36
Barrett v. Bank of Vancouver 7.82, 7.87
Barrett v. Hartley 10.69
Barrette v. Crabtree Estate 11.267
Barron v. Potter 9.13, 10.7, 12.37
Barrow v. Ontario, Simcoe & Huron Rlwy. 14.58
Barsh v. Feldman 12.44, 12.50
Barthels, Shewan & Co. v. Winnipeg Cigar Co. 8.23
Bartlett v. Barclays Bank Trust Co. 8.176
Bartlett v. Bartlett Mines Ltd. 10.71, 12.178
Bartling v. Danby 5.60
Barwick v. English Joint Stock Bank 3.3
Basara v. Carhoun 7.210
Basic Refractory Products Ltd. v. M.N.R. 8.197
Bata Industries Ltd., R. v. 11.305
Batavia Times Publishing Co. v. Davis 8.62
Batchlett v. United Cobalt Mines Ltd. 7.154
Bateman Television Ltd. (in liq.) v. Coleridge Finance Co. 15.43
Bateman v. Service 14.221
Bates v. Dresser 10.135
Bath v. Standard Land Co. 9.2, 13.257

Batten v. Wedgwood Coal & Iron Co. 8.168
Battisti v. Galati 15.85
Baughman v. Rampart Resources Ltd. 7.245
Baumgartner v. Carsley Silk Co. 8.62
Bauscher-Grant Farms Inc. v. Lake Diefenbaker Potato Corp. 13.93
Baxted v. Warkentin Estate... 15.57
Bayhold Financial Corp. v. Clarkson Co. 8.154
Baynes Carriage Co., Re 15.45
Bazley v. Curry... 3.4
Beam ex rel. Martha Stewart Living Omnimedia, Inc. v.
    Stewart 9.90, 11.39.1, 13.224, 13.230
Beamish v. Solnick 11.124, 11.162
Bearcat Exploration Ltd. (Re) 8.43
Beatty v. Neelson 7.107, 7.117
Beatty v. North-West Transportation Co. 9.25
Beaubien v. Campbell... 13.30
Beauchemin v. Beauchemin & Sons Ltd. 12.58
Beaudry v. Read.. 10.69
Beaver Dam Mining Co. v. Larson 7.166
Beaver Truck Co., Re.. 8.20
Beechwood Cemetary Co. v. Graham.. 5.53, 12.8
Beechy Savings & Credit Union v. Warwaruk 8.46
Bell & Black, Re 5.153
Bell Canada v. Quebec... 4.50
Bell ExpressVu Limited Partnership v. Rex 1.27
Bell Houses Ltd. v. City Wall Properties Ltd. 6.13
Bell Insurance Agencies Ltd. v. Bell & Cross Insurance Agency Ltd. 5.123
Bell Oil & Gas Co. v. Allied Chemical Corp. 2.49
Bell v. British Columbia (Director of Employment
    Standards)...11.208, 11.269, 11.276, 11.278
Bell v. Lever Bros. Ltd. 2.70, 11.132
Bell v. Milner... 10.5
Bell v. Source Data Control Ltd. 11.194, 12.123
Bell, R. v. 5.59
Bellerby v. Rowland & Marwood's Steamship Co. 7.255
Belleville Driving & Athletic Assn., Re 7.224, 12.204
Bellman v. Western Approaches Ltd. 13.201
Bellows v. Porter... 12.27
Belman v. Belman..13.27, 13.127, 13.133
Belmont Finance Corp. v. Williams Furniture Ltd. (No. 2) 11.92, 13.18
Beman v. Rufford.. 4.77
Benallack v. Bank of British North America 8.328
Bendix Home Systems Ltd. v. Clayton 11.152
Benjamin Cope & Sons Ltd., Re 8.141
Benner v. Currie.. 7.162
Bennett v. British Columbia (Securities Commission) 4.51
Bennett v. Ogston... 8.29
Bennett v. Riem 13.31

Bennetts v. Board of Fire Commissioners of New South Wales 11.135
Benson & Hedges (Canada) Ltd. and Liquor Control Board of Ontario, Re 5.146
Benson v. Department of Revenue 14.189
Benson v. Heathorn 11.170
Benson v. Third Canadian General Investment Trust Ltd. ... 12.129, 13.63, 14.43
Bentley-Boudreau v. Red Knight Enterprises (1987) Ltd. 13.267
Bentley-Stevens v. Jones 12.58, 12.61, 12.78
Bergeron v. Cie de meubles de Jonquière 7.198
Bergner & Engel Brewing Co. v. Dreyfus 6.107
Berkey Photo (Canada) Ltd. v. Ohlig 11.151
Berkinshaw v. Henderson 7.224, 12.202
Berlei Hestia (N.Z.) Ltd. v. Fernyhough 9.13, 11.140
Bermuda Cablevision Ltd. v. Colica Trust Co. 13.70
Bernard v. Montgomery 13.20, 13.92
Bernardin v. Municipality of North Dufferin 5.152
Bernhardt v. Main Outboard Centre Ltd. 13.103
Berry v. Indian Park Association 6.10, 6.12, 6.16
Berry v. Pulley 1.51
Berryere v. Fireman's Fund Insurance Co. 6.50
Berryland Canning Co. v. Toronto Dominion Bank 8.221
Berryman v. Wise 12.169
Bessette v. Bessette 13.5
Bessette v. Equitable Mutual Fire Insurance Co. 6.79
Besta International Corp. v. Watercraft Offshore Canada Ltd. 11.234
Better-off-Dead Productions v. Pendulum Pictures 4.28
Betts & Co. v. Macnaghten 12.77, 12.118
Beverly Hills Motor Car Co., Re 5.113
Bexwell v. Christie 11.299
Biakanja v. Irving 9.190.6
Bially v. Churchill Electric & Associates (1987) Ltd. 13.34
Bianco v. I.H. Mathers & Son 6.99
Bickman v. Smith Motors Ltd. 3.9
Big M Drug Mart Ltd., R. v. 4.67, 4.68
Big Sky Marketing Co. v. Glengor International Pty Ltd. 5.193
Biggerstaff v. Rowatt's Wharf Ltd. 6.50, 6.71
Biggs v. James Hardie & Co. Pty. Ltd. 2.50
Bigley v. Haffey 7.24, 11.191
Bily v. Arthur Young & Co. 9.190.6, 9.190.7
Bindra v. Falotico 5.142
Bing Crosby Minute Maid Corp. v. Eaton 7.154
Biondi v. Scrushy 11.35, 13.229
Biondich v. Kingscroft Investments Ltd. 5.203, 6.38
Birch v. Cropper 7.26, 7.40, 7.284, 7.304, 7.331, 11.90, 12.12
Bird v. Hussey-Ferrier Meat Co. 6.78
Bird v. Merchants Telephone Co. 5.156
Bird v. Warnock Hersey Professional Services Ltd. 2.60
Birks v. Birks 12.105
Birmingham & Gloucester Rlwy. Co., R. v. 3.23

Birmingham Midshires Mortgage Services Ltd. v. Sabherwal 13.189
Birney v. Toronto Milk Co. 10.69
Birt v. St. Mary Mercy Hospital of Gary, Inc. 2.22
Birtchnell v. Equity Trustees Executors & Agency Co. 11.154
Bishop Engraving & Printing Co., Re... 12.19
Bishop v. Smyrna & Cassaba Rlwy. Co. 7.321
Bishopgate Investment Management Ltd. v. Maxwell (No. 2) 11.8
Bisset v. Wilkinson 7.96
Bitter v. Canada (Secretary of State)... 7.25
Black & Decker Manufacturing Co., R. v. 14.89, 14.133
Black Estate v. Ontario (Attorney General)... 15.167
Black v. Black... 14.71
Black v. Smallwood...5.189, 5.201, 5.204, 9.2
Black, White & Grey Cabs Ltd. v. Fox.. 9.17, 12.31
Black, White & Grey Cabs Ltd. v. Reid... 7.196
Blacklaws v. 470433 Alberta Ltd. 2.33, 3.55, 11.216
Blackmere v. United States... 10.166
Blackmore v. Richardson... 13.42
Blackwater v. Plint.. 3.4, 11.299
Blair Open Hearth Furnace Co. v. Reigart.. 12.43
Blair v. Consolidated Enfield Corp. 11.306, 12.86
Blake v. Blake Agency.. 14.195
Blaker v. Herts and Essex Waterworks Co. 4.76
Blasius Indus., Inc. v. Atlas Corp. 14.8
Blattgerste v. Heringa 15.49
Bleau v. Perruquier français Inc. 15.64
Bligh v. Brent... 1.49
Bloomenthal v. Ford 7.153
Blue Band Navigation Co. (Trustee of) v. Price Waterhouse (No. 2)........... 9.183
Blue Range Resource Corp., Re... 13.178, 13.189
Bluebird Corp., Re... 7.77
Bluechel v. Prefabricated Buildings Ltd. 12.85
Bluestein v. R. 7.142
BNZ Finance Ltd. v. Commissioner of Inland Revenue................................ 5.1
Boak v. Woods... 9.73
Board of Directors of the Washington city Orphan Asylum v. Board of
    Trustees 5.65
Boardman v. Phipps.. 10.42
Boddam v. Ryley 8.29
Boeing Co. v. Van Gemert... 12.79
Bogart v. King (Township).. 8.132
Bogle v. Kootenay Valley Co. 7.288
Boland v. Bear Exploration & Radium Ltd. 15.27
Bolt & Iron Co., Re... 7.77, 7.79, 10.85
Bolton v. County of Wentworth... 9.15, 11.253
Bolton v. Natal Land & Colonisation Co. 7.310
Bolton v. Stone.. 11.28
Bomac Batten Ltd. v. Pozhke... 12.85

Bonanza Creek Gold Mining Co. v. R. 4.14, 4.23, 6.11, 6.13
Bonar Inc. v. Smith 11.152
Bonavista (Town) v. Atlantic Technologies Ltd. 8.201
Bond v. Barrow Haematite Steel Co. 7.298, 7.303, 7.310, 7.319
Bond Worth Ltd., Re.. 8.68, 8.138
Bondi Better Bananas Ltd., Re...3.2, 6.79, 9.134, 12.86
Bonds & Securities (Trading) Pty. Ltd. v. Glomex Mines NL...................... 7.211
Bonisteel v. Collis Leather Co. 11.112
Border Cities Press Club v. Ontario (Attorney General)................ 15.151, 15.154
Borg-Warner Acceptance Canada Ltd. v. Gentleman.................................. 8.143
Borsook v. Broder.. 13.42
Boschoek Pty. Co. v. Fuke.. 5.48, 10.103
Bosman v. Doric Holdings Ltd. 13.98
Boston Deep Sea Fishing & Ice Co. v. Ansell 11.178
Boston Shoe Co. v. Frank 11.173
Boswell & Co. (Steels) Ltd., Re.. 13.133
Bottoms v. Brent Petroleum Industries Ltd. 11.180
Boulet v. Hudon 7.77, 7.80, 7.289
Boultbee v. Wills & Co. 7.208
Boulting v. Association of Cinematograph, Television & Allied
 Technicians 11.136, 11.200, 13.258
Boutique Andre Bibeau Inc. (Syndicate) v. Ernst & Whinney Inc. 8.221
Bove v. Community Hotel Corp. of Newport R.I. 14.1
Bovey Hotel Ventures Ltd., Re.. 13.156
Bow Valley Husky (Bermuda) Ltd. v. Saint John Shipbuilding
 Ltd. 5.164, 9.190.4, 11.299
Bowater Canadian Ltd. v. R.L. Crain Inc. 7.331, 12.109
Bowden v. Cumberland County.. 9.129
Bowditch v. Jackson Company 10.17
Bowie, Re.. 6.112
Bowles v. City of Winnipeg... 1.60
Bowling & Welby's Contract, Re 12.5
Bowman v. Secular Society Ltd. 5.17, 5.159
Bowman v. Solway 15.128
Box v. Bird's Hill Sand Co. 7.334
Boyd v. International Utility Structures Inc. 8.43
Boyer v. Wilmington Materials Inc. 10.58
Boyle v. Rothschild.. 11.135
Bradbury v. English Sewing Cotton Co. 7.17, 7.19
Bradford Investments plc, Re.. 7.44
Bradford Roofing Industries Property Ltd., Re.. 14.42
Bradley Egg Farm Ltd. v. Clifford... 5.162
Bradstone Equity Partners Inc., Re 12.54
Brady v. Brady 11.80
Brant Dairy Co. v. Ontario (Milk Commission) 5.63

Brant Investments Ltd. v. KeepRite Inc. 11.17, 11.192, 11.196, 11.189,
                12.122, 12.128, 13.5, 13.15, 13.20, 13.22, 13.30, 13.63,
                13.138, 13.140, 13.155, 13.157, 14.50, 14.67, 14.69
Braun Estate v. Canada (Custodian) 7.25
Bray v. Ford 10.69, 11.117
Brazilian Rubber Plantations and Estates Ltd., Re............................. 11.17, 11.28
Breckland Group Holdings Ltd. v. London & Suffolk
    Properties Ltd 10.35, 12.32, 13.212
Breen v. Williams 11.117
Brehm v. Eisner 9.33, 10.113
Brenfield Squash Racquets Club Ltd., Re... 13.127
Brettingham-Moore v. Christie 9.93
Bre-X Minerals Ltd. (Trustee of) v. Verchere 15.109
Bridge City Electric (1981), Ltd. v. Robertson 5.207
Bridges v. California 1.49, 6.22
Bridport Old Brewery Co., Re 12.78
Bright Pine Mills Pty. Ltd., Re... 13.35
Bright v. Hutton 5.182
Brightlife Ltd., Re 8.115, 8.138, 8.200, 8.201
Brinds Ltd. v. Offshore Oil N.L. (No. 3) 15.43
Brio Industries Inc. v. Clearly Canadian Beverage Corp. 11.23
Bristol Athenaeum, Re 1.2
British & American Trustee & Finance Corp. v. Couper........ 7.255, 7.275, 12.12
British America Corp., Re... 10.50
British America Nickel Corp. v. M.J. O'Brien
    Ltd. 12.102, 12.128, 12.129, 14.264
British American Elevator Co. v. Bank of British North America................ 11.31
British American Timber Co. v. Jones... 7.260
British Asbestos Co. Ltd. v. Boyd... 6.66
British Bank of the Middle East v. Sun Life Assurance Co. of Canada (U.K.)
    Ltd. 6.62
British Cattle Supply Co., Re.. 7.153
British Columbia v. Consolidated Churchill Copper Corp. 8.146, 8155
British Columbia v. Federal Business Development Bank 8.141, 8.218
British Columbia v. Imperial Tobacco Canada Ltd. 4.21
British Columbia v. Lega Fabricating Ltd. 8.141
British Columbia v. Yu 3.2
British Columbia Aircraft Propeller & Engine Co., Re 15.67
British Columbia Bond Corp. v. Lang 6.60
British Columbia Electric Rlwy. Co. Ltd. v. The King.............................. 10.166
British Columbia Permanent v. Wootton 5.117
British Columbia Power Corp. v. A.G. British Columbia..................... 4.58, 4.59
British Columbia Power Corp. v. B.C. Electric Co. 4.58
British Columbia Red Cedar Shingle Co. v. Stoltze Manufacturing Co. 7.271
British Columbia Timber Co. v. Jones... 7.345
British Consolidated Oil Corp., Re 8.193
British Diabetic Association v. Diabetic Society Ltd. 5.85
British Empire Steel Corp., Re.. 15.53

British India, etc. Co. v. CIR... 8.130
British International Finance (Canada) Ltd., Re 9.110, 12.43
British Pacific Properties Ltd. v. British Columbia (Minister of Highways
 and Public Works).. 8.46
British Telecommunications plc., Re 14.165
British Thomson-Houston Co. v. Federated European Bank
 Ltd. 6.44, 6.50, 6.60, 6.72
British Thomson-Houston Co. v. Sterling Accessories, Ltd. 3.55, 11.216
British Union for the Abolition of Vivisection, Re 12.45
Briton Medical & General Life Assn., Re.. 6.78
Briton Medical & General Life Association v. Jones 9.112
Broadcasting Station 2GB Pty. Ltd., Re 9.64, 11.141
Brock District Council v. Bowen, Re.. 5.80
Brodeur Co. v. Merrill... 7.60, 7.80
Brodie, Re 8.304
Broken Hill South Ltd. v. Commissioner of Taxation 4.22
Brokx v. Tattoo Technology Inc. 13.30, 13.141
Bronson, Re 8.207
Brooks Steam Motors Ltd., Re... 11.109
Brothers of the Christian Schools (Canada), Re 4.40
Brown v. Alberta & Great Waterways Rlwy. 8.63
Brown v. Beleggings-Societeit N.V. 7.25
Brown v. Can-Erin Mines Ltd. 13.203, 13.211
Brown v. Cole 8.80
Brown v. L.A. Brown Ltd. (Trustee of) 11.180
Brown v. Maxim Restoration Ltd. 13.262, 13.267
Brown v. McLanahan... 12.104, 14.10
Brown v. Menzies Bay Timber Co. 13.196
Brown v. Moore 6.5, 6.15
Brown v. Shearer 9.120, 11.266
Brown v. Shyne... 11.28
Brown v. Tenney.. 13.241
Brown v. Weil... 8.332
Browne v. La Trinidad 12.58, 12.61, 12.78
Bruce (Township) v. Thornburn 13.249
Bruell, ex p. 6.112
Brumley v. Touche, Ross & Co. 9.196.7
Brunton v. Electrical Engineering Corp. 8.143
Bryant, Powis & Bryant Ltd. v. Quebec Bank... 6.98
Brydges v. Dominion Trust Co. 7.85
Brydon Marine Products Ltd. v. ITT Industries of Canada Ltd. 5.120
BSB Holdings Ltd. (No. 2), Re 11.59, 11.61, 13.37
Buchler v. Talbot 8.140
Buckley v. B.C.T.F. 13.29, 13.66, 13.149
Buckley v. British Columbia Teachers' Federation 15.70
Buckner v. Bourbon Farming Co. 15.53
Budd v. Gentra Inc. 1.1, 3.60, 11.291, 13.104
Buenos Ayres Great Southern Rlwy. Co., Re 7.321

Buff Pressed Brick Co. v. Ford 7.108
Buff Pressed Brick Co., Re 5.153, 7.88
Builders Supplies Ltd. v. Fraser 2.17
Bulawayo Market & Offices Co., Re 9.72
Bulkeley v. Schutz 14.221
Bull HN Information Systems Ltd. v. L.I. Business Solutions Inc. 13.69
Bulut v. City of Brampton 13.178
Bumper Development Corporation v. Comm. of Police of the Metropolis 4.19
Bumper's, The Beef House (Banff) Ltd. v. Alberta Registrar of Companies 5.111
Burdon v. Zellers Ltd. 14.158
Burland v. Earle 7.298, 7.325, 10.21, 10.51, 10.54, 11.155, 13.255
Burn v. London & South Wales Coal Co. 10.29
Burnett v. Tsang 13.32, 13.119, 13.123
Burns v. Ambler 7.107
Burnsland Ltd., Re 7.107
Burrows v. Becker 13.203
Burt v. The Irvine Co. 11.102
Burton v. Contributories of Home Assurance of Canada 15.145
Bury v. Bell Gouinlock Ltd. 13.57, 13.123
Bury v. Famatina Development Corp. 7.176
Bushell v. Faith 7.32, 9.106.9, 9.135, 12.211
Butler v. Manchester Sheffield & Lincolnshire Rlwy. Co. 3.3
Butterworth, Re 8.339
Byng v. London Life Association Ltd. 12.37, 12.86, 12.181, 14.24
Byrne v. Van Tienhoven 7.79

C

C Chemicals, Re 5.120
C. & H. Electric v. Robinson 5.196
C. & J. Enterprises (1971) Ltd. v. Curtis 14.134
C. Cole & Co., Re 5.34, 5.118
C. Evans & Sons Ltd. v. Spritebrand Ltd. 3.55
C.A. Fitzsimmons & Co. v. A.H. Fitzsimmons & Co. 5.96
C.C. Chemicals Ltd., Re 5.120, 5.123
C.C. Petroleum Ltd. v. Allen 13.178, 13.189
C.E. Plain Ltd. (Trustee of) v. Kenley 6.12, 6.25, 8.323, 11.6, 11.106
C.I. Covington Fund Inc. v. White 13.30, 13.38
C.I.R. v. Crossman 7.5
C.I.R. v. Duke of Westminster 2.31
C.L. McClain Fuel Corp. v. Lineinger 6.60
C.P.C. Valve & Investment, Ltd. v. Scott 5.159
C.P.H.C. Holding Co. v. Western Pacific Trust Co. 15.48, 15.128
C.P.R. v. Ottawa Fire Insurance Co. 4.25
C.P.R. v. Western Union Telegraph 4.24
C.S.M. v. Bell Telephone Co. of Canada 4.50
Cadbury Schweppes Inc. v. FBI Foods Ltd. 11.219
Cadillac Fairview Corp., Re 14.165

Cadwell's Ltd., Re 15.203
Cadwells Ltd. (Trustee of) v. Royal Bank of Canada 8.19
CAE Industries, R. v. 2.35
Cahall v. Lofland 10.114, 10.115
Cai v. Mo 13.59
Cairney v. Golden Key Holdings Ltd. 13.116, 13.220
Cairney v. MacQueen 4.60
Cairns v. Canadian Kennel Club 10.7
Caisse populaire de Notre Dame Ltée v. Moyen.. 4.14
Caldwells Ltd., Re.. 8.319
Caleron Properties Ltd. v. 510207 Alberta Ltd. 5.51, 13.260
Callander v. Eveline Holdings Ltd. 13.92
Calmont Leasing Ltd. v. Kredl................................. 11.116, 13.29, 13.73, 13.139
CALPERS v. Cooper 10.14
Calvin Church v. Logan 5.4, 5.160
Cambrian Peat, Fuel & Charcoal Co., De La Mott's & Turner's Cases, Re....... 14.24
Cambrian Peat, Fuel & Charcoal Co., Re 12.48, 12.49
Cameron Publications Ltd. v. Piers, Conrod & Allen 9.185
Camino Management Ltd. v. Manitoba (Securities Commission) 4.51
Campbell v. Australia Mutual Provident Society.. 12.76
Campbell v. Lanark (Village) 5.59
Campbell v. Loews Inc. 9.126
Campbell v. Morgan 4.46
Campbell v. Paddington Corp 3.6
Campbell v. Prudential Trust Co. 7.150
Campbell v. Taxicabs Verrals Ltd. 5.166
Campbell v. Vose... 14.43
Campbell-Bennett Ltd. v. Comstock Midwestern Ltd. 4.76
Camroux v. Amstrong.. 13.66
Canada (Attorney General) v. Central Cartage Co. 4.73
Canada (Attorney General) v. Confederation Life Insurance Co. 15.113
Canada (Attorney General) v. Continental Trust Co. (No. 2) 15.154
Canada (Attorney General) v. Grannell 10.40
Canada (Attorney General) v. Security Home Mortgage Corp. 15.69
Canada (Attorney General) v. Standard Trust Co. 13.78, 13.96
Canada (Canadian Human Rights Commission) v. Haynes........................... 4.50
Canada (Minister of National Revenue) v. Cameron 2.31
Canada (Minister of National Revenue) v. Connor....................................... 2.31
Canada (Minister of National Revenue) v. Leon 2.31
Canada (Minister of National Rlwys. & Canals) v. Quebec Southern
   Rlwy. Co. 8.274, 8.319
Canada (Minister of Rlwys. & Canals) v. Quebec Southern Rlwy. Co. 10.69
Canada (Privacy Commissioner) v. Canada (Labour Relations Board).......... 1.27
Canada Bonded Attorney and Legal Directory Ltd. v. Leonard-Parmiter
   Ltd. 10.40, 10.71, 11.151
Canada Bread Co., Re 14.246
Canada Business Corporations Act, Re................. 14.120, 14.131, 14.132, 14.227
Canada Campers Inc. v. British Columbia Registrar of Companies 5.87

Canada Car & Manufacturing Co. v. Harris.. 12.1
Canada Cement LaFarge Ltd. v. British Columbia Lightweight
    Aggregate Ltd. 11.245
Canada Cotton Ltd., Re... 14.249
Canada Deposit Insurance Corp. v. Canadian Commercial Bank...... 8.51, 13.178
Canada Deposit Insurance Corp. v. Commonwealth Trust Co. 15.71
Canada Food Co. v. Stanford.. 7.114
Canada Furniture Co. v. Banning.. 7.165, 10.73, 12.72
Canada Guaranty Trust Co. v. Young... 10.40
Canada Imperial Bank of Commerce v. Hallahan... 7.157
Canada Life Assurance Co. v. CIBC 2.39, 2.42
Canada Morning News Co. v. Thompson... 1.52
Canada Permanent Loan & Savings Co. v. Todd... 8.128
Canada Permanent v. B.C. Permanent 5.111
Canada Plastic Containers Ltd. v. Farkas... 11.48
Canada Safeway Ltd. v. Thompson 11.148
Canada Southern Railway Co. v. Gebhard.. 14.275
Canada Tea Co., Re 7.52, 7.327, 7.343
Canada Trust Co. v. Lloyd... 11.164, 15.176
Canada Trustco Mortgage Corp. v. Port O'Call Hotel Inc. 8.201
Canada v. Antosko... 1.26
Canada v. Fredericton Housing Ltd. 12.154
Canada v. Imperial General Properties Ltd. 8.11
Canada v. Quebec Southern Rlwy. 5.176
Canada West Loan Co. v. Virtue 7.154
Canadian Aero Service Ltd. v. O'Malley................... 6.69, 10.59, 11.118, 11.133,
    11.182, 11.187
Canadian Allis-Chalmers Ltd., R. v. 3.29
Canadian Bank of Commerce v. Martin... 15.125
Canadian Bank of Commerce v. Pioneer Farm Co. & Hall 6.73
Canadian Cereal & Flour Mills Co., Re.. 15.16
Canadian Civil Liberties Association v. Canada (Attorney General) 4.68
Canadian Commercial Bank v. Crawford, Smith & Swallow........................ 2.10
Canadian Commercial Bank v. Prudential Steel Ltd. 8.144, 13.99
Canadian Deposit Insurance Corp. v. Commonwealth Trust Co. 15.71, 15.80
Canadian Diamond Co. (Broad's Case), Re... 5.180
Canadian Dredge & Dock v. The Queen... 3.30
Canadian Druggists' Syndicate Ltd. v. Thompson... 7.85
Canadian Egg Marketing Agency v. Richardson 4.68
Canadian Express Ltd. v. Blair 12.118, 12.153
Canadian Film Development Corp. v. Perlmutter.. 2.9
Canadian Gas & Energy Fund Ltd. v. Sceptre Resources Ltd. 14.66
Canadian General Service Corp. (No. 2), Re 15.45
Canadian Guaranty Trust v. Young 10.42
Canadian Imperial Bank of Commerce v. Dene Mat Construction Ltd. 5.144
Canadian Imperial Bank of Commerce v. Flemming-Gibson Industries Ltd. 8.157
Canadian Imperial Bank of Commerce v. Fletcher.. 8.221
Canadian Imperial Bank of Commerce v. Graat.. 11.220

Canadian Imperial Bank of Commerce v. Grande Cache Motor Inn Ltd. 8.327
Canadian Imperial Bank of Commerce v. Ramsay 8.328
Canadian Imperial Bank of Commercial & Hallahan, Re........................... 7.157
Canadian Indemnity Co. v. A.G. British Columbia 4.60
Canadian Javelin Ltd. v. Boon Strachan Coal Co. 12.44
Canadian Javelin Ltd. v. Sparling 13.271
Canadian Jorex Ltd., Re... 7.59
Canadian Laboratory Supplies Ltd. v. Engelhard Industries of Canada
  Ltd. 6.42, 6.44, 6.79
Canadian Mail Orders Ltd., Re 7.80
Canadian McVicker Engine Co., Re... 7.87
Canadian Metals Exploration Ltd. v. Wiese 11.143
Canadian Motorways Ltd. v. Laidlaw Motorways Ltd. 5.123, 5.124
Canadian National Fire Insurance Co. v. Hutchings 1.56, 7.222
Canadian Newspapers Co. v. A.G. Canada.. 4.67
Canadian Ohio Motor Car Co. v. Cochran.. 7.88
Canadian Opera Co. v. 670800 Ontario Inc. 2.21, 13.66, 13.92
Canadian Pacific Ltd. v. R. 4.50
Canadian Pacific Ltd. v. Telesat Canada... 4.78
Canadian Pacific Ltd., Re 7.296, 7.332, 14.250
Canadian Pacific Railway Company v. Winnipeg (City)............................... 1.11
Canadian Pioneer Management Ltd. v. Saskatchewan
  (Labour Relations Board).. 4.39
Canadian Pittsburg Industries Ltd. v. Roberts & Hall Ltd. 8.19
Canadian Slate Products Ltd., Re.. 7.81
Canadian Tire Corp. v. C.T.C. Dealer Holdings Ltd. 9.123
Canadian Western Bank v. Alberta... 4.50
Canadian Western Millwork Ltd. (Trustee of) v. Royal Bank of Canada..... 8.215
Canadian Western Millwork Ltd. v. Royal Bank of Canada; Flintoft v.
  Royal Bank of Canada, Re 8.242
Canadian Woodmen of the World v. Hooper.. 9.175
Canal Capital Corp. v. French.. 10.114
Canbev Sales & Marketing Inc. v. Natco Trading Corp. 13.47
Cann v. Eakins 12.187
Cannaday v. McPherson 10.62
Cannaday v. Sun Peaks Resort Corp. 10.63
Canson Enterprises Ltd. v. Broughton & Co. 11.134.1, 11.195
Cantrade Sales & Import Co., Re... 5.84, 5.120, 5.123
Cape Breton Co., Re 5.175
Cape Breton Cold Storage Co. v. Rowlings.. 11.159
Capital Community Credit Union Ltd. v. BDO Dunwoody........................ 9.164
Capital Services Ltd., Re.. 15.41
Cappuccitti Potato Co., Re.. 15.61
Cappuccitti v. Bank of Montreal 12.43
Carapark Industries Pty. Ltd. (in. liq.) & the Companies Act, 1961
  (No. 1), Re... 15.41
Caratal (New) Mines Ltd., Re 12.114
Carbon Developments (Pty.) Ltd., Re... 8.291

Cardiff Savings Bank, Re.. 11.13, 11.29
Cardinal Health Inc., Re.. 10.173
Carecon Properties v. 510207 Alberta Ltd. 5.64
Caremark Inc. v. Coram Healthcare Corp. 7.97
Caremark International Inc. Derivative Litigation, Re............ 11.25, 11.39
Cargill v. Bower... 3.55
Carle v. Ranger 10.27
Carlen v. Drury 11.5, 13.199
Carleton Condominium Corp. No. 347 v. Trendsetter Developments Ltd. 10.4
Carlisle's Will, Re... 7.325
Carlton Realty Co. v. Maple Leaf Mills Ltd. 14.158
Carmody v. Toll Brothers, Inc. 10.14, 11.55
Carom v. Bre-X Minerals Ltd. 5.172
Carpenter Ltd., Re.. 9.113
Carr v. Cheng... 13.209
Carron Iron Co. v. Maclaren 6.110
Carruth v. Imperial Chemical Industries 12.129
Carson v. Carson... 6.18
Carson, Re.. 7.296
Cartaway Resources Corp., Re.. 11.37
Carter Dewar Crowe Co. v. Columbia Bitulithic 6.15
Carter v. Wake 8.210
Carton v. Bragg... 8.29
Cartwright v. Lyster... 7.212
Cashin v. The King 10.167
Casino Co., Re 15.136
Casper v. Kalt-Zimmers Mfg. Co. 5.65
Castleman v. Waghorn, Gwynn & Co. 7.208, 7.286
Casurina Limited Partnership v. Rio Algom Ltd. 8.171, 13.147
Caswell v. Jordan.. 11.124
Catalano v. Worrilow.. 10.173
Catalyst Fund General Partner Inc. v. Hollinger Inc. 4.70
Catalyst Fund General Partner I Inc. v. Hollinger
  Inc. 9.31, 9.122, 11.101, 13.267, 13.274
Caufield v. Sunland Biscuit Co. 12.121
Cavalier Oil Corp. v. Harnett... 14.81
Cavell Insurance Co., Re.. 14.274
Cavendish Bentinck v. Fenn 11.179
Cavendish Investing Ltd., Re... 7.294
Cayley v. Coburg, Peterborough & Marmora Rlwy. & Mining Co. 14.133
CBC Pension Plan v. BF Realty Holdings Ltd. 8.130, 8.166
CBI Holding Company Inc., Re.. 9.190.10
CBS Inc. v. Ames Records & Tapes Ltd. 11.218
CDIC v. CCB 7.10
Cede & Co. v. JRC Acquisition Corp. 14.75
Cede & Co. v. Technicolor, Inc. 11.24, 11.25, 14.74
Cedric Kushner Promotions Ltd. v. King................................. 3.52
Cement Products Ltd. v. Forget 7.54

Cement Stone & Building, Re.. 7.76
Cenco Inc. v. Seidman & Seidman 9.190.9
Central Alaska Broadcasting Inc. v. Bracale.. 9.9
Central Bank & Hogg, Re 7.198
Central Capital Corp., Re 7.16, 8.12, 8.14, 12.2, 13.172
Central Gas Utilities Ltd. v. Canadian Western Natural Gas Co. 11.135
Central Georgia Rlwy. Co. v. Central Trust of New York.......................... 8.197
Central Ontario Railway v. Trusts and Guarantee Co. Ltd. 4.76
Central Piggery Co. v. McNicholl & Hurst... 7.49
Central Trust Co. v. Phaseco Ltd. 8.144
Century Industries Ltd. v. Delta (Municipality) Approving Officer 5.59
Century Services Inc. v. ZI. Inc. 6.91
Cha v. 604459 Alberta Ltd. 7.75, 14.64
Chaff & Hay Acquisition Committee v. J.A. Hemphill & Sons Pty. Ltd. 4.19
Chaing v. Heppner 2.25
Chalie v. Duke of York... 8.29
Champagne Perrier-Jouet SA v. H.H. Finch Ltd. 8.7
Champlain Thickson Inc. v. 365 Bay New Holdings Ltd. 5.188, 5.191
Chan v. Zacharia 11.48, 11.177
Chapin v. Benwood Found... 10.113
Chaplin v. Young (No. 1)... 8.81
Charge Card Services Ltd., Re... 8.82
Charlebois v. Bienvenu.. 12.76, 13.203
Charles J. Wilson Ltd. & Nuform Investments Ltd., Re 13.262
Charles Osenton Co. v. Johnston 13.128
Charles P. Kinnell & Co. v. Harding, Wace & Co. 2.11
Charlottetown (City) v. Prince Edward Island... 4.68
Charnley Davies Ltd. (No. 2), Re 13.141
Chartac Small-Business Services Ltd. v. Chartacc Computer Services Inc. 5.87
Charter Oil Co. v. Beaumont 12.31, 12.62
Charterbridge Corp. v. Lloyds Bank Ltd. 11.5, 11.49, 11.68
Chas A. Day & Co. v. Booth... 12.72
Chatham National Bank v. Mabou Coal and Gypsum Co. (Liquidators of)..... 11.113
Chaudhry v. Prabhaker... 11.28
Cheah v. Equicorp Finance Group Ltd. 8.291
Checkovsky v. SEC 10.173
Chen Investments Australia Pty. Ltd. v. Gerrard Corp. of Australia Ltd. ... 12.114
Chenier v. Johnson.. 2.34
Cheong v. Noble China Inc. 12.85
Chequepoint Securities Ltd. v. Claremont Petroleum N.L. 12.77
Chernoff v. Parta Holdings Ltd. 13.72
Chestnut Corp. v. Pestine, Brinati, Gamer, Ltd. 9.190.7
Chetal Enterprises Ltd., Re 15.64
Chez Nico (Restaurants) Ltd., Re 11.22, 13.257
Chiaramonte v. World Wide Importing Ltd. 13.43, 13.136
Chicago Blower Corp. v. 141209 Canada Ltd. 13.19, 13.125
Chiips Inc. Skyview Hotels Ltd 8.287
Chilian v. Augdome Corp. 13.93

Chin Keow v. Government of Malaysia 15.114
China Software Corp. v. Leimbigler 11.178, 11.186
Chiu v. Universal Water Technology Inc. 13.106
Choi v. Sutton Group Central Realty Inc. 3.4
Choppington Collieries Ltd. v. Johnson 12.77, 12.144
Chow Yoong Hong v. Choong Fah Rubber Manufactory 8.7
Christchurch City Corp. v. Flamingo Coffee Lounge Ltd. 6.15
Christian Brothers of Ireland, Re 13, 178, 15.105, 15.107, 15.114
Christopher v. Noxon 11.161, 12.36, 12.91
Chugal Properties Ltd. v. Levine 6.60
Chung v. Chung 13.122
Church of Scientology, R. v. 3.24, 4.73
Churchill Pulpmill Ltd. v. Manitoba 13.206
Chytros v. Standard Life Assurance Co. 3.4
CIBC v. Cedar Hills Properties Ltd. 8.47, 8.49, 8.90
Cie d'immeubles v. St. Amour 7.156
Cie de villas du cap Gibraltar v. Hughes 6.12
Cina v. Ultratech Tool & Gauge Inc. 5.81
Cinapri v. Guettler 13.194, 13.198
Cinerama, Inc. v. Technicolor, Inc. 10.58, 11.35
Cira v. Rico Resources Inc. 6.107
Ciriello v. The Queen 15.109
CIT Financial ltd. v. 1153461 Ontario Inc. 11.235, 11.237
Citadel Industries, Inc., Re 15.157
Citibank Canada v. Chase Manhattan Bank of Canada 14.272
Citibank Canada v. Citicapital Financial Corp. 5.117
Citizens Coal & Forwarding Co., Re 15.61
Citizens Insurance Co. v. Parsons 4.40, 4.46, 4.48, 4.60
Citizens Life Assurance Co. Ltd. v. Brown 3.3
Citizens Savings & Loan Association v. Fischer 11.214
Citron v. E.I. DuPont De Nemours & Co. 14.193
City Branch Group Ltd., Gross v. Rackind, Re 13.37
City Equitable Fire Insurance Co.,
   Re 6.1, 9.183, 10.104, 10.108, 10.111, 10.134, 11.5, 11.13, 11.17, 11.28
City of Barrie v. 1606533 Ontario Inc. 6.52
City of Calgary v. Northland Properties 12.62
City of London, R. v. 15.151, 15.155
City of Toronto v. Consumers' Gas Co. 7.49
City of Toronto v. Toronto Electric Light Co. 14.89
City Parking Canada Ltd. v. Ontario (Min. of Revenue) 7.14
Citytrust v. Joy 13.209
C-L & Associates Inc. v. Airside Equipment Sales Inc. 13.30, 13.76
Clark v. Denton 5.64
Clark v. Supertest Petroleum Corp. 8.110
Clarke v. Rossburger 13.60
Clarke v. Sarnia Street Railway 6.15
Clarke v. Technical Marketing Associates Ltd. Estate 14.137
Clarke v. Union Fire Insurance 4.25, 7.86

Clarkson Co. v. Ace Lumber Ltd. 6.57
Clarkson Co. v. Zhelka 2.3, 2.11, 2.34, 2.43
Clarkson v. Davies 10.72, 11.192
Classic Hosiery Co. v. Fillis 5.48, 12.165
Classic Organ Co. v. Artisan Organ Co. 15.47, 15.67
Clay v. S.P. Powell & Co. 7.85
Clearwater Fine Foods Inc. v. FPI Ltd. 12.193
Cleary v. Brazil Rlwy. Co. 8.169
Clemens v. Clemens Brothers Ltd. 12.131
Clifton v. Ground Engineering Ltd. 10.69
Clippens Oil Co. v. Edinburgh & District Water Trustees 10.14, 12.169
Clough Mill Ltd. v. Martin 8.68
Clough v. London & N.W. Rlwy. 7.107, 7.118
Cloutier v. Dion 11.255
Clow Darling Ltd. v. 1013983 Ontario Inc. 5.206, 5.207
Club Flotilla (Pacific Palms) Ltd. v. Isherwood 10.37
Club Mediterranean Pty. Ltd., Re 15.41
CMS Dolphin Ltd. v. Simonet 11.180
CNR v. Ontario (Director, Environmental Protection Agency) 4.10
Coachman Tavern (1985) Ltd., Re 12.32
Coal Economising Gas Co. Gover's Case, Re 5.175
Coal Gate Oils Ltd. v. Western Petroleum (No. 2) 9.113
Coast Wholesale Appliances Ltd. v. Buffalo 2.25
Cody's Ltd. v. Chester Branch Canadian Legion 6.112
Cogeco Cable Inc. v. CFCF Inc. 14.43
Cohen v. Beneficial Industrial Loan Corp. 13.200
Cohen v. Jonco Holdings Ltd. 13.30, 13.43
Cohen-Herrendorf v. Army & Navy Department Store Holdings
  Ltd. 12.49, 12.211, 13.30, 13.157
Coin-A-Matic v. Coin Automat Washing Machine Corp. 5.107
Cokeman v. Myers 11.180
Colborne Capital Corp. v. 542775 Alberta
  Ltd. 7.204, 7.251, 11.44, 11.73, 12.206
Coleman Taymar Ltd. v. Oakes 11.151
Coleman v. Coleman 12.3
Coleman v. Myers 11.122, 11.192, 11.194, 13.231, 13.257
Coleman v. Toronto & Niagara Power Co. 6.24
Coliseum (Barrow) Ltd., Re 9.194
Collingwood Dry Dock, Ship Building & Foundry Co., Re 7.77
Collins v. Associated Greyhound Racecourses Ltd. 7.112
Collins v. Ontario (Pension Commission) 5.116
Colman v. Eastern Counties Rlwy. Co. 6.17
Colonial Assurance Co. v. Smith 5.57, 5.60, 7.268, 12.114, 12.153
Colonial Bank v. Cady 12.1
Colonial Bank v. Whinney 7.18, 7.21, 7.286
Colonial Building and Investment Association v. A.G. Quebec 4.17, 4.40
Colonial Investment Co. of Winnipeg, Re 15.200
Colonial Trust Corp., ex p. Bradshaw, Re 8.146

Colonist Printing & Publishing Co. v. Dunsmuir.. 12.35
Colorado Constructions Pty. Ltd. v. Platus 12.83
Columbia Bitulithic Co. v. Vancouver Lumber Co. 6.13
Columbia Gypsum Co., Re 15.55
Columbia Mgmt. Co. v. Wyss... 14.80
Columbus Ave. Realty Trust, Re 13.185
Comeau's Sea Foods Ltd. v. Canada (Minister of Fisheries and Oceans) 7.157
Commcorp Financial Services Inc. v. Mark & Kellog Enterprises Ltd. 14.136
Commerce Capital Mortgage Corp. v. Jemmet.. 8.329
Commercial Agencies Ltd., Re 15.45
Commercial Credit Corp. v. Niagara Finance Co. Ltd. 3.3
Commercial Management Ltd. v. Registrar of Companies............................ 9.65
Commission de transport de la communauté urbaine de Québec v. Canada
   (Commission des champs de bataille nationaux) 4.46
Commission v. Seifert... 6.16
Commissioner for Corporate Affairs v. Peter William Harvey................... 15.114
Commissioners of Inland Revenue v. Bew Estates Ltd. 1.58
Commissioners of Inland Revenue v. Sansom... 2.42
Common v. Matt.. 7.80
Common v. McArthur.. 7.154, 7.255
Commonwealth Homes & Investment Co. v. Smith 7.148
Commonwealth Investors Syndicate Ltd. v. KPMG Inc. ..15.102, 15.110, 15.113
Commonwealth Investors Syndicate Ltd., Re... 15.199
Commonwealth Savings Plan Ltd. (Trustee of) v. Commonwealth Trust
   (Bahamas) Ltd. (Trustee of)... 11.180
Commonwealth Trust Co. v. Canada Deposit Insurance
   Corp. 13.206, 13.209, 13.238
Communities Economic Development Fund v. Canadian Pickles Corp. 6.16
Compaction Systems Pty. Ltd., Re... 12. 81
Compagnie de Mayville v. Whitley 10.2
Compagnie de Villas du Cap Gibraltar v. Hughes 11.247, 11.253
Compania Merabello San Nicholas SA, Re 15.79
Compaq Computer Ltd. v. Abercorn Group Ltd. 8.68
Compro Ltd., Re 5.120
Conant v. Miall.. 8.27
Condec Corp. v. Lunkenheimer Co. 7.57
Condotrust Realty Investments Inc. v. 983177 Ontario Inc. 15.46
Cone v. Russell & Mason 10.17
Confectionately Yours Inc., Re... 15.86
Confederation Land Corp. v. Canadian Pacific Rlwy. 15.154
Con-Force Products Ltd. v. Rosen... 5.171
Connecticut & Passumpsic River Rlwy. v. Comstock 7.77
Connecticut General Life Ins. Co. v. Johnson...................................... 1.49, 6.22
Connolly v. Montreal Park & Island Rlwy. 8.32, 8.271
Connolly v. Rudderham.. 11.117
Consolidated Enfield Corp. v. Blair.........................9.146, 12.87, 12.90, 13.267
Consolidated Fastfrate Transport Inc., R. v. 2.46
Consolidated Investments Ltd., Re 7.120

Constitution Insurance Co. of Canada v. Kosmopoulos 2.12, 2.61
Construction Montcalm Inc. v. Minimum Wage Commission 4.5, 4.39, 4.50
Consul-Pak Inc. v. Cheeseman 5.120
Consumers' Coal Co., Re 15.44
Consumers' Cordage Co. v. Molson 7.85
Continental Bank Leasing Corp. v. Canada 6.16
Continental Illinois Securities Litigation 13.209
Continental Salvage Corp., R. v. 4.47
Contract Corporation (Gooch's Case), Re 15.113
Contract Group, Re 8.50
Contributories of Home Assurance Co. v. Burton 12.1
Convert-A-Wall Ltd. v. Brampton Hydro-Electric Commission 8.36
Conway v. Petronias Clothing Co. 10.29
Cook v. Deeks 10.54, 11.155, 11.166, 12.126, 12.128, 13.202, 13.203
Cook v. Hinds 10.70
Cook, R. v. 1.36
Cook's Ferry Band v. Cook's Ferry Band Council 4.76
Coombs v. Dynasty Pty Ltd. 13.134
Cooper v. Cayzor Athabasca Mines Ltd. 12.1, 12.7
Cooper v. Gordon 13.6
Cooper v. Hobart 9.190.5
Cooper v. McIndoe 4.47
Cooper v. The Premier Trust Co. 12.184, 12.185
Coopérants, Mutual Life Insurance Society (Liquidator of) v.
    Dubois 15.80, 15.92
Co-operative Cycle & Motor Co., Re 7.170, 7.181, 7.185
Coopers & Lybrand v. Ford Credit Canada Ltd. 6.63
Coopers & Lybrand v. H.E. Kane Agencies Ltd. 9.185
Coopers & Lybrand v. National Caterers Ltd. 8.146
Cope v. Price Waterhouse 9.190.8
Corkery v. Foster Wedekind 5.128
Corkum v. Lohnes 5.196, 5.206, 5.207
Cornish Silver Mining Co. v. Bull 5.72
Coro (Canada) Inc., Re 8.207
Corona Minerals Corp. v. CSA Management Ltd. 14.147
Corp. de placement Renaud Inc. v. Nor Mix Ltée 7.222
Corpique (No. 20) Pty. Ltd. v. Eastcourt Ltd. 12.85
Corporacion Americana de Equipamientos Urbanos S.L. v. Olifas Marketing
    Group Inc. 11.27, 13.112
Cosslett (Contractors) Ltd., Re 8.67, 8.136, 8.138
Coté v. Lake St. John Distributing Co. 5.144
Coté v. Stadacona Insurance Co. 12.20
Cotman v. Brougham 5.159, 6.15, 6.56
Cottell v. Stratton 8.168
Cotton v. Imperial and Foreign Agency & Investment Corp. ... 14.41
Coulton v. Slaugher 13.81
Country Club of Montreal v. Bell Telephone Co. 6.77
Country Ltd. v. Gironsentrale Securities 7.89

Country Traders Distributors Ltd., Re 15.92, 15.109, 15.188
County Life Assurance Co., Re 6.44, 6.82
County Palatine Loan and Discount Co., Re 10.81
Courchêne v. Cie du parc Viger 12.121
Coutu v. San Jose Mines Ltd. 10.21, 15.50
Coveney v. Glendenning 11.209, 11.267
Covia Canada Partnership Corp. v. PWA Corp. 13.218
Cowan v. Scargill 11.10, 11.105
Cowichan Native Heritage Society v. Toronto Dominion Bank 8.204
Cowie v. Baguley 7.166
Cox Communications Inc., Re 14.194, 14.196
Crabtree (Succession de) v. Barrette 2.30
Crabtree-Vickers Pty. Ltd. v. Australian Direct Mail Advertising &
  Addressing Co. Pty. Ltd. 6.43
Craig v. North Shore Heli Logging Ltd. 3.55, 11.219
Craik v. Aetna Life Insurance Co. of Canada 11.207
Cramer v. Bird 11.92
Cramp Steel Co., Re 15.200
Cravo Equipment Ltd., Re 15.64
Crawford v. Bathurst Land & Development Co. 7.342
Creasey v. Breachwood Motors Ltd. 2.29
Crédit foncier franco-canadien v. C.S.W. Enterprises Ltd. 13.121
Credit Suisse Canada v. 1133 Yonge Street Holdings 8.160, 8.201
Cree v. Somervail 7.255
Creighton Enterprises Ltd. v. Creighton Holdings Ltd. 13.192
Crescent/Mach I Partners, L.P. v. Turner 13.230
Crew v. Dallas 11.271
Crichton's Oil Co., Re 7.321
Crighton v. Roman 10.41
Criterion Properties plc v. Stratford UK Properties LLC 7.59
Croatian Peasant Party of Ontario, Canada v. Zorkin 12.44
Crocker Press Ltd. v. Imperial Trust Co. 8.25
Crocker v. Waltham Watch Co. 7.325
Crockett v. Academy of Music 7.322
Crombie v. Young 8.331
Crompton & Co., Re 8.146
Cross v. Aurora Group Ltd. 14.32
Crossgrove v. Crossgrove 15.63, 15.64
Crossmore Electrical and Civil Engineering Ltd., Re 13.113
Crown Bank, Re 6.15, 15.54
Crown Diamond Paint Co., R. v. 3.9
Crown Lumber Co., Re 5.35
Crown Reserve Consolidated Mines Ltd. v. MacKay 11.177
Crown Trust Co. v. Ontario 13.204, 13.242
Crown Trust Co. v. Rosenberg 15.106
Csak v. Aumon 13.65, 13.66
CTS Corp. v. Dynamics Corp. of America 15.12
CTS Truss, Inc. v. FDIC 13.185

CTS Truss, Inc., Re 13.189
Cuff & Thomson Ltd., Re 5.110
Cuff v. London & County Land and Bldg. Co. Ltd. 9.166
Cullen v. Corporate Affairs Commission 6.69
Cumana Ltd., Re 13.18, 13.157
Currie v. Harris Lithographing Co. 4.23
Curtain Dream plc., Re 8.170
Curtis v. Nevins 13.219, 13.221
Cusack v. Southern Loans & Savings Co. 8.273
Cushing v. Dupuy 4.5
Cuthbert v. Roberts, Lubbock & Co. 8.7
Cutts v. Head 14.73
Cuttwell v. Lee 7.169
CW Shareholdings Inc. v. WIC Western International Communications
    Ltd. 10.52, 11.56, 11.64, 13.27, 14.147
CW Shareholdings Inc., Re 11.56
Cyprus Anvil Mining Corp. v. Dickson 13.135, 14.64, 14.66

D

D & D Holdings, Re 15.67
D. & H. Holdings Ltd. v. Trinity Placentia Mall Ltd. 13.206
D. Investments Ltd. v. Saskatchewan Business Corporations Branch 5.116, 5.119
D.R. Chemicals Ltd., Re 13.157
D'Addario v. Environmental Management Solutions Inc. 12.160, 13.263
D'Amore v. McDonald 11.178, 12.11, 13.203
D'Ivry v. World Newspaper Co. 3.27
D'Jan of London Ltd., Re 11.296
Daimler Co. v. Continental Tyre & Rubber Co. (Great Britain)
    Ltd. 2.45, 6.106, 6.109, 7.195, 10.36
Daimler Motor Car Co. v. British Motor Traction Co. 5.112
Dairy Containers Ltd. v. N.Z. Bank Ltd. 10.95, 11.141
Dairy Corp. of Canada Ltd., Re 12.152, 14.242, 14.245, 14.246
Dale & Plant Ltd., Re 2.14
Dalex Mines Ltd. (N.P.L.) v. Schmidt 12.42, 12.144
Dalhousie Lumber Co. v. Walker 5.144
Dallas & Briks v. Dallas Oil Co. & Webster 7.210
Dana v. McLean 8.340
Dancey v. 229281 Alberta Ltd. 13.99
Daniel v. Dow Jones & Co., Inc. 9.190.7
Daniel v. Gold Hill Mining Co. 6.23, 11.159
Daniels v. Daniels 12.32, 13.232
Daniels v. Fielder 13.83, 13.120, 13.122
Daniels v. Noxon 12.13
Danish Mercantile Co. Ltd. v. Beaumont 6.87
Daon Development Corp., Re 7.313, 13.72
Darby, ex p. Brougham, Re 2.32
Darrah v. Wright 11.261

Dartford Union Guardians v. Trickett 5.150
Dartmouth College v. Woodward 1.2, 1.36
Darvall v. North Sydney Brick & Tile Co. ...10.33, 11.56, 11.74, 11.112, 11.122
Dashney v. McKinlay 13.33
Dassen Gold Resources Ltd. v. Royal Bank 6.12, 6.17, 6.20
Data Business Forms Ltd. v. MacIntosh 5.206
Davey & Co. v. Williamson & Sons 8.146
Davey v. Gibson 11.272, 15.41
David Payne & Co., Re 3.11, 6.56
Davidson v. Brooker 7.208
Davidson v. Grange 9.97
Davis v. Jones 7.86
Davis v. Keilsohn Offset Co. 10.29
Davis v. Louisville Gas & Electric Co. 11.5
Davison v. Douglas 8.339
Davison v. Priest 7.102
Davrose Holdings Ltd. v. Phoenix Leasing Ltd. 2.28
Dawson International plc v. Coats Patons plc 3.14, 12.76, 13.231
Day v. Ogdensburg & Lake Champlain Railroad Co. 8.197
Daymond Motors Ltd. v. Thistletown Developments Ltd. 5.206
DC Foods (2001) Inc. v. Planway Poultry Inc. 5.82, 5.206
DCD Industries (1995) Ltd., Re 8.287
DCF Systems Ltd. v. Gellman 11.120, 11.152
De Jetley Marks v. Lord Greenwood 11.242
de la Giroday v. Giroday Sawmills Ltd. 13.26, 13.149
Deacon v. Kemp Manure Spreader 7.32
Dealers Finance Corp. v. Masterson Motors 8.128
Dean v. John Menzies (Holdings) Ltd. 3.43
Dean-Willcocks v. Soluble Solution Hydroponics Pty Ltd. 14.238
DeBeers Consolidated Mines Ltd. v. Howe 1.149, 6.114
Deep v. M.D. Management 11.15, 11.194
Deering v. Hyndman 8.293
Degelder Construction Co. v. Dancorp Developments Ltd. 8.44
Deguise v. Lesage 9.120, 9.121
Deloitte & Touche Inc. v. 1035839 Ontario Inc. 8.88
Delrina Corp. v. Triolet Systems Inc. 11.175
Deluce Holdings Inc. v. Air Canada 11.139, 13.95
Denault v. Stewart, Denault & Co. 5.52, 5.58
Denham & Co., Re 10.116, 11.29
Denischuk v. Bonn Energy Corp. 14.54, 14.70
Denison Mines Ltd. and Ontario Securities Commission, Re 9.195
Denison Mines Ltd. v. Minister of National Revenue 1.43
Denison v. Leslie 7.162
Denison v. Smith 7.76
Denman Street Restaurant Corp., Re 14.132
Denman v. Clover Bar Coal Co. 10.40, 10.42, 10.69
Dennis Willcox Pty. Ltd. v. FCT 2.34
Denver & R.G.W. Rlwy. Co., Re 8.127

Deptuck v. The Queen 3.15
Deputy Federal Commissioner of Taxation v. Status Constructions Pty. Ltd. ... 15.41
Derbach v. Shaw 11.273
Derry v. Peek 7.114
Desbiens v. Mordini... 1.26
Design House Assoc. v. Ravin.. 5.192, 5.193
Deslaurier, R. v. 2.61
Deutsche Bank of Canada v. Oxford Properties Group Inc. 7.238, 13.152
Deutsche Genossenschaftsbank v. Burnhope............................. 1.27, 1.49, 3.40
DeVall v. Wainwright Gas Co. 7.319
Deveraux Holdings Pty. Ltd. v. Pelsart Resources N.L. 12.63
DeVigier v. IRC 8.7
Devlin v. Slough Estates Ltd. 13.232
Devries v. Royal Bank of Canada.. 8.219
Devry v. Atwood's Furniture Showrooms Ltd. 13.76
Dewey & O'Heir Co., Re... 15.65
DeWitt Truck Brokers v. W. Ray Flemming Fruit Co. 2.27, 2.35
DeWitt v. M.N.R. 9.61
Dex Resources Ltd. v. Alberta Registrar of Corporations 5.123
DFS Ventures Inc. v. Manitoba (Liquor Control Commission).................... 4.50
Dhanjoon v. Unicity Taxi Ltd. 13.62
Dhillon v. Bonny's Taxi Ltd. 9.60
DHN Food Distributors Ltd. v. Tower Hamlets London Borough Council.... 2.11
Diamond Dog Management Inc. v. DMM Biehn Holdings Ltd. 6.18
Diamond Fuel Co., Re... 15.92
Dibble v. Wilts & Somerset Farmers Ltd. 7.196, 7.236
Dickson Co. v. Graham... 6.63
Dickson v. McMurray... 12.37, 12.115
Dicore Resources Ltd. v. Goldstream Resources Ltd. 13.99
Diehl v. Carritt 14.264
Digex Inc. Shareholders Litigation, Re.. 11.12
Diligenti v. RWMD Operations Kelowna Ltd. 9.62, 13.22, 13.82, 13.101, 13.123
Dimbleby & Sons Ltd. v. National Union of Journalists 2.28, 2.30
Dimbula Valley (Ceylon) Tea Co. v. Laurie 7.310, 7.311
Dimes v. Grand Junction Canal Proprietors... 2.45
Dimo Holdings Ltd. v. H. Jager Developments Inc. 10.42
Director General of Fair Trading v. Pioneer Concrete (U.K.) Ltd. 3.18
DiRisio v. DeLorenzo 15.67
Discount & Loan Corp. of Canada v. Canada (Superintendent of
    Insurance).. 2.3, 2.17
Discoverers Finance Corp., Re... 7.221
Discovery Enterprises Inc. v. Ebco Industries Ltd. 13.236, 13.244
Discovery Enterprises Inc. v. ISE Research Ltd. 12.185
Discovery Enterprises v. Hong Kong Bank of Canada............................. 8.221
Distribulite Ltd. v. Toronto Board of Education Staff Credit Union Ltd. .. 10.133
Dixon v. Deacon Morgan McEwan Easson 3.13
DNH Food Distributors Ltd. v. Tower Hamlets London Borough Council.... 2.67
Dobie v. Temporalities Board 4.61

Doctor v. People's Trust Co. 6.46
Dodge v. Ford Motor Co. 7.325, 11.5, 11.97
Dohme v. Pacific Coast.. 7.323
Doiron v. Caisse populaire d'Inkerman Ltée 11.217
Doloswella Rubber & Tea Estates Ltd., Re 7.276
Domanski v. Wilson... 11.271
Dome Oil Co. v. Alberta Drilling Co. 6.20
Domglas Inc. v. Jarislowsky Fraser & Co. 14.66, 14.70
Dominion Bank v. Cowan.. 8.339
Dominion Bridge Co. v. R. 2.35
Dominion Combing Mills Ltd., Re (1928)... 7.209
Dominion Combing Mills Ltd., Re (1930).. 7.170
Dominion Cotton Mills Co. v. Amyot 6.5, 6.13
Dominion Creosoting Co. v. T.R. Nickson Co., ... 8.20
Dominion Distillery Products Co. v. Canada.. 15.156
Dominion Fire Brick & Clay Products Ltd. v. Pollock................................. 6.63
Dominion High-Rise Ltd. v. Night-Hawk Cleaning & Supply Co. 11.133
Dominion Marble Co., Re... 4.40, 8.20, 7.76
Dominion Permanent Loan Co., Re.. 7.162
Dominion Radiator v. Steel Co. of Canada.. 7.118
Dominion Royalty Corp. v. Goffatt 2.34, 5.176, 5.180, 11.128, 11.171
Dominion Salvage & Wrecking Co. v. Canada (Attorney General) 15.155
Dominion Shipbuilding & Repair Co., Re 15.44
Dominion Steel & Coal Corp., R. v. 3.29
Dominion Steel Corp., Re... 15.46
Dominion Textile Co. v. MNR 7.166
Dominion Trust Co. v. Boyce; Dominion Trust Co., Re........................... 15.51
Don King Productions Inc. v. Warren (No. 2) 8.73
Donahue v. Rodd Electrotype Co. of New England Inc. 7.325, 7.333, 13.5
Donald v. Suckling... 8.210
Donly v. Holmwood.. 9.18
Donnelly v. Steward.. 12.209
Donohue v. Hull Brothers & Co. 8.326, 8.330
Dorchester Electric Co. v. Thompson 8.161
Dorchester Finance Co. v. Stebbing....................................... 11.8, 11.32, 11.296
Dorman, Long & Co., Re.. 14.245
Douglas v. Maritime United Farmers Co-op Ltd. 8.23
Dovey v. Cory.. 7.310, 10.119
Downtown Eatery (1993) Ltd. v. Ontario 2.65
Doyle v. Blake 8.168
Doyle v. Canada (Restrictive Trade Practices Commission) 4.39
Doyle v. Smith 7.314
DPC Estates Pty. Ltd. v. Grey.. 6.69
DPP v. Kent and Sussex Contractors Ltd. 2.32, 3.29, 3.43
Drabinsky v. KPMG 11.132
Drax, Re.. 8.34
Dreyfus v. Commissioners of Inland Revenue... 4.19
Driedger v. Schmidt... 8.128

Drive-in Development Corp., Re 6.85
Druckerman v. Harbord 13.243
Dryco Building Supplies Inc. v. Wasylishyn 5.203, 15.159
Dublin City Distillery Ltd. v. Doherty 8.204
Duck v. Tower Galvanizing 6.68
Dudnik (No. 1) v. York Condominium Corp No. 216 .... 9.14
Duff v. S.S. Overdale Co. 9.58
Duffy v. Super Centre Development Corp. 15.117
Dufour v. Dufour-Wilson Motors Ltd. 10.70
Duha Printers (Western) Ltd. v. Canada 3.65, 12.207
Duke of Portland v. Lady Topham 11.160
Duke v. Andler 15.172
DuMart Packing Co. v. DuMart 9.114, 10.36
Duncan & Gray Ltd. (Liquidator of) v. Silver Spring Brewery 15.17
Duncan Gilmour & Co. Ltd., Re 5.51
Duncan v. Duncan 7.22
Dundas (Town) v. Desjardins Canal Co. 8.79, 8.87
Dunham and Apollo Tours (No. 1), Re 7.182
Dunham v. Apollo Tours Ltd. 7.163
Dunham v. Apollo Tours Ltd. (No. 1) 7.153
Dunham v. Apollo Tours Ltd. (No. 2) 15.61
Dunham, Re 8.304
Dunlop Pneumatic Tyre Co. v. Dunlop Motor Co. 5.96
Dunlop v. Woollahra Municipal Council 15.123
Dunne v. Quebec (Sous-Ministre du Revenu) 4.22
Dunsmuir v. Colonist Printing & Publishing Co. 9.16
Dunston v. Imperial Light & Coke Co. 1.32
Dunwoody Ltd. v. 358074 Ontario Ltd. 15.65
Duomatic Ltd., Re 12.36
Dupont v. Taronga Holdings Ltd. 4.20
Dusik v. Newton 11.192, 11.203, 12.123
Dyck v. Sweeprite Manufacturing Inc. 5.69

E

E D White Ltd., Re 14.232
E L Management Incorporated, Re 14.322
E.B. v. Order of the Oblates of Mary Immaculate in the Province of
    British Columbia 3.3
E.B.M. Co. v. Dominion Bank 2.8, 2.11, 2.34
E.H. McGuire & E.H.J. Forester Ltd. v. Cadzow 12.63
E.K. Buck Retail Stores v. Harkert 10.19, 13.197
E.W. Savory Ltd., Re 7.43
Eagle Insurance Co., ex. p. 6.56
East Anglian Rlwys. v. Eastern Counties Rlwy. Co. 6.13
East Chilliwack Agricultural Cooperative, Re 7.11, 8.11
East v. Bennett Bros. 12.36, 12.49
East West Promotions Pty Ltd., Re 13.7

Eastern & Chartered Trust Co. v. Leland Publishing Ltd. 8.153
Eastern Archipelago Co. v. The Queen.. 15.155
Eastern Canada Coal Gas Venture Ltd. v. Cape Breton Development
 Corp. 10.26, 10.35
Eastern Counties Rlwy. Co. v. Hawkes 6.13
Eastern Telegraph Co., Re 15.54
Eastern Trust Co. v. Cushing Sulphite Fibre Co. 8.30, 8.87
Eastern Union Rlwy. v. Cochrane.. 14.136
Eastview (Town) v. Roman Catholic Episcopal Corp. of Ottawa............... 5.150
Eau Claire Sawmills Ltd., Re... 14.240
Eaves v. Hickson.. 11.204
EBC I Inc. v. Goldman Sachs & Co. 11.116
EBM Co. v. Dominion Bank.. 5.163
Ebrahimi v. Westbourne Galleries Ltd. 13.18, 13.26, 13.149, 15.58, 15.66
Ebsco Investments Ltd. v. Ebsco Subscription Services Ltd. 5.87
Ebsworth & Tidy's Contract, Re...15.92, 15.188
Ed Miller Sales & Rentals Ltd. v. Caterpillar Tractor Co. 11.238
Eddystone Marine Insurance Co., Re... 7.161
Edelman v. Phillips Petroleum Co. 11.55
Edelstein v. Schuler & Co. 8.263
Edelweiss Credit Union and Cobbett, Re..11.192, 15.80
Eden v. Ridsdale's Rlwy. Lamp and Lighting Co. 9.79
Edgar v. MITE Corp. 15.12
Edgington v. Fitzmaurice.. 7.76, 7.101, 7.103
Edman v. Ross 10.29
Edmonds v. Blaina Furnaces Co. 8.130
Edmonton Country Club Ltd. v. Case.. 7.196, 7.236
Edmonton Journal v. Alberta (Attorney General).. 4.73
Edmonton Telephones Corp. v. Monette 5.28
Edward Nelson & Co. v. Faber & Co. 8.146
Edwards v. Blackmore 6.1, 6.11
Edwards v. Carter... 7.197
Edwards v. Edwards Dockrill Horwich Inc. 13.117, 14.68
Edwards v. Halliwell...13.199, 13.255, 13.257
Edwards v. Law Society of Upper Canada 9.190.5
Egyptian International Foreign Trade Co. v. Soplex Wholesale Supplies Ltd.
 (The Raffaella)... 6.62
Egyptian Salt & Soda Co. Ltd. v. Port Said Salt Association Ltd. 6.5
Einhorn v. Westmount Investments Ltd. 11.237
Eiserman v. Ara Farms Ltd. 13.89, 13.123
El Ajou v. Dollar Land Holdings plc 3.11
El Sombrero Ltd., Re 12.44
Elan Development Ltd., R. v. 4.73
Elar Construction Ltd., Re 15.203
Elcano Acceptance Ltd. v. Richmond, Richmond, Stambler & Mills......... 8.46
Elder v. Elder & Watson Ltd. 13.24
Electrical Contractors Assn., R. v. 3.42

Electrical, Electronic, Telecommunications & Plumbing Union v. Times
  Newspapers Ltd. 1.58
Electrohome Ltd., Re 14.47
Electromobile Co. v. British Electromobile Co. 5.112
Elgindata Ltd., Re 13.57, 13.160
Elliot v. Baker 11.106
Elliot v. Hatzic Prairie Ltd. 12.16
Elliott v. Expansion of Trade, Ltd. 5.112
Elliott v. Opticom Technologies Inc. 13.25, 13.30
Elms v. Laurentian Bank of Canada 5.172
Elrae Estates Ltd. v. P.J. Industries 8.152
ELS Ltd., Re 8.145
Embree v. Miller 12.10
Emco Ltd. v. Union Insurance Society of Canton Ltd. 11.124
Emerald Partners v. Berlin 11.199
Emergent Capital Inv. Mgmt., LLC v. Stonepath Group, Inc. 7.97
Emerging Communications, Inc. Shareholders' Litigation, Re 114.75
Emerson v. New Brunswick (Provincial Secretary-Treasurer) 5.33
Emerson v. New Brunswick (Secretary-Treasurer) 1.56
Emma Silver Mining Co. v. Lewis & Son 5.171, 5.172, 5.176
Emmadart Ltd., Re 10.24
Empire Timber, Lumber & Tie Co., Re 15.200
Empress Engineering Co., Re 5.183, 5.186
Encana Corp. v. Douglas 12.172
English & Scottish Mercantile Investment Co. v. Brunton 6.32, 8.115
English v. Sylvan Lands Development Corp. 13.81
Enterprise Gold Mines N.L., Re 13.108
Enterprises A.B. Rimouski v. Canada 1.32
Enterprises Payment Solutions Inc. v. Soft Tracks Enterprises Ltd. 14.67
Envirodrive Inc. v. 836442 Alberta Ltd. 11.302, 13.30, 13.98
Equitable Tr. Co. v. Prentice 7.335
Erlanger v. New Sombrero Phosphate Co. 5.176, 5.177, 5.181
Ernest v. Nicholls 6.32
Esam Construction Ltd., R. v. 2.3
Esberger & Son Ltd. v. Capital & Counties Bank 8.82
Escott v. Bar Chris Construction Corp. 7.116, 7.127
Esheleman v. Keena 7.301
Esley's Frosted Foods Ltd. v. Mid White Oak Square Ltd. 7.222
Espirit Communications Inc., Re 5.113
ESS Production Ltd. v. Sully 1.25, 11.3
Essex Centre Manufacturing Co., Re 15.17
Essex Provision Co., Re 12.7
Esskay Farms Ltd., R. v. 2.31
Esso Standard (Inter-America) Inc. v. J.W. Enterprises Ltd. 4.39
Estate of Mixon v. U.S. 7.13
Estates Investment Co., Re 7.106
Estmanco (Kilner House) Ltd. v. Greater London Council ... 12.131, 13.232
Estonian State Cargo & Passenger Steamship Line v. S.S. Elise ... 15.169

Estrabrooks Pontiac Buick Ltd., Re 1.25
Ethical Funds Inc. v. Mackenzie Financial Corp. 5.119
Etna Foods of Windsor Ltd. v. Caradonna 13.106
Euroclean Canada Inc. v. Forest Glade Investments Ltd. 8.287
European & North American Railway v. McLeod 7.18, 7.75
European Bank, Re 7.204
European Life Assurance Society, Re 15.52
Evans v. Bartlam 11.304
Evans v. Rival Granite Quarries Ltd. 8.140, 8.141, 8.146
Evenden v. Standard Art Manufacturing Co. 8.60
Evening Standard Co. Ltd., R. v. 3.27
Everfresh Beverages Inc., Re 14.147
Evetts v. Evetts 2.46
Evling v. Israel & Oppenheimer Ltd. 7.319
Ex p. Belchier 10.108
Ex p. Bevan 8.29
Exchange Banking Co., Re 7.310
Exco Corp. v. Nova Scotia Savings & Loan
    Co. 11.48, 11.62, 11.63, 11.11, 11.125, 12.86
Executive Life Ins. Co., Re 15.129
Exeter & Crediton Railway Co. v. Buller 12.33
Exide Canada Inc. v. Hilts 11.128
Export Brewing & Malting Co. v. Dominion Bank 6.11, 11.6, 11.48, 11.218
Express Engineering Works Ltd., Re 8.23, 12.36, 12.60
Ezekiel Ray v. Homewood Hospital, Inc. 10.18

F

F. Dalkeith Investments Pty Ltd., Re 13.23
F. deJong & Co., Re 7.43
F. Goldsmith (Sicklesmere) Ltd. v. Baxter 5.72
F. Pinet & Cie v. Maison Louis Pinet Ltd. 5.96
F. Stacey & Co. Ltd. v. Wallis 5.145
F.D.I.C. as receiver for Buena Vista Bank & Trust Company v. American
    Casualty Co. of Reading 15.103
F.P. Chapple Co., Re 5.112
F.R. Diesel Electric Co. v. Farkas 11.164
Fabian v. Bud Mervyn Construction Ltd. 3.4
Fabricators, Inc. v. Technical Fabricators, Inc. 13.185
Faehndrich Petition, Re 12.3
Fahlman v. Independent Northern Laboratories Ltd. 11.271
Fairhall v. White Star Refining Co. (1927) 7.298, 7.325
Fairhall v. White Star Refining Co. (1928) 7.321, 7.328
Fairline Shipping Corp. v. Adamson 11.210, 11.230
Famatina Development Corp., Re 11.300
Famous Players Canadian Corp. v. Hamilton United Theatres Ltd. 12.47
Fan Flame Spark Plug Co. v. Morin 12.10
Fane Robinson Ltd., R. v. 3.29

Fanshawe v. Amav Industries Ltd. 8.141
Farmers Bank v. Sunstrum.. 7.77
Farmers Mutual Hail Insurance Association of Iowa v. Whittaker................. 4.25
Farmers Packing Co. v. Tully 7.76, 7.81, 7.83
Farmers' Loan & Savings Co., Re 8.18, 8.130
Farnham v. Fingold.. 13.206
Farquharson Bros. & Co. v. C. King & Co. 6.49, 6.81
Farrell v. Caribou Gold Mining Co. 8.18
Farrow's Bank Ltd., Re.. 15.21, 15.92
Farvolden v. Algorithmics Inc. 12.60
Faure Electric Accumulator Co., Re 9.23
FCMI Financial Corporation v. Curtis International Ltd. 5.12
Federal Bank of Australia Ltd., Re 15.133
Federal Business Development Bank v. Belyea.. 15.90
Federal Business Development Bank v. Prince Albert Fashion Bin
 Ltd. 8.146, 8.154
Federal Election Comm. v. Beaumont 4.74
Fedoruk v. Fedoruk Holdings Ltd. 15.64
Fedsure International v. NSP Financial Services Group................................ 7.253
Fee v. Turner... 11.263
Feit v. Leasco Data Processing Corp. 7.127
Feld v. Glick 13.211
Feldbaum v. McCory 8.189
Fellowes v. Ottawa Gas Co. 8.32, 8.271
Ferguson v. Imax Systems Corp. ...7.297, 13.18, 13.23, 13.24, 13.27, 13.262, 13.271
Ferguson v. Lastewka 8.330
Ferguson v. Wilson 9.2
Fergusson v. Fyffe 8.30
Ferland v. Sun Life Assurance Co. 8.46
Fern Brand Waxes Ltd. v. Pearl.. 2.8, 11.48, 11.181
Ferrari Furniture Co. Pty. Ltd. & Cos. Act, Re.. 9.66
Feuchter v. Smolek 11.273
FFM Holdings Ltd. v. Lilydale Cooperative Ltd. 7.26
FG (Films) Ltd., Re... 2.45
Fiber Connections Inc. v. SVCM Capital Ltd. 12.209, 13.81
Fidelity Developments v. Northwest Territories (Chief of Resources)........... 2.10
Fidelity Investments International plc. v. Mytravel Group plc. 8.289
Fidelity Manufacturing & Research Co. v. Gulf Canada Resources Ltd. 7.319
Field v. Bachynski 12.103
Field v. Galloway... 7.162
Financial Corp., Goodson's Claim, Re 12.23.1
Financial Management Inc. v. Associated Financial Planners Ltd. 6.46
Fine Cotton Spinners & Doublers Assoc. Ltd. & John Cash & Sons Ltd. v.
 Harwood Cash & Co. 5.96
Finger's Will Trust, Re 15.164
Finnemore v. T. Underwood, Ltd. 9.25
Firbank's Executors v. Humphreys.. 6.100
Fire Valley Orchards Ltd. v. Sly 5.176, 5.180, 6.15, 6.20

Fireproof Doors Ltd., Re 10.7, 10.86
Firestone Tyre & Rubber Co. Ltd. v. Lewellin 2.34
First Alliance Mortgage Company, Re 11.7
First Bank & Trust Co. v. Zagoria 2.22
First City Capital Ltd. v. 105383 British Columbia Ltd. 6.66
First Edmonton Place Ltd. v. 315888 Alberta Ltd. ..13.66, 13.73, 13.204, 13.205
First Empire Bank v. FDIC 8.51
First Investors Corp. v. Prince Royal Inn Ltd. 10.26
First Investors Corp., Re 13.267, 13.271
First Marathon Inc., Re 14.243
First Mortgage Fund (V) Inc. (Receiver and Manager of) v. Boychuk 13.78
First Natchez Bank v. Coleman 10.5
Firstbrook Boxes Ltd., Re 12.105
Fischer v. Borland Carriage Co. 6.82, 10.81
Fish and Game League (Regina), Re 13.9
Fisher v. St. John Opera House Co. 13.203
Fitch v. Churchill Corp. 14.57
Fitzherbert v. Dominion Bed Manufacturing Co. 7.107
Five Minute Car Wash Service Ltd., Re 13.102
Flame Bar-B-Q Ltd. v. Hoar's Estate 10.69
Flanagan Sailmakers v. Walker 11.119
Flatley v. Algy Corp. 13.83
Fleischer, Re 14.80
Flewitt v. Agravoice Productions Ltd. (Trustee of) 6.59
Flintoft v. Royal Bank 8.217
Flitcroft's Case 9.21
Florence Land & Public Works Co., Re 7.79
Florida Mining Co., Re 15.55
Fluet v. McCabe 10.33
Foley v. Commercial Cars Ltd. 6.79, 6.99
Fomento (Sterling Area) Ltd. v. Selsdon Fountain Pen Co. Ltd. 9.179
Food Giant Markets v. Watson Leaseholds Ltd. 2.23
Footitt v. Gleason 13.90, 13.108, 13.127
Fopex Discount Ltd., Re 15.73
Ford Motor Co. of Canada v. Manning Mercury Sales Ltd. 8.218, 8.219
Ford Motor Co. of Canada v. Ontario Municipal Employees Retirement
    Board 13.30, 13.61, 13.75, 14.73, 14.86
Ford v. Courier-Journal Job Printing Co. 14.80
Forest of Dean Coal Mining Co., Re 9.22
Foriter v. Laurin 11.266
Formento (Sterling Area Ltd.) v. Selsdon Fountain Pen Co. Ltd. 9.164
Forrester v. Stockstill 11.241
Fortier v. Spafax Canada Inc. 11.119
Foss v. Harbottle 2.99, 7.133, 8.318, 11.192, 11.207, 13.160,
                                13.199, 13.200, 13.202, 15.209
Foster v. Foster 10.7, 10.69, 10.70
Foster v. Oxford, etc. Rlwy. Co. 10.46
Four-K Western Equipment Ltd. v. CIBC 8.149

Four-Maids Ltd. v. Dudley Marshall (Properties) Ltd. 8.81
Fowell v. Tranter.. 6.5
Fowlers Vacola Manufacturing Co., Re.. 7.276
Fox & Son v. Morrish Grant & Co. 9.183
Fox, Walker & Co., Re 8.34
Frame v. Smith.. 11.196
Framlington Group plc. v. Anderson 11.153
Francis v. United Jersey Bank... 10.118, 11.9
Frantz Manufacturing Co. v. EAC Industries 12.106
Fraser Inc. v. Aitken... 14.72
Fraser v. Hartt Group Ltd. 8.152
Fraser v. Whalley 11.193
Fred T. Brooks Ltd. v. Claude Neon General Advertising
  Ltd. 6.64, 6.83, 10.83, 10.85
Fredericton Boom Co., Re 15.203
Freeman & Lockyer v. Buckhurst Park Properties (Mangal) Ltd. 6.39, 6.43, 6.45
Freemont Canning Co. v. Wall 9.73, 12.83
French Protestant Hospital, Re... 13.257
Freudiana Music Co., Re... 13.160
Fridman v. Chesapeake & Ohio Rlwy. Co. 8.185
Friedman Equity Developments Inc. v. Final Note Ltd. 5.207
Friedman v. Beway Realty Corp. 14.80
Friedmann Equity Developments Inc. v. Final Note Ltd. 6.95
Friends of the Oldman River Society v. Canada (Minister of Transport)... 13.128
Friese v. Superior Court of San Diego County 14.275
Frinton & Walton UDC v. Walton & District Sand & Mineral Co. 2.11
Froebel v. Claxton... 3.6
FSLIC v. Texas Real Estate Counselors, Inc. 9.190.1
Fuches v. Hamilton Tribune Printing & Publishing Co. (Copp's Case) 6.2
Fulham Football Club Ltd. v. Cabra Estates plc 11.200
Fuller v. Bruce 12.102, 12.128
Fullerton v. Crawford... 13.209
Fulmer v. Peter D. Fulmer Holdings Inc. 13.57
Fund of Funds Ltd., Re 8.29, 15.110, 15.115, 15.136
Furmanek v. Community Futures Development Corp. 8.114
Furry Creek Timber Corp. v. Laad Ventures Ltd. 13.235

G

G & E Vending Ltd. v. 700748 Alberta Ltd. 13.31
G. & T. Earle Ltd. v. Hemsworth Rural District Council 8.114, 8.115
G.T. Campbell & Associates Ltd. v. Hugh Carson Co. 2.21, 15.125
G.T.R. v. A.G. Canada... 4.5
G.W. Turner v. Lauze 5.196
Gabco Ltd. v. M.N.R. 11.94
Gabriel v. Gabriel.. 2.9
Gaby v. Federal Packaging & Partition Co. 12.1
Gadsden v. Bennetto 11.120, 11.161

Gagliardi v. TriFoods International Inc. 11.24
Gagne v. Red Diamond Taxi.. 11.104
Gagnon v. Tremblay 7.165
Gaiman v. National Association for Mental Health 11.68, 11.112
Gainers Inc. v. Pocklington 2.15, 13.31, 13.73, 13.81, 13.96
Galbraith v. Merito Shipping Co. 15.54
Galea v. Khosravi... 13.112
Gallelli Estate v. Bill Gallelli Investments Ltd. 13.31
Galler v. Galler... 13.5
Galloway v. Halle Concerts Society 7.236
Galpin, ex p. Chowilla Timber Supply Co., Re 7.225
Galway & Salthill Tramways Co., Re.. 10.24, 12.32
Gandalman Investments Inc. v. Fogle... 13.66
Garamendi v. Golden Eagle Insurance Company 15.129
Gardiner v. Iredale 7.175
Gardner v. London, Chatham and Dover Railway Co. 4.76
Gardner v. Parker 13.199
Garey v. Dominion Manufacturers Ltd. 8.274
Garland v. Consumers' Gas Co. 7.55, 8.40, 8.44, 13.189
Garner & Gavan 4.38
Gartside v. Silkstone & Dodsworth Coal & Iron Co. 8.133
Garvie v. Axmith 12.62, 12.76, 12.153
Garvin v. Edmondon.. 12.202
Garvin v. Edmondson 5.182
Gasque v. I.R.C. 6.109
Gasquoine, Re... 11.12
Gatineau Power Co. v. Crown Life Insurance Co. 8.62, 8.64, 8.131
GATX Corp. v. Hawker Siddeley Canada Inc. 14.43
Gauntlet Energy Corp., Re... 7.168
Gauthier v. Woollatt.. 8.331
Gazit (1997) Inc. v. Centrefund Realty Corp. 13.44, 13.112, 13.152
Gearing v. Kelly... 14.24
Geddes v. Toronto Street Rlwy. Co. 8.134
Gelhorn Motors Ltd. v. Yee 5.207
General Accident Assurance Co. of Canada v. Lornex Mining Co. ...14.156, 14.165
General Dairies Ltd. v. Maritime Electric Co. 7.286, 8.270
General Motors of Canada Ltd. v. Brunet............................... 11.306, 13.215
General Radio Co. v. General Radio (Westminster) Ltd. 5.112
General Rolling Stock Co., Re... 15.26
Geneva Steel Co., Re 13.184
Gentel v. Rapps.. 5.60
Georbay Developments Inc. v. Smahel... 13.205
George Fisher (Great Britain) Ltd. v. Multi-Construction Ltd. 2.10, 13.232
George Newman & Co., Re 7.334, 12.36
George v. Strong 11.272
George W. Griffiths Co., Re 7.315
George Whitechurch Ltd. v. Cavanagh.. 6.79
German Mining Co., Re.. 11.300

Gertzenstein Ltd., Re 15.114
Gesco Industries Ltd. v. Hongkong Bank of Canada 14.133
Gething v. Kilner 12.175, 13.231
Getty Oil Co. v. Skelly Oil Co. 11.148
Ghimpelman v. Bercovici 9.111
Gibbons v. Darvill 8.332
Gibson Pelican Lake v. Traders Trust Co., Re 7.175
Gibson v. Doeg 12.170
Gibson v. Manitoba Development Corp. 13.238
Giegy (Canada) Ltd. v. B.C. Min. of Finance 4.28
Giffels & Vallet of Canada Ltd. v. R. 4.48
Gifford-Hill & Co. v. Stoller 8.330
GIGA Investments Pty. Ltd., Re 12.181
Gignac, Sutts and Woodall Construction Co. v. Harris 11.291
Giguère v. Colas 10.72
Giles v. Rhind 13.195
Gilford Motor Co. v. Horne 2.29, 2.45
Gill v. Bhandal 15.65
Gillespie v. Clover Bar Coal Co. 7.87
Gillespie v. Overs 12.210
Gillespie v. Retail Merchants' Assn. of Canada (Ontario) Inc. 7.163, 7.182, 7.288
Gillespie, v. Schneider, Arthur Andersen & Co. 9.190.7
Gillett v. Deloitte & Touche Inc. 15.100
Gimbel v. Signal Cos., Inc. 11.25
Ginter, Re 11.264
Ginther v. Rainbow Management Ltd. 13.93, 13.236
Glace Bay Printing Co. v. Harrington 10.3, 11.111
Glasgow Lumber Co. v. Fettes 6.14
Glasvon Great Dane Sales Inc. v. Qureshi 13.76
Glaxo v. Glaxowellcome Ltd. 5.74, 5.85
Glay Adhesives, Re 6.98
Glazer v. Zapata Corp. 11.102
Glen Brick Co. v. Shackwell 8.24
Glimmer Resources Inc. v. Exall Resources Ltd. 7.199
Global Equity Corp. v. MKG Enterprises Corp. 4.28
Global Leak Detection Inc. v. Van 5.142
Global Securities Corp. v. British Columbia Securities Commission 4.20, 4.22
Globe Fire Insurance Co., Re 7.83
Glossop v. Glossop 9.121
Gloucester, Aberystwith & South Wales Rlwy. Co. (Maitland's Case), Re ... 9.20
Gluckstein v. Barnes 5.171, 5.181
Godbout v. Longueuil 4.79
Godfrey Phillips Ltd. v. Income Investment Trust Corp. 7.321, 7.330
Goerz & Co. v. Bell 6.112
Goft v. 1206448 Ontario Ltd. 13.106
Goh Kim Hai Edward v. Pacific Can Investmemt Holdings Ltd. 11.62
Gold Key Pontiac Buick (1984) Ltd. v. 464750 B.C. Ltd. (Trustee of) 5.84
Gold v. Maldaver 6.5, 12.113

Goldberg v. Western Approaches Ltd. 2.60
Golden Star Resources Ltd. v. IAM-Gold Corp. 12.174, 13.65
Golden West Restaurants Ltd. v. CIBC 10.26
Goldex Mines Ltd. v. Revill.......... 11.203, 12.76, 12.122, 12.175, 13.206, 13.234
Goldhar & Quebec Manitou Mines Ltd., Re... 13.260
Goldhar v. D'Aragon Mines Ltd. 12.153, 12.191
Goldhar v. JM Publications Inc. 13.30
Goldin, Re... 13.189
Gold-Rex Kirkland Mines Ltd. v. Morrow... 12.42
Good & Jacob Y. Shantz, Son & Co., Re....................... 5.73, 6.8, 7.207, 7.222
Good v. Lackawanna Leather Co. 14.43
Goodman v. J. Eban Ltd. 12.154
Goodwin v. East Hartford 1.2
Goodwin v. Ottawa & Prescott Rlwy. Co. 3.2, 7.22
Goodwin, Re 5.69
Goodwood Recoveries Ltd. v. Breen 3.55, 11.1
Goodyear Tire & Rubber Co. of Canada, R. v. 4.42
Goold v. Gillies... 7.85
Gord v. Iowana Farms Milk Co. 12.27
Gorden Gully United Quartz Mining Co. v. McLister............................... 9.113
Gordon Glaves Holdings Ltd. v. Care Corp. of Canada............................ 13.152
Gordon Leaseholds Ltd. v. Metzger.. 11.49, 12.8
Gordon MacKay & Co. v. J.A. Laroque Co. 4.47, 8.140
Gordon v. Gaby... 7.192
Gordon v. Street.. 7.100
Gorman v. Littlefield 7.288
Gosman, Re.. 8.29
Gottlieb v. Adam... 3.60, 11.291, 13.29
Gougen v. Metro Oil Co. 13.123
Gough's Garages Ltd. v. Pugsley... 15.28
Gould v. Gillies.. 11.135
Gould v. Mount Oxide Mines Ltd. 11.28
Gould v. Yukon Order of Pioneers 1.27
Government of India v. Taylor 15.115
Governments Stock & Other Securities Investment Co. v. Manila
   Rlwy. Co. 8.140, 8.146, 8.155
Govind Narayan v. Rangnath Gopal 11.32
Gow v. Consolidated Coppermines Corp. 12.106
Grace v. Biagioli.. 13.42
Graham v. Allis-Chalmers Manufacturing Co. 11.39.1
Graham v. Green, Inspector of Taxes 1.31
Graham v. Technequip Ltd. 15.67
Grammas v. Kensington Cafe Ltd. 11.163
Gramophone & Typewriter Ltd. v. Stanley.............. 2.8, 2.11, 9.13, 10.21, 12.188
Grand Junction Rlwy. Co. v. Midland Rlwy. Co. 5.70, 5.149
Grant (c.o.b. Cougar Pool League) v. Rathy (c.o.b. Panther Pool
   League) 5.116, 5.124
Grant Thornton LLP v. Federal Deposit Insurance Corporation...... 9.164, 10.173

Grant v. Dominion Loose Leaf Co. 6.1
Grant v. Gold Exploration & Development Syndicate Ltd. 11.129
Grant v. United Kingdom Switchback Railways Co. 6.87, 13.145, 13.253
Gray Eisdell Tims Pty Ltd. v. Combined Auctions Pty Ltd. 13.258
Gray Tractor Co. v. Van Troyen 8.127
Gray v. Gray... 7.18
Gray v. New Augarita Porcupine Mines Ltd. 10.40, 10.42, 11.146, 13.258
Gray v. Yellowknife Gold Mines Ltd. ... 11.46, 12.83, 12.85, 12.86, 5.171, 5.176
Gray v. Yellowknife Gold Mines Ltd. (1947)... 11.135
Gray v. Yellowknife Gold Mines Ltd. (No. 2) (1946) 11.135
Great America Leasing Co. v. Yates... 8.43, 8.44
Great North of England Rlwy., R. v. 3.23
Great Northern Assurance Co., Re.. 7.86
Great Northern Grain Terminals Ltd. v. Axley Agricultural Installations
    Ltd. 6.41, 11.81
Great Northern Railway Co. v. The Eastern Counties Railway Co. 4.77
Great Northern Salt Co., Re 10.7
Great Prairie Investment Co., Re 15.128
Great West Permanent Loan Co., Re 15.45
Great West Saddlery Co. v. R. 4.13, 4.43, 4.46, 4.47
Great Western Insurance Co. v. Cunliffe 8.29
Great Western Natural Gas Co. v. Central Gas Utilities Ltd. 2.126
Great Wheal Polgooth Co., Re 5.168, 5.171
Greathead v. Bromily.. 8.38
Grebely v. Seven Mile High Group Inc. 13.271
Green Gables Manor Inc., Re... 8.333
Green v. Bestobel Industries Pty Ltd. 2.29, 6.70
Green v. Charterhouse Group Canada Ltd. 12.123
Green v. New York United Hotels Inc. 8.185
Green v. Victor Talking Machine Co. 13.196
Greene, Re 7.229
Greenhalgh v. Arderne Cinemas Ltd. 11.66, 12.129
Greenlight Capital Inc. v. Stronach................... 11.44, 13.39, 13.42, 13.220
Greenpeace Foundation of Canada v. Inco 12.97
Greenstreet v. Paris Hydraulic Co. 8.318, 11.127, 11.161
Greenwell v. Porter 12.103
Greenwich Pier Co. v. The Conservators of the River Thames 4.78
Greenwood v. Doceray 7.267
Greenwood v. Leather Shod Wheel Co. 7.100
Greenwood v. Martins Bank 6.104
Gregorio v. Intrans-Corp. 2.44
Gregory & Co. v. Imperial Bank of Canada 4.51
Griffin Hotel Co., Re 8.145
Grigson v. Taplin & Co. 8.143
Grimes v. Donald 10.113, 10.114, 10.115
Grimm's Foods Ltd., Re 15.67, 15.73
Grimwade v. B.P.S. Syndicate Ltd. 10.29
Grimwade v. Mutual Society 9.22, 11.13

Grinrod & District Credit Union v. Cumis Insurance Society Inc. 10.134
Grobow v. Perot.. 11.21
Grondin v. Tisi & Turner 12.154
Gruia v. Canada 11.37
Grundt v. Great Boulder Proprietary Mines Ltd. 10.120, 12.31, 12.188
Guantlet Energy Corp., Re.. 8.287
Guarantee Co. of North America v. Aqua-Land Exploration Ltd. 2.12
Guardian Ins. Co. of Canada v. Sharp... 9.187
Guardian Insurance Co. v. Sharp 9.164
Guardian Press Ltd., Re 8.139
Guccio Gucci S.P.A. v. Gucci Investments Inc 5.117
Guenard v. Coe 11.266, 11.273
Guerin v. Canada 11.196
Guildford v. Anglo-French Steamship Co. 12.11
Guillot v. Sandwich & Windsor Gravel Road Co. 7.22
Guinness Mahorn & Co. v. Kensington & Chelsea London Borough
  Council.. 6.13
Guinness plc v. Saunders 10.44, 10.51, 10.62, 10.69, 11.155
Guinness v. Land Corp. of Ireland................................. 5.51, 5.62, 7.150
Gulland v. Fed. Comm. of Taxation 5.16
Guttman v. Huang.. 11.25
Guy Major Co. v. Canadian Flaxhills Ltd. 1.36

H

H & Others, Re 2.32, 2.36
H. (Restraint Order: Realisable Property), Re... 11.210
H. Flagal (Holdings) Ltd., Re 13.267
H. Timber Protection Ltd. (In Receivership) v. Hickson International
  plc.. 7.299, 11.141
H.A. Fawcett & Son Ltd. v. R. 3.68
H.A. Stephenson & Son Ltd. v. Gillanders, Arbuthnot & Co. 6.15, 15.54
H.E.P.C. and Thorold, Re 2.3
H.J. Logan Co., Re.. 10.119
H.L. Bolton (Engineering) Co. v. T.J. Graham & Sons Ltd. 3.18, 3.29
H.M. Coroner for East Kent, ex p. Spooner, R. v. 3.24
H.R. Harmer Ltd., Re................. 9.64, 12.130, 13.24, 13.26, 13.84, 13.89, 13.156
H.W. Thomas Ltd., Re 13.15, 13.21, 13.102, 13.155
Haberman v. Washington Public Power Supply System 13.239
Haggart Construction Ltd. v. Canadian Imperial Bank of Commerce 8.55
Hague v. Cancer Relief & Research Institute 1.33
Haig v. Bamford... 9.157, 9.179
Halifax (City) v. Jones 4.25
Halifax Carette Co. v. Moir 7.76
Halifax Steet Carette Co. v. McManus 7.76
Halifax Yacht Co., Re 15.56
Halket v. Merchant Traders' Ship Loan & Insurance Assoc. 2.73
Hall-Chem Inc. v. Vulcan Packaging Inc. 3.24, 3.52, 11.219, 11.245

Hallett v. Dowdall	2.73
Hallmac Ltd., Re	8.304
Halt Garage (1964) Ltd., Re	7.334, 10.72, 11.98
Hambro v. Burnand	6.42
Hamer v. London City & Midland Bank	8.145
Hamer v. National Forest Products	7.283
Hamilton & Flamborough Road Co. v. Townsend	7.197
Hamilton Bridge Co., Re	14.249
Hamilton Harbour Commissioners v. Hamilton (City)	4.46
Hamilton v. Grant	7.208
Hamilton v. Stewiacke Valley & Lansdowne Rlwy.	7.162
Hamilton v. Wright	11.158
Hammond v. Bank of Ottawa	5.61
Hampshire Land Co., Re	6.63, 11.43
Hampstead Carpets Ltd. v. Ivanovski	5.196
Hansen v. Eberle	13.81
Hanson v. Clifford	11.294
Harben v. Phillips	10.35, 12.132, 12.135, 12.139
Harbert Distressed Investment Master Fund, Ltd. v. Calpine Canada Energy Finance II ULC	15.76
Harbor Finance Partners v. Huizenga	13.230
Hardman Group Ltd. v. Alexander	12.208
Hardoon v. Belilios	12.1, 12.4
Hardwick, Re	8.82
Hardy Lumber Co. v. Pickerel River Improvement Co.	15.13
Harhen v. Brown	11.35, 13.208
Harker v. Britannic Assurance Co.	3.29
Harlowe's Nominees Pty. Ltd. v. Woodside (Lake Entrance) Oil Co. N.L.	7.58, 11.56, 11.112
Harmony and Montague Tin and Copper Mining Co., Re	7.165, 7.172, 7.241
Harold Holdsworth & Co. (Wakefield) Ltd. v. Caddies	10.85, 10.104
Harper & Co. v. Vigers Bros.	5.187
Harris Maxwell Larder Lake Gold Mining Co., Re	15.55, 15.65
Harris Scientific Products Ltd. v. Araujo	11.119
Harris v. Brunette Saw Mill Co.	3.7
Harris v. Dry Dock Co.	7.162, 11.80
Harris v. English Canadian Co.	12.37
Harris v. Harris	11.204
Harris v. Knight	12.169
Harris v. Nugent	2.28
Harris v. Sumner	7.151
Harris v. Tong	8.206
Harrison v. Nepisiguit Lumber Co.	8.79, 8.184, 15.199
Harry D. Shields Ltd. v. Bank of Montreal	8.162
Harry Simpson & Co. Pty, Re	2.14
Hart v. Felsen	11.249
Hartford Accident & Indemnity Co. v. Millsons Construction & Equipment Ltd.	1.44, 2.17

Hartga v. Bank of England.. 7.192
Hartley Baird Ltd., Re.. 14.24
Harvey Dodds Ltd. v. Royal Bank of Canada.. 8.145
Hassel v. Merchant Traders' Ship Loan & Insurance Assoc. 2.73
Hastings v. International Paper Co. 7.319
Hatch v. Rowland... 3.2
Haven Gold Mining Co., Re 15.54
Hawkins v. Allied Truck Co. 15.126
Hawkins v. Huron, Perth & Bruce (United Counties), Re 5.80
Haycraft Gold Reduction & Mining Co., Re 5.48, 12.58, 12.61
Hayes v. Bristol Plant Hire Ltd. 10.29
Hazell v. Hammersmith & Fulham London Borough Council 6.13
Hazzard, R. v.. 4.40, 4.54
Heap Noseworthy Ltd. v. Didham 10.74, 13.77
Heather's House of Fashion Inc., Re 8.19
Heaton's Steel & Iron Ore Co., Re 7.54, 12.4
Hedican v. Crows Nest Pass Lumber Co. 6.74
Hedley Byrne & Co. v. Heller & Partners Ltd. 7.114, 9.190.2
Heidelberg Canada Graphic Equipment Ltd. v. Arthur Anderson Inc. 14.135
Heil v. ROAM I.T. (Canada) Holdings Inc. 14.57
Heil v. T.E.N. Private Cable Systems Ltd. 12.89, 12.99
Heinhuis v. Black Sheep Charters... 5.193
Helby v. Matthews.. 8.69
Heller-Natofin (Western) Ltd. v. Carlton Developments Ltd. 8.38
Helmore v. Smith (No. 2).. 11.151
Helo Enterprises Ltd. v. Liquidators of Standard Trust Co. 8.42
Helping Hands Agency Ltd. v. British Columbia (Director of Employment
    Standards)... 11.276
Help-U-Sell Inc. v. Help-U-Sell Real Estate Ltd. 5.87
Helwig v. Siemon... 7.255, 7.268
Hely-Hutchinson v. Brayhead Ltd. 6.40, 6.50, 6.61, 6.99, 11.155
Hemmerling v. IMTC Systems 6.119
Henderson v. Australian Royal Mail Steam Navigation Co. 5.152
Henderson v. Bank of Australasia... 11.98, 12.37, 12.118
Henderson v. James Loutitt & Co. 14.24
Henderson v. Strang... 7.171, 13.202, 13.209
Henderson, R. v.. 4.52
Hendin v. Cadillac Fairview Corp. 13.75
Hendricks v. Montague.. 5.85
Henry Bentley & Co. & Yorkshire Breweries Ltd., ex p. Harrison, Re........... 3.4
Henry Hope & Sons of Canada Ltd. v. Sinclair................................... 5.186, 7.108
Henry Squire Cash Chemist Ltd. v. Ball Baker & Co. 9.183
Henry v. Great Northern Rlwy. 7.322
Hercules Insurance Co. (Brunton's Claim), Re.. 8.322
Hercules Managements Ltd. v. Ernst & Young 2.10, 9.190.4, 13.193, 13.198
Heriteau v. W.D. Morris Realty Ltd. 5.80
Herman v. Wilson 11.271
Hermanns v. Ingle... 15.87

Hern v. Nichols 6.81
Heron International Ltd. v. Lord Grade 7.33, 11.68
Heslop v. Paraguay Central Rlwy. Co. 8.66, 8.197
Hess Manufacturing Co., Re 5.168, 7.156
Hess Mfg. Co. (Sloan's Case), Re 5.172, 5.180
Hevenor v. Canada 11.37
Heymann v. European Central Ry. Co. 7.106
Higgins v. Brock & Higgins Insurance Agencies Ltd. 15.59, 15.63
Higgins v. Nicol 12.181
Highfield Commodities Ltd., Re 15.70
Highfields Capital ILP v. Telesystems International Wireless Inc. 13.106, 13.114
Highland Queen Sportswear Ltd., Re 14.165
Highway Advertising Co. of Canada v. Ellis 5.176, 5.179
Hill v. Bellevue Gardens Inc. 12.3
Hill v. Permanent Trustee Co. of New South Wales Ltd. 7.296
Hillcrest General Leasing Ltd. v. Guelph Investments Ltd. 11.298
Hillcrest Housing Ltd., Re 13.114, 15.64, 15.72, 15.112
Hillside Investments Ltd. v. Boychuck 13.30
Hilton v. Tucker 8.209
Hindle v. John Cotton Ltd. 11.63, 11.108, 11.243
Hirsche v. Sims 11.254
Hirsh & Co. v. Burns 7.242
HMG/Courtland Props., Inc. v. Gray 11.121
Ho Tung v. Man On Insurance Co. Ltd. 12.36
Hobbs v. Dempsey 13.81
Hodge v. R. 4.1, 4.5
Hodson v. Tea Co. 8.146
Hoffman Products Ltd. v. Karr 11.172, 13.211
Hogg v. Cramphorn Ltd. 7.58, 11.60, 11.63, 11.109, 11.111, 13.254
Holden v. Construction Machinery Co. 12.3
Holden v. Infolink Technologies Ltd. 13.106
Holders of Investment Trust Ltd., Re 12.131
Holdex Group Ltd., Re 7.52, 14.249
Hole v. Garnsey 7.196, 7.236
Holland v. Hodgson 8.137
Hollebone's Agreement, Re 11.297
Hollinger Bus Lines Ltd. v. Ontario (Labour Relations Board) 1.59
Hollinger International, Inc. v. Black 11.121, 12.106, 14.152
Hollister v. Porchet 8.127
Holloway v. Skinner 11.241
Holly Farms Corp. Shareholders Litigation, Re 11.27
Holman v. Calgary Properties Inc. 7.295
Holmes v. Blogg 7.197
Holmes v. Lord Keyes 5.53, 12.113
Holmes v. R. 2.31
Holmested v. Annable 11.134
Holmstead v. Alberta Pacific Grain Co. (1927) 7.285
Holmstead v. Alberta Pacific Grain Co. (1928) 7.320

Holund Holdings Ltd. v. Lewicky 5.169
Home & Colonial Insurance Co., Re 15.113, 15.119
Home Bank of Canada, Re 15.45
Home Mortgage Co. v. Ramsey 8.185, 8.189
Home Treat Ltd., Re 12.36
Homestead Development Ltd. v. Lehman Resources Ltd. 9.62
Hong Kong & China Gas Co. v. Glen 7.166
Hongsathavij v. Queen of Angels etc. Medical Center 10.115
Honsberger v. Weyburn Townsite Co. 4.25
Hood v. Caldwell 7.107, 7.170, 7.180
Hood v. Eden 12.165
Hooper Grain Co. v. Colonial Assurance Co. 4.25
Hooper v. Kerr, Stuart & Co. 12.58
Hope v. International Financial Society 7.255, 13.202
Hôpital du Sacré Coeur v. Lefebvre 1.33
Hopkinson v. Mortimer, Harley & Co. 7.275, 7.345
Horbury Bridge Coal, Iron & Waggon Co., Re 12.108
Horn v. Henry Faulder & Co. 6.24, 10.86, 10.104
Horne v. Chester & Fain Property Developments Pty. Ltd. 8.294
Horsefield v. Ontario (Registrar of Motor Vehicles) 4.11
Horsley & Weight Ltd., Re 6.15, 6.87, 11.80, 11.99, 13.253, 13.258
Hoskin v. Price Waterhouse Ltd. 13.193, 13.206, 13.238
Hoskinson, Re 15.90
Hospes v. Northwestern Mfg. & Car. Co. 7.8
Hospital Products Ltd. v. United States Surgical Corp. 11.115, 11.116, 11.120
Hotton v. Joyce 14.73
Houghton & Co. v. Nothard Lowe & Wills Ltd. 10.84, 10.85
Houldsworth v. City of Glasgow Bank 3.3, 7.83, 7.106
Houle v. Low 948
Houle v. National Bank of Canada 2.75
House of Fraser plc v. A.C.G.E. Investments Ltd. 7.43
Household Fire & Carriage Accident Insurance Co. v. Grant 7.78
Household Products Co. v. Federal Business Development Bank 8.146
Hovey v. Whiting 10.24, 15.13
Hovsepian v. Westfair Foods Ltd. 14.43
Howard Smith Ltd. v. Ampol Petroleum Ltd. 7.57, 9.13, 10.21,
       11.5, 11.49, 11.61, 11.63, 11.108, 11.113, 11.243, 11.253, 12.31
Howard Stove Mfg. Co. v. Dingman 5.182
Howard v. Patent Ivory Manufacturing Co. 6.98
Howard's Case 10.103
Howbeach Coal Co. v. Teague 14.24
Howell Lithographic Co. v. Brether 5.145
HSB Holdings Ltd., Re 9.13
HSBC Capital Canada Inc. v. First Mortgage Alberta Fund (V) Inc. 13.75, 13.79
Hubbard & Co., Re 8.132, 8.133
Hubbuck v. Helms 8.146
Huber v. Lion Mead Rubber Co. 6.98, 7.107
Hudson v. Benallack 8.335, 13.64

Huggard v. Prudential Life Insurance Co. 11.159
Huggins, R. v. 3.27
Hughes v. Bob Tallman Investments Inc. 13.30
Hughes v. Mutual Fire Insurance Co. 5.73
Hughes v. Northern Electric & Manufacturing Co. 6.5, 7.255
Hughes v. Oakes 15.81
Hugh-Pam Porcupine Mines Ltd., Re 15.65
Hulme v. Brigham... 8.137
Humber Ironworks & Shipbuilding Co., Re 8.50
Humber Valley Broadcasting Co., Re... 15.63, 15.67
Humberbank Investment & Development Ltd., Re...................................... 15.61
Humfrey v. Hickey... 8.136
Humphreys v. Winous.. 9.100
Hunt Estate v. Canada.. 7.25
Hunt v. LAC d'Amiante du Quebec 6.128
Hunt v. T&N plc 4.22, 5.67
Hunt v. TD Securities Inc. 11.134.1
Hunter v. Southam Inc. 4.67
Hurely v. Ornsteen... 10.5
Hurlbut Co. v. Hurlburt Shoe Co. 5.94
Hurley v. BGH Nominees Pty. Ltd. 2.29, 13.232, 13.257
Hurley v. Ornsteen... 6.88
Hurley v. Slate Ventures Inc. 13.77, 13.78
Hurst v. Mersea (Township) 5.59
Hurst v. Societe Nationale de L'Amiante 13.41, 13.48, 13.143
Husky Oil Operations Ltd. v. Canada (Minister of National Revenue) 4.10
Hutchins v. State Bank... 7.192
Hutton v. West Cork Rlwy. Co. 10.69, 11.5, 11.49, 11.83, 11.94, 11.96, 12.78
Hyman v. Velsicol Corp. 11.109

I

I. Browns Packaging Inc. v. Canada (Department of Consumer &
  Corporate Affairs).. 5.95
I. Ramjit Inc. v. 3-for-1 Pizza & Wings (Canada) Inc. 2.32
I.C.B.C. v. Eurosport Auto Co. 11.129
I.C.B.C. v. Sanghera 11.129
I.C.R. Haulage Ltd., R. v. 3.25, 3.29, 3.42
I.O.S. Ltd. (No. 2), Re... 15.44
Ian Chisholm Textiles Ltd. v. Griffiths.. 8.114
ID Biomedical Corp. v. Glaxo Smith Kline plc 12.130
Illingworth v. Houldsworth... 8.138, 8.140
Impenco Ltd. v. M.N.R. 11.93
Imperial Bank of Canada v. Dennis 6.60
Imperial Bank of Canada v. McLellan 8.19
Imperial Bank of China, India & Japan, Re 12.113
Imperial Canadian Trust Co. v. Potter 15.29
Imperial Hydropathic Hotel Co., Blackpool v. Hampson 9.23, 12.32, 12.35

Imperial Land Co. of Marseilles, Re 7.79
Imperial Mercantile Credit Association v. Coleman 11.106, 11.155, 13.253
Imperial Oil Co. v. A.S. McDonald 15.27
Imperial Oil Ltd. v. C & G Holdings Ltd. 3.5, 11.210, 11.238
Imperial Oil Ltd. v. Westlake Fuel Ltd. 13.38
Imperial Starch Co., Re 7.222
Imperial Tobacco Co. v. Younger 7.329
Imperial Trust Co. v. Canbra Foods Ltd. 10.41, 10.54, 14.260
In Re Enron Corporation Securities 7.97
Independence Tube Corp. v. Levine 14.80
Indian & General Investment Trust Ltd. v. Union Bank of Halifax 8.143
Indian Head Credit Union Ltd. v. R. & D. Hardware Ltd. 8.149
Industrial Development Bank v. Valley Dairy Ltd. 8.146
Industrial Development Consultants Ltd. v. Cooley 11.188
Industrial Equity Ltd. v. Blackburn 2.10, 2.66
Inex Pharmaceuticals Corp., Re 8.329, 14.238
Inglewood Pulp Co. v. New Brunswick (Electric Power Commission) 8.34
Inglis v. Wellington Hotel Co. 7.175
Inland Kenworth Ltd. v. Commonwealth Insurance Co. 7.96
Inland Rev. Comm. v. Fisher's Executors 1.49
Innocan Inc. v. Canadian Pacific Air Lines Ltd. 13.30
Inrig Shoe Co., Re 7.8
Insight Venture Associates III, LLC v. Rampart Securities Inc.
    (Trustee of) 13.193
Insight Venture Associates III, LLC v. SlimSoft Inc. 7.240
Insight Venture Associates III, LLC v. Trustee of Rampart Securities Inc.
    (Trustee of) 13.195
Insomnia (No. 2) Pty. Ltd. v. F.C.T. 14.24
Installations Ltd., Re 15.44
Insurance Act of Canada, Re 4.40, 4.43
Insurance Contracts, Re 4.25, 4.40, 4.46
Insurance Corp. of British Columbia v. Dragon Driving School Canada
    Ltd. 11.129
Int'l Pulp Equip. Co. v. St. Regis Kraft Co. 15.157
Inter City Baking Co. v. Rosenblood 5.150
Intercontinental Precious Metals Inc. v.
    Cooke 12.3, 13.33, 13.215, 13.216, 13.220, 13.249
Interlake Packers Ltd. v. Vogt 5.206
International Baslen Enterprises Ltd. v. Kirwan 12.57
International Brotherhood of Electrical Workers' Union, Local 2345 v.
    Callahan 11.274
International Brotherhood of Teamsters v. Therien 1.51
International Casualty Co. v. Thomson 7.107
International Corona Resources Ltd. v. LAC Minerals Ltd. 11.116, 11.196
International Electric Co., Re 7.283
International Home Purchasing Contract Co. v. Alberta (Registrar of
    Joint Stock Companies) 4.14

International Laboratories Ltd. v. Dewar (Peat, Marwick,
   Mitchell & Co.) 9.154, 9.156, 9.170, 9.176
International Railway Co. & Niagara Parks Commission, Re 4.28
International Rlwy. v. Ontario (Niagara Parks Commission) 8.34
International Soc. for Krishna Consciousness v. Lee 4.79
International Text-Book Co. v. Brown 4.25
Intertech Model Fixtures Inc. v. Rusch 11.152, 11.176
Intl. Brotherhood of Teamsters v. Therien 5.162
Intl. Longshoremen's Association v. Maritime Employer's Association 5.162
Introductions Ltd. v. National Provincial Bank 6.12
Introductions Ltd., Re 6.15
Inversiones Montforte S.A. v. Javelin International Ltd. 13.121
Investissements Mont-Soleil Inc. v. National Drug Ltd. 14.69
Investment Trust Corp. v. Singapore Traction Co. 7.32
IRC v. Black 7.326
IRC v. Holder 8.29
IRC v. Rowntree & Co. 8.7
Irma Co-operative Co., Re 15.16
Iron Clay Brick Manufacturing Co., Re 11.186, 15.199
Iroquois Falls Community Credit Union Ltd. (Liquidation of) v.
   Co-operators General Insurance Co. 9.190.9
Irvin v. Irvin Porcupine Gold Mines Ltd. 12.62
Irvine v. Irvine 13.138
Irvine v. Union Bank of Australia 6.33, 6.87, 8.22, 12.78
Irving Oil Ltd. v. Colbourne 5.206
Irving Ungerman Ltd. v. Galanis 14.73
Irvington Holdings Ltd. v. Black 8.36
Irwin Toy Ltd. v. A.G. Quebec 4.50, 4.67
Isaac v. Cook 8.145
Isaacs v. Chapman 12.136
Island Export Finance Ltd. v. Umunna 11.189, 11.205
Island Getaways Inc. v. Destinair Airlines Inc. 11.222
Island Recreational Properties Ltd. v. Dyck 15.160
Isle of Thanet Electricity Supply Co., Re 7.43, 7.285
Isle of Wight Rlwy. Co. v. Tahourdin 9.13, 10.7, 12.33
Italia (Azzuri) Soccer Club Inc. v. Manitoba (Director of Corporations
   Branch) 5.87
Item Software (UK) Ltd. v Fassihi 11.43
Iverson v. Westfair Foods Ltd. 13.74, 13.105

J

J. Gillespie & Co. v. Sheady 7.210
J. McCarthy & Sons Co. of Prescott Ltd., Re 15.5
J.C. Harris Groceteria Ltd., Re 10.69
J.C. Houghton & Co. v. Northard, Lowe & Wills Ltd. 3.11, 6.34, 6.45, 11.43
J.D. MacArthur Co. v. Alberta & Great Waterways Rlwy. Co. 11.132, 11.135
J.D. Wain Ltd., Re 15.56

J.E. Cade & Son Ltd., Re 13.55
J.F. Cunningham & Son Ltd., Re 15.73
J.H. Ashdown Hardware Co. v. Residential Building Co. 15.44
J.H. McKnight Construction Co. v. Vansickler 10.85
J.I. Thornycroft & Co. v. Thornycroft 7.322
J.J. Beamish Const. Co., R. v. 3.24
J.N. Taylor Holdings, Re 15.41
J.R. Auto Brokers Ltd. v. Hillcrest Auto Leasing Inc. 8.138
J.R. Morgan Ltd., Re 5.186
J.S. Darrell & Co. v. The Ship American 6.109
J.V. Boudrias Fils Ltée v. Boudrias Frères Ltée 5.95
Jackman v. Jackets Enterprises Ltd. 12.12, 13.116, 13.123
Jackson v. Trimac Industries Ltd. 2.33, 11.124, 11.238
Jackson v. Turquand 7.79
Jacobi v. Griffiths 3.4
Jacobs Farms Ltd. v. Jacobs 13.69, 13.71, 13.205
Jacobus Marlet Estates Ltd. v. Marler 5.175
Jacques Cartier Water & Power Co. v. Quebec Railway Light & Power Co. 6.24
Jacques Furniture Co., Re 6.11
James Lumbers Co., Re 15.59
James Offenbecher v. Baron Services, Inc. 14.76
James Street Hardware & Furniture Co. v. Spizziri 3.4
James v. Beaver Consolidated Mines Ltd. 5.52, 7.327, 7.329
James v. Beuna Ventura Nitrate Grounds Syndicate Ltd. 7.228, 12.5
James v. Eve 7.255, 9.59
James, Re 11.280
Jameson, R. v. 4.20
Jamieson v. Hotel Renfrew (Trustees of) 12.62
Jamieson v. Jamieson 5.94
Jamieson's Foods Ltd. v. Ontario (Food Terminal Board) 6.11
Janson v. Driefontein Consolidated Mines Ltd. 6.109
Jarman v. Brown 13.99, 15.46
Jarvis Construction Co., Re 15.202
Jaska v. Jaska 13.101, 13.103, 13.153
Jasper Liquor Co., Re 15.27
Jeannette BBQ Ltée v. C.P. de Tracadie Ltée 8.149
Jefferson v. Omnitron Investments Ltd. 14.69
Jeffery, Re 11.203
Jeffree v. National Companies and Securities Commission 11.80
Jenice Ltd. v. Dan 2.24
Jennings v. Bernstein 13.237
Jenny Lind Candy Shops, Re 7.78
Jenson v. South Trail Mobile Ltd. 6.50
Jepson v. Canadian Salt Co. 14.57
Jermyn Street Turkish Baths Ltd., Re 13.19
Jerry v. Gillard 13.210
Jesuit Fathers of Upper Canada v. Guardian Insurance Co. of Canada 11.312
Jewell v. Ross 2.9

Table of Cases

Jim Landry Pontiac Buick Ltd. v. CIBC 8.149
Jirna v. Mister Donut of Canada Ltd. 12.123
Joel v. Morison 3.9
Johansen v. St. Louis Union Trust Co. 7.155
John A. McAfee Law Corp. v. Willey 4.28
John Brinsmead & Sons v. T.E. Brinsmead & Sons 5.96
John Deere Credit Inc. v. Doyle Salewski Lemieux Ltd. 8.304
John Deere Plow Co. v. Agnew 4.28
John Deere Plow Co. v. Wharton 4.7, 4.8, 4.13, 4.45, 4.49
John Doe v. Bennett 1.7, 5.4
John E. Hayes & Sons v. Turner 7.156, 7.170
John Henshall Quarries Ltd. v. Harvey 3.29
John J. Starr (Real Estate) Pty. Ltd. v. Robert R. Andrew (A'Asia) Pty. Ltd. ... 12.88
John Labatt Ltd. v. Lucky Lager Breweries Ltd. 14.160
John Shaw & Sons (Salford) Ltd. v.
 Shaw 9.13, 9.17, 10.20, 10.35, 10.36, 12.31, 12.188
John Ziner Lbr. v. Kotov 6.87
Johnson v. Bialick State Treasurer, Custodian of Special Compensation
 Fund 13.174
Johnson v. Canada Theaters Ltd. 7.86
Johnson v. Gore Wood & Co. 13.199
Johnson v. Hall 12.84, 12.85
Johnson v. Meyer 13.211, 13.218, 13.249
Johnson v. Newton 11.12
Johnson v. Trueblood 11.125, 11.127
Johnson v. W.S. Johnson & Sons Ltd. 15.67
Johnson Woollen Mills Ltd. v. Southern Canada Power Co. 13.270
Johnston v. Wade 8.140
Johnston, R. v. 5.171
Joint Application of the Great Northern Railway Company and the Great
 Central Railway Company, Re 4.78
Joint Receivers & Managers of Niltan Carson Ltd. v. Hawthorne 11.190
Joint Stock Discount Co. v. Brown 6.6, 10.131, 11.29
Joint Stock Discount Co., Re 8.50
Jolicoeur v. Boivin & Cie 15.92
Jolin v. Lart Investments Ltd. 15.167
Jolub Construction Ltd., Re 13.210
Jon Beauforte (London) Ltd., Re 6.13
Jonah v. Quinte Transport (1986) Ltd. 11.276
Jonathan Alexander Ltd. v. Proctor 2.11
Jones & Moore, Re 7.153, 7.154, 7.166
Jones v. Jones and others; Re Incasep Ltd. 13.113
Jones v. Lipman 2.29
Jones v. Skinner 7.168
Jones, Re 1.2, 11.11
Jordan Inc. v. Jordan Engineering Inc. 13.30
Jordan v. McKenzie 15.63
Jostens Canada Ltd. v. Gibsons Studio Ltd. 11.115

Journet v. Superchef Food Industries Ltd. 13.42, 13.123
Joy v. North 10.130, 13.209
Joyce v. DPP 10.168
JP Morgan Chase Bank v. Mystras Maritime Corp. 13.178
JP Morgan Chase Bank v. Traffic Stream (BVI) Infrastructure Ltd. 4.26
Jubilee Cotton Mills Ltd. v. Lewis 5.176, 5.181
Jubilee Theatre Ltd., Re 9.111
Junction Contracting Services Ltd. v. Allen 2.22
Jury Gold Mine Development Co., Re 15.55

K

K.L.B. v. British Columbia 3.4
Kabat Pty Ltd., Re 15.113
Kaffarian Steam Mill Co., Re 15.149
Kahn v. Lynch Communications, Inc. 10.58, 14.193
Kahn v. Roberts 11.57
Kalef v. Canada 10.28
Kalenczuk v. Kalenczuk 4.22
Kammin's Ballrooms Co v. Zenith Investments (Torquay) 1.27
Kanagaratnam v. Li 11.262
Kaplan v. Block 10.17
Kaplan v. Wyatt 13.228
Kare v. North West Packers 8.152
Kary Investment Corp. v. Tremblay 12.1, 12.5, 12.64, 12.209
Katz v. Chevron Corp. 13.230
Katzowitz v. Sidler 11.109
Kavanagh v. Norwich Union 10.5
Kavcar Industries Ltd. v. Aetna Financial Services 8.149
Kawai Canada Music Ltd. v. Encore Music Ltd. 8.219
Kawakita v. United States 10.168
Kaye v. Croydon Tramways Co. 12.76, 12.78
Keating v. Bragg 11.19, 11.140, 13.33, 13.74
Keating, Re 7.303
Kebet Holdings Ltd. v. 351173 B.C. Ltd. 8.41
Keddy Motor Inns Ltd., Re 12.114
Keddy Motor Inns, Re 14.268
Keech v. Sandford 11.185
Keewatin Tribal Council Inc. v. Thompson (City) 2.3, 2.11
Keho Holdings Ltd. v. Noble 13.22, 13.24, 13.26, 13.30, 13.149, 13.157
Keith Spier Ltd. v. Mansell 5.169
Keith v. Kilmer (In re Nat'l Piano Co.) 13.184
Kelaw Pty v. Catco Developments Pty Ltd. 15.28
Kelley v. Electrical Construction Co. 6.5
Kellogg Brown & Root Inc. v. Aerotech Herman Nelson Inc. 8.63
Kelly v. Condon 15.60
Kelly v. Electrical Construction Co. 5.56, 5.57, 5.60
Kelner v. Baxter 5.1, 5.187, 5.201, 12.202

Kendall v. Hamilton 5.207
Kennedy v. Acadia Pulp & Paper Mills Co. 7.14, 8.6
Kennedy v. Williams 7.208
Kenson Holdings Ltd. v. Kennedy 2.9
Kent v. Communauté des Soeurs de Charité de la Providence 15.13
Kentucky Fried Chicken Canada, a Division of Pepsi-Cola Canada Ltd. v.
 Scott's Food Services Inc. 2.11, 2.34, 7.266
Kentwood Construction Ltd., Re 15.115
Kepert v. West Australian Pearlers Association 15.149
Kepic v. Tecumseh Road Builders 3.58, 11.210, 11.239
Keppel v. Wheeler 11.298
Kerr v. Danier Leather Inc. 7.128
Kerr v. Fleming Financial Corp. 7.242
Kerr v. John Mottram Ltd. 12.165
Kethwar v. Duncan 8.32
Kettle River Mines Ltd. v. Bleasdel 7.164
Kettle v. Borris 5.191
Key Investments Ltd., Re 15.41
Keyes v. Hope Trading Syndicate 12.50
Keystone Leasing Corp. v. Peoples Protective Life Insurance 6.85
Khanna v. McMinn 10.2
Khayraji v. Safaverdi 13.27, 13.88, 13.131
Khotim v. Mikheev 15.177
Kiely v. Kiely 9.58
Kiely v. Smyth 7.18, 8.318
Kilgoran Hotels Ltd. v. Samek, Re 8.46
Kindree v. Canada (Minister of National Revenue) 2.31
Kinexus Holdings Ltd. v. Kineter Pharmaceuticals Inc. 14.63
King City Holdings Ltd. v. Preston Springs Gardens Inc. 15.58
King v. Merrill Lynch Canada Inc. 3.4
Kingston Cotton Mill Co. (No. 2), Re 9.21, 9.183
Kingstone v. Dominion Alloy Steel Corp. 7.114
Kinookimaw Beach Assn. v. Saskatchewan 2.28
Kinsela v. Russell Kinsela Pty. Ltd. 11.80, 11.82, 13.257
Kippen v. Bongard, Leslie & Co. 7.4
Kirby v. Wilkins 7.255
Kirkpatrick v. Cornwall Electric Street Rlwy. 8.23
Kirpps v. Touche Ross 7.96
Kitson & Co., Re 15.54
KL Tractors Ltd., Re 6.13
Klassen v. Klassen 9.62, 9.136
Klein v. James 9.73-9.113
Klianis v. Poole 12.184, 12.185
Knappton Towboat Co. v. Chambers 14.189
Knight v. Ducklow Motors Ltd. 8.127
Knight's Case 10.7
Knightsbridge Estates Trust Ltd. v. Byrne 8.280
Knowles v. Scott 15.113, 15.114

Knudsen v. Knudsen 8.29, 8.94
Koch Transport Ltd. v. Class Freight Lines Ltd. 12.219, 14.99
Koffyfontein Mines Ltd. v. Mosely 7.53
Kokotovich Constructions Pty Ltd. v. Wallington 13.261
Konamaneni v. Rolls-Royce Industrial Power (India) Ltd. 13.252
Kong Thai Sawmill (Miri) Sdn Bhd., Re 11.5, 13.6
Kont Vanis v. O'Brien (No. 2) 6.46
Kooragang Investments Pty. Ltd. v. Richardson & Wrench Ltd. 3.9
Kootenay Valley Fruit Lands Co., Re 12.14, 13.262
Kornblum v. Dye 11.271
Korogonas v. Andrew 13.94
Korz v. St. Pierre 11.131
Kramer v. Humfrey 11.261
Kraus v. J.G. Lloyd Pty Ltd. 13.259
Kreditbank Cassel, GmbH v. Schenkers Ltd. 6.44
Kreglinger v. New Patagonia Meat & Cold Storage Co. 8.66, 8.80, 8.110
Kremlin Canada Inc. v. Turner 11.180
Krendel v. Frontwell Investments Ltd. 11.10
Krepchin v. Barclay-Arrow Holding Corp. 8.185
Kripps v. Touche Ross & Co. 7.95
Kronson v. Metro Drugs Manitoba Ltd. (Trustee of) 8.323
Kronvic v. Lamarche-Craven 11.152
Kruger Inc. v. Kruco Inc. 13.126
Kruger v. Harwood 7.83
Krumm v. McKay 13.178
Krynen v. Bugg 13.31, 13.152
Kuin v. 238682 Alberta Ltd. 2.3
Kummen v. Kummen-Shipman Ltd. 13.123, 15.46
Kussner, R. v. 11.249
Kuwait Asia Bank EC v. National Mutual Life Nominees
   Ltd. 10.21, 11.137, 11.147
Kylsant, R. v. 7.99
Kyshe v. Alturas Gold Co. 10.29

L

L&B Electric Ltd. v. Oickle 13.15, 13.214
L.A. Brown Ltd. v. Brown 11.177
L.C.C., ex p. London & Provincial Electric Theaters Ltd., R. v. 2.45
L.K. Bros Pty Ltd. (Receivers and Managers Appointed) v. Gerald Collins and
   Philip Jefferson and Landmara Pty Ltd. 6.75
L.K. Oil & Gas Ltd. v. Canalands Energy Corp. 7.96
L.L. Constantin & Co. v. R.P. Holding Co. 7.302, 7.323
La Compagnie de Mayville v. Whitley 10.23
La Compagnie Hydraulique de St. François v. Continental Heat and Light Co. ... 4.6
Labatt Brewing Co. v. Trilon Holdings Inc. 12.185
Lacey v. Stoyles 12.123
Ladd v. Roane Hosiery, Inc. 11.241

Ladies Dress Association Ltd. v. Pulbrook 5.159
Ladies of the Sacred Heart of Jesus v. Armstrong's Point Association 1.52
Ladore v. Bennett 4.22
Lady Forrest (Murchinson) Gold Mine Ltd., Re 5.175
Ladywell Mining Co. v. Brookes 5.177
Laemthong International Lines Co. Ltd. v. Artis 4.19, 4.30
LaFontaine v. Drynan 13.249
Lagunas Nitrate Co. v. Lagunas Syndicate 5.176, 5.181, 11.13
Lagunas Nitrate Co. v. Schroeder & Co. & Schmidt 7.327
Lajoie v. Lajoie Brothers Contracting Ltd. 13.123
Lake & Co. v. Calex Resources Ltd. 14.47, 14.111
Lake Mechanical Systems Corp. v. Crandell Mechanical Systems
    Inc. 11.165, 11.179
Lake Superior Navigation Co. v. Morrison 12.20
Lake Winnipeg Transportation, Lumber & Trading Co., Re 4.14
Lakeway Heights Developments Inc. v. Royal Bank 2.47
Lala Indra Sen, R. v. 1.31
Lamb v. Canada (Minister of National Revenue) 2.31
Lambert v. Great Eastern Rlwy. Co. 3.3
Lampolier Manufacturing Co. v. Manitoba 5.74
Land Commissioner v. Pillai 2.72
Land Credit Co. of Ireland v. Lord Fermoy 3.55, 10.117
Land Loan Mortgage Co., Re 7.82
Lands & Homes of Canada Ltd., Re 12.54
Lands Allotment Co., Re 6.17, 11.92, 11.104
Lang Michener v. American Bullion Minerals Ltd. 11.15
Langley's Ltd., Re 12.152, 14.242, 14.245
Laniere de Roubaix S.A. v. Craftsmen Distributors Inc. 4.28
Laprise v. Julio's Pizza & Spaghetti Parlour 11.269
LaRoche v. HARS Systems Inc. 13.213, 13.252
Larocque v. Beauchemin 5.179, 5.181
Laronge Realty Ltd. v. Golconda Investments Ltd. 8.323
Larouque v. Beauchemin 7.161
Laserworks Computer Services Inc., Re 12.125
Laskin v. Bache & Co. 11.196, 12.123
Latchford Premier Cinema, Ltd. v. Ennion 9.121
Lauman v. Lebanon Valley R.R. Co. 14.45
Laurentian Bank of Canada v. Princeton Mining Corp. 14.253
Lavigne v. Robern 11.186, 12.123
Law Society of British Columbia v. Mangat 4.50
Lawson Mardon Wheaton, Inc. v. Smith 14.80
Lawyers' Advertising Co. v. Consolidated Railway, Lighting &
    Refrigeration Co. 12.161
Laxon & Co. (No. 2), Re 5.38
Lay v. Genevest Inc. 14.111
Lazard Bros. & Co. v. Midland Bank Ltd. 4.19, 15.13, 15.151
LB Holliday & Co., Re 2.14
Le Groupe Visuel (1990) Inc. v. Trustus International Trading Inc. 3.55

Learoyd v. Whiteley 11.11
Leavens v. Great West Permanent Loan Co. 12.102
Lebeault v. Venant Lebeault Ltée 6.79
LeBlanc v. Corporation Eighty-Six Ltd. 13.43, 13.122
LeBlanc, Re 8.304, 8.305
Lebron v. National R.R. Passenger Corp. 4.79
Leby Properties Ltd. v. Manufacturers Life Insurance 8.100
Lecce v. Lecce 13.120
Leclerc Ltd. v. Pouliot 7.303, 7.327
Leclerc v. Beaulieu 10.27, 11.272
Lee Panavision Ltd. v. Lee Lighting Ltd. 10.44, 11.112
Lee v. Block Estates Ltd. 13.199
Lee v. Chou Wen Hsien 9.125, 11.192, 13.232
Lee v. Friedman 11.271
Lee v. International Consort Industries Inc. 13.69, 13.205
Lee v. Jenkins Bros. 6.78
Lee v. Lee 13.129
Lee v. Lee's Air Farming Ltd. 2.11, 2.13, 5.163
Lee v. Neuchatel Asphalte Co. 7.310, 7.341
Lee, Behrens & Co., Re 11.83, 11.95
Leeds & Hanley Theatres of Varieties Ltd., Re 5.178, 5.180, 5.181
Leeds Banking Co., Re 10.81
Leeds Estate Building & Investment Co. v. Shepherd 9.183, 10.132
Lefebvre v. Lefebvre Frères Ltée 15.59
Legg v. Evans 8.74
Legion Credit Union (Co-liquidators of) v. British Columbia (Minister of
   Finance and Corporate Relations) 5.35
Legion Oils Ltd. v. Barron 12.85
Legion Oils Ltd. v. Barron (No. 2) 11.49, 11.106
Lehndorff Canadian Pension Properties Ltd. v. Davis & Co. 3.57, 11.238
Lehr v. Bassano (Town) 5.59
Lei v. Noble China Inc. 12.63
Leiser v. Popham Brothers Ltd. 7.223
Lemay Ltd., Re 12.86
Lemon v. Austin Friars Investment Trust Ltd. 8.130
Lemonides, R. v. 4.11
Len Plumbing & Heating Co., Re 5.80, 5.146
Lenart, R. v. 4.50
Lennard's Carrying Co. v. Asiatic Petroleum Co. 3.10, 3.24, 3.42, 9.2
Leon Chevrolet, Inc. v. Trapp 9.89, 10.2
Leslie v. Canadian Birkbeck Co. 7.315
Lester & Orpen Dennys Ltd. v. Canadian Broadcasting Corp. 13.171
Letain v. Conwest Exploration Co. 4.39, 5.156
Levi v. Chartersoft Canada Inc. 11.238
Levin v. Clark 11.144
Levis County Rlwy. v. Fontaine 8.171, 8.270
Levy v. Abercorris Slate and Slab Co. 8.130

Levy-Russell Ltd. v. Shieldings
Inc. 8.18, 8.28, 11.82, 11.135, 13.30, 13.31, 13.66, 13.73
Levy-Russell Ltd. v. TecMotiv Inc. 2.36, 10.42, 11.44
Lewis v. Fuqua...11.35, 13.229, 13.230
Lewis v. Vogelstein 11.102
Lewis, R. v. 4.50
Lickbarrow v. Mason... 6.81
Lifschultz Fast Freight, Re... 13.189
Limberlost Club, Re... 8.10
Lindgren v. L. & P. Estates Ltd. 2.70, 11.168, 11.123
Lindsay Petroleum Co. v. Hurd 5.176, 5.180
Lindsay v. Imperial Steel & Wire Co. 7.166
Lindthaler v. Minister of National Revenue... 2.30
Lindzon v. International Sterling Holdings Inc. 11.49, 13.98, 14.41
Linedata Services SA v. Katatakis.. 12.209
Lion Breweries Ltd. v. Scarrott... 13.257
Lion Mutual Marine Insurance Assoc. Ltd. v. Tucker 7.196, 7.236
Lippitt v. Ashley 9.20, 11.14, 11.35
Liquidator of Coopérants, Mutual Life Insurance Society v. Dubois 15.39
Liquidator of Iroquois Falls Community Credit Union Ltd. v. Co-Operators
General Insurance Co. 15.21
Liquidator of Markham General Insurance Co. v. Bennett.......................... 15.80
Lister v. Dunlop 8.148, 8.151
Litemor Distributors (Ottawa) Ltd. v. W.C. Somers Electric Ltd. ... 5.203, 15.159
Little Olympian Each-ways Ltd., Re.. 13.147
Little v. Spreadbury 6.46
Littlewoods Mail Order Stores Ltd. v. McGregor... 2.69
Litwin Construction (1973) Ltd. v. Pan 11.115, 11.123, 12.123
Litwin v. Allen 10.22, 11.19, 11.208
Litz v. R. Litz & Sons Co. 7.224
Liu v. Sung.. 13.233
Liverpool Household Stores Asso. 10.116
Livingstone v. Temperance Colonization Society 7.283
Lloyd v. European & North American Rlwy. 5.70, 5.73
Lloyd v. Grace, Smith & Co. 3.2, 3.4, 6.81, 6.104
Lloyd's Bank Canada v. Canada Life Assurance Co. 13.65
Lloyds Estate v. Roets Estate.. 15.176
Lobstick Golf & Tennis Club Inc. v. Harris....................................... 12.40, 12.41
Loch v. John Blackwood Ltd. 15.64, 15.66
LoCicero v. B.A.C.M. Industries Ltd. 14.69
Locke & Smith Ltd., Re... 8.193
Locke v. Queensland Investment Co. 8.66
Lockhart v. C.P.R. 3.4
Lockharts Ltd. v. Excalibur Holdings Ltd. 2.29
Loeb v. Provigo Inc. 7.301, 13.233
Loewen Group Inc., Re.. 14.239
Logging Co. v. Random Services Corp. 6.20
Logicrose Ltd. v. Southend United Football Club Ltd. 11.155

Lollypops (Harbourside) Pty. Limited v. Werncog Pty. Ltd. 7.245
London & General Bank (No. 2), Re 9.160, 9.168, 9.176, 9.183
London & Mashonaland Exploration Co. v. New Mashonaland Exploration
    Co. 11.132
London & New York Investment Corp., Re 6.33
London & Northern Bank, ex p. Jones, Re 7.78
London Assurance v. Mansel 7.100
London Chatham & Dover Rlwy. v. South Eastern Rlwy. 8.29
London County & Westminster Bank Ltd. v. Tompkins 8.86
London Drugs Ltd. v. Kuehne & Nagel International Ltd. 3.14, 3.55, 11.231
London Finance Corp. v. Banking Service Corp. 9.122
London Guarantee & Accident Co. v. Abrams 11.164
London India Rubber Co., Re 7.321
London Loan & Savings Co. of Canada v. Brickenden 10.41
London Pressed Hinge Co., Re 8.81
London School of Electronics Ltd., Re 13.18, 13.42, 13.157
London Speaker Printing Co., Re 396, 397
London, Brighton & South Coast Rlwy. v. Goodwin 14.136
London, Hamburg & Continental Exchange Bank (Emmerson's Case),
    Re 7.76, 7.255, 15.41
Long Acre Press Ltd. v. Odhams Press Ltd. 8.197
Long Park Inc. v. Trenton-New Brunswick Theaters Co. 12.203
Long v. Guelph Lumber Co. 12.22
Long v. Hancock 8.23
Long v. The Guelph Lumber Co. 7.275, 7.325, 7.341
Lonrho Ltd. v. Shell Petroleum Co. 11.80
Lopez v. TDI Services, Inc. 11.35
Loranger v. Dorion 1.52
Lord Corporation Pty. Ltd. v. Green 15.92
Loudon v. Archer-Daniels Midland Co. 11.199
Lough v. Canadian Natural Resources Ltd. 14.69
Louis K. Liggett Co. v. Lee 1.30
Louis v. Smellie 11.151
Love Hill v. Spurgeon, Re 8.168
Lovenheim v. Iroquois Brands Ltd. 112.192, 12.196
Lovibond v. Grand Truck Railway Co. of Canada 7.20. 7.208
Low v. Ascot Jockey Club 13.18, 13.82, 13.123
Lowry v. Commercial & Farmers Bank 7.192
LSI Logic Corp. of Canada, Inc. v. Logani 13.75, 14.156
Lubin, Rosen & Associates Ltd., Re 15.154
Lucking's Will Trusts, Renwick v. Lucking, Re 13.199
Ludlow v. McMillan 13.27
Lukey v. Ruthenian Farmers' Elevator Co. 4.52
Lumbers v. Fretz 10.72, 12.49, 12.62
Lundy Granite Co., Re 10.72
Lunn v. B.C.L. Holdings Inc. 12.3, 13.28
Lunness, Re 7.168
Lunney v. Welland Securities Ltd. 12.11

Luther v. C.J. Luther Co. 11.112
Luther v. Sagor & Co. 15.169
Lycette v. Green River Gorge, Inc. 12.3
Lydney & Wigpool Iron Ore Co. v. Bird 5.171, 5.173
Lyford v. Media Portfolio Ltd. 6.63
Lyle & Scott's Trustees v. British Investment Trust Ltd. 7.225
Lymburn v. Mayland 4.40, 4.41, 4.46, 4.51, 4.55, 4.56
Lynde v. Anglo-Italian Hemp Spinning Co. 7.112

M

M. (K.) v. M. (H.) 11.196, 11.197
M. v. H. 13.110
M.G. Bancorporation v. LeBeau 14.78
M.H. Smith (Plant Hire) Ltd. v. Mainwaring 15.161
M.J. O'Brien Ltd. v. British America Nickel Corp. (1925) 14.264
M.P. Guimaraens & Son v. Fonseca & Vanconcellos Ltd. 5.95
M.P.M. Enterprises, Inc. v. Gilbert 14.75
Mabou Coal & Gypsum Co., Re 11.134
Macaura v. Northern Assurance Co. 2.12
Macdonald v. Drake 11.266, 11.271
Macdonald v. Georgian Bay Lumber 15.171
Macdonald v. Master Cartage Inc. 15.58
Macdonald v. Soulis 7.87
MacDougall v. Gardiner 5.48, 13.199, 13.256
MacDougall v. Johnson 7.18
MacDougall v. Union Navigation Co. 4.14
MacFarlane, Re 1.49
MacKay & Hughes (1973), Ltd. v. Martin Potatoes Inc. 8.145
MacKay v. Commercial Bank of New Brunswick 3.3
MacKenzie & Co., Re 12.81
Mackenzie v. Craig 11.172, 13.65, 13.205, 15.51
MacKenzie v. MacKenzie 5.36
Mackenzie v. Maple Mountain Mining Co. 5.51, 5.52. 5.58
Maclaine Watson & Co. v. ITC 5.162
MacLean v. Portland Masonry Ltd. 5.208
MacMillan Bloedel Ltd. v. Binstead 11.48, 11.165
MacMillan, R. v. 7.145
MacMullin v. A. & B. Miller Contracting Ltd. 5.208
MacPhail v. Tackama Forest Products Ltd. 2.58, 2.60
MacPherson v. Boyce 15.51
MacPherson v. deWinter 5.169
MacPherson v. Ritz Management Inc. 15.90
MacRae v. Broder 15.158
Macro (Ipswich) Ltd., Re 13.157, 13.160
Macson Development Co. v. Gordon 10.25, 12.31
Madden v. Dimond 11.48, 11.104, 11.115, 11.185, 11.281
Madden v. Nelson & Fort Sheppard Rlwy. Co. 4.4

Madi Pty. Ltd., Re 6.43
Madrid Bank Ltd. v. Bayley 15.71, 15.92
Maelor Jones Investments (Noarlunga) Pty Ltd. v. Heywood
    Smith 15.118, 15.123
Magdalena Steam Navigation Co., Re 8.25
Magical Waters Fountains Ltd. v. Sarnia (City) 5.8
Magnacrete Ltd. v. Douglas-Hill 12.36, 12.181
Magog Textile & Print Co. v. Price 7.77
Mahony v. East Holyford Mining Co. 6.46, 6.54, 9.112
Maiklem v. Springbank Oil & Gas Ltd. 11.43
Main St. Brewing Co., Re 13.184
Main v. Delcan Group Inc. 11.23, 13.152
Major (Inspector of Taxes) v. Brodie 4.19
Malcolm v. Transtec Holdings Ltd. 11.194
Malleson v. National Insurance & Guarantee Corp. 14.45
Malone v. Brincat 11.199
Maloney v. Maloney 13.88
Malouf v. Labad 7.21, 7.24
Mammone v. Doralin Investments Ltd. 15.64
Mamone v. Pantzer 15.102
Mancetter Developments Ltd. v. Garmanson Ltd. 3.55
Manchester & Milford Rlwy., Re. 8.250
Manchuck v. Byle 1.60
Manco Home Systems Ltd., Re 14.133
Manes Tailoring Co. v. Willson 5.51, 5.60, 5.144, 10.85
Mangan v. Terminal Transport System 2.51
Manitoba Commission Co., Re 15.45
Manitoba Securities Commission v. Versatile Cornat Corp. 14.47
Manitoulin Quartzite Ltd., Re 7.76, 7.88
Manley Inc. v. Fallis 2.59, 2.68
Mann v. Goldstein 15.70
Mannai Limited v. Eagle Star Association Company Ltd. 7.245
Manning v. Harris Steel Group Inc. 14.54, 14.62, 14.63, 14.66
Manson v. Curtis 10.17, 12.201
Mantei v. Morris 2.28
Manulife Financial Services Ltd. v. BTK Holdings Ltd. 11.210
Manurewa Transport Ltd., Re 8.155
Maple Engineering & Construction Canada Ltd. v. 1373988 Ontario
    Inc. 5.203, 6.38
Maple Leaf Foods Inc. v. Schneider
    Corp. 7.67, 13.19, 13.43, 13.48, 13.49, 13.157, 14.142, 14.148, 14.150
Maranda-Desaulniers v. Peckham 15.80
Marblestone Industries Ltd. v. Fairchild 5.201
Marc-Jay Investments Inc. v. Levy 13.209
Maredelanto Compania Naviera S.A. v. Bergbau-Handel Gmbh,
    The Mihalis Angelos 13.162
Mareva Compania Naviera, SA v. International Bulk Carriers, SA 2.46
Mariani v. Price Waterhouse 9.190.7

Maritime National Fish Ltd. v. Ocean Trawlers, Ltd. 15.125
Maritime United Farmers Co-op Ltd. v. Dickie... 7.114
Mark Developments Ltd. v. Big White Ski Developments Ltd. 6.25
Marks & Spencer v. One in a Million and Others.. 5.74
Marks v. Rocsand Co. 10.69
Marr v. Tumulty... 3.47, 6.22
Marshall v. Marshall Boston Iron Mines Ltd. 12.98
Marshall v. South Staffordshire Tramways Co. 4.76
Marshall's Valve Gear Co. v. Manning Wardle & Co. 9.13, 10.35
Marstar Trading International Inc., R. v. 2.61
Martello & Sons Ltd., Re.. 13.270, 15.65
Martin Ruby Ltd. v. National Upholstering Manufacturing Co. 8.130
Martin v. Artyork Investments Ltd. 6.59, 8.25
Martin v. Columbia Metals Corp. 11.173
Martin v. F.P. Bourgault Industries Air Seeder Division Ltd. 14.41, 14.42
Martin v. Gibson 7.51, 11.111
Martin v. Goldfarb 11.132, 13.143
Martin v. Martin.. 8.332
Martin v. Perrie 15.162
Martin, R. v. 3.42
Marv-Eon Signs Ltd. v. Vogue Shoppe (1977) Ltd. 11.235
Marzetti's Case 11.13
Marzitelli v. Verona Construction Ltd. 15.60
Masecar v. McKenzie & Son 15.146
Mason v. Intercity Properties Ltd. 13.99, 13.101, 13.138, 14.70
Massey Manufacturing Co., Re... 5.4
Massey v. Sladden 8.149
Massey v. Wales 12.32
Massey-Harris Co., R. v... 4.14
Master Records Inc. v. Backman 9.121
Mathers v. Mathers 10.6, 12.8
Matheson Brothers Ltd., Re... 6.107
Matthew Guy Carriage & Automobile Co., Re.. 7.335
Matthew v. Guardian Assurance Co. 4.24, 4.25
Matthews Bros. v. Pullen 13.184
Matthews v. Maurice 5.182
Maxwell Communications Corp. plc (No. 2), Re 8.291, 8.294
Maxwell Taylor's Restaurants Inc. v. Carcasole.. 14.96
Maxx Petroleum Ltd. v. Amercian Eagle Petroleum Ltd. 12.24
Maxymych v. Kleinstein... 13.211
Mayor of Colchester v. Brooke... 15.13
Mazzotta v. Twin Gold Mines Ltd. 13.105
MC United Masonry Ltd., Re... 3.2
McAlister v. Eclipse Oil Co. 7.167
McAlister v. McAlister 7.168
McArthur v. Imperial Trust Co. 3.6
McAskill v. Northwestern Trust Co. 7.83
McAteer v. Devoncroft Developments Ltd. 6.63, 6.82, 6.89, 10.56, 12.209

McAusland v. Deputy Commissioner of Taxation.................................... 15.188
McClurg v. Canada 7.62, 7.297, 7.301, 7.331
McConnachie v. M.N.R. 11.289
McConnell v. NEWCO Financial Corp. 14.58
McCormack v. Carman 15.13
McCoubrey, Re.. 8.303
McCracken v. McIntyre 7.164
McCulloch v. State of Maryland.. 1.33
McCullough v. M.N.R. 11.289
McCurdy v. Gorrie.. 12.92, 12.112
McCurdy v. Oak Tire & Rubber Co. 7.55, 7.226
McCutcheon Lumber Co. v. Minitonas (Municipality) 8.210
McDermott, Inc. v. Lewis 15.1174
McDonald v. Dickenson 3.4
McDonald v. Great Western Rlwy. Co. 8.32, 8.271
McDonald v. Klondike Government Concession Ltd. 4.25
McDonnell, R. v. 3.24, 3.42, 3.52
McDougall Segur Exploration Co. v. Solloway, Mills & Co. 7.210
McDougall v. Black Lake Asbestos & Chrome Co. 12.59, 12.63
McDougall v. Gamble... 15.73
McDowell v. Macklem 7.76
McEwen v. Goldcorp Inc. 13.41, 13.48, 13.143, 14.257
McFadden v. 481782 Ontario Ltd. 3.57, 11.244
McGaffigan v. National Husker Co. 7.114
McGauley v. British Columbia 13.202
McGill Chair Co., Re 7.335
McInerney v. MacDonald 11.195
McInnis v. Tignish Fisheries Ltd. 7.255
McIntosh, R. v. 1.27
McIntyre Ranching Co. v. Cardston (Municipality) 5.59
McKain v. Canadian Birkbeck Investment & Savings Co. 7.346
McKain, Re 7.223
McKee v. Dumas 3.4
McKenna v. Spooner Oils Ltd. 5.40, 9.65, 12.135
McKenzie v. Montreal & Ottawa Junction Rlwy. Co. 8.66, 8.270
McKeown v. Boudard-Perveril Gear Co. 7.101
McKinnon v. Doran 8.131
McKnight Construction Co. v. Vansickler... 5.152
McLachlan v. Canadian Imperial Bank of Commerce................................ 8.219
McLaughlin v. Solloway.. 11.227
McLennan Holdings Pty. Ltd., Re 15.41
McLennan v. Newton.. 11.158
McMan Oil & Gas Co. v. Hurley 6.60
McMaster v. Byrne 11.131
McMullin v. Beran... 11.27, 11.45, 11.199
McMurrich v. Bond Head Harbour Co. 7.344
McNamara (No. 1), R. v. 3.13
McNaughton v. Exchange National Bank.. 1.44

McNaughton, R. v.	7.148
McNeil v. Fultz	8.131
McPherson v. Forlong	11.163
McQuade v. Stoneham	10.17, 12.31
McRae v. Corbett	5.69
McRobb, R. v.	8.44
McWilliams v. Geddes & Moss Undertaking Co.	12.9
Meade, Re	8.323
Meadow Farm Ltd. v. Imperial Bank of Canada	2.3, 6.79
Measures Brothers Ltd. v. Measures	15.92, 15.188
Medical Committee for Human Rights v. SEC	12.192
Meditrust Healthcare Inc. v. Shoppers Drug Mart	13.195, 13.233
Meinhard v. Salmon	11.115
Meltzer v. Western Paper Box Co.	13.119, 15.63
Memec plc v. Inland Revenue Commissioners	4.19
Mendl v. Smith	8.34
Menegon v. Philip	7.134
Menell et Cie, Re	7.326
Menier v. Hooper's Telegraph Works	10.71, 12.131, 13.232, 13.257
Mentmore Manufacturing Co. v. National Merchandise Manufacturing Co.	3.55, 3.56, 3.59, 11.210, 11.216
Menzies-Gibson Ltd., Re	5.120
Mercantile Bank v. Leon's Furniture Ltd.	8.219
Mercantile Investments & General Trust Co. v. International Co. of Mexico	14.264
Mercator Enterprises Ltd. v. Harris	12.153
Merchandise Transport Ltd. v. British Transport Commission	2.26, 2.30
Merchant Commercial Real Estate Services Inc. v. Alberta (Registrar of Corporations)	5.96
Merchants Bank of Canada v. Handcock	5.55
Mercury Marine Ltd. v. Dillon	11.152, 11.175
Mercury Partners & Co. v. Cybersurf Corp.	12.85
Meridian Global Funds Management Asia Ltd. v. Securities Commission	3.11, 3.18, 11.43
Merkur Bros. v. W.J. McCart & Co.	5.151
Merrimac Paper Co., Re	13.185, 13.187
Merryweather v. Nixon	11.299
Mesheau v. Campbell	11.261
Metal Constituents Ltd., Re	7.112
Metal Manufacturers Ltd. v. Lewis	1.30
Metera v. Financial Planning Group	5.81, 5.172
Metropolis Motorcycles Ltd; Hale v. Waldock, Re	13.37
Metropolitan Commercial Carpet Centre Ltd. v. Donovan	11.152, 11.176, 13.125
Metropolitan Life Assurance Co. v. Urel	11.103
Metropolitan Mortgage & Savings Co., Re	8.20
Metropolitan Toronto Condo. Corp. No. 1000 v. Ontario	15.167
Metropolitan Toronto Police Widows & Orphans Fund v. Telus Comm.	7.240

Metropolitan Trust Co. of Canada v. Henneberry 8.293
Meunier v. National Finance Corp. 7.173
Mexican Light & Power Co. v. Shareholders of Mexican Light & Power
  Co. 15.18
Meyers v. Lucknow Elevator Co. 7.51, 7.223, 15.155
Meyers v. Richards 7.206
Michael P. Georgas Ltd., Re 15.73
Michael v. Bank of Montreal 8.20
Michalak v. Biotech Electronics Ltd. 13.30, 13.122
Mickshaw v. Coca Cola Bottling Co. 6.88
Middelkamp v. Fraser Valley Real Estate Board 14.73
Midland Counties & Shannon Junction Ry. Co., R. v. 7.196
Midland Counties District Bank v. Attwood 15.125
Mid-West Collieries Ltd. v. McEwen 8.23, 9.137, 10.24, 11.246
Milam v. Cooper Co. 12.3
Milani v. Banks 8.41
Milburn v. Wilson 5.182
Millard v. North George Capital Management Ltd. 5.172
Miller v. Diamond Light & Heating Co. 10.32, 11.180
Miller v. F. Mendel Holdings Ltd. 12.5, 12.12, 12.52, 12.95, 13.23, 13.123
Miller v. Thompson 5.165
Miller, Court & Manley Ltd. (in Liquidation), Re 15.130
Millgate Financial Corp. v. BF Realty Holdings Ltd. 8.171, 8.186, 8.189, 11.212
Millheim v. Barewa Oil and Mining NL 13.261
Milligan v. Bergman 12.104, 12.153
Mills Acquisition Co. v. Macmillan, Inc. 11.24, 11.121
Mills v. Dowdall 2.48
Mills v. Mills 7.56, 11.68, 11.08, 11.160, 11.193, 13.6
Mills-Hughes v. Raynor 11.267
Milne v. Durham Hosiery Mills Ltd. 7.83
Milowski and Director of the Employment Standards Division, Re 11.270
Mimico Sewer Pipe & Brick Mfg. Co., Re 11.159
Ming Minerals Inc. v. Blagdon 12.205
Minister of National Revenue v. Cameron 1.43
Minister of National Revenue v. Eldridge 1.31
Minister of Rlwys. & Canals for Dominion of Canada v. Quebec Southern
  Rlwy. Co. & South Shore Rlwy. Co. 8.169
Minneapolis-St. Paul & S.S.M., Re 8.197
Minton v. Cavaney 2.35
Misener v. H.L. Misener & Son Ltd. 11.48, 11.128
Missalla v. Brown 1.43
Mission Hill Tire & Auto Centre Ltd. v. Killerney Group Ltd. 2.3
Mississauga (City) v. Greater Toronto Airports Authority 4.50
Mister Broadloom Corp. (1968) v. Bank of Montreal 8.149
Mitchell & Hobbs (U.K.) Ltd. v. Mill 10.35, 10.85
Mizel v. Connelly 13.230
MM Companies Inc. v. Liquid Audio Inc. 14.8
Mobile Steel Co., Re 13.185

Moco Management Ltd. v. Llernam Holdings Ltd. 12.49, 12.50, 12.74
Modern Livestock Ltd. v. Kansa General Insurance Co. 15.162
Modstock Mining Co. v. Harris 9.113, 9.114
Mogil v. Abelson 11.150
Mohan v. Philmar Lumber (Markham) Ltd. 13.69, 13.83, 13.205
Molchan v. Omega Oil & Gas Ltd. 10.41, 11.148
Molineux v. London, Birmingham & Manchester Insurance Co. 10.5
Molson Bank v. Halter 8.341
Molson Inc., Re 14.200
Molyneux v. Hamm 12.18
Monarch Bank of Canada, Re 7.77, 7.87
Monarch Life Assurance Co. v. Brophy 7.87
Mondor v. Fisherman 5.172
Monsanto Canada Inc. v. Schmeiser 3.55, 11.216
Montel v. Groupe de consultants P.G.L. Inc. 4.39
Montgomery & Wrights Ltd., Re 3.2, 7.24, 7.208
Montgomery v. Mitchell 7.344
Montgomery v. Shell Canada Ltd. 14.67
Montreal & St. Lawrence Light & Power Co. v. Robert 10.34
Montreal (City) v. Montreal Street Railway Co. 4.42
Montreal Trust Co. of Canada v. Call-Net Enterpreises Inc. 3.67
Montreal Trust Co. of Canada v. ScotiaMcLeod Inc. 2.33, 3.55, 3.57, 11.210
Montreal Trust Co. v. Abitibi Power & Paper Co. 8.30, 8.61, 8.271
Montreal Trust Co. v. Oxford Pipe Line Co. 12.49, 12.128
Montreal Trust Co. v. Stanrock Uranium Mines Ltd. 8.33
Moodie v. W. & J. Sheppard Ltd. 7.222
Moore & Port Bruce Harbour Co., Re 9.97, 9.114
Moore v. Gurney 7.77
Moore v. I. Bresler Ltd. 3.18, 3.45, 6.104
Moore v. Murphy 7.86
Moore v. Northwood 7.283
Moore v. Ontario Investment Association 7.107
Moore v. Texaco Canada Ltd. 8.110
Moore v. Valder 9.164
Moorgate Mercantile Holdings Ltd., Re 12.77, 12.118
Moose Securities Ltd. v. Minister of National Revenue 2.58
Moran v. Household International. Inc. 11.53
Moran v. Pyle National (Canada) Ltd. 4.21, 4.22
Morden Woollen Mills Co. v. Heckles 12.59
Moreland Metal Co. v. Comlinshaw 5.71
Morgan v. 45 Flyers Avenue Pty. Ltd. 5.1, 13.21, 13.36, 13.156
Morgan v. A. G. P.E.I. 4.57
Morgan v. Saskatchewan 2.33
Moriarity v. Slater 13.66, 13.93
Morin v. Anger 7.107
Morlock and Cline Ltd., Re 11.9
Morris Funeral Services Ltd., Re 12.43
Morris v. C.W. Martin & Sons Ltd. 3.6

Morris v. Call the Car Alarm Guys Inc. 2.17
Morris v. Kanssen 6.66, 9.112
Morrisburgh & Ottawa Electric Rlwy. v. O'Connor 7.117
Morrison & Mahoney v. New Brunswick 5.8
Morrison v. New Brunswick 1.2
Morrison, Jones & Taylor Ltd., Re 8.149
Morritt, Re 8.82
Morrow v. Hayes 8.3
Morrow v. Peterborough Water Co. 15.136
Morse Electro Products (Can.) Corp. v. Central Discount House Ltd. 5.207
Mortgage Insurance Co. of Canada v. Innisfil Landfill Corp. 15.167
Mortimer v. Harley & Co. 7.260
Morton v. Asper 12.123
Morton v. Cowan 7.21
Mosely v. Koffyfontein Mines Ltd. 7.49
Moskowitz v. Bantrell 11.148
Moss Steamship Co. v. Whinney 10.26
Motherwell v. Schoof 11.200, 11.202
Motor Car Supply Co. of Canada v. A.G. Alberta 4.47, 4.51
Motor Mfrs. & Traders, Ltd. v. Motors Mfrs. & Traders Mutual Insurance
  Co. 5.110
Moto-Sway Corp. of America v. Standard Steel Construction Co. 15.154
Mountain State Steel Foundries Inc. v. C.I.R. 8.11
Mountain State Steel Foundries Inc. v. CIR 7.273
Movitex Ltd. v. Bulfield 10.44, 11.155
Moxham v. Grant 7.342
Moyes v. Fortune Financial Corp. 5.172
Mozley v. Alston 12.35, 13.199, 13.202
MTC Leasing v. National Bank Leasing Inc. 8.207
Mueller Canada Inc. v. State Contractors Inc. 14.73
Muir v. City of Glasgow Bank 12.13
Muldowan v. German Canadian Land Co. 9.57
Muljardi v. O'Brien 13.93
Muljo v. Sunwest Projects Ltd. 7.62, 7.284
Mulligan v. Lancaster 11.271
Mulliner v. Florence 8.74
Mullins v. Collins 3.23
Multinational Gas & Petrochemical Co. v. Multinational Gas & Petrochemical
  Services Ltd. 3.10, 11.5, 11.80, 11.192, 12.36
Multiple Access Ltd. v. McCutcheon 4.10, 4.39, 4.57
Multiponics Inc., Re 13.185
Murano v. Bank of Montreal 8.55
Murray Hill Limousine Service Ltd. v. Batson 4.50
Music Corpn. of America v. Music Corpn. (Gt. Britain), Ltd. 5.113
Musselwhite v. C.H. Musselwhite & Son Ltd. 12.80
Mutchenbacker v. Dominion Bank 6.55
Mutter v. Eastern & Midlands Railway Co. 6.122

Mutual Life Insurance Co. of New York v. Rank Organization
Ltd. 5.53, 7.251, 9.13, 11.59, 11.63
Myers v. Aquarell Pty. Ltd. 6.93
Myers v. Union Natural Gas Co. 6.79

N

N. Rattenbury Ltd. v. Winchester 11.48
N. Slater Co., Re 12.62, 14.245
N.A. Properties (1994) Ltd. v. D.I.A. Holdings Ltd. 13.31
N.B. Power Co. v. Maritime Transit Ltd. 6.7
N.W. Robbie & Co. v. Witney Warehouse Co. 8.145
NA Properties (1994), Ltd. v. DIA Holdings Ltd. 7.318
Naaykens v. Bayes Equipment (Neepawa) Ltd. 13.24, 13.148
Nadeau v. Nadeau & Nadeau Ltd. 7.222, 12.92, 12.153
Nagrella Manufacturing Co., Re 7.54
Nagy v. M.N.R. 11.289
Nalcap Holdings Inc. v. Kelvin Energy Ltd. 12.43
Naneff v. Con-Crete Holdings
Ltd. 13.83, 13.91, 13.104, 13.105, 13.128, 137, 13.140
Narnard v. Duplessis Independent Shoe Machinery Co. 5.60
Nash Brick & Pottery Manufacturing Co., Re 8.23
Nash v. Lancegaye Safety Glass (Ireland) Ltd. 12.71
Nasmith v. Manning.. 7.76, 12.7
Nassau Phosphate Co., Re.. 5.38
Natal Land & Colonization Co. v. Pauline Colliery & Development
Syndicate Ltd. 5.186, 12.202
National Acceptance Co. of America v. Pintura Corp. 11.214, 11.226
National Australia Bank Ltd. v. Composite Buyers Ltd. 8.146
National Bank of Australasia v. Falkingham 8.200
National Bank of Canada v. Merit Energy Ltd. 13.179
National Bank of Greece, SA. v. Pinios Shipping Co. (No. 1) and Another,
The Maria.. 8.29
National Bank of Wales, Re.. 7.310, 10.117
National Building Maintenance Ltd. v. Dove 15.46, 15.63
National Building Maintenance Ltd., Re 13.23, 15.15.46, 15.63
National Can. Corp. v. Liberato 8.19
National Coal Board v. Gamble 3.43
National Debenture & Assets Corp., Re 5.159
National Drive-in Theaters Ltd., Re... 15.64
National Dwellings Society v. Sykes 12.84, 12.86
National Funds Assurance Co., Re 7.296
National Grocers Co., Re 12.153, 14.249
National Insurance Co. v. Egleson 7.76
National Land & Loan Co. v. Rat Portage Lumber Co. 5.60
National Malleable Castings Co. v. Smiths' Falls Malleable Castings Co. 5.144
National Manure Co. v. Donald 6.13
National Savings Bank Association, Re... 7.79

National Stadium Ltd., Re 7.83, 7.87
National Telephone Co., Re 7.41
National Trust Co. v. Ebro Irrigation & Power Co. ...4.61, 6.109, 15.109, 15.151
National Trust Co. v. Gilbert 7.19, 7.328
National Trust Co. v. H & R Block Canada Inc. 1.27
National Trust Co. v. Mead 14.133
National Trust Co. v. Vancouver Kraft Co. 8.164, 8.184, 8.192
National Trust v. Bouckhuyt 7.157
National Trustees Co. of Australasia v. General Finance Co. of Australasia 8.176
National Westminster Bank Ltd. v. Halesowen Presswork & Assemblies
    Ltd. 8.293
National Westminster Bank plc v. I.R.C. 7.54
National Westminster Bank plc v. Inland Revenue Comm. 12.4
National Westminster Bank plc v. Spectrum Plus Ltd. 8.202
Natural Sodium Products Ltd. v. Holland 11.185
NBD Bank, Canada v. Dofasco Inc. 7.96, 8.108, 11.225
NCR Australia v. Credit Connection 6.69
Neato Employment Services v. Australian Securities and Investments
    Commission 14.139
Nedco Ltd. v. Clark 2.28
Neil M'Leod & Sons Ltd., Re 12.178
Nelles v. Ontario Investment Association 7.107
Nelson Coke & Gas Co. v. Pellatt 7.54, 7.77, 7.79, 7.83, 12.7
Nelson v. CTC Mortgage Corp. 8.140
Nelson v. Rentown Enterprises Inc. 7.263, 7.267, 7.273, 8.11
Neonex International Ltd. v. Kolasa 14.69
Neptune (Vehicle Washing Equipment) Ltd. v. Fitzgerald 10.44, 10.50
Neri v. Finch Hardware (1976) Ltd. 12.3, 13.27, 13.56, 13.130, 13.135
Nesbitt Thompson v. Pigott & Pigott Construction Co. 7.114
Netupsky v. Canada 9.120
Neumann, R. v. 10.168
New Brunswick & Canada Rlwy. & Land Co. v. Muggeridge 7.91, 7.99
New Brunswick Assn. of Real Estate Appraisers v. Poitras 6.16
New Bullas Trading Ltd., Re 8.201
New Cedos Engineering Co., Re 12.35
New Chile Gold Mining Co., Re 2.14
New Era Packaging, Inc., Re 13.184
New Federal Oils Ltd. v. Rowland 7.157
New Lambton Land & Coal Co. v. London Bank of Australia Ltd. 7.204
New Land Design Inc., Re 5.120
New Quebec Raglan Mines v. Blok-Anderson 13.138
New South Wales Henry George Foundation v. Booth 12.132
New Westminster (City), R. v. 4.47
New World Alliance Pty Ltd., Re 11.76
New World Pictures v. New World Video Inc. 5.117
New York Trust Co. v. American Realty Co. 10.65
New York, Lake Erie & Western Railroad v. Nicklas 7.319

New Zealand Conference of Seventh Day Adventists v. Registrar of
Companies 5.87
New Zealand Farmers' Co-operative Distributing Co. v. National Mortgage &
Agency Co. of New Zealand 11.298
New Zealand Gold Extraction Co (Newbery-Vautin Process) Ltd. v.
Peacock 12.5
New Zealand Netherlands Society "Oranje" Inc. v. Kuys 11.153
Newborne v. Sensolid (Great Britain) Ltd. 5.187, 5.189, 5.201
Newhart Developments Ltd. v. Co-operative Commercial Bank Ltd. 10.26
Newman & Co., Re 12.178
Newman v. Gint 7.80
Newman v. Warren 9.22, 10.5
News Ltd. v. Australian Rugby Football League Ltd. 11.117
Newton National Bank v. Newbegin 13.175
NFU Development Trust Ltd., Re 14.238
Ngurli Ltd. v. McCann 11.160, 12.130, 13.258
Niagara Falls Heating & Supply Co., Re 12.20
Niagara Falls Road Co. v. Benson 5.35
Nicholas v. Soundcraft Electronics Ltd. 13.37
Nicholls v. Tavistock U.D.C. 5.60
Nicholson v. Permakraft (N.Z.) Ltd. 11.80, 11.82
Nieforth v. Nieforth Bros. Ltd. 15.60
Nielsen Estate v. Epton 11.220.1
Nixon v. Blackwell 10.58
NMRA Insurance Group Ltd. v. Spragg 12.174
Noble v. Cameron 12.47
Nocton v. Lord Ashburton 12.123
Nolan v. Parsons 10.34, 10.72
Norcan Oils Ltd. v. Fogler 14.118
Norcen International Ltd. v. Sunco Inc. 14.133
Nord Resources Corp. v. Nord Pacific Ltd. 13.111
Norman v. Theodore Goddard 11.168
Normandy v. Ind, Cooper & Co. 10.70
Normart Management Ltd. v. West Hill Redevelopment Co. 3.58, 11.245
Norris v. Wright 11.10
Norris, Re 8.336
Norseman Products Ltd., Re 14.267
North American Co. v. SEC 13.240
North American Life Assurance Co. v. Silver's Ltd. 6.15
North Bay Supply Co., Re 7.166
North Queensland Auto Spares Co., Re 5.71
North Sydney Mining & Transportation Co. v. Greener 7.86
North West Battery Ltd. v. Hargrave 10.8
North West Electric Co. v. Walsh 5.63
North Western Railway Co. v. McMichael 7.197
Northern & Central Gas Corp. v. Hillcrest Collieries 11.227
Northern Construction Ltd., Re 7.162
Northern Counties Securities Ltd. v. Jackson & Steeple Ltd. ... 12.76, 12.102, 12.124

Northern Creameries Ltd. v. Rossington Produce Co. 7.315
Northern Crown Bank v. Great West Lumber Co. 2.8
Northern Electric Co. v. Frank Warkentin Electric Ltd. 2.3
Northern Life Assurance Co. v. McMaster, Montgomery, Fluery & Co. .. 11.208
Northern Meat Packers Ltd. v. Roynat Ltd. 8.149
Northern Office Micro Computers Ltd. v. Rosenstein.............................. 11.175
Northern Ontario Power Co. v. LaRoche Mines Ltd. 15.125
Northern Ontario Power Co., Re.. 7.327, 15.26
Northern Telecom Canada Ltd. v. Communication Workers of Canada 4.1
Northern Telecom Ltd. v. Communications Workers of Canada................... 4.50
Northern Trust Co. v. Butchart 9.114, 11.13
Northland Bank v. G.I.C. Industries Ltd. 8.146
Northland Bank v. Willson 3.9, 11.17
Northland Bank, Re 8.301
Northland Office Systems Group Inc. v. Northland Stationers (1963) Ltd. 5.124
Northland Superior Supply Co. and S.M.W. Local 397, Re 11.262, 11.268
Northrop Mining Co. v. Dimock... 5.176
Northside Developments Pty. Ltd. v. Registrar-General............. 6.43, 6.45, 6.79
Northumberland Insurance Ltd. (in liq.) v. Alexander & Ors..................... 9.187
Northwest Forest Products Ltd., Re 13.210, 13.213
Northwest Trading Co. v. Northwest Trading Co. 5.113
North-West Transportation Co. v. Beatty 10.51, 12.127, 11.155, 13.6, 13.257
Northwestern Trust Co., Re 6.11, 7.55
Norwich Corp. v. Norfolk Rlwy. Co. 6.13
Nova Scotia (Attorney General) v. Bergen 15.155
Nova Scotia (Attorney General) v. Canada (Attorney General) 4.1
Nova Scotia Central Rlwy. v. Halifax Banking Co. 8.161, 8.163, 8.169
Nova Scotia Human Rights Commission v. County of Annapolis 4.79
Nova Scotia Trust Co. v. Auto Parts Co. 11.179, 11.248
Novel Energy (North America) Ltd. v. Glowicki 13.31
NPV Management Ltd. v. Anthony 11.8, 13.193, 13.231
NRMA Insurance Group Ltd. v. Spragg 12.88
NRMA v. Stewart Geeson 10.15
Nunachiaq Inc. v. Chow... 14.63
Nunachiaq v. Chow.. 13.138
Nutter Brewery Ltd., Re.. 7.86
Nystad v. Harcrest Apartments Ltd. 13.123
NZI Bank Ltd. v. Euro-National Corporation Ltd. 5.163

O

O'Bear-Nester Glass Co. v. Anti-Explo Co. 7.168
O'Connor v. Winchester Oil & Gas Inc. 13.18
O'Hara v. Arkipelago Architecture Inc. 13.111
O'Neill v. Phillips 13.40, 13.50, 13.51, 13.152
O'Sullivan v. Clarkson... 5.179, 5.181
Oakbank Oil Co. v. Crum 5.53, 7.329, 12.12
Oakes v. Turquand & Harding 2.17

Oakes v. Turquand	7.83, 7.243
Oakley v. McDougall	7.153, 13.57, 13.123, 15.47
Oceatain Investments Ltd. v. Canadian Commercial Bank	11.237
Odessa Waterworks Co., Re	7.321
Office Overload Co. v. Driver Overload Ltd	5.111, 5.113
Official Assignee of Madras v. Mercantile Bank of India Ltd.	8.209
Official Assignee v. 15 Insoll Avenue Ltd.	2.32
Official Receiver of Jubilee Cotton Mills Ltd. v. Lewis	5.157
Official Receiver v. Tailby	8.200
Olds Discount Co. v. Cohen	8.7
Oliver v. Dalgleish	12.139, 12.140
Oliver v. Elliott	9.113
Oliver v. McLaughlin	8.329
Oliver v. Ruge	12.122
Olson v. Machin	11.267
Olson v. Phoenix Industrial Supply Ltd.	11.48, 11.50, 11.62, 11.112, 11.193
Olympia & York Developers Ltd. v. Price	11.259
Olympia & York Development Ltd. v. Royal Trust Co.	13.78
Olympia & York Developments (Trustee of) v. Olympia & York Realty Corp.	13.37
Olympia & York Developments Ltd., Re	14.265, 14.272
Olympia & York Enterprises Ltd. v. Hiram Walker Resources Ltd.	11.49, 11.73, 14.43
Olympia & York, Re	13.125
Olympia Co., Re	10.24
Olympia Ltd., Re	5.180, 5.181
Omista Credit Union Ltd. v. Thomson	2.3
Ontario (Attorney General) v. Electrical Development Co.	14.89
Ontario (Attorney General) v. Toronto Junction Recreation Club	15.155
Ontario (Milk Control Board) v. Wawanesa Mutual Insurance Co.	15.203
Ontario (Ministry of Labour) v. Ivaco Inc.	5.79
Ontario (Securities Commission) v. Xantrex Management Corp.	15.125
Ontario (Treasurer) v. Blondé	7.286
Ontario Accident Insurance Co., Re	12.20
Ontario Bank v. Merchant's Bank	11.209
Ontario Equipment (1976) Ltd., Re	8.207
Ontario Express & Transport Co., Re	7.51
Ontario Fire Insurance Co., Re	7.154
Ontario Forge & Bolt Co., Re	15.203
Ontario Investment Assn. v. Sippi	7.222
Ontario Jockey Club Ltd. v. McBride	7.207, 7.221
Ontario Ladies' College v. Kendry	6.98, 7.86
Ontario Marine Insurance Co. v. Ireland	7.162
Ontario Metal Products Co. v. Mutual Life Insurance	7.96
Ontario Power Generation, R. v.	3.5
Ontario Salt Co. v. Merchants Salt Co.	6.16
Ontario Securities Commission v. McLaughlin	13.66
Ontario Sprinkler Sales Ltd. v. Emco Ltd.	15.162

Ontario Store Fixtures Inc. v. Mmmuffins Inc. 3.57
Ontario v. Policyholders of Wentworth Insurance Co. 4.41
ONTI, Inc. v. Integra Bank 14.80, 14.82
Ooregum Gold Mining Co. of India Ltd. v. Roper 1.25, 2.21, 7.77
Opera Ltd., Re 8.146
Oppenheimer & Co. v. United Grain Growers Ltd. 12.57
Oppenheimer v. Cattermole 15.173
Oracle Corp. Derivative Litigation, Re 13.228, 13.230
Orchard v. Tunney 5.162
Ordon Estate v. Grail 4.50
Osborne v. Kane... 11.28
Osborne v. Preston & Berlin Rlwy Co. 8.32, 8.271
Oshkosh B'Gosh Inc. v. Dan Marbel Inc. 14.32
Ottawa Cement Block Co., Re 7.171
Outset Media Corp. v. Stewart House Publishing Inc. 11.237
Overend, Gurney & Co. (Oakes v. Turquand), Re....................................... 5.159
Overend, Gurney & Co. v. Gibb 9.22, 11.13, 11.17
Overton Holdings Pty Ltd., Re.. 13.24
Ovey v. Ovey 11.12
Owen Sound Dry Dock Shipping & Navigation Co., Re............................... 5.55
Owen Sound General & Marine Hospital v. Mann..................................... 8.330
Owen Sound Lumber Co.,
   Re 7.325, 7.341, 9.114, 9.168, 10.54, 10.125, 11.28, 11.32
Owens Corning, Re... 13.183
Owston v. Grand Trunk Rlwy. Co. 11.204
Oxford Building & Investment Co., Re 15.133
Oxnard Financing SA v. Rahn 4.19
Oxweld Acetylene Co. v. Oxyweld Co. of Canada....................................... 5.108
Ozesezginer v. Royal Bank of Canada... 13.192, 13.238

P

P & J Macrae Ltd., Re.. 15.56
P. & O. European Ferries (Dover) Ltd., R. v. 3.18, 3.28
P.L. Robertson Manufacturing Co., Re.. 14.158, 14.240
Pace Savings and Credit Union v. CU Connection Ltd. 6.92, 12.182
Pacific Acceptance Corp. v. Forsyth & Ors 9.160, 9.163, 9.181, 9.186
Pacific Coast Coal Mines Ltd. v.
   Arbuthnot 6.56, 7.275, 12.62, 12.76, 12.77, 14.264
Pacific National Investments Ltd. v. City of Victoria............................. 5.8, 6.52
Pacific Rim Installations Ltd. v. Tilt-Up Construction Ltd. 2.35
Pacifica Papers Inc. v. Johnstone 12.142
Pacifica Papers Inc., Re... 14.248
Packenham Pork Packing Co., Re 12.1, 12.20
Page v. Austin 7.51, 7.164, 12.20
Pahmer (St. George Lumber Co.), Re 5.146
Pahmer, Re.. 5.206
Painblanc v. Kastner 3.59

Table of Cases

Paintin & Nottingham Ltd. v. Miller, Gale & Winter 8.68
Pakenham Pork Packing Co. (Liquidator of) v.
    Kendrick 7.161, 7.166, 10.40, 10.51
Pakenham Pork Packing Co., Re 5.56, 7.40, 10.85
Pakistan v. Zardari 15.77
Paley v. Leduc 15.58
Palmer v. Carling O'Keefe Breweries of Canada
    Ltd. 11.68, 13.73, 13.75, 13.85, 13.123
Palmolive Manufacturing Co. (Ontario) v. R. 1.43
Panama, New Zealand & Australian Royal Mail Co., Re 8.139, 8.146
Panorama Developments (Guildford) Ltd. v. Fidelis Furnishing Fabrics
    Ltd. 6.50, 6.79
Pantheon Inc. v. Global Pharm Inc. 13.39
Panton & Cramp Steel, Re 7.221, 7.222
Papercraft Corp., Re 13.185, 13.189
Papp v. Papp 4.5
Pappaioannoy v. The Greek Orthodox Community of Melbourne 5.48
Pappas v. Acan Windows Inc. 11.8, 13.217
Parallels Restaurant Ltd. v. Yeung's Enterprises Ltd. 7.95
Paramount Acceptance Co. v. Souster 10.26
Paramount Communications, Inc. v. QVC Network, Inc. 14.143, 14.148
Pardee v. Humberstone Summer Resort Co. 10.34
Parfi Holding AB v. Mirror Image Internet, Inc. 13.224
Parisian Cleaners & Laundry Ltd. v. Blondin 14.266
Park v. Anglo-Canadian Lands Ltd. 8.193
Parke v. Daily News Ltd. 11.68, 11.74, 11.97, 11.99
Parker v. Camden London Borough Council 4.76
Parker v. McKenna 11.177, 11.179
Parker-Knoll v. Knoll International, Ltd. 5.112
Parras v. FAI General Insurance Company Ltd. 7.245
Partington v. Cushing 15.21
Pasnak v. Chura 13.106, 13.204, 13.205
Past v. Past 13.31
Patent Ivory Manufacturing Co., Re 6.63
Patent Word Key Syndicate Ltd. v. Pearse 12.113
Patmore, Re 7.22
Paton v. IRC 8.30
Patricia Appliance Shops Ltd., Re 12.10
Patrick Corp. Ltd. v. Toll Holdings Ltd. 12.208
Patten v. Outerbridge 12.134
Patterson & Sons Ltd., Re 7.319
Patterson v. Turner 7.78, 7.82
Patterson v. Vulcan Iron Works 7.271
Patton v. Yukon Consolidated Gold Corp. 2.11, 5.172, 5.176, 9.26
Paul D'Aoust Construction Ltd. v. Markel Insurance Co. of Canada 6.95
Paul v. Kobold 5.48
Pavlides v. Jensen 12.32, 13.232, 13.258
Paws Pet Food & Accessories Ltd. v. Paws & Shop Inc. 5.123

PCM Construction Control Consultants Ltd. v. Heeger................. 11.244, 13.122
Peak Mechanical Ltd. v. Lewko... 2.38
Pearson Finance Group v. Takla Star Resources 7.182
Peat Moss Plant Foods Ltd. v. Sutherland (1923).. 7.79
Peat Moss Plant Foods Ltd. v. Sutherland (1983).. 7.107
Pectel Ltd., Re.. 13.52
Peddie v. Peddie... 13.210
Pedlar v. Road Block Gold Mines of India Ltd. 6.15
Peek v. Gurney.. 7.98
Peel v. London & N.W. Rlwy. Co. 12.161
Pelham v. Griesheimer.. 9.190.7
Pelissiers Ltd., R. v. 5.70, 5.72
Pelley v. Pelley.. 13.36
Pelling v. Pelling.. 11.192
Pender v. Lushington 12.129, 13.232
Peninsular Co. Ltd. v. Fleming 7.196, 7.236
Pennell Securities Ltd. v. Venida Investments Ltd. 11.109
Pennelly Y Ltd. v. 449483 Ontario Ltd. 5.142
Penner's Construction Ltd. v. Ancel... 8.328
Pennington v. Motor Works Ltd. 8.74
Pente Investment Management Ltd. v. Schneider
   Corp. 13.19, 13.43, 13.48, 13.49, 14.142, 14.148, 14.150
People v. Pullman Co. 12.23
Peoples Department Stores Inc. (Trustee of) v.
   Wise 7.57, 10.128, 11.20, 11.73, 11.74, 11.75
Pepper (Inspector of Taxes) v. Hart 1.27
Pepper v. Litton... 13.181
Percival v. Wright 11.192, 11.194, 13.257
Performing Right Society Ltd. v. Ciryl Theatrical Syndicate
   Ltd. 2.33, 3.55, 11.210, 11.245
Pergamon Press Ltd., Re... 13.271
Perishables Transport Co. v. Spyropoulos (London) Ltd. 11.297
Perlman v. Permonite Mfg. Co. 14.80
Permanent Houses (Holdings) Ltd., Re... 8.155
Perreault v. Milot 7.56
Persona Communications Inc. v. Mahoney... 14.63
Perth Electric Tramways Co., Re.. 8.132
Peso Silver Mines Ltd. (N.P.L.) v. Cropper................................. 11.189, 11.190
Peter's American Delicacy Co. v. Heath....................5.61, 11.68, 13.6, 14.45
Pethybridge v. Unibifocal Co. 8.185
Petre v. Duncombe... 8.34
Petrie Mfg. Co., Re 6.77
Petrie v. Guelph Lumber Co. 7.107, 7.117
Petro-Canada v. 366084 Ontario Ltd. 7.95
Petro-Canada v. Cojef Ltd. 6.82
Petten v. E.Y.E. Marine Consultants.. 2.59
Pezim v. British Columbia Superintendent of Brokers 7.132
Phillippou, R. v. 2.12

Phillips v. La Paloma Sweets Ltd. 3.2, 7.24, 7.222, 7.223, 7.226, 11.85
Phillips v. Montana Educational Association 11.24
Phipps v. Boardman 10.62, 11.125, 11.128
Phoenix Electric Light & Power Co., Re 12.114
Phonogram Ltd. v. Lane 2.40, 5.202
Photo Production Ltd. v. Securicor Transport Ltd. 3.8
Piccadilly Hotel; Paul v. Piccadilly Hotel Ltd., Re 8.194
Pick v. LSI Logic Corp. of Canada Inc. 14.63, 14.65
Pictou (County) Board of Education v. Cameron 10.36
Pierson v. Egbert 7.54, 7.79, 7.80
Piller Sausages & Delicatessens Ltd. v. Cobb International Corp. 13.30, 13.106
Pineau v. Neigette Co. 7.107
Pine-Vale Investments Ltd. v. McDonnell & East Ltd. 11.112
Pioneer Bancorporation, Inc. v. Waters 14.80
Pioneer Concrete Services Ltd. v. Yelnah Pty. Ltd. 2.68
Pioneer Distributors Ltd. v. Bank of Montreal 2.27, 7.172, 13.178
Pioneer Laundry & Dry Cleaners Ltd. v. Minister of National Revenue 2.29
Pioneer Savings & Loan Society, Re 5.35, 12.40
Piroth v. Kalinocha 11.220
Pitchford v. Canada 11.37
Pitrie v. Racey 5.169
Pitt River Lumber Co. v. Schaake 6.79
Pittsburgh Terminal Corp. v. Baltimore and Ohio Railroad 11.106
Pizza Pizza Ltd. v. Gillespie 11.151
Pizzo v. Crory 13.234
Plains Engineering Ltd. v. Barnes Security Services Ltd. 3.4, 3.9
Plantation Patterns Inc. v. Commissioner 7.13
Platts v. Canada 15.167.1
Plummer v. Terra Mining & Exploration Ltd. 13.202
Ply Gem. Industries Inc. Shareholders' Litigation, Re 11.45
PMSM Investments Ltd. v. Bureau 13.75, 13.84
Pocklington Goods Inc. v. Alberta (Provincial Treasurer) 14.64
Pogostin v. Rice 11.100
Polar Heating Ltd. v. Banque Nationale de Paris (Canada) 13.194
Polly Peck International plc, Re 2.11, 2.26, 2.27, 2.37
Pople v. Evans 5.207
Port Arthur Wagon Co., Re 7.77, 7.78, 12.1, 12.19
Port Arthur Waggon Co., Re 7.86
Portbase Clothing Ltd., Re 8.291
Portland & Lancaster Steam Ferry Co. v. Pratt 7.76, 12.37, 12.39
Porto Rico Power Co.; International Power Co. v. McMaster
   University, Re 15.135
Portugese Consolidated Copper Mines Ltd., Re 12.36
Posluns v. Toronto Stock Exchange, ... 11.238
Possfund Custodian Trustee v. Diamond 7.96
Potts Executors v. IRC 8.8
Poulton v. London & South Western Rlwy. Co. 3.6
POW Services Ltd. v. Clare 9.121

Powell Rees Ltd. v. Anglo-Canadian Mtge. Corp. 6.2
Power v. Vitrak Systems Inc. 12.205
Prairie Fibreboard Ltd., Re 15.137
Prairie Palace Motel Ltd. v. Carlson 15.89
Prairie Realty Ltd. v. J.M. Sinclair Co. 7.255, 7.257
Pramatha Nath Mullick v. Pradyumna Kumar Mullick 2.72, 4.19
Pre-Delco Machine & Tool Ltd., Re 15.61
Préfontaine v. Société des arts du Canada 12.11
Premier Trust Co. v. McAlister 10.40
Premor Ltd. v. Shaw Bros. 8.7
Prenor Trust Co. of Canada v. Hills of Columbia 8.48
Prescott Group Small Cap, L.P. v. Coleman Co. 14.83
President of Westfield Bank v. Corner 6.43
Pressello v. Venture Pacific Development Corp. 12.84
Price v. Dept. of Rev. 14.186
Priceville Fox Co. v. Jordan 7.329
Prichard & Constance (Wholesale), Ltd. v. Amata, Ltd. 3.55, 11.216
Prickett v. Allen 7.168
Priestley's Contract, Re 8.34
Prim Investments Ltd. v. Madison Development Corp. 5.159
Primary Distributors Ltd., Re 12.51
Prime Locations Ltd. v. Prime Realty Inc. 5.111, 5.120
Primex Investments Ltd. v. Northwest Sports Enterprises Ltd. 13.210, 13.215
Princess Copper Mines Ltd. v. Trelle 7.87
Princess of Reuss v. Bos 6.106, 7.194
Principal Savings & Trust Co. v. Principal Group Ltd. (Trustee of) 8.48
Prism Hospital Software Inc. v. Hospital Medical Records Institute 11.210
Proctor & Gamble Co., Re 4.47
Producers Real Estate & Finance Co., Re 15.46
Professional Sign Crafters (1988) Ltd. v. Wedekind 2.47
Profit Sharing Investors of Canada Ltd. v. Coffee Vending Services
   (Ottawa) Ltd. 15.162
Proprietary Articles Trade Association v. A.G. Canada 4.42
Proprietary Industries Inc. v. eDispatch.com Wireless Data 12.41, 12.174
Proprietary Mines Ltd. v. MacKay 5.176, 5.180
Proud v. National Bank of Canada 8.149
Proulx v. Sahelian Goldfields Inc. 11.266
Providence & Worcester Co. v. Baker 12.94
Provigo Inc. & Consumers Distributing Co., Re 14.165
Provincial Bank of Canada v. Gagnon 8.225
Provincial Electric (1969) Ltd. v. Registered Holdings Ltd. 2.34
Provincial Insurance Co. v. Cameron 5.70, 5.149
Provincial Machine & Supply Co., Re 7.86
Provincial Plating Ltd. v. Steinkey 11.117, 11.119
Provisional Corp. of the County of Bruce v. Cromar 5.80
Prudential Assurance Co. v. Chatterly-Whitfield Collieries Co. 7.8
Prudential Assurance Co. v. Newman Industries Ltd.
   (No. 2) 13.203, 13.232, 13.257

Prussin v. Park Distributors Inc. 15.61
Public Accountants Council (Ontario) v. Premier Trust Co. 4.48
Publishers' Syndicate, Re (1902)... 7.83, 7.86
Publishers' Syndicate, Re (1903).. 10.69
Puddephatt v. Leith 12.103
Pulbrook v. Richmond Consolidated Mining Co. 9.79, 13.231
Pulsford v. Devenish 15.35
Puma v. Marriott, Inc. 14.193
Punt v. Symons & Co. 6.24, 11.107, 11.193
Purdom v. Doherty 3.62
Pure Resources, Inc. Shareholders Litigation, Re 11.35, 11.87
Purvis Fisheries Ltd., Re 15.64
PWA Corp. v. Gemini Group Automated Distribution Systems
   Inc. 11.139, 11.143, 15.62
Pye v. Metro Credit Union Ltd. 13.193
Pyle Works, Re 12.165
Pylypchuk v. Dell Hotel Ltd. 10.22
Pym v. Campbell 7.86
Pyramid Building Society, Re 2.21

Q

Qintex Australia Finance Ltd. v. Shroders Australia Ltd. 2.66
Quaglieri v. 374400 Ontario Ltd. 13.57
Quantum Management Services Ltd. v. Hann 11.152, 11.175
Quarter Master UK Ltd. v. Pyke 11.180
Quebec Steel Products (Industries) Ltd. v. James United Steel Ltd. 13.69, 13.205
Queen City Plate Glass Co., Re 10.69, 12.178
Queen v. Cognos Inc. 9.190.2
Queensland Mines Ltd. v. Hudson 11.190, 13.257
Queensland Press Ltd. v. Academy Instruments No. 3 Pty. Ltd. 12.32, 12.188
Quelamine Co., Inc. v. Stewart Title Guaranty Co. 9.190.6
Quickturn Design Systems Inc. v. Shapiro 11.155, 11.158
Quin & Axtens Ltd. v. Salmon 7.32, 9.17
Quintex Ltd., Re 6.78

R

R. ex rel. Enid Jubilee Mines Ltd. v. British Columbia Registrar of
   Companies 5.35
R. ex rel. Wong v. British Columbia Registrar of Companies 5.35
R.C. Young Insurance Ltd., Re 15.58, 15.64
R.E. Jones Ltd., Re 12.113
R.J. Jowsey Mining Co., Re 11.19, 15.57, 15.63, 15.67, 15.75
R.M. Dalley & Co. Pty Ltd., Re 13.105
R.P. Clarke & Co. (Vancouver) Ltd., Re 7.157
R.P. Howard Ltd. v. Woodman, Matthews & Co. 13.232
R.S. v. RW-LB Holdings Ltd. 13.141

R.V. Demmings & Co. v. Caldwell Construction Co. 8.201
R.W. Hamilton Ltd. v. Aeroquip Corp. 11.119
Raab v. Villager Industries 14.47
Rabinowitz v. Kaiser-Frazer Corp. 8.189
Rackham v. Peek Foods Ltd. 12.76
Radiology Associates, Inc., Re 14.75
Rafuse v. Bishop 15.67
Raia v. Transworld Simcoe Inc. 11.219
Raicevic v. Nancy G. Dress Corp. 15.63
Railway & General Light Improvement Co. (Marzetti's Case) 9.23
Rainbow Industrial Caterers v. C.N.R. 2.23
Rainham Chemical Works Ltd. v. Belvedere Fish
    Guano Co. 2.11, 2.34, 2.36, 2.40, 2.43, 3.55, 11.216
Raintree Financial Ltd. v. Bell 8.47, 8.48
Rainy Lake River Boom Corp. v. Rainy River Lumber Co. 4.24
Rales v. Blasband 11.45
Ralph v. Bieberstein 11.261
Rama Corporation Ltd. v. Proved Tin & General Investments Ltd. 6.34, 9.14
Ramirez v. Amstead Industries Inc. 14.133
Ramrakha v. Zimmer 5.168
Ramsey Estate v. Royal Bank of Canada 8.336
Ramsgate Victoria Hotel Co. v. Montefiore 7.78
Rands v. Hiram Walker, Gooderham & Worts Ltd. 7.330
Rapid-American Corp. v. Harris 14.80
Rathie v. Montreal Trust Co. 4.39, 4.41, 14.47, 14.160
Rauchman v. Mobil Corp. 12.196
Ravelston Corp., Re 15.108
Rayment Estate v. Rayment & Collins Ltd. 13.39
Rayner (Mining Lane) Ltd. v. DTI 5.162
RCM Securities Fund, Inc. v. Stanton 11.102
Read v. Astoria Garage (Streatham) Ltd. 9.128
Reader v. Crown Laundry & Dry Cleaning Co. 15.116, 15.134
Real Estate Investment Co. v. Metro Building Society 6.5
Real Property Act of Manitoba, Re 8.23
Reay v. Landcorp Ontario Ltd. 13.114
Receiver of Javelin Intl. Ltd. v. Hillier 7.153
Reckitt v. Barnett, Pembroke & Slater Ltd. 6.42
Red Deer Mill & Elevator Co. (Liquidators of) v. Hall 15.143
Red Deer Mill & Elevator Co., Re 8.22
Red Hot Video Ltd. v. Vancouver (City) 5.59
Redekop v. Robco Construction Ltd. 13.18
Reed Stenhouse Ltd. v. Foster, Re 11.152
Reference re Upper Churchill Water Rights Reversion Act 1980
    (Newfoundland) 4.21, 4.22
Reg. of Companies, ex p. A.G., R. v. 5.17
Reg. of Companies, ex p. Central Bank of India, R. v. 5.159
Regal (Hastings) Ltd. v. Gulliver 11.20, 11.157, 11.171, 11.177
Regal Constellation Hotel Ltd., Re 15.106

Regehr v. Ketzakey Silver Mines Ltd. 12.102, 12.177
Regina Fur Co. v. Bossom 3.11
Regina Steam Laundry Ltd. v. Saskatchewan Government Insurance Office 8.39
Regina Windmill & Pump Co., Re.. 15.27
Regional Steel Works (Oshawa) Ltd., Re 9.112
Registrar of Companies, ex p. A.G. (Miss Whiplash & Hookers Ltd.), R. v. 5.17
Registrar of Joint Stock Companies, ex p. Moore, R. v. 5.17, 5.34
Regulvar Canada Inc. v. Ontario 3.64
Rehm v. DSG Communications Inc. 8.159
Reid Crowther & Partners Ltd. v. Simcoe & Erie General Insurance Co. 11.311
Reid v. Purity Farms Ltd. 8.22
Reid, R. v. 1.49
Reider v. Sair 7.19
Reinhardt v. Interstate Telephone Co. 8.189
Reitzman v. Grahame-Chapman & Derustit Ltd. 11.210
Reliable Manufacturing Co., Re.. 7.81
Relmar Holding Co. v. Paramount Public Corp. 8.185
Remambrose Lake Tin Mining Co., Re 5.180
Rempel Bros. Concrete Ltd. v. Mission (District) 5.59
Rendle v. Edgcumbe J. Rendle & Co. 5.96
Rendle v. Stanhope Dairy Farms Ltd. 15.43
Republic of Bolivia Exploration Syndicate Ltd., Re.. 9.62
Resfab Manufacturier de Ressort Inc. v. Archambault 11.132
Residues Treatment & Trading Co. v. Southern Resources Ltd. 12.76, 13.232
Reuss (Princess) v. Bos., Re 1.52
Revelstoke Credit Union v. Miller 9.164, 9.184, 10.129, 10.134
Reversion Fund & Insurance Co. v. Maison Casway Ltd. 8.25
Revlon, Inc. v. MacAndrews & Forbes Holdings, Inc. 14.143, 14.144
Reynolds Extrusion Co. v. Cooper... 8.102
Reynolds v. Ashby & Son.. 8.137
Reynolds v. Atherton 9.14
Reznick v. Bilecki 15.64
Rhodian River Shipping Co. v. Halla Maritime Corp. 6.62
Rhude et al. v. Corbett 5.36
Richard Brady Franks Ltd. v. Price... 11.49
Richardson Greenshields of Canada Ltd. v. Kalmacoff 13.207, 13.244
Richardson v. Control Fire Holdings Inc. 12.209
Richardson v. English Crown Spelter Co. 7.326
Richardson v. Landecker.. 9.2
Richardson, Re... 8.82
Richelieu Oil Co., Re 7.171
Richmond Hill Hotel Co., Re... 7.77, 7.166, 7.170
Richmond London Borough Council v. Pinn & Wheller 1.49
Richmond v. Branson & Son 10.136
Richter v. Battle 13.132
Ricketts v. Ad Valorem Factors Ltd. 1.25, 5.88, 11.3
Rico Enterprises Ltd., Re 8.300
Rideau Carleton Raceway Holdings Ltd., Re 14.263

Ridout Real Estate Ltd. (Trustee of) v. Bank of Nova Scotia 8.23
Rielle v. Reid 2.3, 2.9
Rigaud-Vaudreuil Gold Fields Co. v. Bolduc 12.11
Rights & Issues Investment Trust Ltd. v. Stylo Shoes Ltd. 13.6
Ringling Bros.-Barnum & Bailey Combined Shows v. Ringling 12.103
Ringuet v. Bergeron 11.138, 11.201, 12.127
Rio Hotel Ltd. v. New Brunswick (Liquor Licensing Board) 4.6
Ripley International Ltd., Re 14.158, 14.240, 14.245
Riptide Technologies Inc., Re 14.254
Ritchie v. Central Ontario Rlwy. 8.171
Ritchie v. Vermillion Mining Co. 2.125, 12.34, 12.102, 12.127
River Stave Co. v. Sill 6.82, 9.14
Rizzo & Rizzo Shoes Ltd., Re 1.27, 11.262, 11.267
RJR-MacDonald v. Canada (Attorney General) 13.111
Roadmakers Pty Ltd., Re 15.41
Robb v. Green 11.151
Robert M. Bass Group Inc. v. Evans 13.230
Robert v. Montreal Trust Co. 7.107, 7.118
Roberts & Cooper Ltd., Re 7.43
Roberts Clinics Ltd., Re 5.72
Roberts v. Ball, Hunt, Hart, Brown & Baerwitz 9.190.7
Roberts v. Elwells Engineers Ltd. 11.151
Robertson & Carlisle Ltd., Re 8.50
Robertson v. Canadian Canners Ltd. 14.69
Robertson v. FTC 7.229
Robertson v. North-Western Register Co. 6.65
Robertson-Durham v. Inches 7.43
Robin Hood Mills Ltd. v. Paterson Steamships Ltd. 6.77
Robins v. National Trust Co. 13.98
Robinson v. Countrywide Factors Ltd. 4.10, 8.338
Robinson v. Jenkins 7.286
Robinson v. Pittsburgh Oil Refining Corp. 14.143
Robinson v. Toronto General Trusts Corp. 12.58
Robinson v. Wangemann 7.267, 8.11
Robitaille v. Canada 11.290
Roblin v. Jackson 11.204
Robson v. Smith 8.144
Roccograndi v. Unemployment Comp. Bd. of Review 2.58
Roessler v. Security Savings & Loan Co. 14.67
Rogers & Agincourt Holdings Ltd., Re 15.59, 15.67
Rogers & Co. v. British & Colonial Colliery Supply Association 8.169, 8.185
Rogers Trusts, Re 8.32
Rogers v. Bank of Montreal 13.192, 13.195, 13.233
Rogers v. Colvert 12.172
Rogers v. Wood 11.273
Rogers-Majestic Corp. v. Toronto 2.3
Rogerson Lumber Co. v. Four Seasons Chalet Ltd. 8.220
Rohani v. Rohani 2.46

Rohe v. Reliance Training Network, Inc. 9.91
Rolled Steel Products (Holdings) Ltd. v. British Steel
    Corp. 6.12, 6.15, 11.92, 11.99
Rolls Razor Ltd. v. Cox 8.293
Roman Corp. v. Peat Marwick Thorne 2.10
Roman Hotels Ltd. v. Desrochers Hotels Ltd. 12.60
Ronald Elwyn Lister Ltd. v. Dunlop Canada Ltd. 8.148, 8.150
Rooney v. Cree Lake Resources Corp. 10.62, 10.63
Roper v. Murdoch 11.65
Roray v. Howe Sound Mills & Logging Co. 10.69
Rose v. British Columbia Refinery Co. 13.202
Rosemont Enterprises Ltd. v. Mercury Industrial Inc. 13.262
Rosenblatt v. Getty Oil Co. 10.114, 11.35, 11.199
Rosenfeld v. Fairchild Engine & Airplane Corp. 12.161
Ross Steel Fabricators & Contractors v. Loaring Construction Co. 8.36
Ross v. Fleet 7.255
Ross v. Imperial Life Assurance Co. 8.127
Rothlish Investments Ltd., Re 15.73
Rothmans, Benson & Hedges Inc. v. Saskatchewan 4.6
Roundwood Colliery Co., Re 8.146
Rourke v. Robinson 8.80
Routley v. Gorman... 10.111
Routley's Holdings Ltd., Re 12.44, 12.90
Rover International Ltd. v. Cannon Film Sales Ltd. 5.201
Rowe v. Brandon Packers Ltd. 15.74
Rowe v. National Wholesalers Ltd. 13.125
Rowlings v. Cape Breton Cold Storage Ltd. 10.69
Roxborough Gardens of Hamilton Ltd. v. Davis 11.135, 11.191
Royal Bank of Canada v. Cal Glass Ltd. 8.149
Royal Bank of Canada v. Central Capital Corp. 7.11, 7.12
Royal Bank of Canada v. First Pioneer Investments Ltd. 11.192
Royal Bank of Canada v. Flemming 6.11
Royal Bank of Canada v. GM Homes Inc. 8.159
Royal Bank of Canada v. Roles 8.328
Royal Bank of Canada v. Saulnier 7.157
Royal Bank of Canada v. Soundair Corp. 15.107
Royal Bank of Canada v. Starr... 5.203, 6.38
Royal Bank of Canada v. Sullivan 8.341
Royal Bank of Scotland plc v. The Golden Trinity... 13.178
Royal Bank v. British Columbia Accident and Employers' Liability
    Insurance Co. 8.23
Royal Bank v. Cadillac Fairview/JMB Properties 14.73
Royal Bank v. Cal Glass Ltd. 8.19, 8.271
Royal Bank v. Larry Creighton Professional Corp 8.29
Royal Bank v. Madill.. 8.87
Royal Bank v. McMahon 6.110, 6.114
Royal Bank v. Nobes 8.162
Royal Bank v. Port Royal Pulp & Paper Co. 10.25

Royal Bank v. Stewart 6.25, 6.32
Royal Bank, R. v. 8.60
Royal British Bank v. Turquand 6.53, 15.209
Royal Canadian Insurance Co. v. Montreal Warehousing Co. 4.5
Royal Canadian Legion v. Hamilton War Veterans' Poppy Fund
    Inc. 5.116, 5.120
Royal Heaters Ltd., Re 14.267
Royal Mutual Benefit Building Society v. Sharman 12.81
Royal Stores Ltd. v. Brown 2.3, 2.8, 2.25, 2.38
Royal Trust Bank v. National Westminster Bank plc. 8.201
Royal Trust Co. v. Atlantic & Lake Superior Rlwy. 8.191, 8.270
Royal Trust Co. v. Baie des Chaleurs Rlwy. Co. 8.318
Royal Trust Co. v. Great Northern Elevator Co. 8.23
Royal Trust Co. v. H.A. Roberts Group Ltd. 8.286, 8.289, 8.291
Royal Trust Corp. of Canada v. Hordo 13.69, 13.70, 13.76, 13.205
Royal Trustco Ltd. (No. 3), Re 13.267, 13.268
Royalite Oil Co., Re 4.40, 4.46, 4.54
Royfor & Co. v. Skye Resources Ltd. 14.54
Rozeik, R. v. 3.11
Rubas v. Parkinson 7.32
Rubber & Produce Investment Trust, Re 15.133
Ruben v. Great Fingall Consolidated 6.79
Rudkin v. British Columbia Automobile Assn. 12.62
Ruethel Mining Co. v. Thorpe 5.181, 11.191
Ruffo v. I.P.C.B.C. Contractors Canada Inc. 13.99
Rumford v. Hinton 5.176, 5.186
Runciman v. Walter Runciman plc 10.44, 10.50
Rundle v. Miramichi Lumber Co. 10.85
Ruskin v. Canada All-News Radio Ltd. 13.118, 14.90
Russell Institution, Re 1.2
Russell Kinsela Pty Ltd. v. Kinsela 11.62
Russell v. Northern Bank Development Corp. 8.96, 12.211, 14.23
Russell v. Wakefield Waterworks Co. 11.92
Russian & English Bank v. Baring Brothers Ltd. 15.169
Russian (Vyksounsky) Iron Works Co., Re 7.106
Russian Bank for Foreign Trade, Re 15.169
Russian Commercial & Industrial Bank v. Comptoir d'Escompte de
    Mulhouse 10.36
Russo-Chinese Bank v. Li Yau Sam 6.48
Rylands v. Fletcher 11.245

S

S. Solomont & Sons Trust, Inc. v. New England Theatres Operating
    Corp. 13.243
S.E. Walker Co., Re 15.126
Saarnok-Vuus v. Teng 13.30
Safarik v. Ocean Fisheries Ltd. 13.22, 13.50, 13.135, 13.138

Safety-Kleen Canada Inc., R. v.	3.23, 3.29
Safeway Insurance Co. v. Daddono and Khano	11.226
Said v. Butt	11.242
Saint John River Log Driving Co., Re	15.125
Salada Tea Co. of Canada v. Kearney	5.74
Salih v. Atchi	2.72
Salisbury G.M. Co., Re	12.92, 12.107
Salisbury Railway and Market House Co. Ltd., Re	4.76
Salmon v. Quin & Axtens Ltd.	10.25, 11.252, 12.31, 12.32, 12.33
Salomon v. Salomon & Co.	2.3, 2.4, 2.5, 2.6, 2.7, 2.8, 2.39, 2.42, 2.66, 13.165
Salt Lake Tribune Publishing Company, L.L.C., v. AT &T Corp.	10.114
Saltdean Estate Co., Re	7.43
Sam Weller & Sons Ltd., Re	7.319
Sammi Atlas Inc., Re	13.80
Sammon, Re	8.166
Samos Investments Inc. v. Pattison	14.245
Samuel Tak Lee v. Cho Wen Hsien	9.135
Sanata Clara Co. v. Southern Pacific Railroad	4.66
Sanders v. British Columbia Milk Board	7.157
Sanders v. Cuba Railroad Co.	7.42
Sanders v. Wang	9.9
Sandilands v. Powell	5.18, 5.30
Sands Motor Hotel Ltd., R. v.	7.313, 13.66
Sandusky Coal Co. v. Walker	5.182, 12.21
Sanitary Carbon Co., Re	14.24
Santley v. Wilde	8.80
Santos Ltd. v. Pettingell	9.57
Santos v. Wood	13.192
Sapphire Petroleums Ltd., Re	7.250
Sarnia Ranching Co., Re	13.268
Saskatchewan Land & Homestead Co. v. Moore	10.40, 10.81, 11.164
Saskatchewan Wheat Pool v. Manitoba	5.116
Saskatoon Auction Mart Ltd. v. Finesse Holsteins	7.157
Sasko-Wainwright Oil & Gas Ltd. v. Old Settlers Oils Ltd.	12.95
Sass v. St. Nicholas Mutual Benefit Association of Winnipeg (City)	4.61
Saul D. Harrison & Sons plc, Re	13.40, 13.45, 13.51, 13.152, 13.156, 13.157
Saunders v. Oceanus Marine Inc.	8.41
Saunders v. South Eastern Rlwy.	5.63
Savage v. Amoco Acquisition Co.	14.251
Sawers v. American Phenolic Corp.	12.172
Saxe v. Brady	11.102
Sazio v. Canada (Minister of National Revenue)	2.31
Scales v. Irwin	7.165
Scandinavian Bank Group, Re	7.150, 7.158
Scarborough Harbour Commrs. v. Robinson Coulson Kirby & Co.	9.183
Schafer v. International Capital Corp.	13.218
Schapp, Hochberg & Sommers v. Nislow	2.22
Schauenburg Industries Ltd. v. Borowski	11.118

Schelew v. Moncton Family Outfitters, Ltd. 12.184
Schelew v. Schelew 11.117, 12.35, 13.217
Scherer v. Paletta 3.4
Schicchi v. Orveas Bay Estates Ltd. 13.34
Schiller Estate v. Canada (Minister of National Revenue) 7.25
Schiowitz v. I.O.S. Ltd. 13.211
Schlensky v. Wrigley 10.22
Schmaltz v. Avery 5.187
Schmeichel v. Lane 11.237
Schnell v. Chris-Craft Indus., Inc. 10.14
Schnell v. Chris-Craft Industries Inc. 7.57, 11.106
Schouls v. Canadian Meat Processing Corp. 2.68
Schuppan (No. 2), Re 11.222
Schurek v. Schnelle 11.114, 12.34
Schwartz v. Scott 11.267
SCI Systems, Inc. v. Gornitzki Thompson & Little Co. 13.45, 13.79, 13.137
SCMLLA Properties Ltd. v. Gesso Properties (BVI) Ltd. 15.167.1
Scotch Granite Co., Re 15.114
ScotiaMcLeod Inc. v. Peoples Jewellers Ltd. 3.14, 3.58, 7.109, 11.222,
                                                                                                  11.225, 11.231
Scott v. Frank F. Scott (London) Ltd. 2.125, 14.3
Scott v. Pilliner 5.63
Scott v. Riehl 11.233
Scott v. Robb 13.129
Scott v. Scott 9.17, 12.188
Scott, R. v. 6.69
Scottish Co-operative Wholesale Society Ltd. v.
    Meyer 11.132, 11.135, 11.137, 11.202, 13.20, 13.26
Scottish Insurance Corp. v. Wilson & Clyde Coal Co. 7.8, 7.41, 7.43, 7.285
Scottish Loan & Finance Co. Ltd., Re 6.50
Scottish Petroleum Co., Re 7.106
Scottish Widows' Fund & Life Assurance Society v. Canada Permanent
    Mortgage Corp. 8.195
Scozzafava v. Prosperi 15.60
Sculthorpe v. Tipper 11.11
Seaboard Life Insurance Co. v. British Columbia (Attorney General) 14.89
Sealand of Pacific Ltd. v. Robert C. McHaffie Ltd. 2.23
Seaton v. Federal Hotels Pty. Ltd. 7.43
Seawater Products (Nfld.) Ltd. v. Royal Bank of Canada 8.149
SEC v. May 12.144
Second Consolidated Trust Ltd. v. Ceylon Amalgamated Tea &
    Rubber Estates Ltd. 12.86, 12.140
Second Standard Royalties Ltd., Re 12.77, 12.78, 12.108, 14.249
Secretary of State for Trade & Industry v. Swan 11.324
Secretary of State for Trade & Industry v. Taylor 13.190
Secretary of State for Transport, ex p. Factortame Ltd., R. v. 2.45
Securitibank Ltd. (in liq.) & Ors, Re 2.67
Seel v. Seel 13.57

Segenhoe Ltd. v. Akins 2.62
Seibert v. Harper & Row, Publishers, Inc. 13.230
Seidel v. Kerr 13.107
Seiffert v. Irving 5.182
Seinfeld v. Coker 13.193
Selangor United Rubber Estates Ltd. v. Cradock (No. 3) 11.200, 11.233
Selby's Electrical Ltd. v. Bruce 5.207
Selkirk, Re 15.107
Sepp's Gourmet Foods Ltd. v. Janes 14.203
Sepp's Gourmet Foods Ltd., Re 14.153, 14.163, 14.260
Servers of the Blind League, Re 15.164
Setter v. Mander 7.55
Severn and Wye & Severn Bridge Rlwy. Co., Re 7.313, 7.321
Shack v. Matthews Construction Co. 7.86
Shacket v. Universal Factors Corp. 15.63
Shacter, R. v. 9.162
Shahinian v. Precinda Inc. 7.264, 7.266
Shaker v. Al-Bedrawi 13.199
Shalfoon v. Cheddar Valley Co-Operative Dairy Co. Ltd. 7.176, 7.236
Shamrock Holdings, Inc. v. Polaroid Corp. 11.10
Shankman and Mutual Life Assurance Co. of Canada, Re 8.99
Shannex Health Care Management Inc. v. Nova Scotia
  (Attorney General) 13.66, 13.81
Shapiro (c.o.b. ISR Ent. in Trust) v. 1086891 Ontario Inc. 5.188
Sharon Golf & Country Club Ltd., Re 15.45
Sharp v. Dawes 12.49, 12.178
Sharp v. Wakefield 5.34
Sharp, R. v. 8.163
Shaughnessy v. Imperial Trusts Co. 8.171
Shaw v. BCE Inc. 13.31
Shaw v. Tati Concessions Ltd. 12.113
Shawinigan Lake Recreation Association v. Hansen 12.116
Sheffield & South Yorkshire Permanent Building Society v. Aizlewood .. 10.129
Sheffield & South Yorkshire Permanent Building Society, Re 2.16
Shell Canada Products Ltd. v. Vancouver (City) 1.27
Shell v. Hensley 11.6
Shepherd (Trustee) v. Shepherd 15.109
Sheppard v. Bonanza Nickel Mining Co. of Sudbury 8.18, 8.25
Sherbrooke Clothing Co. v. Lemieux 7.78
Sherwood Design Services Inc. v. 872935 Ontario Ltd. 5.192
Sherwood Village Optical Ltd. v. Allied Lumberland Ltd. 13.123
Shibamoto & Co. v. Western Fish Producers Inc. 11.219
Shield Development Co. v. Snyder 12.41
Shillingford v. Dalbridge Group Inc. 2.26, 11.222
Shimmin v. Clark 7.164
Shindler v. Northern Raincoat Co. Ltd. 9.128, 9.135
Shipman Boxboards Ltd., Re 8.20, 8.79
Shipway Iron Bell & Wire Manufacturing Co., Re 15.59

Shirim v. Fesena 13.134
Shirlaw v. Southern Foundries (1926) Ltd. 10.102
Shoom v. Great-West Lifeco Inc. 14.58
Shrewsbury & Birmingham Rlwy. Co v. North Western Rlwy. Co. 6.13
Shuttleworth v. Cox Bros. & Co. (Maidenhead) Ltd. 9.128, 11.49, 14.45
Shymka v. Smokey Lake United Farmers Co. 7.76, 7.255
Sidaplex-Plastic Suppliers Inc. v. Elta Group
    Inc. 3.60, 11.291, 13.18, 13.23, 13.27, 13.68, 13.77, 13.79, 13.157
Sidebottom v. Kershaw, Leese & Co. 14.45
Sidmay Ltd. v. Wehttam Investments Ltd. 5.32
Siebe Gorman & Co. v. Barclays Bank Ltd. 8.138, 8.201
Siemens v. Manitoba Attorney General 4.12
Sifneos v. M.N.R. 6.114
Sign O-Lite v. Bugeja 3.4
Signal Hill Oils Co. v. London Oil Securities Ltd. 11.135, 11.161
Silber v. BGR Precious Metals Inc. 14.64, 14.67, 14.69
Silber v. Pointer Exploration Corp. 14.54
Silkstone & Haigh Moor Coal Co. v. Edey 15.113, 15.114
Silver's Garage Ltd. v. Bridgewater (Town) 5.8, 6.52
Silverman v. Goldman 13.251
Simons v. Cogan 8.185
Simpson Balkwill Co. v. Canadian Credit Men's Trust Assn. 8.193
Simpson v. Gillespie 7.192, 12.17
Simpson v. Montreal Trust Co. 2.38
Simpson v. Westminster Palace Hotel Co. 6.17
Sinclair Oil Corp. v. Levien 11.148
Sinclair v. Blue Top Brewing Co. 7.21, 7.24
Sinclair v. Sutton Resources Ltd. 6.122, 10.29
Singh v. Bhasin 8.168
Singh v. Moody Shingles Ltd. 15.64
Singhania v. Uttarwar 14.46
Sir John Moore Gold Mining Co., Re 15.133
Siscoe & Savoie v. Royal Bank 14.266
Si-Thoo v. Berry 8.38
Skeen v. Jo-Ann Stores, Inc. 11.199
Skrien v. Waterloo Junction Rail Tours Ltd. 12.28, 13.96
Skyepharma PLC v. Hyal Pharmaceutical Corp. 15.107
Slappey Drive Industrial Park v. U.S. 7.12
Slate Ventures Inc. v. Hurley 11.154
Slingsby v. District Bank 6.81, 6.103
Sloan v. United States Department of Housing & Urban Dev. 9.164
Smart v. Bowmanville Machine & Implement Co. 7.76
Smeenk v. Dexleigh Corp. 14.45, 14.67, 14.69
Smith & Fawcett Ltd., Re 2.8, 11.49, 11.85
Smith & Goldberg Ltd. v. Moyer & Co. 6.77
Smith (Administrator of Cosslett (Contractors)) v. Bridgend County
    Borough Council 8.136
Smith Transportation Co., Re 6.115

Smith v. Anderson	9.21
Smith v. Atlantic Properties Inc.	13.5
Smith v. Canada Car Co.	7.222
Smith v. Canada	11.37
Smith v. Chadwick	7.96, 7.103
Smith v. Croft (No. 2)	12.32, 13.257
Smith v. ECO Grouting Specialists Ltd.	12.185
Smith v. First Merchant Equities Inc.	14.243
Smith v. Hamelin	7.222
Smith v. Hanson Tire & Supply Co.	11.106, 11.193
Smith v. Hull Glass Co.	3.4
Smith v. Kay	7.100
Smith v. National Money Mart Co.	11.210
Smith v. National Trust Co.	8.84
Smith v. Paringa Mines Ltd.	12.52
Smith v. R.	4.51
Smith v. Van Gorkom	11.19, 11.25, 11.27
Smith v. Walkerville Malleable Iron Co.	7.286
Smith, Stone & Knight Ltd. v. Birmingham Corp.	2.11, 5.164
Sneyd, ex p. Fewings, Re	8.38
Snook v. London & West Riding Investments Ltd.	2.34
Snow v. Benson	11.209
Snyder Dynamite Projectile Co., Re	7.106
Sobey's Inc., R. v.	3.24
Sobrinho v. Oakville Portugese Canadian Club	15.67
Societa Caruso v. Tosolini	9.119
Société Asbestos Ltée v. Société National de l'Amiante	4.60
Société Eram Shipping Co. Ltd. v. Compagnie Internationale de Navigation	15.171
Société Général (Canada) v. 743823 Ontario Ltd.	10.26
Société Générale de Paris v. Walker	12.8
Society of Composers, Authors and Music Publishers of Canada v. 1007442 Ontario Ltd.	3.55, 11.216
Society of Composers, Authors and Music Publishers of Canada v. Canadian Association of Internet Providers	4.20
Society Shirt Co., Re	4.29
Soden v. British & Commonwealth Holdings plc	2.14, 7.110, 7.111
Soft Tracks Enterprises Ltd., Re	12.76
Solloway v. Blumberger	7.288
Solmon v. Elkin	13.215
Solomon v. Solomon	8.330
Sommers, R. v.	3.29
Soper v. Littlejohn	2.126
Soper v. The Queen	11.36, 11.37
Soplex Wholesale Supplies Ltd. v. Egyptian International Foreign Trading Co.	6.50
Sorrel 1985 Partnership v. Sorrel Resources	3.9
South African Supply & Cold Storage Co., Re	14.89

South African Territories v. Wallington 8.131
South High Development Ltd. v. Weiner, Lippe & Crawley Co. 2.22
South Hinds Water Co. v. Mississippi Public Service Comm. 7.14
South Llaharran Colliery Co., ex p. Jegon, Re.. 7.326
South Shore Development Ltd. v. Snow.. 12.41
South Yorkshire Rlwy. & River Dun Co. v. Great Northern Railway Co. 6.13
Southern Brazilian Rio Grande do Sul Rlwy. Co., Re 8.280
Southern Counties Deposit Bank Ltd. v. Rider................................ 12.58, 12.61
Southern Cross Biscuit Co., Ltd., Re 5.77
Southern Foundries (1926) Ltd. v. Shirlaw........................... 9.128, 9.135, 12.11
Southern Lumber & Coal Co. v. M. P. Olson Real Estate and Construction
 Co., Inc. 8.330
Southern Music Publishing Co. v. Southern Songs Ltd. 5.112
Southern Pacific Transportation Co. v. Dept. of Revenue 14.189
Southside Property Management (London) Inc. v. Sibold Estate 5.194, 5.205
Southwestern Tool Co. v. Hughes Tool Co. 3.56, 11.210
Sovereign Bank, Re 7.197
Sovereign Life Assurance Co. v. Do.. 7.62
Sovereign Oil Co., Re 15.64
Spackman v. Evans.. 9.162
Sparling v. Javelin Internationale Ltee.. 13.142
Sparling v. Royal Trust Co. 13.93, 14.243
Sparling v. Southam Inc. 13.146
Speckling v. Kearney.. 3.4
Spectrum Plus Ltd. (in liq.), Re.. 8.142
Speedrack Ltd., Re 8.207
Spiers, R. v. 7.22
Spies v. The Queen 11.76
Spilsbury Communications Ltd. v. Fentronics-NSI Ltd. 5.206
Spirax Sarco Ltd. v. Sarco Canada Ltd. 5.120
Spitz v. Canada (Secretary of State) 7.25
Spitzel v. Chinese Corp. 12.1
Spivak v. Lee 15.100
Sportscope Television Network Ltd. v. Shaw Communications
 Inc. 12.216, 12.219
Spratt v. Wilson 11.12
Srebot Farms Ltd. v. Bradford Co-operative Storage Ltd. 1.28, 3.57, 11.210
Sri Lanka Omnibus Co. v. Perera... 7.210
SSSL Realizations (2002) Ltd., Re 8.920
St. Elizabeth Home Society v. City of Hamilton 3.4
St. James Recreation, LLC v. Rieger Opportunity Partners, LLC 11.35
St. Jerome (Town) v. Commercial Rubber Co. 8.23
St. John v. Fraser.. 13.271
St. Lawrence & Hudson Railway Co., Re.. 14.242
St. Lawrence Corp. & Mayer, Re.. 14.245
St. Lawrence Corp., R. v. 3.29, 3.52
St. Lawrence Transport Ltd. v. Buchanan... 6.113

St. Stanislaus-St. Casimir's Parish (Toronto) Credit Union v. Ontario
   Credit Union League Ltd. 5.63
Stabile v. Milani Estate 13.100, 13.106
Stadacona-Rouyn Mines Ltd., Re 7.255
Standard Bank of Australia Ltd., Re 12.32
Standard Chartered Bank v. Pakistan National Shipping Corp. (No. 2). ... 11.224
Standard Chartered Bank v. Walker 12.126
Standard Construction Co. v. Crabb 10.5
Standard Fire Insurance Co., Re 12.7
Standard Investments Ltd. v. CIBC 3.5
Standard Manufacturing Co., Re 8.146
Standard Mutual Fire Insurance Co., Re 12.13
Standard Trust Co. 13.169
Standard Trust Co. (Liquidator of) v. Cattanach 9.190.2
Standard Trust Co. v. South Shore Rlwy. 6.77
Standard Trustco Ltd., Re 11.32, 11.202, 11.296
Stanham v. National Trust of Australia (New South Wales) 13.259
Stankovic v. Leighton 13.211
Stanley L. Block v. Klein 9.183
Stanton v. Republic Bank of S. Chicago 14.80
Stanward Corp. v. Denison Mines Ltd. 14.133
Staples v. Eastman Photographic Materials Co. 7.42, 7.322
Stark v. Flemming 2.69
Star-Link Entertainment Inc. v. Star Quest Entertainment Inc. 11.177
State Dep't of Revenue v. Acker 13.172
State Dep't of Revenue v. Birmingham Realty Co. 14.195
State of Wyoming Syndicate, Re 12.58, 12.61
State Tax Commissioners of Utah v. Aldrich 1.31
State, ex rel. Pillsbury v. Honeywell, Inc. 12.172
Stavert v. McMillan 7.255
Stech v. Davies 13.22, 13.123, 15.46
Steel Co. of Canada v. Ramsay 7.292, 7.295, 7.303, 7.305, 7.320, 7.332
Steel Service Ltd., Re 6.63, 7.79
Steen v. Gunnar Mining Ltd. 7.330
Steeplejack Services (Sarnia) Ltd. v. Stowe Nut & Bolt Co. 11.219
Steinberg v. Amplica, Inc. 14.46
Steinberg v. Scala (Leeds) Ltd. 7.197
Steinhart v. Moledina 3.59, 11.216
Stelco Inc., Re 9.122, 13.141
Stephens v. McArthur 8.328
Stephens v. Mysore Reefs (Kangundy) Mining Co. Ltd. 6.17
Stephens v. Riddell 7.83
Stephens, R. v. 3.27
Stephenson v. Vokes 5.56, 9.122, 12.153
Stern v. Imasco Ltd. 13.147
Sternberg v. O'Neil 13.243
Stethem v. Feher 13.30
Stevens v. Spencer 11.270

Stewart v. LePage 15.95, 15.99, 15.103
Stiles v. Aluminum Product Co. 14.43
Stirling Homex Corporation, Re 13.175
Stone v. Stonehurst Enterprises Ltd. 13.84, 13.89, 13.99
Stoody v. Kennedy 13.106
Stothers v. William Steward (Holdings) Ltd. 12.124
Stott v. Merit Investment Corp. 8.64
Strachan v. MacCosham Administrative Services Ltd. 10.26
Strategic Capital Resources v. Citrin Cooperman & Co. 9.158
Stratford Fuel, Ice, Cartage & Construction Co. v. Mooney 2.8, 5.181
Strickland v. Hayes 5.64
Strickland v. Tricom Associates (1979) Ltd. 15.67
Strilec v. Alpha Pipe Fittings Ltd. 13.114
Stroud v. Grace 11.199
Structural Dynamics Research Corp. v. Engineering Mechanics Research
  Corp. 11.175
Struthers v. MacKenzie 11.208
Strutzenegger v. K. Peters Industries Northern Ltd. 5.206, 6.87
Stubart Investments Ltd. v. The Queen 2.35
Su v. Canada Eighty-Eight Fund Ltd. 7.265
Suburban Hotel Co., Re 15.54
Such v. RW-LB Holdings Ltd. 13.15, 13.20, 13.99, 13.155
Suddaby v. 864226 Ontario Inc. 7.204
Sukloff v. A.H. Rushforth & Co. Estate 8.323, 13.170
Suleiman v. Saffuri 15.58
Sullivan Resources Ltd. and Sullivan Mines Inc., Re 14.165
Summerside Electric Co., Re 6.54
Sun Life Assurance Co. of Canada v. Elliott 8.331
Sun Life Assurance Co. of Canada v. Sisters Adorers of Precious Blood 4.61
Sun Ray Manufacturing Co., Re 7.83, 7.84
Superior Acceptance Corp., Re 14.165
Superstein v. Albertawest Forest Products Corp. (Liquidators of) 15.135
Susan Hosiery Ltd. v. Minister of National Revenue (No. 2) 2.34
Sutherland v. Birks 13.43
Sutton's Hospital Case 1.36, 1.49, 6.22
Swager v. Couri 11.215, 13.173, 13.174
Swire v. Francis 3.3
Sydney & Whitney Pier Bus Service Ltd., Re 15.65
Sydney Cooperative Society Ltd. v. Coopers & Lybrand 9.164, 9.190.10
Sydney Land & Loan Co. v. Solicitor 8.135
Sylvester v. McCuaig 5.182, 12.21
System Controls plc v. Munro Corporate plc 7.173
System Theater Operating Co. v. Pulos 15.200
Systemcorp A.L.G. Ltd., Re 14.254
Szczerba v. St. Stanislaus-St. Casimir's Polish Parishes Credit Union Ltd. 9.125
Szecket v. Huang 5.196, 5.201

T

T&N Ltd., Re 15.2
T.D. Bank v. Coopers & Lybrand Ltd. 6.59
T.E. O'Reilly Ltd., Re 7.76
T.E.A.P. International Inc. v. Murphy 12.54, 12.61
T.F.P. Investments Inc. (Trustee of) v. Beacon Realty Co. 8.45
T'Ease Fashions Ltd. v. Flory 5.117
Tabbi v. Pollution Control Industries 14.47
Tailby v. Official Receiver 8.138, 8.145, 8.199
Tal v. Lifemark Health Inc. 12.209
Taldua Rubber Co., Re 15.54
Tamlin v. Hannaford 1.31, 5.3
Tangier Amalgamated Mining Co., Re 15.56
Tanguay v. Royal Paper Mills Co. 10.85, 11.29
Tanner v. Canada 11.37
Tanning Research Laboratories v. O'Brien 15.115
Tara Exploration & Development Co. v. Minister of National Revenue 1.31
Tarel Hotel Ltd. v. Saskatchewan Co-operative Financial Services Ltd. 8.46
Tate Access Floors Inc. v. Boswell 2.66
Tato Enterprises Ltd. v. Rode 2.25
Taunton v. Warwickshire Sheriff 8.146
Taurine Co., Re 10.81
Tavistock Ironworks Co., Re 15.114, 15.117
Taylor v. Alberta (Registrar, South Alberta Land Registration District) 4.50
Taylor v. Borger 12.153
Taylor v. Chichester & Midhurst Rlwy. Co. 6.13
Taylor v. London Guarantee Insurance Co. 13.39
Taylor v. Standard Gas & Electric Co. (Deep Rock) 13.183
TCT Logistics Inc. v. Osborne (c.o.b. Key-West Storage &
    Distribution) 5.81, 5.142
Teck Corp. v. Millar 7.57, 9.17, 10.21, 11.50, 11.59, 11.63, 11.74,
                                            11.111, 11.112, 12.31, 14.144
Teede & Bishop Ltd., Re 12.118
Telegram Publishing Co. Ltd. and Marc Zwelling & Gottlob Essig, Re 11.262
Téléphone Guévremont Inc. v. Quebec 4.14
Telsten Services Ltd., Re 7.296, 7.317
Teltronics Servs., Inc., Re 13.189
Tembro Truck & Auto Services Ltd. v. Brown 11.153
Tennant v. Trenchard 8.82
Teperman & Sons Ltd., R. v. 3.29
Teperman & Sons Ltd., Re 13.268
Terranex Information Services v. Canada (Canada Business Corporations Act,
    Director) 5.116
Tesco Supermarkets Ltd. v. Nattrass 3.43
Testa v. MacDonnell 11.49, 13.66
Thacker v. Hardy 11.298
THC Financial, Re 13.176

The Albazero 2.64
The Bank of Hindustan, China & Japan Ltd. v. Alison 7.48
The Isle of Thanet Electricity Supply Co., Re 7.43
The Koursk 11.299
The Queen in Right of Manitoba v. Air Canada 4.22
The Queen v. Cognos Inc. 7.133
The Russell-Cooke Trust Co. v. Elliott 8.136
The Schooner Exchange v. McFaddon 10.166
The Walt Disney Company Derivative Litigation, Re 11.24, 11.117
Theatre Amusement Co. v. Stone 5.47
Themadel Foundation v. Third Canadian General Investment
    Trust Ltd. 13.86, 13.151, 13.152
Thérien v. Brodie 11.217
Thermo King Corp. v. Provincial Bank of Canada 8.201
Thero v. Wijewardena 2.72
Theseus Exploration N.L. v. Mining & Associated Industries Ltd. 9.64
Thibault Auto Ltd. (Trustee of) v. Thibault 6.12, 6.25
Thiess Watkins White v. Equiticorp Australia Ltd. 8.17
Thomas Equipment Ltd., R. v. 4.21, 4.22
Thomas Franklin & Sons Ltd. v. Cameron 15.113
Thomas Gerrard & Son Ltd., Re 9.62, 9.183
Thomas Ltd. v. Standard Bank 5.145
Thomas v. Equipment Rebuilders Ltd. 5.196
Thomas v. Thomas Health Care Corp. 13.106
Thomas v. Walke 6.63
Thompson & Sutherland Ltd. v. Redden 5.206
Thompson & Sutherland v. Nova Scotia Trust Co. 8.22
Thompson v. Big Cities Realty & Agency Co 5.145
Thompson v. Brantford Electrical & Operating Co. 6.59
Thompson v. Goold & Co. 1.26
Thompson v. Northern Trusts Co. 8.192
Thompson v. Skill 7.77
Thompson v. Victoria Rlwy. Co. 8.262, 8.271
Thomson Motors Co. v. British Columbia 15.167
Thomson v. Quality Mechnical Services Inc. 13.38
Thor Power Tool Co. v. Comm. of Internal Revenue 9.146
Thorby v. Goldberg 11.200
Thorne v. Silverleaf 5.88
Thorpe v. CERBCO, Inc. 11.121
Thorpe v. Tisdale 10.75
Three Point Oils Ltd. v. Glencrest Energy Ltd. 13.31, 13.32
Tiessen v. Henderson 12.76
Tilden Rent-a-Car v. Keffer 5.80
Tilley v. Hails 13.127
Tilsonburg Agricultural Manufacturing Co. v. Goodrich 7.76, 7.77
Timbers Ltd., Re 15.59
Tip Top Canners Ltd., Re 14.249
Title Estate v. Harris 13.93

Tkatch v. Heide 13.82, 13.215
TNT Australia Pty Ltd. v. Poseidon Ltd. 12.76
TNT Canada Inc., R. v. 4.46
Tober Enterprises Ltd., Re 15.199
Tolofson v. Jensen 4.20, 4.22
Tombill Gold Mines Ltd. v. Hamilton 11.133, 11.154
Tomczak v. Morton Thiokol, Inc. 11.25
Toms v. Cinema Trust Co. 10.50
Toms v. Wilson 8.147
Torbock v. Lord Westbury 12.118
Toronto & Regional Crime Stoppers Inc. v. Crimestoppers Security
   Systems Inc. 5.120
Toronto (City) v. Bell Telephone Co. 4.47
Toronto Board of Education v. Brunel Construction 2000 Ltd. 2.61
Toronto Bocciofila Club, Re 5.120
Toronto Brewing & Malting Co. v. Blake 12.175
Toronto Dairies Ltd., Re 15.116
Toronto Dominion Bank v. Fortin 10.26
Toronto Dominion Bank v. Park Foods Ltd. 15.87
Toronto Finance Corp. v. Banking Service
   Corp. 7.153, 7.166, 7.170, 7.175, 7.180
Toronto General Trusts Corp. v. Bartram 1.36, 1.49
Toronto General Trusts Corp. v. Central Ontario Rlwy. Co. . 8.134, 8.161, 8.192
Toronto General Trusts Corp. v. Lake Superior Corp. 8.302
Toronto Harbour Commissioners v. Disero 13.204
Toronto Rlwy. Co. v. Toronto 8.31
Toronto v. Consumers' Gas Co. 7.14
Toronto Wood & Shingle Co., Re 15.21
Toronto-Dominion Bank v. Crosswinds Golf & Country Club Ltd. 15.107
Toronto-Dominion Bank v. Leigh Instruments Ltd. 11.129
Toronto-Dominion Bank v. Prichard 8.55
Totten G. Publishers Ltd., Re 8.303
Tough Oakes Gold Mines Ltd. v. Foster 7.208, 12.1, 12.90, 12.98
Touquoy Gold Mining Co., Re 8.10
Tourangeau v. Taillefer 12.123
Towers v. African Tug Co. 7.315, 12.35
Town Topics Co., Re 13.262, 13.266
Townend v. Graham 8.127
Townsend v. Ontario Forge & Bolt Co. 9.154
Township of Montague v. Page 4.79
Toys "R" Us Inc. Shareholder Litigation, Re 14.148
Tracy v. Mandalay Pty. Ltd. 5.171
Traders Group Ltd. v. Mason 8.338
Traders Trust Co. v. Goodman 9.113
Traders' Trust Co. and Kory, Re 11.228
Trail Tire Service Ltd. v. Scobie 5.207
Trans World Airlines Inc. Shareholders Litigation., Re 14.193

Transamerica Commercial Finance Corp. v. Imperial TV & Stereo Centre
  Ltd. (Receiver/Manager of) 8.301
Trans-American Airlines Inc. v. Kenton 5.85
Trans-Canada Resources Ltd. v. Bobella 11.48
Transmountain Pipeline Co. v. Inland Natural Gas 12.174
Transplanters (Holding Co.) Ltd., Re 9.162, 9.194
Transport & General Credit Corp. v. Morgan 8.7
Transport North American Express Inc. v. New Solutions Financial
  Corp. 5.64, 13.172
Transport Rober (1973) Ltée., R. v. 4.66
Transvaal Lands Co. v. New Belgium (Transvaal) Land & Development
  Co. 11.170
Transwest Energy Inc., Re 12.96, 14.247
Travel 2000 Ltd. v. iTravel2000.com.Inc. 5.116
Travel West (1987) v. Langdon Towers Apt. 7.172
Travellers Insurance Co. v. Travellers Life Assurance Co. 5.108
Traverse de Lévis v. Lemieux 4.17, 4.40
Treadway Cos., Inc. v. Care Corp. 11.52
Treasurer of Ontario v. Blondé 7.25
Trebanog Working Men's Club & Institute Ltd. v. MacDonald 2.34
Tree Savers International Ltd. v. Savoy 11.152, 11.175
Trefethen v. Amazeen 10.17
Trefor Ivory Ltd. v. Anderson 3.55
Trembert v. Mott 10.130
Tremblay v. Vermette 15.140
Tremblett v. SCB Fisheries 13.215
Trent & Frankford Road Co. v. Marshall, Re 5.80
Trepca Mines Ltd., Re 15.115
Trevor Ivory Ltd. v. Anderson 5.163, 11.229, 11.230
Trevor v. Whitworth 7.8, 7.255, 7.275, 7.325
Tri Level Claims Consultant Ltd. v. Koliniotis 4.38
Triad Oil Holdings Ltd. v. Manitoba 14.132
Tri-Con Concrete Finishing Co. Ltd. v. Caravaggio 5.142
Trident Holdings Ltd. v. Danand Investments Ltd. 9.21
Tridont Leasing (Canada) Ltd. v. Saskatoon Market Mall Ltd. 5.163
Trillium Computer Resources Inc. v. Taiwan Connection Inc. 13.70, 13.79
Trimac Ltd. v. C-I-L Inc. 12.122
Triple "L" Construction Ltd. v. Aikens Lake Lodge Ltd. 13.122
Tri-State Developers Inc. v. Moore 5.154
Tritonia Ltd. v. Equity & Law Life Assurance Society 2.11
Trizec Corp., Re 14.246, 14.247
Trnkoczy v. Shooting Chrony Inc. 13.141
Trost v. Cook 11.11
Trudell Partnership Holdings Ltd. v. Retirement Counsel of Canada Inc. 12.209
Trustee of A. Zimet Ltd. v. Woodbine Summit Ltd. 3.66
Trustee of C.G. Plain Ltd. v. Kenley 7.8, 7.56, 7.276
Trustee of Dylex Ltd. v. Anderson 13.76

Trustee of Olympia & York Developments Ltd v. Olympia & York Realty
   Corp. 13.78
Trustee of Peoples Department Stores Inc. v. Wise 13.169, 14.143
Trustee of Standard Trustco Ltd. v. Standard Trust Co. 13.169
Trustees of Gray & Farr Ltd. v. Carlile 12.178
Truster v. Tri-lux Fine Homes Ltd. 5.142
Trusts & Guarantee Co. v. Continental Supply Co. 8.29
Trusts & Guarantee Co. v. Continental Supply Ltd. 8.30
Trusts & Guarantee Co. v. Grand Valley Rlwy. Co. 8.32, 8.66, 8.190, 8.270
Trusts & Guarantee Co. v. Smith 7.83
Tunstall v. Steigmann 2.8, 2.70
Turf Care Products Ltd. v. Crawford's Mower & Marine Ltd. 8.20
Turkawski v. 738675 Alberta Ltd. 8.333
Turner v. Corney 10.108
Turner v. Mailhot 13.250
Turquand, Re 8.319, 15.209
Turvey v. Lauder 12.105
Twigg v. Thunder Hill Mining Co. 6.1
Twiggco Financial Ltd. v. Peat Marwick Thorne 2.10
Twin City Oil Co. v. Christie 10.5, 10.6, 10.85
Tyne Mutual Steamship Insurance Association v. Brown 9.112
Tytler v. C.P.R. 6.110

U

U.S. Financial Incorporated, Re 13.176
U.T.U. v. Central Western Railway 4.50
Ultra Petroleum Corp., Re 14.260
Ultraframe (UK) Ltd. v. Fielding 11.7
Ultramares Corp. v. Touche 9.190.3
Ultramares Marine v. Touche Niven and Co. 2.74
UNA v. Alberta (Attorney General) 5.162
Unified Freight Services Ltd. v. Therriault 11.175
Unifund Assurance Co. v. Insurance Corp. of British Columbia 4.20, 4.22
Union Bank of Canada v. A. McKilliop & Sons Ltd. 6.5
Union Bank of Canada v. Cross 11.236
Union Bank of Canada v. Morris 7.164
Union Bank v. Gourley 12.19
Union Colliery Co. v. Bryden 4.4
Union Colliery Co. v. R. 3.29
Union Corp. Ltd. v. IRC 6.114
Union Enterprises Ltd., Re 12.109
Union Fire Insurance Co. v. O'Gara 6.117, 14.38
Union of India v. Azadi Bachao Andolan 6.111
Unisoft Group Ltd. (No. 3), Re 13.49, 13.157
Unisource Canada Inc. (c.o.b. Barber-Ellis Fine Papers) v. Hong Kong
   Bank of Canada 7.63
Unit Construction Co. Ltd. v. Bullock 6.114

United Canso Oil & Gas Ltd., Re 12.86, 12.159
United Copper Securities Co. v. Amalgamated Copper Co. 13.218
United Fuel Investments Ltd., Re 14.249
United Mills Agencies Ltd. v. R.E. Harvey 11.298
United Shoe Machinery Co. v. Brunet 7.117
United States Trust v. Australia & New Zealand Banking Group 8.296, 8.300
United States v. Arthur Young & Co. 10.173
United States v. Noland 3.49, 13.182
United States v. Reorganized CF & I Fabricators of Utah, Inc. 3.50
United Steel Industries Inc. v. Manhart... 7.175
United Used Auto Truck Parts Ltd., Re 8.90
Unitel International Inc. v. Unitel Communications Inc. 5.116
Unitrin, Inc. v. American General Corp. 11.57
Unity Insurance Brokers (Windsor) Ltd. v. Unity Realty & Insurance Inc. 5.121
Universal Banking Corp., Re 7.78, 12.7
Unocal Corp. v. Mesa Petroleum Co. 11.57, 11.87, 13.226, 14.144
UPM-Kymmene Corp. v. UPM-Kymmene Miramachi
  Inc. 10.43, 10.55, 10.62, 10.63, 11.23, 13.66, 13.81
Upper Churchill Water Rights Reversion Act 1980 (Newfoundland), Re 4.60
Upper Yonge Ltd. v. CIBC 8.46
Ursel Investments Ltd., Re 14.272
US v. Bestfoods 2.53
US v. Dunn 5.80
Uscan Engineering Corp., R. v. 2.45
USF Red Star Inc. v. 1220103 Ontario Ltd. 13.190
Uxbridge Permanent Benefit Building Society v. Pickard 6.49

V

V.F. Erickson Consultants Ltd. v. Ventures West Minerals Ltd. 13.101
V/O Sovfracht v. Gebr Van Udens Scheepvaart en Agentuur Maatschapij 2.45
Vacation Brokers Inc. v. Joseph 5.189, 5.201
Vacuum Oil Co. v. Ellis 8.82
Vadeko International Inc. v. Philosophe 13.206, 13.217
Valin v. Lion Nead Rubber Co. 8.23
Valuation of Common Stock of Libby, McNeil & Libby, Re 13.134
Value Investment Corp. v. Caldwell Gundy Inc. 12.152
Value Liquor Mart Ltd. v. Werkman 5.142
Van Alstyne v. Rankin 9.135
Van Hummell v. International Guarantee Co. 5.183
Van Laun, ex p. Chatterton, Re 15.115
Vancouver (City) v. Burchill 11.28
Vancouver Engineering Works v. Columbia Bitulithic Co. 6.15
Vancouver Life Insurance Co. v. Richards 7.107
Vantagepoint Venture Partners 1996 v. Examen, Inc. 15.12
Van-Tel T.V. Ltd., Re 12.12, 12.13, 15.46
Varity Corp. v. Jesuit Fathers of Upper Canada 12.196
VCS Holdings Ltd. v. Helliwell 14.70

Vedova v. Garden House Inn Ltd. 13.215
Veilleux v. Atlantic & Lake Superior Railway Co. 8.25, 6.55
Venezuela Rlwy. Co. v. Kisch 7.102
Venner v. Chicago City R. Co. 10.17
Ventures West Capital Ltd. v. Bethlehem Copper Corp. 12.104
Verdun v. Toronto-Dominion Bank 12.98, 12.197
Verner v. General & Commercial Investments Trust 7.310
Victor (Can.) Ltd. v. Farbetter Addressing & Mailing Ltd. 5.206
Victoria Onion & Potato Growers' Association Ltd. v. Finnigan, Re 5.63
Victoria Steamboat Co., Re 8.146
Victoria Wood Works Ltd., Re 12.20
Victorov v. Davison 9.13, 10.41, 13.99
Viner v. Poplaw 6.107
Virani v. Virani 13.275
Vitomen Cereal Ltd. v. Manitoba Grain Co. 5.176, 5.180
Vivian Agencies Ltd. v. Butler 5.206
Vizzard v. E.W. Lancaster 7.88
Vladi Private Islands Ltd. v. Haase 11.120, 11.194, 13.202
Vollick v. Sheard 3.4
Von Hellfeld v. Rechnitzer 1.58
Vopni v. Groenewald 11.267, 11.273
Vought v. Republic-Franklin Insurance Co. 14.67

W

W. & M. Roith Ltd., Re 11.95
W. McKenzie Securities Ltd., R. v. 4.51
W. Noall & Co. v. Wan 7.211
W.C. Pitfield & Co. v. Jormac Gold Syndicate Ltd. 7.210
W.D. Latimer Co. v. Dijon Investments Ltd. 2.23, 2.28
W.H. Dey Enterprises Ltd. v. Volvo Canada Ltd. 13.93
W.J. Christie & Co. v. Greer 11.132, 11.152
W.N. McEachern & Sons Ltd. 6.14, 6.34
W.W. Duncan & Co., Re 8.29
Wabash Railway Co. v. Barclay 7.42, 7.298, 7.302
Wachovia Shareholders Litigation, Harbor Finance Partners v.
    Balloun, Re 13.3, 13.193
Wade v. Murray 8.30
Wagman, Re 15.107
Wagon Stop Inc., Re 13.238
Wah Tat Bank Ltd. v. Chan Cheng Kum 2.33, 3.55, 11.245
Waiakei Ltd. v. Cleave 10.14, 12.169
Waiser v. Deahy Medical Assessments Inc. 11.235
Waite Hill Holdings Ltd. v. Marshall 8.7
Waite's Auto Transfer Ltd. v. Waite 11.133
Wakley, Re 7.301, 7.330
Walbridge Grain Co. (Liquidator of) v. Walbridge Grain Co. 7.275
Waldron v. Hogan 2.3

Waldron v. Royal Bank.. 8.149
Walker v. Jones... 8.80
Walker v. WA Personnel Ltd. 11.74
Walker v. Wimborne... 2.10, 2.66, 11.80, 11.140, 11.145
Walker Youth Homes Inc. v. Ottawa-Carleton District School Board 1.25
Walkerton Binder Twine Co. v. Higgins... 7.345
Walkovsky v. Carlton 2.52
Wall & Redekop Corp. v. W. & R. Properties Ltd. 14.70
Wallace v. Universal Automatic Machines Co. 8.146
Wallersteiner v. Moir 2.69, 13.200, 13.247
Wallinder v. Target Tunnelling Ltd. 7.273
Wallis v. Littell 7.86
Walmsley v. Rent Guarantee Co. 8.24, 11.248
Walt Disney Co. Derivative Litigation, Re 9.90, 13.230
Walter Symons Ltd., Re... 7.43
Walters v. Woodbridge 8.168
Waltham Motors Corp. of Canada Ltd., Re 15.200
Walton v. Bank of Nova Scotia... 6.34, 12.36
Ward v. Lewis.. 13.196
Ward v. Simeon 7.107, 7.118
Wark v. Kozicki 13.110
Warrant Finance Co.'s Case, Re 15.26
Warren v. People's Finance Corp. 7.260
Warren v. Superior Engravers Ltd. 5.64, 7.170, 7.176, 10.73
Warren, R. v. 8.209
Waschysyn v. Kildonan Ice and Fuel Co. 12.103
Washburn v. National Wallpaper Co. 7.169
Washer v. Smyer... 7.168
Watergroup Companies Inc. v. Stevens 13.48
Waterman's Will Trust, Re 10.72
Waterous Engine Works Co. v. McLean... 5.144
Waterous Engine Works Co. v. Palmerston.. 5.8
Waterous v. Koehring-Waterous Ltd. 14.160
Waters and Water Powers, Re.. 4.5
Watfield International Enterprises Ltd. v. 655293 Ontario Ltd. 11.260
Watkin v. Open Window Bakery Ltd. 12.43, 13.110, 13.114
Watson v. Barrett 12.177
Watson v. Imperial Steel Corp. 8.165, 8.171, 8.184
Watt v. Commonwealth Petroleum Ltd. 12.175
Wawanesa Mutual Insurance Co. v. J.A. (Fred) Chalmers & Co. 11.227
Waxman v. Waxman... 11.134.1, 11.194, 13.143, 13.160
Wayde v. New South Wales Rugby League 13.15, 13.155
Webb Distributors (Aust.) Pty v. State of Victoria 2.14
Webb v. Earle.. 7.42, 7.322
Weber Feeds Ltd. (Trustee) v. Weber.......................... 11.168, 11.177, 11.182
Weber's Hardware (Huntsville) Ltd. v. Home Hardware Ltd. 13.113
Wedderburn's Trusts, Re 11.12
Wedge v. McNeill... 10.78

Wedtech Inc. v. Wedco Technology Inc. 10.38
Weidman Brothers v. Guaranty Trust Co. 8.273
Weight Watchers International Inc. v. Weight Watchers of Ontario Ltd. 4.29
Weiller & Williams Ltd. v. Peterson... 13.218
Weinberger v. UOP Inc. 10.57, 10.59, 11.115, 14.195
Weir v. Bell... 11.299
Weisser v. Mursam Shoe Corp. 2.24, 2.35
Weitzen Land & Agricultural Co. v. Winter.. 11.173
Welch v. Bowmaker (Ireland) Ltd. 8.114, 8.115
Welch v. Ellis.. 11.266
Welcome Investments Ltd. v. Sceptre Investment Counsel Ltd. 6.98
Welichka v. Bittner Investments Ltd. 13.23
Wellburn's Market Ltd. v. Pacific Green Grocers Ltd. 8.318
Wellman v. Dickinson... 11.52
Wells Fargo Bank v. Superior Court of San Francisco 9.9, 9.129, 9.131
Wells v. Dane.. 13.197
Welport Investments Ltd., Re 13.93, 15.60, 15.61
Welton v. Saffery 7.162, 12.211
Wessex Dairies Ltd. v. Smith.. 11.151
West City Motors Ltd. v. Delta Acceptance Corp. 5.150
West Cumberland Iron & Steel Co. v. Winnipeg & Hudson's Bay Rlwy. ... 8.162
West Fraser Builder Supplies v. Vandler Horst 5.142
West Humber Apartments Ltd., Re.. 14.240, 14.249
West Mercia Safetywear Ltd. (in liq.) v. Dodd 11.74, 11.78, 11.81
West Toronto Stereo Center Ltd., Re... 15.90
Westburn Sugar Refineries Ltd. v. IRC 7.311
Westcom Radio Group Ltd. v. MacIsaac 5.189, 5.203, 5.204
Westdeutsche Landesbank Girozentrale v. Islington London Borough
    Council 6.13, 10.66
Western Air Lines, Inc. v. Sobieski 14.275
Western Bank Ltd. v. Schindler 8.81
Western Canada Fire Insurance Co., Re 7.83
Western Canada Flour Mills Ltd., Re 14.246, 14.249
Western Canada Investment Co. v. McDiamid... 8.127
Western Canadian Place Ltd. v. Con-Force Products Ltd. 2.67
Western Coal Co., Re.. 15.126
Western Finance Co. v. Tasker Enterprises Ltd. 11.80, 11.92, 11.192
Western Fire Insurance Co. v. Alexander 7.83
Western Hemlock Products Ltd., Re... 15.202
Western Mines Ltd. v. Shield Development Co. 9.65, 12.219
Western National Corp. Shareholders' Litigation, Re 11. 45
Western Ontario National Gas Co. v. Aikens 11.49
Western Rock Co. v. Davis.. 2.51
Western-National Drug Services and R.W.D.S.U, Local 580................... 11.262
Westfair Foods Ltd. v. Watt...11.203, 13.133, 13.148, 13.152
Westfair Properties Ltd. v. Wilson.. 5.39
Westlake v. Ontario 1.60
Westminster Corp. v. London and North Western Railway Co. 13.128

Westminster Road Construction and Engineering Co., Re 9.183
Westmore v. Old MacDonald's Farms Ltd. 13.18
Westover v. Turner 1.49
Weyburn Townsite Ltd. v. Honsberger 4.23, 4.24
WH Eutrope Pty., Re 2.14
Whaley Bridge Calico Printing Co. v. Green 5.171, 5.176
Wharlton v. Kirkwood 8.149
Wheeler & Wilson Manufacturing Co. v. Wilson 7.107
Wheeler v. Annesley 13.204
Wheeliker v. Canada 11.14
Whicher v. National Trust Co. 11.11
While v. True North Springs Ltd. 9.57
Whistle Co., Re 7.83
White Horse Distillers Ltd. v. Gregson Associates Ltd. 11.210
White Star Line Ltd., Re 7.155
White v. Bank of Toronto 2.8
White v. Brompton Pulp & Papers Co. 10.22
Whitehorse Lounge Ltd. v. Bennett 6.55, 6.59
Whitehouse v. Carlton Hotel Pty. Ltd. 7.59, 11.108, 11.293
Whitehouse v. Jordan 15.120
Whitlam v Australian Securities and Investment Commission 12.162
Whitney v. Small 2.125
Wholesale Travel Group Inc., R. v. 4.68
Wiarton Beet Sugar Manufacturing Co., Re 7.87, 7.164, 7.166, 12.19
Wicken (Litigation guardian of) v. Harssar 1.25
Wickham v. New Brunswick & Canada Rlwy. 8.87, 8.139
Wiggins v. Savics 13.120
Wilkes v. Springside Nursing Home, Inc. 13.5
Wilkes v. Teichmann 13.93
Wilkinson v. West Coast Capital 13.141
Will v. Engerbreston & Co. 13.227
Will v. United Lankat Plantations Co. 7.41, 7.42, 7.305, 7.306, 7.3320, 7.332
William A. Flemming Ltd. v. Fisher 5.207
William B. Sweet & Associates Ltd. v. Copper Beach Estates Ltd. 12.122
William Bedford Ltd., Re 7.43
William E. Thomson Associates Inc. v. Carpenter 8.42, 8.45
Williams & Glyn's Bank Ltd. v. Barnes 8.55
Williams v. Gaylord 14.275
Williams v. Natural Life Health Food Ltd. 3.14, 11.211, 11.229, 11.230
Williams v. Peel River Land Co. 7.120
Williams v. R. 7.286
Williams v. Rice 1.52
Williams v. Scott 10.41, 11.10
Williams, Re 4.51
Williamson v. Williamson 8.30
Willis v. Association of Universities of the British Commonwealth 15.25
Will-Kare Paving Construction Ltd. v. Canada 1.27
Willmott v. London Celluloid Co. 8.143, 8.146

Willoughby v. Chicago Junction Rlwy. 8.197
Wilson v Whitehouse 15.121
Wilson v. British Columbia Refining Co. 12.13
Wilson v. Conley 13.114
Wilson v. Hotchkiss 7.109
Wilson v. London & Globe Finance Corp. 7.210
Wilson v. London, Midland & Scottish Rlwy. Co. 11.128
Wilson v. Woollatt 10.8
Wilsons & Clyde Coal Co. v. Scottish Insurance Corp. 7.43
Wiltse v. Excelsior Life Ins. Co. 8.80
Winch v. The Birkenhead, Lancashire and Cheshire Junction Railway Co. 4.77
Winchell v. Del Zotto 13.234
Wind Ridge Farms v. Quadra Group Investments 14.50
Winding-up Act (Canada), Re 12.20
Winding-up Act and Canadian etc., Tractor Co., Re 7.76, 7.77, 7.83
Winding-Up Act and Panama Pacific Grain Terminals Ltd., Re 11.179
Winding-up Act and Summerside Electric Co., Re 8.25
Windsor Steam Coal Co. (1901), Ltd., Re 8.176, 15.114, 15.117
Winfield v. Daniel 13.214, 13.218
Wing v. Woodstock Ltd. 7.252
Winkworth v. Edward Baron Development Co. 11.44, 11.80, 11.192
Winnipeg Electric Railway v. City of Winnipeg 6.15
Winnipeg Hedge & Wire Fence Co., Re 7.153, 7.154, 7.162, 7.289
Winnipeg Saddlery Co., Re 15.53
Winnipeg Winter Club v. Thorsteinson 14.6
Winpar Holdings Ltd. v. Goldfields Kalgoorlie Ltd. 14.220
Winthrop Investments Ltd. v. Winns Ltd. 12.30
Wise, ex p. Mercer, Re 8.330
Wismer v. Javelin International Ltd. 13.121
Witcomb v. Toronto General Trusts Corp. 7.85
Wittlin v. Bergman 13.135, 15.47
Wm M'Culloch & Co., ex p. Trevascus, Re 3.2
Wolfdale Electric Ltd. v. RPM's Systems Automation and Design 5.200
Wolfe v. Moir 2.8, 2.25
Wondoflex Textiles Pty. Ltd., Re 13.40, 13.51, 15.67
Wood v. Odessa Waterworks Co. 7.329
Wood v. Pan-American Investment Ltd. 12.57
Wood v. W. & G. Dean Pty. Ltd. 7.204
Wood v. Wood 12.209
Wood, Skinner & Co., Re 7.43
Wood, Vallance & Co., Re 2.125
Woodford v. Johnston Equipment (1998) Ltd. 13.267
Woodgers & Calthorpe Ltd. v. Bowring 7.86
Woodroffes (Musical Instruments), Re 8.146
Woodruff v. Harris 7.223, 7.226
Woodson v. Russell 4.51
Woolf v. East Nigel Gold Mining Co. 10.69
Woolfson v. Strathclyde Regional Council 2.34, 2.58

Wotherspoon v. Canadian Pacific Ltd. 11.202, 13.26, 13.149
Wouk v. Merin 7.42
Wragg Ltd., Re 7.155, 7.166, 7.170
Wright v. Rider Resources Inc. 10.69
Wrightson v. McArthur & Hutchinson (1919) Ltd. 8.209
Wurzel v. Houghton Main Home Delivery Service Ltd. 2.34

X

Xerox Canada Finance Inc. v. Wilson's Industrial Auctioneers Ltd. 3.55, 11.219

Y

Yakimishyn v. Canada 11.37
Yoakham v. Providence Biltmore Hotel Co. 12.26
Yokohama Enterprises Inc. v. Mascot Enterprises Inc. 14.118
York & North Midland Rlwy. v. Hudson 9.20
York Region Condo. Corp. No. 921 v. Atop Comm. Inc. 5.187
Yorkshire Woolcombers Association Ltd., Re 8.128, 8.136, 8.140
Young v. Alberta Petroleum Consolidated 10.6
Young v. Dannecker 11.261
Young v. Newfoundland Dried Squid Exporters Association 5.48
Young v. South African & Australian Exploration and Development
    Syndicate 12.49, 12.118
Yuille v. B. & B. Fisheries (Leigh) Ltd. 11.210

Z

Zanny Ltd. v. Vero-Kim Developments Inc. 8.46
Zapata Corp. v. Maldonado 10.75, 11.22, 13.209, 13.218, 13.219, 13.225, 13.228
Zavitz v. Brock 11.271
Zephyr Holdings Pty Ltd. v. Jack Chia (Australia) Ltd. 13.102
Zething v. Kilner 12.76
Zimmerman v. Andrew Motherwell of Canada Ltd. (Trustee of) 8.25, 12.77
Zion v. Kurtz 12.210
Zoological & Acclimatization Society of Ontario, Re 7.82
Zubik v. Zubik 2.34
Zuckerman v. Zuckerman 13.231
Zurich Insurance Co. v. Troy Woodworking Ltd. 8.146
Zwicker v. Stanbury 7.18, 7.276
Zwicker v. Turnbull Estate 7.19, 11.180, 11.190
Zwicker, R. v. 12.154
Zwig v. Schupack 15.60, 15.61
Zysko v. Thorarinson 10.42

TABLE OF CONCORDANCE

References
- CA: Canada Business Corporations Act RSC 1985, c. C-44 (as amended to 2007, c. 6)
- AB: Business Corporations Act RSA 2000, c. B-9 (as amended to 2006, c. S-4.5)
  - * Securities Transfer Act SA 2006, c. S-4.5
- BC: Business Corporations Act SBC 2002, c. 57 (as amended to 2006, c. 12)
  - * Securities Transfer Act SBC 2007, c. 10
- MB: Corporations Act RSM 1987, c. C.225 (as amended to 2006, c. 10)
- NB: Business Corporations Act RSNB 1981, c. B-9.1 (as amended to 2004, c. 6)
- NF: Corporations Act RSNL 1990, c. C-36 (as amended to 2004, c. 14)
- NS: Companies Act RSNS 1989, c. 81 (as amended to 2004, c. 3)
  - * Companies Winding Up Act RSNS 1989, c. 82
- NW/NU: Business Corporations Act S.N.W.T. 1996, c. 19 (as amended to 2006, c. 23)
- ON: Business Corporations Act RSO 1990, c. B.16 (as amended to 2006, c. 8)
  - * Securities Transfer Act SO 2006, c. 8
- PE: Companies Act RSPEI 1988, c. C-14 (as amended to 2003, c. 33)
  - * Winding up Act RSPEI 1988, c. W-5 (as amended to 1994, c. 48)
- QC: Companies Act RSQ 1979, c. C-38 (as amended to 2004, c. 37)
  - * Winding up Act RSQ 1979, c. L-4 (as amended to 2003, c. 29)
- SK: Business Corporations Act RSS 1978, c. B-10 (as amended to 2006, c. 26)
- YK: Business Corporations Act RSY 2002, c. 20

* These acts have been presented in the table with the letter W preceding the section number

	CA	AB	BC	MB	NB	NF	NS	NW	ON	PE	QC	SK	YK
Title	1					1	1					1	
Part I Interpretation and application													
Definitions	2	1-4	1, 2	1	1	2, 7-10	2	1, 5	1	1	123.1	2	1, 2
Application	3		4	4	2	4	138(1)		2, 3.2		123.3	3	
Purposes	4			4		3							
Part II Incorporation													
Incorporators	5	5	10	5	3	11	9	5	4	4, 6	123.9, 123.10	5	5, 7
Articles of incorporation	6	6	11, 12, 58	6	4	12	20, 22	6	5	6, 7	123.11, 123.12	6	7, 8
Delivery of articles of incorporation	7	7	10	7	5	14	25	7	6	8	123.14	7	9
Certificate of incorporation	8	8	13	8	6	15	26(1)	8	6	10	123.27	8	10
Effect of certificate	9	9	13, 17	9	7	16		9	7			9	11
Name of corporation	10	10	23, 24, 25, 27	10	8	17-19	15, 80	10	10	12, 84	123.22, 123.23, 123.24	10, 267	12
Reserving name	11	11	22	11	9	20, 403		11	8	12	9.2	11, 292, 294, 294.1	13
Prohibited names	12	12, 13	22, 28	12	10	21, 22, 404	16	12	9, 12	10	9.1	12	14, 15
Certificate of amendment	13	14		13	11	25		13	12	16	123.27.1	13, 293, 294	16
Personal liability	14	15	20	14	12	26		14	21		123.7, 123.8	14	17
Part III Capacity and powers													
Capacity of a corporation	15	16	30, 32	15	13	27	26	15	15, 16	15	123.29	15	18
Powers of a corporation	16	17	33	16	14	28, 29		16	17	14, 20	123.29	16	19

	CA	AB	BC	MB	NB	NF	NS	NW	ON	PE	QC	SK	YK
No constructive notice	17	18	421	17	15	30	31	17	18		123.30	17	20
Authority of directors, officers and agents	18	19	136, 146	18	16	31	30	18	19	60	123.31	18	21
Part IV Registered office and records													
Registered office	19	20	34, 35	19	17	33, 34	79	19, 20	14	67	123.34-123.36	19	22
Corporate records	20	21, 22	42, 179, 196, 426, 428	20	18	36-39	42, 88, 89, 90, 120	21	140, 144	50	123.111-123.113	20	23
Access to corporate records	21	23	46, 47, 48, 49, 426	21	19	42-45	29, 43, 88, 90	22	145, 146	52, 53	123.114	21	24
Form of records	22	24	44	22	20	40	89	23	139			22	25
Corporate seal	23	25	194	23	21	32	104	24	13		123.165	23	26
Part V Corporate finance													
Shares	24	26	52, 53, 56, 58, 59	24	22	46-48	32, 17, First Schedule	25	22	13, 39	123.38, 123.39	24	27
Issue of shares	25	27	62, 63, 64, 65, 87	25	23, 24	49-51		27	23	32-36	123.17	25, 25.1	28
Stated capital account	26	28	72	26	25	52, 53		28	24	37	123.47	26	29
Shares in series	27	29	60	27	26	54		29	25		123.47	27	30
Pre-emptive right	28	30		28	27	55		30	26			28	31
Options and rights	29	31		29	28	56		31	27	47, 48	123.40, 123.41	29	32
Corporation holding its own shares	30	32	85	30	29	58		32	28	88.1	123.43	30	33
Exception	31	33	85	31	30	59		33	29	88.2	123.44	31	34
Exception relating to Canadian Ownership	32					60			29		31.1		
Voting shares	33		177			61		34	29	59, 88.3		31.2	
Acquisition of Corporation's own shares	34	34	77, 78	32	31	62	51	35	30	88.4	123.42, 123.52	32	35
Alternative acquisition of corporation's own shares	35	35		33	32	63	51	37	31	88.5	123.50	33	36
Redemption of shares	36	36	77, 79	34	33	64	51	38	32	88, 88.6	123.53	34	37
Donated shares	37	37	75	35	34	65		39	33			35	38
Other reduction of stated capital	38	38	74, 75	36	35	67	57	40	34		123.51	36	39
Adjustment of stated capital account	39	39, 40	73, 76, 82, 104	37	36, 37	68-73	51, 113	41	35, 44		123.61-123.65	37	40, 41
Enforceability of contract to buy shares	40	41		38	39	74	114	43	36			38	42
Commission for sale of shares	41	42	67	39	40	75	110	44	37			39	43
Dividends	42	43	70	40	41	76		45	38	62	81, 123.72	40	44
Form of dividend	43	44	70	41	42	77		45	38	63	81	41	45
Shareholder immunity	45	46	87, 89	43	44	81, 82		47	40	57, 58	41, 123.67-123.69	43	47
Part VI Sale of constrained shares													
Sale of constrained shares by corporation	46					83			45		43.1		

Table of Concordance   **CXXXV**

	CA	AB	BC	MB	NB	NF	NS	NW	ON	PE	QC	SK	YK
Proceeds of sale to be trust fund	47					84			45			43.2	
Part VII Security certificates, registers and transfers													
Application of Part	48		W106.1	44	45, 46	85-88		48				44	48
Rights of holder	49	48	57, 69, 83, 107, 108, 110	45	47, 50	89-95		49	42, 54-57	49, 51	53	45	49
Securities records	50	49	111	46	48	96-101	42, 46	50	141-143	50	123.113	46	50
Dealings with registered holder	51	50	115, 118, 119	47	49	102-106		51	67			47	51
Overissue	52	51		48		107		52	58			48	52
Burden of proof	53	W53	W53	49		108		53	W53			49	53
Securities fungible	54			50		109		54				50	54
Notice of defect	55	W56-59	W56-59	51		110-112		55	W56-59			51	55
Staleness as notice of defect	56	W61	W61	52		113		56	W61			52	56
Unauthorized signature	57	W57	W57	53		114		57	W57			53	57
Completion or alteration	58	W63	W63	54		115, 116		58	W63			54	58
Warranties of agents	59	W65	W65	55		117		59	W65			55	59
Title of purchaser	60	W69, 70	W69, 70	56		118		60	W69, 70			56	60
Deemed notice of adverse claim	61	W18-22	W18-22	57		119, 120		61	W18-22			57	61
Staleness as notice of adverse claim	62	W20	W20	58				62	W20			58	62
Warranties to issuer	63	W33-43	W33-43	59		121		63	W33-43			59	63
Right to compel endorsement	64	W74	W74	60		122		64	W74			60	64
Definition of 'appropriate person'	65	W1, 29, 33, 34, 77	W1, 29, 33, 34, 77	61		123		65	W1, 29, 33, 34, 77			61	65
Effect of endorsement without delivery	66	W73	W73	62		124		66	W73			62	66
Endorsement in bearer form	67	W75	W75	63		125		67	W75			63	67
Effect of unauthorized endorsement	68	W90, 91	W90, 91	64		126		68	W90, 91			64	68
Warranties of guarantor of signature	69	W79-84	W79-84	65		127		69	W79-84			65	69
Constructive delivery of a security	70	W68	W68	66		128, 129		70	W68			66	70
Delivery of security	71	W68	W68	67				71	W68			67	71
Right to reclaim possession	72			68		132		72				68	72
Right to requisites for registration	73	W85	W85	69		133		73	W85			69	73
Seizure of security	74	W48-51	W48-51	70		134		74	W48-51			70	74
No conversion if good faith delivery by agent	75							75			70.1		75
Duty to register transfer	76	W86	W86	71	48	135		76	W86			71	76
Assurance that	77	W86, 87	W86, 87	72		136		77	W86, 87			72	77

	CA	AB	BC	MB	NB	NF	NS	NW	ON	PE	QC	SK	YK
endorsement effective													
Limited duty of inquiry	78			73		137, 138		78				73	78
Limitation of issuer's liability	79	W86(2), 90, 91	W86(2), 90, 91	74		141, 142		79	W86(2), 90, 91			74	79
Notice of lost or stolen security	80	W92, 93	W92, 93	75		143		80	W92, 93			75	80
Agent's duty, rights, etc.	81	W94	W94	76		144		81	W94			76	81
Part VIII Trust indentures													
Definitions	82	81	90, 91	77		145, 146		82	46			77	82
Conflict of interest	83	82	92	78		147		83	48			78	83
Qualification of trustee	84	83	92	79		148		84				79	84
List of security holders	85	84	93, 94	80		149, 503		85	52			80	85
Evidence of compliance	86	85	95	81		150		86	49			81	86
Contents of declaration, etc.	87	86	96	82		151		87	49			82	87
Further evidence of compliance	88	87	96	83		152		88	49			83	88
Trustee may require evidence of compliance	89	88	97	84		153, 154		89	47			84	89
Notice of default	90	89	98	85		155		90	51			85	90
Duty of care	91	90	99	86		156		91	47			86	91
Reliance on statements	92	91	100	87		157		92	47			87	92
No exculpation	93	92	101	88		158		93	47			88	93
Part IX Receivers and receiver-managers													
Functions of receiver	94	93		89	52	159	71	94					94
Functions of receiver-manager	95	94		90	53	160, 505	72	95					95
Directors' powers cease	96	95	105	91	54	161	73	96				91	96
Duty to act	97	96		92	55	162	74	97					97
Duty under instrument	98	97		93	56	163	75	98					98
Duty of care	99	98		94	57	164	76	99					99
Directions given by court	100	99		95	58	165	77	100					100
Duties of receiver and receiver-manager	101	100	106	96	59	166	78	101					101
Part X Directors and officers													
Duty to manage or supervise management	102	101, 103	120, 136, 137	97	60	167-169	93	102	115	21, 28	123.72	97	102
By-laws	103	102		98	61	170		103	116	29, 30, 38, 87	91	98	103
Organization meeting	104	104		99	62	171		105	117	22	123.17, 123.19	99	105
Qualifications of directors	105	105	124, 125	100	63	172-174	95	106	118	23	123.73, 123.74	100	106
Notice of directors	106	106	1, 121, 122, 123	101	64	175	94	107	119		123.18, 123.76	101	107
Cumulative voting	107	107		102	65	176		108	120	25		102	108

Table of Concordance

	CA	AB	BC	MB	NB	NF	NS	NW	ON	PE	QC	SK	YK
Ceasing to hold office	108	108	128	103	66	177, 178		109	121		89	103	109
Removal of directors	109	109	128, 130, 131, 138	104	67	179		110	122		123.77, 123.79	104	110
Attendance at meeting	110	110		105	68	180		111	123	26	123.85, 123.86	105	111
Filling vacancy	111	111	130, 131, 132, 133, 134, 135	106	69	181		112	124	21	123.78	106	112
Number of directors	112	112		107	70	182		113	125	27	123.80	107	113
Notice of change of directors or director's address	113	113	127	108	71	183	98	114	125		123.81	108	114
Meeting of directors	114	114	140	109	72	184		115	126		123.20	109	115
Delegation	115	115		110	73	185-188	103	116	127		89.91	110	116
Validity of acts of directors and officers	116	116	143	111	74	189	97	117	128		123.31	111	117
Resolution in lieu of meeting	117	117	140	112	75	191	89, 91	118	129		89.3	112	118
Directors' liability	118	118	154, 156	113	76	192		119	130	54, 65, 66, 83, 88.7	72, 123.59, 123.69, 123.71, 123.121	113, 301	119, 120
Liability of directors for Wages	119	119		114		193-197		120	131		96	114	121
Disclosure of interest	120	120	147-153	115	77	198-201	99	121	132			115	122
Officers	121	121	141	116	78	202		122	133		89.91	116	123
Duty of care of directors and officers	122	122	142	117	79	203		123	134		123.84	117	124
Dissent	123	123	154, 157	118	80	204		124	135		123.85	118	125
Indemnification	124	124	159-165	119	81	205-209		125	136	64	123.87-123.89	119	126
Remuneration	125	125		120	82	219		126	137		123.75	120	127
Part XI Insider trading													
Definitions	126	126	192	125	83	211		127	138			125	128
Prohibition of short sale	130							131					
Definitions	131	121, 125	192	121-125	83	211-214		132	138			121-125	129-132
Part XII Shareholders													
Place of meetings	132	131	166	126	84	215, 216		133			98	126	133
Calling annual meetings	133	132	181, 182	127	85	217	83, 84, 85	134	94	31	123.94	127	134
Fixing record date	134	133	171	128	86	218-220		135	95		98	128	135
Notice of meeting	135	134	169	129	87	221, 222	135A	136	96		97	129	136
Waiver of notice	136	135	170	130	88	223		137	98		123.94	130	137
Proposals	137	136	187-191	131	89	224-232	135A	138	99			131	138
List of share-holders entitled to receive notice	138	137	112	132	90	233, 234		139	100			132	139
Quorum	139	138	172	133	92	235		140	101			133, 274	140
Right to vote	140	139	173	134	93	236-238	86	141	102			134	141
Voting	141	140	173, 174	135	94	239		142	103		101, 123.95	135	142
Resolution in lieu of meeting	142	141	180, 182	136	95	240	91, 92	143	104		123.96	136	143

	CA	AB	BC	MB	NB	NF	NS	NW	ON	PE	QC	SK	YK
Requisition of meeting	143	142	167	137	96	241	84	144	105		99	137	144
Meeting called by court	144	143	186	138	97	242		145	106			138	145
Court review of election	145	144		139	98	243		146	107			139	146
Pooling agreement	145.1	145	175	140	99	244, 245		147	108		123.91-123.93	140	147
Unanimous shareholder Agreement	146	146	137					148			123.91		148
Part XIII Proxies													
Definitions	147	147		141		246	85A	149	109			141	149
Appointing proxyholder	148	148		142	91	247-249	85B	150	110		103	142	150
Mandatory solicitation	149	149		143		250, 506	85C	151	111			143	151
Soliciting proxies	150	150		144		251, 252, 507	85D	152	112			144	152
Exemption	151	151		145		253	85E	153	113			145	153
Attendance at meeting	152	152, 153		146		254, 508	85F	154	114		103	146	154
Duty of intermediary	153	152, 153		147		255, 256		155				147	155
Restraining order	154	154		148		257, 509		156	253			148	156
Part XIV Financial disclosure													
Annual financial statements	155	155	185, 198	149	100	258	121	157	154		98	149	157
Exemption	156	156		150		259	123, 124	158				150	158
Consolidated statements	157	157		151	101	260	121, 135A	159	157		98	151	159
Approval of financial statements	158	158	199	152	102	261	122	160	159			152	160
Copies to shareholders	159	159	185	153	103	262, 510	121	161	154	79		153	161
Copies to director	160	160		154		263, 511		162				154, 154.1	162
Qualification of auditor	161	161	205, 206, 208	155	104	264	119A	163	152			155	163
Appointment of auditor	162	162	203, 204, 207	156	105	265	117	164	149		123.97	156	164
Dispensing with auditor	163	163	203	157		266	118	165	148		123.98-123.100	157	165
Ceasing to hold office	164	164		158	106	267	117	166				158	166
Removal of auditor	165	165	209	159	107	268	117	167	149			159	167
Filling vacancy	166	166		160	108	269	117	168				160	168
Court appointed auditor	167	167		161		270	117	169				161	169
Right to attend meeting	168	168	209, 210, 211, 214, 219	162	109	271-273, 512	117, 119	170	151			162	170
Examination	169	169	212	163	110	274	119B	171	153			163	171
Right to information	170	170	217, 218	164	111	275	119B	172	153			164	172
Audit committee	171	171	216, 223-226, 426, 428	165		276	119B	173	153, 158			165	173
Qualified privilege (defamation)	172	172	217-220	166	112	278	119, 119B	174	151			166, 271	174

Table of Concordance cxxxix

	CA	AB	BC	MB	NB	NF	NS	NW	ON	PE	QC	SK	YK
Part XV Fundamental changes													
Amendment of articles	173	173	54, 58, 60, 139, 257, 259, 263	167	113	279	17, 19, 23, 51	176	168	17	123.101-123.106	167	175
Constraints on shares	174	174		168		280-282			42			168	176
Proposal to amend	175	175		169	114	283		177	169			169	177
Class vote	176	176	60,61	170	115	284	135A	178	170		49	170	178
Delivery of articles	177	177	257	171	116	285		179	171	18	123.104	171	179
Certificate of amendment	178	178	257, 263	172	117	286	17	180	172	19	123.105	172	180
Effect of certificate	179	179	259, 263	173	118		17, 18	181			123.106	173	181
Restated articles	180	180		174	119	287		182	173			174	182
Amalgamation	181	181	269, 275, 285	175, 319	120	288	26, 134	183	174	77	123.115, 123.116	175, 295	183
Amalgamation agreement	182	182	270	176	121	289	134	184	175		123.122, 123.123	176	184
Shareholder approval	183	183	271	177	122	290	134, 135A	185	176		123.124-123.127	177	185
Vertical short-form amalgamation	184	184	273	178	123	291, 292		186	177		123.129	178	186
Sending of articles	185	185	275, 277, 278, 279, 281, 286	179	124	293	134	187	178		123.117, 123.119	179	187
Effect of certificate	186	186	282, 286	180	125	294	134	188	179		123.120	180	188
Amalgamation under other federal Acts	186.1	187						189					
Continuance (import)	187	188	284, 285, 302-307	181	126	295-298	133	190	180	85	123.131-123.139	181	190
Continuance (other jurisdictions)	188	189	308, 310, 311	182	127	299-301	133, 135A	191	181	86		182	191
Borrowing powers	189	190	301	183	130	302, 303	26, 135A	192	184	78		183	104, 192
Right to dissent	190	191	237-247, 260, 272, 309	184	131	304, 313	135A	193	185			184	193
Definition of 'reorganization'	191	192		185	132	314	131	194	186			185, 186	194
Definition of 'arrangement'	192	193	288-299	185	128, 129	315	130, 131	195	182, 183		49, 123.107	186.1	195
Part XVI Going-private transactions and squeeze-out transactions													
Going-private transactions	193												
Squeeze-out transactions	194												
Part XVII Compulsory and compelled acquisitions													
Definitions	206	194	300					196			51		
Obligation to acquire shares	206.1	195						197, 201					
Part XVIII Liquidation and dissolution													
Definition of "court"	207						W2		W1				
Application of part	208	207	313				W3	209				201	209
Revival	209	208-210	355, 356, 357, 358, 364, 365, 367	200, 202	136	331		210, 211		73		202, 296	210, 211

Table of Concordance

	CA	AB	BC	MB	NB	NF	NS	NW	ON	PE	QC	SK	YK
Dissolution before commencing business	210	211		203	137	332-335	W4		237-239	W4		203	212
Proposing liquidation and dissolution	211	212	314-319, 321, 323	204	138	336-340	W4	213	193, 198, 239	W5-W7	W3, W9, W18	204	213
Dissolution by director	212	213	422	205	139	341	136, 137	212	240	72		205	212
Grounds for dissolution	213	214		206	140	342			241			206	214, 215
Further grounds	214	215	324	207	141	343		216	207			207	216
Application for supervision	215	216		208	142	344		217				208	217
Application to court	216	217		209	143	345	W5	218		W21	W24	209	218
Powers of court	217	218	325, 326	210	144	346	W42, W48, W58, W62, W63	219	211, 233	W25		210	219, 220
Effect of order	218	219		211	144	347	W9	220	213	W22-W24	W25	211	221
Cessation of business and powers	219	220	282, 339, 340	212	145	348	W9, W50	221		W6	W4	212	
Appointment of liquidator	220	221	324	213	146	349	W10	222	210	W9, W15, W26	W5, W6, W8	213	222
Duties of liquidator	221	222	329, 330, 331, 338	214	147	350	W40	223	202, 223			214, 269.1	223
Powers of liquidator	222	223	334, 335, 339	215	148	351	W16	224	223	W11, W17-W19	W10	215	224
Costs of liquidation	223	224	338, 341, 342, 343, 344, 345	216	149	352	W67	225	212, 218, 222	W10, W36	W12-W14, W16	216	225
Right to distribution in money	224	225	336	217	150	353	W20	226	204			217	226
Custody of records	225	226	351-353	218	151	354, 502	W71	227	236		W21	218	227
Definition of 'shareholder'	226	227	346, 348	219	152	355		228	243			219, 277	228
Unknown claimants	227	228	337, 349	220	153	356	W70	229	234, 238	W39	W20	220	229
Vesting in Crown	228	229	337, 368	221	154	357, 358	W70	230	244	W39	W20	221	230
Investigation	229	223	248, 249	222	155	359	115	231	161			222	231, 232
Powers of court	230	232	253	223	156	360	115	233	162			223	233
Power of inspector	231	233	248, 249, 251	224	157	361	115	234	163			224	234
Hearing in Camera	232	234		225	158	362		235	164			225	235
Criminating statements	233	235		226	159	363		236				226	236
Part XIX Investigation													
Absolute privilege (defamation)	234	236	255	227	160	364		237	165			227	237
Information respecting ownership and control	235		426	228		365, 515						228	
Solicitor-client privilege	236	237	252	229	161	366		238	166			229	238
Inquiries	237			230	162	367		239	167		110	230	

Table of Concordance cxli

	CA	AB	BC	MB	NB	NF	NS	NW	ON	PE	QC	SK	YK
Part XIX.1 Apportioning award of damages													
Definitions	237.1												
Application of part	237.2												
Degree of responsibility	237.3												
Exception – fraud	237.4												
Individual or personal body corporate	237.5												
Equitable grounds	237.6												
Value of security	237.7												
Court determines value	237.8												
Application to determine value	237.9												
Part XX remedies, offences and punishment													
Definitions	238	239	227, 232	231	163	368	135A	240	245			231	240
Commencing derivative action	239	240	232, 233	232	164	369	135A	241	246			232	241
Powers of court	240	241	233	233	165	370	135A	242	247			233	242
Application to court re oppression	241	242	227	234	166	371	135A	243	248			234	243
Evidence of shareholder approval not decisive	242	243	233, 235, 236	235	167	372, 373	135A, 152	244	249			235	244
Application to court to rectify records	243	244		236	168	374		245	250			236	245
Application for directions	244	245		237	169	375		246				237	246
Notice of refusal by director	245	246		238	170	376	16	247	251			238	247
Appeal from director's decision	246	247	406	239	171	377	16	248	252			239	248
Restraining or compliance order	247	248	228	240	172	378		249				240	249
Summary application to court	248	249	235	241	173	379		250				241	250
Appeal of final order	249	250			174	380		251	255		242		
Offences with respect to reports	250	251	427	242	175	504		252	256		108, 114	300	251
Offence	251	252	426	243	176	516		253	258		123	302	252
Order to comply	252	253	430	244, 245		517-519		254	259, 261			303	253
Part XX.1 Documents in electronic or other form													
Definitions	252.1												
Application	252.2												
Use not Mandatory	252.3												
Creation and provision of information	252.4												
Creation of information in writing	252.5												

	CA	AB	BC	MB	NB	NF	NS	NW	ON	PE	QC	SK	YK
Statutory declarations and affidavits	252.6												
Signatures	252.7		418										
Part XXI General													
Notice to directors and shareholders	253	255	6, 7	246	177	385-387		256	262			247-249	255
Notice to and service on corporation	254	256	6, 7, 9	247	178	402	154	257	263	68		269, 269.01	256
Waiver of notice	255	258	7	248	179	388		259	264			250	258
Certificate of director	256	259	282, 364, 365, 419	249	180	399	28	260				286	259
Certificate of corporation	257	260	194	250	181	389, 391		261	266			251, 253	260
Copies	258	261		251	182	392		262	267		1.2	254	261
Contents and form of notices and documents	258.1							263	273(4), 273.1, 273.2				
Exemption	258.2							264					
Proof required by director	259	262		252	183	396		265	268			289	262
Appointment of Director	260	263	400	253	184	381	3	266	278	2		279	263
Regulations	261	266	432	254	185	409	7	267	272	81, 82	123.169	304	265
Fee to be paid before service performed	261.1		431					269					
Definition of 'statement'	262	267		255	186	393		268	273			255	266
Signature	262.1	267		255(6)		393(4)			273(4)(a), 273.2(2)			255(4)	266
Annual return	263	268		273	187	408		270		80		273	267
Certificate	263.1		411				28	271					
Alteration	264	269		256	188	394		272			123.162	256	268
Corrections at request of Director	265	270	229, 230, 413, 420	257	189	395		273	275		123.140, 123.163	257	269
Cancellation of articles by director	265.1												
Inspection	266	271	416	284, 285	190	384	4	273	270		110	284, 285	270, 271
Records of director	267	272	412	288	191	383, 397, 398		274	276		1.2, 2.5	288	272
Form of publication	267.1							275					
Definition of charter	268	276		258	192							258	

Chapter 1

THE CORPORATE CONCEPT

A. OVERVIEW OF CORPORATE LAW

§1.1 Briefly stated, a corporation is an artificial or juristic entity created by or under the authority of the laws of a state, province or nation, that is regarded in law as being a legal person separate and distinct from the person or persons who comprise its membership. Many of the essential issues of corporate law were summarized in but a single paragraph by Doherty J.A. in *Budd v. Gentra Inc.*:

> A corporation is a discrete legal entity. It has rights and obligations, can contract, commit torts, and even commit crimes. When a corporation acts, it must act through the persons who are fixed with the power to act as the corporation, principally, its officers, directors and senior management. Where a director or officer does something which harms another, the question sometimes becomes — who should be responsible for that action, the company or the individual? Our jurisprudence answers that question by determining whether, in the circumstances, the act is properly attributable to the company or to the individual.[1]

In addition to these matters, corporate law also deals with the procedure for creating the corporation, and for effecting fundamental changes in the corporation, the rules and procedures governing the raising of capital by a corporation, the distribution of its profits, the relationship among a corporation and those who hold an interest in it, the rules governing the exercise of its powers, and the procedure for winding-up and liquidating a corporation at the end once it has served its purpose or is no longer viable. It is with these matters that this text is concerned.

§1.2 The focus of this book is on the Canadian law and practice relating to business corporations.[2] As the following chart indicates, they comprise but one of

---

[1] [1998] O.J. No. 3109 at para. 25 (C.A.).
[2] The principles discussed in this text have little application to corporations exercising a governmental or other public responsibility, such as municipal corporations. The latter have been characterized as follows:
> A municipal corporation is a creature of provincial legislation.
> A "municipal corporation" or "municipality" is defined as a public corporation created by the government for political purposes and having subordinate or local powers of legislation. It can exercise its corporate powers only within its defined limits.
> It does not own its defined territorial area, but is limited thereto as to its jurisdiction.
> *Morrison v. New Brunswick*, [1994] N.B.J. No. 597 at para. 9, 158 N.B.R. (2d) 161, 406 A.P.R. 161 (Q.B.), *per* Riordon J.

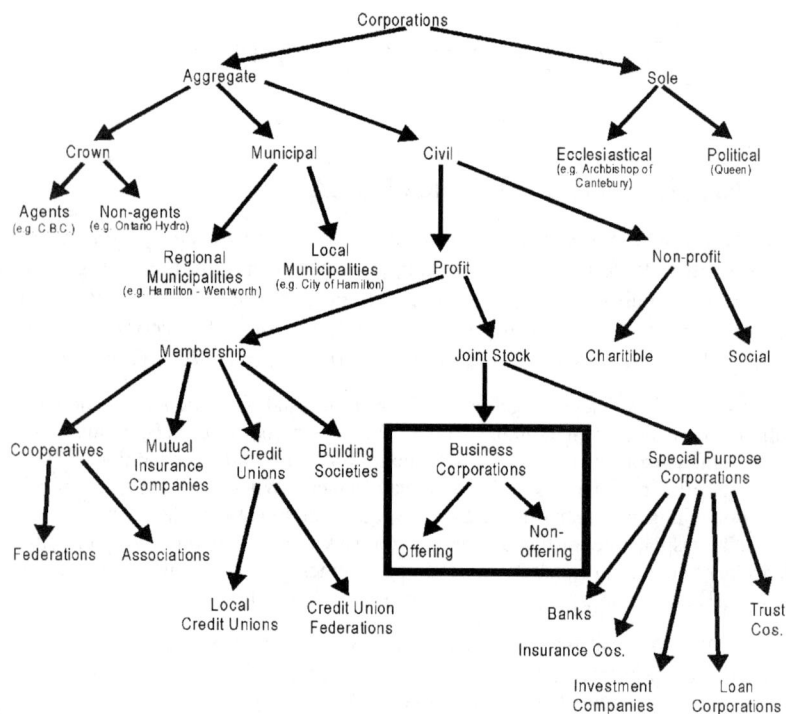

many different forms of corporate entity. In many cases, corporations represent associations of individuals or other persons, joined together by their voluntary action or by legal compulsion, to accomplish some purpose — pecuniary, ideal or governmental — authorized or permitted by or under the law which created the corporation. At least as frequently, however, a corporation is not an association of persons, but is merely an administrative vehicle through which one and only one person carries on some activity: thus the very large number of corporations that are wholly owned subsidiaries of other corporations, or that are owned by the Crown or a single individual. Historically, the law has recognized several different types of corporation. Public corporations are those that are created by the state for some political or other public purpose, and which often act as agencies of the government.[3] Private corporations (which term, in this context, includes corporations whose securities are publicly traded) are those that are founded by private individuals or other corporations for some private purpose.[4] Private corporations may be further divided into ecclesiastical and lay corpora-

---

[3] See, for instance, *Goodwin v. East Hartford* (1897), 70 Conn. 18 (S.C. Errors), 38 A. 876 (S.C. Conn. 1897).
[4] See, for instance, *Dartmouth College v. Woodward* (1819), 4 Wheat 518, 4 L.Ed. 629.

tions, benevolent and civil, domestic and foreign, and trading and non-trading. Within the category of trading corporations lies the sub-category of business corporations, which for the moment may be defined as private corporations formed for the purpose of transacting business in the widest sense of that term on a for-profit basis, with the profits so earned to be distributed among the members of the corporation concerned, in accordance with their respective membership interest as represented by investment in share capital.[5]

B. THE NATURE OF A CORPORATION

§1.3 The English noun "corporation" and the verb "to incorporate" are both derived from the Latin verb *corporare*, which means to form into or furnish with a body or to infuse with substance. To understand the meaning of "corporation" it is necessary to understand the meaning of "legal personality". At law, a person is a being or entity that has the capacity to:

- enjoy by virtue of its existence, or to acquire in some other way, enforceable legal rights or property; or
- be by virtue of its existence, or to become in some other way, subject to enforceable legal obligations or liabilities.

At law, therefore, a person is a being or entity having legal substance. There are two classes of person: natural and juristic. Under Ontario law (and in other common law jurisdictions), every individual live-born human being is a natural person. Corporations are juristic persons: the term "juristic" meaning no more than they are entities that are considered to be persons for the purposes of the law. In common law jurisdictions, the term corporation is universally and exclusively linked to artificial or juristic persons. If an entity is said to be a corporation, then it is presumed conclusively to be a legal person. Any entity, other than a human being, that is recognized as enjoying legal personality is a corporation.[6] To confer personal status on an entity is to make it a corporation.[7]

§1.4 Entities that perform a similar function to the modern business corporation (in the sense of carrying on a collective enterprise) can be traced back long into history. References to such collective entities have been found in Babylonian texts dating back as far as 2100 BC. However, while collective enterprise is ancient, the concept of the juristic person is of much more recent vintage. It appears to date back not much further than the 13th century, at which time one may find a reference by Pope Innocent IV to a corporation as being *"persona ficta"*.

§1.5 As will be discussed in greater detail below, in Canada, all corporations other than the Crown are created by or under statute. The consequences of incorporation are governed to a very large extent by the terms of the legislation

---

[5] See, generally, *In Re Bristol Athenaeum* (1889), 43 Ch. D. 236; *In Re Russell Institution*, [1898] 2 Ch. 72; *Re Jones*, [1898] 2 Ch. 83.
[6] See, generally, *Bank of Montreal v. Bethune* (1836), 4 O.S. 341 (U.C.C.A.), *per* Robinson C.J.
[7] See, for instance, the *Atlantic Canada Opportunities Agency Act*, R.S.C. 1985, c. 41 (4th Supp.), which confers the right to sue and enter into contracts.

under which each corporation respectively is incorporated, but in general the consequences reflect the fact that the creation of a corporation gives rise to a distinct legal person. For example, section 27 of the *Interpretation Act* provides:

> In every Act, unless the contrary intention appears, words making any association or number of persons a corporation or body politic and corporate,
>
> (a) vest in the corporation power to sue and be sued, to contract and be contracted with by its corporate name, to have a common seal, to alter or change the seal at its pleasure, to have perpetual succession, to acquire and hold personal property or movables for the purpose for which the corporation is constituted, and to alienate the same at pleasure;
>
> (b) vest in a majority of the members of the corporation the power to bind the others by their acts; and
>
> (c) exempt individual members of the corporation from personal liability for its debts, obligations or acts if they do not contravene the provisions of the Act incorporating them.[8]

(i) The Different Classes of Corporation

§1.6 The two classes of corporation are corporations sole and corporations aggregate. Most corporations are corporations aggregate. As a practical matter, the distinction between the two classes of corporation relates to the numbers of members that each corporation may possess. Although they are comparatively rare, it is worthwhile to begin any survey of the forms of corporation with a brief description of the nature of a corporation sole, which in common law jurisdictions was the first recognized class of corporation. For this reason, many of the concepts first worked out with respect to such corporations eventually came to be adapted and applied to corporations aggregate as they began their evolution.

(ii) Corporations Sole

§1.7 As the moniker suggests, a corporation sole is limited by law to one member at a given time. The membership of the corporation is attached as an incident to a particular office. The corporation is identified with the current holder of the office from time to time. The property associated with the office passes from one incumbent to the next, without need of any specific conveyance, and any contracts entered into by the incumbent in his or her official capacity are identified with the corporation sole, rather than with the incumbent personally. There are four basic principles that apply with respect to such corporations:

1. All corporations sole are either public officers or dignitaries of the established church (in some provinces, the status of corporation sole has also been conferred upon Episcopal officers in other churches).

2. According to some authorities, under the ancient common law, the corporation sole could claim title to real property only. This principle never seems to have been formally abrogated, but it is doubtful if it is still applicable. No one

---

[8] R.S.O. 1990, c. I.11.

would suggest, for instance, that the Royal Navy or the Crown jewels belong to the Queen in Her personal capacity.
3. Property and powers of a corporation sole are transferred on the death of an incumbent to successors in the office, not to heirs or through executors.
4. The corporation sole lacks the usual trappings of a corporation. It does not have a board of directors, officers, stock, by-laws, official minutes, seal, or corporate name. At least in the United Kingdom and Ireland, the older corporations sole are also devoid of any royal charter or other formal authorization, characteristics that are required in later corporations.

Official acts undertaken by the individual holder of such an office attach to the office rather than to the individual personally. Alternatively stated: when the holder of an office acts in an official capacity, it is seen to be the corporation sole that is acting. When the holder of the office changes, every right, property or other asset, privilege, duty, obligation, and liability associated with or consequent to the exercise of the office concerned, passes to the successor in office automatically by transmission of law. No conveyance, assignment, transfer, bequest or novation is required for this purpose. In the case of a corporation sole, the holder of the individual office is shielded from liability in his or her personal capacity for the liabilities and obligations associated with the office to which the corporation is attached. However, the property associated with that office is subject to those liabilities and obligations.[9]

§1.8 As Blackstone indicates, it was under the canon law that the notion of a corporate person originated.[10] Indeed, it must have become evident to the church early that it was essential to find some way of differentiating the individual acts of priests, bishops or abbots from those carried out in their official capacity. Once the notion of a separate corporate person had evolved to even an elementary level within the ecclesiastical sphere, it was highly likely that it would be exported into the secular realm, given the extent to which the clergy controlled the early administrative regime of the English Crown. At common law, corporations sole were attached to the following offices: the Crown, archbishoprics, bishoprics, and parish priests of the established church.[11] Although the Crown is

---

[9] *John Doe v. Bennett*, [2002] N.J. No. 218 (C.A.).

[10] See, generally, *The Code of Canon Law (English Translation)* (London: Collins Liturgical Publications and the Canon Law Society of Great Britain & Ireland, 1983), Title VI, c. 2, Juridical Persons, canon 113 § 2:

> In the Church, besides physical persons, there are also juridical persons, that is, in canon law subjects of obligations and rights which accord with their nature.

> There is one major difference between the canon law concept of a corporation and the common law concept. At canon law, a corporation could be an aggregate of things as well as of other persons. Thus canon 115 § 3 provides:

> An aggregate of things, or an autonomous foundation, consists of goods or things, whether spiritual or material, and is directed, in accordance with the law and the statutes, by one or more physical persons or by a college.

[11] Curiously, abbots of religious orders were not considered to be corporations sole. Religious orders occupied a kind of middle ground position between corporations sole and corporations aggregate. At common law, the membership of a religious order comprised the corporation, but

a corporation sole, individual ministers, ministries and offices of the Crown do not enjoy that status unless conferred by statute. A number of statutory corporations sole have also been created. The Public Guardian and Trustee is continued as a corporation sole under subsection (2) of the *Public Guardian and Trustee Act*.[12] The Accountant of the Supreme Court would appear to remain a corporation sole, by virtue of the old *Judicature Act*,[13] unless and until the status of the office as such is formally dissolved. By virtue of being corporations sole, these officers have a right to sue or be sued in their corporate capacity and to acquire property, which may be held in a fiduciary capacity for the benefit of another person.[14]

(iii) Corporations Aggregate

§1.9 Most corporations belong to the second class of corporation, which is known as the corporations aggregate. This class includes all business corporations and companies and corporations under the Ontario *Corporations Act*,[15] municipalities and regional municipalities. Corporations aggregate are distinct from partnerships and other forms of unincorporated association in that the corporation aggregate (whether it consists of one person or a million or more persons) possesses its own separate personality from its members. The first corporations aggregate were the deans and chapters of cathedrals, universities and municipalities. The modern business corporation began to divert from such ecclesiastical and religious corporations at a very early period. It is not entirely clear whether medieval guilds constituted corporations as such, although at least some such guilds seem to have had corporate status conferred upon them by Royal charter. For instance, in 1505, Henry VII granted a charter to The Company of Merchant Adventurers, giving the members of that company a monopoly on trade in export of English manufactures. Although the charter was issued at the request of London merchants, membership in the company was (by terms of the charter) open to any English merchant who paid a fee. The charter authorized the company (which, curiously, was headquartered on the Continent, rather than in England) to elect "Four and Twenty of the most sadd discreet and honest Persons of divers fellowships" to be "Assistants" to the governor. The governor and the assistants were empowered to resolve disputes among merchants and to enact ordinances for the regulation of the members of the company. During the first half of the 16th century, merchant adventurers in other English cities obtained their own corresponding companies of merchant adventurers. These companies often also employed a board governance structure, with elected governors and 12 or 18 assistants. In 1564, however, Elizabeth I issued a new charter to the Merchant Adventurers which confirmed governance of the company in a governor, a deputy governor, and 24 assistants. In this case, it was

---

the power to act on behalf of the corporation was tied to the office of abbot. However, since the passage of the (second) *Act of Dissolution, 1539*, the unusual nature of such corporations has been largely a matter of only historic interest. Modern monasteries and convents are usually the subject of a private Act, or are incorporated under non-profit corporation legislation.

[12] R.S.O. 1990, c. P.51.
[13] R.S.O. 1970, c. 288, s. 108(1).
[14] See, for instance, the *Crown Administration of Estates Act*, R.S.O. 1990, C. 47.
[15] R.S.O. 1990, c. C. 38.

made clear that the company had jurisdiction over merchant adventurers wherever they operated. Despite these early precedents, it would not be until the 19th century, that the modern business corporation began to come into its own.

§1.10 As these developments were slowly taking place, changes began to take place in the method of incorporation. Historically, corporations in Britain (and, by succession, most of the rest of the former British Empire) have been created in a variety of ways:

- prior to the *Act in Restraint of Appeals, 1533*,[16] by papal bull—as in the case of the University of Glasgow in 1451;
- by Royal charter or patent;
- by public or private statute;
- by letters patent issued under the authority of a general statute of incorporation; and
- by registration under a general statute of incorporation.

With the exception of incorporation by way of papal bull, all of these forms of incorporation may be encountered in Canadian corporations active in Ontario today.

§1.11 Even before the Reformation, incorporation by Royal charter was the most common method of incorporation. The Hudson Bay Company, which is Canada's oldest corporation, was so established in 1670.[17] The creation of such a corporation involved the exercise of the royal prerogative and was usually coupled with the grant by the Sovereign of some exclusive monopoly or a related franchise. For example, the patent creating the Hudson Bay Company gave that company a monopoly on the fur trade in the Hudson Bay basin (an area that eventually became known as Rupert's Land); the patent creating the Virginia Company gave that company exclusive rights to colonize and trade in Virginia. The East India Company (created by the Royal charter of Elizabeth I in 1600) enjoyed a monopoly on tea sales that continued in British North America well into the 19th century. The sale of monopolies was one of the Crown's methods of raising revenue other than through taxation, and was greatly resented by Parliament for two reasons. First, it led to price gouging and to the other inconveniences generally associated with monopolies. Second, it reduced the control that Parliament exercised over the Sovereign through its control over taxation.

§1.12 Incorporation by Royal charter fell into disfavour with the enactment of the *Statute of Monopolies, 1624*.[18] This statute is reproduced as part of the law of

---

[16] 24 Henry VIII, c. 12.
[17] It is sometimes assumed that the Canadian Pacific Railway was incorporated by Royal charter, but in fact this does not appear to be the case. The authority for the incorporation was a federal enactment, even though the charter for the corporation was issued under the Great Seal of Canada: *Canadian Pacific Railway Company v. Winnipeg (City)*, [1952] 1 S.C.R. 424.
[18] 21 Jac. I, c. 3.

Ontario in *An Act concerning Monopolies, and Dispensation with Penal Laws.*[19] Section 1 of that Act provides:

> All monopolies, and all commissions, grants, licenses, charters, and letters patents, heretofore made ... or hereafter ... granted ... for the sole buying, selling, making, working, or using, of any thing ... or of any other monopolies, ... are altogether contrary to the laws of Ontario, and so are and shall be utterly void and of no effect, and in no wise to be put in use or execution.

The Sovereign could still create a corporation (and, in fact, retains that prerogative today), but since the corporation could not be granted any exclusive right, there was little in the way of Crown revenue to be derived from so doing.

§1.13 After the *Statute of Monopolies* was enacted, corporations tended to be created by Royal patent only for the purposes of foreign trade (as with the Hudson Bay and Virginia companies), since the *Statute of Monopolies* did not touch or concern that area of commerce. That use itself fell into disfavour following the South Sea Bubble. This company is considered in detail later in the chapter, but for the moment it is sufficient to say that the South Sea Company was essentially the Enron of its day. A good deal of restrictive legislation followed the collapse of this company, which remained in effect until the middle of the 19th century. During this period, the creation of corporations by way of Sovereign patent fell into almost complete disfavour and very few such corporations have been so created since. However, Parliament would occasionally create a corporation by way of special or private Act.

§1.14 With the Industrial Revolution and the rapid expansion of the British economy that followed, it became necessary to find a more expeditious method of creating corporations than by way of special or private Act. Similar pressures followed in the major British colonies, particularly those undergoing rapid economic and population expansion. In Britain, the solution settled upon was to create a scheme for the creation of companies by way of registration under a general statute of incorporation—the forerunner of the modern *Companies Act.*

(iv) The Evolution of Incorporation in Ontario

§1.15 Both such methods of incorporation continue to be used frequently in Ontario today. Subsection 4(1) of the *Corporations Act* follows the old Upper Canada approach. It provides that:

> The Lieutenant Governor may in his or her discretion, by letters patent, issue a charter to any number of persons, not fewer than three, of eighteen or more years of age, who apply therefor, constituting them and any others who become shareholders or members of the corporation thereby created a corporation for any of the objects to which the authority of the Legislature extends, except those of railway and incline railway and street railway corporations and corporations within the meaning of the *Loan and Trust Corporations Act.*

---

[19] R.S.O. 1897, c. 323.

However, most corporations in Canada are now created by way of registration. Both the *Canada Business Corporations Act* (CBCA) and the *Ontario Business Corporations Act* (OBCA) follow this approach. Subsection 4(1) of the OBCA provides that:

> One or more individuals or bodies corporate or any combination thereof may incorporate a corporation by signing articles of incorporation and complying with section 6.

Articles of incorporation must follow the prescribed form and set out the prescribed information.[20] However, provided the appropriate form is correctly completed and delivered to the registrar, incorporation becomes a matter of right, section 6 of the OBCA providing:

> An incorporator shall send to the Director articles of incorporation and, upon receipt of the articles, the Director shall endorse thereon, in accordance with section 273, a certificate which shall constitute the certificate of incorporation.

§1.16 The present approach to incorporation was a long time in evolving. The pre-colonial legislatures of the United States had the capacity to create corporations and occasionally did so by way of special Act. According to Wegenast, none of the pre-colonial constitutions provided for incorporation by charter of the colonial governor. Crown charter was nevertheless possible, and indeed much of the original effort at colonization in North America was carried out by English companies created under such a charter. The colonial legislatures were also considered to have the power to incorporate. Curiously, after the Revolution many state constitutions were amended to prohibit the creation of a corporation by way of special Act. However, in 1811, New York became the first state to create a general incorporation Act. That Act significantly influenced the development of all subsequent corporate legislation across the continent.

§1.17 During its early years, Upper Canada followed the established practice of the original 13 Colonies. Incorporation of business entities of various kinds began in Upper Canada around the 1820s. Prior to that date, domestic incorporation was limited to a handful of educational and institutional corporations, most of which were fairly well established by the time they acquired corporate status. The Law Society of Upper Canada was perhaps the earliest. It was founded in 1797, but was only incorporated in 1822.[21] An attempt to incorporate the Upper Canada College of Physicians and Surgeons failed in 1839, when the Act of incorporation was disallowed. The Midland District School Society was incorporated in 1815, and the Legislative Assembly Library was incorporated in 1816.

§1.18 The first domestic corporation created with the object of carrying on a business for profit was the Bank of Kingston, which was incorporated in 1819.[22] However, the charter was forfeited for non-user. The early incorporation process was fraught with confusion. The Bank of Upper Canada would have been incorporated

---

[20] R.S.O. 1990, c. B.16, s. 5(1) [hereinafter "OBCA"].
[21] By 37 Geo. III, c. 13.
[22] By 59 Geo. III, c. 15.

the same year,[23] but the Act was reserved. Jumping the gun somewhat, this bank nevertheless commenced operations and is therefore sometimes referred to as the "Pretended Bank of Upper Canada". It operations were discontinued in 1823, but its land holdings were not disposed of until 1826.[24] Another Bank of Upper Canada was incorporated in 1821. It went bankrupt in 1866.

§1.19 As might be expected, the types of corporation established reflected the changing economic and social conditions within the province. Early commercial transportation in Upper Canada was mostly by water, and the corporations created reflect the importance of that mode of transportation. The incorporation of canal companies began with the Burlington Bay Canal Construction Company in 1823.[25] This was followed by the Welland Canada Company Inc. (1824), the Desjardin Canal Company (1826), and the Rideau Canal Construction Company (1827). A number of companies were incorporated to construct or operate harbours and bridges, beginning with the Kettle Creek Harbor Construction Company (1827)[26] and the Burlington Bay Harbor Company (1828).[27] Five navigation companies were incorporated in Upper Canada prior to 1840.

§1.20 The most significant economic development of the 19th century was, however, the railway — and the growing importance of this method of transportation becomes evident in mid-19th century legislation creating corporate entities. The Cobourg Railway Company became the first incorporated railroad in 1834.[28] It seems to have been a fairly diverse transportation company, because it eventually operated under the name Cobourg and Rice Lake Plank Road and Ferry Co. The London and Gore Railroad Company (which became the Great Western Railroad) was also incorporated in 1834.[29] The first manufacturing company was not incorporated until 1831, when the Marmora Foundry Company was incorporated.[30] There would only be nine such companies incorporated between 1831 and the creation of the United Provinces of Canada in 1840, only one of which was based in Toronto (and its charter expired by reason of non-user).

§1.21 For many years, the Imperial Parliament continued to create corporations that were intended to carry on business in Ontario. These included the Canada Company (1825), the Bank of British North America (1836), the British America Fire and Life Assurance Company (the forerunner to the modern Royal Insurance Company) (1833). The Bank of British North America would merge with the Bank of Montreal in 1918. The Canada Company was incorporated to purchase and develop lands. It purchased the Crown reserve, comprising almost

---

[23] By 59 Geo. III, c. 24.
[24] See 6 Wm IV, c. 32. Apparently, the effort was not entirely successful: see 10 Geo. IV, c. 7.
[25] By 4 Geo. IV, c. 8.
[26] By 8 Geo. IV, c. 18.
[27] By 9 Geo. IV, c. 12.
[28] By 4 Wm. IV, c. 29.
[29] By 4 Wm. IV, c. 29.
[30] By 1 Wm. IV, c. 11.

1.4 million acres, and received a special grant of a further 1.1 million acres in the Huron County area.

§1.22 Non-profit corporations were also created by Royal charter. King's College (the oldest of the constituent university colleges comprising the University of Toronto) was incorporated by Royal charter in 1827; Victoria College was incorporated as Upper Canada Academy in 1836. An attempt to incorporate Kingston University in 1840[31] failed when the Act was disallowed.

C. BUSINESS CORPORATIONS

§1.23 By the end of the 19th century, Canadian commerce was becoming increasingly dominated by corporations—so much so, that there was a growing populist concern with respect to the extent of their control of the economy. In 1889, the Federal Parliament enacted *An Act for the Prevention and Suppression of Combinations Found in Restraint of Trade*, the forerunner of the *Combines Investigation Act* and today's *Competition Act*. Canada's 1889 legislation preceded the American *Sherman Antitrust Act*,[32] by almost a full year. Neither the Canadian nor American efforts at controlling the growth of business corporations were particularly successful. In Canada, America and every other modern economy incorporated entities have spread across the entire economy, and have continued to grow in both size and scope. Few major corporations today confine their operations to but a single country. As Parkinson[33] has pointed out, the world's 10 largest business corporations employ approximately 4.3 million people, and some 21 million people are directly dependent upon them. The total of their assets is approximately equal to Canada's Gross National Product. Generally speaking, Canadian business corporations operate on a much smaller scale, but their dominance of the domestic market is equally significant in relative terms.

---

[31] Under 2 Vic., c. 35.
[32] 1890, 26 Stat. c. 647.
[33] J.E. Parkinson, *Corporate Power and Responsibility, Issues in the Theory of Company Law* (Oxford: Clarendon Press, 1993) at 5.

THE TEN LARGEST CORPORATIONS IN CANADA, 1990[34]

Name	Revenue (millions)	Assets (millions)	Profit (Loss) (millions)	Employees
General Motors of Canada	$18,458	$5,961	$45	42,555
BCE Inc.	$18,373	$41,987	$1,147	120,000
Ford Motor Co. of Canada	$13,706	$3,564	($57)	28,000
George Weston Ltd.	$10,856	$3,707	$125	55,000
Canadian Pacific Ltd.	$10,500	$20,224	$355	72,200
IMPERIAL OIL LTD.	$10,223	$15,196	$493	14,702
Alcan Aluminum Ltd.	$10,217	$12,352	$634	57,000
Noranda	$9,565	$14,917	$120	56,000
Brascan Ltd.	$7,163	$5,718	$80	20
Chrysler Canada Ltd.	$7,067	$2,845	$16	14,000
Total	$116,128	$126,471	$2,958	459,477

By way of comparison, the combined revenues of Canada's 10 largest corporations in 1990 accounted in total for approximately 17.29 per cent of the Gross Domestic Product for Canada — more than that of all provinces other than Ontario and Quebec.

(i) The Corporate Legislative Realm

§1.24 In this book, we will examine the basic nature of a business corporation, dealing with such questions as: what is a business corporation? How can such an entity be identified? What differentiates a corporation from other forms of business enterprise? From where did the law of business corporations originate? We shall concentrate study on the two statutes in Canada under which the vast majority of business corporations operate, namely the Ontario *Business Corporations Act*[35] and the *Canada Business Corporations Act*,[36] with secondary consideration, by way of illustration, being given to corresponding legislation in other provinces.

§1.25 Few areas of law are so heavily influenced by legislation as corporate law. The primary source of the rules of law governing corporate entities is the statute by or under which each of them respectively incorporated or (where applicable) continued. In the words of Lord Halsbury, L.C.:

---

[34] Figures taken from *The Canadian Global Almanac, 1992* (Toronto: Global Press, 1991) at 610.
[35] OBCA, originally enacted as S.O. 1982, c. 4.
[36] R.S.C. 1985, c. C-44, originally enacted as S.C. 1974-75-76, c. 33.

... the whole structure of a limited company owes its existence to the Act of Parliament and it is to the Act of Parliament one must refer to see what are its powers, and within what limits it is free to act.[37]

Given the influence of statute law on corporate operations, it is therefore appropriate to spend a brief moment summarizing the key rules of statutory interpretation recognized in Canadian law. No special rules of statutory interpretation apply with respect to either corporate or securities law. The general rule with respect to statutory interpretation is that the words of an Act are to be read in their entire context and in their grammatical and ordinary sense in a manner that is harmonious with the scheme of the Act, the object of the Act, and the intention of Parliament. From a practical perspective, the difficulty is settling upon that apparent object of the Act and the intention of Parliament. Certain basic principles of interpretation may be quickly summarized and are of obvious importance. They include:

- Legislation that abrogates a common law right is given a narrow construction.[38]

- The words of each specific provision must be construed within the context of the statute in its entirety: as integral parts of a complete whole.

- When different wording is used in different provisions of an enactment, that variation of wording will generally be taken to indicate a different meaning.

- Where there are two or more statutes or regulations that may be relevant to a given situation, they are to be interpreted in a way that avoids any absurd or inconsistent result. A result is absurd where it leads to unworkable or impractical result; an inconvenient result; an anomalous or illogical result; a futile or pointless result; an artificial result; or a disproportionate countermischief.[39] It is not to be readily assumed that the legislature intends an unreasonable result or to perpetrate an injustice or absurdity.[40] If a statute is susceptible to two interpretations, the interpretation that avoids absurdity is to be preferred.[41]

- As a general rule, specific provisions are seen to qualify general provisions, and subsequently enacted provisions are seen to modify prior inconsistent statutory provisions.

- The scope of a regulation making power conferred under a statute is constrained by that enabling legislation.

---

[37] *Ooregum Gold Mining Co. of India Ltd. v. Roper*, [1892] A.C. 125 at 133.
[38] As to the approach to statutory interpretation that should be taken with respect to the construction of legislation under which personal liability is imposed on a director, officer or employee, see: *ESS Production Ltd. v. Sully*, [2005] All E.R. (D) 158 (C.A.) — such legislation to be given a fair interpretation, construing the rules set down therein in coherent and rational manner. See also: *Ricketts v. Ad Valorem Factors Ltd.*, [2004] 1 B.C.L.C. 1 (C.A.).
[39] *Walker Youth Homes Inc. v. Ottawa-Carleton District School Board*, [2004] O.J. No. 2307 (S.C.), *per* Caputo J.
[40] *Re Estrabrooks Pontiac Buick Ltd.*, [1982] N.B.J. No. 397, 44 N.B.R. (2d) 201 at para. 21 (C.A.).
[41] See, for instance, *Wicken (Litigation guardian of) v. Harssar*, [2004] O.J. No. 1935, 73 O.R. (3d) 600 (S.C.J.).

- Legislation is presumed to have been enacted in conformity with applicable constitutional limitations, and (to a somewhat more qualified degree) also the norms embodied in human rights legislation.
- When material is incorporated by reference into a statute or regulation it becomes an integral part of that enactment as if reproduced in its entirety within it.

§1.26 The search for legislative purpose can be an extremely difficult task and may require resorting to a number of sources apart from the text of the legislation itself, including legislative debates and the history of the legislation.[42] Most common law jurisdictions have enacted Interpretation Acts that guide courts as to the rules to be followed in construing the meaning of legislation. Subsection 9(5) of the Nova Scotia *Interpretation Act*,[43] is particularly detailed in directing how the courts are to discern the Legislature's intent. It provides that:

> Every enactment shall be deemed remedial and interpreted to insure the attainment of its objects by considering among other matters
>
> (a) the occasion and necessity for the enactment;
>
> (b) the circumstances existing at the time it was passed;
>
> (c) the mischief to be remedied;
>
> (d) the object to be attained;
>
> (e) the former law, including other enactments upon the same or similar subjects;
>
> (f) the consequences of a particular interpretation; and
>
> (g) the history of legislation on the subject.

Only rarely can all of these matters be resolved from the wording of the legislation itself. In a given case, one critical question to resolve is the extent to which a court may depart from the apparent literal meaning of a legislative provision in order to give effect to the "object" or "legislative purpose" of the legislature as revealed in extrinsic sources. At one time, the courts took a narrow view of their authority to depart from the apparent literal meaning of legislation. So, for instance, in *Thompson v. Goold & Co.*,[44] it was said:

> It is a strong thing to read into an Act of Parliament words which are not there, and in the absence of clear necessity it is the wrong thing to do.

Similarly in *Canada v. Antosko,* it was said that:

> While it is true that the courts must view discrete sections of the *Income Tax Act* in light of the other provisions of the Act and of the purpose of the legislation, and that they must analyze a given transaction in the context of economic and commercial reality, such techniques cannot alter the result where the words of the stat-

---

[42] *Desbiens v. Mordini*, [2004] O.J. No. 4735 (S.C.J.), *per* Spiegel J.
[43] R.S.N.S. 1989, c. 235.
[44] [1910] A.C. 409 at 420 (H.L.), *per* Lord Mersey.

ute are clear and plain and where the legal and practical effect of the transaction is undisputed.[45]

§1.27 In recent years, however, courts have begun to move away from a literal approach to statutory construction to what is sometimes described as a "purposive" approach. While there are other cases which presaged it, this change in direction can be traced at least to Lord Diplock's decision in *Kammin's Ballrooms Co v. Zenith Investments (Torquay)*.[46] In *Pepper (Inspector of Taxes) v. Hart*,[47] Lord Browne-Wilkinson referred to "the purposive approach to construction now adopted by the courts in order to give effect to the true intentions of the legislature", while in *Deutsche Genossenschaftsbank v. Burnhope*,[48] Lord Steyn referred to "the shift during the last two decades from a literalist to a purposive approach to the construction of statutes." A similar trend shift in approach has also been embraced by the Supreme Court of Canada,[49] and also by other courts.[50] In *Gould v. Yukon Order of Pioneers*, Iacobucci, J. described this approach as follows:

> A true purposive approach looks at the wording of the statute itself, with a view to discerning and advancing the legislature's intent. Our task is to breathe life, and generously so, into the particular statutory provisions that are before us.[51]

Obviously such a liberal approach to statutory construction would, if abused, allow a court considerable latitude to recast the language of the statute in any direction that largely suited itself.[52] However, there is considerable body of case law supporting the general proposition that absent ambiguity or an apparent absurdity, there is a definite logic and fairness in holding that when the language used in an enactment is plain and clear, the plain meaning should be followed.[53]

(ii) Special Legislation Governing Business Corporations

§1.28 In contrast to the U.K. *Companies Act, 1985*,[54] which is a statute governing virtually all companies generally that operate within the U.K., for several

---

[45] [1994] S.C.J. No. 46, [1994] 2 S.C.R. 312 at 326-27.
[46] [1971] A.C. 850 at 879 (H.L.).
[47] [1993] A.C. 593 at 635 (H.L.).
[48] [1995] H.L.J. No. 44, 4 All E.R. 717 at 726 (H.L.).
[49] *Shell Canada Products Ltd. v. Vancouver (City)*, [1994] S.C.J. No. 15, [1994] 1 S.C.R. 231; *Bell ExpressVu Limited Partnership v. Rex*, [2002] S.C.J. No. 43, [2002] 2 S.C.R. 559; *Re Rizzo & Rizzo Shoes Ltd.*, [1998] S.C.J. No. 2, [1998] 1 S.C.R. 27.
[50] *Canada (Privacy Commissioner) v. Canada (Labour Relations Board)*, [1996] F.C.J. No. 1076, [1996] 3 F.C. 609 (T.D.).
[51] [1996] S.C.J. No. 29 at para. 7, [1996] 1 S.C.R. 571.
[52] For an extreme example of this tendency, and critical comment upon it, see the dissenting judgment of LeBel and Deschamps JJ. in *National Trust Co. v. H & R Block Canada Inc.*, [2003] S.C.J. No. 70, [2003] 3 S.C.R. 160.
[53] See, generally, for instance: *Will-Kare Paving Construction Ltd. v. Canada*, [2000] S.C.J. No. 35 at para. 54, [2000] 1 S.C.R. 915, 188 D.L.R. (4th) 242, *per* Binnie J.; *R. v. McIntosh*, [1995] S.C.J. No. 16, [1995] 1 S.C.R. 686 at 697, *per* Lamer J.
[54] While this book was in the course of final editing and typesetting, the *Companies Act 1985* was replaced by the *Companies Act 2006*, which received Royal Assent on November 8, 2006. The new Act substantially revised UK company law. Given the late date of the enactment of the new legislation, and since the references to the former *Companies Act 1985* are included in this text

decades the Canadian approach to corporate legislation has been to enact more specialized legislation. The *Canada Business Corporations Act* and the Ontario *Business Corporations Act* deal with only one type of corporation: specifically, the general business corporation. Accordingly, not all corporations carrying on business are subject to either the CBCA or the OBCA; specialized types of business (*e.g.*, insurance companies, banks, credit unions, and trust companies) are subject to their own legislation. Although there was at one time a clear distinction between cooperatives and business corporations, in recent years that distinction has blurred.[55] Nevertheless, these two types of corporations remain governed by separate legislation, and it cannot necessarily be assumed that one type of corporation possesses the same rights and powers as another merely because the two types of corporation carry on comparable lines of business.

§1.29 The separation of the law relating to business corporations from the general law of corporations is comparatively recent. Until the 1970s, such corporations were generally regulated across Canada under the same statutes as charitable and non-profit corporations. Business corporations were not seen either to need or merit a special statute. It was only with the enactment of the first *Business Corporations Act* in Ontario in 1970,[56] that a clear trend began to emerge in favour of a specialized statute dealing solely with business corporations. Although repealed, many of the provisions of that Act (the "former OBCA") still appear in the more recent legislation which replaced it.[57] It is also worth noting that the Ontario *Corporations Act*[58] continues to govern non-profit companies in Ontario. Generally, we have excluded the *Corporations Act* from the scope of this study. At the federal level, the *Canada Business Corporations Act* was enacted in 1975. As in Ontario, the CBCA replaced the provisions of the *Canada Corporations Act*[59] dealing with business companies, although certain non-profit and special Act companies continue to be governed by the *Canada Corporations Act*.

§1.30 Thus, neither the Ontario *Business Corporations Act* nor the *Canada Business Corporations Act* came into being in a vacuum. Rather, they each stand at the end of a long and steady evolution in corporate law that has stretched over

---

purely for the purpose of comparison, it was not considered necessary to update the references to the new statute. Readers interested in UK company law are advised to consult a current edition of one of the many texts on that subject.

[55] See, generally, *Srebot Farms Ltd. v. Bradford Co-operative Storage Ltd.*, [1997] O.J. No. 313, 145 D.L.R. (4th) 331 at 339 (Gen. Div.), *per* Epstein J.
[56] S.O. 1970, c. 25.
[57] As the foregoing list makes clear, the law of business corporations has been the subject of frequent amendment in Canada over the past few decades. This has not been an exclusively Canadian phenomenon. In England, major revisions to company law were made in 1948, 1967, 1976, 1980, 1981, 1985, 1989 and 2006. A similar process of extensive amendment has occurred in Australia. The approach taken towards law reform has varied not only over time and from one jurisdiction to another, but also with respect to different aspects of company law. For instance, broadly speaking, England has opted for a much more regulated approach to company law than has Canada or its provinces. However, all Canadian jurisdictions impose much greater regulation upon the issue of corporate securities to the public than does England.
[58] R.S.O. 1990, c. C.38.
[59] R.S.C. 1970, c. C-32 (R.S.C. 1985, c. C-1.8).

a period of several hundred years, and which has involved judges and legislators whose views of the benefits of corporate organization have ranged from the wildly enthusiastic to the overtly critical.[60] The present OBCA is patterned on the CBCA (paradoxically, the CBCA was itself heavily influenced by the former OBCA). The CBCA has also influenced the business corporations legislation in Alberta,[61] New Brunswick,[62] Manitoba[63] and Saskatchewan,[64] along with a variety of more specialized corporate law statutes, from the *Bank Act*[65] to the *Trust and Loan Companies Act*,[66] and even the Saskatchewan *Co-operatives Act.*[67] The CBCA and the original Ontario *Business Corporations Act*, were themselves heavily influenced by the *Model Business Corporations Act*,[68] prepared by the Committee on Corporate Laws of the American Bar Association.[69]

---

[60] For an example of a supportive judgment, see *Metal Manufacturers Ltd. v. Lewis* (1988), 13 A.C.L.R. 357 at 359 (N.S.W.C.A.), *per* Kirby P. For a critical view of corporations, see the dissenting decision of Brandeis J. (who was never a great friend of big business) in *Louis K. Liggett Co. v. Lee* (1933), 288 U.S. 517.
[61] *Business Corporations Act,* S.A. 1981, c. B-15.
[62] *Business Corporations Act,* S.N.B. 1981, c. B-9.1.
[63] *Corporations Act,* R.S.M. 1987, c. C225.
[64] *Business Corporations Act,* R.S.S. 1978, c. B-10.
[65] S.C. 1991, c. 46.
[66] S.C. 1991, c. 45.
[67] S.S. 1983, c. C-37.1.
[68] The label "model" is something of a misnomer. The original model Act was first published in 1950 and eventually influenced legislation in more than 36 states. However, no state adopted it in its entirety and over the years the statute was modified significantly on numerous occasions, so that there is considerable variation among even those states which have adopted it. Some states have also revised their statutes in light of changes that have subsequently been made to the model Act: See Robert W. Hamilton, *Statutory Supplement to Corporations*, 3rd ed. (St. Paul, Minn.: West Publishing, 1986), at 57.
[69] There is no general federal corporate law statute in the United States. The United States Supreme Court avoids making pronouncements with respect to matters that are within the exclusive jurisdiction of the states, and, accordingly, rarely makes statements of legal principle relating specifically to the corporate law area. However, the United States Supreme Court does often consider cases relating to American federal securities laws and antitrust laws, many of which necessitate some discussion of corporate law related matters. Federal district courts and circuit courts of appeal will often consider corporate law issues when dealing with state law based cases that are brought within the federal courts under Article 3, s. 2(1) of the Constitution, which provides that the federal judicial power shall extend to disputes between citizens of two or more states, or between the citizens of a state and foreign citizens.

(iii) Business Corporations as a Species of Business Enterprise

§1.31 A business corporation is first and foremost a type of business organization.[70] While the term "business" has no definite legal meaning, a business organization may be defined as being an enterprise organized for the purpose of making a profit through trade or service, including agriculture, fishing, forestry, mining, refining and processing, the conduct of trade in goods or other property, the manufacture of products of any type or description, the construction of improvements to, maintenance or repair of real or personal property, or the provision of a service.[71] A business organization may be owned by the state or a municipality (as for instance, in the case of Ontario Hydro[72] or Canadian National Railway Company,[73] the former being at one time owned by the Province of Ontario and the latter by the Crown in right of Canada),[74] but in Canada it is more common for such enterprises to be owned by private citizens. Although there has been a tremendous growth within the last 50 years in the portion of the population who are employed in non-business enterprises such as government

---

Among the various states, decisions emanating from the courts of New York and Delaware enjoy the highest prestige in corporate law matters. New York is, of course, the principal commercial jurisdiction in the United States. The prominence of the Delaware courts requires some explanation. Delaware has long been the jurisdiction of choice for incorporation of national enterprises in the United States. In early years, Delaware's corporate laws were viewed as being favourable to management and control groups. Consequently, many large corporations were set up or continued under its laws. Over time, the expertise of its courts grew to the point that they have come to be considered expert in corporate law matters. There is also an extensive body of corporate jurisprudence emanating from Delaware courts. The Delaware court system remains divided between the Court of Chancery, which is a superior court of equitable jurisdiction, and the Superior Court, which is a common law court. In the late 19th century, the Delaware legislature (following a similar decision in England) gave the Court of Chancery jurisdiction over Delaware corporations. Although that jurisdiction is not strictly in equity, it is highly influenced by equitable principles. Appeals from the Court of Chancery lie to the Supreme Court of Delaware and there is no further appeal from that court.

Although Delaware is the current jurisdiction of choice for incorporation in the United States, this has not always been so. In the late 19th and early 20th centuries, New Jersey enjoyed this pride of place. Delaware became prominent after 1913, when New Jersey amended its laws in ways that made them less attractive to large business. See W.E. Kirk, "A Case Study in Legislative Opportunism: How Delaware Used the Federal-State System to Attain Corporate Preeminence" (1984) 10 J. of Corp. Law 233.

[70] There are numerous factors that will influence selection among the various types of business organization vehicle that will be selected by the promoters of a business in a given case. See, generally, C.W. Maughan, Kevin McGuinness, "Towards an Economic Theory of the Corporation" (2001) 1 J.C.L.S. 141, which provides a comprehensive survey of much of the literature in this area.

[71] See, generally, *Tara Exploration & Development Co. v. Minister of National Revenue*, [1970] C.T.C. 557 (Ex.), *per* Jackett P., aff'd [1972] S.C.J. No. 136, [1972] C.T.C. 328; *Graham v. Green, Inspector of Taxes*, [1925] 2 K.B. 37, *per* Rowlatt J.; *R. v. Lala Indra Sen*, [1940] 8 I.T.R. 187 at 219 (Ind.), *per* Braund J.; *Ryall v. Hoare*, [1923] 2 K.B. 447, *per* Rowlatt J.; *Minister of National Revenue v. Eldridge*, [1964] C.T.C. 545 (Ex.).

[72] See the *Power Corporation Act*, R.S.O. 1990, c. P.18 and the *Energy Competition Act*, S.O. 1998, c. 15.

[73] See the *Canadian National Railways Act*, R.S.C. 1985, c. C-19 [Repealed S.C. 1995, c. 24, s. 19].

[74] *Canadian National Railways Act*, R.S.C. 1985, c. C-19, s. 4(1) [Repealed S.C. 1995, c. 24, s. 19].

agencies,[75] business organizations of one form or another continue to provide the largest source of employment for the Canadian population.[76]

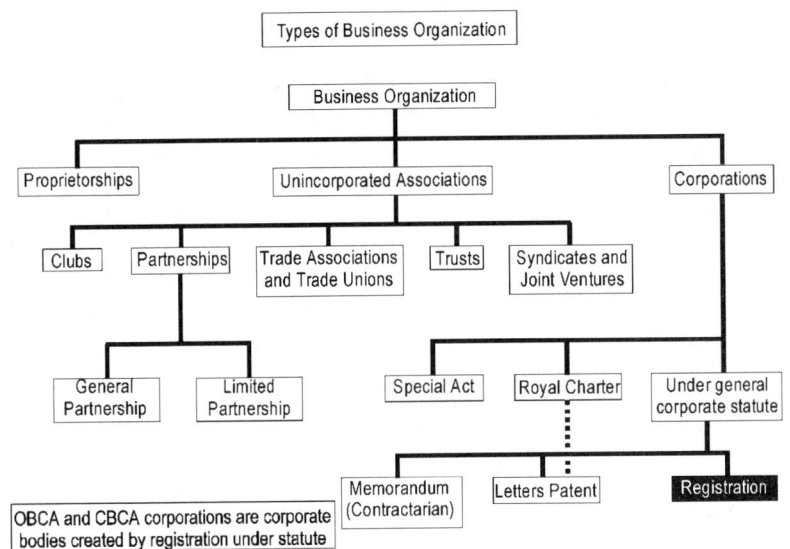

(iv) The Distinguishing Feature of a Corporate Entity

§1.32 A business corporation is merely one type of corporate body. Unlike partnerships, corporations are not exclusively a business vehicle, but may be organized for a variety of public and private purposes. Charitable corporations, for instance, are the complete antithesis of the business corporation — they exist for the purpose of giving money away, rather than making it. A corporation is a group of persons or a series of holders of an office, who are deemed in law to constitute collectively a single, separate legal entity. The corporation has a legal personality, existence, rights and duties that are distinct from those of the individuals comprising that group or series of persons who collectively constitute the corporation. Thus a corporation is sometimes described as an artificial or

---

[75] In *Bank Voor Handel en Scheepvaart N.V. v. Slatford*, [1953] 1 Q.B. 248 (C.A.), Denning L.J. stated that Crown corporations enjoy no special immunity by virtue of their public ownership. See also *Tamlin v. Hannaford*, [1950] 1 K.B. 18 at 21 (C.A.).
[76] The views expressed by Jackson J. in *State Tax Commissioners of Utah v. Aldrich* (1942), 316 U.S. 174 at 192 are as applicable in Canada today as they were in the United States when he pronounced them:
    The corporation has become almost the unit of organization of economic life. Whether for good or ill the stubborn fact is that in our present system the corporation carries on the bulk of production and transportation, is the chief employer of both labor and capital, pays a large part of our taxes, and is an economic institution of such magnitude and importance that there is no present substitute for it except the state itself.

juristic person (*i.e.*, a legal person), since it is seen in law as having a separate personality. As an entity recognized in law as having a personality separate from the person or persons who comprise it,[77] the corporation is capable of acquiring, enjoying, enforcing and disposing of rights and obligations that are legally separate from, and possibly inimical to, the rights and obligations of the person or persons who comprise the corporation.[78]

§1.33 In describing a corporation as a person, the law adopts and gives substantive effect to a fiction.[79] The fiction of the corporation has come to be seen as necessary in the interest of efficient administration of assets and the raising and administration of capital. Long before the evolution of the business corporation as a common means of carrying on trade, the law was prepared to recognize incorporation as an administrative necessity.[80] The recognition of corporate personality does not mean that the courts have lost sight of the fact that only the people who stand behind the corporation are real. Thus it has been said that:

> According to our system of law, a corporation is a group or series of persons which by a legal fiction is regarded and treated as a person itself. It is a legal entity composed of persons. In law a "person" is any being that is capable of having rights and duties, and is confined to that. Persons are of two classes only — natural persons and legal persons. A natural person is a human being who has the capacity for rights or duties. A legal person is anything to which the law gives a legal or fictitious existence and personality, with capacity for rights and duties. The only legal person known to our law is the corporation — the body corporate. ...
>
> It must follow that there can be no corporation, that is no legal person, unless and until there is first a group or series of natural persons to compose or constitute the corporation, because although later corporations may be formed of existing corporations, these component corporations in the first instance must consist exclusively of natural persons.[81]

§1.34 Section 14 of the British Columbia *Company Act*[82] prohibited a company from carrying on business unless it has members and imposes upon the directors and officers of the company a personal liability for the debts of the company where it is in breach of this prohibition. There is no corresponding provision in either the Ontario *Business Corporations Act* or the *Canada Business Corporations Act*. In view of the fact that the members of a company enjoy limited liability, it is not at all clear why liability should be imposed on the directors if no such members exist.

---

[77] See, for instance, *Dunston v. Imperial Light & Coke Co.* (1831), 3 B. & Ad. 125 at 132, 110 E.R. 47 (K.B.), *per* Parke J.; *Enterprises A.B. Rimouski v. Canada*, [1998] F.C.J. No. 1308, 40 B.L.R. (2d) 189 (F.C.T.D.).

[78] See, generally, 1 *Blackstone's Commentaries on the Laws of England* (Chicago: University of Chicago Press, 1979, reprint) at 463-64.

[79] See, generally, *Hôpital du Sacré Coeur v. Lefebvre* (1891), 17 Q.L.R. 35, 14 L.N. 202, *per* Andrews J.

[80] *McCulloch v. State of Maryland* (1819), 4 Wheat 316 at 411 (U.S.S.C.), *per* Marshall C.J.U.S.

[81] See *Hague v. Cancer Relief & Research Institute*, [1939] 3 W.W.R. 1 at 5, additional reasons at 160 (K.B.), *per* Dysart J.

[82] R.S.B.C. 1996, c. 27 (now repealed). Now largely repealed by the *Business Corporations Act*, S.B.C. 2002, c. 57, s. 445(*a*), in force March 29, 2004.

§1.35 While principle dictates otherwise, it is at least theoretically possible for corporations to exist without any natural person standing behind them at any point in the line of ownership. However, such a situation would be exceedingly rare. It would also be an arrangement that would be very difficult to structure under either the OBCA or the CBCA, given the restrictions which each statute imposes on a corporation holding shares in itself or in a holding body corporate.[83]

§1.36 Even if it is possible to create a memberless corporation under the OBCA and CBCA, there would seem to be little reason for doing so. Corporations themselves are only administrative conveniences, employed for the purpose of furthering the needs of their members. The existence of a corporation is completely artificial and notional. Although it has legal attributes, it has no substance and no material existence. Thus it has been said that a corporation is invisible, intangible and exists only in the contemplation of the law.[84] The abstract nature of a corporation was recognized in *Toronto General Trusts Corp. v. Bartram*,[85] where it was held that the intention of a corporation must be inferred from what it does alone. Thus the form of a company's resolutions and instruments is also their substance — there can be no secret intention within the company itself.

§1.37 The concept of a corporation or company[86] is recognized in the legal systems of all industrialized (and many non-industrialized) nations, and the existence of any corporate body duly incorporated in its domicile will be recognized by the courts of any common law jurisdictions, even though the right of a foreign corporation to carry on business or conduct its affairs in another jurisdiction will often be regulated[87] and restricted (and sometimes prohibited)[88] in that jurisdiction.

---

[83] Subsection 1(3) of the Ontario *Business Corporations Act*, R.S.O. 1990, c. B.16 provides:

For the purposes of this Act, a body corporate shall be deemed to be another's holding body corporate if, but only if, that other is its subsidiary.

[84] *Sutton's Hospital Case* (1612), 10 Co. Rep. 1a at 32b, *per* Coke C.J. 77 E.R. 937 (Ch.):

They cannot commit treason, nor be outlawed nor excommunicated, for they have no souls, neither can they appear in person but by an attorney. ... A corporation aggregate of many cannot do fealty, for an invisible body can neither be in person nor swear.

A similar view was repeated by Marshall C.J.U.S. in *Dartmouth College v. Woodward* (1819), 4 Wheat 518. See also: *R. v. Cook*, [1932] 1 D.L.R. 88 at 262 (Alta. C.A.), *per* McGillivray J.A. dealing with the right of a corporation to appear in person. See also *Guy Major Co. v. Canadian Flaxhills Ltd.* (1912), 3 O.W.N. 1058 (H.C.).

[85] (1954), 11 W.W.R. 409 at 416 (B.C.S.C.), *per* Coady J.

[86] The terms "company" and "corporation" are often used interchangeably. Strictly speaking, the two terms are not synonymous. A company is an association of two or more persons formed to conduct a business or some other activity in the name of that association. A corporation is one type of such association and differs from the others in that it is incorporated. Despite this technical distinction, in this text the word "company" has been used to refer to a corporate body incorporated by or under some statute other than the OBCA or CBCA, while the term "corporation" refers to those corporations which are incorporated under either of those statutes.

[87] See the *Loan and Trust Corporations Act*, R.S.O. 1990, c. L.25, which regulates extraprovincial trust corporations in Ontario.

[88] See, for instance, the *Bank Act*, S.C. 1991, c. 46, s. 508(1), which prohibits foreign banks from engaging in the business of banking in Canada.

§1.38 As with so many other legal innovations, some writers have attempted to trace the concept of the corporation (*i.e.*, of an artificial legal personality) back to antiquity, some to the Romans,[89] others even farther into the past, perhaps as far back as Babylon.[90] Yet ultimately it is difficult to view these attempts as little more than unlikely conjecture. Even at a relatively recent point in legal history,[91] it becomes very difficult to separate true corporate entities from organizations more closely resembling partnerships (*e.g.*, in the case of the *commenda* and *societas,* long recognized in continental jurisdictions.) Unfortunately, corporations are not a logical outgrowth of the partnership concept, for partnership is fundamentally based on agency, whereas a corporation is fundamentally based upon the status of personality. As noted earlier in this Chapter, the first unequivocal reference to a corporation as a legal person did not occur until the 13th century—although no doubt the broad concept had emerged somewhat earlier. It seems doubtful that primitive systems of law would have possessed the sophistication to grapple with the concept of artificial personality, but until such an understanding was available, no true law of corporations could develop.

D. CORPORATE THEORY

§1.39 The development of a theory of the corporation as an economic phenomenon lies largely outside the scope of this work.[92] To date, the principal difficulty in development of a unifying economic theory has been identifying common characteristics that underlie most corporations, even of a given class. For instance, most business corporations are operated with a view towards profit, but a profit motive among the incorporators is not essential and it is incorrect to assume that such an intention will always exist. Many corporations will be incorporated for no other purpose but to hold a non-income earning asset. In other cases, the business and affairs of a corporation will be structured so as to render its net income to zero (a useful tax planning approach where profits might otherwise be earned at a subsidiary level while a parent corporation continues to suffer from tax losses). Tax planning approaches must be employed with care, since the general anti-avoidance rule under the *Income Tax Act*[93] gives considerable latitude to the Canada Revenue Agency to disregard artificial transactions. However, while income tax law may ignore efforts to use a corporate device to split or park income or to create the false illusion of a tax loss, for all other purposes a corporation that is used for such a purpose is a valid corporation.

---

[89] 1 *Blackstone's Commentaries on the Laws of England* (Chicago: University of Chicago Press, 1979, reprint), at 456.

[90] See, for instance, J.H. Farrar, N.E. Furey, B. Hannigan, P. Wylie, *Farrar's Company Law,* 7th ed. (London: Butterworths, 1988), at 15.

[91] So, for instance, R.W.M. Dias, who suggests that the Romans did not develop a clear legal concept of personality: *Jurisprudence*, 3rd ed. (London: Butterworths, 1970), at 304.

[92] For a survey of the literature and a discussion as to what a comprehensive theory would need to contain, see C.W. Maughan and K. McGuinness, "Towards An Economic Theory of the Corporation" (2001) 1 Journal of Corporate Law Studies 141.

[93] R.S.C. 1985, c. (hereinafter "ITA") s. 245. But see, Brian J. Arnold, "The Long, Slow, Steady Demise of the General Anti-Avoidance Rule" (2004) 52 Can. Tax J. 488 as to the limited effectiveness of this rule.

§1.40 A further obstacle to the development of an economic theory of the corporation has been the confusion of the legal concept of a corporation with the economic concept of a firm. In economic parlance, a "firm" is an organization through which entrepreneurs combine resources for the production and supply of goods and services. It is thus a device used to organize economic output. Suffice to say that not all firms are corporations (*e.g.*, partnerships, joint ventures, limited partnerships and trusts are not) and not all corporations are firms.

§1.41 Business corporations range in size from small corporations, with a single shareholder, no employees and nominal capital, to huge multinational enterprises with hundreds of thousands of shareholders and employees, and issued capital in the billions of dollars. It is obviously significant that the corporation has become such a dominant vehicle in the world of business organization. Since this is a text on the law, rather than on economics, no detailed attempt will be made to deal in detail with the various roles that corporations play in the modern Canadian economy. It is necessary, however, to have some general understanding of the purposes that they may serve, in order to analyze the laws that apply to them.

§1.42 To some writers, the primary purpose of the company is to provide a method of solving problems encountered in raising substantial amounts of capital.[94] This assertion is undoubtedly true in the case of some corporations, but the percentage of all corporations that it accurately describes is minuscule. Relatively few corporations are in the least way concerned with the raising of capital. Instead, most corporations are wholly owned by a single shareholder (very often another corporation), and have only notional share capital and no term debt. A substantial number of other corporations are owned by a handful of investors, all of whom are insiders to the company and directly involved in its management. The access of all such corporations to outside financing (aside from bank and similar financing which is for all intents and purposes entirely dependent upon shareholder guarantees) ranges from very limited to non-existent.

§1.43 Rather than being concerned with raising capital, the primary function of such corporations is the administration of assets and liabilities — and indeed this administrative characteristic is one that nearly all corporations have in common. But even then, it would oversimplify matters to suggest that the primary purpose of corporations is to achieve some administrative purpose, because there are many different types of administrative purpose that a company may serve, some of which are entirely inconsistent with each other. For instance, a corporation may be incorporated: (a) to hold securities in other corporations; (b) to carry on some active business such as manufacturing or trade; (c) to acquire[95] or hold a particular asset, such as title to a specific piece of real estate; (d) to provide

---

[94] See, for instance, Richard Posner, *Economic Analysis of Law*, 2nd ed. (Boston: Little, Brown, 1977), at 290.
[95] See, for instance, *Minister of National Revenue v. Cameron*, [1972] S.C.J. No. 137, [1972] C.T.C. 380, 72 D.T.C. 6325.

services to its members; (e) to isolate the business of the corporation from the claims of the creditors of some of the shareholders; (f) to protect the shareholders of the corporation from the claims of creditors of the business; (g) for some tax purpose;[96] (h) to qualify for some form of government aid; or (i) to circumvent some contractual or regulatory restriction.[97] A corporation may also afford more flexibility than other types of business enterprise for accommodating different roles, skills, and resources of the persons who will stand behind the enterprise.[98] These are but a few of the functions that a corporation may serve. It follows that to speak of the economic purpose or role of the corporation is misleading. There is no such thing as the typical corporation. Not only does their size vary, the activities in which they engage are nearly limitless, and the roles that they may perform are limited only by the restrictions that arise from the attributes of incorporation itself.

E. JURISPRUDENTIAL CONCEPTIONS OF A CORPORATION

§1.44 Our main concern here, however, is not with corporations as an economic phenomenon, but instead, with the corporation as a creature of the law. The various attributes now associated with the corporate form of organization evolved over time, and many have fairly ancient roots. The concept of separate personality may be traced back to early corporations sole. The use of a corporation for the conduct of trade dates back directly at least to 1530, and indirectly may be traced back further to the medieval guilds. The notion of self-government and the authority of the majority of the members of the corporation to bind the minority grows from the medieval municipal corporation. The notion that the members hold a share in the capital of the corporation, rather than in the assets that are owned by the corporation[99] stems from the joint stock company, as does the concept of management through a board of governors or directors. Even the methods of incorporation are much older than is widely appreciated. Incorporation by way of registration, the modern method of incorporation employed under the OBCA and CBCA, may actually be traced back as far as the *Hospitals for the Poor Act, 1597*.[100]

§1.45 In 1800, corporate law dealt mostly with municipalities, churches and charities. Only a few business operations were conducted through the instrumentality of a corporation. Within a century all this had changed. The business

---

[96] See, for instance, *Palmolive Manufacturing Co. (Ontario) v. R.*, [1933] S.C.R. 131.
[97] See, for instance, *Denison Mines Ltd. v. Minister of National Revenue*, [1971] C.T.C. 640, 71 D.T.C. 5375, aff'd [1972] F.C. 1324, [1972] C.T.C. 521 (F.C.A.), aff'd [1974] S.C.J. No. 148, [1974] C.T.C. 734.
[98] *Missalla v. Brown*, [2001] O.J. No. 3028, 107 A.C.W.S. (3d) 146 (S.C.J.).
[99] See, generally, *Re Corlet*, [1939] 3 W.W.R. 83 (Alta. Q.B.); and *McNaughton v. Exchange National Bank* (1891), M.L.R. 7 Q.B. 180 (Que. C.A.); and in the case of a corporation owned by a single person, see: *Hartford Accident & Indemnity Co. v. Millsons Construction* (1939), 44 Que. P.R. 170.
[100] 39 Eliz. I, c. 5.

corporation had become the dominant form of corporate entity and the dominant form of business enterprise.

§1.46 Over the years, jurisprudence scholars have sometimes attempted to draw up comprehensive theories of corporations that explain them as a legal phenomenon. The contractarian school argues that the corporation is the result of a contract among the members of the corporation and those with whom it deals.[101] The "fiction" school argues that the corporation is an entity that exists only in the contemplation of the law.[102] Realists argue that corporations are not artificial or abstract entities but have an independent existence that distinguishes them from their members.[103] Concessionists argue that corporate status is essentially a franchise or privilege granted by the state, without which the corporation could not exist.[104]

§1.47 None of these theories is universally compelling, although some of the arguments of each school have their uses in particular contexts. The concessionist theory is tautological. The recognition of a corporation as a separate legal entity only requires the grant of a franchise or charter by the state because that is what the common law says. It is easily possible to envisage a legal system in which the existence of a corporation would be determined as a matter of fact, much as the existence of a partnership is often so determined.[105] While separate corporate existence may in fact reflect contractual arrangements among shareholders and other stakeholders in the corporation, contract theory offers no explanation as to why this arrangement should be effective *vis-à-vis* third parties. Moreover, the contractarian school offers little explanation for the vast majority of corporations that are wholly owned by a single person (often another corporation).

§1.48 With respect to the realist school, there can be little argument that the modern multinational corporation is an entity in its own right, operating not only to a very large extent independently of its members, but also to at least some extent independently from its jurisdiction of incorporation.[106] Yet such corporations are

---

[101] See, for instance, R. Posner, *Economic Analysis of Law*, 2nd ed. (Boston: Little, Brown & Co; 1977), at 302.
[102] J. Dewey, "The Historical Background of Corporate Legal Personality" (1926) 35 Yale Law Journal 655 at 667: "The fiction theory is ultimately a philosophical theory that the corporate body is but a name, a thing of intellect ...".
[103] See, for instance, A.A. Berle, *Studies in the Law of Corporation Finance* (Chicago: Callaghan & Co., 1928).
[104] See, generally, J. Kent, *Commentaries on American Law* (Boston: Little, Brown, 1873).
[105] For instance, the definition of "partnership" in the *Partnerships Act,* R.S.O. 1990, c. P.5, s. 2 provides that:

> Partnership is the relation that subsists between persons carrying on a business in common with a view to profit, but the relation between the members of a company or association that is incorporated by or under the authority of any special or general Act in force in Ontario or elsewhere, or registered as a corporation under any such Act, is not a partnership within the meaning of this Act.

[106] Despite its age, the leading work dealing with this phenomenon of modern political-economics remains Anthony Sampson, *The Sovereign State of ITT* (Greenwich Conn.: Fawcett Publications,

few in number. It is only their vast size and omnipresence that makes them familiar to us. Further, they represent the end product of 150 years of corporate evolution, rather than its foundation. Most corporations have few assets, and many have no employees and operate at the very fringe of existence; yet even so the law recognizes them as entities that can acquire rights and obligations.

§1.49 The fiction school was alluded to earlier in this chapter. It is the school to which most legal practitioners subscribe and is unquestionably the most influential. However, even it has its limitations. It is correct in saying that the existence of the corporation is dependent upon the extent to which the law recognizes it as an entity capable of enjoying legal rights and being subject to legal obligations. Corporations may enjoy personal status,[107] but numerous rules of law recognize the artificial or "metaphysical"[108] nature of that status and the fact that they are nothing more than legal fictions.[109] It is accepted that a corporation does not "live",[110] cannot eat or sleep,[111] cannot marry, or drive a vehicle.[112] A corporation may be seen to possess an intention only in the very qualified sense that such an intention may be inferred from what it has done, the statements that can in some way be attributed to it, or the contracts into which it has entered.[113] It has been said that a corporation cannot claim "liberty" within the meaning of the Due Process clause of the U.S. Constitution;[114] that corporations have neither race nor colour;[115] that they cannot commit treason, nor be outlawed, nor excommunicated, and that they have no souls;[116] Perhaps most importantly, it is accepted that a corporation cannot act except through the agency of some other person. As it lacks a physical body, it can be difficult in some cases to decide where a corporation may be said to be present. While the wording of relevant legislation may vary from one case to another, under many statutes a company is deemed to be present at a place where an employee of any grade is present on its behalf.[117]

§1.50 Each of these legal propositions re-inforces the apparent fictional character of a corporation. They reflect the fact that the legal consequences of incorporation derive not so much from theoretical principles as from the statutes that

---

1974). See also J.K. Galbraith, *The New Industrial State*, 2nd ed. (New York: Houghton-Mifflin, 1971).

[107] See, for instance, *R. v. Reid* (1873), 15 N.B.R. 26 dealing with the question of whether a provision in a statute conferring a voting right on all "persons" who were ratepayers applied with respect to a corporation.

[108] *Bligh v. Brent* (1837), 2 Y. & C. 268.

[109] Corporations may be legal fictions, but they are far from the only such entities recognized in law. Government departments, provinces and even nation states are similar legal fictions.

[110] *Westover v. Turner* (1876), 26 U.C.C.P. 510 *per* Gwynne J.

[111] *DeBeers Consolidated Mines v. Howe*, [1906] A.C. 455 at 458; *Re MacFarlane*, [1933] O.R. 44 (C.A.).

[112] *Richmond London Borough Council v. Pinn & Wheller*, [1989] R.T.R. 354.

[113] See, generally, *Toronto General Trusts Corp. v. Bartram* (1954), 11 W.W.R. 409 (B.C.S.C.); *Inland Rev. Comm. v. Fisher's Executors*, [1926] A.C. 395 at 411 (H.L.) *per* Lord Sumner.

[114] *Bridges v. California*, 314 U.S. 252 (1941) at 280-81, *per* Frankfurter J.

[115] *Connecticut General Life Ins. Co. v. Johnson*, 303 U.S. 77 (1938) at 87, *per* Black, J.

[116] *Sutton's Hospital Case*, [1612] 10 Co. Rep. 23 at 32b.

[117] *Deutsche Genossenschaftsbank v. Burnhope*, [1995] B.C.C. 488 (C.A.).

provide for incorporation, and from the rules of case law that have evolved in response to those statutes. There are no inherent attributes of corporate status common across the world. The rules vary, and what a corporation can do in one jurisdiction, it may not be able to do in another jurisdiction, even if the legal systems of the two jurisdictions are very similar. For instance, in England, one corporation will often act as the director of another. In Canada, this is not normally possible. The shareholder-members of an OBCA business corporation may take over its management under a unanimous shareholder agreement. This opportunity is not available to the members of a Part III corporation under the Ontario *Corporations Act*.

§1.51 Yet it is important not to stretch these points too far. Corporations themselves may not be able to act, think, believe or make decisions on their own behalf. But they nevertheless do act: they acquire and dispose of assets, organize productive activity, employ workers and spend money. It may be true that they can do so only through the agency of one or more actual physical beings; yet individuals often will also act through agents. When a corporation acts through an agent, the acts in question are as effective *vis-à-vis* both the corporation and others as if the corporation itself carried them out personally. The foregoing aspects of corporate existence do not make corporations a fiction, any more than denying rights to individuals is sufficient to rob those individuals of their reality (although different systems of law have from time to time tried to accomplish exactly that result). As 19th century business discovered, denying trade unions legal recognition did not make those entities disappear. They reflected an economic reality with which the business community was eventually forced to deal.[118] Corporations are no more fictions than are the nations and, provinces and states that create them: each has no physical existence, but they each can exert considerable influence, and each reflects a range of differing underlying interests that are real by any measure, other than tangibility.

F. CREATION A SOVEREIGN ACT

§1.52 At common law, the creation of a corporation is a sovereign act.[119] Although a few companies in England are recognized on the basis of prescription or of lost grant, it has always been clear that in Canada no company can be created by prescription, or as a result of a course of dealing under which two or more persons carry on business as if they were a corporate entity.[120] Since corporations are mere manifestations of the law, and exist only by virtue of their charter, there can be no right for persons to arrogate to themselves the character

---

[118] See, generally, *Berry v. Pulley*, [2002] 2 S.C.R. 493; *International Brotherhood of Teamsters v. Therien* (1960), 22 D.L.R. (2d) 1 (S.C.C.).

[119] Perhaps for this reason, the authority to confer corporate status on aliens was in doubt until the decision of the House of Lords in *Reuss (Princess) v. Bos* (1871), L.R. 5 H.L. 176.

[120] *Loranger v. Dorion* (1881), 4 L.N. 108, aff'd 4 L.N. 372 (Que. C.A.). Where an unincorporated enterprise carries on business as a corporation, it may be challenged in *quo warranto* proceedings: *Askew v. Manning* (1876), 38 U.C.Q.B. 345.

of a company or to assume to act as a company.[121] There must be a legal authority for acting as a corporate entity. Since it lacks legal personality, an unincorporated association of individuals (or other persons) cannot acquire property, and so cannot become a lessee, nor can it otherwise assert any position which is maintainable in law only by a legal entity.[122]

§1.53 It is not the creation of a group of individuals carrying on business collectively that requires sovereign approval. Two or more individuals may combine their efforts at any time, and certain legal consequences may well flow from doing so (even if the sole effect is to render them each liable in conspiracy). Partnerships and joint ventures offer obvious examples of collective enterprise that the parties to a transaction are able to create without any governmental permission — indeed, the legal characteristics of a joint venture concept are so poorly defined, that neither statute law nor the common law properly provide for the use of this structure, with the result that it is difficult to provide clear advice as to the consequences that will flow from its use. What individuals cannot do without the approval of the state – at least in modern common law jurisdictions – is confer legal personality on themselves as a collective group. When a corporation acquires an asset, the entity itself does so rather than its members; when a corporation enters into a contract, the rights and obligations arising under it belong to the corporation rather to its members; when a corporation earns taxable income (or incurs a tax deductible expense), it does so rather than the members who stand behind it. All of these consequences are vastly different from those that result through the conduct of trade by a partnership.

§1.54 Historically, the sovereign act of incorporation took the form of the issue of a charter, usually in the form of letters patent issued under the Great Seal. As our earlier review of early Ontario corporate law makes clear, this method of incorporation, while not entirely unknown during the early colonial period, was used very sparingly across North America. The English settlement of Canada followed the political upheavals of 17th century, which had resulted in the transfer of much of the sovereign authority to the legislative branch of government. This trend was evidenced in the incorporation process. Parliamentary incorporation emerged during the 17th century.[123]

§1.55 For a long period, the sovereign act of incorporation was exercised primarily by way of special Act. By the mid-19th century, this approach was recognized as impractical: the pressure brought about by the Industrial Revolution (particularly railway construction) for an expeditious means of allowing busi-

---

[121] *Bank of Montreal v. Bethune* (1836), 4 O.S. 341 at 356 (U.C.C.A.), *per* Sherwood J. Note, however, that where persons carry on business as a corporation, they are estopped from denying its corporate status: *Williams v. Rice* (1926), 7 C.B.R. 699 at 704 (Man. K.B.), *per* Dysart J. Such an entity is known as a *de facto* corporation.
[122] *Canada Morning News Co. v. Thompson*, [1930] S.C.R. 338 at 342 *per* Anglin, C.J.C.; *Ladies of the Sacred Heart of Jesus v. Armstrong's Point Association* (1961), 29 D.L.R. (2d) 373 (Man. C.A.), leave to appeal ref'd [1962] S.C.R. viii, *per* Schultz J.A.
[123] See, for instance, the *Act creating the New River Company 1606* (U.K.), 3 Jac. 1, c. 18.

ness to be conducted through a corporate organization was inexorable.[124] In response, the English Parliament passed its first *Joint Stock Companies Act* in 1844,[125] setting out a procedure under which companies could be incorporated by mere registration without need of a Royal Charter or a special Act. Separate statutes to a similar effect were enacted for Upper and Lower Canada a few years later.[126] This approach to incorporation remains the dominant approach across the entire common law world today. By statute, the legislature creates the authority for incorporation. Actual incorporation, however, is carried out through the administrative process under the authority of that legislation.

§1.56 In modern Canada, most companies are now incorporated by an administrative act under a general corporations statute. There are three systems of such incorporation in use in Canada. The most modern system — and the one in widest use — is the certificate of incorporation system, under which a company is incorporated by filing articles of incorporation. Upon registration, a certificate of

---

[124] The development of English company law was side-tracked as a result of a scandal known as the South Sea Bubble. It came about primarily as a result of the activities of the South Sea Company, which was founded in 1711 with the object of obtaining a monopoly on the trade with colonies in South America. As the company grew, it put forward an ambitious plan to purchase the national debt, by buying out government creditors by way of the issue of stock in the company — a special statute (the *South Sea Act*) being enacted for this purpose. The proposal attracted wide interest, and the market value of South Sea Company stock soared from £136 in 1719, to £1,000 in 1720. This surge had touched off a speculative boom in the trading of shares in other companies. Sadly, the boom collapsed when the South Sea Company itself proved unable to meet its own obligations. This collapse led that same year to the passage of the *Bubble Act 1720* (U.K.), 6 Geo. 1, c. 18, which was intended to impose strict regulation on the creation of joint stock companies. The combination of the *Bubble Act* and the public distrust of speculative investment delayed the evolution of the business corporation in England (and its Empire) by perhaps 125 years. The *Bubble Act* was repealed in 1825, but the first true general corporate Act, the *Joint Stock Companies Act* would not be enacted until 1844, by 7 & 8 Vic., cc. 110 and 111 and it is that Act which is the predecessor of all corporate statutes in the modern world. Limited liability would be introduced (or made clear that it was conferred by virtue of incorporation) under the *Limited Liability Act, 1855*, 19 Vic., c. 133. The two Acts were rolled together in the *Joint Stock Companies Act, 1856*.

[125] The first Canadian general statutes for incorporation of trading and industrial enterprise were enacted first for Upper Canada in 1849, and then later that year by way of separate legislation for Lower Canada. Further statutes followed in 1850 and 1864. However, the Canadian legislation adopted a different approach from that in England. In the mother country, incorporation was made a matter of contract. The incorporators entered into a memorandum of association, which was then registered with the government. The two Canadian provinces adopted a more regulated approach (based upon similar regimes widely employed in the United States), under which incorporation was by way of the discretionary issue letters of patent following a formal application to the government. Considerable oversight was exercised in the decision to create the corporation, which included a detailed review of the application. This approach was ultimately adopted by the Federal government, and also in New Brunswick and Prince Edward Island. In contrast, Nova Scotia, British Columbia, and eventually Alberta, Saskatchewan and Newfoundland adopted the English memorandum of association and registration approach. It was only in the 1970s that a firm trend emerged in Canada away from discretionary incorporation, to a less regulated approach.

[126] For example, *An Act for the Formation of Incorporated Joint-Stock Companies, for Manufacturing, Mining, Mechanical or Chemical Purposes 1850*, 13-14 Vict., c. 28. Statutes for companies constructing roads and bridges had been passed the previous year: (1849), 12 Vict., c. 56; (1849), 12 Vict., c. 84.

incorporation is issued as a matter of right. An older system, the letters patent system, still exists in respect of some types of corporation in every jurisdiction in Canada. According to the Ontario Select Committee on Company Law, the letters patent system originated in Canada in 1864, when an Act was passed providing for the incorporation of companies at the discretion of the Governor-in-Council. Thus the Ontario *Corporations Act* (which continues to employ the letters patent system for Part II and III corporations) retains a measure of departmental discretion over the incorporation of companies.[127] A third method of incorporation, known as the registration or memorandum of association system, remained in effect until recently in three provinces. Under this last system (which is derived from English corporate law practice), the company comes into existence upon the registration of a memorandum of association. The major distinction between the registration and certificate systems lies not so much in the method of incorporation as in the rules of law generally applicable to the corporations incorporated under each of these systems, once these corporations have been created. For instance, companies incorporated under a memorandum of association regime are deemed to embody a contractual arrangement among the members of the company,[128] whereas corporations under the Ontario *Business Corporations Act* or *Canada Business Corporations Act* are pure creatures of statute,[129] and thus the rights and obligations flowing from incorporation are defined by statute rather than being contractual in origin.

§1.57 From time to time the legislature may create a corporation indirectly, not by declaring it to be a corporation, but rather by vesting in it the attributes of a corporation. Either the direct or the indirect approach to incorporation is effective, and each has the same consequence in terms of creating a juristic person. In *Bank of Montreal v. Bole*,[130] a garnishee summons was directed to the Liquor Board of Saskatchewan. Justice Taylor noted that the Board's governing statute conferred upon it the power to contract, to buy, sell and accept a grant (and therefore implicitly, a power to take property in its own name and transfer any property so taken), may pledge its credit for money borrowed. It was also possible for a guarantee to be given for the corporation. Justice Taylor concluded that the statute had created a Board that was distinct entity from its members thereof,

---

[127] Specifically, the *Corporations Act*, R.S.O. 1990, c. C.38, s. 4(1) provides:

> The Lieutenant Governor may in his or her discretion, by letters patent, issue a charter to any number of persons, not fewer than three, of eighteen or more years of age, who apply therefor, constituting them and any others who become shareholders or members of the corporation thereby created a corporation for any of the objects to which the authority of the Legislature extends, except those of railway and incline railway and street railway corporations and corporations within the meaning of the *Loan and Trust Corporations Act*.

[128] See, for instance, *Canada Cooperative Associations Act*, R.S.C. 1985, c. C-40, s. 43(6) [Repealed S.C. 1998, c. 1, s. 385].

[129] *Emerson v. New Brunswick (Secretary-Treasurer)* (1940), 15 M.P.R. 406, [1941] 2 D.L.R. 232 at 413 (N.B.C.A.), *per* Baxter C.J.; see also *Canadian National Fire Insurance Co. v. Hutchings*, [1918] A.C. 451 (P.C.).

[130] [1931] 1 W.W.R. 203 at 206-207 (K.B.).

and it necessarily followed the statute, that the Board was amenable to the ordinary processes of the Court.

§1.58 From time to time the legislature will expressly confer on a particular unincorporated entity some but not all of the attributes of a corporation.[131] Such entities are sometimes referred to as quasi-corporations,[132] but the implications of this term must be properly understood. Where legislation clearly deems that a particular entity shall be a corporation, then all of the common law attributes associated with corporate status are implicitly conferred upon it.[133] In contrast, where one or more of the specific attributes of a corporation is conferred upon an unincorporated entity, there is no presumption that the other attributes of incorporation are intended to apply to that entity.[134]

§1.59 So jealously is the power of incorporation guarded by the courts that they are even reluctant to infer a right to carry on business or conduct affairs as a corporation in the case of emanations of the Crown itself. Accordingly, there is no presumption that an administrative agency of either the Federal or Provincial government necessarily enjoys corporate status. In *Hollinger Bus Lines Ltd. v. Ontario (Labour Relations Board)*, Roach J.A. discussed the nature of the Ontario Securities Commission, and concluded that it was not an entity that could be sued in an action for damages. He said:

> The whole scheme and purpose of the Act is to deal with certain phases of the employer-employee relationship. The Board does not carry on any business. Its function is primarily administrative and it has been given power to exercise certain functions of a judicial nature. There is nothing in the Act remotely suggesting that it was intended by the Legislature that the Board should have the capacity either to sue or be sued.[135]

§1.60 More generally, companies are to be distinguished from bare administrative agencies that are created by a wide range of Federal and Provincial legislation, that exist without property, assets or funds of their own out of which any judgment recovered against it could be realized, and that have no direct means of raising funds, whether by way of the conduct of a business or levying any taxes or rates or acquiring any property or creating any fund for the discharge of a judgment. Generally, there is no right to sue such entities nor for them to commence any action in their own name, since any judgment against such an entity would be absolutely futile.[136]

---

[131] See, for instance, *Commissioners of Inland Revenue v. Bew Estates Ltd.*, [1956] Ch. 407.
[132] See, for instance, *Amalgamated Society of Railway Servants v. Osborne*, [1910] A.C. 87 at 102 (H.L.), *per* Lord Atkinson.
[133] See, generally, *Bank of Montreal v. Bethune* (1836), 4 O.S. 341, *per* Robinson C.J.
[134] *Electrical, Electronic, Telecommunications & Plumbing Union v. Times Newspapers Ltd.*, [1980] Q.B. 585; see also *Von Hellfeld v. Rechnitzer*, [1914] 1 Ch. 748 at 754 (C.A.), *per* Phillimore L.J.
[135] [1952] 3 D.L.R. 162 at 166, [1952] O.R. 366 (C.A.).
[136] *Bowles v. City of Winnipeg* (1919), 45 D.L.R. 94 at 111-12 (K.B.), *per* Mathers C.J.K.B. See also *Westlake v. Ontario*, [1971] 3 O.R. 533 (H.C.J.), aff'd [1972] 2 O.R. 605 (C.A.), *per* Houlden J.; and *Manchuck v. Byle*, [1978] M.J. No. 116, 93 D.L.R. (3d) 426 (Q.B.), *per* Nitikman J.

G. CONCLUSION

§1.61 In this chapter we have briefly surveyed the nature of a corporation, the various theories that relate to corporations as a legal entity and the general requirements for incorporation. Each of these subjects has touched upon the basic attributes of a corporation. In the next chapter, we shall examine these attributes in detail, as we move to the subject of corporations as legal persons.

Chapter 2

PERSONALITY AND ITS IMPLICATIONS

A. INTRODUCTION

§2.1 In Chapter 1, we discussed the evolution of corporations as a legal phenomenon and the many methods by which such entities are brought into being. As we noted in that chapter, what sets a corporation apart from partnerships and other forms of unincorporated association (whether organized for the purpose of business or not) is the consequence of legal personality. In this chapter, we will look at the concept of personality in detail and explore its legal implications.

§2.2 Generally, all business corporations and other companies serve as administrative devices, and are employed in connection with the acquisition, ownership, holding and controlling the use of assets. Because corporations have been found to be very successful for these purposes, the vast majority of the productive assets of the economy are now owned by corporations. However, a company may just as easily be used as a device for collecting and controlling liabilities. In either case, corporations are useful as an administrative device largely because the law recognizes them as being separate persons.

§2.3 Not only is personality the basic attribute of a company that separates it from other forms of organization, it is that unique personality that distinguishes that company from its members,[1] and most of the other attributes of corporate existence are no more than a logical outgrowth of this separate personality. It has been said that corporate personality is essentially a metaphorical use of language, clothing the group which comprises the corporation with a separate legal identity by analogy with a natural person.[2] However, the implications of separate personality are far from metaphorical. The separate personality of the company is relevant in determining to whom particular acts, rights, duties, liabilities, powers and capacities are to be attributed: the company or its members,[3] for separate personality implies that any of these which belong to the company or its members are distinct

---

[1] *Meadow Farm Ltd. v. Imperial Bank of Canada*, [1922] 2 W.W.R. 909, 66 D.L.R. 743 (Alta. C.A.).

[2] J.H. Farrar, *Company Law* (London: Butterworths, 1985) at 56. See also L.L. Fuller, *Legal Fictions* (Stanford, CA: Stanford University Press, 1967) at 19.

[3] *Meadow Farm Ltd. v. Imperial Bank of Canada*, [1922] 2 W.W.R. 909, 66 D.L.R. 743 (Alta. C.A.); *Discount & Loan Corp. of Canada v. Canada (Superintendent of Insurance)*, [1938] Ex. C.R. 194, aff'd [1939] S.C.R. 285.

from those which belong to the other.[4] Similarly, where two corporations are owned by the same shareholder, the acts, rights, duties, liabilities, powers and capacities of each are distinct from those which are attributable to the other.[5] For instance, a corporation is not bound by any principle of *res judicata* or *issue estoppel* as a result of a judgment obtained against one of its shareholders.[6] From the time when a company is legally incorporated,[7] it is considered to be a legal person and will be bound by any rule of law applying to persons generally.[8] It will be treated as an independent person with rights and liabilities belonging to itself,[9] even where there is only a single owner of the corporation.[10]

B. THE SALOMON CASE

§2.4 The defining case in the area of separate personality was the decision of the House of Lords in *Salomon v. Salomon & Co*. The facts in that case were as follows: a man named Aron Salomon operated a successful business that he decided to sell to a limited company, in which he would have a controlling interest. The company had authorized capital of £40,000, divided into £1 par value shares. On the organization of the company, 20,007 of these shares were issued, of which Salomon held 20,001, with the other signatories of the memorandum of association holding one share each. The company had seven shareholders (the minimum then permitted under the *Companies Act, 1862*) who were Aron, his wife and daughter and four sons. At the first meeting of the board of directors, which consisted of the appellant and two of his sons, the pre-incorporation business was transferred to the company for £38,782, of which £16,000 was to be paid in cash or debentures. The board approved payment to Aron of £6,000 in cash and £10,000 by way of debentures.

---

[4] *Meadow Farm Ltd. v. Imperial Bank of Canada*, [1922] 2 W.W.R. 909, 66 D.L.R. 743 (Alta. C.A.); *Keewatin Tribal Council Inc. v. Thompson (City)*, [1989] M.J. No. 295, 5 W.W.R. 202 (Q.B.).

[5] *Northern Electric Co. v. Frank Warkentin Electric Ltd.*, [1972] M.J. No. 21, 27 D.L.R. (3d) 519 at 530 (C.A.), *per* Dickson J.A. But compare *Bagby v. Gustavson International Drilling Co.*, [1980] A.J. No. 743, 24 A.R. 181 at 199 (C.A.), var'g [1979] A.J. No. 767, 20 A.R. 244 (S.C.T.D.), *per* Laycraft J.A.

[6] See, generally, *Kuin v. 238682 Alberta Ltd.*, [1997] A.J. No. 1115, 56 Alta. L.R. (3d) 329 (M.C.); compare, however, *Barakot Ltd. v. Epiette Ltd.*, [1997] B.C.L.C. 303.

[7] A company cannot become subject to a legal obligation (*e.g.*, by entering a contract) prior to its incorporation: *Omista Credit Union Ltd. v. Thomson*, [1982] N.B.J. No. 389, 43 N.B.R. (2d) 628 at 631, 113 A.R. 628 (C.A.), *per* La Forest J.A. See Chapter 3 re pre-incorporation contracts at para. 3.149, *et seq.*

[8] See, for instance, *R. v. Esam Construction Ltd.*, [1973] O.J. No. 2266, 2 O.R. (2d) 344 (H.C.J.) (corporation bound by by-law requiring all persons to obtain a building permit).

[9] *Salomon v. Salomon & Co.* [1897] A.C. 22 (H.L.); see also *Rielle v. Reid* (1899), 26 O.A.R. 54 at 60; *Clarkson Co. v. Zhelka*, [1967] 2 O.R. 565 (H.C.); *Re H.E.P.C. and Thorold* (1924), 55 O.L.R. 431, leave to appeal ref'd 26 O.W.N. 386 (C.A.); *Rogers-Majestic Corp. v. Toronto*, [1943] S.C.R. 440; *Mission Hill Tire & Auto Centre Ltd. v. Killerney Group Ltd.*, [1989] A.J. No. 904, 38 C.P.C. (2d) 64 (Master).

[10] *Salomon v. Salomon & Co.* [1897] A.C. 22 (H.L.); *Waldron v. Hogan*, [1934] 3 D.L.R. 800 at 801 (B.C. Co. Ct.), *per* Swanson Co. Ct. J. Compare, however, the decision of Winter J. in *Royal Stores Ltd. v. Brown* (1956), 5 D.L.R. (2d) 146 (Nfld. T.D.).

§2.5 After the transfer of the business, the company experienced a series of setbacks. While the business was solvent and prosperous at the time of the sale, as a result of a series of strikes, it ultimately failed. In the meantime, prior to its ultimate failure, Aron had advanced further funds from his own resources to the company; when these gave out he had borrowed a further £5,000 from a lender named Broderip, which was also advanced to the company. The original debentures were mortgaged by Salomon to Edmund Broderip as a security for an advance of £5,000 which was used to fund the company. Subsequently, the initial debentures were cancelled, and £10,000 in fresh debentures was issued to Broderip. In October 1898, the company went into liquidation. At that time, the company's realizable assets amounted to only £6,000. Broderip claimed £5,000 of this, with Aron claiming the remaining £1,000 under his debenture. No money remained for the unsecured creditors, whose claims amounted to £7,773. An action was brought by the liquidator of the company against Aron, which was tried before Vaughan Williams J., who held that the company was entitled to be indemnified by Aron to the amount of £7,733. This decision was affirmed by the Court of Appeal.[11]

§2.6 The case was appealed to the House of Lords. There, after considering these facts, Lord Davey rejected the notion that a corporation owned by a single shareholder was a mere alias of its shareholder. Similarly, even though the legislation required seven shareholders and six of the seven had only a nominal interest, Lord Macnaghten rejected the notion that the separate status of the corporation was in any way compromised.[12] If the creditors chose to deal with a limited company, they took the risk as to whether it would prove creditworthy. The number of shareholders could have no effect on the risk that they ran in this regard.[13] Since the Ontario *Business Corporations Act* and *Canada Business Corporations Act* require only a single incorporator, the points put forward by the Law Lords in the *Salomon* case would seem even more valid now than they did when they were first pronounced.

§2.7 While the *Salomon* decision has been highly influential, and settled many formerly contentious points of law by reason of its being a decision of the House of Lords, it is important to understand that this case did not radically alter the law, but merely made clear that one set of legal rules governs the separate personality of a company, whether it has one or countless shareholders. The case did not establish the proposition that a corporation was a separate legal person from its members. This was already a principle clearly established by statute law. Nor did the case create limited liability. That principle was again set out in statute. The main ruling in the case was that the statutory requirement for seven incorporators was satisfied even though only one of them had any real interest in the corporation, and the others held only a nominal share, and even that interest was held by them largely as the nominees of the controlling shareholder. Fur-

---

[11] [1895] 2 Ch. 328.
[12] *Salomon v. Salomon & Co.*, [1897] A.C. 22 at 53 (H.L.).
[13] *Ibid.*, at 44-45, *per* Lord Herschell.

ther, the case did not give rise to the sole-shareholder corporation, since the corporation had more than one shareholder. Instead, the case recognized that it was not contrary to the true intent and meaning of the *Companies Act, 1862* for a trader to sell his business to a limited company consisting only of himself and six members of his own family, in order to limit his liability and obtain the preference of a debenture-holder over other creditors, where at the time of the sale the business was solvent, all the terms of sale (even if one-sided in favour of the vendor) were known to and approved by the shareholders, and all the requirements of the Act governing incorporation had been satisfied. The effect of the decision was to bring home the critical consequences that flowed as a result of the recognition of incorporated entities as separate legal persons.

C. THE IMPLICATIONS OF SEPARATE PERSONALITY

§2.8 A corporation has the capacity to own its own property, have and enforce its own rights and is subject to its own liabilities. As the *Salomon* case makes clear, as a separate person the company is entitled not only to acquire rights and become subject to obligations independently from its members,[14] it is also able to acquire rights against, and become subject to enforceable obligations that favour, the persons who stand behind it. The business carried on by the corporation is its own.[15] Thus the owner of a corporation will not be seen to be engaging in a particular business merely because a corporation of which he or she is the

---

[14] Note, however, the necessity of proper organization of the corporation: *Tato Enterprises Ltd. v. Rode*, [1979] A.J. No. 496, 17 A.R. 432 (Dist. Ct.), in which Dea D.C.J. commented upon the potential liability of a director, officer or shareholder of a corporation who purports to contract on behalf of a corporation that has been incompletely organized (at 438; see also 436):

> In this case ... the corporate formalities have clearly been offended and, in fact, there has been a wide and broad failure of compliance with corporate formalities. The failure of the defendant Rode to take the time and trouble to determine the correct name of the corporation and to conduct his business in that name is simply a further evidence of his failure to comply with those requirements of the *Companies Act* which are necessary if a person purporting to be an agent of a corporation is to avoid personal liability. Accordingly, the limited liability otherwise available ... is not available to the defendant Rode and it is my view that the contracting parties in the matter before me are the plaintiff and the defendant Rode personally.

> Yet this decision is not without its problems: the creditor plaintiff had not been misled into thinking that it was dealing with Rode personally. On the contrary, it believed that it was dealing with a corporate entity, albeit one with a different name than the one given by Rode (Scott Bradley Ltd.). The real company (Scott Bradley Marketing Ltd.) may never have been properly organized, and in particular may never have appointed Rode as its secretary or agent for the purposes of negotiating the contract in question. But that company did not dispute its liability under the contract. Therefore, it is difficult to see what prejudice it had suffered, or why it was in the interests of justice to impose liability on Rode. In effect, Dea D.C.J.'s judgment allowed the plaintiff to take advantage of slipshod corporate administration by Rode so as to enjoy the benefit of a right of action against Rode personally that it had never been expected to enjoy. Nevertheless, the language employed by Dea D.C.J. is consistent with other case law in the area: see *Wolfe v. Moir* (1969), 69 W.W.R. 70 (Alta. T.D.); and *Royal Stores Ltd. v. Brown* (1956), 5 D.L.R. (2d) 146 (Nfld. T.D.).

[15] *Tunstall v. Steigmann*, [1962] 2 Q.B. 593 (C.A.), *per* Willmer L.J.

owner is engaged in that business.[16] From a legal perspective, a closely held private company is just as much a separate legal person from its owner as is a widely held public company, although from a commercial perspective the private company may be seen to be more closely analogous to a sole proprietorship or partnership than a public corporation.[17] Because of their separate personality, it is of utmost importance to mark, observe and maintain clearly the distinction between the assets and liabilities of the corporation and those of its shareholders.[18] The assets of the corporation are reserved for the satisfaction of its obligations and liabilities. Consequently, the assets of a corporation are not available in execution to the creditors of the owner of that corporation even where it is alleged that the corporation is an agent of the owner,[19] although it may be possible to attack a transfer of assets to the corporation as a fraudulent conveyance.[20]

§2.9 In most cases, however, separate personality protects the shareholder. Thus a sole shareholder is not liable for the debts, obligations and liabilities of the company,[21] nor is the company liable for the debts, obligations and liabilities of the shareholders.[22] Similarly, a judgment against the company does not operate as a judgment against the shareholder, nor does a judgment against the shareholder operate as a judgment against the company, and by the same token a stay of proceedings against a shareholder does not affect enforcement of a judgment against a corporation.[23] The motives of the shareholders in forming the company are irrelevant to its status as an independent entity.[24] However, there are limits on a shareholder's ability to isolate transactions within a corporation, particularly where fraud or other wrongdoing can be shown. In *Canadian Film Development Corp. v. Perlmutter*[25] the plaintiff claimed that the defendant defeated his creditors by setting up shell corporations to receive payments that otherwise would have been made to him. By virtue of these devices, the plaintiff was unable to recover any money by way of legal execution. Justice Gray held that equitable execution could be granted where special circumstances exist that made it impractical or impossible to obtain execution by legal means. In the circumstances, there was no reasonable prospect of recovery for the plaintiff

---

[16] *Northern Crown Bank v. Great West Lumber Co.* (1914), 7 Alta. L.R. 183 (C.A.); *White v. Bank of Toronto*, [1953] O.R. 479 at 491 (C.A.), *per* Aylesworth J.A.; *Gramophone & Typewriter Ltd. v. Stanley*, [1908] 2 K.B. 89 (C.A.). However, a separate corporate personality may not be used as an instrument for fraud: *Fern Brand Waxes Ltd. v. Pearl* (1972), 29 D.L.R. (3d) 662 at 669 (Ont. C.A.), *per* McGillivray J.A.
[17] *Re Smith & Fawcett Ltd.*, [1942] Ch. 304 at 306 (C.A.), *per* Lord Greene M.R.
[18] *E.B.M. Co. v. Dominion Bank*, [1937] 3 All E.R. 555 at 564-65 (P.C.); see also *White v. Bank of Toronto*, [1953] O.R. 479 at 491 (C.A.), *per* Aylesworth J.A.
[19] *Rielle v. Reid* (1899), 26 O.A.R. 54 at 60, *per* Osler J.A.
[20] *Ibid.*; see also *Stratford Fuel, Ice, Cartage & Construction Co. v. Mooney* (1909), 21 O.L.R. 426 at 443 (C.A.), *per* Moss C.J.O.
[21] *390346 Ontario Ltd. v. Malidav Holdings Ltd.*, [1980] N.B.J. No. 158, 31 N.B.R. (2d) 72, 75 A.P.R. 72 (Q.B.).
[22] *Gabriel v. Gabriel*, [1980] A.J. No. 39, 12 Alta. L.R. (2d) 1, 14 R.F.L. (2d) 174 (C.A.); *Kenson Holdings Ltd. v. Kennedy* (1980), 20 R.F.L. (2d) 113 (Alta. Q.B.).
[23] *Jewell v. Ross*, [1987] O.J. No. 1416, 16 C.P.C. (2d) 46 (Dist. Ct.).
[24] *Rielle v. Reid* (1899), 26 O.A.R. 54, *per* Osler J.A.
[25] (1986), 6 C.P.C. (2d) 262 (Ont. H.C.).

other than by the appointment of a receiver. Accordingly, Gray J. concluded that it was just and convenient to appoint a receiver on the facts of the case.

§2.10 Separate personality is purchased at a price: corporations are subject to tighter regulatory control on their operations than are other forms of business enterprise. Moreover, generally speaking the separate personality of a company is recognized even where it would be in the interests of the shareholders to treat the corporation and its shareholders as one.[26] So, for instance, a shareholder may not sue to enforce a contract belonging to the corporation,[27] nor for a breach of a duty of care owed to the corporation.[28] Similarly, the sole shareholder of a company may not deduct business losses incurred by the corporation from his or her own taxable income. As we shall see, the fiction of separate personality has particular force where the directors of one corporation belonging to a group of associated corporations[29] wish to make use of the resources of that corporation for the benefit of other members of the group. For instance, in *Walker v. Wimborne*[30] the court considered the liability of directors of a number of associated companies who had caused funds to be moved among the companies to pay various debts of each, and who had used assets of one company as security for loans obtained by others. The companies went into liquidation, and the liquidator sued the directors on the grounds that the directors had been guilty of fraud, negligence, default, breach of trust and breach of duty. Justice Mason rejected the arguments that where two or more companies were associated, the directors could disregard their duties to each individual company so as to benefit the group as a whole.[31]

---

[26] *Fidelity Developments v. Northwest Territories (Chief of Resources)*, [1979] 1 W.W.R. 151 (N.W.T. S.C.).

[27] However, the sole shareholder of a corporation may recover for breach of contract for damages resulting to the corporation as a result of a failure by the defendant to perform properly a contract between the shareholder and defendant. Such losses are not too remote, and the claim in such a case is based upon an obligation owed to the shareholder personally: *George Fisher (Great Britain) Ltd. v. Multi-Construction Ltd.*, [1995] B.C.C. 310 (C.A.).

[28] For cases holding that no duty is owed by corporation's auditors to a controlling block of shareholders or other persons investing in the corporation, see: *Hercules Managements Ltd. v. Ernst & Young*, [1997] S.C.J. No. 51, [1997] 2 S.C.R. 165; *Roman Corp. v. Peat Marwick Thorne*, [1993] O.J. No. 694, 12 B.L.R. 10 (Gen. Div.), see also [1992] O.J. No. 2207, 8 B.L.R. (2d) 43 (Gen. Div.); no such duty even where corporation is essentially wholly owned: *Twiggco Financial Ltd. v. Peat Marwick Thorne*, [1994] O.J. No. 462, 12 B.L.R. (2d) 1, leave to appeal ref'd [1994] O.J. No. 4192, 12 B.L.R. (2d) 34 (Gen. Div.); no such duty owed to creditors: *Canadian Commercial Bank v. Crawford, Smith & Swallow*, [1993] O.J. No. 726, 9 B.L.R. (2d) 311, affd [1994] O.J. No. 632, 21 C.C.L.T. (2d) 89 (C.A.), leave to appeal to S.C.C. ref'd [1994] S.C.C.A. No. 261, 21 C.C.L.T. (2d) 89*n*.

[29] Discussed in Chapter 11, Duties and Liabilities of Directors and Officers.

[30] (1976), 137 C.L.R. 1 (H.C. Aust.). For a case dealing with the use of a mirror account system, in which a group of related corporations essentially pooled their banking resources, see: *Arthur Andersen Inc. v. Toronto Dominion Bank*, [1994] O.J. No. 427, 14 B.L.R. (2d) 1, leave to appeal to S.C.C. ref'd [1994] S.C.C.A. No. 189, 16 B.L.R. (2d) 254*n*. See also: *Re A Company (No. 002470 of 1988), ex p. Nicholas*, [1992] B.C.C. 895 (C.A.).

[31] See also *Industrial Equity Ltd. v. Blackburn* (1977), 137 C.L.R. 567 (H.C. Aust.).

§2.11 The separate legal personality recognized to exist in respect of a corporation does not mean that corporations have all the characteristics of, and no characteristics not shared by, individuals.[32] Although it is a separate legal person, like any other person, a corporation may act as the agent of its owner.[33] However, there is a strong presumption that in carrying on business it is not doing so. The presumption against agency applies even where one shareholder controls the corporation.[34] Where a corporation holds property or engages in contracts or other transactions it is presumed to be acting for itself and for its own account rather than as agent for its owner, unless there is clear evidence to the contrary.[35] Whether an agency relationship does exist is a question of fact, which is answered by deciding whether the corporation is acting on its own behalf as an independent entity (so that the benefit of the contract or transaction flows primarily to its own account) or whether it is acting simply for and on behalf of some other person.[36] To establish such a relationship, the facts must be such that a finding of agency would be made even if the purported principal had no shareholding in the corporation.[37] Moreover, where a person believes that he or she is contracting with a corporation rather than its owner, a claim of agency is untenable.[38]

§2.12 Separate personality also implies that the shareholder of a corporation has no legal or equitable interest in the assets of the corporation. So strictly is this rule applied that at one time a shareholder was seen to possess no insurable interest in the assets belonging to the corporation,[39] although this extreme view no

---

[32] *Re Polly Peck International plc*, [1995] B.C.C. 486 at 495 (Ch.), *per* Robert Walker J. Concerning the right of a corporation to appear "in person" before a court, through one of its officers or directors, see *Charles P. Kinnell & Co. v. Harding, Wace & Co.*, [1918] 1 K.B. 405 at 413 (C.A.), *per* Swinfen Eady L.J.; *Frinton & Walton UDC v. Walton & District Sand & Mineral Co.*, [1938] 1 All E.R. 649; *Tritonia Ltd. v. Equity & Law Life Assurance Society*, [1943] A.C. 584 at 586 (H.L.), *per* Viscount Simon L.C. at p. 586; *Jonathan Alexander Ltd. v. Proctor*, [1995] B.C.C. 598 (C.A.).

[33] *Gramophone & Typewriter Ltd. v. Stanley*, [1908] 2 K.B. 89 (C.A.), *per* Sir H.H. Cozens-Hardy M.R.

[34] *Clarkson Co. v. Zhelka*, [1967] 2 O.R. 565 (H.C.).

[35] *Canada Life Assurance Co. v. CIBC* (1974), 3 O.R. (2d) 70 (C.A.), leave to appeal to S.C.C. ref'd [1974] S.C.R. viii; *Lee v. Lee's Air Farming Ltd.*, [1961] A.C. 12 (P.C.); *R. v. B.C. Brick & Tile Co.*, [1936] 3 D.L.R. 23 (Ex. Ct.).

[36] *Rainham Chemical Works Ltd. v. Belvedere Fish Guano Co.*, [1921] 2 A.C. 465 (H.L.); *Patton v. Yukon Consolidated Gold Corp.*, [1934] O.W.N. 321 at 324, *per* Middleton, J.A., additional reasons at [1936] O.R. 308 (C.A.); *Kentucky Fried Chicken Canada v. Scott's Food Services Inc.*, [1997] O.J. No. 3773 (H.C.J.), [1998] O.J. No. 4368, 41 B.L.R. (2d) 42 (C.A.).

[37] See, generally, *E.B.M. Co. v. Dominion Bank*, [1937] 3 All E.R. 555 at 564 (P.C.), *per* Lord Russell of Killowen; *Clarkson Co. v. Zhelka*, [1967] 2 O.R. 565 at 578 (H.C.), *per* Thompson J.; *Keewatin Tribal Council Inc. v. Thompson (City)*, [1989] M.J. No. 295, [1989] 5 W.W.R. 202 (Q.B.); *Pioneer Concrete Services Ltd. v. Yelnah Pty. Ltd.* (1987), 5 A.C.L.C. 467, 11 A.C.L.R. 108 (S.C.N.S.W.). Compare, however, *Smith, Stone & Knight Ltd. v. Birmingham Corp.*, [1939] All E.R. 116, *per* Atkinson J.; *DHN Food Distributors Ltd. v. Tower Hamlets London Borough Council*, [1976] 1 W.L.R. 852, [1976] 3 All E.R. 462 (C.A.).

[38] *Bank of Montreal v. Canadian Westgrowth Ltd.*, [1990] A.J. No. 125, 102 A.R. 391 (Q.B.), aff'd [1992] A.J. No. 371, 135 A.R. 49 (C.A.).

[39] *Macaura v. Northern Assurance Co.*, [1925] A.C. 619 at 626 (H.L.). The problem was not simply one of lack of a proprietary (and therefore insurable interest), but also the difficulty of accurately measuring loss — *per* Lord Buckmaster. See also *Guarantee Co. of North America v.*

longer represents the law in Canada.[40] The sole shareholder of a corporation may be convicted of theft of the property of the corporation.[41]

§2.13 It is an elementary principle of contract law that a person may not enter into a contract with himself or herself. However, a corporation may enter into a contract with one or all of its members and may enforce that contract with the member to the same extent as if the contract had been made with a stranger.[42] As discussed in detail in Chapters 3 and 8, because corporations are legally distinct from their members, it is necessary, when entering into a contract with a corporation, to show that the contract was approved by the corporation as opposed to one of its members, for unlike a partnership, a member of a corporation does not possess the implied authority to bind the corporation to a contract.

§2.14 If a corporation and its shareholder(s) may enter into a contract with each other, it follows that each may enforce the rights that flow from that contract or which arise out of its formation against the other. The extent to which a shareholder may sue the corporation in which he or she owns shares was brought home forcefully in the English case of *Soden v. British & Commonwealth Holdings plc*.[43] The relevant facts in that case were as follows: Atlantic Computers plc had been acquired by British & Commonwealth Holdings plc ("B & C"), who were advised by Barclays de Zoete Wedd ("BZW"), for a total consideration in cash and shares of more than £400-million. Subsequently, Atlantic failed

---

[40] *Aqua-Land Exploration Ltd.*, [1965] S.C.J. No. 65, [1966] S.C.R. 133; *Constitution Insurance Co. of Canada v. Kosmopoulos*, [1987] S.C.J. No. 2, 36 B.L.R. 283 at 291, *per* Wilson J.

See, generally, *Constitution Insurance Co. of Canada v. Kosmopoulos*, [1987] S.C.J. No. 2, 36 B.L.R. 283. In that case Wilson J. (giving the opinion of the majority) held that the restriction of the scope of insurable interest to a direct proprietary interest was not realistic in the modern economy. The policies underlying the requirement for an insurable interest (prevention of wagering; lack of risk to the insured if the property is damaged) were held not to require such a restrictive view of insurable interest. Where an insured can demonstrate some relation to or concern in the insured property, the insured has a sufficient insurable interest. A person has an insurable interest where that person has a normal expectation of deriving an advantage or benefit from the insured property, but for the risk or damages against which the insurance is obtained, or where that person benefits from the existence of the property and would suffer from its loss. In a separate concurring judgment, McIntyre J. took a narrower view, holding only that a sole shareholder of a corporation had an insurable interest in the property of the company, arising from the identity of interest between the corporation and the shareholder. From a corporate law perspective, McIntyre J.'s narrower approach seems preferable to that of Wilson J. It would be difficult to find the exact point at which the shareholding of a shareholder who is not the sole beneficial owner of the corporation would drop to a point that his or her advantage, benefit or suffering in respect of corporate property would fall below the point of an insurable interest. This question aside, where a shareholder holds less than all the shares of a corporation purchases insurance over the assets of the corporation, it may be possible (on the facts of a given case) to argue that the insurance so purchased was obtained on an agency or trust basis on behalf of the corporation.

[41] *Re A.G.'s Reference (No. 2 of 1982)*, [1984] Q.B. 624 (C.A.), *per* Kerr L.J.; *R. v. Phillippou* (1989), 89 Cr. App. R. 290 (C.A.), *per* O'Connor L.J.

[42] In *Lee v. Lee's Air Farming Ltd.*, [1961] A.C. 12 (P.C.) it was necessary to decide whether the sole beneficial owner of a corporation could be an employee of a company, so as to entitle his widow to claim under workers' compensation legislation. The Board upheld the contract of employment.

[43] [1995] B.C.C. 531 (Ch. D.).

and was placed under administration. The collapse of Atlantic led to the collapse of B & C, which also went into administration. B & C commenced two actions, the first against Atlantic and its directors for negligent misrepresentation and the second against BZW for breach of duty. BZW sought indemnification from Atlantic, by way of a third party proceeding. The administrator of Atlantic complained that the effect of these proceedings was to attempt to elevate B & C's claim against Atlantic from that of a shareholder to a creditor. Justice Robert Walker concluded that the validity of this defense turned upon whether the claim being made by B & C was sufficiently closely related to the corporate nexus as to be characterized as a member's claim.[44]

§2.15 A law firm is not barred from acting against a former owner of a corporation merely because it acted for that corporation while that former owner owned that corporation. Access to confidential information belonging to the corporation is not equated with access to confidential information of the client. Although on the facts of a given case the arrangements between the former owner and the corporation may have been of such a nature that it would be necessary to prohibit the law firm from acting against the former client, there is no presumption of disqualification.[45]

§2.16 To summarize the points made above, the separate personal status of a corporation is one of the chief defining characteristics which differentiates it from other forms of business enterprise. In practical terms, two major consequences grow out of this separate status, namely limited liability[46] and the separate taxation of the company, and it is to the nature of limited liability that we shall now turn.

---

[44] *Ibid.*, at 534-35; see also *Re Dale & Plant Ltd.* (1889), 43 Ch. D. 255 at 258-59, *per* Kay J.; *Re LB Holliday & Co.*, [1986] 2 All E.R. 367, 2 B.C.C. 99,031; *Re Harry Simpson & Co. Pty* (1963), 81 W.N. (Pt. 1) N.S.W. 207, 84 W.N. (Pt. 1) N.S.W. 455; *Re WH Eutrope Pty,* [1932] V.L.R. 453; *Re Harlou Pty,* [1950] V.L.R. 499; *Re New Chile Gold Mining Co.* (1890), 45 Ch. D. 598 at 605, *per* Stirling J.; *Webb Distributors (Aust.) Pty v. State of Victoria* (1993), 11 A.C.L.C. 1178 (H.C. Aust.).

[45] *Gainers Inc. v. Pocklington,* [1995] A.J. No. 438, 20 B.L.R. (2d) 289 at 295 (C.A.), *per* Côté J.A.

[46] *Re Sheffield & South Yorkshire Permanent Building Society* (1889), 22 Q.B.D. 470 at 476 (Div. Ct.), *per* Cave J.:

> [It was] argued that persons who unite together for trading or making profits are, at common law, liable for all debts which are incurred during the time they are members of the association, and that, if the association has ultimately to be wound up, past members must pay their shares of the debts. As a general rule–apart from legislation–that is perfectly true with respect to partners, and with respect to associations in the nature of partnership where there is no incorporation, but with respect to corporations the case is entirely different where the legislation has not thought fit to intervene, or where the charter under which the body is incorporated does not provide otherwise. A corporation is a legal *persona* just as much as an individual; and, if a man trusts a corporation, he trusts the legal *persona,* and must look to its assets for payment: he can only call upon the individual members to contribute in case the Act or charter has so provided.

D. LIMITED LIABILITY

§2.17 Limited liability[47] is the regime which applies where the liability of a participant in a business or undertaking for the debts or other obligations incurred with respect to that business or undertaking is limited to his or her capital investment in that business or undertaking.[48] Under a limited liability regime, the business organization, rather than its members, is responsible for the debts and other obligations and liabilities of the corporation.[49] Perhaps the most widely recognized feature of the separate existence of a corporation is the principle of limited liability, and it is expressly conferred upon shareholders by both the OBCA and the CBCA.[50] Thus subsection 92(1) of the OBCA provides:

> The shareholders of a corporation are not, as shareholders, liable for any act, default, obligation or liability of the corporation except under subsection 34(5), subsection 108(5) and section 243.

The corresponding provision of the CBCA is substantially the same.[51] It follows that the fact that A Inc. owns all the shares of B Ltd. will not make A Inc. liable for any act or obligation of B Ltd.; still less will A Inc. be liable for the acts or obligations of B Ltd. on the sole ground that A Inc. and B Ltd. both have the

---

[47] The Ontario *Business Corporations Act* and the *Canada Business Corporations Act* provide for only one basic type of corporation, namely the corporation limited by shares. In contrast, in England and Australia, it is possible to create other several distinct types of company, including no liability companies (in Australia), companies limited by guarantee, and unlimited companies. These other options have not proved particularly popular and in each country comprise less than one per cent of all corporations organized. Companies limited by guarantee have not been widely adopted in Canada, but both Nova Scotia and Alberta provide for unlimited liability companies. Ontario is considering enacting such legislation. Currently no Province in Canada provides for incorporated partnerships as outlined in the U.K. *Limited Liability Partnerships Act, 2000*. The primary advantage derived from using such an entity is to enjoy the tax treatment of a partnership, while having the benefits of incorporation. The federal structure of the Canadian political system complicates any effort to create a similar regime here.

[48] For this reason it may be said that the liability of the shareholder is not extinguished, but is merely restricted to the fully paid-up value of the shares or (in the case of a subscriber or person to whom shares have been issued — improperly — otherwise than on a fully paid-up basis) to the amount for which the shareholder is liable to contribute for those shares: *Oakes v. Turquand & Harding* (1867), L.R. 2 H.L. 325.

[49] In *Oakes v. Turquand & Harding* (1867), L.R. 2 H.L. 325 at 357 Lord Cranworth said:

> There is no doubt that the direct remedy of a creditor is solely against the incorporated company. He has no dealing with any individual shareholder, and if he is driven to bring any action to enforce any right he may have acquired, he must sue the company, and not any of the members of whom it is composed.

For general discussions of the policy implications of the doctrine of limited liability, see: F.H. Easterbrook & D.R. Fishel, "Limited Liability and the Corporation" (1985) 52 U. Chi. L. Rev. 89; Landers, "A Unified Approach to Parent, Subsidiary and Affiliate Questions in Bankruptcy" (1975) 42 U. Chi. L. Rev. 589; R. Posner, "The Rights of Creditors of Affiliated Corporations" (1976) 43 U. Chi. L. Rev. 499; Landers, "Another Word on Parents, Subsidiaries and Affiliates in Bankruptcy" (1976) 43 U. Chi. L. Rev. 527.

[50] Surprisingly, the concept was firmly introduced into English corporate law only in 1855, with the enactment of the *Limited Liability Act*, which granted limited liability to companies with at least 25 members holding shares to a minimum value of £10, with at least one-fifth being fully paid up on those shares. See, generally, P. Ireland, I. Grigg-Spall, D. Kelly, "The Conceptual Foundations of Modern Company Law" [1987] J. Law & Soc. 149 at 150.

[51] CBCA, s. 45(1).

same shareholders.[52] As a general rule, a shareholder will only be liable for the debts and obligations of a corporation where the shareholder has given a guarantee of those debts and obligations.[53]

(i) The Evolution of Limited Liability

§2.18 Limited liability may be a logical consequence of separate personality. However, it is a curious fact that these two concepts which are today so closely linked together, actually evolved separately. As discussed in Chapter 1, in England it was only settled that limited liability resulted from incorporation under the *Joint Stock Companies Act, 1844* by the 1855 enactment of the *Limited Liability Act*. In contrast, in France and other civilian jurisdictions, it was possible to confer limited liability on investors long prior to the evolution of true corporations, using a form of business organization known as the *société en commandite simple* (the forerunner of the statutory limited partnership, now available in most common law jurisdictions). It consists of one or more general partners with unlimited liability, and one or more limited partners, who are liable only to the extent of their capital contributions. Except for the limited liability of the investor-partners, a *société en commandite simple* is subject to the same principles of law and governance as a general partnership. An alternative form of business organization, known as a *société en commandite par actions*, offers enhanced mobility of capital: the limited partners are issued with shares that may be traded. In early 19th century England, there was resentment among many commercial interests of the continental ability to enter into limited liability investment arrangements, and there was intensive lobbying in favour of copying these civilian schemes by way of legislation. Ultimately, these efforts to create limited liability partnerships failed. By the time common law jurisdictions began to introduce such regimes by statute in the early 20th century, the limited liability corporation was already a well-established feature of their law. Even when the limited partnership was adopted, it was initially subject to such strict restrictions on its manner of operation that it proved useless for most commercial purposes.[54] Liberalization in this area around the common law world would only occur in the late 20th century.[55]

---

[52] *Hartford Accident & Indemnity Co. v. Millsons Construction & Equipment Ltd.* (1939), 44 Que. P.R. 170; see also *Discount & Loan Corp. of Canada v. Canada (Superintendent of Insurance)*, [1938] Ex. C.R. 194, aff'd [1939] S.C.R. 285.

[53] See, generally, *Builders Supplies Ltd. v. Fraser*, [2005] O.J. No. 1540, 3 B.L.R. (4th) 1 (S.C.J.); and compare *Morris v. Call the Car Alarm Guys Inc.*, [2004] O.J. No. 5896, 3 B.L.R. (4th) 72 (S.C.J.) against the decision on appeal at [2005] O.J. No. 85 (C.A.).

[54] See F.B. Palmer, *The Companies Act 1907 and the Limited Liability Partnerships Act 1907, With Explanatory Notes* (London: Steven & Sons, 1908), at 71.

[55] Ontario liberalized its limited partnership regime in the 1980s, following the earlier lead of Alberta. In the U.K., reform would not occur until the enactment of the *Limited Liability Partnerships Act, 2000*.

(ii) The Limits of Limited Liability

§2.19 It is clear from the wording of subsection 92(1) of the Ontario *Business Corporations Act* that the shareholders or members of a limited liability corporation are not fully immune from liability for the debts, obligations and liabilities of the corporation. In particular, the shareholders are liable under subsections 34(5), 108(5) and 243 of the OBCA. Subsection 34(5) imposes liability upon shareholders where there has been an improper reduction in share capital. It reads:

> A creditor of a corporation is entitled to apply to the court for an order compelling a shareholder or other recipient,
>
> (a) to pay to the corporation an amount equal to any liability of the shareholder that was extinguished or reduced contrary to this section; or
>
> (b) to pay or deliver to the corporation any money or property that was paid or distributed to the shareholder or other recipient as a consequence of a reduction of capital made contrary to this section.

Subsection 38(4) of the CBCA is identical. The restrictions referred to in subsections 34(5) and 38(4) relate to the extinguishment or reduction in liability of amounts unpaid on any share, or to the reduction of a corporation's stated capital. In general terms, such steps may not be taken where the corporation is or would become insolvent by reason thereof.[56] Subsection 108(5) of the OBCA imposes liability on a shareholder who is a party to a unanimous shareholder agreement. Essentially, it transfers to such shareholders the potential liability of directors in respect of any discretion or power of the directors that is assumed by the shareholders under the terms of the unanimous shareholder agreement. Subsection 146(5) is the corresponding provision of the CBCA.[57] Subsection 243(1) of the OBCA imposes a liability upon shareholders where a distribution of property is made to the shareholders of a corporation following its dissolution. The corresponding provision of the CBCA is subsection 226(5).[58]

§2.20 The principle of limited liability is qualified by subsection 77(1) of the *Bankruptcy and Insolvency Act*.[59] It provides that:

> Every shareholder or member of a bankrupt corporation is liable to contribute the amount unpaid on his shares of the capital or on his liability to the corporation, its

---

[56] See Chapter 14, Fundamental Changes. The CBCA provision (in s. 146(5)) was amended in 2001 to read:

> To the extent that a unanimous shareholder agreement restricts the powers of the directors to manage, or supervise the management of, the business and affairs of the corporation parties to the unanimous shareholder agreement who are given that power to manager or supervise the management of the business and affairs of the corporation have all the rights, powers, duties and liabilities of a director of the corporation, whether they arise under this Act or otherwise, including any defenses available to the directors, and the directors are relieved of their rights, powers, duties and liabilities, including their liabilities under section 119, to the same extent.

[57] The liability imposed under these provisions is discussed in Chapter 12, Shareholders and Their Rights.

[58] These provisions are discussed in Chapter 15, Winding-up and Dissolution.

[59] R.S.C. 1985, c. B-3.

members or creditors, as the case may be, under the Act, charter or instrument of incorporation of the company or otherwise.

§2.21 The limited liability of the shareholders of a corporation involves exemption, at a price, from what would otherwise be an unlimited liability.[60] The dominant and cardinal principle of virtually all statutes creating corporations limited by shares is that the investor purchases immunity from liability beyond a certain limit, on the term that there is and shall remain a liability up to that limit.[61] It follows that a shareholder's claim for the return of share capital on liquidation is subordinate to the claims of the creditors against the estate of a bankrupt or insolvent company. Since under both the Ontario *Business Corporations Act* and the *Canada Business Corporations Act*, only shares that are "fully paid and non-assessable" may be issued (*i.e.*, the shares may be issued only upon payment of their full issue price), the amount paid by the shareholder for his or her shares is normally the only amount that he or she is liable to contribute towards the debtors of the company. However, shareholders will be subject to claims as contributories where shares have been issued for an inadequate property consideration or where less than their full subscription price has been paid, and also where distributions of capital or dividends have been improperly made to those shareholders. Moreover, under the oppression remedy, shareholders may occasionally be required to return funds or property to the corporation where they had depleted or removed assets from the corporation with a deliberate intent to defeat the claims of creditors.[62]

§2.22 The effect of limited liability is that although the creditors of a corporation may petition it into bankruptcy or apply to have the corporation wound up if it becomes insolvent, the creditors have no right of claim against the shareholders for any debts that may be owed to them.[63] Thus those persons who deal with corporations must base their dealings upon the creditworthiness of the corporation itself, rather than on its members. They must look to the assets of the corporation to determine whether credit may be safely granted. If they are concerned with the under-capitalization of a corporation, creditors should insist that a guarantee is provided. The limited liability of a corporation that has only nominal issued capital

---

[60] For a useful summary of the law relating to the liability of partners, see: *3464920 Canada Inc. v. Strother*, [2005] B.C.J. No. 1655, 8 B.L.R. (4th) 4 (C.A.).

[61] *Re Pyramid Building Society* (1992), 10 A.C.L.C. 1205 at 1217 (S.C. Vict.), *per* Tadgell J.; *Ooregum Gold Mining Co. of India v. Roper,* [1892] A.C. 125 at 145, *per* Lord Macnaghten.

[62] *G.T. Campbell & Associates Ltd. v. Hugh Carson Co.*, [1979] O.J. No. 4248, 24 O.R. (2d) 758 (Div. Ct.); *Canadian Opera Co. v. 670800 Ontario Inc.*, [1990] O.J. No. 2270, 75 O.R. (2d) 720 (Div. Ct.).

[63] For an interesting American case in this area, dealing with professional corporations, see *First Bank & Trust Co. v. Zagoria*, 250 Ga. 844, 302 S.E.2d 674 (S.C. Geo. 1983) where a lawyer-shareholder was held liable to a client of a professional corporation for funds misappropriated by another lawyer-shareholder. But *cf. Birt v. St. Mary Mercy Hospital of Gary, Inc.*, 175 Ind. App. 32, 370 N.E.2d 379 (1977) where a doctor-shareholder was held not liable for malpractice of another doctor-shareholder in the corporation. As to the liability of lawyers for obligations of a professional corporation that are not related to some aspect of professional practice, compare: *South High Development Ltd. v. Weiner, Lippe & Crawley Co.*, 4 Ohio St. (3d) 1, 445 N.E.2d 1106 (Ohio S.C. 1983) (liable for lease); and *Schapp, Hochberg & Sommers v. Nislow*, 431 N.Y.S.2d 324 (1980).

is a special concern where dealing with litigation brought in the name of the corporation,[64] since such an entity may not be able to meet any award of costs against it. Nevertheless, as a legal person a corporation should not be denied resort to the courts on the basis that it is impecunious, any more than the poor should be denied such access. Provided that a proceeding is instituted in good faith, and is not clearly without merit, it is doubtful whether it can or should be restrained, merely because the corporation that instituted it has only nominal assets.

§2.23 The limited liability conferred in respect of the corporation's debts, obligations and liabilities upon the shareholders (or members) of a corporation exist only in their capacity as such. It may be lost where a shareholder acts in some other capacity, as for instance if the shareholder is a director or officer of the corporation and breaches some duty owed to it, or commits some wrong on the corporation's behalf. But the tendency in the law is against imposing any such liability.[65] A shareholder, employee or officer of a corporation is not liable for a breach of contract unless he or she induced that breach of contract.[66] Moreover, an employee or officer of a corporation is not necessarily personally liable for a tort committed by the corporation merely because he or she participates incidentally in it in that capacity;[67] however, liability will attach where the officer becomes a party to the tort in question.[68]

§2.24 The failure to follow proper corporate formalities and procedures (*e.g.*, such as the holding of meetings and the adoption of formal resolutions) is sometimes invoked in justification for ignoring the corporate veil. If, by reason of the informal way in which a corporation carries on its business or conducts its affairs, it becomes difficult for an outsider to tell whether he or she is dealing with a corporation or its shareholder(s), then there may be some justification for ignoring the corporate veil.[69] There are, however, clear risks in the courts taking a too aggressive approach along these lines. Many corporations carry on small-scale businesses. Their shareholders are not particularly sophisticated and lack ready access to legal and other relevant professional advice. Often, merely running the business is a full-time occupation, leaving the owner little time to take care of formalities.[70] Generally speaking, the courts shy away from imposing personal liability merely due to some innocent error on the part of corporate

---

[64] See *Junction Contracting Services Ltd. v. Allen*, [2003] A.J. No. 777 (Q.B.), *per* Lee J. and the cases cited therein.
[65] *W.D. Latimer Co. v. Dijon Investments Ltd.*, [1992] O.J. No. 2909, 12 O.R. (3d) 415 (Gen. Div.).
[66] *Sealand of Pacific Ltd. v. Robert C. McHaffie Ltd.*, [1974] 6 W.W.R. 724 (B.C.C.A.).
[67] See, generally, *Rainbow Industrial Caterers v. C.N.R.*, [1988] B.C.J. No. 1710, 46 C.C.L.T. 112 (C.A.); *B & A Log Homes Ltd. v. Evans* (1988), Doc. Nos. 13/87/CA, 14/87/CA (N.B.C.A.), varying Doc. Nos. F/C/69/86, F/C/589/86.
[68] *Rainbow Industrial Caterers v. C.N.R.*, [1988] B.C.J. No. 1710, 46 C.C.L.T. 112 at 137 (C.A.), *per* Esson J.A. It is also necessary to show that the employee caused the damages suffered by the victim and owed an independent duty of care towards the victim: *Food Giant Markets v. Watson Leaseholds Ltd.*, [1987] A.J. No. 1125, 43 C.C.L.T. 152 at 157 (Q.B.), *per* Picard J.
[69] See, generally, *Weisser v. Mursam Shoe Corp.*, 127 F.2d 344 (2d Cir. 1942).
[70] See, generally, *Zubik v. Zubik*, 384 F.2d 267 (3rd Cir. 1967).

directors or shareholders. For instance, in *Jenice Ltd. v. Dan*,[71] the name of a company was misspelled on its cheques. The directors of the company were held not to be liable personally despite the spelling or typographical error.

§2.25 Even where the corporation has been properly organized, the shareholder will not enjoy limited liability where he or she enters into a specific transaction in his or her personal capacity, rather than through the corporation.[72] Similarly, the shareholder will be personally liable if there is an incomplete transfer of a pre-existing unincorporated business to a newly formed corporation, so that the shareholder continues to carry on business in his or her personal name, without any indication that the business is being operated by a corporation.[73] In *Chaing v. Heppner*,[74] a watch was left with a jeweler for repair. The claim ticket gave no indication that the business was being operated by a limited corporation. All the dealings between the shop and the customer were conducted on a personal basis. It was held that the jeweler was personally liable for the negligent repair of the watch.[75] Personal liability may also result where the corporation is not properly identified. For instance, in *Tato Enterprises Ltd. v. Rode*,[76] the shareholder did not properly identify the corporation in its correspondence, contracts and dealings. It was held that this was sufficient to deny the shareholder the benefit of limited liability. Furthermore, accrued rights of action subsisting against proprietors or partners of an unincorporated business are not affected by the subsequent transfer of the business to an unincorporated entity.[77]

(iii) Piercing (Lifting) the Corporate Veil

§2.26 The terms "lift the corporate veil" and "pierce the corporate veil" are synonyms describing the practice of ignoring the separate personality (and liability) of a corporation in certain situations.[78] The expression "pierce the corporate veil" has been dismissed as a vivid but imprecise metaphor.[79] Be that as it may, the phrase and the concept to which it relates are so entrenched in corporate law, that it is impossible now to move away from them.[80]

§2.27 Whatever the factual relationship between a corporation and its shareholders might be, the corporation cannot simply be regarded as a creature or

---

[71] [1994] B.C.C. 43 at 45 (Q.B.).
[72] *Coast Wholesale Appliances Ltd. v. Buffalo*, [1990] A.J. No. 21, 103 A.R. 307 (Q.B.). In that case, the plaintiff agreed to supply goods to the defendant under a credit agreement which identified the defendant as a sole proprietor. Subsequently, the defendant incorporated the business. He argued that as a result of the incorporation, he was not personally liable for credit that was subsequently extended by the plaintiff. Master Fundunk rejected this argument (at 309).
[73] *Royal Stores Ltd. v. Brown* (1956), 5 D.L.R. (2d) 146 (Nfld. T.D.).
[74] (1978), 6 B.C.L.R. 76, 85 D.L.R. (3d) 487 (Co. Ct.).
[75] See also *Wolfe v. Moir* (1969), 69 W.W.R. 70 (Alta. T.D.).
[76] (1979), 17 A.R. 432 (Dist. Ct.).
[77] *Alers-Hankey v. Solomon*, [1997] B.C.J. No. 1869, 35 B.L.R. (2d) 264 (S.C.).
[78] *Shillingford v. Dalbridge Group Inc.*, [1996] A.J. No. 1063, 28 B.L.R. (2d) 281 (Q.B.).
[79] *Re Polly Peck International plc*, [1995] B.C.C. 486 at 497 (Ch.), *per* Robert Walker J.
[80] The general basis for piercing the corporate veil was explained by Devlin L.J. in *Merchandise Transport Ltd. v. British Transport Commission*, [1962] 2 Q.B. 173 at 202 (C.A.).

puppet of its shareholders in point of law, for the law deems it to be a separate person. Corporations are by definition a legal fiction: a mere construct of the law, which exists only in the eyes of the law.[81] While widely held corporations may deal with their shareholders on an arm's length basis, narrowly held corporations only rarely do so. When one looks at a narrowly held corporation to inquire into its economic character, it may well appear to be the alter ego of its shareholders. But the legislation does not limit the benefits of incorporation to widely held corporations. On the contrary, corporations wholly owned by a single shareholder are expressly envisaged under the Act.[82] Mere control is not sufficient to justify piercing the corporate veil.[83] It is settled law that the separate personality of a company and its shareholders will not be ignored merely because it might be said on some basis to be fair in the circumstances for this to be done.[84]

§2.28 Thus the courts are generally unwilling to pierce the corporate veil[85] and will normally do so only where required to do so by statute[86] or where extraordinary circumstances exist.[87] Cases falling within the latter category are confined within a narrow compass.[88] Taking advantage of the limited liability of a corporation *per se* is not improper. If a person chooses to deal with a corporation, then he or she is limited in recourse to whatever assets the corporation may itself own.[89] The occasional judgment suggests that courts are particularly unwilling to pierce the corporate veil where the corporation concerned has been in business for a considerable period of time, it is solvent, and there is no evidence of dis-

---

[81] *DeWitt Truck Brokers v. W. Ray Flemming Fruit Co.*, 540 F.2d 681 (4th Cir. 1976), *per* Donald Russell Cir. J.
[82] *Pioneer Distributors Ltd. v. Bank of Montreal*, [1994] B.C.J. No. 2093, 28 C.B.R. (3d) 266 at 278 (S.C.), *per* Holmes J.
[83] *W.D. Latimer Co. v. Dijon Investments Ltd.*, [1992] O.J. No. 2909, 12 O.R. (3d) 415 (Gen. Div.).
[84] See, generally, *Re Polly Peck International plc*, [1996] 2 All E.R. 433.
[85] See, for instance, *Gregorio v. Intrans-Corp.*, [1994] O.J. No. 1063, 15 B.L.R. (2d) 109, additional reasons at 109n (C.A.); *Re Polly Peck International plc*, [1996] 2 All E.R. 433 (Ch.), *per* Robert Walker J.
[86] *Bank Voor Handel en Scheepvaart NV v. Slatford*, [1953] 1 Q.B. 248 at 278 (C.A.), *per* Devlin J.; *Dimbleby & Sons Ltd. v. National Union of Journalists*, [1984] 1 All E.R. 751 at 758 (H.L.), *per* Lord Diplock: a statutory authority to pierce the corporate veil must be set out in clear and unequivocal language.
[87] For instance, the courts will sometimes ignore the corporate veil where necessary to prevent a statutory scheme of entitlement from being thwarted. So, for example, the courts have been prepared to ignore the corporate veil in family law cases, for the purposes of attributing income to a spouse: *Arsenault v. Arsenault*, [1998] O.J. No. 1423, 78 A.C.W.S. (3d) 745 (Fam. Ct.). See also *Mantei v. Morris*, [1997] S.J. No. 448, 157 Sask. R. 43 (Q.B.) dealing with a decision by a Workers' Compensation Board to impose liability as an employer on the individuals who stood behind a corporation.
[88] See, generally, *Kinookimaw Beach Assn. v. Saskatchewan*, [1979] S.J. No. 255, [1979] 6 W.W.R. 84 at 88 (C.A.), *per* Culliton C.J.S., leave to appeal to S.C.C. ref'd 30 N.R. 267. The fact that the court does lift the corporate veil for a specific purpose does not affect the status of the corporation as an independent and autonomous entity for other purposes: *Nedco Ltd. v. Clark*, [1973] 6 W.W.R. 425 at 433 (Sask. C.A.), *per* Culliton C.J.S.
[89] *W.D. Latimer Co. v. Dijon Investments Ltd.*, [1992] O.J. No. 2909, 12 O.R. (3d) 415 at 426 (Gen. Div.), *per* Mandel J.

honesty relating to the conduct of its business or affairs.[90] The courts are also unwilling to lift the corporate veil where to do so would contravene the express terms of a contract entered into by the party who is seeking to have it lifted.[91] However, the weight of these factors and the circumstances when they will apply are not at all clear.

§2.29 It is difficult to discern any general principle that the courts have followed in the handling of such cases. However, one unifying thread of reasonably broad application is that the separate personality of a corporation will be disregarded where the corporation has been used as a cover for deliberate wrongdoing.[92] So, for instance, the courts are prepared to lift the veil:

- where the company has been used as a cloak for fraud[93] or manifestly improper conduct[94] — although in such cases there is no need to lift the corporate veil in order to affix liability on the shareholder who perpetrated the fraud, as the shareholder will be personally liable for the fraud as a co-party;[95]

- where there is a trust relationship,[96] especially where the target who will be attached by lifting the veil has benefitted from a breach of that trust;[97]

- where the company is involved in criminal activity directed by its shareholders.

Absent such abuse, the instances in which the courts are prepared to ignore the separate personality of the corporate entity are very rare, and are for the most part limited to cases where the corporation has carried on business as an agent for its shareholders, or has appeared in the circumstances to do so. What follows is a more detailed consideration of the law as summarized in this general synopsis.

---

[90] See, generally, *Harris v. Nugent*, [1995] A.J. No. 719, 32 Alta. L.R. (3d) 126 (Q.B.), rev'd [1996] A.J. No. 1068, 32 Alta. R. (3d) 126 (C.A.), leave to appeal to S.C.C. ref'd, [1997] S.C.C.A. No. 77, 221 N.R. 160*n*.

[91] See, generally, *Davrose Holdings Ltd. v. Phoenix Leasing Ltd.*, [1993] B.C.J. No. 1444, 80 B.C.L.R. (2d) 289 (C.A.).

[92] See, generally, *Gilford Motor Co. v. Horne*, [1933] Ch. 935 at 956 (C.A.), *per* Lord Hanworth M.R.; *Jones v. Lipman*, [1962] 1 All E.R. 442 (Ch.); *Green v. Bestobell Industries Ltd.*, [1982] W.A.R. 1 (S.C. West. Aust.); *Creasey v. Breachwood Motors Ltd.*, [1992] B.C.C. 638 (Q.B.); *Re A Company* (1985), 1 B.C.C. 99,421 (C.A.). In *Barle v. Home Owners Cooperative*, 309 N.Y. 103, 127 N.E.2d 832 (C.A.N.Y. 1955), *per* Froessel J.

[93] *Pioneer Laundry & Dry Cleaners Ltd. v. Minister of National Revenue*, [1940] A.C. 127 at 137 (H.L.).

[94] *Lockharts Ltd. v. Excalibur Holdings Ltd.*, [1987] N.S.J. No. 450, 47 R.P.R. 8 (T.D.); *Gilford Motor Co. v. Horne*, [1933] Ch. 935; *Smith v. Hancock*, [1894] 2 Ch. 377 (C.A.).

[95] *B.G. Preeco I (Pacific Coast) Ltd. v. Bon Street Holdings Ltd.*, [1989] B.C.J. No. 1032, 43 B.L.R. 67 at 79 (C.A.), *per* Seaton J.A.

[96] *Jones v. Lipman*, [1962] 1 W.L.R. 832 (Ch.); *Abbey Malvern Wells Ltd. v. Ministry of Local Government & Planning*, [1951] Ch. 728.

[97] *Hurley v. BGH Nominees Pty Ltd.* (1982), 6 A.C.L.R. 791 (S.C.S. Aus.).

(1) Where Provided by Statute

§2.30 In a good many cases the legislature has provided an express authority for piercing the corporate veil[98] and affixing liability on shareholders,[99] directors[100] or other persons in effective control of the corporation,[101] or some relevant aspect of its activities.[102] Many such situations are specified under tax legislation, but such provisions crop up in many different contexts, including where the principals behind a company fail to describe it as a "limited" company.[103] In general, it is more common for statutes to impose liability upon directors than shareholders, as in the case of the personal liability imposed upon director for wages.[104] The scope of statutory liability is a matter of statutory interpretation, and in each case is decided in accordance with the normal rules governing the construction of legislation.

§2.31 Various tax laws expressly provide for the penetration of the corporate veil.[105] Except where one of the other corporate veil-piercing criteria is satisfied,[106] the extent of the authority so conferred appears to be primarily a matter

---

[98] *Bank Voor Handel en Scheepvaart NV v. Slatford,* [1953] 1 Q.B. 248 at 278 (C.A.), *per* Devlin J.
[99] OBCA, s. 243(1).
[100] *Income Tax Act,* R.S.C. 1985, c. 1 (5th Supp.), s. 227.1.
[101] See, for instance, subsection 13(1) of the *Construction Lien Act,* R.S.O. 1990, c. C.30:

13(1) In addition to the persons who are otherwise liable in an action for breach of trust under this Part,

(a) every director or officer of a corporation; and

(b) any person, including an employee or agent of the corporation who has effective control of the corporation or its relevant activities,

who assents to, or acquiesces in, conduct that he or she knows or reasonably ought to know amounts to breach of trust by the corporation is liable for the breach of trust.

[102] See, for instance, s. 99(2) of the *Environmental Protection Act,* R.S.O. 1990, c. E.19, as amended:

99(2) Her Majesty ... has the right to compensation,

(a) for loss or damage incurred as a direct result of,

(i) the spill of a pollutant that causes or is likely to cause an adverse effect,

(iii) neglect or default in carrying out a duty imposed or an order or direction made under this Part,

from the owner of the pollutant and the person having control of the pollutant.

[103] Early case law was to the effect that a statute could give express or implicit authority to lift the corporate veil: *Merchandise Transport Ltd. v. British Transport Commission,* [1962] 2 Q.B. 173 (C.A.). Compare however, *Dimbleby & Sons Ltd. v. National Union of Journalists,* [1984] 1 All E.R. 751 at 758 (H.L.), *per* Lord Diplock: a statutory authority to pierce the corporate veil must be set out in clear and unequivocal language.

[104] *Crabtree (Succession de) v. Barrette,* [1993] S.C.J. No. 37, 10 B.L.R. (2d) 1; liability imposed under CBCA; personal liability of director for tax deducted at source under the *Income Tax Act*: *Lindthaler v. Minister of National Revenue* (1992), 8 B.L.R. (2d) 159 (T.C.C.).

[105] See, for instance, *R. v. Myers,* [1977] C.T.C. 507 (Dist. Ct.); *Appleby v. Minister of National Revenue,* [1974] S.C.J. No. 127, [1974] C.T.C. 693, 74 D.T.C. 6514.

[106] See, for instance, *R. v. Esskay Farms Ltd.,* [1976] C.T.C. 24, 76 D.T.C. 6010 (Fed. T.D.); *C.I.R. v. Duke of Westminster,* [1936] A.C. 1 (H.L.).

of statutory interpretation,[107] which turns upon the wording of the statute in question. However, in contrast to the various rules applicable for piercing the corporate veil in order to collect additional tax, at least one jurisdiction has adopted the approach of deeming certain non-corporate entities as corporations. Under Treasury Regulation 301.7701-2 made under the United States *Internal Revenue Code,* a partnership may be treated as a company where it has more than two of the following corporate characteristics: (1) limited liability; (2) centralized management; (3) free transferability of interests; (4) continuity of life. Furthermore, under section 7704 of the *Internal Revenue Code,* certain types of publicly traded limited partnerships are treated as companies for tax purposes.[108] These rules take the alleged justification for piercing the corporate veil to an illogical extreme. An argument may be made for piercing the corporate veil in order to overcome an entirely artificial organization created solely or primarily with the objective of reducing the amount of tax payable. But it is entirely another thing to deem a particular type of entity to exist on the basis that it might have been used, and, that if it had been used, it would have increased the amount of tax recovered.

(2) Fraud

§2.32 As noted above, the corporate veil will be pierced where the corporation is used as a cover for fraud by the persons who stand behind the corporation.[109] The case law in this area is extensive, and therefore worthy of being examined in detail.[110] There is no question that the corporation can itself be seen to have acted fraudulently.[111] In *Re Darby*[112] Darby and Glyde registered a company in Guern-

---

[107] Although in tax cases the courts have been particularly careful when deciding whether it is the corporation or the individual shareholder who stands behind it, in determining who is carrying on the business giving rise to income: *Kindree v. Canada (Minister of National Revenue),* [1964] C.T.C. 386, 64 D.T.C. 5248 (Ex. Ct.) — the diversion of income of a doctor to a corporation was held ineffective; *cf. Lamb v. Canada (Minister of National Revenue),* [1963] 34 Tax A.B.C. 79, 63 D.T.C. 975; *Sazio v. Canada (Minister of National Revenue),* [1968] C.T.C. 579, 69 D.T.C. 5001 (Ex. Ct.); *Holmes v. R.,* [1974] F.C. 353, [1974] C.T.C. 156, 74 D.T.C. 6143 (Fed. T.D.); *Canada (Minister of National Revenue) v. Cameron,* [1972] S.C.J. No. 137, [1972] C.T.C. 380, 72 D.T.C. 6325; *Canada (Minister of National Revenue) v. Leon,* [1977] F.C. 249, [1976] C.T.C. 532, 76 D.T.C. 6299 (C.A.); *Canada (Minister of National Revenue) v. Connor,* [1975] C.T.C. 2132, 75 D.T.C. 85 (T.R.B.).

[108] For instance, a partnership whose interests are traded on an established market or are readily tradeable on a secondary market. In general, real estate partnerships are excluded from this treatment, provided at least 90 per cent of its gross income constitutes qualifying income (such as rent).

[109] See, for instance, *Aveling Barford Ltd. v. Per Ion Ltd.,* [1989] B.C.L.C. 626 (Ch.); *I. Ramjit Inc. v. 3-for-1 Pizza & Wings (Canada) Inc.,* [2004] O.J. No. 5539, 6 B.L.R. (4th) 43 (S.C.).
See also *Re H & Others,* [1996] 2 All E.R. 391 (C.A.), where the corporate veil was lifted so as to treat the property of a company as realizable property of shareholder defendants where the company was used for fraudulent evasion of excise duty on a large scale from which the defendants had benefited.

[110] See, for instance, *Official Assignee v. 15 Insoll Avenue Ltd.,* [2001] 2 N.Z.L.R. 492 (H.C.) which discusses the general approach of the courts in such cases.

[111] *DPP v. Kent and Sussex Contractors Ltd.,* [1944] K.B. 146 (D.C.); *R. v. I.C.R. Haulage Ltd.,* [1944] K.B. 551 (C.A.).

[112] *Re Darby, ex p. Brougham,* [1911] 1 K.B. 95.

sey called City of London Investment Corporation ("CLI"). They were CLI's only directors even though they were un-discharged bankrupts, with a number of convictions for fraud. CLI purported to register an English company under the name Welsh Slate Quarries Ltd. A prospectus was issued to raise funds from the public. With the funds so raised, they sold a trivial interest in a Welsh slate quarry to the English company. Welsh Slate failed and the liquidator brought an action against Darby on the basis that he had made a secret profit from the company, contrary to the fiduciary duties imposed upon him as a promoter. Darby objected that he was not a promoter; Welsh Slate had been promoted by CLI. Phillimore J. held that in such a case the corporate veil could be disregarded.

§2.33 It is a fair question whether the "fraud" cases actually involve a lifting of the corporate veil at all. An alternative view is that they involve a particular manifestation of the rule that a corporate shareholder, director or officer who is personally a party to the commission of a tort (specifically fraud) is not shielded from personal liability for that tort merely because a corporation was used as a tool in the perpetration of that tort. The mere fact that a corporation has itself committed a fraud does not lead to the liability of its shareholder(s) for that fraud. Rather, liability attaches to a shareholder (or director or officer) only where it can be shown that this person also was involved in the fraud. So, for instance, in *Wah Tat Bank Ltd. v. Chan Cheng Kum*,[113] Lord Salmon observed:

> A tort may be committed through an officer or servant of a company without the chairman or managing director being in any way implicated. There are many such cases reported in the books. If, however, the chairman or managing director procures or directs the commission of the tort he may be personally liable for the tort and the damage flowing from it ... Each case depends upon its own particular facts.

Where the actions of a shareholder (or other person standing behind a corporation or acting as its operative) are themselves tortious or exhibit a separate identity or interest from that of the corporation so as to make the act or conduct that forms the basis of the claim the act or conduct of that shareholder or other person, personal liability will flow.[114] This approach is consistent with the notion that everyone should be answerable for his or her own tortious acts.[115]

(3) The Corporation as Agent

§2.34 As we have seen, on the right facts a corporation may be held to have acted as the agent of its owner. In order for limited liability to apply, the company must act for itself rather than as an agent of the shareholder.[116] However,

---

[113] [1975] A.C. 507 at 514-15 (P.C.); *Performing Right Society Ltd. v. Ciryl Theatrical Syndicate Ltd.*, [1924] 1 K.B. 1 at 14-15 (C.A.), *per* Atkin L.J.
[114] See, generally, *Blacklaws v. 470433 Alberta Ltd.*, [2000] A.J. No. 725, 1 C.C.L.T. (3d) 149, 261 A.R. 2 (C.A.); *Montreal Trust Co. of Canada v. ScotiaMcLeod Inc.*, [1995] O.J. No. 3556, 26 O.R. (3d) 481 (C.A.), leave to appeal denied [1996] S.C.C.A. No. 40, 205 N.R. 314*n* (S.C.C.); *Jackson v. Trimac Industries Ltd.* [1994] A.J. No. 445, 155 A.R. 42 (C.A.).
[115] *Morgan v. Saskatchewan*, [1985] S.J. No. 124, 31 B.L.R. 173 (C.A.).
[116] *Clarkson Co. v. Zhelka*, [1967] 2 O.R. 565 (H.C.).

there is a presumption that a transaction is what it purports to be[117] and so as a general rule a contract made by it will not be impugned back to the owner of the corporation on an agency basis unless it can be shown that both parties so intended at the time of the formation of the contract.[118] Clear evidence of agency will be required to defeat the presumption that the company is acting on its own behalf.[119] The courts are loath to find that a company was acting as the agent of its shareholders.[120] The overwhelming current in the case law is that the separate status of a corporation must be respected.[121] It is appropriate to lift the corporate veil only where special circumstances exist indicating that the corporation is a mere facade concealing the true facts.[122]

(4) The Corporation as Facade or Alter Ego

§2.35 In some cases, the courts have also ignored the separate existence of a corporation in cases where the corporation can be said to be a sham[123] or simulacrum or a facade[124] or alter ego of its shareholders.[125] Generally, in order to a corporation

---

[117] *Snook v. London & West Riding Investments Ltd.*, [1967] 2 Q.B. 786 at 804 (C.A.), *per* Russell L.J. and at 801 *per* Diplock L.J.; *Susan Hosiery Ltd. v. Minister of National Revenue (No. 2)*, [1969] C.T.C. 533 (Ex. Ct.).

[118] *J.H. Rayner (Mincing Lane) Ltd. v. Department of Trade & Industry*, [1989] Ch. 72 at 189 (C.A.), *per* Kerr L.J. For an example of a case involving an express agency agreement, see *Rainham Chemical Works Ltd. v. Belvedere Fish Guano Co.*, [1921] 2 A.C. 465 (H.L.).

[119] *Export Brewing & Malting Co. v. Dominion Bank*, [1934] O.R. 560 at 579, *per* Masten J.A., rev'd on other grounds *(sub nom. E.B.M. Co. v. Dominion Bank)*, [1937] 3 All E.R. 555 (P.C.); *Kentucky Fried Chicken Canada v. Scott's Food Services Inc.* (1998), 35 B.L.R. (2d) 21, rev'd 41 B.L.R. (2d) 42 (C.A.).

[120] See, generally, *Chenier v. Johnson* (1964), 48 D.L.R. (2d) 380 at 383-84 (B.C.S.C.), *per* Ruttan J.; but see *Provincial Electric (1969) Ltd. v. Registered Holdings Ltd.* (1977), 34 N.S.R. (2d) 100 at 105, *per* Anderson Co. Ct. J. See also *Firestone Tyre & Rubber Co. Ltd. v. Lewellin*, [1957] 1 All E.R. 561 (H.L.); *Trebanog Working Men's Club & Institute Ltd. v. MacDonald*, [1940] 1 K.B. 576 (Div. Ct.): liquor bought by incorporated club in its own name was held to have been bought on behalf of its members; but compare: *Wurzel v. Houghton Main Home Delivery Service Ltd.*, [1937] 1 K.B. 380 (Div. Ct.). See also *Dennis Willcox Pty. Ltd. v. FCT* (1988), 14 A.C.L.R. 156 at 163 (F.C.), *per* Jenkinson J.

[121] See, generally, *Dominion Royalty Corp. v. Goffatt*, [1935] O.R. 169, aff'd [1935] S.C.R. 565, *per* Masten J.A.

[122] *Woolfson v. Strathclyde Regional Council*, [1978] 38 P. & C.R. 521 at 526 (H.L.), *per* Lord Keith.

[123] *Ascot Investments Pty. Ltd. v. Harper* (1981), 148 C.L.R. 337 (H.C. Aust.), *per* Gibbs J. As to the meaning of "sham" see *Stubart Investments Ltd. v. The Queen*, [1984] S.C.J. No. 25, [1984] 1 S.C.R. 536 at 545, *per* Estey J. Note also the warning given by Diplock L.J. in *Snook v. London & West Riding Investments Ltd.*, [1967] 1 All E.R. 518 at 528 (C.A.) as to the narrowness of the term.

[124] See, for instance, *Pacific Rim Installations Ltd. v. Tilt-Up Construction Ltd.* (1978), 5 B.C.L.R. 231 (Co. Ct.). The term "simulacrum" (which is certainly not in popular usage) means an effigy, image or representation. While the terms sham, simulacrum, facade and alter ego are used by the courts as if they describe different circumstances, they are virtually undefined, and, if for no other reason, can therefore be treated as if they are synonymous.

[125] *DeWitt Truck Brokers v. W. Ray Flemming Fruit Co.*, 540 F.2d 681 (4th Cir. 1976), *per* Donald Russell Cir. J.:

> ...[I]n applying the "instrumentality" or "alter ego" doctrine, the courts are concerned with reality and not form, with how the corporation operated and the individual defendant's relationship to that corporation. One court has suggested that courts should ab-

to be so held, the evident appearance to those who have been said to have dealt with the corporation must be that it is the shareholder that is carrying on business, rather than the corporation itself. For instance, liability may attach to a parent corporation, when it and its subsidiary conduct themselves as if they were a single entity.[126] In *Dominion Bridge Co. v. R.*,[127] the taxpayer was a Canadian steel manufacturer which purchased part of its steel requirements from foreign mills. A wholly owned subsidiary was incorporated in the Bahamas in order to act as a supplier of foreign steel. The purpose was found by the court to be "to put aside part of [Dominion Bridge's] profits in the hands of Span for safekeeping in a tax-free country and [it] could always repatriate these profits to Canada tax free". Accordingly, the corporate veil was disregarded.

§2.36 The question which arises in such cases is whether the sham, facade, *etc.*, cases add anything to the fraud,[128] breach of trust[129] and agency cases — for instance, the Bahamas subsidiary in the Dominion Bridge case might just as easily have been viewed as the agent of its Canadian parent. The authorities are divided on this point. As the courts themselves have noted, it is no easy task to decide when to lift the corporate veil on the grounds that the corporation is such a facade.[130] This is with good reason: for as the corporation is by definition an artificial entity — that is, a legal fiction — it is necessarily a sham, alter ego,

---

jure "the mere incantation of the term 'instrumentality'" in this context and, since the issue is one of fact, should take pains to spell out the specific factual basis for its conclusion. ... And the authorities have indicated certain facts which are to be given substantial weight in this connection. One fact which all the authorities consider significant in the inquiry, and particularly so in the case of the one-man or closely-held corporation, is whether the corporation was grossly under-capitalized for the purposes of the corporate undertaking. ... Other factors that are emphasized in the application of the doctrine are failure to observe corporate formalities, non-payment of dividends, the insolvency of the debtor corporation at the time, siphoning of funds of the corporation by the dominant stock holder, non-functioning of other officers or directors, absence of corporate records, and the fact that the corporation is merely a facade for the operations of the dominant stock holder or stock holders. The conclusion to disregard the corporate entity may not, however, rest on a single factor ... but must involve a number of such factors; in addition, it must present an element of injustice or fundamental unfairness.

Other considerations beyond those listed above include whether creditors provided credit on the basis of some informal assurance from the shareholder: *Weisser v. Mursam Shoe Corp.*, 127 F.2d 344 (2nd Cir. 1942); *American Wholesale Corp. v. Mauldin*, 128 S.C. 241, 122 S.E. 576 (1924). See also *Minton v. Cavaney*, 15 Cal. Rptr. 641, 364 P.2d 473 (S.C. Calif. 1961).

[126] *R. v. CAE Industries* (1989), 20 D.L.R. (4th) 347 (Fed. C.A.).
[127] [1977] C.T.C. 554 (Fed. C.A.).
[128] For a case where the veil was lifted where a corporation used it as a device or facade to facilitate criminal activity on the part of the persons standing behind it, see: *Re H & Others*, [1996] 2 All E.R. 391 (C.A.).
[129] For a recent case involving a conspiracy to breach trust, sufficient to justify the lifting of the corporate veil, see: *Levy-Russell Ltd. v. Tecmotiv Inc.*, [1994] O.J. No. 650, 13 B.L.R. (2d) 1 (Gen. Div.).
[130] See, for instance, the decision of Rand J. in *Aluminum Co. of Canada v. Toronto (City)*, [1944] S.C.R. 267 at 271-72.

simulacrum or facade for its shareholders, and this becomes more and more true as the number of shareholders approaches the limit of one.[131]

§2.37 Neither agency nor "nomineeship", still less a sham, will be inferred merely because a subsidiary corporation has a small amount of issued capital and has a board of directors all or most of whom are also directors or senior officers of the parent company.[132] A subsidiary corporation will necessarily be under the control of the parent and will be especially so where the parent governs the corporation directly under a unanimous shareholder agreement. In such a case how else can the corporation be characterized other than as a puppet? Yet subsection 4(1) of the Ontario *Business Corporations Act* expressly permits one person to incorporate a corporation, and subsection 92(1) of the OBCA provides: "The shareholders of a corporation are not, as shareholders, liable for any act, default, obligation or liability of the corporation ...". Thus control by one person should have no effect upon the limited liability of the shareholder.

§2.38 As we have seen, if the corporation is not carrying on business, then there can be no liability of the corporation from which the shareholder can be insulated.[133] This, however, is a question entirely separate from that of whether or not it is a sham. The shareholder may have entered into liabilities of his or her own, but in such a case the shareholder's liability is unlimited not because the corporation itself is not effective, but rather because the corporation is not involved as a party to the transaction concerned.[134] If, however, the corporation carries on business and while so acting enters into a contract, it can only do so in one of two capacities: either it may contract in the capacity of an agent or it may contract for its own benefit. If the corporation contracts as an agent, it is not necessary to enter into a consideration of whether the corporation is a façade; the shareholder will be liable as a principal solely on the basis of the law of agency. Yet as we have seen, in order to hold that a corporation is an agent of its shareholders, it must be possible to conclude that the corporation would be an agent even if the purported principal had no interest in the corporation at all.

§2.39 There are a number of sham-based corporate veil cases that are difficult to fit into the mainstream of Canadian case law. For instance, in *Canada Life Assurance Co. v. CIBC*,[135] Gale C.J.O. reviewed prior cases, and then attempted to devise a schedule of criteria that could be applied in deciding whether or not to disregard the separate existence of a corporation as a mere sham. He said:

> I do not suggest that the foregoing represent all of the cases relating to whether, in particular circumstances, the corporate form and independence are to be respected. They do not, however, provide sufficient basis on which to tentatively catalogue

---

[131] *Rainham Chemical Works Ltd. v. Belvedere Fish Guano Co.*, [1921] 2 A.C. 465 at 475 (H.L.), *per* Lord Buckmaster.
[132] *Re Polly Peck International plc*, [1995] B.C.C. 486 at 496 (Ch.), *per* Robert Walker J.
[133] *Simpson v. Montreal Trust Co.* (1915), 21 R.L.N.S. 206 (Que. K.B.).
[134] See, for instance, *Royal Stores Ltd. v. Brown* (1956), 5 D.L.R. (2d) 146 (Nfld. T.D.); *Peak Mechanical Ltd. v. Lewko*, [2005] S.J. No. 201, 3 B.L.R. (4th) 75 (Q.B.).
[135] [1974] O.J. No. 1839, 3 O.R. (2d) 70 at 84-85 (C.A.).

factors relevant to this determination. By way of a tentative catalogue, I offer the following relevant criteria:

(1) the capitalization of the subsidiary;

(2) the degree of observance of corporate formalities;

(3) the extent of the relationship between the business of the parent and subsidiary;

(4) the nature and extent of the business dealings between parent and subsidiary;

(5) the corporate histories of both parent and subsidiary;

(6) the relationship between the boards of directors and upper management personnel of parent and subsidiary; and

(7) the extent of the ownership interest of the parent in the subsidiary.[136]

While the existence of several of these factors might be significant, it is doubtful whether any of them individually is sufficient to justify the piercing of the corporate veil. For instance, the capitalization of the subsidiary can scarcely be relevant, for as Lord Davey observed in *Salomon*,[137] the legislature has not seen fit to impose a minimum capitalization requirement, nor is there any restriction, as there is in the case of many types of regulated financial institutions, on the extent to which a corporation may leverage its share capital. Since the legislature has chosen to leave the appropriate capitalization of a corporation to the market, there is no apparent basis on which the courts may impose their own requirements.

§2.40 The degree of observance of corporate formalities is clearly important, but it is doubtful whether formalities add any real substance to the "sham" concept, so as to vary the law from what would exist and apply in its absence. If the corporation has not been validly incorporated and organized, then it cannot carry on business no matter how much the corporate form may be used.[138] Where the corporation has been validly incorporated and organized the sole question is whether it is carrying on business, and if it is, whether it is doing so on an agency basis. Thus the façade question does not come into play.[139]

§2.41 Considerable caution would seem to be justified before ignoring the corporate veil on the basis of the relationship between the board and officers of the parent and subsidiary, for in this area of intra-corporate affairs, the legislature itself has been quite active. Subsection 92(1) of the Ontario *Business Corporations Act* — which provides for the limited liability of a shareholder — expressly provides that a shareholder will be liable under three specific provisions of the Act, namely subsections 34(5) and 108(5) and section 243. Significantly, however, it makes no suggestion that a sole shareholder of a corporation will be

---

[136] *Canada Life Assurance Co. v. CIBC*, [1974] O.J. No. 1839, 3 O.R. (2d) 70 at 84-85 (C.A.), leave to appeal to S.C.C. ref'd, [1974] S.C.R. viii.
[137] *Salomon v. Salomon & Co.*, [1897] A.C. 22 (H.L.).
[138] See, for instance, *Phonogram Ltd. v. Lane*, [1982] Q.B. 938 (C.A.), *per* Lord Denning M.R.
[139] *Rainham Chemical Works Ltd. v. Belvedere Fish Guano Co.*, [1921] 2 A.C. 465 at 475 (H.L.), *per* Lord Buckmaster.

liable as a shareholder where the shareholder enters into a unanimous shareholder declaration under subsection 108(4), even though subsection 108(5) of the OBCA does provide that where such a declaration is made, the shareholder will be liable for the duties and liabilities of a director under the Act, to the extent that the declaration in question relates to a matter to which those duties and liabilities pertain. Since the question of shareholder liability has clearly been considered by the legislature and provided for in the Act, any further implication of liability — except where it can be done under general principles of agency law — would seem to be excluded on the basis of the *expressio unius* rule of statutory construction.

§2.42 The last factor touched upon in Gale C.J.O.'s list[140] — the extent of minority interest — can be particularly difficult to apply. A *bona fide* minority share-holding may preclude a finding that the corporation is a facade.[141] But that does not mean that a corporation without such a share-holding is a facade.[142]

§2.43 In conclusion, it would therefore seem to follow that there is no basis on which the separate personality of a corporation may be disregarded on the grounds that the corporation is a mere sham, simulacrum, facade or alter ego of its shareholders, merely because the benefits derived from its operations ultimately flow back to the people by whom it has been called into existence, since the OBCA and the CBCA expressly contemplate that people may substitute the limited liability of the company for the unlimited liability of the individual, with the object that by this means enterprise and adventure may be encouraged.[143] In general, save in the case of fraud (which provides a separate basis for penetrating the corporate veil), creditors who deal with a corporation that has not acted as an agent have no ground for complaint that they have no claim against its shareholders. If they do not wish to deal with the corporation on a limited liability basis, they may insist on a guarantee or take their business elsewhere. Having decided to contract with a limited liability corporation, they cannot afterwards be heard to complain of its limited liability.[144]

§2.44 Although the unifying principles of the sham cases are difficult to identify, the following propositions would nonetheless seem to provide a reasonable approach to guide courts as to when it is appropriate to disregard the separate personality of a single shareholder corporation *vis-à-vis* its shareholder. A corporation should not be viewed as an agent (in the absence of an actual agency agreement) or alter ego or sham where:

---

[140] *Canada Life Assurance Co. v. CIBC*, [1974] O.J. No. 1839, 3 O.R. (2d) 70 (C.A.), leave to appeal ref'd [1974] S.C.R. viii.
[141] *Commissioners of Inland Revenue v. Sansom*, [1921] 2 K.B. 472 at 509 (C.A.), *per* Scrutton L.J.
[142] See the judgment of Lord Herschell *Salomon v. Salomon & Co.* [1897] A.C. 22 (H.L.).
[143] *Rainham Chemical Works Ltd. v. Belvedere Fish Guano Co.*, [1921] 2. A.C. 465 at 475 (H.L.), *per* Lord Buckmaster.
[144] *Clarkson Co. v. Zhelka*, [1967] 2 O.R. 565 (H.C.), *per* Thompson J., approved by Gale C.J.O. in *Canada Life Assurance Co. v. CIBC*, [1974] O.J. No. 1839, 3 O.R. (2d) 70 (C.A.), leave to appeal ref'd [1974] S.C.R. viii.

(a) the shareholders of the corporation respect the separate ownership by the corporation of its own property, thereby recognizing in effect that it is to that property that the creditors of the corporation must look for their payment; and

(b) the corporation's board of directors can be seen to be performing their duties as directors to act in good faith, with a view to its best interests, and are performing their other duties owed to that corporation by law (and thereby implicitly to all other persons interested in the corporation, including its creditors and security holders).

Since it is perfectly permissible under the Ontario *Business Corporations Act* and the *Canada Business Corporations Act* for a corporation to have a single shareholder, and since such a shareholder must necessarily be exposed to the moral certainty of profit if that corporation succeeds, or loss should it fail, it is not sufficient to show only that the shareholder's interest is inescapably linked to the fortunes of the corporation.[145] On the other hand, if the shareholder(s) of a corporation:

(c) treat the property of the corporation as it it belonged to the shareholders to do with as they wish, without regard to the interests of other persons dealing with the corporation; or

(d) cause the board of that corporation to disregard the interests of the corporation and act instead solely in the interests of the shareholder, without regard to other persons having an interest in or claim against the corporation,

so that in effect the corporation becomes a mere instrumentality employed by the shareholder in pursuit of his or her own interest, then there is, no doubt, good reason to disregard the separate personality of the corporation. In so doing, the court would merely be adopting the same approach to the corporation as that which has been adopted by the shareholder personally.

(5) Miscellaneous Cases Involving Lifting the Veil

§2.45 The courts have on occasion lifted the veil in cases that involve no evident element of wrong-doing, as for instance:

- where it is necessary to determine the residence of the company;
- in the interest of defence or national security;[146]
- where to recognize the veil would be contrary to public policy.[147]

---

[145] See, generally, *Gregorio v. Intrans-Corp.*, [1994] O.J. No. 1063, 18 O.R. (3d) 527 (C.A.).
[146] *Daimler Co. v. Continental Tyre & Rubber Co. (Great Britain) Ltd.*, [1916] 2 A.C. 307 (H.L.); *V/O Sovfracht v. Gebr Van Udens Scheepvaart en Agentuur Maatschapij*, [1943] A.C. 203 (H.L.).
[147] *Re FG (Films) Ltd.*, [1953] 1 All E.R. 615 (Ch.); see also *R. v. Secretary of State for Transport, ex p. Factortame Ltd.*, [1992] Q.B. 680 (E.C.J.); *Gilford Motor Co. v. Horne*, [1933] Ch. 935; *Dimes v. Grand Junction Canal Proprietors* (1852), 3 H.L. Cas. 759; *Barakot Ltd. v. Epiette Ltd.*, [1997] B.C.L.C. 303 — *res judicata*: whether a corporation can bring an action when a previous action by a shareholder was dismissed.

The separate personality of a corporation may also be pierced for the purpose of determining whether the corporation is an enemy alien. A company incorporated within Canada will assume an enemy character in time of war if it is controlled by enemy aliens or by persons who are situate within enemy territory.[148] Perhaps on a somewhat related basis, separate corporate personality is also sometimes disregarded in deciding whether a particular corporation qualifies for a benefit provided by the state to its citizens.[149]

§2.46 The limited liability of a corporation may sometimes justify a court in granting *Mareva*[150] type relief to restrain the corporation from dealing with its assets pending the resolution of litigation, where the effect of the dealings in question would be to place assets necessary to do justice to a plaintiff in the litigation beyond the reach of the plaintiff.[151] For instance, in *R. v. Consolidated Fastfrate Transport Inc.*[152] the respondent was charged with an offence under the *Competition Act*. If convicted, the Crown intended to seek a fine of $8-million. The respondent had recently sold its assets to a newly incorporated company for $6.8-million. The Crown applied for an injunction prohibiting the respondent from disposing of the proceeds of sale of its assets until after the criminal trial was completed, arguing that such an injunction was required in the public inter-

---

[148] *R. v. Uscan Engineering Corp.* (1949), 7 C.R. 417, [1949] 1 W.W.R. 780 (N.W.T. Mag. Ct.); *Daimler Co. v. Continental Tyre & Rubber Co. (Great Britain) Ltd.*, [1916] 2 A.C. 307 (H.L.); *R. v. L.C.C., ex p. London & Provincial Electric Theaters Ltd.*, [1915] 2 K.B. 466.
[149] *Re FG (Films) Ltd.*, [1953] 1 All E.R. 615 (Ch.).
[150] *Mareva Compania Naviera, SA v. International Bulk Carriers, SA*, [1980] 1 All E.R. 213 (C.A.).
[151] In *Rohani v. Rohani*, [2004] B.C.J. No. 2493, 135 A.C.W.S. (3d) 672 (C.A.) a trial judge ordered that a husband's company post security for a compensation order made in a family law dispute. The judgment was appealed. It was held that the real issue was whether the corporate veil should be pierced. Since the company had been used as a corporate vehicle before the separation and had legitimate business, succession, and tax planning objectives, it was a genuine corporation. The company had not been used to defeat the wife's claims, although there had been an irregular use of corporate funds to cover the personal expenses of its principals. It was held that the order granting security directly against the assets of the company could not be supported, but that injunctive relief could be ordered to protect the wife's interest. See also *Evetts v. Evetts*, [1996] B.C.J. No. 2614, rev'd [1995] O.J. No. 1855 (C.A.).
[152] [1995] O.J. No. 61, 22 O.R. (3d) 172 (Gen. Div.). On appeal, at [1995] O.J. No. 1855, the Court of Appeal overruled the issue of the injunction on the ground that McCombs J. had incorrectly equated the committal for trial alone with the establishment of a strong *prima facie*. It was necessary for the Court to examine the transcripts of the evidence taken at the preliminary hearing. Galligan J.A. (giving the majority judgment) held that the following principles apply to the granting of a Mareva type of injunction issued in aid of a criminal prosecution:

  (1) The Crown must demonstrate that the accused person has assets within the jurisdiction of the court.

  (2) The Crown must demonstrate a strong *prima facie* case (i) that the accused person will likely be convicted of the offence with which it is charged, and (ii) that the amount of the fine will likely equal or exceed the value of the assets sought to be attached.

  (3) The Crown must demonstrate that the accused person is or has been dissipating, removing or disposing of its assets for the improper purpose of making them unavailable to pay a fine in the event of conviction.

  (4) The Crown must give the usual undertaking respecting damages.

est to ensure that there would be sufficient funds available to pay the fine. After concluding that there was a jurisdiction to grant the injunction sought in a criminal case, McCombs J. provided the following summary of the considerations relevant to the decision as to whether to issue the injunction:

> ... I have concluded that the following questions are appropriate to be asked in determining whether the relief sought should be granted:
>
> 1. Has the applicant established that there is a strong *prima facie* case on the merits?
>
> 2. Is the respondent disposing of its assets in a manner out of the ordinary course of business, so as to make tracing of assets remote or impossible?
>
> 3. Would there be irreparable harm suffered if the injunction is not granted?
>
> 4. In balancing the relative inconvenience of the applicant and the respondent, whose interests should prevail?[153]

(6) Principal Appearing in Court

§2.47 As a mere fiction, a corporation cannot truly appear in person before a court or tribunal. Ordinarily, leave will not be given to a director or shareholder of a corporation to appear in person on behalf of the corporation.[154] However, it has been held that a corporation should be permitted to be represented by a director or shareholder where it is unable to afford a lawyer, and its rights are likely to be affected by a proceeding.[155]

(7) Contract vs. Tort

§2.48 Where the creditor (or other person) who is seeking to lift the corporate veil has entered into a contractual relationship with the corporation, it can be argued strongly that the separate existence of even a minimally capitalized corporation causes no injustice to the creditor. At least in the normal case, the parties to a transaction are free to choose whatever lawful arrangement will suit their purpose. Where they do so in circumstances where there is no deception of one part by the other, effect should be given to the true nature of the transaction, including the legal forms and arrangements actually entered into. A party should not be permitted to dismiss as mere machinery for effecting the purposes of the parties the form of the transaction adopted by them.[156]

§2.49 If a person knowingly deals with a corporation, it is open to him or her to inquire into its capital strength. Where the capital of a corporation is considered by that person to be inadequate, he or she can refuse to deal with the corporation unless a personal guarantee is provided (as, for instance, by a shareholder or

---

[153] *Ibid.*, at 179-80.
[154] *Professional Sign Crafters (1988) Ltd. v. Wedekind*, [1993] A.J. No. 35, 8 Alta. L.R. (3d) 11 (Master).
[155] See, generally, *Lakeway Heights Developments Inc. v. Royal Bank*, [1992] B.C.J. No. 255, 65 B.C.L.R. (2d) 132 (C.A.), leave to appeal to S.C.C. ref'd 68 B.C.L.R. (2d) xxxiw (S.C.C.).
[156] See, generally, *Mills v. Dowdall*, [1983] N.Z.L.R. 154 at 159 *per* Richardson J.

director) or until the under-capitalization of the corporation is corrected. Indeed, transactions are often entered into in the name of a shell corporation, precisely because the shareholders do not wish to assume the risk of loss associated with a particular enterprise. By entering into a contract with a corporation in such circumstances, the creditor must be taken to have assumed the risk of loss. When the parties have apportioned the risk of loss between themselves, upon the terms and through the mechanisms by which the transaction was structured, there is no reason for the court to disturb this allocation of risk.[157] Nevertheless, there are often complaints that it is not practical for suppliers of goods, services or finance to inquire into the question of the capitalization of the corporations with which they deal. This point would seem more valid, if it was unusual for corporations to be inadequately capitalized. In fact, however, the vast majority of corporations have only minimal capital.[158] Thus if anything, a person dealing with a corporation has no reason to believe that it has more than nominal capital behind it. The natural assumption where dealing with a corporation would surely be that it is only nominally capitalized. Presumably, those corporations which are sufficiently capitalized, will go out of their way to signal this fact to their suppliers, so as to obtain more favorable credit terms.

§2.50 Academic commentators have occasionally raised the question of whether the courts should be more willing to pierce the corporate veil in the case of involuntary creditors, such as the victims of a tort which does not arise out of a pre-existing contractual relationship between the corporation and the victim.[159] Where a person voluntarily deals with an under-capitalized corporation, he (or she) may be seen to take on the risk that the corporation will be unable to repay the credit provided. On the other hand, the victim of a tort often has no choice over who causes injury or damage. Surprisingly little attention has been paid in the case law to this apparently fundamental distinction in the case law, although in recent years there has been some suggestion that it may be a factor in deciding whether the veil ought to be lifted.[160]

§2.51 One problem in seeking to differentiate tort from contract claims is that in many cases a tort claim may arise within the context of a contractual relation-

---

[157] See, for instance, *Bell Oil & Gas Co. v. Allied Chemical Corp.*, 431 S.W.2d 336 (Tex. C.C.A. 1968).
[158] In England, the Registrar of Companies maintains a public record of the issued capital of companies incorporated under the *Companies Act, 1985*. These records (for 1992-93) show that approximately 62 per cent have issued capital of less than £100. While corresponding statistics are not available for Ontario *Business Corporations Act* or *Canada Business Corporations Act* corporations, similarly low capitalization of most corporations would undoubtedly be true in Canada.
[159] See, generally, H. Hansmann, R. Kraakman, "Toward Unlimited Shareholder Liability for Corporate Torts" (1991) 100 Yale L.J. 1879; Hamilton, "The Corporate Entity" (1971) 49 Texas L. Rev. 979 at 985; see also: Robert Zimet, "The Validity of Limited Tort Liability for Shareholders" (1973) 23 Am. U.L. Rev. 208; *Biggs v. James Hardie & Co. Pty. Ltd.* (1989), 7 A.C.L.C. 841 (N.S.W.C.A.), per Rogers A.J.A.
[160] See, for instance, *Alvi v. Misir*, [2004] O.J. No. 5088, 73 O.R. (3d) 566, 50 B.L.R. (3d) 175 at 196 (S.C.), per Cameron J.; *ADGA Systems International Ltd. v. Valcom Ltd.*, [1999] O.J. No. 27, 43 O.R. (3d) 101 (C.A.).

ship. In *Mangan v. Terminal Transport System*[161] the plaintiff was injured as a result of the negligent operation of a cab. It was found that the cab was owned and operated by one of four operating companies which were all affiliated with the defendant TTS. The owners of TTS were essentially the same as the owners of the four operating companies, and the name of TTS was displayed on the sides of all of the cabs used by the companies concerned. TTS serviced, inspected, repaired and dispatched the cabs. To an outsider, it would have appeared that he or she was dealing with TTS rather than with the separate cab-owning companies. On these facts, it was held that there was sufficient cause to pierce the corporate veil of the company which operated the cab which injured the plaintiff, so as to attach liability to TTS.[162]

§2.52 However, later cases have indicated that the TTS case was limited by its unusual facts. In *Walkovsky v. Carlton*[163] a claim was brought by a tort plaintiff against the sole shareholder of a corporation which owned a cab which had injured the plaintiff in a car accident. The assets of the corporation concerned consisted of only two cabs. The shareholder-defendant owned 10 such corporations. On a preliminary motion by the shareholder-defendant, Fuld J. indicated that the courts were less willing to pierce the corporate veil where the effect would be to attach liability to an individual, rather than to another corporation. The court seems to have taken the view that not only must the tortfeasor take his or her victim as found, but so too the victim must take his or her tortfeasor. Following this decision, Walkovsky amended his pleading to allege that Carlton was "conducting the business of the taxicab fleet in [his] individual capacity". A motion to dismiss for failure to state a cause of action was dismissed, and the action was then settled.[164]

§2.53 In *US v. Bestfoods*[165] the Untied States Supreme Court considered the liability of a parent corporation under the *Comprehensive Environmental Response, Compensation, and Liability Act of 1980* ("CERCLA"), for environmental damage caused by a subsidiary corporation. Section 107(*a*)(2) of CERCLA authorizes claims against "any person who at the time of disposal of any hazardous substance owned or operated any facility". The trial focused on the question of whether the parent corporation ("CPC"), had "owned or operated" the plant of its subsidiary ("Ott II") within the meaning of section 107(*a*)(2). The District Court said that operator liability may attach to a parent corporation both indirectly, when the corporate veil can be pierced under common law, and directly, when the parent has exerted power or influence over its subsidiary by actively participating in, and exercising control over, the subsidiary's business during a period of hazardous waste disposal. Applying that test,

---

[161] 247 App. Div. 853, 286 N.Y.S. 666, leave to appeal denied 272 N.Y. 676 (C.A. 1936).
[162] See also *Western Rock Co. v. Davis*, 432 S.W.2d 555 (Tex. Civ. App. 1968).
[163] 18 N.Y.2d 414, 276 N.Y.S.2d 585, 223 N.E.2d 6 (C.A. 1966).
[164] *Walkovsky v. Carlton (No. 2)*, 287 N.Y.S.2d 546 (App. Div.), affd 23 N.Y.2d 714, 296 N.Y.S. (2d) 362, 244 N.E. (2d) 565 (C.A. 1968).
[165] 524 U.S. 51 (1998).

the court held that CPC could be held liable, taking into account the following facts:

- CPC had selected Ott II's board of directors and had appointed its executive officers;
- An officer of CPC had played a significant role in shaping Ott II's environmental compliance policy.

§2.54 The Sixth Circuit reversed this decision, concluding that a parent corporation's liability for operating a facility ostensibly operated by its subsidiary depends on whether the degree to which the parent controls the subsidiary and the extent and manner of its involvement with the facility amount to the abuse of the corporate form that will warrant piercing the corporate veil and disregarding the separate corporate entities of the parent and subsidiary. Since the two corporations maintained separate personalities and CPC did not utilize the subsidiary form to perpetrate fraud or subvert justice, CPC could not be held liable.

§2.55 At the Supreme Court, it was held that CERCLA liability applied against a parent corporation only when the corporate veil could be pierced. The court noted that it is a general principle of corporate law that a parent corporation is not liable for the acts of its subsidiaries. Subject to the range of cases in which the veil could be lifted, the court would not ignore that principle in the absence of a clear legislative intent, since to abrogate a common-law principle, a statute must speak directly to the question addressed by the common law.

§2.56 Nevertheless, the court made clear that a parent corporation that actively participated in, and exercised control over, the operations of its subsidiary's facility could be held directly liable in its own right under section $107(a)(2)$ as an operator of the facility. In such cases, the parent would be liable for its own actions, rather than on some derivative basis as a result of the actions of the subsidiary. The court held that under the plain language of section $107(a)(2)$, any person who operates a polluting facility is made directly liable for the costs of cleaning up the pollution, and this is so even if that person is the parent corporation of the facility's owner. The court concluded that to "operate" a facility had its ordinary meaning: to direct the workings of, manage, or conduct the affairs of the facility. It was necessary to show that the purported operator managed, directed, or conducted operations specifically related to the leakage or disposal of hazardous waste, or decisions about compliance with environmental regulations.

§2.57 The Supreme Court concluded that the Sixth Circuit was right to reject imposing direct liability analysis on little more than CPC's ownership of Ott II and its majority control over Ott II's board of directors. Instead, the question of liability should have focused on the relationship between CPC and the facility itself, *i.e.*, on whether CPC "operated" the facility, as evidenced by its direct participation in the facility's activities. The District Court's focus on the relationship between parent and subsidiary (rather than on whether there was a relationship between parent and the facility), combined with its automatic attribution of the actions of dual officers and directors to CPC was erroneous, given the absence of any legislative intent to alter common law principles regarding the separate nature of corporate enterprise. However, the Supreme Court also commented that the ordinary meaning of the verb "to operate" extends also to situations in which joint officers or directors of a parent and subsidiary conduct the affairs of the facility on behalf of the parent, or agents of the parent with no position in the subsidiary manage or direct activities at the subsidiary's facility. Norms of corporate behaviour were held to be crucial reference points, both for determining whether a dual officer or director has served the parent in conducting operations at the facility, and for distinguishing a parental officer's oversight of a subsidiary from his or her control over the operation of the subsidiary's facility. For instance, it was relevant whether the direction given by the joint officers and directors departed from accepted norms of parental oversight of a subsidiary's facility, so that the direction could be attributed back to the parent.

(8) Where the Shareholder Will Benefit from Lifting the Veil

§2.58 While in most cases it is contrary to the interests of the shareholders of a company for the courts to lift the corporate veil, on occasion, the courts have considered whether to lift the corporate veil where it is necessary to do so in order to protect the company or its shareholders.[166] For instance, by incorporating, the shareholders will lose their personal interest in the business transacted by the corporation.[167] However, there are exceptions.

§2.59 In *Manley Inc. v. Fallis*[168] the defendant was employed by one plaintiff, which was a wholly owned subsidiary of the second plaintiff. The defendant established his own business which competed with the parent company, but not against his employer. In defense of a claim by his employer and parent company for breach of fiduciary duty, it was argued that his activities were not injurious to his employer and he owed no fiduciary duty to the parent company of his employer. On these facts, the court was prepared to ignore the separate corporate personality of the employer and parent company and allow the claim for breach of fiduciary duty.[169]

---

[166] See for instance *Roccograndi v. Unemployment Comp. Bd. of Review*, 197 Pa. Super. 372, 178 A.2d 786 (S.C. Penn. 1962); *Moose Securities Ltd. v. Minister of National Revenue* (1963), 31 Tax A.B.C. 145, 63 D.T.C. 182 (T.A.B.). In *MacPhail v. Tackama Forest Products Ltd.*, [1993] B.C.J. No. 2170, 11 B.L.R. (2d) 19 (S.C), Leggatt J. held that the owner of a professional service corporation could bring an action for wrongful dismissal against an employer which had hired the personal service corporation rather than the owner. He concluded that in the circumstances there was an independent employment relationship between the plaintiff owner and the defendants that existed collaterally to the formal agreement between the defendant and the professional service corporation. Where such a collateral relationship exists, it is not necessary to lift the corporate veil.

[167] *Roccograndi, ibid.*, at 178-79. See also *Woolfson v. Strathclyde Regional Council*, [1978] 38 P. & C.R. 521, [1978] S.L.T. 159, [1978] S.C. (H.L.) 90, *per* Lord Keith.

[168] (1977), 2 B.L.R. 277, 38 C.P.R. (2d) 74 (Ont. C.A.).

[169] See also *Petten v. E.Y.E. Marine Consultants*, [1998] N.J. No. 369, 180 Nfld. & PE.I.R. 1 (S.C.).

§2.60 In *MacPhail v. Tackama Forest Products Ltd.*[170] the plaintiff was employed by the defendant Tackama as an accountant. Some years after starting work for the defendant, he arranged (for tax reasons) for his salary to be paid to a company (Longspur Management) that he owned. After he was fired, he sued for wrongful dismissal. The defendant argued that it had no contract with the plaintiff. Its relationship was with Longspur Management. Justice Leggett concluded[171] that on the facts it was not necessary to lift the corporate veil. There was an independent employment relationship between the defendant and the plaintiff, existing collaterally to the formal agreement between Longspur and the defendant. The use of the corporation was "only a mode of payment".[172]

§2.61 The *Manley* and *MacPhail* cases may perhaps be explained as a reverse application of the corporate group concept sometimes invoked in employment law.[173] Yet in most cases even where it would be beneficial to the shareholders to disregard the separate personality of the corporation, the courts have shown a marked unwillingness to do so,[174] and on some occasions have even gone so far as to suggest that they are less willing to do so for the benefit of the shareholders than for their detriment.[175] The decision of the House of Lords in *Re Bank of Credit and Commerce International S.A. (No. 8)*[176] provides an excellent illustration as to how the separate personality of a corporation may just as easily work against the interests of a shareholder as in his or her favour. In that case, a controlling shareholder ("S") of a corporation ("D") was a depositor in BCCI, an insolvent bank in the process of liquidation. That deposit was pledged to guarantee the repayment of a debt owed by D to BCCI. Instead of enforcing the guarantee given by S and claiming that deposit in payment of the debt owing, BCCI decided to sue D itself (the corporation being quite solvent, and able to pay the debt owing). D argued that there should be a right to set off the deposit in BCCI against the debt owed by D. BCCI argued that no right of set-off was available. The debt owed by it in relation to the deposit was owed to one person (S), the debt that it was trying to enforce was owed by another (D); it was not obliged to enforce the guarantee, but was perfectly entitled to claim against the principal debtor. S's rights with respect to the deposit were limited to whatever

---

[170] [1993] B.C.J. No. 2170, 11 B.L.R. (2d) 19 (S.C.).
[171] *Ibid.*, at 22.
[172] See also *Bird v. Warnock Hersey Professional Services Ltd.*, [1980] B.C.J. No. 2057, 25 B.C.L.R. 95 (S.C.), per Locke J.; *Goldberg v. Western Approaches Ltd.*, [1985] B.C.J. No. 937, 7 C.C.E.L. 127 (S.C.), per Taylor J.
[173] See above at paras. 258 and 259.
[174] See *R. v. Deslaurier*, [1992] M.J. No. 502, 77 C.C.C. (3d) 329 (C.A.); *R. v. Marstar Trading International Inc.*, [1999] O.J. No. 2644, 138 C.C.C. (3d) 87, [1999] C.R.D.J. 377 (C.A.), both dealing with the Charter right to trial within a reasonable time.
[175] *Constitution Insurance Co. of Canada v. Kosmopoulos*, [1987] S.C.J. No. 2, 36 B.L.R. 233 at 240-41 (S.C.C.), per Wilson J. More than one court has expressed the view that anyone who has chosen to pursue the benefits of incorporation must bear the corresponding burdens, so that the veil will not be lifted for the benefit of the principal standing behind a corporation, but only in the interests of third parties who would otherwise suffer as a result of that choice: see, for instance, *Toronto Board of Education v. Brunel Construction 2000 Ltd.*, [1997] O.J. No. 3783, 74 A.C.W.S. (3d) 206 (Gen Div.), per Kiteley J.
[176] [1997] 4 All E.R. 568 (H.L.).

dividend might be paid to the depositors as a result of the liquidation of the bank. The House of Lords agreed with BCCI's position.[177]

§2.62 The decision of the Supreme Court of New South Wales *Segenhoe Ltd. v. Akins*,[178] is a somewhat interesting case that is worth discussing at this juncture. In this case, the court considered a claim brought on behalf of a company, to recover money improperly paid to its shareholders in the form of dividends. The defendants were the auditors of the company, who were to audit its financial statements. The accounts overstated retained profits, and as a result the company paid an additional dividend, $494,111 of which impaired the company's issued capital. The company claimed this amount from DHS in damages for negligence. It was argued that to permit such a claim could result in the shareholders of the company twice receiving the same money. Giles, J. observed:

> ... the company as a separate entity is out of pocket to the extent of the money paid away. The effect of the company being out of pocket may be different: those who ultimately suffer may be the shareholders rather than the creditors. But the effect in the case of a solvent company may vary according to whether or not the company is trading profitably; not having the money paid away may be what takes a solvent company into insolvency; or an insolvent company may nevertheless trade out of its difficulties. To investigate and forecast these effects would be to embark upon a never-ending process. ... [It] does not seem to me that in principle the company is unable to recover the money so paid away because it was paid to shareholders rather than to a third party or third parties. That would negate the company's status as a legal entity separate from its shareholders and the shareholders' lack of any proprietary interest in the company's assets.

The possibility that the shareholders might ultimately receive a double recovery was not seen as a valid answer to the company's claim.

> Further, recovery of the money paid away does not necessarily mean that shareholders will be paid twice over. Even if the shareholders remain the same, the company may or may not distribute the amount recovered by way of further dividend; it may or may not make profits from the use of that amount; it may have suffered in its trading between payment out and recovery such that the recovery only restores its position. Inquiry into these matters would be akin to the never-ending process to which I previously referred. Changes in shareholding may mean that there is a real loss to shareholders occasioned by the company being out of pocket which is not matched by receipt of the dividend wrongly paid. An incoming shareholder will not necessarily pay a price for his shares discounted so as to reflect the company being out of pocket, and thus will not necessarily receive a benefit, or the equivalent of a benefit, twice over if the company recovers the money paid away. If the submission for DHS were to be accepted incoming shareholders may be disadvantaged, and it can not be that the result should differ according to when in relation to changes in shareholding the proceedings were brought to a successful conclusion, or according to an investigation of the position of each of the shareholders.

---

[177] *Ibid.*, *per* Lord Hoffmann at 573.
[178] (1990), 1 A.C.S.R. 691 (S.C.N.S.Q.).

(iv) The Corporate Group Concept

§2.63 Until the enactment of the former Ontario *Business Corporations Act* in 1970, Ontario law required three incorporators to apply for the incorporation of a corporation.[179] At that time, this requirement was repealed, and it became possible for a single incorporator to incorporate a corporation; similarly, a single shareholder was thereafter expressly permitted to own all shares in the corporation. The Ontario Select Committee made clear that it was its intent to bring the law in line with commercial practice and needs, so as to allow a single individual or parent company to carry on business through a wholly owned corporation:

> This Committee, as was the case with the 1952 Select Committee and with the Jenkins Committee, has considered whether the law should permit the so-called "one-man" company, that is, a company having but a single shareholder. For practical purposes, the one-man company has been recognized in law since Salomon's case. Particularly this is true in Ontario and other jurisdictions which provide for private companies. The private or closely-held company is not infrequently beneficially owned by one person or company. The law should be brought in line with reality by giving statutory sanction to the judicial recognition of one-man companies. The limited company, being a separate legal entity distinct from its incorporators and shareholders, it should not matter, in law, whether a company has one beneficial owner or many or whether such one owner is a natural person or a company ...
>
> The majority of corporations in Ontario are no doubt in essence "one-man" companies. The Committee has concluded that the existing statutory minimum number of three incorporators (and, infrequently, of shareholders) is arbitrary and artificial causing unnecessary inconvenience. We do not consider that a reduction in the number of incorporators of companies would encourage "irresponsible incorporations" or facilitate fraud. The concept of one-man companies can be given recognition in the Ontario Act without detrimentally affecting rights of creditors or other persons dealing with corporations. This recommendation would bring Ontario law into line with the laws of 16 of the states of the United States including New York, Pennsylvania, Illinois and Michigan.[180]

This change was eventually adopted across the country.

§2.64 The concepts of limited liability and separate personality have come in for most criticism in the case of parent and subsidiary corporations. More generally, it is sometimes suggested that the commercial realities of corporate group structure necessitates a re-examination of existing corporate liability and entitlement rules.[181] Where a group of corporations with interlocking ownership carry on what is in effect a single combined and integrated economic enterprise, the question arises as to whether the law should disregard the separate corporate vehicles conducting each aspect of the combined enterprise, and treat the group

---

[179] See *The Corporations Act*, R.S.O. 1960, c. 71, s. 3(1).
[180] *Report of the Ontario Select Committee on Company Law* (Toronto: Legislature of Ontario, 1969), 1.2.3 and 1.2.6.
[181] See, for instance, Bob Baxt, "Tensions Between Commercial Reality and Legal Principle — Should the Concept of the Corporate Entity be Re-examined?" (1991), 65 Australian L. Journal 352.

as a single entity. The traditional view with respect to such corporate groups has been summarized as follows:

> ... [E]ach company in a group of companies (a relatively modern concept) is a separate legal entity, possessed of separate legal rights and liabilities so that the rights of one company in a group cannot be exercised by another company in that group even though the ultimate benefit of the exercise of those rights would enure beneficially to the same person or corporate body.[182]

Group enterprise, involving the combined operations of several distinct corporate entities, all of which ultimately are wholly owned by one single shareholder, is a widespread feature of modern commerce. The following schematic illustrates such a relationship involving a British parent holding company, which owns operating companies carrying on an integrated operation in Canada, the United States and Australia. The complex web of corporate relationships illustrated in respect of Canada, might well be mirrored in the United States and Australia.

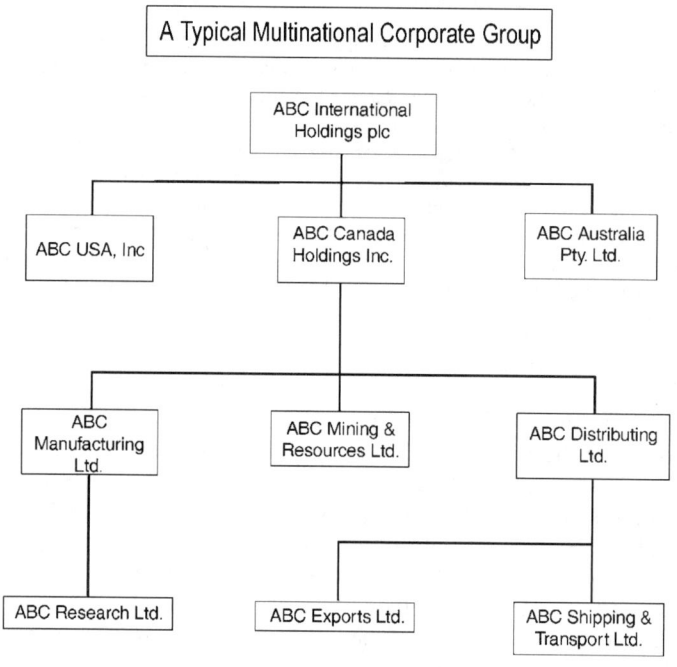

---

[182] *The Albazero*, [1977] A.C. 774 at 807, *per* Roskill L.J.

§2.65 One area in which the corporate group concept has been successfully employed is in the area of employment related claims, including claims for wrongful dismissal. It is now widely accepted that in order to effect to employee rights and obligations, an employer may have more than one employee, and for this purpose the courts are willing to disregard form, formal contractual limits and independent corporate structure. The willingness to do so is not open-ended. Some genuine nexus must be shown between the "employee" and "employer" concerned.[183]

§2.66 The traditional rule is the logical outgrowth of the decision in *Salomon v. Salomon & Co.*,[184] and is clearly consistent with a wide range of basic principles of corporate law, not the least of which are the restrictions on the provision of financial assistance among members of a corporate group.[185] It is also consistent with the notion that the obligation falls upon a creditor to identify the customer with whom he or she is dealing. Nevertheless, it is often suggested that it is inappropriate to treat the members of a corporate group as separate entities. The point is made with most force where two or more corporations carry on related operations which constitute in substance a single joint economic enterprise. As often as not, the question has been raised in connection with the question of whether a particular member is entitled to claim the benefit of a contract[186] or other entitlement, rather than whether a claim can be enforced against it.[187] For instance, in *Qintex Australia Finance Ltd. v. Shroders Australia Ltd.*,[188] the court dealt with the question of which of a group of companies was able to claim the benefit of a contract entered into by the defendant. The facts were that the defendant had received instructions from one member of the group to purchase a forward contract for Japanese yen. A loss occurred on the contract, and the defendant company appropriated funds from an account of the plaintiff company, which was another member of the group, to reduce the debt owed to the defendant. The defendant argued that it had always treated the entire group as its client, and that it did not differentiate between the members of the group. Chief Justice Rogers Comm. D. commented upon the extent to which such practices were common in the business world and continued that it might be beneficial:

> ... for Parliament to consider whether this distinction between the law and commercial practice should be maintained. This is especially the case today when the many collapses of conglomerates occasion many disputes. Regularly, liquidators of subsidiaries, or of the holding company, come to court to argue as to which of

---

[183] See *Downtown Eatery (1993) Ltd. v. Ontario*, [2001] O.J. No. 1879, 14 B.L.R. (3d) 41 (C.A.) and the cases cited therein.
[184] [1897] A.C. 22 (H.L.).
[185] See the Ontario *Business Corporations Act*, R.S.O. 1990, c. B.16, s. 20; *Canada Business Corporations Act*, R.S.C. 1985, c. C-44, s. 44. See also *Walker v. Wimborne* (1976), 137 C.L.R. 1 (H.C. Aust.).
[186] See, however, *Tate Access Floors Inc. v. Boswell*, [1991] Ch. 512 at 531, *per* Browne-Wilkinson V.C.
[187] See, for instance, *Multinational Gas and Petroleum Co. v. Multinational Gas and Petroleum Services Ltd.*, [1983] Ch. 258 (C.A.); *Industrial Equity Ltd. v. Blackburn* (1977), 137 C.L.R. 567 at 577 (H.C. Aust.), *per* Mason J.
[188] (1991), 9 A.C.L.C. 109 at 110 (S.C.N.S.W.), *per* Rogers C.J. Comm. D.

their charges bears the liability ... As well, creditors of failed companies encounter difficulty when they have to select from amongst the moving targets the company with which they consider they concluded a contract. The result has been unproductive expenditure on legal costs, a reduction in the amount available to creditors, a windfall for some, and an unfair loss to others. Fairness or equity seems to have little role to play.

§2.67 Courts have sometimes overcome the separate identity of group members by characterizing the activities of the group as being in the nature of a partnership.[189] The leading case adopting such an approach was the decision of the U.K. Court of Appeal in *DNH Food Distributors Ltd. v. Tower Hamlets London Borough Council*.[190] It was found that DNH ran a wholesale grocery business from premises owned by its wholly owned subsidiary (B). The only asset of B was the premises concerned, which was occupied only by DNH as a licensee. The property was expropriated by the Borough Council. Compensation was paid to B (as owner) of the property, for the value of the land itself. Compensation could be claimed by DNH only if it had an interest in the land greater than that of a bare licensee. Lord Denning M.R. held that in such a case the separate corporate existence of the various members of the group would be ignored, so as to allow DNH to obtain compensation:

> This group is virtually the same as a partnership in which all the three companies are partners. They should not be treated separately so as to be defeated on a technical point. They should not be deprived of the compensation which should justly be payable for disturbance.[191]

As Shaw L.J. noted in his judgment, there was an "utter identity and community of interest" between DNH and B, and the directors of DNH could at any time have caused B to transfer title to the premises from B to DNH itself. He continued:

> Why then should this relationship be ignored in a situation in which to do so does not prevent abuse but would on the contrary result in what appears to be a denial of justice? If the strict legal differentiation between the two entities of parent and subsidiary must, even on the special facts of this case, be observed, the common factors in their identities must at the lowest demonstrate that the occupation of DNH would and could never be determined without the consent of DNH itself. If it was a license at will, it was at the will of the licensee ... The President of the Lands Tribunal took a strict legalistic view of the respective positions of the companies concerned. It appears to me that it was too strict in its application to the facts of this case ...[192]

Goff L.J. came to a similar conclusion, but took care to make clear that as an authority for lifting the corporate veil, the case was confined to its unusual facts:

---

[189] See, for instance, *Western Canadian Place Ltd. v. Con-Force Products Ltd.*, [1997] A.J. No. 1299, [1998] 1 W.W.R. 527 (Q.B.).

[190] [1976] 3 All E.R. 462 at 467 (C.A.); see also *Pioneer Concrete Services Ltd. v. Yelnah Pty. Ltd.* (1986), 5 A.C.L.C. 467, 11 A.C.L.R. 108 at 117-18 (S.C.N.S.W.), per Young J.

[191] *DNH Food Distributors Ltd. v. Tower Hamlets London Borough Council*, [1976] 3 All E.R. 462 at 467 (C.A.).

[192] *Ibid.*, at 473.

... [T]his is a case in which one is entitled to look at the realities of the situation and to pierce the corporate veil. I wish to safeguard myself by saying that so far as this ground is concerned, I am relying on the facts of this particular case. I would not at this juncture accept that in every case where one has a group of companies one is entitled to pierce the veil ...[193]

§2.68 This narrow view of the scope of the *DNH* case has been echoed in Australia, where in *Pioneer Concrete Services Ltd. v. Yelnah Pty. Ltd.*, Young J. said:

> ... [I]t is only if the court can see that there is in fact or in law a partnership between companies in a group, or alternatively where there is a mere sham or facade that one lifts the veil. The principle does not apply in the instant case where it would appear that there was a good commercial purpose for having separate companies in the group performing different functions even though the ultimate controllers would very naturally lapse into speaking of the whole group as "us".[194]

§2.69 Efforts to extrapolate a general corporate group exception to the separate person concept have been less successful. In *Littlewoods Mail Order Stores Ltd. v. McGregor,* Lord Denning M.R. suggested that the courts will pierce the corporate veil in a wide range of situations, primarily on the basis of whether the corporation and its shareholders are factually distinct:

> It has often been supposed to cast a veil over the personality of a limited company through which the courts cannot see. But that is not true. The courts can and often do draw aside the veil. They can, and often do, pull off the mask. They look to see what really lies behind. The legislature has shown the way with group accounts and the rest. And the courts should follow suit. I think we should look at the Fork Company and see it as it really is — the wholly owned subsidiary of the taxpayers. It is the creature, the puppet, of the taxpayers in point of fact; and it should be regarded so in point of law.[195]

But this is far too extreme a position, and has gathered little support in the Commonwealth from the time it was first put forward.[196] What the legislature may have done in piercing the corporate veil offers no support or guidance to the courts. The legislature has made the corporation, and implicit in that power, is the power to unmake or qualify corporate existence. The courts enjoy no such authority. Moreover, they have been told by the legislature that corporations are to be treated as separate persons, and it is not within the province of the courts to ignore this instruction.[197]

---

[193] *Ibid.*, at 468; Justice Shaw also commented on the special nature of the facts; see also *Re Securitibank Ltd. (in liq.) & Ors,* [1978] 1 N.Z.L.R. 97 at 133, *per* Barker J. and at 158, *per* Richmond P.

[194] (1986), 5 A.C.L.C. 467, 11 A.C.L.R. 108 (S.C.N.S.W.). See also *Manley Inc. v. Fallis,* [1977] O.J. No. 1080, 38 C.P.R. (2d) 74 (C.A.), *per* Lacourcière J.A.; *Schouls v. Canadian Meat Processing Corp.,* [1983] O.J. No. 3020, 147 D.L.R. (3d) 81 at 83 (H.C.), *per* Trainor J.

[195] [1969] 1 W.L.R. 1241, [1969] 3 All E.R. 855 at 860 (C.A.); see also *Wallersteiner v. Moir,* [1974] 3 All E.R. 217 at 238 (C.A.), *per* Lord Denning M.R. Significantly, however, the subsidiary in the *Littlewoods* case was established for the sole purpose of obtaining a tax advantage, conducted no other business than holding a property used by the taxpayer shareholder, and was entirely dependent upon the shareholder for its existence.

[196] Lord Denning's views on this question were finally and completely rejected by the Court of Appeal in *Adams v. Cape Industries plc,* [1991] 1 All E.R. 929 at 1025 (C.A.).

[197] See, generally, *Stark v. Flemming,* 283 F.2d 410 (9th Cir. 1960).

§2.70 Although a corporation and its shareholder may have an identity of economic interest, the legal distinction between corporation and shareholder is so fundamental that it cannot be ignored.[198] Generally, the law is not concerned with the functional organization of the group. So long as the law remains as it is currently drafted, it appears that commercial reality in this context must give away to legal formality,[199] for the very purpose of the law is to create a separate legal person in the corporation. In the field of corporate law, form is to a very large extent often the same as substance. Cases in which the members of a corporate group can be regarded as a single entity are a very narrow exception rather than the rule.[200]

§2.71 Whether the exception should be so narrowly defined, is of course a separate question. A strong argument can be made for piercing the corporate veil where the parent corporation has misled the creditors of the subsidiary corporation into thinking that they are dealing with the parent rather than the subsidiary; indeed, it is possible to argue that the sham or alter ego cases can be explained in terms of whether such deceit has in practice been exercised. Such cases are, however, rare. It is less easy to justify the piercing of the corporate veil merely because a particular creditor has deluded itself into thinking that it is dealing with the parent company rather than a mere subsidiary, even where the parent and subsidiary might in some respects be characterized as carrying on a single integrated economic enterprise. In the absence of evidence of deliberate wrongdoing on the part of the parent corporation, it would open the door to the worst kind of self-serving evidence to allow the creditors of a subsidiary to claim that they thought they were dealing with the parent rather than with a separately incorporated subsidiary. It would also encourage sloppy credit-granting, while increasing the risk of penalizing those creditors who were careful in their credit practices. Moreover, the merit in allowing the subsidiary's creditors to pierce the corporate veil is even less clear where there are creditors of the parent who might thereby be prejudiced, when one considers that the parent's creditors may well only have extended credit to the parent on the basis that it was not liable for the risks that were being taken by its subsidiary corporation. It is difficult to understand why it is unreasonable to impose an obligation upon creditors to know the customers with which they are dealing. Leaving aside cases in which they are actually misled, if creditors do not take the time to inquire into this question, they have little cause for complaint if it ultimately turns out that the customer to which they have supplied is significantly less creditworthy than they hoped would be the case.

---

[198] *Bank of Tokyo v. Karoon*, [1986] 3 All E.R. 468 at 486 (C.A.), *per* Robert Goff L.J.; *Tunstall v. Steigmann*, [1962] 2 Q.B. 593 (C.A.), *per* Willmer L.J.: pointing out that the separate personality of the corporation from its shareholder(s) is a matter of substance, not form.

[199] *Bell v. Lever Bros. Ltd.*, [1932] A.C. 161 at 228 (H.L.): a holding company cannot sue to enforce rights belonging to its subsidiary, nor can a subsidiary sue to enforce rights belonging to its parent holding company: *Lindgren v. L. & P. Estates Ltd.*, [1968] Ch. 572 (C.A.).

[200] *Adams v. Cape Industries plc*, [1990] Ch. 433 (C.A.), *per* Slade L.J.

(v) The Veil Cases Are Exceptions

§2.72 Despite these limited exceptions, the overwhelming tendency within the law is to respect the separate existence of corporate enterprises. On occasion, allowing the owners of a corporation to shelter behind that corporation may seem arbitrary or unjust. However, the whole notion of corporate personality is itself arbitrary. The forms of corporation that are recognized, and the steps that must be satisfied in order to attain corporate status, could just as easily have been cast in very different terms. For instance, corporations sole are unique to the common law. The common law legal system also differs from other legal systems in that in common law a corporation must have members who are other persons. Many civilian legal systems have been influenced by the canon law, which recognizes corporations that are aggregates of things[201] — as do other legal systems.[202] Since corporations are inherently artificial in nature, all rules pertaining to them are likely to seem artificial in at least certain contexts. In deciding the scope that should be given to limited liability, an important consideration must be the function that limited liability apparently serves.

§2.73 It is sometimes said that limited liability is a "privilege", in the sense that there is a benefit conferred upon a business person in permitting investment and trade without risk of personal liability. In a sense this is true, but it is equally true that unlimited liability would be a privilege extended to those who deal with a business to allow claims against the owners of the business. There is no *a priori* reason to favour either limited or unlimited liability. In support of unlimited liability, there is a certain logic in the argument that business people who wish to enjoy the chance of profit must be willing to assume the risk of loss. However, in support of limited liability there is also some logic in the argument that creditors are paid interest to compensate them for the risk that a debtor will default, and having been so compensated, they have no legitimate claim to look further than the business to which they have extended credit. Applying the now near legendary Coase theorem[203] to the corporate law sphere, in a world of zero transaction costs, the same final allocation of rights, liabilities and immunities would eventually result through bargaining regardless of whether limited or unlimited liability was initially provided for under corporate law.[204] Assuming a

---

[201] Canon 115: Juridical persons in the Church are either aggregates of persons or aggregates of things ... An aggregate of things, or an autonomous foundation, consists of goods or things, whether spiritual or material, and is directed, in accordance with the law and the statutes, by one or more physical persons or by a college.

[202] *Pramatha Nath Mullick v. Pradyumna Kumar Mullick* (1925), L.R. 2 Ind. App. 245 (P.C.); see also *Thero v. Wijewardena*, [1960] A.C. 842; *Land Commissioner v. Pillai*, [1960] A.C. 854; *Salih v. Atchi*, [1961] A.C. 778.

[203] R.H. Coase, "The Problem of Social Cost" (1960) 3 J. Law & Econ. 1: in a competitive market economy in which transaction costs are nil, brargining will inevitably produce an efficient allocation of property rights, obligations, liabilities and risks, irrespective of the initial entitlement thereto that may be assigned by law to the parties who operate in that market.

[204] As to the economic implications of limited liability, see: R.E. Meiners, *et al.*, "Piercing the Veil of Limited Liability" (1979) 4 Delaware J. Corp. L. 351; P. Halpern, M. Trebilcock, S. Turnbull, "An Economic Analysis of Limited Liability in Corporation Law" (1980) 30 U.T.L.J. 117; F.H. Easterbrook, D.R. Fishel, "Limited Liability and the Corporation" (1985) 52 U. Chi. L. Rev. 89.

limited liability regime if the more efficient allocation of liability was unlimited, then even under a limited liability regime, creditors and suppliers would offer sufficiently lower costs or availability of credit to the principals behind a corporation to induce them to offer a guarantee for the corporation's debts and obligations.[205] If the more efficient allocation was limited liability, then the principals who stand behind a corporation would be prepared to offer higher interest costs and similar incentives to encourage creditors and suppliers to waive their right to claim against the principals personally.[206] Under the present Ontario limited liability corporate law regime, relatively few creditors bargain to obtain guarantees.

§2.74 As we shall discuss in greater detail below, in the United Kingdom, Nova Scotia and Alberta corporations may be created with unlimited liability, yet in practice this is rarely done, except where driven by tax considerations. This unpopularity suggests that suppliers and other creditors offer an insufficient economic incentive to encourage incorporators that adopt such a model.[207] In contrast, limited liability is preferred because it allows the principals behind a corporation to cap their exposure. Under an unlimited liability regime, the transaction of business raises the prospect of potential liability to an indeterminate amount to an indeterminate number of claimants. The problems with liability so broadly conceived have long been appreciated.[208] Given the extent to which limited liability has been employed to encourage economic activity, and the investments that have been made on the strength of this mechanism, it would be highly disruptive to the economy at this late date to second guess the use of limited liability as a risk-insulation mechanism.

§2.75 As E.M. Dodd observed in 1932, business is encouraged primarily because it is of service to the community rather than because it is a source of profit to its owners.[209] Across the whole of the common law world, the prevailing view appears to be that once corporate personality is recognized, it becomes necessary to give effect to it, for the simple reason that people make their investments and plan and carry out their actions on the assumption that such personality will be respected. If investment is to be encouraged it is necessary for stability to prevail. The constant recognition of corporate personality promotes stability, for otherwise investors and business people would be unable to predict when the corporate form would be respected and when it would not, and thus no confidence would be placed in it. It is the need for stability which justifies the limited

---

[205] See, generally, J.A. Grundfest, "The Limited Future of Unlimited Liability" (1992) 102 Yale L.J. 387.
[206] Prior to the evolution of the modern limited liability corporation, such waivers of personal liability were frequently encountered in insurance policies, and were held to be effective in *Halket v. Merchant Traders' Ship Loan & Insurance Assoc.* (1849), 13 Q.B. 960; 116 E.R. 1530; see also *Hassel v. Merchant Traders' Ship Loan & Insurance Assoc.* (1849), 4 Ex. 525, 154 E.R. 1322; *Hallett v. Dowdall* (1852), 18 Q.B. 2, 118 E.R. 1.
[207] See, generally, CW. Maughan, K. McGuinness, "Towards an Economic Theory of the Corporation" (2001) 1 Journal of Corporate Law Studies 141.
[208] *Ultramares Marine v. Touche Niven and Co.*, 255 NY 170, 174 NE 441 (1931), *per* Cardozo J.
[209] "For Whom Are Corporate Managers Trustees?" (1932) 45 Harv. L. Rev. 1145 at 1149.

willingness of the courts to pierce the corporate veil.[210] It may fairly be stated that people will often engage in a dangerous activity only if they can isolate themselves from the risks of liability associated with that activity. One method of such isolation is insurance, but the use of the limited liability corporation is another.

E. UNLIMITED COMPANIES

§2.76 Having discussed the subjected of limited liability at some length, we will now look at an alternative arrangement. Currently, the laws of two provinces (Nova Scotia and Alberta) permit the incorporation of an unlimited liability company. In this section, we will take a brief look at these two regimes (including the primary rationale for the use of such entities), and then discuss the guidance that they afford with respect to more recent proposals to incorporate an unlimited liability corporation into Ontario corporate law.

(i) Overview of the Nova Scotia Regime

§2.77 The Nova Scotia legislation is by far the older of the two existing Canadian regimes. It originated early in the last century, following the adoption by that province of the *Companies Act* then in effect in England. Nova Scotia now employs the general terms of the U.K. *Companies Act, 1948*, which also provided for the unlimited liability company option. Similar provisions remain in the current U.K. *Companies Act, 1985*. In Nova Scotia, unlimited liability companies were not much used prior to the time when the Free Trade Agreement came into effect. However, in recent years they have come to be used as tax planning devices.

§2.78 The Nova Scotia *Companies Act* permits the incorporation of a company that does not limit the liability of the members of the company to its creditors. Such companies are commonly known as "Nova Scotia unlimited liability companies" or "NSULCs". Strictly speaking, unlimited liability results under the Nova Scotia Act partly by reason of the terms of the *Companies Act* itself, and partly by reason of its memorandum of association. More specifically, the memorandum must indicate whether the members of the corporation wish to be incorporated on a limited or unlimited liability basis. Despite the absence of limited liability, an unlimited liability company has all the powers of a natural person, subject to any limitations it may decide to impose in its memorandum of association, and subject also to the Nova Scotia *Companies Act*. In other words, an unlimited liability company is a full corporation, save in the respect that it does not confer limited liability upon its members.

§2.79 Unlimited liability companies have become popular as cross-border tax-planning vehicles in recent years, due to the different manner in which such a company is characterized in Canada and the United States for income tax pur-

---

[210] *Houle v. National Bank of Canada*, [1990] S.C.J. No. 120, [1990] 3 S.C.R. 122 at 178, *per* L'Heureux-Dubé J.

poses. Generally speaking, for income tax purposes, corporations incorporated either federally or provincially are not permitted to flow profits and losses through to their U.S. shareholders, so that losses within the U.S. parent may be set-off against profits on the Canadian subsidiary, or so that losses with the Canadian subsidiary may be set-off against profits in the U.S. parent.

§2.80 Under U.S. tax law, a partnership is a flow-through entity for most purposes so that the partnership is ignored for income tax purposes and the individual partners are taxed directly. Accordingly, any income or loss flows through directly to the partners. Under United States federal tax regulations, a body corporate for U.S. federal tax purposes excludes certain corporations formed under laws that provide for unlimited liability of its shareholders. The tax treatment of unlimited liability companies under U.S. tax law was altered on January 1, 1997, when the United States introduced the "check-the-box" rules which permit a Canadian corporation,[211] formed under federal or provincial law and whose members have unlimited liability, to be treated as a flow-through entity for U.S. tax purposes. As a result, the entity is disregarded completely if there is only one member, and it is treated as a partnership if there is more than one member. The tax treatment desired is decided by the corporation, through the process of "checking the box".

§2.81 In contrast, for Canadian tax purposes, the entity is regarded as a true corporation, with the effect that it does not have a flow-through character but is subject to Canadian federal and provincial corporate income tax. This offers several advantages; for example, because the corporation is deemed resident in Canada by reason of its Canadian incorporation, it is subject to Canadian corporate income tax as opposed to both Part I tax and branch tax of the *Income Tax Act*. At the same time, losses realized on the Canadian operations of the unlimited liability company would be applied against the profits in the U.S. company.

§2.82 The members of an unlimited liability company may elect not to take advantage of flow-through treatment. Partnership or proprietorship status is the default classification for a foreign eligible entities where at least one of the company's members has personal liability for the debts of the organization; otherwise, corporate status is the default classification. The question of member liability for an organization's debts is determined solely by reference to the applicable local statute or law under which the entity is organized. Personal liability exists where a member is personally liable for all or any portion of an organization's debts. An entity's organizational documents may be referred to determine whether members have limited liability. The election must be signed by:

- each member of the electing entity as of the filing date; or

---

[211] See IRS Form 8832, Entity Classification Election.

- any member, officer or owner of the electing entity authorized to make the election who must so represent under penalties of perjury.

However, in order for the election is to be effective prior to its filing date, the election must also be signed by each person who was a member during the effective period who is not also a member on the filing date.

§2.83 Prior to the adoption of the "check the box" approach, a company could qualify for the above tax treatment only by satisfying a four-factor test. The check the box approach simplified the incorporation process, as it means that it is no longer necessary to obtain U.S. tax advice as to whether the four-factor test is satisfied. The following list provides a good sample of some of the various tax planning purposes to which unlimited companies have been put:

- As indicated above, to allow U.S. taxpayers to consolidate losses from a Canadian business with income from other sources in the U.S.
- To avoid so-called toll charges on outbound transfers of assets from the United States to a foreign corporation. Generally, where such transfers are made it is necessary to impose a toll charge or excise tax, unless the taxpayer enters into a gain recognition agreement with the IRS. However, if a U.S. corporation is the sole shareholder in a Unlimited liability companies, then the "Check-the-Box" regulations allow the U.S. parent corporation to elect to have the unlimited company disregarded as an entity, with the result that it is usually possible to transfer assets to the unlimited company without the imposition of the toll charge. The Canadian taxes are considered to have been paid by the U.S. parent for U.S. tax purposes, so as to permit the U.S. parent to claim the U.S. foreign tax credit with respect to them.
- To avoid double taxation in cross-border leasing. Under Canadian tax law, a withholding tax is payable on lease payments to a non-resident lessor. If the unlimited company is the lessor of the leased assets, Canadian withholding tax is not payable since the payments are made within Canada from a Canadian lessee to a Canadian lessor. For United States tax purposes, however, the unlimited company is ignored under the flow-through rules, which allows the real lessor to obtain the tax treatment it could have obtained as if the lease were made from a United States entity.
- To avoid U.S. anti-deferral rules which apply to controlled foreign corporations and foreign personal holding companies. These rules may lead to perceived double taxation. For instance, in the case of an OBCA or CBCA subsidiary, the U.S. parent corporation generally cannot take advantage of taxes paid by the Canadian subsidiary for United States foreign tax purposes. Accordingly, profits of a Canadian subsidiary are taxed when earned and also when distributed to the United States shareholder. Under the flow-through approach, the parent obtains a U.S. foreign tax credit for the taxes which are paid by the Canadian subsidiary and so avoids the U.S. anti-deferral rules.

- Since the practical combined effect of the U.S. and Canadian tax regimes is to treat the Canadian unlimited company as a branch for U.S. tax purposes, but as a separate company for Canadian tax purposes, the principals behind the corporation enjoy the best of both worlds.

- Canadians emigrating to the U.S. can avoid double taxation on their Canadian holdings and secure a higher cost basis for U.S. tax purposes.

To obtain this treatment, section 301.7701-2(b)(8)(ii)(A) of the *Internal Revenue Code 1986* requires:

> With regard to Canada, any corporation or company formed under any federal or provincial law which provides that the liability of all of the members of such corporation or company will be unlimited.

§2.84 In addition to the tax benefit of unlimited liability incorporation, there are a number of other features of such a corporation that may make it attractive to certain investors.[212] The directors of an unlimited liability company do not have to be resident in Canada, but any such company must have a registered office in Nova Scotia. An unlimited liability company may be incorporated with or without share capital. Where it possesses share capital, changes in the share capital may be made by way of a member resolution that becomes effective immediately. The *Companies Act* also allows the issuance of par value shares (non-par value shares are also allowed). In addition, the Act does not bar an unlimited liability company from owning shares of its parent or prohibit a subsidiary from acquiring shares of its parent.

§2.85 An unlimited liability company is formed by filing with the Registrar of Joint Stock Companies under *Companies Act* a signed memorandum and articles of association. As under the U.K. Act, these documents provide a contractual framework for the eventual company that arises. The memorandum and articles must be accompanied by a lawyer's declaration concerning the propriety of the incorporation. Unlimited liability companies must have a corporate name (as opposed to a number name), and the name must include one of the words or abbreviations "Company", "Co.", "Corporation", "Corp.", "ULC" or "Unlimited Liability Company" at the end of the corporate name. The use of the words "Limited" or "Incorporated" are prohibited.

---

[212] For instance: one of the most surprising uses for an unlimited liability company can be to enhance shareholder protection. A ULC may actually prove to be a more effective device to limit a shareholder's potential personal liability than an limited liability corporation. For instance, unlimited liability may be employed as a substitute for a shareholder guarantee. Such an arrangement may be attractive where the company will have only a single creditor, and the shareholder intends to sell off the company relatively quickly should it be a successful venture. In many cases, it will prove easier to extricate a departing shareholder from liability under an unlimited liability regime, than to extricate the shareholder of a limited liability corporation from liability under a personal guarantee. In England, unlimited liability companies are less regulated, and are exempt from the public disclosure of corporate accounts. If any Ontario regime is drafted to relieve from such provisions applicable to limited liability corporations (*e.g.*, with respect to dividend payment), unlimited companies may prove to have a degree of popularity even where tax benefits are not a consideration.

§2.86 A limited company under the Nova Scotia law may not directly convert to an unlimited company, but such a transition can be accomplished indirectly through amalgamation. (In contrast, U.K. companies can migrate directly from unlimited to limited status.) Under the amalgamation method, the limited company amalgamates with an unlimited company to form an unlimited company. As a prelude to such a transaction, both companies must have been incorporated, continued, or must otherwise exist, under the Nova Scotia *Companies Act*.

§2.87 Somewhat surprisingly, there are a number of measures that can be taken to limit the liability of the members of a supposedly unlimited liability company. Some of these arise under the *Companies Act* itself. In particular, a member is only liable for debts of the company existing at the time he or she ceases to be a member and a past member is not liable to contribute at all if he or she has not been a member for a one-year period prior to the wind-up. In addition, a past shareholder, if potentially liable, is not required to contribute unless existing shareholders are unable to satisfy their obligations to pay. These restrictions on liability generally follow the rules of liability applicable under partnership law.

§2.88 The liability of a member of an unlimited liability company can also be limited contractually, which is a useful device where there are only one or two large lenders and sufficient security is in place to address the debt of the unlimited company. If doing business with the company is sufficiently attractive, such creditors may be prepared to contractually agree to not pursue the shareholder in the event of default. Another technique employed to limit liability is to make use of an "S" corporation under U.S. tax law, as an intermediary between the unlimited liability companies and the ultimate investor.

(ii) The Alberta Regime

§2.89 Effective, May 17, 2005, Alberta amended its *Business Corporations Act* ("Alberta BCA")[213] to permit the incorporation of unlimited liability corporations. The Alberta legislation weds the unlimited concept to a pre-existing business corporation that closely resembles that in effect under the OBCA and CBCA.

§2.90 There are a number of important differences, however, between the Alberta and Nova Scotia approach. Under the Alberta legislation, the articles of the corporation must include an express statement that the liability of each of its shareholders "for any liability, act or default of the unlimited liability corporation is unlimited in extent and joint and several in nature". Accordingly, a creditor of an AULC will have a direct claim against all shareholders of the corporation for all liabilities owed to the creditor without having to first seek recourse against the AULC or have it wound up. Under the Nova Scotia regime, although the liability of the members of such a company is not limited, the members have no direct liability to creditors. Instead, their responsibility is acti-

---

[213] R.S.A. 2000 c. B-9.

vated only on the winding up of the company if there are insufficient assets to satisfy the liabilities outstanding at that time. In the event of a deficiency, a call is then made on the members to make good the amount required to pay the creditors in full. Although it has been said that the obligations of the members are akin to that of a guarantor, the true nature of their obligation is that of contributories.

§2.91 The Nova Scotia Act contains no director residence requirements. The Nova Scotia *Companies Act* relies upon the common law restrictions on the payment of dividends, whereas the Alberta legislation maintains the normal OBCA/CBCA approach to dividend declaration. As a result, the Nova Scotia regime allows somewhat greater flexibility with respect to dividend payments. The Nova Scotia regime allows shares to be issued without being fully paid. They may also be issued in exchange for a promissory note or other debt instrument of the subscriber. The Alberta BCA regime adheres to the normal OBCA/CBCA requirement of prohibiting shares to be issued other than as fully paid. Shares may not be issued in consideration of a subscriber debt instrument. The repayment of share capital is also more restricted under the Alberta BCA regime than the Nova Scotia regime.

§2.92 The primary advantage of the Alberta unlimited liability corporation regime is financial. A one-time-only fee for incorporation is payable in Alberta in the amount of $100. In contrast, the incorporation fee in Nova Scotia is $6,000, with an annual renewal fee of $2,000. The Nova Scotia fee was clearly fixed in an effort to secure revenue to the province, but the ability to obtain this benefit eroded quickly once a second jurisdiction entered the picture. It is extremely unlikely that any additional jurisdiction providing for the incorporation of an unlimited liability corporation would be able to derive much revenue from the process. The sole benefit to any new jurisdiction in allowing for such corporations is to permit the residents of that jurisdiction to obtain the tax benefit of unlimited corporation status without the need to use the incorporation laws of some other province.

(iii) A Possible Ontario Regime

§2.93 Since Ontario is the primary commercial law jurisdiction in Canada, there is a strong argument that it should offer investors and entrepreneurs the full range of incorporation options that are offered in other jurisdictions. This would include permitting the incorporation of unlimited liability corporations. However, considerable care needs to be take in crafting any unlimited liability regime. The U.K. precedent employed in Nova Scotia has been little considered in the case law, and therefore offers little guide. In terms of the specific language of the two statutes concerned, both the Alberta and Nova Scotia precedents have serious shortcomings that should be remedied in any Ontario legislation. In this section, we will consider some of the issues that ought to be addressed in any such legislation.

(1) Identification of Unlimited Status

§2.94 The Alberta BCA contains a number of provisions that require notice to be given to persons dealing with an unlimited liability corporation concerning the status of such an entity. While third parties who deal with a corporation are benefited by the fact that it is an unlimited liability entity (since there is now a potential recovery against shareholders) the same is not true in the case of outsiders who may acquire a share interest in such a corporation. Unless care is taken to make clear to potential investors that they are acquiring a potentially open-ended liability, there is considerable risk that the unwary may be taken advantage of. It is not that long ago, for instance, that many investors in certain Lloyd's syndicates (some of whom might have been considered to be highly sophisticated investors) claimed that they were unaware that the interests that they had acquired subjected them to potential unlimited liability.[214]

§2.95 Fair notice under the Alberta BCA is provided in part under section 15.3, which provides that:

> In addition to meeting the requirements of section 6, the articles of incorporation, amalgamation, amendment, continuance or conversion of an unlimited liability corporation shall contain an express statement that the liability of each of the shareholders of the unlimited liability corporation for any liability, act or default of the unlimited liability corporation is unlimited in extent and joint and several in nature.

In addition, subsection 15.4(1) provides that:

> The name of every unlimited liability corporation shall end with the words "Unlimited Liability Corporation" or the abbreviation "ULC", and an unlimited liability corporation may use and may be legally designated by either the full or the abbreviated form.

To circumvent the risk that a person may seek to obtain preferential treatment from creditors by claiming unlimited status where it does not exist, subsection 15.4(2) provides:

> No person other than a body corporate that is an unlimited liability corporation shall carry on business within Alberta under any name or title that contains the words "Unlimited Liability Corporation" or "ULC".

§2.96 Should Ontario create an unlimited liability corporation regime, one key question is whether provisions along these lines should also be incorporated into any Ontario regime, and if so whether they are adequate to their intended purpose. Looking first at subsection 15.4(2), the practical effect of this provision is to prevent any extra-provincial corporation from identifying itself as having unlimited status, to the extent that it is carrying on business in Alberta. It does not, however, prevent any such corporation from carrying on business in that province. The sole effect appears to be to require it to do so under a name that does not include the word "Unlimited". Currently, however, there is no require-

---

[214] *Ibid.*, s. 9. See, for instance, *Arbuthnott v. Feltrim Underwriting Agencies Ltd.* (10 March 1995, Queen's Bench Div., Comm. Ct. before Phillips J.).

ment under Nova Scotia law that the name of an unlimited company include the word "Unlimited", so it is difficult to see what point subsection 15.4(2) is intended to serve.

§2.97 The general intent behind section 15.3 is also unclear. The exact wording ties this provision to the specific liability regime under the Alberta BCA. The merit of that regime is discussed below. If section 15.3 is intended to ensure that notice to a potential investor that the company in which the investor intends to purchase shares has unlimited status, it is far from clear that it is adequate to the purpose. Requiring that fact to be disclosed on share certificates might provide better notice, as might the requirement, under subsection 15.4(1), that the corporation's name must include the words "Unlimited Liability Corporation" or the abbreviation "ULC".

§2.98 To address the above concerns, if Ontario elects to move ahead with an unlimited liability corporation regime, consideration should be given to using language along the lines of the following draft sections in any corresponding provisions of the Ontario Act:

A.(1) The articles of incorporation, amalgamation, amendment, continuance or conversion of an unlimited liability corporation shall contain an express statement that the liability of each of the shareholders of the corporation is unlimited.

(2) The name of every unlimited liability corporation shall end with the words:

(a) "unlimited liability corporation" or the abbreviation "ULC", or

(b) "*société illimitée de responsabilité*" or the abbreviation "SIR",

but an unlimited liability corporation may use and may be legally designated by either the full or the abbreviated form.

(3) The share certificates of every unlimited liability corporation shall bear the legend, "incorporated with unlimited liability under the laws of Ontario" or "*incorporé avec la responsabilité illimitée en vertu des lois d'Ontario*".

To circumvent the risk that a person may seek to obtain preferential treatment from creditors by claiming unlimited status where it does not exist, a provision along the following lines might also be included:

B. No person other than a body corporate that is incorporated with unlimited liability under the laws of Ontario or another jurisdiction shall carry on business within Ontario under any name or title that contains the words:

(a) "unlimited liability corporation" or the abbreviation "ULC", or

(b) "*société illimitée de responsabilité*" or the abbreviation "SIR".

(2) General Liability Regime

§2.99 Neither the Alberta nor the Nova Scotia legislation are particularly clear with respect to the rules governing shareholder liability, and those rules that are set out in the legislation seem to be based on some fairly questionable assumptions. More specifically, subsection 15.2(1) of the Alberta BCA provides that:

> The liability of each of the shareholders of a corporation incorporated under this Act as an unlimited liability corporation for any liability, act or default of the unlimited liability corporation is unlimited in extent and joint and several in nature.

The first question that arises for consideration when examining this provision is whether a shareholder should be liable to creditors and other claimants against a corporation outside the context of the winding-up of a corporation. Liability only on winding up seems the preferable approach for two reasons. First, the undertaking of a shareholder in an unlimited corporation is to make good the liabilities of the corporation that it is unable to discharge itself. Second, since under the rule in *Foss v. Harbottle*[215] shareholders have no right to enforce specific rights of the corporation, it is only fair and reasonable that they should not be subject to have specific obligations of the corporation enforced against them. A further concern in this respect is that the shareholder may not have the practical ability to raise all of the potential defences that may be available to the corporation itself.

§2.100 A person who chooses to deal with an unlimited liability corporation enters into a relationship with that corporation. There is no reason why such a person should be given a direct right of claim against the shareholders as well. Shareholders of an unlimited liability corporation are not guarantors, in the sense that they undertake that the corporation will perform its obligations. Rather, their undertaking is that if the corporation is unable to pay the amount for which it is liable by reason of a default, the shareholders will make good the deficiency.

§2.101 Taking all of the foregoing into account, the suggestion in subsection 15.2(1) that each shareholder should be liable for "any liability, act or default of the unlimited liability corporation" is inappropriate. The liability of the shareholder should be only for the undischarged liabilities of the corporation, as formally determined in a liquidation of the corporation. Except where it is possible to agree upon the extent of that liability, the determination of the amount owing would probably need to be made in one of three specific contexts: bankruptcy (including a proposal under that Act), liquidation under the BCA itself, or in the event of an approved plan of arrangement under the *Companies' Creditors Arrangement Act.*

§2.102 The next questionable aspect of subsection 15.2(1) is whether the shareholders should be jointly and severally liable. In deciding on the appropriate extent of liability, there would seem to be much merit in adopting the common recommendation of the economic analysis of law movement, that any statutory regime that is imposed on the parties to a given transaction should approximate what the parties would bargain for in a transaction cost-free world. Adopting

---

[215] (1843), 2 Hare 461.

that approach here, it is unlikely that such a "joint and several" liability regime for all debts owing would be what a rational investor would intend when agreeing to purchase a share interest in an unlimited liability corporation. Generally, it would seem more reasonable to assume that an investor's willingness to participate in the risk associated with the business would be tied to that investor's entitlement to share in the profit that it might generate. Such an arrangement could be accommodated by tying each shareholder's liability to his or her proportionate share interest in the corporation. By way of example, a shareholder who agrees to take up a five per cent interest in a corporation most likely would not intend to assume more than the risk of liability for five per cent of the un-discharged liabilities of the corporation, because the extent of that interest identifies the share profit that the shareholder would hope to receive.

§2.103 The following proposed section C incorporates the foregoing ideas into a possible legislative scheme:

> C.(1) In this section, "un-discharged liabilities" means, with respect to an unlimited liability corporation, that portion of the fair value of the aggregate debts and other liabilities of a corporation remaining un-discharged after the liquidation of the assets of the corporation, and the application of the proceeds thereof to the satisfaction of the debts and liabilities of the corporation, where the corporation is being wound-up under this Act or is subject to a receiving order under the *Bankruptcy and Insolvency Act* (Canada).
>
> (2) Where an unlimited liability corporation is the subject of an approved plan of arrangement under the *Companies Creditors Arrangement Act* (Canada) or a proposal approved under Division I of Part III of the *Bankruptcy and Insolvency Act* (Canada), the amount for which the shareholders of the corporation are liable in respect of its un-discharged liabilities shall be shall be as provided in the terms of the plan of arrangement or proposal, or in the absence of any such provision, shall be as ordered by the court.
>
> (3) The liability of each of the shareholders of an unlimited liability corporation in respect of the un-discharged debts of the corporation may be determined only in a winding-up under this Act, or in a proceeding under the *Bankruptcy and Insolvency Act* (Canada) or the *Companies Creditors Arrangement Act* (Canada) with respect to that corporation.
>
> (4) A shareholder in an unlimited liability corporation is not a proper party, by reason only of the corporation's unlimited liability status, to a proceeding against the corporation for the purpose for the enforcement an obligation of the corporation or for recovering damages or enforcing any other liability to which it is subject.
>
> (5) The liability of each shareholder of an unlimited liability corporation for the un-discharged liabilities of the corporation unlimited in amount but several in nature and extent, with the relative liability of each shareholder liable being equal to the proportion of all shares of the corporation that are held by that shareholder.
>
> (6) A shareholder of an unlimited liability corporation is a contributory within the meaning of section 191 of this Act, to the extent of that shareholder's liability under this section.

(7) Nothing in this section prevents the shareholders of an unlimited liability corporation from agreeing as among themselves that their respective liability for the un-discharged debts of the corporation shall be otherwise than as provided in this section.

The above regime leads to proportionate liability, and provides a workable package of rules for fixing the amount of the liability of each shareholder at the time of winding-up or an equivalent process.

(3) Limitation on the Term of Shareholder Liability

§2.104 A significant concern where shareholders are liable for the debts and other obligations of a corporation is that shareholders (particularly insiders) will dispose of their share interests, when as the probability of a default by the corporation becomes clear. In such a case, the creditors and other potential claimants against the corporation are likely to find that the remaining shareholders are all judgment proof. On the other hand, one of the driving factors in the use of corporations as a vehicle for business is the opportunity that it allows a shareholder to dispose of his or her shareholding, and to sever connections with the corporation.

§2.105 Subsection 15.2(2) of the Alberta BCA imposes a time limit on any claim against a shareholder of an unlimited liability corporation. It provides a reasonable period for the bringing of any claim, but releases a shareholder from the risk of further liability:

> Notwithstanding subsection (1), but subject to any immunity from liability otherwise available on pleading the *Limitations Act* as a defense, a former shareholder of an unlimited liability corporation is not liable for any liability, act or default of the unlimited liability corporation unless an action to enforce a claim arising out of that liability, act or default is brought within 2 years from the date on which the former shareholder last ceased to be a shareholder of the unlimited liability corporation.

The words "subject to any immunity from liability otherwise available on pleading the *Limitations Act* as a defense" appear to reflect the possibility of a direct claim by creditors and other claimants against the shareholders rather than the corporation. The effect of this wording is that the shareholders may raise any limitation period to which the corporation is itself entitled. The limitation period to which the shareholders are entitled is as set out in subsection 15.2(2) itself.

§2.106 It does not seem unreasonable to impose a sunset provision upon the potential liability of a shareholder of an unlimited liability corporation, who disposes of his or her interest in the corporation. If a two-year limit on liability is assumed to be fair and reasonable, one question to consider is whether it is necessary to include a specific provision in the OBCA itself. The general limitation rule for personal claims in Ontario is set down in section 4 of the *Limitations Act*, 2002, S.O. 2002, c. 24, Sched. B. It provides:

> ... a proceeding shall not be commenced in respect of a claim after the second anniversary of the day on which the claim was discovered.

§2.107 If it is decided to make the shareholders of an unlimited liability corporation liable for the un-discharged debts of that corporation, then this provision would not provide a satisfactory time limit for shareholder liability, because the liability of a shareholder would not be determinable until after the realization of the corporation's assets, *etc*. A second question is whether the shareholder who disposes of a share interest should be liable only where the current shareholder defaults. These issues are addressed in the following draft section D:

> D.(1) A former shareholder of an unlimited liability corporation shall be liable as if still a shareholder of that corporation, upon default in payment by the current holder of the shares of that former shareholder in respect of any un-discharged liability of the unlimited liability corporation, where:
>
> (a) a winding-up of the corporation is commenced, or
>
> (b) a receiving order or interim receiving order is made under the *Bankruptcy and Insolvency Act* (Canada) with respect to the corporation; or
>
> (c) a stay is granted under the *Companies Creditors Arrangement Act* or a stay takes effect with respect to the making of a proposal under Division I of Part III of the *Bankruptcy and Insolvency Act* with respect to the corporation,
>
> within 365 days of the day on which the former shareholder last was shareholder of the unlimited liability corporation.
>
> (2) Where a share in an unlimited liability corporation is redeemed or repurchased by the corporation, the person who was a holder of that share prior to the time of its redemption or repurchase shall be liable in respect of any un-discharged liability of an unlimited liability corporation as if no such redemption or repurchase had occurred, where:
>
> (a) a winding-up of the corporation is commenced, or
>
> (b) a receiving order or interim receiving order is made under the *Bankruptcy and Insolvency Act* (Canada) with respect to the corporation; or
>
> (c) a stay is granted under the *Companies Creditors Arrangement Act* or a stay takes effect with respect to the making of a proposal under Division I of Part III of the *Bankruptcy and Insolvency Act* with respect to the corporation,
>
> within 365 days of the day of the redemption or repurchase of that share.

§2.108 In addition to the foregoing, subsection 15.2(3) of the Alberta BCA protects a former shareholder against liability for obligations that arise after the shareholder has ceased to be involved in the corporation. It provides that:

> A former shareholder of an unlimited liability corporation is not liable for any liability, act or default of the unlimited liability corporation that did not exist on or prior to the date on which the former shareholder last ceased to be a shareholder of the unlimited liability corporation.

Since the former shareholder will have no direct or indirect input into the incurring of such liabilities, it is difficult to argue with the grant of such protection, and it is to be hoped that such a provision is incorporated into any future Ontario regime.

(4) Director Liability

§2.109 The question is sometimes raised as to whether the directors of an unlimited liability corporation should be subject to a lower level of liability than directors of a limited liability corporation. The argument in favour of a different director liability regime is that since the shareholders are themselves liable for the corporation's obligations, there is no reason to impose liability on the directors. However, there are a number of reasons for maintaining liability. First, most of the rules governing director liability are scattered across hundreds of federal and provincial Acts. This fact presents obvious practical difficulties in changing the director liability regime. Second, while the shareholders of an unlimited liability corporation may be nominally liable for its obligations, recovery from those shareholders may be a time-consuming process, particularly where the shareholders are located in a distant jurisdiction. Third, even in an unlimited liability corporation, the shareholders are not subject to any on-going duties with regard to the conduct of the corporation's business and affairs. The directors are subject to those duties. Taking these considerations into account, the better approach would seem to be to leave director liability unchanged.

(5) Issue of Shares for a Debt Instrument, Repayment of Capital, etc.

§2.110 The Nova Scotia *Companies Act* permits the shares of an unlimited liability corporation to be issued in consideration of a debt instrument issued by the subscriber for those shares. The Alberta BCA does not. Any Ontario regime would need to select between these two approaches. Arguments can be made in favour of each approach. For instance, at present, the units in a limited partnership may be issued in exchange for a promissory note. Many lenders have found it difficult to pursue the members of a limited partnership, particularly where the unit holders are scattered across several jurisdictions, and their indebtedness to the corporation is relatively small. If it were permissible to issue shares in an unlimited liability corporation on other than a fully paid basis, a similar problem would likely arise with respect to the holders of shares in such an entity. On the other hand, whether a corporation is limited or unlimited, there is only a small corporate law obligation to invest in the share capital of the corporation. Creditors are unlikely to have much leverage to entice a shareholder in an unlimited liability corporation to tie up his or her own assets in the capital of the corporation, since the prospect of unlimited liability offers little incentive to do so.

§2.111 Generally, where there is no strong theoretical argument for adopting a particular legislative approach, the better option is usually to adopt the approach that imposes the least amount of regulation. With respect to the restrictions applicable under the OBCA with respect to the issue of shares, such an approach would lead to relaxing or suspending altogether the restrictions applicable to the issue of shares on other than a fully paid basis. For obvious reasons, the Act would also have to be amended to make clear that any such shares were assessable.

(6) Continuation and Fundamental Changes

§2.112 There are two types of continuation that would need to be dealt with in any Ontario legislation dealing with limited liability corporations:

- Intra-provincial continuation: the continuation of a corporate body incorporated under a limited liability corporate regime in Ontario as an unlimited liability corporation, or a corresponding reverse migration. Continuation of a limited liability corporation as an unlimited liability corporation (and *vice versa*) are very real possibilities, because in almost all cases the driving rationale for the use of the unlimited liability vehicle is purely one of tax planning. The tax benefit of using unlimited liability is likely to change where there is a change in ownership (*e.g.*, a sale to an ownership interest that is not subject to U.S. taxation). By the same token, the acquisition of a limited liability corporation by a U.S. taxpayer may stimulate a desire to convert the corporation to unlimited status.

- Inter-jurisdictional continuation: The continuation of a corporate body incorporated under the laws of some jurisdiction other than Ontario (whether as a limited or unlimited liability corporation) as an Ontario unlimited liability corporation, or some reverse migration. Inter-jurisdictional continuation may involve considerations similar to those that drive intra-provincial continuation, but it is equally to involve considerations such as:

    - the desire to avoid payment of the annual renewal tax in Nova Scotia (or a similar charge in some other jurisdiction); or

    - the desire to enjoy the benefits of incorporation under a modern corporate law regime.

Whatever the motivation may be, the general goal with respect to continuation under most corporate law statutes is to ensure that the rights of third parties continue unaffected by reason of the continuation. In other words, as a result of the continuation, the rights are neither greater nor less.

§2.113 Sections 15.5 and 15.6 of the Alberta BCA provide for the continuation of extra-provincial corporations as unlimited liability corporations under that Act. The provisions borrow from the general rules regarding continuation, and then incorporate a number of specific rules to deal with the unique attributes of an unlimited liability corporation. A strong argument can be made that these provisions are unduly complex. Moreover, in at least certain aspects, they expand the rights of a creditor who dealt with the corporation prior to its continuation, rather than simply ensuring that they continue unaffected. For instance, subsection 15.5(2) provides that:

> When an extra-provincial corporation that was incorporated as an unlimited liability corporation is continued as a limited corporation,
>
> (*a*) the shareholders of the extra-provincial corporation as it existed prior to the date shown on the certificate of continuance continue to be liable without

limit for any liability, act or default of the extra-provincial corporation that existed as of the date shown on the certificate of continuance,

(b) an existing cause of action, claim or liability to prosecution is unaffected,

(c) a civil, criminal or administrative action pending by or against the extra-provincial corporation may continue to be prosecuted by or against the shareholders of the extra-provincial corporation as it existed prior to the date shown on the certificate of continuance or by or against the limited corporation, and

(d) a conviction against, or ruling, order or judgment in favour of or against, the unlimited liability corporation may be enforced against or by the shareholders of the extra-provincial corporation as it existed prior to the date shown on the certificate of continuance or against or by the limited corporation.

Clause (a) appears to create a right of claim against the shareholders directly by reason of the continuation under the Alberta BCA. In contrast, clause (c) proceeds on the assumption that the shareholders are liable in such actions and prosecutions under the laws of the other jurisdiction, which may well not be the case. It is unclear whether it is sufficient to create a right of claim where the proceeding has commenced prior to continuation, but since such a right is now conferred under clause (d), the issue may be moot. Clause (d) is more troubling, because it has the potential to amend the effect of a judgment granted prior to continuation. On its face, it allows direct enforcement against a shareholder of the corporation, even though the judgment may not have been enforceable in such a way prior to the continuation. It also allows shareholders a direct right of enforcement of rights belonging to the unlimited corporation itself.

§2.114 As with a number of other provisions of the Alberta BCA provisions dealing with unlimited liability, the continuation provisions confuse the concept of "unlimited liability" with that of co-equal responsibility. Unlimited liability does not affect the status of a corporation as a separate legal entity. Its effect is to make the shareholders liable to the extent that the corporation is unable to meet its legal obligations. It is, of course, open to the legislature to provide that the shareholders of a corporate entity will be directly liable for the performance of its obligations and for such wrongs as it may commit. However, that is not unlimited liability. It is concurrent liability, and it is a liability of such a nature as to call into existence the separate personality of the corporation itself.

§2.115 If it is decided to introduce an unlimited liability corporation regime into Ontario law, the possibility of the continuation of a corporate body as an unlimited liability corporation can be easily accomplished, whether Ontario-incorporated or incorporated elsewhere, and whether that corporate body was previously a limited or unlimited liability. A provision along the following lines would seem to be sufficient to meet the foregoing concerns:

> C.(1) In this section, "company" means a corporation incorporated with limited liability under this Act, or a corporate body that is eligible to continue under this Act under section 180 or 181 of this Act.

(2) A company may apply to the Director for a certificate of continuance as an unlimited liability corporation,

    (*a*) upon complying with section 180, in the case of a corporate body incorporated under the laws of any jurisdiction other than Ontario; and

    (*b*) upon complying with section 181, in the case of a corporate incorporated with limited liability under this Act or under another statute of Ontario.

(3) Except as provided in this section, sections 180 or 181, as the case may be, apply with respect to any company continuing as an unlimited liability corporation.

(4) Where a company is continued as an unlimited liability corporation under this Act

    (*a*) such continuation does not affect the liability of any shareholder with respect to any debt, liability or other obligation of the company that arose prior to the time when such continuation took effect.

    (*b*) subject to clause (a), the liability a shareholder of the unlimited liability corporation shall be as provided in section C.

    (*c*) for the purposes of clause (*b*), "shareholder" means a person who was a shareholder of the company at the time when it continued under this Act or who is admitted as a shareholder of the unlimited liability corporation at any time thereafter.

(5) Where a limited liability corporation amalgamates with an unlimited liability corporation so as to create an unlimited liability corporation, subsection (4) applies with the necessary modifications.

§2.116 Subsection 15.5(2) of the Alberta BCA deals with the potential continuation of an unlimited liability corporation as a limited liability corporation. Section 15.6 deals with the possible amalgamation of an unlimited liability corporation by way of amendment of its articles or amalgamation. Broadly similar rules apply in each case. Unfortunately, the rules set down in that section are far from ideal. Aside from maintaining the mistake of confusing unlimited liability with concurrent liability, it is far from clear how the rules that are set down in these sections would work in practice. For instance, clause 15.6(1)(*a*) provides that:

> (a) the shareholders of the unlimited liability corporation as it existed prior to the amendment or amalgamation continue to be liable without limit for any liability, act or default of the unlimited liability corporation that existed as of the date shown on the certificate of amendment or amalgamation.

This provision may seem at first to correspond to proposed clause E(4)(*a*) as set out above. On closer analysis, it does not. When a limited liability entity continues as an unlimited liability entity, third parties are not in any way affected. The existing shareholders of the entity may decide for themselves whether to assume the risk of shareholder liability. In contrast, an unlimited liability corporation that proposes to convert to unlimited liability status may be a party to a wide range of term contracts. Liability under those contracts may relate to supplies ordered after the date of conversion to unlimited liability. It is far from clear whether clause 15.6(1)(*a*) would protect a contractor in such a case. In addition, it may be difficult to decide which contracts and other liabilities predate the continuation of the corporation. While the same is true in the case of shareholder liability under clause E(4)(*a*), the difference is that the shareholder has a right to decide whether to run the risk of liability. The creditor or contractor who loses the right to claim against shareholders by reason of the continuation has no control over the process. Similar concerns apply with respect to amalgamation.

§2.117 The basic problem with provisions such as subsection 15.5(2) section 15.6 of the Alberta BCA is that they do not adequately address the wide range of different circumstances that may apply with respect to fundamental changes of the sort that they contemplate. One corporation to which they apply may be highly solvent. Another may be on the verge of bankruptcy. One may have a comprehensive and credible scheme in mind for discharging its existing liabilities to all creditors and other potential claimants. Another may have given this concern no consideration whatever.

§2.118 Perhaps with so many possibilities in mind, in Nova Scotia, fundamental changes require court approval. Consideration should be considered to adopting a similar regime in Ontario. More specifically, a provision along the following lines would meet the foregoing concerns:

F.-(1) In this section, "reorganization" means:

    (*a*) a continuation of an unlimited liability corporation as a limited liability corporation, whether by way of continuation under this Act or under another Act of Ontario or another jurisdiction; or

    (*b*) an amalgamation of a limited liability corporation with an unlimited liability corporation so as to create a limited liability corporation;

and reorganize has a corresponding meaning.

(2) Where an unlimited liability corporation proposes to reorganize may apply to the court for an order permitting it to do so, on such notice to affected parties or potentially affected as the court may direct.

(3) The directors of an unlimited liability corporation or a majority of the shareholders of such a corporation may by resolution authorize an application under subsection (2).

(4) An unlimited liability corporation making an application under subsection (2) shall file with its application:

    (*a*) an affidavit verified by at least one director of the corporation, listing the names and addresses of the all secured and unsecured creditors of the corporation and other known potential claimants against the corporation, the amount of the indebtedness or other liability due or to become due to those creditors and claimants, the nature of their security (if any) and whether their claims are due or, in the event of sale, become due on the date fixed for the completion of the sale; and

(b) a plan of reorganization explaining why the creditors and claimants listed in the affidavit required under clause (a) will not be prejudiced if the reorganization is allowed to proceed.

(5) A court may make an order permitting a reorganization to proceed where it is satisfied that the proposed reorganization is advantageous to the unlimited liability corporation and will not unreasonably impair the ability of the creditors and other potential claimants against that corporation to recover the amounts owing by that corporation to them in full, and to enforce such other obligations as may be owing to them by the corporation, and in making any such order, the court may

(a) impose such terms and give such directions as it considers appropriate; and

(b) make any order that it considers appropriate with respect to any other person whom it has directed to be served under subsection (2), or who is otherwise properly before the court.

(6) Where an order referred to in subsection (4) has been made, and all terms, directions and conditions of that order have been satisfied,

(a) the unlimited liability corporation may proceed with the proposed reorganization in accordance with that order; and

(b) no proceeding shall be instituted under section 207 (winding-up), 246 (derivative action), or 248 (oppression, etc.) with respect to the reorganization.

F. SEPARATION OF THE OWNERSHIP OF THE CORPORATION AND ITS ASSETS

§2.119 Since a corporation is a separate person, it may have its own property and liabilities,[216] and thus ownership of the corporation itself does not imply ownership of the assets of the corporation. Thus if a corporation carries on a business involving numerous assets (*e.g.*, such as a trucking company) it is pos-

---

[216] Note, however, that it need not necessarily do so. Crown corporations often hold all their property and incur all their liabilities as agents of the Crown. Thus s. 31 of the *Broadcasting Act*, R.S.C. 1985, c. B.9, provides (with respect to the Canadian Broadcasting Corporation):

(1) Except as provided in subsection 29(3), the Corporation is, for all purposes, an agent of Her Majesty, and it may exercise its powers under this Act only as an agent of Her Majesty.

(2) The Corporation may, on behalf of Her Majesty enter into contracts in the name of Her Majesty or in the name of the Corporation.

(3) Property acquired by the Corporation is property of Her Majesty and title thereto may be vested in the name of Her Majesty, or in the name of the Corporation.

(4) Actions, suits or other legal proceedings in respect of any right or obligation acquired or incurred by the Corporation on behalf of Her Majesty, whether in its name or in the name of Her Majesty, may be brought or taken by or against the Corporation in the name of the Corporation in any court that would have jurisdiction if the Corporation was not an agent of Her Majesty.

sible to transfer ownership of that business simply by selling the ownership of the corporation itself without the necessity of transferring ownership of the trucks. Where title to the assets concerned must be registered the transaction costs of selling the enterprise can be considerably less if the corporation — rather than the individual assets themselves — is sold. Yet the transfer of the underlying assets of a corporation is only one aspect of the separation of ownership that has important implications in the selection of the corporate vehicle as a suitable method of organizing a business.

§2.120 The ownership of a corporation is evidenced by shares in the corporation. A share is a defined portion of the capital (*i.e.*, the shareholder's equity interest) in a corporation. In general terms, the ownership of a share entitles its owner to receive a proportionate share in the profits and residual property of a corporation (the property remaining after the satisfaction of the debts and other obligations of a corporation), in accordance with the terms and conditions of the share.

§2.121 The use of the share device allows great flexibility in structuring, dividing and transferring ownership interests in the corporation. By the sale of the shares of a corporation, ownership of the corporation (or a part interest therein) can be transferred from one person to another. Upon the sale of the shares, the previous shareholder may sever all connection with the corporation. Thus new owners may be brought into a corporation by issuing or transferring shares to them; existing owners may step out of the corporation by selling their shares or having their shares redeemed by the corporation. Furthermore, by including different terms and conditions in the case of shares of different classes, it is possible to create an almost unlimited range of different types of ownership interest.

G. SEPARATION OF MANAGEMENT FROM OWNERSHIP

§2.122 The shareholders of a corporation usually have no direct say in the management of a corporation.[217] Instead, management is exercised through the board of directors.[218] Although the board is answerable to the shareholders, they are not agents of the shareholders. The shareholders are not agents of the corporation and may not bind it to a contract.[219] In addition, in most cases, it is not necessary for shareholders to act unanimously when called upon to decide a question (*e.g.*, an amendment to a by-law).[220]

---

[217] Note, however, the possibility of a unanimous shareholder agreement, reserving such control to the shareholders of the corporation: OBCA, s. 108; CBCA, s. 146.
[218] OBCA, s. 115(1); CBCA, s. 102(1); BCCA, s. 117(1).
[219] See Chapter 9, Directors, Officers and the Notion of Corporate Governance.
[220] See Chapter 12, Shareholders and Their Rights.

H. PERPETUAL EXISTENCE

§2.123 A corporation will not die merely by passage of time. It remains in existence from the time of its incorporation until it is dissolved or its certificate of incorporation is canceled for cause.[221] The shareholders of the corporation may change or pass away, but this does not affect the existence of the corporation. Even if all of the shareholders were to die, the corporation would survive, with each shareholder's interest in the corporation forming part of his or her separate estate.

§2.124 Thus a corporation is said to have perpetual succession, which means that despite changes in the ownership of the corporation itself, the corporation continues to own its property and conduct its business and affairs without need for successive conveyances and assignments of that property and business from one owner to the next. In this respect, perpetual existence resembles separation of ownership. Again, this feature of corporate existence is a logical consequence of separate personality. Despite the sale of the corporation it remains in existence unaffected as an artificial person. It continues as title holder and owner of the property and business concerned even though there may be frequent and indeed continuous changes in its membership. The members of the corporation succeed to the property of the corporation. Changes in membership are merely a matter between the corporation and its members. They have no necessary implication with respect to the corporation and its property or with respect to dealings between the corporation and outsiders.

§2.125 By the same token, a corporation is more than the business it conducts. A mining company that sells all of its mining properties does not thereby lose its powers as a mining company and need not necessarily be dissolved.[222] Thus a corporation does not lose or change its objects by selling its assets. It may reinvest the proceeds derived from the sale of its assets and carry on business again. The corporation is also distinguishable from its ownership from time to time. Although a partnership is presumed to dissolve on the death of a partner,[223] there is no such presumption in the case of the death of a shareholder of a corporation.[224] On the contrary, the shareholder's interest is deemed to pass to his or her personal representative.[225] Therefore, unlike other forms of business organization, a corporation is potentially immortal.

---

[221] OBCA, s. 240, CBCA, s. 212.

[222] *Ritchie v. Vermillion Mining Co.* (1902), 4 O.L.R. 588 at 604 (C.A.), *per* Moss, J.A.; see also *per* Maclennan J.A. at 594:

> It is said that the sale of this land is a sale of the company's business and so is *ultra vires*. I do not think so. There is nothing to prevent the business being continued by the purchase of other mines or mining lands afterwards; it is for the company to determine what shall be done afterwards.

[223] *Partnerships Act*, s. 33(1).

[224] *Re Wood, Vallance & Co.* (1915), 34 O.L.R. 278, rev'd on other grounds 53 S.C.R. 51; see also *Whitney v. Small* (1914), 31 O.L.R. 191 (C.A.).

[225] *Scott v. Frank F. Scott (London) Ltd.*, [1940] Ch. 794 (C.A.) per Luxmore, L.J. at 805.

I. LESSER DUTY OF LOYALTY

§2.126 The shareholders of a corporation owe no duty of loyalty to either the corporation or to their fellow shareholders.[226] A shareholder may carry on business with the corporation, may trade with it as if he were a stranger and may compete with it.[227] This rule of arm's length dealing between a corporation and its shareholders stands in contrast to the members of a partnership (who owe many duties among themselves). In the absence of a contract to the contrary, there is no duty of utmost good faith or fiduciary duty owed by the shareholders of a corporation towards the corporation or the other shareholders of the corporation. For instance, in *Great Western Natural Gas Co. v. Central Gas Utilities Ltd.*,[228] the defendant was a substantial creditor and shareholder of the plaintiff corporation, and provided day-to-day management for the plaintiff. In competition with the plaintiff, the defendant obtained a franchise for the distribution of natural gas in an area in which the plaintiff already carried on the business of distributing propane gas. The plaintiff sued the defendant for a declaration that the defendant held the natural gas franchise subject to a constructive trust in favour of the plaintiff. It argued that the defendant's provision of day-to-day management to the plaintiff placed it in a fiduciary relationship to the plaintiff, which prevented it from competing against it. The Supreme Court of Canada rejected these contentions. Even the defendant's management position did not place it in a fiduciary position with the plaintiff or remove legal control over the management of the corporation from the plaintiff's directors.

J. CONCLUSION

§2.127 For the most part, the common law adopts a relatively straightforward approach to the status of personality and the consequences that flow from it. A being or entity is either a legal person or not, and once the personality of a given being or entity is recognized, with few qualifications the full range of rights and obligations associated with personality attach to that being or entity. Among these attributes are the notion that each person is entitled to its own property and other assets and rights, and is subject to its own obligations and liabilities. By extension, one person is not normally liable for the obligations and liabilities of another. The principle of limited liability is thus fully consistent with the basic common law conception of personality.

§2.128 Nevertheless, there are important exceptions to this general approach. One person may sometimes be held to be vicariously liable for the obligations of another. As we shall see, the principle of vicarious liability is one of particular application with respect to corporations. Despite the general presumption of limited liability that we have discussed in this chapter, a shareholder, director or other corporate insider may sometimes so involve himself or herself in the business or affairs of a corporation as to become personally liable in respect of cor-

---

[226] See Chapter 12, Shareholders and Their Rights.
[227] See, generally, *Soper v. Littlejohn* (1901), 31 S.C.R. 572.
[228] [1966] S.C.R. 630.

porate acts or omissions. Such liability may be civil, administrative, criminal or quasi-criminal. Different principles govern each form of liability. And it is to this subject that we shall turn, in the next chapter.

Chapter 3

CORPORATE LIABILITY

A. INTRODUCTION

§3.1 As we have discussed, the primary purpose of nearly all corporations will be related to the holding and administration of some asset or collection of assets. In the case of a business corporation, the assets in question will generally relate to some form of integrated collective enterprise — although this is far less universally true. It is a basic principle of elementary accounting that for every asset, there must be some off-setting liability or obligation. This principle is equally manifest in corporate law practice. Liabilities of various kinds swirl around every corporate form of organization. It follows that a critical part of the study of corporate law is to differentiate between those liabilities and obligations that belong to the corporation, and those that belong to its directors, officers, shareholders and other stakeholders. Many of these principles (*e.g.*, with respect to the director's general duty of care and fiduciary duty) are best deferred until a later point in the text, where they can be studied more in the context of the office or other element of corporate organization to which they relate. However, a study of the following aspects of corporate liability does much to complete the general introduction to the basic concepts of incorporation that have been surveyed in the two previous chapters.

B. LIABILITY OF A CORPORATION FOR THE ACTS OF ITS INSIDERS

§3.2 While it is usual to think of limited liability and separate personality in terms of how these concepts insulate the shareholders of a corporation from liability for the debts and obligations of the corporation, by the same token the separate personality of the corporation also means that the corporation is not, as a rule, itself liable for the wrongdoing of its shareholders. A shareholder's interest in the corporation is, of course, exigible by his or her creditors;[1] but the assets of the cor-

---

[1] Surprisingly, shares were not exigible at common law, but this deficiency was eliminated in Ontario in the early 19th century. As to the procedure which must be followed to execute against shares, see: *Goodwin v. Ottawa & Prescott Rlwy. Co.* (1862), 22 U.C.Q.B. 186; *Malouf v. Labad* (1912), 3 O.W.N. 1235 (Div. Ct.); *Re Patmore* (1962), 39 W.W.R. 460 (B.C.S.C.); *British Columbia v. Yu,* [1984] B.C.J. No. 3029, [1984] 6 W.W.R. 13, aff'd [1985] B.C.J. No. 2759 3 W.W.R. 279 (C.A.); *AACR Enterprises Ltd. v. Grimwood* (1984), 51 B.C.L.R. 13 at 14 (S.C.), *per* Meredith J. As to the effect of a writ of execution on shares, see: *Hatch v. Rowland* (1870), 5 P.R. 223 (Ont. Master); *Re Montgomery and Wrights Ltd.* (1917), 38 O.L.R. 335 (H.C.). The case law is divided as to whether the court can compel the directors of a private company to register a transfer of shares: *Phillips v. La Paloma Sweets Ltd.* (1921), 51 O.L.R. 125 (H.C.); *Re*

poration itself cannot be directly attached by them. Nevertheless, liability may flow back to the corporation where those acts, duties or liabilities can be shown to have been incurred by the shareholder when acting as an agent or employee of the corporation and within the scope of his or her authority. Similarly, a corporation may be held vicariously liable for torts committed by its employees or other agents while acting within the scope of their employment,[2] and where a shareholder acts in the capacity of such an agent, the possibility of vicarious liability must therefore be borne in mind.

§3.3 The liability of a corporation for tort grows out of the general law of agency with respect to the liability of a principal for any torts committed by his or her agent.[3] Generally, the liability of a corporation in tort is vicarious, so that in order for the corporation to be found liable, the agent must have committed the tort while acting within the scope of his or her employment.[4] Vicarious liability is liability imposed on one person for the wrongs committed by another. The underlying principles of vicarious liability was discussed by the Supreme Court of Canada in *E.B. v. Order of the Oblates of Mary Immaculate in the Province of British Columbia*.[5] The court stressed that in order for an employer to be held vicariously liable, there must be a strong connection between what the employer asked the employee to do and the wrongful conduct. To satisfy this test it is necessary to show that features of the employment or agency relationship contributed to the ability of the employee or agent to do what was done (taking into account the power conferred and the nature and extent of the employee's duties, whether the wrongful acts occurred while furthering the employer's aims, etc.). A "mere opportunity" to commit the wrongful act does not suffice.

§3.4 The principles of vicarious liability are the subject of near constant comment and refinement by the courts. The present law may be summarized as follows: Vicarious liability in tort may arise either when a corporation directs an employee to do work for the corporation or where a corporation agrees to make the services of an employee available to a third party.[6] In order to affix the cor-

---

Bondi Better Bananas Ltd., [1951] O.R. 845 (C.A.); *Commercial Credit Corp. v. Niagara Finance Co. Ltd.*, [1940] S.C.R. 420; but *cf. Associates Finance Co. v. Webber*, [1972] 4 W.W.R. 131 (B.C.S.C.); *Re Wm M'Culloch & Co., ex p. Trevascus* (1879), 5 V.L.R. 195 at 199, per Stalwall C.J. Accordingly, where a shareholder judgment debtor has an interest in a company the transfer of the shares of which is restricted, the appointment of a receiver may be a better remedy. See also *Re MC United Masonry Ltd.* (1983), 40 O.R. (2d) 330 (C.A.).
[2] *Lloyd v. Grace, Smith & Co.*, [1912] A.C. 716 (H.L.).
[3] *Citizens Life Assurance Co. Ltd. v. Brown*, [1904] A.C. 423 at 426 (P.C.), per Lord Lindley.
[4] A comprehensive list of the authorities on this subject would fill a volume. For a reasonable cross-section the following cases may be consulted: *Houldsworth v. City of Glasgow Bank* (1880), 5 App. Cas. 317 (H.L.); *MacKay v. Commercial Bank of New Brunswick* (1874), L.R. 5 P.C. 394; *Swire v. Francis* (1877), 3 App. Cas. 106 (P.C.); *Lambert v. Great Eastern Rlwy. Co.*, [1909] 2 K.B. 776 (C.A.); *Butler v. Manchester, Sheffield & Lincolnshire Rlwy. Co.* (1888), 21 Q.B.D. 207 (C.A.); *Barwick v. English Joint Stock Bank* (1867), L.R. 2 Exch. 259.
[5] [2005] S.C.J. No. 61.
[6] *McKee v. Dumas*, [1976] O.J. No. 2157, 12 O.R. (2d) 670 at 672-73 (C.A.), per Dubin J.A.; see also *James Street Hardware & Furniture Co. v. Spizziri*, [1985] O.J. No. 2609, 33 C.C.L.T. 209 (Ont. H.C.), var'd [1987] O.J. No. 1022, 43 C.C.L.T. 9 (C.A.).

poration with liability, it is necessary to show that the employee or agent was acting in the course of his or her employment. This will be presumed where the act was a wrongful act authorized by the corporation, or where the employee adopted a wrongful and unauthorized method of doing some lawful act authorized by the corporation. Thus, the corporation is liable even for acts which it has not authorized, provided they are so connected with acts that it has authorized that they may legitimately be regarded as modes — albeit improper modes — of doing the authorized acts. Put simply, the corporation is liable not only for what it has authorized its agent to do, but also for the way in which the agent does it.[7] A corporation may also be liable for torts committed by a non-agent, where the conduct or words of the corporation estop it from denying the agency of that person.[8] Note should be taken of the following general principles of vicarious liability:

- In contract, an agent renders his or her principal liable when acting within the scope of the apparent authority that has been conferred upon the agent. In tort, the issue of liability is more complex. At one time, tort claims against employers or principals based upon vicarious liability also focused on whether the acts of the agent were within the scope of the agent's apparent authority — and even today, there are cases in which the test of liability is so expressed. Obviously, of course, if acts are authorized by the principal, then liability in tort will flow. However, in *Bazley v. Curry*, the Supreme Court of Canada focused on a broader question of fairness, and whether the use of the agent or employee gave rise to a risk of wrong-doing:

    > The common theme resides in the idea that where the employee's conduct is closely tied to a risk that the employer's enterprise has placed in the community, the employer may justly be held vicariously liable for the employee's wrong.[9]

- While vicarious liability flows through to the principal or employer of the agent or employee, it is not derivative from the liability of that person. For instance, a grant of immunity to the agent or employee under statute, for example, does not automatically immunize the employer from vicarious liability.[10]

- Liability is most likely to arise where there was strong element of control (actual or potential) between the corporation and its agent.[11] However, the presence of actual control is, however, only one consideration.[12] The fact that the tortfeasor was in fact acting outside the practical control of the employer, principal or other defendant alleged to be vicariously liable,

---

[7] *Plains Engineering Ltd. v. Barnes Security Services Ltd.* (1987), 43 C.C.L.T. 129 (Alta. Q.B.).
[8] *Smith v. Hull Glass Co.* (1852), 11 C.B. 897, 138 E.R. 729 at 928 (K.B.), per Maule J.; *Re Henry Bentley & Co. & Yorkshire Breweries Ltd., ex p. Harrison* (1893), 69 L.T. 204 (C.A.).
[9] [1999] S.C.J. No. 35, [1999] 2 S.C.R. 534.
[10] *Vollick v. Sheard*, [2005] O.J. No. 1601, 75 O.R. (3d) 621 at para. 25 (C.A.), per Finlayson J.A.
[11] See, generally, *Speckling v. Kearney* (2006), 147 A.C.W.S. (3d) 810 (B.C.S.C.).
[12] See, generally, *Jacobi v. Griffiths*, [1990] S.C.J. No. 36, [1999] 2 S.C.R. 570.

and indeed contrary to the instructions given by that defendant, is not sufficient to exclude liability: In *Blackwater v. Plint*,[13] McLachlin C.J.C. noted that the fact that wrongful acts may occur through the act of an employee, agent or similar person is a cost of business. Imposing vicarious liability serves the policy ends of providing an adequate remedy to people harmed by the tortfeasor whom the defendant engaged to act on its behalf. So, for instance, a principal is liable for the fraud of his agent where the fraudulent act is within the course of the principal's business and the scope of the agent's authority, notwithstanding the motive of the agent to benefit himself rather than the principal.[14]

- A justification for vicarious liability rests on the principle of deterring the person in control of the activities from acting negligently and also ensuring that the hazards of the business are borne by the party, who was in business on his or her own account, or whose workload was lightened through the employment of the agent.[15] In *Bazley v. Curry*, McLachlin, J. noted:

> The cases based on the employer's creation of a situation of friction rest on the idea that if the employer's aims or enterprise incidentally create a situation of friction that may give rise to employees committing tortious acts, an employee's intentional misconduct can be viewed as falling within the scope of the employment and the employer is vicariously liable for ensuing harm. This rationale was used to extend vicarious liability to intentional torts like a provoked bartender's assault on an obnoxious customer. While it does not rest on ostensible or implied authority, it builds on the logic of risk and accident inherent in the cases imposing vicarious liability on the basis that the employee was acting to further the employer's aims. Intentional torts arising from situations of friction are like accidents in that they stem from a risk attendant on carrying out the employer's aims. Like accidents, they occur in circumstances where such incidents can be expected to arise because of the nature of the business, and hence their ramifications appropriately form part of the cost of doing business.
>
> Neither furtherance of the employer's aims nor creation of situations of friction, however, suffice to justify vicarious liability for employee theft or fraud ... A bank employee stealing a client's money cannot be said to be furthering the bank's aims. Nor does the logic of a situation of friction apply, unless one believes that any money-handling operation generates an inexorable temptation to steal. ...
>
> At the heart of the dishonest employee decisions is consideration of fairness and policy ... The same logic dictates that where the employee's wrongdoing was a random act wholly unconnected to the nature of the enterprise and the employee's responsibilities, the employer is not vicariously liable. Thus an employer has been held not liable for a vengeful assault by its store clerk.[16]

---

[13] [2005] S.C.J. No. 59 at para. 20.
[14] *Lloyd v. Grace, Smith & Co.*, [1912] A.C. 716 (H.L.).
[15] *King v. Merrill Lynch Canada Inc.* (2005), 144 A.C.W.S. (3d) 268 at para. 35 (Ont. Sup. Ct.), per Smith J.
[16] [1999] S.C.J. No. 35, [1999] 2 S.C.R. 534 at paras. 19-21.

- While historically, vicarious liability has been applied primarily in both agency and employment situations, it has recently been held that the categories of relationships in law that attract vicarious liability are neither exhaustively defined nor closed.[17] In *K.L.B. v. British Columbia*,[18] it was held

> To make out a successful claim for vicarious liability, plaintiffs must demonstrate at least two things. First, they must show that the relationship between the tortfeasor and the person against whom liability is sought is sufficiently close as to make a claim for vicarious liability appropriate. ... Second, the plaintiffs must demonstrate that the tort is sufficiently connected to the tortfeasor's assigned tasks that the tort can be regarded as a materialization of the risks created by the enterprise. ... These two issues are of course related. A tort will only be sufficiently connected to an enterprise to constitute a materialization of the risks introduced by it if the tortfeasor is sufficiently closely related to the employer to ground a claim for vicarious liability.

- The principal will be held liable where unauthorized acts were so connected with the authorized acts that must be considered as being inextricably connected with those acts that were authorized. On the other hand, no liability will flow where there is only a tenuous connection between what the agent or employee has been asked or empowered to do, and the tort that has been committed.[19]

- When determining whether vicarious liability should be imposed, the court bases its decision on several factors, which include:[20]

    (a) the opportunity afforded by the corporation's enterprise for the tortfeasor to abuse the power entrusted;

    (b) the extent to which the wrongful act furthered the corporation's interests;

    (c) the extent to which the employment or agency situation created intimacy or other conditions conducive to the wrongful act;

    (d) the extent of power conferred on the tortfeasor in relation to the victim; and

    (e) the vulnerability of potential victims.

Although in the past, the courts have distinguished between the employer-employee relationship and the principal-agent relationship, the distinction has little practical bearing today, and both types of relationship attract vicarious li-

---

[17] *671122 Ontario Ltd. v. Sagaz Industries Canada Inc.*, [2001] S.C.J. No. 61, [2001] 2 S.C.R. 983, at para. 25 *per* Major J.
[18] [2003] S.C.J. No. 51, [2003] 2 S.C.R. 403 at para. 19.
[19] *Bazely* at para. 37.
[20] *Blackwater v. Plint*, [2005] S.C.J. No. 59 at para. 20, *per* McLachlin C.J.C. See also *Jacobi v. Griffiths*, [1990] S.C.J. No. 36, [1999] 2 S.C.R. 570, *per* Binnie J.

ability in appropriate circumstances.²¹ The line between an agent-contractor and an independent-contractor is not clear. There is a considerable volume of case law dealing with the distinction between an independent contractor and an employee. Only a few cases, however, are relevant to the question of potential tort liability, since it is readily possible for an independent contractor to be found to be acting in an agency capacity on behalf of the person who has hired that contractor. To give one obvious example: private sector law firms retained by a corporation in connection with a legal matter may or may not be held to be acting as agents of the corporation, depending on the nature of their retainer. For instance, if such counsel are retained to represent the corporation in a legal proceeding, then they have the same general range of implied agency powers as any other lawyer acting on behalf of a client. On the other hand, if the retainer is purely one for the provision of legal advice to the corporation, there is no implication of agency.²² While the law relating to vicarious liability is some respects of vague and uncertain application, it is possible to summarize certain general principles from the above case law. Specifically, an employer is liable for the torts committed by an employee:

(a) In the performance of work carried out solely for the benefit of the employer, if that work was entrusted by the employer to the employee or it was reasonably foreseeable that the employee might undertake that work, even if in the ordinary course it would not be expected that the work in question or manner of performing it would impact adversely on a third party.

(b) In the performance of work or some other obligation that the employer would otherwise be obliged to perform itself. For instance, in *McDonald v. Dickenson*,²³ a township council appointed two council members to a committee to rebuild a culvert under a municipal highway. It was found that while performing this work, they were servants or agents of the corporation, and the maxim of *respondeat superior* applied.

(c) Where the employee commits a tort while exercising an authority of the employer or performing some duty on behalf of the employer, or acting on behalf of the employer with respect to some matter in which the employer has an interest.

A person who retains an independent contractor would appear to be potentially liable under (b) and (c), but not under (a). So, for instance, a homeowner who hires an independent contractor to paint his or her home is not normally liable to a neighbour, if the contractor negligently spills paint onto a neighbour's car. In contrast, an employer who instructs an employee to paint the employer's store

---

[21] *St. Elizabeth Home Society v. City of Hamilton* (2005), 148 A.C.W.S. (3d) 497 at para. 262 (Ont. Sup. Ct.), *per* Crane J.
[22] See, generally, *Chytros v. Standard Life Assurance Co.* (2006), 83 O.R. (3d) 237 (Sup. Ct.); *Scherer v. Paletta*, [1986] 2 O.R. 524; *Sign O-Lite v. Bugeja*, [1994] O.J. No. 1381 (Gen. Div.); *Fabian v. Bud Mervyn Construction Ltd.*, [1981] O.J. No. 3205, 35 O.R. (2d) 132 (H.C.).
[23] (1897), 24 O.A.R. 31 (C.A.).

front will be liable to a neighbouring owner for paint negligently spilled onto the neighbour's car.[24] The greater the degree of control over the agent, the greater the prospect that the principal will be held vicariously liable.

§3.5 A corporation is personally, as opposed to vicariously, liable in tort for the tortious actions of the person(s) who is its directing mind.[25] In contrast to criminal liability, in the civil sphere, the knowledge and acts of two or more principal officers can be aggregated for the purpose of determining whether the corporation is negligent, irrespective of whether each or any of those individuals behaved negligently. So in *Standard Investments Ltd. v. CIBC*[26] it was said a corporation cannot be found in law to have a split personality. It cannot rely on the lack of knowledge on the part of one of its directing minds of the acts, disregarding any intentions and knowledge of a second directing mind operating in the same sphere, to protect it from liability for the actions of that second directing mind, nor can it escape responsibility for the combined activities of both directing minds. At least in civil cases, where the element of *mens rea* is not applicable, when there are two or more directing minds operating within the same field assigned to both of them, the knowledge, intentions and acts of each become together the total knowledge, intention and acts of the corporation which they represent.

§3.6 It does not matter that the corporation would never have authorized the actual mode of action that the agent adopted, could not lawfully do so,[27] or has prohibited its employees or agents from acting a particular unlawful manner. Thus, a corporation which owns a truck that is negligently driven by one of its truck drivers when making deliveries on behalf of the corporation will be liable for any injury thereby caused. So too, if a corporation entrusts property of which it is bailee to one of its employees, and that employee steals it, the corporation is vicariously liable for theft.[28] Similarly, a corporation is vicariously liable for negligent misrepresentation made by an employee in the course of his or her employment.[29] In *McArthur v. Imperial Trust Co.*,[30] money was entrusted by the plaintiff to an officer and employee of the corporate defendant who subse-

---

[24] See, generally, *Choi v. Sutton Group Central Realty Inc.* (1998), 77 A.C.W.S. (3d) 235 (Ont. Gen. Div.); *Lockhart v. C.P.R.*, [1942] 3 W.W.R. 149 at 157 (P.C.); *Lloyd v. Grace, Smith & Co.*, [1912] A.C. 716 at 725, 735-36, and 742 (H.L.).
[25] *ACA Cooperative Association Ltd. v. Associated Freezers of Canada Inc.*, [1992] N.S.J. No. 255, 93 D.L.R. (4th) 559 (C.A.). *R. v. Ontario Power Generation*, [2006] O.J. No. 4659 (Ct. J.) — determination as to whether a manager was a "directing mind" of the corporation; individual not a directing mind where he or she did not make or design corporate policy, did not have governing executive authority, and worked solely in an operational capacity.
[26] [1985] O.J. No. 2668, 22 D.L.R. (4th) 410 at 430-31 (C.A.), *per* Goodman J.A., leave to appeal to S.C.C. ref'd 53 O.R. (2d) 663*n*.
[27] *Lockhart v. C.P.R.*, [1942] 3 W.W.R. 149 at 157 (P.C.), *per* Lord Thankerton; *Campbell v. Paddington Corp.*, [1911] 1 K.B. 869, *per* Avory J. Compare, however, *Poulton v. London & South Western Rlwy. Co.* (1867), L.R. 2 Q.B. 534 (now taken to mean that the corporation is not seen to have given implied authority to its employees to do a patently unlawful act).
[28] *Morris v. C.W. Martin & Sons Ltd.*, [1966] 1 Q.B. 716 at 731 (C.A.), *per* Diplock L.J.
[29] *Froebel v. Claxton*, [1997] B.C.J. No. 1284, 34 B.L.R. (2d) 276 (S.C.).
[30] (1911), 17 W.L.R. 415 (B.C.S.C.).

quently absconded with the money. In an action for breach of trust against the corporation, it was held that these two persons were acting within the company's corporate powers and within the scope of their employment when they committed their fraud. Therefore the corporation was vicariously liable for their misconduct.

§3.7 In *Adams v. National Electric Tramway & Lighting Co.*,[31] the question arose as to whether a corporation might be liable for tortious conduct committed by an employee contrary to the direction or policies of the corporation. It was held that liability could arise in such circumstances. Thus, where an employee commits a tort in the course of his or her employment for the benefit of an employer, the employer may still be liable irrespective of whether the tort was committed under the employer's order or not, indeed even if it was beyond the power of the company to authorize the act concerned, or the doing of the act was actually forbidden by the corporation.[32]

§3.8 Furthermore, if the agent commits a breach of duty, not in the actual performance of the task entrusted to the agent, but while doing something reasonably incidental to that performance, the corporation will be liable. For instance, in *Photo Production Ltd. v. Securicor Transport Ltd.*,[33] a night patrolman employed by a company (which had contracted to provide security services to the plaintiff) lit a match while inspecting the plaintiff's premises. The match touched off a fire which caused great damage. Although the defendant company was eventually excused from liability under the terms of an exclusion clause, Lord Diplock felt that in the absence of such a clause the company would have been liable.[34]

§3.9 However, where an employee does an act that is completely independent of his or her employment and that is not only unauthorized but prohibited by the corporation, vicarious liability will not apply.[35] So, for instance, where an employee hired to guard a building committed a deliberate act of arson and burned the building down, the corporation that employed the guard was held not to be vicariously liable.[36] A corporation is vicariously liable for what is done by its operative agents while acting on its behalf. It is not an implicit guarantor of their good behavior when they act in any other capacity.[37] Thus, the corporation will

---

[31] (1983), 3 B.C.R. 199 (C.A.).
[32] See, generally, *Harris v. Brunette Saw Mill Co.* (1893), 3 B.C.R. 172 (C.A.).
[33] [1980] A.C. 827, [1980] 1 All E.R. 556 (H.L.).
[34] *Photo Production Ltd. v. Securicor Transport Ltd.*, [1980] A.C. 827, [1980] 1 All E.R. 556 at 568 (H.L.), *per* Lord Diplock. See also Lord Salmon at 569.
[35] *Bickman v. Smith Motors Ltd.*, [1955] 5 D.L.R. 256 (Alta. C.A.); see also *R. v. Crown Diamond Paint Co.*, [1983] 1 F.C. 837 (C.A.).
[36] *Plains Engineering Ltd. v. Barnes Security Services Ltd.*, [1987] A.J. No. 1156, 43 C.C.L.T. 129 (Q.B.). *Quaere* the corporation may be held liable as a principal (rather than vicariously liable) for breach of a duty of care in the hiring of its workers.
[37] With respect to the potential liability of a third party in connection with assisting corporate agents in perpetrating a wrong by or against the corporation, see: *Northland Bank v. Willson*, [1999] A.J. No. 1010, 249 A.R. 201 (Q.B.), cross appeal allowed in part 15 B.L.R. (3d) 5 (C.A.); see also *Alberta Treasury Branches v. Ghermezian*, [1999] A.J. No. 1023, 249 A.R. 240 (Q.B.); *Sorrel 1985 Partnership v. Sorrel Resources*, [2000] A.J. No. 1140, 10 B.L.R. (3d) 61 (C.A.).

not be liable if the employee or agent goes off on some frolic of his or her own, unrelated to the performance of his or her duties.[38] In such cases, the agent clearly departs from the scope of his or her employment and thus there is no basis for holding the corporation vicariously liable.[39]

§3.10 Vicarious liability must be distinguished from liability as a principal. As an artificial entity, a corporation must necessarily act through agents. Vicarious liability arises where the law holds one person accountable for the misconduct of another, although the person so held liable is not personally blameworthy.[40] Where a corporation actively participates in a tort, it is not vicariously liable but rather is itself personally liable for the wrongdoing concerned. Therefore, entirely separate from the question of vicarious liability, there is no doubt that where a corporation authorizes or directs the commission of a tort, it will be liable for that tort. The corporation will be primarily liable where the act complained of can be attributed to its directing mind — to a person who acts not on behalf of the corporation, but rather as the corporation.[41] Thus primary liability for tortious injury attaches to the corporation where the directors of the corporation authorize the tortious act, although in such a case the corporation may be entitled to a claim over against the directors for maladministration of its business.[42]

§3.11 Moreover, a corporation may be found liable for wrongs committed by its officers, agents or employees, where they possess knowledge under circumstances which permit that knowledge to be attributed back to the corporation.[43]

---

[38] *Joel v. Morison* (1834), 6 C. & P. 501 at 503, 172 E.R. 1338 (N.P.), *per* Parke B.
[39] *Kooragang Investments Pty. Ltd. v. Richardson & Wrench Ltd.,* [1982] A.C. 462 (P.C.).
[40] Flemming, *The Law of Torts* (Sydney: The Law Book Co., 1971), at 312.
[41] *Lennard's Carrying Co. v. Asiatic Petroleum Co.,* [1915] A.C. 705 at 713-14 (H.L.), *per* Viscount Haldane L.C.
[42] *Multinational Gas & Petrochemical Co. v. Multinational Gas & Petrochemical Services Ltd.,* [1983] Ch. 258 (C.A.).
[43] The question of whether knowledge possessed by a corporate officer should be attributed back to his or her corporation is complex. If the officer in question is the effective directing mind of the corporation, then any knowledge acquired by the officer will normally be so attributed back: *El Ajou v. Dollar Land Holdings plc,* [1994] 1 B.C.L.C. 464 (C.A.). Knowledge possessed by other (lower ranked) officers may be attributed back, depending upon the circumstances of the case. See, for instance, *Regina Fur Co. v. Bossom,* [1957] 2 Lloyd's Rep. 466 at 468, *per* Pearson J. (on appeal [1958] 2 Lloyd's Rep. 425 (C.A.)):

> ... [I]n deciding whether in a particular case the knowledge of the agent is to be imputed to the company, or other principal, one should consider, mainly at any rate, (1) the position of the agent in relation to the principal and whether the agent had a wide or narrow sphere of operations, and (2) the position of the agent in relation to the relevant transaction and whether he represented the principal in respect of that transaction.

If the information is obtained by the officer privately (*i.e.,* not in his or her capacity as an officer of the company), then the knowledge will not normally be attributed back to the corporation: *Re David Payne & Co.,* [1904] 2 Ch. 608 (C.A.). Similarly, the corporation will not be impressed with knowledge possessed by an officer who is guilty of a wrong against the company. So in *J.C. Houghton & Co. v. Nothard, Lowe & Wills,* [1928] A.C. 1 at 19 (H.L.), Viscount Sumner said:

> It has long been recognized that it would be contrary to justice and common sense to treat the knowledge of such persons as that of the company, as if one were to assume that they would make a clean breast of their delinquency.

The question of attribution back to the corporation is one of construction, rather than metaphysics.[44] The question of what knowledge (and state of mind) could be attributed back to a corporation based upon the knowledge of its officers was considered by the Court of Appeal in *R. v. Rozeik*.[45] This case grew out of dishonest applications made to finance companies for the funds required to purchase equipment to be used by corporations controlled or owned by the appellant. The Crown alleged that false information was provided to the finance companies, although it was accepted by the Crown that the managers of the finance companies were not deceived. In delivering the judgment of the court allowing the appeal against conviction, Leggatt L.J. turned first to the question of whether the two managers were directing minds relative to the transactions in which the fraud was alleged to have occurred:

> For the purposes of determining whether in entering into the hire purchase agreements the company was deceived, whose state of mind stood as the state of mind of the company? The person who in each branch most obviously represented the company was the branch manager. Mr. Shaw drew attention to many examples of employees declaring in evidence that they worked under the supervision and control of Birch. Others similarly worked under Wilkinson. In relation to several of the counts the evidence showed direct implication by one of them. The managers appear to have had the conduct of those transactions, so as to involve their direct indorsement or approval of it. It may also, we think, be said with some force that, once the credit limits had been set by Birch and Wilkinson, all the ensuing transactions within the limits proceeded by their authority. By appointing credit limits Birch and Wilkinson must be taken to have authorized all transactions with the appellant up to and within those limits.[46]

The next and more difficult question was whether the knowledge of Birch and Wilkinson could be attributed back to their respective companies. Leggatt L.J. continued:

> The company may be liable to third parties or be guilty of criminal offences even though that employee was acting dishonestly or against the interests of the company, or contrary to orders. But different considerations apply where the company is the victim, and the employee's activities have caused or assisted the company to suffer loss. The company will not be fixed with knowledge where the employee or officer has been defrauding it. ... It is not a question of the manager having notice of the fraud: his state of mind is the state of mind of the company, and the company is deceived unless the manager is party to the deception. The reason why the company is not visited with the manager's knowledge is that the same individual cannot both be party to the deception and represent the company for the purpose of its being deceived. Unless therefore, it is proved that the managers were party to the fraud, with the result that their knowledge can be disregarded, their knowledge must be imputed to the companies, and the fact that other employees of the company were deceived could not avail the companies.[47]

---

[44] *Meridian Global Funds Management Asia Ltd. v. Securities Commission*, [1995] 2 A.C. 500, [1995] B.C.C. 942 at 945-46 (P.C.), *per* Lord Hoffmann.
[45] [1996] B.C.C. 271 (C.A.).
[46] *Ibid.*, at 274, *per* Leggatt L.J.
[47] *Ibid.*, at 275.

The Court of Appeal held that there was no evidence on which it could be inferred that either of the managers were acting dishonestly. Accordingly, the convictions were quashed.

§3.12 In *Acer v. Percy*[48] the plaintiff alleged that certain individuals had sold shares in the defendant corporation in breach of trust. It was further alleged that this sale had been made with the knowledge of the president of the corporation, who had made a profit on the transaction. The defendant corporation moved to strike out all references in the pleading to the president (who was not a party to the action) on the ground that even if the president was privy to the fraud it did not result in any liability to the company. The motion was rejected and it was held that the pleading was good. The company acquired the shares through the connivance of the president, and therefore his connivance was related back to the corporation.

§3.13 In *Dixon v. Deacon Morgan McEwan Easson*,[49] the president and chief financial officer of National Business Systems Inc. ("NBS") falsified its records in order to improve the appearance of its financial condition. The president issued a press release which presented a false picture of the financial affairs of the corporation. The plaintiff purchased shares of NBS in reliance upon the press release. Following discovery of the true financial position, the share price fell from the $12.50 per share paid by the plaintiff to $1.65 per share. NBS argued that it was not liable for the misconduct of the president and chief financial officer. On appeal, it was held that their acts should be identified with the corporation, and accordingly it was liable. In reaching this conclusion, McEachern C.J.B.C. referred to the following passage from the decision of Estey J. in *R. v. McNamara (No. 1)*:

> ... in my view, the identification doctrine only operates where the Crown demonstrates that the action taken by the directing mind (a) was within the field of operation assigned to him; (b) was not totally in fraud of the corporation, and (c) was by design or result partly for the benefit of the company.[50]

McEachern C.J.B.C. continued:

> The foregoing, of course, is the theory by which a company may be found criminally responsible for the fraudulent acts of its employees. The trial judge concluded that the defendant had failed to bring itself within the exception provided by the above test because, at the very least, it had a better credit relationship with its lenders after the falsely enhanced financial statements were released. While it appears the learned trial judge may have imposed an onus on the defendant in this respect, I think the result is the same ... [The] President and Chief Financial Officer were still operating minds of the Company at the time the Press Release was published and at the time the plaintiff purchased his shares. The findings of the trial judge that the fraud of the officers was the fraud of the company in these cir-

---

[48] (1901), 5 Que. P.R. 401.
[49] [1993] B.C.J. No. 1095, 12 B.L.R. (2d) 184 (C.A.).
[50] [1985] S.C.J. No. 28, 19 D.L.R. (4th) 314 at 351 (Ont. C.A.).

cumstances led inescapably to the conclusion that the fraudulent intent of the officers was also the fraudulent intent of the Company.

> In my judgment, the plaintiff was clearly entitled to succeed on the issue of fraudulent misrepresentation and I would allow the plaintiff's appeal on that issue.[51]

§3.14 Ordinarily, because of the principle of limited liability, a shareholder of a corporation is not liable for the torts committed by the corporation or its agents. Similarly, the directors of a corporation will not normally be liable for torts for which the corporation is responsible. While the subject of director (and officer) liability is discussed in detail below, it can be stated here conveniently that as a general rule, liability will apply to a director (or shareholder) where he or she has breached a duty owed by him or her personally to the victim of the tort.[52]

C. SEPARATE TAXATION

§3.15 Like limited liability, the separate taxation of a company is an outgrowth of the separate personality of a company.[53] Subsection 2(1) of the *Income Tax Act* provides that:

> an income tax shall be payable as hereinafter required upon the taxable income for each taxation year of every person resident in Canada at any time in the year.

Unlike the tax laws of the United States, Canadian income tax law provides very limited opportunity for a tax payer to elect the type of tax treatment that a corporate entity (or near corporation) will receive. While flow-through arrangements are not unknown, they are of limited availability (*e.g.*, in the case of flow-through shares of mineral exploration companies). In nearly all cases, since a company is a separate person, it must pay income tax in accordance with that Act. The liability of the company to pay that tax is separate and personal to the company, and in accordance with Division B of the Act, the company must calculate its income in terms of its own receipts and disbursements.

§3.16 Because a company is a separate person for tax purposes, to at least some extent it may be employed to shelter income or a portion of income from taxation or defer taxation on that income by retaining funds in the company until such time as the shareholder chooses to remove those funds on a tax-free or reduced-tax basis (as, for instance, where the shareholder incurs a business loss

---

[51] *Dixon v. Deacon Morgan McEwan Easson*, [1993] B.C.J. No. 1095, 12 B.L.R. (2d) 184 at 188 (C.A.).

[52] See, for instance, *Williams v. Natural Life Health Food Ltd.*, [1978] 1 W.L.R. 830 (H.L.). Such a personal duty may either be imposed by law under general principles of tort, trust or contract, or may be assumed as a result of the personal conduct of the director or officer in question: *Dawson International plc v. Coats Paton plc*, [1988] S.L.T. 854 at 861, *per* Lord Cullen. See also *London Drugs Ltd. v. Kuehne & Nagel International Ltd.*, [1992] S.C.J. No. 84, [1992] 3 S.C.R. 299; *ScotiaMcLeod Inc. v. Peoples Jewellers Ltd.*, [1995] O.J. No. 3556, 26 O.R. (3d) 481 (C.A.), *per* Finlayson J.A., leave to appeal to S.C.C. ref'd [1996] S.C.C.A. No. 40, 137 D.L.R. (4th) vin.

[53] See, generally, *Deptuck v. The Queen*, [2002] T.C.J. No. 306, [2002] 3 C.T.C. 2396, [2002] Can. Tax Ct. LEXIS 1038 (Tax Ct. Can.).

that may be offset against earned income). However, for two reasons the separate tax liability of a company may also be a disadvantage arising from incorporation. First because income is taxed initially as it is earned by the company and then again when it is distributed to the shareholders of the company, the use of a company may result in some degree of double taxation. Second, even where a company is wholly owned, it remains a separate taxpayer. As a result, where A incorporates B Ltd., it is not possible to offset the losses of A against the taxable income of B Ltd., nor is it possible to offset any losses incurred by B Ltd. against the taxable income of A, at least not directly. Thus, either a parent company or its subsidiary may continue in a tax-paying position even though they would not be in such a position if the two enterprises were considered on a consolidated basis.

D. CRIMINAL LIABILITY OF A CORPORATION

§3.17 Until recently, the liability of a corporation for criminal and quasi-criminal misconduct of its employees, directors or officers was a fairly unsettled area of the law. At the federal level, the situation has now been much clarified by way of amendment to the *Criminal Code*. At the provincial quasi-criminal level, the question of whether a corporation can be convicted of a particular offence continues to be decided by the common law rules governing such liability.

§3.18 Corporate criminal liability involves a consideration of a wide range of factual and public policy issues, including the following: (a) can a corporation possess an independent knowledge of the facts relevant to a crime, and if so in what circumstances should such knowledge be attributed to it?[54] (b) can a corporation properly be seen to carry out the *actus reus* of the crime? (c) can a corporation form the necessary criminal intent?[55] (d) what, if any, public purpose is served by holding a corporation criminally responsible? And (e) should corporations be subject to special rules of criminal liability or merely the same rules which apply to all persons generally?[56] To these difficult legal and factual questions, there is often added a significant measure of emotional response, which clouds and complicates their resolution — as is perhaps only predictable given the great outrage and feelings of pity which often arise naturally from the types of personal injury and death which so often give rise to criminal charges. It is fair to say that none of these considerations has yet been adequately, much less comprehensively, addressed.

---

[54] See, for instance, *R. v. P. & O. European Ferries (Dover) Ltd.* (1990), 93 Cr. App. R. 72; *Director General of Fair Trading v. Pioneer Concrete (U.K.) Ltd.*, [1995] 1 A.C. 456 (H.L.).

[55] See, generally, *Meridian Global Funds Management Asia Ltd. v. Securities Commission*, [1995] 2 A.C. 500 (P.C.); *Moore v. I. Bresler Ltd.*, [1944] 2 All E.R. 515 (K.B.); *H.L. Bolton (Engineering) Co. v. T.J. Graham & Sons Ltd.*, [1957] 1 Q.B. 159 (C.A.).

[56] See, generally, the Law Commission's Consultation Paper, *Criminal Law: Involuntary Manslaughter* (London: HMSO, 1994, No. 135).

(i) Corporate Criminal Liability at Common Law

§3.19 To better understand the new *Criminal Code* approach, it is advisable to consider first the common law rules governing corporate criminal and quasi-criminal liability. Such liability is clearest where specifically provided for by statute. Many statutes that create offences expressly provide that corporations may be convicted of such offences. For instance, subsection 122(1) of the *Securities Act* provides:

> Every person or company that,
>
> (*a*) makes a statement in any material, evidence or information submitted to the Commission, a Director, any person acting under the authority of the Commission or the Executive Director or any person appointed to make an investigation or examination under this Act that, in a material respect and at the time and in the light of the circumstances under which it is made, is misleading or untrue or does not state a fact that is required to be stated or that is necessary to make the statement not misleading;
>
> (*b*) makes a statement in any application, release, report, preliminary prospectus, prospectus, return, financial statement, information circular, take-over bid circular, issuer bid circular or other document required to be filed or furnished under Ontario securities law that, in a material respect and at the time and in the light of the circumstances under which it is made, is misleading or untrue or does not state a fact that is required to be stated or that is necessary to make the statement not misleading; or
>
> (*c*) contravenes Ontario securities law,
>
> is guilty of an offence and on conviction is liable to a fine of not more than $5 million or to imprisonment for a term of not more than five years less a day, or to both.[57]

§3.20 Where there is such a statutory provision, the application of the rule in question is a mere matter of statutory interpretation. However, even in such cases, one critical question is whether prosecutorial effort should focus on the corporation or those individuals who stand behind it, and who are directly or indirectly responsible for the conduct of the relevant aspect of the corporation's business or affairs ought also to be liable. Liability under subsection 122(1) — and similar provisions like it in other legislation — relates only to offences committed directly by a person. Accordingly, a director or officer of a corporation cannot be charged under this provision merely because the corporation with which he or she is connected has committed some offence unless he or she personally also committed one of the specified offences. However, there are many statutes that impose an express liability on the directors, officers or employees of a corporation who implicated in some way in an offence committed by a corporation. Director and officer liability provisions may impose liability as an alternative or in addition to corporate liability. The *Securities Act* contains some

---

[57] R.S.O. 1990, c. S.5.

of the most potentially punitive director and officer liability provisions of any Provincial statute. Subsection 122(3) of that Act provides:

> Every director or officer of a company or of a person other than an individual who authorizes, permits or acquiesces in the commission of an offence under subsection (1) by the company or person, whether or not a charge has been laid or a finding of guilt has been made against the company or person in respect of the offence under subsection (1), is guilty of an offence and is liable on conviction to a fine of not more than $5 million or to imprisonment for a term of not more than five years less a day, or to both.

Subsection 129.2 of that Act further provides:

> For the purposes of this Act, if a company or a person other than an individual has not complied with Ontario securities law, a director or officer of the company or person who authorized, permitted or acquiesced in the non-compliance shall be deemed to also have not complied with Ontario securities law, whether or not any proceeding has been commenced against the company or person under Ontario securities law or any order has been made against the company or person under section 127.

§3.21 Director and officer liability provisions are not limited to offences committed within the core area of corporate activity, such as the issue of securities and the conduct of the affairs of a corporation, but frequently extend to any business in which the corporation may engage. Particular concerns apply with respect to regulated aspects of business. For instance, subsection 43(2) of the *Regulated Health Professions Act, 1991* — dealing with the performance of "controlled acts" by someone other than an authorized health professional — provides that directors of corporate employers may be convicted of an offence where they have "approved of, permitted or acquiesced in the contravention" of the prohibitions set out in subsection 27(1) of the Act with respect to such acts. In whatever type of statute or regulation such provisions may appear, they are conclusive with respect to the question of the potential liability of corporations, their directors and officers to prosecution.

§3.22 It is one thing to provide by statute that a corporation has the potential or capacity to be convicted of an offence. It is quite another to decide when the corporation is guilty of conduct sufficient to justify its conviction. To date, the common law has not produced a single comprehensive theory with respect to this aspect of liability. Different approaches have been taken depending upon the wording of the legislation under which the statute is created, the nature of the offence, and (to be frank) the degree of public outrage associated with the offence that has allegedly been committed.

§3.23 It has long been recognized that a corporation may be convicted of regulatory offences created by statute. For instance, in *R. v. Birmingham & Gloucester Rlwy. Co.*,[58] the Divisional Court upheld an indictment against the defendant company for failing to construct connecting arches over a railway line

---

[58] (1842), 3 Q.B. 223.

that it had built. The deficiency in construction was in breach of an absolute statutory duty imposed upon the corporation. In subsequent case law, a more general conclusion was reached that a corporation would be liable for a statutory offence where the failure to impose such liability would render the statute nugatory, and thereby defeat the will of the legislature.[59] A corporation might also be convicted of public nuisance arising from the misconduct of its operations.[60] Two lines of reasoning underlie these decisions. The first was that liability might be imposed under a delegation principle: a corporation will be liable for the acts or non-performance of another person where it delegates the performance of a statutory duty to that other person and the person in question fails to perform that duty. The second line of reasoning was that liability might be imposed where, as a matter of construction, the corporation could be said to be liable vicariously for the acts of its employees or agents.[61] Since vicarious criminal liability involves the imposition of criminal liability without *mens rea*, it obviously can apply only in the case of strict liability offences.

§3.24 Thus it is clear that criminal liability applies where the act or omission in question can be specifically attributed to the corporation itself[62] (as for instance where the corporation fails to discharge a statutory duty of care or contravenes some other regulatory provision: the normal situation in cases relating to the trading activities of the corporation),[63] or the manner in which it carries on its

---

[59] See, for instance, *Mullins v. Collins* (1874), L.R. 9 Q.B. 292.
[60] *R. v. Great North of England Rlwy.* (1846), 9 Q.B. 315 at 327, *per* Lord Denman C.J.
[61] In *R. v. Safety-Kleen Canada Inc.*, [1997] O.J. No. 800, 145 D.L.R. (4th) 276 at 284 (C.A.), *per* Doherty J.A., a very specific indication was given as to the type of language required to create statutory vicarious liability:

> Had the Legislature intended to impose vicarious liability on corporate employers for all offences committed by employees in the course of their employment, it would have used language such as that found in section 207(1) of the *Highway Traffic Act*. That section reads in part:
>
> > ... the owner of a vehicle may be charged with and convicted of an offence under this Act or the regulations or any municipal by-law regulating traffic for which the driver of the vehicle is subject to be charged unless, at the time of the offence, the vehicle was in the possession of some person other than the owner without the owner's consent ... (emphasis added)
>
> Unlike section 146f of the [*Environmental Protection*] *Act*, section 207 of the *Highway Traffic Act* does not merely attribute the acts or omissions of the driver to the owner of the motor vehicle. Instead, it renders the owner liable for conviction for any offence committed by the driver. By imputing only the acts or omissions of the employee to the corporate employer instead of rendering the employer liable for conviction for any offence committed by the employee, the Legislature stopped short of imposing total vicarious liability on corporate employers for any and all offences ... committed by their employees. The employee's act becomes the employer's by virtue of section 146f, but fault must still be attributed to the corporate employer either through the identification theory doctrine where the offence is one of *mens rea*, or through a failure to establish due diligence where the offence is one of strict liability.

[62] As to the application of the principle of general deterrence where a corporation is convicted of an offence, see *R. v. Church of Scientology*, [1997] O.J. No. 1548, 33 O.R. (3d) 65 (C.A.).
[63] See generally, *R. v. Sobey's Inc.*, [1998] N.S.J. No. 467, 172 D.L.R. (4th) 782 (C.A.).

business.[64] However, in recent years, there has been a steady expansion of the range of corporate criminal liability,[65] and it now seems that on the appropriate facts a corporation might be properly convicted of most crimes.[66]

§3.25 At one time it was believed that a corporation could not be convicted of an offence for which death or imprisonment was the only punishment, such as murder or treason.[67] However, except where otherwise provided by law, section 719 of the *Criminal Code* now provides that a corporation that is convicted of an offence is liable, in lieu of any imprisonment that is prescribed as punishment for that offence, to be fined in an amount:

- that is in the discretion of the court, where the offence is an indictable offence; or

- not exceeding $25,000, where the offence is a summary conviction offence.

Although there are some offences which a corporation would be incapable of committing itself by virtue of its status as an artificial person (*e.g.*, perjury, rape or bigamy),[68] a corporation may still be a party to such an offence under section 21 of the *Criminal Code,* which provides that every one is a party to an offence who:

- actually commits it;

- does or omits to do anything for the purpose of aiding any person to commit it; or

- abets any person in committing it.

Where two or more persons form an intention to carry out an unlawful purpose and to assist each other in that purpose and any one of them, in carrying out the common purpose, commits an offence, each of them who knew or ought to have known that the commission of the offence would be a probable consequence of carrying out the common purpose is a party to that offence.[69]

§3.26 A corporation may also be guilty of counselling the commission of an offence under section 22 of the *Criminal Code*. A person counsels the commission of an offence where he or she procures, solicits or incites its commis-

---

[64] See, for instance, *Lennard's Carrying Co. v. Asiatic Petroleum Co.,* [1915] A.C. 705 at 713 (H.L.), *per* Viscount Haldane; *Re Akiba Investment Ltd.,* [1963] 1 O.R. 513, aff'd [1963] 1 O.R. 517n (C.A.); *R. v. J.J. Beamish Const. Co.,* [1968] 1 O.R. 5, appeal quashed [1968] 1 O.R. 31n (S.C.C.).

[65] See, for instance, *R. v. H.M. Coroner for East Kent, ex p. Spooner* (1987), 3 B.C.C. 636 (D.C.).

[66] So, for instance, it has been held that a director may conspire with corporations of which he or she is the directing mind: *Hall-Chem Inc. v. Vulcan Packaging Inc.,* [1994] O.J. No. 817, 12 B.L.R. (2d) 274 at 297 (Gen. Div.), *per* Spence J.; *cf. R. v. McDonnell,* [1966] 1 Q.B. 233 (Bristol Assizes). The subject of conspiracy between a corporation and its directing mind is discussed in greater detail below at para. 3.52.

[67] *R. v. I.C.R. Haulage Ltd.,* [1944] K.B. 551 at 544 (C.A.), *per* Slade J.

[68] *Ibid.*

[69] *Criminal Code*, R.S.C. 1985, c. C-46, s. 21(2).

sion.[70] Subsection 22(1) provides that where a person counsels another person to be a party to an offence and that person is afterwards a party to that offence, the person who counselled is a party to that offence, even where the offence was committed in a different way from that which was counselled. Similarly, under subsection 22(2) of the *Criminal Code*, every person who counsels another person to be a party to an offence is a party to every offence that the other commits in consequence of the counselling if the person who gave that counsel knew or ought to have known that an offence was likely to be committed in consequence of the counselling.

(ii) Approaches to Liability

§3.27 At common law, the principle of vicarious liability as a basis for imposing criminal liability on a corporation was early rejected by the courts,[71] at least with respect to the "hard core" of criminal offences. Vicarious liability, although considered an acceptable basis for requiring a corporation to compensate a third party injured by reason of the conduct of the corporation's employees, was considered incompatible with the moral basis of criminal liability. Crimes requiring proof of a culpable mental state are said to require proof of *mens rea*. This category of offence includes all of the major criminal offences of theft, fraud, manslaughter[72] and the like. Absent a statutory basis for such liability, a corporation can only be guilty of such an offence if the corporation itself can be shown to have possessed the required *mens rea*. However, the courts accepted three exceptional cases in which criminal liability could arise vicariously, on the basis that liability for these offenses was strict and did not depend upon whether the accused possessed the necessary *mens rea*. These exceptions were: criminal libel,[73] contempt of court[74] and public nuisance.[75] Eventually, these exceptions would be expanded to provide for vicarious corporate criminal liability with respect to all strict liability offenses, which includes the vast majority of regulatory offenses. For offences requiring *mens rea*, two major approaches evolved with respect to the determination of whether a corporation should be held criminally liable (in the absence of clear statutory direction). These are the aggregation principle and the identification principle.

(1) The Aggregation Principle

§3.28 The courts within the Commonwealth have shown no great interest in the adoption of the "aggregation" principle, under which the separate knowledge of two or more corporate agents can be "aggregated" together, so as to form the basis for a finding of a criminal intent. Although it is common to speak of aggregating the separate faults of individual officers or employees, in most cases the aggregation said to justify criminal prosecution pertains to the

---

[70] *Ibid.*, s. 22(3).
[71] See, for instance, *R. v. Huggins* (1730), 92 E.R. 518.
[72] See, for instance, *R. v. OLL Ltd., The Times,* December 9, 1994.
[73] *D'Ivry v. World Newspaper Co.* (1897), 17 P.R. 387 (Ont. C.A.).
[74] *R. v. Evening Standard Co. Ltd.,* [1954] 1 Q.B. 578.
[75] *R. v. Stephens* (1866), L.R. 1 Q.B. 792.

extent of knowledge possessed by individual corporate agents, since in most cases a person can only be guilty of conscious wrongdoing where possessed of sufficient knowledge as to the circumstances in which he or she is acting. Suppose, for instance, that officer A knows fact X while officer B knows fact Y. If both these facts were known by one person, and that person acted in the same manner as the corporation has acted, then the person concerned would be criminally liable. On the other hand, if both the facts were not known by a single person, then the act would not be criminal. In *R. v. P. & O. European Ferries (Dover) Ltd.*[76] the case involved this sort of allegation. Justice Turner rejected the aggregation principle and concluded that before a corporation can be convicted of manslaughter, it is necessary to show that there is at least one person who could be identified with the company who was himself or herself, guilty of manslaughter.

(2) The Identification Theory

§3.29 Historically in Canada, the usual basis on which a corporation has been held criminally liable for the wrongdoing of its employees, directors or officers has been under what is often referred to as the identification principle. Under this theoretical approach, the existence of *mens rea* within the corporation is determined[77] by looking for proof of the corporation's intent in the conduct of those who manage or otherwise control it or its relevant activities.[78] Whether in any particular case there is evidence to go to a jury that the criminal act of an agent, including his or her state of mind, intention, knowledge or belief, is the act of the company, depends upon the nature of the charge, the relative position of the officer or agent and the other relevant facts and circumstances of the case.[79] The basis of the liability of the corporation is not vicarious liability, but that of independent liability arising because the crime of the agent was in fact the crime of the corporation itself.[80] The necessary *mens rea* to support such a charge may be found in any officer, employee or other agent authorized by the corporation to act for it in connection with matters to which the conspiracy pertains.[81] Under the identification principle, a corporation has been convited of conspiring to lessen competition contrary to the *Competition Act*, even where the board of directors has not taken any initiative in that respect.[82] A corporation has

---

[76] (1990), 93 Cr. App. R. 72.
[77] *R. v. Safety-Kleen Canada Inc.,* [1997] O.J. No. 800, 145 D.L.R. (4th) 276 at 281 (C.A.), per Doherty J.A.
[78] *H.L. Bolton Engineering Co. v. T.J. Graham & Sons Ltd.,* [1957] 1 Q.B. 159 at 172-73 (C.A.), per Denning L.J.
[79] *R. v. I.C.R. Haulage Ltd.,* [1944] K.B. 551 (C.A.); see also *John Henshall Quarries Ltd. v. Harvey,* [1965] 2 Q.B. 233 at 241, per Lord Parker C.J.
[80] *"Rhone" (The) v. "Peter A.B. Widener" (The),* [1993] S.C.J. No. 19, [1993] 1 S.C.R. 497 at 520-21, per Iacobucci J.
[81] *R. v. Ash-Temple Co.,* [1949] O.R. 315 at 337 (C.A.), per Robertson C.J.O; *DPP v. Kent and Sussex Contractors Ltd.,* [1944] K.B. 146 (D.C.). As to cases in which *mens rea* is not an ingredient of the offence, see *R. v. Teperman & Sons Ltd.,* [1968] 2 O.R. 174 (C.A.), application for leave to appeal to S.C.C. dismissed, [1968] 2 O.R. 174n.
[82] *R. v. St. Lawrence Corp.,* [1969] O.J. No. 1326, [1969] 2 O.R. 305 (C.A.).

been found guilty of bribing a public official,[83] and criminal negligence causing bodily harm.[84] A corporation may be a party to a conspiracy with an outsider to the corporation.[85] A corporation may not hide behind the *ultra vires* character of a criminal act in order to escape liability for that act or to escape liability under the *Criminal Code*[86] or under any other statute.[87]

§3.30 The terms of the identification theory were outlined in *Canadian Dredge & Dock v. The Queen*,[88] in which four companies were convicted under the *Criminal Code* of offences in relation to contracts entered into with certain public authorities. The bids for these contracts were alleged to have been tendered on a collusive basis, so that the low bidders included in their bids compensation to be paid to high bidders or non-bidders. Each company had a manager who conducted the business of the company relating to the submission of bids for tender. It was argued on appeal that the corporations should not be held liable because these managers:

- were acting in fraud of the appellant-employers;
- were acting throughout for their own benefit; or
- were acting contrary to instructions and hence outside of the scope of their employment with the appellants.

§3.31 The Supreme Court of Canada dismissed these grounds of appeal, holding that liability flowed to the corporations in the circumstances as the wrongdoing could be identified with the corporation. The underlying premise of the identification theory is that where the person actually perpetrating the offence is the same person who is the directing mind of the company, the acts and intentions of that person and the company coincide. As a result, the directing mind who physically commits the offence effectively acts as the corporation. Therefore, even in offences requiring proof of *mens rea,* a company may be convicted if the court finds an officer or managerial level employee was the effective directing mind of the relevant sphere of corporate operations, so that his or her actions and intent can be identified with the company itself. The theory doctrine can be applied with respect to the board of directors, a managing director, an officer or anyone else to whom has been delegated sufficient relevant executive authority to exercise control over the matters concerned. It is implicit in the foregoing that a corporation may have more than one directing mind. However, the person who is alleged to be the directing mind must have been acting within the scope of his or her authority, in the sense that his or her actions are within the sector of the corporate operation that has been assigned to him or her. That sector of opera-

---

[83] *R. v. Sommers*, [1959] S.C.J. No. 49, [1959] S.C.R. 678.
[84] *Union Colliery Co. v. R.* (1900), 31 S.C.R. 81; *R. v. Canadian Allis-Chalmers Ltd.*, [1923] O.J. No. 8, 54 O.L.R. 38 (C.A.).
[85] *R. v. I.C.R. Haulage Ltd.*, [1944] K.B. 551 at 559 (C.A.), *per* Stable J.; *R. v. Dominion Steel & Coal Corp.* (1956), 116 C.C.C. 117, additional reasons at [1956] O.W.N. 753 (H.C.).
[86] *R. v. Fane Robinson Ltd.*, [1941] 2 W.W.R. 235 at 236 (Alta. C.A.), *per* Ford J.A.
[87] *Harker v. Britannic Assurance Co.*, [1928] 1 K.B. 766 at 772, *per* Lord Hewart C.J.
[88] [1985] S.C.J. No. 28, [1985] 1 S.C.R. 662.

tion may be functional, or geographic, or may embrace the entire undertaking of the corporation. It is the ability to direct a particular aspect of corporation's operation that affords the basis of liability, rather than express authority to act in a criminal manner (since a requirement for express authority would rarely be satisfied). The scope of authority is a question of fact. Consequently, liability can arise whether or not there has been formal delegation, and irrespective of whether the board of directors is aware of what is being done, or indeed, even if it has expressly prohibited the actual conduct that amounts to the criminal offence, provided that the "directing mind" can still fairly be said to be acting at least partly in the corporation's behalf.

§3.32 Liability under the identification theory ceases to apply where the directing mind has ceased completely to act, in fact or in substance, in the interests of the corporation, as for instance where the directing mind defrauds the corporation, or when his or her wrongful actions lie outside the regular activities of his or her office. In a case where his or her entire energies are directed to his or her own betterment (so that he or she is effectively undermining the undertaking of the corporation), then it becomes unrealistic to identify the acts of the corporate operative with the corporation. The identification doctrine only operates where the Crown demonstrates that the action taken by the directing mind (a) was within the field of operation assigned to him or her; (b) was not totally perpetrating a fraud against the corporation; but (c) was by design or result acting partly for the benefit of the company.

(3) Impact of Bill C-45

§3.33 At least at the federal level in Canada, the law relating to certain aspects of the criminal liability of corporations have now been codified under amendments to the *Criminal Code,* under what is still popularly referred to as Bill C-45.[89] The new legislative provisions do not extend to all types of criminal and quasi-criminal liability, but only to offences governed by the *Criminal Code.* The result is that one must now take into account the common law rules respecting criminal liability of corporations when dealing with provincial offences, and the new statutory rules when dealing with federal offences governed by the Code.

§3.34 By virtue of the amendments effected by Bill C-45 section 22.1 of the *Criminal Code* sets down a standard of liability for "negligence"-based offences. It provides:

> In respect of an offence that requires the prosecution to prove negligence, an organization is a party to the offence if:
>
> (a) acting within the scope of their authority
>
>   (i) one of its representatives is a party to the offence, or

---

[89] S.C. 2003, c. 21.

(ii) two or more of its representatives engage in conduct, whether by act or omission, such that, if it had been the conduct of only one representative, that representative would have been a party to the offence; and

(b) the senior officer who is responsible for the aspect of the organization's activities that is relevant to the offence departs—or the senior officers, collectively, depart—markedly from the standard of care that, in the circumstances, could reasonably be expected to prevent a representative of the organization from being a party to the offence.

Other offences not based upon "negligence" are governed by section 22.2, which provides:

In respect of an offence that requires the prosecution to prove fault — other than negligence — an organization is a party to the offence if, with the intent at least in part to benefit the organization, one of its senior officers

(a) acting within the scope of their authority, is a party to the offence;

(b) having the mental state required to be a party to the offence and acting within the scope of their authority, directs the work of other representatives of the organization so that they do the act or make the omission specified in the offence; or

(c) knowing that a representative of the organization is or is about to be a party to the offence, does not take all reasonable measures to stop them from being a party to the offence.

While section 22.2 requires the proof of an intent to benefit the corporation, no such proof is required under section 22.1. Also relevant to the new statutory scheme is section 23.1, which provides:

For greater certainty, sections 21 to 23 apply in respect of an accused notwithstanding the fact that the person whom the accused aids or abets, counsels or procures or receives, comforts or assists cannot be convicted of the offence.

§3.35 In explanatory comments to Bill C-45, the Department of Justice has provided the following explanation of the intended operation of section 22.1:

For example, in a factory, an employee who turned off three separate safety systems would probably be prosecuted for causing death by criminal negligence if employees were killed as a result of an accident that the safety systems would have prevented. The employee acted negligently. On the other hand, if three employees each turned off one of the safety systems each thinking that it was not a problem because the other two systems would still be in place, they would probably not be subject to criminal prosecution because each one alone might not have shown reckless disregard for the lives of other employees. However, the fact that the individual employees might escape prosecution should not mean that their employer necessarily would not be prosecuted. After all, the organization, through its three employees, turned off the three systems.

Nevertheless, conviction in such a case would be difficult because of the need to prove that both clause 22.1(*a*) and (*b*) are satisfied. In the ordinary case, it would be difficult to establish that simultaneous independent action on the part of three separate employees could occur because a senior officer responsible for the aspect of the organization's activities concerned departed "markedly from the standard of care that, in the circumstances, could reasonably be expected". The Department of Justice explanation suggested that:

> The organization might be convicted if, for example, the director of safety systems failed to give the one negligent employee basic training necessary to perform the job.

§3.36 The difficulty with this line of reasoning is that it presupposes that the lack of training was the cause of the accident, whereas the facts of the hypothetical example that was stated indicate that the cause of the accident was because each of the representatives concerned thought that "the other two systems would still be in place". On such facts, the lack of training would be collateral to the accident itself. A more realistic hypothetical illustration of where liability might arise would be where there was no system in place to allow each employee to see what other switches were set to. Liability in such a situation would arise if it could be established that the lack of such a system constituted a marked departure from the standard of care expected in the circumstances. Even in such cases, there would likely be no liability for unexpected failure of the system, at least where corporate policy was to discontinue operation of the relevant area or equipment as soon as failure was detected, and reasonable precautions were in place to permit such detection. In all cases, in order to determine whether what the accused organization has done, or allowed to occur, violates the statutory standard, the court would have to consider the practices at other similar organizations, taking into account such factors as compliance with applicable regulatory standards, whether there was normal or abnormal use of the equipment causing injury or damage, the degree of apparent risk, the apparent likelihood of occurrence, the general availability of technology, and the like. In short, although Bill C-45 may have widened the scope of potential corporate criminal liability, there are still considerable obstacles to overcome in securing a conviction.

§3.37 It will be noted that the above provisions deal not so much with corporations as such, but with the broader category of organizations. Bill C-45 thereby avoids one of the basic criticisms of the law concerning corporate crime: that it is not sensible to apply a different regime of law to one form of joint enterprise than the regime that is applicable with respect to others. The term "organization" is defined to mean:

- a public body, a body corporate, a society, a company; and
- a firm, a partnership, a trade union or an association of persons created for a common purpose.

This definition is sufficiently broad to capture most forms of business enterprise but it does not appear to affect informal groups.

§3.38 The definition of "senior officer" in section 2 of the Code includes the directors, the chief executive officer and the chief financial officer of the corporation. Liability in their case is by virtue of the position that they hold. A corporation cannot argue that the individuals occupying these positions actually had no real role in setting policy or managing the organization and therefore were not senior officers. However, the definition also sweeps up everyone else within an organization who has an important role in:

- setting policy; or
- managing an important part of the organization's activities.

The individuals who fall within the scope of this basket provision will vary from case to case, and the extent of their control must be proven.

§3.39 Generally, to prove a charge with respect to an organization, the Crown will usually seek to show that the physical acts were committed by one or more employees of the organization. However, the new provisions are sufficiently flexible to allow a charge to be brought where no employment relationship can be established. This is accomplished through the use of the new term "representative", which is defined to mean directors, partners, members, agents and contractors, as well as employees. These representatives must be acting within the scope of their employment at the time of the alleged crime.

(4) The Innocent Corporate Operative

§3.40 Not infrequently, while the directing mind behind the corporation will be acting with a criminal intent, he or she will make use of well-meaning and entirely innocent subordinates, who have no inkling that they are being employed in the commission of an offence. In such a case, it may be necessary to determine the time and place at which the offence was committed by the corporation. This need was illustrated in an unusual case in the House of Lords decision in *Deutsche Genossenschaftsbank v. Burnhope*.[90] In that case, the respondent bank was insured by the appellant insurers against direct financial losses incurred by reason of, "theft, larceny or false pretences, committed by persons present on the premises of the bank". A fraud was perpetrated by the chairman of a financial company that was a customer of the bank. It had deposited treasury bills and bank certificates of deposit with the bank, having a value of approximately £9 million, as security for a line of credit in that amount. The chairman persuaded the bank to release the security documents to him in exchange for acceptable alternative security documents to be delivered by the close of business on the same day. A junior employee of the company took physical delivery of the security documents but the alternative security documents were never delivered to the bank and three days later the company was suspended by the Bank of England. The chairman was arrested and charged with fraudulent trading. The bank was unable to obtain repayment of its loan of £9 million. It sued for that amount under its insurance policy. The insurers refused to pay, arguing that the theft was not a risk covered by the policy because it had not been committed by "persons present on the [bank's] premises". In an action brought by the bank the judge at first instance held that although it was not disputed that the bank's securities had

---

[90] [1995] 4 All E.R. 717 (H.L.).

been the subject of a theft, the bank was not entitled to recover because the only person connected with the theft who was on the bank's premises at the time was the innocent employee of the company who had collected the documents. He was not alleged to have been in any way dishonest or to have committed any criminal offence. The criminal offence of theft was committed by the chairman and through him by the company. The Court of Appeal allowed an appeal by the bank on the grounds that the company had been present on the bank's premises through its employee. Whether or not that employee was himself culpable, it was he who performed the actual the act of appropriating the securities, by which the company committed the theft. The insurers appealed to the House of Lords, where the majority concluded that the policy required physical presence of the person committing the theft on the bank's property. It contemplated theft by a person physically in the bank and not theft by a corporation or the abstraction of money by electronic means. Since the theft of the bank's securities had not been committed by the company acting through the chairman on bank's premises, the loss caused was not covered under the policy. In discussing the attribution of the theft to the corporation as well as to the dishonest chairman of the company, Lord Keith of Kinkel commented:

> The reason why the company was guilty of theft in the circumstances of this case was that its directing mind and will, Mr. Smith, was himself guilty of theft. It was he who formed the dishonest intention of permanently depriving the bank of the securities, and who arranged for the innocent Mr. Towers to deliver to the bank his letter containing false representations and to uplift the securities against it. If there had been no company involved and if it had been Mr. Smith as an individual to whom the bank had granted the loan and who had deposited his own securities with the bank, so that the theft was committed by Mr. Smith alone, then it could not be said, consistently with the ordinary use of language, that Mr. Smith was present in the bank when the securities were uplifted by Mr. Towers.

(iii) The Logic of Corporate Criminal Liability

§3.41 The conclusion as to whether or not a corporation *can* be convicted of a particular offence, merely begs the question of whether it *ought to be* convicted of that offence. That broader policy question involves a consideration of the proper role to be played by the criminal law. Criminal liability seems at first a natural outgrowth of the separate legal personality of the corporation. It also seems to be consistent with the potential liability of the corporation for tortious conduct. In fact, neither of these considerations provides much support for imposing criminal liability on corporations. Vicarious liability, which provides much of the basis for the tortious liability of a corporation, plays no general role in the criminal law, save to the extent that it has been introduced by statute either expressly or by necessary implication. Thus, historically, in order to affix criminal liability on the corporation at common law, it has been necessary to show that the corporation committed the prohibited act itself and possessed the required mental state to make that act criminal.

§3.42 Although a corporation may be a separate juristic person, it is obviously not a separate decision-making entity. The corporation is purely a matter of form; it has no substance. In order to fix the corporation with the guilty act or mental state, it is necessary to relate that act or mental state back to some individual who stands behind the corporation.[91] The opinion of Viscount Haldane in *Lennard's Carrying Co. v. Asiatic Petroleum Co.*[92] is the starting point for any consideration of these issues, for it has influenced all subsequent case law in the area. While this opinion was given with respect to a claim in tort, it is no less relevant in the criminal context:

> ... [A] corporation is an abstraction. It has no mind of its own any more than it has a body of its own; its active and directing will must consequently be sought in the person of somebody who for some purpose has been called an agent, but who is really the directing mind and will of the corporation, the very ego and centre of the personality of the corporation. That person may be under the direction of the shareholders in general meeting; that person may be the board of directors thereof, or it may be, and in some companies it is so, that that person has an authority co-ordinate with the board of directors given to him under the articles of association, and is appointed by the general meeting of the company, and can only be removed by the general meeting of the company.

Thus it is necessary to trace the crime back not to a person who acts under the direction of the corporation, but rather to someone who causes the corporation to commit the crime. And it is with respect to the question of attribution that one encounters the first of several wider public policy issues: if it is that individual who is in truth responsible for the crime, then why prosecute the corporation? Attributing knowledge or conduct back to a corporation makes sense if the object is to provide compensation for a victim — this, presumably, being the primary objective of tort law. In the criminal law context the same consideration does not apply.

§3.43 A better option would be to prosecute the actual perpetrator: the individual who uses the corporation in the course of committing a crime,[93] rather than to prosecute the corporation. The deterrent effect of prosecution, whatever it may be, is not increased by reason of the corporate prosecution. The argument that the prosecution of the corporation will encourage the corporation to exercise greater control over the "agent" who committed the crime is untenable because the foundation of the criminal liability of the corporation is that the "agent" in question exercised such control over the corporation to such an extent that he or she was able to cause the corporation to commit the crime.[94] Control can only

---

[91] *R. v. I.C.R. Haulage Ltd.*, [1944] K.B. 551 at 559 (C.A.), *per* Stable J.; see also *R. v. Electrical Contractors Assn.*, [1961] O.R. 265 (C.A.); *R. v. McDonnell*, [1966] 1 Q.B. 233 at 244 (Bristol Assizes), *per* Nield J.; *R. v. Martin*, [1933] 1 D.L.R. 434 (Man. C.A.).

[92] [1915] A.C. 705 at 713 (H.L.).

[93] See Tom Onyshko, "Directors' Failure to Act Means Personal Liability for Pollution" *The Lawyer's Weekly*, May 1, 1993 (Markham, Ont.: Butterworths) at 1.

[94] See, for instance, *DPP v. Kent and Sussex Contractors Ltd.*, [1944] K.B. 146 (D.C.), *per* Viscount Caldecote C.J.; *R. v. I.C.R. Haulage Ltd.*, [1944] K.B. 551 (C.A.).

work in one direction.[95] A corporate crime is not comparable to the situation in which one party commits the act under the encouragement or with the assistance of a second party. In corporate crime there is only one wrongdoer: the directing mind. The corporation acts and is implicated solely by reason of the directions given by that person.[96] It is far from an unrealistic conclusion that if the wrongdoer is not deterred by the risk of personal criminal liability, the risk to the corporation will be given scant regard.

§3.44 One justification frequently put forward for the criminal prosecution of the corporation is to prevent the corporation from reaping a profit derived from the commission of a criminal offence. In this regard, the penalty may be said to serve a restitutionary purpose. There are three basic fallacies in this argument. First, it assumes that all crime is profit-motivated; second, it equates crime with civil wrongs; and third, it assumes that criminal punishment compensates or otherwise vindicates the victim. None of these assumptions is true.

§3.45 Even where a crime results in a profit to the wrongdoer, it cannot always be assumed that the corporation will benefit from that profit. In fact, the annals of corporate criminal law are filled with prosecutions of the corporation even though it was the victim of the crime. For instance in *Moore v. I. Bresler Ltd.*,[97] two employees of the respondent company defrauded the company by selling certain goods that belonged to it and pocketing the proceeds. In order to cover their tracks one of them submitted falsified purchase tax returns, which was an offence under section 35 of the *Finance Act (No. 2), 1940*. Unfortunately for the corporation, it was clear that the employees had the authority to sell the goods and that the one who filed the return had the authority to do so. Therefore, Viscount Caldecote L.C.J. concluded that the corporation could be held liable for the falsified tax returns.[98] The public policy interest served in subjecting a corporation to criminal liability in such a case is far from clear. The risk of such liability obviously had no deterrent effect on the commission of the crime. Since the crime was committed against the corporation, the punishment aggravated the victim corporation's loss, rather than compensating or vindicating it. If the remedies against a corporation were limited (as suggested) to the civil sphere, the law would permit the assets of the corporation to be applied in compensation and restitution to the victims of any criminal activity with which it has been connected.

---

[95] *Tesco Supermarkets Ltd. v. Nattrass*, [1972] A.C. 153 (H.L.), *per* Lord Reid; *cf. Dean v. John Menzies (Holdings) Ltd.*, [1981] S.L.T. 50 (H.C.J.).

[96] As to the question of when a particular officer may be seen to act as the corporation, see *DPP v. Kent and Sussex Contractors Ltd.*, [1944] K.B. 146 (D.C.); *Lady Gwendolen (The)*, [1965] 2 All E.R. 283 (C.A.); *National Coal Board v. Gamble*, [1959] Q.B. 11. Generally, the mental state of junior employees and officers will not be attributed to the company: *Tesco Supermarkets Ltd. v. Nattrass*, [1972] A.C. 153 (H.L.).

[97] [1944] 2 All E.R. 515 (K.B.).

[98] *Ibid.*, at 516-17.

§3.46 Furthermore, potential criminal liability of the corporation is not a natural outgrowth of the liability of the corporation in tort. Industrial and commercial activity necessarily entails a degree of risk; some tortious injury to outsiders is almost certain to occur as a result of any such activity. As a basic principle, it is economically desirable to internalize the costs associated with a particular activity to as great an extent as possible. One rationale for corporate liability in tort is that by imposing such liability the social costs of torts committed in the course of corporate activity (*i.e.*, industrial production or commerce) will be reflected in the pricing of the corporation's products and services. In this way, externalities are reduced and the costs and revenues associated with the particular activity carried on by the corporation can be aggregated at the corporate level and balanced against each other. Thus when corporation A manufactures widgets and by so doing causes damage to the property of B, the recovery of damages by B from A allows the cost of those damages to be passed along to A's customers. Thus the price of the widgets that A manufactures reflects the social costs of their production. A further consideration is that corporations generally are better able to pay for damages caused through their operations than are the workers employed by them.

§3.47 In contrast, when criminal liability is imposed upon the corporation, the practical effect is usually to impose an entirely extraneous cost (usually in the form of a fine or forfeiture). Where a corporation is convicted of an offence, it is made to suffer for a wrong committed not by itself but by its directors, officers or employees;[99] the justice of such suffering is that it is from those shareholders that those individuals ultimately draw their authority to act on behalf of the corporation. Where, however, the interest of the shareholders in the corporation is exhausted by reason of losses sustained in the transaction of business, the loss is thrust upon the creditors of the corporation. In such cases, the rationale for criminal punishment is far less compelling.

§3.48 In such a case, the penalty imposed must be paid by persons who are entirely innocent of any wrongdoing. The prosecution of the Bank of Credit & Commerce International ("BCCI") serves as a case in point. By nearly all accounts, the operations of BCCI constituted one of the greatest swindles in corporate history. It was estimated by the bank's liquidators that the bank's liabilities exceeded its assets by some U.S. $9.5 billion. During the course of investigating BCCI's collapse it became evident that BCCI had participated in a number of violations of United States law. A prosecution was launched. As a result of a plea bargain, the liquidator agreed to pay over $550 million in assets as a fine.[100] Thus the creditors of the bank, who already were required to make good the $9.5 billion shortfall, were now required to make good a further $550 million. It is difficult to see how the public interest was served by imposing criminal liability in such a case.

---

[99] *Marr v. Tumulty*, 256 N.Y. 15 (1931) at 24 *per* Cardozo J.
[100] P. Truell, L. Gurwin, *False Profits* (Boston: Houghton Mifflin, 1992) at 453.

§3.49 In the United States, a partial solution to this problem has been arrived by applying the equitable subordination concept, enshrined in American insolvency law. (The availability of this remedy in Canada is more limited, but it is argued in Chapter 13 that such a remedy may sometimes be available under the oppression remedy.) For instance, in *United States v. Noland* the Internal Revenue Service ("IRS") filed a claim for a tax penalty against a bankrupt corporation. Under U.S. insolvency law, such a claim generally is entitled to first priority in bankruptcy as an administrative expense.[101] The court concluded that filing the claim was not inequitable, nor was its collection. However, in the circumstances of the bankrupt company, the impact of the recovery of the penalty would (from the perspective of the other creditors of the bankrupt) lead to an equitable result: their recovery would be vastly reduced by reason of the payment to the IRS. The bankruptcy court concluded that the IRS was guilty of no misconduct in enforcing the penalty, it ordered the penalty claim equitably subordinated under section 510(c) of the *Bankruptcy Code*. The intent was to avoid the perceived unfairness that would result from allowing the IRS to take precedence over secured and unsecured creditors who had given value to the business. The Sixth Circuit affirmed this approach, looking to the legislative history of the *Bankruptcy Code* and holding that a tax penalty claim could be subordinated, even in the absence of inequitable conduct on the claimant's part. The Supreme Court disapproved of the general terms of this reasoning, but held that while penalty claims cannot be categorically subordinated, they could be subordinated on a case-by-case basis where a fit case was made out for doing so. It stated:

> ... although [a bankruptcy court] is a court of equity, it is not free to adjust the legally valid claim of an innocent party who asserts the claim in good faith merely because the court perceives the result as inequitable.[102]

§3.50 In *United States v. Reorganized CF & I Fabricators of Utah, Inc.*,[103] the court dealt with an appeal from the 10th Circuit, in which it had been held that a tax penalty claim by the federal government could be subordinated, where the effect of the penalty was to punish the debtor's innocent creditors by diminishing the dividend payable to them, rather than to achieve the obvious purpose of the punitive fine: to punish the company and its owners for their wrongdoing. The Supreme Court upheld the decision but narrowed its legal basis, cautioning against any "categorical" re-organization of priorities. However, the Supreme Court did allow that lower courts could employ equitable subordination judgment on a case-by-case basis in the absence of any evidence of inequitable conduct to reduce the priority of a penalty claim, where the facts made out a fit case for doing so.

(iv) Sentencing

§3.51 Bill C-45 also created new sentencing options where a corporation is convicted, specifically the possibility of a corporate probation order. This sentenc-

---

[101] See 11 U.S.C. paras. 503(*b*)(1)(C), 507(*a*)(1).
[102] 517 U.S. 535 (1996) at 539.
[103] 518 U.S. 213 (1996).

ing option was effected by way of amendment to section 732.1 of the Code. Subsection (3.1) provides that:

> The court may prescribe, as additional conditions of a probation order made in respect of an organization, that the offender do one or more of the following:
>
> (a) make restitution to a person for any loss or damage that they suffered as a result of the offence;
>
> (b) establish policies, standards and procedures to reduce the likelihood of the organization committing a subsequent offence;
>
> (c) communicate those policies, standards and procedures to its representatives;
>
> (d) report to the court on the implementation of those policies, standards and procedures;
>
> (e) identify the senior officer who is responsible for compliance with those policies, standards and procedures;
>
> (f) provide, in the manner specified by the court, the following information to the public, namely,
>
>   (i) the offence of which the organization was convicted,
>
>   (ii) the sentence imposed by the court, and
>
>   (iii) any measures that the organization is taking — including any policies, standards and procedures established under paragraph (b) — to reduce the likelihood of it committing a subsequent offence; and
>
> (g) comply with any other reasonable conditions that the court considers desirable to prevent the organization from committing subsequent offences or to remedy the harm caused by the offence.

Before making an order under clause (3.1)(b), the court must consider whether it would be more appropriate for another regulatory body to supervise the development or implementation of the policies, standards and procedures referred to in that clause.[104] The Department of Justice explained:

> Courts are not necessarily well equipped to supervise corporate activities and the organization may already be subject to extensive regulation by government bodies. There is no need for a court to get involved in overseeing changes in an organization's safety practices, for example, if a provincial occupational health and safety department is already doing so. Such an agency has trained inspectors and expertise that the courts lack. Therefore, the section requires the court to consider whether another body would be more suitable to supervise the organization.

(v) Conspiracy

§3.52 There has never been much question that the corporation — through its directing minds — may conspire with outsiders of the corporation to commit a criminal offence.[105] Conspiracy between a corporation and its insiders is a more

---

[104] *Criminal Code*, s. 732.1(3.2).
[105] *R. v. St. Lawrence Corp.*, [1969] 2 O.R. 305 (C.A.).

complex question, although here again liability may lie on the correct facts.[106] The terms of such liability were recently considered by the United States Supreme Court in *Cedric Kushner Promotions Ltd. v. King*.[107]

§3.53 In the *King* case, a boxing promotion sued Don King, the president and sole shareholder of a rival corporate promoter, alleging that King had conducted his corporation's affairs in violation of the *Racketeer Influenced and Corrupt Organizations Act* ("RICO").[108] Under section 1962(c) of the *RICO* Act it is unlawful for any person employed by or associated with any enterprise to conduct or participate in the conduct of that enterprise's affairs through a pattern of racketeering activity. The District Court dismissed the complaint, and the Second Circuit affirmed, concluding that section 1962(c) applies only where a plaintiff shows the existence of two separate entities, a "person" and a distinct "enterprise", the affairs of which that "person" has improperly conducted. It was undisputed that on the facts, King was an employee of his corporation and also acting within the scope of his authority. Accordingly, in a strict legal sense, King was part of the corporation, not a "person", distinct from it who was improperly conducting the "enterprise's affairs".

§3.54 The United States Supreme Court disagreed. It held that section 1962(c) requires no more than the formal legal distinction between a "person" and the "enterprise" concerned, which exists by virtue of incorporation. Accordingly, the provision applies when a corporate employee unlawfully conducts the affairs of the corporation of which he or she is the sole owner—whether the employee conducts those affairs within the scope, or beyond the scope, of corporate authority. The Supreme Court concluded that King was distinct from the corporation itself, as he was the owner/employee of the corporation and a natural person in his own right, and the corporation was a legally different entity with separate rights and responsibilities due to its separate legal status. An employee who conducts his or her corporation's affairs through illegal acts comes within the terms of sections 1962(c) forbidding any "person" unlawfully to conduct an "enterprise," particularly as the RICO Act itself explicitly defines the term "person" to include "any individual ... capable of holding a legal or beneficial inter-

---

[106] See, generally, *Hall-Chem Inc. v. Vulcan Packaging Inc.*, [1994] O.J. No. 817, 12 B.L.R. (2d) 274 at 297 (Gen. Div.), *per* Spence J.; *cf. R. v. McDonnell*, [1966] 1 Q.B. 233 (Bristol Assizes).
[107] 533 U.S. 158 (2001).
[108] 18 U.S.C. c. 62:

> (b) It shall be unlawful for any person through a pattern of racketeering activity or through collection of an unlawful debt to acquire or maintain, directly or indirectly, any interest in or control of any enterprise which is engaged in, or the activities of which affect, interstate or foreign commerce.
>
> (c) It shall be unlawful for any person employed by or associated with any enterprise engaged in, or the activities of which affect, interstate or foreign commerce, to conduct or participate, directly or indirectly, in the conduct of such enterprise's affairs through a pattern of racketeering activity or collection of unlawful debt.
>
> (d) It shall be unlawful for any person to conspire to violate any of the provisions of subsection (a), (b), or (c) of this section.

est in property", and defines the term "enterprise" to include a "corporation".[109] A further consideration that appears to have influenced the court was that drawing fine legal distinctions—*e.g.*, between employees acting within and without the scope of corporate authority—would frustrate a basic purpose of the RICO Act, this being to affix liability to high-ranking individuals in an illegitimate criminal enterprise, who acts within the scope of their authority while seeking to further the enterprise's purposes. The Supreme Court further concluded that its approach to the RICO Act was no less consistent than was the lower courts' approach with the principle that a corporation acts only through its directors, officers, and agents; as well as with the principle that a corporation should not be liable for its employees' criminal acts in the absence of a clear legislative intent.

E. LIABILITY OF DIRECTORS, OFFICERS AND OTHERS

§3.55 Much as a corporation is a separate legal person from the shareholders who comprise it, *a fortiori* a corporation enjoys a separate existence from its directors and officers.[110] Directors and officers are not normally personally liable for a corporate tort.[111] Accordingly, in the absence of a guarantee or similar undertaking entered into in their personal capacity, the directors, officers and employees of a corporation are not liable *in the ordinary case*[112] for corporate action or inaction, whether in contract, fiduciary duty or tort.[113] So, for instance, where a tort is committed by a corporation, even a sole director[114] will not be liable merely because he or she conceivably might have exercised his or her authority in some way as a director to prevent the corporation from committing the tort.[115] The corporate veil will not be lifted to permit an action to be brought against the directors of a corporation on the grounds of alleged negligence or breach of statutory duty unless the plaintiff (a creditor of the corporation) can establish that a duty of care was owed to it personally by the directors.[116] A director, who

---

[109] Sections 1961(3), (4).
[110] See, generally: *Le Groupe Visuel (1990) Inc. v. Trustus International Trading Inc.*, [2003] F.C.J. No. 1511, 127 A.C.W.S. (3d) 865 at para. 23 (T.D.) *per* Rouleau, J.
[111] *Blacklaws v. 470433 Alta. Ltd.*, [2000] A.J. No. 725, 7 B.L.R. (3d) 204 (C.A.).
[112] *Monsanto Canada Inc. v. Schmeiser*, [2001] S.J. No. 275, 12 C.P.R. (4th) 204 at paras. 143-45 (F.C.T.D.) *per* McKay J.
[113] *Mentmore Manufacturing Co. v. National Merchandise Manufacturing Co.*, [1978] F.C.J. No. 521, 40 C.P.R. (2d) 164 at 171 (C.A.), *per* LeDain J.
[114] *British Thomson-Houston Co. v. Sterling Accessories, Ltd.* (1924), 41 R.P.C. 311; *Prichard & Constance (Wholesale), Ltd. v. Amata, Ltd.* (1924), 42 R.P.C. 63.
[115] *Rainham Chemical Works Ltd. v. Belvedere Fish Guano Co.*, [1921] 2 A.C. 465 (H.L.); *Society of Composers, Authors and Music Publishers of Canada v. 1007442 Ontario Ltd.*, [2002] F.C.J. No. 876, 20 C.P.R. (4th) 68 (T.D.), *per* Kelen J.:

> It is the necessary implication of this approach, I think, that not only will the particular direction or authorization required for personal liability not be inferred merely from the fact of close control of a corporation but it will not be inferred from the general direction which those in such control must necessarily impart to its affairs.

[116] *Montreal Trust Co. of Canada v. ScotiaMcLeod Inc.*, [1994] O.J. No. 2194, 15 B.L.R. (2d) 160, var'd [1995] O.J. No. 3556, 26 O.R. (3d) 481 (C.A.), leave to appeal to S.C.C. ref'd [1990] S.C.C.A. No. 40, 137 D.L.R. (4th) vin; *London Drugs Ltd. v. Kuehne & Nagel International Ltd.*, [1992] S.C.J. No. 84, [1992] 3 S.C.R. 299; *Alper Development Inc. v. Harrowston Corp.*,

although not committing a tort personally, will be liable for a tort committed by his or her corporation if he or she authorized the acts giving rise to the tort, and knew that they were tortious or did not care whether they were tortious.[117] Similarly, while an employee will not normally be liable to the victim of a tort for which the corporation is responsible, he or she will be so liable where the employee concerned has breached some personal duty of care owed by him or her to the victim. There is no general rule to the effect that an employee acting in the course of his or her employment owes no duty of care to the employer's customers, even when carrying out the very essence of the contract between the employer and the customer.[118] A director will not be held personally liable for fraud committed by the corporation unless he or she has expressly or implicitly authorized the fraud.[119] However, a director will be personally liable for a tort where he or she was personally and directly a party to its commission.[120] More rarely, a director may also be liable as a result of a tort committed by another director (or officer) of the corporation, while acting as an agent for the first director.

§3.56 The practical problem with which the court must grapple in cases in which directors and officers are sued personally for torts committed by the corporation, is that the corporation can only act on the direction of its directors or officers. It would clearly be unrealistic to apply personal liability in all cases. Instead, the courts have attempted to strike a balance between allowing the directors and officers to run the corporation, while at the same time affording recompense to third parties who are injured by the directors and officers who make use of the corporation as a tool for this purpose.[121] The balance is often a difficult one to strike. So, for instance, in *Mentmore Manufacturing Co. v. National Merchandise Manufacturing Co.*, LeDain J. said (in the context of a patent infringement case):

> What is involved here is a very difficult question of policy. On the one hand, there is the principle that an incorporated company is separate and distinct in law from its shareholders, directors and officers, and it is in the interests of the commercial purposes served by the incorporated enterprise that they should as a general rule

---

[1998] O.J. No. 1199, 38 O.R. (3d) 785 (C.A.). As to deliberate wrongdoing by a director or officer, see *ADGA Systems International Ltd. v. Valcom Ltd.*, [1999] O.J. No. 27, 168 D.L.R. (4th) 351 (C.A.); *Craig v. North Shore Heli Logging Ltd.*, [1997] B.C.J. No. 983, 34 B.L.R. (2d) 119 (S.C.). With respect to the jurisdiction of a court to award costs against a corporate director who is responsible for an unsuccessful claim brought in the name of the corporation, see: *Goodwood Recoveries Ltd. v. Breen*, [2005] All E.R. (D) 226 (C.A.).

[117] See, generally, *C. Evans & Sons Ltd. v. Spritebrand Ltd.*, [1985] 1 W.L.R. 317 (C.A.); *Performing Right Society Ltd. v. Ciryl Theatrical Syndicate Ltd.*, [1924] 1 K.B. 1 (C.A.); *Mancetter Developments Ltd. v. Garmanson Ltd.*, [1986] 1 All E.R. 449 (C.A.); *Wah Tat Bank Ltd. v. Chan Cheng Kum*, [1975] A.C. 507 (P.C.); *Xerox Canada Finance Inc. v. Wilson's Industrial Auctioneers Ltd.*, [1997] O.J. No. 210, 34 B.L.R. (2d) 135 (Gen. Div.).

[118] *London Drugs Ltd. v. Kuehne & Nagel International Ltd.*, [1992] S.C.J. No. 84, [1992] 3 S.C.R. 299.

[119] *Cargill v. Bower* (1878), 10 Ch. D. 502; *Land Credit Co. of Ireland v. Lord Fermoy* (1870), L.R. 5 Ch. 763.

[120] *Trefor Ivory Ltd. v. Anderson*, [1992] 2 N.Z.L.R. 517 at 527, *per* Hardie Boys J.

[121] See, generally, *Southwestern Tool Co. v. Hughes Tool Co.* (1938), 98 F. (2d) 42 at 45.

enjoy the benefit of the limited liability afforded by incorporation. On the other hand, there is the principle that everyone should answer for his tortious acts. The balancing of these two considerations in the field of patent infringement is particularly difficult. This arises from the fact that the acts of manufacture and sale which are ultimately held by a Court to constitute infringement are the general business activity of a corporation which its directors and officers may be presumed to have authorized or directed, at least in a general way. Questions of validity and infringement are often fraught with considerable uncertainty requiring long and expensive trials to resolve. It would render the offices of director or principal officer unduly hazardous if the degree of direction normally required in the management of a corporation's manufacturing and selling activity could by itself make the director or officer personally liable for infringement by his company. [122]

§3.57 When a director (or officer) of a corporation engages in discussions and makes decisions relating to the corporation's business, he or she is acting within the scope of his or her authority as the human agent necessary to allow the corporation to carry on any business. In such a case, the director will usually be subject to a personal liability if he or she acts outside the scope of such authority, as for instance by being motivated by the desire to advance some personal interest contrary to the interest of the company, by fraud or with malice.[123] Every director owes a duty to act in the best interests of the corporation. In attempting to do so, a director, although acting in good faith, may in some cases cause the corporation to breach a contract. At least in the ordinary case,[124] provided the director genuinely believes that he or she is acting in the best interest of the corporation, the director will not be liable.[125]

§3.58 However, there are exceptions to this overall approach — the most obvious being where there are statutory rules of liability. Moreover, while directors and officers of a corporation will not normally be personally liable for any breach of contract or tort that the corporation may commit,[126] in recent years, courts have made clear repeatedly that there are limited circumstances in which an action may be brought against the directors or officers of a corporation in respect of alleged corporate wrongdoing. Much of the judicial thinking in this area seems to echo the reasoning applied in deciding whether a directing mind can be implicated in criminal wrongdoing. In Ontario, the current leading authority in this regard is the decision of Finlayson J.A. in *ScotiaMcLeod Inc. v. Peoples Jewellers Ltd.*, in which he stated:

---

[122] [1978] F.C.J. No. 521, 89 D.L.R. (3d) 195 at 202 (C.A.).
[123] *Lehndorff Canadian Pension Properties Ltd. v. Davis & Co.*, [1987] B.C.J. No. 85, 10 B.C.L.R. (2d) 342 at 350-51 (S.C.), per Anderson L.J.S.C.
[124] *Srebot Farms Ltd. v. Bradford Co-operative Storage Ltd.*, [1998] O.J. No. 532, 163 D.L.R. (4th) 190 (C.A.); *923087 NWT Ltd. v. Anderson Mills Ltd.* (1998), 35 B.L.R. (2d) 1 (N.W.T. S.C.).
[125] *Imperial Oil Ltd. v. C & G Holdings Ltd.*, [1989] N.J. No. 228, 62 D.L.R. (4th) 261 at 264-65 (Nfld. C.A.), per Marshall J.A.; see also *McFadden v. 481782 Ontario Ltd.*, [1984] O.J. No. 3268, 47 O.R. (2d) 134 (H.C.); *Ontario Store Fixtures Inc. v. Mmmuffins Inc.*, [1989] O.J. No. 1357, 70 O.R. (2d) 42 (H.C.); *Montreal Trust Co. of Canada Ltd. v. ScotiaMcLeod Inc.*, [1994] O.J. No. 2194, 15 B.L.R. (2d) 160, rev'd in part [1995] O.J. No. 3556, 26 O.R. (3d) 481 (C.A.), leave to appeal to S.C.C. ref'd [1996] S.C.C.A. No. 40, 137 D.L.R. (4th) vin.
[126] See, generally, *Kepic v. Tecumseh Road Builders*, [1985] O.J. No. 410, 29 B.L.R. 85 at 117 (H.C.), per McKinlay J., var'd at 23 O.A.C. 72 (C.A.).

Absent allegations which fit within the categories [of fraud, deceit, dishonesty, want of authority, the use of the corporate structure as a sham, or the principal being privy to the tort of inducing breach of contract between the company and the plaintiff], officers or employees of limited companies are protected from personal liability unless it can be shown that their actions are themselves tortious or exhibit a separate identity or interest from that of the company so as to make the act or conduct complained of their own. [127]

Similarly, in *Normart Management Ltd. v. West Hill Redevelopment Co.*, Finlayson J.A. stated:

> ... The directing minds of corporations cannot be held civilly liable for the actions of the corporations they control and direct unless there is some conduct on the part of those directing minds that is either tortious in itself or exhibits a separate identity or interest from that of the corporations such as to make the acts or conduct complained of those of the directing minds. [128]

§3.59 The exact point at which directors and officers assume a personal liability is not clear. However, in the *Mentmore* case, LeDain, J. provided the following somewhat vague guide:

> ... there must be circumstances from which it is reasonable to conclude that the purpose of the director or officer was not the direction of the manufacturing and selling activity of the company in the ordinary course of his relationship to it but the deliberate, willful and knowing pursuit of a course of conduct that was likely to constitute infringement or reflected an indifference to the risk of it. The precise formulation of the appropriate test is obviously a difficult one. Room must be left for a broad appreciation of the circumstances of each case to determine whether as a matter of policy they call for personal liability. [129]

In *Steinhart v. Moledina*,[130] the plaintiff alleged that he was the photographer and owner of photographs that were posted without permission on the web site of the corporate defendant in the action. The plaintiff also sued an individual on the ground that as an officer, director and shareholder of the corporate defendant, he had personally authorized the infringement of the copyright and moral rights of plaintiff's photographs by authorizing the reproduction, distribution, selling, and renting out of plaintiff's photographs. The action against the individual was struck out. In reaching this decision, Ground J. effectively rejected the argument that there was a special rule with respect to claims involving infringement of intellectual property. He followed the approach adopted in *Painblanc v. Kastner*,[131] and indicated that in order to support a claim against a director or officer, it would be necessary to allege (and ultimately prove) some fact along the following lines:

- the individual defendant knew of the plaintiff's rights and in directing the corporation's conduct acted with indifference to those rights;

---

[127] [1995] O.J. No. 3556, 26 O.R. (3d) 481 at 491 (C.A.).
[128] [1998] O.J. No. 391, 37 O.R. (3d) 97 at 102 (C.A.).
[129] *Mentmore Manufacturing Co. v. National Merchandise Manufacturing Co.*, [1978] F.C.J. No. 521, 40 C.P.R. (2d) 164 at 172-74 (Fed. Ct.).
[130] [2005] O.J. No. 525, 37 C.P.R. (4th) 443 (S.C.J.).
[131] [1994] F.C.J. No. 1671, 58 C.P.R. (3d) 502 (C.A.).

- the individual defendant must in fact be the *alter ego* of the corporation whose conduct or activities was wrong or willful or deliberately reckless; and

- the individual defendant must have known of the infringing activities and counseled and directed the manner in which the activities were being carried out and directly or indirectly ordered, instigated, authorized or procured those activities.

The plaintiff had failed to plead such specific acts. Accordingly, the statement of claim did not state a reasonable cause of action against the individual defendant. A bare allegation that an individual defendant was personally liable as a director, officer and "directing mind" of a corporate defendant for wilfully authorizing the posting, selling and distribution of plaintiff's photographs on the web site did not meet this requirement.

§3.60 In addition to the foregoing principles of liability, the directors and officers of a corporation may be personally liable to a shareholder or other complainant under the oppression remedy provided for in section 241 of the CBCA and 248 of the OBCA. The nature of the oppression remedy and the types of relief available are discussed in detail later in the text. For the moment, it is sufficient to note only that the oppression remedy is intended to serve as a judicial break upon abusive exercises of corporate power. Particular (but not exclusive) emphasis is placed on those in control of the corporation who are thereby in a position to force their will on minority interests within the corporation. Sections 241 and 248 empower the court to intercede in the business and affairs of the corporation. Where a claim is made against the directors or officers of a corporation based upon the oppression remedy, it is essential for the complainant to demonstrate that the claim is of such a nature that the directors (or officers) should be answerable for the wrong forming the basis of the complaint in addition to or in lieu of the corporation itself. An oppression claim against the directors (or officers) does not arise on the basis that the director concerned has acted in his or her personal capacity so as to become personally liable. Instead, it arises where the director has acted oppressively against the complainant, and it is appropriate in the circumstances to rectify that oppression by making an order against the director or officer personally. The conduct of the defendant director (or officer) that forms the basis of the complaint must be conduct *qua* director. An order against the director personally is normally available only where the director must be determined following a consideration of all relevant circumstances, including the nature of oppressive conduct and the corporation. However, any decision as to whether to grant a personal order against the director must be determined following a consideration of all relevant circumstances, including the nature of oppressive conduct and the effects of other possible orders on other persons interested in the corporation. In addition, the director or officer must be personally implicated in that oppressive conduct. The complainant must make specific allegations of wrongdoing against the director or officer. The courts will reject "shot-gun" type pleadings that fail to satisfy this test.[132]

F. RELATED PERSONS, AFFILIATED CORPORATIONS AND ASSOCIATES

§3.61 Before leaving the subject of corporate liability, there are a number of basic definitions and concepts that require consideration. Under numerous statutes, special rules of liability and also qualifications upon the validity of transactions apply where a corporation deals with a person who is in a close relationship to the corporation. A similar principle underlies the arm's length rule under the *Income Tax Act*: which is essentially that any transactions between parties who are not dealing at arm's length should be treated for tax purposes as if it took place upon the terms and at the price that would reasonably be anticipated in the case of a similar transaction between the parties who were dealing at arm's length in similar circumstance.[133] The foundation for much of the law in this area is to be found in the terms of the OBCA and CBCA. Both the OBCA and the CBCA focus considerable attention upon the relationships that may exist between two or more corporations or other persons, and there are a number of terms of art and other definitions included in each of the two statutes that are intended to clarify the types of relationship that are of concern. For instance, subsection 1(1) of the OBCA defines the term "related person":

> "related person", where used to indicate a relationship with any person, means,
>
> (*a*) any spouse, son or daughter of that person,
>
> (*b*) any relative of the person or of the person's spouse, other than a relative referred to in clause (*a*), who has the same home as the person, or
>
> (*c*) any body corporate of which the person and any of the persons referred to in clause (*a*) or (*b*) or the partner or employer of the person, or any combination, beneficially own, directly or indirectly, voting securities carrying more than 50 per cent of the voting rights attached to all voting securities of the body corporate for the time being outstanding.[134]

---

[132] *Budd v. Gentra Inc.*, [1988] O.J. No. 3109 (C.A.), *per* Doherty J.A., see also *Gottlieb v. Adam*, [1994] O.J. No. 2636, 21 O.R. (3d) 248 (Gen. Div.); *Sidaplex-Plastic Suppliers Inc. v. Elta Group Inc.*, [1995] O.J. No. 4048, 131 D.L.R. (4th) 399 (Gen. Div.), var'd [1988] O.J. No. 2910 (C.A.).

[133] Subsection 251 of the *Income Tax Act*, R.S.C. 1985, c. 1 (5th Supp.) provides:

> For the purposes of this Act,
>
> (*a*) related persons shall be deemed not to deal with each other at arm's length;
>
> (*b*) a taxpayer and a personal trust (other than a trust described in any of paragraphs (a) to (*e*.1) of the definition "trust" in subsection 108(1)) are deemed not to deal with each other at arm's length if the taxpayer, or any person not dealing at arm's length with the taxpayer, would be beneficially interested in the trust if subsection 248(25) were read without reference to subclauses 248(25)(*b*)(iii)(A)(II) to (IV); and
>
> (*c*) where paragraph (*b*) does not apply, it is a question of fact whether persons not related to each other are at a particular time dealing with each other at arm's length.

[134] *Cf.* s. 251(2) of the *Income Tax Act*.

It is curious to note that while the child of a person is always a related person, the parent of a person is not related to that person within the meaning of the Act unless they share the same place of abode. A similar distinction is drawn under clause (*b*) in the case of a child of the spouse of the person.

§3.62 The definition of related person is to be compared with the definition of "affiliate", which is defined in subsection 1(4) of the Ontario *Business Corporations Act* as follows:

> For the purposes of this Act, one body corporate shall be deemed to be affiliated with another body corporate if, but only if, one of them is the subsidiary of the other or both are subsidiaries of the same body "corporate" or each of them is controlled by the same person.

In reading this definition, it is necessary to incorporate into it the related definition of control. In all cases, the question of control is determined by reference to subsection 1(5), which provides:

> For the purposes of this Act, a body corporate shall be deemed to be controlled by another person or by two or more bodies corporate if, but only if,
>
> (*a*) voting securities of the first-mentioned body corporate carrying more than 50 per cent of the votes for the election of directors are held, other than by way of security only, by or for the benefit of such other person or by or for the benefit of such other bodies corporate; and
>
> (*b*) the votes carried by such securities are sufficient, if exercised, to elect a majority of the board of directors of the first-mentioned body corporate.

The term "voting securities" indicates that the securities held by a controlling person need not be shares — any type of security to which a vote is attached is sufficient. In contrast, under the CBCA only voting shares are considered. The concept of holding securities upon which subsection 1(5) is based contrasts with the concept of ownership upon which clause (*b*) of the definition of "related person" depends: "holding" suggests that any type of arrangement whereby the controlling person controls the manner in which the shares are voted (*e.g.*, such as a voting trust) is sufficient to bring the person within the definition, even if nominal or beneficial ownership of the securities remains in some other person. However, control for corporate law purposes is generally equated with actual and existing control, rather than hypothetical control or contingent control where there is only a possibility that control may be acquired if certain conditions are satisfied or if certain contingencies work out in a particular way.[135]

§3.63 The question of control of a corporation under the OBCA or the CBCA is (at least as far as those statutes are concerned) one of law rather than fact. The Act gives no regard to the possibility that a person may acquire effective control other than through the holding of voting securities, or to the possibility that less than a 50 per cent holding may be sufficient to secure control in the case of widely held corporations.

---

[135] *Purdom v. Doherty*, [1929] 3 D.L.R. 719 (S.C.C.).

§3.64 The meaning of the statutory test of control under the *Fairness is a Two-Way Street Act (Construction Labour Mobility), 1999* was discussed in *Regulvar Canada Inc. v. Ontario*.[136] Under that Act, a number of restrictions on access to jobs in the Ontario construction industry were imposed on a "person resident in a designated jurisdiction". The only jurisdiction designated under the Act was Quebec. Subsection 1(1) of the Act, defined the term "person resident in a designated jurisdiction" to mean

(i) a person whose head office or registered office is located in that jurisdiction or

(ii) a person controlled directly or indirectly by a person described in sub-clause (i).

Subsection 1(2) of the Act defined the word "controlled" as having the same meaning as the definition in subsection 1(5) of the OBCA. It was determined that Regulvar Canada Inc. ("Regulvar Ontario") carried on business in the construction industry and that it had a head office in Ontario. Regulvar Ontario was closely related to Regulvar Inc. ("Regulvar Quebec"), a corporation whose head office was located in the province of Quebec, in that Regulvar Quebec owned 30 per cent of the shares of Regulvar Ontario. The balance of Regulvar Ontario's shares were held by 14 individuals who, for the most part, were either directors, officers or shareholders of Regulvar Quebec.

§3.65 Regulvar Ontario applied for a declaration that it was not a "person resident in a designated jurisdiction" as defined under the Act. Justice Métivier granted the application following the *de jure* test applied by the Supreme Court of Canada in *Duha Printers (Western) Ltd. v. Canada.* This "*de jure*" approach is essentially the same as the test provided for under the OBCA. The Crown appealed and submitted that Métivier J. interpreted the Act too narrowly by ignoring that the Act allows for control to be "direct or indirect". The appeal was dismissed. It was held that the applications judge was correct in applying the test in Duha Printers, on the basis of the following reasoning:

- If the legislature had intended the appropriate test to be *de facto* rather than *de jure* control, the legislature would have made this explicit. However, the court noted that the Act specifically incorporated the definition of control found in the *Business Corporations Act,* which it concluded was in effect a codification of the common law concept of *de jure* control. The use of the word "indirectly" in the Act did not bring the definition outside the scope of the *de jure* test because the *de jure* control test has been applied even in cases where the relevant legislation includes the word "indirectly".

- Regulvar Ontario was not indirectly controlled by Regulvar Quebec solely due to the fact that many of the individual shareholders of Regulvar Ontario are also directors and officers of Regulvar Quebec. There was no legal authority to support the argument that shareholders of Regulvar Ontario, who were also directors and officers of Regulvar Quebec, were required to vote in their capacity as shareholders of Regulvar Ontario in a manner that was in the

---

[136] [2004] O.J. No. 3298, 70 O.R. (3d) 641 (C.A.).

best interest of Regulvar Quebec (in fact, their fiduciary duty to Regulvar Ontario barred them doing so). Nor was indirect control established by reason of the fact that the sole director of Regulvar Ontario was also a director and officer of Regulvar Quebec. There was no absolute rule regarding multiple directorships. While it was possible that a conflict of interest could arise, a hypothetical conflict of interest was not enough to ground a finding that Regulvar Quebec controls Regulvar Ontario.

The court concluded that the Act did not prevent individual Quebecers from holding shares in a corporation, the head office of which is in Ontario. The legislation was not meant to prevent Quebecers from doing business in Ontario, but rather to encourage them to relocate and do business in Ontario. Regulvar Ontario was effectively relocated to Ontario and was not controlled by a corporation in Quebec. This was sufficient to exempt it from restrictions under the Act.

§3.66 Although the OBCA and CBCA adopt a *de jure* test of control, for many statutes, *de facto* control can have important consequences, even though the requirements of *de jure* control cannot be established.[137] The term *de facto* control is not a clearly defined one. It incorporates any type of informal arrangement under which one person or group in effect controls a corporation. It has been described in the following terms:

> *De facto* control is not necessarily dependent upon share ownership or upon powers derived from share ownership. It can arise as a result of family or personal influence of a benign sort or, on the other hand, from fear of reprisals, or from execution or blackmail, among other causes. ... *de facto* conrol could arise from may things, including extraneous factors and is, in that sense, an open-ended concept.[138]

§3.67 In the context of a change of control agreement, it has been held that a mere accumulation of proxies does not in itself amount to a change in control.[139] Since proxies ordinarily may be revoked at any time, an argument can be made that this is a rule of general application.

§3.68 In *H.A. Fawcett & Son Ltd. v. R.*[140] the controlling shareholder of a corporation died, leaving his shares by will to his son, as sole executor and beneficiary. It was held that the son was the controlling shareholder of the corporation by operation of law from the time of his father's death, and it was irrelevant that the son was unable to probate the will, convene a shareholder's meeting or register shares in his name immediately after the death.[141]

---

[137] See, for instance, s. 13 of the *Construction Lien Act*, R.S.O. 1990, c. C.30 which focuses on the question of "effective control". See also the concept of non-arm's length transactions, as developed in the *Income Tax Act*.

[138] *Trustee of A. Zimet Ltd. v. Woodbine Summit Ltd.*, [1985] O.J. No. 1280, 31 B.L.R. 277 at 302, aff'd [1987] O.J. No. 2392, 64 C.B.R. (N.S.) 89 (C.A.), *per* Sutherland J.

[139] *Montreal Trust Co. of Canada v. Call-Net Enterpreises Inc.*, [2004] O.J. No. 631, 40 B.L.R. (3d) 108 (C.A.).

[140] [1980] C.T.C. 293, 80 D.T.C. 6195 (F.C.A.).

[141] *H.A. Fawcett & Son Ltd. v. R.*, [1980] F.C.J. No. 314, [1980] C.T.C. 293 at 296 (F.C.A.), *per* Ryan J.

§3.69 Closely related to the concept of control is the relationship between a subsidiary and its holding body corporate. Subsection 1(2) of the OBCA sets out the definition of subsidiary:

> For the purposes of this Act, a body corporate shall be deemed to be a subsidiary of another body corporate if, but only if,
>
> (*a*) it is controlled by,
>
>   (i) that other, or
>
>   (ii) that other and one or more bodies corporate each of which is controlled by that other, or
>
>   (iii) two or more bodies corporate each of which is controlled by that other; or
>
> (*b*) it is a subsidiary of a body corporate that is that other's subsidiary.

Thus the test as to whether a particular corporation is a subsidiary is entirely one of control, but direct or indirect control by the same ultimate person is sufficient to establish the required degree of control. The definition of "holding body corporate" is provided in subsection 1(3), which reads:

> For the purposes of this Act, a body corporate shall be deemed to be another's holding body corporate if, but only if, that other is its subsidiary.

§3.70 Akin to the concepts of related person and affiliate corporations is the concept of association. Both the Ontario *Business Corporations Act* and the *Canada Business Corporations Act* contain a definition of "associate", with subsection 1(1) of the OBCA providing:

> "associate" where used to indicate a relationship with a person means,
>
> (*a*) any body corporate of which the person beneficially owns, directly or indirectly, voting securities carrying more than 10 per cent of the voting rights attached to all voting securities of the body corporate for the time being outstanding,
>
> (*b*) any partner of that person,
>
> (*c*) any trust or estate in which the person has a substantial beneficial interest or as to which that person serves as trustee or liquidator of the successor or in a similar capacity,
>
> (*d*) any relative of the person, including the person's spouse, where the relative has the same home as the person, or
>
> (*e*) any relative of the spouse of the person where the relative has the same home as the person.

In contrast, the definition found in subsection 2(1) of the CBCA reads:

> "associate" in respect of a relationship with a person means,
>
> (*a*) a body corporate of which that person beneficially owns or controls, directly or indirectly, shares or securities currently convertible into shares carrying more than ten per cent of the voting rights under all circumstances or by rea-

son of the occurrence of an event that has occurred and is continuing, or a currently exercisable option or right to purchase such shares or such convertible securities,

(b) a partner of that person acting on behalf of the partnership of which they are partners,

(c) a trust or estate in which that person has a substantial beneficial interest or in respect of which that person serves as a trustee or liquidator of the succession or in a similar capacity,

(d) a spouse of that person or an individual who is cohabiting with that person in a conjugal relationship, having so cohabited for a period of at least one year,

(e) a child of that person or of the spouse or individual referred to in paragraph (d), and

(f) a relative of that person or of the spouse or individual referred to in paragraph (d), if that relative has the same residence as that person.

Chapter 4

CONSTITUTIONAL CONSIDERATIONS

A. INTRODUCTION

§4.1 The Canadian Constitution provides for a federal form of government, with original and sovereign legislative jurisdiction being divided between a national or federal government and 10 provincial governments.[1] While the federal Parliament and provincial Legislatures are each generally sovereign within their respective spheres,[2] their sovereignty is limited by the *Canadian Charter of Rights and Freedoms* and by certain other provisions set out in the *Constitution Act, 1867,* as variously amended.[3] Under the 1867 Act, jurisdiction over business matters (and over the corporations that engage in business) is divided between the federal and provincial levels of government. Due to this division, there are several key areas of constitutional concern with respect to business corporations, including: (a) which level of government has jurisdiction to incorporate a particular corporation; (b) to what extent may the federal and provincial governments, respectively, regulate the business and affairs of a corporation incorporated by the other level of government; (c) what are the powers of eminent domain of the respective levels of government with respect to corporations incorporated by the other; (d) which level of government has jurisdiction over the winding-up and liquidation of corporations and under what circumstances; (e) to what extent, if any, are corporations entitled to the benefit of the *Canadian Charter of Rights and Freedoms* and other protections conferred upon persons under the *Constitution Act, 1867.* These questions form the subject of this chapter.

B. PARAMOUNTCY

§4.2 The most basic constitutional issue concerning business corporations concerns which level of government (federal or provincial) has jurisdiction to incorporate such corporations. A number of supplementary questions flow from this issue, such as: whether there are any limitations on the ability of the federal or provincial governments to incorporate specific types of business corporations;

---

[1] *Hodge v. R.* (1883), 9 App. Cas. 117 at 132 (P.C.), *per* Sir Barnes Peacock; *Nova Scotia (Attorney General) v. Canada (Attorney General)*, [1951] S.C.R. 31.

[2] In *Northern Telecom Canada Ltd. v. Communication Workers of Canada*, [1983] S.C.J. No. 54, [1983] 1 S.C.R. 733 at 741, Estey J. stated that the courts are:

> the authority in the community to control the limits of the respective sovereignties of the two plenary governments, as well as to police agencies within each of these spheres to ensure their operations remain within their statutory boundaries.

[3] *Hodge v. R.* (1883), 9 App. Cas. 117 (P.C.).

which level of government has jurisdiction to regulate the raising of money by way of the issue of securities; which level of government has the jurisdiction to regulate the business activities in which a corporation engages.

§4.3 Any effort to answer these questions, is complicated by the structure of the Canadian Constitution itself. The foundation of the Canadian Constitution is the *Constitution Act, 1867* (formerly the *British North America Act*). Among the earliest attempts at a written Constitution enacted by the British Parliament, it was the result of lengthy negotiation among Canadian power brokers that took place during the 1860s. The language employed in the Constitution reflects both the novel character of the document at the time, and the process of negotiation that gave birth to it. In contrast to many other federal constitutions, the Canadian Constitution makes no clear and sharp division of jurisdiction between the federal and provincial governments. Instead, both levels of government have certain general areas of jurisdiction along with a number of specific fields of jurisdiction.

§4.4 It is well established that the distribution of powers under the Canadian Constitution is (with a few limited exceptions such as agriculture and immigration) mutually exclusive: the federal government possesses exclusive jurisdiction in some areas, the province in others. The fact that one level of government has not legislated to the full extent of its powers does not permit the other level of government to enact laws to fill the void,[4] nor may one level of government delegate legislative responsibility to the other.[5] Thus the federal government, and only the federal government, has jurisdiction over bills of exchange and promissory notes,[6] while only provincial governments may legislate with respect to the incorporation of companies with provincial objects.[7]

§4.5 It is possible in certain cases, however, for a law enacted by one level of government in one field to relate incidentally to some other field of law that is reserved for the jurisdiction of the other level of government. So it has been said that "subjects which in one aspect and for one purpose fall within section 92 of the *Constitution Act, 1867*, may in another aspect and for another purpose fall within section 91."[8] In such cases, both the federal and provincial[9] governments may validly enact laws pertaining to the matter,[10] provided that each stays within

---

[4] *Union Colliery Co. v. Bryden*, [1899] A.C. 580 at 588 (P.C.), *per* Lord Watson; *Madden v. Nelson & Fort Sheppard Rlwy. Co.*, [1899] A.C. 627 at 628 (P.C.), *per* Lord Herschell L.C. See also *A.G. Canada v. A.G. Ontario*, [1898] A.C. 700 (P.C.).

[5] *A.G. Nova Scotia v. A.G. Canada*, [1951] S.C.R. 31 at 34, *per* Rinfret C.J.C.; although either level may adopt and incorporate valid legislation of the other by reference, when enacting laws within its own sphere of jurisdiction.

[6] *Constitution Act, 1867*, s. 91, para. 18.

[7] *Ibid.*, s. 92, para. 11.

[8] *Hodge v. R.* (1883), 9 App. Cas. 117 (P.C.), *per* Sir Barnes Peacock.

[9] *A.G. Ontario v. A.G. Canada*, [1894] A.C. 189 at 200, *per* Lord Herschell L.C.

[10] *A.G. Ontario v. A.G. Canada*, [1896] A.C. 348 (P.C.); *G.T.R. v. A.G. Canada*, [1907] A.C. 65 at 68 (P.C.), *per* Lord Dunedin.

the area of exclusive jurisdiction respectively assigned to each.[11] Whether the encroachment is federal or provincial, its validity depends upon whether it is an integral element in an overall scheme of legislation that on balance falls within the jurisdiction of the level of government concerned.[12] For instance, there is no question when the province enacts a law providing for the incorporation of companies that it may provide in those laws that the corporation is competent to borrow money and pay interest, even though the regulation of interest is in general a matter of federal jurisdiction.[13]

§4.6 It follows from this reasoning that a particular law may have a double aspect: it may in one respect fall within provincial jurisdiction and in another respect fall within federal jurisdiction. Where such a situation exists, it is possible that there may be a conflict between the provincial and federal laws,[14] even though each of these laws was validly enacted by the level of government concerned. In such a case, the federal enactment will prevail over that of the province to the extent of the conflict, so that the provincial law will be rendered inoperative to that extent.[15] This rule of constitutional law is often described as the doctrine of federal legislative paramountcy.[16]

§4.7 An illustration of the paramountcy of federal legislation in the corporate law context can be found in *John Deere Plow Co. v. Wharton*.[17] In that case the Privy Council considered the constitutional validity of British Columbia legislation which purported to restrict the right of a federally incorporated company (namely, the John Deere Plow Company) to carry on business within the prov-

---

[11] *Re Waters and Water Powers*, [1929] S.C.R. 200 at 217, *per* Duff J.; *A.G. Canada v. C.P.R. and C.N.R.*, [1958] S.C.R. 285 at 290, *per* Rand J.; see also *A.G. British Columbia v. Smith*, [1967] S.C.R. 702; *Cushing v. Dupuy* (1880), 5 App. Cas. 409 at 415 (P.C.), *per* Sir Montague Smith.
[12] *Construction Montcalm Inc. v. Minimum Wage Commission*, [1978] S.C.J. No. 110, [1979] 1 S.C.R. 754 at 768-69, *per* Beetz J.; *Papp v. Papp*, [1970] 1 O.R. 331 at 335, *per* Laskin J.:

> The Constitution is a working instrument addressed to legislative bodies, and its implementation in legislation must be seen as a social assessment by the enacting body of the scope of the power which is involved in any particular cases. Where there is admitted competence, as there is here, to legislate to a certain point, the question of limits (where that point is passed) is best answered by asking whether there is a rational, functional connection between what is admittedly good and what is challenged.

[13] *Royal Canadian Insurance Co. v. Montreal Warehousing Co.* (1880), 3 L.N. 155 (Que.).
[14] *Rio Hotel Ltd. v. New Brunswick (Liquor Licensing Board)*, [1987] S.C.J. No. 46, 44 D.L.R. (4th) 663 at 667 (S.C.C.), *per* Dickson C.J.
[15] *La Compagnie Hydraulique de St. François v. Continental Heat and Light Co.*, [1909] A.C. 194 at 198 (P.C.), *per* Sir Arthur Wilson. The federal government cannot repeal provincial law, but the provincial law ceases to have effect so long as the inconsistency exists: *A.G. Ontario v. A.G. Canada*, [1896] A.C. 348 at 366 (P.C.), *per* Lord Watson. Should the conflicting federal law be repealed, the provincial law will revive.
[16] *Rothmans, Benson & Hedges Inc. v. Saskatchewan*, [2005] S.C.J. No. 1, [2005] 1 S.C.R. 188 at para. 11, *per* Major, J.
[17] [1915] A.C. 330 (P.C.). In *La Compagnie Hydraulique de St. François v. Continental Heat and Light Co.*, [1909] A.C. 194 (P.C.), the respondent company was incorporated by federal special Act which empowered it to manufacture, supply, sell and dispose of gas and electricity. It was held that it could not be restricted under a provincial statute which purported to grant an exclusive privilege of producing and selling electricity in a locality.

ince. John Deere's federal corporate charter expressly permitted the company to carry on the business of a dealer in agricultural implements throughout Canada. The federal *Interpretation Act* provided that:

> ... words making any association or number of persons a corporation shall vest in such corporation the power to sue and be sued, to contract by their corporate name, and to acquire and hold personal property.

The British Columbia legislation required every company incorporated other than under the law of that province (including a federally incorporated company) to be licensed under provincial law. Until so doing an extra provincial company was not capable of carrying on business in the province or of maintaining an action in the courts of the province. The practical effect of the licence procedure contemplated by the British Columbia legislation was to impose a "dual incorporation" requirement — the federal Charter in and of itself would have permitted the company to do nothing, unless a provincial licence was obtained. Therefore, the issue that the Privy Council confronted was whether the province was competent to interfere with the carrying on of business in British Columbia by a federally incorporated company.

§4.8 In giving its decision, the Privy Council commented first upon the structure of sections 91 and 92 of the *Constitution Act, 1867*, Viscount Haldane stating:

> The language of these sections and of the various heads which they contain obviously cannot be construed as having been intended to embody the exact disjunction of a perfect logical scheme. The draftsman had to work on the terms of a political agreement, terms which were mainly to be sought for in the resolutions passed at Quebec in October, 1864. ... [I]f there is at points obscurity in language, this may be taken to be due, not to uncertainty about general principle, but to that difficulty in obtaining ready agreement about phrases which attends the drafting of legislative measures by large assemblages. It may be added that the form in which provisions in terms overlapping each other have been placed side by side shows that those who passed the Confederation Act intended to leave the working out and interpretation of these provisions to practice and to judicial decision.[18]

Given the *ad hoc* nature of the division of powers, the Privy Council expressly rejected the notion that any firm rule of universal application could be given to all cases:

> An abstract logical definition of their scope is not only ... impracticable, but is certain, if attempted, to cause embarrassment and possible injustice in future cases. It must be borne in mind in construing the two sections that matters which in a special aspect and for a particular purpose may fall within one of them may in a different aspect and for a different purpose fall within the other. In such cases the nature and scope of the legislative attempt of the Dominion or the Province ... have to be examined with reference to the actual facts if it is to be possible to determine under which set of powers it falls in substance and in reality.[19]

Thus each case falls to be decided on its own facts. He continued:

---

[18] *John Deere Plow Co. v. Wharton*, [1915] A.C. 330 at 338 (P.C.).
[19] *Ibid.*, at 339.

...[I]f it be established that the Dominion Parliament can create such companies, then it becomes a question of general interest throughout the Dominion in what fashion they should be permitted to trade. Their Lordships are therefore of opinion that the Parliament of Canada had power to enact the sections relied on in this case in the Dominion Companies Act. and the Interpretation Act.[20]

§4.9 In the corporate law context, the paramountcy issue most often arises where the province interferes with the conduct of business by a federal corporation in the course of regulating some aspect of property and civil rights (or some other matter within provincial jurisdiction) rather than interfering with the status and corporate capacity of a federal corporation. In such cases, the Board saw no necessary inconsistency between the federal and provincial legislation:

> They do not desire to be understood as suggesting that because the status of a Dominion company enables it to trade in a province and thereby confers on it civil rights to some extent, the power to regulate trade and commerce can be exercised in such a way as to trench, in the case of such companies, on the exclusive jurisdiction of the provincial Legislatures over civil rights in general. ... It is enough for present purposes to say that the Province cannot legislate so as to deprive a Dominion company of its status and powers. This does not mean that these powers cannot be exercised in contravention of the laws of the Province restricting the rights of the public in the Province generally. What it does mean is that the status and powers of a Dominion company as such cannot be destroyed ...[21]

Ultimately, the Privy Council refused[22] to set down a precise statement of the extent to which the province may restrain the activities of federal companies. It was clear from the decision, however (particularly in the last two sentences of the passage quoted above), that some form of balance must be struck between the competing legislative objectives of the two jurisdictions.

§4.10 In recent years, the courts have significantly clarified the circumstances in which the paramountcy of federal legislation comes into play. The courts no longer inquire whether federal legislation "fully occupies" the field. Instead, they now focus upon the practical effect of any conflict between the federal and provincial legislation within the context of the purpose underlying the federal law.[23] There are two approaches which may be taken towards the identification of instances of such conflict. Under the narrower of these approaches, paramountcy applies only where compliance with provincial law would entail an actual breach of federal law. On occasion, the courts have tended towards this

---

[20] *Ibid.*, at 340.
[21] *Ibid.*, at 340-41.
[22] *Ibid.*, at 343.
[23] See, generally, *Husky Oil Operations Ltd. v. Canada (Minister of National Revenue)*, [1995] S.C.J. No. 77, 128 D.L.R. (4th) 1 at 48, *per* Gonthier J.; *Robinson v. Countrywide Factors Ltd.*, [1977] S.C.J. No. 76, 72 D.L.R. (3d) 500 at 538, *per* Beetz J.; *CNR v. Ontario (Director, Environmental Protection Agency)*, [1991] O.J. No. 684, 47 O.A.C. 47 at 64 (Div. Ct.):

> The test today is clearly such that mere duplication by the provincial legislature of laws enacted by Parliament is no longer sufficient to invoke the doctrine of paramountcy. Actual conflict between two pieces of legislation is required.

This case was affirmed at [1992] O.J. No. 317, 54 O.A.C. 367 (C.A.).

view.[24] The mere fact that both federal and provincial laws provide for similar rights of recovery is not sufficient to raise a paramountcy issue, since the courts have the ability to control and prevent possible double recovery as they are able to control and prevent any abusive proceedings.[25] However, impossibility of dual compliance is only one of two tests of inconsistency. Under the second (and broader) approach to the paramountcy question, the courts will not only look at the terms of the two laws, but will also inquire whether the policy underlying the federal law would be frustrated if compliance was required with the provincial law.[26] Where provincial legislation would have such a frustrating effect, it may also be held inoperative under the doctrine.[27]

§4.11 The first test is considerably easier to apply than the second. The courts exercise restraint when attempting to apply the second test, and will normally rule provincial legislation inoperative only if and to the extent that compliance with provincial legislation would frustrate a clear federal policy objective. There are abundant good reasons for exercising such restraint. As the courts have often noted in the context of statutory interpretation, the identification of the purpose of legislation by methods other than by reviewing the express wording of the statutes concerned is no easy matter. The mere fact that the federal law does not impose a restriction does not necessarily give rise to a conflict of policy if the provincial law does introduce such a restriction. It is a general principle of common law that freedom is presumed, so that the citizen is free to do anything that is not prohibited or restricted by law. It is only where the federal law confers a privilege or right that would otherwise not exist, that federal policy would be thwarted by the introduction of a provincial restriction or prohibition. In enacting their separate laws, the federal and provincial governments are dealing with the same subject matter, but are approaching that subject matter from different perspectives. It is more than likely that from time to time the province will find it necessary to impose an additional restriction or prohibition beyond those that were felt to be necessary when the subject matter was viewed exclusively from the different federal perspective. It cannot be inferred in such a case that the silence of the federal law concerning such a restriction means that the federal policy would be defeated if the provincial restriction is imposed.[28]

§4.12 In summary, when invoking the paramountcy concept, it is not enough for a person who disputes the effectiveness of a provincial law to show that the provincial law says X while the federal law says Z. It is necessary to show that X and Z are irreconcilable, so that compliance with X necessitates the violation of Z

---

[24] *Multiple Access v. McCutcheon*, [1982] S.C.J. No. 66, [1982] 2 S.C.R. 161 at 190, *per* Dickson J. See also *Aeroguard v. A.G. British Columbia*, [1998] B.C.J. No. 910, [1998] 10 W.W.R. 155 (S.C.).
[25] *Ibid.*
[26] *Bank of Montreal v. Hall*, [1990] S.C.J. No. 9, [1990] 1 S.C.R. 121 at 153-54, *per* La Forest J.
[27] *Bank of Montreal v. Hall*, [1990] S.C.J. No. 9, [1990] 1 S.C.R. 121 at 155, *per* La Forest J.
[28] See generally, *R. v. Lemonides*, [1997] O.J. No. 3562, 35 O.R. (3d) 611 (Gen. Div.); *Horsefield v. Ontario (Registrar of Motor Vehicles)*, [1997] O.J. No. 3183, 34 O.R. (3d) 509 (Gen. Div.), rev'd [1997] O.J. No. 3388, 35 O.R. (3d) 304 (C.A.).

or that the purpose of Z would be defeated if effect were to be given to X. Instances of such conflict are rare, and in recent years the courts have become increasingly unwilling to hold provincial laws ineffective on the basis of whether the effect of compliance with the provincial law would be to thwart the underlying perceived purpose of the federal law. As will be explained below, this new approach to the issue of paramountcy places a distinct hue upon much of what was said in earlier cases dealing with federal/provincial conflicts in the corporate and securities law areas.[29]

C. JURISDICTION TO INCORPORATE

§4.13 Most countries with a federal structure empower both the federal and provincial governments to incorporate corporate entities of at least some sort, and in this respect Canada is no exception. The federal and provincial powers of incorporation exist in separate spheres.[30] The provincial power of incorporation is express, under section 92, paragraph 11 of the *Constitution Act, 1867*, which states that:

> 92. In each Province the Legislature may exclusively make Laws in relation to Matters coming within the Classes of Subjects next hereinafter enumerated; that is to say, ...
>
> 11. The Incorporation of Companies with provincial Objects.

Except in the case of banks,[31] the federal incorporation power is implicit. It is mostly seen as emanating from the general power of the federal government under section 91 of the *Constitution Act, 1867* over peace, order and good government.[32] However, in the case of corporations carrying on certain activities, the power of incorporation is also implicit in certain of the enumerated powers of the federal government as well.[33]

§4.14 Both the federal and provincial powers of incorporation have been broadly construed, and there have been few, if any, instances in which the incorporation of a particular type of corporation has been seen to fall outside the legislative jurisdiction of either — quite probably because the effects of any such ruling would undoubtedly be highly disruptive to Canada's overall economic activity. The precise demarcation between the federal and provincial power has never been fully determined, but it now seems clear that both the federal and provincial governments may enact legislation providing for the incorporation of busi-

---

[29] Although paramountcy is not entirely excluded where federal legislation contemplates valid provincial legislation with respect to a dual aspect matter, the prospect of a paramountcy problem is unlikely to arise, and it would take a clear indication of incompatibility in such a case to support the invocation of the doctrine so as to invalidate the provincial legislative scheme. See, generally, *Siemens v. Manitoba Attorney General*, [2002] S.C.J. No. 69, [2003] 1 S.C.R. 6.
[30] *Great West Saddlery Co. v. R.*, [1921] 2 A.C. 91 at 114 (P.C.), *per* Viscount Haldane.
[31] *Constitution Act, 1867*, s. 91, para. 15.
[32] *John Deere Plow Co. v. Wharton*, [1915] A.C. 330 (P.C.).
[33] E.g., the power to legislate with respect to navigation and shipping, under s. 91, para. 10, and the trade and commerce clause, s. 91, para. 2. See, generally, *Re s. 110 of Dominion Companies Act*, [1934] S.C.R. 653.

ness corporations, as both the provinces and Canada have done. Of the two levels of government, it is the provincial government's power of incorporation which has often been suggested to be more limited, since the Constitution grants the provinces only the power for the incorporation of corporations having "provincial objects". The meaning of this phrase is not clear; what is clear is that any implicit limitation that flows from it has been narrowly construed.[34] There is no question that a corporation may be provincially incorporated where it is to carry on a business that is closely related to that most closely guarded area of federal jurisdiction, banking;[35] *a fortiori*, a provincial corporation may engage in other federally regulated lines of business, such as navigation.[36]

§4.15 In 1867, the incorporation of business enterprise was very much atypical. For this reason, the widespread incorporation of business likely was the furthest thing from anyone's mind, at the time when the (then entitled) *British North America Act* was drafted. Even in the United States and Great Britain, such industry and commerce as existed was operated on a local basis — often on a scale little larger than traditional cottage industry and the village shop. The conduct of business on a continental or international scale was still in its infancy. In Europe, Mayer Rothschild had died only in 1812, and his son James was still very much in charge of the Paris branch of the family's banking empire. In the United States, the transcontinental railway would not be complete until 1869, the Standard Oil Company was not created until 1870, the Carnegie Steel Co. would not be founded until 1873, and the Federal Steel Co. would not come into existence until 1898. Even in 1867, Cornelius Vanderbilt was only beginning to assemble his railway empire. It was within this context that paragraph 11 of section 92 was enacted.

§4.16 It is always a matter of speculation when seeking to divine the meaning of the original text of the *British North America Act*. Very often, individual Fathers of Confederation placed widely different interpretations on the same language in the same provisions. Further, even where the written record evidences only one intended meaning, it is far from certain that the written record is complete. Others involved in shaping the Constitution may well have understood the provisions concerned to mean something entirely different. The final text of the Act was the product of a great deal of give and take, and what was ultimately en-

---

[34] *Bonanza Creek Gold Mining Co. v. R.*, [1916] 1 A.C. 566 (P.C.); see also *R. v. Massey-Harris Co.* (1905), 1 W.L.R. 45, 9 C.C.C. 25 (N.W.T.S.C.); *International Home Purchasing Contract Co. v. Alberta (Registrar of Joint Stock Companies)* (1912), 3 W.W.R. 806 (Alta. T.D.), per Harvey C.J.

[35] *Re Bergethaler Waisenamt* (1949), 29 C.B.R. 189 (Man. C.A.); see also *Alberta (Provincial Treasurer) v. Long* (1973), 49 D.L.R. (3d) 695 (Alta. T.D.); *Caisse populaire de Notre Dame Ltée v. Moyen* (1967), 59 W.W.R. 129 (Sask. Q.B.). For a case involving a provincially incorporated entity carrying on a telephone and telecommunications business, see: *Téléphone Guévremont Inc. v. Quebec*, [1992] Q.J. No. 2213, 99 D.L.R. (4th) 241, aff'd [1994] S.C.J. No. 31, 112 D.L.R. (4th) 127.

[36] *Re Lake Winnipeg Transportation, Lumber & Trading Co.* (1891), 7 Man. R. 602 (Q.B.); see also *MacDougall v. Union Navigation Co.* (1877), 21 L.C. Jur. 63, 1 L.N. 210 (Que. C.A.). The only exception is in the case of a bank, which must be federally incorporated.

acted was language with which people were prepared to live for the moment — reserving the right to argue about its meaning at some later date. Nevertheless, the traditional method of interpreting statutes by way of contrasting provisions enacted at the same time does provide an indication of what was probably meant by the phrase "the incorporation of companies with provincial objects". First, this line appears in paragraph 11 of section 92, and it follows immediately a paragraph that confers upon the provinces jurisdiction over:

> 10. Local Works and Undertakings other than such as are of the following Classes:
>
> (*a*) Lines of Steam or other Ships, Railways, Canals, Telegraphs, and other Works and Undertakings connecting the Province with any other or others of the Provinces, or extending beyond the Limits of the Province;
>
> (*b*) Lines of Steam Ships between the Province and any British or Foreign Country;
>
> (*c*) Such Works as, although wholly situate within the Province, are before or after the Execution declared by the Parliament of Canada to be for the general Advantage of Canada or for the Advantage of Two or more of the Provinces.

Most likely, any corporate enterprise falling in clauses (a) or (b) of paragraph 10 would have been seen as outside the scope of provincial authority under paragraph 11. By extension, everything else — excepting the one line of business specifically assigned to the federal government under section 91 — would have been seen as being within the scope of the provincial incorporation power. Indeed, it is significant to note that it was considered necessary in clauses 92 10(*a*) and (*b*) to exclude expressly both international steam ship lines and interprovincial railways from the scope of the term local works and undertakings. Only one type of business was expressly contemplated in the BNA Act as being conducted on an incorporated basis and that is banking, which section 91(15) specifically grants to the federal government. However, if this a correct interpretation of what was originally intended, it is suffice to say that it has not been interpreted this way. Instead, both federal and provincial powers of incorporation have been broadly construed.

§4.17 Since section 92, paragraph 11 of the *Constitution Act, 1867* gives the province exclusive jurisdiction over the incorporation of companies having provincial objects, and since the powers of the province under section 92 are exclusive, the question arises as to whether the federal government may validly create a corporation which chooses to limit its operations to an object or purpose that is provincial in nature. This question was answered in *Colonial Building and Investment Association v. A.G. Quebec*,[37] where a company was incorporated by federal Act with the express power to deal with real estate throughout Canada. In actuality, all of the dealings of the company were limited to Quebec. It was held that the *de facto* limitation of business to a single province did not affect the validity of the federal incorporation, so long as the com-

---

[37] (1883), 9 App. Cas. 157 (P.C.).

pany was not limited in its powers or objects to dealing only within a single province.[38]

(i) The Territorial Limits of Corporate Law

§4.18 In the modern global economy, it is an unusual corporate entity that does not on occasion engage in some transaction under which it comes within the orbit of a jurisdiction other than the one under which it was incorporated. For instance, a company may order goods or services from a supplier in another jurisdiction, or retain a sales representative in another jurisdiction and commence the supply of its own goods or services into that other jurisdiction. Many corporations invest directly in foreign subsidiaries. Other corporations will seek to raise capital in one or more jurisdictions other than the jurisdiction of incorporation. In each of these cases, it is necessary to consider the rules governing such extraterritorial operation. In Canada, extraterritoriality raises constitutional questions in the case of provincial legislation or legal action.

§4.19 It is a general principle of private international law that the courts of one jurisdiction will recognize the corporate status of an entity incorporated under the laws of another jurisdiction.[39] So in *Lazard Bros. & Co. v. Midland Bank Ltd.,* Lord Wright said:

> English courts have long since recognized as juristic persons, corporations established by foreign law in virtue of the fact of their creation and continuance under and by that law.[40]

Whether a particular foreign entity has been validly incorporated is determined in accordance with the relevant rules of the foreign legal system under which incorporation purportedly occurred.[41] It is not necessary for this purpose that the rules governing the formality of incorporation under the laws of the foreign jurisdiction approximate those of the domestic jurisdiction or even those of common law jurisdictions generally. What applies with respect to actual foreign corporate entities also applies with respect to foreign near-corporations with respect to such attributes of corporate personality as may be conferred upon them under the jurisdiction of domicile. For instance, in some jurisdictions, separate legal personality may be conferred without any grant of status by the government of the jurisdiction concerned. To give one example: it is often said that under Scots law, a partnership attains legal personality[42] by virtue of the private partnership contract between the members of the firm, rather than as a

---

[38] See also *Traverse de Lévis v. Lemieux* (1940), 79 Que. S.C. 52.
[39] *Dreyfus v. Commissioners of Inland Revenue* (1929), 14 T.C. 560; *Chaff & Hay Acquisition Committee v. J.A. Hemphill & Sons Pty. Ltd.* (1947), 64 C.L.R. 375 (H.C. Aust.).
[40] [1933] A.C. 289 (H.L.).
[41] See, for instance, *Laemthong International Lines Co. Ltd. v. Artis*, [2005] All E.R. (D) 157 (Q.B. Comm. Ct.).
[42] One may debate whether a Scot's partnership truly is a separate person, for it lacks certain of the attributes of separate personality. It clearly has the right to sue and be sued in its own name. However, a Scottish firm cannot hold heritable property in its own name but can only be in the names of its partners.

result of any act of the state. Nevertheless, the personality of Scots partnerships is still recognized in England.[43] Nor is it necessary that the body or entity upon which corporate status is conferred under the laws of the foreign jurisdiction be a body or entity that would be capable of incorporation under the laws of the domestic jurisdiction. So, for instance, it has been held that a foreign temple that enjoys legal personality or corporate status under the law of the place in which it is situate should be recognized as an incorporated entity in other jurisdictions.[44] A similar ruling was made with respect to a foreign idol.[45]

(1) The Canadian Approach to Extraterritoriality

§4.20 One critical area of concern with respect to the validity of legislation dealing with corporations is the extent to which such laws may have extraterritorial effect. It is a settled principle of international law that each sovereign jurisdiction is presumed in its legislative and regulatory action to have intended to respect the sovereignty of other jurisdictions. Accordingly, there is a strong presumption that all laws are intended to be confined in their operation to the territorial jurisdiction of the enacting state. So, in *R. v. Jameson*, it was said:

> ... if any construction otherwise be possible, an Act will not be construed as applying to foreigners in respect to acts done by them outside the dominions of the sovereign power enacting. That is a rule based on international law by which one sovereign power is bound to respect the subjects and the rights of all other sovereign powers outside its own territory.[46]

In *Tolofson v. Jensen*, La Forest J. stated as follows:

> Ordinarily people expect their activities to be governed by the law of the place where they happen to be and expect that concomitant legal benefits and responsibilities will be defined accordingly. The government of that place is the only one with power to deal with these activities. The same expectation is ordinarily shared by other states and by people outside the place where an activity occurs. If other states routinely applied their laws to activities taking place elsewhere, confusion would be the result. In our modern world of easy travel and with the emergence of a global economic order, chaotic situations would often result if the principle of territorial jurisdiction were not, at least generally, respected.[47]

The application of this principle in Canada has been more considered in the context of provincial legislation and regulatory activity than with respect to federal. It is settled principle of Canadian constitutional law that the provincial legislatures have no jurisdiction to legislate extraterritorially.[48] The legislative power of the

---

[43] See, generally, *Memec plc v. Inland Revenue Commissioners*, [1998] S.T.C, 754 (C.A.); *Major (Inspector of Taxes) v. Brodie*, [1998] S.T.C. 491 (Ch.); see also *Oxnard Financing SA v. Rahn*, [1998] 3 All E.R. 19 (C.A.) pertaining to a Swiss partnership which also enjoyed separate personality.
[44] *Bumper Development Corporation v. Comm. of Police of the Metropolis*, [1991] 1 W.L.R. 1362.
[45] *Pramatha Nath Mullick v. Pradyumna Kumar Mullick* (1925), L.R. 52 Ind. App. 245 (P.C.).
[46] [1896] 2 Q.B. 425 at 430, per Lord Russell of Killowen C.J.
[47] [1994] S.C.J. No. 110, [1994] 3 S.C.R. 1022 at 1050-51.
[48] *Unifund Assurance Co. v. Insurance Corp. of British Columbia*, [2003] S.C.J. No. 39, [2003] 2 S.C.R. 63 at para. 50; *Dupont v. Taronga Holdings Ltd.* (1986), 49 D.L.R. (4th) 335 at 337 (Que.

provinces is territorially limited as a result of the words "in each Province" in the introductory paragraph of section 92 of the *Constitution Act, 1867*. In contrast, unlike the legislative assemblies of the provinces, the federal Parliament has the legislative competence to enact laws having extraterritorial effect, in the sense that Canadian courts[49] will recognize legislation that purports to have such effect as valid and enforceable. However, Parliament is presumed not to intend to legislate extraterritorially, in the absence of clear words or necessary implication to the contrary.[50]

§4.21 While a province may not legislate with the specific purpose of regulating some extra-territorial subject matter, provincial legislation is not necessarily invalid to the extent that it has some extra-provincial effect, where that effect is incidental to some valid intra-provincial purpose.[51] The courts now recognize that the circumstances of modern life, including the increasing globalization of economic relationships, often mean that provincial legislation must necessarily be given valid extraterritorial effect to the extent required to attain a legitimate provincial legislative goal. To be effective in its extra provincial aspect, the interjurisdictional elements affected by the provincial legislation in question must have a meaningful connection to the province that enacted that legislation. Where the validity of provincial legislation is challenged on the basis that it violates territorial limitations on provincial legislative competence, the analysis centers on the pith and substance of the legislation. If its pith and substance is in relation to matters falling within the field of provincial legislative competence, the legislation is valid. Incidental or ancillary extraprovincial aspects of such legislation are irrelevant to its validity.[52] So, for instance, where one party to a transaction resides in one jurisdiction and the second in another, the law governing the transaction will necessarily have some spill-over extraterritorial effect. The out-of-province party is not entitled to be isolated from the reach of provincial law, merely on the basis of being externally resident. It follows that provincial tax and regulatory regimes are generally applicable to out-of-province entities that engage in business within the province.[53]

§4.22 What amounts to a sufficient connection to support an extraprovincial effect can be difficult to determine, particularly whether where there is only a

---

S.C.), per Guerin J. See also *Global Securities Corp. v. British Columbia Securities Commission*, [1998] B.C.J. No. 1597, 162 D.L.R. (4th) 601 (C.A.), rev'd [2000] S.C.J. No. 5.

[49] The extent to which a foreign court would recognize legislation clearly drafted to accomplish an extra-territorial purpose depends upon the nature of the legislation in question, and also principles comparable to those discussed in this section with respect to the extraterritorial application of provincial laws.

[50] *Society of Composers, Authors and Music Publishers of Canada v. Canadian Association of Internet Providers*, [2004] S.C.J. No. 44, [2004] 2 S.C.R. 427.

[51] *Reference re Upper Churchill Water Rights Reversion Act 1980 (Newfoundland)*, [1984] S.C.J. No. 16, [1984] 1 S.C.R. 297.

[52] See *British Columbia v. Imperial Tobacco Canada Ltd.*, [2005] S.C.J. No. 50, 257 D.L.R. (4th) 193; *Reference re Upper Churchill Water Rights Reversion Act 1980 (Newfoundland)*, [1984] S.C.J. No. 16, [1984] 1 S.C.R. 297 at 332.

[53] *R. v. Thomas Equipment Ltd.*, [1979] 2 S.C.R. 529; *Moran v. Pyle National (Canada) Ltd.*, [1973] S.C.J. No. 149, [1975] 1 S.C.R. 393 at 409.

fleeting connection between the parties or other subject matter of a law and a particular province.⁵⁴ However, recent Supreme Court of Canada case law indicates the extent to which a provincial law may have valid extraprovincial consequence:⁵⁵

- The connection must be a "real and substantial" one. What constitutes a "sufficient" connection depends on the relationship among the enacting jurisdiction, the subject matter of the legislation and the individual or entity sought to be regulated by it. The required strength of the relationship varies with the type of jurisdiction being asserted. A relationship that is inadequate to support the application of regulatory legislation may nevertheless provide a sufficient "real and substantial connection" to permit the courts of the forum to take jurisdiction over a dispute.

- The assessment of sufficient connection must take into account the requirements of order and fairness that underlie a federal arrangement of government. The principles of order and fairness, being purposive, must be applied flexibly according to the subject matter of the legislation. Many activities within one state necessarily have impact in another, but a multiplicity of competing exercises of state power in respect of such activities should be avoided so far as possible.⁵⁶ For instance, in *Hunt v. T&N plc*,⁵⁷ a Quebec statute prohibited the removal from Quebec of business records required by judicial process a British Columbia court with documentary production. The court noted that such a rule would effectively immunize the business concerns located in Quebec from ever having to produce documents sought for the purposes of litigation in other provinces. Justice La Forest held that the Quebec "blocking statute" was "constitutionally inapplicable" on fairness and order criteria insofar as it interfered with the extraprovincial legal proceeding. It was also decided that is not only the view of the enacting legislature that must be considered, but the collective interest of the Canadian federation as a whole in assessing the impact of a given law on order and fairness.

- Actual physical presence within a jurisdiction is only one consideration to take into account in deciding upon the validity of extraterritorial effect, on the basis of substantial connection. Other considerations include residence, domicile,⁵⁸ carrying on business there,⁵⁹ or even remoter connections.⁶⁰ An incidental connection with the parties will not confer such jurisdiction.⁶¹

---

⁵⁴ *The Queen in Right of Manitoba v. Air Canada*, [1980] S.C.J. No. 69, [1980] 2 S.C.R. 303.
⁵⁵ *Unifund Assurance Co. v. Insurance Corp. of British Columbia*, [2003] S.C.J. No. 39, [2003] 2 S.C.R. 63.
⁵⁶ *Tolofson v. Jensen*, [1994] S.C.J. No. 110, [1994] 3 S.C.R. 1022 at 1051, *per* La Forest J.
⁵⁷ [1993] S.C.J. No. 125, [1993] 4 S.C.R. 289.
⁵⁸ *Kalenczuk v. Kalenczuk* (1920), 52 D.L.R. 406 (Sask. C.A.).
⁵⁹ *Moran v. Pyle National (Canada) Ltd.*, [1973] S.C.J. No. 149, [1975] 1 S.C.R. 393 at 409; *R. v. Thomas Equipment Ltd.*, [1979] S.C.J. No. 57, [1979] 2 S.C.R. 529.
⁶⁰ *Broken Hill South Ltd. v. Commissioner of Taxation (N.S.W.)* (1936-1937), 56 C.L.R. 337 at 375, *per* Dixon, J.
⁶¹ *The Queen in Right of Manitoba v. Air Canada*, [1980] S.C.J. No. 69, [1980] 2 S.C.R. 303 at 316, *per* Laskin C.J.C.

Provincial regulatory schemes governing a transaction that has a genuine footprint within the province (*e.g.*, where the transaction occurred within the province, or where the law of the province is the proper law of the law of the transaction) will be valid even though it affects the rights of other parties to the transaction that are outside the province. For instance, in *Ladore v. Bennett*,[62] Ontario legislation that reduced the rate of interest payable on Ontario municipal bonds was upheld although it affected the out-of-province holders of those bonds. There was a sufficient relationship between Ontario and the bond holders to afford the province jurisdiction in respect of the legislation. A province may also cooperate with out-of-province regulators to enhance the effectiveness of inter-jurisdictional regulation. In *Global Securities Corp. v. British Columbia Securities Commission*,[63] the Supreme Court upheld provincial legislation that permitted a securities regulator to exchange information with out-of-province securities regulators. The decision was based squarely on the proposition that statutory authorization of voluntary cooperation with foreign securities regulators "does not attempt to extend the reach of provincial legislation outside its borders". Similarly, provincial taxation laws may apply to an out-of-the province corporation where they relate to property or transactions that occur within the province, or to benefits that are paid to the out-of-province corporation from within the province.[64]

(2) Conduct of Business Outside the Province

§4.23 The creation of a corporation that may potentially operate outside the borders of a Province of incorporation is an example of an act of a provincial government that has a potential incidental extraprovincial consequence. There seems to be no practical problem with provincially incorporated companies carrying on business outside their provinces of incorporation.[65] It has now been clearly established that the provincial legislature may empower a corporation to enter transactions outside Ontario,[66] and that the province may empower a corporation to exercise its powers in other jurisdictions as may be permitted under the laws of those other jurisdictions.[67] Both the *Canada Business Corporations Act* ("CBCA") and the Ontario *Business Corporations Act* ("OBCA") purport to confer such capacity upon the corporations to which each respectively applies.[68] In this regard, section 16 of the OBCA provides:

---

[62] [1939] A.C. 468 (P.C.); see also *Reference re Upper Churchill Water Rights Reversion Act 1980 (Newfoundland)*, [1984] S.C.J. No. 16, [1984] 1 S.C.R. 297.
[63] [2000] S.C.J. No. 5, [2000] 1 S.C.R. 494.
[64] *Dunne v. Quebec (Sous-Ministre du Revenu)*, [2005] J.Q. No. 11812, 142 A.C.W.S. (3d) 699 (C.A.).
[65] *Weyburn Townsite Ltd. v. Honsberger* (1919), 59 S.C.R. 281 at 313, per Brodeur J.
[66] *Bonanza Creek Gold Mining Co. v. R.*, [1916] 1 A.C. 566 (P.C.).
[67] *Weyburn Townsite Ltd. v. Honsberger* (1919), 59 S.C.R. 281.
[68] A federal corporation is not a foreign corporation when operating in any province, and is therefore not acting extraterritorially: *Currie v. Harris Lithographing Co.* (1917), 40 O.L.R. 290 at 294 (H.C.), *per* Masten J. However, a corporation created under the laws of another province is a foreign corporation when carrying on business in a second province.

16. A corporation has the capacity to carry on its business, conduct its affairs and exercise its powers in any jurisdiction outside Ontario to the extent that the laws of such jurisdiction permit.

While subsection 15(2) of the CBCA expressly confers upon each corporation to which that Act applies the right to "carry on business throughout Canada", subsection 15(3) corresponds exactly to section 16 of the OBCA with respect to conducting business outside Canada:

> A corporation has the capacity to carry on its business, conduct its affairs and exercise its powers in any jurisdiction outside Canada to the extent that the laws of such jurisdiction permit.

§4.24 A close reading of these sections shows that both levels of government adopt a similar approach towards extraterritorial capacity, depending more upon principles of international comity more than upon any claim to be able to legislate extraterritorially.[69] The practical limits of the power of any government to confer capacity on a corporation end at the border of the jurisdiction over which it exercises authority, it being a general principle of public international law that no legislation of a foreign power can confer power on a corporation to infringe the rights of or impose obligations upon a person or corporation of and within another country.[70] Indeed, in *Matthew v. Guardian Assurance Co.*[71] it was held that a British company could not carry on business in Canada if so doing would be contrary to a law of the Canadian Parliament made within an area of its jurisdiction. While this statement was open to debate at the time when it was made, it has clearly been correct since the enactment of the *Statute of Westminster, 1931*.[72]

§4.25 Thus while the authority of the Canadian government to legislate extraterritorially may be recognized within Canada, beyond its borders, any capacity, powers and existence purportedly conferred upon a corporation under federal legislation exist only to the extent that other jurisdictions are prepared to give recognition to them.[73] The same rule applies with respect to provincially incor-

---

[69] *C.P.R. v. Western Union Telegraph* (1889), 17 S.C.R. 151 at 155; *Weyburn Townsite Ltd. v. Honsberger* (1918), 43 O.L.R. 451 at 459 (H.C.), rev'd 45 O.L.R. 176 (C.A.), aff'd 59 S.C.R. 281.
[70] *Rainy Lake River Boom Corp. v. Rainy River Lumber Co.* (1912), 27 O.L.R. 131 (H.C.).
[71] (1919), 45 D.L.R. 32 at 34 (S.C.C.), *per* Idlington J.
[72] (U.K.), 22 Geo. V, c. 4, ss. 2 and 4.
[73] Similarly, foreign companies may engage in business in Canada (or a province) only to the extent permitted to do so under the laws of Canada or the province concerned: see, generally, *Halifax (City) v. Jones* (1896), 28 N.S.R. 452 at 459 (C.A.), *per* Graham E.J.; *International Text-Book Co. v. Brown* (1907), 13 O.L.R. 644 (C.A.). The federal government may prohibit foreign corporations from carrying on business in Canada, even where those companies are licensed by a provincial government to do so: *Matthew v. Guardian Assurance Co.* (1919), 58 S.C.R. 47 at 49, *per* Davies C.J.C. — provided that in so doing the federal government is not seeking to meddle in a particular business which is outside its jurisdiction (*e.g.*, insurance), but is legislating generally with respect to dealings with aliens: *Re Insurance Act of Canada*, [1932] A.C. 41 (P.C.); *Farmers Mutual Hail Insurance Association of Iowa v. Whittaker*, [1917] 3 W.W.R. 750 (Alta. C.A.); *Re Insurance Contracts* (1926), 58 O.L.R. 404 (C.A.). As to the position of a foreign company carrying on business in a territory, see *McDonald v. Klondike Government Concession Ltd.* (1906), 4 W.L.R. 151 (Y.T.).

porated entities;[74] and also by implication, to foreign companies carrying on business within Canada.[75]

(3) Regulation of Extraprovincial Corporations

§4.26 A corporation incorporated outside a jurisdiction is foreign to that jurisdiction, irrespective of whether the jurisdiction of incorporation is recognized as a sovereign entity.[76] In other words, jurisdiction A may recognize the power of jurisdiction B to create a corporate entity. It does not automatically follow, however, that jurisdiction A will necessarily give effect to the full range of corporate powers (or, indeed, any of the powers) conferred by jurisdiction B upon any such entity that it may have created. More specifically, a company incorporated outside a jurisdiction has no general right to carry on business within that jurisdiction. In a federal country, such as Canada, this rule is qualified insofar as a federally incorporated company, such as a CBCA corporation, may carry on business across Canada. A federal corporation is not foreign to Ontario or any other province of Canada. However, this is not to say that a federal corporation is immune from provincial law, such as the need to comply with provincial registration requirements. Moreover, as discussed in detail below, federal incorporation affords no guarantee of a right to conduct of a particular line (or lines) of business, when such business is subject to provincial regulation. In such cases, a federal entity may be required to obtain a provincial licence. The raising of funds by such a corporation will also be generally subject to provincial securities laws. In contrast, companies incorporated at the provincial level in one province are "foreign" to the other provinces, and as such have no inherent right to carry on business in another province. Companies incorporated outside Canada have no inherent right to carry on business anywhere in Canada.

§4.27 Generally, extraprovincial corporations are regulated at the provincial level. In Ontario, corporations incorporated at the federal level or under the laws of a jurisdiction other than Ontario are governed by the *Extra-Provincial Corporations Act*[77] (the "EPCA"). Although broadly similar legislation is in force in other provinces, the Ontario legislation fills in many gaps that are left open elsewhere.

§4.28 Subsection 1(1) of EPCA defines the term "extra-provincial corporation" to mean a corporation, with or without share capital, incorporated or continued otherwise than by or under the authority of a province of Ontario statute. It also makes clear that the term "business" includes undertaking and non-profit activi-

---

[74] *Clarke v. Union Fire Insurance* (1883), 10 P.R. 313, aff'd 6 O.R. 223 (H.C.); *C.P.R. v. Ottawa Fire Insurance Co.* (1907), 39 S.C.R. 405 at 447-48, *per* Idlington J.
[75] A corporation has no right to carry on business outside its jurisdiction of incorporation if that power has not been conferred by that jurisdiction: *Hooper Grain Co. v. Colonial Assurance Co.*, [1917] 1 W.W.R. 1226 (Man. K.B.). However, such powers need not be expressly conferred. There is no presumption that a provincial corporation is limited to carrying on business within the province: *Honsberger v. Weyburn Townsite Co.* (1919), 59 S.C.R. 281, *per* Duff J.
[76] *JP Morgan Chase Bank v. Traffic Stream (BVI) Infrastructure Ltd.*, 536 U.S. 88 (2002).
[77] R.S.O. 1990, c. E.27.

ties. Subsection 1(2) of the EPCA provides the following explanation of when a corporation will be considered to be carrying on business in Ontario:

> For the purposes of this Act, an extra-provincial corporation carries on its business in Ontario if,
>
> (a) it has a resident agent, representative, warehouse, office or place where it carries on its business in Ontario;
>
> (b) it holds an interest, otherwise than by way of security, in real property situate in Ontario; or
>
> (c) it otherwise carries on its business in Ontario.

In construing the scope of clause (c), it is worthwhile to consider some of the rulings made under earlier legislation, and under comparable legislation in other provinces. The question of whether a company is carrying on law in a province is a question of fact.[78] In resolving this question, the courts will take into account such factors as whether there is an established physical presence in the province, and if so whether it is of a permanent or enduring nature; where contracts are being made;[79] where contracts are to be performed;[80] the number of transactions that occur within a province (whether transactions were isolated or part of an organized pattern, for instance); and the currency of the transactions in which a company may have engaged.[81] Generally, a company engaging in isolated transactions is not carrying on business in a province.[82] It has also been held that a foreign company that discontinues its operations in Ontario is not required to maintain its prior licence status in order to institute or continue legal proceedings in Ontario.[83] As with any question of fact, generally no one factor will necessarily be determinative. It is the overall picture that the aggregate facts present that is determinative. For obvious reasons, physical presence within a jurisdiction (in the form of an office or branch) is highly indicative. However, it is possible for a company to be notionally based in one jurisdiction while carrying on all of its business and affairs elsewhere. Many companies incorporated in tax havens (or, in the admiralty context, under flags of convenience) may maintain a notional residence in the jurisdiction of incorporation but otherwise have no connection with it.

§4.29 The foregoing general principles should be taken as being qualified by certain specific provisions of the EPCA itself. Subsection 1(3) provides that:

---

[78] *Laniere de Roubaix S.A. v. Craftsmen Distributors Inc.*, [1991] B.C.J. No. 767, 55 B.C.L.R. (2d) 103 (C.A.).
[79] *Giegy (Canada) Ltd. v. B.C. Min. of Finance* (1968), 66 W.W.R. 689 at 690-92 (B.C.S.C.), *per* Wilson C.J.S.C.
[80] *John Deere Plow Co. v. Agnew* (1913), 48 S.C.R. 208.
[81] *John A. McAfee Law Corp. v. Willey*, [2002] B.C.J. No. 29, 20 B.L.R. (3d) 147 at 153 (B.C.S.C.), *per* Wilson J.
[82] *Better-off-Dead Productions v. Pendulum Pictures*, [2002] B.C.J. No. 626, 22 B.L.R. (3d) 122 (S.C.); *Global Equity Corp. v. MKG Enterprises Corp.*, [1997] B.C.J. No. 1423 (S.C.).
[83] *Re International Railway Co. & Niagara Parks Commission*, [1936] 2 D.L.R. 405 (C.A.).

An extra-provincial corporation does not carry on its business in Ontario by reason only that,

(a) it takes orders for or buys or sells goods, wares and merchandise; or

(b) offers or sells services of any type,

by use of travelers or through advertising or correspondence.

Under prior legislation it was also held that the institution of a bankruptcy petition in Ontario did not constitute carrying on business so as to require a licence.[84] The sale of franchises by a foreign company to Ontario residents may or may not constitute carrying on business in Ontario, depending upon the circumstances of the transaction.[85]

§4.30 The EPCA is decidedly minimalist in the approach that it embodies towards the regulation of extraprovincial corporations. Section 2 of the EPCA divides extraprovincial corporations into three distinct classes:

Class 1 corporations are those incorporated or continued by or under the authority of an Act of a legislature of a province of Canada.

Class 2 corporations are those incorporated or continued by or under the authority of an Act of the Parliament of Canada or of the legislature of a territory of Canada.

Class 3 corporations incorporated or continued under the laws of a jurisdiction outside of Canada.

Corporations incorporated under the laws of the Northwest Territories or of Nunavut but governed by the corporation laws of a territory are corporations within Class 1.[86] Whether a particular foreign entity has been validly incorporated is determined in accordance with the relevant rules of the foreign legal system under which incorporation purportedly occurred.[87]

§4.31 Subject to any specific statutory requirement to the contrary, a class 1 or 2 extraprovincial corporation may carry on any of its business in Ontario without obtaining a licence under the EPCA.[88] In contrast, no extraprovincial corporation within class 3 is permitted to carry on any of its business in Ontario without a licence under the EPCA. In addition, no person acting as representative for or agent for any such extraprovincial corporation may carry on any of its business in Ontario unless the corporation has a licence under the EPCA.[89] By virtue of section 22 of the EPCA, every corporation within class 1 or 2, or that holds a licence as a class 3 extraprovincial corporation has the power to acquire, hold and convey any land or interest therein in Ontario necessary for its actual use and occupation or for carrying on its undertaking.

---

[84] *Re Society Shirt Co.*, [1932] O.R. 104 (C.A.).
[85] *Weight Watchers International Inc. v. Weight Watchers of Ontario Ltd.*, [1973] 1 O.R. 549.
[86] EPCA, s. 2(2).
[87] See, for instance, *Laemthong International Lines Co. Ltd. v. Artis*, [2005] All E.R. (D) 157 (Q.B. Comm. Ct.).
[88] EPCA s. 4(1).
[89] *Ibid.*, s. 4(2).

§4.32 A licence under the EPCA is made by way of endorsement by the Director upon a formal application made in prescribed form. The application must be made in duplicate and signed by a director or officer of the corporation, and be accompanied by all other required documents as well as the required fee. The licence may be dated as of the date the Director receives the originals of any application together with all other required documents and the prescribed fees or as of any later date acceptable to the Director, where such a date was specified by the person who submitted the application.[90]

§4.33 Subsection 5(2) of the EPCA indicates that the grant of a licence is discretionary. Subsection 5(5) provides that the Director may make a licence (or an amended licence) subject to restrictions on the business of a corporation and to such other limitations or conditions as are specified in the licence or amended licence. Where the Director refuses to endorse any application required by this Act to be endorsed by the Director before it becomes effective, he or she is required give written notice to the person who delivered the application of the refusal, specifying the reasons therefor.[91] The Director is allowed up to six months to decide whether or not to grant the licence. If the Director fails or refuses to grant the licence for six months, then the Director is deemed to have refused the grant of the licence.[92] Section 7 of the EPCA confers upon the Director a power to cancel a licence granted under the Act, where "sufficient cause is shown". Before doing so, the Director must give the extraprovincial corporation an opportunity to be heard. Cancellation takes effect upon such date as is fixed in the order. The term "sufficient cause" includes:

(*a*) failure to pay any required fee,

(*b*) failure to comply with section 19,

(*c*) failure to comply with a filing requirement under the *Corporations Information Act,* and

(*d*) a conviction of the extra-provincial corporation for an offence under the *Criminal Code* (Canada) or an offence as defined in the *Provincial Offences Act* in circumstances where cancellation of the license is in the public interest.

§4.34 Section 12 of the EPCA requires an extraprovincial corporation to apply for an amended licence where:

(*a*) it has changed its name or has been ordered to change its name under section 11 of the EPCA; or

(*b*) it has continued under the laws of another jurisdiction.

Where a class 3 extraprovincial corporation has not carried on any of its business in Ontario for any two consecutive years, it is required make application for

---

[90] *Ibid.*, s. 5.
[91] *Ibid.*, s. 6 (1).
[92] *Ibid.*, s. 6(2).

termination of its licence. If it does not do so, the Director, upon giving the corporation an opportunity to be heard, may cancel the licence by order.[93]

§4.35 Section 8 of the EPCA creates an appeal procedure. Specifically, subsection 8(1) provides that:

> A person aggrieved by a decision of the Director,
>
> (*a*) to refuse to endorse an application;
>
> (*b*) to make or refuse to make an order under section 11;
>
> (*c*) to cancel a license under section 7 or subsection 12(2);
>
> (*d*) to require that a corrected licence be endorsed under section 13; or
>
> (*e*) to impose conditions on a licence or amended licence,

may appeal that decision to the Divisional Court. Where such an appeal is brought, the Director must certify to the Divisional Court:

> (*a*) the decision of the Director together with a statement of the reasons therefor;
>
> (*b*) the record of any hearing; and
>
> (*c*) other material that is relevant to the appeal.

The Director is entitled to be heard by counsel or otherwise upon the argument of an appeal under this section. After hearing the appeal, the Divisional Court may direct the Director to make such decision or do such other act as the court thinks proper having regard to the material and submissions before it, provided that the Director is empowered to do so under the EPCA. However, despite any order made in such an appeal, the Director has power to make any further decision where he or she is presented with new material or where there is a material change in the circumstances and every such decision is subject to this section.

§4.36 In addition to the foregoing provisions, there are a number of other provisions in the EPCA that deal with such matters as the name under which an extraprovincial corporation may carry on business, the order that may be made by the Director where there is a contravention of the Act, the correction of licences issued in error, as well as a variety of procedural and administrative matters. The EPCA also contains a number of enforcement mechanisms. Subsection 14(1) of the EPCA provides that:

> The Director may apply to the court for an order prohibiting an extra-provincial corporation within class 1 from carrying on its business in Ontario or such other order as the Director may think fit and, where sufficient cause exists, the court may make an order under subsection (2).

Subsection 14(2) provides that upon such an application, the court may make any interim or final order it thinks fit.

---

[93] *Ibid.*, s. 12(2).

§4.37 A violation of the Act can result in penal, administrative and civil consequences. Subsection 21(1) provides:

> An extra-provincial corporation within class 3 that is not in compliance with section 19 or has not obtained a licence when required by this Act, is not capable of maintaining any action or any other proceeding in any court or tribunal in Ontario in respect of any contract made by it.

This general provision is significantly qualified by subsection 21(2), which provides a mechanism for correcting a default under the Act:

> Where a default referred to in subsection (1) has been corrected, an action or other proceeding may be maintained as if the default had been corrected before the institution of the action or other proceeding.

§4.38 Subsection 20(1) creates a number of offences. It provides that:

> Every person who, without reasonable cause,
>
> (a) contravenes the Act or the regulations;
>
> (b) contravenes a condition of a licence; or
>
> (c) fails to observe or comply with an order, direction or other requirement made under the Act or the regulations,
>
> is guilty of an offence and on conviction is liable to a fine of not more than $2,000 or if such person is a corporation to a fine of not more than $25,000.

In addition, subsection 20(2) provides that:

> Where an extra-provincial corporation is guilty of an offence under subsection (1), every director or officer of the corporation and every person acting as its representative in Ontario who authorized, permitted or acquiesced in such offence is also guilty of an offence and on conviction is liable to a fine of not more than $2,000.

The main civil sanction is a denial of standing to bring a proceeding in an Ontario court. Subsection 21(1) provides:

> An extra-provincial corporation within class 3 that is not in compliance with section 19 or has not obtained a licence when required by this Act, is not capable of maintaining any action or any other proceeding in any court or tribunal in Ontario in respect of any contract made by it.

However, the action is not a nullity, since subsection 21(2) permits the default to be corrected after the institution of the proceeding. Recent case law with respect to the impact of illegality on a contract,[94] together with the foregoing provisions, suggest strongly that transactions entered into by a company contrary to regulatory statutes such as the *Extra-provincial Corporations Act* are not, in general, void. Under the previous legislation, it was held that an unlicensed extra-

---

[94] See, for instance, *Tri Level Claims Consultant Ltd. v. Koliniotis*, [2005] O.J. No. 3381, 141 A.C.W.S. (3d) 860 (C.A.).

provincial corporation may acquire an interest in land,[95] and may convey any interest previously acquired so as to confer good title.

(ii) Limitation on Federal Incorporation Power

§4.39 The federal power over incorporation extends beyond the simple act of incorporation, to encompass all aspects of the status of the corporation,[96] including the nature and terms of its share capital and other securities,[97] and all other aspects of the internal affairs of the corporation.[98] Accordingly, it includes the power to provide for: the constitution of the corporation; the conditions under which membership may be acquired; its management; the terms and conditions upon which profits should be divided;[99] the conditions under which the capital of the company could be increased or diminished; the responsibility of the members of the corporation in respect of debts of the corporation; the responsibility of directors in respect of such debts;[100] and the investigation of the manner in which the affairs of the corporation are conducted.[101] However, federal jurisdiction does not extend to the regulation of the business in which the corporation engages[102] or its labour relations, unless it is engaging in a federally regulated field of business so as to constitute a federal undertaking.[103]

§4.40 A federally incorporated company is not improperly constituted merely because it chooses to exercise its powers only in one province,[104] nor because the business which it conducts is limited to a matter falling entirely within provincial jurisdiction. It is doubtful, however, that a corporation may be incorporated at the federal level if it has exclusively provincial objects, and some provincial legislation appears to exclude a federally incorporated entity from engaging in certain types of provincially regulated business.[105] By the same token, a provincially incorporated company may engage in business in two or more provinces

---

[95] See, generally, *Re Garner & Gavan*, [1952] O.R. 385 (C.A.).
[96] *Letain v. Conwest Exploration Co.*, [1961] S.C.R. 98 at 105-06, *per* Ritchie J.
[97] *Rathie v. Montreal Trust Co.* (1952), 5 W.W.R. (N.S.) 675 at 683 (B.C.S.C.), *per* Coady J., aff'd 6 W.W.R. (N.S.) 652 (C.A.), rev'd on other grounds [1953] 4 D.L.R. 289 (S.C.C.).
[98] *Montel v. Groupe de consultants P.G.L. Inc.* (1982), 20 B.L.R. 159 (Que. C.A.). Federal jurisdiction also encompasses imposing compulsory acquisition of minority shares in the event of a take-over bid: *Esso Standard (Inter-America) Inc. v. J.W. Enterprises Ltd.*, [1963] S.C.R. 144 at 153, *per* Judson J.
[99] *Re s. 110 of the Dominion Companies Act*, [1934] S.C.R. 653.
[100] *Multiple Access Ltd. v. McCutcheon*, [1982] S.C.J. No. 66, [1982] 2 S.C.R. 161 at 178, *per* Dickson J.; see also *Re s. 110 of the Dominion Companies Act*, [1934] S.C.R. 653 at 658, *per* Duff C.J.C.
[101] *Doyle v. Canada (Restrictive Trade Practices Commission)* (1983), 7 D.L.R. (4th) 524 at 529-30 (F.C.T.D.), *per* Pratte J., leave to appeal to S.C.C. ref'd 51 N.R. 223 (C.A.).
[102] *Re Board of Commerce Act*, [1922] 1 A.C. 191 (P.C.).
[103] *Canadian Pioneer Management Ltd. v. Saskatchewan (Labour Relations Board)*, [1979] S.C.J. No. 115, 107 D.L.R. (3d) 1; *Construction Montcalm Inc. v. Minimum Wage Commission*, [1978] S.C.J. No. 110, [1979] 1 S.C.R. 754 at 768, *per* Beetz J.
[104] *Colonial Building and Investment Association v. A.G. Quebec* (1883), 9 App. Cas. 157 (P.C.); *Traverse de Lévis v. Lemieux* (1940), 79 Que. S.C. 52. As to whether the federal government may incorporate a corporation that is limited by its charter to dealing in one province, see *Re Dominion Marble Co.* (1917), 35 D.L.R. 63 (Que. S.C.).
[105] For instance, in Ontario, see the *Public Hospitals Act*, R.S.O. 1990, c. P.40, s. 4.

and carry on a federally incorporated business other than the business of banking. Incorporation and regulation are two separate matters.[106] Still, section 92 of the *Constitution Act, 1867* provides that the powers conferred on the provinces under that section are exclusive to the provinces, and thus some exclusive area of provincial jurisdiction must necessarily exist with respect to certain areas of incorporation, just as the courts have held that exclusive areas exist in the case of federal jurisdiction.[107]

D. REGULATORY JURISDICTION

§4.41 The power of incorporation neither includes nor precludes the power of regulation, and the fact that a particular corporation is created either federally or provincially does not exempt it from regulation by the other level of government that is imposed within their respective spheres of competence. Incorporation and regulation are separate issues. Neither the federal nor provincial governments expand their regulatory jurisdiction over the subject matters allocated to each of them by the Constitution merely by reason of incorporating a corporation that carries on a business relating to a subject of jurisdiction belonging to the other.[108] However, where the federal or provincial government may incidentally regulate the manner in which that corporation conducts its business or affairs, to the extent that in so doing, the regulation pertains to the constitution of the corporation in question, aspects of its membership, the division of profits or changes in its capital, the protection of its assets, or the liability of shareholders or directors for particular acts or liabilities of the corporation, or its capacity or powers. For instance, in *Re s. 110 of the Dominion Companies Act*,[109] the Supreme Court of Canada considered the validity of a provision of the federal corporations legislation that provided that the directors of a company who declared and paid a dividend that had the effect of rendering the company insolvent or that impaired its capital, should be jointly and severally liable to the shareholders, the company and its creditors for all debts then owing or thereafter contracted by the company. The Supreme Court of Canada held that this provision was *intra vires* the federal government.[110]

---

[106] See, for instance, *Citizens Insurance Co. v. Parsons* (1881), 7 App. Cas. 96 (P.C.); *Lymburn v. Mayland*, [1932] A.C. 318 (P.C.); *Re Insurance Act of Canada*, [1932] A.C. 41 (P.C.); *Re Royalite Oil Co.*, [1931] 1 W.W.R. 484 (Alta. C.A.); *R. v. Hazzard*, [1932] O.R. 139 (C.A.); *Re Insurance Contracts* (1926), 58 O.L.R. 404 (C.A.).
[107] As to education, for instance, see *Re Brothers of the Christian Schools (Canada)* (1876), Cout. S.C. 1 (S.C.C.).
[108] *Lymburn v. Mayland*, [1932] A.C. 318, [1932] 2 D.L.R. 6 at 11 (P.C.), per Lord Atkin; *Ontario v. Policyholders of Wentworth Insurance Co.*, [1969] S.C.R. 779, per Judson J.
[109] [1934] S.C.R. 653.
[110] See also *Rathie v. Montreal Trust Co.* (1952), 5 W.W.R. (N.S.) 675, aff'd 6 W.W.R. (N.S.) 652, rev'd on other grounds [1953] 4 D.L.R. 289 (S.C.C.).

(i) Federal Regulation of Provincially Incorporated Corporations

§4.42 While the regulation of federally incorporated businesses by the province may raise the question of paramountcy, that issue does not apply in the case of provincially incorporated corporations. Accordingly, the federal government may regulate activities carried on by provincially incorporated companies to the extent of its general legislative jurisdiction. Thus the federal government may enact legislation preventing the formation of industrial combines, trusts and other anti-competitive cartels and may extend the application of any such legislation to provincially incorporated companies.[111] Although the federal government may not regulate the corporate affairs of a provincial corporation as such, it may enact legislation controlling the sale of a controlling interest to foreigners, relying in such a case on its jurisdiction over international trade or over aliens. However, the jurisdiction of the federal government to regulate the activities of provincial companies is limited to those matters which are necessarily incidental to the exercise of the federal government's law-making powers under section 91 of the *Constitution Act, 1867*.[112] The federal government may not invade areas of provincial regulatory jurisdiction and attempt to regulate a particular type of business within provincial competence, by invoking under the colour of a licensing requirement,[113] the criminal law[114] or legislation with respect to aliens.[115]

(ii) Provincial Regulation of Federal Companies

§4.43 More complex constitutional issues arise in the case of provincial regulation of federally incorporated entities. The fixing of conditions of local trade, the regulation of the form and formalities of contract, and the prescription of restrictions under which property can be acquired all fall within the general jurisdiction of the province under property and civil rights.[116] As a general rule, within its fields of jurisdiction, a province may validly regulate the conduct of business by a federally incorporated company.[117] It follows that the jurisdiction to incorporate and the jurisdiction to regulate are entirely separate questions.

§4.44 Where one level of government enjoys regulatory jurisdiction over the business of a corporation or the activities that it chooses to pursue, while the other level of government is the jurisdiction of incorporation, it is necessary to decide what law will govern where there is a conflict between the laws of the

---

[111] *Proprietary Articles Trade Association v. A.G. Canada*, [1931] A.C. 310 (P.C.); *R. v. Goodyear Tire & Rubber Co. of Canada*, [1956] S.C.R. 303.
[112] See *Montreal (City) v. Montreal Street Railway Co.*, [1912] A.C. 333 at 343 (P.C.), *per* Lord Atkinson.
[113] *A.G. Canada v. A.G. Alberta*, [1916] A.C. 588 (P.C.).
[114] *A.G. Ontario v. Reciprocal Insurers*, [1924] A.C. 328 (P.C.).
[115] *Re Insurance Act of Canada*, [1932] A.C. 41 (P.C.).
[116] *A.G. Manitoba v. A.G. Canada*, [1929] A.C. 260 at 268 (P.C.), *per* Viscount Sumner.
[117] *Re Insurance Act of Canada*, [1932] A.C. 41 (P.C.), *per* Viscount Dunedin; *Great West Saddlery Co. v. R.*, [1921] 2 A.C. 91 (P.C.).

two jurisdictions that apply to the corporation. As noted earlier in the chapter, in general terms (but only very general terms) under the doctrine of paramountcy in the case of any such conflict, federal law prevails. But the federal government has no jurisdiction to exempt its corporations from provincial regulation in a field of endeavour subject to provincial regulation.[118]

§4.45 In drawing that balance between federal competence over incorporation and provincial competence over the regulation of a particular industry or activity, either the provincial requirements or the powers purportedly conferred by the federal government might be seen as ousted — a point made clear in this subsequent passage of Viscount Haldane's judgment in the *John Deere* case:

> It is true that even when a company has been incorporated by the Dominion Government with powers to trade, it is not the less subject to provincial laws of general application enacted under the powers conferred by s. 92. Thus, notwithstanding that a Dominion company has capacity to hold land, it cannot refuse to obey the statutes of the Province as to mortmain ... or escape the payment of taxes, even though these may assume the form of requiring, as the method of raising a revenue, a license to trade which affects a Dominion company in common with other companies. ... Again, such a company is subject to the powers of the Province relating to property and civil rights under s. 92 for the regulation of contracts generally.[119]

Although reluctant to attempt a description of the full range of provincial powers to regulate a federal company, the Privy Council went on to suggest the manner in which the provincial regulatory objective might have been accomplished in the *John Deere* case:

> In the opinion of their Lordships it was not within the power of the provincial Legislature to enact these provisions in their present form. It might have been competent to that legislature to pass laws applying to companies without distinction, and requiring those that were not incorporated within the Province to register for certain limited purposes, such as the furnishing of information. It might also have been competent to enact that any company which had not an office and assets within the Province should, under a statute of general application regulating procedure, give security for costs. But their Lordships think that the provisions in question must be taken to be of quite a different character, and to have been directed to interfering with the status of Dominion companies, and to preventing them from exercising the powers conferred on them by the Parliament of Canada, dealing with a matter which was not entrusted under s. 92 to the provincial Legislature. ... They think that the legislation in question really strikes at capacities which are the natural and logical consequences of the incorporation by the Dominion Government of companies with other than provincial objects.[120]

§4.46 It follows that federally incorporated entities are subject to provincial regulatory jurisdiction so long as that jurisdiction does not hinder the corpora-

---

[118] *A.G. Ontario v. Reciprocal Insurers*, [1924] 1 D.L.R. 789 (P.C.), *per* Viscount Haldane.
[119] *John Deere Plow Co. v. Wharton*, [1915] A.C. 330 at 342-43 (P.C.), *per* Viscount Haldane.
[120] *Ibid.*, at 343-44.

tion's operation or lead to its dissolution.[121] Destruction of the federal corporation must be distinguished from destruction of its business. Despite the views expressed in some earlier decisions that a provincial government may not exclude corporations from carrying on business, the better view is that provincial regulation may completely prohibit or destroy the conduct of a particular line of business by a federal company[122] — a situation that might well result, for instance, from provincial environmental regulation.[123] On this basis it has been held that a province may require a federal company to obtain a provincial licence as a condition of engaging in *a particular* business,[124] or *particular* activity such as the holding of land.[125] Similarly, federal corporations are subject to municipal zoning by-laws made under the authority of provincial law.[126] Likewise, a federally incorporated insurance company may be regulated in the conduct of its insurance business by a provincial government,[127] and a federally incorporated trust company will be subject to provincial debt moratorium legislation.[128] But the province oversteps its jurisdiction where it imposes a general requirement that federal corporations obtain a provincial license as a precondition to the conduct of *any* business.[129]

§4.47 Although a province may not enact a general licence requirement for all corporations:

- to prevent a federal corporation from carrying on business of any kind in the province; or

- to deny or negate its corporate existence or capacity,

federally incorporated corporations enjoy no special protection from provincial taxation,[130] must comply with provincial title registration laws,[131] and must comply with provincial licensing requirements applicable to the conduct of a line of business subject to provincial regulation.[132] For instance, in *Cooper v. McIndoe*[133]

---

[121] *Commission de transport de la communauté urbaine de Québec v. Canada (Commission des champs de bataille nationaux)*, [1988] R.L. 146 (Que. C.A.), rev'd on other grounds [1990] 2 S.C.R. 838.
[122] See, for instance, *Lymburn v. Mayland*, [1932] A.C. 318 at 324 (P.C.), per Lord Atkin; *Motor Car Supply Co. of Canada v. A.G. Alberta*, [1939] 3 W.W.R. 65 (Alta. T.D.).
[123] See, generally, *R. v. TNT Canada Inc.*, [1986] O.J. No. 1322, 58 O.R. (2d) 410 (C.A.) .
[124] *R. v. Continental Salvage Corp.*, [1930] 2 W.W.R. 562 (Man. C.A.).
[125] *Campbell v. Morgan*, [1919] 1 W.W.R. 268 (Man. K.B.).
[126] *Hamilton Harbour Commissioners v. Hamilton (City)* (1978), 21 O.R. (2d) 459 (C.A.).
[127] *Citizens Insurance Co. v. Parsons* (1881), 7 App. Cas. 96 (P.C.).
[128] *Abitibi Power & Paper Co. v. Montreal Trust Co.*, [1943] A.C. 536 (P.C.). See also *Re Royalite Oil Co.*, [1931] 1 W.W.R. 484 (Alta. C.A.); *Re Insurance Contracts* (1926), 58 O.L.R. 404 (C.A.).
[129] *Great West Saddlery Co. v. R.*, [1921] 2 A.C. 91 (P.C.).
[130] *Bank of Toronto v. Lambe* (1887), 12 App. Cas. 575 (P.C.); *R. v. Continental Salvage Corp.*, [1930] 2 W.W.R. 562 (Man. C.A.). However, a province may not discriminate against federally incorporated corporations: *Re Proctor & Gamble Co.*, [1937] 3 W.W.R. 680 (Sask. K.B.), per Taylor J.
[131] *Gordon MacKay & Co. v. J.A. Laroque Co.* (1926), 7 C.B.R. 53 (Ont. S.C.), var'd 7 C.B.R. 384, rev'd in part [1927] S.C.R. 374.
[132] *Motor Car Supply Co. of Canada v. A.G. Alberta*, [1939] 3 D.L.R. 660 (Alta. T.D.).
[133] (1887), 15 R.L.O.S. 276, M.L.R. 7 Q.B. 481, aff'g M.L.R. 2 S.C. 388, 10 L.N. 35 (Que. C.A.).

it was held that a company incorporated by special Act of the federal Parliament with the power to do business in Quebec was nevertheless subject to the laws of that province in conducting that business.[134] In particular, the company was required to comply with articles 346 and 366 of the Quebec *Civil Code* which governed the acquisition of land by all corporations, wherever incorporated. Federal companies are bound by provincial laws of general application,[135] whether enacted directly by the province or by some subordinate law-making body such as a municipality.[136] It follows that in regards to matters within the scope of provincial regulatory authority, a federally incorporated company is in no better position than any other corporation.[137]

§4.48 Moreover, in the course of regulating an industry (although there is some uncertainty on this point), the better view would appear to be that a province may prohibit all corporations (including federally incorporated corporations) from engaging in particular lines of business relating to that industry or the general scheme of regulation adopted.[138] For instance, in *Public Accountants Council (Ontario) v. Premier Trust Co.*[139] the defendant federally incorporated trust company argued that it was entitled to act as an accountant and auditor (which under its federal charter it was empowered it to do) despite a provincial law forbidding the practice of accountancy by a corporation. Justice Schatz suggested that the law was valid because it did not restrict any fundamental aspect of the corporation's operations. However, taking a stronger line on the question of provincial regulatory powers, it may be argued that the general power of the federal government to incorporate in such a case cannot be held to overrule the specific provincial power of regulation. If a particular business is subject to provincial regulation, then federal incorporation is not an effective device for circumventing or frustrating any general scheme of regulation properly adopted by the province. Thus, federal incorporation provides no guarantee whatsoever that the company concerned will be permitted to engage in particular lines of business at all.[140] By the same token, federally incorporated corporations are subject to general laws of the province regulating, prescribing or prohibiting the exercise of property or civil rights.[141] Indeed, the *Constitution Act, 1867* would employ a most strange (and wholly unworkable) division of powers between the federal and provincial governments if it permitted the federal government to overcome provincial regulation concerning any matter merely by conducting (or empowering a person to conduct) that matter through the instrumentality of a corporation.

---

[134] The regulatory law must, of course, be with respect to a subject matter over which the province is competent to legislate: *Toronto (City) v. Bell Telephone Co.*, [1905] A.C. 52 (P.C.) — province purporting to regulate interprovincial telephone company.
[135] *R. v. Arcadia Coal Co.*, [1932] 1 W.W.R. 771 (Alta. C.A.), *per* McGillivray J.A.
[136] *R. v. New Westminster (City)* (1965), 54 W.W.R. 238, aff'g 53 W.W.R. 373 (B.C.C.A.).
[137] *Great West Saddlery Co. v. R.*, [1921] 2 A.C. 91, *per* Viscount Haldane.
[138] *Giffels & Vallet of Canada Ltd. v. R.*, [1952] 2 D.L.R. 720, aff'g [1952] 1 D.L.R. 620 (Ont. C.A.).
[139] [1964] 1 O.R. 386 at 392 (H.C.).
[140] *A.G. Ontario v. A.G. Canada*, [1896] A.C. 348 at 361 (P.C.), *per* Lord Watson.
[141] *Citizens Insurance Co. v. Parsons* (1881), 7 App. Cas. 96 (P.C.), *per* Sir Montague Smith.

§4.49 In deciding whether provincial legislation is operative insofar as it applies to a federal corporation, the key question is not whether the regulatory legislation in question is concerned with the conduct of corporate activity or with the conduct of the regulated activity. If the legislation deals with the conduct of corporate activity, then to the extent that it extinguishes what the federal government has conferred, the provincial legislation would be inoperative. However, if it is the latter (and the province has exclusive jurisdiction over the regulation of that activity), then the legislation will be effective irrespective of whether the effect is to extinguish the regulated activity, so long as the province has plenary regulatory jurisdiction over the line of business concerned. If the province shares regulatory jurisdiction (a relatively rare situation in the case of general business corporations), the federal legislation would prevail to the extent that the federal law was prescriptive (*i.e.*, that it required a particular thing to be done) or if the basic purpose of the federal law would be defeated if the provincial law were to apply. Otherwise, the provincial law would apply, and the permissive power or capacity granted by the federal government would be seen to be qualified by the provincial law. This approach reconciles the corporate law cases with modern interpretations of the paramountcy doctrine, on which cases such as *Arcadia Coal* and *John Deere Plow* are ultimately dependent.[142]

(iii) The Vital Part Doctrine

§4.50 The power of a province to regulate an industry or some aspect of corporate activity subject to provincial regulation, and in so doing to affect consequentially the activities of federally incorporated corporations carrying on regulated business or activities within the province, arises only insofar as the province possesses the constitutional authority to regulate the subject matter concerned. Moreover, provincial laws dealing with a matter normally subject to provincial regulation will be inoperative where the so-called "vital part doctrine" comes into play. The power of the federal government to make laws touching upon a vital part[143] of a federally regulated undertaking[144] is exclusive.[145] Accordingly, the provinces cannot regulate or interfere with a vital part of the management and operation of a federally regulated undertaking (or line of business), such as an airline, telephone company or bank.[146] So, for instance, the labour

---

[142] *R. v. Arcadia Coal Co.*, [1932] 1 W.W.R. 771 (Alta. C.A.); *John Deere Plow Co. v. Wharton*, [1915] A.C. 330 (P.C.). Under the modern approach to paramountcy, a provincial law is not affected merely by showing that it is inconsistent with a validly enacted federal law. Assuming that both the federal and provincial laws are validly enacted, the provincial law is inoperative only to the extent that compliance with the provincial law would prevent compliance with the federal law or defeat the object of the federal law.

[143] As to the tests to apply to determine whether a particular enterprise is a vital part of a federally regulated undertaking, see *U.T.U. v. Central Western Railway*, [1990] S.C.J. No. 136, 76 D.L.R. (4th) 1 at 8, *per* Dickson C.J.C.; *Northern Telecom Ltd. v. Communications Workers of Canada*, [1979] S.C.J. No. 98, 98 D.L.R. (3d) 1 at 14, *per* Dickson J.

[144] As determined by one of the heads of federal jurisdiction either general or specific: *Canada (Human Rights Commission) v. Haynes*, [1983] F.C.J. No. 106, 144 D.L.R. (3d) 734 at 736 (C.A.), *per* Le Dain J.

[145] *Bell Canada v. Quebec*, [1988] S.C.J. No. 41, [1988] 1 S.C.R. 749.

[146] *C.S.M. v. Bell Telephone Co. of Canada*, [1966] S.C.R. 767.

relations of federally regulated undertakings are subject to federal rather than provincial law, even though labour relations is ordinarily a subject matter subject to provincial legislative jurisdiction. It is equally clear that a provincial law will be invalid to the extent that it impairs, sterilizes or paralyzes a federally regulated undertaking.[147] However, a provincial law may apply to some incidental aspect of a federally regulated undertaking, as for instance the sale of alcohol by airlines[148] or the operation of an airport limousine service.[149] Similarly, a provincial law will not be invalid where any effect upon the federally regulated undertaking is indirect, such as in the case of environmental regulation,[150] or where provincial labour laws apply to a contractor building a runway for an airport[151] or the supply of printing to the Bank of Canada or post office.[152] More generally, outside the scope of its "vital parts", a federally regulated corporation that enters into a provincially regulated line of business enjoys no special protection from provincial regulation. For instance, it has been held that banks under the *Bank Act* enjoy no immunity from provincial regulation of insurance.[153] The exact point at which the vital part doctrine ceases to apply is not entirely clear. To give one obvious illustration: the procurement of goods and consulting services by a bank or broadcast facility is clearly no less "vital" to the conduct of the bank or broadcast facility than is the procurement of labour. Yet no one has ever seriously argued that banks operate under some sort of federal law of contract. It appears, therefore, that to bring the vital part doctrine into application, there must be some competing federal regulatory regime that could apply, in lieu of the provincial scheme.[154]

---

[147] *Irwin Toy Ltd. v. A.G. Quebec*, [1989] S.C.J. No. 36, [1989] 1 S.C.R. 927. In cases in which this principle is invoked, the court must decide whether the provincial statutory provision at issue has the effect of regulating a core aspect of a federal jurisdiction. If the provincial law has this effect, it is read down so as not to exceed legitimate provincial power by intruding on the federal. If the law does not have this effect, then in the ordinary case it will be applicable as valid provincial law: see *Ordon Estate v. Grail*, [1998] S.C.J. No. 84, 166 D.L.R. (4th) 193. Stated differently, if a provincial law affects the basic, minimum and unassailable core of a federal subject, then an interjurisdictional immunity is said to apply to the federal subject, with the effect that the application of the provincial law is restricted (or is "read down") so as to exclude the federal subject. If on the other hand, the provincial law does not intrude heavily on the federal subject, then the "pith and substance" doctrine permits the provincial law to continue to have application: *Law Society of British Columbia v. Mangat*, [1998] B.C.J. No. 2756, 167 D.L.R. (4th) 723 (C.A.), per Mackenzie J.A. See also *R. v. Lewis*, [1997] O.J. No. 5075, 155 D.L.R. (4th) 442 (C.A.); *R. v. Lenart*, [1998] O.J. No. 1105, 158 D.L.R. (4th) 508 (C.A.).

[148] *Air Canada v. Ontario (Liquor Control Board)*, [1997] S.C.J. No. 66, 148 D.L.R. (4th) 193 at 212, per Iacobucci J.

[149] *Murray Hill Limousine Service Ltd. v. Batson*, [1965] Que. Q.B. 778.

[150] *Canadian Pacific Ltd. v. R.*, [1995] S.C.J. No. 62, 125 D.L.R. (4th) 385 — Ontario Environmental Protection Act, R.S.O. 1980, c. 114 was held applicable to a railroad burning brush on a railway right of way, resulting in extensive smoke interfering with use of adjacent property.

[151] *Construction Montcalm Inc. v. Minimum Wage Commission*, [1979] S.C.J. No. 110, [1979] 1 S.C.R. 754.

[152] *Canadian (Human Rights Commission) v. Haynes*, [1983] F.C.J. No. 106, 144 D.L.R. (3d) 734 (C.A.).

[153] *Canadian Western Bank v. Alberta*, [2003] A.J. No. 1166 (Q.B.), aff'd [2005] A.J. No. 21 (C.A.), leave to appeal to S.C.C. granted [2005] S.C.C.A. No. 121.

[154] For more recent case law in this area, see: *Taylor v. Alberta (Registrar, South Alberta Land Registration District)*, [2005] A.J. No. 696, 141 A.C.W.S. (3d) 212 (C.A.); *Mississauga (City) v.*

(iv) Regulation of Securities

§4.51 Perhaps in no other area within the field of corporate law has the battle over provincial and federal jurisdiction been so pronounced as with respect to the regulation of securities. Provincial competence over the terms, issue and trading in securities is inherent in the jurisdiction of the province over property and civil rights.[155] Thus, the province may: require the registration of brokers and others dealing in securities;[156] impose standards of conduct upon such registrants and investigate their adherence to those standards without entering into federal jurisdiction over criminal law;[157] impose a freeze on the bank and other accounts of those under investigation;[158] and require that a given level of disclosure be made to investors.[159] The province may also regulate the activities of dealers in securities who solicit business within a province from an office outside that province.[160] Federal incorporation affords no shield against provincial regulation as such.[161]

§4.52 In general, the early case law dealing with provincial security laws suggested that such laws did not apply to federally incorporated companies. For instance, in *Lukey v. Ruthenian Farmers' Elevator Co.*[162] it was held that Saskatchewan's *Sale of Shares Act*,[163] was *ultra vires*. The Act purported to prohibit a Dominion company from selling or attempting to sell its shares in Saskatchewan without first having complied with certain regulatory formalities. It was held that the power to sell its own shares throughout Canada goes to the root of

---

Greater Toronto Airports Authority, [2000] O.J. No. 4086, 192 D.L.R. (4th) 443 (C.A.), leave to appeal to S.C.C. refused [2001] S.C.C.A. No. 83; *DFS Ventures Inc. v. Manitoba (Liquor Control Commission)*, [2001] M.J. No. 416, 159 Man. R. (2d) 55 (Q.B.), aff'd [2003] M.J. No. 73 (C.A.), leave to appeal to S.C.C. refused [2003] S.C.C.A. No. 209.

[155] *Lymburn v. Mayland*, [1932] A.C. 318 (P.C.); *Re Williams*, [1961] O.R. 657 at 659 (C.A.), *per* Roach J.A.
[156] *Woodson v. Russell*, [1961] Que. Q.B. 349 (C.A.).
[157] *Re Williams*, [1961] O.R. 657 (C.A.); *Camino Management Ltd. v. Manitoba (Securities Commission)*, [1979] 2 W.W.R. 594 (Man. Q.B.). Nor is it an abuse of process for a provincial securities commission to conduct its own investigation of alleged misconduct, after the dismissal of a criminal charge based on the same allegations: *Bennett v. British Columbia (Securities Commission)*, [1992] B.C.J. No. 1655, [1992] 5 W.W.R. 481 (C.A.), leave to appeal to S.C.C. ref'd [1992] 6 W.W.R. lviin.
[158] *Gregory & Co. v. Imperial Bank of Canada*, [1960] Que. S.C. 204.
[159] *Smith v. R.*, [1960] S.C.R. 776, *per* Kerwin C.J.C.
[160] *R. v. W. McKenzie Securities Ltd.* (1966), 55 W.W.R. 157 (Man. C.A.).
[161] *Motor Car Supply Co. of Canada v. A.G. Alberta*, [1939] 3 W.W.R. 65 (Alta. T.D.).
[162] [1924] S.C.R. 56.
[163] R.S.S. 1920, c. 199, s. 4, which provided:

> 4. No person shall sell or offer or attempt to sell in Saskatchewan any shares, stocks, bonds or other securities of a company, other than securities hereinbefore excepted, without first obtaining from the board a certificate, and in the case of an agent, a license, as hereinafter provided.

> Significantly the Act afforded few exemptions, and there were none comparable to the private company, seed capital and private placement exemptions so frequently relied upon under modern securities legislation. As a result, it was accurate to view the legislation as effectively preventing federal companies from raising capital completely if they did not obtain the required certificate.

the essential powers and capacities of a federally incorporated corporation, and that, therefore, any provincial law which prohibited altogether the sale of those shares, whether absolute in nature or where related to compliance with provincial regulatory requirements, was beyond the powers of the province.[164] As late as 1929, the Privy Council would reject the need for investor protection as being sufficient justification for interference with the basic corporate powers of share and security issuance. Although the objective of investor protection might be worthy, the interference with the corporate capacity of federal corporations was seen as being too great.[165]

§4.53 The attitude of the courts began to change with the coming of the Depression. In *A.G. Manitoba v. Rosenbaum*,[166] the Attorney General for Manitoba applied to the court for an injunction restraining the defendant and a company incorporated under the *Dominion Companies Act* from trading in securities of the company contrary to the *Manitoba Security Frauds Prevention Act*.[167] The court granted the injunction. It was held that a statute which aims at preventing fraudulent trading in securities was *intra vires* the province even when it applied to the sale of shares by a federal corporation. The statute did not impair the essential capacities of the company, nor did it invade the field of criminal law. Instead, it was held to be in pith and substance a statute dealing with property and civil rights and a matter of a merely local or private nature.[168]

§4.54 The *Rosenbaum* case[169] left open the question of prior restraint — that is, whether a province might validly require regulatory clearances prior to the issue of securities by a federal corporation. This question was addressed two years later by the Alberta Court of Appeal in *Re Royalite Oil Co.*,[170] which involved section 145 of the Alberta *Companies Act*.[171] Section 145 in part required the filing of a prospectus as a pre-condition to any trade in shares by a federal company. The requirement was held invalid.[172] In contrast, in the Ontario case of *R. v. Hazzard*,[173] which dealt with similar provisions under Ontario law, it was held that such regulatory requirements did not impair the status of a federal corporation operating within a province, but merely fixed certain conditions of trading within the province and accordingly, the legislation was within the powers of the province.

---

[164] A similar result was reached in *R. v. Henderson* (1924), 51 N.B.R. 346 (C.A.).
[165] *A.G. Manitoba v. A.G. Canada*, [1929] A.C. 260 (P.C.), *per* Viscount Sumner.
[166] [1929] 1 W.W.R. 148 (Man. K.B.).
[167] S.M. 1928, c. 46.
[168] *A.G. Manitoba v. Rosenbaum*, [1929] 1 W.W.R. 148 at 163 (Man K.B.), *per* Donovan J.
[169] *Ibid.*
[170] [1931] 1 W.W.R. 484 (Alta. C.A.).
[171] S. A. 1929, c. 14.
[172] *Re Royalite Oil Co.*, [1931] 1 W.W.R. 484 at 502 (Alta. C.A.), *per* Harvey C.J.A.
[173] [1932] O.R. 139 at 139-40 (C.A.), *per* Riddell J.A.

§4.55 The issue came before the Privy Council in *Lymburn v. Mayland*,[174] which dealt with the Alberta *Security Frauds Prevention Act*.[175] This Act required all persons trading with the public in securities to be licensed. It further authorized examinations in order to ascertain whether any fraudulent act or offence against the Act had been, was being or was about to be committed. In upholding the validity of these provisions, Lord Atkin rejected the argument that the whole Act was invalid so far as it related to Dominion companies, because it destroyed their status by making it impossible for them to issue their share capital; and that it was invalid because under the colour of dealing with the prevention of fraud in share transactions, it was assuming to legislate as to criminal law, a class of subject reserved to the Dominion.

§4.56 Lord Atkin then went on to deal with the question of whether the province might validly restrict dealings in shares to licensed traders and corporations. In upholding the validity of such restrictions, he stated that a federal corporation constituted with powers to carry on a particular business is subject to the competent legislation of a province as to that business and may find its activities completely paralyzed, as by legislation against traffic in alcohol or by the laws as to holding land. He continued:

> If it is formed to trade in securities there appears no reason why it should not be subject to the competent laws of the Province as to the business of all persons who trade in securities. As to the issue of capital there is no complete prohibition, as in the *Manitoba* case in 1929; and no reason to suppose that any honest company would have any difficulty in finding registered persons in the Province through whom it could lawfully issue its capital. There is no material upon which their Lordships could find that the functions and activities of a company were sterilized or its status and essential capacities impaired in a substantial degree.[176]

Unfortunately, this passage cast some doubt on whether a province may validly require compliance with provincial regulatory requirements such as a prospectus filing or continuous disclosure as a precondition to the issue of securities by a federal corporation.

§4.57 Those doubts have been all but eradicated in more recent decisions of the Supreme Court of Canada. While the Supreme Court has never entirely repudiated the earlier case law suggesting a limited provincial power over securities dealings involving federal corporations, in practical terms the effect has been the same. For instance, in *Morgan v. A. G. P.E.I.*, Laskin J. made the following observations concerning provincial securities regulation:

> ... [F]ederally-incorporated companies are not constitutionally entitled, by virtue of their federal incorporation, to any advantages, as against provincial regulatory legislation, over provincial corporations or over extra-provincial or foreign corporations, so long as their capacity to establish themselves as viable corporate entities (beyond the mere fact of their incorporation), as by raising capital through

---

[174] [1932] A.C. 318 (P.C.).
[175] S.A. 1930, 20 Geo. V., c. 8.
[176] *Lymburn v. Mayland*, [1932] A.C. 318 at 324-25 (P.C.).

issue of shares and debentures, *is not precluded* by the provincial legislation. Beyond this, they are subject to competent provincial regulations in respect of businesses or activities which fall within provincial legislative power. *(emphasis added)*[177]

The most important case in confirming provincial jurisdiction over securities regulation was the decision of the Supreme Court of Canada in *Multiple Access v. McCutcheon*.[178] Although the majority opinion took care to keep the door open for possible federal entry into this field,[179] the court gave broad recognition to the jurisdiction of the provinces to regulate in securities dealings. A key question to be decided in that case was whether provincial regulation of insider trading was within the powers of the provinces. In upholding the validity of the legislation in question, Dickson J. stated:

> The argument against the validity of ss. 113 and 114 of the Ontario *Securities Act* is that they are beyond the legislative power of the Province in that they purport to apply to companies incorporated under the laws of Canada ... I do not think this argument is tenable. It is well established that the provinces have the power, as a matter of property and civil rights, to regulate the trade in corporate securities in the province, provided the statute does not single out federal companies for special treatment or discriminate against them in any way. There must be no impairment of status or of the essential power to raise capital for corporate purpose. But federal incorporation does not render a company immune from securities regulation of general application in a province.[180]

Later in his decision, he returned to a discussion of the extent to which a province might regulate securities dealings in respect of federally incorporated companies:

> Federally-incorporated companies are subject, with one important exception, to provincial regulation with respect to trading in securities. The legislative powers of the Province are restricted so that "the status and powers of a Dominion company as such cannot be destroyed" and legislation will be invalid if a Dominion company is "sterilized in all its functions and activities" or "its status and essential capacities are impaired in a substantial degree" ... Subject to that exception, a federal company empowered to carry on a particular business in a province is subject to the competent legislation of the province as to that business. If it wishes to raise capital through the sale of securities there is no reason why it should not be subject to the laws of the province applicable to all those in the province who wish to raise capital through security sales, and subject thereafter to rules requiring honest dealings in securities, so that the public be not defrauded.[181]

---

[177] (1975), 55 D.L.R. (3d) 527 at 539 (S.C.C.).
[178] [1982] S.C.J. No. 66, [1982] 2 S.C.R. 161.
[179] *Ibid., per* Dickson J. at 173.
[180] *Ibid.*, at 183.
[181] *Ibid.*, at 184.

(v) Nationalization of Federal Corporation by Provincial Government

§4.58 The liability of a federally incorporated corporation to provincial expropriation was considered by the British Columbia Supreme Court in *British Columbia Power Corp. v. A.G. British Columbia*.[182] In that case, all of the shares of a provincially incorporated company, the B.C. Electric Company ("BCE"), were owned by a federally incorporated company, the B.C. Power Corporation ("BCP"). The province of British Columbia enacted legislation purporting to expropriate BCE. The three statutes in question provided: first that the ownership of the shares of the B.C. Electric Company was vested in the Crown in right of British Columbia, with the compensation payable to BCP being specified in that statute; second, that the ownership of the physical and financial assets of BCE was vested in a newly created B.C. Hydro Authority, which was a provincial Crown corporation; third, that BCP was not entitled to question either the divesting of share ownership or the amount of compensation payable for its shares in the courts. BCP alleged that this expropriation was *ultra vires* the province, but since a petition of right was denied, it was prevented from challenging the legislation directly. BCP then sought court protection by seeking a declaration that the action was *ultra vires*, and the appointment of a receiver for the assets of BCE. The receivership action went to the Supreme Court of Canada, where the majority of the court held that a receiver should be appointed and the declaration proceeding should proceed.[183]

§4.59 The declaration proceeding was then heard by Lett C.J.,[184] who held that it was *ultra vires* for the province to expropriate the shares of BCE because it effectively sterilized the federally incorporated parent company. He concluded that in making it impossible for BCP to exercise its powers, the province had sterilized the federal corporation, and thereby impaired its status and capacities to a substantial degree. He was particularly concerned that if one province might effectively block a federal corporation from carrying on the line of business for which it was incorporated, so might the others, with the result that the company would be unable to carry on its business anywhere in Canada. The legislation was directed primarily at BCP and was designed to interfere with the exercise of the powers conferred on it under federal legislation.

§4.60 The *B.C. Power*[185] case contains perhaps the most extreme position ever advanced concerning the privileged position relative to provincial legislation that is sometimes claimed by or alleged on behalf of federally incorporated companies. In the position for which it stands, however, it stands quite alone.[186]

---

[182] (1963), 44 W.W.R. 65 (B.C.S.C.).
[183] *British Columbia Power Corp. v. B.C. Electric Co.*, [1962] S.C.R. 642.
[184] *British Columbia Power Corp. v. A.G. British Columbia* (1963), 47 D.L.R. (2d) 633 (B.C.C.A.).
[185] *British Columbia Power Corp. v. B.C. Electric Co.*, [1962] S.C.R. 642.
[186] See, for instance, *Société Asbestos Ltée v. Société National de l'Amiante* (1981), 128 D.L.R. (3d) 405 (Que. C.A.); *Re Upper Churchill Water Rights Reversion Act 1980 (Newfoundland)*, [1982] N.J. No. 8, 134 D.L.R. (3d) 288 (Nfld. C.A.), rev'd on other grounds [1984] S.C.J. No. 16.

More recent cases have taken a markedly different approach from that adopted by Lett C.J. in the *B.C. Power* case. The most important of these cases was the decision of the Supreme Court of Canada in *Canadian Indemnity Co. v. A.G. British Columbia*.[187] In that case, the province of British Columbia established a universal compulsory automobile insurance scheme, and granted a monopoly over the sale of such insurance to a Crown corporation. The appellants were insurance companies that had previously carried on the business of automobile insurance. They argued that the provincial insurance legislation was an unconstitutional interference with interprovincial trade and commerce, and that as federally incorporated companies it was not open to the province to deny them access to the business for which they were incorporated. The Supreme Court rejected both these arguments. With respect to the interprovincial commerce argument, Martland J. stated:

> The impact of the legislation upon the appellant's automobile insurance business in British Columbia could not be more drastic. However, that effect of the legislation upon companies whose operations are inter-provincial in scope does not mean that the legislation is in relation to inter-provincial trade and commerce. The aim of the legislation relates to a matter of provincial concern within the Province and to property and civil rights within the Province.[188]

Martland J. then turned to the question of whether a federal Charter gave the insurance companies in question a vested right to engage in the business of insurance. He said:

> Parliament can create and maintain the legal existence of a corporate entity, with which a Province cannot interfere. But a provincial Legislature within its own field of legislative power can regulate, in the Province, a particular business or activity. The fact that a federally-incorporated company has, by federal legislation, derived existence as a legal person, with designated powers, does not mean that it is thereby exempted from the operation of such provincial regulation. It is subject to such regulation in the same way as a natural person or a provincially-incorporated company.[189]

Thus it was open to the province to nationalize automobile insurance business in British Columbia, and federally incorporated insurance companies were powerless to prevent it. In taking this position, Martland J. echoed previous decisions running back at least as far as the decision of the Privy Council in *Citizens Insurance Co. v. Parsons*,[190] where as noted above, Sir Montague Smith stated with respect to mortmain legislation:

> ... [I]f a company were incorporated for the sole purpose of purchasing and holding land in the Dominion it might happen that it could do no business in any part

---

Therefore it should be considered with some caution. As Kerwin C.J.C. stated in *Cairney v. MacQueen* (1956), 3 D.L.R. (2d) 481 at 484 (S.C.C.), "it cannot be said that one decision of a single judge is a clear judicial interpretation ..." of the law.
[187] (1976), 73 D.L.R. (3d) 111 (S.C.C.).
[188] *Canadian Indemnity Co. v. A.G. British Columbia* (1976), 73 D.L.R. (3d) 111 at 117 (S.C.C.).
[189] *Ibid.*, at 122.
[190] (1881), 7 App. Cas. 96 (P.C.).

of it, by reason of all of the provinces having passed Mortmain Acts, though the corporation would still exist and preserve its status as a corporate body.

(vi) Applying for Provincial/Federal Powers

§4.61 A federally incorporated entity may apply to the province (or to some non-Canadian jurisdiction) for the grant of a power to be exercised in Ontario with regard to its property and civil rights additional to the powers with which it was invested on incorporation, provided that additional power is not inconsistent with the powers conferred by the federal government.[191] However, the laws of the incorporating jurisdiction (federal or provincial) govern not only the creation and continuing existence of the corporation,[192] but also all matters of internal management,[193] the creation of share capital and related matters.[194]

E. CONCLUSION RE DIVISION OF JURISDICTION

§4.62 Based upon the foregoing review of the law, the following general principles may be stated with respect to the constitutional authority of the federal and provincial governments to incorporate:

- With limited exceptions, either the federal or provincial governments may incorporate all general business corporations within the meaning of the Ontario *Business Corporations Act* or the *Canada Business Corporations Act*, including corporations that intend to engage in activities that are within the exclusive regulatory jurisdiction of the other level of government, as the jurisdiction to regulate does not preclude the jurisdiction to incorporate.

- Neither the provincial or federal government may incorporate a corporation in an area within the exclusive jurisdiction of the other level of government, where either under the terms of the *Constitution Act, 1867* itself or under the laws passed by that government preclude incorporation except by that government (*e.g.*, banks as such,[195] which must be incorporated under the *Bank Act*).

- The federal government may not incorporate a corporation the objects of which are entirely intraprovincial in nature (*e.g.*, if the corporation is restricted in its objects to doing business only in Ontario).[196]

---

[191] *Sun Life Assurance Co. of Canada v. Sisters Adorers of Precious Blood*, [1942] O.R. 708 (C.A.), but compare *Dobie v. Temporalities Board* (1882), 7 App. Cas. 136 (P.C.).
[192] *Sass v. St. Nicholas Mutual Benefit Association of Winnipeg (City)*, [1937] S.C.R. 415.
[193] However, current thinking is that a jurisdiction may require the existence of a particular management structure and regime of shareholder rights as a condition of permitting the sale of securities to residents of that jurisdiction.
[194] *National Trust Co. v. Ebro Irrigation & Power Co.*, [1954] O.R. 463 (H.C.).
[195] As opposed to near banks such as trust companies and credit unions. See para. 4.14.
[196] Unless the object in question can be declared to be a work for the general advantage of Canada. It has never been particularly clear whether there is a limit on the power of the federal Parliament to so declare a work, but the experience with other general powers suggests that such a limit does indeed exist.

- The provincial government may not incorporate a corporation the objects of which are entirely extraprovincial in nature (*e.g.*, if the corporation is restricted in its objects to doing business only outside of Ontario).
- Federal incorporation does not insulate a corporation from provincial regulatory laws enacted within fields of provincial jurisdiction, but the province may not sterilize a federal corporation under the guise of regulation.
- Provincially incorporated corporations are subject to federal regulatory laws enacted within fields of federal jurisdiction.

§4.63 Having reviewed the theoretical power of the federal and provincial governments to incorporate, it is worthwhile to give some consideration to the practical benefits of incorporation at either level. Clients will often ask a lawyer whether it is preferable to incorporate a corporation at the federal or provincial level. There is no clear answer to this question. The OBCA and CBCA have each been amended frequently, and whatever momentary advantage one secures in being more "modern" than the other is quickly wiped out when the other is brought up to date. For most corporations the practical differences between the two regimes are negligible. For corporations that realistically expect to carry on business (in the sense of having permanent places of business) in more than two provinces or territories, federal incorporation may result in slightly lower administrative costs. For corporations that expect to carry on their activities (other than an isolated trade) in only one or two provinces, the administrative burden is reduced through provincial incorporation, as it eliminates filing at the federal level. If the corporation is only to carry on business in Ontario, provincial incorporation is preferable, particularly if the corporation will engage in a provincially regulated activity. Federal regulation, on the other hand, may tip the balance in favour of federal incorporation. Another consideration is the time required to incorporate: incorporation under the OBCA can be obtained more quickly than under the CBCA. For most lawyers (and residents of Ontario) the offices of the provincial Ministry are more accessible than those of the federal Department.

F. CORPORATIONS AND THE CANADIAN CHARTER OF RIGHTS AND FREEDOMS

§4.64 The rights of a corporation to claim the protection of the *Canadian Charter of Rights and Freedoms* have continued to develop over the years since the publication of the first edition of this text, but there are still many areas of the law with respect to this question that remain unclear. Much of the defining case law remains at the inferior court level.[197]

§4.65 As noted in Chapter 2, the personal status of a corporation does not imply that the corporation will be entitled to all of the rights of a natural person. This is particularly true in the Charter area. The argument against extending Charter

---

[197] See, for instance, *R. v. 741290 Ontario Inc.*, [1991] O.J. No. 215, 1 B.L.R. (2d) 279 (Prov. Ct.).

protection to corporations is essentially that the purpose of the Charter is to protect human rights — that is, the rights of citizens, and to a lesser extent immigrants and visitors to the country. Corporations are administrative devices. They exist only in theory, and therefore they do not have human rights that can be infringed. Moreover, corporations are creatures of the state. In deciding to create them, the state decides what rights to confer upon corporations. If the state has the power to confer full rights on corporations (which it must necessarily possess if corporations are to be held to be entitled to rights under the Charter) then it must surely have the right to confer less than full rights — and therefore it follows that the state may withhold Charter rights from a corporation.

§4.66 The argument in favour of extending Charter protection to corporations is that although they are artificial entities created by the state, they represent (either directly or indirectly) the human beings who stand behind them as shareholders and other stakeholders. If the corporation is not allowed to assert rights under the Charter, then those human beings may be prejudiced as a result. The state should not be permitted to take advantage of the citizens' use of a lawful administrative device such as a corporation, and so deny (albeit indirectly) those people who make use of that device the rights to which they are entitled under the *Canadian Charter of Rights and Freedoms*.[198] In other words, citizens are not to be put to a choice between administrative efficiency and their fundamental liberties.[199] That which the state cannot do directly, it should not be allowed to do indirectly.

§4.67 Neither of these arguments has completely carried the day. It is now clear that a corporation may invoke the protection of the Charter in at least some circumstances. For instance in *Hunter v. Southam Inc.*[200] a corporation was held to be entitled to seek an injunction to prevent the Director of Investigation and Research of the Combines Investigation Branch from continuing with a search of the corporation's premises. Similarly, in *Canadian Newspapers Co. v. A.G. Canada*[201] the Supreme Court of Canada ruled that certain provisions of the *Criminal Code* infringed the rights to which the corporation was entitled under paragraph 2(*b*) of the Charter with respect to freedom of the press.[202] In both of these cases, the court did not specifically state that corporations as such were entitled to invoke the Charter. However, in *R. v. Big M Drug Mart Ltd.*,[203] Dickson C.J.C. observed in passing that subsection 24(1) of the Charter sets out a remedy for individuals (whether real persons or artificial ones such as corporations) whose rights under the Charter have been infringed.

---

[198] *R. v. Transport Rober (1973) Ltée.*, [2003] O.J. No. 4306, 234 D.L.R. (4th) 546 at para. 12 (C.A.).
[199] See, generally, *Sanata Clara Co. v. Southern Pacific Railroad* (1886), 118 U.S. 394.
[200] [1984] S.C.J. No. 36, 27 B.L.R. 297.
[201] [1988] S.C.J. No. 67, [1988] 2 S.C.R. 122.
[202] See also *Irwin Toy Ltd. v. A.G. Quebec*, [1989] S.C.J. No. 36, [1989] 1 S.C.R. 927.
[203] [1985] S.C.J. No. 17, [1985] 1 S.C.R. 295.

§4.68 On the other hand, there are certain rights under the Charter that a corporation may not invoke, because by their very nature they relate to human rather than corporate activity and therefore can have no relevance to corporations.[204] Some rights may also not apply since by their very nature they cannot extend to an artificial entity such as a corporation (*e.g.*, the right not to be subject to arbitrary arrest). Thus it has been held that since a corporation cannot be a witness, a corporation cannot invoke the protection against self-incrimination provided under clause 11(*c*) of the Charter.[205] Nor may a corporation claim the protection of section 7 of the Charter.[206] But this general statement is subject to an important qualification:[207] In some circumstances, a corporation may rely on a section of the Charter notwithstanding that corporations lie outside the scope of the section's protection. No accused, human or artificial, may be convicted under a law that has the practical effect of infringing the constitutional rights of a human being. Thus a corporation can argue that legislation under which it is charged infringes, for example, the rights of an individual under section 7 of the Charter, provided there are facts before the court sufficient to establish the peril to the liberty of the individual(s) concerned.[208]

(i) Corporate Investigations and Charter Rights

§4.69 One key area of concern in constitutional law as it pertains to corporations is the extent to which corporate law procedures may be applied without violating the Charter rights of the individual directors and shareholders who stand behind such corporations. Part XIII of the OBCA and Part XIX of the CBCA provide for an investigation remedy. Under this procedure, security holders may apply to the court for an order directing an investigation of the corporation. The investigator may be empowered to "conduct a hearing, administer oaths and examine any person upon oath", subject to such rules as may be prescribed by the court for the conduct of the hearing. The order may also require attendance for the purpose of giving such evidence. Since one of the specific purposes for which an investigation may be made is to determine whether the business affairs of the corporation have been conducted in a manner that is "fraudulent or unlawful", the question is often raised as to the extent to which an investigation may be carried on without violating Charter protection against self-incrimination.

---

[204] In *R. v. Big M Drug Mart*, [1985] S.C.J. No. 17, [1985] 1 S.C.R. 295, Dickson C.J.C. held that corporations are not entitled to freedom of conscience. Quaere whether such a finding would be reached in a case where the corporation was incorporated in furtherance of a religious purpose, such as in an ecclesiastical corporation.

[205] *R. v. Amway of Canada Ltd.*, [1989] S.C.J. No. 3, [1989] 1 S.C.R. 21.

[206] *Irwin Toy Ltd. v. A.G. Quebec*, [1989] S.C.J. No. 36, [1989] 1 S.C.R. 927.

[207] *R. v. 741290 Ontario Inc.*, [1991] O.J. No. 215, 1 B.L.R. (2d) 279 at 286 (Prov. Ct.), *per* MacDonnell J. See also *R. v. Wholesale Travel Group Inc.*, [1989] O.J. No. 1971, 63 D.L.R. (4th) 325, var'd [1991] S.C.J. No. 79, 84 D.L.R. (4th) 161.

[208] *Canadian Civil Liberties Association v. Canada (Attorney General)*, [1998] O.J. No. 2856, 161 D.L.R. (4th) 225 (C.A.); see also *Canadian Egg Marketing Agency v. Richardson*, [1998] S.C.J. No. 78, 166 D.L.R. (4th) 1; *Charlottetown (City) v. Prince Edward Island*, [1998] P.E.I.J. No. 88, 167 D.L.R. (4th) 268 (C.A.).

§4.70 This question was addressed squarely by the Ontario Court of Appeal in *Catalyst Fund General Partner Inc. v. Hollinger Inc.*[209] The decision in the *Hollinger* case indicates that the circumstances of an investigation or the manner in which it is conducted may raise Charter issues. However, the decision also makes clear that the hypothetical possibility of such issues is not be a sufficient argument to frustrate the utilization of the investigation procedure.

§4.71 The issue in the case was whether an inspector appointed under section 229 of the CBCA to inquire into the affairs of Hollinger Inc. infringed the rights of certain former senior officers and directors of Hollinger under sections 7 and 13 of the *Charter of Rights*. The appellants argued that the investigation procedure would violate their Charter self-incrimination protection, since they were the target of an ongoing criminal an investigation into their conduct in the United States. The appellants sought a declaration that an investigation order compelling them to submit to questioning was premature because the inspector had not exhausted other sources of information. They also asked that the order to compel them to answer questions should be set aside and dismissed or, in the alternative, stayed pending the outcome of criminal proceedings in the United States.

§4.72 The court was not overly receptive to the Charter argument. It was noted that many of the areas of inquiry in the CBCA investigation were outside the scope of the American criminal investigation. The claim of a violation of Charter rights was too abstract, and not tied to any specific concern:

> The protection under the Charter is witness-specific and fact-specific. The balancing of potential prejudice to a particular appellant against the necessity of obtaining the evidence must be undertaken in context. For example, by his plea of guilty in the United States, Mr. Radler may be in a different position in some respects than the other two appellants and may not need protection from the use that can be made of his answers at least in respect of the matters to which he has already pled guilty. Campbell J. indicated that he was prepared to rule on whether the appellants should be compelled to answer specific questions and we regard that as the appropriate context in which to consider the appellants' rights. Also, like Campbell J., we are not persuaded that Canada is completely powerless to protect those under its jurisdiction.[210]

The court also noted that the investigation order incorporated a procedure specifically to deal with the self-incrimination problem. Taking these factors into account, the Court of Appeal declined to order a stay of his order.

(ii) Laws of Special Application

§4.73 Section 15 of the Charter of Rights, guaranteeing equality of treatment under the law, does not apply to corporations.[211] Accordingly, statutes subjecting

---

[209] [2005] O.J. No. 4666, 79 O.R. (3d) 70, 143 A.C.W.S. (3d) 478 (C.A.).
[210] *Ibid.*, at para. 12
[211] *Edmonton Journal v. Alberta (Attorney General)*, [1989] S.C.J. No. 124, 45 C.R.R. 1, [1989] 2 S.C.R. 1326; *Canada (Attorney General) v. Central Cartage Co.*, [1990] F.C.J. No. 407, [1990]

corporations to differential tax treatment are not open to challenge under the Charter. Similarly, provisions of a statute creating an offence and subjecting a corporation to higher penalties than individuals would also seem to be acceptable, and indeed may in some cases be argued as being necessary to provide a genuine deterrent to corporate wrongdoing.[212]

§4.74 From time to time, courts have also recognized that it is necessary to curb the exercise by corporations of what for individuals would constitute democratic rights, in order to protect the democratic nature of society. For instance, in *Federal Election Comm. v. Beaumont*,[213] the U.S. Supreme Court considered the constitutionality of certain prohibitions against contribution or expenditure by corporations in connection with certain federal elections,[214] although indirect support is permitted through so-called political action committees. The respondents in the case, North Carolina Right to Life, Inc., was a non-profit advocacy corporation ("NCRL"). It sued the Federal Election Commission (FEC), challenging the constitutionality of the prohibition as applied to NCRL. The U.S. Supreme Court held that the prohibition was consistent with the First Amendment, even given the express advocacy purpose of the corporation. The Court noted that since 1907, American federal law has barred such direct corporate contributions. The prohibition was found to have a number of specific legitimate governmental objectives, including to respond to the characteristics of corporate structure that could threaten the integrity of the political process, such as giving the wealthy and powerful exclusive access to government, as well as the need to discourage corruption or the appearance of corruption. The ban also protects individuals who have paid money into a corporation or union for other purposes from having their money used to support political candidates to whom they may be opposed. The ban also prevented corporations from being used as conduits for circumventing valid contribution limits.

G. PUBLIC AND QUASI-PUBLIC CORPORATIONS

(i) Corporations Charged with a Statutory Mandate

§4.75 While a corporate entity may have been cloaked with the powers of a natural person, the exercise of those powers may be restricted under various principles of public law, where the corporation is charged with carrying out a specific statutory mandate or some governmental function. This possibility raises a number of concerns, especially where one is dealing with an OBCA or CBCA entity that is government owned—and these concerns are of an even higher level of magnitude when dealing with a Crown agent.

---

2 F.C. 641, 109 N.R. 357 (C.A.); *R. v. Elan Development Ltd.* (1998), 55 C.R.R. (2d) 34 (T.C.C.).
[212] See, generally, in this area *R. v. Church of Scientology*, [1996] O.J. No. 2870, 42 C.R.R. (2d) 284 (C.A.).
[213] (2003), 539 U.S. 146.
[214] 2 U.S.C., s. 441b(a).

§4.76 Generally, the members of a corporate body have the right to decide when to windup the operations of that entity. This rule is substantially qualified where dealing with a corporation that has a statutory mandate. In *Re Salisbury Railway and Market House Co. Ltd.,* Buckley J., stated:

> It has long been recognized that where a company has been incorporated by a special Act of Parliament for the purpose of providing some service, such as a railway, for the public benefit, the incorporating statute may, by inference if not expressly, impose a statutory duty on the company to establish and maintain the service in question, with the consequence that the company cannot properly dispose of any asset, such as part of its railway line, which is necessary for the maintenance of that service.[215]

In *Gardner v. London, Chatham and Dover Railway Co.*, the plaintiffs applied to the court for the appointment of a receiver-manager over the assets of a company against which they held a mortgage. The company in question was a railway company, incorporated by statute. The court held that it could not appoint such a receiver-manager. Lord Cairns L.C. explained:

> When Parliament, acting for the public interest, authorizes the construction and maintenance of a railway, both as a highway for the public, and as a road on which the company may themselves become carriers of passengers and goods, it confers powers and imposes duties and responsibilities of the largest and most important kind, and it confers and imposes them upon the company which Parliament has before it, and upon no other body of persons. These powers must be executed and these duties discharged by the company. They cannot be delegated or transferred.[216]

§4.77 There is also a long line of case law relating to the delegation of a statutory authority or duty. As a general rule, a statutory corporation that has been given certain statutory powers cannot delegate those powers to another, particularly where after the proposed delegation would take effect, the corporate entity subject to the statutory responsibility would exercise little or no supervision or control over the performance of the statutory responsibility. Most of these cases related to the leasing of certain statutory rights to another company for a period of years. For instance, in *Great Northern Railway Co. v. The Eastern Counties Railway Co.*[217] one railway company gave what was in effect a lease of its rail lines and related assets to another such company. The court stated:

---

[215] [1967] 1 All E.R. 813 at 819 (Ch. D.).

[216] (1867), 2 Ch. App. 201 at 212. See also: *Blaker v. Herts and Essex Waterworks Co.* (1889), 41 Ch. D. 399; *Marshall v. South Staffordshire Tramways Co.*, [1895] 2 Ch. 36 at 50 (C.A.), *per* Lindley L.J.; *Parker v. Camden London Borough Council*, [1986] 1 Ch. 162 (C.A.). This line of reasoning seems to have been incorporated into the law of Ontario (and, presumably, the rest of Canada as well) by the Privy Council in *Central Ontario Railway v. Trusts and Guarantee Co. Ltd.*, [1905] A.C. 576, and it has been followed repeatedly since: See *Allan v. The Manitoba and Northwestern Railway Co.* (1894), 10 Man. R. 106 at 120 (C.A.); *Campbell-Bennett Ltd. v. Comstock Midwestern Ltd.*, [1954] S.C.R. 207 at 215, and *Cook's Ferry Band v. Cook's Ferry Band Council*, [1989] F.C.J. No. 458, [1989] 3 F.C. 562 at 569-571, 30 F.T.R. 180 (T.D.).

[217] (1851), 9 Hare 306 at 310-312. See also *Beman v. Rufford* (1851), 1 Sim. (N.S.) 550 at 569; and also *Winch v. The Birkenhead, Lancashire and Cheshire Junction Railway Co.* (1852), 5 DE. G. & SM. 562 at 579.

It is impossible to read the agreement between the plaintiffs and the East Anglian Railways Company without being satisfied that it amounts to an entire delegation to the plaintiffs of all the powers conferred by Parliament upon the East Anglian Company. All the stock of that company is to be taken by the plaintiffs without any obligation to restore it. The plaintiffs are to manage and regulate the railways of the East Anglian Company for the purposes of the agreement; and, although in form it is declared that the instrument shall not operate as a lease, or agreement for a lease, it amounts in substance either to one or the other. It is framed in total disregard of the obligations and duties which attach upon these companies; and is an attempt to carry into effect, without the intervention of Parliament, what cannot lawfully be done except by Parliament in the exercise of its discretion with reference to the interests of the public.

§4.78 Generally, it is not possible for a statutory corporation charged with the performance of a statutory duty to enter into a pooling arrangement under which property or rights vested in the corporation for a statutory purpose is shared with some other entity.[218] In *Re the Joint Application of the Great Northern Railway Company and the Great Central Railway Company*,[219] two rail companies (each of which were statutory corporations) entered into an agreement by which the affairs of both companies were to be managed by a joint committee of directors chosen from amongst the two companies. All the receipts and profits of the companies were to be put into a common fund, to be distributed according to a certain formula. Despite a provision in the *Railways Act* authorizing the two statutory corporations to make agreements to work the rail lines of another company, it was held that the arrangement was *ultra vires*. However, in all cases, the question of what can and cannot be done depends upon a fair and realistic interpretation of the statutory provisions concerned.[220]

(ii) Government Owned Corporations

§4.79 A Crown corporation or other incorporated entity discharging a governmental authority may also be obliged to respect the Charter rights of the persons with whom it deals, to the same extent as the government would be required to do so, if it was itself dealing with those persons directly. This constitutional responsibility has been extensively discussed in the United States. There, it has been held that where a government creates a corporate entity that is owned by the government and is used for the purposes of carrying out a declared public purpose of the government, it forms part of the government for the purposes of constitutional law, irrespective of whether that purpose is of a commercial nature.[221] A generally similar approach has been adopted in Canada with respect to

---

[218] See, for instance, *Greenwich Pier Co. v. The Conservators of the River Thames* (1905), 21 T.L.R. 669 (Ch.).
[219] (1908), 24 T.L.R. 417 (C.A.),.
[220] See, for instance, *Canadian Pacific Ltd. v. Telesat Canada*, [1982] O.J. No. 3210, 133 D.L.R. (3d) 321, at 329 (C.A.).
[221] *Lebron v. National R.R. Passenger Corp.* (1995), 513 U.S. 374, but *cf. International Soc. for Krishna Consciousness v. Lee* (1992), 505 U.S. 672 — ban on solicitation of contributions at airports operated by the New York Port Authority.

such corporate entities as municipalities,[222] and presumably would also apply to Crown-owned business corporations and other corporate entities discharging a governmental function.

---

[222] See, for instance, *Godbout v. Longueuil*, [1997] S.C.J. No. 95, [1997] 3 S.C.R. 844 (municipal governments were subject to the Charter); *Township of Montague v. Page*, [2006] O.J. No. 33 (Ont. S.C.) *per* Pedlar J. (with respect to a libel action against a municipality); *Nova Scotia Human Rights Commission v. County of Annapolis*, [2005] N.S.J. No. 469, 144 A.C.W.S. (3d) 157 at para. 98 (S.C.) (human rights commission investigation), *per* Warner J.

Chapter 5

INCORPORATION

A. INTRODUCTION

§5.1 The term "incorporation" describes the procedure by which a corporation is created. Upon incorporation, the company comes into being as a legal person; prior to its incorporation, the corporation is a non-entity.[1] Incorporation confers upon the members of a company the privilege of acting together in concert as a collective body.[2]

§5.2 As discussed in Chapter 1, there are various ways in which a company may come into existence, the principal methods recognized at common law being by charter, by prescription, or by or under statute. The incorporation procedure varies depending upon which of these methods is employed. A chartered company is formed by the grant of a charter by the Crown (or Royal patent) either under the prerogative powers of Her Majesty, or under special statutory powers conferred upon Her.[3] At one time, incorporation by charter (in the form of letters patent) issued under the authority of statute was the most widely employed method of incorporation in Canada, but the trend is now overwhelmingly away from this method of incorporation, except in the case of charitable and other not-for-profit companies. It appears that no corporation in Canada (other than the Crown itself) is seen to have been incorporated on the basis of prescription.

§5.3 A statutory company is a company formed by statute or a company formed by administrative act under the authority of a statute. Statutory companies may be created for a public or private purpose, with Crown corporations being the most obvious example of public, and the typical business corporation being the most obvious example of private purpose entities. Crown corporations are often created by special Act. The ownership of such companies is vested in the Crown by law rather than by shareholding.[4] Where the Crown corporation is made an agent of the Crown (so that all property of the corporation belongs to the Crown and the business that it transacts is carried on behalf of the Crown), the effect

---

[1] *Kelner v. Baxter* (1866), L.R. 2 C.P. 174. As to statutory exceptions, see *BNZ Finance Ltd. v. Commissioner of Inland Revenue*, [1997] J.C.J. No. 51 (P.C.).
[2] *Morgan v. 45 Flyers Avenue Pty. Ltd.* (1986), 10 A.C.L.R. 692.
[3] See, for instance, U.K. 1698, 9 Wm. III, c. 44; U.K. 1710, 9 Anne, c. 15. For a Canadian example, see N.S. Stats. 1796, 36 Geo. III, c. 7.
[4] However, there are exceptions. The Ontario Infrastructure Projects Corporation was originally incorporated under the OBCA, but was subsequently continued by special Act, see S.O. 2006, c. 9, Schedule I. The distinction between Crown companies and ordinary business corporations was explained by Denning L.J. in *Tamlin v. Hannaford*, [1950] 1 K.B. 18 at 23 (C.A.).

would appear to render the Crown liable for the debts and obligations of the corporation — on the basis of the statutory agency relationship.[5] Where the Crown corporation is not an agent of the Crown, the presumption of limited liability would appear to apply, since the concepts of limited liability and agency are mutually exclusive.

§5.4 Although new companies are still incorporated from time to time by special Act, virtually all new business corporations in Ontario are now incorporated under the authority of the Ontario *Business Corporations Act* ("OBCA") or the *Canada Business Corporations Act* ("CBCA"), and it is those corporations with which we are primarily concerned in this work. As we have seen, at common law, the members of a body may not by themselves confer corporate status upon that body, except by act of the sovereign.[6] However, the incorporation of a corporation does depend to a degree upon the will of its members, for it is a principle of common law that no group of persons can be incorporated without their consent.[7] Thus under the OBCA and the CBCA, the creation of a corporation involves a two-step procedure, involving first an application made for incorporation made by one or more persons (which evidences their consent to incorporation), and then the issue of a certificate of incorporation by the Director (which evidences the consent of the sovereign).[8] In this chapter, we shall examine the procedure for incorporating a corporation under the CBCA or OBCA.

(i) Types of Corporate Enterprise

§5.5 As discussed in Chapter 1, the OBCA and CBCA (and other business corporations statutes in force in other provinces) deal with only one particular type of corporation. Neither the CBCA nor the OBCA is a statute of general application in the same sense as the U.K. *Companies Act, 1985*. Instead, different legal regimes govern different types of corporation. The OBCA applies to most Ontario incorporated entities that have share capital. Subsection 2(1) of the OBCA provides:

> This Act, except where it is otherwise expressly provided, applies to every body corporate with share capital,

---

[5] See Chapter 2, para. 2.34.
[6] *Bank of Montreal v. Bethune* (1836), 4 O.S. 341 at 356 (U.C.C.A.), *per* Sherwood J. Although it is the state that creates and gives legal recognition to a corporate entity, for both the corporation sole and the corporation aggregate, the citizens who bring about the creation of the entity play an equally important role in giving birth to it. By the issue of a corporate charter, the state may confer corporate status on the incorporators and those who are admitted to the corporation afterwards. However, only the incorporators and the directors as their successors can identify who those persons are. In like manner with a corporation sole, the state may chose to confer the status of a corporation on a bishop, but only the church can identify who the bishop is. This point is made in *John Doe v. Bennett*, [2002] N.J. No. 218 (C.A.) with respect to corporations sole, but it applies equally with respect to corporations aggregate as well. Under the OBCA and CBCA, the incorporation power of the sovereign has been delegated to an administrative officer, namely the Director under each Act: see, generally, *Re Massey Manufacturing Co.* (1886), 13 O.A.R. 446 (C.A.), *per* Burton J.A. See also Chapter 1.
[7] *Calvin Church v. Logan* (1884), Trueman's Equity Cases 221 (N.B.S.C.).
[8] CBCA, R.S.C. 1985, c. C-44, ss. 5(1), 7, 8; OBCA, R.S.O. 1990, c. B.16, ss. 4(1), 6.

(a) incorporated by or under a general or special Act of the Parliament of the former Province of Upper Canada;

(b) incorporated by or under a general or special Act of the Parliament of the former Province of Canada that has its registered office and carries on business in Ontario; or

(c) incorporated by or under a general or special Act of the Legislature,

but this Act does not apply to a corporation within the meaning of the *Loan and Trust Corporations Act* except as provided by that Act.

In the case of Ontario incorporate entities, most Crown corporations,[9] cooperatives[10] and creditor unions,[11] and a number of special purpose corporations including insurance companies[12] are all governed by their own legislation. Formerly, the Ontario *Loan and Trust Corporations Act* created a separate corporate law regime to govern the incorporation of provincial loan or trust corporations, but Ontario no longer incorporates such entities, and all of the old Ontario corporate entities of this type have continued under federal legislation. The OBCA also does not apply to Part III corporations under the Ontario *Corporations Act*.[13] (which include all not-for-profit corporations, such as social clubs, public hospitals and charities).

§5.6 To complete the overall picture, under Ontario law, the statute governing most non-share corporations is the *Corporations Act*, section 272 of which provides:

Subject to section 2, this Part, except where it is otherwise expressly provided, applies,

(a) to every corporation incorporated by or under a general or special Act of the Parliament of the late Province of Upper Canada;

(b) to every corporation incorporated by or under a general or special Act of the Parliament of the late Province of Canada that has its head office and carries on business in Ontario and that was incorporated with objects to which the authority of the Legislature extends; and

(c) to every corporation incorporated by or under a general or special Act of the Legislature,

but this Part does not apply to a corporation incorporated for the construction and working of a railway, incline railway or street railway, or to a corporation within the meaning of the *Loan and Trust Corporations Act* except as provided by that Act.

---

[9] See, for example, *Capital Investment Plan Act, 1993*, S.O. 1993 c. 23.
[10] See the *Cooperative Corporations Act* R.S.O. 1990, c. C.35.
[11] *Credit Unions and Caisses Populaires Act, 1994*, S.O. 1994, c. 11.
[12] OBCA, s. 2(3)(c). In the case of railways, see OBCA, s. 2(2) and *The Railways Act*, R.S.O. 1950, c. 331.
[13] R.S.O. 1990, c. C.38. Part VI of the OBCA, which applies to a wide range of corporate entities issuing securities in Ontario is an exception to this general rule.

Section 272 and then Part VII of the *Corporations Act* set down a large number of general corporate law rules and presumptions that apply to all Ontario incorporated corporate entities unless expressly excluded (section 2 excludes the application of Part VII to any OBCA corporation). By virtue of this arrangement, in Ontario the *Corporations Act* rather than the OBCA remains the general corporate law statute of broadest *potential* effect (although the number of corporations actually subject to that Act is dwarfed by the number governed by the OBCA).

§5.7 Nevertheless, there are corporate entities that operate outside both regimes. For instance, neither the OBCA nor the *Corporations Act* applies with respect to municipal corporations, which in Ontario and other provinces are subject to their own statutory regime. In Ontario, the procedure for the creation of a municipal corporation is generally by way of private Act, although a handful (*e.g.*, Toronto,[14] Ottawa[15] and Hamilton)[16] are governed by their own public statutes.[17] A few regional municipalities also continue to be governed by their own public statutes. The constitution of all municipalities in Ontario is the *Municipal Act, 2001*[18] — although this will soon change in the case of Toronto,[19] and may change within the foreseeable future for other major municipalities as well.

§5.8 A municipal corporation is a creature of provincial legislation, created for political purposes and having subordinate or local powers of legislation. Municipalities differ from business corporations in several important respects. A municipality can exercise its corporate powers only within its defined limits. It does not own its specified territorial area, but is limited thereto as to its jurisdiction. Its powers, authorities, liberties, franchises, capacities and objects are as defined by provincial legislation.[20] Subject to provincial law, its citizens can neither add to them nor take away from them. Nor can the federal government, but to the extent that provincial law permits, federal law may delegate federal responsibilities to the municipal level of government. In several provinces, municipalities recently have been given natural person powers. However, it is questionable whether the extension of such powers will have any effect on long-standing conventions of municipal law, such as the general rule that a municipality can only Act by or under the authority of a by-law.[21] Municipalities are corporate entities that perform a defined statutory role and exercise a govern-

---

[14] *City of Toronto Act, 2006*, S.O. 2006, c. 11, Sched. A (not yet in force).
[15] *City of Ottawa Act, 1999*, c. 14, Sched. E.
[16] *City of Hamilton Act, 1999*, c. 14, Sched. C.
[17] *Regional Municipality of Peel Act, 2005*, c. 20.
[18] S.O. 2001, c. 25.
[19] *City of Toronto Act*, S.O. 2006, c. 11.
[20] *Morrison & Mahoney v. New Brunswick*, [1994] N.B.J. No. 597, 158 N.B.R. (2d) 161 (Q.B.), per Riordon J.
[21] *Municipal Act, 2001*, S.O. 2001, c. 25, s. 5(3). Purported contracts that are not so authorized are void: *Pacific National Investments Ltd. v. City of Victoria*, [2000] S.C.J. No. 64, [2000] 2 S.C.R. 919, 15 M.P.L.R. (3d) 1; *Waterous Engine Works Co. v. Palmerston* (1892), 21 S.C.R. 556; *Silver's Garage Ltd. v. Bridgewater (Town)*, [1970] S.C.J. No. 93, [1971] S.C.R. 577; *Magical Waters Fountains Ltd. v. Sarnia (City)*, [1992] O.J. No. 1320, 10 M.P.L.R. (2d) 253 (Div. Ct.).

mental mandate. Consequently, there are public law considerations that militate in favour of requiring tight compliance with the procedures and restrictions on authority that are not germane in the business corporation setting.

(ii) Terminology

§5.9 In both the OBCA and the CBCA, the term "corporation" is used to describe a corporation that is subject to each of the Acts respectively; the term "body corporate" is used to describe any corporate entity, whether or not it is subject to the Act in question.[22] This distinction in terminology is of obvious importance in ascertaining the scope of particular provisions, and in particular in determining whether specific provisions of each statute are intended to govern all corporate bodies, or only those that are corporations under the Act.

§5.10 As was discussed in earlier chapters, generally in law the term "person" ibis used only when describing beings or entities that enjoy full legal status. Thus there is a certain irony in the fact that one of the most expansive legal definitions of "person" is to be found in the OBCA. Subsection 1(1) of the OBCA provides that the term "person", when used in that Act,

> includes an individual, sole proprietorship, partnership, unincorporated association, unincorporated syndicate, unincorporated organization, trust, body corporate, and a natural person in his or her capacity as trustee, executor, administrator, or other legal representative.

The CBCA contains a similar, but narrower, definition of this term. These extended definitions allow non-corporate collective entities to exercise the powers and rights allowed to true persons under the OBCA and CBCA, including the right (it would appear) to incorporate a corporation under either of those statutes. It is thus hypothetically possible for an unincorporated association to incorporate a corporation, even though it cannot own one, except through the facilitating mechanism of one or more trustees who hold the shares of the corporation for the collective benefit of its members from time to time.

§5.11 Under the laws of many jurisdictions, a clear status distinction is drawn between public and private companies[23] — that is, companies whose securities may be distributed to the public and those whose securities may not. For instance, under the English *Companies Act, 1985*, a public company must be specifically incorporated as such,[24] and must include the words "public limited company" or the abbreviation "plc" in its corporate name.[25] Under that Act, public companies are also subject to a minimum capitalization requirement of

---

[22] See OBCA, s. 1(1); CBCA, s. 2(1).
[23] The State of Victoria in Australia introduced such a distinction in 1896.
[24] *Companies Act, 1985* (U.K.), c. 6, s. 3(1).
[25] *Ibid.*, s. 26(1)(*a*). Technically, if the company's registered office is to be situate in Wales, the public company may also be designated using the Welsh term "cwmni cyfyngedig cyhoedus" or the corresponding abbreviation "ccc", but there are few if any companies so designated.

£50,000, and cannot carry on business until such time as they receive a trading certificate from the registrar of companies.[26]

§5.12 In contrast, the OBCA and CBCA do not draw any status distinction between public and private corporations. However, both the OBCA and the CBCA do contain a number of special rules applicable to corporations that offer their securities to the public.[27] Subsection 1(6) of the OBCA provides:

> For the purposes of this Act, a corporation is offering its securities to the public only where,
>
> (a) in respect of any of its securities a prospectus, statement of material facts or securities exchange take-over bid or issuer bid circular has been filed under the *Securities Act* or any predecessor thereof, or in respect of which a prospectus has been filed under *The Corporations Information Act*, being chapter 72 of the Revised Statutes of Ontario, 1960, or any predecessor thereof, so long as any of such securities are outstanding or any securities into which such securities are converted are outstanding; or
>
> (b) any of its securities have been at any time since the 1st of May, 1967, listed and posted for trading on any stock exchange in Ontario recognized by the Commission regardless of when such listing and posting for trading commenced,
>
> except that where, upon the application of a corporation that has fewer than fifteen security holders, the Commission is satisfied, in its discretion, that to do so would not be prejudicial to the public interest, the Commission may order, subject to such terms and conditions as the Commission may impose, that the corporation shall be deemed to have ceased to be offering its securities to the public.

The "Commission" referred to in the definition is the Ontario Securities Commission. It is clear from this definition that once a corporation becomes an offering corporation, it remains so unless and until it is released from that status by the Commission. However, in order to become an offering corporation, the corporation must at some point have initiated a public distribution of securities in Ontario. If a corporation issues securities to the public, but always outside Ontario so that it was never required to file a prospectus with the Commission and its securities are not and were never posted for trading on an Ontario stock exchange, then the corporation will not be an offering corporation within the meaning of the Act.[28] Given the requirement for an Ontario distribution (which, it must be conceded, does seem somewhat parochial), there are some corporations that, although not technically within the definition of an "offering corporation",

---

[26] *Companies Act, 1985* (U.K.), c. 6, s. 117. This requirement was introduced into U.K. law under the E.U.'s *Second Company Law Directive*. In Australia and New Zealand, private companies are designated through the use of the abbreviation "Pty." (for "proprietary"). The practice in the U.K. is to abbreviate the relevant status designation in the lower case for public companies: ABC plc. In contrast, the word "Limited" is usually capitalized when abbreviated, as is also the practice in Canada.

[27] The OBCA, s. 1(1) describes any such corporation as an "offering corporation".

[28] For example, where securities are issued into the Euromarket or are traded on some foreign exchange.

cannot be compared to the typical closely held private corporation. These include corporations that issue securities to the public in a foreign jurisdiction.[29]

§5.13 One of the 2001 amendments of the CBCA was to delete the term "offering corporation" and to replace it with the term "distributing corporation". The primary intent behind this change appears to have been to bring the requirements of the CBCA more into conformity with the requirements of provincial securities laws. In Ontario, and other jurisdictions employing the so-called "closed system" of securities regulation, the determining consideration in securities regulation is not whether a corporation is issuing securities "to the public" but rather whether it has made a "distribution" to which the securities regulatory regime applies. The definition of "distributing corporation" is set out in section 2 of the *Canada Business Corporations Regulations*. It provides:

> For the purpose of the definition "distributing corporation" in subsection 2(1) of the Act and subject to subsections 2(6) and (7) of the Act and subsection (2) of this section, "distributing corporation" means:
>
> (a) a corporation that is a "reporting issuer" under any legislation that is set out in column 2 of an item of Schedule 1; or
>
> (b) in the case of a corporation that is not a "reporting issuer" referred to in paragraph (a), a corporation:
>
> > (i) that has filed a prospectus or registration statement under provincial legislation or under the laws of a jurisdiction outside Canada,
> >
> > (ii) any of the securities of which are listed and posted for trading on a stock exchange in or outside Canada, or
> >
> > (iii) that is involved in, formed for, resulting from or continued after an amalgamation, a reorganization, an arrangement or a statutory procedure, if one of the participating bodies corporate is a corporation to which subparagraph (i) or (ii) applies.

§5.14 A corporation that is subject to an exemption under provincial securities legislation, or to an order of the relevant provincial securities regulator that provides that the corporation is not a "reporting issuer" for the purposes of the applicable legislation, is not a "distributing corporation" for the purpose of the CBCA. Moreover, subsection 2(6) of the CBCA provides as follows:

> On the application of a corporation, the Director may determine that the corporation is not or was not a distributing corporation if the Director is satisfied that the determination would be prejudicial to the public interest.

Subsection (6) allows an individual corporation to obtain relief from the special regulatory rules applicable to distributing corporations. Subsection 2(7) contemplates a class wide exemption:

---

[29] See, for instance, *FCMI Financial Corporation v. Curtis International Ltd.*, [2004] O.J. No. 4262, 134 A.C.W.S. (3d) 407 (S.C.J.), dealing with a NASDAQ listed corporation.

The Director may determine that a class of corporations are not or were not distributing corporations if the Director is satisfied that the determination would be prejudicial to the public interest.

B. RESTRICTIONS ON INCORPORATION

§5.15 The OBCA prohibits corporations under that Act from carrying on the business of a loan or trust corporation.[30] Corporations incorporated under the CBCA must not carry on[31] the business of a bank, a company to which the *Insurance Companies Act*[32] applies or a company to which the *Trust and Loan Companies Act*[33] applies.[34] There is no express prohibition against the incorporation of a credit union under the CBCA (although there are, in fact, no federally incorporated credit unions in Canada), nor does the CBCA in any way reconcile itself with the *Canada Cooperatives Act*[35] or the *Cooperative Credit Associations Act*.[36] Subsection 3(5) of the CBCA further provides that:

> No corporation shall carry on business as a degree-granting educational institution unless expressly authorized to do so by a federal or provincial agent that by law has the power to confer degree-granting authority on an educational institution.

§5.16 There are only a handful of cases across the Commonwealth in which the impact of such provisions and restrictions have been considered by the courts, and even where those courts have commented upon that issue it has been only tangentially. The general rule seems to be that while statutory restrictions on, or prohibitions against, the incorporation of particular types of business must be respected and will be given fair effect by the courts, there is nothing inherently improper in a person arranging his or her business or affairs in such a way as to circumvent any applicable restriction or prohibition. Efforts to do so should not be disregarded as artificial or a sham merely because they are unusual or highly technical or complex.[37]

(i) Legality of Purpose

§5.17 It is implicit in the law that a corporation may only be incorporated for a lawful purpose.[38] Nevertheless, the certificate of incorporation is conclusive evi-

---

[30] OBCA, s. 2(1).
[31] CBCA, s. 3(4).
[32] S.C. 1991, c. 47.
[33] S.C. 1991, c. 45.
[34] CBCA, s. 3(4).
[35] S.C. 1998, c. 1. There are only a handful of federally incorporated cooperatives, most of which are owned by provincially incorporated cooperatives.
[36] S.C. 1991, c. 48. There is only one company incorporated under this statute, although there are a number of others which hold licences and are regulated under it.
[37] See, generally, *Gulland v. Fed. Comm. of Taxation* (1984), 55 A.L.R. 65 (Fed. Ct. Aust.), *per* Fisher J.
[38] See, for instance, *R. v. Registrar of Joint Stock Companies, ex p. Moore*, [1931] 2 K.B. 197; *R. v. Reg. of Companies, ex p. A.G. (the "Lindi St. Clair Case")*, [1991] B.C.L.C. 476 at 478-79 (Div. Ct.), *per* Ackner L.J.

dence of incorporation.[39] It relieves all persons dealing with the corporation from any duty to inquire as to whether all steps required for incorporation have been taken and releases them from any actual or constructive notice of a deficiency in the incorporation procedure. The mere fact that a corporation can be shown to have been incorporated on the application of an unauthorized person (*e.g.*, a person under 18),[40] or incorporated for an unlawful purpose, or is operated illegally, does not affect the validity of incorporation or the status of the corporation itself, but it may afford grounds for the corporation to be dissolved.[41] Instances in which corporations have been incorporated for an overtly illegal purpose are rare, but not entirely unknown. In *R. v. Registrar of Companies, ex p. A.G. (Miss Whiplash & Hookers Ltd.)*[42] the court considered a case in which a company had been set up "to carry on the business of prostitution". Strictly speaking, the business of prostitution is not illegal in England. Nevertheless, Ackner L.J. held that the registration of the company would be quashed. Where after incorporation it is subsequently learned that a particular corporation is organized for an illegal purpose, both the CBCA and OBCA permit the registrar to apply to have the incorporation cancelled for cause.[43] However, until that step is taken, the corporation remains in existence.

(ii) Incorporation of Professional Practices

§5.18 At one time, there was a general prohibition against the incorporation of a professional practice[44] — one apparent policy perception being that since professions were practised by gentlemen, and since a gentleman would as a matter of honour eschew limited liability, there was no need for incorporation. In Canada, the concept of the professional corporation was introduced into Alberta law in 1975.[45] Since then, several other provinces have adopted the concept. The legislation differs in detail from one province to another, but the general scheme of law is much the same. In *Sandilands v. Powell*[46] Wittman J.A. provided the following description of the distinguishing features of Alberta professional corporation:

> Professional corporations are distinct persons in the law akin to any corporation... but they differ from normal corporations in that they are regulated by their respective professions. A professional corporation cannot register as a licensed member of the profession nor can it be a registered practitioner of a profession. It may obtain a permit that allows it to engage in the practice of the profession. Professional corporations also differ from other corporations in that only a licensed member or

---

[39] OBCA, s. 7; s. 9 of the CBCA is less clear in this respect.
[40] See, generally, *Ex p. Bread Manufacturers Ltd., Re Truth & Sportsman Ltd.* (1937), 37 S.R. (N.S.W.) 242.
[41] See, generally, *Bowman v. Secular Society Ltd.*, [1917] A.C. 406 at 439 (H.L.).
[42] [1991] B.C.L.C. 476 (Div. Ct.).
[43] Discussed below in Chapter 15, Winding-up and Dissolution.
[44] The rationale behind this provision is discussed in detail in the *Interim Report of the Select Committee on Company Law* (the *"Lawrence Report"*), (Toronto: Queen's Printer for Ontario, 1967), ¶¶2.2.1 to 2.2.6.
[45] *Attorney General Statutes Amendment Act (No. 2)*, S.A. 1975, c. 44.
[46] [2003] A.J. No. 855 at para. 17, 330 A.R. 92(C.A.).

registered practitioner of a profession may be a shareholder in a professional corporation. Professional corporation can sue and be sued in their own name.

§5.19 Professional corporations are now specifically contemplated in sections 3.1 to 3.4 of the OBCA,[47] which were enacted in 2000.[48] Section 3.1 sets down two definitions that apply in sections 3.2, 3.3 and 3.4:

> "member" means a member of a profession governed by an Act that permits the profession to be practised through a professional corporation;
>
> "professional corporation" means a corporation incorporated or continued under this Act that holds a valid certificate of authorization or other authorizing document issued under an Act governing a profession.

The basic rule with respect to the incorporation of a professional practice is set out in subsection 3.1(2):

> Where the practice of a profession is governed by an Act, a professional corporation may practise the profession if,
>
> (a) that Act expressly permits the practice of the profession by a corporation and subject to the provisions of that Act; or
>
> (b) the profession is governed by an Act named in Schedule 1 of the *Regulated Health Professions Act, 1991,* one of the following Acts or a prescribed Act:
>
>   1. *Certified General Accountants Association of Ontario Act, 1983.*
>   2. *The Chartered Accountants Act, 1956.*
>   3. *Law Society Act.*
>   4. *Social Work and Social Service Work Act, 1998.*
>   5. *Veterinarians Act.*

§5.20 Since many statutes relating to individual professions have been amended over the years to permit incorporation,[49] most if not all, of the major regulated professions would seem to fall within the scope of subsection 3.1(2). Any entity incorporated under this provision is designated a "professional corporation" for the purposes of the Act. The general rule is that:

> This Act and the regulations apply with respect to a professional corporation except as otherwise set out in this section and sections 3.1, 3.3 and 3.4 and the regulations.[50]

§5.21 Nevertheless, there are a number of important restrictions applicable to the incorporation of such entities. In particular, it must hold a valid certificate of authorization or other authorizing document issued under the Act which governs the profession in question. Subsection 3.2(2) provides:

---

[47] Since the regulation of professions is fundamentally a matter of provincial responsibility, some question must be raised as to whether a professional practice may be incorporated under the CBCA, even where it is intended to carry on business in two or more provinces of Canada.
[48] S.O. 2000, c. 42, Sched. 2.
[49] See, for instance the *Professional Engineers Act*, R.S.O. 1990, c. P.28; the *Pharmacy Act*, S.O. 1991, c. 36; the *Architects Act*, R.S.O. 1990, C.A. 26 (am. S.O. 2006, c. 19, Sched. B, c. 1).
[50] OBCA, s. 3.2(1).

Despite any other provision of this Act but subject to subsection (6), a professional corporation shall satisfy all of the following conditions:

1. All of the issued and outstanding shares of the corporation shall be legally and beneficially owned, directly or indirectly, by one or more members of the same profession.
2. All officers and directors of the corporation shall be shareholders of the corporation.
3. The name of the corporation shall include the words "Professional Corporation" or "Société professionnelle" and shall comply with the rules respecting the names of professional corporations set out in the regulations and with the rules respecting names set out in the regulations or by-laws made under the Act governing the profession.
4. The corporation shall not have a number name.
5. The articles of incorporation of a professional corporation shall provide that the corporation may not carry on a business other than the practice of the profession but this paragraph shall not be construed to prevent the corporation from carrying on activities related to or ancillary to the practice of the profession, including the investment of surplus funds earned by the corporation.

In addition, a unanimous shareholder agreement in respect of a professional corporation is void unless each shareholder of the corporation is a member of the professional corporation,[51] and an agreement or proxy that vests in a person other than a shareholder of a professional corporation the right to vote the rights attached to a share of the corporation is void.[52]

§5.22 Subsection 3.2(6) contemplates regulations setting down detailed special rules, with respect to health profession corporations. It provides:

The Lieutenant Governor in Council may make regulations,

(a) exempting classes of health profession corporations, as defined in section 1(1) of the *Regulated Health Professions Act, 1991,* from the application of subsections (1) and (5) and such other provisions of this Act and the regulations as may be specified and prescribing terms and conditions that apply with respect to the health profession corporations in lieu of the provisions from which they are exempted;

(b) exempting classes of the shareholders of those health profession corporations from the application of subsections 3.4(2), (4) and (6) and such other provisions of this Act and the regulations as may be specified and prescribing rules that apply with respect to the shareholders in lieu of the provisions from which they are exempted;

(c) exempting directors and officers of those health profession corporations from the application of such provisions of this Act and the regulations as may be specified and prescribing rules that apply with respect to the directors and officers in lieu of the provisions from which they are exempted.

---

[51] *Ibid.*, s. 3.2(5).
[52] *Ibid.*, s. 3.2(4).

The *Health Professions Corporations Regulation* under the OBCA embodies these special rules.[53] Section 2 of the Regulation deals with physician corporations; section 3 with dentist corporations. Briefly, the regulatory provisions permit family members to hold shares in the professional corporation as well as permitting such holdings by members of the regulated professions. Provisions of the OBCA that would prevent such an arrangement are rendered inapplicable.

§5.23 Section 3.3 of the OBCA sets out a number of special rules that govern the consequences of a change in the composition of the membership of a professional corporation. Subsection 3.3(1) states:

> Despite any other Act, a professional corporation's certificate of authorization or other authorizing document remains valid and the corporation does not cease to be a professional corporation despite,
>
> (a) the death of a shareholder;
>
> (b) the divorce of a shareholder;
>
> (c) the bankruptcy or insolvency of the corporation;
>
> (d) the suspension of the corporation's certificate of authorization or other authorizing document; or
>
> (e) the occurrence of such other event or the existence of such other circumstance as may be prescribed.

Subsection 3.3(2) deals with the invalidity of certificate. It provides:

> Subject to the regulations, a certificate of authorization or other authorizing document becomes invalid and the corporation ceases to be a professional corporation on the revocation of the certificate.

While subsection 3.3(2) may result in the revocation of the status of an entity as a "professional corporation" it does not, however, cease to be a corporation. This is made clear by subsection 3.3(4), which provides:

> A corporation that ceases to be a professional corporation shall change its name to remove from it the word "professional" or "professionnelle".

Moreover, subsection 3.2(3) provides that:

> No act done by or on behalf of a professional corporation is invalid merely because it contravenes this Act.

Continued existence is essential to permit the corporation to recover debts owed to it, and to enforce its other rights, and to allow outsiders to enforce rights against the corporation. It also leaves the tax situation of the corporation intact.

§5.24 The above provisions are reinforced by subsection 3.3(3), which creates a further specific regulation making power:

---

[53] O. Reg. 665/05.

For the purposes of subsection (1), the Lieutenant Governor in Council may make regulations,

(a) prescribing events and circumstances for the purposes of clause (1)(e);

(a.1) providing that, despite clause (1)(a), (b), (c), (d) or (e), whichever applies, a professional corporation's certificate of authorization or other authorizing document ceases to be valid and the corporation ceases to be a professional corporation because of a failure to meet the terms and conditions described in the regulation;

(a.2) prescribing terms and conditions that apply with respect to the events and circumstances referred to in clauses (1)(a), (b), (c), (d) and (e);

(a.3) prescribing exceptions to the events and circumstances referred to in clauses (1)(a), (b), (c), (d) and (e);

(b) prescribing the manner in which shares of a shareholder are to be dealt with on the occurrence of any event mentioned in clauses (1)(a) to (e), the time within which they are to be dealt with and any other matter related to dealing with the shares.

However, to date no such regulations have been adopted.

§5.25 One important distinction between a professional corporation and an ordinary OBCA corporation is the partial exclusion of limited liability. In this regard, subsection 3.4(1) provides:

Subsection 92 (1) shall not be construed as limiting the professional liability of a shareholder of a professional corporation under an Act governing the profession for acts of the shareholder or acts of employees or agents of the corporation.

For the purposes of professional liability, the acts of a professional corporation shall be deemed to be the acts of the shareholders, employees or agents of the corporation, as the case may be.[54] The liability of a member for a professional liability claim is not affected by the fact that the member is practising the profession through a professional corporation.[55] A person is jointly and severally liable with a professional corporation for all professional liability claims made against the corporation in respect of errors and omissions that were made or occurred while the person was a shareholder of the corporation.[56] Thus the shareholder-professionals who stand behind a professional corporation remain liable both for their own individual negligence or other relevant breach of professional duty, and for the negligence or other breach of other professionals who are employed by the corporation, to the same extent as they would be if the profession were being practised through the medium of a partnership. Any doubt in this respect is eliminated by subsection 3.4(5), which provides:

The liability of a member under subsection (4) cannot be greater than his or her liability would be in the circumstances if he or she were not practising through the professional corporation.

---

[54] *Ibid.*, s. 3.4(2).
[55] *Ibid.*, s. 3.4(3)(c).
[56] *Ibid.*, s. 3.4(4).

In addition, subsection 3.4(6) provides:

> If a professional corporation is a partner in a partnership or limited liability partnership, the shareholders of the corporation have the same liability in respect of the partnership or limited liability partnership as they would have if the shareholders themselves were the partners.

§5.26 The scope of the corresponding liability provisions under the Alberta legislation has been considered in a number of cases. Under Alberta law, each profession continues to be governed by separate legislation, but the provisions of the various statutes are generally the same. For instance, section 34 of the *Dental Profession Act*[57] provided:

> Notwithstanding any provision to the contrary in the *Companies Act* or the *Business Corporations Act,* every person who is a shareholder of a corporation during the time that it is the holder of a permit or of a corporation during the time that it acts in contravention of this Act or a predecessor of this Act is liable to the same extent and in the same manner as if the shareholders of the corporation were, during that time, carrying on the business of the corporation as a partnership or, where there is only one shareholder, as an individual practicing dentistry.

One obvious consequence of such provisions was stated by Mahoney J. in *599291 Alberta Ltd. v. Luff*[58] with respect to the corresponding provision of the *Engineering, Geological and Geophysical Professions Act:*

> A corporation, or the facade of a corporation, cannot protect an individual professional engineer practicing engineering from liability for professional negligence against a member of the public.

A more difficult question is how much further liability extends.

§5.27 In *Bancorp. Financial Ltd. v. Thomas N. Mather Professional Corp.,*[59] a claim for payment of a mortgage debt was brought against the sole shareholder of an incorporated dental practice. The issue was whether the shareholder was personally liable by operation of the predecessor to section 77. Stratton J. said:

> The critical words are "as an individual practicing dentistry or dental surgery". Giving these words their plain, ordinary meaning I find his liability is limited to that arising from his practice of dentistry or dental surgery. To find otherwise would render the words "practicing dentistry or dental surgery" meaningless. If the legislature intended the shareholder to be personally liable for all the corporation's acts it would have drafted the section to read "liable as an individual", so that the section would end with the words "as an individual".

After further discussion of the provision, Stratton J. concluded:

> The result of this interpretation is that the dentist in a professional corporation is liable only for those activities related to his dental practice such as a breach of his professional duties. The agreed statement of facts makes it clear that the indebted-

---

[57] R.S.A. 2000, c. D-10. Repealed R.S.A. 2000, c. H-7, s. 156(*c*).
[58] [2005] A.J. No. 633 (Q.B.) regarding R.S.A. 2000, c. E-11 (am. 2006, c. 14, s. 2).
[59] [1985] A.J. No. 608, [1985] 3 W.W.R. 190 (Q.B.).

ness in issue is not related, directly or indirectly, to the practice of dentistry or dental surgery.[60]

§5.28 In contrast, in *Corkery v. Foster Wedekind*,[61] Virtue J. considered the equivalent section of the *Legal Profession Act*[62] with respect to liability for unpaid employee benefits for work done for the professional corporation. He said:

> In my view the plain meaning of the words of the section are that the sole shareholder of a professional corporation is personally liable for debts arising from the practice of law. Costs associated with maintaining the operation of an office for the practice of law including the wages and benefits of employees who are lawyers are costs directly related to carrying on the business of the practice of law and are matters for which the sole shareholder of a professional corporation remains personally liable.[63]

§5.29 In *Attorney General of Canada v. Roger M. Bourbonnais Professional Corp.*,[64] the Attorney General claimed against both the corporation and the shareholder professional for federal income tax for the 1982 year. The shareholder had practised law through his professional corporation from 1976 to 1981 when he sold his law practise and ceased to practise law in Alberta. In 1984, his professional corporation was struck-off by the Registrar of Companies for failing to file annual reports. The Attorney General claimed that subsection 116(1) of the *Legal Profession Act* rendered the shareholder personally liable for the taxes owing, plus interest and costs. Foisy J.A. rejected this approach:

> The issue on this appeal therefore, is the interpretation of subsection 116(1). Should it be interpreted narrowly to only catch those obligations that arise directly out of the practice of law, such as liability arising from professional negligence, or should it be interpreted more broadly? ... In my view the obligation of a professional corporation to pay income taxes does not arise from the practice of accountancy, or in the case before us, from the practice of law. Rather, the obligation flows from provisions of the *Income Tax Act* (Canada) which impose a tax on business income after it has been earned and without reference to the character of the business in which it was earned.

Foisy J.A. concluded that the shareholder was not personally liable for the income tax liability of his professional corporation.

§5.30 Most recently, in *Sandilands v. Powell*,[65] two shareholders of an incorporated dental practice entered into a contract for the sale of the shares, under the terms of which the practice would be purchased by another dentist. The purchaser (another incorporated practice) did not close the transaction on time or at all. The vendor shareholders brought an action against Dr. Powell P.C. and a consent judgment was given in favour of them. They then sued the appellant,

---

[60] *Ibid.*, at 192.
[61] [1987] A.J. No. 949, 88 A.R. 232 (Q.B.).
[62] R.S.A. 1980 c. L-9 (now R.S.A. 2000, c. L-8).
[63] [1987] A.J. No. 949, 88 A.R. 232 at 233 (Q.B.); see also *Edmonton Telephones Corp. v. Monette*, [1994] A.J. No. 755, 160 A.R. 72 (Q.B.).
[64] [1996] A.J. No. 378, [1996] 6 W.W.R. 571 (C.A.).
[65] [2003] A.J. No. 855, 330 A.R. 92 (C.A.).

Douglas B. Powell personally, as the shareholder of the purchaser, arguing that since Powell was the sole shareholder of Dr. Powell P.C., and since the judgment was unpaid, they were entitled to recover from Powell personally. The Alberta Court of Appeal concluded that Powell was not liable, as the purchase of the shares was not within the scope of the practice of dentistry.

§5.31 Each of the foregoing Alberta cases turned upon the specific wording in the Alberta legislation that tied liability to the practice of a profession. Whether courts construed differently worded provisions, such as section 3.4 of the OBCA, in a similarly narrow manner remains to be seen. However, it is significant that the Ontario Legislative Assembly chose not to employ the words of the Alberta legislation that have led to a narrow finding of liability.

(iii) "Three-Two" Corporations

§5.32 As noted above, paragraph 3(4)(*a*) of the CBCA prohibits corporations under that Act from engaging in the business of a company to which the *Loan and Trust Corporations Act* applies. In contrast, subsection 3(2) of the OBCA provides that a corporation may be incorporated under that Act with its powers restricted by its articles to lending and investing money on mortgage of real estate, or otherwise with its powers restricted by its articles to accepting and executing the office of liquidator, receiver, assignee, trustee-in-bankruptcy or trustee for the benefit of creditors and to accepting the duty of and acting generally in the winding-up of corporations, partnerships and estates, other than estates of deceased persons. Such a corporation is not deemed to be a corporation within the meaning of the *Trust and Loan Corporations Act*[66] by reason of conducting that business,[67] but the number of its shareholders, exclusive of persons who are in the employment of the corporation, is limited to five. No such corporation may issue debt obligations, except to its shareholders, or borrow money on the security of its property, except from its shareholders, or receive money on deposit or offer its securities to the public. In general terms, the effect of this provision is to

---

[66] Under s. 1 of the *Trust and Loan Corporations Act*, R.S.O. 1990, c. L.25, a loan corporation is:

> ... a body corporate incorporated or operated for the purpose of borrowing money from the public by receiving deposits and lending or investing such money but does not include a bank, a bank mortgage subsidiary, an insurance corporation, a trust corporation, a credit union, caisse populaire or league under the *Credit Unions and Caisses Populaires Act, 1994* or a retail association under the *Cooperative Credit Associations Act* (Canada) ...

A trust corporation is defined to be:

> ... a body corporate incorporated or operated,
>
> (a) for the purpose of offering its services to the public to act as trustee, bailee, agent, executor, administrator, receiver, liquidator, assignee, guardian of property or attorney under a power of attorney for property, and
>
> (b) for the purpose of receiving deposits from the public and of lending or investing such deposits.

[67] See also *Sidmay Ltd. v. Wehttam Investments Ltd.*, [1967] O.J. No. 946, [1967] 1 O.R. 508, aff'd [1968] S.C.J. No. 63, [1968] S.C.R. 828.

permit a private corporation to engage in some functions reserved to companies under the *Loan and Trust Corporations Act,* provided that such a private corporation does not raise funds by public subscription.

(iv) The Procedure for Incorporation

§5.33 As discussed in Chapter 1, both the OBCA and the CBCA employ what is known as a registration regime of incorporation, under which a corporation comes into existence upon the registration with a specified government agency of certain prescribed documents. This method of incorporation was unrecognized at common law. An early version of this method, sometimes called the memorandum of association regime, was introduced into the law of England by statute in 1844, and came into Canadian law shortly thereafter by way of a statute for Upper Canada.[68] The present legislation succeeds to the registration approach, but adopts a markedly different procedure from that which applies in memorandum jurisdictions. It makes use of few conventions that historically have been employed in corporate law regimes. For instance, under a memorandum of association regime (as in Nova Scotia), the creation of a company inherently involves the formation of a contract of incorporation among its members. In contrast, the formation of a corporation under either the OBCA or the CBCA is not a matter of contract, but instead is purely a matter of statute.[69]

§5.34 Both the OBCA and the CBCA require the Director to incorporate a corporation where the required statutory and regulatory conditions are met. There is no discretion to refuse incorporation,[70] and thus neither the Minister nor any departmental official may refuse to incorporate on any criteria, other than a failure to comply with the statutory requirements. The absence of such discretion has important regulatory implications. For instance, a wrongful refusal by the registrar to create a corporation following the submission of a properly completed application for incorporation, and compliance by the incorporators with all other requirements for incorporation, will be subject to judicial review.[71]

---

[68] See Stats. U.C. 12 Vic. 56; see also *An Act for the Formation of Incorporated Joint-Stock Companies for Manufacturing, Mining, Mechanical or Chemical Purposes,* 1850, S.U.C. 13-14 Vic., c. 28.
[69] *Emerson v. New Brunswick (Provincial Secretary-Treasurer),* [1941] 2 D.L.R. 232, 15 M.P.R. 406 (N.B.C.A.).
[70] Thus s. 8 of the CBCA provides that "on receipt of articles of incorporation, the Director *shall* issue a certificate of incorporation in accordance with section 262". See also OBCA, s. 6. Under the old Ontario *Corporations Act,* R.S.O. 1960, s. 3(1), a discretionary power was conferred upon the Lieutenant Governor (acting through the Provincial Secretary). For cases providing guidance as to the manner in which the discretion was to be exercised, see *Sharp v. Wakefield,* [1891] A.C. 173 (H.L.) and *Re C. Cole & Co.,* [1965] 2 O.R. 243 (C.A.). Subsection 8(2) of the CBCA does empower the Director to refuse to issue a certificate "if a notice that is required to be sent ... indicates that the corporation, if it came into existence, would not be in compliance with the Act".
[71] See, for instance, *R. v. Registrar of Joint Stock Companies, ex p. Moore,* [1931] 2 K.B. 197; *R. v. Reg. of Companies, ex p. Brown,* [1914] 3 K.B. 1161 (Div. Ct.).

§5.35 Furthermore, as practical matter, the incorporation procedure under the OBCA and CBCA involves little in the way of administrative review or oversight of the incorporation process, beyond confirmation that:

(a) all required incorporation documents have been filed and appear on their face to be properly completed; and

(b) there is no other patent impediment to incorporation, such as an unsuitable name.

In contrast, for many other types of companies (especially regulated financial institutions such as banks, insurance companies, trust and loan companies and credit unions), public authorities play a much more active role[72] in assessing the apparent viability of the proposed corporate entity (including whether there is a realistic business plan), its proposed capital structure, and other critical aspects proposed with respect to its internal affairs and proposed business.[73] However, even though such regulatory discretion has been eliminated under the OBCA and the CBCA, the incorporators may not obtain an order in the nature of *mandamus* compelling the incorporation of the corporation until they have complied fully with all statutory and regulatory formalities and requirements in respect of a proposed corporation.[74] Once these steps have been taken, the Director may not impose additional requirements.[75] As a result of the elimination of the element of discretion, the incorporation procedure has become streamlined, and requires little time.[76] Ontario corporate charters can usually be obtained on the day of application, provided the application is in order.[77]

---

[72] See, for instance, *R. ex rel. Wong v. British Columbia Registrar of Companies*, [1950] 2 W.W.R. 665 (B.C.S.C.); *Re Crown Lumber Co.*, [1943] 2 W.W.R. 679 (Alta. T.D.).

[73] See, generally, *Legion Credit Union (Co-liquidators of) v. British Columbia (Minister of Finance and Corporate Relations)*, [1994] B.C.J. No. 379, 45 A.C.W.S. (3d) 1204 (S.C.).

[74] *Re Pioneer Savings & Loan Society*, [1928] 1 W.W.R. 361 (B.C.C.A.); see also *Niagara Falls Road Co. v. Benson* (1852), 8 U.C.Q.B. 307 (Ont. C.A.).

[75] *R. ex rel. Enid Jubilee Mines Ltd. v. British Columbia Registrar of Companies*, [1934] 1 W.W.R. 393 at 394 (B.C.C.A.), *per* Macdonald C.J.B.C.

[76] For an example of the bureaucratic obstacles placed in the way of companies under the old discretionary regime, see *Re Crown Lumber Co.*, [1943] 2 W.W.R. 679 (Alta. T.D.). In that case a company sought to amend its memorandum of association, to correct certain errors made when rules set out in Table A to the *Companies Act*, R.S.A. 1942, c. 240, s. 38(1) had been improperly copied. The alterations would have enabled the company to carry on its business more economically and better attain its principal object. Nevertheless, the Registrar rejected the proposed amendments.

[77] It was the extraordinary delay in the time required to incorporate a company, together with the practical absurdity of any meaningful review of applications for incorporation (given the numbers concerned) which provided much of the impetus to the enactment of the original OBCA. The *1967 Interim Report of the Select Committee on Company Law* (the "Lawrence Report") (Toronto: Queens Printer) made the following observations, at ¶¶ 1.1.6-1.1.7:

> 1.1.6 Over 700 applications for incorporation and over 1300 applications for supplementary letters patent are filed with the Provincial Secretary's Department each year and these numbers will likely increase. The Committee has concluded that the duty and responsibility imposed upon the Minister by the Ontario Act in the exercise of his discretionary power to grant or amend charters of companies cannot be discharged in a meaningful way; that the Ontario system of incorporation by ministerial act is an historical anachronism which ought not to be preserved; and that modern public policy no longer requires that a corporation can come into being only by ministerial act.

§5.36 Generally speaking the incorporation of an OBCA or CBCA corporation is a fairly routine matter that frequently is handled quite competently by untrained lay-people with little or no legal assistance beyond the instructions provided in the packages of incorporation documents that may be purchased at any office supply store. Nevertheless, the incorporation of a company can go wrong. It is essential to make sure that the documents are filed properly and that they record the intent of the incorporators with respect to such matters as internal governance, the say that each incorporator or subsequent shareholder is to enjoy in the corporation, the nature of the capital structure and so forth. Restrictions on the lines of business in which the corporation may engage need to be very carefully provided for. The more numerous and complex the matters to be dealt with (*e.g.*, where it is intended to provide for redeemable or retractable shares, or it is intended to confer some preferential right on the shares of a given class), the greater the need to obtain professional advice. Where property is to be transferred to the corporation by a shareholder, getting tax planning advice is usually worth while. Such advice is also wise where the incorporators and subscribers for shares in the corporation are expected to pay different types of consideration for the shares that are issued to them, or the time at which the shares are to be paid for and allotted is likely to vary. Unless the incorporators are sophisticated business people, they are well-advised to seek professional advice as to the adequacy of capitalization, regulatory controls and prohibitions on the business in which they propose to engage, the implications of shareholder guarantees and the like. This need increases where it is intended to carry on business in two or more jurisdictions, especially where one of them will be a foreign (*i.e.*, non-Canadian) jurisdiction. Tax planning advice is prudent for any corporation; it is especially necessary where there is an international element. Unless there is a substantial identity of interest among the various incorporators, individual (*i.e.*, independent) advice will usually be worth while — both from the perspective of the individuals concerned, as well as from the perspective of their associates and the professionals who are advising them. The main areas of concern in the incorporation process are to:

- ensure that the incorporation documents reflect the incorporators' underlying business objectives and provide a workable set of rules for the conduct of the corporation's business and affairs;
- ensure that the corporation is properly organized as well as incorporated;

1.1.7 The present Ontario method of incorporation and charter amendment results in administrative procedures which are unnecessarily cumbersome and invite unwanted administrative interference. The existing practice of engrossing letters patent and supplementary letters patent for ministerial signature results in further delay. As a practical illustration, the Committee is advised that to incorporate a company in Ontario under the letters patent system requires at least three weeks and that to incorporate a company by way of certificate of incorporation in New York requires not more than 48 hours, in each case assuming no undue difficulty as to the proposed corporate name.

- ensure that any pre-existing business is properly assumed by the corporation, and that any residual liabilities of the incorporators with respect to that business are mitigated to the greatest extent possible;
- avoid unexpected adverse tax consequences;
- provide properly for routine business hazards that are almost certain to be encountered at some point in the life of the corporation (*e.g.*, the death of a participant in the incorporation, or the desire of one of the incorporators to move on to some new opportunity);
- anticipate the possibility that the relationship between the parties may ultimately not work out, and so far as possible provide mechanisms that permit the incorporators to
    - allow them to identify, assess and deal appropriately with the types of risk that are likely to be encountered in carrying on a business;
    - deal with small problems as they arise in a business-like manner, with minimal friction and disappointed expectations; and
    - extricate themselves from the business where problems of a substantial nature are encountered that cannot be resolved through negotiation in good faith.

Where there are incorporators of different bargaining strength or degrees of sophistication, or where one has greater access to information or will have greater control over the corporation than the other(s), further specific areas of professional responsibility are to:[78]

- ensure that the weaker party understands the risks that arise in such a situation;[79]
- confirm (so far as possible) that the weaker party is making an independent and informed decision; and
- mitigate (so far as possible) the risk that the stronger party will abuse his or her position of strength.

§5.37 To some extent the value of even the best legal advice ultimately turns upon the ability of the client to make effective use of that advice. Clients (and prospective clients) should be educated to understand that:

- While the cost of legal advice is obviously a concern to most clients, it is often dangerous to choose a lawyer based purely on an estimate of fees. An equally important consideration is to confirm that the a lawyer is suitably

---

[78] For a case illustrating the kinds of things that can go wrong even where lawyers are involved in the incorporation of a business, see *Rhude et al. v. Corbett*, [1981] N.S.J. No. 464, 47 N.S.R. (2d) 472, 90 A.P.R. 472 (S.C.).

[79] For a case illustrating the potential problems associated with an imbalance in the sophistication of the incorporators, see *MacKenzie v. MacKenzie*, [1980] P.E.I.J. No. 58, 6 A.C.W.S. (2d) 70 (S.C.).

- Clients need to provide a proper description and explanation of their objectives and concerns to their lawyers, in order for the lawyers to be able to provide advice that is tailored to their situation.

- It is ill-advised for someone to pretend to have training or experience that they do not possess.

- To ensure that the documentation prepared will reflect client intentions, clients need to provide to the lawyer copies of any written documents records that explain previous dealings and the overall intent underlying the creation of the corporation.

- There are serious risks in seeking simple, quick answers to complex questions.

(v) The Role of Incorporators

§5.38 An incorporator is a person who seeks to set the incorporation process in motion so as to bring about the incorporation of a company. The active application of one or more incorporators is required for a corporation to be created. The incorporator need not be a natural person, nor need he or she be a citizen of Canada or a resident of Ontario. Under the present law, as a general rule a person (including both an individual and a corporation) may incorporate a corporation alone or in combination with another person. Where an individual seeks to incorporate a corporation, the individual must (1) be at least 18 years of age;[80] (2) not have been found to be of unsound mind by a court in Canada or elsewhere; and (3) not have the status of a bankrupt.[81] These restrictions do not apply where the incorporator is a body corporate.

§5.39 The motive of an incorporator in bringing about the creation of a corporation is almost always irrelevant to the question of whether the courts will recognize the separate corporate existence of the entity so created. In particular, even where it is clear that the sole intent was to obtain the benefit of limited liability, or the sometimes preferential tax treatment to which incorporation can lead, the courts will still recognize the separate existence of the corporation. So, for instance, in *Westfair Properties Ltd. v. Wilson*,[82] Nurgitz J. commented:

> ... the establishment of a corporation was indeed to limit its liability but that it is a legal device open and available to these directors and to any other person pursuing a legal and legitimate purpose.

The only real exception to this general rule is where the intent in creating a corporation is fraudulent.

---

[80] As to the effect of a minor signing the articles as an incorporator, see *Re Nassau Phosphate Co.* (1876), 2 Ch. D. 610; and *Re Laxon & Co. (No. 2)*, [1892] 3 Ch. 555.
[81] CBCA, s. 5(1); OBCA, s. 4(1).
[82] (1998), 133 Man. R. (2d) 191 (Q.B.).

C. THE CORPORATE CONSTITUTION

§5.40 Every company has certain basic charter documents that constitute the fundamental terms of the corporation concerned. In exercising its powers, carrying on its business and organizing its affairs, every company must stay within the boundaries traced out by that constitution.[83] The nature of the documents comprising the corporate constitution depends upon the statute under which the company is incorporated, and may take the form of letters patent, a special Act, articles of incorporation or a memorandum of incorporation. There are certain common aspects to the constitution of every company: it will specify rights to the capital of the company, provide for the distribution of profit and risk among the members of the company, and set out the division of control within the company. In so doing, the corporate constitution may contain any number of provisions relating to the officers of the company. More importantly, the corporate constitution will usually contain: the name of the company and of its incorporators; the place of the registered or head office; a description of the capital that the corporation is authorized to issue, including the terms of all shares; any restrictions on share transfer; the size of the board of directors and the names of the first directors; any restrictions on the objects or business of the company (in some jurisdictions, it is necessary to specify the actual objects of the company); and any restrictions on the exercise of the powers of the company.

§5.41 Some jurisdictions (*e.g.*, Ontario, Canada, Alberta and Saskatchewan) also provide in their business corporations legislation for unanimous shareholder agreements. A unanimous shareholder agreement is an agreement among the shareholders of a corporation that restricts in whole or in part the powers of the directors to manage the business and affairs of the corporation. Such an agreement is also one of the basic charter documents of the corporation and binds the corporation and its board of directors as well as the shareholders who are parties to it.[84]

(i) The Articles of a Corporation

§5.42 For most OBCA and CBCA corporations, the basic charter documents consist of the articles of incorporation. Articles of continuation, where the corporation was originally incorporated under some other statute and then continued under the OBCA or CBCA, as the case may be); articles of amalgamation are also frequently encountered, together with any amendments or other variations to each of the foregoing types of articles. The definition of the term "articles" found in subsection 2(1) of the CBCA is narrower than the corresponding definition found in the OBCA. The CBCA definition reads:

> "articles" means the original or restated articles of incorporation, articles of amendment, articles of amalgamation, articles of continuance, articles of reorgani-

---

[83] *McKenna v. Spooner Oils Ltd.*, [1934] 1 W.W.R. 255 at 256 (Alta. T.D.), *per* Ives J.
[84] The subject of unanimous shareholder agreements is discussed in detail in Chapter 12, Shareholders and Their Rights.

zation, articles of arrangement, articles of dissolution, articles of revival and includes any amendments thereto;

A more expansive definition of the term "articles" is found in subsection 1(1) of the OBCA, which reads:

> "articles" means the original or restated articles of incorporation, articles of amendment, articles of amalgamation, articles of arrangement, articles of continuance, articles of dissolution, articles of reorganization, articles of revival, letters patent, supplementary letters patent, a special Act and any other instrument by which a corporation is incorporated.

The difference in the wording of the definition that exists between the two statutes arises in part from the fact that when the OBCA was enacted, corporations to which it applied which were incorporated prior to the date when it came into effect were not required to continue under the OBCA. In contrast, such continuation was required under the CBCA, with the result that all CBCA corporations operate either under articles of incorporation, articles of amendment, articles of amalgamation, articles of arrangement, articles of continuance, articles of dissolution, articles of reorganization, or articles of revival, which in each case must have been issued under the CBCA. In addition, the wider definition under the OBCA clarifies the meaning of certain provisions of the Act which apply to non-OBCA corporations.[85]

§5.43 Incorporation under both the OBCA[86] and the CBCA[87] is by way of certificate of incorporation, issued (or, in the case of the OBCA, endorsed) by the Director under whichever of the Acts is concerned. Subsection 273(1) of the OBCA further explains that:

> 273.(1) Where this Act requires that articles relating to a corporation be sent to the Director, unless otherwise specifically provided,
>
> (a) two duplicate originals of the articles shall be signed by a director or an officer of the corporation or, in the case of articles of incorporation, by an incorporator; and
>
> (b) upon receiving duplicate originals of any articles in the prescribed form that have been executed in accordance with this Act, any other required documents and prescribed fees, the Director shall, subject to ... subsection (2),
>
> > (i) endorse on each duplicate original a certificate, setting out the day, month and year of endorsement and the corporation number,
> >
> > (ii) file a copy of the articles with the endorsement certificate thereon, and
> >
> > (iii) send to the corporation or its representative one duplicate original of the articles with the endorsement of the certificate thereon. ...

Subsection 273(4) now contemplates the filing of articles in electronic form. Subsection 273(2) provides that certificates of the type described in subsection

---

[85] For instance, s. 180(3) of the OBCA, dealing with continuance. Compare s. 187(2) of the CBCA.
[86] OBCA, ss. 6, 7.
[87] CBCA, ss. 8, 9.

(1) shall be dated as of the day the Director receives the duplicate originals of any articles together with all other required documents executed in accordance with the Act and the prescribed fee, or as of any later date acceptable to the Director and specified by the person who submitted the articles or by the court. Where there are several integral steps that must be taken to complete a mandatory procedure, it is necessary for the legislation to specify at which point in the chain of steps the procedure becomes effective. In the context of incorporation, subsection 273(3) makes clear that articles endorsed with a certificate are effective on the date shown in the certificate, even if any action required to be taken by the Director with respect to the endorsement of the certificate and filing by the Director is taken at a later date.[88]

§5.44 Subsections 5(1) of the OBCA and 6(1) of the CBCA provide that in the case of each Act, the articles of incorporation must follow the prescribed form.[89] Only articles in the prescribed form will be accepted.[90] The two forms are similar. However, the form prescribed under the OBCA requires the street address of the registered office and the name and address of the incorporators and first directors[91] are set out in the articles, while under the CBCA, the names and addresses of the first directors[92] and the street address of the registered office are provided in separate notices filed together with the articles of incorporation.[93] Section 6 of the CBCA does not specifically require the names and addresses of the incorporators to be set out in the articles of incorporation, but this information is required under Form 1, the form of articles of incorporation prescribed by the regulations. Despite these mandatory requirements, considerable flexibility is permitted in the structuring the terms of the articles.

§5.45 Clause 273(1)(*a*) of the OBCA requires the articles to be filed in duplicate and signed by an incorporator.[94] While this clause and subsection 4(1) of that Act suggests that it is not necessary for all incorporators to sign, Form 1 under the OBCA *General Regulation*[95] (the prescribed form of articles) suggests that every incorporator must sign. The normal practice is for all incorporators to sign the articles of incorporation. Subsection 24(4) of the *General Regulation* provides that articles, applications or statements filed with the Director signed by one or more persons shall be signed manually by each such person and not by an

---

[88] See also CBCA, s. 262.
[89] OBCA, s. 4(1).
[90] CBCA, s. 6(1); OBCA, s. 5(1).
[91] Subsection 5(2) of the OBCA provides that where the articles name as a first director an individual who is not an incorporator, the consent of that individual in prescribed form must accompany the articles. The prescribed form of consent is set out in Form 2 under the Regulations.
[92] Historically, it has been necessary to disclose the residence address, and it is not difficult to understand why. The purpose for the disclosure is so that an originating court process may be served on each person concerned. By virtue of Rule 16.03(5) of the *Rules of Civil Procedure*, R.R.O. 1990, Reg. 194, the normal place for service is an individual's address. A business address is not.
[93] CBCA, ss. 19, 106.
[94] An electronic signature may be employed in electronic filing: OBCA, s. 273(4).
[95] R.R.O. 1990, Reg. 62.

attorney. However, where a body corporate is an incorporator, the articles may be signed by a director or an officer of that body corporate.[96]

§5.46 Under subsection 6(1) of the CBCA there are four specific subjects that must be dealt with in the articles, namely: (a) the name of the corporation; (b) the place within Canada where the registered office is to be situated; (c) the number of directors, or the maximum or minimum number of directors; (d) the classes and any maximum number of shares that the corporation is authorized to issue. The prescribed requirements under the OBCA are similar. If there are to be two or more classes of shares, the articles must specify the rights, privileges, restrictions and conditions attaching to each class of shares; if the shares of a class may be issued in series, then the articles must provide the directors with the authority to fix the number of shares in a series and to determine the designation of, and the rights, privileges, restrictions and conditions attached to each series. In addition to the foregoing, (if the incorporators are inclined to include such restrictions) the articles must also contain certain specific types of provision relating to the conduct of the business and affairs of the corporation, namely: (a) the nature of any restriction on the right to transfer shares, and (b) any restrictions on the businesses that the corporation may carry on.[97] In other words, in order for provisions of this type to be valid, they must be set out in the articles — a provision in the by-laws of the corporation is not satisfactory. The CBCA also permits the articles of a corporation (or a unanimous shareholders' agreement) to increase the number of votes of directors or shareholders of a corporation above any requirement set out in the Act. Once again, it would seem that a provision in the by-laws to this effect would not be satisfactory, but the articles may contain any provisions that are permitted by the Act or by law to be set out in the by-laws of the corporation or in a unanimous shareholder agreement.[98]

§5.47 The status of the articles of a corporation under the OBCA and the CBCA is unclear. While the articles of the corporation clearly bind the corporation,[99] and its directors and officers,[100] both Acts are silent as to their effect upon the members of the corporation. In memorandum of association corporate law regimes, the company's constitution is usually deemed by statute to be binding and effective between the company and its members, and among the members of

---

[96] OBCA, s. 272(1)(*a*): the use of the term "corporation" in this clause rather than "body corporate" is probably a simple misnomer, and it is unlikely that the section would be interpreted as dispensing with the need for a signature in the case of an application for incorporation filed by a body corporate that was not a "corporation" within the meaning of the OBCA.
[97] CBCA, s. 6(1).
[98] CBCA, s. 6(2); OBCA, s. 5(3).
[99] CBCA, s. 16(2); OBCA, s. 17(2):

(2) A corporation shall not carry on any business or exercise any power that is restricted by its articles from carrying on or exercising, nor shall the corporation exercise any of its powers in a manner contrary to its articles.

[100] CBCA, s.122(2); OBCA, s. 134(2):

(2) Every director and officer of a corporation shall comply with this Act, the regulations, articles, by-laws and any unanimous shareholder agreement.

the company themselves, as a contract.[101] The use of contract theory as a basis for the corporate constitution seemed a logical progression: it appears to have originated in the deed of settlement employed before the reforms to English corporate law in 1844.

§5.48 In contrast, there is no such contract under the OBCA and CBCA — which begs the question of whether the shareholders of the corporation are bound to observe the articles or by-laws, or whether they may simply ignore them.[102] There is some indication in the case law that a by-law may not be binding on a corporation where the shareholders of the corporation decide unanimously to ignore it. Thus in *Classic Hosiery Co. v. Fillis*[103] it was held that the shareholders of the company, when assembled in a general meeting, constituted the supreme forum of the company concerning everything relating to its internal affairs. If the shareholders unanimously resolved to ignore the company's by-laws or the provisions contained in them, a shareholder who consented to the resolution would not subsequently be allowed to complain of the irregularity.[104] However, subsections 5(3) of the OBCA and 6(2) of the CBCA provide that the articles may set out any provisions permitted by the Act or by law to be set out in the by-laws of a corporation, and where any provision is so included in the articles, it is undoubtedly binding upon the corporation.[105]

§5.49 Despite the uncertainty surrounding the articles and by-laws of a corporation with respect to their application to dealings among the shareholders, their actual status and effect may well be moot. Under section 253 of the OBCA[106] a complainant may apply to the court for an order directing the corporation or any person to comply with its articles, by-laws or a unanimous shareholder agreement. Similarly, a complainant may seek relief under section 248 of the OBCA — the oppression remedy — where the complainant's interests (as opposed to the narrower term "rights") have been oppressed, treated in an unfairly prejudicial manner or unfairly disregarded. Complainants also have standing to seek court authority to institute a derivative action on behalf of the corporation where a right of the corporation has been transgressed. These various statutory remedies provide protection to shareholder interests at least equivalent to that afforded under those statutes which deem the articles and by-laws of a company to be a contract among the members of the company. Moreover, the term "com-

---

[101] See, for instance, *Theatre Amusement Co. v. Stone* (1914), 50 S.C.R. 32 at 36, *per* Duff J.
[102] See, generally, *Young v. Newfoundland Dried Squid Exporters Association* (1949), 24 M.P.R. 245, [1950] 2 D.L.R. 772 (Nfld. T.D.).
[103] (1920), 18 O.W.N. 17 at 18 (H.C.), *per* Logie J.
[104] Compare, however, *Paul v. Kobold* (1906), 3 W.L.R. 407 (N.W.T.C.A.), where only a majority (as opposed to all) approved the violation of the by-laws. Arguably, a matter approved by a sufficient majority of shareholders to amend the articles would be sufficient. See, generally, *MacDougall v. Gardiner* (1875), 1 Ch. D. 13 at 25 (C.A.), *per* Mellish, L.J. but cf. *Re Haycraft Gold Reduction & Mining Co.*, [1900] 2 Ch. 230; *Boschoek Proprietary Co. Ltd. v. Fuke*, [1906] 1 Ch. 148; *Pappaioannoy v. The Greek Orthodox Community of Melbourne* (1978), 3 A.C.L.R. 801.
[105] CBCA, s. 16(2); OBCA, s. 17(2).
[106] CBCA, s. 247.

plainant" is broadly defined, and extends the protection of these remedies to outsiders, rather than limiting them to shareholders.

(ii) By-laws

§5.50 For the most part, the articles of a corporation contain only the most basic provisions concerning the corporation: its name, the structure of its share capital, the place of its registered office, the size of the board of directors, and any restrictions on the business in which it may engage. It is unusual for the articles to contain any provisions concerning the administration of the corporation, or the general conduct of its business and affairs. It often happens, however, that a corporation may set out fairly detailed rules with respect to such matters in a collection of rules known as the by-laws of the corporation. Thus if the articles of a corporation set out the area beyond which the actions of a corporation cannot go, the by-laws of the corporation set out the regulations governing conduct within the areas permitted by the articles; and in so doing the general rule is that the shareholders may make such regulations for their own government as they consider fit.[107]

§5.51 A by-law[108] is a regulation, rule or ordinance adopted by a company for the regulation of its own actions and concerns, and of the rights and duties of its members among themselves.[109] As such, it regulates or controls the conduct of the company's business or affairs, or some aspect thereof.[110] The by-laws of a corporation may not be contrary to its articles.[111] Somewhat differently stated: the by-laws of a corporation are subordinate to the articles in the sense that the by-laws cannot confer powers that are excluded by or not conferred under the articles.[112] If there is any inconsistency between the two, the articles will prevail and any purported alteration of the articles made by way of by-law is void to the extent of the inconsistency.[113] The by-laws cannot be used to fill in a gap in an area which must by law be dealt with in the articles, first, because the terms and conditions set out in the articles are there for the protection of the creditors of the corporation and other outsiders, as well as for the shareholders,[114] and second, because both the OBCA and the CBCA impose certain procedural safeguards to preserve the rights of dissenting shareholders in the case of

---

[107] *Ashbury Railway Carriage & Iron Co. v. Riche* (1875), L.R. 7 H.L. 653 at 671, *per* Lord Cairns L.C.
[108] According to Wegenast, *Canadian Companies*, reprint (Toronto: Carswell, 1979), the term is derived from "bye" (a synonym for village) to denote a local law as distinct from a law of the country (at 243).
[109] *Manes Tailoring Co. v. Willson* (1907), 14 O.L.R. 89 at 96 (H.C.), *per* Magee J.
[110] *Mackenzie v. Maple Mountain Mining Co.* (1910), 20 O.L.R. 615 at 618 (C.A.), *per* Osler J.A.
[111] *Guinness v. Land Corp. of Ireland*, (1882), 22 Ch. D. 349.
[112] *Caleron Properties Ltd. v. 510207 Alberta Ltd.*, [2000] A.J. No. 1237, 9 B.L.R. (3d) 218 (Q.B.).
[113] See, generally, *Ashbury v. Watson* (1885), 30 Ch. D. 376 at 383 (C.A.), *per* Baggallay L.J., *per* Fry L.J. at 384-85.
[114] *Guinness v. Land Corp. of Ireland* (1882), 22 Ch. D. 349 (C.A.).

amendments to the articles.[115] More generally, the articles of the corporation will be construed without reference to its by-laws.[116]

§5.52 Within these general limits, the function of the by-laws of a company is to prescribe the rights and duties of shareholders and directors with reference to the internal government of the company, the management of its affairs, and the rights and duties existing between the members themselves. Thus by-laws will normally deal with the following matters:

- the form of share certificate and corporate seal;
- the procedure to be followed in subscribing for, allotting and recording the issue of shares;
- the records and books to be kept by the corporation, and the responsibility of particular senior officers (*e.g.*, the secretary and the treasurer) with respect to such records and books;
- signing authorities and the appointment, remuneration, function, duties, and removal of agents, officers and employees of the corporation, and the security, if any, to be given by them in respect of the performance of their duties;
- the time, place and notice to be given for the holding of meetings of the directors (including telephone meetings), the quorum at such meetings, and the procedures to be followed at those meetings;
- the time, place and notice to be given for the holding of meetings of the shareholders and other security holders, the quorum at such meetings, and the procedures to be followed at those meetings;
- the qualification and remuneration of directors, the indemnification of directors, and the time and manner for the election of directors;
- standing committees of the directors, and in particular the executive committee and the audit committee;

---

[115] *Alexander v. Bar SP Ranches Ltd.*, [1990] S.J. No. 876, 190 Sask. R. 1 at para. 49 (Q.B.), *per* Baynton J., aff'd [2000] S.J. No. 723 (C.A.):

> Although closely held corporations are permitted to enact by-laws and resolutions to expedite directors and shareholders meetings and to facilitate operational decisions, there are a few basic statutory requirements that must be met. Most of them pertain to the content and length of notices that must be sent to shareholders before certain actions can be validly taken on behalf of the corporation ... These statutory requirements apply even though a minotiry shareholder may well be out-voted by the majority sahreholders at a duly called and constituted meeting. But at a minimum they guarantee that minority shareholders must be advised of the proposal in question and have the right to attend the meeting, speak to the proposal and attempt to influence the decision that will ultimately be made respectivng it. If the directors and shareholders of a corporation ignore these basic requirements, they do so not only at their own peril, but they put the interests of the corporation at risk as well.

[116] *Re Duncan Gilmour & Co. Ltd.*, [1952] 2 All E.R. 871: If it were otherwise, then provisions of the articles could be amended without compliance with the procedures governing changes to the articles of the corporation.

- dealings with the property of the corporation and certain aspects of the banking operations of the corporation;
- controls and restrictions upon the exercise of corporate powers;
- execution of instruments by the corporation.

For the most part, a by-law differs from a resolution in that a by-law is a permanent and continuing rule, whereas a resolution usually relates to a single act of the company.[117] By-laws may also be enacted to confer a particular authority of either a one-time or continuing nature on the directors.

§5.53 In general, the normal rules of documentary construction will govern the interpretation of the articles and by-laws of a corporation.[118] So far as practical, effect will be given to the plain English meaning of a by-law.[119] However, the by-laws of a corporation are given a liberal as opposed to a technical construction by the courts, as explained by Jenkins L.J.:

> I think that the articles of association of the company should be regarded as a business document and should be construed so as to give them reasonable business efficacy, where a construction tending to that result is admissible on the language of the articles, in preference to a result which would or might prove unworkable.[120]

Thus the courts avoid drawing fine distinctions, and, in an appropriate case, the court will imply a term into a by-law in order to give effect to its apparent intention.[121] When different interpretations are open, the court will choose that which is most practical and workable.[122]

(1) Enactment of By-laws

§5.54 Although under many company law statutes, corporate entities are required to have by-laws (or similar rules otherwise described) in addition to their fundamental charter document, there is no such requirement under either the OBCA or the CBCA. On the contrary, both Acts expressly provide that:

> It is not necessary for a by-law to be passed in order to confer any particular power on the corporation or its directors.[123]

In fact, this provision is misleading, for there are a number of powers that by the express wording of the Act must be conferred by by-law (or by the articles),[124] such as the power to conduct meetings of the board at a place other than the

---

[117] *James v. Beaver Consolidated Mines Ltd.* (1927), 60 O.L.R. 420 at 423 (H.C.), *per* Wright J.; see also *Mackenzie v. Maple Mountain Mining Co.* (1910), 20 O.L.R. 615 (C.A); *Denault v. Stewart, Denault & Co.* (1918), 54 Que. S.C. 209 (Ct. of Rev.).
[118] See, for instance, *Oakbank Oil Co. v. Crum* (1882), 8 App. Cas. 65 (H.L.).
[119] *Beechwood Cemetery Co. v. Graham*, [1998] O.J. No. 5289, 41 B.L.R. (2d) 171 (C.A.).
[120] *Holmes v. Lord Keyes*, [1959] Ch. 199 at 215 (C.A.), *per* Jenkins L.J.
[121] *Mutual Life Insurance Co. of New York v. Rank Organization Ltd.*, [1985] B.C.L.C. 11 at 21.
[122] *Holmes v. Lord Keyes*, [1959] Ch. 199 at 219 (C.A.), *per* Ormerod L.J.
[123] CBCA, s. 16(1); OBCA, s. 17(1).
[124] OBCA, s. 5(3); CBCA, s. 6(2).

registered office of the corporation.[125] Other powers may be taken away by by-law.[126] Still others must be authorized by special resolution.[127] Where, however, the corporation is prepared to operate without the benefit of these few powers (as many corporations do), there is no need for by-laws at all.

§5.55 To be effective, a corporate by-law must be adopted in the manner specified in the applicable legislation (*i.e.*, the OBCA or CBCA),[128] and any by-law not so adopted will fall. The directors of a corporation are given extensive by-law making powers. For instance, subsection 116(1) of the OBCA provides that unless the articles, the by-laws or a unanimous shareholder agreement otherwise provide, the directors may by resolution make, amend or repeal any by-laws that regulate the business or affairs of a corporation. Where they do so, they must submit the by-law, *etc.*, for shareholder confirmation to the next meeting of shareholders.[129] During the interim period, the new by-law or amendment or repeal is effective.[130] If the shareholders reject a proposed by-law, amendment or repeal, then:

> ... no subsequent resolution of the directors to make, amend or repeal a by-law having substantially the same purpose or effect is effective until it is confirmed or confirmed as amended by the shareholders.[131]

The shareholders of a corporation have a direct power to enact by-laws on their own initiative by way of shareholder proposal. Where such a proposal is approved, the by-law (or amendment or repeal) "is effective from the date of its adoption and requires no further confirmation".[132]

§5.56 In *Re Pakenham Pork Packing Co.*,[133] the Act under which a company was incorporated provided that in order to create preference shares it was necessary for the directors to pass a by-law for that purpose and for the by-law to be unanimously approved by the shareholders at a meeting duly called for the purpose of considering the by-law. Instead of following this procedure, the shareholders purported to pass a resolution to create the preference shares at a meeting called for another purpose. This resolution was held to be insufficient, as the statutory requirements had not been satisfied.[134] Nevertheless, the by-laws

---

[125] OBCA, s. 125(3).
[126] See, for instance, s. 127(1) of the OBCA under which the power of delegation to a managing director is made subject to the articles or by-laws of the corporation.
[127] See, for instance, s. 125(3) of the OBCA, which empowers the directors to fix the number of directors where the articles provide for a maximum and minimum number of directors.
[128] But see *Re Owen Sound Dry Dock Shipping & Navigation Co.* (1891), 21 O.R. 349 at 351-52 (H.C.), *per* the Master's Report (confirmed by Robertson J. at 354). See also *Merchants Bank of Canada v. Handcock* (1883), 6 O.R. 285 at 289-90 (H.C.), *per* Boyd C.
[129] OBCA, s. 116(2).
[130] *Ibid.*, s. 116(3).
[131] *Ibid.*, s. 116(4).
[132] *Ibid.*, s. 116(5).
[133] (*Galloway's Case*) (1906), 12 O.L.R. 100 at 109 (C.A.), *per* Moss C.J.O.
[134] *Kelly v. Electrical Construction Co.* (1907), 16 O.L.R. 232 at 238-39 (H.C.), *per* Mullock C.J. Ex.

of a corporation can only be enacted in the manner expressly or impliedly provided by the legislation to which the corporation is subject.[135]

§5.57 Neither the OBCA nor the CBCA provide much in the way of guidance as to what a by-law may contain. To determine the scope of the by-law making power of a corporation one may refer to the pre-CBCA case law to determine the types of matter that might be included within their scope for some limited guidance, taking into account differences in the terms of the legislation.[136] For instance, in the absence of express provision, it is assumed that a corporation has the implied power to pass such by-laws as are necessary[137] or considered advisable for the proper management of its business or affairs. Similarly, in his *Commentaries on the Laws of England,* Blackstone explained that every corporation has the implied (or common law) power:

> ... to make by-laws or private statutes for the better government of the corporation; which are binding upon themselves, unless contrary to the laws of the land and then they are void. This is also included by law in the very act of incorporation: for, as natural reason is given to the natural body for the governing of it, so by-laws or statutes are a sort of political reason to govern the body politic.[138]

§5.58 In other words, the function of a by-law is to provide for or regulate the government of the corporation. The government of the corporation means the general conduct, rather than the manner of dealing with any specific aspect, of its business or affairs, for as noted above, a by-law is a general governance provision that prescribes the rights and duties of the members with respect to the internal government of the corporation or the management of its affairs, and the rights and duties existing between the members themselves.[139] Thus it is not generally within the scope of a by-law for it to deal with a specific matter of administration.[140]

§5.59 As with every power to enact subordinate legislation, the power to enact by-laws must be exercised in good faith so that any by-law made in bad faith is invalid.[141] Bad faith may be inferred from the circumstances, such as a breach of a voluntary undertaking.[142] Every by-law must be made in the best interest of the corporation.[143] Like all corporate powers, the power to enact by-laws must be exercised for its proper purpose, and therefore a hidden improper purpose affords a ground for attacking the validity of the by-law.[144] A by-law that is passed for the same purpose as a previous by-law which was declared invalid on the

---

[135] See also *Stephenson v. Vokes* (1896), 27 O.R. 691 at 696 (H.C.), *per* Street J.
[136] See, for instance, *Colonial Assurance Co. v. Smith* (1912), 2 W.W.R. 699 (K.B.).
[137] See, generally, *Kelly v. Electrical Construction Co.* (1907), 16 O.L.R. 232 (H.C.).
[138] William Blackstone, *1 Commentaries on the Laws of England,* reprint ed. (Chicago: University of Chicago Press, 1979).
[139] *Mackenzie v. Maple Mountain Mining Co.* (1910), 20 O.L.R. 615 at 618 (C.A.), *per* Osler J.A., rev'g 20 O.L.R. 170 (Div. Ct.).
[140] See, generally, *Denault v. Stewart, Denault & Co.* (1918), 54 Que. S.C. 209 (Ct. of Rev.).
[141] *Ashby v. Prince Albert (City)*, [1984] S.J. No. 68, [1984] 6 W.W.R. 93 (Q.B.).
[142] *McIntyre Ranching Co. v. Cardston (Municipality)*, [1984] A.J. No. 780, 1 W.W.R. 36 (C.A.).
[143] *Hurst v. Mersea (Township)*, [1931] O.R. 290 (C.A.).
[144] *Campbell v. Lanark (Village)* (1893), 20 O.A.R. 372 (C.A.).

grounds of its improper purpose is invalid as well.[145] By-laws may not be discriminatory,[146] nor may they be unreasonable or oppressive.[147] Moreover, a by-law must not be ambiguous or uncertain, so that its meaning cannot be determined in accordance with general principles of statutory interpretation.[148]

§5.60 A by-law may have a retroactive operation so as to validate a step previously taken by the directors or officers of the corporation.[149] A by-law need not be in any particular form;[150] moreover, subsection 116(6) of the OBCA provides that a by-law need not be so described,[151] but to be effective as such, it must be enacted in the manner specified in either the OBCA or the CBCA, as applicable. More broadly stated, the by-laws of a corporation must be consistent with any statute governing the corporation,[152] including the manner of its enactment.[153] In contrast to municipal by-laws and other by-laws made by a public authority, in the case of by-laws made by a business corporation, the courts do not assume good faith but are prepared to guard against unnecessary or unreasonable exercise of a by-law making power to public disadvantage.[154]

(2) Judicial Review of By-laws

§5.61 The grounds upon which the courts are prepared to review a by-law of a corporation extend logically from the criteria outlined above that govern the preparation and adoption of that by-law. The courts are prepared to inquire into the circumstances surrounding the adoption or repeal of a by-law, and are not bound to accept any factual or legal assertions contained in the recitals of the by-law, and, even where the assertions are true, the court may disregard the form if they are irrelevant to the transaction at which the by-law is directed.[155] However, as with all matters pertaining to the internal government of a corporation, the

---

[145] *Lehr v. Bassano (Town)*, [1976] W.W.D. 14 (S.C.).
[146] *Rempel Bros. Concrete Ltd. v. Mission (District)*, [1989] B.C.J. No. 2027, 40 B.C.L.R. (2d) 393 (S.C.). As to the test for discrimination, see *Century Industries Ltd. v. Delta (Municipality) Approving Officer*, [1991] B.C.J. No. 3222, 5 M.P.L.R. (2d) 315 (S.C.).
[147] *R. v. Bell*, [1979] S.C.J. No. 44, [1979] 2 S.C.R. 212.
[148] *Red Hot Video Ltd. v. Vancouver (City)*, [1985] B.C.J. No. 2157, 18 C.C.C. (3d) 153 (C.A.).
[149] See, generally, *National Land & Loan Co. v. Rat Portage Lumber Co.*, [1917] 3 W.W.R. 269 at 274 (Man. K.B.), *per* Mathers C.J.K.B.
[150] See, for instance, *Manes Tailoring Co. v. Willson* (1907), 14 O.L.R. 89 (H.C.).
[151] In *Narnard v. Duplessis Independent Shoe Machinery Co.* (1907), 31 Que. S.C. 362, the shareholders of a corporation entered into an agreement which was not submitted to a meeting of the corporation, nor entered into the minutes of corporate proceedings. It was held that this agreement was merely a contract among the members and was not a by-law even though the agreement was deposited in the archives of the company. Thus the company was not able to raise or rely upon the agreement as it was not a party to it.
[152] *Bartling v. Danby* (1911), 1 W.W.R. 428 (Sask. Dist. Ct.).
[153] *Colonial Assurance Co. v. Smith* (1912), 2 W.W.R. 699 (Man. K.B.); *Kelly v. Electrical Construction Co.* (1907), 16 O.L.R. 232 (H.C.). As to inconsistency with other statutes and principles of common law, see *Nicholls v. Tavistock U.D.C.*, [1923] 2 Ch. 18; *Gentel v. Rapps*, [1902] 1 K.B. 160 at 166, *per* Channell J.
[154] *Kruse v. Johnson*, [1898] 2 Q.B. 91 at 99 (Div. Ct.), *per* Lord Russell of Killowen C.J.
[155] *Hammond v. Bank of Ottawa* (1910), 22 O.L.R. 73 at 80 (C.A.), *per* Moss C.J.O.

courts are loath to intervene in the exercise of a by-law making power unless a clear case is made out for so doing.[156]

§5.62 The most obvious basis on which a by-law may be struck down by the court is that the by-law is inconsistent with the OBCA or the CBCA. The by-laws of a corporation are also subordinate to the articles of the corporation, and are void to the extent of any inconsistency between the two.[157] Moreover, where there is a provision included in the articles under subsection 5(3) of the OBCA or 6(2) of the CBCA, that provision will also prevail over any conflicting provision of the by-laws, even though the text of that provision might properly have been set out in the by-laws of the corporation.[158]

§5.63 The courts have struck down by-laws that were seen to be unreasonable,[159] or were illegal or contrary to public policy.[160] Furthermore, any by-law enacted by a corporation must be sufficiently certain in its form and effect, positive in its meaning,[161] and equal and uniform in its operation, so that the persons bound by it shall not fall into a legislative trap or be made the victim of caprice or of favouritism. In other words, a person bound by a by-law must be able to understand its effect before taking action.[162] Moreover, a by-law must operate equally[163] between the members of every class affected by the by-law[164] (unless, of course, inequality of treatment is authorized by the articles, the Act or otherwise by law).[165]

§5.64 Where there is a partial inconsistency between a by-law and applicable statute, it may be possible to sever the offending part of the by-law from the balance, so as to permit the balance to continue in force.[166] Historically, the courts took the view that in order for an offending provision to be severed from the by-law, the offending portion of the text must be capable of deletion in a single stroke, while leaving the rest of the text intelligible. More recently, the courts have tended towards a more flexible approach to the question of sever-

---

[156] *Peter's American Delicacy Co. v. Heath* (1939), 61 C.L.R. 457 at 506-08 (H.C. Australia), *per* Dixon J.
[157] See, generally, *Guinness v. Land Corp. of Ireland* (1882), 22 Ch. D. 349 (C.A.).
[158] See, generally, *Ashbury v. Watson* (1885), 30 Ch. D. 376 (C.A.).
[159] *Saunders v. South Eastern Rlwy.* (1880), 5 Q.B.D. 456 at 463, *per* Cockburn C.J.; Sir Charles Odgers, *The Construction of Deeds and Statutes*, 4th ed. (London: Sweet & Maxwell, 1956) at 305.
[160] See, for instance, *Re Victoria Onion & Potato Growers' Association Ltd. v. Finnigan*, [1922] V.L.R. 384.
[161] *Scott v. Pilliner*, [1904] 2 K.B. 855 at 858, *per* Lord Alverstone C.J.
[162] *Good & Jacob Y. Shantz, Son & Co., Re* (1911), 23 O.L.R. 544 at 552 (C.A.), *per* Garrow J.A.
[163] *North West Electric Co. v. Walsh* (1898), 29 S.C.R. 33 at 49, *per* Sedgewick J.
[164] See, generally, *Re Good & Jacob Y. Shantz & Son Co.* (1910), 21 O.L.R. 153, aff'd 23 O.L.R. 544 (C.A.); *St. Stanislaus-St. Casimir's Parish (Toronto) Credit Union v. Ontario Credit Union League Ltd.*, [1989] O.J. No. 845 (C.A.), *per* Houlden J.A.
[165] *Brant Dairy Co. v. Ontario (Milk Commission)*, [1972] S.C.J. No. 82, [1973] S.C.R. 131.
[166] *Warren v. Superior Engravers Ltd.*, [1941] 1 D.L.R. 323 at 327 (Ont. C.A.), *per* Robertson C.J.O.; *Strickland v. Hayes*, [1896] 1 Q.B. 290 at 292 (C.A.), *per* Lindley L.J.; *Clark v. Denton* (1830), 1 B. & Ad. 92 at 95, 109 E.R. 721 (K.B.), *per* Bayley J.

ance.[167] Even so, the court will not rewrite the by-law. Furthermore, the inconsistency must not go to the root of the by-law, for if it does, no severance is possible. More specifically, in deciding whether a particular provision is severable it is necessary to decide whether that provision deals with a distinct matter from the balance of the by-law, or whether it is one and entire with the balance of the by-law—in which case it is not possible to sever.[168]

§5.65 While there is no authority directly on point, there is a certain logic in construing the articles and by-laws of an OBCA or CBCA corporation in accordance with the normal rules governing the construction of private contracts, rather than statutes and other public instruments. As private instruments such documents are closely related to contractual documents. However, because corporate charter documents are of more general application than contractual documents, and also tend to be brief, there would also seem to be considerable practical benefit in allowing the generous use of extrinsic evidence as a guide to their intended meaning. Nevertheless, there is American authority to the effect that the corporate constitution of an entity created by legislative charter should be construed in accordance with the prevailing rules of statutory construction. In *Board of Directors of the Washington city Orphan Asylum v. Board of Trustees*, Belson J.A. stated:

> The legislation in question here enacted a particular corporate charter. Legislation confers corporate power through general or special statutes. ... To examine charters granted by special acts of a legislature we use the same rules of construction that we use to examine articles of incorporation adopted pursuant to general law. ... The intent of the legislature governs the interpretation of both a special and a general act of incorporation, as both constitute legislative acts.[169]

Similarly, in *Casper v. Kalt-Zimmers Mfg. Co.,* the Supreme Court of Wisconsin stated:

> The charter of a corporation is a legislative grant—just as much so when incorporated under a general law as by special act. An amendment to a charter is a legislative act just as much so when made in pursuance of a provision in its charter or in a general law as by special act.[170]

(3) Record of By-laws

§5.66 Under the laws of many jurisdictions, companies are required to place a copy of their by-laws (or equivalent internal rules of government) on the public record. For instance, under section 25 of the Nova Scotia *Companies Act*, the incorporators of a company under that Act must deliver a copy of the "articles" of the proposed company to the Registrar under that Act, together with the

---

[167] *Transport North American Express Inc. v. New Solutions Financial Corp.*, [2004] S.C.J. No. 9, [2004] 1 S.C.R. 249.
[168] *Carecon Properties v. 510207 Alberta Ltd.*, [2000] A.J. No. 1237, 9 B.L.R. (3d) 218 at 233 (Q.B.), *per* McIntyre J.
[169] (2001), 798 A.2d 1068 (Dis. Col. C.A.).
[170] (1914), 159 Wis. 517, 149 N.W. 754 at 756 (Wis. S.C.).

memorandum of association of the company, at the time of applying for its incorporation. The Act also requires copies of any alterations to the articles to be filed with the Registrar. No such public filing requirement is imposed under either the OBCA or the CBCA with respect to the by-laws of a corporation.

§5.67 Nevertheless, paragraph 20(1)(*a*) of the CBCA provides that every corporation shall prepare and maintain at its registered office or at any other place in Canada designated by its directors, records containing the articles and by-laws and all amendments to them, and also a copy of any unanimous shareholder agreement. Clause 140(1)(*a*) of the OBCA is to a similar effect, except the required records must be kept within Ontario.[171] Where a corporation is continued under either Act, the records maintained by that corporation must include any similar records required by law to be maintained by the corporation prior to its continuation.[172] Under the OBCA, the records may be kept in a bound or looseleaf book, or may be entered or recorded by any system of mechanical or electronic data processing or any other information storage device.[173] Under the CBCA, a similar latitude is allowed, but the manner of storage must be capable of reproducing any required information in intelligible written form within a reasonable time.[174] Both statutes require corporations to take reasonable precautions to guard against the falsification of records.[175] The CBCA also requires that reasonable steps be taken to prevent the loss or destruction of records and to facilitate detection and correction of inaccuracies.[176]

D. CORPORATE NAMES

§5.68 The determination of the precise legal name of a corporation is often a matter of importance, particularly in the case of the registration of security interests and conveyancing, and especially where the registration is to be made under the *Personal Property Security Act*,[177] where the failure to use the proper name can invalidate a registration.[178] Despite the legal problems that may result, many corporations do not employ their actual corporate name in the conduct of their business, so it is advisable to clarify the actual corporate name of a party whenever a security search or registration is to be made. In addition to the possibility of trade styles, it is also necessary to take into account the fact that a corporation may have more than one legal name.

---

[171] Such a provision cannot be invoked so as to frustrate a right of discovery in a judicial proceeding in another province of Canada: *Hunt v. T&N plc*, [1993] S.C.J. No. 125, [1993] 4 S.C.R. 289.
[172] CBCA, s. 20(3); OBCA, s. 140(3).
[173] OBCA, s. 139(1).
[174] Section 22(1). Note, however, clause 139(2)(*b*) of the OBCA which requires the corporation to "provide means for making the information available in an accurate and intelligible form within a reasonable time to any person lawfully entitled to examine the records".
[175] OBCA, s. 139(2); CBCA, s. 22(2).
[176] See s. 22(2)(*a*) and (*c*).
[177] R.S.O. 1990, c. P.10.
[178] *Personal Property Security Act, General Regulation*, R.R.O. 1990, Reg. 912, ss. 3, 16.

§5.69 Like all companies, every corporation under either the OBCA or the CBCA has a corporate name, that is given to it at its creation or that is subsequently recognized and approved by the applicable regulatory authority. At common law, it is by that name the corporation is known and must be designated and may sue and be sued, and do all its acts, and exercise all the rights which belong to it.[179] That general rule has been eroded to a very large extent, however. As discussed below, it is now clear that a corporation may conduct much of its business under a trade name (although certain documents must contain a statement of its proper name). Moreover, there are many cases in which it has been held that a corporation is sufficiently described if it is named in language sufficient to identify it and no other body. For instance, in *Re Goodwin*,[180] a corporation was identified in its old corporate name in a writ of *fieri facias*. The description was held to be sufficient. Similarly in *McRae v. Corbett*,[181] an action was brought to set aside a deed for certain lands sold at a tax sale. It was argued that the municipal corporation that had sold the land had been incorrectly named in the deed, and that for this reason the deed was invalid. The Manitoba Court of Appeal held that the deed was valid, for where the identity of a company is readily known, either the instrument which it has executed or from the averments and proofs, any variation in or omission from the correct name is immaterial.[182]

§5.70 A change in the name of a corporation has no effect upon its status or continuity. Where the name of a corporation is changed, no right of the corporation is lost or diminished, nor is any obligation of the corporation affected.[183] In one case in which, while an application for a name change was pending, the company entered into an agreement with another company in which it was described by its old name. The new agreement was executed in the new name of the company. It was held that the name of a company is merely a means of identification.[184] The change of name did not affect the identity of the company nor its continued existence as the original corporation.[185]

§5.71 A change in the name of a corporation or the use of an improper name in a document will usually have no effect on the right of the other party to enforce the contract with the corporation.[186] Despite these general rules respecting the

---

[179] William Blackstone, *1 Blackstone's Commentaries on the Laws of England*, reprint ed. (Chicago: University of Chicago Press, 1979), at 462.
[180] (1863), 13 U.C.C.P. 254 at 259, *per* Draper C.J.
[181] (1890), 6 Man. R. 426 (C.A.).
[182] Perhaps the most extreme case in this vein was the decision of the Manitoba Court of Appeal in *Dyck v. Sweeprite Manufacturing Inc.*, [1989] M.J. No. 657, [1990] 1 W.W.R. 673 (C.A.), aff'g [1989] M.J. No. 148, 33 C.P.C. (2d) 230 (C.A.), esp. Huband J.A. at 679.
[183] *Provincial Insurance Co. v. Cameron* (1881), 31 U.C.C.P. 523 at 539 (Ont. H.C.), *per* Wilson C.J., aff'd 9 O.A.R. 56.
[184] Compare, however, *R. v. Pelissiers Ltd.*, discussed in detail below, at § 5.72.
[185] Compare, however, *Grand Junction Rlwy. Co. v. Midland Rlwy. Co.* (1882), 7 O.A.R. 681 at 686, *per* Patterson J.A.; and *Lloyd v. European & North American Rlwy.* (1878), 18 N.B.R. 194 (C.A.).
[186] *Moreland Metal Co. v. Comlinshaw* (1919), 19 S.R. (N.S.W.) 231; *Re North Queensland Auto Spares Co.* (1983), 8 A.C.L.R. 547 at 566.

continuation of contractual and property rights and obligations, where the name of a corporation is changed, certain procedural problems may arise under property (and security) registration statutes.[187]

§5.72 While there are many decided cases across the Commonwealth that have indicated that the use of the proper name of a corporation is only one of several different means of identifying a particular corporate body — so that it is equally possible to identify the corporation by reference to such criteria as its place of business, shareholders, directors and employees[188] — there are also occasional cases going the other way. The special character of a corporate name was stressed in *R. v. Pelissiers Ltd.*,[189] in which a company named in the information and described in the proceedings as Pelissiers Brewing Co. was convicted of a liquor offence. Afterward, a conviction was entered against Pelissiers Ltd., on the basis of evidence at trial. There was no evidence before the court to establish that Pelissiers Ltd. and Pelissiers Brewing Co. were one and the same (*e.g.*, to show that there was no such company or firm as Pelissiers Brewing Co.). Justice Dennistoun held that the conviction was bad. It appears that if there is confusion as to the parties before the court, it is not possible to proceed.[190] It is prudent, therefore, to use the proper name of a corporation wherever possible.

§5.73 The name of a corporation is part of its corporate charter and therefore cannot be changed except in the manner provided by law.[191] Where a corporation includes the name of a municipality or other geographic district, the name of the corporation is not changed by implication merely as a result of a change in the name of that municipality or district.[192] Instead, the corporation continues to bear its original name, including the now anachronistic municipal or geographic label. Perhaps the ultimate illustration of this rule is the name of the governing body of Ontario lawyers (the Law Society of Upper Canada), which continues to be known by the old name for Ontario, more than 160 years after that name was changed.

(i) General Requirements and Restrictions

§5.74 In selecting a corporate name it is necessary to address a number of interconnected issues. First, what are the specific basic requirements re content and form that a proposed corporate name must meet in order to be acceptable under the OBCA or the CBCA, as the case may be? Second, what are the prohibitions

---

[187] The correct procedure to follow in the case of land where the name of a corporate owner has changed was explained by the Saskatchewan Master of Titles in *A. MacDonald Co. v. Western Grocers Ltd.*, [1922] 3 W.W.R. 662 (Sask. Mast. Titles).
[188] See, for instance, *F. Goldsmith (Sicklesmere) Ltd. v. Baxter*, [1970] Ch. 85; *Re Roberts Clinics Ltd.*, [1934] St. R. Qld. 85.
[189] [1926] 1 W.W.R. 189 at 192 (Man. C.A.).
[190] See, generally, *Cornish Silver Mining Co. v. Bull* (1874), 21 Gr. 592 (Ont. Ch.), although the plaintiff was allowed to amend on payment of the costs of the objection.
[191] *Lloyd v. European & North American Rlwy.* (1878), 18 N.B.R. 194 (C.A.); *R. v. Pelissiers Ltd.*, [1926] 1 W.W.R. 189 (Man. C.A.).
[192] *Hughes v. Mutual Fire Insurance Co.* (1852), 9 U.C.Q.B. 387 at 392 (C.A.), *per* Robinson C.J.

and restrictions, if any, that limit the selection of a name that otherwise meets those basic requirements? Third, what are the procedures in place in the name approval process to protect a name that has already been adopted or proposed by one person from being adopted by a second person? Fourth, in the event that two or more persons adopt identical or overly-similar names, what procedures are in place to deal with that conflict? In answering this last question, it is necessary to consider not only the relevant provisions of the CBCA and the OBCA and the regulations thereunder, but also the procedures of the directors under each Act and the protection afforded to the user of a trade name under trade mark law[193] and the law of passing off.[194]

§5.75 The regulations under the CBCA and the OBCA set out similar rules of general application with respect to corporate names. Although considerable freedom is given with respect to the names that are proposed, the name of a corporation must not exceed 120 characters in length, including punctuation marks and spaces.[195] In addition, no word or expression that misdescribes (in any language) the business, goods or services in association with which the corporate name is proposed to be used may be included in the name. Similar prohibitions apply concerning the place of origin of the goods or services produced or supplied by the corporation, or with respect to the conditions under which the goods or services will be produced or supplied or concerning the employment of the persons who will be employed in the production or supply of those goods or services.[196]

§5.76 Subsection 11(1) of the *General Regulation* under the OBCA[197] contains a prohibition against overly general or non-descriptive names. It reads:

A corporate name shall not be,

---

[193] Corporate names that are registered trade-marks are protected under the *Trade Marks Act*, R.S.C. 1985, c. T-13. For other corporate names, the protection afforded to the name is determined by the terms of the OBCA or the CBCA, as the case may be, the regulations thereunder and by the common law action of passing off. See, for instance, *Salada Tea Co. of Canada v. Kearney*, [1925] Ex. C.R. 119. The term "passing off" describes a common law tort in which one person conducts business in such a way as to mislead the public into thinking that his or her goods or services are those of another person. It is not necessary to show an intention to deceive, for innocent passing off is also actionable. See, generally, *Glaxo v. Glaxowellcome Ltd.*, [1996] F.S.R. 388 (Ch.), *per* Lightman J. However, the mere registration of a deceptive company name or a deceptive internet domain name is not passing off: *Marks & Spencer v. One in a Million and Others* (1997), 147 N.L.J. 1809; The Times, 2 December 1997 (Ch.).

[194] Whatever the decision of the Director as to the validity of the name, his or her regulatory approval of that name has no effect upon the trade-mark rights of any other user, nor does such approval affect the protection afforded to another user under the law of passing off. The approval of a name by NUANS or the Director merely evidences that there is no regulatory objection raised to the name. It is not a guarantee by the Government that the name does not infringe the name of any other corporation or trade-mark, nor does it grant the applicant authority to make use of the name in derogation of the goodwill of a prior user. See, generally, *87118 Canada Ltd. v. Canada* (1981), 13 B.L.R. 272, 56 C.P.R. (2d) 209 (Fed. C.A.); *Lampolier Manufacturing Co. v. Manitoba* (1967), 60 W.W.R. 459 (Man. Q.B.).

[195] OBCA, *General Regulation*, R.R.O. 1990, Reg. 62, s. 21.

[196] *Ibid.*, s. 17.

[197] R.R.O. 1990, Reg. 62.

(a) too general;

(b) only descriptive, in any language, of the quality, function or other characteristics of the goods or services in which the corporation deals or intends to deal;

(c) primarily or only the name or surname of an individual who is living or has died within thirty years preceding the date of filing the articles; or

(d) primarily or only a geographic name used alone,

unless the proposed corporate name has been in continuous use for at least twenty years prior to the date of filing the articles or the proposed corporate name has through use acquired a meaning which renders the name distinctive.

It would seem to follow that the general intent behind the rules relating to corporate names is to ensure that the names used by corporations differentiate them from the products that they sell, the places where they carry on business, and other persons. A further prohibition exists against the use of names that, although distinctive in a certain sense, consist entirely or primarily of symbols and marks, rather than words. Thus subsection 11(2) of the regulation reads:

11.(2) A corporate name shall not be primarily or only a combination of punctuation marks or other marks that are permitted under section 20 and the first character of the name shall be a numeral or an Arabic character.

Hence it is not permitted to name a corporation, "#£$! Ltd.". The precise rationale for this rule is not clear, although one explanation that springs to mind is a possible concern that the human eye is unable to distinguish names that consist entirely of symbols.[198] As noted below, the perceived difficulty to the public in distinguishing between names that closely resemble the sound or appearance of each other is one of the rationales for restricting the use of similar names.

§5.77 There is no requirement that the name be descriptive of the nature of the business in which the corporation is engaged,[199] or of the persons who comprise its membership. Yet while a name need not be descriptive of the business or make-up of a corporation, the regulations under both the CBCA and the OBCA contain prohibitions on the use of deceptively misdescriptive names. A name is deceptively misdescriptive if it misleads the public with respect to:

(a) the business, goods or services in association with which it is proposed to be used;

(b) the conditions under which the goods or services will be produced or supplied or the persons to be employed in the production or supply of those goods or services; or

(c) the place of origin of those goods or services.[200]

---

[198] Consider the apparent similarity of "$%^& Ltd". and "%$&^ Ltd.", for instance.
[199] *Re Southern Cross Biscuit Co., Ltd.* (1907), 26 N.Z.L.R. 557.
[200] CBCA Reg. SOR/2001-512, s. 32; see also OBCA *General Regulation*, R.R.O. 1990, Reg. 62, s. 17, which is to a similar effect.

A name may be deceptively misleading even where there is no intentional or accidental element of passing off. For instance, a name is misleading where it indicates that the members of a corporation or its employees have a professional qualification that they do not possess, or where it suggests that the corporation is a type of specially regulated company (*e.g.*, a bank or insurance company) which it is in fact not. However, a name is not sufficiently misleading to justify its disallowance merely because it misdescribes the nature of the business in which the corporation is engaged, when that decision is not likely to be material to the decision of the public as to whether to provide credit to the corporation or as to how much to pay for its goods or services. So, for instance, it would probably not be misleading for a corporation in the business of selling fish to have a name that suggests that it is in the business of selling books.[201]

§5.78 While all corporations are required to have a name distinct from the name of any other corporation, in recent years requirements with respect to names have been relaxed so that both the federal or provincial Acts now permit the use of number names. For instance, subsection 8(2) of the OBCA provides that where no name is specified in the articles that are delivered to the Director, the corporation shall be assigned a number name. The use of a number name greatly simplifies the incorporation process, particularly where the corporation is being set up as a financing or similar vehicle, and it is not intended for the corporation to engage in trade with the public. In such a case, there is little advantage in securing a proper corporate name, and the time and expense required to obtain the approval of a proper name would be wasted.

§5.79 Subsections 10(5) of the OBCA and the CBCA require a corporation to set out its name in legible characters in all contracts, invoices, negotiable instruments and orders for goods or services issued or made by or on behalf of the corporation.[202] Subsection 10(5) of the OBCA further requires the proper corporate name to be set out in all documents sent to the Director under the Act.[203] Although historically many corporation statutes have imposed personal liability on the directors and officers in the case of contracts entered into in contravention of this requirement, the present CBCA and OBCA do not.

---

[201] *Association of Certified Public Accountants of Britain v. Secretary of State for Trade & Industry*, [1997] 2 B.C.L.C. 307, *per* Jacob J.

[202] As to misnomer of a corporation in a prosecution under the *Provincial Offences Act*, R.S.O. 1990, c. P.33, see: *Ontario (Ministry of Labour) v. Ivaco Inc.*, [2001] O.J. No. 1329, 104 A.C.W.S. (3d) 326 (S.C.J.).

[203] Section 9 of the *Extra-Provincial Corporations Act*, R.S.O. 1990, c. E.27, provides that an "extra-provincial corporation may, subject to its incorporating instrument, the *Corporations Information Act* and any other Act, use and identify itself in Ontario by a name other than its corporate name" and, in the case of an extraprovincial corporation within class 3 (*i.e.*, corporations incorporated or continued under the laws of a jurisdiction outside of Canada), may be licensed to use such name.

(ii) Use of a Name Other Than the Legal Name

§5.80 At common law, it is entirely lawful for a person to carry on a business under an assumed or fictitious name provided that the purpose of using such a name is not to defraud or otherwise mislead the person with whom the user of the name is dealing.[204] Historically, the courts have been prepared to permit a corporation to depart from the use of its proper corporate name in its day-to-day commercial dealings and (to a certain extent) in its legal dealings as well, provided that the name that is used by the corporation is substantially correct and there is no ambiguity as to the entity that is identified.[205] This leniency originally developed to deal with cases of inadvertent misnomer, but eventually it was extended to cover a much wider range of cases. For instance, in *Re Len Plumbing & Heating Co.*[206] the court expressly held that it was permissible for a corporation to carry on business under an assumed name.[207] By the time the Ontario Select Committee came to consider the subject of corporate names, it found that there was already a widespread practice of using trade styles other than the official corporate name in the conduct of business. While it was generally prepared to accept the practice, it expressed some concern that unofficial trade styles might be used as a device for circumventing legal restrictions on the selection of corporate names.[208]

§5.81 The *Business Names Act*[209] now gives statutory recognition to the right of a corporation to make use of a name other than its proper corporate name, although any such name must now be registered in accordance with that Act, subsection 2(1) of which provides:

> No corporation shall carry on business or identify itself to the public under a name other than its corporate name unless the name is registered by that corporation.

By the same process of registration, the use of an assumed name is legitimized—although not entirely. As noted above, Canadian corporations have long been required by statute to use their proper corporate names in contracts and instruments such as promissory notes and bills of exchange. Under the present law, subsection 2(6) of the *Business Names Act* continues this approach, but softens it to an extent. It provides:

> A corporation and such other persons as are prescribed carrying on business under a registered name or, in the case of a corporation, identifying itself to the public under a registered name, shall set out both the registered name and the person's

---

[204] See, generally, *US v. Dunn*, 564 F.2d 348 (9th Cir. 1977).
[205] See, generally, *Re Hawkins v. Huron, Perth & Bruce (United Counties)* (1852), 2 U.C.C.P. 72 at 83, *per* Macaulay J.; *Re Brock District Council v. Bowen* (1850), 7 U.C.Q.B. 471 at 475, *per* Robinson C.J.; *Re Trent & Frankford Road Co. v. Marshall* (1861), 10 U.C.C.P. 325 (C.A.); *Provisional Corp. of the County of Bruce v. Cromar* (1870), 22 U.C.Q.B. 321.
[206] [1969] 2 O.R. 698 (S.C.).
[207] See also *Heriteau v. W.D. Morris Realty Ltd.*, [1943] O.R. 724 (H.C.); *Tilden Rent-a-Car v. Keffer*, [1964] 2 O.R. 80 (Co. Ct.).
[208] *Interim Report of the Select Committee on Company Law* (the "Lawrence Report") (Toronto: Queens Printer, 1967) at para. 3.1.1.
[209] R.S.O. 1990, c. B.17.

name in all contracts, invoices, negotiable instruments and orders involving goods or services issued or made by the person.

Contravention of this requirement constitutes an offence under the Act[210] on the part of the corporation and on the part of the directors or officers of the corporation who authorized, permitted or acquiesced in the offence by the corporation.[211] However, in contrast to much of the earlier legislation of this type, a contravention of subsection 2(6) does not result in the imposition of personal liability on those directors or officers under the contracts, invoices, negotiable instruments and orders concerned (although personal liability may result where it is determined that the contract, *etc.* is not a corporate undertaking, but rather one entered into by an unincorporated person).[212] In addition, no contract is void or voidable by reason only that it was entered into by a person who was in contravention of the *Business Names Act* or the regulations at the time the contract was made.[213]

§5.82 Nevertheless, there are civil impediments that may result from a failure to register. In particular, subsection 7(1) of the *Business Names Act* provides that:

> A person carrying on business in contravention of subsection 2 (1), (2) or (3) or subsection 4 (4) or (6) is not capable of maintaining a proceeding in a court in Ontario in connection with that business except with leave of the court.

Subsection 7(2) goes on to clarify the circumstances in which leave should be granted:

> The court shall grant leave if the person seeking to maintain the proceeding satisfies the court that,
>
> (*a*) the failure to register was inadvertent;
>
> (*b*) there is no evidence that the public has been deceived or misled; and

---

[210] Thus s. 10(1) of the *Business Names Act* provides:

> 10.(1) Every person who, without reasonable cause, contravenes section 2 ... is guilty of an offence and on conviction is liable to a fine of not more than $2,000 or, if the person is a corporation, to a fine of not more than $25,000.

[211] Thus s. 10(2) of the *Business Names Act* provides:

> 10.(2) If a corporation is guilty of an offence under subsection (1), every director or officer of the corporation and every person acting as its representative in Ontario who authorized, permitted or acquiesced in such an offence is also guilty of an offence and on conviction is liable to a fine of not more than $2,000.

[212] *TCT Logistics Inc. v. Osborne (c.o.b. Key-West Storage & Distribution)*, [2001] M.J. No. 460, 159 Man. R.(2d) 147 (Q.B.), *per* Clearwater J.:

> ..., persons who wish to carry on business through a corporation for the express purpose of limiting their personal liability for business debts will not, in the absence of either actual or deemed notice of the existence of the corporation and the fact that it is the owner and operator of the business, have the benefit of limited liability.

As to the implications of two or more members of the same corporate group carrying on business under the same trade name, see *Cina v. Ultratech Tool & Gauge Inc.*, [2001] O.J. No. 4383, 56 O.R. (3d) 338 (S.C.J.); but compare *Metera v. Financial Planning Group*, [2002] A.J. No. 1483 (Q.B.).

[213] *Business Names Act*, s. 7(3).

(c) at the time of the application to the court, the person is not in contravention of this Act or the regulations.

In *DC Foods (2001) Inc. v. Planway Poultry Inc.*[214] Glithero J. concluded that leave to proceed with an action in respect of a business should not be given to a corporation that had failed to register its trade name under the Act where the aim of the corporation in not registering was apparently to maintain its ability to draw upon the goodwill of a defunct company, and yet not properly identify to suppliers and others contracting with the corporation that they were dealing with the new entity.

§5.83 Clause 11(*e*) of the *Business Names Act* permits the Lieutenant Governor in Council to make regulations exempting any class of person or business from the application of section 2 of the Act, and imposing conditions upon any such regulation. Section 12 of the Regulation under the Act[215] provides that subsection 2(6) of the Act does not apply with respect to corporations carrying on business in Ontario, or identifying themselves to the public in Ontario, in any form of partnership or business association if three conditions are met. First, the partnership or association must consist of at least two corporations. Second, the name of the partnership or association must be registered under the *Business Names Act*. Third, the name of the partnership or business association, together with the words "Registered Name", "nom enregistré", or the abbreviations "Reg'd Name" or "nom enr." must be set out in all contracts, invoices, negotiable instruments and orders involving goods or services issued or made by the association or partnership.

(iii) Each Name Must Be Unique

§5.84 Every corporation, whether provincially or federally incorporated, is required by law and by administrative policy to have a name that is different from the name currently used in Canada by any other body corporate.[216] An exhaustive summary of the various principles of law that have evolved with respect to the use of similar corporate names is beyond the scope of this text, therefore only a cursory summary has been provided. Proposed corporate names may be refused by the Director under each Act, prior to incorporation (or the amendment of the articles of a corporation, where the purpose of the amendment is to effect a name change). The Director also has the jurisdiction to require a change of a name that was previously accepted for registration. However, the grounds on which a proposed name may be rejected are broader than the grounds which permit the Director to order the change of an existing name.[217]

---

[214] [2004] O.J. No. 3327, 46 B.L.R. (3d) 148 (S.C.).
[215] *Business Names Act, General Regulation*, O. Reg. 121/91.
[216] While the general approach embodied in applicable legislation across Canada is that corporate names must be unique, the same is not true with respect to business names. Such trade names are not unique, and there may be many persons doing business under the same or at least very similar names: *Gold Key Pontiac Buick (1984) Ltd. v. 464750 B.C. Ltd. (Trustee of)*, [2000] B.C.J. No. 1460, 189 D.L.R. (4th) 668, (C.A.).
[217] *Re Cantrade Sales & Import Co.*, [1977] O.J. No. 2194, 15 O.R. (2d) 562 (Div. Ct.).

§5.85 One major area of concern with respect to corporate names is that a new corporation will seek to pass off its goods and services as those of an existing corporation, or perhaps secure access to credit facilities and other supplies on more favourable terms than would otherwise be possible, on the basis of the supplier's mistaken belief that the new corporation is (or is associated with) an established corporation. The possibility of such passing-off raises both public and private rights issues. The tort of passing-off permits a corporation that is concerned that some other company is trading on its reputation to obtain a remedy in the form of damages or an injunction.[218] Generally speaking, the responsibility for restraining passing-off can be left to those other business entities who are likely to be injured as a result. In many American jurisdictions,[219] the responsibility of the relevant government office with respect to corporate names is specifically limited to determining whether a proposed name appears distinguishable from the names of other corporations on the records of the government department concerned. However, from a wider public perspective, a strong argument exists that the OBCA and CBCA Directors have a clear duty to ensure that the public is not likely to be misled by the deceptive similarity of two corporate names, even in cases where the two corporations concerned do not object to the similarity.[220]

§5.86 Clause 9(1)(b) of the OBCA provides that a corporation shall not have a name that is the same as or similar to the name of a known body corporate, trust, association, partnership, sole proprietorship or individual, whether in existence or not, and also the "known name" under which any body corporate, trust, association, partnership, sole proprietorship or individual carries on business or identifies itself. The prohibition against identical names is for all intents and purposes self-explanatory and absolute. Unfortunately, the law relating to similar corporate names is neither self-explanatory, nor (given the number of exceptions which exist) is it absolute. The various restrictions that apply to similar corporate names are partly an outgrowth of trademark law and the law of passing-off, and partly an outgrowth of the administrative practices of the Director's office. The provisions of both the OBCA and the CBCA respecting corporate names are greatly expanded and detailed by the regulations under those Acts.

---

[218] See, generally, *Hendricks v. Montague* (1881), 17 Ch. D. 638; *British Diabetic Association v. Diabetic Society Ltd.*, [1995] 4 All E.R. 812; *Glaxo v. Glaxowellcome Ltd.*, [1996] F.S.R. 388 (Ch.).

[219] *E.g.*, Delaware. Section 4.01(b) of the *Model Business Corporation Act* provides:

4.01(b) Except as authorized by subsections (c) and (d), a corporate name must be distinguishable upon the records from,

(1) the corporate name of a corporation incorporated or authorized to transact business in this state;

(2) a corporate name reserved or registered under section 4.01 or 4.03;

(3) the fictitious name adopted by a foreign corporation authorized to transact business in this state because its real name is unavailable; and

(4) the corporate name of a not-for-profit corporation incorporated or authorized to transact business in this state.

[220] See, for instance: *Trans-American Airlines Inc. v. Kenton*, 491 A.2d 1139 (Del. 1985).

Yet even if administrative practice has now been codified by regulation, the approval of a corporate name is to a large extent a matter of administrative discretion, since the application of the regulations to particular fact situations is not always clear.

§5.87 One important consideration in deciding whether two names are distinct is whether the proposed corporate name and the existing name of another corporation contain a unique and distinctive coined word.[221] The key question to resolve is whether the two names are so confusingly similar[222] that there is a reasonable possibility that the public would[223] be deceived into believing that two corporations were associated by reason of the similarity of their names.[224] The fact that both corporations make use of the same unique and distinctive coined word increases the likelihood of such confusion, and that likelihood is not diminished by reason of the different types of business indicated in each of the two names concerned (*e.g.*, investment and subscription services).[225]

§5.88 Potential civil liability for trading under a deceptively similar name is not limited to liability to the owner of the original name for passing off. Liability may also arise vis-à-vis those who deal with the corporation that makes improper use of the corporate name. The availability of such a claim was considered recently in England in the decision of the Court of Appeal in *Ricketts v. Ad Valorem Factors Ltd.*,[226] In that case, the appellant had served as a director of a company, The Air Component Co. Ltd. (Air Component), that had gone into creditors' voluntary liquidation in early 1998. Shortly afterward, the appellant became a director of another company, Air Equipment Co. Ltd. (Air Equipment), which like Air Component traded in the West Midlands region in the field of air compressors, providing parts in the case of Air Component and apparatus and tools in the case of Air Equipment. On October 21, 1999 Air Equipment went into creditors' voluntary liquidation. The respondent claimed payment of the debt and interest directly from the appellant on the ground that he was personally liable for the debts of Air Equipment by virtue of sections 216

---

[221] For instance, in *Ebsco Investments Ltd. v. Ebsco Subscription Services Ltd.*, it was held that the name Ebsco Subscription Services Ltd. was similar to Ebsco Investments Ltd., and therefore likely to deceive the public: [1975] O.J. No. 2246, 7 O.R. (2d) 741 at 748 (Div. Ct.) *per* Goodman J. aff'd [1975] O.J. No. 2571, 11 O.R. (2d) 305 (C.A.).

[222] *Italia (Azzuri) Soccer Club Inc. v. Manitoba (Director of Corporations Branch)*, [1988] M.J. No. 433, 55 Man. R. (2d) 273 at 274 (Q.B.), *per* Kennedy J.

[223] As to the meaning of "would", see *New Zealand Conference of Seventh Day Adventists v. Registrar of Companies*, [1997] 1 N.Z.L.R. 751 at 759 (H.C.).

[224] But see *Canada Campers Inc. v. British Columbia Registrar of Companies*, [1989] B.C.J. No. 1707, 28 C.P.R. (3d) 137 (S.C.); *Help-U-Sell Inc. v. Help-U-Sell Real Estate Ltd.*, [1988] S.J. No. 435, 69 Sask. R. 142, aff'd [1988] S.J. No. 787, 72 Sask. R. 76 (C.A.).

[225] *Ebsco Investments Ltd. v. Ebsco Subscription Services Ltd.*, [1975] O.J. No. 2246, 7 O.R. (2d) 741, aff'd [1975] O.J. No. 2571, 11 O.R. (2d) 305 (C.A.); *cf. Chartac Small-Business Services Ltd. v. Chartacc Computer Services Inc.*, [1983] B.C.C.O. No. 9, 44 B.C.L.R. 259 (C.F.S. Comm.).

[226] [2004] 1 B.C.L.C. 1 (C.A.).

and 217 of the *Insolvency Act, 1986*.[227] Under subsection 216(2) a company name was "prohibited" if it was a "name which is so similar" to the name by which the name of Air Component "as to suggest an association with that company". The district judge gave summary judgment for the respondent on the grounds that the name of Air Equipment was a prohibited name because the words "equipment" and "component" were interchangeable. The appellant appealed, contending that the court ought to adopt a purposive approach to the construction of the legislation. He argued that the object of sections 216 and 217 was to curb the so-called phoenix syndrome (*i.e.*, companies being set up with minimal capital, incurring debts by taking deposits from consumers for goods and services that were never delivered, then transferring the assets at an undervalue to a second company and allowing the first company to cease trading—leaving the creditors with little or no assets against which to have recourse). It was common ground that there was no transfer of assets by Air Component to Air Equipment at an undervalue, and no evidence that the companies were used to run up debts or to avoid their payment or that creditors of Air Equipment or anyone else had been misled by the similarity of the two companies' names or by the fact that the appellant was a director of both of them.

§5.89 The Court of Appeal held that in the natural and ordinary meaning of the language of subsection 216(2) the name Air Equipment was a prohibited name. A comparison of the names Air Equipment and Air Component in the context of all the circumstances in which they were actually used or likely to be used—specifically the types of products they manufactured, the location of the businesses, the types of customers and the persons involved in the operation of the two companies—suggested an association between the two companies or that they were part of the same group. Whether the words "equipment" and "component" were considered to be interchangeable was irrelevant as was the fact that Air Equipment was not a phoenix company. The court found the appellant personally liable for the company's debts.

§5.90 From a practical perspective, there are some difficulties with this approach to the legislation. Although the degree of similarity of any two names is a matter of opinion, it is far from clear that a reasonable person dealing with a company named Air Component Co. Ltd. would confuse it with a second company known as Air Equipment Co. Ltd., or vice versa. In the absence of a probability of such confusion, it is difficult to see why a director should be held liable to the creditors of a company, particularly where (as here) the company that was purported to have a similar name was itself already in liquidation. The names Air Equipment and Air Component seem no more similar than Coca-Cola

---

[227] In the U.K., a special statutory liability is imposed under ss. 216 and 217 of the *Insolvency Act, 1986*, as a device to prevent people from using different companies with similar names in a decpetive manner. It imposes personal liability where it is established that two companies have traded under similar names and one of them has gone into insolvent liquidation, on a director or officer or other person concerned with the management of the insolvent company. The intent is to deter giving the impression of continuity or substance by using similar names. See, for instance, *Thorne v. Silverleaf*, [1994] B.C.C. 109 (C.A.).

and Pepsi Cola, but it seems doubtful that anyone would conclude that there is an association between those two companies. Nevertheless, the decision in *Ricketts* underscores the need to exercise care in the selection and use of a corporate name.

(1) NUANS Search

§5.91 The unique character of the name submitted by an applicant for incorporation or for the issue of articles of amendment effecting a name change is demonstrated through the submission of a NUANS name search. Under the OBCA, every such applicant must submit an original Ontario biased or weighted computer printed NUANS search for the proposed name dated not more than 90 days prior to the submission of the articles,[228] which confirms that the proposed name is not objectionable. Where the proposed name is in an English form and a French form or a combined English and French form, and the English and French names are phonetically dissimilar, a separate computer-printed search report must be provided for both the English form and the French form of the name.[229] Subsection 18(4) of the OBCA *General Regulation*[230] provides that no name that is identified in a NUANS search report as proposed may be used in a corporate name by a person other than the person who proposed it, unless the written consent of the proposer is obtained.

§5.92 The name of every proposed corporation, and any proposed new name of an existing corporation, must be approved by the Director prior to the issue of the relevant certificate incorporating the corporation or amending its articles of incorporation. In either case, the approval procedure involves the submission of a "clean" NUANS name search, confirming that the proposed name does not conflict with the name of any existing corporate entity or any prior submitted proposed corporate name. In practice, the search is performed by a private search house approved for that purpose by the Director under the OBCA or the CBCA, as the case may be.

§5.93 In some cases, a name similar to that of an existing entity will be approved, provided a consent or undertaking of the existing user is obtained, and the existing user undertakes to discontinue the use of a name as filed by the applicant. In such a case, any consent or consent and undertaking that is required by the OBCA, or the *General Regulation* thereunder must also accompany the articles of incorporation.[231]

---

[228] OBCA, *General Regulation*, R.R.O. 1990, Reg. 62, s. 18(1). The NUANS name search system is operated and maintained by the Department of Consumer and Corporate Affairs, Canada. In the case of electronic filing, see O. Reg. 62, s. 18(1.1).
[229] *Ibid.*, s. 18(2).
[230] *Ibid.*, s. 18(4).
[231] *Ibid.*, s. 18(1), para. 2.

(2) Use of Personal Names

§5.94 It is a basic principle that a person is entitled to carry on business under his or her or her own name.[232] The general rule with respect to the use of a personal name was set down by Lord Lindley M.R. in *Jamieson v. Jamieson*:

> The Court ought not to restrain a man from carrying on business in his own name simply because there are people who are doing the same and who will be injured by what he is doing. It would be intolerable if the Court were to interfere, and to prevent people from carrying on business in their own name in rivalry to others of the same name. There must be something more than that, *viz.*, that the person who is carrying on business in his own name is doing it in such a way as to pass off his goods as the goods of somebody else.[233]

§5.95 In earlier cases there was some doubt as to whether this principle permitted an individual to incorporate a company having a name that included the incorporator's own name; but those doubts no longer seem of concern, at least where the incorporator in question has a legitimate connection with the corporation. For instance, in *I. Browns Packaging Inc. v. Canada (Department of Consumer & Corporate Affairs)*,[234] the respondent director ordered the applicant I. Browns Packaging Inc. to change its name on the ground that it could be confused with the name of an older corporation, Browns Bottle (Canada) Ltd. The older company had sold bottles and packaging materials for over 50 years. The owner of the new corporation was the former president and co-owner of the older corporation, and it was intended that the new corporation would engage in the business of designing packaging products, so that the markets and products of the two corporations would overlap, even though they were not identical. Nevertheless, it was held that the two corporate names were sufficiently distinct that the proposed name for the new corporation was acceptable. The applicant had a right to use his own name as part of the business name, so long as there was no passing-off. In the circumstances, the inclusion of the word "Bottle" in the name of the one corporation and the initial "I" in the name of the other was seen to be sufficient to distinguish the two corporations.[235]

§5.96 Therefore subject to the prohibitions against identical and deceptive names,[236] the common law rule with respect to personal names also applies in the case of corporations, to the extent that the personal name of the owner of a cor-

---

[232] A person may use his (or her) own name as a trade name in a business carried on by him personally, irrespective of similarity to the trade or legal name of some other person unless his purpose in so doing is to pass off his goods or services as those of that other trade, or if it can be shown that irrespective of the intent of the person concerned, such usage by him or her has that effect: *Hurlbut Co. v. Hurlburt Shoe Co.*, [1925] S.C.R. 141.

[233] (1897), 15 R.P.C. 169 at 181 (C.A.); see also *Hurlbut Co. v. Hurlburt Shoe Co.*, [1925] S.C.R. 141, *per* Duff J. at 142-43.

[234] (1982), 24 B.L.R. 44 (Que. S.C.); see also *J.V. Boudrias Fils Ltée v. Boudrias Frères Ltée*, [1934] Ex. C.R. 88.

[235] (1982), 24 B.L.R. 44 at 48 (Que. S.C.), *per* Rothman J. Compare, however, *M.P. Guimaraens & Son v. Fonseca & Vanconcellos Ltd.* (1921), 38 R.P.C. 388.

[236] *Rendle v. Edgcumbe J. Rendle & Co.* (1890), 63 L.T. 94 at 96 (Ch.), *per* Kay J.

poration may form part of the corporate name,[237] even where the name is similar to that of another corporation.[238] For instance, in *C.A. Fitzsimmons & Co. v. A.H. Fitzsimmons & Co.*[239] the plaintiff and defendant both carried on business in the same region. Despite this overlap, it was held that the defendant was entitled to use the name of its owner in its corporate name. The different initials which appeared in the name were seen to create a sufficient distinction between the two corporate names.[240] But it is quite clear that there is no right for a person to change his or her name in order to make it similar to that of another trader, and then to carry on business under that name: such names of conveniences provide a clear instance of the misuse of a personal name in order to pass off goods or services as those of another person.[241]

§5.97 Despite the foregoing general principles, the regulations under both the OBCA and the CBCA do place restrictions upon the use of personal names by themselves. Subsection 11(1) of the OBCA *General Regulation*[242] provides that a corporation name must not be primarily or only the name or surname of an individual who is living or has died within 30 years preceding the date of filing of the articles, unless the proposed corporate name has been in continuous use for at least 20 years prior to the date of filing, or the proposed corporate name has, through use, acquired a meaning which renders the name distinctive. A similar restriction is found in section 24 of the CBCA Regulations.[243] It follows that although a new business may be incorporated as "John White Industrial Supply Ltd." on the basis that it is not "primarily or only" the name of an individual, it may not be incorporated under a name such as "John White's Ltd." unless the prolonged use test is satisfied, even if the owner of the business is in fact a person named John White. Moreover, where a person transfers the goodwill of a business to a purchaser, along with the name of the business, that person forgoes the right to trade under his or her own name.

(3) Permitted Similar Names

§5.98 Since there is no prohibition against two individuals having the same name or trading under the same name, it is somewhat curious that such an extensive body of law has developed to prevent such an occurrence in the case of corporations. As indicated above, the ostensible purpose behind the law is to prevent the public from being deceived as to the identity of the corporation with

---

[237] See, for instance, *John Brinsmead & Sons v. T.E. Brinsmead & Sons* (1896), 13 T.L.R. 3 (C.A.), but compare *Fine Cotton Spinners & Doublers Assoc. Ltd. & John Cash & Sons Ltd. v. Harwood Cash & Co.*, [1907] 2 Ch. 184 at 189-90, *per* Joyce J.
[238] *Dunlop Pneumatic Tyre Co. v. Dunlop Motor Co.*, [1907] A.C. 430 at 438 (H.L.), *per* Lord James of Hereford.
[239] (1975), 20 C.P.R. (2d) 285 (Ont. Div. Ct.).
[240] Even so, where the names of two corporations are so similar that confusion is probable, the confusing name cannot be saved merely because it includes the name of one of the shareholders of the corporation concerned: *Merchant Commercial Real Estate Services Inc. v. Alberta (Registrar of Corporations)*, [1997] A.J. No. 47, 48 Alta. L.R. (3d) 119 (Q.B.).
[241] *F. Pinet & Cie v. Maison Louis Pinet Ltd.*, [1898] 1 Ch. 179 at 181, *per* North J.
[242] R.R.O. 1990, Reg. 62.
[243] *Canada Business Corporation Regulations, 2001*, SOR/2001-512.

whom they are dealing. In this respect, the rule is a further manifestation of the concern that because a corporation is an intangible person it can only be identified by its name. Yet if the purpose of the law is to prevent such deception, many of the exceptions built into the regulations seem to work against this purpose. Permitting affiliated corporations to use similar names often leads to abuse; many a person has done business with a corporation having a name such as ABC Inc., believing it to be ABC Ltd.

§5.99 Although both the OBCA and CBCA contain broad prohibitions against similar names, the *General Regulation* under the OBCA provides a number of exemptions from this general prohibition, where the conditions prescribed by regulation are satisfied. The most elementary exceptions to the general prohibition of similar or identical names are those relating to successor corporations. For instance, where two or more corporations amalgamate, the name of the amalgamated corporation may be identical to the name of one of the amalgamating corporations.[244]

§5.100 With the exception of amalgamating corporations, the extent to which one corporation may have a name that is similar to that of another corporate body or other entity depends upon the extent to which the corporation seeking to use the name is affiliated with the prior user, and whether the prior user is prepared to consent to, and in some cases discontinue the use of, the name in question. Section 5 of the *General Regulation* under the OBCA[245] provides that a corporation may have a name similar to that of another body corporate where the corporation is affiliated with that other body corporate. The word "similar", however, must be contrasted with "identical". In this respect it is necessary to consider the effect of section 6 of the Regulation, which provides that except in the case of an amalgamation, no corporation may acquire a name identical to the name or former name of another body corporate, whether in existence or not, unless the body corporate was incorporated under the laws of a jurisdiction outside Canada and has never carried on any activities or identified itself in Canada. The degree of previous activity in Canada that is required to bring the prohibition into play is not clear. To raise some obvious questions: is the mere owning of property in Canada an activity; do passive operations, such as the conduct of research in Canada, constitute activities; if the corporation advertises in a foreign magazine that is sold in Canada, does that constitute identifying itself in Canada? In practice, approval will likely be given for a corporate name that is the same as that of a foreign company unless the name is so well-known that confusion would be obvious (*e.g.*, "British Petroleum") or the name is recorded in the NUANS list. Except in these two situations, there likely would be no evidence before the Director on which he or she might decline the registration of a name.

---

[244] R.R.O. 1990, Reg. 62, s. 10. This exemption does not apply in the case of corporations with number names, because the name given to such corporations is the Ontario Corporation Number (a sequential number indicating its rank in the total of all corporate charters issued).

[245] R.R.O. 1990, Reg. 62.

§5.101 Section 7 of the Regulation[246] further provides that the addition or deletion of punctuation marks or other symbols does not make a name different. Thus two corporations carrying on business in Canada cannot use similar names such as "ABC, Limited" and "ABC Limited" — although such similar names are not unusual in the case of a foreign parent and Canadian subsidiary, and *vice versa*. However, a name is not identical for the purposes of section 6 if words, numerals or initials are added, deleted or substituted or the legal element of the name (*e.g.*, "Ltd." or "Inc.") is varied by substituting one of the other legal elements required under subsection 10(1) or their corresponding abbreviations. Thus "ABC Ltd." may be used by an affiliate of "ABC Corp.", as may "ABC Inc." The regulations do not make clear whether two corporations may have the names "ABC Ltd." and "ABC Ltée", although it would seem clear from section 7 of the Regulations and subsection 10(1) of the OBCA that two corporations may not carry on business with the names "ABC Ltd." and "ABC Limited."

§5.102 Under the OBCA, a corporation may have a name similar to that of another body corporate where the corporation is not or will not be affiliated with the body corporate, only if the following conditions are met: first, neither the corporation nor the other body corporate may be an offering corporation;[247] and second, either,

- that corporate name must relate to a corporation that is the successor to the business of the corporate body and the corporate body must have ceased or will cease to carry on business under that name; or

- the body corporate must undertake in writing to dissolve forthwith or to change its name before the corporation proposing to use the name commences to use it.

The first of these exemptions is sometimes called the "goodwill exemption" and deals with successor corporations, and is often used where the assets of a business are sold, rather than the corporation operating a business.[248] For instance, if the assets of a business operating as ABC Tailors Ltd., including the goodwill and trademarks of the business, are sold to a new corporation, clause 4(*a*) of the OBCA *General Regulation*[249] permits the new corporation to have a name such as ABC Tailors (2006) Inc.

§5.103 The second of the above exemptions often comes into play where the corporate names involved relate to a premises that has been sold. For instance, if a restaurant operating under the name "100 Park Lane Ltd." was sold, the purchaser might obtain the right to use the name "100 Park Lane (2005) Inc.", even if the business carried on at that location is different from that of the previous

---

[246] *Ibid.*
[247] An offering corporation is a corporation that offers its securities to the public: see OBCA, ss. 1(1) and (6).
[248] Clause 8(*e*) of the OBCA *General Regulation*, R.R.O. 1990, Reg. 62, creates a corresponding exemption where the corporation is a successor to a known trust, association, partnership or sole proprietorship.
[249] R.R.O. 1990, Reg. 62.

business. However, where reliance is placed upon this exemption, clause 4(*b*) of the OBCA *General Regulation*[250] stipulates that the original corporation must undertake in writing to dissolve forthwith or to change its name. The undertaking to discontinue use or dissolve the previous user is necessary to preserve the unique character of the name. Subsection 12(2) of the OBCA provides that where an undertaking to dissolve or change a corporate name is given by a corporation (*i.e.*, a corporation under the Act) and the undertaking is not carried out within the specified time, the Director may issue a certificate of amendment to the articles of the corporation, changing the name of that corporation. Where the undertaking is given by a body corporate that is not a corporation under the Act, the Director has no power to compel that body corporate to comply with its undertaking. The Director is also empowered under subsection 12(3) of the OBCA to issue a certificate of amendment to the articles, changing the name of the new user. In both cases, the practice is to substitute a number name for the offending name. It is, of course, open to the corporation affected by such a move to apply for the issue of articles of amendment, changing the number name to some other name.

§5.104 A third requirement is that the corporate name must set out in numerals the year of acquisition of the name in parentheses, words, numbers or initials must be added, deleted or substituted, as the case may be, or the name must be varied by substituting one of the legal elements required under subsection 10(1) of the OBCA or their corresponding abbreviations. Thus ABC Ltd. may be succeeded by a corporation that uses the name ABC (1993) Ltd.; White Auto Supply Inc. may be succeeded by a corporation that uses the name J.A. White Auto Supply; and XYZ Ltd. may be succeeded by XYZ Inc.

§5.105 Corresponding rules apply in the case of names that are similar to the name of a known trust, association, partnership or sole proprietorship, or a business name under which any of them carries on business or identifies itself. A corporation cannot have a name that is identical to that of a known trust, association, partnership or sole proprietor, because under subsection 10(1) of the OBCA the name of a corporation must include a corporate status identifier such as "Limited" or "Incorporated". Since the name of a trust, association, partnership or sole proprietor may not include such a status term, the only issue with respect to the names of corporations and trusts, associations, partnerships or sole proprietors is whether they may possess similar names. In general, similar names are permitted provided one of the following two requirements are satisfied. First the corporate name must relate to a proposed corporation that is the successor to the business carried on under the name and the user of the name must either have ceased to carry on the business or will cease to carry on business under that name. Second (and in the alternative), the known trust, association, partnership or sole proprietor must undertake in writing to dissolve forthwith or to change its name before the corporation proposing to use the name commences to use it. However, in contrast to the rules governing the use

---

[250] *Ibid.*

of names by one corporation that succeeds to the business of another, there is no requirement in the case of a corporate successor to a known trust, association, partnership or sole proprietor that the corporation include in its name the year of acquisition of the name in parentheses.

§5.106 Section 9 of the Regulation under the OBCA sets out a rule of special application where a corporate name contains a word that is the same as or similar to the distinctive element of a trade-mark or name of another corporate body. It provides that the new similar name shall not be prohibited by reason only of the similarity if the body corporate consents to the use of the name and the corporate name contains additional words or expressions to differentiate it from the body corporate and other users of the trade-mark or name. Where such a name is proposed, the owner of the trade-mark must ensure that the new user enters into a registered user agreement with respect to the trade-mark in question, otherwise the distinctiveness of the trade-mark may be lost.

(4) Passing-off and Trade-marks

§5.107 The subject of passing-off was touched upon briefly above in the context of a discussion of the duties of the Director when approving a proposed corporate name. The fact that the Registrar or Director has permitted incorporation under a given name does not prevent a person whose business is adversely affected by reason of that name from seeking protection in an action for passing-off, where the facts indicate that confusion has occurred or is likely.[251] The subjects of passing-off and trade-mark protection lie outside the scope of this work and accordingly readers interested in these subjects should refer to a standard work or tort or trade-mark.

(5) Use of Names Under Executive and Legislative Sanction

§5.108 Where a corporation is incorporated by special Act, and the name of the corporation is set out in the special Act,[252] the courts have no power to prevent the use of that name by that corporation through the issue of an injunction.[253] The statutory authority to use the name is conclusive. In contrast, in *Oxweld Acetylene Co. v. Oxyweld Co. of Canada*[254] it was held that the court had no power to compel the amendment or cancellation of letters patent of a corporation where the name included in letters patent infringed on the name of another company, except at the instance of the Attorney General suing on behalf of the Crown or upon the relation of an interested party. However, in that case an injunction was granted against the corporation, prohibiting it from making use of the name in question. Thus the administrative act of granting letters patent in a particular name did not provide an authority for making use of the name in question, and could not extinguish the rights of the prior user of that name.

---

[251] *Coin-A-Matic v. Coin Automat Washing Machine Corp.* (1966), 35 Fox Pat. Cas. 46.
[252] See, for example, the *Human Resources Professional Association Act*, S.O. 1990, c. Pr. 28.
[253] *Travellers Insurance Co. v. Travellers Life Assurance Co.* (1910), 20 Que. K.B. 437 (C.A.).
[254] (1923), 53 O.L.R. 455 (C.A.).

§5.109 There are a large number of para-professional designations that are prohibited except to members of a designated organization. For instance, subsection 7(2) of the *Human Resources Professionals Association of Ontario Act*[255] provides that:

> 7.2 Any person in Ontario who, not being a registered member of the Association, takes or uses the designation "Certified Human Resources Professional" or its abbreviation "C.H.R.P." alone or in combination with any other words, name, title, or description, or implies, suggests or holds out that the person is a certified human resources professional is guilty of an offence.[256]

The absence of the name of any person from a copy of the membership register maintained by such organizations is usually deemed by statute to be proof (in the absence of evidence to the contrary) that the person is not a member.[257]

(6) Geographic and Descriptive Names

§5.110 A corporation may obtain a proprietary right in its name, but it cannot remove a word from the English language (*i.e.*, a descriptive or generic word) merely by registering that word as part of its name, even when that word constitutes virtually the entire name.[258] Accordingly, existing competitors may continue to make use of such words, and in this respect, new entrants into a field enjoy the same rights as the old competitors. It is not necessary for the new user to show that a particular word is the only word that will do or even to show that it is the most suitable word. It is sufficient to show that the word is in general usage or within the usage of a particular trade or business in a generic sense rather than in connection with the products or services of the first user. Thus in *Re Cuff & Thomson Ltd.*,[259] the use of the word "Precision" in the names of two engineering concerns was held not to be infringement.

§5.111 The distinction between descriptive, generic and ordinary words is not clear-cut, nor is it always easy to distinguish between such words and "fancy",

---

[255] S.O. 1990, c. Pr. 28.
[256] See also *Association of Municipal Clerks and Treasurers of Ontario Act*, S.O. 1985, c. Pr. 24; *Ontario Association of Speech Language Pathologists and Audiologists Act*, S.O. 1986, c. Pr. 9; *Ontario Mortgage Brokers Act*, R.S.O. c. M. 39, *Mortgage Brokers Association Act*, S.O. 1989, c. Pr. 46; *Association of Translators and Interpreters Act*, S.O. 1989, c. Pr. 2; *Chartered Institute of Marketing Management of Ontario Act*, S.O. 1988, c. Pr. 13; *Institute of Certified Management Consultants of Ontario Act*, S.O. 1986, c. 25; *Institute of Municipal Assessors of Ontario*, S.O. 1987, c. 20; *Ontario Institute of the Purchasing Management Association of Canada Inc. Act*, S.O. 1987, c. 21; *Ontario Municipal Management Institute Act*, S.O. 1988, c. 20; *Association of Registered Wood Energy Technicians of Ontario Act*, S.O. 1988, c. 5; *Chiropody Act, 1991*, S.O. 1991, c. 20; *Chiropractic Act, 1991*, S.O. 1991, c. 21; *Dental Hygiene Act, 1991*, S.O. 1991, c. 22; *Dental Technology Act, 1991*, S.O. 1991, c. 23; *Denturism Act, 1991*, S.O. 1991, c. 25; *Dietetics Act, 1991*, S.O. 1991, c. 26; *Massage Therapy Act, 1991*, S.O. 1991, c. 27; *Medical Laboratory Technology Act, 1991*, S.O. 1991, c. 29; *Midwifery Act, 1991*, S.O. 1991, c. 31; *Occupational Therapy Act, 1991*, S.O. 1991, c. 33; *Opticianry Act, 1991*, S.O. 1991, c. 34; *Physiotherapy Act, 1991*, S.O. 1991, c. 37.
[257] S.O. 1990, c. 28, s. 7(5).
[258] See, for instance, *Motor Mfrs. & Traders, Ltd. v. Motors Mfrs. & Traders Mutual Insurance Co.*, [1925] Ch. 675 (C.A.); *Aerators Ltd. v. Tollitt*, [1902] 2 Ch. 319 at 323, *per* Farwell J.
[259] [1933] N.Z.L.R. 313.

"contrived" or "coined" words. A word is descriptive when it is used in a sense that describes the business in which the corporation is engaged.[260] For instance, in *Office Overload Co. v. Driver Overload Ltd.*[261] the applicant (Office) sought an order compelling three corporations with names including the word "Overload" to change their name. The application was refused. The court rejected the argument that the word "overload" was a coined term, and held that in order for such an order to be granted, it was necessary to show that the visual and auditory qualities of the names were so similar that it was probable that a prospective customer would be induced to deal with a company other than the one intended.[262]

§5.112 A coined term is a term developed especially to describe the products or services of a particular trader. During the earliest stages of their use, such words are invariably associated with their originator.[263] But if the product with which they are associated is both novel and successful, the public may well come to use that coined term in association with all similar products, irrespective of their manufacturer. Whether a particular word has acquired such a generic meaning is a question of fact,[264] and the onus of proof is upon the person claiming that the words are distinctive of his or her goods, that this is in fact the case.[265]

§5.113 While fancy words are more likely to receive the protection of law, on the other hand, even a word that is normally a part of ordinary English usage may come to be associated with a particular corporation, at least with respect to a particular kind of product as a result of its long and widespread association with that corporation. Where this is the case, injunctive relief is available to prevent a competitor from using that word in its corporate name.[266] To obtain relief, however, there must be present or immediately pending competition between the plaintiff and defendant. Relatively little protection is afforded under the law of passing-off where the only similarity between two corporate names are descriptive words or other words in general English usage or geographical place names.[267] In order to obtain protection for a geographic based name, it is neces-

---

[260] *Prime Locations Ltd. v. Prime Real Estate Ltd.*, [1976] O.J. No. 23, 30 C.P.R. (2d) 38 at 39 (Div. Ct.), *per* Grange J.; *Bumper's, The Beef House (Banff) Ltd. v. Alberta Registrar of Companies*, [1977] A.J. No. 497, 4 Alta. L.R. (2d) 68 (T.D.).
[261] [1968] 1 O.R. 292 (H.C.).
[262] Compare *Canada Permanent v. B.C. Permanent* (1898), 6 B.C.R. 377 (S.C.).
[263] The "fancy" word concept includes family names as well as contrived words: *Re F.P. Chapple Co.*, [1960] O.R. 531 (C.A.); *Parker-Knoll v. Knoll International, Ltd.*, [1962] R.P.C. 243 (C.A.).
[264] *Daimler Motor Car Co. v. British Motor Traction Co.* (1901), 18 R.P.C. 465.
[265] See, for instance, *General Radio Co. v. General Radio (Westminster) Ltd.*, [1958] R.P.C. 68; *Southern Music Publishing Co. v. Southern Songs Ltd.*, [1966] R.P.C. 137; *Elliott v. Expansion of Trade, Ltd.* (1909), 54 So. Jo. 101; *Electromobile Co. v. British Electromobile Co.* (1907), 98 L.T. 258, 24 T.L.R. 192, 25 R.P.C. 149 (C.A.).
[266] *Albion Motor-Car Co. Ltd. v. Albion Carriage & Motor Body Works Ltd.* (1917), 33 T.L.R. 346, 34 R.P.C. 257 (Ch.); *Music Corpn. of America v. Music Corpn. (Gt. Britain), Ltd.* (1964), 64 R.P.C. 41.
[267] *Office Overload Co. v. Driver Overload Ltd.*, [1968] 1 O.R. 292 (H.C.); *Northwest Trading Co. v. Northwest Trading Co.*, [1920] 1 W.W.R. 353 (B.C.S.C.), aff'd [1920] 3 W.W.R. 729 (B.C.C.A.); see also *Re Beverly Hills Motor Car Co.* (1987), 18 C.P.R. (3d) 334 (Ont. Comp. Br.); *Re Espirit Communications Inc.* (1987), 18 C.P.R. (3d) 345 (Ont. Comp. Br.).

sary to show that the name has acquired a secondary meaning or become so associated with the plaintiff's business that usage would be misleading to the public. The Hudson Bay Company, Canada Trust, and the Bank of Montreal are likely examples of such an association.

(7) Objections to Names

§5.114 The similarity of a corporate name may become an issue either prior to or after the acceptance of the articles for filing containing the name in question. Such acceptance may be loosely termed the "approval" of the name by the Director, but that label is somewhat misleading: the Director does not actually approve the name, but merely proceeds to record the name as the name of the corporation concerned. The recording by the Director is for all practical purposes a rubber stamp that follows virtually automatically upon the submission of a clean NUANS name search prepared by a recognized private name search company. If that name search company raises no objection to the name, no further inquiry will be made at the time when the articles are accepted for filing. Moreover, in general, once a name is approved, the Director will not take further issue with it unless the name is objected to by some third party.

§5.115 The relevant statutory authority for the objection procedure is found in subsection 12(1) of the OBCA, which provides:

> 12.(1) If a corporation, through inadvertence or otherwise, has acquired a name contrary to section 9 or 10, the Director may, after giving the corporation an opportunity to be heard, issue a certificate of amendment to the articles changing the name of the corporation to a name specified in the certificate and, upon the issuance of the certificate of amendment, the articles are amended accordingly.

The CBCA makes no express provision for the holding of such a hearing.

§5.116 Where the Director proposes to change the name of a corporation under subsection 12(1) of the OBCA on the grounds that it is objectionable, he or she is required to hold a hearing into the suitability of the name concerned. The OBCA hearing procedure is generally informal. There is no statutory power of decision and a hearing officer can only make a recommendation to the Minister, who then makes the determination as to whether a name contravenes the Act or Regulation. Accordingly, the *Statutory Powers Procedure Act*[268] does not apply to the proceeding.[269] Insofar as the Director has developed a specialized approach to the issue of names and the likelihood of confusion arising over the use of similar names, absent any manifest or patent error in applying the statutory tests to the facts of the case, the courts will not interfere with the judgment of the Director.[270] The objector is entitled to the status of a party to the hearing as a person whose interest is directly and substantially affected by the decision that is

---

[268] R.S.O. 1990, c. S.22.
[269] *Royal Canadian Legion v. Hamilton War Veterans' Poppy Fund Inc.* (1987), 15 C.P.R. (3d) 472 (Ont. Comp. Br.), *per* McPhail, Hearing Officer.
[270] *Saskatchewan Wheat Pool v. Manitoba*, [1997] M.J. No. 282, 32 B.L.R. (2d) 201 (Q.B.).

to be made.[271] There is no procedure set out in the OBCA for seeking a court order to change the name of the corporation. However, the Divisional Court may review any decision made under subsection 12(1) under the *Judicial Review Procedure Act*;[272] in addition, any decision to change the name is subject to review by the Divisional Court under section 252 of the OBCA.[273] In *Unitel International Inc. v. Unitel Communications Inc.*[274] Justice Kennedy surveyed the relevant case law respecting the review of a decision of the Director, and based upon that review set down the following guidelines: (1) The power of review by a court is on the merits of the decision. The hearing is not a hearing *de novo* but is related to the prior administrative decision. (2) The power of review is not to be read as authorizing a substitution of a judicial for an administrative opinion on no other basis than disagreement with the administrative opinion. (3) The record of the hearing will be considered to see if the decision was founded on grounds that have a rational relation to the statutory standard. (4) Undoubtedly in deciding an appeal, the court must accord great weight to the decision of the Director, but it must not rely on that decision to the extent of allowing it to relieve the court of its ultimate responsibility of determining the issue in light of the evidence and the proceedings before it. (5) The Director will be given all the curial deference due to one who acts in the nature of a specialized judge.[275]

§5.117 The courts will not lightly review the Director's finding with respect to the acceptability of a name on the basis of new evidence.[276] The proper procedure in such a case is to seek a new hearing before the Director.[277] However, the courts are not bound by the Director's findings of fact,[278] and are prepared to overturn the finding of the Director in an appropriate case,[279] as for instance where the Director fails to give appropriate weight to the similar elements of a name.[280]

---

[271] *Collins v. Ontario (Pension Commission)*, [1986] O.J. No. 769, 56 O.R. (2d) 274 (Div. Ct.).
[272] R.S.O. 1990, c. J.1.
[273] CBCA, s. 246.
[274] [1992] S.J. No. 177, [1992] 3 W.W.R. 548 at 569 (Q.B.).
[275] See also: *Terranex Information Services v. Canada (Canada Business Corporations Act, Director)*, [1995] O.J. No. 78, 20 B.L.R. (2d) 192 at 201 (Gen. Div.), *per* Feldman J. See also: *Travel 2000 Ltd. v. iTravel2000.com.Inc.*, [2003] O.J. No. 770 (Div. Ct.); *Bargain Tire Centre Ltd. v. Registrar of Business Corporations Act and Pro-Western Tire Corp.*, [1984] S.J. No. 951, 32 Sask. R. 12 (Q.B.); *Grant (c.o.b. Cougar Pool League) v. Rathy (c.o.b. Partner Pool League)*, [1995] S.J. No. 587, 136 Sask. R. 151 (Q.B.). An appeal court may receive new evidence concerning the question of confusion: *D. Investments Ltd. v. Saskatchewan Business Corporations Branch*, [2000] S.J. No. 102, 95 A.C.W.S. (3d) 473 (Q.B.).
[276] *Guccio Gucci S.P.A. v. Gucci Investments Inc.*, [1988] O.J. No. 326, 29 O.A.C. 241 at 242 (Div. Ct.), *per* Galligan J.; *Balaton Hungarian Dancers Inc. v. Saskatchewan (Director of Corporations)*, [1981] S.J. No. 1302, 10 Sask. R. 147 at para. 5 (Q.B.), *per* Noble J.; *T'Ease Fashions Ltd. v. Flory*, [1980] S.J. No. 285, 6 Sask. R. 133, 55 C.P.R. (2d) 217 (Q.B.).
[277] *Citibank Canada v. Citicapital Financial Corp.* (1988), 24 C.P.R. (3d) 221 at 223 (Ont. Div. Ct.), *per* Potts J.
[278] *British Columbia Permanent v. Wootton* (1898), 6 B.C.R. 382 (B.C.S.C.).
[279] *Action Plumbing Ltd. v. Alberta (Registrar of Companies)*, [1976] A.J. No. 338, 1 A.R. 296 at 310 (C.A.), *per* Clement J.A.
[280] *New World Pictures v. New World Video Inc.*, [1986] O.J. No. 2346, 53 O.R. (2d) 794 at 799 (H.C.), *per* Anderson J.

§5.118 In a name change application, the grievance of the prior user is merely a catalyst that brings the subject of the new user's name up for review. The process does not lead to an award of compensation for any loss of trade. If the prior user believes that the new user is injuring its trade, the appropriate remedy is for that prior user to commence a passing-off procedure. The sole consideration at the hearing of the application is whether the public is being disadvantaged:

> ... [T]he court must act for the benefit of the public who are likely to be deceived, the grievance of a party being an entirely secondary result. Under this Act, this is a matter respecting the public primarily, *i.e.*, is the public likely to be deceived, and therefore in my opinion the principles of a passing-off action are not applicable.[281]

It follows that it is not necessary to establish that actual damages have flowed from the use of the similar name, or that the name has been used with the intent of misleading the public into believing that the products or services of the new user are those of the prior user. However, while a name change application (whether before the Director or a court on judicial review) is not a passing-off action, evidence relevant in a passing-off action (*e.g.*, instances of actual confusion or evidence of an actual intent of the part of the new user to mislead) is nevertheless admissible in the name change application to substantiate the claim that the names are likely to lead to public confusion.[282]

§5.119 In *D. Investments Ltd. v. Saskatchewan Business Corporations Branch*,[283] the court discussed the alleged similarity between the names "Diana's Restaurant" and "Friendly Dianas Place" The Registrar concluded that:

> In our opinion the names Diana's Restaurant and Friendly Dianas Place are not so similar as to confuse or mislead. In reaching our decision, the tests established by judicial precedent were applied-that is, the visual and oral similarities of the names, the natures of the business and proximity of the entities and the persons or class of persons who ordinarily deal with or might be expected to deal with both entities were considered. The reasons for our decision are as follows:
>
> 1. There has been no evidence of confusion other than an indication of two inquiries from suppliers about "double orders". This cannot be viewed as overwhelming evidence of confusion.
>
> 2. The businesses appear to have little, if any, overlap of clientele, i.e. Friendly Dianas Place is a restaurant open to the public whereas Diana's Restaurant cannot be accessed by any public.
>
> Therefore, no one should be induced to deal with someone they had no intention to deal.

---

[281] *Re C. Cole & Co. (sub nom. Cole's Sporting Goods Ltd. v. C. Cole & Co.)* (1964), 44 C.P.R. 65 at 71, *per* Schultz J., aff'd 46 C.P.R. 244 (C.A.).
[282] *Action Plumbing Ltd. v. Alberta (Registrar of Companies)*, [1976] A.J. No. 338, 1 A.R. 296 at 310 (C.A.), *per* Clement J.A.
[283] [2000] S.J. No. 102 at para. 9, 95 A.C.W.S. (3d) 473 (Q.B.). As to the availability of an interlocutory injunction barring the use of an allegedly similar corporate name that may be confusing with the name of another corporation, see *Ethical Funds Inc. v. Mackenzie Financial Corp.*, [2000] F.C.J. No. 244, 6 C.P.R. (4th) 92 (T.D.).

On appeal from the Registrar, Smith J. was of a different view:

> It would seem beyond question that if both restaurants were currently operating 'on the street' the potential for confusion would be beyond doubt. I agree with the appellant's submission that the thrust of both names lies in the name 'Diana's' and that the distinction in spelling between 'Diana's' and 'Dianas' is unlikely to be generally appreciated. The word 'Friendly' is just an adjective and the difference between 'Place' and 'Restaurant', for two restaurants, is insignificant. There was some admitted initial confusion among suppliers. While the Registrar quite reasonably concluded that this confusion, in itself, could as a practical matter easily be rectified, this does not diminish its evidential value as to the potential for confusion in the two names for similar businesses. It is obvious that both names are likely to be reduced to merely 'Diana's' in the minds of consumers, and, indeed, before me the appellant submitted into evidence photographs of the sign outside of Friendly Dianas Place which gives significant prominence to the name, 'Dianas' while relegating the words 'Friendly' and 'Place' to much smaller and less visible print.

§5.120 The courts have long recognized that it is a serious matter to require a corporation to change its name.[284] Consequently, although in theory the Director enjoys a broad discretion in deciding whether to approve a proposed name,[285] a more limited jurisdiction exists where an application is made for a compulsory name change of an existing corporation.[286] There are obvious direct costs to a corporation if it is required to change its name (*e.g.*, new letterhead and signs, changes to advertising, an inevitable loss of at least some of the goodwill and custom related to the old name).[287] Given these burdens, there is a great reluctance to order a name change where the name to which objection is taken has had substantial use.[288] In order for a name change to be ordered there must be actual evidence of confusion or such a real likelihood[289] of deception to the public[290] so as to make a name change in the public interest.[291] The question is one of probability, not possibility.[292]

---

[284] See, generally, *Re C Chemicals*, [1967] O.J. No. 1007, [1967] 2 O.R. 248 (C.A.).

[285] *Consul-Pak Inc. v. Cheeseman* (1986), 12 C.P.R. (3d) 394 at 401 (Ont. Comp. Br.), *per* Barrows Q.C.

[286] See, for instance, *Re Cantrade Sales & Import Co.*, [1977] O.J. No. 2194, 1 B.L.R. 179 (Div. Ct.); see also *Brydon Marine Products Ltd. v. ITT Industries of Canada Ltd.* (1986), 10 C.P.R. (3d) 361 (Ont. Comp. Br.).

[287] *Re Menzies-Gibson Ltd.*, [1955] O.W.N. 657 at 658-59 (H.C.), *per* McRuer J.

[288] *Prime Locations Ltd. v. Prime Realty Inc.* (1987), 14 C.P.R. (3d) 457 at 483 (Ont. Comp. Br.), *per* Ross, Hearing Officer.

[289] An example of a case in which a sufficient likelihood of deception was found to exist, so as to justify a court-ordered name change, may be found in the decision of Wells C.J.H.C. in *Re Compro Ltd.*, [1974] O.J. No. 1831, 2 O.R. (2d) 671 at 674 (Div. Ct.).

[290] *Toronto & Regional Crime Stoppers Inc. v. Crimestoppers Security Systems Inc.* (1986), 13 C.P.R. (3d) 323 (Ont. Comp. Br.); *Re Ashrae Controls Inc.* (1987), 16 C.P.R. (3d) 273 (Ont. Comp. Br.); *Royal Canadian Legion v. Hamilton War Veterans' Poppy Fund Inc.* (1987), 15 C.P.R. (3d) 472 (Ont. Comp. Br.); *Re Toronto Bocciofila Club* (1985), 7 C.P.R. (3d) 328 (Ont. Comp. Br.).

[291] *Re New Land Design Inc.* (1987), 18 C.P.R. (3d) 495 (Ont. Comp. Br.); *Spirax Sarco Ltd. v. Sarco Canada Ltd.* (1985), 8 C.P.R. (3d) 465 (Ont. Comp. Br.).

[292] *Re C.C. Chemicals Ltd.* (1967), 52 C.P.R. 97 (Ont. C.A.).

§5.121 In *Unity Insurance Brokers (Windsor) Ltd. v. Unity Realty & Insurance Inc.*,[293] the Director under the OBCA required the appellants to file articles of amendment changing their name to names that were distinguishable from "Unity Insurance". It was determined that Unity Insurance Toronto had provided brokerage services in the Toronto area since 1974. The appellants, who carried on an insurance brokerage in the Windsor area had changed their corporate names to their present names, which included "Unity Insurance" in 2000. Neither the appellants nor the respondents had registered their names under the *Business Names Act*. However, there was evidence that there was confusion about the two companies in the minds of insurers, re-insurers and insurance brokers with whom the parties had business dealings but there was only one recorded instance of confusion on the part of a customer. The Director had concluded that the use of the phrase "Unity Insurance" by the appellants would be likely to deceive in the sense of leading someone who had an interest in dealing with Unity Insurance in Toronto to deal with Unity Insurance in Windsor and *vice versa*. She ordered the appellants to file articles of amendment changing their corporate names to names that were distinguishable from "Unity Insurance".

§5.122 The appellants appealed to the Divisional Court of Ontario, where their appeal was dismissed. The focus of the hearing before the Director and on appeal was not on damage to the parties but on protection of the public who would likely be deceived by similarity of names. While there was limited jurisprudence on the meaning of the term "someone who has an interest in dealing with that person" as now used in section 2(1) of the Regulation, more recent authorities have not limited the class of persons to be considered in determining whether corporate names are likely to deceive to customers of the corporation. It was held that the Director made no error in concluding the use of the name "Unity Insurance" by the appellants would be likely to deceive and in ordering the appellants to file articles of amendment changing their corporate names.

§5.123 In summary, the following factors must be considered in compulsory name change applications:[294]

- to what degree is there visual or auditory similarity between names of the two entities;

- does the similarity arise solely or primarily because of a mutual use of a common, generic or descriptive word, or a common abbreviation of such words;

- are the two users active in the same line of business and active in the same market, so that the two are competitors;

---

[293] [2005] O.J. No. 1069, 138 A.C.W.S. (3d) 273 (Div. Ct.).
[294] See, generally, *Re C.C. Chemicals Ltd.* (1967), 52 C.P.R. 97 at 108-109 (Ont. C.A.), *per* Kelly J.A.; *Canadian Motorways Ltd. v. Laidlaw Motorways Ltd.*, [1973] S.C.J. No. 103, 11 C.P.R. (2d) 1 at 13-14, *per* Laskin J.; *Re Cantrade Sales & Import Co.* (1977), 1 B.L.R. 179 at 186 (Ont. Div. Ct.), *per* Robins J.

- if not, is there a likelihood of expansion by one user into the market of the other user, so that they may well become competitors;
- the person or class of persons who ordinarily might be expected to deal with each — *i.e.*, are the two entities active in a sophisticated market in which potential suppliers and customers would recognize even subtle differences between the two names;
- the extent to which there have been actual instances of confusion;
- whether both users are active.

The best evidence of undue similarity between two corporate names exists where actual confusion can be shown to have occurred. The fact that customers have indicated that they believed that the place of business of one corporation is in fact the place of business of another corporation is good evidence that the names of the two corporations are in fact confusing.[295] In most name-related cases, the courts must speculate as to whether confusion is likely. Where actual confusion on the part of prospective customers can be shown, such speculation is no longer necessary. By the same token, where actual experience indicates little if any confusion between the two names, a finding of undue similarity is unlikely to be made.[296] Moreover, a name change should not be ordered where the person objecting to the use of the name is a dormant corporation, for in such cases the prospect of public confusion is slight.[297] On the other hand, it is not necessary to show that actual confusion has occurred if two names are sufficiently similar that confusion seems very likely to occur.[298]

§5.124 An appeal lies to the Divisional Court under section 252 of the OBCA[299] from any order of the Director with respect to the rejection of a proposed name or the issue of articles compelling the change of a name of a corporation. As noted above, such a "review" is not a hearing *de novo*. The Act does not authorize substitution of a judicial opinion for an administrative opinion on any other basis but disagreement with the administrative decision, nor does it permit a court to come to a different conclusion merely on the basis of its conclusion as to the weight of the evidence which was before the administrative authority.[300] The decision of the Director with respect to a name change or the rejection of a proposed name will not lightly be interfered with by the courts.[301] Generally,

---

[295] *Paws Pet Food & Accessories Ltd. v. Paws & Shop Inc.*, [1992] A.J. No. 1026, 6 Alta. L.R. (3d) 22 (Q.B.), *per* Prouse J.
[296] See, generally, *Bell Insurance Agencies Ltd. v. Bell & Cross Insurance Agency Ltd.*, [1983] M.J. No. 97, [1983] 4 W.W.R. 38, 21 B.L.R. 306 (Q.B.).
[297] *Re Cantrade Sales & Import Co.*, [1977] O.J. No. 2194, 15 O.R. (2d) 562 (Div. Ct.).
[298] *Dex Resources Ltd. v. Alberta Registrar of Corporations*, [1992] A.J. No. 33, 1 Alta. L.R. (3d) 240 (Q.B.).
[299] CBCA, s. 246.
[300] *Per* Laskin J. in *Canadian Motorways Ltd. v. Laidlaw Motorways Ltd.*, [1973] S.C.J. No. 103, 11 C.P.R. (2d) 1.
[301] *Northland Office Systems Group Inc. v. Northland Stationers (1963) Ltd.*, [1989] S.J. No. 585, 80 Sask. R. 153 at 154-55 (C.A.).

such a decision will not be altered or overturned by the court unless it is clear that the decision was wrong or unfair.[302]

(8) Other General Prohibitions and Restrictions

§5.125 A corporate name may not contain a word that, in any language, "is obscene or connotes a business that is scandalous, obscene or immoral" or that is otherwise objectionable on public grounds.[303] Nor (should there be any doubt) may a name contain any word, expression or abbreviation which is prohibited or restricted under an Act or regulation of the Parliament of Canada, a province other than Ontario or a territory, unless (in the case of the restriction), the restriction is satisfied.[304] Sections 15 and 16 of the OBCA *General Regulation*[305] also impose certain restrictions on corporate names, that for the most part are intended to prevent members of the public from confusing a corporation with another type of business enterprise, or in misleading the public into thinking that an unlicensed corporation is licensed to carry on a professional practice or that its business operations are subject to public regulation. More specifically, section 15, paragraph 1 provides that the following words and expressions shall not be used in a corporate name:

> "Amalgamated"... unless the corporation is an amalgamated corporation resulting from the amalgamation of two or more corporations.

The reason for this prohibition is not clear, since there is no additional benefit which accrues to a corporation from the use of the word "amalgamated". Since amalgamated corporations are not required to include the word "amalgamated" in their corporate names, the prohibition can hardly be attributed to the goal of making sure that all amalgamated corporations are identified as such in a distinct manner that prevents confusion with other types of corporate entity. Nevertheless, an apparently related prohibition may also be found in section 15, paragraph 13, which prohibits the use in a corporate name of "[n]umerals indicating the year of incorporation unless section 4 applies or it is a year of amalgamation of the corporation". The reference to section 4 in paragraph 13 is to section 4 of the OBCA *General Regulation* rather than to section 4 of the Act itself, which as noted above, deals with the names of successor corporations and in general requires any successor corporation that has a name that is similar to its predecessor to include the year in which it acquired the similar name. Thus if "ABC Limited" is superseded by a successor corporation in 1995, and that successor also wishes to make use of the name ABC, the successor corporation must be called "ABC (1995) Limited." Such names are often employed when the assets of a corporation in receivership are sold as a going concern.

---

[302] *Grant (c.o.b. Cougar Pool League) v. Rathy (c.o.b. Panther Pool League)*, [1995] S.J. No. 587 at para. 10 (Q.B.), *per* Lang J.
[303] R.R.O. 1990, Reg. 62, s. 13.
[304] *Ibid.*, s. 14.
[305] *Ibid.*, ss. 15, 16.

§5.126 Paragraphs 2 and 10 of section 15 of the OBCA General Regulation[306] restrict the use of the words "architect", "architectural", "engineer" and "engineering" in a corporate name:

> "Architect"... [or] "architectural"... or any variation thereof where such word suggests the practice of the profession, except with the written consent of the Council of the Ontario Association of Architects.

> "Engineer"... [or] "engineering"... or any variation thereof where such word suggests the practice of the profession, except with the written consent of the Association of Professional Engineers of Ontario.

The restriction imposed under these paragraphs apply only where the implication is that the corporation is engaged in the practice of the regulated profession concerned. Where the word is used in a purely descriptive sense, the restriction does not apply. Thus, section 15 would not seem to prevent the incorporation of a pub under a name such as "The Plastered Engineer Tavern" for in such a case there is no suggestion that the pub is engaged in the practice of engineering.

§5.127 Paragraph 3 of section 15 of the OBCA General Regulation[307] places a general prohibition on the use of the word "association", while a similar prohibition is imposed under paragraph 8 on the use of the word "council". The probable rationale for the prohibition against the use of the term "association" is that it is most often used in connection with non-incorporated business enterprises — although that is not always the case, for federally incorporated cooperatives known as "cooperative associations", even though they are incorporated and confer limited liability on their members.[308] If this is the concern which underlies the prohibition, it is curious that none of the other legal terms commonly associated with non-limited liability enterprises are prohibited under the section, such as "firm", "partnership" or "proprietorship".

§5.128 Significantly the prohibition under paragraph 3 of section 15 of the OBCA General Regulation[309] applies only where the full word "association" is used — in contrast to the prohibition on the use of the word "cooperative" for instance, which also includes any abbreviation or derivation of that term. The narrower scope of paragraph 3 can be attributed to the fact that one common abbreviation for association ("assoc.") is also a common abbreviation for associates — and the word "associate" (and its abbreviation) are often used in the names of corporations that are owned or affiliated with persons prominent in particular fields, such as "Al Capone & Associates Limited."

§5.129 Formerly, paragraph 4 of section 15 of the *General Regulation* under the OBCA restricts the use of the word club in a corporate name, so that no corporation may make use of the word "club":

---

[306] R.R.O. 1990, Reg. 62.
[307] *Ibid.*
[308] *Canada Cooperatives Act*, S.C. 1998, c. 1, s. 29.
[309] R.R.O. 1990, Reg. 62.

... unless the corporation carries on a sporting or athletic business and there is no inference that a member of the public may become a member of the corporation.

This restriction was repealed effective April 1, 1999.[310]

§5.130 In recent years there has been considerable concern in Ontario and elsewhere about bogus academic institutions. This concern is reflected in paragraph 5 of section 15 of the OBCA *General Regulation*[311] which restricts the use of certain words commonly associated with genuine places of higher learning. It provides that the words "college", "institute" or "university" shall not be used in the name of a corporation if the use of the word would lead to the inference that the corporation is a university, college of applied arts and technology or other post-secondary institution. Surprisingly, however, there is no restriction on the use of the word "school" itself. A related prohibition is found in clause 16(1)(*b*) of the *General Regulation*, which provides that no word or expression may be used in the name of a corporation that suggests that the corporation "is sponsored or controlled by or associated or affiliated with a university or an association of accountants, architects, engineers, lawyers, physicians, surgeons or any other professional association recognized by the laws of Canada or a province or territory of Canada" unless the consent in writing of the appropriate authority, university or professional association is obtained.[312]

§5.131 The Regulations governing name use display a general concern with the possibility that one type of corporate entity may be confused with another. Thus paragraph 6 of section 15 of the OBCA *General Regulation*[313] prohibits the use of the word "'Condominium' or any abbreviation or derivation thereof" in the name of an OBCA corporation, while paragraph 7 imposes a prohibition against the use of the word "'Co-operative' or any abbreviation or derivation thereof". A somewhat similar prohibition is found in paragraph 9 of section 15 which prohibits the use of digits or words that would lead to the inference that the name is a number name.

§5.132 Under clause 16(1)(*c*) of the OBCA *General Regulation*[314] a prohibition is placed upon the use of words or expressions that suggests that the corporation carries on the business of a bank, loan company, insurance company, trust company, other financial intermediary or a stock exchange that is regulated by a law of Canada or a province or territory of Canada. This prohibition can be attributed to the general regulatory goal, identified above, of preventing the use of names that deceive the public into believing that it is dealing with a regulated entity, when in fact it is not.

---

[310] O. Reg. 190/99, s. 1.
[311] R.R.O. 1990, Reg. 62.
[312] See *Canada Business Corporations Regulations, 2001*,SOR/2001-512, s. 22(*c*).
[313] R.R.O. 1990, Reg. 62.
[314] *Ibid.*

§5.133 Section 16 of the OBCA *General Regulation*, prevents a corporation from suggesting that it has any government sanction or affiliation. Thus clause 16(1)(*a*) provides that:

> No word or expression that suggests that a corporation
>
> (a) is connected with the Crown or the Government of Canada, a municipality, any province or territory of Canada or any department, Ministry, branch, bureau, service, board, agency, commission or activity of any such government or municipality;

shall be used in a corporate name unless that authority has consented in writing. Similarly, subsection 16(2) restricts the use of names that suggest political affiliation:

> No word or expression that suggests that a corporation is connected with a political party or leader of a political party, where the purpose for which the corporation is incorporated is of a political nature, shall be used in a corporate name.

The corresponding provisions under the CBCA Regulation[315] take a different approach. In particular, paragraphs 22(*a*) and (*b*) of the CBCA Regulation provide that a corporate name is prohibited where the name connotes that the corporation:

> (*a*) carries on business under royal, vice-regal or government patronage, approval or authority, unless the appropriate government department or agency consents in writing to the use of the name;
>
> (*b*) is sponsored or controlled by or is connected with the Government of Canada, the government of a province, the government of a country other than Canada or a political subdivision or agency of any such government, unless the appropriate government, political subdivision or agency consents in writing to the use of the name.

There is no prohibition under the CBCA or the Regulation under that Act corresponding to the prohibition on suggestions of political affiliation, which is set out in subsection 16(2) of the OBCA Regulation.

§5.134 Finally, paragraph 12 of section 15 of the OBCA *General Regulation*[316] imposes restrictions on the use of "veteran" in a corporate name:

> "Veteran"... or any abbreviation or derivation thereof unless there has been continuous use of the name for a period of at least twenty years prior to the acquisition of the name.

In the years immediately following World War II, of course, the use of the word "veteran" in a business name provided a certain competitive advantage. Whether it still confers such an advantage is uncertain, but the prohibition remains.

---

[315] *Canada Business Corporations Regulations, 2001*, SOR/2001-512.
[316] R.R.O. 1990, Reg. 62.

(9) Language of Name

§5.135 Both the CBCA and the OBCA govern the language in which a corporate name may be expressed. It would seem that under the CBCA a corporation's name must either be in English or in French, or some combination of the two, for subsection 10(3) of the CBCA provides that a corporation may set out its name in an English form, a French form, an English form and a French form (*i.e.*, a separate English form and French form), or in a combined English and French form, and it may be legally designated by any such form.[317] In other words, a corporation may have the name "XYZ Ltd.", "XYZ Ltée", "XYZ Ltd. or XYZ Ltée" or "XYZ Ltd. and XYZ Ltée", and may be legally designated by any of those forms. The phrase "any of those forms" is significant, because it suggests that in the case of the name "XYZ Ltd. and XYZ Ltée", the corporation may be legally designated by either of "XYZ Ltd." or "XYZ Ltée" or by the full and proper name "XYZ Ltd. and XYZ Ltée". Thus under the CBCA there would seem to be no practical distinction between a corporation that has a name in an English form and a French form, and a corporation that has a name that is a combined English and French form.

§5.136 A somewhat different approach to the language of the corporate name is taken under the OBCA. Subsection 10(2) of the OBCA provides that:

> Subject to this act and the regulations, a corporation may have a name that is in,
>
> (*a*)   an English form only;
>
> (*b*)   a French form only;
>
> (*c*)   a French and English form, where the French and English are used together in a combined form;
>
> (*d*)   a French form and an English form where the French and English forms are equivalent but are used separately.

Subsection 2.1 provides that a corporation that has a form described in clause (2)(*d*) may be legally designated by the French or English version of its name. Subsection 10(3), which is the corresponding provision of that Act, reads as follows:

> Subject to subsection 12(1), the name of a corporation may be set out in its articles in an English form, a French form, an English form and a French form, or a combined English and French form, so long as the combined form meets the prescribed criteria. The corporation may use and may be legally designated by any such form.

Section 10(2.1) of the OBCA provides that a corporation may be legally designated by any such name. Thus under the OBCA, a corporation that has a combined English and French language name may be legally designated only by the full combined name, that is by the name "XYZ Ltd. and XYZ Ltée". It follows that somewhat greater care must be taken under the OBCA than the CBCA to make clear whether a particular bilingual name arrangement is intended to create

---

[317] *Cf.* s. 10(1) dealing with use of Limited and Ltd., *etc.*, which permits the corporation to *use* and be legally designated by either the full or the abbreviated term.

two separate English and French names or a combined English and French name. The practical value of a combined name is far from clear.

§5.137 The requirement that names must be in English or French seems to be applied in a liberal manner, as is for all practical purposes essential, given the extent of cultural diversity in Canada and the number of international corporations carrying on business through Canadian subsidiaries. In many cases, translation of a foreign name into English or French would be positively misleading: as for instance, requiring Heinrich Schwartz Ltd. to use the name Henry Black Ltd. Furthermore, given the extent to which technical terms or industrial jargon now form part of the Queen's English (downlink, sat-com, beamscope, cablevision, simware, firmware, AI, bio-tech, fax, hot-point, tele-direct), and the extent to which contrived words (*e.g.*, RE/MAX) and acronyms, and other abbreviations (*e.g.*, Stelco, IBM) are employed in corporate names throughout the world, it would obviously be impractical to restrict Canadian corporate names to only those words that are found in the *Oxford English Dictionary* or *Webster's Dictionary of the English Language*. If an incorporator can use as a corporate name a letter combination that is not a word in any language, it would be the height of caprice to prevent the use of a letter combination on the sole ground that although it is not a word in English it happens to be a word in some other language, such as Lapp, Magyar or Basque. Thus in practice, the only requirement with respect to the language of a name is that the name must be generally intelligible (in the sense of capable of expression) in either the English or French alphabet.

§5.138 It may happen, however, that an English or French name may be entirely or at least partly unsuited to a corporation, given the customers with which it intends to deal or because it intends to carry on business both inside and outside Canada. In such a case, the corporation may prefer to have a foreign language name. The approaches taken towards the use of languages other than English and French under the OBCA and the CBCA are entirely different. The CBCA is quite restrictive of foreign language usage. Subsection 10(4) provides that a corporation may set out its name in any language form *for use outside Canada,* and it may be legally designated by any such form outside Canada, but no permission is given to use a foreign language name within Canada. In contrast, the OBCA does not require the use of either a French or English name within Canada. Instead, subsection 10(4) of the OBCA provides that:

> Subject to the provisions of this Act and the regulations, a corporation may have in its articles a special provision permitting it to set out its name in any language and the corporation may be legally designated by that name.

Where a corporation takes advantage of this provision, section 22 of the OBCA *General Regulation*[318] provides:

---

[318] R.R.O. 1990, Reg. 62.

A name set out in the articles pursuant to subsection 10(4) of the Act shall be a direct translation of the corporate name but changes may be made to ensure that the name is idiomatically correct.

From these two provisions it would appear that the corporation must have a French or English name, but once its name is included in the articles, a corporation may include a further special provision authorizing the use of a foreign translation of that name not only outside Canada, but within Canada as well, so that for all intents and purposes it is possible for an OBCA corporation to have and carry on business under a non-English and non-French name. While this provides broad latitude in the selection of a name, subsection 10(3) of the OBCA does provide that only letters from the English language alphabet, Arabic numerals, and such punctuation and other marks as may be permitted by regulation, may form part of the name of a corporation.[319]

(10) Number Names

§5.139 The former OBCA was the first corporations legislation in Canada to give formal legal recognition to the widespread administrative practice of assigning companies a number name, consisting of their corporation number plus an appropriate status identifier. This was carried forward into both the present OBCA and the CBCA. Section 11(2) of the CBCA now provides that:

> If requested to do so by the incorporators or a corporation, the Director shall assign to the Corporation as its name a designated number followed by the word "Canada" and a word or expression, or the corresponding abbreviation, referred to in subsection 10(1).

Since the "corporation" may apply under this section for the issue of a number name wording, it is now clear that a corporation may change its name to a number name after it has commenced operation. The issue of such a name is not restricted to newly incorporated entities.

(11) Identifying the Status of a Corporate Entity

§5.140 Subsection 10(1) of the CBCA sets out the corresponding provisions of that Act with respect to the designation of legal status. It provides that words of expression such as "Limited", "*Limitée*", "Incorporated", "*Incorporée*", "Corporation", or "*Société par actions de régime fédéral*" or the corresponding abbreviations shall be part of the name of every corporation (other than only in a figurative or descriptive sense). Subsection 10(1) of the OBCA is to a similar effect, but does not provide for a corresponding status identifier to "*Société par actions de régime federal*". Corporations incorporated prior to 2001 that were

---

[319] Although the Act is silent on the point, the approved marks include all of the diacritical marks and diphthongs found within the foreign words imported into the language (*e.g.*, ø, å, æ, œ), particularly those of the French alphabet that are no part of the English or the Roman alphabets *per se* (*e.g.*, ç, é, è, ê). The following other symbols have also been prescribed: ! " " # $ % & ' ( ) * +, _ . / : ; > = < ? [ ] \ ^ . As a result of these additions to the basic English alphabet, almost all names in a language derived from Latin or Old High German would be permissible under the OBCA.

described by the expression "*Société commerciale canadienne*" or the corresponding abbreviation of "S.C.C." may continue to use these expressions in their name, but no new corporations may be created using this form of status identifier.

§5.141 The status identifier requirement dates from the 19th century, when limited corporations were a comparatively rare form of commercial enterprise. The inclusion of these status terms within the corporate name is intended to put all persons dealing with the corporation on notice as to the nature of the entity with which they are dealing.[320] The concern at the time the requirement originated was that unless the agents of an entity made clear to the contractors dealing with it that the entity was a limited corporation, those contractors might be misled into believing that the owners of the corporation were personally liable for its debts. At a time when most business organizations were sole proprietorships or partnerships, this was no doubt a serious concern. Given the prevalence of the limited corporation in modern economy, it seems doubtful that any contractor today would assume that the owners of a commercial enterprise were personally liable.

§5.142 Nevertheless, the requirement for the use of "limited" or a corresponding word or abbreviation remains,[321] and even today an agent of a corporation who fails to identify the status of the corporation properly risks personal liability un-

---

[320] As to improper use of these status terms, s. 11 of the OBCA provides:

11.(1) No person, while not incorporated, shall trade or carry on a business or undertaking under a name in which "Limited", "Incorporated" or "Corporation" or any abbreviation thereof, or any version thereof in another language, is used.

(2) Where a corporation carries on business or identifies itself to the public by a name or style other than as provided in the articles, that name or style shall not include the word "Limited", "Incorporated", or "Corporation" or any abbreviation thereof or any version thereof in another language.

[321] *In Re Asphalt Products (B.C.) Ltd.* (1961), 36 W.W.R. 526 (B.C.S.C.), a corporation reduced its paid-up capital from $22,500 to $2. Justice Collins upheld a direction by the registrar to the corporation to add the word "and reduced" to its corporate name. It was held that since there was a possibility that the company might recommence business operations in the near future while its business reputation as a successful company with adequate paid-up capital would still be remembered, it was only fair that the public receive some warning of the reduced, and for all practical purposes extinguished, financial status of the corporation. The fallacy of this reasoning, of course, is that it is doubtful anyone would have understood the point the judge was trying to make through the name change. Moreover, it is difficult to identify any practical concern, since any corporation's capital base is liable to be extinguished at any time as a result of losses, but in such cases there would be no notice given by the corporate name.

der any contract that the agent enters into on the corporation's behalf.[322] Indeed, courts still are prepared to state that:

> It is an essential principle of the concept of limited liability in company law that a person doing business with a limited corporation must have this fact brought to their attention in order that they be bound by the law related to the limitations of liability of companies.[323]

The premise, practicality and fairness of this statement may be individually questioned. To begin with, a corporation may carry on business (as many numbered companies do) under a properly registered trade name, in which case the failure to bring the limited liability status of the business to the attention of those with whom it may deal has no effect on limited liability. Moreover, the various corporate labels employed in Canada do not necessarily make clear that the use of a particular entity confers limited liability. The implications of dealing with an entity designated as "Limited" or "Incorporated" may be clear to most business people of even limited experience, but it is doubtful whether one business person in 50 outside Quebec would be aware the implications of dealing with an entity designated (as the CBCA permits) only as a "SARF" or *"Société par actions de regime fédéral"*. In the modern economy, in which even an increasing number of partnerships operate behind a shield of limited liability, it can hardly come as a surprise to a supplier or other creditor to discover that the form of entity with which it has dealt confers limited liability on the principals who stand behind it. Indeed, often those principals will be no more than a matter of speculation: a supplier or other creditor has no way of knowing who or what may be behind a trade name such as, "Stoney Creek Industrial and Contractor Supply": the trade name may belong to an individual, a partnership or a limited company of some kind. Imposing personal liability in such a case merely gives the supplier or creditor the windfall benefit of allowing it to sue some other person when it determines that the entity with which it was dealing is unable to pay. A more realistic approach would be to disregard the corporate veil only where the supplier or other creditor appears to have been misled concerning the person with whom it was dealing. For instance, if Joseph White orders goods using his own name, it would be perfectly reasonable to disregard the fact that he intended

---

[322] *West Fraser Builder Supplies v. Vandler Horst*, [1990] B.C.J. No. 146 (C.A.). Subsections 10(5) and 10(6) of the CBCA provide:

> (5) A corporation shall set out its name in legible characters in all contracts, invoices, negotiable instruments and orders for goods or services issued or made by on behalf of the corporation.
>
> (6) Subject to subsections (5) and 12(1), a corporation may carry on business under or identify itself by a name other than its corporate name if that other name does not contain, other than in a figurative or descriptive sense, either the word or expression "Limited", *"Limitée"*, Incorporated, *"Incorporée"*, corporation or *"Société par actions de régime federal"*.

[323] *Tri-Con Concrete Finishing Co. Ltd. v. Caravaggio*, [2002] O.J. No. 2771 at para. 48, (S.C.J.) *per* Wilkins J. See also: *Pennelly Y Ltd. v. 449483 Ontario Ltd.*, [1986] O.J. No. 2672, 20 C.L.R. 145 (H.C.J.); *Truster v. Tri-lux Fine Homes Ltd.*, [1995] O.J. No. 415 (Gen. Div.), aff'd [1998] O.J. No. 2001 (C.A.); *Bindra v. Falotico*, [2002] O.J. No. 2077, (S.C.J.); *TCT Logistics Inc. v. Osborne (c.o.b. Key-West Storage & Distribution)*, [2001] M.J. No. 460, 159 Man. R. (2d) 147 (Q.B.).

to order the goods on behalf of a corporation named "Joseph White Ltd.", since the supplier would have no way of anticipating this fact at the time of accepting an order.[324] In contrast, where on the facts the supplier or other creditor was apparently indifferent as to the nature of the entity with which it was dealing, and had reasonable opportunity to determine whether it was contracting with a corporation or a non-incorporated business, then the failure to disclose expressly the limited liability status of the corporation should give no entitlement to sue either the agent of the corporation personally or the owner of the corporation.[325]

§5.143 Subsection 10(2) of the CBCA provides that the Director may exempt a body corporate continued as a corporation under the Act from the provisions of subsection 10(1). No corresponding provision is found in the OBCA. It is not clear on what basis such an exemption would be given, although one likely basis would be where the body corporate is well known, and has traditionally traded under a name that does not include the required words or abbreviations.

§5.144 As noted above, both the CBCA and the OBCA require the inclusion of one of the words "Limited", "Limitée", "Incorporated", "Incorporée" or "Corporation" or the abbreviation "Ltd.", "Ltée", "Inc." or "Corp." in the name of every corporation. There is a considerable volume of case law dealing with the question of whether the name of a corporation includes the word "Limited"[326] (or the corresponding terms and abbreviations — corporation, incorporated, etc.), *i.e.*, whether it constitutes part of the name of a corporation. It is now clear under both of the Acts[327] that these words do form part of the corporate name, and therefore it is a misnomer to omit such words when naming or identifying the corporation. However, the misnomer is not a fatal one,[328] for it has been held that where a contract made by a company is in other respects enforceable, the omission of the word "Limited" from the company's name will not affect the validity or enforceability of the contract,[329] or of a promissory note in the company's favour.[330]

§5.145 It is a grand but erroneous oral tradition of Ontario law — so widely circulated that it deserves correction — that a corporation with the name XYZ Limited may not be designated legally by the name XYZ Ltd., on the basis that XYZ Limited is not the same name as XYZ Ltd. This absurd view appears to

---

[324] See, for instance, *Value Liquor Mart Ltd. v. Werkman*, [1999] A.J. No. 613 (Alta. Q.B.) *per* Master Quinn.
[325] See, generally, *Global Leak Detection Inc. v. Van*, [2000] A.J. No. 1081 (P.C.).
[326] See, *e.g.*, *Waterous Engine Works Co. v. McLean* (1885), 2 Man. R. 279 at 288 (C.A.), *per* Taylor J.; *Coté v. Lake St. John Distributing Co.*, [1956] Que. P.R. 314 (S.C.).
[327] OBCA, s. 10(1); CBCA, s. 10(1).
[328] *Dalhousie Lumber Co. v. Walker* (1916), 44 N.B.R. 81, 30 D.L.R. 498 (C.A.); *Canadian Imperial Bank of Commerce v. Dene Mat Construction Ltd.*, [1988] 4 W.W.R. 344 (N.W.T. S.C.).
[329] *National Malleable Castings Co. v. Smiths' Falls Malleable Castings Co.* (1907), 14 O.L.R. 22 at 23 (C.A.), *per* Falconbridge C.J.
[330] *Manes Tailoring Co. v. Willson* (1907), 14 O.L.R. 89 at 98 (H.C.), *per* Magee J.

have derived from the peculiar wording of older legislation[331] as interpreted in *Howell Lithographic Co. v. Brether.*[332] It is now completely contradicted by the express wording of both the CBCA and the OBCA. Subsections 10(1) of the CBCA and of the OBCA each provide that a corporation may use and be legally designated by either the full or the abbreviated form.

(12) Alternate Name

§5.146 With the exception of the allowance made for foreign language names (for use outside Canada under the CBCA or generally in the case of the OBCA), and for English and French names, the general rule is that a corporation must have one name and one name only. There is no provision in either the OBCA or the CBCA which allows a corporation to have alternate names — although such alternate names might be desirable in such cases as where there is an amalgamation between two corporations carrying on distinct lines of business or which were active in two or more areas. However, as noted above, it is permissible for a corporation to carry on business under a trade name,[333] so to the extent that alternate names are necessary in order to exploit the goodwill of a corporation or its predecessors, the trade name option may be employed.

(13) Change of Name

§5.147 Both the OBCA and the CBCA permit a corporation to change its name, in each case by way of an amendment to the articles of incorporation.[334] Generally speaking, like all amendments to the articles of a corporation, a change of the corporate name must be approved by a special resolution of the shareholders of the corporation. However, subsection 168(4) of the OBCA provides a simplified procedure for amending the articles of a corporation to change the name of the corporation from a number name to a name that is not a number name. It provides that where a corporation has a number name, the directors may amend its articles to change that name to a name that is not a number name. Subsection 168(4) goes on to provide that only a simple resolution of the directors is required for that purpose. Subsection 173(3) of the CBCA is to a similar effect.

§5.148 As noted above, in certain cases a corporation may also be required to change its name by the Director, as for instance where a name has been acquired in contravention of the Act or the Regulations. In such cases, the change of name is compulsory, and there is no need for the change to receive either the approval of

---

[331] As to the common law position, see *F. Stacey & Co. Ltd. v. Wallis* (1912), 106 L.T. 544 at 547 (C.A.), *per* Scrutton L.J.; *Thompson v. Big Cities Realty & Agency Co.* (1910), 21 O.L.R. 394 at 404 (Div. Ct.), *per* Riddell J.

[332] (1899), 30 O.R. 204 at 207, *per* Street J. However, that case turned upon the peculiar wording of s. 22(1) of the Ontario *Companies Act*, which at the time expressly required the use of "the unabbreviated word 'Limited'". Compare: *Thomas Ltd. v. Standard Bank* (1910), 15 O.W.N. 188, 1 O.W.N. 379 at 382, *per* Teetzel J., aff'd 1 O.W.N. 548 (C.A.).

[333] *Re Len Plumbing & Heating Co.*, [1969] 2 O.R. 698 at 701 (S.C.), *per* Lacourcière J.; *Re Pahmer (St. George Lumber. Co.)* (1969), 12 C.B.R. (N.S.) 261 (Ont. S.C.); *Re Benson & Hedges (Canada) Ltd. and Liquor Control Board of Ontario* (1974), 3 O.R. (2d) 378 (C.A.).

[334] OBCA, s. 167(1)(*a*); CBCA, s. 173(1)(*a*).

the shareholders or the directors of the corporation — indeed, the change will take effect even if the directors and shareholders vigorously oppose it.

§5.149 A change in the name of a corporation is a mere housekeeping measure, although it is obviously one that may have a significant impact upon the business of the corporation. The change does not affect the status or continuity of a corporation. The same corporation remains in existence despite the name change, for the name of a corporation is merely a means of identification.[335] Therefore, the corporation may continue to assert the same rights to which it was previously entitled and is subject to the same liabilities and obligations, and so it may continue to maintain actions in the same manner as if its name had not been changed.[336] While legal proceedings must be brought in the new name of the corporation, where the original name is used by mistake in a deed or other instrument, the corporation may still bind itself and obtain rights to acquire or convey good title.[337]

E. CORPORATE SEAL

§5.150 Great weight was placed by the common law on the corporate seal, for at common law, a corporation could evidence its assent to a document only through the affixing of its corporate seal to that document. The right to possess and use a corporate seal was seen to be an essential attribute of every corporation.[338] At common law, a corporation executed a document by sealing it; the affixing of a seal to a document by a corporation had the same effect relative to the corporation that the signing of a document had in the case of an individual.[339] Any signatures of corporate officers endorsed under the seal were inserted primarily to indicate which persons affixed the seal to the document, so as to facilitate inquiry into whether the person who affixed the seal was authorized to do so. In this respect, the presence of a seal might well be misleading, for if the seal was affixed by an unauthorized person it was of no effect.[340]

§5.151 The general rule at common law was that a corporation was not bound by a contract unless it was made under the seal of the corporation. However, that rule was subject to three main exceptions. First, a seal was not required in the case of contracts or agreements entered into by trading corporations in the ordinary course of their business. Second, a seal was not required in the case of

---

[335] *Alliance Securities Ltd. v. Posnikoff*, [1922] 3 W.W.R. 1201 (Sask. K.B.).
[336] *Provincial Insurance Co. v. Cameron* (1881), 31 U.C.C.P. 523 at 539, *per* Wilson C.J., aff'd 9 O.A.R. 279.
[337] *Grand Junction Rlwy. Co. v. Midland Rlwy. Co.* (1882), 7 O.A.R. 681 (C.A.).
[338] William Blackstone, *1 Commentaries on the Laws of England*, reprint ed. (Chicago: University of Chicago Press, 1979), at 463.
[339] *Eastview (Town) v. Roman Catholic Episcopal Corp. of Ottawa* (1918), 44 O.L.R. 284 at 295-96 (C.A.), *per* Riddell J.; *Dartford Union Guardians v. Trickett* (1889), 59 L.T. 754 at 757 (Q.B.), *per* Pollock B.
[340] *West City Motors Ltd. v. Delta Acceptance Corp.*, [1963] 2 O.R. 683 (H.C.), although it was presumed that any seal that was affixed was valid: *Inter City Baking Co. v. Rosenblood*, [1954] O.W.N. 531 (C.A.).

contracts or agreements relating to matters trivial in their nature and of frequent occurrence. Third, no seal was required in the case of contracts or agreements to which the equitable doctrine of part performance applied, or when the corporation had received the benefit of an executed agreement or had acted upon the contract.[341]

§5.152 The cumbersome requirement for the use of a seal was a hold-over from a time when corporations were primarily ecclesiastical or public bodies such as municipalities or agencies of the Crown. These bodies rarely engaged in contractual dealings. Even allowing the ordinary course of trade exception, the requirement for the use of a seal could not long survive in an age when corporations had become a common form of trading enterprise; the courts soon recognized its impracticality.[342] Eventually the requirement was abolished by statute. In this regard, section 23(2) of the CBCA now provides:

> 23(2). A document executed on behalf of a corporation is not invalid merely because a corporate seal is not affixed to it.

The present version of the OBCA contains no similar provision, although section 13 of the Act does provide:[343] "A corporation may, but need not, have a corporate seal". In contrast, the previous OBCA (which required every corporation under that Act to have a seal)[344] expressly authorized unsealed written and parol contracts, and provided:

> 18.(2) A contract that if entered into by an individual person would be by law required to be in writing signed by the parties to be charged therewith may be entered into on behalf of the corporation in writing signed by any person acting under its authority, express or implied.
>
> (3) A contract that if entered into by an individual person would be valid although made by parol only and not reduced into writing may be entered into by parol on behalf of a corporation by any person acting under its authority, express or implied.

Despite the deletion of the above provisions, it nevertheless is implicit in the permissive wording of section 13 that a corporation may conduct its business (or otherwise signify its consent to contracts, *etc.*) other than by way of affixing its corporate seal — for the very purpose of a business corporation is to carry on business, and if a seal were required to carry on that business, the permissive nature of section 13 would be entirely defeated.[345]

§5.153 Until recently, certain contracts (*e.g.*, deeds of land) were required by law to be made under seal by both individuals and corporations. Under the law

---

[341] *Merkur Bros. v. W.J. McCart & Co.*, [1944] O.W.N. 671 at 673 (M.C.), *per* Marriott M.
[342] *Henderson v. Australian Royal Mail Steam Navigation Co.* (1855), 5 El. & Bl. 409 at 417, 119 E.R. 533 (Q.B.), *per* Erle J.; approved by Duff J. in *McKnight Construction Co. v. Vansickler* (1915), 24 D.L.R. 298, 51 S.C.R. 374 at 390.
[343] Am. 2001, c. 14, s. 12. CBCA, s. 23(1): "A corporation may but need not have a seal, and may change a seal that it has adopted".
[344] R.S.O. 1970, c. 53.
[345] See, generally, *Bernardin v. Municipality of North Dufferin* (1891), 19 S.C.R. 581.

of Ontario, there no longer appear to be any contracts that must be entered into under seal, although the same cannot be said of many other jurisdictions.[346] Subsection 18(1) of the former OBCA dealing with contracts required by law to be under seal, was declarative of the general law. It provided that:

> A contract that if entered into by an individual person would be by law required to be in writing and under seal may be entered into on behalf of a corporation in writing under the seal of the corporation.

Where a seal is required by all parties, but the corporation possesses no actual corporate seal, the contract is sufficiently sealed if it is sealed in the same manner as it would be sealed by an individual — as, for instance, through the affixing of a wafer seal on the document. Where there is no seal on a document, the fact of sealing will be presumed (even in cases where no mark or impression on the paper appears) provided that the attestation indicates that the solemnity of affixing a seal has been satisfied.[347]

F. MINIMUM CAPITALIZATION

§5.154 In the United Kingdom, section 118 of the *Companies Act, 1985* (which incorporates into British law the minimum capital requirements of the E.U.'s *Second Company Law Directive*) provides that a public limited company must have a minimum authorized and allotted capital of £50,000. At one time, many North American jurisdictions also imposed a minimum capitalization requirement on corporations, under which a company was obliged to issue a minimum amount of capital as a condition of attaining either limited liability or being validly organized. For instance, until 1972, the Kentucky legislation required a company to have a minimum capital base of $1,000. In *Tri-State Developers Inc. v. Moore*,[348] it was found that a corporation had begun operations with only $500 rather than $1,000 in capital. It was held that the company's members lost their right to limited liability as a result. A few such jurisdictions continue to impose such a requirement, but across North America the trend is strongly away from such requirements, particularly since the requirement for minimum capital was removed from the *Model Business Corporation Act* in 1969. Neither the OBCA nor the CBCA impose a minimum capitalization requirement for either public or private companies.[349] As a practical benefit, it is difficult to see what benefit flows from the imposition of such a requirement.

G. CERTIFICATE OF INCORPORATION

§5.155 The ancient Roman civil law allowed three or more persons to form a primitive form of company capable of acting as a collective body by mere voluntary association. In contrast, under the common law, it has always been abso-

---

[346] See, for instance, the *Companies Act*, 1985 (U.K.), s. 36.
[347] *Re Bell & Black* (1882), 1 O.R. 125 (Ch.); *Re Buff Pressed Brick Co.* (1924), 56 O.L.R. 33 at 35 (H.C.), *per* Mowat J.
[348] 343 S.W. (2d) 812 (Ky. 1961).
[349] In its *1967 Interim Report* (Toronto: Queens Printer), the Ontario Select Committee on Company Law explained its reasons for not requiring a minimum capital base at paras. 1.4.1 to 1.4.3.

lutely necessary for the king to consent to the incorporation of a company.[350] Such Royal consent might be express (as where the king created a company by Royal Charter under letters patent) or implied (as for instance where the company was created by statute) to which royal assent was a necessary ingredient. Under the OBCA and the CBCA, the Crown's consent to incorporation remains in vestigial form, both in the fact that when enacted each of these statutes necessarily required royal assent, and as well as the requirement that a certificate of incorporation be issued by the responsible ministry of the Crown, in order for any corporation to come into existence.

§5.156 The requirement for a certificate of incorporation is set out in section 6 of the OBCA, which provides that upon receipt of the articles, the Director shall endorse thereon a certificate which shall constitute the certificate of incorporation.[351] It is the certificate of incorporation (rather than the articles themselves) that is the basic incorporating instrument of the corporation,[352] so that the mere submission of the articles to the Director in and of itself is no more than an application for incorporation which sets the incorporation procedure in motion. Until the certificate of incorporation is endorsed (or issued under the CBCA) no corporation exists.

§5.157 The form of certificate is governed by clause 273(1)(*b*) of the OBCA, and must contain the day, month and year of the endorsement and the corporation number. The certificate of incorporation is endorsed on both duplicate copies of the articles of incorporation. One of the two duplicate copies of the articles of incorporation must be filed, the other is returned to the corporation or its representative. Formerly, the Director was required to publish forthwith a notice of the endorsement of the certificate in *The Ontario Gazette*, but this requirement has now been repealed.[353] Articles of incorporation are effective on the date shown in the certificate.[354] The certificate may be dated as of the day the Director receives the duplicate originals of the articles together with all other required documents executed in accordance with the Act and the prescribed fee, or upon any later date acceptable to the Director that is specified by the person who submitted the articles of incorporation.[355] A corporation is deemed to be in existence for the whole of the day on which it is incorporated.[356]

---

[350] William Blackstone, *1 Commentaries on the Laws of England*, reprint ed. (Chicago: University of Chicago Press, 1979), at 460. In England and Scotland, a handful of corporations predate this rule, but it is nevertheless presumed that they received the authority of the Crown to act as a corporate entity under a lost grant.

[351] The Legislature has the power to so delegate its powers of incorporation: *Bird v. Merchants Telephone Co.* (1894), 5 Que. S.C. 445.

[352] See, generally, *Letain v. Conwest Exploration Co.*, [1961] S.C.R. 98.

[353] OBCA, ss. 273(1)(*b*)(iv), repealed S.O. 1994, c. 27, s. 71(38).

[354] *Ibid.*, s. 273(3).

[355] *Ibid.*, s. 273(2). Subsection (2) also provides that the court may request that the certificate of articles be dated on some other day, but this provision would seem to have no application in the case of articles of incorporation.

[356] *Official Receiver of Jubilee Cotton Mills Ltd. v. Lewis*, [1924] A.C. 958 at 999 (H.L.), *per* Lord Dunedin.

§5.158 The corresponding CBCA provisions take a somewhat different approach. Instead of endorsing a certificate of incorporation on the articles themselves, the certificate of incorporation is a separate document that is issued by the Director.[357] Since it is obviously desirable to have some actual indication on the face of documents submitted to the Director that evidences their receipt, on the actual articles a simple filing endorsement is made.[358] By analogy to the OBCA, it is the issue of the certificate rather than the filing endorsement that creates the corporation. The balance of the incorporation procedure under the CBCA resembles that under the OBCA. For instance, a notice of the issue of the certificate of incorporation is published in a publication generally available to the public (until 2001, publication was in the *Canada Gazette*).[359] The corporation comes into existence on the date set out in the certificate of incorporation,[360] and following the issue of the certificate, a copy of the filed articles is returned to the corporation or its representative.[361]

§5.159 The courts have long recognized that people who deal with a corporation need to be able to do so in the confidence that the existence of the corporation will not be easily disturbed.[362] Under the OBCA, a certificate of incorporation is conclusive proof that the corporation has been incorporated on the date set out in the certificate, except in a proceeding under section 240 to cancel the certificate for cause.[363] The CBCA contains no corresponding provision, section 9 of that Act providing no more than that the corporation comes into existence on the date set out in the certificate. However, the case law indicates that a certificate of incorporation issued under that Act should be treated as conclusive proof of incorporation.[364] Third parties act on the strength of the certificate of incorporation. It would be unfairly prejudicial to their interests if it were possible to look behind such certificates.

§5.160 At one time it was necessary to show not only that a corporation had been granted a charter, but also that the incorporators had accepted the incorporation, in order to give the charter full force and effect. The reason for this re-

---

[357] CBCA, s. 8.
[358] *Ibid.*, s. 262(2)(*b*)(i).
[359] *Ibid.*, s. 262(2)(*b*)(v).
[360] *Ibid.*, s. 9.
[361] *Ibid.*, s. 262(2)(*b*)(iv).
[362] *Cotman v. Brougham*, [1918] A.C. 514 at 591 (H.L.); *R. v. Reg. of Companies, ex p. Central Bank of India*, [1986] Q.B. 1114 (C.A.). See also *Re amalgamation of Aylwards (1975) Ltd.*, [2001] N.J. No. 195, 16 B.L.R. (3d) 34 at 41 (S.C.), *per* Green C.J.
[363] OBCA, s. 7; *Prim Investments Ltd. v. Madison Development Corp.*, [1982] A.J. No. 572, [1983] 1 W.W.R. 697 (Q.B.) — dealing with a certificate of incorporation under the Alberta *Business Corporations Act*. At common law, a wrongful decision by the Registrar to incorporate an entity where the statutory requirements have not been satisfied could be the subject of judicial review but only where sought by the Attorney General: *Bowman v. Secular Society Ltd.*, [1917] A.C. 406 (H.L.).
[364] *Re Barned's Banking Co. (Peel's Case)* (1867), 2 Ch. App. 674 (L.JJ.); *Re Overend, Gurney & Co. (Oakes v. Turquand)* (1867), 36 L.J. 949 at 965 (H.L.), *per* Lord Chelmsford L.C.; but compare *C.P.C. Valve & Investment, Ltd. v. Scott* (1979), 9 Alta. L.R. (2d) 35 (T.D.); *Re National Debenture & Assets Corp.*, [1891] 2 Ch. 505 at 575 (C.A.), doubted in *Ladies Dress Association Ltd. v. Pulbrook*, [1900] 2 Q.B. 376 (C.A.), *per* Romer L.J.

quirement was that "persons cannot be incorporated without their consent".[365] Under the present OBCA and CBCA, the requirement that incorporators sign the articles of incorporation[366] would seem to be sufficient evidence of such consent, so it is not now necessary to show that the incorporators have "accepted" the incorporation of the company.[367]

H. ONTARIO CORPORATION NUMBER

§5.161 All corporations carrying on business in Ontario are required to have a corporation number. In the case of corporations incorporated under the OBCA, section 8 of the Act provides that every corporation shall be assigned a number by the Director and that number shall be specified as the corporation number in the certificate of incorporation[368] and in any other certificate relating to the corporation endorsed or issued by the Director. Where the Director assigns a number to a corporation that is the same as the number of any other corporation previously assigned, the Director may issue a certificate of amendment to the articles of the corporation changing the number, and upon the issuance of the certificate of amendment, the articles are amended accordingly.[369] Similarly, where the Director has endorsed a certificate on articles that set out the corporation number incorrectly, the Director may substitute a corrected certificate that bears the date of the certificate it replaces.[370]

I. EFFECT OF INCORPORATION

§5.162 The primary effect of incorporation, as that concept is understood at common law, is to create a juristic person.[371] As noted above, in this regard, section 27 of the Ontario *Interpretation Act*[372] provides that:

> 27. In every Act, unless the contrary intention appears, words making any association or number of persons a corporation or body politic and corporate,

---

[365] *Calvin Church v. Logan* (1884), Trueman's Equity Cases 221 (N.B.S.C.).
[366] OBCA, s. 4(1); CBCA, s. 5(1).
[367] *Baldwin Iron & Steel Works Ltd. v. Dominion Carbide* (1903), 2 O.W.R. 6 at 8 (H.C.), per Meredith C.J.
[368] The file number that was assigned to a corporation by the Minister prior to s. 8 coming into force is deemed to be the corporation number of that corporation: OBCA, s. 8(5).
[369] OBCA, s. 8(3).
[370] *Ibid.*, s. 8(4).
[371] *Orchard v. Tunney* (1957), 8 D.L.R. (2d) 273 at 278 (S.C.C.). The law does not necessarily ignore the existence of unincorporated associations however, particularly where an unincorporated association has been implicated in criminal or tortious conduct: see for instance, *UNA v. Alberta (Attorney General)*, [1992] S.C.J. No. 37, 89 D.L.R. (4th) 609; *Intl. Brotherhood of Teamsters v. Therien*, [1960] S.C.J. No. 6, 22 D.L.R. (2d) 1; *Intl. Longshoremen's Association v. Maritime Employer's Association*, [1978] S.C.J. No. 79, 89 D.L.R. (3d) 289 (S.C.C.); *Bradley Egg Farm Ltd. v. Clifford*, [1943] 2 All E.R. 378 (C.A.); *Alberta Government Telephones v. CRTC*, [1989] S.C.J. No. 84, 61 D.L.R. (4th) 193. For some fairly recent cases dealing with various aspects of corporate personality generally, see *Rayner (Mining Lane) Ltd. v. DTI*, [1989] Ch. 72 (C.A.), rev'd [1990] 2 A.C. 418 (H.L.); and see also *Maclaine Watson & Co. v. ITC*, [1989] Ch. 253, 286 (C.A.); *Re ITC*, [1989] Ch. 309 (C.A.); *Arab Monetary Fund v. Hashim (No. 3)*, [1912] 2 A.C. 114 (H.L.).
[372] R.S.O. 1990, c. I.11.

(a) vest in the corporation power to sue and be sued, to contract and be contracted with by its corporate name, to have a common seal, to alter or change the seal at its pleasure, to have perpetual succession, to acquire and hold personal property or movables for the purpose for which the corporation is constituted and to alienate the same at pleasure;

(b) vest in a majority of the members of the corporation the power to bind the others by their acts; and

(c) exempt individual members of the corporation from personal liability for its debts, obligations or acts if they do not contravene the provisions of the Act incorporating them.

Section 21(1)(b) of the Canada *Interpretation Act*[373] is to like effect, but contains the following additional presumption:

in the case of a corporation having a name consisting of an English and a French form or a combined English and French form, as vesting in the corporation power to use either the English or the French form of its name or both forms and to show on its seal both the English and French forms of its name or have two seals, one showing the English and the other showing the French form of its name.

For the most part, these general presumptions are expanded rather than constrained under both the OBCA and the CBCA. There are, however, certain exceptions. In particular, the power of the majority of shareholders to bind the minority is now constrained under both the OBCA and the CBCA by virtue of the statutory class voting rights, the oppression remedy and the right of shareholder dissent given in respect of certain fundamental changes to the corporation.

§5.163 The nature and implications of separate legal personality are fully discussed in Chapter 1, and therefore need not be repeated here in detail.[374] Suffice it to say that the separate personality of a corporation from its shareholders or other members is a matter of law, not judicial convention. It arises from the express wording of statute and accordingly cannot be lightly ignored, except in the clearest cases where agency or some other overriding consideration can be shown.[375] The court will not ignore the separate personality of a corporation merely because it might seem fair to do so according to some abstract notion of justice,[376] or because the persons standing behind the corporation might not seem to have "clean hands" according to some manner of reckoning. In the words of McKay J.:[377]

It is not enough for a party to cry "equity" and expect to be compensated. One must identify the relevant principle of equity on which a claim can be properly founded.

---

[373] R.S.C. 1985, c. I-21.
[374] For a case which illustrates the practical implications of the rule, see *Tridont Leasing (Canada) Ltd. v. Saskatoon Market Mall Ltd.*, [1995] S.J. No. 297, 24 B.L.R. (2d) 105 (C.A.).
[375] *Lee v. Lee's Air Farming Ltd.*, [1961] N.Z.L.R. 325 (P.C.); *EBM Co. v. Dominion Bank*, [1937] 3 All E.R. 555 (H.L.); *Trevor Ivory Ltd. v. Anderson*, [1992] 2 N.Z.L.R. 517 (C.A.).
[376] *NZI Bank Ltd. v. Euro-National Corporation Ltd.*, [1992] 3 N.Z.L.R. 538 at 539, *per* Richardson J.
[377] *A.G. v. Equitycorp Industries Group Ltd.*, [1996] 1 N.Z.L.R. 528 at 537.

§5.164 A number of American cases have adopted what is known as the "group enterprise doctrine" as a basis for ignoring the separate liability of parent and subsidiary corporations in certain cases. If broadly applied, the principle would seem to ignore the express effect of both the OBCA and the CBCA, each of which provides for wholly owned subsidiary corporations and confers limited liability on all shareholders of corporations, irrespective of the individual make-up of their shareholder constituencies. Nevertheless, there is some Commonwealth case law which is at least partly supportive of a group enterprise approach. For instance, in *Smith, Stone & Knight Ltd. v. Birmingham Corp.*[378] Atkinson J. listed six factors which were relevant to the question of whether it was appropriate to ignore the separate legal identity of a subsidiary corporation, specifically:

- whether the profits of the subsidiary are treated as the profits of the parent;
- whether the persons conducting the business of the subsidiary were appointed by the parent company;
- whether the parent was the head and brains of the subsidiary;
- whether the parent governed the adventure of the subsidiary, in that it decided what should be done and what capital should be embarked on the venture;
- whether the subsidiary makes its profits by its own skill and director or by that of its parent;
- whether the parent was in effectual and constant control of the subsidiary.

This list was examined and discussed by Reed J. in *Alberta Gas Ethylene Co. v. R.*:

> As I read the jurisprudence, it does not establish that it is sufficient to consider the six criteria and when they are all met (as they are in the present case), to ignore the separate legal existence of the subsidiary company. One has to ask for what purpose and in what context is the subsidiary being ignored. What is more, I do not interpret the jurisprudence as ignoring the existence of subsidiary corporations *per se*. Rather, it seems to me that the jurisprudence proceeds on the basis that in certain circumstances, consequences will be drawn *despite* the legal existence of separate subsidiary corporations.[379]

A similar sentiment was expressed by Cameron J.A. in *Bow Valley Husky (Bermuda) Ltd. v. Saint John Shipbuilding Ltd.*[380] As noted in Chapter 1, the group enterprise doctrine has been adopted in the labour/employment context in Canada but elsewhere the doctrine has little if any application at all. In England, the Court of Appeal seems to have rejected the doctrine entirely in *Adams v. Cape Industries plc,* in which Slade L.J. wrote:[381]

---

[378] [1939] 4 All E.R. 116 (K.B.).
[379] [1989] F.C.J. No. 1104, 24 F.T.R. 309 at 313-14, 41 B.L.R. 117 (T.D.), aff'd [1990] F.C.J. No. 549, 90 D.T.C. 6419 (C.A.).
[380] [1995] N.J. No. 150, 126 D.L.R. (4th) 1 at 15 *et seq.* (C.A.), var'd [1997] S.C.J. No. 111, 153 D.L.R. (4th) 385.
[381] [1990] Ch. 433 at 544 (C.A.).

... [W]e do not accept as a matter of law that the court is entitled to lift the corporate veil as against a defendant company which is the member of a corporate group merely because the corporate structure has been used so as to ensure that the legal liability (if any) in respect of particular future activities of the group (and correspondingly the risk of enforcement of that liability) will fall on another member of the group rather than the defendant company. Whether or not this is desirable, the right to use a corporate structure in this manner is inherent in our corporate law.

J. ORGANIZATION OF THE CORPORATION

§5.165 Upon incorporation, the corporation comes into existence, but in order for it to carry on its business and affairs, a further step (known generally as organization) is required. The organization process includes the adoption of necessary by-laws or governing resolutions by the corporation, the receipt of initial share subscriptions from the proposed shareholders of the corporation, the approval of by-laws by the shareholders, the authorization to open bank accounts, and so forth. Even where the incorporators or intended shareholders sign a unanimous shareholder agreement reserving to themselves all powers of management, it is still necessary to conduct an organizational meeting of the directors, for until such time as shares are allotted to them, those persons are not shareholders in the corporation.[382]

§5.166 As a practical matter, the holding of an organizational meeting is a prerequisite to the conduct of business and affairs by the corporation. In the absence of such a meeting (or unanimous written resolutions of the directors in lieu thereof), there would be no validly appointed signing officers for the corporation, and no authorities given to deal on the corporation's behalf. While certain acts and contracts of the corporation might possibly be saved by invoking the concept of ostensible authority, the legitimacy of corporate acts would clearly be open to question. However, despite the general requirement for organization, once the corporation is incorporated it is a legal entity and therefore has the necessary power to defend (and presumably, initiate and prosecute) an action.[383]

§5.167 Sections 104 of the CBCA and 117 of the OBCA make express provision concerning the holding and conduct of the organizational meeting of directors (which is called a "first meeting of directors" under the OBCA) in the case of every newly incorporated corporation.[384] Each Act allows this meeting to be called on five days' notice by any incorporator or director.[385] Subsection 104(1) of the CBCA reads:

---

[382] See, generally, *Miller v. Thompson* (1866), 16 U.C.C.P. 513 at 522, *per* Wilson J.
[383] *Campbell v. Taxicabs Verrals Ltd.* (1912), 27 O.L.R. 141 (H.C.).
[384] It is not necessary under either Act to hold an organizational meeting of the corporation where the corporation is one to which a certificate of amalgamation has been issued or a certificate of continuance has been issued: OBCA, s. 117(3); CBCA, s. 104(2). There is no express exemption granted where a corporation is revived or reorganized, or where articles of arrangement are issued. However, it is doubtful that an organizational meeting is required in such cases, since the issue of such articles does not create a new corporation but merely affects the constitution of an existing corporation.
[385] OBCA, s. 117(4); CBCA, s. 104(3).

104.(1) After the issue of the certificate of incorporation, a meeting of the directors of the corporation shall be held at which the directors may,

(a) make by-laws;

(b) adopt forms of security certificates and corporate records;

(c) authorize the issue of securities;

(d) appoint officers;

(e) appoint an auditor to hold office until the first annual meeting of shareholders;

(f) make banking arrangements; and

(g) transact any other business.

Subsection 117(1) of the OBCA is similar, but provides that the meeting must be held "after incorporation". Since incorporation occurs at the time of the issue of the certificate of incorporation, it follows that there is no significant difference between the two statutes. As the statute specifically provides that the organizational meeting may not be held until after incorporation, any purported organizational meeting that was held prior to that time will be invalid. Subsection 117(2) of the OBCA expressly permits unanimous written resolutions in lieu of an organizational meeting. Section 104 of the CBCA contains no express provision in this regard, but subsection 117(1) of the CBCA would seem to be sufficiently broad to permit unanimous written resolutions under that Act as well.

K. PROMOTERS

§5.168 Under the present OBCA and CBCA, the incorporators of a corporation are the person or persons who sign the articles of incorporation submitted to the Director to secure its incorporation. Historically, the incorporators of a company have been seen to number among the promoters of the company. Broadly stated, a promoter is a person who is engaged (as the instigator or an active participant rather than in a professional capacity) in the formation of a corporation or the floatation of its securities. A person will only be a promoter of a proposed corporation if he or she is concerned in some way in the management or preparation for management of that corporation's business or affairs, so that his position or the functions that he is performing are analogous to the position or functions of a director.[386] A promoter is not a trustee *per se*, but he or she may well become subject to the full range of the duties of a trustee on the facts of a given case.[387] In the ordinary case, the promoter stands in a fiduciary relationship to the corporation and owes a duty to deal fairly with the corporation.[388] The promoter may not transfer assets to the corporation at an exorbitant price. He or she may not conceal relevant facts from the directors of the corporation — that is, facts that the directors must know in order to make a fair judgment concerning their dealings

---

[386] *Re Great Wheal Polgooth Co.* (1883), 53 L.J. Ch. 42.
[387] *Re Hess Manufacturing Co.* (1894), 23 S.C.R. 644, *per* Strong C.J.C.
[388] *Ramrakha v. Zimmer*, [1994] A.J. No. 816, 24 Alta. L.R. (3d) 240 (C.A.) — a promoter must account for a secret profit.

with the promoter. Furthermore the promoter may neither misrepresent nor conceal material facts. Perhaps most importantly, to be safe from impeachment, dealings between a promoter and the corporation must be independently approved.

§5.169 The incorporators and other promoters of a corporation are not normally considered to be partners in the business of the corporation.[389] A different conclusion may be reached where the incorporators carry on trade prior to incorporation — effectively conducting the business that they intend for the corporation eventually to carry on itself. Pending the incorporation of a business, the incorporators may be held to have conducted the business as partners, and they will be liable as such for the obligations of the business leading up to the time of incorporation.[390] The transfer of the pre-existing business to the corporation does not release the incorporators from liability as partners for the debts and liabilities incurred before the transfer, but there will not normally be any such liability for debts and liabilities that arise after the time of the transfer of the business to the corporation.[391]

(i) Identification of Promoters

§5.170 In drafting the former OBCA in the late 1960s, the Ontario Select Committee expressly rejected the idea that the incorporators of a company should be deemed to be promoters, as being inconsistent with prevailing commercial practice.[392] Very often, the association of the named incorporators with the corporation is nominal. Accordingly, the Select Committee concluded both that the incorporators should not be required to subscribe for shares in the corporation, and that they not be required to serve as its first directors.

§5.171 The articles of incorporation must identify the incorporators of a corporation under the OBCA and the CBCA, but it is not necessary to disclose any other promoter of the corporation. Therefore, in order to decide whether a particular person is or is not a promoter, as that term is understood at law, it is necessary to look beyond the OBCA and the CBCA. Although defined under the *Securities Act*, the term "promoter" is not a term of art for corporate law purposes, but rather is a business term that usefully provides a single word designation for persons who perform a number of business functions in connection with bringing a corporation into existence.[393] In each case, it is necessary to inquire into the real connection that the person has in connection with the incorporation of the company in order to decide whether that person is a promoter.[394] There

---

[389] *MacPherson v. deWinter*, [1997] N.B.J. No. 166, 188 N.B.R. (2d) 31 (Q.B.); *Keith Spier Ltd. v. Mansell*, [1970] 1 All E.R. 462 at 464 (C.A.), per Edmund Davies L.J.
[390] *Holund Holdings Ltd. v. Lewicky* (1970), 12 D.L.R. (3d) 398 (B.C.S.C.).
[391] *Pitrie v. Racey* (1963), 37 D.L.R. (2d) 495 (B.C.S.C.).
[392] *Interim Report of the Select Committee on Company Law* (Toronto: Queen's Printer, 1967), para. 1.2.5.
[393] *Whaley Bridge Calico Printing Co. v. Green* (1880), 5 Q.B.D. 109 at 111, per Bowen J.
See also *Con-Force Products Ltd. v. Rosen* (1967), 61 W.W.R. 129 at 133 (Sask. Q.B.), per Disbery J.
[394] *Lydney & Wigpool Iron Ore Co. v. Bird* (1886), 33 Ch. D. 85 at 93 (C.A.), per Lindley L.J.

may be (and often are) several promoters of a company. In addition to covering a person who plays an active part in setting up the company, it can also cover those who play a more passive role, provided they have been involved in the setting up of the company or organization of its business on the understanding that they will profit from its establishment.[395] However, ordinarily a person will not fall within the definition of "promoter" unless there has been some exertion on his or her part for the purpose of either organizing or substantially reorganizing the business, structure and affairs of a corporation.[396] Summarizing the foregoing, it follows that a person *may* be held to be a promoter where he or she:

- raised the idea of forming the corporation for the purpose in question, and solicited the interest of others in that idea;

- had control over the terms set out in the articles of incorporation, by-laws and any unanimous shareholder agreement, not in the sense of providing legal, financial or technical advice,[397] but in the sense of deciding which of the advice so provided should be acted upon;

- paid or undertook an absolute or contingent obligation to pay the costs of preparing the incorporation and organization documents, and signed those documents as an incorporator;

- was named as a first director or sought out the people who agreed to act as first directors;

- solicited subscriptions for capital investment in the corporation;

- directly benefited from the formation of the corporation.[398]

But these are mere considerations that will be taken into account; none of them is by itself conclusive. A corporation may be the promoter of another corporation,[399] and a person who acts as agent for another may also be held to be a promoter.[400]

(ii) The Duties of Promoters

§5.172 Though difficult to resolve, the question of whether a particular person falls within the concept of a promoter is an important one. As noted above, equity has long been concerned with restraining the conduct of promoters, to ensure that they do not misconduct themselves in the formation or flotation of their

---

[395] See, for instance, *Tracy v. Mandalay Pty. Ltd.* (1953), 88 C.L.R. 215 (H.C. Aust.).
[396] *Emma Silver Mining Co. v. Lewis & Son* (1879), 4 C.P.D. 396 at 407, *per* Lindley J.
[397] *Re Great Wheal Polgooth Co.* (1883), 53 L.J. Ch. 42 at 47, *per* Bacon V.C.
[398] On this basis, vendors of property to a corporation have often been held to be promoters: See, for instance, *Gluckstein v. Barnes*, [1900] A.C. 240 at 249 (H.L.), *per* Lord Macnaghten.
[399] *Gray v. Yellowknife Gold Mines Ltd.*, [1947] O.R. 928 (C.A.), but compare *R. v. Johnston*, [1932] O.R. 79 at 82 (C.A.).
[400] See *Lydney & Wigpool Iron Ore Co. v. Bird* (1886), 33 Ch. D. 85 at 94-95 (C.A.), *per* Lindley L.J.

companies.[401] The primary mischief at which equity has aimed is that a promoter may use his or her position to secure a secret profit through some trade between the promoter and the company. For instance, a promoter personally may buy a property and then sell it on to the company at a higher price. Equity prohibits the promoter from making a secret profit in such a case.[402] Because a breach of these duties may result in liability, the wisest course for anyone who *may* be a promoter is to act on the assumption that he or she *is* a promoter, and to comply with the duties concerned.

§5.173 The fiduciary duty of a promoter[403] arises as soon as the promoter begins to act in promotion of the corporation. These duties extend not only to the corporation, but also to subscribers for capital in the corporation during the process of its incorporation. In this respect, the fiduciary duties of the promoters stand in contrast to those of the directors, as the director's fiduciary duties (*i.e.*, those duties that are imposed upon them under corporate law) are always owed to the corporation. The duties, and hence the potential liability, of promoters to the corporation constitute one of the few aspects of corporate law left almost entirely untouched by the OBCA and the CBCA. As a result, there is no statutory codification of the liability of promoters, and therefore in order to ascertain the nature and extent of their duties and liability it is necessary to canvass the extensive body of law which has been handed down in this area over the past century or so.

§5.174 The reason why promoters are subjected to a fiduciary duty can be quickly explained. It is common for the promoters of a corporation to exercise an extraordinary degree of control over a corporation during its formative stages. All too frequently in the past they have been found to abuse the particular advantages which their early involvement with the corporation affords to them. So long as promoters retain exceptional control, the following types of transaction involving promoters give rise to concern:

---

[401] Much of the common law insofar as it pertains to reporting issues has been superceded by statutory and other rules imposed under applicable securities regulation regimes. However, the common law rules remain relevant when dealing with private companies and other non-reporting issuers. As to the availability of class action proceedings in claims against promoters, see *Metera v. Financial Planning Group*, [2003] A.J. No. 468 (Q.B.); *Abdool v. Anaheim Management Ltd.*, [1995] O.J. No. 16, 21 O.R. (3d) 453, 121 D.L.R. (4th) 496, 31 C.P.C. (3d) 197 (Div. Ct.); *Carom v. Bre-X Minerals Ltd.*, [2001] O.J. No. 4014, 51 O.R. (3d) 236, 196 D.L.R. (4th) 344, 1 C.P.C. (5th) 62, 11 B.L.R. (3d) 1 (C.A.), rev'g [1999] O.J. No. 5114, 46 O.R. (3d) 315, 6 B.L.R. (3d) 82, 1 C.P.C. (5th) 82 (Div. Ct.), aff'g [1999] O.J. No. 1662, 44 O.R. (3d) 173, 46 B.L.R. (2d) 247, 35 C.P.C. (4th) 43 (S.C.J.); *Millard v. North George Capital Management Ltd.*, [2000] O.J. No. 1535, [2000] O.T.C. 305, 47 C.P.C. (4th) 365 (S.C.J.); *Elms v. Laurentian Bank of Canada*, [2001] B.C.J. No. 1284, 90 B.C.L.R. (3d) 195, 5 C.P.C. (5th) 201 (C.A.); *Mondor v. Fisherman*, [2002] O.J. No. 1855, [2002] O.T.C. 317, 26 B.L.R. (3d) 281, 22 C.P.C. (5th) 346 (S.C.J.); *Moyes v. Fortune Financial Corp.*, [2002] O.J. No. 4297, 61 O.R. (3d) 770 (S.C.J.).

[402] *Emma Silver Mining Co. v. Lewis & Son* (1879), 4 C.P.D. 396 at 407, per Lindley J.; *Re Hess Mfg. Co. (Sloan's Case)* (1894), 21 O.A.R. 66 at 85, per Haggarty C.J.O., aff'd 23 S.C.R. 644; *Patton v. Yukon Consolidated Gold Corp.*, [1934] O.W.N. 321, additional reasons [1936] O.R. 308 at 324 (C.A.) — controlling shareholder of a promoter is also a promoter; see also the remarks of Middleton J.A. at 322.

[403] *Lydney & Wigpool Iron Ore Co. v. Bird* (1886), 33 Ch. D. 85 at 94 (C.A.), per Lindley L.J.

- the negotiation and payment of a commission to the promoters by a person who is selling or who intends to sell property to the corporation;
- the creation and issue of "golden shares" and similar rights which give the promoters effective control over the corporation or a degree of control disproportionate to the investment that they are making in the corporation;
- the sale or other transfer of property to the corporation, including any business transferred, and in particular all aspects of the valuation of the property so sold or transferred;
- the assumption by the corporation of the debts of a pre-existing business, particularly where those debts are not entirely related to the business that is being acquired by the corporation;
- the grant of options to acquire shares in the corporation at some time in the future or under certain conditions where the issue price is set unreasonably low;
- reimbursement of costs and expenses incurred in the promotion of the corporation;
- misrepresentation or concealment of relevant facts either from the corporation itself or from potential or existing investors in the corporation.

With the exception of misrepresentation, some of the above transactions may well be legitimate.

§5.175 Not all dealings between a promoter and his or her company give rise to an opportunity for dishonesty. There will be no such opportunity if suitable precautionary mechanisms are put in place. In general terms, by deeming promoters to be fiduciaries, equity imposes the following requirements as a precautionary mechanism to protect the corporation: first, a need for full and truthful disclosure; second, a need for independent decision-making in all transactions directly or indirectly conferring a benefit on the promoter; and third, a general duty of fair dealing. While the risk of dishonesty gives rise to the fiduciary duty, it is important to note that the liability of a promoter does not turn upon proof of actual dishonesty. A cause of action is still made out where the corporation or (in certain cases) its shareholders can establish that the high standards of a fiduciary have not been satisfied.[404]

§5.176 A promoter usually makes one of two mistakes in his (or her) dealings with the corporation. Either he will deal with the corporation as if it were at arm's length, disclosing only such information as is considered expedient to advance his interests, and exacting whatever bargain he is able to drive; or he will deal with the corporation as if it was an extension of himself so that he was

---

[404] See, in this regard, *Re Coal Economising Gas Co. Gover's Case* (1875), 1 Ch. D. 182 at 187 (C.A.), *per* James L.J.; *Re Lady Forrest (Murchinson) Gold Mine Ltd.*, [1901] 1 Ch. Ch. 582; *Jacobus Marlet Estates Ltd. v. Marler* (1913), 85 L.J. P.C. 167; *Re Cape Breton Co.* (1885), 29 Ch. D. 795, aff'd 12 App. Cas. 652 (H.L.).

allowed to deal with its property and resources as if they were his own. Essentially the fiduciary duty of a promoter gives rise to an obligation of fair dealing with the corporation, which means that the promoters must act with utmost good faith towards the corporation.[405] This duty arises from the time (but not before) each of them respectively became a promoter — this time being a question of fact,[406] irrespective of whether those acts were done prior to incorporation[407] or afterward.[408] The duty of fair dealing has implications with respect to both the manner of negotiation and the terms of any transaction between the promoter and the corporation. For instance, where a promoter sells property to the corporation[409] he or she must do so at a fair price and must conceal nothing that it was proper for the directors of the corporation to know in order to form a fair judgment as to the value of the property concerned. The promoter must make no misrepresentation of facts that are material to the purchase, nor may the promoter structure the transaction (*e.g.*, through the use of a nominee vendor) so as to conceal that he or she is the beneficial vendor of the sale.[410] An incorporator may not make a secret profit[411] through any dealing with the corporation, [412] and will be liable for damages or to account for those profits if any are earned[413] and must make good any damages suffered by the corporation in any event.[414] Both with respect to profits and other critical aspects of the transaction, the promoter's disclosure must be full and fair.[415] A promoter who seeks to sell property[416] to the corporation at a profit must normally disclose the acquisition cost of that property,[417] and will be liable if the promoter misrepresents the value of the property.[418]

§5.177 The point at which the duty of disclosure arises is a matter of some uncertainty: specifically whether it is sufficient for the duty to arise where the

---

[405] See, for instance, *Fire Valley Orchards Ltd. v. Sly* (1914), 6 W.W.R. 934 (B.C.S.C.).
[406] The person who sells property to the corporation must be a promoter at the time of the sale in order to be subject to these duties: *Highway Advertising Co. of Canada v. Ellis* (1904), 7 O.L.R. 504 (C.A.).
[407] *Emma Silver Mining Co. v. Lewis & Son* (1879), 4 C.P.D. 396.
[408] *Erlanger v. New Sombrero Phosphate Co.* (1879), 3 App. Cas. 1218 at 1236 (H.L.), per Lord Cairns L.C. and per Lord Blackburn at 1269; *Lagunas Nitrate Co. v. Lagunas Syndicate*, [1899] 2 Ch. 392 at 422 (C.A.), per Lindley M.R.; *Gray v. Yellowknife Gold Mines Ltd.*, [1947] O.R. 928 (C.A.).
[409] *Erlanger v. New Sombrero Phosphate Co.* (1879), 3 App. Cas. 1218 at 1269 (H.L.), per Lord Blackburn.
[410] *Proprietary Mines Ltd. v. MacKay*, [1939] O.R. 461 (C.A.).
[411] *Lindsay Petroleum Co. v. Hurd* (1874), L.R. 5 P.C. 211; *Jubilee Cotton Mills Ltd. v. Lewis*, [1924] A.C. 958 (H.L.).
[412] *Patton v. Yukon Consolidated Gold Corp.*, [1934] O.W.N. 321 (C.A.).
[413] *Rumford v. Hinton* (1922), 52 O.L.R. 47 (C.A.).
[414] *Vitomen Cereal Ltd. v. Manitoba Grain Co.*, [1928] 4 D.L.R. 440 (B.C.S.C.); *Northrop Mining Co. v. Dimock* (1894), 27 N.S.R. 112 (C.A.).
[415] *Dominion Royalty Corp. v. Goffatt*, [1935] 1 D.L.R. 780 at 795, aff'd [1935] S.C.R. 565.
[416] The rule against secret profits also applies with respect to brokerage and similar fees charged by a promoter to a vendor selling assets to a company: *Whaley Bridge Calico Printing Co. v. Green* (1880), 5 Q.B.D. 109.
[417] *Canada v. Quebec Southern Rlwy.* (1908), 12 Ex. C.R. 11.
[418] *Alexandra Oil & Development Co. v. Cook* (1907), 10 O.W.R. 781, aff'd 11 O.W.R. 1054 (C.A.).

promoter has an intent to incorporate a company at the time of acquisition.[419] In *Erlanger v. New Sombrero Phosphate Co.*, Lord Cairns in the House of Lords, expressed a strong view that no duty arises unless the company is in the process of formation/floatation at the time when the property is acquired. Similarly, in *Ladywell Mining Co. v. Brookes*[420] five persons were found to have purchased a leasehold mine for £5,000 on February 1, 1873, with a view towards reselling it to a company to be formed. At the time, no steps had been taken toward formation. The purchase was completed on March 17, the purchase price being paid out of their own money. On April 4, the five persons concerned entered into a provisional contract with the trustee of an intended company, for the sale of the mining property at a price of £18,000. The company was registered on April 8. The contract of April 4 was adopted by the company. Four of the five vendors were named as directors. The contract of February 1 was not disclosed to the company. In 1882, the company was wound up voluntarily. During the course of liquidation, the facts relating to the purchase became known. In 1884, the company commenced an action against the vendors and their estates (three of them being dead) to recover the secret profits made. The Court of Appeal held that there was no right of recovery. In the course of his judgment, Cotton L.J. indicated that on the right facts promoters might be subject to a duty to disclose and to account even if the company was not in the process of incorporation at the time of purchase, but that it would be an unusual case in which this was so.[421] On the facts, this situation did not apply in the *Ladywell*.[422]

§5.178 In *Re Leeds & Hanley Theatres of Varieties Ltd.*,[423] it was found that the promoters of a company purchased property for the purpose of selling it to the company when formed. The property was conveyed to a trustee nominated by the promoters. Afterwards, it was conveyed by that trustee to a second trustee for the company, on the direction of the promoters. The promoters also nominated the first directors of the company, and prepared the prospectus for the raising of capital. The prospectus did not disclose the fact that the promoters were the real vendors of the property to the company, but instead represented that the promoter's own trustee was the vendor. In the course of the company's liquidation, the liquidator brought an action calling upon the promoters to account for their profit. It was held on these facts that the promoters stood in a fiduciary duty to the investors who were invited to take shares in the company, and that accordingly the promoters were obliged to disclose their interest. The prospectus was found to be fraudulent, containing statements deliberately intended to mislead. Accordingly, the promoters were liable to account for the profit that they had made. In the course of his judgment, Vaughan Williams L.J. expressly rejected the suggestion that the property was purchased for the benefit

---

[419] *Erlanger v. New Sombrero Phosphate Co.* (1878), 3 App. Cas. 1218 at 1234 (H.L.), *per* Lord Cairns L.C.; and *per* Lord Hatherley at 1242.
[420] (1887), 35 Ch. D. 400 (C.A.).
[421] *Ibid.*, at 411.
[422] As to the type of evidence required, see Lindley L.J., *ibid.*, at 414.
[423] [1902] 2 Ch. 809 (C.A.).

of the company.[424] This fact did not, however, preclude the promoters from being found to stand in a fiduciary position.[425]

§5.179 A person may also be liable as a promoter where he or she brings about an amalgamation of the corporation. By extension of the secret profit rule, a person promoting an amalgamation will be liable if he or she misrepresents the liabilities of a company in which the promoter is concerned in order to make sure that the amalgamation proceeds.[426] If, however, the corporation acts with full knowledge of the relevant facts and the promoter acts in good faith, the transaction will not be open to attack even if the promoter does earn a profit.[427] Moreover, a person will not be held to be a promoter merely by accepting shares in exchange for property, and unless a transferor was involved as a promoter at the time that the impugned transaction took place, there is nothing wrong with that person profiting from a sale of property to the corporation.[428]

§5.180 The promoter must also ensure that the judgment made by the board of directors is entirely independent of the promoters.[429] Where the promoter fails to take these steps, the corporation may repudiate the purchase within a reasonable time of the facts being discovered, even where the contract has been completely carried out, provided that it is able to restore the property transferred to the vendor.[430] If payment and transfer of the property has already been made, rescission may be ordered.[431] Where rescission is not available or has been denied, the corporation may still succeed in an action for damages against the promoter.[432] The measure of damages to the corporation is the loss that the corporation has suffered by reason of the transfer at the inflated price and thus will be equal to the difference in the value of the property in fact and the value represented to the corporation.[433] If any part of the promoter's profits consists of paid-up shares of the corporation, those shares may be treated as unpaid shares in a winding-up,[434]

---

[424] Note, however, the guarded manner in which his opinion was expressed, *ibid.*, at 822.
[425] [1902] 2 Ch. 809 at 823.
[426] *O'Sullivan v. Clarkson* (1907), 9 O.W.R. 46 (C.A.).
[427] *Larocque v. Beauchemin*, [1897] A.C. 358 (P.C.).
[428] *Highway Advertising Co. of Canada v. Ellis* (1904), 7 O.L.R. 504 (C.A.).
[429] *Re Hess Mfg. Co. (Sloan's Case)* (1894), 23 S.C.R. 644 at 667-78, *per* Strong C.J.; see also *Alexandra Oil & Development Co. v. Cook* (1907), 10 O.W.R. 781 (C.A.).
[430] *Dominion Royalty Corp. v. Goffatt*, [1935] 1 D.L.R. 780, *per* Masters J.A. at 795, aff'd [1935] S.C.R. 565.
[431] *Lindsay Petroleum Co. v. Hurd* (1874), L.R. 5 P.C. 221 (P.C.).
[432] See *Re Leeds & Hanley Theatres of Varieties Ltd.*, [1902] 2 Ch. 809 (C.A.), where it was held that the measure of damages in that case was the profit which the promoter had obtained upon the flip of the property: *per* Vaughan Williams L.J.
[433] *Vitomen Cereal Ltd. v. Manitoba Grain Co.*, [1928] 4 D.L.R. 440 at 460 (B.C.S.C.), *per* Murphy J.; *Re Olympia Ltd.*, [1898] 2 Ch. 153; *Re Remambrose Lake Tin Mining Co.* (1880), 14 Ch. D. 390 at 398 (C.A.), *per* Cotton L.J.. Both the corporation and its shareholder may be entitled to separate causes of action: *Alexandra Oil & Development Co. v. Cook* (1907), 10 O.W.R. 781 at 785 (C.A.), *per* Riddell J.
[434] *Re Hess Mfg. Co. (Sloan's Case)* (1894), 21 O.A.R. 66 at 85 (C.A.), *per* Haggarty C.J.O., aff'd 23 S.C.R. 644; but compare *Re Canadian Diamond Co. (Broad's Case)* (1913), 4 W.W.R. 578 (Alta. T.D.).

or may be cancelled if the corporation is not being wound-up and the shares have not been transferred to a purchaser in good faith.[435]

(iii) Protecting Promoters

§5.181 A promoter may protect himself or herself from liability by making full, plain and true disclosure of all relevant (*i.e.*, material) particulars in the course of his or her dealings with the corporation.[436] The disclosure must be made to an independent body of directors or shareholders, who then decide whether to approve the transaction on behalf of the corporation.[437] Where at the time the transaction takes place, the promoter intends to sell off interests in the corporation, the promoter may not approve the transaction on behalf of the corporation, although the promoter may hold at the time a controlling interest in the corporation, or even if he or she is the sole beneficial shareholder at the time. Thus the duty of disclosure is no mere formality.[438] It inures to the benefit of all shareholders of the corporation other than the promoter, and also for all future shareholders of the corporation.[439] Unless all shareholders of the corporation are fully aware of the nature of the promoter's interest and approve the transaction,[440] the promoter must ensure that the board of directors makes an independent decision.[441] Independence is a question of fact, but it is unlikely that nominee directors[442] or directors who stand to share in the profits of the transaction[443] could be seen to be independent.

(iv) Liability of Promoters Among Themselves

§5.182 Except in unusual circumstances,[444] two or more promoters of a corporation are not jointly or jointly and severally liable as partners with respect to the corporation, and thus there is no presumption that one promoter is the agent of

---

[435] *Proprietary Mines Ltd. v. MacKay*, [1939] O.R. 461, aff'd [1941] 1 D.L.R. 240 (S.C.C.); *Fire Valley Orchards Ltd. v. Sly* (1914), 6 W.W.R. 934 (B.C.S.C.).
[436] *Lagunas Nitrate Co. v. Lagunas Syndicate*, [1899] 2 Ch. 392 at 428 (C.A.), *per* Lindley M.R.
[437] *Gluckstein v. Barnes*, [1900] A.C. 240 (H.L.); *Jubilee Cotton Mills Ltd. v. Lewis*, [1924] A.C. 958 (H.L.).
[438] *Erlanger v. New Sombrero Phosphate Co.* (1872), 5 Ch. D. 73, aff'd 3 App. Cas. 1218 (H.L.); see also *Proprietory Mines Ltd. v. MacKay*, [1938] O.R. 508 at 514 (H.C.), *per* McTague J., var'd [1939] O.R. 461, aff'd [1941] 1 D.L.R. 240 (S.C.C.).
[439] *Bagnall v. Carlton* (1877), 6 Ch. D. 371 at 406 (C.A.), *per* Cotton L.J.; *Erlanger v. New Sombrero Phosphate Co.* (1878), 3 App. Cas. 1218 at 1255 (H.L.), *per* Lord O'Hagan.
[440] *Larocque v. Beauchemin*, [1897] A.C. 358 at 364 (P.C.), *per* Lord Macnaghten; *A.G. Canada v. Standard Trust Co. of New York*, [1911] A.C. 498 at 505 (P.C.), *per* Viscount Haldane.
[441] See, generally, *Gluckstein v. Barnes*, [1900] A.C. 240 at 249 (H.L.), *per* Lord Macnaghten; *Ruethel Mining Co. v. Thorpe* (1907), 9 O.W.R. 942, aff'd 10 O.W.R. 222 (Div. Ct.); *O'Sullivan v. Clarkson* (1907), 9 O.W.R. 46 (C.A.); *Stratford Fuel, Ice, Cartage & Construction Co. v. Mooney* (1909), 21 O.L.R. 426 (C.A.).
[442] *Re Olympia Ltd.*, [1898] 2 Ch. 153, aff'd [1900] A.C. 240 (H.L.).
[443] *Re Leeds & Hanley Theatres of Varietes Ltd.*, [1902] 2 Ch. 809 (C.A.).
[444] See, for instance, *Matthews v. Maurice* (1923), 54 O.L.R. 64 at 69 (H.C.); *Sandusky Coal Co. v. Walker* (1896), 27 O.R. 677 (C.A.); *Howard Stove Mfg. Co. v. Dingman* (1907), 10 O.W.R. 127 (Div. Ct.). Generally, the promoters do not enjoy the rights of partners among themselves: *Bright v. Hutton* (1852), 3 H.L. Cas. 341.

the others.[445] However, where the promoters of a corporation collectively authorize one or more of their number to solicit subscriptions for shares in the corporation, and those persons make a misrepresentation to the subscribers, the other promoters will also be liable, if the misrepresentation was within the scope of the agents' authority, or if the other promoters ratify or derive a profit or benefit from the misrepresentations so made.[446] Similarly, if the promoters collectively authorize one of their number to make purchases on behalf of the proposed corporation, they will be liable as partners if that corporation is never incorporated and therefore does not adopt the contract.[447]

(v) Promotion Expenses

§5.183 A promoter has no right to require a corporation to reimburse him or her for the expenses of promotion and incorporation unless, after incorporation, the corporation makes a binding agreement with the promoter to do so.[448] However, a corporation may make payments of this sort of its own volition, and it appears from subsection 23(5) of the OBCA[449] that the directors may issue shares for this purpose. Although any such agreement must have all the requisites of a legally binding contract (including new consideration to support the promise), the agreement need not be in writing, although some form of express agreement to reimburse the promoter is required.[450]

(vi) Pre-incorporation Contracts

(1) Overview

§5.184 As noted above, the OBCA and CBCA do not deal with promoters of a corporation as such. However, there is one particular area in which both of these Acts touch upon the activities of promoters, and that is with respect to pre-incorporation contracts. A pre-incorporation contract is a contract entered into in the name of or on behalf of a proposed corporation prior to the time when the corporation comes into existence. Given the fact that corporations today can be incorporated with relative ease (often in less than a day) pre-incorporation contracts within the scope of the OBCA and CBCA are actually quite rare.

§5.185 At one time, the lengthy delays inherent in the incorporation process often made it necessary for corporate promoters to enter into contracts on behalf of a corporation, prior to its actual incorporation, in order to secure necessary supplies, franchises, a suitable premises for the conduct of its business, and the like. Since it is now possible to incorporate quickly, and to buy corporations "off-the-shelf", where speed is especially of the essence, the extent of pre-

---

[445] *Garvin v. Edmondson* (1909), 14 O.W.R. 435, aff'd 15 O.W.R. 210 (C.A.); *Sylvester v. McCuaig* (1878), 28 U.C.C.P. 443 at 474-75 (C.A.), *per* Hagarty C.J.O.
[446] *Milburn v. Wilson* (1901), 31 S.C.R. 481 at 483, *per* Stong C.J.
[447] *Seiffert v. Irving* (1888), 15 O.R. 173 at 175 (C.A.), *per* Boyd C.
[448] *Re Empress Engineering Co.* (1880), 16 Ch. D. 125 (C.A.).
[449] CBCA, s. 25(4).
[450] *Van Hummell v. International Guarantee Co.* (1913), 3 W.W.R. 941 (Man. K.B.).

incorporation contracting has been greatly reduced. Even so, it may still happen that the promoter of a proposed corporation will seek to acquire some property or right on behalf of the corporation prior to the time when it is incorporated. As a practical business matter, if an opportunity is not seized when it presents itself, it may not be there by the time the corporation is actually incorporated and organized. Accordingly, the subject of pre-incorporation contracts remains relevant despite improvements made in the time required to incorporate a corporation.

(2) Common Law and Pre-incorporation Contracts

§5.186 The subject of pre-incorporation contracts is one with which the common law long had difficulty. Although the promoter of a corporation has an obvious interest in its success, a promoter is not presumed to be the agent of a corporation either before or after its incorporation. Prior to incorporation, the corporation does not exist and therefore can have no agents.[451] After its incorporation, a promoter may become an agent of the corporation, but only if authorized to act on its behalf — the promoter has no deemed authority to contract or otherwise deal on behalf of the corporation. Thus at common law the corporation is not generally bound by representations made by its promoter "X" with a contractor "Y" prior to incorporation,[452] although such liability may be imposed by statute. Adopting a similarly mechanical approach to the question of agency, on much the same basis, the common law would not permit the newly incorporated entity to ratify a contract purportedly made prior to its incorporation on its behalf by X.[453] However, post-incorporation novation of the contract was possible,[454] provided (of course) that the consent of Y to such an arrangement could be obtained. Short of an actual novation, the benefit of the contract might be assigned so as to permit the corporation to enforce the contract, but that did not give the contractor (Y) the right to enforce the contract against the corporation nor did it release the promoter (X) from the liability that the promoter had assumed under it.

§5.187 The common law approach to pre-incorporation contracts was settled by the decision of the Court of Common Pleas in *Kelner v. Baxter*.[455] In that case, Kelner sold wine to Baxter and others who described themselves as acting on "behalf of the proposed Gravesend Royal Alexander Hotel Company Limited". The wine was delivered and used, but not paid for. When the company failed, Kelner sued Baxter personally. Erle C.J. upheld the claim, saying:

> I agree that if the Gravesend Royal Alexander Hotel Company had been an existing company at this time, the persons who signed the agreement would have

---

[451] *Rumford v. Hinton* (1922), 52 O.L.R. 47 (C.A.).
[452] *Henry Hope & Sons of Canada Ltd. v. Sinclair* (1920), 17 O.W.N. 459 (H.C.), *per* Lennox J.
[453] *Re Empress Engineering Co.* (1880), 16 Ch. D. 135 (C.A.); *Natal Land & Colonization Co. v. Pauline Colliery & Development Syndicate Ltd.*, [1904] A.C. 120 at 126 (P.C.), *per* Lord Davey.
[454] *Re J.R. Morgan Ltd.*, [1927] 1 D.L.R. 882 (Ont. S.C.); *Bagot Pneumatic Tyre Co. v. Clipper Pneumatic Tyre Co.*, [1902] 1 Ch. 146 (C.A.).
[455] (1866), L.R. 2 C.P. 174. See also: *York Region Condo. Corp. No. 921 v. Atop Comm. Inc.*, [2003] O.J. No. 5255, 40 B.L.R. (3d) 317 (S.C.J.).

signed as agents of the company. But, as there was no company in existence at the time, the agreement would be wholly inoperative unless it were held to be binding on the defendants personally. The cases referred to in the course of the argument fully bear out the proposition that, where a contract is signed by one who professes to be signing "as agent," but who has no principal existing at the time, and the contract would be altogether inoperative unless binding upon the person who signed it, he is bound thereby; and a stranger cannot by a subsequent ratification relieve him from that responsibility. When the company came afterwards into existence it was a totally new creature, having rights and obligations from that time, but no rights or obligations by reason of anything which might have been done before. It was once, indeed, thought that an inchoate liability might be incurred on behalf of the proposed company, which would become binding on it when subsequently formed: but that notion was manifestly contrary to the principles upon which the law of contract is founded. There must be two parties to a contract; and the rights and obligations which it creates cannot be transferred by one of them to a third person who was not in a condition to be bound by it at the time it was made. ... It was no doubt the notion of all the parties that success was certain: but the plaintiff parted with his stock upon the faith of the defendants' engagement that the price agreed on should be paid on the day named. It cannot be supposed that he for a moment contemplated that the payment was to be contingent on the formation of the company on the 28th of February. The paper expresses in terms a contract to buy. And it is a cardinal rule that no oral evidence shall be admitted to shew an intention different from that which appears on the face of the writing.[456]

The determination of the intention of the parties to the contract was thus a matter of contractual interpretation. If the persons contracting on the company's behalf purported to contract personally, then they (rather than the company) obtained rights and were liable under the contract. On the other hand, if they purported to contract solely for the company and in its name, then no contract would be made. While this latter conclusion is not immediately evident in the *Kelner* case, it was settled in *Newborne v. Sensolid (Great Britain) Ltd.*[457] In *Newborne,* it was held that an individual who purported to contract as agent on behalf of a non-existent company had no right to sue in his or her own name to enforce the contract. This question was complicated somewhat by an old rule of agency law, which allows a person to sue on a contract made by him or her purportedly as an agent, by subsequently claiming to be the principal.[458] In giving judgment for the defendant (who sought to avoid liability under the contract purportedly made with the company), Lord Goddard held that this rule did not apply in the case of ordinary corporate contracts. He said:

> The contract was one which he was making for the company, and although Mr. Diplock has argued that in signing as he did Mr. Newborne must have signed as agent, since the company could only contract through agents, that was not really the true position.
>
> The company makes the contract. No doubt the company must do its physical acts, and so forth, through the directors, but it is not the ordinary case of principal

---

[456] *Ibid., per* Erle C.J. at 183.
[457] [1954] 1 Q.B. 45 (C.A.).
[458] See, generally, *Schmaltz v. Avery* (1851), 16 Q.B. 655; *Harper & Co. v. Vigers Bros.*, [1909] 2 K.B. 549.

and agent. It is a case in which the company is contracting and the company's contract is authenticated by the signature of one of the directors. This contract purports to be a contract by the company; it does not purport to be a contract by Mr. Newborne. He does not purport to be selling his goods but to be selling the company's goods. The only person who had any contract here was the company, and Mr. Newborne's signature merely confirmed the company's signature....

In my opinion, unfortunate though it may be, as the company was not in existence when the contract was signed there never was a contract, and Mr. Newborne cannot come forward and say, "Well, it was my contract." The fact is, he made a contract for a company which did not exist. It seems to me, therefore, that the defendants can avail themselves of the defense which they pleaded and the appeal must be dismissed.[459]

This approach to pre-incorporation contracts was widely condemned,[460] and it has now been abolished in its entirety in most jurisdictions.

(3) The Statutory Regime

§5.188 At least with respect to business corporations, the common law rules with respect to pre-incorporation contracts have been supplanted by a statutory package of rules under both the OBCA and the CBCA. Under the current law, pre-incorporation contracts are essentially a statutory form of obligation, and as such they depart significantly from the normal rules of contract in several important respects.[461] The OBCA and CBCA each create their own regime for governing the formation of pre-incorporation contracts, and for determining whether and when rights and obligations arise under them, which operate independently of the common law of contract. In particular, the requirements for mutuality and consideration are substantially modified by the statutory rules, as is the normal limitation with respect to an offer to contract that it may be accepted only by the person to whom it is directed. Most importantly, the statutory rules significantly modify the law of agency as it applies to nascent corporations. Even so, the statutory pre-incorporation contract provisions must be seen as a gloss upon the law of contract. They cannot properly be characterized as a comprehensive code.[462]

§5.189 The two Acts deal with pre-incorporation contracts in similar terms — although there are differences in matters of detail. Subsection 21(1) of the OBCA provides that:

---

[459] [1954] 1 Q.B. 45 at 51 (C.A.), *per* Lord Goddard C.J.
[460] See, for instance, *Report of the Company Law Committee* (London: HMSO, 1962, Cmnd. 1749) at para. 44.
[461] *Shapiro (c.o.b. ISR Ent. in Trust) v. 1086891 Ontario Inc.*, [2006] O.J. No. 302 (S.C.J.), *per* Perell J.
[462] So, for instance, the pre-incorporation contract provisions of the OBCA do not affect the requirement under the *Statute of Frauds* that contracts for the sale of an interest in land must be in writing. See, for instance, *Champlain Thickson Inc. v. 365 Bay New Holdings Ltd.*, [2006] O.J. No. 541, 145 A.C.W.S. (3d) 596 (S.C.J.).

Except as provided in this section, a person who enters into an oral or written contract in the name of or on behalf of a corporation before it comes into existence is personally bound by the contract and is entitled to the benefits thereof.[463]

In consequence, *prima facie* the effect of such a contract is to bind the promoter and not the corporation.[464] The major change to the law is effected by subsection 21(2) of the OBCA,[465] which permits a newly incorporated corporation to adopt a pre-incorporation contract made on its behalf. It provides:

> A corporation may, within a reasonable time after it comes into existence, by any action or conduct signifying its intention to be bound thereby, adopt an oral or written contract made before it came into existence in its name or on its behalf, and upon such adoption,
>
> (a) the corporation is bound by the contract and is entitled to the benefits thereof, as if the corporation had been in existence at the date of the contract and had been a party thereto; and
>
> (b) a person who purported to act in the name of or on behalf of the corporation ceases, except as provided in subsection (3) to be bound by or entitled to the benefits of the contract.

Thus it is no longer necessary to show novation, or to show that the contract has been assigned. It is necessary, however, to show that the corporation has adopted the contract, but this can be shown to have taken place by conduct as well as by formal resolution within the corporation itself.[466]

§5.190 Subsection 14(1) of the CBCA provides that a person who enters into, or purports to enter into, a written contract in the name of or on behalf of a corporation before it comes into existence is personally bound by the contract and is entitled to its benefits. It is not exactly clear what additional force is added to the provision by the words "or purports to enter into". However, the reach of this provision is qualified by subsection 14(3) of the CBCA, which provides that:

> Subject to subsection (4), whether or not a written contract made before the coming into existence of a corporation is adopted by the corporation, a party to the

---

[463] CBCA, s. 14(1).
[464] Contrast, however, *Westcom Radio Group Ltd. v. MacIsaac*, [1989] O.J. No. 1902, 63 D.L.R. (4th) 433, 45 B.L.R. 273 (Div. Ct.).
[465] CBCA, s. 14(2).
[466] For a case in which a very narrow interpretation was given to s. 21(2) of the OBCA and, by implication, s. 14(2) of the CBCA, see *Vacation Brokers Inc. v. Joseph*, [1993] O.J. No. 1654, 14 O.R. (3d) 183 (Gen. Div.), in which it was held that if the parties believed that the corporation existed at the time when the contract was made, but it did not, then no contract exists. See also *Newborne v. Sensolid (Great Britain) Ltd.*, [1954] 1 Q.B. 45 (C.A.); *Black v. Smallwood*, [1966] A.L.R. 744 (H.C. Aust.). In *Black*, a vendor of land agreed to sell it to what was believed to be a corporate purchaser. Both the individual vendor and the persons who signed under the corporate name believed that the purchaser had been incorporated. When it was discovered that no such corporation existed, the vendor sued the directors for specific performance. The High Court held that there was no contract and dismissed the action. It found that the intention of the plaintiff was to contract with a corporation and not personally with the directors. See also *Westcom Radio Group Ltd. v. MacIsaac*, [1989] O.J. No. 1902, 70 O.R. (2d) 591 at 598 (Div. Ct.), *per* Austin J.

contract may apply to the court for an order respecting the nature and extent of the obligations and liability under the contract of the corporation and the person who entered into, or purported to enter into, the contract in the name or on behalf of the corporation, On application, the court may make any order it thinks fit.

§5.191 The OBCA and CBCA provisions differ in one critical respect: the CBCA rules apply only with respect to written contracts. The OBCA covers all contracts.[467] However, where under the general law of contract, a particular agreement must be in writing in order to be valid or enforceable (*e.g.*, with respect to the sale of land), that requirement will also apply with respect to any pre-incorporation contract.[468] Moreover, there are obvious problems in seeking to enforce any pre-incorporation contract that is not in writing with respect to proving exactly what was intended by the parties.

(a) ADOPTION OF A PRE-INCORPORATION CONTRACT

§5.192 Both the OBCA and the CBCA require the corporation to adopt the pre-incorporation contract in order for it to become a party to it. The Act provides little guidance as to the steps that must be satisfied in order for a corporation to be deemed to have adopted the pre-incorporation contract. In *Sherwood Design Services Inc. v. 872935 Ontario Ltd.*,[469] in a divided judgment of the Ontario Court of Appeal, Abella J.A. commented upon the practical environment within which OBCA section 21 operates, and the need for the law to adopt an approach to the interpretation of section 21 that recognizes the practical needs of the business community:

> ... [I]t is difficult to see how the January 11, 1990 letter escapes a common-sense interpretation of section 21(2) of the *Business Corporations Act*. ...There is nothing in the language of the section to suggest a requirement of formal documentation before any such intention can be extracted. Nor is there any suggestion emerging from the language that only on closing can one be certain that the prior contract has been adopted, or that there is any necessity that the ultimate shareholders and directors be in place. ... It is irrelevant that at the moment the letter was sent, the company was not actually transferred to the individual purchasers. It was in existence, it was identified as being designated for the purpose of closing the purchase, and it awaited only the formal documentation transferring the shares. The letter was an unequivocal expression of 872935 Ontario Limited's adoption and intention to complete the agreement of purchase and sale.[470]

A contract may not be assigned to a corporation prior to its incorporation. Any such purported assignment is a nullity.[471]

---

[467] *Kettle v. Borris*, [2000] O.J. No. 4167, 10 B.L.R. (3d) 122 (S.C.J.).
[468] *Champlain Thickson Inc. v. 365 Bay New Holdings Ltd.*, [2006] O.J. No. 541 (S.C.J.).
[469] (1998), 109 O.A.C. 77, 158 D.L.R. (4th) 440 (C.A.). See also *Design Home Associates v. Raviv*, [2004] O.J. No. 1710, 44 B.L.R. (3d) 124 (S.C.J.).
[470] *Ibid.*, [2006] O.J. No. 116, 109 O.A.C. 77 at 80-81.
[471] *Arbutus Garden Homes Ltd. v. Arbutus Apartments Corp.*, [1996] B.C.J. No. 456, 20 B.C.L.R. (3d) 292 (S.C.).

§5.193 The courts have generally rejected any highly formal approach towards the adoption of a pre-incorporation contract. In *Design Home Associates v. Raviv*,[472] Karakatsanis J. observed:

> There is no requirement for a formal adoption of a pre-incorporation contract or of formal advice to the other party. Section 21(2) of the OBCA does not set out the manner of adoption of a pre-incorporation contract and there is no principled basis for imposing a stringent requirement of formality. The section permits adoption 'by any action or conduct signifying its intention to be bound thereby.' ... A simple notification of intent is all that is required.

There must, however, be some evidentiary basis for concluding that the contract has in fact been adopted by the newly incorporated entity. Entry into possession, the making of payments under the contract, the assertion of rights of ownership with respect to the subject matter of the contract would all seem to be sufficient for this purpose. It is unclear whether such acts must actually come to the notice of the other party to the contract. For instance, the purchase of insurance may be seen to constitute the assertion of a right of ownership, but it is unlikely that the other party would be aware that the corporation has purchased insurance. In the absence of evidence demonstrating such an intention, the promoter normally will continue to be bound, unless there is a disclaimer of liability as contemplated in subsection 21(4).[473] Evidence of adoption cannot arise until the corporation has in fact been created.[474]

(b) EXCLUDING LIABILITY OF THE PROMOTER

§5.194 Under subsection 21(4) of the OBCA, a promoter may choose to exclude liability under the pre-incorporation contract altogether.[475] Where a promoter enters into an oral or written contract on behalf of a corporation to be incorporated under a stipulation that he or she is not bound by the contract or entitled to the benefits thereof, then the promoter is not in any event bound by or entitled to the benefits of the contract.[476] However, there is a serious risk of surviving liability unless the provision in question is clear and unequivocal, since the disposition of the courts with respect to attempts to exclude liability is not favourable.[477]

§5.195 The usual practice is to state expressly that the contract is made "without personal liability". The effect of such a provision was discussed in *1394918 Ontario Ltd. v. 1310210 Ontario Inc.*, in which Carthy J.A. said:

> If a promoter enters into an oral or written contract on behalf of a corporation to be incorporated and that oral or written contract expressly provides that the promoter

---

[472] [2004] O.J. No. 1710 (S.C.J.).
[473] *Big Sky Marketing Co. v. Glengor International Pty Ltd.*, [2004] B.C.J. No. 2242, 125 A.C.W.S. (3d) 426 (S.C.).
[474] *Heinhuis v. Black Sheep Charters*, [1987] B.C.J. No. 2238, 19 B.C.L.R. (2d) 239 (C.A.).
[475] CBCA s. 14(4).
[476] *1394918 Ontario Ltd. v. 1310210 Ontario Inc.* [2002] O.J. No. 18 (C.A.), *per* Carthy J.
[477] See, for instance, *Southside Property Management (London) Inc. v. Sibold Estate*, [2004] O.J. No. 1701 (C.A.).

is not bound by the contract or entitled to the benefits thereof, then the promoter is not in any event bound by or entitled to the benefits of the contract. ... Section 21(4) of the OBCA permits the defendant to expressly provide that he not be bound by the contract. The defendant clearly expressed this intention and therefore his personal liability is excluded. The fact that the defendant may have received some benefit is not relevant as this does not nullify the effect his express intention not to be bound by the offer to lease.[478]

Thus where subsection 21(4) applies, the party with whom the promoter contracts is bound by the agreement from the moment that it is made, but there is no counterparty who is also bound unless and until the intended corporation is incorporated and the contract is made. The question has been raised as to whether such a conclusion follows if there is no down payment. If some form of down payment is provided this would seem to be sufficient consideration to bind the party dealing with the promoter to the contract, in the same sense that a payment to secure an option made by the person to whom the option is granted binds the party who grants the option. Given the wording of the statute, the better view where there is no down payment, is that the party dealing with the promoter is still bound. As noted above, section 21 effectively creates its own scheme for deciding upon the existence of rights and liabilities. To this extent, the requirement for consideration under the law of contract has been modified in the case of a pre-incorporation contract.

§5.196 Subsection 21(4) of the OBCA requires an express disclosure that no personal liability is assumed.[479] The burden is upon the agent to prove that sufficient disclosure was made.[480] Express disclosure would seem to have a narrower meaning in the pre-incorporation contract context than it does in the context of notification of corporate status. In the notification of corporate status cases, sufficient disclosure was seen to be made in cases where there was correspondence between the corporation and the supplier,[481] where goods were ordered on corporate letterhead or on an order form bearing the proper corporate name or a trade name registered to the corporation,[482] or where the corporation repeatedly paid for the supplies that were made by issuing cheques in its proper corporate name.[483] In the pre-incorporation contract context, something more would be required: the question is not merely one as to the identity of the person with which the supplier is dealing; rather, the supplier is undertaking to supply to a corporation which may never come into being. If the promoter is not liable and there is no corporation, then the supplier will have no right of recovery at all. Because of this exceptional risk, a heavy onus should fall upon the promoter to make clear that no personal liability is assumed.

---

[478] [2002] O.J. No. 18 (C.A.).
[479] *Szecket v. Huang*, [1998] O.J. No. 5197, 42 O.R. (3d) 400 (C.A.).
[480] *G.W. Turner v. Lauze*, [1981] M.J. No. 470, 25 Man. R. (2d) 35 at 39 (Co. Ct.), *per* Krindle Co. Ct. J.; *Hampstead Carpets Ltd. v. Ivanovski*, [1981] S.J. No. 1201, 12 Sask. R. 173 at 177 (Q.B.), *per* Maurice J.; *C. & H. Electric v. Robinson* (1979), 14 B.C.L.R. 16 (S.C.).
[481] *Thomas v. Equipment Rebuilders Ltd.* (1974), 10 N.S.R. (2d) 225 (C.A.).
[482] *Vanier v. Learmonth* (1976), 23 N.S.R. (2d) 387 (Co. Ct.).
[483] *Vivian Agencies Ltd. v. Butler* (1978), 22 Nfld. & P.E.I.R. 256 (Nfld. Dist. Ct.); but compare *Corkum v. Lohnes*, [1981] N.S.J. No. 325, 121 D.L.R. (3d) 761 (C.A.).

(c) OLD STYLE CONTRACTS

§5.197 It would seem to follow that where a person wishes to contract on behalf of a proposed corporation, that person must make very clear that the corporation is not in existence and that no liability is assumed. Nevertheless, purchasers will often enter into an agreement of purchase and sale for real property under the style "in trust for a corporation to be incorporated". The practice appears to have originated under section 273 of the Ontario *Corporations Act,* which provides that:

> A corporation is, upon its incorporation, invested with all the property and rights, real and personal, theretofore held by or for it under any trust created with a view to its incorporation.

There is no direct equivalent provision in either the OBCA or the CBCA, and thus the effect of an arrangement of this sort will turn upon how it can be fit within the pre-incorporation contract rules. The apparent effect of such an agreement would seem to be to create a binding legal agreement of sale between the named vendor and purchaser, at least until that corporation is incorporated and adopts the contract. A trustee who enters into a contract on behalf of a beneficiary is not shielded from personal liability: the liability of the trustee is not limited to the assets of the trust, unless the trustee clearly so indicates. Further, there cannot be a valid trust in favour of a corporation that has not been incorporated. However, the vendor in such a transaction is also at risk. Subject to the possibility of a court order restoring the "trustee's" liability under subsection 21(4), the trustee could cease to be liable to perform the contract personally upon its adoption by the corporation. Accordingly, care should be taken by the vendor to make sure that the purchaser-trustee is obliged to put the corporation into sufficient funds to enable it to perform the contract.

(d) POWER OF THE COURT TO MAKE ORDERS

§5.198 Subsection 21(3) of the OBCA[484] provides that whether or not an oral or written contract made before the incorporation of a corporation is adopted by the corporation, a party to the contract may apply to the court for an order fixing obligations under the contract as joint or joint and several, or apportioning liability between the corporation and the person who purported to act in the name of or on behalf of the corporation. On such an application, the court may make such order as it thinks fit. The right to bring an application of this type is subject to subsection 21(4),[485] which states that if it is expressly so provided in an oral or written pre-incorporation contract, a person who purported to act in the name of or on behalf of the corporation before it came into existence is not in any event bound by the contract or entitled to the benefits of the contract.

---

[484] CBCA, s. 14(3).
[485] *Ibid.*, s. 14(4).

(4) Mistake Made as to Corporate Status

§5.199 The pre-incorporation provisions of the OBCA and CBCA are clear enough where it is evident at the time when the contract is made that it is intended to be a pre-incorporation contract. Complications arise where the corporate existence is assumed by one or both of the individuals who negotiate the contract, but in fact it does not exist.

§5.200 In most cases, the agent will know at the time of entering the contract whether or not the corporation on whose behalf the agent is purporting to act has yet been incorporated. Where the agent knows that the corporation has not yet been incorporated, the agent is under a duty to disclose that fact, if the agent wishes to avoid personal liability[486] — the only exception being where it is made clear that the contract is made as a pre-incorporation contract without personal liability under subsection 21(4).

§5.201 A different rule must necessarily apply where the agent believes that the corporation has been incorporated, but in fact no incorporation has taken place.[487] Where it is mistakenly assumed that a corporation exists when in fact it does not, the policy argument for holding the purported agent personally liable is far less compelling. In a limited range of cases, liability may be imposed upon the purported corporate "agent" on the basis of negligence, but in order to raise a claim on this basis, the person with whom the contract was made must establish a breach of duty of care that was owed to him or her by the purported corporate agent. Absent a basis for a finding of negligence, the courts have been less certain in their approach. Earlier case law suggested that if the promoter (X) contracted with the contractor (Y) on the basis that X was acting as the agent of a non-existent corporation, then X would be personally liable to Y under the contract.[488] More recent cases have backed away from this clear but Draconian rule, and have held that whether X will be liable to Y depends upon the intention of the parties. In some cases, the courts have sought to identify the apparent intention of the parties as to whether the purported agent would be liable.[489] In most cases, however, this is a pointless inquiry: if the parties had known that the corporation did not exist most likely they would not have made the contract. It seems reasonably clear on this basis that if both parties knew that the corpora-

---

[486] *Wolfdale Electric Ltd. v. RPM's Systems Automation and Design*, [2004] O.J. No. 4663, 47 B.L.R. (3d) 1 (S.C.); *1080409 Ontario Ltd. v. Hunter*, [2000] O.J. No. 2603, 9 B.L.R. (3d) 198 (S.C.J.).

[487] For a case in which a very narrow interpretation was given to s. 21(2) of the OBCA and, by implication, s. 14(2) of the CBCA, see *Vacation Brokers Inc. v. Joseph*, [1993] O.J. No. 1654, 14 O.R. (3d) 183 (Gen. Div.), in which it was held that if the agent and contractor believe that the corporation existed at the time when the contract was made, but it did not, then no contract exists. *Cf. Szecket v. Huang*, [1998] O.J. No. 5197, 42 O.R. (3d) 400 (C.A.). See also *Newborne v. Sensolid (Great Britain) Ltd.*, [1954] 1 Q.B. 45 (C.A.); *Black v. Smallwood*, [1966] A.L.R. 744 (H.C. Aust.).

[488] *Kelner v. Baxter* (1866), L.R. 2 C.P. 174; *Marblestone Industries Ltd. v. Fairchild*, [1975] 1 N.Z.L.R. 529. Compare, however, *Re Murray* (1970), 14 C.B.R. (N.S.) 142 (Ont. S.C.); *Black v. Smallwood* (1966), 117 C.L.R. 52 (H.C. Aust.).

[489] See, for instance, *Black v. Smallwood* (1966), 117 C.L.R. 52 (H.C. Aust.).

tion did not exist, then any contract purportedly entered between Y and X acting on the corporation's behalf would be no contract at all.[490] A contract could arise in such a case only if it was a fair inference that X intended to incur a personal liability.

§5.202 Where X and Y are both mistaken as to the existence of the corporation, the strict wording of subsection 21(1) of the OBCA might at first seem to suggest that the purported agent should be held liable in such a case.[491] However, a strong argument can be made that section 21 was intended to apply only where the parties to a contract make it knowing that the corporate party has not yet been incorporated. Under this view, section 21 does not apply in cases where this is unknown to the parties at the time. Indeed, to impose liability on an agent who did not know that the corporation was non-existent and who would not have made any contract had this fact been known, seems to run counter to the basic principle of contract law that the burden of a contract must be willingly assumed. Quite often a corporation will be dissolved due to a default in regulatory or tax filings. It seems hard to believe that the legislature would intend to impose personal liability on well-meaning corporate employees who might enter into contracts on behalf a dissolved corporation, not knowing (and not really having any practical way of discovering) that the corporation has in fact been dissolved by administrative act of the Ministry of Government Services.

§5.203 At least three distinct approaches have evolved in such cases. Under one line of authority, the individuals who have acted on behalf of the corporation have been held liable on the contract in such cases, on the basis of a breach of a warranty of authority.[492] This approach has obvious shortcomings where the purported agent is relatively low ranking, and even in other cases, doubts must be expressed as to whether this principle of agency law is properly applicable. It is not the authority that is lacking in such a case; rather it is the existence of the corporate principal. In yet a further branch of the case law, the courts have treated the non-existence of the corporation as a mistake.[493] Another line of case law adopts an almost restitutionary approach. It looks at whether the individual who has signed on behalf of the non-existent corporation has drawn a personal

---

[490] *Newborne v. Sensolid (Great Britain) Ltd.*, [1954] 1 Q.B. 45 (C.A.); *Rover International Ltd. v. Cannon Film Sales Ltd.*, [1987] B.C.L.C. 540, revd on other grounds [1988] B.C.L.C. 710 (C.A.). Similarly, where the agent and supplier both believe that the corporation is in existence, but in fact it is not, the contract is a nullity and the agent is not liable on it: *Westcom Radio Group Ltd. v. MacIsaac*, [1989] O.J. No. 1902, 63 D.L.R. (4th) 433, 45 B.L.R. 273 (Div. Ct.).

[491] Such a conclusion was reached in England, albeit on different wording, in *Phonogram Ltd. v. Lane*, [1982] Q.B. 938 (C.A.).

[492] *Biondich v. Kingscroft Investments Ltd.*, [2002] O.J. No. 4742 (S.C.J.); *Royal Bank of Canada v. Starr (c.o.b. Ettmor Ltd.)*, [1985] O.J. No. 1763, aff'd [1986] O.J. No. 1061 (C.A.); *Maple Engineering & Construction Canada Ltd. v. 1373988 Ontario Inc.*, [2004] O.J. No. 5025 (S.C.J.).

[493] See, for instance, *Westcom Radio Group Ltd. v. MacIsaac*, [1989] O.J. No. 1902, 70 O.R. (2d) 591 (Div. Ct.).

benefit from the contract. If not, then that person is not held liable under the contract.[494]

§5.204 The third approach focuses on mutual intent. In *Black v. Smallwood*,[495] a vendor of land agreed to sell it to what was believed to be a corporate purchaser. Both the individual vendor and the persons who signed under the corporate name believed that the purchaser had been incorporated. When it was discovered that no such corporation existed, the vendor sued the directors for specific performance. The High Court of Australia held that there was no contract and dismissed the action. It found that the intention of the plaintiff was to contract with a corporation and not personally with the directors.[496]

(5) Where Pre-incorporation Rules Not Applicable

§5.205 The pre-incorporation contract provisions of the OBCA and CBCA have no application with respect to corporations already in existence at the time when the contract was made.[497] In such cases, the question as to who is liable under the contract is governed by the normal rules of the law of agency. One question that sometimes arises in practice is the effect of a contract made by a promoter, who subsequently purchases an existing shelf-contract from his or her lawyer, accountant or other business advisor. Obviously, in such cases, there will be no authority in favour of the promoter to enter into the contract as an agent. Where the promoter purchases the corporation, and it ratifies the contract entered into on its behalf, then the matter is largely moot (although the fact that the specific corporation probably was not known at the time when the contract was made, and could not have been identified by the parties means that the matter is not without some difficulty). Where no corporation is ever acquired by the promoter, then in the ordinary case the promoter will remain liable under the contract by virtue of subsection 21(1).

(6) Corporate Status Must Be Disclosed

§5.206 The onus is on the person who contracts on behalf of a business to make clear that the business is an incorporated entity. The courts routinely impose personal liability on individuals who contract on behalf of a business without disclosing that it is incorporated (at least in the case of individuals who have an ownership interest in the business).[498] This issue often arises where corporations

---

[494] See, for instance, *Dryco Building Supplies Inc. v. Wasylishyn*, [2002] A.J. No. 919 (Q.B.); *Kelner v. Baxter* (1866), L.R. 2 C.P. 174; *Litemor Distributors (Ottawa) Ltd. v. W.C. Somers Electric Ltd.*, [2004] O.J. No. 4686, 49 B.L.R. (3d) 143 at 149 (S.C.) per Panet, J.
[495] [1966] A.L.R. 744 (H.C. Aust.).
[496] A similar approach was adopted in *Westcom Radio Group Ltd. v. MacIsaac*, [1989] O.J. No. 1902, 70 O.R. (2d) 591 at 598 (Div. Ct.), per Austin J.
[497] See, for instance, *Southside Property Management (London) Inc. v. Sibold Estate*, [2004] O.J. No. 1701 (C.A.).
[498] *Sturzenegger v. K. Peters Industries Northern Ltd.*, [2004] Y.J. No. 42, 45 B.L.R. (3d) 91 (S.C.); *DC Foods (2001) Inc. v. Planway Poultry Inc.*, [2004] O.J. No. 3327, 46 B.L.R. (3d) 148 (S.C.); *3253791 Canada Inc. v. Armstrong*, [2002] O.J. No. 3424, 27 B.L.R. (3d) 230 (S.C.J.).

engage in business under a trade name rather than their proper corporate name.[499] Persons acting on behalf of a corporation must make the corporate status of the corporation clear to the persons with whom they deal if they wish to avoid liability under the contracts which they enter.[500] For instance, in *Interlake Packers Ltd. v. Vogt*[501] the owners of a corporation purchased products from a supplier, using invoices and cheques marked with the name of the corporation or variants of that name. However, these documents did not indicate that the business was operated by a limited corporation. The supplier sued the owners personally for the price of the products supplied and the owners were held liable. They had not brought home to the supplier that it was dealing with a corporation even though they had ample opportunity to do so. It is also necessary to inform suppliers of a change in status where a previously unincorporated business is incorporated.[502] If the owner of the new corporation fails to make clear that supplies are now being made to the corporation rather than to the owner personally, the owner will be liable.[503]

§5.207 The basis for this rule is that *prima facie* an agent is personally liable where he or she fails to disclose the existence of a principal.[504] In the corporate

---

[499] *Re Pahmer* (1969), 12 C.B.R. (N.S.) 261 (Ont. S.C.); *Victor (Can.) Ltd. v. Farbetter Addressing & Mailing Ltd.*, [1978] O.J. No. 2687, 3 B.L.R. 312 (H.C.J.). In that case, it was found that Farbetter Addressing & Mailing Ltd. carried on business as Farbetter Business Products — an unregistered trade name. The president of the corporation was found personally liable on contracts that he had made on behalf of the corporation. See also s. 51 of the *Bills of Exchange Act*, R.S.C. 1985, c. B-4. Any ambiguity (at least in the case of cheques or other bills of exchange) will be resolved against the agent: *Alliston Creamery v. Grosdanoff*, [1962] O.R. 808 (C.A.); *Daymond Motors Ltd. v. Thistletown Developments Ltd.*, [1956] O.W.N. 867 (C.A.).
[500] *Irving Oil Ltd. v. Colbourne* (1983), 44 Nfld. & P.E.I.R. 132, 130 A.P.R. 132 at 149-50 (Nfld. Dist. Ct.), per Inder D.C.J.; *Corkum v. Lohnes* (1981), 43 N.S.R. (2d) 477, 81 A.P.R. 477 at 486 (C.A.), per Cooper J.A.; cf. *Vivian Agencies Ltd. v. Butler* (1978), 22 Nfld. & P.E.I.R. 256, 55 A.P.R. 256 (Nfld. Dist. Ct.), per Stone J.
[501] [1987] M.J. No. 130, 47 Man. R. (2d) 268 (Q.B.).
[502] See, for instance, *Thompson & Sutherland Ltd. v. Redden*, [1978] N.S.J. No. 763, 34 N.S.R. (2d) 91, 59 A.P.R. 91 (Co. Ct.).
[503] *Clow Darling Ltd. v. 1013983 Ontario Inc.*, [1997] O.J. No. 3655, 36 B.L.R. (2d) 137 (Gen. Div.), var'd [1998] O.J. No. 2299 (Div. Ct.); *Data Business Forms Ltd. v. MacIntosh*, [1986] N.S.J. No. 472, 76 N.S.R. (2d) 418, 189 A.P.R. 418 (T.D.); see also *Spilsbury Communications Ltd. v. Fentronics-NSI Ltd.*, [1986] N.S.J. No. 64, 73 N.S.R. (2d) 86 (T.D.).
[504] *Bridge City Electric (1981), Ltd. v. Robertson*, [1986] S.J. No. 396, 49 Sask. R. 58 (Q.B.). But cf. *Friedman Equity Developments Inc. v. Final Note Ltd.*, [1997] O.J. No. 2003, 42 O.R. (3d) 712 (C.A.), re contracts executed under seal. The burden is on the agent to show that the contractor knew it was dealing with a corporation and not the agent: *William A. Flemming Ltd. v. Fisher*, [1978] N.S.J. No. 624, , 29 N.S.R. (2d) 338, 45 A.P.R. 338 at 343 (T.D.), per Morrison J. It was suggested in *Morse Electro Products (Can.) Corp. v. Central Discount House Ltd.* (1978), 5 B.C.L.R. 340 (Co. Ct.) that the reason for the rule was that the concept of limited liability was such a significant departure from the common law that it was necessary to protect the public by imposing an obligation to provide clear notice. Under present market conditions this position is untenable. The concept of limited liability is now widely recognized, and except for very small businesses and those which are prohibited from incorporating by law, there are few businesses that are not incorporated. Because limited liability corporations are so common it would be more logical for a supplier to assume that he or she is dealing with a corporation than that he or she is not. Where, however, a person does not make clear that he or she is acting as an agent, there is no reason for the supplier to assume that the person is an agent. On the contrary, concealing corporate status is tantamount to a representation that there is no agency.

context the rule may be summarized as follows: if a person incorporates a business he or she must make it clear to the persons with whom that business deals that he or she is negotiating a contract on behalf of the corporation and that the person assumes no personal responsibility.[505] By so doing, the other party then has the option to decide whether he or she is prepared to deal with the corporation, insist upon a personal guarantee, or walk away from the transaction. If the owner of the business fails to provide this opportunity, the owner is taken to have signed in his or her personal capacity, and therefore will not be allowed to hide behind the corporate veil.[506] However, the supplier must elect to sue either the agent or the corporation; it cannot claim against both.[507]

§5.208 It is not essential to disclose corporate status during the early stages of negotiation, so long as corporate status is disclosed before the contract is entered. As long as the party with whom the contract has notice that he or she is dealing with a corporate entity at the time when the contract is made, the agent will be protected. For instance, in *MacMullin v. A. & B. Miller Contracting Ltd.*[508] the agent did not disclose that he was acting on behalf of a corporation during the negotiations. However, this fact became evident when the contract itself was executed, for it was printed on the corporation's stationary and otherwise clearly indicated that it was a corporate contract. Consequently, it was held that there was sufficient disclosure to protect the agent.[509] By extrapolation, so long as the promoter of a proposed corporation makes clear that he or she is contracting without personal liability before the contract is formed, the promoter will be able to claim the benefit of OBCA subsection 21(4). Otherwise, liability will apply.

---

[505] *Clow Darling Ltd. v. 1013983 Ontario Inc.*, [1997] O.J. No. 2115, 36 B.L.R. (2d) 192 (Gen. Div.), var'd [1998] O.J. No. 2299 (Div. Ct.); *Trail Tire Service Ltd. v. Scobie*, [1976] A.J. No. 343, [1976] 5 W.W.R. 409 (Dist. Ct.); *Gelhorn Motors Ltd. v. Yee*, [1969] M.J. No. 4, 71 W.W.R. 526 (C.A.).
[506] *Corkum v. Lohnes*, [1981] N.S.J. No. 325, 121 D.L.R. (3d) 761 (C.A.).
[507] *Selby's Electrical Ltd. v. Bruce*, [1984] N.J. No. 138, 3 C.L.R. 314 (Dist. Ct.); *Kendall v. Hamilton* (1879), 4 App. Cas. 504 at 514 (H.L.), per Earl Cairns L.C.; see also *Pople v. Evans*, [1969] 2 Ch. 255.
[508] (1887), 78 N.S.R. (2d) 48 at 50-51 (S.C.), per Nunn J.
[509] See also *MacLean v. Portland Masonry Ltd.*, [1982] N.S.J. No. 570, (1982), 55 N.S.R. (2d) 666, 114 A.P.R. 666 (T.D.).

Chapter 6

THE CAPACITY AND POWERS OF CORPORATIONS AND THE MANNER OF THEIR EXERCISE

A. INTRODUCTION

§6.1 As we have seen, corporations are artificial or juristic persons, and as such, they are entitled to acquire property, rights, obligations and liabilities of their own, separate and distinct from those of their owners. A corporation is not the trustee of its property and rights on behalf of its shareholders; it is the owner of that property and those rights itself and holds them for its own account.[1] Nevertheless, as a creation of the law, it stands to reason that the capacity and powers of a corporation are defined by the law.[2]

§6.2 The fundamental objective of corporate law is to create or provide for the creation of juristic persons. In this chapter, we will see that both the Ontario *Business Corporations Act* ("OBCA") and the *Canada Business Corporations Act* ("CBCA") confer upon the corporations subject to each of them respectively, the capacity, rights, powers and privileges of a natural person (although under the CBCA those rights, powers and privileges are expressly made subject to that Act). Moreover, there are certain basic powers that are incidental to corporate status, and these powers will exist in the case of every company (however incorporated) except where provided to the contrary. For instance, by virtue of its status as a legal person, a company has certain inherent powers which are necessarily and inseparably incident to it, among which are the power to sue or be sued in its corporate name,[3] along with the power to compromise and settle disputes.[4] Many of these inherent powers and capacities of a company are now codified in both the federal and provincial *Interpretation Acts*, which confer

---

[1] *Re City Equitable Fire Insurance Co.*, [1925] Ch. 407 at 530 (C.A.), *per* Sargant L.J.
[2] Thus in *Twigg v. Thunder Hill Mining Co.*, Drake J. rejected the novel argument that a company was not bound by the statute under which it was incorporated, provided the company acted in accordance with its memorandum of association: (1893), 3 B.C.R. 101 at 112 (S.C.); see also *Grant v. Dominion Loose Leaf Co.* (1924), 56 O.L.R. 43 at 48 (H.C.), *per* Wright J., rev'd on other grounds 56 O.L.R. 508 (C.A.); compare *Edwards v. Blackmore* (1918), 42 O.L.R. 105 (C.A.).
[3] *Powell Rees Ltd. v. Anglo-Canadian Mtge. Corp.* (1912), 26 O.L.R. 490 at 493 (H.C.), *per* Riddell J., aff'd 27 O.L.R. 274 (C.A.).
[4] *Bath's Case* (1878), L.R. 8 Ch. D. 334 at 340 (M.R.), *per* Jessell M.R.; but it does not follow that this power may necessarily be exercised by the directors: *Fuches v. Hamilton Tribune Printing & Publishing Co. (Copp's Case)* (1885), 10 O.R. 497 at 503 (Ch.), *per* Boyd C.

upon every corporate body (including corporations under the CBCA and OBCA respectively):

- the power to sue and be sued, to contract and be contracted with by its corporate name, to have a common seal and to alter or change it at pleasure, to have perpetual succession, to acquire and hold personal property or movables for the purpose for which the corporation is established and to alienate that property at pleasure;
- the power to vest in a majority of the members of the corporation the power to bind the others by their acts;
- the power to exempt from personal liability for its debts, obligations or acts such individual members of the corporation as do not contravene the provisions of the enactment establishing the corporation.

In addition to those powers and capacities, it would appear that at common law every body corporate has the following additional powers and capacities:[5]

- the power to purchase and hold such property as is required to conduct the business of the corporation contemplated within its objects, including any lands, although this power is subject to mortmain legislation;
- the power to make by-laws.

§6.3 As noted above, it is presumed that OBCA and CBCA corporations enjoy the powers and capacities of a natural person.[6] As a result, for the vast majority of such corporations it is unnecessary to consider the extensive body of case law relating to the express and implied powers conferred upon corporations under the terms of earlier corporate law regimes. However, both the OBCA and CBCA permit the articles of a corporation to set out prohibitions and restrictions on the exercise of corporate powers.[7] They thereby allow the statutory grant of powers to be curtailed, perhaps even completely ousted, and replaced by powers settled by the incorporators or shareholders. As the articles may be amended with relative ease, it is quite possible for the powers of an OBCA or CBCA corporation to be expanded and contracted over time, by express decision of the members of the corporation concerned.

§6.4 In addition to the OBCA and CBCA, there are a number of statutes that confer specific powers and capacities upon corporate entities. Dealings with property represent a key area of concern. For instance, section 20 of the *Conveyancing and Law of Property Act* provides:

> Any corporation capable of taking and conveying land in Ontario shall be deemed to have been and to be capable of taking and conveying land by deed of bargain and sale in like manner as a person in his natural capacity, subject to any general

---

[5] *Bank of Montreal v. Bethune* (1836), 4 O.S. 341 at 352 (U.C.C.A.), *per* Robinson C.J.
[6] OBCA, s. 15; CBCA, s. 15(1).
[7] OBCA, s. 17(2); CBCA, s. 16(2).

limitations or restrictions and to any special provisions as to holding or conveying land that are applicable to the corporation.[8]

Subsection 43(1) of that Act deals with the possibility of a corporation holding property in joint tenancy. It provides:

> A corporation is and has been capable of acquiring and holding real or personal property in joint tenancy in the same manner as if it were an individual, and, where a corporation and an individual, or two or more corporations, became or become entitled to any such property under circumstances or by virtue of any instrument that would, if the corporation had been an individual, have created a joint tenancy, they are and have been entitled to the property as joint tenants, but the acquisition and holding of property by a corporation in joint tenancy has been and is subject to the like conditions and restrictions as attach to the acquisition and holding of property by a corporation in severalty.

The distinguishing characteristic of joint tenancy is, of course, the right of survivorship on the death of one of the joint tenants. As artificial entities, corporations cannot die in any meaningful sense. However, subsection 43(2) of the Act goes on to provide that:

> Where a corporation is joint tenant of property and the corporation dissolves, the property devolves on the other joint tenant.

§6.5 Where prohibitions and restrictions are imposed under the articles, reference may be made to the old case law to determine their scope and effect, as may the normal rules of documentary construction. The general rule of construction with respect to the construction of corporate constitutional documents is that they are to be read fairly, with their import being derived from a reasonable interpretation of the language used.[9] The words used are construed according to their natural meaning, unless such a construction would render them senseless, or would be opposed to the general scope and intent of the instrument, or unless there is some other compelling reason in favour of a different interpretation.[10] It would also seem from the old case law that where it is intended to limit only a particular power of a corporation, or to prohibit the conduct of only a particular business, the general presumption of power arising from the statutory grant of the powers and capacities of a natural person will continue to apply, and the specific exclusion imposed under the articles will not be interpreted as ousting that presumption further than necessary in order to give effect to the literal meaning of the words used in the prohibition or limitation concerned. On the other hand, where the articles give a corporation express powers that are to be exercised only for a particular purpose, it would seem that the exercise of that power for a purpose not expressly or implicitly authorized will be prohibited.[11] In such a case, the corporation will enjoy the benefit of all powers that are necessary or reasonably incidental to the attainment of the specified purpose over

---

[8] R.S.O. 1990, c. C. 34, s. 20.
[9] *Egyptian Salt & Soda Co. Ltd. v. Port Said Salt Association Ltd.*, [1931] A.C. 677 at 682, *per* Lord Macmillan.
[10] *Fowell v. Tranter* (1804), 3 H. & C. 438 at 461, 159 E.R. 610, *per* Bramwell B.
[11] *A.G. v. Great Eastern Rlwy Co.* (1880), 5 App. Cas. 473 at 481 (H.L.), *per* Lord Blackburn.

and above those powers which are expressly conferred.[12] Implied powers are only relevant in the absence of an express power, and where an express power is conferred with respect to a particular matter (*e.g.*, the power to pass by-laws), then that express power will be seen to be exhaustive.[13] The old case law holds that a power is incidental where:

- it may be derived by reasonable implication from the language used in the relevant statute or incorporating instrument conferring the power;[14]
- it is necessary to give effect to the express power conferred[15] or to enable that power to be exercised;[16]
- it is incorporated within the scope of an express power that is actually conferred (*e.g.*, a power to lease property being subsumed within a power to sell).[17]

However, a power is not incidental merely because it is in the interests of the company to possess such a power.[18]

§6.6 While the foregoing principles may be of assistance in assessing how restrictions on the powers of a corporation are likely to be construed, they must nevertheless be resorted to with caution. At the time when these rules of interpretation were laid down, the doctrine of *ultra vires* was the order of the day. At that time, the courts were of the view that implied powers should be narrowly construed.[19] It is not clear whether such a narrow construction would be adopted under the modern statutes, given their apparent intent to confer power except to the extent that the shareholders or incorporators decree that the power is not to be exercised.

§6.7 From time to time, a corporation may be created by Parliament or the legislature and granted an exclusive franchise (usually time-limited) to conduct a particular activity, such as the operation of a ferry or other quasi-public service. Such corporations are often made subject to a general corporate law statute, such as the OBCA or the CBCA. Where a corporation is granted such an exclusive but time-limited franchise, its powers, capacity and status as a corporation are

---

[12] *A.G. v. Great Eastern Rlwy. Co.* (1880), 5 App. Cas. 473 (H.L.).
[13] *Kelley v. Electrical Construction Co.* (1907), 16 O.L.R. 232 at 238 (C.A.), *per* Mulock J.A.
[14] *Union Bank of Canada v. A. McKillop & Sons Ltd.* (1913), 30 O.L.R. 87 at 98 (C.A.), *per* Hodgins J.A., aff'd 51 S.C.R. 518; See also *Amalgamated Society of Rlwy. Servants v. Osborne*, [1910] A.C. 87 at 97 (H.L.), *per* Lord Macnaghten.
[15] *Brown v. Moore* (1921), 62 S.C.R. 487.
[16] *Real Estate Investment Co. v. Metro Building Society* (1883), 3 O.R. 476 at 492 (C.A.), *per* Osler J.; including commercial necessity: *Hughes v. Northern Electric & Manufacturing Co.* (1915), 50 S.C.R. 626 at 654, *per* Duff J.
[17] *Dominion Cotton Mills Co. v. Amyot*, [1912] A.C. 546 (P.C.); but compare *Gold v. Maldaver* (1912), 4 O.W.N. 106 (H.C.).
[18] See, for instance, *A.G. v. Mersey Rlwy.*, [1907] A.C. 415 (H.L.).
[19] *Joint Stock Discount Co. v. Brown* (1866), L.R. 3 Eq. 139.

not lost at the expiration of the term of the franchise, but the franchise granted to the corporation does cease to be exclusive at the end of that time.[20]

§6.8 In many jurisdictions, the law distinguishes between closely held and widely held corporations in terms of their capacity and powers. Neither the OBCA nor the CBCA adopt such an approach. Although the *Securities Act* imposes certain safeguards to protect people who invest in widely held corporations, as indeed (to a lesser extent) do the OBCA and the CBCA, a corporation is a corporation for all purposes, no matter how many shareholders it may possess. In terms of the capacities and powers that flow from incorporation, all OBCA and CBCA corporations are equal no matter how great or small they may be.[21]

§6.9 It is sometimes objected that it is not appropriate to grant the same rights to small, closely held corporations as are given to widely held corporations — particularly with respect to limited liability. Yet there is no strong case for introducing any distinctions in the law between the capacities and powers of what in other jurisdictions are called "proprietary" or "public limited" companies. For instance, it is said that closely held corporations are often undercapitalized. That fact is no doubt true, but it is equally true of a good many widely held corporations and is universally true of insolvent corporations whether widely or closely held. It is said that limited liability often prevents people injured through the tortious conduct of a corporation from recovering adequate compensation for their injuries. Yet the limited liability afforded by a corporation is not the only way of making the owners of a business judgment proof — as many a disappointed judgment creditor will attest. If there is a public concern in ensuring that people who engage in certain activities are able to make good any injury or loss that they cause, minimum capitalization requirements (such as those applied in the case of banks, insurance companies and trust companies) or mandatory insurance requirements (such as the insurance required in the case of automobiles) are a more effective method of dealing with the problem of inadequate compensation than are amendments to the basic principles of corporate law.

(i) The Doctrine of Ultra Vires

§6.10 Although the powers conferred under the OBCA, the CBCA and relevant *Interpretation Acts* are broad, the question arises as to the consequences that flow where a corporation exceeds the powers that are conferred upon it, as for instance by acting in a manner contrary to the Act under which it is incorporated, or otherwise in contravention of the law, or contravenes some prohibition or restriction or fails to comply with some essential procedure set out in its articles or by-laws or a unanimous shareholder agreement relating to the corpora-

---

[20] *N.B. Power Co. v. Maritime Transit Ltd.* (1936), 11 M.P.R. 174, aff'd 12 M.P.R. 152 (N.B.C.A.).

[21] *Securities Act*, R.S.O. 1990, c. 55. Subject, of course, to any such prohibition or limitation on the exercise of capacities or powers as may be set out in the articles of a corporation. See generally: *Re Good & Jacob Y. Shantz, Son & Co.* (1911), 23 O.L.R. 544 at 547 (C.A.), *per* Moss C.J.O.

tion. In order to undertake an inquiry into this question it is necessary to consider briefly the doctrine of *ultra vires* and the vestigial remains of that doctrine which continue to affect OBCA and CBCA corporations.[22]

§6.11 The Latin term *"ultra vires"* describes a class of acts of a body that were beyond its powers or jurisdiction. The term is derived from a doctrine of administrative law under which bodies created by a sovereign legislature are not permitted to exercise powers beyond those which have been conferred upon them. The doctrine renders ineffective not only acts which are beyond the powers actually conferred, but also the exercise of powers which are conferred, where these powers are exercised irregularly.[23] At common law, the doctrine applied in full force to companies incorporated by or under statute, such as special Act companies and registration companies. Historically, the doctrine of *ultra vires* has applied in full force to companies incorporated by or under statute, such as special Act companies[24] and registration companies, rather than to companies created by Royal charter[25] or under a letters patent regime,[26] even if incorporated in such a manner under a general statutory authority. Over the years, the application of the doctrine came to involve several questions: first, had the company exceeded the powers conferred upon it; second, if the company had exercised a power which it possessed in order to attain the objects for which it was incorporated, in exercising that power had the company acted contrary to or inconsistently with its objects clause; and third, had the directors exceeded their authority in exercising the powers in question.

§6.12 The term *"ultra vires"* was used to describe a number of different classes of corporate act.[27] These included:

- acts that were contrary to law (*i.e.*, illegal);[28]

- acts that, although not illegal, were outside the powers conferred upon the company;

---

[22] The doctrine remains relevant for many non-OBCA and non-CBCA companies. See, for instance, *Berry v. Indian Park Association*, [1997] O.J. No. 1873, 33 O.R. (3d) 522 (Gen. Div.).
[23] The extension and effect of the doctrine of *ultra vires* to companies is briefly described in Howard Street, *A Treatise on the Doctrine of Ultra Vires* (London: Sweet & Maxwell, 1930) at 1.
[24] *Jamieson's Foods Ltd. v. Ontario (Food Terminal Board)*, [1959] O.W.N. 141 (C.A.); *Re Northwestern Trust Co.*, [1926] 1 W.W.R. 426 (Man. C.A.), *per* Perdue C.J.M.
[25] *Bonanza Creek Gold Mining Co. v. R.*, [1916] 1 A.C. 566 at 583-84, *per* Viscount Haldane.
[26] *Royal Bank of Canada v. Flemming*, [1933] O.R. 601 (C.A.); *Edwards v. Blackmore* (1918), 42 O.L.R. 105 (C.A.), *per* Ferguson J.A.; *cf.* Davies J.A. in *Export Brewing & Malting Co. v. Dominion Bank*, [1934] O.R. 560, rev'd on other grounds [1937] 3 All E.R. 555 (P.C.). See also *Re Jacques Furniture Co.* (1933), 14 C.B.R. 316 (Ont. C.A.).
[27] See generally, *Cie de villas du cap Gibraltar v. Hughes* (1884), 11 S.C.R. 537 at 547, *per* Ritchie C.J.
[28] *Dassen Gold Resources Ltd. v. Royal Bank of Canada*, [1997] A.J. No. 777, 33 B.L.R. (2d) 220 (C.A.).

- acts that, although legal and involving the exercise of a power conferred upon the company, were beyond its stated objects;[29]
- acts that, although legal and within the powers and objects of the company, were beyond the powers of the directors or other functionaries who purported to act on behalf of the corporation,[30] as for instance where that power had been conferred upon someone else (such as the members of the company in general meeting), or where the power was exercised for an improper purpose or in breach of a fiduciary duty;[31]
- acts that were legal, within the company's powers and objects and within the powers of the functionaries purporting to execute them, but which were defectively executed due to some failure to comply with some prescribed procedure or other formality.

Corporate acts that were *ultra vires* within the first three of the above classes were beyond the powers of the company, and accordingly even the members acting in general meeting had no power to ratify the act concerned.[32] However, *ultra vires* acts of the fourth and fifth class could be ratified by the members of the company and therefore were potentially curable.[33] Illegal acts on the part of a corporation are open to attack on the same grounds as illegal acts on the part of an individual. Therefore, illegal acts need not concern us here.

§6.13 The *ultra vires* doctrine was inherently connected both with the administrative law objective of constraining the exercise of powers by statutory bodies and with the desire of the courts to place some control on the range of activities carried on by corporations, which at the time the doctrine evolved were still a questionable form of business enterprise.[34] The rationale of many of the earlier cases applying the doctrine to private corporations may well have been[35] that many of the companies concerned in those cases were performing a quasi-public function, such as railway companies,[36] which had the power to interfere with

---

[29] *Berry v. Indian Park Association*, [1997] O.J. No. 1873, 33 O.R. (3d) 522 (Gen. Div.). So, for instance, in *Introductions Ltd. v. National Provincial Bank*, [1970] Ch. 199 (C.A.), a statement in the objects clause of the memorandum of a company that it had the power to borrow money, was held insufficient to support a loan made to finance pig-breeding activities, when the memorandum of the company limited its objects to tourism.

[30] *C.E. Plain Ltd. (Trustee of) v. Kenley* (1930), 12 C.B.R. 66 at 77, aff'd 12 C.B.R. 492 (Ont. C.A.), *per* Orde J.

[31] But see *Rolled Steel Products (Holdings) Ltd. v. British Steel Corp.*, [1986] Ch. 246 (C.A.).

[32] *Ashbury Railway Carriage & Iron Co. v. Riche*, [1874-80] All E.R. Rep. Ext. 2219 (H.L.); *Thibault Auto Ltd. (Trustee of) v. Thibault* (1962), 33 D.L.R. (2d) 317 at 332, 334-35 (N.B.C.A.), *per* Ritchie J.A.

[33] For this reason, *ultra vires* acts within the fourth and fifth class are sometimes described as "voidable".

[34] These dual aspects of the doctrine were made clear in *Ashbury Railway Carriage & Iron Co. v. Riche* (1875), L.R. 7 H.L. 653.

[35] R.R. Pennington, *Company Law*, 4th ed. (London: Butterworths, 1979) at 93.

[36] See, for instance, *East Anglian Rlwys. v. Eastern Counties Rlwy. Co.* (1851), 11 C.B. 775, 138 E.R. 680 (C.P.); *Taylor v. Chichester & Midhurst Rlwy. Co.* (1867), L.R. 2 Exch. 356; *Norwich Corp. v. Norfolk Rlwy. Co.* (1855), 4 El. & Bl. 397, 119 E.R. 143 (Q.B.); *Ashbury Railway Carriage & Iron Co. v. Riche* (1875), L.R. 7 H.L. 653; *Shrewsbury & Birmingham Rlwy. Co v.*

private rights in order to carry out their undertaking. The rationale for the doctrine of *ultra vires* was explained by Parke B. in *South Yorkshire Rlwy. & River Dun Co. v. Great Northern Railway Co.*[37] by reference to a presumed legislative intention. Since the rule was derived from a presumed legislative intention, it might be ousted by legislative provision to the contrary.[38] As originally conceived, the doctrine permitted members of the corporation to bring proceedings to restrain the corporation from exceeding its powers. However, in *Taylor v. Chichester & Midhurst Rlwy. Co.*[39] the doctrine was extended (despite a vigorous dissent by Blackburn J.) to render void any contract entered into by a company that either was beyond its powers, or which was not necessary or incidental to the carrying out of its objects.[40] The duty therefore fell upon persons dealing with a corporation to make sure that the powers that the corporation was purporting to exercise in its dealings were truly held by it, and that those powers were being exercised for a purpose consistent with the objects of the company.[41] According to some (but not all) authorities, the doctrine could also work against the company: for not only might the company escape liability under an *ultra vires* contract, but so too might the other party.[42] Thus the practical effect of the doctrine was to render void any act, contract or dealing by the corporation which ran afoul of the *ultra vires* prohibitions,[43] and also the irregular exercise of any powers conferred on the corporation, as for instance where such an exercise possessed the character of a fraud.[44]

North Western Rlwy. Co. (1857), 6 H.L. Cas. 113; *A.G. v. Great Eastern Rlwy Co.* (1880), 5 App. Cas. 473 (H.L.); *Eastern Counties Rlwy. Co. v. Hawkes* (1855), 5 H.L. Cas. 331, 10 E.R. 928.

[37] (1853), 22 L.J. Ex. 305, 9 Exch. R. 55, 156 E.R. 23 at 84. Similarly, Pollock C.B. in *National Manure Co. v. Donald* (1859), 4 H. & N. 8, 157 E.R. 737 at 741 (Q.B.); see also Wigram V.C. in *Bagshaw v. Eastern Union Rlwy. Co.* (1849), 7 Hare 114 at 129, 68 E.R. 46 (V.C.).

[38] *Bonanza Creek Gold Mining Co. v. R.*, [1916] 1 A.C. 566 at 577-78, *per* Viscount Haldane.

[39] (1867), L.R. 2 Exch. 356.

[40] As to the right of a creditor to recover money advanced to a borrower under an *ultra vires* contract as money had and received, see *Guinness Mahorn & Co. v. Kensington & Chelsea London Borough Council*, unreported, March 2, 1998, *The Times* (C.A.); see also *Hazell v. Hammersmith & Fulham London Borough Council*, [1992] 2 A.C. 1 (H.L.);*Westdeutsche Landesbank Girozentrale v. Islington London Borough Council; Kleinwort Benson Ltd. v. Sandwell Borough Council* (1993), 92 L.G.R. 323.

[41] *Re Jon Beauforte (London) Ltd.*, [1953] Ch. 131.

[42] *Bell Houses Ltd. v. City Wall Properties Ltd.*, [1966] 1 Q.B. 207, rev'd [1966] 2 Q.B. 656 (C.A.); *Columbia Bitulithic Co. v. Vancouver Lumber Co.* (1915), 8 W.W.R. 132, 21 D.L.R. 91 (B.C.C.A.), *cf. Re KL Tractors Ltd.*, [1961] A.L.R. 410 (H.C. Aust.), *per* Fullagar J.

[43] For instance, in *Re Jon Beauforte (London) Ltd.*, [1953] Ch. 131, the company was incorporated to carry on the business of a tailor and manufacturer of clothes and materials. It subsequently entered into the manufacture of veneered panels. The company ordered a quantity of coke on letterhead which identified the company as a manufacturer of veneered panels. An action by the supplier to recover the price of the coke was dismissed because the contract was *ultra vires*. The manufacture of veneered panels fell outside the scope of the company's objects. The fact that the coke could have been used in connection with the business provided for in the objects clause of the memorandum did not save the transaction. The supplier was held to have notice that the coke that was supplied would be used in connection with the veneered panels business.

[44] *Dominion Cotton Mills Co. v. Amyot*, [1912] A.C. 546 at 552 (P.C.), *per* Lord Macnaghten.

§6.14 Unfortunately, in extending the doctrine of *ultra vires* so that it affected the validity of dealings with third parties, the doctrine undermined the ability of companies to conduct commerce — a substantial flaw in a law governing business corporations, since commerce was their very purpose. The doctrine was further expanded (under the doctrine of constructive notice) by impressing the whole world with knowledge of the contents of all documents which were a matter of public record.[45] The fact that it was not practical for business people to make reference to such documents was no defence.[46] In economic terms, the problem with the doctrine of *ultra vires* was that it greatly increased the transaction costs associated with the contracting process. Since the cost of inquiry was high, in many cases third parties had little practical option but to proceed in ignorance and simply hope for the best.

§6.15 Given the extensive changes that have been made to the common law by statute, it is no longer necessary to consider in detail the specific rules of law laid down under the *ultra vires* rule, much less its often peculiar or eccentric features and the creative devices employed by lawyers in an attempt to circumvent it.[47] It is sufficient to say that the doctrine was found to cause considerable inconvenience to the conduct of commerce, which led eventually to widespread calls for its abolition, not only in Canada, but across the common law world. Most such jurisdictions have now attempted to rid themselves of the doctrine. The general Canadian legislative approach towards the empowerment of a corporation begins by conferring upon the corporation the powers of a natural person. As might be expected, it is this approach which has been adopted in the CBCA and the OBCA, subsection 15(1) of the CBCA providing:

> A corporation has the capacity and, subject to this Act, the rights, powers and privileges of a natural person.[48]

---

[45] See, for instance, *Glasgow Lumber Co. v. Fettes*, [1932] 1 W.W.R. 195 (Sask. C.A.); *Re W.N. McEachern & Sons Ltd.*, [1933] O.R. 349 (C.A.). There was no duty, however, to inspect other documents which were not a matter of public record, such as the books or accounts of the corporation: *Re Banker's Trust* (1915), 7 W.W.R. 171, aff'd 8 W.W.R. 38 (B.C.C.A.).

[46] As Robert Pennington explains in *Company Law*, 4th ed. (London: Butterworths, 1979) at 96-97.

[47] For those interested in these questions, reference may be made to *Cotman v. Brougham*, [1918] A.C. 514 at 519-20 (H.L.), especially *per* Lord Parker of Waddington and at 522-23, *per* Lord Wrenbury; *Re Crown Bank* (1890), 44 Ch. D. 634 at 644, *per* North J.; see also *Pedlar v. Road Block Gold Mines of India Ltd.*, [1905] 2 Ch. 427 at 439, *per* Warrington J.; *Re Horsley & Weight Ltd.*, [1982] Ch. 442 at 448 (C.A.), *per* Buckley L.J.; *Rolled Steel Products (Holdings) Ltd. v. British Steel Corp.*, [1986] Ch. 246 (C.A.); *Re Introductions Ltd.*, [1970] Ch. 199; compare, however, *Christchurch City Corp. v. Flamingo Coffee Lounge Ltd.*, [1959] N.Z.L.R. 986; *H.A. Stephenson & Son Ltd. v. Gillanders, Arbuthnot & Co.* (1931), 45 C.L.R. 476 (H.C. Aust.), *per* Dixon J.; *Clarke v. Sarnia Street Railway* (1877), 42 U.C.Q.B. 39 at 45 (Ont. C.A.), *per* Harrison C.J.; *North American Life Assurance Co. v. Silver's Ltd.*, [1921] 2 W.W.R. 540 at 544 (Alta. C.A.), *per* Stuart J.; *Vancouver Engineering Works v. Columbia Bitulithic Co.* (1914), 6 W.W.R. 413 (B.C.S.C.) — implied power to take and grant chattel mortgages; *Winnipeg Electric Railway v. City of Winnipeg*, [1912] A.C. 355; *Brown v. Moore* (1921), 62 S.C.R. 487 at 497, *per* Anglin J.; *Carter Dewar Crowe Co. v. Columbia Bitulithic* (1914), 6 W.W.R. 1215 at 1217 (B.C.C.A.), *per* Macdonald C.J.A.; *Fire Valley Orchards Ltd. v. Sly* (1914), 6 W.W.R. 934 at 936 (B.C.S.C.), *per* Clement J.

[48] OBCA, s. 15.

The rights, powers, privileges and capacities of natural persons are theoretically unbounded: except where prohibited by statute, any power that may be held or exercised may be held or exercised by a natural person; anything that can be done, can be done by a natural person; any right or privilege which a person can enjoy can be enjoyed by a natural person. Thus it is implicit in the grant of the rights, powers and privileges of a natural person that corporations are unlimited in the powers, rights and privileges which they possess or may acquire, and like natural persons corporations will be presumed to possess or be capable of acquiring all rights, powers and privileges except to the extent that such possession or acquisition is denied to them by law.

§6.16 It has been held by the Supreme Court of Canada that the doctrine of *ultra vires* has been abolished with respect to business corporations, and also with respect to other companies (*e.g.*, banks) incorporated under legislation that contain similar provisions conferring the rights of a natural person upon the incorporated entities to which they apply. The doctrine cannot be revived in some residual form by demonstrating that in entering into a particular transaction (or performing it in some way), a corporation under the OBCA or CBCA has acted outside the scope of its declared objects or contrary to the legislation by which it is governed.[49] It may be argued that this is a rather strained interpretation of the natural powers provisions of the OBCA and CBCA — since at common law the *ultra vires* doctrine also came into play where the powers conferred upon the corporation were used for a purpose not authorized by the objects of the corporation.[50] However, both the OBCA and the CBCA do not require any statement of corporate objects in the articles of incorporation. Although such objects may be included if the incorporators so wish, it is very unusual for this to be done. More importantly, outsiders to a corporation are no longer impressed with knowledge or notice of the contents of publicly recorded documents concerning a corporation, such as its articles. Moreover, subsection 17(3) of the OBCA expressly provides that:

> ... No act of a corporation including a transfer of property to or by the corporation is invalid by reason only that the act is contrary to its articles, by-laws, a unanimous shareholder agreement or this Act.[51]

§6.17 Nevertheless the doctrine of *ultra vires* has still not been fully laid to rest. While outsiders need not be concerned with whether an act is beyond the powers

---

[49] *Communities Economic Development Fund v. Canadian Pickles Corp.*, [1991] S.C.J. No. 89, [1991] 3 S.C.R. 388 at 406, *per* Iacobucci J.; *Continental Bank Leasing Corp. v. Canada*, [1998] S.C.J. No. 63. In contrast, the doctrine of *ultra vires* continues to apply to Crown and other public corporations, created to carry out a statutory mandate, even when vested with the powers of a natural person. Public corporations run afoul of the doctrine where they exceed the powers that have been conferred upon them, or when they exercise those powers for a purpose that is inconsistent with their statutory objects. See, for instance, *British Columbia Securities Commission v. Seifert*, [2006] B.C.J. No. 225 (S.C.), *per* Kelleher J.; *New Brunswick Assn. of Real Estate Appraisers v. Poitras*, [2005] N.B.J. No. 545, 144 A.C.W.S. (3d) 475 (N.B.C.A.); see *Canadian Pickles*, *ibid*.

[50] *Berry v. Indian Park Association*, [1997] O.J. No. 1873, 33 O.R. (3d) 522 (Gen. Div.); *Ontario Salt Co. v. Merchants Salt Co.* (1871), 18 Gr. 540 (Ont. Ch.), *per* Strong V.C.

[51] CBCA, s. 16(3).

or outside the objects of the corporation, the directors of the corporation itself must continue to be. Thus subsection 17(2) of the OBCA[52] provides that a corporation must not carry on business or exercise any power that it is restricted by its articles from carrying on or exercising, nor may the corporation exercise any of its powers in a manner contrary to its articles. Moreover, subsection 134(2) of the OBCA[53] requires the directors and officers of the corporation to comply with the Act, the regulations, articles, by-laws and any unanimous shareholder agreement.[54] It is implicit in clause 19(*a*) of the OBCA[55] that any person who enters into a contract with or concerning the corporation knowing that it involves or contemplates the violation of the articles, by-laws or any unanimous shareholder agreement cannot enforce that contract against the corporation or any guarantor of the corporation.[56] Even in the absence of actual knowledge, a similar rule applies where that person ought to have known of that violation by virtue of his or her position with or relation to the corporation. Moreover, under subsection 253(1) of the OBCA:

> Where a corporation or any shareholder, director, officer, employee, agent, auditor, trustee, receiver and manager, receiver or liquidator of a corporation does not comply with this Act, the regulations, articles, by-laws, or a unanimous shareholder agreement, a complainant or a creditor of the corporation may, despite the imposition of any penalty in respect of such non-compliance and in addition to any other right the complainant or creditor has, apply to the court for an order directing the corporation or any person to comply with, or restraining the corporation or any person from acting in breach of, any provisions thereof, and upon such application the court may so order and make any further order it thinks fit.[57]

Although a corporation may be restrained from contravening a restriction on its business before it has entered into a contract that would have that effect,[58] it is doubtful whether such an order may be made after the formation of the contract, unless the other party to the contract can be shown to be implicated in some way in the contravention.

§6.18 The power of the court to issue a compliance order is discretionary. In *Carson v. Carson*[59] a corporate by-law prohibited shareholders from disposing of their shares without at least one month's notice to the company. Other shareholders had a pre-emptive right to acquire the shares where such notice was give, at the book value of the shares. Justice Creghan granted an order enforcing

---

[52] *Ibid.*, s. 16(2).
[53] *Ibid.*, s. 122(2).
[54] Concerning the potential liability of a director who sanctions a breach of a restriction set out in the articles of the corporation, see: *Re Lands Allotment Co.*, [1894] 1 Ch. 616 (C.A.).
[55] CBCA, s. 18(1)(*a*).
[56] See, generally, *Dassen Gold Resources Ltd. v. Royal Bank*, [1997] A.J. No. 777, 33 B.L.R. (2d) 220 (C.A.).
[57] CBCA, s. 247. The wording of the CBCA provision varies slightly from that of the OBCA provision, but there is no apparent significance in those differences in wording.
[58] *Simpson v. Westminster Palace Hotel Co.* (1860), 8 H.L. Cas. 712; *Colman v. Eastern Counties Rlwy. Co.* (1846), 10 Beav. 1, 50 E.R. 481 (M.R.); *Stephens v. Mysore Reefs (Kangundy) Mining Co. Ltd.*, [1902] 1 Ch. 745.
[59] [2000] N.B.J. No. 305, 6 B.L.R. (3d) 242 (Q.B.).

the restriction on transfer, but refused to order the sale at book value since this was substantially lower than the real value of the shares. In *Diamond Dog Management Inc. v. DMM Biehn Holdings Ltd.*,[60] the court concluded that the equivalent provision of the Saskatchewan *Business Corporations Act*[61] did not authorize the court to make orders with respect to an anticipated breach.

(ii) Restrictions Set out in the Articles

§6.19 As noted above, both the OBCA and CBCA permit a corporation to include restrictions on the conduct of a corporation or its activities in its articles. However, there is a subtle difference in the language and the approach taken under each of the two statutes with respect to this question. The prescribed form of articles under section 168 of the OBCA allows a corporation to include in its articles any restrictions:

> ... on the business or businesses that the corporation may carry on *or* upon *the powers* that the corporation may exercise. (emphasis added).

In contrast, paragraph 6(1)(*f*) of the CBCA allows the corporation to set out restrictions on the *business* that the corporation may carry on, but not on the *powers* that it may exercise. Nevertheless, despite this omission from clause 6(1)(*f*) of the CBCA, it would appear that restrictions on the exercise of a corporate power may be included in CBCA articles since subsection 16(2) of the CBCA provides:

> A corporation shall not carry on any business *or exercise any power* that it is restricted by its articles from carrying on or exercising, nor shall the corporation *exercise any of its powers in a manner contrary to its articles*. (emphasis added).[62]

§6.20 Although it is exceedingly rare for new corporations incorporated under either the OBCA or the CBCA to have clauses in their articles of incorporation setting out the objects for which the corporation is incorporated, many corporations that were incorporated under the previous legislation in Ontario still contain such provisions in their articles of incorporation.[63] Where there is an exercise of a power contrary to the articles (or the Act), the remedy of an aggrieved party is to enjoin that exercise.[64] However, a considerable degree of protection is given to third parties in respect of provisions of that type by clause 19(*a*) of the OBCA,[65] which provides that a corporation or guarantor of an obligation of a corporation may not assert against a person dealing with the corpo-

---

[60] [2003] S.J. No. 297, 32 B.L.R. (3d) 292 (Q.B.), *per* Koch J.
[61] 1978, c. B 10, s. 240.
[62] Subsection 17(2) of the OBCA is identical.
[63] Fortunately, most objects clauses were drafted in extremely broad terms, and usually contain basket provisions allowing the corporation to carry on any other business (in addition to that specifically mentioned in the objects clause) "that can conveniently be carried on in connection with" the specified business. For cases construing the meaning of such a provision, see *H. & H. Logging Co. v. Random Services Corp.* (1967), 60 W.W.R. 619 (B.C.C.A.); *Dome Oil Co. v. Alberta Drilling Co.* (1916), 52 S.C.R. 561, aff'g 27 D.L.R. 118; *Fire Valley Orchards Ltd. v. Sly* (1914), 6 W.W.R. 934 (B.C.S.C.).
[64] OBCA, s. 247; CBCA, s. 253.
[65] CBCA, s. 18(1)(*a*).

ration or with any person who has acquired rights from the corporation that "the articles, by-laws or any unanimous shareholder agreement have not been complied with". Further protection is afforded by subsection 17(3) of the OBCA, which provides:

> Despite subsection (2) and subsection 3(2), no act of a corporation including a transfer of property to or by the corporation is invalid by reason only that the act is contrary to its articles, by-laws, a unanimous shareholder agreement or this Act.[66]

Thus, from the perspective of third parties dealing with the corporation, it is no longer necessary for them to confirm that the powers being exercised by a corporation are necessary or incidental to the attainment of the objects of the corporation. However, the protection afforded under clause 19(*a*) does not apply to any person who has or ought to have[67] knowledge of the contravention in question.[68]

§6.21 Both the OBCA and the CBCA provide that it is not necessary for a by-law to be passed in order to confer a particular power on the corporation and its directors.[69] The presumption is that a corporation is vested with all powers that any person may possess, and it is further presumed that any power that may be exercised by the corporation may be exercised by its directors on behalf of the corporation. By virtue of paragraph 6(1)(*f*) of the CBCA, any restriction on the exercise of powers by the directors in derogation of that presumption must be set out in the articles. The prescribed form of articles under OBCA is to a similar effect. It would therefore appear that restrictions contained in the by-laws are ineffective.

(iii) Excluded Rights

§6.22 Although corporations for the most part enjoy the rights of natural person, there are numerous rights from which they are excluded. For instance, as discussed in Chapter 4, a corporation cannot claim "liberty" within the meaning of the Due Process clause of the U.S. Constitution;[70] that corporations have neither race nor colour;[71] that they cannot commit treason, nor be outlawed, nor excommunicated, and that they have no souls.[72] As completely artificial entities, corporations are not themselves capable of committing crime; but they may be held responsible for the crimes that are committed by others. Where a corporation is convicted of an offence, the shareholders and other stakeholders who stand be-

---

[66] *Ibid.*, s. 16(3).
[67] *Dassen Gold Resources Ltd. v. Royal Bank*, [1997] A.J. No. 777, 33 B.L.R. (2d) 220 (C.A.). See the discussion of Constructive Notice, below, at § 6.32 *et seq.*
[68] The precise wording of the exclusion is: "… except where the person has or ought to have, by virtue of the person's position with or relationship with the corporation, knowledge to that effect". See OBCA, s. 19; CBCA, s. 18.
[69] CBCA, s. 16(1); OBCA, s. 17(1).
[70] *Bridges v. California* (1941), 314 U.S. 252 at 280-81, *per* Frankfurter J.
[71] *Connecticut General Life Ins. Co. v. Johnson* (1938), 303 U.S. 77 at 87, *per* Black J.
[72] *Sutton's Hospital Case*, [1612] 10 Co. Rep. 23 at 32b.

hind the corporation are made to suffer for a wrong committed not by itself but by its directors, officers or employees.[73]

(iv) Special Legislative Grants of Power

§6.23 In some cases a provincial Legislature or the federal Parliament may by special legislation confer extraordinary powers upon a corporation that is otherwise subject to the OBCA or the CBCA, as the case may be, such as a power of expropriation or a power to pass by-laws affecting strangers to the corporation. The question of whether a grant of specific powers to a corporation affects the powers that it would otherwise enjoy under the OBCA or the CBCA is one of statutory interpretation. The general presumption with respect to statutory provisions conferring powers upon corporations is that they are enabling rather than prescriptive, so that the corporation may exercise them, but is not obliged to do so.[74] However, OBCA and CBCA corporations already enjoy broad powers under those two statutes, so unless it can be argued that the particular powers were conferred by the legislature upon special purpose corporations out of an abundance of caution, the continued applicability of that general presumption may be open to question.

§6.24 Where the legislature confers similar powers to be exercised in the same territory upon two or more corporations, it is assumed that the legislature intended those powers to be concurrent, and that neither possesses exclusive powers. Therefore the courts will not restrain either of those corporations from exercising the powers so conferred except to the extent that in exercising those powers one is preventing the other from exercising the powers conferred on it.[75] It has been held that a corporation may not enter into a contract under which it binds itself not to exercise a power specifically granted to it by statute.[76] This view is certainly correct insofar as the statute appears to require the corporation to exercise a particular power[77] or where it appears that the continuance of that power in the corporation is required as part of the general scheme of the legislation concerned.[78] However, it is difficult to see on principle why a corporation should not be allowed to restrict its right to use a permissive power.

---

[73] *Marr v. Tumulty* (1931), 256 N.Y. 15 at 24, *per* Cardozo J.
[74] *Daniel v. Gold Hill Mining Co.* (1899), 6 B.C.R. 495 (C.A.).
[75] *Jacques Cartier Water & Power Co. v. Quebec Railway Light & Power Co.* (1902), 11 Que. K.B. 511 (C.A.).
[76] *Ayr Harbour Trustees v. Oswald* (1883), 8 App. Cas. 623 (H.L.); *Coleman v. Toronto & Niagara Power Co.* (1917), 40 O.L.R. 130 at 134 (C.A.), *per* Hodgins J.A.
[77] See, generally, *Horn v. Henry Faulder & Co. Ltd.* (1908), 99 L.T. 524 at 525-26, *per* Neville J.
[78] See, for instance, *Punt v. Symons & Co. Ltd.*, [1903] 2 Ch. 506, *per* Byrne J., where it was held that a company could contract out of the right to amend its articles (the equivalent of Canadian by-laws), although it might enter into a contract under which an amendment of the by-laws would be a breach of contract. See also *Allen v. Gold Reefs of West Africa*, [1900] 1 Ch. 656 (C.A.).

(v) Financial Assistance by Corporation

§6.25 In general a corporation must use its property only for it own corporate purposes, but within that restriction can otherwise do what it likes with its property, provided that it deals with that property according to the laws governing its constitution. A corporation cannot give away its property either to shareholders or others except where the board concludes in good faith that to do so is in the best interests of the corporation and in furtherance of its objects.[79] The best interest requirement essentially prevents the major or controlling shareholders of a corporation (or even all its shareholders) from misappropriating the assets of the corporation for their own benefit.[80] However, the benefit derived by a corporation from a particular transaction may sometimes be indirect. In certain cases, it may be in the interest of a corporation to provide financial assistance (or even make gifts) to its shareholders, employees, officers or their dependants, or to members of its corporate group, such as its subsidiaries, holding company or sister subsidiaries. Gifts to outsiders, particularly charities and similar organizations, may often be justified in the interest of promoting the goodwill of the corporation. Gifts or financial assistance to directors, officers or employees may often be justified as being in the nature of remuneration for services rendered or to be provided, or as being an integral aspect of promoting a good employer-employee relationship.

§6.26 Historically, Canadian corporate laws imposed extensive restrictions with respect to the provision of financial assistance by one member of a corporate group to another (*e.g.*, by way of a guarantee). In recent years, these restrictions have been greatly cut back. Section 44 of the CBCA, which regulated the provision of financial assistance by a corporation to its affiliates, was repealed by section 26 of S.C. 2001, c. 14. There are currently no specific restrictions on or prohibitions against the provision of such financial assistance by a CBCA corporation. However, on the facts of a specific case the giving of such assistance may be sufficient to give rise to a remedy under section 248 of the OBCA as conduct that is "oppressive or unfairly prejudicial to or that unfairly disregards the interests of any security holder, creditor, director of officer of the corporation... "

§6.27 The financial assistance provisions of the OBCA were revised in 2000.[81] Subsection 20(1) of the OBCA sets down the general rule that: "A corporation may give financial assistance to any person for any purpose by means of a loan, guarantee or otherwise." The principal obligation now imposed under the OBCA

---

[79] *C.E. Plain Ltd. (Trustee of) v. Kenley* (1930), 12 C.B.R. 66 at 77 (H.C.), *per* Orde J.A., aff'd [1931] O.R. 75 (C.A.); *Mark V. Developments Ltd. v. Big White Ski Developments Ltd.*, [1985] B.C.J. No. 112, 31 B.L.R. 169 (S.C.); *Royal Bank v. Stewart*, [1979] B.C.J. No. 550, 8 B.L.R. 77, aff'd, [1981] B.C.J. No. 378, 31 B.L.R. 33 (C.A.).
[80] The necessity to act in the best interest of the corporation being a consideration that often comes into play where a corporation provides financial assistance to its sole or controlling shareholder: *Thibault Auto Ltd. (Trustee of) v. Thibault* (1962), 33 D.L.R. (2d) 317 at 332, 334-35 (N.B.C.A.), *per* Ritchie J.A.
[81] S.O. 2000, c. 26, Sched. B, s. 3(4).

where such assistance is provided is a disclosure requirement.[82] In this respect, subsection 20(2) provides:

> Subject to subsection (3), a corporation shall disclose to its shareholders all material financial assistance that it gives to,
>
> (a) a shareholder, a beneficial owner of a share, a director, an officer or an employee of the corporation, an affiliate of the corporation, or an associate of any of them; or
>
> (b) a person for the purpose of, or in connection with, the purchase of a share or a security convertible into or exchangeable for a share issued or to be issued by the corporation or an affiliate of the corporation.

The disclosure must include a brief description of the financial assistance given, including its nature and extent, the terms on which the financial assistance was given; and a statement the amount of the financial assistance initially given and the amount, if any, outstanding.[83] Where the corporation is not an offering corporation it must make the disclosure by giving a notice to all shareholders no later than 90 days after giving the financial assistance.[84] An offering corporation must make the required disclosure:

> (*a*) in each management information circular that it is required to send to its shareholders in respect of the first annual meeting called and held after it gives the financial assistance and in respect of each annual meeting thereafter so long as the financial assistance remains outstanding; or
>
> (*b*) in a financial statement that the directors are required to place before the shareholders under subsection 154(1) at the first annual meeting called and held after it gives the financial assistance and at each annual meeting thereafter so long as the financial assistance remains outstanding.[85]

Subsection 20(3) provides that:

> a corporation is not required to disclose to its shareholders material financial assistance that it gives,
>
> (*a*) to a person in the ordinary course of business if the lending of money is part of the corporation's ordinary business;
>
> (*b*) to a person on account of expenditures incurred or to be incurred on behalf of the corporation;
>
> (*c*) to its holding body corporate if the corporation is a wholly owned subsidiary of the holding body corporate;
>
> (*d*) to a subsidiary body corporate of the corporation; or
>
> (*e*) to employees of the corporation or any of its affiliates in accordance with a plan for the purchase of shares of the corporation or any of its affiliates.

---

[82] Subsection 20(7) of the OBCA provides that: "A contract made by a corporation in contravention of subsection (2), (3), (4), (5) or (6) may be enforced by or against the corporation."
[83] OBCA, s. 20(4).
[84] *Ibid.*, s. 20(5).
[85] *Ibid.*, s. 20(6).

§6.28 The Ontario Ministry of Government Services has recently published a discussion paper asking whether the financial assistance provisions of the OBCA should be repealed in the same manner as occurred in 2001 with the CBCA. A similar legislative initiative is already underway in Manitoba. The current OBCA provisions were modeled on the regime in force under the Saskatchewan *Corporations Act*, and a similar regime is also in place in British Columbia and Alberta. According to the Ministry, the current disclosure provisions serve two goals:

- to protect minority shareholders from practices by corporate directors and officers that would jeopardize the financial position of the corporation; and

- to protect creditors of a corporation from having their interests compromised by the corporation's decision to provide financial assistance that would detrimentally deplete the financial assets of the corporation.

A serious question must be raised as to whether a mere disclosure requirement is satisfactory for either of these objectives. Thus far, there appear to have been no adverse consequences from the complete repeal of financial assistance restrictions under the CBCA.

§6.29 It is difficult to understand what benefit is obtained by imposing ineffective regulatory restrictions at the provincial level that do not apply to CBCA corporations. In the absence of even a theoretical argument — much less any hard evidence — to indicate that a practical benefit is derived from the current regulatory regime, it is to be hoped that the Ontario government proceeds with the repeal of the above provisions.

(vi) Statutory and Contractual References to "Persons"

§6.30 Both the federal and provincial *Interpretation Acts* make clear that the term "person", when used in a statute, includes corporate entities. In England, the *Law of Property Act, 1925* expressly provides that the word "person" when used in a contract includes corporations. No corresponding provision appears in the statute law of Ontario. However, it is doubtful whether the oversight is of much practical consequence. When a contract or other private legal document employs a legal term of art such as "person", it is natural to assume that the parties to that document enjoy its ordinary legal meaning. As a general principle, what does and what does not constitute a person is determined by the law of the land rather than by the parties to a contract. If they intend a particular contractual provision to apply or relate to "persons" then the logical inference is that they intend to include within that term all such beings and entities as are recognized under the law as constituting persons.

§6.31 Section 20 of the *Conveyancing and Law of Property Act*[86] provides that any corporation capable of taking and conveying land in Ontario shall be deemed to have been and to be capable of taking and conveying land by deed of

---

[86] R.S.O. 1990, c. C. 34 ("CLPA").

bargain and sale in like manner as a person in his or her natural capacity, subject to any general limitations or restrictions and to any special provisions as to holding or conveying land that are applicable to the corporation.[87]

B. CONTRACTS AND CORPORATE UNDERTAKINGS

§6.32 Constructive notice is knowledge of a fact that is presumed or imputed by law. The doctrine (which originated in the law of conveyancing)[88] can apply only where the means of information is available to the person impressed with the knowledge concerned. It applies in respect of facts which would have become known to a person, or his or her agent, if proper inquiries had been made; or where such facts did come to the knowledge of that person's agent, but for some reason did not come to the knowledge of that person.[89] In the corporate law context, the doctrine of constructive notice has been applied with respect to restrictions on the authority of certain agents or officers of a corporation that are set out in a public document.[90]

§6.33 At common law, a person who dealt with a corporate body was deemed to have notice of the contents of all documents that the corporation was required to file with, and did file with, a public office that were open to public inspection[91] (such as the articles of incorporation filed with the registrar), and also any documents or notices that the corporation was required to publish and did publish in an official journal such as *The Ontario Gazette*. For the most part, these documents and notices would deal with such matters as the objects of the corporation, the share capital of the corporation, the structure of the board and the names and addresses of its directors, the place of the corporation's head office and any limits upon the powers of the corporation or the manner in which those powers were to be exercised. Essentially, the effect of the rule of constructive notice was that no person could make a valid contract (or enter into any other transaction with a corporation) that was in patent conflict with one of the public documents or notices relating to the corporation.

§6.34 The doctrine of constructive notice operated entirely for the benefit of the companies to which it applied. It afforded the corporation a shield, but gave no protection to third parties who dealt with a corporation (*e.g.*, to avoid liability under a contract that proves disadvantageous to those third parties).[92] The onus

---

[87] As noted above at §6.4.
[88] See, generally, *English & Scottish Mercantile Investment Co. Ltd. v. Brunton*, [1892] 2 Q.B. 700 (C.A.).
[89] See, for instance, *Royal Bank v. Stewart* (1979), 8 B.L.R. 77, aff'd 31 B.C.L.R. 33 (C.A.).
[90] See, for instance, *Ernest v. Nicholls* (1857), 6 H.L. Cas. 401; *Irvine v. Union Bank of Australia* (1877), 2 App. Cas. 366 (P.C.).
[91] See, generally, *Re London & New York Investment Corp.*, [1895] 2 Ch. 860; *Irvine v. Union Bank of Australia* (1877), 2 App. Cas. 366 (P.C.).
[92] *Rama Corporation Ltd. v. Proved Tin & General Investments Ltd.*, [1952] 2 Q.B. 147 at 149, *per* Slade J. Inasmuch as the articles of a corporation prescribed internal rules and regulations governing the exercise of a company's powers, or prohibited the exercise of certain powers, that provision was binding upon outsiders and shareholders alike. The theory underlying the doctrine was that a person who dealt with a corporation had no right to complain about the invalidity of a

was on the outsider to satisfy himself or herself that the transaction was not in apparent conflict with a public document or notice.

§6.35 Given the interplay between the doctrine of *ultra vires* and the doctrine of constructive notice, it was perhaps not surprising that when the Ontario Select Committee on Company Law proposed the abolition of the former, it also proposed the abolition of the latter.[93] The present OBCA now contains an express provision abolishing the doctrine of constructive notice. In this regard section 18 provides:

> No person is affected by or is deemed to have notice or knowledge of the contents of a document concerning a corporation by reason only that the document has been filed with the Director or is available for inspection at an office of the corporation.

Aside from a slight procedural variation (*i.e.*, "filed *by* the Director" as opposed to "filed *with* the Director"), section 17 of the CBCA is to the same effect. Nevertheless, certain of the common law exceptions to the rule of constructive notice continue to be of importance in determining the extent to which outsiders are required to inquire into the internal affairs of a corporation before entering into a transaction with the corporation. Those exceptions are embodied in a rule of corporate law known as the indoor management rule, to which we will turn momentarily. In order to understand that rule, it is first necessary to appreciate the general principles of the law of agency governing the authority of an agent, and accordingly it is that subject to which we will now turn.

(i) The Authority of Corporate Agents

§6.36 Since it is an artificial person, a corporation may act only through agents. For this reason, the principles of the law of agency are highly relevant to any dealing with a corporation. A principal (such as a corporation) will be bound by a contract entered into by its agent on behalf of the principal in any of four

---

transaction entered into with the corporation, where there was a patent conflict with the provisions or requirements of a document that the person could have inspected: R.R. Pennington, *Company Law*, 4th ed. (London: Butterworths, 1979) at 114. See also *J.C. Houghton & Co. v. Northard, Lowe & Wills Ltd.*, [1927] 1 K.B. 246 at 266 (C.A.), *per* Sargant L.J., aff'd [1928] A.C. 1 (H.L.). Therefore a contravention of a prohibition or restriction could be raised as a defence by a corporation in answer to a claim made against the corporation by any person who dealt with a company in a transaction which violated that prohibition or restriction, but not the by-laws of the corporation to the extent that the contravention was or would have been patently evident to a person who took the trouble to read those public documents: *Re W.N. McEachern & Sons Ltd.*, [1933] O.R. 349 at 367 (C.A.), *per* Davies J.A.; *Walton v. Bank of Nova Scotia*, [1964] 1 O.R. 673 (H.C.). So if the articles required all contracts to be signed by two directors or officers of the corporation and it was only signed by one such person, the corporation might raise the doctrine of constructive notice in defence.

[93] Thus it stated at ¶ 4.2.3 of its Report:

> In order to make effective the recommendation in Section 1 of this Chapter that the *ultra vires* doctrine be removed from Ontario law, the Committee recommends that by appropriate amendment to the Act the rule or doctrine of constructive notice be abolished as it might otherwise relate to the certificate of incorporation and amendments thereto ...

situations: (1) where the agent does what he or she is actually authorized to do; (2) where an agent does what an agent of his or her type would normally have the authority to do; (3) where the agent does what he or she has been held out by the principal as having the authority to do, even though no such authority has actually been conferred; (4) where unauthorized acts of an agent are subsequently ratified. In cases falling under (2) and (3), it is necessary to show that the other party did not know that the agent was exceeding his or her actual authority. It is upon these principles that the indoor management rule is based.

§6.37 Closely akin to the question of whether a corporation has the power to act regarding a particular matter is the question of whether or not the corporate agent, functionary or operative (usually an employee or director) has the authority to act in a particular matter. Determining the extent to which a particular corporate agent, functionary or operative has the authority to bind a corporation involves as many as five successive legal questions, specifically:

(a) the extent of the authority of an agent or putative agent under the general law of agency;

(b) the extent of the authority of a corporate agent, functionary or operative under the common law indoor management rule;

(c) the extent to which the law as determined under (a) and (b) is modified by section 19 of the OBCA[94] (the statutory indoor management rule);

(d) the extent to which the law as determined under (a), (b) and (c) is modified by any specific provision of the OBCA or the CBCA, such as section 65 of the OBCA[95] dealing with unauthorized signatures on a security certificate before or in the course of its issue;

(e) the extent to which the law as determined under (a), (b), (c) and (d) is modified by some other statutory provision.

(ii) Actual, Implied and Ostensible Authority

§6.38 Under the general law of agency, in order for an agent to bind the principal he or she must possess the authority to act on the principal's behalf — that is, the agent must be acting within the scope of his or her authority. There are three types of authority that an agent may possess: actual, apparent or deemed.[96] Where an agent purports to act for a principal, and the agent has the principal's actual or ostensible authority, the principal is liable to the third party and the agent ordinarily is not.[97] If, however, the agent does not have such authority, the principal cannot be made liable to the third party. In such a case, the agent may

---

[94] CBCA, s. 18.
[95] Ibid., s. 57.
[96] Agency of necessity is of limited application and may be ignored for the purposes of the general analysis provided here.
[97] The agent may be liable for the principal, where the agent has exceeded his or her actual authority.

be personally liable to the third party, on the basis of the breach of an implied warranty of authority, even though that breach may be entirely innocent. These principles have a particular application in the corporate content, where a person purports to act on behalf of a non-existent corporation, it is necessary to determine whether or not personal liability for the contract flows back to that agent. Frequently, liability has been imposed.[98]

§6.39 Each form of authority is independent of the others, although they may co-exist and coincide.[99] However, where one form of authority exists, it is not necessary to show that either of the other forms also exists. A person who is presumed to possess certain authority by law has deemed authority. The scope of a deemed authority is determined by construction of the law under which it is conferred. Under the OBCA and the CBCA, the board of directors as a collective entity has deemed authority to act on behalf of the corporation,[100] as does a liquidator.[101] It need not be shown that the corporation has actually conferred any particular authority on its board;[102] instead, it is presumed that such authority exists unless it can be shown that in fact the authority has been removed. In contrast, the officers, employees and other agents of a corporation possess no comparable deemed authority, but they may be cloaked with either actual or apparent authority to deal on the corporation's behalf.

§6.40 Actual authority is a legal relationship between a principal and agent created by a consensual agreement to which they alone are parties. Its scope is to be ascertained by applying ordinary principles of construction to the contract creating the agency, including any proper implications that may be inferred from the express words used, the usages of the trade in which the parties are engaged or the course of business between the parties. To this contract, the person dealing with the agent (the "obligee") is a stranger. The obligee dealing with the agent may be totally ignorant of the existence of any authority on the part of the agent — and such ignorance is frequently the case where a person contracts as an agent for an undisclosed principal. But if the agent does enter into a contract under the actual authority of the undisclosed principal, his or her so doing will create contractual rights and liabilities between that principal and the obligee.[103] Actual authority may be express or implied. It is express when it is given by express words, such as when a board of directors passes a resolution which authorizes two of the directors to sign cheques or to execute a guarantee (or some other contract) on the part of the corporation. It is implied when it is in-

---

[98] See, for instance, *Royal Bank of Canada v. Starr*, [1985] O.J. No. 1763 (Dist. Ct.); *Biondich v. Kingscroft Investments Ltd.*, [2002] O.J. No. 4742 (S.C.J.); *Maple Engineering & Construction Canada Ltd. v. 1373988 Ontario Inc.*, [2004] O.J. No. 5025, 135 A.C.W.S. (3d) 823 (S.C.J.).
[99] *Freeman & Lockyer v. Buckhurst Park Properties (Mangal) Ltd.*, [1964] 2 Q.B. 480 at 502 (C.A.), *per* Diplock L.J.
[100] OBCA, s. 17(1) provides: "It is not necessary for a by-law to be passed in order to confer any particular power on the corporation or its directors". See also CBCA, s. 16(1).
[101] See, for instance, OBCA, ss. 202, 203, 204, 223.
[102] OBCA, s. 17.
[103] *Freeman & Lockyer v. Buckhurst Park Properties (Mangal) Ltd.*, [1964] 2 Q.B. 480 at 503 (C.A.), *per* Diplock L.J.

ferred from the conduct of the parties and the circumstances of the case, such as when the directors appoint one of them to be a managing director. If a person is appointed to an office in the corporation, by making that appointment the directors implicitly authorize the person so appointed to do all such acts and things as fall within the usual scope of that office.[104]

§6.41 Where a person who has no authority to act as an agent claims to act as agent for another person and makes a contract on that person's behalf, or where a person who is an agent exceeds the authority actually conferred upon him or her and enters into a contract when not authorized to do so, it is not acceptable for the alleged principal concerned to sit back and do nothing. Clear notice of repudiation must be given to the other party to the contract purportedly made by the agent as soon as possible after notice of the making of the contract comes to the attention of the alleged principal, and any benefit received under that contract must be returned. Failure to act promptly may result in the alleged principal being held to have ratified the contract even if the alleged agent was not authorized to act on its behalf. For instance, in *Great Northern Grain Terminals Ltd. v. Axley Agricultural Installations Ltd.*[105] the Alberta Court of Appeal held that there was a duty of an alleged surety to disclaim promptly any contract purportedly made on its behalf by a putative agent or an agent who has exceeded his authority.[106] Ideally, the contract should be disclaimed as soon as it comes to the notice of the purported principal, but disallowance within a reasonable time afterward is also effective.

§6.42 There are two possible situations in which an agent may exceed the authority actually conferred upon him or her by the principal. First, the agent may innocently misunderstand the limits of the authority that has been conferred. Second, the agent may be motivated by an ulterior purpose, such as the commission of a fraud for his or her personal benefit. In general, the liability of the principal is not affected by whichever of these situations applies. The principal cannot escape from liability merely because the agent may have abused the authority or betrayed the trust.[107] The law of agency is of necessity a highly practical branch of the law. It must operate consistently with the requirements and expectations of reasonable commercial practice.[108]

§6.43 In the case of apparent or ostensible authority, the agent may be a stranger to the impression of authority that the principal has created, although in most cases the agent will be at least generally aware of the existence of the representation. But the agent must not purport to make the agreement as principal personally. The representation, when acted upon by the obligee by entering into a contract with the agent, operates as an estoppel, preventing the principal from

---

[104] *Hely-Hutchinson v. Brayhead Ltd.*, [1968] 1 Q.B. 573 (C.A.).
[105] [1990] A.J. No. 817, 76 Alta. L.R. (2d) 156 (C.A.).
[106] *Ibid.*, at 159-61.
[107] *Hambro v. Burnand*, [1904] 2 K.B. 10 (C.A.), *per* Romer L.J.; see also *Reckitt v. Barnett, Pembroke & Slater Ltd.*, [1929] A.C. 176 at 185, *per* Viscount Dunedin.
[108] See, generally, *Canadian Laboratory Supplies Ltd. v. Engelhard Industries of Canada Ltd.* (1979), 97 D.L.R. (3d) 1 at 24 (S.C.C.), *per* Estey J.

denying that he or she is not bound by the contract.[109] The principle of ostensible or apparent authority comes into play where a person is held out as an agent when that person is not an agent, or being an agent is held out to possess an extent of authority greater than that which has actually been conferred. It seems a reasonable proposition to say that the representation of authority must emanate from the principal.[110] However, certain difficulties arise in applying this general principle to a corporation.[111] Since corporations can only act through agents, it is not possible to show that the representation emanated from the corporation itself, but only that it emanated from some corporate agent who had the authority to provide such a representation.[112] One basic question to resolve is whether the representation may be made by the same person who purports to act as agent. Except in very unusual cases, the answer is that representations made by an agent as to the scope of his or her authority are not binding on the principal.[113] Even in the exceptional case where an agent does possess the authority to represent the scope of his or her agency, the authority to make such representations must itself emanate from the principal. In the normal case, the impression of authority on the strength of which the third party acts must be *directly* attributable to some representation made by the principal concerning the scope or existence of the purported authority in question, rather than to a representation made by the purported agent. The principal may make such representations in essentially one of two ways: by words or by conduct.

§6.44 A corporation may represent authority by conduct in a variety of different ways, but the three most common are: (1) where the corporation allows a particular person to exercise the authority associated with a particular office held by that person, even though that authority was denied to or not conferred upon that person under the terms of his or her appointment; (2) where the corporation allows a person to represent that he (or she) holds an office to which a particular type of authority is attached when in fact he does not; (3) where the corporation

---

[109] *Freeman & Lockyer v. Buckhurst Park Properties (Mangal) Ltd.*, [1964] 2 Q.B. 480 (C.A.), *per* Diplock L.J.; *President of Westfield Bank v. Corner* (1891), 37 N.Y.R. (10 Tiff), 322 (N.Y.C.A.), *per* Andrews J.; approved [1893] A.C. 180.

[110] *Freeman & Lockyer v. Buckhurst Park Properties (Mangal) Ltd.*, [1964] 2 Q.B. 480 at 503, 505 (C.A.), *per* Diplock L.J.

[111] See, for instance, *Crabtree-Vickers Pty. Ltd. v. Australian Direct Mail Advertising & Addressing Co. Pty. Ltd.* (1976), 50 A.L.R. 527 (H.C. Aust.). In *Re Madi Pty. Ltd.* (1987), 5 A.C.L.C. 847 (Vic. S.C.), the Madi company was found to have entered into a deed under which it guaranteed the payment of a loan made to its parent company. Madi's corporate seal was affixed to the deed, and its execution was attested to by a director and one McCorley, who signed as company secretary, and another director who signed as a witness. When the creditor sought to enforce the guarantee, Madi argued that McCorley was not the company secretary, and therefore the guarantee was not executed in accordance with the company's articles. Justice Southwell rejected this defence, on the basis the records filed by the company with the state government indicated that McCorley was its company secretary. Significantly, there was no evidence before the court that the creditor had relied on this publicly filed record. *Cf. Northside Developments Pty. Ltd. v. Registrar-General* (1990), 8 A.C.L.C. 611 (H.C. Aust.).

[112] *Freeman & Lockyer v. Buckhurst Park Properties (Mangal) Ltd.*, [1964] 2 Q.B. 480 at 504-505 (C.A.).

[113] *Armagas Ltd. v. Mundogas S.A. (The Ocean Frost)*, [1985] 3 W.L.R. 640 at 652-53 (C.A.), *per* Goff L.J., aff'd [1986] A.C. 717, [1986] 2 All E.R. 385 (H.L.).

allows a particular person to act generally on its behalf with respect to a particular matter and the act in question pertains to that matter. In each case the corporation is estopped from denying the truth of the impression that it has created, which is that the ostensible authority in fact has been conferred. An example of such agency arises where a corporation allows a person to act as a director even though that person is not qualified to so act or has not been validly appointed to the office.[114] Moreover, a director validly appointed may bind the corporation by exercising the type of authority that a director would normally possess even though the board of directors has decided that directors individually should not so act.[115] Similarly, if the corporation effectively allows the agent to act as a plenipotentiary, it may not subsequently deny the existence of authority. As Greer L.J. observed:

> In the case before us the guarantee was signed by a person who was the chairman of the board of directors. Some one must represent the Company for the purpose of conducting correspondence, it may be a secretary, or the managing director, or some other officer; and he must have authority to bind the Company by letters written on its behalf. The person chosen by the defendants for this purpose was the chairman of the board, and the defendants have represented by their chairman that the plaintiffs could rely on the guarantee of the defendants as the act of the defendants and are responsible for those acts which they have held him out as having authority to perform.[116]

Apparent authority created by representation is similar. Strictly speaking, such authority cannot arise by words expressly declaring the authority to exist — for in such a case the authority of the agent would be actual, not apparent. However, an implied authority may arise where the words used by a corporation create the impression that such authority exists.[117] The ostensible or apparent authority that the corporation confers is the impression that the corporation conveys to outsiders as to the scope of authority that the agent possesses.

§6.45 An illustration of the application of the apparent authority concept in the corporate context can be found in the decision of the Court of Appeal in *Freeman & Lockyer v. Buckhurst Park Properties (Mangal) Ltd.*[118] In that case a company was set up by two men, Kapoor and Hoon, for the purpose of buying and reselling the Buckhurst Park Estate. These two men and a nominee of each were appointed as the directors of the company. The articles of the company permitted it to appoint a managing director, although none was ever appointed. However, Kapoor instructed the plaintiff architects to carry out certain work in connection with the development of the estate. In an action by the plaintiffs for

---

[114] *Re County Life Assurance Co.* (1870), L.R. 5 Ch. 288; *Mahony v. East Holyford Mining Co.* (1875), L.R. 7 H.L. 869 at 895 (H.L.), per Kelly L.C.B.
[115] *Kreditbank Cassel, GmbH v. Schenkers Ltd.*, [1927] 1 K.B. 826 (C.A.), per Atkin L.J.; see also *British Thomson-Houston Co. v. Federated European Bank Ltd.*, [1932] 2 K.B. 176 at 183 (C.A.), per Slesser L.J.
[116] *British Thomson-Houston Co. v. Federated European Bank Ltd.*, [1932] 2 K.B. 176 at 182 (C.A.), per Greer L.J.
[117] See, generally, *Canadian Laboratory Supplies Ltd. v. Engelhard Industries of Canada Ltd.* (1979), 97 D.L.R. (3d) 1 at 24-25 (S.C.C.), per Estey J.
[118] [1964] 2 Q.B. 480 (C.A.).

their fees, the Court of Appeal held the company liable. The directors had known that Kapoor had been acting as the managing director and had permitted him to do so. By allowing him to conduct himself in such a manner, they had represented that Kapoor had the authority to enter into contracts of a kind which a managing director would normally be authorized to enter on the company's behalf. Lord Diplock stated:

> The commonest form of representation by a principal creating an "apparent" authority of an agent is by conduct, namely, by permitting the agent to act in the management or conduct of the principal's business. Thus, if in the case of a company the board of directors who have "actual" authority under the memorandum and articles of association to manage the company's business permit the agent to act in the management or conduct of the company's business, they thereby represent to all persons dealing with such agent that he has authority to enter on behalf of the corporation into contracts of a kind which an agent authorized to do acts of the kind which he is in fact permitted to do usually enters into in the ordinary course of such business. The making of such a representation is itself an act of management of the company's business. Prima facie it falls within the "actual" authority of the board of directors. ...[119]

Where, however, there is an unusual character to the acts of a director or officer, or the contract that the director or officer is purporting to make is so usual as to take it beyond the range of a normal transaction, the creditor is put on notice and must inquire as to whether the director or officer possesses actual authority.[120] A creditor who does not do so will not be able to rely upon apparent authority.[121]

§6.46 In rare cases, the impression that a person possesses the apparent authority to do a particular thing may be so great that even that person may misunderstand (and reasonably misunderstand) that he or she possesses that particular authority, despite the subsequent claim by the principal not to have conferred the authority in question. Apparent authority of this manifest type may be styled "implied authority". Conceptually, implied authority can be distinguished from more limited forms of ostensible or apparent authority that will protect a third party but not the agent. Implied authority is the authority that the agent might naturally assume to follow from those authorities that have actually been conferred.[122] Implicit authority of an agent to enter into a contract includes what is commercially customary,[123] and while the point is not entirely clear, it appears that such authority may be presumed both by the agent and with the person with whom the agent is dealing on behalf of the principal, unless specifically withheld. For instance, where a person is hired to fill a particular office of a common type, that person may reasonably assume that he or she has been authorized to exercise the functions normally incumbent upon a person who holds such an office unless properly advised to the contrary. The position might be quite junior

---

[119] *Ibid.*, at 505.
[120] *Northside Developments Pty. Ltd. v. Registrar-General* (1990), 8 A.C.L.C. 611 (H.C. Aust.).
[121] *J.C. Houghton & Co. v. Northard, Lowe & Wills Ltd.*, [1927] 1 K.B. 246 (C.A.).
[122] See *Kont Vanis v. O'Brien (No. 2)*, [1958] N.Z.L.R. 516 (S.C.); *Little v. Spreadbury*, [1910] 2 K.B. 658.
[123] *Financial Management Inc. v. Associated Financial Planners Ltd.*, [2006] A.J. No. 132 (C.A.).

yet nonetheless confer an implied authority. Thus a person hired to act as a teller at a bank might naturally assume that he or she is authorized to receive deposits on the bank's behalf, to give receipts for those deposits, and to make the required entries in the customer accounts to reflect deposits that are received. More generally, an agent hired to perform a particular task might naturally assume that he or she possesses the authority necessary to carry out the task that the principal has requested the agent to perform.[124] Obviously, implied authority has no application where the agent knows that he or she lacks that authority. But outsiders in such a case are unlikely to know of those limits on the agent's authority. And if the circumstances are such that the agent would be entitled (in the absence of actual knowledge to the contrary) to assume that a particular authority has implicitly been conferred, then an even stronger case can be made for allowing outsiders to assume the existence of the authority in question.

§6.47 The question of apparent authority often arises where the agent commits a wrong for which the third party seeks to hold the principal responsible. No agent possesses the actual authority to misappropriate the principal's property or to commit other torts or actionable wrongs either against the principal or (in most cases) a third party. However, an agent may sometimes misappropriate property or otherwise behave wrongfully while acting in a manner that appears to be within the scope of the authority conferred upon the agent;[125] in other words, the agent acts within the scope of his or her ostensible authority. The key question for the law to resolve is how the scope of that ostensible authority is to be determined. This question is of particular importance in the corporate context, because in many cases the only or key operative of the corporation with whom outsiders have any contact is the very agent who is guilty of the wrongdoing, and who is therefore alleged by the corporation to have exceeded his or her authority. In the guarantee context, for instance, a corporate officer may sign a guarantee on behalf of the corporation in respect of some principal debtor in which that officer has an interest. The guarantee purportedly given by the corporation enables that principal debtor to obtain credit that otherwise would not be available, and thus the corporate officer obtains a benefit for himself.

§6.48 The scope of an agent's ostensible authority turns in large measure upon the capacity in which a corporation presents that agent to the public and the responsibilities that have been given to the agent by the principal. In *Russo-Chinese Bank v. Li Yau Sam*[126] it was found that it was the custom of European businesses doing business in China to employ a Chinese intermediary, known as a compradore, to assist in the negotiations between Chinese customers and their European customers. The position was relatively junior, somewhat analogous to a translator. The respondent-plaintiff wished to arrange for the appellant-

---

[124] *Associated Growers of B.C. Ltd. v. B.C. Fruit Land Ltd.*, [1925] 1 D.L.R. 871 at 875 (B.C.S.C.), *per* McDonald J.; *Doctor v. People's Trust Co.* (1913), 16 D.L.R. 192 (B.C.C.A.).
[125] This statement is tautological, for if a person has been authorized to "misappropriate" property in a particular way, then dealing with it in that way (*e.g.*, donating it to charity) is not a misappropriation, even though it would be in the absence of such authorization.
[126] [1910] A.C. 175 at 184-85 (P.C.), *per* Lord Atkinson.

defendants (a Russian-owned bank) to wire-transfer 30,000 taels (a unit of silver currency in Imperial China) to Shanghai. He went to the office of the appellant, where he dealt with the compradore. The compradore asked the respondent for payment of $40,961.30 U.S. Instead of transferring the money as requested, the compradore misappropriated it. It was clear from the evidence at trial that the compradore had no authority to receive money on behalf of the appellant-defendant, either for the purposes of deposit or for the purpose of a wire-transfer of funds. However, the compradore pretended that he did have such authority. He even went to the length of pretending to check certain aspects of the transaction with the manager of the bank. It was held on these facts that the bank was not bound. It had done nothing to suggest that the compradore had the authority to act as he did.

§6.49 Thus on the facts of the *Russo-Chinese Bank* case, the agent was known by the plaintiff to possess only the limited authority of a translator (a position that would not normally imply a contracting authority), and thus the compradore's authority did not extend to the receipt of money on the defendant's behalf. Therefore the plaintiff could not be said to have relied upon an impression of agency created by the defendant.[127] In order to bind the principal, there must, in other words, be some statement, act or omission on the part of the principal which creates the impression that the agent had the authority to act as he or she did, and the creditor must have relied upon the impression so conveyed.[128]

§6.50 It follows that the ostensible authority of an agent is the appearance of authority conveyed to outsiders by the actual authority that is conferred.[129] Where an agent who is known to have only a limited authority represents that he or she possesses actual authority to enter into a transaction lying outside the scope of that limited authority, the representation will not be binding upon the principal.[130] In the absence of an implied authority, the onus is on the creditor to determine whether actual authority exists. The more limited the agent's actual authority, the less will be the appearance of ostensible authority; conversely the broader or more general the actual authority, the greater the appearance of ostensible authority. For instance, it has been held that a managing director of a corporation has the implied authority to borrow money and give security over the corporation's property;[131] give guarantees on behalf of the corporation in respect to the debts of subsidiaries of the corporation and indemnify other persons who have provided such guarantees;[132] or guarantee the payment of debts owed by outsiders at least to the extent that those guarantees appear to relate to

---

[127] *Farquharson Bros. & Co. v. C. King & Co.*, [1902] A.C. 325 at 341 (H.L.), *per* Lord Lindley.
[128] *Uxbridge Permanent Benefit Building Society v. Pickard*, [1939] 2 All E.R. 344 at 348 (C.A.), *per* Sir Wilfred Greene M.R.
[129] *Berryere v. Fireman's Fund Insurance Co.* (1965), 51 D.L.R. (2d) 603 (Man. C.A.).
[130] *Jenson v. South Trail Mobile Ltd.* (1972), 28 D.L.R. (3d) 233 (Alta. C.A.); *Armagas Ltd. v. Mundogas S.A. (The Ocean Frost)*, [1986] A.C. 717, [1986] 2 All E.R. 385 (H.L.).
[131] *Biggerstaff v. Rowatt's Wharf Ltd.*, [1896] 2 Ch. 93 (C.A.).
[132] *Hely-Hutchinson v. Brayhead Ltd.*, [1968] 1 Q.B. 549 (C.A.).

the ordinary course of business of the corporation.[133] In contrast, the contract-making powers of a more junior officer, such as the corporate secretary, would seem to be limited to those contracts that are concerned with the administrative side of the corporation's operations: *i.e.*, with the area of corporate activity for which the corporate secretary is customarily responsible.[134] However, the scope of a specific officer's authority will vary based upon the nature of the corporation's business.[135]

§6.50.1 Trade custom also plays a role, as does the creation of risk. The cashier in a supermarket clearly has the ostensible authority to receive payment and convey title, but probably has no ostensible authority to depart from the sticker price. However, the same individual may quite possibly be assigned to affix sticker price labels to the goods offered for sale. Should an incorrect price be mistakenly affixed to one of those goods, and it be sold, the store owner would be bound by the sale. When a cashier purports to change the sticker price at the check-out desk, he or she is not carrying out any part of the assignment of acting as a cashier. When that same individual is asked to affix prices to goods, and makes a mistake in doing so, the mistake that is made is within the scope of the assignment given. Borrowing the language recently employed by the Supreme Court of Canada in connection with vicarious liability,[136] by asking the cashier to affix price tags, the owner of the store creates the risk that the wrong price tag will be affixed, and having created that risk, is bound by any mistake that is made in doing so.

§6.51 In summary, the scope of apparent authority of a corporate (or other) agent is essentially a question of fact. It depends not only on the nature of the contract involved, but also the position held by the officer or other agent negotiating it, the corporation's usual manner of conducting business, the size of the corporation, the circumstances that give rise to the contract, the nature and character of the contract and whether it is apparently in the best interest of the corporation, the amounts involved, and the contracting party and its relationship and history of dealings with the corporation. The foregoing is not an exhaustive list.

(iii) The Indoor Management Rule

§6.52 The principles of agency applicable under the general law of contract are modified in the context of *business* corporations by the indoor management rule.[137] Quite early in the development of corporate law, the courts began to dif-

---

[133] *British Thomson-Houston Co. v. Federated European Bank Ltd.*, [1932] 2 K.B. 176; see also *Re Scottish Loan & Finance Co. Ltd.* (1944), 44 S.R.N.S.W. 461 (S.C.).
[134] *Panorama Developments (Guildford) Ltd. v. Fidelis Furnishing Fabrics Ltd.*, [1971] 2 Q.B. 711 (C.A.).
[135] For a case in which a credit manager of a bank was held to have the apparent authority to execute guarantees of bank customers on behalf of the bank, see *Soplex Wholesale Supplies Ltd. v. Egyptian International Foreign Trading Co.*, [1985] Fin. L. R. 123 (C.A.).
[136] See §3.4.
[137] The rule does not apply to municipal corporations: *Pacific National Investments v. City of Victoria*, [2000] S.C.J. No. 64, [2000] 2 S.C.R. 919 at para. 68, per Lebel, J.; *City of Barrie v.*

ferentiate between those transactions that were patently defective and those transactions that contained only a latent defect. It was appreciated that a transaction with a corporation might be defective, not because of a patent conflict with the corporate charter, by-laws or other public document, but because some condition required to be satisfied under one of those documents was not taken. Under the rule of constructive notice, the existence of the condition was deemed to be known by every person dealing with the corporation. The question that remained unanswered was whether any such person was obliged to determine whether the condition had been satisfied. Stating the question slightly differently, was a person dealing with a corporation obliged to inquire into whether a condition upon the exercise of a power by a corporation had been satisfied, or might that person assume such compliance and enter into a binding transaction with the corporation, unless he or she knew that there had been no such compliance? Even during the heyday of the doctrine of *ultra vires*, the courts were loath to require third parties dealing with a corporation to inquire into compliance by a corporation or its directors and officers or into the internal rules of management governing the conduct of the business or affairs of a corporation. Such rules might govern the directors and officers, and might entitle the corporation or its shareholders to restrain them from acting in contravention or to seek damages should those rules be broken, but they were not a matter with which the general public had need to concern itself.[138]

§6.53 The general principle known as the indoor management rule received its earliest articulation in clear form in *Royal British Bank v. Turquand*[139] — the eponymous case by the name of which the rule is sometimes described. In that case, the registered deed of settlement under which the company was established authorized the directors of the company to borrow such amounts as might from time-to-time be authorized by a resolution of the company in general meeting. The board borrowed money from the plaintiff bank, and in connection with that borrowing issued a bond to the company bearing the company's seal. In fact, however, no resolution was ever adopted by the company authorizing the borrowing or the issue of the bond. The court thus confronted the question of whether the bank (which was required under the doctrine of constructive notice to read the deed of settlement) was obliged to determine whether the company resolution required under the deed of settlement had actually been adopted. Chief Justice Jervis rejected this notion in categorical terms:

1606533 Ontario Inc., [2005] O.J. No. 2953 (S.C.); *City of Ottawa v. Letourneau*, [2005] O.J. No. 305 (S.C.). It is probable that the rule also has no application to Crown corporations, at least where governed by specific legislation regulating the manner in which it may exercise its powers, and information relating to the exercise of those powers is generally available to the public. See also: *Silver's Garage Ltd. v. Bridgewater (Town)*, [1970] S.C.J. No. 93, [1971] S.C.R. 577 at 586-87.

[138] For a reasonably current case, see *Antle v. Stratos Global Corp.*, [2005] N.J. No. 135, 4 B.L.R. (4th) 14 (S.C.), var'd [2006] N.J. No. 248 (C.A.).

[139] (1855), 5 El. & Bl. 248, 119 E.R. 886, aff'd 6 El. & Bl. 327, 25 L.J.Q.B. 317. For this reason, the rule is sometimes called the Rule in *Royal British Bank v. Turquand* or more simply, the Rule in *Turquand's Case*.

We may now take for granted that the dealings with these companies are not like dealings with other partnerships and that the parties dealing with them are bound to read the statute and the deed of settlement. But they are not bound to do more. And the party here, on reading the deed of settlement, would find, not a prohibition from borrowing, but a permission to do so on certain conditions. Finding that the authority might be made complete by a resolution, he would have a right to infer the fact of a resolution authorizing that which on the face of the document appeared to be legitimately done.[140]

§6.54 In *Mahony v. East Holyford Mining Co.*,[141] the House of Lords approved of the rule put forward by Jervis C.J., and applied the "indoor management" title to it by which it has subsequently come to be known:

> [T]he articles and by-laws of a corporation] are open to all who are minded to have any dealings whatsoever with the company, and those who so deal with them must be affected with notice of all that is contained in those two documents.
>
> After that ... all that the directors do with reference to what I may call the indoor management of their own concern, is a thing known to them and known to them only; subject to this observation, that no person dealing with them has a right to suppose that anything has been or can be done that is not permitted by the [articles or by-laws]. ...
>
> [W]hen there are persons conducting the affairs of the company in a manner which appears to be perfectly consonant with the articles of association, then those so dealing with them, externally, are not to be affected by any irregularities which may take place in the internal management of the company.[142]

The indoor management rule was soon being applied throughout the Empire, including within Canada.[143]

§6.55 Two explanations have been advanced for the indoor management rule. The first is that since no outsider has the right to insist on proof by the directors that the requirements of the articles or by-laws of a corporation have been satisfied, the outsider cannot therefore be deemed to have notice of any failure to satisfy those requirements.[144] The second is that the imposition of such a burden of verification upon outsiders would impose an intolerable burden on the business community.[145] It is the latter view which has attracted most support in Canada.[146]

---

[140] *Ibid.*, 119 E.R. 886 at 888.
[141] (1875), L.R. 7 H.L. 869.
[142] *Ibid.*, at 893-94 *per* Lord Hatherley.
[143] For instance, in *Re Summerside Electric Co.* (1908), 5 E.L.R. 129 (P.E.I.S.C.), *per* Fitzgerald J.
[144] R.R. Pennington, *Company Law*, 6th ed. (London: Butterworths, 1990) at 115. This view is consistent with the frequently advanced explanation as to why the indoor management rule does not apply to a municipal corporation, since municipal council decisions are generally a matter of public record.
[145] *Whitehorse Lounge Ltd. v. Bennett* (1984), 51 Nfld. & P.E.I.R. 91 at para. 24 (S.C.), *per* Steele J., and see, generally, C.C.B. Gower, *Principles of Modern Company Law*, 5th ed. (London: Sweet & Maxwell, 1992), 86 *et seq.*
[146] See, for instance, *Veilleux v. Atlantic & Lake Superior Rlwy.* (1910), 39 Que. S.C. 127, *per* Greenshields J.; *Mutchenbacker v. Dominion Bank* (1910), 13 W.L.R. 282 (Man. K.B.).

§6.56 The indoor management rule has been applied in numerous different contexts.[147] In *Pacific Coast Coal Mines Ltd. v. Arbuthnot*, Viscount Haldane stated:

> No doubt where some act, such as the granting of an obligation in the course of [the corporation's] business is put by the constitution of the company within its power, and certain formalities of administration are prescribed by the articles of association which for domestic purposes regulate the duties of the directors to the shareholders, the mere failure to comply with a formality, such as a proper appointment or the presence of a quorum of directors, will not affect a person dealing with the company from outside and without knowledge of the irregularity. He is presumed to know the constitution of the company, but not what may or may not have taken place within doors that are closed to him.[148]

Following a similar line of thinking, in *Re Athenaeum Life Assurance Society, ex p. Eagle Insurance Co.*, Page Wood V.C. stated:

> There is, no doubt, an important distinction to be drawn ... between that which, upon the face of it, is manifestly imperfect when tested by the requirements of the deed of settlement of the company, and that which contains nothing to indicate that those requirements have not been complied with. Thus, where the deed requires certain instruments to be under the common seal of the company, every person contracting with the company can see at once whether that requisition is complied with, and he is bound to do so; but where ... the conditions required by the deed consist of certain internal arrangements of the company — for instance, resolutions at meetings, and the like — if the party contracting with the directors find the acts which they undertake to do to be within the scope of their powers under the deed, he has a right to assume that all such conditions have been complied with. In the case last supposed he is not bound to inquire whether the resolutions have been duly passed, or the like, otherwise he would be bound to go further back, and to inquire whether the meetings have been duly summoned, and to ascertain a variety of other matters, into which, if it were necessary to make such inquiry, it would be impossible for the company to carry on the business for which it is formed.[149]

(1) Codification of the Indoor Management Rule

§6.57 Both the OBCA and the CBCA contain a codified version of the indoor management rule. It is not clear under either statute whether the statutory rule excludes the common law rule, or is merely intended to supplement it. However, the general principle of statutory interpretation that the common law remains unaffected by a statute except to the extent that it is repugnant to the statute[150] may be invoked to support the conclusion that the statutory rules merely supplement the common law rule. Accordingly, in any particular case, consideration

---

[147] *Cotman v. Brougham*, [1918] A.C. 514 at 521 (H.L.), per Lord Parker; *Re David Payne & Co.*, [1904] 2 Ch. 608 (C.A.) — where a company has a general power to borrow money for the purpose of its business, a lender is not bound to inquire into the purpose for which the money is intended to be applied, and the misapplication of the money by the company does not avoid the loan in the absence of knowledge on the part of the lender that the money was intended to be misapplied.
[148] [1917] A.C. 607 at 616 (P.C.).
[149] (1858), 4 K. & J. 549, 70 E.R. 229.
[150] *Clarkson Co. v. Ace Lumber Ltd.* (1963), 36 D.L.R. (2d) 554 at 558 (S.C.C.), per Ritchie J.

must be given both to the common law indoor management rule (discussed above) and also the statutory indoor management rule to which we will now turn, in order to determine whether a corporation is bound. The statutory rule does not appear to limit any of the circumstances in which a corporation would be held bound under the common law rule, but instead appears to expand the grounds on which a corporation may be held bound.

§6.58 Although the scope and limits of the common law rule were considered in numerous cases handed down by Canadian, English and other Commonwealth courts, there has been little judicial consideration of the present statutory rules set down in sections 19 of the OBCA and 18 of the CBCA. As discussed above, clause 19(*a*) of the OBCA provides that neither a corporation nor a guarantor of a corporation may assert against a person dealing with the corporation or with any person who has acquired rights from the corporation that "the articles, by-laws or any unanimous shareholder agreement have not been complied with". Paragraph 18(1)(*a*) of the CBCA is identical. In the case of the articles and by-laws, the effect of paragraph (*a*) is no more than to reaffirm the abolition of the doctrine of constructive notice. It has never been suggested that outsiders could be bound by internal private arrangements such as a unanimous shareholder agreement.

§6.59 Aside from OBCA clause 19(*a*), clause 19(*d*) is the clause of the statutory rule that would appear to have the broadest application. It provides that a corporation or guarantor of an obligation of a corporation may not assert against a person dealing with the corporation or with any person who has acquired rights from the corporation that:

> (*d*) a person held out by the corporation as a director, an officer or an agent of the corporation has not been duly appointed or does not have the authority to exercise the powers and perform the duties that are customary in the business of the corporation or usual for such director, officer or agent ...

Paragraph 18(1)(*d*) of the CBCA is to a similar effect. These provisions partly codify both:

- the common law rules governing *de facto* directorship and officership — which, essentially, state in effect that a creditor is entitled to assume the regularity of appointment; and

- the general law of agency relating to apparent authority.[151]

They allow the obligee to assume that actual authority exists where the purported agent is doing what a person in his or her position and circumstances would normally do.[152] Moreover, although as noted above, there is some uncer-

---

[151] See, for instance, *Thompson v. Brantford Electrical & Operating Co.* (1898), 25 O.A.R. 340. In that case, the defendant authorized its manager to purchase from the plaintiff a machine required for its business. The resolution authorizing the purchase stipulated that the purchase was to be made on certain terms, but this fact was unknown to the seller. The manager purchased the machine on different terms. The contract was held binding on the defendant. See also: *Martin v. Artyork Investments Ltd.*, 29 A.C.W.S. (3d) 792 (Gen. Div.).

[152] *Whitehorse Lounge Ltd. v. Bennett*, [1984] N.J. No. 199, 6 C.P.R. (3d) 219 (S.C.).

tainty under the common law indoor management rule as to the extent to which it applies to acts by persons other than directors, clause 19(*e*) makes clear that there is no such uncertainty under the statutory rule. It prevents a corporation from disputing that:

(*e*) a document issued by any director, officer or agent of a corporation with actual or usual authority to issue the document is not valid or not genuine ...

Paragraph 18(1)(*e*) of the CBCA is identical. When clauses 19(*d*) and (*e*) of the OBCA are read in conjunction with section 18 of that Act[153] — which abolishes the doctrine of constructive notice — it becomes clear that even outright prohibitions against directors or officers exercising certain powers will no longer bind a person dealing with the corporation, at least where the creditor lacks actual knowledge of the contravention. Moreover, it is not necessary for the creditor to inquire whether the directors of a corporation have passed a resolution authorizing the dealing in question,[154] provided the document is regular on its face,[155] and if certified copies of a purported resolution of the directors are obtained, the creditor may rely upon those certified copies.[156]

§6.60 Clause 19(*d*) of the OBCA[157] refers to the authority of a director or officer that is "customary in the business of the corporation". Similarly, clause (*e*) refers to the "usual authority" of directors, officers and agents to issue certain documents.[158] Both of these references would appear to refer to the apparent authority of an agent; if a corporate agent purports to exercise authority which an agent in his or her position would usually possess, the corporation will be bound by what the agent does on its behalf.[159] However, clause 19(*d*) goes somewhat further when it speaks of the usual authority "for such director, officer or agent". Thus there may exist both apparent authority in the context of a particular office generally (*e.g.*, chief executive officer[160] or secretary-treasurer)[161] and the apparent authority of a particular office holder, on the basis of historic dealings between the corporation, the agent and the creditor.

---

[153] CBCA, s. 17.
[154] *Flewitt v. Agravoice Productions Ltd. (Trustee of)*, [1985] M.J. No. 666, 61 C.B.R. (N.S.) 280 (Q.B.).
[155] *T.D. Bank v. Coopers & Lybrand Ltd.*, [1982] A.J. No. 1020, 42 C.B.R. (N.S.) 120 (Q.B.).
[156] *Bank of Nova Scotia v. LeBlanc*, [1954] 2 D.L.R. 579 at 584 (N.B.C.A.), *per* Harrison J.
[157] CBCA, s. 18(1)(*d*).
[158] *Ibid.*, s. 18(1)(*e*).
[159] *British Thomson-Houston Co. v. Federated European Bank Ltd.*, [1932] 2 K.B. 176 (C.A.).
[160] See, for instance, *British Columbia Bond Corp. v. Lang* (1931), 12 C.B.R. 213 (B.C.S.C.); *Chugal Properties Ltd. v. Levine*, [1970] O.J. No. 1756, [1971] 2 O.R. 331, rev'd on other grounds [1971] O.J. No. 1746, [1972] 1 O.R. 158 (C.A.).
[161] See, for instance, *Imperial Bank of Canada v. Dennis* (1925), 57 O.L.R. 203, var'd 59 O.L.R. 20 (C.A.). In *McMan Oil & Gas Co. v. Hurley* (1928), 24 F.2d 776 (5th Cir.), resolutions of the executive committee and full board of directors were challenged as not having been approved. The court concluded (at 778) that there was sufficient authority for the execution of documents on the strength of the purported resolutions. See also *C.L. McClain Fuel Corp. v. Lineinger* (1941), 341 Pa. 364, 19 A.2d 478 at 480.

§6.61 The basis of apparent authority is a representation by the corporation, which may be either by words or conduct. However, one question that must frequently be answered is whether the corporation can properly be said to have made any representation at all. This question was confronted by Lord Pearson in his decision in *Hely-Hutchinson v. Brayhead Ltd.* In that case, the chairman of the defendant company acted as its *de facto* managing director. The remainder of the board knew that the chairman frequently entered into contracts on the company's behalf, since he later reported the contracts to the board. In effect, they had acquiesced in the chairman acting as he did. The chairman signed a contract with the plaintiff on behalf of the company, under which the company gave certain indemnities and guarantees to the plaintiff. The Court of Appeal held that the defendant company was liable to the plaintiff on the basis that the chairman had the apparent authority to act for the company which could be implied from the surrounding circumstances. Of particular interest, however, were the comments of Lord Pearson with respect to the possibility that the agent personally may be the voice of the corporation in making the representation of authority to the creditor:

> Now there is not usually any direct communication in such cases between the board of directors and the outside contractor. The actual communication is made immediately and directly, whether it be express or implied, by the agent to the outside contractor. It is, therefore, necessary in order to make a case of ostensible authority to show in some way that such communication which is made directly by the agent is made ultimately by the responsible parties, the board of directors. That may be shown by inference from the conduct of the board of directors in the particular case by, for instance, placing the agent in a position where he can hold himself out as their agent and acquiescing in his activities, so that it can be said they have in effect caused the representation to be made. They are responsible for it and, in the contemplation of law, they are to be taken to have made the representation to the outside contractor.[162]

§6.62 In *British Bank of the Middle East v. Sun Life Assurance Co. of Canada (U.K.) Ltd.*[163] the bank sought to enforce undertakings signed by a junior employee (a unit manager) of the defendant insurance company. The authority of the junior employee to give the undertakings in question had been confirmed to the bank by his supervisor, the branch manager — the request for that confirmation being sent to the defendant's general manager. The defendant claimed that the unit manager had no authority to sign on behalf of the corporation and further contended that the branch manager had no authority to represent that the unit manager did possess such authority. The House of Lords agreed. It found that insurance companies did not customarily give branch managers the authority to sign or make representations on their behalf. Therefore the bank could have no basis on which it might assume that the claimed authority of the unit manager or branch manager existed.[164]

---

[162] [1968] 1 Q.B. 549 at 593 (C.A.).
[163] [1983] B.C.L.C. 78, [1983] 2 Lloyds R. 9 (H.L.); see also *Rhodian River Shipping Co. v. Halla Maritime Corp.*, [1984] B.C.L.C. 139.
[164] See also *Egyptian International Foreign Trade Co. v. Soplex Wholesale Supplies Ltd. (The Raffaella)*, [1985] B.C.L.C. 404, [1985] 2 Lloyd's R. 36 (C.A.) in which it was held that it was not

§6.63 The protection afforded under section 19 of the OBCA to a person dealing with a corporation or acquiring rights from it does not apply where that person has knowledge[165] of the deficiency in the authority of a director or officer or a contravention of the articles, by-laws or a unanimous shareholder agreement, or reasonably ought to have such knowledge by virtue of his or her position with or relationship to the corporation.[166] Three obvious questions arise from these limitations: first, when may a person be said to possess knowledge of a deficiency;[167] second, when will a person be impressed with such knowledge on the basis that he or she reasonably ought to know of it by virtue of his or her position with or relationship to the company; and third, when will a corporation be impressed with knowledge of one of its officers or directors? There is no general rule that the knowledge of one person who is an officer of two companies is always the knowledge of both companies. Knowledge which has been acquired by a person as an officer of corporation A will not be imputed to corporation B unless that officer has some duty to communicate that knowledge to B and was obliged to receive the information concerned on B's behalf.[168]

§6.64 Clause 19(*d*) of the OBCA protects an outsider who deals with a corporate agent with respect to a type of matter which would usually fall within the authority of an agent of that type. From this it follows that where there is something out of the ordinary in a transaction, a person dealing with an officer or other agent of the corporation is put upon inquiry to determine whether the officer has the authority to enter into that transaction on behalf of the corporation.[169] Unfortunately, the case law provides little real guidance as to the factors that a creditor who deals with an agent should take into account in deciding whether there is something out of the ordinary in connection with the transaction. One situation which perhaps might alert the creditor is where the transaction does not confer any apparent benefit upon the corporation — although it is necessary to recognize that the benefits that arise from a transaction may be direct or indirect.

---

appropriate simply to inquire into the normal authority within an industry of a particular type of officer. Instead, the whole of the corporation's conduct must be examined to determine whether it has held out a person as possessing a particular authority.

[165] See, for instance, *Dickson Co. v. Graham* (1913), 23 O.W.R. 749, 4 O.W.N. 670, 9 D.L.R. 813, *per* Hodgins J.A.; see also *Coopers & Lybrand v. Ford Credit Canada Ltd.*, [1983] N.S.J. No. 70, 48 C.B.R. (N.S.) 155 at 163 (S.C.T.D.), *per* Burchell J. Where a contractor possessing such knowledge acts through an agent who does not possess that knowledge, the contractor cannot claim the benefit of the agent's ignorance: *Abana Mines Ltd. v. Wall* (1935), 58 Que. K.B. 352 (C.A.), *per* Hall J. See also *Re Patent Ivory Manufacturing Co.* (1888), 38 Ch. D. 156.

[166] Case law in this area is obviously fact specific. See, generally, *Lyford v. Media Portfolio Ltd.* (1989), 7 A.C.L.C. 271 (S.C. West. Aust.), *per* Nicholson J.; *McAteer v. Devoncroft Developments Ltd.*, [2001] A.J. No. 1481, 124 A.C.W.S. (3d) 680 (Q.B.); *2671914 Manitoba Ltd. v. Suncorp Pacific Ltd. et al.*, [2001] M.J. No. 124, 154 Man. R. (2d) 261 (Q.B.).

[167] See, for instance, *Thomas v. Walker* (1910), 16 O.W.R. 751 (H.C.); *Baldwin Iron & Steel Works Ltd. v. Dominion Carbide Co.* (1903), 2 O.W.R. 170 (H.C.).

[168] *In Re Hampshire Land Co.*, [1896] 2 Ch. 743 at 748, *per* Vaughan Williams J.; *Re Steel Service Ltd.* (1935), 16 C.B.R. 231 at 236 (Ont. S.C.), *per* Cook Reg.; *Dominion Fire Brick & Clay Products Ltd. v. Pollock*, [1919] 2 W.W.R. 245 (Sask. K.B.).

[169] *Fred T. Brooks Ltd. v. Claude Neon General Advertising Ltd.*, [1931] O.R. 92 at 107-08 (H.C.), *per* Garrow J.

§6.65 Where an unauthorized instrument is negotiable, the fact that the original holder of the instrument knew of the lack of authority will not protect the corporation from liability to a subsequent holder in due course. Innocent holders of negotiable securities are not bound to inquire whether appropriate authorization has been obtained.[170]

§6.66 The primary object of clause 19(*d*)[171] is to make the honest acts of *de facto* directors and officers as good as the honest acts of *de jure* directors and officers. Although there may be some deficiency in the manner of their appointment, so long as it was genuinely intended that they hold such an appointment, then the clause upholds the validity of their acts.[172] However, it is not possible to invoke the protection of this clause where the person purporting to act as an officer or director has not even the colour of such a position. Unless the corporation has in some way held out a person as a director or officer, then the clause has no application.[173] If the corporation never holds out a person as a director, officer or other agent, then there is no basis on which the corporation can be bound by the acts of that purported agent (in the absence of ratification), even though that purported agent may have claimed to possess the authority to act on the corporation's behalf.[174]

§6.67 This conclusion, however, merely begs the question of when a corporation may be said to hold out a person as a director or officer. The Act deals with this question in only one respect, which is set out in clause 19(*b*) of the OBCA. It provides that a corporation or a guarantor of a corporation may not assert as a defence that:

> (*b*) the persons named in the most recent notice filed under the *Corporations Information Act*, or named in the articles, whichever is more current, are not the directors of the corporation ...

Paragraph 18(*b*) of the CBCA, which is the equivalent provision in that Act, is to the same effect, but contains no reference to any person named in the articles, in view of the fact that no such persons are so named under that Act. The apparent purpose of paragraph (*b*) is to make any person whose name is so filed a *de facto* director of the corporation, irrespective of whether that person is actually a director. The onus is on the corporation to keep its filings under the Act current, and if it fails to do so, then it runs the risk that persons who have retired may continue to bind the corporation. This, in effect, turns the doctrine of constructive notice on its head: the law now is not that outsiders are deemed to have no-

---

[170] *Robertson v. North-Western Register Co.* (1910), 13 W.L.R. 613 at 617 (Man. C.A.), *per* Cameron J.A.
[171] CBCA, s. 18(*d*).
[172] *British Asbestos Co. Ltd. v. Boyd*, [1903] 2 Ch. 439 at 445, *per* Farwell J.
[173] *Morris v. Kanssen*, [1946] A.C. 459 at 471-72 (H.L.), *per* Lord Simmonds.
[174] See, for instance, *First City Capital Ltd. v. 105383 British Columbia Ltd.*, [1985] B.C.J. No. 1901, 28 B.L.R. 274 (C.A.).

tice of documents filed with the Director, but rather that the corporation is bound by the list of its directors or officers that it has placed upon the public record.[175]

§6.68 The indoor management rule protects creditors who deal with corporate agents who act within the scope of their apparent authority from a defence being raised by the corporation as to the agent's want of actual authority. It also protects such creditors from having the validity of their contracts attacked by outsiders. So in *Duck v. Tower Galvanizing*,[176] it was held that the rights of a holder in good faith of a debenture that was in proper form and charged all of the property of the corporation as security for the debt that it evidenced was entitled to prevail over an execution creditor. In that case it was shown that the debenture was issued without authority, as no directors of the company had been appointed and no resolution to issue the debentures had been passed. Even so, the debenture holder was entitled to prevail.

(2) The Authority of Corporate Officers

§6.69 Thus far we have focused attention on dealings by and with directors. It is also necessary to consider dealings by and with officers. Relatively few corporate contracts involve any active participation by the board of directors or even an individual director. The courts have long accepted that as a practical matter the day-to-day operations of a company are likely to be under the effective control of senior employees, variously described as the officers or managers of a company. The identification of the officers and other employees of a corporation whose acts are sufficient to bind it is not always clear-cut. In attempting to answer this question, the courts tend towards a functional approach.[177] A person may be considered to be a *de facto* officer of a corporation despite some defect in his or her appointment.[178]

§6.69.1 Since corporate officers are at least in theory the delegates of the directors, appointed by them to act as agents on behalf of the corporation, there is considerable less case law relating to the inherent managerial responsibility of the directors. However, as agents, the officers of a corporation owe a fiduciary duty in connection with the responsibilities assigned to them, and more generally with respect to their custodianship and other dealings with corporate property. The determination of the specific responsibilities that flow from these

---

[175] See also clause 19(c) of the OBCA, which provides that a corporation or guarantor of an obligation of a corporation may not assert against a person dealing with the corporation or with any person who has acquired rights from the corporation that:

(c) the location named in the most recent notice filed under subsection 14(3) or named in the articles, whichever is more current, is not the registered office of the corporation.

[176] [1901] 2 K.B. 314 at 317-18.
[177] *Re A Company*, [1980] Ch. 138 at 144 (C.A.), *per* Shaw L.J. See also *Cullen v. Corporate Affairs Commission* (1989), 7 A.C.L.C. 121 (N.S.W.S.C.), *per* Young J.; *R. v. Scott* (1990), 8 A.C.L.C. 752 at 758 (Ct. Cr. App. N.S.W.), *per* Gleeson J.
[178] *Canadian Aero Service Ltd. v. O'Malley*, [1973] S.C.J. No. 97, 40 D.L.R. (3d) 371; *DPC Estates Pty. Ltd. v. Grey*, [1974] 1 N.S.W.L.R. 470. The *de facto* director concept is discussed at §9.109.

general responsibilities requires an inquiry into the scope of the authority actually or apparently conferred. The approach that should be taken in assessing the scope of such authority was considered by Austin J. of the New South Wales Supreme Court in *NCR Australia v. Credit Connection*.[179] The case related to the national credit manager of NCR. CC, which was a supplier to NCR sought to justify a change in its accounting and billing practices by relying upon the apparent acceptance of these changes under two deeds purportedly signed by the national manager on August 11, 1998 and November 18, 1998. On the basis of the evidence, Austin J. concluded that the two deeds were not executed until at least the second half of December 1998, and that they were created primarily for the purpose of justifying the changes made by CC to its accounting and billing procedures. In deciding whether the national credit manager had ostensible authority, Austin J. stated the relevant test was whether NCR had "by representation or other conduct, or acquiescence in a state of affairs, held [the national credit manager] out to have the authority so to act on its behalf, notwithstanding the absence of actual authority". He then identified two steps that must be taken into consideration:

1. Examination of whether the agent possessed usual authority by virtue of the office he held, or assumed to occupy with the acquiescence of the principal, and whether any limitations imposed by the principal upon the scope of the office were communicated to the third party with whom the agent dealt; and

2. Consideration of whether there was, on the part of the principal, any specific representation, other conduct or acquiescence in a state of affairs having the effect of clothing the agent with the appearance of authority going beyond the usual authority of a person holding the office occupied by the agent.

Justice Austin held that the office of national credit manager does not imply any authority to commit a company to the institution of legal proceedings or any authority to bind the company to a formal written agreement or deed with a supplier of services. However, there was an implied authority to give specific instructions to a credit collection agency for the recovery of debts under pre-existing arrangements. It was held that the question is not whether the agent with whom the third party dealt made any representation about his or her authority to bind the principal, but whether a person with actual authority to bind the principal did so.

§6.70 As discussed in detail below, large companies often have hundreds or more officers who act in an effective managerial capacity to a greater or lesser extent. Even small companies may have several.[180] For most public companies, the great majority of the contracts are made by junior employees. There is no question that the directors of The Bay or any other major retailer will not often turn their minds to the selling price placed upon their products, the need for a promotional sale, or the question of whether a person who returns a product for some reason may exchange it for another product. Commerce would grind to a

---

[179] [2004] N.S.W.S.C. 1.
[180] See, generally, *Green v. Bestobel Industries Pty Ltd.*, [1982] W.A.R. 1.

halt if contracts entered into by a corporation in the ordinary course of its business required formal director approval. However, even relatively major contracts falling near but beyond the ordinary course of business often will be entered into by senior officers with little direct participation by the board of directors. As noted above, it was not clear at common law whether the indoor management rule case extends to the acts of officers of a corporation, although some support for this proposition may be found in cases dealing with the acts of persons acting as the managing directors of a corporation. While the OBCA and the CBCA have to some extent addressed this issue, the law governing the authority of corporate officers remains unsettled.

§6.71 There are certainly cases that take a broad view of the scope of the authority of corporate officers and employees. For instance, in *Biggerstaff v. Rowatt's Wharf Ltd.*,[181] it was held that where a director of a corporation purports to act as managing director, and in so doing does a thing that is within the powers of the corporation and within the powers of the full board to delegate to him or her, a person who deals with the managing director in good faith and in the ordinary course of business of the corporation may assume that he or she has the power which that person claims to possess and is not bound to inquire whether or not those powers have in fact been delegated to that person. A person will not be bound by an informality, irregularity or deficiency in the appointment of an agent or a delegation of a power of which that person has no notice.

§6.72 Similarly, in *British Thomson-Houston Co. v. Federated European Bank Ltd.*,[182] the articles of association empowered the directors of a corporation to delegate to any one or more of their number the powers conferred upon them generally as they might consider "requisite for carrying on the business of the company". The directors were further empowered to authorize persons to sign contracts and documents on the corporation's behalf. A document purporting to be a guarantee was given to the plaintiffs, and was executed in the form: "Federated European Bank Limited, signed N. Pal". It was found that N. Pal was a director of the corporation and chairman of the board. During the negotiation of the giving of the guarantee he had written to the plaintiffs and had signed the letter "for and on behalf of" the company "N. Pal Chairman". On the facts, it was held that the plaintiffs were entitled to assume that the board had authorized N. Pal to sign contracts on behalf of the corporation, and the corporation was held liable on the guarantee.

§6.73 In *Canadian Bank of Commerce v. Pioneer Farm Co. & Hall*,[183] the president and manager of a company was personally indebted to the bank. The manager told the bank that the company was indebted to him. The bank caused the manager to endorse in favour of the bank a note of the company that was payable to the manager. In an action on the note, the company argued that there was

---

[181] [1896] 2 Ch. 93 (C.A.).
[182] [1932] 2 K.B. 176 (C.A.).
[183] [1927] 4 D.L.R. 772 (Sask. K.B.).

no debt due to the manager because no resolution authorizing payment of a salary had been passed. It was held that the adoption of such a resolution was a matter of internal management, and the bank was not bound to see whether that procedure had been taken.

§6.74 Based on the foregoing case law, it would seem to follow that an outsider may act in reliance upon the authority that has actually been delegated to the officer, and may assume that the officer has the customary authority usually possessed by an officer of a particular type (that is, may rely upon the officer's apparent authority), unless there is something in the circumstances to suggest that the officer's authority is more limited.[184] The powers of the officers of a corporation are determined by the scope of the authority that has been delegated to them. In reviewing the case law in this area, it is important to distinguish between disputes between a corporation and its officer, and between a corporation and a person who has acted on reliance with respect to an act of the officer. Even if the conferral of a particular title upon a particular officer is sufficient to cloak that officer with apparent authority on which third parties who deal with the officer may rely,[185] between the corporation and the officer, it is usually necessary to show that the required authority was actually conferred in order to protect the officer from claims by the corporation (except, as discussed above, where the disputed authority is implicit within the express authority that was conferred on the agent in question).

§6.75 The authority of a director to make a contract on behalf of a corporation was recently considered in the Australian case, *L.K. Bros Pty Ltd. (Receivers and Managers Appointed) v. Gerald Collins and Philip Jefferson and Landmara Pty Ltd.*[186] The decision in that case well illustrates the extent to which the courts are prepared to construe statutory rules governing the formation of contracts by a corporation in a realistic manner, taking into account the environment in which corporations operate. In this case, a company purportedly entered into a franchise agreement for the operation of a store forming part of a convenience store chain. A debenture was also signed in respect of this agreement. The company had two directors. When it became apparent that the company was unable to properly administer the business, the respondent receivers sought to enforce the debenture. The company argued that the debenture was improperly executed, and therefore unenforceable. It had been executed by only one of the directors. The signature of the Brisbane resident director appeared in two places: once above the word "Director" and once above the words "Director/Secretary". The corporate constitution required two distinct persons' signatures.

§6.76 The court determined that the director who signed resided in Brisbane and was involved in the day-to-day management of the company and its business, while the other resided in Japan. The court held that in signing, the director was

---

[184] *Hedican v. Crows Nest Pass Lumber Co.* (1914), 6 W.W.R. 969 (B.C.C.A.).
[185] OBCA, s. 19; CBCA, s. 18.
[186] [2004] Q.S.C. 026.

acting within the section 126(1) of the *Corporations Act, 2001* (Australia), which provides:

> A company's power to make, vary ratify or discharge a contract may be exercised by an individual acting with the company's express or implied authority and on behalf of the company.

It will be noted that this language merely reflects the common law regarding the agency of a director. Justice Chesterman concluded that even though there was no director's resolution appointing the signing director as agent for the company, a number of facts suggested there was implied authority for him to act its behalf. Specifically:

- The signing director owned 83 per cent of the issued shares and therefore could exercise effective control at general meetings.

- The other director could not understand the language of the jurisdiction of the business, and could not read or comprehend the relevant business and company documents.

- The signing director did not communicate with Mr. Komoto with regard to the company, and according to his testimony, "he simply never discussed such matters with him in person, through other people or over the telephone".

- The other director essentially played no part in the company's business activity.

- There was a patent of conduct over the course of which the signing director signing effectively made all the decisions for the applicant company.

Taking these factors into account, Chesterman J. held that the signing director had the authority to act as agent for the company in signing the charge deed. Accordingly, the company was bound by the mortgage debenture, despite the irregularities in the execution of the debenture.

§6.77 However, there are other cases which have taken a much more restrictive approach, holding that the apparent authority of corporate officers is extremely limited, and that the onus is upon the person dealing with the corporation to determine whether actual authority existed.[187] For instance, it has been held that the president of a corporation has no more authority than any other director, unless the by-laws of the corporation expressly give him wider powers.[188] Thus it has been held that the president of a corporation has no power to give away property of the corporation[189] or to give an undertaking on behalf of the corporation that rent will be paid[190] — both of these cases having obvious relevance in the guarantee context. The courts have been more willing to find authority where the president has acted in a manner that is necessarily in the best interests of the

---

[187] See, for instance, *Smith & Goldberg Ltd. v. Moyer & Co.* (1928), 63 O.L.R. 388 (C.A.), aff'd [1929] S.C.R. 625; compare however *Robin Hood Mills Ltd. v. Paterson Steamships Ltd.*, [1935] Ex. C.R. 207, aff'd [1937] 3 D.L.R. 1 (P.C.).

[188] *Re Petrie Mfg. Co.* (1923), 4 C.B.R. 65, aff'd [1924] 4 D.L.R. 1038 (C.A.).

[189] *Country Club of Montreal v. Bell Telephone Co.* (1920), 58 Que. S.C. 56 (C.A.).

[190] *Almon v. Law* (1894), 26 N.S.R. 340 (C.A.).

corporation, as for instance, in the case of an action to protect the rights of the corporation.[191]

§6.78 The general rule is that the authority of a manager or other officer of a corporation is not co-extensive with the authority of the directors in respect of contracts. An officer will be seen to possess the authority to carry on business in an ordinary way, but the courts will not extend apparent authority to include dealing outside the ordinary course for the company,[192] even where it is possible that the authority in question might be delegated to the officer.[193] Moreover, in this context, "ordinary course of business" is given a narrow interpretation — at least relative to the broad interpretation that the term is given in the context of floating charge. A *fortiori* it is assumed that since officers are generally appointed to carry on the business of a corporation — to manage it as a going concern — they therefore do not possess the authority to wind up the corporation.[194]

§6.79 In the case of other more junior officers, an even more restrictive interpretation of authority was given under the pre-statutory case law to the implied authority of corporate officers. Thus it was held that the secretary-treasurer of a corporation had no legal right to call a general meeting of the shareholders, except as directed by the directors or in accordance with the by-laws,[195] to terminate a lease,[196] to sign a power of attorney on behalf of the corporation,[197] to execute a guarantee on behalf of the corporation,[198] to make representations on behalf of the corporation,[199] or agree to the variation of a contract.[200] More junior officers possessed an even more limited apparent

---

[191] See, for instance, *Standard Trust Co. v. South Shore Rlwy.* (1903), 5 Que. P.R. 257.
[192] *Lee v. Jenkins Bros.* (1959), 268 F. (2d) 357 (2d Cir.), *per* Medina Cir. J.
[193] *Bird v. Hussey-Ferrier Meat Co.* (1913), 25 O.W.R. 13, 5 O.W.N. 60 (H.C.).
[194] *Re Briton Medical & General Life Assn.* (1886), 11 O.R. 478 (H.C.). In *Re Quintex Ltd.* (1990), 8 A.C.L.C. 811, Underwood J. concluded that the managing director of a company did not have apparent authority to make "critical" decisions following the presentation of a petition to wind-up the company. In that case the managing directors purported to appoint solicitors to oppose the petition. This conclusion is difficult to accept, for since the successful opposition of the petition was crucial to the company remaining in business, and since the managing director was responsible for it doing so, the appointment would seem to be implicit within the scope of the authority conferred.
[195] *Re Bondi Better Bananas Ltd.* (1951), 32 C.B.R. 74, rev'd on other grounds [1951] 1 D.L.R. 277 (Ont. C.A.).
[196] *Lebeault v. Venant Lebeault Ltée*, [1944] Que. S.C. 275.
[197] *Bessette v. Equitable Mutual Fire Insurance Co.* (1907), 10 Que. P.R. 260.
[198] *A.R. Williams Machinery Co. v. Crawford Tug Co.* (1908), 16 O.L.R. 245 (C.A.).
[199] *Meadow Farm Ltd. v. Imperial Bank of Canada*, [1922] 2 W.W.R. 909 (Alta. C.A.).
[200] *Myers v. Union Natural Gas Co.* (1922), 53 O.L.R. 88 (H.C.).

authority.[201] Recent cases, however, have tended to take a more liberal view of the question.[202]

§6.80 Although it is not reasonable to assume that a person who is appointed as an agent for a limited and specific purpose has any authority to do anything beyond that purpose, such an inference may be justified where an agent appears to have been cloaked with a general authority to act on behalf of a corporate principal concerning a wide range of matters. In the world of modern corporate commercial dealing, it is popular these days for relatively junior corporate officers and other agents to be given grandiose titles. Large corporations often seem to have a dozen or more vice-presidents, backed up by many more assistant vice-presidents, directors and associate and assistant directors of various departments, and an almost limitless supply of managers.[203] Each division of a corporation is likely to operate under the control of a divisional general manager or president. Where a corporate agent is given such a grand title, it creates an obvious impression that the agent in question enjoys a broad authority to deal on behalf of the principal.

§6.81 Corporations confer grand sounding titles because if they do not, they often find that their junior officers are ignored by the customers and suppliers with whom they must deal. Such outsiders may doubt the authority of the agent to speak on behalf of the corporation if they appear to have a lesser title. Thus the very object behind giving the grand sounding title is to create the impression that the agent does indeed possess the authority to deal on behalf of the principal. But once the corporation commits to this strategy, it is not then open to the corporation to come along at some later date and say "We know that we created

---

[201] *Pitt River Lumber Co. v. Schaake* (1914), 6 W.W.R. 994 (B.C.S.C.) — accountant has no authority to give notice of cancellation of agreement for sale. The decision of Ferguson J.A. in *Foley v. Commercial Cars Ltd.* (1922), 52 O.L.R. 174 (C.A.) provides a fairly concise summary of the approach taken in older cases by the courts with respect to the apparent authority of officers. See also *George Whitechurch Ltd. v. Cavanagh*, [1902] A.C. 117 at 124 (H.L.), *per* Lord Macnaghten; *Ruben v. Great Fingall Consolidated*, [1906] A.C. 439 (H.L.).

[202] In Canada it is a question whether the old decisions respecting the authority of officers remain good law: see *Canadian Laboratory Supplies Ltd. v. Engelhard Industries of Canada Ltd.*, [1979] S.C.J. No. 72, 97 D.L.R. (3d) 1 at 24 (S.C.C.), *per* Estey J., var'd [1980] S.C.J. No. 84. For the current approach in England, see *Panorama Developments (Guildford) Ltd. v. Fidelis Furnishing Fabrics Ltd.*, [1971] 2 Q.B. 711 (C.A.); *cf. Northside Developments Pty. Ltd. v. Registrar-General* (1990), 8 A.C.L.C. 611 (H.C. Aust.).

[203] The Royal Bank of Canada serves to illustrate this point. In its 1990 Annual Report, it listed some 211 executive officers — that is, persons who held the office of vice-president or higher in its overall hierarchy of officers. In addition to a chief executive officer and a president and chief operating officer, the Bank listed the following:

Designation	Head Office	Other	Total
Senior Executive Vice President	5	0	5
Executive Vice President	7	0	7
Senior V.P. & General Manager	0	9	9
Senior Vice President	19	7	26
Vice President	73	89	162
Total	104	105	209

the impression that this person could speak for us, but if you had read our bylaws and minutes of director meetings, you would see that the person had no authority to do so". Long ago it was established that "seeing somebody must be a loser by this deceit, it is more reason that he that employs a trust and confidence in the deceiver should be a loser than a stranger".[204] The reason that the law takes this approach is that it provides for certainty in dealings with agents. Since corporations can only act through agents, and corporations dominate the economy, it is obviously necessary for people who deal with such agents to be able to place confidence in the agents entrusted by a corporation to deal on its behalf.[205]

(3) Exceptional Cases Where Outsiders Are Not Protected

§6.82 Despite the indoor management rule and the general flexibility of the courts on the question of corporate agency, it remains fairly clear that there are a number of circumstances in which third party contractors who deal with a corporate agent must either inquire into the existence of actual authority or act at their own peril.[206] Sadly, nothing in the case law suggests a clear point at which such dangers arise. As we have seen, there are clear parallels between the exceptions to the common law indoor management rule and the exceptions that apply to the statutory rules set down in sections 17 and 18 of the CBCA and sections 18 and 19 of the OBCA. A person contracting with a corporation may not rely upon either of these where the circumstances put that person on inquiry that there is some irregularity or impropriety in the manner in which the contract is being made.[207] For instance, a person may not rely on the indoor management rule where he or she has notice of the defect in authority.[208] More generally, at common law, a person is not entitled to rely upon apparent authority where the circumstances are such as to put a reasonable person on notice that something is out of the ordinary and that there may be a defect in authority.[209] Moreover, the indoor management rule does not relieve creditors from formal registration requirements governing the perfection of security interests, for such requirements are not part of the indoor management of the corporation, but are intended for the protection of outsiders.[210]

---

[204] *Hern v. Nichols* (1701), 1 Salk. 289; 90 E.R. 1154 (K.B.). See also *Lickbarrow v. Mason* (1787), 2 Term Rep. 63, [1775-1802] All E.R. Rep. 1 at 3 (K.B.), *per* Ashurst J., but note the qualifications on this principle set out in *Farquharson Bros. & Co. v. C. King & Co.*, [1902] A.C. 325 at 342 (H.L.), *per* Lord Lindley; *Slingsby v. District Bank*, [1932] 1 K.B. 544 at 560 (C.A.), *per* Scrutton L.J.

[205] *Lloyd v. Grace, Smith & Co.*, [1912] A.C. 716 at 740 (H.L.), *per* Lord Shaw.

[206] See, generally, *McAteer v. Devoncroft Developments Ltd.*, [2001] A.J. No. 1481, 124 A.C.W.S. (3d) 680 (Q.B.); *2671914 Manitoba Ltd. v. Suncorp Pacific Ltd. et al.*, [2001] M.J. No. 124, 154 Man. R. (2d) 261 (Q.B.).

[207] *B. Liggett (Liverpool) Ltd. v. Barclays Bank Ltd.*, [1928] 1 K.B. 48. However, a corporation may ratify an unauthorized act, and where it does so, it will be bound: *Fischer v. Borland Carriage Co.* (1906), 8 O.W.R. 579, aff'd 9 O.W.R. 193 (Div. Ct.).

[208] *Re County Life Assurance Co.* (1870), 5 Ch. App. 288; but compare *Petro-Canada v. Cojef Ltd.*, [1992] M.J. No. 575, [1993] 3 W.W.R. 76 (C.A.).

[209] *Fred T. Brooks Ltd. v. Claude Neon General Advertising*, [1931] O.R. 92 at 108 (H.C.), *per* Garrow J.

[210] *River Stave Co. v. Sill* (1886), 12 O.R. 557 (C.A.).

§6.83 As noted above, an agent does not normally possess the authority to represent the existence or scope of his or her authority. Thus the onus lies on the creditor to satisfy itself that a person who represents that he or she is an officer does in fact hold the office in question. In *Fred T. Brooks Ltd. v. Claude Neon General Advertising Ltd.*, Garrow J. rejected the notion that a creditor might assume that a person was actually an officer of a corporation.[211] Nevertheless, where the corporation is aware that a person is acting as its agent and sits back and does nothing to prevent that person from continuing to do so, or to correct the mistaken impression that this person is conveying to third parties, the corporation will be estopped from denying the authority of that person to act as its agent. Similarly, it may not raise a defect in the manner of an agent's appointment as a defence to a claim.

§6.84 The protection afforded to outsiders who deal with corporate agents under the strength of sections 18 and 19 of the two Acts is further limited by the following proviso found at the conclusion of each of the sections:

> ... except where the person has or ought to have, by virtue of the person's position with or relationship to the corporation, knowledge to that effect.

The intent of the statutory indoor management rule, therefore, is to protect those who act in innocent ignorance, and not those who act with blind disregard or in wilful contravention or whose position allowed ample opportunity to determine whether the agent possessed the required authority. There can be little debate that those who act in wilful contravention should not enjoy the protection of the indoor management rule.

§6.85 More controversial is the exclusion from the protection of all persons who by virtue of their relationship to the corporation "ought to have" knowledge, particularly since the statute gives no indication as to the type of relationship that would meet this description. One situation where section 19 would afford no protection is where the creditor or other outsider deals with an officer even though he or she must have been aware that there was a lack of authority.[212] But it is not always clear whether a person has actual knowledge of the lack of authority or ought to possess such knowledge. For instance, as noted above, where the contractor is a corporate body it remains unclear whether it would be appropriate to affix knowledge upon that entire corporate body merely because one of its officers has knowledge, or whether it must be shown that the officers who acted for it in the transaction that is being impugned possessed the required knowledge.[213] If the former, then it is also necessary to decide at what point a duty is imposed upon one officer of a contractor to determine if there are other officers of the contractor who have knowledge concerning a particular corpora-

---

[211] [1931] O.R. 92 at 107 (H.C.).
[212] *Keystone Leasing Corp. v. Peoples Protective Life Insurance* (1981), 514 F. Supp. 841 (E.D.N.Y.); *American Union Financial Corp. v. University National Bank of Peoria* (1976), 44 Ill. App.3d 566, 358 N.E.2d 646.
[213] See, for instance, *In Re Drive-in Development Corp.* (1966), 371 F. (2d) 215 (7th Cir.), *per* Swygert Cir. J.

tion with which the contractor intends to deal, that may call into question the validity of the acts of that corporation.

§6.86 In summary, while there has been a considerable clarification of the law respecting the apparent authority of corporate officers, there is much that remains unsettled. These areas are clearly among the most important to which law reformers should turn, the next time the OBCA or the CBCA are revised.

(iv) Ratification

§6.87 The principle of ratification is a rule of agency law that permits a principal to come in after the fact and give antecedent authority to a contract that has already been made.[214] So, where a non-agent purports to act on behalf of a corporation but does so without authority, or an agent acts in excess of his or her authority, then in the normal case the act may be ratified by the corporation. If the act of the agent or putative agent lies outside the authority of the board of directors, then the general rule is that the act may be ratified by the shareholders of the corporation in general meeting.[215] Where the actual authority to act on behalf of the corporation rests in the directors, then they may ratify the act.[216] Ratification rectifies the original lack of authority and adopts the act as that of the corporation.[217] Ratification appears to be possible even the agent acted on behalf of a non-disclosed principal.[218]

§6.88 The extent of formality required for ratification remains unsettled. Clearly, there must be some evidence in the record to support a finding of ratification.[219] In many cases, however, the courts must grapple with corporations that conduct their business in a highly informal manner. In *Mickshaw v. Coca Cola Bottling Co.*[220] it was found that the following text appeared in an article in the Sharon Herald:

> The Coca-Cola Bottling Co. Inc. of Sharon today took a place among the outstanding patriotic firms of the Shenango Valley. William Feinberg, Manager, announced that any employee called to the colors through the conscription law will not lose a cent in wages. The company is prepared to pay the difference between the government wages and the amount the employee received before he went to camp. Feinberg said this ruling will protect every man employed by the company and the "pay while away" plan will be continued as long as the man is in service.

The plaintiff testified that Feinberg (the manager and secretary of the defendant) showed the article to him and two other employees. The plaintiff was subse-

---

[214] *John Ziner Lbr. v. Kotov*, [2000] O.J. No. 3793 (C.A.).
[215] *Grant v. United Kingdom Switchback Railways Co.* (1888), 40 Ch. D. 135 (C.A.); *Irvine v. Union Bank of Australia* (1877), 2 App. Cas. 366 (P.C.).
[216] *Re Horsley & Weight Ltd.*, [1982] Ch. 442 (C.A.).
[217] *Danish Mercantile Co. Ltd. v. Beaumont*, [1951] Ch. 680 (C.A.).
[218] *Strutzenegger v. K. Peters Industries Northern Ltd.*, [2004] Y.J. No. 42, 45 B.L.R. (3d) 91 at 98 (S.C.) *per* Gower, J.
[219] See, for instance, *Hurley v. Ornsteen* (1942), 311 Mass. 477, 42 N.E.2d 273 (S.J.C. Mass.), *per* Dolan J.
[220] (1950), 166 Pa. Super. 148, 70 A.2d 467 (S.C. Penn.).

quently drafted. Following the end of the war, he claimed for the promised pay. In upholding the judgment of $1,000 made in the plaintiff's favour, Dithrich J. wrote:

> It would be grossly unjust to require a claimant against a corporation to prove his case by formal corporate records. It is well known that corporations which include few stockholders do not often act with as much formality as larger companies. This is especially so where members of the board, actually and directly, personally conduct the business. ... Plaintiff's suit is based upon an oral proposal alleged to have been made to him by Feinberg. The substance of the proposal was embodied in the newspaper item published at the direction of Feinberg. This publication was, tacitly at least, approved by Myer Ackerman. There was no disavowal by Samuel Ackerman, the third director, or by the corporation, of Feinberg's authority to make the published proposal. If the circumstances warranted the inference that the corporation by previous authorization, or by subsequent ratification, or by acquiescence with knowledge of the facts, approved Feinberg's published offer, we think it may be assumed that he could bind his company by an oral proposal of substantially the same terms to the same persons. It was undisputed that the proposal was published; that the publication was directed by Feinberg; that Myer Ackerman approved it; that Samuel Ackerman did not disavow it; and that no officer of the company had disavowed it to the date of the trial.

§6.89 It is customary in major commercial corporations to employ officer's certificates confirming due authorization of transactions and the existence of signing authority. Such certificates supplement rather than supplant the protection afforded by the indoor management rule.[221]

(v) Evidentiary Issues

(1) Plenipotentiary Authority

§6.90 Although it is common practice (and is generally wise, where significant amounts of money are involved) for major corporate transactions to be submitted for board approval when the final details of the transaction are settled through negotiation, generally there is no specific requirement that such specific approval actually be obtained, provided that it can be established that the requisite authority to negotiate and conclude a contract was delegated to the person who made the contract on the corporation's behalf. Both sections 127 of the OBCA and 115 of the CBCA give the board of a corporation very broad powers of delegation. Subject to the any statutory exception, a corporation may delegate virtual plenipotentiary powers to an agent, authorizing the agent to negotiate and approve the terms of a transaction on the part of the corporation. Indeed, many corporations will delegate such broad powers, at least with respect to transactions of a given type (especially in the case of transactions falling within the scope of the ordinary business of the corporation). For instance, the manager of an auto dealership, will usually have plenipotentiary powers to negotiate the selling price for a car. As the transaction takes on more of an exceptional, out of

---

[221] *McAteer v. Devoncroft Developments Ltd.*, [2001] A.J. No. 1481, 24 B.L.R. (3d) 1 at 63-64 (Q.B.) *per* Rooke J.

the ordinary course quality, it becomes progressively less realistic for any person dealing with the corporate officer to assume that full authority to negotiate and approve the transaction exists. In such cases, evidence of actual board approval for the specific contract should be obtained. Generally, such evidence is obtained in the form of a certified copy of a board resolution. However, any clear representation of authority that may be attributed back to the corporation as being given by a person who would normally have the authority to give such a representation would seem to suffice.

§6.91 Where a corporate agent is conferred with a broad and plenary authority to negotiate a given transaction and (on his or her own initiative) specified during negotiation that any deal tentatively concluded must be ratified by the corporate board or approved by corporate counsel, the agent may waive these requirements. Where it is the corporation that limits the authority of the agent in this way, and the agent notifies the person with whom he or she is dealing of the limit of the authority conferred, the requirement for board (or counsel) approval may not be waived by the agent.[222]

(2) Director Resolutions

§6.92 Even where a contract must be submitted for board approval, and such approval is obtained, it is customary for a director resolution to incorporate a provision allowing some discretion to corporate management to approve amendments, deletions *etc.* to any contract or other instrument to which the resolution relates. Care must be taken in drafting any such discretion, otherwise the approval apparently obtained by way of that resolution may be declared ineffective.[223] Although the issue does not yet seem to have been decided by the courts, it is reasonable to assume that the courts would give a narrow construction to any such provision. If a proposed amendment departs significantly from what was approved, fresh authorization should be obtained.

(3) Execution by Same Person in Two Capacities

§6.93 A person who is a director and an officer in a corporation may sign a document on behalf of the corporation in both capacities.[224]

(4) Corporate Seal

§6.94 As discussed in Chapter 5, the common law rule that required many corporate contracts to be executed under the seal of the corporation has now been abrogated by statute. Section 13 of the OBCA provides that a corporation may, but need not, have a corporate seal. The corporate seal provisions of the CBCA were replaced during the 2001 amendments. Section 23 of the CBCA now provides:

---

[222] *Century Services Inc. v. ZI. Inc.*, [1998] A.J. No. 1192, 47 B.L.R. (2d) 41 (C.A.).
[223] *Pace Savings and Credit Union v. CU Connection Ltd.*, [2000] O.J. No. 3830, 9 B.L.R. (3d) 266 (S.C.).
[224] *Myers v. Aquarell Pty. Ltd.*, [2000] V.S.C. 429, *per* Gillard J.

(1) A corporation may, but need not, adopt a corporate seal, and may change a corporate seal that is adopted.

(2) A document executed on behalf of a corporation is not invalid merely because a corporate seal is not affixed to it.

§6.95 Where a contract requires a corporate seal to be attached, consideration should be given to the so-called sealed contract rule, which substantially departs from the normal rules of agency. As a general rule, under the law of agency, an undisclosed principal may sue or be sued under a simple contract that is entered into on the principal's behalf by an agent. However, where a contract is executed under seal, only the named parties may sue and be sued under it, since only the parties to a sealed instrument enjoy enforceable rights and obligations under it (the rule is an extension of the principle that sealed instruments are enforceable by virtue of their form). Accordingly, where a contract is entered into under corporate seal, with the intention that it will be a sealed instrument (a logical inference where the document is said to be "signed, sealed and delivered"),[225] the rule will apply. In addition, by virtue of subsection 13(1) of the *Land Registration Reform Act*, all documents in Ontario transferring an interest in land fall within the scope of the rule, whether or not executed under seal.[226]

C. FRAUD BY AN AGENT OR FORGERY OF A CORPORATE DOCUMENT

§6.96 A corporate document may appear on its face to be authentic, and it may appear to have been signed by a person who would normally possess the authority to execute and deliver the document on behalf of the corporation. However, such appearances are not conclusive of the question of whether the corporation is bound by the document, for one must also consider the possibility of forgery or fraud committed by an agent in connection with its execution.

§6.97 A fraud is an intentional perversion of the truth (a false misrepresentation deliberately made or made recklessly without regard for the truth) for the purpose of inducing another in reliance upon it to part with some valuable thing belonging to him or her or to surrender a legal right. The term is sufficiently broad to encompass any kind of artifice employed by one person to deceive another. Fraud may be either actual or constructive. Actual fraud consists of deceit, artifice, or design, and involves some direct and active operation of the mind. Constructive fraud consists of any act or omission contrary to a legal or equitable duty or trust or confidence properly reposed, which is contrary to good conscience and operates to the injury of another. In order for an act or omission to be viewed as being a constructive fraud it must be of a type which if it were generally permitted would be prejudicial to the public welfare.

---

[225] See also, *Paul D'Aoust Construction Ltd. v. Markel Insurance Co. of Canada*, [2001] S.C.J. No. 78, [2001] 3 S.C.R. 744, aff'g [1999] O.J. No. 1837, 45 C.L.R. (2d) 65 (C.A.).

[226] R.S.O. 1990, c. L. 4. *Friedmann Equity Developments Inc. v. Final Note Ltd.*, [2000] S.C.J. No. 37, 7 B.L.R. (3d) 153.

§6.98 Under the general law of agency, a principal is not allowed to profit from the fraudulent act of an agent.[227] This rule applies with full vigour in the case of corporations and their agents. Thus if an agent of a corporation induces a person to subscribe for and purchase shares in a corporation by making misrepresentations to potential purchasers, the corporation will be liable for those representations.[228] The corporation will be so bound even where an agent was motivated (while acting within the scope of his or her employment or authority) by some improper motive such as the intention to make a personal profit.[229] In such a case it is not necessary to show that the corporation has benefited from the wrongdoing; indeed, it will remain liable even if it also was injured by the wrongdoing in question. The fact that an agent abuses the trust which is placed in him or her cannot affect an outsider who has no notice of that wrongdoing.

§6.99 Similarly, if the agent does an act that is within the ordinary scope of the agent's authority, the corporation will be bound by that act or representation even if it expressly forbade the agent from so acting.[230] If the corporation knows that the agent is misrepresenting his or her authority to outsiders, the corporation will be bound by those representations.[231] Similarly, the corporation will be liable for the acts of an agent within the scope of the agent's authority despite any informality or irregularity in the agent's appointment.[232] However, a corporation is not liable to a third party for an unauthorized representation made by an agent of the corporation, where the representation in question was unusual in nature, either because it was beyond the ordinary business carried on by the corporation,[233] or beyond the normal responsibility of an agent of that type. Moreover, a corporation is clearly not liable for an act or representation in excess of an agent's authority where the third party knows that the agent lacks that authority[234] or knows that the representation was wrong.

§6.100 An agent acting on behalf of a corporation who makes a contract in the name of a corporation or otherwise indicates that the contract is being made on the corporation's behalf incurs no liability to the other contracting party unless the agent exceeds his or her authority, or that authority is otherwise defective. The agent will be liable if the agent fails to make clear that he or she is signing in an agency capacity only. If a corporation repudiates a contract entered into by an officer or agent without authority, the officer or agent will be liable to the

---

[227] *Re Gloy Adhesives* (1912), 4 O.W.N. 350 (H.C.).
[228] See, for instance, *Ontario Ladies' College v. Kendry* (1905), 10 O.L.R. 324 (C.A.); *Huber v. Lion Mead Rubber Co.* (1923), 25 O.W.N. 72 (Co. Ct.).
[229] *Bryant, Powis & Bryant Ltd. v. Quebec Bank*, [1893] A.C. 170 (P.C.); *Welcome Investments Ltd. v. Sceptre Investment Counsel Ltd.*, [2000] O.J. No. 2807, 98 A.C.W.S. (3d) 1014 (S.C.J.).
[230] *Foley v. Commercial Cars Ltd.* (1922), 52 O.L.R. 174 (C.A.).
[231] *Allen v. Ontario & Rainy River Rlwy.* (1898), 29 O.R. 510 (C.A.). As to what is sufficient evidence of agency to bind a corporation, see *O'Brien v. Credit Valley Rlwy.* (1875), 25 U.C.C.P. 275 (C.A.); *Albert Cheese Co. v. Leeming* (1880), 31 U.C.C.P. 272 at 279 (C.A.).
[232] *Hely-Hutchinson v. Brayhead Ltd.*, [1968] 1 Q.B. 549 (C.A.) — chairman of the board never formally appointed as managing director or expressly authorized to act for corporation.
[233] *Bianco v. I.H. Mathers & Son* (1938), 12 M.P.R. 444 (N.S.C.A.).
[234] *Howard v. Patent Ivory Manufacturing Co.* (1888), 38 Ch. D. 156.

other contracting party in damages for breach of the agent's implied warranty of authority.[235]

§6.101 Somewhat different rules apply in the case of a forged corporate document. To forge is to fabricate by false imitation. A forged document is essentially a counterfeit. Forgery occurs where a person

- alters a document made by another person without the authority of that other person;
- purports to make, complete, execute, authenticate, issue or transfer a document in the name of another person who did not authorize the act in question;
- falsely dates, numbers or otherwise inserts information into a document in order to mislead as to its effect or the time or place of its execution, authentication, issue or transfer,

with the intent to defraud or injure another person, or with the knowledge that he or she is facilitating a fraud or injury being committed by one person against another.

§6.102 As a general rule, a forged document is a nullity, but there are certain exceptions to that rule. The most important of these grows out of clause 19(*e*) of the OBCA[236] which provides that a corporation or a guarantor of an obligation of a corporation may not assert against a person dealing with the corporation or with any person who has acquired rights from the corporation that: "a document issued by any director, officer or agent of a corporation with actual or usual authority to issue the document is not valid or genuine". However, in order for clause 19(*e*) to apply it is necessary to show at least that the person who issued the document had the usual authority to do so.

§6.103 In *Ruben v. Great Fingall Consolidated*,[237] it was found that the company secretary had issued a share certificate to which he had affixed the company's seal and forged the signatures of the directors. A transferee claimed damages from the company on the basis that the company was estopped from denying the validity of a security certificate that it had issued. The document was held to be a forgery, and accordingly it would not bind the company unless it was issued by an agent who was authorized to warrant its authenticity. It was held that even if the secretary could be taken to have given a warranty of authenticity in issuing the certificate, he had no apparent or express authority to give that warranty on the corporation's behalf. Lord Loreburn stated that the certificate was[238]

> ... a pure nullity. It is quite true that persons dealing with limited companies are not bound to inquire into their indoor management and will not be affected by irregularities of which they have no notice. But this doctrine, which is well estab-

---

[235] *Firbank's Executors v. Humphreys* (1886), 18 Q.B.D. 54 (C.A.).
[236] CBCA, s. 18(1)(*e*).
[237] [1906] A.C. 439 (H.L.).
[238] *Ibid.*, at 443; see also 444 *per* Lord Macnaghten.

lished, applies only to irregularities that otherwise might affect a genuine transaction. It cannot apply to a forgery.

In *Slingsby v. District Bank*[239] the court attempted to read into Lord Loreburn's statement a much broader principle of public policy:

> Though a man may be estopped by conduct from denying that a forgery is his signature, yet as forgery is a crime he cannot authorize in advance (if indeed it is not a contradiction in terms to authorize a forgery) without being an accessory before the fact. Nor can he agree to be bound by it subsequently, so as to shield a criminal or compound a felony. Hence an act of forgery is a nullity and outside any actual or ostensible authority ...

§6.104 One must express some doubts about the validity of the extreme view advanced in the *Slingsby* case.[240] It is far from unusual for one person (*e.g.*, a secretary or personal assistant) to be given the authority by another person (usually a superior) to sign documents on that superior's behalf using that superior's name. There is nothing inherently fraudulent in such a practice, although it is one that clearly does give rise to a degree of risk, since the writing of the person so authorized will eventually be taken to be the writing of the superior who gave the authorization. Having created the risk that others will be misled, it seems most sensible to impose the risk of wrong-doing (and loss) on the person who created the risk.[241] Despite the general presumption that a forged document is a nullity, in the corporate context, the existence of apparent authority may prevent a corporation from escaping liability under a forged document. The legal basis of apparent authority is not the existence of any actual authority, but rather an estoppel which prevents the principal from denying the existence of authority. It arises from a representation or other conduct on the part of the corporation that prevents it from denying the validity of what has transpired. The mere fact that an agent has committed a fraud against his or her principal is not sufficient to entitle the principal to disclaim the authority of the agent (*vis-à-vis* a third party) in acting as the agent did[242] — particularly where the victim-principal has created the very circumstances that allow the fraud to be committed. Much as a person may be estopped from denying that the forged signature on a document is his or her own,[243] it follows naturally that the same person may be estopped by the circumstances from denying that the document itself was forged, if the document was issued by a person who is customarily or actually authorized to issue genuine documents of the same sort. By placing security certificates and the corporate seal in the custody of an agent, the corporation creates the opportunity for a fraud against it, and therefore must be seen to take the risk that the agent will misuse the trust that has been reposed. It is only when a document is entirely forged or fraudulent — in that it is not only bogus, but was issued by a

---

[239] [1932] 1 K.B. 544 (C.A.).
[240] *Ibid.*
[241] See the discussion of vicarious liability in Chapter 3, Corporate Liability.
[242] *Lloyd v. Grace, Smith & Co.*, [1912] A.C. 716 (H.L.); *Moore v. I. Bresler Ltd.*, [1944] 2 All E.R. 515 (K.B.).
[243] See *Greenwood v. Martins Bank*, [1933] A.C. 51 (H.L.).

person who had no authority to issue documents of the type in question — that it is open to a corporation to deny authority and repudiate the document as a forgery.

D. CORPORATE DOMICILE

§6.105 It is sometimes necessary to determine the domicile of a corporation.[244] In the case of individuals, a clear and sharp distinction has always been drawn among nationality, residence and domicile. An individual may have only one domicile, which in general terms is the jurisdiction that the person treats as his or her permanent home and to which he or she has the closest legal attachment. No individual can be without a domicile — since on leaving a domicile of choice without an intent to return, the domicile of birth revives. Moreover, no one at any given time can have more than one domicile. However, an individual may have several residences — a residence being merely a place in which a person makes a home — and at least in theory it is possible for a person to have no country of residence at all.

§6.106 In addition to dealing with the authority of officers and directors, the statutory indoor management rules set out in the OBCA and the CBCA also make limited provision with respect to the residence and domicile of the corporation. Thus clause 19(c) of the OBCA provides that no objection may be taken that:

> the location named in the most recent notice filed under subsection 14(3) or named in the articles, whichever is more current, is not the registered office of the corporation.

Paragraph 18(c), the equivalent provision in the CBCA, is similar but is cast in slightly different terms. It reads:

> the place named in the most recent notice sent to the Director under section 19 is not the registered office of the corporation.

The differences between the OBCA and the CBCA provisions largely reflect the administrative differences that exist under those two statutes, and in substance the two provisions are to the same purpose and effect. The rule that each sets down is of obvious importance in the case of notices and other documents that are required by law or contract to be sent to or kept at the registered office of the corporation. In addition, the provision may be of importance in determining the jurisdiction of a court or tribunal. For instance, under section 207 of the CBCA, the court having jurisdiction over the liquidation and dissolution of a corporation is the "court having jurisdiction in the place where the corporation has its registered office". By virtue of paragraph 18(1)(c), if an application is brought before

---

[244] For example, in order to establish jurisdiction over a corporate debtor that does not carry on business in Canada under the *Bankruptcy and Insolvency Act*, R.S.C. 1985, c. B-3, the definition of "debtor" in s. 2 of the Act provides:

> "debtor" includes an insolvent person and any person who, at the time an act of bankruptcy was committed by him, resided or carried on business in Canada and, where the context requires, includes a bankrupt.

the proper court according to the recorded place of the registered office, then it will not be open to the corporation to challenge the jurisdiction of the court on the ground that the registered office of the corporation is in fact elsewhere. During time of war, the domicile or nationality of the principals who stand behind an incorporated entity may be highly relevant for many purposes.[245] However, at common law,[246] there is no requirement that the incorporators of a corporation under the OBCA or CBCA be resident in Canada or (in the case of the OBCA) within the province of Ontario. In general, a corporation incorporated outside Canada may incorporate a wholly-owned subsidiary within Canada, and all of the shares of a corporation incorporated within Canada may be owned by persons resident outside Canada.

§6.107 It has sometimes been put forward that a corporation has its domicile in the place where it is incorporated and nowhere else.[247] This view must still be considered to be the doctrinally received position,[248] but is it doctrinally sound? One advantage to the "domicile equals place of incorporation" rule is that it is certain: there can be little confusion as to the domicile of a corporation under that rule. Equating the domicile of a corporation with the jurisdiction of its incorporation presents certain problems in Canada, where many corporations have been incorporated at the Federal level. The domicile of an individual is tied to the particular province with which the individual has his or her closest connection. As a general rule, the courts of one jurisdiction will not issue orders purporting to direct or regulate the internal affairs or governance of a corporation that was incorporated in another jurisdiction.[249] However, it has been held that an oppression action in respect of a CBCA corporation that has its registered office in Quebec may be brought in another province.[250] The related question of the limited authority of the courts of one jurisdiction to wind up the business and affairs of a foreign corporate entity that are being carried out within the jurisdiction of that court, was explained by Kay J. in *Re Matheson Brothers Ltd.*, in the following terms:

> a company formed in a foreign country, which chooses to carry on business, have assets, and contract debts in this country does not come within the spirit as it clearly comes within the letter of the 199th section. It is argued that this is a company which cannot be 'dissolved,' and reference has been made to sect. 111 of the same Act, which provides that when the affairs of the company have been completely wound up the Court shall make an order that the company shall be dissolved from the date of such order, and the company shall be dissolved accordingly, and the contention is that no company is within the scope of this Act unless the Court has jurisdiction to dissolve it. But the dissolution of a company is

---

[245] See, for instance, *Daimler Co. v. Continental Tyre & Rubber Co. (Great Britain) Ltd.*, [1916] 2 A.C. 307 (H.L.).
[246] See, for instance, *Princess of Reuss v. Bos* (1871), L.R. 5 H.L. 176.
[247] *Bergner & Engel Brewing Co. v. Dreyfus*, 70 Am. St. Rep. 251 (1898).
[248] P.M. North, *Cheshire's Private International Law*, 9th ed. (London: Butterworths, 1974) at 197-98.
[249] *Cira v. Rico Resources Inc.*, [2004] O.J. No. 3981, 41 B.L.R. (3d) 206 at 208 (S.C.J.), per Ground J. This rule is subject to any statutory provision to the contrary, the most obvious being with respect to securities legislation.
[250] *Viner v. Poplaw*, [2003] O.J. No. 3981, 38 B.L.R. (3d) 134 (S.C.J.).

brought about by a separate order of the Court, and it by no means follows that because the Court has no power to make an order to dissolve a company that it has no power to make an order to wind it up, and, as a matter of fact, wound up companies very seldom are dissolved.[251]

§6.108 Ultimately, linking domicile to incorporation confuses domicile with nationality (or citizenship). A distinction has always been drawn in the case of individuals between nationality and domicile, and there is no apparent reason for not drawing a similar distinction in the case of corporations. If for certain legal purposes it is necessary to distinguish between the place with which an individual has the closest connection and the place of which that individual is a national (and this, presumably, is the whole rationale which underlies the entire concept of domicile), it seems likely that a similar need will sometimes present itself in the case of a corporation.

§6.109 It is clear that the nationality of a corporation may be changed only to the extent permitted by the legislation of its incorporating jurisdiction[252] — as, for instance, by continuing under the laws of some other jurisdiction.[253] However, analogies between humans and corporations are generally not a sound basis for analysis, and so it is in the case of determining corporate nationality. There is only one citizenship in Canada for individuals. In contrast, a company is a national of the jurisdiction in which it was incorporated.[254] A company incorporated by or under the laws of Canada is a citizen of Canada generally and also of every province in which it resides or operates.[255] The same is not true of provincially incorporated companies. Such companies are citizens only of their province of incorporation. Elsewhere, even in another province of Canada, they are foreign, although in some cases are entitled to preferential treatment relative to other foreign corporations.[256]

---

[251] (1884), 27 Ch. D. 225.
[252] *Gasque v. I.R.C.*, [1940] 2 K.B. 80 at 84, *per* Macnaghten J.; *National Trust Co. v. Ebro Irrigation & Power Co.*, [1954] O.R. 463 (H.C.); but compare *J.S. Darrell & Co. v. The Ship American*, [1925] Ex. C.R. 2.
[253] Macnaughton J.'s famous statement in *Gasque v. I.R.C.*, [1940] 2 K.B. 80 at 84 that "the domicil of origin, or domicil of birth [of a corporation] ... clings to it throughout its existence" so that it cannot be changed. This clearly is not applicable to either CBCA or OBCA corporations, since their governing legislation expressly contemplates the continuation of a corporation under the laws of another jurisdiction.
[254] *Janson v. Driefontein Consolidated Mines Ltd.*, [1902] A.C. 484 at 485 (H.L.), *per* Lord Lindley; *Daimler Co. v. Continental Tyre & Rubber Co. (Great Britain) Ltd.*, [1916] 2 A.C. 307 (H.L.).
[255] See Chapter 4. Where a provincially incorporated entity is declared by the federal Parliament to be a work for the general advantage of Canada, it thereupon becomes a federal entity: *A.G. British Columbia v. Vancouver, Victoria & Eastern Rlwy. Navigation Co.* (1902), 9 B.C.R. 338.
[256] See, for instance, the *Extraprovincial Corporations Act*, R.S.O. 1990, c. E.27, which relieves companies incorporated under the laws of a province other than Ontario of the need to obtain a licence under that Act as a condition of carrying on business in Ontario. Such a licence is required in the case of companies incorporated in other countries.

§6.110 While the old case law indicated that corporate residence and domicile were synonymous,[257] in later cases[258] the courts began to distinguish between the two. Thus in *Royal Bank v. McMahon* it was held that while a corporation could have only one domicile, which was where its head office was located, it could be said to be resident in each place where it maintained a branch office.[259] In *Tytler v. C.P.R.*[260] Meredith J. went even further, holding that a corporation resides wherever it carries on business.

§6.111 The distinction between residence and domicile is sometimes of particular importance in determining liability to taxation, although under the present Canadian income tax regime, liability for tax turns upon residence rather than domicile or nationality. As noted in Chapter 1, in common law jurisdictions, the existence of a company is usually determined under the law of the jurisdiction of incorporation. On the other hand, the tax status of a corporation is determined under the law of each of the jurisdictions in which it "carries on business" or is "resident" or "non-resident" as determined by the laws of each such jurisdiction respectively. Tax residence usually results in the application of the principle of universality of taxation, under which a taxpayer is taxed within a jurisdiction on its worldwide taxable income (subject to such credits as may be allowable under the laws of that jurisdiction). Historically, fixing the residence of a corporation has been complicated by the fact that a corporation may have administrative activities, directors and managers who reside, meet and take decisions in one or several places. It has activities and carries on business. Finally, it has shareholders who control it. When all of these elements of control are situate in the same country, no complications arise. As soon as they are dissociated and "scattered" in different states, each country may want to subject the company to taxation on the basis of an element to which it gives preference: incorporation procedure, management functions, running of the business, shareholders' controlling power *etc*. Depending on the criteria adopted, residence for tax purposes may arise in one or the other country.[261]

§6.112 Under Canadian tax law, the scope of corporate residence has been expanded so that now any corporation incorporated in Canada after April 26, 1965 is deemed to be resident in Canada for income tax purposes[262] (irrespective of

---

[257] *Carron Iron Co. v. Maclaren* (1855), 5 H.L. Cas. 416 at 459 (H.L.), *per* Lord St. Leonards.
[258] See, for instance, *Bank of Toronto v. Pickering* (1919), 46 O.L.R. 289 (H.C.), although Middleton J. was prepared to acknowledge a limited concept of residence for certain specific purposes, such as fixing venue. Wegenast, *Canadian Companies* (Toronto: Carswell, 1979 reprint), seems to have shared this view, at 168.
[259] (1934), 8 M.P.R. 363 at 365 (P.E.I.S.C.), *per* Arsenault J. See also Rule 16.02 of the Ontario *Rules of Civil Procedure*, R.R.O. 1990, Reg. 194, which provides that where a document is to be served personally on a corporation, it shall be made "by leaving a copy of the document with an officer, director or agent of the corporation, or with a person at any place of business of the corporation who appears to be in control or management of the place of business".
[260] (1899), 29 O.R. 654 at 657 (H.C.).
[261] *Union of India v. Azadi Bachao Andolan*, [2003] 4 L.R.I. 172 (S.C. Ind. Civ. App.).
[262] ITA, R.S.C. 1985, c. 1 (5th Supp.), s. 250(4).

where it may be domiciled). It follows that result that a corporation may now also be resident in more than one jurisdiction,[263] and may be resident in one jurisdiction for one purpose while resident in another jurisdiction for some different purpose.[264]

§6.113 Although the determination of corporate residence is primarily of importance for tax purposes, it may also be important in the litigation context, where the determination of residence is often relevant in fixing the appropriate location for a trial or application.[265] Residence in this context, however, seems more broadly conceived. For instance, in *Bank of Toronto v. Pickering*[266] it was held that a bank doing business through its branches is resident in each of the locations of the branches, so that where a defendant fails to make a payment on a promissory note, the cause of action arises at the branch where the loan transaction took place.[267] In contrast, residence may be more narrowly construed where the issue is whether a corporate plaintiff should be required to post security for costs.[268] Since multiplicity of domicile is not acceptable, it must now be taken as settled that the concepts of corporate residence and domicile are distinct.

§6.114 What then is the domicile of a corporation? As noted above, in *Royal Bank v. McMahon* it was held that a corporation had only one domicile, which was where its head office was located.[269] This suggests a view of corporate domicile closely approximating that applicable to individuals: namely that domicile is the place of permanent residence — the place with which the individual has the closest legal attachment. The term "head office" is meaningless under the present OBCA and CBCA, but there is a considerable amount of case law which would tie the domicile of a corporation to the place where effective control of the corporation was exercised. Under this approach, a corporation is not domiciled in Canada by reason only that it is incorporated under the CBCA or the OBCA, or even if it carries on a majority (or the whole) of its business in Canada. Instead, domicile is a question of fact, decided primarily by reference to the place where the corporation's central management and control abides.[270] That place is identified by scrutinizing the whole course of business and trading of the company in question, rather than by reference to any particular provision of the articles or by-laws of the company.[271] In general, management abides at the

---

[263] But this is subject to any applicable tax treaty; see, for instance, *Canada-United States Tax Convention*, Article IV(3), which deems a corporation that is resident in both Canada and the United States to be resident in the country in which it is incorporated for the purposes of the treaty.
[264] *Ex p. Bruell, In Re Bowie* (1880), 16 Ch. D. 484 at 486-87 (C.A.), per James L.J.; see also *Goerz & Co. v. Bell*, [1904] 2 K.B. 136 at 194, per Channell J. This possibility was stated unequivocally by Ilsley C.J. in *Cody's Ltd. v. Chester Branch Canadian Legion* (1962), 47 M.P.R. 203 (N.S.C.A.), not only with respect to the question of taxation, but as a general principle.
[265] *St. Lawrence Transport Ltd. v. Buchanan* (1931), 39 O.W.N. 528 (H.C.).
[266] (1919), 46 O.L.R. 289 (H.C.).
[267] *Bank of Montreal v. Perry*, [1981] O.J. No. 2904, 31 O.R. (2d) 700 (H.C.).
[268] *Ashland Co. v. Armstrong* (1906), 11 O.L.R. 414 at 415 (H.C.), per Boyd C., aff'd 62 O.A.R. 467.
[269] (1934), 8 M.P.R. 363 at 365 (P.E.I.S.C.), per Arsenault J.
[270] *DeBeers Consolidated Mines Ltd. v. Howe*, [1906] A.C. 455 at 458 (H.L.), per Lord Loreburn.
[271] *Ibid.*

place where the board of directors meets and exercises its authority, but other factors — such as the location of the registered or head office of the company or the place where its official records (share registry, *etc.*) are kept — may also be relevant to the question. Where the corporation is subject to a unanimous shareholder agreement under which the bulk of management power is reserved to the shareholder, the residence of the controlling shareholder presumably would be determinative. It is possible for corporate management and control to abide in two different jurisdictions, as for instance where *de facto* control resides in one jurisdiction while *de jure* control resides in another.[272] The place where actual management and control abides, rather than where it is legally supposed to reside, is the question which must be decided in order to fix the corporation's domicile.[273]

E. REGISTERED OFFICE OF A CORPORATION

§6.115 All corporations under both Acts are required to have a registered office.[274] The concept of a registered office was introduced into Canadian corporate law by the CBCA. Until the CBCA, corporate law statutes generally required that a corporation have a "head office",[275] but the CBCA makes no reference to the head office of the corporation, and in the OBCA, the only reference to the head office of a corporation is found in subsection 14(2), which merely provides that the head office of every corporation incorporated prior to the day on which the Act comes into effect shall be deemed to be the registered office of the corporation. The change from "head office" to "registered office" is largely one of terminology, as the purpose of the registered office is much the same as that of the head office under the old legislation. However, one fact is now clear: the registered office of a corporation is the place specified in the manner described above, rather than the chief place of business of the corporation.[276]

§6.116 The provisions of the CBCA and the OBCA with respect to the registered office are similar but differ in administrative detail. Under the standard form of articles under the OBCA, the municipality or geographic township in Ontario; and the address including the street name and number, if any; and

---

[272] *Union Corp. Ltd. v. IRC*, [1952] 1 All E.R. 646 (C.A.), aff'd [1953] A.C. 482 (H.L.).
[273] *Unit Construction Co. Ltd. v. Bullock*, [1960] A.C. 351 (H.L.); but compare *Sifneos v. M.N.R.*, 68 D.T.C. 522 at 528 (T.A.B.), *per* Roland St-Onge, Member:

> One should not be misled by appearances whereby the power behind the throne seems to originate in another country. They are not really powerful if they cannot act according to the laws of this country. Otherwise the company would be completely useless. Only an exercise of authority within the framework of the constitution of a company should matter.
>
> In view of the fact that the law now permits shareholders to assume direct control through a unanimous shareholders' agreement, this question may well need to be revisited.

[274] OBCA, s. 14(1); CBCA, s. 19(1).
[275] See, for instance, s. 14 of the former OBCA.
[276] *Re Smith Transportation Co.* (1928), 10 C.B.R. 48 (Ont. H.C.).

where the registered office is to be located must all be designated.²⁷⁷ Under the CBCA, the articles need only set out the place in Canada in which the registered office is to be located (the office must, however, be in the province specified in the articles),²⁷⁸ but a notice of registered office in prescribed form must be sent to the director together with any articles that designate or change the place of the registered office of the corporation.²⁷⁹ Both Acts empower the directors of a corporation to change the address of the registered office within the place specified in the articles.²⁸⁰ Subsection 19(2) of the CBCA allows the directors to authorize a change of the registered office anywhere within the same province.²⁸¹ Where the address of the registered office is changed, subsection 19(4) of the CBCA requires that the corporation send to the director a notice of the change in the prescribed form within 15 days of the change of address. Upon receipt, this notice is filed by the director. Under the OBCA a notice of change must be filed under the *Corporations Information Act* within 10 days after the passing of the resolution.²⁸²

§6.117 Under both Acts, a more cumbersome procedure must be followed in order to change the municipality or place in which the registered office is required to be located. Both Acts recognize that a change in the location of the registered office may inconvenience the shareholders of the corporation, and therefore any such change requires substantial shareholder support. Subsection 14(4) of the OBCA provides that a corporation may change the municipality or geographic township in which its registered office is located to another place in Ontario.²⁸³ As an alternative, clause 167(1)(*b*) of the Act permits such a change to be made by way of amendment to the articles of the corporation. In contrast, under the CBCA, paragraph 173(1)(*b*) requires any change in the province in which the registered office is required to be situated to be made by way of amendment to the articles of incorporation.²⁸⁴

F. RECORDS OF A CORPORATION

§6.118 Although the laws governing the keeping of records by a corporation are not specifically related to the capacity and powers of a corporation as such, those records are often the only method for determining how the powers of a corporation have in fact been exercised. Accordingly, there is considerable logic in including a discussion of the relevant provisions governing the maintenance

---

[277] See OBCA, s. 14(1).
[278] See CBCA, s. 19(1).
[279] *Ibid.*, s. 19(2).
[280] CBCA, s. 19(3); OBCA, s. 14(3).
[281] This presumed authority may be problematic for many corporations, and should be borne in mind when drafting a unanimous shareholder agreement or any other restriction on the exercise of director powers.
[282] OBCA, s. 14(3).
[283] Where it does so, it is required to file a certified copy of the resolution with the Director within 10 days after the passing of the resolution, but a failure to file does not affect the validity of the resolution: OBCA, s. 14(4), (5).
[284] See, generally, *Union Fire Insurance Co. v. O'Gara* (1883), 4 O.R. 359 (H.C.).

of records relating to the business and affairs of corporations, at this point in the text.

(i) OBCA and CBCA Requirements

§6.119 When all is said and done, a corporation is really little more than an administrative convenience: it is a bundle of rights, assets, liabilities and obligations built around a legal fiction. Given the ethereal nature of a corporation, it is not surprising that corporate law statutes generally impose detailed requirements with respect to the records that a corporation must keep concerning the rights, assets, liabilities and obligations to which it is entitled or subject. In this respect, the OBCA and the CBCA are no exception. Section 140 of the OBCA requires every corporation to maintain:

> at its registered office, or at such other place in Ontario designated by the directors,
>
> (a) the articles and the by-laws and all amendments thereto, and a copy of any unanimous shareholder agreement known to the directors;
>
> (b) minutes of meetings and resolutions of shareholders;
>
> (c) a register of directors in which are set out the names and residence addresses while directors, including the street and number, if any, of all persons who are or have been directors of the corporation with the several dates on which each became or ceased to be a director;
>
> (d) a securities register complying with section 141.[285]

---

[285] Section 141 of the OBCA provides:

> 141.(1) A corporation shall prepare and maintain at its registered office, or at any other place in Ontario designated by the directors, a securities register in which it records the securities issued by it in registered form, showing with respect to each class or series of securities,
>
> (a) the names, alphabetically arranged of persons who,
>
>> (i) are or have been within six years registered as shareholders of the corporation, the address including the street and number, if any, of every such person while a holder, and the number and class of shares registered in the name of such holder,
>>
>> (ii) are or have been within six years registered as holders of debt obligations of the corporation, the address, including the street and number, if any, of every such person while a holder, and the class or series and principal amount of the debt obligations registered in the name of such holder, or
>>
>> (iii) are or have been within six years registered as holders of warrants of the corporation, other than warrants exerciseable within one year from the date of issue, the address including the street and number, if any, of every such person while a registered holder, and the class or series and number of warrants registered in the name of such holder; and
>
> (b) the date and particulars of the issue of each security and warrant.
>
> (2) A corporation shall cause to be kept a register of transfers in which all transfers of securities issued by the corporation in registered form and the date and other particulars of each transfer shall be set out.

Unless the legislation specifically requires the disclosure of a residence address (as in the case of directors), an accommodation address — or address of convenience — is sufficient for the purposes of a securities register.[286] Subsection 20(1) of the CBCA is similar, but instead of a register of directors, the corporation is required to maintain copies of all notices of elections or appointments of directors required to be sent to the Director by section 106 or 113. In addition to the foregoing, every corporation is required under section 140(2) of the OBCA to prepare and maintain:

(a) adequate accounting records; and

(b) records containing minutes of meetings and resolutions of the directors and any committee thereof ...

Section 20(2) of the CBCA is to like effect. However, subsection 140(2) of the OBCA goes on to state that provided the retention requirements of any taxing authority of Ontario, the government of Canada or any other jurisdiction have been satisfied, the accounting records mentioned in clause (a) need only be retained by the corporation for six years from the end of the last fiscal period to which they relate. No corresponding provision is to be found in the CBCA. Both the OBCA and the CBCA provide that where a body corporate is continued under either Act, the required records include similar records that the body corporate was required to maintain by law before it was so continued.[287]

§6.120 Subsection 20(2.1) of the CBCA now provides that subject to any federal or provincial statute imposing a longer retention period, a corporation must retain its accounting records for six years after the end of the financial year to which those records relate. The CBCA now permits both accounting and corporate records outside Canada, but where this is done:

- ... accounting records adequate to enable the directors to ascertain the financial position of the corporation with reasonable accuracy on a quarterly basis must be kept at the registered office or at another place in Canada designated by the directors [; and]

  .....

- ... the records are available for inspection, by means of computer terminal or other technology, during regular hours at the registered office or any other place in Canada designated by the directors.[288]

§6.121 Having required the maintenance of the above records, subsection 20(4) of the CBCA goes on to provide that the records described in subsection (2) shall be kept at the registered office of the corporation or at such other place as the directors think fit and shall at all times be open to inspection by the directors. A similar provision is found in subsection 144(1) of the OBCA, except that the right of inspection is limited to the normal business hours of the corporation.

---

[286] *Hemmerling v. IMTC Systems*, [1993] B.C.J. No. 2570, 109 D.L.R. (4th) 582 (C.A.).
[287] OBCA, s. 140(3); CBCA, s. 20(3).
[288] CBCA, s. 20(5) and (5.1).

§6.122 In *Sinclair v. Sutton Resources Ltd.*[289] it was suggested that the right to inspect a securities register did not imply a right to take notes and make copies. That suggestion was quickly and soundly rejected.[290]

(ii) Canada Revenue Agency Requirements

§6.123 For most corporations, the key rules governing the retention of records are those specified by the Canada Revenue Agency.[291] The general rule is that all records relevant to a tax return filed in a given year must be kept for a minimum of six years after the end of the taxation year to which they relate. The six-year retention period begins at the end of the tax year to which the records relate. Records and supporting documents concerning long-term acquisitions and disposal of property, the share registry, and other historical information that would have an impact upon sale or liquidation or wind-up of the business must be kept indefinitely. Since a tax return relates to an entire financial year, and since a tax return for a year may be filed properly up to six months after the end of the year to which it relates, at least some of the records concerned will be close to seven years old before the obligation to retain ends. If a tax return is filed late, the six-year period runs from the date of filing, rather than the end of the relevant taxation year.

§6.124 When a corporation is dissolved, the following records must be kept for two years after the date of dissolution:

- all records and supporting documents to verify the tax obligations and entitlements; and

- all the additional records that corporations have to keep, as listed above.

When a corporation amalgamates or merges, business records must be retained as if the new corporation is a continuation of each of the original corporations.

§6.125 A taxpayer may apply for permission to destroy business records before the expiration of the above periods. It is necessary to obtain written permission from the director of the relevant tax services office. Applications for such permission are made using Form T137, Request For Destruction of Books and Records. Care must be exercised in relying upon any such permission. It will apply only to records that are required to be kept under the legislation administered by the CRA. The CRA has no authority to approve the destruction of records that you are required to keep under other federal, provincial/territorial, and municipal laws.

---

[289] [1996] B.C.J. No. 1849, 28 B.L.R. (2d) 258 at 262 (S.C.), *per* Harvey J.
[290] See also *Mutter v. Eastern & Midlands Railway Co.* (1888), 38 Ch. D. 92 at 107 (C.A.), *per* Lindley L.J.
[291] See CRA Publication No RC4409, *Keeping Records*, which governs accounting and other financial documents generally required in respect of a business undertaking, including ledgers, journals, vouchers, financial statements and accounts, and income tax records. They are generally supported by source documents, or their computer equivalents.

§6.126 The CRA specifies that all records must:

- be reliable and complete;
- provide correct information necessary to calculate tax obligations and entitlements;
- be supported by source documents to verify the information contained in the records;
- include other documents, such as appointment books, logbooks, income tax and GST/HST returns, and certain accountants' working papers, that assist in determining obligations and entitlements; and
- be kept in English or French.

Business corporations are directed to keep:

- the minutes of meetings of the directors of a corporation;
- the minutes of meetings of the shareholders of a corporation;
- any record of a corporation containing details about:
    - the ownership of the shares of the capital stock of the corporation; and
    - any transfers of these shares;
- the general ledger or other books of final entry, in paper or electronic format, containing the summaries of the year-to-year transactions of the corporation; and
- any special contracts, agreements, or other documents necessary to understand the entries in the general ledger or other books of final entry.

Corporations should also retain related documentation to support their transactions. This is particularly important for businesses engaged in international non-arm's length transactions. These businesses should retain documentation related to their transfer pricing policies.

§6.127 As an alternative to retention of the original paper copy of a relevant record, the CRA also permits records to be kept in an acceptable microfiche, microfilm, or electronic image format, but if any source documents are initially created, transmitted, or received electronically, they must be retained in an electronic format. In addition, where a taxpayer has filed a tax objection or appeal, it is necessary to keep the relevant records until the issue is settled, and until the time limit for filing any further appeal has expired. The combined effect of these rules is that records must normally be kept for a minimum of between six and seven years.

(iii) Business Records Protection

§6.128 In Ontario, the *Business Records Protection Act*,[292] also regulates the keeping of corporate records. Section 1 of the Act provides that:

> No person shall, under or under the authority of or in a manner that would be consistent with compliance with any requirement, order, direction or summons of any legislative, administrative or judicial authority in any jurisdiction outside Ontario, take or cause to be taken, send or cause to be sent or remove or cause to be removed from a point in Ontario to a point outside Ontario, any account, balance sheet, profit and loss statement or inventory or any resume or digest thereof or any other record, statement, report, or material in any way relating to any business carried on in Ontario, unless such taking, sending or removal;
>
> (a) is consistent with and forms part of a regular practice of furnishing to a head office or parent company or organization outside Ontario material relating to a branch or subsidiary company or organization carrying on business in Ontario;
>
> (b) is done by or on behalf of a company or person as defined in the *Securities Act,* carrying on business in Ontario and as to a jurisdiction outside Ontario in which the securities of the company or person have been qualified for sale with the consent of the company or person;
>
> (c) is done by or on behalf of a company or person as defined in *the Securities Act,* carrying on business in Ontario as a dealer or salesperson as defined in the *Securities Act,* and as to a jurisdiction outside Ontario in which the company or person has been registered or is otherwise qualified to carry on business as a dealer or salesperson, as the case may be; or
>
> (d) is provided for by or under any law of Ontario or of the Parliament of Canada.

Where the Attorney General or any person having an interest in a business as mentioned in section 1 has reason to believe that a requirement, order, direction or summons as mentioned in section 1 has been or is likely to be made, issued or given in relation to that business, the Attorney General or that person, as the case may be, may apply to the Superior Court for an order requiring any person, whether or not that person is named in the requirement, order, direction or subpoena, to furnish an undertaking and recognizance for the purpose of ensuring that the person will not contravene section 1 and the court may make such order as the court considers proper.[293] Every person who, having received notice of such an application under this section, is deemed to be in contempt of court and is liable to one year's imprisonment.[294] Every person required to furnish an undertaking or recognizance who contravenes this Act may also be found in contempt of court and in addition to any penalty provided by the recognizance is liable to one year's imprisonment.[295]

---

[292] R.S.O. 1990, c. B.19 ("BRA"). See however, *Hunt v. LAC d'Amiante du Quebec*, [1993] S.C.J. No. 125, [1993] 4 S.C.R. 289.
[293] BRA, s. 2(1).
[294] *Ibid.*, s. 2(2).
[295] *Ibid.*, s. 2(3).

(iv) Electronic Provision of Information

§6.129 Part XX.1 of the CBCA deals with the provision of information by a corporation in electronic form. It was enacted in self-evident response to the growing trend to use electronic service and electronic documents as an alternative mechanism to the more traditional paper based system of past generations. For the purpose of Part XX.1, the term "electronic document" means:

> except in section 252.6, any form of representation of information or of concepts fixed in any medium in or by electronic, optical or other similar means and that can be read or perceived by a person or by any means.[296]

In section 252.6(2), the term "electronic document" has the following alternative definition:

> For the purposes of this section, "electronic document" and "secure electronic signature" have the same meaning as in subsection 31(1) of the *Personal Information Protection and Electronic Documents Act*.[297]

§6.130 There are clear risks to policy makers when deciding upon the extent to which a legal system should embrace technological innovation. These include the risk that the law will be tied to a technology that quickly becomes obsolete. When one considers how quickly command line operating systems such as DOS and CPM were supplanted by graphic user interface based operating systems, the extent of this risk becomes clear. A different but equally serious risk is that the law will be tied to a technology that never catches on. In the late 1970s and early 1980s, the Canadian government invested heavily in promoting a teletext system known as Telidon. It never became popular. In contrast, the explosion of the Internet as a means of business communication caught most governments by complete surprise. Perhaps with these experiences in mind, Part XX.1 adopts more of an enabling than a prescriptive approach towards the use of electronic communications. Section 252.3(1) provides that "nothing in this Act or the regulations requires a person to create or provide an electronic document". Subsection 252.3(2) sets out both consent and other requirements that must be met before electronic communications may be used:

> Despite anything in this Part, a requirement under this Act or the regulations to provide a person with a notice, document or other information is not satisfied by the provision of an electronic document unless
>
> (a) the addressee has consented, in the manner prescribed, and has designated an information system for the receipt of the electronic document; and
>
> (b) the electronic document is provided to the designated information system, unless otherwise prescribed.

§6.131 Thus the Act permits both the providers and recipients of information to "opt-in" to the electronic system. However, a requirement under this Act or the

---

[296] CBCA, s. 252.1.
[297] *Ibid.*, s. 252.6(2).

regulations to provide a document by registered mail is not satisfied by the sending of an electronic document unless prescribed.[298]

§6.132 The basic rules with respect to the creation and provision of information are set out in subsection 252.4. Which provides:

> A requirement under this Act or the regulations that a notice, document or other information be created or provided, is satisfied by the creation or provision of an electronic document if
>
> (a) the by-laws or the articles of the corporation do not provide otherwise; and
>
> (b) the regulations, if any, have been complied with.

Clause 252.4(a) effectively prevents reliance upon electronic documents unless the shareholders or incorporators have approved such a method of documentation. Clause (b) contemplates possible regulatory oversight, but does not make the issue of regulations a condition precedent to the use of electronic documentation. In addition to the foregoing, subsections 252.5(1) and (2) impose accessibility requirements. Under subsection (1), any information created in writing must be accessible so as to be usable for subsequent reference. Under subsection (2), any information provided electronically must be accessible by the addressee and capable of being retained by the addressee, so as to be usable for subsequent reference. Subject to these requirements, subsection 252.5(3) provides that:

> A requirement under this Act or the regulations for one or more copies of a document to be provided to a single addressee at the same time is satisfied by the provision of a single version of the electronic document.

Requirements as to signature are dealt with in section 252.7. Which provides:

> A requirement under this Act or the regulations for a signature or for a document to be executed, except with respect to a statutory declaration or an affidavit, is satisfied if, in relation to an electronic document, the prescribed requirements pertaining to this section, if any, are met and if the signature results from the application by a person of a technology or a process that permits the following to be proven:
>
> (a) the signature resulting from the use by a person of the technology or process is unique to the person;
>
> (b) the technology or process is used by a person to incorporate, attach or associate the person's signature to the electronic document; and
>
> (c) the technology or process can be used to identify the person using the technology or process.

§6.133 Perhaps the most controversial provision is subsection 252.6, dealing with statutory declarations and affidavits. Subsection 252.6(1) provides that:

> A statutory declaration or an affidavit required under this Act or the regulations may be created or provided in an electronic document if

---

[298] *Ibid.*, s. 252.5(4).

(a) the person who makes the statutory declaration or affidavit signs it with his or her secure electronic signature;

(b) the authorized person before whom the statutory declaration or affidavit is made signs it with his or her secure electronic signature; and

(c) the requirements of sections 252.3 to 252.5 are complied with.

For the purpose of complying with clause (1)(c), the references to an "electronic document" in sections 252.3 to 252.5 are to be read as references to an "electronic document" as defined in subsection 31(1) of the *Personal Information Protection and Electronic Documents Act*.[299]

---

[299] *Ibid.*, s. 252.6(3).

Chapter 7

EQUITY FINANCE

A. INTRODUCTION

§7.1 In commercial parlance, the term "corporate finance" describes the methods and devices by which a corporation obtains and employs the money that it requires in order to conduct its operations.[1] That money constitutes the capital of the corporation. Like many terms used in the corporate law area, the term "capital" unfortunately has several distinct meanings, each of which is applied only in a limited context. In the context of the corporate constitution, the term "capital" (as in authorized capital and stated capital) describes the various classes of shares that the corporation is authorized to issue and the authorized number or amount thereof, if any. In other contexts, the term "capital" can have a quite different meaning. For instance, many loan agreements will permit a corporation to borrow up to a stated percentage of the corporation's aggregate capital. Similarly, legislation governing deposit-taking financial institutions and insurance companies regulates the amount that such corporations may borrow or take in as deposits, by fixing a maximum ratio between the debt and capital of the company concerned. In each of these contexts, the term "capital" will normally be used to describe the net worth of a business, so that the term includes not only the amount in each stated capital account of the corporation (*i.e.*, the amount obtained by the corporation through the issue of its shares), but also any contributed surplus, general reserves and retained earnings of the corporation. Finally, for capital tax purposes[2] and, in the case of some financial institutions for regulatory purposes,[3] certain types of long-term debt may be counted as capital.

§7.2 The function of the laws regulating corporate finance is to provide a suitable framework within which capital-raising methods and devices can operate.[4] In this chapter, we will examine the rules governing the raising of equity capital.

---

[1] So, for instance, in England the accounting standard FRS 4 provides the following definition of the term "capital instruments":

> All instruments that are issued by reporting entities as a means of raising finance, including shares, debentures, loans and debt instruments, options and warrants that give the holder the right to subscribe for or obtain capital instruments. In the case of consolidated financial statements the term includes capital instruments issued by subsidiaries except those that are held by another member of the group included in the consolidation.

[2] *Corporations Tax Act*, R.S.O. 1990, c. C.40, s. 61(1).
[3] See, generally, Donald Davis and Kevin Lee, "A Practical Approach to the Capital Structure for Banks" (1997) 10 J. of App. Corp. Finance (no. 1) 33.
[4] R. Burgess, *Corporate Finance Law* (London: Sweet & Maxwell, 1985), 1.

There are four basic aspects to corporate finance law that must be considered in any financing transaction relating to a corporation. First, since different rules of law govern different classes of capital, it is necessary to classify the type of capital that is being employed by the corporation. We shall see that essentially, there are two types of capital that a corporation may utilize, namely equity and debt. Second, it is necessary to consider the various types of instrument that may be fashioned in order to raise each class of capital, which involves a consideration of the various terms and conditions that are permitted by law. We shall see that subject to a few general limitations (*e.g.*, restrictions on the redemption of share capital) the law allows corporations and their investors considerable freedom with respect to these matters — so much freedom in fact that the entire equity/debt dichotomy has become blurred. Third, consideration must be given to the procedures that must be followed in connection with the issue of those instruments. We shall see that there are essentially two types of procedure that must be taken into account. One type of procedure — which will be dealt with in this chapter — represents general corporate law requirements that must be satisfied in order to issue a particular type of capital-raising instrument, namely shares[5] in a corporation. The second type of procedure — which lies outside the focus of this work — involves the special steps that must be taken under the *Securities Act*[6] in connection with public security issues. Fourth, consideration must be given to the relative rights of the holders of different types of instrument. As we shall see, there are considerable differences in the priority of the claims against the corporation to which holders of debt and equity are respectively entitled.

(i) Equity and Debt

§7.3 Broadly stated, a business, whether or not incorporated, has three potential sources of funding. First, it may be funded by the persons who own it, either by way of the direct investment of funds by those persons, or alternatively, by those persons providing guarantees or similar comfort to third parties to encourage them to provide funding to the business. Second, it may be funded out of the

---

[5] In Canada and the United States, the terms "shares" and "stock" are used interchangeably. Etymologically, these terms are in fact synonymous, both being contractions of the original term "shares in the capital stock" of a corporation. In other jurisdictions, the terms are distinct. For instance, in England, a company may decide to treat its paid-up share capital as stock, held by the members and having a value equal to the total nominal value of those paid-up shares. Each member is regarded as being the holder of an amount of stock of a certain nominal value, rather than of a number of shares with that nominal value. In principle, a member may transfer any amount of stock he or she wishes, though in practice it is usual to specify a stock unit and require the nominal amount of the amount transferred to be a multiple of the stock unit. In the past, the advantage of stock over shares was that shares had to be numbered and this caused a great deal of extra work in public companies when registering transfers. However, under s. 182(2) of the *Companies Act 1985* (U.K.), distinguishing numbers are no longer required if all issued shares of a class are fully paid up and rank equally for all purposes. Thus stock has largely fallen into disuse in England. See: S.W. Mayson, D. French & C. Ryan, *Company Law*, 14th ed. (London: Blackstone, 1997), 163-64. See also H.A.J. Ford, *Principles of Company Law* (Sydney: Butterworths, 1990), 158.

[6] R.S.O. 1990, c. S.5.

surplus generated from its own trading activities. Since the owners of the business may ultimately withdraw any surplus from a business, in effect, this second method is merely a subset of the first method of financing. Third, the business may be funded by borrowing funds or obtaining credit from outsiders (creditors) who have no actual ownership interest in the business. The first method of financing may be described as equity financing, and in the case of a corporation, funding raised by way of equity financing may be described as the equity capital of the corporation.

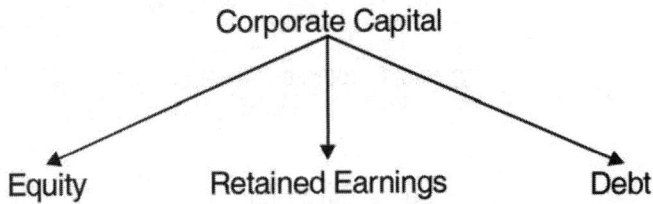

§7.4 In view of the principle of limited liability applicable to corporations, it is necessary to find some method of distinguishing between equity and debt investments to a far greater degree extent than in the case of other business enterprises. In general terms, the equity capital of a corporation is the amount that the shareholders of a corporation have invested in it on a relatively permanent basis, in order to provide the corporation with the basic asset base which it requires in order to conduct its business. In contrast, the debt of the corporation is the amount that the corporation owes to its creditors. Unfortunately, this distinction is not hard and fast, for as the corporation is a separate legal person from the shareholder(s) who owns it, the law permits a shareholder to lend money to the corporation as a creditor as well as to invest in it as a shareholder. Partly due to this possibility, in the modern legal world, the distinction between equity and debt has become blurred.[7] Many types of corporate securities (particularly those involving institutional lenders and investors) possess features of both equity and debt.

§7.5 At the most basic level, a share in the equity stock of a corporation represents a proportionate interest in the corporate entity.[8] The value of certain shares may increase with increases in the value of the corporation. However, there are many types of shares that have a fixed value, and that therefore do not appreciate in value with the corporation. In this respect, they represent a kind of subordinated debt, and indeed in the case of banks and trust companies, indebtedness created under subordinated debentures is treated as a form of "equity" for regulatory purposes. A further distinction between equity and debt is that the interest

---

[7] Discussed in the annotation to *Kippen v. Bongard, Leslie & Co.*, [1977] O.J. No. 154, 1 B.L.R. 57 (H.C.J).
[8] *C.I.R. v. Crossman*, [1937] A.C. 26 at 66 (H.L.), *per* Lord Russell of Killowen, dissenting.

payments due on debt are usually (although not invariably) an obligation which the corporation must pay whether it is profitable or not, whereas dividends on shares depend upon profitability. However, on some types of indebtedness (known as "income bonds") the obligation to pay interest is contingent upon profitability; while a default in the payment of interest on some types of shares may give rise to consequences quite similar to those which ordinarily flow from a default in the payment of a creditor. Although equity is viewed to be long-term investment, it is not uncommon to find even secured indebtedness of very long duration, whereas many "term preferred shares" provide for redemption within a relatively short period.

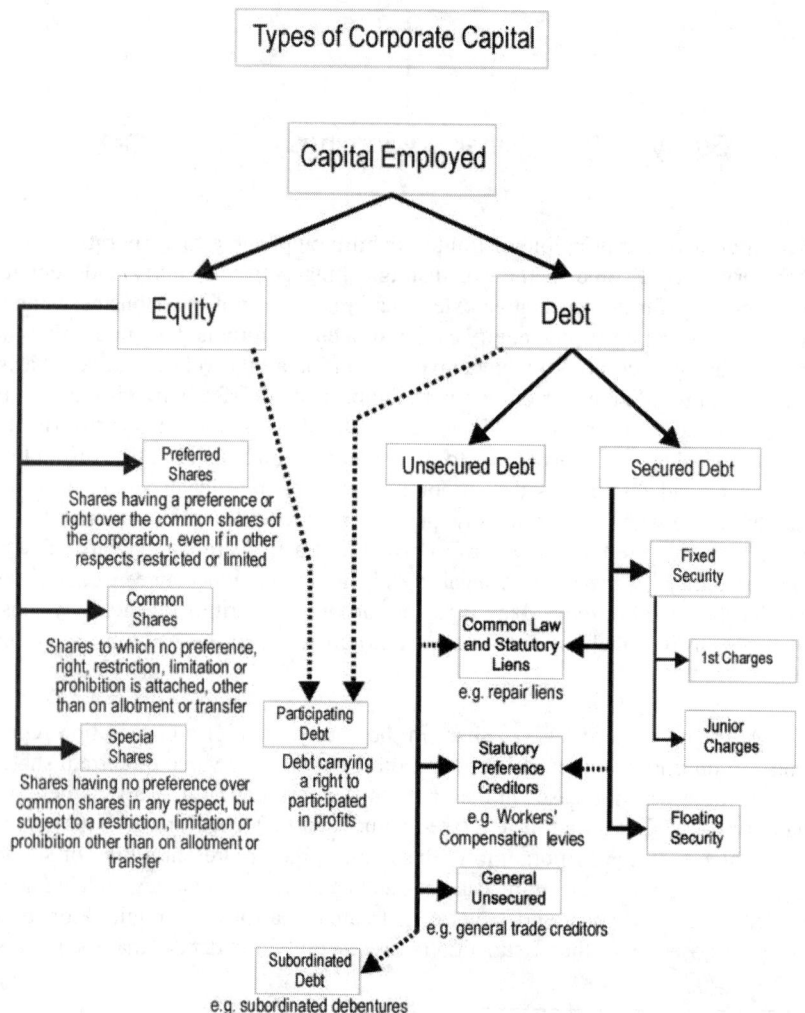

Equity Finance

§7.6 Securities possessing features of both debt and equity investments are known as hybrid securities or mezzanine financing. Where mezzanine financing is employed, limited "ownership" interests may be created in a corporation and assigned to outside investors. Such interests, although structured in the form of an equity interest, are in many respects more in the nature of debt. Alternatively, a creditor may sometimes agree to take a hybrid debt instrument under the terms of which its normal priority entitlement to payment is subordinated to the claims of general creditors, in exchange for the right to participate in profits. In recent years, hybrid securities have played an increasingly important role in corporate financing. Flexible and desirable as hybrid securities may be from a commercial perspective, they often raise complex legal issues that are difficult to resolve.

§7.7 While the distinction between equity and debt has to some extent become blurred, that distinction remains important, due to the large number of legal rules and restrictions that apply to equity interests. First, the equity (share capital) of a corporation must be provided for in the articles of a corporation; debt, in contrast, is purely a matter of contract. Second, while a corporation may normally pay interest on its debt according to the terms agreed between the parties (subject only to the laws governing preferences) and the authority to approve and pay both interest and principal may be delegated to the officers of a corporation, the payment of a dividend on share capital is generally[9] permitted only where the corporation satisfies prescribed solvency and liquidity tests,[10] and may only be made where approved by way of formal resolution[11] on the part of the full board of directors.[12] Third, even greater restrictions apply where part of the stated capital in respect of any class of shares is to be repaid to the holders of those shares.[13]

§7.8 Thus from a legal if not always from a commercial perspective, equity and debt are conceptually distinct. Although the equity interest of the shareholders of a corporation is in a sense a liability, it is not in the nature of a debt owed by the corporation.[14] Under Canadian bankruptcy laws, the obligation of a corporation to repay the equity investments of its shareholders is subordinate to the obligation of the corporation to repay the holders of its debt. The creditors of a corporation have a right to look to the paid-up capital or equity of the corporation as the source from which the corporation will pay its debts,[15] and they have a right to rely on the capital of the corporation remaining intact except for that purpose.[16] The capital of a corporation is a secure fund or safety net. It does not follow from that characterization that the corporation may never impair its

---

[9] *Ontario Business Corporations Act*, R.S.O. 1990, c. B.16 ("OBCA"), s. 39.
[10] OBCA, s. 38(1); *Canada Business Corporations Act*, R.S.C. 1985, c. C-44 ("CBCA"), ss. 42 and 43.
[11] OBCA, s. 38(1); CBCA, s. 43(1).
[12] OBCA, s. 127(3)(*d*); CBCA, s. 115.
[13] See OBCA, s. 24(9) to (11) — reduction of share capital; s. 32 — redemption of share capital; s. 35 — purchase of shares by issuing corporation.
[14] Dennis Keenan, *Smith & Keenan's Company Law*, 7th ed. (London: Pitman Publishing, 1987), 135.
[15] See, generally, *Hospes v. Northwestern Mfg. & Car. Co.*, 48 Minn. 174, 50 N.W. 117 (1895), dealing with the issue of bonus shares for no consideration.
[16] *Re Inrig Shoe Co.* (1924), 27 O.W.N. 110 (S.C. in bankruptcy), *per* Fisher J.

capital in the sense that it must always be maintained intact and topped up by the shareholders should any impairment occur. On the contrary, it is at best a once and for all investment.[17] However, the uses of equity capital are limited to expenditures in connection with the conduct of the business of the corporation, and so, except as authorized by law, it is not available for redistribution among the shareholders of a corporation until the creditors of the corporation have been paid in full.[18] For this reason, as a general rule the capital of a corporation cannot be impaired by the declaration of dividends. In dealing with the capital of the corporation, the directors must respect not only the rights of the shareholders, but also the rights of the creditors of the corporation.[19] The claim of the shareholders with respect to the capital is subordinate to the rights of the creditors. Therefore the directors of the corporation must not permit the capital of the corporation to be used for any purpose other than a capital purpose — that is, for a purpose authorized under the OBCA or CBCA[20] (or, perhaps more to the point, for a purpose inconsistent with the restrictions and prohibitions imposed under those Acts).

§7.9 A further important distinction between equity and debt arises from the differing methods by which each of these types of claim may be enforced. Where debt is unpaid at the time when due, the person who is owed the debt may sue for it, and compel the corporation to pay the amount owed. If the corporation fails to do so, its assets may be seized in execution. A holder of equity has more limited remedies. The only option is to move for the judicial liquidation and wind-up of the corporation, which is not only more time-consuming, but is also an equitable (or discretionary) remedy of the court, and hence, one which will not necessarily be granted in all cases. In recent years, the oppression remedy has also been employed on occasion, with varying degrees of success. However, it too is both discretionary and time consuming in comparison to an action for debt.

---

[17] Indeed, since ss. 23(2) of the OBCA and 25(2) of the CBCA provide that:

(2) Shares issued by a corporation are non-assessable and the holders are not liable to the corporation or to its creditors in respect thereof.

It would be difficult to structure the terms of shares so that any such top-up could be required.

[18] *Trevor v. Whitworth* (1887), 12 App. Cas. 409 at 415 (H.L.), *per* Lord Herschell. Generally speaking, the rule in *Trevor v. Whitworth* cannot be circumvented directly or indirectly, through the use of shell or holding companies and other devices. See, generally, *Barclays Bank plc v. British & Commonwealth Holdings plc*, [1996] 1 B.C.L.C. 1 (C.A.).

[19] *Scottish Insurance Corp. v. Wilson & Clyde Coal Co.*, [1949] A.C. 462 at 486 (H.L.), *per* Lord Simmonds.

[20] *Re Anglo-French Exploration Co.*, [1902] 2 Ch. 845 at 853, *per* Buckley J.; *Trustee of C.G. Plain Ltd. v. Kenley*, [1931] O.R. 75 at 79 (C.A), *per* Hodgins J.A.; *Prudential Assurance Co. v. Chatterly-Whitfield Collieries Co.*, [1949] A.C. 512 at 516 (H.L.), *per* Viscount Maugham at; see also *Scottish Insurance Corp. v. Wilson & Clyde Coal Co.*, [1949] A.C. 462 (H.L.). At one time, there was a widespread view (particularly in the United States) that the equity capital of a corporation constituted a trust fund for the benefit of its creditors. This view was soundly rejected in *Hospes v. Northwestern Mfg. & Car. Co.*, 48 Minn. 174, 50 N.W. 117 (1895).

§7.10 The characterization of a particular investment can be problematic. In *CDIC v. CCB*[21] it was found that a participation agreement was entered into by the governments of Canada and Alberta, the CDIC, and six major banks in an effort to rescue the Canadian Commercial Bank from insolvency. The agreement provided for the sale of a portfolio of assets to the participants for $225 million. Under the terms of the agreement, the participants were indemnified against loss by the CCB in an amount up to their individual shares of the purchase price, and the participant banks were said to be entitled to rank as depositors (*i.e.*, creditors) to the extent of any amount owing to them should the bank be placed in liquidation. It was also agreed that each participant would receive either (a) a proportionate share of any amount received on account of each portfolio asset plus a proportionate share of 50 per cent of the CCB's pre-tax income, or (b) a proportionate share of CCB's pre-tax income plus interest. Thus it was agreed that the $225 million advanced by the participants would be repaid by CCB, and after that repayment, all payments from the portfolio of assets of CCB would cease. So described, the transaction was in effect a loan made in the form of a purchase of doubtful accounts. However, the arrangement also conferred upon the bank a right to subscribe for more than 24 million shares in the CCB at a stipulated price of 25¢ per share. It was argued that the $225 million paid by the participant banks constituted an equity capital investment in the CCB, rather than a loan, given the right conferred upon the banks to purchase shares in the CCB. In giving the judgment of the court, Iacobucci J. held the investment to be a loan. He explained that where the equity features of a transaction are nothing more than supplementary to and not definitive of the essence of the transaction, the court must search for the substance of the transaction, and should not be too easily distracted by aspects which, in reality, are only incidental or secondary in nature to the main thrust of the agreement.[22]

§7.11 In *Royal Bank of Canada v. Central Capital Corp.*,[23] the court was called upon to distinguish between debt and equity within the context of preference share redemption. It was found in that case that the shareholders of an insolvent corporation (Central) had a right of retraction in respect of their shares, entitling them to require the corporation to redeem their shares. The shareholders had each filed a proof of claim with respect to a Plan of Arrangement under the *Companies' Creditors Arrangement Act*,[24] in accordance with the order of the court seized of the CCAA proceeding. The order required all creditors of Central Capital who wished to participate in a newly incorporated company called Canadian Insurance Group Limited ("CIGL") to submit claims by a specified date. The claims of the preferred shareholders were disallowed by the administrator as they were not creditors of Capital. It was argued by the preference shareholders that their right to have the shares retracted accrued before the reorganization, and that as they had exercised this right, their claim against the corporation con-

---

[21] [1992] S.C.J. No. 96, 97 D.L.R. (4th) 385.
[22] *Ibid.*, at 406.
[23] [1996] O.J. No. 359, 88 O.A.C. 161, 26 B.L.R. (2d) 88 (C.A.).
[24] R.S.C. 1985, c. C-36.

stituted a present debt or liability entitling them to rank as creditors.[25] Justice Feldman held that the preferred shareholders' claims were not those of creditors.

§7.12 The case was appealed to the Ontario Court of Appeal. There the majority held that the preferred shares were an equity, not a debt investment. In reaching this conclusion, they noted that the articles of the corporation (and in particular the share terms) provided that the shares would be redeemed only where not "contrary to law". Given the insolvency of Central, it could not lawfully redeem its shares. The articles also provided a continuing right to receive dividends so long as the company could not pay for the shares. Thus the characterization of the shares as equity rather than debt essentially turned upon the rights conferred and restrictions imposed upon those shares under the articles. Significantly, in both the CCB and Central Capital cases, the courts focused primarily on the substance of the transactions, rather than upon the form in which they were cast, or the labels by which the instruments in question were identified. Clearly, therefore, the description that the parties have placed upon a particular security is not conclusive as to its nature.[26] At best, the formal designation of a particular security as debt or equity does no more than create a rebuttable presumption that the security in question possesses the character formally described.

§7.13 It follows that while the distinction between equity and debt is primarily a legal one, it is not an abstract question of legal theory. As indicated above, the character of a particular investment can have important practical consequences, not only in the debtor and creditor context, but also for tax purposes. In *Slappey Drive Industrial Park v. U.S.*[27] Goldberg Cir. J. identified a wider range of (non-exhaustive) factors that the courts should take into account in deciding whether a particular investment is in the nature of debt or equity, namely:[28]

- the names given to the certificates evidencing the indebtedness;
- the presence or absence of a fixed maturity date;
- the source of principal repayment;
- the right to enforce payment of principal and interest;
- the status of the contribution in relation to regular corporate creditors;
- the intent of the parties;
- thin or otherwise inadequate capitalization;
- the identity of interest between creditor and investor;
- the source of interest payment;

---

[25] See, generally, *Re East Chilliwack Agricultural Cooperative*, [1989] B.C.J. No. 705, 74 C.B.R. (N.S.) 1 (C.A.).
[26] See the dissenting judgment of Finlayson J.A. in *Royal Bank of Canada v. Central Capital Corp*, [1996] O.J. No. 359, 26 B.L.R. (2d) 88 at 105 (C.A.).
[27] 561 F.2d 572 (5th Cir. 1977).
[28] See also *Estate of Mixon v. U.S.*, 464 F.2d 394 (5th Cir. 1972).

- the ability of the corporation to obtain loans from outside lending institutions;
- the extent to which the advance was used to acquire capital assets;
- the failure of the debtor to repay on the date due or to seek a postponement.

Other factors that might also be considered include the rigour with which the investor enforces its rights (a willingness to tolerate breaches of those rights suggesting that the relationship is not one of a debtor-creditor),[29] whether the investment was used to finance the initial (or start-up) operations of the enterprise,[30] and the rate of interest payable and the question of whether interest payment will be suspended in given circumstances, for "a true lender is concerned with interest".[31] The question of the true character of an investment ultimately turns upon the intent of the parties, as evidenced not only in the terms in which they have drafted the instrument of investment, but also in the manner in which they have conducted themselves with respect to the investment.

(ii) Working Capital Distinguished

§7.14 The normal meaning usually associated with the term "the capital of a corporation" is the proceeds received by the corporation from the sale of its capital stock.[32] However, as noted above, the word "capital" is used in numerous different ways both in legislation (and other relevant legal contexts) and also by commerce, so that the meaning of the term can often vary widely from one statute or context to another.[33] One particular special meaning of capital is worthy of specific mention. The term "working capital" is often used to describe the money used in the corporation's business to fund its ongoing operations, regardless of the source of that money, although it is not a term that has an exact legal meaning.[34] In contrast to the "shareholder's equity" account on the balance sheet of a corporation, the working capital of a corporation is neither an income nor an asset account, but rather is the result obtained through the off-setting of two accounts: it is the difference between the current assets and the current liabilities of the corporation,[35] and thus approximates to the corporation's projected net cash flow. Given the transitory nature of working capital — describing only the pool of net liquid assets at any time — it is not equity or capital in the sense that "capital" is used in this chapter.

---

[29] *Slappey Drive Industrial Park v. U.S.*, 561 F.2d 572 (5th Cir. 1977), *per* Goldberg Cir. J.
[30] See, generally, *Plantation Patterns Inc. v. Commissioner*, 464 F.2d 712 (5th Cir. 1972); *Acqualane Shores Inv. v. Commissioner*, 269 F.2d 116 (5th. Cir. 1959).
[31] *Curry v. U.S.*, 396 F.2d 630 at 634 (5th Cir. 1968) *certiorari* denied 393 U.S. 967.
[32] *Toronto v. Consumers' Gas Co.*, [1927] 4 D.L.R. 102 at 105 (P.C.), *per* Duff J.
[33] See, for instance, *City Parking Canada Ltd. v. Ontario (Min. of Revenue)*, [1973] O.J. No. 2324, 1 O.R. (2d) 425 (C.A.) as to the meaning of capital under the *Corporations Tax Act*.
[34] *Kennedy v. Acadia Pulp & Paper Mills Co.* (1905), 38 N.S.R. 291 at 206-07 (C.A.), *per* Graham C.J.
[35] *South Hinds Water Co. v. Mississippi Public Service Comm.*, 422 So. 2d 275 at 283 (Miss. S.C.), the general formula being: current assets – current liabilities = working capital.

(iii) Fixed and Circulating Capital

§7.15 Confusion over the relationship between working capital and true capital arises in part due to a distinction often drawn in the old case law between the fixed and circulating capital of a corporation. In *Ammonia Soda Co. v. Chamberlain*,[36] Swinfen Eady L.J. defined fixed capital to mean:

> That which a company retains in the shape of assets upon which the subscribed capital has been expended, which assets either themselves produce income independent by of any further action by the company, or, being retained by the company are made use of to reproduce income or gain profits.

For its part, the circulating capital of the corporation was defined to mean:

> [A] portion of the subscribed capital of the company intended to be used by being temporarily parted with and circulated in business in the form of money, goods, or other assets, and which or the proceeds of which are intended to return to the company with an increment and are intended to be used again and again, and to always return with some accretion. Thus the capital with which a trader buys goods circulates; he parts with it and with the goods bought by it, intending to receive it back again with profit arising from the resale of the goods.

These two concepts of fixed and circulating capital were purely notional and transitory. The distinction then was relevant in the determination of whether a company was in a position to pay dividends. Unfortunately, while appearing conceptually clear, the distinction was notoriously difficult to draw in practice. A corporation might sell a capital asset and purchase circulating assets in exchange; it might use the profits derived from the sale of circulating assets to purchase capital assets such as plant and equipment. As will be explained later in this chapter, under the OBCA and CBCA the right to pay dividends no longer turns upon profitability, but rather upon solvency and liquidity. Thus the distinction between fixed and circulating capital, although useful for some accounting and analytical purposes, is no longer of any particular significance under Ontario law.

B. SHARES

§7.16 Civil corporations are often described as falling into one of two classes: corporations with share capital and those without share capital. For the most part, corporations with share capital are essentially profit oriented enterprises, while corporations without share capital are non-profit in nature. Corporations with share capital constitute by far the largest in number of corporations and in the business area; they fully occupy the field. The share capital of a corporation is the capital investment of the shareholders in the corporation. It is the amount for which the shareholders are at greatest risk. In the event of the liquidation of a corporation, the claims of the shareholders with respect to their shares are deferred to the claims of the creditors of the corporation.[37] Ordinarily, the share-

---

[36] [1918] 1 Ch. 266 at 296-97 (C.A.).
[37] *Re Central Capital Corp.*, [1996] O.J. No. 359, 132 D.L.R. (4th) 223 at 237-38 (C.A.), *per* Finlayson J.A. dissenting.

holders of a corporation cannot recover the amount invested by them in the share capital of the corporation except by way of the transfer of the shares.[38] Even so, in many cases, the articles of incorporation of a corporation will provide that one class of shares will be repaid in priority to another class. Such provisions are perfectly lawful, because they do not affect the rights of creditors. However, the articles may not confer upon shareholders a prior claim against the property of a corporation over the claims of its creditors.

§7.17 Many definitions have been offered for the term "share." While the most frequently cited definitions are generally similar, there is a certain difference in focus or emphasis in the approach that each takes. For instance, *Black's Law Dictionary*[39] defines the term "share" to mean a part or definite portion of a thing owned by a number of persons in common, and thus a share in a corporation may be said to constitute an ownership interest in the corporation in the form of a definite portion of the subscribed capital of the corporation, so that the focus is on membership and ownership. Alternatively, the term "share" has been defined to mean a unit of measure of the interest of a member of a corporation, first for the purpose of determining the potential liability of the member and second for the purpose of determining the member's right of participation in the capital and income of the corporation, but also consisting of a series of mutual covenants entered into by all the shareholders of the corporation.[40] In this definition, the focus is on liability and rights of participation. A share has also been described as a fractional part of the capital of a corporation which confers upon the holder a certain right to a proportionate part of the assets of the corporation, whether by way of dividend or of distribution of the assets in a winding-up.[41] It is not a sum of money, but is an interest measured by a sum of money, and made up of various rights contained in the share terms, including the right to receive a sum of money (*e.g.*, on the liquidation of the corporation or upon redemption of the shares), which may be greater than or less than the amount of the original investment.[42] Under this definition, the focus is on the relationship between the monetary value of the share (its stated capital) and the entitlement of its holder.

§7.18 Under each of the preceding definitions, it is clear that a share is a type of chose in action,[43] in the nature of intangible[44] personal property.[45] Shares have

---

[38] *Ibid.*, at 251 *per* Weiler J.A.
[39] 6th ed. (St. Paul, Minn., 1990).
[40] *Borland's Trustee v. Steel Brothers & Co.*, [1901] 1 Ch. 279 at 288, *per* Farwell J.
[41] *Bradbury v. English Sewing Cotton Co.*, [1923] A.C. 744 at 767 (H.L.), *per* Lord Wrenbury.
[42] *Borland's Trustee v. Steel Brothers & Co.*, [1901] 1 Ch. 279 at 288, *per* Farwell J.
[43] *Kiely v. Smyth*, [1879] O.J. No. 236, 27 Gr. 220 at 226 (Ch.), *per* Spragge C.
[44] *MacDougall v. Johnson*, [1946] 3 W.W.R. 143 (B.C.S.C.); *Colonial Bank v. Whinney* (1886), 11 App. Cas. 426 (H.L.). However, although the shares themselves are intangible, an equitable transfer occurs by the physical delivery of the certificate: *per* Wilson J. at 148 in *MacDougall v. Johnson*.
[45] OBCA, s. 41. There is no equivalent provision in the CBCA. As a form of property, shares may be sold or otherwise alienated. The prospect of such dealings in shares tends to connote trading through a stock exchange, but in practice only a small percentage of companies are listed for trading on any exchange. In Canada (as in other countries with advanced economies), recent years have witnessed a thinning out in the number of recognized stock exchanges. Canada's first stock ex-

also been described as fractions of potential interest in the assets and active life of a corporation.[46] However described, it is necessary to distinguish between the share and the tangible share certificate which represents it.[47] As noted earlier in the chapter, a shareholder's interest differs from that of a holder of a debt security. In the case of a debt security, the relationship between the corporation and the holder is that of debtor and creditor. In the case of a share, the relationship between the corporation and its holder is one of membership and ownership. The right of ownership may be limited to a stated amount; the membership may be qualified in the sense that the share confers only the most limited say in the

---

change, the Montreal Stock Exchange, was incorporated in 1874, followed by the Toronto Stock Exchange, which was incorporated under a special Act of the Province of Ontario in 1878. For many years, rival exchanges operated in a number of major cities across the country.

In 1999, Canada's stock exchanges agreed to restructure their operations along lines of market specialization. The Toronto Stock Exchange (TSE) became the only exchange for the trading of senior equities. The Montreal Exchange agreed to focus on the trading of derivatives, and the Canadian Venture Exchange (CDNX), created through a merger of the Vancouver and Alberta (and later Winnipeg) stock exchanges, took responsibility for the trading of junior equities. The Toronto Stock Exchange Group now includes two distinct exchanges: the main Toronto Stock Exchange (TSX), which is Canada's primary exchange and remains the focus of senior equity trading, and also the Toronto Venture Exchange, which is discussed below. Together, these two exchanges represent the third largest stock market in North America, and eighth largest in the world in terms of market capitalization. As of September 2005, there were more than 1,500 issuers listed on the TSX and another 2,200 venture issuers listed on the TSXV. The TSX has the strictest listing requirements in Canada, and all top Canadian companies are listed on the TSX. The TSX is regulated by the Ontario Securities Commission. The TSXV is subject to joint regulatory oversight by the Alberta Securities Commission and the British Columbia Securities Commission.

The Montreal Curb Market was created in 1926 as a stock exchange specializing in stocks that were considered to be too speculative or junior to be traded on the Bourse de Montréal. As these companies matured, trading in their shares was transferred to the Bourse. In 1953, the Montreal Curb Market changed its name to Canadian Stock Exchange. In 1974, the Canadian Stock Exchange merged with the Bourse de Montréal (or Montreal Stock Exchange). In 1982, the name was changed to the Montreal Exchange to reflect the growing importance of financial instruments other than stocks (primarily options and futures) being traded through the exchange. The Canadian Venture Exchange (CDNX) was created in 1999 through the merger of the Vancouver Stock Exchange (VSE) and the Alberta Stock Exchange (ASE). It specialized in small, resource exploration companies and high technology companies. The Winnipeg Stock Exchange and the equities market of the Bourse de Montréal were also later merged into the CDNX. In May 2001 the TSE acquired full ownership of the CDNX, with the result that all equity trading was consolidated into the TSX Group. In April 2002 the CDNX was renamed the TSX Venture Exchange.

Other key exchanges in the Canadian securities industry are as follows: In 2004 the Ontario Securities Commission recognized the Canadian Trading and Quotation System Inc. (CNQ) as a stock exchange. It provides an Internet-based quotation and trade reporting system for companies that cannot meet the listing requirements of the Toronto Stock Exchange and TSX Venture Exchange or that do not wish to list on either of those exhanges. In addition, NASDAQ Canada (a wholly owned subsidiary of The NASDAQ Stock Market Inc.) originally operated out of Montreal, where it commenced business in November 2000. However, since 2004, Nasdaq Canada's operations have been now run out of New York. Finally, the Winnipeg Commodity Exchange (WCE), operates Canada's national agricultural futures and options exchange. This exchange can be traced back to 1887, when the Winnipeg Grain & Produce Exchange was created.

[46] Shares are simply fractions of potential interest in the assets and active life of the company: *Zwicker v. Stanbury*, [1953] 2 S.C.R. 438 at 439, *per* Rand J.
[47] *European & North American Railway v. McLeod* (1875), 16 N.B.R. 3 at 82 (C.A.), *per* Allen J. *Gray v. Gray*, [1944] O.W.N. 399 (M.C.).

running of the corporation; but no matter how the share may be structured, the holder stands in a fundamentally different relationship to the corporation and enjoys wholly different rights than would be the case if the holder held even a subordinated debt security instead.

§7.19 Each share of a corporation constitutes a separate, fractional part of the authorized capital of the corporation and is issued from that authorized capital — the authorized capital in corporations subject to the OBCA, the CBCA and similar regimes being the classes and any maximum number of shares of each class that the corporation is authorized to issue under its articles.[48] A share confers upon its holder a defined right to a proportionate share of the assets of the corporation. The profits of a corporation are available for distribution as dividends; any residual profits of the corporation not so distributed and any capital remaining after payment of the creditors of the corporation may be distributed among the shareholders in accordance with their respective rights at the time of the winding-up of the corporation. But in these respects, the shares of a corporation are a right of claim for dividend and distribution only. They confer no right or title in the underlying assets of the corporation themselves. The property of the corporation belongs to the corporation alone, not to its shareholders.[49] The aggregate of all shares together if collected into the hands of a single person does not constitute the shareholder the owner of the property of the corporation.[50] Instead, the share is simply a property interest in the capital of the corporation itself.

§7.20 The location of the company is not tied to its shareholder(s) nor to the physical location of the assets with which it carries on business. Much as an individual may reside in one country and own assets in another, a corporation may carry on business elsewhere than the place in which it is incorporated. For instance, in *Lovibond v. Grand Truck Railway Co. of Canada*,[51] the plaintiff was a resident of England who owned shares in the Grand Trunk Railway, a company incorporated in Canada and having the bulk of its assets there, along with its executive offices. However, the share registry was kept in London, England, where the principal office of the company was also established and where meetings of its directors and shareholders took place. The shares of the corporation (including those of the plaintiff) were expropriated under Canadian legislation. The plaintiff contended that the statute did not extend to certain assets of the company which were located in the United States or to the shares on the London registry, which he argued should be regarded as being situate in Eng-

---

[48] CBCA, s. 6(1)(c); standard form of articles under the OBCA. Since the OBCA and the CBCA now permit corporations to provide in their articles that the authorized capital shall be unlimited, the authorized capital rule is no longer the force that it once was.

[49] *Reider v. Sair*, [1922] 2 W.W.R. 1271, aff'd [1923] 1 W.W.R. 307 (Sask. C.A.); see also *National Trust Co. v. Gilbert*, [1921] 1 W.W.R. 359 at 360 (Sask. C.A.), *per* Newlands J.A.

[50] *Bradbury v. English Sewing Cotton Co.*, [1923] A.C. 744 at 767 (H.L.), *per* Lord Wrenbury; *Lovibond v. G.T.R. & C.N.R.*, [1939] O.R. 305 (C.A.); *Zwicker v. Turnbull Estate*, [1953] 2 S.C.R. 438.

[51] [1939] O.J. No. 473, [1939] O.R. 305 at 326-27 (C.A.), *per* Masten J.A.

land. It was held that the plaintiff possessed no property or right to the American physical assets. As for the shares, the company itself was a Canadian company incorporated in Canada. The entry of certain shares on a registry maintained in England did not divest the shares of their Canadian character or make those shares foreign property. The London registry was nothing more than a notation of ownership.

§7.21 As shares are a chose in action,[52] the shares held by a person may be the subject of an equitable assignment.[53] Such an assignment may be good as against the assignor's execution creditors even though the assignee has failed to complete the transfer of title by recording the transfer on the books of the corporation.[54] By statute,[55] shares in a corporation may also be seized in execution.[56] In Ontario, the procedure for seizing shares in execution is set out in sections 14 and 16 of the *Execution Act*. Subsection 14(1) provides:

> 14.(1)The interest of an execution debtor in a security or security entitlement may be seized by the sheriff in accordance with sections 47 to 51 of the *Securities Transfer Act, 2006*.

The procedure for effecting seizure is essentially by way of notice to the issuer, rather than by way of seizure of the share certification. Thus subsection 14(2) provides:

> 14.(2) If a seizure under subsection (1) is by notice to an issuer of securites intermediary, the seizure becomes effective when the issues or securities intermediary has had a reasonable opportunity to act on the seizure, having regard to the time and manner of receipt of the notice.

§7.22 Compliance with the statutory procedure is mandatory: no other approach to seizure is effective.[57] However, it appears that share certificates (rather than the shares themselves) may be seized in execution in the same manner as any other property, at least where the certificate is in "street form", and seizure may be effected at any bank, trust company, brokerage or other depository at which it is located.[58] Even when share certificates in street form are seized, it is necessary to notify the issuer of the seizure to enjoy the full protection of section 14 (*e.g.*,

---

[52] OBCA, s. 41; but consider *Colonial Bank v. Whinney* (1886), 11 App. Cas. 426 at 434 (H.L.), *per* Lord Blackburn.
[53] *Bank of N.T. Butterfield & Son Ltd. v. Golinksy*, [1926] A.C. 733 at 736 (P.C.), *per* Viscount Haldane.
[54] *Bank of N.T. Butterfield & Son Ltd. v. Golinsky*, [1926] A.C. 733 (P.C.).
[55] See s. 15 of the *Execution Act*, R.S.O. 1990, c. E. 24, which formerly provided:

> 15. If a sheriff seizes the shares of an execution debtor in a private company, he or she shall first offer them for sale to the other shareholders ... and if none of them will purchase the shares for a reasonable price, the sheriff may then offer the debtor's interest therein for sale to the public generally and sell and convey to the highest bidder.

Shares were not exigible at common law: *Morton v. Cowan*, [1894] O.J. No. 168, 25 O.R. 529 at 534 (C.A.), *per* Armour J.; *Malouf v. Labad* (1912), 3 O.W.R. 1235 at 1236 (Div. Ct.), *per* Riddell J.
[56] See for instance, *Sinclair v. Blue Top Brewing Co.*, [1947] 4 D.L.R. 561 (S.C.C.).
[57] *R. v. Spiers*, [1896] B.C.J. No. 49, 4 B.C.R. 388 at 395 (S.C.), *per* Davies C.J.
[58] *Re Patmore*, [1962] B.C.J. No. 20, 39 W.W.R. 460 at 462 (S.C.), *per* Sullivan J. A certificate is in street-form when it is endorsed for transfer by the holder.

with respect to the subsequent payment of dividends).[59] Subsection 14(3) specifies the place at which such service may be made:

> 14.(3) Every seizure and sale made by the sheriff shall include all dividends, distributions, interest and other rights to payment or otherwise organized under Ontario law, or in respect of the security entitlement and, after the seizure becomes effective, the issuer or securities intermediary shall not pay the dividends, distributions or interest or give effect to other rights to payment to or on behalf of anyone except the sheriff or a person who acquires or takes the security or security entitlement from the sheriff.

Subsection 14(4) contemplates a deferral of effect where there is more than one place at which service may be made under subsection (3):

> 14.(4) In this section and sections 15, 16 and 19, "endorsement", "entitlement order", "instruction", "issuer", "securites intermediary", "security" and "security entitlement" have the meaings given to such terms in the *Securities Transfer Act, 2006*.

The Act does not deal with the manner of effecting sale in the case of a non-private company, but subsection 14(5) does specify the mode of proceeding after sale. Where the corporation fails to comply, a court may direct a corporation by order to adjust its share records to reflect the sale.[60] The corporation's board and officers are not obliged or entitled to review what the sheriff has done to determine whether he or she has followed the correct sale procedure or was properly authorized to seize the shares.[61]

§7.23 Section 15 of the *Execution Act* was revised in 2006 and now sets out a special rule applicable to shares in a private company[62] provides:

> 15.(1) If an execution debtor's interest in a security or security entitlement is seized by a sheriff, the sheriff shall be deemed to be the appropriate person under the *Securities Transfer Act, 2006* for the purposes of dealing with or disposing of the seized property and, for the duration of the seizure, the execution debter is not the appropriate person under that Act for the purposes of dealing with or disposing of the seized property.
>
> (2) Upon seizure of an execution debtor's interest in a security or security entitlement, the sheriff may,
>
> (a) do anything that would otherwise have to be done by the execution debtor; or
>
> (b) execute or endorse any document that would otherwise have to be executed or endorsed by the exection debtor.
>
> (3) If the sheriff makes or originates an endorsement, instruction or entitlement order as the appropriate person pursuant to subsection (1), the sheriff shall provide the issuer or securities intermediary with a certificate of the sheriff stating that the

---

[59] *Duncan v. Duncan*, [1984] B.C.J. No. 1875, 27 A.C.W.S. (2d) 471 (S.C.).
[60] *Goodwin v. Ottawa and Prescott Railway Co.*, [1863] O.J. No. 143, 13 U.C.C.P. 254 (C.P).
[61] *Guillot v. Sandwich & Windsor Gravel Road Co.*, [1867] O.J. No. 1, 26 U.C.Q.B. 246, at 250, per Draper C.J.
[62] Presumably this term has the same meaning in the *Execution Act* as in the *Securities Act*, but the point never appears to have been addressed.

sheriff has the authority under this Act to make that endorsement, instruction or entitlement order and any subsequent endorsements, instructions and entitlement orders in respect of the same execution debt.

§7.24 In Ontario, it has been held an execution creditor[63] or assignee of shares of a corporation can only take whatever interest the debtor may possess.[64] Where the shares of a corporation cannot be transferred without the consent of the directors of the corporation, the assignee or any purchaser of shares seized and sold under an execution cannot compel the corporation to register them in his or her name. If the directors refuse their consent in good faith, the only remedy is to have a receiver appointed to receive all dividends and other distributions payable under or with respect to the shares.[65] A different view was put forward in British Columbia by Anderson J. in the *Associates Finance Co. v. Webber*.[66] He held that when the Sheriff seizes and sells the shares in a private corporation that are registered in the name of a judgment debtor, the only effect of a restriction upon share transfer contained in the articles of association may be to give the remaining shareholders the privilege, in accordance with the expressed terms, of purchasing from the Sheriff. A discretion granted to the board to refuse to register an intended transferee is ineffective against the Sheriff and the purchaser from him. In that case, the articles of the company (the equivalent to the by-laws of an OBCA or CBCA corporation) provided that:

> The directors may refuse to register as a member any transferee of shares of whom they do not approve.

Justice Anderson relied upon the Australian decision in *Ex p. Trevascus*,[67] in which Stawell C.J., stated:

> The power of the company to decline to register a transfer, can apply only to a voluntary transfer, not to a transfer *in invitum*. The conditions must not be construed so as to defeat the common law rights of a judgment creditor, unless the words of the Act leave no alternative. The condition allowing the company to decline to register a transfer by a shareholder indebted to it, applies only to an indebtedness qua member. The whole purview of the Act is confined to matters among the members inter se. It was never intended to give the company, as to debts outside the constitution of the company, a preferential claim above all other creditors.

The logic of this paragraph is not especially compelling. Requiring the other shareholders to accept the purchaser into membership the corporation interferes with their rights. Why their rights should be prejudicially affected, and why they

---

[63] An execution creditor will take the shares subject to any perfected security interest: *Re Montgomery & Wrights Ltd.*, [1917] O.J. No. 133, 38 O.L.R. 335 at 336 (H.C.), *per* Middleton J.
[64] *Sinclair v. Blue Top Brewing Co.*, [1947] 4 D.L.R. 561 at 566 (S.C.C.), *per* Estey J.; but see *Bigley v. Haffey*, [1941] O.W.N. 261 (C.A.). As to where execution on the shares may be levied, see *Malouf v. Labad* (1912), 3 O.W.R. 1235 and the cases cited below under "Location (Situs) of Shares."
[65] *Phillips v. La Paloma Sweets Ltd.*, [1921] O.J. No. 21, 51 O.L.R. 125 at 127-28 (H.C.), *per* Middleton J.
[66] (1972), 28 D.L.R. (3d) 673 (B.C.S.C.).
[67] (1879), 5 V.L.R. 195 at 199 (S.C. Law).

should be compelled to enter into a commercial relationship without their consent, merely because another shareholder is the subject of an adverse judgment is far from clear. The argument that the other shareholders are given the right to purchase the judgment debtor's shares is beside the point: if the judgment debtor is not entitled to require the other shareholders to buy out his (or her) interest, why should his judgment creditor? There is no particular reason to favor the rights of the judgment creditor to payment, over those of the other members of the corporation to have control over their own business dealings. In recent years, numerous cases have referred to the partnership character of a private company. Partnership is a relationship of trust and utmost good faith. Compelling the members of a corporation to accept a new shareholder runs counter to that relationship. It is, of course, true that the satisfaction of judgments is an important goal of public policy. However, it is not the only goal, nor the most important goal.

(i) Location (Situs) of Shares

§7.25 The location of the share certificates relating to particular shares is the place in which they are to be found from time to time. However, the location of shares of a corporation for the purpose of determining a dispute as to their ownership is the domicile of the corporation, for that is where the court has jurisdiction over the corporation, and power to order a rectification of its register, where rectification is necessary, and to enforce that order by personal decree against it.[68] Thus where share certificates relating to shares in a corporation having its head office in Canada are located outside of Canada, seizure of the shares in Canada is effective irrespective of where the share certificates are located. The shares themselves constitute a bundle of legal rights conceptually distinct from the physical share certificate,[69] and therefore could have a different location from the certificates even where those shares are not transferable within Canada but only at a registry elsewhere.[70] The dominant consideration for the purpose of determining the location of the shares (as opposed to the share certificates) is the jurisdiction to which the corporation itself is subject. If the corporation is domiciled within Canada it is subject to the jurisdiction of a Canadian court, and thus the shares are situate within Canada, irrespective of where the share certificates may be located.[71]

---

[68] *Braun Estate v. Canada (Custodian)*, [1944] S.C.R. 339 at 346; *Spitz v. Canada (Secretary of State)*, [1939] 2 D.L.R. 546 (Ex. Ct.); see also *Bitter v. Canada (Secretary of State)*, [1944] Ex. C.R. 61; *Schiller Estate v. Canada (Minister of National Revenue)*, [1969] S.C.J. No. 42, [1969] C.T.C. 348; *Treasurer of Ontario v. Blondé*, [1941] O.R. 227, aff'd [1946] 3 W.W.R. 683 (P.C.); *Brown v. Beleggings-Societeit N.V.*, [1961] O.J. No. 598, [1961] O.R. 815 (H.C.); *Hunt Estate v. Canada*, [1966] C.T.C. 474, aff'd [1968] S.C.J. No. 18, [1968] S.C.R. 323.
[69] *Hunt Estate v. Canada*, [1966] C.T.C. 474 at 479, per Jackett J., aff'd [1968] S.C.J. No. 18, [1968] S.C.R. 323.
[70] *Braun Estate v. Canada (Custodian)*, [1944] Ex. C.R. 30, aff'd [1944] S.C.R. 339 at 345, especially *per* Kerwin J.
[71] *Hunt Estate v. Canada*, [1966] C.T.C. 474, aff'd [1968] S.C.J. No. 18, [1968] S.C.R. 323 at 345, *per* Abbot J.

(ii) Classification of Shares

§7.26 The starting presumption with respect to the shares of a corporation is that all shares of the corporation are in all respects equal[72] and that (subject to such differences as flow naturally and inevitably from differences in the extent of their respective shareholdings), the holders of the shares of a corporation are entitled to be treated alike. Equality is equity.[73] However, it is possible to defeat this presumption of equality by dividing shares into different classes or series. Under the OBCA and the CBCA, all shares in a corporation are classified — that is, all shares must belong to one and only one class of shares in the corporation. All shares in a corporation are designated, identified and described in their rights, terms, conditions and restrictions on a class-by-class basis. There is no upper limit on the number of classes of share possible, and accordingly a corporation may have as many classes of share as its incorporators (or shareholders) consider necessary or desirable — although in practice very few corporations possess more than four classes of share.

§7.27 Under the present OBCA and CBCA, where a corporation has only one class of shares, the rights of the holders thereof are equal in all respects and include the right to vote at all meetings of the shareholders and to receive the remaining property of the corporation upon dissolution.[74] Put another way, unless there is some provision in the share terms that would suggest the contrary, the holder of a share is seen to be a part owner of the corporation that issued the share, and as such is entitled to a full right of participation in the corporation, including a proportionate say in the selection of the management of the corporation and in all other matters to be decided by the shareholders as members of the corporation, together with an unrestricted right to participate in dividends and upon distribution of the remaining property of a corporation upon dissolution.

§7.28 When a corporation has more than one class of share, each class constitutes a distinct subdivision within the total share capital of the corporation. The shares belonging to each class may, but need not, have rights, terms, conditions and restrictions attached to them that distinguish them from the shares belonging to other classes. Indeed, the goal of creating such distinctions is one purpose behind issuing different classes of share — although it is not the only one, for paid-up capital considerations under the *Income Tax Act*[75] will often justify the issue of two or more classes of share. As discussed in greater detail below, there may be further subdivisions within a class of shares, which are known as series. In the corporate law legislation of the United States, the distinction between classes and series of shares is often obscure. Under the OBCA and the CBCA a clear distinction is drawn. Series are subdivisions within a class, and limits are drawn on the extent to which one series of shares may have rights, terms, condi-

---

[72] *Birch v. Cropper* (1889), 14 App. Cas. 525 at 543 (H.L.), *per* Lord Macnaghten.
[73] *FFM Holdings Ltd. v. Lilydale Cooperative Ltd.*, [1998] A.J. No. 1491, [1999] 4 W.W.R. 211 (Q.B.).
[74] OBCA, s. 22(3).
[75] R.S.C. 1985, c. 1 (5th Supp.).

tions and restrictions that prefer it over another series within the same class. Where the articles provide for more than one class of shares, the rights, privileges, restrictions and conditions attaching to each class of shares must be set out in the articles. Where there are two or more classes of shares, the right to vote at all meetings of the shareholders and the right to receive the remaining property of the corporation upon dissolution must be attached to at least one class of shares, but both rights need not be attached to the same class.[76] Therefore, in order to determine the rights to which shares are entitled, it is necessary to look at the articles to see what specific rights, privileges, conditions and restrictions are attached to each class of shares.

§7.29 It is quite common for corporate articles to provide for two or more different classes of share, and for the holders of each different class of shares to have very different rights. The practice of creating different classes or series of shares with different rights, privileges, conditions and restrictions attached to each class appears to have originated in England around 1830. In general, where there are two or more classes of shares, it is very unusual for all classes of shares in a corporation to carry exactly the same rights, and when all is said and done, some classes or series of shares will seem to confer greater rights than others. Often, some shares of a corporation will be designated as "common" while others will bear the label "preference", "special", or "restricted", as a kind of shorthand notice (albeit an extremely inexact one) of the relative priority of the rights conferred. In the case of corporations that are not offering corporations (or "reporting issuers" to use the terminology of the *Securities Act*),[77] these designations no longer have any particular legal significance. However, in the case of offering corporations, the use of these terms is limited in each case to shares that meet certain specified criteria.

(1) Common and Preference Defined

§7.30 In Canadian and American corporate finance practice, the term "common shares" has traditionally been used to describe shares that confer a full right of participation in the corporation that issues them,[78] and thus unrestricted rights to participate in dividends and in the distribution of the remaining property of a corporation upon dissolution. If all the company shares are issued without differentiation among them, then all of those shares are considered to be common shares. Common shares are often referred to as "equity shares" because they are entitled to the equity of the company, that is the residue remaining after the payment of all,

- profits after all prior claims, such as the loan interest and preference dividends; and

---

[76] OBCA, s. 22(4).
[77] R.S.O. 1990, c. S.5. The term "distributing corporation" is now used in the CBCA.
[78] In England, the term "ordinary shares" is used. The terms "common shares" and "ordinary shares" are synonymous.

- capital after repayment of all prior claims as to capital, such as tax, creditors, loan capital, and (generally) preference shares.

§7.31 Since the holders of common shares may only be paid dividends or repaid capital after the satisfaction of other claims against the company, ordinary shares are more risky than loans or other forms of debt investment, and are even more risky than preference shares. However, common shares give the investor who holds them, as a part owner of the business, an unlimited right to share in the profits and growth of the company. Across the economy as a whole, the total return on common shares generally runs significantly in excess of inflation, and (over the long term) other types of investment.

§7.32 The present working definition of "common share" is a legacy of the earlier legal definitions of the term, such as that found in subsection 26(1) of the former OBCA,[79] which provided:

> 26.(1) The common shares of a corporation shall be shares to which there is attached no preference, right, condition, restriction, limitation or prohibition set out in the articles of the corporation, other than a restriction on the allotment, issue or transfer.

In contrast, the term "preference share" has been used to describe special shares[80] to which was attached some preferential right which caused the share in question to rank ahead of the common shares of a corporation in some way. Thus subsection 26(4) of the former OBCA provided:[81]

> 26.(4) No class of special shares shall be designated as preference shares or by words of like import, unless that class has attached thereto a preference or right over the common shares.

Thus although all preference shares were special shares, some special shares could not properly be described as preference shares, because they lacked the preference or right over the common shares of the corporation. Typical preferences include

- a prior right to receive a dividend (usually at a fixed rate, such as a percentage of par value or alternatively at a stated amount; preferential dividend rights might be cumulative or non-cumulative);
- priority in the repayment of capital upon winding-up;[82]
- special and quite often separate class voting rights, either generally with respect to all matters to be decided by shareholders, or with respect to the election of directors, or concerning some matter of particular importance, such as (in the case of privatized former Crown corporations), a change in the busi-

---

[79] R.S.O. 1970, c. 53.
[80] That is, shares that were not common shares.
[81] Prior to the enactment of this provision, the governing definition appears to have been that provided in *Rubas v. Parkinson*, [1929] O.J. No. 22, 64 O.L.R. 87 at 91 (C.A.), *per* Masten J.A.
[82] See, for instance, *Deacon v. Kemp Manure Spreader* [1907] O.J. No. 37, 15 O.L.R. 149 at 155 (Div. Ct.), *per* Anglin J.

ness of the corporation, any sale of a significant portion of its undertaking, or in the location of the head office;

- a right of redemption or retraction, either at a specified time or in specified circumstances, as, for instance, upon the death of the holder;
- conversion rights;
- poison pill rights, which augment the rights attached to the shares in the event of a take-over bid.

An individual "golden share" may sometimes be encountered, that allows the holder of that single share some sort of a special class right to veto specified types of corporate act or change in its basic constitution.[83] The concept of a golden share is more developed in England than in North America.

§7.33 In certain cases, a share will be subject to a limitation rather than a right. It is not appropriate to describe special shares of this sort as preference shares. The following types of non-preference special share are reasonably common:

- deferred shares, in which the right to receive income or capital comes after the ordinary shares of the company;
- non-voting shares: although preference shares generally carry no or very limited voting rights, non-voting ordinary shares which confer no off-setting preference may also be issued where the goal is to restrict control of the company in some way — for instance, in some cases, a regulatory body may insist that particular shareholders (*e.g.*, foreign residents) have no voting rights, and in such cases non-voting shares may offer a mechanism to accomplish the desired purpose;[84]
- shares with limited voting rights;
- employee shares are usually not specially designated as such, but are acquired by a trustee under an employees' share plan (such shares may be subject to special restrictions with respect to such matters as the right of transfer);
- deferred shares or founder's shares, which defer the right to receive income or return on capital until after repayment of the all ordinary shareholders.

§7.34 Although there are no restrictions under the present OBCA and CBCA on the use of the terms "common," "preference" and "restricted" in connection with the shares of non-offering corporations, such restrictions do exist in the case of offering corporations. Specifically, OSC Rule 56-501 Restricted Shares under

---

[83] See, for example, *Investment Trust Corp. v. Singapore Traction Co.*, [1935] Ch. 615; *Quin & Axtens Ltd. v. Salmon*, [1909] A.C. 442 (H.L.); *Bushell v. Faith*, [1970] A.C. 1099 (H.L.). Devices of this kind have been employed in many privatization issues, where the former government owner wishes to retain some form of limited control (*e.g.*, restriction on take-over, a change in business, or a relocation of the main offices of the business) over a denationalized industry following privatization.

[84] See, for instance, *Heron International Ltd. v. Lord Grade*, [1983] B.C.L.C. 244 (C.A.).

section 143 of the *Securities Act* differentiates among types of share as follows:[85] It defines the term "common shares" to mean:

> ... equity shares to which are attached voting rights exercisable in all circumstances, irrespective of the number or percentage of shares owned, that are not less, on a per share basis, than the voting rights attaching to any other shares of an outstanding class of shares of the issuer, unless the Director makes a determination under section 4.1 that the shares are restricted shares.

The definition is further refined by the use of the incorporated term "equity shares", which is itself defined to mean:

> ... shares of an issuer that carry a residual right to participate in the earnings of the issuer and, upon the liquidation or winding up of the issuer, in its assets.

One qualification is obviously implicit in this definition: the right to participate in earnings may be qualified by the subordination of the right to receive dividends on the shares concerned to some prior preferential right to receive dividends that is given to some other class of shares; if not, then no corporation that had shares which provided for a preferential dividend could have common shares. However, once that prior preferential dividend has been paid, the right to participate in the remaining earnings must be unlimited. The definition of "preference shares" harkens back to the definition found in the former OBCA. It provides that:

> "preference shares" means shares to which there is attached a preference or right over any class of shares of the issuer, but does not include equity shares.

(2) Popular Share Designations Within the Securities Industry

§7.35 There are a number of other share classifications that are commonly used in the securities industry and broader investment community. Although these designations have no legal significance whatsoever, they are frequently encountered in practice and accordingly corporate law practitioners do need at least a general understanding of their meaning. The term "income stock" is used to describe shares of a corporation that has a history of stable growth in sales and earnings and that has a track record of dividend payments above the average in the market. Income stocks are invariably issued by well-established corporations. The term "blue chip" describes stocks issued by corporations that are the most solidly capitalized, have had a respectable earnings record for a substantial period of time, and are the leading players in the industry in which they are engaged.

---

[85] The Rule provides holders of restricted shares and prospective purchasers of such shares with rights similar rights to those formerly available to them under OSC Policy 1.3. It requires holders of restricted shares and prospective purchasers of restricted shares to be made informed that restricted shares have rights that differ from those attached to an issuer's common shares. It also requires that holders of restricted shares be sent all material required to be sent to holders of common shares. The Rule also removes prospectus exemptions and provides that the Director shall not issue a receipt for a prospectus for a distribution of restricted shares unless shareholder approval, on a majority of the minority basis, was obtained for the distribution or the reorganization that resulted in the creation of the restricted shares.

§7.36 The term "income stock" is used primarily on the basis of the prior track record of the issuing corporation — it being assumed (in the absence of any reason to think otherwise) that the future will reflect the past. In contrast, the term "growth stock" describes shares of a corporation that is perceived to have a rosy future. The corporations issuing such stocks are often engaged in new and expanding lines of business that appear to have significantly above average growth potential in the foreseeable future. It is usually expected that such corporations will pay limited or no dividends, but will instead reinvest profits in expansion, product research and development and other growth of the business. However, there is a good potential for capital gain on such stocks. The term "performance stocks" describes those stocks of corporation that have so far performed in accordance with market expectations, and that therefore enjoy widespread popularity with investors.

§7.37 "Cyclical stocks" are shares of a corporation that engages in an industry that is subject to pronounced cyclical trends. Virtually all businesses suffer from some cyclical fluctuation in earnings and demand, but in cyclical industries (*e.g.*, cars, machinery, and construction related products) the fluctuation is more severe. Historically, corporations engaged in cyclical industries tend to enjoy periods of boom (during which they out-perform corporations in other fields) followed by periods of bust (during which they experience a severe downturn in their fortunes). Corporations engaged in cyclical industries generally require more solid capitalization than those that are not, in order to ride out the periodic downturns that they are likely to suffer. The terms "cyclical stock" and "blue chip" are not mutually exclusive. Provided a corporation makes adequate provision for the downturn that will eventually come, its stock may be considered "blue chip" despite the fact that it is engaged in a cyclical industry.

§7.38 The term "speculative stock" describes shares in a corporation that has a highly erratic earnings record or that has an insufficient record on which any assessment may be made as to its probable prospects. Quite often the corporations that issue such shares are involved in high risk industries in which participants will enjoy very high returns on original investments if everything works out as hoped, but (in most cases) there is also a very high risk of investors losing all or substantially all of their investment. The most obvious example of speculative stocks are those issued by junior mining, oil and gas companies. For instance, if a junior oil corporation strikes recoverable quantities of oil, then its shareholders will likely enjoy a substantial return on their original investment — far beyond that which is available in less speculative industries. However, if no oil is found, then investors stand a good chance of losing their entire investment. Speculative stocks often "take off" as word of a rumoured success spreads through the market. If the rumour proves unfounded, people who invested in those stocks in reliance on the rumour are also liable to suffer significant loss. It follows that speculative stocks are considered to be a high risk investment.

§7.39 There are also a number of common investment industry terms that describe shares not by reference to the perceived investment grade of their issuers, but rather by reference to special rights that they carry. For instance, a "stripped common share" is an instrument that separates the potential capital gain associated with the purchase of common shares from the right to receive dividend income on those shares. A variety of different arrangements may be employed to achieve this effect, but the original instrument of this type issued in Canada was developed by McLeod, Young, Weir & Co. with respect to shares in Bell Canada Enterprises. In that case, the underwriter created a corporation which issued two types of securities, which may be designated as Class "A" shares and installment receipts. The proceeds received from the issue of all of these shares were invested in common shares of Bell Canada Enterprises. The Class "A" shares entitled the holders to receive all of the dividends paid out by Bell Canada Enterprises. The installment receipts gave the holder an option to buy the Bell Canada shares at a fixed price.

(iii) The Presumption of Equality and the Creation of Preferences

§7.40 There is a general presumption that the shares issued by a corporation, even if designated as belonging to different classes, are intended to be equal.[86] Unless the constitution of a corporation so provides or allows (and then only to the extent so provided or allowed), the directors have no power to grant a preference to one class or series of shares over another class or series of shares.[87] *A fortiori* the directors possess no authority to confer any preference on the holders of any particular shares forming part of a series or class of shares (except, in the latter case, if those shares constitute a distinct series within a class). Under the present legislation and at common law, the articles are the sole authority for determining the terms, conditions, rights, privileges and restrictions attached to the shares. The directors have no inherent authority to add to, subtract from or otherwise vary those terms, whether for the purpose of creating a preference or for conferring rights less than those with respect to the shares previously issued. Under the OBCA and the CBCA, the directors of a corporation may be empowered under the articles of the corporation to create a distinct series of shares within a class and to confer terms, conditions, rights, privileges and restrictions upon that series.[88] If that power is not conferred in the articles then the power does not exist.[89] It makes no difference that in varying the share terms the directors have acted in good faith in what they perceive to be the best interests of the corporation; nor does it matter if the shareholders overwhelmingly approve of the preference granted unless in the course of giving approval they formally amend the articles.[90] If the preference is not properly authorized, it may be challenged by any shareholder who is prejudiced by it, and, possibly, under the

---

[86] See, generally, *Birch v. Cropper* (1889), 14 App. Cas. 525 (H.L.).
[87] *Re Banker's Trust* [1915] B.C.J. No. 20, 8 W.W.R. 38 (C.A.).
[88] OBCA, s. 25(1); CBCA, s. 27(1), but note the limitation on this power imposed under OBCA, s. 25(3) and CBCA, s. 27(3).
[89] *Re Pakenham Pork Packing Co.*, [1906] O.J. No. 27, 12 O.L.R. 100 at 109 (C.A.), *per* Moss C.J.O.
[90] *Re Banker's Trust*, [1915] B.C.J. No. 20, 8 W.W.R. 38 (C.A.).

OBCA section 253 compliance remedy, by any complainant under that section who objects to it.

§7.41 The ordinary meaning of a "preference" is that it is something in addition to that which is otherwise available. Accordingly, one might assume that any preferential right is in addition to those rights which would otherwise apply to the common or ordinary shares of a company, so that if the holder of preferred shares was entitled to a preferential dividend of $1 per share, that dividend would be paid in addition to any other dividend paid to the holders of the ordinary shares. Any special voting rights would be in addition to the voting rights of the holders of the ordinary shares. However, early in the evolution of corporate law, preferential rights were (as a matter of interpretation) held to be in substitution for, rather than additional to the rights of, ordinary shareholders. Where the terms of a share contain an express provision as to the rights attached to the share with respect to any particular matter, such as dividends, the return of capital or voting, that provision is presumed to be an exhaustive statement of the rights of the holder of that share with respect to the matter concerned.[91]

§7.42 Nevertheless, these presumptions are merely the starting point for determining the actual rights of the holders of preferred shares in any given case. The rights to which a particular class of preference shares are entitled are always a matter of construction, that turns upon the wording of the memorandum or articles or the terms of the shares themselves. Where the wording of the share terms is clear and unambiguous, effect will be given to the preference conferred by those terms, even where it is inconsistent with the normal presumptions that the courts have placed upon the meaning of certain preference clauses. Where there is ambiguity, it is necessary to fall back upon the case law, setting out those normal presumptions. For instance, it is often particularly important to determine whether any preferential right to a dividend is *cumulative* (*i.e.*, if no dividend is declared in one year, is the undeclared dividend carried forward as a charge against future profits, so that no dividend may be paid on a share ranking junior to the preference share until all previous years' undeclared dividends are paid).[92] There is a loose presumption that dividend entitlements are intended to be cumulative in the absence of provision to the contrary,[93] but a shareholder would be foolish to rely on an implied provision.[94] Instead, an express entitlement to cumulative dividends should be obtained. An express provision is cer-

---

[91] *Will v. United Lankat Plantations Co.*, [1914] A.C. 11 (H.L.); *Re National Telephone Co.*, [1914] 1 Ch. 755, *per* Sargant J.; see also *Scottish Insurance Corp. v. Wilsons & Clyde Coal Co.*, [1949] A.C. 462 (H.L.).

[92] See, for instance, *Wabash Railway Co. v. Barclay*, 280 U.S. 197 (1930).

[93] See, for instance *Webb v. Earle* (1875), L.R. 20 Eq. 556. It can be argued with some force, however, that the presumption that dividends are cumulative ought to be strong, so that it would require the clearest language to overcome. See also: *Sanders v. Cuba Railroad Co.*, 21 N.J. 78, 120 A.2d 849 at 852 (1956); *Arizona Western Insurance Co. v. L.L. Constantin Co.*, 247 F.2d 388 (3d Cir. 1957); *Bank of America National Trust & Savings Association v. West End Chemical Co.*, 37 Cal. App. (2d) 685, 100 P.2d 318 (1940). For a case taking a narrow view of a cumulative right, see *Wouk v. Merin*, 283 A.D. 522, 128 N.Y.2d 727 (S.C.N.Y.A.D. 1954).

[94] See, generally, *Staples v. Eastman Photographic Materials Co.*, [1896] 2 Ch. 303 (C.A.).

tainly required if the holders of preference shares wish to participate in residual dividend payments made by a corporation to the holders of its other shares after payment of the preference dividend. The presumption is that there is no such right to participate.[95]

§7.43 Unless it is otherwise provided, it is assumed that preference shares confer no priority in the repayment of capital on liquidation;[96] moreover, it is presumed that the right to be paid undeclared cumulative dividends will lapse upon liquidation.[97] In general, however, preference share terms will usually contain express provisions conferring such entitlements.[98] The extensive volume of reported case law concerning this aspect of the rights of the preference shareholders demonstrates eloquently the great practical need for clarity in the drafting of share terms. Where preference shares confer a priority in the repayment of capital, they are presumed to be *non-participating,* meaning that they do not confer any right to participate in the surplus property of the corporation after the repayment of capital.[99] Therefore, if some other intention exists, the share terms should expressly confer a right of participation.[100]

§7.44 The general rule is that the shareholders of a corporation vote together as a single decision-making body with respect to any proposed amendment, with every voting share being entitled to the same number of votes (*i.e.*, one vote) per share. Unless the articles, memorandum or the share terms themselves otherwise provide, preference shares will be presumed to carry the same voting rights at general meetings as the ordinary shares of the corporation. It is customary, however, for the share terms connected with a preference share issue to specifically provide that there will be no right to vote in respect of those shares, although an exception will often be made where there is a persistent breach in the obligation to pay dividends.[101] As a general rule, complete prohibitions on voting preference shares will be respected by the courts. However, to this general rule there are a number of important exceptions. In particular, there are certain share terms which are available by operation of law to the shareholders of a given class. In

---

[95] *Will v. United Lankat Plantations Co.*, [1914] A.C. 11 (H.L.).
[96] *Wilsons & Clyde Coal Co. v. Scottish Insurance Corp.*, [1948] S.C. 360; [1949] S.C. 90 (H.L.); *Re The Isle of Thanet Electricity Supply Co.*, [1950] Ch. 161 (C.A.).
[97] See, for instance, *Re Roberts & Cooper Ltd.*, [1929] 2 Ch. 383.
[98] See, for instance, *Re Walter Symons Ltd.*, [1934] Ch. 308; *Re F. deJong & Co.*, [1946] Ch. 211 (C.A.); *Re Wood, Skinner & Co.*, [1944] Ch. 323; *Robertson-Durham v. Inches* (1917), 1 S.L.T. 267 (O.H.); *Re William Bedford Ltd.*, [1967] V.R. 490; *Re E.W. Savory Ltd.*, [1951] 2 All E.R. 1036; *Re Wharfedale Brewery Co.*, [1952] Ch. 913.
[99] See, generally, *Scottish Insurance Corp. v. Wilsons & Clyde Coal Co.*, [1949] A.C. 462 (H.L.); *Re Isle of Thanet Electricity Supply Co.*, [1950] Ch. 161. In the *Thanet* case, the preference shareholders were entitled to participate in profits beyond their fixed preferential dividend while the company remained a going concern. Despite that entitlement, the preference shareholders were held not to be entitled to participate in the distribution of surplus assets in the widing-up of the company. See also: *Re William Bedford Ltd.*, [1967] V.R. 490; *Re Collie Power Co. Pty. Ltd.* (1952), 54 W.A.L.R. 44; *Seaton v. Federal Hotels Pty. Ltd.* (1981), 6 A.C.L.R. 214.
[100] See, generally, *Re Saltdean Estate Co.*, [1968] 1 W.L.R. 1844; *House of Fraser plc v. A.C.G.E. Investments Ltd.*, [1989] H.L.J. No. 17, [1987] A.C. 387.
[101] *Re Bradford Investments plc*, [1990] B.C.C. 740.

addition, the terms of a particular class of preference share may sometimes confer special rights on the holders of those shares. For instance, in the case of corporations with only a few shareholders (*i.e.*, what are sometimes called "closely held" corporations), preference shares are often used to distribute control among those concerned in the corporation.

§7.45 Where the terms of a share specifically provide that the holders of shares of that class or series are entitled to vote separately from the shareholders of the other classes or series of the corporation, effect must be given to that provision. Where such class voting rights apply, the special resolution approving a proposed amendment must be approved by the holders of each class or series entitled to vote separately. A right to vote separately by class obviously increases the degree of control that the holders of each class of shares possesses over the corporation, for in order for a resolution to be approved, it must be passed by the holders of each class of shares. Such a system of voting is negative; it allows each class a veto, but that same veto necessarily encumbers any effort that the shareholders might make to change the articles of the corporation.

§7.46 Subsection 22(5) of the OBCA provides it is not necessary for the articles to make express provision in respect of the right to vote at all meetings of the shareholders and to receive the remaining property of the corporation upon dissolution. The section does not give an express explanation of the consequence where there is no express provision. However, other provisions of the Act do answer this question: under subsection 102(1) of the OBCA,[102] unless the articles otherwise provide, each share of a corporation entitles the holder of that share to one vote at a meeting of the shareholders. Thus, if the articles are silent, all shares are voting shares. The general rule that all shares are equal would suggest that in the absence of an express provision, all classes of shares are entitled to equal voting rights. Similarly, clause 221(1)(*a*) of the OBCA provides that upon a winding-up,

> (*a*) the liquidator shall apply the property of the corporation in satisfaction of all its debts, obligations and liabilities and, subject thereto, shall distribute the property rateably among the shareholders according to their rights and interests in the corporation ...

Here again, the normal presumption of equality of shares would appear to be relevant.

(iv) Interpretation of Share Terms, etc.

§7.47 The construction of share terms, conditions and restrictions is governed by the ordinary rules of contractual interpretation. While the rules of contractual interpretation generally follow the rules of statutory interpretation, there are some important differences. For instance, the federal and provincial *Interpretation Acts* provide that a citation of, or reference to, an enactment is deemed to be

---

[102] CBCA, s. 140.

a citation of, or reference to, the enactment as amended. Unless the intent appears otherwise, there is no similar assumption made with respect to references to statutes, by-laws and other enactments in corporate constitutional documents (such as the articles of incorporation or amendment), nor do the provisions of the *Interpretation Acts* apply with respect to the interpretation of private documents. Where the parties wish to incorporate current legislation into their agreements (or a corporation wishes to incorporate such legislation into the interpretation of its articles, by-laws and other governing instruments), the best option is to state specifically that the reference to a statute includes a reference to all amendments and substitutions as may be made to that Act from time to time.

(v) Key Concepts

(1) Authorized and Issued Capital

§7.48 The authorized capital of a company is the amount and type of capital that the corporation is empowered to raise. At one time (and still today in the United Kingdom and Australia), it was customary to include in a company's constitutional charter documents a statement of both a monetary amount and a maximum number of shares that the company was authorized to issue. In most Canadian jurisdictions, this practice is no longer followed. Instead, the articles of incorporation of most modern Canadian business corporations usually will be found to contain provisions such as "the corporation is authorized to issue in one or more series, an unlimited number of Class A shares without par value". Where this approach is followed there is no limit on the capital that the corporation is authorized to raise through the issue of shares. However, if the authorized capital is limited to a specific number of shares, then no more than that number of shares may be issued by the corporation, and any allotment in excess is void.[103]

§7.49 In general terms, the issued capital[104] of a corporation — to which the stated capital under the OBCA and the CBCA is a corresponding analogue — constitutes the consideration received by a corporation in respect of the issue by it of shares to its shareholders, expressed as a monetary amount.[105] The issued capital of a corporation bears no necessary relationship to the market value of the shares of the corporation: the market value of shares in a corporation may

---

[103] *The Bank of Hindustan, China & Japan Ltd. v. Alison* (1871), L.R. 6 C.P. 222.
[104] The terms "issued" and "allotted" are often sued interchangeably, and indeed under the OBCA and CBCA, there seems to be no meaningful distinction between the two terms. In other jurisdictions, there is a vague distinction between the terms. See, for instance, in *Mosely v. Koffyfontein Mines Ltd.*, [1911] 1 Ch. 73 at 84, *per* Farwell L.J., aff'd [1911] A.C. 409; *cf. Commonwealth Homes & Investment Co. v. Smith* (1937), 59 C.L.R. 443 (H.C. Aust.), *per* Dixon J.; *Central Piggery Co. v. McNicholl & Hurst* (1949), 78 C.L.R. 594 at 599 (H.C. Aust.); *Re Amrose Lake & Tin Copper Co. (Clarke's Case)* (1878), 8 Ch. D. 635 at 638, *per* Cockburn C.J., at 641, *per* Cotton L.J., at 642, *per* Thesiger L.J.
[105] *City of Toronto v. Consumers' Gas Co.*, [1927] 4 D.L.R. 102 (P.C.) at 105, *per* Duff J., aff'g [1927] O.J. No. 37, 60 O.L.R. 336 (P.C.).

exceed or be less than the issue price for those shares. The issued capital of a particular share is the amount that was paid to the corporation at the time of its issue. In some jurisdictions, although not under the OBCA or the CBCA, shares may still have par value. In such a case, the issued capital of a corporation with respect to those shares is equal to the number of shares issued times the par value of those shares. Any amount received over the par value is termed the "premium".

§7.50 Both the CBCA and the OBCA permit a corporation to raise equity through the issue of shares. Subsection 22(1) of the OBCA provides that shares of a corporation shall be in registered form[106] and shall be without nominal or par value.[107] Consequently it is not possible to have bearer shares in a corporation under the OBCA and the CBCA, or to have par value shares under those Acts. Shares with nominal or par value of a corporation incorporated before section 22 of the OBCA came into effect are deemed to be shares without nominal or par value.[108] Moreover, in the case of an OBCA corporation a share certificate issued prior to the 29th day of July, 1993 does not contravene the Act merely because the certificate refers to the share or shares represented thereby as having a nominal or par value.[109]

(2) Alteration of Share Capital

§7.51 A corporation may increase, reduce or otherwise modify its authorized capital only in accordance with the provisions of the OBCA or the CBCA, as the case may be. With limited exceptions, any such modification will require an amendment to the articles of the corporation concerned.[110] As discussed in Chapter 14, subject to the power of the directors to create a new series of shares under subsection 25(1) of the OBCA,[111] such amendments generally require prior shareholder approval. Where a meeting of the shareholders is held for the purpose of considering an amendment to the articles of a corporation in order to create a new class of shares or in order to amend the terms and conditions of the shares of an existing class, the notice must state that such is the purpose of the meeting. If the notice does not provide adequate information, there is no compliance with the statute, and therefore any special resolution approving the amendment in question is invalid. In such a case, a perpetual injunction may be granted restraining the corporation from allotting any of the new shares,[112] and

---

[106] In contrast, s. 43 of the OBCA provides that "Nothing in this Act prohibits the issue of debt obligations in bearer form." No comparable provision is found in the CBCA.
[107] CBCA, s. 24(1).
[108] To the same effect: CBCA, s. 24(2).
[109] OBCA, s. 56(6).
[110] OBCA, s. 5(1); CBCA, s. 6(1).
[111] CBCA, s. 27(1).
[112] *Meyers v. Lucknow Elevator Co.*, [1905] O.J. No. 523, 6 O.W.R. 291 at 293-94 (H.C.), per MacMahon J.; *Martin v. Gibson*, [1907] O.J. No. 85, 15 O.L.R. 623 (H.C.); see also *Bonisteel v. Collis Leather Co.*, [1919] O.J. No. 125, 45 O.L.R. 195 at 199 (H.C.), per Rose J.

preventing the addition of the names of the persons who have subscribed for those shares from being added to the list of shareholders.[113]

§7.52 In some cases, the corporation may reserve a right within the terms of the shares themselves to modify the rights of shareholders in some way, as for instance, where the articles confer the right to create a new series of shares upon the directors. Occasionally, the dividend to which particular shares are entitled may be subject to periodic revision by the corporation (the shareholder being protected by some form of put option, if the rate is set unrealistically low). Whether the rights of the holders of any class or series of shares can be so modified depends on the terms and conditions of those shares,[114] although given the presumption against unilateral rights to modify the terms of a contract, there would seem to be a strong presumption against any such right. Irrespective of whether provisions for modification appear in the articles of the corporation, the rights of the holders of shares may be modified in accordance with an amendment to the articles of the corporation (although in certain cases any such modification would be subject to a right of dissent by any shareholder who objects to the modification),[115] or by way of a compromise or arrangement effected under the OBCA or the CBCA.[116]

(3) Creation and Issue of Shares

§7.53 The shares of a corporation must be authorized by the articles of the corporation (*i.e.*, by articles of incorporation, continuation, amalgamation or amendment). The mere provision in the articles for shares of a particular class or series creates the shares[117] and empowers their issue. While the original shares that a corporation is authorized to issue must be provided for in the articles of incorporation,[118] a corporation may at any time amend its articles in order to provide for further classes of share.[119] Subject to any unanimous shareholder agreement to the contrary, shares authorized under the articles of a corporation may only be issued by the board of directors of the corporation. This approach is to be contrasted with that taken in the United Kingdom, where sections 80 and 80A of the *Companies Act 1985* go to great lengths to limit the control of the directors over share issuance. The question of whether control over share issuance should reside with the directors exclusively or be qualified in some way is an important policy matter, to which some attention should be given in the next review of the OBCA and the CBCA, for the question involves many important corporate governance considerations.[120]

---

[113] *Re Ontario Express & Transport Co.* (1894), 21 O.A.R. 646 at 654 (C.A.), *per* Hagarty C.J.O. and at 657, *per* Osler J.A.; *Page v. Austin* (1882), 10 S.C.R. 132.
[114] *Re Canada Tea Co.*, [1959] O.W.N. 378 at 379 (H.C.), *per* Danis J.
[115] See Chapter 10, Fundamental Changes.
[116] *Re Holdex Group Ltd.*, [1972] O.J. No. 1871, [1972] 3 O.R. 425, at 427 (H.C.), *per* Holden J.
[117] See, generally, *Koffyfontein Mines Ltd. v. Mosely*, [1911] A.C. 409 (H.L.).
[118] See Form 1 under the OBCA; CBCA, s. 6(1)(*c*).
[119] See Chapter 14, Fundamental Changes.
[120] The problems inherent in leaving the directors with full control over the issue of shares could be no better illustrated than by reference to the struggle between Cornelius Vanderbilt, on the one hand,

§7.54 Shares are issued when they are segregated from the authorized but unissued shares of a corporation which remains in its treasury awaiting possible future issue. A formal board resolution authorizing the issue of shares is not required, and any action on their part which is tantamount to an acceptance of a share subscription will suffice,[121] as will entry of the name of the subscriber on the register of shareholders.[122] Furthermore, the issue of a share certificate is not necessary in order for a share to be validly issued.[123] The executive officers of a corporation are not presumed to possess the power or authority to issue shares.[124] Nor may the directors delegate their power to issue shares, except in the manner and on terms that the full board of directors has authorized.[125] However, the officers of a corporation may possess the authority to solicit subscriptions and represent that shares have been validly issued, in which case such a representation will be binding on the corporation.[126]

§7.55 An issue of shares contrary to the *Securities Act*[127] is both illegal and (at least potentially) fraudulent[128] and the illegality will render the issue of the shares concerned void rather than voidable unless an exemption from those requirements applies.[129] The articles of a corporation that is seeking the benefit of the private company exemption under the *Securities Act* will provide that shares in the corporation may only be transferred with the approval of the board of directors.[130] Where the articles so provide, the directors must specifically authorize a transfer. A general note in the minutes of the directors such as "all shares of stock subscribed for and transferred to date be hereby allotted and allotment is hereby confirmed" is too vague and therefore insufficient for this purpose, un-

---

and the team of Jim Fisk, Daniel Drew and Jay Gould, on the other, for control of the New York and Erie Railroad Company. See J.K. Galbraith, *The Age of Uncertainty* (London: BBC/André Deutsch, 1977), 49-53.

[121] *Pierson v. Egbert* (1916), 10 W.W.R. 1068 at 1069 (Alta. C.A.), *per* Stuart J.A., aff'd [1917] 2 W.W.R. 1175 (S.C.C.). See also *Cement Products Ltd. v. Forget* (1916), 28 D.L.R. 717 (P.C.); *cf. National Westminster Bank plc v. I.R.C.*, [1995] 1 A.C. 119 (H.L.).

[122] *Re Heaton's Steel & Iron Ore Co.* (1876), 4 Ch. D. 140.

[123] *Associated Stevedoring Co. v. Callanan* (1968), 70 D.L.R. (2d) 687 at 692 (B.C.S.C.), *per* Hickson Co. Ct. J. See also *Nelson Coke & Gas Co. v. Pellatt*, [1902] O.J. No. 179, 4 O.L.R. 481 at 489 (C.A.), *per* Maclennan J.A.

[124] *Re Nagrella Manufacturing Co.*, [1915] O.J. No. 522, 8 O.W.N. 452 (H.C.), *per* Britton J.

[125] OBCA, s. 127(3)(*c*).

[126] *Anglo-American Lumber Co. v. McLellan*, [1908] B.C.J. No. 5, 7 W.L.R. 422 at 423 (S.C.), *per* Hunter C.J. aff'd [1908] B.C.J. No. 58, 9 W.L.R. 469, 14 B.C.R. 93 (C.A.).

[127] R.S.O. 1990, c. S.5.

[128] *Setter v. Mander* (1952), 6 W.W.R. (N.S.) 577 at 581 (Man. Q.B.), *per* Beaubien J.

[129] *Re Northwestern Trust Co.*, [1924] 3 W.W.R. 625 at 630 (Man. C.A.), *per* Fullerton J.A. It is worth noting that more recent cases have taken a more flexible view of the effect of illegality upon contractual rights, and it may well be that this statement must be modified in the light of those cases. See, generally, *Garland v. Consumers' Gas Co.*, [2004] S.C.J. No. 21, [2004] 1 S.C.R. 629 and also Kevin McGuinness, *The Law of Guarantee*, 2nd ed. (Toronto: Carswell, 1996) §§4.5 to 4.15. It is certainly true that in some cases the putative shareholder may not wish to repudiate the share subscription despite the violation of the *Securities Act*. See, generally, *Kerr v. Fleming Financial Corp.*, [1998] M. J. No. 140, [1998] 9 W.W.R. 176 (Q.B.).

[130] For corporations considering the issue of shares or other securities in Ontario, the private company exemption no longer applies. It has been superceded by the Rule 45-501 closely held issuer exemption, the requirements and limitations of which are discussed below.

less it can be shown that a particular transfer must have been within the contemplation of the directors at the time when that resolution was passed.[131]

§7.56 The directors of a corporation may wish to issue shares in the corporation for a variety of different purposes, including:

- to raise funds required by the corporation;
- to consolidate the existing capital structure of the corporation;
- to change control within the corporation;
- to prevent a change of control within the corporation.

For many years the prevailing view was that the power of the directors to issue shares was limited so that it might be used only for a capital related purpose, such as raising the capital reasonably required by the corporation in order to carry out its objects. Thus the directors of a corporation could not use their power to issue shares so as to perpetuate their control over the corporation against the will of the majority of shareholders,[132] or to allow one group of shareholders to acquire control as opposed to another.[133] This limitation on the directors' share-issuing power was part and parcel of the general rule that the powers of the directors may not be exercised in order to obtain some private advantage or for any purpose foreign to the power[134] — a rule which can be traced back at least as far as the decision of Lord Northington in *Aleyn v. Belchier*,[135] where he held that the power of a trustee was required to be exercised "*bona fide* for the end designed, otherwise it is corrupt and void". So strictly was the rule applied that it was even held that the directors could not issue shares in order to effect a change of control in the corporation, although the directors considered such a change of control to be in the best interests of the corporation.[136]

§7.57 It is clear that as a general principle the directors of a corporation cannot issue shares or otherwise manipulate the machinery of a corporation in order to perpetuate their control of the corporation.[137] However, in *Teck Corp. v. Millar*[138]

---

[131] *McCurdy v. Oak Tire & Rubber Co.*, [1918] O.J. No. 51, 44 O.L.R. 571 at 574 (H.C.), per Middleton J.
[132] *Perreault v. Milot* (1886), 12 Q.L.R. 248 (C.A.).
[133] *Trustee of C.E. Plain v. Kenley*, [1931] O.J. No. 393, 12 C.B.R. 492 at 497-98 (Ont. C.A.), per Hodgins J.A.
[134] *Mills v. Mills* (1938), 60 C.L.R. 150 (H.C. Aust.), per Dixon J.
[135] (1758), 1 Eden 132 at 132, 28 E.R. 634.
[136] *Bonisteel v. Collis Leather Co.*, [1919] O.J. No. 125, 45 O.L.R. 195 at 199 (H.C.), per Rose J.
[137] See, for instance, *Condec Corp. v. Lunkenheimer Co.*, 230 A.2d 769 (Del. Ch. 1967); *Schnell v. Chris-Craft Industries Inc.*, 285 A.2d 437 (Del. Ch. 1971).
[138] (1972), 33 D.L.R. (3d) 288 (B.C.S.C.). It is worth noting that although the *Teck* case has been widely discussed in academic, professional and judicial circles both in Canada and abroad — in an effort to try and reconcile the decision with both the prior and subsequent case law — little attention has ever been given to one obvious possibility: the case may simply have been wrongly decided. The case was cited with approval by the Supreme Court of Canada in *Peoples Department*

Berger J. held that it was a valid exercise of the directors' powers for them to issue shares for the purpose of defeating a take-over bid, where they honestly believed that to do so was in the best interests of the corporation. Neither the OBCA nor the CBCA contains a provision that can fairly be construed as limiting the share issuance power to capital-raising purposes. On the contrary, subsection 134(1) of the OBCA[139] imposes an express and unrestricted duty upon the directors to act honestly and in good faith with a view to the best interests of the corporation. It follows that directors are permitted to issue shares for a non-capital purpose if it is in the best interest of the corporation that this be done. Consequently, the narrow view that it is a hard and fast rule that the share issuance power may not be issued for a non-capital purpose can no longer be accepted.[140] Under the law as it now stands, the raising of capital continues to be the normal purpose of the issuance of shares, but it is permissible for the directors to issue shares if some other need of the corporation besides its capital requirements necessitates the issue of the shares concerned.

§7.58 The context in which such extraordinary (non-capital raising) share issues have usually been encountered has been where the shares have been issued to thwart a hostile take-over.[141] As they did in the *Teck* case, directors may invoke the best interests of the corporation as justification for their decision to issue shares so as to defeat a hostile take-over. However, the extent to which the directors may rely upon the best interests of the corporation when interfering with a take-over bid is limited[142] and exists only in very unusual circumstances. Directors act at their peril when they issue shares in the context of a take-over bid, because of the obvious conflict of interest to which they are subject. The directors have no right to issue shares merely because they believe that the bid should be rejected. In the ordinary situation it would be difficult for the directors to demonstrate that the frustration of the take-over bid was motivated by any "best interest of the corporation" beyond the directors' subjective assessment that it would be in the best interest of the corporation for them to remain in office. Unless some exceptional situation exists that takes the take-over bid beyond a mere contest for control, it would not seem proper for the directors to be allowed to utilize their power over share issuance to substitute their decision as to corporate control for that of the shareholders.

§7.59 A board may not justify the misuse of its power by making vague, self-serving references to the need to act in the corporation's best interest. On the contrary, the primary public interest lies in giving shareholders the right to respond to rival take-over bids by selling their shares as they wish, without undue hindrance from defensive tactics on the part of directors who (while sincere in

---

Stores Inc. (Trustee of) v. Wise, [2004] S.C.J. No. 64 at para. 42, 134 A.C.W.S. (3d) 548 and so it must therefore continue to be accepted as good law.

[139] CBCA, s. 122(1).
[140] See, for instance, *Howard Smith Ltd. v. Ampol Petroleum Ltd.*, [1974] A.C. 821 (H.L.).
[141] See, generally, *Hogg v. Cramphorn*, [1967] Ch. 254; *Bamford v. Bamford*, [1970] Ch. 212.
[142] *Harlowe's Nominees Pty. Ltd. v. Woodside (Lake Entrance) Oil Co. N.L.* (1968), 121 C.L.R. 483 (H.C. Aust.), *per* Barwick C.J. Aust.

their opposition to a bid) are misguided or have outlived their usefulness. It is for the shareholders of a corporation, not its board of directors, to decide whether the bid should be accepted. The various provincial securities commissions have indicated that where the directors attempt to introduce some form of "shareholders' rights plan" (*i.e.*, a poison pill) which interferes with the shareholder's right to choose, a cease trading order may be made in any rights or securities issuable under the plan.[143] The improper purpose need not be the dominant purpose in order to invalidate an exercise of the share-issuance power; if the improper purpose was a "causative" one — in the sense that it was one of a number of significantly contributing causes, so that but for this improper purpose the power would not have been exercised — the issue of shares will be held improper.[144] However, from a corporate law perspective, provided that the directors of a corporation have acted honestly, the question of whether they have the authority to enter into a "poison pill" agreement intended to deter outsiders from making a hostile take-over bid to shareholders that provides for the contingent divesting of company assets turns solely on whether the directors who signed the agreement did so within the actual or apparent scope of their authority. This issue, in turn, depends upon an application of ordinary agency principles.[145]

(4) Classes and Series of Shares

§7.60 Both the OBCA and the CBCA permit corporations to divide their share capital into distinct classes of share, and where such a division has been made, both Acts permit the corporations subject to each of them to further subdivide one or more classes of shares into series of shares. The division of shares into separate classes, and to a lesser extent series, overcomes the general requirement of corporate law that all shareholders be treated alike. Where some shareholders of a corporation hold shares of one class, while another hold shares of another class, it is permissible for the corporation to confer preferential rights upon one class, to the detriment of the other, provided those preferences are within the contemplation of the articles. Specifically, subsection 27(1) of the CBCA was amended in 2001, to clarify the series issuance procedure. It now provides that:

> 27.(1) The articles may authorize, subject to any limitations set out in them, the issue of any class of shares in one or more series and may do either or both of the following,
>
> > (*a*) fix the number of shares in, and determine the designation, rights, privileges, restrictions and conditions attaching to the shares of, each series; or
> >
> > (*b*) authorize the directors to fix the number of shares in, and determine the designation, rights, privileges, restrictions and conditions attaching to the shares of, each series.

---

[143] *Re Canadian Jorex Ltd.* (1992), 4 B.L.R. (2d) 1 (Ont. Sec. Comm.).
[144] *Whitehouse v. Carlton Hotel Pty. Ltd.* (1987), 5 A.C.L.C. 421 (H.C. Aust.).
[145] *Criterion Properties plc v. Stratford UK Properties LLC*, [2004] U.K.H.L. 28.

Where the directors exercise their authority under paragraph (1)(b), they must send to the Director articles of amendment in a form that the Director fixes, that designate the series of shares, before the issue of shares of that series.[146]

§7.61 Except as provided in section 25 of the OBCA, each share of a class must be the same in all respects as every other share of that class.[147] However, subsection 25(1) of the OBCA provides that the articles subject to the limitations set out in them:

(a) may authorize the issue of any class of shares in one or more series and may fix the number of shares in, and determine the designation, rights, privileges, restrictions and conditions attaching to the shares of, each series; and

(b) may, where the articles authorize the issue of any class of shares in one or more series, authorize the directors to fix the number of shares in, and to determine the designation, rights, privileges, restrictions and conditions attaching to the shares of each series.[148]

§7.62 What constitutes a class of security holders is partly a matter of contract and (where a vote is taken under legislation such as the *Companies, Creditors Arrangement Act* or the OBCA or CBCA) partly a matter of law. If particular shares of a corporation are declared to be a class of shares under the articles of the corporation, that statement would appear to be determinative, even where the rights of other shares are exactly the same. So, for instance, in *McClurg v. Canada*[149] the designation of a class of shares in the articles of a corporation was described as being "the accepted means by which differential treatment of shares is recognized". Leaving aside for a moment the division of a class of shares into different series, the general rule with respect to the shares of class is that all members of the class are entitled to the same treatment by the corporation, irrespective of the fact that different shareholders of that class may have paid a vastly different amount for the shares that they hold.[150] The same rule would seem to apply with respect to debt securities. In such cases, the right to vote as a class is a proprietary right to which the holders are entitled (proprietary, because the right passes to subsequent holders of the security). In some cases, legislation declares that the holders of each class of securities to be entitled to vote with respect to a matter. In such cases, a common law concept of class applies, which was summarized by Bowen L.J. in *Sovereign Life Assurance Co. v. Dodd:*

> [A class] must be confined to those persons whose rights are not so dissimilar as to make it impossible for them to consult together with a view to their common interest.[151]

---

[146] CBCA, s. 27(4).
[147] OBCA, s. 22(6).
[148] CBCA, s. 27(1).
[149] [1990] S.C.J. No. 134, [1990] 3 S.C.R. 1020.
[150] *Muljo v. Sunwest Projects Ltd.*, [1990] B.C.J. No. 3332, 60 B.C.L.R. (2d) 343 at 346-49 (C.A.).
[151] [1892] 2 Q.B. 573 (C.A.).

§7.63 Series of share are not common in the case of non-offering corporations, but they do provide a measure of flexibility in structuring the capital of a corporation that would otherwise not be present. Where the articles permit the issue of shares in a series, the power of the directors to affix rights, privileges, restrictions and conditions on the shares of a series is qualified by subsection 25(3) of the OBCA, which provides that no rights, privileges, restrictions or conditions attached to a series of shares authorized under section 25 may confer upon the shares of a series a priority in respect of,

- dividends; or
- return of capital in the event of the liquidation, dissolution or winding-up of the corporation,

over the shares of any other series of the same class. In contrast, subsection 27(3) of the CBCA provides:

> 27.(3) No rights, privileges, restrictions or conditions attached to a series of shares authorized under this section shall confer on a series a priority in respect of dividends or return of capital over any other series of shares of the same class *that are then outstanding.*

(Emphasis added.)
Thus while the OBCA prohibits such priorities in the case of all shares of the same class, the CBCA imposes the prohibition only in respect of outstanding shares. As a result, under the OBCA it is not possible to provide that a new series of shares in a class shall be subordinate to the rights of the holders of shares of an existing series of shares of that class with respect to dividends or return of capital, for in doing so a priority would be conferred on the existing series. In contrast, under the CBCA a subsequent series may be made subordinate to an existing series.

§7.64 The prohibition against the conferring of a priority in respect of dividends does not restrain the directors from fixing the rate or amount of dividend payable with respect to the shares of a series, since no priority is conferred by reason of so providing. Thus it is permissible for the directors to resolve, for instance, that the shares of series 1 of the class A shares of a corporation shall be entitled to a fixed dividend of $1.50 per annum payable quarterly, while the shares of series 2 of that class shall be entitled to a fixed dividend of $1.75 payable annually, because the priority of the dividend entitlement of both series is not affected. However, it would not be permissible for the directors to resolve that the series 2 shares will be entitled to the payment of their dividend before any dividend is payable to the series 1 shareholders, since that would confer a priority upon the series 2 dividend.

§7.65 Where the directors exercise the authority conferred upon them to create a series of shares within a class, they must send the Director articles of amendment in the prescribed form designating the series before any shares of that series are issued.[152] On receipt of articles of amendment, the Director must endorse on that certificate a certificate of amendment in accordance with section 273 of the OBCA (section 262 of the CBCA).[153]

(5) Coattail Provisions

§7.66 Many widely held corporations (particularly those with different classes of share) have adopted so-called coattail provisions into their share terms. Often, stock exchanges require the inclusion of such a provision as a condition of listing.[154] Such provisions are designed to ensure that if the common (voting) shareholders of a corporation wish to accept an offer that will lead to a change in control, and if the price or terms offered to the common shareholders are more favorable than those offered to the holders of non-voting shares, then the non-voting shareholders will have an opportunity to participate in the premium paid for the transfer in control. Arrangements of this type can be justified because the holders of restricted voting shares agree to buy into a corporation that has an existing ownership and control structure. Any take-over bid will effectively alter the terms of that deal.

§7.67 Such provisions generally work as follows: if the holders of the non-voting shares are excluded from participating in a take-over bid for the voting shares, the holders of the non-voting shares will be given a right to convert their non-voting shares into voting shares. Thus coattail provisions discourage exclusionary bids.[155] Under current TSX policy, the actual wording of a coattail is the responsibility of the issuer, but the terms of any such arrangement must be approved by the TSX. The following general requirements apply:

(1) If there is a published market for the Common Securities, the coattails must provide that if there is an offer to purchase Common Securities that must, by reason of applicable securities legislation or the requirements of a stock exchange on which the Common Securities are listed, be made to all or substantially all holders of Common Securities who are in a province of Canada to which the requirement applies, the holders of Restricted Securities will be given the opportunity to participate in the offer through a right of conversion, unless:

(i) an identical offer (in terms of price per security and percentage of outstanding securities to be taken up exclusive of securities owned immediately prior to the offer by the offeror, or associates or affiliates of the offeror, and in all other material respects) concurrently is made to purchase Restricted Securities, which identical offer has no condition attached other that the right not to take up and pay for securities tendered if no securities are purchased pursuant to the offer for Common Securities; or

---

[152] OBCA, s. 25(4); CBCA, s. 27(4).
[153] OBCA, s. 25(5); CBCA, s. 27(5), (6).
[154] See, for instance, *TSX Venture Exchange Corporate Finance Manual,* Policy 3.5.
[155] *Maple Leaf Foods Inc. v. Schneider Corp.*, [1998] O.J. No. 4142 at paras. 130-31, *(sub nom. Pente Investment Management Ltd. v. Schneider Corp.)* 42 O.R. (3d) 177 (C.A.).

(ii) less than 50% of the Common Securities outstanding immediately prior to the offer, other than Common Securities owned by the offeror, or associates or affiliates of the offeror, are deposited pursuant to the offer.

(2) If there is no published market for the Common Securities, the holders of at least 80% of the outstanding Common Securities will be required to enter into an agreement with a trustee for the benefit of the holders of Restricted Securities from time to time, which agreement will have the effect of preventing transactions that would deprive the holders of Restricted Securities of rights under applicable take-over bid legislation to which they would have been entitled in the event of a take-over bid if the Common Securities had been Restricted Securities.[156]

Where there is a material difference between the equity interests of the Common Securities and Restricted Securities, or in other special circumstances, the TSX may permit or require appropriate modifications to the above criteria.

(vi) Abolition of Par Value

§7.68 In some jurisdictions, the shares that a company is authorized to issue may have or be required to have a "par value".[157] Par value is the monetary face value assigned to a share in a corporation under the corporate constitution. Although the par value has no significance in fixing the market value of a share, the amount of the issued capital of a corporation is determined by multiplying the number of issued shares by the par value of those shares. Par is a synonym for equal, and in this context, par value means that all shares of a given class in a corporation were issued for at least an equal consideration. Thus where the articles of a corporation provide for par value shares, the governing statute usually requires the corporation to issue those shares for no less than their stated par value. For instance, subsection 44(2) of the former OBCA provided:

> 44.(2) Shares with par value shall not be allotted or issued except for a consideration at least equal to the product of the number of shares allotted or issued or multiplied by the par value thereof.

This requirement posed certain obstacles where the par value of a share was less than its market value at the time of its issue — as would be the case where the corporation had accumulated losses or a poor earnings history. The Nova Scotia *Company Act* still permits par value shares as do most cooperative corporation statutes.[158] Since par value shares remain an integral aspect of such law, it is worthwhile discussing the strengths and weaknesses of the par value approach.

§7.69 The issued capital of a corporation with respect to the shares of a par value class that it has issued is equal to the number of shares issued times the nominal value of those shares. The nominal or par value of a share is the face

---

[156] TSX Company Manual, s. 624.
[157] In England and Australia, the term "nominal value" is more common.
[158] In the U.K., the *Companies Act 1985*, still requires shares of a corporation to have a stated nominal (or par) value.

value of a share. Under English company legislation, every company with share capital must state the amount of the share capital with which it proposes to be registered in its memorandum of association — this amount being the authorized capital of the company. The authorized (share) capital so stated must be divided into shares of fixed amount.[159] The fixed amounts so stated constitute the nominal or par value of the shares so concerned.

§7.70 In practice, the par or nominal value concept is an arbitrary one, and for the most part has limited commercial significance.[160] British practice is to keep the par value of a share relatively low. Although the company may issue shares at a price above par, and many shares trade at prices well above their par value, there is a widespread belief that a high par value significantly reduces the market for a share. While it is possible that there would be practical problems in issuing shares at very high par values (*e.g.*, more than £20), the concern that moderately high par values significantly affect the attraction which shares offer to investors is probably over-stated. Be that as it may, as a general rule British companies usually have large numbers of shares of relatively low par value. Par values of a few pennies are common,[161] and even lower par values are not unknown. The par or nominal value of the share capital of a company must, of course, be specified in monetary terms.

§7.71 The former OBCA and its predecessor permitted par value shares, but did not require them. The practice of issuing par value shares was widely abandoned during the 1970s. However, many par value shares issued before this time remained. In order to accommodate the two regimes of capitalization, the Act required very detailed accounting rules, to govern the statement of corporate capital in the financial statements of a corporation which had a mixture of par and no-par value shares. When it was enacted four years later, the CBCA abolished the par value concept, and this approach has subsequently been followed by most corporate law statutes — although par value shares continue to exist for certain special purpose corporations such as cooperatives and even banks and trust companies. Thus subsection 22(1) of the present OBCA provides:

> 22.(1) Shares of a corporation shall be in registered form and shall be without nominal or par value.

---

[159] *Companies Act 1985* (U.K.), s. 2(5)(*a*).
[160] Critics of par value shares are common. Few speak in its defence. The complaint most frequently voiced is that the par value concept is misleading to unsophisticated investors. In 1954, the Gedge Committee in England recommended allowing no par value common shares; in 1962, the Jenkins Committee extended the proposal to shares of all types. Although an effort was made in 1967, these proposals have still not found their way into English company law. Similar proposals were brought forward in Australia in 1990. See also L.C.B. Gower, *Principles of Modern Company Law*, 5th ed. (London: Sweet & Maxwell, 1992), 242. There is little to say in favour of par value, but the complaints made against it are excessive. Bonds, promissory notes and other debt securities invariably bear a specified face value and no one has ever complained about that feature of such securities (although the market value of such an instrument will also vary, due to fluctuations in prevailing interest rates and the bond rating of the insurer).
[161] R.R. Pennington, *Company Law*, 4th ed. (London: Butterworths, 1979), 28.

Instead of requiring the shares of a corporation to be issued at a predetermined value, the current approach embodied in the OBCA and CBCA is to allow the directors a broad discretion in fixing the price to be paid upon the issue of shares. Thus subsections 25(1) of the CBCA and 23(1) of the OBCA provide that in general shares may be issued at such times and to such persons and for such consideration as the directors may determine.

§7.72 Although par value has been abolished, quite often in practice a lawyer may encounter share certificates and articles of incorporation that state a par value for the shares of a corporation. In the case of such shares, subsection 22(2) of the OBCA provides:[162]

> 22.(2) Shares with nominal or par value of a corporation incorporated before the 29th day of July, 1983, shall be deemed to be shares without nominal or par value.

Any new amendments to articles or articles of incorporation which are now submitted to the Director for endorsement and filing will not be accepted if they contain a reference to par value or nominal value.

§7.73 The abolition of the par value concept has resulted in a number of modifications to the recording of the issued capital of a corporation. Issued capital is the amount received by a corporation in exchange for the shares which it has issued to its shareholders. Under a par value regime, the issued capital of a corporation is equal to the number of shares issued times the par value of the shares concerned. The issued capital of a corporation bears no necessary relationship to the market value of the shares of the corporation: the market value of shares in a corporation may exceed or be less than the issue price for those shares. The issued capital of a particular share is the amount that was paid to the corporation at the time of its issue in consideration of the issue of the share. Under the CBCA and the OBCA, the issued capital in respect of each share is credited to a stated capital account maintained in respect of each class and series of shares.

§7.74 The concept of stated capital is more fully explored below, and at this point we shall examine only the rules respecting the presentation of the stated capital account. As a balance sheet account, each stated capital account is a "real account" within the meaning of accounting parlance, as it represents a portion of the equity obligations of the corporation that are actually owed to its creditors. Nevertheless, these accounts are notional in operational terms: they do not constitute impressed funds that the corporation is required to keep in some liquid or other suspended form; instead a stated capital account merely describes the character of that portion of the corporation's aggregate employed capital to which it relates. In the case of CBCA corporations, the basic rule governing the manner in which stated capital accounts are to be maintained is set down in subsections 26(1) and (2) of the CBCA, which provides that:

---

[162] CBCA, s. 24(2).

> 26.(1) A corporation shall maintain a separate stated capital account for each class and series of shares it issues.
>
> (2) A corporation shall add to the appropriate stated capital account the full amount of any consideration it receives for any shares it issues.

The wording of the OBCA provisions is somewhat different. Subsection 24(1) of the OBCA provides that a corporation shall maintain a separate capital account for each class and series of shares, while subsection 24(2) goes on to provide:

> 24.(2) A corporation shall add to the appropriate stated capital account in respect of any shares it issues the full amount of the consideration it receives as determined by the directors which, in the case of shares not issued for money, shall be the amount determined by the directors in accordance with clause 23(4)(*a*) or, if a determination is made by the directors in accordance with subclause 23(4)(*b*)(i), the amount so determined.

The concept of "paid up capital" which is imposed upon shareholders under the *Income Tax Act*[163] presented certain administrative problems if the approach required under CBCA subsection 26(1) and OBCA subsection 24(2) were rigourously followed, where shares were issued in exchange for property transferred by the subscriber to a corporation. Accordingly, in 1977 the CBCA was amended[164] to allow a more flexible approach in the accounting treatment of share capital in certain cases, with a similar approach being adopted in the OBCA from the time of its enactment. Specifically, subsection 24(3)(*a*) of the OBCA provides that despite subsection 24(2) and subsection 23(3), where a corporation issues shares in exchange for,

(i) property of a person who immediately before the exchange does not deal with the corporation at arm's length within the meaning of that term in the *Income Tax Act* (Canada), or

(ii) shares of a body corporate that immediately before the exchange or that, because of the exchange, does not deal with the corporation at arm's length within the meaning of that term in the *Income Tax Act* (Canada);

the corporation may add all or any portion of the consideration it received for the shares to the appropriate stated capital account. This provision effectively allows the corporation to record the stated capital at an amount equal to the "elected amount", where property is rolled-over to a corporation under section 85 of the *Income Tax Act*. Similar latitude is allowed in the case of an amalgamation or arrangement.[165] However, on the issue of a share, a corporation must not add to the stated capital account in respect of the share an amount greater than the full amount of the consideration that it received in exchange for the share.[166]

---

[163] R.S.C. 1985, c. 1 (5th Supp.).
[164] CBCA, s. 26(3) and (4).
[165] OBCA, s. 24(3)(*b*).
[166] OBCA, s. 24(4).

§7.75 It has been said that "a negative share value is a legal impossibility".[167] Generally speaking, this is true when dealing with a limited liability corporation in the absence of impropriety, but the value of the equity capital investment made by the shareholders in a corporation may both in fact and in law erode to a negative value, by reason of accumulated losses. In such cases, the stated capital account(s) of the corporation still records the original equity investment made, but it also shows the effect of the losses as an accumulating amount that must be subtracted from that investment. So, for instance, the capital account for a given corporation may show:

Class "A" Shares

(1 million authorized, 150,000 outstanding)	$1,500,000
Less Accumulated Losses on Operations	($2,000,000)
Total Deficit	($500,000)

(vii) Subscription

§7.76 There are several ways in which a person may become a shareholder in a corporation, but the two most common methods are by purchase of shares from an existing shareholder or by subscription.[168] A subscription for shares is a written offer made to a corporation by a prospective purchaser to take up and pay for shares in the corporation.[169] Such an offer may be conditional or absolute.[170] The term is somewhat archaic, and describes two old practices: first, the signing by an incorporator[171] of an undertaking contained in an application for incorporation to purchase shares in a prospective company,[172] or the signing

---

[167] *Cha v. 604459 Alberta Ltd.* (2001), 110 A.C.W.S. (3d) 642 (Alta. Q.B.) *per* Moen J.

[168] A person may also make an oral application for shares, and if in response to that application shares are issued and taken up by the shareholder, the issue is perfectly valid, and the shareholder may not subsequently challenge its validity: *National Insurance Co. v. Egleson*, [1881] O.J. No. 223, 29 Gr. 406 at 408-409 (Ch.), *per* Boyd C.

[169] See, generally, *Re Richelieu Oil Co.* (1950), 31 C.B.R. 221 at 225 (Que. C.A.), *per* Casey J.; see also *Re London Speaker Printing Co. (Pearce's Case)*, [1889] O.J. No. 38, 16 O.A.R. 508 at 515 (C.A.), *per* Osler J.A. Under some earlier legislation an incorporator-subscriber would be liable for the subscription price even if those shares were not subsequently issued to him: *European & North American Railway v. McLeod* (1875), 16 N.B.R. 3 (C.A.), but in the absence of a statutory provision to this effect, a subscription is no more than an offer to contract which must be accepted by the corporation to become binding: *Pearce's Case*. One justification for the former rule was that such subscriptions (when included in the corporation's basic charter) constituted a public representation that the shares in question would be taken up and paid for: *Farmers Packing Co. v. Tully*, [1927] 1 W.W.R. 902 at 907 (Man. K.B.), *per* Curran J., quoting *Mitchell on Corporations* (Toronto, 1916). Under the present OBCA and CBCA, there is no subscription for shares included in the application for incorporation (indeed, there is no requirement that the incorporators ever subscribe for shares), and therefore the only applicable rules as to whether a subscription is binding are those of the laws of contract. As to the identity of the subscriber, see *Smart v. Bowmanville Machine & Implement Co.*, [1875] O.J. No. 148, 25 U.C.C.P. 503.

[170] But see *Re Manitoulin Quartzite Ltd.*, [1933] 4 D.L.R. 132 (Ont. C.A.).

[171] As to the liability of persons wrongly named as incorporators, see *Portland & Lancaster Steam Ferry Co. v. Pratt* (1850), 7 N.B.R. 17 (C.A.).

[172] *Re T.E. O'Reilly Ltd.*, [1927] O.J. No. 77, 60 O.L.R. 649 at 651 (H.C.), *per* Fisher J.; see also *Re Cement Stone & Building Co.*, [1906] O.J. No. 626, 8 O.W.R. 264; *Re George W. Griffiths Co.*,

of a stock book by a prospective incorporator.[173] The term "subscription" is now equated with any written application to a corporation for the issue of new shares to the applicant. The subscription is a mere application[174] and therefore constitutes an offer to contract and creates no obligation in the corporation until it is accepted.[175] There is no prescribed wording that must be used in order to constitute a valid subscription.[176] In contrast to the laws in some jurisdictions, a prospective shareholder may subscribe to a corporation for shares at any time after the incorporation of a corporation or before incorporation;[177] however, it is doubtful that the pre-incorporation contract provisions of the two Acts permits a share subscription to be accepted prior to incorporation because prior to incorporation there is no way to perform the obligation to issue shares in the corporation concerned.[178]

§7.77 A person subscribing for shares in a corporation has no right to insist that his application for shares be accepted. The subscription is an offer to the corporation which is open to the corporation to accept or reject, and if not accepted there is no contract.[179] The subscriber may withdraw the offer at any time until it is accepted.[180] In general, even where the corporation solicits subscriptions, the

---

[1924] D.L.R. 1031 (Man. K.B.); *Alberta Improvement Co. v. Everett*, [1914] A.J. No. 4, 6 W.W.R. 709 (S.C.), aff'd 7 W.W.R. 757 (Alta. C.A.); *Re Richelieu Oil Co.* (1950), 31 C.B.R. 321 (Que. C.A.).

[173] See, for example, *Denison v. Smith*, [1878] O.J. No. 114, 43 U.C.Q.B. 503 at 506 (C.A.), per Armour J.

[174] *Nasmith v. Manning* (1880), 5 S.C.R. 417. But there can be some confusion in this respect, for in *McDowell v. Macklem*, [1904] O.J. No. 418, 4 O.W.R. 482 (H.C.), Teetzel J. held that in the circumstances of a particular case, the subscription amounted to an acceptance of the corporation's offer to sell.

[175] *Shymka v. Smoky Lake United Farmers Co.* (1922), 66 D.L.R. 729 at 731-32 (Alta. S.C.), per Tweedie J.; *Re Dominion Milling Co.*, [1915] O.J. No. 550, 8 O.W.N. 496 (H.C.).

[176] See, generally, *Brodeur Co. v. Merrill* (1918), 57 Que. S.C. 137.

[177] See also *Re Winding-up Act and Canadian etc., Tractor Co. (Svaigher's Case)* (1914), 7 W.W.R. 562 at 564 (Sask. S.C.), per Parker M.; see also *Re London Speaker Printing Co. (Pearce's Case)*, [1889] O.J. No. 38, 16 O.A.R. 508 at 517 (C.A.) per Osler J.A. This is a practical but theoretically weak result, for the subscription can only be accepted by the corporation, and until the corporation exists it is an offer made to a non-existent person. However, any other rule would be so wholly impractical that the rule can be justified despite its weak foundation.

[178] *Re London Speaker Printing Co. (Pearce's Case)*, [1889] O.J. No. 38, 16 O.A.R. 508 at 512, per Osler J.A.; *Tilsonburg Agricultural Manufacturing Co. v. Goodrich* (1885), 8 O.R. 565 (H.C.); *Halifax Carette Co. v. Moir* (1895), 28 N.S.R. 45 (C.A.); *Halifax Steet Carette Co. v. McManus* (1894), 27 N.S.R. 173 (C.A.).

[179] *Re Bolt & Iron Co. (Hovenden's Case)* (1884), 10 P.R. 434 at 435 (H.C.), per Master Hodgins; *Re Richmond Hill Hotel Co. (Pellatt's Case)* (1867), L.R. 2 Ch. 527 (L.JJ.), per Lord Cairns L.J.; *Re Bluebird Corp.* (1926), 7 C.B.R. 522 (C.A.); *Re Monarch Bank of Canada (Murphy's Case)*, [1919] O.J. No. 156, 45 O.L.R. 412 at 420 (C.A.), per Riddell J. Where the subscription is made under seal, the applicant cannot withdraw the application: *Nelson Coke & Gas Co. v. Pellatt*, [1902] O.J. No. 179, 4 O.L.R. 481 (C.A.). The intention to make a subscription under seal must be proved as a fact: *Thompson v. Skill* (1909), 13 O.W.R. 887 at 888 (C.A.), per Moss C.J.O. Even though a standard form application for shares in a corporation has a form of seal printed at the foot of the application, it may still be held that any subscription made using the form was not intended to be made under seal — this being a question of substantive intent rather than form: *Farmers Bank v. Sunstrum* (1909), 14 O.W.R. 288 (H.C.).

[180] *Re Port Arthur Wagon Co.* (1918), 57 S.C.R. 388 at 391, per Idlington J.

solicitation is a mere invitation to treat and therefore is not open to acceptance by the subscriber in order to create a valid contract. Once accepted[181] a subscription for shares constitutes a binding contract[182] which may be enforced by[183] or against the corporation. In *Connecticut & Passumpsic River Rlwy. v. Comstock*,[184] an American railway company was requested by the inhabitants of a county in Quebec to extend its line north to the Canadian border. The cost of the extension was estimated at $1.2 million. The company agreed to build the line if the inhabitants of the county subscribed for a total of $300,000 in the capital of the corporation. The defendant was one such subscriber. The company raised the balance of the funds required by issuing preference shares, which were offered initially to its shareholders and then to the public. The defendant refused to take up and pay for the shares for which he had subscribed, arguing that by issuing the preference shares the corporation had diminished the value of the shares for which he had subscribed, thus releasing him from his agreement. It was held that even if this contention was true, it did not release the defendant from his obligation to take the shares, although it might have given rise to a cause of action for damages against the company or its directors.

§7.78 To bind the corporation, the requisites of a valid contract must be satisfied. There must be a consensus between the two parties to the subscription (the corporation and the subscriber) in the form of an offer and an acceptance.[185] Thus where a person subscribes for the issue of preference shares, the corporation may not accept that subscription by issuing common shares to that person:[186] providing the subscriber with the next best thing is not acceptance of the offer that has been made; it is at best a counter offer. Consensus requires a certainty of terms.[187] Any subscriptions submitted to the corporation must also be accepted

---

[181] Under some corporation law statutes, incorporators were required to subscribe for stock in the application for incorporation. Where a person so subscribed, it was necessary for the subscription to be accepted in order to hold that person bound to take up and pay for the shares of the corporation: see, for instance, *Alberta Improvement Co. v. Everett*, [1914] A.J. No. 4, 6 W.W.R. 709 (S.C.), aff'd 7 W.W.R. 757 (Alta. C.A.). In all other cases, however (including pre-incorporation subscriptions not appended to the application for incorporation), the normal rules of contract law relating to offer and acceptance applied to subscriptions: *Magog Textile & Print Co. v. Price* (1887), 14 S.C.R. 664 at 671, *per* Ritchie C.J.C.; *Tilsonburg Agricultural Manufacturing Co. v. Goodrich*, [1885] O.J. No. 291, 8 O.R. 565 (H.C.).

[182] See, for instance, *Boulet v. Hudon* (1916), 51 Que. S.C. 29; *Ooregum Gold Mining Co. of India Ltd. v. Roper*, [1892] A.C. 125 at 134, *per* Lord Halsbury L.C.

[183] *Re Winding-up Act and Canadian, etc., Tractor Co. (McWatt's Case)* (1914), 7 W.W.R. 562 (Sask. S.C.). As to a claim against a partnership, see *Moore v. Gurney*, [1861] O.J. No. 27, 21 U.C.Q.B. 127; (Ont. C.A.); *Re Collingwood Dry Dock, Ship Building & Foundry Co.*, [1890] O.J. No. 74, 20 O.R. 107 (H.C.).

[184] (1870), 1 R.L.O.S. 589, 20 R.J.R.Q. 392 (C.A.).

[185] But the acceptance need not be formal. It is sufficient if it is in writing, verbally or by conduct sufficient to show the subscriber that there was a response by the company to the offer: *Universal Banking Corp. (Gunn's Case)* (1867), 3 Ch. App. 40 at 45 (L.JJ.), *per* Rolt L.J. As to the application of the postbox doctrine, see *Household Fire & Carriage Accident Insurance Co. v. Grant* (1879), 4 Ex. D. 216 (C.A.); *Re London & Northern Bank, ex p. Jones*, [1900] 1 Ch. 220.

[186] *Re Port Arthur Wagon Co.* (1918), 57 S.C.R. 388 at 394-95, *per* Anglin J.

[187] *Re Jenny Lind Candy Shops* (1935), 16 C.B.R. 209 (Ont. S.C. in bank.); *Re Universal Banking Corp. (Gunn's Case)* (1867), 3 Ch. App. 40; *Baker v. Guaranty Savings & Loan Association*, [1931] S.C.R. 199.

within a reasonable period of time.[188] Finally, in order for a person to have a right to enforce the subscription contract, there must also be privity of contract: so where A and B agree between themselves that they will subscribe for shares in a corporation, only A or B may enforce that agreement; the corporation itself has no right to do so unless the corporation is a party to that agreement and has given consideration to support the promises of A and B.[189]

(1) Offer and Acceptance

§7.79 The subscription procedure weds the corporate law governing the issue of shares to the ordinary law of contract, for through the subscription process, a contract is made for the issue of shares to a specific subscriber. Generally speaking, the offer to contract is seen as being made by the subscriber-applicant.[190] Until accepted, a subscription for shares is no more than an offer to contract, and as such, acceptance of a subscription is governed by the general law of contract with respect to the making of offers.[191] Some of the early case law suggests that the offer is not accepted until there is a formal allotment of shares to the subscriber,[192] but this is no longer good law. Allotment means no more than acceptance,[193] and it is now generally understood that a subscription may be accepted in any manner as any other offer to contract.[194] Thus a subscription may be withdrawn by the applicant at any time prior to the time when it is accepted, although a revocation is not effective at the time when it is mailed, but only when it is actually communicated to the corporation.[195] The subscription must be accepted in its entirety and on the terms in which it is presented. So if an issue is over-subscribed, the corporation has no general right to allot fewer shares than the applicant has applied for unless the applicant has agreed to accept such a fewer number. However, it is now customary for corporations to include in the application forms provided in connection with the sale of shares a statement that the applicant shall agree to accept on allotment any lesser number of shares than the number of shares than that subscribed for.

---

[188] *Patterson v. Turner*, [1902] O.J. No. 75, 3 O.L.R. 373 at 377 (H.C.), per Britton J.; *Ramsgate Victoria Hotel Co. v. Montefiore* (1866), L.R. 1 Ex. 109.

[189] *Sherbrooke Clothing Co. v. Lemieux*, [1942] Que. S.C. 108.

[190] *Re National Savings Bank Association (Hebb's Case)* (1867), L.R. 4 Eq. 9; *Re Imperial Land Co. of Marseilles (Harris' Case)* (1872), 7 Ch. App. 587. Where a corporation makes a rights issue, offering a specified number of shares to an existing security holder at a specified price, the offer to contract may be seen to be made by the corporation: *Jackson v. Turquand* (1869), L.R. 4 H.L. 305.

[191] *Re Bolt & Iron Co. (Hovenden's Case)*, [1884] O.J. No. 443, 10 P.R. 437 (H.C.); and see, generally, *American Seamless Tube Corp. v. Goward*, [1931] B.C.J. No. 107, [1931] 1 W.W.R. 509 (C.A.); *Re Steel Service Ltd.* (1935), 16 C.B.R. 231 at 235 (Ont. S.C. in Bkrptcy.), per Cook Reg.

[192] See, for instance, *Peat Moss Plant Foods v. Sutherland* (1923), 23 N.B.L.R. 215 at 225 (C.A.), per Stratton J.A.

[193] *Re Florence Land & Public Works Co. (Nicol's Case)* (1885), 29 Ch. D. 421 at 427, per Chitty J.

[194] See, for instance, *Nelson Coke & Gas v. Pellatt*, [1902] O.J. No. 179, 4 O.L.R. 481 at 489 (C.A.), per McLellan J.A.; *Pierson v. Egbert* (1916), 29 D.L.R. 569, aff'g 28 D.L.R. 759 (Alta. C.A.), aff'd [1917] 2 W.W.R. 1253 (S.C.C.).

[195] *Byrne v. Van Tienhoven* (1880), 5 C.P.D. 344 at 347, per Lindley J.

§7.80 There are a number of special rules governing the acceptance of a subscription: first, a corporation cannot accept a subscription where in order to satisfy that subscription it would be necessary for the corporation to exceed its authorized capital.[196] Second, as we have seen, a subscriber must receive notice of the acceptance of the subscription so that he or she can know that a contract has been formed;[197] although it is customary for subscriptions to be accepted formally by director resolutions, subscriptions may also be accepted by equivalent acts such as the acceptance of money tendered in payment of the subscription price,[198] the issue of share certificates to the subscriber, or the subscriber is notified that his offer has been accepted if he is so notified by the secretary of the corporation or some other authorized person.[199]

§7.81 Now that shares are no longer assessable and are not supposed to be issued until they are fully paid, the primary liability that a subscriber is exposed to with respect to a share subscription is the obligation to take up and pay for shares in a corporation that subsequently proves to be insolvent. However, if carried into effect, the proposed introduction of an unlimited liability corporation regime into the OBCA will increase the relevance of the old case law regarding subscription contracts. It is clear that a subscriber for shares is liable to be named as a contributor in a bankruptcy[200] or wind-up of a corporation,[201] although a subscription may also form a basis for an action for specific performance between the corporation and the subscriber.[202] The question of whether a particular subscriber is so liable is likely to be most contentious in cases where the subscription is alleged to be so old that it is stale or where the subscriber (getting wind of the corporation's ill health) has purported to withdraw the subscription.

§7.82 If a subscription does not provide that it is open for acceptance for a specified period of time, the subscription must be accepted within a reasonable time,[203] and if not accepted lapses.[204] Where the corporation purports to accept the subscription, but the subscription is voidable at the instance of the sub-

---

[196] *Re Banker's Trust*, [1915] B.C.J. No. 20, 8 W.W.R. 38 at 38-39 (C.A.), *per* Irving J.A.
[197] *Re Canadian Mail Orders Ltd.*, [1911] O.J. No. 853, 18 O.W.R. 834 at 835 (H.C.), *per* Boyd C.
[198] There must either be a verbal or written response, or conduct of a sort which communicates to the subscriber that the corporation has accepted his or her application: *Newman v. Ginty*, [1878] O.J. No. 259, 29 U.C.C.P. 34, *per* Gwynne J.; see also *Boulet v. Hudon* (1916), 51 Que. S.C. 29.
[199] *Brodeur Co. v. Merrill* (1918), 57 Que. S.C. 137, but compare *Common v. Matthews* (1898), 8 Que. Q.B. 138 (C.A.). See also *Pierson v. Egbert* (1916), 29 D.L.R. 569 (Alta. C.A.), *per* Stuart J. aff'd [1917] 2 W.W.R. 1253 (S.C.C.).
[200] Unless the subscription can be voided on some basis, see *Re Reliable Manufacturing Co.* (1936), 17 C.B.R. 235 (Ont. S.C. in bank.), var'g 17 C.B.R. 157 (Reg.).
[201] See, for instance, *Re Canadian Slate Products Ltd.*, [1939] O.J. No. 128, 20 C.B.R. 397 (S.C. in bkrptcy.).
[202] Where a liquidator brings such an action, it appears that the subscriber may raise a broader range of defences than would be available if the action were brought to compel payment of a contribution in a liquidation. In particular, the subscriber may raise any defences which render the subscription voidable. Such defences are not normally available in a contribution proceeding: see, for instance, *Farmers Packing Co. v. Tully*, [1927] 1 W.W.R. 902 at 909 (Man. K.B.), *per* Curran J.
[203] *Patterson v. Turner*, [1902] O.J. No. 75, 3 O.L.R. 373 (H.C.).
[204] *Re Zoological & Acclimatization Society of Ontario (Cox's Case)*, [1889] O.J. No. 41, 16 O.A.R. 543 (C.A.).

scriber, he or she must be vigilant and prompt in asserting that right to repudiate the earlier subscription for the shares, otherwise the subscriber will be bound to accept them, particularly if creditors intervene by petitioning the corporation into bankruptcy or seeking its wind-up in the interim.[205]

§7.83 Prior to its acceptance, the rules respecting the withdrawal of a share subscription are also generally the same as those governing the withdrawal of any offer to contract.[206] After a subscription is purportedly accepted — that is, after the corporation sends the subscriber notice of the acceptance of the subscription or otherwise accepts that subscription[207] — the offer may be withdrawn only if the subscription was a nullity or if there is some right afforded under the subscription or at law that makes the offer voidable or otherwise terminable by the subscriber. If the subscription is a nullity, that fact may be raised in defense to a claim under the subscription at any time.[208] Where the subscription is not a nullity, but the subscriber wants to withdraw it — as, for instance, where the subscription is voidable — the subscriber must assert that right prior to the bankruptcy, insolvency or commencement of the liquidation of the corporation.[209] In all cases, the notice of withdrawal must be given to the corporation or

---

[205] *Barrett v. Bank of Vancouver*, [1917] B.C.J. No. 48, 24 B.C.R. 241 at 244 (C.A.), *per* McPhillips J.A.; *Re Land Loan Mortgage Co.* (1885), 54 L.J. Ch. 550 at 559, *per* Jay J.
[206] *Re Publishers' Syndicate*, [1902] O.J. No. 202, 3 O.L.R. 552 (H.C.).
[207] *Kruger v. Harwood* (1906), 4 W.L.R. 401, 16 Man. R. 433 (C.A.).
[208] See, for instance, *McAskill v. Northwestern Trust Co.*, [1926] S.C.R. 412, 7 C.B.R. 440 , *per* Duff J.; see also *Farmers Packing Co. v. Tully*, [1927] 1 W.W.R. 902 (Man. K.B.). As indicated briefly above, the right of a subscriber to recover the subscription price of shares purchased as a result of fraudulent misrepresentation is limited in a winding-up or bankruptcy. The principle of the intervention of the rights of third parties applies to bar a defense by a contributory of the insolvent corporation: *Trusts & Guarantee Co. v. Smith*, [1923] O.J. No. 24, 4 C.B.R. 195, 54 O.L.R. 144 (C.A.). The general rule is that where a contract for shares is voidable on the ground of misrepresentation or fraud, a shareholder who does not seek relief until after the company is in bankruptcy or liquidation will not be entitled to relief: *Stephens v. Riddell*, [1910] O.J. No. 152, 21 O.L.R. 484 (H.C.). However, this rule can have no application where there has in fact been no contract formed between the corporation and the subscriber: *Western Fire Insurance Co. v. Alexander*, [1918] 2 W.W.R. 546 (B.C.S.C.). In *Milne v. Durham Hosiery Mills Ltd.*, [1925] O.J. No. 33, 57 O.L.R. 228 (C.A.), the plaintiff subscribed and paid for shares as a result of a fraudulent misrepresentation by an agent of the company. After the company had gone into voluntary liquidation, the plaintiff brought an action against the liquidator for damages for deceit. It was held that in so doing, the plaintiff elected to retain his shares and therefore (being a shareholder) could not recover. The principle which entitles a person who has been induced by fraud to purchase goods to retain those goods and sue for damages does not apply in the case of a subscription for shares in a company because of the subordinate status of the shareholder's claim: see, generally, *Oakes v. Turquand* (1867), L.R. 2 H.L. 325. The subscriber for shares is a member as a shareholder in the company itself, and his only remedy is *restitutio in integrum*, and rescission of the contract. If that becomes impossible (by the winding-up of the company or otherwise) an action for damages cannot be maintained: *Houldsworth v. City of Glasgow Bank* (1880), 5 App. Cas. 317 (H.L.); see also *Re National Stadium Ltd.*, [1924] O.J. No. 9, 55 O.L.R. 199 (H.C.).
[209] As to the steps required to repudiate, see *Re Sun Ray Manufacturing Co.*, [1924] O.J. No. 545, 4 C.B.R. 615 at 621-22 (S.C. in Bkrptcy.), *per* Fisher J.; and *Re Winding-up Act and Canadian Tractor, etc., Co.* (1914), 7 W.W.R. 562 (Sask. S.C.); *Kruger v. Harwood* (1906), 4 W.L.R. 401 at 402, 16 Man. R. 433 (C.A.), *per* Mathers J.; *Re Globe Fire Insurance Co.* (1909), 11 W.L.R. 45, aff'd 11 W.L.R. 293 (Sask. C.A.).

an agent of the corporation authorized to receive such a notice (*e.g.*, the corporate secretary). The notice of the withdrawal of the subscription must be irrevocable and unequivocal in nature.[210] If an accepted subscription is not voidable and there is no right to withdraw it after acceptance under its terms, any notice of withdrawal purportedly given after the acceptance of the subscription is ineffective.[211] The subscriber may not undo what is then an accepted offer (*i.e.*, a contract); moreover, the corporation may release the subscriber from his or her obligation only in accordance with section 34 of the OBCA.[212]

§7.84 The form of consideration tendered in payment of the subscription price does not improve the shareholder's position in the event of a bankruptcy. If a debt is cancelled in exchange for shares, the shareholder is relegated to the position of a shareholder. Similarly, a person who tenders goods in payment of the subscription price for shares may not subsequently reclaim those goods should the corporation make an assignment for the general benefit of its creditors[213] or otherwise become the subject of bankruptcy proceedings. It is extremely doubtful that the rights of revendication now conferred upon unpaid suppliers under section 81.1 of the *Bankruptcy and Insolvency Act*[214] in any way alter this rule.

§7.85 It has been held that a subscription is an application for the issue of new shares, and consequently where a corporation accepts a subscription for its shares, it does not perform its obligation by arranging for the transfer of pre-existing shares to the subscriber. Presumably the subscriber seeks to strengthen the capital base of the corporation, not arrange for the retirement of an existing shareholder.[215] However, there would appear to be no difference in issuing treasury stock[216] to a subscriber rather than newly created shares. Such stock cannot be shown as a part of shareholder equity[217] and consequently the effect of pur-

---

[210] *Re Western Canada Fire Insurance Co.* (1915), 7 W.W.R. 1365 (Alta. C.A.).
[211] *Nelson Coke & Gas Co. v. Pellatt*, [1902] O.J. No. 179, 4 O.L.R. 481 (C.A.). However, where a corporation purports to issue shares to a creditor in satisfaction of a debt without any request by the creditor that it do so, the creditor may dispute the validity of that share issue as a satisfaction of the debt: *Re Whistle Co.* (1925), 5 C.B.R. 495 (Ont. S.C. in Bkrptcy.).
[212] CBCA, s. 38. Note that a special resolution of the corporation is required, not simply a resolution of the directors.
[213] *Re Sun Ray Manufacturing Co.*, [1924] O.J. No. 545, 5 C.B.R. 303 (S.C. in Bkrptcy.).
[214] R.S.C. 1985, c. B-3.
[215] *Witcomb v. Toronto General Trusts Corp.*, [1931] B.C.J. No. 133, [1931] 2 W.W.R. 545 (S.C.).
[216] Briefly defined, treasury stock is the term used to describe shares in the capital stock of a corporation that has been issued and fully paid for, only to be reacquired by the corporation and held by it for future reissue. Treasury stock is permissible under the OBCA and CBCA only in limited cases, subsection 35(6) of the OBCA providing:

> 35.(6) Shares of any class or series or fractional shares issued by a corporation and purchased, redeemed or otherwise acquired by it shall be cancelled or, if the articles limit the number of authorized shares of the class or series, may be restored to the status of authorized but unissued shares of the class.

See also CBCA, s. 39(6).
[217] OBCA, s. 35(1); CBCA, s. 39(1).

chasing it is identical to the purchase of newly issued stock.[218] Like all contract offers, an offer to purchase shares may be accepted only by the person to whom it is made. Therefore, an offer to purchase existing shares from a shareholder is not a subscription for new shares in a corporation and may not be accepted by the corporation.[219]

(2) Conditional Subscriptions

§7.86 Although there is a presumption that share subscriptions are not subject to any conditions,[220] a subscription for shares (or other securities) may be made subject to a condition precedent[221] in which case the subscription will not be binding, even if accepted, until that condition is satisfied.[222] So where an applicant for shares in a corporation agrees to take them conditionally upon his or her receiving certain moneys to pay for them, that applicant has a right to withdraw the application by informing the corporation of his or her non-receipt of those moneys, and in such cases the subscriber will not be liable as a contributory.[223] Similarly, the corporation may make its acceptance of a subscription conditional upon the satisfaction of some condition precedent, and where it does so, the corporation is not bound to issue shares to the subscriber until that condition is satisfied.[224] It has been held that where there is a written agreement to take shares in a corporation and contemporaneously therewith a collateral oral agreement is made that the written agreement is not to take effect until some other event happens, parol evidence is admissible to prove that contemporaneous oral agreement.[225]

§7.87 The general law of contract distinguishes between a condition precedent and a condition subsequent. These distinctions influence the corporate law respecting conditional share subscriptions, but the rules must be modified in line with the restrictions applicable to the reduction of share capital (and liability in

---

[218] *Goold v. Gillies* (1908), 1 E.L.R. 440, aff'd 42 N.S.R. 28, aff'd 40 S.C.R. 437; see also *Clay v. S.P. Powell & Co.*, [1932] S.C.R. 210; *Brydges v. Dominion Trust Co.*, [1919] O.J. No. 58, [1919] 2 W.W.R. 510 (S.C.).

[219] *Canadian Druggists' Syndicate Ltd. v. Thompson*, [1911] O.J. No. 56, 24 O.L.R. 108 (Div. Ct.); see also *Consumers' Cordage Co. v. Molson* (1912), 2 D.L.R. 451 (Que. C.A.).

[220] See, for instance, *Re Port Arthur Waggon Co.*, [1916] O.J. No. 697, 9 O.W.N. 358 (C.A.); *Moore v. Murphy* (1862), 11 U.C.C.P. 444 (Ont. C.A.); and see generally *North Sydney Mining & Transportation Co. v. Greener* (1898), 31 N.S.R. 41 (C.A.); but compare *Re Nutter Brewery Ltd.*, [1910] O.J. No. 569, 15 O.W.R. 265 (H.C.).

[221] *Johnson v. Canada Theaters Ltd.* (1955), 15 W.W.R. 41 (Alta. C.A.); *Woodgers & Calthorpe Ltd. v. Bowring* (1935), 35 S.R. (N.S.W.) 483 at 485, *per* Jordan C.J. As to the meaning of condition precedent, see *Clarke v. Union Fire Insurance Co.*, [1884] O.J. No. 413, 10 P.R. 339 at 334 (H.C.), *per* Master Hodgins.

[222] *Re Great Northern Assurance Co.* (1915), 9 W.W.R. 240 (Man. K.B.).

[223] *Re Publishers' Syndicate*, [1902] O.J. No. 202, 3 O.L.R. 552 (H.C.). It would appear that in such a case, there is no obligation on the subscriber to inform the corporation that the condition in question has not been met: *per* Street J. at 554.

[224] *Shack v. Matthews Construction Co.*, [1962] O.J. No. 578, [1962] O.R. 556 (C.A.).

[225] *Ontario Ladies' College v. Kendry*, [1905] O.J. No. 63, 10 O.L.R. 324 at 328 (C.A.), *per* Moss C.J.O. *Re Provincial Machine & Supply Co.*, [1923] O.J. No. 423, 4 C.B.R. 148 (S.C. in Bkrptcy.); see also *Wallis v. Littell* (1861), 11 C.B.N.S. 309, 142 E.R. 840 (C.P.); *Davis v. Jones* (1856), 17 C.B. 625, 139 E.R. 635; *Pym v. Campbell* (1856), 6 E. & B. 370, 119 E.R. 903 (K.B.).

respect of unpaid share capital) that apply to corporations. Either type of condition may be set out on the face of the subscription or in a side document or may even be expressed orally, provided in every case that it is clear that the condition is an integral part of the subscription.[226] In contrast to a condition precedent, the non-satisfaction of a condition subsequent[227] may not normally be raised by a subscriber in defense of a claim[228] against the subscriber as a contributor,[229] or in respect of any other type of claim that a creditor or creditor's representative may be entitled to bring against the subscriber.[230]

§7.88 A condition of a subscription contract may be such that it ceases to be operative as a condition when the subscriber becomes a shareholder in fact. The terms of the subscription will be dependent for effect upon the status of the term concerned as a collateral agreement for the surrender of the shares and a return of the money paid for them — meaning that the subscriber's right will be subject to the general law respecting reduction of share capital.[231] The key consideration is whether the subscriber's present intent is to become a shareholder or is instead an intent to become a shareholder only when a particular condition is met. It is the latter which makes a condition a condition precedent. Where a person takes up shares without regard to whether the conditions on which he or she subscribed for those shares have been satisfied, that person will not be allowed to complain of the non-satisfaction of that condition where a claim is brought against him or her as a contributory in a bankruptcy[232] or winding-up of a company. However, if the subscriber is misled into believing that a condition precedent has been satisfied, where it has not been, he will not be considered to have waived the condition.[233]

§7.89 In *Country Ltd. v. Gironsentrale Securities*,[234] the plaintiff bank agreed to underwrite the issue of some 26 million shares in a publicly traded company. The bank advised the company and its brokers that it would only proceed with the issue if institutional investors agreed to subscribe for all of the shares. The bank's letter of engagement required the brokers to offer the shares to prospec-

---

[226] *Re Canadian McVicker Engine Co.*, [1909] O.J. No. 712, 13 O.W.R. 916 (H.C.); *Macdonald v. Soulis* (1925), 58 N.S.R. 134, [1925] 2 D.L.R. 926 (H.C.).
[227] As to the distinction between the two in the context of share subscriptions, see *Monarch Life Assurance Co. v. Brophy*, [1907] O.J. No. 100, 14 O.L.R. 1 (C.A.); *Gillespie v. Clover Bar Coal Co.* (1911), 16 W.L.R. 534, 3 Alta. L.R. 238 (T.D.).
[228] *Re National Stadium Ltd.*, [1924] O.J. No. 9, 55 O.L.R. 199 (C.A.).
[229] *Alberta Rolling Mills Co. v. Christie*, [1919] 1 W.W.R. 572, 58 S.C.R. 208 at 211, *per* Idlington J; and see, generally, *Re Wiarton Sugar Beet Manufacturing Co.*, [1905] O.J. No. 388, 5 O.W.R. 542 (H.C.); *Princess Copper Mines Ltd. v. Trelle*, [1922] 3 W.W.R. 59 (Alta. S.C.).
[230] *Barrett v. Bank of Vancouver*, [1917] B.C.J. No. 48, [1917] 3 W.W.R. 53 at 54, 36 D.L.R. 158 (C.A.), *per* McPhillips J.A; *Re Monarch Bank*, [1919] O.J. No. 156, 45 O.L.R. 412 (C.A.).
[231] *Alberta Rolling Mills Co. v. Christie*, [1919] 1 W.W.R. 572, 58 S.C.R. 208 at 213, *per* Anglin J.
[232] *Vizzard v. E.W. Lancaster*, [1925] O.J. No. 482, 28 O.W.N. 433 (H.C.); *Re Buff Pressed Brick Co.*, [1924] O.J. No. 85, 56 O.L.R. 33 (H.C.); *Re Manitoulin Quartzite Ltd.*, [1933] 4 D.L.R. 132 at 138 (Ont. C.A.), *per* Riddell J.A.
[233] *Canadian Ohio Motor Car Co. v. Cochrane*, [1915] O.J. No. 653, 7 O.W.N. 698 (H.C.), *per* Latchford J., aff'd [1915] O.J. No. 434, 8 O.W.N. 242 (C.A.).
[234] [1966] 3 All E.R. 834 (C.A.)

tive investors strictly on the terms and conditions contained in certain issue documents, which did not include disclosure of the bank's intention to proceed only on an "all or nothing" basis. The brokers obtained indicative commitments from certain investors, but in so doing informed those investors that the issue would go ahead only if it was fully subscribed. An indicative commitment for some 6 million shares was also made by the chairman of the company, on behalf of unnamed investors. When the issue was made, the chairman was unable to provide subscriptions from those unnamed investors, with the result that nearly 4.5 million shares were not taken up. Certain of the investors who had subscribed on the basis that the offer was fully subscribed then withdrew. As a result the bank lost nearly £6.9 million on the deal as underwriter. The bank sued the brokers claiming that they had acted outside their authority and in breach of the terms of their engagement letter. At trial, the judge held that the terms of the letter did not prohibit the brokers from telling potential investors of the bank's intentions. Moreover, the representation was not the sole cause of the loss; a number of factors had contributed to it, not least of which was the bank's decision to accept the vague indicative commitments provided by the chairman of the company without making proper inquiries to confirm the existence of actual investors. The bank appealed. On appeal it was held that the letter made it clear that the brokers were not free to give information to investors beyond that specified in the issue documents. It was fundamental to the success of the placement that the brokers did not do or say anything at the time of obtaining an indicative commitment that might enable an investor to back out of the transaction. By disclosing the bank's intent to proceed only on an "all or nothing" basis, they had provided investors with an escape route. This breach of contract by the brokers was the effective cause of the bank's loss. The fact that another cause also contributed to the bank's loss did not require the judge to choose which cause was the more effective. It was sufficient that the broker's breach of contract was an effective cause, and it remained effective despite the fact that the bank had not made sufficient inquiries into the nature of the commitments obtained by the chairman.

C. MISREPRESENTATION AND SHARE SUBSCRIPTIONS

§7.90 It is no longer practically possible to extricate the law relating to misrepresentation as it applies to shares from the law with respect to other securities. Increasingly, specific securities regulatory statutes — such as (in Ontario) the *Securities Act* and the various rules, policies and regulations promulgated under it — are supplanting the older rules of contract and tort. Moreover, since many of the principles of law that are relevant with respect to misrepresentation in the context of share issuance, are also of relevance in other contexts, it is convenient to digress momentarily from the discussion of share capital in order to summarize in one place the relevant principles with respect to misrepresentation, and therefore to digress from the on-going discussion with respect to the equity capital of a corporation.

§7.91 The governing principle with respect to misrepresentation in the case of solicitation of share subscriptions was laid down long ago by Kindersley V. in *New Brunswick & Canada Rlwy. Co. v. Muggeridge*.[235] He said:

> ... [I]t appears to me that it is quite necessary to uphold this as a principle: that those who issue a prospectus holding out to the public the great advantages which will accrue to persons who will take shares in a proposed undertaking and inviting them to take shares on the faith of the representations therein contained, are bound to state everything with strict and scrupulous accuracy, and not only to abstain from stating as facts that which is not so, but to omit no one fact within their knowledge, the existence of which might in any degree affect the nature, or extent, or quality of the privileges and advantages, which the prospectus holds out as inducements to take shares.[236]

Since that oft-quoted statement of principle was laid down, the law has tightened greatly.[237] Unfortunately, the modifications that have been made to the law have not been uniformly applied to all corporations. Instead, in considering the law with respect to misrepresentations inducing subscriptions for shares, it is necessary to differentiate between corporations whose securities are distributed to the public ("publicly traded corporations") and those which are not ("privately held corporations").

§7.92 In the case of publicly traded corporations, considerable rights are afforded to subscribers under the *Securities Act*[238] and *Securities Act General Regulation*.[239] In particular, a person who subscribes for securities in a corporation where the prospectus relating to the securities contain a misrepresentation is entitled to a number of remedies under section 126 of the Act.[240] With one important exception[241] subscribers for shares in privately held corporations are limited to: (a) those remedies which are provided in respect of misrepresentation at common law; (b) to the remedy available under sections 248 of the OBCA and 241 of the CBCA — the shareholder oppression remedy; and (c) an application for the wind-up of the corporation. This section reviews the common law remedies arising from misrepresentations in connection with a share subscription.

(i) The Common Law

§7.93 The modern law relating to fraud and misrepresentation is complex, being an amalgam of common law, equity and in some respects statute, particularly (as noted above) in the case of securities transactions subject to the *Securities Act*.[242]

---

[235] (1860), 1 Dr. & Sm. 363, 62 E.R. 418.
[236] *Ibid.*, at 485.
[237] Dishonesty in share transactions may have criminal as well as civil consequences. Concerning potential criminal consequences, see Michael Brent Henderson, *Commercial Crime in Canada* (Toronto: Carswell, 1990), c. 6.
[238] R.S.O. 1990, c. S.5.
[239] R.R.O. 1990, Reg. 1015.
[240] Discussed below at §7.112, *et seq.*
[241] Except in the case of a distribution of securities exempt from the *Securities Act* under s. 72(1)(*d*) of the Act.
[242] R.S.O. 1990, c. S.5.

It is further complicated by the fact that some types of misrepresentation constitute an actionable tort, while others are innocent in nature.

§7.94 At common law both fraud and misrepresentation may render a contract voidable at the option of the injured party. Where a misrepresentation (fraudulent, negligent or innocent) forms a term of a contract, an action lies for breach of contract against the party guilty of the misrepresentation in favour of the other party to the contract (but not in favour of a non-party). The plaintiff in an action for damages based upon fraud may seek to recover on two grounds. First, he or she may sue to receive the "benefit-of-the-bargain" — that is to recover the difference between the actual market value of what was actually received and the value of what was supposed to have been received. Alternatively, a plaintiff may sue for his "out-of-pocket" loss, and seek to recover the amount expended as a result of the fraud, and any other loss attributable to the fraud. In some cases, punitive damages may also be available, particularly where the fraud was malicious, wanton, willful, or made with a total disregard of the consequences of the fraud. The precise legal effect of a material misrepresentation made during the course of the negotiations of the contract depends upon the nature of the statement. A misrepresentation may be collateral to the contract or may become embodied in the contract as one of its terms. Where the statement becomes a term of the contract, it may be either a condition or a warranty. If the statement is a condition, then the falsity of the statement will make it possible for the other party to treat the contract as repudiated. If it is a mere warranty, then only damages will be available. Where a misrepresentation is material to a transaction, the court may set aside the transaction at the request of the innocent party, if that innocent party can be shown to have acted on the strength of it. If the representation is fraudulent, an action will also lie for deceit. If the misrepresentation was negligent, a claim may be brought for negligence, provided the person injured by the misrepresentation was owed a duty of care by the speaker. There is no tortious liability where there is neither negligence or fraud involved in the misrepresentation (*i.e.*, in the case of innocent misrepresentation), although where the untruth of a representation breaches a term of the contract, a claim for damages may be made for breach of contract.

§7.95 Where the misrepresentation does not form a term of the contract, or a non-party to a contract wishes to sue in respect of that misrepresentation, the claim must be based in tort. An action in tort for fraud or deceit may be brought at common law where the following conditions are met:

- There must have been a false representation which was fraudulent. In general terms, fraud is the obtaining of a material advantage by unfair or wrongful means.
- In order to prove fraud, it is necessary to show dishonesty. It is not, however, necessary to show that the person making the statement intended to cause the other person harm: fraud may be committed even though the statement was made in the belief that no one would suffer a loss.

- The maker must have known that the representation was false or have been recklessly indifferent as to whether it was true or false. However, a statement is not fraudulent if it is made with an honest belief in its truth, even if that belief was unreasonable.

- The maker must have intended that the representation would be relied upon by the person to whom it was made.

- That person must have relied upon it and suffered damages as a consequence. However, where the misrepresentation in question is one which is calculated to be, or would naturally tend to be, relied upon, the plaintiff's reliance may be inferred. The inference may be rebutted, but the onus of proof lies on the person who made the misrepresentation.[243]

Breach of contract for fraudulent misrepresentation entitles the wronged party not only to avoid the contract but to sue in tort for damages to compensate for his or her out-of-pocket loss, including consequential damages.[244]

§7.96 Misrepresentation is wider conceptually than fraud, for the term describes any false statement of fact.[245] Fraud involves a degree of willful misconduct; however, misrepresentation does not necessarily imply moral obloquy on the part of the person who made the misrepresentation: a person may negligently misrepresent the facts material to a transaction,[246] and indeed a misrepresentation may still occur even when the speaker takes reasonable care to ensure the truth of all statements made. It follows that misrepresentation may be innocent, negligent or fraudulent in nature.[247] The character of misrepresentation may change during the course of a transaction. For instance, innocent or negligent misrepresentation becomes fraudulent where the untruth of the statement becomes known to its maker and he fails to inform the other party, when it is possible to do so before the time when the other party suffers injury. To establish a claim in tort for negligent misrepresentation at common law, it is necessary to show that:

- There was an untrue, misleading, inaccurate or otherwise false representation which is material. The determination of materiality is an objective question of fact to be made on a fair consideration of all the evidence.[248] The question is not, however, whether a reasonable individual would have objected, but rather

---

[243] *Kripps v. Touche Ross & Co.*, [1997] B.C.J. No. 968, [1997] 6 W.W.R. 421, 89 B.C.A.C. 288 (C.A.); *Parallels Restaurant Ltd. v. Yeung's Enterprises Ltd.*, [1990] B.C.J. No. 1861, 49 B.L.R. 237 at 245 (C.A.), *per* Anderson J.A.

[244] *Petro-Canada v. 366084 Ontario Ltd.*, [1995] O.J. No. 3994, 25 B.L.R. (2d) 19 at 33 (Gen. Div.), *per* Cumming J.

[245] As to statements of opinion at common law, see *Bisset v. Wilkinson*, [1927] A.C. 177 (P.C.). As to statements of intention, see *Edgington v. Fitzmaurice* (1885), 29 Ch. D. 459 (C.A.) — declared intent that was never the true intent of the directors was held to be a misrepresentation.

[246] *Smith v. Chadwick* (1882), 20 Ch. D. 27 (C.A.).

[247] For a case dealing with liability for negligent misrepresentation in a prospectus, see *Possfund Custodian Trustee v. Diamond*, [1996] 2 All E.R. 774, [1996] 2 B.C.L.C. 665, *per* Lightman J.

[248] *Ontario Metal Products Co. v. Mutual Life Insurance*, [1925] 1 W.W.R. 362 at 368 (P.C.).

whether the statements were reasonably capable of affecting the mind of a reader.[249]

- The misrepresentation must have been made by a person who owed a duty of care arising from a special relationship between the person making the representation and the person to whom the representation was made.

- The misrepresentation must have arisen as a result of negligence on the part of the person making the representation (*i.e.*, a failure to exercise reasonable care).

- The person to whom the representation was made must have relied on the misrepresentation to an extent and in circumstances where it was reasonable to do so.

- Damages or loss must have resulted as a consequence of that reliance.[250]

§7.97 There are two elements of causation that must be alleged in a claim based upon misrepresentation leading to loss in a securities related case, these being transaction causation and loss causation.[251] The respective scope of these two distinct requirements were briefly summarized in *Caremark Inc. v. Coram Healthcare Corp.*[252] where it was said:

> To plead transaction causation, the plaintiff must allege that it would not have invested in the instrument if the defendant had stated truthfully the material facts at the time of sale. To plead loss causation, the plaintiff must allege that it was the very facts about which the defendant lied which caused its injuries.

In *Emergent Capital Inv. Mgmt., LLC v. Stonepath Group, Inc.*, the court provided more specific guidance:

> ... transaction causation refers to the causal link between the defendant's misconduct and the plaintiff's decision to buy or sell securities. ... It is established simply by showing that, but for the claimed misrepresentations or omissions, the plaintiff would not have entered into the detrimental securities transaction. ... Loss causation, by contrast, is the causal link between the alleged misconduct and the economic harm ultimately suffered by the plaintiff. ... We have often compared loss causation to the tort law concept of proximate case, "meaning that the damages suffered by plaintiff must be a foreseeable consequence of any misrepresentation or material omission." ... Similar to loss causation, the proximate cause element of common law fraud requires that plaintiff adequately allege a causal connection between defendants' nondisclosures and the subsequent decline in the value of the [the] securities ... Of course, if the loss was caused by an intervening event, like a general fall in the price of Internet stocks, the chain of causation will not have

---

[249] *Inland Kenworth Ltd. v. Commonwealth Insurance Co.*, [1990] B.C.J. No. 1858, 48 B.C.L.R. (2d) 305 at 309 (C.A.); *Kirpps v. Touche Ross*, [1997] B.C.J. No. 968, [1997] 6 W.W.R. 421 (C.A.); but *cf. L.K. Oil & Gas Ltd. v. Canalands Energy Corp.*, [1989] A.J. No. 577, 60 D.L.R. (4th) 490 at 498 (C.A.), leave to appeal to S.C.C. refused (1990), 65 D.L.R. (4th) viii.

[250] *NBD Bank, Canada v. Dofasco Inc.*, [1997] O.J. No. 1803, 34 B.L.R. (2d) 209 at 228 (Gen. Div.), *per* Crane J.

[251] *In Re Enron Corporation Securities*, 310 F. Supp. 2d 819 (S.D. Tex. 2004).

[252] 113 F.3d 645 at 648 (7th Cir. 1997).

been established. But such is a matter of proof at trial and not to be decided on a Rule 12(b)(6) motion to dismiss.[253]

§7.98 In the ordinary case, the common law of misrepresentation does not protect anyone who may learn of a misrepresentation, but only those persons to whom the misrepresentation is made. Thus, as a general rule under the common law, where a misrepresentation is set out in a prospectus, that misrepresentation will entitle a subscriber for shares who relies on the prospectus to rescind the contract, but will not entitle a person who purchases the shares from the subscriber to obtain rescission.[254] However, an exception to this general rule applies where the intent of the prospectus was not only to create a primary market among potential subscribers for shares, but also a secondary market.[255] Where third parties who hear of the misrepresentation are protected, their remedy is in damages rather than rescission, for there is no contract to which they are party that is capable of being rescinded.

§7.99 To constitute misrepresentation, it is usually necessary that the statement be unambiguous.[256] However, the decision in the criminal case of *R. v. Kylsant*[257] places an important qualification upon this rule. In that case, a prospectus was found to have been issued by a shipping company with respect to a series of debentures. During several years, the company had suffered a series of losses, but had continued to pay dividends out of its retained earnings and reserves for future taxes. The prospectus made reference to the dividend payments, but carefully concealed their source. It was carefully worded to create the impression that the dividends had been paid out of current trading profits and that the earning power of the corporation was sufficient to meet the requirements of the debenture. Nevertheless, despite conveying a misleading impression, none of the statements contained in the debenture was literally and strictly untrue. Even so, the court held that the prospectus contained false statements of fact. It follows that an ambiguous statement will amount to misrepresentation where it is made in a manner that is calculated to deceive, or when it is misleading no matter in which of all possible meanings it is understood. Representations must fairly and fully present the truth in the apparent sense and meaning conveyed by the terms in which they are expressed.[258]

§7.100 To entitle the innocent party to a remedy the misrepresentation must be material.[259] A statement is material if it is one of fact that could reasonably be

---

[253] 343 F.3d 189 at 196-97 (2d Cir. 2003).
[254] *Peek v. Gurney* (1873), L.R. 6 H.L. 377.
[255] *Andrews v. Mockford*, [1896] 1 Q.B. 372.
[256] But see *Aaron's Reefs Ltd. v. Twiss*, [1896] A.C. 273 at 281 (H.L.), *per* Lord Halsbury L.C.
[257] [1932] 1 K.B. 442.
[258] *New Brunswick & Canada Rlwy. & Land Co. v. Muggeridge* (1860), 1 Dr. & Sm. 363 at 381, *per* Kindersley V.C.
[259] It is argued that where a statement is made with a fraudulent intent, the party who made the representation will not be allowed to deny its materiality: see, for instance, *Smith v. Kay* (1859), 7 H.L. Cas. 750. However, if the representation is clearly immaterial, and if it was the only misrepresentation that was made, it is difficult to see how the court could sustain a finding of fraudulent intent.

expected to influence the decision of the person to whom it is made as to whether to enter into a transaction — that is, where it is of a kind which would affect the judgment of a reasonable person in deciding whether or not to enter into a contract.[260] The subjective belief of the statement by the person making the representation as to the influence that a representation is likely to have is irrelevant to the determination of its materiality.[261] In contrast, the subjective assessment of materiality to the victim may have a bearing on the materiality of a representation, at least where the party making an apparently immaterial misrepresentation knew that the victim would be influenced by it. Quite clearly, where a contract includes a provision that a particular representation made to one party by another party will be deemed to be material, the materiality of that provision will be binding on the party making the representation, however unimportant it might otherwise seem.[262]

§7.101 A misrepresentation must be as to some existing fact. Generally, it is not sufficient to prove a false statement of opinion, a promise of future conduct (*i.e.*, intention) or a misstatement of law. However, a statement of future intention will amount to misrepresentation, where it can be shown that the person making the statement did not possess that intention at the time when the statement was made.[263] For instance, it would obviously be a misrepresentation to tell potential subscribers that funds raised through the issue of securities would be put to a specified purpose, when, in fact, there was no intent to so use them. As noted above, the general rule is that non-disclosure does not constitute misrepresentation — although this statement can only be made in a qualified sense, since corporate and securities laws impose numerous disclosure obligations. Even tacit acquiescence by one party in the other party's self-deception is acceptable, provided that self-deception was not caused by a representation made by the party. Moreover, the conduct of a person may be sufficient to constitute a representation.[264] In addition, although total non-disclosure does not normally amount to misrepresentation, partial non-disclosure may do so; one cannot tell only the good and ignore the bad.

§7.102 Despite receiving a misrepresentation, a person will not be permitted to avoid liability where he or she had actual knowledge of the facts.[265] A person must be not only a recipient of misinformation, but a victim of it. However, where there is an express misrepresentation of fact, it is not an answer to a claim based upon it to say that the person to whom the representation was made had the opportunity to discover that the statement was incorrect, or that he or she might have discovered the truth through the exercise of reasonable care. For instance, in *Venezuela Rlwy. Co. v. Kisch*[266] a prospectus of a railway company

---

[260] See, for instance, *Greenwood v. Leather Shod Wheel Co.*, [1900] 1 Ch. 421 (C.A.).
[261] *Gordon v. Street*, [1899] 2 Q.B. 641.
[262] See, generally, *London Assurance v. Mansel* (1879), 11 Ch. D. 363.
[263] *Edgington v. Fitzmaurice* (1885), 29 Ch. D. 459 (C.A.).
[264] See, generally, *McKeown v. Boudard-Perveril Gear Co.* (1896), 65 L.J. Ch. 735 (C.A.).
[265] *Davison v. Priest* (1920), 53 N.S.R. 426 at 437, 51 D.L.R. 158 (S.C.), *per* Harris C.J.
[266] (1867), L.R. 2 H.L. 99.

contained untrue representations of material fact. However, the prospectus went on to say that "the engineer's report, maps, plans, etc. may be inspected and further information obtained at the offices of the company". Trusting to the representations set out in the prospectus, Kisch did not examine the underlying reports, etc. of the engineer. It was held that his neglect to do so did not disentitle him from being released from the contract. However, if a potential investor tests the truth of a representation that has been made, but fails to discover the truth, he or she will lose the right to relief for misrepresentation in cases where the representation was innocent or negligent, but not if the misrepresentation was fraudulent.[267]

§7.103 A person will only be released from a contract where he or she relied upon a misrepresentation which was made. For instance, in *Smith v. Chadwick*[268] the prospectus of a company listed a James J. Grieve M.P. as a director. In fact, he was not. The plaintiff Smith bought shares in the company and subsequently sought to have the agreement set aside on the ground of misrepresentation. At trial, he stated in evidence that he had never heard of Grieve before, and when asked if seeing the name had any effect upon him he answered with a shake of the head. It was held that the misrepresentation in the prospectus did not induce Smith to enter into the contract.[269] It is not necessary, however, that the misrepresentation be the sole motivating factor in the decision to enter into the contract; it is sufficient if it is a factor. Thus in *Edgington v. Fitzmaurice*,[270] the plaintiff was induced to purchase debentures partly because of a misrepresentation and partly because of his mistaken belief as to the rights conferred by the debentures. He was held to be entitled to rescind the contract, even though the misrepresentation was not the sole motivating factor in his decision to purchase the debentures. This case is also significant in that it stands for the proposition that a statement of intention can amount to a misstatement of fact (as, for instance, where it amounts to a misrepresentation of the present intentions of the speaker, or of the present intentions of some other person that are known to the speaker).

§7.104 In order for a party to avoid liability under a contract on the ground of fraud or misrepresentation, the fraud or misrepresentation must be that of the other party to the contract. The misstatement of a person who is a stranger to the contract is insufficient. If A is induced by B's fraud or negligence to enter into a contract with C, A's remedy is by way of an action for deceit or negligence against B. However, where B is the agent of C, then C is bound by the misrepresentation or fraud of B as if he (or she) had made it himself.

§7.105 Misrepresentation and fraud both render a contract voidable rather than void. A voidable contract cannot be set aside if the person who was entitled to

---

[267] See, generally, G.H. Teote, *The Law of Contract*, 5th ed. (London: Stevens & Sons, 1979), 253.
[268] (1882), 20 Ch. D. 27 (C.A.), aff'd (1883-84) 9 App. Cas. 187 (H.L.).
[269] *Per* Jessell M.R. at 52.
[270] (1885), 29 Ch. D. 459 (C.A.).

apply for relief ratifies the contract. Ratification takes place where the person who has the right of rescission indicates his or her approval or satisfaction with the contract. Such an indication may be express or implied. Retention of the consideration given by the other party, or of the benefits of the contract, combined with an act or statement that evidences an overt expression of approval will constitute ratification. Ratification will not be seen to have taken place unless the party ratifying the contract knew or had notice of all relevant facts.

§7.106 At common law, a shareholder could not sue the corporation for damages relating to an alleged misrepresentation by the corporation that induced the shareholder to subscribe for his or her shares in the corporation, unless he or she first rescinded the contract. Once the corporation goes into liquidation, such rescission is impossible.[271] A subscriber who delays in repudiating his or her subscription or seeking rescission of the subscription contract for an unreasonable period of time will lose that remedy under the doctrine of laches.[272] In *Re Estates Investment Co. (Ashley's Case)*,[273] the plaintiff had been present at a meeting at which allegations of misrepresentation were made. Some of the members of the company formed a committee to commence legal proceedings against the company, but the plaintiff did not join them. Only one of the group actually instituted proceedings, but when the case was ultimately decided in his favour, the plaintiff sought to recover as well. It was held that the plaintiff had lost his right to rescission by reason of his delay.[274]

§7.107 On the basis of the foregoing, it is clear that where a subscription for shares is induced by misrepresentation made by the corporation or its agents,[275] the purchaser has a right to rescind the subscription or any purchase resulting from it and also is entitled to recover any damages suffered,[276] particularly in a case of fraud,[277] but also in the case of negligence.[278] In the case of innocent misrepresentation, there is no right to recover damages for tort, but there is a right of rescission. In all these cases the right of rescission must be exercised with respect to all shares to which the misrepresentation pertained; the subscriber cannot both approve and disapprove.[279] Where the subscriber would be entitled

---

[271] *Houldsworth v. City of Glasgow Bank* (1880), 5 App. Cas. 317 (H.L.).
[272] See, for instance, *Re Scottish Petroleum Co.* (1883), 23 Ch. D. 413 at 434 (C.A.), *per* Baggallay L.J.; *Re Russian (Vyksounsky) Iron Works Co. (Taite's Case)* (1867), L.R. 3 Eq. 795; *Heymann v. European Central Ry. Co.* (1868), L.R. 7 Eq. 154; *Re Snyder Dynamite Projectile Co. (Skelton's Case)* (1893), 68 L.T. 210; *cf. Armstrong v. Jackson*, [1917] 2 K.B. 822.
[273] (1870), L.R. 9 Eq. 263.
[274] *Ibid.*, *per* Lord Romilly at 268-69. See also *Re Estates Investment Co. (Pawle's Case)* (1869), L.R. 4 Ch. App. 497.
[275] *International Casualty Co. v. Thomson* (1913), 48 S.C.R. 167; *Ruck v. McLeod*, [1985] B.C.J. No. 2266, 3 B.C.L.R. (2d) 35 (C.A.); *Huber v. Lion Mead Rubber Co.*, [1923] O.J. No. 215, 25 O.W.N. 72 (Co. Ct.); *Fitzherbert v. Dominion Bed Manufacturing Co.*, [1915] B.C.J. No. 33, 8 W.W.R. 743 (C.A.).
[276] *Petrie v. Guelph Lumber Co.* (1886), 11 S.C.R. 450 at 463, *per* Gwynne J.
[277] *Burns v. Ambler*, [1963] B.C.J. No. 31, 42 W.W.R. 254 (S.C.); *Wheeler & Wilson Manufacturing Co. v. Wilson*, [1884] O.J. No. 160, 6 O.R. 421 (H.C.).
[278] *Peat Moss Plant Foods Ltd. v. Sutherland*, [1983] N.B.J. No. 38, 23 B.L.R. 215 (C.A.).
[279] *Ward v. Simeon*, [1918] O.J. No. 113, 43 O.L.R. 113 (H.C.).

to rescission if the purchase had been completed, the corporation may not sue to enforce the subscription.[280] However, there is no right of rescission where the subscriber did not rely upon the representation in question or where the misrepresentation was waived by the subscriber.[281] The subscriber will also lose his (or her) right of rescission where he takes up the shares and delays in asserting his claim for rescission for an unreasonable time[282] after learning the true facts.[283] A right of rescission will also be lost where the subscriber asserts his rights as a shareholder (*e.g.*, by attending and voting at meetings)[284] or enters into a subsequent agreement to sell the shares concerned.[285]

§7.108 The general rule with respect to misrepresentations made by the promoters of a privately held corporation is that each promoter is responsible for his or her own misrepresentations, but the corporation itself is not liable for that misrepresentation since any misrepresentation made prior to its incorporation cannot be attributed to it.[286] The implications of a promoter's misrepresentation after incorporation turns on whether there is a finding of agency. However, where the misrepresentation is contained in a prospectus, the corporation will be liable for the misrepresentation, for in issuing securities the corporation adopts the prospectus as its own.[287]

§7.109 As an alternative to seeking recovery from the corporation, a victim of misrepresentation may of course also pursue the corporate promoter who was actually guilty of the misrepresentation in question.[288] Where there are two or more promoters of a proposed corporation, it is possible in very limited circumstances to fix one of them (A) with liability in respect of misrepresentations made by the other (B). Such liability arises only where an agency relationship between A and B can be proved, so that it is possible to show that in making a

---

[280] *Vancouver Life Insurance Co. v. Richards*, [1919] 3 W.W.R. 907 (B.C.C.A.); *Moore v. Ontario Investment Association*, [1888] O.J. No. 127, 16 O.R. 269 (H.C.).
[281] *Baker v. Guaranty Savings & Loan Association*, [1931] S.C.R. 199 at 208, *per* Lamont J. The normal standard of proof in civil actions applies to the determination of this question: *Nelles v. Ontario Investment Association*, [1889] O.J. No. 157, 17 O.R. 129 at 151 (H.C.), *per* Ferguson J.
[282] *Morin v. Anger*, [1930] O.J. No. 50, 66 O.L.R. 327 (C.A.); *Hood v. Caldwell*, [1921] O.J. No. 222, 50 O.L.R. 387 (C.A.). *Roberts v. Montreal Trust Co.* (1918), 56 S.C.R. 342 at 360, *per* Anglin J. Long delay in asserting a claim for rescission may also be taken into account in deciding whether there was any misrepresentation or whether the subscriber relied upon it, if in fact a misrepresentation was made: *Beatty v. Neelson* (1886), 13 S.C.R. 1 at 6-7, *per* Ritchie C.J.C., aff'g 12 O.A.R. 50; but compare the vigorous dissent of Strong J. at 8. Such delay may also furnish evidence of ratification of the agreement: *Aaron's Reefs v. Twiss*, [1896] A.C. 273 at 294 (H.L.), *per* Lord Davey; *Clough v. London & N.W. Rlwy.* (1871), L.R. 7 Exch. 26.
[283] *Nelles v. Ontario Investment Association*, [1889] O.J. No. 157, 17 O.R. 129 at 152 (H.C.), *per* Ferguson J.
[284] *Petrie v. Guelph Lumber Co.* (1886), 11 S.C.R. 450 at 476, *per* Gwynne J. (again, providing the relevant facts are known); see also *Pineau v. Neigette Co.* (1911), 22 R.L.N.S. 154 (Que. C.A.).
[285] *Re Burnsland Ltd. (Barr's Case)*, [1920] 2 W.W.R. 933 (Alta. S.C.).
[286] *Henry Hope & Sons of Canada Ltd. v. Sinclair*, [1920] O.J. No. 631, 17 O.W.N. 459 (H.C.), *per* Lennox J.; see also *Bergeron v. Cie de meubles de Jonquière* (1913), 22 Que. K.B. 341 (C.A.).
[287] *Buff Pressed Brick Co. v. Ford*, [1915] O.J. No. 173, 33 O.L.R. 264 at 266 (C.A.), *per* Riddell J.
[288] See, for instance, *Scotia McLeod v. Peoples Jewellers Ltd.*, [1995] O.J. No. 3556, 129 D.L.R. (4th) 711 (C.A.).

representation concerning the proposed corporation or its shares, B acted as the agent of A. The common interest that A and B have in the organization of the company itself is not sufficient to establish such an agency relationship.[289]

§7.110 In *Soden v. British & Commonwealth Holdings plc*[290] it was found that in 1988, British and Commonwealth Holdings plc (B) had purchased the whole of the share capital of Atlantic Corporation plc (A) in a take-over bid at a price of some £434 million. The acquisition proved to be disastrous. A went into administration in 1990; B followed it shortly afterward. B sued A for negligent misrepresentation said to have been made by A so as to induce B to acquire its shares. A related claim was brought by B against Barclays deZoet Wedd Ltd. for damages for negligent advice given in relation to the acquisition of A. The question to be decided was whether the claim for damages against A in respect of the alleged misrepresentation was subordinate to the claims of the general creditors of A. In this respect, clause 74(2)(f) of the U.K. *Insolvency Act, 1986* provided that:

> (f) a sum due to any member of the company (in his character of a member) by way of dividends, profits or otherwise is not deemed to be a debt of the company, payable to that member in a case of competition between himself and any other creditor not a member of the company, but any such sum may be taken into account for the purpose of the final adjustment of the rights of the contributories among themselves.

§7.111 Counsel for the administrator of A argued that this provision created a general rule — albeit one subject to several exceptions — that "members come last"; that is, that the members or shareholders of a company can take nothing until the outside creditors have been paid in full. It was noted that in *Re Addlestone Linoleum Co.*[291] the provision corresponding to clause 74(2)(f) of the U.K. *Insolvency Act 1986* that was then in effect covered a claimant who was induced to subscribe for shares by misrepresentation. In that case, it was found that shares purporting to be fully paid had actually been issued by the company at a discount of £2 10s off their stated par value. At the trial level in that case, Kay J. had said:

> Now, unquestionably — the Applicants — retaining their shares and claiming damages because the shares are not exactly what they were represented to be, are making such claims in the character of members of the company, and the only question is whether such claims are for sums due "by way of dividends, profits or otherwise" . . . Practically, what these Applicants are seeking to recover by their

---

[289] The conditions which must be satisfied in order for such vicarious liability to apply were outlined by Osler J.A. in *Wilson v. Hotchkiss*, [1901] O.J. No. 305, 2 O.L.R. 261 at 269-70 (C.A.), aff'd (1901), 31 S.C.R. 481 at 483, *per* Strong C.J.C. (The acts, statements and letters of one member of a committee formed for getting up a company cannot prejudice any other member, unless the former can be shown to be the agent of the others by some other circumstance than their common object. It is a question in each case whether the party whose acts are relied upon as giving rise to a liability can be said to have been the agent.)
[290] [1997] H.L.J. No. 41, [1997] 4 All E.R. 353.
[291] (1887), 37 Ch. D. 191 (C.A.).

proof is a dividend in respect of the £2 10s per share which they have been compelled to pay in the winding-up. But as shareholders they have contracted that they will pay this money, and that it shall be first applied in payment of the creditors whose debts are not due to them as members of the company — that is, they are practically admitting their liability to pay the £2 10s per share to such other creditors and yet seeking to get part of it back out of the pockets of those very creditors themselves. I confess it seems to me that the money so claimed is not only claimed in the character of members but that claim is just as unreasonable as if it were a claim of dividends or profits, and that accordingly, comes within the words "or otherwise", which I have read from section 38.[292]

In giving the unanimous judgment of the House of Lords in favour of the claim of B against A, Lord Browne-Wilkinson commented upon the different nature of the claim being made by B from that made in the *Addlestone* case:

> There is nothing in the Addlestone case to justify the application of that decision to cases where the claim against the company is founded in a misrepresentation made by the company on the purchase of existing shares from a third party. To allow proof for such a claim in competition with the general body of creditors does not either directly or indirectly produce a reduction of capital. The general body of creditors are in exactly the same position as they would have been had the claim been wholly unrelated to the shares in the company.[293]

In the *Addlestone* case, the shareholders were attempting to reduce the company's capital account. In the *British & Commonwealth Holdings* case, the capital account would remain intact, but the liabilities of the company would be increased.

(ii) Liability for Misrepresentation Under the Securities Act and Securities Act Regulation

§7.112 In the case of publicly traded corporations that are reporting issuers under the *Securities Act*,[294] the common law rules respecting misrepresentation have been greatly expanded by the various rules set out in the *Securities Act* and the *Securities Act Regulation*.[295] In particular, the *Securities Act* and Regulation have imposed a broader statutory duty of disclosure replacing the limited duty applicable under the common law of contract,[296] have clarified the responsibility of the issuer for misrepresentation made by its officers, directors, promoters, etc. (for not all promoters of a corporation will be among its agents, nor will a misrepresentation of an agent of the corporation necessarily have occurred within

---

[292] *Ibid.*, at 197-98.
[293] *Soden v. British & Commonwealth Holdings plc*, [1997] H.L.J. No. 41, [1997] 4 All E.R. 353 at 359-60.
[294] R.S.O. 1990, c. S.5.
[295] R.R.O. 1990, Reg. 1015.
[296] In Canadian securities law, there is a distinction between information that is "filed" and information that is "delivered". Section 140 of the *Securities Act* provides that any material filed under that Act will be made available for public inspection by the OSC, unless it decides to hold the material in confidence on the ground that it "discloses intimate financial, personal or other information." In contrast, the term "deliver" is generally used to describe documents that must be provided by a reporting issuer to its security holders.

the scope of his or her authority),[297] and have clarified the responsibility of one person engaged in the issue of a prospectus for a misrepresentation made by another person in connection with its issue.

(1) Disclosure of Material Facts

§7.113 Subsection 56(1) of the *Securities Act* requires a prospectus to provide full, true and plain disclosure of all "material facts relating to the securities issued or proposed to be distributed". Subsection 57(1) of the Act provides:

> 57.(1) Subject to subsection (2), where a material adverse change occurs after a receipt is obtained for a preliminary prospectus filed in accordance with subsection 53 (1) and before the receipt for the prospectus is obtained or, where a material change occurs after the receipt for the prospectus is obtained but prior to the completion of the distribution under such prospectus, an amendment to such preliminary prospectus or prospectus, as the case may be, shall be filed as soon as practicable and in any event within ten days after the change occurs.

§7.114 Section 130 of the *Securities Act*[298] imposes a civil liability where there is a misrepresentation in a prospectus or an amendment to a prospectus. As we have seen, equity affords the remedy of rescission whenever a person is induced to enter into a contract by a misrepresentation, whether innocently, recklessly or fraudulently made so long as the contract is executory; but once the contract becomes executed, rescission will only be available where the contract was induced by reckless or fraudulent misrepresentation.[299] However, until recently, at common law the mere fact that statements in a prospectus were false was insufficient to render the corporation or its promoters liable in damages. In order to establish liability it was necessary to prove that the false representation was made knowingly or without belief in its truth, or with reckless disregard as to whether it was true or false. Thus if the person making the representation was indifferent as to whether the statements in the prospectus were true or false, that frame of mind would support civil liability.[300] With the evolution of the doctrine of negligent misstatement under the rule in *Hedley Byrne & Co. v. Heller & Partners Ltd.*[301] liability for damages might also be established if it could be shown that a misrepresentation was negligently made by a person who owed a duty to the plaintiff to take reasonable care to ensure that any statements made by him or her were accurate — although in such a case the liability would be limited to the economic loss suffered as a result of the negligence. In any of

---

[297] See, generally, *Lynde v. Anglo-Italian Hemp Spinning Co.*, [1896] 1 Ch. 178; *Collins v. Associated Greyhound Racecourses Ltd.*, [1930] 1 Ch. 1; *Re Metal Constituents Ltd. (Lord Lurgan's Case)*, [1902] 1 Ch. 707.
[298] R.S.O. 1990, c. S.5.
[299] See, for instance, *Abrey v. Victoria Printing Co.* (1912), 21 O.W.R. 444 (C.A.); *Kingstone v. Dominion Alloy Steel Corp.*, [1939] O.J. No. 471, [1939] O.R. 286 at 292-93 (C.A.), per Gillanders J.A.; *McGaffigan v. National Husker Co.*, [1911] O.J. No. 753, 2 O.W.N. 600 (H.C.); *Adams v. Newbigging* (1883), 13 App. Cas. 308 (H.L.).
[300] *Nesbitt Thompson v. Pigott & Pigott Construction Co.*, [1941] S.C.R. 520 at 530, per Taschereau J; *Derry v. Peek* (1889), 14 App. Cas. 337 (H.L.).
[301] [1964] A.C. 465 (H.L.).

these cases it was necessary to establish that the plaintiff had known of the representation and had relied upon it.[302]

§7.115 Section 130 of the *Securities Act* has largely swept away the narrow common law protection afforded with respect to misrepresentation, although strictly speaking the rights conferred by section 130 are in addition to, and without derogation from, any other right the purchaser may have at law.[303] Subsection 130(1) of the Act provides:

> 130.(1) Where a prospectus together with any amendment to the prospectus, contains a misrepresentation, a purchaser who purchases a security offered thereby during the period of distribution or distribution to the public has, without regard to whether the purchaser relied on the misrepresentation, a right of action for damages against,
>
> (a) the issuer or a security holder on whose behalf the distribution is made;
>
> (b) each underwriter of the securities who is required to sign the certificate by section 59;
>
> (c) every director of the issuer at the time the prospectus or the amendment to the prospectus was filed;
>
> (d) every person or company whose consent has been filed pursuant to a requirement of the regulations but only with respect to reports, opinions or statements that have been made by them; and
>
> (e) every person or company who signed the prospectus or the amendment to the prospectus other than the persons or companies included in clauses (a) to (d),
>
> or, where the purchaser purchased the security from a person or company referred to in clause (a) or (b) or from another underwriter of the securities, the purchaser may elect to exercise a right of rescission against such person, company or underwriter, in which case the purchaser shall have no right of action for damages against such person, company or underwriter.

Perhaps the most striking departure from the common law embodied in subsection 130(1) is the scope of the liability that is imposed. It gives a right to recover damages not only from the person who was guilty of the misrepresentation, but also from others directly concerned in the distribution of the security. Specifically, joint and several[304] liability is imposed on five distinct classes of person. In practical terms, the effect of this broad cast of liability is to impose a positive duty upon persons falling in each of those classes to exercise due diligence in order to prevent any misrepresentation taking place. In this respect, section 130 may be seen to be a proactive rather than a reactive remedy.

---

[302] *Baker v. Guaranty Savings & Loan Association*, [1931] S.C.R. 199; see also *Canada Food Co. v. Stanford* (1916), 50 N.S.R. 252 (C.A.); *Maritime United Farmers Co-op Ltd. v. Dickie* (1925), 52 N.B.R. 42 (C.A.).

[303] *Securities Act*, R.S.O. 1990, c. S.5, s. 130(10).

[304] *Ibid.*, s. 130(8).

§7.116 The persons made liable by statute cannot simply hide behind each other, each claiming that the onus was on the others to discover the truth. So in *Escott v. Bar Chris Construction Corp.*, the District Court stated with respect to the equivalent American provision:

> The underwriters say that the prospectus is the company's prospectus, not theirs. Doubtless this is the way they customarily regard it. But the *Securities Act* makes no such distinction. The underwriters are just as responsible as the company if the prospectus is false. And prospective purchasers may rely on the reputation of the underwriters in deciding whether to purchase the securities.[305]

It was not enough that the underwriters were unaware of any misrepresentation. It was their duty to make reasonable inquiries to confirm that no misrepresentation existed. Nor were superficial inquiries enough to protect them:

> The purpose of section 11 is to protect investors. To that end, the underwriters are made responsible for the truth of the prospectus. If they may escape that responsibility by taking at face value representations made to them by the company's management, then the inclusion of underwriters among those liable under section 11 affords the investors no additional protection. To effectuate the statute's purpose, the phrase "reasonable investigation" must be construed to require more effort on the part of the underwriters than the mere accurate reporting in their prospectus of the "data presented" to them by the company. It should make no difference that this data is elicited by questions addressed to the company's officers by the underwriters, or that the underwriters at the time believe that the company's officers are truthful and reliable. In order to make the underwriter's participation in this enterprise of any value to the investors, the underwriters must make some reasonable attempt to verify the data submitted to them. They may not rely solely on the company's officers or on the company's counsel. A prudent man in the management of his own property would not rely on them. It is impossible to lay down a rigid rule suitable for every case defining the extent to which such verification must go. It is a question of degree, a matter of judgment in each case.

§7.117 In order to establish a claim under section 130 of the *Securities Act* arising out of a misrepresentation in a prospectus, it is no longer necessary to prove reliance on the representation; such reliance is presumed as a matter of law.[306] Thus it is no defence that there is no evidence either that the purchaser did read the prospectus or that the purchaser did rely upon the misrepresentation, or could have discovered the truth through the exercise of reasonable diligence. The presumption of detrimental reliance is conclusive, unless the defendant[307] can prove that the purchaser purchased the securities with knowledge of the misrepresentation.[308] Nor is any distinction drawn under the present legislation be-

---

[305] 283 F. Supp. 643 at 696-97 (S.D.N.Y. 1968).
[306] *Securities Act*, R.S.O. 1990, c. S.5, s. 130(1).
[307] Subs. 130(8) of the *Securities Act*, R.S.O. 1990, c. S.5, provides that "[a]ll or any one or more of the persons or companies specified by subseciton (1) are jointly and severally liable, and every person or company who becomes liable to make any payment under this section may recover a contribution from any person or company who, if sued separately, would have been liable to make the same payment provided that the court may deny the right to recover such contribution where, in all the circumstances of the case, it is satisfied that to permit recovery of such contribution would not be just and equitable."
[308] *Securities Act*, R.S.O. 1990, c. S.5, 130(2).

tween negligent, reckless or deliberate misrepresentation; the term includes any untrue statement of material fact or omission to state a material fact that is required to be stated or that is necessary to make a statement not misleading in the light of the circumstances in which it was made.[309] However, it is necessary for the plaintiff to establish that the representations complained of were made; that they were false in fact; and that within a reasonable time after the plaintiff's discovery of the misrepresentation he or she elected to avoid the contract and accordingly repudiated it.[310] This last requirement grows out of the fact that, like any contract arising from a misrepresentation, a subscription for securities is not void but merely voidable at the election of the person mislead.[311]

§7.118 Although based in statute, it is widely assumed that the remedies afforded by section 130 of the *Securities Act* are subject to the same general principles that govern equitable relief in general — although this point has never been conclusively decided. If so, it would follow that a person entitled to avoid a subscription for securities under section 130 cannot indefinitely withhold his or her election in order to exercise it as may ultimately prove most advantageous.[312] Moreover, where the desired remedy is rescission, the subscriber cannot both approve and disapprove; the subscriber must elect either to walk away from the contract in its entirety or stand beside it.[313] Prolonged silence will be taken to amount to acquiescence and such an unreasonable delay will estop the subscriber from attacking the validity of the prospectus.[314] Although, strictly speaking, a distinction is drawn between laches (which is merely a defence to a claim founded in equity) and acquiescence (which involves an election to affirm or an abandonment of the right to avoid), prolonged silence will give rise to a conclusive presumption of acquiescence.[315]

§7.119 The potential liability thrust upon the securities industry by subsection 130(1) of the *Securities Act* is clearly broad, and likely would be intolerable if no limit were placed on the amount recoverable and if certain due diligence and reasonable reliance defences were not built into it. Therefore, it is not surprising to discover that a number of constraints are built into the statutory remedy. Where the plaintiff proves that a prospectus contains a misrepresentation, he or she establishes a *prima facie* case against the defendant. It is then open to the defendant to prove that the plaintiff purchased the securities with knowledge of

---

[309] *Ibid.*, s. 1(1) definition of "misrepresentation".
[310] See, for instance, *Robert v. Montreal Trust Co.* (1918), 56 S.C.R. 342 at 355, *per* Anglin J.; *United Shoe Machinery Co. v. Brunet*, [1909] A.C. 330 (P.C.); *Beatty v. Neelson* (1886), 13 S.C.R. 1; *Petrie v. Guelph Lumber Co.* (1885), 11 S.C.R. 450.
[311] *Morrisburgh & Ottawa Electric Rlwy. v. O'Connor*, [1915] O.J. No. 57, 34 O.L.R. 161 (C.A.).
[312] *Robert v. Montreal Trust Co.* (1918), 56 S.C.R. 342.
[313] *Ward v. Simeon*, [1918] O.J. No. 113, 43 O.L.R. 113 at 119 (H.C.), *per* Meredith C.J.C.P.
[314] *Robert v. Montreal Trust Co.* (1918), 56 S.C.R. 342; whether there has been an actual repudiation is a question of fact: *Freedman v. French*, [1921] O.J. No. 224, 50 O.L.R. 432 at 441 (C.A.); *Re Rubel Bronze & Metal Co. and Vos*, [1918] 1 K.B. 315 at 322, *per* McCardie J.; *Dominion Radiator v. Steel Co. of Canada*, [1918] O.J. No. 141, 43 O.L.R. 356 at 369-70 (C.A.), *per* Meredith C.J.O.
[315] *Clough v. London & N.W. Rlwy.* (1872), L.R. 7 Ex. 26 at 35, *per* Mellor J.

the misrepresentation.[316] There are also a number of defences potentially available to persons connected with the prospectus process other than the issuer or selling security holder.

§7.120 The first important limitation on the apparent scope of section 130 of the *Securities Act* is found in subsection (7), which imposes a substantial limit on the amount recoverable. It provides that:

> 130.(7) In an action for damages pursuant to subsection (1), the defendant is not liable for all or any portion of such damages that the defendant proves do not represent the depreciation in value of the security as a result of the misrepresentation relied upon.

Thus if a security is worth $X less than the issue price if a particular representation is true, but $X + $Y less than the issue price both because that representation is not true and because of certain other adverse developments, the defendant is liable only for $X. While subsection (7) is not clearly worded, it places the onus on the defendant to prove that any portion in the decline in the value of the security was attributable to some fact other than the representation being untrue. In many cases, of course, it will be quite difficult to allocate any decline in value in the manner contemplated by subsection (7); however, at least in theory, it does place a potential limit on the liability of a defendant.

§7.121 A second limit on the amount recoverable is set out in subsection 130(9) of the *Securities Act*, which provides:

> 130.(9) In no case shall the amount recoverable under this section exceed the price at which the securities were offered to the public.

The initial temptation is to interpret this provision as meaning that an investor cannot recover consequential damages, such as the opportunity cost of the investment, or damages relating to the loss of expected profits. However, that is not what subsection (9) says. It does not limit the plaintiff's right of recovery to a particular class of damages. Instead, it merely limits the absolute amount that may be recovered for damages of all classes, namely the price at which the securities were offered to the public. Thus if the purchaser sells the securities at a loss of 50 per cent, the purchaser may still claim for the decline in value by reason of the misrepresentation (*i.e.*, 50 per cent of the purchase price), plus any consequential damages relating to the investment, provided that the aggregate amount recovered does not exceed the price at which the securities were offered to the public — an amount could conceivably be more or less than the price of the securities to the purchaser. What is less clear is whether subsection (9) limits the discretion of the court to award pre-judgment and post-judgment interest, where the amount of damages awarded equals the price at which the securities were offered to the public.

---

[316] *Securities Act*, R.S.O. 1990, c. S.5, s. 130(2).

§7.122 In addition to constraining the potential liability of defendants by limiting the amount recoverable, the section also provides a limited range of defences to persons other than the issuer or selling security holder. The first level of defence is set out in clause 130(3)(*a*) of which provides:

> 130.(3) No person or company, other than the issuer or selling security holder, is liable under subsection (1) if he, she or it proves,
>
> (*a*) that the prospectus or the amendment to the prospectus was filed without his, her or its knowledge or consent, and that, on becoming aware of its filing, he, she or it forthwith gave reasonable general notice that it was so filed;

Clause (*a*) does not deal so much with the misrepresentation that the document contains as with the fact that a prospectus was filed without the knowledge or consent of the defendant. Furthermore, clause (*a*) gives no guidance as to what is meant by "reasonable general notice". *Black's Law Dictionary* defines "reasonable notice" to mean "such notice or information of a fact as may fairly and properly be expected or required in the particular circumstances". Although this definition is somewhat circular, it does provide some guidance as to how clause (*a*) might be interpreted. Given the purpose of the notice required under clause (*a*), the notice must be sufficiently public so that it is likely to come to the attention of potential investors. Furthermore, the statute requires that it be "general", which suggests that it must be made widely available to persons who would be interested in it. One option which might suffice would be to notify dealers participating in the distribution. A second option would be to publish a notice in a business newspaper that most investors would be likely to read. A third option would be to notify the Ontario Securities Commission ("OSC") of the unauthorized filing. In this regard, it is intriguing that clause (*a*) makes no reference to advising the OSC, whereas subclause (*d*)(i) expressly requires that such notice be given.

§7.123 A second defence to an action under subsection 130(1) of the *Securities Act* is given by clause 130(3)(*b*), which provides:

> 130.(3) No person or company, other than the issuer or selling security holder, is liable under subsection (1) if he, she or it proves, ...
>
> (*b*) that, after the issue of a receipt for the prospectus and before the purchase of the securities by the purchaser, on becoming aware of any misrepresentation in the prospectus or an amendment to the prospectus he, she or it withdrew the consent thereto and gave reasonable general notice of such withdrawal and the reason therefor;

Clause (*b*) may be described as a last clear chance defense. It allows the defendant to escape potential liability in essence by bringing the misrepresentation to the notice of potential investors. However, in order to invoke the defense provided by clause (*b*), the defendant must bring the misrepresentation to light upon his or her "becoming aware" of it. If he or she delays, then the defence may be lost, and it will certainly be lost against any person who purchases the securities before the defendant withdraws his or her consent to the prospectus or amendment and gives reasonable notice of that withdrawal.

§7.124 Clause 130(3)(*c*) of the *Securities Act* goes on to provide a defence where reliance is placed upon expert opinion. It reads:

> 130.(3) No person or company, other than the issuer or selling security holder, is liable under subsection (1) if he, she or it proves,
>
> . . . . .
>
> > (*c*) that, with respect to any part of the prospectus or the amendment to the prospectus purporting to be made on the authority of an expert or purporting to be a copy of or an extract from a report, opinion or statement of an expert, he, she or it had no reasonable grounds to believe and did not believe that there had been a misrepresentation or that such part of the prospectus or the amendment to the prospectus did not fairly represent the report, opinion or statement of the expert or was not a fair copy of or extract from the report, opinion or statement of the expert;

Clause (*c*) does not protect a person simply because that person is relying upon a report, opinion or statement. It merely protects a defendant where the alleged misrepresentation is contained in a report, opinion or statement. Furthermore, the defendant must show that he or she did not believe and had no reason to believe that the report, opinion or statement was misleading. Clause (*c*) does not state expressly whether the defendant is under an obligation to determine if a copy of a report or extract from a report, opinion or statement is fairly representative of that document, although it does say that the person must have "no reasonable grounds to believe" that the extract is not fair. Even a person who has read the full report and the prospectus might not be able to judge the fairness of an extract unless that person possesses a degree of expertise in the subject matter of the report.

§7.125 Clause 130(3)(*d*) of the *Securities Act* is the counterbalance to clause 130(3)(*c*), and protects experts whose reports, opinions or statements are contained in a prospectus. It provides:

> 130. (3) No person or company, other than the issuer or selling security holder, is liable under subsection (1) if he, she or it proves,
>
> . . . . .
>
> > (*d*) that, with respect to any part of the prospectus or the amendment to the prospectus purporting to be made on his, her or its own authority as an expert or purporting to be a copy of or an extract from his, her or its own report, opinion or statement as an expert but that contains a misrepresentation attributable to failure to represent fairly his, her or its report, opinion or statement as an expert,
> >
> > > (i) the person or company had, after reasonable investigation, reasonable grounds to believe and did believe that such part of the prospectus or the amendment to the prospectus fairly represented his, her or its report, opinion or statement, or
> > >
> > > (ii) on becoming aware that such part of the prospectus or the amendment to the prospectus did not fairly represent his, her or its report, opinion or statement as an expert, he, she or it forthwith

advised the Commission and gave reasonable general notice that such use had been made and that he, she or it would not be responsible for that part of the prospectus or the amendment to the prospectus;

Clause (*d*) applies only where there was a misrepresentation of the expert's report, opinion or statement (*i.e.*, a failure to represent fairly the report, opinion or statement). It provides no protection where the report, opinion or statement itself is misleading. If an expert's report, opinion or statement itself was a bad one, then the expert may be liable nonetheless for negligent misstatement despite clause 130(3)(*c*) or (*d*).

§7.126 Subsection 130(4) of the *Securities Act* goes on to provide:

> 130.(4) No person or company, other than the issuer or selling security holder, is liable under subsection (1) with respect to any part of the prospectus or the amendment to the prospectus purporting to be made on his, her or its own authority as an expert or purporting to be a copy of or an extract from his, her or its own report, opinion or statement as an expert unless he, she or it,
>
> (*a*) failed to conduct such reasonable investigation as to provide reasonable grounds for a belief that there had been no misrepresentation; or
>
> (*b*) believed that there had been a misrepresentation.

In addition, subsection 130(5) of the Act provides a further defence:

> 130.(5) No person or company, other than the issuer or selling security holder, is liable under subsection (1) with respect to any part of the prospectus or the amendment to the prospectus not purporting to be made on the authority of an expert and not purporting to be a copy of or an extract from a report, opinion or statement of an expert unless he, she or it,
>
> (*a*) failed to conduct reasonable investigation as to provide reasonable grounds for a belief that there had been no misrepresentation; or
>
> (*b*) believed that there had been a misrepresentation.

Subsections (4) and (5) provide the statutory foundation for what has come to be known as the due diligence defence — a defense which was touched upon briefly above. They are derived from clause 11(b) of the United States *Securities Act* of 1933. The American legislation contains a further clause 11(c) which gives a clearer picture of standard of care required:

> 11. (c) In determining, for the purposes of paragraph (3) of subsection (b) of this section, what constitutes reasonable investigation and reasonable ground for belief, the standard of reasonableness shall be that required of a prudent man in the management of his own property.

Although this clause is omitted from the Ontario *Securities Act*, it is likely that the courts would impose a similar standard here, for the American clause (c) appears to codify the common law concept of a standard of reasonable care.

§7.127 The case law in the United States (there appear to be no reported Canadian cases pertaining to the due diligence defence) is not particularly helpful as a guide to the steps that an underwriter or professional advisor must take in order to exercise "due diligence" with respect to an issue of securities. As noted above, in the *Bar Chris*[317] case the court said only that the extent of inquiry required depended upon the facts of each case. Some limited guidance as to what is necessary can be gleaned from the decision in *Feit v. Leasco Data Processing Corp.*, where the court said:

> Dealer-managers cannot, of course, be expected to possess the intimate knowledge of corporate affairs of inside directors, and their duty to investigate should be considered in light of their more limited access. Nevertheless, they are expected to exercise a high degree of care in investigation and independent verification of the company's representations. Tacit reliance on management assertion is unacceptable; the underwriters must play devil's advocate.[318]

§7.128 The statement of rights required under section 60 of the *Securities Act* is usually given in the form of a brief summary of the rights, rather than by quoting the relevant provisions (although a full quote would be acceptable). A typical statement of the rights may read:

> Securities legislation in certain of the provinces and territories provides purchasers of the securities with the right to withdraw from an agreement to purchase the securities within two business days after the receipt or deemed receipt of a prospectus and any amendment to the prospectus. In several of the provinces and territories, securities legislation entitles the purchaser to the remedies of rescission or damages where the prospectus or any amendment contains a misrepresentation or is not delivered to the purchaser within the time allowed. Such remedies must be exercised within the time limits prescribed by the securities legislation of the province or territory of the purchaser. The purchaser should refer to any applicable provisions of the securities legislation of his province or territory for the particulars of these rights, or consult with a legal advisor.

In *Kerr v. Danier Leather Inc.*[319] the Ontario Court of Appeal considered the impact of the foregoing disclosure requirements under the *Securities Act* where the prospectus for a public offering contains a forecast of the company's anticipated revenue and earnings (a type of information often described as future-oriented financial information, or "FOFI"). The facts of the case were as follows: in May 1998, the appellant, Danier Leather Inc., made an initial public offering of its shares through a prospectus (for which a receipt was issued on May 6) that contained a forecast concerning Danier's projected revenue and earnings for the last quarter of its fiscal year. An internal company analysis prepared a few days before its public offering closed (May 20) showed that Danier's fourth quarter revenue and earnings were lagging behind the forecasted figures. Danier did not disclose these results before closing, but it did disclose them after closing in a revised forecast. That disclosure led to a significant decline in its share price. However, Danier's sales rebounded, and by the end of the fiscal year it had substantially achieved its original forecast. Despite the re-

---

[317] *Escott v. Bar Chris Construction Corp.*, 283 F. Supp. 643 (S.D.N.Y. 1968).
[318] 332 F. Supp. 544 (S.D.N.Y. 1971).
[319] [2005] O.J. No. 5388, 261 D.L.R. (4th) 400 (C.A.).

covery in value, the plaintiffs began a class proceeding for prospectus misrepresentation under subsection 130(1) of the SA.

§7.129 Justice Lederman found Danier and its chief officers liable for statutory misrepresentation. It was held that the prospectus embodied an implicit representation that the forecast was objectively reasonable, both on the date Danier's prospectus was issued, and on the date its public offering closed. It was also held that the poor fourth quarter revenue and earnings were material facts that Danier was required by statute to disclose before closing. Since Danier's failed to do so, its implied representation that the forecast was objectively reasonable was false on the closing date, even though it was true on the date that the prospectus was issued.

§7.130 On appeal, the Ontario Court of Appeal reversed this decision. It held that while investor protection was a key objective of the *Securities Act*, it did not impose on issuers an ongoing obligation to disclose material facts. While the Act required an issuer to amend its prospectus for a "material change" occurring after it obtained a receipt for its final prospectus, no provision expressly required an issuer to disclose material facts during that period. Neither section 130 of the Act nor the definition of misrepresentation in subsection 1(1) of the Act imposed any obligations on an issuer to disclose material facts occurring after the date a receipt for a final prospectus was issued and before the end of the distribution period. Although poor intra-quarterly results could, under some circumstances, in themselves amount to a material change, there was no such finding on the evidence. The Court of Appeal also rejected Lederman J.'s conclusion that the prospectus contained an implied representation of objective reasonableness. The prospectus indicated that the forecast represented only management's best judgment. Moreover, the fact that the forecast was substantially achieved was material as to whether it was reasonably achievable when it was issued.

§7.131 Central to the decision of the Court of Appeal was its treatment of subsection 130(1) of the *Securities Act,* which creates a cause of action for misrepresentation within a prospectus. At the time it provided:

> 130.(1) Where a prospectus together with any amendment to the prospectus, contains a misrepresentation, a purchaser who purchases a security offered during the period of distribution or offered by the prospectus during distribution to the public [shall be deemed to have relied on such misrepresentation if it was a misrepresentation at the time of purchase and has] a right of action for damages against,
>
> (a) the issuer or a selling security holder on whose behalf the distribution is made;
>
> . . . . .
>
> (e) every person or company who signed the prospectus or the amendment to the prospectus. ...

The court gave these provisions a narrow reading:

Our application of this "modern approach" to statutory interpretation leads us to conclude that neither section 130 nor the definition of misrepresentation in subsection 1(1) of the OSA imposes any disclosure obligations on an issuer. On our view of an issuer's statutory disclosure obligations, the respondents and other purchasers of Danier shares were entitled to assume that:

(a) at May 6, 1998, Danier's prospectus, including the Forecast, provided full, true and plain disclosure of all facts that would reasonably be expected to have a significant effect on the market price or value of Danier's securities ...; and

(b) no change in the business operations or capital of Danier that would reasonably be expected to have a significant effect on the market price or value of any of Danier's securities occurred between May 6 and May 20, 1998. ...

The purchasers of Danier shares, however, were not entitled to assume that no facts had occurred after May 6 and before May 20 that would reasonably be expected to have a significant effect on the market price or value of Danier's securities. Danier had no obligation to disclose material facts occurring between May 6 and May 20 (unless those material facts amounted to a material change, in which case the material change would have had to have been disclosed). In short, Danier had no obligation to update its Forecast by disclosing its Q4 results to May 16, 1998.[320]

The court thus drew a distinction between "material facts" (which were not as such subject to a duty of disclosure) and a "material change" which would fall within the scope of the statutory requirement:

The Legislature made a policy choice. It engaged in a line-drawing exercise. It decided to require issuers to update prospectuses for material changes but not for material facts. No doubt it weighed the considerations for and against broader continuous disclosure: on the one hand, the advantage of giving investors more information; on the other, the disadvantages of cost and inconvenience that flow from flooding the market with transitory information. We see nothing inconsistent between the Legislature's express choice in s. 57(1) and a statutory regime aimed at investor protection. United States securities legislation has drawn a similar line. And, as Mr. Zarnett aptly pointed out in oral argument, the proposition that more transitory information is good for the market is not shown by this case, where the original forecast was substantially achieved and the revised forecast proved inaccurate.[321]

§7.132 The question of liability for misrepresentation is, however, only one aspect of the legal obligation to disclose information. Section 4.5 of National Policy 51-201, which governs timely disclosure, adopts the TSX policy of requiring listed companies to make timely disclosure of all "material information" (a term that includes both "material facts" and "material changes" relating to the business and affairs of the company). Failure to provide such disclosure may have administrative consequences. In addition, subsection 7.1(1) of National Policy 48 (governing the preparation of, and disclosure required in, future-oriented financial information), provides:

---

[320] *Ibid.*, at paras. 86, 87.
[321] *Ibid.*, at para. 100.

When a change occurs in the events or in the assumptions used to prepare FOFI that has a material effect on such FOFI, such a change shall be reported in a manner identical to that followed when a material change occurs as defined under the Securities Legislation and Securities Requirements.

The Court of Appeal referred to both of these policy instruments, but concluded that while they could be raised in proceedings before a securities regulator, they cannot be used to found an action for prospectus misrepresentation under subsection 130(1).[322]

(iii) Liability for in the Secondary Market

§7.133 Approximately 90 per cent of all securities trading relates to the secondary market for securities. Historically, little protection has been afforded for purchasers in that market with respect to negligently mistaken information. In *The Queen v. Cognos Inc.*,[323] it was held that in order to make out an action for negligent misrepresentation it as necessary for the plaintiff to establish the following:

- there must be a duty of care based on a special relationship between the plaintiff and defendant;
- the representation in question must be untrue, inaccurate, or misleading;
- the defendant must have acted negligently in making the misrepresentation;
- the plaintiff must have relied, in a reasonable manner, on the negligent misrepresentation; and
- the reliance must have resulted in damages to the plaintiff.

These requirements limited the availability of relief in the case of claims against auditors, directors, officers and other professionals, in deciding upon the application of the Rule in *Foss v. Harbottle,* and in many other contexts.

§7.134 The effect of the *Cognos* rules with respect to misrepresentation in a prospectus or other disclosure document was considered in *Menegon v. Philip Services Corp.*[324] In that case, the plaintiff (Menegon) purchased shares of the Philip corporation on the open or secondary market. Philip later became insolvent. Menegon commenced an action on his own behalf and on behalf of other purchasers of such shares against the auditors and underwriters of Philip, claiming damages for misrepresentation under the *Securities Act* and for negligent misrepresentation at common law. He brought a motion for certification as a class proceeding. The underwriters and auditors brought cross-motions to dismiss, arguing that Menegon's statement of claim disclosed no reasonable cause of action. Menegon conceded that he did not personally have a cause of action

---

[322] *Ibid.*, at para. 104. See also: *Pezim v. British Columbia Superintendent of Brokers*, [1992] B.C.J. No. 957, 96 D.L.R. (4th) 137 at 150 (C.A.), rev'd on other grounds [1994] S.C.J. No. 58, [1994] 2 S.C.R. 557.
[323] [1993] S.C.J. No. 3, [1993] 1 S.C.R. 87 at 110.
[324] [2003] O.J. No. 8, 31 B.L.R. (3d) 29 (C.A.).

under the *Securities Act* because he bought the shares on the secondary market. However, he argued that he could be a representative for the class of purchasers who had such a cause of action because of his common law action for negligent misrepresentation. The motions judge found that there was no cause of action for the benefit of purchasers in a secondary market in the absence of a special relationship. On appeal to the Ontario Court of Appeal, it was held that Menegon's pleadings did not set out allegations of the kind of facts that would give rise to a duty of care to Menegon on the part of the auditors or the underwriters.

§7.135 In Ontario and British Columbia, a statutory liability regime for secondary market transactions has now been enacted. In Ontario, the new regime (popularly known as Bill 198)[325] became effective on December 31, 2005. The following is a brief overview of the new liability regime: Potential plaintiffs include any investors who acquired or sold an issuer's securities between the time the misrepresentation was made and the time when it was publicly corrected. Investors dealing with securities in the secondary market are entitled to a claim against "responsible issuers" (i.e. a reporting issuer in Ontario or an issuer whose securities are publicly traded outside Ontario if the issuer has a substantial connection to Ontario), directors, and certain officers, experts and influential persons (such as promoters, controlling persons and certain other insiders) of such an issuer, for misrepresentation in

- a "core document" such as an financial statement, securities filing, management discussion and analysis statement,[326] or press release; or
- a "non-core" document, such as a speech, conference call or other public oral statement;

Liability also exists for a failure to make timely disclosure of material changes (with such liability running until the time when actual disclosure is made).

§7.136 Where a misrepresentation is contained in a document, the following are potentially liable:

- the issuer;
- all directors;
- any officer who authorized, permitted or acquiesced in the release of the document;
- any influential person or director or officer of an influential person who influenced the release of the document;

---

[325] See Part XXIII.I of the Ontario *Securities Act*. For the British Columbia legislation (not yet in force at the time of writing) see: S.B.C. 2004, c. 43.

[326] The MD&A statement will provide an overview of the previous year of operation and explain the reasons why the company faired as it did during in that time period. It will usually also forecast the coming year, outlining future goals and projects and any new approaches that will be implemented.

- any expert, where the misrepresentation is in a statement, opinion or report of that expert summarized or quoted in the document, provided the expert consented in writing to the inclusion of the summary or quotation and did not withdraw that consent prior to publication.

Where a misrepresentation is made in a public oral statement made by a person with authority to speak on behalf of the issuer the list of potential defendants is the same, but the directors are only liable if they authorized, permitted or acquiesced in the making of the statement. Where the misrepresentation is made in a document released by or public oral statements made by an influential person, the issuer is only liable if an officer or director of the issuer authorized, permitted or acquiesced in the release of the document or the making of the statement. In addition, the following are liable:

- the person who made the statement;
- any director or officer of the issuer who authorized, permitted or acquiesced in the release of the document or making of the statement;
- the influential person;
- any director or officer of the influential person who authorized, permitted or acquiesced in the release of the document or the making of the statement;
- any expert, in the same circumstances as for a misrepresentation in a document released by the issuer.

§7.137 Claimants are not require to prove that they acquired or disposed of securities in reliance on the particular misrepresentation or failure to make timely disclosure in order to establish liability. In the case of a "core" document, once an investor-plaintiff proves that a misrepresentation has been made, the defendant must establish certain statutory defences in order to escape liability. For "non-core" documents and failures to make timely disclosure, the investor-plaintiff must prove (with certain exceptions) knowledge, willful blindness or gross misconduct on the part of the defendant, before the burden shifts to the defendant to establish a defence. The key defences are:

- Due diligence: To make out this defence, the defendant must establish that after a reasonable investigation, the defendant had no reasonable grounds to believe that a misrepresentation had been made or that there had been a failure to make timely disclosure. In deciding whether the defendant's investigation was reasonable, the amendments require the court to consider "all relevant circumstances" including a list of specified factors. In particular, issuers are expected to have a system in place that is designed to ensure compliance with the continuous disclosure requirements.

- Reliance upon the report of an expert, but this defense is available only if the defendant can demonstrate that the misrepresentation is contained in a report, statement or opinion made by an expert who consented to its use.

- There is no liability for losses to the extent that they were due to market factors not related to the disclosure failure.

- A "safe harbor" defense for forward-looking information. Projections and other forward looking information are inherently speculative. A reasonable investor will understand that characteristic. However, to avoid liability for a misrepresentation in forward-looking information, the defendant must establish that the document or oral statement included cautionary language identifying the information as forward-looking, a statement identifying the material factors that could cause actual results to differ from what was forecasted and a statement of material factors or assumptions that were applied in making the forecast or projection. In addition, there must be a reasonable basis for making the forecast or projection in the forward-looking information.

- Derivative Information: A person is not liable merely for repeating information that is contained in a document filed by another person with a securities regulator or stock exchange, provided (in Ontario) that the re-publication of that information expressly identifies the source. In British Columbia, there is no need for the re-publication to disclose the source of the information. However, in both Ontario and British Columbia, a defendant must not know, and must not have reasonable grounds to believe, that he or she is repeating a misrepresentation.

§7.138 Damages are recoverable to the extent that they can be shown to have resulted from the impact of the misrepresentation or non-disclosure on market value, subject to a potential cap. The liability of each defendant is proportionate rather than joint or joint and several, meaning that a defendant who is only 15 per cent at fault can only be required to pay 15 per cent of the damages. As a result, a plaintiff must collect from each defendant in proportion to the degree of fault ascribed by the court to each respective defendant. Since it is quite possible that a defendant may be unable to satisfy his, her or its share of the damages proved, there is a serious risk of under-recovery. However, defendants who knew of the misconduct, or who were reckless or willfully blind are not entitled to the benefit of proportionate liability.

§7.139 Except in a case in which a misrepresentation was made knowingly, the liability for an issuer is capped at the greater of a maximum of 5 per cent of an issuer's market capitalization and $1 million. In the case of individual defendants, the cap is fixed at the greater of $25,000 or 50 per cent of the aggregate of the individual's compensation from the issuer. Liability of an expert is limited to the greater of $1 million and the revenue that the expert earned from the issuer during the preceding 12 months. The British Columbia legislation will permit an awards of punitive damages if a defendant had knowledge or recklessly avoided knowledge of the misconduct.

§7.140 Before commencing an action, leave of the court must be obtained and the court may only grant leave where it is satisfied that the action is being brought in good faith and that there is a reasonable possibility that the action will be decided in favor of the plaintiff at trial. No stay, discontinuance, settlement, or dismissal of the action for delay may take place without approval of the court given on such terms as it sees fit. No action for damages may be commenced after three years. This limitation period is reduced to six months once leave is granted to commence an action in any recognized jurisdiction.

(iv) Securities Disclosure Obligations

§7.141 The significance of the principles of liability discussed above is best appreciated when they are considered in the context of the disclosure obligations imposed under the *Securities Act*, and the Regulations, policies and rules that have been promulgated under that Act. These are summarized in Chapters 10 and 11.

(v) Wash Trading, etc.

§7.142 Liability for misrepresentation also underlies the provisions of the *Criminal Code*[327] dealing with stock and other security manipulation. Section 382 of the *Criminal Code* provides:

> 382. Every one who, through the facility of a stock exchange, curb market or other market, with intent to create a false or misleading appearance of active public trading in a security or with intent to create a false or misleading appearance with respect to the market price of a security,
>
> > (*a*) effects a transaction in the security that involves no change in the beneficial ownership thereof;
> >
> > (*b*) enters an order for the purchase of the security, knowing that an order of substantially the same size at substantially the same time and at substantially the same price for the sale of the security has been or will be entered by or for the same or different persons, or
> >
> > (*c*) enters an order for the sale of the security, knowing that an order of substantially the same size at substantially the same time and at substantially the same price for the purchase of the security has been or will be entered by or for the same or different persons,
>
> is guilty of an indictable offense and is liable to imprisonment for a term not exceeding ten years.

It has been held that the words "or other market" are sufficiently broad to encompass the over-the-counter market.[328]

§7.143 The clear purpose behind section 382 is to prevent the apparent market value of a security from being artificially inflated through bogus transactions, simulating a series of market trades — what is commonly known as "wash trading" or a "wash sale". The term "wash trading" describes the practice of buying and selling securities, improperly taking both sides of the trade at the same time. It constitutes one of the classic ways of rigging a market. The trades look legitimate but there is no real change in ownership; meaning that in street parlance, the transaction is a "wash" (*i.e.*, the sale washes out the buy").

---

[327] R.S.C. 1985, c. C-46.
[328] *Bluestein v. R.* (1982), 36 C.R. (3d) 46, 70 C.C.C. 336 (Que. C.A.).

§7.144 For instance, a group of conspirators (B, C, and D) may agree to purchase shares in a particular corporation, and to engage in a series of "sales" among themselves, which create the illusion that there is a substantial market for the shares, and that the true value of the shares is substantially in excess of their market value. The following table provides simple illustration of how the swaps can be arranged among the conspirators, until eventually, an innocent investor (mistakenly believing that he or she has spotted a hot item) puts in a buy-bid at a price well in excess of the true value of the manipulated securities.

Date	Transaction	Price	Price Per Share
Monday	B purchases 100 shares at true market price from a non-conspirator	$100	$1.00 per share
Tuesday	B sells 100 shares to C, a co-conspirator	$125	$1.25 per share
Wednesday	C sells 100 shares to D, a co-conspirator	$250	$2.10 per share
Thursday	D sells 100 shares to B	$325	$3.50 per share
Friday	B sells 100 shares to C, a co-conspirator	$400	$4.00 per share
Monday	C sells 100 shares to a non-conspirator (F) at a price of $4.50 per share	$450	$4.50 per share

Thus B, C, and D, obtain a profit of $350 on their investment of $100, and dispose of the shares at four and one half times their true value. The trick works because F is convinced by all the reported trades that the company has great prospects and that the people making the trade have access to inside information that is not generally available.

§7.145 Wash trading depends for its success upon the conspirators finding a mark who is both gullible and greedy — a person more intent upon speculative gain than return upon investment: in short someone who is out for the fast buck and the windfall profit. Except in the case of breach of trust, there is something to be said for letting the chips fall where they lie in the world of investment, for the simple reason that once one decides to interfere in the market place, it becomes very difficult to draw the line. But such a *laissez-faire* attitude has not been well-received by the courts. Instead, they have given a broad construction to the section, believing that by so doing they will protect the integrity of securities markets.[329] For instance, it has been held that although a charge under section 382 will normally relate to a series of trades involving either fictitious persons or conspirators, it is not essential that the Crown prove either the existence of a conspiracy or fictitious persons. The Crown need only show that there

---

[329] See, generally, *R. v. MacMillan*, [1968] O.J. No. 1045, 2 C.C.C. 289 (C.A.).

was a fraudulent misuse of the market, as for instance by engaging in a series of wash sales.[330]

§7.146 In order to be convicted of an offense under section 382, the accused must have intended to create a false or misleading appearance of active public interest. If a series of trades are entered into a by an investor for the purpose of stabilizing the market price, there is no offence.[331] For instance, if the trading price of a stock is declining, it is not improper for a person having an investment in the corporation to attempt to counter that trend by putting in purchase bids at a higher price than others might be willing to pay. Nevertheless, it is important when structuring a series of stock transactions to ensure that the wash trading prohibition is not contravened. Hedging transactions in particular need to be carefully structured.[332]

§7.147 A further prohibition is contained in section 380 of the *Criminal Code*. It provides that:

> 380.(1) Every one who, by deceit, falsehood or other fraudulent means, whether or not it is a false pretense within the meaning of this Act, defrauds the public or any person, whether ascertained or not, of any property, money or valuable security or any service,
>
> . . . . .
>
> (b) is guilty
>
>   (i) of an indictable offence and is liable to imprisonment a term not exceeding two years
>
>   (ii) of an offence punishable on summary conviction,
>
> where the value of the subject-matter of the offence does not exceed five thousand dollars.

A broker was convicted of a conspiracy to commit fraud under this subsection where the broker conspired to obtain money and securities by false pretenses. The broker carried on a policy of failing to disclose information to clients and to carry out their instructions properly and was paid secret commissions for so doing.

§7.148 Subsection 380(2) of the *Criminal Code* creates a further offense regulating dealings with securities. It reads:

> 380.(2) Every one who, by deceit, falsehood or other fraudulent means, whether or not it is a false pretense within the meaning of this Act, with intent to defraud, affects the public market price of stocks, shares, merchandise or anything

---

[330] *R. v. Lampard*, [1968] O.J. No. 1177, [1968] 2 O.R. 470 (C.A.), rev'd on procedural grounds [1969] S.C.J. No. 31, [1969] S.C.R. 373; see also *R. v. MacMillan*, [1968] O.J. No. 1045, [1968] 1 O.R. 475 (C.A.).

[331] *R. v. Jay*, [1965] O.J. No. 997, [1966] 1 C.C.C. 70, [1965] 2 O.R. 471 at 474 (C.A.), *per* Roach J.A.

[332] See, for instance, "RBC traders face 'wash trading' allegations", CBC News, May 30, 2005, available through the CBC web site at <http://www.cbc.ca/news/>.

that is offered for sale to the public is guilty of an indictable offence and is liable to imprisonment for a term not exceeding fourteen years.

Prosecutions under subsection 380(2) have been rare. In *R. v. McNaughton*,[333] the accused was one of several people involved in operating a box set up to maintain an orderly marketing in speculative shares. A box is essentially a reservation of shares (usually by or on behalf of the principals in a corporation) for the purpose of using them in stabilization of the market for those shares. The nature of the scheme was described in the following terms:

> ... the operator of the box, who could be a broker or an ordinary individual, had to have at his disposal a certain number of shares of the company and a certain amount of money. When the price of the stock or rather of the security rose in an excessive way because of a large demand, the operator of the box sold in the market through the agency of the Exchange a part of the shares which he had in his possession. On the other hand, when the ... shares declined in an undue fashion as a result of too large a number of shares being offered for sale, the operator of the box bought those shares at the Exchange with a view to stabilizing the market, it is good to point out that according to the practices of the Exchange, the box was not to be used to enrich the person or persons who operated it. Its role was essentially to assure an orderly market of securities, that is an "orderly market".[334]

However, on the facts of the case it was found that the box was used to give the illusion of arm's length transactions in the trading of the shares. This usage gave the impression that the shares were continually rising in value. The conviction of the accused was upheld. The box had generated a profit of $750,000 for the people standing behind the scheme. In upholding the conviction, Mayrand J.A. commented:

> Like [Turgeon, J.A.] I am equally of the view that the appellant McNaughton could not have known that his manipulations of the market were prohibited by the *Criminal Code*. The appellant however was unable not to know that by using the "box" ... in such a way as to bring about an artificial and disorderly increase in prices, he was distorting the ordinary operation which is rather the stabilization of prices. The false appearance of a real increase in the value of shares was created in order to deceive the public for the gain of a small group of speculators.[335]

§7.149 In addition to the foregoing, it is an offence for a broker to sell short against the margin purchases of a client.[336] To obtain a conviction it is necessary to prove first that the accursed was employed by a broker, whether in an individual capacity or as a member or employee of a partnership. Second it must be proved that the accused carried shares on margin for his or her customers. The shares in question may be in an incorporated or unincorporated entity — which suggests that limited partnership units might also be caught by the section. The accused must then sell the shares or cause them to be sold for any account in which the accused (or the accused's firm, partner, corporation or a director thereof) has a direct or indirect interest. The effect of the sale must be the reduc-

---

[333] (1976), 43 C.C.C. (2d) 293 (Que. C.A.).
[334] *Ibid.*, per Turgeon J.A. at 297.
[335] *Ibid.* at 309.
[336] *Criminal Code*, s. 384.

D. PRICE

§7.150 Subject to the articles, the by-laws and any unanimous shareholder agreement, shares in either a CBCA[337] or an OBCA[338] corporation may be issued at such time and to such persons and for such consideration as the directors may determine.[339] Upon payment of the purchase price of shares, the money so paid belongs to the corporation and is in no sense the property of the shareholders.[340] In *Campbell v. Prudential Trust Co.*,[341] the money paid by the shareholders was deposited to an escrow account. Although withdrawal from that account was restricted, the payments by the shareholder appear to have been absolute, with the shares being issued in consequence. Had the money in that case been held in suspense — the subscription being made conditionally — with no shares being issued to the shareholders, they might have been successful in their attempt to recover the money, by raising the failure of the corporation to satisfy the condition of their subscription. The absolute nature of the payment made the money irrecoverable.

§7.151 Both the power to issue shares and the determination of the issue price are discretionary powers normally reserved to the directors (although a unanimous shareholder agreement may provide otherwise). As with all statutory powers of discretion, these powers must be exercised in the best interests of the corporation and it is not appropriate for the directors to fetter the exercise of their discretion. However, while the directors are obliged to get a fair price for the shares, they are not obliged to put the shares of a corporation up for auction at the time of their issue, so as to raise the maximum amount of stated capital.[342] A fair price is not necessarily the maximum price, for a wide range of considerations may be relevant to the decision as to whom to issue shares to, beyond the simple question of who is prepared to pay the most for them. The responsi-

---

[337] CBCA, s. 25(1).
[338] OBCA, s. 23(1). Subsection (1) is also subject to s. 26 (s. 28 in the case of the CBCA), which deals with the pre-emptive rights of existing shareholders, but since any such right must be provided for in either the articles or a unanimous shareholder resolution, the reference to s. 26 is unnecessary.
[339] The issue price assigned to shares may be very low (*e.g.*, in the case of so called "penny stocks") — so low, indeed, that the subscription price for an individual share will be less than the lowest denomination of legal currency: *Re Scandinavian Bank Group*, [1988] Ch. 87 at 99-100. In *Re Australian Pacific Technology Ltd.*, [1995] 1 V.R. 457, the court approved the issue of shares that had a per share issue price of 0.01 cent.
[340] *Campbell v. Prudential Trust Co.*, [1944] B.C.J. No. 34, [1944] 3 W.W.R. 456 at 489 (C.A.), *per* O'Halloran J.A. at 489; *Guinness v. Land Corporation of Ireland* (1883), 22 Ch. D. 349 at 375, *per* Cotton L.J.
[341] [1994] B.C.J. No. 34, [1944] 3 W.W.R. 456 (C.A.).
[342] *Harris v. Sumner* (1909), 39 N.B.R. 204 (C.A.).

bility of the directors of a corporation is to manage it according to its best interests in the widest sense, not merely its immediate best financial interest.

§7.152 Although in general shares may be issued for any consideration determined by the directors, no share may be issued until the consideration for it has been fully paid.[343] One justification for the fully paid requirement is that it reduces the transaction costs of a winding-up. Before this requirement was introduced (and even today in the case of limited partnership unit interests, where there is no fully paid requirement), in many cases the creditors found it impractical to attempt to pursue the shareholders of a corporation to recover the unpaid portion of the subscription price of shares. The costs of enforcement were disproportionately high relative to the probable recovery.

§7.153 Any shares that are not fully paid are still validly issued, but the holder of those shares is liable to the corporation for the subscription price.[344] A corporation cannot be estopped by its conduct from asserting that a share is not fully paid *vis-à-vis* the person to whom it was issued.[345] The fully paid requirement prevents a corporation from issuing shares in consideration of the supply of future services[346] or the future supply of goods.[347]

§7.154 Shares in a corporation that were purportedly issued as fully paid, but that were in fact issued at less than its fully paid amount (or for no consideration at all) fall within the definition of watered stock. No specific statutory liability is imposed upon the directors in respect of the issue of watered stock *per se*, although such a liability is imposed where the shares are issued for a consideration

---

[343] CBCA, s. 25(3); OBCA, s. 23(3).
[344] *Oakley v. McDougall*, [1987] B.C.J. No. 272, 37 B.L.R. 31 (C.A.), additional reasons at [1987] B.C.J. No. 1226, 37 B.L.R. 47 (C.A.); but compare *Receiver of Javelin Intl. Ltd. v. Hillier*, [1988] Q.J. No. 928, 40 B.L.R. 249 (S.C.) and *Dunham v. Apollo Tours Ltd. (No. 1)*, [1978] O.J. No. 3381, 20 O.R. (2d) 3 (H.C.), which take the opposite position. The argument that a person improperly shown on the books as a shareholder should remain liable as such is as follows. It has always been the law that a corporation cannot enter into a contract with a shareholder under which it undertakes to limit the liability to an amount less than the issue price of the share that the shareholder takes up: *Toronto Finance Corp. v. Banking Service Corp.*, [1926] O.J. No. 34, 59 O.L.R. 278 at 284 (C.A.), per Ferguson J.A. If the corporation cannot exonerate the shareholder directly, then it should not be able to do so by simple defiance of the statutory requirement to issue shares only when they are fully paid. It cannot be open to the corporation (which has wrongly issued the share) to dispute liability; nor can the shareholder (who knowingly received the share partly or wholly unpaid) deny liability: *Re British Cattle Supply Co. (Hisey's Case)*, [1920] O.J. No. 239, 19 O.W.N. 147 (C.A.). But if the initial shareholder is subject to that liability, it is then only reasonable that he or she is entitled to the rights of a shareholder. If the share is transferred to a purchaser in good faith without notice, both the corporation and its liquidator are estopped from claiming that the share is not fully paid: see, generally, *Bloomenthal v. Ford*, [1897] A.C. 156. In such a case the OBCA and CBCA then provide that the directors who issued the shares are liable for the deficiency.
[345] *Re British Cattle Supply Co. (Hisey's Case)*, [1920] O.J. No. 239, 19 O.W.N. 147 (C.A.).
[346] See, generally, *Hirsche v. Sims*, [1894] A.C. 654 at 659-60 (P.C.), per Lord Herschell, for a discussion of the implications of such an issue. See also *Re Winnipeg Hedge & Wire Fence Co.* (1912), 1 D.L.R. 316 (Man. K.B.).
[347] See *Re Jones & Moore* (1909), 18 Man. L.R. 549, 10 W.L.R. 210 (C.A.), for an illustration of such a share issue.

other than money. It does not follow that directors are free from liability to the corporation where they issue shares without securing full payment for them. The corporation is bound to comply with the Act, and under subsection 134(2) of the OBCA every director and officer is similarly obliged. At common law, where the directors of a corporation issued and allotted shares of the corporation without consideration, they were required to make good the value of those shares to the corporation.[348] On this basis, the directors of a corporation would be liable if they issued shares and showed the corporation having been paid for them in full, when in fact no payment or only a part payment was made. The directors may not simply revise the issue price of the shares downward, and so relieve themselves and the shareholders from liability.[349] There can be little doubt that the shareholder to whom the share was issued (so long as he or she remains the shareholder) is liable to make good any deficiency in the paid-up capital of a share,[350] as for instance where payment for a share has been tendered by cheque, and that cheque is subsequently dishonoured. The shareholder may not escape this liability by (a) transferring a worthless property to the corporation or (b) returning the excess value of the shares received to the corporation for cancellation.[351] The onus lies upon the shareholder to establish that full payment has been made for his or her shares. It is at least arguable that a person who fails to pay fully for shares is liable for interest in respect of the deficiency between the time

---

[348] *Batchlett v. United Cobalt Mines Ltd.*, [1953] O.W.N. 425 at 427 (H.C.), *per* Marriott S.M. See also *Re Ontario Fire Insurance Co.* (1915), 8 W.W.R. 1081 (Alta. T.D.). Note, however, s. 130(1) of the OBCA which provides:

> 130.(1) Directors of a corporation who vote for or consent to a resolution *authorizing the issue of a share for a consideration other than money contrary to section 23* are jointly and severally liable to the corporation to make good any amount by which the consideration received is less than the fair equivalent of the money that the corporation would have received if the share had been issued for money on the date of the resolution.
>
> (Emphasis added)

See also CBCA, s. 118(1); *Bing Crosby Minute Maid Corp. v. Eaton*, 46 Cal.2d 484, 297 P.2d 5 at 8 (1956).

[349] *Re Jones & Moore* (1909), 18 Man. L.R. 549, 10 W.L.R. 210 at 216 (C.A.), *per* Howell C.J.

[350] In the case of corporations continued under the OBCA or under the former OBCA, s. 92(2) of the OBCA provides:

> 92.(2) The provisions of the *Corporations Act* relating to the liability of a holder of shares that are not fully paid and to the enforcement of such liability apply in respect of shares that were not fully paid,
>
> (a) on the 1st day of January, 1971, in the case of shares of a corporation that then became subject to *The Business Corporations Act*, being chapter 53 of the Revised Statutes of Ontario, 1970; or
>
> (b) on the day upon which any other body corporate was continued under *The Business Corporations Act*, being chapter 53 of the Revised Statutes of Ontario, 1970, or under this Act, in the case of shares of such other body corporate.

[351] *Re Winnipeg Hedge & Wire Fence Co.* (1912), 1 W.W.R. 853 (Man. K.B.); *Common v. McArthur* (1898), 29 S.C.R. 239: any right of lien to which the corporation is entitled exists for its benefit, and the decision of whether to utilize the lien or seek some other remedy belongs to the corporation. It is not open to the shareholder to insist that the corporation rely upon the lien.

when the shares were first taken up and the time when he or she is called upon to pay for them.[352]

§7.155 In most cases the consideration paid in respect of a share will constitute either money or property.[353] The value of a monetary consideration will rarely present a problem. However, in the case of a consideration other than money, the directors are subject to a specific duty to value the consideration that is being received. In this regard, subsection 23(3) of the OBCA[354] requires that where shares are issued for property or past services, that consideration must have a value that is not less than the fair equivalent value of the money that the corporation would have received if the share had been issued for money.[355] Subsection 23(4) of the OBCA[356] further provides that in connection with the issue of any share not issued for money, the directors must determine the amount of money the corporation would have received if the share had been issued for money; and either

- the fair value of the property or past service in consideration of which the share is issued, or
- that such property or past service has a fair value that is not less than that amount of money.

These procedures set down a modern embodiment of the true value rule under which a subscriber for stock is required to pay the fair value thereof in money or money's worth, so that the amount received by the corporation is at least square with stated capital as shown in the books of the corporation. Implicit within this rule is the notion that where by fraud, accident or mistake the true value paid by the subscriber is less than the stated capital, the stock is considered to be unpaid for the extent of the difference and the holder is liable to the creditors of the corporation for that difference, irrespective of the good faith of the parties concerned.[357]

§7.156 Subsection 23(4) of the OBCA imposes a two-step process. The directors must determine first the value of the share they are issuing and then the value of the consideration that they are receiving.[358] There is no obligation upon the di-

---

[352] See *Canada West Loan Co. v. Virtue*, [1920] B.C.J. No. 9, 1 W.W.R. 730 (S.C.). There is no question as to liability for interest after the time when the shareholder is called to pay the deficiency.
[353] *Re Wragg Ltd.*, [1897] 1 Ch. 796 (C.A.), *per* Lindley L.J.
[354] CBCA, s. 25(3).
[355] See, generally, *Re White Star Line Ltd.*, [1938] 1 All E.R. 607 (C.A.).
[356] No comparable provision exists in the CBCA, but the steps required under subs. 23(4) of the OBCA would seem to be implicit in the requirement — set out in subs. 25(3) of the CBCA — that no share may be issued until the consideration for it has been fully paid in money or in property or past service that is not less in value than the money that the corporation would have received if the share had been issued for money.
[357] See *Johansen v. St. Louis Union Trust Co.*, 345 Mo. 135, 131 S.W.2d 599 at 603.
[358] Directors who vote for or consent to a resolution authorizing the issue of a share for a consideration other than money contrary to s. 23 of the OBCA (or s. 25 of the CBCA, as the case may be) are jointly and severally liable to the corporation to make good any amount by which the consideration received is less than the fair equivalent of the money that the corporation would have re-

rectors to obtain a formal appraisal of the value of the property, but it is clear that they are required to make a reasonable estimate. In valuing property, the directors may refer to the amount paid by the shareholder for the property in question.[359] Where, however, there has been a substantial interval of time since the time when the property was acquired by the shareholder, that amount is not likely to provide much of a guide. Provided the directors act in good faith, honestly and reasonably,[360] the courts will not take issue with the valuation placed by the directors on the consideration received.[361]

§7.157 Subject to the true value rule, a corporation may issue shares in exchange for notional property, such as goodwill, and in exchange for time-limited property such as an option or a grant of a franchise.[362] The sole requirement is that the corporation receives something of value in return for its shares. Both the OBCA and the CBCA provide for a money, property or past service consideration — which leaves open the question of whether a shareholder may transfer non-property assets (such as an agricultural quota and also revocable licences and franchises) in exchange for shares.[363]

§7.158 It has been held in England that a company may have its capital denominated in the currency of a foreign nation, or in a combination of different currencies.[364] Neither the OBCA nor the CBCA are clear as to whether a share of a corporation may be denominated in foreign currency (*i.e.*, whether the issue price may be pegged at a certain amount of foreign currency, rather than Canadian currency). Even so, foreign currency denominated shares are quite common, and indeed have been common in Canada since before Confederation. Subsection 24(8) of the OBCA expressly provides that "[s]tated capital accounts of a corporation may be expressed in one or more currencies", which strengthens the conclusion that the term "money" includes both Canadian and foreign

---

ceived if the share had been issued on the date of the resolution: OBCA, s. 130(1); CBCA, s. 118(1).
[359] OBCA, s. 23(5); CBCA, s. 25(4).
[360] *Cie d'immeubles v. St. Amour* (1920), 59 Que. S.C. 391, *per* Howard J.
[361] *Co-operative Cycle & Motor Co.*, [1902] O.J. No. 636, 1 O.W.R. 778 (H.C.); *John E. Hayes & Sons v. Turner*, [1924] O.J. No. 620, 26 O.W.N. 456 at 458 (H.C.), *per* Wright J.; *Re Hess Manufacturing Co.*, [1894] O.J. No. 1, 23 S.C.R. 644, 21 O.A.R. 66.
[362] See, for instance, *Re R.P. Clarke & Co. (Vancouver) Ltd.*, [1938] B.C.J. No. 36, 20 C.B.R. 6 (S.C.); *New Federal Oils Ltd. v. Rowland*, [1929] 1 W.W.R. 263 (Alta. C.A.).
[363] See, generally, *Re Canadian Imperial Bank of Commercial & Hallahan*, [1990] O.J. No. 861, 69 D.L.R. (4th) 449 (C.A.), leave to appeal to S.C.C. refused [1991] 1 S.C.R. vi, 74 D.L.R. (4th) vii; *National Trust v. Bouckhuyt*, [1987] O.J. No. 930, 43 D.L.R. (4th) 543 (C.A.); *Sanders v. British Columbia Milk Board*, [1990] B.C.J. No. 414, 43 B.C.L.R. (2d) 324 (S.C.), *per* Hinds J. See also *Royal Bank of Canada v. Saulnier*, [2006] N.S.J. No. 38, 145 A.C.W.S. (3d) 376 (S.C.), *per* Kennedy C.J.N.S, var'd [2006] N.S.J. No. 307 (C.A.); *Canadian Imperial Bank of Commerce v. Hallahan*, [1990] O.J. No. 861, 1 P.P.S.A.C. (2d) 58 (C.A.), leave to appeal to S.C.C. refused [1991] 1 S.C.R. vi; *Saskatoon Auction Mart Ltd. v. Finesse Holsteins*, [1992] S.J. No. 518, [1993] 1 W.W.R. 265 (Q.B.); *Comeau's Sea Foods Ltd. v. Canada (Minister of Fisheries and Oceans)*, [1997] S.C.J. No. 5 at para. 33, [1997] 1 S.C.R. 12, *per* Major J. In addition to the foregoing see §7.167 *et seq.*
[364] *Re Scandinavian Bank Group plc*, [1987] 2 All E.R. 70, [1987] 2 W.L.R. 752; *Re Anglo-American Insurance Co.*, [1991] B.C.L.C. 564.

currency. Denomination of one class or series of shares in more than one currency presents considerable accounting problems, and therefore this practice should be avoided.[365]

§7.159 Although it is not clear, it is arguable that where one currency is received in payment for shares that are issued in another currency, the true value provisions of the OBCA and the CBCA impose an obligation upon the directors to value the currency that is received relative to the currency of the shares, and to issue shares by reference to that valuation. There is no requirement that the payment actually be converted to the currency of the shares, but any valuation at other than the current exchange rate would clearly be open to question. The relative value of currencies can be extremely volatile — and the possibility that currency may fluctuate in value brings to mind the question of at what time the directors are required to make their valuation. A number of options exist: (1) at the time of subscription; (2) at the time when the directors accept the subscription and direct the issue of the shares; (3) at the time of the issue of the shares. As a practical matter, option (3) would not be workable: the directors must make the valuation before they authorize the issue of the shares.

§7.160 Both Acts also permit the consideration for a share to be paid in past service that is "not less in value than the fair equivalent of the money the corporation would have received if the share had been issued for money".[366] This possibility is discussed in detail below.

(i) Payment of the Price

§7.161 At common law, a company was barred from giving its shares away,[367] although it was accepted that a company was not limited to issuing shares for cash.[368] The present OBCA and CBCA go much further. Although subsection 23(1) of the OBCA[369] provides that shares may be issued "at such time and to such persons and for such consideration as the directors may determine", under subsection 23(3)[370] shares may not be issued until the consideration for their issue is fully paid. As noted above, it is now clear under both Acts that (a) shares may be paid for in money or money's worth in the form of property or past services; and (b) shares may not be issued until they are fully paid. The question may arise, however, as to whether payment has actually been made for the shares that have been issued to a shareholder,[371] and if so, the effect of that payment. Neither statute provides much help in answering either of these questions, and thus in attempting to answer them, it is necessary to go back to the pre-OBCA/CBCA case law.

---

[365] See, generally, *Re Scandinavian Bank Group plc*, [1987] 2 All E.R. 70, [1987] 2 W.L.R. 752.
[366] OBCA, s. 23(3); CBCA, 25(3).
[367] *Re Eddystone Marine Insurance Co.*, [1893] 3 Ch. 9; *Re Baglan Hall Colliery Co.* (1870), 5 Ch. App. 346.
[368] *Pakenham Pork Packing Co. (Liquidator of) v. Kendrick* (1905), 37 S.C.R. 32.
[369] CBCA, s. 25(1).
[370] CBCA, s. 25(3).
[371] See, for instance, *Larouque v. Beauchemin*, [1897] A.C. 358 (P.C.).

§7.162 On the basis of that old case law, it would seem that the requirement that shares not be issued until fully paid does not prevent the corporation from soliciting or accepting subscriptions for shares without payment attached, provided the shares concerned are not actually issued until payment is received.[372] However, the onus lies upon the shareholder to prove that he or she has paid for the shares that have been issued to him,[373] and the shareholder will be liable as a contributory in a winding-up or bankruptcy in the event of any deficiency.[374] The shareholder does not have the option of forfeiting the shares to the corporation and walking away from the deal.[375] However, in reply to a claim for the unpaid balance of a share, the shareholder is entitled to raise the usual defences, including a right of set-off.[376]

§7.163 In *Gillespie v. Retail Merchants Assn. of Canada (Ontario) Inc.*[377] it was alleged that the plaintiff was allotted shares by the defendant while he was employed by it as compensation for work that he had completed. The plaintiff was subsequently fired. The defendant corporation proposed to have the shares valued and transferred as a part of a severance settlement. However, it then refused to deliver a share certificate, claiming that the $250 subscription price of the shares had never been paid. The plaintiff tendered this amount but it was refused. The plaintiff moved for summary judgment requiring the defendant to deliver up the certificate. Judgment was given for the plaintiff. The court noted that no request had ever been made to the plaintiff to pay the $250 before the dispute arose between the parties over severance. The issue was raised only when the plaintiff demanded delivery of the certificate.[378]

§7.164 Historically, it was settled under the former (pre-OBCA) corporate law regime that a shareholder might transfer shares on which that shareholder is liable to pay up a capital deficiency even,

- on the eve of bankruptcy, and
- where the transferee is a man of straw,

---

[372] See, generally, *Denison v. Leslie*, [1879] O.J. No. 102, 3 O.A.R. 536 at 543-45 (C.A.), *per* Moss C.J.A.
[373] *Re Winnipeg Hedge & Wire Fence Co.* (1912), 1 D.L.R. 316, 22 Man. R. 83 (K.B.); *Re Northern Construction Ltd.* (1910), 12 W.L.R. 618 at 619 (Man. K.B.), *per* Macdonald J.
[374] *Welton v. Saffery*, [1897] A.C. 299 at 305 (H.L.), *per* Lord Halsbury L.C.; see, generally, *Re Dominion Permanent Loan Co.* (1920), 47 O.L.R. 87 (C.A.); *Hamilton v. Stewiacke Valley & Lansdowne Rlwy.* (1897), 30 N.S.R. 10 (C.A.).
[375] *Ontario Marine Insurance Co. v. Ireland*, [1855] O.J. No. 114, 5 U.C.C.P. 135. A creditor may obtain an order compelling the corporation to enforce the claim for the amount owing: see *Harris v. Dry Dock Co.* (1859), 7 Gr. 450 (U.C. Ch.).
[376] *Field v. Galloway*, [1884] O.J. No. 236, 5 O.R. 502 (H.C.), but compare *Benner v. Currie*, [1875] O.J. No. 29, 36 U.C.Q.B. 411 at 415 (Ont. C.A.), *per* Gwynne J.
[377] [1997] O.J. No. 956, 33 B.L.R. (2d) 307 (Gen. Div.).
[378] See also *Dunham v. Apollo Tours Ltd.*, [1978] O.J. No. 3380, 20 O.R. (2d) 3 (H.C.).

provided that the transfer is *bona fide* and the transferor retains no interest in the shares.[379] At common law, if an unpaid or partly paid share is transferred,[380] the transferee assumed the liability of the transferor — although that transferee might have been entitled to a right to recover indemnity from the transferor where there was an express or implied warranty that the shares were fully paid. As the law now stands, shares cannot be issued except as fully paid, and thus there would seem to be such an implied warranty in every case. Moreover, in *Kettle River Mines Ltd. v. Bleasdel*[381] it was held that where shares were sold to a transferee, and the share certificate in respect of those shares bore the legend "fully paid", the company was estopped from claiming against them for the unpaid issue price of the shares. Since under the present OBCA and CBCA, corporations are prohibited from issuing shares except fully paid, it would seem to follow that any corporation which issues a share without full payment is similarly estopped from seeking to recover any deficiency from a transferee.[382] Thus under the present law it is not possible to recover a capital deficiency on a share from any transferee unless the transferee took the share with notice of that capital deficiency.

(1) Payment by Cheque

§7.165 Although it is customary to speak of shares being issued for a money consideration, actual cash payment is rare. Usually payment for shares will be made by way of the subscriber tendering payment by cheque. Although a cheque is nothing more than a type of bill of exchange, even if certified, it is doubtful that cheques would be held to be a "document evidencing indebtedness" so as to run afoul of the prohibition in subsection 23(6) of the OBCA,[383] and even if so construed, there seems no doubt that cheques may be accepted as conditional payment of the issue price, which becomes absolute once final payment is made under it.[384] The remarks of James L.J. in *Re Harmony and Montague Tin and Copper Mining Co.*[385] are quite helpful in fixing the meaning of the money payment requirement. In that case, the court was required to interpret section 25 of the *Companies Act*[386] which required shares to be paid for in cash. He said:

> ... [I]t could not be right to put any construction upon that section which would lead to an absurd and unjustifiable result as this, that an exchange of cheques

---

[379] *Shimmin v. Clark*, [1932] B.C.J. No. 28, 14 C.B.R. 138 (C.A.).
[380] *Ross v. Marcher*, [1885] O.J. No. 270, 8 O.R. 417 (H.C.); *Re Wiarton Beet Sugar Manufacturing Co. (Freeman's Case)*, [1906] O.J. No. 35, 12 O.L.R. 149 (H.C.).
[381] [1900] B.C.J. 80, 7 B.C.R. 507 (S.C.), aff'd [1901] B.C.J. No. 66, 8 B.C.R. 350 (C.A.); see also *McCracken v. McIntyre* (1877), 1 S.C.R. 479. As to whether the transferor in such a case remains liable, compare: *Union Bank of Canada v. Morris*, [1900] O.J. No. 40, 27 O.A.R. 396 (C.A.), aff'd 31 S.C.R. 594 and *Re Wiarton Beet Sugar Manufacturing Co.*, [1906] O.J. No. 35, 12 O.L.R. 149 (H.C.), where Meredith C.J. suggests (at 153) that the transferor may be liable where he or she was a party to the breach of trust against the corporation.
[382] See also *Page v. Austin* (1884), 10 S.C.R. 132.
[383] CBCA, s. 25(5).
[384] See, generally, *Gagnon v. Tremblay* (1925), 41 Que. K.B. 58 (C.A.) and also *Canada Furniture Co. v. Banning* (1917), 39 D.L.R. 313 at 315-16 (Man. K.B.), per Mathers C.J.K.B.
[385] (1873), L.R. 8 Ch. App. 407 at 411-12.
[386] 1867, 30 & 31 Vic., c. 131.

would not be payment in cash, or that an order upon a banker to transfer money from the account of a man to the account of a company would not be payment in cash. In truth, it appeared to me that anything which amounted to what would be in law sufficient evidence to support a plea of payment, would be a payment in cash within the meaning of the provision. ... If it came to this, that there was a debt in money payable immediately by the company to the shareholders and an equal debt payable immediately by the shareholders to the company, and that each accepted in full payment of the other, the company could have pleaded payment in an action brought against them, and the shareholder could have pleaded payment in cash in a corresponding action brought by the company against him for calls. [387]

However, the giving of the cheque by itself does not satisfy the shareholder's payment obligation; the cheque must be cashed.[388]

(2) Payment by Transfer of Property

§7. 166 A corporation can agree to purchase property and pay for services at any price it thinks proper and may pay for that property or those services provided it does so honestly and not colourably[389] and has not been so imposed upon as to entitle it to repudiate the bargain.[390] Shares may be issued in consideration of any property so purchased,[391] and likewise shares may also be issued in payment of an existing and genuine debt.[392] Obviously the fully paid requirement prohibits the issue of shares at an inflated value.[393] As discussed in greater detail below, a specific valuation requirement is also imposed under subsection 23(4) of the OBCA where shares are issued in consideration of the transfer of property.[394] Subsection 23(3) specifically requires services to be performed before shares may be issued. This wording would seem to beg the question as to whether an undertaking to transfer property is sufficient consideration, particularly where the undertaking is sufficient to create an equitable interest in the property concerned, and is an obligation which might be specifically enforced. Given the general requirement for full payment, the better view is that such an undertaking is not sufficient.[395]

---

[387] *Re Harmony and Montague Tin and Copper Mining Co.* (1873), L.R. 8 Ch. App. 407 at 411-12.
[388] *Scales v. Irwin*, [1874] O.J. No. 27, 34 U.C.Q.B. 545 at 551 (C.A.), *per* Wilson J.
[389] *Re Wiarton Beet Sugar Co. (Freeman's Case)*, [1906] O.J. No. 35, 12 O.L.R. 149; *Cowie v. Baguley*, [1919] O.J. No. 288, 16 O.W.N. 231 (C.A.); *Re Wragg Ltd.*, [1897] 1 Ch. 796 (C.A.).
[390] *Pakenham Pork Packing Co. (Liquidator of) v. Kendrick* (1905), 37 S.C.R. 32. There must be a reasonable basis to sustain the valuation, as is made clear in the remarks of Davies J. at 44. *Re North Bay Supply Co.*, [1905] O.J. No. 481, 6 O.W.R. 85 at 86 (H.C.), *per* Anglin J.; *Lindsay v. Imperial Steel & Wire Co.*, [1910] O.J. No. 139, 21 O.L.R. 375 (Div. Ct.); *Toronto Finance Corp. v. Banking Service Corp. Ltd.*, [1926] O.J. No. 34, 59 O.L.R. 278 (C.A.). As to the requirements applicable to a contract between promoters and the corporation, see Chapter 3.
[391] *Dominion Textile Co. v. MNR*, [1940] Ex. C.R. 130; *Re Wragg Ltd.*, [1897] 1 Ch. 796 (C.A.).
[392] *Beaver Dam Mining Co. v. Larson*, [1927] O.J. No. 350, 32 O.W.N. 143 (H.C.), aff'd [1927] O.J. No. 224, 33 O.W.N. 19 (C.A.).
[393] OBCA, s. 23(3); CBCA, s. 25(3); and see, generally, *Hong Kong & China Gas Co. v. Glen*, [1914] 1 Ch. 527.
[394] There is no equivalent CBCA provision.
[395] See, generally, *Re Jones & Moore* (1909), 18 Man. L.R. 549, 10 W.L.R. 210 (C.A.); *Re Richmond Hill Hotel Co. (Pellatt's Case)* (1867), L.R. 2 Ch. App. 527.

§7.167 Neither the OBCA nor the CBCA attempt a definition of property, although as noted below, both statutes limit the use of promissory notes and similar undertakings as a means of payment. Subject to any statutory exclusion, it would seem reasonable to conclude that shares may be paid for through the transfer to the corporation of anything falling within the general legal definition of property.[396] Property is sometimes described as consisting of the rights of use, abuse[397] and *fructus*.[398] This rather general and somewhat vague definition provides as useful a starting point as any for a consideration of the nature of property rights. Conceptually, property may be said to exist where one or more persons (including the state, or some emanation of the state) own an interest in a specific asset which confers an entitlement to the benefit of the asset, to the right of management of the asset, or to be entitled to a security interest in it or a remedy against it. In broad terms, the term "property" is generally seen to encompass anything which is capable of ownership; it also includes the rights of a person with respect to the subject matter concerned, as in the phrase "the property in the goods".[399] In this last sense, the term "property" is a synonym for ownership. Ownership is the fullest right which may exist in and over any subject. It is not a single right, but a bundle of rights, some or even many of which may be relinquished without loss of ownership. At its most basic level, ownership exists where a person has a present or future right to use an asset, to withhold it from use, to enjoy the profits or income derived from that asset, to dispose of it, or any combination of two or more of those rights. While the full rights conferred by ownership are so extensive as to be beyond ready description, implicit within control over use are (1) the right to select among uses to which a particular asset may be put (*e.g.*, to possess, use, lend, alienate, use up, enjoy the fruits or profits of, consume, alter and otherwise deal with the asset); (2) the right to exclude others from the use of that asset; (3) the right not to be deprived of that asset (subject, of course, in the case of expropriation, to the payment of just compensation). Property is not restricted to tangible things, but includes incorporeal assets such as choses in action, patents, and copyrights.

§7.168 It is less clear whether a subscriber may pay for shares by transferring to the corporation an asset which has value, but which for some reason fails to satisfy the legal definition of property. There are many "soft assets" of this type,

---

[396] See, generally, *McAlister v. Eclipse Oil Co.*, 128 Tex. 449, 98 S.W.2d 171 (S.C. 1936).
[397] When traced to its etymological roots, "abuse" means non-use rather than misuse — abuse is derived from ab (away from) uti (use); so abuse means holding something away from use (*i.e.*, not using it): and it is in this more etymologically correct sense that the term "abuse" is used in connection with property rights.
[398] The right of *fructus* is the right to enjoy the fruits of property — in other words, the gains that it produces.
[399] At common law, property is divided into two types: (1) real property, consisting of freehold estates in land, legal interests in land attaching to freehold interests, chattels affixed to land so as to become fixtures, and appurtenances to land; and (2) personal property. The category of property known as personal property consists of all other forms of property, whether moveable and immoveable, corporeal or incorporeal forms of property. By historical accident, leasehold interests in land are a form of personal property. Fixtures (*i.e.*, articles which have become attached to land or a building on land) do not constitute personal property.

including farm quota, certain types of government licenses, unpatentable technology including secret know-how,[400] and many types of franchise arrangement. A strict reading of the Act would exclude assets of this type from the scope of acceptable consideration for the issue of shares.[401] A number of cases (construing statutes ranging from the *Personal Property Security Act*[402] to matrimonial property legislation) have reached a range of conclusions when construing the meaning of "property" when used in a statute. Generally, the term property is given a broad definition by the courts. It is sometimes said to incorporate "every possible interest which a party can have".[403] It incorporates partial as well as full interests in a given subject matter.[404] Basic business information has been held to constitute property. For instance, a dentist's patient records were held to be property within the meaning of the Ontario PPSA, Arbour J.A. explaining:

> I see no difference between a dentist's entitlement to sell his or her practice and a dentist's entitlement to pledge records. Both can be accomplished in a manner compatible with the dentist's professional responsibilities, as long as the dentist acts with utmost good faith and loyalty in protecting the patient's confidence. The doctor may use the records to pursue his or her self-interest, so long as it does not conflict with a duty to act in the patient's best interest.

In *Re Gauntlet Energy Corp.*[405] confidential seismic data was held to constitute property. Despite the varying opinions as to the meaning of "property", it is far from clear what benefit would be derived from a policy perspective in taking such a strict approach. A corporation may well require a soft asset, such as farm quota, in order to enter into a particular line of business. There is no question that a shareholder may pay money to the corporation in exchange for shares with the money so paid then being invested by the corporation in the purchase of farm quota. It would be most capricious for the law to be interpreted to mean that a shareholder may not simply transfer the quota to the corporation, and receive back shares in exchange.

§7.169 It seems to be widely accepted that a subscriber may pay for shares by transferring the goodwill of an existing business of the subscriber to the corporation. The goodwill of a business is the whole advantage that flows to a business from its reputation with its customers and the public at large, together with any circumstances that make or tend to make that reputation permanent.[406] It may be described as the favourable reputation that customers or potential customers apply to a particular business, its products and services, or as the attractive force that encourages old customers to return and new customers to seek out the busi-

---

[400] See, for instance, *O'Bear-Nester Glass Co. v. Anti-Explo Co.*, 101 Tex. 431, 108 S.W. 967 (1908); but *cf. Prickett v. Allen* (1971), 475 S.W.2d 308 (Tex. Civ. App.).
[401] See, for instance, *Washer v. Smyer*, 109 Tex. 398, 211 S.W. 985 (S.C. 1919), *per* Philips C.J.
[402] R.S.O. 1990, c. P. 10.
[403] *Re Lunness*, [1919] O.J. No. 51, 51 D.L.R. 114 at 124 (C.A.), *per* Riddell, J.A.; *Jones v. Skinner* (1835), 5 L.J. Ch. 87.
[404] *McAlister v. McAlister*, [1982] A.J. No. 686, 41 A.R. 277 para. 86 (Q.B.), *per* Dea J. at 160.
[405] [2003] A.J. No. 1062, 36 B.L.R. (3d) 250 at 263, *per* Kent J.
[406] See, generally, J.M. Yang, *Goodwill & Other Intangibles* (New York: Ronald Press, 1927).

ness.[407] Although it is a recognized form of property,[408] goodwill has certain unique features that complicate its use as consideration for the issue of shares, namely:[409]

- the value of goodwill has no reliable or predictable relationship to the costs incurred in its creation;
- individual intangible factors that contribute to goodwill often cannot be valued;
- the value of goodwill can fluctuate suddenly and widely because of the innumerable factors which influence that value;
- goodwill attaches only to a business as a whole;
- goodwill is not utilized or consumed in the production of earnings;
- goodwill often appears to be an element of value that relates directly to the management or owner of a business enterprise, rather than to the enterprise itself.

Current accounting practice attempts to discount the present value of goodwill to the expected superior earnings resulting from the presence of goodwill — a process which involves both forecasting future earnings with and without goodwill, and choosing an appropriate discount rate. Obviously calculations of this type are highly speculative. Where the transfer of goodwill involves an arm's length transaction, it may be reasonable to assume that the price paid by the purchaser is a fair approximation of the value of the goodwill transferred. The same assumption cannot be made where a non-arm's length transaction is concerned.

§7.170 The immediate concern under the CBCA and the OBCA is not that an excessive number of shares are issued in exchange for property,[410] but rather that the value of those shares as reflected in the relevant stated capital account is overstated, thus giving the impression of a stronger capital base than actually exists. The reason for such concern is clear. Under normal rules of commercial lending, corporations are permitted to "leverage" their capital: that is, the amount which they can borrow from institutional lenders such as banks is often pegged to a given multiple of their capital base. Thus by inflating the amount that appears in a corporation's stated capital account, its directors can obtain access to greater amounts of credit. For this reason, subsection 23(4) of the OBCA[411] provides that where shares are issued in consideration of the transfer of property to the corporation, the directors must either determine the fair value of the property in consideration of which the share is issued, *or* that the property

---

[407] *Cuttwell v. Lee* (1810), 17 Vesey 335 at 346, *per* Lord Eldon.
[408] See, generally, *Washburn v. National Wallpaper Co.*, 81 Fed. 17 at 20, *per* Lacombe Cir. J.
[409] G.R. Cartlett & N.O. Olson, *Accounting for Goodwill* (New York: American Institute of Certified Public Accountants, 1968), 20-21.
[410] Although such an excess may amount to oppression of the other shareholders if it dilutes their control or dividend entitlement.
[411] There is no equivalent CBCA provision.

has a fair value that is not less than the amount that the corporation would have received if the share had been issued for money. In determining the value of the property, the directors may take into account reasonable payments for that property, as for example, the arm's length purchase price of the property to the transferor to whom the shares are to be issued.[412] The value placed by the directors upon property transferred to the corporation in exchange for shares creates a strong presumption as to the value of the property so transferred, where the shares were issued in the course of an arm's length transfer.[413] Where the transaction is not at arm's length, the valuation is not conclusive so the court will permit an inquiry into whether the consideration given for shares was fictitious,[414] or that a highly inflated value has been placed on the property concerned.[415] If, however, it appears that the directors have acted in good faith, honestly and reasonably, the court will not embark into a further review of the valuation placed on the property exchanged for the shares.[416]

§7.171 Where it is proposed that the subscription price for shares of a corporation may be paid for by way of the cancellation in whole or in part of debt obligations or other liabilities of that corporation,[417] the fair value of the debt or liability concerned must be at least equal to the amount of money the corporation would have received if the shares had been issued for money.[418] In order to satisfy this condition, the debt must be *bona fide* owed by the corporation. The fair value requirement raises an interesting question where shares are issued by an insolvent corporation in exchange for the cancellation of a debt owed by the corporation: must the value placed upon the debt be discounted to reflect the probability of recovery on that debt? Although an unrealizable debt cannot be said to be worth its full face value in terms of what some third party creditor would be willing to pay for it, it would clearly be inequitable to impose a discounting requirement. One possible answer to this question is to focus on what the corporation receives in exchange for its shares: it is released from an obligation to pay the full amount of the debt. Even though the debt had a value to the creditor of a fraction of its face value, the value of the debt to the corporation is its full face value, for that is the extent to which the debt must be satisfied in order to restore the corporation to solvency.

---

[412] OBCA, s. 23(5).
[413] See, for instance, *Hood v. Caldwell*, [1923] S.C.R. 488 at 490, *per* Duff C.J.C.; *Toronto Finance Corp. v. Banking Services Corp.*, [1926] O.J. No. 34, 59 O.L.R. 278 (C.A.), aff'd [1928] A.C. 333, [1928] 3 D.L.R. 1 (P.C.).
[414] *Warren v. Superior Engravers Ltd.*, [1940] O.J. No. 280, [1941] 1 D.L.R. 323 (C.A.), where it was held that the debt cancelled in exchange for shares was not owing.
[415] *Re Richmond Hill Hotel Co. (Pellatt's Case)* (1867), L.R. 2 Ch. App. 527; *Re Wragg*, [1897] 1 Ch. 796 (C.A.); *Re Dominion Combing Mills Ltd.*, [1930] O.J. No. 81, 11 C.B.R. 189 (S.C.).
[416] *John E. Hayes & Sons v. Turner*, [1924] O.J. No. 620, 26 O.W.N. 456 at 457-58 (H.C.), *per* Wright J.; *Jones v. Miller*, [1893] O.J. No. 42, 24 O.R. 268 (H.C.); *Re Co-operative Motor & Cycle Co.* (1902), 1 O.W.R. 778 (H.C.). See also *American Wollastonite Mining Corp. v. Scott* [2003] B.C.J. No. 2621, 44 B.L.R. (3d) 1 (C.A.).
[417] See, for instance, *Re Richelieu Oil Co.* (1950), 31 C.B.R. 221 (Que. C.A.); *Re Ottawa Cement Block Co. (Mascoun's Case)*, [1907] O.J. No. 149, 14 O.L.R. 389 (H.C.); see also *Henderson v. Strang* (1920), 60 S.C.R. 201.
[418] OBCA, s. 23(3).

§7.172 Where a loan pre-dating a subscription for shares is owed to a prospective shareholder, there is nothing improper in the corporation using funds that may be paid to it by that shareholder in respect of a subscription for shares to repay that loan.[419] This possibility is important because such circular flows of funds often form an integral part of complex corporate refinancing. The complexity of a transaction is neither evidence that the transaction is in bad faith or a sham, particularly where the complexity of the transaction is directed by the need to fit squarely within the scope of tax exemption provisions.[420]

(3) Payment for Shares by the Issue of a Promissory Note

§7.173 At common law, a promissory note constitutes a chose in action and thus a form of property. Both Acts require that no share may be issued until fully paid, but since payment may be made in property as well as money, the question arises as to whether a promissory note tendered to the corporation by a person subscribing for shares constitutes payment for the shares through the transfer of property. Obviously the requirement that all shares be fully paid would be substantially undermined if it was permissible to make payment by way of a promissory note drawn by the subscriber. Therefore, both Acts contain provisions intended to prevent such payment.[421] Prior to the 2001 amendments, subsection 25(5) of the CBCA provided:

> 25.(5) For the purposes of this section, "property" does not include a promissory note or a promise to pay.

The corresponding provision of the OBCA adopted a different approach, subsection 23(6) providing:

> 23.(6) For the purposes of subsection (3) and of subsection 24(3), a document evidencing indebtedness of a person to whom shares are to be issued, or of any other person not dealing at arm's length with such person within the meaning of that term in the *Income Tax Act* (Canada) does not constitute property.

In essence, the OBCA permits payment to be made by way of the transfer of a promissory note issued by a person at arm's length, whereas the CBCA prohibits payment by way of the transfer of any promissory note. In 2001, the CBCA was brought to a large extent into line with the OBCA, when subsection 25(5) was amended to read:

> 25.(5)For the purposes of this section, "property" does not include a promissory note, or a promise to pay, that is made by a person to whom a share is issued,

---

[419] *Pioneer Distributors Ltd. v. Bank of Montreal*, [1994] B.C.J. No. 2093, 28 C.B.R. (3d) 266 (S.C.). See also *Travel West (1987) v. Langdon Towers Apt.*, [2002] S.J. No. 208, 27 B.L.R. (3d) 25 at 44-46 (C.A.), *per* Jackson J.A.

[420] *Ibid.* Concerning whether a debt owed by the corporation may be raised in liquidation in set-off to a call made on shares, see *Re Consolidated Investments Ltd.*, [1918] A.J. No. 47, [1918] 2 W.W.R. 581 (Master); *cf. Re Harmony and Montague, Tin and Copper Mining Co.* (1873), L.R. 8 Ch. App. 407.

[421] The rule reflects the Quebec Superior Court in *Meunier v. National Finance Corp.* (1931), 69 Que. S.C. 417.

or a person who does not deal at arm's length, within the meaning of that expression in the *Income Tax Act,* with a person to whom a share is issued.

Of the above approaches, the OBCA seems preferable, because where the subscription price is paid by way of a note drawn by a person at arm's length, true value is given to the corporation. It is true that the note may ultimately prove to have a lower value than its face amount and may possibly be uncollectible, but the same is equally true where payment is made in the form of any type of property, and indeed even where payment is made in money, that money may be lost or squandered. Third parties dealing with the corporation where payment has been made for shares by the transfer of a promissory note drawn by an arm's length party are protected by the requirement that the directors value any property before accepting it as payment and issuing shares.[422]

§7.174 The OBCA prohibits a subscriber from paying for shares by issuing a document evidencing indebtedness, or by negotiating such a document provided by a person at non-arm's length to the subscriber. In contrast, the CBCA prohibits any promissory note or promise to pay. The CBCA provisions provide no guidance as to the meaning of "promissory note". A promissory note within the meaning of the *Bills of Exchange Act*[423] describes only a very narrow class of instrument. Subsection 176(1) of that Act provides:

> 176.(1) A promissory note is an unconditional promise in writing made by one person to another, signed by the maker, engaging to pay, on demand or at a fixed or determinable future time, a sum certain in money, to or to the order of, a specified person, or to bearer.

It has been held that a note containing an obligation to pay interest at a variable rate tied to the prime lending rate of a chartered bank falls outside this definition, as such an instrument does not constitute an obligation to pay a "sum certain in money". It clearly cannot have been intended that the prohibitions in the OBCA and the CBCA could be circumvented simply by adding a requirement that the issuer pay interest at such a variable rate. Therefore it seems likely that the phrase "promise to pay" would be given a sufficiently broad interpretation to cover all non-promissory note documents that evidence indebtedness, as under the OBCA.

(4) Payment for Shares in Services to the Corporation

§7.175 A corporation may not issue shares in consideration of services that (at the time of issue) remain to be performed in the future.[424] However, a corpora-

---

[422] See, generally, *System Controls plc v. Munro Corporate plc*, [1990] B.C.L.C. 659.
[423] R.S.C. 1985, c. B-4.
[424] CBCA, s. 25(3); OBCA, s. 23(3):

> (3) A share shall not be issued until the consideration for the share is fully paid in money or in property or past services that are not less in value than the fair equivalent of the money that the corporation would have received if the share had been issued for money.

See, generally, *United Steel Industries Inc. v. Manhart*, 405 S.W.2d 231 (Tex. Civ. App.).

tion may enter into an agreement under which it takes on an obligation to issue shares in consideration of the performance of services to be performed, provided those shares are not issued until after the performance is rendered.[425] In either case the consideration given by the creditor is neither illusory nor unpaid,[426] and is analogous to an undertaking to issue shares in consideration of the transfer of title to property — that issue to be made at the time of actual transfer. The restriction under subsection 23(3) of the OBCA is that shares cannot be paid for by a covenant, the remedy for which is limited to damages.[427] Once performance is rendered the corporation has received consideration in full, and therefore the fully paid requirement no longer presents an obstacle to the issue of the shares.

§7.176 As noted above, shares of a corporation may be paid for by way of the cancellation in whole or in part of debt obligations or other liabilities of a corporation. By extension, the common law position was that shares could be issued in payment of a debt owed in respect of past services or in order to compromise a genuine claim (even a doubtful claim) with respect to such services.[428] It is doubtful that a corporation may issue shares for a past service when the corporation is not, in any way, obliged to pay for the service that was so rendered, for such a consideration would be past consideration, and past consideration is no consideration at all.[429] However, an argument can be made that the wording of the OBCA permits a corporation to issue shares in consideration of past services for which there is a moral obligation or debt of honour, even though it is not obligated legally to pay for them. First, the fact that the Act separately provides for the issue of shares in consideration of property and in consideration of past service suggests that these two forms of consideration were meant to be distinct. If past services were limited to those for which the corporation is obliged to pay then there would be no distinction between the issue of shares in consideration of property and the issue of shares in consideration of past services — for payment in past services would simply be the cancellation of a debt, which is effectively property in the form of a chose in action.

§7.177 Second, subsection 23(4) of the OBCA requires the directors to place a fair value on the past services accepted in payment of the issue price of shares — which would not seem to be necessary if a debt were owed in respect of those services, since in such a case the liquidated amount of the debt would be its fair value. Similarly, subsection 23(5) of the OBCA[430] gives the directors the discretion to take into account "reasonable charges and expenses of organization and reorganization and payments for...past service reasonably expected to benefit

---

[425] *Inglis v. Wellington Hotel Co.*, [1878] O.J. No. 288, 29 U.C.C.P. 387.
[426] See *Re Gibson Pelican Lake v. Traders Trust Co.* (1929), 11 C.B.R. 100 at 103 (Man. K.B.), *per* Macdonald C.J.K.B.
[427] *Toronto Finance Corp. v. Banking Service Corp.*, [1926] O.J. No. 34, 59 O.L.R. 278 at 286 (C.A.), *per* Ferguson J.A., aff'd [1928] A.C. 333, [1928] 3 D.L.R. 1 (P.C.). See also *Gardiner v. Iredale*, [1916] 1 Ch. 700 at 715-16, *per* Parker J.
[428] But compare *Warren v. Superior Engravers Ltd.*, [1940] O.J. No. 280, [1941] 1 D.L.R. 323 (C.A.).
[429] See, generally, *Bury v. Famatina Development Corp.*, [1909] 1 Ch. 754, aff'd [1910] A.C. 439.
[430] CBCA, s. 25(4).

the corporation". Again, if the corporation were obliged to pay for the charges, expenses and past services concerned there could be no discretion to take those costs into account, for they would constitute debt liabilities of the corporation. The corporate law concern is to ensure that the corporation obtains fair value for the shares that it issues; it is not to see that the corporation honours only those obligations that fit within the doctrine of consideration.

§7.178 A corporation may wish to issue shares at a discount from the cash price at which they are sold to outsiders, to persons who have provided assistance in connection with the establishment of a corporation or a particular securities issue. The term "discount" has normally been used in association with the issue of shares for less than their par value. With the abolition of the par value concept, that concept of discount is now largely irrelevant — although not entirely so, as will presently be explained. However, there is a wider meaning of "discount": it applies wherever the directors issue shares of a particular class or series to one subscriber at a price less than those shares were issued to the another subscriber.

§7.179 As noted earlier, the directors may use their share issuance powers only in the best interests of the corporation. Generally, the directors must seek to issue shares for their fair value. Accordingly, it is certainly not open to them to issue shares to one shareholder ("A") at a lower price than the other ("B"), simply because they like A more than B. As will be discussed in detail in Chapter 10, the directors have no right to use their powers in a discriminatory fashion; they are required to maintain an even hand when dealing with shareholders who hold the same class or series of shares, and this requirement applies with no less force, even at the stage when the shares of the class or series in question are being issued. But the objective of issuing shares at a lower price to B than A is not necessarily inconsistent with the director's duty to maintain an even hand and to seek the best return for the corporation: B may not be prepared to pay as much as A; the price quoted to B may reflect some form of service that B is rendering to the corporation; the financial situation of the corporation may have deteriorated between the time when the shares were issued to A and when they are proposed to be issued to B, so that they no longer command the price which they formerly enjoyed.

§7.180 Under earlier legislation, the issue of shares at a discount (usually from their par value) presented serious problems.[431] Under the present legislation, with the abolition of par value it is possible to issue shares at what is effectively a discount, provided the discount is structured so that it fits within the fully paid requirement and within the directors' duty to obtain a fair price. Under subsection 23(1) of the OBCA[432] the directors may issue shares in the corporation "for

---

[431] See, for instance, *Re Manitoulin Quartzite Ltd.* (1932), 13 C.B.R. 404, aff'd [1933] 4 D.L.R. 132 at 137 (Ont. C.A.), *per* Sedgewick J.; *Auditorium Ltd. v. Lumsden*, [1926] O.J. No. 60, 59 O.L.R. 496 at 503 (C.A.), *per* Masten J.A.; *Hood v. Caldwell*, [1923] S.C.R. 488; *Toronto Finance Corp. v. Banking Service Corp.* (1925), 57 O.L.R. 514 (H.C.), aff'd (1926), 59 O.L.R. 278 (C.A.), aff'd [1928] A.C. 333 (P.C.).

[432] CBCA, s. 25(1).

such consideration as the directors may determine". With two important exceptions, there is no obligation upon the directors to issue the shares for the same consideration to every shareholder. The first is the requirement that the directors deal impartially between the two subscribers. If they sincerely try to obtain $10 from both A and B, but B is only prepared to pay $9, and the corporation needs the funds that B is prepared to invest, then there would seem to be no impropriety in issuing shares at different prices. In such a case, A is not the victim of discrimination. He or she is simply not as effective at bargaining as B. Therefore, at least in certain cases, it is open to the directors to issue class A shares to A at a consideration of $10 per share, while shares of the same class are issued to B at a discounted amount, relative to their street price.[433]

§7.181 The second important exception arises where the shares that are to be issued to B are to be issued for a non-cash consideration. In such a case the directors' hands are tied to some extent by subsection 23(3) of the OBCA which provides that:

> 23.(3) A share shall not be issued until the consideration for the share is fully paid in ... property or past service that is not less in value than the fair equivalent of the money that the corporation would have received if the share had been issued for money.

If A is paying $10 for the shares at the same time that shares are to be issued to B, it would hardly be reasonable for the directors to conclude that the cash value of the shares — which they are required to determine under clause 23(4)(*a*) of the OBCA — is only $9 rather than $10. However, even in such a case it may still be possible to give B what is effectively a discount relative to the cash price. The consideration paid for shares need not be paid entirely in one form of consideration, but may be paid in any combination of cash, property or past services. If the discount from the cash price represents the fair value of services provided by the persons receiving the discount prior to the issue of the shares (*e.g.*, is a reasonable commission payable to a broker for placing shares),[434] the discount will be lawful. Ideally the discount on the shares so issued would be in payment of a debt owing in respect of those services — although this would not seem to be an essential requirement, provided the discount is no greater than the fair value of the services concerned.

§7.182 Despite the statutory prohibition against the issue of shares other than fully paid, the better view appears to be that shares issued contrary to such restrictions are not void,[435] particularly since such a conclusion would be inconsistent with the legal consequences that flow from them. For instance, under

---

[433] Where such a step is considered, attention must be paid to the paid-up capital implications of the *Income Tax Act*.
[434] *Re Co-operative Cycle & Motor Co.* (1902), 1 O.W.R. 778 (H.C.). Where a prospectus is required under the *Securities Act*, R.S.O. 1990, c. S.5, Forms 12, 13 and 14 require the disclosure of any commission paid or payable or discount given by the issuer or selling security holder in respect of the security issue concerned.
[435] See, generally, *Pearson Finance Group v. Takla Star Resources*, [2002] A.J. No. 422, 22 B.L.R. (3d) 174 at 179 (C.A.), *per* Cote J.A.

subsection 103(1) of the OBCA, directors who vote for or consent to the issue of shares at an under-value are liable to the corporation to make good the deficiency. A deficiency in the price paid may be cured by paying up the deficiency, which may even be done after court proceedings have commenced.[436]

(5) Shares in an Unlimited Liability Corporation

§7.183 The Nova Scotia *Companies Act* permits the shares of an unlimited liability corporation to be issued in consideration of a debt instrument issued by the subscriber for those shares. The Alberta BCA does not. Any Ontario regime would need to select between these two approaches. Arguments can be made in favor of each approach. For instance, at present, the units in a limited partnership may be issued in exchange for a promissory note. Many lenders have found it difficult to pursue the members of a limited partnership, particularly where the unit holders are scattered across several jurisdictions, and their indebtedness to the corporation is relatively small. If it were permissible to issue shares in an unlimited liability corporation on other than a fully paid basis, a similar problem would likely arise with respect to the holders of shares in such an entity. On the other hand, whether a corporation is limited or unlimited, there is only a small corporate law obligation to invest in the share capital of the corporation. Creditors are unlikely to have much leverage to entice a shareholder in an unlimited liability corporation to tie up his or her own assets in the capital of the corporation, since the prospect of unlimited liability offers little incentive to do so. Generally, where there is no strong theoretical argument for adopting a particular legislative approach, the better option is usually to adopt the approach that imposes the least amount of regulation.

§7.184 On a more theoretical level: one pervasive change that would need to be made to the OBCA to implement an unlimited liability regime would be to modify the provisions of that Act that require or assume that all shares that are issued will be un-assessable and fully paid. Since the shareholders of an unlimited liability corporation are liable to make good any deficiency on its liquidation, the shares in such a corporation are always potentially assessable, and are never fully paid. Accordingly, it would seem to be necessary to modify subsections 23(2) and (3) of the OBCA as follows:

> (2) Except for shares in an unlimited liability corporation, shares issued by a corporation are non-assessable and the holders are not liable to the corporation or its creditors in respect thereof.
>
> (3) Except in the case of a share in an unlimited liability corporation, a share shall not be issued until the consideration for the share has been fully paid in money or in property or past service that is not less in value than the fair equivalent of the money that the corporation would have received f the share had been issued for money.

---

[436] *Re Dunham and Apollo Tours (No. 1)*, [1978] O.J. No. 3381, 86 D.L.R. (3d) 573, 20 O.R. (2d) 3 (H.C.); *Gillespie v. Retail Merchants' Assn. of Canada (Ontario) Inc.*, [1997] O.J. No. 956, 31 O.T.C. 147, 33 B.L.R. (2d) 307.

(ii) Commission on the Sale of Shares

§7.185 In any public issue of securities, a commission will normally be paid to the underwriter. Underwriting is a guarantee of the sale of securities at a specified minimum price, where those securities are offered for sale to the investing public. It is, therefore, in the nature of a condition subscription for those securities. The underwriter undertakes to purchase unsold securities at the stipulated minimum price, if they are not taken up on or before a specified date, by the public or other person(s) to whom they are offered. The consideration for this guarantee usually takes the form of a certain portion of the price at which it is anticipated that the securities will be sold. If the market is buoyant, the underwriter will usually pocket a substantial profit. However, there are substantial advantages to an issuer in securing an underwriting commitment. The success of the securities flotation is secured from the moment that the underwriting agreement is made (although this statement has been qualified in recent years by so-called "market out" clauses that allow an underwriter to avoid liability, where there is a substantial decline in the overall securities market). In addition, it is often possible to borrow on the strength of the undertaking. Sections 37 of the OBCA and 41 of the CBCA provide that the directors may authorize the corporation to pay a reasonable commission to any person in consideration of his purchasing or agreeing to purchase shares of the corporation from the corporation or from any other person, or procuring or agreeing to procure purchasers for any such shares. What is reasonable as a commission depends upon the circumstances of the case.[437] Where the recipient of the commission is at arm's length to the corporation, it is doubtful that the reasonableness of a commission fixed by contract would be reopened by the court; it can fairly be assumed in such a case that the corporation would not agree to pay more than what was reasonable. Where the recipient of the commission is a promoter of the corporation, in calculating any commission payable consideration should be given to the restrictions applicable to contracts between a corporation and its promoters.[438]

§7.186 In general, no restrictions apply on the payment of a commission where a shareholder retains a broker or other commission agent to sell shares held by the shareholder. In such a case, the payment of the commission will have no direct effect upon the corporation's own accounts, and therefore is purely a matter of contract between the parties concerned, with no corporate law implication. However, this would not be the case if what was truly an issue of shares by the corporation was filtered through a nominal shareholder in a colourable attempt to circumvent sections 37 of the OBCA and 41 of the CBCA. In such a case, the commission would be subject to the statutory requirement that it be reasonable.

(iii) Share Splits and Exchanges

§7.187 Share exchanges and share splits (the latter being sometimes called a "stock split") are two types of relatively common transaction frequently en-

---

[437] *Re Co-operative Cycle & Motor Co.* (1902), 1 O.W.R. 778 at 779 (H.C.), *per* Falconbridge C.J.
[438] The subject of promoters is discussed in detail in Chapter 5, Incorporation.

countered during the course of the reorganization of the share capital of a corporation. In a share split, the number of outstanding shares comprising a class is increased by way of the division of the existing shares into a greater number of shares. For instance, in a two-for-one split, each existing share of a particular class is divided into two new shares of the same class. In a share exchange, a share of one class or series is exchanged (on the basis of some stipulated ratio) for shares of another class or series: the term "share exchange" in this context being used in a limited sense so as to describe a transaction that occurs entirely within the same corporation, rather than the purchase of shares in one corporation through the issue of shares by a second corporation which purchases them, or any similar multiple corporation transaction.

§7.188 Share exchanges and share splits are largely paper transactions: no assets are received by the corporation from the holders of the shares concerned, nor is any property distributed to those shareholders by the corporation. In the share split, an amendment is made to the statement of the number of issued shares of the class concerned, but no change is made in the amount shown in the stated capital account. The sole effect of the transaction is to dilute the value of the shares comprising the class. Where a share exchange takes place, the amount shown in the stated capital accounts of the classes or series of shares will be modified to reflect the exchange.

§7.189 Share splits offer investors an opportunity to have their cake and eat it too: Specifically, if an investor purchased a share at $10, expecting a return of $1, and in fact the return earned per share is in the range of $2.50, then the value of the share will increase. Assuming that the level of earnings can be sustained, a two-for-one share split allows an investor to sell half of his or her interest in the corporation, and yet still retain the expected income stream that encouraged the investment in the corporation in the first place. Viewed from an alternate perspective, the investor manages to recover the amount invested (subject to tax), but nevertheless continues to earn the same level of income. The sale of the extra share results in a capital gain, which has a preferential tax rate. It is for this reason that share splits are most likely to occur where both management and the market have confidence in the earnings prospects of the corporation. For instance, in line with the run-away popularity of its iPod music player, shares in Apple Computer climbed from $23 to $81.99 per share. The company decided to undertake a share split, under which shareholders received one additional share for every outstanding share held. This increased the amount of Apple shares in circulation to 1.8 billion from 900 million.[439]

§7.190 Clause 168(1)(*h*) of the OBCA permits a corporation to amend its articles to

---

[439] See, for instance, Apple Computer picks share split, BBC News, World Edition, February 22, 2005.

(h) change the shares of any class or series, whether issued or unissued, into a different number of shares of the same class or series or into the same or a different number of shares of other classes or series;

Moreover, clause 170(1)(g) of the OBCA provides the holders of a class with a right to vote separately on a proposal to amend the articles of a corporation to "effect an exchange of shares from one class to another". It would seem to follow from these provisions that a share exchange must either be expressly authorized by the existing articles of the corporation — presumably by the terms and conditions of the shares concerned — or alternatively (if there is no such provision in the articles that contemplates such a conversion) must be authorized by way of an amendment to the articles. Otherwise, it would be open to the directors to approve a share exchange without regard to its effect upon the shareholders, a possibility that would seem to be incongruous with the control that the shareholders are entitled to exercise over the amendment of the articles of the corporation. It is worth noting that

- share exchanges may affect the rights and relative priorities of claim of the shareholders among themselves; and
- share exchanges may present tax problems to the shareholders whose shares are converted, and also to any existing holders of shares into which their shares are to be converted.

Thus the structure of the share capital of a corporation cannot be considered as a mere matter of the internal government of the corporation over which the directors of the corporation are entitled to exercise control under their power to manage the business and affairs of the corporation.

E. SPECIAL SHAREHOLDER CONSIDERATIONS

§7.191 The rights and obligations of shareholders are considered in detail in Chapter 12, and therefore will not be considered in this chapter, where the focus is on the share as a species of corporate obligation. However, it is appropriate to give some consideration at this point to three special aspects of the shareholder-corporate relationship, as these aspects have a direct bearing upon shares as corporate obligations. In the vast majority of cases, a person subscribing for or otherwise acquiring shares in a corporation will be *sui generis* and will subscribe for shares in his or her own right. Under both the OBCA and the CBCA, special rules apply where shares are acquired by an infant or by a trustee. In addition, there are also special rules which apply where only certain persons are eligible to own shares of a corporation.

(i) Shares Held in Trust

§7.192 There is no reason why the shares of a corporation may not be held by a trustee rather than by the person beneficially entitled, or why a share certificate should not indicate that the holder is a trustee.[440] Indeed, both the OBCA and the CBCA expressly contemplate this possibility. They provide that as a general rule, the corporation is entitled to treat the registered holder as if that person were the sole beneficial owner of the shares.[441] However, a person who is the beneficial owner of shares, but who is not registered as the owner of those shares, is nevertheless entitled to have the benefit of any agreement or term of the shares requiring shareholders who wish to sell their shares to offer them to other shareholders on a ratable basis.[442]

(ii) Shares Held by an Intermediary (CBCA)

§7.193 Amendments made to the CBCA in 2001 expand the rights of a person whose share interest in a corporation is held by an intermediary. Subsection 153(1) requires the intermediary to send the form of proxy and applicable proxy circulars to the beneficial owner:

> 153.(1) Shares of a corporation that are registered in the name of an intermediary or their nominee and not beneficially owned by the intermediary must not be voted unless the intermediary, without delay after receipt of the notice of the meeting, financial statements, management proxy circular, dissident's proxy circular and any other documents other than the form of proxy sent to shareholders by or on behalf of any person for use in connection with the meeting, sends a copy of the document to the beneficial owner and, except when the intermediary has received written voting instructions from the beneficial owner, a written request for such instructions.

The intermediary seek instructions as to how the shares are to be voted. Subsection 153(2) imposes a prohibition against voting those shares unless such instructions are received:

> 153.(2) An intermediary, or a proxy holder appointed by an intermediary, may not vote shares that the intermediary does not beneficially own and that are registered in the name of the intermediary or in the name of a nominee of the intermediary unless the intermediary or proxy holder, as the case may be, receives written voting instructions from the beneficial owner.

The intermediary must either vote or appoint a proxy-holder to vote any such shares in accordance with such written voting instructions as may be received from the beneficial owner.[443] Breach of these requirements constitutes an offence,[444] but no such breach affects the validity of any meeting or any action taken at a meeting.[445]

---

[440] *Simpson v. Gillespie*, [1930] O.J. No. 180, 38 O.W.N. 103 at 105 (H.C.), *per* Raney J., rev'd on other grounds [1930] O.J. No. 220, 38 O.W.N. 260 (C.A.).
[441] OBCA, s. 67(1); CBCA, s. 51(1). As to the position at common law, see: *Hartga v. Bank of England* (1796), 3 Ves. Jun. 56, 30 E.R. 891 (Ch.); but compare *Lowry v. Commercial & Farmers Bank* (1848), 15 F. Cas. 1040 (C.C.D. Md.); *Hutchins v. State Bank* (1847), 52 Mass. (12 Metc.) 421; *Bank of Virginia v. Craig* (1835), 32 Va. (6 Leight) 399.
[442] *Gordon v. Gaby*, [1966] S.C.J. No. 30, [1966] S.C.R. 527 at 530, *per* Judson J.
[443] CBCA, s. 153(4).
[444] CBCA, s. 153(8).
[445] CBCA, s. 153(6).

(iii) Shares Held by Aliens

§7.194 Subject to any specific statutory restriction, there is no common law or general corporate law limitation on the right of an alien to hold shares in a corporation.[446] However, from time to time specific regulatory requirements are enacted for companies engaged in certain types of business, under which a majority of the voting shares in a corporation are required to be held by Canadians. Both the federal and provincial business corporations statutes contemplate and accommodate such legislative requirements.[447] However, provisions of this sort form no part of the general corporate law of Canada, but are more properly the study of works specifically examining the regulatory regimes concerned.

§7.195 In time of war, where a controlling interest in a corporation is held by one or more enemy aliens, the courts will disregard the separate corporate existence of the corporation, and will treat the corporation as an enemy alien as well.[448]

(iv) Shares Held by a Minor

§7.196 There is no rule at common law that a minor may not be a shareholder of a corporation (*e.g.*, by gift or bequest), although a minor may not be an incorporator.[449] Subsection 67(4) of the OBCA now clearly contemplates the possibility that a minor may acquire shares in a corporation. It was formerly the case that a corporation might refuse to register the transfer of shares to a minor where the shares concerned were only partly paid or assessable.[450] With the abolition of partly paid and assessable shares,[451] there would no longer appear to be any such

---

[446] *Princess of Reuss v. Bos* (1871), L.R. 5 H.L. 176; *R. v. Arnaud* (1846), 9 Q.B. 806.
[447] OBCA, s. 29(4); CBCA, s. 32(1).
[448] *Daimler Co. v. Continental Tyre & Rubber Co. (Great Britain)*, [1916] 2 A.C. 307 (H.L.).
[449] OBCA, s. 4(2)(*a*); CBCA, s. 5(1)(*a*).
[450] *R. v. Midland Counties & Shannon Junction Ry. Co.* (1862), I.C.L.R. 514 (IR).
[451] Incorporators of certain types of company may wish to provide for the payment of an annual sum or other regular payment as a condition of continuing membership in the company. Generally speaking this is not permissible. In *Edmonton Country Club Ltd. v. Case*, [1974] S.C.J. No. 63, 44 D.L.R. (3d) 554, the Supreme Court of Canada held that a corporation cannot require its shareholders to pay an annual contribution. In support of this conclusion Dickson J. invoked (at 562):

> ... the basic jural principle which has given limited liability companies their vitality, namely, that a shareholder who has paid for his shares is thereafter free of pecuniary obligations in respect of those shares.

It appears, however, that such a commitment may be made binding under the terms of a collateral contract, so that it is not one of the share terms: See, for instance, *Peninsular Co. Ltd. v. Fleming* (1872), 27 L.T. 93; *Lion Mutual Marine Insurance Assoc. Ltd. v. Tucker* (1883), 12 Q.B.D. 176; *Re Bangor & North Wales Mutual Marine Protection Association ("Baird's Case")*, [1899] 2 Ch. 593 — although on occasion, this has been doubted: see, for instance, *Dibble v. Wilts & Somerset Farmers Ltd.*, [1923] 1 Ch. 342. The better view is the former, since as a general rule, "an incorporated company is entitled to make with one of its own shareholders any contract which it could lawfully make with an outsider". *Shalfoon v. Cheddar Valley Co-Operative Dairy Co Ltd.*, [1924] N.Z.L.R. 561 at 579-80, *per* Salmond J. See also *Black White & Grey Cabs Ltd. v. Reid*, [1980] 1 N.Z.L.R. 40 (C.A.); *Hole v. Garnsey*, [1930] A.C. 472 (H.L.).

right in favour of a corporation. However, provided that the directors of the corporation are given a sufficiently broad discretion over the approval of any transfer of shares, they may take into account the fact that a transferee is a minor when deciding not to approve a proposed transfer. In any event, as a general rule it is not advisable for shares to be registered in the name of a minor, since such registration will affect the ability to dispose of those shares.

§7.197 Cases involving subscriptions for shares by minors are rare but not unknown. In *North Western Railway Co. v. McMichael*[452] it was held that a minor to whom shares were allotted upon application was to be treated as acquiring an interest in a subject of a permanent nature, with certain obligations attached to it. Accordingly, unless the minor repudiated the contract before or within a reasonable time of attaining majority,[453] the minor would remain bound by the obligations attaching to the share. Also at common law, any contract made by an infant for the purchase or other acquisition of shares is voidable at the option of the infant,[454] but unless and until so repudiated is valid.[455] However, subsection 67(5) of the OBCA now makes clear that if a minor exercises any rights of ownership in the securities of a corporation, no subsequent repudiation or avoidance is effective against the corporation. Moreover, a minor's contracts are voidable only in the sense that by repudiating the contract the minor may free himself (or herself) from further liability. A minor may only recover money paid prior to repudiation where there has been a total failure of consideration. Generally speaking, where shares are issued to the minor, there is no such failure — although if the shares are worthless (or perhaps worth far less than the minor believed), a total failure of consideration will exist.[456]

§7.198 As noted above, subscribers for shares whose subscriptions are voidable will lose their right to repudiate their subscription once a corporation becomes bankrupt or enters into liquidation, or if they delay unreasonably in asserting that right. However, the relevant point for determining whether an infant has delayed unreasonably is the date of the commencement of the insolvency. Thus an infant who attains majority prior to the commencement of winding-up and who remains entitled to repudiate a subscription for shares on the date that winding-up commences is not precluded from repudiating that subscription by any delay subsequent to its commencement.[457]

---

[452] (1850), 5 Ex. 114 at 123, 155 E.R. 49.
[453] *Holmes v. Blogg* (1817), 8 Taunt. 508, 129 E.R. 481 (C.P.). Where the infant delays an unreasonable length of time after attaining majority, he or she will not be allowed to escape liability under the subscription: *Re Sovereign Bank (Clarke's Case)*, [1916] O.J. No. 70, 35 O.L.R. 448 at 456 (C.A.), *per* Garrow J.A.
[454] *Hamilton & Flamborough Road Co. v. Townsend*, [1886] O.J. No. 133, 13 O.A.R. 534 (C.A.).
[455] *Edwards v. Carter*, [1893] A.C. 360 (H.L.).
[456] *Steinberg v. Scala (Leeds) Ltd.*, [1923] 2 Ch. 452 (C.A.).
[457] *Re Central Bank & Hogg*, [1890] O.J. No. 117, 19 O.R. 7 at 8-9 (H.C.), *per* Boyd C.

(v) Restrictions on the Issue and Transfer of Shares

§7.199 Subsection 42(1) of the OBCA provides that a corporation shall not impose restrictions on the issue, transfer or ownership of shares of any class or series, except such restrictions as are authorized by its articles.[458] Moreover, a corporation that has imposed restrictions on the issue, transfer or ownership of its shares of any class or series shall not offer any of its shares[459] to the public unless the restrictions are necessary[460]

(a) by or under any Act of Canada or Ontario as a condition to the obtaining, holding or renewal of authority to engage in any activity necessary to its undertaking;

(b) for the purpose of achieving or preserving its status as a Canadian body corporate for the purpose of any Act of Canada or Ontario;

(c) to limit to a specified level the ownership of its shares by any prescribed class of person for the purpose of assisting the corporation or any of its affiliates or associates to qualify under the *Securities Act* or similar legislation of a province or territory to obtain, hold or renew registration, or to qualify for membership in a stock exchange in Ontario recognized as such by the Commission; or

(d) to attain or maintain a specified level of Canadian ownership or control for the purpose of assisting the corporation or any of its affiliates or associates to qualify to receive licences, permits, grants, payments or other benefits under any prescribed Act of Canada or a province or ordinance of a territory.

Subsection 42(3) provides that nothing in clauses (2)(*c*) or (*d*) authorizes a corporation to impose restrictions on the issue, transfer or ownership of shares of any class or series of which any shares are outstanding unless those shares were already subject to a restriction for a purpose described in those clauses respectively. Thus it would appear that if a share is subject to a restriction under clause (2)(*c*) or (*d*), a further such restriction may be introduced, but if there is no such restriction, the articles may not be amended to introduce a restriction under those clauses.

§7.200 A corporation may limit the number of its shares that may be owned, or prohibit the ownership of its shares, by any person whose ownership would adversely affect the ability of the corporation or any of its affiliates or associates to maintain a level of Canadian ownership or control specified in its articles that equals or exceeds a specified level referred to in clause 42(2)(*d*) of the OBCA. Clause (2)(*d*) authorizes restrictions only where necessary "to qualify to receive licences, permits, grants, payments or other benefits under any prescribed Act of

---

[458] Where restrictions are imposed by the directors of a corporation at the time of creating a series of shares, those restrictions must be set out in the articles sent to the Director under s. 25(4) of the OBCA. Individual shareholders may enter into a contractual restriction on the transfer of shares, but any such restriction is binding only among the parties to that contract: *Glimmer Resources Inc. v. Exall Resources Ltd.*, [1997] O.J. No. 3085, 35 B.L.R. (2d) 297 (Gen. Div.).

[459] It would appear that this prohibition extends to shares of other classes that are not so restricted.

[460] OBCA, s. 42(2); CBCA, s. 49(9).

Canada or a province or ordinance of a territory". However, subsection 49(1) of the CBCA:

> Where the articles of a corporation constrain the issue, transfer or ownership of shares of any class or series in order to assist,
>
> (a) the corporation or any of its affiliates or associates to qualify under any prescribed law of Canada or a province to receive licenses, permits, grants, payments or other benefits by reason of attaining or maintaining a specified level of Canadian ownership or control; or
>
> (b) the corporation to comply with any prescribed law,
>
> the constraint, or a reference to it, shall be conspicuously noted on every security certificate of the corporation evidencing a share that is subject to the constraint where the security certificate is issued after the day on which the share becomes subject to the constraint under this Act.

Subsection 56(8) of the OBCA is differently worded, but to a similar effect.

§7.201 From time to time a corporation may find that shares have come to be held contrary to restrictions to which those shares are subject under the articles, as for instance, where the amount held by any one person or class of persons exceeds a restriction on the aggregate amount that may be so held, or where the number of shares held by non-residents of Canada has exceeded a specified maximum. Part IV of the OBCA sets out a number of provisions providing for the sale of restricted shares.[461] Subsection 45(1) of the OBCA empowers a corporation to sell shares that are held contrary to restrictions on the issue, transfer or ownership of its shares imposed in order to qualify

- under the *Securities Act*[462] or similar legislation of a province or territory to obtain, hold or renew registration or for membership in a stock exchange in Ontario recognized as such by the Commission, in order to limit to a specific level of ownership the shares of any prescribed class or person,[463] or

- under any prescribed Act of Canada or a province or ordinance of a territory to receive licences, permits, grants, payments or other benefits by reason of attaining or maintaining a specified level of Canadian ownership or control,[464]

as if the corporation was the owner of those shares. The power so conferred is one of expropriation, and because of the narrow construction that is given to the exercise of such powers, extreme care should be exercised by the corporation to ensure that the statutory requirements are strictly observed. Any such sale may only be made after the corporation gives the prescribed notice. Both Acts require that where shares are sold by the corporation under the statutory authority, the directors of the corporation must select the shares in good faith and in a manner

---

[461] Part VI of the CBCA contains corresponding provisions dealing with the sale of constrained shares. The terms "restricted" and "constrained" (and all variants thereof) are synonymous.
[462] R.S.O. 1990, c. S.5.
[463] OBCA, s. 45(1)(a) and (b).
[464] OBCA, s. 45(1)(c). Subsection 46(1) of the CBCA contains a similar provision to clause (c). It contains no equivalent to clauses (a) and (b).

that is not unfairly prejudicial to, and does not disregard the interests of, the holders of the shares in the restricted class or series taken as a whole.[465] Where a single person or identifiable group of persons are responsible for the contravention, it would seem to follow that it is their shares that are to be the subject of the sale. In many cases, however, it will not be possible to determine which of many shareholders is responsible for the contravention, and in such a case it will be necessary to find an alternative method of selecting the shares to be sold. The normal practice of corporations in comparable situations (*e.g.*, redemptions under a sinking fund) is to select the shares randomly. A provision along the following lines would be typical:

> Where less than all of a series of Shares that are outstanding are to be redeemed, the Shares of the series that are to be redeemed shall be selected by the Corporation by lot, in such manner as the Corporation may consider equitable, and any drawing by lot so made by the Corporation shall be valid and binding upon all Holders of Shares of that series.

But there are other approaches that would surely meet the requirements of the Act, such as a selection of the shares to be sold on a "last in, first sold" basis. In many respects, such an approach would seem superior to selecting the shares to be sold by lot, because in many cases it would recognize that it is the most recent shares to be acquired that have caused the contravention of the restriction on share ownership.

§7.202 Where shares are sold under the Act, the proceeds of sale constitute a trust fund in the hands of the corporation for the benefit of the person entitled to receive the proceeds of sale. The Act permits the trust funds to be commingled, but they must be invested in the prescribed manner.[466] Any reasonable costs incurred in the administration of the trust fund may be deducted from either the capital or the income of the trust fund.[467]

§7.203 By virtue of the sale, the owner of the share immediately prior to the sale becomes divested of his or her interest in the shares.[468] The person entitled to receive the proceeds held in trust is normally the registered holder of the shares (unless some other person can satisfy the corporation that he should instead properly be treated as the registered holder) and from the time of the sale the registered holder is entitled to receive only the net proceeds of the sale, together with any income earned on those proceeds from the beginning of the month next following the date of the receipt by the corporation of the proceeds of the sale,[469] less any applicable taxes and any applicable costs in ad-

---

[465] See also OBCA, s. 45(2); CBCA, s. 46(2).
[466] OBCA, s. 45(5); CBCA, s. 47(1).
[467] OBCA, s. 45(6); CBCA, s. 47(2). The normal practice in admnistering trust funds of this sort is for the fund to be transferred to a trust corporation, and both Acts specifically permit the employment of a trust corporation in this capacity: OBCA, s. 45(7); CBCA, s. 47(3).
[468] OBCA, s. 45(3); CBCA, s. 46(3).
[469] Income earned during the interim apparently belongs to the corporation, which means that in an appropriate case a corporation may earn a substantial amount from the float, by arranging the settlement for early in a month.

ministering that amount as a trust fund. A receipt signed by a person entitled to receive the proceeds of a sale is a complete discharge of the corporation and of any trust company administering the trust fund in respect of both the trust fund and any income earned on it that is paid to that person.[470] Under both Acts, any amount not claimed within ten years after the date of the sale passes to the Crown.[471]

F. TRANSFER OF SHARES

§7.204 A second common method by which shares in a corporation may be acquired is by transfer from an existing shareholder. The right of alienation is one of the cornerstones of property.[472] Accordingly, the law frowns upon any attempt to restrict the right of an owner to transfer property. Since shares constitute a form of property, it is not surprising that there is a strong presumption that shares are freely transferable.[473] In the absence of a restriction on share transfer in the corporation's articles, the motive of the transferor in disposing of his or her shares is immaterial.[474] The corporation must give effect to the transfer. Not only does the transferor have the right to compel the corporation to register a transfer, so too does the transferee; the right passes to the transferee as an incident of the transferor's equitable interest in the shares.[475]

§7.205 Subsection 60(1) of the CBCA provides that:

---

[470] OBCA, s. 45(8); CBCA, s. 47(4). By virtue of s. 45(4) of the OBCA, the following provisions apply in respect of the person who is entitled under the Act to receive the proceeds of a sale of shares, as if the proceeds were a security and the person were a registered holder of the security:

> 67.(4) An issuer is not required to inquire into the existence of, or see to the performance or observance of, any duty owed to a third person by a registered holder of any of its securities or by anyone whom it treats, as permitted or required by this section, as the owner or registered holder thereof.

> (5) If a minor exercises any rights of ownership in the securities of an issuer, no subsequent repudiation or avoidance is effective against the issuer.

> (6) Where a security is issued to several persons as joint holders, upon satisfactory proof of the death of one joint holder, the issuer may treat the surviving joint holders as owner of the security.

[471] OBCA, s. 45(9); CBCA, s. 47(5) and (6). The "Crown" means the Crown in right of Canada in the case of the CBCA and the Crown in right of Ontario in the case of the OBCA.

[472] *Colborne Capital Corp. v. 542775 Alberta Ltd.*, [1995] A.J. No. 538, 22 B.L.R. (2d) 226 at 275 (Q.B.), *per* Virtue J.:

> Short of some statutory right, which is not asserted here, the law proceeds upon the basis that rights with respect to property are acquired by entering into an agreement with the owner.

> The law recognizes legal ownership in shares as property which can be bought and sold.

[473] See, generally, *New Lambton Land & Coal Co. v. London Bank of Australia Ltd.* (1904), 1 C.L.R. 524 at 544.

[474] *Re European Bank (Master's Case)* (1872), 7 Ch. App. 292.

[475] *Suddaby v. 864226 Ontario Inc.*, [2003] O.J. No. 471, 31 B.L.R. (3d) 119 (S.C.J.). See also OBCA, s. 81; *Wood v. W. & G. Dean Pty. Ltd.* (1929), 43 C.L.R. 77 (H.C. Aust.).

60.(1) On delivery of a security the purchaser acquires the rights in the security that the transferor had or had authority to convey, except that a purchaser who has been a party to any fraud or illegality affecting the security or who as a prior holder had notice of an adverse claim does not improve their position by taking from a later *bona fide* purchaser.

As we have seen, the OBCA and CBCA protect the issuer of a security from liability in respect of any breach of trust growing out of securities that are held in trust by the registered holder. Subsection 61(2) of the CBCA extends this protection to persons who acquire securities from a trustee:

61.(2)Notwithstanding that a purchaser, or any broker for a seller or purchaser, has notice that a security is held for a third person or is registered in the name of or endorsed by a fiduciary, they have no duty to inquire into the rightfulness of the transfer and have no notice of an adverse claim, except where they know that the consideration is to be used for, or that the transaction is for, the personal benefit of the fiduciary or is otherwise in breach of the fiduciary's duty, the purchaser or broker is deemed to have notice of an adverse claim.

§7.206 As a general rule, a person who sells or otherwise transfers his or her interest in a security gives no guarantee to the transferee that the issuer will make the payments evidenced by the security, or otherwise will perform its obligations under the security. However, there is an implied warranty on the part of the transferee that the security is genuine.[476] In contrast, the endorser of a negotiable instrument undertakes that the drawer of the instrument will pay as the instrument specifies, unless it is specifically noted that the endorsement is without recourse.[477]

§7.207 In general, a shareholder is entitled to transfer his or her shares to anyone else upon compliance with the provisions of the governing Act and the articles and by-laws of the corporation and any unanimous shareholder agreement relating to it.[478] There is no law which precludes the shareholders from contracting to submit the shares they hold to a reasonable restriction on the right of transfer, although an outright contractual prohibition on transfer is not valid. So, for instance, a restriction which does no more than give a right of pre-emption is perfectly valid.[479] Where the corporation is offering its shares to the public, the

---

[476] *Meyers v. Richards*, 163 U.S. 385 (1896).
[477] A blank endorsement of a negotiable instrument (consisting of only the holder's signature) generally converts an instrument made out to "order" to one that is in "bearer" form. A restrictive endorsement includes a restriction on how the instrument may be used by transferee in addition to holder's signature (the most common of such an endorsement is the addition of the words "for deposit only", which is frequently made when depositing a cheque to a bank account; the depository must apply the check to the holder's deposit account). A special endorsement names the next holder and requires that person's endorsement for further negotiation. The usual of a special endorsement is "pay to the order of ...". A qualified endorsement includes the words "without recourse", and makes clear that the endorser assumes no personal liability with respect to the honor of the instrument. In all cases, an endorsement requires a signature, subject to any statutory relaxation of the rule. A without recourse endorsement does not affect the negotiability of the instrument.
[478] *Re Good & Jacob Y. Shantz, Son & Co.*, [1911] O.J. No. 51, 23 O.L.R. 544 (C.A.).
[479] *Ontario Jockey Club v. McBride*, [1927] A.C. 916 at 923 (P.C.), *per* Lord Wrenbury.

corporation may not include in its articles restrictions on the transfer of shares, even where the shareholders or incorporators may approve of them.[480] However, the shareholders of an offering corporation may agree among themselves to restrict their right to transfer its shares.

§7.208 The ownership of a share may be transferred so as to create rights between the vendor and purchaser without having an effect on registered ownership for corporate law purposes. In the absence of a special agreement it is not the duty of a vendor of shares to procure the registration of the transfer in the corporation's books; he or she need only complete all requisite steps within his or her control to permit the transfer to be registered.[481] Although a transfer is incomplete until it is registered, prior to that registration, the transferor holds the shares as trustee for the transferee,[482] and thus the transferee has an equitable title (but only an equitable title) to the shares.[483] The transferee does not become the legal owner until the name of the transferee is entered on the register in respect of the shares so transferred.[484] Thus the corporation may continue to treat the registered holder of shares as the owner of those shares.[485] Moreover, the transferor remains the person entitled to vote those shares until the transfer is registered.[486]

§7.209 As a general rule, claims that the original subscriber for shares is entitled to make against the corporation with respect to those shares do not pass to the

---

[480] OBCA, s. 42(2); CBCA, s. 49(9). Note, however, that the corporation may include in its articles restrictions on the issue, transfer or ownership of shares that are necessary:

(a) by or under any Act of Canada or Ontario as a condition to the obtaining, holding or renewal of authority to engage in any activity necessary to its undertaking;

(b) for the purpose of achieving or preserving its status as a Canadian body corporate for the purpose of any Act of Canada or Ontario;

(c) to limit to a specified level the ownership of shares by any prescribed class of person for the purpose of assisting the corporation or any of its affiliates or associates to qualify under the *Securities Act* or similar legislation of a province or territory to obtain, hold or renew registration, or to qualify for membership in a stock exchange in Ontario recognized as such by the Commission; or

(d) to attain or to maintain a specified level of Canadian ownership or control for the purpose of assisting the corporation or any of its affiliates or associates to qualify to receive licences, permits, grants, payments or other benefits under any prescribed Act of Canada or a province or ordinance of a territory.

[481] *Castleman v. Waghorn, Gwynn & Co.* (1908), 41 S.C.R. 88 at 96, *per* Duff J.; *Boultbee v. Wills & Co.*, [1907] O.J. No. 51, 15 O.L.R. 227 (H.C.); *Davidson v. Brooker*, [1924] O.J. No. 340, 27 O.W.N. 195 at 197 (C.A.), *per* Mulock C.J.O. In the absence of evidence to the contrary, it may be assumed that the required consent was given: *Hamilton v. Grant* (1900), 30 S.C.R. 566 at 573, *per* Sedgewick J.

[482] OBCA, s. 67(1); CBCA, s. 51(1); *Re Montgomery & Wrights Ltd.*, [1917] O.J. No. 133, 38 O.L.R. 335 at 336 (H.C.), *per* Middleton J.

[483] *Lovibond v. Grand Trunk Rlwy.*, [1939] O.J. No. 473, [1939] O.R. 305 (C.A.), *per* Masten J.A.

[484] OBCA, s. 67(1); CBCA, s. 51(1); *Tough Oakes Gold Mines Ltd. v. Foster*, [1917] O.J. No. 221, 39 O.L.R. 144 at 152 (H.C.), *per* Kelly J.

[485] *Re Montgomery & Wrights Ltd.*, [1917] O.J. No. 133, 38 O.L.R. 335 (H.C.); *Kennedy v. Williams* (1937), 75 Que. S.C. 65.

[486] *Tough Oakes Gold Mines Ltd. v. Foster*, [1917] O.J. No. 221, 39 O.L.R. 144 (H.C.).

transferee of those shares.[487] Nor is the corporation entitled to assert claims relating to the transferor against the transferee of the shares. However, where the shares are subject to a lien, and a proper warning of the existence of that lien is provided by conspicuously noting it on the share certificate,[488] the corporation may enforce the lien in accordance with its articles and by-laws.[489]

§7.210 Specific performance of a contract for the sale of shares may be granted[490] or the court may award damages in lieu of but not in addition to[491] specific performance.[492] Where there is a breach of contract to allot shares, the aggrieved subscriber's position is fully restored where the shares are allotted to the subscriber and he or she has received the equivalent of any dividend that would have been received if the contract had been duly performed, plus interest for non-payment. A subscriber complaining of such a breach is not entitled to be put in a better position than he or she would have enjoyed if the contract had been performed according to its terms.[493]

§7.211 Although it can be said that the buyer of shares has an equitable interest in the shares from the time when the contract of sale is made[494] until the transfer of the shares to the buyer is registered by the corporation (at which time the equitable title will merge with the legal title to the shares), there are certain qualifications that must be put upon this general proposition. First, where a contract is made for the sale of unascertained shares, there can be no interest in those shares until such time as specific shares are appropriated to the contract (*e.g.*, by the execution of a transfer document). Until payment is made or the transfer is effected (whichever occurs first), the seller retains a vendor's lien against the shares for the unpaid portion of the purchase price. It is only when the seller has been paid in full that he or she becomes a passive trustee for the benefit of the buyer.[495] Where shares are sold through the instrumentality of a stock exchange, the sale contract will usually incorporate the rules and regulations of the stock exchange concerned. In such a case, the rights of the parties will be as specified in the rules.[496]

---

[487] *Re Dominion Combing Mills Ltd.* (1928), 10 C.B.R. 153 (Ont. S.C.).
[488] OBCA, s. 56(8); CBCA, s. 49(8).
[489] OBCA, s. 40(3); CBCA, s. 45(3).
[490] See, for instance, *Baird v. Red Bluff Inns Ltd.*, [1997] B.C.J. No. 1152, 32 B.L.R. (2d) 249 (S.C.); *Basara v. Carhoun* (1993), 82 B.L.R. 71 (C.A.); *W.C. Pitfield & Co. v. Jormac Gold Syndicate Ltd.*, [1938] O.J. No. 438, [1938] O.R. 427 (C.A.); *McDougall Segur Exploration Co. v. Solloway, Mills & Co.*, [1931] 2 W.W.R. 516 (Alta. S.C.). See also *J. Gillespie & Co. v. Sheady* (1929), 24 Alta. L.R. 245 (C.A.), aff'd [1931] S.C.R. 232; *Dallas & Briks v. Dallas Oil Co. & Webster*, [1930] 2 W.W.R. 301, aff'd [1931] S.C.R. 220.
[491] *Williams v. Peel River Land Co.* (1886), 55 L.T. 689 (Ch. D.).
[492] In an action for damages, the measure of the damage is the difference between the contract price and the market price at the date of the breach of contract: *Wilson v. London & Globe Finance Corp.* (1897), 14 T.L.R. 14.
[493] *Sri Lanka Omnibus Co. v. Perera*, [1952] A.C. 76 (P.C.).
[494] See, for instance, *Baden Pacific Ltd. v. Portreeve Pty. Ltd.* (1988), 14 A.C.L.R. 677.
[495] *Avon Downs Pty. Ltd. v. F.C.T.* (1949), 78 C.L.R. 353 (H.C. Aust.).
[496] See, generally, *W. Noall & Co. v. Wan*, [1970] V.R. 683; *Bonds & Securities (Trading) Pty. Ltd. v. Glomex Mines NL*, [1971] 1 N.S.W.L.R. 879.

§7.212 While section 69(1) of the OBCA[497] provides that a good faith purchaser acquires good title to securities free of any adverse claim, that protection does not apply where the purchaser acquires the security for value but in circumstances that ought to have put him or her on inquiry as to the existence of an adverse claim. For instance, in *Cartwright v. Lyster*,[498] a bank was given a stock certificate as additional security for a loan owed by one of its customers. The certificate stated on its face that it was owned by the estate of the customer's father (the customer and his brother being executors of the father's estate). The manager of the bank made no inquiries as to the right of the customer to pledge the certificates as security for his own indebtedness. It was held that in these circumstances, the manager was under a duty to inquire, and accordingly the bank was required to return the certificates to the estate.

(i) Restrictions on Transfer

§7.213 A great many corporations (including nearly all small corporations) have restrictions upon the transfer of their shares set out in their articles. Any such restrictions are considered to be a restraint on alienation, and therefore are strictly construed by the courts.

§7.214 The most commonly encountered restriction on share transfer is the so-called private company restriction required to enjoy the benefit of the private company exemption under provincial securities legislation.[499] Until recently, the securities laws of each of the provinces provided a general exemption from the regulatory regimes that they created in the case of private companies. To secure the benefit of this exemption it is necessary to include in the articles of the corporation a restriction on share transfer and ownership along the following lines:

> The right to transfer shares in the Corporation is subject to the restriction that no shares shall be transferred without either,
>
> (a) the consent of the directors of the Corporation expressed by a resolution passed by the directors or an instrument in writing signed by a majority of the directors; or
>
> (b) the consent of the holders of shares of the Corporation to which are attached at least 51 per cent of the votes attaching to all shares of the Corporation for the time being outstanding carrying a voting right either under all circumstances or under circumstances that have occurred and are continuing at that time, that consent to be expressed by a resolution of those shareholders or by an instrument in writing signed by those shareholders,
>
> which consent may be given either prior to or subsequent to the time of transfer of the shares.

§7.215 In Ontario, the "private company" exemption now has been largely superceded by the closely held issuer exemption, which is provided for in Rule 45-

---

[497] [1934] O.J. No. 231, CBCA, s. 60(2).
[498] [1934] O.R. 161 (C.A.).
[499] R.S.O. 1990, c. S.5.

501[500] — although the *Securities Act* itself continues to provide for the former. The term "closely-held issuer" is defined in Rule 45-501 to mean:

> ... an issuer, other than a mutual fund or non-redeemable investment fund, whose
>
> (a) shares are subject to restrictions on transfer requiring the approval of either the board of directors or the shareholders of the issuer "(or the equivalent in a non-corporate issuer) contained in constating documents of the issuer or one or more agreements among the issuer and holders of its shares.

This requirement for a restriction on share transfer is similar to the old requirement for the private company exemption. Currently, the closely-held issuer exemption is unique to Ontario. Other provinces continue to make use of the older private company exemption. There are steps that an issuer may take to ensure that it qualifies under both the closely-held issuer exemption in Ontario and the private company exemption in other Canadian jurisdictions. Among the important distinctions, the closely-held issuer exemption broadens the scope of potential investors to include members of the public. Where an issuer wishes to retain the private company exemption for other provinces, then it must include in its constating documents a provision prohibiting it from offering its securities to the public. The down-side of this approach is that the issuer thereby forfeits the opportunity to issue securities to members of the public, which is the one offsetting benefit that the closely-held issuer exemption offers to small corporations.

§7.216 The new exemption differs from the old, first in the number of shareholders who are permitted, second by removing the requirement for that number to be specified formally in the constating documents, and third in the manner of calculating the number of shareholders. These matters are dealt with in clause (b) of the definition:

> (b) outstanding securities are beneficially owned, directly or indirectly, by not more than 35 persons or companies, exclusive of
>
>> (i) persons or companies that are, or at the time they last acquired securities of the issuer were, accredited investors;
>>
>> (ii) current or former directors or officers of the issuer or of an affiliated entity of the issuer; and
>>
>> (iii) current or former employees of the issuer or of an affiliated entity of the issuer, or current or former consultants as defined in MI 45-105, who in each case beneficially own only securities of the issuer that were issued as compensation by, or under an incentive plan of, the issuer or an affiliated entity of the issuer;
>
> provided that:
>
>> (A) two or more persons who are the joint registered holders of one or more securities of the issuer shall be counted as one beneficial owner of those securities; and

---

[500] OSC Rules, see website <http://www.osc.gove.on.ca>.

(B) a corporation, partnership, trust or other entity shall be counted as one beneficial owner of securities of the issuer unless the entity has been created or is being used primarily for the purpose of acquiring or holding securities of the issuer, in which event each beneficial owner of an equity interest in the entity or each beneficiary of the entity, as the case may be, shall be counted as a separate beneficial owner of those securities of the issuer;

The Commission's Companion Policy 45-501CP confirms that current and former directors and officers are excluded regardless of the manner in which they acquired their securities of the issuer. It also confirms that securities issued as an incentive on a "one-off" basis — *i.e.*, not under an incentive plan — are securities issued as compensation by the issuer.

§7.217 Subsection 2.1(1) of the Rule provides what is in effect a three-part test that must be satisfied to enjoy the benefit of the exemption. The first two parts of this test are as follows:

(1) Sections 25 and 53 of the Act do not apply to a trade in a security of an issuer if

(a) in the case of a trade by the issuer, following the trade, the issuer will be a closely-held issuer; or in the case of a trade by a selling security holder, the selling security holder has, upon reasonable inquiry, no grounds to believe that following the trade the issuer will not be a closely-held issuer;

(b) in the case of a trade by the closely-held issuer, following the trade the aggregate proceeds received by the closely-held issuer, and any other issuer engaged in common enterprise with the closely-held issuer, in connection with trades made in reliance upon this exemption will not exceed $3,000,000.

Clause (b) amounts to a major departure from the old private company exemption. Under the new approach, there is a maximum aggregate limits on the value of the issues that may be made in reliance upon the exemption. A closely-held issuer may no longer use the closely-held issuer exemption once it has received aggregate proceeds of $3 million from trades made in reliance upon the exemption. This represents a major change in policy and is obviously intended to limit the exception to relatively small issuers.

§7.218 Subsection 2.1(1) of the Rule continues by adding the further requirement, as the third component of the test:

(c) no selling or promotional expenses are paid or incurred in connection with the trade, except for services performed by a dealer registered under the Act.

The scope of clause (c) is significantly qualified by the Companion Policy. Closely-held issuers are one of the two private placement exemptions discussed in the policy. Section 2.1 of the Companion Policy states:

The Commission recognizes that a seller of securities may, in connection with any distribution of securities, rely concurrently on more than one private placement exemption. The Commission notes that where the seller is paying or incurring selling or promotional expenses in connection with the distribution, other than for the services of a dealer registered under the Act, the seller may not be able to rely on the exemption in section 2.1. The Commission takes the view that expenses incurred in connection with the preparation and delivery of an offering memorandum do not constitute selling or promotional expenses in this context.

In addition, paragraph (c) does not prohibit legitimate selling or promotional expenses, such as printing, mailing and other administrative or nominal expenses incurred in connection with the trade.

§7.219 The Companion Policy further clarifies that the closely-held issuer exemption is available to the closely-held issuer itself in respect of an issue of its own securities, and also to any holder of a closely-held issuer's securities in respect of a resale of the securities. The closely-held issuer may issue its own securities in reliance upon the exemption so long as it is able to meet the criteria for the availability of the exemption in paragraphs (a), (b) and (c) of subsection 2.1(1). In contrast, a holder of securities of a closely-held issuer may rely upon the exemption in section 2.1 in connection with any resale of the securities provided that paragraphs (a) and (c) of subsection 2.1(1) are satisfied. In particular, paragraph (a) of subsection 2.1(1) requires the issuer to continue to be a closely-held issuer after the re-sale. However, the $3 million aggregate cap on the value of issues made in reliance on the exemption, set out in paragraph 2.1(1)(b), does not apply to re-sales of securities in reliance upon this exemption. Once the issuer no longer meets the paragraph (a) and (c) requirements of the definition, a re-sale of securities distributed under the exemption in section 2.1 may only be made in reliance upon another exemption or by complying with the applicable provision of Multilateral Instrument 45-102 Resale of Securities.

§7.220 Determination of whether the cap of $3 million has been reached, is made by reference to the aggregate of all proceeds received by the issuer at any time from trades made in reliance upon the closely-held issuer exemption since it was introduced in November 2001. Proceeds received by the issuer from trades made in reliance upon other exemptions, including exemptions available prior to the date when the closely-held issuer exemption first became available, are not relevant. In particular, the proceeds realized by the issuer from trades to accredited investors need not be included in determining whether the $3 million threshold would be exceeded in respect of any proposed trade under section 2.1. One important qualification on this rule relates to the issuer's obligation to file a Form 45-501F1 report in respect of a trade with an accredited investor. Where such a filing is required, but for some reason is not made, it will be presumed that the trade was made in reliance upon section 2.1. Consequently, the proceeds received through that issue must be counted for purposes of the aggregate proceeds limit.

(ii) Presumption Against Restriction

§7.221 In general, the rules governing the transfer of shares are the same as the rules governing the transfer of other corporate securities. In the absence of a provision to the contrary, shares are presumed to be capable of transfer.[501] The motive of the present holder in seeking to transfer his or her shares is irrelevant. Unless the right of transfer is restricted under the memorandum, articles or share terms, the company may not prevent a shareholder merely because they believe that the shareholder is acting in bad faith in effecting the transfer. For instance, in *Lindlar's Case*[502] a shareholder sought to transfer partly paid shares to a impecunious third party, while the company teetered on the verge of financial failure. Once the transfer was made, the transferor would cease to be liable for the unpaid amount. The question before the court was whether such a transfer might properly be made. Buckley L.J. held that the transfer was effective.

§7.222 In the absence of a provision to the contrary, shares are presumed to be capable of transfer.[503] Such restrictions as are imposed upon the transfer of shares must be authorized in the articles of a corporation.[504] Therefore the directors of a corporation have no authority to introduce such restrictions.[505] Restrictions on the transfer of shares that are set out in the articles of a corporation are subject to a narrow construction.[506] So, for instance, it has been held that the creation of a security interest in shares by delivery of the share certificates in pledge to a secured creditor does not constitute a trade in shares.[507] Although the present OBCA and CBCA permit a corporation (other than an offering corporation) to set out in its articles restrictions on the transfer of shares, the power to impose restrictions is broader than a mere power to regulate share transfer.[508] Such a power cannot be exercised arbitrarily.[509] A pre-emptory refusal to approve a transfer, combined with a refusal of an explanation, is unacceptable.[510]

---

[501] *Re Panton & Cramp Steel*, [1904] O.J. No. 2, (1904), 9 O.L.R. 3 (C.A.), *per* Osler J.A. See also *Ontario Jockey Club Ltd. v. McBride*, [1927] A.C. 916 (P.C.).
[502] *Re Discoverers Finance Corp. (Lindlar's Case)*, [1910] 1 Ch. 312 (C.A.).
[503] *Re Panton & Cramp Steel*, [1904] O.J. No. 2, 9 O.L.R. 3 (H.C.), *per* Osler J.A.; *Ontario Jockey Club Ltd. v. McBride*, [1927] A.C. 916 (P.C.).
[504] See the prescribed form of articles under the OBCA — although it appears that where the articles or by-laws of a corporation provide in accordance with s. 40(1) of the OBCA that the corporation is entitled to a lien against shares registered in the name of a particular shareholder, the articles or by-laws may provide that the corporation need not transfer those shares while the lien remains undischarged: OBCA, s. 40(3); *Esley's Frosted Foods Ltd. v. Mid White Oak Square Ltd.*, [1976] O.J. No. 2339, 14 O.R. (2d) 479 (H.C.).
[505] *Re Good & Jacob Y. Shantz, Son & Co.*, [1910] O.J. No. 117, 21 O.L.R. 153 (H.C.), aff'd [1911] O.J. No. 158, 23 O.L.R. 544 at 547-49 (C.A.), *per* Moss C.J.O.
[506] See, for instance, *Nadeau v. Nadeau & Nadeau Ltd.*, [1972] N.B.J. No. 178, 6 N.B.R. (2d) 512 at 530 (Q.B.), *per* Dickson J.; *Moodie v. W. & J. Sheppard Ltd.*, [1949] 2 All E.R. 1044.
[507] *Smith v. Hamelin*, [1992] B.C.J. No. 2453, 75 B.C.L.R. (2d) 360 (S.C.).
[508] See, for instance, *Re Imperial Starch Co.*, [1905] O.J. No. 179, 10 O.L.R. 22 at 25 (H.C.), *per* MacMahon J.; *Ontario Investment Assn. v. Sippi*, [1890] O.J. No. 103, 20 O.R. 440 (H.C.); *Canadian National Fire Insurance Co. v. Hutchings*, [1918] A.C. 451 (P.C.).
[509] *Canadian National Fire Insurance Co. v. Hutchings*, [1918] A.C. 451 at 457 (P.C.), *per* Sir Walter Phillimore.
[510] *Smith v. Canada Car Co.* (1876), 6 P.R. 107.

The power to refuse the transfer of shares must be exercised in the best interests of the corporation. Although any such jurisdiction must be exercised reasonably,[511] the court will not interfere where the directors refuse in good faith to register a transfer of the shares of a corporation, particularly where the corporation is a virtual partnership.[512] Any restriction on share transfer cannot be exercised for the personal benefit of the directors, as, for instance, so as to force the sale of those shares at less than their market price.[513] In *Australian Metropolitan Life Assurance Co. v. Ure*[514] Isaacs J. made the following observations concerning the types of factors that the directors might take into account before deciding whether to approve a transfer of shares:

> The general character of such a regulation is clear, but the ambit of the purpose of the power of course varies with the circumstances of each particular case. The nature of the company, its constitution and the scheme of its regulations as a whole must be taken into account in determining whether a given factor comes within its range. Solvency of a transferee is, of course, important; for otherwise the mutual undertaking to contribute would be ineffectual, and creditors would be unjustly dealt with. But his solvency is not necessarily the only consideration. The reputation of the company may be an essential element of success ... the maintenance of a board of directors against whom not even a suggestion of reproach can be made is manifestly a high business consideration, which no person charged with the beneficial administration of the corporate affairs would be likely to overlook, in the interests of the shareholders as a whole. ... It follows that if the directors honestly acted upon the business consideration mentioned, it was within their power, even though a transient majority thought differently or desired differently. It is possible, of course, that the directors were not really moved by that legitimate consideration, but acted upon some extraneous reason, perhaps some unworthy reason. If they did, then their power is gone, and the court would ... hold that the right had become absolute and would direct registration.

§7.223 A restriction on share transfer may be introduced to the terms and conditions of a particular class of shares after their issue only by way of an amendment to the articles of a corporation. Since section 185(2) of the OBCA now provides a right of dissent where any such amendment is made, the principle set down in earlier case law that any such alteration must be accepted as one of the contingencies of investments in share capital[515] must now be taken as abrogated. Moreover, a purchaser for value without notice of any restriction as to transfer is entitled to have the transfer registered on the books of the corporation.[516] Where the transfer of the shares of a corporation requires the approval of the directors of a corporation, and certain shares of that corporation are seized and sold in

---

[511] *Re Panton & Cramp Steel*, [1904] O.J. No. 2, 9 O.L.R. 3 (H.C.).
[512] *Phillips v. La Paloma Sweets Ltd.*, [1921] O.J. No. 21, 51 O.L.R. 125 at 127 (H.C.), *per* Middleton J.
[513] *Corp. de placement Renaud Inc. v. Nor Mix Ltée*, [1980] C.S. 980.
[514] (1923), 33 C.L.R. 199 (H.C. Aust.).
[515] See, for instance, *Leiser v. Popham Brothers Ltd.*, [1912] B.C.J. No. 38, 17 B.C.R. 187 at 188 (S.C.), *per* Clement J.
[516] *Re McKain*, [1904] O.J. No. 131, 7 O.L.R. 241 (H.C.); see also OBCA, s. 56(8) and (10); CBCA, s. 49(10) and (11); *Meyers v. Lucknow Elevator Co.*, [1905] O.J. No. 523, 6 O.W.R. 291 at 296 (H.C.), *per* MacMahon J.

execution, the purchaser of those shares has no right to compel the corporation to register the transfer of the shares. The purchaser of the shares acquires no greater rights than were possessed by the original shareholder.[517]

§7.224 Restrictions on transfer may also be set out in a shareholder agreement. Where such an agreement applies, the scope of the restriction is a matter of contractual construction.[518] The restrictions imposed under a shareholder agreement may be greater than those imposed under the articles of the corporation.[519] Except in the case of a unanimous shareholder agreement, however, a shareholder agreement is a mere matter among the shareholders who are parties to that agreement, and unless the corporation is itself a party, the directors of the corporation have no right to refuse to register a transfer of shares merely because it violates the terms of a shareholder agreement.[520]

§7.225 In *Lyle & Scott's Trustees v. British Investment Trust Ltd.*[521] the articles of a company required a shareholder who wished to transfer his or her shares to inform the secretary of the company. The other shareholders were then entitled to buy the shares of the intended retiree at a price fixed by the company's auditor. Some of the shareholders of the company entered into a contract with an outside buyer, under which they agreed to put the buyer in as full control of the company as they could, even though they would not seek the registration of a transfer. The company sought a declaration that the shareholders were bound to comply with the articles. The declaration was granted. It was held that even if the sellers intended to retain legal title and to transfer only their equitable interest to another person, they were still within the contemplation of the provision.

§7.226 The articles of a corporation will often provide that shares in the corporation may only be transferred with the approval of the board of directors, granting to the directors an absolute discretion over the approval of a transfer. Where the articles so provide, the directors must specifically authorize a transfer. A general note in the minutes of the directors such as "all shares of stock subscribed for and transferred to date be hereby allotted and allotment is hereby confirmed" is too vague and therefore insufficient for this purpose, unless it can be shown that a particular transfer must have been within the contemplation of the directors at the time when that resolution was passed.[522] Where the transfer of the shares of a corporation requires the approval of the directors of a corporation, and certain shares of that corporation are seized and sold in execution, the

---

[517] *Woodruff v. Harris*, [1854] O.J. No. 112, 11 U.C.Q.B. 490; *Phillips v. La Paloma Sweets Ltd.*, [1921] O.J. No. 21, 51 O.L.R. 125 (H.C.).
[518] *Litz v. R. Litz & Sons Co.* (1957), 65 Man. R. 103 (Q.B.). As to the evidence required to establish such an agreement, see *Berkinshaw v. Henderson*, [1909] O.J. No. 417, 1 O.W.N. 97 (C.A.), per Osler J.A.
[519] *Ontario Jockey Club Ltd. v. McBride*, [1927] A.C. 916 (P.C.).
[520] *Re Belleville Driving & Athletic Assn.*, [1914] O.J. No. 15, 31 O.L.R. 79 at 85 (C.A.), per Meredith C.J.O.
[521] [1959] A.C. 763 (H.L.).
[522] *McCurdy v. Oak Tire & Rubber Co.*, [1918] O.J. No. 51, 44 O.L.R. 571 at 574 (H.C.), per Middleton J.

purchaser of those shares has no right to compel the corporation to register the transfer of the shares. Such a purchaser acquires no greater rights than were possessed by the original shareholder.[523]

(iii) Transmission of Shares

§7.227 It is customary to distinguish between the voluntary transfer of shares and the involuntary transmission of shares from one owner to another which occurs as a result of act of law. Transmission occurs (a) upon bankruptcy, where the property of a bankrupt shareholder vests in his or her trustee; (b) upon death, where title passes to the executor, administrator or personal representative of the bankrupt; (c) where an order is made by the court placing the estate of a mentally incompetent person under guardianship. Subsection 67(2) of the OBCA provides that:

> 67.(2) ... an issuer whose articles restrict the right to transfer its securities shall, and any other issuer may, treat a person referred to in clause (*a*), (*b*) or (*c*) as a registered security holder entitled to exercise all the rights of the security holder that the person represents, if that person furnishes evidence as described in subsection 87(3) to the issuer that the person is,
>
> > (*a*) the executor, administrator, estate trustee heir or legal representative of the heirs, of the estate of a deceased security holder;
> >
> > (*b*) a guardian, attorney under a continuing power of attorney with authority, guardian of property, committee, trustee, curator or tutor representing a registered security holder who is a minor, an incompetent person or a missing person; or
> >
> > (*c*) a liquidator of, or a trustee in bankruptcy for, a registered security holder.[524]

Moreover, where a person upon whom the ownership of a security devolves by operation of law, other than a person referred to in subsection 67(2), furnishes proof of his or her authority to exercise rights or privileges in respect of a security of the issuer that is not registered in the person's name, the issuer "shall treat the person as entitled to exercise those rights or privileges".[525] So, for instance, if an equitable receiver is appointed over shares held by a shareholder, the receiver becomes the person entitled to receive any dividends or other distributions payable by the corporation, upon furnishing proof of his or her appointment to the corporation.

§7.228 The personal representative does not automatically become a member-shareholder of the corporation unless a proper application for registration as such

---

[523] *Woodruff v. Harris*, [1854] O.J. No. 112, 11 U.C.Q.B. 490; *Phillips v. La Paloma Sweets Ltd.*, [1921] O.J. No. 21, 51 O.L.R. 125 (H.C.).
[524] CBCA, s. 51(2).
[525] OBCA, s. 67(3); CBCA, s. 51(3).

is made and, where a transfer restriction applies, the application is approved.[526] Even so, the personal representative has the same rights as a member or shareholder for the purpose of determining entitlement to participate in both profit and liability,[527] but he or she does not enjoy the rights of a full member for the purpose of enjoying a say in the running of the company. So, for instance, the personal representative is entitled to receive dividends payable on the class of shares held by the deceased shareholder, or to participate in any pre-emptive right existing for the benefit of the members of the company generally.[528] It would also appear that the personal representative has the right to transfer the shares or other securities which have been transmitted to him or her by law.

§7.229 In *Re Greene*[529] a provision of the articles of a company provided that on the death of a director, his shares would pass to his widow. It was held that the provision was invalid as a testamentary instrument. Accordingly, the shares passed to the personal representative of the director. However, the articles may provide that shares will be stripped of valuable incidents as a result of death or some other contingency. For instance, in the Australian case of *Robertson v. FTC*,[530] a shareholder held a block of shares in a private company. The articles of the company provided that on his death those shares would be divided into two

---

[526] In this regard, OBCA, s. 67(7) provides:

> 67.(7) Subject to any applicable law of Canada or a province of Canada relating to the collection of taxes, a person referred to in clause (2)(*a*) is entitled to become a registered holder or to designate a registered holder, if the person deposits with the issuer or its transfer agent,
>
> (*a*) the original grant of probate or of letters of administration, or a copy thereof certified to be a true copy by,
>
>   (i) the court that granted the probate or letters of administration,
>
>   (ii) a trust corporation incorporated under the laws of Canada or a province, or
>
>   (iii) a lawyer or notary acting on behalf of the person; or
>
> (*b*) in the case of transmission by notarial will in the Province of Quebec, a copy thereof authenticated under the laws of that Province;
>
> together with,
>
> (*c*) an affidavit or declaration of transmission made by the person stating the particulars of the transmission;
>
> (*d*) the security certificate that was owned by the deceased holder,
>
>   (i) in the case of a transfer to the person, with or without the endorsement of that person, and
>
>   (ii) in the case of a transfer to any other person, endorsed in accordance with section 73; and
>
> (*e*) any other assurance the issuer may require under section 87.

[527] *James v. Buena Ventura Nitrate Grounds Syndicate Ltd.*, [1896] 1 Ch. 456 at 466 (C.A.), per Rigby L.J.

[528] *A.L. Campbell & Co. Pty. Ltd. v. FCT* (1951), 82 C.L.R. 452 at 460 (H.C. Aust.).

[529] [1949] Ch. 333.

[530] (1952), 86 C.L.R. 463 (H.C. Aust.).

classes. Certain preferential rights were conferred on the second of these classes, which had the effect of lowering the value of the first class. It was held that the provision of the articles was valid.

§7.230 Section 51 of the CBCA was amended in 2001 to clarify the rights of a personal representative upon the transmission of shares. Specifically, subsection 51(2) of the CBCA now provides:

> 51.(2) Notwithstanding subsection (1), a corporation whose articles restrict the right to transfer its securities shall, and any other corporation may, treat a person as a registered security holder entitled to exercise all the rights of the security holder that the person represents, if the person furnishes the corporation with evidence as described in subsection 77(4) that the person is,
>
> (*a*) the heir of a deceased security holder, or the personal representative of the heirs, or the personal representative of the estate of a deceased security holder;
>
> (*b*) a personal representative of a registered security holder who is an infant, an incompetent person or a missing person; or
>
> (*c*) a liquidator of, or a trustee in bankruptcy for, a registered security holder.

Subsection 51(8) of the CBCA provides:

> 51.(8) Despite subsection (7), if the laws of the jurisdiction governing the transmission of a security of a deceased holder do not require a grant of probate or of letters of administration in respect of the transmission, a personal representative of the deceased holder is entitled, subject to any applicable law relating to the collection of taxes, to become a registered holder or to designate a registered holder, if the personal representative deposits with the corporation or its transfer agent
>
> (*a*) the security certificate that was owned by the deceased holder; and
>
> (*b*) reasonable proof of the governing laws of the deceased holder's interest in the security and of the right of the personal representative or the person designated by the personal representative to become the registered holder.

G. ACCOUNTING FOR SHARE CAPITAL — THE STATED CAPITAL ACCOUNT

§7.231 Earlier we touched upon the subjects of authorized and issued capital, and it was noted that in general terms the issued capital of a corporation constitutes the consideration received by a corporation in respect of the issue of its shares, expressed as a monetary amount. The OBCA and the CBCA do not deal with issued capital as such, but rather with stated capital. Subsection 24(1) of the OBCA provides that a corporation shall maintain a separate stated capital account for each class and series of shares it issues.[531] Thus, on the balance sheet of a corporation, its stated capital will be set out along following lines:

---

[531] Note that s. 24 does not apply to an "open-ended mutual fund", a term defined to mean an offering corporation that carries on only the business of investing the consideration it receives for the shares it issues, and all or substantially all of the shares of which are redeemable upon the

Shareholder's Equity	1989	1988
Stated Capital		
Class A		
series 1	$10,000	$7,000
series 2	25,000	0
Class B shares	5,000	2,000
Retained Earnings	5,000	3,500
TOTAL	$45,000	$12,500

A corporation is required to add to the appropriate stated capital account the full amount that it receives in respect of any share it issues, so that if additional series 2 shares are issued, the consideration received for them (the "subscription price") will be added to the stated capital account for that series. If, however, a new series of shares is created, then a new stated capital account must be created as well, even where the rights, privileges, conditions and restrictions attached to the two series are exactly the same.

§7.232 Where shares are issued for a consideration other than money, the appropriate amount is determined by the directors in accordance with subsection 23(4) of the OBCA. This obligation is subject, however, to subsection 24(3)(*a*),[532] which provides that despite subsection 24(2) and subsection 23(3), where a corporation issues shares in exchange for

(i) property of a person who immediately before the exchange does not deal with the corporation at arm's length within the meaning of that term in the *Income Tax Act* (Canada); or

(ii) shares of a body corporate that immediately before the exchange or that, because of the exchange, does not deal with the corporation at arm's length within the meaning of that term in the *Income Tax Act* (Canada).

the corporation may, subject to subsection 24(4), add all or any portion of the consideration it received for the shares to the appropriate stated capital account. A similar treatment may be followed where the corporation issues shares

- under an agreement referred to in subsection 175(1) of the OBCA; or

- under an arrangement referred to in clause 182(1)(*c*) or (*d*) of the OBCA; or

- to shareholders of an amalgamating corporation who receive the shares in addition to or instead of securities of the amalgamated corporation.

Subsection 175(1) deals with amalgamation agreements, while clause 182(1)(*c*) relates to an arrangement in the form of an amalgamation of the corporation with another corporation; subsection 24(4) provides that on the issue of a share, a corporation shall not add to a stated capital account in respect of the share an amount greater than the amount referred to in subsection 24(2). Thus under sub-

---

demand of the holders of such shares. See also s. 26(11) and (12) of the CBCA, which are of like effect.

[532] CBCA, s. 26(3).

section 24(3), where there is a roll-over of property or shares between non-arm's length parties, or an amalgamation, it is not necessary that the full amount of the consideration received be allocated to a stated capital account.

§7.233 Subsection 26(3) of the CBCA, which corresponds to subsection 24(3) of the OBCA provides as follows:

> 26.(3) Despite subsection (2), a corporation may, subject to subsection (4), add to the stated capital accounts maintained for the shares of classes or series the whole or any part of the amount of the consideration that it receives in an exchange if the corporation issues shares,
>
> (a) in exchange for
>
>> (i) property of a person who immediately before the exchange did not deal with the corporation at arm's length within the meaning of that expression in the *Income Tax Act*; or
>>
>> (ii) shares of, or another interest in, a body corporate that immediately before the exchange, or that because of the exchange, did not deal with the corporation at arm's length within the meaning of that expression in the *Income Tax Act*, or
>>
>> (iii) property if a person who, immediately before the exchange, dealt with the corporation at arm's length within the meaning of that expression in the *Income Tax Act*, if the person, the corporation and all the holders of shares in the class or series of shares so issued consent to the exchange; or
>
> (b) pursuant to an agreement referred to in subsection 182(1) or an arrangement referred to in paragraph 192(1)(b) or (c) or to shareholders of an amalgamating body corporate who receive the shares in addition to or instead of securities of the amalgamated body corporate.

§7.234 Under the former OBCA, the concept of the stated capital account was unknown: corporations had authorized capital and issued capital only. This led to somewhat complicated rules of accounting where a corporation had two or more classes of shares, particularly where some of the shares were with par value, while others were not. Subsection 24(5) of the new OBCA sets out a transitional rule, applicable to corporations operating under the old Act, and also to corporations that are continued under the new OBCA, to govern the transition to the stated capital accounting concept:

> 24.(5) Despite subsection (2) on the 29th day of July, 1983 or at such time thereafter as a corporation has been continued under this Act, as the case may be, the amount in the stated capital account maintained by a corporation in respect of each class or series of shares then issued shall be equal to the aggregate amount paid up on the shares of each such class or series of shares immediately prior thereto, and, after such time, a corporation may, upon complying with subsection (6), add to the stated capital account maintained by it in respect of any class or series of shares any amount it has credited to a retained earnings or other surplus account.

Subsection 24(6) of the OBCA[533] governs additions to a stated capital account. It provides that where a corporation proposes to add any amount to a stated capital account that it maintains in respect of a class or series of shares otherwise than by way of a stock dividend, the addition to the stated capital account must be approved by a special resolution of the shareholders, if the two following conditions are met:

(a) the amount to be added,

  (i) was not received by the corporation as consideration for the issue of shares, or

  (ii) was received by the corporation as consideration for the issue of shares but does not form part of the stated capital attributed to such shares; and

(b) the corporation has outstanding shares of more than one class or series.

Where a class or series of shares would be affected by the addition of an amount to any stated capital account in a manner different from the manner in which any other class or series of shares of the corporation would be affected by that action, the holders of the differently affected class or series of shares are entitled to vote separately as a class or series, as the case may be, on the proposal to take the action, whether or not those shares otherwise carry the right to vote.[534]

§7.235 In the past, there has often been confusion as to the precise application of the stated capital concept where a company incorporated under the laws of a jurisdiction that does not employ the stated capital concept is continued under the CBCA or the OBCA. In the case of the CBCA, this question was partly answered in 2001, with the enactment of subsection 26(9), which provides:

> 26.(9) For the purposes of subsection 34(2), sections 38 and 42 and paragraph 185(2)(a), when a body orporate is continued under this Act its stated capital is deemed to include the amount that would have been included in stated capital if the body corporate had been incorporated under this Act.

H. SPECIAL RIGHTS

(i) Shares Non-Assessable

§7.236 Subsections 23(2) of the OBCA and 25(2) of the CBCA provide that "[s]hares issued by a corporation are non-assessable and the holders are not liable to the corporation or to its creditors in respect thereof". A strong argument can be made that a corporation may enter into a collateral agreement with any shareholder under which the shareholder agrees to contribute sums to the corporation, although in *Edmonton Country Club Ltd. v. Case*[535] it was held that a company could not require some of its shareholders to pay an annual contribution. Across the Commonwealth, the case law is divided concerning the validity

---

[533] CBCA, s. 26(5).
[534] OBCA, s. 24(7).
[535] [1974] S.C.J. No. 63, 44 D.L.R. (3d) 554.

of contractual undertakings to contribute further capital to a corporation which is given outside the terms of the shares themselves, although the preponderant weight of authority seems tipped in favour of such undertakings.[536] Assuming that such undertakings are binding, two further points may be stated: first, any such obligation is a personal contractual obligation to which only the shareholders who have become parties to the agreement are subject; second, the power of the directors to call for such additional contributions to be paid would presumably be subject to the general principle that all shareholders of the same class must be treated equally.[537]

§7.237 Leaving aside whether the corporation and a shareholder may enter into a contract providing for the infusion of additional capital, there would seem to be no doubt that two or more shareholders may enter into an agreement under which they agree to contribute to the capital requirements of the corporation; and a similar arrangement may be made between a shareholder and a creditor, under which the shareholder undertakes to provide a certain amount of capital from time to time. In any of these cases, the agreement is interpersonal and will not pass to or bind any other persons who subsequently acquire the shares of the shareholder who entered into the agreement.

(ii) Securities Convertible to Shares

§7.238 A corporation will often confer upon the holder of a particular security a right to convert that security to a security of another type, or an option to acquire a security of a particular type. Such a right or option may be a term of a security, or may be an entirely separate obligation assumed by the corporation. In either case, the scope and meaning of the conversion right are matters of contractual interpretation, to be resolved in accordance with the general legal rules governing the interpretation of contract.[538] Both the OBCA and the CBCA contain a number of special rules relating to securities that are convertible to or from shares. Where a corporation has granted privileges to convert any securities, other than shares issued by the corporation, into shares of the corporation or has issued or granted options or rights to acquire shares of the corporation, and the articles limit the number of authorized shares, the corporation must reserve a sufficient number of authorized shares to meet the exercise of that conversion privilege, option or right.

---

[536] For cases upholding or supportive of such undertakings, see *Agricultural Wholesale Society Ltd. v. Biddulph & District Agricultural Society*, [1925] Ch. 769, aff'd [1927] A.C. 76 (H.L.); *Hole v. Garnsey*, [1930] A.C. 472 (H.L.); *Peninsular Co. v. Fleming* (1872), 27 L.T. 93; *Lion Mutual Marine Insurance Assoc. Ltd. v. Tucker* (1883), 12 Q.B.D. 176; *Re Bangor & North Wales Mutual Marine Protection Association (Baird's Case)*, [1899] 2 Ch. 593. For cases taking a hostile view of the idea, see *Shalfoon v. Cheddar Valley Co-operative Dairy Co.*, [1924] N.Z.L.R. 561 at 577, per Salmond J.; *Dibble v. Wilts & Somerset Farmers Ltd.*, [1923] 1 Ch. 342. None of these cases, however, appear to have addressed a specific statutory provision such as s. 23(2) of the OBCA.

[537] *Galloway v. Halle Concerts Society*, [1915] 2 Ch. 233.

[538] See generally, *Deutsche Bank Canada v. Oxford Properties Group Inc.*, [1998] O.J. No. 4375, 40 B.L.R. (2d) 302 (Gen. Div.).

§7.239 In addition to the possibility that non-share securities may be convertible into shares. it is also possible that shares may be convertible from one class to another. By virtue of subsections 35(8) of the OBCA and 39(9) of the CBCA, where shares are converted in accordance with their terms into the same or another number of shares of another class or series, those shares become the same in all respects as the shares of the class or series into which they are converted and, if the articles limit the number of shares of either of such classes or series, the number of authorized shares of the class or series is changed and the articles are amended accordingly.

§7.240 Where a corporation enjoys the right to convert a debt security into shares, effect will be give to the procedure set out in the debt instrument for so doing. Upon compliance with that procedure, the corporation is released from liability in debt.[539] In general, courts apply a liberal approach towards the interpretation of conversion and redemption rights, so as to afford them the greatest degree of flexibility with respect to their capital structure.[540]

(1) Conversion Rights and Options

§7.241 The OBCA does not deal specifically with the adjustment that must be made to a stated capital account where debt or non-share securities of a corporation are converted into shares. Presumably in such a case, the normal rules regarding the issue of shares for a property consideration apply.[541] However, both Acts deal expressly with the adjustments that must be made upon a conversion of shares in accordance with their terms into shares of another class or series. Specifically, the CBCA and the OBCA[542] provide that upon a conversion of issued shares in accordance with the terms into shares of another class or series, the corporation must deduct from the stated capital account maintained for the class or series of shares converted an amount equal to the result obtained by multiplying the stated capital account of the shares of that class or series by the number of shares of that class or series converted, and by dividing by the number of issued shares of that class or series immediately before the conversion. The corporation is then required to add the result so obtained plus any additional consideration received as a result of the exercise of the conversion privilege to the stated capital account maintained in respect of the shares of the class or series into which the conversion is made. The Acts further provide that subject to the articles of a corporation, where a corporation issues two classes or series of shares and there is attached to each class or series a right to convert a share of the one class or series into a share of the other class or series, the amount of stated capital attributable to a share in either class or series is the amount obtained when the sum of the stated capital of both classes or series of shares is

---

[539] *Insight Venture Assoc. III, LLC v. SlimSoft Inc.*, [2003] O.J. No. 3701, 43 B.L.R. (3d) 227 at 234 (S.C.J.), *per* Ground J.

[540] See, generally, *Metropolitan Toronto Police Widows & Orphans Fund v. Telus Comm.*, [2006] O.J. No. 4520, 75 O.R. (3d) 784 (C.A.).

[541] See, generally, *Re Harmony, Montague Tin & Copper Mining Co.* (1873), L.R. 8 Ch. App. 407 at 411-12, *per* James L.J.

[542] OBCA, s. 35(4) and (5); CBCA, s. 39(4) and (5).

divided by the number of issued shares of both classes or series of shares immediately before the conversion. All of these provisions apply, however, only where shares are converted in accordance with their terms. Where the share terms provide no right of conversion, but the shares of one class are merely exchanged for shares of another on a contractual basis, the normal rules respecting the issue of shares for a property consideration apply.[543]

(2) Warrants and Options

§7.242 A corporation may grant an existing shareholder or an outsider an option to take up its shares (as, for instance, will be the case where a debt security is issued with a warrant attached). The option may be structured in the form of a binding contract.[544] Subject to the terms of the option granted, the beneficiary of an option may even subscribe for and take up the shares after the commencement of the winding-up of the company[545] (a possibility which would be attractive where the expected distribution of the shares concerned exceeds the option price). However, an option holder as such is not a member or shareholder of the corporation granting the option.

§7.243 A warrant is simply a form of coupon that is presented by the holder as evidence of an entitlement to exercise a particular right. Warrants are often issued by corporations as a sweetener in a securities offering, in order to make the offering more attractive to potential investors. For instance, a corporate bond may come with a warrant that entitles the holder of the bond to purchase shares of a corporation at a given price. While shares are required to be in registered form,[546] there is no such requirement in the case of warrants, since until their exercise, warrants represent inchoate rather than vested rights in the corporation.

§7.244 Section 27 of the OBCA[547] provides that a corporation may issue warrants as evidence of conversion privileges or options or rights to acquire securities of the corporation. Where a warrant is so issued, the corporation must set out the conditions of the warrant either in a certificate evidencing the securities to which the conversion privileges, options or rights are attached, or in separate certificates or other documents. The Act expressly permits the corporation to structure conversion privileges and options or rights to purchase securities of a corporation as transferable or non-transferable rights, or to make them separable or inseparable from any securities to which they are attached.[548] Where the articles of a corporation limit the number of authorized shares of a series or class and the corporation has granted any privilege to convert any securities other than shares into such shares, or has issued or granted options or rights to acquire such

---

[543] OBCA, s. 23(4).
[544] *Kerr v. Fleming Financial Corp.*, [1998] M.J. No. 140, [1998] 9 W.W.R. 176 (Q.B.); *Hilder v. Dexter*, [1902] A.C. 474.
[545] *Hirsh & Co. v. Burns* (1877), 77 L.T. 377.
[546] OBCA, s. 22(1); CBCA, s. 24(1). The rationale for the registered form requirement was given in *Oakes v. Turquand* (1867), L.R. 2 H.L. 325 at 367, *per* Lord Cranworth.
[547] CBCA, s. 29.
[548] OBCA, s. 27(2); CBCA, s. 29(2).

shares, the corporation must reserve a sufficient number of shares to meet the exercise of the conversion privilege, option or right.[549]

§7.245 An option to acquire (or sell) shares may only be exercised in accordance with its terms, and proper compliance with those terms is a condition precedent to the bringing of any action under or in respect of the option. However, an exception to this general rule applies where there is conduct amounting to an anticipatory breach, so that any effort to exercise the option would inevitably have been in vain.[550] At one time, the courts inclined to the view that a person who sought to exercise an option was required to comply strictly with its terms. More recently, this view has been relaxed, with the adoption of more of a standard of commercial reasonableness.[551]

(3) Back-Dating Stock Options

§7.246 In order to obtain the most favourable tax and accounting treatments, stock options are usually granted with an exercise price at least equal to the market value of the underlying stock at the time of the grant (indeed, the employee stock plans of many public companies prohibit the granting of below-market options). In Canada, the Toronto Stock Exchange (TSX) imposes the following rules for its listed companies:

(i) the exercise price for options granted by listed issuers must not be less than the market price of the underlying securities when the options are granted;

(ii) the exercise price must not be based on market prices that do not reflect undisclosed material information; and

(iii) all option grants must be reported to the TSX within 10 days of the end of the month in which the grant was made.

The TSX Venture Exchange (TSX-V) imposes similar rules, though it allows an issuer to set the exercise price at a discount (ranging from 15 per cent to 25 per cent) from the market price, which is specified by the TSX-V. Canadian securities legislation generally requires insiders of reporting issuers to file a report on SEDI within 10 days of any change in their direct or indirect beneficial ownership of or control or direction over securities of the issuer, including options.

§7.247 The term "back-dating" describes a range of practices involving the grant of stock options. Back-dating schemes include the following:

---

[549] OBCA, s. 27(3); CBCA, s. 29(3).
[550] *Baughman v. Rampart Resources Ltd.*, [1995] B.C.J. No. 752, 4 B.C.L.R. (3d) 146 (C.A.).
[551] See, for instance, *Parras v. FAI General Insurance Company Ltd.*, [2001] N.S.W.S.C 1077; *Mannai Limited v. Eagle Star Association Company Ltd.*, [1997] 2 W.L.R. 945 (H.L.); *Lollypops (Harbourside) Pty. Limited v. Werncog Pty. Limited* (1998), 9 B.P.R. 16,361, *per* Young J. (communication of acceptance is satisfied when the relevant letter or notice is opened "in the ordinary course of business or would have been so opened if the ordinary course were followed").

- cherry-picking a grant date when the stock price was low, rather than using the price on the date the options were actually awarded;
- changing dates on employment letters to make it appear that new hires started on a date before in-the-money options were granted;
- retroactively adding employees to existing grant contracts; and falsifying documents to hide back-dating from auditors and investors;
- granting options to fictitious employees when the company's stock price was low, and then altering the records to substitute the names on the grants with the names of newly hired executives;
- granting options in compensation for fictitious "part-time" work performed by newly hired executives purportedly done after they were offered employment, but before they actually commenced working for the corporation.

The practice of back-dating appears to have been going on for some time, but only recently came to light due to changes in the manner of reporting the grant of options. Until the *Sarbanes Oxley Act of 2002* came into effect, the SEC's did not require public disclosure of option grants until 45 days after the company's fiscal year-end. Since August, 2002, such grants have been required to be disclosed within two days — a time limit that has greatly reduced the possibility for back-dating.

§7.248 The practice is inherently deceptive, because it involves the manufacture of events that never took place, such as concocting minutes for a board meeting that never occurred. When back-dating is employed, the effect is to reposition the timing of the grant of the stock option to a time when the company's stock was trading at a lower market price. The result is to create an immediate gain that can instantly be realized by exercising the option and then selling the stock purchased under it. Since the purpose of a stock option is to align executive compensation (and thus their interests) with those of shareholders, back-dating is counter-productive. It is also deceptive. It gives the appearance that executives have incentive compensation, but in fact the back-dating often constitutes little more than a gift.

§7.248.1 With certain limits, backdating is legal (though certainly controversial) if properly accounted for and disclosed. However, back-dating is illegal if it is not disclosed or if taxes are evaded. Back-dating may also violate the terms of a company's equity compensation plan. Regardless of whether back-dating was intentional or inadvertent, financial statements must be adjusted to reflect compensation expense resulting from the difference between the stock price on the measurement date and the option's exercise date. If the impact of a misstatement is material the company will be required to restate its financial statements. The SEC takes the view that misstatements that increase management compensation may be material even though they involve a "quantitatively small misstatement".

§7.248.2 The SEC is currently probing dozens of companies concerning the back-dating of stock options to employees as compensation. One of the most high profile cases involves Apple, Inc., which recently announced $84 million in restated revenue owing to back-dating irregularities. However, it is believed that hundreds of companies have actually participated in back-dating arrangements. In the first successful prosecution by the SEC, former Take Two Interactive CEO and chairman Ryan Brant pled guilty to charges that he back-dated stock option grants to increase their value to himself, other company executives and employees. The scheme created an off-the-books windfall of millions of dollars for himself, none of which was recorded as compensation. He was sentenced to a fine of $7.26 million and serve five years' probation.

§7.248.3 It is unclear whether the practice of back-dating has been as widely followed in Canada as in the United States. The reason for the difference between Canada and the United States appears to be more the result of the lesser opportunity afforded by Canadian insider trading rules, in comparison to those which formerly applied in the United States. Since the TSX requires option grants to be reported to the TSX within 10 days of the end of the month in which the grant was made, there is little opportunity to back-date to a significant extent. Nevertheless, in a September, 2006, the Canadian Securities Administrators advised as follows with respect to the question of back-dating:

> The board of directors of an issuer is responsible for ensuring that the issuer prices options appropriately and discloses them properly. The following guidance may reduce concerns about the timing of option grants and the risk of non-compliance with securities legislation:
>
> - establish a compensation committee that follows the guidance contained in National Policy 58-201 — Corporate Governance Guidelines;
>
> - consider the guidance in National Policy 51-201 — Disclosure Standards including adopting a corporate disclosure policy, adopting an insider trading policy, and establishing "blackout periods" around earnings announcements; and
>
> - ensure that, following a grant of options to insiders, the issuer provides them with details of their grants so that they can comply with their legal obligation to file insider reports on SEDI within 10 days.
>
> CSA staff recommend that all issuers assess current policies, procedures and controls for option grants and equity-based awards to ensure that they comply with relevant stock exchange rules and securities legislation. If CSA staff become aware, through disclosure reviews, tips, or otherwise, of abuses by reporting issuers, they may take enforcement action against the issuers or their directors and officers. In considering the appropriate course of action, CSA staff may take into account what steps, if any, such issuers took to ensure their policies and controls complied with regulatory requirements.

(iii) Sinking Funds

§7.249 Capital investments in a corporation which are made for a fixed period of time, such as term shares or bonds, often contain a requirement under which the corporation is required to redeem or repurchase a stated percentage or amount of those instruments over a period of time prior to the final expiration of the term. Such a requirement is known as a sinking fund. There are several basic objectives behind the inclusion of a sinking fund provision, including:

- the continuous reduction that it leads to in the outstanding redemption obligation of the corporation provides a measure of increased safety to the holders of the securities concerned;
- by providing for the redemption of the securities over time, the corporation is afforded a degree of cash flow relief;
- the periodic repurchase of the securities by the corporation for the purposes of the sinking fund stabilizes their value within the market and creates some form of secondary market — albeit a very limited one — for the securities concerned;
- where the corporation's requirements for the funds obtained through the issue of the securities will decline over time, the sinking fund will allow the corporation to repay the unnecessary portion of those funds, and thereby reduce the cost of financing its operations;
- by reducing the outstanding number of securities, there is some enhancement of the ability of the corporation to meet its interest or dividend payment obligations.

Usually a sinking fund provision will not take effect during the first few years that a security is outstanding. Once it does become operative, the mechanics of the sinking fund are essentially governed by the terms of the contract under which the sinking fund is created. However, there are two basic types of sinking fund and nearly all sinking funds operate under one or other of these two approaches. Under the first, the corporation is required to set aside annually or at specified dates a stipulated sum sufficient to redeem a percentage of the securities concerned. Under the second, the corporation is required to set aside a stipulated percentage of its net annual income for the purposes of the sinking fund. Quite often the sinking fund obligations will be made cumulative, so that if a sinking fund redemption is not made in one year (as, for instance, where to do so would contravene some legal restriction), the obligation to perform that obligation is carried forward to the next year in which it is possible for the obligation to be discharged.

§7.250 In *Re Sapphire Petroleums Ltd.*,[552] certain debentures to which a sinking fund requirement applied also carried a conversion privilege under which the holder of such a debenture was entitled to convert the debenture into common shares in the company, which might be exercised either before or after the debenture was called for redemption. The trust deed provided that the company was required to make payments to a trustee each year for the purposes of the sinking fund. The sinking fund provision stated that the company might either

---

[552] [1956] O.J. No. 551, [1956] O.R. 581 (C.A.).

purchase or redeem the debentures or that the trustee might purchase or redeem them through the sinking fund. Any debentures purchased or redeemed by the company itself were to be credited to the principal reduction requirement under the sinking fund. A number of the debenture holders elected to exercise the conversion privilege. The company sought a declaration as to whether it was entitled to have the principal amount of the debentures so converted credited against the sinking fund requirement. It was held that the company was not entitled to do so. It was held that the conversion of debentures into shares was not a redemption within the meaning of the sinking fund provisions.[553]

(iv) Pre-emptive Rights

§7.251 The most common right or option existing with respect to the shares of a corporation (and less frequently, with respect to other types of securities) is a pre-emptive right held by the holder of an existing share or security. A right of pre-emption is a right to purchase property before or in preference to another person. Section 26 of the OBCA provides that if it is so provided in the articles or a unanimous shareholder agreement, no shares of a class or series shall be issued unless the shares have first been offered to the shareholders of the corporation holding shares of that class or series or of another class or series on such terms as are provided in the articles or unanimous shareholder agreement.[554] While subsection 28(1) of the CBCA is to a similar effect, subsection 28(2) goes on to provide that shareholders can have no pre-emptive right in respect of shares to be issued:

(*a*) for a consideration other than money;

(*b*) as a share dividend; or

(*c*) pursuant to the exercise of conversion privileges, options or rights previously granted by the corporation.

The OBCA contains no corresponding limitation. The directors of a corporation cannot give a third party a right of first refusal to purchase the shares of a shareholder. That right can only be given by the shareholder concerned, or under the terms of the articles of the corporation setting out the terms of the shares concerned.[555]

§7.252 In practical terms, a pre-emptive right affords current shareholders a right of first refusal where new shares are issued by a corporation, so that their existing participatory interest and voting right and share of dividends will not be diluted without their consent. Each shareholder may acquire a proportionate share of any new shares proposed to be issued by a corporation, the extent of that right being determined by reference to the shareholder's existing share-

---

[553] *Ibid., per* Pickup C.J.O. at 587-88.
[554] There is no presumption that the shareholders of a corporation are entitled to a pre-emptive right: *Mutual Life Insurance Co. of New York v. Rank Organization Ltd.*, [1985] B.C.L.C. 11.
[555] *Colborne Capital Corp. v. 542775 Alberta Ltd.*, [1995] A.J. No. 538, 22 B.L.R. (2d) 226 at 275 (Q.B.), *per* Virtue J.

holding.[556] In many jurisdictions, a statutory preemptive right is conferred on shareholders, but while some jurisdictions afford this right only in the case of publicly traded corporations, others afford it only with respect to private companies. As indicated above, the OBCA and CBCA permit but do not require pre-emptive rights, and thus in the absence of a provision in the articles of a corporation affording such a right, the matter will be decided by the common law. There is no common law pre-emptive right in favour of a shareholder. At common law, a company was free to issue its shares to whomever it might choose, and if the effect of a particular issue was that a shareholder might discover his or her interest reduced from, say, a one-third interest to a small minority interest, there was nothing that could be done.

§7.253 In *Fedsure International v. NSP Financial Services Group*,[557] the shareholders in NSP were bound by a pre-emptive rights arrangement which required each shareholder to offer its shares to the other shareholders, accompanied by a proposed sale price. The other shareholders had 30 days from receipt of the offer to exercise their rights. Clause 14 of the agreement provided for the situation where there was a change in the control of a corporate shareholder, it was deemed to have made an offer to sell its shares to the other shareholders on the day before control of the corporate shareholder changed. Clause 14 also authorized the company's auditors to determine the price at which the shares were to be offered to the remaining shareholders. One shareholder, Fedsure, underwent a change of control on June 5th. A few days before and after the change of control, NSP communicated that fact to its shareholders and to its auditors. The auditors were asked to value Fedsure's share interest. It took two months for the auditors to produce a valuation. A month later, the remaining shareholders indicated their acceptance of the deemed offer under the pre-emption agreement.

§7.254 Fedsure argued that the offer had lapsed, since the 30 days for acceptance had started to run on June 4th (*i.e.*, the day before its change of control). Since the remaining shareholders had not notified their acceptance of the deemed offer until September, their acceptances were too late. The remaining shareholders argued that the requirement that an offer to remaining shareholders had to be accompanied by an offer price, and that there was no such price until the valuation was received. The court rejected this argument, giving the wording of the pre-emptive right a strict reading, focusing in particular on the use of the past tense in clause 14 (specifically, the words "deemed to have made an offer"). These it construed to mean the deemed offer was made on the day before the change of control. In answer to the complaint that this interpretation of the agreement would lead to strange results, the court commented that deeming provisions often run contrary to reality.

---

[556] See, generally, *Wing v. Woodstock Ltd.*, 56 Sol. J. 412 (1912).
[557] [2001] N.S.W.S.C. 910.

I. TRAFFICKING, REDUCTION IN CAPITAL, AND RELATED QUESTIONS

§7.255 A corporation traffics in its shares where it provides an incentive to a potential investor (in order to procure his or her subscription for its shares) in such a way or on such terms that the subscriber is released from the financial hazard normally inherent in an investment in share capital. The share investment becomes, for all practical purposes, a sham — although it matters not whether there was any improper motive underlying the giving of the incentive. At common law, a company was prohibited from trafficking in its own shares,[558] whether directly or indirectly.[559] It could not sell shares under a "buy back" contract whereby the shareholder is, in effect, guaranteed against loss, and put on a parity with creditors in a winding-up, as this was seen as breaching the understanding on which the shareholder was granted an exemption from personal liability for the debts of the company.[560] Thus the rule grew out of the fundamental concern of the courts with respect to maintaining the integrity of the corporate capital base.[561] Akin to the prohibition against trafficking in shares was the common law prohibition against a corporation owning shares in itself, for if the object of the acquisition was to sell the shares again, that was trafficking in the shares; if the object was to retain them, that was an indirect method of reducing share capital.[562]

§7.256 Although these rules have now been modified by statute,[563] they remain an undercurrent to the present legislation: the stated capital of a corporation rep-

---

[558] *Hope v. International Financial Society* (1876), 4 Ch. D. 327 (C.A.); *Stavert v. McMillan*, [1911] O.J. No. 87, 24 O.L.R. 456 (C.A.).

[559] *James v. Eve* (1873), L.R. 6 H.L. 335, where Lord Chelmsford held (at 344) that a corporation could not impair its capital base by repayment to its shareholders by an indirect method. See also the judgment of Lord Cairns at 350-51.

[560] *Hamer v. National Forest Products Ltd.* (1964), 47 W.W.R. 375 at 378 (B.C.S.C.), *per* Wilson C.J.S.

[561] *Trevor v. Whitworth* (1882), 12 App. Cas. 409 at 423-24 (H.L.) *per* Lord Watson; *McInnis v. Tignish Fisheries Ltd.* (1961), 30 D.L.R. (2d) 749 (P.E.I.S.C.); *Common v. McArthur* (1898), 29 S.C.R. 239 at 245, *per* Sedgewick J. The judgment of Riddell J.A. in *Hughes v. Northern Electric & Manufacturing Co.*, [1914] O.J. No. 29, 31 O.L.R. 221 (C.A.), rev'd 50 S.C.R. 626, provides a concise explanation of the rule forbidding a company from buying its own shares, either in its own name or in that of a trustee (at 254). As to the scope of the rule, see, for instance, *British & American Trustee & Finance Corp. v. Couper*, [1894] A.C. 399 at 399 (H.L.), *per* Lord Herschell L.C.; *Re Galpin, ex p. Chowilla Timber Supply Co.*, [1967] 11 F.L.R. 155; but *cf. Kirby v. Wilkins*, [1929] 2 Ch. 444, *per* Romer J.; *Shymka v. Smokey Lake United Farmers Co.* (1922), 66 D.L.R. 729 at 731 (Alta. S.C.), *per* Tweedie J.; *Bellerby v. Rowland & Marwood's Steamship Co.*, [1902] 2 Ch. 14 (C.A.); *Guinness v. Land Corp. of Ireland* (1882), 22 Ch. D. 349 at 375, *per* Cotton L.J.; *Re London, Hamburg and Continental Exchange Bank (Evan's Case)* (1867), L.R. 2 Ch. 427; *Helwig v. Siemon*, [1916] O.J. No. 609, 10 O.W.N. 296 (C.A.), but *cf. Hughes v. Northern Electric Mfg. Co.* (1913), 50 S.C.R. 626; *Hart v. Felsen* (1924), 30 R.L. 109; *Ross v. Fleet* (1882), 8 Q.L.R. 251; *Cree v. Somervail* (1879), 4 App. Cas. 648 (H.L.); *Re Stadacona-Rouyn Mines Ltd.*, [1942] Que. S.C. 275.

[562] *Prairie Realty Ltd. v. J.M. Sinclair Co.*, [1967] S.J. No. 79, 63 D.L.R. (2d) 555 at 557 (Q.B.), *per* Tucker J.

[563] For a discussion of the related rules governing financial assistance, see Chapter 4 ot the First Edition of this text.

resents the equity investment made by the shareholders in the corporation. If a corporation were permitted to hold shares, so that they continued to be shown on its balance sheet as a shareholder investment, it would obviously take very little effort to mislead creditors as to the capital strength of the corporation — the corporation could issue shares, subsequently repurchase them from the shareholders, and still show the subscription price of those shares as an investment in itself, even though that amount had been repaid at the time of the repurchase of the shares by the corporation.

§7.257 To prevent such abuses from occurring, the general rule is that a corporation may hold shares neither in itself nor in its holding body corporate,[564] nor may any corporation permit any of its subsidiaries to hold shares in the corporation.[565] Where a corporate body becomes a subsidiary of a corporation and holds shares in the corporation at the time when it becomes a subsidiary, the corporation must cause the subsidiary to sell or otherwise dispose of the shares within five years from the date on which it became a subsidiary.[566] It follows from this requirement that, although improper, the acquisition by a corporation of shares in its holding corporation does not affect the validity of those shares. If the subsidiary is subsequently sold, or if the subsidiary subsequently sells the shares to a third party, the purchase of those shares by the subsidiary may no longer be set aside and the restrictions imposed with respect to those shares no longer apply.[567]

§7.258 The general prohibition against a corporation holding shares in itself or in its parent corporation in subsection 29(1) of the OBCA does not prevent a corporation from holding shares in itself or in a holding corporate body in the capacity of a legal representative, provided neither the corporation nor the holding corporate body, nor a subsidiary of either of them has a beneficial interest in the shares. Similarly, under the OBCA (but not the CBCA), a corporation may permit a subsidiary to hold shares in the corporation in the capacity of a legal representative, unless the corporation or the subsidiary corporate body or a subsidiary of either of them has a beneficial interest in the shares.[568]

§7.259 The restrictions on inter-corporate shareholding under the current CBCA (as amended in 2001) resemble those applicable to OBCA corporation. Subsection 30(2) of the CBCA sets down the general rule that a corporation must cause a subsidiary to sell shares within the same five year period as applies under the OBCA. However, this general rule is subject to the following exceptions set out in section 31 of the CBCA. Subsection 31(3) provides that:

---

[564] Subsection 1(3) of the OBCA provides:

    1.(3) For the purposes of this Act, a body corporate shall be deemed to be another's holding body corporate if, but only if, that other is its subsidiary.

Compare CBCA, s. 2(3), (4) and (5).

[565] OBCA s. 28(1); CBCA, s. 30(1).
[566] OBCA, s. 28(2); CBCA, s. 30(2).
[567] *Prairie Realty Ltd. v. J.M. Sinclair Co.*, [1967] S.J. No. 79, 63 D.L.R. (2d) 555 at 557 (Q.B.), *per* Tucker J.
[568] OBCA, s. 29(2); CBCA, s. 31(3).

31.(3) A corporation may permit any of its subsidiary bodies corporate to acquire shares of the corporation,

(a) in the subsidiary's capacity as a legal representative, unless the subsidiary would have a beneficial interest in the shares; or

(b) by way of security for the purposes of a transaction entered into by the subsidiary in the ordinary course of a business that includes the lending of money.

Subsection 31(4) continues by allowing further permissible inter-corporate shareholdings to be authorized by regulation. It provides:

31.(4) A corporation may permit any of its subsidiary bodies corporate to acquire shares of the corporation through the issuance of those shares by the corporation to the subsidiary body corporate if, before the acquisition takes place, the conditions prescribed for the purposes of this subsection are met.

To prevent the circumvention of the restrictions set out in the Act by orchestrating arrangements so that the prescribed conditions are met before the shares are acquired under subsection (4), but not afterwards, subsection 31(5) provides:

31.(5) After an acquisition has taken place under the purported authority of subsection (4), the conditions prescribed for the purposes of this subsection must be met.

§7.260 There is one important exception to the beneficial interest exclusion described in subsection 29(1) of the OBCA[569] and the corresponding provision of the CBCA.[570] A corporation may hold shares in itself or in its holding body corporate by way of security for the purpose of a transaction entered into in the ordinary course of business that includes the lending of money.[571] Although it would appear that the corporation may not take and hold shares in itself in respect of any business other than the lending of money, the Act does contemplate the exercise by the corporation of a lien right over its shares. Such a right normally entitles the corporation to seize the shareholder's interest in shares and to sell those shares anew to some new investor, applying the proceeds to any debt owed to the corporation.[572]

---

[569] OBCA, s. 29(3).
[570] CBCA s. 31(2).
[571] See, for instance, *British American Timber Co. v. Jones*, [1943] B.C.J. No. 43, [1943] 2 W.W.R. 654 at 663 (S.C.), per Bird J. var'd on other grounds [1944] 2 D.L.R. 481 (C.A.). See also *Warren v. People's Finance Corp.* (1961), 36 W.W.R. 627 (Man. C.A.). Compare, however, a power of forfeiture for debts owing: *Mortimer v. Harley & Co.*, [1917] 1 Ch. 646. It is one thing for the shareholder and corporation to agree that the corporation shall have a right to seize and sell the shareholder's interests in the shares (applying the proceeds obtained from the purchaser to the reduction of the balance owing). Such a procedure enhances the corporation's prospect of recovering the amount owing. It is quite another thing to enter into an arrangement under which the equity interest of the shareholder is effectively set off against a debt due to the corporation. The shareholder's interest in the corporation as a shareholder is not the equivalent of an offsetting debt. The effect of a set-off achieved through forfeiture is to raise the status of the shareholder to the level of a creditor.
[572] See, generally, *Bank of Africa v. Salisbury Gold Mining Co.*, [1892] A.C. 281.

§7.261 Subsection 29(4) of the OBCA provides that for the purpose of assisting the corporation or any of its affiliates or associates to qualify under any prescribed Act of Canada or a province or ordinance of a territory to receive licences, permits, grants, payments, or other benefits by reason of attaining or maintaining a specified level of Canadian ownership or control, hold shares in itself that,

(a) are not restricted for the purpose of assisting the corporation or any of its affiliates or associates to so qualify; or

(b) are shares into which shares under clause (a) were converted by the corporation that are restricted for the purpose of assisting the corporation to so qualify and that were not previously held by the corporation.

Subsection 29(5) goes on to provide that a corporation may not transfer shares held under subsection (4) to any person unless the corporation is satisfied on reasonable grounds that the ownership of the shares as a result of the transfer would assist the corporation or any of its affiliates or associates to achieve the purpose set out in subsection (4). Subsections 32(1) and (2) of the CBCA are to like effect.

§7.262 Subsection 29(8) of the OBCA provides that a corporation holding shares in itself or in its holding body corporate, or a subsidiary body corporate of a corporation holding shares of the corporation, shall not vote or permit those shares to be voted unless the corporation or subsidiary body corporate, as the case may be, holds the shares in the capacity of a legal representative, and has complied with section 49 of the *Securities Act*[573] (which, in essence, requires the legal representative to notify the beneficial owner of the vote to be taken and to vote in accordance with the written instructions given by the beneficial owner). Section 33 of the CBCA is similar but makes no express reference to "a subsidiary body corporate of a corporation holding shares of the corporation".[574] It provides that a corporation holding shares in itself or in its holding body corporate shall not vote or permit those shares to be voted, unless the corporation holds those shares as a legal representative and has complied with section 153 (which is a provision comparable to section 48 of the *Securities Act*).

(i) Redemption and Retraction

§7.263 In some cases, a corporation may wish to issue a time-limited share, that may be called in at some future point; in others, investors may demand a right to require the corporation to repay their investment at a future date as a condition of agreeing to invest in the share capital. Shares which provide such rights are said to be redeemable or retractable (the two terms being largely interchangeable, despite the heroic efforts of some writers to draw a distinction between them). Redeemable shares are a popular method of venture capital financing,

---

[573] R.S.O. 1990, c. S.5.
[574] Given the scope of the definition of subsidiary, it is not clear how these words expand the scope of the prohibition set out in the OBCA.

and are also frequently encountered in estate freeze transactions in the case of private corporations. Both Acts deal with purchases in respect of share redemptions separately from other purchases of shares by a corporation. Subsection 32(1) of the OBCA provides:

> 32.(1) Despite subsection 30(2) and subsection 31(3), but subject to subsection (2) and to its articles, a corporation may purchase or redeem any redeemable shares issued by it at prices not exceeding the redemption price thereof stated in the articles or calculated according to a formula stated in the articles.

However, subsection 32(2) goes on to qualify this general authority by imposing solvency and liquidity tests that must be satisfied before a redemption may be made:

> 32.(2) A corporation shall not make any payment to purchase or redeem any redeemable shares issued by it if there are reasonable grounds for believing that,
>
> (a) the corporation is or, after the payment, would be unable to pay its liabilities as they become due; or
>
> (b) after the payment, the realizable value of the corporation's assets would be less than the aggregate of,
>
>   (i) its liabilities, and
>
>   (ii) the amount that would be required to pay the holders of shares who have a right to be paid, on a redemption or in a liquidation, rateably with or prior to the holders of the shares to be purchased or redeemed.

The purpose of these and related provisions is to prevent any shareholder(s) in a corporation from recouping their investment to the detriment of creditors and other shareholders.[575]

§7.264 Since the shares of a corporation do not constitute debt obligations, no action in debt can normally be brought to enforce an obligation to redeem those shares. However, declarative relief may be available.[576] Similarly in a suitable case, an oppression action may lie, and a failure to redeem may be sufficient to justify the winding-up of the corporation. In addition, as discussed below, recent amendments to the CBCA now suggest an obligation to repurchase shares. Nevertheless, since the courts are reluctant to require the directors of a corporation to pay dividends even where the wording of shares suggests an obligation to do so, and since a redemption is essentially no more than an alternative form of distribution to shareholders, the holder of a redeemable share who has the right to demand that the corporation redeem his or her shares in accordance with their terms, faces an up-hill fight should the corporation refuse to do so. In *Re*

---

[575] *Nelson v. Rentown Enterprises Inc.*, [1992] A.J. No. 917, 96 D.L.R. (4th) 586 at 589 (Q.B.), aff'd [1994] A.J. No. 127 (C.A.); *Unisource Canada Inc. (c.o.b. Barber-Ellis Fine Papers) v. Hong Kong Bank of Canada*, [1998] O.J. No. 5586 (Gen. Div.), aff'd [2000] O.J. No. 947 (C.A.).

[576] See, for instance, *Shahinian v. Precinda Inc.*, [2004] O.J. No. 476, 128 A.C.W.S. (3d) 1115 (C.A.).

Cavendish Investing Ltd.[577] a shareholder sought to have the corporation wound up on the grounds that shares were not retracted by it in accordance with their terms. It was held that although the court will consider the terms of a unanimous shareholder agreement providing such a right, the court's decision as to whether to order a winding-up in such a case remains discretionary.[578] There may be factors which justify the court in declining to order liquidation. To circumvent this problem, it may be considered wise to insert an express right to apply for the winding-up of the corporation, in a unanimous shareholder agreement since subclause 207(1)(*b*)(i) of the OBCA provides expressly that the court may order the winding-up of a corporation where:

(i) a unanimous shareholder agreement entitled a complaining shareholder to demand dissolution of the corporation after the occurrence of a specified event and that event has occurred ...

As the *Cavendish* case indicates, if the right to apply for a winding-up of the corporation is only set out in the share terms, then it will be necessary to satisfy the court that the failure to comply with the redemption requirement was oppressive or unfairly prejudicial or was in unfair disregard of the shareholder's rights, or that it is just and equitable that the corporation should be wound up. However, even where there is such a unanimous shareholder agreement, it does not automatically follow that a winding-up order will be made by the court in the event that shares are not redeemed at the time specified. The decision as to whether to order the liquidation of the corporation remains discretionary under section 207 of the OBCA. While the court will give due weight to any such contractual arrangement, it will not be treated as conclusive. The discretionary, equitable nature of a court-supervised winding-up, means that conduct of the shareholder in seeking such an order must meet the normal standards applicable to the granting of equitable relief. Due attention must also be given to the rights of other persons interested in the corporation, particularly where they did not have the opportunity to approve the terms of the shares or agreement.

§7.265 In *Su v. Canada Eighty-Eight Fund Ltd.*[579] the plaintiff, Su, was a member of the Canada 88 fund, holding one Class A voting share and 250 preferred shares in its capital. Each holder of a preferred share was entitled to require Canada 88 to redeem the preferred shares at a minimum price of $1,000 per share, that obligation being made expressly "subject to the availability of funds". Under the terms of the redemption right, a holder was required to give 90 days' notice of his or her intention to redeem, and the corporation was required to redeem the shares of the holder concerned at the end of that 90-day period. Su gave notice in accordance with the share terms, but his shares were not redeemed because other shareholders had also given notice and there were insufficient funds on hand for the corporation to meet all of their claims (the assets of Canada 88 being illiquid). Su was the first shareholder to institute an action to recover the amount owing. As there were sufficient funds available to pay his

---

[577] [1996] A.J. No. 743, 42 Alta. L.R. (3d) 345 (Q.B.).
[578] *Ibid.*, *per* McMahon J. at 353.
[579] [1996] B.C.J. No. 599, 28 B.L.R. (2d) 116 (S.C.).

claim (although insufficient to pay all of the relevant preferred shares), he moved for summary judgment. The reasons advanced by Shabbit J. in rejecting this motion were instructive as to the nature of the rights of the holder of a preferred share, and the obligation of a corporation that issues such shares to consider all shareholders who hold those shares when performing its redemption obligations:

> The plaintiff is confusing his right of action with the enforcement of that right. The obligation of the defendant company to holders of preferred shares to redeem those shares is an obligation owed to all the holders of preferred shares entitled to such redemption. A condition precedent to the right of redemption was the availability of funds. ... I accept the submissions advanced on behalf of the defendant company that the defendant company's obligation to redeem shares was limited to an obligation to make use of funds on hand, or to make use of funds available without undue loss. ... The plaintiff is not a creditor of the defendant company, but a shareholder and member of the defendant company. His rights in respect of the defendant company are not yet a claim in debt. Even if the defendant company did not redeem shares which it ought to have redeemed, the relief to which the plaintiff is entitled is not a judgment for a liquidated sum.[580]

Thus in contrast to a claim in debt where (subject to legislation such as the *Creditors' Relief Act*)[581] the race is generally to the swiftest, in the case of redeemable shares, both the corporation and, it would appear, the court are required to give consideration to the rights of other shareholders of the same class,[582] at least to the extent that there are reasonable grounds to believe that those other shareholders may wish to redeem their shares as well.

§7.266 Whatever relief may be available with respect to the breach of a redemption or retraction requirement, the onus lies on the party seeking to enforce right in question to establish that all conditions governing the right of redemption or retraction have been satisfied. Such rights are interpreted in accordance with the ordinary rules governing the construction of contracts — in particular, generally. courts will give effect to the ordinary meaning and plain reading of the agreement into which the parties have entered.[583] For instance, in *Shahinian v. Precinda Inc.*[584] the Ontario Court of Appeal considered an appeal by a company from decision in which declared that it was obliged to redeem respondent's shares immediately in accordance with a redemption obligation set out in the Articles of Amalgamation of the company. The respondent had acquired his preference shares in a restructuring of the business affairs of the company. The Amalgamation Agreement provided that the redemption rights of Class X preference shareholders were unconditional, requiring only thirty days notice to the company, but in a separate Shareholders' Agreement, the respondent had agreed

---

[580] *Ibid.*, at 119-20.
[581] R.S.O 1990, c. C.45.
[582] This being a further illustration of the general principle that all shareholders of a class must receive equal treatment.
[583] *Kentucky Fried Chicken Canada, a Division of Pepsi-Cola Canada Ltd. v. Scott's Food Services Inc.*, [1998] O.J. No. 4368 at para. 25, 114 O.A.C. 357.
[584] [2004] O.J. No. 476, 128 A.C.W.S. (3d) 1115 (C.A.).

that the company would not be required to redeem Class X preference shares except in three specified circumstances. The second of these exceptions was the failure of the appellant to remedy a default in the payment of dividends on Class X preference shares. The company went into default in the payment of dividends on the Class X shares on September 30, 2002 (although it had sufficient funds to make the payment), because it was concerned that the respondent was acting in breach of confidentiality and non-competition obligations owed to the appellant company. At trial, Blair J. found that there was no evidence of any such breaches and that the non-payment of the dividends met the requirements of the second exception permitting redemption of the respondent's shares. His declaration that the respondent was entitled to immediate redemption of all his Class X preference shares was upheld on appeal. The Court of Appeal refused to accept that the plain meaning of the relevant documents should be over-looked.

(ii) Purchase by a Corporation of Its Shares

§7.267 While a corporation may not ordinarily hold shares in itself, both the OBCA and the CBCA give a general right to a corporation to purchase its own shares and warrants, subject to general solvency restrictions set out in the legislation and to any provision in the articles.[585] The solvency and liquidity restrictions are intended to protect creditors and other stakeholders from a reduction in share capital where the corporation is likely to be unable to meet its obligations in full on a timely basis.[586] Despite the language used in expressing this statutory power to purchase, where such a purchase is made it is unrealistic to characterize the transaction as a sale in economic terms. The corporation does pay a sum of money to the shareholder whose shares are purchased, but it receives no equivalent or comparable consideration in return. The repurchase of the share constitutes no more than a way of distributing assets of the corporation to a shareholder.[587] The solvency and liquidity restrictions on such purchases are broad enough to cover non-monetary forms of payment.[588]

§7.268 Except as provided under the OBCA and the CBCA, as the case may be, a corporation has no other power to purchase its own shares.[589] Generally speaking, under both of these Acts the right to repurchase capital is given to permit the corporation to perform redemption obligations, exercise rights of retraction and to satisfy dissident shareholders who withdraw from the corporation. The potential stated capital problems alluded to above are avoided by effectively removing repurchased capital from the corporation's balance sheet. Nevertheless, such reductions present clear risks to creditors. For instance, a

---

[585] OBCA, s. 30(1); CBCA, 34(1).
[586] *Nelson v. Rentown Enterprises Inc.*, [1992] A.J. No. 917, 96 D.L.R. (4th) 586 (Q.B.), aff'd [1994] A.J. No. 127, 109 D.L.R. (4th) 608 (C.A.); see also *Greenwood v. Dockeray* (1993), 41 A.C.W.S. (3d) 78 (Ont. Gen. Div.).
[587] *Robinson v. Wangemann*, 75 F.2d 756 at 757 (5th Cir. 1935), *per* Foster Cir. J.
[588] *Nelson v. Rentown Enterprises Inc.*, [1992] A.J. No. 917, 96 D.L.R. (14th) 586 (Q.B.), aff'd [1994] A.J. No. 127, 109 D.L.R. (4th) 608 (C.A.).
[589] *Helwig v. Siemon*, [1916] O.J. No. 609, 10 O.W.N. 296 (C.A.); *Colonial Assurance Co. v. Smith* (1913), 4 W.W.R. 295 (Man. K.B.).

creditor may lend to a corporation on the assumption that it has a given level of capital, and a certain debt-to-equity ratio, only to find that the level of capital has been reduced and that the debt-equity ratio has been increased. To prevent this from happening, it is necessary for creditors to secure a negative covenant from the corporation not to redeem its capital below a fixed amount or to allow its debt-equity ratio to exceed a specified level.

(1) Repurchase

§7.269 From time to time, corporations may wish to purchase shares that they have issued in the past either in the market or by way of private contract. The reasons for such purchases vary. Tax considerations may sometimes be relevant to the decision as to whether to purchase shares.[590] Occasionally, a corporation will have more cash on hand than it can profitably employ. In such a situation, retirement of share capital may provide a way of distributing that surplus cash back to the shareholders of the corporation. Offering corporations may often find it attractive to eliminate small share holdings, since the costs of printing and mailing annual reports, information circulars and notices to small shareholders are the same as for larger shareholders. Private corporations may wish to buy out the interest of a retiring shareholder.

§7.270 In some jurisdictions, different rules govern market and off-market purchases. Under the OBCA and the CBCA, only one set of rules apply. The primary restriction on the purchase of shares by a corporation is that a corporation may not, as a general rule, make any payment to purchase or otherwise acquire shares issued by it if there are reasonable grounds for believing that,[591]

(a) the corporation is or, after the payment, would be unable to pay its liabilities as they become due; or

(b) after the payment, the realizable value of the corporation's assets would be less than the aggregate of,

  (i) its liabilities, and

  (ii) its stated capital of all classes.

The words "realizable value of the corporation's assets" are significant because they suggest that the right to purchase is not dependent upon the profit history of the corporation. Where there has been a substantial appreciation in the realizable value of the assets of a corporation, it appears that the corporation may purchase shares in reliance upon that appreciation, irrespective of whether it has earned sufficient profits to allow it to fund the purchase.

§7.271 Subclause 30(2)(*b*)(ii) of the OBCA is of particularly wide import, because it prohibits the purchase of shares even where the shares that are being

---

[590] In the United States during the mid-1970s, there were tax advantages to the purchase of shares, as an alternative to the payment of a dividend. At that time, the total amount of share purchase was approximately equal to one-fifth the total amount of dividend payment in the United States.

[591] OBCA, s. 30(2); s. 34(2) of the CBCA is to like effect.

purchased are payable in priority to other shares of the corporation. However, in certain cases a looser restriction applies. In particular, a corporation may purchase or acquire shares issued by it to[592]

(a) settle or compromise a debt or claim asserted by or against the corporation;[593]

(b) eliminate fractional shares; or

(c) fulfill the terms of a non-assignable agreement under which the corporation has an option or is obliged to purchase shares owned by a current or former director, officer or employee of the corporation,

unless there are reasonable grounds for believing that,

(a) the corporation is or, after the payment, would be unable to pay its liabilities as they become due; or

(b) after the payment, the realizable value of the corporation's assets would be less than the aggregate of,

(i) its liabilities, and

(ii) the amount that would be required to pay the holders of shares who have a right to be paid, on a redemption or in a liquidation, prior to the holders of the shares to be purchased or acquired.

The important distinction between the first of these rights of repurchase and the second is that under the second, the exercise of the right is not barred under subclause 30(2)(b)(ii) if there are insufficient assets to repay the stated capital of all classes, but only where there are insufficient assets to repay the holders of those shares who have a right to be paid prior to the holders of the shares to be purchased.

§7.272 In addition to the foregoing, subsection 31(2) of the OBCA[594] permits a corporation to purchase or otherwise acquire shares issued by it to satisfy the claim of a dissenting shareholder,[595] or to comply with an order of the court made by the court on an application in respect of oppressive conduct by the corporation.[596] The power to purchase or otherwise acquire shares under this section is not subject to the solvency tests set out in either subsection 30(2) or 31(3) of the OBCA. However, the repurchase or other acquisition of shares in such cases are subject to somewhat looser solvency and liquidity restrictions that are imposed under subsections 185(3) and 248(6). In particular, subsection 185(30) provides:

> 185.(30) A corporation shall not make a payment to a dissenting shareholder under this section if there are reasonable grounds for believing that,

---

[592] OBCA, s. 31(1), (3); CBCA, s. 35(1).
[593] At common law this power existed but only where the purchaser did not effect a reduction in the assets of the corporation: *British Columbia Red Cedar Shingle Co. v. Stoltze Manufacturing Co.*, [1932] B.C.J. No 84, [1932] 1 W.W.R. 164 (C.A.); *Patterson v. Vulcan Iron Works*, [1930] B.C.J. No 16, [1930] 1 W.W.R. 640 at 640 (C.A.), per Martin J.A.
[594] Subsection 35(2) of the CBCA is to like effect.
[595] See, generally, OBCA, s. 185, and Chapter 13, Shareholder Remedies.
[596] See, generally, OBCA, s. 248, and Chapter 13, Shareholder Remedies.

(*a*) the corporation is or, after the payment, would be unable to pay its liabilities as they become due; or

(*b*) the realizable value of the corporation's assets would thereby be less than the aggregate of its liabilities.

Subsection 248(6) is substantially the same. The significant difference between these provisions and the solvency and liquidity tests discussed above is that subsections 185(30) and 248(6) make no reference to the ability of the corporation to repay share capital, and therefore, provided all liabilities can be paid punctually and in full, the repurchase must proceed.

§7.273 In *Nelson v. Rentown Enterprises Inc.*[597] the court was required to decide whether section 34 of the CBCA prohibited a corporation from performing an agreement to purchase its own shares. At the time when the agreement was made, the corporation satisfied both the solvency and liquidity tests imposed under that section. However, by the date specified for the performance of the purchase obligation, it no longer satisfied those tests. Justice Hunt (whose reasons were adopted by the Alberta Court of Appeal) held that it was not sufficient for the solvency and liquidity tests imposed under section 34(2) to be satisfied at the date of the agreement; they also had to be satisfied at the time specified for performance.[598] Any other interpretation would defeat the purpose of section 34.[599]

(2) Effect of the Purchase by a Corporation of Its Shares

§7.274 As discussed above, corporations are generally prohibited from holding shares in themselves or in their holding bodies corporate. The reason is that a reduction in capital results where a corporation purchases its shares. A brief consideration of the accounting entries involved proves this to be the case. If the shares are purchased, there is a credit to the cash account. But it is also necessary to make an off-setting entry, and the only appropriate account to which that entry can be made is to the stated capital (shareholder equity) account, where it must be shown as a debit. Thus the result of the transaction is to reduce the balance of the shareholder equity account. Following this reasoning, subsection 35(6) of the OBCA provides that:

> 35.(6) Shares of any class or series or fractional shares issued by a corporation and purchased, redeemed or otherwise acquired by it shall be cancelled or, if the articles limit the number of authorized shares of the class or series, may be restored to the status of authorized but unissued shares of the class.

Subsection 39(6) of the CBCA is to like effect. Under both Acts, the corporation is required to deduct from the stated capital account maintained for the class or series of shares to which the acquired shares belong, an amount equal to the result obtained by multiplying the stated capital of the shares of that class or series

---

[597] [1992] A.J. No. 917, 96 D.L.R. (4th) 586 (Q.B.), aff'd [1994] A.J. No. 127, 109 D.L.R. (4th) 608*n* (C.A.).
[598] *Ibid.*, at 589-90 (Q.B).
[599] See also *Mountain State Steel Foundries Inc. v. CIR*, 284 F.2d 7373 (4th Cir. 1960); *Wallinder v. Target Tunnelling Ltd.* [1988] A.J. No. 846, 92 A.R. 267 (Q.B.).

by the number of shares of that class or series or fractions thereof that were acquired, divided by the number of issued shares of that class or series immediately before the acquisition.[600] The option of restoring the shares to the unissued shares of the corporation (what is sometimes called treasury stock of the corporation) permits the corporation to reissue those shares at some subsequent point in time, and thereby reduces the likelihood that the authorized capital will be exhausted.

(iii) Reduction in Share Capital

§7.275 The distinction between a reduction in share capital and a repurchase by the corporation of its shares is slight; indeed, the one is merely a form of the other. Nevertheless, the two subjects are treated separately under both the OBCA and the CBCA. At common law, corporations had no power to reduce their stated capital even where the articles of the company provided for such a right at the time of the issue of those shares (*i.e.*, where the shares provided for a right of redemption or retraction).[601] The courts consistently took the position that any such power must be conferred by statute and in exercising that power the company must follow the procedure laid down in its statute of incorporation,[602] adhering strictly to all prescribed conditions, restrictions and prohibitions set out in that legislation.[603] Under earlier legislation and at common law, it was improper for a corporation to enter into a collateral agreement with a shareholder or subscriber outside the terms and conditions of the shares concerned under which the corporation would agree to accept a surrender of the shares and repay the money invested by the shareholder or subscriber, as, for instance, where the purpose for which the subscription is sought is abandoned.[604] Under the OBCA and the CBCA, there is no outright prohibition on such side agreements. On the contrary, subsections 30(1) of the OBCA and 34(1) of the CBCA create a general right in favour of the corporation to purchase or otherwise acquire any of its issued shares or warrants, subject to the respective liquidity and solvency tests set out in subsections 30(2) and 34(2). Therefore it may be concluded that the earlier prohibition no longer applies.

§7.276 As we have seen, the common law took the view that a company could not purchase its own shares both because of the underlying obligation to use the

---

[600] OBCA, s. 35(1); CBCA, s. 39(1). No such deduction is made in the case of shares acquired by gift (s. 33 of the OBCA) or in the case of shares acquired as a legal representative (under s. 29 of the OBCA) or in respect of shares held to meet a Canadian ownership requirement (also s. 29 of the OBCA).

[601] *Long v. The Guelph Lumber Co.*, [1880] O.J. No. 242, 31 U.C.C.P. 129 at 137-38 (H.C.), per Osler J.

[602] *Walbridge Grain Co. (Liquidator of) v. Walbridge Grain Co.*, [1916] A.J. No. 47, [1918] 2 W.W.R. 886 at 889 (S.C.), per Clarry M.C.; *Pacific Coast Coal Mines Ltd. v. Arbuthnot*, [1917] A.C. 607.

[603] See, generally, *Trevor v. Whitworth* (1887), 12 App. Cas. 409 (H.L.).

[604] See, for instance, *Alberta Rolling Mills Co. v. Christie* (1919), 58 S.C.R. 208; *Trevor v. Whitworth* (1887), 12 App. Cas. 409 at 419 and 433 (H.L.); *British & American Trustee & Finance Corp. v. Couper*, [1894] A.C. 399 at 403 (H.L.); *Hopkinson v. Mortimer, Harley & Co.*, [1917] 1 Ch. 646 at 653.

funds of the company for the objects for which the company was created, and because it would mean an abstraction of assets of the company on the strength of which creditors deal with it.[605] In *Trustee of C.E. Plain Ltd. v. Kenley*[606] it was held that a corporation has a duty to its creditors and shareholders to maintain the equity account of its balance sheet so that it is not used except for capital purposes. These positions have now been modified by statute. Consistent with the rules pertaining to redemption and retraction, a corporation under either the CBCA or the OBCA may reduce its stated capital only in accordance with the Act to which it is subject.[607] A corporation may choose to do so, for instance, where it retires from a particular line of business, sells off its related assets, and as a result has capital in excess of its needs.[608] The rules governing reduction of share capital are set out in subsection 34(1) of the OBCA, which provides that:

> 34.(1) Subject to subsection (4), a corporation may by special resolution,
>
> (a) extinguish or reduce a liability in respect of an amount unpaid on any share; or
>
> (b) reduce its stated capital for any purpose including, without limiting the generality of the foregoing, for the purpose of,
>
> > (i) distributing to the holders of issued shares of any class or series of shares an amount not exceeding the stated capital of the class or series, or
> >
> > (ii) declaring its stated capital to be reduced by,
> >
> > > (A) an amount that is not represented by realizable assets, or
> > >
> > > (B) an amount otherwise determined in respect of which no amount is to be distributed to holders of issued shares of the corporation.

Although OBCA and CBCA corporations are prohibited from issuing shares unless fully paid, clause (a) appears to recognize the possibility that such improper issues may from time to time occur, and so provides that a corporation may extinguish or reduce the liability of shareholders in respect of the amount unpaid.[609] The ability to effect such a result reinenforces the view put forward previously, that the issue of shares that are not fully paid is not a void transaction.

§7.277 Subsection 34(4) of the OBCA provides that the corporation shall not take any action to extinguish or reduce liability in respect of an amount unpaid on a share or to reduce its stated capital for any purpose other than the purpose mentioned in sub-subclause 34(1)(b)(ii)(A) where there are reasonable grounds for believing that,

---

[605] *Zwicker v. Stanbury*, [1953] 2 S.C.R. 438.
[606] [1931] O.J. No. 393, 12 C.B.R. 492 at 494-95 (C.A.), per Hodgins J.A.
[607] OBCA, s. 24(9); CBCA, s. 26(10).
[608] *Re Fowlers Vacola Manufacturing Co.*, [1966] V.R. 97 — the company was found to have abandoned the food-canning business due to intense competition.
[609] See, generally, *Re Doloswella Rubber & Tea Estates Ltd.*, [1917] 1 Ch. 213.

- the corporation is, or after taking such action, would be unable to pay its liabilities as they become due; or
- after the taking of such action, the realizable value of the corporation's assets would be less than the aggregate of its liabilities.

Subsections 38(1) and (3) of the CBCA are generally to a similar effect, except that the CBCA contains no equivalent to sub-subclause (B). Both Acts expressly require that any special resolution must specify the stated capital account or accounts from which the reduction of stated capital effected by the special resolution will be made.[610]

§7.278 A creditor of a corporation is entitled to apply[611] to the court for an order compelling a shareholder or other recipient to pay to the corporation an amount equal to any liability of the shareholder that was extinguished or reduced contrary to section 34 of the OBCA or 38 of the CBCA, as the case may be, or to pay or deliver to the corporation any money or property that was paid or distributed to the shareholder or other recipient as a consequence of a reduction of capital made contrary to the applicable section.[612] The OBCA permits a class action for this purpose, where it appears that there are numerous shareholders who may be liable.[613] A two-year limitation period (running from the date of the act in respect of which the complaint is made) is imposed under both the OBCA and the CBCA upon actions to enforce such a liability.[614]

§7.279 While the provisions of the OBCA and CBCA are similar, there are two key differences between the two Acts. First, by virtue of subsection 34(8) of the OBCA, a person who is registered as a shareholder of a corporation as a personal representative of a named person is not personally liable under section 34, although any such personal representative is otherwise subject to all liabilities imposed by the section.[615] The following consequences would appear to result from this provision:

- Until amounts received by the personal representative are distributed to the beneficial owner of the share, the creditor may obtain an order requiring the personal representative to repay the amount in question. In such a case the claim is made for the personal representative to account for the amount improperly received, and provided the personal representative is still holding it, there is no personal liability.

---

[610] OBCA, s. 34(3); CBCA, s. 38(2). The stated capital account of the corporation must be adjusted accordingly: OBCA, s. 35(3); CBCA, s. 39(3).
[611] In the case of both the OBCA and the CBCA, the word "apply" is inappropriate. The correct procedure is by way of action rather than originating application.
[612] OBCA, s. 34(5); CBCA, s. 38(4).
[613] OBCA, s. 34(7). There is no equivalent provision in the CBCA.
[614] OBCA, s. 34(6); CBCA, s. 38(5).
[615] No equivalent provision is found in the CBCA.

- Once the personal representative distributes the payment received by the personal representative to the beneficiary, any further claim against the personal representative is blocked.

- A claim may, however, be made against the beneficial owner, as such a person would fall within the scope of an "other recipient" as provided in subsection 34(5).

§7.280 Second, on a procedural level, subsection 34(7) of the OBCA provides that where it appears that there are numerous shareholders who may be liable under the section, the court may permit an action to be brought against one or more of them as representatives of the class and, if the plaintiff establishes his claim as a creditor the court may make an order of reference and add as parties in the referee's office all such shareholders as may be found. In such a reference, the referee is required to determine the amount that each shareholder should contribute towards the plaintiff's claim, which amount may not, in the case of any particular shareholder, exceed the amount of the liability of the shareholder that was extinguished or reduced contrary to the section, or paid, delivered or distributed to the shareholder. The referee is expressly empowered to direct payment of any sum so determined by him. The class action procedure clearly simplifies the bringing of multi-party actions (which, as noted above, was one of the administrative problems inherent in the use of partially paid shares as a method of corporate financing).

(iv) Contract Re the Purchase of Shares

§7.281 Under both Acts, a contract with a corporation providing for the purchase of shares of the corporation by the corporation is specifically enforceable against the corporation, except to the extent that the performance of such a contract cannot be performed without a contravention of the restrictions set out in the Act upon the purchase of shares by the corporation.[616] In an action brought on a contract respecting the purchase of shares by the corporation, the burden of proving that the purchase would result in such a contravention lies upon the corporation.[617] Until the corporation has fully performed the contract, the other party retains the status of a claimant entitled to be paid as soon as the corporation is lawfully able to do so. Where the corporation is liquidated, the claim of that party ranks subordinate to the rights of creditors, but in priority to the other shareholders.[618]

§7.282 The 2001 amendments to the CBCA introduced a *prima facie* statutory obligation to purchase shares, and granted a priority to any seller who is entitled to require the corporation to purchase shares under that obligation. Specifically, subsection 40(1) of the CBCA now provides:

---

[616] OBCA, s. 36(1); CBCA, s. 40(1).
[617] OBCA, s. 36(2); CBCA, s. 40(2).
[618] OBCA, s. 36(3); The Corresponding provision CBCA, s. 40(3) was repealed by 2001, c. 14.

> 40.(1) A corporation shall fulfill its obligations under a contract to buy shares of the corporation, except if the corporation can prove that enforcement of the contract would put it in breach of any of sections 34 to 36.

The wording indicates that a court may now issue some sort of binding order to compel a corporation to comply with the repurchase obligation — although the wording of subsection 40(1) could be clearer on the point. Subsection 40(2) further provides:

> 40.(2)Until the corporation has fulfilled all its obligations under a contract referred to in subsection (1), the other party retains the status of claimant entitled to be paid as soon as the corporation is lawfully able to do so or, in a liquidation, to be ranked subordinate to the rights of creditors and to the rights of holders of any class of shares whose rights were in priority to the rights given to the holders of the class of shares being purchased, but in priority to the rights of other shareholders.

(v) Gifts of Shares

§7.283 A corporation may accept for any shareholder a share of the corporation surrendered to it as a gift.[619] Thus in *Hamer v. National Forest Products*[620] it was held that a voluntary surrender by a shareholder of fully paid shares to the corporation did not constitute trafficking in shares. No reduction in share capital resulted from the surrender, even though the number of issued shares was reduced. Both the OBCA and the CBCA provide that a surrender of shares may not extinguish or reduce a liability in respect of an amount unpaid on any such share except in accordance with the rules set out in the Act respecting the reduction of share capital.[621] However, in *Re International Electric Co.*,[622] the court was prepared to uphold a surrender of shares where the surrender was part of an otherwise valid settlement of a genuine dispute between the corporation and shareholder as to the liability of the holder in respect of those shares[623] — a power now expressly granted to the corporation by statute not only in respect of disputes pertaining to the liability to take up shares, but in the case of any dispute.

(vi) Entitlement to Repayment of Share Capital

§7.284 The general rule respecting the repayment of share capital is that unless the share terms set out in the articles otherwise provide, the shareholders of a corporation are entitled to be repaid their capital ratably in a winding-up.[624] The principle of equality of shares within a class can sometimes lead to unequal results. One of the objectives behind the abolition of the no par value concept was to permit the shares of a class or series to be issued for different amounts, as the circumstances of a corporation change. However, on the winding-up of a corpo-

---

[619] OBCA, s. 33; CBCA, s. 37. See, for instance, *Moore v. Northwood* (1960), 31 W.W.R. 241 (Man. C.A.).
[620] (1964), 47 W.W.R. 375 (B.C.S.C.).
[621] OBCA, s. 33; CBCA, s. 37.
[622] [1914] O.J. No. 36, 31 O.L.R. 348 (H.C.).
[623] But compare *Livingstone v. Temperance Colonization Society*, [1890] O.J. No. 28, 17 O.A.R. 379 (C.A.).
[624] *Birch v. Cropper* (1889), 14 App. Cas. 525 (H.L.).

ration, subject to the articles, the holders of the shares of a class are entitled to receive a ratable distribution of the amount remaining after payment of creditors, determined by reference to the number of shares held by each, irrespective of the amount that each may have paid for his or her shares in consideration of their issue.[625] Therefore, one shareholder will be entitled to receive back a greater consideration paid for the shares of that class before a ratable distribution is made among all shareholders of that class only if the articles so provide. This may confer a windfall on those shareholders who paid less for the issue of their shares than other members of the same class, and may just as easily result in the shareholders who paid more receiving less than they originally paid.

§7.285 Where the assets of the corporation are insufficient to repay all shareholders in full, all shareholders are repaid a proportionate amount. The holder of a share providing for the payment of a preferential dividend is presumed not to be entitled to any priority in the repayment of share capital over the holders of other classes or series of shares of a corporation. However, it frequently happens that the terms of the preference shares of a corporation will make express provision for a priority in the repayment of share capital. Such a provision is a two-edged sword. Although it entitles the preference shareholders to priority in repayment,[626] those shareholders are presumed not to be entitled to any further share of the surplus assets of the corporation, even where those share terms allow the preference shareholders to participate in the residual profits of the corporation after the stipulated preference dividend has been paid.[627] But in each case, it is a matter of construction — the rights of the various classes of shareholder being determined by the terms of their respective shares as set out in the articles of the corporation.

J. SHARE CERTIFICATES

§7.286 The shares in a corporation are personal property and constitute a chose in action.[628] In contrast, the share certificate is a chattel in the nature of a documentary evidence of title.[629] The share certificate is not the title in itself, but it is proof, in the absence of evidence to the contrary, of the title of the shareholder to the shares to which it relates.[630] Share certificates do not constitute any express obligation or promise, and although they may be issued under the seal of the corporation, they are not specialties. They are no more than an evidence of

---

[625] *Muljo v. Sunwest Projects Ltd.*, [1991] B.C.J. No. 3332, 2 B.L.R. (2d) 221 at 226 (C.A.), per Goldie J.A.
[626] *Holmstead v. Alberta Pacific Grain Co.*, [1927] 3 W.W.R. 230 (Alta. S.C.), aff'd [1927] 3 W.W.R. 707 (Alta. C.A.).
[627] *Re Isle of Thanet Electric Supply Co.*, [1950] Ch. 161 (C.A.), per Wynne-Parry J.; see also *Scottish Insurance Corp. v. Wilsons & Clyde Coal Co.*, [1949] A.C. 462 (H.L.).
[628] *Colonial Bank v. Whinney* (1886), 11 App. Cas. 426 at 439-40 (H.L.), per Lord Blackburn; see also *Robinson v. Jenkins* (1890), 24 Q.B.D. 275 (C.A.).
[629] *Gray v. Gray*, [1944] O.W.N. 399 (Master).
[630] *Société Générale de Paris v. Walker* (1885), 11 App. Cas. 20 (H.L.); *General Dairies Ltd. v. Maritime Electric Co.*, [1935] S.C.R. 519 at 525, per Dysart J., rev'd [1937] 1 W.W.R. 591 (P.C.).

entitlement.[631] The certificate is not a negotiable instrument and is distinct from the shares that it represents.[632]

§7.287 The enactment of the *Securities Transfer Act, 2006* ("STA")[633] will further the steady current drifting towards a world in which shares (and other corporate securities) will be almost entirely uncertificated. A number of complementary amendments were made to the OBCA at the time when the STA was enacted, to provide a supporting foundation for an uncertificated regime. Although these provisions have not yet been proclaimed into effect, on proclamation, subsection 54(1) of the OBCA will provide that a security issued by a corporation may be represented by a security certificate or may be an uncertificated security. In practice, it is unlikely that uncertificated securities will be much employed by other than by reporting issuers under the *Securities Act,* for some years to come. Nevertheless, subsection 54(2) will provide that:

> 54.(2) Unless otherwise provided by the corporation's articles, the directors of a corporation may provide by resolution that any or all classes and series of its shares or other securities shall be uncertificated securities, provided that such resolution shall not apply to securities represented by a certificate until such certificate is surrendered to the corporation.

Within a reasonable time after the issuance or transfer of an uncertificated security, the corporation shall send to the registered owner of the uncertificated security a written notice containing the information required to be stated on a share certificate under subsections 56(1) and (2) of the OBCA.[634] Except as otherwise expressly provided or authorized by law, the rights and obligations of the registered owners of uncertificated securities and the rights and obligations of the holders of certificated securities of the same class and series shall be identical.[635]

§7.288 The shares of a class or series of a corporation are fungible, as are the share certificates that represent them. When shares are bought and sold, it is sufficient to deliver certificates representing the agreed quantity of shares of the same class and series; it is not necessary to deliver a specific share certificate.[636] The OBCA sets down a number of general rules which apply to all security certificates, including share certificates, and a number of special rules which apply only to share certificates. Looking first at the general rules, each holder of a security is entitled upon request to receive a certificate in respect thereof that is held by that holder, or to receive a non-transferable written acknowledgment of the security holder's right to obtain a security certificate from the corporation in respect of the securities of the corporation that are held by the security holder.

---

[631] *Ontario (Treasurer) v. Blondé*, [1941] O.R. 227 (C.A.), aff'd [1946] 3 W.W.R. 683 (P.C.); *Williams v. R.*, [1942] A.C. 541 (P.C.); *Castleman v. Waghorn, Gwynn & Co.* (1908), 41 S.C.R. 88.
[632] *Smith v. Walkerville Malleable Iron Co.*, [1896] O.J. No. 15, 23 O.A.R. 95 at 103 (C.A.), per Burton J.A.
[633] S.O. 2006, c. 8.
[634] OBCA, s. 54(3).
[635] OBCA, s. 54(4).
[636] *Gorman v. Littlefield*, 229 U.S. 19 (1908), per Day J.; quoted with approval by Rinfret J. in *Solloway v. Blumberger*, [1933] S.C.R. 163 at 167.

Where the corporation refuses to issue a share certificate, the shareholder may obtain a declaration that he or she is a shareholder in the corporation.[637]

§7.289 However, since a corporation may not issue shares until the shares are fully paid, it follows that a subscriber for shares is not entitled to demand the issue of a share certificate until those shares have been paid for.[638] Moreover, a corporation is not bound to issue more than one security certificate in respect of a security held jointly by several persons, and delivery of a security certificate to one of several joint security holders is sufficient delivery to all.[639] No charge may be made for the original security certificate, but where the security that it represents is transferred, the corporation may charge a fee of not more than $3 for the issue of a new certificate.[640]

§7.290 A security certificate must be signed manually by at least one director or officer of the corporation or by, or on behalf of, a registrar, transfer agent, branch transfer agent or issuing or other authenticating agent of the corporation, or a trustee who certifies it in accordance with a trust indenture. Any additional signatures required on the security certificate may be printed or otherwise mechanically reproduced on the certificate.[641] However, a manual signature is not required on a promissory note that is not issued under a trust indenture, a scrip certificate, a security certificate representing a fractional share or a warrant.[642] Where a security certificate contains a printed or mechanically reproduced signature of a person, the corporation may issue the security certificate even though the person has ceased to be a director or an officer of the corporation, and the security certificate is as valid as if the person were a director or an officer at the date of its issue.[643]

§7.291 A corporation must state upon the face of each share certificate issued by it the name of the corporations and the words "incorporated under the law of the Province of Ontario" or "incorporated under the laws of Canada", as the case may be, or words of like effect.[644] The certificate must bear the name of the person to whom it was issued,[645] as well as the number and class of shares and the designation of any series that the share certificate represents.[646] Where a corpo-

---

[637] *Gillespie v. Retail Merchants' Assn. of Canada (Ontario) Inc.*, [1997] O.J. No. 956, 33 B.L.R. (2d) 307 (Gen. Div.); *Bogle v. Kootenay Valley Co.* (1906), 5 W.L.R. 139 at 139 (Man. K.B.), *per* Macdonald J.
[638] This being inherent in the requirement that the shares not be issued until they are fully paid. For a general discussion of this question, see *Boulet v. Hudon* (1917), 51 Que. S.C. 29. The issue of a certificate does not estop the corporation from contesting whether the consideration has been paid: *Re Winnipeg Hedge & Wire Fence Co.* (1912), 1 D.L.R. 316 (Man. K.B.).
[639] OBCA, s. 54(1) [am. 2006, c. 8, s. 111]; CBCA, s. 49(1).
[640] OBCA, s. 54(2) [am. 2006, c. 8, s. 111]; CBCA, s. 49(2).
[641] OBCA, s. 55(1) [am. 2006, c. 8, s. 112]; CBCA, s. 49(4).
[642] OBCA, s. 55(3) [am. 2006, c. 8, s. 112]; CBCA, s. 49(5).
[643] OBCA, s. 55(2) [am. 2006, c. 8, s. 112]; CBCA, s. 49(6). It is still customary to pass a directors' resolution to this effect, but in view of s. 55(2) of the OBCA, such a resolution is no longer necessary.
[644] OBCA, s. 56(1)(*a*) [am. 2006, c. 8, s. 113]; CBCA, s. 49(7)(*b*).
[645] OBCA, s. 56(1)(*b*) [am. 2006, c. 8, s. 113]; CBCA, s. 49(7)(*c*).
[646] OBCA, s. 56(1)(*c*) [am. 2006, c. 8, s. 113]; CBCA, s. 49(7)(*d*).

ration is authorized to issue more than one class or series of shares, the corporation must legibly state on each share certificate issued by it, the rights, privileges, restrictions and conditions attached to the shares of each class and series that exists when the share certificate is issued, or state that the class or series of shares that it represents has rights, privileges, restrictions or conditions attached to it, and that the corporation will furnish to a shareholder a full copy of the text of[647]

- the rights, privileges, restrictions and conditions attached to that share and to each class authorized to be issued and to each series in so far as the same have been fixed by the directors; and
- the authority of the directors to fix the rights, privileges, restrictions and conditions of subsequent series, if applicable.

The corporation must furnish any such description on demand by, and without charge to, the shareholder.[648]

§7.292 The general rule is that a share certificate may not vary the rights, conditions, privileges and restrictions to which a share is entitled under the articles of incorporation.[649] Under the OBCA and the CBCA, this general rule has been modified in at least two important respects, however. First, even against a purchaser for value who has no notice of a defect going to the validity of a security,[650] the terms of a security include those stated on the security certificate and those incorporated in it by reference to another instrument, statute, rule, regulation or order to the extent that the terms so referred to do not conflict with the stated terms. However, such a reference is not of itself notice to a purchaser for value of a defect going to the validity of the security, even if the security expressly states that a person accepting it admits such notice.

§7.293 Second, subsection 56(2) of the OBCA provides that where the articles of a corporation restrict the issue, transfer or ownership of shares of any class or series for a purpose set out in clause 42(2) (c) or (d) of the OBCA,[651] the restriction or a reference to it must be noted conspicuously on every share certificate of

---

[647] OBCA, s. 56(2) [am. 2006, c. 8, s. 113]; CBCA, s. 49(13).
[648] *Ibid.*; OBCA. s. 56(7); CBCA, s. 49(14).
[649] *Steel Co. of Canada v. Ramsay*, [1931] A.C. 270 at 273 (P.C.), *per* Viscount Dunedin.
[650] OBCA, s. 63(1); CBCA, s. 55(1).
[651] Clauses 42(2)(c) and (d) of the OBCA provide that a corporation that has imposed restrictions on the issue, transfer or ownership of its shares of any class or series shall not offer any of its shares to the public unless the restrictions are necessary,

> (c) to limit to a specified level the ownership of its shares by any prescribed class of person for the purpose of assisting the corporation or any of its affiliates or associates to qualify under the *Securities Act* or similar legislation of a province or territory to obtain, hold or renew registration, or to qualify for membership in a stock exchange in Ontario recognized as such by the Commission; or
>
> (d) to attain or to maintain a specified level of Canadian ownership or control for the purpose of assisting the corporation or any of its affiliates or associates to qualify to receive licences, permits, grants, payments or other benefits under any prescribed Act of Canada or a province or ordinance of a territory.

the corporation evidencing a share that is subject to the restriction of the certificate. To this general rule, there is one important qualification: it applies only in respect of certificates issued after the day on which the share becomes subject to the restriction under the Act. Any reference to the restriction must include a statement that the corporation will furnish to a shareholder a full copy of the text of the restriction.[652] The corporation is obliged to furnish a full copy of the text of the restriction concerned on demand by, and without charge to, the shareholder.[653] However, a failure to note the restriction or to provide a reference to it neither invalidates the share or share certificate nor renders the restriction ineffective against any owner, holder or transferee of the share or share certificate.[654]

§7.294 A corporation may issue a certificate for a fractional share. Alternatively, the corporation may issue a scrip certificate in bearer form that entitles the holder to receive a certificate for a full share by exchanging scrip certificates aggregating a full share.[655] The holder of such scrip certificates, as such, is not a shareholder even where sufficient certificates are held to entitle the holder to receive a full share, and in this respect subsection 57(4) of the OBCA expressly provides that the holder of a scrip certificate is not entitled to exercise voting rights or to receive a dividend in respect of the scrip certificate. The directors may attach conditions to any scrip certificates that the corporation may issue, including conditions that the scrip certificates will become void if not exchanged for a certificate representing a full share before a specified date and that any shares for which such scrip certificates are exchangeable may be issued by the corporation to any person, and the proceeds thereof distributed ratably to the holders of the scrip certificates, despite any pre-emptive right.[656]

K. DIVIDENDS

§7.295 A dividend may be defined as a distribution of earnings made by a corporation among its shareholders, the procedure for the declaration of which is as provided in the corporate constitution (*i.e.*, its articles, by-laws and any unanimous shareholder resolution), including any specification of the respective rights of various classes of share that are created under the articles of the corporation.[657] They constitute the normally anticipated stream of payments that will be made by a corporation to its shareholders in consideration of the use of the capital contributed by those shareholders (or their predecessors) to the corporation. In England, it is customary for control over the payment of dividends to be divided between the shareholders and directors (with the directors having an exclusive authority to recommend the amount of dividend payable, and the shareholders the final say on the approval of the dividend). In North American

---

[652] OBCA, s. 56(8); CBCA, s. 49(10).
[653] *Ibid.*; OBCA, s. 56(9); CBCA, s. 49(11).
[654] OBCA, s. 56(10).
[655] OBCA, s. 57(1); CBCA, s. 49(15).
[656] OBCA, s. 57(2); CBCA, s. 49(16).
[657] See, generally, *Holman v. Calgary Properties Inc.*, [2003] A.J. No. 260 (Q.B.).

jurisdictions,[658] dividends are usually declared by director resolution[659] (although under both the OBCA and the CBCA the shareholders of a corporation may reserve the power to declare dividends to themselves under a unanimous shareholder agreement). Thus subsection 38(1) of the OBCA provides:

> 38.(1) Subject to its articles and any unanimous shareholder agreement, the directors may declare and a corporation may pay a dividend by issuing fully paid shares of the corporation or options or rights to acquire fully paid shares of the corporation and, subject to subsection (3), a corporation may pay a dividend in money or property.[660]

§7.296 The term "dividend" has no specific legal meaning, but in the corporate law context, the term usually refers to a payment made to the shareholders of a corporation out of the profits and other amounts available for distribution.[661] A payment which fits within this description will be held to be subject to the rules set out in the OBCA and the CBCA pertaining to the dividends, no matter how it is described.[662] In *Hill v. Permanent Trustee Co. of New South Wales Ltd.*,[663] Lord Russell of Killowen said:

> A limited company not in liquidation can make no payment by way of return of capital to its shareholders except as a step in an authorized reduction of capital. Any other payment made by it by means of which it parts with moneys to its shareholders must and can only be made by way of dividing profits. Whether the payment is called "dividend" or "bonus" or any other name, it still must remain a payment on division of profits.

In *Re Canadian Pacific Ltd.*[664] it was found that the directors of Canadian Pacific had decided to distribute 80 per cent of the shares of its subsidiary Marathon Realty Company Ltd. to its shareholders as a dividend. Canadian Pacific had two kinds of shareholders: preference and ordinary. The proposed distribution was opposed by some of the holders of the preference shares. The court was required to determine whether the transfer of the shares might properly be char-

---

[658] In the United Kingdom, the payment of a dividend is normally authorized by ordinary resolution of the members of the company, but only upon and in accordance with a recommendation for the payment of dividends made by the directors. The members may reject the recommendation of the directors and authorize the payment of a lesser dividend than that recommended. However, they may not authorize the payment of a dividend that was not recommended, nor may they authorize an increase in the dividend beyond the amount that was recommended. Thus under the U.K. *Companies Act 1985*, control over the payment of dividends is divided between the directors and members of the company. Or at least, such are the rules set out in article 102 of Table A of the Act. It is unclear whether this particular provision of Table A can be substantially modified, so as to confer upon the directors full control over the payment of dividends, or to give the shareholders full control. A case can be made in either direction, and until such time as the question comes fully before a court, it would be ill-advised to assume that either option would necessarily be followed.
[659] See, for instance, *Steel Co. of Canada v. Ramsay*, [1931] A.C. 270 at 273 (P.C.), *per* Viscount Dunedin.
[660] CBCA, s. 43(1).
[661] *Re Carson*, [1963] O.J. No. 661, [1963] 1 O.R. 373 at 379 *et seq.* (H.C.), *per* Wells J.
[662] So, in *Re National Funds Assurance Co.* (1878), 10 Ch. D. 118 (M.R.), it was held that "interest" on share capital amounted to a type of dividend.
[663] [1930] A.C. 720 at 731 (P.C.).
[664] [1990] O.J. No. 606, 47 B.L.R. 1 (H.C.J.).

acterized as a dividend. Justice Austin held that a corporation could only make two kinds of distribution to its shareholders: retained income and capital. A distribution of retained income is a dividend.[665] After tracing the history of the corporation, he concluded that the proposed transfer was in essence a division of profits and therefore a dividend. However, to constitute a dividend, the payment must be a distribution made to a person in his or her capacity as a shareholder. A payment in the nature of employee remuneration, even when in the form of a performance bonus, does not fall within the scope of the term.[666]

(i) Nature of Dividend Entitlement — Are Dividends Gifts?

§7.297 Dividends are sometimes characterized as a gift of corporate property made by a corporation to its shareholders,[667] but such a characterization is too extreme. They are "gifts" in so far as they possess a discretionary character, and the corporation is not legally obliged to pay them. However, there the similarity to a gift ends. In the normal case shareholders invest in a corporation on the understanding that dividends will be paid as and when the corporation is in a fit position to pay them. Since that question requires a fuller knowledge concerning the condition and business of the corporation than any outsider (including the court) can ever possess, the decision as to whether to pay dividends at any particular time is properly reserved to the directors. However, it must never be forgotten that the corporation has use of the shareholders' funds, and it would be commercially unrealistic for the shareholders not to expect compensation for that use at some point. Where payment is withheld indefinitely, or the directors' control over dividend payments are otherwise abused for the apparent purpose of benefiting the controlling shareholder at the expense of a minority, the directors may be seen to have exceeded their authority. Thus it has been held that it is oppressive for the majority shareholders to misuse their control over the board of directors and thus the payment of dividends to force a minority shareholder to sell his shares.[668] If dividends were truly gifts, the oppression remedy could never apply by reason of their non-payment.

(ii) Director Discretion over Dividend Declaration

§7.298 The determination as to when and in what amount a corporation should pay a dividend rests in the honest discretion of the directors of a corporation or other relevant decision-maker under the articles of the corporation. A corporation and its directors are not obliged to declare a dividend, this being a matter of internal management within the corporation.[669] This basic principle is known as the rule in *Burland v. Earle,* where it was said:

---

[665] *Ibid.,* at 29.
[666] *Re Telsten Services Ltd.,* [1981] O.J. No. 2393, 39 C.B.R. (N.S.) 68 at 74-75 (Ont. S.C. in bnkrptcy.), *per* Anderson J.
[667] *McClurg v. Canada,* [1990] S.C.J. No. 134, 50 B.L.R. 161 at 186, *per* Dickson J.
[668] *Ferguson v. Imax Systems Corp.,* [1983] O.J. No. 3156, 43 O.R. (2d) 128 (C.A.), leave to appeal to S.C.C. refused (1983), 2 O.A.C. 158*n*.
[669] *Fairhall v. White Star Refining Co.,* [1928] S.C.R. 369; *Burland v. Earle,* [1902] A.C. 83 (P.C.).

> Their Lordships are not aware of any principle which compels a joint stock company while a going concern to divide the whole of its profits amongst its shareholders. Whether the whole or any part should be divided, or what portion should be divided and what portion retained, are entirely questions of internal management which the shareholders must decide for themselves, and the Court has no jurisdiction to control or review their decision, or to say what is a "fair" or "reasonable" sum to retain undivided, or what reserve fund may be properly required.[670]

The directors of a corporation are perfectly within their rights in setting aside profits of the corporation to meet its general needs as they may arise from time to time.[671] Indeed, the law presumes that the directors may well consider the payment of dividends even by a profitable corporation to be contrary to the best interest of the corporation over the long term. The risk that there will be a long, perhaps indefinite delay, in the distribution of dividends is inherent in an equity investment.[672]

§7.299 In the ordinary case, the dividends paid by a corporation will be paid out of the profits earned by the corporation from its ongoing operations. Alternatively, profits may be credited to a general reserve account or to a reserve for specific contingent liabilities that have not yet crystallized. The directors may re-invest profits in the business, whether by way of the purchase of new capital assets or in research and development. In deciding whether to declare dividends, the directors must strike a compromise between the competing purposes that retained earnings and dividends serve in the financing of the corporation. There is no rule of company law which prohibits a corporation from distributing its retained earnings and other reserves to its shareholders, provided that at the time of its so doing, it complies with restrictions imposed under corporate law on the payment of dividends and return of share capital, and does not otherwise improperly prejudice the interests of its creditors.[673] Nevertheless, most successful corporations withhold a portion of their net income in the form of retained earnings, generally for at least one of the following five basic reasons:

- to provide the corporation with a "no-cost" source of funds, since there is no dividend or interest payable on retained earnings, and in particular to reduce the corporation's need for borrowed funds;

- to strengthen the capital base of the corporation, including the ratio of current assets to current liabilities and of equity to debt;

- to fund capital expansion, plant modernization and other growth of the corporation;

- to provide a contingency fund against future losses or requirements;

---

[670] [1902] A.C. 83 at 95 (P.C.).
[671] *Bond v. Barrow Haematite Steel Co.*, [1902] 1 Ch. 353.
[672] *Wabash Rlwy. Co. v. Barclay* (1930), 280 U.S. 197 at 203 (S.C.), *per* Holmes J.
[673] *H. Timber Protection Ltd. (In Receivership) v. Hickson International plc*, [1995] 2 N.Z.L.R. 8 (C.A.).

- to provide a reserve from which dividend payments can be made during down-turns in the corporation's economic cycle.

While it is clearly desirable for a corporation to retain a reasonable portion of its net income in the form of retained earnings, there is also a need to implement a balanced policy of dividend payment. Corporations also pay dividends on their share capital for several reasons, which include:

- to meet legal obligations of the corporation;
- to attract future investment in share capital;
- to maintain shareholder satisfaction with existing corporate management by providing a competitive return on investment to the holders of the shares of the corporation, not only to provide those investors with a stream of income, but also to maintain the value of those shares.

§7.300 The dividend history of a corporation will significantly affect the value of its equity securities and its ability to raise funds through the issue of such securities should a need arise. To a large extent, the value of equity securities (particularly common shares) is determined by the discounted (to present value) income stream represented by the history of dividend payments on such securities. Thus dividends play the dominant role in fixing the market price of common shares. In general, companies that pay higher dividends have more marketable shares than those companies with a similar earnings record that pay lower dividends.

§7.301 Striking the appropriate balance among the foregoing objectives requires the exercise of business judgment and a degree of understanding of the peculiar business and affairs of a corporation that no outsider can reasonably be expected to possess. It follows that at least in the ordinary case, the courts will not second-guess a decision by the directors of a corporation not to pay a dividend. So long as they do not exercise their power over the declaration of dividends in an oppressive or otherwise unjust manner, the directors' control will not be subject to review. One reason why the courts are particularly unwilling to review the decision of the directors not to declare a dividend is that the declaration of a dividend exposes the directors of a corporation to a risk of personal liability.[674] However, the directors' power over the payment of dividends is subject to the same fiduciary obligations as the exercise of any other aspect of their managerial control over the corporation.[675] The courts will review and overrule the judgment of the board of directors where there is clear evidence of fraud or gross abuse of discretion.[676] In *Baron v. Allied Artists Pictures Corp.*[677] the preferred shareholders of a company were entitled to elect the majority of the board of directors

---

[674] *Loeb v. Provigo Inc.*, [1978] O.J. No. 3455, 4 B.L.R. 272 at 277 (H.C.J), *per* Steele J.
[675] See *McClurg v. Canada*, [1990] S.C.J. No. 134, 50 B.L.R. 161 at 185-86, *per* Dickson J.
[676] *Moskowitz v. Bantrell*, 41 Del. Ch. 177, 190 A.2d 749 (1963); *Baron v. Allied Artists Pictures Corp.*, 337 A.2d 653 (Del. Ch. 1975), *per* Brown V.C.; *Esheleman v. Keena*, 22 Del. Ch. 82, 194 A. 40, aff'd 23 Del. Ch. 234, 2 A.2d 904 (1937).
[677] 337 A.2d 653 (Del. Ch. 1975).

where the company failed to pay a dividend for six or more consecutive quarters — a common type of provision frequently inserted into preferred share terms to protect the holders of preferred shares from abuse at the hands of the holders of the common shares of a corporation. In the *Baron* case, however, it was argued that the provision had been turned upon its head; after the preferred shareholders obtained such control, they refused to cause the board to declare a dividend for a period of nine years even though (according to the plaintiff) the company was well able to afford to pay one. The plaintiff was a common shareholder who sought to require a new election of directors, arguing that the preferred shareholders had "fraudulently perpetuated itself in office by refusing to pay the accumulated dividend arrears." Brown V.C. refused to make the order, concluding that the action was tantamount to an action to compel the payment of a dividend. While it was accepted that a persistent refusal to pay dividends might constitute a breach of fiduciary duty, the facts as they stood were not sufficient to show that there was an abuse of control.

§7.302 There is no question that a corporation may not enter into a binding contract to pay a dividend where it would contravene the statutory restrictions on dividend payments imposed under the OBCA or the CBCA. Any contract between a corporation and its shareholders must be construed as being made in the light of and subject to the corporation's governing legislation. As a general rule, there is no contractual right to receive dividends even where corporate income is sufficient so that funds are available for the purpose, and the share terms indicate an obligation to pay.[678] If this general rule can be circumvented, it can only be through the use of clear and unequivocal language. So, for instance, in one American case where the share terms provided that "the holders of the preferred stock shall be entitled to receive, and the Company shall be bound to pay thereon, ... a fixed yearly dividend" it was held that the directors might still decide not to pay a dividend.[679] This decision and the wording of the OBCA would seem to leave open the possibility that the discretion of the directors may be ousted by a suitably worded provision, which in effect would permit recourse to the courts to compel payment where the specified criteria are satisfied. However, given the reluctance of the courts to interfere in the internal management of a corporation, it is doubtful whether any provision mandating the payment of compulsory dividends would be effective, unless both the criteria are particularly clear, and so too is their application to the facts of the case at hand.

(iii) Form of Declaration

§7.303 The declaration of a dividend is the *sine qua non* of a dividend payment, for until such time as a dividend is declared, no dividend is payable.[680] In the case of most OBCA or CBCA corporations, a dividend will be declared by di-

---

[678] *Srebot Farms Ltd. v. Bradford Cooperative Storage Ltd.*, [1998] O.J. No. 532, 163 D.L.R. (4th) 190 (C.A.); *Wabash Rlwy. Co. v. Barclay*, 280 U.S. 197 at 203, *per* Holmes J. (U.S.S.C. 1930); but see *Arizona Western Insurance Co. v. L.L. Constantin Co.*, 247 F.2d 388 (3d. Cir. 1957).
[679] *L.L. Constantin & Co. v. R.P. Holding Co.*, 56 N.J. Super. 411, 153 A.2d 378 (Ch. 1959).
[680] See, generally, *Bond v. Barrow Haematite Steel Co.*, [1902] 1 Ch. 353.

rector resolution.[681] No special form of wording is necessary in order to declare a dividend provided it is clear that the intention was to distribute the profits to a certain extent among the shareholders concerned. Until the board declares a dividend out of the profits of a corporation they remain an integral part of the assets of the corporation, and should the corporation enter into liquidation, they form part of the capital of the corporation available for distribution among the shareholders of the corporation upon winding-up but are not income to the shareholders.[682] Once the company goes into liquidation, the power to declare dividends is gone.[683] Where, however, a dividend has been legally declared, it constitutes a debt owing by the corporation (albeit one that can only be paid where the statutory conditions are met) and cannot subsequently be revoked or reduced by the board of directors.[684]

§7.304 Rights of participation in dividends and other distributions are generally determined on a class-by-class basis. With the abolition of par value and unpaid shares, most offering corporations now declare dividends in the form of a specified amount per share (*e.g.*, "$1.50 per Class A Share of the Corporation"). Some private corporations discriminate among shareholders of the same class, adjusting dividends payable to reflect shares issued during the course of a year. The practice has a certain logic to it, but in the absence of authorization being given for it in the articles, is of dubious validity. Under English company law, it is clear that there is no right to differentiate in the payment of dividends among the holders of shares of the same class. So, for instance, unless the articles or memorandum otherwise provide, any dividend declared must be paid at a uniform rate on all shares of the same class. Thus at one time it was held that dividends must be paid proportionately on the nominal value of shares, and could not be prorated to reflect the amount paid up.[685]

§7.305 Among different classes, the normal rule is that preferential dividends must be paid in full before any dividend is paid on the ordinary shares (the right to receive cumulative dividends is discussed in detail below).[686] There is no presumption that the shares of one class are entitled to receive a dividend merely because a dividend has been declared or paid in respect of some other class of shares, even when there are sufficient funds available to allow both classes of share to be paid a dividend. Preferential dividend rights are presumed to be exhaustive. Ordinarily speaking, when a preferred shareholder receives his or her preferential dividend, there is no entitlement to participate further in profits.[687]

---

[681] See, for instance, *Steel Co. of Canada v. Ramsay*, [1931] A.C. 270 at 273 (P.C.), *per* Viscount Dunedin.
[682] *Re Keating*, [1933] O.J. No. 403, [1934] O.R. 71 at 76 (C.A.), *per* Mullock C.J.O., aff'd [1934] S.C.R. 698.
[683] *Re Armitage*, [1893] 3 Ch. 337 (C.A.), *per* Lindley L.J.
[684] *Leclerc Ltd. v. Pouliot*, [1924] 1 D.L.R. 361, 35 Que. K.B. 175.
[685] *Birch v. Cropper* (1889), 14 App. Cas. 525 (H.L.). Article 104 of Table A under the U.K. *Companies Act 1985* now excludes this rather anomalous rule.
[686] As discussed below in grater detail at §7.319.
[687] *Will v. United Lankat Plantations Co.*, [1914] A.C. 11 at 17-18 (H.L.), *per* Viscount Haldane L.C., at 19, *per* Earl Loreburn.

However, the terms of a particular class of preference shares may confer a right of further participation in profits.[688]

§7.306 There are several types of dividend, among the most common of which are (a) cash dividends (*i.e.*, dividends paid in currency); (b) stock dividends (*i.e.*, dividends paid by way of the issue of additional stock in the corporation); (c) preferential dividends (*i.e.*, a dividend that must be paid to the holders of shares of a particular class in priority to the holders of the shares of other classes, particularly the common shares of the corporation); (d) cumulative dividends (*i.e.*, a preferential dividend that if not fully paid in one year must be paid out of subsequent profits, in priority to any dividend to the holders of the shares of other classes). In Canada, dividends are normally paid on a quarterly basis during each fiscal year. Ordinarily speaking, when a preferred shareholder receives his or her preferential dividend, there is no entitlement to participate further in profits.[689] However, the terms of a particular class of preference shares may confer a right of further participation in profits.[690]

§7.307 It is unusual for dividends to be paid in cash (*i.e.*, in actual currency). Nor, since shares in OBCA and CBCA corporations must be registered, is it common for dividend payments to require the presentation of a coupon. Standard form share terms invariably provide that any dividend or other moneys payable in respect of a share may be paid by cheque sent by mail to the registered address of the person entitled to payment, or if two or more persons are the holders of the share or are jointly entitled to it by reason of the death or bankruptcy of the holder, to the registered address of whichever of them is first named in the register of members, or to such person and to such address as the person or persons entitled may direct in writing. Every cheque must be made payable to the order of the person entitled to it, or to such other person as that person may direct in writing. Payment of the cheque is a good discharge of the liability of the company in respect of the amount so paid.

§7.308 In the modern investment marketplace, an increasing number of corporations are encouraging the use of a direct deposit system, in which payment is directed into a designated bank account of the shareholder. Any such payment system should be provided for in the articles or share terms, but if in fact credit is received by the shareholder for the amount payable that fact would presumably constitute sufficient discharge of the company's liability even if the method of payment was not so authorized.

(iv) Restrictions on the Declaration and Payment of Dividends

§7.309 There are a number of important qualifications on the extent of the directors' control over the declaration and payment of dividends. First, both the

---

[688] *Steel Co. of Canada v. Ramsay*, [1931] A.C. 270 at 274 (P.C.), *per* Viscount Dunedin.
[689] *Will v. United Lankat Plantations Co.*, [1914] A.C. 11 at 17-18 (H.L.), *per* Viscount Haldane L.C., at 19, *per* Earl Loreburn.
[690] *Steel Co. of Canada v. Ramsay*, [1931] A.C. 270 at 274 (P.C.), *per* Viscount Dunedin.

dividends that the directors declare and their payment must be authorized under the terms of the OBCA or the CBCA, whichever governs the corporation in question. Second, the dividends must also be authorized under the articles of the corporation. For instance, if class 1 shares are entitled to a preferential dividend over class 2 shares, it clearly would be inconsistent with the preference so conferred for the directors to purport to pay a dividend on the class 2 shares before paying the preferential dividend on the class 1 shares; similarly if only a $1 dividend per share is authorized under the articles, payment of a $2 dividend would be improper. Third, the control of the directors over the payment of dividends may be restricted or reserved to the shareholders, as for instance under a unanimous shareholder agreement.

§7.310 At common law,[691] corporations were prohibited from paying a dividend out of capital.[692] Alternatively stated, dividends were payable only out of profits or net income. So in *Re Exchange Banking Co. (Flitcroft's Case)*, directors who knowingly paid dividends out of fictitious profits were held liable to pay to the corporation the amount of dividends so improperly paid, Jessel M.R. stating:

> The creditor has no debtor but that impalpable thing the corporation, which has no property except the assets of the business. The creditor, therefore, I may say, gives credit to that capital, gives credit to the company on the faith of the representation that the capital shall be applied only for the purposes of the business, and he has therefore a right to say that the corporation shall keep its capital and not return it to the shareholders.[693]

The implicit assumption underlying this statement, of course, is that there is a clear and sharp meaning for the terms "profits" and "capital." In fact there is not — a point noted by Lindley L.J. in *Lee v. Neuchatel Asphalte Co.*

> There is nothing at all in the Acts about how dividends are to be paid, nor how profits are to be reckoned; all that is left, and very judiciously and properly left, to the commercial world. It is not a subject for an Act of Parliament to say how accounts are to be kept; what is to be put into a capital account, what into an income account, is left to men of business.[694]

Unfortunately these concepts are not especially clear or precise. From an accounting perspective, the capital of a corporation may be seen to include not only the stated capital account, but also any contributed surplus and general reserves. Since the general reserves of a corporation represent retained profits, it would not seem reasonable to prevent a corporation from paying a dividend out of such accounts. Furthermore, the whole concept of profit is itself ambiguous, because the profits earned during a particular accounting period may be operating or extraordinary in nature. Accounting practice generally requires unrealized losses on capital assets to be reflected in the books of a corporation; in contrast, unrealized gains are not generally recognized. Thus the use of a profit-based test can lead to certain problems: would it be reasonable to restrain the hands of di-

---

[691] See B.S. Yamey, "The Law Relating to Company Dividends" (1941) 4 Modern Law Rev. 273.
[692] *Bond v. Barrow Haematite Steel Co.*, [1902] 1 Ch. 353 at 365, *per* Farwell J.
[693] *Re Exchange Banking Co. (Flitcroft's Case)* (1882), 21 Ch. D. 519 at 533-34 (C.A.).
[694] (1889), 41 Ch. 1 at 21 (C.A.).

rectors to prevent them from paying a dividend where there is an unrealized loss,[695] but not to permit them to pay dividends where there is an unrealized gain.[696] Moreover, as noted above, there is also the question of whether dividends might properly be paid where there is a trading profit during the current accounting period, but the amount of that profit is insufficient to make good trading losses suffered in earlier accounting periods. The common law was prepared to permit dividends to be paid in such a case;[697] yet such a determination of profit would be entirely inconsistent with accounting theory. Given these uncertainties, it is fortunate that the false dichotomy of profit and capital has largely been abandoned under the OBCA and the CBCA and replaced by the twin tests of solvency and liquidity.

§7.311 The OBCA contains more detailed provisions respecting the payment of dividends than are found in the CBCA, but the general approach of the two Acts is similar. Subsection 38(1) of the OBCA provides that subject to its articles and any unanimous shareholder agreement, the directors may declare and a corporation may pay a dividend by issuing fully paid shares of the corporation or options or rights to acquire fully paid shares of the corporation and, subject to subsection (3), a corporation may pay a dividend in money or in property.[698] Subsection 38(3) imposes a general solvency and liquidity restriction upon the payment of dividends, and provides that the directors shall not declare and the corporation shall not pay a dividend if there are reasonable grounds for believing that,

(*a*) the corporation is or, after the payment, would be unable to pay its liabilities as they become due; or

(*b*) the realizable value of the corporation's assets would thereby be less than the aggregate of,

   (i) its liabilities, and

   (ii) its stated capital of all classes.

Section 42 of the CBCA is to a similar effect. Thus both the OBCA and the CBCA have moved away from the old profit-based approach to the permissibility of dividends. Under the OBCA and the CBCA, the governing issues are solvency and liquidity. Dividend eligibility is governed by the balance sheet rather

---

[695] Surprisingly, the common law view was that there was no restriction on paying dividends in such a case: *Bolton v. Natal Land & Colonisation Co.*, [1892] 2 Ch. 124 at 131-32, *per* Romer J. This rule was of particular importance in the case of corporations that operated wasting assets, such as mines — where the value of the assets of the corporation would decline steadily over the life of the corporation: *Lee v. Neuchatel Asphalt Co.* (1889), 41 Ch. D. 1 (C.A.). See also *Verner v. General & Commercial Investments Trust*, [1894] 2 Ch. 239 (C.A.).

[696] See, generally, *Dimbula Valley (Ceylon) Tea Co. v. Laurie*, [1961] Ch. 353 at 372-74, *per* Buckley J., as to the common law position with respect to this question.

[697] *Re National Bank of Wales*, [1899] 2 Ch. 629 (C.A.); *Ammonia Soda Co. v. Chamberlain*, [1918] 1 Ch. 266 (C.A.), *per* Swinfen-Eady L.J.; but see the doubts expressed by Lord Davey in *Dovey v. Cory*, [1901] A.C. 477 at 493 (H.L.).

[698] Subsection 43(1) of the CBCA is similar, but does not provide for a dividend in the form of an option or right to acquire fully paid shares.

than the income statement.[699] This change in approach was and is most welcome. It is no easy feat to compute profit correctly for any given period. The determination of profit requires allocations of receipts, expenses, losses and gains to the specified fiscal period. While such allocations may sometimes be based on fact, in many if not most cases they are based on no more than an estimate, an accounting convention, or even an assumption as to what may occur in the future. Accounting principles are not fundamental truths, capable of scientific proof. Changes that have been made to accounting principles show that income is not a fixed concept, but is one subject to reasonable differences of opinion, with the view that enjoys prominence at any given time subject to possible variation from year to year.[700]

§7.312 As noted above, once declared, a dividend constitutes a debt owed by the corporation to the shareholders of the corporation as of the record date. The debt is due and payable as of the date specified in the resolution declaring the dividend, or in the absence of such a specification, upon the date of the resolution.

§7.313 The OBCA and the CBCA solvency and liquidity tests apply both to the declaration and payment of the dividend. It follows that the nature of a declared dividend as a debt is a modified one for corporations under those statutes.[701] Payment of a dividend in circumstances where the corporation cannot satisfy the solvency or liquidity tests constitutes oppressive conduct towards the creditors of the corporation.[702] Thus if the financial condition of the corporation deteriorates between the date of declaration and payment, the corporation may not pay, if by so doing it would contravene clauses 38(3)(*a*) or (*b*). Since the actual payment of a dividend is usually carried out by the officers of a corporation, those officers risk liability where they make a payment where the corporation is not

---

[699] To give some illustration of the significance of the shift: in the UK, where an income statement approach is used to govern the payment of dividends, there is conflicting case law as to whether a company may pay a cash dividend where it has sufficient liquid funds available to do so and the company has an unrealized capital gain. In the Scottish case of *Westburn Sugar Refineries Ltd. v. IRC*, [1960] S.L.T. 197, [1960] T.R. 105 it was held that no such payment might be made. In contrast, in the English case *Dimbula Valley (Ceylon) Tea Co. v. Laurie*, [1961] Ch. 353, the court reached the opposite conclusion. Section 263 the U.K. *Companies Act 1985,* now expressly provides that dividends may be paid only out of accumulated realized profits less accumulated realized losses. However, under the OBCA and the CBCA balance sheet approach, there would appear to be no problem with the payment of the dividend, provided the recognition of the gain would be in accordance with generally accepted accounting principles. However, a balance sheet approach necessarily requires losses from prior years to be taken into account in deciding whether any dividend may be paid (since such prior year losses will be charged against the company's equity account). Thus the decision in *Ammonia Soda Co. v. Chamberlain*, [1918] 1 Ch. 266 to the effect that a dividend may be paid to the extent of current year profits, without taking into account prior year losses, would not represent good law under either the OBCA or the CBCA.

[700] See, generally, Hackney, "The Financial Provisions of the Model Business Corporations Act" (1957) 70 Harv. L. Rev. 1357 at 1368-69.

[701] Compare, however, *Re Daon Development Corp.*, [1984] B.C.J. No. 2945, 26 B.L.R. 38 at 46 (S.C.), *per* Wallace J.; see also *Re Severn and Wye & Severn Bridge Rlwy. Co.*, [1896] 1 Ch. 559.

[702] *R. v. Sands Motor Hotel Ltd.*, [1984] S.J. No. 56, 28 B.L.R. 122 at 128 (Q.B.), *per* McLellan J.

permitted to do so. In this respect, the officers must make an independent assessment; it is not enough for them to say that they were carrying out the directors' instructions.

§7.314 The declaration of a dividend where the financial circumstances of a corporation are such that the dividend cannot be paid also amounts to a misrepresentation by the directors,[703] that may give rise to a cause of action against the directors concerned. To provide the basis for an action, the declaration of the dividend must have been false and dishonest; it must have been made with the intent that it be acted upon; and the plaintiff must have acted upon the strength of it.

§7.315 In deciding whether it is possible to declare a dividend, the directors must use reasonable judgment as to the financial condition of the company,[704] taking into account the corporation's expenses, contingencies and actual and probable losses, as well as the necessity to provide reasonable reserves.[705] However, the directors do not guarantee that the value of the corporation's assets will not be eroded by losses that were not anticipated at the time concerned. If such losses do eventually arise, neither the directors nor the shareholders are liable to repay the dividend to the corporation.[706]

§7.316 In 1997, the *Bankruptcy and Insolvency Act*[707] was amended to clarify the liability of directors for improperly paid dividends or for other wrongful distributions to the shareholders of a corporation, in the event of the bankruptcy of the corporation.[708] Specifically, subsection 101(1) of that Act now provides that (on the application of the trustee in bankruptcy of a corporation) where the corporation,

- paid a dividend, other than a stock dividend, or

- redeemed or purchased for cancellation any of the shares of the capital stock of the corporation

within the period beginning on the day that is one year before the date of the initial bankruptcy event and ending on the date of the bankruptcy (both dates included), the court charged with the bankruptcy proceeding in respect of the

---

[703] *Doyle v. Smith* (1897), 40 N.S.R. 157 (S.C.), *per* Graham E.J.
[704] See, for instance, *Northern Creameries Ltd. v. Rossington Produce Co.*, [1922] 1 W.W.R. 1150 (Alta. C.A.).
[705] *Leslie v. Canadian Birkbeck Co.* (1913), 24 O.W.R. 407 at 414, 10 D.L.R. 629 (H.C.), *per* Britton J., aff'd 25 O.W.R. 513, 15 D.L.R. 78 (C.A.).
[706] *Towers v. African Tug Co.*, [1903] 1 Ch. 558 (C.A.); *Re George W. Griffiths Co.*, [1924] 4 D.L.R. 1031 at 1035 (Man. K.B.), *per* Macdonald J. On the other hand, if the shareholders authorize the directors to transfer to a general reserve account funds which might be distributed to them as dividends, they cannot claim as creditors of the corporation in respect of the amount so transferred. The fact that those amounts might properly have been distributed as dividends had they not been transferred is irrelevant: *Re Atlas Loan Co.*, [1904] O.J. No. 266, 7 O.L.R. 706 at 714-15, *per* Britton J., aff'd [1905] O.J. No. 140, 9 O.L.R. 468 (C.A.).
[707] R.S.C. 1985, c. B-3.
[708] S.C. 1997, c. 12, s. 82.

corporation may inquire into the transaction to ascertain whether it occurred at a time when the corporation was insolvent or whether it rendered the corporation insolvent. The court may give judgment to the trustee against the directors of the corporation, jointly and severally, in the amount of the dividend or redemption or purchase price (plus interest thereon) that has not been paid to the corporation where the court finds that,[709]

(a) the transaction occurred at a time when the corporation was insolvent or the transaction rendered the corporation insolvent; and

(b) the directors did not have reasonable grounds to believe that the transaction was occurring at a time when the corporation was not insolvent or the transaction would not render the corporation insolvent.

In making a determination under paragraph 101(2)(b), the court must consider whether the directors acted as prudent and diligent persons would have acted in the same circumstances and whether the directors in good faith relied on[710]

(a) financial or other statements of the corporation represented to them by officers of the corporation or the auditor of the corporation, as the case may be, or by written reports of the auditor to fairly reflect the financial condition of the corporation; or

(b) a report relating to the corporation's affairs prepared pursuant to a contract with the corporation by a lawyer, notary, accountant, engineer, appraiser or other person whose profession gave credibility to the statements made in the report.

Where a transaction referred to in subsection 101(1) has occurred and the court makes a finding referred to in paragraph 101(2)(a), the court may give judgment to the trustee against a shareholder who is related to one or more directors or to the corporation, or who is a director not liable by reason of paragraph (2)(b) or subsection (3), in the amount of the dividend or redemption or purchase price referred to in subsection (1) and the interest thereon, that was received by the shareholder and not repaid to the corporation.[711] A judgment under subsection (2) may not be entered against, and is not binding on, a director who protested against the payment of the dividend or the redemption or purchase for cancellation of the shares of the capital stock of the corporation in accordance with any applicable law governing the operation of the corporation, so as to thereby exonerate himself or herself under that law from any such liability.[712] The onus of proof lies upon the directors to show that,[713]

(a) the corporation was not insolvent at the time the transaction occurred and that the transaction did not render the corporation insolvent, or

---

[709] *Bankruptcy and Insolvency Act*, R.S.C. 1985, c. B-3, s. 101(2).
[710] *Ibid.*, s. 101(2.1).
[711] *Ibid.*, s. 101(2.2).
[712] *Ibid.*, s. 101(3).
[713] *Ibid.*, s. 101(5). Where a claim is brought against a shareholder, the onus of proof lies on the shareholder: s. 101(6).

(b) the directors had reasonable grounds to believe that the transaction was occurring at a time when the corporation was not insolvent or that the transaction would not render the corporation insolvent.

The Act further provides that nothing in section 101 affects any right, under any applicable law governing the operation of the corporation, of the directors to recover from a shareholder the whole or any part of any dividend, or any redemption or purchase price, made or paid to the shareholder when the corporation was insolvent or that rendered the corporation insolvent.[714]

§7.317 The solvency and liquidity restriction set out in the OBCA and the CBCA with respect to the payment of dividends and repurchase of share capital do not prevent the corporation from paying debts other than dividends that are owed to the shareholder, as for instance debts arising in respect of services rendered.[715]

§7.318 Where it is intended to allow the holders of redeemable or retractable shares to recover all unpaid cumulative dividends — whether or not they have been formally declared — on those shares at the time of their redemption or retraction, it is strongly advisable to make that obligation express. Unless this is done, there is a risk that the corporation will not be held obliged to pay undeclared cumulative dividends.[716] The question of which of these alternatives was intended to apply is one of contractual interpretation, and as is always the case with respect to such questions, where there is any room for debate, it is better to err on the side of express provision.

(v) Preferential Dividends

§7.319 At least in the ordinary case, a right set out in the terms and conditions of a share to receive a preferential dividend does not bind the corporation to pay such a dividend, even when sufficient funds are on hand that might be used for that purpose.[717] The general rule is that such a right bars only the payment of any junior ranking dividend. In the absence of any provision to the contrary in the statute governing a corporation or in its articles,[718] the directors of a corporation are always entitled to exercise an honest judgment in deciding whether to pay dividends, or use funds available for that purpose to set up a reserve.[719] As discussed below, absent express statutory authority it is doubtful whether a corporation may bind itself contractually to pay a dividend even if that undertaking is limited to where there are sufficient funds available. Any right to receive a preferential dividend at a specified rate out of profits of each year is but a right to

---

[714] *Bankruptcy and Insolvency Act*, R.S.C. 1985, c. B-3, s. 101(4).
[715] *Re Telsten Services Ltd.* (1981), 39 C.B.R. (N.S.) 68 (Ont. S.C. in Bnkpty.).
[716] See, generally, *NA Properties (1994), Ltd. v. DIA Holdings Ltd.* (1995), 33 Alta. L.R. (3d) 284 (Q.B.).
[717] *Bond v. Barrow Haematite Steel Co.*, [1902] 1 Ch. 353 at 362 and 368, *per* Farwell J.
[718] *New York, Lake Erie & Western Railroad v. Nicklas*, 119 U.S. 363 at 367 (1886).
[719] See *Re Patterson & Sons Ltd.*, [1916] W.N. 352 (H.L.) where the articles of association stated specifically how the profits of the company were to be applied and left no discretion to the directors. See also *Evling v. Israel & Oppenheimer Ltd.*, [1918] 1 Ch. 101.

receive a dividend in priority to any dividend in respect of shares ranking junior to the preferred shares in question, should the corporation have funds that may properly be applied to this purpose and should the directors resolve to pay dividends. The preferential right is not one that the directors must give effect to by declaring dividends, but rather a right in the form of a ranking of priority to payment among shareholders.[720] However, the directors do not have absolute discretion. On the one hand it is the duty of the board of directors to set aside funds for depreciation and for all contingencies that may be reasonably expected to arise, as well as sufficient funds and property to enable the corporation to carry on its ordinary business.[721] On the other hand, it may be argued that where the directors of a corporation persistently refuse to declare a preferential dividend even though the corporation is well able to do so, that persistence may be sufficient to give rise to a claim for oppression under section 248 of the OBCA or 241 of the CBCA.[722]

§7.320 The question often arises as to whether the terms of a preferred share providing for the payment of a fixed dividend also entitle the holder of that share to participate in any further dividends paid by the corporation.[723] Generally speaking, there is a presumption that where the terms of a share provide for the payment of a preferential dividend, that share is intended to be non-participating.[724] Thus preferential dividend rights are presumed to be exhaustive, so that once a preferred shareholder receives his or her preferential dividend, there is no entitlement to participate further in profits.[725] However, where the terms of a particular class of preference shares clearly indicate a right of further participation in profits, effect will be given to that provision.[726] In the absence of such a provision, the directors have no authority to pay a dividend to a preferred shareholder over and above his or her contractual entitlement, even where there are sufficient funds on hand to do so. Any surplus over the amount required for the payment of the preferred shareholders belongs to the holders of the common shares of the corporation — although the directors may set aside a reserve out of those funds in respect of the corporation's preferred dividend payment obligations in future years.

(1) Cumulative Dividends

§7.321 As noted above, where a preferential dividend specifies that a dividend will be paid out of the profits of the corporation or the profits or other funds

---

[720] *Fidelity Manufacturing & Research Co. v. Gulf Canada Resources Ltd.*, [1996] O.J. No. 2508, 27 B.L.R. (2d) 135 (Gen. Div.); *DeVall v. Wainwright Gas Co.*, [1932] 2 D.L.R. 145 at 156 (Alta. C.A.), *per* McGillivray J.A. See also *Hastings v. International Paper Co.*, 175 N.Y.S. 815 (1919).
[721] *Hastings v. International Paper Co.*, 175 N.Y.S. 815 (1919).
[722] See, for instance, *Re Sam Weller & Sons Ltd.*, [1990] B.C.L.C. 80, [1990] Ch. 682, *per* Gibson J.; *Re A Company (No. 00370 of 1987)*, [1988] 1 W.L.R. 1068, *per* Harman J.
[723] See, generally, *Holmstead v. Alberta Pacific Grain Co.*, [1928] 1 D.L.R. 135 (C.A.).
[724] *Will v. United Lankat Plantations Co.*, [1914] A.C. 11 (H.L.).
[725] *Ibid.*, at 17-18, *per* Viscount Haldane L.C., at 19, *per* Earl Loreburn.
[726] *Steel Co. of Canada v. Ramsay*, [1931] A.C. 270 at 274 (P.C.), *per* Viscount Dunedin.

available for dividend payments, the payment obligation is still discretionary to the corporation.[727] Some protection may be given to a shareholder by making the preferential dividend cumulative, so that if the dividends are not declared in a particular year, or are declared only in part, the undeclared dividend is carried forward and added to the preferential dividend entitlement for the next following year, and so on in like fashion until the preferential dividend for each completed year has been paid in full.[728] In this way, the dividend accumulates as a charge against the moneys available for payment as dividends to junior shareholders.[729] However, even where the dividend is cumulative, the liability of the corporation with respect to that dividend is not in the nature of a debt unless and until the dividend is declared.[730]

§7.322 Strictly speaking the question of whether preferential dividends are cumulative or non-cumulative is a matter of construction, but in construing particular share terms there is a presumption that an entitlement to be paid preferential dividends is cumulative.[731] That presumption will be defeated where it is inconsistent with the terms of the shares concerned. The presumption is not a strong one: even share terms that provided only for an annual entitlement to dividends have been interpreted to be inconsistent with a cumulative right.[732] Where a share carries a non-cumulative preferential right to a dividend, that preferential right lapses in each year (or other relevant dividend period) if no dividend is in fact declared.[733]

§7.323 The protection of the holders of non-cumulative preference shares from abuse by common shareholders who control the board and thereby the payment of dividends is an issue that has not yet been addressed by Canadian courts. Where the share terms allow little doubt that a particular preferential dividend was intended to be non-cumulative, it is necessary to decide whether the holder

---

[727] *Re Buenos Ayres Great Southern Rlwy. Co.*, [1947] Ch. 384.
[728] See, for instance, *Re Wakley*, [1920] 2 Ch. 205 (C.A.); *Godfrey Phillips Ltd. v. Income Investment Trust Corp.*, [1953] Ch. 449. However, there is no presumption that the holder of a cumulative preference share is entitled to be paid dividend arrears in a winding-up even where the corporation has earned sufficient profits from the sale of assets on liquidation to pay them: *Re London India Rubber Co.* (1868), L.R. 5 Eq. 519; *Re Odessa Waterworks Co.*, [1901] Ch. 190; *Re Crichton's Oil Co.*, [1902] 2 Ch. 86 (C.A.). The preference share shareholder will be entitled to so claim where:

   (a) the share terms so provide: *Bishop v. Smyrna & Cassaba Rlwy. Co.*, [1895] 2 Ch. 265;

   (b) the dividend in question was declared but not paid: *Re Severn and Wye & Severn Bridge Rlwy. Co.*, [1896] 1 Ch. 559; *Re Artisan's Land & Mortgage Corp.*, [1904] 1 Ch. 796.

[729] *Fairhall v. White Stare Refining Co.*, [1928] S.C.R. 369 at 374, per Mignault J.
[730] *Re Wakley*, [1920] 2 Ch. 205 at 221-22 (C.A.), per Warrington L.J.
[731] *Crockett v. Academy of Music* (1902), 22 C.L.T. 301 (N.S.T.D.); *Henry v. Great Northern Rlwy.* (1857), 1 De. G. & J. 606 at 638-39, 45 E.R. 858 (Ch.), per Lord Cranworth L.C.; *Webb v. Earle* (1875), L.R. 20 Eq. 556.
[732] *Adair v. Old Bushmills Distillery Co.*, [1908] W.N. 24.
[733] See, for instance, *Staples v. Eastman Photographic Materials Co.*, [1896] 2 Ch. 303 (C.A.); *J.I. Thornycroft & Co. v. Thornycroft* (1927), 44 T.L.R. 9.

of such a share has any right to legal redress should the board never choose to declare and pay a dividend on that share. It is quite clear that non-cumulative dividends give rise to a potential for abuse. The common shareholders of a corporation will have every interest in not declaring dividends on non-cumulative shares, as by so doing the amounts withheld become available for eventual distribution to the common shareholders. In New Jersey, the courts have evolved what has come to be known as the "dividend credit rule" under which the holders of shares carrying a right to a non-cumulative preferred dividend are seen to be entitled (in the absence of express exclusion) to an "inchoate right" to the unpaid dividends from all earlier years in which there were sufficient corporate earnings to pay the dividends in question.[734] The dividend credit rule does not override the general control of the directors over the payment of dividends, but merely vests the rights of the holders of the preferred shares *vis-à-vis* other shareholders, should the directors ultimately decide to pay dividends on the share capital of the corporation.[735] Despite this precedent, it seems doubtful that a Canadian court would follow a similar approach, for it effectively negates the "non-cumulative" character of the share. While non-cumulative shares may be a bad bargain, if that is the bargain that a shareholder has struck, on what basis can the court revise it? The sole statutory authority for undertaking any revision would appear to lie in the shareholder oppression remedy. However, in order to invoke that remedy, the non-payment of dividends would have to be so abusive in nature as to justify the court interfering with the internal management of the corporation. As noted above, in the area of dividends, such interference is something that the courts are normally most unwilling to undertake.

(2) Proportionate Abatement

§7.324 Subsection 25(2) of the OBCA provides for the proportionate abatement of rights to cumulative dividends. It provides:

25.(2) If any amount,

(*a*) of cumulative dividends, whether or not declared, or declared non-cumulative dividends; or

(*b*) payable on return of capital in the event of the liquidation, dissolution or winding up of a corporation,

in respect of shares of a series is not paid in full, the shares of the series shall participate rateably with the shares of all other series of the same class in respect of,

(*c*) all accumulated cumulative dividends, whether or not declared, and all declared non-cumulative dividends; or

(*d*) all amounts payable on return of capital in the event of the liquidation, dissolution or winding up of the corporation,

as the case may be.

---

[734] *Dohme v. Pacific Coast*, 5 N.J. Super. 477, 68 A.2d 490 (1949).
[735] *L.L. Constantin & Co. v. R.P. Holding Co.*, 56 N.J. Super. 411, 153 A.2d 378 at 384 (Ch. 1959).

See subsection 25(2) qualifies the general right of the directors, where empowered by the articles, to assign rights and privileges to series of shares in a class. The OBCA provisions considerably expand upon the wording found in subsection 27(2) of the CBCA, which provides only that:

> 27.(2) If any cumulative dividends or amounts payable on return of capital in respect of a series of shares are not paid in full, the shares of all series of the same class participate rateably in respect of accumulated dividends and return of capital.

(3) "Guaranteed" Dividend Payments

§7.325 A corporation cannot agree to pay interest on its share capital irrespective of whether or not there are profits or other resources that permit it to do so, nor can it guarantee a specific dividend to the holders of its shares,[736] irrespective of whether that guarantee is placed in the share terms themselves (*i.e.*, in the articles) or in some collateral contract between the corporation and any one or more of the shareholders. This prohibition is clear where compliance with the "guarantee" would contravene the above liquidity and solvency restrictions: subject to the wasting assets exception, dividends cannot be paid out of capital.[737] It follows that any contract to pay dividends whether or not such dividends are permitted under the terms of the OBCA or the CBCA is *ultra vires* the corporation and void.[738] As noted above, the question of whether a corporation may contractually commit to pay dividends when there are adequate funds on hand to support such payments is less straightforward. The better answer appears to be that a contractual commitment guaranteeing that dividends will be paid whenever sufficient funds are on hand to satisfy the statutory test is unenforceable as a contractual obligation — although that failure maybe sufficient to give rise to a remedy for oppression on the specific facts of the case. Ordinarily the decision as to whether or not to recommend payment of a dividend is seen as lying within the province of the directors' managerial mandate. At least in the ordinary case, until such times as a dividend is approved, a member is not entitled to claim or be paid a dividend by the corporation.[739] There can be little doubt it would take clear and compelling evidence before a court would second-guess the decision of the directors. Generally speaking, the payment of a dividend is a matter of business judgment, which the courts recognize as being best left to the directors.[740] Clause 127(3)(*d*) of the OBCA prohibits the directors from delegating

---

[736] *Long v. The Guelph Lumber Co.*, [1880] O.J. No. 242, 31 U.C.C.P. 129 (H.C.).
[737] *Re Owen Sound Lumber Co.*, [1917] O.J. No. 144, 38 O.L.R. 414 at 432 (C.A.) *per* Hodgins J.A., *Trevor v. Whitworth* (1887), 12 App. Cas. 409 (H.L.).
[738] See, generally, *Long v. The Guelph Lumber Co.*, [1880] O.J. No. 242, 31 U.C.C.P. 129 (H.C.).
[739] *Burland v. Earle*, [1902] A.C. 83 (P.C.); *Crocker v. Waltham Watch Co.*, 315 Mass. 397, 53 N.E.2d 230 at 233 (S.C. 1944). But *cf. Dodge v. Ford Motor Co.*, 204 Mich. 459, 170 N.W. 668 (1919) — dividend decision made in bad faith or for purposes unrelated to the best interests of the corporation may be set aside by the court; see also *Donahue v. Rodd Electrotype Co. of New England Inc.*, 367 Mass. 589, 328 N.E.2d 505 (S.C. 1975). Whether or not the dividend decisions of directors are subject to review by the courts, the corporation may still be obliged to disclose the unpaid dividends as a liability in certain cases: see *Fairhall v. White Star Refining Co.* (1927), 61 O.L.R. 306 (S.C.), aff'd [1928] S.C.R. 369.
[740] The reason for this approach was explained in *Re Carlisle's Will*, 53 Misc. 2d 546, 278 N.Y.S.2d 1011 at 1017 (Surr. 1967).

their authority to declare dividends. If the power to declare dividends may not be delegated, it would seem to follow that the board cannot abdicate its authority over dividends entirely by entering into a contractual undertaking.

§7.326 Nevertheless, a guarantee of dividend payments may be provided by another person; moreover, there is nothing wrong in one person entering into an agreement to purchase the shares of a shareholder if specified dividend payments are not made. Similarly, the corporation may enter into a contract with a third party (such as another shareholder) under which the third party undertakes to pay dividends on behalf of the corporation.[741] In such a case, the corporation would enforce that right as trustee on behalf of the shareholders. Although a payment by a third party under such a guarantee does not constitute a distribution of dividends by the corporation, it has been held in England that any such payment is taxable as a dividend in the hands of the recipient.[742]

(vi) Entitlement to Dividends

§7.327 As indicated above, a dividend once it has been declared on a share constitutes a debt of the corporation to the holder of that share.[743] After the dividend is declared, the directors cannot revoke it,[744] nor can they correct a mistaken or improper declaration by way of a subsequent declaration of dividend repealing the first.[745]

§7.328 Any dividend purportedly paid by a corporation without the authorization of its directors will be improper and may be recovered by an assignee for the benefit of creditors, a trustee in bankruptcy or liquidator of the corporation.[746] The same rule applies in the case of both cumulative and non-cumulative dividends.[747] However, although undeclared cumulative dividends are not a liability of the corporation, the amount of any such dividends should be included as a note to the corporation's balance sheet, as a warning to the purchasers of shares of other classes.

§7.329 A director's resolution declaring a dividend should do so expressly, and should set out the amount of the dividend. In the absence of express authority, a corporation must pay its dividends in cash,[748] but that authority is now expressly given under both the OBCA and the CBCA. Thus subsection 38(1) of the

---

[741] See, generally, *Re South Llaharran Colliery Co., ex p. Jegon* (1879), 12 Ch. D. 503; *Richardson v. English Crown Spelter Co.*, [1855] W.N. 31; *Re Menell et Cie*, [1915] 1 Ch. 759.
[742] *IRC v. Black*, [1940] 4 All E.R. 445.
[743] *Re Canada Tea Co.*, [1959] O.W.N. 378 (H.C.J.). In Canada the debt is not a specialty debt: *Re Northern Ontario Power Co.*, [1954] O.W.N. 106; although it is in England: *Re Artisan's Land & Mortgage Corp.*, [1904] 1 Ch. 796.
[744] *Leclerc Ltd. v. Pouliot*, [1924] 1 D.L.R. 361 (Que. C.A.).
[745] *James v. Beaver Consolidated Mines Ltd.*, [1927] O.J. No. 46, 60 O.L.R. 420 (H.C). As to the right to rescind an interim dividend, see *Lagunas Nitrate Co. v. Schroeder & Co. & Schmidt* (1901), 85 L.T. 22.
[746] *National Trust Co. v. Gilbert*, [1921] 1 W.W.R. 359 (Sask. C.A.).
[747] *Fairhall v. White Star Refining Co.*, [1928] S.C.R. 369 at 374, *per* Mignault J.
[748] *Wood v. Odessa Waterworks Co.* (1889), 42 Ch. 636 at 645, *per* Stirling J.

OBCA[749] allows a dividend to be paid in money, property, shares, or options or rights to acquire fully paid shares. It is not improper for the corporation to offer shareholders the option of taking the dividend in cash or shares,[750] provided all shareholders of the same class or series are given the same option. A dividend must be declared at a uniform rate on all shares of the same class[751] or series,[752] and each shareholder is entitled to receive the dividend through the same method(s) of payment.[753] Where the articles themselves fix the amount of a dividend, or some aspect of it, such as the exchange rate, the directors have no authority to depart from the provisions set out in the articles.[754]

§7.330 Subsection 95(1) provides that for the purpose of determining the shareholders entitled to receive a dividend, the directors may fix a date as the record date for that determination, but the record date must not precede the payment of the dividend by more than 50 days. Where no record date is so fixed, dividends are payable to the persons who are registered in the books of the corporation as on the date when the dividend is declared.[755] The by-laws of a corporation will often provide that dividend obligations are satisfied by the mailing of a cheque to the registered address of a shareholder.[756] Where the by-laws so provide, a shareholder cannot recover from the corporation if the cheques are stolen and cashed after they are so mailed.[757]

§7.331 Despite the general presumption that the holders of different classes of share are entitled to equal rights,[758] and therefore to equal dividends,[759] that presumption does not apply where the share terms of a particular class make specific provision with respect to the rights of the holders of shares of that class. Therefore, although it may constitute oppression where the shareholders concerned object, there appears to be nothing wrong (from an income tax perspective) in the directors paying all dividends to the holders of one class of shares, and paying no dividends to the holders of the other classes of shares.[760] The divi-

---

[749] CBCA, s. 43(1).
[750] *James v. Beaver Consolidated Mines Ltd.*, [1927] O.J. No. 46, 60 O.L.R. 420 (H.C.).
[751] *Oakbank Oil Co. v. Crum* (1882), 8 App. Cas. 65.
[752] Subsection 25(3) of the OBCA prohibits the giving of a priority to dividends in favour of one series of shares of a class over another series of shares of the same class. Thus, although the rate of dividend may vary from one series to another under the OBCA, the priority of claim must be the same. Under subsection 25(3), the prohibition on priority of dividends between two series of shares of the same class applies only in respect of series of shares outstanding. Thus Series 1 shares may be given a first priority; Series 2 shares a second priority, *etc.*
[753] *Priceville Fox Co. v. Jordan*, [1929] O.J. No. 32, 64 O.L.R. 172 (C.A.).
[754] See generally *Imperial Tobacco Co. v. Younger* (1935), 58 Que. K.B. 310 (C.A.).
[755] See, generally, *Re Wakley*, [1920] 2 Ch. 205 (C.A.); *Godfrey Phillips Ltd. v. Income Investment Trust Corp.*, [1953] Ch. 449 at 459, *per* Wynne-Parry J.; *Munro v. Mullen*, 100 N.H. 128, 121 A.2d 312 (S.C. 1956), *per* Duncan J.
[756] See *Steen v. Gunnar Mining Ltd.*, [1963] O.J. No. 656, [1963] 1 O.R. 329 (C.A.).
[757] *Rands v. Hiram Walker, Gooderham & Worts Ltd.*, [1936] O.J. No. 226, [1936] O.R. 488 (H.C.J.).
[758] *Birch v. Cropper* (1889), 14 App. Cas. 525 (H.L.).
[759] *Wunderlich Brothers v. Norwestern Mutual Fire Assn.*, [1936] 1 W.W.R. 297 (Sask. C.A.).
[760] *McClurg v. Canada*, [1990] S.C.J. No. 134, 50 B.L.R. 161, *per* Dickson J.

sion of shares into separate classes defeats the common law presumption that the shareholders concerned are to be treated equally.[761]

§7.332 Despite the elimination of preference shares as a statutory concept under the OBCA and the CBCA, it still seems clear that the holder of a share which provides for the payment of a fixed preferential dividend is presumed not to be entitled to share in any residual profits of the corporation after that dividend has been paid.[762] However, there is no absolute rule of law that the holders of dividends carrying a fixed dividend shall not be entitled to participate in residual profits. Where it is intended to confer such a right of participation, the share terms should make clear whether the right of participation extends to the whole of the residual profit of the corporation, or whether a stipulated dividend must first be paid on the other shares of the corporation before the right of participation of the preference shares takes effect.[763]

(vii) Dividends to Controlling Shareholder/Directors

§7.333 It is permissible for a corporation to pay its directors and officers the salary to which they are entitled in that capacity even though the corporation has no distributable profits from which a dividend might be paid. Indeed, such payments may even be made when the company is insolvent, provided no fraudulent preference results from the making of the payments. However, payments of salary and other remuneration to directors and officers are at least potentially subject to impeachment on two criteria: first, where payments are made to directors and officers who are shareholders, but no dividend payments are made, the other shareholders who hold shares of the same class may object that the company is not dealing equally with its shareholders.[764]

§7.334 Second, the creditors of an insolvent corporation may object that the payment to the director or officer constitutes a disguised gift or an unlawful return of capital.[765] For instance, in *Re Halt Garage (1964) Ltd.*[766] payments were made to a director (Mrs. Charlesworth) for services rendered as a director after she had become ill and had ceased to take an active part in the business of the company. She was required to refund that portion of the payments made to her which did not represent a genuine award of remuneration, but which were instead a disguised gift out of capital.[767] Although some nominal payment might be made in respect of

---

[761] *McClurg v. Canada*, [1990] S.C.J. No. 134, 50 B.L.R. 161 at 187, *per* Dickson J.; see also *Bowater Canadian Ltd. v. R.L. Crain Inc.*, [1987] O.J. No. 1157, 62 O.R. (2d) 752 at 754 (C.A.), *per* Holden J.A.
[762] *Re Canadian Pacific Ltd.*, [1990] O.J. No. 864, 73 O.R. (2d) 212 (H.C.); *Will v. United Lankat Plantations Co.*, [1914] A.C. 11 (H.L.).
[763] See *Steel Co. of Canada v. Ramsay*, [1931] A.C. 270 (P.C.).
[764] See, for instance, *Donahue v. Rodd Electrotype Co. of New England Inc.*, 367 Mass. 578, 328 N.E.2d 505 (S.C. 1975).
[765] *Re George Newman & Co.*, [1895] 1 Ch. 674 at 686 (C.A.).
[766] [1982] 3 All E.R. 1016 (Ch. D.).
[767] In fact, Mrs. Charlesworth held only a single share, although her husband's holding was more substantial.

the bare service of lending one's name as a director, payments beyond what might reasonably be made in such a case could be recovered. The case is sometimes alleged to stand for the proposition that gifts may never be made to directors. Other courts have taken a more conservative position, arguing only that "if an *insolvent* company may not properly give assets to its members it is difficult to see why it should be able to give them to anyone else".[768]

(viii) Stock Dividends

§7.335 Under both Acts, the solvency restriction on the payment of dividends applies only in the case of dividends paid in money or property; no such restriction applies in the case of a stock dividend,[769] or (in the case of an OBCA corporation) a dividend paid in the form of an option or right to acquire fully paid shares.[770] Subsections 38(1) of the OBCA and 43(1) of the CBCA expressly permit a corporation to pay a dividend "by issuing fully paid shares of the corporation". Where such a dividend is declared, subsection 38(2) of the OBCA provides:

> 38.(2) If shares of a corporation are issued in payment of a dividend, the corporation shall add to the stated capital account maintained or to be maintained for the shares of the class or series issued in payment of the dividend the declared amount of the divided stated as an amount of money.

In contrast to the OBCA and the CBCA, subsection 6.23(*a*) of the *Model Business Corporations Act* provides:

> 6.32.(*a*) Unless the articles of incorporation provide otherwise, shares may be issued *pro rata* and without consideration to the corporation's shareholders or to the shareholders of one or more classes or series. An issuance of shares under this subsection is a share dividend.

It is sometimes said that a stock dividend constitutes little more than merely exchanging one coin of a given denomination for another.[771] Along these lines, the commentary to the *Model Act* explains that:

> A share dividend is solely a paper transaction: No assets are received by the corporation for the shares and any "dividend" paid in shares does not involve the distribution of property by the corporation to its shareholders. ... Such transactions were treated in a fictional way under the old "par value" and "stated capital" statutes, which treated a share dividend as involving transfers from a surplus account to stated capital and assumed that par value shares could be issued without receiving any consideration by reason of that transfer of surplus.

---

[768] *ANZ Executors & Trustee Co. v. Qintex Australia Ltd.* (1990), 2 A.C.S.R. 676 at 684 (S.C. Qld.), per McPherson J.; *Re George Newman & Co.*, [1895] 1 Ch. 674 at 686 (C.A.).

[769] Consider, however, as to whether the declaration and payment of such a dividend may amount to misrepresentation by the directors.

[770] As to the liability of a shareholder in respect of a stock dividend where there were no profits out of which such a dividend might have been paid, see *Re McGill Chair Co.*, [1912] O.J. No. 126, 26 O.L.R. 254 (H.C.J.), leave to appeal granted 22 O.W.R. 222, but compare *Re Matthew Guy Carriage & Automobile Co.* (1912), 21 O.W.R. 842 (H.C.).

[771] *Equitable Tr. Co. v. Prentice* (1928), 250 N.Y. 1 at 9, per Cardozo J.

This commentary is partly but not entirely applicable under the OBCA and the CBCA, depending upon how the stock dividend is structured. In order to consider the consequences of a stock dividend it is necessary to examine its impact on the shareholders of the corporation and the impression that the dividend conveys to outsiders.[772]

§7.336 In all cases, the payment of a stock dividend has the effect of increasing the number of shares outstanding. For example, if a 25 per cent stock dividend is declared, each shareholder will receive one-quarter of a new share for each share previously held. Where necessary, fractional shares may be issued. Since each shareholder receives a number of new shares corresponding to his or her existing percentage interest in the corporation, the proportionate ownership of the corporation remains unchanged unless and until one of those shareholders elects to sell the shares concerned. The value of the pre-existing shares is nonetheless diluted: previously each share represented a 1 per cent interest in the corporation. After the dividend is paid, it represents a 0.8 per cent interest in the corporation. Thus, the practical consequence of the stock dividend is to lower the value of each share in the corporation.

§7.337 Still, shareholders may benefit as a result of the issue of the stock dividend. The market value of shares relates largely, but not entirely, to the percentage interest that they confer in the underlying value of the corporation. However, high value shares often have a very limited market. The reduction in the per share value of the corporation achieved by issuing further shares may increase the size of the market for those shares, and as a result will lead to an increase in the number of trades involving such shares. In other words, a dilution in per share value may increase their liquidity. In such a case, although the underlying value of the corporation remains the same, the aggregate market value of the shares of the corporation may increase because of the larger number of potential buyers who are now willing to invest in them.

§7.338 Stock dividends are similar to but are distinguishable from dividend reinvestment options sometimes offered by corporations. In a dividend reinvestment option, the corporation declares a cash dividend but instead of sending cheques in payment immediately to the shareholders, offers them an opportunity to elect to reinvest the dividend in new shares of the corporation. This type of dividend arrangement became popular as a result of changes to the *Income Tax*

---

[772] Stock dividends often create an illusion of dividend, but provide no real income to, nor confer any other benefit upon, the shareholders who "receive" them. Where such dividends represent true earnings, they may allow the shareholders to whom they are paid to cash in on the retained earnings of the corporation while keeping those earnings within the corporation to fund its continued growth or operations or as a hedge against future risks. However, where the amount of a stock dividend does not equate to the earnings of a corporation, the sole effect of the dividend will be to dilute the earnings of the corporation and thereby cause the price of the shares of the corporation to drop by a percentage of their aggregate market value corresponding to the amount of the dividend: C.A. Barker, "Evaluation of Stock Dividends" (1958) 36 Harvard Bus. Rev. 99-114.

Act[773] which had the effect of making stock dividends unpopular with investors. Until May 1985, stock dividends issued by most public corporations had a zero tax cost as a result of the issue of the dividend shares themselves. When the shares acquired through the issue of the dividend were sold, the shareholder to whom they were issued received a capital gain. Under the present treatment, stock dividends receive the same treatment as any other dividend paid by a corporation. Since shareholders may not have sufficient liquid resources to permit them to meet the tax liability arising from the payment of a stock dividend, it is obviously preferable to allow them the option of taking the dividend in cash, if they prefer.

§7.339 Corporations considering the payment of a stock dividend would be well advised to consider the tax implications of such a dividend to the shareholders of the corporation. If the shares paid out as a dividend are illiquid, either because of restrictions on the transfer of the shares concerned, or because there is no secondary market for those shares, the practical consequence of the dividend may be to impose what is in effect a tax penalty on the shareholders. The definition of "dividend" in subsection 248(1) of the *Income Tax Act*[774] includes most "stock dividends" within the scope of that term. As a result, the amount of any such dividend must be grossed-up and included in the taxable income of the shareholder when calculating his or her own taxable income. Although the dividend tax credit reduces the tax bite of that inclusion, if the stocks cannot be converted to cash, a shareholder may find that tax must be paid on the amount of the dividend remaining after the credit, even though no actual benefit has been received as a result of its payment.

§7.340 Where the shares on which a stock dividend is paid are part of a trust property, the stock dividend constitutes income rather than an increase in the capital of the trust property.

(ix) Corporations With Wasting Assets

§7.341 As we have seen, the declaration or payment of dividends out of capital is illegal in most cases since in order to pay such a dividend it will be necessary to violate the solvency restriction.[775] However, the OBCA contains a further exception to the solvency restriction upon the payment of dividends in the case of corporations with wasting assets.[776] Subsection 39(1) provides:

> 39.(1) Despite anything in this Act, a corporation,

---

[773] R.S.C. 1985, c. 1 (5th Supp.).
[774] *Ibid.*
[775] See, for instance, *Long v. The Guelph Lumber Co.*, [1880] O.J. No. 242, 31 U.C.C.P 129 at 134 (H.C.), *per* Osler J.; but compare *Re Owen Sound Lumber Co.*, [1917] O.J. No. 144, 38 O.L.R. 414 (C.A.).
[776] The foundation for this approach would appear to lie in the decision in *Lee v. Neuchatel Asphalte Co.* (1889), 41 Ch. D. 1 at 24 (C.A.), *per* Lindley L.J.

(a) that for the time being carries on as its principal business the business of operating a producing mining, gas or oil property owned and controlled by it;

(b) that has at least 75 per cent of its assets being of a wasting character; or

(c) that is incorporated for the purpose of acquiring the assets or a substantial part of the assets of a body corporate and administering such assets for the purpose of converting them into cash and distributing the cash among the shareholders of the corporation,

may declare and pay dividends out of the funds derived from the operations of the corporation.

The powers conferred under subsection 39(1) are of particular importance in the mining industry and other extractive industries. They may be exercised irrespective of whether the value of the net assets of the corporation may be reduced as a result to less than the corporation's stated capital of all classes, provided the payment of the dividend does not reduce the value of its remaining assets to an amount insufficient to meet all the liabilities of the corporation, exclusive of its stated capital of all classes.[777] Any such dividend must be authorized by special resolution.[778] No comparable provision is found in the CBCA.

(x) Liability for Dividends Improperly Paid

§7.342 Under clause 130(2)(d) of the OBCA, the directors of a corporation who vote for or consent to the payment of a dividend contrary to section 38 of that Act are jointly and severally liable to restore to the corporation any amounts so distributed or paid that are not otherwise recovered by the corporation.[779] An action to recover that amount must be brought against the director within two years of the date of the resolution in question.[780] A director who satisfies a judgment in respect of such an unlawful dividend is entitled to contribution from the other directors who voted for or consented to the declaration of that dividend.[781] In addition, the director may apply to the court for an order compelling a shareholder or other recipient of the dividend to pay or deliver to the director any amount paid by the director that was received by that person.[782]

(xi) Unclaimed Dividends

§7.343 A surprising amount of dividends are never claimed by the persons entitled to them: cheques in payment of the dividends are mailed but remain un-

---

[777] OBCA, s. 39(2).
[778] OBCA, s. 39(3).
[779] No such claim may be brought by a shareholder who knowingly received payment in contravention of s. 38, even if brought both on his own behalf and on behalf of innocent shareholders: *Crawford v. Bathurst Land & Development Co.*, [1916] O.J. No. 166, 37 O.L.R. 611 (H.C.), aff'd [1918] O.J. No. 88, 42 O.L.R. 256 (C.A.), rev'd on other grounds 59 S.C.R. 314.
[780] Although formerly provided in s. 130(7) of the OBCA, a corresponding limitation is now found in the *Limitations Act, 2002*, s. 4. See also CBCA, s. 118(7).
[781] OBCA, s. 130(3); CBCA, s. 118(3).
[782] OBCA, s. 130(4); CBCA, s. 118(4). See also *Moxham v. Grant*, [1900] 1 Q.B. 88 (C.A.).

cashed or are returned to sender. The reasons why this is the case vary, but quite frequently it is because the payee has died, and the executor or administrator of his or her estate was simply not aware that the deceased shareholder owned the shares on which the dividend was paid. It is common for share terms to provide that such unclaimed dividends will be deposited in a commercial depository. If the dividends remain unclaimed after a specified period time, they will be forfeited back to the corporation.[783] In Ontario, the *Unclaimed Intangible Property Act* would effectively negate such arrangements, when and if this legislation comes into force. It provides that where a dividend is unclaimed within five years after the date on which a dividend becomes payable, the amount of the dividend must be transferred to Her Majesty in right of Ontario.[784] However, the Act has now been on the books for many years without being proclaimed, and so far as can be determined, there is no current intention that this Act ever will be proclaimed in force.

L. LIEN ON SHARES AND RELATED CONSIDERATIONS

§7.344 Subsection 40(1) of the OBCA[785] provides that the articles or by-laws of a corporation may provide that the corporation has a lien on a share registered in the name of a shareholder or a shareholder's legal representative for a debt of that shareholder to the corporation.[786] Lien provisions will generally grant the corporation:

- a right to refuse to register the transfer of a share until a debt owed to the corporation by the transferring shareholder is paid in full;
- a right in favour of the corporation to seize and sell the shareholder's interest in the share so as to convey the share to the purchaser and to apply the proceeds to the debt owing;
- a right to apply dividend payments to the debt;
- a provision that any transferee will take the share subject to the foregoing rights.

Except in the case of a corporation that has shares listed on a stock exchange,[787] the articles or by-laws of a corporation may provide that the corporation has a lien on a share registered in the name of a shareholder or his legal representative for a debt of that shareholder to the corporation.[788] Any such lien may be en-

---

[783] See, for instance, *Re Canada Tea Co.*, [1959] O.W.N. 378.
[784] *Unclaimed Intangible Property Act*, R.S.O. 1990, c. U.1, s. 4(2), 8, 9; s. 17.
[785] CBCA, s. 45(2).
[786] There is no entitlement to such a lien in the absence of a provison in the articles or by-laws: *Box v. Bird's Hill Sand Co.* (1913), 4 W.W.R. 961 (Man. C.A.); *Montgomery v. Mitchell* (1908), 7 W.L.R. 518 (Man. K.B.); *McMurrich v. Bond Head Harbour Co.*, [1851] O.J. No. 134, 9 U.C.Q.B. 333.
[787] This exclusion appears in s. 40(2) of the OBCA but not in the CBCA; nevertheless, it is of equal application in the case of shares issued by CBCA corporations, because the by-laws of stock exchanges invariably prohibit the listing of any share that is subject to such a lien.
[788] OBCA, s. 40(1); CBCA, s. 45(2), (3).

forced in the manner provided in the articles or by-laws.[789] To be effective against a transferee of the share, the lien or a reference to it must be noted conspicuously on the face of the share certificate.[790]

§7.345 It is a rule of common law, set down in *Hopkinson v. Mortimer, Harley & Co.*[791] that a power of forfeiture of fully paid shares for debts that are generally due to the corporation is illegal and void as a clog on the equity of redemption. However, liens on shares for debts due to the corporation which permit the sale of the shareholder's interest have long been recognized.[792] A corporation whose articles or by-laws contain such a provision may enforce the lien in accordance with the articles or by-laws.[793] Where such lien provisions are conferred, the courts have given a broad interpretation to the meaning of debt.[794]

§7.346 To bind a transferor, notice of the existence of a lien right must appear on the face of a share certificate in accordance with subsection 56(2) of the OBCA.[795] Where a corporation is entitled to a lien against the shares of a particular shareholder it will lose that lien if it registers a transfer of the shares before the debt giving rise to the lien is paid.[796]

---

[789] OBCA, s. 40(3).
[790] OBCA, s. 56(3); CBCA, s. 49(8).
[791] [1917] Ch. 646 at 655, *per* Eve J.
[792] See, for instance *Bank of Africa v. Salisbury Gold Mining Co.*, [1892] A.C. 281 (P.C.); *British Columbia Timber Co. v. Jones*, [1943] 4 D.L.R. 686 (B.C.S.C.), var'd [1944] 2 D.L.R. 481 (B.C.C.A.).
[793] OBCA, s. 40(3).
[794] See, for instance, *Walkerton Binder Twine Co. v. Higgins*, [1902] O.J. No. 453, 1 O.W.R. 403 (H.C.J.).
[795] Where the lien is set out in the by-laws, a reference to restrictions and conditions set out in the articles of the corporation is not adequate notice of the right of lien: *McKain v. Canadian Birkbeck Investment & Savings Co.*, [1904] O.J. No. 131, 7 O.L.R. 241 (C.A.).
[796] *Bank of Africa v. Salisbury Gold Mining Co.*, [1892] A.C. 281 (P.C.).

Chapter 8

DEBT FINANCING

A. INTRODUCTION

§8.1 Virtually all corporations require medium-term and long-term financing. Chapter 7 examined the various rules governing the raising of financing through the issue of shares. Equity financing constitutes one of the two basic sources of corporate and commercial financing. The other basic source of financing is debt, and indeed it is this source which has given rise to the most widely varied types of specific investment. This chapter examines the raising of medium- and long-term capital through the issue of debt instruments. Consideration is also given to line-of-credit financing, as it often is provided by a bank or other financial institution to finance the day-to-day operations of the corporation. Although line-of-credit financing is theoretically of a short-term nature, in practice, such financing tends to continue from year to year without interruption.

§8.2 The focus of this chapter is on specific corporate law aspects of debt financing, rather than with the general debtor-creditor relationship. It is not practical in a text devoted to the study of corporate law to tackle in detail the law relating to mortgages, personal property security, bills of exchange, banking, guarantees, letters of credit, debtor and creditor rights and remedies, and bankruptcy and insolvency. While such subjects are obviously relevant to the financing of corporations, reference must be made to specialist texts devoted to these subjects for a complete statement of the law. In this chapter, it is possible to provide only some introductory notes sufficient to place the rules of corporate law discussed herein into a meaningful, practical context.

(i) The Nature of Debt

§8.3 The word "debt" has no fixed legal meaning, but takes shades of meaning from the occasion of its use and the context in which it appears.[1] In general terms, however, a debt is a certain sum of money that is owed by one person (the "debtor") to another (the "creditor"). All debts are a species of liability. The basic character of a debt that distinguishes it from other liabilities is that a debt is an obligation to pay a liquidated sum of money — that is a sum that is fixed and certain, and is due at an ascertainable time. In contrast, a liability to pay damages constitutes an inchoate liability, the precise extent of which remains to be ascertained. Because of their uncertain extent, damages have a contingent

---

[1] *Morrow v. Hayes*, 226 Mich. 301, 197 N.W. 554 at 555 (Supp. Ct. 1924).

character: the amount claimed is not necessarily the same as the amount owed to the creditor concerned. However, all liabilities of a corporation or other person, whether liquidated or not and whether absolute or contingent, ultimately may be reduced to some form of debt, if in no other manner than by way of judgment (in which case the amount of the judgment constitutes a judgment debt).

§8.4 The term "debt" denotes not only the obligation of the debtor to pay, but also the right of the creditor to receive and enforce payment. This right constitutes a chose in action, and thus a debt is a form of intangible property of which the creditor is the owner. Debts may be divided into the following classes: (1) statutory debts or penalties; (2) debts of record (*i.e.*, judgment debts), which are debts proved to exist by the record of a court or other tribunal; (3) debts arising by simple contract; (4) debts arising by deed; (5) debts arising from an estate. As discussed below, a debt may be either secured or unsecured — a secured debt being a debt for which the creditor has some security in addition to the mere personal liability of the debtor. Debts are assignable both in equity and by statute. Under a statutory assignment, where the assignment is absolute and in writing and notice of the assignment has been given to the debtor, then the assignee may sue the debtor to enforce the payment of the debt, without joining the assignor as a party to the action.

§8.5 Despite its breadth in certain contexts, in the context of corporate financing the word "debt" has a much narrower meaning: it describes liabilities of a corporation arising through loans to the corporation, the sale or other disposition by the corporation of its debt securities, and trade credit extended to the corporation by its suppliers. Other liabilities (*e.g.*, potential liability for damages, judgment debts and contingent or absolute liability under guarantees for the debts of third parties) are no doubt important, and may reduce, extinguish or otherwise qualify the amount that the corporation is entitled or able to borrow from its lenders. But those liabilities are not incurred by the corporation in the course of financing its operations.

§8.6 In theory the capital of a corporation may consist entirely of equity (*i.e.*, share capital) or may consist of a combination of equity and debt.[2] No matter how strong their equity base, virtually all active corporations have some debt, if only in the form of trade credit. Moreover, in practice, the equity of a corporation may have been eroded through losses of various sorts. Not infrequently, the point is reached where the equity of a corporation has been entirely eroded away, so that all that remains is a notional deficit account on the balance sheet of a corporation: the equity account represents no money, but rather the estimated extent of the shortfall between the value of the assets of the corporation and the extent of its liabilities. In such a case, the debt liabilities of the corporation are

---

[2] In *Kennedy v. Acadia Pulp & Paper Mills Co.* (1905), 38 N.S.R. 291 (C.A.), a prospectus in respect of a new issue of shares said that part of the proceeds raised through the issue would be applied in replacing working capital already spent. The money to be replaced had in fact been borrowed from a bank. Graham E.J. held that it was not improper to describe such borrowed funds as part of the capital of the corporation.

the only real funds that support the continued existence of the corporation and its asset base. In such a situation, business logic dictates that the interests of the shareholders have been extinguished, so that the corporation may properly be said to belong to its creditors. Surprisingly, however, the law does not correspond exactly with this logic. The creditors may petition the corporation into bankruptcy. The directors are required to consider the interests of the creditors in making their decisions. Nevertheless, the law continues to treat the shareholders as the owners of the corporation.

§8.7 A loan is a sum of money lent for a period of time that is required to be repaid either in money or in money's worth, with or without interest.[3] Generally, the undertaking to repay is absolute, but there is nothing improper in the parties agreeing that the obligation to repay shall be contingent.[4] The obligation to repay may also be limited by the parties to a particular income stream, and the creditors' right of recovery may be limited to a particular asset.[5] It is common among financial analysts to refer to the loans that have been made to a corporation as being its loan capital. Loan capital is capital in the sense that it constitutes part of the financial basis on which a corporation conducts its operations and constructs its business. From time to time, there have been cases in which the courts have attempted to distinguish loans from other types of credit. For instance, it has been suggested that a purchase of credit does not constitute a loan from the seller,[6] nor hire-purchase transactions,[7] nor is the discounting of bills of exchange drawn under an acceptance credit.[8] In contrast, payments made by bankers on overdrawn cheques,[9] and even perpetual debentures, have been held to constitute loans. For the most part, distinctions between loans and other types of credit serve only to confuse. Generally, they are drawn only for the purpose of bringing a particular transaction within, or casting it outside, taxation, registration or regulatory laws. Distinctions drawn for such limited purpose have little to offer as general principles of law.

§8.8 From an economic perspective, virtually all forms of credit may be employed as a method of corporate financing, and all expose the parties to the credit transaction to similar types of risk, which may be handled by employing similar techniques, such as the provision of security. It is true that not all of the liabilities and obligations of a corporation amount to an extension of credit, and that not all types of credit amount to a loan. However, whether a particular form of credit constitutes a loan is more determined by the circumstances in which the credit is provided, and the intentions of the parties, than the form that the credit

---

[3] See, generally, *Champagne Perrier-Jouet SA v. H.H. Finch Ltd.*, [1982] 3 All E.R. 713 at 717, *per* Walton J.
[4] See, generally, *Waite Hill Holdings Ltd. v. Marshall* (1983), 133 N.L.J. 745.
[5] See, generally, *DeVigier v. IRC*, [1964] 2 All E.R. 907 (H.L.).
[6] *Chow Yoong Hong v. Choong Fah Rubber Manufactory*, [1962] A.C. 209 at 216 (P.C.).
[7] *Olds Discount Co. v. Cohen*, [1938] 3 All E.R. 281 (H.L.); *Transport & General Credit Corp. v. Morgan*, [1939] Ch. 531; *Premor Ltd. v. Shaw Bros.*, [1964] 2 All E.R. 583 (C.A.).
[8] *IRC v. Rowntree & Co.*, [1948] 1 All E.R. 482 (C.A.).
[9] See, for instance, *Looker v. Wrigley* (1982), 9 Q.B.D. 397 (D.C.); *Cuthbert v. Roberts, Lubbock & Co.*, [1909] 2 Ch. 226 (C.A.).

takes.[10] If a particular extension of credit is intended to finance the operations of a corporation, it may properly be viewed as comprising part of the corporation's loan capital (although it may or may not be held to constitute a "loan" within the specific meaning of a particular statute).

(1) Importance of the Distinction Between Debt and Equity

§8.9 Equity and debt represent two different methods of financing corporate activity. As explained in Chapter 7, there is no clear and sharp distinction between them, for in many cases securities issued by a corporation will have a hybrid debt and equity character. The features of an obligation which tend to characterize it as being in the nature of equity are: (1) permanence; (2) subordinated status relative to the general unsecured liabilities of the corporation; (3) no right to receive interest on the principal sum advanced or invested, but rather an entitlement to participate in such distributions of the profits of the corporation as may be declared by the directors of the corporation.[11] Yet each of these characteristics may be modified to some extent without destroying the basic equity character of an investment. For instance, term preferred shares are not permanent; the holders of preference shares may enjoy a priority in the repayment of share capital over the holders of other shares issued by a corporation; cumulative dividends, if unpaid, must ultimately be discharged by the corporation even if their payment cannot be compelled. By the same token, a debt obligation of the corporation may possess some of these characteristics and yet still constitute a debt obligation. For instance, a debt security may be of very long term, and even perpetual debt obligations are not unknown. A debt may be subordinate by its terms to the right of the general and unsecured creditors of a corporation to be repaid amounts owing to them as such; and the entitlement of a creditor to interest on a debt obligation may be contingent upon the profitability of the corporation or there may be no such entitlement at all.

§8.10 There is little case law indicating how to distinguish between hybrid debt and equity obligations of a corporation, or with respect to the rules which govern such investments. In practice, the tendency is to treat those obligations of a corporation which are styled as shares as equity investments,[12] and to subject them to the restrictions imposed upon such investments under the OBCA or the CBCA, while hybrid obligations of a corporation which are styled as debt obligations are treated as such, although being limited in accordance with their terms. Distinguishing between equity and debt becomes important in the event of the insolvency or illiquidity of a corporation. If a particular investment is

---

[10] See, generally, *Potts Executors v. IRC*, [1951] A.C. 443 (H.L.).
[11] Because of its permanence, subordinated status and the limited right to receive dividends rather than interest, equity is sometimes described as the shareholders' "at risk" investment in the corporation. This term is misleading; "at greater risk" would be more appropriate, for as many a creditor will attest, all money advanced or otherwise owing on credit is to some extent at risk, for there is no certainty that even secured and guaranteed debt will ever be repaid in full.
[12] But see *Re Touquoy Gold Mining Co.* (1906), 1 E.L.R. 142 (N.S.T.D.), where an investment styled as a "preferred share" was held on its true construction to be a loan secured by a mortgage.

characterized as a share, the right of the corporation to redeem it or otherwise refund the investor's capital investment and the right to pay dividends on it is subject to the restrictions set out in Part III of the OBCA or Part V of the CBCA, as the case may be.[13] In particular, dividends may not be paid by the corporation, nor may shares be repurchased or otherwise acquired by the corporation where there are reasonable grounds for believing (in the case of repurchase) that,

- the corporation is, or after the payment would be, unable to pay its liabilities as they become due (*i.e.*, the corporation is illiquid); or
- after the payment the realizable value of the corporation's assets would be less than the aggregate of its liabilities and the amount that would be required to pay the holders of shares who have a right to be paid, on a redemption on liquidation, prior to the holders of the shares concerned (*i.e.*, the corporation is insolvent).

These restrictions do not apply in the case of debt obligations, although payments on such obligations are restricted under the general law concerning fraudulent preferences. Moreover, the shares of a corporation may not be issued until they are fully paid, and they may not be paid for by way of the issue of a promissory note by the person to whom they are issued, but these prohibitions do not apply in the case of debt securities.[14] So far there has been no reported Canadian case in which a corporate obligation styled as a subordinated debt has been treated as a share for corporate law purposes. But at least conceptually it is possible that such a finding might be made, and there is some authority for so doing (at least where those obligations provide that entitlement to interest is contingent on profitability), for section 139 of the *Bankruptcy and Insolvency Act* ("BIA")[15] provides:

> 139. Where a lender advances money to a borrower engaged or about to engage in trade or business under a contract with the borrower that the lender shall receive a rate of interest varying with the profits or shall receive a share of the profits arising from carrying on the trade or business, and the borrower subsequently becomes bankrupt, the lender of the money is not entitled to recover anything in respect of the loan until the claims of all other creditors of the borrower have been satisfied.

---

[13] See Ontario *Business Corporations Act*, R.S.O. 1990, c. B.16 ("OBCA"); *Canada Business Corporations Act*, R.S.C. 1985, c. C-44 ("CBCA"). Thus clause 221(1)(*a*) of the OBCA provides that upon a winding up,

> (*a*) the liquidator shall apply the property of the corporation in satisfaction of all its debts, obligations and liabilities and, subject thereto, shall distribute the property rateably among the shareholders according to their rights and interests in the corporation ...

[14] See *Re Limberlost Club*, [1973] O.J. No. 2243, , 2 O.R. (2d) 139 at 143-44 (H.C.J.), *per* Lerner J.
[15] R.S.C. 1985, c. B-3.

(2) The Nature of the Obligation Arising Under an Exercise of Redemption or Retraction Rights

§8.11 The overlap that exists between debt and equity comes into sharp focus when dealing with such hybrid rights as the right of a holder of a redeemable preferred share. Shares providing their holder with a right to require the corporation to redeem the shares may contain a provision which expressly confers a right to cause the corporation to be wound up, in the event that the corporation fails or refuses to redeem the shares as required.[16] Whether or not such a provision is present, it appears that the serving of a notice requiring the corporation to redeem shares gives rise to a binding obligation owed by the corporation to the shareholder whose shares are to be redeemed for the redemption price.[17] The precise nature of this obligation is, however, a matter of some uncertainty, for a key question to resolve is whether the obligation of the corporation to pay that obligation gives rise to

- a debt subject to an overriding condition that the solvency and liquidity tests governing redemption of share capital[18] are satisfied (so that upon the failure to satisfy the condition, the obligation lapses);

- a debt the performance of which is suspended for so long as the tests are unsatisfied (so that once the condition is satisfied, the binding force of the obligation revives and must be performed);

- a non-debt contingent obligation which is subordinate to the claims of the ordinary creditors of the corporation.[19]

In resolving this uncertainty, the courts have sometimes cautioned themselves that it is necessary to take care to ensure that the controlling shareholders of a corporation do not and are not permitted to recoup their investment in the corporation to the detriment of the creditors and minority shareholders of the corporation.[20]

§8.12 In *Re Central Capital Corp.*[21] the three justices hearing the case each adopted a different approach to the question of the nature of the corporation's payment obligation. The facts in that case were as follows: the two appellants had sold shares in Canadian General Securities Limited to the corporation, Central Capital, in 1987 and 1989, respectively. The appellants were issued preferred shares in the corporation in payment for those shares. The articles of the corporation provided that in the event of the liquidation, dissolution or winding up of Central Capital, the holders of the preferred shares were only entitled to rank after the creditors but ahead of the junior shareholders of the corporation.

---

[16] See generally, *Canada v. Imperial General Properties Ltd.*, [1985] S.C.J. No. 64, 21 D.L.R. (4th) 741.
[17] *Re East Chilliwack Agricultural Co-operative*, [1989] B.C.J. No. 705, 58 D.L.R. (4th) 11, 42 B.L.R. 236 (C.A.).
[18] OBCA, s. 32(2); CBCA, s. 36(2).
[19] See, for instance, *Robinson v. Wangemann*, 75 F.2d 756 at 757 (5th. Cir. 1935), *per* Foster Cir. J.
[20] *Nelson v. Rentown Enterprises Inc.* (1992), 96 D.L.R. (4th) 586 at 589 (Alta. Q.B.), *per* Hunt J.; see also *Mountain State Steel Foundries Inc. v. C.I.R.*, 284 F.2d 737 at 741 (1960).
[21] [1996] O.J. No. 359, 132 D.L.R. (4th) 223 (C.A.).

Unfortunately, the share terms of the articles made no express provision with respect to the rights of the appellants in the event of a reorganization of the corporation.

§8.13 The preferred shares contained a retraction clause entitling their holders to call upon the corporation to redeem the shares at a specified price. Central Capital became insolvent before the right was exercised. An order was made appointing Peat Marwick Thorne Inc. as interim receiver and administrator ("IRA") under the *Companies' Creditors Arrangement Act* ("CCAA"). Ultimately, a plan of arrangement was approved. Under the plan, the corporation's creditors were entitled to elect to exchange part of the debt owed them for shares and debentures in a new corporation, to which some of the assets of the insolvent corporation were transferred. The remainder of the debt was to be satisfied by the issuance of new debentures and shares in Central Capital. Prior to the order, Central Capital notified the appellants that it would not redeem the preferred shares because it was insolvent. Both appellants deposited the shares for redemption, even though the redemption date in the case of the second vendor was two years in the future at the time of that deposit. When the corporation failed to pay the redemption price, the appellants filed proofs of claim with the IRA, as creditors of the corporation. The IRA disallowed the claim, holding that the redemption would be contrary to law. On appeal to Feldman J., it was held at first instance[22] that the administrator was correct. An appeal was taken to the Ontario Court of Appeal, where three separate judgments were delivered.

§8.14 In a strong dissenting judgment, Finlayson J.A. was prepared to allow the appeal. In his eyes, the issue was a simple one: did the retraction clause in the preferred share terms create a debt owed by Central Capital as of June 15, 1992. Finlayson J.A. was of the opinion that a debt was so created.[23] After referring to the definition of debt in *Black's Law Dictionary, Jowitt's Dictionary of English Law* and *The Shorter Oxford English Dictionary*, he continued:

> ... I believe that the fundamental error that has been made in these proceedings arises from the conception that the preferred shares in question can either be debt instruments or equity participation instruments but they cannot have the attributes of both. ... [Feldman J.] is in effect stating that these instruments are preferred shares in the corporation because the parties have so described them. In the first place, I do not think that describing the documents as preferred shares is conclusive as to what instrument the parties thought they were creating. In the second place, it is not what the parties call the documents that is determinative of their identity, but rather it is what the facts require the court to call them. The character of the instrument is revealed by the language creating it and the circumstances of its creation. Although these instruments may "remain in place as shares" until they are actually redeemed, they also contain a specific promise to pay at a specified date. This is the language of debt. I cannot accept the proposition that a corporate

---

[22] [1995] O.J. No. 19, 29 C.B.R. (3d) 33, 22 B.L.R. 210 (Gen. Div.).
[23] [1996] O.J. No. 359, 132 D.L.R. (4th) 223 at 235 (C.A.).

share certificate cannot create a corporate debt in addition to the certificate holder's rights as a shareholder.[24]

There are, unfortunately, a number of problems inherent in the foregoing analysis. For instance, Finlayson J.A. appears to argue not that the label of "preferred shares" which was applied by the parties to the instruments in question, is inconclusive as to their nature of the rights created, but more that it is entirely irrelevant. Given that the parties in the *Re Central Capital* case were all sophisticated, it seems more logical to assume that they intended the term "share" to have its normal equity meaning rather than the debt meaning that Finlayson J.A. ascribed to it. The argument that the preferred shares should be treated as debt since the shares were accepted in part payment for capital assets transferred to Central Capital[25] is difficult to follow, since it is just as possible for a vendor to accept shares in payment of the transfer price as a debt obligation. The fact is at best inconclusive as to the true nature of the transaction, and where such uncertainty exists, it is far more consistent with the objective intent approach to contract interpretation to give effect to the form of a transaction (*i.e.*, to treat the preferred shares as having a debt character) than to some suspected hidden intent of the parties.

§8.15 As Weiler J.A. noted in her judgment dismissing the appeal, there was little in the documentation or record relating to the transaction to indicate an intention to create a debt obligation.[26] Moreover, the description of an investment in a corporation as being in the nature of preferred shares constitutes a representation to outsiders that the investment forms part of the equity capital base to which creditors and others with claims against the corporation may look for their payment.[27] She continued:

> The appellants submit that a winding-up or liquidation is not the same as a reorganization. This is true. Both, however, are methods of dealing with insolvency. Both are methods for secured creditors to enforce their claims by seizing the assets in which they hold security interests. If the value of the corporation as a going concern exceeds the liquidation value of the assets, it is in the interest of all the debt holders that the corporation be preserved as a going concern. The purpose of both a liquidation and a reorganization is to permit the rehabilitation of the insolvent person unfettered by debt. ... On a reorganization, among other things, the articles may be amended to alter or remove rights and privileges attaching to a class of shares and to create new classes of shares. ... These statutory provisions provide a clear indication that, on a reorganization, the interests of all shareholders, including shareholders with a right of redemption, are subordinated to the interests of the creditors. Where the debts exceed the assets of the company, a sound commercial result militates in favour of resolving this problem in a manner that allows creditors to obtain repayment of their debt in the manner which is most advantageous to them. ... In the case of an insolvency where the debts to creditors clearly exceed the assets of the company, the policy of federal insolvency legislation appears to be clear that

---

[24] *Ibid.*, at 236-37.
[25] *Ibid.*, at 239.
[26] *Ibid.*, at 256.
[27] *Ibid.*, at 252.

shareholders do not have the right to look to the assets of the corporation until the creditors have been paid.[28]

The promise of the corporation to repay the redemption price was dependent upon its ability to pay that price in accordance with the rules set down in the Act governing repayment of capital.[29] The obligation of the corporation to pay for the preferred shares was without effect to the extent that it conflicted with the statutory obligation under section 36 of the CBCA, not to reduce Central Capital's equity base.[30] The relevant date for determining whether there was a claim against Central Capital enforceable as a debt was September 8, 1992, at which time the corporation was insolvent, and section 36 barred payment. Thus even if Central Capital's obligation to redeem the shares of the appellants created a debt or liability, the appellants did not have claim provable within the meaning of section 121 of the *Bankruptcy and Insolvency Act*.[31]

§8.16 The judgment of Laskin J.A. dismissing the appeal came to a similar conclusion, but followed a different route. With respect to the attempt to distinguish between liquidation and reorganization he noted:

> It is illogical to conclude that the appellants could claim only as shareholders on a liquidation and yet can claim as creditors on the reorganization. Whether Central Capital's financial difficulties led to a liquidation or a reorganization, the issue is the same and the analysis and the result should also be the same. ... if when the appellants exercised their retraction rights the company were insolvent and were to be subsequently liquidated (or dissolved or wound up), the appellants would rank as shareholders on the liquidation. And as I have indicated above the result should be no different on the reorganization.[32]

While Laskin J.A. was prepared to accept that a hybrid investment interest could be created in a corporation that possessed certain of the features of both debt and equity,[33] he went on to hold that either in liquidation or reorganization it would ultimately be necessary to classify the interest of the investor concerned as being either debt or equity:

> It seems to me that these appellants must be either shareholders or creditors. Except for declared dividends, they cannot be both. Once they are characterized as shareholders, their rights of retraction do not create a debtor-creditor relationship. These rights enable them to call for repayment of their capital on a specific date (and at an agreed upon price) provided the company is solvent. Ordinarily shareholders have to recoup their investment by selling their shares to third parties. If they have retraction rights, however, they can compel the company (if solvent) to repay their investment at a given time for a given price. But the right of retraction provides for the return of capital not for the repayment of a loan. Certainly the *Canada Business Corporations Act* treats a redemption of shares as a return of capital because s. 39 of the statute requires a company on a redemption to deduct

---

[28] *Ibid.*, at 256-57.
[29] *Ibid.*, at 258.
[30] *Ibid.*, at 261.
[31] *Ibid.*, at 262.
[32] *Ibid.*, at 267-68.
[33] *Ibid.*, at 264-65.

from its stated capital account an amount equal to the value of the shares redeemed. The shares redeemed are then either cancelled or returned to the status of authorized but unissued shares.[34]

Later in his judgment, Laskin J.A. declared:

> Putting it differently, a preferred shareholder exercising a right of retraction on terms that exist here must rank behind the company's creditors.[35]

He explained:

> Holding that the appellants do not have provable claims accords with sound corporate policy. On the insolvency of a company, the claims of creditors have always ranked ahead of the claims of shareholders for the return of their capital. Case law and statute law protect creditors by preventing a company from using their funds to prejudice creditors' chances of repayment. Creditors rely on these protections in making loans to companies. Permitting preferred shareholders to be turned into creditors by endowing their shares with retraction rights runs contrary to this policy of creditor protection.[36]

(3) Debt and Trust

§8.17 In general, money lent to a debtor becomes the property of the debtor upon receipt, subject to a personal obligation on the part of the debtor to repay the amount so lent (perhaps backed up by a security interest against property of the debtor). In contrast, money received in trust by the debtor does not form part of the property of the debtor for distribution among the borrower's creditors, and may be traced by the beneficiary and recovered from the estate of the debtor in the event that the debtor is adjudged bankrupt.[37] It is therefore of utmost importance to determine whether a particular sum advanced to a debtor was advanced in the form of a loan or on trust. Such a trust need not be express, although in the absence of express provision, a trust must clearly have been intended.[38] Where money is advanced by A to B under the mutual intention that it should not become part of the assets of B but should be used exclusively for a specific purpose, the money is seen to have been advanced subject to an implied stipulation that if that purpose fails the money will be repaid, and that arrangement is sufficient to impress the money so advanced with a trust obligation.[39]

(ii) Secured and Unsecured Debt

§8.18 A secured debt entitles the creditor (by way of a lien, charge, mortgage or pledge) to look to some asset or assets of the corporation (including the whole of

---

[34] *Ibid.*, at 268.
[35] *Ibid.*, at 268.
[36] *Ibid.*, at 274.
[37] *Bankruptcy and Insolvency Act*, R.S.C. 1985, c. B-3, s. 67(1).
[38] *Thiess Watkins White v. Equiticorp Australia Ltd.*, [1991] 1 Qd. 82 at 84 (S.C.), *per* Jersey J.
[39] See *Barclays Bank Ltd. v. Quistclose Investments Ltd.*, [1970] A.C. 567 (H.L.); *Australian Conference Association Ltd. v. Mainline Constructions Pty. Ltd. (in liq.)* (1978), 141 C.L.R. 335 at 353 (H.C. Aust.), *per* Gibbs A.C.J.; *Re Associated Securities and the Companies Act*, [1981] 1 N.S.W.L.R. 742 (S.C.), *per* Needham J.

the undertaking of the corporation) for the satisfaction of the debt owed to him should the corporation default in payment.[40] A secured debt is thus a debt claim against the creditor coupled with a proprietary interest in one or more assets of the debtor. The right of a debtor to grant such a proprietary interest is inherent in the debtor's right to carry on business and to deal with its property in the ordinary course of that business. If a debtor has the right to sell its assets outright (which it surely must, for otherwise business is impossible), it must equally possess the more limited right to grant proprietary interests falling short of full ownership.[41] By simple logic, if there is a power to part with the whole of a property, there must necessarily be a power to part with its component elements and interests.

§8.19 Where a security interest is granted to secure a genuinely new indebtedness, it would be unusual for there to be any doubt as to its propriety. There is nothing improper *per se* with respect to the grant of a security interest to secure an existing indebtedness provided that in so doing the debtor does not create an unlawful preference in favour of the creditor to whom the security is granted, and provided the grant of the security interest is supported by fresh consideration.[42] The security will take effect not only against subsequent unsecured creditors, but also against unsecured creditors whose claims arose before the grant of the security.[43] Where a security is granted in consideration of an increase in an existing (but previously unsecured) line of credit, there is sufficient consideration to support the security.[44] Similarly, an act of forbearance may be sufficient consideration to support the grant of security.[45] Where funds are advanced on the understanding that a certain type of security interest will be provided, the fact that this security interest is not actually granted until after the advance is made does not mean that the security interest is inoperative for want of consideration.[46] The onus is upon the person attacking the validity of a security to prove a lack of consideration or some other defect in the security, unless

---

[40] The definition of secured creditor found in the *Bankruptcy and Insolvency Act*, R.S.C. 1985, c. B-3, s. 2(1) reads:

> 2.(1) "secured creditor" means a person holding a mortgage, hypothec, pledge, charge, lien on or against the property of the debtor or any part of that property as security for a debt due or accruing due to the person from the debtor, or a person whose claim is based on, or secured by, a negotiable instrument held as collateral security and on which the debtor is only indirectly or secondarily liable...

[41] *Levy-Russell Ltd. v. Shieldings Inc.*, [2004] O.J. No. 4291, 48 B.L.R. (3d) 28 at 45 (S.C.J.), *per* Cumming J.; see also, generally, *Farrell v. Caribou Gold Mining Co.* (1897), 30 N.S.R. 199 (C.A.); *Sheppard v. Bonanza Nickel Mining Co. of Sudbury*, [1894] O.J. No. 141, 25 O.R. 305 (Div. Ct.); *Re Farmers' Loan & Savings Co.*, [1899] O.J. No. 150, 30 O.R. 337 at 348 (C.A.), *per* Meredith C.J.

[42] *National Can Corp. v. Liberato*, [1978] O.J. No. 1315, 29 C.B.R. (N.S.) 108 (C.A.).

[43] *Re Heather's House of Fashion Inc.*, [1977] O.J. No. 2152, 23 C.B.R. (N.S.) 161 (C.A.).

[44] *Royal Bank v. Cal Glass Ltd.*, [1979] B.C.J. No. 1406, 9 B.L.R. 1 at 6-7 (S.C.), *per* Fawcus J., aff'd [1980] B.C.J. No. 2422, 22 B.C.L.R. 328 (C.A.).

[45] *Cadwells Ltd. (Trustee of) v. Royal Bank of Canada*, [1933] O.J. No. 205, 14 C.B.R. 497 (H.C.J.), aff'd [1934] O.J. No. 233, 15 C.B.R. 293 at 298 (C.A.), *per* Masten J.A.

[46] *Canadian Pittsburg Industries Ltd. v. Roberts & Hall Ltd.*, [1973] 2 W.W.R. 341, 32 D.L.R. (3d) 766 (Alta. C.A.).

the creditor and debtor are affiliated and the circumstances are so suspicious as to give rise to doubts as to the legitimacy of the transaction.[47]

§8.20 In order to create perfected security interests binding against third parties and trustees in bankruptcy, it is necessary to comply with registration requirements which apply to all security interests generally or of a particular type, such as the *Personal Property Security Act*,[48] the *Bank Act*,[49] and (in the case of security interests against land or interests in land), the *Registry Act*[50] or *Land Titles Act*.[51] There is no question that provincial registration requirements apply to federally incorporated corporations.[52] Disguising a security agreement in the form of an absolute conveyance or assignment does not circumvent the requirement for registration.[53] However, an incomplete or otherwise deficient legal charge of collateral may sometimes be sufficient to create an equitable charge of that collateral.[54] Where the same security agreement covers two different classes of property subject to different registration or perfection requirements, defective registration or perfection against one class of property does not affect the validity of registration or the perfection of a security interest against any other class of property.[55]

§8.21 In contrast to secured debt, an unsecured debt is a debt claim against the creditor to which no such proprietary interest is coupled. As a result, unsecured creditors enjoy no specific claim against the property of the debtor. Instead, they are entitled to look for their payment only to such property of the corporation as remains where all persons having interests in that property have enforced or abandoned their interests. This limit is inherent in the *Bankruptcy and Insolvency Act,* which provides for the gathering in of the property of a bankrupt, its realization and distribution among the creditors of a bankrupt, but subject to the rights of secured creditors. The general rule is that the unsecured debts of a corporation rank rateably,[56] but there are numerous preferences[57] and postponements[58] which depart from that general rule.

---

[47] *Imperial Bank of Canada v. McLellan* (1919), 12 Sask. R. 415 at 417 (T.D.), *per* McKay J.
[48] R.S.O. 1990, c. P.10.
[49] S.C. 1991, c. 46.
[50] R.S.O. 1990, c. R.20.
[51] R.S.O. 1990, c. L.5.
[52] See *Re Dominion Marble Co.* (1917), 35 D.L.R. 63 (Que. S.C.).
[53] *Dominion Creosoting Co. v. T.R. Nickson Co.*, [1916] B.C.J. No. 57, 35 D.L.R. 272 (C.A.), aff'd [1917] 2 W.W.R. 350, 55 S.C.R. 303; *Re Metropolitan Mortgage & Savings Co.*, [1915] B.C.J. No. 144, 7 W.W.R. 1204 (S.C.).
[54] See, generally, *Re Shipman Boxboards Ltd.*, [1940] O.J. No. 418, [1942] O.R. 118 (H.C.J.), but any such equitable charge will still be subject to applicable registration requirements: *Re Beaver Truck Co.*, [1926] 1 D.L.R. 71 at 73 (Ont. Master), *per* Garrow M.
[55] *Michael v. Bank of Montreal*, [1982] P.E.I.J. No. 46, 38 Nfld. & P.E.I.R. 398, 108 A.R. 398 at 400, 141 D.L.R. (3d) 169 (S.C.), *per* Campbell J.; but see *Turf Care Products Ltd. v. Crawford's Mower & Marine Ltd.*, [1978] O.J. No. 3686, 5 B.L.R. 89 (H.C.J.), leave to appeal refused 23 O.R. (2d) 292*n* (Div. Ct.).
[56] *Bankruptcy and Insolvency Act*, R.S.C. 1985, c. B-3, s. 141.
[57] *Ibid.*, s. 136.
[58] *Ibid.*, ss. 137, 138, 139 and 140.

(iii) Book Value

It is very rare for there to be an equivalence, between the book value of an asset and its market value (as determined by its actual selling price); moreover, there is not even a predictable relationship. In a number of recent sales of real property in Southern Ontario, the following book values and selling prices were recorded. Generally, the market value will exceed the book value of a non-depreciable asset, but in two of the following transactions, the book value was above the selling price (although one of these transactions was for a nominal sum to a non-arm's length party).

Property	Book Value	Sold For	Difference	Market Value As a percentage of Book Value
A	$133,652	$4,670,000	4,536,348	3494.149%
B	$1	$163,000	162,999	16,300,000.000%
C	$557,200	$3,570,000	3,012,800	640.704%
D	$148,000	$1	(147,999)	0.001%
E	$4,834,888	$21,000,000	16,165,112	434.343%
F	$296,024	$240,000	(56,024)	81.075%
G	$190,463	$2,000,000	1,809,537	1050.073%
Average	$880,033	$4,520,429	3,640,396	513.666%

(iv) Authority to Borrow

§8.22 The authority of the corporation and its directors and officers to incur debt is synonymous with the authority of the corporation to borrow.[59] Subsection 184(1) of the OBCA[60] provides that:

> 184.(1) Unless the articles or by-laws or a unanimous shareholder agreement otherwise provide, the articles of a corporation shall be deemed to state that the directors of a corporation may, without authorization of the shareholders,
>
> (a) borrow money upon the credit of the corporation;
>
> (b) issue, reissue, sell or pledge debt obligations of the corporation;
>
> (c) subject to section 20, give a guarantee on behalf of the corporation to secure performance of an obligation of any person; and
>
> (d) mortgage, hypothecate, pledge or otherwise create a security interest in all or any property of the corporation, owned or subsequently acquired, to secure any obligation of the corporation.

---

[59] *Irvine v. Union Bank of Australia* (1877), 2 App. Cas. 366 at 380 (P.C.), per Sir Barnes Peacock; *Thompson & Sutherland v. Nova Scotia Trust Co.*, [1971] N.S.J. No. 158, 19 D.L.R. (3d) 59 at 65 (S.C.), per Dubinsky J.; but see *Re Red Deer Mill & Elevator Co.* (1907), 7 W.L.R. 284 at 286 (Alta. T.D.), per Beck J.

[60] CBCA, s. 189(1).

Furthermore, unless the articles or by-laws of a corporation or a unanimous shareholder agreement relating to a corporation otherwise provide, the directors may, by resolution, delegate all or any of these powers to a director, a committee of directors or an officer.[61] It is a common and acceptable practice[62] for the directors of a corporation to approve a proposed loan to the corporation and the giving of security in respect of that loan, while delegating to the officers of the corporation the actual form (*i.e.*, terms and conditions) of the loan and security agreements.

§8.23 The power of a corporation to borrow for purposes connected with its business is generally presumed to exist.[63] Moreover, where specific borrowing powers are conferred, the statutory and by-law provisions granting those powers receive a broad interpretation, so as to permit the corporation to carry on its business with reasonable flexibility.[64] For instance, it is accepted that the power to borrow implies a power to grant security in respect of a borrowing,[65] and that power to grant security applies both with respect to new and existing indebtedness.[66] Similarly, security may be granted over after acquired property.[67] Furthermore, the courts do not inquire whether there has been strict compliance with such restrictions as apply, but rather whether there has been substantial compliance.[68]

§8.24 Despite this flexible attitude, the courts do require the directors and officers[69] to respect any limitation which is placed upon their borrowing powers

---

[61] OBCA, s. 184(2).
[62] *Reid v. Purity Farms Ltd.*, [1937] O.J. No. 267, [1937] O.R. 248 at 253 (C.A.), *per* Henderson J.A.
[63] *Long v. Hancock* (1885), 12 S.C.R. 532 at 545, *per* Gwynne J., rev'g [1885] O.J. No. 16, 12 O.A.R. 137 (C.A.), aff'd [1884] O.J. No. 31, 7 O.R. 154 (H.C.J.); see also *Royal Bank v. British Columbia Accident and Employers' Liability Insurance Co.*, [1917] 2 W.W.R. 898 at 899 (B.C.C.A.), *per* Galliher J.; *St. Jerome (Town) v. Commercial Rubber Co.* (1908), 17 Que. K.B. 274, [1908] A.C. 444 at 450-51 (P.C.), *per* Sir Henri Taschereau.
[64] See, for instance, *Royal Trust Co. v. Great Northern Elevator Co.* (1906), 30 Que. S.C. 499; *Re Atlas Loan Co.*, [1905] O.J. No. 119, 9 O.L.R. 250 (H.C.J.).
[65] *Re Nash Brick & Pottery Manufacturing Co.* (1873), 9 N.S.R. 254 (T.D.).
[66] *Mid-West Collieries Ltd. v. McEwen*, [1925] S.C.R. 326; *Re Real Property Act of Manitoba*, [1922] 1 W.W.R. 1043 (Man. K.B.); see also *Barthels, Shewan & Co. v. Winnipeg Cigar Co.* (1909), 10 W.L.R. 263 (Alta. T.D.).
[67] *Kirkpatrick v. Cornwall Electric Street Rlwy.*, [1901] O.J. No. 174, 2 O.L.R. 113 (C.A.).
[68] *Ridout Real Estate Ltd. (Trustee of) v. Bank of Nova Scotia*, [1965] S.C.J. No. 41, 7 C.B.R. (N.S.) 264, [1965] S.C.R. 681 at 694, *per* Spence J.; *Re Express Engineering Works Ltd.*, [1920] 1 Ch. 466 (C.A.). See generally, *Douglas v. Maritime United Farmers Co-op Ltd.*, [1928] 3 D.L.R. 166 (C.A.); but compare *Valin v. Lion Nead Rubber Co.* (1927), 65 Que. S.C. 410; *Barthels, Shewan & Co. v. Winnipeg Cigar Co.* (1909), 10 W.L.R. 263 (Alta. T.D.) — all shareholders signing chattel mortgage held to dispense with need for a meeting to authorize the security in question; *Adams and Burns v. Bank of Montreal*, [1899] B.C.J. No. 3, 8 B.C.R. 314 at 319-20 (C.A.), *per* Martin J., aff'd 32 S.C.R. 719 — ratification by shareholders rather than prior authorization.
[69] See, for instance, *Glen Brick Co. v. Shackwell* (1870), 2 R.L.O.S. 625, 15 R.J.R.Q. 230, aff'd 2 Rev. Crit. 470 (Que. C.A.).

under the articles or by-laws of the corporation,[70] although subsection 16(3) of the OBCA provides that acts of a corporation are not invalid by reason only that the act is contrary to its articles, by-laws or a unanimous shareholder agreement and clause 19(*a*) of that Act prohibits a corporation from asserting as a defence that the articles, by-laws or a unanimous shareholder agreement respecting the corporation have not been satisfied.

(v) Identifying Contracts of the Corporation

§8.25 The question may arise as to whether a transaction entered into by an officer purportedly on behalf of a corporation was in fact a transaction of that corporation.[71] Suppose for instance, that funds are lent to a corporation as a result of a loan agreement purportedly entered into on the corporation's behalf by someone connected with it. As a general rule, it is difficult to affix liability to a corporation for money purportedly borrowed in its name where the funds in question never reach the corporation.[72] In *Bank of Montreal v. Petrobuild Ltd.*[73] a line of credit in favour of a corporation was increased under the authority of a single signing officer of the debtor company. The banking by-law of that company required borrowings to be authorized by two officers. The defendant company was nonetheless held liable with respect to advances under the increased line, for the company had received the money advanced under it and had used it for legitimate purposes of its business. In such circumstances, the company was not entitled to deny the validity of the increase on the basis that it was an unauthorized borrowing.[74]

§8.26 Along the same lines, in *Re Guaranteed Hardware Co.*[75] the banking resolution of a corporation provided that any two officers or directors acting together were authorized to borrow money on the corporation's behalf. The corporation obtained a loan from a bank, giving as security a chattel mortgage and a debenture, both of which documents were executed by a single person

---

[70] *Walmsley v. Rent Guarantee Co.* (1881), 29 Gr. 484 at 488-89 (Ont. H.C.). See also *Anderson Lumber Co. v. Canadian Conifer Ltd.*, [1976] A.J. No. 358, [1976] 3 W.W.R. 255 (S.C.), aff'd [1977] A.J. No. 179, 77 D.L.R. (3d) 126 (C.A.).

[71] As to the difficulty of identifying contracts of a corporation where a corporate agent has acted to defraud both the corporations and the contractor with whom he or she has dealt, see clause 19(*d*) of the OBCA and CBCA, s. 18(*d*); *Martin v. Artyork Investments Ltd.*, [1995] O.J. No. 2829, 25 O.R. (3d) 705 (C.A.), rev'd [1997] S.C.J. No. 54, 33 O.R. (3d) 64; *Sheppard v. Bonanza Nickel Mining Co. of Sudbury*, [1894] O.J. No. 141, 25 O.R. 305 (C.A.), per Boyd C.; *Veilleux v. Atlantic & Lake Superior Railway Co.* (1910), 39 Que. S.C. 127, per Greenshields J.; see also *Re Winding-up Act and Summerside Electric Co.* (1908), 5 E.L.R. 129 (P.E.I.S.C.); *Re Magdalena Steam Navigation Co.* (1860), Johns 690, 70 E.R. 597 at 694, per Wood V.C.; *Zimmerman v. Andrew Motherwell of Canada Ltd. (Trustees of)*, [1923] O.J. No. 48, 54 O.L.R. 342 at 350 (C.A.), per Logie J., aff'd [1925] 3 W.W.R. 42, [1925] 3 D.L.R. 953 (P.C.); *Reversion Fund & Insurance Co. v. Maison Casway Ltd.*, [1913] 1 K.B. 364.

[72] *Martin v. Artyork Investments Ltd.*, [1995] O.J. No. 2829, 25 O.R. (3d) 705 (C.A.), rev'd [1997] S.C.J. No. 54. On the other hand, where funds do reach the corporation, it will not normally be permitted to escape liability to repay them merely because the loan was not authorized.

[73] [1981] N.B.J. No. 247, 36 N.B.R. (2d) 375, 94 A.P.R. 375 (Q.B.).

[74] See also *Crocker Press Ltd. v. Imperial Trust Co.*, [1921] O.J. No. 427, 20 O.W.N. 409 (H.C.).

[75] [1972] O.J. No. 1831, [1972] 3 O.R. 138 (H.C.J.).

who held the offices of president and secretary of the corporation. The bank making the loan and receiving the security had actual notice of the resolution. The corporation argued that the loan was unauthorized. Even so, it was held that the bank's claim was good. Under general equitable principles the corporation was bound by the lending arrangement: it had borrowed money which was used to pay debts owed by the corporation.[76]

§8.27 A corporation may be seen to have adopted a contract improperly made by its directors or officers in exercise of their authority either by its express words or by its conduct. For instance, in *Conant v. Miall*,[77] the defendant company was incorporated in England but carried on business in Ontario, where it had a resident managing director. Its board meetings were held in England, where most of its directors lived. The managing director bought property in his own name for the use of the company, giving a mortgage back. The reason given for the use of his own name rather than the company's was that the company's seal was in England. In an action brought against the company to enforce the transaction, it was contended by the company that it had neither authorized nor ratified the transaction, and that its managing director had not been acting as such but had entered into the transaction personally. The evidence showed that the managing director had notified the company as to what he had done, and although the other directors disapproved, they had not repudiated the transaction. Instead they had occupied the property and instructed the managing director to insure the property against fire. It was held that in so doing the company had adopted the contract made by its managing director as its own. Although it was doubtful whether the managing director had the authority to enter into the transaction, the company had by ratification and part performance rendered itself liable on the mortgage.[78]

§8.28 Restitutionary principles may also come into play, if there is a dispute over whether a corporate borrowing has been properly authorized. More specifically, where a corporation borrows money and uses the borrowing to pay its debts or uses the moneys otherwise in the normal course of its business, the loan is repayable, and applicable security is enforceable, even though the lender may know of the want of power of the corporation to borrow.[79] Any other approach than to hold the corporation obliged to repay would lead to an unjust enrichment.

(vi) Interest

§8.29 Interest is the payment made by a borrower to the lender as compensation for the use of the lender's money over the period of the loan.[80] It is a general rule of common law that, except in limited cases, interest is not payable on a debt or

---

[76] *Ibid.*, at 141.
[77] [1870] O.J. No. 289, 17 Gr. 574 (Ch.).
[78] *Ibid.*, *per* Spragge C. at 584.
[79] *Levy-Russell Ltd. v. Shieldings Inc.*, [2004] O.J. No. 4291 at para. 102 (S.C.J.) *per* Cumming J.
[80] See, generally, *Bennett v. Ogston* (1930), 15 Tax Cas. 374 at 379, *per* Rowlatt J.

loan unless there is an express or implied agreement to that effect,[81] a statute so provides,[82] or there has been a course of dealing between the parties under which the obligation to pay interest has been recognized.[83] Trade custom may also give rise to an implied agreement to pay interest.[84] If an agreement provides for the payment of interest, but does not specify a rate, then interest is payable only at a rate of 5 per cent per annum.[85] Compound interest is interest charged upon arrears in the payment of interest. The lawfulness of compound interest has been settled since at least the 18th century.[86]

§8.30 A loan agreement may provide for the payment of interest both before and after maturity[87] and judgment.[88] Where interest is payable under an agreement, it is presumed that only simple interest is contemplated unless compound interest is expressly provided for[89] or can be inferred from trade custom or past dealing.[90] It has been held that where the debt instrument is silent, interest may be claimed on overdue interest at the legal rate — that is the 5 per cent interest rate provided for in the *Interest Act*.[91]

§8.31 It follows that as a general rule a loan agreement or debt instrument must provide for the payment of interest in order for any interest to be recoverable under it[92] — although the courts have a residual discretion to allow interest

---

[81] See, for instance, *Carton v. Bragg* (1812), 15 East. 223, 104 E.R. 828 at 227 (K.B.), per Lord Ellenborough L.J.; *Chalie v. Duke of York* (1806), 6 Esp. 45, 170 E.R. 826 (N.P.). In *Re Fund of Funds Ltd.*, [1986] O.J. No. 497, 59 C.B.R. (N.S.) 310 (H.C.J.), Houlden J.A. held that interest was payable at common law as damages for breach of contract where the contract, if performed, would to the knowledge of the parties have entitled the plaintiff to receive interest.

[82] *Re Gosman* (1881), 17 Ch. D. 771 (C.A.); *Trusts & Guarantee Co. v. Continental Supply Co.*, [1932] 1 W.W.R. 921 (Alta. T.D.).

[83] *London Chatham & Dover Rlwy. v. South Eastern Rlwy.*, [1893] A.C. 429 at 438 (H.L.), per Lord Herschell L.C. For cases in which such courses of dealing have been recognized, see *Re Anglesey (Marquis); Wilmot v. Gardner*, [1901] 2 Ch. 548 (C.A.); *Great Western Insurance Co. v. Cunliffe* (1874), L.R. 9 Ch. App. 525; *Re W.W. Duncan & Co.*, [1905] 1 Ch. 307.

[84] See, for instance, *IRC v. Holder*, [1931] 2 K.B. 81 (H.L.); *National Bank of Greece, SA. v. Pinios Shipping Co. (No. 1) and Another, The Maria*, [1990] 1 All E.R. 78 (H.L.).

[85] *Interest Act*, R.S.C. 1985, c. I-15, s. 3 provides:

> 3. Whenever any interest is payable by the agreement of parties or by law, and no rate is fixed by the agreement or by law, the rate of interest shall be five per cent per annum.

For an instance where this section was applied, see *Royal Bank v. Larry Creighton Professional Corp.*, [1989] A.J. No. 129, 45 B.L.R. 217 (C.A.). For a recent case involving the interpretation of an ambiguous interest payment provision, see *Knudsen v. Knudsen*, [1998] O.J. No. 6474, 37 O.R. (3d) 676 (Gen. Div.).

[86] See generally *Boddam v. Ryley* (1787), 4 Bro. P.C. 561 (H.L.); *Ex p. Bevan* (1803), 9 Ves. 223 (L.C.); *Fergusson v. Fyffe* (1841), 8 Cl. & Fin. 121, 8 E.R. 121 (H.L.).

[87] *Trusts & Guarantee Co. v. Continental Supply Co.*, [1932] 1 W.W.R. 921 (Alta. T.D.).

[88] *Eastern Trust Co. v. Cushing Sulphite Fibre Co.* (1906), 3 N.B. Eq. 392, 2 E.L.R. 93 (S.C.).

[89] *Fergusson v. Fyffe* (1841), 8 Cl. & Fin. 121, 8 E.R. 121 at 140 (H.L.), per Lord Cottenham L.C.; *Williamson v. Williamson* (1869), L.R. 7 Eq. 542 (V.C.); *Wade v. Murray*, [1940] O.J. No. 376, [1940] O.R. 239 (H.C.J.); *Eastern Trust Co. v. Cushing Sulphite Fibre Co.* (1906), 3 N.B. Eq. 392 at 402 (S.C.).

[90] *Paton v. IRC*, [1938] A.C. 341 (H.L.).

[91] *Montreal Trust Co. v. Abitibi Power & Paper Co.*, [1944] O.R. 515 (H.C.J.).

[92] See, generally, *Montreal Trust Co. v. Abitibi Power & Paper Co.*, [1944] O.R. 515 (H.C.J.).

where payment had been wrongfully withheld.[93] However, much of the case law pertaining to the limited availability of pre- and post-judgment interest must now be read subject to the *Courts of Justice Act*, which, as detailed below, provides a broad discretion to the court to award interest on judgment debts.

§8.32 In the case of publicly traded medium- and long-term debt securities (particularly non-registered debt securities) it is common for interest to be payable upon presentation of coupons which are attached to and form part of the debt instrument at the time of its issue.[94] Coupons were developed as a convenient method of obtaining payment of interest as it became due under a debenture. They were of particular value where the holders were mostly foreign residents, as they eliminated the need to forward the entire bond to the place of payment each time interest was payable under the bond. In time, the coupons themselves came to be recognized as articles of commerce. They may be separated from the bond or instrument to which they were attached and sold separately (usually at a discount) to third parties.[95] The coupon is entitled to the benefit of any security interest securing payment of the principal under the debenture or instrument to which it was originally attached.[96] Although interest coupons may provide for the payment of interest at monthly, quarterly, half-yearly or yearly intervals, interest accrues from day-to-day, so that if the debenture is redeemed between interest payment dates, interest must be paid up to the date of redemption.[97]

§8.33 Where a creditor refuses to accept payment of an amount owing, the creditor forfeits the right to compound interest. For instance, in *Montreal Trust Co. v. Stanrock Uranium Mines Ltd.*[98] the defendant corporation was in default in the payment of principal and interest on a bond. It offered to pay the holders of the bond principal and interest to a stated date. This payment would be made without prejudice to any claim that the bond holders might have for the payment of compound interest — the defendant's proposal providing for that question to be submitted to court. Certain of the bond holders accepted this offer while others rejected it. It was held that those bond holders who refused the offer could not claim compound interest beyond the stated date of payment.

---

[93] *Toronto Rlwy. Co. v. Toronto*, [1906] A.C. 117 (P.C.).
[94] Generally, presentment is required before any payment will be made: *Osborne v. Preston & Berlin Rlwy Co.*, [1859] O.J. No. 218, 9 U.C.C.P. 241 (C.A.); *McDonald v. Great Western Rlwy. Co.*, [1861] O.J. No. 40, 21 U.C.Q.B. 223 (C.A.). However, it is not a condition precedent to the bringing of an action to enforce bonds that bonds be presented for payment, where there would have been no funds available to pay the bonds in any event: *Fellowes v. Ottawa Gas Co.*, [1869] O.J. No. 109, 19 U.C.C.P. 174 (C.A.).
[95] See, generally, *Connolly v. Montreal Park & Island Rlwy.* (1901), 20 Que. S.C. 1 (C.A.); *Kethwar v. Duncan*, 96 U.S. 659 at 662 (1877).
[96] *Trusts & Guarantee Co. v. Grand Valley Rlwy. Co.*, [1919] O.J. No. 84, 44 O.L.R. 398 at 412-13 (C.A.), *per* Hodgins J.A.
[97] *Re Rogers Trusts* (1860), 1 Dr. & Sm. 338 at 342, 62 E.R. 408 at 412-13 (V.C.), *per* Kindersley V.C.
[98] [1965] O.J. No. 1170, [1966] 1 O.R. 258 at 283 (H.C.J.), *per* Evans J.

§8.34 The limited cases in which interest is payable by operation of law in the absence of a provision in the lending agreement or an established practice between the parties are: first, that interest is payable on a mortgage debt even though the deed is silent as to interest;[99] second, that interest is payable to a guarantor who has paid the creditor under a guarantee — this right arising from the guarantor's right to indemnification by the principal debtor;[100] third, that interest is payable in relation to a sale of land which is specifically enforceable.[101]

§8.35 In contrast to shares, debt securities generally have a nominal face value — the equivalent to the par value which was formerly common in the case of shares. The trading value of a debt security may easily be greater or less than the face value of that security — the trading value depending upon such factors as the credit rating of the issuer and the rate of interest provided for in the instrument relative to the rates that are then prevailing in the market. Debentures, promissory notes, bills of exchange (particularly bankers' acceptances) and other debt instruments of a corporation may be issued at a discount.[102] The discount amount is not interest, although the practical effect of any such discount is to impose a cost of borrowing on the corporation: for the corporation receives only the discounted amount, but must repay the full face amount of the debenture or other instrument upon its maturity.

(1) The Effect of Default and Judgment on Interest Entitlement

§8.36 Commercial lending agreements usually include a provision extending the contractual rate of interest until the time when the full balance owing to the lender is paid. A typical provision may read:

> The Borrower shall pay the Lender interest on any amount advanced under the Line of Credit and upon all arrears of interest and costs and fees payable under this Agreement at the rate specified above, that interest to be calculated not-in-advance and compounded monthly and payable on the amount outstanding from day to day both before and after default and judgment, until payment is made.

Although section 128 of the *Courts of Justice Act* provides for pre-judgment interest, it has been held that where pre-judgment interest is payable at a rate specified in a contract, the court has no jurisdiction to alter the contract rate.[103] This is consistent with the Court of Appeal's ruling in *Irvington Holdings Ltd. v.*

---

[99] See *Mendl v. Smith* (1943), 112 L.J. Ch. 279, 169 L.T. 153; *Re Drax*, [1903] 1 Ch. 781 at 795 (C.A.), *per* Cozens-Hardy L.J.

[100] See *Petre v. Duncombe* (1851), 20 L.J.Q.B. 242; *Re Fox, Walker & Co.* (1880), 15 Ch. D. 400 (C.A.).

[101] *International Rlwy. v. Ontario (Niagara Parks Commission)*, [1941] A.C. 328 (P.C.); *Re Priestley's Contract*, [1947] Ch. 469. Interest is payable not only in the case of voluntary sale, but also in the case of expropriation: *Inglewood Pulp Co. v. New Brunswick (Electric Power Commission)*, [1928] A.C. 492 (P.C.).

[102] *Bank of Toronto v. Cobourg, Peterborough & Marmara Rlwy.*, [1885] O.J. No. 86, 10 O.R. 376 (Ch.).

[103] *Convert-A-Wall Ltd. v. Brampton Hydro-Electric Commission* (1988), 65 O.R. (2d) 385 (Div. Ct.); *Courts of Justice Act*, R.S.O. 1990, c. C.43.

Black[104] that interest is not to be used as either a reward or penalty, but is meant to reflect the value of the money wrongfully held.

§8.37 Section 129 of the *Courts of Justice Act* empowers a court to award post-judgment interest, but subsection 129(5) goes on to provide:

> 129.(5) Interest shall not be awarded under this section where interest is payable by a right other than under this section.

In an action for debt it is therefore necessary to decide whether the contractual right survives the judgment. If it does, subsection (5) bars an award of interest at the rate provided under section 129, and the contract rate will continue.

§8.38 The question of whether a contractual rate of interest will survive a judgment given with respect to the principal debt involves a consideration of the doctrine of merger as it applies to judgment debts.[105] Broadly stated, merger is the absorption of a lesser right into a greater right, so that the lesser right is sunk or drowned in the greater right. When judgment has been given in an action, the cause of action in respect of which it was given is merged in the judgment and its place is taken by the rights created by the judgment, so that a second action may not be brought on that cause of action.[106] The concept of merger is an outgrowth of the principle of *res judicata,* which prevents the relitigation of matters and questions that have previously been the subject of final judgment in another action or proceeding.[107] The principle has been greatly extended, however, so that upon final judgment with respect to a particular breach of contract, all rights of the injured party under the contract with respect to that breach merge in the judgment.[108] The rule is not confined (either by logic or by law) to the sole question of interest, but extends by inference to all contractual rights relevant to the contract that was the subject of the action. However, whether the rule applies on the facts of a given case is primarily a question of construction.[109] The parties to a contract may agree that the contract rate will survive any judgment and remain in effect until actual payment is received by the creditor.[110] Moreover, if a covenant to pay interest at a specified rate appears in a fresh agreement (*e.g.*, an agreement relating to the payment of the judgment) made between the parties after the giving of the judgment, that contract rate will apply, because although the old contract rate may have merged in the judgment, the subsequent (post-judgment) agreement creates a new debt.[111] The clearest situation in which the right to receive interest at the contract rate will survive judgment is where the

---

[104] [1987] O.J. No. 56, 58 O.R. (2d) 449 (C.A.). See also *Ross Steel Fabricators & Contractors v. Loaring Construction Co.*, [1986] O.J. No. 1122, 15 C.P.C. (2d) 27 (H.C.J.).

[105] See, for instance, *Heller-Natofin (Western) Ltd. v. Carlton Developments Ltd.*, [1979] B.C.J. No. 666, 16 B.C.L.R. 64 (S.C.).

[106] 26 Hals. (4th ed.), 551.

[107] *Greathead v. Bromily* (1798), 7 Term Rep. 455 at 456, 101 E.R. 1073 (K.B.), *per* Lord Kenyon C.J.

[108] *Re Sneyd, ex p. Fewings* (1883), 25 Ch. D. 338 at 355 (C.A.), *per* Fry L.J.

[109] *Economic Life Assurance Society v. Ushborne*, [1902] A.C. 147 at 151 (H.L.).

[110] *Ibid.*, at 153.

[111] *Ibid.*, at 151.

parties expressly so provide.[112] However, the continuation of the contract rate may be seen to be implicit in the language that the parties have used, even where the question of merger is not expressly dealt with in the contract.

§8.39 At one time it was accepted that where the contract did not provide for a continuation of the contract rate of interest after judgment, the court could allow interest only at the legal rate.[113] By virtue of subsection 127(1) of the *Courts of Justice Act*[114] the post-judgment interest rate in Ontario is the Bank of Canada bank rate at the end of the first day of the last month of the quarter preceding the quarter in which the date of the judgment falls, rounded to the next higher whole number where the bank rate includes a fraction, plus 1 per cent. Subject to an adverse fluctuation in interest rates between the date of default and judgment, for most borrowers and in most cases this is still a favourable rate and will likely be less than the contract rate. However, clause 130(1)(*b*) of the *Courts of Justice Act* would appear to allow the court to continue the contract rate until payment is made, despite the merger of the interest payment provision of the contract into the judgment of the court. It provides that:

> 130.(1) The court may, where it considers it just to do so, in respect of the whole or any part of the amount on which interest is payable under section 128 or 129,

> . . . . .

> (*b*) allow interest at a rate higher or lower than that provided in either section.

(2) Usury

§8.40 The charging of interest was illegal at common law, and while the law has changed significantly, there are still fairly strict prohibitions under Canadian law. However, throughout the common law world, the meaning of usury and the approach taken towards it varies significantly from one jurisdiction to another. In Canada, the law respecting usury is found in subsection 347(1) of the *Criminal Code*,[115] which makes it an indictable offence punishable by up to five years' imprisonment to enter into an agreement to receive interest at a criminal rate, or to receive a payment or partial payment of interest at a criminal rate.

> 347.(1) Notwithstanding any Act of Parliament, everyone who

> (*a*) enters into an agreement or arrangement to receive interest at a criminal rate, or

> (*b*) receives a payment or partial payment of interest at a criminal rate,

> is guilty of,

---

[112] See, for instance, *Si-Thoo v. Berry*, [1978] 2 W.W.R. 641 (Man. Q.B.).
[113] *Regina Steam Laundry Ltd. v. Saskatchewan Government Insurance Office*, [1971] 1 W.W.R. 96 at 99 (Sask. C.A.).
[114] R.S.O. 1990, c. C.43.
[115] R.S.C. 1985, c. C-46.

(c) an indictable offence and is liable to imprisonment for a term not exceeding five years, or

(d) an offence punishable on summary conviction and is liable to a fine not exceeding twenty-five thousand dollars or to imprisonment for a term not exceeding six months or to both.

Subsection 347(2) defines a criminal rate to be an effective annual rate of interest that exceeds 60 per cent on the credit advanced:

> "criminal rate" means an effective annual rate of interest calculated in accordance with generally accepted actuarial practices and principles that exceeds sixty per cent on the credit advanced under an agreement or arrangement ...

The scope of the prohibition is considerably expanded as a result of the wide definition given to the term "interest":

> "interest" means the aggregate of all charges and expenses, whether in the form of a fee, fine, penalty, commission or other similar charge or expense or in any other form, paid or payable for the advancing of credit under an agreement or arrangement, by or on behalf of the person to whom the credit is or is to be advanced, irrespective of the person to whom any such charges and expenses are or are to be paid or payable, but does not include any repayment of credit advanced or any insurance charge, official fee, overdraft charge, required deposit balance or, in the case of a mortgage transaction, any amount required to be paid on account of property taxes ...

The courts have had some difficulty in deciding whether profit-sharing arrangements[116] and late-payment penalties[117] are caught by the definition, but the current approach taken by the courts is to give the definition a broad interpretation. Nevertheless, not all amounts payable to a creditor are caught. For instance, prepayment penalties have been held to fall outside the definition.[118] As with late payment fees, pre-payment fees are in many respects elective at the borrower's discretion (for the borrower need not pay them if he or she keeps the loan outstanding for the term agreed). Moreover, pre-payment fees are not amounts charged "for the advancing of credit", but rather are payable because of the early repayment of a term loan, as compensation for the lost income of the lender.

§8.41 It is not possible to circumvent the prohibition against usury by disguising interest payments as fees.[119] In *Milani v. Banks*[120] it was found that the plaintiff had lent the defendant $35,000 for one month on terms that required the defendant to pay an up-front fee of $3,000 (so that the defendant received only

---

[116] *677950 Ontario Ltd. v. Artell Developments Ltd.*, [1992] O.J. No. 1548, 93 D.L.R. (4th) 334 (C.A.), aff'd [1993] S.C.J. No. 61, 64 O.A.C. 161.

[117] *Garland v. Consumer's Gas Co.* (1995), 122 D.L.R. (4th) 377 (Gen. Div.), aff'd [1996] O.J. No. 3162, 155 D.L.R. (4th) 671 (C.A.), rev'd [1998] S.C.J. No. 76, 165 D.L.R. (4th) 385.

[118] *Nelson v. CTC Mortgage Corp.*, [1984] B.C.J. No. 3161, 16 D.L.R. (4th) 139 (C.A.), aff'd [1986] S.C.J. No. 35, [1986] 1 S.C.R. 749.

[119] As to the charging of issuance fees for letters of credit, see *Kebet Holdings Ltd. v. 351173 B.C. Ltd.*, [1992] B.C.J. No. 2735, 8 B.L.R. (2d) 89 (C.A.).

[120] [1992] O.J. No. 2297, 98 D.L.R. (4th) 104 (Gen. Div.), rev'd in part [1997] O.J. No. 1171, 145 D.L.R. (4th) 55 (C.A.).

$32,000), plus interest at 18 per cent on the $35,000. A promissory note was given in respect of the loan, secured by a collateral mortgage. The fee of $3,000 was held to be within the definition of "interest" and thus the total interest payment obligation was held to be contrary to the *Criminal Code* and illegal. Nevertheless, the principal amount of $32,000 was recoverable. In addition, at the trial level, the collateral mortgage was set aside under the *Unconscionable Transactions Relief Act*,[121] because of the excessive interest payment obligation.[122] On appeal to the Ontario Court of Appeal, interest was allowed at 18 per cent per annum and the mortgage was reinstated. The disallowance of the $3,000 fee was left in place.[123]

§8.42 In *William E. Thomson Associates Inc. v. Carpenter*,[124] A agreed to provide a loan of U.S. $750,000, with $250,000 of that amount being advanced immediately (to be repaid within three months), and the balance to be advanced at A's discretion. Interest was to be charged at 2 per cent above the U.S. Base Rate of a designated bank. In addition, the borrower was to pay a facility fee of $37,500 in respect of services and expenses, that amount being deductible from the first advance. The borrower also agreed to pay legal fees and disbursements of $7,500, so that in total the borrower received only $205,000 of the first advance. After paying $17,000 in interest, the borrower defaulted. The first question that the court had to decide was whether the various fees were within the scope of the term "interest", in which respect Blair J.A. stated that the definition is intended to be all-inclusive and covers charges of any kind or in any form paid or payable under an agreement or arrangement for the advancing of credit. However, while the definition of interest is broad, brokerage fees payable to a third party broker rather than to the lender do not fall within the definition of interest.[125]

§8.43 Section 347 of the *Criminal Code* has been extensively interpreted by the courts, and there is now a detailed body of case law governing the correct manner of applying the provision to the facts of a given case. In terms of its general objective, it has been held that section 347 is an anti-usury law, intended to prevent both agreements for the payment of excessive interest and the actual receipt of such interest. As with any allegation of criminality, the party asserting the illegality bears the onus of proving it.[126] Section 347 has been described by the Supreme Court of Canada as a "a deeply problematic law". The law was originally designed to deal with the problem of loan sharking, but because of the comprehensive terms in which it is drafted, the section applies it applies to a

---

[121] R.S.O. 1990, c. U.2.
[122] See also *Saunders v. Oceanus Marine Inc.*, [1997] N.S.J. No. 162, 32 B.L.R. (2d) 97 (C.A.).
[123] [1997] O.J. No. 1171, 145 D.L.R. (4th) 55 (C.A.).
[124] [1989] O.J. No. 1459, 44 B.L.R. 125 (C.A.), leave to appeal to S.C.C. refused 37 O.A.C. 398*n*.
[125] *Helo Enterprises Ltd. v. Liquidators of Standard Trust Co.*, [1993] B.C.J. No. 2662, 108 D.L.R. (4th) 415 (C.A.), aff'd [1996] S.C.J. No. 18.
[126] *Great America Leasing Co. v. Yates*, [2003] O.J. No. 4689 (C.A.); *618469 Ontario Ltd. v. Szanto*, [1990] O.J. No. 2407 (Gen. Div.).

broad range of commercial transactions involving the advancement of credit.[127] Due to its broad scope:

> Ironically, this criminal law is often 'enforced' by a sophisticated borrower defending a civil claim, seeking to avoid payment of a charge imposed in a freely negotiated commercial financing transaction.[128]

It has recently been held that the legality or illegality of an arrangement under section 347(1)(b) should not be made in a summary proceeding without a complete record.[129]

§8.44 In effect, section 347 creates two offences respecting criminal interest rates. Under clause (1)(a) it is an offence to enter into an agreement to receive interest at a criminal rate. In deciding whether there has been a breach of section 347(1)(a) it is necessary to determine the rate of interest that the agreement *requires*.[130] The Supreme Court of Canada has directed that the clause is to be narrowly construed, and that for the purposes of this clause the critical time for determination of whether the interest rate is illegal is when the lender enters into the agreement. An interest rate is illegal under clause (1)(a) only if the agreement "expressly imposes an annual rate of interest above 60%, or if the agreement requires payment of interest charges over a period which necessarily gives rise to an annual rate exceeding the legal limit". It is not sufficient to show that there is mere possibility that the rate could become illegal if a payment is made at a particular time. If the effective annual rate of interest remains speculative until such time as a payment is made, then there can be no conviction under clause (1)(a). The question of whether there has been a contravention of clause (1)(b) is entirely separate. Clause (1)(b) makes it illegal to *receive* a payment or partial payment of interest at a criminal rate. The following are the elements of an offence under clause 347(1)(b):

- The charges in question must fit within the statutory definition of interest.

- As a result of those charges, the accused <u>must actually receive</u> a payment or partial payment of interest at a criminal rate.

- Payment must be made under an agreement or arrangement for the advancement of credit.

- At the actual time of receipt, the effective annual interest rate generated by reason of receipt must be a criminal rate (*i.e.*, must exceed 60 per cent per annum on the credit advanced).

---

[127] *Bearcat Exploration Ltd. (Re)*, [2004] A.C.W.S.J. LEXIS 5831 (Q.B.).
[128] *Boyd v. International Utility Structures Inc.*, [2002] B.C.J. No. 1770, 216 D.L.R. (4th) 139 (C.A.), *per* Levine J.A.
[129] *Bearcat Exploration Ltd. (Re)*, [2003] ABCA 365 (C.A.).
[130] See *Degelder Construction Co. v. Dancorp Developments Ltd.*, [1998] S.C.J. No. 75, [1998] 3 S.C.R. 90; *Garland v. Consumers' Gas Co.*, [1998] S.C.J. No. 76, [1998] 3 S.C.R. 112.

- The effective annual rate of that interest is to be calculated in accordance with generally accepted actuarial practices and principles.[131]

The Supreme Court has held that clause 347(1)(b) should be broadly construed. A payment of interest may be illegal under section 347(1)(b) even if the loan agreement under which it is made did not itself violate section 347(1)(a) at the time it was entered into. The relevant time frame for calculating the interest rate is the period over which credit is actually repaid. This often requires a wait-and-see approach to determining the lender's liability. A lender who enters into an agreement to receive interest under ambiguous terms bears the risk that the agreement, in its operation, may in fact give rise to a violation of section 347.[132]

Under neither paragraph is it necessary to prove that the accused knew that charging a rate above 60 per cent was unlawful.[133] Likewise, it is no defence to show that the borrower was a willing participant in the agreement or that the borrower understood that the rate was above the 60 per cent ceiling.

§8.45 The fact that a loan or other credit agreement provides for the charging of interest at a criminal rate does not necessarily render that agreement void or unenforceable in its entirety. Principal may still be recovered, where the obligation to repay principal is severable from the obligation to pay the criminal rate of interest.[134] This specific question came up for consideration by the Ontario Court of Appeal in the *Thomson* case.[135] In that case, the Court of Appeal held that in certain circumstances the obligation of the borrower to repay the principal advanced under the loan agreement might be severed from the obligation to repay interest. In deciding whether the obligation to repay may still be enforced, it was held that a court must exercise its discretion based upon the four following considerations:

- whether the purpose and policy of section 347 (that being to suppress loan sharking) would be subverted by severance;

- whether the parties entered into the agreement for an illegal purpose or with an illegal intention (*e.g.*, was the very purpose of the loan agreement to exact a usurious return, or was the rate of interest merely collateral to the main purpose of the agreement);

- whether the borrower and lender occupied relatively equal bargaining positions;

---

[131] See, generally, *Great American Leasing Co. v. Yates*, [2003] O.J. No. 4689 (C.A.), per Borins, J.A.; *Degelder Construction Co. v. Dancorp Developments Ltd.*, [1998] S.C.J. No. 75, [1998] 3 S.C.R. 90; *Garland v. Consumers' Gas Co.*, [1998] S.C.J. No. 76, [1998] 3 S.C.R. 112.

[132] See *Degelder Construction Co. v. Dancorp Developments Ltd.*, [1998] S.C.J. No. 75, [1998] 3 S.C.R. 90; *Garland v. Consumers' Gas Co.*, [1998] S.C.J. No. 76, [1998] 3 S.C.R. 112.

[133] *R. v. McRobb* (1984), 20 C.C.C. (3d) 493 at 500-501 (Co. Ct.), per Ferguson Co. Ct. J., var'd (1986), 32 C.C.C. (3d) 479n (Ont. C.A.).

[134] See, for instance, *T.F.P. Investments Inc. (Trustee of) v. Beacon Realty Co.*, [1994] O.J. No. 775, 114 D.L.R. (4th) 541 (C.A.).

[135] *William E. Thomson Associates Inc. v. Carpenter*, [1989] O.J. No. 1459, 44 B.L.R. 125 (C.A.), leave to appeal to S.C.C. refused 37 O.A.C. 398n.

- whether the borrower would be unjustly enriched at the expense of the lender if the principal was not repaid.

§8.46 The *Criminal Code* imposes substantive restrictions on the extent to which a creditor may charge and recover interest under a loan agreement or other credit facility, and renders any agreement to charge interest over the amount allowed illegal. However, the charging of interest is also subject to regulation as to form. Specifically, interest must be disclosed to the borrower in a specified manner. Depending upon the wording of the applicable legislation, the failure to make proper disclosure of the interest chargeable under an agreement may render the interest payment obligation partly or wholly unenforceable.[136]

(3) Interest After Default

§8.47 Section 8 of the *Interest Act*[137] provides that no fine, penalty or rate of interest shall be provided for on a mortgage against real property that has the effect of increasing the charge on amounts in arrears beyond the rate that is payable on principal money that is not in arrears.[138] However, this prohibition does not prevent a contract for the payment of interest on arrears of interest or principal at a rate that is not greater than the rate payable on principal money that is not in arrears. In *Raintree Financial Ltd. v. Bell*[139] the mortgage provided that one week before the maturity date of the mortgage, the rate of interest payable under the mortgage would increase from 18½ per cent to 24 per cent. The mortgage debt was not paid on maturity. In a foreclosure action, the mortgagor complained that the increase in the rate violated section 8. Justice Ryan rejected the argument and held that as the effect of the provision was to increase the interest rate on both the principal in default and that not in default, section 8 could have no application.

---

[136] The federal *Interest Act* is the oldest statute in Canada regulating the form in which the disclosure of interest must be made (R.S.C. 1985, c. I-15). The Act has been interpreted in a very large number of cases, but unfortunately it is not possible within the confines of this book to deal with these cases in detail. Those interested in the Act should refer generally to *British Pacific Properties Ltd. v. British Columbia (Minister of Highways and Public Works)*, [1980] S.C.J. No. 67, [1980] 2 S.C.R. 283; *Elcano Acceptance Ltd. v. Richmond, Richmond, Stambler & Mills*, [1989] O.J. No. 340, 68 O.R. (2d) 165 (H.C.J.), supp. reasons at 641 (H.C.J.), aff'd [1991] O.J. No. 1139, 79 D.L.R. (4th) 154, 3 O.R. (3d) 123 (C.A.) — interest was held to include promissory notes. See also *Zanny Ltd. v. Vero-Kim Developments Inc.* (1994), 47 A.C.W.S. (3d) 160 (Ont. Gen. Div.); *Bank of Nova Scotia v. Dunphy Leasing Enterprises Ltd.*, [1991] A.J. No. 1021, [1992] 1 W.W.R. 577 (C.A.), aff'd [1994] S.C.J. No. 25; see also *Upper Yonge Ltd. v. CIBC*, [1990] O.J. No. 1614, 75 O.R. (2d) 98 (H.C.J.); *Beechy Savings & Credit Union v. Warwaruk*, [1992] S.J. No. 500, [1993] 1 W.W.R. 765 (Q.B.); *Re Kilgoran Hotels Ltd. v. Samek*, [1967] S.C.J. No. 72, 65 D.L.R. (2d) 534; *Tarel Hotel Ltd. v. Saskatchewan Co-operative Financial Services Ltd.*, [1994] S.J. No. 467, 118 D.L.R. (4th) 629 (C.A.); *Ferland v. Sun Life Assurance Co.*, [1974] S.C.J. No. 49, [1975] 1 S.C.R. 266. Provincial cost of borrowing laws may also govern the manner in which interest must be disclosed, although most of these laws apply only in respect of consumer transactions.

[137] R.S.C. 1985, c. I-15.

[138] See, for instance, *CIBC v. Cedar Hills Properties Ltd.*, [1997] B.C.J. No. 1052, 32 B.L.R. (2d) 277, 47 C.B.R. (3d) 153 (C.A).

[139] [1993] B.C.J. No. 2845, 11 B.L.R. (2d) 202 (S.C.).

§8.48 Section 8 of the *Interest Act* does not prevent a change in the rate of interest after a mortgage goes into default (*e.g.*, where a variable rate increases in accordance with an adjustment in the prime lending rate or some other reference rate). Nor does it affect increases in the rate of a mortgage that occur before the mortgage goes into default. It provides only that the rate of interest on the portion of the mortgage that is in default must be no greater than the rate of interest on that portion which is not in default.[140]

§8.49 There is no contravention of section 8 where a lender charges an administrative fee to a borrower who is in default, by reason of or in connection with the variation of the mortgage at the borrower's request.[141]

(4) Interest and Bankruptcy

§8.50 Although a corporation and its creditor may agree that interest shall be payable at a specified contract rate until such time as full payment is made, that contractual undertaking will be suspended where the corporation is placed into bankruptcy and is wound up for that purpose. Generally, the rights of all creditors are fixed as of the date on which a bankruptcy proceeding commences (although this rule does not apply where a solvent corporation is wound up, or where an insolvent corporation makes a proposal under the *Bankruptcy and Insolvency Act*[142] or under the *Companies' Creditors Arrangement Act*).[143] It is a fundamental principle that debts are ascertained as of the date of bankruptcy. Accordingly, interest due as of that date on each debt payable is then deemed to be part of the principal indebtedness owed to each creditor concerned. Further interest is not allowed under that date unless there is a surplus.[144] Differences in the contract rates of interest payable to individual creditors justify no departure from this rule, the governing principle being "as the tree falls, so it must lie".[145]

§8.51 However, further interest will be allowed when it is necessary to achieve a ratable and equitable distribution among creditors, as for instance where the payment of a particular claim is accidentally or deliberately deferred.[146] In *Principal Savings & Trust Co. v. Principal Group Ltd. (Trustee of)*[147] the payment of

---

[140] *Raintree Financial Ltd. v. Bell*, [1993] B.C.J. No. 2845, 11 B.L.R. (2d) 202 at 204 (S.C.), *per* Ryan J.; see also *Prenor Trust Co. of Canada v. Hills of Columbia*, [1994] B.C.J. No. 299, 12 B.L.R. (2d) 180 (S.C.), *per* Cowan J.

[141] *CIBC v. Cedar Hills Properties Ltd.*, [1997] B.C.J. No. 1052, 47 C.B.R. (3d) 153, 32 B.L.R. (2d) 277 (C.A.).

[142] R.S.C. 1985, c. B-3.

[143] R.S.C. 1985, c. C-36.

[144] *Re Humber Ironworks & Shipbuilding Co.* (1869), 4 Ch. App. 643, 38 L.J. Ch. 712 (L.JJ.); *Re Robertson & Carlisle Ltd.*, [1949] 2 D.L.R. 529 (Alta. C.A.); *Re Joint Stock Discount Co.* (1869), 38 L.J. Ch. 565; *Re Contract Group*; *(Ebbw Vale Co.'s Case)* (1869), 39 L.J. Ch. 363 (L.C.).

[145] *Re Humber Ironworks & Shipbuilding Co.* (1869), 4 Ch. App. 643, 38 L.J. Ch. 712 at 712-14 (L.JJ.), *per* Selwyn L.J.; *Re Amalgamated Investment & Property Co. Ltd.*, [1984] 3 All E.R. 272 (Ch. D.).

[146] See, generally, *First Empire Bank v. FDIC*, 572 F.2d 1361 at 1372 (9th Cir. 1978), *per* Merrill J.

[147] [1993] A.J. No. 845, 109 D.L.R. (4th) 390 (C.A.), *per* Conrad J.A.

the claims of certain creditors were deferred by court order to allow for the completion of an inquiry into the affairs of the insolvent corporate debtor. Other funds were distributed and the liquidator retained an interest-bearing cash reserve for the payment of the postponed claims. The Alberta Court of Appeal held that the deferred creditors should receive the interest earned on that account (*i.e.*, interest on the amount reserved in respect of their deferred claims) from the date of the earlier distribution.[148]

B. COMMON TYPES OF DEBT

§8.52 There are many different types of debt that a corporation may incur and credit facility of which it may enjoy the benefit. Since the legal restrictions on lending to corporations are few, the range of possible lending arrangements that may be encountered in practice is limited to a large extent only by the imagination of lenders and borrowers. In this section we shall review the basic types of debt arrangement most frequently encountered in corporate and commercial practice.

§8.53 Direct lending of funds by a bank or other institutional lender to a corporation is usually made under a formal loan agreement. There are two basic types of loan agreement, namely a term loan agreement and a demand loan agreement, the most common form of the latter being the line of credit agreement. A typical term loan arrangement will provide that the lender is obliged to make advances to a borrower up to a specified amount throughout a stipulated commitment period. The advances so made will be repayable either at specified intervals (an installment payment facility) or at the end of the commitment period (in which case the repayment will be made in a single "bullet" payment). In some cases, installments will be payable during the commitment period, but a large balance will remain unpaid at its end, in which case the agreement will often provide for the outstanding balance to be paid on the expiration of the commitment (a "balloon" payment).

§8.54 One aspect of a term loan which distinguishes it from other types of credit is that funds may not be repaid by a borrower and then drawn again as a fresh advance from the lender. As funds are repaid, the amount of the credit is reduced. Even if an early payment is made, the borrower has no right to a re-advance of those funds. Term loans thus constitute a discrete rather than continuing facility.

§8.55 A line of credit or revolving credit facility provides for the periodic repayment of advances by the borrower, with a right to redraw them during the remaining commitment period. Generally speaking, such a facility will be repayable on demand;[149] there may be a fixed date at which the commitment period

---

[148] *Ibid.*, per Conrad J.A. at 393. See also *Canada Deposit Insurance Corp. v. Canadian Commercial Bank*, [1993] A.J. No. 512, 21 C.B.R. (3d) 12 at 23-24 (Q.B.), per Wachowich A.C.J.Q.B.

[149] In Canada there is an enormous and ever-growing body of jurisprudence dealing with the obligation of a lender to provide a reasonable opportunity to repay demand debt before taking steps

expires, but repayment of the loan may be demanded by the lender at any time during that period. The advantage of demand loan or line of credit financing is that borrowing under such an arrangement will usually lead to lower aggregate interest charges. Interest will be paid only on the advances outstanding from time to time; however, the borrower will also be required to pay a commitment fee to the lender, in consideration of keeping the undrawn portion of the facility open for the borrower, should it choose to draw upon it. Lines of credit may be used as a source of working capital[150] for the corporation, to allow it to meet expected sluggish periods during its cash flow cycle to meet its ongoing payment obligations. Alternatively, it may be held in reserve by the borrower as a standby facility, to be drawn upon only if the corporation has an exceptional requirement for funds. In some cases, a revolving credit facility will be set up as a swing-line facility, which will provide the borrower with very short-term (seven days or less) advances, required to meet maturing commercial paper obligations. A multiple option facility allows a borrower to select among a variety of these options, and perhaps others as well. Where no time is specified for repayment of a loan, it is presumed to be repayable on the demand of the lender, unless a contrary intent is evident.

§8.56 In some cases the loan will be evidenced by a promissory note, so that only the terms and conditions of the agreement will be set out in the loan agreement itself. However, the use of a promissory note is not necessary. So long as there is sufficient evidence of an advance of funds and a covenant to repay those funds on the part of the borrower, there is sufficient evidence of a debt to support the term loan agreement. Nor is it essential that all funds that are to be advanced under a term loan be advanced at one time. While it is common for the entire amount of the loan to be advanced at a single time under a term loan, it is equally possible (and relatively common) for the loan to be structured so that the amount of the loan is advanced in separate tranches.

§8.57 In the case of a line of credit (sometimes called a "revolving credit"), a certain level of credit is offered by the lender to the borrower. The borrower draws upon the credit from time to time as required and repays the advances made under the credit in accordance with the line of credit agreement. As with a term loan, advances are subtracted from the available amount of credit, but under a revolving credit when the principal amount of an advance is repaid, that amount is added back to the amount available to the borrower for future advances. In some cases, the borrower may be required to do no more than pay

---

to enforce its security. It is impossible in a general work such as this to do justice to that subject. For recent cases, see *Toronto-Dominion Bank v. Prichard*, [1997] O.J. No. 4622, 154 D.L.R. (4th) 141 (Div. Ct.); *Murano v. Bank of Montreal*, [1998] O.J. No. 2897, 163 D.L.R. (4th) 21 (C.A.); *Haggart Construction Ltd. v. Canadian Imperial Bank of Commerce*, [1998] A.J. No. 20, [1998] 5 W.W.R. 586 (Q.B.), aff'd [1999] A.J. No. 685 (C.A.). Where a loan agreement is silent as to repayment, then it is presumed that the loan is repayable on demand. So in *Williams & Glyn's Bank Ltd. v. Barnes*, [1981] Com. L.R. 205, *per* Gibson J.

[150] The working capital of a business represents the net current assets of the business: the surplus of current assets over current liabilities. It is the primary source to which the business may turn to meet its ongoing expenses of operation.

interest on the outstanding balance, although the lender will normally enjoy the right to demand repayment of that balance at any time. Where the line of credit is provided by a bank (and other clearing financial institutions) the line of credit will often be combined with an overdraft facility on a current account. Lines of credit provided by institutional lenders were at one time documented using grid-form promissory notes, but the use of such evidentiary devices is becoming increasingly rare. Generally, in place of the grid promissory note, loan agreements now provide that the accounts maintained by the lender shall be accepted as *prima facie* evidence as to the state of accounts between the parties.

§8.58 Lines of credit are also provided by suppliers to corporations in the form of running accounts. For instance, a trade creditor may allow a customer to purchase a given value of goods on credit. As the customer pays for goods previously supplied, the amount so paid (less interest) is added back to the credit available to the customer for future purchases of supplies. Except where the supplier retains a security interest in the goods supplied, it is unusual for credit of this type to be advanced beyond a very simple credit agreement, and in some cases there is no formal loan agreement at all — the only evidence of debt being the invoices for goods or services supplied.

§8.59 Debt may also be incurred under a variety of investment securities that are sold to the public. Historically, among the most common forms of such securities in Ontario are commercial paper, in the form of promissory notes or bills of exchange maturing not more than one year from the date of issue, which (to gain the benefit of a *Securities Act* exemption) have a denomination or principal amount of not less than $50,000.[151] The most common type of bill of exchange employed in raising funds in this manner is known as the banker's acceptance, which is no more than a bill of exchange drawn on and accepted for payment by a bank. Banker's acceptances are usually issued in denominations of $100,000. While commercial paper is normally unsecured, it is also possible for a corporation to raise debt financing through the sale of secured debt instruments, a number of common such instruments being discussed below.

§8.59.1 Although this specific exemption has been eliminated, there is a similar exemption still in effect. Section 2.35 of National Instrument 45-106 pertaining to prospectus and registration exemptions now provides:

(1) The dealer registration requirement does not apply in respect of a trade in a negotiable promissory note or commercial paper maturing not more than one year from the date of issue, if the note or commercial paper traded

   (a) is not convertible or exchangeable into or accompanied by a right to purchase another security other than a security described in this section, and

   (b) has an approved credit rating from an approved credit rating organization.

(2) The prospectus requirement does not apply to a distribution of a security in the circumstances referred to in subsection (1).

---

[151] See, generally, *Securities Act*, R.S.O. 1990, c. S.5, s. 23(2), para. 4 (since repealed).

Securities within the scope of this provision are free-trading under NI 45-102, dealing with resale of securities.

§8.60 However the raising of debt may be structured, it is important to distinguish between debt incurred for general corporate purposes and debt incurred for a specific purpose of the corporation. Where debt is incurred for general corporate purposes, the corporation is free to employ that debt as it considers best, although in so doing it must be careful to observe any restrictions, performance covenants and other undertakings that it may have provided to the lender with respect to the use of the funds. In contrast, where money is advanced to a corporation for a specific purpose and that purpose is not carried out, the creditor advancing that money is entitled to reclaim the amount advanced as money held to its use.[152]

§8.61 One recent development in the lending field has been the increased use of securitization as a method of corporate finance. A securitization occurs where cash flow producing assets (*e.g.*, the accounts receivable of a credit card company or a portfolio of mortgages owned by a mortgage lender) are packaged or bundled together and transferred to a special purpose corporate vehicle ("SPV"). The SPV pays for the transfer by issuing securities to investors who would not normally be able or willing to purchase assets of the type concerned. The securities issued by the SPV are in a tradable form, suitable for the public or institutional investor market. The securities are supported by a charge against the package of assets and the cash flow generated by those assets. In some cases, additional assets will be put into place to support the payment obligations of the SPV on the securities, in order to give investors enhanced protection against default. The original owner of the transferred assets (the "originator") will continue to administer the transferred assets as agent on behalf of the SPV, charging a fee for this service. Since the SPV has only one line of business, assuming that the assets transferred are collectible, it can generally obtain a good credit rating, and therefore will have a low cost of funds. Securitization can be used for a variety of different purposes, including to improve capital adequacy by removing the transferred assets from the originator's balance or to improve the originator's working capital.

(i) Foreign Currency Debt

§8.62 It is common for major Canadian corporations — and some not so major corporations — to borrow in foreign currency. The borrowing of foreign currency itself presents no legal problem.[153] However, the debtor's obligation to repay in foreign currency should be clearly stated in the loan documentation, for it is presumed that unless the agreement otherwise specifies, the debt is payable

---

[152] *R. v. Royal Bank*, [1913] A.C. 283 at 296 (P.C.), *per* Viscount Haldane. See also *Evenden v. Standard Art Manufacturing Co.*, [1906] O.J. No. 670, 8 O.W.R. 392 (Div. Ct.).

[153] See, generally, *Gatineau Power Co. v. Crown Life Ins. Co.*, [1945] S.C.R. 655; *Montreal Trust Co. v. Abitibi Power & Paper Co.*, [1944] O.J. No. 467, [1944] O.R. 515 (H.C.J.).

in Canadian currency.[154] Under section 12 of the *Currency Act*,[155] judgments in a Canadian court must be given in Canadian currency.[156] For this reason, legal opinions relating to foreign currency loans are usually qualified to reflect the fact that the covenant to repay the loan cannot be enforced in the currency of the loan.

§8.63 The manner in which the exchange rate is determined for the purposes of giving judgment is governed by section 121 of the *Courts of Justice Act*.[157] Subsection 121(1) of the Act provides that where a person obtains an order to enforce an obligation in a foreign currency, the order shall require payment of an amount in Canadian currency sufficient to purchase the amount of the obligation in the foreign currency at a chartered bank in Ontario at the close of business on the first day on which the bank quotes a Canadian dollar rate for the purchase of the foreign currency before the day payment of the obligation is received by the creditor.[158] However, subsection 121(4) of the *Courts of Justice Act* qualifies this general provision. It states that where an obligation enforceable in Ontario provides for a manner of conversion to Canadian currency of an amount in a foreign currency, the court shall give effect to the manner of conversion in the obligation. For instance, in *Brown v. Alberta & Great Waterways Rlwy.*,[159] the interest coupon of a debenture provided for payment of interest in London England at a fixed rate of exchange of $4.86⅔ per £1. At the time when a particular payment was to be made, Canadian currency was trading at a premium over sterling. In an action for a declaratory judgment as to the amount payable, it was held that the company should pay at the rate settled in the contract.

§8.64 A further qualification on the general rule set out in subsection 121(1) of the *Courts of Justice Act*[160] is found in subsection (3) of that section. It provides that where the court is satisfied that conversion of the amount of the obligation to Canadian currency at the rate provided in subsection (1) would be inequitable to any party, the order may require payment of an amount in Canadian currency sufficient to purchase the amount of the obligation in the foreign currency at a chartered bank in Ontario on such other day as the court considers equitable in the circumstances. In deciding whether to depart from the general rule laid down under subsection (1), the court might consider that the debtor has control over the making of payment, while the creditor may only obtain payment by enforcement of the debt. Thus if the amount recoverable decreases significantly between the date when payment is due and the date of recovery under the judg-

---

[154] *Currency Act*, R.S.C. 1985, c. C-52, s. 13.
[155] R.S.C. 1985, c. C-52.
[156] *Batavia Times Publishing Co. v. Davis*, [1978] O.J. No. 3450, 88 D.L.R. (3d) 144 (H.C.J.); *Baumgartner v. Carsley Silk Co.* (1971), 23 D.L.R. (3d) 255 (Que. C.A.).
[157] R.S.O. 1990, c. C.43.
[158] In the absence of corresponding legislation, see: *Kellogg Brown & Root Inc. v. Aerotech Herman Nelson Inc.*, [2004] M.J. No. 181, 238 D.L.R. (4th) 594 (C.A.), leave to appeal to S.C.C. refused [2004] S.C.C.A. No. 344.
[159] [1921] 1 W.W.R. 1216 at 1217-18 (Alta. C.A.), *per* Harvey C.J.
[160] *Courts of Justice Act*, R.S.O. 1990, c. C.43.

ment, it would be inappropriate to limit the creditor's recovery to the amount contemplated in subsection (1).[161]

§8.65 Where a writ of seizure and sale or a notice of garnishment is issued under an order to enforce an obligation in a foreign currency, the day the sheriff, bailiff or clerk of the court receives money under the writ or notice is deemed to be the date payment is received by the creditor, for the purposes of section 121.

(ii) Participatory Loans and Similar Interests

§8.66 Interest owed by a corporation itself constitutes a debt of the corporation and may be recovered as such. So, for instance, interest coupons may be detached from the bond to which they were originally affixed and an action may be brought by the holder of the coupon for the time being, without presentation of that original bond.[162] As discussed in Chapter 7, in the case of shares, as a general rule, there is no right to receive dividends unless and until they are declared. In contrast, in the case of debt obligations, there is a presumption that interest is payable whether there are profits or not.[163] Nor in the ordinary case is there any discretion in the directors as to the timing of interest payments: the date on which interest is due will normally be specified in the debt instrument, and that obligation is binding on the corporation as a matter of contract. However, there is no rule that a lender cannot agree that any right to recover interest shall be contingent upon the profitability of the corporation, and where such an agreement has been made, the creditor is not entitled to receive interest unless the required profits are earned.[164] In much the same way, in theory, a debt instrument may provide an element of discretion to the borrower, in the timing of interest payments — although any such discretion would be very rare. Much more frequently, a mortgagee or other lender may agree to forgo all or part of the interest normally payable in respect of a loan in exchange for a share in the anticipated profits that will be earned from the subject-matter relating to the loan (such as the purchase and resale of the property subject to a mortgage). Although care must be exercised in drafting such provisions so as not to contravene the usury prohibitions of the *Criminal Code*,[165] there is no general prohibition against such participatory arrangements.[166]

---

[161] See, generally, *Stott v. Merit Investment Corp.*, [1988] O.J. No. 134, 63 O.R. (2d) 545 at 566 (C.A.), *per* Finlayson J.A., leave to appeal to S.C.C. refused (1988), 63 O.R. (2d) x; *Gatineau Power Co. v. Crown Life Insurance Co.*, [1945] S.C.R. 655.
[162] See, generally, *McKenzie v. Montreal & Ottawa Junction Rlwy.* (1878), 20 U.C.C.P. 333; *Trusts & Guarantee Co. v. Grand Valley Rlwy. Co.*, [1919] O.J. No. 84, 44 O.L.R. 398 (C.A.).
[163] *Locke v. Queensland Investment Co.*, [1898] A.C. 700 at 715 (P.C.).
[164] See, for instance, *Heslop v. Paraguay Central Rlwy. Co.* (1910), 54 Sol. J. 234.
[165] See, generally, *677950 Ontario Ltd. v. Artell Developments Ltd.*, [1992] O.J. No. 1548, 93 D.L.R. (4th) 334 (C.A.), aff'd [1993] S.C.J. No. 61, 64 O.A.C. 161.
[166] *Kreglinger v. New Patagonia Meat & Cold Storage Co.*, [1914] A.C. 25 at 54-55 (H.L.), *per* Lord Parker.

C. TYPES OF SECURITY INTEREST

§8.67 Although there are many different types of security agreement that are utilized in present day commerce, the common law recognizes essentially only a limited range of methods by which security can be created in property by contract. The exact number of types of security interest recognized by the common law is the subject of some debate. In his monograph, *Legal Problems of Credit and Security*,[167] Roy Goode identified only three types of security: the mortgage, charge and pledge.[168] However, reservation of title, leases and trusts are also commonly used as security devices, and none of them fit within the three categories identified by Goode. In addition, there are a number of specific types of consensual security arrangement provided for by statute (in Canada, the most important being the security rights contemplated under sections 426 and 427 of the *Bank Act*)[169] which are difficult to categorize into traditional common law classifications. What is clear is that there are only a limited number of different types of security interest.[170] While all have in common the notion of conferring upon a creditor a right to look to some or all of the assets of a debtor in priority to his or her general creditors for the payment of the debt owed to the creditor, the approach that each type of security interest takes toward the attainment of this goal varies significantly.

§8.68 A reservation of title arrangement exists where the seller of property inserts a term in the sale contract to the effect that title to the property shall not pass to the buyer unless and until the purchase price has been paid in full.[171] The most common form of reservation of title is the conditional sale agreement, under which the purchase price is payable in installments, the agreement providing that the title to the property will not pass until the final installment is paid.[172] While the buyer will be allowed use of the property during the term of the contract, if the buyer defaults in payment, the sale agreement is taken to be repudiated by the buyer, and the seller is entitled to recover the property.[173]

---

[167] (London: Sweet & Maxwell, 1982).
[168] In contrast, in *Re Cosslett (Contractors) Ltd.*, [1997] E.W.J. No. 371, [1997] 4 All E.R. 115 at 126 (C.A.), Millett J. said that there were four different types of consensual security known to common law.
[169] S.C. 1991, c. 46.
[170] In addition to true security interests, there are a variety of quasi-security interests that a lender may seek to obtain, such as expanded rights of contractual set-off, *e.g.*, the right to apply compensating or other deposits placed by the borrower with the lender in reduction of the debt owed by the borrower.
[171] See, for instance, *Aluminium Industrie Vaassen BV v. Romalpa Aluminium Ltd.*, [1976] 1 W.L.R. 676 (C.A.); *Clough Mill Ltd. v. Martin*, [1985] 1 W.L.R. 111 (C.A.); *Compaq Computer Ltd. v. Abercorn Group Ltd.*, [1991] B.C.C. 484 (Ch.), *per* Mummery J. While useful in terms of statements of general principle, English case law in the area of retention of title agreements should be referred to with great caution, due to the absence of any English legislation directly comparable to the *Personal Property Security Act*, R.S.O. 1990, c. P.10 or the *Uniform Conditional Sales Act* (draft Act prepared by the Uniform Law Commission).
[172] See, generally, *Armour v. Thyssen Edelstahlwerke AG*, [1990] H.L.J. No. 46, [1991] 2 A.C. 339.
[173] As to the difference between title reservation and charges, see *Paintin & Nottingham Ltd. v. Miller, Gale & Winter*, [1971] N.Z.L.R. 164; *Re Bond Worth Ltd.*, [1980] Ch. 228.

§8.69 Leases of property may be used in much the same way to secure the interest of the creditor. A typical manner in which leasing arrangements may be used to provide contract security is through a hire-purchase arrangement, under which the borrower "rents" a good until he or she has paid specified rent payments equal in sum to the aggregate of the purchase price of the asset and an implicit rate of interest. The borrower then has the option of buying title to the good for a nominal sum. If the borrower defaults, the creditor is entitled to recover the leased property as an unpaid lessor.[174] However, as discussed in greater detail below, sale and lease-back arrangements have also been a popular method of providing contract security.

§8.70 A mortgage is a transfer (*i.e.*, a conveyance) of an estate or interest in property from a debtor or other obligor to a creditor or other obligee for the purpose of securing the performance of an obligation or the payment of a debt owed to the creditor or obligee, that transfer being made subject to the condition (known as the equitable right of redemption) that upon the performance of the obligation or payment of the debt, as the case may be, the property so transferred will be transferred back to the debtor or obligor.[175] Since the mortgage is granted by the debtor, he or she is known as the mortgagor, and the creditor or other obligee to whom it is granted is known as the mortgagee. In the very early days of the common law, the property was actually taken by the creditor or obligor and the rents or profits arising from it belonged to the creditor and (in contrast to the pledge) were not applied to the reduction of the debt — and hence the term "mortgage" arose, for it meant that from the debtor's perspective, the land or other mortgaged property was dead or profitless. However, in modern practice, the mortgagor will normally remain in possession of the mortgaged property and enjoys the benefit of any profit or income that it may yield until such time as there is a default and the mortgagee enters into possession.

§8.71 While a mortgage is a conveyance of the full title of the mortgagor subject to an equitable right of redemption, in a charge a limited property interest in the subject matter of the property is created by a debtor or other obligor (the "chargor") in favour of the creditor to whom the debt or obligation is owed (the "chargee"). In general terms, a charge is an encumbrance[176] against the debtor's title to property which creates a proprietary interest in the property concerned that entitles the creditor in whose favour it is granted the right to be paid from the income of that property or to cause the sale or other disposition of that property and to be paid from the proceeds thereby generated. The charge exists so long as the obligation(s) to which it relates remains unperformed — although the

---

[174] *Helby v. Matthews*, [1895] A.C. 471 (H.L.).
[175] See, generally, *Re Curtain Dream plc.*, [1990] B.C.L.C. 925: debtor sold its entire stock to creditor for cash under an agreement which permitted debtor to repurchase that stock in 90 days on credit, subject to a title retention in favour of the creditor. Justice Knox held that the transaction should be looked at as a whole. Transaction held to be a charge requiring registration under governing English legislation.
[176] Originally, charges were seen to be equitable interests in property, but now a good many interests of this type are specifically contemplated by statute.

obligation may be structured (as in the case of a revolving loan) so that it will continue to secure a running or revolving account, despite periodic repayment of even the full balance outstanding at any particular time. As will be discussed in greater detail below, a charge may be either fixed or floating, but as with a mortgage, the chargor will normally remain in possession unless and until there is a default and the chargee elects to enforce the security to which he or she is entitled. Whatever the nature of the charge, where the chargor defaults in performance or payment, the property subject to the charge may be seized and sold.

§8.72 A pledge is a form of bailment. In a pledge, possession, but not the ownership, of property is transferred from a debtor or other obligor (the "pledgor") to the creditor or other obligee to whom payment or some other obligation is owed (the "pledgee"). Where the pledgor defaults in the payment of that debt or the performance of that obligation, the subject matter of the pledge may be sold and the proceeds applied to the payment of the debt or other amount owing.

§8.73 Trusts may be used as a security device either as an alternative to a mortgage, or in cases where the property to be made subject to a charge cannot for some reason be assigned or transferred to the creditor.[177] In a trust, the debtor or other obligor creates a trust over certain property in favour of the creditor or other obligee to whom payment or some other obligation is owed. The debtor will then either transfer that property to a named trustee who undertakes to hold that property in trust for the benefit of the beneficiary so named. Alternatively, the debtor may continue to own the property, but subject to an express trust in favour of the creditor. In either case, beneficial ownership of the secured property will belong to the creditor and will stand as security for the debt. Where the trust property is left in the hands of the debtor, the trust agreement will often provide that it must be kept separate and apart from the debtor's own property that is not subject to the trust. Moreover, there will usually be an undertaking that the debtor will hold not only the subject matter of the trust, but also any income received from, under or by virtue of it in trust for the creditor, as well as a further obligation to pay that income (either on demand or at specified intervals) to the creditor for whose benefit the trust exists.

§8.74 In addition to contractual forms of security, both common law and statutory law provide for various types of lien.[178] There are essentially two types of lien. A common law lien is a right to retain possession of property (either a specific property or, more rarely, any property generally of the debtor) until the debt to which the lien relates is repaid. Such a lien is contingent upon continuous possession and except as provided by statute confers no power of sale.[179] In the absence of a statutory power of sale, a common law lien is a mere defence to

---

[177] See, generally, *Don King Productions Inc. v. Warren (No. 2)*, [1998] E.W.J. No. 4513, [1998] 2 All E.R. 608, *per* Lightman J.
[178] See, generally, Kevin McGuinness, "Liens," Title 86 of the *Canadian Encyclopedic Digest, Ontario*, 3rd ed. (Toronto: Carswell, 1983).
[179] See, generally, *Legg v. Evans* (1840), 6 M. & W. 36; *Mulliner v. Florence* (1878), 3 Q.B.D. 484 (C.A.), and *Pennington v. Motor Works Ltd.*, [1923] 1 K.B. 127.

a claim for recovery of the property concerned. In contrast, an equitable lien is not dependent upon possession. Moreover, it confers the additional right of allowing the property subject to the lien to be seized and sold, so that the proceeds may be applied to the repayment of the debt to which the lien relates. Since liens are not consensual forms of security, they are beyond the concern of this work.

§8.75 Whatever form of security interest may be created, the fundamental purpose of all security interests remains generally the same: they entitle the creditor to look to the assets (or class of assets) against which the security interest is created for payment in priority to the claims of the general creditors of the borrower. Where a major capital expenditure is financed on a project financing basis, the terms of the lending/security agreements will normally provide that there is no Right of Rrecourse against the borrower once the assets pledged as security have been realized by the creditor. In some jurisdictions, legislation has been enacted which specifically forces a secured creditor to elect either to enforce its rights as to security or to sue for the debt owing. If the debtor chooses to enforce its security, then it forgoes any personal claim against the borrower. Subject to such legislation, the normal common law presumption is the reverse. Except in the case of so-called no-recourse financing (where the creditor specifically agrees that it shall have no right to recover against the borrower personally, but shall be limited in its recovery to the collateral pledged as security to the creditor), the creditor is presumed to be entitled to enforce its claim for the debt owing by realizing on its security, by way of ordinary civil action for the recovery of the debt owing by the borrower (coupled with normal execution proceedings), or both. There is a strong presumption that the collateral pledged as security for a debt is intended to supplement, rather than define or limit, the rights of the creditor to recovery.[180]

D. TYPES OF SECURITY AGREEMENT

§8.76 The forms of security agreement in common use in Ontario are largely derived from English precedents that evolved during the 19th century, although some types of security (*e.g.*, real property mortgages) are of much older vintage. It is a curious feature of the most common forms in Ontario that they have undergone little evolution in commercial practice despite substantial modifications of the law which have been made during the 20th century, primarily through statutory amendment. The most significant of these statutory changes have been the enactment of the *Personal Property Security Act*[181] (the "PPSA" — which came into force in 1976 and was substantially amended in 1989) and the *Land Registration Reform Act*.[182] While there are various types of security agreement, most share a number of common features: the grant of the security; the nature of the obligation secured; the giving of certain undertakings concerning dealings with the charged assets; the making of certain warranties related to the security

---

[180] *Re Bank of Credit and Commerce International S.A. (No. 8)*, [1997] 4 All E.R. 568 at 572 (H.L.), *per* Lord Hoffman.
[181] Now R.S.O. 1990, c. P.10.
[182] R.S.O. 1990, c. L.4.

that is given; a list of certain acts and events the occurrence of which will constitute a default under the agreement; the granting of contractual remedies where there is a default.

(i) Real Property Charges and Mortgages

§8.77 Although mortgages and charges are conceptually distinct, the legal distinction between such interests has become significantly blurred in Ontario because of the various changes which have been made to the law by the *Personal Property Security Act* and the *Land Registration Reform Act*. Despite this fact, both real property and personal property (chattel) mortgage forms remain in common use throughout Ontario. While the pledge is the oldest form of security known to the common law, the real property mortgage is also of great antiquity and has had a greater effect upon the evolution of the common law, equity and statute law relating to security interests than all other forms of security interest combined. Because such interests have played so prominent a role, what follows is a fairly detailed overview of their nature.

(1) The Nature of a Mortgage and a Charge and the Distinction Between Them

§8.78 A mortgage is a conveyance of property from a debtor or other obligor (known as the mortgagor) to a creditor or other obligee (known as the mortgagee) as security for the payment of a debt or the performance of some other obligation, on the express or implicit understanding that upon payment of the debt or performance of the obligation concerned, that property will be conveyed back to the debtor by the creditor. Thus a mortgage is not a debt itself, but is only a security for repayment. If the debt or other obligation is not performed, then the mortgagee (the creditor to whom the mortgage is given) may look to the land charged for the recovery of the amount which he is owed. Mortgages can be created with respect to real or personal property, or conceivably with respect to both. However, since different regimes of law now govern real and personal property mortgages,[183] it is convenient to consider mortgages against each class of property separately.

§8.79 Historically, two types of real property mortgage were recognized: legal mortgages and equitable mortgages. A legal mortgage arose only where a legal estate was conveyed to the mortgagee. In all legal mortgages, the legal ownership of the real property vests in the mortgagee. There is only one class of legal mortgage (that being a mortgage created by deed) and the owner of a particular estate can create only one such mortgage. In contrast, there are several distinct types of equitable mortgage.

- Equitable mortgages of the first class arise where an owner whose interest is already subject to a legal mortgage grants a further mortgage to a creditor. Any such mortgage constitutes a transfer of the mortgagor's equitable right of

---

[183] The mortgages of certain types of property (*e.g.*, ships) are regulated by special statutory regimes, and are not considered in this text. See K. McGuinness & G. Bowtle, *The Law of Ship Mortgages* (London: LLP, 2001).

redemption to the mortgagee. Thus all second and other subordinate mortgages are equitable mortgages.

- Equitable mortgages of the second class comprise any mortgage created by a person who has only an equitable interest in the real property.

- A third class of equitable mortgage arises where the owner deposits the title deeds to the real property with a creditor.

- Finally, a fourth class of equitable mortgage arises where the owner enters into a contract to grant a mortgage to a creditor.[184] An equitable mortgage exists pending the due delivery of an effective legal mortgage. The equitable charge remains in effect if for some reason a purported legal mortgage is ineffective.[185]

Mortgages may be granted by the owner of any kind of interest in real property. There are, for instance, not only mortgages of fee simple interests, but also mortgages of leasehold interests and mortgages of mortgages.

§8.80 The essential feature of a mortgage is the transfer of ownership to the creditor. In a legal mortgage, the legal estate of the owner vests in the creditor. At common law, a mortgage is simply a conveyance of land or an assignment of chattels as a security for the discharge of some obligation.[186] There is no reason, at common law, that one mortgage cannot secure several debts or other obligations.[187] The vesting of the title implicit in a mortgage is conditional. It is subject to a contractual right of redemption — provided the mortgagor pays the debt or performs the obligation secured — meaning that where the secured obligation is discharged without need of recourse to the security provided, then the transfer of property to the creditor automatically terminates.[188] From very early times, the courts of equity expanded this general equitable right of redemption, so that it would apply even where the contractual right of redemption had lapsed or was otherwise suspended, whether by law or under the terms of the contract. So, for instance, if the mortgagor failed to pay the secured mortgage debt on the agreed date, he or she might still redeem the property by paying the agreed amount at some later date.[189] Eventually the mortgagor came to be seen as being entitled to redeem despite any provision to the contrary. Indeed, a mortgage may not include a provision that is contrary to the right of redemption — any such provi-

---

[184] See, for instance, *Dundas (Town) v. Desjardins Canal Co.* (1870), 17 Gr. 27, *per* Mowat V.C.
[185] See, generally, *Harrison v. Nepisiguit Lumber Co.* (1911), 41 N.B.R. 1 (C.A.): mortgage granted to trust company as security for bond holders. Trust company incompetent to take a mortgage, as an unlicensed foreign company. Bond holders held entitled to an equitable charge on the property as security for the payment of their bonds. However, the equitable mortgage concept cannot be invoked to cure a breach of a mandatory registration requirement with respect to a mortgage: *Re Shipman Boxboards Ltd.*, [1940] O.J. No. 418, [1942] O.R. 118 (H.C.J.).
[186] *Santley v. Wilde*, [1899] C.A. 474.
[187] *Wiltse v. Excelsior Life Ins. Co.* (1916), 10 W.W.R. 1166 at 1173 (Alta. C.A.).
[188] See, for instance, *Walker v. Jones* (1866), L.R. 1 P.C. 50 (P.C.); *Rourke v. Robinson*, [1911] 1 Ch. 480.
[189] See, for instance, *Brown v. Cole* (1845), 14 Sim. 427, 60 E.R. 424.

sion being void as a clog on the equity.[190] The right of redemption remains until it is terminated by foreclosure, power of sale or the exercise of some other remedy inconsistent with redemption.

§8.81 Because mortgages involve at least a notional conveyance of title, it is necessary to determine the respective rights of the mortgagor and mortgagee concerning possession of the mortgaged property. Since the conveyance is intended only for the purposes of giving security, it seems surprising that the holder of a legal[191] mortgage has an immediate right to take possession of the property,[192] even where there has been no default by the mortgagor.[193] However, the *prima facie* right of the mortgagee to take immediate possession may be excluded by contract, and for the most part mortgage agreements will always contain a provision to this effect. Moreover, a mortgagee who enters into possession may do so only for the purpose of protecting or enforcing the security to which he or she is entitled, and must do so diligently.[194]

§8.82 Having briefly considered the nature of mortgage rights, we shall now turn to the subject of charges. A charge is a contractual arrangement entered into between a debtor and creditor under which the creditor is granted an interest in land or other property of the debtor,[195] that confers upon the creditor the right to pay the debt or other obligation owed to the creditor out of income derived from that property or the proceeds of the sale or other disposition of that property.[196] In conceptual terms, charges represent a less exacting form of security than a mortgage, insofar as they do not involve the conveyance of title to the property charged, but merely the grant of an encumbrance against the title of the debtor. Since charges involve no conveyance of title, they confer no inherent right to possession of the charged property.[197]

§8.83 While the distinction between mortgages and charges is both of ancient origin and conceptual, in Ontario the distinction between real property mortgages and charges has now been substantially blurred and modified by the enactment of subsection 6(1) of the *Land Registration Reform Act*.[198] It provides that a charge does not operate as a transfer of the legal estate to the chargee. However, subsection 6(3) of that Act goes on to provide:

---

[190] *Kreglinger v. New Patagonia Meat & Cold Storage Co.*, [1914] A.C. 25 (H.L.).
[191] *Re London Pressed Hinge Co.*, [1905] 1 Ch. 576 at 583, *per* Buckley J.
[192] *Four-Maids Ltd. v. Dudley Marshall (Properties) Ltd.*, [1957] Ch. 317 at 320, *per* Harman J.
[193] *Western Bank Ltd. v. Schindler*, [1977] Ch. 1 (C.A.).
[194] *Chaplin v. Young (No. 1)* (1864), 33 Beav. 330 at 337-38, *per* Romilly M.R.
[195] *Re Charge Card Services Ltd.*, [1987] Ch. 150, *per* Millett J. A charge arises at the time when the contract conferring the charge is made, even where the obligation to which it relates has not yet been incurred, but is expected to arise at some point in the future: *Esberger & Son Ltd. v. Capital & Counties Bank*, [1913] 2 Ch. 366.
[196] See, generally, *Re Morritt* (1886), 18 Q.B.D. 222 (C.A.); *Re Richardson* (1885), 30 Ch. D. 396 (C.A.); *Re Hardwick* (1886), 17 Q.B.D. 690 at 698 (C.A.), *per* Bowen L.J. and Fry L.J. at 701.
[197] See, generally, *Tennant v. Trenchard* (1869), L.R. 4 Ch. App. 537; *Vacuum Oil Co. v. Ellis*, [1914] 1 K.B. 693.
[198] R.S.O. 1990, c. L.4.

6.(3) Despite subsection (1), a chargor and chargee are entitled to all the legal and equitable rights and remedies that would be available to them if the chargor had transferred the land to the chargee by way of mortgage, subject to a proviso for redemption.

The term "charge" is defined in section 1 of that Act as follows:

"charge" means a charge on land given for the purpose of securing the payment of a debt or the performance of an obligation, and includes a charge under the *Land Titles Act* and a mortgage, but does not include a rent charge ...

§8.84 Since the term "charge" includes a mortgage, and no charge operates as a transfer of a legal estate to the chargee, the combined effect of these provisions would appear to be to abolish legal mortgages entirely in Ontario, at least in the case of real property. The question is, what takes the place of such mortgages? Subsection 6(1) states that the legal estate is not transferred; but what then of the owner's equitable interest? Subsection 6(3) suggests that there is no transfer *per se* of even the equitable interest, because it provides that the rights and remedies of the parties are "as if" the land had been transferred, subject to a proviso for redemption — a wording which suggests that there is no actual transfer. If this is correct, the effect of the section is to replace the concept of legal and equitable mortgages with a new form of statutory right that incorporates the rights and remedies provided to a mortgagor and mortgagee under the old law of mortgages, but largely abolishes the concept of transfer of ownership.[199]

§8.85 In some cases, lenders may find that there are several different charges registered against the same property. During the 1970s and 1980s, the value of land and buildings increased quickly, due to high rates of inflation. At that time it became common for corporations to take out second and sometimes third mortgages on their property, each secured by a separate charge, quite often granted to a different lender from the previous charges. A second charge is a charge that is subordinate to a prior charge (*i.e.*, a first charge) on a property. A second charge is a charge against the chargee's residual interest in the property — that interest broadly corresponding to what, under the law of mortgages, was known as the borrower's equity of redemption. Whereas the rights of second mortgagees were equitable, the rights of a second chargee under the *Land Registration Reform Act* are based upon the statute. The rights of a second chargee are similar to those of a first chargee, subject only to the priority of the first chargee. While it is true that the position of a second chargee is not so secure as that of the first chargee, because of the different priority of their respective charges, if a first chargee commences foreclosure proceedings, the second chargee may redeem the property.

§8.86 Since the *Land Registration Reform Act* uses the term "charge" rather than mortgage, and since the rights of the parties under both a mortgage and a charge are now made the same by virtue of section 6 of the Act, in the balance of this

---

[199] See, generally, *Smith v. National Trust Co.* (1912), 45 S.C.R. 618 at 639-41, *per* Duff J.

section only the term "charge" has been used in the case of security interests in real property.[200] It is important to note, however, that charges may also be created against personal property, and indeed, a charge agreement may cover both personalty and realty. In such a case, the *Personal Property Security Act*[201] ("PPSA") contains a number of provisions intended to reconcile the differences between the registration requirements applicable to personal property charges and real property charges,[202] and also with respect to the methods of enforcement. In this latter respect, subsection 59(6) of the PPSA provides:

> 59.(6) Where a security agreement covers both real and personal property, the secured party may proceed under this Part as to the personal property or may proceed as to both the real and the personal property in accordance with the secured party's rights, remedies and duties in respect of the real property, with all necessary modifications, as if the personal property were real property, in which case this Part does not apply.

(2) Property Subject to the Charge

§8.87 Under the PPSA, the security agreement must contain a description of the collateral sufficient to enable it to be identified. To secure a fixed charge against a specific parcel of land, that parcel must be described with sufficient particularity[203] to permit its registration under the *Land Registration Reform Act*.[204] The general rule is that no specific form of words is required in order to create a charge, provided that the parties make clear that it was their intention to confer such an interest.[205] The extent of any charge so created is a matter of contractual interpretation.[206]

§8.88 Except where otherwise agreed, a charge of real property attaches to the land and to all buildings, structures and appurtenances on the land. Where a chargor makes an improvement to the land after the granting of a charge, the charge will also extend to that improvement. Similarly, if any chattel is annexed

---

[200] For most practical purposes, there has long been little difference between a mortgage and a charge: *London County & Westminster Bank Ltd. v. Tompkins*, [1918] 1 K.B. 515 at 528-29 (C.A.), *per* Scrutton L.J.
[201] R.S.O. 1990, c. P.10.
[202] *Ibid.*, ss. 34, 36.
[203] *Royal Bank v. Madill*, [1979] N.S.J. No. 769, 9 B.L.R. 61, 33 C.B.R. (N.S.) 40 (S.C.), aff'd [1981] N.S.J. No. 328, 37 C.B.R. (N.S.) 80 (C.A.).
[204] R.S.O. 1990, c. L.4.
[205] *Dundas (Town) v. Desjardins Canal Co.*, [1870] O.J. No. 198, 17 Gr. 27 at 30 (Ont. H.C.), *per* Mowatt V.C.
[206] See, generally, *Wickham v. New Brunswick & Canada Rlwy.* (1865), 11 N.B.R. 175, aff'd L.R. 1 P.C. 64. Thus in *Eastern Trust Co. v. Cushing Sulphite Fibre Co.* (1906), 3 N.B. Eq. 378 (S.C.) it was held that the word "plant" in a mortgage securing debentures did not include the office furniture, or a horse and carriage used for occasional errands, or the material kept on hand for repairs to machinery. However, it did include scows used for lightering and the output of the mill from its wharf to the steamers, and in lightering coal for the use of the mill, as well as such stores as axes, shovels and other articles complete in themselves that were used in carrying on the mill business.

to the land so as to render it a fixture, the charge will also extend to the fixture.[207] However, the rights acquired by the chargor in respect of any such fixture may be subordinate to the rights of the holder of a security interest under the PPSA, depending upon the date of the registration of the competing interests against the title to the real property and the attachment of the security interest under the PPSA, and the date on which advances were made.[208]

(3) Personal Covenant to Pay

§8.89 The chargor is usually personally liable for the charge debt not by reason of the grant of the charge, but either because of a specific term that is included in the charge that makes the chargor so liable, or because there is a note or other contract collateral to the charge under or by virtue of which the chargor is so liable. The personal covenant found in many standard form charges is deceptively simple in appearance. For instance, a typical provision reads:

> The chargor covenants with the chargee that the chargor will pay the money and interest secured by the charge.

The effect of the provision is far wider than its comparative brevity would suggest. It amounts to a continuing undertaking by the chargor to pay the amounts secured by the principal and interest due under the charge. That covenant remains in force even where the chargor has sold or otherwise transferred his or her interest in the subject property. Should any purchaser who has assumed the mortgage fail to make the payments required under the mortgage, the chargee may then claim against the chargor on the personal covenant.[209]

§8.90 Loans or guarantees will usually oblige the borrower (or guarantor) to pay the lender's costs of enforcing or defending its security and recovering the amount owing. This obligation does not extend to the costs incurred by a lender in connection with a *Companies' Creditors Arrangement Act* proceeding pertaining to the borrower.[210]

(4) Right to Remain in Possession

§8.91 As long as the chargor complies with his or her covenants under the charge, the chargor is entitled to remain in possession of the charged property during the term of the charge. Payment of the debt or performance of any other obligation to which the charge relates terminates the charge and entitles the chargor to receive a discharge of the charge. A chargee has the right to receive payment in the manner provided under the charge, and has the right to pay off

---

[207] See, generally, *Deloitte & Touche Inc. v. 1035839 Ontario Inc.*, [1996] O.J. No. 874, 28 O.R. (3d) 139 (Gen. Div.), aff'd [1998] O.J. No. 2672, 39 O.R. (3d) 607*n* (C.A.).
[208] See s. 34 of the *Personal Property Security Act*, R.S.O. 1990, c. P.10.
[209] As to the rights of the chargee relative to the person who purchases the property, see s. 20 of the *Mortgages Act*, R.S.O. 1990, c. M.40.
[210] *CIBC v. Cedar Hills Properties Ltd.*, [1997] B.C.J. No. 1052, 35 B.C.L.R. (3d) 1 (C.A.); *Re United Used Auto Truck Parts Ltd.*, [2003] B.C.J. No. 1535, 35 B.L.R. (3d) 110 (S.C.), aff'd [2005] B.C.J. No. 164 (C.A.).

senior chargees and other encumbrancers whose claim ranks in priority to his own claim against the property. The amount so paid is chargeable to the chargor. Where a charge is properly registered, it will run with the land and bind any subsequent encumbrancer or purchaser.

§8.92 A person who purchases land that is subject to a charge does not thereby become personally liable under the charge (although his interest in the land will be subject to that charge if it was properly registered). When the grantee assumes the charge (*i.e.*, agrees to become contractually bound by it and to observe its terms), then he or she will become liable under the charge as if the grantee was an original party to it. Such an assumption must be established by clear evidence.

(5) Foreclosure and Powers of Sale

§8.93 A chargor is in default where the chargor fails to pay off the charge debt within the allowed time or to satisfy the other obligations of the chargor under the charge. In such a case, the chargee may pursue any of the following remedies: (1) it may go into possession of the charged property; (2) it may sue the chargor on his personal covenant to pay the debt to which the charge relates; (3) it may proceed with an action for foreclosure; (4) it may exercise a power of sale either under the *Mortgages Act* or the terms of the charge itself; (5) in some cases, depending upon the law of the province,[211] after obtaining an order of foreclosure, it may sue the chargor on the personal covenant to pay provided it is in a position to re-convey the property. Where a chargor defaults under a charge, the chargee will usually elect between foreclosure and the exercise of a power of sale.

§8.94 Historically, the remedy of foreclosure arises in answer to the equitable right of redemption. Because mortgagees (and, by extension, debtors) were able to redeem their interests in land, lenders began to appeal to the courts for a declaration that the redemption period had expired and the debtor's right to redeem was forever "foreclosed". Thus foreclosure is a method by which a lender may obtain title to the property free of the equity of redemption.[212] The lender was then able to treat the land as his own. The meaning of the term "foreclosure" is the same today. In contrast, a power of sale is a right given to the lender to sell the land subject to the charge where there is a default. The amount realized in the sale is used first to pay the costs of the sale owed, second to pay the debt owed to the lender, third to pay the debts owed to subsequent encumbrancers; any amount remaining belongs to the debtor. Such a power may be conferred by law, as under the *Mortgages Act*[213] (in which case a judicial sale must be conducted) or may be conferred by contract (in which case a judicial sale is not necessary).

---

[211] Ontario permits such actions if the parties have so contracted; generally speaking the western provinces do not.
[212] See, generally, *Knudsen v. Knudsen*, [1998] O.J. No. 6474, 37 O.R. (3d) 676 (Gen. Div.).
[213] R.S.O. 1990, c. M.40, s. 24.

§8.95 It is worth noting that the equitable right of redemption is not limited solely to the debtor. It may also be exercised by a subsequent encumbrancer (*i.e.*, an encumbrancer whose rights against the charged property are subordinate to those of the person who is seeking to foreclose). Hence, if a first lender commences foreclosure proceedings, the second lender may redeem the property.

(6) Charge Terms

§8.96 Subsection 7(1) of the *Land Registration Reform Act*[214] sets out a number of standard charge terms that are presumed to form part of every charge. It provides:

> 7.(1) A charge in the prescribed form shall be deemed to include the following covenants by the chargor, for the chargor and the chargor's successors, with the chargee and the chargee's successors and assigns:
>
> 1. In a charge of freehold or leasehold land by the beneficial owner:
>   i   That the chargor or the chargor's successors will pay, in the manner provided by the charge, the money and interest it secures, and will pay the taxes assessed against the land.
>   ii. That the chargor has the right to give the charge.
>   iii. That the chargor has not done, omitted or permitted anything whereby the land is or may be encumbered, except as the records of the land registry office disclose.
>   iv. That the chargor or the chargor's successors will insure the buildings on the land as specified in the charge.
>   v.   That the chargee on default of payment for the number of days specified in the charge or in the *Mortgages Act*, whichever is longer, may on giving the notice specified in the charge or required by that Act, whichever is longer, enter on and take possession of, receive the rents and profits of, lease or sell the land.
>   vi. That where the chargee enters on and takes possession of the land on default as described in subparagraph v, the chargee shall have quiet enjoyment of the land.
>   vii. That the chargor or the chargor's successors will, on default, execute such assurances of the land and do such other acts, at the chargee's expense, as may be reasonably required.
>   viii. That the chargee may distrain for arrears of interest.
>   ix. That on default of payment of interest secured by the charge, the principal money shall at the option of the chargee, become payable.
> 2. In a charge of freehold land by the beneficial owner, that the chargor has a good title in fee simple to the land, except as the records of the land registry office disclose.
> 3. In a charge of leasehold land by the beneficial owner:

---

[214] R.S.O. 1990, c. L.4.

i. That, despite anything done, omitted or permitted by the chargor, the lease or grant creating the term or estate for which the land held is, at the time the charge is given, a valid lease or grant of the land charged, in full force, unforfeited and unsurrendered, and that there is no subsisting default in the payment of the rents reserved by or in the performance of the covenants, conditions and agreements contained in the lease or grant at the time the charge is given.

ii. That the chargor or the chargor's successors will, while the money secured by the charge remains unpaid, pay, observe and perform all the rents reserved by and all the covenants, conditions and agreements contained in the lease or grant and will indemnify the chargee against all costs and damages incurred by reason of any non-payment of rent or non-observance or non-performance of the covenants, conditions and agreements.

However, these presumed terms may be waived or varied by the parties, for subsection 7(3) of the Act goes on to provide that:

> 7.(3) A covenant deemed to be included by subsection (1) may, in a schedule to the charge, or in a set of standard charge terms filed under subsection 8(1) and referred to in the charge by filing number, be expressly excluded or varied by setting out the covenant, appropriately amended.

Thus the parties to a charge have a number of options: they may rely in whole or in part upon the statutory covenants; they may exclude the statutory covenants and formulate appropriate charge terms between themselves, and register these on title as a schedule to the charge; or they may adopt the terms and conditions set out in any standard charge terms filed under the Act, whether by one of those parties or by another person. Despite this apparent freedom, consideration must always be given to the possibility of whether a provision in a loan or security agreement is binding upon a borrower-corporation where it is inconsistent with a direct statutory power conferred upon that corporation.[215]

§8.97 In practice, most institutional lenders insist upon the exclusion of the statutory covenants in the place of their own standard charge terms. Therefore most charges will contain a provision along the following lines.

> The implied covenants deemed to be included in the charge under subsection 7(1) of the *Land Registration Reform Act* are hereby excluded from this charge and are replaced by the terms and conditions set out in these Standard charge Terms.

The procedure for creating standard charge terms is set out in subsection 8(1) which provides that:

> 8.(1) A person may file with the Director, in the prescribed manner and form, a set of standard charge terms and, with the consent of the Director, may file a set of standard charge terms in a form other than the prescribed form.

---

[215] See, generally, *Russell v. Northern Bank Development Corp.*, [1992] 3 All E.R. 161 (H.L.).

There are now several hundred variations of standard charge terms on file with the Director, and the text of each of these charge terms is published in an annual volume.

§8.98 For the most part, the terms and conditions set out in standard charge terms are self-explanatory. There are, however, a few provisions that have certain hidden features that may come as a surprise to the uninitiated. For instance, most charges contain an acceleration of payment provision along the following lines:

> Where there is a default under this charge, the entire outstanding balance of the Principal Amount shall immediately become due and payable at the option of the chargee.

While acceleration of payment is also a common consequence of default in the case of unsecured loans and loans secured by a charge against personal property, there are a number of statutory rules with respect to the acceleration of payment under a mortgage within the meaning of the *Mortgages Act*[216] that are unique. In particular, section 22(1) of the *Mortgages Act* provides that:

> 22.(1) Despite any agreement to the contrary, where default has occurred in making any payment of principal or interest due under a mortgage or in the observance of any covenant in a mortgage and under the terms of the mortgage, by reason of such default, the whole principal and interest secured thereby has become due and payable,
>
> (a) at any time before sale under the mortgage; or
>
> (b) before the commencement of any action for the enforcement of the rights of the mortgagee or of any person claiming through or under the mortgagee,
>
> the mortgagor may perform such covenant or pay the amount due under the mortgage, exclusive of the money not payable by reason merely of lapse of time, and pay any expenses necessarily incurred by the mortgagee, and thereupon the mortgagor is relieved from the consequences of such default.

Thus despite any contractual right to accelerate the debt, the chargor may pay all arrears and expenses or otherwise cure a default under the charge and return the charge to good standing, and thereby defeat the operation of the acceleration provision. In addition to the protection afforded to a chargor under section 22, subsection 23(1) of the *Mortgages Act* provides:

> 23.(1) Despite any agreement to the contrary, where default has occurred in making any payment of principal or interest due under a mortgage or in the observance of any covenant in a mortgage and under the terms of the mortgage, by reason of such default, the whole principal and interest thereby secured has become due and payable, in an action for enforcement of the rights of the mortgagee or of any person claiming through or under the mortgagee, the mortgagor, upon payment into court of the sum of $100 to the credit of the action as security for costs, may apply to the court and, conditional upon performance of such covenant or upon payment of the money due under the mortgage, exclusive of the money not

---

[216] R.S.O. 1990, c. M.40.

payable by reason merely of lapse of time, and upon payment of the costs of the action, the court,

(a) shall dismiss the action if judgment has not been recovered; or

(b) may stay proceedings in the action, if judgment has been recovered and if no sale or recovery of possession of the land or final foreclosure of the equity of redemption has taken place.

However, the apparently broad scope of subsection (1) is partly qualified by subsection 23(2) of the *Mortgages Act*, which provides:

23.(2) Despite clause (1)(b), where judgment has been recovered and recovery of the possession of the land has taken place, the court may stay proceedings in the action upon the application of a person added as a party in the master's office, made under subsection (1) within ten days after service of notice of the judgment has been made upon the person.

Thus under section 23 it is possible to obtain relief from acceleration even after judgment, but not after a sale of the land. Finally, subsection 17(1) of the *Mortgages Act* provides:

17.(1) Despite any agreement to the contrary, where default has been made in the payment of any principal money secured by a mortgage of freehold or leasehold property, the mortgagor or person entitled to make such payment may at any time, upon payment of three months interest on the principal money so in arrear, pay the same, or the mortgagor or person entitled to make such payment may give the mortgagee at least three months notice, in writing, of the intention to make such payment at a time named in the notice, and in the event of making such payment on the day so named is entitled to make the same without any further payment of interest except to the date of payment.

However, subsection (1) is qualified by subsection 17(3), which reads:

17.(3) Nothing in this section affects or limits the right of the mortgagee to recover by action or otherwise the principal money so in arrear after default has been made.

§8.99 Acceleration of payment by the lender must be distinguished from early repayment by the borrower. Most fixed term lending requires the payment of an interest penalty or bonus if the borrower elects to prepay ahead of schedule. The purpose of the penalty is to compensate the lender for the "breakage costs" of early termination, including the replacement of its investment and any reduction in the anticipated stream of income resulting from adverse variation (from the lender's perspective) in prevailing rates of interest in the market. Generally, where a lender elects to demand repayment of a loan and enforce the security for that loan by reason of default, the lender foregoes the right to receive the payment of that penalty.[217] However, in *Re Shankman and Mutual Life Assurance Co. of Canada*[218] the mortgagee commenced an action only for the arrears and for an order for possession for the limited purpose of collecting the amount in

---

[217] *Municipal Savings & Loan Corporation v. Wilson*, [1981] O.J. No. 118, 127 D.L.R. (3d) 127 (C.A.).
[218] [1985] O.J. No. 2630, 52 O.R. (2d) 65 (C.A.).

arrears. When the mortgagor tendered the full amount owing and asked for the security to be discharged, the mortgagee refused. The Court of Appeal concluded that so long as the mortgagee was seeking only payment of the arrears, and not to accelerate repayment of the full amount secured by the mortgage, it did not trigger the equitable right to redeem.[219]

§8.100 A similar approach was followed in *Leby Properties Ltd. v. Manufacturers Life Insurance*[220] where a lender demanded payment of a demand loan from borrower who was in default under a mortgage. The lender served a notice of intention to enforce security under section 244 of the *Bankruptcy and Insolvency Act* ("BIA"), but it referred to only arrears owing and not full amount outstanding. The borrower filed a notice of intention to make a proposal under the BIA. The borrower entered into agreement to sell the mortgaged property to third party. The lender issued a payout statement that included a prepayment penalty. Borrower brought motion for declaration that it was not obligated to pay prepayment penalty. The motions judge ruled that the notice of intention to enforce security did not trigger the equitable right to redeem, and accordingly the borrower was required to pay prepayment penalty. This conclusion was upheld on appeal, where it was noted that the lender had not invoked acceleration by demanding full payment of loan. It was held that the purpose of section 244 was to provide the borrower with time to meet demand for payment. A section 244 notice was not the equivalent to a notice of mortgage sale.

§8.101 One provision commonly found in charges that requires some explanation is the clause permitting the chargee to grant extensions and otherwise vary the terms of the charge. A typical provision may read:

> No amendment of the terms or conditions of the charge or of these Standard charge Terms, or renewal of the charge or other extension of time given by the chargee to the chargor or anyone claiming under him, or other dealing by the chargee with the Property shall release, discharge or otherwise prejudicially affect the rights of the chargee against the chargor or any other person liable for the payment of the Principal Amount.

This provision is included to permit the chargee to agree to amendments to the charge with any subsequent owner of the property, without releasing the original chargor from its obligations under the personal covenant to pay. In the absence of such a provision, any material amendment to the charge made without the consent of the chargor will release the chargor from the personal covenant to pay. Similarly, an extension of time under the charge will release the original chargor from that covenant.

---

[219] *Cameo Developments Ltd. v. National Life Assurance Co. of Canada*, [1984] B.C.J. No. 6, 56 B.C.L.R. 363 (C.A.); *Prudential Insurance Co. of America v. Hollyburn Properties (Alberta) Ltd.*, [1984] B.C.J. No. 18, 58 B.C.L.R. 211 (C.A.).

[220] [2006] N.B.J. No. 17, 145 A.C.W.S. (3d) 316 at paras. 26 *et. seq.* (C.A.), leave to appeal to S.C.C. refused [2006] S.C.C.A. No. 99.

§8.102 Many charges also contain a provision expressly permitting the chargee and the chargor to agree to renew the charge at a higher rate of interest than was provided under the original charge:

> Whether or not there are subsequent encumbrances against the Property, the charge may be renewed by an agreement in writing at maturity for any term with or without an increased rate of interest, and it shall not be necessary to register that renewal in order to retain the priority of this charge over any subsequent instrument or encumbrance.

In *Reynolds Extrusion Co. v. Cooper*,[221] it was held that where the charge contains such a provision, any subsequent encumbrancer must accept the amended rate of interest as it takes effect.

(a) WARRANTIES

§8.103 Representations (or warranties) relate to the present state of facts, or to a state of fact at a particular time. Covenants are ongoing obligations that are assumed by the borrower, that are meant to preserve the assumed state of fact. From the perspective of both the borrower and the lender, the test as to whether there should be a warranty and covenant with respect to a particular matter should depend entirely upon whether that matter is material to the transaction. If that matter is likely to influence the lender's decision as to whether to enter the transaction, the rate of interest that will be payable, or the security that will be required, then the borrower cannot fairly object to a warranty and covenant with respect to that matter. If, on the other hand, a particular consideration is of a class entirely collateral to the transaction that is contemplated, then it should not be within the scope of the warranties or covenants, even though that consideration may quite possibly influence the general business of the borrower.

§8.104 Before discussing the conditions, covenants, warranties and events of default that should be contained in lending documents, it is necessary to decide which such provisions belong in the loan agreement and which in security agreements, and indeed whether it is preferable to have separate loan and security agreements or a single comprehensive agreement. Many lawyers adopt the practice of including all terms and conditions relating to the loan and its attendant security in a single comprehensive document. This approach has both strengths and weaknesses. On the positive side, a single comprehensive document can be easier to follow than a series of interrelated documents. Secondly, by using a single document it is unnecessary to duplicate similar provisions, as will often be required where two or more documents are used. Not only does the avoidance of duplication reduce the overall length of the documentation, it also avoids the risk of inconsistency among the various documents. The major drawback with the use of a single comprehensive document is that if the document is required to be registered in a public registry in order to perfect the security, then that document is available for anyone to review. At least in theory, such public access may be detrimental to the interest of both the lender and the borrower, as

---

[221] [1978] O.J. No. 3551, 21 O.R. (2d) 416 at 419 (H.C.J.), *per* Grange J.

exposing the details of the borrower's financing may give the competitors of each an unnecessary advantage. A further problem arises where an effort is made to combine different types of security into a single document in order to accommodate two or more different legislative regimes. The consequence of any such combination is almost certainly to be confusion; it may also render the documents ineffective. In an effort to balance the competing goals of eliminating unnecessary duplication, without over-consolidating the documentation, a number of rules of thumb can be recommended:

- Subject to any statutory requirement that must be satisfied to perfect the security interest, the terms of the credit facility should be included only in the loan agreement (*e.g.*, the authorized line of credit, the rate of interest, fees payable, manner of drawing, method repayment).
- The required security should be identified only in general terms in the loan agreement.
- A specific reference should be made to the loan agreement in the security agreement.
- Covenants and warranties relating to security should be in the security agreement rather than the loan agreement.
- Covenants and warranties relating specifically to the loan (*e.g.*, capitalization requirements, and other balance sheet and income statement tests that must be satisfied) should be in the loan agreement.
- Acts and events of default that relate specifically to the security interest or the collateral should be in the security agreement.
- Acts and events of default under the loan agreement should be in the loan agreement.
- Cross default provisions should be inserted in both the loan and security agreements.
- Remedies relating to realization upon collateral should be in the security agreement.
- Remedies relating to the termination of the credit facility should be in the loan agreement.
- Security agreements that are subject to inconsistent legislation should be contained in separate agreements.

A further complication that militates against both unnecessary duplication and over-consolidation is that where a document is registered, the amendment of that document will often require the registration of the amendment. Since such registration can be both time-consuming and expensive, it should be avoided to the greatest extent practicable.

§8.105 In a loan agreement or security agreement, warranties relate to the factual assumptions that underlie the lending transaction. While certain specific warranties are likely to be limited to individual transactions, there are a number of warranties that are encountered in most lending or security documents.

§8.106 A group of related standard warranties included in virtually all loan and security agreements involving a corporate borrower require a representation by the borrower that it is duly incorporated and that all necessary powers exist and all requisite steps have been taken to enable it to enter into the transaction:

> The borrower expressly warrants that it is a duly incorporated, organized and subsisting corporation, and has all requisite powers, capacities, licences and permissions under its governing legislation and the other laws applicable to it, and under its articles of incorporation, by-laws and governing resolutions to,
>
> (i) own the assets which the borrower has represented as belonging to the borrower in any financial statement or representation made by the borrower to the lender,
>
> (ii) carry on all businesses in which the borrower is engaged,
>
> (iii) enter into, exercise its rights and perform and comply with its obligations under this agreement,
>
> and that all actions, conditions and things have been done, taken or fulfilled with respect thereto, that are required by law, contract or otherwise.

While it is important for the borrower to provide the above warranty, no such warranty reduces the need for the counsel to both the borrower and the lender to satisfy themselves that the above warranty is factual.

§8.107 It is customary for the borrower to warrant that neither the borrower's participation in the loan agreement nor in the security agreements violates any contractual prohibition or restriction:

> The borrower expressly warrants that it is not a party to any agreement under the terms of which the borrower is prohibited or restricted from entering into any of the obligations assumed, liabilities imposed, or restrictions accepted by the borrower under this agreement.

Unlike the warranty of corporate status, it would be difficult in most cases even for the counsel to the borrower to express a firm opinion with respect to the possibility of contractual breach. Nevertheless, it is not unusual to require the counsel to the borrower to include in their opinion that they are aware of no such breach.

§8.108 A third standard warranty relates to the non-existence of any encumbrance on the assets of the borrower. While most encumbrances are required to be registered, even in the case of corporate securities, the possibility exists that there may be valid encumbrances that are registered against an older corporate name or against a predecessor corporation. Since there may also be a variety of inchoate liens in effect against various assets, such as liens in favour of repairers, the borrower is also likely to be expected to warrant that there are no outstanding judgments, orders or similar processes that may have an adverse impact upon the borrower or the collateral, as in the following provision:

The borrower expressly warrants that

(a) no encumbrance exists on or over any of its assets or revenues or the assets or revenues of any of its subsidiaries, except as disclosed in writing to the lender;

(b) there are no outstanding judgments, writs of execution, work orders, injunctions, or administrative or regulatory directives against the borrower or any of its assets which might reasonably be seen to have a materially adverse impact upon the borrower, its assets, prospects or condition. [222]

§8.109 Although lending agreements are not contracts of utmost good faith, they have at least one common characteristic with most such agreements: the lender is largely dependent upon the borrower for its knowledge concerning the borrower's affairs. Therefore it is not surprising that most standard loan documents include an express representation by the borrower concerning the accuracy of the financial and other information provided by the borrower to the lender:

The borrower expressly warrants as follows:

(a) the borrower's financial statements present fairly the financial position of the borrower and the results of its operations in accordance with generally accepted accounting principles applied on a consistent basis with that of the preceding year, or other relevant financial period, except for such changes or departures from such principles as are expressly identified by the auditors of the borrower in their report on the financial statements, or are expressly noted in the notes to the financial statements;

(b) to the best of the borrower's information and belief and after making diligent inquiries,

   (i) the information concerning the business, affairs and financial and other condition of the borrower that are contained in all documents, memoranda, records, statements made, sent or given by the borrower to the lender during the course of the negotiation of this agreement, its application for a credit facility of any kind with the lender, or in connection with the renewal of this agreement, and in its current regulatory filings, are true and accurate in all material respects; and

   (ii) the borrower is not aware of any material facts or circumstances which have not been disclosed.

Similarly, it is customary to include a warranty that there has been no significant deterioration in the borrower's position since the time when the loan application was made:

The borrower expressly warrants as follows:

---

[222] See, generally, *NBD Bank, Canada v. Dofasco Inc.*, [1997] O.J. No. 1803, 34 B.L.R. (2d) 209 (Gen. Div.), aff'd [1997] O.J. No. 4749 (C.A.), leave to appeal to S.C.C. refused [2000] S.C.C.A. No. 96.

(a) no event of default has occurred since the date on which the borrower applied for a credit facility to which this agreement applies, or appears reasonably likely to occur as of the date of this agreement;

(b) no litigation, arbitration or administrative proceeding is current or pending, so far as the borrower is aware, in respect of the borrower or any of its subsidiaries, which appears reasonably likely to have a materially adverse effect on the borrower and its subsidiaries taken as a whole;

(c) there has been no material adverse change, since the date of the borrower's most recently audited financial statements, or the date of the borrower's loan application, whichever is more recent.

(b) Covenants

§8.110 Covenants are undertakings made by the borrower to the lender that the borrower agrees to abide by so long as the loan remains outstanding. In general terms, covenants, other than the covenant to pay, are collateral undertakings given by the borrower. There is no rule in equity that precludes a secured creditor from stipulating for any collateral advantage other than the repayment of the principal, interest and costs, provided that collateral advantage is not (1) unfair and unconscionable; (2) in the nature of a penalty clogging the equity of redemption;[223] or (3) inconsistent with or repugnant to the contractual or equitable right to redeem.[224] Covenants generally focus on six key areas:

- the preservation of the identity and integrity of the borrower;
- the preservation of the security;
- the uses to which the loan may be put;
- the maintenance of the collateral and permitted uses of the charged assets by the borrower;
- maintaining the condition of the borrower;
- provision of information in both the ordinary course and in the event of an extraordinary circumstance.

Essentially, the wider the credit, the wider the range of material considerations. In the case of a defined purpose credit (*e.g.*, lease financing for the purchase of a computer), material considerations are likely to be limited to the ability of the borrower to service the lease and, except in rare cases, the lease of the computer is unlikely to constitute a substantial portion of the borrower's overall business. A lawyer reviewing proposed covenants should consider and advise the client concerning the potential practical impact of any proposed covenant on the business, affairs and other aspects of the operations of the borrower. The longer the term of the proposed loan or security agreement, the more closely that impact

---

[223] See *Moore v. Texaco Canada Ltd.*, [1965] O.J. No. 980, [1965] 2 O.R. 253 (H.C.J.).
[224] *Kreglinger v. New Patagonia Meat & Cold Storage Co.*, [1914] A.C. 25 at 61 (H.L.), *per* Lord Parker; *Clark v. Supertest Petroleum Corp.*, [1958] O.J. No. 527, [1958] O.R. 474 (H.C.J.).

should be considered. A restriction in a long-term debt instrument that can only be redeemed upon the payment of a premium may complicate the raising of future finance, or may result in unexpected costs to the borrower, once the borrowed funds are no longer required. The following paragraphs discuss some typical types of covenant that appear in loan and security documentation.

§8.111 The covenant to pay the debt we have already considered. In addition to that covenant, a number of further payment covenants will be included, to ensure that the value of the collateral is not compromised. A lengthy list of taxes, rates, duties, assessments, rents, fees or appropriations constitute or are capable of becoming charges ranking in priority to security interests. To protect the lender's security against encroachments by such interests, a variety of covenants are often included, such as:

> The borrower covenants that so long as this agreement remains in effect, the borrower shall:
>
> (a) pay all taxes, rates, duties, assessments, rents, fees or appropriations, and all other moneys due or to become due or charged or hereafter to be charged upon the collateral or upon the borrower on account thereof as and when the same become payable;
>
> (b) pay all tax installments withheld or collected by the borrower on time and remit to the appropriate taxing authority all amounts deemed by any rule of law to be held on trust for the benefit of that taxing authority, and
>
> (c) from time to time, provide to the lender proof that all such payments and remittances have been made.

Clause (a) relates to the tax liabilities of the borrower. Clause (b) refers to tax withholdings retained by the borrower for remittance to the taxing authority. An alternative to the covenant to pay taxes is for the security agreement to require the borrower to pay an amount to the lender, for remittance by the lender to the taxing authority.

§8.112 Where money is advanced in trust, generally it must be used for the purpose intended, and any failure to use it for that purpose constitutes a breach of trust. In contrast, money loaned to a debtor belongs to that debtor (subject to a mere contractual commitment for its repayment). Until such time as the debt is repayable, the debtor is generally free to deal with that money as he or she chooses. The creditor has no ownership of it or inherent legal right to require it to be used in a particular manner. This rule is obviously unacceptable to creditors in many cases. Fortunately it may be overcome by contractual provision.

§8.113 Accordingly, where the funds are being advanced to the borrower for a specific purpose, the lender will often insist on an express covenant that the funds be used for that specific purpose and no other. When coupled with a properly drafted default provision, the consequence of using the funds for any other purpose would be to place the borrower in default, and thereby permit the acceleration of the lender's right to repayment.

The borrower covenants that the borrower shall use the funds advanced to the borrower under this agreement for lawful purposes and only in accordance with the terms and restrictions set out any agreement relating thereto between the borrower and the lender, provided that the fact that an advance is used for a purpose other than that specified in the agreement shall not affect the obligation of the borrower to repay that advance, but shall render that advance repayable on demand.

Although often included as a warranty, this provision is more in the nature of a covenant: it is a promise concerning the use to which the funds will be put after they are advanced.

§8.114 Except in the case of subordinated debt, it is usual for loan and security agreements to contain a prohibition against granting or permitting the existence of any security that ranks in priority to the claim of the lender. This covenant (often abbreviated as a "negative covenant") is particularly important in the case of unsecured loan agreements, since any creditor who subsequently acquires a security will rank ahead of the unsecured creditors. It is also of importance in the case of floating charges, since any fixed charge granted before the crystallization of the floating charge will have priority over the floating charge. Unfortunately, such provisions do little to protect the lender if a security interest is granted in contravention of the negative covenant, unless it can be shown that the creditor who acquired the security interest had notice of that negative covenant.[225]

§8.115 In the case of a fixed charge, it is not possible to create a prior ranking security interest except with the consent of the holder of the charge (although there are numerous statutes that give rise to liens by operation of law, that are not subject to this restriction). Much the same rule appears to apply in provinces with *Personal Property Security Acts* with respect to any kind of perfected security interest. Elsewhere, a floating charge enjoys no such priority. A company that creates a floating charge over an asset may continue to deal with those assets in the ordinary course, and since it may sell an asset in the ordinary course, it would seem to follow that it may also encumber those assets by way of a fixed charge.[226] Under general principles of equity, where the equities are equal, the legal right prevails. However, under the doctrine of constructive notice, the holder of the subsequent fixed charge will not take priority over the holder of the floating charge if

- the floating charge contained a negative covenant prohibiting the grant of competing security; and
- the holder of the fixed charge had notice of this prohibition.

---

[225] See, generally, *G & T Earle Ltd. v. Hemsworth Rural District Council* (1928), 140 L.T. 169, aff'd 44 T.L.R. 758 (C.A.), per Wright J; *Welch v. Bowmaker (Ireland) Ltd.*, [1980] I.R. 251; *Ian Chisholm Textiles Ltd. v. Griffiths*, [1994] 2 B.C.L.C. 291; *Re Automatic Bottle Makers Ltd.*, [1926] Ch. 412; *Furmanek v. Community Futures Development Corp.*, [1998] B.C.J. No. 1536, 162 D.L.R. (4th) 501 (C.A.).

[226] A subsequently granted floating charge will normally rank after a prior granted floating charge, although where the second charge relates to a specific asset, the second charge may enjoy priority: *English & Scottish Mercantile Investment Co. v. Brunton*, [1892] 2 Q.B. 700 (C.A.).

Knowledge (or deemed notice) of the existence of the floating charge is not the same as knowledge of the existence of the negative covenant.[227]

§8.116 The probability that a competing security will be granted is not limited to situations where there is a deliberate intent on the part of the borrower to defraud the lender. A total prohibition on the grant of security is normally inconsistent with the practical working requirements of the borrower. Consequently, any such provision is normally qualified to permit the borrower to grant a number of itemized permitted encumbrances — a list that will be sufficiently comprehensive to permit the borrower to carry on its day-to-day business. For instance, in the case of borrowing by financial institutions, it is common to include a right in favour of the financial institution to grant security to institutions such as the Bank of Canada, the Canada Deposit Insurance Corporation and similar liquidity support agencies, to cover borrowings to meet short term liquidity requirements of the financial institution. Such borrowings may, of course, quickly become a substantial charge against the assets of an insolvent or illiquid borrower, with the result that the protection afforded to the lender by the negative covenant against the grant of security may be more illusory than real. That much said, the following is an example of such a negative covenant:

> The borrower covenants that so long as this agreement remains in effect, the borrower shall not, without the prior consent in writing of the lender create or permit the existence of any mortgage, charge, lien or other encumbrance upon the collateral or any part thereof ranking or purporting to rank in priority to or equally with the charges created by this agreement, except for permitted encumbrances.

In certain cases the business realities of a proposed transaction may render it impossible or impractical to obtain a negative covenant against the grant of securities. As an alternative, loan agreements occasionally contain a positive covenant to the effect that the indebtedness of the lender will rank at least *pari passu* with competing creditors, other than statutory preferred creditors. The following is an example of such a "most favoured lender" provision:

> The lender shall at all times be entitled to rights against the borrower at least equal to the rights granted by the borrower to any other lender with respect to security and priority of claim, so that,
>
> (a) the obligation of the borrower to make payment shall at all times rank *pari passu* and at least equally and rateably in all respects with all other unsubordinated obligations of the borrower except for statutory preferred exceptions; and
>
> (b) the borrower shall not grant security or a preference to any other creditor without granting a similar security or preference on a rateable basis to the lender.

§8.117 In the case of floating charges, the security interest in particular collateral is also likely to be defeated if that collateral is seized in execution before the

---

[227] *G & T Earle Ltd. v. Hemsworth Rural District Council* (1928), 140 L.T. 169, aff'd 44 T.L.R. 758 (C.A.), *per* Wright J.; see also *Welch v. Bowmaker (Ireland) Ltd.*, [1980] I.R. 251.

crystallization of the security interest. To protect a lender's floating charge against that risk, it is common for the loan documents to include a covenant to pay all amounts that are capable of being realized against the collateral:

> The borrower covenants that so long as this agreement remains in effect, the borrower shall:
>
> (a) pay all amounts secured by and observe and perform all covenants and conditions contained in all other charges on the whole or any part of the collateral in accordance with their terms, whether those other charges rank prior to or subsequent to the charges granted by this agreement;
>
> (b) defend the whole and every part of the collateral against the claims and demands of all other persons claiming to have an interest in the collateral and against every charge, lien, encumbrance, execution, sequestration, extent or analogous process.

§8.118 Under numerous statutes and regulations particular types of collateral are liable to seizure or forfeiture if they are not used in accordance with applicable legislation. A further risk, particularly in the case of conditional sale agreements and leases, is that the lender may be affixed with liability, if the collateral causes injury to a third party.

> The borrower covenants that so long as this agreement remains in effect, the borrower shall observe all laws and conform to all valid requirements of any governmental authority with respect to all or any part of its business, the collateral and all covenants, terms and contracts upon or under which the whole or any part of the collateral is held.

This covenant goes beyond the standard covenant to preserve and maintain the collateral insofar as it requires the entire business of the borrower to be conducted in a lawful manner. Reported cases involving provisions of this sort are, however, very rare, and therefore it is far from clear whether such provisions are particularly effective (or necessary) in protecting the lender from the borrower. On the other hand, for obvious reasons a prospective lender may well wish to reconsider whether to become involved with a prospective borrower where that borrower refuses to provide a covenant to act in a lawful manner.

§8.119 Most security documents contain an undertaking by the borrower to take such additional steps and provide such further assurances as the lender may reasonably request in order to carry out the intent of the parties under the agreement. A provision of this type will permit the lender to remedy any defect in the documentation that is discovered after the closing of the transaction, although, of course, any such remedy will often be subject to rights acquired by third parties who act in good faith prior to the time when the corrective step is taken. A typical provision will read:

> The borrower covenants that from time to time upon request by the lender, so long as this agreement remains in effect, the borrower shall do, execute, acknowledge and deliver, or cause to be done, executed, acknowledged and delivered, all and every such further acts, deeds, mortgages, transfers and assurances in law as the lender may require

(i) to perfect the security of the lender on all or part of the collateral,

(ii) to charge specifically any or all of the property now or hereafter subject to the floating charge created by this agreement, and

(iii) to carry into effect the intentions of the parties as set out in this agreement.

In many cases, the covenant will also confer an express power of attorney upon the lender, to complete, sign, deliver and register on behalf of the borrower any agreement or other document within the scope of the section.

§8.120 The need to protect the collateral against undue waste is clear. On the other hand, the borrower will require the right to use the collateral, and any such use is bound to result in some depreciation in the value of the collateral. To balance the competing interests of the lender and the borrower, security agreements usually provide that the borrower shall maintain the collateral in a good state of repair, but allow for the wear and tear that results from ordinary usage. Similarly, a borrower engaged in business will require the right to dispose of and acquire new furniture and equipment in the ordinary course of business.

> The borrower covenants that so long as this agreement remains in effect, the borrower shall:
>
> (a) refrain from and prevent waste from being committed on the collateral and the borrower shall maintain the collateral in good order and repair to the satisfaction of the lender and where the borrower fails to keep the collateral so repaired, the lender may take possession of the collateral and have such repairs made, and the cost incurred by the lender in effecting any such repair shall be secured by the security interest provided for in this agreement;
>
> (b) not sell or otherwise dispose of furniture, machinery, equipment, vehicles and accessories (other than those that may become worn out or otherwise unsuitable), unless equivalent replacement collateral are acquired.

The basic commitment, therefore, is to maintain the collateral in a steady state of condition, so as not to undermine the value of the collateral as a security to the lender.

§8.121 The need for insuring the collateral against the normal risk of damage is fairly obvious, as any damage to the collateral may substantially undermine the value of the security interest. However, merely imposing an obligation to insure is not sufficient. The lender should have an express right to insure if the borrower fails to do so, and the security agreement should provide that any amount paid in respect of such insurance may be charged against the collateral. The rights of the lender are significantly enhanced if the lender is named as a named insured, rather than as a loss payee, for where the lender is a named insured, it is protected against breaches of the conditions of the insurance policy by the debtor which would otherwise release the insurer from the obligation to indemnify.

> The borrower covenants that so long as this agreement remains in effect, the borrower shall insure and keep insured under an insurance policy issued by a licensed insurance company approved by the lender, all of the property hereby charged against loss or damage by fire and against loss or damage by tempest, tornado, cy-

clone, flood, lightning and other risks, hazards or perils as the lender may require, to the extent that such collateral is insurable for its full insurable value, and the borrower shall forthwith assign, transfer and deliver to the lender the policy or policies of such insurance and the receipts therefor, provided that:

> (a) where the borrower fails or refuses to keep the collateral or any part of it insured as aforesaid and to deliver such policies and receipts or to produce to the lender at least ten days before the termination of any of such insurance, evidence of renewal thereof, the lender may (but shall not be obliged to) insure the collateral or any of part of it; and
>
> (b) on all such policies (except in respect of collateral specifically charged to such other lenders as may be permitted) the lender shall be an additional insured, and indemnity shall be payable first to the lender as its interest shall appear.

Insurance provisions often provide the lender with the option to require any amount paid under an insurance policy to be applied to the reduction of the loan, rather than to the purchase of replacement assets. The reason for this is that the purchase of replacement assets will not always be sufficient to maintain the security of the lender, particularly where the destruction of the collateral undermines the ability of the borrower to generate the income required to service the debt. In this regard, where the collateral is real property, consideration must be given to section 6 of the *Mortgages Act*,[228] which provides:

> 6.(1) All money payable to a mortgagor on an insurance of the mortgaged property, including effects, whether affixed to freehold or not, being or forming part thereof, shall, if the mortgagee so requires, be applied by the mortgagor in making good the loss or damage in respect of which the money is received.
>
> (2) Without prejudice to any obligation to the contrary imposed by law or by special contract, a mortgagee may require that all money received on an insurance of the mortgaged property be applied in or towards the discharge of the money due under his mortgage.

Akin to the requirement for insurance, most loan documents require the borrower to make insurance claims promptly, so as not to prejudice the right to recover under the policy, or the amount payable as a result of the damage to the collateral:

> The borrower covenants that so long as this agreement remains in effect, the borrower shall forthwith on the happening of any loss or damage, furnish at its own expense all necessary proofs and do all necessary acts to enable the lender to obtain payment of the insurance money.

§8.122 Under corporate law, dividends may be paid by a corporation out of earnings, including retained earnings. To prevent retained earnings from being used for such a purpose, it is common for loan documents to provide:

> The borrower covenants that so long as this agreement remains in effect, the borrower shall not issue any dividends, patronage refunds or bonuses in any financial year except out of current earnings or with the prior written consent of the lender.

---

[228] R.S.O. 1990, c. M.40.

The intent behind provisions of this sort is to ensure that retained earnings are used by the corporation primarily for the repayment of debt.

§8.123 In order to monitor the performance of a borrower, it is necessary to have assurance that the accounts and records of the borrower will be kept in an intelligible manner, that permits comparison to an objective standard or at least to a comparable enterprise. There must also be ongoing access to the accounts and records, both in the form of routine disclosure of financial information, and the ability to make on-premises inspections of records, where the lender considers it advisable to do so.

> The borrower covenants that so long as this agreement remains in effect, the borrower shall:
>
> (a) keep proper books of account and maintain therein in accordance with generally accepted accounting principles true and faithful entries of all dealings and transactions in relation to its business;
>
> (b) permit the lender, by its officers or agents, to enter the premises of the borrower and to inspect the books and records of the borrower and to make extracts therefrom;
>
> (c) provide the lender with audited annual and unaudited semi-annual financial statements within 60 days of the end of these fiscal periods, such statements to be certified by a senior financial officer of the borrower as truly and accurately representing the financial condition of the borrower.

In addition to the disclosure of routine financial information, the borrower should also be required to disclose the occurrence of any exceptional circumstances that jeopardize the ability of the borrower to perform its obligations:

> The borrower covenants that so long as this agreement remains in effect, the borrower shall notify the lender promptly of:
>
> (a) any change in the information contained herein or in the schedules hereto relating to the borrower, its business or the Assets;
>
> (b) the details of any significant acquisition of any further Assets;
>
> (c) the details of any claims or litigation affecting the borrower or the Assets;
>
> (d) any damage to the whole or a material part of the Assets or any other material adverse change in the financial or other condition of the borrower or of the borrower and its subsidiaries taken as a whole since the date of this agreement which affects or is likely to affect the ability of the borrower to perform its obligations under this agreement or in respect of any relevant indebtedness.

§8.124 A wide range of different types of performance measurement can be imposed under a loan agreement, but the most common involve covenants to maintain a specified current ratio position, to maintain current liabilities below a certain level, to maintain at least a stated minimum net worth, and to restrict borrowings external to the loan agreement to a specified amount or a specified type of debt. The following provisions illustrate these types of covenant:

1. The borrower and its subsidiaries shall at all times have at least $••• in their consolidated aggregate current assets in excess of their consolidated current liabilities and shall at all times maintain a ratio of consolidated current assets to consolidated current liabilities of at least •• to ••.

2. The borrower shall not permit its consolidated aggregate liabilities to exceed $•• and shall not permit its consolidated aggregate liabilities to exceed •• per cent of its consolidated net worth.

3. The borrower shall at all times maintain a minimum consolidated tangible net worth of at least $••.

4. The borrower shall not have, and shall not permit its subsidiaries to have, any indebtedness, except for,

    (a) the indebtedness provided for in this agreement;

    (b) short term indebtedness in any combination of notes or lines of credit with a bank or other lending institution, not exceeding $••• in aggregate principal amount;

    (c) current trade credit and other debts incurred in the ordinary course of business, not exceeding $••• in aggregate principal amount,

    and all such indebtedness shall be paid when due, in accordance with customary trade terms.

The advantage derived by the lender from the inclusion of such provisions is that they fix specific performance milestones that must be satisfied in order for the loan to remain in good standing. They are more precise than standards such as "material adverse change" provisions, which involve a subjective assessment by the lender, and that consequently may become a source of friction and litigation. The disadvantage is that they are inflexible, and it is always possible that a genuinely material adverse change will occur that is not caught within the scope of one of the performance covenants.

§8.125 In addition to direct performance covenants, loan agreements will typically contain certain negative covenants restricting aspects of the business operation. For instance, over-investment in capital assets is a frequent cause of illiquidity, which can often result in the failure of a business. Consequently, it is not surprising that many lenders will seek to restrict capital investment by borrowers by introducing covenants along the following lines:

> The borrower covenants that so long as this agreement remains in effect, the borrower shall not incur capital expenditures greater than such amounts as may be agreed from time to time between the parties without the prior approval of the lender.

Another common loan covenant restricts the right of the issuer to pay dividends or make distributions to its shareholders unless certain performance standards are satisfied, usually related to a ratio of total debt to net worth. A key concern underlying a covenant of this type will be to maintain a minimum standard of debt service capability in the borrower. The following is an example of such a provision:

(1) The Corporation shall not declare or pay any dividend, redeem or purchase or otherwise acquire any of its shares, or make any other distribution to its shareholders, where immediately after the making of that payment, redemption, repurchase or distribution, as the case may be, the aggregate principal amount of the Funded Obligations of the Corporation would be •• or more times the Shareholders' Equity.

(2) In subsection (1),

  (a) "Funded Obligations" means in respect of any particular date the aggregate of the indebtedness of the Corporation in respect of any borrowed money or otherwise that by its terms is due and payable within the 12 months next following that date, and in the case of any debt payable in a currency other than Canadian dollars, for the purposes of making the calculation required under subsection (1), the amount of the indebtedness shall be the Canadian dollar Equivalent Amount of that currency as of that date;

  (b) "Shareholders' Equity" means the aggregate of,

    (i) the amount in the stated capital accounts of the shares of all classes and series of the Corporation;

    (ii) any contributed surplus in the Corporation;

    (iii) any earned surplus or deficit, as the case may be,

  but does not include any appraisal surplus or provision for deferred income taxes.

A provision of this sort is clearly less restrictive to the borrower than a total prohibition upon the payment of dividends, but will be equally unrealistic from the borrower's perspective if the multiple of Funded Obligations to Shareholders' Equity is set at too high a level. Although generally considered to be protective of the lender's interest, restrictions upon the payment of dividends may actually weaken the lender's position in certain cases, because any such restriction may deter investment in the capital of the borrower.

(7) Defeasance

§8.126 As noted above, a mortgage or charge is a security interest conferred on a lender or other creditor to secure the payment of a debt or the performance of some other obligation. Where that debt is paid or other obligation is performed, the security interest is discharged. In the case of charges against real property, defeasance of the security interest now takes place by operation of subsection 6(2) of the *Land Registration Reform Act*,[229] which provides:

---

[229] R.S.O. 1990, c. L.4.

6.(2) A charge ceases to operate when the money and interest secured by the charge are paid, or the obligations whose performance is secured by the charge are performed, in the manner provided by the charge.

Despite this statutory provision, it is common for charges and other security agreements to contain an express provision relating to discharge, particularly in the case of continuing security arrangements, so as to clarify when the security interest is discharged by performance, and to provide an express right to obtain the necessary discharge documents.

(8) Waiver

§8.127 A creditor may waive or release security to which the creditor is entitled prior to the performance of the secured obligation, and similarly, the creditor may waive or release rights that arise under a security or loan agreement by reason of the occurrence of a particular act or event. Briefly stated, waiver is the forgoing of some right, claim or privilege or the giving up of an advantage to which a party is entitled. It may arise by reason of action or inaction on the part of the creditor that is inconsistent with the right, claim or privilege in question, and may be express or implied.[230] Where there is said to have been an implied waiver, the circumstances must warrant an inference that such a release has occurred.[231] Whether a creditor has waived its rights is a question of intention,[232] which must be clearly and unequivocally evident on the facts.[233] Unless supported by consideration, conduct alleged to amount to a waiver will not bar the enforcement of the right unless it amounts to a release.[234] For conduct of a creditor to amount to such a waiver, it is necessary to satisfy two conditions. First, it must be shown that the creditor knew of the right, claim or privilege alleged to have been waived. Second, the facts must evidence a clear intention that the creditor intended to forgo that right, claim or privilege.[235]

(ii) Chattel Mortgage

§8.128 The chattel mortgage is the personal property analog of the real property mortgage. It may cover both existing and future property of a corporate debtor.[236] Although the term has an extended definition in the legislation of some provinces, a chattel mortgage is a transfer of the debtor's ownership or title to a chattel to a creditor, subject to a right of redemption,[237] as security for the payment of a debt or the performance of an obligation.[238] If the conditions of the agreement are not satisfied, then the sale becomes absolute (although any such

---

[230] *Gray Tractor Co. v. Van Troyen*, [1925] 1 D.L.R. 718 (Sask. K.B.).
[231] *Ross v. Imperial Life Assurance Co.*, [1929] 1 D.L.R. 324 at 328 (Alta. C.A.), *per* Lunney J.A.
[232] *Townend v. Graham*, [1899] B.C.J. No. 33, 6 B.C.R. 539 at 544 (S.C.), *per* Martin J.
[233] *Hollister v. Porchet* (1922), 66 D.L.R. 579 at 591 (Alta. C.A.), *per* Hyndman J.A.
[234] *Knight v. Ducklow Motors Ltd.*, [1926] 4 D.L.R. 1111 at 1113 (Sask. C.A.), *per* Lamont J.A.
[235] *Western Canada Investment Co. v. McDiamid* (1922), 66 D.L.R. 457 at 460-61 (Sask. C.A.), *per* Lamont J.A.
[236] *Canada Permanent Loan & Savings Co. v. Todd*, [1895] O.J. No. 64, 22 O.A.R. 515 (C.A.).
[237] *Driedger v. Schmidt*, [1931] 3 W.W.R. 514 (Sask. C.A.).
[238] *Dealers Finance Corp. v. Masterson Motors*, [1931] 2 W.W.R. 214 (Sask. C.A.).

transfer of title would now be subject to the provisions of the PPSA relating to the enforcement of security interests). For a valid chattel mortgage to exist, the debtor must have had a right or title to the chattel that is transferred. Chattel mortgages confer fixed and specific security interests in the subject collateral. Except in the case of a consumer transaction, a chattel mortgage may extend to present and future acquired property.[239]

(iii) Debentures and Bonds

§8.129 Historically, debentures and bonds of various kinds were the most common type of corporate debt security instrument. Their importance has lessened in recent years, with the gradual extension of legislation based upon the Ontario *Personal Property Security Act* across the country. Nevertheless, they are still common nonetheless.

§8.130 Although many valiant and imaginative attempts have been made to distinguish between the two, the term "debenture" is for all intents and purposes a synonym for the term "bond". Debentures of one form or another have been in use in England for nearly 600 years. While debentures of various sorts are among the most frequently encountered type of corporate security interest, the term "debenture" is not clearly defined either in law or in commerce,[240] and the nature of the interest and rights conferred by such instruments vary widely.[241] In *CBC Pension Plan v. BF Realty Holdings Ltd.*, Cronk J.A. said:

> Debentures, by definition, either create or acknowledge a debt. They are often, but not invariably, coupled with a charge or security interest against the debtor's property.[242]

Thus while the term "mortgage" is always used to describe an agreement that confers a security interest, this is not so the term "debenture": it is used with equal ease to describe instruments that create a fixed or floating charge upon some or all of the assets of a corporation, to describe unsecured debt, and (particularly in the case of banks and trust companies) to describe subordinate debt instruments.[243] It is sometimes said that the term "debenture" imports a debt — an acknowledgment of a debt, and that generally, if not always, the instrument imports an obligation or covenant to pay.[244] However, not every acknowledgment of indebtedness and covenant to pay constitutes a debenture; a simple promissory note, for instance, would never be called a debenture. To differenti-

---

[239] *Re Yorkshire Woolcombers Association Ltd.*, [1903] 2 Ch. 284 (C.A.).
[240] *Levy v. Abercorris Slate and Slab Co.* (1887), 37 Ch. D. 260 at 264, *per* Chitty J.
[241] Many of the cases in which the meaning of the term has been considered are cases involving questions of statutory interpretation rather than the general meaning of the term at common law. See, for instance, *Martin Ruby Ltd. v. National Upholstering Manufacturing Co.* (1964), 47 W.W.R. 211 (Sask. Dist. Ct.).
[242] [2002] O.J. No. 2125, 214 D.L.R. (4th) 121 (C.A.).
[243] The imprecision of the term has received judicial recognition: *British India, etc. Co. v. CIR* (1881), 7 Q.B.D. 165 at 172-73, *per* Lindley J. See also *Re Farmers' Loan & Savings Co.*, [1899] O.J. No. 150, 30 O.R. 337 (C.A.).
[244] *Edmonds v. Blaina Furnaces Co.* (1887), 36 Ch. D. 215 at 219, *per* Chitty J.; see also *Lemon v. Austin Friars Investment Trust Ltd.*, [1926] Ch. 1 (C.A.).

ate debentures from other debt instruments, the following other common (but not universal) characteristics of debentures have also been noted judicially: debentures are (a) usually issued by corporations; (b) sometimes issued in series;[245] (c) often under a trust deed and (d) usually under corporate seal. But these are merely rules of thumb, and in individual cases, the courts are freely prepared to depart from them. For instance, although the term "debenture" usually describes a corporate debt instrument, it has been widely recognized by the courts that unincorporated associations sometimes issue them, and on occasion even instruments issued by individuals have been held to constitute debentures.[246] The case law indicates that the fact that the parties to a particular instrument have described it as a debenture creates a heavy presumption that the instrument is such[247] but in contrast, the fact that an instrument is not so described seems to be of far less import.[248]

§8.131 Like a share, a debenture is a chose in action. But unlike a share, the court will not ordinarily grant a decree of specific performance of a contract to purchase debentures.[249] Instead, the normal remedy in such a case is damages.[250] Debentures are very often made redeemable. In contrast to shares, few restrictions (other than those relating to fraudulent preferences) apply to the redemption of debentures. A corporation that is required to redeem debentures that it was issued must be ready and willing to pay the debt on the day fixed, and must maintain that readiness until the debt is discharged.[251] For this reason, it is customary to include in debentures a clause permitting the issuer to pay the amount payable at maturity into a depositary, where the debenture holder fails to present the debenture at that time. Upon that payment, the liability of the debenture holder will be extinguished.

§8.132 A debenture may be issued in consideration of a past-due debt. It has even been held that a new debenture may be issued where other security holders have begun an action to enforce their own security under an earlier debenture.[252] Where the debenture is granted by a corporation in insolvent circumstances and secures a past indebtedness, the issue may well give rise to questions of fraudulent preference. Debentures are not issued until such time as they are signed,

---

[245] A series of debentures is a set of identical debt instruments (although sometimes varying in amount), each of which ranks rateably and in equal priority as a claim against the corporation (or, where the debenture is secured, the charged assets of the corporation). As an alternative to the issue of series debentures, it is possible to issue a single debenture to a trustee, with unit interests in the trust debenture being issued by the trustee to investors.

[246] *Bank of Toronto v. Cobourg, Peterborough & Marmora Rlwy.*, [1884] O.J. No. 17, 7 O.R. 1 at 7 (H.C.J.), *per* Boyd C.

[247] *Lemon v. Austin Friars Invst. Trust*, [1926] Ch. 1 at 18 (C.A.), *per* Sargant L.J.

[248] See, for instance, *Martin Ruby Ltd. v. National Upholstering Manufacturing. Co.* (1964), 47 W.W.R. 211 (Sask. D.C.).

[249] *South African Territories v. Wallington*, [1898] A.C. 309 at 312 (H.L.), *per* Earl of Halsbury L.C.; *Dorchester Electric Co. v. Thompson* (1915), 48 Que. S.C. 471.

[250] *McKinnon v. Doran*, [1915] O.J. No. 98, 34 O.L.R. 403 (S.C.), aff'd [1916] O.J. No. 64, 35 O.L.R. 349 (C.A.), aff'd 53 S.C.R. 609; see also *McNeil v. Fultz* (1906), 38 S.C.R. 198.

[251] *Gatineau Power Co. v. Crown Life Insurance Co.*, [1945] S.C.R. 655.

[252] *Re Hubbard & Co.* (1898), 68 L.J. Ch. 54 at 57, *per* Wright J.

sealed and delivered. However, delivery of a debenture by a corporation to the person entitled to the charge that it creates will normally be presumed to complete the issue of the debenture.[253]

§8.133 As noted in Chapter 7, the shares of a class or series are presumed to be equal. In contrast, where debentures are issued in series and are not expressed to rank on an equal footing, each ranks in priority to those that are subsequently issued.[254] Unless the terms of the debentures provide for equal priority for all debentures in a series, once the corporation creates a security it is no longer able to confer an equal priority on any subsequently issued debenture.[255]

§8.134 While it was at one time held that debentures were non-assignable[256] and even where assignable could be transferred only subject to such equities as might exist between the issuer and the transferor, this view no longer represents the law.[257] On the contrary, the present presumption is that transfers of debentures will not be subject to such equities, for subsection 53(3) of the OBCA now provides that except where a transfer is restricted and noted on a security in accordance with subsection 56(3), a security is a negotiable instrument. However, debentures may be drafted so as to exclude negotiability. Whether a particular debenture is non-negotiable, or even non-assignable, is a matter of interpretation.

(1) Fixed and Floating Charges

§8.135 A debenture may be secured or unsecured,[258] or as we shall see presently, may even relate to a subordinated debt. However, a good many debentures are secured and one of the most elemental distinctions between some of the various types of debentures that are encountered in practice is with respect to whether the debenture provides for a fixed charge, a floating charge or a combination of the two.

§8.136 Under a fixed charge the security interest attaches to a specific item of property and binds that property so that any further dealing with the property may be made only in accordance with the terms of the charge so conferred or with the consent of the creditor to whom that charge is given.[259] A fixed charge is sometimes called a specific charge, or a fixed or specific charge, but in each case the nature of the security interest concerned is the same. At one time there

---

[253] *Re Perth Electric Tramways Co.*, [1906] 2 Ch. 216, and see *Bogart v. King (Township)*, [1901] O.J. No. 96, 1 O.L.R. 496 at 501 (C.A.), *per* Osler J.A.
[254] *Gartside v. Silkstone & Dodsworth Coal & Iron Co.* (1882), 21 Ch. D. 762 at 767, *per* Fry J.
[255] *Re Hubbard & Co.* (1898), 68 L.J. Ch. 54.
[256] *Geddes v. Toronto Street Rlwy. Co.*, [1864] O.J. No. 211, 14 U.C.C.P. 513 at 520, *per* Richards C.J.
[257] *Toronto General Trusts Corp. v. Central Ontario Rlwy. Co.*, [1905] O.J. No. 68, 10 O.L.R. 347 at 351 (C.A.), *per* Maclennan J.A.
[258] For an example of a case considering an unsecured debenture, see *Sydney Land & Loan Co. v. Solicitor* (1910), 7 E.L.R. 549 (N.S.T.D.).
[259] *The Russell-Cooke Trust Co. v. Elliott*, [2007] All E.R. (D) 166 (Ch.); *In Re Cosslett (Contractors) Ltd.*, [1988] ch. 495 at 510 (C.A.), *per* Millett L.J.; *Smith (Administrator of Cosslett (Contractors)) v. Bridgend County Borough Council*, [2002] 1 A.C. 336 (H.L.).

was doubt as to whether a fixed charge could be created over property not owned by the borrower at the time when the charge was created, particularly in the case of property the acquisition of which was not even contemplated at that time. This question was resolved in the *Yorkshire Woolcombers*[260] case in which a purportedly fixed charge was created in all the borrower's equipment, including not only that owned by the borrower at the time when that charge was created, but also any equipment that was subsequently acquired by the borrower.[261] Thus the specific property subject to a fixed charge may be present or future,[262] and indeed the charge may attach to all property answering a general description or only that property described in an itemized list set out in or attached to the charge itself.

§8.137 A fixed charge will normally extend not only to the property in respect of which it is created, but also (in the case of land) to any new asset that becomes affixed or (in the case of personalty) attached to it. However, the question will often arise as to whether the degree of annexation of the new asset to the charged property is sufficient to bind the new asset with the charge. Each case must be considered and decided on its own facts, but over the years a number of general principles have emerged from the case law which clearly provide guidance.[263] In deciding when the extent of attachment is sufficient to bind the attached assets or fixtures with the charge, attention must be paid not only to the nature of the thing and to the mode of attachment, but to the circumstances under which it was attached, the purpose to be served by making the attachment, and also the position of the rival claimants to the things in dispute.[264] In all cases, the question of whether the new asset is annexed to the old is dependent upon some degree of physical attachment. It is very difficult, if not impossible to say with precision what constitutes an annexation sufficient to give rise to attachment.[265]

§8.138 Historically, the disadvantage of a fixed charge was that the assets covered by the charge could not be disposed of without the consent of the debenture holder. This limitation on use presented severe problems in the case of the circulating assets of a borrower — that is, in the case of the cash, inventory and receivables. The cash and receivables of a borrower generate the cash flow which must be used not only to service the secured debt of the borrower but to satisfy all other debts and money liabilities of the borrower. The inventory of the borrower must, of course, be sold in order to generate those receivables and that cash. Consequently, it was not considered appropriate to place a fixed charge over circulating assets of this type. If security was to be provided against those assets, it must be of a sort that allowed the borrower the right to deal with the assets concerned in the ordinary course of its business: to sell or otherwise dispose of its inventory and so pass good title to its customers, to receive payment

---

[260] *Re Yorkshire Woolcombers Association Ltd.*, [1903] 2 Ch. 284 (C.A.).
[261] *Ibid.*, *per* Vaughan Williams L.J.
[262] *Humfrey v. Hickey*, [1972] 3 W.W.R. 389 (Alta. C.A.).
[263] *Hulme v. Brigham*, [1943] 1 All E.R. 204.
[264] *Reynolds v. Ashby & Son*, [1904] A.C. 466 at 473-74 (H.L.), *per* Lord Lindley.
[265] *Holland v. Hodgson* (1872), L.R. 7 C.P. 328, *per* Blackburn J.

on accounts owed to it and apply the amount so received to its general indebtedness. The floating charge evolved as a method of providing security against circulating assets, while allowing the borrower the flexibility to deal with the assets concerned in the ordinary course of its business. While the nature of a fixed charge can be quickly stated and is readily conceptualized, the nature of a floating charge is not so straightforward. A floating charge is an equitable charge[266] upon the assets subject to the charge. The composition of the assets may change from time to time.[267] However, the main distinction between a floating and a fixed charge that is under a floating charge, the borrower retains the power to manage and deal with the charged assets; if a security contemplates such a right of management and dealing, then the charge is floating; if not then the charge is fixed.[268]

§8.139 Floating charges are usually granted over the whole of the assets and undertaking[269] for the time being of a business, or over the inventory of a business or its accounts receivable.[270] In contrast to fixed charges, floating charges are almost always granted by corporations. It appears that the first case in which a clear floating charge came before a court for consideration was *Re Panama, New Zealand and Australian Royal Mail Company*.[271] In *Re Panama*, the debtor had given a charge against its undertaking and all sums of money arising therefor. Sir G.M. Giffard analyzed the nature and scope of the charge in the following terms:

> ... I have no hesitation in saying that in this particular case, and having regard to the state of this particular company, the word "undertaking" had reference to all the property of the company, not only which existed at the date of the debenture, but which might afterwards become the property of the company. And I take the object and meaning of the debenture to be this, that the word "undertaking" necessarily infers that the company will go on, and that the debenture holder could not interfere until either the interest which was due was unpaid, or until the period had arrived for the payment of his principal, and that principal was unpaid. I think the meaning and object of the security was this, that the company might go on during that interval, and, furthermore, that during the interval the debenture holder would not be entitled to any account of mesne profits, or of any dealing with the property of the company in the ordinary course of carrying on their business. I do not refer

---

[266] *J.R. Auto Brokers Ltd. v. Hillcrest Auto Leasing Inc.*, [1968] O.J. No. 1191, [1968] 2 O.R. 532 at 537 (H.C.J.), *per* Lief J.

[267] *Tailby v. Official Receiver* (1888), 13 App. Cas. 523 at 543 (H.L.), *per* Lord Macnaghten; see also *Illingworth v. Houldsworth*, [1904] A.C. 355 at 358 (H.L.), *per* Lord Macnaghten; *Re Bond Worth Ltd.*, [1980] Ch. 228, *per* Slade J.

[268] Compare *Siebe Gorman & Co. v. Barclays Bank Ltd.*, [1979] 2 Lloyd's Rep. 142 (Ch.) and *Re Brightlife Ltd.*, [1986] 3 All E.R. 673 (Ch.); *Re Cosslett (Contractors) Ltd.*, [1997] 4 All E.R. 115 at 126 (C.A.), *per* Millett L.J.; see also *Re Bond Worth*, [1979] 3 All E.R. 919 at 953 (C.A.), *per* Slade L.J.

[269] There is no fixed meaning to the term "undertaking"; its meaning in any given case depends upon the apparent intent of the parties, determined in accordance with the normal rules of contractual interpretation: *Wickham v. New Brunswick & Canada Rlwy.* (1865), L.R. 1 P.C. 64, aff'g 11 N.B.R. 175 (C.A.).

[270] See, for instance, *Re Guardian Press Ltd.*, [1953] 3 D.L.R. 127 (Nfld. S.C.).

[271] (1870), 5 Ch. App. 318.

to such things as sales or mortgages of property, but to the ordinary application of funds which came into the hands of the company in the usual course of business. I see no difficulty or inconvenience in giving that effect to this instrument. But the moment the company comes to be wound up, and the property has to be realized, that moment the rights of these parties, beyond all question, attach ... I hold that under these debentures they have a charge upon all property of the company, past and future, by the term "undertaking," and that they stand in a position superior to that of the general creditors, who can touch nothing until they are paid.[272]

§8.140 Two decisions given by Lord Macnaghten at the turn of the century continue to influence modern legal thinking concerning the nature and scope of floating charges. In *Governments Stock and Other Securities Investment Co. v. Manila Rlwy. Co.*,[273] he stated:

A floating security is an equitable charge on the assets for the time being of a going concern. It attaches to the subject charged in the varying condition in which it happens to be from time to time. It is the essence of such a charge that it remains dormant until the undertaking charged ceases to be a going concern, or until the person in whose favour the charge is created intervenes. His right to intervene may of course be suspended by agreement. But if there is no agreement for suspension, he may exercise his right whenever he pleases after default.

In *Re Yorkshire Woolcombers Association Ltd.*,[274] Vaughan Williams L.J. criticized the above passage, particularly the word "dormant", as imprecise. On the appeal of that case,[275] Lord Macnaghten stated that his comments in the *Manila Rlwy.* case were intended to be a description of a floating security rather than a definition. He then went on to define a floating security in the following terms:

I should have thought there was not much difficulty in defining what a floating charge is in contrast to what is called a specific charge. A specific charge ... is one that without more fastens on ascertained and definite property or property capable of being ascertained and defined; a floating charge, on the other hand, is ambulatory and shifting in its nature, hovering over and so to speak floating with the property which it is intended to affect until some event occurs or some act is done which causes it to settle and fasten on the subject of the charge within its reach and grasp.

A similar definition was adopted by Ferguson J.A. in *Gordon MacKay & Co. v. J.A. Laroque Co.*,[276] when he quoted verbatim the definition of "floating security" found in the judgment of Buckley L.J. in *Evans v. Rival Granite Quarries Ltd.*:

A floating security is not a future security; it is a present security, which presently affects all the assets of the company expressed to be included in it. On the other hand, it is not a specific security; the holder cannot affirm that the assets are specifically mortgaged to him. The assets are mortgaged in such a way that the

---

[272] *Ibid.*, at 322-23.
[273] [1897] A.C. 81 at 86 (H.L.). See also *Buchler v. Talbot*, [2004] 2 A.C. 298 (H.L.).
[274] [1903] 2 Ch. 284 (C.A.).
[275] *Illingworth v. Houldsworth*, [1904] A.C. 355 at 358 (H.L.).
[276] [1926] O.J. No. 35, 59 O.L.R. 293 at 314 (C.A.). Ferguson J.A.'s dissenting judgment was affirmed by the Supreme Court of Canada: [1927] S.C.R. 374. See also *Johnston v. Wade*, [1908] O.J. No. 65, 17 O.L.R. 372 at 378 (C.A.), *per* MacMahon J., where he also adopted the definition given by Lord Macnaghten in the *Manila Rlwy.* case.

mortgagor can deal with them without the concurrence of the mortgagee. A floating security is not a specific mortgage of assets plus a license to the mortgagor to dispose of them in the course of his business, but is a floating mortgage applying to every item comprised in the security, but not specifically affecting any item until some event occurs or some act on the part of the mortgagee is done which causes it to crystallize into a fixed security. ... It is a mortgage presently affecting all the items expressed to be included in it, but not specifically affecting any item till the happening of the event which causes the security to crystallize as regards all the items.[277]

§8.141 In practical terms, the most important distinction between a fixed and a floating charge is that a floating charge does not prevent the debtor from dealing with its assets in the ordinary course of business.[278] Generally speaking, the authorities draw a clear distinction between fixed and floating charges, recognizing nothing between and taking the view that any charge which permits dealing in the ordinary course of business must be regarded as floating.[279] Although it is possible to create fixed and floating charges within the same security agreement against different assets, it is not possible to take both floating charges and fixed charges against the same assets, for the rights of the parties with respect to each type of security are mutually inconsistent. By the same token, a charge is either fixed or floating. The same language cannot create a fixed charge against some assets and a floating charge against others.[280]

§8.142 The general adoption of the regimes of law comparable to the Ontario *Personal Property Security Act* has reduced the extent to which floating charges are now encountered in Canadian lending practice.[281] The PPSA substantially modifies the rules of priority governing floating charges, and largely eliminates the requirement for crystallization, except — although this is not entirely clear — with respect to charges against accounts receivable and deposits held at financial institutions (which must necessarily be floating in most cases, in order to allow the debtor to continue in business).[282] Accordingly, for a detailed discussion of the law relating to those charges, reference should be made to the First Edition of this work.

§8.143 The essence of the floating charge is that the debtor will be allowed to deal with its assets in an ordinary way, which means that the debtor has the right to buy new assets, sell or otherwise dispose of existing assets, pay its other se-

---

[277] [1910] 2 K.B. 979 at 999 (C.A.).
[278] *British Columbia v. Federal Business Development Bank*, [1985] B.C.J. No. 3001, [1986] 2 W.W.R. 255 (S.C.), aff'd [1987] B.C.J. No. 1834, 17 B.C.L.R. (2d) 273 (C.A.); *British Columbia v. Lega Fabricating Ltd.*, [1981] B.C.J. No. 970, 126 D.L.R. (3d) 148 (C.A.); *Re Benjamin Cope & Sons Ltd.*, [1914] Ch. 800 at 806-807, *per* Sargant J.
[279] *British Columbia v. Federal Business Development Bank*, [1987] B.C.J. No. 1834, 17 B.C.L.R. (2d) 273 at 303 and 307 (C.A.), *per* Maclachlin J.A.; *Evans v. Rival Granite Quarries Ltd.*, [1910] 2 K.B. 979 at 999 (C.A.), *per* Buckley L.J. and *per* Fletcher-Moulton L.J. at 995.
[280] *Fanshawe v. Amav Industries Ltd.*, [2006] EWHC 486 at para. 33 (Ch.), *per* Blackburne J.
[281] See below at §8.157.
[282] See In *Re Spectrum Plus Ltd. (in liq.)*, [2005] 2 A.C. 680 (H.L.). This matter is discussed in detail at §§8.201 seq.

cured and unsecured creditors and (in some cases, depending upon the terms of the contract) even grant fixed charges in the ordinary course of business.[283] However, it has not always been clear at what point the floating charge crystallizes, and the debtor's authority to so deal with the assets terminates. The law is clear that a floating charge is an equitable charge on a part or the whole of the assets from time to time of a debtor, which remains dormant and allows a debtor to deal with the assets subject to the charge in the ordinary course of business, so long as the charge remains floating.[284] Until crystallization, the assets to which the charge relates may in general be dealt with as if no such charge had ever been given. But this right of usage is limited to dealings in the ordinary course. The right of dealing is intended to permit the debtor to carry on its business, not act to the prejudice of the lender. As noted above, the licence to deal is contractual. Accordingly, it must be construed in terms consistent with the purpose and language of the security agreement to which it relates. It can never be construed so as to negate the rights of the creditor under that agreement, although in practice the licence to deal may frustrate the creditor's rights or compromise its powers on the facts of a given case. Similarly, while the licence may permit a right to deal, the parties are free to determine the scope of dealings that will be considered to be in the ordinary course — which is simply another way of saying that the licence given to the debtor is a matter of contractual interpretation.[285]

§8.144 The very purpose of a floating charge is to enable a debtor to carry on his business as a going concern, and as a result the floating charge does not prevent dealings with the assets in the ordinary course of business. Under this principle, legitimate (*i.e.*, good faith) dealings by the debtor in the ordinary course of business may not be impeached by the secured creditor.[286] In deciding whether particular dealings are within the ordinary course of business, the courts look not only at the nature of the transaction but the circumstances in which it takes place. This flexible approach is revealed in the following passage from the decision of Virtue J. in the *Prudential Steel* case, where he said:

> The fact that a person is in insolvent circumstances, or unable to pay his debts in full or knows that he is on the eve of insolvency does not render void a transaction which is a *bona fide* sale or payment made in the ordinary course of trade to an innocent party where there is sufficient consideration.

---

[283] *Indian & General Investment Trust Ltd. v. Union Bank of Halifax* (1908), 42 N.S.R. 353 (C.A.), aff'd 40 S.C.R. 510; *Borg-Warner Acceptance Canada Ltd. v. Gentleman*, [1982] N.B.J. No. 341, 42 N.B.R. (2d) 449, 110 A.P.R. 449 (C.A.), *per* Stratton J.A. However, the mere reservation of a right to grant further charges is not sufficient in itself to convert a fixed charge to a floating charge. The question of whether a charge is floating or fixed must be determined upon a construction of the security document in its entirety: *Grigson v. Taplin & Co.* (1915), 85 L.J. Ch. 75. Note that the loan and security agreement to which UMF and Bluenose were subject expressly prohibited the grant of further charges.
[284] *Brunton v. Electrical Engineering Corp.*, [1892] 1 Ch. 434; *Robson v. Smith*, [1895] 2 Ch. 118.
[285] See, generally, *Willmott v. London Celluloid Co.* (1886), 34 Ch. D. 147 (C.A.).
[286] *Canadian Commercial Bank v. Prudential Steel Ltd.*, [1986] A.J. No. 1142, 49 Alta. L.R. (2d) 58 (Q.B.).

In determining what is "in the ordinary course of trade", I am of the view that one can consider what is ordinary in light of all the circumstances, including the difficult financial condition in which a business finds itself at the time of the transaction impugned.

If an objective viewer would reasonably conclude that the impugned transaction is one which a company would ordinarily do in the course of trade, including a transaction made to keep its business going in difficult times then so long as the transaction is a *bona fide* one made for the purpose of carrying on the business and not one which either the vendor or the purchaser intended to be primarily for the purpose of preferring one creditor over another, it meets the test...[287]

The "ordinary course" requirement is essentially a limitation on the scope of the licence allowed to the debtor to continue dealing with the property. But the floating charge would obviously confer little security if it never took complete effect upon the assets subject to the charge, so as to bar the borrower from further dealing with the pledged assets. Therefore it is implicit within such charges that the authority retained by the debtor to deal with the assets will cease upon the occurrence of certain events. Such a termination of the debtor's right to deal with the assets is known as the crystallization of the charge.[288]

§8.145 A floating charge remains ambulatory until such times[289] as it crystallizes, at which point it becomes affixed to the assets[290] then held by the debtor that are within its terms at the time of crystallization.[291] The effect of crystallization is to convert the floating inchoate charge into a fixed one attaching to the subject property then in the hands of the debtor.[292] From the moment of crystallization the charge is as effective an encumbrance upon the debtor's assets as if it had been a fixed charge from the time of its inception, but subject to any right in the assets that, prior to crystallization, was transferred to a person who took it in good faith and for value.[293] Thus where a floating security crystallizes prior to the time when judgment creditors realize upon their judgment,[294] or prior to payment under a garnishee,[295] the security holder will have priority. However, despite the crystallization of a floating charge it will still extend to assets acquired after the time of crystallization[296] and to assets relating to new business

---

[287] *Ibid.*, at 62.
[288] See, generally, *Central Trust Co. v. Phaseco Ltd.*, [1988] N.B.J. No. 535, 91 N.B.R. (2d) 107, 232 A.P.R. 107 (Q.B.), aff'd [1988] N.B.J. No. 1059, 93 N.B.R. (2d) 157, 238 A.P.R. 157 (C.A.).
[289] In *Re Morrison, Jones & Taylor Ltd.*, [1914] 1 Ch. 50, aff'd [1914] 1 Ch. 55 at 57 (C.A.), per Cozens-Hardy M.R., per Eve J. at 55; see also the decision of Bayda J.A. in *Harvey Dodds Ltd. v. Royal Bank of Canada*, [1979] S.J. No. 317, 8 B.L.R. 215 at 223 (C.A.).
[290] R.M. Goode, *Commercial Law* (London: Penguin, 1982), 790.
[291] *Tailby v. Official Receiver* (1888), 13 App. Cas. 523 at 541 (H.L.), per Lord Macnaghten.
[292] *Re Griffin Hotel Co.*, [1941] Ch. 129; *Re ELS Ltd.*, [1995] Ch. 11.
[293] *Hamer v. London City & Midland Bank* (1918), 87 L.J.K.B. 973 at 975, per Sankey J.
[294] *Isaac v. Cook* (1983), 44 C.B.R. (N.S.) 39 at 51 (N.W.T.S.C.), per deWeerdt J.
[295] *MacKay & Hughes (1973), Ltd. v. Martin Potatoes Inc.*, [1984] O.J. No. 3205, 46 O.R. (2d) 304 at 309 (C.A.), per Blair J.A.
[296] *N.W. Robbie & Co. v. Witney Warehouse Co.*, [1963] 3 All E.R. 613 (C.A.).

entered into after the time when the floating charge was created.[297] Crystallization binds the property of the debtor; it does not limit the scope of the charge.

§8.146 Although the case law on point is not entirely clear there are at least four types of situation in which the debtor's power to deal with the assets will be lost:

(1) Where the debtor's business ceases to be conducted as a going concern: The power reserved to the debtor to continue dealing with the secured property is restricted to dealings in the ordinary course of business. It follows that where the debtor ceases to carry on business it no longer may deal with the assets under the terms of the authority reserved. A debtor may cease business voluntarily[298] or by court order in response to a bankruptcy petition or an application to wind up the debtor.[299] Any cessation of business is sufficient to crystallize the charge,[300] even where the cessation is for the purposes of a reorganization.[301] Similarly the appointment of a receiver (whether or not also a manager) will have this effect, whether that appointment is made by the debtor, the court or by another creditor.[302] In the case of a winding up, crystallization takes place the moment the winding up commences,[303] for at that mo-

---

[297] *Tailby v. Official Receiver* (1888), 13 App. Cas. 523 (H.L.).
[298] *Edward Nelson & Co. v. Faber & Co.*, [1903] 2 K.B. 367 at 376-77, *per* Joyce J.
[299] See the judgment of Kekewich J. in *Re Victoria Steamboat Co.*, [1897] 1 Ch. 158. For crystallization to occur as a result of wind-up proceedings, the presentation of a petition to wind up the company is not in itself sufficient. It must be shown that the debtor has in fact ceased to carry on business. In most cases, the issue is moot because the appointment of a liquidator will bring about the crystallization of security. However, the *Victoria Steamboat* case does make it clear that even prior to crystallization the court may appoint a receiver where circumstances warrant, in order to protect the interests of the creditor entitled to the floating charge. Upon such an appointment being made, the charge would crystallize.
[300] *Hubbuck v. Helms* (1887), 56 L.J. Ch. 536; see also *Davey & Co. v. Williamson & Sons*, [1898] 2 Q.B. 194, as explained by Fletcher-Moulton L.J. in *Evans v. Rival Granite Quarries Ltd.*, [1910] 2 K.B. 979 at 997 (C.A.).
[301] *Re Crompton & Co.*, [1914] 1 Ch. 954 at 963-64, *per* Warrington J.
[302] At least, such will be the case where the floating charge concerned covers all of the business and undertaking of the debtor (as will normally be the case), for the intent of receivership is the liquidation of the assets subject to the charge, either piecemeal or by way of a sale as a going concern. Since liquidation is inconsistent with the continuation of business *by the debtor* it follows that the appointment of a receiver by any creditor is sufficient to terminate the condition on which the debtor's licence to deal operates, and accordingly all other floating charges will crystallize, subject to any agreement in the contract. Unfortunately, the case law on this point is not particularly clear: See, generally, *Evans v. Rival Granite Quarries*, [1910] 2 K.B. 979 (C.A.); *Re Woodroffes (Musical Instruments)*, [1986] Ch. 366 (D.C.), *per* Nourse J.; *National Australia Bank Ltd. v. Composite Buyers Ltd.* (1991), 6 A.C.S.R. 94; *Federal Business Development Bank v. Prince Albert Fashion Bin Ltd.*, [1983] S.J. No. 181, [1983] 3 W.W.R. 464 (C.A.); *Northland Bank v. G.I.C. Industries Ltd.*, [1986] A.J. No. 435, [1986] 4 W.W.R. 482, 36 Alta. L.R. (2d) 200 (Master); *Household Products Co. v. Federal Business Development Bank*, [1981] O.J. No. 3039, 124 D.L.R. (3d) 325, 33 O.R. (2d) 334 (H.C.J.).
[303] *Wallace v. Universal Automatic Machines Co.*, [1894] 2 Ch. 547 (C.A.); *Re Panama, New Zealand & Australian Royal Mail Co.* (1870), L.R. 5 Ch. App. 318; *Re Crompton & Co.*, [1914] 1 Ch. 954. But see *Re Roundwood Colliery*, [1897] 1 Ch. 373, as to when the winding up is deemed to take place. See also *Re Colonial Trust Corp., ex p. Bradshaw* (1879), 15 Ch. D. 465 at 473 (M.R.), *per* Jessel M.R.

ment[304] the company ceases to be carrying on business,[305] irrespective of whether the security agreement makes the winding up an express event of default accelerating the right to receive repayment.[306]

(2) Where the creditor takes a positive step to crystallize the security: The general rule is that mere default under the terms of an agreement,[307] and even the insolvency of the debtor,[308] are not sufficient in themselves to crystallize any floating charge conferred by the agreement. Furthermore, except where the parties have otherwise agreed, a mere demand for payment does not result in the crystallization of security.[309] On the other hand, where there is a default under the terms of the security agreement, that occurrence will (in the absence of an agreement to the contrary) entitle the creditor to take such steps as are necessary to crystallize the security.[310] In order to crystallize the security there must normally be some positive and unequivocal[311] act on the part of the creditor.[312] The fact that the creditor is entitled to act is not enough; the creditor must undertake some action to crystallize the security.[313]

(3) Where the security crystallizes as a result of an act being taken by some person other than the creditor. Under this criteria, the floating charge of one creditor will crystallize where another creditor appoints a receiver over the property of the debtor.

---

[304] *Hodson v. Tea Co.* (1880), 14 Ch. D. 859 (V.C.); *Wallace v. Universal Automatic Machines Co.*, [1894] 2 Ch. 547 (C.A.).
[305] *Re Crompton & Co.*, [1914] 1 Ch. 954; *Edward Nelson & Co. v. Faber & Co.*, [1903] 2 K.B. 367 at 377, *per* Joyce J.
[306] *Wallace v. Universal Automatic Machines Co.*, [1894] 2 Ch. 547 (C.A.).
[307] *Governments Stock & Other Securities Investment Co. v. Manila Rlwy. Co.*, [1897] A.C. 81 (C.A.).
[308] *Willmott v. London Celluloid Co.* (1886), 34 Ch. D. 147 (C.A.).
[309] *Evans v. Rival Granite Quarries Ltd.*, [1910] 2 K.B. 979 (C.A.).
[310] *Governments Stock & Other Securities Investment Co. v. Manila Rlwy. Co.*, [1897] A.C. 81 at 86 (C.A.), *per* Lord Macnaghten.
[311] *British Columbia v. Consolidated Churchill Copper Corp.*, [1978] 5 W.W.R. 652 at 659 (B.C.S.C.), *per* Berger J. The secured creditor must either crystallize its security in whole or not at all. See also *Edward Nelson & Co. v. Faber & Co.*, [1903] 2 K.B. 367 at 377.
[312] *Evans v. Rival Granite Quarries Ltd.*, [1910] 2 K.B. 979 at 993 (C.A.), *per* Fletcher-Moulton L.J.: "Mere default on the part of the company does not change the character of the security; the debenture-holder must actually intervene."
[313] *Governments Stock & Other Securities Investment Co. v. Manila Rlwy. Co.*, [1897] A.C. 81 (C.A.); *Bank of Montreal v. Woodtown Development Ltd.*, [1979] O.J. No. 4263, 25 O.R. (2d) 36 at 40 (H.C.J.), *per* Osler J. See also *Bank of Montreal v. Union Gas Co.*, [1969] 2 O.R. 776 (C.A.); *Re Roundwood Colliery Co.*, [1897] 1 Ch. 373. Compare, however, *Re Opera Ltd.*, [1891] 3 Ch. 260 (C.A.); *Taunton v. Warwickshire Sheriff*, [1895] 2 Ch. 319 (C.A.); *Re Standard Manufacturing Co.*, [1891] 1 Ch. 627 at 641 (C.A.), *per* Lord Halsbury L.C. and Fry L.J.; *Industrial Development Bank v. Valley Dairy Ltd.*, [1953] O.J. No. 648, [1953] O.R. 70 (H.C.J.). See also *Alberta Paper Co. v. Metropolitan Graphics Ltd.*, [1983] A.J. No. 969, 24 B.L.R. 134 (Q.B.); *Coopers & Lybrand v. National Caterers Ltd.*, [1982] B.C.J. No. 1331, 47 C.B.R. (N.S.) 57 (S.C.); *Zurich Insurance Co. v. Troy Woodworking Ltd.*, [1984] O.J. No. 3113, 26 B.L.R. 141 (C.A.).

(4) Possibly, where the floating charge crystallizes automatically under the terms of the debenture.[314] This last criteria is controversial.

(a) THE RULE IN LISTER V. DUNLOP

§8.147 It is now widely known and understood that the lender on a demand loan must allow the borrower a reasonable period for the repayment of the balance outstanding following any demand for repayment on that loan. The idea that a creditor on a demand loan was required to make not only a demand but give a reasonable time to repay such a loan originated at least as long ago as 1863.[315] As implied terms go, a requirement for some reasonable period of notice seems a fairly sensible one. A borrower does not take on credit in order to stockpile the money so that it will be able to repay that money should the lender demand it back. The credit is invested and otherwise employed, quite often in illiquid form — a fact of which the lender is obviously aware, for usually the borrower must disclose the use to which the credit advanced will be applied as an integral part of applying for the credit in the first place. On the other hand, in every lending transaction it is the lender rather than the borrower who is most at risk. The lender has provided the credit to the borrower. Whether its loan is secured or unsecured, at best all the lender has is an expectation of repayment, and the confidence that it may place in that expectation obviously depends on the confidence in which it may place in the borrower.

§8.148 The requirement for reasonable notice on demand is often called the rule in *Lister v. Dunlop*.[316] That rule may be summarized briefly: where a contract provides that payment of a sum owing is to be made "immediately upon demand", "forthwith" or in like terms, those words are construed to mean "within a reasonable time following demand". The question of whether a reasonable time has been allowed is one of fact turning upon the circumstances of each case, but the time allowed must not be illusory unless the creditor is in imminent peril by reason of the debtor's fraud or other misconduct or, possibly, other circumstances as well.

§8.149 The rule restricts the seizure of collateral by the creditor, whether directly or by way of the appointment of a receiver. Since the creditor may not seize collateral until the expiration of the required period of reasonable time, *a fortiori* the creditor may not sell or otherwise realize on the collateral during that time period. It extends to the seizure of collateral of every type and the enforcement of every type of security, including conditional sale agreements,[317] assignments of book

---

[314] See below at §8.155.
[315] See *Toms v. Wilson* (1863), 4 B. & S. 455; 122 E.R. 529 (Q.B.), *per* Pollock, C.B., aff'g 4 B. & S. 442, 122 E.R. 524.
[316] *Ronald Elwyn Lister Ltd. v. Dunlop Canada Ltd.*, [1982] S.C.J. No. 38, 135 D.L.R. (3d) 1.
[317] *Jim Landry Pontiac Buick Ltd. v. CIBC*, [1987] N.S.J. No. 273, 40 D.L.R. (4th) 343 (S.C.).

debts,[318] pledges;[319] and security under sections 426 and 427 of the *Bank Act*.[320] Breach of the rule constitutes an actionable tort. However, the rule does not affect other rights of the creditor, such as the right to initiate an action to recover the amount owing, to petition the debtor into bankruptcy, to seek the appointment of a receiver and receiver-manager by the court, to cancel further credit, to demand payment under a stand by line of credit or to call upon a guarantor to pay. The rule has been notoriously difficult to apply in practice.[321]

§8.150 In 1992, the *Bankruptcy and Insolvency Act*[322] was amended to require certain creditors having broad security interests against commercial debtors to give a notice of intention to enforce the security interest prior to the appointment of a receiver or the seizure of the collateral subject to a security interest. Subsection 244(1) of the BIA now provides:

244.(1) A secured creditor who intends to enforce a security on all or substantially all of

(*a*) the inventory,

(*b*) the accounts receivable, or

(*c*) the other property

of an insolvent person that was acquired for, or is used in relation to, a business carried on by the insolvent person shall send to that insolvent person, in the prescribed form and manner, a notice of that intention.

---

[318] *Barclay Construction Corp. v. Bank of Montreal*, [1989] B.C.J. No. 2257, [1990] 2 W.W.R. 489 (C.A.).

[319] *Proud v. National Bank of Canada*, [1985] P.E.I.J. No. 8, 57 Nfld. & P.E.I.R. 14, 170 A.P.R. 14 (C.A.).

[320] S.C. 1991, c. 46; *Waldron v. Royal Bank* (1991), 53 B.C.L.R. 294 (C.A.).

[321] While the leading case in this regard is *Ronald Elwyn Lister Ltd. v. Dunlop Canada Ltd.*, [1982] S.C.J. No. 38, [1982] 1 S.C.R. 726, the rule is based on the decisions in *Massey v. Sladden* (1868), L.R. 4 Ex. 13 and *Wharlton v. Kirkwood* (1873), 29 L.T. 644 (Ex.). A complete catalogue of the cases in which this rule has been invoked would take up several pages. A general understanding of its application can be obtained from a review of the following cases: *Jim Landry Pontiac Buick Ltd. v. CIBC*, [1987] N.S.J. No. 273, 40 D.L.R. (4th) 343 (S.C.); *Barclay Construction Corp. v. Bank of Montreal*, [1989] B.C.J. No. 2257, [1990] 2 W.W.R. 489 (C.A.); *Proud v. National Bank of Canada*, [1985] P.E.I.J. No. 8, 57 Nfld. & P.E.I.R. 14, 170 A.P.R. 14 (C.A.); *Waldron v. Royal Bank* (1991), 53 B.C.L.R. 294 (C.A.); *Kavcar Industries Ltd. v. Aetna Financial Services*, [1989] O.J. No. 1723, 70 O.R. (2d) 225 (C.A.); *Banque Nationale du Canada v. Houle*, [1987] J.Q. no. 1200, 66 C.B.R. (N.S.) 241 (C.A.), aff'd [1990] S.C.J. No. 120; *Indian Head Credit Union Ltd. v. R. & D. Hardware Ltd.*, [1986] S.J. No. 598, 54 Sask. R. 161, aff'd [1988] S.J. No. 203, 66 Sask. R. 90 (C.A.); *Mister Broadloom Corp. (1968) v. Bank of Montreal*, [1983] O.J. No. 3271, 44 O.R. (2d) 368 (C.A.), leave to appeal to S.C.C. refused (1984), 55 N.R. 160 (S.C.C.); *Northern Meat Packers Ltd. v. Roynat Ltd.*, [1986] N.B.J. No. 82, 60 C.B.R. (N.S.) 1 (C.A.), aff'd 77 N.R. 158n; *Jeannette BBQ Ltée v. C.P. de Tracadie Ltée*, [1989] N.B.J. No. 819, 100 N.B.R. (2d) 374, 252 A.P.R. 374 (Q.B.), var'd [1991] N.B.J. No. 556 (C.A.); *Seawater Products (Nfld.) Ltd. v. Royal Bank of Canada*, [1980] N.J. No. 36 C.B.R. (N.S.) 21 (S.C.); *Four-K Western Equipment Ltd. v. CIBC*, [1983] B.C.J. No. 702, 46 C.B.R. (N.S.) 146 (S.C.); *Royal Bank of Canada v. Cal Glass Ltd.*, [1979] B.C.J. No. 1406, 18 B.C.L.R. 55 (C.A.). See also *ANZ Banking Group (N.Z.) Ltd. v. Gibson*, [1981] N.Z.L.R. 513.

[322] S.C. 1992, c. 27.

Where a notice is required to be sent under subsection (1), the secured creditor must not enforce the security in respect of which the notice is required until the expiry of 10 days after sending that notice, unless the insolvent person consents to an earlier enforcement of the security.[323] It has been held that the delivery of such a notice of intention is sufficient to crystallize a floating charge.[324]

§8.151 While it is sometimes assumed that section 244 codifies the rule in *Lister v. Dunlop,* the section actually serves an entirely different purpose. The rule in *Lister v. Dunlop* was based upon a presumed intent of the parties. It was assumed that the lender and borrower must have understood that the lender's rights to demand repayment could be exercised only in a reasonable manner, including allowing a sufficient opportunity for repayment. Section 244 is not tied to any concept of reasonableness. Notice is required even where the lender is jeopardized by the borrower's behaviour. The intent of the notice is not so much to allow the borrower an opportunity to repay, as to decide whether or not to proceed with a proposal under the CCAA or plan of arrangement under the BIA. Nevertheless, as a practical matter, the enactment of the section 244 notice requirement has reduced the volume of litigation arising with respect to the termination of credit and similar arrangements. Furthermore, the 10-day notice required under section 244 before the enforcement of security easily meets the "reasonable notice" requirements of the common law rule.

(b) WAIVER OF DEFAULT

§8.152 Although the general principles applicable to waiver were discussed above, it remains necessary to apply those principles in the context of waivers of default. It is customary for debentures and other security agreements to contain a provision entitling the creditor to waive any default that occurs under the debenture. Subject to the terms of the agreement in question, a waiver of default may be express or implied. Generally, a waiver of a breach prevents the creditor from crystallizing the floating charge in consequence of that breach. A creditor cannot waffle in deciding whether to realize upon its security as a result of a default.[325] However, a debtor is not entitled to the benefit of waiver of a default where it is procured by fraud, even where the debtor is not responsible for that fraud.[326] A waiver of a default by reason of a failure to exercise the remedy to which the creditor is entitled does not prejudice the creditor's right to its security.[327]

§8.153 In *Eastern & Chartered Trust Co. v. Leland Publishing Ltd.*[328] the debentures of a company were secured under a trust deed. A meeting of the de-

---

[323] BIA, s. 244(2). A consent to earlier enforcement of a security may not be obtained by a secured creditor prior to the sending of the notice referred to in subsection (1): BIA, s. 244(2.1).
[324] *Access Advertising Management Inc. v. Servex Computers Inc.,* [1993] O.J. No. 2439, 15 O.R. (3d) 635 at 639-40 (Gen. Div.), *per* Saunders J.
[325] *Kare v. North West Packers,* [1955] 2 D.L.R. 407 at 414-15 (Man. Q.B.), *per* Adamson J.
[326] *Elrae Estates Ltd. v. P.J. Industries* (1973), 38 D.L.R. (3d) 94 (B.C.S.C.).
[327] *Fraser v. Hartt Group Ltd.,* [1984] N.B.J. No. 191, 55 N.B.R. (2d) 284, 144 A.P.R. 284 at 286 (Q.B.), *per* Stevenson J.
[328] [1966] O.J. No. 610, 9 C.B.R. (N.S.) 265 (S.C.).

benture holders was called to consider a proposal to waive a default, and a resolution to that effect was unanimously passed by the debenture holders. The resolution directed the trustee to take all necessary steps for this purpose, but the trustee failed to do so. Shortly afterwards, the company went into bankruptcy. It was held that the debenture holders could not take advantage of an administrative slip by the trustee to undo their waiver.

(c) Action by Some Third Parties

§8.154 In *Federal Business Development Bank v. Prince Albert Fashion Bin Ltd.*[329] two creditors each held floating charges covering the same assets of a company. One of those creditors appointed a receiver over the company who then took possession of the company's assets. It was held that the appointment of the receiver caused the crystallization of both floating charges, for the effect of the appointment was that the company was no longer able to carry on business.[330]

(d) "Automatic" Crystallization Under the Terms of the Security Agreement

§8.155 The fact that the debtor's right to deal with the collateral that is subject to a floating charge is contractual begs the question of whether the terms of the contract can provide that the floating charge shall crystallize automatically upon the occurrence of specified events or conditions without the necessity for immediate intervention by the creditor. Although Canadian case law has generally taken a hostile view of automatic crystallization it is not entirely clear that such hostility is either consistent with authority or business efficacy.[331] It is significant to note that English[332] and other Commonwealth[333] courts are prepared to accept it. In the *Manila Rlwy.* case,[334] the House of Lords appears to have regarded the question as merely one of construction.

§8.156 The arguments against recognizing the effectiveness of an automatic crystallization provision are as follows:[335]

- automatic crystallization puts at risk anyone who purchases the charged property from the debtor, or who otherwise acquires rights in that property;

---

[329] [1983] S.J. No. 181, [1983] 3 W.W.R. 464, 47 C.B.R. (N.S.) 1 at 9 (C.A.), *per* Tallis J.A.
[330] But *cf. Bayhold Financial v. Clarkson Co.*, [1991] N.S.J. No. 488, 86 D.L.R. (4th) 127 (C.A.).
[331] See, generally, *British Columbia v. Consolidated Churchill Copper Corp.*, [1978] B.C.J. No. 505, [1978] 5 W.W.R. 652 at 665 (S.C.), *per* Berger J.; *Access Advertising Management Inc. v. Servex Computers Inc.*, [1993] O.J. No. 2439, 15 O.R. (3d) 635 (Gen. Div.); *Bayhold Financial Corp. v. Clarkson Co.*, [1991] N.S.J. No. 488, 86 D.L.R. (4th) 127, 10 C.B.R. (3d) 159 (C.A.).
[332] *Re Brightlife Ltd.*, [1986] 3 All E.R. 673 (Ch.), *per* Hoffmann J.; *Re Permanent Houses (Holdings) Ltd.*, [1988] B.C.L.C. 563 (Ch.).
[333] *Re Manurewa Transport Ltd.*, [1971] N.Z.L.R. 909 (S.C.).
[334] *Governments Stock & Other Securities Co. v. Manila Rlwy. Co.*, [1897] A.C. 81 (C.A.).
[335] *Insolvency Law and Practice: Report of the Review Committee* (the "Cork Report") (London: HMSO, 1982, Cmnd. 8558) paras. 1570 *et seq.*

- there is no way in which a third party can determine whether or not automatic crystallization has occurred;
- it is highly inconvenient for a floating charge to crystallize in circumstances in which it is unknown to any of the parties;
- automatic crystallization may occur contrary to the wishes of the parties (*e.g.*, in the case of a technical default).

None of the foregoing points presents a particularly convincing argument against the recognition of automatic crystallization. General principles of estoppel would appear to provide a complete answer to the alleged "risk" to third parties which arises where automatic crystallization occurs and the creditor does nothing to assert its rights. Since the creditor has allowed the debtor to have control of the charged assets pending crystallization, it is only reasonable that the creditor should take the loss if the debtor sells or otherwise disposes of those assets to a third party acting in good faith before the creditor takes control of them. It may well be true that a third party cannot determine whether or not automatic crystallization has occurred. However, if that party is protected under the rules of estoppel, then he or she has no reason to care about its occurrence. There may well be a certain inconvenience to the parties in respect of automatic crystallization provisions. However, the parties to any contract must generally weigh the benefits obtained under one term of the agreement against the costs that such a term entails. Since the law of contract generally leaves it to the parties to decide what is in their best interest, there is no reason to depart from that approach with respect to automatic crystallization. Finally, a creditor who does not wish to take advantage of the automatic crystallization of its security may waive the term concerned, much as the breach of any loan condition may be waived by a creditor.

(e) Floating Charges under the Personal Property Security Act

§8.157 As noted above, the extent to which Ontario law continues to recognize a floating charge is now an open question. A floating charge against land will not bind subsequent encumbrancers or purchasers of that land until it is registered against a particular land title (in which case it would amount to a fixed charge), but it will bind unsecured claims against that land (*e.g.*, those of execution creditors) from the time that it crystallizes.[336] As noted above, the traditional legal justification for recognition of a floating charge was the need to balance the conflicting needs of the creditor and debtor. If the creditor was to fund the ongoing operations of the debtor by providing working capital financing, such as an operating line of credit, the creditor required security over the bulk of the assets of the debtor, including its circulating assets. The ability of the creditor to realize advantageously on the collateral of the debtor was governed in large measure by whether the assets comprising the business could be sold as a going

---

[336] *Canadian Imperial Bank of Commerce v. Flemming-Gibson Industries Ltd.*, [1981] N.B.J. No. 300, 37 N.B.R. (2d) 196, 97 A.P.R. 196 at 199 (Q.B.), *per* Dickson J.

concern. Such realization was not possible unless the circulating assets of the debtor could be made subject to the creditor's security interest. However, the debtor required the freedom to deal with circulating assets subject to such a charge in order to carry on business. Without that freedom it could neither earn income nor pay its bills. Thus the crystallization of the charge is seen to be postponed until such time as the debtor ceases to carry on business in the ordinary course.

§8.158 These considerations no longer apply under the *Personal Property Security Act* ("PPSA").[337] The ability of the debtor to deal with circulating assets is now conferred by statute. In particular, section 28 of the PPSA provides that:

> 28. A buyer of goods from a seller who sells the goods in the ordinary course of business takes them free from any security interest therein given by the seller even though it is perfected and the buyer knows of it, unless the buyer also knew that the sale constituted a breach of the security agreement.

Thus in the case of dealings with inventory, good title may be passed without regard as to whether the charge is described as fixed or floating. Similarly, in the case of an assignment of book debts, the right to apply income towards the general expenses of the debtor would seem to be implicit within the terms of the security agreement — for there is no other way that the debtor can remain in business and meet its obligations to the secured creditor who holds the assignment in the ordinary course. Thus again the licence conferred by the floating charge is not necessary. This, of course, does not necessarily lead to the conclusion that floating charges as such no longer exist. In any event, such charges remain important from the perspective of Ontario-based corporations because they are often conferred with respect to assets owned by such corporations but lying outside Ontario.

§8.159 It is sometimes said that the concept of a floating charge does not exist under the *Personal Property Security Act*,[338] but given the fact that subclause 2(*a*)(i) of the PPSA specifically states that the Act applies to a floating charge, that statement must be rejected as far too strong. What is true is that the PPSA sets down a comprehensive code on perfection and priority, so that the old common law rules about crystallization and the relative priority of a floating charge no longer apply.[339] Unfortunately, while the PPSA refers to floating charges, it does so in terms that blur the distinction between floating and fixed charges.

§8.160 The relationship of floating charges to the *Personal Property Security Act* regime formed the subject of *Credit Suisse Canada v. 1133 Yonge Street*

---

[337] R.S.O. 1990, c. P.10.
[338] R.S.O. 1990, c. P.10; see, for instance, *Rehm v. DSG Communications Inc.*, [1995] S.J. No. 126, 9 P.P.S.A.C. (2d) 114 (Q.B.), *per* Hunter J.
[339] *Royal Bank of Canada v. GM Homes Inc.*, [1984] S.J. No. 443, 4 P.P.S.A.C. 116 at 124 (C.A.).

Holdings[340] in which the Toronto Dominion Bank sought clarification as to whether the requirement for crystallization continued to apply under the PPSA. By virtue of subsection 11(1) of the PPSA, a security interest is not enforceable against a third party until it has attached. Attachment occurs when all steps necessary to create a security interest in the collateral as between the immediate parties to the security agreement has been completed. Subsection 11(2) sets out the rules governing attachment:

> 11.(2) A security interest, including a security interest in the nature of a floating charge, attaches when,
>
> (a) the secured party or a person on behalf of the secured party other than the debtor or the debtor's agent obtains possession of the collateral or when the debtor signs a security agreement that contains a description of the collateral sufficient to enable it to be identified;
>
> (b) value is given; and
>
> (c) the debtor has rights in the collateral,
>
> unless the parties have agreed to postpone the time for attachment, in which case the security interest attaches at the agreed time.

The claim of a secured creditor will be subordinate against many interests acquired by third parties in collateral unless and until the security interest in the collateral is perfected — most often by way of the registration of a financing statement. Although the steps required to perfect a security interest may be taken before the security interest attaches, the security interest will not be perfected until attachment occurs. The question that the court had to decide was whether these rules meant that attachment did not occur until a crystallization event had occurred. Justice Day conducted a comprehensive review of the case law and legislative history of the provisions concerned, and concluded that crystallization was irrelevant under the PPSA.

(2) Pledging of Debentures

§8.161 At one time it was common for debentures to be formally pledged to the lender. The original reason for pledging debentures was to provide a method of recovering the amount owing; there was a practice upon default of attempting to realize upon the security afforded by debentures by selling them. Upon such a sale, the purchaser (which might be the original holder) became absolute owner of the debentures concerned with no right of redemption existing in favour of the debtor corporation.[341] Though this practice is now declining, it is worth considering some of the cases decided with respect to that practice because they do afford some indication of the judicial attitude towards realization on security that has prevailed over the years. In general, the courts require a pledgee to adhere strictly to the terms of the pledge when selling the debentures. Thus it was stated that the court would watch any sale other than a judicial sale with jealousy

---

[340] [1996] O.J. No. 1264, 26 B.L.R. (2d) 282 (Gen. Div.), var'd [1998] O.J. No. 4468, 41 O.R. (3d) 632 (C.A.).

[341] *Nova Scotia Central Rlwy. v. Halifax Banking Co.* (1892), 21 S.C.R. 536 at 549, *per* Strong J.

and would not permit any irregularities to take place in such a process.[342] The pledgee was also limited in the sale of debentures to an amount sufficient to repay the loan owed by the corporation.[343]

§8.162 Apparently, the pledge of the bonds did not prevent the holder of the bonds (even if the original pledgee) from enforcing the security interest granted under the bonds, at least if the debenture so provided.[344] In many respects, the use of a pledge coupled with a debenture seems to serve little practical purpose. Nevertheless, until the repeal of the *Corporation Securities Registration Act* ("CSRA"),[345] there was some argument that a formal pledge was required in order to meet the requirements of a very strict interpretation of clause 3(2)(*a*) of that Act — although views as to whether an actual pledge was required differed.[346] This view was an extremely technical one and not universally held. At the very least, it involved an interpretation of the legislation which placed form over substance and seemed to lack any commercial justification. Since the repeal of the CSRA, the number of lenders requiring a formal pledge has decreased. Under the present PPSA, there is no longer any reason for the use of a pledge with a properly drafted debenture that provides for revolving advances, and it is likely that formal pledges of debentures will become progressively more rare in the future, as efforts continue to simplify overall loan documentation.

(3) Trust Deeds

§8.163 Where a bond or debenture is issued by a corporation in favour of more than a few lenders, it is common for that instrument to be issued under a trust indenture or deed, under which the trustee will be vested with certain powers to act on behalf of the holders of the instrument, and any security granted in respect of the instrument will be vested in the trustee on behalf of the holders. The purpose behind the use of the trust indenture vehicle is to simplify the administration of the bonds or debentures, as the corporation may deal with the trustee, rather than with the holders at large. Such simplicity obviously has great value where the debentures are secured.[347] The use of a trustee to hold the security on behalf of several (or even one) creditor-beneficiaries who are actually funding

---

[342] See, for instance, *Toronto General Trusts Corp. v. Central Ontario Rlwy.*, [1905] O.J. No. 68, 10 O.L.R. 347 at 352 (C.A.), *per* Maclennan J.A.

[343] *Toronto General Trusts Corp. v. Central Ontario Rlwy.*, [1905] O.J. No. 68, 10 O.L.R. 347 at 352 (C.A.); see also *Nova Scotia Central Rlwy. v. Halifax Banking Co.* (1892), 21 S.C.R. 536 at 549, *per* Strong J.

[344] *West Cumberland Iron & Steel Co. v. Winnipeg & Hudson's Bay Rlwy.* (1890), 6 Man. R. 388 (C.A.); *Anderson v. McNair Lumber & Shingle Co.*, [1929] B.C.J. No. 114, [1929] 2 D.L.R. 209 (C.A.); *Royal Bank v. Nobes*, [1981] N.S.J. No. 510, 48 N.S.R. (2d) 635 (S.C.), aff'd [1982] N.S.J. No. 45, 16 B.L.R. 289 at 694 (C.A.), *per* Cowan C.J.T.D.; *Harry D. Shields Ltd. v. Bank of Montreal*, [1992] O.J. No. 68, 8 B.L.R. (2d) 169 (Gen. Div.).

[345] R.S.O. 1980, c. 94, repealed 1989, c. 16, s. 84.

[346] See, generally, Peter Lewarne, "The Bank Wants a Debenture as Security — What's it all about?" (1975), Canadian Bar Association (New Brunswick), reproduced in W. Grover & D. Ross, eds., *Materials on Corporate Finance* (Toronto: Richard De Boo Limited, 1975), 275.

[347] See, generally, *R. v. Sharp* (1901), 35 N.B.R. 470 (C.A.).

the corporation in no way prejudices the validity of the security concerned.[348] While limited discretionary powers are normally conferred upon the trustee, the decision of the trustee with respect to any important matter will require the approval of the holders, and the trust indenture will normally provide a procedure for convening meetings of the holders, and will also specify that any decision made at such a meeting will be binding upon all holders.

§8.164 The decision of Murphy J. in *National Trust Co. v. Vancouver Kraft Co.*,[349] involved a claim for remuneration by a trust company. The following remarks from the judgment are of particular interest with respect to the role of corporate trustees. Justice Murphy commented first upon the different roles of trustees in Canada and the United States, saying:

> ... it is admitted that trustees in [the United States] ... are regarded by the law there as stake-holders. Under our law, however, the position of a trustee is very different. It places upon the trustee the primary responsibility for the protection of all bondholders and holds such trustee to strict account at the suit of any particular bondholder suing on behalf of himself and other bondholders for all his actions in the carrying out of the trust.[350]

He then proceeded to consider the advantage of using a corporate trustee:

> ... it is to be noted that there are advantages to a company in having a corporation act as trustee for bondholders under a trust deed, which are not existent if such a trustee is an individual. In the first place continuity is an important factor. In the next place the fact that the trustee is a well-known financial corporation carrying on an extensive trust business is likely to be an assistance in the selling of the bonds. Further, a trustee, such as the plaintiff herein, has through its extensive business relations and through its organization of a complete trust department, and maintenance of same for many years, advantages in carrying out the trusts beneficially for the bondholders which are not always or indeed frequently possessed by individual trustees.

§8.165 In Canadian lending practice, the trustee is invariably a trust corporation, but it is legally permissible for any individual to act as such a trustee. Among companies, only trust corporations may so act. The relationship among the corporation issuing the instruments, the trustee and the holders of the instruments is normally an arm's length one, although in many cases the trustee will be expressly permitted to invest in the instruments to which the trust relates. The corporation usually chooses the trustee, and the rights and duties of the trustee will normally be exhaustively set out in the trust document. Even so, the court may substitute a new trustee for the trustee appointed under a deed, on the application of a bond holder relating to that deed.[351] Where a corporation has more than one trust indenture arrangement in place, it may seek to appoint the same trustee to serve in respect of two or more of those arrangements. A clear risk in such a

---

[348] *Nova Scotia Central Rlwy. v. Halifax Banking Co.* (1892), 21 S.C.R. 536.
[349] [1983] B.C.J. No. 91, [1938] 2 W.W.R. 32 (S.C.).
[350] *Ibid.* at 38, *per* Murphy J.
[351] *Watson v. Imperial Steel Corp.*, [1925] O.J. No. 410, 28 O.W.N. 242, aff'd [1925] S.C.R. 703.

case is that by accepting the second appointment, the trustee may be held to have entered into a conflict of interest *vis-à-vis* the creditors for whose benefit the first trust indenture is held.

§8.166 Trust indentures are interpreted in accordance with the ordinary rules of contract. The various terms of the contract are read in their entirety so as to accord with the purpose of the contract. The court seeks to give effect to the reasonable expectations of the parties as indicated by the terms that they have used in drafting the agreement.[352] In *Re Sammon*,[353] it was held that for a deed to be effective it must be "delivered". The party whose deed the document is expressed to be must by words or conduct or impliedly acknowledge his intention to be immediately and unconditionally bound. In other words, delivery is a matter of intention, which may be manifested by acts or words.

§8.167 Trust indenture agreements normally contain elaborate provisions respecting the day-to-day administration of the trust. The practice is to leave as few matters uncovered as possible. The trustee will usually possess a discretionary power to grant waivers to the borrower, and to consent to modifications and substitutions of charged assets, where the trustee concludes that there is no material risk involved in so doing. Provisions of this sort add an important element of flexibility into securitized lending, since the alternative would be to summon a meeting of the holders of unit interests in the secured debt — almost always a very expensive proposition. The trustee will also be the focal point for the delivery of information from the borrower to the lenders and, accordingly, will usually be entitled to receive specified information from the borrower at regular intervals during the term of the commitment.

§8.168 Due to the commercial nature of the transaction, the trust indenture will usually make provision for the remuneration of the trustee (although the exact amount of remuneration is often dealt with in a side agreement) and will also provide for the various indemnities to which the trustee is entitled with respect to costs and potential liabilities.[354] The trustee will be empowered to employ bankers, seek legal or other professional advice, and will be given an express permission to act on the strength of their advice.[355] The trustee will also be per-

---

[352] See, for instance, *CBC Pension Plan v. BF Realty Holdings Ltd.*, [2000] O.J. No. 2487, 10 B.L.R. (3d) 188 at 198 (S.C.J.), aff'd [2002] O.J. No. 2125 (C.A.).

[353] (1979) 22 O.R. (2d) 721 (C.A.).

[354] *Cottell v. Stratton* (1872), L.R. 8 Ch. App. 295, *per* Lord Selborne; *Walters v. Woodbridge* (1878), 7 Ch. 504 (C.A.), *per* James L.J. In actions relating to the administration of the trust, the trustee is entitled to legal costs on a solicitor and client basis: *Re Love Hill v. Spurgeon* (1885), 29 Ch. D. 348 (C.A.); but *cf. Singh v. Bhasin*, [1998] The Times, 21 August (H.L.). However, in a debenture holders' action, the trustee's costs are postponed to the costs of realization (including the costs and remuneration of a receiver), but have priority over the costs of the plaintiff: *Batten v. Wedgwood Coal & Iron Co.* (1884), 28 Ch. D. 317.

[355] In the absence of such a provision, the wisest course is for the trustee to seek directions from the court (*i.e.*, to confirm advice received from counsel, by way of an application to court): *Doyle v. Blake* (1804), 2 Sch. & Lef. 243, *per* Lord Redesdale. See, however, the *Trustee Act*, R.S.O. 1990, c. T.23.

mitted to employ agents and to rely upon such agents, and will be absolved from liability where it so acts (these provisions generally expanding upon the equitable rules permitting trustees to employ and rely upon brokers, bankers, solicitors, accountants and bailiffs). The indenture is also likely to provide an authority to the trustee to delegate certain of its responsibilities with respect to the administration of the trust. Most trust indentures contain a provision for the removal of trustees and the appointment of substitute trustees. Where there is no such provision, resort must be taken to the court under the *Trustee Act*.[356]

§8.169 In most cases, a trust indenture will confer a security interest on the trustee, to be held in favour of the holders of the instruments to which it relates. In such cases, the trust indenture will include the normal range of security agreement provisions relating to events of default and the remedies (*e.g.*, the appointment of a receiver) that may be taken upon default. The right to enforce the security will normally belong to the trustee rather than to the unit holders.[357] The trustee is the trustee for the benefit of the unit holders, and between the trustee and the debtor corporation, the trustee will enjoy the same rights as would be possessed by any secured creditor.[358] In addition, in its role as the holder of security, the trustee may play a key role in the issue of bonds, as trust indentures will often provide that the bonds issued under them shall not be effective until certified by the trustee under the indenture.[359]

§8.170 The purpose behind the use of the trust indenture vehicle is to simplify the administration of the bonds or debentures, as the corporation may deal with the trustee, rather than with the holders at large. While limited discretionary powers are normally conferred upon the trustee, the decision of the trustee with respect to any important matter will require the approval of the holders, and the trust indenture will normally provide a procedure for convening meetings of the holders, and will also specify that any decision made at such a meeting will be binding upon all holders. Generally, trustees will waive serious infractions by the corporation only with the consent of the unit holders, but it is customary for the trustee to have the power to waive minor or technical defaults, without the need to consult with the holders.

§8.171 Since the reason for the use of the trust vehicle is to allow the debenture-issuing corporation to deal with a single trustee rather than with a large group of bond holders, the normal rule is that it is for the trustee rather than the individual bond holders or interest coupon holders to sue to enforce rights relating to the

---

[356] R.S.O. 1990, c. T.23.
[357] *Amaranth LLC v. Counsel Corp.*, [2003] O.J. No. 4674, 40 B.L.R. (3d) 212 (S.C.J.); *Rogers & Co. v. British & Colonial Colliery Supply Association* (1898), 68 L.J.Q.B. 14; *Cleary v. Brazil Rlwy. Co.* (1915), 85 L.J.K.B. 832, [1914-15] All E.R. Rep. 790.
[358] See, generally, *Nova Scotia Central Rlwy. v. Halifax Banking Co.* (1892), 23 N.S.R. 172, aff'd 21 S.C.R. 536.
[359] Where a new trustee is appointed, and that trustee certifies the bonds by signing the name of the original trustee and adding its own name as successor, the irregularity does not affect the validity of the bonds: *Minister of Rlwys. & Canals for Dominion of Canada v. Quebec Southern Rlwy. Co. & South Shore Rlwy. Co.* (1908), 12 Ex. C.R. 152.

debenture or the security it confers.[360] In this respect, rule 9.01(1) of the *Rules of Civil Procedure* provides that:

> 9.01(1) A proceeding may be brought by or against an executor, administrator or trustee representing an estate or trust and its beneficiaries without joining the beneficiaries as parties.[361]

However, under rule 9.01(4), the court may order that any beneficiary, creditor or other interested party be made a party to a proceeding brought by or against a trustee. Moreover, the courts have made clear that they will permit individual bond holders to act for their own protection where the trustee fails to do so, with the trustee being added to any such action as a party defendant.[362] So, for instance, a bond holder may bring a class action to have the provisions of the trust deed enforced where the debtor is in default and the trustee fails to take any initiative to enforce the security.[363] On the other hand, where the proceeding (or the order sought) is contrary to the wishes of the majority of the bond holders, except in a case of fraud or oppression the court will not permit the minority to act against those wishes.[364]

§8.172 Part V of the Ontario *Business Corporations Act* ("OBCA") and Part VIII of the *Canada Business Corporations Act* ("CBCA") each contain provisions regulating the terms upon which any such trust indenture may be structured. The term "trust indenture" is defined broadly in both of the Acts. Clause 46(1) of the OBCA defines the term "trust indenture" to mean "any deed, indenture or other instrument, including any supplement or amendment thereto, made by a body corporate under which the body corporate issues or guarantees debt obligations and in which a person is appointed as trustee for the holders of the debt obligations issued or guaranteed thereunder". The definition in section 82 of the CBCA is similar, but is limited to trust indentures made by "corporations".

§8.173 Part V of the OBCA applies to a trust indenture (including trust indentures that were entered into before the Act came into force) if, in respect of any debt obligations outstanding or guaranteed under the trust indenture or to be issued or guaranteed under the trust indenture,[365]

---

[360] See, for example, *Levis County Rlwy. v. Fontaine* (1904), 13 Que. K.B. 523 (C.A.); *Casurina Limited Partnership v. Rio Algom Ltd.*, [2004] O.J. No. 177 (C.A.), leave to appeal to S.C.C. refused [2004] S.C.C.A. No. 105; *Amaranth L.L.C. v. Counsel Corp.* (2004), 131 A.C.W.S. (3d) 578 (Ont. C.A.). The right of the trustee to control proceedings does not extend to rights enjoyed by a unit holder outside the context of the trust and its related security: *Millgate Financial Corp. v. BF Realty Ltd.*, [1994] O.J. No. 1968, 15 B.L.R. (2d) 212 (Gen. Div.).

[361] R.R.O. 1990, Reg. 194; under rule 9.01(2), a number of exceptions are created, specifically with respect to a proceeding to remove or replace a trustee, in a proceeding in respect of the alleged fraud or misconduct of the trustee, or for the execution of the trust by the court.

[362] *Shaughnessy v. Imperial Trusts Co.* (1904), 3 N.B. Eq. 5 (S.C.).

[363] See, generally, *Watson v. Imperial Steel Corp.*, [1925] O.J. No. 410, 28 O.W.N. 242 (C.A.), aff'd [1925] S.C.R. 703. See also *Shaughnessy v. Imperial Trusts Co.* (1904), 3 N.B. Eq. 5 (S.C.).

[364] See, for instance, *Ritchie v. Central Ontario Rlwy.*, [1904] O.J. No. 268, 7 O.L.R. 727 (H.C.J.).

[365] OBCA, s. 46(2).

(a) a prospectus or securities exchange corporation take-over bid circular has been filed under the *Securities Act* or any predecessor to that Act; or

(b) in respect of which a prospectus has been filed under the *Corporations Information Act*[366] or any predecessor to that Act.[367]

The OBCA does not expressly state whether the provisions of Part V apply only in the absence of any provision negating their application, or whether they will apply despite any provision in the trust indenture to the contrary. However, the Act does permit the Ontario Securities Commission to exempt a trust indenture issued by a corporate body not incorporated under the laws of Canada, a province or a territory from the application of Part V (subject to such terms and conditions as the OSC may impose), where the OSC is satisfied to do so would not be prejudicial to the public interest.[368] Since the requirement for a formal order from the OSC exempting the security would seem to be inconsistent with a contractual right to exclude the operation of the part, the logical inference would be that Part V will apply despite any provision in the trust indenture purporting to negate its operation.

§8.174 The CBCA trust indenture provisions are similar to those of the OBCA, but there are a number of important differences between the provisions of the two Acts. Subsection 82(2) of the CBCA provides that Part VIII of the CBCA applies to a trust indenture "if the debt obligations issued or to be issued under the trust indenture are part of a distribution to the public". The OBCA contains no equivalent restriction. However, since trust indentures are normally used in connection with widely held securities, this distinction between the two statutes may lack much in the way of practical significance. The CBCA provisions do not apply to any trust indenture entered into prior to the date when the Act came into effect. Like the OBCA, the CBCA contemplates regulatory exemptions. However, under the CBCA the exemption is granted by the Director, who is empowered to exempt a trust indenture from Part VIII if the trust indenture, the debt obligations under it, and the security interest effected thereby are subject to a law of a province or a country other than Canada that is substantially equivalent to Part VIII of the CBCA.[369]

§8.175 In the case of every trust indenture to which Part V of the OBCA applies, the person appointed as trustee under the trust indenture, or at least one of those

---

[366] R.S.O. 1960, c. 72.

[367] Since Part V apparently applies to all bodies corporate that have filed a prospectus, securities exchange issue or take-over bid under the *Securities Act*, R.S.O. 1990, c. S.5, or a prospectus under the old *Corporations Information Act*, the Part clearly applies irrespective of whether or not the body corporate is a corporation under the OBCA. Given the scope of the Part, it is not clear why it was included in the *Business Corporations Act* as opposed to the *Securities Act*, which would seem to be the natural place for its inclusion. The CBCA provisions are limited to those corporations that are subject to that Act (as, indeed, they would have to be, since the federal government has no general jurisdiction with respect to securities), and therefore are properly located in a corporate law statute.

[368] OBCA, s. 46(4).

[369] CBCA, s. 82(3).

persons if there is more than one trustee appointed, must be resident or authorized to do business in Ontario.[370] Since it is customary to employ only corporate trustees in the case of any trust indenture relating to a public issue of securities, in effect this restriction means that for all practical purposes at least one trustee under the trust indenture must be licensed to carry on the business of a trust company under the *Loan and Trust Corporations Act*.[371]

(a) STANDARD OF CARE

§8.176 Under both the OBCA and CBCA, every trustee is required to act honestly and in good faith with a view to the best interests of the holders of the debt obligations issued under the trust indenture and exercise the care, diligence and skill of a reasonably prudent trustee,[372] despite any term of a trust indenture or any agreement between the holders of debt obligations to the contrary.[373] Trust corporations and other professional corporate trustees are liable for breach of trust if loss is caused to the trust fund because they neglect to exercise the special care and skill which they are seen to hold themselves out as possessing. They are expected to demonstrate a high level of professional expertise in their discharge of their duties.[374] However, a trustee is not in contravention of the required standard of care, diligence and skill if it relies in good faith upon statements contained in a statutory declaration, certificate, opinion or report that complies with the Act or with the trust indenture,[375] provided at any rate that the reliance so placed is consistent with general commercial practice for trustees in a similar position.[376] Subject to any applicable statutory restriction, the general rule in equity is that the liabilities of a trustee may be limited or excluded under a properly worded exclusion clause set out in the trust instrument.[377]

(b) CONFLICT OF INTEREST

§8.177 Both the OBCA and the CBCA prohibit the appointment of a person as trustee where "there is a material conflict of interest between the person's role as trustee and the person's role in any other capacity".[378] Although neither Act gives any illustration of the type of conflict of interest that is prohibited, there are numerous situations where the conflict of interest would be sufficiently clear and of such obvious materiality, that they would almost certainly be seen to contravene the prohibition. For example, it is doubtful that an employee or director of the corporation could act as trustee, or its legal counsel, auditor or other

---

[370] OBCA, s. 46(3).
[371] R.S.O. 1990, c. L.25.
[372] OBCA, s. 47(1). A similar standard of care is imposed under s. 91 of the CBCA.
[373] OBCA, s. 47(2). Section 93 of the CBCA is to the same effect.
[374] *Bartlett v. Barclays Bank Trust Co.*, [1980] 1 All E.R. 139 at 152, *per* Brightman J.
[375] OBCA, s. 49(6); CBCA, s. 92.
[376] See, generally, *National Trustees Co. of Australasia v. General Finance Co. of Australasia*, [1905] A.C. 373 at 381 (P.C.); *Re Windsor Steam Coal Co. (1901), Ltd.*, [1929] 1 Ch. 151 at 164 (C.A.), *per* Lawrence L.J.
[377] *Armitage v. Nurse*, [1997] E.W.J. No. 2577, [1997] 3 W.L.R. 1046 (C.A.).
[378] OBCA, s. 48(1); CBCA, s. 83(1).

professional advisor, or a principal banker to the issuer. In each of those cases, the person would owe a duty of loyalty and confidentiality to the corporation that would be entirely inconsistent with the trustee's duty to the holders of the debt obligations secured by the trust indenture. On the other hand, there are certain types of minor conflict of interest that are generally accepted within the standards of the investment industry, and that would probably not contravene the prohibition of the section. For instance, it is probably acceptable under the Act for the trustee to be and exercise the rights of a holder of the debt obligations secured by the trust indenture. Similarly, it is probably acceptable for the trustee to provide limited banking or custodial services to the issuer.

§8.178 In certain cases, a person may become aware of the existence of a material conflict of interest only after being appointed as trustee, or the facts giving rise to that conflict may only come into being after the person has taken up that appointment. For instance, a conflict of interest may arise due to the merger of the trustee with another person whose interests conflict with those of the beneficiaries of the trust. In such cases, the trustee must either eliminate the conflict of interest or resign from office within 90 days of its becoming aware that the material conflict of interest exists. Moreover, under subsections 48(4) of the OBCA and 83(4) of the CBCA, any interested person (a term surely broad enough to include either a holder of a debt obligation or the issuer) may apply to court for an order replacing the trustee, and upon such an application the court may make any order that it thinks fit.

§8.179 Subsection 49(1) of the OBCA provides that the corporation or a guarantor of debt obligations issued or to be issued under a trust indenture must furnish the trustee with evidence of compliance with the conditions of the trust indenture relating to,

(a) the issue, certification and delivery of debt obligations under the trust indenture;

(b) the release or release and substitution of property subject to a security interest constituted by the trust indenture;

(c) the satisfaction and discharge of the trust indenture; or

(d) the taking of any other action to be taken by the trustee at the request of or on the application of the corporation or guarantor.

before any of the steps referred to in the above clauses is taken.[379] The effect of subsection (1) is to make the delivery of such evidence of compliance a condition precedent to the doing of the acts in question, irrespective of any provision to that effect in the trust indenture itself. For instance, the corporation must first satisfy the trustee of its compliance with all conditions relating to the issue of debt obligations before the corporation may proceed with the issue of those obligations. Subsection 49(2) provides that the required evidence of compliance must consist of:

---

[379] Subsection 86(1) of the CBCA is similar, but omits para. (d).

(a) a statutory declaration or certificate made by a director or an officer of the issuer or guarantor stating that the conditions referred to in that section have been complied with in accordance with the trust indenture; and

(b) where the trust indenture requires compliance with conditions that are subject to review,

   (i) by legal counsel, an opinion, and

   (ii) by an auditor or accountant, an opinion or report of the auditor of the issuer or guarantor, or any accountant licensed under the *Public Accountancy Act, 2004* or comparable legislation of the jurisdiction in which the accountant practises based on the examinations or enquiries required to be made under the trust indenture,

in each case approved by the trustee, that the conditions have been complied with in accordance with the terms of the trust indenture.

Section 87 of the CBCA is to the same general effect, but is less specific:

87. Evidence of compliance required by section 86 shall consist of,

(a) a statutory declaration or certificate made by a director or an officer of the issuer or guarantor stating that the conditions referred to in that section have been complied with; and

(b) where the trust indenture requires compliance with conditions that are subject to review,

   (i) by legal counsel, an opinion of legal counsel that such conditions have been complied with, and

   (ii) by an auditor or accountant, an opinion or report of the auditor of the issuer or guarantor, or such other accountant as the trustee may select, that such conditions have been complied with.

The failure to define the term "accountant" in the CBCA is unfortunate, because unlike the terms "solicitor", "legal counsel" or "lawyer" (which are always identified with a member of the bar), the term "accountant" has no clear legal meaning. Also unfortunate is the ambiguity in paragraph (b), which leaves it uncertain as to whether the trustee has any control over the selection of the person providing the opinion or report, or the form of that opinion or report. In contrast, under the OBCA, it is clear that the trustee must be satisfied as to the source and form of the opinion and report.

§8.180 Under both Acts, each evidence of compliance must include a statement by the person giving the evidence declaring that he or she has read and understands the applicable conditions of the trust indenture, describing the nature and scope of the examination or investigation upon which he (or she) based the statutory declaration, certificate, opinion or report, as the case may be, and declaring that he has made such examinations or investigations as he believes to be necessary to enable him to make the statement or give the opinions contained or expressed in the statutory declaration, certificate, opinion or report.[380]

§8.181 Under both the OBCA and the CBCA, an obligation is imposed upon every corporation issuing debt obligations under a trust indenture to provide ongoing disclosure to the trustee. More specifically, at least once in each 12-month period beginning on the date debt obligations are first issued under the trust indenture, and at any other reasonable time upon the demand of the trustee, the corporation or guarantor of debt obligations issued under a trust indenture must furnish the trustee with a certificate that the corporation or guarantor has complied with all requirements contained in the trust indenture that, if not complied with, would, after the giving of notice, lapse of time or otherwise, constitute an event of default. Where there has been a failure to meet those requirements, the certificate must give particulars of that failure.[381] In addition, at any time the trustee may require the corporation or any guarantor to furnish evidence in such form as the trustee may require as to compliance with any condition of the trust indenture relating to any action required or permitted to be taken by the corporation or any guarantor under the trust indenture as a result of any obligation imposed by the trust indenture.[382]

§8.182 Both the OBCA[383] and the CBCA[384] provide that the trustee must give the holders of debt obligations issued under a trust indenture notice of every event of default arising under the trust indenture and continuing at the time the notice is given, unless the trustee reasonably believes that it is in the best interest of the holders of the debt obligations to withhold the notice.[385] Any notice so required must be given within 30 days of the trustee becoming aware of the occurrence of the default.[386] Where the trustee determines that it is in the best interest of the holders of the debt obligations to withhold the notice, it must so inform the issuer and the guarantor in writing. The OBCA contains the additional requirement that where notice of the occurrence of a default has been given and the default is cured, notice that the default is no longer continuing must be given by

---

[380] OBCA, s. 49(3); CBCA, s. 88. In 2001, the wording of the CBCA provision was revised as follows:

> 88. The evidence of compliance referred to in section 87 shall include a statement by the person giving the evidence
>
> (a) declaring that they have read and understand the conditions of the trust indenture described in section 86;
>
> (b) describing the nature and scope of the examination or investigation on which the certificate, statement or opinion is based; and
>
> (c) declaring that they have made the examination or investigation that they believe necessary to enable them to make their statements or give their opinions.

[381] OBCA, s. 49(4); CBCA, s. 89(2).
[382] OBCA, s. 49(4); CBCA, s. 89(1).
[383] Subsection 51(1).
[384] Section 90.
[385] Under s. 51(1) of the OBCA, this belief must be held by the trustee in good faith; the same wording appeared in the former Act.
[386] Under the OBCA, the notice must be given within a reasonable time not exceeding 30 days.

the trustee to the holders of the debt obligations within a reasonable time not exceeding 30 days after the trustee becomes aware that the default has been cured.

§8.183 Subsection 52(1) of the OBCA provides that any person may require the trustee to furnish a list setting out the names and addresses of the registered holders of the outstanding debt obligations, the principal amount of outstanding debt obligations owned by each holder, and the aggregate principal amount of debt obligations outstanding, as shown on the records maintained by the trustee on the day that the statutory declaration is delivered to the trustee. In contrast, under subsection 85(1) of the CBCA, the right to obtain such information is limited to a holder of a debt obligation issued under a trust indenture. Under both Acts, the issuer is obliged to furnish the trustee with the information required to enable the trustee to comply with the obligation imposed upon it.[387] The procedure for requisitioning such information is the same under both Acts: the applicant[388] must provide a statutory declaration setting out its name and address and providing an undertaking that the list will be used only for the purposes authorized in the Act, namely in connection with,

(a) an effort to influence in writing the holders of the debt obligation secured by the trust indenture;

(b) an offer to acquire debt obligations secured by the trust indenture; or

(c) any other matter relating to the debt obligations or the affairs of the issuer or any guarantor of the debt obligations.[389]

Given the fact that (c), above, is so broad, it is difficult to understand why any statutory declaration is required; moreover, the provision of an undertaking in the form of a statutory declaration does not make the undertaking any more binding than if it was not in such a solemnized form. Statutory declarations verify the truth of the facts therein declared, not the sincerity or enforceability of the declarant's promise.

§8.184 Equity will not allow a trust to fail for want of a trustee,[390] and where the appointment of a trustee is defective, the court has an inherent power to substitute a new trustee in the place of the original trustee appointed under a trust deed securing a debenture issue.[391] The appointment of a receiver under the trust indenture does not oust the trustee, and despite any such appointment the trustee remains bound to discharge its duties and is entitled to its remuneration.[392] The trustee is the trustee for the bondholders and it is the primary responsibility of

---

[387] OBCA, s. 52(2); CBCA, s. 85(2).
[388] Where the applicant is a corporate body, the statutory declaration must be made by a director or officer of the corporate body.
[389] OBCA, s. 52(5); CBCA, s. 85(5).
[390] *Harrison v. Nepisiguit Lumber Co.* (1911), 41 N.B.R. 1 at 23-24 (C.A.), *per* White J.
[391] *Watson v. Imperial Steel Corp.*, [1925] O.J. No. 410, 28 O.W.N. 242 (C.A.), aff'd [1925] S.C.R. 703.
[392] *Balkwill v. Burrard Saw Mills Ltd.*, [1921] 3 W.W.R. 831 (B.C.S.C.).

the trustee to act for their protection. The trustee is held to strict account for any failure to carry out this responsibility.[393]

(c) NO ACTION CLAUSES

§8.185 Debentures issued under a trust indenture frequently contain a provision (known as a "no action clause") restricting — or, more accurately, barring — the institution of proceedings by individual debenture holders in most cases. Instead, subject to certain exceptions proceedings must be instituted by the trustee. The purpose of provisions of this sort is to avoid the possibility of multiplicity of proceedings and to allow the issuer to deal with a single plaintiff, albeit one who may well be acting under the direction of a large number of debenture holders.[394] While the validity and effect of such provisions has not been much litigated in Canada, it has been extensively considered in the United States[395] and in England. In *Relmar Holding Co. v. Paramount Public Corp.*[396] Wasservogel J. said:

> The plaintiff as a bond holder holds his securities subject to the condition of this underlying trust agreement and can maintain an action only upon the conditions specified in the trust agreement. ... The complaint contains no allegations showing compliance with these provisions of the trust agreement. The plaintiff as an individual creditor holding this small number of bonds had no capacity to maintain this action and his complaint should have been dismissed.

The suggestion that no action clauses are barred as an attempt to oust or control the jurisdiction of the court has also been rejected:

> The plaintiff argues that these provisions are void because it is an attempt to oust the jurisdiction of the courts. We do not so regard them. Under the terms of the bonds and indenture, the trustee is the representative of the plaintiff and entitled to bring suit. The provisions are merely reasonable conditions precedent to the right of the plaintiff to bring the suit herself. They are intended for security of all the bond holders, and no doubt rendered the bonds more saleable. They were devised for just such a case as is presented here, where one bond holder, or a small minority, is determined upon action which a large majority believe is hostile to their interests.[397]

It follows that there is nothing illegal or contrary to the public interest in a no action clause, and that generally speaking effect will be given to both the literal meaning and apparent intent of such clauses.[398] Similarly, effect will be given to clauses which allow the majority of debenture holders to decide that no action

---

[393] *National Trust Co. v. Vancouver Kraft Co.*, [1938] B.C.J. No. 91, [1938] 2 W.W.R. 32 at 38 (S.C.), *per* Murphy J.
[394] See, generally, *Green v. New York United Hotels Inc.*, 261 N.Y. 698, 185 N.E. 798 (1933).
[395] See, for instance, *Krepchin v. Barclay-Arrow Holding Corp.*, 1236 A.D. 777, 258 N.Y.S. 1031 (1932); *Fridman v. Chesapeake & Ohio Rlwy. Co.*, 395 F.2d 663 (2nd Cir. 1968); *Simons v. Cogan*, 542 A.2d 785 at 793 (Del. Ch. 1987), *per* Allen C.
[396] 147 Misc. 824, 263 N.Y.S. 776 at 778, aff'd 237 A.D. 870, 261 N.Y.S. 959 (1993).
[397] *Home Mortgage Co. v. Ramsey*, 49 F.2d 738 at 743 (4th. Cir. 1931), *per* Cochran J.
[398] See, for instance, *Rogers & Co. v. British and Colonial Colliery Supply Association* (1899), 68 L.J.Q.B. 14 (Q.B.); *Atlantic Acceptance Corp. v. Burns & Dutton Construction (1962), Ltd.*, [1971] 1 W.W.R. 84 (Alta. C.A.).

will be brought at all, or that an action already instituted will be discontinued, even though the effect of such a decision may be to prejudice the rights of a dissident minority of the debenture holders, although any such provision must be clearly expressed.[399]

§8.186 In *Millgate Financial Corp. v. BF Realty Holdings Ltd.*,[400] the defendant BF issued a prospectus relating to an issue of $100 million, 8 per cent convertible subordinated debentures. The defendant BCE Inc. purchased $25 million of these debentures, with the remaining $75 million being sold to three investment dealers as underwriters for resale to members of the public. The debentures were issued under a trust indenture between BF and National Trust, another defendant in the action. The trust indenture contained a typical "no action" clause, which provided that unless four conditions were met, any proceeding to enforce the debenture could be instituted only by National Trust, specifically:

- a debenture holder had given notice to National Trust that an event of default had occurred;

- the debenture holders had by extraordinary resolution requested National Trust to institute proceedings and National Trust had been given a reasonable opportunity to do so;

- National Trust had been provided with sufficient funds for the proceeding, security and indemnity against liability for costs, etc.; and

- National Trust had failed to act within a reasonable time after the foregoing three conditions were met.

It was alleged that at the end of 1989 and early in 1990, all of the assets owned by BF Ltd. were transferred to Brookfield Developments Corporation ("BD"), a subsidiary of BF, this transfer being made without consultation with National Trust and without its consent.

§8.187 In 1991, National Trust commenced legal proceedings in British Columbia against BF, alleging default under the trust indenture. In 1992, National Trust sought the appointment of a debenture holders' committee under the terms of the trust indenture to represent the debenture holders. Ultimately no indemnity was secured. The trial of the British Columbia action was adjourned, and in 1994 those proceedings were dismissed for want of prosecution.

§8.188 The plaintiff Millgate Financial Corporation Limited ("MFC") commenced an action in Ontario in 1993, naming all of the same defendants as in the British Columbia action as well as the National Trust Company and some of the directors and officers of the BF group of companies. The allegations of MFC included one to the effect that the transfer of the properties from BF to BD constituted a breach of trust. A claim for $150 million was made against National

---

[399] *Pethybridge v. Unibifocal Co.*, [1918] W.N. 278 at 279 (K.B.), *per* Lush J.
[400] [1994] O.J. No. 1968, 15 B.L.R. (2d) 212 (Gen. Div.).

Trust for breach of fiduciary duty and negligence in improperly commencing and conducting the British Columbia action. National Trust argued that the procedures under the trust indenture were a condition precedent to the institution of proceedings by MFC and that since they had not been followed, MFC had no standing. Accordingly, National Trust sought a stay of the proceedings or alternatively an order for security for costs.

§8.189 There was no dispute among the parties that the conditions set out in the "no action clause" of the trust indenture had not been satisfied. However, in considering the merits of National Trust's motion, Farley J. noted that American case law supports the proposition that a "no action clause" in a debenture will not prevent a debenture holder from instituting an action where the trustee has been guilty of incompetence, mismanagement, misconduct or has put itself in a position where it cannot faithfully and competently discharge its duties.[401] He then stated:

> One may question whether it is appropriate or truly possible to meet such conditions when Millgate is seeking a class action proceeding against the defendants including National. Ordinarily one would think it peculiar if a plaintiff with an (apparent) just cause were to be prevented from proceeding because the party who was to initially take the proceedings did not do so. It would of course be unusual for such a party to encourage litigation against itself. If the precondition simply came down to a situation in which the "gatekeeper" could prevent (or even retard or otherwise impede) litigation against itself, then I would generally think that the Court would find that such a precondition was superfluous.[402]

He concluded that the no action clause could not be invoked by National Trust in order to stay proceedings against it:

> ... it appears to me that the only defendant which is able to rely on the precondition clause is BF and then only to the extent that Millgate is alleging that it is in breach of its contractual obligations pursuant to the payment of principal and interest on the Debentures being in default.[403]

§8.190 In *Trusts & Guarantee Co. v. Grand Valley Rlwy. Co.*[404] the manager of the trust company acting for the bond holders was appointed by court order as the receiver of the corporation which issued the debenture. It was held that in such circumstances, the trustee did not represent the bond holders with respect to the passing of the receiver's accounts and his right to remuneration. Therefore, the bond holders were allowed to be heard upon the passing of accounts and the fixing of remuneration.

---

[401] *Rabinowitz v. Kaiser-Frazer Corp.*, 111 N.Y.S.2d 539 (Sup. Ct. 1952); *Feldbaum v. McCory*, Del. Ch. (1992), online: *LEXIS* 113 at 22; *Home Mortgage Co. v. Ramsey*, 49 F.2d 738 at 741 and 743 (4th Cir. 1931). See also *Reinhardt v. Interstate Telephone Co.*, 71 N.H. Eq. 70, 63 A. 1097 (1906).

[402] *Millgate Finance Corp. v. BF Realty Holdings Ltd.*, [1994] O.J. No. 1968, 15 B.L.R. (2d) 212 at 219-20 (Gen. Div.).

[403] *Ibid.*, at 225.

[404] (1915), 34 O.L.R. 87 (C.A.).

(d) Fees and Expenses of the Trustee

§8.191 There is a presumption in equity that a trustee is entitled to be indemnified out of the trust estate against expenses incurred in the administration of the trust. However, historically there was no presumption of entitlement to remuneration for serving as trustee.[405] On the contrary, the normal presumption of equity was that the trustee was not entitled to remuneration for its services. But the presumption against a right of remuneration has long been expressly over-turned by section 61 of the *Trustee Act*,[406] subsection (1) of which provides:

> 61.(1) A trustee, guardian or personal representative is entitled to such fair and reasonable allowance for the care, pains and trouble, and the time expended in and about the estate, as may be allowed by a judge of the Superior Court of Justice.

Any order may be made under subsection (1) even though the trust estate is not before the court in an action.[407]

§8.192 Although section 61 of the *Trustee Act*[408] permits a court to allow remuneration to a trustee, it would hardly be practical for commercial trustees to depend for their remuneration upon the discretion of the courts. As a result, the nearly invariable practice in Canadian commercial trust indentures is for a right of remuneration to be provided as a matter of contract. The compensation settled between the trustee and beneficiaries (or the corporation) is binding upon the trustee: the court has no power to authorize additional compensation if the amount payable subsequently proves to be unreasonable given the nature of the services required.[409] On the other hand, even where remuneration is expressly provided, it appears that the courts have the jurisdiction to review that compensation where it is argued that the remuneration in question is unconscionable. In resolving this question, the courts will consider: (1) the magnitude of the trust; (2) the care and responsibility springing from the trust; (3) the time occupied by the trustee in performing its duties; (4) the skill and ability displayed by the trustee; (5) the success of the trustee's administration.[410]

§8.193 In most cases, the extent of remuneration to which a trustee is entitled will be purely a matter of contractual construction. Disputes over remuneration entitlement most often arise where a receiver and manager is appointed with respect to the property of the debtor corporation. The appointment of a receiver and manager over the assets charged in favour of the trustee does not necessarily result in the termination of the appointment of the trustee or extinguish the trustee's obligations; whether it will have this effect depends upon the terms of the

---

[405] See, for instance, *Royal Trust Co. v. Atlantic & Lake Superior Rlwy.* (1908), 13 Ex. C.R. 42.
[406] R.S.O. 1990, c. T.23.
[407] *Ibid.*, s. 61(2).
[408] R.S.O. 1990, c. T.23.
[409] *Thompson v. Northern Trusts Co.*, [1925] 4 D.L.R. 184 at 187 (Sask. C.A.), *per* Lamont J.A.; *French v. Toronto General Trusts Corp.*, [1923] O.J. No. 134, 53 O.L.R. 336 (H.C.).
[410] *Toronto General Trusts Corp. v. Central Ontario Rlwy.*, [1905] O.J. No. 536, 6 O.W.R. 350 at 354 (H.C.J.), *per* Teetzel J.; see also *National Trust Co. v. Vancouver Kraft Co.*, [1938] B.C.J. No. 91, [1938] 2 W.W.R. 32, 52 B.C.R. 552 (S.C.).

trust itself.[411] Such an appointment may, however, prejudice the trustee's entitlement to remuneration — although again this question will turn upon the wording of the relevant documents. In one case, a receiver and manager was appointed and the property was realized, with conduct of the sale being given to the trustee who had executed the required conveyancing documents. Under the terms of their trust, the trustee was entitled to be paid a specified salary "as remuneration for their services". It was held that although the trustee was entitled to remuneration up to the date of the appointment of the receiver, the services performed after that date were not those contemplated by the deed. Therefore, there was no right to remuneration. Similarly, in *Re Locke & Smith Ltd.*[412] it was held that the trustees were not entitled to be paid after the appointment of the receiver, for they had not performed any services. However, the trustee will be allowed to claim remuneration where the terms of its contract clearly provide for such payment.[413]

§8.194 The mere fact that a deed of trust provides that a trustee is entitled to remuneration does not in and of itself entitle the trustee to any security with respect to that remuneration. Ordinarily, the trust indenture will expressly provide the trustee with a lien against any proceeds obtained on the realization of the security held by the trustee for any fees or disbursements owing to the trustee.[414] Where the relevant documents are silent, the trustee cannot demand payment of remuneration in priority to repaying the debt owed to the trust beneficiaries.[415] Ordinarily, it is the corporate debtor rather than the beneficiary debenture holders who stands charged with the payment of the trustee's remuneration. It may be argued, however, that section 61 of the *Trustee Act*[416] permits the court to award remuneration at the contract rate, and to charge the beneficiaries of the trust with its payment.

(4) Debenture Stock

§8.195 Although the term "debenture stock" is common in England, it is not frequently encountered in Canadian practice. In both Canada and England it is a term of loose definition.[417] For most purposes, the distinction between debentures and debenture stock is not particularly significant. In some contexts, it has been used to describe a perpetual debt security.[418] In other contexts, the term debenture stock has been used to identify the unit interests in a consolidated single debt security, so that the whole stock constitutes a single debt, and the

---

[411] See, generally, *Simpson Balkwill Co. v. Canadian Credit Men's Trust Assn.*, [1921] B.C.J. No. 55, [1921] 3 W.W.R. 831, 30 B.C.R. 347, 79 D.L.R. 731 (S.C.).
[412] [1914] 1 Ch. 687.
[413] *Re British Consolidated Oil Corp.*, [1919] 2 Ch. 81; *Park v. Anglo-Canadian Lands Ltd.*, [1918] 2 Ch. 287.
[414] See, for instance, *Re Piccadilly Hotel; Paul v. Piccadilly Hotel Ltd.*, [1911] 2 Ch. 534.
[415] See, generally, *Re Accles Ltd.; Hodgson v. Accles* (1902), 51 W.R. 57, 18 T.L.R. 786, per Farwell J.
[416] R.S.O. 1990, c. T.23.
[417] *Scottish Widows' Fund & Life Assurance Society v. Canada Permanent Mortgage Corp.*, [1929] O.J. No. 133, 63 O.L.R. 637 at 639 (H.C.), per Rose J.
[418] *Attree v. Hawe* (1878), 9 Ch. D. 337 at 349 (C.A.).

interest of each investor a several share of it. When so used, the term "debenture" is the name given to the instrument that constitutes the debenture. In contrast, the term "debenture stock" is the name given to the debt to which a debenture created under a trust deed relates. In this respect, debentures differ from debenture stock in the same way that a mortgage deed differs from the mortgage debt.[419] The use of debenture stock is seen to facilitate division of the debt relating to the debenture into unit interests in a debenture that can be sold to public investors, with the debenture itself being held by a trustee on their behalf.[420] The funds advanced by individual unit holders or their predecessors in title need not be for the same amount or for any predefined amount.

(5) Income Bonds

§8.196 Income bonds and debentures differ from most debt instruments in that interest is payable only out of the net profits of the borrower. If there is no net profit then no interest is payable, although such bonds (in a manner analogous to dividends upon preference shares) may provide that unpaid interest shall accumulate from one year to another, and shall be paid out of net earnings in subsequent years. The popularity of income bonds is greatest when interest rates are high, because in such cases, there is an enormous potential for tax saving.

§8.197 For corporate law purposes, there is no special restriction upon the ability of a corporation to raise funds through the issue of income-based debt instruments, such as income bonds and debentures.[421] However, there are certain practical limitations on the issue of such bonds that arise under the *Income Tax Act* (Canada).[422] From the perspective of the issuer of the income bond or debenture, paragraph 18(1)(*g*) of the Act provides that:

> 18.(1) In computing the income of a taxpayer from a business or property, no deduction shall be made in respect of,
>
> …..
>
> (*g*) an amount paid by a corporation as interest or otherwise to holders of its income bonds or income debentures unless the bonds or debentures have been issued or the income provisions thereof have been adopted since 1930,
>
> > (i) to afford relief to the debtor from financial difficulties, and

---

[419] A.F. Topham & A.M.R. Topham, *Debentures and Debenture Stock* (3 Palmer's Company Precedents) (London: Stevens & Sons, 1933), 6. See *Scottish Widows' Fund & Life Assurance Society v. Canada Permanent Mortgage Corp.*, [1929] O.J. No. 133, 63 O.L.R. 637 (H.C.), per Rose J.
[420] *Attree v. Hawe* (1878), 9 Ch. D. 337 (C.A.).
[421] For cases dealing with the use of income bonds, see American cases: *Re Minneapolis-St. Paul & S.S.M.*, 48 F. Supp. 330 (D.C. Minn. 1943); *Central Georgia Rlwy. Co. v. Central Trust of New York*, 69 S.E. 708 (1910); *Re Denver & R.G.W. Rlwy. Co.*, 48 F. Supp. 330 (D.C. Colo. 1940); *Willoughby v. Chicago Junction Rlwy.*, 25 A. 277 (1892); *Day v. Ogdensburg & Lake Champlain Railroad Co.*, 13 N.E. 765 (1887). Canadian cases: *Basic Refractory Products Ltd. v. M.N.R.* (1951), 4 Tax A.B.C. 94. English Cases: *Heslop v. Paraguay Central Rlwy. Co.* (1910), 54 So. J. 234 (Ch.); *Long Acre Press Ltd. v. Odhams Press Ltd.*, [1930] 2 Ch. 196.
[422] R.S.C. 1985, c. 1 (5th Supp.).

(ii) in place of or as an amendment to bonds or debentures that at the end of 1930 provided unconditionally for a fixed rate of interest.

From the perspective of the holder of the income bond or debenture, subsection 15(3) of the *Income Tax Act* (Canada) provides:

> 15.(3) An amount paid as interest or a dividend by a corporation resident in Canada to a taxpayer in respect of an income bond or income debenture shall be deemed to have been paid by the corporation and received by the taxpayer as a dividend on a share of the capital stock of the corporation, unless the corporation is entitled to deduct the amount so paid in computing its income.

Subsection 15(4) contains a similar provision in respect of non-resident corporations.

§8.198 The combined effect of these provisions is to subject the payment of interest on income bonds to dividend tax treatment: it is non-deductible to the issuing corporation; its treatment in the hands of the recipient depends upon the recipient's tax status. Generally, the purpose of the issue is to allow the interest to be paid and received out of after-tax earnings. In the short and medium term, the issue of such instruments will have a neutral effect on corporate issuers that have large tax losses. They have no need to deduct the interest payable in respect of those instruments because their accumulated tax losses may be off-set against any profits that they earn. From the perspective of the holder, however, the issue of such bonds is attractive because the income received by the holder is non-taxable in the hands of the holder. The holder may reduce the amount of interest payable by the borrower, yet still receive the same or a greater net after-tax income on the instrument because of this tax treatment. Needless to say, this possibility has occurred to Canada Revenue Agency, and consequently a detailed definition has been included in section 248 of the *Income Tax Act* (Canada), which has the effect of narrowing the eligibility of instruments qualifying for the tax treatment provided in sections 18 and 15 to a relatively narrow range. Section 248 provides that in the *Income Tax Act* (Canada):

> "income bond" or "income debenture" of a corporation (in this definition referred to as the "issuing corporation") means a bond or debenture in respect of which interest or dividends are payable only to the extent that the issuing corporation has made a profit before taking into account the interest or dividend obligation and that was issued,
>
> (*a*) before November 17, 1978;
>
> (*b*) after November 16, 1978 and before 1980, pursuant to an agreement in writing to do so made before November 17, 1978 (in this definition referred to as an "established agreement");
>
> (*c*) by an issuing corporation resident in Canada for a term that may not, in any circumstances, exceed five years,
>
> > (i) as part of a proposal to or an arrangement with its creditors that had been approved by a court under the *Bankruptcy and Insolvency Act*,

(ii) at a time when all or substantially all of its assets were under the control of a receiver, receiver-manager, sequestrator or trustee in bankruptcy, or

(iii) at a time when by reason of financial difficulty, the issuing corporation or another corporation resident in Canada with which it does not deal at arm's length was in default, or could reasonably be expected to default, on a debt obligation held by a person with whom the issuing corporation was dealing at arm's length and the bond or debenture was issued in either wholly or in substantial part and either directly or indirectly in exchange or substitution for that obligation or a part thereof,

and in the case of a bond or debenture issued after November 12, 1981, the proceeds from the issue may reasonably be regarded as having been used by the issuing corporation or a corporation with which it was not dealing with at arm's length in the financing of its business carried on in Canada immediately before the bond or debenture was issued ...

While paragraphs (c)(i) and (ii) have a straightforward application, subparagraph (iii), the financial difficulty test, requires a subjective assessment of the "financial condition" of the borrower. To protect the parties, it is customary to obtain an advance tax ruling from Revenue Canada as to whether a proposed issue will meet the requirements of an income bond or debenture under the Act, particularly where reliance is placed upon subparagraph (iii).

(iv) Assignment of Debts (or Accounts)

§8.199 The terms "assignment of debts" and "assignment of accounts" are synonymous. An assignment of debt is a transfer to the assignee of the right to receive payment in respect of the debt, and where granted as security for a loan, it is understood that the amount received by the assignee shall be applied to the repayment of the loan owed by the assignee to the assignor. The assigned debts need not be owing at the time when they are assigned.[423] There are in fact two different types of assignment of book debt (or assignment of account), and each generally confers a different type of security interest. These are: (a) the general assignment, and (b) the assignment of a specific debt.

(1) General Assignment of Book Debts (General Assignment of Accounts)

§8.200 A general assignment of book debts (or general assignment of accounts, the latter term now replacing the former due to the increased use of computerized accounting systems which do not employ books as such) is a transfer by the debtor of its beneficial interest in the general debts and accounts that are owed to it in the ordinary course of its business.[424] Essentially, a general assignment of book debts is intended to attach all account debts arising in a business which it is the proper and usual course to record in books of account relating to the business,[425] and will include all present and future accounts of this type as they arise

---

[423] *Tailby v. Official Receiver* (1888), 58 L.J.Q.B. 75 at 79 (H.L.), *per* Lord Watson.
[424] *National Bank of Australasia v. Falkingham*, [1902] A.C. 585.
[425] *Official Receiver v. Tailby* (1886), 18 Q.B.D. 25 at 79 (C.A.), *per* Lord Esher M.R. at 29; but *cf.* *Re Brightlife Ltd.*, [1987] Ch. 200, *per* Hoffmann J. as to bank accounts.

from time to time. Ancillary security is usually granted over all books and other records evidencing such accounts. Pending default and enforcement, the debtor is allowed to collect its accounts and use and apply the proceeds in the ordinary course of its business. Consequently the nature of the security given by a general assignment of book debts would appear to be that of a floating charge. A general assignment of book debts usually includes a power to appoint a receiver to collect in the debts owing to the borrower.

§8.201 In recent years, there has been a fair amount of discussion as to whether assignments of book debts can take the form of a specific charge. Although there is case law to this effect,[426] there is substantial *obiter* to the contrary, and the proposition has been the subject of some doubt.[427] Recent U.K. case law dealing with floating charges has been greatly influenced by the fact that the *Insolvency Act, 1986* creates a number of preferred creditors, whose claims are entitled to priority as against a floating charge. To avoid the effective subordination of a floating security to the claims of preferred creditors, it has become widespread practice in England to attempt to draft all charges so that they resemble fixed rather than floating charges.[428] In Ontario and other PPSA jurisdictions this is to a large extent moot, since the PPSA contains a comprehensive code governing the priority of all security interests; elsewhere the question remains more relevant. Generally speaking, Canadian case law has rejected the notion that a general assignments of book debts can take the form of a fixed charge,[429] at least in the ordinary case.[430] Moreover, even where absolute (*i.e.*, fixed) assignments are said to have been created, the manner in which the parties conduct themselves, and the rights reserved to the borrower under the terms of the fixed charge, are often quite inconsistent with the nature of a fixed charge.[431]

§8.202 The categorization of a general assignment of receivables as a fixed or floating charge was considered by the House of Lords in *National Westminster Bank plc. v. Spectrum Plus Ltd.*[432] In *Spectrum* a company obtained an overdraft facility and provided a debenture to secure its indebtedness to the bank. The debenture purportedly conferred a specific (fixed) charge of all book debts and

---

[426] *Siebe Gorman & Co. v. Barclays Bank Ltd.*, [1979] 2 Lloyds Rep. 142 (Ch.); see also *Barclays Bank plc. v. Willowbrook International Ltd.*, [1987] 1 F.T.L.R. 386 (C.A.); *Re New Bullas Trading Ltd.*, [1994] 1 B.C.L.C. 485 (C.A.).

[427] J.R. Lingard, *Bank Security Documents*, 2nd ed. (London: Butterworths, 1988), 119. See also *Re Brightlife Ltd.*, [1986] 3 All E.R. 673 (Ch.).

[428] See, generally, *Re New Bullas Trading Ltd.*, [1994] 1 B.C.L.C. 485; *Royal Trust Bank v. National Westminster Bank plc.*, [1996] 2 B.C.L.C. 682.

[429] See also *Bank of Montreal v. Century Ltd. (Trustee)*, [1979] N.J. No. 32, 33 C.B.R. (N.S.) 256 (C.A.); *R.V. Demmings & Co. v. Caldwell Construction Co.*, [1956] 4 D.L.R. (2d) 465 (N.B.C.A.); *Credit Suisse Canada v. 1133 Yonge St. Holdings Ltd.*, [1998] O.J. No. 4468, 41 O.R. (3d) 632 (C.A.).

[430] *Canada Trustco Mortgage Corp. v. Port O'Call Hotel Inc.*, [1996] S.C.J. No. 45, 27 B.L.R. (2d) 147 at 161-62 and 166, *per* Cory J.

[431] *Thermo King Corp. v. Provincial Bank of Canada*, [1981] O.J. No. 3136, 34 O.R. (2d) 369 (C.A.); *Bonavista (Town) v. Atlantic Technologies Ltd.*, [1994] N.J. No. 28, 117 Nfld. & P.E.I.R. 19 at 24 (T.D.), *per* Osborn J.

[432] [2005] 2 A.C. 680, [2005] 4 All E.R. 209, [2005] 2 B.C.L.C. 269.

other debts then and from time to time due or owing to the company and a floating security of its undertaking and all its property assets and rights, including those for the time being charged by way of specific charge if and to the extent that such charges failed as specific charges. Section 5 of the debenture required the company to pay into its account with the bank:

> ... all moneys which it may receive in respect of such debts and shall not without the prior consent in writing of the Bank sell factor discount or otherwise charge or assign the same in favor of any other person or purport to do so...

After the company went into voluntary liquidation, the bank applied for a declaration that the debenture had created a fixed charge over the company's book debts (under U.K. insolvency law, certain of the company's creditors, were entitled to the proceeds of the book debts in priority to the bank if the charge was held to be a floating charge).

§8.203 It was held that the essential and distinguishing characteristic of a floating charge was that the asset subject to the charge was not finally appropriated as a security for the payment of the debt until the occurrence of some future event. In the meantime the debtor was left free to use the charged asset and to remove it from the security. If part of the arrangement between the company and the bank was that the company was free to collect the book debts but had to pay the collected money into a specified bank account, the categorization of the charge would turn upon what (if any) restrictions were placed on the use that the company could make of the funds paid into the account. If the account was treated as a blocked account, so long as it had remained overdrawn, it would have been easy to infer from a combination of that treatment and the description of the charge as a fixed charge that the company had no right to draw on the account until the debit on the account had been discharged. However, on the facts the account had never been so treated. The overdraft facility allowed the company to draw on the account at will. The company's right, until notice might be received from the bank terminating the overdraft facility and requiring immediate repayment of the indebtedness, was to draw freely on the account. Such a right was inconsistent with the charge being a fixed charge and the label placed upon the debenture could not be prayed-in-aid to detract from that right. Accordingly, the debenture, although it expressly purported to grant the bank a fixed charge over the company's book debts, was held to grant only a floating charge.

(2) Assignment of Specific Debts and Accounts

§8.204 As the term suggests, in an assignment of specific debts, the borrower assigns its interest in a specific, ascertainable debt (which may be present or future) rather than to such debts and accounts as may be owing to the borrower from time to time.[433] There can be little doubt that an assignment of specific debts normally creates a fixed and specific charge, and indeed in most cases it

---

[433] See, for instance, *Cowichen Native Heritage Society v. Toronto Dominion Bank*, [1993] B.C.J. No. 1872, 106 D.L.R. (4th) 126 (C.A.).

would be hard to characterize the security as other than a fixed charge. Often the proceeds of such a charge must be applied by the borrower to a defined purpose, normally to repay the loan in respect of which the specific charge is given.

(v) General Security Agreement

§8.205 The general security agreement is a recent evolution under the *Personal Property Security Act*,[434] and is essentially a simplified form of fixed and floating debenture, as it provides both fixed and floating charges over the general assets of the borrower. However, one difference between a general security agreement and a debenture is that a debenture always secures the payment of a debt acknowledged in the debenture, whereas a general security agreement may secure the performance of any obligation. In some provinces, a general security agreement may not be registered against title to real property. In Ontario, no obstacle prevents such registration, provided the agreement is appended to the appropriate land registration form, which may be either a form of charge or a general form.

(vi) Conditional Sale Agreement

§8.206 A conditional sale agreement is a title reservation agreement, under which delivery of the good to the purchaser is made immediately, while the purchase price is paid over a period of time. To protect the seller, title to the good is transferred to the buyer only upon the full payment of the purchase price and the satisfaction of the other terms and conditions of the conditional sale agreement.[435] While conditional sale contracts are usually entered into between a merchant and the purchaser of a good, it is common for contracts of this type to be assigned by the merchant to a lending institution. Such assignments may be with recourse to the merchant in the event of a default by the purchaser of the good (in which case the merchant must buy back the conditional sale agreement from the lending institution), or without recourse (in which case the lending institution assumes the risk of default).

(vii) Leases

§8.207 There are various types of leases, only some of which are truly credit arrangements. Generally speaking, an arrangement under which one person leases property to another is not a security agreement. However, because a lease can be used as a method of retaining title in a creditor while allowing a borrower to make use of the leased property, there is an obvious temptation to use such an arrangement as a security device.[436] The terms "capital lease" and "financing lease" are used to describe any lease in which the lessee will (or is very likely

---

[434] R.S.O. 1990, c. P.10.
[435] *Harris v. Tong*, [1930] O.J. No. 86, 65 O.L.R. 133 (C.A.).
[436] See, generally, *Re Bronson*, [1996] B.C.J. No. 216, 39 C.B.R. (3d) 33 (S.C.) dealing with the distinction between true leases and financing leases. See also *Re Coro (Canada) Inc.*, [1997] O.J. No. 4704, 36 O.R. (3d) 563 (Gen. Div.); *MTC Leasing v. National Bank Leasing Inc.*, [1997] M.J. No. 384, 34 B.L.R. (2d) 20 (Q.B.), aff'd [1998] M.J. No. 453 (C.A.).

to) acquire title to the leased asset at the end of the lease term, either automatically, or at a very low option price.[437] In such a lease, the term of the lease will normally be 75 per cent or more of the anticipated life of the leased asset, and the present value of the minimum lease payments will be at least 90 per cent of the fair value of that asset. In many cases a lease will provide for the eventual acquisition of ownership by the lessee. Such a contract (which is often called a hire-purchase agreement) differs from a conditional sale contract, in that under a conditional sale contract, the buyer is contractually committed to purchase, while under a hire-purchase contract, the lessee merely has a right to do so. Where the buy-out price is nominal, however, this distinction is of little import.[438] For this reason, the law often treats leases and conditional sales as if they were the same.[439] Moreover, in many cases business people treat leases as the equivalent of a conditional sale agreement as well. For instance, leases, like conditional sale contracts, may be assigned by the lessor to a lending institution.

(viii) Equipment Trust Certificates

§8.208 Equipment trust certificates are a form of security instrument frequently employed by airlines, railroads, truck companies and shipping companies to finance the purchase of new equipment. Title to the transportation equipment concerned is registered in the name of a trustee and participation in the debt is evidenced by the issue of a certificate to each investor. Although the debtor corporation has the right to use the equipment unless and until there is a default, the trust is for the benefit of the lenders whose credit is secured by the certificates. The certificate entitles the holder to participate as a beneficiary in the trust, and therefore constitutes the equivalent of a first charge on the equipment subject to the trust. Because there is only one title holder to the equipment,[440] this type of lending simplifies realization on the subject equipment, which is often readily marketable to other companies engaging in the same line of business.

(ix) Pledge

§8.209 A pledge is the delivery or transfer of possession of a chattel by its owner to a creditor or a person acting on the creditor's behalf as security for the payment of a debt or the performance of another obligation that is owed to the creditor.[441] Delivery may be actual or constructive.[442] A pledge is nearly the opposite of a mortgage. Under a mortgage, ownership of the collateral vests in the

---

[437] See, for instance, *Adelaide Capital Corp. v. Integrated Transportation Finance Inc.*, [1994] O.J. No. 103, 111 D.L.R. (4th) 493 (Gen. Div.).
[438] *Re Ontario Equipment (1976) Ltd.* (1981), 14 B.L.R. 113 (Ont. S.C.), aff'd [1982] O.J. No. 3105 (C.A.).
[439] *Re Speedrack Ltd.*, [1980] O.J. No. 141, 11 B.L.R. 220 (S.C.), but *cf. Ontario Equipment (1976) Ltd.* (1981), 14 B.L.R. 113 (Ont. S.C.), aff'd [1982] O.J. No. 3105 (C.A.).
[440] The ownership of equipment of this type must often be formally registered with a government agency.
[441] *R. v. Warren* (1911), 17 C.C.C. 504 (Ont. Co. Ct.), per Denton Jun. Co. J.
[442] See, for instance, *Hilton v. Tucker* (1888), 39 Ch. D. 669; *Wrightson v. McArthur & Hutchinson (1919) Ltd.*, [1921] 2 K.B. 807; *Dublin City Distillery Ltd. v. Doherty*, [1914] A.C. 823; *Official Assignee of Madras v. Mercantile Bank of India Ltd.*, [1935] A.C. 53.

lender, but possession remains with the borrower. Under a pledge, ownership remains with the borrower, but possession of the collateral is transferred to the lender. Upon taking possession, the lender is said to acquire a special proprietary interest in the collateral pledged to the lender. Where the borrower fails to perform the secured obligation, that special proprietary interest permits the lender to realize upon the pledged collateral. Thus a pledge differs from a common law lien, in that a lien affords only a right to remain in possession until performance is rendered. Under Ontario law, a pledge is the only form of contract security that is not required to be in writing.

(x) Hypothecation Agreement

§8.210 The term "hypothecation" is one borrowed from the civil law. In common law jurisdictions, it describes a form of equitable charge, corresponding to a pledge, but under which possession of the collateral is not delivered to the creditor or to any person acting on behalf of the creditor, but instead remains in the hands of the debtor.[443] Such a security interest may be created either by a hypothecation agreement, or by the delivery of documents of title to goods to the lender. Hypothecations are useful where delivery cannot be made of property, so as to permit it to be pledged. For instance, while securities payable to a bearer may be pledged by deposit, securities in registered form may not (since the delivery of the security certificate does not constitute delivery of the underlying security).[444] Thus a hypothecation is used, generally accompanied by a completion of the form of transfer relating to the securities in blank.

§8.211 The distinction between hypothecations and pledges has become confused in practice, so that many documents that are styled hypothecation agreements are actually pledges, under which it is contemplated that possession of the collateral will be given to the creditor. However, there is an important distinction between the two types of security. In the case of a true pledge, where possession of the collateral is transferred, possession is sufficient to perfect the security interest of the lender in collateral that constitutes chattel paper, goods, instruments, securities, negotiable documents of title and money within the meaning of the *Personal Property Security Act* ("PPSA").[445] However, if the security agreement is a hypothecation, and possession of the collateral is not transferred to the lender (or to a trustee for the lender, being a person other than the borrower) then the security interest must be perfected by registration. Furthermore, a lender who obtains a security interest by the pledge of chattel paper, an instrument, a negotiable document of title or a security (as those terms are defined in the PPSA) will constitute a "purchaser" of the collateral concerned, and except where that security interest was acquired with "knowledge" of a prior registered security interest, the pledge will have priority over prior

---

[443] *McCutcheon Lumber Co. v. Minitonas (Municipality)* (1912), 2 D.L.R. 117 at 118 (Man. K.B.), per Pendergast J.
[444] *Donald v. Suckling* (1886), L.R. 1 Q.B. 585; *Carter v. Wake* (1877), 4 Ch. D. 605.
[445] R.S.O. 1990, c. P.10, s. 22.

registered security interests.[446] In contrast, in the case of a true hypothecation, priority is normally by order of the registration of the security interests.[447]

§8.212 Although the term "hypothecation" is borrowed from civil law terminology, there is a distinction between the common law concept of a hypothecation (which is used to describe a relatively narrow class of security agreement) and the civil law term "hypothec", which under article 2016 of the Quebec *Civil Code* describes any "real right upon immovables made liable for the fulfillment of an obligation, in virtue of which the creditor may cause them to be sold in the hands of whomsoever they may be, and have a preference upon the proceeds of the sale in order of date as fixed by this Code".

(xi) Assignment of Specific Securities

§8.213 Conceptually, an assignment of specific securities is similar to an assignment of specific accounts, the primary difference being that securities are not generally viewed as falling within the accounts of an enterprise — the accounts being limited to debts owed to the debtor in the ordinary course of its business. In contrast, securities are investment instruments. Like an assignment of specific debts, an assignment of specific securities is in the nature of a specific charge.

(xii) Bank Act Security

§8.214 Sections 426 and 427 of the *Bank Act*[448] permit banks subject to that Act[449] to take special forms of security from certain classes of borrower, and to lend money on the strength of such security. The Act also creates a registration scheme in respect of such security and provides a basis for determining the relative priority of securities granted under these provisions. Section 426 or 427 security can be given only by those types of borrowers named in each section respectively and only in respect of the types of assets identified in that section. The possibility that such security exists should be considered by any lender in any transaction involving one of the named classes of borrower, especially if

---

[446] The reason why this is so cannot be explained briefly, but turns upon the construction of the following provisions of the PPSA: subss. 28(3), (4), (6) and (7), and the definitions of "purchaser" and "purchase" in subs. 1(1) of the Act.
[447] Note that although actual possession of uncertificated securities is not possible, the PPSA contemplates the constructive transfer of the possession of such securities: see subss. 28(6), (7) and (8).
[448] S.C. 1991, c. 46; formerly s. 178 of the *Bank Act*, R.S.C. 1985, c. B.1; and s. 88 of the previous version of the *Bank Act*. A provision along the same lines was introduced into Canadian banking law in 1890 as s. 74 of the *Bank Act* then in force.
[449] In certain cases, the term "bank" has been expanded to encompass virtually every class of financial institution: see, for instance, the *Canada Wheat Board Act*, R.S.C. 1985, c. C-24. The federal Business Development Bank may take security under s. 427 of the *Bank Act*, but not, it would appear, under s. 426 of the *Bank Act*: *Federal Business Development Bank Act*, R.S.C. 1985, c. F-6, s. 25 [now *Business Development Bank of Canada Act*, S.C. 1995, c. 28]. Even under s. 427, its power to take security is limited to bills of lading, warehouse receipts and goods, wares and merchandise. Sections 426 and 427 security may not be taken by other types of financial institution (*e.g.*, trust companies) engaged in bank-type activities. There are no longer any institutions operating under the *Quebec Savings Bank Act*.

such a transaction contemplates the giving of security over a class of asset included within the section. Despite the limitation of *Bank Act* security to certain defined classes of borrower, the classes of eligible borrower and the type of security allowed have both expanded steadily since the concept was first introduced in the 1890 *Bank Act*, so that it is now at least arguable that section 427 security may be granted even by consumer borrowers (as retail purchasers of goods) under the strength of paragraph 427(1)(*a*).

(1) Section 427 Security

§8.215 Section 427 of the *Bank Act*[450] allows banks to take a unique form of security over eligible collateral from certain designated types of borrower. As will be discussed in detail below, the general purpose of section 427 is to allow farmers, manufacturers, traders, mine operators and the like to borrow from banks on the security of their current assets (such as inventory and produce) to finance their ongoing operations.[451] The nature of the security conferred by section 427 is not clear under the Act. The express wording of the statute would appear to confer a fixed charge. However, from the beginning it appears to have been assumed that section 427 (and its antecedents) is intended to permit the borrower to continue dealing with the property charged in the ordinary course of business, pending default and seizure by the bank. Indeed, the section 427 security regime could barely be interpreted in any other way, for if the change was interpreted as being fixed in nature, the effect of a grant of section 427 security would be to bring the commercial activities of the borrower practically to a halt. In *Canadian Western Millwork Ltd. (Trustee of) v. Royal Bank of Canada*[452] Judson J. suggested that dispositions made by the borrower in the ordinary course are made with the implied consent of the bank. He went on to hold that the security given against the charged assets of the borrower (*e.g.*, inventory, etc.) attaches by implication — even in the absence of express agreement — to any proceeds arising from the sale, including book debts and other accounts receivable, and to proceeds collected, so long as they remain traceable.[453]

§8.216 The origins of *Bank Act* section 427 security, can be traced back to the 1890 revisions of the *Bank Act*. The original purpose behind section 427 was to provide:

> ... a convenient and suitable means for the provision and application of capital to industry with the object that thus manufacturing and commercial enterprise in Canada may be encouraged.[454]

---

[450] S.C. 1991, c. 46.
[451] See, generally, *Bank of Montreal v. Hall*, [1990] S.C.J. No. 9, 65 D.L.R. (4th) 361 at 369-70, *per* La Forest J.
[452] [1964] S.C.J. No. 40, 47 D.L.R. (2d) 141 at 166.
[453] *Ibid.*, at 145: the reasoning adopted by that learned judge seems more inclined towards making the terms of the legislation conform to the obvious requirements of business, than in giving effect to the strict wording of the statute.
[454] *Bank of Montreal v. Guaranty Silk Dyeing & Finishing Co.*, [1935] O.J. No. 254, [1935] 4 D.L.R. 483 at 489 (C.A.), *per* Masten J.A.

It did so, first, by expanding the power of a bank to lend on certain types of security and, second, by providing a statutory prescribed form of security agreement and a simplified method of registering any security so taken. By these methods the transaction costs of security were reduced: section 427 permits a bank officer to complete the documentation required to obtain the security without legal assistance. Unfortunately, simplicity has been bought at a price. Section 427 security is to some extent incompatible with provincial personal property security legislation, provides a cumbersome second system of registration which largely negates the transaction costs savings that the PPSA system was intended to afford, and gives comparatively little protection to debtors and other parties interested in the collateral against which the security is taken.

§8.217 A strong argument can be made that the special *Bank Act* security provisions are anachronistic and ought to be repealed. The only apparent rationale for their continuation is that banks consistently lobby in support of them because they allow banks a slight competitive advantage over non-bank financial institutions in such areas as agricultural financing and field warehousing. Since overconcentration in the Canadian financial industry is self-evident, there is little general economic advantage in providing banks with such a competitive edge. As Judson J. noted in *Flintoft v. Royal Bank*,[455] no other country in the world provides for this sort of security. None of them seem to have suffered by its absence. The Supreme Court of Canada had the opportunity to strike down the whole scheme as unconstitutional in *Bank of Montreal v. Hall*,[456] but it shied away from doing so. Given the economic and political clout of Canada's banks, it seems likely that special *Bank Act* security will be with us for some time to come.

(a) Nature of Section 427 Security

§8.218 The nature of the security conferred under section 427 of the *Bank Act*[457] and the rights that flow from it are not easily described. To say the least, the relevant provisions are not clearly drafted. Although courts have occasionally tried to categorize it within the traditional common law fixed/floating charge dichotomy and to compare it to one of the traditionally recognized forms of security,[458] the most appropriate description would be that it is a security of a special and specific statutory nature which incorporates selectively individual features of both fixed and floating charges. Section 427(2) of the *Bank Act* provides that:

---

[455] [1964] S.C.J. No. 40, [1964] S.C.R. 631 at 634.
[456] [1990] S.C.J. No. 9, 65 D.L.R. (4th) 361 (S.C.C.).
[457] S.C. 1991, c. 46.
[458] *Ford Motor Co. of Canada v. Manning Mercury Sales Ltd.*, [1996] S.J. No. 657, 43 C.B.R. (3d) 84 at 101 (C.A.), *per* Jackson J.A., leave to appeal to S.C.C. refused [1996] S.C.C.A. No. 627. See also *British Columbia v. Federal Business Development Bank*, [1987] B.C.J. No. 1834, [1988] 1 W.W.R. 1 at 12-13 (C.A.), *per* Lambert J.A.

427.(2) Delivery of a document giving security on property to a bank under the authority of this section vests in the bank in respect of the property therein described,

(a) of which the person giving the security is the owner at the time of the delivery of the document, or

(b) of which that person becomes the owner at any time thereafter before the release of security by the bank, whether or not the property is in existence at the time of delivery,

the following rights and powers, namely,

(c) if the property is property on which security is given under paragraph (1)(a), (b), (g), (h), (i) (j) or (o) under paragraph (1)(c) or (m) consisting of aquacultural implements, under paragraph (1)(d) or (n) consisting of agricultural implements or under paragraph (1)(p) consisting of forestry implements, the same rights and powers as if the bank had acquired a warehouse receipt or bill of lading in which that property was described, or

(d) if the property

   (i) is property of which security is given under paragraph (1)(c) consisting of aquacultural stock growing or produced in the aquacultural operation or aquacultural equipment,

   (ii) is property on which security is given under paragraph (1)(d) consisting of crops or agricultural equipment,

   (iii) is property on which security is given under any of paragraphs (1)(e), (f), (k) and (l),

   (iv) is property on which security is given under paragraph (1)(m) consisting of aquacultural equipment,

   (v) is property on which security is given under paragraph (1)(n) consisting of agricultural equipment, or

   (vi) is property on which security is given under paragraph (1)(p) consisting of forestry equipment,

a first and preferential lien and claim thereon for the sum secured and interest thereon, and as regards a crop as well before as after the severance from the soil, harvesting or threshing thereof, and, in addition thereto, the same rights and powers in respect of the property as if the bank had acquired a warehouse receipt or bill of lading in which the property was described, and all rights and powers of the bank subsist notwithstanding that the property is affixed to real property and notwithstanding that the person giving the security is not the owner of that real property,

and all such property in respect of which such rights and powers are vested in the bank under this section is for the purposes of this Act property covered by the security.

Subsection 428(1) goes on to provide that the rights and powers of a bank in respect of property covered by a security given to the bank under section 427 are the same as if the bank had acquired a warehouse receipt or bill of lading in which that property was described, and subject to the registration requirements imposed under subsections 427(4) and 428(3) to (6) have priority over all rights subsequently acquired in or in respect of that property, and also over the claim of any unpaid vendor. However, in the case of an unpaid vendor, subsection 428(2) further provides:

> 428.(2) The priority referred to in subsection (1) does not extend over the claim of any unpaid vendor who had a lien on the property at the time of the acquisition of the bank of the warehouse receipt, bill of lading or security, unless the same was acquired without knowledge on the part of the bank of that lien, and where security is given to the bank under paragraph 427(1)(c) or (m) consisting of aquacultural equipment, under paragraph 427(1)(d) or (n) consisting of agricultural equipment, under paragraph 427(1)(k) consisting of aquacultural equipment or aquacultural electric system, under paragraph 427(1)(l) consisting of agricultural equipment or a farm electric system or under paragraph 427(1)(p) consisting of forestry equipment, that priority shall exist notwithstanding that the property is or becomes affixed to real property.

The power of the bank to take possession of the property is generally deferred by the Act until such time as there is a default by the borrower, subsection 427(3) providing:

> 427.(3) Where security on any property is given to a bank under any of paragraphs (1)(c) to (p), the bank in addition to and without limitation of any other rights or powers vested in or conferred on it, has full power, right and authority, through its officers, employees or agents, in the case of,
>
> (a) non-payment of any of the loans or advances for which the security was given,
>
> (b) failure to care for or harvest any crop or to care for any livestock covered by the security,
>
> (c) failure to care for or harvest any aquatic stock growing or produced in the aquaculture operation or to care for any aquatic plants and animals covered by the security,
>
> (d) failure to care for any property on which security is given under any of paragraphs (1)(i) to (p),
>
> (e) any attempt, without the consent of the bank, to dispose of any property covered by the security, or
>
> (f) seizure of any property covered by the security,
>
> to take possession of or seize the property covered by the security, and in the case of aquacultural stock growing or produced in the aquacultural operation or a crop growing or produced on the farm to care for it and, where applicable, harvest it or thresh the grain therefrom, and, in the case of livestock or aquatic plans and animals to care for them, and has the right and authority to enter any land, premises or site whenever necessary for any such purpose and to detach and remove such property, exclusive of wiring, conduits or piping incorporated in a building, from any real property to which it is affixed.

§8.219 These rather convoluted provisions have been much discussed in the case law. It has been held on the highest authority that a bank taking security under section 427 of the *Bank Act* effectively acquires legal title to the borrower's interest in the present and after-acquired property assigned to it by the borrower.

The bank's interest attaches to the assigned property upon the later of the time when the security is given or when the borrower acquires the property[459] and remains attached until released by the bank, despite changes in the attributes or composition of the assigned property. The borrower retains an equitable right of redemption, but the bank effectively acquires whatever legal title or other rights the borrower holds in the assigned property from time to time.[460] The bank does not, however, acquire rights greater than those of the debtor.[461] So, for instance, any receivables against which the bank acquires security are subject to all set-offs to which the customers are entitled against the borrower.[462] Similarly, if the debtor acquires assets subject to a section 427 security under a conditional sale agreement or comparable title retention arrangement, the bank's claim against those assets is subject to the right of the seller or its assignee (assuming that all steps have been taken to perfect the seller's or assignee's interest),[463] although by virtue of its "first lien" the bank will enjoy priority over subsequently registered security interests — including non-title retention purchase money security interests — despite the fact that such interests would enjoy priority against *Bank Act* type security if it were perfected under legislation comparable to Ontario's *Personal Property Security Act*. On the other hand, there is now a growing body of case law which holds that proceeds derived from inventory subject to a security under the *Bank Act* may be applied to meet expenses arising in the ordinary course of business.[464]

(b) Procedure for Taking the Security — Overview

§8.220 At the present time, the *Bank Act*[465] permits section 427 security to be taken from: (a) wholesale or retail purchasers, shippers or dealers; (b) manufacturers; (c) farmers; (d) fishermen; (e) foresters. The types of asset against which security may be taken may generally be divided into three classes: (1) tangible personal property, particularly property used for productive purposes; (2) inventory and similar goods, including growing crops, minerals and hydrocarbons; (3) proceeds from the sale or disposition of the foregoing.

§8.221 In comparison to the PPSA,[466] the *Bank Act* security provisions impose a somewhat inflexible security regime upon the parties to a secured lending trans-

---

[459] *Devries v. Royal Bank of Canada*, [1975] O.J. No. 2290, 58 D.L.R. (3d) 43 (H.C.J.), aff'd [1975] O.J. No. 2610 (C.A.).
[460] *Bank of Montreal v. Hall*, [1990] S.C.J. No. 9, 65 D.L.R. (4th) 361 at 370, *per* La Forest J.
[461] See, generally, *McLachlan v. Canadian Imperial Bank of Commerce*, [1985] B.C.J. No. 886, 58 C.B.R. (N.S.) 113 (S.C.).
[462] *Mercantile Bank v. Leon's Furniture Ltd.*, [1992] O.J. No. 2753, 98 D.L.R. (4th) 449 (C.A.).
[463] *Rogerson Lumber Co. v. Four Seasons Chalet Ltd.*, [1980] O.J. No. 3651, 113 D.L.R. (3d) 671 (C.A.); *Bank of Nova Scotia v. International Harvester Credit Corp.*, [1990] O.J. No. 1702, 73 D.L.R. (4th) 385 (C.A.); *Kawai Canada Music Ltd. v. Encore Music Ltd.* (1993), 101 D.L.R. (4th) 1 (Alta. C.A.).
[464] *Ford Motor Co. of Canada v. Manning Mercury Sales Ltd.*, [1996] S.J. No. 657, 43 C.B.R. (3d) 84 at 109 (C.A.), *per* Jackson J.A., leave to appeal to S.C.C. refused [1996] S.C.C.A. No. 627.
[465] S.C. 1991, c. 46.
[466] R.S.O. 1990, c. P.10.

action. The following steps must be taken in correct sequence in order to create a valid section 427 security.

- A prospective borrower from a bank must complete an application for credit which contains an undertaking or promise to give section 427 security.

- A notice of intention to give section 427 security, in the form of Schedule III to the *Registration of Bank Special Security Regulations*,[467] must be filed with the Bank of Canada or an agent of the Bank of Canada. The notice must be filed no more than three years prior to the actual giving of security (*i.e.*, a notice filed after the giving of security is invalid),[468] but this is the only registration that is required (*i.e.*, it is not necessary to make any filing once the security is actually given nor of the security agreement itself). The registration of the notice of intention lapses five years after the date of initial registration unless it is renewed or earlier terminated.

- The borrower must execute an assignment of the relevant collateral in the form of Schedule II to the *Registration of Bank Special Security Regulations*. The completion of this form by the borrower constitutes the actual grant of section 427 security. It would appear that any substantial deviation from this form will take the security outside the scope of the *Bank Act*, although both subsection 427(1) of the Act and the federal *Interpretation Act* would appear to countenance minor variations.[469]

- At the time of granting the section 427 security, the borrower also completes a loan agreement concerning loans and advances with the bank, which governs the lending relationship between the bank and the borrower. It is not entirely clear whether a bank may convert an unsecured loan to a secured loan by opening a second secured loan which is used to "pay" the first unsecured loan.[470]

The failure of a bank to register a notice of intention before taking security under section 427 does not invalidate the security for all purposes. It remains valid against the debtor corporation and against the holder of a prior registered floating security[471] (at least in non-PPSA provinces; in PPSA provinces, the priority provisions of the *Personal Property Security Act* would appear to subordinate the unregistered *Bank Act* security to the claim of the holder of the PPSA interest, as the old law regarding crystallization and the priority of floating charges no longer applies).

---

[467] SOR/92-301.
[468] *Bank Act*, s. 427(4)(*a*).
[469] Section 32 of the *Interpretation Act*, R.S.C. 1985, c. I-21 provides:

32. Where a form is prescribed, deviations from that form, not affecting the substance or calculated to mislead, do not invalidate the form used.

[470] See *Boutique Andre Bibeau Inc. (Syndicate) v. Ernst & Whinney Inc.*, [1987] J.Q. no. 1405, [1987] R.J.Q. 1694 (C.A.); *Berryland Canning Co. v. Toronto Dominion Bank*, [1971] S.J. No. 106, 20 D.L.R. (3d) 3; *Canadian Imperial Bank of Commerce v. Fletcher*, [1978] O.J. No. 3222, 82 D.L.R. (3d) 257 (H.C.J.).
[471] *Discovery Enterprises v. Hong Kong Bank of Canada*, [1994] B.C.J. No. 1205, 20 B.L.R. (2d) 34 at 41-43 (S.C.), *per* Edwards J., rev'd [1995] B.C.J. No. 1362 (C.A.).

§8.222 Subsection 427(1) of the *Bank Act* sets out both the permitted classes of borrower and the permitted classes of security. The section is drafted in somewhat archaic language (*e.g.*, "products of agriculture" as opposed to a more contemporary "agricultural products"), which tends to make it difficult to read and understand. Traditionally section 427 security has been used to finance agricultural, fisheries and industrial production, particularly by small and medium sized enterprises. In 1954, the *Bank Act* was amended to permit security of this type to be taken in respect of hydrocarbons and related rights, licences and permits. The 1980 revisions allowed such security to be taken on minerals and on goods acquired by retail purchasers as well. The primary change in the 1991 revision to the *Bank Act* was to allow security to be taken over aquacultural operations.

(c) Loans and Advances

§8.223 Subsection 427(1) of the *Bank Act*[472] provides that a bank may lend money and make advances on the security set out in the section. It follows that the section is only applicable in respect of loans and advances. Neither of these terms is defined in the Act, and surprisingly the scope of these two terms has not been judicially considered, either in the context of section 427 itself or its statutory forebears. While it cannot be stated categorically, it is possible that the section would be interpreted broadly to include within "advance" most types of credit accommodation provided by a bank to a borrower. For instance, a payment made by a bank to a third party on the strength of a section 427 security (*e.g.*, under a letter of credit) presumably would constitute an advance. Whether there is a commitment to make such payments is far less clear. Even more uncertain is the question of whether the person granting the security must draw a direct benefit in order to be brought within the scope of section 427. For instance, is the term "advance" sufficiently broad to include credit accommodation granted to a third party on the strength of a guarantee by a person giving the security?

(d) Conditions Precedent

§8.224 Subsection 429(1) of the *Bank Act*[473] specifies certain conditions that must be satisfied before a bank may take or hold a section 427 security, or a warehouse receipt or bill of lading as security:

> 429.(1) A bank shall not acquire or hold any warehouse receipt or bill of lading, or any security under section 427, to secure the payment of any debt, liability, loan or advance unless the debt, liability, loan or advance is contracted or made,
>
> (*a*) at the time of the acquisition thereof by the bank, or
>
> (*b*) on the written promise or agreement that a warehouse receipt or bill of lading or security under section 427 would be given to the bank, in which case the

---

[472] S.C. 1991, c. 46.
[473] *Ibid.*

debt, liability, loan or advance may be contracted or made before or at the time of or after that acquisition,

and such debt, liability, loan or advance may be renewed, or the time for the payment thereof extended, without affecting any security so acquired or held. It is this provision which results in the practice of requiring the borrower to sign a promise to give security. But this provision also prevents section 427 security from being taken to secure past advances, unless those advances were made on a written promise that such security would be given.

(e) PERMITTED BORROWERS AND SECURITY

§8.225 Under section 427 of the *Bank Act*[474] security may be granted to a bank only by specifically mentioned eligible borrowers and is further restricted in the case of each type of borrower it may be granted to only in respect of the specific type of collateral designated for that class. In this regard, paragraph 427(1)(*a*) provides that:

> 427.(1) A bank may lend money and make advances
>
> (*a*) to any wholesale or retail purchaser or shipper of, or dealer in, products of agriculture, products of aquaculture, products of the forest, products of the quarry and mine, products of the sea, lakes and rivers or goods, wares and merchandise, manufactured or otherwise, on the security of such products or goods, wares and merchandise and of goods, wares and merchandise used in or procured for the packing of such products or goods, wares and merchandise, ...

Paragraph (*a*) is by far the broadest of the various paragraphs of subsection 427(1), its scope contrasting significantly with a number of the other paragraphs in the section. Unlike several of the other paragraphs, paragraph (*a*) does not contain any wording suggesting that a person who gives security under that paragraph must be engaged in a business-related activity, either with respect to the asset over which the security is granted or otherwise. Until the 1980 revisions to the *Bank Act*, the clause had been limited to wholesale purchasers, shippers of, or dealers in inventory. The present paragraph permits a loan to be given "to any wholesale or retail purchaser ... of ... goods, wares and merchandise ... on the security of" such property. The result of this change in wording has been a significant broadening of the scope of the section. *Prima facie*, there would be few persons, indeed, who could not be brought within the category of retail purchaser of goods. In the previous version of the *Bank Act*, the term "goods" was given a very broad meaning, including all "articles of commerce".[475] This definition does not appear in the most recent revision of the Act, but subsection 425(1) of the present Act is to like effect. It is possible that the scope of the term "retail purchaser" might be given a narrow interpretation by the courts so as to restrict it to those who purchase at the retail level in connection with some commercial activity, and given the legislative history of the section, it might possibly be con-

---

[474] *Ibid.*
[475] *Bank Act*, R.S.C. 1970, c. B-1. s. 2(1).

fined to purchases made with a view to resale. However, there is no express requirement under the wording of the paragraph that the security given must relate to the purchase of the goods over which the security is granted, and the loan need not be for the purposes of financing the purchase; it is sufficient if it is granted by a person who is a wholesale or retail purchaser of goods. These two aspects of paragraph (*a*) would tend to militate against any such narrow construction.[476]

§8.226 Paragraph 427(1)(*b*) goes on to include manufacturers among the list of persons eligible to give security under the *Bank Act*. It provides that:

> 427.(1) A bank may lend money and make advances
>
> . . . . .
>
> (*b*) to any person engaged in business as a manufacturer, on the security of goods, wares and merchandise manufactured or produced by him or procured for such manufacture or production and of goods, wares and merchandise used in or procured for the packing of goods, wares and merchandise so manufactured or produced,

In contrast to paragraph 427(1)(*a*), paragraph 427(1)(*b*) permits security only where a person is "engaged in business" as a manufacturer. It would seem, therefore, that security may be given under this paragraph only if the borrower meets the test for carrying on business. Furthermore, it is clear from the wording of paragraph (b) that security may not be granted under it in respect of any assets that may be held by the borrower, but only in respect of those goods, wares and merchandise that are concerned with the manufacturing business. The term "manufacturer" is described broadly in subsection 425(1) of the *Bank Act* to mean:

> ... any person who manufactures or produces by hand, art, process or mechanical means any goods, wares and merchandise and without restricting the generality of the foregoing, includes a manufacturer of logs, timber or lumber, maltster, distiller, brewer, refiner and producer of petroleum, tanner, curer, packer, canner, bottler and a person who packs, freezes or dehydrates any goods, wares and merchandise.

§8.227 In addition to those engaged in the mining and manufacturing sectors, section 427 contains a number of paragraphs relating to the provision of security by farmers. The first of these is paragraphs 427(1)(*d*), which provides that:

> 427.(1) A bank may lend money and make advances
>
> . . . . .
>
> (*d*) to any farmer, on the security of crops growing or produced on the farm or on the security of agricultural equipment or agricultural implements,

The term "farmer" is broadly defined in subsection 425(1). It includes not only the actual farmer (*i.e.*, the person who raises the livestock, operates a dairy,

---

[476] As to the meaning of a security over "products of the quarry and mine", see *Provincial Bank of Canada v. Gagnon*, [1981] S.C.J. No. 66, [1981] 2 S.C.R. 98.

keeps bees, grows fruit or trees or who tills the soil), but also the owner, occupier, landlord or tenant of the farm on which these activities are conducted.

§8.228 It is again significant to note that paragraph (*d*) contains no purpose test. Security may be granted by any farmer under this section in respect of crops growing or produced on the same. There is no requirement that the security be given for a loan related to the farm enterprise. Thus it is arguable that security may be granted under section 427 by a farmer to secure a loan for any type of purpose.[477]

§8.229 Over and above providing for credit to farmers, paragraphs 427(1)(*c*) and (*e*) of the 1991 revisions to the *Bank Act* added a further new category of eligible borrower and security, namely that of the aquaculturist. Paragraph 427(1)(*c*) provides that:

> 427.(1) A bank may lend money and make advances
>
> . . . . .
>
> (*c*) to any aquaculturist, on the security of aquacultural stock growing or produced in the aquaculture operation or on the security of aquacultural equipment or aquacultural implements,

Subsection 425(1) defines the term "aquaculture" to mean the cultivation of aquatic plants and animals, with the term "aquaculturist" being given a broad definition comparable to that given to the term "farmer". Further capacity to make loans in the aquaculture field is conferred under paragraph 427(1)(*e*), which provides that:

> 427.(1) A bank may lend money and make advances
>
> . . . . .
>
> (*e*) to any aquaculturist
>
> > (i) for the purchase of aquatic broodstock or aquatic seedstock, on the security of the aquatic broodstock or aquatic seedstock and any aquatic stock to be grown therefrom,
> >
> > (ii) for the purchase of pesticides on the security of the pesticide and any aquatic stock to be grown from the site on which the pesticide is to be used, and
> >
> > (iii) for the purchase of feed, veterinary drugs, biologicals or vaccines, on the security of the feed, veterinary drugs, biologicals or vaccines and any aquatic stock to be grown in the aquaculture operation on which the feed, veterinary drugs, biologicals or vaccines are to be used,

Essentially, paragraphs (*d*) and (*e*) fill in the gap between the provisions of section 427 pertaining to farmers and fishermen. As should be fairly clear, while

---

[477] The scope of para. 427(1)(*d*) was considered by the Ontario Court of Appeal in *Bank of Montreal v. Elgin Co-operative Services*, [1983] O.J. No. 3227, 48 C.B.R. (N.S.) 245 at 247 (C.A.).

paragraph (*c*) imposes no purpose test, such a test is imposed under paragraph (*e*).

§8.230 The next provision dealing with the giving of security by farmers is paragraph 427(1)(*f*) which provides that:

> 427.(1) A bank may lend money and make advances
>
> . . . . .
>
> (*f*) to any farmer
>
> > (i) for the purchase of seed grain or seed potatoes, on the security of the seed grain or the seed potatoes and any crop to be grown therefrom, and
> >
> > (ii) for the purchase of fertilizer or pesticide, on the security of the fertilizer or pesticide and any crop to be grown from land on which, in the same season, the fertilizer or pesticide is to be used,

Viewed in the juxtaposition to paragraph (*c*), it is difficult to understand why paragraph 427(1)(*f*) is drafted in such restrictive terms. Not only must a loan or advance under paragraph (*f*) be advanced for a specific purpose, the security is limited by time so that the credit is effectively limited to a single growing season. Perhaps the narrow scope of paragraph (*f*) was intended to protect farmers from being tied to a single source of credit from one growing season to another, although the breadth of paragraph (*c*) effectively undermines any protection so afforded. Thus paragraph (*c*) stands in contrast to subsection 32(1) of the PPSA, which effectively prevents the extension of crop financing for two or more crop-growing seasons. It is hard to imagine a situation in which security might be granted under paragraph (*f*) but not under paragraph (*c*). However, the section does permit a farmer to provide single-season security only if he (or she) is able to convince his bank to grant credit on the strength of such limited security.

§8.231 Following paragraph (*f*), paragraph 427(1)(*h*) goes on to provide that:

> 427.(1) A bank may lend money and make advances:
>
> . . . . .
>
> (*h*) to any farmer or to any person engaged in livestock raising, on the security of feed or livestock, but security taken under this paragraph is not effective in respect of any livestock that, at the time the security is taken, by any statutory law that is then in force, is exempt from seizure under writs of execution and the farmer or other person engaged in livestock raising is prevented from giving as security for money lent to the farmer of the other person,

Paragraph 427(1)(*g*) contains a similar provision with respect to aquaculturalists and aquatic plants and animals. Paragraphs 427(1)(*g*) and (*h*) are the animal husbandry equivalents to paragraph 427(1)(*f*). The term "livestock" is normally taken to include all domestic animals, such as horses, cattle and sheep, that are kept for farm purposes. The *Bank Act* definition in subsection 425(1) is more specific but would seem to be equally broad. It includes,

> (*a*) horses and other equines;

(b) cattle, sheep, goats and other ruminants; and

(c) swine, poultry, bees and fur-bearing animals.

For its part, the term "aquatic plants and animals" is also given a broad definition in subsection 425(1). It means "plants and animals that, at most stages of their development or life cycles, live in an aquatic environment". The words "at most stages of their development" may be quite significant in the case of certain types of amphibious creatures, which spend the bulk of their lives living on land, but spend most of their developmental stages in water.

§8.232 In contrast to paragraph 427(1)(*f*), paragraph 427(1)(*h*) contains no purpose qualification — the security need not relate to the financing of any aspect of the farmer's farm operations. However, the livestock to which the security relates must be the livestock that the farmer is engaged in "raising". This results in the somewhat arbitrary distinction that a horse breeder may give section 427 security on his horses, but a fruit farmer who keeps a stable of horses on his farm may not.

§8.233 Paragraph 427(1)(*j*) of the Act provides that:

> 427.(1) A bank may lend money and make advances,
>
> . . . . .
>
> (*j*) to any farmer for the purchase of agricultural implements, on the security of those agricultural implements,

Paragraph (*i*) provides a comparable power in the case of acquacultural implements. Like paragraph (*f*), paragraphs 427(1)(*i*) and (*j*) would also seem to be subsumed within the scope of paragraph 427(1)(*d*). Paragraphs (*i*) and (*j*) are clearly purpose related: the security must relate to the purchase of the agricultural implements in respect of which the security is given. The Act draws an apparent but unclear distinction between agricultural "implements" and "equipment". As discussed below, a section 427 security interest in agricultural "equipment" must be registered under the land registry/land titles system, as well as under the *Bank Act* in order to be perfected. This would seem to suggest that agricultural "equipment" consists only of those things which attach to the land as fixtures.

§8.234 Paragraph 427(1)(*l*) of the Act next provides that:

> 427.(1) A bank may lend money and make advances
>
> . . . . .
>
> (*l*) to any farmer for the purchase or installation of agricultural equipment or a farm electric system, on the security of such agricultural equipment or farm electric system, ...

Paragraph (*k*) provides a comparable power in the case of acquacultural equipment. As with paragraph (*i*), paragraphs (*k*) and (*l*) are purpose limited — the security must relate to the purchase of agricultural equipment and only that agricultural equipment that is being financed may be included in the security under paragraphs (*k*) and (*l*). Because of these purpose restrictions, paragraphs (*k*) and (*l*) would seem to be redundant given the scope of paragraphs (*c*) and (*d*).

§8.235 Paragraph 427(1)(*n*) of the Act provides that:

> 427.(1) A bank may lend money and make advances
>
> . . . . .
>
> (*n*) to any farmer for
>
> > (i) the repair or overhaul of an agricultural implement, agricultural equipment or a farm electric system,
> >
> > (ii) the alteration or improvement of a farm electric system,
> >
> > (iii) the erection or construction of fencing or works for drainage on a farm,
> >
> > (iv) the construction, repair or alteration of or making of additions to any building or structure on a farm,
> >
> > (v) any works for the improvement or development of a farm for which a farm improvement loan as defined in the *Farm Improvement Loans Act* may be made, and
> >
> > (vi) any purpose for which a loan as defined in the *Farm Improvement and Marketing Cooperatives Loans Act* may be made,

on the security of agricultural equipment or agricultural implements, but security taken under this paragraph is not effective in respect of agricultural equipment or agricultural implements that, at the time security is taken, by any statutory law that is then in force, are exempt from seizure under writs of execution and the farmer is prevented from giving as security for money lent to the farmer,

Paragraph (*m*) sets out a similar power in the case of an aquaculturist. For the most part these provisions do little more than extend the purchase money security provided for in other clauses to cover the repair or improvement of the equipment or implements. However, they also allow security to be given in the case of virtually any improvement to the farm or farm property.

§8.236 Leaving the fields of farm and acquaculture financing, paragraph 427(1)(*o*) of the *Bank Act* permits a fisherman to obtain credit by way of section 427 security, as it provides that:

> 427.(1) A bank may lend money and make advances
>
> . . . . .
>
> (*o*) to any fisherman, on the security of fishing vessels, fishing equipment and supplies or products of the sea, lakes and rivers, but security taken under this paragraph is not effective in respect of any such property that, at the time the security is taken, by any statutory law that is then in force, is exempt from seizure under writs of execution and the fisherman is prevented from giving as security for money lent to the fisherman, . . .

Much like paragraph (*c*), paragraph (*o*) contains no purpose requirement. A fisherman may obtain a loan or advance under security granted under this paragraph irrespective of whether the loan or advance so obtained relates to his fishing operation.

§8.237 Paragraph 427(1)(*p*) completes the industrial cycle begun with wholesalers and retailers in paragraph (*a*) by extending the availability of section 427 security to forestry producers, as it provides that:

> 427.(1) A bank may lend money and make advances
>
> . . . . .
>
> (*p*) to any forestry producer on the security of fertilizer, pesticide, forestry equipment, forestry implements or products of the forest, but security taken under this paragraph is not effective in respect of any such property that, at the time the security is taken, by any statutory law that is then in force, is exempt from seizure under writs of execution and the forestry producer is prevented from giving as security for money lent to the forestry producer,

The effect of section 427 therefore is that financing under that section is now available to virtually all primary and secondary Canadian industries, but such financing remains unavailable in the service industry (which paradoxically is the fasting growing sector of the economy).

(2) Section 426 Security

§8.238 Section 426 of the *Bank Act*[478] creates a scheme of security applicable to hydrocarbons, minerals and the rights relating thereto. Although appearing first in sequence, section 426 security is very much an extension of section 427 security. The forerunner to section 426 was introduced into the *Bank Act* in 1954 to permit banks to finance the development of the petroleum industry following the major oil discoveries of the late 1940s. When the *Bank Act* was revised in 1980, section 426 (then section 177) was expanded to include "minerals" as well as hydrocarbons. There has been little if any case law with respect to the meaning of this section, and (in Ontario at least) security is only rarely taken under this section.

§8.239 The *Bank Act*'s scheme of security for hydrocarbons and minerals is created in subsection 426(1) of the Act, which provides:

> 426.(1) A bank may lend money and make advances on the security of any or all of the following, namely,
>
> (*a*) hydrocarbons or minerals in, under or on the ground, in place or in storage,
>
> (*b*) the rights, licences or permits of any person to obtain and remove any such hydrocarbons or minerals and to enter on, occupy and use lands from or on which any of such hydrocarbons or minerals are or may be extracted, mined or produced,

---

[478] S.C. 1991, c. 46.

(c) the estate or interest of any person in or to any such hydrocarbons or minerals, rights, licences, permits and lands whether the estate or interest is entire or partial, and

(d) the equipment and casing used or to be used in extracting, mining or producing or seeking to extract, mine or produce, and storing any such hydrocarbons or minerals,

or of any rights or interests in or to any of the foregoing whether the security be taken from the borrower or from a guarantor of the liability of the borrower or from any other person.

Section 426 differs from section 427 of the Act in that it expressly contemplates a grant of security under its provisions by a guarantor.

§8.240 The term "hydrocarbons" is defined in section 425(1) of the Act to mean:

... solid, liquid and gaseous hydrocarbons and any natural gas, whether consisting of a single element or of two or more elements in chemical combination or uncombined and, without restricting the generality of the foregoing, includes oil-bearing shale, tar sands, crude oil, petroleum, helium and hydrogen sulphide;

For its part, the term "minerals" is defined in subsection 425(1) as follows:

"minerals" includes base and precious metals, coal, salt and every other substance that is an article of commerce obtained from the earth by any method of extraction, but does not include hydrocarbons or any animal or vegetable substance other than coal;

In contrast, the term "products of the quarry and mine" (a term appearing in section 427) includes:

... stone, clay, sand, gravel, metals, ores, coal, salt, precious stones, metalliferous and non-metallic minerals and hydrocarbons, whether obtained by excavation, drilling or otherwise.

There is thus a fair degree of overlap among the three provisions, particularly when one considers the possibility that coal may be gasified or liquefied.

§8.241 Security may be given under section 426 separately under each of the paragraphs. In other words, the same debtor may give security separately and to different lenders with respect to hydrocarbons, the licence which it holds to remove those hydrocarbons and the equipment used to extract them. If it is intended to obtain security against the entire mining or drilling operation, it is important to ensure that security is obtained under all of the clauses. If not, the bank may find that it has only partial security, which may greatly complicate the process of realization.

§8.242 Security may be given under section 426 over both hydrocarbons or minerals that are in place or those that are in storage. This again raises the possibility that different lenders may obtain security with respect to the same hydrocarbons at particular stages of production. The risk of splitting security is augmented because under paragraph 427(1)(a) of the *Bank Act*, security may be taken in products of the quarry and mine. As the definition of "products of the quarry and mine" expressly includes minerals and hydrocarbons, it would also appear that security may be taken against minerals or hydrocarbons "in storage" under section 427. It is not clear whether the availability of section 427 security with respect to such hydrocarbons is intended to exclude the giving of security under section 426. Obviously the safest course from the perspective of the lender is to ensure that valid security is obtained under both sections and in particular to see that the appropriate steps are taken to perfect the security under both sections. If, however, such double security is not obtained it is at least arguable that valid security may be obtained under either section. There is a fair amount of redundancy within section 427 itself, and the view which the courts have taken is that the availability of security under one clause does not prevent the taking of security in the same subject matter under another clause. By extension, it would follow that the availability of security under section 426 does not prevent security being taken in the same collateral under section 427. One potential problem with relying upon section 426 only is that the section makes no provision that any security granted under it will extend to any proceeds realized on the disposition of the collateral. However, the decision of the Supreme Court of Canada in *Re Canadian Western Millwork Ltd. v. Royal Bank of Canada*; *Flintoft v. Royal Bank of Canada*[479] would suggest that irrespective of this omission, the security will so extend.

§8.243 Subsection 426(2) of the Act provides that security given under that section may extend to property,

 (a) of which the person giving the security is the owner at the time of the delivery of the instrument, or

 (b) of which that person becomes the owner at any time thereafter before the release of the security by the bank, whether or not the property is in existence at the time of the delivery,

all of which property is for the purpose of this Act property covered by the security.

In contrast to section 427, section 426 of the Act does not provide that the bank becomes the legal owner of the secured property once security is given. Instead, the bank's interest is in the nature of a fixed charge. Once the section 426 security interest is duly registered, it will have priority over subsequently registered interests or rights.

§8.244 Subsection 426(11) of the Act provides that when making a loan or advance on section 426 security, a bank may take any further security it sees fit on any property covered by the security. The Act does not specify whether the effect of taking such further security is to merge the section 426 security into the new security so taken. Presumably subsection (11) was intended to permit the bank to take further security without risk of such merger.

---

[479] [1964] S.C.J. No. 40, [1964] S.C.R. 631, 7 C.B.R. (N.S.) 78.

§8.245 Subsection 426(12) of the Act makes specific provision with respect to the substitution of security. It reads:

> 426.(12) Notwithstanding anything in this Act, where the bank holds any security covering hydrocarbons or minerals, it may take in lieu of that security, to the extent of the quantity covered by the security taken, any security covering or entitling it to the delivery of the same hydrocarbons or minerals or hydrocarbons or minerals of the same or a similar grade or kind.

(a) Procedure for Taking and Perfecting Section 426 Security

§8.246 The procedure set out in section 426 of the *Bank Act*[480] for taking such security is similar in approach to the procedure set out in section 427 for taking security under that section. A section 426 security is created where a borrower signs and delivers to a bank an assignment in the form set out in Schedule I to the *Registration of Bank Special Security Regulations*,[481] or in a form to like effect.[482] Although it is clear that it is not absolutely necessary to use the statutory form, great care should be exercised in departing from that form as any deviation may result in a dispute as to whether the form used is truly "to like effect" as required by the statute. Schedule I provides that the borrower assigns the property described in the schedule to the bank as a continuing security for the payment of all loans and advances made or to be made to the borrower by the bank.

§8.247 It follows that section 426 security is not appropriate (from the borrower's perspective) as security for a discrete indebtedness, such as a term loan. If section 426 security is provided for such a loan, the borrower should insist upon a covenant by the bank to deliver up and cancel the security upon repayment.

(b) Priority of Section 426 Security

§8.248 The relative priority of the bank's claim once a Schedule I security under the *Registration of Bank Special Security Regulations*[483] has been given is set out in subsection 426(7) of the *Bank Act*,[484] which reads:

> 426.(7) Subject to subsections (8), (9) and (10) all of the rights and powers of a bank in respect of the property covered by security given under this section have priority over all rights subsequently acquired in, or in respect of such property and also over the claim of any mechanics' lien holder or of any unpaid vendor of equipment or casing but this priority does not extend over the claim of any unpaid vendor who had a lien on the equipment or casing at the time of the acquisition by

---

[480] S.C. 1991, c. 46.
[481] SOR/92-301.
[482] *Bank Act*, S.C. 1991, c. 46, s. 426(2).
[483] SOR/92-301.
[484] S.C. 1991, c. 46.

the bank of the security, unless the security was acquired without knowledge on the part of the bank of that lien.

Thus the bank acquires a superior right in the collateral to that of the borrower in respect of any subsequent interest — a far broader grant of priority than that which applies under section 427.

§8.249 The scheme of perfecting the security (*i.e.*, registration) provided for in section 426 of the *Bank Act* differs significantly from the corresponding scheme set out in section 427. In contrast to section 427, section 426 does not provide for the registration of a notice of intention with the Bank of Canada. Instead, the perfection of section 426 security depends entirely upon provincial registration schemes. Essentially, subsection 426(8) of the Act provides that unless a bank has registered its security in the appropriate provincial land registry or land titles office or other provincial office in which the relevant rights, licences or permits are recorded, its security interest will be subordinate to the interests or rights of other persons in the same collateral. More specifically, in most cases the bank is required to register or file one of the following,

- an original of the instrument giving the bank its security interest;
- a copy of that instrument, certified by an officer or employee of the bank; or
- a caution, caveat or memorial in respect of the rights of the bank,

the appropriate method in each case depending upon the registration or filing requirements of the office in which the registration or filing is to be made. These registration or filing requirements do not apply (1) where the province does not permit the registration of the interests in question (in point of fact, Ontario and most if not all of the other provinces do permit the registration of these interests); or (2) in the case of unpatented Crown land owned by the Crown in right of Canada, as there is no registration scheme in effect with respect to such lands.

(xiii) Receivers and Receiver-Managers

§8.250 In the case of most commercial loans, especially lines of credit, the lender's remedy of choice is the appointment of a receiver-manager to take custody of the borrower's assets, so that the assets may be sold on a going-concern basis, or otherwise liquidated in an orderly fashion. Historically, a distinction has been drawn between receivers and receiver-managers. A receiver is a person appointed to collect and receive rents, debts and other amounts payable to the borrower and to realize upon the existing inventory of the borrower. In contrast, a receiver-manager possesses the additional power of assuming management of the borrower's business and affairs.[485] As a general rule, every security agreement that provides for a receiver should be drafted to make it clear that a receiver-manager may be appointed, as this accords the creditor much greater flexibility and control in the enforcement of the security and the realization of the collateral.

---

[485] *Re Manchester & Milford Rlwy.* (1880), 14 Ch. D. 645 at 653 (C.A.), *per* Jessell M.R.

§8.251 In the absence of an agreement permitting the lender to do so, it has no power to appoint a private receiver merely because it holds a security interest over even the whole of the borrower's property. Where the agreement confers no such right, the lender must seek the appointment of a receiver-manager by the court. Where the security agreement provides for the appointment of a receiver-manager, the lender first must notify the debtor of any of the events of default, and (except in the case of a default in payment on a term loan) allow a reasonable time to rectify the default.[486]

§8.252 There are a number of restrictions upon the appointment of a receiver-manager. For instance, section 50 of the OBCA provides that a trustee under a trust indenture and any related person to the trustee shall not be appointed a receiver or receiver-manager or liquidator of the assets or undertaking of the issuer or guarantor of the debt obligations under the trust indenture. In addition, although the *Personal Property Security Act*[487] permits a lender and borrower to provide a right to appoint a receiver in a security agreement, subsection 60(2) of that Act provides that:

> 60.(2) Upon application of the secured party, the debtor or any other person with an interest in the collateral, and after notice to any other person that the court directs, the Superior Court of Justice, with respect to a receiver or receiver and manager however appointed, may,
>
> (a) remove, replace or discharge the receiver or receiver and manager;
>
> (b) give directions on any matter relating to the duties of the receiver or receiver and manager;
>
> (c) approve the accounts and fix the remuneration of the receiver or receiver and manager;
>
> (d) make any order with respect to the receiver or receiver and manager that it thinks fit in the exercise of its general jurisdiction over a receiver or receiver and manager.

§8.253 Part IX of the CBCA contains a number of provisions respecting any receiver or receiver-manager appointed with respect to a corporation to which that Act applies. The Act maintains the traditional distinction between receivers and receiver-managers. Section 94 of the Act provides that a receiver of any property of a corporation may receive the income from the property and pay the liabilities connected with the property and realize the security interest of those on behalf of whom the receiver is appointed, but, except to the extent permitted by a court, the receiver may not carry on the business of a corporation.[488] In contrast, section 95 of the Act provides that a receiver of a corporation may, if he or she is also appointed receiver-manager of the corporation, carry on any business of the corporation to protect the security interest of those on whose behalf the

---

[486] See s. 244 of the *Bankruptcy and Insolvency Act*, R.S.C. 1985, c. B-3, discussed below at §8.256.

[487] R.S.O. 1990, c. P.10.

[488] The section also provides that the powers of the receiver are "subject to the rights of secured creditors".

receiver is appointed. Where a receiver-manager is appointed by a court or under an instrument, the powers of the directors of the corporation that the receiver-manager is authorized to exercise may not be exercised by the directors until the receiver-manager is discharged.[489] This provision would seemingly apply where a receiver is permitted to carry on the business of the corporation by an order of the court under section 94, for in such a case the receiver would be characterized as a receiver-manager, at least to the extent of the court order.

§8.254 The CBCA adheres to the traditional division between court appointed and privately appointed receivers. Section 97 of the Act provides that a receiver or receiver-manager appointed by a court must act in accordance with the directions of the court. In contrast, section 98 provides that a receiver or receiver-manager appointed under an instrument must act in accordance with the instrument but in so acting, the receiver or receiver-manager must act honestly and in good faith and deal with the property of the corporation in his possession or control in a commercially reasonable manner.[490] Thus the primary source of authority of a privately appointed receiver is the instrument under which he is appointed. However, those powers must be exercised in a manner consistent with the duties of the privately appointed receiver. Section 101 of the CBCA sets out the following specific duties applicable to every receiver and receiver-manager:

> 101. A receiver or receiver-manager shall,
>
> (*a*) immediately notify the Director of their appointment and discharge;
>
> (*b*) take into their custody and control the property of the corporation in accordance with the court order or instrument under which they are appointed;
>
> (*c*) open and maintain a bank account in their name as receiver or receiver-manager of the corporation for the moneys of the corporation coming under their control;
>
> (*d*) keep detailed accounts of all transactions carried out as receiver or receiver-manager;
>
> (*e*) keep accounts of their administration that shall be available during usual business hours for inspection by the directors of the corporation;
>
> (*f*) prepare at least once in every six month period after the date of their appointment financial statements of their administration as far as is practicable in the form required by section 155; and
>
> (*g*) on completion of their duties, render a final account of their administration in the form adopted for interim accounts under paragraph (f).

§8.255 The above provisions have now been supplemented by the receivership provisions set out in Part XI of the *Bankruptcy and Insolvency Act* ("BIA").[491] Under these provisions, the creditors and any trustee in bankruptcy may monitor the appointment of a receiver and review the receiver's conduct after the ap-

---

[489] CBCA, s. 96.
[490] CBCA, s. 98.
[491] R.S.C. 1985, c. B-3.

pointment, as well as the enforcement of security by a secured creditor. The BIA provisions apply only where the debtor is bankrupt or insolvent. While bankruptcy is a matter of legal status, insolvency is a question of fact on which opinions may differ. In certain cases, it may be unclear whether a debtor is insolvent. Receiverships in the absence of insolvency are possible but relatively rare. As a matter of prudence insolvency should normally be presumed whenever a receiver is appointed. However, in any proceeding where it is alleged that a secured creditor or a receiver contravened or failed to comply with any provisions of Part XI, it is a defence for the secured creditor or receiver to show that at the time of the alleged contravention or failure to comply he or she had reasonable grounds to believe that the debtor was not insolvent.

§8.256 Subsection 244(1) of the BIA provides that a secured creditor who intends to enforce a security on all or substantially all of the inventory, the accounts receivable or the other property of an insolvent person that was acquired for, or is used in relation to, a business carried on by the insolvent person shall send a notice of that intention to that person in the prescribed form and manner. The Act provides no explanation of the meaning of "enforce". Broadly construed it would include the appointment of a receiver or receiver-manager. Narrowly construed, it would be limited to actual realization on the collateral pledged as security.

§8.257 The term "receiver" is defined for the purposes of Part XI of the BIA (which deals with secured creditors and receivers) to mean a person who has been appointed to take, or has taken, possession or control of all or substantially all of the inventory, accounts receivable or other property of an insolvent person or a bankruptcy that was acquired for, or is used in relation to, a business carried on by the insolvent person or bankrupt. The receiver may be appointed either under a security agreement or a court order made under any law that provides for or authorizes the appointment of a receiver or receiver-manager.[492]

§8.258 Subsection 245(1) of the BIA provides that a receiver must send a notice of his or her appointment to the Superintendent and, in the case of a bankrupt, to the trustee, or in the case of an insolvent person, to the insolvent person and to all creditors of the insolvent person that the receiver, after making reasonable efforts, has ascertained. Subsection 245(2) further provides that a receiver in respect of property of an insolvent person must forthwith send a notice of his or her appointment to any creditor whose name and address he or she subsequently ascertains after sending the original notice. To facilitate the sending of notices, the insolvent person is required to provide the receiver with the names and addresses of all creditors forthwith after being notified that the receiver has been appointed.[493] These notices must be sent in the prescribed form and manner as soon as possible and in any event not later than 10 days after the appointment of

---

[492] *Bankruptcy and Insolvency Act*, s. 243(2).
[493] *Ibid.*, s. 245(3). In practical terms, this obligation is meaningless, because where a receiver is appointed his first step will be to exclude the debtor from the debtor's place of business.

the receiver. The notice to the Superintendent must be accompanied by the prescribed fee. With the exception of the payment of a fee to the Superintendent, none of these steps is particularly burdensome — nor are they particularly novel, since they are simply the steps that have usually been taken in a prudently conducted receivership.

§8.259 The receiver is required to prepare a number of formal statements concerning the conduct of the receivership which must be provided to interested parties. More particularly, subsection 246(1) provides that the receiver shall prepare a statement containing the prescribed information relating to the receivership and shall forthwith provide a copy of that statement to the Superintendent and to the insolvent person or its trustee, and to any creditor of the insolvent person or bankrupt who requests a copy of the statement at any time up to six months after the end of the receivership. The statement must be prepared forthwith after the receiver takes possession or control of the property of an insolvent person. It is not clear how a receiver would take possession of property yet not assume control of it, or take control of property but not be in possession of it, but should either unlikely event occur the obligation to prepare the statement is imposed upon the occurrence of the earlier of those two steps. The statement must contain the following information:[494]

- the name of each creditor of the insolvent person or bankrupt, the amount owed to each creditor and the total amount owing to the creditors;
- a list of the assets in the possession or under the control of the receiver and the book value of each asset; and
- the intended plan of action of the receiver during the receivership, to the extent that such a plan has been determined.

§8.260 In addition to the initial statement provided to the Superintendent, the insolvent debtor, and its creditors and trustee, the receiver is required under subsection 246(5) to provide further interim reports to those same persons. These reports provide for limited ongoing accounting with respect to the conduct of the receivership. They must set out an interim statement of receipts and disbursements, a statement of all property of which the receiver has taken possession or control that has not yet been sold or realized, and any other significant information about the operation of the receivership.[495] These statements must be prepared in the prescribed form and provided at least semi-annually to the persons entitled to them. At the conclusion of the receivership, the receiver is required to prepare a final report and statement of accounts to the Superintendent, the insolvent, its trustee and any creditor of the insolvent who request a copy of the statement at any time up to six months after the receivership. This statement must contain a final statement of receipts and disbursement, with such modifications as the circumstances require, an explanation of how the proceeds realized from the property of which the receiver had taken control or possession

---

[494] *Bankruptcy and Insolvency General Rules*, C.R.C. 1978, c. 368, s. 125.
[495] *Ibid.*, s. 126.

were distributed, details of the disposition of that property that is not accounted for in the final statement of receipts and disbursements, and any other significant information about the operation of the receivership.[496]

§8.261 The BIA also imposes a uniform minimum standard of conduct upon all receivers and empowers the court (which, in Ontario, means the Superior Court of Justice when the debtor is not a bankrupt)[497] to supervise the conduct of the receivership. In particular, section 247 of the BIA provides that a receiver shall act honestly and in good faith and deal with the property of the insolvent or bankrupt debtor in a commercially reasonable manner. Under section 248 of the BIA, the court has the power to make orders, on such terms as it considers appropriate, directing the secured creditor, receiver or insolvent person to carry out a duty imposed under sections 244 to 247. The court may also restrain the secured creditor or receiver, as the case may be, from realizing or otherwise dealing with the property of the insolvent or bankrupt until that duty has been carried out. The court has a further power to require a receiver to submit the receiver's final report and statement of account to the court for review, and to adjust the fees and charges of the receiver in such manner and to such extent as it considers appropriate.[498] Under section 249 of the Act, the receiver is entitled to apply to the court for directions in relation to any provision of Part XI of the BIA and where such an application is made, the court is required to give such written directions, if any, as it considers proper in the circumstances. Where there is any inconsistency between any order made or direction given by the court under these provisions and the terms of the security agreement or court order under which the receiver is appointed, the direction or order under section 248 or 249 of the BIA prevails to the extent of that inconsistency.[499]

E. REGISTERED DEBT SECURITIES

§8.262 One major contrast between shares and debt securities is that there is no requirement that the debt securities of a corporation be in registered form, although they quite often will be. One advantage of having a debt security in registered form is that it affords the corporation an opportunity to monitor dealings in its securities. This ability facilitates compliance by the corporation with the limitations that it must satisfy in order to continue to qualify for the private company exemption under the *Securities Act*.[500] The disadvantage of registered securities is that registration imposes the transaction costs associated with the maintenance of a registry. Moreover, a registration requirement may reduce the marketability of the securities concerned. Where a debt security is in registered form and an event has occurred which entitles the registered holders of

---

[496] *Ibid.*, s. 127.
[497] *Bankruptcy and Insolvency Act*, s. 243(1)(*b*).
[498] *Ibid.*, s. 248(2). This provision does not apply with respect to a court-appointed receiver: s. 243(3).
[499] *Ibid.*, s. 250(2).
[500] R.S.O. 1990, c. S.5.

the securities to vote, *mandamus* lies to compel the corporation to register securities in the names of their current holders, so as to permit them to vote.[501]

F. NEGOTIABLE DEBT SECURITIES

§8.263 As a trade facilitation mechanism, the early mercantile law evolved the concept of negotiability of certain types of instrument, as an alternative to assignment. Under the negotiability concept, the transferee of the contractual right acquires greater rights *vis-à-vis* the obligor under the contract, and may in fact be able to enforce the rights which it acquires even though the transferor would not have been able to enforce them. Moreover, the procedure for transfer under negotiability is greatly simplified. Specifically, it is not necessary to give notice of the transfer to the obligor. In addition, where an instrument is made negotiable by delivery, the transfer may be made without any kind of formal record being made of the transfer taking place. Originally, negotiability was limited to bills of exchange[502] and promissory notes,[503] but eventually the concept came to be extended to documents of title and certain corporate debt and equity securities. Subsection 53(3) of the OBCA formerly created a rebuttable presumption that the debt securities of a corporation are negotiable. This provision was repealed upon the enactment of the *Securities Transfer Act, 2006*.[504] However, long before this statutory rule was enacted the courts had held that the time was passed when the negotiability of corporate debt securities could be open to serious challenge.[505]

§8.264 Negotiability facilitates the making of payment and the transfer of funds. It reflects the clear commercial need for a method of making payment other than the actual delivery of cash. In the corporate securities area, negotiable instruments facilitate the granting of credit by simplifying trading within secondary securities markets. In the past century, their role in the economy has changed greatly. At present, their primary use lies in the money market, where they are traded under the name "commercial paper".

§8.265 In order to understand how the money market works it is important to remember that banks do not really lend borrowers their own money; rather, they lend money that they have themselves borrowed from other people. In most industrialized nations, there will be many non-bank financial institutions and trading companies that enjoy a general credit reputation on a par with or comparable to the credit reputation of a typical bank. For such a company, bank credit may be an expensive method of raising funds: the company might just as easily raise funds from the public as the bank. If it borrows from the bank, it will not only pay the bank's cost of credit, but will also be required to pay the bank a premium over the cost at which the bank borrowed funds from the public (oth-

---

[501] *Thompson v. Victoria Rlwy. Co.*, [1881] O.J. No. 345, 8 P.R. 423 (H.C.).
[502] As defined in the *Bills of Exchange Act*, R.S.C. 1985, c. B-4, s. 16(1).
[503] *Bills of Exchange Act*, R.S.C. 1985, c. B-4, s. 176(1).
[504] S.O. 2006, c. 8.
[505] *Edelstein v. Schuler & Co.*, [1902] 2 K.B. 144 at 155, *per* Bingham J.

erwise the bank will not make a profit). For small scale borrowers, it would not be practical to try to raise funds outside the banking system, since the transaction costs associated with the identification of potential lenders and the raising of funds from those lenders would exceed the cost saving achieved by borrowing from the public directly rather than from a bank. For large scale borrowers, the interest rate differential between the cost of bank borrowing and non-bank borrowing is likely to be sufficient to offset the transaction costs incurred by stepping outside the banking system.

§8.266 In order to raise funds from the investing public, borrowers issue commercial paper (*i.e.*, promissory notes and bills of exchange — the latter being usually in the form of a bankers' acceptance)[506] to public investors. Although interest-bearing notes may be issued, normally the paper is sold to investors at a discount. The discount represents the difference between the redemption price on the face of the note and the issuing price. The interest rate or discount amortized over the term of the note represents the issuer's cost of funds, and it will generally reflect the issuer's credit risk profile, with no "lender's premium" added. Either demand or term notes may be issued. In the latter case, maturities range from overnight to one year. In the United States, most commercial paper has an original maturity under 270 days, in order to qualify for an exemption from the regulatory requirements of the *Securities Act, 1933*.

§8.267 The principal investors in commercial paper include securities dealers, insurance companies, banks and near-bank financial institutions. It has long been recognized that there is a substantial secondary market for such instruments with the result that a substantial percentage of the total amount of commercial paper issued in any given year is bought with a view towards resale. The existence of this secondary market enhances the liquidity of the money market, and accordingly further reduces the cost of funds to issuers who seek to raise funds in that market. However, in order for the money market to work it is necessary for a great deal of protection to be given by the law to investors who deal in that market. They must have reasonable assurance of repayment. They must

---

[506] A bankers' acceptance is a special type of draft drawn on a bank that is issued by a borrower that has been approved by a bank for that purpose. The bill is then accepted by the bank. By accepting the bill, the bank assumes a liability for the underlying debt. The bill can then be sold to investors in the secondary market under the bank's name and credit rating. The investor thus enjoys the benefit of two payment commitments: that of the underlying borrower and also that of the bank. Bankers' acceptances are sold in bearer form at a discount to their face value. As a negotiable instrument, they can be resold freely in the secondary market at any time prior to maturity. It is not unusual for the accepting bank to repurchase its own acceptances. Such instruments are available in a variety of maturity dates out to a maximum of one year. They have a minimum investment amount of $100,000. Under the *Depository Bills and Notes Act*, S.C. 1998, c. 13 ("DBNA"), which is discussed briefly below, comparable obligations similar in substance to conventional bankers' acceptances may now be created by non-bank financial institutions. Under s. 11 of the DBNA, the acceptor of a depository bill is liable to provide the clearing house to which it is payable with funds so that the clearing house can pay on the due date and in accordance with its terms, the participants who have an interest in the depository bill. A depository bill under the *Depository Act* differs from a bankers' acceptance in that the bill must be made payable to a clearing house and deposited with the clearing house to which it is payable.

know that they can buy negotiable instruments without inquiry into the state of accounts between the issuer and the named payee or any other intervening holder. They must be able to determine with precision exactly what the note is worth.

§8.268 An instrument is negotiable where any person who acquired it in good faith and for value may enforce in his or her own name the contract in it or the proprietary right that it evidences against the persons liable on it. By long tradition, negotiable instruments have characteristics which separate them from other classes of legal obligation. The following are the key characteristics of such instruments: (1) negotiable instruments must be in writing; (2) they are presumed to be supported by good consideration, and therefore the consideration for such instruments need neither be stated nor proved; (3) they are transferable either by delivery (in the case of instruments payable to the bearer) or by endorsement and delivery (in the case of instruments payable to order) without more formal assignment, and upon transfer, the transferee is entitled to sue upon those instruments in his own name; (4) a transferee who takes the instrument in good faith for value and without notice of any defect in the title of the transferor obtains a good title despite any defect in the title of the transferor.

§8.269 A negotiable instrument may either be absolute or qualified in nature. The instrument is absolute where it is transferable so as to give the transferee all the rights originally created by it, free of any equities existing between the prior holders and the drawer of the instrument. Bills of exchange, promissory notes and cheques fall into this category of negotiable instrument. Where an instrument is transferable only to certain persons, or in a certain manner, or so as to make the transferee take it subject to the equities affecting it in the hands of prior holders, but otherwise preserving the other attributes of negotiability, it is qualified in nature. An instrument, such as a bill of lading, which is transferable by delivery or by delivery and endorsement from one person to another, but which otherwise lacks the attributes of negotiability (*e.g.*, conferring good title despite defects in title of a prior holder) is called a "quasi-negotiable" instrument. True negotiability turns upon whether the instrument is transferable — like cash — by delivery, is capable of being sued upon by the person holding it for the time being for the full rights evidenced by the instrument, and whether full property in it passes to a good faith transferee for value. If any of these requisites is wanting, it is not a negotiable instrument.[507]

§8.270 The liability of an issuer under a negotiable security is said to be autonomous. Where an instrument is negotiable, the benefit of the contract or right is attached to the document itself; the document is not merely evidence of that right. As a result, rights belong to the holder of the instrument from time to time. The autonomy of a negotiable instrument has four immediate implications: first, the liability of the issuer of the negotiable security to the holder of the security is the face amount of the security, rather than the amount of the debt actu-

---

[507] Maurice Megrah, *Byles on Bills of Exchange*, 22nd ed. (London: Sweet & Maxwell, 1965), 85.

ally owed to the creditor to whom the bond was originally issued;[508] second, payment of the debt to which a negotiable security relates does not discharge the security itself; third, (as noted above) holders in due course without notice of an equity between the debtor and original creditor take free of any such equity as may exist;[509] fourth, the issuer of a negotiable security is estopped from denying the truth of any representations contained in the text of the security or set out in the recitals to the security against innocent holders for value.[510]

§8.271 Thus possession is required in order to be entitled to enforce a negotiable instrument. Because of the autonomous character of a negotiable security, its issuing corporation must exercise care in making payment. More particularly, it should pay the principal owing under the debenture principal only upon presentation of the debenture[511] and should pay interest only upon presentation of a coupon. Unless these steps are taken, the corporation will not normally be able to raise payment in defence of any payment made to the original holder, should the security or coupon subsequently be presented by a holder in due course.[512] There is one important exception to this general rule: the liability of the debtor may be discharged without presentation and cancellation of the security or coupon where payment is made in some other way and in accordance with provisions set out in the security which specify that the payment in question will give the issuer a good discharge to the extent of all payments made. In all other cases, there is a risk of double liability if payment is made.[513] However, where the corporation does not have money to pay the amount owing on a security or coupon, its presentation is not a condition precedent to the bringing of an action for payment.[514]

---

[508] Although if the original creditor is the holder of the bond, its claim is limited to the amount actually owing to it: *Royal Trust Co. v. Atlantic & Lake Superior Rlwy.* (1908), 13 Ex. C.R. 42. See also *Trusts & Guarantee Co. v. Grand Valley Rlwy. Co.*, [1919] O.J. No. 84, 44 O.L.R. 398 (C.A.).

[509] Thus in *Re Winding-up Act* (1908), 5 E.L.R. 129 (P.E.I.S.C.), Fitzgerald J. stated:

> Debentures in this form pass as freely as bank notes. The company contract to pay not any particular person, but any one who may be the bearer, and provided always there was authority for their issue, holders for value without notice of the equities are entitled to prove in ... [a] liquidation for the amount due free from equities.

See also *McKenzie v. Montreal & City of Ottawa Junction Rlwy. Co.*, [1878] O.J. No. 282, 29 U.C.C.P. 333 (C.A.). However, the holder will take subject to any terms and conditions set out in the negotiable instrument itself: *Levis County Rlwy. v. Fontaine* (1904), 13 Que. K.B. 523 (C.A.).

[510] *General Dairies Ltd. v. Maritime Electric*, [1935] S.C.R. 519 at 526, *per* Dysart J., rev'd on other grounds [1937] 1 D.L.R. 609 (P.C.).

[511] *Royal Bank v. Cal Glass Ltd.*, [1979] B.C.J. No. 1406, 9 B.L.R. 1 (S.C.), aff'd 22 B.C.L.R. 328 (C.A.); *Osborne v. Preston & Berlin Rlwy. Co.*, [1859] O.J. No. 218, 9 U.C.C.P. 241 (C.A.).

[512] Where the debenture contains such a provision, presentation of the coupon is sufficient to obtain payment of interest; it is not necessary to present the bond as well: *Connolly v. Montreal Park & Island Rlwy.* (1901), 20 Que. S.C. 1 (C.A.).

[513] Where there is a delay in presenting the bonds, the corporation is not liable for interest between the maturity date and the time of their actual presentment: *McDonald v. Great Western Rlwy. Co.*, [1861] O.J. No. 40, 21 U.C.Q.B. 223 (C.A.).

[514] *Fellowes v. Ottawa Gas Co.*, [1869] O.J. No. 109, 19 U.C.C.P. 174 (C.A.); *Montreal Trust Co. v. Abitibi Power & Paper Co.*, [1944] O.J. No. 467, [1944] O.R. 515 at 523 (H.C.J.), *per* Kellock J.A. See also *Thompson v. Victoria Rlwy. Co.*, [1881] O.J. No. 339, 9 P.R. 119 at 122 (H.C.J.), *per* Osler J.

§8.272 Negotiable instruments satisfy many of the requirements of the market for high-speed, low-transaction cost, transferable rights. Since negotiable instruments are transferable either by delivery or by delivery and endorsement, without notice of the transfer being required to be given to the debtor, a person acquiring such an instrument need deal only with the person from whom it is being acquired. It is not necessary to notify the debtor in order to lock in the acquired rights. Nor is there any need to confirm the state of accounts existing between the parties, since first, a transferee in good faith for value (*i.e.*, a holder in due course) obtains good title despite any defect in the title of the transferor; and second, a holder in due course takes free of any equity existing between the debtor and the transferor or any other prior holder. The primary benefits derived from making an instrument negotiable are the simplicity of passing title from one holder to the next, and the fact that a holder in due course will obtain a good title despite any defect in the title of a prior holder.

§8.273 The commercial necessity of presentation can present obvious problems in certain cases, as for instance where the security in question has been lost or destroyed. In *Cusack v. Southern Loans & Savings Co.*[515] the plaintiff made a statutory declaration that she had burned a negotiable debenture of the defendant company by mistake. It was held that she was entitled to recover the amount of the debenture upon the delivery of an indemnity bond protecting the corporation against subsequent liability to a holder in due course.

§8.274 The desire to improve the transferability of negotiable instruments often results in the insertion of an agreement to waive presentation of the instrument for payment. Such an agreement may present considerable risk to the issuer. A negotiable security that is stolen prior to maturity is valid in the hands of a purchaser for value who acquires it in good faith.[516] The liability of the issuer of a negotiable bond to a holder in due course of stolen bonds was considered by the High Court of Ontario in *Garey v. Dominion Manufacturers Ltd.*[517] The facts in that case were that bonds payable to bearer were stolen and sold to the plaintiff who purchased them in good faith and without knowledge of the theft. In holding that the corporate issuer was liable on the bonds to the purchaser, Riddell J. stated that the fact that the bonds were stolen was no defence. Such a rule may at first blush seem an overly strict one, yet its adoption is essential if the integrity of the negotiable instrument system is to be maintained. In many cases where there is a wrongdoing stranger, one of two innocent parties must necessarily suffer a loss. In such cases, the loss may be assigned either arbitrarily, or rationally by reference to the context in which the risk of loss arose. In the case of stolen negotiable instruments, the need to protect third parties from fraud (which is almost impossible for them to detect) justifies the imposition of the loss on the

---

[515] [1903] O.J. No. 338, 2 O.W.R. 179 at 180 (H.C.J.), *per* Meredith C.J.; see also *Weidman Brothers v. Guaranty Trust Co.*, [1955] O.J. No. 579, [1955] O.R. 644 (H.C.J.), aff'd [1955] O.W.N. 851 (C.A.).

[516] *Canada (Minister of Rlwys. and Canals) v. Quebec Southern Rlwy. Co.* (1908), 12 Ex. C.R. 152.

[517] [1924] O.J. No. 99, 56 O.L.R. 159 (H.C.).

party from whom those instruments were stolen. A person may prevent theft by making sure that negotiable instruments are secure. In contrast, the third party purchaser may not protect against fraud other than by conducting precisely the type of expensive, time-consuming inquiry that the negotiable instrument system was intended to circumvent.

G. THE DEPOSITORY BILLS AND NOTES ACT

§8.275 The *Depository Bills and Notes Act* modified the law relating to negotiable instruments to accommodate electronic settlement and dealings in money market securities. Generally, the Act updates the law relating to negotiable instruments, to reconcile that law with electronic transactions effected through a clearing house operation. It creates two new classes of investment securities that can be traded and delivered via screen-based systems as an alternative to the traditional negotiable instrument. The first of these is provided for under section 4 of the Act, which provides that a "depository bill" is an unconditional order in writing that is:

(*a*) signed by the drawer and addressed to another person, requiring the person to whom it is addressed to pay, at a fixed or determinable future time, a sum certain in money to, or to the order of, a specified person;

(*b*) accepted unconditionally by the signature of the person to whom it is addressed;

(*c*) marked prominently and legibly on its face and within its text, at or before the time of issue, with the words "This is a depository bill subject to the *Depository Bills and Notes Act*" or "Lettre de dépôt assujettie à la *Loi sur les lettres et billets de dépôt*";

(*d*) not marked with any words prohibiting negotiation, transfer or assignment of it or of an interest in it;

(*e*) made payable, originally or by endorsement, to a clearing house; and

(*f*) deposited with the clearing house to which it is made payable.

In contrast, a depository note as provided under section 5 of the Act is an unconditional promise in writing that is

(*a*) signed by the maker, promising to pay, at a fixed or determinable future time, a sum certain in money to, or to the order of, a specified person;

(*b*) marked prominently and legibly on its face and within its text, at or before the time of issue, with the words "This is a depository note subject to the *Depository Bills and Notes Act*" or "Billet de dépôt assujetti à la *Loi sur les lettres et billets de dépôt*";

(*c*) not marked with any words prohibiting negotiation, transfer or assignment of it or of an interest in it;

(*d*) made payable, originally or by endorsement, to a clearing house; and

(*e*) deposited with the clearing house to which it is made payable.

It will be noted that these definitions correspond closely to those provided for bill and note in the *Bills of Exchange Act*.

§8.276 A depository bill or note is deposited with a clearing house if it is accepted for deposit by the clearing house to which it is payable and is in the possession of that clearing house or, subject to the instructions of the clearing house, in the possession of the clearing house's custodian, or a nominee of either of them.[518] A depository bill or note is payable to a clearing house if it is made payable to the clearing house or its nominee, originally or by endorsement.[519] For the purposes of sections 4 and 5, an order or a promise to pay is not conditional by reason only that it is limited to payment from the assets of a partnership, unincorporated association, trust or estate.[520] The *Bills of Exchange Act* does not apply in respect of depository bills and notes.[521]

§8.277 A transaction related to a depository bill or note recorded by a clearing house, or related to an interest in such a depository bill or note, may be effected by the making of appropriate entries in the records of the clearing house.[522] The transaction has the same effect as a delivery of a bill of exchange in bearer form under the *Bills of Exchange Act*.[523] The transaction, including the time it takes effect, is governed by the laws of the jurisdiction agreed to by the clearing house and its participants.[524] A participant in whose favour the transaction is effected is deemed to be in possession of the depository bill or note. If the transaction relates to an interest in a depository bill or note, the participant in whose favour the transaction is effected is deemed to be in possession of a depository bill or note representing the interest.[525]

§8.278 Transactions related to like depository bills or notes, or related to interests in like depository bills or notes, may be recorded by a clearing house as part of a fungible bulk and the entries may refer merely to a quantity of like depository bills or notes.[526] When there is more than one transaction in depository bills or notes that are part of a fungible bulk, a clearing house may make entries in respect of those transactions on a net basis.[527] The term "fungible bulk" describes a bulk of depository bills or notes of which any unit is, by usage of trade, the equivalent of any other unit.

---

[518] DBNA, s. 2(2).
[519] DBNA, s. 2(3).
[520] DBNA, s. 5.1.
[521] DBNA, s. 6.
[522] DBNA, s. 8(1).
[523] DBNA, s. 8(2).
[524] DBNA, s. 8(3).
[525] DBNA, s. 8(4).
[526] DBNA, s. 9(1).
[527] DBNA, s. 9(2).

H. PERPETUAL DEBT SECURITIES

§8.279 Corporate borrowers occasionally issue debt securities of perpetual duration, under the terms of which the principal amount of those securities becomes payable only in the event of a default or some other remote contingency. The two most common securities of this type are perpetual debentures and perpetual promissory notes, although the market for both in recent years has diminished. In general, perpetual debentures and notes are employed as a substitute for an equity issue, and therefore will not provide for a security interest.

§8.280 Corporations possessed no power to issue perpetual debentures or other securities at common law.[528] However, subsection 44(1) of the OBCA now provides that:

> 44.(1) A condition contained in a debt obligation or in an instrument for securing a debt obligation is not invalid by reason only that the debt obligation is thereby made irredeemable or redeemable only on the happening of a contingency, however remote, or on the expiration of a period, however long.

Thus perpetual debentures, notes and other debt securities are now clearly permitted under the OBCA.[529] While a similar provision was found in section 55 of the *Canada Business Corporations Act*, for some reason no comparable provision was included in the CBCA at the time when it was enacted. Perpetual debentures are repayable by the corporation at their face (or par) value, in the event that the corporation is wound up.[530]

§8.281 Where the intention is to create a perpetual debenture, considerable care should be taken to make the true character of the debenture clear, otherwise the debenture may be misinterpreted to provide for payment at an indefinite time (which will result in the debenture becoming payable upon reasonable notice — a result that would near fully defeat the intent of the borrower). Furthermore, from the borrower's perspective, it is desirable to include a right to retract the debenture upon a specified notice period. For instance, a suitable acknowledgment of indebtedness clause in a perpetual debenture would read:

> The Corporation acknowledges itself indebted to the Registered Holder in the Principal Amount stated above, that amount to be payable only,
>
> (a) upon the occurrence of an act or event of default within the meaning of this Debenture; or
>
> (b) where the Corporation gives six months notice of its intention to retract this Debenture, but in any such case a bonus of $•• shall be payable in addition to the Principal Amount, Interest and Costs secured under this Debenture.

Perpetual debentures and notes may contemplate the use of interest coupons, but because of the duration of such securities, where such provision is made, it is

---

[528] *Re Southern Brazilian Rio Grande do Sul Rlwy. Co.*, [1905] 2 Ch. 78.
[529] For a case dealing with very long term debentures, see *Knightsbridge Estates Trust Ltd. v. Byrne*, [1940] A.C. 613 (H.L.).
[530] *Re Southern Brazilian Rio Grande do Sul Rlwy. Co.*, [1905] 2 Ch. 78.

also necessary to provide for the issue of additional coupons, once the coupons originally attached have been used up. A typical provision of this type would read:

1. Attached to this Debenture are •• Coupons, each providing for the payment of interest at the rate provided in the Debenture on the interest payment date to which it relates, and each payment of interest shall be payable only upon presentation and surrender to the paying agent of the Coupon relating to the payment that is to be made.

2. So long as this Debenture remains outstanding, upon the •• anniversary of the issue of this Debenture, and upon the expiration of each succeeding period of •• years, the Corporation shall issue and deliver to the registered holder on presentation of this Debenture to the paying agent for endorsement, ••• additional Coupons providing for the payment of interest during the ensuing •• year period.

I. OTHER CRITICAL CONCERNS

(i) Priority of Future Advances

§8.282 Under the *Personal Property Security Act* ("PPSA"),[531] it is possible to structure a security agreement so that it gives security in respect of future advances. Three provisions of the Act are of particular importance in this regard. First, section 13 of the PPSA expressly provides that a security agreement may secure future advances. Second, subsection 9(1) of that Act provides that except as provided by the PPSA or some other Act, a security agreement is effective according to its terms between the parties to it and against third parties. Third, subsection 30(3) of the Act sets down the following general rule with respect to future advances made under a security agreement:

> 30.(3) Subject to subsection (4), where future advances are made while a security interest is perfected, the security interest has the same priority with respect to each future advance as it has with respect to the first advance.

Thus in general terms, the priority of a security interest under the PPSA depends not upon the state of the title to the collateral subject to the security interest at the time when advances are made under the secured debt, but rather upon the order of perfection of the security interest relative to other security interests.[532] It

---

[531] R.S.O. 1990, c. P.10.
[532] However, subs. 30(3) is qualified by subs. 30(4) of the Act, which provides:

> 30.(4) A future advance under a perfected security interest is subordinate to the rights of persons mentioned in subclauses 20(1)(*a*) (ii) and (iii) if the advance was made after the secured party received written notification of the interest of any such person unless,
>
> (*a*) the secured party makes the advance for the purpose of paying reasonable expenses, including the cost of insurance and payment of taxes or other charges incurred in obtaining and maintaining possession of the collateral and its preservation; or

follows that future advances made under a security agreement to which the PPSA applies will normally enjoy priority over any intervening security interest that is perfected prior to the time when the advance in question is made.

§8.283 In contrast, future advances under a real property mortgage or charge will often be subordinate to intervening security interests; this result arises from a curious interplay between the *Construction Lien Act*[533] and the *Land Titles Act*[534] or *Registry Act*,[535] whichever is applicable to the land in question. A review of the provisions of the two land registration statutes would first suggest that the future advances under the prior charge will enjoy priority. Thus subsection 93(4) of the *Land Titles Act* provides that:

> 93.(4) A registered charge is, as against the chargor, the heirs, executors, administrators, and assigns of the chargor and every other person claiming by, through or under the chargor, a security upon the land thereby charged to the extent of the money or money's worth actually advanced or supplied under the charge, not exceeding the amount for which the charge is expressed to be a security, although the money or money's worth, or some part thereof, was advanced or supplied after the registration of a transfer, charge or other instrument affecting the land charged, executed by the chargor, or the heirs, executors, administrators or estate trustees of the chargor and registered subsequently to the first-mentioned charge, unless, before advancing or supplying the money or money's worth, the registered owner of the first-mentioned charge had actual notice of the execution and registration of such transfer, charge or other instrument, and the registration of such transfer, charge or other instrument after the registration of the first-mentioned charge does not constitute actual notice.

Section 73 of the *Registry Act* is to like effect in requiring "actual notice" of the subsequent charge. Very often, however, such notice will exist. The reason is that section 78 of the *Construction Lien Act* departs from the normal rules of priority applicable under these two land registration statutes. In particular, subsection 78(1) of the Act provides that except as provided in section 78, the liens arising from an improvement have priority over all conveyances, mortgages or other agreements affecting the owner's interest in the premises. Subsection 78(4) then goes on to deal with the relative priority between lien claims and the interest of a chargor in respect of subsequent advances made under a prior registered charge. It provides:

> 78.(4) Subject to subsection (2), a conveyance, mortgage or other agreement affecting the owner's interest in the premises that was registered prior to the time when the first lien arose in respect of an improvement, has priority, in addition to the priority to which it is entitled under subsection (3), over the liens arising from the improvement, to the extent of any advance made in respect of that conveyance, mortgage or other agreement after the time when the first lien arose, unless,

---

    (b) the secured party is bound to make the advance, whether or not a subsequent event of default or other event not within the secured party's control has relieved or may relieve the secured party from the obligation.

[533] R.S.O. 1990, c. C.30.
[534] R.S.O. 1990, c. L.5.
[535] R.S.O. 1990, c. R.20.

(a) at the time when the advance was made, there was a preserved or perfected lien against the premises; or

(b) prior to the time when the advance was made, the person making the advance had received written notice of a lien.

It follows from this provision that in order for a chargor to be sure of priority relative to construction lien claimants it is necessary to undertake a subsearch of the title to the property in order to determine if any lien claims have been preserved or perfected. Any such subsearch will necessarily reveal the presence of other subsequent charges, from which it follows that the chargor will then have actual notice of the existence of those charges. Thus any further advance on the prior registered charge will likely be subordinate to the interest of the subsequent encumbrancer.

(ii) Securing Revolving Debt

§8.284 Commercial lending agreements between a corporation and an institutional lender, such as a line of credit, will often provide a revolving credit under which the lender agrees to advance funds from time to time to the borrower up to a stipulated aggregate amount of advances. The borrower may repay those advances, and any amount so repaid may subsequently be redrawn under the credit. Where a security interest is conferred to secure a specific advance, the normal rule is that the security interest is discharged upon the repayment of that advance. However, it is possible to structure the terms of a security agreement so that it continues with respect to subsequent advances, despite the repayment from time to time of the whole or any part of the balance outstanding. Moreover, subsection 44(2) of the OBCA provides that debt obligations, issued, pledged, hypothecated or deposited by a corporation are not redeemed by reason only that the indebtedness evidenced by the debt obligations or in respect of which the debt obligations are issued, pledged or hypothecated is repaid. This provision is complemented by subsection 44(3) of the OBCA which provides:

> 44.(3) Debt obligations issued by a corporation and purchased, redeemed or otherwise acquired by it may be cancelled or, subject to any applicable trust indenture or other agreement, may be reissued, pledged or hypothecated to secure any obligation of the corporation then existing or thereafter incurred, and any such acquisition and reissue, pledge or hypothecation is not a cancellation of the debt obligations.

Subsections 39(11) and (12) of the CBCA are to a similar effect.

(iii) Subordination Agreements

§8.285 As indicated above, the evolution of mezzanine financing has led to the creation of a range of debt subordination arrangements.[536] There are two basic types of debt subordination agreement. In the first (a "specified creditor subordi-

---

[536] See generally *Bank of Montreal v. Dynex Petroleum Ltd.*, [1997] A.J. No. 341, 31 B.L.R. (2d) 44 (Q.B.).

nation"), one creditor of a borrower agrees that its debt shall rank after the claim of some other specified creditor, so that in the event of insolvency, the claim of the first creditor will not be repaid until the second creditor has been repaid in full. Such an arrangement will normally take the form of an agreement between the creditors concerned, but security agreements will often permit a borrower to grant prior charges to certain specified classes of creditor (*e.g.*, to secure purchase money financing), in which case there is no direct contractual relationship between the creditors, but instead a permission to grant priority is given to the debtor. In the second type of common debt subordination arrangement (a "general creditor subordination"), a creditor agrees that its claim against the borrower will rank after the claims of the general and unsecured creditors of the borrower.

§8.286 Standard form bank guarantees can be looked to for an illustration of a specified creditor subordination. Such documents often include an undertaking by the surety to subordinate any indebtedness owed to the surety by the principal, to the debt owed by the principal to the bank. Any amount received by the surety from the principal in respect of a debt owed by the principal is deemed to be received in trust for the bank. A subordination or postponement agreement is not a guarantee, but is instead a distinct form of inter-creditor relationship under which one creditor, whose claim against a debtor apparently under general principles of law is entitled to rank equally or in priority to the claim of another creditor or class of creditors, agrees that its claim shall in fact rank after the claim of that other creditor or class of creditors.[537] Where the liability of the surety is unlimited, the surety will be liable to make good the entire indebtedness of the principal, and thus the existence of the subordination agreement might seem to make little difference to the creditor. In fact, however, the subordination agreement normally will have the effect of requiring the surety to retain funds in the principal (so as thereby to prop up the solvency of the principal) until such time as the creditor is paid in full. Thus the chances of a default by the principal are reduced. Moreover, so long as funds remain in the principal, rather than being repaid to the surety, they are available for the payment of the principal's creditors alone, and need not be shared among the surety's own creditors. Where the guarantee is limited in amount, the subordination agreement will often increase significantly the protection afforded by the surety to the creditor. The amounts left in the principal by the surety normally will not reduce the liability of the surety to the creditor. Thus by obtaining the subordination agreement, the creditor enjoys the benefit of the security afforded by the guarantee, plus the investment in the principal made by the surety in leaving the subordinated debt in the principal.

---

[537] See, generally, *Royal Trust Co. v. H.A. Roberts Group Ltd.*, [1995] S.J. No. 96, 44 R.P.R. (2d) 254 at 273-74 (Q.B.), *per* Baynton J.: where the terms of a security agreement or loan agreement provide that the rights of the creditor under that agreement shall be subordinate to the rights of some other creditor or group of creditors, the clause is known as a subordination agreement or clause. In contrast, the term "postponement" is generally used to describe a document that subordinates a second separate and distinct document to a third separate and distinct document.

§8.287 Subordination agreements entered into between a surety and a creditor are a simple matter of contract. They are obviously effective as a contract between the creditors concerned on the basis of the privity of contract subsisting between them. In contrast, a permission granted to a debtor to allow the debtor to confer a prior charge to that held by the existing secured creditor who grants the permission, do not create privity of contract between the two lenders. They will be effective either by reason of estoppel in favour of the third party creditor who takes a prior ranking security interest, or because of the implied license to deal with third party creditors that is conveyed upon the borrower to convey such a prior ranking charge to a third party (in which case, it is not necessary to show that the subsequent creditor knew of the subordination arrangement). In addition, section 38 of the *Personal Property Security Act* gives statutory effect to provisions within security agreements to which that Act applies, under which one secured creditor under that Act concedes priority to another.[538] It provides:

> 38. A secured party may, in the security agreement or otherwise, subordinate the secured party's security interest to any other security interest and such subordination is effective according to its terms.

Obviously, this provision has no effect upon the relative priority of security interests outside the scope of that Act (most specifically, security interests against real property). Nor does it have any bearing upon "general" subordination arrangements, under which a creditor enjoys no security interest whatever, but rather agrees that its claim will rank after the claims of the general, unsecured debt of the borrower.

§8.288 The legal status of a general subordination agreement differs significantly from both of these two types of arrangement. By definition, unsecured creditors enjoy no specific claim against the property of the debtor. Instead, they are entitled to look for their payment only to such property of the corporation as remains where all persons having interests in that property have enforced or abandoned their interests. This limit is inherent in the *Bankruptcy and Insolvency Act*,[539] which provides for the gathering in of the property of a bankrupt, its realization and distribution among the creditors of a bankrupt, but subject to the rights of secured creditors. The general rule is that the unsecured debts of a corporation rank rateably,[540] but there are numerous preferences[541] and postponements[542] that depart from that general rule.

---

[538] For cases in which this provision has been applied, see: *Re Guantlet Energy Corp.* (2003), 36 B.L.R. (3d) 266; *Euroclean Canada Inc. v. Forest Glade Investments Ltd.*, [1985] O.J. No. 2307, 16 D.L.R. (4th) 289 (C.A.); *Chiips Inc. Skyview Hotels Ltd.*, [1994] A.J. No. 562, 155 A.R. 281 (C.A.), leave to appeal to S.C.C. refused [1994] S.C.C.A. No. 444; *Re DCD Industries (1995) Ltd.*, [2002] A.J. No. 1594 (Q.B.), aff'd [2005] A.J. No. 329 (C.A.) — this last case making the important point that careful consideration must be given to the wording of the purported subordination clause, to ascertain its scope and intended effect.

[539] R.S.C. 1985, c. B-3.

[540] *Ibid.*, s. 141.

[541] *Ibid.*, s. 136.

[542] *Ibid.*, ss. 137, 138, 139, and 140.

§8.289 Subordinated debt is not contemplated in the *Bankruptcy and Insolvency Act*[543] (although certain debts are postponed under that Act) or in the OBCA or the CBCA; nevertheless, such debt is often encountered in practice, where it arises by virtue of the debt contract between the creditor and debtor. From time to time, the argument has been advanced that the holder of a subordinated debt cannot be held to his (or her) subordinated status by a general creditor of a corporation, unless there is privity of contract between them. Yet this argument misses the point: the claims of the various creditors against an insolvent corporation arise not as a result of arrangements between them, but rather because of an arrangement between the corporation and each creditor. If a person agrees with the corporation that he is not to be repaid until such time as all general creditors of a corporation have been repaid in full, then until the general creditors are so paid there is no amount owing to the subordinated creditor. The subordinated creditor's right of payment is contingent upon the satisfaction of that condition. Thus privity between the general and subordinated creditors of the corporation is not relevant. In this respect, the status of a subordinated creditor may be analogized to the status of a secured creditor. The secured creditor's right to look to specific property of the corporation is not contingent upon the consent of the unsecured creditors to his acquiring that right. It arises by virtue of a contract between the corporation and the secured creditor.[544]

§8.290 The essence of a subordination agreement is that the enforceability of the debt to which it relates is made dependent if not upon the solvency of the debtor then at least upon the prior repayment of the general and unsecured creditors of the debtor. Issues of priority only matter if the debtor is insolvent. In an insolvency, whether individual or corporate, and leaving aside secured debts, the order is prescribed by legislation, which gives priority to, for example, costs and expenses of the insolvency, and to certain preferential debts. Otherwise, the general rule is that all debts are to be treated equally, with ratable distribution of the available funds between all creditors. It is, however, established that one creditor's rights can be subordinated to those of another or others by contract. Such subordination arrangements are a common feature of commercial dealings (they have a particular relevance to the capital adequacy of banks and other financial institutions under the regulatory regime applying to them, but such arrangements are in fact used in the case of many types of indebtedness). Such arrangements have been considered on a number of occasions by the courts, and their effectiveness should by now be considered to be settled.[545] Even so, it is worthwhile to consider the evolution of subordination arrangements, and the facts that have influenced the courts in dealing with such arrangements.

---

[543] R.S.C. 1985, c. B-3.
[544] See, for instance, *Fidelity Investments International plc. v. Mytravel Group plc.*, [2004] E.W.C.A. Civ 1734 (C.A.); *Royal Trust Co. v. H.A. Roberts Group Ltd.*, [1995] S.J. No. 96, 44 R.P.R. (2d) 254 at 276 (Q.B.), *per* Baynton J.
[545] See, generally, *Re SSSL Realizations (2002) Ltd.*, [2004] E.W.H.C. 1760, [2004] B.P.I.R. 1334 (Ch.).

§8.291 There are many different forms of subordination agreement.[546] Some of them are bilateral arrangements between the debtor and the creditor who holds the subordinated debt. It may be an agreement between two creditors.[547] The agreement may be a multi-party one between the debtor, the subordinated creditor and other creditors of the debtor, and perhaps a trustee.[548] In almost all cases, every form tends to the same effect: the debt is not a contingent one;[549] it comes into existence immediately, but the right of repayment and enforcement on default of repayment arises if and only if the value of the debtor's assets is sufficient to meet the demands of the general unsecured creditors of the debtor in full.[550]

§8.292 In *Re Maxwell Communications Corp. plc. (No. 2)*,[551] the corporation MCC was found to have guaranteed convertible bonds issued by Maxwell Finance Jersey Ltd. ("MFJ"). The guarantee provided that MCC's liability under the guarantee was on a subordinated basis so that if MCC was liquidated, the claims of the unsubordinated creditors would be entitled to be paid before any payment was made to the holders of the MFJ bonds. The question arose as to whether the subordination agreement was valid. Justice Vinelott held that the agreement was effective on the basis of the overriding need for uniformity in international bankruptcies.[552]

§8.293 It was argued that subordination agreements were unenforceable as they conflicted with the scheme of priorities provided for under insolvency legislation.[553] In support of this argument, reference was made to the decision of the House of Lords in *National Westminster Bank Ltd. v. Halesowen Presswork & Assemblies Ltd.*[554] and the decisions of the Court of Appeal, both in *Halesowen* and in *Rolls Razor Ltd. v. Cox*.[555] In those cases, it had been held that the provisions for mutual set-off provided for in section 31 of the *Bankruptcy Act 1914* could not be excluded by agreement between a debtor and its creditors. Accordingly, a creditor could not make a valid agreement that the debtor would not be entitled to set off a debt due to him against a debt due to him from the debtor, nor could a creditor waive his right to set-off after the commencement of a bankruptcy or winding up.[556]

---

[546] See, generally, *Royal Trust Co. v. H.A. Roberts Group Ltd.*, [1995] S.J. No. 96, 44 R.P.R. (2d) 254 (Q.B.) concerning the identification of such agreements.
[547] *Cheah v. Equicorp Finance Group Ltd.*, [1991] 4 All E.R. 989, [1992] 1 A.C. 472 (P.C.).
[548] See, for instance, *Re Portbase Clothing Ltd.*, [1993] B.C.L.C. 796 (Ch.).
[549] *Re Maxwell Communications Corp. plc. (No. 2)*, [1992] 1 B.C.L.C. 1 at 18 (Ch.), *per* Vinelott J.
[550] See *Re Carbon Developments (Pty.) Ltd.*, [1993] 1 S.C. 493 at 504 (C.A. South Africa), *per* Goldstone J.A.
[551] [1992] 1 B.C.L.C. 1 (Ch.).
[552] *Ibid.*, at 5 to 6; see also 20.
[553] As to conflicts with legislation governing the registration of security interests, see *Metropolitan Trust Co. of Canada v. Henneberry*, [1995] O.J. No. 922,, 44 R.P.R. (2d) 161 (C.A.).
[554] [1972] 1 All E.R. 641, [1972] A.C. 785 (H.L.).
[555] [1967] 1 Q.B. 552 (C.A.); *cf.*, however, *Deering v. Hyndman* (1886), 18 L.R. (Ir.) 323 (C.A.).
[556] *Rolls Razor Ltd. v. Cox*, [1967] 1 Q.B. 552 at 570 (C.A.), *per* Lord Denning M.R.

§8.294 Justice Vinelott ultimately concluded that subordination agreements were valid and effective and were not prejudiced by any consideration of public policy.[557] In reaching this conclusion, he first determined that there was no absolute rule that the parties to a contract could not contract out of the scheme of priorities under insolvency legislation. On the contrary, the rule adopted by the House of Lords with respect to section 31 of the *Bankruptcy Act, 1914* turned both upon the mandatory language employed in that section *and* "the proposition that the liquidator and general body of creditors might have an interest in ensuring that the debts due to and from a creditor arising from mutual dealings are set off". Unless the existence of a subordinated debt arrangement would prejudice the general body of creditors on an insolvency there was no reason to hold it as invalid because it was inconsistent with the language of insolvency legislation.[558] Justice Vinelott continued:

> That proposition, it seems to me, must rest upon the inconvenience and potential unfairness to the trustee or liquidator and so to other creditors that might arise if a creditor was entitled either to exercise or, at his option, not to exercise the right of set-off. For otherwise, the creditor might prove in the bankruptcy ... leaving it to the trustee ... to recover the debt due to the estate in proceedings which might be protracted and expensive, and which might not result in the recovery of the full amount due. In the meantime the distribution of the insolvent estate might be held up and a question might arise whether a creditor had waived his right of set-off and would be entitled to a dividend while proceedings to recover the debt due to him was still afoot. An agreement between the debtor and the creditor excluding the creditor's right of set-off, or the waiver by the creditor of his right of set-off, even after the commencement of the bankruptcy ... might thus equally hinder the rapid, efficient and economical process of bankruptcy.[559]

No similar public policy justification existed for barring subordination agreements between a creditor and debtor:

> It seems to me plain that after the commencement ... of a bankruptcy ... a creditor must be entitled to waive his debt just as he is entitled to decline to submit a proof. There might, in any given case, be a question whether a waiver was binding on him but that is irrelevant for this purpose. If the creditor can waive his right altogether I can see no reason why he should not waive his right to prove, save to the extent of any assets remaining after the debtors of other unsecured creditors have been paid in full; or if he is a preferential creditor, to agree that his debt will rank equally with unsecured non-preferential debts. So also, if the creditor can waive his right to prove or agree to the postponement of his debt after the commencement of the bankruptcy ... I can see no reason why he should agree with the debtor that his debt will not be payable or will be postponed or subordinated in the event of a bankruptcy or winding-up. The reason for giving effect to an agreement in these terms seems to me to be if anything stronger than that for allowing the creditor to waive, or postpone, or subordinate his debt after the commencement of

---

[557] *Re Maxwell Communications Corp. plc. (No. 2)*, [1992] 1 B.C.L.C. 1 at 21 (Ch.).
[558] See also *Horne v. Chester & Fain Property Developments Pty. Ltd.* (1986), 11 A.C.L.R. 485 at 489, *per* Southwell J.
[559] *Re Maxwell Communications Corp. plc. (No. 2)*, [1992] 1 B.C.L.C. 1 at 10 to 11 (Ch.).

a bankruptcy ... for other creditors might have given credit on the assumption that the agreement would be binding.[560]

§8.295 Justice Vinelott went on to point out that in many cases, the availability of subordinated debt is crucial to the ability of a company to remain in business. The validity of subordinated debt arrangements was, therefore, essential to this very important aspect of capital planning within a corporate enterprise.[561] For tax and various other reasons (including, but not limited to, ownership concentration restrictions and other regulatory considerations) it may not be suitable for a shareholder to invest funds in the share capital of a corporation. If subordination agreements were not effective *vis-à-vis* third parties, the practical consequence would be that many companies capable of remaining in business would fail.

§8.296 Further complications arise where a subordinated debt instrument purports to subordinate the claim of the holders of that instrument to some but not all of the general unsecured debt of the corporation. In *United States Trust v. Australia & New Zealand Banking Group*[562] a company, Linter Textiles Corporation, issued certain securities (the "Securities") under an indenture. Article 10 of that indenture contained the following provisions:

> ... each person holding any Security, whether upon original issue or upon transfer, assignment or exchange thereof accepts and agrees that the payment of (i) the principal of and interest on the Securities and (ii) all amounts, if any, due ... by the Company shall, to the extent and in the manner herein set forth, be subordinated and junior in right of payment to the prior payment in full of the Senior Indebtedness. ...

> This Article shall constitute a continuing offer to all persons who, in reliance upon such provisions, become holders of, or continue to hold, Senior Indebtedness, and such provisions are made for the benefit of the holders of Senior Indebtedness, and such holders are made obligees hereunder and any one or more of them may enforce such provisions. ...

In addition to the foregoing language, section 10.03 set out the following rules:

> (a) Upon any payment or distribution of assets of the Company ... to creditors upon any dissolution or winding up or total or partial liquidation ... in bankruptcy, insolvency, receivership or other proceedings, all amounts due or to become due upon all Senior Indebtedness shall first be paid in full, or such payment duly provided for before any payment is made on account of the principal of or interest on the Securities. Upon any such dissolution, winding up, liquidation or reorganization, any payment ... to which the Holders of the Securities ... would be entitled, except for the provisions hereof, shall be paid by the Company ... directly to the holders of Senior Indebtedness (*pro rata* to such holders on the basis of the respective amounts of Senior Indebtedness held by such holders) ... as their respective interests may appear, for application to the payment of Senior Indebtedness remaining unpaid until all such Senior Indebtedness has been paid in full after giving effect to any concurrent

---

[560] *Ibid.*, at 11.
[561] *Ibid.*, at 16.
[562] (1993), 11 A.C.S.R. 7 (N.S.W.S.C. Eq.).

payment, distribution or provision therefore to or for the holders of Senior Indebtedness.

(b) In the event that, notwithstanding the foregoing, any payment or distribution of assets of the Company of any kind ... shall be received by ... any Holder when such payment or distribution is prohibited by Section 10.02(a), such payment ... shall be held in trust for the benefit of ... the holders of Senior Indebtedness ... as their respective interests may appear, for application to the payment of Senior Indebtedness remaining unpaid until all such Senior Indebtedness has been paid in full ...

A priority deed to which the plaintiff, the company and certain financial institutions, including the defendant, were parties, also included provision for the subordination of the securities to the senior debt. It mirrored the subordination provisions in the indenture.

§8.297 There were three classes of creditors concerned in the proceeding, these being the Senior Creditors, who held the Senior Indebtedness, the Junior Creditors, who were subject to the subordination provisions, and the other unsecured creditors of the insolvent company, the Ordinary Creditors. The plaintiff in the proceeding represented holders of the securities and the defendants were the holders of the Senior Indebtedness, the company and the liquidators of the company and subsidiaries of the company. Declaratory orders were sought relating to the effect in a winding up, of these subordination provisions. It was argued on behalf of the holders of the Junior Creditors that the liquidators should distribute available funds ratably among all the creditors, in disregard of the subordination provisions.

§8.298 The court concluded that general rule of ratable payment applicable on a corporate insolvency would not prevent the first sentence of paragraph (a) from taking effect according to its terms. The court interpreted the purpose behind this sentence as follows:

> The intended effect of the second sentence is ... that in the event of a winding up of the Company, the liquidator is to pay to the Senior Creditors, in addition to any payment or distribution to which they are otherwise entitled, (until they are all paid in full), amounts equal to the amounts which would have been payable to the Junior Creditors if the Company's liability to them had remained unaffected by paragraph (a) including the contingency provided for by the first sentence.

This second aspect of the subordination was found to be invalid on the following grounds:

> ... it is inconsistent with the principles of law governing distribution in a winding up and is thus invalid and ineffective. ... [to put] it another way, it would require the liquidators to make payments to the Senior Creditors of moneys which would otherwise be available for distribution to the Ordinary Creditors. Such a requirement is open to successful challenge on two grounds. In the first place, it infringes s 440 of the Code which provides:

> Except as otherwise provided by this Code, all debts provable in a winding up rank equally and, if the property of the company is insufficient to meet them in full, they shall be paid proportionately.
>
> It is unnecessary to decide whether this provision can be effectively varied by contract, because it is quite clear that no such contractual variation could effectively operate to the prejudice of a creditor or class of creditors not a party to the contract ... Accordingly, the second sentence of para (a) cannot operate to the prejudice of the Ordinary Creditors, which it would do for reasons already explained if it were to be given its intended effect.
>
> Secondly, such a requirement contravenes the principle illustrated by the rule "that an insolvent estate ... ought not to pay two dividends in respect of the same debt" ... It would be similar in principle to a contractual stipulation between debtor and creditor to the effect that in the event of a winding up of the debtor, the debtor's liability to the creditor is to increase to such amount as will entitle the creditor to receive 100 in the dollar on his original debt or, if this is impossible, to some other specified amount.

In sum, the court concluded that while creditor "A" could agree to subordinate its claim to that of creditor "B", it was not open to creditor "A" to agree that the share to which it would be entitled would be paid over to creditor "B". The subordination arrangement could not be enforced to provide an unsecured creditor (or any subset of unsecured creditors) an advantage in an insolvency proceeding that is denied to other unsecured creditors. The subordinating creditor cannot direct that the resulting benefit shall be distributed preferentially to some unsecured creditors and not others.

§8.299 The problem with this approach is that it is always open for "A" and "B" to agree between themselves outside the scope of the insolvency proceeding. In other words, if a dividend in an insolvency is distributed between "A", "B" and "C" (each being entitled to rank on a par under the general law of insolvency), there is no reason why "A" cannot pay the amount that it receives to "B". There is no prejudice to "C" where this is done: "C" receives precisely the same payment to which it is entitled under insolvency law. In contrast, it would be inequitable to "B" to require it to share the amount that it receives from "A" with "C" — for "B" presumably will have given "A" a consideration in order to purchase the right to receive "A's" share of the dividend; "C", in contrast, will have paid nothing. Since "A" and "B" may effect this arrangement between themselves after the dividend payment is made in the insolvency, it is difficult to understand why they should not be allowed to do so through a valid and effective subordination agreement beforehand, that simply directs the dividend payment to be distributed in the same manner.

§8.300 Not surprisingly, therefore, other courts that have dealt with this problem have come to different conclusions from those adopted in *United States Trust*. In *Re Rico Enterprises Ltd.*[563] Tysoe J. said

---

[563] [1994] B.C.J. No. 415, 24 C.B.R. (3d) 309 at 322-23 (S.C.).

If one creditor subordinates its claim to the claim of another party without subordinating to other claims ranking in priority to the claim of the other party, it is my view that a distribution of the assets of the bankrupt debtor should be made as if there was no subordination except to the extent that the share of the distribution to which the subordinating creditor would otherwise be entitled should be paid to the party in whose favour the subordination was granted.

It is not appropriate to simply take the subordinating creditor out of the class to which it belongs and put it in the class ranking immediately behind the holder of the subordination right.

Under this approach, the only situation in which a subordination arrangement would be objectionable, would be in the unlikely case in which the effect of the arrangement would be to reduce the amount received by the third party creditors (*i.e.*, "C") below what would otherwise be received by them in the absence of the subordination arrangement. It is difficult to conceive of how such a problem would arise.[564]

§8.301 There are relatively few cases that have involved the construction of debt subordination arrangements. It has been held that a subordination undertaking will not be interpreted more broadly than was apparently intended by the parties, as determined by the language that they used.[565] A creditor will not be permitted to employ self-help remedies so as to improve the ranking of his or her claim. Thus subordinated debt owed by A to B may not be set-off against a general unsecured debt owed by B to A, at least where A, the company owing the subordinated debt, is insolvent.[566]

(iv) Proof of Claim

§8.302 Courts possess no general authority to require the holder of a bond or debenture to prove his claim within a limited time, or forfeit his rights under the bond.[567] A debt may be enforced in accordance with applicable limitations legislation. However, bond holders are required to comply with the proof of claim provisions under the *Bankruptcy and Insolvency Act*.[568] By virtue of subsection 124(1) of that Act, every creditor is required to prove his claim in accordance with the procedure set out in the Act and if the creditor does not, it is not entitled to share in any distribution that may be made under the Act. The failure to file a proof of claim does not prevent a secured creditor from realizing upon its security, but will prevent the secured creditor from claiming for any deficiency owing to it after the disposition of the collateral subject to that security.[569]

---

[564] See also *Re Air Canada*, [2004] O.J. No. 1909 (S.C.J.).
[565] *Transamerica Commercial Finance Corp. v. Imperial TV & Stereo Centre Ltd. (Receiver/Manager of)*, [1993] A.J. No. 740, 13 Alta. L.R. (3d) 99 (Q.B.).
[566] See, generally, *Re Northland Bank* (1994), 25 C.B.R. (3d) 160 at 178 (Alta. Q.B.), *per* Kennedy J.
[567] *Toronto General Trusts Corp. v. Lake Superior Corp.*, [1935] O.J. No. 57, [1935] O.W.N. 325 (C.A.).
[568] R.S.C. 1985, c. B-3.
[569] *Ibid.*, s. 127(1).

§8.303 A claim is proved by delivering to the trustee a proof of claim in prescribed form.[570] The proof of claim must have a statement of account attached to it in order to show the trustee some particulars of the creditor's claim against the bankrupt.[571] Where the amount of the claim is not yet known, the amount of the claim must be estimated with reasonable accuracy.[572] The effect of the proof of claim procedure is to make each creditor's claim against the bankrupt a matter of public record in the bankruptcy procedure. Every creditor who has lodged a proof of claim is entitled to see and examine the proofs of the other creditors.[573] It is also the first step in the process of determining the creditors entitled to participate in the bankruptcy and the respective entitlement of each. If a proof of claim is not properly filed so that the creditor's status (*i.e.*, whether the creditor is preferred or secured) is not clear, the proof of claim is invalid and the creditor will not be entitled to vote as a creditor.[574]

§8.304 Subject to the commercial proposal provisions of the *Bankruptcy and Insolvency Act*[575] and to the *Companies' Creditors Arrangement Act*,[576] a secured creditor may proceed to realize on its security without interference by the trustee and without seeking leave of the court,[577] subsection 69.3(2) of the *Bankruptcy and Insolvency Act* providing:

> 69.3(2) Subject to sections 79 and 127 to 135 and subsection 248(1), the bankruptcy of a debtor does not prevent a secured creditor from realizing or otherwise dealing with his security in the same manner as he would have been entitled to realize or deal with it if this section had not been passed, unless the court otherwise orders, but in so ordering the court shall not postpone the right of the secured creditor to realize or otherwise deal with his security, except as follows:
>
> (*a*) in the case of a security for a debt that is due at the date the bankrupt became bankrupt or that becomes due not later than six months thereafter, that right shall not be postponed for more than six months from that date; and
>
> (*b*) in the case of a security for a debt that does not become due until more than six months after the date the bankrupt became bankrupt that right shall not be postponed for more than six months from that date, unless all instalments of interest that are more than six months in arrears are paid and all other defaults

---

[570] *Ibid.*, s. 124(2).
[571] *Re McCoubrey* (1924), 5 C.B.R. 248 (Alta. S.C.). The Official Receiver may reject a proof of claim if there are no vouchers or a statement of account attached to it giving particulars: *Re Corduroys Unlimited Inc.* (1962), 4 C.B.R. (N.S.) 250 (Que. S.C.).
[572] The filing of a false claim is an offence under s. 201 of the *Bankruptcy and Insolvency Act*, R.S.C. 1985, c. B-3. Moreover, s. 125 of the *Bankruptcy and Insolvency Act* provides:

> 125. Where a creditor or other person in any proceedings under this Act files with the trustee a proof of claim containing any wilfully false statement or wilful misrepresentation, the court may, in addition to any other penalty provided in this Act, disallow the claim in whole or in part as the court in its discretion may see fit.

[573] *Bankruptcy and Insolvency Act*, R.S.C. 1985, c. B-3, s. 126(1).
[574] *Re Totten G. Publishers Ltd.*, [1975] O.J. No. 1631, 20 C.B.R. (N.S.) 140 (S.C. in Bnkptcy.).
[575] R.S.C. 1985, c. B-3, ss. 50.4, 69, 69.1 to 69.4 and 224. See, generally, *John Deere Credit Inc. v. Doyle Salewski Lemieux Ltd.*, [1997] O.J. No. 4672, 153 D.L.R. (4th) 572 (C.A.).
[576] R.S.C. 1985, c. C-36.
[577] *Re LeBlanc* (1966), 11 C.B.R. (N.S.) 13 (Que. S.C.).

of more than six months standing are cured, and then only so long as no instalment of interest remains in arrears or defaults remain uncured for more than six months, but, in any event, not beyond the date at which the debt secured by the security becomes payable under the instrument or law creating the security.

If the trustee wishes to obtain a court order staying the secured creditor under section 63, the trustee must apply to the court before the secured creditor has entered into a legally binding contract for the sale of the collateral.[578] Subsection 128(1) of the *Bankruptcy and Insolvency Act* permits the trustee to require a secured creditor to file a proof of security:

> 128.(1) Where the trustee has knowledge of property that may be subject to a security, the trustee may, by serving notice in the prescribed form and manner, require any person to file, in the prescribed form and manner, a proof of the security that gives full particulars of the security, including the date on which the security was given and the value at which that person assesses it.

In addition, the trustee in bankruptcy is entitled to review the validity and enforceability of any security interest and the manner in which the secured creditor realizes upon the collateral.[579] The trustee may redeem the collateral so valued on payment to the secured creditor of the debt or the value of security as set out in the creditor's proof of security.

§8.305 As noted above, a secured creditor who wishes to claim in a bankruptcy for any deficiency remaining after the realization of collateral must file a proof of claim in the bankruptcy proceeding.[580] The creditor may request an extension of time to file its proof of claim.[581] A secured creditor who values its security in response to a notice received from the trustee under subsection 128(1) is entitled to receive a dividend out of the estate of the bankrupt only after deducting the assessed value of the security, so that if the creditor eventually realizes less than that amount, then the creditor's right of claim will be reduced by the amount of the deficiency.[582]

(v) Bond and Other Credit Rating

§8.306 Legal counsel advising with respect to corporate finance need to be generally familiar with the role of bond rating in modern commercial lending and investment practice.[583] A bond rating constitutes an independent assessment by a recognized bond rating agency of the probability of the timely repayment of principal and interest by the issuer, and allows the securities of various issuers to

---

[578] *Re Hallmac Ltd.*, [1973] O.J. No. 2142, 1 O.R. (2d) 143 at 147 (S.C. in Bnkptcy.), *per* Houlden J.A.; see also *Re Dunham*, [1981] O.J. No. 2370, 40 C.B.R. (N.S.) 25 (S.C. in Bnkptcy.); *Re Brodie*, [1984] O.J. No. 2295, 51 C.B.R. (N.S.) 81 (S.C. in Bnkptcy.).
[579] *Ibid.*
[580] *Bankruptcy and Insolvency Act*, R.S.C. 1985, c. B-3, s. 127(1).
[581] *Re LeBlanc* (1966), 11 C.B.R. (N.S.) 13 (Que. S.C.).
[582] *Bankruptcy and Insolvency Act*, R.S.C. 1985, c. B-3, s. 128(3).
[583] See, generally, U.S. Securities and Exchange Commission, *Report on the Role and Function of Credit Rating Agencies in the Operation of the Securities Markets* (Washington: January 2003).

be compared easily. In the United States, SEC has designated five rating agencies as Nationally Recognized Statistical Rating Organizations ("NRSROs"). They are AM Best, Dominion Bond Rating Service ("DBRS"), Fitch Ratings ("Fitch"), Moody's Investors Service ("Moody's"), and Standard & Poor's ("S&P"). Internationally, the two most prominent rating agencies are Moody's Investors Service ("Moody's") and the Standard & Poor's Company ("S&P"). At one time, there were seven NRSROs. By the mid-1990s, there were only three. DBRS was added in 2003, and A.M. Best, which focuses its rating activity on insurance firms was added in 2005. The SEC has stated that:

> The single most important factor in the Commission staff's assessment of NRSRO status is whether the rating agency is "nationally recognized" in the United States as an issuer of credible and reliable ratings by the predominant users of securities ratings. The staff also reviews the operational capability and reliability of each rating organization. Included within this assessment are: (1) the organizational structure of the rating organization; (2) the rating organization's financial resources (to determine, among other things, whether it is able to operate independently of economic pressures or control from the companies it rates); (3) the size and quality of the rating organization's staff (to determine if the entity is capable of thoroughly and competently evaluating an issuer's credit); (4) the rating organization's independence from the companies it rates; (5) the rating organization's rating procedures (to determine whether it has systematic procedures designed to produce credible and accurate ratings); and (6) whether the rating organization has internal procedures to prevent the misuse of nonpublic information and whether those procedures are followed. The staff also recommends that the agency become registered as an investment adviser.

§8.307 In many countries, there are smaller rating agencies which rate debt securities that are not issued into the international securities market. In Canada, DBRS carries on business as a full-service rating agency. It was established in 1976, and is privately owned and operated without affiliation to any financial institution. As well as DBRS, Canadian Bond Rating Services (or "CBRS") — now part of Standard and Poors — formerly was also active in this field. CBRS Inc. was incorporated in 1972, for the purpose of providing credit ratings and financial analysis of Canadian corporations and governments. CBRS was the first credit rating agency to be established in Canada and is the largest in terms of number of staff, as well as in the number of issuers rated. CBRS was the first non-U.S. rating agency to gain international acceptance through its active involvement in the Eurobond Market. CBRS specializes in the analysis and rating of Canadian corporations and governments and their agencies.

§8.308 These organizations review information about selected issuers, especially financial information, such as the issuer's financial statements, and assign a rating to an issuer's bonds (the grades being as explained below). A securities issuer is not required to obtain a rating, but the securities of unrated issuers often cannot be traded widely. Most institutional investors restrict their bond investments to issuers that have a satisfactory bond rating well above the lowest rated grade. Technically bond ratings relate only to the term debt of a company. However, corresponding ratings are often also available with respect to commercial paper and other securities issued by a company, and many investors equate such ratings with the overall financial health of the issuers to which they relate.

§8.309 Before issuing a rating, the agencies must evaluate the financial health of the issuer. Their investigation goes beyond a mere review of the financial statements. It usually incorporates meetings with senior management, discussions with significant creditors and shareholders and the like. Bond rating agencies constantly monitor corporate performance, and revise their rating of individual issuers in accordance both with changes in the overall market and with changes in the specific issuer as well. Even so, the quality of a particular bond may deteriorate overnight because of a sudden material adverse change in its issuer. Such changes are only rarely caught quickly by bond rating agencies.

§8.310 Rating agencies generally offer different ratings for government, corporate debt and investment funds, and differentiate the ratings that they give for short-term debt, long-term debt and preferred shares. For instance, CBRS provides the following

Commercial Paper & Short-term Debt	Long-term Debt	*PREFERRED SHARES*
Highest Quality A-1+TM	Highest Quality A++TM	Credit-Enhanced Preferred SharesP-1+
Very Good Quality A-1	Very Good Quality A+	Highest Quality P-1TM
Good Quality A-1(Low)	Good Quality A	Good Quality P-2
Medium Quality A-2	Medium Quality B++	Medium Quality P-3
Poor Quality A-3	Lower Quality B+	Lower Quality P-4
Rating Suspended: suspended	Poor Quality B	Poor Quality P-5
Unrated	Speculative Quality C	Rating Suspended: Suspended
	Default D	
	Rating Suspended: Suspended	

Although each rating service uses a slightly different range of symbols to rate corporate issuers, their ratings have virtually the same meaning. The following chart compares the ratings of the SEC recognized bond rating agencies:

Moody	Fitch	Dominion	AM Best	S & P
Aaa	AAA	AAA	aaa	AAA
Aa	AA	AA	aa	AA
A	A	A	a	A
Baa	BBB	BBB	bbb	BBB
Ba	BB	BB	bb	BB
B	B	B	b	B
Caa	CCC	CCC	ccc	CCC
Ca	CC	CC	cc	CC
C	C+, C	C	c	C
No rating	D	D	d	D

§8.311 Bond rating is anything but an exact science. In practice, it is possible for the same bond to receive a rating that differs, sometimes substantially, from one ratings agency to the next. The first four categories for each investment agency (S & P AAA to BBB)[584] are sometimes described as "investment grade" securities. Most institutional investors will usually restrict their bond purchases to bonds falling in the investment grade category, and many limit their investments to the top three categories. Issuers falling into this category are considered to have a strong capacity to pay interest and principal.[585]

§8.312 The categories BB to C are considered to be speculative, which means that the issuer's ability to meet interest and principal repayment obligation is less certain. In order to attract investment for their bonds (widely known as "junk bonds"), their issuers must offer higher rates of interest, in some cases coupled with the guarantee of a more creditworthy issuer. Although junk bonds have developed a bad reputation in some quarters, it is worth noting that investment in these securities can often provide an excellent return, for those who are prepared to take the additional risk associated with them.

§8.313 Bonds of issuers falling in category D are bonds on which payment of principal, interest or both is in arrears or which are otherwise in default. Surprisingly, a secondary market still exists for such bonds, among a group of investors known as "vulture funds". These funds specialize in the purchase of the securities of insolvent companies (at a substantial discount against the face value of the securities concerned), and in the liquidation of those companies.

---

[584] Moody's also uses the symbols AA1, A1, Baa1, Ba1 and B1 as subcategories within each of the relevant classes, to identify the corporations within each class which present the strongest investment attributes. S & P uses plus and minus signs to provide a similar calibration within its categories.

[585] The explanations of the various ratings provided in this section are taken from NASD, *Guide to Smart Bond Investing*, online at: <http://apps.nasd.com/investor_Information/smart/bonds/204100.asp>.

§8.314 More exacting definitions for each of these grades are as follows. The highest grade (S & P AAA) describes securities that are of the highest quality with minimal risk of default. Companies in this category are believed to have an "extremely strong capacity to meet financial commitments". The second grade (S & P AA) describes securities that have a superior to very high risk credit quality. Such securities must be issued by companies that have a "very strong capacity to meet financial commitments". The third category (S & P A) describes securities that are considered of medium credit quality, but which are associated with "some risk factors that could contribute to default". The agencies advise, however, that such securities are "still considered to be in little danger of default".

§8.315 Such at least is the theory. The reality is considerably more harsh. Historically, bond ratings have often significantly lagged behind the actual deterioration of the financial quality of the companies to which they relate. To cite a few well-known examples:

- Enron was rated investment grade by the two main bond rating agencies four days before its bankruptcy;

- WorldCom was rated investment grade three months before filing for bankruptcy;

- Global Crossing was rated investment grade in March 2002 but defaulted on its loans in July 2002.

One published study[586] states that only 29 per cent of the bond fund managers they surveyed believe that agencies update their ratings in a timely manner. Taking the probability of lag into account, even BBB issuers (and, some would argue A issuers) should be considered as marginally speculative. This is especially true in times of high interest rates or during sluggish economic conditions, where the prospect of default can only be viewed as higher.

§8.316 The need for caution is brought home as one focuses on the actual meaning behind the labels that are applied. As one moves down the table of security ratings, it becomes increasingly clear that even "investment grade" securities of the BBB class represent what might best be described as a highly courageous investment. Grade BBB applies to investments that present:

> "Adequate to medium credit quality ... Could be susceptible to default risk in the long term or there may be other adverse conditions present which reduce credit quality."

This is considered "investment grade"? At the BB level, the advice is even less sanguine:

> "Questionable to speculative financial security, with additional factors that may contribute to default, such as ability to meet debt obligations, especially during periods of economic recession."

---

[586] H. Kent Baker & Sattar A. Mansi, "Assessing Credit Rating Agencies by Bond Issuers and Institutional Investors" (June 18, 2001).

By the time one reaches CCC grade issues, the rating agencies caution that they are:

> "Very highly speculative with danger of default, or default probable, or may have recently occurred."

By grade C, the securities are:

> "Very highly speculative, often accompanied by bankruptcy petitions; default immanent or has recently occurred."

§8.317 Given the deficiencies associated with reliance only on bond rating, many financial analysts suggest reference to the risk premium associated with the securities of each issuer. The risk premium is the difference between the average yield to maturity for the bonds of an issuer of each rating, and the actual yield with respect to any actual issuer of that rating, for the unexpired balance of the term to maturity. Often changes in the risk premium exacted in the bond market reflect the deteriorating condition of an issuer before any change is made to its rating. For instance, Enron's risk premium jumped from 5 per cent to 7 per cent during the month prior to its filing for bankruptcy. In 1997 two-thirds of debt rated triple-B by S&P was priced within 20 basis points of the average bond with the same rating. By 2001, the range had widened more than six-fold. The growing gap suggests an increasing dissatisfaction with the quality of information provided by bond rating agencies.

(vi) Project Financing

§8.317.1 In recent years, many major corporate capital projects have been financed on what is known as a project financing basis, including large-scale natural resource projects, such as refineries and pipelines, power plants, hydroelectric dams and other electric generating facilities and ports and airport terminals.[587] Essentially, where a project financing model is employed, the project is financed on the strength of its anticipated revenue stream and the underlying value of the assets that will be used in the project. Project financing is thus not so much a form of security, as a description of the sources to which the lenders may look for payment.

§8.317.2 Project financing is a highly technical field. It requires lenders who have extensive knowledge of the industry to which the project relates, so that they are able to prepare a suitable financial plan integrated with the borrower's business plan, and to assess the risks and appropriate financing mix (the blend of equity and debt, and the forms of debt and terms of repayment) that are suited to the project. Only when this is done, is it possible to raise the funds needed. To validate a project's feasibility lenders must determine the project's borrowing capacity, using rigorous cash flow projections to assess measure expected rates

---

[587] See, generally, P.K. Nevitt, F.J. Fabozzi, *Project Financing* (London: Euromoney, 2005 7th ed.); J. Finnerty, *Project Financing* (London, Wiley, 1996); E.C. Buljevich, Y.S. Park, *Project Financing and the International Financial Markets* (Norwell, Mass.: Kluwer, 1999); R.F. Sullivan, *International Project Financing* (London: Juris, 2002, 3rd ed.).

of return; using appropriate analytical techniques. It is essential to factor into the financing mix, the cyclical features of the industry to which the project relates, and anticipated pricing trends (often taking into account projected world wide supply as well as anticipated growth in demand for this purpose. In addition, project financing is very sensitive to legal and regulatory risk, including tax and accounting considerations.

§8.317.3 Since the lenders have only one source of repayment (the project and the revenues that it generates), lending on this basis is often described as "no-recourse". In contrast in conventional lending, the lender usually has recourse to the borrower's other assets for repayment, as well as to guarantees provided in respect of the borrower. Guarantees are not unknown in project financing, but in contrast to more traditional financing, they tend to relate to specific portions of debt and to be capped at a fixed amount. The no recourse feature of the debt makes it essential for the lender to identify, analyze and properly manage all forms of risk associated with the project. Key areas of risk include:

- credit risk (*i.e.*, risks associated with the borrower that is sponsoring the project itself, such as whether the borrower has the right combination of experience, expertise and capital financing to make the project work);

- technical risk (*i.e.*, the difficulties associated with building and operating the project's plant and equipment, and the risk of latent defects in design and construction), as well as the availability of financing resources required to meet such risk (usually this need is provided for by way of a maintenance retention account in which a portion of net cash-flow will be set aside to cover projected maintenance expenditure);

- currency risk (where borrowers and lenders are dealing in different currencies, there are risks associated with adverse fluctuation in the respective currency values);

- regulatory and related approvals risk (often the industries to which projects of this nature are highly regulated, and thus there are risks that the government licences and approvals required to construct or operate the project, or to export its product, will not be issued, or will only be issued subject to onerous conditions;

- other legal risk (*e.g.*, the risk that the project will be subjected to excessive taxation, royalty payments, or rigid requirements as to local supply or distribution by the government of the jurisdiction in which the project will be built);

- political risk (*i.e.*, the risk of political instability in the host country, or of the introduction of some adverse policy such as the suspension or restriction of foreign exchange transactions, or a process of expropriation or nationalization;

- sovereign risk (*i.e.*, the risk that a government may be nullify its contractual obligations through legislative change);

- *force majeure* risk (the risk that the project or its value may be adversely affected by forces beyond the control of any party to the transaction, such as severe weather events).

J. CHALLENGING THE VALIDITY OF A SECURITY AGREEMENT

§8.318 The right of the corporation to impeach security agreements that it has entered, and the corresponding rights of shareholders and corporate outsiders such as creditors to do the same, has received extensive judicial consideration. In the case of the corporation, it seems settled that it may not impeach its own securities; nor may its directors[588] or shareholders. Thus in *Kiely v. Smyth*[589] Spragge J. stated:

> I take it to be very clear that in any question between a bondholder and the company, or any then member of the company, neither of the latter could be heard to allege any fact that would invalidate the bonds, or any fact that would bring their validity into question.

While this principle has no application against a corporations trustee in bankruptcy, it would appear to be applicable to any privately appointed Receiver since such an office holder is usually described as acting as the corporations agent. As the above passage suggests, the rule of non-contestability often combines with the rule in *Foss v. Harbottle*,[590] so as to prevent an indirect challenge by the corporation to the validity of its security by way of a shareholder derivative action. For instance, in *Greenstreet v. Paris Hydraulic Co.*[591] an action was brought against a company on a mortgage made by it. A subsequent encumbrancer objected that the mortgage was invalid because it was taken by the plaintiff (who was a director of the company) in breach of the fiduciary duties owed by the director to the company. The court refused to entertain the creditor's objection. However, as explained below, the creditors of a corporation may impeach a security agreement where it constitutes a fraudulent conveyance or preference.[592]

§8.319 The general principle that a corporation may not deny the validity of a security that it issues applies with respect to any technical defect in the security[593] or with respect to any substantive ground other than a defence generally available to an obligor under a contract, such as duress, undue influence, non-satisfaction of a condition or *non est factum*. Because a corporation is an artificial entity it must necessarily act through agents. The corporation may in certain

---

[588] *Royal Trust Co. v. Baie des Chaleurs Rlwy. Co.* (1907), 13 Ex. C.R. 1.
[589] [1879] O.J. No. 236, 27 Gr. 220 at 229.
[590] (1843), 2 Hare 461.
[591] [1874] O.J. No. 208, 21 Gr. 229 (H.C.).
[592] *Wellburn's Market Ltd. v. Pacific Green Grocers Ltd.*, [1981] B.C.J. No. 829,, 39 C.B.R. (N.S.) 226 (C.A.).
[593] See, for instance, *Re Caldwells Ltd.*, [1934] O.J. No. 233, [1934] O.R. 178 (C.A.), aff'g 14 C.B.R. 497 (H.C.J.).

cases raise agency defences, such as want of authority, in challenging the validity of its security, but its right to do so is substantially curtailed both at common law (under the rule in *Turquand*'s case)[594] and by statute (under sections 19 of the OBCA and 20 of the CBCA). Irrespective of authority, a corporation will also be estopped from denying the validity of a security where the corporation left signed securities in the hands of an agent who then sold them to an innocent holder for value without notice.[595]

§8.320 The reason why corporations are not generally permitted to contest the validity of their securities is that in most cases the corporation will have been subject to a contractual duty to provide the creditor with a valid security. Failure to do so constitutes a breach of contract, and it is clear that the corporation may not invoke its own breach of contract in defence of a claim under the security that it purported to confer. Moreover, the creditor may also invoke the rule of equity that equity considers that to be done which ought to have been done. Thus a promise to give a security interest is sufficient to create an equitable security — although the enforceability of that equitable interest against third parties may be in doubt where there has been a failure to comply.

§8.321 The rule barring corporations from challenging the validity of their own securities comes into play only where the person to whom the security was issued had no knowledge of its defective character. Once so validated, the security remains validated. For instance, in *Re Bank of Syria*[596] the articles of a company provided that it should be managed by a council of three persons. The number of councillors fell to two, but nevertheless, the remaining members purported to issue debt securities to Lloyd's Bank, which had no knowledge of the irregularity in the constitution of the board. One of the members of the council (who had provided a personal guarantee) subsequently paid off the bank and took an assignment of the security. Chief Justice Lord Alverstone ruled that the security was valid not only in the hands of Lloyd's but also in the hands of the councillor to whom it was assigned.[597]

§8.322 Moreover, in *Re Hercules Insurance Co. (Brunton's Claim)*,[598] a non-negotiable bond was issued through a fraud and was subsequently assigned for value to Brunton, who was an innocent third party. Brunton did not inquire as to the validity of the bond before taking the assignment. He then notified the company of the assignment. The company accepted the notice but did not register it. Before the money secured by the bond became payable, the company was ordered to be wound up. It was held that the company was liable on the bond to the assignee Brunton. The company, and not the persons dealing with it, were responsible for the failure of its officers to register the assignment. Whatever equity the company might have raised against the original holder, once the com-

---

[594] (1869) L.R. 4 Ch. 376.
[595] *Canada (Minister of Rlwys. and Canals) v. Quebec Southern Rlwy. Co.* (1908), 12 Ex. C.R. 152.
[596] [1901] Ch. 115 (C.A.).
[597] *Ibid.*, at 121.
[598] (1874), L.R. 19 Eq. 302 (V.C.).

pany accepted notice of the assignment, it was precluded from setting up those equities against the assignee.

§8.323 In recent years, a number of attempts have been made by trustees in bankruptcy to downgrade the claims of secured creditors by invoking the purported doctrine of "equitable subordination", a concept recognized under the bankruptcy laws of the United States. The availability of this remedy in Canada is discussed in Chapter 13, in the context of the oppression remedy. On occasion, Canadian courts have indicated some willingness to permit a trustee in bankruptcy of a corporation to postpone corporate securities that were granted in contravention of restrictions imposed under the statute of incorporation[599] or in breach of the fiduciary duties of directors.[600] Similarly, the courts have also been prepared occasionally to treat shareholder advances as equity investments in the corporation, rather than loans.[601]

K. FRAUDULENT PREFERENCES, CONVEYANCES AND RELATED ISSUES

§8.324 At various points in this chapter, reference has been made to the possibility of attacking a transfer of property or security interest granted to a creditor on the grounds that it constitutes a fraudulent conveyance or preference to or in favour of that creditor. Given the extent to which such questions arise, it is worthwhile to consider briefly the law relating to such conveyances and preferences. A fraudulent preference may be distinguished from a fraudulent conveyance as follows. For a preference, the debtor must have been insolvent or "on the eve of insolvency", and the transaction must have had the effect of conferring a preference on the party receiving the property relative to other creditors of the debtor. A fraudulent is a conveyance of property that is not made for good consideration and that is made with an intention to defraud the debtor's creditors. The language of the *Fraudulent Conveyances Act*[602] is broad enough on its terms to cover both a conveyance and preference.

§8.325 In general terms, a fraudulent conveyance is a transfer of property by a debtor to a third party, whether or not a creditor, made so as to put it beyond the reach of the general creditors of the debtor; whereas a preference is a direct or indirect payment to one, but not all, of the creditors of the debtor. As the financial condition of a corporation deteriorates, the persons in control of the corporation (which in any particular circumstances may be the directors, shareholders

---

[599] *Kronson v. Metro Drugs Manitoba Ltd. (Trustee of)*, [1985] M.J. No. 61, 61 C.B.R. (N.S.) 312 (Q.B.).
[600] *C.E. Plain Ltd. (Trustee of) v. Kenley*, [1931] O.J. No. 393, [1931] O.R. 75 at 78 (C.A.).
[601] *Laronge Realty Ltd. v. Golconda Investments Ltd.*, [1986] B.C.J. No. 848, 7 B.C.L.R. (2d) 90 at 94 (C.A.), and see also R.W. Wasiuk, "Defeating Shareholders' Loans" (1985) 25 Alta. L. Rev. 504; *Sukloff v. A.H. Rushforth & Co. Estate*, [1964] S.C.J. No. 26, [1964] S.C.R. 459; *Re Meade*, [1951] Ch. 774.
[602] R.S.O. 1990, c. F.29.

or officers of the corporation) may attempt to cause the corporation to transfer property, create security interests and otherwise deal with its business and affairs so as to confer an undue advantage on one creditor relative to the other creditors of the corporation. In certain circumstances it may be possible to attack any such dealing under the *Fraudulent Conveyances Act*,[603] the *Assignments and Preferences Act*[604] or the *Bankruptcy and Insolvency Act*.[605]

§8.326 A transfer made without valuable consideration and with the intent of defeating, hindering, delaying or defrauding creditors is known as a fraudulent conveyance. Such conveyances may be made by any debtor, but they are particularly likely to occur in the case of corporate debtors, because of the artificial nature of corporate personality and the control exercised over the business and affairs of the corporation by its insiders. Indeed, it is quite common for a failing corporation (especially a closely held corporation) to attempt to transfer some or all of its assets to one of its shareholders in order to prevent the loss of those assets to the creditors of the corporation. Such transfers are subject to attack under section 2 of the *Fraudulent Conveyances Act*, which provides:

> 2. Every conveyance of real property or personal property and every bond, suit, judgment and execution heretofore or hereafter made with intent to defeat, hinder, delay or defraud creditors or others of their just and lawful actions, suits, debts, accounts, damages, penalties or forfeitures are void as against such persons and their assigns.

Although section 2 provides that the conveyance or other transaction is void, the courts have consistently interpreted this word to mean voidable: the transaction is good between the parties themselves until it is impeached by a creditor.[606]

§8.327 It is self-evident that section 2 of the *Fraudulent Conveyances Act* is quite broad in scope. It applies not only to direct conveyances from the corporation, but also covers devices intended to give the transaction the appearance of legitimacy, such as a default judgment in an action by the transferor of the property. However, the scope of the protection afforded is qualified by section 3 of the Act, which provides:

> 3. Section 2 does not apply to an estate or interest in real property or personal property conveyed upon good consideration and in good faith to a person not having at the time of the conveyance to the person notice or knowledge of the intent set forth in that section.

In order for section 3 to apply, it is necessary to show both that consideration was given and that the conveyance was in good faith to a person without notice or knowledge of the fraudulent intent. Any doubt in this respect is eliminated by section 4 of the Act, which provides:

---

[603] *Ibid.*
[604] R.S.O. 1990, c. A.33.
[605] R.S.O. 1985, c. B-3.
[606] *Donohue v. Hull Brothers & Co.* (1895), 24 S.C.R. 683. For a recent case in which it was not possible to restore the transferee to her original position after the transfer was set aside, see *Bank of Montreal v. Bray*, [1997] O.J. No. 4277, 153 D.L.R. (4th) 490 (C.A.).

4. Section 2 applies to every conveyance executed with the intent set forth in that section despite the fact that it was executed upon a valuable consideration and with the intention, as between the parties to it, of actually transferring to and for the benefit of the transferee the interest expressed to be thereby transferred, unless it is protected under section 3 by reason of good faith and want of notice or knowledge on the part of the purchaser.

While section 4 appears to differentiate between want of notice and good faith, it is difficult to see how a purchaser could act in good faith if he or she had notice of the fraudulent intent; by the same token, it is difficult to see how a person could act in bad faith (at least in a relevant respect) if there was no notice or knowledge of the fraud being perpetrated by the transferor.

§8.328 There has been a considerable volume of case law in which the meaning of the *Fraudulent Conveyances Act* has been considered, and since the subject of fraudulent conveyances and preferences lies primarily in the field of debtor and creditor law, rather than corporate law, it is possible only to touch on that case law here. In *Stephens v. McArthur*[607] it was held that the Manitoba equivalent of the above provisions apply only with respect to a voluntary preference. They do not apply to a case where the transfer has been induced by the pressure of the creditor. A mere demand by the creditor without even a threat of legal proceedings, was held to be sufficient pressure to rebut the presumption of a preference. In order to render such an assignment void there must be knowledge of the insolvency on the part of both parties and concurrence of intention to obtain an unlawful preference over the other creditors.[608] In *Canadian Imperial Bank of Commerce v. Ramsay*,[609] Bayda J., said:

> A plaintiff, in an action instituted pursuant to the *Fraudulent Preferences Act* is in effect saying to the defendant who is at the present time the registered owner of the land "you have acquired your title to the land fraudulently; you have no right to retain title and I am asking the Court to rectify matters by declaring void the transaction which gave rise to your title". An action of this kind squarely brings into question the title to the land. I find that it is not necessary that the plaintiff claim title or an interest or a lien for himself.

In *Canadian Imperial Bank of Commerce v. Grande Cache Motor Inn Ltd.*,[610] Miller J. held that

> ... any allegation of fraudulent intent is a serious one and should not be found as a fact without the presence of substantial evidence on which to base such a finding.

§8.329 Of particular importance is the distinction drawn under the Act between those conveyances that are supported by consideration and those that are not. Where there is no consideration, the plaintiff attacking the transfer need show

---

[607] (1891), 19 S.C.R. 446.
[608] *Benallack v. Bank of British North America* (1905), 36 S.C.R. 120.
[609] [1973] S.J. No. 95, 38 D.L.R. (3d) 618 at 619 (Q.B.); see also *Penner's Construction Ltd. v. Ancel*, [1979] M.J. No. 104, (1979), 106 D.L.R. (3d) 634 (C.A.); *Bank of Montreal v. Ewing*, [1982] O.J. No. 3120, 135 D.L.R. (3d) 382 (Div. Ct.); *Royal Bank of Canada v. Roles*, [1989] S.J. No. 169, 76 Sask. R. 191 (Q.B.).
[610] [1977] A.J. No. 496, 4 Alta. L.R. (2d) 319 at 330 (S.C.).

only that the transferor intended to defeat its creditors. It is not necessary to show that the transferee either knew of or conspired in that attempt.[611] Where consideration was given, it is then necessary to prove a mutual intent to defraud, hinder, defeat or delay on the part of both the transferor and the transferee. Not every transaction that results in some preferential treatment is necessarily fraudulent. Among the legitimate factors that may coincidentally result in a preference are the following:

- A desire to avoid time consuming litigation that would undermine efforts to maintain corporation in operation.[612]
- A payment made in order to maintain the availability of a critical source of supply.
- A transfer of property at fair value used to generate funds needed to meet maturing financial commitments of the debtor corporation. Fair value for this purpose should be established by way of an independent professional appraisal or some corresponding objective process.[613]

§8.330 The question of whether the required intent to prefer existed (be it on the part of both transferee and transferor, or of just the transferor) is one of fact. The intent must exist at the time of the transfer: subsequent acts are irrelevant to the determination of this question,[614] for the obvious reason that it can generally be presumed that a transferee to whom property has been transferred upon payment of valuable consideration will wish to hold onto that property and will be prepared to do everything possible to accomplish that purpose. Over the years the courts have established a number of tests (known as badges of fraud) to assist in determining whether or not the parties had the intent to defeat, delay, hinder or defraud the creditors of the transferor.[615] These include:

- that the transaction was conducted in secrecy — this would appear to be a highly probative factor, for such secrecy raises an obvious inference that there was something inappropriate concerning the transaction;
- unusual haste in closing — this is a rather subjective assessment and for that reason would tend to be less probative than secrecy. However, if combined with other badges of fraud (particularly secrecy), it may be particularly convincing that the transaction was not carried out in good faith;
- the transaction was carried out while an action was pending or after execution had been issued;

---

[611] *Oliver v. McLaughlin*, [1893] O.J. No. 11, 24 O.R. 41 (C.A.); *Commerce Capital Mortgage Corp. v. Jemmet*, [1981] O.J. No. 1242, 37 C.B.R. (N.S.) 59 (H.C.J.).
[612] See, for instance *Re Inex Pharmaceuticals Corp.*, [2006] B.C.J. No. 472 (C.A.).
[613] See, generally, *Re Atlantic Ova Pro Ltd.*, [2006] N.S.J. No. 73, 146 A.C.W.S. (3d) 15 (S.C.).
[614] *Donohue v. Hull Brothers & Co.* (1895), 24 S.C.R. 683.
[615] *Solomon v. Solomon*, [1977] O.J. No. 2349, 16 O.R. (2d) 769 (H.C.J.); *Bank of Montreal v. Vandine*, [1953] 1 D.L.R. 456 (N.B.C.A.); *Ferguson v. Lastewka*, [1946] O.J. No. 646, [1946] O.R. 577 (H.C.J.).

- where the transaction involved a conveyance of substantially all of the debtor's assets — such a transfer is less probative, for there are many alternate legitimate explanations as to why the corporation might have disposed of its assets. For instance, the sale may have been made in the course of a "soft receivership";
- the debtor corporation has continued in possession or has retained some benefit in the property conveyed;
- the transferee is not at arm's length to the transferor.

The badges of fraud raise an evidentiary presumption of fraud, but they are not conclusive of the fact. Once they are shown to be present, the onus of proof shifts to the party seeking to uphold the conveyance.[616] The court must consider not only the effect of the transaction, but also the surrounding circumstances in which it took place.[617] Alternatively stated, the badges of fraud are not acts of fraud in themselves but, rather, afford circumstantial evidence of fraud. They are facts having a tendency to show the existence of fraud, although their value as evidence is relative not absolute. They are not usually conclusive proof, but proof of their presence is sufficient to require an explanation. When several are found in the same transaction, strong, clear evidence will be required to repel the conclusion of fraudulent intent.[618]

§8.331 In contrast to the other statutes in the fraudulent conveyance and preference area, there is no limitation period under the *Fraudulent Conveyances Act*.[619] An action under the Act may be brought by the trustee in bankruptcy of the corporation or by a creditor of the corporation. A secured creditor has no standing under the Act, however, unless the collateral held as security by that creditor is insufficient to repay the creditor in full.[620] Moreover, the deficiency in security must exist at the time when the conveyance or other transaction takes place. So in *Crombie v. Young*, MacMahon J. said:

> If at the time a mortgage is given, payable, say in five years, the mortgaged property is regarded by both the mortgagor and the mortgagee as ample security for the mortgage debt, then if the mortgagor cannot make a voluntary settlement (although otherwise financially in a position so to do), because he may possibly become a debtor to the mortgagee by reason of the depreciation of the mortgaged property, just before the expiration of the five years, the arrangement must hold good as to a mortgage having ten years to run, and a like result happening.[621]

---

[616] See, for instance, *Owen Sound General & Marine Hospital v. Mann*, [1953] O.J. No. 679, [1953] O.R. 643 at 647 (H.C.J.), *per* Anger J.
[617] *Re Wise, ex p. Mercer* (1886), 17 Q.B.D. 290 (C.A.).
[618] *Gifford-Hill & Co. v. Stoller*, 221 Neb. 757, 380 N.W.2d 625 (S.C. Neb. 1986); *Southern Lumber & Coal Co. v. M. P. Olson Real Estate and Construction Co., Inc.*, 229 Neb. 249; 426 N.W.2d 504 (S.C. Neb. 1988).
[619] R.S.O. 1990, c. F.29.
[620] *Sun Life Assurance Co. of Canada v. Elliott* (1900), 31 S.C.R. 91; *Arnold v. Fleming*, [1923] 1 D.L.R. 1026 (Alta. S.C.).
[621] [1894] O.J. No. 90, 26 O.R. 194 at 207 (C.A.).

By logical extension, it might be argued that a creditor who seeks to set aside a transaction must show that he or she was a creditor of the debtor at the time when the transaction occurred. However, in *Gauthier v. Woollatt*[622] Roach J. held that a subsequent creditor could impeach the transaction in two situations: first, where at the time when the action to impeach the transaction is brought, there remains at least one unpaid creditor whose claim existed at the date of the conveyance; second, where the debtor's objective was to put its assets beyond the reach of its creditors, so that its motive was to defraud its creditors generally. Even so, this latter proposition must be stated with some reservation: a debtor is not obliged to maintain a pool of assets that its creditors can attach nor to build up its assets while in business. A subsequent creditor is in no way prejudiced by the debtor's lack of property; the creditor's prejudice stems from its own lack of caution in not limiting its dealings to those customers who had the wherewithal to pay.

§8.332 In contrast, under the *Assignments and Preferences Act*,[623] it is clear that only a creditor whose claim exists at the time of the challenged preference has standing.[624] Moreover, a person who has an unliquidated claim may not attack a preference until such time as that claim has been reduced to judgment. A judgment creditor may maintain an action in his or her own name;[625] any other creditor must bring a representative action on behalf of all creditors.[626] The action is commenced by statement of claim. The transferee is a necessary party defendant, but the debtor corporation is not.[627]

§8.333 A fraudulent preference is a favouring by an insolvent debtor of a particular creditor over others whose claims are entitled by law to rank equally against the debtor. A payment by a debtor to one creditor in full at a time when there is no prospect of making equal payments to its other creditors is a textbook example of a fraudulent preference. Fraudulent preferences may be attacked under the *Bankruptcy and Insolvency Act*[628] or the *Assignments and Preferences Act*.[629] A preference may be structured so that it operates directly or indirectly. Generally, where a creditor receives a payment from a third party in satisfaction of its claim, that payment cannot be attacked as a preference because the money used is not property of the debtor.[630] On the other hand, where the debtor directs a payment owing to it by a third party to be made to a particular creditor instead, that can constitute a preference provided the other requirements of a preferential payment are satisfied.

---

[622] [1940] O.J. No. 39, [1940] 1 D.L.R. 275 (S.C.).
[623] R.S.O. 1990, c. A.33.
[624] *Ashley v. Brown*, [1890] O.J. No. 36, 17 O.A.R. 500 (C.A.).
[625] *Brown v. Weil*, [1927] O.J. No. No. 86, 61 O.L.R. 55 (C.A.).
[626] *Gibbons v. Darvill*, [1888] O.J. No. 299, 12 P.R. 478 (H.C.J.).
[627] *Martin v. Martin*, [1937] O.J. No. 313, [1937] O.R. 759 (H.C.J.).
[628] R.S.C. 1985, c. B-3. See, generally, *Re Green Gables Manor Inc.*, [1998] O.J. No. 2608, 41 B.L.R. (2d) 299 (S.C. in Bnkptcy) (related-party transaction).
[629] R.S.O. 1990, c. A.33.
[630] *Turkawski v. 738675 Alberta Ltd.*, [2006] A.J. No. 469, 69 W.C.B. (2d) 176 at para. 7 (C.A.), per Veit J.

§8.334 Subsection 95(1) of the BIA provides:

> 95.(1) Every transfer of property, every charge made on property, every payment made, every obligation incurred and every judicial proceeding taken or suffered by any insolvent person in favour of any creditor or of any person in trust for any creditor with a view to giving that creditor a preference over the other creditors is, when it is made, given, incurred, taken or suffered within the period beginning on the day that is three months before the date of the initial bankruptcy event and ending on the date the insolvent person became bankrupt, both dates included, deemed fraudulent and void as against, or in the Province of Quebec, may not be set up against, the trustee in the bankruptcy.

If the transfer, charge, payment, obligation or judicial proceeding mentioned in section 95 is in favour of a person related to the insolvent person, the period referred to in subsection 95(1) is increased to one year from the normal three months.[631] If a person has acquired property of a bankrupt under a transaction that is void or voidable and set aside or, in the Province of Quebec, null or annullable and set aside, and has sold, disposed of, realized or collected the property or any part of it, the money or other proceeds, whether further disposed of or not, shall be deemed the property of the trustee.[632] The trustee may recover the property or the value thereof or the money or proceeds there from the person who acquired it from the bankrupt or from any other person to whom he may have resold, transferred or paid over the proceeds of the property as fully and effectually as the trustee could have recovered the property if it had not been so sold, disposed of, realized or collected.[633]

§8.335 Subsection 95(2) creates the following factual presumption:

> 95.(2) If any transfer, charge, payment, obligation or judicial proceeding mentioned in subsection (1) has the effect of giving any creditor a preference over other creditors, or over any one or more of them, it shall be presumed, in the absence of evidence to the contrary, to have been made, incurred, taken, paid or suffered with a view to giving the creditor a preference over other creditors, whether or not it was made voluntarily or under pressure and evidence of pressure shall not be admissible to support the transaction.

In *Hudson v. Benallack*,[634] a company assigned its interest as purchaser in an agreement for conveyance of certain lands to the respondents. The consideration for the assignment was stated to be $15,250. At the time the assignor company was indebted to the assignees in the amount of $15,000 with interest and this indebtedness was used to offset the purchase price of the assignor's interest in the agreement of sale. All of the issued shares of the company were owned by the son and daughter-in-law of the respondents. The company made an assignment in bankruptcy within a 12-month period, and the appellant was named as trustee. The question at issue was whether the words "with a view to giving such

---

[631] BIA, s. 96.
[632] BIA, s. 98(1).
[633] BIA, s. 98(2).
[634] [1975] S.C.J. No. 71, [1976] 2 S.C.R. 168.

creditor a preference" contained in what was then 73(1) of the *Bankruptcy Act* — the precursor to the present section 95 — required only an intention on the part of the insolvent debtor to prefer or a concurrent intent on the part of both debtor and creditor. In allowing the appeal, the Supreme Court concluded that a finding of concurrent intent was not necessary in order to set aside a payment as a fraudulent preference under section 73. The knowledge of the creditor or its absence is not relevant. An innocent creditor who accepts a preferential payment of a debt even in good faith, gains no rights over the other innocent creditors of the bankrupt debtor.

§8.336 However, in *Re Norris*[635] the court pointed out the need to distinguish between what constitutes a preference in fact and fraudulent preference as that latter is defined in the Act.

> There can be no doubt in this case that Revenue Canada received a preference in fact from the payment of tax made by this debtor on November 25, 1992. Its debt was paid where the debts owing to other ordinary creditors were not. What would render that preference in fact a fraudulent one under section 95 is the accompanying intent of the insolvent debtor who in the face of imminent bankruptcy is moved to prefer or favour, before losing control over his assets, a particular creditor over others who will have to wait for and accept as full payment their rateable share on distribution by the Trustee in the ensuing bankruptcy. It is called fraudulent because it prejudices other creditors who will receive proportionately less, or nothing at all, and upsets the fundamental scheme of the Act for equal sharing among creditors. That accompanying intent to favour one creditor over another is what makes a preference in fact a fraudulent preference and is referred to in the cases as the "dominant intent". The state of mind of the debtor at the time of making the payment is ultimately the paramount consideration to be addressed by the court. The intent or state of mind of the preferred creditor is irrelevant.

The second subsection presumes that if all the other matters have been established, the payment is fraudulent in the absence of evidence to the contrary. The present wording of subsection 95(2) places the onus on the bankrupt to introduce some compelling evidence that allows the court to override the presumption. If after consideration of all of the evidence before it the court is satisfied on a balance of probability that the debtor was pursuing a purpose other than that of favouring the particular creditor over others, the presumption is displaced and the application fails. The finding of a court on that particular issue is one of fact which will not be disturbed on appeal, unless relevant evidence has not been taken into account by the trier of fact.[636]

§8.337 In contrast, subsection 4(1) of the *Assignments and Preferences Act* provides:

> 4.(1) Subject to section 5, every gift, conveyance, assignment or transfer, delivery over or payment of goods, chattels or effects, or of bills, bonds, notes or securities, or of shares, dividends, premiums or bonus in any bank, company or

---

[635] [1996] A.J. No. 975 at para. 16, 44 C.B.R. (3d) 218, 193 A.R. 15 (C.A.).
[636] *Ramsey Estate v. Royal Bank of Canada*, [2006] A.J. No. 628 (Q.B.), *per* Wilson J.

corporation, or of any other property, real or personal, made by a person when insolvent or unable to pay the person's debts in full or when the person knows that he, she or it is on the eve of insolvency, with intent to defeat, hinder, delay or prejudice creditors, or any one or more of them, is void as against the creditor or creditors injured, delayed or prejudiced.

Section 5 of the Act deals with assignments for the general benefit of creditors and with sales in good faith. In addition to the general basis for attack on gifts and transfers made with an intent to defeat or prejudice creditors which is provided for in subsection (1), subsection 4(2) of the Act provides a basis for attack on any unjust preference:

> 4.(2) ... every such gift, conveyance, assignment or transfer, delivery over or payment made by a person being at the time in insolvent circumstances, or unable to pay his, her or its debts in full, or knowing himself, herself or itself to be on the eve of insolvency, to or for a creditor with the intent to give such creditor an unjust preference over other creditors or over any one or more of them is void as against the creditor or creditors injured, delayed, prejudiced or postponed.

§8.338 Although the operation of the *Assignments and Preferences Act* is premised upon the insolvency of the debtor, the Supreme Court of Canada has held that it is valid provincial legislation with respect to property and civil rights.[637] However, the insolvency requirement does present a number of problems of interpretation. One question is the extent to which future and contingent liabilities must be taken into account in deciding whether a corporation is or is not solvent. In *Traders Group Ltd. v. Mason*[638] Gills J. held that a contingent liability such as a guarantee should be taken into account; but the rule seems to depend upon the remoteness of contingent liability. It cannot have been the intention of the legislature to tie up the hands of debtors merely because extravagant claims are made against them in lawsuits, or because of a very remote possibility of liability which no one seriously expects to materialize.

§8.339 A second question of interpretation turns upon how the assets of a debtor are to be valued in order to determine whether the debtor is or is not insolvent or on the eve of insolvency. There are a number of cases in which the courts have leaned towards valuation on a sale-under-distress basis, rather than to a going-concern, fair-market valuation.[639] Such an approach is excessively conservative. While it results in the maximum protection for creditors, for several reasons it is nonetheless almost wholly unrealistic. First, while the market valuation of assets is relatively straightforward it is virtually impossible to provide a sale-under-distress value of an asset. It is a truism that the sale-under-distress is significantly less than the fair market value; while over the course of time it is possible to provide a ball-park estimate of sale-under-distress value as a percentage of

---

[637] *Robinson v. Countrywide Factors Ltd.*, [1977] S.C.J. No. 76, [1978] 1 S.C.R. 753.
[638] [1973] N.S.J. No. 155, 43 D.L.R. (3d) 76 (S.C.), var'd [1974] N.S.J. No. 256, 53 D.L.R. (3d) 103 (C.A.).
[639] *Re Butterworth* (1882), 19 Ch. D. 588; *Davison v. Douglas* (1868), 15 Gr. 347 (Ch.); *Dominion Bank v. Cowan*, [1887] O.J. No. 178, 14 O.R. 465 (H.C.J.).

fair market value, any such valuation is simply that: an estimate. There is no guarantee that the percentage so estimated will be realized, nor is there any certainty that only that percentage will be realized. Second, unless a debtor is under virtual siege by its creditors, there is no reason for the debtor to assume that its operations will not continue: that its inventory will not be sold in the ordinary course and that its receivables will not be collected in an orderly and businesslike manner. Generally accepted accounting principles call for valuation on a going-concern basis, unless there is some reason to believe that the debtor will not continue in operation. By extension a going-concern valuation should be used for fraudulent preference purposes as well. Third, sale-under-distress prices are subject to wild fluctuations as overall economic conditions vary. For instance, during the recession of the early 1990s, used office equipment and furniture and store fittings had virtually no value at all. It is not realistic to subtract the value of such items from the assets of a corporation, where there is no reason to doubt that the corporation will continue in operation.

§8.340 In order to attack a preference successfully under the *Assignments and Preferences Act* it is necessary to establish that there was a joint intention between the debtor and the creditor to give and receive a preference. Where an attack is made against an alleged preference within 60 days of the time when it was given, subsections 4(3) and (4) of the Act apply. Subsection 4(3) provides:

> 4.(3) ... if such a transaction with or for a creditor has the effect of giving that creditor a preference over the other creditors of the debtor or over any one or more of them, it shall, in and with respect to any action or proceeding that, within sixty days thereafter, is brought, had or taken to impeach or set aside such transaction, be presumed, in the absence of the evidence to the contrary, to have been made with the intent mentioned in subsection (2), and to be an unjust preference within the meaning of this Act whether it be made voluntarily or under pressure.

Thus creditors prejudiced by a particular payment, etc. obtain a significant procedural advantage where they attack that payment within 60 days of it being made. The onus of proof in such a case falls upon the creditor to whom the payment is made to show that the payment was not made with an intent to give that creditor a preference.[640] A similar procedural advantage applies where the debtor becomes bankrupt during the 60-day period following a particular payment, subsection 4(4) providing:

> 4.(4) ... if such a transaction with or for a creditor has the effect of giving that creditor a preference over the other creditors of the debtor or over any one or more of them, it shall, if the debtor within sixty days after the transaction makes an assignment for the benefit of creditors, be presumed, in the absence of evidence to the contrary, to have been made with the intent mentioned in subsection (2), and to be an unjust preference within the meaning of this Act whether it be made voluntarily or under pressure.

Under both subsections 4(3) and (4) it is not sufficient to rebut the presumption of intention by showing that the creditor exerted pressure. However, it is open to

---

[640] *Dana v. McLean*, [1901] O.J. No. 221, 2 O.L.R. 466 (C.A.).

the creditor to whom the preference was given to show that there was no intent to give a preference.

§8.341 Subsections 4(3) and (4) of the *Assignments and Preferences Act* expressly provide that within the 60-day period of a preferential payment, etc. it shall "be presumed, in the absence of evidence to the contrary, to have been made with the intent mentioned in subsection (2), and to be an unjust preference within the meaning of this Act whether it be made voluntarily or under pressure". It follows from this wording that outside the 60-day period, payments made as a result of pressure, force, demands or requests coming from the creditor do not constitute a preference contrary to the Act. The nature of the pressure required was discussed by the Ontario Law Reform Commission in the following terms:

> While the nature and scope of the pressure that is required to validate a transaction is by no means clear, most of the cases speak in terms of pressure that impairs the debtor's spontaneity or will, thereby making it impossible to assert — at least as a matter of law — that he had an intention to give an unjust preference. The facts involved in determining whether a preference was voluntary or made under pressure have been summarized succinctly in the New Brunswick Report to include "who originally proposed the preference, how much the creditor knows about the debtor's financial situation, to what extent the parties deal at arm's length, and the exact tone of any demand for payment made by the creditor."[641]

It has been said that the pressure must be a pressure to reduce the debt rather than to give a preference, but this is a test that is difficult to apply in practice.[642] What is clear is that in order to run afoul of the Act, the preference must be given voluntarily by the debtor.[643]

§8.342 The protection afforded by the *Assignments and Preferences Act* is to some extent undermined by the exceptions afforded under section 5 of the Act. Subsection 5(1) begins by granting an exception in the case of assignments for the general benefit of creditors and also sales and other transactions in good faith:

> 5.(1) Nothing in section 4 applies to an assignment made to the sheriff for the area in which the debtor resides or carries on business or, with the consent of a majority of the creditors having claims of $100 and upwards computed according to section 24, to another assignee resident in Ontario, for the purpose of paying rateably and proportionately and without preference or priority all the creditors of the debtor their just debts, nor to any sale or payment made in good faith in the ordinary course of trade or calling to an innocent purchaser or person, nor to any payment of money to a creditor, nor to any conveyance, assignment, transfer or delivery over of any goods or property of any kind, that is made in good faith in consideration of a present actual payment of money, or by way of security for a

---

[641] *Report on the Enforcement of Judgment Debts and Related Matters* (Toronto: Queen's Printer, 1983), 164.
[642] *Molson Bank v. Halter* (1890), 18 S.C.R. 88.
[643] *Molson Bank v. Halter* (1890), 18 S.C.R. 88, but compare *Royal Bank of Canada v. Sullivan*, [1957] O.W.N. 68, aff'd [1957] O.W.N. 520 (C.A.).

present actual advance of money, or that is made in consideration of a present actual sale or delivery of goods or other property where the money paid or the goods or other property sold or delivered bear a fair and reasonable relative value to the consideration therefor.

Assignments for the general benefit of creditors under subsection (1) are rare, since the normal practice now is to seek protection under the *Bankruptcy and Insolvency Act*.

§8.343 Section 5 of the *Assignments and Preferences Act* also contains a number of provisions protecting the position of secured creditors. In particular, subsection 5(4) provides

> 5.(4) Where a payment has been made that is void under this Act and any valuable security was given up in consideration of the payment, the creditor is entitled to have the security restored or its value made good to him before, or as a condition of, the return of the payment.

Moreover, clause 5(5)(*b*) provides that nothing in the Act affects any payment of money to a creditor where the creditor, by reason or on account of the payment, has lost or been deprived of, or has in good faith given up, any valuable security that he held for the payment of the debt so paid unless the security is restored or its full value made good to the creditor. Clause 5(5)(*c*) allows securities to be exchanged. Clause 5(5)(*d*) of the Act provides that nothing in the Act:

> (*d*) invalidates a security given to a creditor for a pre-existing debt where, by reason or on account of the giving of the security, an advance in money is made to the debtor by the creditor in the belief that the advance will enable the debtor to continue the debtor's trade or business and to pay the debts in full.

Thus creditors who provide lender-of-last-resort assistance to a debtor are protected under clause 5(5)(*d*) of the Act.

Chapter 9

DIRECTORS, OFFICERS AND THE NOTION OF CORPORATE GOVERNANCE

A. CONTROL OF THE CORPORATION

§9.1 In this and the two chapters that follow, we will discuss the subject of corporate governance, and the role that the board of directors and the officers of a corporation play in that process. In this chapter, we will first look at the underlying problem that gives rise to concerns with respect to corporate control. We shall then discuss the control responsibilities of the board of directors, and then turn to the question of how the directors of a corporation are elected or appointed to play a role in that control process. The role and appointment of the officers of a corporation will be discussed as an adjunct to the discussion of the role of the Board.[1] As we shall see, in most corporations of any size, it is the officers of the corporation who are the persons charged by the directors with day-to-day managerial and administrative responsibility for the corporation.

§9.2 In an age in which so much wealth has come to be held by corporations whose power and influence stretch around the globe, one often loses sight of the fact that a corporation is a legal fiction. It is, by definition, an artificial person. It has neither body nor soul, and although it may acquire rights, liabilities and obligations, it cannot act for itself, but is entirely dependent upon and must, of necessity, act through human agents, proxies or other operatives.[2] Given the

---

[1] See, generally, in this area: Roger H. Ford, *Boards of Directors and the Privately Owned Firm: A Guide for Owners, Officers, and Directors* (Westport, Conn.: Quorum Books, 1992); Charles N. Waldo, *Boards of Directors: Their Changing Roles, Structure, and Information Needs* (Westport, Conn.: Quorum Books, 1985); Kevin Keasey, Steve Thompson & Michael Wright, *Corporate Governance: Accountability, Enterprise and International Comparison* (Chichester, Eng.: John Wiley & Sons Ltd., 2005); Jay A. Conger, Edward E. III Lawler & David Finegold, *Corporate Boards: New Strategies for Adding Value at the Top* (San Francisco: Jossey-Bass, 2001); Fredmund Malik, Effective Top Management: *Beyond the Failure of Corporate Governance and Shareholder Value* (Weinheim: Wiley-VCH, 2006); William A. Dimma, *Excellence in the Boardroom: Best Practices in Corporate Directorship* (Etobicoke, Ont.: John Wiley & Sons, 2002); Colin B. Carter & Jay William Lorsch, *Back to the Drawing Board: Designing Corporate Boards for a Complex World* (Boston: Harvard Bus. School Pub., 2003); Ram Charan, *Boards At Work: How Corporate Boards Create Competitive Advantage* (San Francisco: Jossey-Bass, 1998); Christopher L. Culp & William A. Niskanen (eds.), *Corporate Aftershock: The Public Policy Lessons from the Collapse of Enron and Other Major Corporations* (Hoboken, N.J.: John Wiley & Sons, 2003); Susan Shultz, *The Board Book: Making Your Corporate Board a Strategic Force in Your Company's Success* (New York: AMACOM, 2001).

[2] *Ferguson v. Wilson* (1866), L.R. 2 Ch. App. 77 at 89, *per* Cairns L.J. Where a corporation acts through its directors, the act is taken to be personal to the corporation, as opposed to an act of its

abstract character of the corporation, there must be some provision set out in law to regulate the corporate decision-making process and determine when corporate decisions have been made.[3] Nevertheless, the identification of the person or persons entitled to act on behalf of a corporation is often a difficult question. As a matter of practice, modern corporations of any significant size will be collective bodies, representing divided spheres of interest, control and activity, with the extent of centralized coordination varying from case to case.

§9.3 As a matter of law, under the Ontario *Business Corporations Act* ("OBCA") and the *Canada Business Corporations Act* ("CBCA") the control of the corporation, and therefore its ability to act, are divided among the shareholders, directors and (potentially at any rate), the officers of a corporation. Each of the statutes sets down a general framework specifying which powers of the corporation must be exercised by either the directors or the shareholders of the corporation. The statutes then go on to permit the delegation of certain powers of the shareholders to the directors and of certain powers of the directors to the officers of the corporation. In addition, both of these statutes permit extensive restructuring of the internal government of a corporation through the use of a unanimous shareholder agreement.

§9.4 The board of directors, officers and shareholders comprise the internal governance and control mechanisms employed by corporate role to regulate corporate behaviour. However, it is also important to understand that there are external control mechanisms in place as well. For all corporations, the courts exercise a superintending function. In addition, the Director under the OBCA and CBCA play an important public governance role. Finally, for offering corporations, securities commissions play a steadily growing role as corporate regulators. The various internal and external regulatory mechanisms and agencies governing OBCA corporations are illustrated in the following chart:

---

agents: *Richardson v. Landecker* (1950), 50 S.R. (N.S.W.) 250; *Black v. Smallwood* (1966), 117 C.L.R. 52 at 60.

[3] *Lennard's Carrying Co. v. Asiatic Petroleum Co.*, [1915] A.C. 705 at 713-14 (H.L.), *per* Viscount Haldane L.C.; *Bath v. Standard Land Co.*, [1910] 2 Ch. 408 at 416, *per* Neville J., on appeal [1911] 1 Ch. 618 (C.A.).

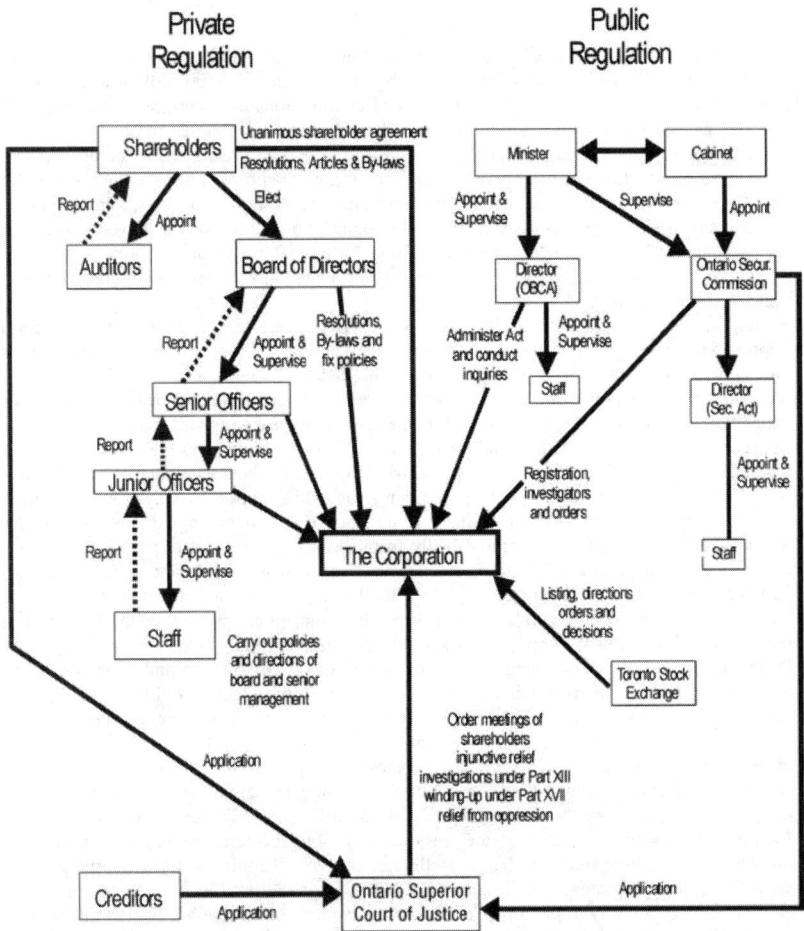

B. THE GENERAL PROCESS OF CORPORATE CONTROL

§9.5 In recent years, investors in Canada and most other major commercial jurisdictions have suffered billions of dollars in losses as a direct result of the weak corporate governance practices in companies, that have led to waste, fraud and other forms of abuse. For instance, in Canada, individual events and even long-running sagas such as those relating to Adscam,[4] Westray,[5] Hollinger International,[6] the Red Cross tainted blood scandal,[7] and Bre-X,[8] have done much to discredit the integrity of the corporate governance process, even in the charitable sector. Globally, the worst corporate governance scandal was almost certainly

---

[4] On February 10, 2004, Canada's federal Auditor General Sheila Fraser confirmed that the federal government's Public Works Department had paid a total of $100 million to a variety of communications agencies in the form of fees and commissions in the course of running an advertising and sponsorship program in Quebec. The program was supposed to boost the image of Canada in that province, but in fact the program did little other than generate commissions for the companies to which the grants were paid. The program had been in the spotlight since 2002, when Fraser recommended that the RCMP should investigate how $1.6 million in federal government advertising contracts were awarded to Groupaction Inc., a Montreal advertising agency. Fraser concluded that officials in Canada's Public Works Department had broken "just about every rule in the book" in contracts. These and other related allegations remain under investigation at the time of writing.

[5] At 5:18 a.m. on May 9, 1992 the Westray coal mine exploded in Pictou County, Nova Scotia, killing 26 miners. The explosion was so strong it blew the top off the mine entrance (more than a mile above), and blew away steel roof supports throughout the mine. In the nearby towns, windows shattered and houses shook. Westray had been planned to mine coal from the Foord seam, which was known for its high-quality coal but also for being exceptionally gassy. The mine was financed through massive federal and provincial government support in the form of loans and loan guarantees. The federal contribution consisted of an 85 per cent guarantee of a $100 million bank loan and the Province of Nova Scotia contributed $12 million by way of a subordinated loan. Although the mine was said to incorporate state of the art mining technology this claim was later called into doubt. It suffered badly from serious ground control problems related directly to the geological configuration of the Foord seam, worsened by incompetent planning. The Westray Mine Public Inquiry, held following the disaster, concluded that "the cost of operating in such an adverse environment and the inherent uncertainties would suggest that the financial viability of the Westray project should have been in doubt from the very beginning". Production was erratic during the few short months of the life of Westray and production quotas were never realized. The provincial government loan was never repaid, and the federal government was called upon to pay up the full amount of its guarantee. There were widespread complaints about the manner in which the incident was investigated.

[6] In November, 2005, prominent Canadian businessman Conrad Black was charged with eight counts of mail fraud and wire fraud in relation to Hollinger International, the publishing company he used to head, by the U.S. Attorney's Office in Chicago. Charges were also laid against John Boultbee, a former executive vice-president of Hollinger International, Peter Atkinson, another former executive vice-president at Hollinger, and Mark Kipnis, the former corporate counsel at Hollinger International. U.S. Attorney Patrick Fitzgerald said in a statement "Insiders at Hollinger — all the way to the top of the corporate ladder — whose job it was to safeguard the shareholders, made it their job to steal and conceal". The charges were still pending at the time of writing.

[7] In 1997, a federally-appointed judicial commission criticized a range of officials, including the federal government, various provincial governments and the Canadian Red Cross for mistakes that left about 1,200 Canadians infected with blood-borne HIV and 10,000 to 20,000 contaminated with hepatitis C.

[8] Bre-X was a Canadian based mining concern which touted properties that it controlled in the Busang area of East Kalimantan, Indonesia, claiming they held the richest gold deposit ever discovered. On February 17, 1997, Freeport-McMoRan Copper & Gold (which had been retained by the Indonesian government to operate mining operations) began its own due-diligence drilling. Four weeks later, Bre-X's geologist Michael de Guzman, fell from his helicopter in an apparent suicide. On March 26, 1997 Freeport reported that four of its due-diligence cores, drilled only a metre and a half from those of Bre-X, showed "insignificant amounts of gold". The next day, Bre-X stock lost almost all of its value. In early May 1997, independent experts confirmed that, in fact, no recoverable gold exists at Busang. Thousands of investors had been defrauded.

the Enron debacle.[9] Based in Houston, Enron was a marketer of electricity and natural gas, that also provided financial and risk management services to customers on a global basis. It sold energy, primarily in the wholesale market, managed pipelines, and owned and operated a telecom network. Its most significant activities were of a trading nature, in the role of a market maker. Enron's corporate strategy focused on a core energy trading business, an energy management business and the outsourcing of business and communications. In 2000, Enron claimed to have earned revenues of $101 billion. In the fourth quarter of 2000 alone, its revenues purportedly rose from $11 billion in the corresponding quarter of 1999 to $40.8 billion. Income before interest, minority interests and taxes was $777 million, almost triple the 1999 figure. The energy services business reported $33 million in income before interest and taxes for the fourth quarter and signed contracts worth $4.5 billion, up 73 per cent from the fourth quarter of 1999.

§9.6 Within a year, the company had filed for bankruptcy. Enron's failure was attributable both to a combination of outright accounting fraud and to more legitimate (although questionable) off-balance-sheet transactions. Collectively, these accounting manipulations grossly misrepresented the company's true financial position. Much of the company's activity was highly leveraged. The full debt load of the company was concealed through the use of off-shore subsidiaries. In a February, 2002 Report to Congress, it was alleged that Enron systematically manipulated its results and deceived shareholders. It had followed a pattern of overstating earnings that dated back to 1997. While this was going on, the top management team was paid millions in unearned entitlements. During 2001 alone, Enron paid $309.8 million to a group of 144 of its executives, while over the same period many of those same executives cashed in stock options worth $311.7 million. It spent extravagantly on real estate and furnishings, such as the $300 million spent on its Enron Center South building, and filled it with expensive sculptures and paintings, including a glass globe in its lobby that had itself cost $2 million. Enron executives used a fleet of seven corporate jets (often for personal travel) that cost more than $5,000 per hour to operate. There were other allegations of improper payments to friends and relatives, of millions being paid in unjustified consulting fees, and on questionable political donations to both of the major political parties.

§9.7 As a result, both large and small scale investors, market regulators and mainstream business groups, as well as various agencies of government, have pressured corporate boards to enhance governance practice. Most corporations that issue securities to the public have responded to this pressure by increasing director independence and creating boardroom structures that are able to hold the corporate management team more accountable to its investors. It has been

---

[9] See, generally, Bethany McLean & Peter Elkind, *Smartest Guys in the Room: The Amazing Rise and Scandalous Fall of Enron* (New York: Penguin USA, 2003); Robert Bryce, *Pipe Dreams: Greed, Ego, and the Death of Enron* (Cambridge, Mass.: Perseus Books, 2002); Mimi Swartz & Sherron Watkins, *Power Failure: The Inside Story of the Collapse of Enron* (Doubleday Books, 2003).

said that one cannot legislate ethics. It is nevertheless possible to legislate that a given set of conditions must be maintained that are conducive to ethical conduct, and that deter improper behaviour to a corresponding degree. As recently as 15 years ago, the role and responsibilities of a board of directors were defined almost entirely by corporate law. Today, securities laws (including regulatory policy and stock exchange listing requirements) are becoming the dominant influence on the role, structure and operation of boards of directors, at least in the case of major corporations. This change has resulted from the growing focus on corporate governance as a tool of effective securities regulation.

§9.8 The importance of the board of directors to effective corporate governance seems at first fairly clear. Subsection 102(1) of the CBCA provides that subject to any unanimous shareholder agreement, the directors shall manage, or supervise the management of, the business and affairs of a corporation. The problem is moving from this general declaration of principle to a more specific understanding of responsibility. While subsection 102(1) clearly confers a broad mandate, it is far from a precise one. Indeed, there is no definitive statement of the various responsibilities of the board of directors of a corporation. The role of the board very clearly extends to an active effort to make the corporation both ethically and financially sound. To an increasing extent, boards are called upon to play a proactive rather than reactive role in corporate management. Yet most commentators on corporate governance are sufficiently astute to perceive that an overly active board of directors (particularly in the case of a large, widely held company) could easily undermine corporate performance through a process of micro-management.

§9.9 The role of the board is often seen to be that of ultimate decision-maker. In this regard, it encompasses serving as the shareholders' chosen arbiter concerning the corporation's interests, whether they be legal, commercial or otherwise.[10] Accordingly, it is within the board's mandate to decide what course of action or inaction is best calculated to protect and advance the interests of the corporation.[11] The board may exercise active control over the business, operations and internal affairs of the corporation, and is entitled to exercise financial control and management of the funds of the corporation, as well as the method of raising such funds. The board is entitled to instruct the officers of the corporation as to how to carry on its business and affairs, and they are entitled to remove an officer from his or her position for failing to act in accordance with any lawful instructions that they may give.[12] A board may establish protocols and policies to govern the manner in which corporate powers are to be exercised. The board may create the offices that are to exist under the corporation, and subject to any statutory restriction or prohibition (or a corresponding constraint imposed under the articles, by-laws or a unanimous shareholder agreement) may define the authority and responsibilities that are to be exercised and discharged by any per-

---

[10] *Sanders v. Wang*, [1999] Del. Ch. LEXIS 203.
[11] *Auerbach v. Wallenstein*, 47 N.Y.2d 619, 393 N.E.2d 994 (N.Y.C.A. 1979).
[12] *Central Alaska Broadcasting Inc. v. Bracale*, 637 P.2d 711 (S.C. Alask. 1982).

sons appointed to those offices.[13] However, despite these broad authorities, there are set limits upon the authority that the directors exercise: they must act in accordance with the legislation governing the corporation, as well as its articles, by-laws and any unanimous shareholder agreement.

§9.10 As we will discuss in detail below, for virtually all corporations, the selection of directors is (at least in theory) controlled by the shareholders of the corporation. They elect or appoint the directors. They may also remove them from office.[14] However, while the shareholders of a corporation may control election or appointment to the board, even the majority of shareholders are not supreme over the board. The board does not exist at the pleasure of those shareholders. Subject to any unanimous shareholder agreement to the contrary that complies with the requirements for such an agreement, the board exercises a statutory authority. As we shall see, these restrictions on shareholder authority also derive from concerns with respect to effective corporate governance.

C. NATURE OF DIRECTORSHIP

§9.11 In legal theory, the most important corporate operatives are usually its directors; in practice, the most important operatives are quite often the officers of the corporation — *i.e.*, the senior employees of the corporation. The position of the shareholders is less clear. In closely-held corporations (including subsidiaries of major corporations) the shareholders may be the *de facto* controlling authority within the corporation, with the directors being little more than the nominees of the shareholders. On the other hand, in most widely held corporations, the shareholders as such operate in the background. As the electoral college controlling the election of directors, they are the source of the authority of the board of directors. However, in practice they play little direct governance role.

§9.12 For a very brief time during the formative years of company law,[15] the courts toyed with the idea that the members of the corporation might directly manage it — but that notion was soon abandoned. Instead, it has long been recognized that in all but the smallest corporations, the needs of commercial efficacy require the shareholders of a corporation to delegate[16] at least some portion (in many cases all) of the management of the corporation to a team of managers capable of relatively quick and continuous decision-making. Indeed, one of the inherent aspects of the corporate form of organization is the ability to separate the management of corporate enterprise from its ownership. In many cases, one important goal of delegation of the control of the corporation to a managing

---

[13] *Wells Fargo Bank v. Superior Court etc. of San Francisco*, 3 Cal. 3d 1082, 811 P.2d 1025, 282 Cal. Rptr. 841 (S.C. Calif. 1991).
[14] OBCA, R.S.O. 1990, c. B.16, s. 122; CBCA, R.S.C. 1985, c. C-44, s. 109.
[15] See, for instance, *A.G. v. Davy* (1741), 2 Atk. 212, *per* Lord Harwicke L.C.
[16] As will be explained below in greater detail, the word "delegate" is not used here in its strict legal sense, for there is considerable authority that the directors do not act as the delegates of the shareholders. Although they represent the shareholder interests, they are not the agents of the shareholders.

board is to entrust the management of the corporate property and business to those with specialized skills. In other cases, delegation is necessitated purely because of the number of assets to be administered or size of the business to be conducted. Delegation may also be needed because of conflicting demands on the time of the shareholders. Whatever factor(s) may give rise to the need for delegation, its effect is to subject the shareholders to the risks common to all agency relationships, namely that

- the managers (or some of them) will act in their own interest rather than in the interest of the shareholders who appointed them; and

- actions taken by the managers to whom a corporation is entrusted may differ from the actions that would have been taken had the shareholders directly administered the business of the corporation themselves.

The laws relating to the powers, responsibilities and liabilities of directors are in large measure designed to deal with these risks arising from delegation.

§9.13 Under the U.K. *Companies Act 1985*, and earlier British (and Canadian) legislation, control over the management of the business and affairs of a company is firmly divided under a fixed set of rules between the board of directors and its shareholders. The OBCA and the CBCA depart from this approach. They continue to divide control, but only as an opening proposition; the shareholders of a corporation are free to depart from the scheme of divided control set out in the legislation. Thus subsection 115(1) of the OBCA provides:

> 115.(1) Subject to any unanimous shareholder agreement, the directors shall manage or supervise the management of the business and affairs of a corporation.[17]

Under subsection 116(1),[18] a provision of the articles, by-laws or a unanimous shareholder agreement may limit or exclude the power of the directors to amend any by-laws that regulate the business or affairs of a corporation; under subsection 17(2) of the OBCA[19] the articles may restrict the exercise of powers by a corporation. However, in the absence of such a departure from the ordinary scheme of arrangement, then subject to the compliance order and oppression remedies, no one shareholder has the right to interfere with the directors' management of the corporation, and the courts will not assist a shareholder if he or she seeks their assistance.[20] The remedy of a shareholder who is dissatisfied with the manner in which the directors are carrying on the business and affairs of the corporation is to vote for a change in its management,[21] and seek proxies for this purpose. So long as they are acting in good faith and in what they believe to be

---

[17] CBCA, s. 102(1).
[18] CBCA, s. 103(1).
[19] CBCA, s. 16(2).
[20] Note, however, the residual power of the shareholders to act where the directors are unable to do so: see, for instance, *Barron v. Potter*, [1914] 1 Ch. 895 (deadlocked board); *Foster v. Foster*, [1916] 1 Ch. 532; but *cf. Berlei Hestia (N.Z.) Ltd. v. Fernyhough*, [1980] 2 N.Z.L.R. 150; *Marshall's Valve Gear Co. v. Manning Wardle & Co.*, [1909] 1 Ch. 267 (conflict of interest).
[21] *Isle of Wight Rlwy. Co. v. Tahourdin* (1883), 25 Ch. D. 320 at 331 (C.A.), *per* Cotton L.J.; *John Shaw & Sons (Salford) Ltd. v. Shaw*, [1935] 2 K.B. 113 at 134 (C.A.), *per* Greer L.J.

the best interests of the corporation, the directors may take a decision that is contrary to the interests of either the majority shareholders[22] or the minority shareholders.[23] Indeed, insofar as the interests of the shareholders differ from the best interests of the corporation, the directors are obliged to do so.[24] Thus it has been held that a shareholder is not a director of a corporation, nor may he or she exercise the powers of a director (unless first elected or appointed) even where a shareholder has sufficient shares to control the election of the board.[25]

§9.14 Individually, the directors of a corporation are not in general seen to possess any particular contracting authority,[26] beyond, perhaps, the widespread presumption that they are normally appropriate signing officers to sign any contract that has been duly approved by the corporation. At common law, the directors of a corporation collectively constitute the managing body of the corporation. When acting collectively, the directors are known as the "board of directors" (or "board"). The board is not itself a legal person; it is merely the governing body of a legal person (namely the corporation), and as such has no existence separate from that of the corporation.[27] The board of directors of a corporation is the board for the time being, rather than the members of the board at any particular time.[28] Thus if A, B and C comprise a board of directors at the time when an offer to contract is made to the corporation, and they are replaced by D, E and F, the new board may accept that offer, for the offeree remains at all times the same person, namely the corporation.

§9.15 *Mandamus* may be directed to a corporation to compel it to perform an act that it is obliged to perform. One question to resolve is whether the *mandamus* should be directed to the corporation or to its board of directors. The criteria governing this choice were explained by Middleton J. in *Bolton v. County of Wentworth* in the following terms:

> The corporation can act only through its officers, and when the corporation is required to act, all the officers of the corporation upon whom devolves the duty of acting as and for the corporation are, in substance and in effect, called upon to do what is necessary to carry the decree of the Court into operation. ... Where the act to be done is a "corporate function", the *mandamus* must be directed to the corporation — when the duty appertains to the officer of the corporation in his official capacity, then the *mandamus* must be to the officer himself.[29]

---

[22] *Howard Smith Ltd. v. Ampol Petroleum Ltd.*, [1974] A.C. 821 at 837 (H.L.).
[23] See, for instance, *Mutual Life Insurance Co. of New York v. Rank Organization Ltd.*, [1985] B.C.L.C. 11; *Re HSB Holdings Ltd. (No. 2)*, [1996] 1 B.C.L.C. 155.
[24] *Gramophone & Typewriter Ltd. v. Stanley*, [1908] 2 K.B. 89 (C.A.).
[25] *Victorov v. Davison*, [1988] O.J. No. 190, 20 C.P.R. (3d) 481 (H.C.J.).
[26] *Rama Corp. v. Proved Tin & General Invts. Ltd.*, [1952] 2 K.B. 147. See also *River Stave Co. v. Sill*, [1886] O.J. No. 86, 12 O.R. 557 at 569 (C.A.), *per* Armour J.
[27] *Dudnik (No. 1) v. York Condominium Corp No. 216* (1988), 9 C.H.R.R. D/5080 (case 792) (Ont. Bd. Inq.).
[28] See, however, *Reynolds v. Atherton* (1922), 127 L.T. 189 (H.L.), as to offers made to members of a board in their individual capacities (*i.e.*, to them personally) rather than to the corporation.
[29] [1911] O.J. No. 139, 23 O.L.R. 390 (H.C.J.).

§9.16 Although the members of the managing body of a corporation will usually be called directors, there is no magic in the term and they need not necessarily be so described: they may sometimes be called managers, councillors,[30] governors,[31] trustees[32] or management committee members, and a variety of other different terms.[33] Thus both the OBCA and the CBCA provide that the term "director" when used in the Act means a person who occupies the position of a director of a corporation, by whatever name called.[34] While this wording would seem to suggest that the meaning of the term "director" is a relatively settled one, in fact, the concept of directorship is not clearly defined. The lack of a clear definition of the term "director" complicates any effort to describe the exact nature of the office.

(i) Theories of Directorship

§9.17 There are five basic theories of directorship,[35] purporting to explain the powers, authority and responsibilities of directors, but none of them are entirely satisfactory. Under the agency theory, the directors are seen to be the delegates of the shareholders, and thus the source of the powers of the directors is seen as being with the shareholders themselves.[36] The deficiency in this theory is that the powers are conferred on the directors more by law than by any pronouncement of the shareholders. In 1906, the Court of Appeal in England effectively held that within the sphere of management vested upon them by statute, the directors of a company were not subject to the direction of the shareholders,[37] and there were many powers of the directors that could not be taken away by the shareholders even when they acted unanimously.[38] There is a broad distinction between the relationship between the board of directors to the corporation and that of an ordinary agent to its principal.[39] It follows that this version of the agency theory is not valid.[40]

---

[30] See, for instance, *Re Bank of Syria*, [1901] 1 Ch. 115 (C.A.).
[31] See, for instance, *Toronto Stock Exchange Act*, R.S.O. 1990, c. T.15, s. 6(1) [rep. 1999, c. 9, s. 224].
[32] See, for instance, *Dunsmuir v. Colonist Printing & Publishing Co.*, [1902] B.C.J. No. 57, 9 B.C.R. 290 (S.C.).
[33] *Parsons v. M.N.R.*, [1983] F.C.J. No. 703, [1984] 1 F.C. 804 (T.D.), rev'd [1984] 2 F.C. 331 (C.A.).
[34] OBCA, s. 1(1); CBCA, s. 2(1).
[35] In the first edition of this text, it was said that there were four such theories, but in reality one of them comprises two different theories wrapped up together.
[36] Subject to any statutory provision to the contrary — see ss. 127 of the OBCA and 115 of the CBCA — the board of directors may not sub-delegate the authority and discretion conferred upon them: *Howard's Case* (1866), 1 Ch. App. 561.
[37] *Automatic Self-Cleansing Filter Syndicate Co. v. Cuninghame*, [1906] 2 Ch. 34 (C.A.); see also *Quin & Axtens v. Salmon*, [1909] 1 Ch. 311, aff'd [1909] A.C. 442 (H.L.).
[38] *John Shaw & Sons (Salford) Ltd. v. Shaw*, [1935] 2 K.B. 113 at 134 (C.A.), *per* Greer L.J.; see also *Scott v. Scott*, [1943] 1 All E.R. 582 (Ch.); *Black, White & Grey Cabs Ltd. v. Fox*, [1969] N.Z.L.R. 824 (C.A.).
[39] *Teck Corp. v. Millar*, [1972] B.C.J. No. 566, [1973] 2 W.W.R. 385 at 405 (S.C.), *per* Berger J.
[40] *Teck Corp. v. Millar*, [1972] B.C.J. No. 566, [1973] 2 W.W.R. 385 at 405 (S.C.), *per* Berger J.

§9.18 A second variant of the agency theory argues that the directors are the agents of the corporation. But here again agency is an inadequate explanation. An agent acts on behalf of a principal and carries out the principal's instructions. In contrast, the board is the body that decides how the corporation will act. Quite often the corporation does not act through the directors but rather through officers, under only a general authority conferred by the board. Thus the board is not the agent of the corporation, but rather is the source from which flows the authority of corporate agents. The powers of the board are not delegated by the shareholders, but are derived and measured by the corporation's charter,[41] and exist by virtue of and according to the terms of their office.[42] However, directors are largely independent in the manner in which they exercise their powers. Thus there is a deficiency in this second branch of the agency theory.

§9.19 Given the deficiencies in the agency theory, a third theory known as the concession theory developed, which explained that the directors were public functionaries whose powers were derived from the state. In creating the corporation, the state authorized the directors to perform the functions and exercise the powers conferred upon them by law, so that the power and authority of the directors flows as a concession from the state, rather than from a delegation by the shareholders. The deficiency in this theory is that the directors of a corporation are answerable to the shareholders rather than to the state (except for breach of law). The shareholders have the power to elect (or appoint) the directors and to terminate their appointment. Moreover, under the OBCA and the CBCA unanimous shareholder agreement provisions, the shareholders have the power to remove authority from the directors, and to some extent this power may also be exercised by way of provisions in the articles and by-laws of the corporation.

§9.20 A fourth theory, sometimes called the Trustee or Platonic Guardian theory, views the directors as a group of statutory supervisors who are required to be appointed by law, whose obligation is to ensure that the corporation conducts its operations in accordance with law.[43] One of the clearest articulations of the trust theory may be found in the American case of *Lippitt v. Ashley*.[44] There it was said with respect to the directors of a savings bank:

> The incorporators of this bank were self-perpetuating and appointed themselves directors, and the directors always constituted a large majority of the incorporators. The depositors had no part, and could have no part, in the management of the bank, or the selection of the incorporators, or directors. A bank of this character is organized for the benefit of its depositors and conducted by its directors without profit to the corporation or directors. The undertaking held out by the bank to every depositor is to receive and invest his deposit through its officers, in the exercise of their reasonable fidelity, diligence and skill, and in the observance of legal

---

[41] *Donly v. Holmwood*, [1880] O.J. No. 104, 4 O.A.R. 555 at 558 (C.A.), *per* Moss C.J.A.
[42] See, generally, *Gramophone & Typewriter Ltd. v. Stanley*, [1908] 2 K.B. 89 (C.A.).
[43] See, for instance, *Re Gloucester, Aberystwith & South Wales Rlwy. Co. (Maitland's Case)* (1853), 4 De G.M. & G. 769, 43 E.R. 708 at 712 (L.JJ.), *per* Turner L.J.; *York & North Midland Rlwy. v. Hudson* (1853), 16 Beav. 485 at 491, 51 E.R. 866 (R.C.), *per* Romilly M.R.
[44] 89 Conn. 451, 94 A. 995 (S.C. Errors, Conn. 1915).

requirements, and to pay him its increment and to return him his deposit on demand, less the expense of management and the maintenance of a surplus as limited by law. The bank is conducted by its directors, and their undertaking toward the depositors is identical with that of the bank. The bank and its directors hold themselves out to the depositors to the performance of this duty. The depositor parts with his title to the specific form of his deposit, and in its stead obtains an equitable ownership in the funds of the proportioned to his deposit. Our whole rigorous statutory system for the government and regulation of savings-banks is based upon the theory that the bank and its directors or trustees are administering a trust. The deposits in the bank constitute a trust fund for the benefit of its owners, the depositors. The institution was created by law to administer a trust. Its directors are by its charter "sworn to a faithful discharge of their duties". This indicates the quasi-public character of the trust. Since the bank is managed by directors or trustees, they, upon assumption of office, become the administrators of a trust fund and necessarily, in virtue of their office and duty, trustees on fact, and each depositor comes into a trust relation with the directors who administer the trust fund created by the deposits. Out of this relation arises the right of the depositor to have his deposit managed with reasonable care and in accordance with the statutory requirements, and on the part of the director a correlative obligation so to manage this trust fund.

In the Canadian context, some support for this theory can be found in subsection 134(2) of the OBCA[45] which provides that:

> 134.(2) Every director and officer of a corporation shall comply with this Act, the regulations, articles, by-laws and any unanimous shareholder agreement.

Under this theory the directors exercise power not as delegates, but more as trustees: they are answerable for their custodianship should they breach their duty as trustees, but they are not subject to the direction of the shareholders.

§9.21 Yet the analogy is only partly justified,[46] for there are significant differences between the position that directors occupy and that of a true trustee. Directors have legal control of the corporation much as trustees have legal control over the trust property, which resembles the fact that a trustee is not normally subject to the control of the beneficiary[47] but is under a duty to act in accordance with the terms of the trust for the benefit of the beneficiary. However, the theory breaks down when one considers both the title of the corporation to its property and the manner in which its powers are exercised. A true trustee is the legal

---

[45] CBCA, s. 122(2).
[46] Thus in *Flitcroft's Case* (1882), 21 Ch. D. 519 at 534 (C.A), Jessell M.R. refers to directors not as trustees, but as quasi-trustees.
[47] A person may be both agent of and trustee for another if the person is to act under the other's control and also hold property for the other; in that case, the agency relationship and its consequences to the principal predominate. That is the case where there is a "bare trust". The distinguishing characteristic of the bare trust is that the trustee has no independent powers, discretions or responsibilities. The trustee's only responsibility is to carry out the instructions of his or her principals — the beneficiaries. If the trustee is not required to accept those instructions, but instead has any significant independent powers or responsibilities, he or she is not a bare trustee: M.C. Cullity, "Liability of Beneficiaries: A Rejoinder" (1985), 7 E. & T.Q. 35 at 36; *Trident Holdings Ltd. v. Danand Investments Ltd.*, [1988] O.J. No. 355, 64 O.R. (2d) 65 (C.A.). Since directors are required to exercise independent judgment, they are not bare trustees.

owner of property and is the principal who deals with the property as such, subject only to an overriding equitable obligation to account to the beneficiary of the trust. The directors are not the owners of the corporation, and much less are they the owners of the assets of the corporation.[48] Both legal and beneficial title to that property belongs to the corporation itself. Nor do the directors exercise the powers of the corporation on its behalf. The corporation exercises its powers itself; the role of the directors is merely to decide when and how those powers will be exercised,[49] and so they are merely the hand that guides the corporation through its business and affairs.

§9.22 Directors are also subject to a lesser duty of care and accountability for their dealings with corporate property than are trustees with respect to trust property.[50] For instance, in *Overend, Gurney Co. v. Gibb*[51] it was held that in a company formed for the purchase of a business, the directors would not be personally responsible for the purchase of that business unless its ruinous character was obviously apparent at the time when the purchase was made.[52] Such a rule reflects the risk nature of business. Business involves taking on properly managed risk in an effort to earn profit. In contrast, a critical aspect of the responsibility of a trustee is risk avoidance. Similarly, directors have a discretion as to whether to sue to enforce debts, which is not a discretion possessed by trustees as such.[53] Trustees have a duty to conserve the trust property. While they may choose not to pursue a questionable claim or to pursue a claim where the debtor is unlikely to satisfy a judgment, they do not have the discretion to take into account the kind of broad strategic interests of a corporation: such considerations as the need for commercial alliance, the prospect of successful joint venture; risk sharing and the like that may prompt a board to forego a potential claim.[54]

§9.23 Most importantly, to apply to directors the strict rules of equity with respect to ordinary trustees might fetter their action to an extent which would be exceedingly disadvantageous to the corporations they represent.[55] It follows that the description of "trustee" is not appropriate,[56] and provides little guidance as to the true characterization of the office, although various rules governing trustees have from time to time been borrowed and imported into the law governing directors.[57]

---

[48] *Smith v. Anderson* (1880), 15 Ch. D. 247 at 275 (C.A.), *per* James L.J.
[49] See *Re Kingston Cotton Mill Co. (No. 2)*, [1896] 2 Ch. 279 at 295, *per* Williams J.
[50] *Grimwade v. Mutual Society* (1884), 52 L.T. 409, 1 T.L.R. 115 (Ch.).
[51] (1872), L.R. 5 H.L. 480, 42 L.J. Ch. 67 (H.L.).
[52] *Re Forest of Dean Coal Mining Co.* (1878), 10 Ch. D. 450 at 451-52, *per* Jessell M.R.
[53] *Ibid.*, at 453.
[54] See, for instance, *Newman v. Warren*, 684 A.2d 1239 (Del. Ch. 1996).
[55] *Re Faure Electric Accumulator Co.* (1888), 40 Ch. D. 141 at 151, *per* Kay J.
[56] See also *Railway & General Light Improvement Co. (Marzetti's Case)* (1880), 42 L.T. 206, 28 W.R. 541 (C.A.).
[57] *Imperial Hydropathic Hotel Co., Blackpool v. Hampson* (1882), 23 Ch. D. 1 at 12 (C.A.), *per* Bowen L.J.

§9.24 The fifth theory, known as the *sui generis* theory, essentially ties the four other theories together. It sees the powers and authority of directors as unique. It explains the powers and responsibilities of directors as growing out of statute and common law, and recognizes that while in certain respects the directors resemble agents, public office holders, trustees and other fiduciaries, the office of director is a creature unto itself. As the law relating to directors is now established under its own body of case law, the duties, liabilities and rights of directors can largely be determined by reference to (and analogy from) that body of law. Only rarely is it necessary to refer to or invoke principles from other fields of law, such as trust or agency. In deciding the extent to which particular principles applicable in other areas of law can be applied in the corporate director context, it is necessary to consider the extent to which those principles can be reconciled with the statutory duties to which directors are subject, and the commercial context in which directors must function. For instance, in deciding whether a corporation can enter into a contract, the directors must first decide whether the contract is in fact in the best interests of the corporation, and in so doing, they owe a fiduciary duty to the corporation in the sense of the shareholders of the corporation as a collective whole. In deciding whether to assent to the provisions of the contract, the directors exercise an original decision-making power in which they act not for the corporation but as the corporation. However, when individual directors sign a contract on the corporation's behalf, they act not as agents of the shareholders or the other directors, but as agents of the corporation itself. The office of director, then, is a unique one. In determining the extent to which the principles of law applicable to trustees (and others) may apply, it is necessary to determine whether those principles are compatible with the expectations placed on directors by the world of commerce and the duties entrusted by law to them. Purists may complain that the *sui generis* theory is no theory at all. It does not explain why a given rule should apply, and it provides no predictive guidance as to what rule will apply in a novel situation. Nevertheless, it is the explanation of the office of director that is the least prone to error.

(ii) The Term "Director" Defined

§9.25 Generally speaking, the directors of a corporation are the body of individuals selected to manage as a collective the business and affairs of the corporation for the benefit of the shareholders.[58] Directors are often described as agents, officers and fiduciaries of the corporations for which they serve, but while each of these descriptions is accurate to an extent, they are also somewhat mis-descriptive. For instance, while an individual director may be empowered to act as an agent of the corporation, when acting collectively as the board, the directors are not subject to the control of the corporation. They are instead the controlling body of their principal. Under normal English usage, the term "director" describes a person who controls, regulates, superintends, guides or orders a particular matter. In the context of corporate law, the term "director" is

---

[58] *Beatty v. North-West Transportation Co.* (1885), 12 S.C.R. 598, rev'd (1887), 12 App. Cas. 589 (P.C.); *Finnemore v. T. Underwood, Ltd.*, [1930] 3 D.L.R. 939 (Alta. C.A.).

used to designate the class of persons given the primary (and in some cases exclusive) responsibility for the management of a corporation. In this respect, subsection 115(1) of the OBCA provides that:

> 115.(1) Subject to any unanimous shareholder agreement, the directors shall manage or supervise the management of the business and affairs of a corporation.

Thus the OBCA begins with the initial presumption that responsibility for management is normally vested with the directors of a corporation. In managing the corporation, the directors do not act as the delegates or agents of the shareholders who elected or appointed them.

(iii) Promoters and Directors Distinguished

§9.26 Promoters, like directors of a corporation, stand in a fiduciary position relative to the corporation. The word "promoter" is not used in either the OBCA or the CBCA, although it does appear in the *Securities Act*,[59] where it is defined in subsection 1(1) to mean:

> (a) a person or company who, acting alone or in conjunction with one or more other persons, companies or a combination thereof, directly or indirectly, takes the initiative in founding, organizing or substantially reorganizing the business of an issuer, or
>
> (b) a person or company who, in connection with the founding, organizing or substantial reorganization of the business of an issuer, directly or indirectly receives in consideration of services or property, or both services and property, 10 per cent or more of any class of securities of the issuer or 10 per cent or more of the proceeds from the sale of any class of securities of a particular issue, but a person or company who receives such securities or proceeds either solely as underwriting commissions or solely in consideration of property shall not be deemed a promoter within the meaning of this definition if such person or company does not otherwise take part in founding, organizing or substantially reorganizing the business.

For the most part, the term "promoter" is simply a convenient way of designating a person who sets in motion the process by which the corporation is created[60] — although as the *Securities Act* definition makes clear, it may also be used to describe a person who procures a corporation's reorganization. While promoters and directors are both corporate fiduciaries, their respective positions and obligations are distinct. A person does not become a director of a corporation merely because he (or she) promoted its incorporation (even if he was the only such promoter) and, consequently, the powers and liabilities of a director do not fall upon him unless and until he assumes office as a director.

(iv) The Requirement for a Board of Directors

§9.27 So vital is the role of the board of directors in the administration of the business and affairs of a corporation, that it is impossible for a corporation to be

---

[59] R.S.O. 1990, c. S.5.
[60] *Patton v. Yukon Consolidated Gold Corp.*, [1934] O.W.N. 321 at 322 (C.A.), *per* Davis J.A.

properly organized without one. Whether a board of directors is still required once the corporation has been properly organized is less clear (for a comprehensive unanimous shareholder agreement reserving all power to the shareholders would nullify the function of the board), but as a matter of practice virtually all corporations — if not all — retain a board with at least a residue of authority, even where operating under a unanimous shareholder agreement that reserves most effective powers to the shareholders.

§9.28 The first board of directors draws its authority as such neither from the shareholders (for there can be no shareholders until the first board of directors admits them as such, accepts their subscriptions and allots shares to them) nor even from the incorporators of the corporation, but from law and the articles of incorporation itself. The OBCA and the CBCA provide slightly different terms with respect to the designation of the first directors of a corporation (that is, the directors who comprise its initial board of directors). Both statutes make the designation of first directors a mandatory part of the incorporation process. Under the OBCA, the first directors of a corporation are the persons named in that capacity in the articles of incorporation. Subsection 119(1) of the OBCA provides that each director named in the articles shall hold office from the date of endorsement of the certificate of incorporation until the first meeting of shareholders. Subsection 119(2) of the OBCA then goes on to provide that no director named in the articles may resign his or her office unless, at the time the resignation is to become effective, a successor is elected or appointed. In the case of the CBCA, section 106 requires the first directors to be named in Form 6, Notice of Directors, which must be submitted at the time of sending the articles of incorporation to the Director. As under the Ontario Act, the first directors so named hold office from the time of the issue of the certificate of incorporation until the first meeting of shareholders, but the CBCA has no equivalent restriction to that set out in subsection 119(2) of the OBCA on the resignation of directors.

§9.29 In *Re Bulawayo Market & Offices Co.*,[61] the court concluded that there was no common law requirement that a corporation possess a board of directors, and that therefore any such requirement must be imposed by statute. Quite possibly with this case in mind, the CBCA requires every corporation operating under that statute to have directors.[62] It provides that:

> 102.(2) A corporation *shall have one or more directors* but a distributing corporation, any of the issued securities of which remain outstanding and are held by more than one person, shall have not fewer than three directors, at least two of whom are not officers or employees of the corporation or its affiliates.

(Emphasis added.)

The different wording of the corresponding provision of the OBCA creates a certain ambiguity with respect to the question of the necessity for a board, subsection 115(2) of the OBCA providing:

---

[61] [1907] 2 Ch. 458 at 463, *per* Warrington J.
[62] CBCA, s. 102(2).

115.(2) A corporation shall have a board of directors which shall consist of,

(a) in the case of a corporation that is not an offering corporation, at least one individual; and

(b) in the case of a corporation that is an offering corporation, not fewer than three individuals.[63]

Despite this difference in wording, since the OBCA and the CBCA specifically require the articles of a corporation to provide for a board of directors, and since under each Act the minimum number at which the board may be pegged under either Act is one, it would seem to follow that it is not possible to dispense entirely with a board under either Act. However, as a matter of policy, it is a fair question whether there should be any insuperable requirement for a corporation to have a board of directors.

§9.30 Both the OBCA and the CBCA charge the board with management responsibility "subject to any unanimous shareholder agreement".[64] Where there is a comprehensive unanimous shareholder agreement, that reserves all managerial power to the shareholders, no strong argument can be made for retaining a vestigial board. In such a case, the managerial powers of the directors would be suspended by reason of the agreement, while the obligations of the directors would be assumed by the shareholders themselves. These consequences are evidenced by subsection 108(5) of the OBCA which provides:

> 108.(5) A shareholder who is a party to a unanimous shareholder agreement has all the rights, powers, duties and liabilities of a director of the corporation, whether arising under this Act or otherwise, to which the agreement relates to the extent that the agreement restricts the discretion or powers of the directors to manage or supervise the management of the business and affairs of the corporation and the directors are thereby relieved of their duties and liabilities, including any liabilities under section 131, to the same extent.

Subsection 146(5) of the CBCA is substantially the same as to the extent of a unanimous shareholder agreement, but it does not provide that the shareholders assume the directors' liabilities. Be that as it may, given the effect of a comprehensive unanimous shareholder agreement, it would seem preferable to dispense with the requirement for a board where all managerial powers are reserved to the shareholders. There is no practical benefit in requiring the existence of a vestigial entity that neither exercises authority nor is liable for any aspect of the business or affairs of the corporation. Even under the CBCA, there would seem to be little benefit in retaining a vestigial board, where the directors have no power remaining to control the corporation and (in all likelihood) are not consulted as

---

[63] The term "offering corporation" is defined in s. 1(1) of the OBCA to mean a corporation that is offering its securities to the public within the meaning of s. 1(6) and that is not the subject of an order of the Ontario Securities Commission deeming it to have ceased to be offering its securities to the public.

[64] OBCA, s. 115(1); CBCA, s. 102(1).

to the manner in which it is run. Nevertheless, as things stand, it appears that some sort of vestigial board is required.[65]

D. THE GROWING ROLE OF THE BOARD

§9.31 Historically, public corporations have often had boards that were dominated by corporate officers, or individuals who represented the principal shareholder. For instance, in *Catalyst Fund General Partner I Inc. v. Hollinger Inc.*[66] a board of 12 directors of an offering corporation included only four independent directors. Recent changes to the *Securities Act* provide a foundation for radical reform in this area. Section 121.3 was inserted into the *Securities Act* by way of the *Budget Measures Act (No. 2), 2005*, to give the OSC greater control over the board of directors of a reporting issuer:

> 121.3 For the purposes of this Act, a reporting issuer shall comply with such requirements as may be prescribed with respect to the governance of reporting issuers, including requirements relating to,
>
> (*a*) the composition of its board of directors and qualifications for membership on the board, including matters respecting the independence of members;
>
> (*b*) the establishment of specified types of committees of the board of directors, the mandate, functioning and responsibilities of each committee, the composition of each committee and the qualifications for membership on the committee, including matters respecting the independence of members;
>
> (*c*) the establishment and enforcement of a code of business conduct and ethics applicable to its directors, officers and employees and applicable to persons or companies that are in a special relationship with the reporting issuer, including the minimum requirements for such a code; and
>
> (*d*) procedures to regulate conflicts of interest between the interests of the reporting issuer and those of a director or officer of the issuer.

Subsection 143(1) of the *Securities Act* also permits the Commission to issue rules imposing requirements with respect to the governance of reporting issuers. The relevant rules making powers include:

> 56.1 Prescribing requirements with respect to the governance of reporting issuers for the purposes of section 121.3.
>
> 57. Requiring reporting issuers to appoint audit committees and prescribing requirements relating to the functioning and responsibilities of audit committees, including requirements in respect of,
>
>> i. the standard of review to be applied by audit committees in their review of documents filed under Ontario securities law,
>>
>> ii. the certification or other evidence of review by audit committees,
>>
>> iii. the scope and content of an audit committee's review, and

---

[65] See, generally, *Canada Business Corporations Act, Discussion Paper Unanimous Shareholder Agreements* (Ottawa: Industry Canada, April 1996).
[66] [2004] O.J. No. 3886, 48 B.L.R. (3d) 194 (S.C.J.).

iv. the composition of audit committees and the qualifications of audit committee members, including independence requirements.

58. Requiring reporting issuers to devise and maintain a system of internal controls related to the effectiveness and efficiency of their operations, including financial reporting and asset control, sufficient to provide reasonable assurances that,

   i. transactions are executed in accordance with management's general or specific authorization,

   ii. transactions are recorded as necessary to permit preparation of financial statements in accordance with generally accepted accounting principles or any other criteria applicable to those statements,

   iii. transactions are recorded as necessary to maintain accountability for assets,

   iv. access to assets is permitted only in accordance with management's general or specific authorization, and

   v. the recorded accountability for assets is compared with the existing assets at reasonable intervals and appropriate action is taken with respect to any differences.

59. Requiring reporting issuers to devise and maintain disclosure controls and procedures sufficient to provide reasonable assurances that,

   i. information required to be disclosed under Ontario securities law is recorded, processed, summarized and reported, within the time periods specified under Ontario securities law, and

   ii. information required to be disclosed under Ontario securities law is accumulated and communicated to the reporting issuer's management, including its chief executive and financial officers, as appropriate, to allow timely decisions regarding required disclosure.

60. Requiring chief executive officers and chief financial officers of reporting issuers, or persons performing similar functions, to provide a certification that addresses the reporting issuer's internal controls, including a certification that addresses,

   i. the establishment and maintenance of the internal controls,

   ii. the design of the internal controls, and

   iii. the evaluation of the effectiveness of the internal controls.

61. Requiring chief executive officers and chief financial officers of reporting issuers, or persons performing similar functions, to provide a certification that addresses the reporting issuer's disclosure controls and procedures, including a certification that addresses,

   i. the establishment and maintenance of the disclosure controls and procedures,

   ii. the design of the disclosure controls and procedures, and

iii. the evaluation of the effectiveness of the disclosure controls and procedures.

§9.32 The foregoing provisions constitute but one recent salvo in the long running battle over corporate control. In the 19th century, as the law of business corporations began to evolve, the courts steadily expanded the role of the board of directors at the expense of the shareholders of the corporation. As a consequence of the mechanism of delegation of managerial authority, as a practical matter, the extent of director control came to be eclipsed by the influence of the first tier of officers within the corporation.

§9.33 The general requirements of good corporate governance practice are steadily evolving in response to changing conditions and demands within the investment market and to public expectations with respect to business ethics. They may influence the evolution of the law, but they do not define it. Corporate stakeholders and board of directors are at liberty to demand (and frequently do demand) higher standards from the corporate officers and agents who are entrusted with the ongoing administration of a corporation than are required under corporate law. Corporate law comes into play only when the bare minimum standard has not been met. This point was made clear in *Brehm v. Eisner*[67] in which the court observed that:

> All good corporate governance practices include compliance with statutory law and case law establishing fiduciary duties. But the law of corporate fiduciary duties and remedies for violation of those duties are distinct from the aspirational goals of ideal corporate governance practices. Aspirational ideals of good corporate governance practices for boards of directors that go beyond the minimal legal requirements of the corporation law are highly desirable, often tend to benefit stockholders, sometimes reduce litigation and can usually help directors avoid liability. But they are not required by the corporation law and do not define standards of liability.

§9.34 The evolution of corporate governance in Canada has been heavily influenced by developments in other jurisdictions, such as the Enron scandal in the United States and the collapse of the Bank of Credit and Commerce International ("BCCI") in Europe. BCCI ultimately became one of the most thoroughly corrupted business organizations in history. Whether it was originally intended to achieve such a distinction is less clear. Whatever the intent might have been the growth and ultimate collapse of the bank did much to reveal the limitations of the regulatory process as a tool for the control of actual criminal conduct. The bank originated in Pakistan in 1972. Its founder (Agha Hasan Abedi) had previously set up the United Bank of Pakistan, which was nationalized in 1971. With the thought of nationalization still fresh in his mind, Abedi intended to create a new type of banking entity that would operate at a supranational level.[68] The

---

[67] 746 A. (2d) 244 at 256 (Del. Ch. 2000).
[68] BCCI expanded rapidly throughout the 1970s. Between 1973 and 1976, it expanded from 19 branches operating in five countries to 108 branches operating in 1976. Over the same period, assets grew from $200 million to $1.6 billion. It is now known that the bank was insolvent by

Kerry-Brown Report, prepared for the U.S. Senate following the collapse of the bank would describe BCCI as having a "unique criminal structure" that was managed "for the specific purpose of evading regulation or control by governments". The Report continued:[69]

> Unlike any ordinary bank, BCCI was from its earliest days made up of multiplying layers of entities, related to one another through an impenetrable series of holding companies, affiliates, subsidiaries, banks-within-banks, insider dealings and nominee relationships. By fracturing corporate structure, record keeping, regulatory review, and audits, the complex BCCI family of entities created by Abedi was able to evade ordinary legal restrictions on the movement of capital and goods as a matter of daily practice and routine. In creating BCCI as a vehicle fundamentally free of government control, Abedi developed in BCCI an ideal mechanism for facilitating illicit activity by others, including such activity by officials of many of the governments whose laws BCCI was breaking.

§9.35 Beyond these foreign influences, Canadian thinking with respect to corporate governance has been influenced by the corresponding Canadian scandals referred to above. In 1994, the Toronto Stock Exchange published the *Dey Report*, which recommended the adoption of 14 corporate governance practices by listed companies on that exchange. In 1995, the TSX adopted these as best practice guidelines. It adopted what is sometimes a "comply or explain" rule, under which compliance with the guidelines was not made mandatory but companies were required to disclose where their approach to corporate governance varied

---

1977, at which time it began funding its operating expenses by drawing upon its deposits. The bank would nevertheless continue to operate for several years. By 1980, BCCI reached assets of over $4 billion and had more than 150 branches operating in 46 countries. While most of its funding came from the Middle East, the bulk of its operations were run out of Europe through BCCI S.A. (which was based in Luxembourg), and BCCI Holdings, which operated out of London. The division of operations among so many countries helped the bank to avoid rigorous regulatory supervision, in part because its footprint in any given country was relatively small, and in part because each country's regulators seemed to assume that the bank was being properly monitored by regulators in other countries.

It would take many years before the true character of the bank became evident. Bank of England officials warned privately of possible fraud at BCCI in 1984, at which time it was described as "a disaster waiting to happen" and "the SS Titanic". In 1985, following significant reported losses in the commodity and financial markets, the Bank of England and the Central Bank of Luxembourg required BCCI to appoint a single auditor for its overall operations, but this would not actually occur until 1987, when Price Waterhouse took over that position. In 1988, BCCI was implicated in a drug money laundering scheme. In 1990, a Price Waterhouse audit of BCCI revealed an unaccountable loss of hundreds of millions of dollars. Even then the bank remained in operation by securing an additional investment in its share capital.

In March 1991, the Bank of England retained Price Waterhouse to conduct an inquiry into the business and affairs of BCCI, under the codename of "Sandstorm". The Sandstorm Report was issued on June 24, 1991, and alleged that BCCI had engaged in "widespread fraud and manipulation". It also disclosed that the Abu Nidal terrorist group had operated accounts at a BCCI branch office in London, and that it had provided letters of credit for this group to fund the purchase of millions of dollars worth of arms from Iraq. On July 5, 1991, the Bank of England closed down the operations of BCCI. At that time, it had more than £7 billion in undeclared debt. More than one million investors would lose money.

[69] See the *Report to the Committee on Foreign Relations of the United States Senate on The BCCI Affair* (the "Kerry-Brown Report") (Washington: December 1992, 102d Congress 2d Session Senate Print 102-140); see also the *Report of the Inquiry into the Supervision of the Bank of Credit and Commerce International* (the "Bingham Report"), (London: HMSO, 1992).

from the guidelines, and to provide an explanation of those differences. In 1999, the Institute of Corporate Directors and the TSX issued a further report, *Five Years to the Dey*. It examined the extent of compliance with the Dey best practices and identified some shortcomings. In July 2000, the Canadian Institute of Chartered Accountants, the TSX and the Canadian Venture Exchange (the forerunner to the TSX Venture Exchange) established a Joint Committee on Corporate Governance (the "Saucier Committee"). In its November 2001 report, the Saucier Committee proposed a number of amendments to the guidelines to bring them into line with international developments. At the federal level in Canada, on June 23, 2002, the Senate Committee on Banking, Trade and Commerce issued a report recommending changes to the CBCA to enhance corporate governance in Canada and to restore investor confidence.

§9.36 When the American *Sarbanes-Oxley Act* was enacted in July 2002, as the legislative response to the collapse of Enron and MCI, the OSC initiated a review of this Act and international reform efforts in the corporate governance area, with a view towards their possible adoption into Ontario law, to see what regulatory changes the OSC should adopt. A further important American development occurred on November 4, 2003, when the SEC approved new corporate governance rules for companies with securities listed on the New York Stock Exchange and NASDAQ. Since many of the larger Canadian issuers are also listed on the NYSE or NASDAQ, and many Canadian investors hold shares in companies traded on those markets, the requirements of those exchanges will inevitably influence the evolution of Canadian and practice, as well investor expectations.

§9.37 Despite a degree of Canadian innovation in the corporate governance field, in comparison to the U.K. and U.S., the adoption of mandatory enhanced corporate governance procedures in Canada has been comparatively slow. In early 2004, the OSC proposed a corporate governance rule and a related policy based upon specific best corporate governance practices and requiring specific disclosure with respect to those best practices. This standardized package of Canadian corporate governance requirements came into effect on June 30, 2005, with the intention of providing a consistent regulatory framework for Canadian issuers concerning corporate governance matters. It replaces the Toronto Stock Exchange corporate governance guidelines and disclosure requirement that formerly applied to Canadian listed corporations. The new regime is set down in the Canadian Securities Administrators National Instrument 58-101 (the "Rule"), *Disclosure of Corporate Governance Practices* and National Policy 58-201, the *Corporate Governance Guidelines* (the "Policy").[70]

---

[70] Compliance with American stock exchange corporate governance listing requirements does not relieve a Canadian reporting issuer listed on a U.S. stock exchange from compliance with Canadian disclosure requirements. However, Canadian issuers that are foreign private issuers in the United States may seek exemptions from certain American stock exchange corporate governance listing requirements (in general, other than those that relate to SEC audit committee requirements). Where such an exemption is granted, the issuer must disclose any divergences from the otherwise applicable American requirements.

§9.38 The underlying thrust of the Rule and Policy was explained by the OSC as being to confirm as best practice, certain governance standards and guidelines that have evolved through legislative and regulatory reforms and the initiatives of other capital market participants, in order to provide greater, transparency for the marketplace regarding the nature and adequacy of issuers' corporate governance practices. The Rule and Policy built upon earlier rules and policies either adopted or proposed for adoption by the OSC and the other Canadian securities regulators, such as:

- the December, 2003 rule and policy adopted by the Canadian Securities Administrators concerning continuous disclosure requirements for reporting issuers.

- the March, 2004, Investor Confidence Rules (which require chief executive officers and chief financial officers to certify certain statements contained in the annual and interim filings made by issuers, and also impose certain rules with respect to audit committees and auditors).

The securities administrators undertook to review the Policy and Rule after their adoption to ensure that they remained appropriate for issuers in the Canadian marketplace.

§9.39 The Policy applies to most reporting issuers in Canada, other than certain foreign issuers, investment funds, issuers of asset-backed securities and issuers of certain guaranteed securities. As with previous Canadian efforts, the Rule and the Policy opts in favour of reliance upon guidelines. However, while the Policy generally applies to all reporting issuers, the provisions of the Policy are not intended to be prescriptive. Instead, they are intended to encourage issuers to adopt the suggested measures, while allowing deviations from the specified standards to be implemented flexibly and sensibly to fit the situation of individual issuers. An issuer must include in its annual information form a disclosure in prescribed form, as to whether it is in compliance with the recommended practices. If it is not, then the issuer must state that fact and explain why the board believes it is appropriate to depart from the practice in question. When management solicits a proxy from the security holders for the purpose of electing directors, the management information circular must also include a cross-reference to the issuer's annual information form that contains such information.

§9.40 In summary, the recommended best practices around which the Policy and Rule are structured incorporate the following measures:

> The majority of the Board of Directors should be independent. For the purpose of the Policy, a director is considered to be independent if he or she has no direct or indirect material relationship with the issuer. A "material relationship" is one that, in the view of the board, could reasonably interfere with the exercise of an independent judgment by the director. However, the Policy also specifies that individuals falling within the following categories are considered to have a material relationship with an issuer:

(a) an individual who is or has been an employee or executive officer of the issuer, unless a "prescribed" three year period has since elapsed;

(b) an individual whose immediate family member is or has been an executive officer of the issuer, unless a three year period has elapsed;

(c) an individual who is, or has been, an affiliate of a partner or employed by, a current or former internal or external auditor of the issuer, unless a three year period has elapsed with the person's relationship with the internal or external auditor, or the auditing relationship has ended;

(d) an individual whose immediate family member is, or has been, an affiliated entity of, partner of, or employed in a professional capacity by, a current or former internal or external auditor of the issuer, unless the three year period has elapsed;

(e) an individual who is, or has been or whose immediate family member is, or has been, an executive officer of an entity if any of the issuer's current executive officers serve on the entity's compensation committee, unless the three year period has elapsed;

(f) an individual who receives, or whose immediate family member receives, more than $75,000 per year in direct compensation from the issuer, other than his remuneration for acting in his or her capacity as a member of the board of directors or any board committee or is a part-time chair or vice chair of the board or any board committee, unless the three year period has elapsed since he or she ceased to receive more than $75,000 per year in such compensation.

This definition of independence is derived from the comparable term in the audit committee rule and policy. The requirements of the Policy further provide that the independent board members should hold separate, regularly scheduled meetings separate from management. In addition, the chair of the board should be an independent director, who should act as effective leader of the board and ensure that the Board's agenda will enable it to successfully carry out its duties. Where for some reason it is not possible for the chair to be an independent director, there should be a designated independent director appointed to act as the "lead director", who should play substantially the same role.

§9.41 Across the world, opinions differ as to the merit of requiring the chair of the board to be an independent director, with some authorities arguing that a separation of the role of the chair from corporate management is essential to good corporate governance, while others argue just as vehemently that good corporate governance is promoted by having the chief executive officer also serve as the chair of the board. The Policy therefore adopts something of a middle course, with a weak preference in favour of an independent chair, but permitting alternative arrangements through an independent "lead director".

(i) Creation of a Suitable Governance Regime

§9.42 It is now widely accepted that a proper corporate governance regime based upon sound principles of business management and the oversight of subordinates is critical to obtaining and maintaining the trust of investors, as well as to creating an environment in which the rights and interests of all investors, employees, customers and other stakeholders of a corporation are given appropriate consideration and respect.[71] Although the specific requirements of a corporation will vary from case to case, as a general rule the key components of a suitable governance structure will include the creation of:[72]

- Appropriate oversight mechanisms to ensure that the business and affairs of the corporation are properly managed, and that appropriate supervision and oversight of management is exercised by the board of directors of the corporation.

- A formalized process for discussion between the CEO, the board and other key management officers, including the review of sufficient regular and special purpose reports, statements and other materials provided to the board to allow them to be familiar with its business and affairs, the environment of the corporation and the issues that arise from that environment and the state of its business and affairs.

- An adequate regime of regular board meetings, supplemented by special meetings where required. As recently as the early 1990s, full board meetings even for sizeable offering corporations were declining to as rarely as once a quarter. It is now common for boards to meet at least monthly. Some will meet even more frequently — particularly where the circumstances of the corporation are such as to require close attention or the environment in which it operates is particularly dynamic. The general nature of the typical board meeting may be quickly summarized. In any corporation, the board's most basic responsibility is to act in a manner that they reasonably believe is in the best interest of the corporation, as determined through the exercise of their collective business judgment and such special expertise as they may each possess. At board meetings, the board will review the reports prepared by management on corporate operations, and discuss those reports with the relevant

---

[71] For a range of the thinking in this area, see: Stephen G. Austin & Mary Steelman, *Rise of the New Ethics Class: Life After Enron: Not Business As Usual* (Lake Mary, Fla.: Charisma House, 2004); Philip Stiles & Bernard Taylor, *Boards at Work: How Directors View their Roles and Responsibilities* (Oxford: Oxford Univ. Press, 2002); Kenneth A. Kim & John R. Nofsinger, *Corporate Governance*, 2nd ed. (Englewood Cliffs, N.J.: Prentice Hall, 2006); Donald H. Chew & Stuart L. Gillan, *Corporate Governance at the Crossroads: A Book of Readings* (New York: McGraw Hill-Irwin, 2005); Robert A.G. Monks & Nell Minow, *Corporate Governance* (London: Blackwell, 2004); Walter J. Salmon et al., *Harvard Business Review on Corporate Governance* (Cambridge, Mass.: Harv. Univ. Press, 2000); John L. Colley et al., *Corporate Governance* (New York: McGraw-Hill, 2003).

[72] See, generally, Business Roundtable, *Principles of Corporate Governance* (White Paper, 2005); Calpers, *US Corporate Governance Core* (2006); Council of Institutional Investors, *Corporate Governance Polices* (2006), *Recommendations of the National Association of Corporate Directors* (2002).

members of the management team. A proper board meeting should consider the financial and operating performance of the corporation over the period to which the meeting relates, as well as its plans and prospects, and any immediate or emerging issues facing the corporation. The purpose of such meetings is not to second-guess the decisions made by management, or to interfere in the day-to-day running of the corporation to an unreasonable extent, but rather to exercise a general oversight over management.

Other important aspects of a comprehensive corporate governance regime include:

- Fixing the board at an appropriate size. The board of a public corporation should not be unwieldy, but it needs to include a sufficient number of members to provide for a proper committee structure. If the board is not large enough, then all members of the board may be required to devote more time to the business and affairs of the corporation than is practical (particularly in the case of outside directors). If the board is too small, then it will often lack focus and a sufficient depth of skill and experience.

- Since new directors have little day-to-day contact with the corporation, it can be difficult for them to get up to speed with respect to the issues facing the corporation. To enhance their ability to perform at the expected level, many corporations have now formalized the process of director orientation. For instance, senior management may now be specifically directed to provide new directors with materials, briefings and additional educational or briefing opportunities to permit them to become familiar with the corporation.

Measures should be adopted to ensure that the corporation will comply with all applicable federal and provincial laws and regulations and stock exchange listing standards; there should be appropriate governance procedures and policies, an ethics code that applies to all employees and directors, and (to make it more than mere window dressing) effective provisions for its enforcement.

§9.43 The creation of a suitable governance regime really requires corporations to introduce a proper process of critical review into decision-making within the corporation, and the manner in which business (and financial) results are reported to shareholders. All too often, corporate frauds occur because people willingly chose to believe what in retrospect must obviously have appeared to them to be a lie. Claims of above-market growth and profitability should be inherently suspect, yet all too often in retrospect it appears that boards of directors have willingly been duped into believing that remarkable results are being achieved. Highly leveraged acquisitions and mismatching of revenues and expense may on occasion result in exceptional return, but they also result very frequently in financial catastrophe. When a person claims to be able to purchase dimes for nine cents a piece (or less), he is probably either lying or mistaken. Losses can only be made good by earning profits on other business, but again (as with Canadian Commercial Bank and the Northland Bank), very often boards have allowed themselves to be convinced that accounting trickery was sufficient for the purpose. In 1985, the Committee of the Sponsoring Organizations of the Treadway Commission COSO was established to investigate fraudulent financial reporting. In its report on financial frauds that occurred over the period 1987 to 1997, it noted that:

> Over half the frauds involved overstating revenues by recording revenues prematurely or fictitiously. Many of those revenue frauds only affected transactions recorded right at period end (i.e., quarter end or year end). About half the frauds also involved overstating assets by understating allowances for receivables, overstating the value of inventory, property, plant and equipment and other tangible assets, and recording assets that did not exist.

For the most part, there are no genuinely new types of fraud. The collapse of Equity Funding Corporation of America,[73] and before that, Robert Vesco and Investors Overseas Services, may have played out in a different industry than the collapse of Enron and Worldcom MCI, but the causes of the collapse were surprisingly similar. An appropriate corporate governance structure will not necessarily ensure that common sense is brought to bear on corporate decision-making, but it can enhance the prospect that this will occur.

§9.44 Corporate governance structures and practices should protect and enhance accountability to, and ensure equal financial treatment of, shareholders. It should allow shareholders to participate in the major fundamental decisions that affect corporate viability, and meaningful opportunities to suggest or nominate director candidates and to suggest processes and criteria for director selection and evaluation. A corporate governance regime should encourage responsible business practices and the practice of good corporate citizenship in a manner consistent with the fiduciary responsibility of the board and officers of the corporation to protect long-term investment interests.

(ii) Strategic Role

§9.45 The requirements of the Policy then turn to the subject of institutionalizing an appropriate overall approach to Board responsibility. The Policy further provides that the board should adopt a written mandate that explicitly identifies its responsibility for the stewardship of the issuer. The mandate should identify those decisions that require prior board approval and the board's expectation of management. It should also specify measures by which security holders can provide feedback. Other key areas of concern include the need for the board to assume responsibility for:

(a) satisfying itself as to the integrity of the senior officers of the corporation;

(b) creating a culture of integrity throughout the corporation (including developing a set of corporate governance principles and guidelines that are specifically applicable to the issuer);

---

[73] Raymond L. Dirks, *The Great Wall Street Scandal* (New York: McGraw-Hill, 1974).

(c) adopting a strategic planning process, including approval, at least annually, of a strategic plan which takes into account, among other things, the opportunities and risks of the business;

(d) identifying the principal risks of the issuer's business and ensuring implementation of appropriate systems to manage them;

(e) succession planning (including appointing, training and monitoring senior management);

(f) adopting a corporate communication policy;

(g) ensuring the integrity of the corporation's internal control and management information systems.

The Policy anticipates that the board will develop clear job descriptions for directors, including the chairs of the board and each board committee. The board, together with the CEO, is also expected to develop a clear position job description for the CEO, including delineating management's responsibilities. The board is also expected to develop or approve the corporate goals and objectives that the CEO is responsible for meeting.

§9.46 The strategic role of a board incorporates reviewing, monitoring and, where appropriate, approving fundamental financial and business strategies and major corporate action, reviewing and approving the corporation's budget, supervision of the general risk management approach (discussing the assessments that have been made of the major risks facing the corporation and the options proposed for dealing with them or mitigating their effect. This discussion is also likely to include a critical review of the realism of the risk management scheme); ensuring that appropriate processes are in place for maintaining the integrity of the corporation, that confidence can be placed in the reliability and integrity of the corporation's financial statements; that there are appropriate procedures in place to result in compliance with law and a proper respect for business ethics, and that relationships with customers, suppliers, and other stakeholders are conducted with integrity.[74]

§9.47 The above guidelines focus on ensuring the proper supervision of corporate management by clearly delineating the scope of board authority. In essence, the assumption is that by institutionalizing a specific role for the board, it will become clear to the members of the board when they should intervene and criticize developments within the corporation. In essence, it is now assumed that a board will be made up of senior and experienced outside business people. The apparent hope is that by clearly delineating the roles of the Board and management, the directors will exercise independent judgment concerning critical high level decision-making areas of responsibility, and will be free to part company with the Chief Executive with respect to those matters concerning those areas

---

[74] See, generally, the National Association of Corporate Directors, *Report of the Blue Ribbon Commission on the Role of the Board in Corporate Strategy* (2000).

that are reserved to the board. The goal is for the board to play an active role in the development of an appropriate business strategy, as well as to see that the board has a clearer mandate to hold management accountable for the execution of that strategy. In the past, the outside directors of many failed companies have not played such a role (or, at least, have begun to play such a role only late in the day), believing that once they had appointed a competent CEO with sufficient experience to run the corporation, their responsibility was to support that individual unless and until it became clear that he or she was unable to perform properly. However, it is necessary for there to be an appropriate balance. There is no question that an active board has a role to play in good governance practice, but effective governance also requires teamwork between the board and the executive officers. They must share leadership responsibilities. While the willingness to engage in critical debate to reach a better outcome has a role, few see the appropriate role of the board being to micromanage or interfere in day-to-day operation.

§9.48 The next set of guidelines focus on developing board expertise. The policy expects that the board will ensure that all new directors receive a comprehensive orientation, ensuring that all new directors fully understand the role of the board and its committees, the contribution expected from individual directors (including commitment and time and energy) and the nature and operations of the issuer's business. The board is also expected to provide continuing education opportunities for all directors, so that they can maintain or enhance their skills and abilities and ensure that their knowledge and understanding of the issuer's business remains current.

§9.49 The process of director training has long been actively pursued in the non-profit and cooperative sector of the economy, where board members often lack any significant business experience prior to election and appointment. The assumption in the case of private sector corporate boards is that directors will already possess sufficient training upon their appointment. Often, however, there is reason to doubt this assumption, particularly where directors for an organization in one industry are recruited from among senior managers in corporations that engage in other industries. Where the members of a board of directors all lack any kind of significant experience in the industry in which a corporation carries on its business, it is difficult to see how they can instill confidence much less guarantee shareholders and other stakeholders good governance of the corporation. When new directors come onto the board, there is a risk that they will feel sufficiently intimidated that they will be drawn into supporting the existing culture and practices within the corporation. Training new directors encourages them to play a more independent role from the time of their appointment. However, the requirement for continuing education is not limited to just new members. It is intended to be an ongoing developmental process to generate a board that is both engaged and informed. Boards should not be inward looking, and a proper process of director education tends to promote the importation of new ideas into the overall governance process.[75]

§9.50 The next collection of guidelines focus on promoting proper behaviour within the corporation, through formalized corporate policies and the like:

> The board should adopt a written code of business conduct and ethics, applicable to directors, officers, and employees of the issuer. This code should constitute written standards that are reasonably designed to deter wrongdoing and should address the following issues:
>
> (a) conflicts of interest;
>
> (b) protection and proper use of corporate assets and opportunities;
>
> (c) confidentiality of corporate information;
>
> (d) fair dealing with the issuer's security holders, customers, suppliers, competitors and employees;
>
> (e) compliance with laws, rules and regulations; and
>
> (f) reporting of any illegal and unethical behaviour (commonly called "whistle blowing").

The overall goals in this area may be summarized as being to enhance transparency, and overall corporate integrity in management, to increase the visibility of the board in overall governance, to encourage the board to play an active leadership role in setting, both by action and the adoption of appropriate policy, the tone and face of their organization, to create a "constructive tension" between the board and management, to increase accessibility to the board and from it, by permitting the board to reach each and every level within the operation of the corporation.

(iii) The Role of the Board of Directors in Corporate Governance

§9.51 The next guidelines deal with the overall supervisory role of the board. It is stated that board should be responsible for monitoring compliance with the above code. Waivers, including implicit waivers, in favour of directors or senior officers should be granted by the board (or a board committee) only. The above principles are now reflected in widely different perceptions of the appropriate role of the board of directors from those that were generally accepted even as recently as the end of the Clinton administration. Today, the more specific responsibilities of the board of an offering corporation with respect to supervision of management are generally seen to include:

- providing guidance to management; and

---

[75] Accredited education programs include those offered by the National Association of Corporate Directors, the University of Wisconsin/State of Wisconsin Investment Board, the Wharton/Spencer-Stuart Directors' Institute, Dartmouth's Center for Corporate Governance, and the Stanford Directors' College, although there are many other such programs on offer.

- actively and regularly reviewing and monitoring:
    ○ all materials distributed to them in advance of each board meeting; and
    ○ the general effectiveness of management's policies and decisions, including the execution of its strategies, with a view toward enhancing shareholder value over the long term.

At one time directors might attend only a majority of meetings held during their term of office, and yet still might be considered to be discharging their responsibilities well. Today, board members are expected to make every effort to attend all meetings of the board and board committees of the board on which they serve. They are also expected to attend shareholder meetings.

(iv) Board Composition

§9.52 The next collection of best practice guidelines in the above Policy relates specifically to the make-up of the board itself. They appear intended to give rise to a board that is more autonomous than has historically been the case:

- The board should appoint a nominating committee composed entirely of independent directors.

- The nominating committee should adopt a written charter that clearly establishes the committee's purpose, responsibilities, member qualifications, member appointment and removal, structure and operations, and manner of reporting to the board. The nominating committee should have authority to engage and compensate any outsider advisor that it determines to be necessary to permit it to carry out its duties.

- Prior to nominating or appointing individuals as directors, the board should, firstly, consider what competencies and skills the board, as a whole, should possess; and secondly, assess what competencies each existing director possesses, considering the board as a group and paying attention also to the personality and other qualities of each director, as these may ultimately determine the boardroom dynamic. The board should also consider the appropriate size of the board, with the view to facilitating effective decision-making. In carrying out each of these functions, the board should consider the advice and input of the nominating committee.

- The nominating committee should be responsible for identifying individuals qualified to become new board members and recommending to the board the new director nominees for the next annual meeting of shareholders.

- In making its recommendations, the nominating committee should consider the competencies and skills that the board considers necessary for the board as a whole, to possess, that it considers each director to possess and those which each new nominee would bring to the board.

For nearly all corporations, it is a challenge to create a board that includes an appropriate mix of directors who are able to offer a balanced range of expertise.

All but the largest corporations can have difficulty recruiting individuals to the board, individuals who are qualified to serve in the role of a director, whether as a result of formal education or business experience.

§9.53 Historically, for many widely-held corporations, it was the executive committee of the board (and frequently the CEO) that controlled nomination as a director. The rationale of this approach was to secure a board that would practice "cabinet solidarity" and support the policies and overall strategy of the executive team. The downside of the approach was that it reduced the board to something akin to a rubber stamp. Frequently, investigations into the collapse of a corporation revealed a link between a board's lack of independence and the corporation's ultimate failure. For instance, in the case of Northland Bank, directors who did not support the business policies that eventually led to the bank's failure were removed from the board.[76] While it is far from certain that a nominating committee made up of independent directors will fully correct this tendency, the revised approach contemplated in guidelines 10 to 14 is at least a start. The revised approach will not create a truly independent board, but rather implements a "first degree of separation" model, in which the sitting directors draw upon their contacts to fill board vacancies. Nevertheless, the risk is that in most cases the replacements will prove to be no more than trusted friends drawn from a limited demographic and experience background.[77]

(v) Executive and Board Compensation

§9.54 The next collection of best practice guidelines pertain to the subject of senior officer compensation. In Canada, senior executive compensation must be disclosed as part of the annual proxy solicitation process. Section 86 of the *Securities Act* requires the delivery of an information circular when any person or company solicits proxies from the holders of the voting securities of an issuer, and a statement of executive compensation is set out in that document.[78] Although concerns have been raised with respect to the manner in which disclosure is made of such compensation,[79] a more controversial issue is the manner in which such compensation is set.

§9.54.1 On January 27, 2007, the TSX published proposed amendments to its Company Manual intended to clarify certain provisions in Part VI of that Manual, particularly rule 613. If implemented, the amendments would clarify the determination of whether an insider who is entitled to the benefit of a security-based arrangement may vote to approve the institution of, or a change in, that security-based arrangement. The amendments would also require security holder

---

[76] *Report of the Inquiry into the Collapse of the CCB and Northland Bank* (the "Estey Report") (Ottawa: Ministry of Government Services, 1986), 183.
[77] For more thinking in this area, see: the Canadian Coalition for Good Governance, *Corporate Governance Guidelines for Building High Performance Boards* (November 2005).
[78] See Form 51-102F6 Statement of Executive Compensation.
[79] See, generally, Ontario Securities Comm., Report on Staff's Review of Executive Compensation Disclosure, November, 2002, CSA Notice 51-304. The staff Report was based on a sample of 76 issuers, and weaknesses were identified in the disclosure provided by 75 of them.

approval for certain arrangements and prohibit some arrangements even if security holders did approve of them. On March 29, 2007, the Canadian Securities Regulators published Proposed Form 51-102F6 Statement of Executive Compensation, to enhance the level of disclosure regarding such director and officer salaries in Canada. It will require disclosure of key aspects of executive compensation, such as salary, bonus, stock and option awards, payments upon termination or change in control, and pension entitlements. These initiatives return public attention to the question of the importance of proper control over director and officer remuneration as a central issue in corporate governance.

§9.54.2 At the beginning of the 21st Century, the average annual retainer for a non-executive director among Canada's largest companies was less than $20,000, with additional payments in the $1,000 to $3,000 range usually being made to such individuals for attendance at board and committee meetings. Most directors were also given shares or options to allow them to attain a minimum level of stock ownership over a defined period (many boards expect directors to have a share interest fixed as a multiple of each director's annual retainer).

§9.54.3 The increasing responsibilities and risks associated with the role of non-executive directors, have begun forcing up the annual retainers payable to such directors. For instance, it is reported that effective January 1, 2003, BCE Inc. established an annual flat fee of $150,000 for all outside directors, a flat fee of $225,000 for the chair of its audit committee and $300,000 for the non-executive chair of the board. Outside directors for BCE are expected to own at least 10,000 BCE common shares or share units and have five years to reach this threshold. Until the minimum level is attained, the annual fee for a director will be paid in share units, after which a director may elect to receive his or her fee either in cash or in additional share units.[80] Most of the attention with respect to director and officer compensation applies, however, not with respect to non-executive or outside directors, but rather with respect to the compensation payable to executive directors.

§9.54.4 The goal of aligning the long-term interests of corporate insiders with those of shareholders applies equally to directors and executives. Director and senior officer compensation is usually built around five elements. Base salary, benefits and perquisites are readily quantifiable and predictable. In contrast, the various long and short-term performance incentives which comprise the other two elements of total compensation, are more difficult to value, and often have a discretionary element to them. In general, short-term incentives usually are tied to some specific formula relating to a specific aspect of corporate operations. The vice president of sales, for instance, will usually have a bonus scheme that is tied to the growth in sales over the year. Long-term incentives are now usually tied to shares. Such incentives may be structured either as the issue of shares as a bonus, or the grant of an option. Payment in shares has a more immediate tendency to align director and shareholder interest, but there is a tax disadvantage

---

[80] Nadine Winter, "Fair Pay for Fair Play" *CA Magazine* (December 2004).

from the director's perspective, in that the value of such shares is added to the director's taxable income. This tax cost was one reason for a drift toward the use of share options. A second reason was that until recently, such options were not disclosed on a corporation's financial statements. Whether shares or options are granted, to maximize their value as a long-term incentive, share entitlements will often be made subject to a vesting term — a period of time before the recipient has the right to transfer shares and therefore realize value. Vesting can be based on time, performance or some combination of both. In view of this timing element, it is readily possible that the ultimate benefit of share based compensation will prove to be vastly more (or far less) than what was expected when the compensation was awarded.

§9.54.5 While director and officer remuneration is often presented primarily as a corporate governance issue, for the most part it is usually more a matter of an internal equity with respect to the distribution of income between senior officers and rank and file workers. Nevertheless, as explained below, there is very often a governance side to it. In 2005, median weekly earnings for full-time American workers rose by 1.9 per cent. In real terms, however, such workers suffered a decline in pay, because inflation for the year was at 3.8 per cent. In contrast, USA Today reported that CEO remuneration had increased by 25 per cent over the same period. Other reports indicated a widening gap between senior executive and average worker pay. In 2005, the average CEO in the United States made 170 times more than the average worker. During the 1970s, the multiple was only 40 times.[81] In Britain, CEOs now earn 22 times the salary of an average worker. In Japan the multiple is 11.[82] Among America's Fortune 500 companies, chief executive officer remuneration totaled $3.3 billion during 2003, or $6.6 million on average.

---

[81] The disparity between average worker salary and executive compensation may well have been worse before widespread disclosure of executive compensation. In 1935, America was in the grip of the worst depression in history. At about that time, the SEC asked directors to start disclosing their remuneration. The information was supposed to be kept confidential, but the SEC published some figures anyway. In a December 16, 1935, article, *Time Magazine* noted who was doing well. Topping the charts were the salaries at General Motors. S.W.P. Knitdsen, GM's executive vice president, was paid $211,128 — a man who had all of $30 in his pocket when he arrived in America in 1900, as an immigrant from Denmark. His boss, A.P. Sloan Jr. — the President of GM — picked up a mere $201,743. GM's head of research, former Ohio farm-boy C.F. Kettering, pocketed a measly $140,495. Former blacksmith Larry Fisher, got paid $125,219 for his expertise in auto-body design. In those days, finance officers took a back seat to production and innovation. CFO Donaldson Brown (whose ancestors arrived on the Mayflower) got $134,688. Sales also did not do too well in the 1930s. R.H. Grant, the vice president for sales, got only $98,003.

According to an article by Sidney Fine on "The Toledo Chevrolet Strike of 1935" (1998), 67 *Ohio History* 326, in 1935, the average American auto worker earned 72.8¢ per hour; but the average worker at the Toledo Chevrolet plant got only 69.6¢ per hour. Assuming a 44 hour week, a Toledo worker would earn $1,592 per year, while the average auto worker nationwide would earn $1,666. It would have taken the average Toledo GM worker more than 132 years to make what Knitdsen did in 1935. On the other hand, such workers might be lucky enough to get overtime. Being on salary, the GM Board members did not qualify for that.

[82] Sharda Prashad, "Puzzle the CEO Pay" *The Toronto Star* (4 June 2006).

§9.54.6 Averages have a tendency to be misleading. In 2005, the CEO of Capital One Financial, Richard Fairbank, purportedly earned $280.1 million. To put that number in its proper perspective, that income exceeded the annual profits of more than half of the thousand largest corporations in the United States. Occidental Petroleum's CEO, Ray Urani, received $63 million pay and benefits, plus an additional $37.6 million in stock option profits. It is said that some nine CEOs earned more than $100 million each. Oracle's CEO Larry Ellison was paid over $868.9 million during the five-year period ending in 2005 (the equivalent of 18,566 average annual salaries).[83]

§9.54.7 High director salaries are not a uniquely American phenomenon. The heads of major Canadian corporations do not make as much as their American counterparts, but by no sensible perspective can they be viewed as self-sacrificing. According to figures widely circulated by the Canadian Center for Policy Alternatives, by 12:13 p.m. on New Year's Day, 2007, the 100 highest paid Canadian CEOs had already earned on average an amount equal to the annual salary of a worker on minimum wage. In a January 3, 2007, article that picked up on the CCPA estimate, the Montreal *Gazette* posed the question, "Are CEOs really worth so much?" It began:

> By 9:46 a.m. yesterday, Canada's highest-paid executives had already been paid as much in 2007 as the average Canadian worker will be for the entire year, about $38,000.

The highest-paid CEO in Canada in 2005 was Hank Swartout of Precision Drilling Trust, who received more than $74 million. Hunter Harrison of Canadian National Railway was paid about $56 million; Magna's Frank Stronach about $40 million. On average, the CEO of Canada's five largest banks make nearly $15 million a year, with the poorest paid making more than $8 million. The federal deputy minister of finance (who administers a budget of $224 billion) has a maximum earning of $341,000.[84] When John Hunkin stepped down as head of the Canadian Imperial Bank of Commerce in July, 2005, he received an annual retirement benefit of $1.3 million to add to the $25.7 million he had accumulated over the years in share based term incentive plans.[85] According to its Annual Proxy Circular, Mike Zafirovski, president and Chief Executive Officer of Nortel received a base salary of $1.2 million in 2006 (unchanged), which was topped up in March, 2007, by a cash bonus of $1,174,263 "in recognition of his accomplishments and personal effectiveness during 2006". However, many senior executives make well below these amounts. The SEDAR database reveals that in 2005, Courtney Pratt, CEO of Hamilton's beleaguered Stelco, was paid a salary of $810,000 (unchanged from 2004). Even so, Pratt did much better than the average Stelco worker.

---

[83] *Forbes Magazine* (8 May 2006).
[84] Brett Gartner, You Get What You Pay For (Canada West Foundation Occasional Paper, March 2007).
[85] John Gray "How much is too much: do consultants promote excessive executive compensation?" *Canadian Business Magazine* (July 17-August 13, 2006).

§9.54.8 Do salaries of this magnitude give rise to governance concerns? There is certainly reason to believe that the non-executive directors of corporations are less than rigorous, when it comes to setting executive compensation. According to one widely circulated report originating in the New York Times, when it was discovered that the CEO of one Las Vegas corporation had been paid more than $1 million in error over what he was entitled to, the board decided that he deserved the extra pay and let him keep it. Director and executive compensation most obviously presents a governance problem when it is structured in such a way as to create a conflict between the payee's own interest and the best interests of the corporation itself. It also raises an obvious governance issue when there are serious doubts as to whether the compensation that is being given is a proper reflection of executive performance, or where a disproportionate share of corporate property is being diverted to pay executives. However, it also presents a more subtle governance problem where the disparity in earning is so great as to breed resentment and hostility on the part of rank and file workers. It is not difficult to find evidence of such resentment. To quote John Monks, the general secretary of Britain's Trade Union Congress:

> Why should a director be worth 15 times as much as an average employee one year, and 20 times as much five years later? Have directors really been improving their performance four times faster than the people who work for them? The answer to that must be no.

Yet criticism of excessive executive compensation is not limited to trade union activists. As American investment guru, Warren Buffett, has noted:

> Too often, executive compensation in the United States is ridiculously out of line with performance. ... A mediocre-or-worse CEO — aided by his hand-picked VP of human relations and a consultant from the ever-accommodating firm of Ratchet, Ratchet and Bingo — all too often receives gobs of money from an ill-designed compensation agreement.

In Canada Stephen Jarislowsky, the founder of Montreal-based investment firm Jarislowsky Fraser Ltd. has said:

> The board of directors is to blame for granting these completely outrageous sums, but the people that are causing all the harm are these compensation consultants. ... The more they can give the CEO, the more other CEOs will be attracted to them as consultants.[86]

§9.54.9 There is anecdotal evidence that high director salaries are beginning to alienate investors. For instance, in May 2004, shareholders at the annual meeting of Glaxo-Smith-Kline in the UK voted against the company's senior executive compensation package of its chief executive officer. The focal point of shareholder concern was the golden parachute to be provided for CEO Jean-Pierre Garnier, which would have entitled him to receive an amount in excess of £22 million if his employment with GSK were terminated during the two-year term of his contract.

---

[86] The Buffett and Jarislowsky quotes are both taken from John Gray "How much is too much: do consultants promote excessive executive compensation?" *Canadian Business Magazine* (July 17-August 13, 2006).

While the vote was advisory only, following this vote the board made significant changes to its compensation regime.

§9.54.10 Top flight executive talent is obviously worth paying for. This is especially true when one compares the present high levels of executive compensation to the earnings of top tier entertainers and major league athletes. People whose innovative thinking, strategic planning, and general managerial skills provide the basis for the generation of great wealth for others, are obviously worth a good deal more than the average employee — but there is an enormous leap in logic from that basic proposition to the conclusion that the 100 highest paid CEOs in Canada are worth more for a day's labour than most Canadian workers earn in a year. The difficulty is knowing how and when to draw the line: if 500 or 1,000 times the salary of the average employee is excessive, would 90 times the average be too much? If it is, then would paying senior executives 10 times the national average wage be sufficient to entice them to take on the risks and time commitment that senior management entails?

§9.54.11 The higher earnings that top entertainers enjoy are tied to box office and record sales. Major league athletes who fail to produce on the field are rarely major league athletes for long. In contrast, the case is far from clear that investors are actually getting the level of results that they have been paying for. Between 1997 and 2002, American GDP grew year to year by between 2 per cent and 4.5 per cent. In contrast, over the same period executive compensation among major American corporations rose by between 5.5 per cent and 11 per cent. Since then, the rate of economic growth has declined, while the rate of increase in executive compensation has increased. In May, 2006, the Ontario Teachers' Pension Plan published a study of executive compensation at 65 of Canada's largest companies, covering the period since 2001. It found no statistically significant relationship between executive compensation and shareholder returns. The report concluded:

> Companies with the greatest increase in CEO pay provide only median levels of excess total returns.

§9.54.12 If this is indeed the case, one must question why boards are not doing a better job of keeping executive compensation in line. In part, one reason may be an unexpected consequence of an intended cure. When the disclosure of executive compensation was introduced (in Ontario) in 1994, it was widely assumed that disclosure would help to keep the lid on excessive increases. In terms of actual experience, there is at least some reason to believe that increased disclosure has only increased the demand by senior executives for higher pay. A CEO at Company A looks at what his counterpart is making at Company B, and says to the board: "if Harry is worth that much, why not me?"

§9.54.13 The members of a board of directors often have little incentive to keep down the compensation of senior management. In many cases, the non-executive directors of one corporation ("A") will also be executive directors at another corporation ("B"). Although such individuals do not benefit directly by raising the salary of the principal executive officers at A, any such increase will be fed into the comparator pool, when it comes time to fix the salaries of the executive directors at B. Finally, to justify their decision making, boards often refer compensation issues to outside consultants for advice. However, all too often, such consultants are found to have material links to the corporations that they are advising (and, of more concern, to the management of those corporations), in that they provide a wide range of personnel related advice. Such connections create an impression of dependency on a good relationship with senior management.

§9.54.14 The appropriate amount and make-up of compensation remains illusive. It is not clear when compensation moves beyond serving as a fair compensation for time committed, to a motivator for excellence, to little more than an expensive and unnecessary fringe benefit, to a misappropriation of corporate profit. The guidelines do not really address these questions, but they do require the board to take an appropriate level of ownership of the overall corporate compensation plan.[87]

- The board should appoint a compensation committee composed entirely of independent directors.

- The compensation committee should have a written charter. It should establish the committee's purpose, responsibilities, member qualifications, member appointment and removal, structure and operations (including any authority to delegate to individual members or subcommittees) and manner of reporting to the board. The compensation committee should be given authority to engage and compensate any outside advisors that it considers necessary.

- The compensation committee should be responsible for:

    (a) Reviewing and approving corporate goals and objectives relevant to CEO compensation, evaluating the CEO's performance in the light of these and making recommendations to the board with respect to the CEO's compensation level based on this evaluation;

    (b) Making recommendations to the board with respect to non-CEO compensation, incentive or compensation plans and equity-based plans; and

    (c) Reviewing executive compensation disclosure before the issuer publicly discloses this information.

- The board should regularly assess its own effectiveness, as well as the effectiveness and contribution of each board committee and each individual director.

§9.55 Somewhat different rules apply with respect to a "venture issuer", that is "an issuer that does not have any of its securities listed or quoted on any of the capital TSX, a U.S. marketplace, or a marketplace outside of Canada or the United States of America". By virtue of this definition, any issuer whose securities are listed or quoted on any stock exchange in Canada other than the TSX is

---

[87] See the Canadian Coalition for Good Governance, *Good Governance Guidelines for Principled Executive Compensation* (Working Paper, June 2006).

a venture issuer. In the interest of brevity, these special rules are excluded here. Readers interested in those rules should consult an appropriate reference work on securities laws.

(vi) The Board and the CEO

§9.56 The board's primary responsibility continues to be to provide for the on-going management of the corporation, by selecting and supervising a well-qualified chief executive officer who will be charged with running the corporation on a daily basis. In a widely-held corporation, the board and its members will not be directly involved in on-going management, but they will be expected to monitor management's performance diligently, on behalf of shareholders and other affected stakeholders. Directors are also expected to serve as effective counsellors to management, and for this purpose they must be knowledgeable concerning trends in the corporation's business. They are also responsible for high level decision-making: for understanding and approving the corporation's principal activities and for monitoring the effectiveness of their implementation. More specifically, the board will usually:[88]

- Provide input into the development of corporate policies, and review and approve all such policies.

- Require and approve the corporate mission statement for the board, its strategic plan for accomplishing that mission, and all amendments to that plan, and the critical aspects of the tactical methods to be employed to implement the strategic plan (these matters will usually be as set out in the board's business plan).

- Require and approve an appropriate program of internal corporate governance and control with respect to the day-to-day operation of the corporation. Many corporations now provide that the board is entitled to access to any member of management to discuss any subject any time it wishes. Except where the nature of the circumstances otherwise require, it remains customary for the CEO to be made aware of such discussions.

- Set performance targets and devise an appropriate system of measures with respect to those targets.

- Monitor compliance with respect to the foregoing by receiving regular reports from the management of the board.

We will discuss many of these concepts in greater detail in Chapter 10, when we examine emerging standards with respect to board committee structure and the responsibility of the board for specific management and governance matters.

---

[88] For more detailed thinking on the role of the corporate CEO, see Canadian Council of Chief Executives, *Governance, Values and Competitiveness: A Commitment to Leadership* (September 2002).

E. APPOINTMENT OR ELECTION TO OFFICE

§9.57 Directors may obtain office in one of four ways: (1) by election; (2) by appointment;[89] (3) by virtue of some other office; (4) by operation of law. Of these four classes of director, three are common. Directors elected by the shareholders of a corporation at an annual meeting are one example of directors of the first class. Directors appointed by the board of directors of a corporation to fill a casual vacancy on the board provide an example of the second class. The first directors of a corporation, who obtain office as a result of the operation of subsection 119(1) of the OBCA, are an example of the fourth class.[90] The articles or by-laws of a corporation may prescribe conditions precedent that must be satisfied before a person may assume a position as a director, and except to the extent that such conditions are contrary to the OBCA or CBCA, as the case may be, such conditions will be binding.[91]

§9.58 *Ex officio* directors (*i.e.*, directors of the third class) are not expressly contemplated by either the CBCA or the OBCA, but may be provided for under the terms of a unanimous shareholder resolution.[92] For instance, in *Kiely v. Kiely*,[93] the private Act of incorporation of the Toronto Street Railway Company provided that there should be not less than three directors, each of whom was required to be a shareholder. There were only three shareholders. Upon the death of one of them, a meeting was called to appoint a new director. The legatee of the deceased director's shares was declared elected by one of the other two shareholders, but the other refused to concur. It was held that the new shareholder was entitled to take his position as a director. No election was necessary, as there were only three persons eligible to be directors and three directors were required.

§9.59 Under both Acts, except where the shareholders of a corporation have entered into a unanimous shareholder agreement, every corporation must be managed by a board consisting of one or more directors. The power to elect or appoint directors must be exercised in accordance with the corporate constitution. In the case of virtually all business corporations that have boards of directors, the power to appoint or elect directors is a right that is reserved to the shareholders of the corporation. Thus in *James v. Eve*,[94] it was held that a corporation could not enter into a contract that permitted an outsider to appoint directors, where the articles provided that the directors were to be elected by the members at a general meeting.

---

[89] See, for instance, *Santos Ltd. v. Pettingell* (1979), 4 A.C.L.R. 110.
[90] See, for example, *Muldowan v. German Canadian Land Co.* (1909), 10 W.L.R. 561 at 562-63 (Man. K.B.), *per* Cameron J.
[91] See, generally, *While v. True North Springs Ltd.*, [2002] N.J. No. 24, 22 B.L.R. (3d) 224 (S.C.).
[92] See, generally, *Duff v. S.S. Overdale Co.* (1915), 52 Sc. L.R. 849.
[93] [1878] O.J. No. 46, 3 O.A.R. 438 at 444 (C.A.), *per* Moss C.J.A.
[94] (1873), L.R. 6 H.L. 335.

§9.60 Where there is a dispute concerning an election of directors, the corporation must keep the ballots cast safe and secure, so that they cannot be tampered with or destroyed. Where the corporation fails to do so, adverse inferences may be drawn by a court. However, an election will not be overturned on the basis of minor tampering, where the majority supporting the elected group of shareholders was overwhelming.[95]

§9.61 A person may not be elected or appointed as a director of a corporation without his or her consent.[96] The first directors of a corporation under the OBCA or the CBCA assume office by operation of law.[97] Except in the case of the first directors, the directors of a corporation are normally elected to office, subsection 119(4) of the OBCA providing:

> 119.(4) Subject to clause 120(*a*), shareholders of a corporation shall elect, at the first meeting of shareholders and at each succeeding annual meeting at which an election of directors is required, directors to hold office for a term expiring not later than the close of the third annual meeting of shareholders following the election.[98]

While the Act speaks of the election of directors, where a single person has the right to "elect" a director, it is more appropriate to speak of that person appointing the director concerned. In some circumstances a direct power to appoint directors is conferred by the statute itself. For instance, subsection 124(1) of the OBCA[99] empowers a quorum of the board of directors to fill casual vacancies on the board. Where such a vacancy occurs by reason of an increase in the number of directors on a board of variable size,[100] the power of the directors to fill a vacancy is limited by subsection 124(2), which provides:

> 124.(2) Where a special resolution passed under subsection 125(3) empowers the directors of a corporation the articles of which provide for a minimum and maximum number of directors to determine the number of directors, the directors may not, between meetings of shareholders, appoint an additional director if, after such appointment, the total number of directors would be greater than one and one-third times the number of directors required to have been elected at the last annual meeting of shareholders.

The relevant yardstick under subsection 124(2) is not the total number of directors on the board, but rather the number required to be elected at the previous annual meeting. Thus, assuming that the minimum number of directors on a particular board is nine members, with a maximum of 15, and the number of directors on a variable sized board is increased by the directors from 10 to 13 members, it would be possible for the board to appoint the three new directors, and still stay within the one and one-third limit imposed under subsection (2). However, if the term of the directors on that board is two years instead of one

---

[95] *Dhillon v. Bonny's Taxi Ltd.*, [2003] B.C.J. No. 1451, 35 B.L.R. (3d) 231 (S.C.).
[96] *DeWitt v. M.N.R.*, [1989] T.C.J. No. 1101, [1990] 1 C.T.C. 2098 at 2107, *per* Kempo T.C.J.
[97] OBCA, s. 119(1); CBCA, s. 106(2).
[98] CBCA, s. 106(3).
[99] CBCA, s. 111(1).
[100] Note s. 125(3) of the OBCA.

year, one-half of the board being elected every two years, the board would be able to appoint only one new director to fill the vacancy occurring by reason of an increase in its size, since two directors would be 40 per cent of the number of directors elected at the previous annual meeting.

§9.62 Subsection 108(1) of the OBCA provides that a written agreement[101] between two or more shareholders may provide that in exercising voting rights, the shares held by them shall be voted as provided in the agreement. It follows that where there is an agreement providing that two shareholders, A and B, shall vote their shares to cause each of them to be elected to the board, that agreement is binding between them.[102] What is less clear is whether A and B (being less than all the shareholders) may go further and agree between themselves that once elected, they shall cooperate on the board so as to secure appointments for each other to individual offices, or to otherwise influence or control the management of the corporation in some way. The only argument against the enforceability of such agreement would appear to be that it might conflict with their individual respective duties as directors to act in the best interest of the corporation. The question to resolve is whether the possibility of a conflict between a statutory duty and a contractual one is sufficient to negate the contract under which the contractual duty arises, or whether the contractual duty remains binding until such time as an actual conflict arises with the statutory duty. In most cases, there would not likely be any conflict between A's and B's duty to the corporation and their contractual obligation, and therefore there would seem to be no reason to prevent the enforcement of the contract. In any event, where the agreement in question is a unanimous shareholder agreement, the provision respecting appointment to offices appears binding both upon the corporation and upon A and B.[103]

§9.63 In general, the law imposes only loose restrictions upon the provisions that may be included in the constitution of a corporation with respect to the manner of electing or appointing directors. In many cases, the share capital of the corporation will be subdivided among various classes, with the holders of each class of shares being given a right to elect a specified number of directors. In contrast, it is at least equally common for certain classes of shareholder to be denied any say in the election of directors. Other corporations will provide for the election of the board by the shareholders at large, while some corporations permit specified shareholders or other persons to appoint directors directly to the board. It is customary to provide an expeditious means of filling casual vacancies on a board of directors, that occur because of death or resignation. Most companies have by-laws which permit the remaining directors to fill such vacancies for the balance of the remaining term of the director who is replaced.

---

[101] *Homestead Development Ltd. v. Lehman Resources Ltd.*, [1988] B.C.J. No. 1582, 40 B.L.R. 1 (S.C.), indicates that an oral agreement concerning board structure may also be binding. See also *Diligenti v. RWMD Operations Kelowna Ltd.*, [1976] B.C.J. No. 38, 1 B.C.L.R. 36 at 43-51 (S.C.), *per* Fulton. J.

[102] *Klassen v. Klassen*, [1989] M.J. No. 174, 42 B.L.R. 261 (Q.B.).

[103] *Ibid.*

However, in the case of OBCA corporations, such a by-law is not necessary, as subsection 124(1) of that Act[104] provides:

> 124.(1) Despite subsection 126(6), but subject to subsections (2), (4) and (5) of this section, a quorum of directors may fill a vacancy among the directors, except a vacancy resulting from,
>
> (a) an increase in the number of directors otherwise than in accordance with subsection (2), or in the maximum number of directors, as the case may be; or
>
> (b) a failure to elect the number of directors required to be elected at any meeting of shareholders.

Any director so appointed holds office for the unexpired balance of the term of the director whom the new appointee replaces.[105]

§9.64 There is case law to the effect that any power possessed by a shareholder to elect or appoint directors must be exercised for the benefit of the corporation as a whole, rather than to secure a personal advantage.[106] On this basis, in one Australian case, an interlocutory injunction was granted to prevent the election of certain directors where there was evidence that they would use their control over the company's assets for the sole benefit of the majority shareholder.[107]

(i) Qualification of Directors

§9.65 Although both the OBCA and the CBCA permit boards of variable size, where the articles fix the number of directors, the shareholders cannot increase the size of the board other than by way of amendment to the articles;[108] nor may they increase the maximum number of directors (or decrease the minimum number of directors) other than by amendment. The obligations of a director are personal; accordingly joint appointment of two or more persons to a single position as a director is not permissible.[109] Neither the OBCA nor the CBCA provides for the appointment of auxiliary, assistant or temporary directors who may act during the temporary absence of a full director.

§9.66 As a general rule there are few qualifications that a person must have in order to be a director. There is no requirement for previous business experience, nor for any professional qualification, even in the case of widely held corporations with significant assets. The apparent assumption is that the shareholders of a corporation are best qualified to determine to whom they will entrust the management of their corporation. Instead of specifying minimum criteria that a di-

---

[104] Compare CBCA, s. 111(1).
[105] CBCA, s. 111(5); OBCA, s. 124(6).
[106] See, generally, *Re H.R. Harmer Ltd.*, [1959] 1 W.L.R. 62 at 82, per Jenkins L.J.; *Re Broadcasting Station 2GB Pty. Ltd.*, [1964-65] N.S.W.R. 1648 at 1662 (S.C.), per Jacobs J.
[107] *Theseus Exploration N.L. v. Mining & Associated Industries Ltd.*, [1973] Qd. R. 81, per Hoare J.
[108] *Western Mines Ltd. v. Shield Development Co.* (1975), 65 D.L.R. (3d) 307 at 310 (B.C.S.C.), per Anderson J.; see also *McKenna v. Spooner Oils Ltd.*, [1934] 1 W.W.R. 255 at 256 (Alta. T.D.), per Ives J. However, it is possible for a unanimous shareholder agreement to transfer power from the existing board to an enlarged board that is provided for in the agreement.
[109] *Commercial Management Ltd. v. Registrar of Companies*, [1987] 1 N.Z.L.R. 744 at 747.

rector must meet, both the OBCA and the CBCA specify certain criteria on which a person may be disqualified from being a director. For instance, section 118(1) of the OBCA provides that the following persons are disqualified from being a director of a corporation:[110]

- a person who is less than 18 years of age;
- a person who is of unsound mind and has been so found by a court in Canada or elsewhere;
- a person who is not an individual;
- a person who has the status of a bankrupt.

In many jurisdictions, there are additional criteria on which a person is excluded from serving as a director, or where the rights of certain persons are substantially restricted, such as a prior conviction for fraud or dishonesty,[111] but there are no comparable prohibitions under the OBCA or the CBCA. As a matter of business practice, the following are among the considerations frequently taken into account when deciding whether a particular person is suitable to serve as a director:

- does the individual have a reputation for honesty, diligence, integrity and good business and ethical judgment;
- does the individual have broad experience at a senior managerial level in business or in the policy formulation field in government;
- does the individual possess any technical or professional skill that would provide useful support to the board;
- is he or she politically astute;
- is the individual believed to be a good listener;
- is he or she an independent and deliberate thinker who speaks his or her mind;
- is the individual able to make decisive judgments and give clear directions to his or her subordinates;
- does the individual have sufficient time available;
- is the individual's health apparently sound;
- is the individual believed to be compassionate and fair;
- does the individual own or represent a significant interest in the corporation;
- can the individual be said to represent some other constituency (*e.g.*, customers or a class thereof) that is important to the corporation;

---

[110] CBCA, s. 105(1).
[111] See, for instance, *Re Ferrari Furniture Co. Pty. Ltd. & Cos. Act*, [1972] 2 N.S.W.L.R. 790.

- does the appointment serve any strategic interest or tactical objective of the corporation (*e.g.*, does the individual offer the corporation useful connections in the business world, government or public administration);
- are there any known or suspected circumstances with respect to an individual or those closely connected to the individual that might compromise his or her reputation, independence or ability to act effectively;
- to what extent is the individual interested in acting as a director;
- is it believed that the individual will be able to work well with the other directors and management;
- has the individual confirmed that he or she is free from any conflict of interest (this question involves more than a consideration of whether there is a commercial conflict of interest; it requires consideration of whether the individual has an existing or prior relationship with any other member of the board, or any officer of the corporation that might compromise his or her ability to act fairly and objectively with respect to any decision that it might be necessary to make, or that might tend to create a political alliance within the management of the corporation);
- is the stature of the individual comparable to that of the other directors;
- would the individual raise the profile or enhance the public image of the corporation?

Few directors of any corporation are likely to satisfy all of the foregoing criteria, but a strong director will satisfy most of them. A negative answer with respect to some of the foregoing factors would invariably justify the rejection of a particular candidate, such as a reputation for dishonesty, an insufficiency of time, or the existence of a significant, pervasive and insurmountable conflict of interest.

§9.67 Surprisingly, familiarity with the line of business in which the corporation is engaged is rarely an important consideration in director selection among public corporations. Such familiarity is not seen to be necessary because non-executive directors rarely have much day-to-day involvement in the business of the corporation. Instead, the director is expected to bring to the table a broad experience in dealing with management problems. The directors' role is seen as being to guide and monitor the corporation, in the sense of setting the overall managerial policy and philosophy of the corporation.[112] The task of developing

---

[112] In *AWA Ltd. v. Daniels* (1991-92), 7 A.C.S.R. 759, on appeal 16 A.C.S.R. 607 (N.S.W.C.A.), Rogers C.J. stated (at trial, 859) that in addition to discharging their statutory duties, directors were usually seen as being charged with carrying out the four following functions:
- to set the goals for the corporation;
- to appoint the corporation's chief executive officer;
- to oversee the plans of managers for the acquisition and organization of the financial and human resources required to attain the corporation's goals;
- to review at reasonable intervals the corporation's progress towards those goals.

specific management strategies for the implementation of that policy and philosophy is the proper role of management, who are involved with the corporation on a day-to-day basis and consequently are familiar with its business and affairs. Unfortunately, directors who possess little expertise in an industry can be ill-qualified to manage or even supervise the management decisions of the corporation.[113] They can complain that the level of profitability of the corporation is unacceptably low, and may even make general recommendations as to changes that may be made to improve the position (*e.g.*, discontinue unprofitable lines of business, sell surplus assets, constrain capital expenditure within limits that the corporation can bear). However, beyond the level of the business axiom, they are less able to evaluate and critique proposals brought to them by management for approval, and may have little or no understanding as to whether particular accounting policies employed by management in the preparation of the financial statements are fair in the circumstances.

§9.68 As a general rule, public corporations tend to select directors in the expectation that each will make a unique contribution to the corporation. Since the requirements of individual corporations vary, it is difficult to catalogue the specific "unique" contributions that corporations are likely to seek. However, there are certain classes of director that are represented on the boards of directors of many public corporations, and the general expertise of the members of those classes can be easily described.[114] In recent years, many public corporations have come to rely more heavily on what may be termed "professional directors" — *i.e.*, business people with a broad background in senior management and consulting. Directors belonging to this class are widely perceived as being effective, since because of their previous experience they do not need to be schooled in the art of management. They know what questions to ask. They understand the difference between the role of the board and the role of management. They also tend to be familiar with the risks associated with being a director and accordingly may be less likely to allow management a completely free rein. A related class of director consists of those persons who are senior officers of other corporations, often major customers and suppliers of the corporation. Although they usually possess the expertise to serve well as directors, quite often they are so preoccupied with their own companies that they have little real time to devote to the corporation.

---

[113] See, *Report of the Inquiry into the Collapse of CCB and Northland Bank* (Ottawa: Min. of Gov. Serv., 1986), 226 *et seq.*

[114] A 1998 survey of annual reports published by several widely held Canadian corporations showed the following breakdown among directorships by category of director:

Professional Directors	10%
Senior Officers of Suppliers or Customers	51%
Lawyers	8%
Chief Executive Officers of a Corporation	3%
Other Senior Officers of a Corporation	7%
Representatives of Major Shareholders	18%
Other	3%

While the precise breakdown depends on the companies included in the survey and will also vary from year to year, the general pattern tends to remain constant.

§9.69 The boards of major corporations will often include one or two senior partners from major law firms — a fact that is perhaps not surprising given the extent to which legal considerations now influence virtually every important policy decision that a board may be called upon to make. However, the practice of having lawyers serve as directors is controversial. Many law firms forbid their partners to assume directorships, others require formal approval by the partnership before any such position may be assumed. Lawyers complain that serving in the capacity of director can compromise their professional independence; it can also give rise to a conflict of interest. Their firms worry about possible liability. Many chief executive officers complain that lawyer-directors are too cautious and hesitant, often lack a sufficient grounding in business, other than its legal aspect, and consequently tend to focus discussion within the board solely on legal issues rather than the underlying commercial merit of a proposal.

§9.70 The inclusion of the chief executive officer as a member of the board is a near universal practice among public corporations. Where the chief executive officer is not the chief operating officer of the corporation, both of those officers will usually serve on the board. Many corporations also appoint other senior officers, such as the chief financial officer, to the board, but although the practice is widespread, there are many who disagree with it. Since these officers usually report to the chief executive officer, it is difficult for them to separate their function as director from that of employee, and it is particularly difficult for them to take a position different from that of the chief executive officer to whom they report. If directors are expected to be independent, objective and bring into the corporation outside expertise, the appointment of executive officers (other than those at the very top rung) to the position of director accomplishes none of these goals. However, one advantage of including a core of executive officers on the board is that this permits the creation of a board level executive officers' committee, that can exercise delegated board authority. In consequence, a board level decision may be made on a more routine basis than is otherwise possible.

§9.71 Though the qualifications required of a director are few, they must continue to be satisfied throughout the period during which a director serves. However, it does not necessarily follow that a failure to qualify as a director will invalidate acts done by a putative director in his or her capacity as a non-director senior officer of the corporation. For instance, in *Re Regional Steel Works (Ottawa-1987) Inc.*[115] it was found that the sole director (D) and shareholder of a corporation made a personal assignment into bankruptcy in March, 1993. The next month he purported to assign P Inc. — a corporation of which he was the president, sole director and shareholder — into bankruptcy. By virtue of paragraph 105(1)(*d*) of the CBCA, D was precluded from serving as a director by reason of his personal bankruptcy, and under paragraph 108(1)(*c*) of that Act was deemed to cease holding the office of director upon being so disqualified. Justice Charron ruled that the disqualification as a director did not prevent D

---

[115] [1994] O.J. No. 559, 25 C.B.R. (3d) 135 (Bkrptcy.).

from continuing to act as the president of P Inc. and that therefore the assignment of P Inc. into bankruptcy was valid.[116]

§9.72 There was no common law requirement that a director must be an individual — on the contrary, it was quite possible for a corporation to be appointed as the director of another corporation.[117] The notion of a corporation serving as a director may seem unusual, but there would be a clear administrative benefit in permitting such directorships in the case of wholly owned subsidiaries. In England, where the practice is still allowed, the perceived benefit of having one company (the "director company") serve as a director of another company (the "subject company") is that it is not necessary to file notice of a change in directorship of the subject company, where there is a change in the officer of the director company assigned to perform the director company's role on the board of the subject company. This simplification is particularly useful where the director company owns a large number of subsidiaries, with the same officer performing its directorial role with respect to each of those subsidiaries. When that officer leaves the director company, there is no need to amend the lists of directors in respect of each of the subject companies concerned. Moreover, allowing corporations to serve as directors would reflect existing practice: it is not unusual for a subsidiary to enter into a management contract with its parent corporation under which the latter is appointed the general manager of the former. It is also common for a parent corporation to sign a declaration under subsection 108(3) of the OBCA[118] effectively reserving to itself all powers of the directors.

§9.73 As noted above, there is no legal requirement that a director possess any particular training or expertise nor is it legally necessary (as a condition precedent to appointment) that a director know anything about the line of business in which the corporation is engaged. While it is sometimes suggested that a formal program of training should be required at least for the directors of public corporations, it is difficult to see why such a requirement should be imposed. It need hardly be said that some of the most successful business people in history have been high school and college drop-outs. While a director must be at least 18, there is no maximum age following which a director must retire.[119] Nevertheless, it remains open to the corporation itself to specify additional qualifications that must be possessed by directors (such as share ownership, training, experience, years of association with the corporation),[120] or grounds of exclusion, such as

---

[116] *Ibid.*, at 138.
[117] See, for instance, *Re Bulawayo Market & Offices Co.*, [1907] 2 Ch. 458 at 463, *per* Warrington J. See also *Bank of Ireland v. Cogry Spinning Co.*, [1900] 1 I.R. 219 (R.C.).
[118] CBCA, s. 146(3).
[119] Other jurisdictions have opted to limit the age at which directors may be appointed. For instance, in the U.K. in the case of public companies, s. 293(2) of the *Companies Act 1985* restricts the appointment of directors over 70 years of age.
[120] See, for instance, *Klein v. James*, [1986] B.C.J. No. 997, 36 B.L.R. 42 (S.C.), aff'd (1987), 37 B.L.R. xxvii (B.C.C.A.).

conviction of a criminal offence,[121] and where such qualifications or grounds are set out the in by-laws of the corporation they will be respected by the courts as a matter relating to the internal government of the corporation.[122]

(1) Resident Canadians

§9.74 The extent to which the Canadian economy is controlled by non-residents of Canada was a preoccupation of Canadian law makers during the 1970s and 1980s. Interest waned during the 1990s, and recently several jurisdictions have drastically scaled back regulation in this area. Ontario remains the sole holdout. To ensure at least a minimum degree of local control over corporate activity, the OBCA requires that at least a majority of the board of directors of every corporation be resident Canadians.[123] In contrast, the CBCA was amended in 2001 to reduce the general requirement with respect to resident Canadians to a mere 25 per cent of the board.

§9.75 Looking first at the OBCA requirements, the term "resident Canadian" is defined in subsection 1(1) of that Act[124] to mean an individual who is:

(a) a Canadian citizen ordinarily resident in Canada,

(b) a Canadian citizen not ordinarily resident in Canada who is a member of a prescribed class of persons, or

(c) a permanent resident within the meaning of the *Immigration Act* (Canada) and ordinarily resident in Canada.

Section 26 of the OBCA General Regulation[125] prescribes the following class of person as being resident Canadians for the purposes of clause (b) of the above definition:

1. Full-time employees of the Government of Canada, a province or a territory of Canada or of an agency of any such government or of a federal or provincial Crown corporation.

2. Full-time employees of a body corporate,

    i. of which more than 50 per cent of the voting securities are beneficially owned or over which control or direction is exercised by resident Canadians, or

    ii. a majority of directors of which are resident Canadians,

---

[121] *Boak v. Woods*, [1926] 1 D.L.R. 1186 (B.C.C.A.). Note, however, that the other directors may not presume to impose such a qualification or prohibition without shareholder authorization for so doing.

[122] *Freemont Canning Co. v. Wall*, [1940] 4 D.L.R. 86 at 99 (Ont. H.C.J.), *per* Rose C.J.H.C., aff'd [1941] 3 D.L.R. 96 (Ont. C.A.). The CBCA and the OBCA make no provision for formal disqualification orders preventing those who have repeatedly been involved in failing businesses from continuing to use the corporate vehicle as a device to defeat or delay those with whom they carry on business. Compare, however, the law in the United Kingdom, the *Company Directors Disqualification Act 1986*, c. 46.

[123] CBCA, s. 105(3); OBCA, s. 118(3).

[124] The definition in s. 2(1) of the CBCA is virtually identical.

[125] R.R.O. 1990, Reg. 62.

where the principal reason for the residence outside Canada is to act as such employees.

3. Full-time students at a university outside of Canada or at another educational institution outside of Canada recognized by the province.

4. Full-time employees of an international association or organization of which Canada is a member.

5. Persons who were, at the time of reaching their 60th birthday, ordinarily resident in Canada and have been resident outside of Canada since that time.

It is evident that section 26 of the OBCA General Regulation creates what is in effect a series of very broad exceptions to the resident Canadian requirement. Given the scope of these exemptions, it is a fair question whether there is any benefit in maintaining the resident Canadian requirement at all.[126]

§9.76 There are certain constitutional questions that may be raised with respect to the foregoing provisions. One is whether the legislation may validly restrict the right of landed immigrants who have not taken out Canadian citizenship. Given the very dubious nexus between citizenship status and corporate responsibility and accountability, there is at least some doubt as to whether these provisions would withstand judicial review. The question is whether requirements of this type can be upheld under clause 6(2)(*b*) and subsection 15(1) of the *Canadian Charter of Rights and Freedoms*. The former grants every citizen of Canada and every person who has the status of a permanent resident of Canada the right "to pursue the gaining of a livelihood in any province". The latter provides that:

> 15.(1) Every individual is equal before and under the law and has the right to equal protection and the equal benefit of the law without discrimination and, in particular, without discrimination based on race, national or ethnic origin, color, religion, sex, age, or mental or physical disability.

In *Andrews v. Law Society of British Columbia*,[127] a citizenship requirement for admission into the profession of law was held to contravene subsection 15(1). It may be argued that a requirement that a majority of directors be resident in a certain locale is not a denial of equality in the same sense that prohibiting a non-resident from serving as a director would deny equality. On the other hand, given the practical burden that such a requirement imposes, it might be equally argued that there is a conflict between subsection 15(1) and the citizenship requirements of the various corporate law statutes.

§9.77 When the CBCA was revised in 2001, the resident director requirements under that Act were scaled back considerably. Section 105(3) of the CBCA now provides:

---

[126] See, generally, *Canada Business Corporations Act: Discussion Paper on Directors' and Other Corporate Residency Issues* (Ottawa: Industry Canada, 1995).
[127] [1989] S.C.J. No. 6, [1989] 1 S.C.R. 143.

105.(3) Subject to subsection (3.1) at least twenty-five per cent of the directors of a corporation must be resident Canadians. However, if a corporation has less than four directors, at least one director must be a resident Canadian.

For corporations involved in the airline industry and other sectors in which majority Canadian ownership is required by federal law, the following special rule is set down under subsection 105(3.1):

105.(3.1) If a corporation engages in an activity in Canada in a prescribed business sector or if a corporation, by an Act of Parliament or by a regulation under an Act of Parliament, is required, either individually or in order to engage in an activity in a particular business sector, to attain or maintain a specified level of Canadian ownership or control, or to restrict, or to comply with a restriction in relation to, the number of voting shares that any one shareholder may hold, own or control, then a majority of the directors of the corporation must be resident Canadians.

If a corporation to which subsection 3.1 applies has only one or two directors, then those directors must be resident Canadians. The foregoing provisions are reinforced by subsection 114(3) of the CBCA:

114.(3) Directors, other than directors of a corporation referred to in subsection 105(4), shall not transact business at a meeting of directors unless,

(a) if the corporation is subject to subsection 105(3), at least twenty-five per cent of the directors present are resident Canadians, or if the corporation has less than four directors, at least one of the directors present is a resident Canadian; or

(b) if the corporation is subject to subsection 105(3.1), a majority of the directors present are resident Canadians or if the corporation has only two directors, at least one of the directors present is a resident Canadian.

Subsection 105(3.1) is subject to the following qualification, set out in subsection 105(4), with respect to certain holding corporations:

105.(4) Despite subsection (3.1), not more than one third of the directors of a holding corporation referred to in that subsection need be resident Canadians if the holding corporation earns in Canada directly or through its subsidiaries less than five per cent of the gross revenues of the holding corporation and all of its subsidiary bodies corporate together as shown in

(a) the most recent consolidated financial statements of the holding corporation referred to in section 157; or

(b) the most recent financial statements of the holding corporation and its subsidiary bodies corporate as at the end of the last completed financial year of the holding corporation.

(2) Qualifying Shareholding

§9.78 For many years, directors were required to maintain a minimum share investment in the corporation, known as the director's qualifying share. For instance, at one time section 103 of the *Canadian Companies Act* provided:

103. No person shall be elected as a director or appointed as a director to fill any vacancy unless he, or a corporation of which he is an officer or director, is a share-

holder, and if the by-laws of the company so provide, owning shares of the company absolutely in his own right to an amount required by the by-laws of the company, and not in arrears in respect of any calls thereon.[128]

Similar provisions are still found in the business company legislation of some provinces and in other corporate legislation, particularly that pertaining to cooperatives and credit unions.

§9.79 The qualifying share requirement was imposed in the belief that in order for directors to represent interests of the corporation properly, they had to be shareholders in the corporation themselves. The obvious intent was to ensure that all directors were "at-risk", by compelling them to make at least a specified minimum share investment in the corporation. Unfortunately, the problem with any rule of this sort is that it is too easy to circumvent. For instance, in many cases (particularly in the case of subsidiary corporations) the shareholding requirement was substantially circumvented by having the directors hold shares in trust, as nominees for the parent corporation.[129] Secondly, the prevailing practice was to keep the requirement for qualifying shares at the statutory minimum, and since the true value of any such investment would likely be minimal (in terms of the commitment required of a conscientious and diligent director), the practical value of the shareholding requirement was negligible. Third, even where shares were issued to directors and those shares were beneficially held by the directors concerned, there could be no guarantee that genuine consideration would ever be paid by the directors for those shares.[130] Fourth, in many cases directors received shares in the corporation as part of their remuneration package, which further undermined the at-risk philosophy underlying the requirement.

§9.80 Given the limited practical value to the practice, subsections 118(2) of the OBCA and 105(2) of the CBCA have largely eliminated the requirement for directors to hold a qualifying share:

> (2) Unless the articles otherwise provide, a director of a corporation is not required to hold shares issued by the corporation.

Thus under the present law it is now possible to separate entirely the management and ownership of a corporation. However, it will be noted that the statutes do not dispense completely with the need for qualifying shares, but instead merely provide that there is no statutory requirement that such shares be held. It remains open to incorporators or shareholders to introduce such a requirement in the articles of a corporation. Consequently, the ghost of that requirement continues to haunt corporate boardrooms, for in a number of older corporations, such requirements remain entrenched in corporate articles, which replicated provisions of the old corporate law statutes. Such articles may become problematical where a lawyer is asked to opine about the validity of a particular corporate

---

[128] Enacted by 1930, 20-21 Geo. V, c. 9, s. 28.
[129] See, for instance, *Pulbrook v. Richmond Consolidated Mining Co.* (1878), 9 Ch. D. 610.
[130] Although the director would remain liable to the corporation if a call was made: see, for instance, *Eden v. Ridsdale's Rlwy. Lamp and Lighting Co.* (1889), 23 Q.B.D. 368 (C.A.).

action, because the failure to hold a qualifying share that is required under the by-laws may be seen to disqualify a director who does not hold such a share. Moreover, in many cases, the ownership of qualifying shares in subsidiaries has never been transferred back to the parent corporation, which may complicate some types of transaction.

(ii) Number of Directors

§9.81 Neither the OBCA nor the CBCA imposes a limit on the maximum number of directors, so that in theory very large boards of directors are possible. A few corporations which have diverse membership and no clear control group do provide in their articles for large boards of directors, but in general this practice will be discouraged by a prudent solicitor. The recent trend to a more diverse and active committee structure has increased the optimum board size, but, boards having more than 15 members tend to be cumbersome and unwieldy and can also result in undue cost to the corporation. In practical terms, where there is a large board of directors it is usually necessary for effective decision-making power to be delegated to an executive committee of directors. Such delegation may well leave the remaining directors open to director liability claims even where they have little direct involvement in the management of the corporation.

§9.82 While the maximum number of directors is left open, subsection 115(2) of the OBCA provides that the board of directors of a corporation must consist of at least one director in the case of a corporation that is not an offering corporation, and at least three directors where the corporation is an offering corporation.[131] Until quite recently, it was mandatory to fix the size of the board at a specified number of directors. Under the present federal and provincial Acts, a corporation may have a board of directors of variable size, unless the articles provide for cumulative voting. Where there is a variable size board, the articles must authorize a maximum and a minimum number of directors.[132] Such an arrangement permits the number of directors to be altered without the necessity of an amendment to the articles, where the circumstances of the corporation (or the board) change, so as to make it advantageous to increase or decrease the size of the board of directors.

§9.83 Subsection 125(3) of the OBCA provides that where there is a variable size board of directors, the number of directors of the corporation and the number of directors to be elected at the annual meeting of the corporation must be determined from time to time by special resolution. Where no resolution has been passed, the number of directors is the number named in the articles.[133] Thus the general rule is that the number of directors must be established and cannot be changed without the approval of the holders of at least two-thirds of the voting shares of the corporation. However, it is permissible for the shareholders to adopt a special resolution authorizing the directors to determine the number of

---

[131] Compare CBCA, s. 102(2).
[132] Standard Form of Articles under the OBCA; CBCA, s. 6(1)(*e*).
[133] OBCA, s. 125(4).

directors from time to time. In the case of most corporations that have provided for a variable size board, this authority has been conferred on the board, and thus in most cases, it is not necessary for the shareholders of an OBCA corporation to authorize or otherwise be involved in periodic changes in the size of the board of directors.

§9.84 A variable number of directors permits the governance structure of a corporation to be adjusted to reflect changes in the make-up of the corporation, such as the issue of a significant new tranche of shares or the acquisition of a significant interest by one investor. It is of particular use in the case of quasi-partnership corporations, where the device permits new directors to be placed on the board in much the same way as new partners may be admitted into a firm. It also facilitates departure by retiring members of the business. However, even publicly traded corporations may find a variable size board to be a useful device. For instance, it may ease adjustment in the internal management structure of the corporation, without necessitating the costly procedure of a full amendment to the articles of the corporation. Recently, changes have been made to the law to simplify the use of this device. Until 1998, it was necessary to file with the Director a copy of any special resolution determining the number of directors within 10 days of that resolution being adopted.[134] Since any change in directors necessitates the filing of a notice of change under the *Corporations Information Act*,[135] it is difficult to see what purpose was served by the old requirement for filing a copy of the special resolution.

§9.85 Where the corporation has a fixed size of directors, the size of the board may be changed only by an amendment to the articles of the corporation.[136] Subsection 125(1) of the OBCA provides that where an amendment is passed reducing the size of the board, the decrease in the number of directors does not shorten the term of any incumbent director. Thus the effect of the amendment is suspended until the appropriate number of terms of the members of the board then sitting end, whether by the expiration of the term of office, resignation, death or otherwise.

(iii) Selecting Among Candidates

(1) Independent Directors

§9.86 In the case of stock-exchange listed companies, it is now necessary for certain types of decision to be decided by directors who are independent of the management or other control group within the corporation.[137] In this area the

---

[134] OBCA, s. 125(5), repealed S.O. 1998, c. 18, Sched. E, s. 22(1).
[135] R.S.O. 1990, c. C.39.
[136] OBCA, s. 125(1).
[137] As to growing concerns respecting ensuring director independence and the range of different perspectives on the subject, see: Arthur R. Pinto, "Corporate Governance: Monitoring the Board of Directors in American Corporations" (1998) 46 Am. J. Comp. L. 317; "When Is a Mutual Fund Director Independent? The Unexplored Role of Professional Relationships Under Section

New York Stock Exchange has been particularly active. The New York Stock Exchange requires that independent directors comprise a majority of the board of each issuer listed on the Exchange and defines independence to be the absence of a "material relationship" with the issuer.[138] Accordingly, many larger corporations have adopted an aggressive approach to the determination of the independence of directors adopting procedures heavily influenced by the NYSE rules. These take into account a wide range of factors in an effort to determine affirmatively whether a director lacks a direct or indirect material relationship with the corporation, that might compromise the director's ability to make an independent assessment of corporate management or the material placed by the Board by such management. For instance, such a review could include the following considerations (usually within a relevant time frame of recent occurrence, such as three years):

- Recent or current involvement in corporate operations: whether the director is or has been an officer or employee of the corporation, or whether an immediate family member is or has been such an officer or employee?

- Whether the director, or an immediate family member of the director, has received a material payment of direct compensation from the corporation in respect of services other than as a director or in the form of deferred compensation for prior service performed during that specified period?

- Whether the director, or an immediate family member, is or has been a current partner, officer or employee of a firm that is the corporation's auditor?

- Whether the director, or an immediate family member of the director, provided to the corporation audit, legal or tax compliance or tax planning advice, or whether the director or an immediate family member, is or has been an employee, officer or partner of a firm that has provided such advice?

- Whether the director, or an immediate family member, is or has been employed as an executive officer of another corporation where any of the corporation's present executive officers at the same time serves or served on that corporation's compensation committee?

- Whether the director, or an immediately family member, is or has been a party to a material transaction with the corporation (*e.g.*, the sale of property or some similar transaction for an amount that exceeds a stipulated minimum sum, or a stipulated percentage of the corporation's consolidated total assets

---

2(a)(19) of the Investment Company Act" (2006) 4 DePaul Bus. & Comm. L.J. 155; Larry D. Barnett, "Social Productivity, Law, and the Regulation of Conflicts of Interests in the Investment Industry" (2006) 3 Cardozo Pub. L. Policy & Ethics J. 701; Grover C. Brown *et al.*, "Director and Advisor Disinterestedness and Independence under Delaware Law" (1998) 23 Del. J. Corp. L. 1157; Eric Landau *et al.*, "Director Independence: Impartiality or Isolation" (2004) 1418 Prac. L. Inst. 111; Sanjai Bhagat & Bernard Black, "The Non-Correlation Between Board Independence and Long-Term Firm Performance" (2002) 27 Iowa J. Corp. L. 231.

[138] See the New York Stock Exchange, Listed Company Manual Standard, at <http://www.nyse.com/listed/1022221393251.html>.

or gross revenues)? Even relationships created by way of charitable contribution may be relevant for this purpose.

The foregoing points reflect the fact that one of the fundamental goals of enhanced corporate governance is to create boards that exercise active diligence and operate independently from corporate management. Traditionally, the Board has acted under the leadership of the executive officers of the corporation. Such an arrangement can present obvious problems where the chief executive is an especially strong-willed individual. Many corporations have now provided a formal method of permitting the independent directors of the corporation to exercise active diligence and to operate to at least some degree independently of the executive officers. For instance, the governance polices of a corporation may provide that the independent members of the Board must hold regular sessions without the presence of management or non-independent directors. To ensure that such meetings take place, the policy may create a shadow chair: an independent director who will act as the "lead outside director" to chair those sessions and to make sure that they are called. When necessary, that individual may represent the independent directors in dealings with the executive of the corporation.

(2) Board Evaluation

§9.87 Another recent emphasis in corporate governance has been to adopt a more systematic approach towards the evaluation of the board itself. To that end, each director will now usually be subject to an individual director performance assessment. The collegial nature of board decision-making tends to foster team like behaviour. Moreover, the director selection process often takes into considerations, such qualities of a given candidate as compatibility and the ability to fit in with other members of the board. Most boards prefer to work on the basis of consensus, rather than conflict, at least until it becomes clear there is a crisis.[139] It is a fair question at what point team play begins to compromise board effectiveness. There is considerable reason to believe that compatibility within the board has both positive and negative outcomes for a corporation. In an ideal case, the positive will outweigh the negative.[140] The difficulty for any corporation is to identify some method of screening out the negative, while promoting the positive.

---

[139] See, generally, in this area: Donald C. Langevoort, "The Human Nature of Corporate Boards: Law, Norms, and the Unintended Consequences of Independence and Accountability" (2001) 89 Geo. L.J. 797; Donald Polden, "Forty Years After Title VII: Creating an Atmosphere Conducive to Diversity in the Corporate Boardroom" (2005) 36 U. Mem. L. Rev. 67.

[140] Compare, for instance, Harry L. Munsinger, "Bias in the Boardroom: Psychological Foundations and Legal Implications of Corporate Cohesion" (1985) 48 Law & Contemp. Prob. 83; Lynne Dallas, "The Relational Board: Three Theories of Corporate Boards of Directors" (1996) 22 J. Corp. Law 1; Ranjay Gulati & James D. Westphal, "Cooperative or Controlling? The Effects of CEO-Board Relations and the Content of Interlocks on the Formation of Joint Ventures" (1999) 44 Admin. Sci. Q. 473; James D. Westphal, "Collaboration in the Boardroom: Behavioral and Performance Consequences of CEO-Board Social Ties" (1999) 42 Acad. Mgmt. J. 7.

§9.88 In principle, a systematic practice of board member assessment could play such a role, but it is uncertain whether the herd mentality of board life inherently undermines proper assessment for this purpose. The criteria of assessment vary from one corporation to another, but the following considerations are frequently employed. It is left to the reader to make his or her own assessment as to whether criteria of the following kind are sufficient or likely in themselves to lead to a board that properly balances a willingness to undertake critical review of management, with the ability to work together as an effective and cohesive team:

- Quality of representation of shareholder and other stakeholder interests. For instance: is the director sufficiently informed and knowledgeable to contribute effectively to the discharge of the Board's responsibilities; does the director possess sufficient judgment and knowledge to have practical input into overall corporate strategy, as well as its business plans, management evaluation and other key matters to be resolved at board level? Does the director make an appropriate time commitment to Board service? Is the director diligent and faithful in attending Board and committee meetings?

- Satisfaction of the legal requirements for holding a directorship. The following questions are relevant: Is the director able to fulfill the legal and fiduciary responsibilities of a director? Is there a potential conflict of interest in having the director serve on the Board?

- Ability to balance proper representation of stakeholder interests against a proper respect for the role of corporate management.

- Effective and meaningful participation in Board decision-making. Critical concerns in this area include the following: Does the performance of the director at Board and committee meetings evidence an active interest in corporate business and affairs? Does the director possess the confidence and willingness to express ideas and engage in constructive discussion? Is the director willing to make tough decisions? Is the director willing and able to respond to appropriate requests for advice and support? Is the director knowledgeable concerning and sensitive to the future direction of industry?

- Expertise: Does the director bring necessary or otherwise useful expertise to the Board? Is the director able to draw upon his or her relevant training and experience in addressing issues facing the company?

- General leadership skill: Is the director able to communicate effectively? Is the director a team player: does he or she work well with the other directors while not necessarily sharing their views? Does the director listen with an open mind?

- Critical ability: Does the director challenge management assumptions and those being made by fellow directors? Does the director ask thought-provoking questions of management that introduce a fresh perspective into decision-making? Does the director evidence an intent to hold management accountable for corporate performance and results?

- Status: Does the director have the appropriate standing and reputation required for a director? Does the director have the proper network of connections in the business, professional and social communities, or with government, so that the director can provide appropriate representation for the corporation?

§9.89 Such performance requirements require a director to strike a difficult balance between providing critical review of management decision making while at the same time not undermining the cohesive management structure of the corporation. The roles of the board and management must be complementary. Little is served by having the board act as a voice of strident opposition within the corporation, second-guessing corporate management at every turn and questioning every decision. On the one hand, as the primary representative of the shareholders and other stakeholders, the board must have a prominent role in setting the corporate vision. On the other hand, no director should perceive his or her mandate as being to impose his own vision of the corporation. Many directors find it difficult to strike the appropriate balance between interference (getting overly involved in operational details)[141] and providing appropriate oversight of corporate operations. It often proves difficult to know when and how to draw the line between dominating discussion and making no contribution at all. A director must support the corporation's philosophy, mission, strategy and values.

(3) Close Personal Relationships and Director Independence

§9.90 Under Delaware law, a shareholder may not pursue a derivative action to assert a claim against the company unless (a) the shareholder has first demanded that the directors pursue the corporate claim and they wrongfully refused to do so; or (b) such demand is excused because the directors are deemed incapable of making an impartial decision regarding the pursuit of the litigation — a provision that is clearly similar to the requirement set out in clause 239(3)(*a*) of the CBCA. Courts have wavered over the question of whether extensive personal relationships can compromise the ability of the directors of a corporation to review each other's behaviour. In *Re Oracle Corp. Derivative Litigation*[142] the court accepted the possibility that social and institutional connections among the directors and officers of a corporation might be so extensive and deep as to bring into doubt the ability of the majority of nominally independent directors to assess the merit of a claim against a director who is alleged to have acted in breach of duty. In *Beam v. Martha Stewart*,[143] the plaintiff who was a shareholder in the company Martha Stewart Living Omnimedia, Inc ("MSLO") brought a derivative action against certain officers and directors of MSLO. The plaintiff argued that a demand on the Board of Directors to pursue the litigation was futile be-

---

[141] *Leon Chevrolet, Inc. v. Trapp*, 391 So. 2d 1371 (C.A. La. 4th Cir. 1980) *per* Schott J.: "If the corporation is to function smoothly these officers must be permitted to perform their duties without interference from individual members of the board once they have been selected by the board as a whole."

[142] 824 A.2d 917 (Del. Ch. 2003).

[143] Supreme Court of Delaware, March 31, 2004, Veasey C.J., Holland, Burger, Steele and Jacobs JJ.

cause the majority of the directors were not independent by virtue of their personal friendships with Martha Stewart, the CEO of the company. It was also argued that the directors were not independent as the CEO could remove directors from office by virtue of the extent of her share ownership. The court rejected these allegations of the plaintiff and said, in relation to social friendships, that:

> Allegations of a mere personal friendship or a mere outside business relationship, standing alone, are insufficient to raise a reasonable doubt about a director's independence.

As evidence of the lack of independence, the plaintiff observed that one director had attended a wedding reception for the daughter of Stewart's lawyer. Stewart was also present at this wedding. In addition, a business magazine article had discussed the close personal relationship between this director and Stewart. The court stated that these social relationships did not create a reasonable doubt of independence.[144]

(iv) Director Election

(1) General

§9.91 It is an inherent right of the shareholders, as the ultimate owners of the corporation to elect, and remove the directors of the corporation, and this authority is fundamental to ensuring managerial accountability. Director election is the primary manner (and for many years was the only direct manner) in which the shareholders might influence the governance of the corporation and its management decisions and corporate policies. The integrity of the election process is essential for good corporate governance. There is no question that two or more shareholders of a corporation may enter into a lawful agreement among themselves, governing the manner in which each shall vote his or her shares, with respect to the election of directors. Generally, such agreements will be legally binding. However, a shareholder will be released from an agreement to vote for a director if the director concerned engages in material misconduct that would justify his or her removal.[145]

§9.92 For most corporations, the directors are elected annually and by all of the shareholders voting as a single class. However, many corporations stagger the election of the full board over a period of up-to-three years, in order to ensure continuity on the board from one year to the next (the same rule also deters radical reconstitution of the board, which might otherwise result from a single year's poor performance). Where this approach to election is employed, each director will be elected for a three-year term, and one-third of the board will be elected in each year. This approach is similar to the rules governing the election of the

---

[144] See also *In re Walt Disney Co. Derivative Litigation*, 731 A.2d 342 at 361 (Del. Ch. 1998).
[145] *Rohe v. Reliance Training Network, Inc.*, [2000] Del. Ch. LEXIS 108 (Del. Ch.).

United States Senate, and appears to be derived from the constitution and customs of that legislature.

§9.93 The director election procedure is usually set down in the corporation's organizational by-law. Where the number of persons nominated is the same or fewer than the number of vacancies on the board, it is customary for the nominated individuals to be acclaimed to office. Where there are more candidates than vacancies, a vote must be taken to ensure that all candidates nominated have a chance of selection by the majority or plurality of the shares that are voted at the meeting.[146] Under the most elementary approach to director election, election is by plurality of shares being voted in favour of election. Each share will be granted a single vote for each position that is to be filled, and the vote for each position is taken separately. Assuming that one director is to be elected from a slate of three candidates, the candidate receiving the most votes cast will be declared elected. Under most standard organizational by-laws, plurality is determined by reference to both the shares present in person and those that are represented by proxy at the meeting. Shares withheld are not considered to be a vote against, but are merely disregarded. Under a plurality of the vote standard, a nominee for election can be elected or re-elected with as little as a single affirmative vote, even while a substantial majority of the votes cast are withheld from voting. With increasing concerns about director accountability and the credibility of the overall corporate governance regime applicable to a corporation, many corporate entities have begun adopting a "majority vote" requirement. Under this approach, a director will not be elected unless he or she receives a majority of the votes cast, whether in person or by proxy.[147]

§9.94 Directors elected at an annual meeting of shareholders will normally hold office until the following annual meeting. Under subsection 106(5) of the CBCA, a director not elected for an express term ceases to hold office at the close of the first annual meeting of shareholders following the director's election. Subsection 106(9) of the CBCA deals with the need for consent to election — a matter that apparently presented itself as a significant concern at the time when the 2001 amendments to the CBCA were enacted:

> 106.(9) An individual who is elected or appointed to hold office as a director is not a director and is deemed not to have been elected or appointed to hold office as a director unless,

---

[146] *Brettingham-Moore v. Christie* (November 21, 1969, Supreme Court of Tasmania). In that case, the company employed what is known as a sequential system of election. Under this approach, each candidate nominated was voted on separately in sequence of nomination. After a majority of votes had been cast in favour of the first three candidates, the presiding officer at the meeting declared that they were elected and that all board positions had been filled, even though two other candidates had still not been considered. Justice Neasey held that the first three candidates had been validly elected.

[147] In Australia, this form of election was supported by the Companies & Securities Advisory Committee (CASAC) *Report on Shareholder Participation* (June 2000), which may be found at: <http://www.camac.gov.au/camac/camac.nsf>.

(a) he or she was present at the meeting when the election or appointment took place and he or she did not refuse to hold office as a director; or

(b) he or she was not present at the meeting when the election of appointment took place and,

   (i) he or she consented to hold office as a director in writing before the election or appointment or within ten days after it, or

   (ii) he or she consented to hold office as a director pursuant to the election or appointment.

Although it is difficult to believe that many people have effectively been conscripted into the office of director, given the responsibilities (and potential liability) that entails, it is hard to argue with the general thrust of subsection (9).

§9.95 The CBCA also provides that:

> 106.(7) If a meeting of shareholders fails to elect the number of the minimum number of directors required by the articles by reason of the lack of consent, disqualification, incapacity or death of any candidates, the directors elected at that meeting may exercise all the powers of the directors if the number of directors so elected constitutes a quorum.[148]

This provision is in some respects troubling, because it begs the question of whether the elected directors may not act if for some other reason than the considerations listed in the above provision the election of a director is invalidated (*e.g.*, by reason of the wrongful exclusion of a proxy, where the effect is limited to one of several elected directors).

(2) Appointment

§9.96 Occasionally an individual shareholder will have the right to appoint a person directly to the board (a process sometimes described in corporate by-laws and shareholder agreements using the somewhat misleading term of "nomination" — for if the effect of the nomination is to make the individual concerned a director, then that person is appointed, not nominated). Most frequently when an appointment is made to the board, it will be by the board itself, in order to fill a casual vacancy that occurs upon the board by reason of the death, retirement or resignation of a member. Section 111 of the CBCA[149] confers upon the directors a limited authority to appoint directors where a casual vacancy occurs. Subsection 111(1) provides:

> 111.(1) Despite subsection 114(3), but subject to subsections (3) and (4), a quorum of directors may fill a vacancy among the directors, except a vacancy resulting from an increase in the number or the minimum or maximum number of directors or a failure to elect the number or minimum number of directors provided for in the articles.

---

[148] CBCA, s. 106(7).
[149] OBCA, s. 124.

The main objective of the section, however, is to retain among the shareholders the principal authority to elect and appoint directors. The procedure for dealing with an increase in the number or the minimum or maximum number of directors is set out in subsection 112(2):

> 112.(2) Where the shareholders at a meeting adopt an amendment to the articles of a corporation to increase or, subject to paragraph 107(*h*) and to subsection (1), decrease the number or minimum or maximum number of directors, the shareholders may, at the meeting, elect the number of directors authorized by the amendment, and for that purpose, notwithstanding subsections 179(1) and 262(3), on the issue of a certificate of amendment the articles are deemed to be amended as of the date the shareholders adopt the amendment.[150]

Subsection 111(2) continues:

> 111.(2) If there is not a quorum of directors or if there has been a failure to elect the number or minimum number of directors provided for in the articles, the directors then in office shall without delay call a special meeting of shareholders to fill the vacancy and, if they fail to call a meeting or if there are no directors then in office, the meeting may be called by any shareholder.

Where the holders of a particular class or series of shares have an exclusive right of election, then subsection 111(3) provides the following rule for filling a vacancy:

> 111.(3) If the holders of any class or series of shares of a corporation have an exclusive right to elect one or more directors and a vacancy occurs among those directors,
>
> (*a*) subject to subsection (4), the remaining directors elected by the holders of that class or series of shares may fill the vacancy except a vacancy resulting from an increase in the number or the minimum or maximum number of directors for that class or series or from a failure to elect the number or minimum number of directors provided for in the articles for that class or series; or
>
> (*b*) if there are no remaining directors any holder of shares of that class or series may call a meeting of the holders of shares of that class or series for the purpose of filling the vacancy.

(3) Invalid Appointment or Election

§9.97 Where the board of directors is invalidly elected, the court may direct a new election to be held. Although the court is reluctant to interfere with the internal management of a corporation, it has the jurisdiction to interfere where it is necessary to do so to prevent the perpetration of a fraud upon the shareholders or any part of the body of shareholders, and such a suit may be brought either as a derivative action or by the aggrieved shareholders themselves.[151] However, the

---

[150] OBCA, s. 125(1).
[151] *Davidson v. Grange*, [1854] O.J. No. 200, 4 Gr. 377 (U.C.C.A.).

court will not interfere where an objection is not taken to the election of the directors concerned within a reasonable period of time.[152]

(v) Cumulative Voting

§9.98 Unless the articles of a corporation otherwise provide, each share of a corporation entitles its holder to one vote on each matter to be decided by the shareholders. Strictly speaking, the election of each director is a separate matter, and accordingly unless there is some provision in the articles to vary the presumed voting arrangement, it is possible for shareholders who individually or collectively hold more than 50 per cent of the voting shares to cast their votes so as to elect all of the directors of the corporation. For obvious reasons, minority shareholders frequently object to a voting scheme which effectively excludes them from having a say in the administration of the company, and not surprisingly a number of methods have been developed to ensure that minority shareholders will have a proportionate say in the election of the board of directors, and a representation on the board that is elected, that is proportional to the total number of votes that they hold.

§9.99 The simplest method of ensuring minority representation on a board of directors is to issue a special class or series of shares to those shareholders, that will entitle them to an exclusive right to elect a stated number of directors. This technique is most often applied in the case of small corporations (options are to vest rights of director appointment under a unanimous shareholder resolution, or to employ a voting trust or similar arrangement to ensure that shares are voted in a particular manner). However, there may be many reasons which militate against the issue of such a class or series of shares, or the employment of entrenched rights of appointment or voting. A more flexible option, and one well-suited to widely held corporations, is to provide in the articles for the cumulative voting of shares.

§9.100 Cumulative voting is a system of voting under which each elector has a number of votes determined by reference to the number of offices that are to be filled by election, with the elector being free to distribute those votes among such number of persons or concentrate those votes upon any one person, as the elector may see fit.[153] For example, if there are 10 directors to be elected by the shareholders, then each share will entitle its shareholder to 10 votes. The practical effect of cumulative voting is to permit one or more shareholders who vote their shares in an appropriate manner to cause the election of a percentage of the board of directors equal to the percentage of the shares held by those shareholders, irrespective of how the other shareholders of the corporation may vote. In

---

[152] *Re Moore & Port Bruce Harbour Co.*, [1856] O.J. No. 122, 14 U.C.Q.B. 365 at 368 (C.A.), *per* Robinson C.J.O., although he equivocated somewhat on this point.
[153] It is called cumulative voting, because it allows any shareholder to cumulate such voting powers as he or she possesses and give one candidate votes equal to the number of directors multiplied by the number of his or her votes: *Humphreys v. Winous*, 165 Ohio 45, 133 N.E.2d 780 (S.C. Ohio 1956), *per* Bell J.

other words, cumulative voting is a device employed to achieve proportional representation on the board of directors.

§9.101 Section 120(a) of the OBCA expressly permits cumulative voting, and clause (a) states that where the articles provide for cumulative voting

> (a) each shareholder entitled to vote at an election of directors has the right to cast a number of votes equal to the number of votes attached to the shares held by the shareholder multiplied by the number of directors to be elected, and the shareholder may cast all such votes in favour of one candidate or distribute them among the candidates in any manner.

The effect of this provision is to permit minority shareholders to elect a number of directors proportionate to the percentage of shares that they hold in the corporation. To do so, they must vote all their shares for only that percentage of the total number of spots to be filled as is approximately equal to their shareholding.

§9.102 Under a cumulative system of voting, the number of directors who receive the largest number of votes are elected, up to the maximum number of positions required to be filled. For instance, if there are 10 directors to be elected by shareholders who collectively hold 185,000 shares, the vote distribution is as set out below:

Holder	Number of Shares	Number of Directors to be Elected	Number of Votes	Percentage of All Shares Held	Number of Directors Electable	Number of Votes Remaining
A	10,000	10	100,000	5.4 %	0	100,000
B	20,000	10	200,000	10.8 %	1	0
C	50,000	10	500,000	27.0 %	2	100,000
D	5,000	10	50,000	2.7 %	0	50,000
E	100,000	10	1,000,000	54.1 %	5	0
Total	185,000	10	1,850,000	100.0 %	8	250,000

Cumulative voting does not guarantee that a minority shareholder will be represented on the board — it is possible for a minority shareholder to vote so irrationally that he or she will lose the benefit that cumulative voting provides. However, under the above vote distribution, any shareholder may guarantee one representative on the board for each block of shares of the corporation held by the shareholder that is equal to 10 per cent of the total number of shares, by voting all of the shares in that block for a single candidate. If this strategy is adopted, no matter how the other shareholders may vote, it will be impossible to block the election of a director by a shareholder who possesses such a block. After all such votes have been cast, there are 250,000 votes remaining, to elect the last two directors. Consequently, both A and C will be able to secure the election of a director to one of the remaining vacancies by voting each block of the remaining shares held by them respectively for a single candidate. D is unable to secure the election of any representative.

§9.103 Clause 120(*b*) of the OBCA[154] further provides that a separate vote shall be taken with respect to each candidate nominated for director unless a resolution is passed unanimously permitting two or more persons to be elected by a single resolution. This provision simplifies the administration of cumulative voting, although it is possible for a cumulative system of voting to work even if all directors are elected simultaneously. In considering the impact of clause (*b*) on the director selection process it is important to remember that votes once cast are spent.

§9.104 Clauses 120(*c*) and (*d*) of the OBCA[155] further provide that

(*c*) if a shareholder has voted for more than one candidate without specifying the distribution of the shareholder's votes among the candidates, the shareholder is deemed to have distributed the shareholder's votes equally among the candidates for whom the shareholder voted;

(*d*) if the number of candidates nominated for director exceeds the number of positions to be filled, the candidates who received the least number of votes shall be eliminated until the number of candidates remaining equal the number of positions to be filled; ...

These provisions make clear that cumulative voting does not guarantee that every minority shareholder will be represented on the board of directors. As a general rule, a minority shareholder will only be certain of representation where the percentage of shares held by the shareholder (of the total number of voting shares) is equal to or greater than the percentage that one director constitutes of the total number of shareholders to be elected.

§9.105 Clause 120(*e*) of the OBCA[156] provides that where the articles provide for cumulative voting:

(*e*) each director ceases to hold office at the close of the first annual meeting of shareholders following his or her election; ...

Clause (*e*) is mandatory in all cases where there is cumulative voting, for the simple reason that any other rule would defeat the purpose of the cumulative vote. Unless the term of all directors expired at the same time, proportional representation would not result from a cumulative vote. Consequently, all directors must be elected at the same meeting. Thus there is no possibility of a term of office for directors of longer than one year, where there is such a voting

---

[154] CBCA, s. 107(*c*).
[155] CBCA, s. 107(*d*) and (*e*).
[156] CBCA, s. 107(*f*).

scheme;[157] nor is it possible to stagger the terms of directors so that only a portion of the board is up for re-election each year.[158]

§9.106 Under clause 120(*f*) of the OBCA[159] a director may not be removed from office if the votes cast against the director's removal would be sufficient to elect him or her and such votes could be voted cumulatively at any election at which the same total number of votes were cast and the number of directors required by the articles were then being elected.[160] The intent behind clause (*f*) is to prevent a recall vote from being used to undo the proportional representation that is achieved through the use of cumulative voting. The wording of the corresponding CBCA provision, clause 107(*g*), is slightly different:

> (*g*) a director may be removed from office only if the number of votes cast in favour of the director's removal is greater than the product of the number of directors required by the articles and the number of votes cast against the motion; ...

§9.107 To prevent the board from being gerrymandered, clause 120(*g*) of the OBCA[161] provides:

> (*g*) the number of directors required by the articles may not be decreased if the votes cast against the motion to decrease would be sufficient to elect a director and such votes could be voted cumulatively at an election at which the same total number of votes were cast and the number of directors required by the articles were then being elected; ...

§9.108 This raises the obvious question of whether it is possible to combine cumulative voting with a variable number (*i.e.*, a maximum and minimum number) of directors — a question which is answered by clause 120(*h*),[162] which provides:

> (*h*) the articles shall require a fixed number and not a minimum and maximum number of directors.

Thus where a corporation introduces a system of cumulative voting, there is a fair cost to the corporation in terms of lost flexibility in the manner in which it may structure its board of directors. Clause 107(*a*) of the CBCA is to a similar effect as clause (*h*) of the OBCA. Moreover, the corresponding wording of clause 107(*h*) of the CBCA is less ambiguous than clause 120(*g*) of the OBCA:

> 107.(*h*) the number of directors required by the articles may be decreased only if the votes cast in favour of the motion to decrease the number of directors is

---

[157] Strictly speaking, identical multi-year terms would have worked as well, but this option does not seem to have been considered.
[158] In widely held corporations, staggered elections are sometimes seen as advantageous since they ensure some measure of continuity from one year to another.
[159] CBCA, s. 107(*g*). As to the ambiguity of this provision, see *Canada Business Corporations Act Discussion Paper Proposals for Technical Amendments* (Ottawa: Industry Canada, September 1995), 45-48.
[160] See, generally, *Bushell v. Faith*, [1970] A.C. 1099 (H.L.).
[161] CBCA, s. 107(*h*).
[162] CBCA, s. 107(*a*).

greater than the product of the number of directors required by the articles and the number of votes cast against the motion.

(vi) De Facto Directors

§9.109 From the earliest days of corporate law, it must have been apparent that from time to time persons would act in the capacity of directors even though (a) they lacked some qualification for that office; or (b) they were not validly elected or appointed. Where either situation occurred, the question would arise as to whether the acts of such directors were valid and binding upon the corporation. The concept of the *de facto* director came into being in response to this concern. Simply defined, a *de facto* director is no more than a person who is not a director (or has ceased to be a director) but who nevertheless purports to act in the capacity of a director.

§9.110 There are now three distinct classes of *de facto* director — the last class having been recently added by statutory amendment. One class comprises former directors whose term of office have expired but who have continued to act as directors of the corporation after the expiration of their term of office. The OBCA contains two provisions that generally permit an outsider to treat such directors as validly appointed. First, clause 19(*b*) of the OBCA provides that the corporation may not assert against a person dealing with the corporation or with any person who has acquired rights from the corporation that the persons named in the most recent notice filed under the *Corporations Information Act*,[163] or named in the articles, whichever is more current, are not directors of the corporation. Second, and more importantly, subsection 119(7) of the OBCA provides that where directors are not elected at a meeting of shareholders, the incumbent directors continue in office until their successors are elected. Thus if the election of a new board is declared invalid, the old board remains in office until a valid election is held.[164]

§9.111 A related doctrine of holding over applies in the case of corporate officers. There is no provision in either the OBCA or the CBCA that deems offices (other than those of director and auditor) to expire after a period of time. On the contrary, the assumption is that the officers of a corporation hold office at the pleasure of the board and, so long as they continue to enjoy that pleasure (or, more accurately, until the board's displeasure becomes manifest), the officers continue in office from year to year despite changes in the make-up of the board itself. Unless the directors resolve to remove them, the officers continue in office uninterrupted.[165] However, this general rule may be modified in the circumstances of a particular case.[166]

---

[163] R.S.O. 1990, c. C.39.
[164] See *Re British International Finance (Can.) Ltd.*, [1968] O.J. No. 1139, [1968] 2 O.R. 217 at 220 (C.A.), *per* Aylesworth J.A.
[165] *Re Jubilee Theatre Ltd.* (1956), 3 D.L.R. (2d) 624 at 626-27 (N.S.C.A.), *per* Doull J.
[166] See, for instance *Ghimpelman v. Bercovici*, [1957] S.C.J. No. 5, [1957] S.C.R. 128, 7 D.L.R. (2d) 193, which turned upon the specific wording of the Quebec *Companies Act*, R.S.Q. 1941, c.

§9.112 The second class of *de facto* directors are those who take upon themselves the office of director without proper election of appointment. In their case, section 128 of the OBCA[167] provides that:

> 128. An act done by a director or by an officer is not invalid by reason only of any defect that is thereafter discovered in his or her appointment, election or qualification.

Section 116 of the CBCA is to a similar effect, but employs counter-positive language to that set out in the OBCA provision:

> 116. An act of a director or officer is valid notwithstanding an irregularity in their election or appointment or a defect in their qualification.

The meaning and effect of a comparably worded provision was considered by Lord Simmonds in *Morris v. Kanssen*,[168] where it was given a fairly narrow construction. It was held that the section can be invoked only where the defect in appointment or qualification is discovered after the act of the director in question.[169] On the basis of this authority, in *Re Regional Steel Works (Oshawa) Ltd.*[170] Charron J. concluded that section 116 of the CBCA would not validate the acts of a director who continued to act in that capacity despite his personal bankruptcy (which rendered him unqualified for office under section 105(1)(*d*) of that Act).[171]

§9.113 Section 128 of the OBCA does not validate the appointment of such directors but rather validates the acts which they undertake and the things which they do.[172] It not only applies between the corporation and third parties, but between the corporation and the directors themselves, so that the corporation is barred from suing the directors for intermeddling, provided they were not aware of the defect in their appointment or election.[173] In order to bind the corporation with the acts of such directors, however, the corporation itself must in some way have held them out to be directors in the sense that there has been at least apparent compliance with the requirements of the Act, articles and by-laws in the manner of their appointment, so that they may be said to have acted under at least some colour of right.[174] The precise point at which there is a sufficient color

---

276, s. 86(1), but compare the vigorous dissenting judgment of Rand J., in which he expressed the opinion that continuity of office is essential to the proper functioning of corporations.
[167] CBCA, s. 116.
[168] [1946] A.C. 459 (H.L.).
[169] *Ibid.*, at 472.
[170] (1994), 25 C.B.R. (2d) 135 (Ont. Bnkrptcy.).
[171] See also *Tyne Mutual Steamship Insurance Association v. Brown* (1896), 74 L.T. 283 (Q.B.); but cf. *Briton Medical & General Life Association v. Jones* (1889), 61 L.T. (N.S.) 384 (Q.B.); *Mahony v. East Holyford Mining Co.* (1875), L.R. 7 H.L. 869.
[172] *Oliver v. Elliott* (1960), 30 W.W.R. 641 at 644-45 (Alta. T.D.), *per* Egbert J.
[173] *Traders Trust Co. v. Goodman*, [1917] 2 W.W.R 1235 at 1240, 37 D.L.R. 31 (Man. C.A.), *per* Perdue J.A.
[174] See, generally, *Re Carpenter Ltd.*, [1916] O.J. No. 86, 35 O.L.R. 626 at 629 (H.C.), *per* Clute J., leave to appeal refused [1916] O.J. No. 523, 10 O.W.N. 122 (C.A.). See also *Gorden Gully United Quartz Mining Co. v. McLister* (1875), 1 App. Cas. 39 (P.C.); *Modstock Mining Co. v. Harris* (1902), 40 N.S.R. 336 (S.C.).

of right to protect the actions of the director is uncertain. In general, the courts seem to lean towards protecting both directors and outsiders who have acted in good faith. Thus for instance, it has been held the corporation will be bound by the acts of directors who are elected and who assume positions on the board despite being disqualified or unqualified for office.[175] However, where a person enters into a contract with a corporation knowing of the defective appointment of the *de facto* directors who approved the contract, the corporation is not bound by that contract.[176]

§9.114 A *de facto* director cannot maintain his office where the corporation demands that he (or she) step down and cease presenting himself as a director.[177] However, outsiders to a corporation have no standing to attack the validity of the appointment of *de facto* directors[178] — although they are not obliged to deal with a corporation where they doubt the validity of the appointment of the incumbent board. Nor may the *de facto* directors themselves escape liability as directors by arguing that their appointment was invalid.[179] By acting as directors, they are estopped from challenging the validity of their appointment.[180]

§9.115 In 1994, the OBCA was amended to add subsections (4) and (5) to section 115, to deal with the responsibility for the management of the corporation, in the event that all directors have resigned or been removed from office. Subsection (4) provides:

> 115.(4) Where all of the directors have resigned or have been removed by the shareholders without replacement, any person who manages or supervises the management of the business and affairs of the corporation shall be deemed to be a director for the purposes of this Act.

However, subsection (5) qualifies this rule:

> 115.(5) Subsection (4) does not apply to,
>
> (*a*) an officer who manages the business of the corporation under the direction or control of a shareholder or other person;
>
> (*b*) a lawyer, accountant or other professional who participates in the management of the corporation solely for the purposes of providing professional services; or

---

[175] See, for instance, *Klein v. James*, [1986] B.C.J. No. 997, 36 B.L.R. 42 (S.C.), aff'd (1987), 37 B.L.R. xxvii (C.A.).

[176] *Coal Gate Oils Ltd. v. Western Petroleum (No. 2)* (1952), 7 W.W.R. (N.S.) 91 at 93-94 (Sask. C.A.), *per* Gordon J.A.

[177] *Modstock Mining Co. v. Harris* (1902), 40 N.S.R. 336 at 338 (S.C.), *per* Graham E.J., but compare *Re Moore & Port Bruce Harbour Co.*, [1856] O.J. No. 122, 14 U.C.Q.B. 365 (C.A.).

[178] *DuMart Packing Co. v. DuMart*, [1927] O.J. No. 140, 61 O.L.R. 478 at 480 (H.C.), *per* Middleton J.A.

[179] *Northern Trust Co. v. Butchart*, [1917] 2 W.W.R. 405 at 421, 35 D.L.R. 169 (Man. K.B.), *per* Mathers C.J.K.B.

[180] *Re Owen Sound Lumber Co.*, [1915] O.J. No. 116, 34 O.L.R. 528 (H.C.), var'd [1917] O.J. No. 144, 38 O.L.R. 414 at 421 (C.A.), *per* Hodgins J.A.

(c) a trustee in bankruptcy, receiver, receiver-manager or secured creditor who participates in the management of the corporation or exercises control over its property solely for the purposes of enforcement of a security agreement or administration of a bankrupt's estates, in the case of a trustee in bankruptcy.

Similar amendments were introduced into section 109 of the CBCA in the 2001 amendment of that Act. To date, these provisions have not been considered by the court, and there can be little doubt that they would present serious difficulties if they were to come before a court. Looking at the provisions initially from a policy perspective, it is difficult to see why a person should become subject to a range of liabilities and duties that the person in question has not agreed to assume. However, that basic question aside, there are a very large number of practical problems that would arise in trying to apply the provisions in the kind of situation that would be likely to arise.

§9.116 To cite but a few of the problems with subsection (4): First, its express terms, subsection (4) applies only in a very limited range of cases: where the director "resigns" or is "removed from office by the shareholders without replacement". It does not apply where a director dies, becomes incapacitated or absconds. Second, the person who takes control is said to be a director, but only "for the purposes of this Act". This narrow wording raises many questions: does it mean that the individual concerned possesses all of the common law authority of a director (*e.g.*, the authority to institute a legal proceeding), as well as the authority conferred upon directors by the by-laws of the corporation? Or is the sole intent of the provision to affix the duties and liabilities of a director upon the hapless individual who takes over day-to-day control of a corporation that suddenly finds itself plunged into crisis. For instance, if a vice president of a business takes over day-to-day operation following the apparent disappearance of the president and sole director of the business, does the vice president then become liable for unpaid wages? If so, does the vice president have the authority to dismiss all of the employees of the corporation, in order to forestall potential wage claims? Third, for most statutory purposes a director may escape further liability by resigning. It is unclear how a subsection (4) *de facto* director could escape further liability.

§9.117 Fourth, as a factual matter it would be difficult to decide when a person would be said to be managing or supervising the management of the business of the corporation. For instance, in the case of the resignation of the sole director of a corporation that operates a manufacturing business, would the plant and office manager of the business have sufficient control over the day-to-day operation of the business (simply by continuing to perform their existing obligations) to come within the scope of subsection (4)? Or is it necessary that such individuals take on some responsibility beyond that which they were previously expected to exercise as officers of the corporation? Complicating this question even further is the fact that these individuals may not even be aware that the sole director has resigned. At what point is it intended for liability as a director to arise? Clause (a) is especially problematic. Specifically, it raises the question of what rule applies where the management officers of the corporation follow the directions of a majority shareholder, but provides no indication of the consequence. For instance, if the general manager of a business routinely consults with the majority shareholder before acting, does that constitute acting under the direction and control of the shareholder? If so, does the majority shareholder then become responsible as a director? If so, at what point: when does consultation amount to direction? A related question is whether a mere officer of a corporation has the proper authority to disregard the express wishes of the majority shareholder: it is far from clear whether subsection (4) is sufficient to clothe an officer who takes over the day-to-day operation of a business pending a shareholder meeting with the same kind of authority as the common law confers upon directors. Next, it is unclear whether a person who is initially caught by subsection (4) remains responsible under it until such time as a replacement director is elected or appointed. A further question is whether liability expands as other people become involved in management of the business. To return to the previous example: if the general manager of a business consults with the majority shareholder, are both brought within the scope of subsection (4) or only one? If one, which one? Does consultation relieve the general manager of responsibility? If so, at what point?

(vii) Assumption of Office

§9.118 The time at which the directors of a corporation assume office as such, and the manner in which they are appointed to that office, depend upon (a) whether the corporation is subject to the OBCA or the CBCA; and (b) whether the directors are first directors. The first directors of a CBCA corporation are named in a notice of directors in the prescribed form, that is filed with the Director together with the articles of incorporation.[181] The first directors hold office from the date of the issue of the certificate of incorporation until the first meeting of directors.[182] The procedure under the OBCA is generally similar. The first directors of an OBCA corporation must be named in the articles of incorporation, and they hold office from the date of the endorsement of the certificate of incorporation until the first meeting of the shareholders of the corporation.[183] Subsection 119(3) of the OBCA goes on to provide specifically that the first directors of a corporation have all the powers and duties and are subject to all of the liabilities of directors generally under the Act. However, there is no reason to believe that any other result would apply, so even though the CBCA is silent with respect to these matters, it is likely that a similar finding would be made under that Act.

§9.119 Aside from the first directors, the time at which and the manner in which the directors of a corporation assume office, and the term for which they hold it, are partly a matter regulated by the Act and are partly regulated by the articles and by-laws of each corporation.[184] The general rule is that the shareholders of a

---

[181] CBCA, s. 106(1).
[182] CBCA, s. 106(2).
[183] OBCA, s. 119(1).
[184] See, generally, *Societa Caruso v. Tosolini*, [2005] O.J. No. 2364, 7 B.L.R. (4th) 222 at 230 (S.C.J.), *per* Gauthier J.

corporation elect the directors of the corporation, those elections commencing with the first meeting of shareholders, and continuing thereafter at each succeeding annual meeting at which an election of directors is required. However, both the OBCA and the CBCA permit directors to have a term of office of up to three years.[185] As noted above, many corporations take advantage of these provisions by staggering the terms of their directors, so as to ensure at least some continuity from one year to another. So, for instance, one third of the positions on the board will be up for election at each annual meeting. Both statutes clearly sanction this practice, as each provides that it is not necessary for all directors elected at a meeting of shareholders to hold office for the same term.[186] As a practical matter, in most cases, it will only be at the first meeting following the introduction of the staggered election system that the directors will be elected for different terms.

(viii) Resignation and Removal of Directors

§9.120 Subsection 119(2) of the OBCA provides that no director named in the articles may resign his office unless at the time the resignation becomes effective a successor has been elected or appointed.[187] The prohibition on resignation does not apply to successor directors who may be elected or appointed once the corporation has been organized, but the wording of the provision is such that it is at least arguable that a first director named in the articles who remains in office following organization is also barred from resigning unless and until a successor is appointed or elected.[188] From time to time, consideration has been given to expanding the scope of the section to prohibit any resignation of directors where the effect would be to reduce the number of directors remaining to less than a quorum, but to date no such change has been made in the legislation. Given the range of duties to which directors are subject, and their potential liability in respect of those duties, any such change would be undesirable, as it could prevent a director who is dissatisfied with the manner in which a corporation is conducting its business or affairs from taking the only real step that is available for his or her own protection.[189] Nor is it clear why a person should be required to continue acting as a director when he or she is not being remunerated as such. There is no equivalent provision to subsection 119(2) in the CBCA, nor is this provision found in certain of the other provincial business corporations statutes. In *Brown v. Shearer*, the Manitoba Court of Appeal held that there was no implied restriction under the CBCA on director resignations.[190]

---

[185] OBCA, s. 119(4); CBCA, s. 106(3).
[186] OBCA, s. 119(5); CBCA, s. 106(4). Such staggered elections may not be held where the articles provide for cumulative voting. See §9.100 *seq*.
[187] OBCA, s. 119(2).
[188] See, generally, *Deguise v. Lesage*, [1945] Que. S.C. 40.
[189] See, generally, *Netupsky v. Canada*, [2003] T.C.J. No. 30, 30 B.L.R. (3d) 46 as to the effective time of a resignation.
[190] *Brown v. Shearer*, [1995] M.J. No. 182, 19 B.L.R. (2d) 1 at 7 (C.A.), *per* Huband J.A.

§9.121 By virtue of subsection 121(2) of the OBCA[191] the resignation of a director becomes effective at the time his or her written resignation[192] is sent to the corporation, or at the time specified in the resignation, whichever is later. The question of whether a director has manifested an intention to resign is one of fact.[193] A director resignation need not be accepted in order for the resignation to be complete and effective.[194] Once a director has submitted his or her resignation, it cannot be withdrawn except with the agreement of the corporation.[195] It is not necessary for the resignation to be accepted or that it be entered on the corporate minutes or that someone be elected or appointed to take the place of the person who is resigning, in order to make the resignation effective. Instead, the officer's resignation is complete when it is tendered, without more. A director (or officer) is not obliged to state his or her reasons for resigning. The inaction or refusal of a board of directors to accept a resignation cannot impose upon the officer any future liability or responsibility.[196]

§9.122 At common law, there was no procedure for the removal of a director during his or her term of office.[197] This entrenched position was unlikely to survive the move towards democratization of corporate law effected under the former OBCA, so it is not surprising that both the current OBCA and the CBCA now provide such a procedure. The right of the shareholders to remove directors seems natural enough; although directors are responsible to the corporation, they are nonetheless elected by and are the representatives of the shareholders. Because of that representative status, the only real question should be the conditions under which the directors of a corporation may be removed. A court has no inherent jurisdiction to remove a director from office (although such a jurisdiction does exist where oppression and related abuse can be proven),[198] nor is there any general implied jurisdiction to do so under the *Companies' Creditors Arrangement Act*.[199]

§9.123 For corporations that are reporting issuers in Ontario, the Ontario Securities Commission is given a statutory authority to remove a director from office. The jurisdiction in question is set out in subsection 127(1) of the *Securities Act*. The relevant portions of this subsection provide:

---

[191] CBCA, s. 108(2).
[192] Oral resignations are not effective: *Latchford Premier Cinema, Ltd. v. Ennion*, [1931] 2 Ch. 409.
[193] *POW Services Ltd. v. Clare*, [1995] 2 B.C.L.C. 435.
[194] See, generally, *Deguise v. Lesage*, [1945] Que. S.C. 40.
[195] *Glossop v. Glossop*, [1907] 2 Ch. 370.
[196] *Master Records Inc. v. Backman*, 133 Ariz. 494, 652 P.2d 1017 (S.C. Ariz. 1982), *per* Feldman J.
[197] *London Finance Corp. v. Banking Service Corp.*, [1922] O.J. No. 378, 23 O.W.N. 138 at 139 (H.C.), *per* Middleton J.; *Stephenson v. Vokes*, [1896] O.J. No. 191, 27 O.R. 691 (H.C.J.).
[198] For instance, directors who improperly favour their own or a majority or controlling shareholder's interest over the interests of other shareholders, or who otherwise oppress the minority interest may be removed from office: *Catalyst Fund General Partner I Inc. v. Hollinger Inc.*, [2004] O.J. No. 4722, 1 B.L.R. (4th) 186 at 197 (S.C.J.), *per* Campbell J., aff'd [2006] O.J. No. 944 (C.A.).
[199] R.S.C. 1985, c. C-36. See *Re Stelco Inc.* (2005), 2 B.L.R. (4th) 328 (Ont. C.A.). The court left open the question of whether such a jurisdiction might arise in an unusual case.

127.(1) The Commission may make one or more of the following orders if in its opinion it is in the public interest to make the order or orders:

.....

7. An order that a person resign one or more positions that the person holds as a director or officer of an issuer.

8. An order that a person is prohibited from becoming or acting as director or officer of any issuer.

Such an order may be made even where the individual in question has not breached a specific provision of the *Securities Act* itself, since the OSC has the jurisdiction to make a preventative order in the public interest where necessary to prevent future harm.[200] There must, however, be an evidentiary record that justifies the making of such an order in the public interest. The term "public interest" for this purpose means the need to protect investors from unfair, improper or fraudulent practices and the need to foster fair, efficient capital markets as well as confidence in those markets. In deciding whether these requirements are satisfied, the OSC must have regard to the fundamental principles set out in section 2.1 of the *Securities Act*, including the maintenance of high standards of fitness and business conduct to ensure honest and responsible conduct by market participants — a term that includes both reporting issuers and their directors and officers.[201] In the *Banks* case, the OSC stated:

> ... where a respondent has egregiously failed to adhere to existing standards or principles of corporate governance, and a respondent's past conduct has convinced us that without one or more orders, future harm is likely to occur, it is appropriate for us to make an order ... Not every lapse in the duty of a director or officer ... will raise a public interest concern. However, a public interest concern will arise ... over a lapse that demonstrates (i) an inability to adhere to high standards of fitness and business conduct which ensure honest or responsible conduct; (ii) a careless disregard for, or indifference to, reasonably foreseeable, serious consequences of a failure to meet highs standards of fitness and business conduct; or (iii) unfair, improper or fraudulent practices impacting participants in the capital market ... [If] a person ahs committed securities fraud in Ontario or another jurisdiction ... we should carefully consider the need for an order ...[202]

§9.124 Subsection 122(1) of the OBCA permits the shareholders of a corporation to remove a director by ordinary resolution at an annual or special meeting. In contrast, under subsection 109(1) of the CBCA, a director may be removed only upon an ordinary resolution passed at a special meeting. However, the distinction in the wording of the two Acts is of little practical importance, since subsection 96(5) of the OBCA provides that:

> 96.(5) All business transacted at ... an annual meeting of shareholders, except consideration of the minutes of an earlier meeting, the financial statements and the

---

[200] *Canadian Tire Corp. v. C.T.C. Dealer Holdings Ltd.*, [1987] O.J. No. 221, 59 O.R. (2d) 79 (Div. Ct.).
[201] *Re Banks* (2003), 34 B.L.R. (3d) 292 (Ont. Sec. Comm.).
[202] *Ibid.* at 306.

auditor's report, election of directors and reappointment of the incumbent auditor, shall be deemed to be special business.

Thus it is necessary to comply with the notice requirements pertaining to special business under both Acts, in order to remove a director. Where the shareholders resolve to remove a director, they may either fill the consequent vacancy on the board themselves, or leave it to the remaining directors to appoint a substitute.[203]

§9.125 In England, it appears to be common for companies to provide in their articles that a director may be required to vacate office where requested to do so in writing by all other members of the board.[204] In view of the requirements of section 122 and the right of a director to appeal his or her proposed removal under subsection 123(1) of the OBCA, it is doubtful whether such a provision would be valid in Canada. In *Szczerba v. St. Stanislaus-St. Casimir's Polish Parishes Credit Union Ltd.*[205] the court considered the interpretation of section 99 of the *Credit Unions and Caisses Populaires Act, 1994*,[206] which provides:

> 99. If a director fails to attend three consecutive board meetings without, in the opinion of the board, reasonable cause or fails to perform any duties allotted to him or her as a director, the board may by resolution, declare the director's position vacant.

It was held that this provision should not be construed so narrowly as to apply only to duties specifically delegated to a director to undertake. It extended to any duty inherent in the position of a director.

§9.126 Under both the OBCA and the CBCA, the right to remove a director is limited where the articles of the corporation either provide for cumulative voting or confer an exclusive right on the holders of a class or series of shares to elect a director. In particular, clause 120(*f*) of the OBCA[207] provides that where the articles provide for cumulative voting:

> (*f*) a director may not be removed from office if the votes cast against the director's removal would be sufficient to elect him or her and such votes could be voted cumulatively at an election at which the same total number of votes were cast and the number of directors required by the articles were then being elected;

In the case of shares of a series or class that confer an exclusive right to elect a director, subsections 122(2) of the OBCA and 109(2) of the CBCA provide:

> 122.(2) Where the holders of any class or series of shares of a corporation have an exclusive right to elect one or more directors, a director so elected may only be removed by an ordinary resolution at a meeting of the shareholders of that class or series.

---

[203] OBCA, s. 122(3); CBCA, s. 109(3).
[204] See, generally, *Lee v. Chou Wen Hsien*, [1984] 1 W.L.R. 1202 (P.C.).
[205] [2003] O.J. No. 5945, 31 B.L.R. (3d) 252 (S.C.J.).
[206] S.O. 1994, c. 11, s. 99.
[207] CBCA, s. 107(*g*).

Thus the right to remove a director may not be used to undo the provisions built into the articles of a corporation to ensure that certain shareholders are represented on the board. However, cumulative voting does not prevent the removal of a director for cause.[208]

§9.127 Historically, the power to remove directors has sometimes been employed by the management committee to remove an outside director who intrudes too much into the business or affairs of the corporation.[209] The usual tactic was for the name of the director in question to be deleted from the management slate. In the case of offering corporations, this practice has now been made more difficult by the introduction of nomination committees made up of independent directors. In addition, both the OBCA and the CBCA provide that a director who receives a notice or otherwise learns of a meeting of shareholders called for the purpose of removing him from office is entitled to submit to the corporation a written statement giving the reasons why he opposes that resolution.[210] Where the director submits such a statement, the corporation is obliged to send a copy of it to every shareholder and to the Director, unless the statement is included in or attached to a management proxy circular.[211] Unfortunately, these procedures do little to protect a director who is removed from the management slate at the end of his or her term. The failure of a number of financial institutions in the 1980s and 1990s gave considerable indication that some such protection is necessary. In the 2001 amendments to the CBCA, a further clause (*c*) was added to section 110(2) of CBCA which extended a corresponding right where a director:

> (*c*) receives a notice or otherwise learns of a meeting of directors or shareholders at which another person is to be appointed or elected to fill the office of director, whether because of the director's resignation or removal or because the director's term of office has expired or is about to expire.

This clause affords some protection where a director is effectively being forced off a board, by reason of asking difficult questions.

§9.128 Although an employee, whose conditions or contract of employment incidentally require or result in his or her service as a director, remains entitled to the same reasonable notice of the termination of employment as any other employee, such notice is not required in the case of a person whose sole connection with the company is in the capacity of a director.[212]

---

[208] See, generally, *Campbell v. Loews Inc.*, 36 Del. Ch. 563, 134 A.2d 852 (1957).
[209] See, for instance, W.Z. Estey, *Report of the Inquiry into the Collapse of the CCBC and Northland Bank* (the "Estey Report") (Ottawa: Ministry of Supply & Services Canada, 1986), 182-83.
[210] OBCA, s. 123(1); CBCA, s. 110(2).
[211] OBCA, s. 123(3); CBCA, s. 110(3).
[212] *Allish v. Allied Engineering of B.C. Ltd.* (1957), 22 W.W.R. 641 (B.C.C.A.); *Shuttleworth v. Cox Bros. & Co. (Maidenhead)*, [1927] 2 K.B. 9 (C.A.); *Southern Foundries (1926) Ltd. v. Shirlaw*, [1940] A.C. 701 (H.L.); *Shindler v. Northern Raincoat Co. Ltd.*, [1960] 1 W.L.R. 1938; *Read v. Astoria Garage (Streatham) Ltd.*, [1952] Ch. 637 (C.A.).

F. OFFICERS

(i) The Meaning of "Officer"

§9.129 Assuming that the directors of a corporation may delegate certain of their responsibilities to officers of a corporation, it remains necessary to identify the persons who fall within the class of officer to whom such powers may be delegated. Surprisingly, the law has never drawn a clear and sharp distinction between officers and other employees of a corporation. There is very little Canadian, or indeed Commonwealth, case law concerning the nature of corporate offices and the distinction between corporate officers and other employees of a corporation.[213] Like so many concepts in corporate law, the officer concept is borrowed from the constitutional and administrative laws of England, and like so many constitutional concepts, the officer concept is essentially military in origin. All military organizations distinguish between officers and ordinary ranks, the former having command of the latter, and (subject to the supervision and supervening orders of their superiors) having the authority to decide upon the course of action of the ordinary ranks under their command. At a relatively early stage in the evolution of the modern English constitution, it was accepted that there was a clear distinction between the type of work, responsibilities and general function of junior level functionaries in the employ of the Crown, who operated under the close supervision of their superiors, and certain more senior persons who operated more independently and who possessed a greater importance and dignity.[214] These more senior personages were seen to be officers of the Crown. A similar distinction may be seen to exist between certain senior corporate functionaries and the more junior employees of a corporation. Conceptually, therefore, the officers of a corporation are those of its employees or directors who enjoy executive decision-making authority.

§9.130 The term "officer" is defined in subsection 1(1) of the OBCA to mean:

> ... an officer designated under section 133 and includes the chair of the board of directors, a vice-chair of the board of directors, the president, a vice-president, the secretary, an assistant secretary, the treasurer, an assistant treasurer and the general manager of the corporation, and any other individual designated an officer of a corporation by by-law or by resolution of the directors or any other individual who performs functions for a corporation similar to those normally performed by an individual occupying any such office ...

None of the offices specifically designated in the definition are described by the Act itself, so whatever meaning that those terms carry must be gleaned from other sources.

---

[213] In the United States cases on this point are also rare, but see *Wells Fargo Bank v. Superior Court of San Francisco*, 228 Cal. App. (3d) 288, 267 Cal. Rptr. 49 (C.A. 1st App. Dist. Div. III 1990).
[214] See, generally, *Bowden v. Cumberland County* (1924), 123 Me. 359, 123 A. 166 at 169.

§9.131 It is clear from the statutory definition of "officer" that all directors of a corporation are not officers. However, since every chair and vice-chair of the board of directors must necessarily be a director, it is clear that certain directors are also officers of the corporation. To the extent that there may be any uncertainty, clause 133(*b*) of the OBCA specifically provides that "a director may be appointed to any office of the corporation". Subsection 127(1) of the OBCA provides (in part) that:

> 127.(1) Subject to the articles or by-laws, directors of a corporation may appoint from their number a managing director, who is a resident Canadian ...

It is curious, therefore, that the statutory definition of "officer" makes no express reference to a managing director. The 2001 amendments to the CBCA added the following definition of the term "officer" to section 2 of that Act:

> "officer" means an individual appointed as an officer under section 121, the chairperson of the board of directors, the president, a vice-president, the secretary, the treasurer, the comptroller, the general counsel, the general manager, a managing director, of a corporation, or any other individual who performs functions for a corporation similar to those normally performed by an individual occupying any of those offices.

The officers of a corporation must also be distinguished from outside agents who act on behalf of a corporation and upon whom may be conferred a considerable degree of authority. However, such outside agents are not part of its internal management structure. The officers of a corporation are agents of the corporation, but not all agents of the corporation are officers.[215]

(ii) Appointment of Officers

§9.132 Subsection 141(1) of the former OBCA required every corporation to have a president and a secretary, as well as such other officers as may be provided for by by-law or by a resolution of the directors. It also permitted one person to hold two or more such offices. Unless the articles or by-laws otherwise provided, the president was to be elected by the directors from among themselves, while the secretary and all other officers might be selected by election or by appointment of the directors.[216] Unless the articles or by-laws otherwise provided, no person might be the president of a corporation unless he was a director.[217]

§9.133 In contrast to the former OBCA, neither the CBCA nor the present OBCA require a corporation to have officers of any specific type or designation. Instead, section 133 of the OBCA provides:

> 133. Subject to the articles, the by-laws or any unanimous shareholder agreement,
>
> (*a*) the directors may designate the offices of the corporation, appoint officers, specify their duties and delegate to them powers to manage the business and

---

[215] *Wells Fargo Bank v. Superior Court etc. of San Francisco*, 3 Cal. 3d 1082, 811 P.2d 1025, 282 Cal. Rptr. 841 (S.C. Calif. 1999).
[216] Subsection 141(2) of the former OBCA, R.S.O. 1980, c. 53.
[217] Section 143 of the former OBCA.

affairs of the corporation, except, subject to section 184, powers to do anything referred to in subsection 127(3);

(b) a director may be appointed to any office of the corporation; and

(c) two or more offices of the corporation may be held by the same person.

Section 121 of the CBCA is generally similar.

§9.134 Subject to any unanimous shareholder agreement, the officers of a corporation are the delegates of the directors, and such powers as they possess are held only in the capacity of delegates.[218] Therefore ultimately, the officers of a corporation are appointed either by or under the authority of the board and are responsible to the board of directors of the corporation, although that responsibility may be either direct or indirect. There is no other construction that can fairly be placed upon the wording of the current legislation, which confers upon the directors a direct statutory responsibility for the management or (in the case of the OBCA) supervision of the management of the corporation.[219] It is significant to note, however, that a similar view was also taken under the common law, even where there was a contract between the corporation and an officer to the contrary.

§9.135 Generally, the officers of a corporation hold office at the pleasure of the board and may be removed by it at any time, but subject to the right of the officer to recover damages for wrongful dismissal.[220] Even the chairman of the board of directors holds office at the pleasure of the board, despite any contract entitling the chairman to tenure in that office.[221] The termination of an officer is effective, even where the directors are improperly motivated in taking this step.[222] The articles or a unanimous shareholder agreement may, however, give a particular individual an entrenched position as an officer of the corporation.[223] The officers of a corporation remain in office despite the end of the term of the directors who appointed them. However, where the board becomes deadlocked so that board cannot remove a director from office, the court may intervene to do so.[224]

§9.136 However, in exceptional cases, it appears that reinstatement of an officer after dismissal (or injunctive relief before dismissal) may be available to a

---

[218] *Re Bondi Better Bananas Ltd.*, [1951] O.J. No. 445, 32 C.B.R. 74 at 79 (H.C.J.), *per* Ferguson J., rev'd in part on other grounds [1951] O.J. No. 510, 32 C.B.R. 171 (C.A.).

[219] OBCA, s. 115(1); CBCA, s. 102(1).

[220] *Southern Foundries (1926) Ltd. v. Shirlaw*, [1940] A.C. 701 (H.L.); *Shindler v. Northern Raincoat Co. Ltd.*, [1960] 2 All E.R. 239.

[221] *Van Alstyne v. Rankin*, [1952] Que. S.C. 12, *per* Collins J.

[222] *Samuel Tak Lee v. Cho Wen Hsien*, [1984] 1 W.L.R. 1202 (P.C.). This particular case dealt with a removal of a director under a specific authority contained in the company's articles. However, the principle would seem to apply equally with respect to corporate officers. It is unclear whether s. 122 of the OBCA precludes any grant of power to the full board to remove a director.

[223] See, for instance, *Bushell v. Faith*, [1970] A.C. 1099 (H.L.).

[224] *Anderson v. Envoy Realty Ltd.*, [2002] B.C.J. No. 23, 19 B.L.R. (3d) 87 (C.A.).

corporate officer under the oppression remedy.²²⁵ Moreover, even where the oppression remedy is not available, it may be possible to prevent the removal of a person from a particular office where, for instance, such removal would prejudice some contractual right extending beyond the office itself (*e.g.*, under a unanimous shareholder agreement or the articles of the corporation).²²⁶

§9.137 The authority possessed by any particular officer is determined under the laws of agency and the rules of construction of contracts. Two particular offices are worthy of mention because of their overall importance in the corporate governance structure. A general manager of a corporation has general charge, direction and control of the business of the corporation for the carrying out of the purposes for which it was incorporated. His or her authority is therefore presumed to be broad. A person who is a managing director is presumed to possess even wider authority: it extends to the full powers of the board save to the extent that the delegation of their powers is prohibited by law or under the articles or by-laws of the corporation, albeit subject to such direction and control as it is the duty of the full board to exercise.²²⁷ Where, however, a person is only a manager of a department or branch of a business, a lesser authority is implied.²²⁸

G. DIRECTOR DISCLOSURE, AUDIT AND RELATED OBLIGATIONS

(i) Overview

§9.138 There are two distinct currents in the law relating to directors and corporate governance. The first is the responsibility of the directors to assume control over the corporation: to manage or supervise the management of the corporation themselves. The second is to report to the shareholders whom they represent on the business and affairs of the corporation, and to account for the manner in which the corporation has performed. It is this second current on which we will focus in this section.

§9.139 The reporting obligations of the directors reflect their duty to account to the shareholders of the corporation who put them into office. The philosophical basis of the various other rules regarding disclosure that expand this entitlement in favour of other stakeholders is not so clear, but no one can dispute the need for the security holders in a reporting issuer to receive a regular ongoing flow of information with respect to the business and affairs of the corporation, if they are to be put into a position in which they can assess the possible erosion of the

---

²²⁵ See OBCA, s. 248; CBCA, s. 241.
²²⁶ *Klassen v. Klassen*, [1989] M.J. No. 174, 42 B.L.R. 261, 62 Man. R. (2d) 106 (Q.B.) (a case involving an application for an interim injunction).
²²⁷ *Mid-West Collieries Ltd. v. McEwen*, [1925] S.C.R. 326 at 330, *per* Rinfret J.
²²⁸ *Mid-West Collieries Ltd. v. McEwen*, [1924] 2 W.W.R. 1027 at 1029, *per* Beck J.A. (Alta. C.A.), aff'd [1925] S.C.R. 326.

value of their security. It is, however, a fair question as to whether the present law is fully meeting this need. Historically, both corporate and securities laws have focused upon the reporting of transaction related or transaction derived information (*e.g.*, the purchase or disposition of assets, the generation of revenue through the conduct of trade, the incurring and payment of operating liabilities, etc.). The provision of such information is fine as far as it goes, but the critical question is whether it goes far enough: there are many who argue that this focus is overly limiting, and that there should be a broader obligation to report with respect to providing social and environmental disclosure. In the United States, the SEC specifically requires environmental reporting under Regulation S-K, items 101 to 103. In particular item 101 requires disclosure of the material effects that complying with federal, state and local environmental provisions may have upon an issuer's capital expenditures, earnings and competitive position. The failure to provide this information in Canada may create an unrealistic impression of the break-up value of a corporation, because it allows no assessment to be made of the cost of remedying potential environmental problems. More generally, a recent OSC staff review of continuous disclosure[229] identified frequent instances in which issuers failed to discuss adequately key "qualitative and quantitative risk factors that could have an effect on future operations and financial position".

§9.140 In England, the *Cadbury Report* provided the following description of the duties of directors with respect to the financial reporting activities of their corporation:

> Company law requires the directors to prepare financial statements for each financial year which give a true and fair view of the state of affairs of the company and the group and of the profit or loss of the group for that period. In preparing those financial statements, the directors are required to
>
> - select suitable accounting policies and then apply them consistently;
> - make judgments and estimates that are reasonable and prudent;
> - state whether applicable accounting standards have been followed, subject to any material departures disclosed and explained in the financial statements;
> - prepare the financial statements on the going concern basis unless it is inappropriate to presume that the company will continue in business.
>
> The directors are responsible for keeping proper accounting records which disclose with reasonable accuracy at any time the financial position of the company and of the group and to enable them to ensure that the financial statements of comply with the *Companies Act, 1985*. They are also responsible for safeguarding the assets of the company and hence for taking reasonable steps for the prevention and detection of fraud and other irregularities.

The same general observations may fairly be made with respect to the duties of the directors of a corporation under the OBCA or CBCA.

---

[229] OSC Staff Notice 51-708.

§9.141 The theory behind the financial disclosure reporting requirements is essentially that corporate decision-making and the behaviour of management are best regulated through the mandatory disclosure of information, rather than through government intervention or supervision.[230] Unfortunately, modern financial managers have proven to be masters at playing games with numbers in order to make accounts suit their purpose — even when still remaining inside the law and acceptable accounting practice.[231] It is at least arguable that audited financial statements can contribute to a false sense of security among investors. That much said, there are three principal functions which corporate financial statements are intended to fulfill, these being:[232]

- to require the management of the corporation to report to investors in the corporation on management's custodianship of the property of the corporation, and particularly in the case of shareholders, to decide whether a change in management is required;

- to allow management to assess its own efforts and performance, particularly in the area of the relationship between management objectives and budget forecasts and actual results;

- to allow prospective investors in the corporation to make an informed decision concerning their proposed investment, and to allow current investors to make an informed decision concerning the retention or disposal of their investment.

§9.142 The regular flow of information is also critical to the effectiveness of the insider trading rules, which control dealings in securities by corporate and other insiders who might otherwise be able to exploit their particular access to corporate information for their own benefit to the prejudice of members of the public who have invested in the corporation. In dealing with these aspects of disclosure NI 51-201 provides that:

> It is fundamental that everyone investing in securities have equal access to information that may affect their investment decisions. The Canadian Securities Administrators ("the CSA" or "We") are concerned about the selective disclosure of material corporate information by companies to analysts, institutional investors, investment dealers and other market professionals. Selective disclosure occurs when a company discloses material nonpublic information to one or more individuals or companies and not broadly to the investing public. Selective disclosure can create opportunities for insider trading and also undermines retail investors' confidence in the marketplace as a level playing field.

The perceived abuses of insider trading encompass the possibility that insiders will pass on information selectively to their friends and other confederates, so as

---

[230] J. Weiss, "Disclosure and Corporate Accountability" (1990) 34 The Business Lawyer 575.
[231] For an excellent treatment of this subject, see Ian Griffiths, *Creative Accounting* (London: Unwin Paperbacks, 1986).
[232] A.H. Slater, "The Accounts Provisions and Accounting Standards", in R.P. Austin & R.J. Vann (eds.), *The Law of Public Company Finance* (Sydney: The Law Book Co., 1986), 100 at 106-107.

to obtain indirect advantage from the corporate information that comes to their notice. With respect to such information, NI 51-201 provides:

> Companies are required by law to immediately disclose a "material change" in their business. For changes that a company initiates, the change occurs once the decision has been made to implement it. This may happen even before a company's directors approve it, if the company thinks it is probable they will do so. A company discloses a material change by issuing and filing a press release describing the change. A company must also file a material change report as soon as practicable, and no later than 10 days after the change occurs. This policy statement does not alter in any way the timely disclosure obligations of companies.
>
> Announcements of material changes should be factual and balanced. Unfavourable news must be disclosed just as promptly and completely as favourable news. Companies that disclose positive news but withhold negative news could find their disclosure practices subject to scrutiny by securities regulators. A company's press release should contain enough detail to enable the media and investors to understand the substance and importance of the change it is disclosing. Avoid including unnecessary details, exaggerated reports or promotional commentary.

Although the various insider trading rules to which corporate insiders are subject are of obvious relevance in corporate finance practice, the detail relating to such rules are so lengthy as to make it impractical to cover this subject within the context of this text. Instead, readers are advised to consult the usual standard references in the securities law field, in which the subject of insider trading will be dealt with in suitable detail.

§9.143 The law regarding the disclosure of financial and other material information by a corporation to its shareholders, other securities holders and other third parties is a complex amalgam of securities law and corporate law, the listing requirements of any stock exchange on which the securities of a particular corporate issuer may be listed, and supplemented in many cases by direct contractual obligations. The extent of disclosure required is frequently amended under securities laws and listing rules in particular are subject to frequent revision as practices and concerns with the securities marker evolve. In this section, we set out a brief synopsis of some of the key rules, beginning with the basic provisions set out in the OBCA and CBCA. It will be noted that these provisions apply to all corporations under those Acts (unless relief from compliance is obtained) and therefore are of relevance even in the case of private companies.

(ii) OBCA and CBCA Disclosure Requirements

§9.144 In broad terms, the directors and relevant officers of a company are responsible for its financial statements. They have a duty to take reasonable care that the statements are true and fair. In each financial year, the directors are required to prepare a report containing a fair review of the development of the business of the company and its subsidiary undertakings during the financial year and of their position at the end of it.

(1) OBCA Requirements

§9.145 Under clause 154(1)(a) of the OBCA,[233] in the case of a corporation that is not an offering corporation, the directors of a corporation must place before the annual meeting of shareholders, financial statements for the period that began on the date the corporation came into existence and ended not more than six months before the annual meeting. If the corporation has completed a financial year, the statements must pertain to the period that began immediately after the end of the last completed financial year and ending not more than six months before the annual meeting.[234] The financial statements placed before the meeting must include four items: a balance sheet, an income statement, a statement of changes in financial position and a retained earnings statement.

§9.146 By virtue of section 44 of the Regulation under the CBCA, the financial statements of a corporation under that Act must be prepared in accordance with the standards as they exist from time to time of the Canadian institute of Chartered Accountants set out in the *CICA Handbook*. The requirement that the financial statements of a corporation be prepared in accordance with generally accepted accounting principles suggests that in the preparation of the financial statements of a corporation, every effort should be made to adhere to the most orthodox accounting treatment, rather than to exotic or creative approaches. While recognizing that GAAP cannot possibly be expected to provide for every contingency,[235] and that on occasion it may be necessary to depart from customary treatment in order to present the financial condition of a corporation fairly, as one court has said:

> Common sense dictates that financial statements prepared for the benefit of the investing public should be drafted in a manner which the average member of the investing public can understand. Few persons have sufficient resources to employ accounting professionals to explain the work of other accounting professionals.[236]

To the extent that a corporation finds it necessary to depart from customary treatment, it is not imposing an unrealistic burden on that corporation to make this fact clear, and to provide an explanation to the reader of the statement as to the reasons for the departure and the impact of that departure upon the impression conveyed.

§9.147 The manner of preparing the financial statements of a corporation is a concern of the accounting profession more than the legal; by the same token, the appropriate content for such statements is more a matter of accounting conven-

---

[233] See *Canadian Business Corporations Regulations, 2001*, SOR/2001-512, s. 46.
[234] OBCA, s. 154(3); CBCA, s. 155(1)(a).
[235] *Thor Power Tool Co. v. Comm. of Internal Revenue* (1979), 439 U.S. 522: "Accountants long have recognized that 'generally accepted accounting principles' are far from being a canonical set of rules that will ensure identical accounting treatment of identical transactions. 'Gernerally accepted accounting principles,' rather, tolerate a range of 'reasonable' treatments, leaving the choice among alternatives to management."
[236] *Consolidated Enfield Corp. v. Blair*, [1994] O.J. No. 850, 19 B.L.R. (2d) 9 (Gen. Div.) *per* Logan J. at 36.

tion than a matter of law. Although the provision of proper financial statements is a legal obligation imposed upon OBCA and CBCA corporations, so that general familiarity with the nature and content of financial statements is clearly required on the part of a corporate lawyer, for information relating to the required content for such statements, reference should be made to a standard accounting text.

§9.148 In the case of an offering corporation, clause 154(1)(*b*) of the OBCA requires the directors to place before the annual meeting of shareholders the financial statements required to be filed under the *Securities Act* and the regulations under that Act relating separately to,

(i) the period that began on the date the corporation came into existence and ended not more than six months before the annual meeting or, if the corporation has completed a financial year, the period that began immediately after the end of the last completed financial year and ended not more than six months before the annual meeting; and

(ii) the immediately preceding financial year, if any.

In either case, these financial statements must be accompanied by the report of the auditor to the shareholders, if any and any further information respecting the financial position of the corporation and the results of its operations required by the articles, the by-laws or any unanimous shareholder agreement.[237] The financial statements must be prepared as prescribed by regulation and in accordance with generally accepted accounting principles,[238] and the auditor's report on those statements must be prepared in accordance with the standards, as they exist from time to time, set forth in the Handbook of the Canadian Institute of Chartered Accountants (the "*CICA Handbook*").

§9.149 Under subsection 154(3) of the OBCA, every corporation must send a copy of its financial statements to each shareholder of the corporation not less than 21 days before the annual meeting in the case of an offering corporation, and not less than 10 days before the annual meeting in the case of a non-offering corporation.[239] It is not necessary to send a copy of these statements to a shareholder who has informed the corporation in writing that the shareholder does not wish to receive a copy of those documents.

(2) CBCA Requirements

§9.150 The subject of financial disclosure is dealt with in Part XIV to the CBCA, which in general terms resembles the corresponding part of the OBCA. Subsection 155(1) of the CBCA provides that the directors of a corporation must place before the shareholders at every annual meeting:

(*a*) comparative financial statements as prescribed relating separately to

---

[237] OBCA, s. 154(1)(*c*), (*d*); CBCA, s. 155 (1)(*b*).
[238] OBCA, s. 155, see also OBCA Reg., R.R.O. 1990, Reg. 62, s. 40.
[239] See also CBCA, s. 159(1).

> (i) the period that began on the date the corporation came into existence and ended not more than six months before the annual meeting or, if the corporation has completed a financial year, the period that began immediately after the end of the last completed financial year and ended not more than six months before the annual meeting, and
>
> (ii) the immediately preceding financial year;
>
> (b) the report of the auditor, if any; and
>
> (c) any further information respecting the financial position of the corporation and the results of its operations required by the articles, the by-laws or any unanimous shareholder agreement.

The financial statements referred to in subparagraph (1)(a)(ii) may be omitted if the reason for the omission is set out in the financial statements, or in a note thereto, to be placed before the shareholders at an annual meeting.[240] The general requirements imposed under subsection 155(1) are subject to the following regulatory exception:

> 156. The Director may, on application of a corporation, authorize the corporation to omit from its financial statements any item prescribed, or to dispense with the publication of any particular financial statement prescribed, and the Director may, if the Director reasonably believes that disclosure of the information contained in the statements would be detrimental to the corporation, permit the omission on any reasonable conditions that the Director thinks fit.[241]

§9.151 Section 158 of the CBCA imposes a statutory duty on the directors of a corporation to approve the financial statements referred to in section 155. The approval must be evidenced by the manual signature of one or more directors or a facsimile of the signatures reproduced in the statements. Subsection 158(2) supplements this requirement by providing that:

> 158.(2) A corporation shall not issue, publish or circulate copies of the financial statements referred to in section 155 unless the financial statements are
>
> (a) approved and signed in accordance with subsection (1); and
>
> (b) accompanied by the report of the auditor of the corporation, if any.

The 1995 Industry Canada *Discussion Paper on Technical Amendments to the CBCA* considered but rejected the idea of dispensing with the requirement for a signature, arguing:

> While audited financial statements will be accompanied by the report of an auditor, most CBCA corporations do not have an auditor. Directors' liability appears to be expanding at common law, including potential liability to third parties for incorrect information in financial statements. Given this potential liability, a director's signature may serve to both caution and protect the director. Moreover, one signature annually does not appear overly burdensome.[242]

---

[240] CBCA, s. 155(2).
[241] CBCA, s. 156.
[242] *Canada Business Corporations Act Discussion Paper: Proposals for Technical Amendments* (Ottawa: Industry Canada, 1995), 62.

§9.152 Once the financial statements have been properly approved, the corporation is required to send copies of those statements to each shareholder, except to a shareholder who has informed the corporation in writing that he or she does not want a copy of those documents. The statements must be sent not less than 21 days before each annual meeting of shareholders or before the signing of a resolution under paragraph 142(1)(b) in lieu of the annual meeting.[243] Failure to comply with this distribution requirement is an offence.[244] Where the corporation is a distributing corporation, a copy of the financial statements must also be sent to the Director under the CBCA.[245]

(3) The Audit Process and Requirement

(a) THE PLACE OF THE AUDIT IN THE GOVERNANCE PROCESS

§9.153 One key object of corporations law is to separate the ownership of a corporation from its management. It is true, of course, that in many corporations, particularly the smaller corporations, the owners and managers of a corporation will be the same persons. But in the absence of a unanimous shareholder agreement, both the OBCA and the CBCA entrust the management of the corporation not to its owners, but to its board of directors. And in practice, in most corporations of any size, the effective management of the corporation (at least on a day-to-day basis) will be exercised not by its board of directors, but by its officers. Given the divergence between management and ownership, it is necessary for corporations law to provide mechanisms to ensure that the persons exercising management control will be accountable to the owners of the corporation. The basic technique used for this purpose under both the OBCA and the CBCA is the audit process.

(b) THE NATURE OF AN AUDIT

§9.154 At its most elementary level, an audit is a check by one person of the work of another person. The term "audit" derives from the ancient practice of listening to each clerk's recital of the tallies and parchment roll records that the clerk had maintained during the audit period. During that recital, the clerk might be called upon to explain any of the records concerned. *Webster's Dictionary* defines "audit" to mean a formal, often periodic examination and checking of accounts or financial records to verify their correctness, and it would seem that this is the meaning of the term under Ontario law.[246] Perhaps understandably, within the accounting profession itself there has been considerably more effort made to devise a more precise definition of audit. For instance, a standard reference text on auditing defines the term "auditing" as:

---

[243] CBCA, s. 159(1).
[244] CBCA, s. 159(2).
[245] CBCA, s. 160.
[246] In *Townsend v. Ontario Forge & Bolt Co.*, [1896] O.J. No. 125, 27 O.R. 230 at 232 (H.C.J.), *per* Robertson J.; *International Laboratories Ltd. v. Dewar (Peat, Marwick, Mitchell & Co.)*, [1932] 3 W.W.R. 174 at 177-78 (Man. K.B.), *per* Donovan J., rev'd on other grounds [1933] 2 W.W.R. 529 (Man. C.A.).

... the process by which a competent independent person accumulates and evaluates the evidence about quantifiable information related to a specific economic entity for the purpose of determining and reporting on the degree of correspondence between the quantifiable information and established criteria.[247]

The same text goes on to differentiate between accounting and auditing in the following terms:

Accounting is the process of recording, classifying and summarizing economic events in a logical manner for the purpose of for the purpose of providing financial information for decision making. The function of accounting ... is to provide certain types of quantitative information that management and other cans use to make decisions. ... In auditing accounting data, the concern is with determining whether recorded information properly reflects the economic events that occurred during the accounting period.[248]

§9.155 In modern accounting practice, an auditor is an independent accountant whose function is to examine and pass an opinion upon the accounts and accounting practices of a company or other business enterprise. The auditor's opinion attests to the general accuracy and conformity of the statements and practices under generally accepted accounting principles and legislation. The opinion is expressed following a review of the accounts, records and practices of the business enterprise that is the subject of the audit conducted in accordance with generally accepted auditing standards (or "GAAS"). Thus auditing is essentially a verification procedure, but it is directed more towards verification of method and arithmetic accuracy rather than of the honesty of the financial statements — although some verification of honesty is implicit in the verification of method. An audit is not an inquisition into the financial records of a corporation, but is an examination of accounts and of the evidence of the transactions relating to those accounts.

§9.156 There are three objects to this examination: first, the detection of fraud; second, the detection of technical errors; third, the detection of errors of principle.[249] To carry out the audit function, the auditor must first be able to interpret the accounting records of the corporation, and second test the procedures that were followed in the production of those accounting records to make sure that they provide an accurate picture of the events to which those records relate. But an auditor is an accountant hired to verify that the books and other account records are in apparent order, not a police constable conducting a criminal investigation or a government regulator ensuring rigid adherence by the corporation to some prescribed code of conduct. Criminal irregularities or deviation from GAAP may be discovered through the audit process, and in such a case must obviously be brought to light and dealt with, but as will be discussed below, it is

---

[247] W.M. Lemon, A.A. Arens & J.K. Loebbecke, *Auditing: An Integrated Approach*, 4th ed. (Scarborough: Prentice-Hall Canada Inc. 1987), 2.
[248] *Ibid.* at 4-5.
[249] *International Laboratories Ltd. v. Dewar (Peat, Marwick, Mitchell & Co.)*, [1932] 3 W.W.R. 174 (Man. K.B.), *per* Donovan J. at 177-78, rev'd on other grounds [1933] 2 W.W.R. 529 (Man. C.A.).

neither necessary nor appropriate for the auditor to act on the assumption that some fraud is being perpetrated, nor is it appropriate to second-guess every decision made by management.

§9.157 The financial statements of a corporation may only be audited by an external accountant licensed under the *Public Accountancy Act*.[250] However, not every financial statement prepared for a corporation by a such an accountant is an audited financial statement, for public accountants also provide general accounting services to their customers. As Dickson J. explained:

> From the expert testimony, it appears that the engagement of a chartered accountant can be on either an "audit" basis or a "non-audit" basis. If the engagement is for an audit, the accountant does what he considers necessary by way of auditing procedures, tests and verification of internal controls, accounts and records to permit him to give an opinion on the financial statements. In an engagement of the non-audit type, the accountant merely helps the client in the preparation of the financial statement on terms which permit him to accept the client's records and dispense with the checks and verifications expected in an audit. The product of an audit is a financial statement accompanied by an auditor's report expressing an opinion on the financial statement. At the end of a non-audit engagement a financial statement is issued to which is appended a comment in which the auditor expressly disclaims responsibility.[251]

Where an accountant prepares a non-audited financial statement, the statement will usually be accompanied by a letter bearing a caveat along the following lines:

> The attached financial statements have been prepared from the books, records and information furnished by the Corporation, without audit, and we are not able to express an opinion as to the financial position of the business.

Despite this caveat, where the accountant includes a report with the financial statements that follows the form of report expected in the case of an audited financial statement, the accountant risks being held to an audit standard.[252]

(c) INDEPENDENCE

§9.158 Section 161[253] sets out the general qualifications required of an auditor of a CBCA corporation. Subsection 161(1) provides that subject to subsection (5), a person is disqualified from being an auditor of a corporation if the person is not independent of the corporation, any of its affiliates, or the directors or officers of any such corporation or its affiliates. The definition of independence is set out in subsection 161(2), which provides that:

(a) independence is a question of fact; and

(b) a person is deemed not to be independent if he or his business partner

---

[250] R.S.O. 1990, c. P.37.
[251] *Haig v. Bamford*, [1976] S.C.J. No. 31, 72 D.L.R. (3d) 68 at 71.
[252] *Ibid.*, per Dickson J. at 73.
[253] OBCA, s. 152.

(i) is a business partner, a director, an officer or an employee of the corporation or any of its affiliates, or a business partner of any director, officer or employee of any such corporation or any of its affiliates,

(ii) beneficially owns or controls, directly or indirectly, a material interest in the securities of the corporation or any of its affiliates, or

(iii) has been a receiver, receiver-manager, liquidator or trustee in bankruptcy of the corporation or any of its affiliates within two years of his proposed appointment as auditor of the corporation.

For the purposes of subsection (2), a person's business partner includes a shareholder of that person.[254]

§9.159 Subsection 161(5) empowers the court to exempt from this requirement. More specifically, it provides that

> 161.(5) An interested person may apply to a court for an order exempting an auditor from disqualification under this section and the court may, if it is satisfied that an exemption would not unfairly prejudice the shareholders, make an exemption order on such terms as it thinks fit, which order may have retrospective effect.

Unless an order is made under subsection (5), an auditor who becomes disqualified under this section must resign forthwith after becoming aware of the disqualification.[255] The counterbalance to subsection (5) is the authority of the court to remove an auditor who is determined not to be independent. In this respect, subsection 161(4) of the CBCA provides:

> An interested person may apply to a court for an order declaring an auditor to be disqualified under this section and the office of auditor to be vacant.

§9.160 The auditor of a corporation reports to the shareholders of the corporation, not to its directors, nor is it appropriate for the auditors to make their report to the shareholders indirectly through the directors.[256] In order for the auditor to discharge this obligation properly, the auditor must be and remain independent of the corporation. The theoretical paradigm of perfect independence is rarely attained, as Moffit J. explained:

> The task of being independent ... is always a difficult one. ... Although the shareholders appoint the auditor ... in many cases management is in a position in a practical way to influence the appointment and replacement of auditors. ... Moreover, of necessity, the persons in true communication with the auditor are management and the directors and not the shareholders. ... [Where the auditor warns] management of a proposal to qualify the audit opinion so as to give management the opportunity of persuading the auditor he is wrong, and, in default the opportunity of altering the accounts to overcome the qualification ... the auditor,

---

[254] The requirement for auditor independence implies that the auditor does not normally owe a fiduciary duty to the corporation, although there could be extraordinary circumstances in which a fiduciary relationship would exist. See *Strategic Capital Resources v. Citrin Cooperman & Co.*, [2007] U.S. App. LEXIS 243 (11th Cir.) and the cases cited therein.

[255] CBCA, s. 161(3).

[256] *In Re London & General Bank (No. 2)*, [1895] 2 Ch. 673 at 684 (C.A.), per Lindley L.J.; but cf. *Re Allen, Craig & Co. (London) Ltd.*, [1934] Ch. 483.

unfortunately for him and no doubt much to his concern, is put in a position where there must often be a real and practical conflict or at least an apparent conflict, between his duty to the shareholders and his interest not to take action which may prejudice his re-appointment or his relations with those whom he works.[257]

§9.161 Although in theory the auditors of a corporation are selected by its shareholders, in practice the management of the corporation plays a very influential role in both the selection of the auditors and in setting their remuneration. Both the CBCA and OBCA permit a sitting auditor to circulate a statement to the shareholders of a corporation where it is proposed to remove the auditor from office. However, in 2001, a number of new measures were introduced into the CBCA to regulate the degree of control exercised by the management of a corporation over the director selection process.

> In the case of a proposed replacement of an auditor, whether through removal or at the end of the auditor's term, the following rules apply with respect to other statements:
>
> (a) the corporation shall make a statement on the reasons for the proposed replacement; and
>
> (b) the proposed replacement auditor may make a statement in which he or she comments on the reasons referred to in paragraph (a).

The corporation is required to send a copy of the statements referred to in subsections (5) and (5.1) without delay to every shareholder entitled to receive notice of a meeting referred to in subsection (1) and to the Director, unless the statement is included in or attached to a management proxy circular.

(d) STATUS OF THE AUDITOR

§9.162 In carrying out their duties, the auditors of a corporation are neither agents of the corporation[258] nor of the shareholders.[259] Although retained by the corporation under contract, they are not officers of the corporation within the meaning of either the OBCA or the CBCA.[260] Instead, auditors are statutory functionaries. As such, they are obliged to know their duties under the OBCA, CBCA, *Securities Act* or other relevant statute under which they function.[261] It is their duty to review the corporation's financial statements, including their manner of preparation and the accounting system through which they were prepared, and in so doing to conduct such tests and undertake such investigations. They must conduct such investigations as are necessary in order to be able to make their report, and if they are prevented from so doing by the directors or employees, they must either refuse to make a report at all or make an appropriately

---

[257] *Pacific Acceptance Corporation Ltd. v. Forsyth & Ors* (1967), 92 W.N. 29 at 75, *per* Moffit J.
[258] *Re Transplanters (Holding Co.) Ltd.*, [1958] 1 W.L.R. 822 (Ch.).
[259] *Spackman v. Evans* (1868), L.R. 3 H.L. 171 — hence facts coming to the notice of the auditors are not imputed back to the shareholders.
[260] *R. v. Shacter*, [1960] 2 Q.B. 252 (C.C.A.).
[261] See, generally, *Re Republic of Bolivia Exploration Syndicate Ltd.*, [1914] 1 Ch. 139 at 171, *per* Astbury J.

qualified report.[262] Where evidence of irregularity surfaces, there is a corresponding increase in the duty to inspect[263] and report. Thus in *Re City Equitable Fire Insurance Co. Ltd.*, Romer J. stated:

> ... an auditor is not ... ever justified in omitting to make personal inspection of securities that are in the custody of a person or company with whom it is not proper that they would be left, whenever such personal inspection is practicable. And whenever an auditor discovers that securities of the company are not in proper custody, it is his duty to require that the matter be put right at once, or, if his requirement be not complied with, to report the fact to the shareholders, and this whether he can or cannot make a personal inspection.[264]

(e) THE DUTIES OF AN AUDITOR

§9.163 Numerous duties are now imposed upon auditors both under the OBCA and CBCA, and also under the *Securities Act* and the various rules and policies under that Act. The general responsibilities of the auditor are subsection 153(1) of the OBCA, which provides as follows:

> 153.(1) An auditor of a corporation shall make such examination of the financial statements required by this Act to be placed before shareholders as is necessary to enable to auditor to report thereon and the auditor shall report as prescribed and in accordance with the generally accepted auditing standards.[265]

Both the OBCA and CBCA confer upon the auditor a statutory right to receive notice of every meeting of shareholders and, at the expense of the corporation, to attend and be heard on matters relating to the auditor's duties. A director or shareholder of the corporation may also require the attendance of the auditor at any other meeting. It follows from the foregoing that auditors are subject to two legal duties of equal import: first to examine the financial records of the corporation; second to report on the findings obtained through that examination to the shareholders:

> Prima facie the duty of the auditor is to audit the books and accounts of the company ... for the very nature of the statutory duty to report pre-supposes that on appointment during the term of office there will be performed duties of an auditing nature. ... In the absence of express terms the scope of the audit will depend on what is directly or indirectly required or indicated by the particular provisions of the [statute] and of the articles and any relevant surrounding circumstances. However, whatever the precise content of his audit duty, the auditor promises to provide a report of his opinion based upon his audit work ... and also impliedly agrees to exercise reasonable care and skill in the conduct of the audit and in the making of the report.[266]

§9.164 The general duties of the auditor may be summarized as follows: The auditor should carry out an independent audit of the company's financial

---

[262] *Re Thomas Gerrard & Son Ltd.*, [1968] Ch. 455 at 477, *per* Pennychuck J.
[263] *Re Thomas Gerrard & Son Ltd.*, [1968] Ch. 455 at 476, [1967] 2 All E.R. 525, *per* Pennychuck J.
[264] [1925] 1 Ch. 407 at 498 (C.A.).
[265] CBCA, s. 169.
[266] *Pacific Acceptance Corporation Ltd. v. Forsyth & Ors* (1967), 92 W.N. 29 at 51, *per* Moffit J.

statements by verifying the arithmetical accuracy of the accounts and the proper vouching of entries in the company's financial accounts. Second, the auditor should make checks to test whether the accounts mask errors or dishonesty. Third, the auditor should report on whether the accounts give to the shareholders reliable information respecting the true financial position of the company. Fourth, a suitable and professional approach should be taken to the conduct of the audit.[267] The auditor has the responsibility to plan and perform the audit to obtain reasonable assurance about whether the financial statements are free of material misstatement, whether caused by error or fraud. The auditor should specifically assess the risk of material misstatement due to fraud and should consider that assessment in designing the audit procedures to be performed.[268] In all cases, an auditor should have a "show me" attitude, and not accept unsubstantiated assertions by management.[269] If there is a high risk of fraud, the auditor ought to employ a heightened professional skepticism. An understanding of the substance of the corporation's arrangements and transactions with third parties is an important factor in determining the information to be confirmed.[270] The staff assigned to the task should collectively possess adequate professional proficiency for their assignment. The manner of conducting the audit should incorporate an appropriate internal quality control system. GAAS requires an auditor to obtain the best evidence available within the time constraints and money constraints applicable to the engagement.[271] The staff conducting the audit should be properly supervised.[272] Sufficient, competent, and relevant evidence should be obtained to afford a reasonable basis for the auditors' findings and conclusions. Auditors should identify potential sources of data that may be used as audit evidence and consider the validity and reliability of these data. While certain decisions in the audit process will involve the mechanical application of mathematical calculation, others (and the overall audit process in its totality) involve the exercise of choice and judgment. There is no discretion not to undertake *any* investigation, but there is discretion with respect to the *manner and extent* of investigation.[273] When applying generally accepted auditing standards, the auditor must exercise an independent professional judgment in determining which auditing procedures are necessary and determining the time and inquiry needed in the circumstances to afford a reasonable basis for his opinion. Exercising due professional care means using sound judgment in establishing the scope, selecting the methodology, and choosing tests and procedures for the audit. Thus, the conduct of an audit involves the exercise of a substantial meas-

---

[267] See, generally, *Sydney Cooperative Society Ltd. v. Coopers & Lybrand*, [2002] N.S.J. No. 578 (S.C.); *Revelstoke Credit Union v. Miller* (1984), 28 C.C.L.T. 17 (B.C.S.C.); *Capital Community Credit Union Ltd. v. BDO Dunwoody*, [2000] O.J. No. 65 (Sup. Ct. J.); *Guardian Insurance Co. v. Sharp*, [1941] 2 D.L.R. 417 (S.C.C.).
[268] *Grant Thornton LLP v. Federal Deposit Insurance Corporation*, [2007] U.S. Dist. LEXIS 19379 (S.D. Virg.), *per* Faber C.J. at paras. 22-23.
[269] *Ibid.* at paras. 19-20.
[270] *Ibid.* at para. 46.
[271] *Ibid.* at para. 27.
[272] See, for instance, *Moore v. Valder* (1995), 314 U.S. App. D.C. 209, 65 F.3d 189, 196 (D.C. Cir.) at 197.
[273] See, for instance, *Appley Brothers v. United States* (1999), 164 F.3d 1164 (8th Cir.) at 1172.

ure of discretion.[274] Having said that, it is not expected that an auditor will intrude into the operations of the corporation that is being audited in a manner analogous to the Spanish inquisition. An auditor is not a detective, nor is the auditor directly responsible for the content of the accounts or financial statements. He or she must approach the financial records of the company:

> ... with an inquiring mind—not suspicious of dishonesty ... but suspecting that someone may have made a mistake somewhere and that a check must be made to ensure that this has not been done.[275]

§9.165 On the other hand, where evidence of wrongdoing comes to the auditor's attention, the auditor must exercise extra care. If suspicious circumstances come to light, they must be investigated by the auditor. Proper disclosure must also be made. So the Institute of Chartered Accountants has advised its members that:

> A member who acquires knowledge indicating that a client may have been guilty of some default or unlawful act should normally raise the matter with the management of the client at an appropriate level. If his concerns are not satisfactorily resolved, he should consider reporting the matter to non-executive directors or to the clients audit committee where these exist. Where this is not possible or he fails to resolve the matter a member may wish to consider making a report to a third party.[276]

The duties of the auditors with respect to the financial statements of a corporation are secondary to those of the company's directors and officers. The auditors of a company are required to provide a signed report to the company's members on all annual accounts of the company of which copies are to be laid before the company in general meeting during their tenure of office.

§9.166 The performance of these obligations is supported by sections 153 of the CBCA and OBCA, which each provide the auditor with a direct right to receive certain information. In particular, subsection 170(1) of the CBCA provides that:

> 170.(1) On the demand of an auditor of a corporation, the present or former directors, officers, employees or agents of the corporation shall furnish such
>
> (a) information and explanations, and
>
> (b) access to records, documents, books, accounts and vouchers of the corporation or any of its subsidiaries
>
> as are, in the opinion of the auditor, necessary to enable the auditor to make the examination and report required under section 169 and that the directors, officers, employees or agents are reasonably able to furnish.

These basic rights to information are expanded under subsection 170(2):

---

[274] *Sloan v. United States Department of Housing & Urban Dev.* (2000), 44 U.S. App. D.C. 389, 236 F.3d 756 (D.C. Cir.).

[275] *Formento (Sterling Area Ltd.) v. Selsdon Fountain Pen Co. Ltd.*, [1958] 1 W.L.R. 45 (H.L.) per Lord Denning

[276] *Statement on Unlawful Acts or Defaults By Clients of Members.*

170.(2) On the demand of the auditor of a corporation, the directors of the corporation shall

> (a) obtain from the present or former directors, officers, employees and agents of any subsidiary of the corporation the information and explanations that the present or former directors, officers, employees and agents are reasonably able to furnish and that are, in the opinion of the auditor, necessary to enable the auditor to make the examination and report required under section 169; and
>
> (b) furnish the auditor with the information and explanations so obtained."

Section 170 remedies the common law rule that the auditor had no right to insist that the directors or officers of the corporation permit him or her to enter its premises.[277]

§9.167 A fairly comprehensive overview of the common law duties of an auditor was provided by Lindley L.J. in *Re London & General Bank (No. 2)*.[278] In that case, the bank had advanced most of its capital to a small group of borrowers on security that was found to be insufficient and difficult to realize. The auditors had informed the directors of the problem with these loans. However, their report to the shareholders provided only that the auditors had:

> ...examined the above balance sheet and compared it with the books of the company; and certify that it is a correct summary of the accounts therein recorded. The value of the assets as shown on the balance-sheet is dependent upon realization.

Lindley L.J. began by making clear that an auditor is not retained as a business consultant or advisor to the corporation:

> It is not part of an auditor's duty to give advice, either to directors or shareholders, as to what they should do. An auditor has nothing to do with the prudence or imprudence of making loans with or without security. It is nothing to him whether the business of the company is being conducted prudently or imprudently, profitably or unprofitably, ... provided he discharges his own duty to the shareholders.

An audit, therefore, is not a business review, nor is an audit report expected to provide advice as to how the profitability or general operation of the corporation might be enhanced. Instead, it is an inspection of the records of the corporation to ascertain whether they are reliable, as Lindley L.J. went on to make clear:

> His business is to ascertain the true financial position of the company at the time of the audit, and his duty is confined to that. But then comes the question. How is he to ascertain that position? The answer is, by examining the books of the company. But he does not discharge his duty by doing this without inquiry, and without taking trouble to see that the books themselves show the company's true position. He must take reasonable care to ascertain that they do. Unless he does this his audit would be worse than an idle farce. Assuming that the books to be so kept as to show the true position of the company, the auditor has to frame a balance sheet showing that position according to the books and to certify that the balance sheet presented is correct in that sense. But his first duty is to examine the books, not merely for the

---

[277] *Cuff v. London & County Land and Bldg. Co. Ltd.*, [1912] 1 Ch. 440 (C.A.).
[278] [1895] 2 Ch. 673 at 682-683 (C.A.).

purpose of ascertaining what they do show, but also for the purpose of satisfying himself that they show the true financial position of the company.

§9.168 It follows that the auditor is not a mere passive functionary. The auditor has a duty of vigilance which requires the exercise of reasonable diligence and the possession of sufficient skill to permit the audit to be properly performed. The auditor may not simply sit back passively and accept the financial statements prepared by the management of the corporation:

> ... he must be honest–i.e., he must not certify what he does not believe to be true, and he must take reasonable care and skill before he believes what he certifies is true. What is reasonable care in any particular case must depend upon the circumstances of the case. Where there is nothing to excite suspicion very little inquiry will be reasonably sufficient, and in practice I believe business men select a few cases at haphazard, see that they are right and assume that others like them are correct also. Where suspicion is aroused more care is obviously necessary; but, still, an auditor is not bound to exercise more than reasonable care and sill, even in a case of suspicion, and he is perfectly justified in acting on the opinion of an expert when special knowledge is required.[279]

(f) REASONABLE RELIANCE UPON MANAGEMENT

§9.169 Despite the general obligation to be vigilant, auditors may also place reasonable reliance upon the information with which they are provided by the officers, directors and employees of the corporation itself. Auditors are not expected to be experts in the business of the corporation, nor are they expected to second-guess every decision made by the corporation and its agents:

> It is not the duty of an auditor to take stock; he is not a stock expert; there are many matters in respect of which he must rely on the honesty and accuracy of others ...; similarly an auditor may need to obtain expert legal advice on relevant matters ... but he must be careful to ensure that the informant is an appropriate person to rely on for that information.[280]

§9.170 In deciding upon how much reliance are the auditors permitted to place in "reasonable" reliance upon others, it is important to bear in mind that what is reasonable in one context is not always reasonable in all. The earlier cases included quite general statements which suggest that considerable reliance may be placed. So in *Re Kingston Mills Co.*, Lopes L.J. said:[281]

> He is justified in believing tried servants of the company in whom confidence is placed by the company. He is entitled to assume that they are honest, and to rely upon their representations, provided he takes reasonable care. If there is anything calculated to excite suspicion he should probe it to the bottom; but in the absence of anything of that kind he is only bound to be reasonably cautious and careful.

---

[279] *Re London & General Bank, ibid.*, at 683; approved *Re Owen Sound Lumber Co.*, [1917] O.J. No. 144, 38 O.L.R. 414 (C.A.), *per* Hodgins J.A.
[280] *In Re Kingston Cotton Mill Company (No. 2)*, [1896] 2 Ch. 279 at 289 (C.A.), *per* Lopes L.J.
[281] [1896] 2 Ch. 279 (C.A.), appd *International Laboratories v. Dewar (Peat, Marwick, Mitchell & Co.)*, [1933] 2 W.W.R. 529, [1933] 3 D.L.R. 665 (Man. C.A.).

More recent cases have been considerably more exact in describing the extent to which reliance is reasonable. In his lengthy decision in *Re Pacific Acceptance* concerning the duties of auditors, for instance, Moffit J. said:

> *Prima facie* the duty of the auditor is to satisfy himself on material matters by such checks and procedures as are commonly understood to comprise an audit. He does not satisfy himself merely by being content that management is responsible and is satisfied about the matter. Of course, the fact that management is satisfied about some matter may be relevant in aiding to produce an apparent state of regularity which may justify some reduction in the auditor's checks. *Prima facie* the auditor's job is to check all material matters for himself and he does not ordinarily do his job or "audit" if he merely seeks the assurance of another as to the check that the other has made or as to his views as to the effect of documents.[282]

§9.171 The auditor is not obliged to cover the entire field already covered by management, but is instead obliged to make sure that management has undertaken a sufficiently thorough and honest review that error or fraud are unlikely to be present. It is acceptable for an auditor to evaluate the corporation's internal system of controls, sample and test its results and on that basis draw a reasonable conclusion that the entirety of the financial information with which he or she has been provided is in all probability accurate in all material respects.[283] Once such tests have been made:

> An auditor may properly rely a great deal on inquiries made and explanations sought of the company's staff and management at the appropriate level, but *prima facie* this is in aid of his couching and checking procedures and not in substitution for them. In appropriate cases it may be reasonable to go no further as a result of an explanation, even although there are other documents that could be inspected. ... However, it is clear ... that if the existence of the document which is under the control of the company is material to the audit, it is the duty of the auditor acting reasonably to examine the document for himself unless there are some specific circumstances which make it reasonable to accept something less than proof by inspection.[284]

§9.172 Inquiries to management must be addressed to the appropriate level: in no circumstance is it appropriate to call upon an employee or officer to vouch for his or her own integrity or competence. If a matter concerning the authority or conduct of an employee calls for an explanation, in the absence of documentary verification it is not sufficient to rely upon a mere oral explanation provided by that employee.[285] The duty of an auditor is to check so far as the auditor reasonably can. He (or she) should not expect somebody else to reveal something which the auditor could find out for himself by dint of reasonable effort and the exercise of due diligence.[286] Justice Moffit concluded by saying:

> There are three essentials that must be met before an auditor can reasonably rely on the company's system of internal control. First, there must be a proper inquiry

---

[282] (1967), 92 W.N. 29 at 67 (N.S.W.S.C.).
[283] *Ibid.*, at 70.
[284] *Ibid.*
[285] *Ibid.*, at 71.
[286] *Ibid.*, at 87.

to ascertain the company's system. This would include ascertaining such features as indicate the strength and weaknesses of the system and hence its reliability. Second, there must be an appraisal of it, in that a person of sufficient auditing competence should make a decision as to the extent, if any, that the auditors can properly rely upon it. ... Third, there must be a testing of its operation. All these essentials may call for revision in the course of the audit.

(g) UPON DETECTION OF ERROR

§9.173 The duties of directors who discover an accounting error are express under both the OBCA and the CBCA. In this regard, section 153(2) of the OBCA provides:

> 153.(2) A director or officer of a corporation shall forthwith notify the audit committee and the auditor or former auditor any error or misstatement of which he becomes aware in a financial statement that the auditor or former auditor has reported upon if the error or misstatement in all the circumstances appears to be significant.

Although it is not clear, the words "in all the circumstances appears to be significant" suggest that there is an objective standard for determining whether a director is under an obligation to report the error or misstatement.

§9.174 Upon receipt of a notice under subsection 153(2), or where the auditor otherwise becomes aware of any error or misstatement on which he or she has reported, the auditor or former auditor must notify each director of the corporation of that error or misstatement, if in his opinion it is material.[287] The fact that the Act imposes an obligation on a director to notify the auditor of "significant" errors or misstatements, while the auditor is required to pass this information along only if the error or misstatement is "material" raises an obvious question as to whether the two obligations are different. While the OBCA itself provides little guidance in resolving this question, some help may perhaps be obtained from the definition of "material fact" in subsection 1(1) of the *Securities Act*, where the materiality is equated with "significant" effect upon the value of securities.

§9.175 The duty to pass along information concerning material errors that the auditor discovers or of which the auditor becomes aware in previously audited financial statements is simply part of the broader duty of the auditor to bring to the corporation's attention information that the auditor obtains concerning any errors, lies, or other irregularities in the financial statements. So in *Canadian Woodmen of the World v. Hooper*[288] Middleton J.A. said:

> The liability of Edwards, Morgan & Co. does not depend upon negligence at all. Their liability depends upon a positive act amounting to misconduct of the office of auditor. Upon discovering the so-called irregularity it was the auditors' duty to at once report the true facts to the company. ... the auditors are responsible for any

---

[287] OBCA, s. 153(3).
[288] [1933] 1 D.L.R. 168 at 171 (Ont. C.A.) (annotated).

loss which resulted from Edward's failure to report the true fact to the plaintiff at the time he acquired this information.

§9.176 The auditors must provide the required notice in a clear and unequivocal manner.[289] In *International Laboratories Ltd v. Dewar*, Donovan J. related the duty to report irregularities in the books to Lopes L.J.'s bloodhound metaphor:

> As I understand it, the useful work of a watch-dog is based on the fact that he is expected, particularly if he be in the dark, to raise an alarm whenever he sees or hears anything usual, and if a possible marauder appears to be approaching, to continue his combined protests and threats with two objects in view: (1) that the cause of the fancied threat may be withdrawn; and (2) that his master may be aroused to his danger; and only when one of these objects has been accomplished will he be considered to have discharged the position which he assumed. He will not have performed the functions of his office if after one howl he retreats "under the barn", or if he confines this protest to a fellow watch-dog.[290]

§9.177 In any event, once the auditor informs the directors of an error or misstatement under subsection 153(3), the obligations of the directors are clear enough. The directors are obliged under subsection 153(4) to get this information to the shareholders:

> 153.(4) When under subsection (3) the auditor or former auditor informs the directors of an error or mis-statement in a financial statement, the directors shall within a reasonable time,
>
> (*a*) prepare and issue revised financial statements; or
>
> (*b*) otherwise inform the shareholders.

It is interesting that no express obligation is imposed upon the directors to send the revised statements to creditors or other non-shareholders who may have relied upon the previous erroneous statements. Since this matter is not dealt with, lawyers acting for creditors and non-share security holders would be well-advised to include a requirement that such revised statements be provided to their clients, in any case where subsection 153(4) applies.

§9.178 The corresponding provisions of the CBCA are similar,[291] and differ only in slight detail. First, a failure by the directors or officers of a corporation to comply with subsections 171(6) or (8) — the notice and revised financial statement requirements — constitutes an offence punishable by a fine not exceeding $5,000 or to imprisonment for a term not exceeding six months or both. There is no such offence expressly created under the Ontario Act, although the general offence provision of the Act would appear to apply.[292] Second, under clause 171(8)(*b*), the directors of a corporation that is required to comply with section 160 of the Act must send a copy of the revised financial statements to the Di-

---

[289] *Re London & General Bank (No. 2)*, [1895] 2 Ch. 673 at 684 (C.A.).
[290] [1933] 1 D.L.R. 34 at 41 (Man. K.B.), rev'd [1933] 3 D.L.R. 665 (Man. C.A.).
[291] See CBCA, s. 171(6) to (9).
[292] OBCA, s. 258(1)(*j*).

rector, as well as to the shareholders. Since there is no corresponding provision to section 160 in the Ontario Act, there is obviously no equivalent to clause 171(8)(*b*).

(h) STANDARD OF CARE

§9.179 The general standard of care (and consequent implicit duties) expected of an auditor was touched upon briefy above. In this section, we shall examine that subject in greater detail. Even in cases where there is no reason to suspect fraud or other wrong-doing, an auditor is not retained merely to check and confirm the arithmetic accuracy of the accounts — although arithmetic accuracy is obviously important and any error that is detected should be corrected. As noted above, the auditor's duties go well beyond this mechanical function. When offering audit services to the public, accountants hold themselves out as being persons possessing special qualifications, skill and competence, which they are prepared to place at the disposal of the public for reward.[293] Upon accepting their retainer as the auditor of a corporation, accountants become subject to a duty to apply those special skills to the audit of that corporation's financial statements. Thus in *Fomento (Sterling Area) Ltd. v. Selsdon Fountain Pen Co. Ltd.*,[294] Lord Denning made the following observations concerning the duties of an auditor:

> He is not to be written off as a professional "adder-upper and subcontractor." His vital task is to take care to see that errors are not made, be they errors of computation, or errors of omission or commission, or downright untruths. To perform this task properly he must come to it with an inquiring mind—not suspicious of dishonesty, I agree—but suspecting that someone may have made a mistake somewhere and that a check must be made to ensure that there has been none.

§9.180 The proper attitude, therefore, is one of healthy and honest skepticism. The auditor must seek out proof of the statements that are made, to the point of reasonable satisfaction rather than absolute certainty. Yet on the other hand, it is not the task of the auditor to engage in aggressive combat with the management or directors of a corporation, to substitute his or her judgment or opinion for the *reasonable* business judgment or opinion of the management or directors, or to insist on excessively conservative accounting treatment — a treatment not in the interest of ensuring a fair representation of the financial condition of the corporation, but rather with a view towards excluding the slightest possibility of an unfavourable variance.

§9.181 The decision of Moffit J. in *Pacific Acceptance Corporation Ltd. v. Forsyth & Ors*[295] provides somewhat more exact guidance as to the type of inquiry that an auditor is obliged to undertake. In that case, Moffit J. began first by commenting upon the need for a systematic audit inquiry: for a process that is both planned and deliberate, and which is sufficiently broad to take into account the possibility that error or some impropriety may have occurred. He said:

---

[293] *Haig v. Bamford*, [1976] S.C.J. No. 31, 72 D.L.R. (3d) 68 at 78, *per* Dickson J.
[294] [1958] 1 W.L.R. 45 at 61 (H.L.).
[295] (1967), 92 W.N. 29 at 63-66 (N.S.W.S.C.).

...it is clear that in planning and carrying out his work an auditor must pay due regard to the possibility of error or fraud. Once it is accepted that the auditor's duty requires him to go behind the books and determine the true financial position of the company and so to examine the accord or otherwise of the financial position of the company, the books and the balance sheet, it follows that the possible causes to the contrary, namely, error, fraud or unsound accounting, are the auditor's concern. ... An auditor pays due regard to the possibility of fraud or error by framing and carrying out his procedures, having in mind the general and particular possibilities that exist, to the intent that if a substantial or material error or fraud has crept into the affairs of the company he has a reasonable expectation that it will be revealed. The problems is an intensely practical one. On the other hand, it may be unjust to criticize a procedure, particularly with hindsight, merely because it was not apt to reveal some fraud or error.... In such instances in particular it is important with resolution to exclude the operation of hindsight, because after the event it is often easy to think of procedures that could have been adopted that would have revealed even the ingenious fraud, whereas in fact the auditor looking at the matter as it then presented itself was acting reasonably.

§9.182 Thus the audit plan must incorporate procedures sufficient to determine whether further inquiry may be merited. The gist of the plan should be to obtain an overview of the corporation's financial situation and to determine whether there are grounds to suggest whether problems may exist. The auditor is expected to possess the expertise to anticipate the problems that are likely to exist, and to be able to design an audit plan which will accommodate the likelihood of such problems, by devising checks that will provide a good indication with respect to their presence. It is not necessary, however, for the auditor to conduct a comprehensive investigation so that the possibility of fraud and error can be categorically ruled out. So Moffit J. continued:

> On the other hand, it should be recognized that an auditor has an opportunity to plan much of his work in advance and to work out a program, which is often built up over a period of time, having some general application, based on some understanding of the possible points of danger in the financial affairs of an organization. He therefore has an opportunity, with some deliberation and forethought, to design procedures which take some account at least of the fact that experience has shown that frauds or their concealment commonly involve manipulation at particular points in the financial operations of a business—for example, cash manipulations near a balance date, which manipulations often fall into various well-known patterns.

§9.183 In specific terms, it has been held that an auditor is obliged to verify the corporation's cash account with its banker and against the appropriate bank statements.[296] In England it has been held that the auditor is not obliged to verify the corporation's inventory,[297] but in Canada and elsewhere in North America this is a common practice.[298] An auditor must confirm that a corporation possesses an appropriate security certificate or other evidence of any investment that is shown on its books as belonging to the corporation.[299] Where loans made

---

[296] *Fox & Son v. Morrish Grant & Co.*, (1918), 35 T.L.R. 126 (K.B.).
[297] *Re Kingston Cotton Mill Co. (No. 2)*, [1896] 2 Ch. 279 (C.A.), although it has been doubted whether that ruling would be followed today. Palmer at 970.
[298] *Stanley L. Block v. Klein*, 258 N.Y.S. (2d) 501 (1965).
[299] *Re City Equitable Fire Insurance Co.*, [1925] 1 Ch. 407 at 514 (C.A.), *per* Pollock M.R.

by the corporation are secured, the auditor must carry out a reasonable investigation to confirm that the security is valid,[300] and in the case of all loans and investments must make some determination as to the probability of payment by the party indebted to the corporation.[301] The auditor must also check into the trade debts owing to or by the corporation,[302] as for instance by confirming with the persons concerned as to the existence of the recorded debts.[303] More generally, the auditor's duty is to examine the corporation's books or other records of original entry, the supporting invoices and vouchers pertaining to the entries in those books or records, and to examine the final accounts (the balance sheet, income statement, and so forth) based upon them, to determine with reasonable certainty that each conforms with the others, and to report on those financial statements to the shareholders or other members of the corporation.[304] The auditor's duty of inquiry is limited, however, to an examination of the types of accounts, records and vouchers that a corporation will ordinarily maintain. The auditor is not obliged to check into informal or unusual records that a particular corporation does maintain.[305]

§9.184 Like all professional skills, the audit process is one that undergoes continuous refinement. Over time, the steps that may be expected of a reasonable and competent auditor advance with the general standards of the procession. As Pennychuck J. noted *In Re Thomas Gerrard & Son Ltd.*[306] the standards of reasonable care and skill are more exacting today than those which prevailed in 1896. Thus in deciding whether a particular auditor acted reasonably, the courts will have regard not only to previous case law, but also to contemporary practice and standards within the accounting profession.[307]

---

[300] *Scarborough Harbour Commrs. v. Robinson Coulson Kirby & Co.* (1934), 78 Acct. L.R. 65.
[301] *Leeds Estate Building & Investment Co. v. Shepherd* (1887), 36 Ch. D. 787; *Re London & General Bank (No. 2)*, [1895] 2 Ch. 673 (C.A.). In *Blue Band Navigation Co. (Trustee of) v. Price Waterhouse (No. 2)*, [1934] B.C.J. No. 82, [1934] 2 W.W.R. 49 at 77-78 (C.A.), per M.A. Macdonald J.A.:

> The auditors should not insert the amount involved as an asset unless reasonably sure it could be realized. They should not report it as such, not knowing anything about the primary debtor unless acting reasonably they might assume that the guarantor was good for the amount ... If, on the other hand, it was perfected by what, in view of all the known facts, might reasonably be regarded as a good guarantee, the indebtedness of the primary debtor might be considered a good asset.

[302] *Scarborough Harbour Commrs. v. Robinson Coulson Kirby & Co.* (1934), 78 Acct. L.R. 65.
[303] *Re Westminster Road Construction and Engineering Co.* (1932), 76 Acct. L.R. 38; *Re Thomas Gerrard & Son Ltd.*, [1968] 1 Ch. 455, [1967] 2 All E.R. 525.
[304] OBCA, s. 153(1):

> 153.(1) An auditor of a corporation shall make such examination of the financial statements required by this Act to be placed before shareholders as is necessary to enable the auditor to report thereon and the auditor shall report as prescribed and in accordance with generally accepted auditing standards.

[305] *Henry Squire Cash Chemist Ltd. v. Ball Baker & Co.* (1911), 106 L.T. 197 (C.A.).
[306] [1968] 1 Ch. 455 at 475.
[307] See, generally, *Revelstoke Credit Union v. Miller*, [1984] B.C.J. No. 2819, [1984] 2 W.W.R. 297, 28 C.C.L.T. 17, 24 B.L.R. 271 (S.C.). In that case, the plaintiff's manager had made unauthorized loans to two customers, commencing in 1977. In 1978, the defendant performed a systematic review of the business and records of the credit union that should have disclosed the

§9.185 In *Coopers & Lybrand v. H.E. Kane Agencies Ltd*,[308] the facts were that an officer of the plaintiff extended credit to a customer contrary to the policy of the plaintiff. The customer subsequently became insolvent and the plaintiff suffered a substantial loss. In conducting its audit, the defendant had relied on the airline and the plaintiff's president to report any ticket sale discrepancies. No such report had been made. The court found that the defendant was liable for accepting the books at face value and for relying on the absence of a report of missing funds. Had the defendant been more alert, the problem would have been sooner discovered and the plaintiff's loss would have been less. The defendant was obliged to protect the plaintiff from schemes of its employees that were easily discoverable.

§9.186 It would seem, therefore, that while an auditor need not suspect that fraud has taken place, he or she cannot simply ignore the possibility that something is wrong — indeed, such an assumption would seem to be contrary to the very purpose of an audit. The auditor must strike a reasonable balance between undue suspicion and indifference to the possibility of improper conduct. As Moffit J. stated in *Pacific Acceptance Corp. Ltd. v. Forsyth & Ors*:

> ... it is clear that in planning and carrying out his work an auditor must pay due regard to the possibility of error or fraud. Once it is accepted that the auditor's duty requires him to go behind the books and determine the true financial position of the company and so to examine the accord or otherwise of the financial position of the company, the books and the balance sheet, it follows that the possible causes to the contrary, namely error, fraud or unsound accounting, are the auditor's concern ...[309]

§9.187 Generally, the auditor will meet the required standard of care so long as the auditor adheres to general standards of auditing practice within the accounting profession. For instance, in *Guardian Ins. Co. of Canada v. Sharp*,[310] the cashier of a corporation had misappropriated money over a long period of time, in such a way that it could not be ascertained by ordinary audit checks. However, had the auditors taken the exceptional step of examining duplicate deposit slips, the fraud would have been discovered. It was proven that it was not general auditing practice to examine those slips, because they were not original documents and in an ordinary case would not have been likely to reveal a fraud. Consequently, it was held that the auditor was not liable for negligence. However, the question of whether the auditor has exercised reasonable care is one for the court, and the fact

---

improper loans, but the defendant failed to discover them. When the loans eventually came to light, the plaintiff sued the auditor. It was held that the action should be allowed. The auditors had a duty to investigate, once they became aware of facts that should have aroused their suspicion. This they failed to do. Consequently, they were liable for all unauthorized loans made after the date of the 1978 audit.

[308] [1983] N.B.J. No. 37, 44 N.B.R. (2d) 374; 23 C.C.L.T. 233 (Q.B.), *per* Hoyt J., rev'd in part on other grounds [1985] N.B.J. No. 161, 32 C.C.L.T. 1, 17 D.L.R. (4th) 695, 62 N.B.R. (2d) 1 (C.A.); *cf. Cameron Publications Ltd. v. Piers, Conrod & Allen*, [1985] N.S.J. No. 311, 69 N.S.R. (2d) 180 (S.C.), aff'd [1986] N.S.J. No. 253, 73 N.S.R. (2d) 211, 35 B.L.R. 32 (C.A.).

[309] (1967), 92 W.N. 29 at 63 *et seq.*

[310] [1941] S.C.R. 164, [1941] 2 D.L.R. 417.

that an auditor has adhered to the standards of the profession will not preclude a finding of negligence, where those standards are themselves deficient.[311]

(i) Dispensing with the Audit Requirement

§9.188 Under both the OBCA and CBCA, the initial presumption is that every corporation that is a reporting issuer will have an auditor. Section 162(1) of the CBCA provides that:

> 162.(1) Subject to section 163, shareholders of a corporation shall, by ordinary resolution, at the first annual meeting of shareholders and at each succeeding annual meeting, appoint an auditor to hold office until the close of the next annual meeting.

Section 148 of the OBCA is slightly different in approach:

> 148. In respect of a financial year of a corporation, the corporation is exempt from the requirements of this Part regarding the appointment and duties of an auditor if,
>
> (a) the corporation is not an offering corporation; and
>
> (b) all of the shareholders consent in writing to the exemption in respect of that year.

Despite this different wording, the starting presumption is that all corporations are required to have an auditor. For corporations that are not offering or distributing corporations, the shareholders may elect to dispense with this requirement. Under both Acts, unanimous consent is required to effect this purpose.[312]

(j) Change of Auditor

§9.189 Both the OBCA and CBCA set out detailed rules that must be followed in order to change an auditor. For reporting issuers, it is also necessary to comply with the numerous requirements set out in section 4.11 of NI 51-102. Since these requirements are normally primarily of concern to securities law practitioners, as opposed to corporate practitioners, they are not discussed in this section.

(k) Audit Committees

§9.190 Both the OBCA and the CBCA include provisions contemplating the creation and operation of audit committees. However, for reporting issuers these provisions have for all intents and purposes been left behind by the more demanding requirements imposed under securities laws and stock exchange listing rules. These requirements are discussed in Chapter 10, and therefore shall not be considered in this section.

---

[311] *Northumberland Insurance Ltd. (in liq.) v. Alexander & Ors* (1984), 8 A.C.L.R. 882 at 889, *per* Clarke J., aff'd 13 A.C.L.R. 170.

[312] CBCA, s. 163(3).

(l) Auditor Liability

§9.190.1 There is no question that an auditor is liable in contract to the corporation where the auditor fails to meet the expected standard of care in carrying out an audit. Where one person enters into a contract with another under which he or she agrees to perform some service for or on behalf of that other person, then ordinarily (*i.e.*, in the absence of express provision to the contrary or clear implication) there is an implied undertaking that reasonable care will be taken by the person performing the service. So, for instance, in *FSLIC v. Texas Real Estate Counselors, Inc.*[313] it was said that:

> ... the duty owed by a professional to his client derives from their contractual relationship and requires that the professional "use the skill and care in the performance of his duties commensurate with the requirements of his profession.

In such cases, liability flows from the voluntary assumption of this risk *vis-à-vis* the known counter-party to the contract.

§9.190.2 Third parties who have relied upon the audit report of the auditor in their dealings with the corporation may in limited cases have a right to claim against the auditor of the corporation based upon negligent misstatement. There are five required elements for a successful negligent misrepresentation claim. The plaintiff must establish that:[314]

- there was a duty of care based on a "special relationship" between the auditor and the plaintiff;
- the representation in question was untrue, inaccurate, or misleading;
- the auditor must have acted negligently in making that misrepresentation;
- the plaintiff must have placed reasonable reliance on that misrepresentation; and
- the reliance must have been detrimental to the plaintiff in the sense that damages resulted.

§9.190.3 Such are the basic principles. However, in the case of claims against auditors, the courts have always been heavily influenced by the concerns raised by Cardozo J.C. in *Ultramares Corp. v. Touche*,[315] In that case, Touche Niven & Co. were employed by Fred Stern & Co., to audit its financial statements. Touche was negligent in conducting the audit and overlooked $700,000 of accounts receivable that were based on fictitious sales and other suspicious activities. It gave an unqualified opinion and provided 32 copies of the audited financial statements to Stern. Stern gave one copy to Ultramares Corporation,

---

[313] (1992), 955 F.2d 261, 265 (5th Cir.).
[314] *Standard Trust Co. (Liquidator of) v. Cattanach*, [1995] O.J. No. 1939, 24 O.R. (3d) 492 (Gen. Div.), *per* MacPherson J.; *Hedley Byrne & Co. v. Heller & Partners Ltd.*, [1964] A.C. 465, [1963] All E.R. 575 (H.L.); *Queen v. Cognos Inc.*, [1993] S.C.J. No. 3, [1993] 1 S.C.R. 87 at 110.
[315] (1931) 174 N.E, 441 (N.Y.S.C.).

which then made a loan to Stern on the basis of the information contained in the audited statements. When Stern failed to repay the loan, Ultramares sued Touche for negligence. Cardozo C.J. stated:

> If liability for negligence exists, a thoughtless slip or blunder, the failure to detect a theft or forgery beneath the cover of deceptive entries, may expose accountants to a liability in an indeterminate amount for an indeterminate time to an indeterminate class. The hazards of a business conducted on these terms are so extreme as to enkindle doubt whether a flaw may not exist in the implication of a duty that exposes to these consequences.

§9.190.4 The *Ultramares* case was expressly referred to by the Supreme Court of Canada, in what has become the leading case in Canada with respect to auditor liability. In *Hercules Managements Ltd. v. Ernst & Young*,[316] the plaintiff was one of a number of shareholders in Northguard Acceptance Ltd. ("NGA") which, together with Northguard Holdings Ltd. ("NGH"), carried on the business of lending and investing money on the security of real property mortgages. Ernst & Young was originally hired by NGA and NGH in 1971 to perform annual audits of their financial statements and to provide audit reports to the companies' shareholders. Both NGA and NGH went into receivership in 1984. A number of shareholders then sued Ernst & Young alleging the audit reports for the years 1980, 1981 and 1982 were negligently prepared, and that they had suffered losses in reasonable reliance on these reports. At the Supreme Court of Canada, La Forest J. noted that in deciding whether the auditors should be liable to such a claim a critical issue was that of proximity. He continued:

> The label 'proximity' ... was clearly intended to connote that the circumstances of the relationship inhering between the plaintiff and the defendant are of such a nature that the defendant may be said to be under an obligation to be mindful of the plaintiff's legitimate interests in conducting his or her affairs.[317]

La Forest J. expressed concern that the extension of auditor liability to too great an extent would impose an intolerable burden upon the accounting profession. He said:

> ... deterrence of negligent conduct is an important policy consideration with respect to auditors' liability. Nevertheless, I am of the view that, in the final analysis, it is outweighed by the socially undesirable consequences to which the imposition of indeterminate liability on auditors might lead. Indeed, while indeterminate liability is problematic in and of itself inasmuch as it would mean that successful negligence actions against auditors could, at least potentially, be limitless, it is also problematic in light of certain related problems to which it might give rise.

The Court went on to hold that the claim against the auditors was one that properly belonged to the corporation.[318]

---

[316] [1997] S.C.J. No. 51, [1997] 2 S.C.R. 165.
[317] At para. 24
[318] See also *Bow Valley Husky (Bermuda) Ltd. v. Saint John Shipbuilding Ltd.*, [1997] S.C.J. No. 111, [1997] 3 S.C.R. 1210.

§9.190.5 The decision in *Hercules* was subsequently refined and elaborated upon in a series of Supreme Court of Canada decisions.[319] The most important of these would seem to be *Cooper v. Hobart*,[320] in which McLachlin C.J. and Major J. (giving the judgment of the Court) adopted a multi-step approach in deciding whether liability should be imposed on particular facts against a defendant. They adopted a two-stage approach, based upon a consideration of two questions:

- Was the harm that occurred the reasonably foreseeable consequence of the defendant's act?
- Are there reasons, notwithstanding the proximity between the parties established in the first part of this test, that tort liability should not be recognized here?

They continued:

> The proximity analysis involved at the first stage ... focuses on factors arising from the relationship between the plaintiff and the defendant. These factors include questions of policy, in the broad sense of that word. If foreseeability and proximity are established at the first stage, a *prima facie* duty of care arises. At the second stage ... the question still remains whether there are residual policy considerations outside the relationship of the parties that may negate the imposition of a duty of care. It may be ... that such considerations will not often prevail. However, we think it useful expressly to ask, before imposing a new duty of care, whether despite foreseeability and proximity of relationship, there are other policy reasons why the duty should not be imposed.

§9.190.6 There are a number of American cases that illustrate in the specific context of auditor and similar claims. The appropriate balancing of policy considerations ought to take into account. In California, for instance, it has been held that the determination of whether in a specific case the defendant should be held liable to a plaintiff who was not in privity of contract is a matter of policy and involves the balancing of various factors, including:[321]

- the extent to which the transaction was intended to affect the plaintiff,
- the foreseeability of harm to the plaintiff,
- the degree of certainty that the plaintiff suffered injury,
- the closeness of the connection between the defendant's conduct and the injury suffered,
- the moral blame attached to the defendant's conduct, and
- the policy of preventing or deterring future harm.

However, in addition to the foregoing factors, which focus upon what the defendant has done and what results have flowed from it, there are other factors that

---

[319] See, for instance, *Edwards v. Law Society of Upper Canada*, [2001] S.C.J. No. 77, [2001] 3 S.C.R. 562.
[320] [2001] S.C.J. No. 76, [2001] 3 S.C.R. 537 at 551-53.
[321] *Biakanja v. Irving* (1958), 49 Cal. 2d 647 at 650, 320 P.2d 16 (Calif. S.C.).

are relevant to the ultimate decision regarding liability, that take into account the conduct of the plaintiff or the extent of the damage suffered. These include that:[322]

- liability may in particular cases be out of proportion to fault;
- parties should be encouraged to rely on their own ability to protect themselves through their own prudence, diligence and contracting power; and
- the potential adverse impact on the class of defendants upon whom the duty is imposed.

Finally, in *Quelamine Co., Inc. v. Stewart Title Guaranty Co.*,[323] the court noted that:

> ... in the business arena it would be unprecedented to impose a duty on one actor to operate its business in a manner that would ensure the financial success of transactions between third parties. With rare exceptions, a business entity has no duty to prevent financial loss to others with whom it deals directly. *A fortiori*, it has no greater duty to prevent financial losses to third parties who may be affected by its operations.

This passage has also been cited in a number of American cases dealing with claims against auditors by third parties.

§9.190.7 While the matter is still unresolved in some states, the prevailing American view seems to be very similar to that in Canada.[324] Specifically, as a matter both of policy and reality there are no express third party beneficiaries of an ordinary, "white-bread" audit engagement contract, but only incidental beneficiaries who have no legal rights arising from the contract.[325] Nevertheless, in a narrow band of cases, persons other than the corporation may enjoy a direct right of claim against the auditor, as for instance where an audit is carried out for the express purpose of providing financial information to a third party.[326] Any claim for liability must be balanced against the complexity of the professional opinions rendered in audit reports, and the difficult and potentially tenuous causal relationships between audit reports and any economic loss suffered. A further consideration is whether the plaintiff belonged to a "sophisticated class" able to make effective use of contract rather than tort liability to control and ad-

---

[322] *Bily v. Arthur Young & Co.* (1992), 3 Cal. 4th 370, 11 Cal. Rptr. 2nd 51, 834 P. 2nd 745 (Calif. S.C.).
[323] (1998), 19 Cal. 4th 26, 77 Cal. Rptr. 2d 709, 960 P.2d 513 (Calif. S.C.).
[324] In addition to those cases discussed here, see also *Brumley v. Touche, Ross & Co.* (1984), 123 Ill. App. 3d 636, 463 N.E.2d 195 (2nd Dist.); *Pelham v. Griesheimer* (1982), 92 Ill.2d 13, 440 N.E.2d 96 (Ill. S.C.); *Brumley v. Touche, Ross, & Co.* (1985), 139 Ill. App. 3d 831, 487 N.E.2d 641 (2nd Dist.); *Chestnut Corp. v. Pestine, Brinati, Gamer, Ltd.* (1996), 281 Ill. App. 3d 719, 667 N.E.2d 543 (1st Dist); *Daniel v. Dow Jones & Co., Inc.* (1987), 520 N.Y.S. 2d 334, 137 Misc. 2d 94 (N.Y.C. Civ. Ct.) — liability of a news service for information reported.
[325] *Mariani v. Price Waterhouse* (1998), 70 Cal. App. 4th 685, 82 Cal. Rptr. 2d 671 at 681 (Calif. S.C.).
[326] *Roberts v. Ball, Hunt, Hart, Brown & Baerwitz* (1976), 57 Cal. App. 3d 104, 128 Cal. Rptr. 901 (Calif. S.C.) — attorney liable for a written opinion to a client, where the attorney knew it would be transmitted to and relied upon by a third party in dealing with the client

just the relevant risks through private ordering, or to carry out its own audit or investigation. In addition, the court should consider the risk that imposing liability on the facts of a given case could lead to increased expense and decreased availability of auditing services in some sectors of the economy. Generally, in order for a third-party to recover against an auditor for negligent misrepresentation the plaintiff must establish that:[327]

- the defendant made a representation;
- with the intent to induce the plaintiff to act in reliance upon it in a specific transaction.

The intent to influence is a threshold issue. In its absence of such proof there is no liability even though a plaintiff has relied on the misrepresentation to his or her detriment, and even if such reliance was reasonably foreseeable.[328]

§9.190.8 In addition to the foregoing broad principles, there are a number of specific rules governing auditor liability that also tend to restrict the range of valid claims. First, any claim against an auditor must normally be based upon some oversight that has a direct bearing on the audit opinion. For instance, audits relate to financial records and statements of a corporation relating to actual transactions that have occurred, and thus in the normal case an audit opinion will not be construed to extend to *pro forma* financial statements containing estimates of expected performance or other forward looking information.[329]

§9.190.9 A further area of concern involves the role played by the corporation (and its staff) in any oversight that occurred. The typical auditor claim relates to a failure to discover some unlawful conduct or other serious irregularity during the conduct of the audit. In almost all cases, the wrong-doing in question will have been covered up by the employees of the corporation. Generally speaking, it is the responsibility of the corporation to supervise its employees, and accordingly it seems questionable whether a corporation should be entitled to shift any loss resulting from a failure to do so to its auditors. In *Cenco Inc. v. Seidman & Seidman*,[330] *per* Posner Cir. J indicated, in an action against an auditor for negligent breach of contract, that breach by the auditor will be excused where it results from a breach on the part of the corporation (in the form of hindrance or failure to cooperate) that prevented the auditor from performing the contract. In an action in tort, the corresponding defense is one of contributory negligence. The general rule in Canada is that contributory negligence is not a full defence to a tort claim, but results in only partial release from liability taking into account the respective fault of each party. Historically, Canadian law has not recognized

---

[327] *Bily v. Arthur Young & Co.* (1992), 3 Cal. 4th 370, 11 Cal. Rptr. 2nd 51, 834 P. 2nd 745 (Calif. S.C.).
[328] *Gillespie, v. Schneider, Arthur Andersen & Co.*, [1996] U.S. App. LEXIS 5771 (9th Cir.).
[329] *Cope v. Price Waterhouse*, [1993] U.S. App. LEXIS 7795 (9th Cir.).
[330] (1982), 686 F.2d 449, 453-54 (7th Cir.).

contributory negligence as a proper defense to a claim based upon breach of contract, although this proposition has recently been doubted.[331]

§9.190.10 In *Sydney Cooperative Society Ltd. v. Coopers & Lybrand*[332] the defendant auditors were found liable in negligence and breach of contract for failing to detect a theft of money by an employee of the plaintiff. The plaintiffs were found 50 per cent contributory negligent. Despite some theoretical shortcomings, the Sydney Cooperative case has a certain degree of merit to it. Irrespective of whether the *Negligence Act* may be applicable to contract claims, it is difficult to understand why as a matter of principle both parties to a contract cannot each be found to have been in breach of a part of their respective obligations under the contract, so that while the corporation and those interested in it may still recover for the loss, an appropriate adjustment is made for the amount recoverable.[333]

(iii) Securities Law Disclosure Obligations

§9.191 The securities laws of the various provinces impose regular disclosure requirements on reporting issuers that are distributing securities in each of the provinces concerned. In addition, more specific disclosure requirements are imposed where a material change occurs. This section provides a very truncated overview of those requirements. As with respect to all other aspects of securities law covered in this text, the intent of the material set out in this section is only to provide a general overview, so as to sensitize the reader concerning possible securities law concerns. Reference should be made to a standard reference text in the securities laws field for more definitive information.

(1) Financial Information

§9.192 Part XIII of the *Securities Act* sets out a number of ongoing (or "continuous") disclosures of relevant information concerning the business and affairs of corporate and other issuers. These are then expanded upon under Regulation 1015, the General Regulation under the *Securities Act* and under National Instruments 51-102 dealing with continuous disclosure and 52-501 dealing with financial statements.

§9.193 Subsection 78(1) of the *Securities Act* provides that every reporting issuer must file annually within 140 days from the end of its last financial year, comparative financial statements relating separately to:

(a) the period that commenced on the date of incorporation or organization and ended as of the close of the first financial year or, if the reporting issuer or

---

[331] See, generally, *Iroquois Falls Community Credit Union Ltd. (Liquidation of) v. Co-operators General Insurance Co.*, [2006] O.J. No. 3999 (S.C.J.).
[332] [2002] N.S.J. No. 578 (S.C.), 213 N.S.R. (2d) 115, further reasons as [2006] N.S.J. No. 382 (S.C.)
[333] For a discussion of American position in this area with respect to audit liability, see: *In Re CBI Holding Company Inc.* (2004), 311 B.R. 350; 2004 (S.D.N.Y.).

mutual fund has completed a financial year, the last financial year, as the case may be; and

(b) the period covered by the financial year next preceding the last financial year, if any.

These statements must be made up in accordance with generally accepted accounting principles and certified as required by the regulations. Specifically, the annual financial statements must include an income statement, statement of surplus, a statement of changes in financial position and a balance sheet prepared for or as at the end of the period, as applicable. The financial statements must be approved by the board of directors of the issuer and that approval must be evidenced by the manual or facsimile signatures of two directors duly authorized by the board to signify its approval.

§9.194 The financial statements distributed by a corporation constitute a public disclosure of its assets and liabilities. A note in the financial statement to the effect that a particular debt is owed constitutes an admission of liability by the corporation with respect to that debt — subject to any supervening or subsequently discovered contra right. However, it is not an admission of liability where the note pertains to a debt or obligation purportedly owed by the corporation to a director of the corporation.[334]

§9.195 The general rule respecting the preparation of financial statements is that all such statements must be prepared in accordance with generally accepted accounting principles,[335] subject of course to any modifications to those principles required under the *Securities Act*, the applicable national policies noted above, or Regulation 1015 under that Act.[336] The term generally accepted accounting principles — customarily abbreviated to "GAAP" — means those pronouncements by the Accounting Research Committee[337] of the Canadian Institute of Chartered Accountants that are set out in the *CICA Handbook* as generally accepted accounting principles.[338] However, subsection 2(4) of the Regulation goes on to qualify this general rule, by providing for alternative regulatory exceptions:

2.(4) Despite subsection (1), where a financial statement is not prepared in accordance with generally accepted accounting principles,

(a) the Director may accept the financial statement for the purposes for which it is to be filed,

---

[334] *In Re Coliseum (Barrow) Ltd.*, [1930] 2 Ch. 44; *In Re Transplanters (Holding Co.) Ltd.*, [1958] 1 W.L.R. 822 at 823 (Ch. D.), *per* Wynne-Parry J.
[335] SAR, s. 2(1).
[336] SAR, s. 2(1).
[337] Prior to June 1973, the Accounting and Auditing Research Committee.
[338] National Policy No. 27. The adoption of GAAP as set out in the *CICA Handbook* is not an *ultra vires* delegation of regulation making authority: *Re Denison Mines Ltd. and Ontario Securities Commission*, [1981] O.J. No. 2966, 32 O.R. (2d) 469 (Div. Ct.).

(i) where the Director is satisfied that it is not reasonably practicable for the issuer to revise the presentation in the financial statement to conform to generally accepted accounting principles, or

(ii) where the Commission by its order under clause (b) has previously accepted a financial statement of the same issuer with a corresponding variation from generally accepted accounting principles and the Director is satisfied that there has been no material change in the circumstances upon which the decision of the Commission was based; or

(b) the Commission may, by order, accept the financial statement after giving interested parties an opportunity to be heard if the Commission is satisfied in all the circumstances of the particular case that the variation from generally accepted accounting principles is supported or justified by considerations that outweigh the desirability of uniform adherence to generally accepted accounting principles and the Commission shall publish written reasons for any acceptance of financial statements under this paragraph.

§9.196 All annual statements must be accompanied by the report of the auditor of the reporting issuer, prepared in accordance with the regulations.[339] The auditor's report must be prepared in accordance with generally accepted auditing standards and with any applicable provision of the *Securities Act*, the applicable national policies or the SAR.

§9.197 Section 79 of the *Securities Act* provides that a copy of each annual statement that is filed in accordance with the *Securities Act* must be concurrently sent to each holder of the securities of the corporation whose latest address as shown on the books of the reporting issuer is in Ontario. However, where the reporting issuer is subject to a corresponding requirement under the laws of the jurisdiction under which it is incorporated, then compliance with that corresponding requirement is deemed to be compliance with the section 79 requirement to distribute information. The fact that the financial statements must be so distributed begs the question of why it is also necessary under the OBCA for those financial statements to be placed before the annual meeting. The apparent reason for the OBCA requirement is to ensure that a discussion of the financial statements is in order at that meeting.

§9.198 The annual financial statements requirements of the *Securities Act* are supplemented by the interim financial statement requirements. More particularly, under subsection 77(1) of the *Securities Act*, every reporting issuer that is not a mutual fund must file (within 60 days of the day to which it made up) an interim financial statement with the OSC. Where the reporting issuer has not completed its first financial year, the interim financial statement must relate to the periods commencing with the beginning of the year then in progress and ending nine, six and three months respectively before the date on which that year ends.[340] No financial statement is required to be filed for any period that is

---

[339] *Securities Act*, s. 78(2).
[340] *Securities Act*, s. 77(1)(*a*).

less than three months in length.[341] Where the reporting issuer has completed its first financial year, the interim financial statements must relate to the end of each of the three-month, six-month and nine-month periods of the current financial year that commenced immediately following the last financial year, and must include a comparative statement to the end of each of the corresponding periods in the last financial year. All such statements must be prepared in accordance with generally accepted accounting principles and certified as required by the regulations. A copy of each such statement must be concurrently sent to each holder of the securities of the corporation (other than debt instruments) whose latest address as shown on the books of the reporting issuer is in Ontario.[342] However, where the reporting issuer is subject to a corresponding requirement under the laws of the jurisdiction under which it is incorporated, then compliance with that corresponding requirement is deemed to be compliance with the section 79 requirement to distribute information.

(2) Management Discussion and Analysis

§9.199 The requirement to provide a management discussion and analysis of the business and affairs of an issuer (generally in Form 51-102F1) ("MD&A") has already been described in broad terms, and what is presented here is essentially no more than a quick summary of the specific filing requirements. Briefly, the MDA is a narrative explanation, through the eyes of management, of how a corporation has performed during the period covered by the financial statements to which it relates, and of what management considers to be the corporation's overall financial condition and future prospects. It is intended to supplement the financial statements, although it does not form part of them. The objective when preparing the MD&A should be to improve the overall level of disclosure by giving a balanced discussion of results and operations and condition, including such aspects of overall financial health as liquidity and capital resources. The document is intended to provide a balanced picture of good and bad news. It is intended to help current and prospective investors understand what the financial statements show and do not show, cover such areas as contingent liabilities, off-balance sheet arrangements, the prospect of default under debt, and other contractual issues. It should also discuss important trends and risks that have affected the financial statements or that are likely to affect them in the future.[343]

§9.200 Section 5.1 of Rule 51-102 provides that an MD&A normally shall be filed by the earlier of:

(a) the filing deadlines for the annual and interim financial statements set out in sections 4.2, 4.4 and 4.7 as applicable; and

(b) the date the reporting issuer files the financial statements under subsections 4.1(1), 4.3(1) or 4.7(1), as applicable.

---

[341] *Ibid.*
[342] *Securities Act*, s. 79.
[343] See, generally, Form 51-102F1.

Generally, board approval is required for the MDA, but the directors may delegate approval for the interim and any supplement to the audit committee.[344] There is no general requirement to deliver the MDA to securities holders, but they may access this information through the SEDAR Internet portal. In addition, securityholders may request that they be provided with any current MDA.[345] The voting rights of shareholders are considered in greater detail in Chapter 12.

(3) Annual Information Form

§9.201 In contrast to the detailed information provided at the time of an initial issue of securities under a prospectus, the annual financial statements and MD&A statement of an issuer provide only limited information to any concerned party with respect to the business and affairs of the corporation. In the United States, far more detailed information is provided under SEC Form 10-K, which in addition to annual financial statements and audit report, includes the related MD&A, as well as other disclosure about the business and affairs issuer. In Canada, the level of disclosure mandated under securities law is now brought closer to the prospectus standard by requiring the filing of an annual information form ("AIF"). Currently, this form is not provided to investors, although access to the information that it contains is available through the SEDAR system.

§9.202 The AIF will include a discussion of the corporate structure of the issuer, and its inter-corporate relationships. It will also provide a discussion of the development of the issuer's business, including a three-year history, a record of any significant acquisitions, a description of its business, including its principal markets, distribution methods, etc. This discussion must include coverage of risk factors, including cash flow and liquidity problems, the general risks inherent in the business in which the corporation is engaged, the regulatory restraints under which it operates, and so forth. Any legal proceedings to which the issuer is subject must be separately discussed. However, the following exception applies:

> You do not need to give information with regard to any proceeding that involves a claim for damages if the amount involved, exclusive of interest and costs, does not exceed ten per cent of the current assets of the company. However, if any proceedings presents in large degree the same legal and factual issues as other proceedings pending or known to be contemplated, you must include the amount involved in the other proceedings in computing the percentage.

The issuer is also required to disclose if it has implemented any social or environmental polices that are fundamental to its operations. In addition to providing a discussion of the issuer's capital structure and dividend history, requirements and restrictions, the corporation is also required to disclose any ratings that have been received from securities rating agencies, as well as information relating to the market for its securities. The directors and executive officers of the corporation must be identified, along with the number of securities of each class held by

---

[344] See NI 51-102, s. 5.5.
[345] See NI 51-102, s. 5.6.

them in the corporation or its subsidiaries. The members of each committee of the board must also be identified.[346]

§9.203 Sections 6.1 and 6.2 of NI 51-102 provides that a reporting issuer that is not a venture issuer must file an AIF. On or before the 90th day after the end of the reporting issuer's most recently completed financial year; or in the case of a reporting issuer that is an SEC reporting issuer filing its AIF in Form 10K, Form 10-KSB, or Form 20-F, on or before the earlier of:

(i) the 90th day after the end of the reporting issuer's most recently completed financial year; and

(ii) the date the reporting issuer files its Form 10-K, Form 10-KSB or Form 20-F with the SEC.

All material incorporated into an AIF that has not been previously filed must be filed at the same time.

(4) Information Circular Requirements

§9.204 Under section 9.1 of NI 51-102, where the management of a reporting issuer gives notice of a meeting to its registered holders of voting securities, then management is required (at the same time as or before giving that notice) to send to each registered holder of voting securities who is entitled to notice of the meeting a form of proxy for use at the meeting. In addition, subject to limited exemptions, a person or company that solicits proxies from registered holders of voting securities of a reporting issuer must,

(a) in the case of a solicitation by or on behalf of management of a reporting issuer, send an information circular with the notice of meeting to each registered securityholder whose proxy is solicited; or

(b) in the case of any other solicitation, concurrently with or before the solicitation, send an information circular to each registered securityholder whose proxy is solicited.[347]

Rule NI 51-102 contains a number of specific requirements regarding the content of proxies and information circulars, particularly with respect to the manner in which any proxy obtained may be revoked, or may or must be voted.

(5) Timely Disclosure Requirements (Material Changes)

§9.205 Generally, a corporation that is a reporting issuer will encourage their directors and executive officers to purchase securities in the corporation, and very often a portion of the remuneration package for such individuals will take the form of share options. For these reasons, trades in corporate securities by insiders to the corporation are quite common. For reasons that need not be discussed here, since the 1970s, there has been steadily mounting concern among

---

[346] Form 51-102F2.
[347] NI 51-102, s. 9.1(2).

securities regulators regarding the possibility that in making such trades, insiders will take advantage of the superior access that they possess to material information relating to the corporation, for their personal trading benefit. The timely disclosure of material change requirements of securities law and policy are intended to address this area of concern.

§9.206 Under the Ontario *Securities Act*, where a material change occurs in the affairs of a reporting issuer, the issuer is obliged to disclose that change forthwith. More specifically, if a material change occurs in the affairs of a reporting issuer, the reporting issuer must,

    (a) immediately issue and file a news release authorized by a senior officer disclosing the nature and substance of the change; and

    (b) as soon as practicable, and in any event within 10 days of the date on which the change occurs, file a Form 51-102F3, Material Change Report with respect to the material change.[348]

These obligations do not apply if,

    (a) in the opinion of the reporting issuer, and if that opinion is arrived at in a reasonable manner, the disclosure required by subsection (1) would be unduly detrimental to the interests of the reporting issuer; or

    (b) the material change consists of a decision to implement a change made by senior management of the reporting issuer who believe that confirmation of the decision by the board of directors is probable, and senior management of the reporting issuer has no reason to believe that persons with knowledge of the material change have made use of that knowledge in purchasing or selling securities of the reporting issuer.[349]

However, in such a case, the reporting issuer must immediately file the report required under paragraph (1)(b) marked so as to include that it is confidential, together with written reasons for non-disclosure. A slightly different formulation of this exception applies in Quebec.[350] Subsection 7.1(5) of NI 51-102 imposes the following sunset on such confidential arrangement:

    If a report has been filed under subsection (2) or (3), the reporting issuer must advise the [securities regulatory authority] in writing if it believes the report should continue to remain confidential, within 10 days of the date of filing of the initial report and every 10 days thereafter until the material change is generally disclosed in the manner referred to in paragraph (1)(a), or if the material change consists of a decision of the type referred to in paragraph (2)(b), until that decision has been rejected by the board of directors of the reporting issuer.

Finally, public disclosure must be made, once it becomes evident that trades are occurring with knowledge of the material change. Specifically, subsection 7.1(7) provides that if a report has been filed under subsection (2),

---

[348] NI 51-102, s. 7.1(1).
[349] NI 51-102, s. 7.1(2).
[350] NI 51-102, s. 7.1(3).

... the reporting issuer must promptly disclose the material change in the manner referred to in paragraph (1)(a) upon the reporting issuer becoming aware, or having reasonable grounds to believe, that persons or companies are purchasing or selling securities of the reporting issuer with knowledge of the material change that has not been generally disclosed.

§9.207 The term "material change" is given a very lengthy definition in subsection 1(1) of the *Securities Act*.

"material change",

(a) when used in relation to an issuer other than an investment fund, means,

  (i) a change in the business, operations or capital of the issuer that would reasonably be expected to have a significant effect on the market price or value of any of the securities of the issuer, or

  (ii) a decision to implement a change referred to in subclause (i) made by the board of directors or other persons acting in a similar capacity or by senior management of the issuer who believe that confirmation of the decision by the board of directors or such other persons acting in a similar capacity is probable, and

(b) when used in relation to an issuer that is an investment fund, means,

  (i) a change in the business, operations or affairs of the issuer that would be considered important by a reasonable investor in determining whether to purchase or continue to hold securities of the issuer, or

  (ii) a decision to implement a change referred to in subclause (i) made,

  (A) by the board of directors of the issuer or the board of directors of the investment fund manager of the issuer or other persons acting in a similar capacity,

  (B) by senior management of the issuer who believe that confirmation of the decision by the board of directors or such other persons acting in a similar capacity is probable, or

  (C) by senior management of the investment fund manager of the issuer who believe that confirmation of the decision by the board of directors of the investment fund manager of the issuer or such other persons acting in a similar capacity is probable.

It is clear that the definition of "material change" under securities legislation is based on a market impact test. In NI 51-201, the Canadian Securities Administrators note that:

> In making materiality judgments, it is necessary to take into account a number of factors that cannot be captured in a simple bright-line standard or test. These include the nature of the information itself, the volatility of the company's securities and prevailing market conditions. The materiality of a particular event or piece of information may vary between companies according to their size, the nature of their operations and many other factors. An event that is "significant" or "major" for a smaller company may not be material to a larger company. Companies should avoid taking an overly technical approach to determining materiality. Under volatile market conditions, apparently insignificant variances between earnings

projections and actual results can have a significant impact on share price once released. For example, information regarding a company's ability to meet consensus earnings published by securities analysts should not be selectively disclosed before general public release.

§9.208 In this chapter we have surveyed the law governing the election or appointment of directors and the officers of a corporation, and discussed the general principles of corporate governance that now are seen to guide and control them in the management of the corporation for which they serve. In Chapter 10, we shall build upon this survey, in a discussion of the detailed rules of law governing the management process within each OBCA and CBCA corporation.

Chapter 10

CORPORATE MANAGEMENT

A. THE BOARD DECISION-MAKING PROCESS

§10.1 As we discussed in Chapter 9, control over the management of the corporation is divided between the shareholders, directors and officers of a corporation. Subject to any unanimous shareholder agreement, the actual involvement of shareholders in day-to-day management is limited. Under the OBCA and CBCA, shareholder involvement in management decisions will usually come into play only with respect to fundamental changes in the business or affairs of a corporation, such as the sale of its business, its continuation under the laws of another jurisdiction, the amendment of the articles or by-laws of the corporation and the like. For most corporations, the directors and officers share effective control over the day-to-day management of the corporation. The terms on which such control are divided varies from one corporation to another, although as we shall see, both the OBCA and the CBCA restrict the extent to which the directors can delegate the entirety of their management responsibility to the officers of the corporation. Moreover, increasingly, legally imposed corporate governance requirements are regulating the overall approach to management within a corporation. Generally, when authority is delegated to the officers of a corporation, it is up to the board of directors of the corporation to fix policy and procedures, and to impose internal controls, that restrict and regulate the manner in which the delegated authority is exercised. In contrast, although specific rules can be introduced with respect to board level management either under the articles or by-laws, or by way of a unanimous shareholder agreement, the OBCA and the CBCA themselves specifically contemplate an overall managerial approach to board level decision-making. And it is to those rules that we will now turn.

(i) Director Meetings

§10.2 As noted in Chapter 9, the directors of a corporation act as a collegial body known as the board of directors.[1] Ordinarily, their decisions are made at

---

[1] *Leon Chevrolet, Inc. v. Trapp* (1980), 391 So. 2d 1371 (C.A. La. 4th Cir.). The collegial nature of the board decision making process has most often been referred to by the courts in a critical way. However, in *Khanna v. McMinn*, [2006] Del. Ch. LEXIS 86 Noble V.C. stated:

> Although there may be instances in which a director's voting history would be sufficient to negate a director's presumed independence, routine consensus cannot suffice to demonstrate disloyalty on the part of a director. To conclude otherwise would simply encourage staged disagreements and non-unanimous decisions for the sake of non-unanimous decisions in the boardroom.

meetings of the board, by way of director resolution. While the shareholders of a corporation are under no obligation to attend shareholder meetings or take any active interest in its business or affairs, the directors of a corporation have a duty to attend the meeting, to familiarize themselves with the business to be conducted, and to take an active interest in the decisions to be made.[2]

§10.3 Neither the OBCA nor the CBCA provides much guidance concerning the formal requirements of director meetings. It is not accurate to draw direct comparisons between the rules governing director meetings and shareholder meetings, for the courts have indicated a markedly greater willingness to tolerate informality and commercial expediency in the case of director meetings than in the case of shareholder meetings. Thus so long as those who are in attendance at their meetings consent, the formalities may be reduced to a minimum.[3] No detailed notice need be given of the business that is to be conducted at director meetings, even where important or extraordinary business is to be conducted.[4] However, where a misleading notice is given or such a brief notice is provided that there is no real opportunity to attend, the meeting may be called into question, particularly where there is reason to suspect an improper motivation.[5]

§10.4 In *Carleton Condominium Corp. No. 347 v. Trendsetter Developments Ltd.*[6] it was found that the condominium corporation ("CC") was incorporated by Trendsetter as declarant. Trendsetter subsequently amalgamated with Thomas C. Assaly Corp. ("TCA") and continued under that name. TCA held more than 15 per cent of the junior mortgages of all units in the high-rise building to which CC related. The president of TCA owned 53 units in the building. The members of the board of directors of CC included the president of TCA and his son (the TCA directors), and three other unit owners (the independent directors). The manager of the building was a corporation affiliated with TCA. The independent directors, constituting the majority of the board of directors, approved a resolution that the management contract should not be renewed. After the president of TCA and his son walked out of the meeting in protest, it was decided to award the management contract to an independent corporation. The following day the TCA directors wrote to the independent directors complaining that the meeting had been conducted contrary to law, and that all business conducted at it was null and void. They further stated that TCA, as the holder of more than 15 per cent of the mortgages in the building, intended to call a special meeting of the unit owners with a view toward removing the independent directors from the board. The independent directors decided to assume control over the finances of CC. They wrote to its banker, notifying it of the dispute, and requesting that no withdrawals from its accounts be permitted without the express written authority

---

[2] *Compagnie de Mayville v. Whitley*, [1896] 1 Ch. 788 (C.A.).
[3] *Re Associated Color Laboratories Ltd.*, [1970] B.C.J. No. 89, 12 D.L.R. (3d) 338 at 351 (S.C.), per Macdonald J.
[4] *Compagnie de Mayville v. Whitley*, [1896] 1 Ch. 788 at 805-806 (C.A.), per Kay L.J.
[5] *Glace Bay Printing Co. v. Harrington* (1910), 45 N.S.R. 268 (T.D.).
[6] [1991] O.J. No. 1268, 4 O.R. (3d) 300 (Gen. Div.), rev'd on other ground [1992] O.J. No. 1767 (C.A.).

of the independent directors. At a subsequent meeting of the independent members of the board, the bank resolution giving the TCA directors and the TCA affiliated former manager control over the bank accounts of CC was revoked and new signing officers were designated. No notice of the meeting was given to the TCA directors or of the intention to pass these resolutions. The court was called upon to decide whether the change in the banking resolution was effective, given the lack of such notice. Justice Isaac held that it was. Since the TCA directors had both given notice, prior to the board meeting dealing with those matters, that they were intent upon removing the independent directors from the board, any notice of the independent directors' meeting would have been a mere formality. The failure to give notice was no more than a procedural irregularity and did not operate to invalidate the resolution.

§10.5 The individual directors of a corporation do not act alone (and, indeed, have no general authority to do so),[7] but instead act collectively[8] as a collegial body known as the board of directors — subject, of course, to the authority vested in the directors to delegate certain of their powers and duties to individual directors and committees of directors.[9] The requirement for collective action by the board is reflected in the requirement that the directors must transact their business by a resolution passed at a duly called meeting of the directors.[10] In acting in an official capacity, the board exercises its authority by way of a vote in favour (or against) a resolution that is properly placed before it. Subject to the specific disclosure requirements that apply with respect to conflict of interest, directors are not obliged to declare or record their reasons for supporting or opposing a given resolution. In *Newman v. Warren*,[11] Allen Ch. discussed the nature of the directors' decision making process:

> ... while "voters" (directors, or legislators or appellate judges or other collective deciders) may agree, according to the rules of their process, on the outcome, they need not agree on reasons. Each member may have a complex set of reasons that lead to his or her vote. Those reasons may or may not overlap with some reasons of other members who also voted in the same way, but they may differ in emphasis, in detail or they may in fact differ radically while leading to the same vote. It is of course not necessary that all directors (or appellate judges or members of a legislature etc) agree on the reasons for an outcome. It is only necessary that, according to the particular institutional rules applicable, at least some part of them do agree on the desirability of the outcome.

For most corporations and for most decisions, the part of the board that must agree on the action to be taken, comprises a majority of the board. The former

---

[7] *Kavanagh v. Norwich Union* (1900), 4 Que. P.R. 229 (C.A.); *Bell v. Milner* (1957), 21 W.W.R. 366 at 367 (B.C.S.C.), *per* Ruttan J.
[8] *Standard Construction Co. v. Crabb* (1914), 7 W.W.R. 719 (Sask. C.A.).
[9] Any such delegation of authority is at the pleasure of the board: *Molineux v. London, Birmingham & Manchester Insurance Co.*, [1902] 2 K.B. 589; *Allish v. Allied Engineering of B.C. Ltd.* (1957), 22 W.W.R. 641 (B.C.C.A.).
[10] *First Natchez Bank v. Coleman* (1903), 2 O.W.R. 358 at 360 (C.A.), *per* Moss C.J.O.; see also *Twin City Oil Co. v. Christie*, [1909] O.J. No. 199, 18 O.L.R. 324 (H.C.J.). See also *Hurely v. Ornsteen*, 311 Mass. 477, 42 N.E.2d 273 (S.J.C. Mass. 1942), *per* Dolan J.
[11] 684 A.2d 1239 (Del. Ch. 1996).

OBCA contained an express provision requiring the business of directors to be transacted at director meetings, subsection 132(2) of the Act providing:

> 132.(2) Subject to section 133 [Executive Committee] and subsection (1) of section 23 [signed directors' resolutions] no business of a corporation shall be transacted by its board of directors except at a meeting of directors at which a quorum of the board is present and, except where the corporation is a non-resident corporation, at which a majority of the directors present are resident Canadians.

Neither the present OBCA nor the CBCA contains an exact equivalent provision, although it is clearly implicit in the provisions of each Act that deal with the conduct of director business that such business will normally be transacted at meetings of directors. Nevertheless, as will be discussed below, both Acts permit a wide range of matters to be delegated to committees of directors or even to individual directors.[12] In the absence of such delegation, a majority of the board of directors acting outside a meeting have no authority to act,[13] although under subsection 129(1) of the OBCA,[14] a unanimous written resolution may be substituted for a meeting of the board. In addition, it may also be possible for absent directors to participate in meetings by way of telephone.[15]

§10.6 It may happen that the number of directors elected at a particular time will be less than a full complement of directors. While the articles of a corporation may provide that the board of directors shall consist of a specified number of directors, there is nothing improper in the corporation proceeding with a smaller board, provided a quorum of directors remains, even where that arrangement prevails for a period of several years.[16] Differing views have sometimes been expressed, however: for instance, in *Twin City Oil Co. v. Christie*[17] it was suggested that where there were insufficient directors the board was not validly constituted and therefore was incapable of acting.[18] The great impracticality of this second view hardly needs mention. Much of the uncertainty in this area is now removed by legislation, for subsection 119(8) of the OBCA[19] provides:

> 119.(8) If a meeting of shareholders fails to elect the number of directors required by the articles or by section 125 by reason of the disqualification, incapacity or death of one or more candidates, the directors elected at that meeting, if they constitute a quorum, may exercise all the powers of the directors of the corporation pending the holding of a meeting of shareholders in accordance with subsection 124(3).

---

[12] *Bell v. Milner* (1957), 21 W.W.R. 366, 8 D.L.R. (2d) 546 (B.C.S.C.); *Standard Construction Co. v. Crabb* (1914), 7 W.W.R. 719 (Sask. C.A.).
[13] *First Natchez Bank v. Coleman* (1903), 2 O.W.R. 358 (C.A.).
[14] Ontario *Business Corporations Act*, R.S.O. 1990, c. B.16 ("OBCA"), *Canada Business Corporations Act*, R.S.C. 1985, c. C-44 ("CBCA"). See CBCA, s. 117(1).
[15] OBCA, s. 126(13); CBCA, s. 114(9).
[16] *Mathers v. Mathers*, [1989] N.S.J. No. 77, 42 B.L.R. 228 (S.C.), aff'd [1989] N.S.J. No. 164, 90 N.S.R. (2d) 354, 230 A.P.R. 354 (C.A.).
[17] [1909] O.J. No. 199, 18 O.L.R. 324 at 326 (H.C.J.), *per* Meredith C.J.C.P.
[18] Where there is no quorum of directors, the most obvious measure to take would be to apply to the court for the appointment of a receiver and manager: *Young v. Alberta Petroleum Consolidated*, [1930] 1 W.W.R. 87 (C.A.).
[19] Compare CBCA, s. 106(7).

By its express terms subsection 119(8) applies only where the reason to elect the required number of directors was by reason of the disqualification, incapacity or death of one or more candidates. This begs the question of whether the board may continue to act in cases where the incomplete board results from other factors, such as a shortage of candidates. Clause 124(1)(*b*) of the OBCA prohibits the directors from appointing additional directors where a vacancy on the board results from "a failure to elect the number of directors required to be elected at any meeting of shareholders". Instead, subsection 124(3) provides:

> 124.(3) If there is not a quorum of directors, or if there has been a failure to elect the number of directors required by the articles or by section 125, the directors then in office shall forthwith call a special meeting of shareholders to fill the vacancy and, if they fail to call a meeting or if there are no directors then in office, the meeting may be called by any shareholder.

§10.7 Although no clear and certain answer can be given, the better view would seem to be that the rump board may assume office and commence management of the corporation so long as it has sufficient members to make up a quorum, for subsection 126(5) of the OBCA provides:

> 126.(5) Subject to the articles or by-laws, where there is a vacancy or vacancies in the board of directors, the remaining directors may exercise all the powers of the board so long as a quorum of the board remains in office.

It seems doubtful that the Legislature could have intended to exclude the application of subsection 126(5) in cases where subsection 119(8) applies, for the effect of so doing might well be to leave a corporation floating rudderless and without direction until the deficiency in directors is corrected. However, where the number of directors falls below a quorum (or where the number of directors elected never reaches a quorum) those directors who remain may not begin or continue to act until the shortage of directors has been rectified. A court has no jurisdiction to dispense with the requirement for a quorum.[20] When there is no quorum, the directors' management responsibilities would appear to revert to the shareholders of the corporation, acting in general meeting.[21] Alternatively, a shareholder, creditor or other interested party (such as a member of the rump board) may apply for the appointment of a receiver and manager to control the business and affairs of the corporation. Such a step would quite certainly seem to be the most suitable direction to follow where there are a large number of shareholders, so that direct management of the corporation by them is impractical.

§10.8 Ordinarily the decisions made by directors at their meetings are embodied in formal resolutions, that are voted upon by the directors present and then recorded in the minutes of the directors' meetings which are required under clause

---

[20] *Cairns v. Canadian Kennel Club*, [2004] A.J. No. 1136, 2 B.L.R. (4th) 210 (Q.B.).
[21] *Barron v. Potter*, [1914] 1 Ch. 895 at 903, *per* Warrington J.; *Isle of Wight Rlwy. Co. v. Tahourdin* (1883), 25 Ch. D. 320 at 333 (C.A.), *per* Cotton L.J.; *Foster v. Foster*, [1916] 1 Ch. 532 at 551, *per* Peterson J.; see also *Knight's Case* (1867), L.R. 2 Ch. 321 (C.A.); *Re Great Northern Salt Co.* (1890), 44 Ch. D. 472 at 483, *per* Sterling J.; *Re Fireproof Doors Ltd.*, [1916] 2 Ch. 142 at 149, *per* Astbury J.; *Alexander Ward & Co. v. Samyang Navigation Co. Ltd.*, [1975] 1 W.L.R. 673.

140(2)(*b*) of the OBCA. However, an entry of a resolution in the minute book of a corporation is not essential in order to provide the approval of a particular action by the directors.[22] The substance of the directors' decision may be proved by extrinsic evidence.[23]

(ii) Telephone and Similar Meetings

§10.9 As indicated above, the requirement that the business of the directors be transacted at a directors' meeting has been loosened somewhat in recent years. Advances in communications technology now offer corporations a range of options unheard of even 20 years ago. Both the OBCA and the CBCA permit corporations to take advantage of these new advances at least to an extent, subsection 126(13) of the OBCA providing:

> 126.(13) Unless the by-laws otherwise provide, if all the directors of a corporation present at or participating in the meeting consent, a meeting of directors or of a committee of directors may be held by means of such telephone, electronic or other communication facilities as permit all persons participating in the meeting to communicate with each other simultaneously and instantaneously, and a director participating in such a meeting by such means is deemed for the purposes of this Act to be present at that meeting.

Until the 2001 amendments, subsection 114(9) of the CBCA, which is the corresponding provision, provided:

> 114.(9) Subject to the by-laws, a director may, if all the directors of the corporation consent, participate in a meeting of directors or of a committee of directors by means of such telephone or other communications facilities as permit all persons participating in the meeting to hear each other, and a director participating in such a meeting by such means is deemed for the purposes of this Act to be present at that meeting.

The 2001 amended language reads (changes as shown):

> 114.(9) Subject to the by-laws, a director may, <u>in accordance with the regulations, if any,</u> and if all the directors of the corporation consent, participate in a meeting of directors or of a committee of directors <u>by means of a telephonic, electronic or other communication facility that permits all participants to communicate adequately with each other during the meeting.</u> A director participating in such a meeting by such means is deemed for the purposes of this Act to be present at that meeting.

While nearly all corporations now provide in their by-laws for the holding of telephone meetings, both the OBCA and the CBCA would seem to allow much more flexibility than merely authorizing the conduct of a meeting by telephone. The former CBCA requirement that all persons be able to hear each other has

---

[22] *Wilson v. Woollatt*, [1928] O.J. No. 82, 62 O.L.R. 620 at 626-27 (C.A.), *per* Masten J.A., aff'd [1929] S.C.R. 483.

[23] *North West Battery Ltd. v. Hargrave* (1913), 5 W.W.R. 1002, 15 D.L.R. 193 at 203 (Man. K.B.), *per* Curran J. Note, however, s. 139(3) of the OBCA which makes the formal records of the corporation required under the Act "admissible in evidence as proof, in the absence of evidence to the contrary, of all facts stated therein".

been repealed. The only requirement under the current approach is that the persons must be able to communicate with each other "simultaneously and instantaneously" under the OBCA, and "adequately" under the CBCA. From this it would follow that a meeting might be held through the medium of a computer chat service through which written messages can be conveyed in such a manner, as well as by voice communication. One difference between subsection 126(13) of the OBCA and subsection 114(9) of the CBCA is that under the former, telephone and similar meetings may be held unless the by-laws otherwise provide, whereas under the latter, the right to hold a telephone meeting is said to be "subject to the by-laws". This wording may be interpreted by the cautious as meaning that such meetings may be held only where expressly permitted under the by-laws.[24] It is clear that under the OBCA, the directors will be presumed to be entitled to hold telephone meetings, unless the by-laws otherwise provide.

§10.10 It is unfortunate that both the CBCA and the OBCA provisions require "all directors" to consent to the holding of a meeting by telephone, rather than providing that such a meeting will be valid and effectual unless one or more of the directors specifically objects. The practical result of the requirement for consent is that a lawyer who is asked to provide an opinion as to whether such a meeting has been duly held must search for some authorization somewhere for use of a telephone meeting. The normal procedure is for directors to sign a blanket consent to telephone and similar meetings at the time when they become directors. Locating those consents may be difficult in the case of a corporation that has frequent changes in the membership of its board.

(iii) Resolutions in Lieu of Meetings

§10.11 The use of a signed resolution in lieu of an actual meeting was contemplated in the old Act, and remains a feature of the present law. Like the concept of the telephone meeting, the signed resolution is an outgrowth of the common law rather than a statutory innovation. The present law is set out in section 129 of the OBCA,[25] and provides:

> 129.(1) A resolution in writing, signed by all the directors entitled to vote on that resolution at a meeting of directors or a committee of directors, is as valid as if it had been passed at a meeting of directors or a committee of directors.
>
> (2) A copy of every resolution passed under subsection (1) shall be kept with the minutes of the proceedings of the directors or committee of directors.

Unless all directors agree to sign (and actually do sign) the resolution, it will fail to meet the requirements of the section, and consequently a directors' meeting must be held. The rationale for the requirement is that a dissident shareholder (who will presumably refuse to sign) has the opportunity at a meeting to present his or her case to the other directors. No such chance is afforded if the majority

---

[24] See, generally, *Re Associated Color Laboratories Ltd.*, [1970] B.C.J. No. 89, 12 D.L.R. (3d) 338 at 352 (S.C.), *per* Macdonald J.
[25] CBCA, s. 117.

simply signs a written resolution. No doubt there is a certain validity in this assumption, but the requirement for unanimous consent presents obvious problems where, for some reason unrelated to the matter under consideration, a single director is not available to sign a resolution.

(iv) Minutes of Director Meetings

§10.12 Clause 140(2)(*b*) of the OBCA requires each corporation under that Act to prepare and maintain "records containing minutes of meetings and resolutions of the directors and any committee thereof". Subsection 20(2) of the CBCA is to a similar effect. While accounting records need be retained by a corporation for a period of only six years from the end of each respective fiscal period, the record of directors meetings and resolutions is perpetual throughout the life of the corporation. Similar records must be prepared and maintained with respect to shareholder meetings and resolutions. Both director and shareholder minutes are open to inspection by any director of the corporation,[26] and also by the auditor of the corporation. Shareholders and creditors are entitled to access the shareholder minutes and resolutions during the usual business hours of the corporation,[27] but are not entitled to access the director minutes and resolutions. Ordinarily, these records must be kept at the registered office of the corporation.[28]

§10.13 In the course of furnishing a legal opinion, it is customary to review the minutes of shareholder and director meetings to confirm that all requisite steps have been taken throughout the history of the corporation so as to bring it to the point at which it now stands (*e.g.*, that the corporation was properly organized after incorporation, that its shares were properly issued, that all share transfers have been properly recorded and where required approved, that all required meetings have been held or unanimous resolutions obtained in their place, that all directors have been properly elected or appointed, that the auditors have been duly appointed by the shareholders, that all by-laws have been properly passed, that all minutes have been duly approved and are confirmed by the required signatures, that all resolutions in lieu of meetings have been signed by all persons required to sign them — *i.e.*, all directors or shareholders, as the case may be). Where errors, omissions or other deficiencies are detected in the minutes, the solicitor conducting the review attempts to remedy them as best he or she may.

§10.14 The correction of errors and deficiencies in such records is known as "Cooperization". In some cases, complete remedy is possible, at least if one assumes that such corrections may be made on a retroactive basis: for instance, where the signature of a person is required, that signature may be readily obtained if the individual concerned is still associated with the corporation. In other cases, however, it is impossible to correct the error, omission or other deficiency, because some necessary person is dead or otherwise unavailable, or because of some other insurmountable problem. Quite often in such cases, a *pro*

---

[26] OBCA, s. 144(1); CBCA, s. 20(4).
[27] OBCA, s. 145(1); CBCA, s. 20(1).
[28] OBCA, s. 144(1); CBCA, s. 20(1).

forma paper trail will be created so as to provide a record of the occurrence of the necessary "events" that would validate the present situation, if one assumes that they ever took place. For instance, if the transfer of shares by past owners to the current owners in a private company was not approved in the manner specified under the articles, "Cooperized" directors' minutes will be created to validate the current share ownership. The authority for adopting this approach lies in the related common law maxims *omnia præsumuntur rite et solemniter esse acta donec probetur in contrarium* (*i.e.*, all things are presumed to have been right and duly performed until the contrary is proved) and *omnia præsumuntur legitime facta donec probetur in contrarium* (*i.e.*, all things are presumed to be lawfully done until the contrary is proved). Unless there is actual evidence that a required step was not taken, it may be assumed that the step was taken. Thus the Cooperization of the minutes does no more than formally record the assumption that a necessary step was taken.[29] It cannot, obviously, remedy a problem that arises because some necessary event clearly could never have occurred on the basis of the facts that are known. It is a general principle of corporate law that the directors of a corporation are equal, at least in the absence of express language in the articles or a unanimous shareholder agreement — and perhaps not even then. It is certain that the position of one or a class of director may not be downgraded (or upgraded) by unilateral board action.[30] The general principle of equality does not mean that all directors must be paid the same, and that all must exercise the same offices in the day-to-day administration of the corporation. However, the incumbent directors of a corporation may not employ devices to deprive newly elected directors of their voting power or to deprive them of the capacity to exercise that power when necessary.[31]

(v) Board Confidentiality

§10.15 Generally, the proceedings of the board of directors of a corporation are private, and the expectation is that the directors will maintain the confidentiality of the matters discussed at such meetings (or that otherwise come to their notice by virtue of their position as directors). Indeed, in very many cases, the disclosure of the private deliberations of the board could be highly prejudicial both to the corporation and to those who are concerned in it as shareholders, creditors and other stakeholders. However, a moment's consideration is sufficient to convince one that there are many cases in which disclosure of information by one or more directors is not only appropriate, but necessary to the proper governance of the corporation. The scope of the duty of confidentiality of director meetings was considered by the New South Wales court of Appeal in *NRMA v. Stewart Geeson*,[32] In that case Ipp A.J.A. stated that

---

[29] Compliance with a statutory formality may be presumed after a lengthy lapse in time: *Aukland Gas Co. v. Point Chevalier Road Board* (1909), 29 N.Z.L.R. 417; *Clippens Oil Co. v. Edinburgh & District Water Trustees*, [1904] A.C. 64; *Waiakei Ltd. v. Cleave*, [1925] N.Z.L.R. 624.
[30] *Carmody v. Toll Brothers, Inc.*, 723 A.2d 1180 at 1191 (Del. Ch. 1998), but *cf. CALPERS v. Cooper*, [2005] Del. Ch. LEXIS 54.
[31] See, generally, *Schnell v. Chris-Craft Indus., Inc.*, 285 A. (2d) 437 (Del. Ch. 1971).
[32] [2001] N.S.W.C.A. 343.

The mere fact that particular information is of a confidential character does not impose an obligation of absolute confidentiality on every person in possession of it. ... Each case depends on its own circumstances and in each case there has to be an enquiry into the extent and limits of the obligation of confidentiality that may be imposed on an individual in regard to particular pieces of confidential information in his or her possession.

The court clearly favoured disclosure of information to those who have a legitimate and serious interest in learning such information, as opposed to a mere idle curiosity.

B. GENERAL MANAGERIAL RIGHTS OF DIRECTORS

§10.16 Between them, the board of directors and the shareholders exercise all of the powers of the corporation. The directors themselves are seen to possess all authority which is required to enable them to manage the corporation and to enable it to carry out its objects, save to the extent that any specific authority is reserved to the shareholders under the Act, articles or by-laws of a corporation, or under a unanimous shareholder agreement. It follows that as a general rule the directors of a corporation may raise funds through the issue of authorized capital and by borrowing on a secured or unsecured basis, sell or retain part or the whole of the company's assets, purchase or otherwise acquire additional assets, declare and pay dividends, hire and dismiss employees and officers and fix the remuneration thereof, enter into contracts, and initiate and settle legal proceedings. The foregoing list is merely illustrative of the powers of the board.

(i) Sterilized Board of Directors

§10.17 The common law did not permit the shareholders of a corporation to create a sterilized board of directors.[33] So, for instance, the shareholders of a corporation could not structure the decision-making process within the corporation, so that the directors were required to consult with the shareholders before exercising any (or all) of their authority, or were required to act in accordance with such direction as the shareholders might give.[34] *A fortiori*, the shareholders could not reserve to themselves all decision making power so that they directly assumed responsibility for the management of the corporation. Under the unanimous shareholder agreement provisions of the OBCA and the CBCA, such measures now appears to be possible. Even in the absence of unanimity, two or more shareholders may lawfully combine their voting power with respect to the election of directors to secure the election of directors of a given disposition, without in any way breaching the law.[35] Thus in *Manson v. Curtis*, it was said:[36]

---

[33] *Manson v. Curtis*, 223 N.Y. 313 at 323 (1918), *per* Collin J.
[34] *Kaplan v. Block*, 183 Va. 327 at 332, 31 S.E. 2d 893 at 895 (1944).
[35] *McQuade v. Stoneham*, 230 A.D. 57; 242 N.Y.S. 548 (1930); *Venner v. Chicago City R. Co.*, 236 Ill. 349, 86 N.E. 266 (1908): an agreement among shareholders to elect the directors of the corporation so as to secure the management of its property, to ballot among themselves for directors and officers if they could not agree, to cast their vote as a unit as the majority should decide so as to control the election, and not to buy or sell stock except for their joint benefit, is not dishonest, in violation of the rights of others or in contravention of public policy.
[36] 223 N.Y. 313, 119 N.E. 559 (1918).

It is not illegal or against public policy for two or more stockholders owning the majority of the shares of stock to unite upon a course of corporate policy or action, or upon the officers whom they will elect. An ordinary agreement, among a minority in number, but a majority in shares, for the purpose of obtaining control of the corporation by the election of particular persons as directors is not illegal. Shareholders have the right to combine their interests and voting powers to secure such control of the corporation and the adoption of and adhesion by it to a specific policy and course of business. Agreements upon a sufficient consideration between them, of such intendment and effect, are valid and binding, if they do not contravene any express charter or statutory provision or contemplate any fraud, oppression or wrong against other stockholders or other illegal object.

The critical restrictions on this power are that the shareholders cannot use their combined power to defraud the corporation, or to oppress or unfairly prejudice the rights of others concerned in the corporation, so as to give rise to a remedy under sections 248 of the OBCA and 241 of the CBCA. Where such an agreement is directed towards some lawful concern of the shareholders concerned, and works no fraud upon others and violates no statute or recognized public policy "the propriety of the object validates the means".[37] So in *Trefethen v. Amazeen*,[38] it was said with respect to a voting trust arrangement:

> The validity of a contract between stockholders is to be determined by the effects of its provisions. In *Bowditch v. Jackson Company*,[39] this Court upheld a stockholders' agreement for a voting trust applying as a test the conclusions that there was no wrong to the corporation, no special benefit to the parties to the contract and no turning over of management to strangers. The Court did not leave out of consideration other stockholders individually and creditors. ... If we apply the above suggested tests to this agreement, it is clear that it is valid. Holden received no special benefit; his only benefit was the general one of all stockholders derived from a corporation with greater working capital. There was no injury to corporation, stockholders or creditors from the addition of new funds. The only detriment was to the parties to the contract and such as they themselves contemplated in the making of it, namely, the paying out of money by two of the parties and the loss of voting rights agreed to by the third party. There was no transfer of control of corporate management, whether for good or ill, to outsiders. The contract merely called for less voting power on the part of an assenting stockholder and relatively greater voting power on the part of other stockholders for a definite period. The effect of this upon other interests no one can say. It is not in violation of any rule or principle of law nor contrary to public policy for stockholders who own a majority of the stock of a corporation to cause its affairs to be managed in such a way as they may think best calculated to further the ends of the corporation. ... A stockholders' agreement reasonably intended to be beneficial to a corporation and injurious to no one save for the contemplated detriment to the contracting parties is valid. Violation of the present agreement by the defendant trustee would cause irreparable injury to the plaintiff and he is without adequate remedy at law.

§10.18 In contrast, the directors are not permitted to enter into a contract that divests them of their statutory responsibilities. The directors are subject to a

---

[37] *Cone v. Russell & Mason*, 48 N.J. Eq. 208, 21 A. 847.
[38] (1944), 93 N.H. 110, 36 A.2d 266.
[39] (1912), 76 N.H. 351, 82 A. 1014.

personal duty to act for the corporation according to their best judgment, and in so doing they cannot be controlled in the reasonable exercise and performance of such duty. Directors may not agree to exercise their official duties for the benefit of any individual or interest other than the corporation itself, and an agreement by which individual directors, or the entire board, abdicate or bargain away in advance the judgment which the law contemplates they shall exercise over the affairs of the corporation is contrary to public policy and void.[40] While nominee directors, who are selected by a single shareholder and who may be presumed to represent the interest of that shareholder in the corporation, are a perfectly acceptable feature of corporate life (provided that the nominee continues to exercise an independent judgment in accordance with the requirements of the OBCA and CBCA), "dummy" directors (who simply fill out empty places on the board, and who do not participate in the supervision of the corporation's management) are not an acceptable tool for corporate governance.

§10.19 In one leading American authority from the 1950s, it was said:

> A corporation is a creature of the Legislature, and statutes and applicable law prevail over private agreements between stockholders The property of a corporation belongs to the stockholders, but the possession and management thereof is in the hands of the directors. An agreement purporting to control the actions of directors after they are elected, in handling the ordinary business of the corporation, is ordinarily void. ... The law imposes the business management of the corporation on its directors, who represent all the stockholders and creditors, and they cannot enter into agreements among themselves or with stockholders by which they purport to abdicate their independent judgment. Stockholders are powerless in this state to alter or reduce the voting power of any share of stock. As a general rule, stockholders cannot act in relation to the ordinary business of the corporation, nor control the judgment of directors in the performance of their duties.[41]

In broad terms, this passage (as edited) remains good law, but the law has moved on apace since 1954. It is, as noted above, qualified in its application within Canada by the statutory concept of the unanimous shareholder agreement. Moreover, it is clearly acceptable for the articles or by-laws of an OBCA or CBCA corporation to provide that a board decision of a particular type will require more than approval by a bare majority.

(ii) Overview of Managerial Powers

§10.20 As the foregoing makes clear, at one time, the directors of a corporation, and only the directors, were seen to possess the general authority to manage the corporation. The shareholders of the corporation had no authority to instruct the directors of the corporation concerning its management, and indeed were not allowed to interfere in matters assigned by law to the control of the directors.[42] The authority and duty of the directors to manage the corporation was considered to be so pervasive that the directors could not restrict it by entering into any

---

[40] *Ezekiel Ray v. Homewood Hospital, Inc.*, 223 Minn. 440, 27 N.W.2d 409 (S.C. Minn. 1947).
[41] *E.K. Buck Retail Stores v. Harkert*, 157 Neb. 867, 62 N.W.2d 288 (S.C. Neb. 1954).
[42] *Grundt v. Great Boulder Proprietary Mines Ltd.*, [1948] Ch. 145 at 158-59 (C.A.), *per* Cohen L.J.

form of agreement among themselves. By structuring an enterprise as a corporation, the shareholders were seen to waive any right to restrain their directors.[43] Consequently, unless the interference with the discretion of the board was insignificant, agreements among shareholders purporting to govern the management of the corporation were seen to sterilize the board, and so prevent it from exercising its statutory duty of management. On this basis they were void as being an improper interference with the directors' responsibility to manage. For instance, in *Atlas Development Co. v. Calof*[44] the plaintiffs entered into an agreement with the defendant which provided that a decision at a meeting of shareholders or directors had to be unanimous. Even this relatively innocuous provision was held to be improper. The court stated that the directors of a corporation had a duty to decide matters affecting the welfare of the corporation in accordance with their best judgment, and the agreement rendered this impossible. The unanimous shareholder provisions of the OBCA[45] and the CBCA,[46] together with the expanded statutory derivative action procedure, the oppression remedy, the aggressive application of the fiduciary concept, and growing concerns about corporate governance (particularly as reflected in securities laws) significantly alter this aspect of the law. Nevertheless, the statutory authority and duty of the directors to manage the corporation remains a strong undercurrent. Except as provided by statute, the law views the directors and the directors alone[47] as being vested with the authority and duty to manage the corporation.[48]

§10.21 It follows that in the ordinary case, the day-to-day management of the corporation is not subject to review by the courts.[49] So in *Coutu v. San Jose Mines Ltd.* Pitfield J. stated.

> The reality of corporate existence is that those who choose to become shareholders of a company are permitted to participate in its governance by electing a board of directors at a duly constituted meeting of those entitled to elect directors. Once elected, the board is required to act in the interests of the company as a whole and not in the interests of any particular shareholder or group of shareholders. The fact is that shareholders do not always get along but a majority of shareholders have a right to make decisions with which the minority does not agree. The fact of such disagreements without more will not prompt the court to exercise its discretion to order the winding up and dissolution of a company.[50]

It is only where the directors overstep the reasonable bounds upon their authority that the court will act. So Pitfield J. continued:

---

[43] *Abercrombie v. Davies*, 35 Del. Ch., 123 A.2d 893, rev'd on other grounds 130 A.2d 338 (Del. S.C. 1957).
[44] (1963), 41 W.W.R. 575 (Man. Q.B.).
[45] OBCA, s. 108.
[46] CBCA, s. 146.
[47] *John Shaw & Sons (Salford) Ltd. v. Shaw*, [1935] 2 K.B. 113 at 134 (C.A.), *per* Greer L.J.
[48] See, generally, *Automatic Self-Cleansing Filter Syndicate Co. v. Cuninghame*, [1906] 2 Ch. 34.
[49] Lord Davey in *Burland v. Earle*, [1902] A.C. 83 at 93 (P.C.).
[50] [2005] B.C.J. No. 675, 3 B.L.R. (4th) 22 at 30 (S.C.), supp. reasons [2005] B.C.J. No. 2214 (S.C.).

At the same time, a board must act in a manner which is not oppressive of, or prejudicial to, the rights of any shareholder or group of shareholders. Adequate provision is made in the *Business Corporations Act* to forestall or correct that which is truly oppressive or prejudicial conduct insofar as any particular shareholder or group of shareholders is concerned. A wide range of options is available to the court in that regard, perhaps the most draconian of which is an order compelling the winding up and dissolution of the company.

Thus in general, the members of a corporation are bound by its constitution and cannot complain concerning decisions made by the directors as a governing body within the general mandate of the corporate constitution.[51] The directors are not servants to obey directions given by the shareholders as individuals; they are not agents appointed by and bound to serve the shareholders as their principals.[52] Where directors intend to do something that they honestly believe to be for the benefit of the corporation, the courts will not restrain them because a majority of shareholders or a single shareholder holding a majority of the shares disagrees with the step that the directors propose to take.[53]

§10.22 One rationale for the degree of respect accorded to the internal management mechanisms of the corporation in general and to the directors in particular is the desire to prevent excessive resort to the courts every time there is a dispute within the corporation as to the proper course to follow. The directors are held bound to discharge their duties of care, loyalty and good faith to the corporation, but they are not liable for simple errors of business judgment that they may make in the management of the corporation. Nor will the courts assist the shareholders of a corporation in restraining the directors from acting against what the directors considered to be in the best interests of the corporation.[54] At one time, the courts adhered firmly to the rule that they would not interfere with the internal management of a corporation nor with the actions of directors who acted within their powers, save in two limited situations: first, where the directors were defrauding the corporation generally or some of its shareholders; second, where the directors were acting beyond their powers or causing the corporation to exceed its powers.[55] Under the old case law, the courts took the view that to justify interference the facts had to indicate a clear or seriously suspected injustice or damage, calling for the court's intervention.[56] While substantial inroads have now been made into this rule by statute, it remains an influential undercurrent of the law. In the absence of evidence to the contrary, the directors of a corporation are presumed to be acting on an informed basis, in good faith and with a view to the best interests of the corporation.[57] The onus of proof lies on the

---

[51] *Howard Smith Ltd. v. Ampol Petroleum Ltd.*, [1974] A.C. 821 at 837 (P.C.), per Lord Wilberforce. See also *Automatic Self-Cleansing Filter Syndicate Co. v. Cuninghame*, [1906] 2 Ch. 34; *Gramophone & Typewriter Ltd. v. Stanley*, [1908] 2 K.B. 89 at 105-106 (C.A.), per Buckley L.J.
[52] *Kuwait Asia Bank E.C. v. National Mutual Life Nominees*, [1991] 1 A.C. 187 at 222 (P.C.).
[53] *Ashburton Oil N.L. v. Alpha Minerals N.L.* (1971), 123 C.L.R. 614 (H.C. Aust.); *Teck Corp. v. Millar*, [1972] B.C.J. No. 566, 33 D.L.R. (3d) 288, [1973] 2 W.W.R. 385 (S.C.).
[54] See, for instance, *Schlensky v. Wrigley*, 95 Ill.App.2d 173, 237 N.E.2d 776 (App. Ct. Ill. 1968).
[55] See, for instance, *Pylypchuk v. Dell Hotel Ltd.* (1958), 15 D.L.R. (2d) 589 (B.C.S.C.).
[56] *White v. Brompton Pulp & Papers Co.*, [1947] Que. S.C. 124, per Bertand J.
[57] *Aronson v. Lewis*, 473 A.2d 805 (S.C. Del. 1984), per Moore J.

person who denies that such is the case. By extension, in the ordinary case the court will not review or interfere with the business decisions that the directors make, and will do so only when it is beyond question that the directors are not acting in a commercially prudent manner. The reasonableness of the decisions made by directors in the exercise of their business judgment is assessed on the basis of the facts as known to the directors at the time when those decisions were made.[58]

§10.23 The courts are particularly unwilling to take sides in what is clearly a dispute between the majority and minority within a corporation as to how its business or affairs should be conducted. In one of the earliest works to touch upon corporate law theory, Blackstone[59] stated it is an inherent aspect of corporate life that the majority within a corporation has the power to bind the minority. The courts have consistently adhered to this position. They are loath to invite disgruntled minorities to seek their protection every time a dispute arises within the corporation. Instead, those who are dissatisfied with the conduct of the corporation are obliged to seek redress within the internal management mechanisms of the corporation — as, for instance, by voting for a change on the board of directors.[60]

§10.24 It is the duty and right of the board of directors of a corporation to manage its business and affairs,[61] and the court will not lightly interfere with the board in the performance of that duty or the exercise of that right. So broad is their power that the directors may even make an assignment of the corporation into bankruptcy[62] or a general assignment for the benefit of creditors[63] without the consent of the shareholders, even though the practical effect of any such step is to bring to an end the life of the corporation as a functioning entity. However, these broad statements of general principle must be qualified in certain respects. The authority of the directors to manage the corporation may be limited by or under the statute under which a corporation is incorporated or continued, or by the articles or by-laws of the corporation or a unanimous shareholder agreement relating to the corporation, the provisions of which curtail the directors' *prima facie* authority to exercise all powers of the corporation.[64] Such limitations may be express or implicit. For instance, it is implicit under the OBCA and the CBCA that the directors have no power to petition for the winding up of a solvent corporation,[65] since such a step does not constitute the management of the corporation as an ongoing concern, but instead the initiation of the process of

---

[58] *Litwin v. Allen*, 25 N.Y.S.2d 687 (S.C.N.Y. 1940), *per* Shientag J.
[59] 1 *Commentaries on the Laws of England*, reprint ed. (Chicago: University of Chicago Press, 1979), 464.
[60] *La Compagnie de Mayville v. Whitley*, [1896] 1 Ch. 788 at 804 (C.A.), *per* Kay L.J.
[61] OBCA, s. 115(1); CBCA, s. 102(1).
[62] *Re Olympia Co.* (1915), 9 W.W.R. 875 (Man. C.A.).
[63] *Hovey v. Whiting* (1887), 14 S.C.R. 515, aff'g [1886] O.J. No. 100, 13 O.A.R. 7 (C.A.).
[64] *Mid-West Collieries, Ltd. v. McEwen*, [1924] 2 W.W.R. 1027 (Alta. C.A.), aff'd [1925] S.C.R. 326.
[65] *Re Galway & Salthill Tramways Co.*, [1918] I.R. 62; *Re Emmadart Ltd.*, [1979] Ch. 540 at 547, *per* Brightman J., but note OBCA, s. 208(1).

dissolving the corporation. In contrast, where the corporation is insolvent, its continued operation may place the directors at personal risk.

§10.25 Despite the basic premise of director managerial authority, by taking the appropriate steps, the shareholders may limit and perhaps even completely extinguish that authority. The shareholders of a corporation have a clear power under both the OBCA and the CBCA to amend the articles and by-laws of the corporation or to enter into a unanimous shareholder agreement. Where such an amendment is made or is brought into being, it will bind the directors of the corporation.[66] But until such a step is taken, responsibility for the management of the business and affairs of the corporation remains with the directors, and they are not bound to follow the dictates of shareholders, even if embodied in a formal shareholder resolution.[67] A person who controls the shares in a company may not, merely by reason of that fact, assume to act on behalf of the corporation.[68]

(iii) Residual Powers after Receivership, etc.

§10.26 So pervasive and persistent are the directors' powers and authority, that they will even survive the placing of the corporation into receivership — the receivership limiting those powers and authorities only to the extent that they are inconsistent with the powers and rights conferred on the receiver. The rights of the receiver and manager must, of course, be respected; and so it has been said:

> ... [W]here as here a receiver and manager is appointed over the whole of the undertaking, the directors will for most practical purposes become *functus officio*. ... This appointment of a receiver and manager over the assets and business of a company does not dissolve or annihilate the company, any more than the taking possession by the mortgagee of the fee simple of land let to tenants annihilates the mortgagor. Both continue to exist; but it entirely supersedes the company in the conduct of its business, deprives it of all powers to enter into contracts in relation to that business, or to sell, pledge or otherwise dispose of the property put into the possession, or under the control of the receiver and manager. Its powers in this respect are entirely in abeyance.[69]

Nevertheless, the directors retain a residual authority over the corporation to the extent that the authority does not conflict with the terms of the receivership. The reason is that the receivership applies with respect to the assets and undertaking of the corporation; it does not extend to the general management of the corporation.[70]

---

[66] OBCA, s. 108; CBCA, s. 146. As to the position at common law, see *Salmon v. Quin & Axtens Ltd.*, [1909] 1 Ch. 311 (C.A.).

[67] *Macson Development Co. v. Gordon* (1959), 19 D.L.R. (2d) 465 (N.S.S.C.). However, a unanimous written resolution that is actually signed by all shareholders will be binding as a unanimous shareholder agreement. In addition, consideration must be given to the shareholders' proposal rights under s. 99 of the OBCA and s. 137 of the CBCA.

[68] *Royal Bank v. Port Royal Pulp & Paper Co.*, [1937] 4 D.L.R. 254 (N.B.C.A.), rev'd [1939] S.C.R. 186, rev'd [1941] 4 D.L.R. 1 (P.C.).

[69] *Paramount Acceptance Co. v. Souster*, [1981] 2 N.Z.L.R. 38 at 42 (C.A.), *per* Davidson C.J.; see also *Moss Steamship Co. v. Whinney*, [1912] A.C. 254 at 263 (H.L.), *per* Lord Atkinson.

[70] *Golden West Restaurants Ltd. v. CIBC*, [1989] S.J. No. 284, [1989] 5 W.W.R. 471, 75 C.B.R. (N.S.) 170 (Q.B.), aff'd [1990] S.J. No. 31, 81 Sask. R. 312, [1990] 3 W.W.R. 287 (C.A.).

The directors have a general and continuing responsibility to the corporation, as the representative of those who stand behind it, from the shareholders to its creditors, to manage the corporation prudently.[71] As the institution or defence of proceedings by the directors does not stultify the receivership,[72] the directors may retain and instruct counsel on behalf of the corporation to initiate proceedings against a creditor who has appointed a receiver under an instrument,[73] and against the receiver-manager so appointed,[74] provided in all cases that the corporation is given an adequate indemnity against costs.[75] These residual rights of the directors reflect their continuing obligation to the shareholders and other stakeholders of the corporation to manage the corporation prudently and to the fullest extent of their power.[76] If the receiver alone was entitled to defend the interests of the corporation in such a case, the corporation would be substantially deprived of its ability to retain counsel of its own choosing and effectively dispute matters relating to the agreement under or by virtue of which the receiver-manager is appointed.[77]

§10.27 However, if a liquidator is appointed to wind up the corporation, the effect is not simply to transfer control over the corporation's assets and under-taking to the liquidator. The liquidator supplants the directors, and so upon the liquidator's appointment, the directors cease to hold office.[78] Therefore, where proceedings are commenced to wind up the corporation, the power of instituting actions devolves upon the liquidator, and the directors are fully *functus officio*.[79] This is made clear in clause 223(1)(*a*) of the OBCA which provides that a liquidator may bring or defend any action, suit or prosecution or other legal proceedings, civil or criminal,

---

[71] *Société Générale (Canada) v. 743823 Ontario Ltd.*, [1989] O.J. No. 2365, 41 C.P.C. (2d) 286 (H.C.J.). In *Strachan v. MacCosham Administrative Services Ltd.*, [1986] A.J. No. 556, 46 Alta. L.R. (2d) 146 (Q.B.), it was held that where the debenture gives the receiver control over the conduct of actions, the directors have no authority to bring the action. This seems dubious, since any such contract would seem to constitute improper delegation by the directors of their managerial responsibility. The receiver may have control over the assets of the corporation (which may include its right of action), but it would be absurd to construe that title as extending to actions against the receiver and creditor as well. The receiver does not have the power to interpret or in any manner concern himself with the contract made between the corporation and the creditor: *Toronto Dominion Bank v. Fortin*, [1978] 2 W.W.R. 761 (B.C.S.C.).

[72] *First Investors Corp. v. Prince Royal Inn Ltd.*, [1988] A.J. No. 521, 60 Alta. L.R. (2d) 269, 69 C.B.R. (N.S.) 50 (C.A.).

[73] As to whether security for costs should be ordered where the principals behind an insolvent corporation are funding ongoing litigation, see: *ABI Biotechnology Inc. v. Apotex Inc.*, [2000] M.J. No. 14, 94 A.C.W.S. (3d) 242 (C.A.). See also *Eastern Canada Coal Gas Venture Ltd. v. Cape Breton Development Corp.*, [2002] N.S.J. No. 465 (S.C.).

[74] *Golden West Restaurants Ltd. v. CIBC*, [1989] S.J. No. 284, [1989] 5 W.W.R. 471, 75 C.B.R. (N.S.) 170 (Q.B.), aff'd [1990] S.J. No. 31, 81 Sask. R. 312, [1990] 3 W.W.R. 287 (C.A.).

[75] *Newhart Developments Ltd. v. Co-operative Commercial Bank Ltd.*, [1978] Q.B. 814 at 819.

[76] *Société Général (Canada) v. 743823 Ontario Ltd.*, [1989] O.J. No. 2365, 41 C.P.C. (2d) 286 (H.C.J.). See also *Strachan v. MacCosham Administrative Services Ltd.*, [1986] A.J. No. 556, 46 Alta. L.R. (2d) 146, 73 A.R. 9 (Q.B.).

[77] *First Investors Corp. v. Prince Royal Inn Ltd.*, [1988] A.J. No. 521, 60 Alta. L.R. (2d) 269 (C.A.); *Toronto Dominion Bank v. Fortin*, [1978] 2 W.W.R. 761 (B.C.S.C.).

[78] See, generally, *Leclerc v. Beaulieu* (1924), 63 Que. S.C. 90.

[79] See, generally, *Carle v. Ranger*, [1961] Que. Q.B. 405 (C.A.).

in the name of the corporation.[80] It follows that if the directors wish to dispute a winding-up proceeding they must do so before the liquidator is appointed.

§10.28 The bankruptcy of a corporation does not remove the directors from office, although the effect of the appointment of a trustee is to suspend the control of the directors over the assets of the corporation.[81] From the date of the receiving order or assignment, the directors have no authority to interfere with the bankruptcy administration, save as contemplated by the proposal provisions of the *Bankruptcy and Insolvency Act* and the arrangement provisions of the *Companies' Creditors Arrangement Act*.

(iv) Specific Rights Enabling Directors to Carry out Duties

§10.29 It is the statutory responsibility of directors as a collective (*i.e.*, as the board) to manage[82] or to supervise the management of the business and affairs of the corporation,[83] and thus it follows that every director is vested with the rights that are necessary to enable each director to carry out that responsibility.[84] For instance, at common law,[85] a director is entitled to inspect all of the documents of a corporation, both at meetings and at other times during regular business hours.[86] The director cannot be called upon to furnish his or her reasons before being allowed to exercise these rights.[87] The director's right of inspection is broadly construed[88] and may be exercised personally by each director, or by the director's agent. However, where the inspection is made by an agent, it may be permissible to require the agent to provide an undertaking that any knowledge so acquired will not be misused.[89] As a general rule, every director has the right to receive notice of every directors' meeting, and may attend any such meeting.[90]

---

[80] CBCA, s. 222(1)(*b*).
[81] *Kalef v. Canada*, [1996] F.C.J. No. 269, 39 C.B.R. (3d) 1 (C.A.), leave to appeal to S.C.C. refused [1996] S.C.C.A. No. 219, 204 N.R. 400*n*.
[82] CBCA, s. 102(1); OBCA s. 115(1).
[83] OBCA, s. 115(1). The wording of the CBCA was brought into conformity with the OBCA in 2001.
[84] Section 102 of the CBCA was amended to include the words "or supervise the management of" in 2001.
[85] *Conway v. Petronias Clothing Co.*, [1978] 1 All E.R. 185 at 201 (Ch. D.), *per* Slade J.
[86] *Burn v. London & South Wales Coal Co.* (1890), 7 T.L.R. 118, *per* North J.
[87] *Edman v. Ross* (1922), 22 S.R. (N.S.W.) 351 at 360 (S.C.), *per* Stuart J.
[88] *Sinclair v. Sutton Resources Ltd.* (1996), 29 B.L.R. (2d) 258 at 262 (B.C.S.C.), *per* Harvey J.
[89] *Edman v. Ross* (1922), 22 S.R. (N.S.W.) 351 (S.C.).
[90] Subsection 126(9) and (10) of the OBCA provide:

> 126.(9) In the absence of any other provision in that behalf in the by-laws of the corporation, notice of the time and place for the holding of the meeting called under subsection (8) shall be given to every director of the corporation by sending the notice ten days or more before the date of the meeting to each director's latest address as shown on the records of the corporation.
>
> (10) A director may in any manner and at any time waive a notice of a meeting of directors and attendance of a director at a meeting of directors is a waiver of notice of the meeting, except where a director attends a meeting for the express purpose of objecting to the transaction of any business on the grounds that the meeting is not lawfully called.

An injunction will be granted on application by a director against his fellow directors, should they attempt to prevent him or her from participating as a director of the corporation, even where they do so on the basis that they believe the director in question to be unfit to serve as a director by reason of his misconduct,[91] and even if they consider the director to have an improper motive in conducting the inspection.[92]

§10.30 Since they act on a collective basis, directors are held collectively responsible for their acts. A director who is present at a meeting of directors or a committee of the directors is deemed to have consented to any resolution passed or action taken at the meeting, unless the director formally dissents in accordance with the procedures set out in section 135 of the OBCA and section 123 of the CBCA. Both statutes provide that a director who has voted for or consented to a resolution is not entitled to enter a formal dissent.[93] The distinction between "vote for" and "consent to" is not immediately clear, but these terms would seem to imply that a director must actually object to a proposed resolution or action as a precondition to registering a dissent. Passive abstention is insufficient to support a formal dissent, as the general rule of law is that silence implies consent.

§10.31 A director who opposes a particular resolution or step may formally request that his or her dissent be entered in the minutes of the corporation.[94] Alternatively, the director may send a written dissent to the secretary of the meeting before the meeting is adjourned, or send a dissent by registered mail or by personal delivery to the registered office of the corporation immediately after the meeting is adjourned. Where the dissenting director fails to follow the statutory procedure, he or she will remain liable as if actually consenting to the matter in question. There are a number of decisions that suggested that at common law no liability attached to a director who was not present at a meeting of directors. Subsections 135(3) of the OBCA and 123(3) of the CBCA would now seem to place a formal obligation on a director who is not present at a meeting to enter a dissent. Subsection 135(3) of the OBCA provides:

> 135.(3) A director who was not present at a meeting at which a resolution was passed or action taken is deemed to have consented thereto unless within seven days after becoming aware of the resolution the director,
>
> (a) causes his or her dissent to be placed with the minutes of the meeting; or
>
> (b) sends his or her dissent by registered mail or delivers it to the registered office of the corporation.

---

[91] *Kyshe v. Alturas Gold Co.* (1888), 36 W.R. 496, 4 T.L.R. 331 (Ch.), *per* North J. The appropriate remedy for the other directors in such a case is to call a shareholders' meeting and to seek the removal of the dishonest director from the board. See also *Hayes v. Bristol Plant Hire Ltd.*, [1957] 1 All E.R. 685 (Ch.); *Grimwade v. B.P.S. Syndicate Ltd.* (1915), 31 T.L.R. 531 (Ch.).

[92] *Davis v. Keilsohn Offset Co.*, 273 App. Div. 695, 79 N.Y.S.2d 540 at 541 (1948).

[93] CBCA, s. 123(2); OBCA, s. 135(2).

[94] If the director fails to so request, but the dissent is nonetheless entered in the minutes, the formal dissent requirement is satisfied.

Neither statute makes clear whether the absent director is deemed to become aware of the resolution or act at the time when he (or she) reads the minutes, the time when the minutes are sent to him, or the time when he actually receives them, but given the tight time restriction for the registration of a dissent, the starting date for the time period is obviously a matter of some importance. However, it can be argued strongly that in fairness to the director that time period should not begin to run until the minutes are actually read or (if unread) the director has had a reasonable time to read and digest their contents.

(v) Power and Duty to Manage

§10.32 As we have seen, both the OBCA and the CBCA entrust the directors of a corporation with the management of its business and affairs or alternatively with the supervision of that management.[95] The general authority of the directors is subject to certain limitations. For instance, they may not exercise powers that are expressly reserved for the shareholders.[96] Nor, of course, may the directors act contrary to the Act, or the articles or by-laws of a corporation, or a unanimous shareholder agreement.[97] However, subject to these limited exceptions, it is clear that the powers of the directors are very broad and encompass all authority required to conduct the ordinary ongoing operations and business of the corporation.

§10.33 Subsection 115(1) of the OBCA provides that subject to any unanimous shareholder agreement, the directors of a corporation shall manage or supervise the management of the business and affairs of the corporation. Subsection 102(1) of the CBCA is similar, but makes no reference to supervision of the management as an alternative to management by the directors themselves. These two provisions each appear at the beginning of the Part of each Act specifically concerned with the directors of corporations, and the prominence of their position is no accident; for though the directors of a corporation are impressed with many specific duties and general duties of care, the duty to manage the corporation must be seen as the overriding responsibility of the directors. To manage is to take charge of, to control or direct the administration of the corporation.[98] It is implicit in the concept of management that a person will be called upon to make complicated decisions on matters involving skill and judgment, and to exercise discretion in the selection among competing options (*e.g.*, balancing the immediate needs of the corporation against its long-term best interests).[99] These decisions must often be made quickly, on the basis of only limited information under conditions of uncertainty, and will involve subjective value judgments. The courts have recognized that business decisions frequently involve considerable

---

[95] OBCA, s. 115(1); CBCA, s. 102(1).
[96] See, generally, *Miller v. Diamond Light & Heating Co.* (1913), 22 Que. K.B. 411 (C.A.).
[97] OBCA s. 134(2); CBCA, s. 122(2).
[98] *Fluet v. McCabe*, 288 Mass. 173, 12 N.E.2d 89 at 93 (1938).
[99] *Darvall v. North Sydney Brick & Tile Co.* (1987), 12 A.C.L.R. 537 at 554, aff'd 15 A.C.L.R. 230, *per* Hodgson J. (duty of directors where the company becomes subject to a take-over bid at the same time as directors are considering whether to embark on a new venture).

risk of loss, sometimes substantial loss. The directors' duty is to manage, but in discharging that duty they are not expected to attain the standards of deliberation expected of courts or philosophers engaged in a meticulous inquiry into the truth.

§10.34 As noted above, the courts will not interfere with an exercise of power by the directors that falls within their recognized and statutory authority unless a clear or seriously suspected injustice or damage appears to be involved.[100] One obvious justification for the reluctance of the courts to join shareholders in interfering in the management of the corporation is the fact that the duties of the directors are owed to the corporation, rather than to its shareholders. Moreover, they are charged with an express statutory mandate to manage the corporation under subsections 115(1) of the OBCA and 102(1) of the CBCA. Except to the extent that the statute specifically provides to the contrary, it would be inconsistent with this statutory duty to hold that the directors may be restricted in the discharge of their duties to the corporation by the shareholders, since the shareholders do not in general assume the duties and consequent liabilities imposed upon directors, merely by telling the directors how they want things run. Quite clearly the directors are not bound and cannot be bound by an ordinary or special resolution of the shareholders directing them to do something contrary to an express or implied prohibition in the Act, such as giving financial assistance contrary to section 20 of the OBCA. If the directors follow the dictates of such a resolution, they will remain liable for so doing, and it will be no answer to a claim against them to argue that they were merely following the orders of the shareholders.[101]

(vi) Control over Litigation

§10.35 Subject to the derivative action provisions of the OBCA and the CBCA, the directors are generally seen to possess the power to control legal proceedings in which the corporation is involved. Accordingly, unless there is a contrary provision in a unanimous shareholder agreement, the directors need not consult with the shareholders of a corporation before instituting legal proceedings. Indeed, for the most part, the shareholders are seen as having no right to institute[102] or intervene in[103] legal proceedings brought in the name of the corporation.[104]

---

[100] *Pardee v. Humberstone Summer Resort Co.*, [1933] O.J. No. 361, [1933] O.R. 580 at 586 (C.A.), per Armour J.; see also *Montreal & St. Lawrence Light & Power Co. v. Robert*, [1906] A.C. 196 (P.C.), concerning the effect of unreasonable delay on any such right of complaint.
[101] See, for instance, *Alexander v. Automatic Telephone Co.*, [1900] 2 Ch. 56 at 72, per Rigby J.; *Nolan v. Parsons*, [1942] O.J. No. 445, [1942] O.R. 358 (C.A.).
[102] However, where a majority of the shareholders join in a proceeding brought in the name of the corporation, it appears that the action is valid: *Marshall's Valve Gear Co. v. Manning Wardle & Co.*, [1909] 1 Ch. 267, per Neville J.; cf. *Breckland Group Holdings Ltd. v. London & Suffolk Properties Ltd.*, [1996] 2 B.C.L.C. 102, per Harman J.
[103] *John Shaw & Sons (Salford) Ltd. v. Shaw*, [1935] 2 K.B. 113 (C.A.).
[104] See, generally, *John Shaw & Sons (Salford) Ltd. v. Shaw*, [1935] 2 K.B. 113 (C.A.); *Alexander Ward & Co. v. Samyang Navigation Co. Ltd.*, [1975] 1 W.L.R. 673 (H.L.); *Breckland Group Holdings Ltd. v. London & Suffolk Properties Ltd.*, [1989] B.C.L.C. 100; *Mitchell & Hobbs (U.K.) Ltd. v. Mill*, [1996] 2 B.C.L.C. 102.

However, the control of the board over litigation does not entitle any individual director to sue in the name of the corporation.[105]

§10.36 Where an action is brought in the name of a corporation without due authority, the defendant may move to stay the action.[106] The proper approach is to apply as early as possible to have the action stayed.[107] The procedure to be followed in such a case was described in the following terms by Middleton J.A.:

> Where the motion is made by the defendant, he must notify not only the solicitor who is alleged to have acted without authority, but he must also notify the plaintiff. The object of this is, among other things, to enable the plaintiff to affirm or repudiate the action of the solicitors. If there was originally no authority, the plaintiff, on being notified, might elect to affirm that which has been done without authority in his name, and this ratification would then relate back, and, generally speaking, would be equivalent to antecedent authority.
>
> Motions of this kind are somewhat frequent in company cases in which there is some internecine warfare between factions in the company, each claiming to be entitled to represent the company. In these cases the practice of the Court is to direct that the proceedings be stayed until a meeting of the shareholders of the company can be called so as to enable the will of the shareholders, or of the majority, to be ascertained.[108]

It follows that the unauthorized action is not truly a nullity (as it may be ratified); it is however, voidable and will be voided should the required ratification not be obtained. However, the court has an inherent jurisdiction to strike out an action where it becomes evident that the action was brought without authority and presumably should do so if it is quite clear that no proper authority is likely to be obtained.[109]

§10.37 The question sometimes arises as to whether an officer of a corporation has the authority to direct the institution of legal proceedings, without being specifically directed to do so by the board. There appears to be no problem with an officer instituting proceedings if the directors have specifically delegated this authority to the officer in question.[110] In the absence of express delegation, there appears to be no implied authority in favour of any officer to institute a legal action, at least if the articles or by-laws of the corporation are incompatible with any implication of such authority, even where in the circumstances the directors of the corporation are powerless to act.[111] Nevertheless, for some types of corporation (*e.g.*, banks and other companies in the business of lending money), litigation is

---

[105] *Harben v. Phillips* (1883), 23 Ch. D. 14 (C.A.). As to the institution of proceedings by a near insolvent or shell corporation, see *Eastern Canada Coal Gas Venture Ltd. v. Cape Breton Development Corp.*, [2002] N.S.J. No. 465 (S.C.).
[106] *Pictou (County) Board of Education v. Cameron* (1879), 2 S.C.R. 690.
[107] See, generally, *Richmond v. Branson & Son*, [1914] 1 Ch. 968 at 974; *Russian Commercial & Industrial Bank v. Comptoir d'Escompte de Mulhouse*, [1923] 2 K.B. 630 at 672 (H.L.); *John Shaw & Sons (Salford) Ltd. v. Shaw*, [1935] 2 K.B. 113 at 145 (C.A.).
[108] *DuMart Packing Co. v. DuMart*, [1927] O.J. No. 140, [1928] 1 D.L.R. 640 at 641 (H.C.).
[109] *Daimler Co. v. Continental Tyre & Rubber Co. (Great Britain)*, [1916] 2 A.C. 307 (H.L.).
[110] *Ibid.*
[111] *Club Flotilla (Pacific Palms) Ltd. v. Isherwood* (1987), 12 A.C.L.R. 387 at 390, *per* Needham J.

such a routine part of day-to-day business that a corporation would not be able to carry on business without delegating the authority to institute legal proceedings, perhaps to very junior officers of the corporation. Accordingly, a general grant of authority to institute legal proceedings must necessarily be permissible.

§10.38 Where a general delegation of authority to institute legal proceedings has been made to a particular officer of the corporation, it is assumed to be limited to an authority to retain and instruct counsel to institute legal proceedings concerning matters arising in the ordinary course of business of the corporation. It does not extend to exceptional proceedings, such as an application to wind up the corporation in question. Where a lawyer institutes legal proceedings on behalf of a corporate client without proper authorization, he or she risks personal liability in costs, even if the officer whose instructions the lawyer has followed has acted in good faith.[112]

(vii) Statutory Requirements for Disclosure of Conflict of Interest

(1) Generally

§10.39 In this section, we will survey the law relating to the routine and special case disclosure of potential or existing conflict of interest by both directors and officers. While the material in this section is of obvious relevance to the day-to-day management of a business corporation, the principles of law from which the specific disclosure rules of the OBCA and CBCA are derived are those relating to fiduciary duty — a subject discussed in detail in Chapter 11. Accordingly, readers who are interested in the question of director disclosure should also refer to the discussion of director disclosure obligations under general principles of equity, as set out in that chapter.

§10.40 A complete prohibition on contracts between a corporation and its directors (either collectively or individually) would not be practical. The law has long recognized that such contracts are inevitable, and therefore is prepared to permit them provided they are made on a basis of full and complete disclosure[113] and the director (or officer) in question steps aside from that transaction so as to permit the corporation to make an independent decision. Unless these requirements are satisfied, the agreement is voidable at the option of the corporation.[114] However, there is nothing to prevent a director who renders services unconnected with his or her position as a director from receiving reasonable compensation for the services so

---

[112] See, generally, *Wedtech Inc. v. Wedco Technology Inc.*, [1997] O.J. No. 2760, 32 B.L.R. (2d) 145 (Gen. Div.).
[113] See, generally, *Denman v. Clover Bar Coal Co.* (1913), 48 S.C.R. 318.
[114] *Canada Guaranty Trust Co. v. Young*, [1932] 3 W.W.R. 671 (Man. C.A.). See also *Canada (Attorney General) v. Grannell*, [1958] O.W.N. 435 at 437 (H.C.J.), *per* Wells J., but see the *dicta* of Idington J. in *Pakenham Pork Packing Co. (Liquidator of) v. Kendrick* (1905), 37 S.C.R. 32.

provided so long as proper disclosure is made and authorization is obtained.[115] Similarly, directors may be remunerated for their services as directors, and indeed in contrast to much of the earlier legislation,[116] the present OBCA and CBCA impose almost no restriction on the provision of such remuneration.[117] Nevertheless, the onus of proving the regularity of a director-corporation transaction (and in particular that all necessary precautions, such as disclosure, have been taken by the director) falls upon the director.[118]

§10.41 Inherent within the concept of fiduciary duty is the obligation to act in utmost good faith. As a general principle of law, a director or officer, like any fiduciary, may protect himself or herself from the duty to account and other fiduciary-based claims arising from a dealing with the corporation by making full disclosure[119] (characterized in one case as full, plain and fair disclosure),[120] and where applicable obtaining the consent of the corporation to the proposed transgression of fiduciary duty. Thus directors and officers dealing with the corporation must disclose *all* material facts relating to a proposed dealing, as well as the existence of a potential conflict of interest. Where it is determined that a fiduciary has withheld relevant facts from the beneficiary, the court will not entertain any inquiry into the possibility that the beneficiary might still have acted as it did, even if those facts had been disclosed.[121] The duty to disclose is an absolute one, because, without full disclosure, any investigation into whether the beneficiary would have acted in the same manner is impossible.[122]

(a) Full and Fair Disclosure

§10.42 The disclosure that a fiduciary is obliged to make must be full and fair, so as to permit the corporation to make an informed judgment and properly assess its interests.[123] It is not enough for the director to say "I am interested" and leave it at that. The director must enlighten the other members of the board as to the real nature of his or her interest.[124] If the director stands to gain from the

---

[115] *Canada Bonded Attorney and Legal Directory Ltd. v. Leonard-Parmiter Ltd.*, [1918] O.J. No. 79, 42 O.L.R. 141 at 154 (C.A.), per Riddell J.; *Premier Trust Co. v. McAlister*, [1933] O.J. No. 323, [1933] O.R. 195 at 205 (H.C.J.), per Rose C.J.H.C.
[116] See, for instance, *Saskatchewan Land & Homestead Co. v. Moore*, [1914] O.J. No. 331, 6 O.W.N. 100 (C.A.).
[117] However, for offering corporations, see the discussion of director and officer compensation in Chapter 9.
[118] *Gray v. New Augarita Porcupine Mines Ltd.*, [1952] 3 D.L.R. 1 (P.C.).
[119] See, generally, *Victorov v. Davison*, [1988] O.J. No. 190, 20 C.P.R. (3d) 481 (H.C.J.); *Molchan v. Omega Oil & Gas Ltd.*, [1985] A.J. No. 1064, 40 Alta. L.R. (2d) 251 at 259 *et seq.* (C.A.), per Prowse J.A., aff'd on other grounds [1988] S.C.J. No. 12, [1988] 1 S.C.R. 348.
[120] *Imperial Trust Co. v. Canbra Foods Ltd.*, [1987] A.J. No. 156, 50 Alta. L.R. (2d) 375 at 391 (Q.B.), per Moore C.J.Q.B.
[121] *London Loan & Savings Co. of Canada v. Brickenden*, [1934] 3 D.L.R. 465 at 469 (P.C.), per Lord Thankerton; followed in *Crighton v. Roman*, [1960] S.C.J. No. 52, [1960] S.C.R. 858 at 869, per Cartwright J. See also *Williams v. Scott*, [1900] A.C. 499 at 508 (P.C.).
[122] See, generally, *Crighton v. Roman*, [1960] S.C.J. No. 52, [1960] S.C.R. 858 at 869, per Cartwright J.
[123] *Boardman v. Phipps*, [1967] 2 A.C. 46 at 109 (H.L.), per Lord Hodson.
[124] See, for instance, *Denman v. Clover Bar Coal Co.* (1913), 48 S.C.R. 318.

transaction, the director must provide some idea of the gain that he or she stands to make.[125] Both the CBCA and the OBCA contain provisions codifying the manner and extent to which such disclosure must be made. Under the OBCA, the general duty is set out in subsection 132(1), which provides:

132.(1) A director or officer of a corporation who,

(*a*) is a party to a material contract or transaction or proposed material contract or transaction with the corporation; or

(*b*) is a director or an officer of, or has a material interest in, any person who is a party to a material contract or transaction or proposed material contract or transaction with the corporation,

shall disclose in writing to the corporation or request to have entered in the meetings of directors the nature and extent of his or her interest.

The purpose of the disclosure is to enable the remaining directors to make an informed and impartial decision on the basis of the declared relationship.[126] What is sufficiently material is a question of fact.[127] A director should disclose a potential conflict of interest whenever the director has a degree of connection with a transaction (be it legal, equitable, financial, emotional, one of personal relationship or otherwise) that creates a reasonable possibility that the ability of the director to act in the corporation's best interest may be compromised.[128] However, although a director must disclose any material conflict of interest, the mere disclosure of a conflict by itself does not absolve the director from the overriding duty to act in the best interests of the corporation. Full disclosure is a necessary but not sufficient condition to the exoneration of the director.[129]

§10.43 There is surprisingly little case law in which the meaning and application of section 132 has been considered, given the fact that conflicts of interest are likely to arise very frequently in day-to-day practice, particularly in view of the large number of nominee directors and directors who hold two or more directorships. The meaning of the corresponding provision of the CBCA was considered by Lax J. in: *UPM-Kymmene Corp. v. UPM-Kymmene Miramichi Inc.*[130] He observed that section 120 of the CBCA presumes the invalidity of a contract or transaction between a director or officer and the corporation unless it is approved by the directors,[131] the disclosure requirements are met and the contract was reasonable and fair to the company when it was approved. The section appears to contemplate that the contract must meet all three parts of the test.

---

[125] *Gray v. New Augarita Porcupine Mines Ltd.*, [1952] 3 D.L.R. 1 at 14-15 (P.C.), *per* Lord Radcliffe.
[126] *Canadian Guaranty Trust v. Young*, [1932] 3 W.W.R. 671 (Man. C.A.).
[127] *Dimo Holdings Ltd. v. H. Jager Developments Inc.*, [1998] A.J. No. 1781, 43 B.L.R. (2d) 123 (Q.B.).
[128] *Zysko v. Thorarinson*, [2003] A.J. No. 1375, 42 B.L.R. (3d) 75 at 89-91 (Q.B.), *per* Chrumka J.
[129] *Levy-Russell Ltd. v. TecMotiv Inc.*, [1994] O.J. No. 650, 13 B.L.R. (2d) 1 at 187 (Gen. Div.), *per* D. Lane J., additional reasons at 233.
[130] [2002] O.J. No. 2412, 214 D.L.R. (4th) 496 (S.C.J.), aff'd [2004] O.J. No. 636 (C.A.).
[131] CBCA: or shareholders, under subsection (8).

(b) GENERAL DISCLOSURE STATEMENTS

§10.43.1 In the 2001 amendments to the CBCA, the general disclosure provisions of section 120 of the OBCA were amended to require a director or officer who files a general notice of an interest in another party to advise the corporation where there is any material change in the nature of that interest. To date, this change has not been carried forward into section 132 of the OBCA, although the Ministry of Government Services has raised the prospect that it may. Since the effect of filing a notice is to require the director or officer to abstain from any role in the approval of the transaction, it is not clear what further purpose is served by requiring the filing of this additional information. Although the additional requirement to notify of a change may seem innocuous, it must be balanced against the risk that an ill-informed director or officer may simply not know of (or forget) to notify the corporation of the change. Since that director or officer should already be excluded from the decision-making process with respect to the transaction, simply by virtue of the original declaration. This new requirement seems excessive.

(c) SINGLE DIRECTOR CORPORATIONS

§10.44 The OBCA does not specify what must be done where there is only one director of the corporation. Single director corporations obviously pose special problems in the case of any disclosure requirement. In most such cases, the director is likely to be the only person who has a direct interest in the corporation, and therefore the problem is usually of academic than practical interest. There seems to be little point in a director disclosing to himself, and if the director is the only person who can act on the part of the corporation, it is difficult to see how a contract might be made if the director refrains from acting with respect to that contract. Where there is only one director of a corporation, but that corporation has other shareholder interests, the better view is that director should disclose to the other shareholders and seek their approval of any contract in which the director has a material interest, since in such a case disclosure to the board is meaningless.[132] If, on the other hand, there are no (minority) shareholder interests in the corporation, and the corporation remains solvent at the time when the contract is made, and there is no reason to believe that it will become insolvent by reason of the contract, then disclosure would not appear to be required.[133] In cases in which the corporation is insolvent, and a director decision respecting some aspect of corporate operations, its business or affairs affects or is likely to have an adverse effect upon the interests of creditors, workers or some other identifiable worker group, at least some consideration should be given to consultation with those affected stakeholders, before proceeding with a transaction in which the director has a self-interest or other conflict. In all cases, the exis-

---

[132] See, generally, *Movitex Ltd. v. Bulfield*, [1986] 2 B.C.C. 99,403 at 99,428-29, *per* Vinelott J.; but compare *Neptune (Vehicle Washing Equipment) Ltd. v. Fitzgerald (No. 2)*, [1995] B.C.L.C. 1000.

[133] See, generally, *Runciman v. Walter Runciman plc*, [1992] B.C.L.C. 1084 at 1097, *per* Simon Brown J.

Corporate Management 853

tence of the conflict should be recorded in the director's minute book, so as to comply with section 132(4).[134]

(2) Material Contracts and Material Interests

§10.45 The OBCA and the CBCA do not define either the term "material contract" or the term "material interest". Presumably a transaction is material where it represents a significant dealing of the corporation, such as one which would have a significant effect upon the profitability, financial strength or operations of the corporation. There can be little doubt that the materiality of the transaction is determined by reference to its effect upon the corporation, rather than upon the director, officer or other corporation in which the director or officer has an interest.

§10.46 The meaning of the term "material interest" is less clear, but it would seem to suggest that the director's or officer's interest must be of a sufficient magnitude that the contract would have some significant effect upon the value of the director's or officer's interest in the other corporation. If the director has only a small interest in the corporation, it is unlikely that his or her interest would be material, even if the contract or transaction is significant both to the corporation of which he or she is a director, and to the second corporation in which he or she has the interest. The size of that interest would be a relative matter, involving a full consideration of the circumstances of the corporations. A $1 share will be a material interest if that share is the only share in the other corporation, for it means that all profit will flow to the director. Paradoxically, a $1 million share interest may be immaterial if the corporation is so widely held that the profit attributable to any particular shareholder from any particular transaction is negligible to the point of being unmeasurable.[135] Suppose, for instance, that a director of A Ltd. owns $1 million worth of shares in one of Canada's major chartered banks. Even a $100 million line of credit between that bank and A Ltd. might well fail the materiality test, for the benefit to the director of the contract would be so slight as to be below measurement. In such a case, it would well be prudent to disclose; it does not follow that disclosure must necessarily be made.

(3) Disclosure Procedure

§10.47 Section 132 of the OBCA also specifies the procedure in which disclosure is to be made by officers and directors. In the case of directors, subsection 132(2) provides that the disclosure required under subsection 132(1) shall be made:

(*a*) at the meeting at which a proposed contract or transaction is first considered;

(*b*) if the director was not then interested in a proposed contract or transaction, at the first meeting after he or she becomes so interested;

---

[134] See, generally, *Neptune (Vehicle Washing Equipment) Ltd. v. Fitzgerald*, [1996] Ch. 274; *Guinness plc v. Saunders*, [1988] 2 All E.R. 940 at 944 (C.A.), per Fox L.J. but *cf. Lee Panavision Ltd. v. Lee Lighting Ltd.*, [1992] B.C.L.C. 22 at 33 (C.A.), per Dillon L.J.
[135] *Cf. Foster v. Oxford, etc. Rlwy. Co.* (1853), 13 C.B. 200, 138 E.R. 1174 (C.P.).

(c) if the director becomes interested after a contract is made or a transaction is entered into, at the first meeting after he or she becomes so interested; or

(d) if a person who is interested in a contract or transaction later becomes a director, at the first meeting after he or she becomes a director.

Clauses (a), (b) and (c) clearly fall within the scope of the traditional requirement for disclosure by fiduciaries. Both clauses (a) and (b) contemplate a contract under consideration at a time when a fiduciary duty is already owed to the corporation. Clause (c) relates to a contract made before there is any conflict of interest. Nevertheless, there is no doubt that a failure to contemplate the situation encompassed in clause (c) would leave a significant gap in the legislation. Clause (d) is not so easy to explain, because it relates to contracts made before any duty was owed to the corporation, and indeed before the director or officer had any control over decision-making by the corporation. Quite possibly, the director or officer may be unaware of the existence of the contract.

§10.48 If the contract was valid at the time when it was made, it is difficult to see why or how it subsequently becomes invalid by reason of the newly acquired directorship. Perhaps the intent behind such disclosure is to ensure that the director concerned plays no role in dealing with any dispute under the contractor in managing its administration. For instance, it would not be appropriate for the director to play a role in relation to the contract if it subsequently becomes necessary to enforce or amend the contract. However, such a step would be a separate transaction, and would therefore fall within one of the other clauses of subsection 132(2). Quite simply, clause 132(2)(d) seems over-inclusive.

§10.49 In the case of officers who are not directors, subsection 132(3) of the Act requires the disclosure to be made,

(a) forthwith after the officer becomes aware that the contract or transaction or proposed contract or transaction is to be considered or has been considered at a meeting of directors;

(b) if the officer becomes interested after a contract is made or a transaction is entered into, forthwith after he or she becomes so interested; or

(c) if a person who is interested in a contract or transaction later becomes an officer, forthwith after he or she becomes an officer.

As in the case of clause 132(2)(d), the requirement of clause (c) is difficult to understand, for it would be very unusual for the officer to be in breach of a fiduciary duty by reason of a contract concluded prior to the time when he became an officer.

§10.50 It goes without saying that in the case of most corporations (particularly those of any size) only a small number of the contracts entered into by the corporation are actually ever considered by its board of directors. Subsection 132(4) goes on to deal with the manner in which disclosure is to be made in the case of contracts that are not of a type normally considered by the board of directors:

132.(4) Despite subsections (2) and (3), where subsection (1) applies to a director or officer in respect of a material contract or transaction or proposed material contract or transaction that, in the ordinary course of the corporation's business, would not require approval by the directors or shareholders, the director or officer shall disclose in writing to the corporation or request to have entered in the minutes of meetings of directors the nature and extent of his or her interest forthwith after the director or officer becomes aware of the contract or transaction or proposed contract or transaction.

Similarly, the Act permits a director or officer to give a general notice to the directors that he or she is a director or officer of, or has a material interest in, a person and is to be regarded as interested in any contract made or any transaction entered into with that person, and that general notice will be a sufficient disclosure of interest in relation to any contract so made or transaction entered into by the corporation.[136] It has been suggested that the following objectives are served by these disclosure requirements:[137]

> Where a director is interested in a contract, the section secures that three things happen at a directors meeting: first, all the directors should know or be reminded of the interest; second, the making of the declaration should be the occasion for a statutory pause for thought about the existence of the conflict of interest and of the duty to prefer the interests of the company to their own; third, the disclosure or reminder must be a distinct happening at the meeting which therefore must be recorded in the minutes of the meeting ...

Where a material contract is made or a material transaction is entered into between a corporation and a director or officer of the corporation, or between a corporation and another person[138] of which a director or officer of the corporation is a director or officer or in which he has a material interest, the director is not accountable to the corporation or to its shareholders for any profit or gain realized from the contract or transaction; and the contract or transaction is neither void nor voidable, by reason only of that relationship, or by reason only that the director is present at or is counted to determine the presence of a quorum at the meeting of directors that authorized the contract or transaction, if the director or officer disclosed his or her interest in accordance with OBCA subsection 132(2), (3), (4) or (6), and the contract or transaction was reasonable and fair to the corporation at the time it was so approved.[139]

§10.51 In the case of directors, disclosure of the conflict of interest is only the first of the requirements imposed under sections 132 of the OBCA and 120 of the CBCA. The second is a duty to abstain from the decision-making process.

---

[136] OBCA, s. 132(6).
[137] *Neptune (Vehicle Washing Equipment) Ltd. v. Fitzgerald*, [1996] Ch. 274 at 283, *per* Lightman J.
[138] Note the extended definition of the term "person" in subsection 1(1) of the OBCA: "person" includes "an individual, sole proprietorship, partnership, unincorporated association, unincorporated syndicate, unincorporated organization, trust, body corporate, and a natural person in his or her capacity as trustee, executor, administrator, or other legal representative".
[139] OBCA, s. 132(7). See, generally, *Re British America Corp.* (1903), 19 T.L.R. 662; *Toms v. Cinema Trust Co.*, [1915] W.N. 29; *Runciman v. Walter Runciman plc*, [1992] B.C.L.C. 1084.

Specifically, subsection 132(5) of the OBCA[140] also prohibits a director (subject to certain exceptions) from voting on any transaction in which he or she is interested:

> 132.(5) A director referred to in subsection (1) shall not vote on any resolution to approve the contract or transaction unless the contract or transaction is,
>
> (*a*) an arrangement by way of security for money lent to or obligations undertaken by the director for the benefit of the corporation or an affiliate;
>
> (*b*) one relating primarily to his or her remuneration as a director, officer, employee or agent of the corporation or an affiliate;
>
> (*c*) one for indemnity or insurance under section 136; or
>
> (*d*) one with an affiliate.[141]

Although clause (*a*) permits directors to vote on their own remuneration, they must comply strictly with any requirements of the articles or by-laws pertaining to such remuneration when doing so.[142]

(a) ATTENDANCE AT MEETINGS

§10.52 The OBCA and CBCA prohibit a director from voting on a contract or other transaction in which the director has a material interest. They do not specifically prohibit the director from attending at, or participating in, the portion of the meeting at which that transaction or contract is discussed. In the C.W. Shareholdings case[143] the court disregarded the presence of the chief executive officer at a meeting of an "independent committee" set up to consider a take-over bid, even though he was in a conflict of interest. In contrast, the New Brunswick and Quebec statutes prohibit conflicted individuals from such attendance.

§10.53 Despite the silence of the OBCA and CBCA on this point, except in two specific circumstances, it is unusual for a director to remain at and participate in a meeting where the director has a material interest in the subject under discussion, because such attendance and participation can easily give rise to a perception of coercion or undue influence, and certainly would appear irregular if the approval of the matter concerned was ever to be challenged in court. The first exception relates to remuneration (a subject that is considered separately below, as well as Chapter 9.). The second relates to participation by the director purely for the purposes of providing the board with necessary or useful information. Very often, a director who has a material interest in the transaction will also have particular knowledge that the other members of the board would benefit from receiving. Insofar as the director attends solely to provide that information, and then leaves while the merits or weaknesses of the transaction are discussed

---

[140] CBCA, s. 120(5).
[141] See *Pakenham Pork Packing Co. (Liquidator of) v. Kendrick* (1905), 37 S.C.R. 32; *Burland v. Earle*, [1902] A.C. 83; *North-West Transportation v. Beatty* (1887), 12 App. Cas. 589.
[142] See, generally, *Guinness plc v. Saunders*, [1990] H.L.J. No. 16, [1990] 2 A.C. 663.
[143] *CW Shareholdings Inc. v. WIC Western International Communications Ltd.*, [1998] O.J. No. 1886, 39 O.R. (3d) 755 (Gen. Div.).

and decided, there can be no sensible objection to the procedure that has been followed.

(b) Effect of Non-Compliance

§10.54 Where interested directors participate in the approval of the agreement, it is liable to be set aside[144] and in certain cases the director may be required to account,[145] subsection 132(9) of the OBCA providing:

> 132.(9) Subject to subsections (7) and (8), where a director or officer of a corporation fails to disclose his or her interest in a material contract or transaction in accordance with this section or otherwise fails to comply with this section, the corporation or a shareholder of the corporation, or, in the case of an offering corporation, the Commission may apply to the court for an order setting aside the contract or transaction and directing that the director or officer account to the corporation for any profit or gain realized and upon such application the court may so order or make such other order as it thinks fit.

While the standing to seek relief is expanded by subsection 132(9), the remedy it creates is no more than declarative of the common law rule. It is now clear beyond doubt that the contract is not void but only voidable, and if the corporation does not object to it, the contract will stand. In case law predating subsection 132(9) it was held that a corporation could not obtain an accounting for the profits or gain realized by the director (or officer) and yet keep the property.[146] So, for instance, if a director property sold property to a corporation (not acquired originally on the corporation's behalf) at an over-valued price, it was not possible to recover the amount of the overpayment from the director while seeking to keep the property in question (a key concern where that property forms a vital part of the substratum of the corporation). However, since the subsection now permits the court to "make such other order as it thinks fit" it is now at least arguable that the court can order the director to disgorge the profit to the corporation.

§10.55 It is no answer to a claim based upon a failure to disclose in accordance with the statutory requirements, to argue that the corporation or other directors could have discovered the facts easily enough by way of prudent inquiry, or perhaps even that the existence of a conflict was self-evident. In the view of at least one judge:

> The duty to disclose is an absolute one, because, without full disclosure, any investigation into whether the beneficiary would have acted in the same manner is impossible.[147]

---

[144] See, generally, *Imperial Trust Co. v. Canbra Foods Ltd.*, [1987] A.J. No. 156, 50 Alta. L.R. (2d) 375 (Q.B.).
[145] *Re Owen Sound Lumber Co.*, [1917] O.J. No. 144, 38 O.L.R. 414 (C.A.).
[146] *Burland v. Earle*, [1902] A.C. 83; see also *Cook v. Deeks*, [1916] 1 A.C. 554 (H.L.).
[147] *UPM-Kymmene Corp. v. UPM-Kymmene Miramichi Inc.*, [2002] O.J. No. 2412 at para. 116 (S.C.J.), aff'd [2004] O.J. No. 636 (C.A.).

Moreover, the Act imposes a duty on the director or officer who is in conflict to disclose. There is no mention of a corresponding duty on the board (or shareholders) to find out, or even inquire.

§10.56 In *McAteer v. Devoncroft Developments Ltd.*[148] Rooke J. raised, without deciding, the question of whether the onus of proof falls on the director or officer to prove that proper disclosure was made, or whether it is up to the corporation or other claimant to prove the insufficiency of disclosure. For three reasons, the better view would seem to be to impose the obligation upon the fiduciary rather than the complainant. First, such an approach reflects the fact that the fiduciary usually has better access to evidence as to the steps that were taken than will any other person. Second, imposing the obligation upon the complainant puts that person in the position of trying to prove a negative. Third it is also consistent with the principle that the onus of establishing a defence to a *prima facie* claim falls upon the defendant. To ensure that a proper record exists, the wisest course to follow is to make sure that the disclosure is made in writing, and that a copy of that instrument is retained — ideally with proof of actual delivery.

(4) The Fairness Requirements

(a) FAIR DEALING

§10.57 Disclosure is only one concern. Fairness is another. Where directors stand on both sides of a transaction, they have the burden of establishing its entire fairness, sufficient to pass the test of careful scrutiny by a court. There is no "safe harbour" for divided loyalty. Directors will be found to have acted with entire fairness where they can demonstrate their utmost good faith and the most scrupulous inherent fairness of the bargain.[149] The concept of entire fairness has two components: fair dealing and fair price. Fair dealing embraces questions of when the transaction was timed, how it was initiated, structured, negotiated, disclosed to the other directors, and how the approvals of the other directors and the stockholders were obtained. Fair price relates to the economic and financial considerations of the proposed transaction, including all relevant factors: assets, market value, earnings, future prospects, and any other elements that affect the intrinsic or inherent value of the deal.

§10.58 In making a determination as to the entire fairness of a transaction, the court does not focus on one component over the other, but examines all aspects of the issue as a whole.[150] Alternatively stated: while there are two aspects to the questions of fairness, the judgment as to whether a transaction satisfies the test is not a bifurcated one but is a single judgment that considers each of these two

---

[148] [2001] A.J. No. 1481, 24 B.L.R. (3d) 1 (Q.B.).
[149] *Weinberger v. UOP, Inc.*, 457 A.2d 701 at 710 (Del. Supr. Ct. 1983).
[150] *Boyer v. Wilmington Materials Inc.*, 754 A.2d 881 (Del. Ch. 1999).

aspects.[151] In some cases, price may be found to a relatively minor or an inapplicable consideration.[152] In other contexts price may be the predominant concern.[153]

§10.59 Fair dealing requires an open process of negotiation, rather than one in which cards are played closely to the chest. This more general requirement is inherent in the specific duty to disclose the existence of a potential conflict. It incorporates an obligation to conduct any negotiations in which they may participate with the beneficiary in an upright manner. Implicit within the obligations of a fiduciary are strict ethical duties of loyalty, good faith, and avoidance of conflict of duty and self-interest.[154] Directors and officers are, therefore, under a very onerous and universal responsibility. They must act with utmost good faith, provide complete disclosure and also otherwise scrupulously minimize the impact of the conflict of interest inherent in the transaction.[155] Hard bargaining, gamesmanship and other sharp practices employed by the directors would fall short of the standard of integrity required of a fiduciary in its dealing with the corporation.[156] Where the same directors of a corporation are involved on both sides of a transaction involving the corporation for which they serve, they are required to demonstrate that they have acted in the utmost good faith, in part by behaving in a manner that is scrupulously and inherently fair in their dealing with the corporation and in terms of the bargain that was struck.[157]

§10.60 Neither the OBCA nor the CBCA expressly provide whether the director or officer must make sure that the corporation is independently represented in the negotiating of the terms of the relevant transaction, although the requirement for independent approval of the terms of the transaction is clear. Despite this silence, a director or officer would be most ill-advised if he or she did not make every reasonable effort to ensure that the corporation received independent representation beginning with the negotiation stage of the contract process. Particular problems arise where the corporation is effectively relying upon the judgment, integrity and advice of the fiduciary.

(b) Fair Terms

§10.61 Over and above the process of negotiation, there is a separate requirement that the terms of the transaction must also be fair to the corporation. The application of this requirement involves a difficult balance, because in many types of transaction, it is self-evident that the directors cannot be expected to disregard completely their own interests. Directors are not obliged to sell property to the corporation at less than its value, to work for less than a fair wage, or to volunteer for lay-off during any economic downturn. Imposing such require-

---

[151] *Kahn v. Lynch Communications Inc.*, 638 A.2d 1110 (Del. Supr. Ct. 1994).
[152] *Nixon v. Blackwell*, 626 A.2d 1366 at 1376 (Del. Supr. Ct. 1993).
[153] *Cinerama, Inc. v. Technicolor, Inc.*, 663 A.2d 1134 (Del. Ch. 1994).
[154] *Canadian Aero Service Ltd. v. O'Malley*, [1973] S.C.J. No. 97, 40 D.L.R. (3d) 371 at 382, *per* Laskin J.
[155] M.V. Ellis, *Fiduciary Duties in Canada* (Toronto: Deboo, 1988), 11-12.
[156] See, generally, *Weinberger v. UOP Inc.*, 457 A.2d 701 at 711 (Del. Supr. 1985).
[157] *Nixon v. Blackwell*, 626 A.2d 1366 (Del. Supr. Ct. 1993).

ments would make it difficult to attract people who have top quality business talent to serve as directors, and such a result could hardly be in the corporation's long-term interest.

§10.62 The courts have exercised particular care when dealing with director and senior officer arrangements that provide for extraordinary remuneration,[158] such as so-called golden parachutes,[159] golden handshakes,[160] as well as poison pills[161] and suicide pills[162] that are designed to entrench the position of existing management. In *Rooney v. Cree Lake Resources Corp.*[163] the court refused to give effect to a golden parachute provision in a contract, where to do so would have resulted in the payment of unearned compensation in a lump sum equal to over 70 per cent of the corporation's assets. Justice Dilks held that since such a provision would prevent dissatisfied shareholders from removing what they considered to be incompetent management, the provision was neither fair nor reasonable.

> In determining whether a particular contract is reasonable and fair to the corporation, one must examine all the surrounding circumstances including the purpose of the agreement and its possible ramifications for the corporation. It need not be either fair or reasonable to the director. It is his fiduciary duty to the corporation which requires it to be reasonable and fair to the corporation.[164]

§10.63 In *Rooney v. Cree Lake Resources Corp.*,[165] the golden parachute would have triggered the payment of unearned compensation in a lump sum equal to over 70 per cent of the corporation's assets. It was also noted that there was no reasonable prospect of any sudden influx of capital or income to support the payment. In these circumstances, Dilks J. concluded that since such a provision would prevent dissatisfied shareholders from exercising their right to terminate incompetent management, it was neither reasonable nor fair to the corporation. In *Cannaday v. Sun Peaks Resort Corp.*,[166] the court dealt with another "golden parachute" provision. It was held on appeal that in deciding whether a contract

---

[158] See, generally, *Guinness plc v. Saunders*, [1990] H.L.J. No. 16, [1990] 2 A.C. 663; *Phipps v. Boardman*, [1964] 1 W.L.R. 993, aff'd [1967] A.C. 46 (H.L.).
[159] A clause in a director's or officer's employment contract to the effect that he (or she) will be granted a substantial benefit in the event that the company is acquired and his employment is terminated. Often, these benefits will take the form of a substantial cash payment entitlement, a bonus, or stock options.
[160] An entitlement in favour of a director or senior officer to receive a large payment upon the termination or expiration of his or her service with the corporation.
[161] A device employed by a corporation employed to deter a hostile takeover. Generally, it will take the form of some right associated with designated securities of the corporation that makes a hostile takeover prohibitively expensive (for instance, a right to redeem otherwise non-voting shares at a premium where there is a successful takeover bid).
[162] An extreme form of poison pill.
[163] [1998] O.J. No. 3077 (Gen. Div.).
[164] *Ibid.*, at para. 52. See also *Cannaday v. McPherson*, [1995] B.C.J. No. 2231, 25 B.L.R. (2d) 75 (S.C.), rev'd [1998] B.C.J. No. 85, 44 B.C.L.R. (3d) 195 (C.A.); *UPM-Kymmene Corp. v. UPM-Kymmene Miramachi Inc.*, [2002] O.J. No. 2412, 27 B.L.R. (3d) 53 (S.C.J.).
[165] [1998] O.J. No. 3077, 40 C.C.E.L. (2d) 96 (Gen. Div.).
[166] [1998] B.C.J. No. 85, 44 B.C.L.R. (3d) 195 (C.A.), rev'g [1995] B.C.J. No. 2231, 25 B.L.R. (2d) 75 (S.C.).

was reasonable and fair, it was necessary to consider the factual matrix that formed the background to the contract. After referring to these two decisions in *UPM-Kymmene* case (which dealt with director remuneration), Lax J. quotes Dilks J.:

> In determining whether a particular contract is reasonable and fair to the corporation, one must examine all the surrounding circumstances including the purpose of the agreement and its possible ramifications for the corporation. It need not be either fair or reasonable to the director. It is his fiduciary duty to the corporation which requires it to be reasonable and fair to the corporation.

§10.64 It should not be assumed, however, that golden parachute (or, for that matter, "golden hello")[167] arrangements are necessarily invalid on the basis that they are neither fair nor reasonable. A consideration of "all the surrounding circumstances" requires a consideration of the general employment market for directors. For instance, the extent of the severance amount payable needs to be assessed in comparison to what other corporations are offering in terms of liquidated settlement arrangements to their directors. Directors who possess proven ability or some unique skill or network of connections on which a corporation intends to draw may be expected to insist upon a generous compensation package, including a proper scheme for severance payment in the event that they are forced out of the corporation. These considerations will be of most importance in the case of executive directors. A proper consideration of the evidence would also consider the financial circumstances of the corporation at the time when the director in question was hired, its susceptibility to a take-over bid, and also whether the corporation has a poor history of summarily dismissing executive officers. All of these factors may necessitate the provision of a golden parachute, if the corporation is to attract the kind of talented (or otherwise gifted) people that it needs. The mere fact that an arrangement is beneficial to one or more of the directors is not in itself determinative of whether it is reasonable and fair to the corporation.

§10.65 In *New York Trust Co. v. American Realty Co.*,[168] it was alleged by way of counterclaim that a director ("Underwood") breached his fiduciary duties to a company in the sale of certain property. The company argued that Underwood stood in a fiduciary duty to the company, and that, in disregard of this duty, he secretly took, upon the sale, an indirect and exorbitant profit. The court found that during the negotiations Underwood revealed his interest in the property. The land sold consisted of various tracts acquired by Underwood at different times; while some of these tracts had been owned by Underwood for years, others were acquired only the year before the purchase (*i.e.*, in 1919). In dealing with the claims against Underwood, the New York Court of Appeals considered the extent to which a director is accountable for profits earned in dealings between the director and the corporation. Justice Lehman began by considering the distinction between a right to demand an accounting and a right to rescind the contract.

---

[167] For example, a signing bonus or similar upfront payment or an analogous other inducement to take up employment.
[168] 244 N.Y. 209, 155 N.E. 102 (C.A.N.Y. 1926).

The right to rescind arose in any contract with a fiduciary duty, where a breach of duty by the fiduciary caused the corporation to enter into a disadvantageous profit.[169] The court held that the right to demand an accounting is more limited, and turns upon the circumstances in which the property was acquired by the fiduciary prior to its sale to the corporation. However, the court went on to distinguish those situations in which the corporate fiduciary acquires the property for his or her own use, and then subsequently elects to put that property on the market. If at that time the corporation decides to put in an offer for the property, there is no comparable duty to account for the profit so made, so long as adequate disclosure of interest is made.

§10.66 As the foregoing discussion indicates, the courts have recognized the need to temper the demands implicit in the fiduciary duty concept to suit the economic environment in which corporations must operate. It cannot be assumed that directors are subject to all restraints that other classes of fiduciary are subject to in entirely different contexts, where to adopt such an approach would undermine the efficient operation of corporations. As Lord Browne-Wilkinson stated in one case:

> ... [W]ise judges have often warned against the wholesale importation into commercial law of equitable principles inconsistent with the certainty and speed which are essential requirements for the orderly conduct of business affairs. ... If the Bank's arguments are correct, a businessman who has entered into transactions relating to or dependent upon property rights could find that assets which apparently belong to one person in fact belong to another; that there are "off balance sheet" liabilities of which he cannot be aware; that these property rights and liabilities arise from circumstances unknown not only to himself but also to anyone else who has been involved in the transactions. A new area of unmanageable risk will be introduced into commercial dealings. If the due application of equitable principles forced a conclusion leading to these results, your Lordships would be presented with a formidable task in reconciling legal principle with commercial common sense.[170]

(5) Specific Areas of Concern

(a) DIRECTOR REMUNERATION

§10.67 One clear and obvious situation in which the directors of a corporation may find themselves in a conflict between their personal interest and that of the corporation is in fixing the remuneration to which they are entitled. In the case of some companies, the potential conflict in this area has been eliminated by prohibiting the directors from receiving remuneration, whether acting as directors as such, or when acting in a professional capacity on behalf of the corporation,[171] and

---

[169] The right of rescission will be lost where a director or officer declares his or her interest and abstains from taking part in the approval of the contract, or the contract is ratified by a disinterested majority of the shareholders.

[170] *Westdeutsche Landesbank Girozentrale v. Islington London Borough Council*, [1996] H.L.J. No. 15, [1996] 2 W.L.R. 802 at 828.

[171] See, for instance, s. 69(1*a*) of the *Credit Unions and Caisses Populaires Act*, R.S.O. 1980, c. 102.

by prohibiting directors from being in the full-time employ of the corporate body.[172]

§10.68 Both the OBCA and the CBCA permit a director to vote on the remuneration payable to a director "as a director, officer, employee or agent of the corporation or an affiliate". The exception exists because if directors were excluded from participating in such votes, in many cases the board could be left without a quorum. The problem would be especially severe in the case of sole director corporations. For corporations that are distributing corporations, the prevailing requirement for officer remuneration to be approved by the compensation committee of the board to a large extent resolves any potential problem. Nevertheless, the Ministry of Government Services has proposed eliminating the so-called remuneration exception, so as to make the normal disclosure and voting prohibitions apply. As discussed in Chapter 9, recent proposals by the TSX would also tighten the rules in the area.

§10.69 At common law,[173] directors as such[174] had no *prima facie* entitlement to remuneration[175] and therefore could make no claim on a *quantum meruit* basis.[176] Directors were entitled only to such remuneration as the shareholders had authorized, and could make no charge, even for exceptional services.[177] The managerial powers of the directors were not seen as extending to fixing their own remuneration.[178] Moreover, where statutory restrictions on such payment were imposed, payment was prohibited unless and until those restrictions had been satisfied.[179] Both the OBCA and the CBCA have rejected this approach, although both preserve the right of the shareholders to take control over director

---

[172] *Credit Unions and Caisses Populaires Act*, R.S.O. 1980, c. 102, s. 45(3).

[173] *Wright v. Rider Resources Inc.*, [1994] A.J. No. 533, , 21 Alta. L.R. (3d) 149, 15 B.L.R. (2d) 308 at 313 (Q.B.), *per* Hunt J.; *Roray v. Howe Sound Mills & Logging Co.* (1915), 22 D.L.R. 855 (B.C.C.A.); *Foster v. Foster*, [1916] Ch. 532.

[174] In the case of directors who were also officers and employees of a corporation, see *Clifton v. Ground Engineering Ltd.*, [1982] S.J. No. 715, 19 Sask. R. 181 (Q.B.); *Flame Bar-B-Q Ltd. v. Hoar's Estate*, [1978] N.B.J. No. 169, 22 N.B.R. (2d) 595, 39 A.P.R. 595 (S.C.), rev'd on other grounds [1979] N.B.J. No. 222, 106 D.L.R. (3d) 438 (C.A.); *Re Arton Lumber Co.*, [1960] B.C.J. No. 15, 32 W.W.R. 516 (S.C.).

[175] *Bray v. Ford*, [1896] A.C. 44 at 48 (H.L.), *per* Lord Watson; *Beaudry v. Read*, [1907] O.J. No. 624, 10 O.W.R. 622 at 625 (H.C.J.), *per* Riddell J.; *Hutton v. West Cork Rlwy. Co.* (1883), 23 Ch. D. 654 (C.A.), *per* Bowen L.J.; see also *Re Publishers Syndicate*, [1903] O.J. No. 88, 5 O.L.R. 392 (C.A.); *Roray v. Howe Sound Mills & Logging Co.* (1915), 22 D.L.R. 855 (B.C.C.A.); *Birney v. Toronto Milk Co.*, [1902] O.J. No. 2, 5 O.L.R. 1 (C.A.); *Canada (Minister of Railways & Canals) v. Quebec Southern Rlwy. Co.* (1908), 12 Ex. C.R. 11.

[176] See, generally, *Guinness plc v. Saunders*, [1990] H.L.J. No. 16, [1990] 2 A.C. 663 at 689, *per* Lord Templeman; *Woolf v. East Nigel Gold Mining Co.* (1905), 21 T.L.R. 660; *Rowlings v. Cape Breton Cold Storage Ltd.*, [1929] S.C.R. 505; *Re J.C. Harris Groceteria Ltd.* (1940), 14 M.P.R. 588 at 593-94, [1940] 2 D.L.R. 257 (N.S.S.C.), *per* Graham J.; *Denman v. Clover Bar Coal Co.* (1913), 48 S.C.R. 318. There can be no implied contract between a corporation and a director: *Marks v. Rocsand Co.*, [1921] O.J. No. 119, 49 O.L.R. 137 at 141 (C.A.), *per* Riddell J.

[177] *Barrett v. Hartley* (1866), L.R. 2 Eq. 789 at 796, *per* Stuart V.C.

[178] *Foster v. Foster*, [1916] 1 Ch. 532 at 544, *per* Peterson J.

[179] *Re Queen City Plate Glass Co.*, [1910] O.J. No. 235, 16 O.W.R. 336, 1 O.W.N. 863 (H.C.J.).

remuneration should they be so inclined. Sections 125 of the CBCA and 137 of the OBCA each provide:

> Subject to the articles, the by-laws or any unanimous shareholder agreement, the directors of a corporation may fix the remuneration of the directors, officers and employees of the corporation.

By virtue of subsections 17(1) of the OBCA and 16(1) of the CBCA, it is not necessary to pass a by-law in order to confer any particular power on the corporation or its directors. Therefore, unless there is a restriction in the articles, by-laws or a unanimous shareholder resolution, the directors generally have full power to fix their remuneration. Where the directors of a corporation are paid, there is no rule that all directors must receive the same remuneration.[180]

§10.70 Thus the remuneration of directors has now been made a matter of the internal management of the corporation,[181] and in the normal case[182] will not be subject to review by the court.[183] There is no rule that all directors must be paid the same remuneration.[184] For most corporations under the present legislation the only requirement respecting director remuneration is that it must be shown to have been authorized by the board — which means that there must be a director resolution to support the payment.

§10.71 The question of whether there are common law limits upon the power of directors to provide for their own remuneration has often come before the courts. It has long been recognized by the courts that allowing directors to control their own remuneration presents an opportunity for abuse and therefore strict compliance is required with procedures set out in the articles, statute and by-laws in order for remuneration to be properly approved.[185] Directors owe a duty of care to the corporation to see that they are not paid more than reasonable remuneration for the services that they provide.[186] As discussed in Chapter 9, world wide, the subject of director remuneration (particularly for executive directors) has recently come to the very forefront of debate concerning the issue of corporate governance.[187]

§10.72 Historically the courts have taken a very dim view of certain director remuneration schemes, such as gratuitous remuneration in consideration of past

---

[180] *Wright v. Rider Resources Inc.*, [1994] A.J. No. 533, 21 Alta. L.R. (3d) 149, 15 B.L.R. (2d) 308 (Q.B.); *Foster v. Foster*, [1916] 1 Ch. 532.
[181] *Normandy v. Ind, Cooper & Co.*, [1908] 1 Ch. 84 at 90-91, *per* Kekewich J.
[182] Directors may not defraud the corporation under the guise of paying themselves remuneration: *Cook v. Hinds*, [1918] O.J. No. 89, 42 O.L.R. 273, 44 D.L.R. 586 (C.A.).
[183] *Dufour v. Dufour-Wilson Motors Ltd.*, [1949] 2 W.W.R. 593 at 600 (Sask. K.B.), *per* Thompson J.
[184] *Foster v. Foster*, [1916] 1 Ch. 532 at 545, *per* Peterson J.
[185] See, generally, *Bartlett v. Bartlett Mines Ltd.*, [1911] O.J. No. 84, 24 O.L.R. 419 (C.A.).
[186] *Canada Bonded Attorney and Legal Directory Ltd. v. Leonard-Parmiter Ltd.*, [1918] O.J. No. 79, 42 O.L.R. 141 at 154 (C.A.), *per* Riddell J.; see also *Menier v. Hooper's Telegraph Works* (1874), L.R. 9 Ch. 350 at 353 (C.A.), *per* James L.J.
[187] See, generally, *Report of the Committee on Financial Aspects of Corporate Governance* (London Gee, 1992) (the *Cadbury Report*); Committee on Corporate Governance, *Final Report* (London: Gee, 1998) (the *Hample Report*).

services rendered to the corporation[188] or compensation for loss of position, in the event of the amalgamation of the corporation with another corporation.[189] However, it has been held that the directors of a corporation are not limited in their remuneration to the profits of the corporation.[190] Like all director powers, the control of the directors over remuneration must be exercised for a proper corporate purpose, and therefore they may not pay any or all of their number a "bonus" so as to permit the recipient(s) to purchase a controlling interest in the corporation.[191] Moreover, where the directors of a corporation vote themselves remuneration that is excessive given the time, attention and services that they devote to the corporation, the remuneration is liable to be set aside.[192] Even where the remuneration is within acceptable limits, its payment and receipt may be a mixed blessing, for it may subject the directors to a higher standard of care.[193]

§10.73 Although neither the OBCA nor the CBCA requires shareholder approval of the remuneration of any director or officer, such a requirement can be introduced by way of one of the three usual avenues for constraining director authority: by including such a provision in the articles, by-laws or a unanimous shareholder agreement. If such a restriction exists, the directors are bound by it, and they cannot claim the protection of section 19 of the OBCA[194] should they sign an agreement purporting to confer remuneration on themselves contrary to that restriction, because they will be impressed with the knowledge of the limits of their powers by reason of their relationship to the corporation.[195] Where the maximum remuneration of a director or officer is fixed by by-law, the remuneration payable is still a matter of contract, so that if a lesser amount is agreed upon between the corporation and the officer concerned, that lesser amount is the amount that is payable.[196]

(b) PAYMENTS TO DIRECTORS

§10.74 Quite apart from director remuneration, a corporation may sometimes make routine payments to directors in the ordinary course of its business, such as the repayment of a loan made by the director, or the payment of interest at the agreed contract rate. There is no presumption at law that such payments when made by a corporation to one of its directors are fraudulent conveyances or preferences. In general, provided that the transaction was properly disclosed by the director and approved by the corporation, the same rules apply with respect to such payments as with respect to corresponding payments made to creditors at

---

[188] *Lumbers v. Fretz*, [1928] O.J. No. 84, 62 O.L.R. 635 (S.C.), aff'd [1928] O.J. No. 111, 63 O.L.R. 190 (C.A.).
[189] *Clarkson v. Davies*, [1923] A.C. 100.
[190] *Re Lundy Granite Co. (Lewis' Case)* (1872), 26 L.T. 673 at 675 (C.A.), per James L.J., per Mellish L.J.; see also *Re Halt Garage (1964), Ltd.*, [1982] 3 All E.R. 1016 (Ch.).
[191] See, generally, *Giguère v. Colas* (1915), 48 Que. S.C. 198.
[192] *Nolan v. Parsons*, [1942] O.J. No. 445, [1942] O.R. 358 (C.A.).
[193] *Re Waterman's Will Trust*, [1952] 2 All E.R. 1054 at 1055 (Ch.), per Harmon J.
[194] CBCA, s. 18.
[195] *Canada Furniture Co. v. Banning* (1917), 39 D.L.R. 313 (Man. K.B.).
[196] *Warren v. Superior Engravers Ltd.*, [1940] O.J. No. 280, [1941] 1 D.L.R. 323 (C.A.).

arm's length. Nor is there any presumption that such payments are oppressive. A director is entitled to be paid amounts owed to him or her by the corporation, whether as remuneration or in payment for credit extended by the director or otherwise.[197] However, section 140 of the *Bankruptcy and Insolvency Act*[198] provides that:

> 140. Where a corporation becomes bankrupt, no officer or director thereof is entitled to have his claim preferred as provided by section 136 in respect of wages, salary, commission or compensation for work done or services rendered to the corporation in any capacity.

Moreover, the claim of a director who is also a shareholder may be a reviewable transaction under that Act, with the result that payment of that claim will be postponed until all other creditors have been paid in full.[199]

(c) VOTE RENTING

§10.75 One obvious way to circumvent the restrictions imposed under subsection 132(5) of the OBCA is vote-renting. Under a vote-renting scheme, directors abstain from voting on matters in which they personally are interested. However, it is recognized that they will participate in votes held on matters on which a colleague is interested. In true vote-renting, a director will vote in favour of the scheme that benefits his or her colleague in the expectation that the consideration shown to the colleague on that matter will be reciprocated in the future — on the principle, "you scratch my back, I'll scratch yours".[200] While such arrangements are undoubtedly common, they rarely come before the courts for the simple reason that their existence is very difficult to prove. However, such an arrangement was considered by the High Court in *Thorpe v. Tisdale*,[201] where several directors in a corporation were each individually interested in a series of stock issues. The court held that in such a situation it was not sufficient that none of the directors participated in approving the specific transaction in which he personally was interested. The successive motions were all obviously the result of an arrangement made among the directors. Therefore, although the OBCA is silent as to acceptability of vote-renting, it is clear from the case law that such a scheme is not acceptable.

(6) Shareholder Ratification

§10.76 Although the procedure is relatively rare, a contract that is subject to the possibility of being set aside under subsection 132(9) may also be ratified (and therefore validated) by the shareholders of the corporation. The authority for this procedure is set down in subsection 132(8) of the OBCA, which reads:

---

[197] See, generally, *Heap Noseworthy Ltd. v. Didham*, [1996] N.J. No. 8, 38 C.B.R. (3d) 94 (T.D.).
[198] R.S.C. 1985, c. B-3.
[199] See, generally, *Bankruptcy and Insolvency Act*, R.S.C. 1985, c. B-3, ss. 100, 4(2) and 137(1).
[200] *Zapata Corp. v. Maldonado*, 430 A.2d 779 (S.C. Del. 1981), *per* Quillen J.
[201] [1909] O.J. No. 740, 13 O.W.R. 1044 at 1049 (H.C.J.), *per* Latchford J.

132.(8) Despite anything in this section, a director or officer, acting honestly and in good faith, is not accountable to the corporation or to its shareholders for any profit or gain realized from any such contract or transaction by reason only of his or her holding the office of director or officer, and the contract or transaction, if it was reasonable and fair to the corporation at the time it was approved, is not by reason only of the director's or officer's interest therein void or voidable, where,

(a) the contract or transaction is confirmed or approved by special resolution at a meeting of the shareholders duly called for that purpose; and

(b) the nature and extent of the director's or officer's interest in the contract or transaction are disclosed in reasonable detail in the notice calling the meeting or in the information circular required by section 112.

Any such ratification will presumably be subject to the rules that have evolved under the law relating to shareholder derivative actions.

§10.77 The subject of shareholder ratification is dealt with in detail in Chapter 12, Shareholders and Their Rights. In this chapter, we will examine only the specific aspects of shareholder ratification that pertain to the ratification of contracts in which directors have a material interest. Even where the directors or officers of a corporation fail to comply with the disclosure or non-participation requirements set out in section 132 of the OBCA with respect to a contract or transaction in which they are interested, the contract or transaction may still be saved, where it is confirmed by the shareholders. The basis for such confirmation is found in subsection 132(8) of the Act, which provides:

132.(8) Despite anything in this section, a director or officer, acting honestly and in good faith, is not accountable to the corporation or to its shareholders for any profit or gain realized from any such contract or transaction by reason only of his or her holding the office of director or officer, and the contract or transaction, if it was reasonable and fair to the corporation at the time it was approved, is not by reason only of the director's or officer's interest therein void or voidable, where,

(a) the contract or transaction is confirmed or approved by special resolution at a meeting of the shareholders duly called for that purpose; and

(b) the nature and extent of the director's or officer's interest in the contract or transaction are disclosed in reasonable detail in the notice calling the meeting or in the information circular required by section 112.

Subsection 120(7.1) of the CBCA is similar, but specifically requires that the contract or transaction must have been reasonable and fair to the corporation "when it was approved or confirmed". This date seems an unusual point of reference. The critical issue is surely more whether the transaction was fair at the time when it was made.

§10.78 It was clear at common law that shareholder ratification was possible, at least in certain cases. Ratification may be express or by conduct. Thus it would appear that a director's breach of fiduciary duty may be ratified expressly or implicitly by the corporation or (where the board is tainted) by the shareholders of the corporation, after the time when it occurs. Such ratification is as effective in curing the earlier breach, as approval by that same body would be if given prior to the act alleged to constitute the breach of duty. Implicit ratification arises from positive and unequivocal action on the part of the corporation, which is sufficient to demonstrate an intention to treat the act of the director as complete, proper and effective.[202] While it is clear that subsection 120(8) of the CBCA is intended to be a saving provision, the courts have had a difficult time applying it to the facts of individual cases.[203]

(7) Shareholder Access to Disclosure Information

§10.79 The CBCA allows the shareholders of a corporation to examine portions of any minutes of meetings of directors (or a committee of directors) that contains a conflict of interest disclosure, as well as any other documents that contain such a disclosure. The Ministry of Government Services has raised the question of whether such a provision should be carried forward into the OBCA. Some concern must be raised with respect to this proposal. The risk of such access proving prejudicial both to the corporation and the other party to whom the disclosure relates would seem to off-set the limited benefit that is to be derived from permitting such access.

C. DELEGATION OF MANAGERIAL POWERS

§10.80 Corporations are, by their nature, bureaucratic entities. The larger the corporation, the larger the bureaucracy that will be engaged in its operation. The creation of a bureaucratic structure for the administration of the corporation's business and affairs necessarily entails the delegation of authority and responsibility by the board of directors. There are essentially two types of delegation that the directors of a corporation may seek to employ. First, they may seek to delegate some of the powers, duties, authorities and rights conferred upon the board collectively to an individual director or a committee or sub-committee of the board. Delegation of this type may be described as intra-board delegation. Second, the board may wish to delegate some of the aspects of managing or administering the business or affairs of the corporation to one or more persons who are not directors of the corporation. Delegation of this second type may be described as extra-board delegation.

§10.81 The case law often describes the directors of a corporation as the delegates and trustees of the shareholders of their corporation, and there is an inherent assumption in that description that the shareholders who elected or appointed the directors did so in reliance upon their skill and experience. Such a relationship is necessarily one of personal trust. The practical effect of the distinction

---

[202] See, generally, *Balaban v. Bryndon Ventures Inc.*, [1993] A.J. No. 726, 13 Alta. L.R. (3d) 171 (Q.B.).
[203] See, for instance, *Wedge v. McNeill*, [1982] P.E.I.J. No. 31, 39 Nfld. & P.E.I.R. 205, 111 A.P.R. 205, 142 D.L.R. (3d) 133 (C.A.).

between agency relationships of personal trust and those that do not involve personal trust was explained by Buckley J. in the following terms:

> The relation of an agent to his principal is normally at least one which is of a confidential character and the application of the maxim *delegatus non potest delegare* to such relationships is founded on the confidential nature of the relationship. Where the principal reposes no personal confidence in the agent the maxim has no application, but where the principal does place confidence in the agent that in respect of which the principal does so must be done by the agent personally unless either expressly or inferentially he is authorized to employ a sub-agent or to delegate the function to another. If the agent personally performs all that part of his function which involves any confidence conferred on him or reposed in him by the principal it is, in my judgment, immaterial that he employs another person to carry out some purely ministerial act on his behalf in completing the transaction.[204]

Since the directors occupy a position of personal trust, the natural assumption would be that the directors' powers of delegation would correspondingly be limited. Because of the fiduciary nature of the office of director, at common law the directors were not authorized to delegate their general managerial powers,[205] even to a block of their own number such as a finance committee,[206] unless authorized to do so under the articles and by-laws of the corporation.

§10.82 But it is self-evident that the suitability of corporations as a vehicle for organizing productive enterprise would be seriously compromised if the directors of a corporation were fully constrained in their ability to delegate their various responsibilities with respect to the corporation. Consequently the courts have approached the question of delegation not on the basis of whether directors ought to be allowed to delegate their responsibilities, but instead considered only the question of the extent to which such delegation should be permitted. As in so many areas of corporate law, they have sought to strike a delicate balance — in this case between the practical needs of the corporation for delegation, against the goal of preventing directors from delegating away so much of their responsibility that they cease to be liable for the performance of the duties that the law imposes upon them.

§10.83 From earliest times it seems to have been appreciated that the directors of a corporation would find it necessary to delegate day-to-day conduct of the business of a corporation.[207] This implied authority reflects widespread commercial practice. In the case of most corporations of any size, the board will rarely

---

[204] *Allam & Co. v. Europa Poster Services Ltd.*, [1968] 1 All E.R. 826 at 832 (Ch.).
[205] Although a corporation might ratify acts purportedly done on its behalf: *Fischer v. Borland Carriage Co.*, [1906] O.J. No. 727, 8 O.W.R. 579 (H.C.J.), aff'd [1907] O.J. No. 248, 9 O.W.R. 193 (Div. Ct.); see also *Re County Palatine Loan and Discount Co. (Cartmell's Case)* (1874), 9 Ch. App. 691 (L.JJ.).
[206] *Saskatchewan Land & Homestead Co. v. Moore*, [1913] O.J. No. 750, 25 O.W.R. 125 at 131 (S.C.), *per* Britton J., var'd on other grounds [1914] O.J. No. 331, 26 O.W.R. 160 (C.A.). See also *Re Leeds Banking Co.* (1886), L.R. 1 Ch. App. 561 (L.JJ.), but compare *Re Taurine Co.* (1883), 25 Ch. D. 118, 53 L.J. Ch. 271 (C.A.).
[207] See, for instance, *Fred T. Brooks Ltd. v. Claude Neon General Advertising Ltd.*, [1932] O.J. No. 323, [1932] O.R. 205 (C.A.).

exercise any practical control over day-to-day operations. Instead, immediate responsibility for those operations will be under the control of the officers of the corporation who are not members of the board.

§10.84 Yet despite the long-standing realization that the directors of corporations of any size must necessarily delegate their authority, as discussed above, the starting presumption in matters of corporate governance is that the directors manage the corporation and that in so doing they will act collectively as a board.[208] The directors of a corporation act on behalf of the corporation only by or under the authority of a resolution adopted by the board at one of its meetings, or, alternatively, by or under the authority of a resolution that was approved in writing by all of the directors who held office at the time when the resolution was adopted.

§10.85 Unlike the members of a partnership,[209] the individual directors of a corporation (even the chairman of the board of directors of the corporation)[210] possess no implied authority to act on behalf of the corporation. Any power belonging to the board as a whole can only be exercised by a single director if the board delegates those powers to him or her. Whether such a delegation of authority has taken place is a question of fact to be decided by reference to all the circumstances of the case.[211] It follows that the authority of individual directors must ultimately be traced back to a delegation of authority expressly or impliedly made by the board. In every case, the extent of such delegation is a question of fact.[212] So, for instance, even where a director is delegated the authority to sign contracts, there is no necessary inference that the director in question has the authority to negotiate and enter into contracts on the corporation's behalf. The delegation of authority is seen to extend no further than the ministerial act of executing a contract that has already been approved by the corporation's directors.[213] It is true that section 19 of the OBCA absolves outsiders from any duty to inquire whether any such delegation has been made, at least

---

[208] *Houghton & Co. v. Nothard Lowe & Wills Ltd.*, [1927] 1 K.B. 246 at 267 (C.A.), per Sargent L.J.

[209] Sections 6 and 7 of the *Partnerships Act*, R.S.O. 1990, c. P.5 reads:

> 6. Every partner is an agent of the firm and of the other partners for the purpose of the business of the partnership, and the acts of every partner who does any act for carrying on in the usual way business of the kind carried on by the firm of which he or she is a member, bind the firm and the other partners unless the partner so acting has in fact no authority to act for the firm in the particular matter and the person with whom the partner is dealing either knows that the partner has no authority, or does not know or believe him or her to be a partner.
>
> 7. An act or instrument relating to the business of the firm and done or executed in the firm name, or in any other manner showing an intention to bind the firm by a person thereto authorized, whether a partner or not, is binding on the firm and all the partners, but this section does not affect any general rule of law relating to the execution of deeds or negotiable instruments.

[210] R.R. Pennington, *Company Law*, 6th ed. (London: Butterworths, 1990), 125 *et seq.*
[211] See, generally, *Mitchell & Hobbs (U.K.) Ltd. v. Mill*, [1996] 2 B.C.L.C. 102 (Q.B.).
[212] *Harold Holdsworth & Co. (Wakefield) Ltd. v. Caddies*, [1955] 1 W.L.R. 352 (H.L.).
[213] *Rundle v. Miramichi Lumber Co.* (1922), 70 D.L.R. 713, 50 N.B.R. 180 (C.A.).

where the authority that a particular director or officer is purporting to exercise is within that director or officer's apparent authority (presumably, the type of authority that a director would normally be given, in the case of similar types of business entity). But between the officer/director and the corporation itself, the authority to act must be shown to originate (directly or indirectly) in some express or implied delegation made by the board. So long as the authority so delegated is limited to the administration of the ordinary commercial business of the corporation, such delegation is perfectly proper.[214] Problems generally arise only when the directors purport to delegate away their

- powers specifically reserved to them by law, or
- discretionary or general policy-making functions, or
- control over basic aspects of the corporation's affairs, such as the allotment of shares.[215]

§10.86 Sections 127 of the OBCA and 115 of the CBCA each contain detailed provisions respecting the extent to which powers and responsibilities of the board of directors may be delegated to committees of the board and to managing directors. The term "committee" is sufficiently broad to permit the board to delegate powers to a single person.[216] Delegation by the board neither reduces nor extinguishes the power and authority of the full board. The board may act as a whole despite a prior decision to delegate authority; similarly it may remove authority from anyone to whom authority has been delegated.[217]

(i) Board Committee Structure

§10.87 It is common practice, and almost always the case with larger corporations, for boards of directors to delegate a considerable portion of their overall responsibility to committees of the board. On August 1, 2002 the Corporate Accountability and Listing Standards Committee of the New York Stock Exchange issued a proposed Corporate Governance Rule, which has largely determined the overall board committee structure adopted by major companies since that date. The rule requires each such company to have an audit committee, an executive

---

[214] *Re Bolt & Iron Co.*, [1884] O.J. No. 443, 10 P.R. 434 at 436 (H.C.J.), *per* Master Hodgins. See, generally, *J.H. McKnight Construction Co. v. Vansickler* (1915), 51 S.C.R. 374; *Fred T. Brooks Ltd. v. Claude Neon General Advertising Ltd.*, [1931] O.J. No. 396, [1931] O.R. 92 (S.C.), aff'd [1932] O.J. No. 323, [1932] O.R. 205 (C.A.); see also *Houghton & Co. v. Nothard Lowe & Wills Ltd.*, [1927] 1 K.B. 246 at 267 (C.A.), *per* Sargent L.J.

[215] See, for instance, *Re Pakenham Pork Packing Co.*, [1906] O.J. No. 27, 12 O.L.R. 100 at 102 (C.A.) (delegation of directors' power to receive subscriptions and allot shares), *per* Anglin J.; *Manes Tailoring Co. v. Willson*, [1907] O.J. No. 109, 14 O.L.R. 89 (H.C.J.). In *Twin City Oil Co. v. Christie*, [1909] O.J. No. 199, 18 O.L.R. 324 at 326 (H.C.J.) (an action to enforce calls on shares issued and allotted by the president of the corporation), Meredith C.J. stated, that the directors had no power to delegate to the president their authority as to the allotment of shares or to accept the offer of the defendant for the shares for which he applied. See, generally, *Tanguay v. Royal Paper Mills Co.* (1907), 31 Que. S.C. 397.

[216] See, generally, *Re Fireproof Doors Ltd.*, [1916] 2 Ch. 142.

[217] *Huth v. Clarke* (1890), 25 Q.B.D. 391; see also *Horn v. Henry Faulder & Co.* (1908), 99 L.T. 524.

compensation committee and a nominating and public responsibility committee, each of which shall be comprised entirely of "independent directors", as determined by the board under the criteria specified in the rule. Some companies have gone beyond these minimum requirements and have modified their committee structure in a way best suited to the unique circumstances or needs of the companies concerned. Under the rule, each committee is required to have a written charter approved by the board. Committees are required to keep the board fully informed of their activities. The board is required to conduct a self-evaluation at least annually to determine whether it and its committees are functioning effectively. The following is a general description of the typical committee structure now widely employed.

(1) Audit Committee

§10.88 The principal board committee in the corporate governance process will usually be the audit committee of the corporation.[218] The general function of an audit committee is to spearhead the board's general oversight of a corporation's financial reporting, internal controls and audit functions. Such a committee will usually review all financial reports and statements prepared by a corporation, particularly those prepared for filing with a securities regulator or for distribution to shareholders or the wider public. The committee will also review the corporation's internal financial and accounting controls, oversee the appointment, compensation, and work performed by the independent auditor and make recommendations regarding the renewal (or removal) of the auditor at the end of the auditor's term of office. In some cases, a similar oversight will be exercised over any other accounting advisor to the corporation.

§10.88.1 The securities law requirement for an audit committee is to be found in section 2.1 of MI 52-110, which provides that every issuer "must have an audit committee that complies with the requirements" of that Instrument. MI 52-110 was heavily influenced by the requirements of the SEC and the *Sarbanes-Oxley Act of 2002* with respect to audit committees. Section 2.1 to Companion Policy 52-110CP provides that:

> An audit committee is a committee of a board of directors to which the board delegates its responsibility for oversight of the financial reporting process. Traditionally, the audit committee has performed a number of roles, including:
>
> • helping directors meet their responsibilities;
>
> • providing better communication between directors and the external auditors;
>
> • enhancing the independence of the external auditor;

---

[218] See Multilateral Instrument MI 52-110 as to the requirements pertaining to such an entity. See, generally, Louis Jr. Braiotta, *The Audit Committee Handbook* (New York: John Wiley & Sons, 1999); Catherine Bromilow & Barbara Berlin, *Audit Committee Effectiveness — What Works Best*, 3rd ed. (Institute of Internal Auditors Research Foundation); Barry J. Epstein, *Audit Committee Best Practices: Guidance for Corporations and Not-for-Profits* (Hoboken, N.J.: Wiley Pub., 2005); Frank M. Burke, Dan M. Guy & K. Tatum, *Audit Committees: A Guide For Directors, Management, And Consultants* (New York: Aspen, 2004).

- increasing the credibility and objectivity of financial reports;
- strengthening the role of the directors by facilitating in-depth discussions among directors, management and the external auditors.

[MI 52-110] requires that the audit committee also be responsible for managing, on behalf of the shareholders, the relationship between the issuer and the external auditors. ... Although under corporate law an issuer's external auditors are responsible to the shareholders, in practice, shareholders have often been too dispersed to effectively exercise meaningful oversight of the external auditors. As a result, management has typically assumed this oversight role. However, the auditing process may be compromised if the external auditors view their main responsibility as serving management rather than the shareholders. By assigning these responsibilities to an independent audit committee, the Instrument ensures that the external audit will be conducted independently of the issuer's management.

Section 2.2 of MI 52-110 provides that the external auditor of every issuer must report directly to the audit committee of that issuer. Section 2.3 deals with the responsibilities of an audit committee. In the case of each issuer, the audit committee is required to have a written charter that sets out its mandate and responsibilities.[219] However, the balance of section 2.3 sets out a set of threshold requirements applicable to any such committee. For instance, under subsection 2.3(2), it is given charge over nominating the corporation's external auditor as well as determining the compensation of the external auditor. Under subsection 2.3(3), the audit committee must be directly responsible for overseeing the work of the external auditor engaged for the purpose of preparing or issuing an auditor's report or performing other audit, review or attest services for the issuer, including the resolution of disagreements between management and the external auditor regarding financial reporting. Subsection 2.3(4) requires that the audit committee must pre-approve all non-audit services to be provided to the issuer or its subsidiary entities by the issuer's external auditor. Under subsection 2.3(5), the audit committee is required to review the issuer's financial statements, MD&A and annual and interim earnings press releases before the issuer publicly discloses this information. Under subsection 2.3(6), the audit committee must be satisfied that adequate procedures are in place for the review of the issuer's public disclosure of financial information extracted or derived from the issuer's financial statements, other than the public disclosure referred to in subsection (5), and must periodically assess the adequacy of those procedures. The structure of the audit committee is specified in section 3.1 of MI 52-110. It requires every audit committee to have at least three members, each of whom must be a director. Subject to limited exceptions applicable with respect to initial public offerings and controlled companies, every audit committee member must be independent.[220] Under subsection 3.1(45) and section 3.8, every member of the audit committee either must be financially literate,[221] or must become so within a reasonable time following his or her appointment.

---

[219] Section 2.3(1).
[220] See section 1.4 as to the meaning of independence.
[221] Financial literacy is issuer specific. To be more precise, section 1.5 of MI 52-110 provides that an individual is financially literate if he or she has the ability to read and understand a set of fi-

§10.89 The primary function of the committee is to conduct a due diligence level verification of the quality and reliability of the information disclosed by the corporation concerning its financial condition and results of operations. Accordingly, the members of this committee will be expected to possess the skills, experience and financial expertise to fulfill the specialized functions of this committee. In the United States, the rules of the Securities and Exchange Commission provide that an audit committee member cannot be considered independent if he or she receives any consulting, advisory or other compensatory fee from the corporation (other than in the way of director and committee fees and pension or other forms of deferred compensation for prior service, which compensation is not contingent upon continued service) or is otherwise an affiliated person of the corporation. The SEC also requires that:

- each member of the Company's Audit Committee must be financially literate and
- at least one member of the Audit Committee must have accounting or related financial management expertise and qualify as an audit committee financial expert.

§10.90 The committee will also usually serve as a regulatory compliance committee. This role is specifically contemplated in section 307 of the *Sarbanes-Oxley Act of 2002* and the rules and regulations promulgated by the SEC under that Act. Many committees play an active role in supervising internal whistle-blowing arrangements (*e.g.*, processing any complaints relating to accounting, internal accounting controls or auditing matters, and any similar submissions by employees with regard to questionable accounting or auditing matters).

§10.91 Critical to the success of the audit committee is a proper relationship with the corporation's auditor. The functions of the audit committee supplement rather than substitute for the investor protection historically provided through the external audit process. The audit committee should take reasonable steps to satisfy themselves that the corporation's financial statements and other disclosure statements fairly and accurately present the corporation's financial condition and results of its operations. The audit committee is not there to second guess the work of the auditor, nor to assume responsibility for ensuring that the auditor has discharged its own professional obligation to ensure that it is in fact independent, without conflict of interest, and has a properly qualified staff who are competent to carry out the audit. However, the audit committee does serve as the interface between the corporation and the auditor, and is the proper forum for discussion of any concerns that the auditor may have about the appropriateness or quality of significant accounting treatment given to business transactions that affect the corporation's financial condition and results of operations, or weaknesses in internal control systems.

---

nancial statements that present a breadth and level of complexity of accounting issues that are generally comparable to the breadth and complexity of the issues that can reasonably be expected to be raised by the issuer's financial statements.

(2) Nominating and Corporate Governance Committees

§10.92 The Nominating Committee will usually be charged with setting the criteria for the selection of new directors and nominees for vacancies on the board and with the implementation of those criteria.[222] The committee is also likely to evaluate the performance of any director whose term is expiring and to make a recommendation as to whether that director should be invited to stand for re-election. Often, the nominating committee will serve a dual role as the search committee should it prove necessary to replace the chief executive officer, the chair of the corporation, or the chair of the corporate governance committee.

§10.93 The Corporate Governance Committee will be drawn from the independent directors of the corporation. Its main role will be to maintain a proper oversight of the general corporate governance process. To that end, the specific duties of the committee will usually include monitoring developments in the corporate governance field, as well as emerging issues in the corporation, and based upon the views so taken, recommending to the full board any modifications of the corporation's scheme of corporate governance. Frequently, the corporate governance committee will include within its mandate a responsibility for evaluating senior management, including the CEO, and also the performance of the board as a whole. The committee is also likely to serve as a liaison between the full board and the executive officers with respect to governance issues.

(3) Compensation Committee

§10.94 The Compensation Committee will usually be responsible for determining and making recommendations with respect to all forms of compensation payable to executive officers of the corporation. This committee will also usually have oversight with respect to the preparation of any annual report on executive compensation that is required to be included in a corporation's annual report or other material that it is required to distribute to shareholders.[223] Compensation committees frequently review and approve any company-wide compensation program and practice, and also approve the salary, bonus, equity and other compensation arrangements of the corporation's senior executive officers (*i.e.*, those individuals reporting directly to the chief executive officer). Ap-

---

[222] For more detailed discussion on the proper role of this committee, see, generally: Jeremy Bacon, *Corporate Directorship Practices: The Nominating Committee and the Director Selection Process* (Conference Board, 1981); John L. Colley, Wallace Stettinius, Jacqueline L. Doyle & George Logan, *What Is Corporate Governance?* (New York: McGraw-Hill, 2005); Robert Gandossy & Jeffrey Sonnenfeld, *Leadership and Governance from the Inside Out* (Hoboken, N.J.: Wiley Pub. 2004); Martin Lowy, *Corporate Governance for Public Company Directors* (New York: Aspen Pub., 2003).

[223] See, generally, James F. Reda, Stewart Reifler & Laura G. Thatcher, *Compensation Committee Handbook* (Hoboken, N.J.: John Wiley & Sons, 2005); Richard H. Wagner, *Executive Compensation 2004 Guide* (Peterborough, N.H.: Kennedy Inform., 2004); Bruce B. Overton & Susan E. Stoffer, *Executive Compensation Answer Book* (New York: Aspen, 2006); Bruce R. Ellig, *The Complete Guide to Executive Compensation* (New York: McGraw-Hill, 2002); Steven Balsam, *An Introduction to Executive Compensation* (San Diego: Academic Press, 2002); Timothy J. Bartl, *Executive Compensation in Competitive Markets* (Washington: HR Policy Assoc., 2005).

proval of the CEO's salary and other remuneration is now usually decided by the entire board of directors. In some corporations, the compensation committee may also review and approve the professional fees and retention terms for any independent expert or consultant. In other corporations, such approval is considered a budget matter.

(4) Legal Restrictions on Committee Authority

§10.95 Although the two statutes are fairly similar in their treatment of delegation, there are a number of differences in detail between the approaches that each takes. Subsection 127(1) of the OBCA provides a general authority to delegate. It reads:

> 127.(1) Subject to the articles or by-laws, directors of a corporation may appoint from their number a managing director, who is a resident Canadian, or a committee of directors and delegate to such managing director or committee any of the powers of the directors.

Subsection 115(1) of the CBCA is similar, but makes no reference to the authority to delegate being subject to the articles or by-laws of the corporation. However, in view of the fact that subsection 122(2) of the CBCA — like subsection 134(2) of the OBCA — expressly requires the directors to comply with the articles and by-laws of the corporation, this omission is not of any particular significance. In most cases, the effect of delegation within the board of directors is essentially to create a two-tier board, consisting of an executive committee of directors to whom powers to administer and run the company have been delegated, and non-members of that group who constitute a pool of directors sitting outside the internal managerial structure of the corporation. In *Dairy Containers Ltd. v. N.Z. Bank Ltd.*,[224] Thomas J. summarized the relationship between such executive and non-executive directors as follows:

> It should not be necessary to restate that it is the fundamental task of the directors to manage the business of the company. Theirs is the power and the responsibility of that management. To manage the company effectively, of course, they must necessarily delegate much of their power to executives of the company, especially in respect of its day to day operations. Although constantly referred to as "the management," the executives' powers are delegated powers, subject to the scrutiny and supervision of the directors. Responsibility to manage the company in this primary sense remains firmly with the directors. ... It is the function of directors to determine the corporate objectives and strategies and ensure that the management implement those policies to determine the extent and priority of the company's investment in new ventures having regard to the resources available and the risks involved, to approve revenue and capital expenditure budgets, business plans and specific major investments such as joint ventures, equity shareholdings and major fixed assets, to select a chief executive officer, to ensure that the company is well-managed, and that the company's accounting and information systems are adequate to monitor the performance of the company and to provide reliable data for sound decision making by management and the board of directors. It can be seen at once that the directors' role in monitoring the performance and direction of

---

[224] [1995] 2 N.Z.L.R. 30 at 79 (H.C.).

management of the company is vital. The directors provide the company with direction, and act as a check on management to ensure that the direction is adhered to and pursued.

§10.96 Subsection 127(2) of the OBCA goes on to provide that where the directors of a corporation, other than a non-resident corporation, appoint a committee of directors, a majority of the members of the committee must be resident Canadians. Subsection 115(2) of the CBCA imposes a similar requirement, although an exception is given in respect of "holding corporations" as described in subsection 105(4) of the CBCA. The OBCA non-resident corporation is a type of corporation not recognized under the CBCA as such.

§10.97 Although both the CBCA and the OBCA generally permit delegation, each statute contains detailed provisions prohibiting certain specified types of delegation. However, each statute contains a lengthy list of directorial responsibilities which may not be delegated to a committee of directors or a managing director. For instance, no managing director and no committee of directors has authority to submit to the shareholders any question or matter requiring the approval of the shareholders.[225] The apparent rationale for this provision is that the shareholders are entitled to know that matters submitted to them by the directors have the support of the full board. In addition, under clause 127(3)(*b*) of the OBCA, no managing director and no committee of directors has authority to,

> (*b*) fill a vacancy among the directors or in the office of auditor or appoint or remove any of the chief executive officers, however designated, the chief financial officers, however designated, the chair or the president of the corporation ...[226]

The chief executive officer and chief financial officer are the senior officers of a corporation and will make most of the effective decisions within the corporation. As these officers are often delegated substantial authority by the board, it stands to reason that the full board should be involved in their appointment. Presumably the office of auditor is also considered to be too important to be left to a committee. Retaining control over the appointment of a replacement auditor helps to maintain the integrity of the audit process; the auditor reports to the shareholders upon the financial records of the corporation, and those reports are prepared by the executive officers of the corporation. There would be far too obvious a risk of abuse if the executive committee or audit committee were allowed to control the appointment of a replacement auditor. Under the corresponding provision of the CBCA,[227] there is no restriction on the delegation of the directors' authority to appoint or remove any of the chief executive officer, the chief financial officer, the chairman or the president of the corporation.

§10.98 Clause 127(3)(*c*) of the OBCA provides that no managing director and no committee of directors has authority to,

---

[225] OBCA, s. 127(3)(*a*); CBCA, s. 115(3)(*a*).
[226] OBCA, s. 127(3)(*b*).
[227] Section 115(3).

(c) subject to section 184, issue securities except in the manner and on the terms authorized by the directors ...

Paragraph 115(3)(c) of the CBCA imposes an identical prohibition. It is difficult to grasp the problem that paragraph (c) is intended to cure. It prohibits a general delegation of the power to "issue securities". However, it in no way restricts the delegation of the power to approve and enter into contracts, and those contracts may easily have the same effect upon the credit and commercial viability of the corporation. The distinction between a loan and mortgage agreement and a debenture may be little more than semantic, but it appears that the directors may delegate the authority to approve and enter into the former,[228] although they are restricted in the extent to which they may delegate the authority to issue the latter. However, the paragraph (c) prohibition is qualified by an exception that is so broad that it allows the prohibition to be circumvented in a very large number of cases.

§10.99 Clauses 127(3)(d) and (e) of the OBCA provide that no managing director and no committee of directors may declare dividends or purchase, redeem or otherwise acquire shares issued by the corporation. Similar prohibitions are found in the CBCA.[229] Presumably these prohibitions are included because the directors are liable for paying dividends where the profits of the corporation are insufficient, and for permitting the corporation to redeem, purchase or otherwise acquire dividends where by so doing the corporation would contravene an applicable solvency or liquidity restriction.

§10.100 In 1994, clause 127(3)(i.1) of the OBCA was added to prohibit delegation of the directors' powers to,

- approve a short-form amalgamation;
- divide a class of shares;
- change a number name to a verbal name.

---

[228] OBCA, s. 184(1) and (2) (CBCA, s. 189(1) and (2)):

>184.(1) Unless the articles or by-laws of or a unanimous shareholder agreement otherwise provide, the articles of a corporation shall be deemed to state that the directors of a corporation may, without authorization of the shareholders,
>
>(a) borrow money upon the credit of the corporation;
>
>(b) issue, reissue, sell or pledge debt obligations of the corporation;
>
>(c) subject to section 20, give a guarantee on behalf of the corporation to secure performance of an obligation of any person; and
>
>(d) mortgage, hypothecate, pledge or otherwise create a security interest in all or any property of the corporation, owned or subsequently acquired, to secure any obligation of the corporation.
>
>(2) Unless the articles or by-laws of or a unanimous shareholder agreement relating to a corporation otherwise provide, the directors may by resolution delegate any or all of the powers referred to in subsection (1) to a director, a committee of directors or an officer.

[229] CBCA, s. 115(3)(d) and (e).

The apparent reason for this amendment was that such changes were seen to amount to fundamental changes to the corporation, and accordingly ought to require full board approval. Industry Canada, the federal department responsible for the CBCA, considered whether such a change should be made to the CBCA, but recommended against it, on the basis that "to date, there has been no evidence of any problems in these areas under the CBCA".[230]

§10.101 The remaining prohibitions set out in subsection 127(3) of the OBCA are of less general application. They are that no managing director and no committee of directors may,

(*f*) pay a commission referred to in section 37;

(*g*) approve a management information circular referred to in Part VIII;

(*h*) approve a take-over bid circular, directors' circular or issuer bid circular referred to in Part XX of the *Securities Act*;

(*i*) approve any financial statements referred to in clause 154(1)(*b*) of the Act or Part XVIII of the *Securities Act*; or

(*j*) adopt, amend or repeal by-laws.

The corresponding provision of the CBCA are generally similar,[231] but no references are made in it to any provincial *Securities Act*.

§10.102 A managing director is a director to whom the board delegates its general powers of management, or some substantial part of them. This delegation is usually, if not invariably, made subject to the overriding authority of the board. Management here means management of the company's business, or part of it, as the case may be.[232] A managing director must be a resident Canadian.[233] The term "managing director" is more common in English practice than Canadian: in most Canadian corporations which make use of the office, the managing director will be described as the "president" (as opposed to the chairman of the board) of the corporation or as its chief executive officer.[234] Moreover, in some corporations, there will be a second in command (often the designated successor of the chief executive officer), who will be designated the chief operating officer.

§10.103 Subsections 115(2) of the OBCA and 102(2) of the CBCA require an offering corporation to have at least three directors. This requirement begs the question of whether it is permissible for the directors to delegate their managerial control over the business of a corporation to a single managing director. In

---

[230] *Canada Business Corporations Act, Discussion Paper Proposals for Technical Amendments* (Ottawa: Industry Canada, September, 1995), 50.
[231] CBCA, s. 115(3).
[232] *Shirlaw v. Southern Foundries (1926) Ltd.*, [1939] 2 All E.R. 113 (C.A.).
[233] OBCA, s. 127(1); CBCA, s. 115(1).
[234] Note that the chief executive officer need not be a director at all. Indeed, among co-operatives, it is very rare for the chief executive officer to hold a position on the board. Where the chief executive officer is not a director, his position is essentially that of general manager as opposed to that of a managing director.

Welch v. Welch[235] Holland J. concluded that it was consistent with a statutory requirement that a proprietary (closely held) company have a minimum of two directors while a public company was required to have at least three, for the full board to delegate extensive managerial control to a "governing" director. Subsection 127(1) of the OBCA, which permits delegation to a managing director, in no way restricts such delegation to corporations that are not offering corporations.[236] Since this section and subsection 115(2)[237] were enacted at the same time, it seems a logical inference that the requirement for three directors under subsection 115(2) in no way restricts the power of delegation conferred under subsection 127(1).[238]

§10.104 Subject to the above limitations, the board may delegate its powers to a committee or to a single director. However, even where such a power is conferred, the managing director will exercise his or her powers as such as a delegate of the board, and will be subject to its overriding authority. Any delegated authority must be subject to the ongoing supervision of the board,[239] It may not give up its power to direct and control those persons who are so employed,[240] from which it follows that the jurisdiction of a managing director or other officer may be narrowed or revoked at any time by the board — although any such modification may amount to a breach of contract in the circumstances of a particular case for which the corporation will be liable.[241]

(ii) Corporate Responsibility of Management

§10.105 Since the executive officers (or management) of a corporation have effective control over the bulk of its operations, including all day-to-day elements of its business and affairs, it stands to reason that they have an important role to play in the corporate governance process. From both a corporate and securities law perspective, corporate governance is not intended to be a game of fox and hounds, in which the management of the corporation works to see what they can get away with, while the board of directors attempts to find what they are up to. Senior management is responsible for the day-to-day operations of the corporation, for properly informing the board of important developments operations, for providing a general periodic account of its progress, and for identifying and managing the risks that the corporation is likely to undertake or encounter in the course of carrying out its business. The corporation's senior management generally are expected to take the lead in strategic, business and

---

[235] [1971-1973] C.L.C. 40-068.
[236] CBCA, s. 115(1).
[237] CBCA, s. 102(2).
[238] In the absence of an authority in the statute under which the corporation operates or in the articles or by-laws of the corporation, there is no power to appoint a managing director of the corporation: *Boschoek Pty. Co. v. Fuke*, [1906] 1 Ch. 148 at 159, *per* Swinfen-Eady J.; *Howard's Case* (1866), 1 Ch. App. 561.
[239] *Re City Equitable Fire Insurance Co.*, [1925] Ch. 407 (C.A.).
[240] *Horn v. Henry Faulder & Co.* (1908), 99 L.T. 524.
[241] See, generally, *Harold Holdsworth & Co. (Wakefield) Ltd. v. Caddies*, [1955] 1 All E.R. 725 (H.L.).

contingency planning, in risk management, and in the execution of the business plan. They must identify and develop appropriate plans for the company, present those plans to the board, and implement the plans once board review is completed. They are directly responsible for the principal actions of the corporation, and for creating (subject to board review and approval) a proper system of corporate control, general supervision and internal audit, to ensure that the corporation is carrying on business lawfully, and that instructions coming down from the upper echelons of the corporation are being carried out.

§10.106 It is management's responsibility to put in place and supervise the operation of business record keeping and information systems that fairly present the financial condition and results of operations of the corporation. For offering corporations, this regime must be adequate to ensure the timely disclosure to investors required under securities laws to permit them to assess the financial and business soundness and risks of the corporation.

(iii) Reliance on Officers of the Corporation

§10.107 Directors often delegate their collective powers not only to individual directors among themselves but also to non-director officers of a corporation. The governing boards of all but the smallest corporate institutions, whether public or private, confront a similar practical need to provide for the effective day-to-day administration of a complex organization. The number of decisions involved in operating even a small business or administrative program will quickly outstrip the practical deliberative capacity of any governing board, even where the board in question would prefer to consider each contract and other matter itself. Direct board control would be impossible in the case of multi-national multi-function business corporations. Further, over-focus on specific decisions at the board level undermines the ability of the board to focus on broader policy and strategic issues. Accordingly, governing boards must delegate decision-making to the officers, managers and administrators of the corporate entity.

§10.108 The starting point for any inquiry into the extent to which the directors of a corporation may rely upon the directors (or officers) to whom they have delegated authority is the decision of Romer J. in *Re City Equitable Fire Insurance Co.*[242] By way of preface, the right to delegate and the right of reliance are essentially the same thing, since in each case the question for the court to resolve is the extent to which the directors may discharge their duty to manage the corporation (or supervise its management) by the delegation of authority to others. It is perhaps with respect to the issue of delegation that the duties of directors and trustees are most clearly distinguished. A trustee is obliged to see to the administration of the trust, and as a result a person who takes on the position of trustee cannot shift that duty onto other persons.[243] Thus a trustee must manage the trust property personally and is not entitled to delegate away his or her man-

---

[242] [1925] Ch. 407.
[243] *Turner v. Corney* (1841), 5 Beav. 515 at 517, 49 E.R. 677 (R.C.), *per* Lord Longdale M.R.

agement responsibilities — although it was held by Lord Hardwicke L.C. in *Ex p. Belchier* that a trustee may employ an agent when it is reasonably necessary or in conformity with common business practice.[244]

§10.109 As discussed above, a general prohibition on delegation by directors is obviously impractical. The need to delegate beyond the membership of the board, to non-director officers of the corporation is most obvious in the case of large corporations, where the sheer volume of business that is to be transacted would render impossible the personal administration of the business of the corporation by its directors, even if they were many in number and dedicated every waking hour to the assignment.

§10.110 Any such delegation of authority must be mindful of the fundamental duties to which the governing board is subject. In the case of a business corporation, the board must maintain for themselves sufficient control over the policies and operations to allow those duties to be discharged. A number of general principles immediately come to mind to guide any delegation of authority and to ensure an appropriate balance of organizational responsiveness with proper corporate governance. Specifically,

- Any delegation must be consistent with law and with corporate articles, by-laws and any unanimous shareholder agreement.

- Power should only be delegated to competent persons or bodies, and should be delegated no further down the chain of command than is necessary for effective corporate operation. Where hiring authority is delegated by the board to the senior management of the corporation, the board should make clear to the senior management that it will be held responsible for selecting qualified management and staff.

- Formalizing the scope of delegated authority reduces the risks of a blurring of fields of responsibility and lines of accountability.

- Where authority is delegated, proper rules and guidelines should be adopted to direct those who shall exercise the delegated authority. Adopting specific guidelines to define the scope of delegated authority is at the very least a prudent restraint discouraging misconduct.

- Clear terms of reference and other operating instructions should be provided, and effective communications implemented to ensure that delegated operations remain consistent with overall strategic goals.

- Effective controls and monitors should be put into place to ensure that the persons to whom authority is delegated exercise their authority properly (*i.e.*, within specified limits and for appropriate purposes) and consistently with decisions made at the board level or at senior levels of management with respect to corporate mission, strategic and tactical intention, budgetary control and the like.

---

[244] (1754), Amb. 218, 27 E.R. 144 (Ch.).

- The board should implement appropriate procedures to ensure that the exercise of delegated authority is properly reviewed, and that where problems are identified, appropriate corrective measures are implemented.

§10.111 Broadly speaking, the same rules govern delegation to non-director officers as those that govern delegation to individual directors or committees of directors. Thus it is settled that having regard to the exigencies of business, and articles and by-laws of a corporation, the day-to-day administration of the business of the corporation may be properly left to some other officer of the corporation, and where various powers and authorities are delegated by the directors to an officer, in the absence of grounds for suspicion, they are justified in trusting that official to perform such duties honestly.[245] It is not necessary for the directors to show that it was essential for them to retain an officer to perform the function delegated to the officer, nor is it necessary to show that it was customary in the business community for officers to exercise the function concerned. The discretion as to whether to employ an officer to carry out a certain function is left to the reasonable discretion of the board. However, like any trustee who retains an agent, the directors must show that they adequately supervised the agent and that reasonable care was exercised in the agent's selection.[246]

§10.112 As fiduciaries, the directors exercise power in trust for the shareholders and other stakeholders of the corporate entity. There are and must be limits beyond which any further sub-delegation by the board must be viewed as an unlawful abdication of their responsibility. They may not divest themselves of the responsibilities that go along with the trust that has been reposed in them. However, even broad delegation of authority may be justifiable and legally permissible when appropriate accountability and oversight is in place. Reliance on subordinates to formulate recommendations must obviously be permitted, since few boards have the requisite scope and depth of expertise to be able to bring forward their own ideas with respect to corporate opportunities, the risks that confront the corporation, and the range of options that exist for dealing with such opportunities and risks. Even decision-making is justifiable at lower levels, where the basis for decision has been approved at the board, and proper oversight is maintained to ensure that decisions are being made correctly. Retaining a notional right of oversight is probably not sufficient where such oversight is not exercised in practice or cannot be exercised because there are no mechanisms in place for doing so. Also objectionable are schemes in which the board's ability to superintend the exercise of delegated authority is left to the discretion of the person to whom that authority has been delegated. Such an arrangement constitutes what is an abnegation of responsibility for all practical purposes.

---

[245] See *Re City Equitable Fire Insurance Co.*, [1925] Ch. 407, [1925] B. & C. R. 109 (C.A.), *per* Romer J.:

> In respect of all duties that, having regard to the exigencies of business, and the articles of association, may properly be left to some other official, a director is, in the absence of grounds for suspicion, justified in trusting that official to perform such duties honestly.

[246] *Routley v. Gorman*, [1920] O.J. No. 156, 47 O.L.R. 420 at 424, 55 D.L.R. 58 (C.A.), *per* Ferguson J.A.

§10.113 It is sometimes suggested that a board should retain control over the setting of policy. However, the distinction between setting policy and its application is not always clear. Conceptually, the test for determining whether delegation goes beyond a reasonable limit is whether the matter concerned has such important wide-reaching or long-term implications for the corporation, or requires the exercise of such extensive judgment, that no reasonable person would consider it suitable to delegate the authority to make the decision to a single person, but would instead insist that the board as a whole should make the decision.[247] So, for instance, it may be said that a board may not remove itself in a very substantial way from its duty to use its own best judgment to manage a company.[248] In contrast, merely working out the details of a particular scheme approved by the board, or deciding upon the specific application of general (board approved rules) to the facts of a given case constitutes delegation of a very different character. In such cases, active board involvement in decision-making would likely be counter-productive. The primary emphasis with respect to such matters would probably be better directed toward creating an oversight process to ensure that corporate funds and property are not misused, any disciplinary power is not misdirected towards the settlement of personal grievances, that instances of misconduct and abuse of authority are identified, including both willful and serious neglect of duty at issue. Boards must also adopt proper personnel policies with a view towards ensuring that day-to-day operations will be under the control of properly trained, competent professionals and technicians, who have the expertise to deal with the problems that the corporation is likely to confront.

§10.114 To that end, a board should be thoughtful in its appointment of senior officers, fix or approve the overall mission, strategic goals and tactical plans of the corporation and monitor its performance.[249] Decisions with respect to delegation of a task or responsibility should be as informed as any other decision of the board, but where properly made such decisions are entitled to as much respect as is the exercise of any other business judgment by the board.[250] One critical question is likely to be whether the directors retain the ability to terminate the delegation arrangement.[251] Where that ability is unfettered so that the delegation may be terminated at will, the courts are prepared to accept wider grants of delegated authority since the directors may resume their pre-delegation managerial role simply by cancelling the arrangement. On the other hand, where the costs and penalties associated with terminating delegated authority are substan-

---

[247] See, generally, *Chapin v. Benwood Found.*, 402 A.2d 1205 at 1210 (Del. Ch. 1979).
[248] See *Grimes v. Donald*, 673 A.2d 1207 at 1214 (Del. Ch. 1996), overruled on other grounds: *Brehm v. Eisner*, 746 A.2d 244 at 253 (Del. Ch. 2000).
[249] See, for instance, *Cahall v. Lofland*, 114 A.2d 224 (Del. Ch. 1921); *Grimes v. Donald*, W.L. 54441 (Del. Ch. 1995); *Rosenblatt v. Getty Oil Co.*, 493 A.2d 929 (Del. Ch. 1985); *Canal Capital Corp. v. French*, Civ. No. 11,764, [1992] W.L. 159008 (Del. Ch.); *In Re Bally's Grand Derivative Litigation*, Civ. No. 14644, [1997] W.L. 305803 (Del. Ch.); *Salt Lake Tribune Publishing Company, L.L.C., v. AT &T Corp.*, [2001] WL 670928 (D. Utah).
[250] See, for instance, *Rosenblatt v. Getty Oil Co.*, 493 A.2d 929 at 943 (Del. Ch. 1985); *Aronson v. Lewis*, 473 A.2d 805 at 813 (Del. Ch. 1984).
[251] *In Re Bally's*, [1997] W.L. 305803.

tial, so that in practice they cannot be exercised, the propriety of a delegation of authority may be brought into question.

§10.115 It has been held that the board's duty to manage or supervise the management of the business and affairs of a corporation ordinarily entails the duty to establish or approve the long-term strategic, financial and organizational goals of the corporation; to approve formal or informal plans for the achievement of these goals; to monitor corporate performance; and to act, when in the good faith, informed judgment of the board it is necessary or appropriate to act in order for it to carry out its responsibilities in good faith.[252] A board cannot delegate a specific regulatory authority that is conferred upon it by law.[253]

(1) Honesty

§10.116 No person is bound to presume fraud, and therefore as a general rule it is sufficient if the directors appoint persons of good repute and competent skill to conduct its ongoing operations, including the preparation of the financial statements of the corporation, and the directors may rely upon those persons.[254] By extension, the shareholders of the corporation may presume the honesty of its directors.[255]

> Directors are assumed to act for the interests of their stockholders, and the latter have a right to rely upon the assumption that they are acting honesty until the contrary appears.

In *Prefontaine v. Grenier,*[256] the president and board of directors of a bank were held not to be personally liable on the failure of the bank due to unauthorized overdrafts being allowed by the head cashier. The head cashier was an officer of the bank, and had presented the books in such a way that the overdrafts were not readily apparent. It was held that directors could not be rendered personally liable merely because they entrusted the regularly authorized officers of the company, or because they had failed to detect the irregularities in question, and had been misled. Although the misrepresentations or concealment had led to a loss, the directors had no reason for doubting the officers' fidelity.

§10.117 The question of the extent to which a director is entitled to rely upon the apparent honesty of the officers of a corporation and his fellow directors was discussed by Lindley M.R. in *Re National Bank of Wales.*[257] In this decision the Master of the Rolls clearly recognized the impracticality of imposing a duty of inquiry upon a director, where there are no circumstances to put the director on

---

[252] See, generally, *Grimes v. Donald,* C.A. No. 13358 (Del. Ch.); *Cahall v. Lofland,* 114 A.224 at 229 (Del. Ch. 1921).
[253] *Hongsathavij v. Queen of Angels etc. Medical Center* (1998), 62 Cal. App. 4th 1123 at 1143, 73 Cal. Rptr. 2d 695.
[254] *Re Denham & Co.* (1883), 25 Ch. D. 752 at 766, *per* Chitty J.
[255] *In re Liverpool Household Stores Asso.,* 59 L.J. (N.S.) Ch. Div. 616.
[256] [1907] A.C. 101.
[257] [1899] 2 Ch. 629 at 673 (C.A.), *per* Lindley M.R.

notice that anything is amiss.[258] The court came to a similar conclusion in the Chancery Appeal decision in *Land Credit Co. of Ireland v. Lord Fermoy*.[259] The facts in that case were that the company was in the business of lending money. The full board of directors of the company appointed an executive committee. In order to raise the price of the shares of the company in the market, the executive committee caused the company to buy shares in the name of the secretary and another. To pay for these shares, they drew cheques on the bankers of the company. The cheques were reported to a meeting of the directors as having been drawn for a loan and were approved by the directors as such. The question to be decided was whether the directors who were not members of the executive committee were under any duty to inquire into whether the executive committee was guilty of misconduct, before approving what they considered to be a perfectly ordinary transaction. Lord Hatherley L.C. rejected this suggestion.[260] Thus the directors of a corporation are entitled to rely on the skill, integrity and efforts of the corporation's officers and other employees who conduct its day-to-day business. A director does not warrant the truth of the corporation's financial statements.[261] He or she is not the insurer of the corporation's creditors, although the directors must hold an honest belief that the statements which they approve are true.[262]

§10.118 Finally, corporate directors have a continuing duty to monitor the business and affairs of the corporation, and monitoring the exercise of delegated authority is part and parcel of that responsibility. Much as directors may not shut their eyes to corporate misconduct and then claim that because they did not see the misconduct, they did not have a duty to look, directors are under a continuing obligation to keep informed about the activities of the corporation. The proper discharge of directorial management responsibility does not require detailed inspection of day-to-day activities, but it does imply general monitoring of the corporations business and affairs.[263] There should be a routine program for the review of activities conducted under a delegated authority. The board has responsibility for overseeing and understanding the corporation's strategic plans from their inception through their development and execution by management. Once the board reviews a strategic plan, the board should regularly monitor implementation of the plan to determine whether it is being implemented effectively and whether changes are needed.

(2) Verification of Reports, Advice of Outside Experts, etc.

§10.119 Reliance by the directors upon individual officers of a corporation is to be contrasted with reliance upon outsiders who provide technical or professional expertise to the corporation as contractors, and with reliance upon impersonal

---

[258] *Ibid.*, see also at 675.
[259] (1870), L.R. 5 Ch. 763 (L.C.).
[260] *Ibid.*, at 770 and 772.
[261] See, however, the verification and certification requirements discussed at §10.186 below.
[262] *Re National Bank of Wales*, [1899] 2 Ch. 629 at 675 (C.A.), *per* Lord Lindley M.R.
[263] See, generally, *Francis v. United Jersey Bank*, 87 N.J. 15, 432 A.2d 814 at 832 (1981).

sources of information such as the books, records, accounts and financial statements of the corporation. There is no general obligation upon directors to investigate independently and verify reports made by other directors, officers or employees to determine whether they are accurate or honestly made, unless there is something in the circumstances to suggest that there are such inaccuracies, misrepresentations or other irregularities in the material with which they have been provided. To impose any greater burden upon the directors would be wholly impractical, as it would largely defeat the entire object of delegation — not to mention the reason for seeking professional advice — and would interfere with the ongoing operations of corporate business. This specific issue was dealt with in the decision of the Earl of Halsbury L.C. in *Dovey v. Cory*, where he said:

> I cannot think that it can be expected of a director that he should be watching either the inferior officers of the bank or verifying the calculations of the auditors himself. The business of life could not go on if people could not trust those who are put into a position of trust for the express purpose of attending to details of management. If Mr. Cory was deceived by his own officers ... there appears to me to be no case against him at all.[264]

Similarly, in *Re H.J. Logan Co.*, a former director claimed in a bankruptcy for back fees owed to him by the bankrupt company for which he had served. The trustee disallowed the claim on the grounds that the director had not properly performed the duties of his office, and that his negligence had caused the company to suffer certain losses. The substance of these allegations was that the director was responsible for the failure to detect forgeries which had been perpetrated by an officer of the company. The court rejected the view put forward by the trustee and held that the director was not bound in his capacity as a director to go behind the financial statements and examine entries in the company's books.[265] It was noted that the director was not a bookkeeper, and therefore lacked the skill to undertake such an examination.

§10.120 It is recognized that the directors of a corporation "cannot be experts in all aspects of the corporations they manage or supervise". They also cannot do everything that the corporation requires to be done, nor can they be everywhere at once. Accordingly, the directors must from time to time rely upon advice and information given to them by others (who may include officers of the corporation, outside consultants, and professionals). There is a wide range in the types of information that may be presented to the directors, and different rights of reliance apply with respect to each type of information. Subsections 135(4) of the OBCA and 123(4) of the CBCA permit a director to place reasonable reliance on financial statements and professional advice — this wording being broad enough to include advice provided both by internal as well as external professionals. The CBCA provision (as revised in 2001) reads:

> 123.(4) A director is not liable under section 118 or 119 and has complied with his or her duties under subsection 122(2), if the director exercised the care, dili-

---

[264] [1901] A.C. 477 at 486 (H.L.).
[265] *Re H.J. Logan Co.*, [1926] 2 D.L.R. 946 (Ont. H.C.).

gence and skill that a reasonably prudent person would have exercised in comparable circumstances including reliance in good faith on,

(a) financial statements of the corporation represented to him by an officer of the corporation or in a written report of the auditor of the corporation fairly to reflect the financial condition of the corporation; or

(b) a report of a person whose profession lends credibility to a statement made by the professional person.

The words "represented ... fairly to reflect the financial condition of the corporation" suggests that reliance is not permissible unless the statements specifically state that they were prepared in accordance with GAAP. There is thus an argument that the directors of the corporation are obliged to inquire as to whether any financial information that is presented to them was prepared in accordance with GAAP. If this is correct, then it follows that the directors may not simply assume such compliance. In the absence of at least a formal request for confirmation of conformity, they are not protected. It is important to consider this point, because very often the monthly financial information provided to the directors will make no mention of "fair presentation" or "generally accepted accounting principles" at all. The corresponding provision of the OBCA is similar to the pre-2001 CBCA text, but in contrast to the CBCA grants the director no protection against employee wage claims (arising under section 131). To obtain protection the liability to such claims must have arisen by reason of reliance on financial statements or reports.

A director is not liable under section 130 or 134 if the director relies in good faith upon,

(a) financial statements of the corporation represented to him or her by an officer of the corporation or in a written report of the auditor of the corporation to present fairly the financial position of the corporation in accordance with generally accepted accounting principles; or

(b) a report of a lawyer, accountant, engineer, appraiser or other person whose profession lends credibility to a statement made by any such person.[266]

(3) The Due Diligence Defence

§10.121 In a 1995 discussion paper[267] Industry Canada raised a number of proposals for reform in the area of director liability. One of the recommendations made was to amend subsection 123(4) of the CBCA to replace the defence in favour of directors who rely in good faith on financial statements prepared by the officers of a corporation, audit opinions and professional advice. It was said:

The good faith reliance defence permits a director to bring forward a very specific kind of argument in response to a suit. If relying on financial statements in the particular circumstances is unreasonable, then the reliance would not be in good

---

[266] See OBCA, s. 131; cf. CBCA, s. 119.
[267] *Canada Business Corporations Act, Discussion Paper, Directors' Liability* (Ottawa: Industry Canada, 1995), 23 et seq.

faith. The good faith reliance defence is deficient in the limited nature of the circumstances in which it can be used to exonerate a director. The good faith reliance defence allows directors to point to a reliable source of information as justification for their actions, but it does not permit them, in the absence of that specific justification, to show that they acted reasonably under the circumstances.

Based on this recommendation, subsection 123(5) creates a defence of due diligence:

> 123.(5) A director has complied with his or her duties under subsection 122(1) if the director relied in good faith on:
>
> (a) financial statements of the corporation represented to the director by an officer of the corporation or in a written report of the auditor of the corporation fairly to reflect the financial condition of the corporation; or
>
> (b) a report of a person whose profession lends credibility to a statement made by the professional person.

There is no current direct equivalent provision in the OBCA,[268] although a Ministry of Government Services discussion paper has raised the question of whether such protection should be afforded. In explaining the intended purpose of subsection (5), the discussion paper also stated:

> The due diligence defence provides more fairness to directors than does the good faith reliance defence. With a due diligence defence, the directors may act reasonably prudently by relying on financial statements represented to them by an officer of the corporation or by relying on their own assessment of the financial health of the corporation. However, the due diligence defence also recognizes that the nature and extent of the expected precautions will vary under each circumstance. These precautions can include such things as putting in place appropriate controls and systems to monitor and ensure that policies are being implemented, requiring a proper review of periodic reports and taking appropriate action when a problem is brought to the director's attention.[269]

§10.122 There are several points worth making in connection with this reasoning. First, it is not immediately clear how the directors of a corporation could ever be seen to be acting reasonably in connection with the matters described in subsection 123(4) without obtaining financial information or professional advice of the sort contemplated in that section. For instance, it is difficult to see how the directors could conclude that the shares that they were issuing for a non-monetary consideration were being issued in accordance with section 25, unless either,

- the directors had some professional appraisal confirming that the property was the "fair equivalent of a money consideration", or
- the value of the consideration given was self-evidently a fair equivalent.

---

[268] But see s. 136(4), especially as amended (in force on proclamation) by S.O. 2006, c. 34, Sched. B, s. 25.

[269] *Canada Business Corporations Act, Discussion Paper, Directors' Liability* (Ottawa: Industry Canada, 1995), 24.

Yet if the self-evident test was satisfied, there would seem to be no possible basis on which the directors could be found liable.

§10.123 While it is unclear whether the due diligence defence adds anything new to the law, it nevertheless may have a detrimental impact upon director practice. As it effectively deems certain types of reliance to constitute due diligence, there is an inherent risk that subsection 123(5) will encourage greater and greater dependency on staff reporting and professional advice rather than the exercise of an independent professional judgment by the directors. Professional advice, in particular, is not necessarily compatible with the type of risk taking decision making characteristic of a market economy — especially those areas of the economy exploiting new technologies and seeking to create new markets. The position of a director requires analytical skill, financial expertise and business acumen, each of which should be brought into the board (and, ultimately, corporate) decision-making process. Being a director requires active assessment of risk and accurate gauging of the potential for profit, with a view towards forming an independent judgment. It is not sufficient to fall into the passive role or merely receiving and approving reports, recommendations and advice.

§10.124 On the other hand, if a due diligence defence would be available only where a director could establish that he or she had exercised the precaution that a reasonably prudent person would exercise in comparable circumstances, and relied upon the described advice and reports, it may add burdens to the director's load that were not previously there. There are, of course, situations in which a reasonably prudent person would not be prepared to act solely on the basis of financial statements or a professional opinion. In such cases, common sense would require the director to take additional steps beyond mere reliance.

§10.125 We will discuss the question of blind reliance in due course. There are many cases, however, that illustrate where reliance is necessary. In *Re Owen Sound Lumber Co.*,[270] the directors relied on the report of their auditors and officers of the company and paid out dividends while the true condition of the corporation was such that the dividends could not lawfully be paid. The court held that in the absence of willful inattention amounting to misfeasance, the directors were not liable. By extension, since the directors of a corporation cannot realistically be expected to verify the truth of the factual information that is provided to them, they may place reasonable reliance upon any such information that is provided by apparently credible individuals. Credibility, in this context, involves not only a consideration of the individual's personal veracity, but also the extent to which the directors have provided for an internal system of checks and balances on the flow of information to minimize the risk that corporate action will be based upon false belief. Internal auditing, systematic reporting, and the like afford the usual methods of establishing reliability.

§10.126 The directors of a corporation must also place considerable reliance upon the opinions that are provided to them by those involved in the management of the

---

[270] [1917] O.J. No. 144, 38 O.L.R. 414 (C.A.).

corporation. A distinction must be drawn between professional opinions, on the one hand, and business and other opinions of corporate officers, on the other. Both types of opinion will necessary influence board decision-making. Neither Act provides much indication of the extent to which reliance may be placed by the board on general business opinions expressed to them by corporate officers (*e.g.*, with respect to the marketability of products, the prices that the market will bear, the availability of necessary supplies and resources, the cost and manner of best managing capital projects, etc.), although the business judgment rule indicates that the directors enjoy a wide latitude in this regard, provided that the person whose advice or opinion is relied upon enjoys apparent credibility.

§10.127 A further question is whether boards should rely upon experts that report to them through corporate management, or whether they should retain their own experts. In-house professionals almost certainly know more about the corporation than any outsider, and they may often have the greatest expertise with respect to a proposed transaction. However, even the most conscientious in-house professional may lack a degree of objectivity and detachment in providing a professional assessment of a management proposal that he or she has helped to formulate. Whether independent advice is required would appear to turn on the apparent importance of the decision that is to be made, and whether a prudent decision-maker in similar circumstances would require independent professional advice before deciding how to act. An increasing number of corporations now provide that the board and its committees shall have authority to hire their own outside consultants as needed to permit them to fulfill properly their legal duties and other assigned responsibilities. A board should exercise reasonable care in assessing the qualifications of the experts upon whom it relies and also the integrity of the process they have used to reach their conclusions and make recommendations. It should ensure that advice is properly given (*e.g.*, in writing or in other permanent form). Moreover, a board should hold its advisors accountable for the advice that they give.

§10.128 Because paragraph 123(4)(*b*) of the CBCA[271] specifically refers to a person whose "profession" lends credibility to the statement, the question has been raised as to whether the paragraph is limited to the narrow category of recognized professions (*e.g.*, law and accounting), or whether it is sufficiently wide to catch any type of calling (*e.g.*, bookkeeper or financial analyst). The courts have adopted a narrow approach to the extent of permissible director reliance. The current case law holds that any individual on whom the directors rely must possess genuine professional expertise and accreditation, such as a law, accounting or engineering qualification.[272] The mere fact that a person holds a senior office in the corporation, and may possess a good deal of informal expertise with respect to a professional field, does not entitle the directors to rely on

---

[271] OBCA, s. 135(4)(*b*).
[272] *Peoples Department Stores Inc. (Trustee of) v. Wise*, [2004] S.C.J. No. 64, [2004] S.C.C.D.J. 3224.

that person. The formal qualification of the person expressing the opinion or providing the advance is a prerequisite to reasonable reliance.

§10.129 In recent years, there have been a number of cases involving claims against auditors who have failed to detect financial irregularities in a corporation.[273] The auditors have in turn usually cross-claimed against the directors. Most of these cases have been settled prior to trial. In one of the few actions of this type which has led to a reported decision, an action was brought against a firm of auditors who failed to discover unauthorized loans being made by a corporation manager in the course of their investigations. The auditing firm had no knowledge of the manager's activities. The corporation successfully sued the auditors for negligence. The auditors brought a third party proceeding against the directors alleging that the directors were negligent in not discovering the manager's activities. The directors at all times believed the manager to be honest and had no knowledge of the manager's activities. At trial the court held that the directors were not negligent in the circumstances as they were entitled to rely on the manager in the day-to-day operations of the corporation.[274]

(4) Blind Reliance

§10.130 The cases dealing with presumption of honesty and reliance on financial statements show that the board may not place blind reliance in a person to whom authority has been delegated by the corporation. Delegation does not mean abdication of responsibility. A director has an obligation to remain generally aware of the state of the corporation's business and affairs. There are several cases which illustrate the dividing line between reasonable reliance and abdication of responsibility, and from these it is possible to extract a number of general principles. A director must not ignore the reports with which he is provided, nor ignore warnings that are sounded by management, auditors or regulators with respect to the condition of the corporation:[275]

> The director must have a general knowledge of the financial situation of the institution, its system of management and daily workings, and exercise a reasonable degree of oversight and supervision of the bank's affairs. The director cannot disregard matters presented to the board of directors nor a failure to present what should be shown nor close his eyes to suspicious conduct of officers or employees nor conduct which could put an ordinarily carefully person on guard and cause him to inquire.

Directors who sit back and show little regard for what is going on, assume a high risk of liability. In one of the leading American cases in this area, the Second Circuit Court of Appeal stated:

> Lack of knowledge is not necessarily a defense, if it is the result of an abdication of directorial responsibility . . . directors who willfully allow others to make major decisions affecting the future of the corporation wholly without supervision or

---

[273] As to whether the directors of a corporation are required to obtain professional advice before acting, see generally: *Sheffield & South Yorkshire Permanent Building Society v. Aizlewood* (1897), 44 Ch. D. 412 at 457-59, esp. *per* Stirling J.
[274] *Revelstoke Credit Union v. Miller*, [1984] B.C.J. No. 2819, [1984] 2 W.W.R. 297 (S.C.).
[275] *Trembert v. Mott*, 271 Mich. 683, 261 N.W. 109 (S.C. 1935).

oversight may not defend on their lack of knowledge, for that ignorance itself is a breach of fiduciary duty.[276]

§10.131 While the director is not obliged to go behind an apparently regular transaction and determine whether the director, officer or other corporate operative has acted properly, a director who is himself called upon to act on behalf of the corporation cannot act without making sure that it is proper for him to do so. This aspect of the director's duty of care was clearly outlined in the decision of Sir W.M. James V.C. in *Joint Stock Discount Co. v. Brown*,[277] where he considered the duty of a director, before whom a cheque is placed for signing, and said:

> ... Mr. Bravo was not a party to the original resolution. ... He says he signed that cheque as a matter of form. It has been repeated with reference to him and some other of the Defendants here that signing cheques in that way is a mere ministerial act. I am startled at hearing such a statement. A company for its own protection against the misapplication of its funds requires that cheques should be signed by certain persons. Of course it is quite clear that no company of this kind could be carried on if every director were obliged to sign every cheque, and it is therefore required that the cheques should be signed by a certain number of persons for the safety of the company. That implies, of course, that every one of those persons takes care to inform himself, or if he does not take care to inform himself is willing to take the risk of not doing so, of the purpose for which and the authority under which the cheque is signed; and I cannot allow it to be said for a moment that a man signing a cheque can say "I signed that cheque as a mere matter of form; the secretary brought it to me; a director signed it before me, two clerks have countersigned it; I merely put my name to it." Most of us have been obliged to trust in the course of our lives to a great number of persons when we have had to sign deeds and things of that kind; but if we trust, of course, we must take the consequences of our so trusting. Mr. Bravo in this instance signed the £5000 cheque probably relying that it was all right; but, of course, relying that it was all right, he must be responsible for so trusting that it was all right.[278]

§10.132 As a minimum, directors should examine the financial statements and review the general business activities with the executive officers. They are expected to become familiar with the information provided to them. They must require proper statements to be prepared and reports to be submitted to them, and they must review those statements and reports. They must supervise management to ensure that there is at least the appearance of propriety.[279] When asked to approve policies, the directors must use reasonable judgment in deciding whether to provide such approval.

§10.133 One of the most complete explanations of the duties and obligations of directors and officers of corporations may be found in the decision of the High Court of Ontario in *Distribulite Ltd. v. Toronto Board of Education Staff Credit*

---

[276] *Joy v. North*, 692 F.2d 880 (2d Cir. 1982).
[277] (1869), L.R. 8 Eq. 381 (V.C.).
[278] *Ibid.*, at 404.
[279] *Leeds Estate Building & Investment Co. v. Shepherd* (1887), 36 Ch. D. 787.

Union Ltd.,[280] which involved a scheme to defraud a credit union by its administrative manager and certain of its members. The administrative manager issued to a third party a number of letters of guarantee or letters of credit to secure payment of amounts owed to them on account of goods and services supplied to a construction project being built by them. Each letter of credit or guarantee appeared on paper bearing the letterhead of the credit union and guaranteed payment of a stated sum. It was argued that the directors and officers of the credit union had not discharged their duties to a degree of care and skill that was required of them while in office under section 65 (now section 144) of the *Credit Unions and Caisses Populaires Act*.[281] The board of directors had put complete trust in the general manager of the corporation, who had been employed by the credit union for 22 years. The directors failed to follow up suggestions by the auditors, a complaint by a staff member to a board member, and they failed to notice discrepancies in loan figures.

§10.134 In making its decision, the court paid particular attention to the fact that credit unions are run by ordinary members of the community who do not in general possess financial expertise or sophistication.[282] It held that they are entitled to retain employees and other advisors who possess the necessary financial skill and to delegate the everyday running of the organization to them. The directors need not ordinarily meddle in the daily operations of the corporation or supervise or deal with staff below the level of the staff who report to the board. Even so, the board did have the duties:

- to ensure that their senior staff were reasonably competent;
- to supervise them to the extent reasonably required under the circumstances,
- to retain reasonable control and supervision over their employees.

In so doing, they were obliged to pay reasonable heed to any warning signs about the performance of those to whom they delegated their daily work.[283] The distribution of work and function between the board and its servants is a business matter to be decided on business lines. The manner of distribution must be a reasonable one under the circumstances. The board of a corporation is not required to exercise super-human skill or to require absolute perfection from its senior management. The court recognized that minor departures from rules or policies are a fact of life in every business organization.[284] For instance, the court

---

[280] [1987] O.J. No. 974, 62 O.R. (2d) 225 (H.C.J.).
[281] R.S.O. 1980, c. 102, s. 65(1) provided:

> 65(1) Every director, officer, member of a supervisory committee and member of a credit committee of a credit union shall exercise the powers and discharge the duties of his office honestly, in good faith and in the best interests of the credit union, and in connection therewith shall exercise the degree of care, diligence and skill that a reasonably prudent person would exercise in comparable circumstances.

[282] See *Grinrod & District Credit Union v. Cumis Insurance Society Inc.*, [1983] B.C.J. No. 161, 4 C.C.L.I. 47 (S.C.), aff'd [1985] B.C.J. No. 2229, 10 C.C.L.I. 39 (C.A.).
[283] *Re City Equitable Fire Insurance Co.*, [1925] 1 Ch. 407 (C.A.).
[284] *Revelstoke Credit Union v. Miller*, [1984] B.C.J. No. 2819, [1984] 2 W.W.R. 297 (S.C.).

suggested that minor departures from lending limits may, in some circumstances, be regarded as minor matters of little or no significance; it is, however, a most serious matter when neither the general manager nor the staff nor the directors nor, indeed anyone in the organization knows what the lending limits are. Even making these concessions, the court found that the directors had failed to discharge their duties as directors. They had let matters ride and left them in the manager's hands without taking steps to ensure compliance; they had taken no effective steps to deal with the obvious deterioration in the manager's performance and conduct. The court rejected the idea that there was a duty on the directors to maintain continuous oversight of the staff of the credit union. However, once they were put on notice that there were problems, they were bound to act. In reaching this decision, the court acknowledged that the directors could rely upon the financial information with which they were provided, in the absence of evidence of errors or irregularities. But on the facts of the case, the directors had ignored warnings so clear that the right of reliance was lost. It was not open to the directors to argue that they wanted to keep an eye on things, but were thwarted by lack of management cooperation. It was their duty to cause the officers of the corporation to cooperate.

§10.135 The extent to which reliance is reasonable depends upon the facts of each case. While the directors need not mistrust those in whom they place their confidence, they are expected to take reasonable precautions (such as the establishment of internal audit and other monitoring procedures) sufficient to deter and detect any wrongdoing. The directors must not place temptation in the way of those whom they trust, nor may they disregard warnings as they arise. In order to protect themselves against a claim that they have acted in blind reliance upon their subordinates, directors should:

- set (in cooperation with management) corporate performance targets, and monitor the extent to which those targets are met;

- identify the overall goals of the corporation — such statements often being embodied in a formal mission statement — identifying general lines of business and the methods and standards to be met in connection with that business;

- set overall corporate policy;

- approve budgets and monitor whether budget targets are being met;

- establish a comprehensive reporting structure within the corporation, fixing lines of accountability, techniques of supervision and control;

- approve major or unusual transactions (*e.g.*, sales of assets out of the ordinary course of business);

- approve procedures to ensure that at least major decisions within a corporation are subjected to a process of critical review before implementation;

- ensure that adequate monitoring procedures are in place after approval for a proposal is given, to see that the proposal is being properly implemented;

- require and approve necessary personnel policies (*e.g.*, remuneration, promotion, training);
- approve the method of hiring staff to perform specialized functions;
- approve senior staff appointments;
- monitor compliance with the above, by requiring, privately reviewing and discussing at board meetings routine and reasonably detailed reports from officers to whom powers are delegated;
- monitor corporate performance, particularly in comparison to the corporation's competitors;
- require explanations of any deviation from budget or other performance targets, and reports with respect to corrective measures that are being taken or that are proposed to correct deficiencies.

It is quite possible that some directors may be put on notice while others may not, where access or possession of relevant information differs from director to director.[285]

(5) Corporations in Financial Distress

§10.136 As noted above, the extent to which the directors may rely upon persons to whom they have delegated authority turns in large measure upon the extent to which they have notice of the existence of some irregularity. Such notice may pertain to the corporation generally, as well as with respect to specific officers or executive directors of the corporation. More specifically, where a corporation is in financial difficulty, the confidence that the directors of a corporation may reasonably repose in existing management (who must bear at least some of the responsibility for that difficulty) is correspondingly reduced. As a result of this reduction, the directors must exercise more vigilant oversight over the policies and management of the corporation.[286] The directors should require more frequent and more detailed reports from management; the directors should require the management of the corporation to develop workable plans for the recovery of the corporation; clear performance targets should be set; adherence to budgets, plans and forecasts should be closely monitored. Failure to achieve performance targets should be investigated, and, where necessary, management changes should be made. In each of these areas, the board has an important role to play. While maintaining the loyalty and morale of the officers of a corporation is clearly important, the directors must remember that their duty of loyalty is to the corporation rather than to its officers.

§10.137 In the United States, the Securities and Exchange Commission has developed certain rules that should be followed by directors when a corporation is experiencing financial trouble. Although these rules are not generally binding

---

[285] *Bates v. Dresser*, 251 U.S. 524 (1920), *per* Holmes J.
[286] See Deloitte, Haskins & Sells: *Audit Committees 1985 — Financial Disclosures and the Directors' Role*.

upon Canadian corporations (other than those which issue securities into markets regulated by the SEC), as an embodiment of considerable thinking on the subject by a respected body of world-wide reputation, the rules may provide a useful guide to Canadian courts as to the standards which should apply to Canadian directors. The rules oblige the directors:

i. to review for a period of at least five years, prior to release, all earnings, reports and the financial statements that accompany the annual audit and quarterly review reports of the independent auditors and reports of the internal audit department;

ii. to engage the company's independent auditors to review and report to the committee on accounting policies concerning revenue recognition, capitalization of certain costs, inventories, research and development expenses, and accruals;

iii. to engage an accounting firm (advisory accountants), to review the services performed by the company's independent auditors for a period of three years, and to assist the committee in other matters as requested;

iv. to resolve any disputes between management, the internal audit department, independent auditors or advisory accountants, concerning accounting policies, changes in policy or matters relating to internal controls.

These rules seem to be consistent with the obligation of the director to exercise the degree of care that a reasonable person would exercise in comparable circumstances. Once the ill-health of the corporation becomes apparent, the directors must devote greater energy to the corporation, in order to resolve its problems and to inquire into their cause. In so doing, they should work with the auditors of the corporation, and, if necessary, consider a change in the auditors of the corporation and the officers who are in charge of it.

D. THE IMPACT OF FOREIGN LAW ON CORPORATE MANAGEMENT

(i) The Sarbanes-Oxley Act of 2002

(1) Reporting Obligations

§10.138 The obligations of the directors and officers of a corporation to provide a routine accounting to the shareholders of the corporation of their stewardship of its business and affairs were discussed in Chapter 9. Without repeating the discussion in that chapter, it is worth noting that such provisions are essentially the lynch-pin of the overall scheme of corporate governance under most corporate law regimes. In this section, we shall consider how the reporting obligations imposed under the securities laws of non-Canadian jurisdictions can have implications for a Canadian incorporated entity, looking at the US *Sarbanes Oxley*

Act of 2002[287] as an example that well illustrates this aspect of corporate governance. It should be noted that the following discussion of the scope and requirements of this Act is intended to offer only a general summary of the law. The specific application of its provisions to a Canadian corporation is a question of American law, and accordingly any Canadian corporation that may be subject to the following should obtain advice from qualified American counsel as to the specific compliance standards that must be met.[288]

(2) Overview of SOX

§10.139 Since many large Canadian corporations either issue securities in the United States, or are subsidiaries of corporations that do so, it is worthwhile to include a brief overview[289] of the most important features of the *Sarbanes-Oxley Act, 2002*.[290] The Act (often referred to as "SOX") is named after its sponsors, Senator Paul Sarbanes and Representative Michael Oxley. It constitutes one of the most significant revision to the Federal securities laws of the United States for several decades, and incorporates provisions governing financial reporting and disclosure, the audit process, conflicts of interest, and corporate governance at corporations and other issuers that issue securities to the public. It also establishes new supervisory mechanisms, including the Public Company Accounting Oversight Board, for accountants and accounting firms that conduct external audits of public companies. Like many new initiatives in the corporate governance area, SOX was enacted in reaction to the series of corporate financial scandals exemplified by Enron, Arthur Andersen, and WorldCom. It provides perhaps one of the best illustrations of how emerging and often poorly defined general business concepts can evolve quickly into strict and demanding specific rules of law.

---

[287] Pub. L. 107-204, 116 Stat. 745.

[288] Without wishing to bog down in a detailed analysis of American securities requirements, the SEC granted a number of compliance extensions to Canadian and certain other foreign private issuers, certain of which are (as of the date of writing) expected to expire in 2006. Extensions have applied with respect to auditor attestation concerning the issuer's internal control over financial reporting and management reporting requirements.

[289] For more detailed information in this area with respect to the practical requirements of compliance, see: Scott Green, *Sarbanes-Oxley and the Board of Directors: Techniques and Best Practices for Corporate Governance* (Hoboken, N.J.: John Wiley & Sons, 2005); Scott Green, *Manager's Guide to the Sarbanes-Oxley Act: Improving Internal Controls to Prevent Fraud* (Hoboken, N.J.: John Wiley & Sons, 2004); Michael J. Ramos, *The Sarbanes-Oxley Section 404 Implementation Toolkit: Practice Aids for Managers and Auditors* (Hoboken, N.J.: John Wiley & Sons, 2005); Dennis C. Brewer, *Security Controls for Sarbanes-Oxley Section 404 IT Compliance: Authorization, Authentication, and Access* (Indianapolis, Ind.: Wiley Pub. 2006); Robert R. Moeller, *Sarbanes-Oxley and the New Internal Auditing Rules* (Hoboken, N.J.: John Wiley & Sons, 2004); Jay C. Thibodeau & Debbie Freier, *Auditing After Sarbanes-Oxley* (New York: McGraw-Hill/Irwin, 2006); Paul Ali & Greg N. Gregoriou, *International Corporate Governance After Sarbanes-Oxley* (Hoboken, N.J.: John Wiley & Sons, 2006). For specific legal issues relating to *Sarbanes Oxley*, readers should refer to a current standard text on American securities law.

[290] Officially titled the *Public Company Accounting Reform and Investor Protection Act of 2002* and commonly called SOX or Sarbox.

§10.140 While it was enacted with overwhelming support at the time,[291] practical difficulties in applying SOX on a day-to-day basis have caused many to question whether a less demanding approach would not be better. In a study of senior executives at reporting issuers carried out by the accounting and consultancy firm Price Waterhouse Coopers, 79 per cent of the survey group replied that their companies would need to improve its reporting practices to meet the requirements of section 404 of SOX. Respondents identified the following specific areas as requiring improvement, financial processes (55 per cent), computer controls (48 per cent), internal audit effectiveness (37 per cent), security control (35 per cent), audit committee oversight (26 per cent), and fraud programs (24 per cent). More than 60 per cent of respondents indicated that they would need to enhance future compliance activity. Clearly, the practical impact of SOX has not simply been to require enhanced compliance and control among those corporations suffering from lax standards in these areas, but rather to increase substantially the cost of meeting securities related regulatory obligations almost across the board.

§10.141 Nevertheless, as of the date of writing, it seems likely that the general rules set out in the Act will continue to have application for some years to come. For instance, section 404 requires CEOs and CFOs to file Internal Control Over Financial Reporting and Certification of Disclosure in Exchange Act Periodic Reports. Section 404 also requires management to document and assess the effectiveness of their internal controls over financial reporting. The cost of implementing the new requirements[292] has led to doubts about whether the Act is beneficial overall. For instance, the cost of updating information systems to comply with the control and reporting requirements has been significant, due to the enhanced document management, financial data access, and long-term storage of information needed to address enhanced auditing requirements. In many cases, this updating has required the complete replacement, of existing systems that were designed with less detailed and exacting requirements in mind.[293]

§10.142 The overall objectives of SOX are to facilitate the exposure and punishment of corporate corruption, to promote greater accountability by financial auditors, and to protect small investors and pension holders. Given the broad terms in which it is drafted, the impact of the legislation can be overlooked accidentally.[294] Section 302 sets out the annual reporting certification requirements of the Act. Generally, sections 302, 401, 404, 409, 802 and 906 are the central

---

[291] It was approved by the House by a vote of 423-3 and by the Senate 99-0.
[292] In a survey of 217 companies with average revenue above $5 billion, conducted by Financial Executives International, the cost of compliance was found to average of $4.36 million. The survey also determined that the actual costs of compliance were approximately 39 per cent higher than companies expected to spend. The high cost of compliance throughout the first year can be attributed to a sharp increase in the average number of hours required for the annual audit.
[293] The corresponding Canadian requirements are discussed below at §10.169 *seq.*
[294] For instance, although SOX does not deal expressly with mergers and acquisitions as such, it is necessary to consider the implications of the Act in structuring such transactions. In particular, the certification and reporting requirements of sections 302 and 404 apply to the entire operation of an issuer, including those portions obtained by way of acquisition.

provisions of the Act. Section 404 (dealing with internal control reporting requirements including a wide range of new risk avoidance measures) seems to have caused the most difficulties relating to compliance. In general terms, the key features of SOX are as follows:

- Most publicly-traded issuers issuing securities to the public in the United States are required to comply with the legislation in full. This obligation extends to their wholly-owned subsidiaries, including foreign subsidiaries. More specifically, section 2(a)(7) of SOX defines an "issuer" to be an issuer within the meaning of section 3 of the *Securities Exchange Act of 1934* the securities of which are registered under section 12 of that Act or that is required to file reports under section 15(d) of that Act.[295]

- An Issuer that is preparing an initial public offering of securities must comply with certain provisions of SOX.

- The Act created a Public Company Accounting Oversight Board ("PCAOB") which operates under the authority of the SEC.

- Certification of internal auditing by external auditors.

- Increased disclosure regarding all financial statements: Specifically, SOX requires issuers to establish a financial accounting framework to generate financial reports that are readily verifiable with traceable source data. The source data must remain intact and cannot undergo undocumented revisions. In addition, any revisions to financial or accounting software must be fully documented as to what was changed, why, by whom and when.

- A issuer's external auditors are required to audit and report on the internal control reports of management, in addition to the company's financial statements.

- Beginning in 2004, all publicly-traded issuers and other securities issuers have been required to submit an annual report of the effectiveness of their internal accounting controls to the SEC.

The obligations imposed by the Act are supported by a range of criminal and civil penalties for non-compliance. For instance, a corporate officer who does not comply with the Act or who submits an inaccurate certificate is subject to punishment up to a fine of $1 million and 10 years in prison, even for certain types of mistake. If a wrong certification was submitted deliberately, punishment can go up to a $5 million fine and 20 years in prison.

(3) Oversight of Accounting Practice

§10.143 A broad general oversight jurisdiction is vested in the Public Company Accounting Oversight Board ("Board"). Section 102 of SOX provides for the mandatory registration of audit firms with the Board as a pre-condition to the

---

[295] Issuers whose reporting obligations are suspended under section 15(d) because they have fewer than 300 security holders of record at the beginning of their respective fiscal years are not, in general, considered to be 0an "issuer" under SOX.

audit of a public company. The annual registration fees collected under this section are used to meet many of the expenses of the Board itself. Under section 104 of the Act, the Board must conduct annual quality reviews (*i.e.*, inspections) of firms that audit more than 100 issuers. Smaller scale operations must be so reviewed every three years. In addition to this routine periodic review, either the SEC or the Board may order a special inspection of any firm at any time. Foreign public accounting firms that audit a U.S. company are also required to register with the Board. This obligation extends to foreign firms that perform audit work with respect to a foreign subsidiary of a U.S. company, where that work is relied on by the primary auditor. A violation of Rules promulgated by the Board is treated as a violation of the *Securities Exchange Act, 1934* and gives rise to the same penalties as a violation of that Act.

§10.144 The Board itself is subject to the supervision and enforcement authority of the SEC, which is also authorized to give the Board additional responsibilities, either by rule or order. The SEC may require the Board to keep certain records, and it has the power to inspect the Board itself, in the same manner as it can with regard to self-regulatory organizations. The Board is required to file its proposed rules and rule changes with the SEC, which may approve, reject, or amend such proposals. The Board is required to notify the SEC of pending investigations involving potential violations of the securities laws, and coordinate its investigation with the SEC's Division of Enforcement. The SEC may censure or impose limitations upon the activities, functions, and operations of the Board where it finds that the Board has violated the Act or the securities laws, or if the Board has failed to ensure the compliance of accounting firms with applicable rules without reasonable justification.

§10.145 Section 107(c) of the Act requires the Board to notify the SEC when it imposes "any final sanction" on any accounting firm or associated person. The Board's findings and sanctions are subject to review by the SEC. The SEC may enhance, modify, cancel, reduce, or require remission of any such sanction.

(4) Integrity of Financial Statements

§10.146 Section 302 of SOX requires the chief (or principal) executive officer and chief (or principal) financial officer of each issuer to prepare a statement that must accompany the audit report, that certifies the "appropriateness of the financial statements and disclosures contained in the periodic report, and that those financial statements and disclosures fairly present, in all material respects, the operations and financial condition of the issuer". If the same individual is both the chief executive officer and chief financial officer, he (or she) may provide one certification but he must provide both titles underneath his signature. In effect, this provision makes the chief executive officer and chief financial officer jointly responsible for the internal accounting controls of the issuer, and requires them to report any deficiencies in internal accounting controls, or any fraud involving the management of the audit committee and to indicate any material changes in internal accounting controls. However, a violation of this obligation gives rise to liability only if knowing and intentional.

§10.147 Deciding who is responsible for providing the required certificate may be difficult in cases where there is a change of personnel at the relevant time when the certificate is to be provided. Often at such a time, a senior officer will be performing the duties of a CEO or CFO on an interim basis, pending the selection of the new incumbent. In such cases, the person performing the function of the relevant officer at the time of the filing is required to provide the certification. If that person does not hold the title of the relevant officer, then the issuer should disclose in the filing that the other individual is performing that function.[296]

(5) Integrity of Internal Controls

§10.148 Section 404 of SOX governs the management assessment of internal controls. It provides that all *annual* financial reports must include an Internal Control Report stating that management is responsible for an "adequate" internal control structure. The internal control report must:

- state the responsibility of management for establishing and maintaining an adequate internal control structure and procedures for financial reporting; and
- contain an assessment, as of the end of the issuer's fiscal year, of the effectiveness of the internal control structure and procedures of the issuer for financial reporting.

Rules 13a-14(b)(5) and (6) and 15d-14(b)(5) and (6) under the 1934 Act require an issuer's CEO and CFO to certify that:

- Each of them and the other certifying officers have disclosed, based on their most recent evaluation, to the issuer's auditors and the audit committee of the board of directors (or persons fulfilling the equivalent function):
    - All significant deficiencies in the design or operation of internal controls which could adversely affect the issuer's ability to record, process, summarize and report financial data and have identified for the issuer's auditors any material weaknesses in internal controls; and
    - Any fraud, whether or not material, that involves management or other employees who have a significant role in the issuer's internal controls; and
- Each of them and the other certifying officers have indicated in the report whether or not there were significant changes in internal controls or in other factors that could significantly affect internal controls subsequent to the date

---

[296] Rules 13a-14 and 15d-14.

of their most recent evaluation, including any corrective actions with regard to significant deficiencies and material weaknesses.

Item 307(b) of Regulations S-B and S-K requires an issuer to disclose whether or not there were significant changes in the issuer's internal controls or in other factors that could significantly affect these controls subsequent to the date of their evaluation, including any corrective actions with regard to significant deficiencies and material weaknesses. The application of the terms "significant deficiencies" and "material weaknesses" to specific cases are governed by generally accepted auditing standards.[297]

§10.149 Thus the Act and Rules provides for a considerable degree of ongoing review by management of the effectiveness of the internal control structure, as well as a report regarding any shortcomings in those controls. The integrity of this process is reinforced by a requirement that the auditor of each issuer must attest to, and report on, the assessment made by the management of the issuer. This attestation must be in accordance with standards for attestation engagements issued or adopted by the PCAO Board. The issuer must disclose whether it has adopted a code of ethics for its senior financial officers and the contents of that code. Immediate disclosure (in Form 8-K) is required "of any change in, or waiver of" an issuer's code of ethics.

§10.150 Section 103 of SOX requires the board of each issuer to adopt an audit standard to implement the internal control review required under section 404(b). Under this standard the auditor must evaluate whether the internal control structure and procedures include records that

- accurately and fairly reflect the transactions of the issuer,
- provide reasonable assurance that the transactions are recorded in a manner that will permit the preparation of financial statements in accordance with GAAP, and a description of any material weaknesses in the internal controls.

(6) Integrity of the Disclosure Process

§10.151 Section 401(a) of SOX sets out a number of specific disclosure obligations with respect to the periodic reporting requirements of an issuer. Each financial report that is required to be prepared in accordance with GAAP must reflect all material correcting adjustments identified by the auditors. In addition each annual and quarterly financial report must disclose all material off-balance sheet transactions and other relationships with unconsolidated entities that may have a material current or future effect on the financial condition of the issuer. The SEC is required to issue rules providing that *pro forma* financial information is presented in a manner that will not contain an untrue statement or omit to state a material fact necessary in order to make the *pro forma* financial information not misleading. Section 409 of the Act requires issuers to disclose material

---

[297] See generally, AU Section 325.

changes in their financial condition or operations on what in effect amounts to a real-time basis.

(7) Integrity of the Audit Process

§10.152 Section 103 of SOX deals with auditing, quality control, independence standards and rules. It provides that:

> The Board shall:
>
> (1) register public accounting firms;
>
> (2) establish, or adopt, by rule, "auditing, quality control, ethics, independence, and other standards relating to the preparation of audit reports for issuers;"
>
> (3) conduct inspections of accounting firms;
>
> (4) conduct investigations and disciplinary proceedings, and impose appropriate sanctions;
>
> (5) perform such other duties or functions as necessary or appropriate;
>
> (6) enforce compliance with the Act, the rules of the Board, professional standards, and the securities laws relating to the preparation and issuance of audit reports and the obligations and liabilities of accountants with respect thereto;
>
> (7) set the budget and manage the operations of the Board and the staff of the Board.

In setting standards, the Board is required to cooperate on an ongoing basis with designated professional groups of accountants and advisory groups. However although the Board may adopt standards proposed by those bodies (to the extent that it considers them appropriate), it also has the authority to amend, modify, repeal, and reject any standards that are suggested by the groups. The Board must report on its standard-setting activity to the Commission on an annual basis. Section 303 of SOX deals with the possibility of improper influence on the conduct of an audit. It is declared unlawful for any officer or director of an issuer to take any action to "fraudulently influence, coerce, manipulate, or mislead" any auditor engaged in the performance of an audit for the purpose of rendering the financial statements materially misleading.

(8) Integrity of Financial Records

§10.153 SOX also enhances record keeping requirements applicable to the corporations that are subject to it. Specifically, auditors are required to prepare, and maintain for a period of not less than seven years, audit work papers, and other information related to any audit report, in sufficient detail to support the conclusions reached in such report. Section 902 of SOX prohibits the corrupt alteration, destruction, mutilation, or concealment of any document with the intent to impair its integrity or availability for use in an official proceeding. In addition, the *Corporate and Criminal Fraud Accountability Act, 2002* makes it a felony knowingly to destroy or create documents to impede, obstruct or influence any existing or contemplated federal investigation.

(9) Conflict of Interest

§10.154 Section 201 of SOX sets out a number of rules limiting the range of services that audit firms may offer to the issuers that they audit, that fall outside the scope of practice generally associated with an audit. It is declared unlawful for a registered public accounting firm to provide any of the following non-audit service to an issuer while contemporaneously acting as its auditor:

- bookkeeping or other services related to the accounting records or financial statements of the audit client;
- financial information system design and implementation related services;
- appraisal or valuation services, fairness opinions, or contribution-in-kind reports;
- actuarial services;
- internal audit outsourcing services;
- management functions or human resources;
- broker or dealer, investment adviser, or investment banking services;
- legal services and other expert services unrelated to the audit; and
- any other service that the Board determines, by regulation, is impermissible.

However, the Board may, on a case-by-case basis, exempt from these prohibitions any person, issuer, public accounting firm, or transaction, subject to review by the Commission. It is not unlawful to provide other non-audit services if they are pre-approved by the audit committee of the issuer and that fact is disclosed to investors in periodic reports. The pre-approval requirement is waived with respect to the provision of non-audit services for an issuer if the aggregate amount paid for all such non-audit services provided to the issuer amounts to less than 5 per cent of the total revenue paid by the issuer to its auditor during the fiscal year when the non-audit services are performed, if

- such services were not recognized by the issuer at the time of the engagement to be non-audit services; and
- such services are promptly brought to the attention of the audit committee and approved prior to completion of the audit.

The authority to pre-approve services can be delegated to one or more members of the audit committee, but any decision by the delegate must be presented to the full audit committee.

§10.155 Two other provisions of SOX are intended to further the arm's length nature of the audit relationship. Section 206 of SOX provides that the chief executive officer, chief financial officer, controller, chief accounting officer or any person in an equivalent position may not have been employed by the issuer's auditor firm during the one-year period preceding the date of an audit. Section 203 of SOX provides for the rotation of auditors — and represents an effort to prevent the development of an overly cozy relationship between an issuer and its auditors. It requires both the lead audit or coordinating partner and the reviewing partner to be rotated out of the audit of an issuer at least every five years.

§10.156 Controls are also imposed on lending to directors and officers. Generally, it is unlawful for an issuer to extend credit to any director or executive officer. Consumer credit companies may make home improvement and consumer credit loans and issue credit cards to its directors and executive officers, provided that such credit is extended in the ordinary course of business on the same terms and conditions that credit is made to the general public. Directors, officers, and persons owing 10 per cent or more of an issuer must report designated transactions by the end of the second business day following the day on which the transaction was executed.

(10) Audit Committees

§10.157 SOX also strengthens the powers and independence of the audit committee of an issuer. Each member of the audit committee of an issuer must be a member of the board of directors of the issuer, but must otherwise be independent of the issuer. The term "independent" is defined to mean not receiving any consulting, advisory, or other compensatory fee from the issuer, and as not being an affiliated person of the issuer, or any subsidiary of the issuer, other than for service on the board. At least one member of each audit committee must be a financial expert.[298]

§10.158 The audit committee of an issuer is made directly responsible for the appointment, compensation, and oversight of the work of any registered public accounting firm employed by that issuer.[299] The specific duties of an audit committee include the following:

- The audit committee of an issuer is required to establish procedures for the receipt, retention, and treatment of complaints received by the issuer regarding accounting, internal controls, and auditing.

- Each audit committee is required have the authority to engage independent counsel or other advisors, as it determines necessary to carry out its duties.

In addition, each issuer is required provide appropriate funding to the audit committee.

---

[298] *Ibid.*, s. 407.
[299] Many limited partnerships do not have audit committees. In the case of such entities, the SEC has directed as follows: "Many general partners of limited partnerships are themselves limited partnerships. In this case, look through each general partner of the limited partnerships acting as general partner until a corporate general partner or an individual general partner is reached. With respect to a corporate general partner, the registrant should look to the audit committee of the corporate general partner or to the full board of directors as fulfilling the role of the audit committee. With respect to an individual general partner, the registrant should look to the individual as fulfilling the role of the audit committee."

(11) Special Remedies

§10.159 Section 304 of SOX provides that where an issuer is required to prepare a restatement due to material non-compliance with financial reporting requirements, the chief executive officer and the chief financial officer must reimburse the issuer for any bonus or other incentive-based or equity-based compensation received by them during the 12 months following the issuance or filing of the non-compliant document along with any profits realized from the sale of securities of the issuer during that period. In addition in any action brought by the SEC for violation of the securities laws, federal courts are authorized to grant any equitable relief that may be appropriate or necessary for the benefit of investors. Section 305 authorizes the SEC to issue an order prohibiting (conditionally or unconditionally, permanently or temporarily) any person who has violated section 10(b) of the 1934 Act from acting as an officer or director of an issuer if the SEC has found that the person's conduct demonstrates his or her unfitness to serve as an officer or director of any such issuer.

§10.160 An offence of securities fraud is created, for which penalties include fines and up to 10 years imprisonment. Employees of issuers and accounting firms are given whistleblower protection, which prohibits employers from taking certain described action against an employee who lawfully discloses private employer information to, among others, parties in a judicial proceeding involving a fraud claim. Whistle blowers are also granted a further remedy of special damages and attorney's fees.

§10.161 Title IX provides for a number of what are generally described as white collar crime penalty enhancements. It increases the maximum penalty for mail and wire fraud from five to 10 years, and creates a crime for tampering with a record or otherwise impeding any official proceeding. The SEC is given authority to seek a court order freezing any extraordinary payments to directors, officers, partners, controlling persons, agents or employees. In addition, the SEC may prohibit anyone convicted of securities fraud from being an officer or director of any publicly traded company.

(ii) Conflicting International Corporate Behaviour Requirements

§10.162 In Chapter 4, we discussed the subject of extra-territoriality. Many companies today (and almost all of the largest companies) operate internationally. By virtue of those operations, corporate entities may be subject to two or more conflicting corporate governance regimes. As the preceding discussion has noted, given the requirements of SOX and its application to foreign subsidiaries of U.S. corporations, and securities issuers whose securities are traded in the U.S. capital market, it will be readily appreciated that American corporate governance requirements can have a significant impact upon the way in which at least certain Canadian corporations carry on their business and affairs. However, it is far from the only field of law in which the extra-territorial reach of foreign laws governing the manner in which a corporate entity must carry on its business and affairs can have a direct or indirect impact upon a Canadian corporation. At least within the general field of corporate governance, it may be fairly said that international regulators have made an effort to harmonize and otherwise integrate their regulatory approach (*e.g.*, by the creation of exemptions or "disclose and explain" rules), so that a corporation is not placed in the position of being told by one jurisdiction to go left, while the other says go right.

§10.163 Unfortunately, the same is not true in many other areas of economic regulation, particularly those that involve considerations relevant to the conduct of foreign policy. This possibility raises little problem where the regimes in question are compatible. Difficulties arise where the regimes are incompatible: a multinational corporation may be put in a position where it can comply with the rules and requirements of its host or its home jurisdiction, but not both. Conflicting trade laws offer some of the best examples of conflicts of regulatory policy, even when dealing with major trading partners that are close allies. For instance, since February 7, 1962, the United States has applied a trade embargo against Cuba. Until the 1990s, the restrictions on trade were imposed under general trading with the enemy legislation, but in 1992 the regime of control was tightened by the *Cuban Democracy Act of 1992* (the "Torricelli Act"). Further restrictions were imposed by the *Cuban Liberty and Democracy Solidarity Act of 1996* (the "Libertad" or "Helms-Burton Act"). In contrast, Canada is one of Cuba's largest trading partners.

§10.164 Potential problems may arise for Canadian corporations due to American export and re-export controls, and also the Cuban Assets Control Regulations ("CACR"). For instance, American Export Administration Regulations ("EAR") prohibit the exportation or re-exportation of products of U.S. origin (including parts, components, or materials of U.S. origin incorporated abroad into foreign-made products) without a licence from the U.S. Department of Commerce. In addition American technology may not be co-mingled with foreign technology without such a licence. Generally, export or re-export licences are denied for Cuba (although a licence will be granted for export of non-strategic foreign-made products to Cuba, provided that the law of the country of export law requires or local policy favours trade with Cuba and the exporter in that foreign country is not U.S. owned or controlled, and the amount of American origin content is 20 per cent or less of the value of the product to be exported to Cuba).

§10.165 From time to time, disputes have broken out between Canada and the United States with respect to the impact of such American export controls on Canadian subsidiaries of American companies and also on Canadian-owned businesses that makes use of American origin products or technology. The Canadian government has issued an order under the *Foreign Extraterritorial Measures Act* ("*FEMA*") that prohibits Canadian companies, and their directors, officers, managers and employees, from complying with an "extraterritorial measure of the United States" or any directive or other communication relating to such a measure received from a controlling entity, such as a U.S. parent company. The Order also requires notice to the Attorney General of Canada of the receipt of any such communication or directive. This Order applies to any law, guideline or other enactment that operates or is likely to operate so as to prevent, impede or reduce trade or commerce between Canada and Cuba. A violation of *FEMA* can lead to a fine of up to $1.5 million and imprisonment for a term of up to five years.

§10.166 It follows that a Canadian based corporation that is U.S. owned or controlled could be subject to conflicting American and Canadian legal requirements, with the violation of either set of requirements leading to possible sanction. Under general principles of international law, the nationals of a state are subject to its laws wherever they may roam.[300] There is a strong presumption, however, that the laws of a state stop operating at its borders. Thus in *British Columbia Electric Rlwy. Co. Ltd. v. The King,* Viscount Simon said:

> A legislature which passes a law having extraterritorial operation may find that what it has enacted ... is not invalid on that account and the courts of the country must enforce the law with the machinery available to them. ... In the Exchequer Court, Thorson J. stated:
>
>> There is a presumption that parliament does not assert or assume jurisdiction which goes beyond the limits established by the common consent of nations.
>
> And it is a rule that statutes are to be interpreted, provided their language admits, so as not to be inconsistent with the comity of Nations.[301]

The rationale of the presumed intent to legislate only within the territory was explained in the following terms in *The Schooner Exchange v. McFaddon,*[302] where it was said:

> The jurisdiction of the nation within its own territory is necessarily exclusive and absolute. It is susceptible of no limitation not imposed by itself. Any restriction upon it, deriving validity from an external source, would imply a diminution of its sovereignty to the extent of the restriction, and an investment of that sovereignty to the same extent in that power which could impose such restriction. All exceptions, therefore to the full and complete power of a nation within its own territories, must be traced up to the consent of the nation itself. They can flow from no other legitimate source.
>
> The world being composed of distinct sovereignties, possessing equal rights and equal independence, whose mutual benefit is promoted by intercourse with each other, and by an exchange of those good offices which humanity dictates and its wants require, all sovereigns have consented to a relaxation in practice, in cases under circumstances, of that absolute and complete jurisdiction within their respective territories which sovereignty confers. This consent may, in some instances, be tested by common usage, and by common opinion, growing out of that usage.

---

[300] *Blackmere v. United States,* 384 U.S. 421 at 437 (1832).
[301] [1946] A.C. 527 at 542 (P.C.).
[302] 7 Cranch 116 (U.S.S.C. 1812), *per* Marshall C.J.

A notion would justly be considered as violating its faith, although that faith might not be expressly plighted, which would suddenly and without previous notice, exercise its territorial powers in a manner not consonant to the usages and received obligations of the civilized world.

This full and absolute territorial jurisdiction being alike the attribute of every sovereign, and being incapable of conferring extra-territorial power, would not seem to contemplate foreign sovereigns nor their sovereign rights as its objects. Once sovereign being in no respect amenable to another, and being bound by obligation of the highest character not to degrade the dignity of his nation, by placing himself or its sovereign rights within the jurisdiction of another, can be supposed to enter a foreign territory only under an express license, or in the confidence that the immunities belonging to his independent sovereign station, though not expressly stipulated, are reserved by implication and will be extended to him. ...

When private individuals on one nation spread themselves through another as business or caprice may direct, mingling indiscriminately with the inhabitants of that other, or when merchant vessels enter for the purposes of trade, it would be obviously inconvenient and dangerous to society, and would subject the laws to continual infraction, and the government to degradation, if such individuals or merchants did not owe temporary and local allegiance, and were not amenable to the jurisdiction of the country. Nor can the foreign sovereign have any motive for wishing such exemption. His subjects thus passing into foreign countries are not employed by him, nor are they engaged in national pursuits. Consequently, there are powerful motives for not exempting persons of this description from the jurisdiction of the country in which they are found, and no one motive for requiring it. The implied license, therefore under which they enter, can never be construed to grant such exemption.

§10.167 Nevertheless, the principle that laws have no extra-territorial effect is merely a rule of interpretation. A state cannot enforce its laws within the territory of another state, but its subjects remain under an obligation not to disregard them, their social relations for all purposes as within its territory are determined by them, and their home state preserves the power of compelling observance by punishment if a person who has broken one of its laws returns within its jurisdiction. Foreign nationals are subject to a duty to obey the laws of every jurisdiction into which they may enter.[303] However, there is no recognized right under international law for a state to legislate with respect to foreign nationals with respect to their conduct, business or affairs outside the jurisdiction of that state. In principle, this applies with respect to foreign subsidiaries of a corporate entity: they are the subjects of a foreign sovereign.

§10.168 Nevertheless, the obligations imposed under the laws of the country of the parent company's incorporation or control cannot simply be ignored, particularly where an entity or those concerned with its management have a footprint in that country. Particularly in time of war, violation of a restriction on trading may attract severe penalties, since any voluntary compliance with the laws of the host may potentially be construed by the country of incorporation,

---

[303] *Cashin v. The King*, [1925] Ex. C.R. 103 (Ex. Ct. Can.), *per* Angers J. Ships and aircraft passing through the waters or airspace of a foreign nation are subject to special rules.

origin or control to amount to assistance to the enemy state, raising the prospect of liability for treason.[304] At least in the case of individuals, dual citizens have the option of escaping the duty of loyalty to the nation in which they are not resident by renouncing their citizenship in that other state — although there is a strong presumption, however, against such renunciation:[305] This option is not open to corporate entities.

E. ROUTINE DISCLOSURE AND CERTIFICATION OF ACCURACY OF INVESTOR INFORMATION

§10.169 Earlier in this Chapter, we looked at the corporate governance/investor confidence initiatives embodied in the requirements of the US *Sarbanes-Oxley Act* ("SOX"), imposing new governance requirements with respect to financial reporting, auditing and general financial control. In this section, we will review the corresponding key Canadian equivalent investor confidence requirements.[306] The material in this section builds upon the requirements set out in Chapter 9 with respect to OBCA and CBCA corporations generally. The focus of discussion is with respect to the additional rules and requirements to which corporations that are reporting issuers are subject. As previously noted when dealing with securities law requirements, readers are cautioned that such requirements are prone to frequent change in response to evolving market practices and shifting regulatory concerns, and that, therefore, readers are encouraged to refer to a standard reference work on securities law, and to the original source documents, to confirm the requirements applicable to any given case.

§10.170 Additional requirements having an impact on continuous disclosure are set out in a series of CSA materials, which include:

- National Instrument 51-102, which sets down the foundation for the continuous disclosure requirements applicable to reporting issuers;
- National Instrument 52-101 pertaining to future oriented information;
- National Instrument 52-102 pertaining to the use of currencies;
- National Instrument 52-103 pertaining to changes in auditor;
- National Instrument 52-107 pertaining to "Acceptable Accounting Principles, Auditing Standards and Reporting Currency";
- Multilateral Instrument 52-109 pertaining to Certification of Disclosure in Issuers' Annual and Interim Filings;
- Multilateral Instrument 52-110, pertaining to Audit Committees.[307]

---

[304] See, generally, *Joyce v. DPP*, [1946] A.C. 347; *R. v. Neumann*, [1949] 3 S. Af. L.R. 1288.
[305] *Kawakita v. United States*, 343 U.S. 717 (1952), *per* Douglas J.
[306] In light of the subject matter of this book, this section deals only with Canadian incorporated issuers.
[307] As previously discussed, the responsibilities of the audit committee include: the review of the issuer's financial statements, MD&A and earnings press releases before they are publicly dis-

And, in each case, the related forms, companion policies and ancillary notices. Several of these documents are quite lengthy, and the specific requirements that they impose are more a matter of accounting practice than legal concern. However, in certain key respects, they impact the corporate governance process, and it is those respects that form the area of concern here. For instance, under NI 51-102, an issuer must mail its financial statements to any security-holder that requests them. [308]

§10.171 At the time of writing, there has been a flurry of action in the disclosure area. On February 4, 2005, the securities regulatory authorities in every Canadian jurisdiction except British Columbia, published for comment Proposed MI 52-111 together with a proposed amended and restated version of MI 52-109. Proposed MI 52-111, as it was published for comment, pertained to Reporting on Internal Control Over Financial Reporting. It proposed a number of verification obligations substantially similar to the requirements applicable to American issuers under the Sox section 404 Rules. On March 30, 2007, the Canadian Securities Administrators published a notice and request for comment relating to MI 52-111, stating that after extensive review and consultation, and in view of the debate and delay in the United States over the implementation of section 404 of SOX, and that the CSA had decided not to proceed with the implementation of Multilateral Instrument 52-111.[309] Instead, the CSA indicated that it was proposing to expand National Instrument 52-109, to include various additional provisions relating to internal controls over financial reporting ("ICFR").[310] The material in this section reflects the proposed changes indicated in that notice. This section of the text has been prepared on the assumption that these recommendations (or ones substantially similar to them) will be carried forward.

(i) Continuous Disclosure and Certification Requirements

§10.172 As discussed in Chapter 9, both securities and corporate law impose a number of continuous disclosure obligations on offering corporations. Currently, in addition to the specific responsibilities imposed under the OBCA, CBCA and corresponding legislation in other jurisdictions, and under provincial securities legislation, numerous specific requirements and duties relating to financial dis-

---

closed; ensuring that adequate procedures are in place for the review of the issuer's disclosure of financial information either included or derived from the issuer's financial statements; making recommendations to the board of directors with respect to external auditors, including with respect to the compensation to be paid to those auditors; and pre-approving non-audit services to be provided to the issuer or its subsidiary entities by external auditors or the external auditors of the issuer's subsidiary entities. Part 3 of MI 52-110 requires that the members of the audit committee possess both independence and financial literacy of members. It also requires a direct reporting relationship between the audit committee and the external auditors. Audit committee members also must be directors of the issuer.

[308] For some reason, CSA explanatory publications often state that an issuer is exempt from this requirement if it distributes its statements to all its security-holders. Since a bulk distribution to all security holders necessarily involves a distribution to those holders who have requested that they receive copies of the material in question, this is not a true exemption.

[309] See also CSA Notice 52-313.

[310] (2007), 30 O.S.C.B. 2877 at 2893-94.

closure process are imposed under a series of National and Multilateral Instruments of the Canadian Securities Administrators. In this section, we shall set out a brief synopsis of the key requirements.

§10.173 We will begin our review of how continuous disclosure by corporation fits into the corporate management process, by referring to the American case of *Catalano v. Worrilow*, in which Gates, P.J. noted that:

> Business companies periodically have their financial statements and accounting records from which they are produced examined by independent accountants called auditors. After the examination, the results are reported to management in a carefully worded letter, usually in two paragraphs. The first paragraph describes the scope of the audit, and the second paragraph contains the auditor's opinion of the financial statement. If the opinion contains no exceptions or comments, it is characterized as a "clean" opinion. An opinion with exceptions or comments is a "qualified" one. At first blush, the foregoing may appear unnecessarily academic, but it has a purpose. The point is this. Many people have the impression that the auditor is responsible for preparing the financial statements. This is not so. Preparation of the statements is the responsibility of the management, not of the auditor.[311]

Yet while management bear the primary responsibility for the audited financial statements of a corporation, that responsibility is not an exclusive one. Other persons within the corporation and outside it have specific mandates to discharge. For instance, while it is management's responsibility to design and implement an effective system of reporting and internal control, it is the responsibility of the board (through its audit committee) to ensure that management has done so.[312] The auditors are there to provide reasonable assurance to shareholders and other security holders that proper accounting methods are being employed by corporate management,[313] but there is at least a degree of responsibility on the auditor's part to

---

[311] (1972), 55 Pa. D. & C.2d 339 (C.P. Penn.).

[312] Financial reports must be audited by an independent accountant in accordance with generally accepted auditing standards. By examining the corporation's books and records, the independent auditor determines whether the financial reports of the corporation have been prepared in accordance with generally accepted accounting principles. The auditor then issues an opinion as to whether the financial statements, taken as a whole, fairly present the financial position and operations of the corporation for the relevant period. *In Re Cardinal Health Inc.*, 426 F. Supp. 2d 688 at 98 (S.D. Ohio 2006), *per* Marbley Dist. J.

[313] An auditor should cast a skeptical eye on information he or she is required to verify, with a view towards confirming that proper accounting methods have been employed. See *United States v. Arthur Young & Co.*, 465 U.S. 805 at 818 (1984). In *Checkovsky v. SEC* (1994), 23 F.3d 452 (D.C. Cir.), the court stated (authorities omitted):

> Although auditors may make suggestions about financial statements, or even draft them, financial statements remain "management's responsibility. The auditor's responsibility is to express an opinion on the financial statements." ... Auditors must test their client's transactions by obtaining "sufficient competent evidential matter" to confirm whether these have been fairly presented in the financial statements. ... When the audit is finished, GAAS ... require the auditor to give an opinion about whether the audited financial statements fairly present the required information in conformity with GAAP.

advise and warn such management where there appear to be systemic problems with the corporation's accounting, management or financial control practice — auditors are, after all, experts in accounting practice, and the corporation that they are auditing is very much their client. For reporting issuers, the current and proposed regulatory framework relating to financial disclosure, internal control over financial reporting, the audit and financial statement approval process reflect this scheme of interlocking responsibility.

§10.174 As discussed in an Chapter 9, National Instrument 51-102 governs the continuous disclosure obligations of an issuer from a securities law perspective. It covers such aspects of continuous disclosure as the financial statements, management discussion and analysis, annual information forms, business acquisition reports, material change reports, proxy solicitations, restricted security disclosure and certain other filing requirements.[314] NI 51-102 continues the requirement that annual financial statements must be approved by the board. In the case of interim financial statements, this responsibility may be delegated to the audit committee.[315] Even where prepared in strict accord with generally accepted accounting principles, financial statements have serious limitations as a governance tool. Since they are based on historic information, they are backward looking documents. They do not place the information that they provide into any kind of wider context. Proper interpretation of the data contained within them requires an understanding of financial analysis. For this reason, a number of other continuous disclosure documents are now incorporated into the governance process.

§10.175 Specifically, the information provided in the financial statements is supplemented by further disclosure provided in an annual information form ("AIF"), the information circular required to be distributed in connection with proxy solicitation,[316] and the report contained in the management discussion and analysis.[317] An AIF is a disclosure document intended to provide material information about a corporation or other issuer and its business at a point in time in the context of its historical and possible future development. It describes the issuer's nature, operations and prospects, together with the risks and other external factors that impact specifically upon the issuer. The annual disclosure that it affords with respect to these matters is supplemented during the year with such on-going continuous disclosure documents as news releases, material change

---

Grant Thornton LLP v. Federal Deposit Insurance Corporation, [2007] U.S. Dist. LEXIS 19379 at paras. 18-20 (S.D.W.V.) per Faber, C.J. (authorities omitted):

> Due professional care under GAAS requires the auditor to exercise professional skepticism. ... The auditor has the responsibility to plan and perform the audit to obtain reasonable assurance that the financial statements are free of material misstatement, whether caused by error or fraud. ... An auditor should have a "show me" attitude, and not accept unsubstantiated assertions by management. ... If there is a high risk of fraud, the auditor ought to employ a heightened professional skepticism.

[314] It applies to all reporting issuers other than investment funds.
[315] Section 4.5.
[316] Form 51-105F5.
[317] Form 51-102F1.

reports, business acquisition reports, interim financial statements, and also the management discussion and analysis. The current requirements governing the filing of the AIF were introduced effective January 1, 2004 and were intended to govern all non-venture issuers.[318] They must be filed within 90 days of year end.[319] This form includes disclosure of: contracts upon which a business is substantially dependent; social and environmental policies fundamental to operations; specified penalties and sanctions. The AIF will also cover trading information, risk factors, capital structure, bond and similar ratings, significant legal proceedings, the interests of management in the issuer, and any transactions involving promoters.

§10.176 The content of MD&A report is specified in Part 5 of NI 512-102 and in Form 51-102F1. The issuer must provide a discussion of any forward-looking information disclosed in any previous MD&A, commenting upon whether intervening events have altered the picture previously painted (*i.e.*, whether those events have made the earlier impression misleading). In the case of critical accounting estimates, it is necessary to identify and describe each estimate, the methodology used, the underlying assumptions and the range of estimates from which the estimate included was selected. Where new accounting polices have been adopted, these must also be disclosed. Off-balance sheet transactions must be disclosed if they are reasonably likely to have an effect on the results of operations or the overall financial condition of the issuer. The MD&A must also include a discussion of all transactions involving related parties.

§10.177 The MD&A is a narrative explanation of how the corporation or other issuer company performed over the period to which the financial statements relate, and of its financial condition and future prospects, in each case told from

---

[318] Section 1.1 of NI 51-102 (including the March 30, 2007 proposed revisions) defined the term "venture issuer" to mean a reporting issuer that, as at the end of the period covered by its annual or interim filings, as the case may be:

  (a) in the case of a reporting issuer that has distributed only debt securities to the public, other than an issuer of asset-backed securities, had total assets of less than $25 million, and

  (b) in the case of,

   (i) a reporting issuer other than a reporting issuer that has distributed only debt securities to the public, and

   (ii) a reporting issuer that is an issuer of asset-backed securities,

  did not have any of its securities listed or quoted on any of: the Toronto Stock Exchange; a marketplace in the United States of America; or a marketplace outside of Canada and the United States of America other than the alternative Investment Market of the London Stock Exchange or the LUS markets operated by PLUS Markets Group plc.

[319] In Canadian securities law, there is a distinction between information that is "filed" and information that is "delivered". Section 140 of the *Securities Act* provides that any material filed under that Act will be made available for public inspection by the OSC, unless it decides to hold the material in confidence on the ground that it "discloses intimate financial, personal or other information." In contrast, the term "deliver" is generally used to describe documents that must be provided by a reporting issuer to its security holders.

through the perspective of management. The MD&A is intended to complement and supplement the financial statements. The underlying purpose of the MD&A is to enhance overall operational as well as financial disclosure by giving a balanced discussion of the corporation's results of operations and financial condition including, without limitation, its liquidity and capital resources, risks and prospects. The document should fairly present bad news as well as good news. The MD&A is not intended to replicate the financial statements. The underlying purpose is to allow investors to understand what the financial statements show and do not show by providing additional material information beyond that which the financial statements are likely to provide. Some of this information will have a contingent nature, covering such matters as the risk of material default under debt, off-balance sheet financing arrangements, or other contractual obligations. The MD&A must provide information available up to the date of the filing of the MD&A.

§10.178 The MD&A serves as a good basis for explaining how the responsibilities of corporate management, the directors and the auditor inter-relate. CSA Staff Notice 52-316 established a requirement that any weaknesses in the design of internal control over financial reporting must be disclosed in the MD&A. While the primary responsibility rests with the CEO and CFO for designing adequate ICFR and DC&P for an issuer, the audit committee is thus caught up in any disclosure with respect to such weaknesses, by reason of the requirement for the audit committee of the board to approve the MD&A. The MD&A does not form part of the financial statements, and therefore is not subject to the audit opinion. Nevertheless, the auditor has specific responsibilities relating to the MD&A and therefore cannot be indifferent concerning its contents. The auditor must assess whether any of the MD&A information appears to be inconsistent with the financial statements, or with knowledge obtained by the auditor in the course of the audit. In addition to the possibility that the MD&A may contain a material misstatement of fact or misrepresentation, the level of disclosure provided may fail to meet the level required. The auditor not knowingly be associated with an apparent material misstatement of fact or misrepresentation, even where is technically no "inconsistency" with the financial statements (*e.g.*, where critical information is omitted).

§10.179 The external audit does not deal explicitly with violations of securities law requirements as such. However, when conducting the audit or reading the MD&A, the auditor may become aware of an apparent failure to comply with securities regulatory requirements. In such a case, the auditor would be expected to discuss and resolve any such inconsistency with management, and (if this should prove impossible) to raise the matter with the board.

(ii) Distribution of Financial Statements, etc.

§10.180 Both corporate law and securities law impose requirements regarding the distribution of financial information. For the most part, securities law requirements go well beyond those of corporate law. However, there is one apparent inconsistency between the distribution requirements under the OBCA and CBCA (on the one hand) and NI 51-102 on the other, in which securities law is slightly less rigorous. Subsection 154(3) of the OBCA provides that

> A corporation shall not less than twenty-one days, in the case of an offering corporation, and ten days, in the case of a corporation that is not an offering corporation, before each annual meeting of shareholders or before the signing of a resolution under clause 104(1)(b) in lieu of the annual meeting, send a copy of the documents referred to in this section to each shareholder, except to a shareholder who has informed the corporation in writing that the shareholder does not wish to receive a copy of those instruments.

Section 159 of the CBCA is fundamentally the same. The requirements for distribution set out in NI 51-102 differ. Subsection 4.6(3) of that instrument provides that:

> If a registered holder or beneficial owner of securities, other than debt instruments, of a reporting issuer requests the issuer's annual or interim financial statements, the reporting issuer must send a copy of the requested financial statements to the person or company that made the request, without charge, by the later of,
>
> (a) in the case of a reporting issuer other than a venture issuer, 10 calendar days after the filing deadline in subparagraph 4.2(a)(i) or 4.4(a)(i), section 4.7, or subsection 4.10(2), as applicable, for the financial statements requested;
>
> (b) in the case of a venture issuer, 10 calendar days after the filing deadline in subparagraph 4.2(b)(i) or 4.4(b)(i), section 4.7, or subsection 4.10(2), as applicable, for the financial statements requested; and
>
> (c) 10 calendar days after the issuer receives the request.

Thus under the corporations legislation, each shareholder is entitled to receive annual financial statements unless he or she declines to do so. Under subsection 4.6(3), a security holder must request to receive financial statements. Clearly there is no problem with subsection 4.6(3), insofar as it applies to statements not required to be provided under the OBCA or CBCA, or for security holders not entitled to disclosure under those Acts. However, one must question whether securities regulators can reverse the onus for requesting provision of annual statements with respect to shareholders, as they enjoy a specific statutory entitlement. However, in view of the extent to which such information is now readily available via the Internet and other electronic media to anyone who is interested in it, perhaps this is a matter of little import.

§10.181 The procedure for requesting provision of the required statements is set out in subsections 4.6(1) and (2) of NI 51-102. These provide:

> (1) Subject to subsection (2), a reporting issuer must send annually a request form to the registered holders and beneficial owners of its securities, other than debt instruments, that the registered holders and beneficial owners may use to request a copy of the reporting issuer's annual financial statements and MD&A for the annual financial statements, the interim financial statements and MD&A for the interim financial statements, or both.

(2) For the purposes of subsection (1), the reporting issuer must, applying the procedures set out in NI 54-101, send the request form to the beneficial owners of its securities who are identified under that Instrument as having chosen to receive all security-holder materials sent to beneficial owners of securities.

However, subsection 4.6(5) provides that:

Subsection (1) and the requirement to send annual financial statements under subsection (3) do not apply to a reporting issuer that sends its annual financial statements to its security-holders, other than holders of debt instruments, within 140 days of the issuer's financial year-end and in accordance with NI 54-101.

If a reporting issuer sends financial statements under section 4.6, the reporting issuer must also send, at the same time, the annual or interim MD&A relating to the financial statements.[320]

(iii) The Audit Process

§10.182 As in the United States, Canadian audit requirements for reporting issuers were tightened following a series of major securities frauds in the early years of the present century. However, in contrast to the United States, where Congress itself acted to impose a together regulator regime in response to Enron and other scandals, in Canada the response to the problems were handled largely by securities regulators themselves, through their national organization the Canadian Securities Administrators ("CSA"). Nevertheless, the initial Canadian response was influenced heavily by the *Sarbanes-Oxley Act*.[321] One such response was to provide for a Canadian auditing oversight board. The specific requirements in this regard are set out in National Instrument 52-108. Section 2.1 of that instrument provides that:

A public accounting firm that prepares an auditor's report with respect to the financial statements of a reporting issuer must be, as of the date of its auditor's report,

(a) a participating audit firm, and

(b) in compliance with any restrictions or sanctions imposed by the CPAB.

Section 2.2 imposes a requirement on each reporting issuer to see that its audit report is prepared by such an accounting firm. The term "participating audit firm" is defined in section 1.1 essentially to mean a public accounting firm that has entered into a participation agreement and that has not had its participant status terminated (reinstated participants also meet the definition). NI 51-108 also requires public accounting firms to provide notice to securities regulators and the audit committees of its clients if restrictions or sanctions are imposed by the CPAB.

§10.183 The CPAB is the Canadian Public Accountability Board, a corporation without share capital incorporated under the *Canada Corporations Act*. Essen-

---

[320] Subsection 4.6(6).
[321] The key requirements of which were discussed at para. 10.138 *seq.*

tially, the CPAB is the Canadian equivalent to the US Public Company Accounting Oversight Board. It is responsible for developing and implementing an oversight program that includes regular and rigorous inspections of the auditors of Canada's reporting issuers. It carries out a range of functions, such as

- promoting high-quality external audits of reporting issuers;
- conducting inspections of public accounting firms that audit reporting issuers to ensure compliance with applicable standards and requirements;
- imposing appropriate, sanctions and restrictions and requiring remedial action on the part of participating audit firms;
- referring matters to provincial accounting regulatory bodies for discipline purposes, where appropriate or to securities regulators;
- serving as a forum for discussion of accounting standards, assurance standards and governance practices to relevant standard-setting and oversight bodies.

§10.184 One of the earliest areas of concern to the CPAB was with respect to the question of auditor independence.[322] In December 2003, the CICA issued comprehensive new independence standards for auditors. The standards are consistent with the global standard issued in December 2001 by the International Federation of Accountants and the SEC requirements for listed entities. Five general areas of concern addressed in the standards were the:[323]

- Self-review threat, which occurs when a practitioner provides assurance on his or her own work;
- Self-interest threat, which occurs, for example, when a practitioner could benefit from a financial interest in a client;
- Advocacy threat, which occurs when a practitioner promotes a client's position or opinion;
- Familiarity threat, which occurs when a practitioner becomes too sympathetic to a client's interests; and
- Intimidation threat, which occurs when a practitioner is deterred from acting objectively by actual or perceived threats from a client.

An auditor must identify and evaluate the significance of any such threat. If threats are other than clearly insignificant, the practitioner must apply safeguards to eliminate the threats or take action to reduce them to a level that would pose no real or perceived compromise. Where no safeguards are adequate to preserve independence, the practitioner must eliminate the activity, interest or relationship that gives rise to the threat, or cease acting as auditor. It is recognized that the provision of certain non-audit related services and activity is in-

---

[322] See the first report of the CPAB at <http://www.cpab-ccrc.ca/41636b335f6cc.pdf>.
[323] See the CICA web page regarding these standards at: <http://www.cica.ca/index.cfm/ci_id/10022/la_id/1.htm>.

compatible with the independence required to act in an audit capacity, and consequently bard the concurrent provision of such services. For instance, a prohibition is imposed on an auditor investing in securities of an audit client and limitations are placed on any loans and guarantees obtained by auditors from those clients.

§10.185 NI 52-107 pertains to acceptable accounting principles, auditing standards and the reporting of currency. It applies to all issuers other than investment funds that file financial statements with a securities regulatory authority, and also all registrants which deliver financial statements to such an authority. In general, NI 52-107 requires Canadian incorporated issues to follow Canadian GAAP and Canadian GAAS in their financial reporting and audit. However, a number of exemptions are available from this requirement, including in the case of an SEC issuer incorporated in Canada.

(iv) Verification of Financial Disclosure

§10.186 Under the proposed rules (as of the date of writing) as embodied in NI 52-109 and its related forms and Companion Policy an issuer's chief executive officer and chief financial offer[324] will be required personally to certify that:

- the issuer's annual filings and interim filings do not contain any misrepresentation;
- the financial statements and other financial information in the annual filings and interim filings fairly present the financial condition, results of operations and cash flows of the issuer;
- they have designed disclosure controls and procedures ("DC&P") and internal control over financial reporting ("ICFR") or caused them to be designed under their supervision;
- they have evaluated the effectiveness of he issuers DC&P and caused the issuer to disclose the conclusions about their evaluation in the issuer's management discussion and analysis report ("MD&A"); and
- they have caused the issuer to disclose certain specified changes in the ICFR, in the issuer's MD&A.

The certifying officers must take into account the subsidiaries and other underlying entities of the issuer when evaluating the effectiveness of internal controls over financial reporting. They must also confirm (and the issuer must have disclosed in the annual MD&A):

- a description of the process used to evaluate the effectiveness of ICFR;
- a description of any "reportable deficiency" (a concept explained in detail below) relating to operation of ICFR existing at the financial year end; and

---

[324] Or persons performing the normal functions of such officers.

- the issuer's plans, if any, to remediate any such reportable deficiency relating to operation of ICFR.[325]

The term "disclosure controls and procedures" is defined to mean:

> controls and other procedures of an issuer that are designed to provide reasonable assurance that information required to be disclosed by the issuer in its annual filings, interim filings or other reports filed or submitted by it under securities legislation is recorded, processed, summarized and reported within the time periods specified in the securities legislation and include controls and procedures designed to ensure that information required to be disclosed by an issuer in its annual filings, interim filings or other reports filed or submitted under securities legislation is accumulated and communicated to the issuer's management, including its certifying officers, as appropriate to allow timely decisions regarding required disclosure.[326]

The term "internal control over financial reporting" is defined to mean:

> a process designed by, or under the supervision of, an issuer's certifying officers, and effected by the issuer's board of directors, management and other personnel, to provide reasonable assurance regarding the reliability of financial reporting and the preparation of financial statements for external purposes in accordance with the issuer's GAAP and includes those polices and procedures that:
>
> (a) pertain to the maintenance of records that in reasonable detail accurately and fairly reflect the transactions and dispositions of the assets of the issuer;
>
> (b) are designed to provide reasonable assurance that transactions are recorded as necessary to permit preparation of financial statements in accordance with the issuer's GAAP, and that receipts and expenditures of the issuer are being made only in accordance with authorizations of management and directors of the issuer; and
>
> (c) are designed to provide reasonable assurance regarding prevention or timely detection of unauthorized acquisition, use or disposition of the issuer's assets that could have a material effect on the annual financial statements or interim financial statements.[327]

§10.187 MI 52-111 previously contemplated that issuers would be required to obtain an internal control audit report. There was a good deal of opposition from issuers with respect to this requirement. The CSA's March 30, 2007 Notice proposed the elimination of this requirement.[328] Nevertheless, the verification process remains a serious responsibility, and one that is not lightly to be discharged. The requirement for issuers to develop both disclosure controls and procedures and internal control over financial reporting suited to their circumstances imposes a heavy new corporate governance burden. The CSA has indicated that they intend this responsibility to be more risk-based and cost-effective than is the case with the corresponding American SOX requirements. To assist in the development process, they have also attempted to provide issuers with a clearer

---

[325] (2007), 30 O.S.C.B. 2881.
[326] NI 52-109, s. 1.1.
[327] NI 52-109, s. 1.1.
[328] (2007), 30 O.S.C.B. 2894.

guide as to what is required. Specifically, Part 6 of the March 30, 2007 (draft) revised Companion Policy 52-109CP states:

> The Instrument does not prescribe the approach certifying officers should use to design the issuer's DC&P and ICFR. However, we believe that a top-down, risk-based approach is an efficient and cost-effective approach that certifying officers should consider. This approach will allow certifying officers to avoid unnecessary time and effort designing components of DC&P and ICFR that are not required to obtain reasonable assurance. ... Under a top-down, risk-based approach ... certifying officers first identify and understand risks faced by the issuer in order to determine the scope and necessary complexity of the issuer's DC&P and ICFR. A top-down, risk-based approach helps certifying officers to focus their resources on the areas of greatest risk and avoid expending unnecessary resources on areas with little or no risk.
>
> ... Using this approach ... the certifying officers would identify the risks that could reasonably result in a material misstatement, which includes misstatements due to error, fraud or omission in disclosure. Identifying risks involves considering the size and nature of the issuer's business and the structure and complexity of business operations.[329]

Before issuing its March 30, 2007 proposals, the CSA gave consideration to providing specific guidance to issuers as to what was required with regard to the design of DC&P and ICFR procedures. However, it ultimately rejected this approach:

> We acknowledge the comments but have decided that design of ICFR is best left to the judgment of certifying officers, acting reasonably, based on factors that may be particular to the issuer and that we will not mandate the use of a particular control framework.[330]

Nevertheless, Part 5 now refers to the following control frameworks as models for consideration in developing controls and procedures:

(a) the Risk Management and Governance Guidance on Control (COCO Framework), formerly known as Guidance of the Criteria and Control Board, published by the Canadian Institute of Chartered Accountants;

(b) the Internal Control — Integrated Framework (COSO Framework) published by the Committee of Sponsoring Organizations of the Treadway Commission (COSO); and

(c) the Guidance on Internal Control (Turnbull Guidance) published by the Institute of Chartered Accountants in England and Wales.

§10.188 More controversial is the decision by the CSA to proceed with a level playing field approach towards DC&P and ICFR, in which even venture issuers are expected to comply with the same requirements as established issuers.[331] On

---

[329] Section 6.5.
[330] (2007) 30 O.S.C.B. 2907.
[331] Critics of the MI 52-111 proposals that they would be very costly for all issuers. It was noted that small US issuers (having a market capitalization of $500 million or less) have spent on average 2.5% of their revenues in order to comply with the SOX verification rules. Since most Cana-

this aspect of the revised approach, the March 30, 2007 Request for Comments stated:

> We do not propose to distinguish between non-venture issuers and venture issuers, so issuers will have to comply with the additional internal control requirements regardless of where their securities may be listed or quoted. Our proposals recognize that ICFR is important for all reporting issuers, regardless of their size or listing. The concern of small issuers was a key reason for eliminating the requirement for an internal control audit opinion. We have also included a design accommodation in our proposals. This recognizes that certain venture issuers cannot reasonably overcome all the challenges in designing ICFR and allows these issuers to disclose a reportable deficiency in their design without having to remediate it.[332]

The "reportable deficiency" concept is described by the CSA as "the most significant proposed change" to the prior requirements. They continue:

> Part 1 includes a definition of "reportable deficiency", which means a deficiency or combination of deficiencies, in the design or operation of one or more controls that would cause a reasonable person to doubt that the design or operation of ICFR provides reasonable assurance regarding the reliability of financial reporting or the preparation of financial statements for external purposes in accordance with the issuer's generally accepted accounting principles (GAAP).
>
> We developed this term to link the concept of reasonable doubt with the existing definition of ICFR, which incorporates a standard of reasonableness in assessing the reliability of financial reporting and the reparation of financial statements for external purposes in accordance with the issuer's GAAP. Any deficiency that is determined to be a reportable deficiency will be required to be disclosed in an issuer's MD&A.[333]

If a venture issuer cannot reasonably remediate a reportable deficiency relating to design, it must disclose in its MDA what is known as the "ICFR design accommodation". This aspect of its disclosure must set out:

- the reportable deficiency;
- why the issuer cannot reasonably remediate the reporting deficiency;
- the risks the issuer faces relating to the reportable deficiency; and
- whether the issuer has mitigated those risks, and if so, how.

The design accommodation option is limited to venture issuers.

§10.189 As noted above, each certifying officer must certify that the issuer's financial statements and other financial information included in the annual or interim filings fairly present in all material respects the financial condition, results of operations and cash flows of the issuer. This certification applies with respect to prior period comparative financial information as well as to current information. The certificate does not incorporate the phrase "in accordance with

---

dian issuers are smaller than even a small US issuer, the anticipated costs of compliance with the original proposals was expected to be higher. See (2007), 30 O.S.C.B. 2898.
[332] (2007), 30 O.S.C.B. 2898.
[333] (2007), 30 O.S.C.B. 2880.

generally accepted accounting principles", that usually appears in the standard audit report. Consequently, the officer's certificate as to the fairness of the information provided requires them to confirm its fairness in its entirety. Companion Policy 52-109CP states:[334]

> The concept of fair presentation encompasses a number of quantitative and qualitative factors, including:
>
> (a) selection of appropriate accounting polices;
>
> (b) proper application of appropriate accounting policies;
>
> (c) disclosure of financial information that is informative and reasonably reflects the underlying transactions; and
>
> (d) additional disclosure necessary to provide investors with a materially accurate and complete picture of financial condition, results of operations and cash flows.

F. CONCLUSION

§10.190 In this chapter, we have examined the rules governing the corporate decision-making process, including the structure and general managerial role of the board of directors, the statutory requirements for disclosure of conflict of interest, and the delegation of managerial authority to the officers of the corporation, as well as the potential impact of foreign laws on corporate management. In Chapter 11, we will see how the foregoing rules and requirements are reinforced by specific and general duties imposed under the OBCA, CBCA and more specific statutes governing the conduct of particular lines of business. We shall also see how these duties are usually underpinned by potential civil, administrative and criminal or quasi-criminal liability for the directors or officers to whom they apply.

---

[334] Section 4.1.

Chapter 11

DUTIES AND LIABILITIES OF DIRECTORS AND OFFICERS

A. INTRODUCTION

§11.1 Since the directors enjoy general managerial responsibility under both the *Ontario Business Corporations Act* (OBCA)[1] and the *Canada Business Corporations Act* (CBCA),[2] the obvious question arises as to the extent to which they can or should be held accountable for the mismanagement of a corporation, and the losses that are thereby incurred. There is a certain irony in the fact that while the creation of the limited liability corporation has effectively insulated the shareholders of such a corporation from most forms of personal liability for wrongs committed by the corporation itself, the liability of the directors of such a corporation has been steadily expanding almost since the moment when the concept of limited liability first came to be understood. Such director liability (which often extends to officers as well) is still expanding today,[3] and there is every reason to believe that it will continue to expand into the foreseeable future.

§11.2 Conceptually, the directors (or officers) of a corporation may be subject to a range of different liabilities where they are held responsible for corporate wrongdoing. Available options include:

- regulatory or administrative penalties or orders;
- personal civil liability for an undischarged liability of the corporation;
- direct criminal or quasi-criminal liability.

As we shall see, each of these forms of liability are employed under both the OBCA and CBCA, and under a very large number of other statutes enacted at both the federal and provincial level.

B. SPECIFIC DIRECTOR LIABILITY

§11.3 While subsection 134(1) of the OBCA lays down the general duties of a director, it is not exhaustive. In addition, directors are also subjected to numer-

---

[1] R.S.O. 1990, c. B.16.
[2] R.S.C. 1985, c. C-44.
[3] For instance, as to the jurisdiction of a court to award costs against a corporate director who is responsible for an unsuccessful claim brought in the name of the corporation, see: *Goodwood Recoveries Ltd v. Breen*, [2005] All E.R. (D) 226 (C.A.).

ous statutory duties and liabilities under a large number of statutes. Indeed, there are said to be more than 200 federal and provincial statutes in force in Ontario that impose such liability at both the federal and provincial level. To cite some specific examples, section 13(1) of the *Construction Lien Act*[4] provides that in addition to the persons who are otherwise liable in an action for breach of trust under that Act:

> (a) every director or officer of a corporation; and
>
> (b) any person, including an employee or agent of the corporation, who has effective control of a corporation or its relevant activities,

who assents to, or acquiesces in, conduct that he or she knows or reasonably ought to know amounts to breach of trust by the corporation is liable for the breach of trust. Section 52 of the *Consumer Protection Act, 2002*,[5] provides that the officers and directors of an operator are jointly and severally liable for any remedy in respect of which a person is entitled to commence a proceeding against the operator under Part V of that Act. Subsection 137(1) of the *Employment Standards Act, 2002*,[6] provides that:

> 137.(1) If a corporation contravenes this Act or the regulations, an officer, director or agent of the corporation or a person acting or claiming to act in that capacity who authorizes or permits the contravention or acquiesces in it is a party to and guilty of the offence and is liable on conviction to the fine or imprisonment provided for the offence.

Subsection 194(1) of the *Environmental Protection Act*[7] provides that:

> 194.(1) Every director or officer of a corporation has a duty to take all reasonable care to prevent the corporation from,
>
> (a) discharging or causing or permitting the discharge of a contaminant, in contravention of,
>
> > (i) this Act or the regulations, or
> >
> > (ii) a certificate of approval, provisional certificate of approval, certificate of property use, licence or permit under this Act;
>
> (b) failing to notify the Ministry of a discharge of a contaminant, in contravention of,
>
> > (i) this Act or the regulations, or
> >
> > (ii) a certificate of approval, provisional certificate of approval, certificate of property use, licence or permit under this Act;
>
> (c) contravening section 27, 40 or 41 in respect of hauled liquid industrial waste or hazardous waste as designated in the regulations relating to Part V;
>
> (d) contravening section 93 or 184;

---

[4] R.S.O. 1990, c. C.30.
[5] S.O. 2002, c. 30, Sch. A.
[6] S.O. 2000, c. 41.
[7] R.S.O. 1990, c. E.19.

(e) failing to install, maintain, operate, replace or alter any equipment or other thing, in contravention of a certificate of approval, provisional certificate of approval, certificate of property use, licence or permit under this Act; or

(f) contravening an order under this Act, other than an order under section 99.1, 100.1, 150 or 182.1.

Subsection 194(2) reinforces those duties by providing that every person who has a duty under subsection (1) and who fails to carry out that duty is guilty of an offence. When construing legislation under which personal liability is imposed on a director, officer or employee, the courts have held that such legislation is to be given a fair interpretation, interpreting the liability regime provided for in the statutes concerned in coherent and rational manner.[8]

§11.4 Lest anyone believe that the foregoing provides a fair summary of the various types of liability to which directors and officers are subject by statute, it should be noted that this list does not even begin to scratch the surface of potential liability. There is no exhaustive catalogue of the statutes and regulations under which directors may be held specifically liable for the obligations of a corporation. It might well prove easier to compile a list of the statutes that do not impose liability of some kind on directors and officers than it would to compile a list of the statutes that do. Many statutes impose direct penal liability upon the directors of a corporation that usually supplements or complements the penal liability imposed upon the corporation itself, where the corporation is implicated in the commission of an offence. Thus both directors and the corporation may be prosecuted and are liable to separate penalties. In contrast, in the realm of civil liability, directors are usually the final port of call, so that they are liable only upon default by the corporation. In addition to those previously discussed, two critical areas of liability are with respect to unremitted pension contributions and unpaid source deductions. Source deductions are tax liabilities that a corporation is required to collect on behalf of the government from the person who is properly responsible for their payment. The list of such deductions includes income tax withholdings from employees, withholding tax, employment insurance deductions, CPP contributions, and GST, HST and PST charged on the supply of goods or services. Where the corporation fails to remit source deductions to the government, the directors of the corporation may be liable for the amount not remitted by the corporation, including any interest and penalties. Given this broad range of potential liability, it is not practical to attempt even a superficial survey of the statutory rules of law under which directors may be held liable in respect of corporate acts or omissions. Instead, we shall focus our attention upon the potential liability of directors under general principles of corporate law, including the specific areas of liability contemplated under the OBCA and CBCA.

---

[8] *ESS Production Ltd. v. Sully*, [2005] All E.R. (D) 158 (C.A.); *Ricketts v. Ad Valorem Factors Ltd.*, [2004] 1 B.C.L.C. 1 (C.A.).

C. GENERAL PRINCIPLES

§11.5 In the field of general corporate law, it should be understood at the outset that any potential liability of directors and officers for corporate action or omission constitutes an exception to the normal rule. As discussed in detail below, the directors are liable where they breach duties of care, loyalty and good faith to the corporation, but they are not liable for simple errors of business judgment that they may make in the management of the corporation, nor are they liable merely because they authorize the corporation to take on contractual or other responsibilities that it ultimately proves unable to discharge. The directors may exercise business judgment without fear that in so doing they will be second-guessed by officious courts acting with the benefit of perfect hindsight. In the absence of evidence to the contrary, the directors of a corporation are presumed to be acting on an informed basis, in good faith and with a view to the best interests of the corporation.[9] The onus of proof lies on the person who denies that such is the case. The courts are extremely reluctant to interfere in the management of a corporation or the administration or conduct of its business.[10] It is clearly judicial policy to allow the directors considerable discretion in the management of the corporation.[11] Generally, the business decisions of the directors of a corporation are immune from judicial review provided the following three steps are satisfied:

- the directors informed themselves (*e.g.*, made reasonable inquiries) on which they could form a business judgment before making their decision;

- they acted in good faith, in accordance with law, and in accordance with their fiduciary duties;

- their decision appears to have had a rational basis (as opposed to having been "the most rational") at the time when it was made.

However, the courts will intervene where the conduct of directors is of a type that no right-thinking person could honestly believe it to be in the interests of the corporation.[12] A number of policy considerations can be advanced to justify the reluctance of the courts to intervene. They include:

- generally speaking, the judiciary have neither training nor experience in the running of a business;[13]

- management of corporations is entrusted by law to boards of directors elected by the shareholders, not to the courts;[14]

---

[9] *Aronson v. Lewis*, 473 A.2d 805 (S.C. Del. 1984), *per* Moore J.
[10] *Carlen v. Drury* (1812), 1 V. & B. 154, 35 E.R. 61, *per* Lord Eldon.
[11] *Howard Smith Ltd. v. Ampol Petroleum Ltd.*, [1974] A.C. 821, [1974] 121 C.L.R. 483 at 493 (P.C.).
[12] *Charterbridge Corp. v. Lloyds Bank Ltd.*, [1970] Ch. 62; *Hutton v. West Cork Rlwy. Co.* (1883), 23 Ch. D. 654 at 671 (C.A.), *per* Bowen L.J.
[13] *Dodge v. Ford Motor Co.*, 204 Mich. 459, 170 N.W. 668 at 684 (S.C. 1919).
[14] *Davis v. Louisville Gas & Electric Co.*, 16 Del. Ch. 157, 142 A. 654 (1928).

- business inherently involves the taking of risk,[15] and corporate enterprise inherently involves the principle of majority rule;[16] it is therefore logical to allow the directors elected by the majority of shareholders to decide upon the risks that the corporation will take;[17]
- allowing recourse to the courts to dispute the decisions made by directors would open the floodgates to an incalculable number of actions brought by disgruntled shareholders, creditors or other complainants; and
- the directors will frequently have access to information concerning the corporation and its circumstances that could not be provided to the courts except at considerable risk to the corporation.

§11.6 One of the most common grounds on which attacks upon directors have been based is that of unfair dealing with the assets of the corporation. In general terms, the directors of a corporation must use their powers for the common benefit of the corporation,[18] and may not use their power to further their own interest, nor the interest of one group of shareholders over another. Any transaction under which the directors seek to apply the corporation's assets for their own benefit will be treated as unenforceable against the corporation, even if the corporation can be shown to have derived a benefit from the transaction.[19] Still, the mere fact that one person (even a director) owns a majority of the shares in a corporation or is otherwise in a position to control the business or affairs of the corporation is not in itself sufficient to defeat the presumption, so as to shift the burden to the directors of proving that they have conducted themselves properly. The person who alleges that the directors are acting improperly must prove that there are additional facts that show that the directors are failing to discharge their duty.[20]

---

[15] *Re City Equitable Fire Insurance Co.*, [1925] Ch. 407, *per* Romer J.

[16] *Re Kong Thai Sawmill (Miri) Sdn Bhd.*, [1978] 2 M.L.J. 227 at 229 (P.C.), *per* Lord Wilberforce.

[17] It may be argued, however, that while the shareholders of a corporation and their directors may take courageous and perhaps even stupid risks while the corporation remains solvent, their right to do so terminates once the corporation becomes insolvent. See, for instance, *Multinational Gas & Petrochemical Co. v. Multinational Gas & Petrochemical Services Ltd.*, [1983] 3 W.L.R. 492 (C.A.). In England, statutory prohibitions apply in respect of fraudulent trading and wrongful trading, with directors being potentially liable in respect of each. See the U.K. *Insolvency Act, 1986*, c. 45, ss. 213 and 214.

[18] *C.E. Plain Ltd. (Trustee of) v. Kenley*, [1931] O.J. No. 393, 12 C.B.R. 492 at 497 (C.A.), *per* Hodgins J.A.

[19] *Export Brewing & Malting Co. v. Dominion Bank*, [1937] 3 All E.R. 555, [1937] 2 W.W.R. 568 (J.C.P.C.).

[20] Note, however, *Shell v. Hensley*, 430 F.2d 819 at 827 (5th Cir. 1970):

> When the other party to the securities transaction controls the judgments of all the corporation's board members or conspires with them or the one controlling them to profit mutually at the expense of the corporation, the corporation is no less disabled from availing itself of an informed judgment than if the outsider had simply lied to the board. In both situations, the determination of the corporation's choice of action in the transaction in question is not made as a reasonable man would make if possessed of the material information known to the other party to the transaction.

§11.7 Many of the specific statutes that impose liability upon directors either oblige them to exercise "due diligence" with respect to some aspect of corporate activity, or provide them with an immunity from liability where they can demonstrate that they have exercised due diligence. In other cases, the concept of due diligence is specifically evoked by statutory provision. Since the phrase "due diligence" is one that comes up frequently in corporate and commercial law, particularly securities law, it is obviously important to understand its meaning. To introduce some specificity as to meaning, "due diligence" is generally defined as: "the diligence reasonably expected from, and ordinarily exercised by a person who seeks to satisfy a legal requirement".[21] It is therefore closely akin to the concept of reasonable care under the general law of negligence,[22] although it may perhaps be of a somewhat higher standard than the basic negligence standard, given the expectation that a person who knew or ought to know that important legal rights and obligations were likely to be affected by his or her performance would be likely to exercise greater care as a result.

(i) Relationship Between Liability and Duty

§11.8 The liabilities and duties of directors are essentially two sides of the same coin: the liabilities of a director afford the remedial device required to give the duties practical effect. The starting point for determining the scope of the general duties to which directors are subject are the relevant provisions of the OBCA and the CBCA. Subsection 134(1) of the OBCA provides that every director and officer of a corporation in exercising his or her powers and discharging his or her duties shall:

   (a) act honestly and in good faith, with a view to the best interest of the corporation; and

   (b) exercise the care, diligence and skill that a reasonably prudent person would exercise in comparable circumstances.

Subsection 122(1) of the CBCA is identical in terms and effect. While the wording of sections 134 of the OBCA and 122 of the CBCA are vague on the point, it appears that they (and corresponding provisions across Canada) essentially incorporate into the Canadian law of business corporations a principle comparable to the American common law business judgment rule.[23] Whether these statutory duties are greater or the same as those that applied under Canadian and English common law may perhaps be the subject of some debate.[24]

---

[21] *In Re First Alliance Mortgage Company*, [2006] U.S. App. LEXIS 30108 (10th Cir.) *per* Clifton Cir. J.

[22] As to the common law duties of directors, see: *Ultraframe (UK) Ltd. v. Fielding*, [2005] E.W.H.C. 1638 (Ch.) *per* Lewison J.

[23] See, generally, *Pappas v. Acan Windows Inc.*, [1991] N.J. No. 164, 90 Nfld. & P.E.I.R. 126 (T.D.); *NPV Management Ltd. v. Anthony*, [2003] N.J. No. 194, 231 D.L.R. (4th) 681 (C.A.), leave to appeal to S.C.C. refused [2003] S.C.C.A. No. 436.

[24] See, generally, *Dorchester Finance Co. v. Stebbing*, [1989] B.C.L.C. 498, *per* Foster J. — director required to show the degree of skill as may be reasonably expected from a person with his or her knowledge and experience, and required to take such care as an ordinary person might be expected to take when acting on his or her own behalf; *Norman v. Theodore Goddard*, [1992]

What is now clear, however, is that the performance of each director is to be assessed according to an objective standard.

§11.9 In exploring the meaning and scope of subsection 134(1) of the OBCA, certain of its features are readily apparent. First, there are two fundamental branches to subsection 134(1): clause (*a*) essentially summarizes the fiduciary duty of a director to the corporation, while clause (*b*) codifies the director's duty of care. Second, subsection 134(1) imposes a uniform duty and standard of care on directors and officers.[25] These duties extend to all directors. The law does not draw a distinction between a so-called "dummy director", who is appointed only for show or to fill up the complement of the board, and active directors who are expected to actually exercise authority as such.[26] A person who is appointed as a director must carry out the duties of a director on an active basis,[27] and will not be allowed to defend a claim for malfeasance in the discharge of his or her office by relying upon his or her own non-feasance.[28]

(ii) The Director's Duty of Care

§11.10 As we will discuss in due course, directors are fiduciaries with respect to the corporation, and as such they are subject to a duty to act honestly, in good faith and with a view to the best interests of the corporation. It is a further inherent obligation of a fiduciary that he or she must act in a manner that is reasonable and prudent. Honesty and sincerity are not the same as prudence and reasonableness,[29] and it is perfectly possible for a person to be found liable on grounds of unreasonable conduct, even where he or she has behaved with utmost honesty. It follows that directors may also be liable by reason of a failure to exercise the care, diligence and skill expected of them.[30] The burden of proving that a fiduciary has acted reasonably is upon the fiduciary.[31]

B.C.C. 14, *per* Hoffmann J. — director required to exercise reasonable diligence, and to have either the general knowledge, skill and experience that may be reasonably expected of a person carrying out the same functions as that carried out by the director in relation to the company, or such greater level of knowledge, skill and experience as the director actually has; *Bishopgate Investment Management Ltd. v. Maxwell (No. 2)*, [1993] B.C.L.C. 1282 (C.A.), *per* Hoffmann L.J.

[25] It can be complained that the OBCA and the CBCA are not particularly helpful in guiding directors as to what they are required to do. Compare s. 203 of the Ghanaian *Companies Code, 1961*:

> 203. A director shall act at all times in what he believes to be the best interest of the company as a whole so as to preserve its assets, further its business, and promote the purpose for which it was formed, and in such manner as a faithful, diligent, careful and ordinarily skillful director would act in the circumstances.

[26] *Kavanaugh v. Commonwealth Trust*, 223 N.Y. 103, 119 N.E. 237 at 238 (N.Y.C.A. 1918).
[27] *Francis v. United Jersey Bank*, 87 N.J. 15, 432 A.2d 814 at 822-23 (N.J.S.C. 1981).
[28] *Re Morlock and Cline Ltd.*, [1911] O.J. No. 115, 23 O.L.R. 165 at 170 (H.C.J.), *per* Riddell J.
[29] *Cowan v. Scargill*, [1984] 2 All E.R. 750 at 762 (Ch.), *per* Megarry V.C.
[30] OBCA, s. 134(1)(*b*).
[31] *Krendel v. Frontwell Investments Ltd.*, [1967] O.J. No. 1055, [1967] 2 O.R. 579 at 584 (H.C.J.), *per* Stewart J. See also *Norris v. Wright* (1851), 14 Beav. 291, 51 E.R. 298 (R.C.); *Williams v. Scott*, [1900] A.C. 499 at 584, *per* Sir Ford North.

§11.11 Because the consequences of fiduciary status have always been heavily influenced by the principles of law respecting trustees, in order to consider the common law and equitable duty of care owed by trustees, it is necessary first to consider the duties of care owed by trustees to their beneficiaries with respect to the investment of trust property. The basic duty of care of a trustee in making investments with trust money is said to be to take reasonable and proper care.[32] However, the notion of reasonable and proper care — of prudence — that has been developed by the chancery courts with respect to trustees is one of particularly exacting severity.[33] In settling upon a rule to govern investment by trustees, the courts were obliged to choose between protecting honest trustees and innocent beneficiaries, and in making that choice they came down squarely on the side of the beneficiaries.[34] Thus, placing the property of the trust in a "state of security" was said to be the first duty of the trustee.[35]

§11.12 The law respecting investment by trustees was heavily influenced by the collapse of the South Sea Company in the mid-18th century.[36] The amounts invested by the British public in the bubble companies was of astronomic proportions — perhaps totalling as much as £500 million (an amount then equal to about twice the value of all the land in England). A considerable portion of this amount was invested by trustees. As a result of the collapse of the bubble companies, the courts began to insist that unless expressly authorized to invest in some other manner, trustees were required to refrain from any form of speculative investment. A broad view was taken as to what constituted speculation, so that essentially, any investment other than government stock (*i.e.*, debentures and bonds) were considered be speculative in nature, and — subject to a transition period generally limited to a year[37] — if a trustee invested or maintained an investment in commercial (*i.e.*, non-government) investments he or she would be held liable, should the investment ultimately prove bad, irrespective of how carefully those investments were selected.[38]

§11.13 Such an exacting standard could obviously have no application in the corporate context. Business corporations are almost by definition enterprises set up to enter into trade and conduct commerce. Risk and the chance of profit are an integral feature of any such enterprise. Accordingly, it has long been settled that the standards of care expected of a trustee do not apply in the case of a

---

[32] *Re Jones*, [1949] 1 W.W.R. 1093 at 1103 (Man. C.A.).
[33] See, for instance, *Sculthorpe v. Tipper* (1871), L.R. 13 Eq. 232; *Learoyd v. Whiteley* (1887), 12 App. Cas. 727 at 733 (H.L.), *per* Lord Watson.
[34] See, for instance, *Whicher v. National Trust Co.*, [1910] O.J. No. 57, 22 O.L.R. 460 at 483 (C.A.), *per* Magee J.
[35] *Trost v. Cook*, [1920] O.J. No. 46, 48 O.L.R. 278 at 280 (H.C.), *per* Lennox J.
[36] Discussed in Chapter 1.
[37] *Johnson v. Newton* (1853), 11 Hare 160, 68 E.R. 1230 (V.C.); see also *Re Gasquoine*, [1894] 1 Ch. 470 at 476-77 (C.A.), *per* Lindley L.J.
[38] *Spratt v. Wilson*, [1890] O.J. No. 119, 19 O.R. 28 (Q.B.); D.W.M. Waters, *The Law of Trusts in Canada* (Toronto: Carswell, 1974) at 668-76; see also *Re Wedderburn's Trusts* (1878), 9 Ch. D. 112; doubted in *Ovey v. Ovey*, [1900] 2 Ch. 524 at 525 (Ch.), *per* Cozens-Hardy J.

director.[39] But if the normal duties of trustees do not apply to directors, it then becomes necessary to decide what standards do apply. The old case law in this area was very confused. Fortunately, reference to this obscure case law has now been made largely unnecessary thanks to the adoption of an apparently exhaustive statutory standard. Under clauses 134(1)(*b*) of the OBCA and 122(1)(*b*) of the CBCA, the directors of a corporation are required to exercise the "care, diligence and skill" that a "reasonably prudent person" would exercise in "comparable circumstances".[40] It would seem to follow that the directors of a corporation may embark upon a business strategy or venture that exposes the corporation to considerable risk, provided it (a) is the type of risk that a reasonable business person would be prepared to assume, and (b) is not contrary to some restriction on business imposed under the articles or a unanimous shareholders' agreement.

§11.14 It is somewhat surprising to discover that more than 30 years after the statutory standard of care was first introduced under the CBCA, no definitive explanation has yet emerged from the case law as to the meaning of these statutory obligations. This lack of guidance is unfortunate, since the language used in

---

[39] *Grimwade v. Mutual Society* (1884), 52 L.T. 409 at 416 (Ch. D.), *per* Chitty J.
[40] It is often suggested that clause 134(1)(*b*) of the OBCA and paragraph 122(1)(*b*) of the CBCA substantially modify the common law duty of care expected of directors, particularly insofar as it transforms the common law duty of care from a subjective standard to one which is objective in nature, although a detailed review of the case law leaves this question open. It is worth noting that a number of the cases tracing out the common law position involved unusual facts which distance those cases from the modern office of director. For instance, in *Re Cardiff Savings Bank (Marquis of Bute's Case)*, [1892] 2 Ch. 100, a claim was made against a nobleman who had inherited the presidency of a savings bank during his infancy. Over the succeeding period of 38 years, he attended only a single board meeting. The defendant was found not liable for irregularities in the bank's lending operation. Although this decision has been widely criticized, it is difficult to accept the validity of this criticism if consideration is given to the full (and rather exceptional) facts of the case. First, the case dealt not with a claim against the director of a corporation, but rather an unincorporated association. Second, the defendant was not properly a director in the modern sense of the word. His position was more that of a noble patron — as is evidenced by the fact that he attained the position of president at only six months of age, at the time when he inherited his father's title. The board of trustees was enormous (55 members), and it was clear that many of the people who were named as its members had merely lent their names to the organization as it was perceived to be a worthwhile cause. Third, it was not clear on the facts whether the defendant was a member of the board of trustees of the bank. Although he had chaired a single meeting of the board shortly after attaining his majority, the decision is unclear as to whether in so doing he acted in anything more than a formal capacity. The facts presented to the court suggested that the position of president was purely honorific. The president had no power under the rules of the bank to enter into its management. Fourth, the decision in the case turned primarily on whether the defendant was liable under the narrow terms of s. 11 of the *Trustees Savings Bank Act, 1863*, and quite clearly, the wording of that section would not support a claim against the defendant. Finally, there was no way of showing that the defendant's neglect had contributed to the losses of the bank, and consequently even if it could be shown that the defendant had not met the standard of care to which he was subject, there was no basis for making an award of damages against him. Other leading cases setting down the common law position include the following: *Lagunas Nitrate Co. v. Lagunas Syndicate*, [1899] 2 Ch. 392 (C.A.); *Northern Trust Co. v. Butchart*, [1917] 2 W.W.R. 405 at 412 (Man. K.B.), *per* Mathers C.J.K.B.; *Marzetti's Case* (1880), 42 L.T. 206 (C.A.), *per* James L.J. at 208, Brett L.J. at 209; but compare *Overend, Gurney & Co. v. Gibb* (1872), L.R. 5 H.L. 480, *per* the Lord Chancellor; *Grimwade v. Mutual Society* (1884), 52 L.T. 409 at 416 (Ch. D.), *per* Chitty J.; *Re City Equitable Fire Insurance Co.*, [1925] Ch. 407 at 427 *et seq.*, *per* Romer J.

clauses 134(1)(*b*) of the OBCA and 122(1)(*b*) of the CBCA is at least in certain respects confusing; some might say deceptively simple.[41] For instance, do the words "care" and "diligence" refer to one or two different obligations of a director? In answer to this question it can only be said that it is difficult to conceive of how a person might exercise sufficient care, but not be sufficiently diligent; or be sufficiently diligent, but insufficiently careful.[42] In obliging directors to exercise the care "that a reasonably prudent person would", clauses 134(1)(*b*) and 122(1)(*b*) clearly relate the director's standard of care to general principles of negligence. Yet even here the wording of the statutes creates some confusion, since it is not clear whether the words "in comparable circumstances" introduce an element of subjectivity, by relating the director's duty to the particular circumstances of that individual director (although in answer to this doubt, it must be said that what is reasonable behaviour will always turn upon the circumstances of a particular case).[43] A further important question is whether it is open to a corporation to modify its structure for the sole purpose of tailoring the duties of officers and directors in a particular manner. Here, fortunately, the express terms of the OBCA and the CBCA furnish an answer, as subsection 134(3) of the OBCA[44] provides that:

> 134.(3) Subject to subsection 108(5), no provision in a contract, the articles, the by-laws or a resolution relieves a director or officer from the duty to act in accordance with this Act and the regulations or relieves him or her from liability for a breach thereof.

The duties to act honestly, reasonably and in good faith, and to exercise reasonable care, diligence and skill are, of course, statutory duties, and therefore fall squarely within the ambit of subsection 134(3).

---

[41] In his dissenting judgment in *Lippitt v. Ashley*, 89 Conn. 451, 94 A. 995 (S.C. Errors, Conn. 1915), Prentice C.J. stated:

> The true rule is that which prevails under all other conditions, and that is, such diligence and care as the ordinarily prudent man would exercise under like circumstances. Translated into terms applicable to the situation in which a savings-bank director finds himself placed, that means that he owes the duty of exercising such a degree of diligence and care as an ordinarily prudent director of similar institutions, similarly circumstanced, would exercise under similar conditions. The conditions which surround a man in his own business are not the same as those in which a bank director is placed, and the degree of care is not, therefore, to be measured by the same standard.

[42] The notion of reasonable skill, however, is a separate matter from reasonable care, and as will be explained below, inquiry into the skill required of a director raises questions that are not easily addressed. As Fleming notes, while negligence is commonly defined to include both acts and omissions involving an unreasonable risk of harm, in general the common law does not impose liability for inaction. However, as will be discussed in detail below, the area of director and officer liability departs from the general approach, since positive duties are imposed upon both directors and officers to see to the management of the corporation: John G. Fleming, *The Law of Torts*, 4th ed. (Sydney: The Law Book Co., 1971), 140.

[43] In addition to the general statutory duties of care imposed under the OBCA and the CBCA, numerous other statutes impose specific statutory duties of care with respect to particular matters. See, for instance, the *Income Tax Act*, R.S.C. 1985, c. 1 (5th Supp.), s. 227.1. In contrast to the OBCA and CBCA provisions, under the *Income Tax Act* directors of all corporations are subject to the same standard of care: *Wheeliker v. Canada*, [1998] F.C.J. No. 401, 172 D.L.R. (4th) 708, leave to appeal to S.C.C. refused [1999] S.C.C.A. No. 260.

[44] CBCA, s. 122(3).

(1) The Business Judgment Rule

§11.15 The directors' duty to manage the corporation, implies a right to manage, and where in the course of providing such management, the directors make reasonable decisions taking into account the type of considerations that a prudent manager would do in exercising managerial authority, their decisions are not normally open to challenge.[45] Legal academics have often cautioned the courts about the risk of hindsight-bias: the tendency of a court to overestimate the extent to which harm was foreseeable at some past point in time, due to the fact that by the time that a case comes before the court, harm (and often very serious harm) has actually occurred. Such a bias tends to play an important role in steadily expanding liability, and consequently encourages further litigation.[46]

§11.16 The courts have long recognized that it is not realistic to hold directors liable to those interested in a corporation or to the corporation itself merely because it ultimately works out that the decisions that they make in the course of their administration turn out to be wrong. More generally stated — to borrow the words of Romer J. — directors are not held liable for mere errors of judgment.[47] As a general principle, the courts will not usurp the function of the board of directors as the managing body of the corporation, and in particular they will not substitute their own decisions for those legitimately made by the board. Two obvious explanations spring forward to justify this approach: first, if the courts were to adopt a policy of second-guessing each and every incorrect business decision made by a board of directors, the courts would soon plug up with cases seeking such relief; second, if the directors were held liable for every decision that ultimately proved wrong, few people would be willing to take on the task of acting as a director.

§11.17 Accordingly, business decisions of a board of directors that were lawfully made in good faith by the board of directors of a corporation and within the authority conferred upon them under the articles and by-laws of a corporation — and any unanimous shareholder agreement — will be respected by the courts, even where the court considers them to have been unwise in the circumstances.[48] However, given the wording of subsections 134(1) of the OBCA and 122(1) of the CBCA, it is clear that the directors may *not* act in any way that they see fit.[49]

---

[45] See for instance, *Aujla v. Yellow Cab Co.*, [2006] B.C.J. No. 600, 16 B.L.R. (4th) 173 (C.A.); *Lang Michener v. American Bullion Minerals Ltd.*, [2006] B.C.J. No. 685 (S.C.); *Deep v. M.D. Management*, [2006] O.J. No. 221, 13 B.L.R. (4th) 193 (Div. Ct.).

[46] See, for instance, Hal R. Arkes & Cindy A. Schipani, "Medical Malpractice v. the Business Judgment Rule: Differences in Hindsight Bias" (1994) 73 Or. L. Rev. 587.

[47] *Re City Equitable Fire Insurance Co.*, [1925] Ch. 407.

[48] *Brant Investments Ltd. v. KeepRite Inc.*, [1987] O.J. No. 574, 37 B.L.R. 65 at 99 (H.C.J.), aff'd [1991] O.J. No. 683, 1 B.L.R. (2d) 225 (C.A.); *Schelew v. Schelew*, [2004] N.B.J. No. 330, 49 B.L.R. (3d) 68 at 76 (Q.B.), *per* Glennie J.

[49] As to the common law position, see the decision of Romer J. in *Re City Equitable Fire Insurance Co.*, [1925] Ch. 407, in which he rejected the approach (adopted in a number of earlier cases) of attempting to differentiate between the liability of directors and trustees on the basis of gross and simple negligence tests, and went on to hold that a director was required to take the care "that an ordinary man might be expected to take in the circumstances on his own behalf". It

Specifically, taking an excessive risk violates the director's duty of care. Where the degree of risk assumed becomes especially great, the director violates the fiduciary duty as well as the duty of care.[50] It follows from these provisions that in making their decisions, directors are expected to exercise a proper business judgment. They must act on an informed basis, in good faith and in the honest belief that the action that they are taking is in the best interest of the corporation.[51]

§11.18 Although many cases discuss the general need for a board to be informed in its decision making, there is little real guidance offered as to what it means to be informed. The case law simply declares that certain boards made an informed decision, while others are condemned for not doing so. What is necessary, in order to be informed, will vary from case to case. In general, the board must possess the type of factual information that a reasonable business would consider necessary or advisable to making a reasoned decision, supported by technical analysis and relevant professional opinion. Informed decision making will likely require a consideration of the relevant options that are open, in addition to the specific proposal that is the subject of the decision, together with a proper assessment of the apparent strengths and weaknesses of each available approach.

§11.19 Directors make informed decisions not when they possess complete knowledge (the time constraints of modern business would rarely allow for them to acquire such knowledge, if indeed such a level of knowledge is possible) but rather when they have sufficient information on the basis of the facts known to them that a reasonable person could consider it reasonable and prudent in the circumstances to come to a decision.[52] To be a reasonable business judgment, the decision need not be the most reasonable decision that a person might have reached; it is sufficient if it is a rational decision made with a view towards furthering the best interests of the corporation. The decision of Horsey J. in the Delaware case of *Smith v. Van Gorkom*[53] provides a clear articulation of their obligations to make informed business decisions and the relationship of that duty to the overall duty of good faith owed to the corporation:

> The determination of whether a business judgment is an informed one turns on whether the directors have informed themselves "prior to making a business decision, of all material information reasonably available to them." ... Under the busi-

---

can be argued with some force that this standard is for all intents and purposes the same as the statutory standard: the care "that a reasonably prudent person would exercise in comparable circumstances". See also *Re Brazilian Rubber Plantations and Estates Ltd.*, [1911] 1 Ch. 425 (as to the meaning of gross negligence); *Overend & Gurney Co. v. Gibb* (1872), L.R. 5 H.L. 480 at 486, *per* Lord Hatherley L.C. From time to time, the "gross negligence" terminology still is encountered in the case law: see, for instance, *Smith v. Van Gorkom*, 488 A.2d 858 (S.C. Del. 1985).

50 *Northland Bank v. Willson*, [1999] A.J. No. 1010, 249 A.R. 201 (Q.B.), aff'd [2001] A.J. No. 714, 15 B.L.R. (3d) 5 (C.A.), leave to appeal to S.C.C. refused [2001] S.C.C.A. No. 421.
51 *Aronson v. Lewis*, 473 A.2d 805 (Del. S.C. 1984), *per* Moore J.
52 See, generally, *Keating v. Bragg*, [1997] N.S.J. No. 248, 34 B.L.R. (2d) 181 at 205 (C.A.), *per* Hallett J.A.; *Re R.J. Jowsey Mining Co.*, [1969] O.J. No. 1358, 6 D.L.R. (3d) 97 at 100 (C.A.), *per* Laskin J.A., aff'd [1970] S.C.R. v.
53 488 A.2d 858 at ¶31 (Del. S.C. 1985).

ness judgment rule there is no protection for directors who have made an "unintelligent or unadvised judgment." ... A director's duty to inform himself in preparation for a decision derives from the fiduciary capacity in which he serves the corporation and its stockholders ... Since a director is vested with the responsibility for the management of the affairs of the corporation, he must execute that duty with the recognition that he acts on behalf of others. Such obligation does not tolerate faithlessness or self-dealing. But fulfillment of the fiduciary function requires more than the mere absence of bad faith or fraud. Representation of the financial interests of others imposes on a director an affirmative duty to protect those interests and to proceed with a critical eye in assessing information of the type and under the circumstances present here. Thus, a director's duty to exercise an informed business judgment is in the nature of a duty of care, as distinguished from a duty of loyalty. Here, there were no allegations of fraud, bad faith, or self-dealing, or proof thereof. Hence, it is presumed that the directors reached their business judgment in good faith ... and considerations of motive are irrelevant to the issue before us.

The reasonableness of the decisions made by directors in the exercise of their business judgment is assessed on the basis of the facts as known to the directors at the time when those decisions were made.[54]

§11.20 In the *Peoples Department Store* case[55] the Supreme Court of Canada confirmed that the business judgment rule forms part of Canadian corporate law. Nevertheless, there remains some confusion within the literature and case law as to the precise nature of the business judgment. It has been variously described as "a procedural guide", a "substantive rule of law", a "standard of review", a "rule of deference", a "standard of conduct", and a "doctrine of abstention". None of these descriptions is particularly helpful. The rule should not be confused with the common law statutory duties of the directors with respect to the management or supervision of management of the business — although evidence that those duties have been breached is, of course, highly relevant as to whether the rule will protect the directors on the facts of a given case.

§11.21 The business judgment rule is partly an evidentiary presumption. It is manifest in an assumption that the directors of a corporation are entitled to the benefit of any doubt. So conceived, it is often articulated as a presumption that "in making a business decision the directors of a corporation acted on an informed basis, ... and in the honest belief that the action taken was in the best interests of the company".[56] When presented in these terms, the business judgment rule adds little to the ordinary rules of civil procedure: in an ordinary civil case, the burden of proof rests upon the plaintiff to establish on the balance of probability by the preponderance of evidence that the defendant has done some act (or refrained from doing some act in such circumstances) that in law gives rise to a civil liability to the plaintiff. Generally, as well, the plaintiff must also prove that he or she has suffered a loss, and that the defendant's action (or inac-

---

[54] *Litwin v. Allen*, 25 N.Y.S.2d 667 (N.Y.S.C. 1940), *per* Shientag J.
[55] *Peoples Department Stores Inc. (Trustee of) v. Wise*, [2004] S.C.J. No. 64, [2004] 3 S.C.R. 461 at para. 64.
[56] *Aronson v. Lewis*, 473 A.2d 805 at 812 (S.C. Del. 1984).

tion) is the proximate cause of that loss. If there is no or insufficient evidence of this nature, then the dispute is resolved in favour of the plaintiff. When the business judgment rule is considered as a rule of evidence, its main contribution to the law is to make clear that there is no burden upon the directors to prove that they have acted honestly, responsibly, or in the best interests of the corporation; rather, the onus is on the defendant to prove that they have not. Accordingly, this evidentiary presumption will apply only insofar as there is insufficient evidence to rebut it, such as credible evidence (as opposed to a mere allegation or ambiguous set of facts) confirming fraud, bad faith, self-dealing, or the pursuit of personal profit or betterment on the part of the directors.[57] In the absence of this evidence, the board's decision will be upheld unless the evidence establishes that the board's decision was (at the time when it was made) so outlandish that it cannot be "attributed to any rational business purpose".

§11.22 It is this last exception that leads us to the second aspect of the business judgment rule. Under this second aspect, the rule may also be conceived as a necessary recognition on the part of the courts of the limited role that they can and should play in superintending the business and affairs of a corporation. So conceived, the business judgment rule serves to protect and promote the role of the board as the ultimate manager of the corporation.[58] It derives from the fact that in the ordinary case it has a superior ability to assess the merit of proposals and other matters that arise for decision in the operation of the company, due to their deeper understanding of the corporation's business and affairs and the circumstances in which it is operating. Without such recognition the autonomy and integrity of the board of directors as a decision making entity would be seriously compromised.

§11.23 Nevertheless, decisions of the board are not insulated from review where the evidence establishes that the deliberations leading up to the board decisions fell short of the exercise of prudent judgment, or were carried out in a manner contrary to the interest of the corporation.[59] There must be actual evidence of improper decision making, however;[60] the court will not engage in a speculative exercise. In *Brio Industries Inc. v. Clearly Canadian Beverage Corp.*,[61] Newbury J. stated:

> It may even be that where it is shown that corporate machinery is being "manipulated", an evidentiary burden shifts to the directors to justify their conduct.

---

[57] *Grobow v. Perot*, 539 A.2d 180 at 187 (Del. Ch. 1988).
[58] *Zapata Corp. v. Maldonado*, 430 A.2d 779 at 782 (Del. Ch. 1981).
[59] *UPM-Kymmene Corp. v. UPM-Kymmene Miramichi Inc.*, [2004] O.J. No. 636, 42 B.L.R. (3d) 34 at 39 (C.A.).
[60] See, for example, *Main v. Delcan Group Inc.*, [1999] O.J. No. 1961, 47 B.L.R. (2d) 200 (S.C.J. — C.L.), in which the evidence showed a lack of sufficient notice, evasive answers to questions that were asked, and other questionable practice.
[61] [1995] B.C.J. No. 1441, 8 C.C.L.S. 1 at para. 15 (S.C.).

On the facts, Newbury J. concluded that the petitioners had not made out a *prima facie* case of wrongdoing. Although she acknowledged that there could be concerns about the prudence of the actions being taken by management, she said "[T]hose are questions of business judgment on which a court is hardly qualified to comment."

She went on to say that the business judgment of the directors is a question for the shareholders to evaluate. If a majority of them do not approve of what is being done, they may change the directors.

§11.24 If courts were overly willing to interfere in minute re-examination and critique of every type of decision made by a corporate board, the role of a board of directors would change from one of being an active business decision maker — identifying risks and opportunities, creating methods of managing the former while pursuing the latter, and all the while balancing cost against benefit — into one of researching through the precedent books, with the primary if not sole goal of ensuring that every board decision made was compatible with some rule set by courts as to what was permissible. The disadvantageous economic consequences to the business world of wearing such a straightjacket are self-evident. When courts explain that the rule is adopted so that courts will not impose themselves "unreasonably on the business and affairs of a corporation",[62] this is effectively what is meant.[63] So, for instance, *In Re the Walt Disney Company Derivative Litigation*[64] Chandler Ch. observed:

> Even where decision-makers act as faithful servants ... their ability and the wisdom of their judgments will vary. The redress for failures that arise from faithful management must come from the markets, through the action of shareholders and the free flow of capital, and not from this Court. Should the Court apportion liability based on the ultimate outcome of decisions taken in good faith by faithful directors or officers, those decision-makers would necessarily take decisions that minimize risk, not maximize value. The entire advantage of the risk-taking, inno-

---

[62] See, generally, *Cede & Co. v. Technicolor, Inc.* ("Cede III"), 634 A.2d 345 at 360 (Del. Ch. 1993); *Mills Acquisition Co. v. Macmillan, Inc.*, 559 A. 2d 1261 at 1280 (Del. Ch. 1989).

[63] See, for instance, *Gagliardi v. TriFoods International Inc.*, 683 A.2d 1049 at 1052 (Del. Ch. 1996), *per* Allen Ch.

> Corporate directors of public companies typically have a very small proportionate ownership interest in their corporations and little or no incentive compensation. Thus, they enjoy (as residual owners) only a very small proportion of any "upside" gains earned by the corporation on risky investment projects. If, however, corporate directors were to be found liable for a corporate loss from a risky project on the ground that the investment was too risky (foolishly risky! stupidly risky! egregiously risky!—you supply the adverb), their liability would be joint and several for the whole loss (with I suppose a right of contribution). Given the scale of operation of modern public corporations, this stupefying disjunction between risk and reward for corporate directors threatens undesirable effects. Given this disjunction, only a very small probability of director liability based on "negligence", "inattention", "waste", etc. could induce a board to avoid authorizing risky investment projects to any extent! Obviously, it is in the shareholders' economic interest to offer sufficient protection to directors from liability for negligence, etc., to allow directors to conclude that, as a practical matter, there is no risk that, if they act in good faith and meet minimalist proceduralist standards of attention, they can face liability as a result of a business loss.

[64] [2005] Del. Ch. LEXIS 113 (Ch.), *per* Chandler Ch.

vative, wealth-creating engine that is the Delaware corporation would cease to exist, with disastrous results for shareholders and society alike. That is why, under our corporate law, corporate decision-makers are held strictly to their fiduciary duties, but within the boundaries of those duties are free to act as their judgment and abilities dictate, free of *post hoc* penalties from a reviewing court using perfect hindsight. Corporate decisions are made, risks are taken, the results become apparent, capital flows accordingly, and shareholder value is increased.

§11.25 In *Re Caremark International Inc. Derivative Litigation*,[65] Allen Ch. explained that the focus in any review of board decisions is more properly placed on the process by which a decision was made, rather than upon whether it has subsequently proved to have been the best one or a wise one. He said:

> What should be understood, but may not widely be understood by courts or commentators who are not often required to face such questions, is that compliance with a director's duty of care can never appropriately be judicially determined by reference to the content of the board decision that leads to a corporate loss, apart from consideration of the good faith or rationality of the process employed. That is, whether a judge or jury considering the matter after the fact, believes a decision substantively wrong, or degrees of wrong extending through "stupid" to "egregious" or "irrational", provides no ground for director liability, so long as the court determines that the process employed was either rational or employed in a good faith effort to advance corporate interests. To employ a different rule — one that permitted an "objective" evaluation of the decision — would expose directors to substantive second guessing by ill-equipped judges or juries, which would, in the long-run, be injurious to investor interests. Thus, the business judgment rule is process oriented and informed by a deep respect for all good faith board decisions.

Decisions of a board are appropriately subject to criticism for the waste of corporate assets, breach of fiduciary duty, lack of good faith, lack of attention, or lack of oversight,[66] but (since business is related to the assumption of risk in the pursuit of profit) not on the ground that a particular decision has not worked out as well as might have been hoped in the circumstances. Only in cases in which the risk that was assumed was self-evidently excessive at the time when the decision was made, in comparison to the chance of success and the profit that might be earned by success, should the court be prepared to second-guess the decision that was made. Within this last category of cases fall most of the American decisions in which boards have been subject to judicial censure for acting in a manner that was grossly negligent.[67] Gross negligence, for this purpose has been defined as a reckless indifference to, or a deliberate disregard of, the whole body of the shareholders (or other stakeholders whose legitimate interests in the corporation are likely to be adversely affected by a decision), or the

---

[65] 698 A.2d 959 at 967-68 (Del. Ch. 1996).
[66] *Cede & Co. v. Technicolor, Inc.* ("Cede III"), 634 A.2d 345 at 366 (Del. Ch. 1993); *Smith v. Van Gorkom*, 488 A.2d 858 at 883 (Del. S.C. 1985) (a board is not required to read every contract or legal document that it approves, but there must be some credible evidence that the directors knew what they were doing, and ensured that their decisions were given effect).
[67] See, for instance, *Smith v. Van Gorkom*, 488 A.2d 858 (Del. Ch. 1985); *Aronson v. Lewis*, 473 A.2d 805, 812 (Del. S.C. 1984).

taking of actions that are outside the bounds of reason.[68] In order to make out a claim it is necessary to show a wide disparity between the process the directors used and that which would have been followed by a hypothetically reasonable and rational board.[69] Such cases are rarely encountered.

(2) Informed and Independent Decision Making

§11.26 Directors are expected to be informed and independently minded in their decision making. Independence is the particular responsibility of the non-executive directors,[70] as the OECD's *Principles of Corporate Governance*[71] makes clear, in its recommendation that:

> Boards should consider assigning a sufficient number of non-executive board members capable of exercising independent judgment to tasks where there is a potential for conflict of interest. Examples of such key responsibilities are ensuring the integrity of financial and non-financial reporting, the review of related party transactions, nomination of board members and key executives, and board remuneration.

In what would ultimately prove to be a far-reaching declaration, the U.K. Cadbury Committee recommended:

> An essential quality which non-executive directors should bring to the board's deliberations is that of independent judgment. We recommend that the majority of independent executives on a board should be independent of the company. This means that apart from their director's fees and shareholdings, they should be independent of management and free from any business or other relationship which could materially interfere with the exercise of their independent judgment. ... Information about the relevant interests of directors should be disclosed in the Director's Report.[72]

The Italian Preda Committee went even further:

> Independence is required of all directors, executive and non-executive alike: directors who are conscious of the duties and risk associated with their position always bring independent judgment to their work.[73]

---

[68] See, for instance, *Tomczak v. Morton Thiokol, Inc.*, 1990 Del. Ch. LEXIS 47, 1990 WL 42607 (Del. Ch.); *Allaun v. Consolidated. Oil Co.*, 16 Del. Ch. 318, 147 A. 257 at 261 (1929); *Gimbel v. Signal Cos., Inc.*, 316 A.2d 599 at 615 (1974), aff'd 316 A.2d 619 (Del. S.C. 1974).

[69] *Guttman v. Huang*, 823 A.2d 492 at 507 (Del. Ch. 2003).

[70] For reporting issuers in Canada, the CSA's National Policy Form 58-101F1 requires disclosure as to whether or not a majority of the directors are independent. If they are not, then the issuer is required to explain why the board considers this to be appropriate. Independence is determined in accordance with National Policy 58-101, pertaining to Disclosure of Corporate Governance Practices, and the same test of independence applies under National Policy 58-201, the Corporate Governance Guidelines.

[71] Organization for Economic Co-operation and Development (Paris: OECD, 2004), at VI.E.1.

[72] *Report of the Cadbury Committee on the Financial Aspects of Corporate Governance* (London: London Stock Exchange, 1992), para. 4.12 (sometimes "Cadbury Report"). See also the *Report of the AFG-ASFFI Commission on Corporate Governance in France* (European Corporate Governance Institute, 1998) para. II.B.1, "Board Independence".

[73] *Preda Committee for the Corporate Governance of Listed Companies, Code of Conduct* (Rome: Borsa Italiana, 1999) Commentary to Rule 3.

Considerable attention has been paid in American case law, and to a lesser extent in Canada as well, to the role of independent directors in the evaluation of takeover and management buyout proposals, and also with respect to requests for the institution of litigation that might otherwise form the basis of a derivative action proceeding.

§11.27 The question of whether the directors have reached an informed decision is determined upon the basis of the information reasonably available to the directors at the time when their decision was made, and that would have appeared relevant on the basis of the facts that were known or that should have been discovered through reasonable inquiry.[74] The presumption that the directors acted in good faith is irrelevant in determining whether the board exercised an informed business judgment or followed a proper procedure in making its decisions.[75] In the *Corporacion Americana* case, the court stated that:

> ... it is a precondition to the application of the rule that the court must determine that the directors have acted honestly, prudently, in good faith and on a reasonable belief that the transaction is in the best interest of the company.[76]

These factors are, however, relevant to the question of whether the business judgment rule is available as a defence. Even so, the foregoing passage is misleading to the extent that it suggests that the onus of proof is on the defendant: indeed, the rule would be almost valueless if this were the case. The court in *Corporacion Americana* itself appears to have appreciated this point, for later in the judgment it was said that the rule (emphasis added):

> ... is ... *a presumption only ... which may cast doubt* as to the honesty, prudence and good faith of the directors in approving or entering into the challenged transaction.[77]

(3) Knowledge, Skill and Experience

§11.28 The most difficult aspect of clauses 134(1)(*b*) of the OBCA and 122(1)(*b*) of the CBCA to construe is the extent to which it imposes an obligation upon directors to possess a particular degree of skill. Skill is the special degree of competence that is not part of the ordinary equipment of the reasonable man or woman, but which arises from special training and experience to carry out a particular kind of work.[78] In the leading common law case of *Re City Equitable Fire Insurance Co.*[79] Romer J. expressed the view that a director need not exhibit in the performance of his (or her) duties a greater degree of skill than may reasonably be expected from a person of his knowledge and experience,

---

[74] See, generally, *McMullin v. Beran*, 765 A.2d 910 (Del. S.C. 2000).
[75] *Smith v. Van Gorkom*, 488 A.2d 858 at 889 (Del. S.C. 1985); see also *In Re Holly Farms Corp. Shareholders Litigation*, [1988] W.L. 143010 (Del. Ch.).
[76] *Corporacion Americana de Equipamientos Urbanos S.L. v. Olifas Marketing Group Inc.*, [2003] O.J. No. 3368, 66 O.R. (3d) 352 at para. 13 (S.C.J.).
[77] *Ibid.*, at para. 14.
[78] John G. Fleming, *The Law of Torts*, 4th ed. (Sydney: The Law Book Company, 1971) at 109.
[79] [1925] Ch. 407.

giving by way of a specific example, the statement that a director of a life insurance company does not guarantee that he possesses the skill of an actuary or of a physician.[80] Under the general law of negligence, a reasonable person is not possessed of any particular skill,[81] unless the type of work in which he or she engages is of such a character that no reasonable man or woman would undertake it unless possessed of a certain degree of skill[82] — that is, unless having been properly trained to carry out the type of work in question. Given the history of the case law in this area, and the prevailing standards of competence displayed in commerce generally, it is quite clear that directors were not expected at common law to have any particular business skill or judgment. It is far from clear that either the OBCA or the CBCA depart from the general approach, and impose a requirement to possess a degree of skill.[83] Until this question is squarely addressed by the courts, it must remain open,[84] although recent case law in this area does indicate that there has been no radical departure from earlier case law with respect to the skill and knowledge required of directors. For instance, in *Osborne v. Kane*,[85] a company was formed with one director and shareholder agreeing to supply the cash, while the second was to contribute goods and expertise. The business failed and the first director sued the second alleging that the defendant had breached the agreement to provide expertise. The court held that the action should be dismissed, on the basis that the plaintiff had failed to establish that the defendant's failure to give expert advice was the cause of the loss. The plaintiff's cause of action was against the corporation, and not against the second director personally.

(4) Extent of Care

§11.29 Much as reasonable care must be distinguished from degree of skill, similarly each of them is distinct from the extent of care that must be devoted to corporate operations. Extent of care may largely be equated with the amount of time that a director is expected to devote to corporate business. In the *City Equitable Fire Insurance* case,[86] Romer J. held that a director is not bound to give his (or her) continuous attention to the affairs of the company. Subject to an express or implicit contractual undertaking (as, for instance, would apply with respect to the executive officers of a corporation), a director's duties are of an

---

[80] See also *Re Brazilian Rubber Plantations and Estates Ltd.*, [1911] 1 Ch. 425 at 437, *per* Neville J.; *Gould v. Mount Oxide Mines Ltd.* (1916), 22 C.L.R. 490 (H.C. Aust.).

[81] See *Re Owen Sound Lumber Co.*, [1917] O.J. No. 144, 38 O.L.R. 414 at 431 (C.A.), *per* Hodgins J.A. (auditor not expected to possess any particular degree of skill); *Bolton v. Stone*, [1951] A.C. 850 at 867 (H.L.), *per* Lord Reid; *Brown v. Shyne*, 151 N.E. 197 (N.Y.S.C. 1926) (quack judged according to the standards of licensed physician); *Vancouver (City) v. Burchill*, [1932] S.C.J. No. 43, [1932] S.C.R. 620 (failure to hold a mandatory licence was held not to be evidence of negligence).

[82] R.A. Percy, *Charlesworth & Percy on Negligence*, 8th ed. (London: Sweet & Maxwell, 1990), paras. 8-10.

[83] See, however, NI 52-110 regarding the financial expertise expected of members of an audit committee.

[84] See, generally, *Chaudhry v. Prabhaker*, [1988] 3 All E.R. 718 (C.A.).

[85] [1977] N.B.J. No. 236, 19 N.B.R. (2d) 316, 30 A.P.R. 316 (Q.B.).

[86] [1925] Ch. 407 (C.A.).

intermittent nature to be performed at periodical board meetings, and at meetings of any committee of the board upon which he happens to be placed. He is not, however, bound to attend all such meetings, though he ought to attend whenever, in the circumstances, he is reasonably able to do so. In the ordinary case, this view appears to remain correct under clauses 134(1)(*b*) of the OBCA and 122(1)(*b*) of the CBCA. Apart from specific statutory obligations, the general duties of the directors of any corporation include those of policy formation and general supervision.[87] In its *Statement on Corporate Governance*,[88] the Business Roundtable stated that the principal functions of a board of directors are to:

(i) Select, regularly evaluate and, if necessary, replace the chief executive officer, determine management compensation; and review succession planning;

(ii) Review and, where appropriate, approve the major strategies and financial and other objectives and plans of the corporation;

(iii) Advise management on significant issues facing the corporation;

(iv) Oversee processes for evaluating the adequacy of internal controls, risk management, financial reporting and compliance, and satisfy itself as to the adequacy of such processes; and

(v) Nominate directors and ensure that the structure and practices of the board provide for sound corporate governance.

In Canadian commercial practice — at least in the case of major corporations — directors as such are not expected to be involved as such in the day-to-day operations of the corporation. However, they are expected to attend board and relevant committee meetings on a regular basis. The extent to which a director may abdicate his responsibilities as a director and leave it to some or all of his fellow directors to carry on the business of the corporation has frequently come before the courts. The director's duty of care involves positive effort on his or her part. Thus a director cannot deny liability for non-feasance merely because he (or she) would have been protected against liability for misfeasance under the corporate management doctrine, had he made the proper inquiries.[89]

§11.30 It is not appropriate for a board to serve as a rubber stamp routinely approving the recommendations brought forward by management. On this point the *German Code of Corporate Governance* is instructive:

It is only with an engaged argument in each case on pending questions of management and supervision that the managerial duties of the Management Board as

---

[87] See *Tanguay v. Royal Paper Mills Co.* (1907), 31 Que. S.C. 397.
[88] September, 1997, at 4-5.
[89] *Joint Stock Discount Co. v. Brown* (1869), L.R. 8 Eq. 381 at 405 (V.C.), *per* Sir W.M. James V.C. Although it is common to refer to *Re Denham & Co.* (1883), 25 Ch. D. 752, and *Re Cardiff Savings Bank (Marquis of Bute's Case)*, [1892] 2 Ch. 100, when discussing the common law position as to the extent of care that directors were expected to exercise, it can be argued that the facts of these cases were so unusual that they have little bearing in ascertaining the general duty of care to which directors are subject.

well as those of the Supervisory Board can be fulfilled in a well-founded manner. Establishing and furthering a culture of open discussion is therefore essential for the proper functioning of corporate governance. This promotes detailed and balanced discussion of the managerial problems to be solved, and thereby utilizes the expertise of the members ...

The chairpersons ... encourage the members ... to analyze suggestions for decisions and to contribute their experience, in order to seek out possible points of weakness and chances of improvement. They make it clear that relevant analysis of planned measures is not considered to be negative criticism and disloyalty, but an expression of the engagement desired of the officer.[90]

§11.31 It is axiomatic that negligence is only actionable upon proof of damage. Where loss would have been suffered no matter what a particular director did, and there was no factual foundation for concluding that his or her negligence gave rise to the damage which was suffered, a director will not normally be liable for failure to exercise a reasonable extent of care.[91] A director may have acted unreasonably, but proof of unreasonable behaviour is not proof of causality.

§11.32 In *Dorchester Finance Co. v. Stebbing*,[92] liability was imposed on the basis of prolonged non-attendance at meetings, and in *Re Owen Sound Lumber*,[93] it was held that directors are required to be more than honest; they must devote their intelligence and diligence to the business. The Indian case *Govind Narayan v. Rangnath Gopal*[94] stands as authority for the proposition that directors are expected to exercise reasonable diligence. Similarly, in *Re Standard Trustco Ltd.*,[95] a discipline hearing under the *Securities Act*, the Ontario Securities Commission reprimanded a person who was a director of a reporting issuer for a period of two years, who had been elected to the board of directors on an understanding between himself and a shareholder that he would not attend board meetings. The Commission said that the director was required to take affirmative action to involve himself in business transacted at board meetings. A director cannot act in the best interests of the corporation if he or she allows himself or herself to be elected on the basis of such an understanding.

§11.33 Still there are obvious practical constraints upon the time and attention that directors can be expected to devote to the corporation. As noted above, in

---

[90] Berlin Initiative Group, *German Code of Corporate Governance* (Berlin: 2000), paras. 4.1-4.2.
[91] Re Denham & Co. (1883), 25 Ch. D. 752; but compare *British American Elevator Co. v. Bank of British North America* (1914), 20 D.L.R. 944 (Man. K.B.), vard 26 D.L.R. 587 (C.A.), rev'd 46 D.L.R. 326, [1919] A.C. 658 (P.C.) (restoring judgment of King's Bench).
[92] (1977), now reported at [1989] B.C.L.C. 498 (Ch.).
[93] [1915] O.J. No. 116, 34 O.L.R. 528 (H.C.D.), *per* Middleton J. However, judgment was varied on appeal at [1917] O.J. No. 144, 38 O.L.R. 414 (C.A.), *per* Hodgins J.A., who questioned whether Middleton J.'s view was not voicing counsel of perfection (p. 422) and then continued (at p. 430): "The dereliction from duty of these directors, if it existed at all, was in accepting incorrect and misleading statements without themselves investigating their accuracy ...". Hodgins J.A. was not prepared to insist that a director is required to turn into an auditor, managing director and chairman of the board and then revisit their work, in order to determine whether the people actually holding those offices were being deceitful.
[94] [1929] I.L.R. 54 (Bom.) 226.
[95] (1991), 14 O.S.C.B. 1633.

North American business practice, directors of an offering corporation (other than those directors who are executive officers) are not expected to be involved in the business or affairs of the corporation on a day-to-day basis. The outside directors of the corporation are obviously not expected to have more than an intermittent connection with the corporation. Most widely held corporations and a very large number of closely held corporations are large, diversified businesses, operating in several different jurisdictions, perhaps on a worldwide basis. Board meetings have increased in frequency in recent years, but for most corporations they still take place only at monthly intervals.[96] No person can be expected to be intimately familiar with the business and affairs of such a corporation, when his or her involvement in the corporation is limited to a monthly board meeting — and perhaps not even all of those.

§11.34 Relatively few matters can be dealt with in a deliberate manner over a period of several meetings. Even a small corporation must make thousands of business decisions over the course of a month. Very many decisions require a quick response. The board's agenda will usually be so crowded that time will allow the board to deal with individual matters only in a broad-brush manner; discussion is likely to be fragmentary, with little time for debate. In many cases the directors must delegate a substantial portion of the responsibility for the day-to-day management of the corporation to committees of the board and to the officers of the corporation. And it is to the subject of delegation, that we shall now turn.

(5) Degree of Care

§11.35 There are relatively few cases that have construed the meaning of "in comparable circumstances" as it is used in the OBCA or CBCA. In the United States, the scope of the corresponding duty has been discussed in a number of cases, from which the following general principles may be distilled.

A. Directors are each expected to exercise an independent decision making authority. Independence means that a director's decision is based on the corporate merits of the subject before the board rather than extraneous considerations or influences. Directors may confer, debate, and resolve their differences through compromise, or they may choose to be bound by a

---

[96] *Cadbury Report on the Financial Aspects of Corporate Governance* (London: London Stock Excahnge, 1992), at paras. 4.23 and 4.24:

> The basic procedural requirements are that the board should meet regularly with due notice of the issues to be discussed supported by the necessary paperwork, and should record its conclusions. We recommend that boards should have a formal schedule of matters specifically reserved to them for their collective decision, to ensure that the direction and control of the company remains firmly in their hands and as a safeguard against misjudgments and possible illegal practices. ...
>
> ... Boards should lay down rules to determine materiality for any transaction, and should establish clearly which transactions require multiple board signatures. Boards should also agree the procedures to be followed when, exceptionally, decisions are required between board meetings.

majority vote. In forming an opinion, they may place reasonable reliance upon the expertise of their colleagues and other qualified persons. In the end, each director must bring his or her own informed business judgment to bear with specificity upon the corporate merits of each issue to be decided.[97]

B. The directors duty of care incorporates an obligation to become informed about the corporation, its business and environment. The directors are not entitled to relax into the passive role of mere recipients of information. They must take active steps to seek out relevant information (*e.g.*, by reasonable questioning of staff and requiring periodic reporting), and they must seek other information that is available to them.[98] They must seek to be informed about both the strengths and weaknesses of available options.[99]

C. An informed decision to delegate a task is as much an exercise of business judgment as any other. The realities of modern corporate life are such that directors cannot be expected to manage the day-to-day activities of a company. In deciding upon the matters in which it will be directly involved, and those that it will delegate to others, a board's decisions in those areas are entitled to equal consideration as exercises of business judgment.[100]

D. The business judgment rule, which normally protects directors, is a two-edged sword. To benefit from it, the directors must be able to demonstrate that they have exercised a business judgment. There must be a business rationale for their decision, and the decision itself must be one that is sufficiently deliberative to constitute the exercise of a proper judgment.

E. The directors' duty of care means that they must be in a position to demonstrate that they have exercised proper oversight. For instance, they have a duty to require proper accounting practices to be put into place, and to confirm periodically that the accounts are accurate.[101] However, the plaintiff shareholder or other stakeholder bears the burden of showing that the director's negligent breach of duty was the proximate cause of injury suffered by the corporation or the plaintiff as the case may be.[102]

F. Directors may be guilty of negligence in failing to supervise corporate staff properly however, subject to any statutory rule to the contrary, to hold a director or officer personally liable for a fraud or other misrepresentation attributable to the corporation, the plaintiff must demonstrate that the officer or director concerned was an actual participant in the fraud — as for instance by showing, that the officer "was responsible for the delivery of the written

---

[97] *Aronson v. Lewis*, 473 A.2d 805 at 816 (Del. S.C. 1984).
[98] A board should not be reduced to a passive instrumentality: *In Re Pure Resources, Inc. Shareholders Litigation*, 808 A.2d 421 (Del. Ch. 2002).
[99] See, generally, *Cinerama, Inc. v. Technicolor, Inc.*, 663 A.2d 1134 (Del. Ch. 1994), aff'd 663 A.2d 1156 (1995).
[100] *Rosenblatt v. Getty Oil Co.*, 493 A.2d 929 (Del. S.C. 1985), per Moore J.
[101] *Lippitt v. Ashley*, 89 Conn. 451, 94 A. 995 (S.C. Errors, Conn. 1915).
[102] *Cinerama, Inc. v. Technicolor, Inc.*, 663 A.2d 1134 (Del. Ch. 1994), aff'd 663 A.2d 1156 (1995).

material" containing the misrepresentation.[103] Allegations that a director, "must have known" a statement was false or misleading due to his or her position within the corporation are not sufficient pleading of particulars of such involvement. Generalized imputations of knowledge do not suffice, regardless of the defendant's position.[104]

G. Directors are not guarantors of the debts or other obligations of a corporation. On the other hand, they cannot use their control over the corporation to strip the corporation of its assets so that it is put in a position where it cannot pay those debts or discharge those obligations. To do so is a violation of the director's fiduciary duty to the corporation.[105] To fail to introduce reasonable controls on misappropriation of corporate property, or extravagant waste, by the officers and employees of the corporation, or to control reckless commercial action on the part of the officers and employees constitutes a breach of their duty of care.

H. Directors have an obligation to cause a proper investigation to be made with respect to any apparent impropriety in corporate management that comes to their notice. It is not inappropriate for the board to delegate this responsibility. More specifically, the board may appoint a litigation committee of independent directors who are at arm's length to the potential claim to decide upon the merit of instituting proceedings. Such an approach can insulate the corporation's decision making process from the influence of those who are under suspicion.[106] In one American case, the role of such a committee was described and explained in the following terms:

> The value of a special litigation committee is coextensive with the extent to which that committee truly exercises business judgment. In order to ensure that special litigation committees do act for the corporation's best interest, a good deal of judicial oversight is necessary in each case. At the same time, however, courts must be careful not to usurp the committee's valuable role in exercising business judgment. At a minimum, a special litigation committee must be independent, unbiased, and act in good faith. Moreover, such a committee must conduct a thorough and careful analysis regarding the plaintiff's derivative suit. ... The burden of proving that these procedural requirements have been met must rest, in all fairness, on the party capable of making that proof — the corporation.[107]

I. The directors are not obliged to pursue every potential claim to which a corporation may be entitled by reason of some alleged wrongdoing. In deciding whether to pursue a claim, the directors may take into account the wider corporate interests as well as the merit of the claim itself. The business judgment rule "affords protection to the business decisions of directors, including the

---

[103] *St. James Recreation, LLC v. Rieger Opportunity Partners, LLC*, [2003] Del. Ch. LEXIS 126.
[104] *In Re Advanta Corp. Sec. Litig.*, 180 F.3d 525 at 539 (3d Cir. 1999).
[105] See *Lopez v. TDI Services, Inc.*, 631 So.2d 679 (La. C.A. 3d Cir. 1994), writ denied 637 So.2d 501 (La. 1994).
[106] *Biondi v. Scrushy*, 820 A.2d 1148 at 1156 (Del. Ch. 2003).
[107] *Houle v. Low*, 407 Mass. 810 at 822, 556 N.E.2d 51 (1990); but *cf. Lewis v. Fuqua*, 502 A.2d 962 at 967 (Del. Ch. 1985).

decision to institute litigation, because directors are presumed to act in the best interests of the corporation".[108] The directors are not liable merely because they have failed to take such measures, and a loss has occurred. Causality must be shown unless in the circumstances it can be naturally and properly inferred. In the words of the leading American authority on this point:

> The plaintiff must, however, go further than to show that [the director] should have been more active in his duties. This cause of action rests upon a tort, as much though it be a tort of omission as though it had rested upon a positive act. The plaintiff must accept the burden of showing that the performance of the defendant's duties would have avoided loss, and what loss it would have avoided. ... When the corporate funds have been illegally lent, it is a fair inference that a protest would have stopped the loan, and that the director's neglect caused the loss. But when a business fails from general mismanagement, business incapacity, or bad judgment, how is it possible to say that a single director could have made the company successful, or how much in dollars he could have saved? Before this cause can go to a master, the plaintiff must show that, had Andrews done his full duty, he could have made the company prosper, or at least could have broken its fall. He must show what sum he could have saved the company.[109]

§11.36 In addition to the foregoing, reference may be made to cases decided under section 227.1 of the *Income Tax Act*,[110] which affords a director a defence from liability for unremitted tax withholdings where the director exercises the degree of care and diligence and skill to prevent a failure to remit that a reasonably prudent person would have exercised in comparable circumstances. The scope of this defence was considered in *Soper v. The Queen*.[111] In construing the meaning of that provision, Robertson J.A. stated:

> The standard of care laid down in subsection 227.1(3) of the Act is inherently flexible. Rather than treating directors as a homogeneous group of professionals whose conduct is governed by a single, unchanging standard, that provision embraces a subjective element which takes into account the personal knowledge and background of the director, as well as his or her corporate circumstances in the form of, inter alia, the company's organization, resources, customs and conduct. Thus, for example, more is expected of individuals with superior qualifications (e.g. experienced business-persons).
>
> The standard of care set out in subsection 227.1(3) of the Act is, therefore, not purely objective. Nor is it purely subjective. It is not enough for a director to say he or she did his or her best, for that is an invocation of the purely subjective standard. Equally clear is that honesty is not enough. However, the standard is not a professional one. Nor is it the negligence law standard that governs these cases. Rather, the Act contains both objective elements embodied in the reasonable person language and subjective elements inherent in individual considerations like

---

[108] *Harhen v. Brown*, 431 Mass. 838 at 845, 730 N.E.2d 859 (2000).
[109] *Barnes v. Andres* (1924), 298 F. 614 (S.D.N.Y.), per Hand J.
[110] Liability under s. 227.1 is further discussed at §11.289 below.
[111] [1997] F.C.J. No. 881, [1998] 1 F.C. 124 (C.A.).

"skill" and the idea of "comparable circumstances". Accordingly, the standard can be properly described as "objective subjective".[112]

A critical distinction between the director duty provisions of the OBCA and CBCA (on the one hand) and section 227.1 (on the other) is that the former impose a duty upon directors to exercise the care, diligence and skill that a reasonable and prudent person would do in comparable circumstances, while section 227.1 makes it a defence to liability to show that such care, *etc.*, was exercised to prevent a default in payment. Nevertheless, the tax cases do provide a helpful guide. In *Re Banks*[113] the court (construing section 134 of the OBCA) stated:

> While all directors and officers are held to the same standard of care, all directors and officers do not stand in the same position, in that they are not all possessed of the same information and they do not occupy the same "comparable circumstances". The most common distinguishing feature between directors is whether they are inside directors (typically senor officers involved in the management of the company) or outside directors (those who have been brought onto the board so that they can share their expertise and experience with a company in which they do not play a day-to-day managerial role). Inside directors and senior officers ... will ordinarily have a much better knowledge of the affairs of the company. Accordingly, their duty to react diligently to certain events or problems may be higher than that of an outside director. As a result, in ascertaining the actual duty of care in a given circumstance, more will usually be expected of inside directors.

§11.37 Among inside directors, the greatest expectations are placed upon the person who holds the position of chief executive officer, as that individual bears "direct responsibility for establishing the standards of behaviour and processes of the corporation". The CEO may delegate specific duties to other members of the management team, but he or she "will always remain primarily responsible for overseeing the performance" of those other senior officers.[114] At least in the tax cases, the courts have looked for active diligence on the part of all directors.[115] A person who is experienced in business and financial matters is likely to be held to a higher standard than a person with no business experience.[116] There is at least some duty on the directors to anticipate problems that are likely to arise in the business of the corporation.[117] Key considerations include whether the directors have put into place "a good and efficient system" for meeting their responsibilities and ensuring that the corporation is properly run.[118] Liability is likely to flow where the approach taken towards corporate management is haphazard.[119] However, the specific attributes of the individual director must also be considered. In *Hevenor v. Canada*,[120] an elderly father became the sole director

---

[112] *Ibid.*, at paras. 37, 38 F.C.J.
[113] 2003 LNONOSC 192 at para. 98.
[114] *Re Cartaway Resources Corp.* (2000), 9 A.S.C.S. 3092 (Alta. Sec. Comm.).
[115] *Pitchford v. Canada*, [2003] T.C.J. No. 253, [2003] 3 C.T.C. 2853.
[116] *Smith v. Canada*, [2001] F.C.J. No. 448, 2001 D.T.C. 5226 at para. 10 (C.A.).
[117] *Yakimishyn v. Canada*, [2003] T.C.J. No. 220, 2003 TCC 255.
[118] *Gruia v. Canada*, [2005] T.C.J. No. 293, 2005 TCC 406.
[119] *Tanner v. Canada*, [2005] T.C.J. No. 71, 2005 TCC 119.
[120] [1999] T.C.J. No. 65.

of his son's corporation as a favour for his son. He did not fully understand his responsibilities and liabilities as a corporate director and was not involved in the decisions or operations of the company. Had he been shown financial statements, he would not have been able to understand them. In a claim made under section 323 of the *Excise Tax Act,* it was held that his degree of care as a director was limited by his lack of skill. *Hevenor,* however, is an exceptional case. The normal rule is that where a director obtains information, or becomes aware of facts that might lead a reasonable person to conclude that there is, or could reasonably be, a potential problem with the corporation meeting its responsibilities the duty to take a proactive role increases.[121]

(6) Directors' Duty to Create Safeguards

§11.38 Since directors tend not to be involved in the day-to-day operations of the corporation, they are expected to create a proper disclosure and oversight process under which suitable controls are placed on corporate operations and the actions of individual employees. The OECD's *Principles of Corporate Governance* lists a number of specific key functions that a board should be expected to fulfill.[122] The list begins with the statement that:

> Board members should act on a fully informed basis, in good faith, with due diligence and care, and in the best interest of the company and the shareholders.

The OECD — following the language of the American Business Roundtable — then goes on to recommend that the board of directors should review and guide corporate strategy, major plans of action, risk policy, annual budgets and business plans; setting performance objectives; monitoring implementation and corporate performance; and overseeing major capital expenditures, acquisitions and divestitures. The board should also be responsible for selecting, compensating, monitoring and, when necessary, replacing key executives and overseeing succession planning. Another area of responsibility recommended is to monitor and manage potential conflicts of interest relating to management, board members and shareholders, including the misuse of corporate assets and abuse in related party transactions. The OECD also recommend that boards ensure the integrity of the corporation's accounting and financial reporting systems, including the independent audit process.[123]

---

[121] *Soper v. The Queen,* [1997] F.C.J. No. 881, [1998] 1 F.C. 124 (C.A.).
[122] (Paris: OECD, 2004), Part VI, "The Responsibilities of the Board".
[123] *Ibid.* See also *Report of the Cadbury Committee on the Financial Aspects of Corporate Governance* (London: London Stock Exchange, 1992), at para. 4.39.

> We regard it as good practice for companies to establish internal audit functions to undertake regular monitoring of key controls and procedures. Such regular monitoring is an integral part of a company's system of internal control and helps to ensure its effectiveness. An internal audit function is well placed to undertake investigations on behalf of the audit committee and to follow up any suspicion of fraud. It is essential that heads of internal audit should have unrestricted access to the chairman of the audit committee in order to ensure the independence of their position.

§11.39 The directors of a corporation are responsible for implementing reasonable safeguards against wrongdoing, such as the introduction of effective expenditure and budgetary control systems.[124] The board should be clear in the extent of authority delegated to management, the supervision that is required where subdelegation takes place, the limits that apply to delegated powers, the manner in which such powers are to be exercised (and, perhaps more importantly, where the exercise of those powers is prohibited or where special authorization is required).[125] They are responsible for ensuring that the corporation is entrusted to competent and honest managers. They have an obligation to introduce a sufficiently comprehensive and detailed internal inspection and control system,[126] coupled with a proper system of reporting, to deter those honest managers from being tempted to misappropriate corporate assets.[127] The directors have a clear responsibility for the accuracy of accounting records and the corporation's management information system. The Cadbury Report on the Financial Aspects of Corporate Governance specified:

> Directors are responsible ... for maintaining adequate accounting records. To meet these responsibilities directors need in practice to main a system of internal controls over the financial management of the company, including the procedures designed to minimise the risk of fraud ...
>
> ... an effective internal control system is a key aspect of the efficient management of a company ...[128]

In addition, the non-executive directors of a corporation are responsible for reviewing the performance of the board and of the executive. It further stipulated that the non-executive directors have a responsibility to take the lead when potential conflicts of interest arise.[129]

§11.39.1 For most corporations of any size, the role of the board is primarily supervisory. The directors of a corporation have a duty to monitor the manner in which the officers of the corporation carry on the business and affairs of the corporation on a day-to-day basis, but, except in very unusual circumstances, it

---

[124] See, for instance, *In Re Caremark Inc., Derivative Litigation*, 698 A.2d 959 (Del. Ch. 1996).

[125] See, for instance, Preda Committee for the Corporate Governance of Listed Companies, *Report: Code of Conduct* (Rome: Borsa Italiana, 1999), at para. 1.2.

[126] Preda Committee for the Corporate Governance of Listed Companies, *Report: Code of Conduct* (Rome: Borsa Italiana, 1999), at para. 5.4.3:

> It is the task of the directors so encharged to set up and ensure the adequacy and effectiveness of the internal control system. A good control system, provided with adequate human and financial resources, increases the ability to identify, forestall and limit, as far as possible, financial and operating risks...

[127] *Report of the Cadbury Committee on the Financial Aspects of Corporate Governance* (London: London Stock Exchange, 1992) at para. 5.23.

> The prime responsibility for the prevention and detection of fraud (and other illegal acts) is that of the board, as part of its fiduciary responsibility for protecting the assets of the company.

[128] *Report of the Cadbury Committee on the Financial Aspects of Corporate Governance* (London: London Stock Exchange, 1992) at paras. 4.31-4.32.

[129] *Ibid.*, paras. 4.5 and 4.6.

is doubtful that there is a further duty upon them to monitor the manner in which those officers carry on their personal business. Absent a cause for suspicion there is no duty upon the directors to install and operate a corporate system of espionage to ferret out wrongdoing that they have no reason to suspect exists.[130] A board may be expected to introduce a monitoring process to ensure that corporate assets are not misused in the private business of corporate officers and employees, but where such a business is conducted off-premises and without resort to corporate assets, it will normally fall outside the scope of the board's duty of supervision. The mere fact that the personal reputation of a senior corporate officer is of critical importance to the corporation is not sufficient to give rise to such a duty.[131]

(7) Director's Duty of Disclosure

§11.40 As we shall discuss in greater detail later in the chapter, the directors of a corporation owe a fiduciary duty to it, and it is part and parcel of the obligation of a fiduciary to provide an accounting for the discharge of the trust reposed in him or her, to the beneficiary of that duty. Current corporate and securities laws go well beyond the traditional equitable obligation to account and subject directors to a number of distinct reporting and disclosure obligations. In addition to the disclosure obligations that are mandated law, special disclosure obligations apply to listed companies, under the listing rules of exchanges such as the NYSE, NASDAQ, the TSX and TSX Venture. The disclosure policies of such exchanges in general require the timely disclosure of all "material information", which includes both material facts and material changes relating to the business and affairs of a company. In the Canadian Securities Administrators' National Policy 51-201, the following guidance is provided with respect to materiality:

> In making materiality judgments, it is necessary to take into account a number of factors that cannot be captured in a simple bright-line standard or test. These include the nature of the information itself, the volatility of the company's securities and prevailing market conditions. The materiality of a particular event or piece of information may vary between companies according to their size, the nature of their operations and many other factors. An event that is "significant" or "major" for a smaller company may not be material to a larger company. Companies should avoid taking an overly technical approach to determining materiality. Under volatile market conditions, apparently insignificant variances between earnings projections and actual results can have a significant impact on share price once released. For example, information regarding a company's ability to meet consensus earnings published by securities analysts should not be selectively disclosed before general public release.[132]

§11.41 As we have discussed in previous chapters, directors have a duty to provide an accounting of their stewardship of the corporation to its shareholders, and to other investors in its securities, in the form of the annual financial reports

---

[130] *Graham v. Allis-Chalmers Manufacturing Co.*, 188 A.2d 125 at 130 (Del. S.C. 1963).
[131] *Beam ex rel. Martha Stewart Living Omnimedia, Inc. v. Stewart*, [2003] Del. Ch. LEXIS 98 (Del. Ch.), aff'd (*sub nom. Beam v. Stewart*), 845 A.2d 1040 (Del. Sup. Ct. 2004).
[132] CSA National Policy 51-201, para. 4.2.

and continuous disclosure obligations imposed under the *Securities Act* and related regulations, rules and policies,[133] and under the OBCA and CBCA. Without repeating the detail of that prior discussion, the general duties of a board in this regard include:

- reviewing and approving the financial statements, business plan and budget of the corporation;

- overseeing the accurate and timely reporting to shareholders and regulators of the corporation's performance, financial statements and significant developments; and

- overseeing the accurate and timely reporting to shareholders and regulators of the corporation's performance, financial statements and significant developments.

With respect to such reporting in the U.K. context, the Cadbury Report noted first the adverse economic impact of deviation from the required standard of accuracy and detail:

> The lifeblood of markets is information and barriers to the flow of relevant information represent imperfections in the market. The need to sift and correct the information put out by companies adds cost and uncertainty to the market's pricing function. The more the activities of companies are transparent, the more accurately will their securities be valued.[134]

The OECD's *Principles of Corporate Governance* offer an expansive statement of the type of disclosure that should be provided to the shareholders, regulators and other stakeholders of the corporation:

> The corporate governance framework should ensure that timely and accurate disclosure is made on all material matters regarding the corporation, including the financial situation, performance, ownership and governance of the company.
>
> A. Disclosure should include, but not be limited to, material information on:
>
> 1. The financial and operating results of the company.
>
> 2. Company objectives.
>
> 3. Major share ownership and voting rights.
>
> 4. Members of the board and key executives, and their remuneration.
>
> 5. Material foreseeable risk factors.
>
> 6. Material issues regarding employees and other stakeholders.
>
> 7. Governance structures and policies.
>
> B. Information should be prepared, audited and disclosed in accordance with high quality standards of accounting, financial and non-financial disclosure, and audit.

---

[133] See CSA National Instrument 51-102 "Continuous Disclosure Obligations", and the OSC's Rule 52-501 Financial Statements and Companion Policy.

[134] Cadbury Report, at paras. 4.48-4.51.

C. An annual audit should be conducted by an independent auditor in order to provide an external and objective assurance on the way in which financial statements have been prepared and presented.

D. Channels for disseminating information should provide for fair, timely and cost-efficient access to relevant information by users.[135]

An explanation of these requirements is provided in the Cadbury Report:

> What shareholders (and others) need from the report and accounts is a coherent narrative, supported by the figures, of the company's performance and prospects. ... Balance requires that setbacks should be dealt with as well as successes, while the need for the report to be readily understood emphasizes that words are as important as figures.
>
> The cardinal principle of financial reporting is that the view presented should be true and fair. Further principles are that boards should aim for the highest level of disclosure consonant with presenting reports which are understandable and with avoiding damage to their competitive position. They should also aim to ensure the integrity and consistency of their reports and they should meet the spirit as well as the letter of reporting standards.[136]

The explanatory notes to the Canadian Investor Relations Institute, *Model Disclosure Policy*,[137] provide the following helpful guidance:

> Determining the materiality of information is clearly an area where judgement and experience are of great value. If it is a borderline decision, the information should probably be considered material and released using a broad means of dissemination. Similarly, if several company officials have to deliberate extensively over whether information is material, they should err on the side of materiality and release it publicly.

§11.42 Significantly, while most international authorities on corporate governance make clear that the audit process is necessary to sustain investor confidence in the corporate governance system, the primary obligation with respect to corporate financial statements falls upon the board and management, rather than upon the auditors. In this respect, the Cadbury Report is particularly instructive.[138]

> The auditors' role is to report whether the financial statements give a true and fair view, and the audit is designed to provide a reasonable assurance that the financial statements are free of material misstatements. The auditors' role is not (to cite a few of the misunderstandings) to prepare the financial statements, nor to provide absolute assurance that the figures in the financial statements are correct, nor to provide a guarantee that the company will continue in existence.

Mere provision of information is not sufficient. On this point, the Canadian Securities Administrators' National Policy 51-201 provides:

---

[135] Part V. "Disclosure and Transparency".
[136] Cadbury Report, at paras. 4.50-4.51.
[137] February, 2001. This particular paragraph is approved in the Canadian Securities Administrators, National Policy 51-201.
[138] *Report of the Cadbury Committee on the Financial Aspects of Corporate Governance* (London: London Stock Exchange, 1992) at para. 5.14.

Existing case law does not establish a firm rule as to what would be a reasonable amount of time for investors to be given to analyze information. The time period will depend on a number of factors including the circumstances in which the event arises, the nature and complexity of the information, the nature of the market for the company's securities, and the manner used to release the information. We recognize that the case law is dated in this respect and that, if the courts were to revisit these decisions today, they may not find the time parameters set out in the decisions appropriate for modern technology.[139]

§11.43 In addition to the foregoing routine disclosure, directors are subject to specific transactional disclosure responsibilities.[140] For instance, a director is subject to a duty to provide full, complete and timely information to the other directors on matters of serious import and effect on the corporation's financial well-being.[141] In addition, under general principles of equity, as fiduciaries, directors and officers are under a duty to their corporation to bring to its notice all information that comes to their attention that is relevant to its business or affairs. There is no presumption in law, however, that directors or officers will necessarily comply with this duty, so that the corporation is impressed with knowledge (or notice of) every fact that is known to a director. In *Meridian Global Funds Management Asia Ltd v. Securities Commission,* Lord Hoffmann said:

> ... their Lordships would wish to guard themselves against being understood to mean that whenever a servant of a company has authority to do an act on its behalf, knowledge of that act will for all purposes be attributed to the company. It is a question of construction in each case as to whether the particular rule requires that the knowledge that an act has been done, or the state of mind with which it was done, should be attributed to the company.[142]

It was a well-established principle that a company or principal will not be deemed to have the knowledge of an employee, officer or agent who is engaged in defrauding the company or principal.[143] In *J.C. Houghton & Co. v Northard Lowe & Wills* Viscount Dunedin held:

> My Lords, there can obviously be no acquiescence without knowledge of the fact as to which acquiescence is said to have taken place. The person who is sought to be estopped is here a company, an abstract conception, not a being who has eyes and ears. The knowledge of the company can only be the knowledge of persons who are entitled to represent the company. It may be assumed that the knowledge of directors is in ordinary circumstances the knowledge of the company. The knowledge of a mere official like the secretary would only be the knowledge of the company if the thing of which knowledge is predicated was a thing within the ordinary domain of the secretary's duties. But what if the knowledge of the director is the knowledge of a director who is himself *particeps criminis,* that is, if the knowledge of an infringement of the right of the company is only brought home to

---

[139] CSA National Policy 51-201, fn 21.
[140] For a rare case in which such a duty was found to extend to a shareholder, see *Canadian Metals Exploration Ltd. v. Wiese,* [2006] B.C.J. No. 1594, 20 B.L.R. (4th) 9 (S.C.).
[141] *Maiklem v. Springbank Oil & Gas Ltd.,* [1994] A.J. No. 1005, 27 Alta. L.R. (3d) 282 at 293 (Q.B.), *per* Power J.
[142] [1995] 2 A.C. 500 at 511G (P.C.).
[143] *In re Hampshire Land Co.,* [1896] 2 Ch. 743 at 749 (C.A.), *per* Vaughan Williams L.J.

the man who himself was the artificer of such infringement? Common sense suggests the answer, but authority is not wanting.[144]

In the last chapter, we discussed the general duty of disclosure that applies to a director (or officer) where such a person has a material interest in a transaction involving the corporation. In addition to the principles previously discussed in this regard, a fiduciary owes the beneficiary of the fiduciary duty an obligation of disclosure. Accordingly, a director who fails to disclose his or her own breach of fiduciary duty to the corporation may be held to have committed a further breach in failing to make such disclosure.[145]

(iii) Duty to Act Honestly and in Good Faith

§11.44 Clause 134(1)(*a*) of the OBCA[146] requires the directors to act honestly and in good faith with a view to the best interests of the corporation. This duty has no fixed meaning, but takes on its meaning in each particular case depending upon the circumstances of the corporation concerned,[147] taking into account the competing interests of persons who are concerned in the corporation and the relative priority of their claims.[148] While the directors are entitled to reasonable remuneration, they are clearly not entitled to dissipate the assets of a corporation or exploit the property of the corporation for their personal benefit to the prejudice of the shareholders of the corporation or its creditors.[149] The best interests of a corporation is not equated with the desires of its directors or principal shareholder.[150] Where the corporation is solvent and seems likely to remain so, the best interests of the corporation can largely be equated with the best interest of the shareholders taken as a whole, no one sectional interest being allowed to prevail over the others.[151] However, there may well be cases in which the interests of shareholders must be balanced against the interests (and potential claims) of other persons having a stake in the corporation. To the extent that the interests of various stakeholders conflict, it is the obligation of the directors to respect the relative priority and rights of the claims of those stakeholders. Similarly, where the interests of different classes of shareholder conflict, due respect must be given to the relative priority of interest and respective rights of each class of shareholder.

---

[144] [1928] A.C. 1 at 14 (H.L.).
[145] *Item Software (UK) Ltd v Fassihi*, [2004] E.W.C.A. Civ. 1244 (C.A.).
[146] CBCA, s. 122.
[147] See for instance *Greenlight Capital Inc. v. Stronach*, [2006] O.J. No. 4353, 22 B.L.R. (4th) 11 (S.C.) — requirement of good faith satisfied where challenged decision reviewed by independent committee that received legal and financial advice.
[148] *Colborne Capital Corp. v. 542775 Alberta Ltd.*, [1995] A.J. No. 538, 22 B.L.R. (2d) 226 at 281 (Q.B.), *per* Virtue J., var'd [1999] A.J. No. 33 (C.A.), leave to appeal to S.C.C. granted [1999] S.C.C.A. No. 128 (notice of discontinuance filed May 17, 2000).
[149] *Winkworth v. Edward Baron Development Co.*, [1986] W.L.R. 1512 at 1516 (H.L.), *per* Lord Templeman.
[150] *Levy-Russell Ltd. v. Tecmotiv Inc.*, [1994] O.J. No. 650, 13 B.L.R. (2d) 1 at 169 (Gen. Div.), *per* D. Lane J.
[151] *Ibid.*

(iv) Director's Duty of Good Faith

§11.45 The presumption that directors have acted in good faith in the discharge of their office and, in particular, that they have acted consistently with their duty of loyalty to the corporation and have exercised disinterested and independent business judgment, means that a party who alleges otherwise in an action must allege specific facts against them that are sufficient to overcome that presumption. The pleadings must create, at a minimum, a reasonable concern that the board members have not acted honestly and objectively in the circumstances. Speculation on the motives for undertaking corporate action does not satisfy this burden, nor does the mere assertion of a personal or business relationship.[152] In *Re Western National Corp. Shareholders' Litigation*, the court stated:

> ... a director is considered interested when he will receive a personal financial benefit from a transaction that is not equally shared by the stockholders or when a corporate decision will have a materially detrimental impact on a director, but not the corporation or its stockholders.[153]

The best way to avoid allegations of bad faith is for a director (or officer) to avoid any circumstances that is suggestive of self-dealing, and to ensure that in cases where the director is concerned in the transaction, that all decisions with respect to the transaction are made by people who are independent, and who are notified and familiarized by that director of the director's involvement in the transaction, and the material implications of that involvement. On this point, the court made the following additional observations in *Re Western National*:

> Independence, ... means that a director's decision is based on the corporate merits of the subject matter before the board rather than extraneous considerations or influences. To establish lack of independence, a plaintiff meets his burden by showing that the directors are either beholden to the controlling shareholder or so under its influence that their discretion is sterilized.[154]

It has been suggested that in assessing director independence, the court should apply a subjective "actual person" standard to determine whether a given director was likely to be affected in the same or similar circumstances.[155]

§11.46 Under guidelines embodied in National Policy 58-201, reporting issuers in Canada are now expected to adopt a written code of business conduct and ethics applicable to directors, officers, and employees of the issuer. Such codes should constitute written standards that are reasonably designed to deter wrongdoing. They are expected to address at least the following issues:

(a) conflicts of interest;

(b) protection and proper use of corporate assets and opportunities;

---

[152] *In Re Ply Gem. Industries Inc. Shareholders' Litigation*, [2001] Del. Ch. LEXIS 84 (Del. Ch.).
[153] [2000] Del. Ch. LEXIS 82; see also *Aronson v. Lewis*, 473 A.2d 805 (Del. S.C. 1984); see also *Rales v. Blasband*, 634 A.2d 927 at 936 (Del. S.C. 1993).
[154] [2000] Del. Ch. LEXIS 82 at 37-38.
[155] *McMullin v. Beran*, 765 A.2d 910 at 923 (Del. S.C. 2000).

(c) confidentiality of corporate information;

(d) fair dealing with the issuer's security holders, customers, suppliers, competitors and employees;

(e) compliance with laws, rules and regulations; and

(f) reporting of any illegal and unethical behaviour (commonly called "whistle blowing").[156]

Responsibility for monitoring compliance with such a code is imposed on the board. Any waivers of compliance, including implicit waivers, in favour of directors or senior officers should be granted only by the full board or an appropriate board committee. In addition, disclosure of the waiver may well be required. More specifically, National Policy 58-201 provides:

> ... the Canadian securities regulatory authorities consider that conduct by a director or executive officer which constitutes a material departure from the code will likely constitute a "material change" within the meaning of National Instrument 51-102 *Continuous Disclosure Obligations*. National Instrument 51-102 requires every material change report to include a full description of the material change. Where a material departure from the code constitutes a material change to the issuer, we expect that the material change report will disclose, among other things:
>
> • the date of the departure(s),
>
> • the party ... involved in the departure(s),
>
> • the reason why the board has or has not sanctioned the departure(s), and
>
> • any measures the board has taken to address or remedy the departure(s).[157]

(v) Best Interests of the Corporation

§11.47 While the powers given to directors under the OBCA and the CBCA are broad and necessarily confer a great deal of discretion upon them, they must exercise those powers subject to a number of restrictive rules that have evolved through the cases over time. There is a considerable degree of overlap between the two rules governing the exercise of director powers, namely the "best interests of the corporation" rule — that requires the directors of a corporation to exercise their powers always so as to further the best interests of their corporation — and the "proper purpose" rule — that requires directors to exercise all powers conferred upon them for the purpose for which they were conferred. Conceptually, it seems clear that the directors might exercise a particular power in a way which they thought was in the best interests of the corporation, yet in so doing not exercise it in a manner related to the purpose for which that power was originally conferred. Similarly, directors might well exercise a power for the purpose for which it was originally conferred, even though not acting in what appears to be the best interests of the corporation. Given this conceptual

---

[156] CSA, National Policy 58-201, para. 3.8.
[157] *Ibid.*, para. 3.9.

distinction, it is convenient to analyze this case law from the separate perspectives of the "best interest" and "proper purpose" rules. Nevertheless, as the following review of the law makes clear, in most cases where the "best interests" rule has come up for consideration, the court has necessarily been called upon to discuss whether the power exercised by the directors was being exercised for its proper purpose, for cases involving one rule invariably raise issues relating to the other.

§11.48 The *Olson* case[158] may also be cited in support of the proposition that the directors must not only act in an honest manner and within the implied or express terms of their powers,[159] but they must also act in the best interest of the corporation. This duty applies even where the director is the sole[160] or essentially the sole[161] shareholder. Here again, concerns related to self-interest and self-dealing play an important role. Quite clearly the misuse by the directors of their authority for personal profit or other self-advancement is improper and the directors will be liable for so abusing their authority.[162] Where the director has an interest in the subject matter of the transaction, the director must act in good faith.[163] Full disclosure of that interest must be made,[164] and the director will be liable to account for any secret profit made in the absence of such disclosure,[165] even where the corporation enjoys a benefit as a result.[166] The duty to account applies irrespective of whether the director sought the profit that he or she received out of the transaction: so, for instance, where the director receives an unsolicited gift from a third party as a consequence of the corporation entering into a contract or other transaction, the director must account to the corporation for that gift.[167]

---

[158] *Olson v. Phoenix Industrial Supply Ltd.*, [1984] M.J. No. 113, [1984] 4 W.W.R. 498 (C.A.), leave to appeal to S.C.C. refused [1984] S.C.C.A. No. 21.

[159] *Angus v. R. Angus Alberta Ltd.*, [1988] A.J. No. 207, 58 Alta. L.R. (2d) 76 at 90 (C.A.), *per* Bezil J.A., rehearing refused [1988] A.J. No. 834, 62 Alta. L.R. (2d) 33 (C.A.).

[160] *Fern Brand Waxes Ltd. v. Pearl*, [1972] O.J. No. 714, [1972] 3 O.R. 829 (C.A.).

[161] *Export Brewing & Malting Co. v. Dominion Bank*, [1937] 3 All E.R. 555 (P.C.).

[162] *Exco Corp. v. Nova Scotia Savings & Loan Co.*, [1987] N.S.J. No. 56, 35 B.L.R. 149 at 255-63 (T.D.), *per* Richard J.; see also *Baniuk v. Carpenter*, [1988] N.B.J. No. 826, 90 N.B.R. (2d) 1 (Q.B.), rev'd in part [1989] N.B.J. No. 519, 104 N.B.R. (2d) 196, additional reasons at 209 (C.A.).

[163] *Molchan v. Omega Oil & Gas Ltd.*, [1985] A.J. No. 1064, 21 D.L.R. (4th) 253 (C.A.), aff'd [1988] S.C.J. No. 12, [1988] 1 S.C.R. 348.

[164] *Canada Plastic Containers Ltd. v. Farkas*, [1973] O.J. No. 957, 12 C.P.R. (2d) 77 (H.C.J.).

[165] *MacMillan Bloedel Ltd. v. Binstead*, [1983] B.C.J. No. 802, 22 B.L.R. 255 at 293 (S.C.), *per* Dohm J.; *Trans-Canada Resources Ltd. v. Bobella*, [1983] N.J. No. 212, 43 Nfld. & P.E.I.R. 51, 127 A.P.R. 51 at 73 (S.C.), *per* Lang J.; but compare *Misener v. H.L. Misener & Son Ltd.*, [1977] N.S.J. No. 497, 21 N.S.R. (2d) 92, 2 B.L.R. 106 (C.A.); *N. Rattenbury Ltd. v. Winchester*, [1950] 3 D.L.R. 826, aff'd [1953] 3 D.L.R. 660 (P.E.I.C.A.).

[166] *B.C. Timber Industry Ltd. v. Black*, [1934] B.C.J. No. 69, [1934] 2 W.W.R. 161 at 169 (C.A.), *per* McPhillips J.A.; *Madden v. Dimond*, [1906] B.C.J. No. 14, 12 B.C.R. 80 at 87 (C.A.), *per* Martin J.A.

[167] *Chan v. Zacharia* (1984), 154 C.L.R. 178 at 198-99 (H.C. Aust.).

§11.49 The meaning of the phrase "best interests of the corporation" is not clear.[168] In some contexts it can be taken to mean the best interests of the corporation itself (*i.e.*, as an abstract entity),[169] while in others it refers to the shareholders as a collective whole.[170] Directors (and officers) are obliged in the exercise of their powers and discharging their duties to "act honestly and in good faith with a view to the best interests of the corporation",[171] and it is implicit in that obligation that the directors must exercise their powers in utmost good faith.[172] Yet the determination of what is in the best interests of the corporation is to a large extent a subjective matter. In *Re Smith & Fawcett Ltd.*,[173] Lord Greene M.R. set down the general rule that the decision of the directors with respect to what is in the best interest of the company will not normally be subject to review by the court. In following this approach, Lord Greene adopted and applied the long-standing practice of the common law against interference in the internal management of a corporation — a concept that is now embodied in the business judgment rule. This tendency to avoid interference with management raises the question as to whether there is anything required of the directors beyond their subjective belief that they are acting in the best interests of the corporation.[174] As Lord Wilberforce stated in *Howard Smith Ltd. v. Ampol Petroleum Ltd.*:

> There is no appeal on merits from management decisions to courts of law; nor will the courts of law assume to act as a kind of supervisory board over decisions within the powers of management honestly arrived at.[175]

As we shall discuss below in greater detail in the context of the business judgment rule, it is not for the courts to decide whether a particular decision by the directors was wise or whether the court would have taken some other course, unless there can be no question that the directors were not acting properly.[176] In all other cases, the directors are entitled to the benefit of the doubt. In other words, in deciding if the directors have acted in the best interests of the corporation, the courts are not concerned with whether the directors have acted wisely,[177] and they pay no regard to the question of whether the decision of the

---

[168] See, for instance, *Western Ontario National Gas Co. v. Aikens*, [1946] O.J. No. 618, [1946] O.R. 661 (H.C.); *Lindzon v. International Sterling Holdings Inc.*, [1989] B.C.J. No. 1773, 45 B.L.R. 57 at 78-79 (S.C.) — payment and other steps benefitting partly owned subsidiary — *per* Gow J.

[169] See, for instance, *Testa v. MacDonnell*, [1986] O.J. No. 1110, 1 A.C.W.S. (3d) 418 (H.C.J.).

[170] See, for instance, *Olympia & York Enterprises Ltd. v. Hiram Walker Resources Ltd.*, [1986] O.J. No. 679, 59 O.R. (2d) 254 (Div. Ct.).

[171] See, for instance, OBCA, s. 134(1)(*a*).

[172] *Legion Oils Ltd. v. Barron (No. 2)* (1956), 2 D.L.R. (2d) 205, 17 W.W.R. 209 at 221 (Alta. T.D.), *per* Cairns J.

[173] [1942] 1 Ch. 304 at 306 (C.A.).

[174] See *Gordon Leaseholds Ltd. v. Metzger*, [1967] O.J. No. 953, [1967] 1 O.R. 580 at 586-87 (H.C.J.), *per* Thompson J., where it was held that although the directors need not act reasonably in deciding whether to approve a transfer of shares, they must act on beliefs that are honestly and genuinely held.

[175] [1974] A.C. 821 at 832 (P.C.); *Shuttleworth v. Cox Bros. & Co. (Maidenhead)*, [1927] 2 K.B. 9 at 18 (C.A.), *per* Bankes L.J.

[176] *Richard Brady Franks Ltd. v. Price* (1937), 58 C.L.R. 112 at 136, *per* Latham C.J.; *Shuttleworth v. Cox Bros. & Co. (Maidenhead)*, [1927] 2 K.B. 9 at 22-24 (C.A.), *per* Scrutton L.J.

[177] *Richard Brady Franks Ltd. v. Price* (1937), 58 C.L.R. 112 at 136 (H.C. Aust.), *per* Latham C.J.

directors was the best one for the corporation.[178] It is sufficient that in acting as they did the directors were seeking to promote its interests — provided, of course, that the act of the directors is not so ridiculous that no person could possibly believe in good faith that it was in the best interests of the corporation.[179]

(1) Poison Pills and the Best Interests of the Corporation

§11.50 Perhaps the most extreme statement along these lines is to be found in the decision of Berger J. in *Teck Corp. v. Millar*[180] in which he held that provided directors honestly believed that they were acting or had acted in the best interests of the corporation, then their decisions could not be reviewed by the courts.[181] In the *Teck* case, the plaintiff Teck Corporation Ltd. ("Teck") purchased a majority of the voting shares in Afton Mines Ltd. (N.P.L.) ("Afton"). In an effort to thwart this takeover bid, the three directors of Afton caused it to enter into a contract with the defendant Canadian Exploration Ltd. ("Canex") under which Afton agreed to issue Canex sufficient shares to frustrate the Teck takeover bid. Teck sued to set aside the contract, arguing that the defendant directors were motivated by an improper purpose and were not serving the best interests of the corporation. After reviewing the facts of the case, Berger J. rejected the plaintiff's argument, saying:

> I find their object was to obtain the best agreement they could while they were still in control. Their purpose in that sense was to defeat Teck. But, not to defeat Teck's attempt to obtain control; rather it was to foreclose Teck's opportunity of obtaining for itself the ultimate deal. That was, as I view the law, no improper purpose. In seeking to prevent Teck obtaining the contract, the defendant directors were honestly pursuing what they thought was the best policy for the company.
>
> .....
>
> I have put the defendant's purpose in a negative way, that is, I have said that they wanted to foreclose Teck's opportunity of obtaining the development contract. But in a larger sense their purpose was a positive one. They wanted to make a contract with Placer while they still had the power to do so. ...
>
> ... I think it is fair to say that Millar's primary purpose was to make the most advantageous deal he could for Afton. That is as far as the court ought to go in seeking to analyze his motivation.[182]

---

[178] *Charterbridge Corp. Ltd. v. Lloyds Bank Ltd.*, [1970] Ch. 62 at 74, *per* Pennycuick J.:

> The proper test ... must be whether an intelligent and hones man in the position of a director of the company concerned could, in the whole of the existing circumstances, have reasonably believed that the transactions were for the benefit of the company.

[179] *Charterbridge Corp. v. Lloyds Bank Ltd.*, [1970] Ch. 62; *Hutton v. West Cork Rlwy. Co.* (1883), 23 Ch. D. 654 at 671 (C.A.), *per* Bowen L.J.

[180] [1972] B.C.J. No. 566, [1973] 2 W.W.R. 385 (S.C.).

[181] See also *Olson v. Phoenix Industrial Ltd.*, [1984] M.J. No. 113, 9 D.L.R. (4th) 451, leave to appeal to S.C.C. refused [1984] S.C.C.A. No. 21, 31 Man. R. (2d) 8.

[182] [1972] B.C.J. No. 566 at paras. 144, 146 and 147, [1973] 2 W.W.R. 385 at 428-29 (S.C.).

To Berger J. the goal behind the defendants' actions was to further the interests of the shareholders collectively rather than the interests of the majority shareholder:

> The defendant directors were elected to exercise their best judgment. They were not agents bound to accede to the directions of the majority of the shareholders. Their mandate continued so long as they remained in office. They were in no sense a lame duck board. So they acted in what they conceived to be the best interests of the shareholders, and signed a contract which they knew the largest shareholder, holding a majority of the shares, did not want them to sign. They had the right in law to do that. When a company elects its board of directors and entrusts them with the power to manage the company, the directors are entitled to manage it. But they must not exercise their powers for an extraneous purpose. That is a breach of their duty. At the same time, the shareholders have no right to alter the terms of the directors' mandate except by amendment of the articles or by replacing the directors themselves.
>
> The purpose of the directors in their negotiations ... was from the beginning a legitimate one. The purpose was to make a favourable deal for Afton. That purpose continued throughout. Did it become an improper purpose because Teck acquired large shareholdings? Did it become an improper purpose because the directors made a deal with Canex knowing that they had to before Teck acquired the power to stop them? I think on the evidence the answer must be "No."[183]

§11.51 The *Teck* case was one of the first decisions of a common law court dealing with takeover defensive strategies and techniques, now widely identified with the label "Poison Pills". Over the years, corporate management have devised a number of strategies to deter hostile takeover bids. Some of the specific techniques that have been employed successfully in the past include:

- The "flip-in" that permits existing shareholders (except the bidder) to buy more shares at a discount; since the bidder must purchase the new shares at the same price as the existing shares, the shareholders secure an instant profit. If the bidder fails to continue with the bid, then the value of its shareholding will be diluted as a result of the issue of the new shares.

- The "flip-over" that allows shareholders to buy the bidder's shares at a discounted price after the merger.

- Share conversion rights, which allow non-voting shares to be exchanged for voting shares in the event that a hostile bid is made for the corporation. This type of arrangement is often referred to as a "shareholder rights" plan.

- Including a provision in the articles that allows current shareholders the right to put their shares to a hostile bidder at a premium above the current market price (*e.g.*, at twice the recent average share price), where a bidder acquires more than a stipulated percentage of the aggregate outstanding voting shares of the corporation.

- Changing the size and composition of the board's membership, or the procedure for election (*e.g.*, creating special classes of share that are entitled to

---

[183] *Ibid.*, at paras. 148, 149 B.C.J.

- exclusive voting rights, or introducing staggered board terms so that hostile bidders will not be able to replace enough directors to revoke the anti-takeover provisions).

- Borrowing substantial amounts, so as to increase the debt load of the corporation and make it less attractive. The disadvantage of this approach is that if the bid fails, the corporation remains saddled with the debt.

- The purchase of other corporations in exchange for shares in the target corporation, which can dilute the value of the target corporation's stock.

- The grant of rebate entitlements to customers, that become payable in the event of a hostile takeover of the corporation

The goal of each of the foregoing techniques is to make the bidder's takeover attempt more difficult and expensive. In most cases, the "poison pill" only comes into effect when a bidder trips a "trigger" — *e.g.*, by acquiring more than a stipulated percentage of stock. When poison pills were first introduced, the trigger was usually set at around 20 per cent. Today, triggers are often set at 15 per cent, and 10 per cent is increasingly common.[184]

§11.52 When a bid is made for the outstanding shares of a corporation, the directors of the corporation must respond to it in some way, almost as a matter of necessity. In deciding upon the appropriate response, the directors are expected to make the same type of independent, informed judgment as is expected of them with respect to any other matter relevant to the business or affairs of a corporation. It goes without saying that the directors of a corporation should not respond in an instinctive defensive manner to any bid that may be made for control. In evaluating a takeover bid, the board must exercise their own best judgment on behalf of a corporation and its shareholders They should not simply follow management blindly.[185] The directors may promote the takeover of a corporation and have no duty to reveal takeover plans to management.[186] Their role is not to protect the incumbent management from a hostile takeover attempt.[187] On the other hand, the board is quite within its rights to oppose a takeover bid that is contrary to the collective interests of the shareholders — as, for instance, where the board believes that the bid puts too low a value on the corporation, and seeks to capitalize on the shareholder's limited access to relevant information.

§11.53 In the United States, the watershed case concerning poison pills was the decision of the Delaware Court of Chancery in *Moran v. Household International. Inc.*[188] In that case, certain shareholders of Household sought to invalidate

---

[184] Kris Frieswick, "Poison Pill Popping — The latest hostile takeover defenses defy the usual justifications" *CFO Magazine* (October 1, 2001).
[185] *Treadway Cos., Inc. v. Care Corp.*, 638 F.2d 357 at 378 (2d Cir. 1980).
[186] *Treadway Cos., Inc. v. Care Corp.*, 490 F. Supp. 668 at 684 (S.D.N.Y. 1980), aff'd in relevant part 638 F.2d 357 (2d Cir. 1980).
[187] *Amerco, U-Haul International Inc. v. Shoen*, 184 Ariz. 150, 907 P.2d 536 (C.A. 1995); *Wellman v. Dickinson*, 475 F. Supp. 783 at 835 (S.D.N.Y. 1979), aff'd 682 F.2d 355 (2d Cir. 1982).
[188] 490 A.2d 1059 (Del. Ch. 1985), aff'd 500 A.2d 1346 (Del. S.C. 1985).

a preferred stock rights dividend plan (the "Rights Plan") which was adopted by a majority of Household's board of directors. It was argued that the Rights Plan, abridged fundamental rights of the share owners of Household by restricting the alienability and marketability of Household shares and that it severely limited the ability of shareholders to engage in proxy contests. Household (or, more to point, its directors) argued that the Rights Plan provided a "drastic but highly effective deterrent device designed to prevent hostile, bust-up takeovers, for the protection of both the corporation and its shareholders".

§11.54 The court found that in February, 1984, Household's management had begun considering various amendments to the corporation's charter that would render a takeover more difficult. A consultant advised that any such amendment would be approved by the shareholders, but only barely. As it was believed that there was not sufficient time available before the annual meeting to present management's position on the fair price amendment and in view of the predicted closeness of the vote, management decided not to pursue such an amendment. In the meantime, one of Household's own directors, Moran, began to explore the possibility of a takeover, in cooperation with an outside entity. On learning of these plans, the majority of the board of directors created a complicated rights plan in an effort to thwart the proposed bid.

§11.55 Following a detailed review of the terms of the rights plan and the circumstances of its adoption, Walsh V.C. concluded that the plan had been properly adopted. It was "not intended primarily for entrenchment of management" and served "a rational corporate purpose". Although the plan had "the potential for the misuse of directorial authority", it could not be assumed that the board would act contrary to the interests of the shareholders. Accordingly, "those events and plaintiffs' fears must await another day". In conclusion, the adoption of the rights plan constituted an appropriate exercise of managerial judgment under the business judgment rule. Thus the creation of a poison pill arrangement was not improper *per se*, although it could be where it appeared on the facts to be intended for the primary or sole purpose of entrenching existing management or otherwise depriving shareholders of their rights. The possibility that it might have this effect was not sufficient, provided the facts did not indicate that this was the case. It is now accepted that poison pill devices are appropriate where intended to deter hostile acquisitions by third parties that might reasonably be considered by a board to be destructive of shareholder value.[189]

§11.56 No exception may be taken with respect to efforts by the directors to maximize shareholder value in the context of a takeover bid. The directors of a corporation are at liberty to encourage competing offers where they believe a takeover bid understates the value of the corporation.[190] Moreover, on the facts

---

[189] *Edelman v. Phillips Petroleum Co.*, [1986] Del. Ch. LEXIS 406; See also *Quickturn Design Systems, Inc. v. Shapiro*, 721 A.2d 1281 (Del. S.C. 1998); *Carmody v. Toll Brothers Inc.*, 723 A.2d 1180 (Del. Ch. 1998).

[190] See, for instance, *CW Shareholdings Inc. v. WIC Western International Communications Ltd.*, [1998] O.J. No. 1886, 38 B.L.R. (2d) 196 (Gen. Div.); but *cf. Re CW Shareholdings Inc.* (1998),

of a given case, the identity of the shareholders who comprise the membership of a corporation may be relevant to the long-term viability and health of the corporation. Admission of a particular person into a controlling interest in the corporation may affect its eligibility for licences, for certain types of government work, and so forth.[191] It may even be essential to issue shares in the context of a takeover bid to stabilize a deteriorating financial situation within the corporation.[192] Where actual and credible evidence exists to support these concerns, the directors of a corporation may be said to be acting in the best interests of the corporation where they act with the deliberate intent to thwart a particular takeover bid, or issue shares at a time which has this practical effect.

§11.57 A person seeking to challenge the use of such a device still bears the evidentiary burden of establishing that the board was motivated by an improper purpose. However, at least in the United States, it has been held that because there is the "omnipresent specter" that a board "may be acting primarily in its own interests, rather than those of the corporation and its shareholders" in creating a poison pill device, the board's actions must be able to withstand enhanced judicial scrutiny.[193] So, for instance, in *Kahn v. Roberts*[194] it was said:

> Where, however, the board takes defensive action in response to a threat to the board's control of the corporation's business and policy direction, a heightened standard of judicial review applies because of the temptation for directors to seek to remain at the corporate helm in order to protect their own powers and perquisites. Such self-interested behaviour may occur even when the best interests of the shareholders and corporation dictate an alternative course. Thus, where the board perceives a threat, its response will not be upheld merely because the response serves "any rational business purpose".

Instead, the board must establish that:

- there were reasonable grounds for believing that a danger to corporate policy and effectiveness existed; and

- the board of directors' defensive response was reasonable in relation to the threat posed.[195]

§11.58 While poison pills are not *per se* improper, the specific terms of a poison pill may render it open to attack. For instance, where the arrangement is structured so as to fetter the discretion of a newly elected board that succeeds the board that put the plan into place, the plan is liable to be set aside. So in *Quick-*

---

38 B.L.R. (2d) 230 (Ont. Sec. Comm.) dealing with the adoption of a rights plan as part of an effort to thwart a takeover.

[191] See, generally, *Darvall v. North Sydney Brick & Tile Co.* (1989), 16 N.S.W.L.R. 260 (C.A.), per Mahoney J.A.; see also *Australian Metropolitan Life Assurance Co. v. Ure* (1923), 33 C.L.R. 199 (H.C. Aust.), per Isaacs J.

[192] *Harlowe's Nominees Pty Ltd. v. Woodside (Lake Entrance) Oil Co. N.L.* (1968), 121 C.L.R. 483 (H.C. Aust.).

[193] *Unocal Corp. v. Mesa Petroleum Co.* (1985), 493 A.2d 946 at 954 (Del. S.C.).

[194] 679 A.2d 460 (Del. S.C. 1996).

[195] *Unitrin, Inc. v. American General Corp.*, 651 A.2d 1361 at 1373 (Del. S.C. 1995).

turn *Design Systems Inc. v. Shapiro*[196] a rights plan was structured in a manner that amounted to an unacceptable interference with the newly elected board. In finding this aspect of the plan improper, the court stated:

> In discharging the statutory mandate ... the directors have a fiduciary duty to the corporation and its shareholders. This unremitting obligation extends equally to board conduct in a contest for corporate control. The Delayed Redemption Provision prevents a newly elected board of directors from completely discharging its fiduciary duties to protect fully the interests of Quickturn and its stockholders.

§11.59 There are a number of Commonwealth cases in which the courts have applied reasoning similar to that set out above. The decision of Goulding J. in *Mutual Life Insurance Co. of New York v. Rank Organization Ltd.*[197] dealt with similar issues to those considered in *Teck*. In that case, the directors of Rank gave the shareholders of a company other than its North American shareholders the right to subscribe for new shares in the company. The North American shareholders were excluded in order to avoid compliance with the registration and other regulatory obligations of Canadian and American securities laws. The directors of Rank had been advised by their merchant bank that it would not be in the interests of the company to be regulated under those laws. The plaintiffs were among the North American shareholders. They claimed that the directors were discriminating against them unfairly. Goulding J. rejected this argument, concluding that the directors had acted in good faith in what they perceived to be the best interests of the company. In this case, however, there was no attempt on the part of the directors to gerrymander or otherwise interfere with control within the company. It was necessary to raise new capital. The existing shareholders were the logical source of that capital. On the other hand, the directors had to take into account other considerations in guiding their actions than only the goal of raising capital; an equally important consideration was how to go about raising the capital, and it was clearly necessary in deciding that question to take into account the adverse consequences of compliance with the more exacting requirements of North American securities laws in comparison to the corresponding laws of other jurisdictions.

§11.60 In *Hogg v. Cramphorn Ltd.*,[198] Buckley J. interpreted the law as setting down two separate tests. First, the directors must not act contrary to what they believe in good faith to be in the best interests of the corporation — this being a subjective test. Second (as discussed in detail below), the directors must not act for an improper purpose, even though they consider the attainment of that purpose to be in the best interests of the corporation — this being an objective test.[199]

---

[196] 721 A.2d 1281 (Del. S.C. 1998).
[197] [1985] B.C.L.C. 11; see also *Re BSB Holdings Ltd. (No. 2)*, [1996] 1 B.C.L.C. 155.
[198] [1967] Ch. 254.
[199] *Ibid.* Significantly, Buckley J. rejected the notion that directors may exercise their powers to issue shares to overrule the wishes of the existing majority shareholders (at 266-68).

§11.61 In *Howard Smith Ltd. v. Ampol Petroleum Ltd.*[200] the Privy Council dealt with what might be termed an inverse poison pill. In this case, two companies (Ampol and Bulkships) between them owned 55 per cent of the issued share capital of a third company ("Millers"). Howard Smith, announced a takeover offer for Millers. Ampol and Bulkships wished to reject it. However, a majority of the Millers' directors were in favour of the Howard Smith offer. A scheme was concocted to issue sufficient shares to Howard Smith to convert Ampol and Bulkships together into minority shareholders. Ampol initiated a proceeding against Howard Smith and Millers in the Equity Division of the Supreme Court of New South Wales to set aside the issue of shares to Howard Smith. At the trial, the judge found (i) that the allotment had not been made by the Millers' directors for any reason of self-interest; but (ii) that the primary purpose of the allotment was not to satisfy Millers' need for capital but rather to end the majority holding of Ampol and Bulkships, thus opening the way to the success of the Howard Smith offer. On the basis of those findings the judge ordered the issue of shares to be set aside. Howard Smith appealed, on the basis that the directors had not been motivated by self-interest.

§11.62 The Privy Council concurred with the trial judge. It was held that it was improper for directors to use their fiduciary powers over the issue of company shares purely for the purpose of destroying an existing majority, or creating a new majority that did not previously exist; furthermore the exercise by the directors of their fiduciary power solely for the purpose of shifting the power to decide to whom and at what price shares were to be sold could not be related to any purpose for which the power over the share capital had been conferred on them. Consequently, the issue of shares by the directors of Millers for the sole purpose of diluting the majority voting power held by Ampol and Bulkships so as to enable a then minority of shareholders to sell their shares more advantageously was an exercise of the power to issue and allot shares unrelated to any considerations of management and outside the proper sphere of the directors. The power had therefore been improperly exercised.[201]

---

[200] [1974] A.C. 821 (P.C.).
[201] Some doubt may be raised with respect to this conclusion, at least for OBCA and CBCA corporations. Under those Acts, directors' powers are to be exercised in the best interests of the corporation and in good faith. There is no additional statutory qualification requiring the power to issue shares to be tied to the capital requirements of the corporation concerned. Provided the power is exercised in the good faith pursuit of the best interests of the corporation, it seems to satisfy the specific duties of the directors. Further, what is in the best interests must be determined by reference to the corporation as a whole, rather than by reference to what is in the interest of the current majority shareholders. In the words of Arden J. in *Re BSB Holdings Ltd. (No. 2,* [1996] 1 B.C.L.C. 155 "The law does not require the interests of the company to be sacrificed in the particular interests of a group of shareholders." See also in this area: *Re a Company (No. 00370 of 1987)*, [1988] 1 W.L.R. 1068 (Ch.); *Goh Kim Hai Edward v. Pacific Can Investmemt Holdings Ltd.*, [1996] 2 Sing. L.R. 109; *Olson v. Phoenix Industrial Supply Ltd.*, [1984] M.J. No. 113, 9 D.L.R. (4th) 451 (C.A.), leave to appeal to S.C.C. refused [1984] S.C.C.A. No. 21; *Exco Corp. Ltd. v. Nova Scotia Savings & Loan Co.*, [1987] N.S.J. No. 56, 78 N.S.R. (2d) 91 (T.D.); *Russell Kinsela Pty Ltd. v. Kinsela*, [1983] 2 N.S.W.L.R. 452.

§11.63 Lord Wilberforce rejected the purely subjective approach advanced by Berger J. in *Teck*, preferring an objective one — albeit a broader one than that envisaged by Buckley J. in *Hogg*.[202] He added:

> Further it is correct to say that where the self interest of the directors is involved, they will not be permitted to assert that their action was bona fide thought to be, or was, in the interest of the company; pleas to this effect have invariably been rejected ... — as trustees who buy trust property are not permitted to assert that they paid a good price. ... But it does not follow from this, as Howard Smith asserts, that the absence of any element of self interest is enough to make an issue valid. Self interest is only one, though no doubt the commonest, instance of improper motive; and, before one can say that a fiduciary power has been exercised for the purpose for which it was conferred, a wider investigation may have to be made.[203]

Lord Wilberforce then quoted the following passage from the decision of Viscount Finlay in *Hindle v. John Cotton Ltd.*:

> Where the question is one of abuse of powers, the state of mind of those who acted, and the motive on which they acted, are all important, and you may go into the question of what their intention was, collecting from the surrounding circumstances all the material which genuinely throw light upon that question of the state of mind of the directors so as to show whether they were honestly acting in discharge of their powers in the interests of the company or were acting from some bye-motive, possibly of personal advantage, or for any other reason.[204]

§11.64 This approach appears to be in line with the enhanced scrutiny approach favoured by Delaware courts.[205] While the best interest test is generally subjective in nature, it is subject to the qualification that where there is a serious risk that the directors may not be motivated by the best interests of the corporation, the courts will be more willing to review their management decisions. Thus while the courts will not demand proof that a particular decision by the directors was the optimum decision that might have been taken or was the best option available of which the directors were aware, the courts will look at the process of director decision making to determine whether it is apparently sound.

§11.65 In *Re ASI Holdings Inc.*[206] the facts were as follows: Atlantic Seaboard Industries Ltd. ("ASIL") was a subsidiary of ASI Holdings, which had suffered large losses and was in urgent need of funds to meet its payroll and debts. The only available option for saving the company was by way of a rights issue to ASI Holdings. A dispute broke out within the company as to the terms on which the rights offering should be made. Castle Capital Inc. ("CC") held a 51 per cent interest in ASI Holdings, with two other shareholders holding the balance of its shares. One of the directors (Brake) proposed a rights offering of one right per

---

[202] See also *Mutual Life Insurance Co. of New York v. Rank Organization Ltd.*, [1985] B.C.L.C. 11; *Exco Corp. v. Nova Scotia Savings & Loan Co.*, [1987] N.S.J. No. 56, 78 N.S.R. (2d) 91 at 162 et seq. (T.D.), per Richard J.
[203] *Howard Smith Ltd. v. Ampol Petroleum Ltd.*, [1974] A.C. 821 (P.C.).
[204] (1919), 56 S.L.R. 625 at 630-31.
[205] But cf. *CW Shareholdings Inc. v. WIC Western International Communications Ltd.*, [1998] O.J. No. 1886, 39 O.R. (3d) 755 (Gen. Div.), per Blair J.
[206] [1996] N.J. No. 126, 28 B.L.R. (2d) 74, sub nom. *Re Brake* (T.D.).

share with unexercised rights only to be taken up by existing shareholders. Ten rights allowed one share to be purchased for $20,000. The two other directors of ASI (Emery and Weir, both nominees of CC) proposed a rights offering of 200 rights for each share, with each right permitting one share to be purchased for $1, payable either by cash or, in the case of CC, by assignment of outstanding cash advances by CC. The other two shareholders were prepared to invest $198,000 in ASI Holdings under Brake's proposal but were not prepared to do so if CC was allowed to assign cash advances rather than pay cash for new shares. The company was on the verge of securing valuable contracts. Brake alleged that Emery and Weir were attempting to arrange the affairs of ASI Holdings so as to maintain CC's control. Brake sought relief under the oppression remedy of the Newfoundland *Corporations Act*. L.D. Barry J. concluded that the behaviour of Emery and Weir constituted a breach of their fiduciary duty to the corporation and granted relief.[207]

§11.66 Takeover defence strategies in Canada must fit within the scope of the Canadian Securities Administrators' National Policy 62-202. Unfortunately, the terms of the policy are not especially clear. It begins with a motherhood declaration that:

> The Canadian securities regulatory authorities are of the view that the take-over bid provisions of Canadian securities legislation should favour neither the offeror nor the management of the target company, and should leave the shareholders of the target company free to make a fully informed decision. The Canadian securities regulatory authorities are prepared to examine target company tactics in specific cases to determine whether they are abusive of shareholder rights and, if they become aware of defensive tactics that are likely to deny or limit severely the ability of shareholders to respond to a take-over bid or to a competing bid, they will take appropriate action. The National Policy also provides that prior shareholder approval of corporate action would, in appropriate cases, allay the concerns of the Canadian securities regulatory authorities.[208]

Rather than seeking to set down fixed rules, the policy provides that:

> ... it is inappropriate to specify a code of conduct for directors of a target company, in addition to the fiduciary standard required by corporate law. Any fixed code of conduct runs the risk of containing provisions that might be insufficient in some cases and excessive in others. However, the Canadian securities regulatory authorities wish to advise participants in the capital markets that they are prepared to examine target company tactics in specific cases to determine whether they are abusive of shareholder rights. Prior shareholder approval of corporate action would, in appropriate cases, allay such concerns.[209]

Nevertheless, the policy makes clear that securities commissions will take appropriate action if they become aware of defensive tactics that will likely result in shareholders being deprived of the ability to respond to a takeover bid or to a

---

[207] *Ibid.*, at 80-82; see also *820099 Ontario Inc. v. Harold E. Ballard Ltd.*, [1991] O.J. No. 1082, 3 B.L.R. (2d) 113 (Div. Ct.).
[208] CSA National Policy 62-202, "Take-over Bids — Defensive Tactics", *Summary of National Policy*.
[209] *Ibid.*, para. 1.1(3).

competing bid. The policy identifies a number of specific defensive tactics that are likely to come under scrutiny if undertaken during the course of a bid, or immediately before a bid, if the board of directors has reason to believe that a bid might be imminent. These include:

(a) the issuance, or the granting of an option on, or the purchase of, securities representing a significant percentage of the outstanding securities of the target company,

(b) the sale or acquisition, or granting of an option on, or agreeing to sell or acquire, assets of a material amount, and

(c) entering into a contract other than in the normal course of business or taking corporate action other than in the normal course of business.[210]

Despite the middle road position indicated by the National Policy 62-202, at least in the case of the Ontario Securities Commission, shareholder rights provisions are generally subject to tight monitoring. According to one commentator the question in a takeover bid is not if the poison pill will be removed, but when. The decisions of the OSC with respect to cease trading requests brought by bidders to terminate the effectiveness of poison pill rights offerings reflect a strong preference for auctions in takeover situations, the right of shareholders to sell shares.[211] Accordingly, irrespective of the legality of the use of poison pills under general principles of corporate law, the tactic has been considerably less effective in Canada as a defensive device than in the United States.

(2) Best Interests and Stakeholder Theory

§11.67 Both the OBCA and the CBCA require the directors to act in the best interests of the corporation. To say that directors, auditors and officers of a corporation owe a duty to the corporation is to beg the question of who or what comprises the corporation. It is in dealing with this question that the entire artificiality of the corporate personality becomes most evident. A corporation in itself has no interest to protect. The only interests that are capable of protection belong to those persons who have funded or otherwise dealt with the corporation, or who are or may be affected by the activities that it carries on.

§11.68 Historically, when the courts have spoken of the best interests of the corporation, they have referred not to the corporation as an abstract entity, but rather to the shareholders (or members) of the corporation as a collective whole.[212] On this basis it has been held that the directors must consider not only

---

[210] *Ibid.*, para. 1.1(4).
[211] Paul Halpern, "Poison Pills: The Next Round" Canadian Investment Review (Spring, 1999).
[212] *Palmer v. Carling O'Keefe Breweries of Canada Ltd.*, [1989] O.J. No. 32, 67 O.R. (2d) 161 at 168 (Div. Ct.), *per* Southey J.; *Greenhalgh v. Arderne Cinemas Ltd.*, [1950] 2 All E.R. 1120 at 1126 (C.A.), *per* Lord Evershed M.R.; *Parke v. Daily News*, [1962] 2 All E.R. 929 at 948 (Ch.), *per* Plowman J.; H.A.J. Ford, *Principles of Company Law*, 4th ed. (Sydney: Butterworths, 1986) at 340; see also *Peter's American Delicacy Co. v. Heath* (1939), 61 C.L.R. 457 (H.C. Aust.). Note, however, the comments of Latham C.J. in *Mills v. Mills* (1938), 60 C.L.R. 150 (H.C. Aust.).

the immediate interest of existing shareholders of the corporation,[213] but future shareholders as well, unless the circumstances are such (*e.g.*, during a takeover bid) that only the existing shareholders need fairly be considered.[214] The law does not favour short term return over long term. In determining whether the directors have acted properly, the question to ask is whether an honest person of normal intelligence, who was in the position of the director, reasonably could have believed that the transaction or action taken by the directors was for the benefit of the corporation.[215]

§11.69 The direct equivalence between corporate interest and shareholder interest is now in doubt. Significantly, both statutes identify this duty with the "corporation"; they do not refer to "the shareholders". It is now settled that the directors of a corporation owe their statutory duties of honesty and good faith (*i.e.*, their fiduciary duty) to the corporation, rather than to any specific stakeholder interest group as such — although the directors must always bear in mind the interests of each stakeholder group (including the shareholders and creditors) in determining where those interests lie.[216]

§11.70 In adopting this approach, both the OBCA and CBCA may be seen to embrace the notions of stakeholder theory, at least to a limited extent. The term "stakeholder theory" describes an as yet nascent body of thinking with respect to corporate governance. It is argued that equating share ownership with the ownership of the corporation is unjustified because the corporation is an independent entity. Instead, the corporation represents a coalition of divergent interests (shareholders, lenders, trade creditors, customers, workers, *etc.*), each of which has a legitimate concern regarding the manner in which the corporation is operated. Stakeholder theorists reject the argument that the proper role of the directors is to maximize shareholder value, because such an approach to corporate management fails to strike an appropriate balance among these competing interests. In other words, managers should make decisions so as to take into account all of the interests of all stakeholders in a corporation.

§11.70.1 Notions like maximization of corporate value seem clear enough when articulated as abstract principles, but in real world conditions their exact meaning can become obscure. When rumors of a pending take-over bid for BCE Inc. began circulating in April, 2007, share prices increased in the expectation that a bidder would pay a premium above the then-current market price. However, the assumption that any such bid would be structured as a leveraged buy-out caused the value BCE bonds to plummet. Incidents like this make clear how it can be difficult for a board to decide what is the "best interests of the corporation". Even a buy-out of the existing shareholders is not necessarily in the wider corporate interests. Any argument in such a case that shareholders are entitled to be

---

[213] *Gaiman v. National Association for Mental Health*, [1971] Ch. 317 at 330, *per* Megarry J.
[214] *Heron International Ltd. v. Lord Grade*, [1983] B.C.L.C. 244 at 264-65 (C.A.).
[215] *Charterbridge Corp. v. Lloyds Bank Ltd.*, [1970] Ch. 62 at 74, *per* Pennycuick J.; *Lindgren v. L. & P. Estates Ltd.*, [1968] 1 Ch. 572 (C.A.).
[216] *Alvi v. Misir*, [2004] O.J. No. 5088, 50 B.L.R. (3d) 192 (S.C.J.), *per* Cameron J.

compensated for assuming a greater risk than bond-holders would simply be ignoring reality. The effect of a buy-out, is to remove the shareholders from risk. When it is a leveraged one, the impact is to shift the risk from the corporation's shareholders to its creditors.[217]

§11.71 Within certain limits, stakeholder theory is reflected in the law. The directors of a corporation are bound to cause the corporation to comply with the criminal law, employment standards laws, labour relations laws, consumer protections laws, and environmental laws. The directors may not strip a corporation of its assets, so as to deny the creditors of the corporation the prospect of recovery against it. If directors act with disregard for these legal rights, it is no answer to a prosecution or civil claim to argue that they were seeking to maximize shareholder value. The problem with stakeholder theory is that it is far better at offering directors guidance as to what they should not do (*e.g.*, not to engage in a headlong rush in search of short-term shareholder gain) than it is at providing guidance as to what should be done.[218]

§11.72 Exactly how the competing interests of the different stakeholder groups are to be balanced is not entirely clear. One elementary problem with stakeholder notion is that it seems to proceed on the assumption that all claims against, and interests in, the corporation are intended to rank equally. In fact this is self-evidently untrue. To give some specific examples: workers generally accept only the most limited level of risk associated with corporate operations. As we shall discuss in detail later in this chapter, not only do they tend to be paid far

---

[217] Catherine McLean, "LBO Fears Hammer BCE Bonds" *The Globe & Mail* (26 April 2007); Ross Marowits, "BCE Inc. stock jumps on latest reports of possible takeover offers" *Canadian Press* (10 April 2007).

[218] Perhaps this is not surprising. Even the notion of maximization of shareholder value is sufficiently murky that it is difficult to apply in terms of day-to-day management. When one says that value should be maximized, is that to be in terms of short-term return on investment or is the objective of the corporation to maximize total long-term corporate market value? If one selects the latter option, then how long a term should current owners be expected to wait until they begin to see a return on their investment? At some point, further investment in a business begins to generate low marginal returns relative to the initial investment. Should re-investment continue indefinitely? Income streams can, of course, be discounted to present value and compared, but such calculations are inherently speculative. Many of the risks to which a corporation is exposed in carrying on business cannot properly be quantified. Advances in science, technology and understanding change our perceptions of value. In the 1940s, many people considered asbestos a miracle product. Today, it is a known health hazard. Further investment in asbestos productive capacity in the intervening years would not have maximized long-term corporate value. It would have resulted in greater losses to the investors. On the other hand, the market can be equally ignorant about many emerging opportunities. In 1899, Charles H. Duell, a high-ranking official at the U.S. patent office, made the bold prediction that "everything that can be invented has been invented". When the pop singer Madonna's career was beginning, Warner Brothers U.K. felt she had little future. She has sold more than 140 million records, and amassed an unequalled 35 consecutive U.K. Top 10 singles. After the Second World War, the American automobile manufacturer Ford, failed to appreciate that there would be a market for the Volkswagon Beetle. In 1943, Thomas J. Watson, then Chairman of the Board of IBM made the famous declaration that "I think there is a world market for maybe five computers." None of this is to suggest that corporate managers would not like to maximize shareholder value — only that to do so requires a degree of knowledge that no one can possess.

more frequently than other creditors, they have successfully lobbied lawmakers to secure both preferential claims against the corporation, and personal claims against its directors. Trade creditors assume a greater degree of risk, but again that level of risk tends to be moderated by contract. Trade creditors in Canada tend strongly to expect payment within 30 days of delivery of supply. They also have secured a range of statutory protection for the debts owing, including the right of revendication in the *Bankruptcy and Insolvency Act,* and a range of liens, such as the construction lien, the repair and storage lien and the like. Institutional lenders tend to assume a longer term credit risk than many other types of creditor. Capital asset purchase financing is obviously of a long-term nature, and even operating credit (such as lines of credit) tends to be of much longer duration than what is offered by trade creditors. On the other hand, institutional lenders invariably seek contractual security (such as mortgages and general security interests) to support the credit that they are offering. Ultimately, it is the shareholders who take the highest level of risk with respect to corporate operations.

§11.73 The case law with respect to the directors' duty to act in the corporation's best interests seem to reflect the different nature of the interests in the corporation to a very large degree. In the normal case (*i.e.*, while the corporation is operating in the ordinary course of business and is expected to continue as a going concern), the best interests of the corporation is no doubt largely linked to the interests of its shareholders. In *Colborne Capital Corp. v. 542775 Alberta Ltd.*[219] the court stated:

> Only the board acting collectively can decide what is in the best interest of the corporation. The best interests of a corporation include the interests of the shareholders collectively. Where there is but one shareholder, the best interests of the corporation will accord with the interests of that shareholder. ... A director's duty to preserve the value of the corporation does not permit the director to ignore the interests of its shareholders.

In *820099 Ontario Inc. v. Harold E. Ballard Ltd.*[220] Farley J. concluded that in resolving a conflict between majority and minority shareholders, it is appropriate for directors and officers to act to make the corporation a "better corporation". The key question to resolve is the extent to which the directors may properly (or must properly) take into account the interests of stakeholders other than the shareholders in fashioning a better corporation. In *Peoples Department Stores Inc. (Trustee of) v. Wise,*[221] the Supreme Court of Canada stated categorically that:

> From an economic perspective, the "best interests of the corporation" means the maximization of the value of the corporation.[222]

---

[219] [1999] A.J. No. 33 at para. 208, 69 Alta. L.R. (3d) 265 at 315 (C.A.).
[220] [1991] O.J. No. 266, 3 B.L.R. (2d) 113 at 123 (Gen. Div.), aff'd [1991] O.J. No. 1082, 3 B.L.R. (2d) 113 at 171 (Div. Ct.).
[221] [2004] S.C.J. No. 64, [2004] 3 S.C.R. 461.
[222] *Ibid.*, at para. 42.

The court went on to observe that it may be legitimate, given all the circumstances of a case, for a board of directors to consider, *inter alia*, the interests of shareholders, employees, suppliers, creditors, consumers, governments and the environment when determining what was in the best interests of the corporation.[223] Such broad statements must be approached in a guarded manner. It is clearly appropriate for the directors to take into account legal, equitable or statutory interests. It is far less clear that the directors may properly take into account hypothetical interests of such open-ended groups. Moreover, the court cautioned:

> The interests of the corporation are not to be confused with the interests of the creditors or those of any other stakeholders.[224]

Presumably, this statement implicitly includes the shareholders of the corporation.

§11.74 At issue in the *Peoples* case was whether, in the "vicinity of insolvency", the interests of the creditors take precedence over the interests of the shareholders.[225] Noting that the notion of the vicinity of insolvency was undefined and impossible to define with any precision, and that the creditors are protected by other rights of action, including the oppression remedy and the duty of care, the court concluded that the creditors' interests did not suddenly become paramount as the fortunes of the corporation waned. Rather, the directors continued to owe their duty to act in the best interests of the corporation, to the corporation itself.

> In resolving these competing interests, it is incumbent upon the directors to act honestly and in good faith with a view to the best interests of the corporation. In using their skills for the benefit of the corporation when it is in troubled waters financially, the directors must be careful to attempt to act in its best interests by creating a "better" corporation, and not to favour the interests of any one group of stakeholders.[226]

In view of the above re-articulation of the guiding principles of law in this area, one must now read with some caution earlier case law dealing with whether the directors are required to consider the interests of creditors and other non-stakeholder shareholders in the conduct or management of corporate operations.[227]

§11.75 In the *Peoples* decision, the Supreme Court of Canada specifically rejected the notion that the directors of a corporation owed a fiduciary duty to the creditors of that corporation, even when it was in the vicinity of insolvency,

---

[223] See also: *Olympia & York Enterprises Ltd. v. Hiram Walker Resources Ltd.*, [1986] O.J. No. 679, 59 O.R. (2d) 254 (Div. Ct.).
[224] *Peoples Department Stores Inc. (Trustee of) v. Wise*, [2004] S.C.J. No. 64, [2004] 3 S.C.R. 461 at para. 43.
[225] On this point, see: *Walker v. WA Personnel Ltd.*, [2002] B.P.I.R. 621 (Ch.); *West Mercia Safetywear Ltd. v. Dodd*, [1988] B.C.L.C. 250 (C.A.).
[226] *Peoples Department Stores Inc. (Trustee of) v. Wise*, [2004] S.C.J. No. 64, [2004] 3 S.C.R. 461 at para. 47.
[227] See, generally, *Parke v. Daily News Ltd.*, [1962] Ch. 927; *Teck Corp. v. Millar*, [1972] B.C.J. No. 566, 33 D.L.R. (3d) 288 at 314 (S.C.), per Berger J. (re employees). And see also *Darvall v. North Sydney Brick & Tile Co.* (1988), 6 A.C.L.C. 154, per Hodgson J., on appeal 16 N.S.W.L.R. 260 (C.A.) (re creditors).

concluding that such a concept was too nebulous to be workable. The fiduciary obligation of the directors requires them to act so as to make the corporation a "better" (*i.e.*, healthier, stronger) corporation.[228] Nevertheless, the court qualified this statement, noting that:[229]

> At all times, directors and officers owe their fiduciary obligation to the corporation. The interests of the corporation are not to be confused with the interests of the creditors or those of any other stakeholders.
>
> ... The residual rights of the shareholders will generally become worthless if a corporation is declared bankrupt. Upon bankruptcy, the directors of the corporation transfer control to a trustee, who administers the corporation's assets for the benefit of creditors.
>
> ... While shareholders might well prefer that the directors pursue high-risk alternatives with a high potential payoff to maximize the shareholders' expected residual claim, creditors in the same circumstances might prefer that the directors steer a safer course so as to maximize the value of their claims against the assets of the corporation.
>
> ... In assessing the actions of directors it is evident that any honest and good faith attempt to redress the corporation's financial problems will, if successful, both retain value for shareholders and improve the position of creditors. If unsuccessful, it will not qualify as a breach of the statutory fiduciary duty.

The court then proceeded to a discussion of the director's duty of care to creditors, specifically within the context of the oppression remedy.

§11.76 A slightly different (and more specific) formulation of director responsibility with respect to director duties was recently put forward in *Spies v. The Queen*,[230] by the High Court of Australia. In that case, the High Court also held that the directors of a company owe no independent duty to the directors of the company. However, the court quoted with approval the decision of Gummow J. in *Re New World Alliance Pty Ltd.* where he stated:

> It is clear that the duty to take into account the interests of creditors is merely a restriction on the right of shareholders to ratify breaches of the duty owed to the company. The restriction is similar to that found in cases involving fraud on the minority. Where a company is insolvent or nearing insolvency, the creditors are to be seen as having a direct interest in the company and that interest cannot be overridden by the shareholders. This restriction does not, in the absence of any conferral of such a right by statute, confer upon creditors any general law right against former directors of the company to recover losses suffered by those creditors ... the result is that there is a duty of imperfect obligation owed to creditors, one which the creditors cannot enforce save to the extent that the company acts on its own motion or through a liquidator.[231]

---

[228] *Peoples Department Stores Inc. (Trustee of) v. Wise*, [2004] S.C.J. No. 64, [2004] 3 S.C.R. 461 at para. 41.
[229] *Ibid.*, at paras. 43-46.
[230] [2000] H.C.A. 43.
[231] (1994), 122 A.L.R. 531 at 550.

§11.77 The general duty of care to which directors are subject means that the corporation must be operated in a commercially prudent manner at all times (or, at least, not in a manner that is commercially reckless, since it must be recognized that business corporations are very often established to take commercially prudent risks). Moreover, as mounting losses erode the interest of the shareholders in the corporation, the more the directors must factor into their decisions the interests of the creditors, for the simple reason that mounting losses increase the foreseeability of loss to the creditors. Once the share capital of the corporation is fully exhausted, it is no longer appropriate for the directors of the corporation to carry on high risk or otherwise speculative ventures in the hope of earning profits that can be used to restore the corporation to a position in which both the claims and creditors and shareholders can be satisfied in full. In general, the creditors have not agreed to assume the same level of risk as have the shareholders, nor do they stand to enjoy any share in such profits as the corporation may earn. A failure to take into account the creditors interests in such circumstances may amount to oppression against them.

§11.78 In other words, in deciding what may be done in the best interests of the corporation in the particular circumstances of the corporation, it is necessary to consider both the extent of competing legal rights in the corporation, and the relative priority of those interests. Equally important are the questions of whose interest is being placed at risk by a particular corporate activity, and whether those persons may fairly be seen to have agreed (either explicitly or implicitly) to assume the risk in question. It is one thing to say that the duty of the directors is owed to the corporation rather than to any particular group of stakeholders, and that the beneficiary of this duty remains constant irrespective of the corporation. It is quite another to conclude that the directors of a corporation enjoy the same liberty to act irrespective of the situation of the corporation. To give one obvious illustration of how the circumstances of a corporate entity restrict the freedom of its directors: When a company is insolvent, whatever it may own is subject to the claims of its creditors, and must be kept primarily for their benefit. Where a company is profitable, its profits may be divided among its shareholders; and its capital may be returned to them in accordance with the relevant rules governing the liquidation of the corporation, following the discharge of the liabilities of the corporation.[232] Since shareholders effectively take on higher risk in exchange for the chance of higher profit, while it is the shareholders' money that remains at risk, much can be said for allowing the directors to pursue profitability through high risk ventures. The same is less true when the shareholders' investment has been eroded away through accumulated losses — or where the magnitude of the risk that is being assumed in a given venture is so great that the shareholders' investment is not sufficient to cover the chance of loss that is being taken on.

§11.79 As the BCE Inc. example illustrates,[233] the various stakeholders in a corporation do not necessarily share interests that are harmonious or compatible.

---

[232] See, generally, *West Mercia Safetywear Ltd. v. Dodd*, [1988] B.C.L.C. 250 (C.A.).
[233] See §11.70.1

Instead, corporations are generally the focus of competing legal rights and interests, each of which has a fixed priority under the law. Because the rules of priority in the event of insolvency are relatively fixed, each of the various stakeholders in a corporation, and others who are concerned with or affected by its operations, may be seen to have agreed to assume different levels of risk associated with those operations. Where there are various interests in conflict, the question of which of those interests should be the predominate concern in the approval of a particular corporate action (or the selection among competing options) must ultimately depend upon the entire circumstances of each case, taking into account both priority, the potential of profit (or other enhancement of corporate value), and the balancing of risk.

§11.80 For instance, in *Harris v. Dry Dock Co.*[234] the plaintiff was a judgment creditor of the defendant corporation. He filed a bill in equity to compel it to make calls upon its shareholders, to raise funds sufficient to meet its liabilities — something which the directors refused to do. Blake C. found for the plaintiff, even though doing so was entirely contrary to the interests of the shareholders. Since the corporation was insolvent, the interests of the creditors had to be seen to override those of the shareholders. The shareholders' interest had been extinguished due to the accrued losses of the corporation. In the sense that the claims of the creditors were entitled to a first call upon those assets, for all practical purposes the assets of the corporation then belonged to the creditors.[235] The creditors' rights arose not as a result of a breach of a duty owed to them as such — for no such direct duty is owed.[236] They were a derivative claim in respect of the duty owed by the directors to the corporation.[237]

§11.81 In terms of ongoing corporate operations, the directors may approve speculative ventures that offer a prospect of future profit for the benefit of shareholders so long as the property of the corporation is clearly sufficient to satisfy the claims of all creditors and the other obligations (consensual and nonconsensual) that arise from such activity. Where a proposed operation would imperil the ability of the corporation to satisfy the claims against it or otherwise meet its obligations, the risk must be rejected as too great.[238] Thus an appropri-

---

[234] [1859] O.J. No. 333, 7 Gr. 450 (U.C.Ch.).
[235] *Multinational Gas & Petrochemical Co. v. Multinational Gas & Petrochemical Services Ltd.*, [1983] Ch. 258 at 288 *et seq.* (C.A.), *per* Dillon L.J.; *Winkworth v. Edward Baron Development Co.*, [1987] 1 All E.R. 114 at 118 (H.L.), *per* Lord Templeman; *Lonrho Ltd. v. Shell Petroleum Co.*, [1980] 1 W.L.R. 627 at 630 (H.L.); see also *Kinsela v. Russell Kinsela Pty Ltd.* (1986), 10 A.C.L.R. 395 at 401 (N.S.W.C.A.), *per* Street C.J.; *Nicholson v. Permakraft (N.Z.) Ltd.*, [1985] 1 N.Z.L.R. 242 at 249 (C.A.), *per* Cooke J.; *Brady v. Brady*, [1988] 2 W.L.R. 1308 (H.L.); *Walker v. Wimborne* (1976), 137 C.L.R. 1 (H.C. Aust.), *per* Mason J.; *Jeffree v. National Companies and Securities Commission* (1989), 7 A.C.L.C. 556 (W.A.S.C.); *A.N.Z. Executors & Trustee Co. v. Quintex Australia Ltd.* (1990), 8 A.C.L.C. 980 (S.C. Qld.), *per* McPherson J.
[236] *Western Finance Co. v. Tasker Enterprises Ltd.*, [1979] M.J. No. 455, 106 D.L.R. (3d) 81 at 87-88 (C.A.), *per* Huband J.A.
[237] *Re Horsley & Weight Ltd.*, [1982] 3 All E.R. 1045 at 1055 (C.A.), *per* Buckley L.J.
[238] See, generally, *West Mercia Safetywear Ltd. (in liq.) v. Dodd*, [1988] B.C.L.C. 250.

ate approach towards risk management becomes incorporated into the overall statutory duties of the directors.[239]

§11.82 Such an approach to director duties is fully consistent with the extensive body of case law to the effect that where a director's breach of duty to the corporation affects the interests of shareholders, then they can either authorize that breach in prospect or ratify it in retrospect. A corporation can cure a defect in authority relating to the formation of any contract by ratifying that contract, assuming that the contract is otherwise *intra vires* the corporation. A court will determine whether substantive ratification has occurred by the circumstances. If a corporation learns of an unauthorized contract but does not give back any benefits received pursuant to that contract the corporation will be taken to have ratified the contract.[240] However, where the interests at risk are those of the creditors (or other stakeholders), the shareholders have no power or authority to absolve the directors from that breach.[241]

§11.83 Similarly, employee interests may undoubtedly be considered to the extent necessary (a) to promote a harmonious relationship between the corporation as an employer and its workforce; and (b) to ensure that the corporation has a properly trained workforce of competent size to enable it to carry on business and pursue successfully the opportunities that may present themselves to the corporation in the future. Generally, taking those concerns into account is fully consistent with the general goal of maximizing the value of the corporation, at least over the long term. Even the recognition of employee rights on termination (*e.g.*, with respect to statutory severance, accrued vacation pay, and damages for wrongful dismissal), is a legitimate factor to take into account. Problems usually arise only when a corporation is in the process of dissolution, and a payment to the employees or former employees becomes entirely gratuitous, so that the use of corporate property and the furthering of employee interests constitute such a disregard of the interests of shareholders and creditors, that in effect it amounts to a confiscation of corporate property to which they are rightfully intended to look for the satisfaction of their own claims against the corporation, for the betterment of others whose claims are of a lower priority or even discretionary.[242]

---

[239] The Business Roundtable, *Statement on Corporate Governance,* September, 1997 at 7, presents the board's risk management responsibility as part of its broader package of integrated responsibilities:

> The Board must assure that an effective system of controls is in place for safeguarding the corporation's assets, managing the major risks faced by the corporation, reporting accurately the corporation's financial condition and rules of operations, adhering to key internal policies and authorizations, and complying with significant laws and regulations that are applicable to it.

[240] *Levy-Russell Ltd. v. Shieldings Inc.*, [2004] O.J. No. 4291 at para. 103 (S.C.J. — C.L.), *per* Cumming J.; See also *Great Northern Grain Terminals Ltd. v. Axley Agricultural Installations Ltd.*, [1990] A.J. No. 817, 76 Alta. L.R. (2d) 156 at 159 (C.A.).

[241] *Kinsela v. Russell Kinsela Pty Ltd.* (1986), 4 N.S.W.L.R. 722, *per* Street C.J.; see also *Nicholson v. Permakraft (N.Z.) Ltd.*, [1985] 1 N.Z.L.R. 242 (C.A.), *per* Cooke J.

[242] See, generally, *Hutton v. West Cork Rlwy. Co.* (1883), 23 Ch. D. 654 (C.A); *Re Lee Behrens & Co.*, [1932] 2 Ch. 46.

§11.84 The right of shareholders, directors, officers, creditors and security holders to apply for relief under the oppression remedy[243] or under the statutory derivative action procedure both provide a mechanism for giving effect to the responsibilities to each stakeholder group that are implicit in the director's statutory obligations to the corporation itself. Other parties outside the corporation who may be adversely affected by its activities must still be considered to the extent that the adverse effect would violate legal rights. For instance, the directors must clearly take reasonable precautions to ensure that the business and affairs of the corporation are carried on in accordance with applicable laws (such as environmental laws), and may also take into consideration the effect that a particular step may have upon regulatory attitudes towards the activities of the corporation, and even the impact that particular measures may have upon the general goodwill that the corporation enjoys within the community or state. Whether the directors may also take into consideration broader (and therefore less clearly defined) social interests such as the community in which it carries on operations or even the state as a whole is more doubtful, but a strong argument can be made that they may do so to the extent that the adoption of an appropriate policy serves the general goodwill in which the corporation is held by the community.

§11.85 The directors of some corporations are entitled to greater latitude in their discretion in determining what is in the best interests of the corporation.[244] This was made clear by the decision of Lord Green in *Re Smith & Fawcett Ltd.*,[245] where he commented upon the broader latitude allowed to the directors of private corporations[246] in determining whether to approve share transfers:

> [A]nother consideration which I think is worth bearing in mind ... is that this type of article is one which is for the most part confined to private companies. Private companies are, of course, separate entities ... just as much as are public companies, but from the business and personal point of view they are much more analogous to partnerships ... Accordingly, it is to be expected that, in the articles of such a company the control of directors over the membership may be very strict indeed. There are very good business reasons, or there may be very good business reasons, why those who bring such companies into existence should give them a constitution which gives to the directors powers of the widest description.

Thus decisions applicable to one type of corporation (or in the circumstances of one particular corporation) will not necessarily apply to all.

(3) Excessive Generosity, or Giving Away the Farm

§11.86 The duty of directors to act in the best interests of the corporation has clear implications in the area of corporate charitable activity, and the making of other gratuitous payments. In the modern world, it seems to be generally ac-

---

[243] OBCA, s. 248; CBCA, s. 241.
[244] See, generally, *Charterbridge Corp. v. Lloyds Bank Ltd.*, [1970] Ch. 62 at 69, *per* Pennycuick J.
[245] [1942] 1 All E.R. 542 at 544 (C.A.).
[246] See also *Phillips v. La Paloma Sweets Ltd.*, [1921] O.J. No. 21, 51 O.L.R. 125 at 127 (H.C.D.), *per* Middleton J.

cepted that a corporation may make reasonable donations to charity and provide similarly reasonable support to other worthwhile public causes. Indeed, a corporate CEO who today responded to a request for a charitable donation, along the lines of Ebenezer Scrooge with the question of whether there were not sufficient workhouses or prisons for the poor, would almost certainly do the public image of his company a great deal of harm. Nevertheless, it does not necessarily follow that the directors of a corporation may be as charitable as they please when dealing with corporate property.

§11.87 The phrase "to give away the farm" means to squander one's inheritance either by prodigal living or by excessive generosity. Either of these meanings can have application in the corporate context, where the directors and officers of a corporation sometimes deal with corporate property as if it was their own. A board of directors has an obligation to protect the corporate enterprise from harm,[247] and from this general principle one may extrapolate reasonably that the duties of the board include an obligation to avoid unreasonable risk, waste and extravagance. Gold-plated fixtures in the executive washrooms, lavish corporate entertainment, personal use of corporate aircraft, "corporate yachts" and other expensive property bearing no apparent relationship to the business of a corporation, "business trips" taken at company expense which lack any apparent corporate purpose or have a corporate purpose so remote or so minuscule by comparison to the cost that they cannot be justified as reasonable or even in good faith, free rides for spouses on business trips taken by directors and senior officers, all fall into the class of prodigal misuse of corporate property.

§11.88 Where the person(s) who approves an expense of this sort is also the person(s) who benefits from it, the expense is obviously suspect. But even where the person approving the expense draws no personal benefit from it, an expense can still be open to attack where it lacks any proper business purpose, as for instance in the case of extravagant gifts or gratuitous payments to employees (lacking any apparent corporate purpose in maintaining good industrial relations), excessive charitable donations (not being directed towards maintaining the general goodwill of the corporation) and trying to be too good a corporate citizen. While not necessarily morally wrong, from a commercial perspective excessive generosity with corporate property is as objectionable as extravagant expenditures on director and officer remuneration. Directors are free to give away their own shirts at any time; they enjoy no right to be so generous with the shirts belonging to the shareholders and creditors of the corporation.

§11.89 While one's initial inclination might be to believe that such misuse of corporate property is more prevalent in the case of closely held corporations than widely held, in fact it is encountered in both contexts. Indeed, the majority of reported cases dealing with such squandering of assets has involved widely held corporations — although that fact is not surprising, since in the case of

---

[247] See, for instance, *Unocal Corp. v. Mesa Petroleum Co.*, 493 A.2d 946 (Del. Ch. 1985); *In Re Pure Resources Inc. Shareholders Litigation*, 808 A.2d 421 (Del. Ch. 2002).

widely held corporations there are likely to be shareholder interests that do not benefit from the directors' excessive extravagance or share their philanthropic convictions.

§11.90 The requirement that directors act in the best interest of the corporation implicitly limits the power of the directors to make gifts of corporate property. They certainly may not give away property of the corporation to the extent that it jeopardizes the substratum of the corporation. Although the shareholders of a corporation have no direct proprietary interest in the property of the corporation, each of their shareholdings in the corporation constitutes a participatory interest in the corporation itself. The general rule is that on the dissolution of a corporation, any surplus remaining after the payment of all debts, share capital and unpaid dividends belongs to the shareholders of the corporation, and is distributed in accordance with their proportionate interest in the corporation.[248] This participatory interest gives the shareholders an expectation of receiving a distribution of the surplus assets of the corporation on its liquidation, even if there is no immediate claim on those surplus assets.

§11.91 The right of the shareholders to participate in the remaining property of a corporation at the time of its winding-up would apply (in the absence of a contrary provision in the articles or charter by-laws) to the holders of common and other participating shares in a corporation. Moreover, the interest of those shareholders in the surplus assets of the corporation is not simply a right *in futuro*. Because the value of the shares of a corporation reflects the underlying value of the assets held by the corporation, the surplus assets of the corporation do provide a quasi-proprietary interest (albeit indirectly) in those surplus assets. Although this value may not be reflected on the books of the shareholder, it would doubtless be factored into the sale price of the shares, if the shareholder were to choose to dispose of them to a third party.

§11.92 As noted above, if the directors exercise their powers improperly, a cause of action arises against them based upon a breach of their duty to the corporation.[249] Thus while the directors of a corporation may make gifts out of corporate property provided an underlying purpose of those gifts is a proper corporate purpose, they may not dispose of corporate property as they might feel inclined without regard to the general objects of the corporation.[250] In administering the property of the corporation, the directors are in certain respects trustees of its property;[251] they are not free to deal with it as if it was their own, and

---

[248] *Birch v. Cropper* (1889), 14 App. Cas. 525 at 530-33 (H.L.), especially *per* Lord Herschell.
[249] See, generally, *Western Finance Co. v. Tasker Enterprises Ltd.*, [1979] M.J. No. 455, 106 D.L.R. (3d) 81 (C.A.).
[250] See, generally, L.C.B. Gower, in *The Principles of Modern Company Law* (London: Stevens, 1969) at 91.
[251] *Belmont Finance Corp. v. Williams Furniture Ltd. (No. 2)*, [1980] 1 All E.R. 393 at 405 (C.A.), *per* Buckley L.J.; *Rolled Steel Products (Holdings) Ltd. v. British Steel Corp*, [1986] Ch. 246 at 298 (C.A.), *per* Slade L.J. See also *Re Lands Allotment Co.*, [1894] 1 Ch. 616 at 631 (C.A.), *per* Lindley L.J. and King L.J. at 638; *Russell v. Wakefield Waterworks Co.* (1875), L.R. 20 Eq. 474 at 479 (C.A.), *per* Jessell M.R.

they are liable to account to the corporation for misdealing with the property of the corporation.[252]

§11.93 The primary purpose of a *business* corporation is to engage in *business*; generally an OBCA or a CBCA corporation is not organized for philanthropic purposes. Such philanthropic powers as it may possess are merely ancillary to its business objectives. So construed, a corporation might make gifts to charity for the purpose of enhancing the goodwill of the corporation or its general public image; it might make gifts to employees in recognition of good service as an integral aspect of enhancing the morale of its workers and encouraging diligent service by them through the recognition by way of gratuity of the work of others. It might even authorize a payment in the settlement of a doubtful claim — perhaps even a very doubtful claim — if the purpose of that settlement was to prevent adverse publicity to the corporation or the diversion of corporate attention away from more profitable business than litigation. But in all such cases the power of the directors to make gratuitous dispositions is limited and relates to a proper corporate purpose, and is directed towards the growth, maintenance and stability of the corporation.[253]

(4) The Cakes and Ale Case Law

§11.94 The limits imposed by corporate law on director generosity have been considered in a number of cases, but surprisingly in relatively few recent ones. In one of the more memorable passages of English corporate case law, Bowen L.J. declared:[254]

> The law does not say that there are to be no cakes and ale, but there are to be no cakes and ale except such as are required for the benefit of the company.

This passage is often invoked, not only when corporations have engaged in activity that might be described as overtly charitable, but also when they have provided "excessive" remuneration to employees, whether in the form of bonuses or direct salary.[255] Although the prohibition against excessive expenditure by a corporation on "cakes and ale" continues to be good law, it is important to understand decisions of this type within their proper context.

§11.95 In *Re Lee, Behrens & Co.*[256] the board of directors decided that the company should enter into an agreement to pay a pension to the widow of a former managing director. In holding that the agreement was *ultra vires*, Eve J. stated:

> It is not contended, nor in the face of a number of authorities to the contrary effect could it be, that an arrangement of this nature for rewarding long and faithful

---

[252] *Cramer v. Bird* (1868), L.R. 6 Eq. 143 (M.R.).
[253] See, generally, D.L. Goldstein, "Whether a Charitable Donation is Deductible as a Business Expense" (1988) 36 Can. Tax J. 695; *Impenco Ltd. v. M.N.R.*, [1988] T.C.J. No. 121, [1988] 1 C.T.C. 2339.
[254] *Hutton v. West Cork Rlwy. Co.* (1883), 23 Ch. 654 at 672 (C.A.).
[255] See, for instance, *Gabco Ltd. v. M.N.R.*, [1968] 2 Ex. C.R. 511.
[256] [1932] 2 Ch. 46, [1932] All E.R. Rep. 889.

service on the part of persons employed by the company is not within the power of an ordinary trading company such as this company was, and, indeed, in the company's memorandum of association is contained ... an express power to provide for the welfare of persons in the employment in the company ... by granting money or pensions. ... But whether they be made under an express or implied power, all such grants involve an expenditure of the company's money, and that money can only be spent for purposes reasonably incidental to the carrying on of the company's business, and the validity of such grants is to be tested ... by the answers to three pertinent questions:

(i) Is the transaction reasonably incidental to the carrying on of the company's business?

(ii) Is it a *bona fide* transaction? and

(iii) Is it done for the benefit and to promote the prosperity of the company?[257]

It may be that social conditions and attitudes have changed sufficiently since the *Lee, Behrens* decision was given so that a similar case would not be decided the same way today.[258] Even so, the questions raised by Eve J. remain at least partially relevant to the standard of conduct expected by directors. More specifically, it is the duty of directors to act for the benefit of the corporation and to promote its prosperity. Accordingly, any expenditure of corporate funds must have some reasonable expectation of corporate benefit, whether in the form of enhancing the profitability of the corporation or merely enhancing the goodwill of the corporation, or improving employer and employee relations. Gratuitous payments that result in no enhancement of the welfare of the corporation are not permitted.

§11.96 Bowen L.J.'s decision in *Hutton v. West Cork Rlwy. Co.*[259] itself involved unusual facts. In that case the West Cork Railway Company had entered into an agreement to sell its undertaking to another railway. After that sale, it remained in existence solely for the purpose of being wound up, and the shareholders resolved at a meeting to pay £1,050 of the purchase money in compensating salaried employees for the loss of their employment, and a further £1,500 in compensation to the directors. It had always been understood that the directors were not entitled to remuneration. A dissenting shareholder sought to stop the payment. Bowen L.J. held that there was no way in which the payment could work to the benefit of the corporation, and therefore upheld the shareholder's complaint.[260] Where, however, there is some element of doubt, it will be left to the directors to decide whether the payment may be made. The question to resolve is whether an intelligent and honest person in the position of the directors concerned could in the circumstances reasonably believe that the transaction was for the benefit of the corporation.[261] Good faith is not enough. Even though the directors of a corporation may act in good faith when they attempt to make a gift

---

[257] *Ibid.*, at pp. 880-81 All E.R. Rep.
[258] But see *Re W. & M. Roith Ltd.*, [1967] 1 W.L.R. 432 at 438-39 (Ch.), *per* Plowman J.
[259] (1883), 23 Ch. D. 654 (C.A.).
[260] *Ibid.*, at 672-73 and 677.
[261] *Charterbridge Corp. v. Lloyds Bank Ltd.*, [1969] 2 All E.R. 1185 at 1194 (Ch.), *per* Pennycuick J.

of corporate property, except where that gift is or could be related in some specific or general way to the advancement of corporate interest, they will not be acting with a view to the best interests of the corporation.[262]

§11.97 In *Dodge v. Ford Motor Co.* the directors of the corporation had embarked upon a policy of using earnings to support a reduction in the price of automobiles, to the complete exclusion of the payment of dividends. In holding that the directors had no power to deprive the shareholders of the earnings of the corporation, Ostrander J. stated:

> A business corporation is organized and carried on primarily for the profit of its stockholders. ... The discretion of directors is to be exercised in the choice of means to attain that end and does not extend to a change in the end itself, to the reduction of profits or to the non-distribution of profits among stock-holders in order to devote them to other purposes.[263]

Similarly, in *Parke v. Daily News Ltd.*,[264] it was held that the directors of the corporation could not divert the proceeds derived from the sale of assets of a corporation to make an *ex gratia* payment to the employees and pensioners of the corporation. The court held that those proceeds were properly the property of the shareholders of the corporation, Plowman J. saying:

> The conclusions which, I think, follow from these cases are: first, that a company's funds cannot be implied in making *ex gratia* payments as such; secondly, that the Court will enquire into the motives actuating any gratuitous payment, and the objectives which it is intended to achieve; thirdly, that the Court will uphold the validity of gratuitous payments if, but only if, after such enquiry, it appears that the tests enumerated by Eve J. are satisfied; fourthly, that the onus of upholding the validity of such payments lies on those who assert it.

§11.98 Gifts — in the sense of fully gratuitous transfers — are atypical. More common are discretionary payments, as for instance where the amount to be paid must be settled by the directors. As we have seen, as a general rule, the courts will not interfere with a proper exercise of a discretionary exercise of power by the directors in the absence of fraud on the creditors or the shareholders (particularly the minority shareholders). A corporation and its directors are not limited in the use that they may make of funds to paying only those debts that the corporation is clearly legally obliged to pay. So long as a payment is made in good faith and within the ordinary scope of the corporation's business and for the corporation's benefit, any payment will be acceptable.[265] It is not generally the responsibility of the court to decide what is reasonable, and the courts will not engage in abstract considerations of what benefits the corporation.[266] The courts accept that as a general rule the directors of the corporation know a great deal more about the corporation and its business than any judge

---

[262] See, generally, Neil Brooks, "The Principle Underlying the Deductibility of Business Expenses" in V. Krishna *et al.*, *Canadian Taxation*, 2nd ed. (Toronto: De Boo, 1981), c. 5.
[263] (1919), 204 Mich. 459, 170 NW 668 (Mich. S.C.).
[264] [1962] Ch. 927 (Ch.).
[265] *Hutton v. West Cork Railway Co.* (1883), 23 Ch. D. 654 at 672 (C.A.), *per* Bowen L.J.
[266] *Re Halt Garage (1964) Ltd.*, [1982] 3 All E.R. 1016 (Ch.).

can possibly know. Accordingly, they are the body best placed to decide what payment is too large or too small.[267]

§11.99 The directors are not necessarily acting improperly merely because there is no immediate commercial purpose to a payment (*i.e.*, an immediate expectation of profit or the financial enhancement of the corporation). They may look to the long-range interests of the corporation as well as to the short term, provided that there is some basis on which it can be construed that the welfare of the corporation will eventually be enhanced.[268] In certain cases, they may even make completely gratuitous payments — that is, payments that have no prospect of consideration being received in return, or other financial betterment of the corporation. But where such payments are to be made, it is necessary to show that there will be some resulting enhancement or maintenance of the corporation's position, even if only in the area of general public goodwill. Apparently gratuitous payments are always a particular matter of concern.[269] However, it is clear that the benefit to the corporation need not be direct; it is sufficient for the corporation to draw an indirect benefit.[270]

§11.100 It follows from the foregoing that the cakes and ale case law must be properly understood. It provides guidance not relating to the fair treatment of employees or former employees (or even to charitable giving), but rather with respect to the wastage of corporate assets. Implementing reasonable measures with a view towards encouraging or sustaining high level performance by employees serves a legitimate business purpose.[271] So, for instance, payment for training and education may not only encourage worker loyalty but may also improve productivity and competence, even when only distantly related to the specific lines of business in which the corporation is engaged. Similarly, a corporation may pay higher than average salaries to its workers, with a view towards encouraging the recruitment of a top quality staff, or to retaining the good quality staff that it has. Such compensation may include stock options, creating scholarships for the children of employees, the payment of bonuses and other incentive schemes, even though increased loyalty and productivity are ephemeral assets that do not lend themselves to valuation in dollar terms.[272] Payments made in recognition of legal rights (such as indemnification against expenses incurred, statutory severance payments, or settlement payments in compromise of pending or probable claims for wrongful dismissal) are even more obviously permissible, because they relate to the settlement of liabilities that may be enforced against the corporation. Even in the case of the compromise of dubious claims, the board is entitled to a great deal of discretion. A corporation is not bound to litigate every claim against it to the highest court of the

---

[267] *Henderson v. Bank of Australasia* (1881), 40 Ch. D. 170 at 181.
[268] *Re Horsley & Weight Ltd.*, [1982] 3 All E.R. 1045 (C.A.).
[269] *Parke v. Daily News Ltd.*, [1962] 2 All E.R. 927 at 942 (Ch.).
[270] See, generally, *Rolled Steel Products (Holdings) Ltd. v. British Steel Corp.*, [1982] 3 All E.R. 1057 (Ch.), aff'd [1985] 2 W.L.R. 908 (C.A.).
[271] See *Shamrock Holdings, Inc. v. Polaroid Corp.*, 559 A.2d 257 at 272 (Del. Ch. 1989).
[272] *Pogostin v. Rice*, 480 A.2d 619 at 625 (Del. S.C. 1984).

land — nor to litigate every possible claim in its favour — where the board or its management concludes in good faith that the probability of success is so limited as to make defence unrealistic, or where there is or may be some other benefit to the corporation in a compromise of a claim sufficient to justify its settlement.

§11.101 What the directors are not permitted to do, is to waste corporate assets, or divert the assets of the corporation away from the purpose for which they were entrusted to them. Payments that might be perfectly proper when made by a corporation while it is carrying on business as a going concern (*e.g.*, in order to enhance the general goodwill of the corporation) cannot be considered as proper where there is no corporate purpose that the payment will serve. Business development expenses, such as even lavish corporate entertaining, may be permissible when the corporation is actually carrying on business and intends to remain doing so (for through such entertaining important contacts may be made and existing relationships may be strengthened),[273] but such extravagant expenditure cannot be justified when the business is in the process of being shut down. It is also questionable (although, depending on the circumstances, could be defensible) where the expense is incurred at a time when the financial condition of the corporation is known to be precarious.

§11.102 Cases involving actual wastage of corporate assets are extremely rare. A shareholder complaining of corporate waste must allege facts that demonstrate that the directors authorized a transaction that was so one-sided that no business person of ordinary, sound judgment *could* conclude that the corporation has received or will receive adequate benefit, whether directly from the recipient or in some indirect way from a third party or even from the world at large. The transaction must either serve no corporate purpose or be so completely devoid of benefit that it is in effect a gift. A pleading does not meet this test by alleging facts showing that the transaction was lopsided or could have been more beneficial. Rather the pleaded facts must show an absence of benefit, rather than inadequate benefit.[274] Although in some cases it is stated that the lack of benefit must be absolute, this is probably an overstatement. A more appropriate formulation is that the possibility of benefit to the corporation must be so remote or unrealistically contingent that no person of ordinary, sound business judgment would deem it worth what the corporation has paid.[275] As with the review of any other board decision, this question must be addressed not as of the time when the matter comes before a court for adjudication, but rather as of the time when the

---

[273] With respect to the benefit of obtaining independent advice with respect to such payments (as to fairness and reasonable amount, *etc.*) see *Catalyst Fund General Partner I Inc. v. Hollinger Inc.*, [2006] O.J. No. 2818, 20 B.L.R. (4th) 249 (S.C.).

[274] See, generally, *Lewis v. Vogelstein*, 699 A.2d 327 at 336 (Del. Ch. 1997); *Pogostin v. Rice*, 480 A.2d 619 at 625 (Del. S.C. 1984); *Glazer v. Zapata Corp.*, 658 A.2d 176 (Del. Ch. 1993).

[275] *Grobow v. Perot*, 539 A.2d 180 at 189 (1988); *Saxe v. Brady*, 40 Del. Ch. 474, 184 A.2d 602 at 610 (Del. Ch. 1962); see also *RCM Securities Fund, Inc. v. Stanton*, 928 F.2d 1318 at 1334 (2d Cir. 1991).

decision was made, taking into account the context in which the corporation was situate at that time, and such facts as were then known to the board.[276]

(5) The Proper Purpose Rule

§11.103 The cakes and ale cases well illustrate the general principle of corporate — and administrative — law that powers must be exercised in furtherance of the purpose for which they were conferred. Alternatively stated, the rule that the directors of a corporation must act in the best interests of the corporation is bound inextricably to the rule that the directors may exercise their powers only for the purpose for which those powers were granted. In this and other areas of breach of duty by a director, the burden of proof ordinarily lies upon the person who alleges that the directors of a corporation have acted improperly. Where the allegations against the directors appear to have some foundation, the courts may take into account the directors' silence or failure to provide an adequate explanation as to what has occurred.[277]

§11.104 The proper purpose rule is a corollary of the equitable principle that a fiduciary[278] must act in accordance with the terms of his or her appointment.[279] Generally, where the directors fail to exercise their powers for a proper purpose, the corporation to which they owe that duty is entitled in the case of a breach of it to seek the protection of the court to enforce the performance of that duty.[280] The proper purpose rule is a supplement to the requirement that they stay within their powers, and essentially circumscribes the exercise of their powers. Under the proper purpose rule, the directors must exercise their powers for the purpose for which they were conferred, and if they misuse their powers for some other purpose, they risk liability for so doing.[281]

§11.105 The proper purpose test is an implied condition of all the powers of directors, however founded.[282] In *Cowan v. Scargill*,[283] Megarry V.C. reviewed the law concerning the duties of trustees, and the manner in which fiduciary powers were to be exercised, and concluded that fiduciary powers must be exercised fairly and honestly for the purposes for which they are given and not so as to accomplish any ulterior purpose, whether for the benefit of the trustees or otherwise.

---

[276] However, when deliberate wastage of assets is shown, it constitutes a constructive fraud on the dissident shareholders. Wastage of corporate assets by the majority cannot be ratified to the prejudice of dissident minority shareholders: *Burt v. The Irvine Co.*, 237 Cal. App. 2d 828, 47 Cal. Rptr. 392 at para. 18 (C.A. Calif. 1st App. Div. 1965).
[277] *Metropolitan Life Assurance Co. v. Urel* (1923), 33 C.L.R. 199 at 221 (H.C. Aust.), *per* Isaacs J.
[278] The fuduciary duties of directors are discussed at §11.115 *seq.*
[279] *Angus v. R. Angus Alberta Ltd.*, [1988] A.J. No. 207, 58 Alta. L.R. (2d) 76 at 175, 85 A.R. 266, *per* Belzil J.A., additional reasons [1988] A.J. No. 1031, 63 Alta. L.R. (2d) 33 (C.A.); see also *Re Lands Allotment Co.*, [1894] 1 Ch. 616 at 631 (C.A), *per* Lindley L.J.
[280] *Madden v. Dimond*, [1906] B.C.J. No. 14, 12 B.C.R. 80 at 87 (C.A.), *per* Martin J.
[281] *Gagne v. Red Diamond Taxi* (1930), 36 R. de Jur. 274 (Que).
[282] See, generally, Lord Lindley M.R. in *Allen v. Gold Reefs of West Africa Ltd.*, [1900] 1 Ch. 656 at 671 (C.A.).
[283] [1984] 2 All E.R. 750.

§11.106 The views expressed in Megarry V.C.'s decision are echoed in much of the legislation now in force in the corporate director field. The requirement that the powers of directors be exercised for their proper purpose is summarized in the statutory rule that the directors must act honestly, in good faith and in the bests interests of the corporation, on which basis it may be said that they must exercise utmost good faith towards the corporation.[284] They must use their powers for the benefit of the corporation and for its benefit alone.[285] Quite clearly, they may not use their powers with the intention of conferring upon themselves a personal benefit.[286] By virtue of their fiduciary duties, directors must not act in an overtly self-serving manner.[287] On no account may they benefit themselves by surreptitious practices, whatever the nature of the advantage that they may seek to secure.[288] The directors may not manipulate their control over the fixing of the record date for dividend purposes to confer a benefit on one shareholder at the expense of another.[289] Nor may the board manipulate its control over the timing or place of the annual meeting or other meetings of shareholders in order to perpetuate its control of the corporation.[290]

(6) Altruism is Not the Required Standard

§11.107 While the directors of a corporation may exercise their powers only for a proper purpose,[291] it does not necessarily follow that they must act altruistically. In many cases, a particular decision that the directors will be called upon to make will have two or more effects: the decision may benefit the corporation, and yet it may also lead to a benefit to one, some or all of the directors; some persons interested in the corporation may benefit as a result of the decision, others may be prejudiced. It is recognized, of course, that in some cases the directors will have a personal financial interest in the corporation. However, even where the directors hold shares themselves, they must act for the benefit of the corporation as a whole (*i.e.*, of its shareholders as a whole), rather than for themselves. In *Peoples Department Stores Inc. (Trustee of) v. Wise*,[292] the Supreme Court of Canada held:

> ... it is not required that directors and officers in all cases avoid personal gain as a direct or indirect result of their honest and good faith supervision or management of the corporation. In many cases the interests of directors and officers will innocently and genuinely coincide with those of the corporation. If directors and officers are also shareholders, as is often the case, their lot will automatically improve

---

[284] *Legion Oils Ltd. v. Barron (No. 2)* (1956), 17 W.W.R. 209, 2 D.L.R. (2d) 505 (Alta. T.D.).
[285] *C.E. Plain Ltd. (Trustee of) v. Kenley*, [1931] O.J. No. 393, [1931] O.R. 75, 12 C.B.R. 492 at 495 *et seq.* (C.A.), *per* Hodgins J.A.
[286] *Imperial Mercantile Credit Association v. Coleman* (1871), L.R. 6 Ch. 558 at 560, 22 L.T. 357 at 359 (Ch.), *per* Lord Hatherley L.C., rev'd on other grounds (1874), L.R. 6 H.L. 189, 29 L.T. 1 (H.L.).
[287] *Elliot v. Baker*, 194 Mass. 518 at 523, 80 N.E. 450 (1907).
[288] *Smith v. Hanson Tire & Supply Co.*, [1927] 2 W.W.R. 529, [1927] 3 D.L.R. 786 (Sask. C.A.).
[289] *Pittsburgh Terminal Corp. v. Baltimore and Ohio Railroad*, 680 F.2d 933 (3d. Cir. 1982).
[290] *Schnell v. Chris-Craft Industries Inc.*, 285 A.2d 437 at 439 (Del. S.C. 1971).
[291] *Punt v. Symons & Co.*, [1903] 2 Ch. 506.
[292] [2004] S.C.J. No. 64, [2004] 3 S.C.R. 461 at para. 39.

as the corporation's financial condition improves. Another example is the compensation that directors and officers usually draw from the corporations they serve. This benefit, though paid by the corporation, does not, if reasonable, ordinarily place them in breach of their fiduciary duty. Therefore, all the circumstances may be scrutinized to determine whether the directors and officers have acted honestly and in good faith with a view to the best interests of the corporation.

§11.108 In *Mills v. Mills*[293] the plaintiff and his uncle (the defendant) were two of the directors and the largest shareholders of a family company. The defendant (Neilson Mills) was the managing director and held the majority of ordinary shares. The plaintiff Ainslie Mills owned most of the preference shares. A resolution was passed by a majority of the directors (including Neilson) under which accumulated profits were capitalized and distributed to the ordinary shareholders in the form of fully paid bonus shares. The effect of this step was to greatly increase the voting power of the ordinary shareholders and to diminish the rights of the preference shareholders to participate in the distribution of assets on the winding-up of the company. Lowe J. found that the majority of directors had acted in what they believed to be the best interest of the company when they passed the resolution. The judgment was upheld on appeal to the High Court of Australia. There, Latham C.J. commented upon whether directors might take into account their own interests as shareholders of a particular class:

> Directors are required to act not only in matters which affect the relations of the company to persons who are not members of the company but also in relation to matters which affect the rights of shareholders *inter se*. Where there are preference and ordinary shares a particular decision may be of such a character that it must necessarily affect adversely the interests of one class of shareholders and benefit the interests of another class. In such a case it is difficult to apply the test of acting in the interests of the company. The question which arises is sometimes not a question of the interests of the company at all, but a question of what is fair as between different classes of shareholders. Where such a case arises some other test than the "interests of the company" must be applied, and the test must be applied with knowledge of the fact that ... the law permits directors ... to hold shares, ordinary or preference as the case may be. A director who holds one or both classes of such shares is not, in my opinion, required by the law to live in an unreal region of detached altruism and to act in a vague mood of ideal abstraction from obvious facts which must be presented to the mind of any honest and intelligent man when he exercises his powers as a director. It would be setting up an impossible standard to hold that, if an action of a director were in any way affected in any degree by the fact that he was a preference or ordinary shareholder, his action was invalid and should be set aside. ... The question is: what was the "moving cause" of the action of the directors?[294]

In a concurring judgment, Dixon J. said:

> When the law makes the object, view or purpose of a man, or of a body of men, the test of the validity of their acts, it necessarily opens up the possibility of an almost infinite analysis of the fears and desires, proximate and remote, which, in

---

[293] (1938), 60 C.L.R. 150 (H.C. Aust.); see also *Hindle v. John Cotton Ltd.* (1919), 56 Sc. L.R. 625, *per* Lord Shaw.
[294] *Mills v. Mills* (1938), 60 C.L.R. 150 at 164 (H.C. Aust.).

truth, form the founding motives usually animating human conduct. But logically possible as such an analysis may seem, it would be impracticable to adopt it as a means of determining the validity of the resolutions arrived at by a body of directors, resolutions which otherwise are ostensibly within their powers. The application of the general equitable principle to the acts of directors managing the company cannot be as nice as it is in the case of a trustee exercising a special power of appointment. It must ... take the substantial object, the accomplishment of which formed the real ground of the board's action. If this is within the scope of the power, then the power has been validly exercised. But if, except for some ulterior and illegitimate object, the power would not have been exercised, that which has been attempted as an ostensible exercise of the power will be void, notwithstanding that the directors may incidentally bring about a result which is within the purpose of the power and which they consider desirable.[295]

Thus the Australian courts look to the dominant purpose of the directors.[296] Where the directors' dominant motive is the pursuit of their own interest, it is no defence to show that an incidental benefit has flowed to the corporation.[297] Unfortunately, the identification of the dominant purpose is no easy feat. Clearly, the courts cannot give too much weight to self-serving declarations by the board.[298] The question can only be decided by reference to all facts that appear relevant to the case. Thus in *Howard Smith Ltd. v. Ampol Petroleum Ltd.*[299] Lord Wilberforce stated:

... [W]hen a dispute arises whether directors of a company made a particular decision for one purpose or another, or where, there being more than one purpose, one or another purpose was the substantial or primary purpose, the court, in their Lordship's opinion, is entitled to look at the situation objectively in order to estimate how critical or pressing or substantial, or *per contra,* insubstantial an alleged requirement may have been. If it finds that a particular requirement, though real, was not urgent, or critical, at the relevant time, it may have reason to doubt, or discount, the assertions of individuals that they acted solely in order to deal with it, particularly when the action they took was unusual or even extreme.[300]

§11.109 A great deal of the case law concerning the proper purpose question arises out of the issuance of shares.[301] It is now clear that the control that the directors possess over the issue of shares is not unfettered. They may not act unfairly, unjustly or out of self-interest in issuing shares.[302] Quite understandably,

---

[295] *Ibid.,* at 185.
[296] But see *Whitehouse v. Carlton Hotel Pty. Ltd.* (1987), 11 A.C.L.R. 715 (H.C. Aust.), *per* Mason, Deanne and Dawson JJ.
[297] See, generally, *Ashburton Oil N.L. v. Alpha Minerals N.L.* (1971), 123 C.L.R. 614 at 627 (H.C. Aust.), *per* Menzies J.; but *cf. Olson v. Phoenix Industrial Supply Ltd.,* [1984] M.J. No. 113, 9 D.L.R. (4th) 451 (C.A.), leave to appeal to S.C.C. refused [1984] S.C.C.A. No. 21, 31 Man. R. (2d) 8n.
[298] *Advance Bank of Australia Ltd. v. FAI Insurance Australia Ltd.* (1987), 9 N.S.W.L.R. 464, *per* Kirby P.
[299] [1974] A.C. 821, [1974] 1 All E.R. 1126 (P.C.).
[300] *Ibid.,* at 832. See also *Hindle v. John Cotton Ltd.* (1919), 56 Sc. L.R. 625 at 630-31.
[301] See, for instance, *Hogg v. Cramphorn,* [1967] Ch. 254, [1966] 3 All E.R. 420 (Ch.). For a detailed discussion of the share issue subject, see *Howard Smith Ltd. v. Ampol Petroleum Ltd.,* [1974] A.C. 821, [1974] 1 All E.R. 1126 (P.C.).
[302] In *Pennell Securities Ltd. v. Venida Investments Ltd.* (July 25, 1974, unreported but as noted in 44 M.L.R. 40), the directors of a company called a meeting of shareholders to approve a resolu-

the directors of a corporation are not permitted to use their position to issue shares of the corporation to themselves at a lower price than they are offered to other shareholders.[303] This last point must be understood in a qualified sense. It should not be understood to prevent the board from granting directors stock options, as a form of director remuneration; only that in doing so, the option price must not be set unrealistically low.

§11.110 A stock option is an agreement entered into by a corporation with another person (usually with a director or senior officer) under which that other person is entitled to purchase a specified number of shares from the corporation at a fixed price for a specified period of time. If the market price of the shares concerned rises during that period the option may confer a significant benefit on that person. To the extent that such an option may fairly be said to constitute a form of remuneration for the services performed by the person to whom it is granted as an officer or director of the corporation — as for instance by providing an incentive to the directors or officers concerned to improve corporate performance — such schemes would not appear to contravene the proper corporate purpose rule. However, to fit within the "remuneration" exception, the option price should at least equal the market price at the time when it was granted (so that the benefit derived from the exercise will reflect the enhanced performance of the corporation), or alternatively be tied to the fair value of services provided by the director or officer to the corporation between the time when the option is granted and the time when it may be exercised.[304] Although under subsection 132(5) of the OBCA directors are prohibited from voting on contracts in which they have a material interest, an exception is provided under clause (*b*) of that provision with respect to contracts relating primarily to the director's remuneration as a director, officer, employee or agent of the corporation or of an affiliate of the corporation.

§11.111 As noted above, when they issue shares, the directors must be able to show that the considerations that guided them were consistent with the best interests of the corporation. Therefore, where the directors of a corporation issue shares not for the purpose of raising capital or for some other valid purpose,[305] but to thwart a takeover bid in order to perpetuate their own position, they are acting more out of self-interest than in the interests of the company, and the is-

---

tion increasing the company's authorized capital to create new shares that would be offered to existing members on a 9-for-1 basis. The directors knew that the plaintiff (who held a 49 per cent interest) could not afford to take up the new shares. The effect of the scheme would be to lower the plaintiff's interest in the company to less than 10 per cent. Although the company would benefit as a result of the infusion of new capital, Templeman J. granted an injunction against the directors' proceeding. He held that the dominant purpose of the directors was to benefit their own group of companies, and that the proposal would violate a tacit agreement made on the formation of the company that the plaintiff's interest would remain at 49 per cent. See also: *Katzowitz v. Sidler*, 24 N.Y.2d 512, 249 N.E.2d 359 (C.A.N.Y. 1969); but *cf. Hyman v. Velsicol Corp.*, 342 Ill. App. 489, 97 N.E.2d 122 (1951).

[303] *Re Brooks Steam Motors Ltd.*, [1934] 2 D.L.R. 648 (Ont. S.C. Master).
[304] See OBCA, ss. 23(3) and 23(4)(*b*)(i); CBCA, s. 25(3).
[305] See the discussion of *Teck Corp. v. Millar*, [1972] B.C.J. No. 566, 33 D.L.R. (3d) 288 (S.C.) above at § 8.118 *et seq.*

sue is liable to be set aside.[306] Nor may the directors issue additional shares solely for the purpose of obtaining enough votes, so that they can defeat the wishes of shareholders[307] or otherwise seize control of the corporation.[308]

§11.112 By and large it is the shareholders rather than the directors who are entitled to decide who will control the corporation, and the directors may not exercise their powers over various aspects of corporate affairs to prevent the shareholders from making that choice[309] even when the directors believe the shareholders' choice will be the wrong one.[310] However, in unusual cases the directors may be justified in using their share issuance powers to gerrymander control of the corporation.[311] For instance, in *Olson v. Phoenix Industrial Supply Ltd.*[312] the court considered the propriety of an issue of shares made for the sole purpose of wresting control from one shareholder, in the hope of preserving an insolvent corporation. The court concluded that the directors honestly believed that they were acting in the best interests of the corporation, and in the circumstances there were reasonable grounds for that belief, since creditors of the company were threatening its survival unless there was a change in control. Furthermore, even a share issue made in an effort to block a takeover bid will be allowed, where the directors act not in the interest of self-preservation, but out of a concern about the reputation, experience and policies of the person seeking to take over the corporation, provided the director's motive is to protect the corporation rather than their own position.[313] Although in *Olson*, Philp J.A. held that the onus was on the shareholder to show that the directors were not acting in good faith, an argument can be made for imposing the burden on the directors to demonstrate their good faith by showing that they did indeed possess reasonable

---

[306] *Exco Corp. v. Nova Scotia Savings & Loan Co.*, [1987] N.S.J. No. 56, 35 B.L.R. 149, 78 N.S.R. (2d) 91, 193 A.P.R. 91 (T.D.). See also *Bernard v. Valentini*, [1978] O.J. No. 3264, 18 O.R. (2d) 656 (H.C.J.); *Bonisteel v. Collis Leather Co.*, [1919] O.J. No. 125, 45 O.L.R. 195 (H.C.D.); *Hogg v. Cramphorn Ltd.*, [1967] Ch. 254 at 266-68, *per* Buckley J.

[307] *Glace Bay Printing Co. v. Harrington* (1910), 45 N.S.R. 268 (C.A.).

[308] *Martin v. Gibson*, [1907] O.J. No. 85, 15 O.L.R. 623 (H.C.J.).

[309] *Lee Panavision Ltd. v. Lee Lighting Ltd.*, [1992] B.C.L.C. 22 at 30 (C.A.), *per* Dillon L.J.; *Gaiman v. National Association for Mental Health*, [1971] Ch. 317, *per* Megarry J. In the Australian case *Darvall v. North Sydney Brick & Tile Co.* (1989), 15 A.C.L.R. 230 it was held (at 287) that even where the directors believe that the fortunes of the company will decline if a bid is successful, they should do no more than inform the shareholders of this belief, their reasons for it, and provide explanations such as that the present board's long-term plans for the company will result in greater benefits to the shareholders than are offered under the takeover bid.

[310] *Luther v. C.J. Luther Co.*, 118 Wis. 112, 94 N.W. 69 at 73 (1903).

[311] Where the effect upon a takeover bid is incidental to the attainment of some other corporate purpose, there is nothing wrong with the share issue: *Harlowe's Nominees Pty Ltd. v. Woodside (Lakes Entrace) Oil Co. N.L.* (1968), 42 A.L.J.R. 123 (H.C. Aust.) — directors issued shares to stabilize the financial condition of the company; the effect was to defeat a takeover bid; *Pine-Vale Investments Ltd. v. McDonnell & East Ltd.* (1983), 8 A.C.L.R. 199 at 209, *per* McPherson J.

[312] [1984] M.J. No. 113, [1984] 4 W.W.R. 498, 9 D.L.R. (4th) 451 (C.A.), leave to appeal to S.C.C. refused [1984] S.C.C.A. No. 21, 31 Man. R. (2d) 8*n*; but compare *Bonisteel v. Collis Leather Co.*, [1919] O.J. No. 125, 45 O.L.R. 195 (H.C.D.).

[313] *Teck Corp. v. Millar*, [1972] B.C.J. No. 566, [1973] 2 W.W.R. 385 (S.C.).

grounds to believe that a proposed takeover would cause substantial damage to the corporation's interests.

§11.113 Earlier in the Chapter, we examined the law relating to poison pills and similar devices. As noted in that section, despite *dicta* to the contrary in the odd eccentric case, it is difficult to imagine a situation in which the motivation of the directors in blocking a takeover bid would be anything other than to perpetuate their tenure as directors. While the *Securities Act*[314] does not prohibit such defensive measures, Canadian securities law administrators have indicated a clear concern with respect to the issue of shares in defence of a takeover bid.[315] The directors of a corporation have ample opportunity to advise the shareholders of a corporation whether they believe that the takeover bid is favourable to the interests of the shareholders. If the directors of a corporation issue shares to block a takeover bid they may well prevent the shareholders from exploiting an opportunity to realize a profit on their investment. Surely in a corporation that has been capitalized (directly or indirectly) by the shareholders, it is up to the shareholders and not the directors of the corporation to decide whether the takeover bid should succeed.[316]

§11.114 The proper purpose rule is also relevant with respect to the control of the directors over the holding of meetings. Directors are not entitled to defer the holding of a shareholder meeting in order to preserve their position on the board of directors.[317] The directors' control over the meeting process must be exercised in the best interest of the corporation. In this context, the best interest of the corporation is equated with the shareholders (or other relevant group) who are entitled to attend and participate in the meeting in question.

D. THE FIDUCIARY DUTIES OF DIRECTORS

(i) Overview

§11.115 A fiduciary is a person who has agreed, or who has undertaken, to act for or on behalf of, or in the interest of, another person in respect of the exercise of a power or discretion which will affect the interest of that other person in a legal or practical sense.[318] The word "fiduciary" from the Latin, "*fiducia*", which means trust. In general, it is the element of trust or confidence which makes a particular relationship a fiduciary one.[319] Implicit within the notion of fiduciary duty is the idea that the fiduciary may not abuse the trust or confidence that has

---

[314] R.S.O. 1990, c. S.5, as amended.
[315] C.S.A. National Policy No. 62-202.
[316] In *Howard Smith Ltd. v. Ampol Petroleum Ltd.*, [1974] A.C. 821, [1974] 1 All E.R. 1126, it was held to be improper for the directors to issue additional shares to facilitate a takeover bid over the objections of the majority of the shareholders.
[317] *Schurek v. Schnelle*, [2002] A.J. No. 140, 2 B.L.R. (3d) 108 (Q.B.).
[318] *Hospital Products Ltd. v. United States Surgical Corp.* (1984), 156 C.L.R. 41 at 68 (H.C. Aust.), *per* Gibbs C.J.
[319] *Madden v. Dimond*, [1906] B.C.J. No. 14, 12 B.C.R. 80 (C.A.).

been placed in the fiduciary, nor exercise the powers or discretions reposing in him or her as a fiduciary in a manner detrimental to the beneficiary of the fiduciary duty concerned. The effect of being held to be a fiduciary is to subject the person so conceived to the highest burdens[320] of fair dealing[321] beyond those that apply to all persons engaging in contractual dealings.[322]

§11.116 In certain cases, the law deems a relationship to be a fiduciary one. For instance, a solicitor stands in a fiduciary relationship toward his or her client; a trustee is a fiduciary for the beneficiary of the trust. Whether or not a fiduciary relationship exists in other relationships is a question of fact, but in order for an ordinary commercial relationship to be recognized as possessing a fiduciary character, there must be special circumstances that show that one party is entitled to expect that the other will act in his or her interests and for the purpose of the relationship.[323] The critical feature of a fiduciary relationship is that the fiduciary undertakes or agrees to act for or on behalf of or in the interest of another person in the exercise of a power or discretion that will affect the interests of that other person in a legal or practical sense. The relationship is, therefore, one of dependence that gives the fiduciary a special opportunity to exercise the power or discretion conferred upon him or her to the detriment of that other person, and because of that dependence, there is a clear vulnerability to abuse.[324] Given the extent of control that the directors of a corporation possess over the business and affairs of a corporation — and the obvious dependence of the shareholders and creditors of a corporation upon the integrity, good faith and fair dealing of and on the part of the directors — it is not surprising to find that a director is seen to stand in a fiduciary relationship to the corporation on the board on which he or she sits.[325]

§11.117 The general duties of a director to act in good faith and in the best interest of the corporation constitute the foundation of the many specific "fiduciary" duties of directors that are discussed extensively in the case law (a number of which have already been discussed). In more general terms, fiduciary duty imposes obligations of loyalty, good faith, and avoidance of conflict of duty and interest.[326] It bars directors and officers from acting inconsistently with

---

[320] The imposition of a fiduciary obligation is unusual in commercial relationships: *Litwin Construction (1973) Ltd. v. Pan*, [1988] B.C.J. No. 1145, 29 B.C.L.R. (2d) 88 at 105 (C.A.); *Jostens Canada Ltd. v. Gibsons Studio Ltd.*, [1997] B.C.J. No. 2637, [1998] 5 W.W.R. 403 (C.A.).

[321] As to the meaning of fair dealing, see *Weinberger v. UOP, Inc.*, 457 A.2d 701 at 711 (Del. S.C. 1983).

[322] *Meinhard v. Salmon*, 249 N.Y. 458, 164 N.E. 545 (1928), *per* Cardozo C.J.

[323] *International Corona Resources Ltd. v. LAC Minerals Ltd.*, [1989] S.C.J. No. 83, [1989] 2 S.C.R. 574 at 648-69, *per* La Forest J.

[324] *Hospital Products Ltd. v. United States Surgical Corp.* (1984), 55 A.L.R. 417 at 454 (H.C. Aust.), *per* Mason J.

[325] *Calmont Leasing Ltd. v. Kredl*, [1995] A.J. No. 475, 30 Alta. L.R. (3d) 16 at 24 (C.A.), *per curiam*. As to the potential liability of an underwriter as a promoter and for breach of fiduciary duty, see *EBC I Inc. v. Goldman Sachs & Co.*, 832 N.E.2d 26 (N.Y. 2005).

[326] *Provincial Plating Ltd. v. Steinkey*, [1997] S.J. No. 616, [1998] 3 W.W.R. 1 (Q.B.). Some Canadian and other Commonwealth authorities adopt an expansive approach to fiduciary duty, conceiving it to allow remedies to be tailored to the unique circumstances of a given case. Such an

the proper, free and independent discharge of their responsibilities to the corporation.[327] In this section, we will review the nature of those duties. In the recent decision of the Delaware Court of Chancery *In Re the Walt Disney Company Derivative Litigation*,[328] the court offers considerable guidance with respect to the manner in which the fiduciary principle ought to be applied in the corporate law sphere:

> Unlike ideals of corporate governance, a fiduciary's duties do not change over time. How we understand those duties may evolve and become refined, but the duties themselves have not changed, except to the extent that fulfilling a fiduciary duty requires obedience to other positive law. This Court strongly encourages directors and officers to employ best practices, as those practices are understood at the time a corporate decision is taken. But Delaware law does not — indeed, the common law cannot — hold fiduciaries liable for a failure to comply with the aspirational ideal of best practices, any more than a common-law court deciding a medical malpractice dispute can impose a standard of liability based on ideal — rather than competent or standard — medical treatment practices, lest the average medical practitioner be found inevitably derelict.

(ii) Extension of the Fiduciary Concept to Officers of a Corporation

§11.118 Before proceeding to consider directors' fiduciary duties in detail, it is worth stating that except insofar as they depend on statutory provisions expressly limited to directors, the principles discussed in this chapter concerning fiduciary duty apply generally to any senior officer[329] of the corporation who is authorized to act on its behalf in a managerial capacity.[330]

---

approach is consistent with the general American approach towards equitable remedies. See, for instance, *News Ltd. v. Australian Rugby Football League Ltd.* (1996), 64 F.C.R. 410 at 539 (F.C. Aust.), *per* Lockhart, von Doussa and Sackville JJ.:

> It is important to appreciate that the existence of a fiduciary relationship does not determine the content of the duties owed by one fiduciary to another. It has long been recognised that the nature and extent of the duties depend on the circumstances surrounding the particular relationship and the context in which relief is sought.

However, there are other authorities that take a minimalist approach to the scope of fiduciary duty. See *Breen v. Williams* (1996), 186 C.L.R. 71 at 113 (H.C.), *per* Gaudron and McHugh JJ.:

> In this country, fiduciary obligations arise because a person has come under an obligation to act in another's interests. As a result, equity imposes on the fiduciary proscriptive obligations — not to obtain any unauthorised benefit from the relationship and not to be in a position of conflict. If these obligations are breached, the fiduciary must account for any profits and make good any losses arising from the breach. But the law of this country does not otherwise impose positive legal duties on the fiduciary to act in the interests of the person to whom the duty is owed.

[327] *Connolly v. Rudderham*, [2001] P.E.I.J. No. 40, 15 B.L.R. (3d) 114 (T.D.).
[328] [2005] Del. Ch. LEXIS 113 (Ch.), *per* Chandler Ch.
[329] *Schauenburg Industries Ltd. v. Borowski*, [1979] O.J. No. 4349, 25 O.R. (2d) 737 (H.C.J.); *Alberts v. Mountjoy*, [1977] O.J. No. 2334, 16 O.R. (2d) 682 (H.C.J.); *57134 Manitoba Ltd. v. Palmer* (1985), 65 B.C.L.R. 355 (S.C.), aff'd [1989] B.C.J. No. 810, 37 B.C.L.R. (2d) 50 (C.A.).
[330] *Canadian Aero Services v. O'Malley*, [1973] S.C.J. No. 97, 11 C.P.R. (2d) 206, 40 D.L.R. (3d) 371 at 381, *per* Laskin J., quoting L.C.B. Gower, *The Principles of Modern Company Law*, 3rd

§11.119 Only a minority of employees of any given corporation are likely to attain the status of fiduciary. An employee of a corporation will not normally be seen to be a fiduciary duty unless he or she exercises some managerial authority to direct and guide the business of the corporation.[331] However, it is unusual for employees other than the senior officers of a corporation to be classed as fiduciaries, although there are obvious exceptions. In particular:

A. An employee other than a senior officer may not be a fiduciary to the corporation with respect to his or her general duties to the corporation, but may be a fiduciary in some limited aspect so as to attract liability for a particular wrongdoing that relates to that limited aspect of work. Typical cases of this sort arise where a relatively junior level has access to corporate funds, or is given access to proprietary and confidential information of the employer. For instance, in *Fortier v. Spafax Canada Inc.*,[332] a sales representative of a company selling a range of financial services, contemplated retirement and offered to sell to the company his 140-160 accounts (obtained by his own efforts), representing approximately 75 customers. The company was non-responsive to this offer. The plaintiff then sold his accounts to a competitor.

B. In-house counsel and other professionals who are retained by a corporation to perform services of a fiduciary nature will almost certainly be subject to fiduciary liabilities despite their status as employees.

Generally, only key employees will owe the fiduciary duties to avoid conflicts of interest and not compete with the employer.[333] In *Flanagan Sailmakers v. Walker*,[334] the court concluded that whether or not a particular employee is subject to fiduciary duties is dependent upon the individual's position and responsibility within the company. Where the plaintiff company is a small business with few employees it may be in a particularly vulnerable position *vis-à-vis* employee dishonesty, and individuals may often be found to play an important and influential role either generally or with respect to specific transactions. A person does

---

ed. (London: Stevens, 1969), at 518. The following passage from Laskin J.'s decision (at C.P.R. 221) is of particular interest:

> What these decisions indicate is an updating of the equitable principle whose roots lie in the general standards that I have already mentioned, namely loyalty, good faith and avoidance of conflict of duty and self-interest. Strict application against directors and senior management officials is simply recognition of the degree of control which their positions give them in corporate operations, a control which rises above accountability to owning shareholders and which comes under some scrutiny only at annual, general or special meetings. It is a necessary supplement, in the public interest, of statutory regulation and accountability which themselves are, at one and the same time, an acknowledgement of the importance of the corporation in the life of the community and of the need to compel obedience by it and by its promoters, directors and managers to norms of exemplary behaviour.

[331] *Alberts v. Mountjoy*, [1977] O.J. No. 2334, 16 O.R. (2d) 682 (H.C.J.).
[332] [1998] O.J. No. 3016, 71 O.T.C. 47 (Gen. Div.).
[333] See, generally, *Harris Scientific Products Ltd. v. Araujo*, [2005] A.J. No. 1107, 382 A.R. 332 (Q.B.), *per* Veit J.
[334] [2002] N.S.W.S.C. 1125.

not become a fiduciary merely because he or she is given a fancy title. It is the content of a person's job, and the nature of his or her responsibilities in connection with that job[335] that determines whether the person owes a fiduciary duty to the employer, the focus being on whether the job confers the power and ability to direct and guide the business or affairs of the corporation in some aspect.[336] In dealing with the cases that come before them, the courts strive to protect the employer's rights in its confidential information, without imposing excessive duties on employees, "lest the law commit a high proportion of employees in [Ontario] to slavery".[337]

(iii) General Principles

§11.120 It is not difficult to understand why it has been necessary to incorporate the fiduciary concept into corporate law. The corporation as a fictional entity must be directed by the acts and decisions of others, and therefore from time to time the courts have had to look behind the artificial personality of the corporation and focus upon the directors, officers and other agents (as opposed to the shareholders) who stand behind it. Corporate directors are given significant powers ranging from the broad general power to manage or supervise the running of the business and affairs of a corporation, to more specific powers, such as the ability to declare dividends, or issue shares. It is axiomatic that directors and officers when carrying out their duties must exercise discretion and deal with the property of the corporation. Under general principles of equity, the existence of such broad discretionary authority will often be seen to give rise to a fiduciary duty owed by the person on whom the discretion is conferred in favour of the person for whose benefit it is to be exercised. It is clear that with such unfettered discretion there is always a possibility of abuse. Equity has developed the concept of fiduciary duty to deal with the risk of abuse where extensive reliance is placed by one party on another.[338] As noted above, such is the case with directors and officers, and accordingly, it is now settled that the directors and officers of a corporation occupy a fiduciary position *vis-à-vis* the corporation[339] for which they serve.[340]

---

[335] *Provincial Plating Ltd. v. Steinkey*, [1997] S.J. No. 616, [1998] 3 W.W.R. 1 (Q.B.).
[336] *R.W. Hamilton Ltd. v. Aeroquip Corp.*, [1988] O.J. No. 906, 65 O.R. (2d) 345, 40 B.L.R. 79 (H.C.J.).
[337] *Ibid.*, at para. 28.
[338] *Hospital Products Ltd. v. United States Surgical Corp.* (1984), 55 A.L.R. 417 at 454 (H.C. Aust.), *per* Mason J.
[339] As to whether the fiduciary duty extends to the minority shareholders, see *Vladi Private Islands Ltd. v. Haase*, [1990] N.S.J. No. 104, 96 N.S.R. (2d) 323, 253 A.P.R. 323 (C.A.).
[340] *Regal (Hastings) Ltd. v. Gulliver*, [1967] 2 A.C. 134 at 159, *per* Lord Porter. Note that in certain circumstances, the directors may become liable for special fiduciary duties owed to the shareholders directly in addition to those discussed here: *Gadsden v. Bennetto* (1913), 3 W.W.R. 1109 (Man. C.A.); see also *Allen v. Hyatt* (1914), 26 O.W.R. 215, 17 D.L.R. 7 (P.C.). An outsider to the corporation who entices or conspires with a director or officer in connection with a breach of fiduciary duty will be liable to the corporation: *DCF Systems Ltd. v. Gellman* (1978), 5 B.L.R. 98, 41 C.P.R. (2d) 145 (Ont H.C.J.).

§11.121 The fiduciary relationship imposes upon the directors duties of loyalty and good faith, that are akin to those imposed upon trustees properly so called. From these general duties more specific requirements may be derived. So, for instance, it has been held that it is a violation of a director's fiduciary duty of loyalty to deny his (or her) fellow directors the right to consider fairly and responsibly a strategic opportunity; to mislead his fellow directors about his conduct and dealings in relation to corporate assets, to use confidential information belonging to the corporation to advance his own personal interests, without authorization from his fellow directors; and to urge an outside organization to pressure the corporation or those acting on behalf of the corporation with improper inducements to cause the person subjected to that pressure to act against the interests of the corporation.[341] Misleading and deceptive behaviour towards the board of directors is a fraud upon the board.[342]

§11.122 Directors are also under duties of care, diligence and skill, but these duties are very different from the duties to which trustees proper are normally subject, to be cautious and not to take risks with the trust property.[343] The fiduciary duties that grow out of the fiduciary relationship between directors (and officers) and their corporations supplement the statutory duties set out in the OBCA and the CBCA. They are not exhaustive. It is possible for individual directors and officers of a corporation to become subject to separate fiduciary duties on the facts of a given case that may be owed in a fiduciary capacity by the director or officer concerned, either to the corporation generally or to some of its shareholders. It is possible for a director to owe a fiduciary duty to a corporation in more than one capacity (*e.g.*, the director may also act as the corporation's solicitor).[344] Similarly, a director may assume a fiduciary responsibility towards a particular shareholder on the facts of a given case.[345]

§11.123 Although fiduciary status is exceptional[346] in the commercial context, it is justified in the case of the relationship between a corporation and its directors and officers on the obvious basis that they do not deal with the corporation at arm's length. On the contrary, they are the parties who have effective control over the corporation, and because of this fact there is a particular risk to the shareholders and other persons interested in the corporation that their interests

---

[341] *Hollinger International, Inc. v. Black*, 844 A.2d 1022 (Del. Ch. 2004), *per* Strine V.C., aff'd 872 A.2d 559 (Del. S.C. 2005); See also *Thorpe v. CERBCO, Inc.*, 676 A.2d 436 at 442 (Del. S.C. 1996); *In re Digex Inc. Shareholders Litigation*, 789 A.2d 1176 at 1192-93 and n. 7 (Del. Ch. 2000); *Mills Acquisition Corp. v. MacMillan, Inc.*, 559 A.2d 1261 at 1283 (Del. S.C. 1989); *HMG/Courtland Props., Inc. v. Gray*, 749 A.2d 94 at 119 (Del. Ch. 1999); *Agranoff v. Miller*, 1999 WL 219650, at 19 (Del. Ch. 1999), aff'd as modified 737 A.2d 530 (Del. S.C. 1999).

[342] *HMG/Courtland Props., Inc. v. Gray*, 749 A.2d 94 at 119 (Del. Ch. 1999); *Mills Acquisition Co. v. Macmillan, Inc.*, 559 A.2d 1261 at 1283 (Del. 1988).

[343] C.M. Schmitthoff, *Palmer's Company Law*, 23rd ed. (London: Stevens 1982), vol. 1 at 838.

[344] *Darvall v. North Sydney Brick & Tile Co.* (1989), 15 A.C.L.R. 230 at 280.

[345] *Coleman v. Myers*, [1977] 2 N.Z.L.R. 225 (C.A.); *Re Chez Nico (Restaurants) Ltd.*, [1992] B.C.L.C. 192 (Ch.), *per* Browne-Wilkinson V.C.

[346] *Litwin Construction (1973) Ltd. v. Pan*, [1988] B.C.J. No. 1145, 29 B.C.L.R. (2d) 88 at 105 (C.A.).

will be unfairly disregarded unless the directors and officers of the corporation are held to the highest standard of conduct that the law recognizes, namely the fiduciary standard of honesty, selflessness and loyalty. The risk to which the shareholders and other interested persons are exposed arises as soon as a person achieves a position of control. Prior to that time there is no exceptional risk and therefore no justification for imposing a fiduciary obligation, and thus it has been held there is no such liability in the case of a "director-elect".[347]

§11.124 In general terms, the fiduciary obligations of directors include:

- a duty to act in the best interests of the corporation and, correspondingly, not to do anything that undermines or thwarts those best interests;

- a duty to act with the highest degree of honesty, loyalty, good faith and fair dealing;[348]

- a duty not to compete with the corporation, including a prohibition against appropriating its business opportunities and assets;

- a duty to maintain the confidentiality of information received or knowledge obtained through the fiduciary position, including a prohibition against making use of such confidential information for the director's or officer's personal benefit;[349] and

- a duty to disclose material information that is within the knowledge of the fiduciary where it is relevant to the business or affairs of the corporation or some decision that the corporation is called upon to make (this being an implicit aspect of the duty to act in the best interests of the corporation).[350]

The fiduciary duty of directors and officers prohibits the plunder and looting of the corporate assets over which they have been placed in charge.[351] While directors and officers do not become subject to fiduciary obligations until they take up their respective positions in the corporation, their duties are retrospective in so far as they encompass a duty to investigate mistakes and misconduct committed prior to that time by past management in corporate management as well as a duty to supervise present management.[352] The duty of a fiduciary may be breached both by action or by failing to act.[353]

§11.125 In making these general observations, however, it is necessary to exercise some caution. Since the fiduciary concept and the duties and remedies that it gives rise to are equitable, and therefore essentially discretionary and flexible,

---

[347] *Lindgren v. L. & P. Estates*, [1968] 1 Ch. 572 at 596 (C.A.), *per* Dankwerts L.J.
[348] *Amerco, U-Haul International Inc. v. Shoen*, 184 Ariz. 150, 907 P.2d 536 (Ariz. C.A. 1995).
[349] *B. Love Ltd. v. Bulk Steel & Salvage Ltd.*, [1982] O.J. No. 3578, 40 O.R. (2d) 1 (H.C.J.).
[350] *484887 Alberta Inc. v. Faraci*, [2002] A.J. No. 522, 27 B.L.R. (3d) 110 (Q.B.); *Jackson v. Trimac Industries Ltd.*, [1994] A.J. No. 44, 155 A.R. 42 (C.A.).
[351] *Caswell v. Jordan* (1987), 362 S.E.2d 769 (Ga. App.).
[352] *Emco Ltd. v. Union Insurance Society of Canton Ltd.*, [1987] O.J. No. 42, 58 O.R. (2d) 420 (C.A.), leave to appeal to S.C.C. refused [1987] S.C.C.A. No. 160, 61 O.R. (2d) 192*n*.
[353] *Beamish v. Solnick*, [1980] O.J. No. 87, 10 B.L.R. 224 (S.C.).

it is not wise to attempt to lay down hard and fast rules, particularly with respect to the extent of potential obligations or liabilities that flow from such obligations. As Lord Upjohn observed,[354] rules of equity are applied in such a great diversity of circumstances that they can be stated only in the most general terms and applied with particular attention to the exact circumstances of each case. Nevertheless, two particular rules seem to prevail throughout the corporate director context. The first is that a person who acts in a fiduciary capacity must not make a profit out of his or her position of trust. The second, which essentially subsumes the first rule, is that a fiduciary must not place himself or herself in a position where his or her duty and personal interest conflict. Unfortunately, although the general nature of the obligations which flow from fiduciary status can readily be described, the specific obligations that are imposed on the directors and senior officers of a corporation by virtue of their fiduciary position are not settled.[355] So, for instance, in *Johnson v. Trueblood*,[356] Seitz C.J. noted that:

> It is frequently said that directors are fiduciaries. Although this statement is true in some senses, it is also obvious that if directors were held to the same standard as ordinary fiduciaries the corporation could not conduct business. For example, an ordinary fiduciary may not have the slightest conflict of interest in any transaction he undertakes on behalf of the trust. Yet by the very nature of corporate life a director has a certain amount of self-interest in everything he does. The very fact that the director wants to enhance corporate profits is in part attributable to his desire to keep shareholders satisfied so that they will not oust him.

§11.126 The scope of the fiduciary duty to which directors and officers are subject is determined by the law of the place of incorporation, rather than the law of the forum in which the question may be litigated.[357]

(iv) Conflict of Interest

§11.127 Despite the caution sounded by Seitz J., in the *Johnson* case, as a general rule, like any fiduciary, a director or officer[358] of a corporation must not place himself in a position that gives rise to a conflict between the duties that he or she owes to the corporation and some other interest that he or she is bound in law to serve, or that it seems reasonably probable he or she will consider.[359] The scope and effect of the general rule was clearly stated by Blake V.C. in *Greenstreet v. Paris Hydraulic Co.*:

> ... [A] director of a Company is a trustee for the shareholders, and ... a person occupying this fiduciary capacity is not allowed to enter into engagements in which he has or can have a personal interest conflicting, or which possibly conflict, with the interest of those whom he is bound by this duty to protect. This principle is so

---

[354] *Phipps v. Boardman*, [1967] 2 A.C. 46 (H.L.).
[355] *Exco Corp. v. Nova Scotia Savings & Loan Co.*, [1987] N.S.J. No. 56, 35 B.L.R. 149 at 255-56 (T.D.), *per* Richard J.
[356] 629 F.2d 287 at 292 (3d Cir. 1980), *cert.* denied 450 U.S. 999 (1981).
[357] *Amerco, U-Haul International Inc. v. Shoen*, 184 Ariz. 150, 907 P.2d 536 (Ariz. C.A. 1995).
[358] *B.C. Timber Industry Journal Ltd. v. Black*, [1934] B.C.J. No. 69, [1934] 2 W.W.R. 161 (C.A.).
[359] In *Aberdeen Rlwy. Co. v. Blaikie Bros.* (1854), 1 Macq. 461 at 471, [1843-60] All E.R. Rep. 249, *per* Lord Cranworth.

strictly adhered to that no question is allowed to be raised as to the fairness or unfairness of the transaction, and it makes no difference whether the contract relates to realty or personality; in mercantile transactions the disability arising, not from the subject matter of the contract, but from the fiduciary character of the contracting party.[360]

§11.128 There are two basic types of conflict of interest with which the director or officer must be concerned: the first is where the director's personal interest conflicts with that of the corporation;[361] the second is where he undertakes to act on behalf of a person whose interests are not compatible with those of the corporation. Usually, conflicts of intent will involve divergent financial interests, but it can also be problematic for a director to act when a close personal relationship or familial ties bring into question the willingness of the director to act in the best interest of the corporation.[362] The rule against conflicts of interest may be summarized in the following terms: a director has a duty to avoid conflicts of interest;[363] if the director fails to do so, the corporation may obtain an injunction restraining the director from acting in conflict of interest. Where a director or officer acts in a position of conflict of interest and duty, the corporation may recover for any damage suffered as a result. Similarly, if the director makes an unauthorized profit from his (or her) position as an officer or director, then the company has a remedy against him.[364]

§11.129 Where a supplier to a corporation (or other contracting party) bribes one of its directors or officers, the corporation may recover the amount of the bribe from the supplier, since it is assumed that the contract price charged to the corporation was inflated by at least the amount of the bribe.[365] It may also recover the bribe from the director or officer, for that fiduciary is required in such a case to account to his or her principal for the unlawful profit that he earned through the breach of trust.[366] This is not a case of double recovery, as the act of the payer and the recipient constitute separate wrongs against the corporation. The costs of investigation are also a recoverable item.[367]

---

[360] [1874] O.J. No. 208 at para. 11, 21 Gr. 229 at 232 (Ch.).
[361] See, for instance, *Canada Safeway Ltd. v. Thompson*, [1951] 3 D.L.R. 295 (B.C.S.C.); *Dominion Royalty Corp. v. Goffatt*, [1935] O.J. No. 204, [1935] O.R. 169 (C.A.), aff'd [1935] S.C.J. No. 27, [1935] S.C.R. 565.
[362] See, for instance, *Exide Canada Inc. v. Hilts* (2005), 11 B.L.R. (4th) 311 (Ont. Sup. Ct.).
[363] *Phipps v. Boardman*, [1967] 2 A.C. 46 at 124 (H.L.), per Lord Upjohn (commenting upon the duty to avoid potential conflicts of interest); *Wilson v. London, Midland & Scottish Rlwy. Co.*, [1940] Ch. 169.
[364] See *Misener v. H.L. Misener & Son Ltd.*, [1977] N.S.J. No. 497, 21 N.S.R. (2d) 92, 28 A.P.R. 92 (C.A.), for a difficult case involving romantic conflicts of interest.
[365] *Grant v. Gold Exploration & Development Syndicate Ltd.*, [1900] 1 Q.B. 233.
[366] *Insurance Corp. of British Columbia v. Dragon Driving School Canada Ltd.*, [2005] B.C.J. No. 1653, 43 B.C.L.R. (4th) 330 at para. 14 (S.C.), per Groberman J.
[367] *I.C.B.C. v. Sanghera*, [1991] B.C.J. No. 766, 55 B.C.L.R. (2d) 125 (C.A.); *I.C.B.C. v. Eurosport Auto Co.*, [2004] B.C.J. No. 201, 8 C.C.L.I. (4th) 236 (S.C.).

(v) Conflicting Duties

§11.130 A person who owes a fiduciary obligation to one person may not accept a conflicting duty to another person, irrespective of whether the second duty gives rise to any benefit in favour of the fiduciary. The obligation of a director or officer to avoid such a conflict of interest is an extension of the general obligation placed on fiduciaries to avoid such conflicts. Where a fiduciary acts in contravention of this duty, it is not necessary to prove that damage has actually flowed from that contravention. The obligation of the fiduciary is to avoid both actual conflicts of interest and potential conflicts of interest.

§11.131 In essence, the law requires the individual subject to the duty to scrupulously avoid placing himself in a possible or potential conflict of interest. Therefore, the fact that a conflict could have arisen, but did not, does not excuse the fiduciary. Entering into a potential conflict of interest is a breach, whether or not the conflict ever becomes operative or involves conduct that would in the absence of the fiduciary duty be itself wrongful, the potential for conflict itself violates the beneficiary's right to utmost loyalty and avoidance of conflict.[368] The consideration of whether there is a conflict or potential conflict of interest involves both present and former directors. The principle stated by the Ontario Court of Appeal in *Korz v. St. Pierre*[369] with respect to lawyers and their former clients is no less applicable to other fiduciaries, including the directors and senior officers of corporations:

> As a result of the possession by the lawyer of special and confidential information pertaining to clients, he should not take advantage of that position of superiority if he enters into a transaction with them. If he is entering into such a transaction, the lawyer is bound to make full disclosure of his position so that the client is not placed at a disadvantage. The ethics of the profession and fairness require that such a disclosure be made. To hold otherwise would place lawyers in an unfairly advantageous position. They would be able to benefit from special and confidential information obtained from their clients in the course of advising them on legal problems, while permitting lawyers to surreptitiously avoid the very risks they know are being assumed by their clients. This principle must apply in many instances to former clients as well as current clients.

§11.132 Entry into a business competing with that of the corporation may or may not constitute a conflict of interest, depending upon the circumstances of the case.[370] Early decisions in this area tended to support the right of a director to compete with the corporation. For instance, in *London & Mashonaland Exploration Co. v. New Mashonaland Exploration Co.*[371] it was held that present directors could not be restrained from acting as directors of a competing

---

[368] M.V. Ellis, *Fiduciary Duties in Canada* (Toronto: De Boo, 1988).
[369] [1987] O.J. No. 906, 61 O.R. (2d) 609 at 618, *per* Cory J.A., leave to appeal to the S.C.C. refused [1988] S.C.C.A. No. 81, 62 O.R. (2d) ix. See also *McMaster v. Byrne*, [1952] 3 D.L.R. 337 at 344 (P.C.), *per* Lord Cohen.
[370] Discussed in greater detail and as a discrete subject at §11.151 *seq.*
[371] [1891] W.N. 165.

company.[372] It is doubtful that a court would reach a similar conclusion today. The decision in that case predated the evolution of much of the law relating to fiduciary duty. As a fiduciary, a director necessarily owes a duty of confidentiality and of disclosure to the corporation that he or she serves,[373] and must act to maximize return to the shareholders of that corporation.[374] A fiduciary also owes a duty of full disclosure to the beneficiary of the duty.[375] Where one person sits on the board of two competitors (A and B), it would be impossible to reconcile the duty of confidentiality to corporation A with the duty of disclosure to corporation B. Nor could the director balance the conflicting duties to maximize the profits of both corporations. It is worth noting that more recent cases in this area call the decision in *Mashonaland* into question. In *Resfab Manufacturier de Ressort Inc. v. Archambault*,[376] an injunction was granted in favour of a corporation restraining a former director from joining a competitor of the corporation. Similarly, in *W.J. Christie & Co. v. Greer*[377] a former director was successfully sued for damages where he established a new corporation and solicited customers away from the plaintiff. However, the damage award was discounted to take into account the defendant's cost of doing business.[378]

§11.133 The fiduciary duty of a director or officer does not permanently bar that person from becoming involved with a competitor to the corporation. A director may purchase an interest in a company operating in the same line of business as the corporation for which he is a director.[379] Clearly after having done so, however, a former director may not use confidential information of the corporation to assist a competitor,[380] nor (as discussed in detail below) may the director assist the competitor to usurp commercial opportunities that properly belong to the corporation.[381] However, so long as the former director or officer is not misusing confidential information entrusted to him by virtue of his or her position with the corporation, or otherwise abusing the trust reposed, it would seem that it is not improper for the director to go into competition with the corporation, upon retirement. The decision of the Manitoba Court of King's Bench in *Waite's Auto*

---

[372] See also *Bell v. Lever Bros. Ltd.*, [1932] A.C. 161 at 195-96 (H.L.); but compare *Scottish Co-operative Wholesale Society Ltd. v. Meyer*, [1959] A.C. 324 at 368.
[373] See, generally, *Drabinsky v. KPMG*, [1998] O.J. No. 4075, 41 O.R. (3d) 565 (Gen. Div.).
[374] *J.D. MacArthur Co. v. Alberta & Great Waterways Rlwy. Co.*, [1924] 2 D.L.R. 118 at 127 (Alta. C.A.), per Stuart J.A.
[375] See, generally, *Martin v. Goldfarb*, [1998] O.J. No. 3403, 163 D.L.R. (4th) 639 (C.A.), leave to appeal to S.C.C. refused [1998] S.C.C.A. No. 516, 239 N.R. 193n.
[376] (1985), 10 C.P.R. (3d) 102 (Que. C.A.). See also *Dominion High-Rise Ltd. v. Night-Hawk Cleaning & Supply Co.*, [1982] O.J. No. 3291, 37 O.R. (2d) 148 (Co. Ct.).
[377] [1981] M.J. No. 77, 14 B.L.R. 146, 121 D.L.R. (3d) 472 (C.A.). Note, however, that ordinary employees are free to terminate their employment and enter into competition with a former employer.
[378] See also *Alberts v. Mountjoy*, [1977] O.J. No. 2334, 16 O.R. (2d) 682 (H.C.J.).
[379] *Tombill Gold Mines Ltd. v. Hamilton*, [1955] O.J. No. 602, [1955] O.R. 903, aff'd [1956] S.C.J. No. 61, [1956] S.C.R. 858.
[380] See, generally, *Ainley & Associates Ltd. v. Tatham*, [1989] O.J. No. 1556, 46 B.L.R. 104 (H.C.J.); *Dominion High-Rise Ltd. v. Night-Hawk Cleaning & Supply Co.*, [1982] O.J. No. 3291, 37 O.R. (2d) 148 (Co. Ct.).
[381] *Canadian Aero Service Ltd. v. O'Malley*, [1973] S.C.J. No. 97, [1974] S.C.R. 592, 40 D.L.R. (3d) 371, discussed below at §11.187.

Transfer Ltd. v. Waite[382] illustrates the limits that apply to the prohibition against a former director or officer competing with the corporation. In that case it was found that the defendant and his partners had sold the assets of their business to the plaintiff corporation in 1919. The defendant had acted as president and manager of the company until 1928, at which time he resigned as manager but remained as a director. About the same time, he set himself up in the same business and began to solicit business from the plaintiff's customers. The defendant took away from the company no customer lists, although he knew of the names of the company's clients and the nature and extent of their dealings. It was held that the plaintiff was not entitled to an injunction restraining the defendant from so competing, or for damages for the loss of business that it had suffered. The acts of the defendant had not been in breach of any contract made by him with the plaintiff corporation. The defendant's fiduciary relationship with the plaintiff was a bare technical one,[383] having no real ongoing character. The court ruled that the defendant was entitled to compete with the corporation, and placed the onus on the plaintiff to show that the defendant had abused his position as a director.

§11.134 In *Holmested v. Annable*[384] the former directors of a corporation that was being liquidated and wound up purchased the corporation's assets from the liquidators. The applicable legislation[385] provided that upon the appointment of liquidators all the powers of the directors ceased except insofar as the corporation in general meeting or the liquidators might sanction the continuance of such powers. No general meeting had been held, nor had the liquidators sanctioned the continuation of any powers. It was held that the directors breached no fiduciary duty in purchasing the assets and that the sale was valid. Thus in the ordinary course the fiduciary relationship between a director or officer and the corporation ceases upon the appointment of a liquidator in a winding-up.[386] The effect of a winding-up is to make the directors and officers as such strangers to the management and control of the corporation's business and affairs, and therefore their former fiduciary duty no longer stands in their way.[387]

(vi) Remoteness and Related Defences

§11.134.1 Historically, claims for breach of breach of fiduciary duty have paid little attention to such questions of remoteness, causation and intervening act. This approach was rejected by the Ontario Court of Appeal in *Waxman v. Waxman*,[388] where it was observed that:

---

[382] [1928] 3 W.W.R. 649 (Man. K.B.).
[383] Although the defendant was a nominal director, there appear to have been no director meetings.
[384] (1914), 6 W.W.R. 1497 (Sask. T.D.).
[385] *Companies Winding-up Act*, R.S.S. 1909, c. 78, s. 7(5).
[386] *Chatham National Bank v. Mabou Coal and Gypsum Co. (Liquidators of)* (1895), 24 S.C.R. 348.
[387] *Re Mabou Coal & Gypsum Co.* (1894), 27 N.S.R. 305 (C.A.).
[388] [2004] O.J. No. 1765, 44 B.L.R. (3d) 165 at 302 (C.A.), *per curiam*, leave to appeal to S.C.C. refused [2004] S.C.C.A. No. 291.

The rationale for keeping these concerns out of equity has been the desire to enforce fiduciaries' strict standards of good faith. But as Canadian law has changed to permit plaintiffs to sue "in whatever manner they find most advantageous", correspondingly courts have recognized ... that "equity is flexible enough to borrow from the common law". Increasingly, courts seek to achieve similar compensation for "similar wrongs", whether the action is framed in contract or tort or as breach of fiduciary duty. Indeed, as La Forest J. commented in *Canson*[389]...

> ...it would be odd if a different result followed depending solely on the manner in which one framed an identical claim. What is required is a measure of rationalization.

Our former colleague, Finlayson J.A., made the same point in *Martin v. Goldfarb*[390] when he approved the following passage from the reasons of the trial judge in that case:

> Regardless of the doctrinal underpinning, plaintiffs should not be able to recover higher damage awards merely because their claim is characterized as breach of fiduciary duty, as opposed to breach of contract or tort. The objective of the expansion of the concept of fiduciary relationship was not to provide plaintiffs with the means to exact higher damages than were already available to them under contract or tort law.

The court went on to conclude that it may consider the principles of remoteness, causation, and intervening act where necessary to reach a just and fair result, but should apply them only if doing so does not raise any policy concerns.[391]

(vii) Nominee Directors

§11.135 The rule that the directors of a corporation must avoid actual or potential conflicts of interest[392] obviously poses great practical problems in cases where a director has been appointed to the board of directors of a corporation for the specific purpose of protecting the interest of a nominating shareholder.[393] In many cases (*e.g.*, where one corporation is a subsidiary of another) the same persons will serve on the board of directors of two corporations, or all of the directors of one corporation will be officers or employees of the other. While overlapping directorates are common, they worsen rather than mitigate the legal problems arising from a conflict of interest. As a general rule, although a director may be appointed to represent the interest of a single shareholder, any nominee director so appointed must serve the interests of the corporation as a whole.[394] A failure to discharge this responsibility may invalidate transactions

---

[389] *Canson Enterprises Ltd. v. Boughton & Co.*, [1991] S.C.J. No. 91, [1991] 3 S.C.R. 534.
[390] [1998] O.J. No. 3403, 41 O.R. (3d) 161 (C.A.), leave to appeal to S.C.C. refused [1998] S.C.C.A. No. 516.
[391] See also *Hunt v. TD Securities Inc.*, [2003] O.J. No. 3245, 66 O.R. (3d) 481 at 506 (C.A.), leave to appeal to S.C.C. refused [2003] S.C.C.A. No. 473.
[392] *Aberdeen Rlwy. Co. v. Blaikie Bros.* (1854), 1 Macq. 461 at 471-72 (H.L.), *per* Lord Cranworth.
[393] See, generally, *Scottish Co-operative Wholesale Society Ltd. v. Meyer*, [1959] A.C. 324 at 366-67 (H.L.), *per* Lord Denning M.R.
[394] *Bennetts v. Board of Fire Commissioners of New South Wales* (1967), 87 W.N. (Pt. 1) N.S.W. 307 (S.C.); *Re Broadcasting Station 2GB Pty Ltd.*, [1964-65] N.S.W.R. 1648 (S.C.), *per* Jacobs J.

and expose the director concerned to liability. For instance, in *Gray v. Yellowknife Gold Mines Ltd.*[395] the court was required to consider the fiduciary duties that were owed to two corporations where four of five directors of the one corporation also served on the board of directors of the other.[396] In that case, the plaintiff attacked the validity of a transaction between the two corporations because of the lack of independence arising from the identity of the boards of directors of the two corporations.[397] The court held that the transaction was void.[398] However, the mere fact that a particular shareholder is represented by a nominee on the board, and a transaction has been entered into that worked to the benefit of that shareholder does not create a presumption of any breach of fiduciary duty on the part of that nominee-director, particularly where the nominee in question is one of several directors and the rest are independent of the shareholder in question. A nominee director in such a case is subject to statutory disclosure obligations with respect to any potential conflict of interest, but provided there was proper disclosure, the transaction may be set aside only where it is shown to constitute a fraudulent preference or some similar impeachable transaction.[399]

§11.136 It may be complained that to the extent that a nominated director champions the interests of his or her nominating shareholder, the inevitable result will be some fettering of the discretion of that director. Some courts have taken the view that while a shareholder may nominate a director, the director so nominated must remain free to exercise his or her best judgment in the interests of the company for which he or she serves.[400]

(1) The Orthodox Position

§11.137 Historically, Canadian and English case law has tended to favour imposing the same fiduciary duties on nominee directors as apply to directors at large. The decision of Lord Denning in *Scottish Co-operative Wholesale Society Ltd. v. Meyer*[401] is often cited when describing the risks run by nominee directors who attempt to serve two masters: the corporation for which they serve and the shareholder who secured their appointment. He said:

---

[395] [1947] O.J. No. 550, [1947] O.R. 928 (C.A.). See also *Gray v. Yellowknife Gold Mines Ltd. (No. 2)*, [1946] O.J. No. 617, [1946] O.R. 639 (H.C.J.), aff'd [1947] O.J. No. 551, [1947] O.R. 994 (C.A.); *Roxborough Gardens of Hamilton Ltd. v. Davis*, [1920] O.J. No. 99, 46 O.L.R. 615 (C.A.).

[396] See also *Signal Hill Oils Co. v. London Oil Securities Ltd.*, [1927] 3 D.L.R. 984, 2 W.W.R. 392 (Alta. T.D.); *Boyle v. Rothschild*, [1907] O.J. No. 647, 10 O.W.R. 696 (K.B.); *Gould v. Gillies* (1908), 40 S.C.R. 937.

[397] See also *Central Gas Utilities Ltd. v. Canadian Western Natural Gas Co.* (1964), 53 W.W.R. 705, revd [1966] S.C.J. No. 40, [1966] S.C.R. 630 (*sub nom. Canadian Western Natural Gas v. International Utilities Corp.*).

[398] But compare *J.D. MacArthur Co. v. Alberta and Great Waterways Rlwy. Co.*, [1923] 3 W.W.R. 46, aff'd [1924] 2 D.L.R. 118 (Alta. C.A.).

[399] *Levy-Russell Ltd. v. Shieldings Inc.*, [2004] O.J. No. 4291, 48 B.L.R. (3d) 28 (S.C.J. — C.L.), *per* Cumming J.

[400] *Boulting v. Association of Cinematograph, Television and Allied Technicians*, [1963] 2 Q.B. 606 at 626-27 (C.A.), *per* Lord Denning M.R.

[401] [1959] A.C. 324 (H.L.).

What then is the position of the nominee directors here? Under the articles of association of the textile company the cooperative society was entitled to nominate three of the five directors, and it did so. It nominated three of its own directors and they held office as "nominees" of the cooperative society. These then were at one and the same time directors of the cooperative society ... and also of the textile company ... So long as the interests of all concerned were in harmony, there was no difficulty. The nominee directors could do their duty by both companies without embarrassment. But as soon as the interests of the two companies were in conflict, the nominee directors were placed in an impossible situation. ... It is plain that, in the circumstances, these three gentlemen could not do their duty by both companies, and they did not do so. They put their duty to the cooperative society above their duty to the textile company in the sense at least, that they did nothing to defend the interests of the textile company against the conduct of the cooperative society. They probably thought that "as nominees" of the cooperative society their first duty was to the cooperative society. In this they were wrong. By subordinating the interests of the textile company to those of the cooperative society, they conducted the affairs of the textile company in a manner oppressive to the other shareholders.[402]

In *Kuwait Asia Bank EC v. National Mutual Life Nominees Ltd.*,[403] it was found that the Kuwait Asia Bank held 40 per cent of the shares of a New Zealand company, AIC Securities Ltd. ("AICS"). Two of the five directors of AICS were employees of the Kuwait Asia Bank. The Privy Council expressly rejected the notion that these nominee directors were entitled to follow the instructions of their employer.

§11.138 In Canada it has also been held that nominee directors are required to act in the best interests of the corporation for which they serve, irrespective of the wishes of the appointing shareholder.[404] The situation of a director is very different from that of the shareholders whom he or she represents. The director is not the agent of the shareholder who appoints the director. He is an overseer required by law to supervise the corporations' business and affairs. The assets of the corporation do not belong to the director or appointing shareholder but are merely entrusted to the director for management. The director's duties are owed to the corporation itself as distinct from the appointing shareholder. The director must proceed very cautiously in the sole interest of the corporation entrusted to his or her care. The director's decisions must be guided by and conform to what the director perceives to be the best interests of the corporation as this is what the law requires the director to watch over and protect.[405]

§11.139 Thus there is now a substantial body of Canadian and English case law to the effect that a director who serves on the board of directors of a corporation as a nominee of a particular shareholder owes the same duties to the corporation

---

[402] *Ibid.*, at 366-67.
[403] [1991] 1 A.C. 187 (P.C.).
[404] *820099 Ontario Inc. v. Harold E. Ballard Ltd.*, [1991] O.J. No. 266, 3 B.L.R. (2d) 113 at 167 *et seq.* especially at 172 (Ont. Gen. Div.), *per* Farley J., aff'd [1991] O.J. No. 1082 (Div. Ct.).
[405] *Ringuet v. Bergeron*, [1960] S.C.J. No. 40, [1960] S.C.R. 672, 24 D.L.R. (2d) 449 at 457-58, *per* Judson J.

as any other shareholder. Such a director is not accorded an attenuated standard of loyalty to the corporation. The director must exercise his or her judgment in the interests of the corporation alone, and comply with the duties of disclosure that are imposed by law. The director must not subordinate his or her duties to the corporation to any duty that is owed to the shareholder.[406] A nominee director must act in the best interests of the corporation as a whole. He or she may not favour the interest of the shareholder who appointed him or her over the interests of other shareholders, and in particular may not make that shareholder's interest his paramount consideration.[407]

(2) Are the Courts Moving to a More Moderate Stance?

§11.140 Despite these general principles, in recent years, many courts seem to have moved towards a softer position: they have been more willing to recognize the commercial realities of life, specifically the need to protect the interests of a major investor.[408] For instance, it has been held that a nominee director is not necessarily affixed with conflicts of interest to which the nominating shareholder would be subject if it served as a director personally.[409] In *Levin v. Clark*[410] Jacobs J. found that the directors of a company had acted with primary concern for the interests of the mortgagee of shares in the company, who had secured their appointment, and held that the extent of their duties as directors depended upon the circumstances. He took the view that the scope of the directors' fiduciary duties to the company could be modified both by the terms of the constating documents of the company,[411] and also by the wishes of the person whom they represented on the board. However, this is the minority view, even within Australia. For instance, in *Walker v. Wimborne*[412] the High Court rejected the argument that the directors of a company that belonged to a group of affiliated companies that shared common directors were entitled to consider the interests of that group ahead of the individual company, particularly where there was a conflict of interest between the shareholders and the creditors who were interested in the corporation.

§11.141 The express wording of sections 134 of the OBCA and 132 of the CBCA imposes duties on the directors incapable of being overridden by agreement or by the articles of the corporation. A nominating shareholder — while no doubt an important investor — may only be one of several persons whose interests the board of directors of the corporation (and thus, ultimately, each of its

---

[406] *PWA Corp. v. Gemini Group Automated Distribution Systems Inc.*, [1993] O.J. No. 723, 8 B.L.R. (2d) 221 at 265 (Gen. Div.), *per* Callaghan C.J.O.C., aff'd [1993] O.J. No. 1793, 103 D.L.R. (4th) 609 (C.A.), leave to appeal to S.C.C. refused [1993] S.C.C.A. No. 343, 104 D.L.R. (4th) vii.
[407] *Deluce Holdings Inc. v. Air Canada*, [1992] O.J. No. 2382, 98 D.L.R. (4th) 509 (Gen. Div.).
[408] See, for instance, *Berlei Hestia (N.Z.) Ltd. v. Fernyhough*, [1980] 2 N.Z.L.R. 150 at 165-66, *per* Mahon J.
[409] *Keating v. Bragg*, [1997] N.S.J. No. 248, 34 B.L.R. (2d) 181 at 205 (C.A.), *per* Hallett J.A., supp. reasons (1997), 160 N.S.R. (2d) 363 (C.A.).
[410] [1962] N.S.W.R. 686.
[411] See, also, *Berlei Hestia (N.Z.) Ltd. v. Fernyhough*, [1980] 2 N.Z.L.R. 150, *per* Mahon J.
[412] (1976), 137 C.L.R. 1, 3 A.C.L.R. 525, 50 A.L.J.R. 446 (H.C. Aust.).

members) are required to protect — for example, minority shareholders and creditors. Even so, in *Re Broadcasting Station 2GB Pty Ltd*.[413] Jacobs J. went on to reject the argument that nominated directors were conducting the affairs of a company in an oppressive way, by reason of following the wishes of the nominating shareholder. He held that the minority shareholders could not expect that every director of a company would approach the matters to be dealt with by the board with a completely open mind. To adopt such an approach, he said, would be to ignore the realities of company organization. In *Dairy Containers Ltd. v. N.Z. Bank Ltd.*,[414] Thomas J. put forward what might well be an acceptable middle course. He would allow nominated directors to protect the interests of their nominating shareholders so long as the interests of the company and those shareholders were not in conflict. Once a conflict arose, however, it would be necessary for the nominated shareholders to act with the same commitment to the welfare of the company as independent directors.[415]

§11.142 The difficulty of reconciling competing loyalties owed by nominee directors not only arises in the context of wholly owned subsidiaries or controlled corporations, but also where two or more business rivals form a joint venture for some common purpose, making direct or indirect use of a corporate vehicle for that purpose, with each member appointing a representative to the board of the corporation controlling the joint venture. While the fiduciary duty of a director ordinarily carries with it an obligation to disclose information relevant to the business of the corporation, a particular problem arises in the case of joint venture corporations involving business rivals, because any disclosure made to the full board of the joint venture corporation may eventually filter back to the rivals of the member of the corporation whose directors disclose the information concerned. It now appears that nominee directors may be subject to a lesser duty of disclosure than that to which directors in a corporation are ordinarily subject.

§11.143 For instance, in *PWA Corp. v. Gemini Group*[416] the court considered the conduct of nominee directors appointed by PWA to the board of a corporation that acted as the general partner of a limited partnership to which PWA belonged. PWA and the other two members of the limited partnership were equally sophisticated commercial corporations, with two of them (PWA and Air Canada) being the operators of the major national air carriers in Canada. In a divided judgment, the Ontario Court of Appeal held that the nominee directors were in breach of their fiduciary duty to the corporate general partner in that they failed to disclose ongoing negotiations by PWA with American Airlines which affected the limited partnership in a vital aspect of its business. However, on the special facts of the case, the duty of disclosure was a limited one. *Per* Griffiths J.A.:

---

[413] [1964-65] N.S.W.R. 1648.
[414] [1995] 2 N.Z.L.R. 30 at 96-97 (H.C.).
[415] See also *H. Timber Protection Ltd. (In Receivership) v. Hickson International plc*, [1995] 2 N.Z.L.R. 8 (C.A.).
[416] [1993] O.J. No. 1793, 103 D.L.R. (4th) 609 (C.A.), leave to appeal to S.C.C. refused [1993] S.C.C.A. No. 343, 104 D.L.R. (4th) vii.

Because Air Canada and PWA remain competitors outside the partnership, they have no obligation to disclose to each other their business strategies and they are not bound generally to put the interests of the Gemini Partnership ahead of their own. In my view, the directors had a duty of disclosure as directors but subject to a limit. The PWA-appointed directors would not, in the ordinary course, be under a fiduciary duty to disclose confidential PWA negotiations, or solicitor-and-client advice, in connection with a proposed arrangement, even with a rival airline, such as an agreement sought by PWA as a means to improve its competitive position in the airline business.[417]

§11.144 It is beyond doubt that nominee directors may not conspire with the shareholder who appointed them to the board of a corporation against the corporation, but there is nothing improper in nominee directors insisting that the corporation respect the legal rights of that shareholder, nor in their assisting that shareholder to enforce those rights. For instance, in *Levin v. Clark*[418] two directors were appointed to the board of a company by a creditor with a view towards ensuring compliance with a security agreement. Jacobs J. held that they were not in breach of any duty to the company when they acted to enforce that security. The directors of a corporation are obliged to act in its interests, but they are also obliged to cause the corporation to honour its obligations. If the directors do no more than compel the corporation to do so, they commit no wrong merely because the directors concerned also owe a duty to the other party to that contract. However, directors may be in breach of their duty to the company where they cause the corporation to pay off debts that are owed to creditors who hold a guarantee given by the directors, so as to give priority in their repayment over debts owed to other creditors.[419] In such a case, the directors will often be seen to be acting in their own interests rather than that of the corporation. On the other hand, such payments may well be justified where they are made in good faith in an effort to keep the head of the corporation above water, and the creditor paid has been harassing the corporation for payment.

§11.145 In *Walker v. Wimborne*[420] the defendants were directors of a group of associated companies. In order to ease the financial pressure to which various members of the group were subject, the directors sought to shuffle funds between the companies. Such inter-corporate financial assistance could raise concerns under section 20 of the OBCA. However, the Australian financial assistance provisions are not so broad as this Canadian counterpart. Thus, the High Court of Australia dealt with the case primarily on the general principles of a director's duty. In the course of his judgment, Mason J. made the following observation:

> ... the emphasis given by the primary judge to the circumstance that the group derived a benefit from the transaction tended to obscure the fundamental principles that each of the companies was a separate and independent legal entity, and that it was the duty of the directors of Asiatic to consult its interests and its interests

---

[417] *Ibid., per* Griffiths J.A. at 645-46.
[418] [1962] N.S.W.R. 686 at 700.
[419] *West Mercia Safetywear Ltd. v. Dodd*, [1988] B.C.L.C. 250 (C.A.).
[420] (1976), 137 C.L.R. 1, 3 A.C.L.R. 525, 50 A.L.J.R. 446 (H.C. Aust.).

alone in deciding whether payments should be made to the other companies. In this respect it should be emphasized that the directors of a company in discharging their duty to the company must take into account the interests of its shareholders and its creditors. Any failure by the directors to take into account the interests of creditors will have adverse consequences for the company as well as for them. The creditor of a company, whether it be a member of a "group" of companies in the accepted sense of that term or not, must look to that company for payment. His interests may be prejudiced by the movement of funds between companies in the event that the companies become insolvent.[421]

The following comments from Mason J.'s judgment with respect to the benefit derived by Asiatic (the company providing the assistance) are also helpful:[422]

> The transaction offered no prospect of advantage to Asiatic, it exposed Asiatic to the probable prospect of substantial loss, and thereby seriously prejudiced the unsecured creditors of Asiatic. It was more than an improvident transaction reflecting an error of judgment; it was undertaken in accordance with a policy adopted by the board of directors in total disregard of the interests of the company and its creditors.

(3) Material Contracts Involving the Nominating Shareholder

§11.146 Clause 132(5)(*d*) of the OBCA and paragraph 120(5)(*c*) of the CBCA permit directors of a corporation to vote on material contracts or transactions that relate to an affiliate of the corporation of which the director is an officer or director or in which the director has a material interest. It appears, however, that the relationship between the director and the affiliate must still be disclosed by the director — the normal course being by way of a general disclosure under subsections 132(6) of the OBCA and 120(6) of the CBCA.[423] Under subsection 1(4) of the OBCA one corporation is an affiliate of the other if, but only if, "one of them is a subsidiary of the other or both are subsidiaries of the same body corporate or each of them is controlled by the same person". Under subsection 2(2) of the CBCA, the following test of affiliation is set down:

> 2.(2) For the purposes of this Act,
>
> (*a*) one body corporate is affiliated with another body corporate if one of them is the subsidiary of the other or both are subsidiaries of the same body corporate or each of them is controlled by the same person; and
>
> (*b*) if two bodies corporate are affiliated with the same body corporate at the same time, they are deemed to be affiliated with each other.

Where a director participates in an irregular meeting, he may not subsequently set up the invalidity of the meeting in defence of a claim made against the directors in respect of a decision taken at that meeting.[424]

---

[421] *Ibid.*, at 6-7 C.L.R.
[422] *Ibid.*, at 7 C.L.R.
[423] *Gray v. New Augarita Porcupine Mines Ltd.*, [1952] 3 D.L.R. 1 (P.C.).
[424] *Gray v. Yellowknife Gold Mines Ltd.*, [1945] O.J. No. 540, [1945] O.R. 688 (H.C.J.), rev'd on other grounds [1947] O.J. No. 550, [1948] 1 D.L.R. 473 (C.A).

(4) Responsibilities of the Nominating Shareholder

§11.147 Except in unusual cases, the shareholders of a corporation owe no duty to each other as such. By extension from that principle, within the Commonwealth, the position appears to be that although a shareholder may appoint nominee directors, or has sufficient voting power to secure the election of a director, that shareholder owes no duty to the corporation or to other shareholders to see that the director(s) so appointed discharge their duties with due diligence and competence. One shareholder may lock away his or her shares and sleep; another may take an active interest in the corporation, insist that detailed information be provided and deluge the directors with advice. Neither the active nor the passive shareholder is liable. It is the director and not the shareholder who owes the duty to the corporation. The duty is personal to the directors, and therefore the shareholder is not vicariously liable for any default by the director, even if the director is the shareholder's nominee.[425]

§11.148 The general immunity of a nominating shareholder does not apply where the shareholder interferes in the management of the corporation or causes the directors to breach their duty towards it.[426] There are a number of American cases in which such a fiduciary duty has been found to exist in such cases.[427] The existence of such a duty may afford considerably greater protection to the creditors of the subsidiary corporation and other persons interested in it than is afforded by the fiduciary duties imposed on directors, since in most cases the parent is more likely to be able to repay any amount lost to the corporation by reason of the breach of fiduciary duty. Moreover, if it is the parent corporation that benefits from the breach of fiduciary duty committed by its nominee directors, there is a certain logic in requiring the parent corporation to account directly to the subsidiary corporation for the losses concerned.[428] It can be argued with some force that where a parent and subsidiary corporation enter into a dealing in which a benefit is to be conferred upon the parent (*i.e.*, self-dealing), the parent owes a fiduciary duty to the corporation to ensure that the dealing in question is conducted on terms that are intrinsically fair to the subsidiary. Where the element of self-dealing is not present, any decision made by the board, including its nominee directors, within their reasonable business judgment should not be subject to review by the court.

§11.149 More broadly, it can be argued with some force that where a corporation causes a subsidiary to be incorporated, or purchases a subsidiary, and delegates certain of its senior officers or directors to sit on the board of that subsidiary, it gives them implicit authority to act in the interests of that subsidiary in priority to its own should those interests at any time conflict. Having

---

[425] *Kuwait Asia Bank EC v. National Mutual Life Nominees Ltd.*, [1990] 3 W.L.R. 297 at 319 (P.C.), *per* Lord Lowry.
[426] Under U.K. company law, a shareholder who appoints and controls a nominee director may be liable as a shadow director of a corporation.
[427] See, generally, for instance, *Getty Oil Co. v. Skelly Oil Co.*, 267 A.2d 883 (Del. S.C. 1970); *Moskowitz v. Bantrell*, 41 Del. Ch. 177, 190 A.2d 749 (Del. S.C. 1963).
[428] See, generally, *Sinclair Oil Corp. v. Levien*, 280 A.2d 717 (Del. S.C. 1971), *per* Woolcott C.J.

taken advantage of the separate corporate existence of the subsidiary for its own purposes — as, for example, to secure limited liability to itself or to obtain some advantageous tax position — it is only reasonable for the parent corporation to bear the burden that flows from that separate existence, as for instance, by subordinating the fiduciary duties that may incidentally be owed to it by its directors and officers to those that are owed by them with respect to the subsidiary. Such an approach is fully consistent with two ancient and fundamental maxims of law, namely, that he (or she) who has taken a benefit must also take any accompanying burden, and that he who creates a risk (in this case that risk arising from separate corporate existence) must bear that risk.

§11.150 A nominee director who agrees to act as a director at the request of a person who is interested in a corporation is entitled to an implied right of indemnity from that person against any liability arising by reason of his or her so acting. The right of indemnity lapses when the nominee director acquires a personal interest in the corporation.[429] Where a nominating shareholder instructs or otherwise causes a director to breach a fiduciary duty that is owed to the corporation, the shareholder is liable to the corporation for that breach.[430]

(viii) Going into Competition with the Director's Former Corporation

§11.151 As a general principle, an employee is free to leave his or her position of employment and go into competition with his or her former employer. Consequently, in the absence of a non-competition agreement a corporation may not restrain one of its former employees from going into competition with it, unless it can establish a breach of fiduciary duty.[431] The former employee's new business may be the mirror image of that of his or her former employer. The former employee is perfectly entitled to carry on his or her own business in the same way as the former employer carries on the original business, and the former employee may make use of all the skills acquired in his or her former position,[432] other than confidential information.[433] The former employer's only remedy in such a case is to take solace in the fact that imitation is the sincerest form of flattery. Moreover, the employee may prepare the ground before he or she leaves, so that it will be a fertile soil in which his or her new business may prosper,[434] at least provided the extent of preparation is not excessive.[435] After leaving, the employee may also seek out the former employer's customers.[436]

---

[429] *Mogil v. Abelson*, [1992] O.J. No. 2159, 8 B.L.R. (2d) 102 at 106 (Gen. Div.), *per* Lane J.
[430] *Ibid.*
[431] *Berkey Photo (Canada) Ltd. v. Ohlig*, [1983] O.J. No. 3194, 43 O.R. (2d) 518 (H.C.J.).
[432] *Louis v. Smellie* (1895), 73 L.T. 226 at 228 (C.A.), *per* Lindley L.J.; *Pizza Pizza Ltd. v. Gillespie*, [1990] O.J. No. 2011, 75 O.R. (2d) 225 (Gen. Div.).
[433] *Helmore v. Smith (No. 2)* (1886), 35 Ch. D. 449 at 456 (C.A.), *per* Bowen L.J.
[434] *Wessex Dairies Ltd. v. Smith*, [1935] 2 K.B. 80 at 89 (C.A.), *per* Maugham L.J.
[435] *Coleman Taymar Ltd. v. Oakes*, [2001] 2 B.C.L.C. 749.
[436] *Roberts v. Elwells Engineers Ltd.*, [1972] 2 All E.R. 890 at 894 (C.A.), *per* Lord Denning M.R.; see also *Canada Bonded Attorney & Legal Directory Ltd. v. Leonard-Parmiter Ltd.*, [1918] O.J. No. 79, 42 O.L.R. 141 at 157 (C.A.), *per* Riddell J.; *Robb v. Green*, [1895] 2 Q.B. 315.

§11.152 The fiduciary obligation of senior employees to avoid conflicts of interest results in major modifications to the foregoing general statements of principle. The right of a fiduciary who leaves the employment of a corporation to go into competition with that corporation is more limited. The general rule respecting the right of a senior employee has been summarized as follows:[437]

> The law is clear that an employee of a company cannot be restricted from using knowledge gained through the course of his employment to his advantage and that he may enter into competition with his former employer. ... He may not, however, take with him customer lists or other property of his former employer to assist him. ... [Memorization] of such lists in some cases is tantamount to physical appropriation.
>
> The position of "key" employees is somewhat different from that of ordinary employees. It seems that the determining factors in assessing liability for the solicitation of former customers or clients rests upon the following criteria:
>
> 1. Whether a new business was started or substantially considered prior to leaving the employ of the plaintiff company ...
>
> 2. Whether customer lists were appropriated ...
>
> 3. Whether former clients were offered inducement or were actually solicited by the former key employee.

Obviously it is inappropriate for a key employee (and even a more junior employee) to solicit business away from his or her corporate employer while he or she remains in the corporation's employ. On leaving, a junior employee is free to solicit such business. However, the fiduciary duties owed by a former key employee or former director of a corporation continue at least for a reasonable period of time after leaving the corporation.[438] The direct solicitation of former clients by a former key employee or director crosses the boundary of acceptable conduct.[439] However, subject to this qualification, it is clear that in the absence of a non-competition agreement, even former employees who held the most senior management positions in a corporation are free to enter into competition with

---

[437] *Anderson, Smyth & Kelly Customs Brokers Ltd. v. World Wide Customs Brokers Ltd.*, [1993] A.J. No. 614, 10 B.L.R. (2d) 155 at 166-67 (Q.B.), *per* Moshansky J., rev'd [1996] A.J. No. 475, 39 Alta. L.R. (3d) 411 (C.A.). See also *Mercury Marine Ltd. v. Dillon*, [1986] O.J. No. 957, 30 D.L.R. (4th) 627 (H.C.J.); *Alberts v. Mountjoy*, [1977] O.J. No. 2334, 16 O.R. (2d) 682 (H.C.J.); *Quantum Management Services Ltd. v. Hann*, [1989] O.J. No. 542, 43 B.L.R. 93, aff'd [1992] O.J. No. 2393, 11 O.R. (3d) 639n (C.A.); *Bendix Home Systems Ltd. v. Clayton*, [1977] 5 W.W.R. 10 (B.C.S.C.), aff'd [1979] B.C.J. No. 159 (C.A.); *Reed Stenhouse Ltd. v. Foster*, [1989] A.J. No. 604, 98 A.R. 49 (Q.B.); *Tree Savers International Ltd. v. Savoy*, [1992] A.J. No. 61, 84 Alta. L.R. (2d) 384 (C.A.); *Metropolitan Commercial Carpet Centre Ltd. v. Donovan*, [1989] N.S.J. No. 254, 91 N.S.R. (2d) 99 (T.D.); *Bonar Inc. v. Smith*, [1991] B.C.J. No. 57, 35 C.P.R. (3d) 161 (S.C.); *Kronvic v. Lamarche-Craven*, [1991] O.J. No. 907; *DCF Systems Ltd. v. Gellman*, [1978] O.J. No. 1381, 5 B.L.R. 98 (H.C.J.).

[438] *Anderson, Smyth & Kelly Customs Brokers Ltd. v. World Wide Customs Brokers Ltd.*, [1996] A.J. No. 475, 39 Alta. L.R. (3d) 411 at 422 (C.A.), *per* O'Leary J.

[439] *W.J. Christie & Co. v. Greer*, [1981] M.J. No. 77, 121 D.L.R. (3d) 472 at 477 (C.A.), *per* Huband J.A. See also *Anderson, Smyth & Kelly Customs Brokers Ltd. v. World Wide Customs Brokers Ltd.*, [1996] A.J. No. 475, 39 Alta. L.R. (3d) 411 (C.A.).

that corporation upon leaving it.[440] The right of a senior employee to compete includes the right to employ the usual methods of promoting a business, such as advertising targeted at the relevant public generally, mass mailing, grand openings and the like, but it does not extend to the purloining of trade secrets, confidential information nor (as discussed below) other corporate property, including a business opportunity belonging to the corporation.[441]

§11.153 A former director of a corporation who enters into a line of business formerly pursued by the corporation for which he served as a director, but which has been subsequently abandoned by that corporation, does not breach either a fiduciary duty to the corporation or an agreement not to compete with it by taking employment with another company which carries on that discontinued business.[442] By the same token, it is no breach of fiduciary duty for a former director of a corporation or one of its subsidiaries to move to another corporation which buys the line of business in which the director works, at least so long as the former director in question is not a moving force in that sale.[443] Where a director discloses fully and obtains the consent of the corporation from an independent decision making body within the corporation to the conflict in question, then there is no breach of fiduciary duty.[444]

(1) Non-competing Businesses

§11.154 While a director has a duty to avoid potential conflicts of interest, the mere fact that a person is a director of one corporation does not prevent him from acquiring ownership of, or an interest in, another corporation.[445] Directors do not ordinarily undertake to devote their full time and energy to the administration of the corporation, and therefore if the corporation for which they act as director and some other corporation in which they have an interest do not compete, there can be nothing improper in the director's interest in that second corporation.[446] The test of whether the two corporations are in competition, however, is determined by the actual businesses in which they are engaged, rather than by reference to the business for which they were originally incorporated.[447] Clearly there can be no ground for complaint where a former director or

---

[440] *Metropolitan Commercial Carpet Centre Ltd. v. Donovan*, [1989] N.S.J. No. 254, 91 N.S.R. (2d) 99 at 104 (T.D.), *per* Davison J.; *Intertech Model Fixtures Inc. v. Rusch*, [1992] O.J. No. 2252, 8 B.L.R. (2d) 150 at 156 (Gen. Div.), *per* Macfarland J.
[441] *W.J. Christie & Co. v. Greer*, [1981] M.J. No. 77, 121 D.L.R. (3d) 472 at 477 (C.A.), *per* Huband J.A.
[442] *Tembro Truck & Auto Services Ltd. v. Brown*, [1996] O.J. No. 2817, 30 B.L.R. (2d) 263 (Gen. Div.).
[443] *Framlington Group plc. v. Anderson*, [1995] 1 B.C.L.C. 475.
[444] *New Zealand Netherlands Society "Oranje" Inc. v. Kuys*, [1973] 1 W.L.R. 1126 (P.C.).
[445] *Tombill Gold Mines Ltd. v. Hamilton*, [1955] O.J. No. 602, [1955] O.R. 903 (C.A.), aff'd [1956] S.C.J. No. 61, [1956] S.C.R. 858.
[446] See, generally, the remarks of L.D. Barry J. in *Slate Ventures Inc. v. Hurley*, [1996] N.J. No. 88, 27 B.L.R. (2d) 41 at 65-66 (T.D.).
[447] *Birtchnell v. Equity Trustees Executors & Agency Co.* (1929), 42 C.L.R. 384 at 408 (H.C.), *per* Dixon J.

senior officer of a corporation enters into a business that truly does not compete with the corporation.[448]

(2) Self-dealing

§11.155 As noted above, it is a fundamental principle of the obligations of a fiduciary that he or she may not allow his or her personal interest to conflict with the duties owed to the beneficiaries of the fiduciary relationship. Both actual and potential conflicts are prohibited,[449] and any transaction in contravention of this principle is voidable and open to rescission by the corporation.[450] Directors are bound to disregard their own private interests whenever a regard to them conflicts with the proper discharge of that duty.[451] It is a corollary of this general principle that a director may not exert his or her influence over the corporation where the corporation is dealing with the director or with a person in whom the director has a material interest. This rule must not be too broadly understood. It is not that the director cannot enter into a contract with the corporation — there is no such rule.[452] Rather, the true rule is that the director is precluded from dealing on behalf of the company with himself or herself, as for instance by entering into engagements in which his or her personal interest conflicts or may possibly conflict with those of the corporation.[453]

§11.156 The classic decision in this area of the law was that of the House of Lords in *Regal (Hastings) Ltd. v. Gulliver*.[454] Since this decision has played so pivotal a role in the development of the law in this area, it is worthwhile to consider the decision given in that case in detail. The keynote passage of the decision appears in the judgment of Viscount Sankey, where he indicated that the liability of a fiduciary to account for profits does not depend upon the proof that he (or she) acted in bad faith. Instead, the general rule of equity is that no one who has duties of a fiduciary nature to perform is allowed to enter into engagements in which he has or can have a personal interest conflicting with the interests of those whom he is bound to protect. If he holds any property so acquired as trustee, he is bound to account for it to his *cestui que trust*.[455] Similarly, Lord Russell of Killowen rejected

---

[448] *Balston Ltd. v. Headline Filters Ltd.*, [1990] F.S.R. 385 (Ch.), *per* Falconer J.
[449] *Guinness plc. v. Saunders*, [1990] 2 A.C. 663 at 690 (H.L.), *per* Lord Templeman.
[450] *Hely-Hutchinson v. Brayhead Ltd.*, [1968] 1 Q.B. 549 (C.A.); *Movitex Ltd. v. Bulfield*, [1986] 2 B.C.L.C. 99,403 at 99,432, *per* Vinelott J. If a third party other than the director is involved in the transaction, and that third party would be prejudiced by rescission, then it is necessary to show either that the third party is responsible for the director on some agency or like basis, or that the third party knew of or reasonably ought to have known of the breach of duty: *Logicrose Ltd. v. Southend United Football Club Ltd.*, [1988] 1 W.L.R. 1256.
[451] *Imperial Mercantile Credit Association v. Coleman* (1871), 6 Ch. App. 558 at 563, *per* Malins V.-C., and *per* Lord Hatherley L.C. at 566, revd L.R. 6 H.L. 189.
[452] See *Cook v. Deeks*, [1916] 1 A.C. 554 at 564-65 (P.C.), *per* Lord Buckmaster L.C. See also *North-West Transportation Co. v. Beatty* (1887), 12 App. Cas. 589 (P.C.); *Burland v. Earle*, [1902] A.C. 83.
[453] *North-West Transportation Co. v. Beatty* (1887), 12 App. Cas. 589 at 593 (P.C.), *per* Sir Richard Baggallay.
[454] [1942] 1 All E.R. 378, [1967] 2 A.C. 134 (H.L.). The decision was given on February 20, 1942, but for some reason was not reported until 1967.
[455] *Ibid.*, at 137 (A.C.).

the argument that it was necessary to show bad faith on the part of the fiduciary, in order to hold him accountable for the profit made.[456] It is the making of the profit which itself gives rise to the liability to account.[457]

§11.157 The directors in the *Regal (Hastings) Ltd.* case raised a battery of defences to the claims that were made against them. Among them was the argument that the corporation did not have the wherewithal to fully fund the investment that the directors made. That defence was rejected:

> It was then argued that it would have been a breach of trust for the respondents, as directors of Regal, to have invested more than £2000 of Regal's money in Amalgamated, and that the transaction would never have been carried through if they had not themselves put up the other £3000. Be it so, but it is impossible to maintain that because it would have been a breach of trust to advance more than £2000 from Regal and that the only way to finance the matter was for the directors to advance the balance themselves, a situation arose which brought the respondents outside the general rule and permitted them to retain the profits which accrued to them from the action they took. At all material times they were directors and in a fiduciary position, as they used and acted upon their exclusive knowledge acquired as such directors. They framed resolutions by which they made a profit for themselves. They sought no authority from the company to do so, and, by reason of their position and actions, they made large profits for which, in my view, they are liable to account to the company.[458]

§11.158 A director or officer of a corporation is not free to trade for his own advantage upon the information acquired by him in the course of acting for the corporation.[459] It follows that a fiduciary who has acquired confidential information in the course of acting in a professional capacity on behalf of the beneficiary, will not be permitted to make personal investments based upon that information or sell it to other parties, particularly if they are adverse in interest to the beneficiary.[460] Moreover, as the House of Lords ruled in *Aberdeen Rlwy. Co. v. Blaikie Bros.*:

> So strictly is this principle adhered to that no question is allowed to be raised as to the fairness, or unfairness, of the transaction; for it is enough that the parties interested object. It may be that the terms on which a Trustee has attempted to deal with the trust estate are as good as could have been obtained from any other quarter. They may even be better. But so inflexible is the rule that no inquiry into that matter is permitted.[461]

§11.159 A director or officer of a corporation will be liable for self-dealing, where the director or officer misuses the powers or responsibilities that have been entrusted to him so as to confer a personal advantage on himself, and the

---

[456] *Ibid.*, at 143-44 (A.C.).
[457] See, generally, Lord Eldon in *Ex parte James* (1803), 8 Ves. 337, 32 E.R. 385 at 345 (Ch.).
[458] *Regal (Hastings) Ltd. v. Gulliver*, [1942] 1 All E.R. 378, [1967] 2 A.C. 134 at 139 (H.L.), *per* Viscount Sankey.
[459] *Hamilton v. Wright* (1842), 9 Cl. & F. 111 at 124, 8 E.R. 357 (H.L.), *per* Lord Brougham; *Boardman v. Phipps*, [1967] 2 A.C. 46 at 105 (H.L.), *per* Lord Hodson.
[460] *McLennan v. Newton*, [1928] 1 D.L.R. 189 at 191 (Man. C.A.), *per* Fullerton J.A..
[461] [1843-60] All E.R. Rep. 249 at 252 (H.L.).

transaction itself is liable to be set aside.[462] The rule against self-dealing prevents a director from performing services for the corporation and then claiming for payment for those services on a *quantum meruit* basis. For instance, in *Huggard v. Prudential Life Insurance Co.*,[463] it was held that the rule against self-dealing prohibited a director who was a solicitor from recovering legal fees from the corporation, even where the work giving rise to those fees was done under express instructions from the executive committee of the corporation's board of directors, and the corporation received the benefit of the services rendered.[464]

§11.160 However, directors are subject to a somewhat lesser standard than are trustees. A trustee must act with a certain and single view to the real purpose and object of his or her power, namely the interest of the beneficiary.[465] Directors are not held to such an exacting standard. It is quite permissible for a director to take a step that incidentally advances his own best interests, provided that the controlling motivation of the director is the best interests of the corporation.[466] In *Mills v. Mills*, Latham C.J. was prepared to go even further:

> Very many actions of directors who are shareholders, perhaps all of them, have a direct or indirect relation to their own interests. It would be ignoring realities and creating impossibilities in the administration of companies to require that directors should not advert to or consider in any way the effect of a particular decision upon their own interests as shareholders. A rule which laid down such a principle would paralyze the management of companies in many directions.[467]

It is important in considering the scope of this exception from the traditional duties of a fiduciary to remember the difference between the position of a director and that of a trustee. It is exceptional[468] for a trustee to draw a benefit from an act done in the interest of the beneficiary, since the trustee will have no interest in the trust property itself. In contrast, because directors will often have an interest in the corporation, they will often draw an incidental benefit from their acts — as, for instance, where directors fix their remuneration, approve their expenses or even direct payment of a dividend. Such incidental benefits do not cast doubt over the validity of their action. It is only where they cease to look to

---

[462] See, generally, *Daniel v. Gold Hill Mining Co.*, [1899] B.C.J. No. 25, 6 B.C.R. 495 (C.A.).
[463] [1923] 1 W.W.R. 555 at 574-75 (Man. K.B.), *per* Mather C.J.K.B.; *cf. Re Mimico Sewer Pipe & Brick Mfg. Co.*, [1895] O.J. No. 108, 26 O.R. 289 at 296-97 (Ch.), *per* MacMahon J.
[464] A similar decision was reached in *Cape Breton Cold Storage Co. v. Rowlings*, [1929] S.C.J. No. 29, [1929] S.C.R. 505, [1929] 3 D.L.R. 577, *per* Newcombe J.
[465] See *Duke of Portland v. Lady Topham* (1864), 11 H.L. Cas. 32 at 54, 11 E.R. 1242, *per* The Lord Chancellor.
[466] *Ngurli Ltd. v. McCann* (1953), 90 C.L.R. 425 (Aust.). Under the OBCA and the CBCA, there would seem to be nothing objectionable in a solicitor-director being retained and paid to provide legal services to the corporation, provided the solicitor-director complies with ss. 132 of the OBCA and 120 of the CBCA, as the case may be. Specifically, there must be a formal retainer providing for the payment of legal fees. The contract must be approved by the board and the solicitor-director must disclose his or her interest and refrain from taking part in the approval of the retainer arrangement.
[467] (1938), 60 C.L.R. 150 (Aust.).
[468] *E.g.*, where the trustee is entitled to remuneration under the terms of the trust, or where the trustee is also a beneficiary.

the interests of the corporation, and focus instead on their own interests, that directors contravene their duties.

§11.161 The advantage derived from an act of the board that places a director in conflict with his or her duty to the corporation may be either a direct one, that is a benefit conferred on the director or officer personally,[469] or an indirect one, such as a benefit conferred on another corporation in which the director has a material interest,[470] irrespective of the nature of the contract.[471] The director may not justify self-dealing by demonstrating that the transaction was favourable to the corporation. The rule is so inflexible that no inquiry will be permitted into this question, even if the transaction is fair in the circumstances and is as good or better than would have been obtained from some other person.[472] On the other hand, it is open to the corporation to hold the director to the bargain if it cannot obtain a better deal from another source.[473] The rule protects the corporation, not the director.

§11.162 In *Beamish v. Solnick*,[474] the plaintiff and defendant were directors of a corporation, of which each had a 50 per cent interest. The corporation's restaurant business was failing and it was decided to sell it. An agreement of purchase and sale was reached with a third party, but the defendant refused to sign the documents on behalf of the corporation, thereby preventing closing. If the transaction had closed, the proceeds would have been sufficient to cover the corporation's debts, but not to cover an amount of $15,000 which the parties had agreed would be paid out to the defendant. The corporation suffered financially as a result of the postponed closing, as did the plaintiff who was called upon to pay on a personal guarantee given to the corporation's bank. The plaintiff brought a representative action on behalf of the corporation and a personal action for damages against the defendant. Both actions were allowed. It was held that the defendant's refusal to close the transaction was in his own interest, and not that of the corporation. By acting in his own interest, the defendant breached the statutory duty that he owed to act in the corporation's best interest. Furthermore, if a director violated his duty at a time when he knew or ought to have known that he would subject another director to separate special harm or damage from that suffered by the corporation, then he owed a duty to the other director not to subject him to that separate harm or damage.

§11.163 As a general principle, the fiduciary duties owed to the corporation may not be invoked or enforced by a stranger to the corporation.[475] However, a director may not take advantage of his conflict of interest to avoid personal liability. In

---

[469] See, for instance, *Gadsden v. Bennetto* (1913), 3 W.W.R. 1109 (Man. C.A.).
[470] See, for instance, *Signal Hill Oils Co. v. London Oil Securities Ltd.*, [1927] 3 D.L.R. 984, [1927] 2 W.W.R. 392 (Alta. T.D.).
[471] *Greenstreet v. Paris Hydraulic Co.*, [1874] O.J. No. 208, 21 Gr. 229 (C. Ch.), *per* Blake V.-C.
[472] *Aberdeen Rlwy. Co. v. Blaikie Bros.* (1854), 1 Macq. 461, [1943-60] All E.R. Rep. 249 (H.L.), *per* Lord Cranworth.
[473] *Christopher v. Noxon*, [1883] O.J. No. 273, 4 O.R. 672 at 682-83 (Ch. D.), *per* Proudfoot J.
[474] [1980] O.J. No. 87, 10 B.L.R. 224 (H.C.J.).
[475] *Grammas v. Kensington Cafe Ltd.*, [1919] 3 W.W.R. 301 (Man. K.B.).

McPherson v. Forlong,[476] the defendant was the managing director of a loan corporation who also had an interest in an oil company. The oil company borrowed money from time to time from the loan company, giving it promissory notes, including a final note endorsed by the plaintiffs, which consolidated the earlier notes. The plaintiffs claimed against the defendant on the basis that he had agreed to share equally in the liability incurred. The defendant contended that the agreement contemplated a fraud on the loan company and that therefore any agreement to share in the liability on the notes was unenforceable. The court disagreed. Even if the agreement by the loan corporation to loan money to the oil company was voidable by the loan company, that fact did not invalidate the agreement to indemnify the endorsers of the note.

(ix) Misappropriation of Corporate Property

§11.164 There is no question that a director or officer who misappropriates corporate property is accountable for any property so taken,[477] and for interest thereon.[478] The directors of a company — whether collectively or individually — have no authority to steal that company's property.[479] In *London Guarantee & Accident Co. v. Abrams*[480] an officer of the corporate plaintiff had drawn cheques in the plaintiff's name and issued several such cheques to the defendant in payment of personal loans. In an action for conversion brought by the corporation, it was held that the plaintiff was entitled to recover from the defendant. Although the defendants argued that they had received the cheques honestly, believing the officer's statement that they represented money due to him, the defendants were on notice of a breach of trust, because the cheques were made out in the name of the plaintiff. The defendants had no reason to believe that the officer had the authority to draw such cheques.

(1) The Corporate Opportunity Doctrine

§11.165 A related principle to the prohibition against misappropriation of property relates to corporate business and similar opportunities. It is clear that a director or officer must not incur personal profit at the expense of the corporation,[481] whether by way of awarding material contracts or by confiscating or appropriating corporate property for his or her own use. Similarly, it is a breach of fiduciary duty for a director or officer to appropriate for his own

---

[476] [1928] 3 W.W.R. 45, 37 Man. R. 508 (K.B.).
[477] See, for instance, *F.R. Diesel Electric Co. v. Farkas*, [1985] B.C.J. No. 1497, B.C. Corps. L.G. 78,309 (S.C.).
[478] *Canada Trust Co. v. Lloyd*, [1968] S.C.J. No. 16, [1968] S.C.R. 300, 66 D.L.R. (2d) 722. The right to claim interest is of particular importance because of the limited application of the *Statute of Limitations*: *Saskatchewan Land & Homestead Co. v. Moore*, [1913] O.J. No. 750, 25 O.W.R. 125 at 135 (H.C.D.), *per* Kelly J., var'd [1914] O.J. No. 331, 26 O.W.R. 160 (1st Div. Ct.), var'd [1915] O.J. No. 570, 8 O.W.N. 525 (C.A).
[479] *A.L. Underwood v. Bank of Liverpool and Martins*, [1924] 1 K.B. 775 at 796 (C.A.), *per* Atkin L.J.
[480] [1923] 2 W.W.R. 1006 (Sask. K.B.).
[481] *MacMillan Bloedel v. Binstead*, [1983] B.C.J. No. 802, 22 B.L.R. 255 (S.C.).

benefit an economic opportunity that rightly belongs to the corporation.[482] A director cannot escape potential liability in this regard by resigning his or her directorship.[483]

§11.166 The rule that a director or officer may not usurp a business opportunity belonging to the corporation is known as the corporate opportunity doctrine.[484] In *Cook v. Deeks*,[485] Lord Buckmaster L.C. stated the following general principles, which even today provide a firm foundation for this doctrine:

> ... [M]en who assume the complete control of a company's business must remember that they are not at liberty to sacrifice the interests which they are bound to protect, and, while ostensibly acting for the company, divert in their own favour business which should properly belong to the company they represent.[486]

The difficulty has been ascertaining the precise point at which business belongs to the corporation.[487]

§11.167 The tests for the imposition of the corporate opportunity doctrine vary. Some courts limit the doctrine to situations where the corporation is considered to have an expectancy or inchoate interest in the particular transaction (the concept of the maturing business opportunity).[488] Others extended it to all opportunities that fall within the company's line of business,[489] while a third variant is provided by those courts that reject these tests and determine liability by the application of ethical standards of what is fair and equitable on the particular facts of a case.[490] Under all three approaches, there runs a common thread. The question to resolve is the point at which business properly belongs to the company to a sufficient extent that the directors are precluded from usurping it.

§11.168 The clearest type of case in which a director or officer will run afoul of the corporate opportunity doctrine lies where the transaction is originally pur-

---

[482] See, for instance, *Roper v. Murdoch*, [1987] B.C.J. No. 1193, 21 C.P.R. (3d) 468, 39 D.L.R. (4th) 684 (S.C.); *Lake Mechanical Systems Corp. v. Crandell Mechanical Systems Inc.*, [1985] B.C.J. No. 1606, 31 B.L.R. 113 (S.C.); *Coulter v. E.L. Huckerby & Associates Inc.*, [1998] O.J. No. 909, 41 B.L.R. (2d) 264 (Gen. Div.).

[483] *Industrial Development Consultants Ltd. v. Cooley*, [1972] 1 W.L.R. 443 (Ch.); *Roper v. Murdoch*, [1987] B.C.J. No. 1193, 21 C.P.R. (3d) 468, 39 D.L.R. (4th) 684 (S.C.).

[484] For a cross section of recent British cases dealing with the subject of corporate opportunity beyond those considered here, see: *Ultraframe (UK) Ltd. v. Fielding*, [2005] E.W.H.C. 1638 (Ch.); *Brown v. Bennett*, [1999] 1 B.C.L.C. 649 (C.A.); *Plus Group Ltd. v. Pyke*, [2002] 2 B.C.L.C. 201 (C.A.); *Bhullar v. Bhullar*, [2003] E.W.C.A. Civ. 424 (C.A.), per Jonathan Parker L.J.; *Crown Dilmun v. Sutton*, [2004] E.W.H.C. 52 (Ch.); *Lindsley v. Woodfull*, [2004] E.W.C.A. Civ. 165 (C.A.).

[485] [1916] A.C. 554 at 568 (P.C.).

[486] See also *Irving Trust v. Deutsch*, 73 F.2d 121 at 124 (2d Cir. 1934).

[487] See, for instance, *Pacifica Shipping Co. v. Andersen*, [1986] 2 N.Z.L.R. 328 (H.C.).

[488] See, for instance, *Redekop v. Robco Construction Ltd.*, [1978] B.C.J. No. 46, 7 B.C.L.R. 268, 89 D.L.R. (3d) 507 (S.C.).

[489] See, for instance, *Jiffy People Sales (1966) Ltd. v. Eliason*, [1975] B.C.J. No. 26, 58 D.L.R. (3d) 439 (S.C.); *Cranleigh Precision Engineering Ltd. v. Bryant*, [1965] 1 W.L.R. 1293; *Slate Ventures Inc. v. Hurley*, [1997] N.J. No. 252, 37 B.L.R. (2d) 138 (C.A.).

[490] D.B. Prentise, "The Corporate Opportunity Doctrine" (1974) 37 Mod. L.R. 468; *Martin v. Columbia Metals Corp.*, [1980] O.J. No. 146, 12 B.L.R. 72 at 79 (H.C.J.), per Parker A.C.J.H.C.

sued on behalf of the corporation, and then the director or officer elects to complete the transaction for his own benefit.[491] In *Roper v. Murdoch*[492] the defendants were senior officers of a corporation, who had negotiated a contract for the production of television programs. The defendants had resigned from the corporation on the eve of its bankruptcy. Shortly thereafter, they had concluded an agreement on substantially the same terms, but this time for their own benefit. The plaintiff was the assignee of all of the bankrupt corporation's rights to proposed programs. It sued claiming that the defendants had breached their fiduciary duties to the bankrupt corporation by usurping the corporation's maturing opportunity to conclude the contract for its own account. Judgment was given for the plaintiff, it being held that the corporation's bankruptcy did not relieve the defendants of their obligations as fiduciaries.[493]

§11.169 It is worthwhile at this juncture to review four key cases in which the corporate opportunity doctrine has come into play, as these cases do much to illustrate both the scope of the doctrine and its limitations. For instance, in *Aberdeen Rlwy. Co. v. Blaikie Brothers*,[494] a company entered into a contract to purchase a large number of chairs from a partnership. At the time the contract was concluded, one of the directors of the company was also a member of the partnership. In holding that the company was not bound by the contract, the court emphasized that it was the duty of a director of a company to act in a way that best promoted the interests of the company. That duty being of a fiduciary character, no one discharging it could be allowed to enter into transactions in which a personal interest conflicted, or might conflict, with the interests of the company. Consequently, the director was precluded from entering into a contract on behalf of the company with the firm of which he was a member. Furthermore, adherence to the principle was so strict that no argument could be raised as to the fairness of a contract so entered into.

§11.170 A company has the right to the services of a director including the director's undivided loyalty. It has a right to the voice of every director and a right to insist that when a director speaks in board meetings his or her voice is not influenced by personal interest.[495] As noted above, the taint of personal interest may arise from either a direct or indirect benefit. In *Transvaal Lands Co. v. New Belgium (Transvaal) Land & Development Co.*,[496] a person who was a director of company A also owned shares in company B. At a meeting of the board of directors of company A, a proposal was put forward that shares of company B be bought for corporate purposes. The director failed to disclose his interest in

---

[491] See, for instance, *Kendall v. Webster*, [1910] B.C.J. No. 39, 14 W.L.R. 117 (C.A.).
[492] [1987] B.C.J. No. 1193, 14 B.C.L.R. (2d) 385, 39 D.L.R. (4th) 684 at 691 (S.C.), *per* Cohen J. See also *Weber Feeds Ltd. v. Weber*, [1979] O.J. No. 4247, 99 D.L.R. (3d) 176 (C.A.), *per* Houlden J.A.
[493] See also *Abbey Glen Property Corp. v. Stumborg*, [1976] A.J. No. 284, [1976] 2 W.W.R. 495, 65 D.L.R. (3d) 235 (Q.B.), aff'd [1978] A.J. No. 712, 85 D.L.R. (3d) 35.
[494] *Aberdeen Rlwy. Co. v. Blaikie Bros.*, [1843-60] All E.R. Rep. 249 (H.L.).
[495] *Benson v. Heathorn* (1842), 1 Y. & C. Ch. 326, 62 E.R. 909 (V.C.), *per* Knight Bruce V.-C.
[496] [1914] 2 Ch. 488 at 503 (C.A.), *per* Swinfen Eady L.J.

company B and proceeded to vote on the acquisition of the shares. The question before the court was whether a director of a company on behalf of the company can buy shares and other property from himself or from a company in which he has a pecuniary interest. In that case, the court held that it is immaterial as to the amount of shares or the capacity in which they are held. The mere fact that a conflict is apparent on the surface would make that transaction voidable unless the director withdrew himself from the decision-making process.

§11.171 The various principles of law set down in the decision of the House of Lords in the *Regal (Hastings) Ltd.* case[497] were considered in detail above.[498] The facts of that case are also relevant to an understanding of the corporate opportunity doctrine. In that case a group of directors attempted to acquire some property. For this purpose they formed a subsidiary company with a capital of £5,000. In order to lease the properties with a view to purchasing them, the directors had to post a guarantee with the landlord of £5,000. As there was only £2,000 available, each of the directors agreed to take a number of shares, in consideration for money in an attempt to make up the difference. Upon the sale of a property at great profit the directors were called on by the company to account for the profits made on this sale of their shares. The House of Lords held in the circumstances that the directors were in a fiduciary relationship to the company and liable therefore to repay to it the profit they had made on the sale of their shares. However, certain shares had been sold by the directors to private parties and these parties were not liable to account as they were not in a fiduciary relationship to the company.[499]

§11.172 In contrast, in *Hoffman Products Ltd. v. Karr*[500] four individuals incorporated a corporation as equal shareholders, with a view towards purchasing an existing business. Two of the four were unwilling to secure the required financing by providing personal guarantees. Since the other still wished to pursue the venture they joined with a third person to incorporate a second corporation and proceed with the purchase. Money was raised at their own risk. The plaintiff (the original corporation) brought an action for a declaration that the two held their interest in the business in trust. The action was dismissed. There was no duty to account in such a situation. In *Hoffman*, imposing a fiduciary duty to account would have conferred a windfall benefit on the two incorporators who balked at the original proposal. The proposal was not a maturing corporate opportunity, but rather an opportunity that had been abandoned despite the best efforts of the alleged fiduciaries.[501]

---

[497] [1942] 1 All E.R. 378, [1967] 2 A.C. 134 (H.L.).
[498] See §§11.156, *et seq.*
[499] *Regal (Hastings) Ltd. v. Gulliver*, [1942] 1 All E.R. 378, [1967] 2 A.C. 134 (H.L.). See also *Dominion Royalty Corp. v. Goffatt*, [1935] O.J. No. 204, [1935] O.R. 169 (C.A.), aff'd [1935] S.C.J. No. 27, [1935] S.C.R. 565.
[500] [1989] O.J. No. 2280, 70 O.R. (2d) 789 at 797 *et seq.* (H.C.J.), *per* Chadwick J., appeal quashed [1990] O.J. No. 3320, 71 O.R. (2d) 734n, leave to appeal to Div. Ct. refused [1990] O.J. No. 3321, 72 O.R. (2d) 797.
[501] See also *Mackenzie v. Craig*, [1997] A.J. No. 855, 42 B.L.R. (2d) 133 (Q.B.), aff'd [1999] A.J. No. 239, 171 D.L.R. (4th) 268 (C.A.).

(2) Exceptions to the Corporate Opportunity Doctrine

§11.173 It is not improper for the directors or officers of a corporation to seize an opportunity that has been turned down by the corporation, at least where the information on which they act is not acquired by reason only of their position in the corporation and the opportunity has been properly brought to the attention of, and legitimately rejected by, the corporation.[502] The decision to reject must be made by persons independent of the director or officer concerned, Similarly it is not improper for a director or officer to operate a business entirely collateral to that carried on by the corporation. In *Weitzen Land & Agricultural Co. v. Winter*[503] the managing director of a corporation operated a business for his own benefit, that included keeping a store on the premises of the corporation for its accommodation, and buying land in speculation as a possible town site. It was held that these operations were outside the scope of the managing director's responsibilities. This business could not properly be characterized as being conducted by him in breach of his fiduciary responsibilities. He was not in competition with the corporation, since such activities were outside the scope of the powers of the corporation. Moreover, the corporation had knowledge of what the managing director was doing.

§11.174 As the foregoing discussion makes clear, that there are limits to the corporate opportunity doctrine goes almost without saying. The principles set out in cases in which the doctrine has been applied should not be over-extended, so that they begin to apply to corporations in an entirely different context from that in which they were given. The concern in this regard is particularly clear in the case of closely held corporations, where many of the principles relating to the corporate opportunity doctrine can have only a limited application, at least where the director and the controlling shareholder are the same person. For instance, where a corporation is wholly owned by one person, there is certainly no impropriety in that person deciding to book a particular transaction through another corporation, or to take advantage of that transaction for himself, even if the possibility of that transaction first came to light through the corporation itself. Where the corporation is solvent, of course, there can be no breach of fiduciary duty because the interests of the corporation and its shareholders as a whole coincide. However, even where the corporation is insolvent, there is surely no rule which requires the shareholder (and the directors acting on their behalf) to pass by a business opportunity or to assign it to the corporation, for the reason that by so doing the profitability of the corporation may be enhanced, to the salvation of its creditors. In such a case, the interests of the corporation and those of its shareholders are clearly not the same. Even so, if limited liability is to have any meaningful role, the concept of fiduciary duty should not be employed as a mechanism for circumventing it, by requiring shareholder directors to make an investment or to divert business to the corporation, which they would otherwise not be disposed to do.

---

[502] *Martin v. Columbia Metals Corp.*, [1980] O.J. No. 146, 12 B.L.R. 72 at 79 (H.C.J.), *per* Parker A.C.J.H.C. See also *Boston Shoe Co. v. Frank* (1915), 48 Que. S.C. 66 (C.A.).

[503] (1914), 17 D.L.R. 750, 6 W.W.R. 964 at 966(Sask. T.D.), *per* Brown J.

(3) Use of Knowledge Gained During Employment

§11.175 As noted above, the law is clear that a former employee is entitled to use knowledge gained through the course of his or her employment and may as a general rule enter into competition with a former employer.[504] However, a former employee may not abscond with property belonging to the employer and use that in competition against the employer[505] — property being widely defined in this context to include such things as confidential trade secrets and other proprietary know-how, as well customer lists that the employee has memorized.[506] In *Unified Freight Services Ltd. v. Therriault*[507] Erb J. discussed the importance of confidential information to the employer corporation, noting that its:

> ... stock in trade was, and continues to be, its business information. The information itself is a business advantage and it is proprietary. Fiduciary employees who are entrusted with the control of such information have a duty extending beyond the termination of their employment to not solicit business from the customers of their former employer. This duty extends for a reasonable period of time sufficient to permit the former employer to take steps to secure the loyalty of the customers...

The distinction between the information that a former employee may use and that which is forbidden is not entirely clear. It can be argued that former employees are entitled to use generic information relating to the manner of conducting a particular business (even if that information is not generally known to persons not working for the employer), but not specific confidential information relating to their former employer's business.[508] If the subject matter of a trade secret is brought into being because of the initiative of the employee in its creation, innovation or development, even though the relationship is one of confidence, no duty arises since the employee may then have an interest in the subject matter at least equal to that of his employer or in any event, such knowledge is part of the employee's skill and experience.[509] However, each case in this regard is likely to require a unique result in order to prduce a fair balancing of interests. As one court has explained:

> An employer's trade secret may be no more than the result of the application by an employee of his own skill, knowledge and experience. But if the employee was engaged to evolve the secret, it remains the employer's trade secret for all that. The employee may not simply copy it if, by copy, one means literally. For exam-

---

[504] See, for instance, *Mercury Marine Ltd. v. Dillon*, [1986] O.J. No. 957, 30 D.L.R. (4th) 627 (H.C.J.); *Alberts v. Mountjoy*, [1977] O.J. No. 2334, 16 O.R. (2d) 682 (H.C.J.).

[505] *Tree Savers International Ltd. v. Savoy*, [1992] A.J. No. 61, 84 Alta. L.R. (2d) 384 (C.A.); as to the right of the former employer to claim restitution in such a case, see *Barnabe v. Touhey*, [1994] O.J. No. 906, 18 O.R. (3d) 370 (Gen. Div.), rev'd [1995] O.J. No. 3456, 26 O.R. (3d) 477 (C.A.), leave to appeal to S.C.C. refused [1996] S.C.C.A. No. 26.

[506] See, for instance, *Quantum Management Services Ltd. v. Hann*, [1992] O.J. No. 2393, 11 O.R. (3d) 639n (C.A.).

[507] [2006] A.J. No. 125, 14 B.L.R. (4th) 285 at para. 62 (Q.B.).

[508] See, generally, *Delrina Corp. v. Triolet Systems Inc.*, [1993] O.J. No. 319, 9 B.L.R. (2d) 140 (Gen. Div.), per O'Leary J., aff'd [2002] O.J. No. 676, 58 O.R. (3d) 339 (C.A.), leave to appeal to S.C.C. refused [2002] S.C.C.A. No. 189; *Structural Dynamics Research Corp. v. Engineering Mechanics Research Corp.*, 401 F. Supp. 1102 at 1111 (E.D. Mich. 1975).

[509] *Structural Dynamics Research Corp. v. Engineering Mechanics Research Corp.*, 401 F. Supp. 1102 at 1111 (E.D. Mich. 1975).

ple, if he has conducted a confidential market survey for his erstwhile employer to establish what demand, if any, exists in a particular area for a particular type of product, he cannot simply copy the survey and hand it over to his new employer. But *non consta* that the employee may never again set out to establish the market demand for that particular type of product in the same area. Generally speaking, he cannot be prevented from using his own skill and experience to attain a particular result, merely because it is a result which he has achieved before for a previous employer. I say, generally speaking, because one can conceive of cases where the result sought to be achieved is so elusive that only a solution of the kind which legend has prompted Archimedes to say "Eureka" will do, and the employee has been engaged specifically to find it. In such a case, it may well be that the employee who has evolved the solution may have to refrain from solving it in the same way for a future employer.[510]

A former employee is not required to "wipe clean from the slate of his memory" any recollection that he or she may have of the things which he or she learned during the course of working for the former employer. To accept the contrary view would hinder the employee's use of his or her own training, skill and experience to an unacceptable degree.[511]

§11.176 Directors, senior officers and other key employees who occupy a fiduciary position are in a somewhat different position, for the nature of their fiduciary position may give them access to information that other employees lack. Nevertheless, key personnel also may enter into competition with the corporation for which they formerly served,[512] provided that in so doing they do not breach any fiduciary duty. Such key personnel are not permitted to offer inducements or actively solicit former clients while they are in the employ of the corporation. Once they leave, however, it appears that they may compete against their former employer to the same extent as any other employee, provided that they are not trading upon customer lists or other confidential information[513] that belongs to the corporation.[514] If the director, officer or other key employee has established a loyal following among the customers of the corporation, that key employee is not prevented from capitalizing on the personal reputation that he or she has built, should those customers choose to follow him or her.

---

[510] *Northern Office Micro Computers Ltd. v. Rosenstein*, [1982] F.S.R. 124 at 138-40 (S.C. South Africa), *per* Marais J.
[511] *Ibid.*
[512] *Metropolitan Commercial Carpet Centre Ltd. v. Donovan*, [1989] N.S.J. No. 254, 91 N.S.R. (2d) 99 at 104 (T.D.), *per* Davison J.
[513] *Intertech Model Fixtures Inc. v. Rusch*, [1992] O.J. No. 2252, 8 B.L.R. (2d) 150 at 156 (Gen. Div.), *per* Macfarland J.
[514] *Anderson, Smyth & Kelly Customs Brokers Ltd. v. World Wide Customs Brokers Ltd.*, [1993] A.J. No. 614, 10 B.L.R. (2d) 155 at 167 (Alta. Q.B.), *per* Moshansky J., rev'd [1996] A.J. No. 736, 39 Alta. L.R. (3d) 411 (C.A.).

(4) Liability to Account for Profit

§11.177 The remedy provided by equity for breach of fiduciary duty was not a right to recover damages but rather a right to an accounting.[515] In *Bray v. Ford,* Lord Herschell set down the following general rule:

> It is an inflexible rule of a court of equity that a person in a fiduciary position, such as the plaintiff's, is not, unless otherwise expressly provided, entitled to make a profit; he is not allowed to put himself in a position where his interest and duty conflict. It does not appear to me that this rule is, as has been said, founded upon principles of morality. I regard it rather as based on the consideration that, human nature being what it is, there is danger, in such circumstances, of the person holding a fiduciary position being swayed by interest rather than by duty, and thus prejudicing those whom he was bound to protect. It has, therefore, been deemed expedient to lay down this positive rule. But I am satisfied that it might be departed from in many cases, without any breach of morality, without any wrong being inflicted, and without any consciousness of wrongdoing. Indeed, it is obvious that it might sometimes be to the advantage of the beneficiaries that their trustee should act for them professionally rather than a stranger, even though the trustee were paid for his services.[516]

In addition, the High Court of Australia has stated:

> ... [T]he principle of equity is that a person who is under a fiduciary duty must account to the person to whom the obligation is owed for any benefit or gain (i) which has been obtained or received in circumstances where a conflict or significant possibility of conflict existed between his fiduciary duty and his personal interest in the pursuit or possible receipt of such a benefit or gain, or (ii) which was obtained or received by use or by reason of his fiduciary position or of opportunity or knowledge resulting from it. Any such benefit or gain is held by the fiduciary as constructive trustee. ... That constructive trust arises from the fact that a personal benefit or gain has been so obtained or received and it is immaterial that there was no absence of good faith or damages to the person to whom the fiduciary duty was owed.[517]

Generally, the court will not inquire and is not in a position to ascertain whether the person to whom the fiduciary duty is owed has actually lost or not lost by reason of the breach of duty. Instead, the court will look to see whether an improper profit has been made by the fiduciary, and if so it will require the fiduciary to account for that profit.[518] It follows that like all fiduciaries, a director or officer of a corporation has a duty to account to the corporation for any profit made in breach of the director's or officer's fiduciary duties to the corporation.[519]

---

[515] See, generally, *Star-Link Entertainment Inc. v. Star Quest Entertainment Inc.*, [2003] B.C.J. No. 1637, 37 B.L.R (3d) 269 (S.C.). As to the right to recover punitive damages, see *692331 Ontario Ltd. v. Garay*, [1997] O.J. No. 3600, 36 B.L.R. (2d) 231 (Gen. Div.), aff'd [1999] O.J. No. 4008 (C.A.).

[516] [1896] A.C. 44, [1895-99] All E.R. Rep. 1009 at 1011 (H.L.).

[517] *Chan v. Zacharia* (1984), 154 C.L.R. 178 at 199 (H.C. Aust.), *per* Deane J.

[518] *Parker v. McKenna* (1874), L.R. 10 Ch. App. 96 at 118, *per* Lord Cairns L.C.

[519] *Weber Feeds Ltd. (Trustee) v. Weber*, [1979] O.J. No. 4247, 30 C.B.R. (N.S.) 97 (C.A.); *L.A. Brown Ltd. v. Brown*, [1969] N.B.J. No. 120, 1 N.B.R. (2d) 836 (C.A.), var'd [1971] S.C.J. No. 54, [1971] S.C.R. 501.

The liability to account does not depend upon proof of negligence, fraud[520] or bad faith[521] on the part of the director.

§11.178 The courts take a very dim view of any arrangement that permits a director or officer to earn a secret profit.[522] A secret profit made in breach of trust is a fraud on the corporation, and the director or officer will not be permitted to retain it because he believed that he was entitled to do so at law.[523] Furthermore, anyone who participates in the perpetuation of the fraud is similarly liable to account for the profit.[524] In *China Software Corp. v. Leimbigler*,[525] the corporate plaintiff had developed a software system for handling and converting Chinese character text. The directors who had been involved in the development of the software misled the corporation as to the lack of interest of possible customers and concerning the costs of completing the development of the software. The directors induced the plaintiff to sell the system to a college, which resold the software to a company which had an agreement with the directors. The college purchased the software only on the condition that it obtain an indemnity from the directors. A claim by the plaintiff against the college was settled, and the directors alleged that the settlement barred a claim against them for secret profits. The court held that the directors remained liable to account for the secret profits. The settlement of the claim against the college did not bar the action against the directors. The directors and the college were not engaged in a common course and the claims against the directors and the college were differently founded.

§11.179 While it is necessary to show that something has passed from the corporation that properly belongs to it or that it has not received a profit that has been earned by a person who owes it a fiduciary duty (otherwise there is nothing for which the accounting can be given),[526] it is not, however, necessary to show that

---

[520] *Crown Reserve Consolidated Mines Ltd. v. MacKay*, [1941] O.J. No. 171, [1941] O.W.N. 269 at 273 (C.A.), per Robertson C.J.O.; *Regal (Hastings) Ltd. v. Gulliver*, [1942] 1 All E.R. 378, [1967] 2 A.C. 134 (H.L.).

[521] *D'Amore v. McDonald*, [1973] O.J. No. 1860, [1973] 1 O.R. 845 (H.C.J.), aff'd [1973] O.J. No. 2176, 1 O.R. (2d) 370 (C.A.).

[522] Consider also s. 426 of the *Criminal Code*, R.S.C. 1985, c. C-46.

[523] *D'Amore v. McDonald*, [1973] O.J. No. 1860, [1973] 1 O.R. 845 (H.C.J.), aff'd [1973] O.J. No. 2176, 1 O.R. (2d) 370 (C.A.). See also *Rogers Hardware Co. v. Rogers* (1913), 10 D.L.R. 541 at 543-44 (P.E.I.S.C.), per Fitzgerald V.-C. In *Boston Deep Sea Fishing & Ice Co. v. Ansell* (1888), 39 Ch. D. 339 (C.A.) the defendant director was held liable to account to the plaintiff corporation for secret bribes or bonuses that he had received from persons contracting with the corporation. The liability flowed from the fiduciary relationship in which the defendant stood to the corporation (per Bowen L.J. at 367-68).

[524] *D'Amore v. McDonald*, [1973] O.J. No. 1860, [1973] 1 O.R. 845 (H.C.J.), aff'd [1973] O.J. No. 2176, 1 O.R. (2d) 370 (C.A.).

[525] [1989] B.C.J. No. 1138, 27 C.P.R. (3d) 215 (S.C.).

[526] *Regal (Hastings) Ltd. v. Gulliver*, [1942] 1 All E.R. 378, [1967] 2 A.C. 134 at 140 (H.L.), per Viscount Sankey; *Cavendish Bentinck v. Fenn* (1887), 12 App. Cas. 652 at 661 (H.L.), per Lord Herschell; *Re Winding-Up Act and Panama Pacific Grain Terminals Ltd.*, [1940] 4 D.L.R. 194, 21 C.B.R. 445 (Sask. K.B.); *Nova Scotia Trust Co. v. Auto Parts Co.*, [1936] 2 D.L.R. 441 (N.S.T.D.). See also *Lake Mechanical Systems Corp. v. Crandell Mechanical Systems Inc.*, [1985] B.C.J. No. 1606, 31 B.L.R. 113, 7 C.P.R. (3d) 279 (S.C.), dealing with the misappropriation of a computer program.

the corporation has actually suffered a loss. All that must be shown is whether a profit has been made by the fiduciary, without the knowledge of his (or her) principal, in the course and execution of his fiduciary duty.[527]

§11.180 The obligation to account for profit applies whether the profit was earned directly or indirectly.[528] However, the liability to account is not limited to profit *per se,* although the receipt of a profit will necessarily give rise to a duty to account. Liability also applies where corporate property has been improperly misappropriated or dissipated by reason of a conflict of interest. The claim in such a case is for the loss in value, with the result that the remedy very closely resembles a claim for damages (§11.801.1) The no conflict of interest rule inherent in fiduciary duty ceases to apply once a director resigns office, but the no profit rule is more flexible.[529] A resignation of convenience to take advantage of a corporate opportunity is no defence to a claim for misappropriating a corporate opportunity, and from this it may be argued is no defence where the resignation occurred solely to facilitate the receipt of a profit.[530] The obligation of the fiduciary is to account for improper administration in the discharge of the trust. So, as noted above, the fiduciary must make good a loss suffered by the corporation by reason of a breach of fiduciary duty owed to it,[531] whether or not the fiduciary enjoyed a profit. Moreover, the duty to account extends to all property,[532] undertakings, rights,[533] money[534] and things acquired as a result of the breach of fiduciary duty.[535] In an appropriate case, interest may be awarded.[536] Whenever it can be shown that the fiduciary has so arranged matters as to obtain an advantage whether in money or money's worth to himself or herself personally through the execution of the trust, the fiduciary will not be permitted to retain, but will be compelled to pay it over to the beneficiary. However, the amount recoverable by

---

[527] *Parker v. McKenna* (1874), L.R. 10 Ch. App. 96 at 118, *per* Lord Cairns L.C. and at 124-25 *per* James L.J.

[528] *Regal (Hastings) Ltd. v. Gulliver,* [1942] 1 All E.R. 378, [1967] 2 A.C. 134 at 153 (H.L.), *per* Lord Macmillan.

[529] *Quarter Master UK Ltd. v. Pyke,* [2005] 1 B.C.L.C. 245 (Ch.), *per* Paul Morgan Q.C.

[530] *CMS Dolphin Ltd. v. Simonet,* [2001] 2 B.C.L.C. 704 at para. 96 (Ch.), *per* Lawrence Collins J.:

> In my judgment the underlying basis of the liability of a director who exploits after his resignation a maturing business opportunity of the company is that the opportunity is to be treated as if it were property of the company in relation to which the director had fiduciary duties. By seeking to exploit the opportunity after resignation he is appropriating for himself that property. He is just as accountable as a trustee who retires without properly accounting for trust property. In the case of the director he becomes a constructive trustee of the fruits of his abuse of the company's property, which he has acquired in circumstances where he knowingly had a conflict of interest, and exploited it by resigning from the company.

[531] Subject, of course, to the business judgment rule.

[532] *Commonwealth Savings Plan Ltd. (Trustee of) v. Commonwealth Trust (Bahamas) Ltd. (Trustee of),* [1977] A.J. No. 197, 26 C.B.R. (N.S.) 44 *sub nom. Sigurdson v. Langridge* (T.D.).

[533] See, generally, *Zwicker v. Stanbury,* [1953] S.C.J. No. 54, [1953] 2 S.C.R. 438 (*sub nom. Zwicker v. Stanbury*).

[534] See, for instance, *Miller v. Diamond Light & Heating Co.* (1913), 22 Que. K.B. 411 (C.A.).

[535] *Kremlin Canada Inc. v. Turner,* [1990] O.J. No. 268 (C.A.), leave to appeal to S.C.C. refused [1990] S.C.C.A. No. 218, 44 O.A.C. 80n.

[536] *Bottoms v. Brent Petroleum Industries Ltd.,* [1984] B.C.J. No. 1151, 17 E.T.R. 48 (S.C.).

the corporation is ordinarily the net profit improperly earned, after deduction of expenses, rather than the fiduciary's gross receipts.[537]

§11.181 In *Fern Brand Waxes Ltd. v. Pearl*,[538] a director of a corporation made unauthorized loans from the company to two companies under his control. They then subscribed for shares of the creditor company and purported to use part of the proceeds of the loan to pay for the shares. The creditor company issued a call on the shares, and on the debtor company failing to pay, it forfeited its shares. The Court of Appeal held that the shares were properly forfeited, saying that a director should not be allowed to profit from the breach of his fiduciary duty by setting up the separate identities for himself and his companies as a shield. For as long as the unauthorized loans existed, any payment by the debtor corporations purporting to be payment for the shares should be applied to reduce the amount of the loans. Thus the shares were properly forfeited as in effect the shares had not been paid for. Similarly, in *Baniuk v. Carpenter*[539] an officer caused his employer corporation to make a heavy investment in the preferred shares of another corporation. The officer acquired all of the common shares of the other corporation for $1. The court ordered the redemption of the preferred shares and gave a declaration that title to the common shares should be transferred from the officer to the corporation. The officer was not allowed to take advantage of his position to make a personal gain at the expense of the corporation.

§11.182 In determining whether or not a director has committed a breach of fiduciary duty, there is no general rule to be applied. Each case will turn on its own facts.[540] However, the courts are particularly concerned with schemes and dealings that would provide an opportunity to those acting in bad faith to misappropriate property, or defraud the corporation, its shareholders or creditors. For instance, it has been held that where on the eve of bankruptcy a corporation disposes of an asset so that a director acquires a right, the director must account to the trustee in bankruptcy of the company for any profit realized from the disposal of that right, for the simple reason that to hold otherwise would open the door to fraud. The question of whether the corporation could actually have derived some benefit from the transaction is immaterial.[541]

§11.183 Where the company has suffered a loss, but the director has not earned a personal profit as a result of the breach of fiduciary duty, the liability of the directors is limited to the loss that the corporation has suffered; it is not the ob-

---

[537] See, generally, *Abbey Glen Property Corp. (Genstar Corp.) v. Stumborg*, [1981] A.J. No. 877, 37 A.R. 212 (Q.B.); see also *Abbey Glen Property Corp. v. Stumborg*, [1975] A.J. No. 284, [1976] 2 W.W.R. 1 (T.D.), aff'd [1978] A.J. No. 712, [1978] 4 W.W.R. 28 (C.A.); see also *Brown v. L.A. Brown Ltd. (Trustee of)*, [1971] S.C.J. No. 54, [1971] S.C.R. 501 (sub nom. *Brown v. Gentleman*).
[538] [1972] O.J. No. 714, [1972] 3 O.R. 829 (C.A.).
[539] [1988] N.B.J. No. 826, 90 N.B.R. (2d) 1, rev'd in part [1989] N.B.J. No. 519, 104 N.B.R. (2d) 196 (C.A.), additional reasons at 209.
[540] *Canadian Aero Services Ltd. v. O'Malley*, [1973] S.C.J. No. 97, [1974] S.C.R. 592.
[541] *Weber Feeds Ltd. v. Weber*, [1979] O.J. No. 4247, 30 C.B.R. (N.S.) 97 at 101 (C.A.), per Houlden J.A.

ject of equity to inflict punishment. The liability to account in such a case is for the property under the fiduciary's administration, and that property being impaired by reason of a breach of fiduciary duty, the fiduciary must make good the impairment in question.

(5) The Rule in Keech v. Sandford

§11.184 In *Keech v. Sandford*[542] a trustee found that it was impossible to obtain the renewal of a lease for the benefit of an infant beneficiary. Since the property was valuable, he took the lease for his own benefit. It was held by Lord King L.C. that although the trustee was unable to renew the lease for the infant, he was nevertheless bound to hold it for the infant's benefit, since he had secured the lease himself. The Lord Chancellor noted that the adoption of any other rule would undermine the integrity of the trust system, since beneficiaries could far too easily be victimized. In a similar vein, a director was found liable to account where he attempted to negotiate a contract on behalf of his corporation with a third party, and when unable to do so concluded a separate agreement which was beneficial to himself.[543]

§11.185 A director or officer cannot escape the liability to account for his own personal profit by showing that the transaction has worked to the benefit of the corporation.[544] Nor, under the rule in *Keech v. Sandford*[545] (and the subsequent cases which have followed it),[546] is it any defence to show that the corporation was in no position to avoid the loss occasioned by the breach.[547] In general, it is a director's duty to secure the contract or other opportunity for the corporation's benefit,[548] rather than to accept the other party's refusal to deal with feigned remorse and then appropriate that opportunity for his or her own benefit.

§11.186 In *Re Iron Clay Brick Mfg. Co.*[549] the defendant director purchased property of the corporation at a mortgage sale, and subsequently sold the property at a substantial profit. There was no suggestion of any misconduct on his part. Nevertheless, it was held that the defendant was required to account for the profit that he had made. Clearly in certain cases, the strictness of the duty to account may result in a windfall to the corporation.[550] That likelihood is accepted by the courts, and is viewed as an acceptable cost, in order to discourage impropriety on the part of fiduciaries.[551]

---

[542] (1726), Sel. Cas. Ch. 61 at 62, 2 Eq. Cas. Abr. 741, 25 E.R. 223 (L.C.), *per* Lord King L.C.
[543] *Abbey Glen Property Corp. v. Stumborg*, [1976] 2 W.W.R. 495 (Alta. T.D.).
[544] *Madden v. Dimond*, [1906] B.C.J. No. 14, 12 B.C.R. 80 at 87, *per* Martin J.
[545] (1726), Sel. Cas. Ch. 61, 2 Eq. Cas. Abr. 741, 25 E.R. 223 (L.C.).
[546] Discussed below at §8.226 *et seq*. See also *Abbey Glen Property Corp. v. Stumborg*, [1976] 2 W.W.R. 495 (Alta. T.D.).
[547] *B.C. Timber Industry Journal Ltd. v. Black*, [1934] B.C.J. No. 69, [1934] 2 W.W.R. 161 (C.A.).
[548] See *Natural Sodium Products Ltd. v. Holland*, [1946] 1 W.W.R. 605 (Sask. K.B.).
[549] [1889] O.J. No. 131, 19 O.R. 113 at 123 (H.C.), *per* Robertson J.
[550] *China Software Corp. v. Leimbigler*, [1989] B.C.J. No. 1138, 27 C.P.R. (3d) 215 at 232 (S.C.), *per* Callaghan J.
[551] *Lavigne v. Robern*, [1984] O.J. No. 3443, 6 C.P.R. (3d) 54 at 57 (C.A.), *per* MacKinnon A.C.J.O.

§11.187 The decision of Laskin J. in *Canadian Aero Services Ltd. v. O'Malley*[552] is unquestionably one of the pivotal decisions in Canadian law with respect to the duty of a fiduciary to account for profits. In that case, the court dealt with a situation where two senior officers of the corporation had negotiated a proposed contract with a customer of the corporation. Before the contract was signed, they left the employ of the corporation and then proceeded to conclude a contract for their own benefit with the same customer on substantially the same terms. Laskin J. held that the seizure of this maturing business opportunity amounted to a breach of fiduciary duty.[553] He went on to hold that the obligation of a fiduciary to account was both far-reaching and strictly enforced, and cannot be avoided by a resignation of convenience.[554] It is no defence to show that the business opportunity seized might not have truly been available to the corporation:

> The reaping of a profit by a person at a company's expense while a director thereof is, of course, an adequate ground upon which to hold the director accountable. Yet there may be situations where a profit must be disgorged, although not gained at the expense of the company, on the ground that a director must not be allowed to use his position as such to make a profit even if it was not open to the company, as for example, by reason of legal disability, to participate in the transaction.[555]

This last aspect of Laskin J.'s decision is of some significance, because it shows that the true basis of the fiduciary's liability is not that the fiduciary has seized a corporate opportunity or a maturing business prospect (for if the transaction is not available to the corporation, it cannot be said to have matured, or to be a corporate opportunity), but rather because the fiduciary has permitted self-interest to conflict with the duties that are owed to the corporation.

§11.188 A similar result was reached in the English case of *Industrial Development Consultants Ltd. v. Cooley*.[556] The relevant facts in that case were that the defendant was the managing director of the plaintiff corporation, and had entered into a series of negotiations on behalf of the corporation, in an effort to conclude a contract with a potential customer. Unfortunately, the other party disliked the set-up of the corporation, and was not inclined to deal with the plaintiff. They were, however, interested in working with the defendant. The defendant procured permission to resign his position as managing director by claiming ill health. He then obtained the contract for himself. It is quite clear from the decision that the court felt there was something about the case (particularly the feigned illness) which did not smell right. Still, it was prepared to accept as fact that the contract was not one which was truly available to the corporation. It did not matter. Roskill J. went on to hold that the defendant was still liable to account.[557]

---

[552] [1973] S.C.J. No. 97, [1974] S.C.R. 592, 40 D.L.R. (3d) 371.
[553] *Ibid.*, at 382 (D.L.R.).
[554] *Ibid.*
[555] *Ibid.*, at 383-84 (D.L.R.).
[556] [1972] 2 All E.R. 162 (Ch.).
[557] *Ibid.*, at 175.

§11.189 The difficulty is to reconcile all this case law with the decision of the Supreme Court of Canada in *Peso Silver Mines Ltd. (N.P.L.) v. Cropper*.[558] In this case a prospector approached the board of directors of Peso Silver Mines with an opportunity for gain regarding certain mining claims. On consideration of all of the factors and relevant information, and in the light of strained finances, the board of directors rejected the opportunity. Afterwards, the refused offer was taken up by one of the directors of the plaintiff company, through which he enjoyed considerable financial gain. The plaintiff asked for an accounting from the director for the profits earned. The court held that the rejection by the directors of the plaintiff company of the mining claims, because of the strained finances of the company, was done in good faith and that any subsequent taking up of this opportunity by a member of the board of directors after rejection by the company, was quite proper. More specifically, Cartwright J. held that where a board of directors of a corporation considers a new venture which is offered to the corporation by outsiders, and genuinely comes to the conclusion that it is not an investment that the corporation ought to make, then individual directors may then contact the outsider and put up their own money for the venture, without being in breach of their fiduciary duties, and therefore without liability to account for any profits that they make, even though the new venture is closely related to a venture in which the corporation is already engaged.

§11.190 Although the decisions in *Canadian Aero Services Ltd. v. O'Mally*,[559] and *Peso Silver Mines Ltd. v. Cropper*,[560] appear irreconcilable, Laskin J. believed that the two could stand together. He stated:

> There is a considerable gulf between the *Peso* case and the present one on the facts as found in each, and on the issues they respectively raise. In *Peso*, there was a finding of good faith in the rejection by its directors of an offer of mining claims because of its strained finances. The subsequent acquisition of those claims by the managing director and his associates, albeit without seeking shareholder approval, was held to be proper because the company's interest in them had ceased.
>
> .....
>
> I am not to be taken as laying down any rule of liability to be read as if it were a statute. The general standards of loyalty, good faith and avoidance of a conflict of duty and self-interest to which the conduct of a director or senior officer must conform, must be tested in each case by many factors which it would be reckless to attempt to enumerate exhaustively. Among them are the factor of position or office held, the nature of the corporate opportunity, its ripeness, its specificness and the director's or managerial officer's relation to it, the amount of knowledge possessed, the circumstances in which it was obtained and whether it was special or, indeed, even private, the factor of time and the continuation of fiduciary duty where the alleged breach occurs after termination of the relationship with the com-

---

[558] [1966] S.C.J. No. 47, 58 D.L.R. (2d) 1; see also *Island Export Finance Ltd. v. Umunna*, [1986] B.C.L.C. 460, per Hutchinson J.; *Balston Ltd. v. Headline Filters Ltd.*, [1990] F.S.R. 385, per Falconer J.
[559] [1974] S.C.J. No. 97, [1974] S.C.R. 592.
[560] [1966] S.C.J. No. 47, [1966] S.C.R. 673.

pany, and the circumstances under which the relationship was terminated, that is whether by retirement or resignation or discharge.[561]

The *Peso* decision also appears to be inconsistent with the authorities on which it was based,[562] and if indeed it may still be regarded as good law, it can only be so regarded if confined to a relatively narrow type of situation. More specifically, in order to escape liability under the *Peso* decision, a director must show that he or she:

- did everything that was reasonably possible to convince the corporation to accept the offer, including bringing any relevant facts within his or her possession to the attention of the board at the time when the offer was considered, and taking all steps necessary to ensure that all such facts were brought to light;

- opposed the decision to turn down the contract, and that decision was made over his objection; and

- was not in a position to control the outcome of the vote on the offer.

§11.191 Leaving aside the *Peso Silver Mines* decision, it is clear that the duty to account is a powerful remedy in the hands of corporations. The obligation to account should be considered by directors (and officers) whenever they deal with corporate property, or seek to capitalize on a hot tip or other information that has come to them by virtue of their connection with the corporation. The right to insist on an accounting by the director or officer gives the corporation a choice of remedies. Depending in large measure upon which option is more advantageous to the corporation, it may rescind the contract,[563] or alternatively, it may elect to affirm the contract and demand that the director or officer account for the profit that has been made.[564] The practical effect of the duty to account can be far-reaching. For instance, as a general rule, except as authorized by a corporation's articles, by-laws or by the governing legislation, the board of directors of a corporation cannot make a binding contract with any other corporation in which a member of the quorum of the board of directors is interested, and if the second corporation has notice of the irregularity, the first corporation may obtain rescission of the transaction, even after its completion, provided it is possible to restore the parties to their original transaction.[565] Fortunately, as will be

---

[561] [1974] S.C.J. No. 97, [1974] S.C.R. 592 at 618-20.

[562] See, for instance, *Zwicker v. Turnbull Estate*, [1953] S.C.J. No. 54, [1954] 1 D.L.R. 257 at 259 (*sub nom. Zwicker v. Stanbury*), per Kellock J.; but compare *Queensland Mines Ltd. v. Hudson* (1978), 52 A.L.R. 399 (P.C.); *Joint Receivers & Managers of Niltan Carson Ltd. v. Hawthorne* (1987), 3 B.C.C. 455.

[563] *Roxborough Gardens of Hamilton Ltd. v. Davis*, [1920] O.J. No. 99, 46 O.L.R. 615 (C.A.).

[564] *Ruethel Mining Co. v. Thorpe*, [1907] O.J. No. 432, 9 O.W.R. 942 at 968-69 (H.C.J.), per Anglin J., aff'd [1907] O.J. No. 518, 10 O.W.R. 222 (Div. Ct.). Any contract made in contravention of the director's fiduciary duty is not void but only voidable and consequently the corporation must not delay unreasonably in moving to set it aside, and the right to do so will be lost once innocent third parties acquire rights under it. Thus no claim may be made against an innocent third party purchaser for value who acquires an interest in the property through the directors: *Bigley v. Haffey*, [1941] O.J. No. 170, [1941] O.W.N. 261 at 264 (C.A.), per Gillanders J.A.

[565] *Roxborough Gardens of Hamilton Ltd. v. Davis*, [1920] O.J. No. 99, 46 O.L.R. 615 (C.A.).

discussed below, both the OBCA and the CBCA set out procedures for concluding binding contracts in such circumstances.

(x) Director Fiduciary Duty and the Individual Shareholder

§11.192 Directors owe their fiduciary duties to the corporation itself,[566] and as a general rule[567] neither the shareholders[568] nor the creditors[569] of a corporation are beneficiaries of the fiduciary relationship,[570] nor may they enforce those duties[571] other than by way of the derivative action procedure. For instance, in *Western Finance Co. v. Tasker Enterprises Ltd.*,[572] a director of a corporation agreed to buy heavy equipment himself and lease it to the corporation to assist it through difficult financial times. The company failed. A finance company which was creditor of the company and a creditor of the finance company, brought an action against the director claiming an account. The court held that there was no breach of fiduciary duty in the circumstances, but that even if there was, the action should be dismissed as the director owed a duty to account only to his company.[573]

---

[566] *Percival v. Wright*, [1902] 2 Ch. 421. In that case, Swinfen Eady J. held that the directors of a corporation are not trustees for individual shareholders, and consequently may purchase their shares without disclosing pending negotiations for the sale of the corporation's undertaking. While this case still stands as authority for the general proposition that the duty of the directors is owed to the corporation, the effect of the ruling has been substantially modified by the statutory provisions relating to insider trading. See *Securities Act*, R.S.O. 1990, c. S.5, Part XXI; Ontario Securities Commission Form 55-102 F6; CBCA, Part XI; OBCA, s. 138, particularly subsection (5):

> 138.(5) An insider who, in connection with a transaction in a security of the corporation or any of its affiliates, makes use of any specific confidential information for the insider's own benefit or advantage that, if generally known, might reasonably be expected to affect materially the value of the security,
>
> > (a) is liable to compensate any person for any direct loss suffered by that person as a result of the transaction, unless the information was known or in the exercise of reasonable diligence should have been known to that person; and
> >
> > (b) is accountable to the corporation for any direct benefit or advantage received or receivable by the insider as a result of the transaction.

[567] For cases dealing with these limited exceptions, see for instance: *Dusik v. Newton*, [1985] B.C.J. No. 18, 62 B.C.L.R. 1 (C.A.); *Coleman v. Myers*, [1977] 2 N.Z.L.R. 225 (C.A.); *Edelweiss Credit Union v. Cobbett*, [1992] B.C.J. No. 1352, 68 B.C.L.R. (2d) 273 at 280 (C.A.).

[568] *Clarkson v. Davies*, [1923] A.C. 100 (P.C.); *Brant Investments Ltd. v. KeepRite Inc.*, [1991] O.J. No. 683, 1 B.L.R. (2d) 225 at 244 (C.A.).

[569] *Western Finance Co. v. Tasker Enterprises Ltd.*, [1979] M.J. No. 86, [1980] 1 W.W.R. 323, 106 D.L.R. (3d) 81 (C.A.). See also *Royal Bank of Canada v. First Pioneer Investments Ltd.*, [1979] O.J. No. 4501, 27 O.R. (2d) 352 at 354 (H.C.J.), per Parker A.C.J.H.C., aff'd [1981] O.J. No. 3242, 32 O.R. (2d) 121, rev'd on other grounds [1984] S.C.J. No. 34, [1984] 2 S.C.R. 125.

[570] *Pelling v. Pelling*, [1981] B.C.J. No. 1945, 130 D.L.R. (3d) 761 at 762 (sub nom. *Roberts v. Pelling*) (S.C.), per Berger J.

[571] This principle being a derivative of the rule in *Foss v. Harbottle* (1843), 2 Hare 461, 67 E.R. 189. See *Lee v. Chou Wen Hsien*, [1984] 1 W.L.R. 1202 at 1207 (P.C.), per Lord Brightman.

[572] *Western Finance Co. v. Tasker Enterprises Ltd.*, [1979] M.J. No. 86, [1980] 1 W.W.R. 323 (C.A.).

[573] Compare, however: *Winkworth v. Edward Baron Development Co.*, [1987] 1 All E.R. 114 at 188 (H.L.), per Lord Templeman; see also, generally, *Multinational Gas & Petrochemical Co. v. Multinational Gas & Petrochemical Services Ltd.*, [1983] Ch. 258 (C.A.), per Dillon L.J.

§11.193 Far from owing a general fiduciary duty to individual shareholders or creditors, on the contrary, it has often been recognized in the case law that the duty to act in the best interests of the corporation may necessitate a deliberate act against a particular shareholder — possibly even the holder of the largest single block of shares, including the shareholder who secured the election or appointment of the majority of the directors of the corporation. For instance, in *Olson v. Phoenix Industrial Supply Ltd.*,[574] the board of directors of a company in financial trouble issued a number of shares to divest the major shareholder of his control. The former majority shareholder sued for a declaration that the issuance of the shares was invalid. On appeal the court held that the test was whether in issuing the shares the directors honestly believed that they were acting in the best interest of the company and whether there were reasonable grounds for that belief. The company was insolvent, its shares were worthless and its survival was dependent on the removal of control from its majority shareholder. In issuing the shares, the directors exercised their powers believing in good faith that they were acting in the best interests of the company.[575]

§11.194 Although the directors owe no general duty to individual shareholders of a corporation,[576] such a duty may exist in the circumstances of a particular case.[577] Stated another way, the mere status of corporate director imposes no fiduciary duty upon the directors with respect to the individual shareholders of the corporation, but such duties may arise with respect to a specific individual shareholder independently of the director-corporate relationship, because of circumstances of the dealing between the director and the shareholder concerned. A finding of the existence of such a special fiduciary duty typically involves a question of mixed fact and law: the application of the well recognized legal classification of a fiduciary relation to the specific facts of a given relationship.[578] These exceptions to the general rule seem to be limited to situations involving a family or other close special relationship of trust and dependency between the claimant and the defendant director, in which the director was seeking to take advantage of that relationship for personal gain or profit.[579] The standard of conduct required from a director in relation to dealings with a shareholder will differ depending upon all the surrounding circumstances and the nature of the responsibility which in a real and practical sense the director has assumed towards the shareholder. In the one case there may be a need to provide an explicit warning and a great deal of information concerning the proposed transaction. In

---

[574] *Olson v. Phoenix Industrial Supply Ltd.*, [1984] M.J. No. 113, [1984] 4 W.W.R. 498 (C.A.), per Philp J.A., leave to appeal to S.C.C. refused [1984] S.C.C.A. No. 21; see also *Mills v. Mills* (1938), 60 C.L.R. 150, 11 A.L.J. 527 (H.C. Aust.). But compare *Punt v. Symons*, [1903] 2 Ch. 506 at 515, per Byrne J.; *Fraser v. Whalley* (1864), 2 H. & M. 10, 71 E.R. 361 (V.-C.); *Smith v. Hanson Tire & Supply Co.*, [1927] 3 D.L.R. 786, [1927] 2 W.W.R. 529 (Sask. C.A.).
[575] *Ibid.*, at 503 (W.W.R.).
[576] *Percival v. Wright*, [1902] 2 Ch. 421 at 426, per Swinfen Eady J.
[577] *Coleman v. Myers*, [1977] 2 N.Z.L.R. 225 (C.A.).
[578] *Waxman v. Waxman*, [2004] O.J. No. 1765, 44 B.L.R. (3d) 165 at 313 (C.A.), per curiam, leave to appeal to S.C.C. refused [2004] S.C.C.A. No. 291.
[579] *Malcolm v. Transtec Holdings Ltd.*, [2001] B.C.J. No. 413, 12 B.L.R. (3d) 66 at 71 (C.A.), per McEachern C.J.B.C.

another there may be no need to speak at all. There may be intermediate situations.[580] For instance, the director will owe a fiduciary duty to a shareholder where the director acts as the agent of the shareholder,[581] where the director buys shares from the shareholder,[582] and where the director has been dishonest with or misled a minority shareholder.[583] Arguably, the unique facts of a given transaction may give rise to a fiduciary duty in favour of other stakeholders as well, or to a general class of shareholders. However, the specific facts giving rise to a fiduciary duty in favour of an individual shareholder or class of shareholders (or other stakeholders) must be specifically alleged in the pleadings.[584]

§11.195 The possibility that a director may owe a fiduciary duty to an individual shareholder of a corporation in particular circumstances reflects the fact that a fiduciary duty arises on the basis of the actual and unique relationship that exists between the parties in each particular case. Even in two similar but not identical cases where fiduciary duties are seen to exist, the scope of the fiduciary duty and the obligations that flow from it in each case are determined by reference to the facts of each case (using prior decisions as a guide as to what is fair), so as to achieve a just result between the parties on the facts of each case.[585] The fiduciary concept is a flexible one, that varies to meet the circumstances of each situation. Thus a relationship may properly be described as "fiduciary" for some purposes, but not for others.[586] This flexibility applies not only in the director/shareholder context, but also in terms of deciding whether individual employees or officers of a corporation may be said to stand in a fiduciary position relative to the corporation, and if so, in determining the extent of their obligations as such.

§11.196 Unfortunately, the very flexibility of the fiduciary concept is a mixed blessing. Slight differences between cases can lead to different results, and consequently the courts have had some difficulty in identifying the circumstances in which a fiduciary duty should be imposed. Counsel arguing in favour of imposing a fiduciary duty upon a particular defendant invariably refer to the judgment of Arnup J.A. in *Laskin v. Bache & Co.*:

> ... [T]he category of cases in which fiduciary duties and obligations arise from the circumstances of the case and the relationship of the parties is no more "closed" than the categories of negligence at common law.[587]

---

[580] *Cokeman v. Myers*, [1977] 2 N.Z.L.R. 225 at 325, *per* Woodhouse J.
[581] *Allen v. Hyatt* (1914), 17 D.L.R. 7 (P.C.).
[582] *Bell v. Source Data Control Ltd.*, [1988] O.J. No. 1424, 66 O.R. (2d) 78 (C.A.) — unless the proposed sale originated with the shareholder and it is clear that the shareholder is not relying upon the guidance of the director either in deciding whether to sell or in fixing the price at which he is prepared to sell.
[583] *Vladi Private Islands Ltd. v. Haase*, [1990] N.S.J. No. 104, 96 N.S.R. (2d) 323, 253 A.P.R. 323 at 326 (C.A.), *per* Macdonald J.A.
[584] *Deep v. M.D. Management*, [2004] O.J. No. 5897, 3 B.L.R. (4th) 33 (S.C.J.), var'd [2006] O.J. No. 221 (Div. Ct.).
[585] *Canson Enterprises Ltd. v. Boughton & Co.*, [1991] S.C.J. No. 91, [1991] 3 S.C.R. 534, *per* La Forest J.
[586] *McInerney v. MacDonald*, [1992] S.C.J. No. 57, [1992] 2 S.C.R. 138 at 149, *per* La Forest J.
[587] [1972] O.J. No. 1804, [1972] 1 O.R. 465, 23 D.L.R. (3d) 385 at 392 (C.A).

However, while the categories of fiduciary duty may not be closed,[588] neither are they boundless. The courts will impose fiduciary duties only in situations where one person stands in a particular position of trust, either by virtue of an agreement or as a result of the circumstances and the relationship of the parties.[589] One necessary condition for the imposition of a duty has sometimes been said to be that "one party is at the mercy of the other's discretion" — although this may not include all possible grounds for imposing such liability.[590] In *Frame v. Smith*, Wilson J. observed:

> Relationships in which a fiduciary obligation has been imposed seem to possess three general characteristics:
>
> (1) The fiduciary has scope for the exercise of some discretion or power.
>
> (2) The fiduciary can unilaterally exercise that power or discretion so as to affect the beneficiary's legal or practical interests;
>
> (3) The beneficiary is peculiarly vulnerable to or at the mercy of the fiduciary holding the discretion or power.[591]

In *International Corona Resources Ltd. v. LAC Minerals Ltd.* La Forest J. expanded upon this observation:

> There the issue was whether a certain class of relationship, custodial and non-custodial parents, was a category, analogous to directors and corporations, solicitors and clients, trustees and beneficiaries, and agents and principals, the existence of which relationship would give rise to fiduciary obligations. The focus is on the identification of relationships in which, because of their inherent purpose or their presumed factual or legal incidents, the courts will impose a fiduciary obligation on one party to act or refrain from acting in a certain way. The obligation imposed may vary in its specific substance depending upon the relationship, though compendiously it can be described as the fiduciary duty of loyalty and will most often include the avoidance of a conflict of duty and interest and a duty not to profit at the expense of the beneficiary.[592]

§11.197 Even where A can be shown to be in a fiduciary relationship to B, it does not necessarily follow that A will be liable to B for some form of dealing that would be prohibited in the context of some other type of fiduciary relationship. The specific obligations that flow from fiduciary duty vary from one context to another. It is only in relation to breaches of the specific obligations imposed in the context of a particular relationship that a claim for breach of fiduciary duty can be founded. The duties applicable in a particular case are not determined by analogy to the duties that exist in other types of fiduciary relationship, but rather depend upon the factual context in which the relationship

---

[588] The concept was, for instance, recently invoked in a claim for compensation for incest committed by a parent against a child: *M. (K.) v. M. (H.)*, [1992] S.C.J. No. 85, 142 N.R. 321.
[589] *Brant Investments Ltd. v. KeepRite Inc.*, [1991] O.J. No. 683, 1 B.L.R. (2d) 225 at 244 (C.A.).
[590] *Guerin v. Canada*, [1984] S.C.J. No. 45, [1984] 2 S.C.R. 335 at 384, *per* Dickson J., quoting E. Weinrib, "The Fiduciary Obligation" (1975) 25 U.T.L.J. 1 at 7.
[591] [1987] S.C.J. No. 49, [1987] 2 S.C.R. 99 at 136.
[592] [1989] S.C.J. No. 83, [1989] 2 S.C.R. 574 at 646-47.

exists.[593] The question in every case is whether it is necessary to impose a particular obligation in order to give effect to the trust or confidence that has been reposed in, or the discretion that has been conferred upon, the fiduciary. To answer that question, one refers to Wilson J.'s criteria of the scope of the fiduciary's discretion or power, the controls that exist upon its exercise and the vulnerability of the beneficiary to abuse.

§11.198 It may fairly be said that fiduciary duties are not lightly imposed in commercial transactions. They will only be recognized where there is a clear and overriding justification for so doing. One argument against imposing broad fiduciary duties on directors in favour of individual shareholders is that such a duty might conflict with the unquestionable duty of the director to the corporation.[594] The fiduciary concept is not necessary where there are adequate alternative mechanisms to protect the beneficiary of the alleged duty. On this basis, McKinlay J.A. held that the availability of protection under the shareholder oppression remedy makes it unnecessary to resort to the equitable concept of breach of fiduciary duty in order to protect minority shareholders.[595]

(xi) Duty to Inform

§11.199 The fiduciary responsibilities of the directors of a corporation extend to their communications with the shareholders about the corporation's affairs. When shareholder action is requested, directors must provide shareholders with all information that is material to the action being requested and provide a balanced, truthful account of all matters disclosed in the communication with shareholders. The directors must disclose all material facts that under all the circumstances a reasonable person would assume would have actual significance in the deliberations of the reasonable shareholder.[596] An omitted fact is material if there is a substantial likelihood that a reasonable shareholder would consider it important in deciding how to vote. A plaintiff claiming on grounds of material omission must demonstrate a substantial likelihood that, under all the circumstances, the omitted fact would have assumed actual significance in the deliberations of the reasonable stockholder. There must be a substantial likelihood that the disclosure of the omitted fact would have been viewed by the reasonable stockholder as having significantly altered the "total mix" of information made available.[597] From time to time, the duty of disclosure may extend to include information relating to the directors' own errors, omissions or other breaches of

---

[593] *M. (K.) v. M. (H.)*, [1992] S.C.J. No. 85, 142 N.R. 321 at 387 (S.C.C.), *per* La Forest J.
[594] *Brant Investments Ltd. v. KeepRite Inc.*, [1991] O.J. No. 683, 1 B.L.R. (2d) 225 at 244 (C.A.), *per* McKinlay J.A.
[595] *Ibid.*, at 244-45.
[596] See, generally, on this point: *McMullin v. Beran*, 765 A.2d 910 (Del. S.C. 2000); *Malone v. Brincat*, 722 A.2d 5 at 10 (Del. S.C. 1998); *Emerald Partners v. Berlin*, 726 A.2d 1215 at 1223 (Del. S.C. 1999); *Skeen v. Jo-Ann Stores, Inc.*, 750 A.2d 1170 at 1171 (Del. S.C. 2000); *Arnold v. Society for Sav. Bancorp*, 650 A.2d 1270 (Del. S.C. 1994).
[597] See, generally, *Stroud v. Grace*, 606 A.2d 75 at 84 (Del. S.C. 1992); *Arnold v. Society for Savs. Bancorp, Inc.*, 650 A.2d 1270 at 1277 (Del. S.C. 1994); *Rosenblatt v. Getty Oil Co.*, 493 A.2d 929 at 944 (Del. S.C. 1985).

duty. In such a case, the directors' duty of disclosure does not oblige them to characterize their own conduct in such a way as to admit wrongdoing. A board is not required to engage in self-flagellation, nor is it required to draw legal conclusions implicating itself in a breach of fiduciary duty from surrounding facts and circumstances prior to a formal adjudication of the matter.[598]

(xii) Restraining Freedom of Action (Fettering Discretion)

§11.200 In carrying out their duty to manage, the directors of a corporation possess broad discretionary powers. Like most functionaries who possess discretion, directors are obliged to exercise that discretion actively; they must come to a decision on the matters that are placed before them. In doing so, the directors may not fetter their discretion in advance,[599] nor may they act on the directions of an outsider as if they were mere puppets.[600] In other words, because the directors have a statutory obligation to manage or supervise the management of their corporation, they must not contract in such a way as to prevent themselves from carrying out the duties that they owe to the corporation. As Lord Denning M.R. said:

> ... [N]o one who has duties of a fiduciary nature to discharge can be allowed to enter into an engagement by which he binds himself to disregard those duties or act inconsistently with them. No stipulation is lawful by which he agrees to carry out his duties in accordance with the instructions of another rather than on his own conscientious judgment; or by which he agrees to subordinate the interests of those whom he must protect to the interests of someone else.[601]

Despite this general statement of principle, it is important to note that the directors may quite properly cause, or permit, the corporation to enter into contracts restraining the manner in which the business or affairs of the corporation are conducted. Indeed, virtually every contract that the corporation will form will to some extent restrain the freedom of the directors to manage the business or affairs of the corporation, and it would scarcely be possible to conduct commerce if it were not possible to restrain the directors to some degree. Even where broad restrictions are placed upon the discretion of the directors by reason of such a contract, the contract will most likely be supportable.[602] For instance, there can be no doubt that a corporation (and the directors on its behalf) may validly contract with its creditors that it shall not reorganize its debt, restructure its equity, redeem or repurchase any of its share capital, discontinue existing lines of business or dispose of its assets out of the ordinary course. If at the time when they make the agreement, the directors of the corporation believe in good faith that it is in the best interests of the corporation to restrict their freedom to manage the corporation

---

[598] *Loudon v. Archer-Daniels Midland Co.*, 700 A.2d 135 (Del. S.C. 1996).
[599] *Motherwell v. Schoof*, [1949] 4 D.L.R. 812 (Alta. S.C.).
[600] *Selangor United Rubber Estates Ltd. v. Cradock (No. 3)*, [1968] 2 All E.R. 1073 (Ch.). The position of the two directors in question was typical of nominee shareholders — *per* Ungoed-Thomas J. at 1123.
[601] *Boulting v. Association of Cinematograph, Television & Allied Technicians*, [1963] 2 Q.B. 606 at 626 (C.A.).
[602] *Fulham Football Club Ltd. v. Cabra Estates plc*, [1994] 1 B.C.L.C. 363 (C.A.).

in a particular way, then the agreement will be valid.[603] The directors and the corporation cannot circumvent what they subsequently conclude is a disadvantageous agreement merely by alleging that it fetters the directors' discretion.[604]

§11.201 The distinction between proper (contractual) limits upon director discretion and improper restrictions on discretion was considered by the High Court of Australia in *Thorby v. Goldberg*.[605] In that case, the directors of a company agreed as part of a transaction that at a stipulated date they would issue shares on agreed terms. When the time came, the directors refused to carry out this obligation, arguing that it was an improper fetter upon their discretion. In rejecting this argument, Kitto J. stated:

> There are many kinds of transaction in which the proper time for the exercise of the directors' discretion is the time of the negotiation of a contract, and not the time at which the contract is to be performed. A sale of land is a familiar example. Where all the members of a company desire to enter as a group into a transaction such as that in the present case, the transaction being one which requires action by the board of directors for its effectuation, it seems to me that the proper time for the directors to decide whether their proposed action will be in the interests of the company as a whole is at the time when the transaction is being entered into, and not the time when their action under it is required. If at the former time they are *bona fide* of the opinion that it is in the interests of the company that the transaction should be entered into and carried into effect, I see no reason in law why they should not bind themselves to do whatever under the transaction is to be done by the board. In my opinion, the directors' contention that the agreement is void for illegality should be rejected.[606]

Similarly, in a concurring judgment, Owen J. said:

> ... [T]he directors of a company may, before the execution of the agreement, have given proper consideration to the desirability of entering into it and decided that it was in the best interests of the company that it should be made. If so, it would be impossible to argue that they had, by executing the document, improperly fettered the future exercise of their discretion. In fact, they would already have exercised it and, in the absence of an allegation that they had done so improperly, the suggested defense could not be sustained.[607]

A distinction must therefore be drawn between a future discretion improperly fettered, and a present discretion exercised and therefore spent. As a general rule, if the directors cause the corporation to enter into some future obligation in exchange for some present benefit to the corporation (including a present promise concerning future performance by a contractor), they are not fettering their future discretion, but exercising a present discretion with respect to the matter concerned.

---

[603] *Thorby v. Goldberg* (1964), 112 C.L.R. 597 (H.C. Aust.); see also *Fulham Football Club Ltd. v. Cabra Estates plc*, [1994] 1 B.C.L.C. 363 (C.A.).
[604] *Fulham Football Club Ltd. v. Cabra Estates plc*, [1994] 1 B.C.L.C. 363 (C.A.).
[605] (1964), 112 C.L.R. 597 (H.C. Aust.); see also *Ringuet v. Bergeron*, [1960] S.C.J. No. 40, 24 D.L.R. (2d) 449.
[606] *Thorby v. Goldberg* (1964), 112 C.L.R. 597 at 605 (H.C. Aust.).
[607] *Ibid.*, at 617.

§11.202 A further test as to whether the directors have improperly restrained their freedom of action is whether they have entered into an agreement with a person that puts the interests of that person ahead of those of the corporation.[608] This question quite often arises where a particular director holds his position as the nominee or appointee of a particular shareholder. As a general principle, there is no question that a director may properly be an employee of a shareholder.[609] However, it is equally clear that the obligation of such a director is to act in the best interests of the corporation as a whole, rather than in the best interests of the shareholder who secured or made his appointment. To the extent that a director seeks to put the interest of any person ahead of the corporation, the director has contravened the duties owed to the corporation.[610] A director may not simply agree to act as a yes-man for a particular shareholder.[611]

(xiii) Maintaining an Even Hand

§11.203 It is trite law that a fiduciary may not pick and choose among those to whom its duties are owed, and decide which of them he or she will consider or favour and which of them he or she will mistreat or ignore. A fiduciary may not act as the champion and advocate of one party whom he or she represents and contrary to the interests of the others, but must at all times maintain an even hand. The duty to maintain an even hand applies to directors as to other fiduciaries.[612] A director owes his fiduciary duties to the corporation in its entirety — that is, to the shareholders as a collective whole rather than to a particular shareholder or group, even where it was that shareholder or group which secured his election or appointment to the board. A director may not favour the interests of one shareholder over another[613] — this being part of the director's duty to act fairly and honestly.[614] The decision of Wells J. in *Re Jeffery*[615] with respect to the duty of a trustee (or other fiduciary) to deal fairly with all beneficiaries is equally applicable to all persons who owe a fiduciary duty to two or more persons:

> It is, I think, a primary principle, which need not be laboured by me, that one of the trustees' first duties was to hold the balance evenly between the beneficiaries and various groups of beneficiaries and to try to interpret the document and carry

---

[608] *820099 Ontario Inc. v. Harold E. Ballard Ltd.*, [1991] O.J. No. 266, 3 B.L.R. (2d) 113 at 123 (Gen. Div.), aff'd [1991] O.J. No. 1082, 3 B.L.R. (2d) 113 (Div. Ct.); see also *Motherwell v. Schoof*, [1949] 4 D.L.R. 812 (Alta. S.C.).
[609] *Wotherspoon v. Canadian Pacific Ltd.*, [1976] O.J. No. 4020, 22 O.R. (2d) 385 (H.C.J.), var'd [1982] O.J. No. 3148, 35 O.R. (2d) 449 (C.A.), var'd [1987] S.C.J. No. 40, 76 N.R. 241.
[610] See, for instance, *Scottish Co-operative Wholesale Society v. Meyer*, [1958] 3 All E.R. 66.
[611] *820099 Ontario Inc. v. Harold E. Ballard Ltd.*, [1991] O.J. No. 266, 3 B.L.R. (2d) 113 at 123 (Gen. Div.), aff'd [1991] O.J. No. 1082, 3 B.L.R. (2d) 113 (Div. Ct.); see also *Re Standard Trustco Inc.* (1991), 124 O.S.C.B. 1633.
[612] See, generally, *Westfair Foods Ltd. v. Watt*, [1990] A.J. No. 315, 73 Alta. L.R. (2d) 326 (Q.B.), aff'd [1991] A.J. No. 321, 5 B.L.R. (2d) 160 (C.A.), leave to appeal to S.C.C. refused [1991] S.C.C.A. No. 241.
[613] See, generally, *Dusik v. Newton*, [1985] B.C.J. No. 18, 62 B.C.L.R. 1 (C.A.).
[614] *Goldex Mines Ltd. v. Revill*, [1974] O.J. No. 2245, 7 O.R. (2d) 216, 54 D.L.R. (3d) 672 at 679-80 (C.A.).
[615] [1947] O.J. No. 563, [1948] O.R. 735 at 742 (H.C.J.).

out its provisions in the spirit and letter in which it was expressed. They were not, nor are they now, entitled to favour one group of beneficiaries in any way as against another. They were obliged to treat all beneficiaries with fairness and impartiality, always attempting to carry out the expressed intention of the settlor.

§11.204 When a fiduciary fails to maintain an even hand, the fiduciary breaches his or her duty of impartiality and is liable to be held accountable to those against whom the fiduciary has acted. It would seem that not only are the directors liable for a contravention of the duty to maintain an even hand, but any shareholder who is improperly favoured may be required to repay to the general fund available for all shareholders, the amount of any benefit improperly received.[616]

(xiv) Termination of Fiduciary Duty

§11.205 If directors and officers of a corporation are to be held liable as fiduciaries, it is important to determine at what point their fiduciary duties to the corporation terminate. As we have seen, a director's or officer's fiduciary duties do not necessarily come to an end when he or she ceases to be a director or officer.[617] A person is not relieved of fiduciary duty merely by resigning from the corporation solely to take advantage of an opportunity that has come along. Moreover, even where a fiduciary is dismissed from the corporation, it is still improper to take advantage of corporate opportunities that came to the notice of the former director or officer while acting for the corporation. Furthermore, fiduciary duties will continue with respect to general confidential information received from the corporation so long as the information remains confidential information belonging to the corporation.

§11.206 In *Alberts v. Mountjoy*[618] the plaintiff ("A") carried on the business of an insurance agency, while the defendant Mountjoy ("M") was a long-term employee of the plaintiff, holding the position of general manager of the agency. M left A's employ and established his own insurance agency following a change in the ownership of A. The defendant Butt ("B") was a junior employee of A who resigned shortly thereafter. B subsequently joined forces with M in the new business. Although M did not take a list of clients from A at the time of leaving A's employ, M was held to be barred from soliciting business away from A on the basis that to do so would contravene the fiduciary duty to which M was subject as a former senior officer.[619] Although B was not in such a fiduciary position himself, he became impressed with M's fiduciary obligations because he had joined in the new business with M.[620] The fiduciary duty did not produce the same result as would a non-competition agreement: M or B were permitted to

---

[616] *Roblin v. Jackson* (1901), 13 Man. R. 328 at 333 (C.A.), *per* Killam C.J.; *Harris v. Harris* (1861), 29 Beav. 110, 54 E.R. 568 (R.C.); *Eaves v. Hickson* (1861), 30 Beav. 136, 54 E.R. 840 (R.C.); *Owston v. Grand Trunk Rlwy. Co.*, [1881] O.J. No. 145, 28 Gr. 431 (Ct. Ch.).
[617] See, generally, *Island Export Finance Ltd. v. Umunna*, [1986] B.C.L.C. 460.
[618] [1977] O.J. No. 2334, 16 O.R. (2d) 682 (H.C.J.).
[619] *Ibid.*, *per* Estey C.J.H.C.
[620] *Ibid.*, at 689.

compete with A in soliciting new business; they were restrained only in the solicitation of the customers of A.

E. LIABILITY FOR CIVIL WRONGS OF THE CORPORATION

(i) General Principles

§11.207 It is well settled that a corporation has the capacity to commit torts, breach its contractual undertakings and commit other civil wrongs and that it is liable for so doing. The law governing the extent to which the directors and officers of a corporation may be rendered personally liable for the wrongs of a corporation is complex and difficult to summarize. In order to understand the law in this area, it is necessary to reconcile general principles of director and officer duty with the rule in *Foss v. Harbottle*,[621] the twin concepts of the separate personality of a corporation and limited liability and general causes of action under the law of torts. For many years, the relationship between the separate liability of a corporation and the directors, officers and employees who acted on its behalf in connection with some wrongful conduct or omission on the part of the corporation was unsettled, and indeed it is only recently that some clarity has begun to emerge in this area.[622]

§11.208 Since the end of the Second World War, there has been a steady expansion in the scope of director duties and liabilities. Nevertheless, despite this expansion, it is a well-established rule of law that (except as provided by statute or where they have entered into a guarantee or similar undertaking) the directors of a corporation are not as such personally liable for the debts and other civil obligations of the corporation or, in the absence of breach of duty to the corporation, with respect to their exercise of the powers entrusted to them.[623] In short, the directors are not implicit guarantors or underwriters of the business of the corporation.[624] Liability arises only if they act in a negligent manner or in breach of their fiduciary duties.[625]

§11.209 The decision in *Ontario Bank v. Merchant's Bank*[626] illustrates the application of these general principles. In that case, an action was brought against a director of a corporation that operated a warehouse, on the ground that the director had failed to inform the holder of a warehouse receipt of the disappearance of the goods covered by that receipt. The director was unaware of the dis-

---

[621] (1843), 2 Hare 461, 67 E.R. 189.
[622] *Craik v. Aetna Life Insurance Co. of Canada*, [1995] O.J. No. 3286 at para. 14 (Gen. Div.), per Cumming J., aff'd [1996] O.J. No. 2377 (C.A.).
[623] *Northern Life Assurance Co. v. McMaster, Montgomery, Fluery & Co.*, [1928] S.C.J. No. 52, [1928] S.C.R. 512.
[624] See, for instance, *Struthers v. MacKenzie*, [1897] O.J. No. 114, 28 O.R. 381 (Div. Ct.).
[625] *Litwin v. Allen*, 25 N.Y.S.2d 667 (S.C. 1940), per Shientag J.
[626] (1900), 5 Que. P.R. 392; see also *Coveney v. Glendenning*, [1915] O.J. No. 202, 33 O.L.R. 571 (H.C.D.).

appearance of the goods. The action against the director was dismissed. Similarly, in *Snow v. Benson*,[627] certain directors, employees and the only shareholders of a company appropriated the whole assets of the company leaving nothing available for creditors. One of the creditors obtained judgment against the company for damages. Being unable to recover, he sued the directors personally in an attempt to recover his damages. The action was dismissed.

§11.210 The courts have consistently rejected efforts to expand director, officer and employee liability in this manner. In most cases where directors or officers of a corporation are liable for some wrong, they will be liable to the corporation by reason of the breach of a duty owed against the corporation. It is rare for the directors or officers to be liable to some third party dealing with the corporation, and even rarer for lower level employees to be so liable. The general principle with respect to corporate wrongdoing is that it is the corporation that is liable for the wrongs that it commits. So, for instance, the mere fact that a corporation has been guilty of a fraudulent conveyance does not by itself make its directors personally liable for that conveyance.[628] Unfortunately, this principle rule is subject to a number of exceptions and qualifications which make it difficult to state any general rule respecting director and officer liability in clear and concise terms.[629] A survey of the case law suggests that to establish personal liability against a director (or officer) of a corporation in respect of a breach of contract, tort or other actionable wrong of the corporation, it is necessary to establish at least one of the following:[630]

- the director or officer was guilty of fraud, bad faith, lack of authority;[631] or

- he or she has committed a knowing, deliberate or willfully wrongful act amounting to active participation in the wrong committed by the corporation so as to make the act of the corporation his or her own;[632] or

- the director has assumed a personal responsibility for the act constituting the wrong of the corporation; or

---

[627] (1905), 2 W.L.R. 359 (N.W.T.S.C.).
[628] *Manulife Financial Services Ltd. v. BTK Holdings Ltd.*, [1997] A.J. No. 1191, 56 Alta. L.R. (3d) 355 (Master).
[629] Although some courts have certainly been prepared to try — see, for instance, *Srebot Farms Ltd. v. Bradford Co-operative Storage Ltd.*, [1997] O.J. No. 313, 145 D.L.R. (4th) 331 at 344 (Gen. Div.), per Epstein J., aff'd [1998] O.J. No. 532, 163 D.L.R. (4th) 190 (C.A.).
[630] *Montreal Trust Co. of Canada v. ScotiaMcLeod Inc.*, [1994] O.J. No. 2194, 15 B.L.R. (2d) 160, rev'd in part, [1995] O.J. No. 3556, 23 B.L.R. (2d) 165 (C.A.), leave to appeal to S.C.C. refused [1996] S.C.C.A. No. 40; *White Horse Distillers Ltd. v. Gregson Associates Ltd.*, [1984] R.P.C. 61 (Ch.); *Mentmore Manufacturing Co. v. National Merchandise Manufacturing Co.*, [1978] F.C.J. No. 521, 89 D.L.R. (3d) 195 (C.A.); *Prism Hospital Software Inc. v. Hospital Medical Records Institute*, [1987] B.C.J. No. 1807, 18 B.C.L.R. (2d) 34 (S.C.); *Performing Right Society v. Ciryl Theatrical Syndicate Ltd.*, [1924] 1 K.B. 1 at 14-15 (C.A.), per Atkin L.J.; *Reitzman v. Grahame-Chapman & Derustit Ltd.* (1950), 67 R.P.C. 168; *Southwestern Tool Co. v. Hughes Tool Co.*, 98 F.2d 42 (1938); *Fairline Shipping Corp. v. Adamson*, [1975] Q.B. 180; *Yuille v. B. & B. Fisheries (Leigh) Ltd.*, [1958] 2 Lloyd's Rep. 596.
[631] See, for instance, *Re H. (Restraint Order: Realisable Property)*, [1996] 2 All E.R. 391 (C.A.).
[632] See *Smith v. National Money Mart Co.*, [2006] O.J. No. 1807, 18 B.L.R. (4th) 22 (C.A.).

- the director or officer of the corporation has breached a personal duty of care owed by the director or officer to the plaintiff.

Moreover, liability can only be imposed upon a director or officer where to do so would be consistent with his or her general duty to act in the corporation's best interests.[633]

§11.211 Recent cases have indicated a growing tendency within the courts to constrain vexatious proceedings against corporate directors, officers and employees. Allegations of their personal wrongdoing must be specific.[634] In taking this approach, the courts have recognized that in many cases the bringing of a claim against the directors, officers or employees is done for no other purpose than to coerce a more favourable settlement than might otherwise be available. So, for instance, in one recent case, Ground J. said:

> These actions against officers and directors are often, as in this case, totally without foundation and are very often based solely on a pleading that the particular officer or director was the "controlling mind of the corporation." To expose business persons to the considerable inconvenience and expense of being personally involved in litigation, where there is no foundation for the action against them in their personal capacities, is in my view an abuse of the process of the courts.[635]

Similarly, the Divisional Court has stated:

> In commercial cases such as this, our courts are carefully examining the trend of simply suing officers, directors and employees in their personal capacities, without really carefully examining the facts or without carefully pleading the allegations which relate to them personally.[636]

§11.212 Where the directors or officers of a corporation are made defendants in an action that should properly be brought against the corporation solely to gain a tactical advantage, the court should apply a severe sanction. It is one thing to allow the pursuit of arguable claims; quite another to allow a party to pursue a claim that must appear non-meritorious on the evidence known to him or her, merely because it provides a tactical benefit to institute such a proceeding. The courts have a broad authority under rule 57.01(1)(f) of the *Rules of Civil Procedure*,[637] which they can and should use to actively discourage the institution of frivolous proceedings brought solely to hector a director or officer who is clearly not personally liable, in order to coerce that person into settling a possibly legitimate action against the corporation for which he or she serves on more favourable terms to the plaintiff than might otherwise be offered. So it has been said:

---

[633] *Kepic v. Tecumseh Road Builders*, [1985] O.J. No. 410, 29 B.L.R. 85 at 117 (H.C.J.), per McKinlay J., aff'd [1987] O.J. No. 890, 23 O.A.C. 72 (C.A.); *Imperial Oil Ltd. v. C & G Holdings Ltd.*, [1989] N.J. No. 228, 62 D.L.R. (4th) 261 at 264-65 (C.A.), per Marshall J.A.

[634] See, for instance, *Williams v. Natural Life Health Food Ltd.*, [1996] B.C.L.C. 288 (Q.B.), aff'd [1997] B.C.L.C. 131 (C.A.), rev'd on other grounds [1998] 1 B.C.L.C. 689 (H.L.).

[635] *Aspiotis v. Coffee Time Donuts Inc.*, [1995] O.J. No. 419 at para. 14 (Gen. Div.).

[636] *ADGA Systems International Ltd. v. Valcom Ltd.*, [1997] O.J. No. 4110, 105 O.A.C. 209 at 216 (Div. Ct.), per the court, rev'd on other grounds [1999] O.J. No. 27, 43 O.R. (3d) 101 (C.A.), leave to appeal to S.C.C. refused [1999] S.C.C.A. No. 124.

[637] R.R.O. 1990, Reg. 194, as amended.

... the prize for pleading should be in the non-fiction category rather than the fiction category. If pleadings are "fictionalized" merely for the sake of advancing an action on a tactical basis and there is no good factual basis (including reasonable assumptions and conclusions as to facts which may not be directly within the pleader's specific knowledge, provided that they are identified as such) then it strikes me that there should be severe sanctions.[638]

(ii) Torts

§11.213 The subject of director and officer liability for torts involving a corporation was discussed in Chapter 3. Although this subject is clearly related to the subject of this section of the text, we will not repeat the detailed case law review included in Chapter 3, but merely touch on such general principles of the law in this area as are relevant to the general subject of this chapter.

§11.214 The extent to which the directors of a corporation may be held accountable for torts committed by the corporation has frequently come before the courts. Three American cases provide a useful summary both of the kind of innovative claims that are sometimes brought against corporate directors in an effort to render them liable for the debt, default or miscarriage of the corporation, and the general reluctance of the courts to impose such liability. In *National Acceptance Co. of America v. Pintura Corp.*[639] the court observed:

> One of the purposes of a corporate entity is to immunize the corporate officer from individual liability on contracts entered into in the corporation's behalf. In contrast, although the officer is not liable for the corporation's torts simply by virtue of his office, corporate officer status does not insulate him from individual liability for the torts of the corporation in which he actively participates. ... Thus a corporate officer may be liable for the negligence of the corporation; ... for fraud; ... trespass to realty; ... willfully inducing breach of contract; ... and conversion.

Similar views were expressed in *Citizens Savings & Loan Association v. Fischer*,[640] in which it was said:

> As a general rule a corporate officer or director is not liable for the fraud of other officers or agents merely because of his official character, but he is individually liable for fraudulent acts of his own or in which he participates. ... The mere fact that a person is an officer or director does not *per se* render him liable for the fraud of the corporation or of other officers or directors. He is liable only if he, with knowledge, or recklessly without it, participates or assists in the fraud.

§11.215 In *Swager v. Couri*,[641] it was argued that the directors and principals of a corporation were liable for causing the corporation to default upon its obligations, where they filed to dissolve the corporation at a time when it was unable to meet its liabilities. The court replied:

---

[638] *Millgate Financial Corp. v. BF Realty Holdings Ltd.*, [1995] O.J. No. 1089, 19 B.L.R. (2d) 271 at 282 (Gen. Div. — C.L.), *per* Farley J.
[639] 94 Ill. App. 3d 703 at 706 (1981).
[640] 67 Ill. App. 2d 315 at 322-23 (1966).
[641] 60 Ill. App. 3d 192, 376 N.E.2d 456 (1978).

We believe that if a corporation is without funds and if there has been no misappropriation of funds by officers, directors, or shareholders of the corporation, then a dissolution of the corporation is proper. If creditors of the corporation are unpaid at the time of the dissolution they have a remedy in contract but not in tort unless they can prove that the dissolution was unjustified. In this instance dissolution is justified if the decision to dissolve the corporation is not motivated for the benefit of the officers, directors or shareholders. Therefore, we hold that the complaint does not state a cause of action which will support a judgment.

§11.216 The foregoing statements are generally representative of the law in Canada as well. Directors and officers are not normally personally liable for a corporate tort.[642] Accordingly, in the absence of a guarantee or similar undertaking entered into in their personal capacity, the directors, officers and employees of a corporation are not liable *in the ordinary case* for corporate action or inaction, whether in contract, fiduciary duty or tort. So, for instance, where a tort is committed by a corporation, even a sole director[643] will not be liable merely because he conceivably might have exercised his or her authority in some way as a director to prevent the corporation from committing the tort.[644]

§11.217 The general rule is that there is no such liability.[645] For instance, in *Thérien v. Brodie*,[646] a claim was made by the widow of an employee of a joint stock company, who was killed by an explosion during the course of his duties. The court held that directors are simply the agents of a disclosed principal, as respects dealings with other than shareholders, and consequently are not responsible personally for the torts of the company in the absence of gross negligence or fraud on their part. In another case, a corporation arranged with a solicitor to have a mortgage drafted for one of its customers. The documents were prepared by the solicitor in a negligent manner and returned to the corporation for execution. The documents were reviewed by the manager of the corporation and filed accordingly. It was later learned that due to the negligent preparation of the documents, the corporation was liable for a substantially larger sum than it had intended. As a result, the corporation brought an action against the solicitor for negligence. It was contended that the corporation was also negligent since its manager did not take a close look at the documents, and so discover the errors. At trial the court found the solicitor negligent. However, the corporation had to bear a certain amount of the loss due to the contributory negligence of its offi-

---

[642] For recent case law in this area, see, generally, *Mentmore Manufacturing Co. v. National Merchandise Manufacturing Co.*, [1978] F.C.J. No. 521, 40 C.P.R. (2d) 164 (C.A.); *Blacklaws v. 470433 Alta. Ltd.*, [2000] A.J. No. 725, 7 B.L.R. (3d) 204 (C.A.), leave to appeal to S.C.C. refused [2000] S.C.C.A. No. 442; *Monsanto Canada Inc. v. Schmeiser*, [2001] F.C.J. No. 436, 12 C.P.R. (4th) 204 (T.D.), aff'd [2002] F.C.J. No. 1209, 21 C.P.R. (4th) 1 (C.A.), var'd [2004] S.C.J. No. 29, [2004] 1 S.C.R. 902; *Society of Composers, Authors and Music Publishers of Canada v. 1007442 Ontario Ltd.*, [2002] F.C.J. No. 876, 20 C.P.R. (4th) 68 (T.D.); *Steinhart v. Moledina*, [2005] O.J. No. 525, 37 C.P.R. (4th) 443 (S.C.J.).

[643] *British Thomson-Houston Co., Ltd. v. Sterling Accessories, Ltd.* (1924), 41 R.P.C. 311; *Prichard & Constance (Wholesale), Ltd. v. Amata, Ltd.* (1924), 42 R.P.C. 63.

[644] *Rainham Chemical Works Ltd. v. Belvedere Fish Guano Co.*, [1921] 2 A.C. 465 (H.L.).

[645] *Mentmore Manufacturing Co. v. National Merchandise Manufacturing Co.*, [1978] F.C.J. No. 521, 40 C.P.R. (2d) 164 (C.A.).

[646] (1893), 4 Que. S.C. 23.

cer. In this action, the corporation was found contributory negligent, but the officer was not.[647]

(1) Personal Involvement in Wrongdoing

§11.218 Directors and officers will be liable where they knowingly and willfully cause the corporation to pursue a course of conduct that is likely to cause actionable injury to another person — as for instance where they induce the corporation to commit a breach of trust.[648] Whether the directors should be seen as having authorized the corporation so to act is a question of fact.[649] Such authorization is readily inferred where the directors of a corporation cause it to commit a wrong for their own benefit. In such a case, the court will treat the transaction as unenforceable, and will refuse even to inquire whether the company has derived any benefit from it, on the basis that the self-dealing constitutes a breach of the fiduciary duty owed to the corporation.[650]

§11.219 Similarly, an employee (including an officer or director of a corporation) who *personally* commits a tort while performing his or her employment duties is liable in damages to the person injured.[651] To give one obvious example: an officer of a corporation who negligently crashes the company plane will be personally liable to those injured by the crash, even where the plane was flown by the officer in connection with the discharge of his or her duties as an officer of the corporation. The vicarious liability of the corporation does not exonerate the officer from personal liability.[652] Similarly, an officer or other employee who personally commits a breach of trust or fiduciary duty is liable for that breach.[653] The employee's liability is not affected by the fact that the employer may also be liable to the same person in respect of that injury.[654]

---

[647] *Doiron v. Caisse populaire d'Inkerman Ltée*, [1985] N.B.J. No. 148, 32 C.C.L.T. 73 (C.A.).
[648] *Air Canada v. M & L Travel Ltd.*, [1991] O.J. No. 177, 77 D.L.R. (4th) 536 (C.A.), aff'd [1993] S.C.J. No. 118, 159 N.R. 1.
[649] *CBS Inc. v. Ames Records & Tapes Ltd.*, [1981] 2 W.L.R. 973 at 987-88 (Ch.), *per* Whitford J.
[650] See, generally, *Export Brewing & Malting Co. v. Dominion Bank*, [1937] 2 W.W.R. 568, [1937] 3 All E.R. 555 (P.C.); *Madden v. Dimond*, [1906] B.C.J. No. 14, 12 B.C.R. 80 at 87 (C.A.), *per* Martin J.
[651] *Craig v. North Shore Heli Logging Ltd.*, [1997] B.C.J. No. 983, 34 B.L.R. (2d) 119 at 129 (S.C.), *per* Smith J.; see also *Shibamoto & Co. v. Western Fish Producers Inc.*, [1991] F.C.J. No. 243, [1991] 3 F.C. 214 at 236 (T.D.), *per* Rouleau J., aff'd [1992] F.C.J. No. 480, 145 N.R. 91 (C.A.); *Steeplejack Services (Sarnia) Ltd. v. Stowe Nut & Bolt Co.*, [1988] O.J. No. 532, 31 C.L.R. 115 (Dist. Ct.); *Raia v. Transworld Simcoe Inc.*, [1997] O.J. No. 1494, 32 B.L.R. (2d) 81 (Gen. Div.).
[652] See, for instance, *Toronto-Dominion Bank v. Leigh Instruments Ltd.*, [1991] O.J. No. 1787, 40 C.C.E.L. 262 at 290 (Div. Ct.), *per* Rosenberg J.
[653] *Xerox Canada Finance Inc. v. Wilson's Industrial Auctioneers Ltd.*, [1997] O.J. No. 210, 34 B.L.R. (2d) 135 (Gen. Div.), var'd [1999] O.J. No. 1016, 122 O.A.C. 97 (C.A.). For a case in which a director who was the controlling mind of a corporation was held liable for breach of confidence by the corporation: *Cadbury Schweppes Inc. v. FBI Foods Ltd.*, [1994] B.C.J. No. 1191, 93 B.C.L.R. (2d) 318 (S.C.), rev'd [1996] B.C.J. No. 1813, 23 B.C.L.R. (3d) 326 (C.A.), rev'd [1999] S.C.J. No. 6, [1999] 1 S.C.R. 142.
[654] *Toronto-Dominion Bank v. Leigh Instruments Ltd.*, [1991] O.J. No. 1787, 40 C.C.E.L. 262 at 290 (Div. Ct.), *per* Rosenberg J.; *Hall-Chem Inc. v. Vulcan Packaging Inc.*, [1994] O.J. No. 817, 12 B.L.R. (2d) 274 at 290 (Gen. Div.), *per* Spence J.

(2) Separate Duty of Care

§11.220 For negligence and similar torts, in order for a plaintiff to have a valid claim against a director (or officer), it is necessary to show both that the director owed a duty of care to the plaintiff, and that the director breached this duty of care. Breach of a duty by the corporation is not sufficient to implicate its individual directors and officers. There is no presumption that the directors, officers or employees of a corporation necessarily owe a personal duty of care to persons with whom the corporation deals or who are affected by its activities. Where a claim is based in negligence or upon similar tortious or other wrongs[655] growing out of a duty owed by the corporation to the plaintiff, it is necessary to show that the employee himself (or herself) owed a *personal* duty (of care or otherwise) to the plaintiff which was breached by the employee himself. Thus no right of action necessarily arises against an employee merely because the employer committed a breach of its own duty of care to the plaintiff. The fact that the act or omission of the employee concerned gave rise to the breach by the corporation of its own duty is not itself sufficient to establish liability against the employee. Nor is it sufficient to show that the employee breached some duty owed to the employer. More broadly, there is no general rule to the effect that a claim may be made against any officer, employee or director who was indirectly, tangentially, or incidentally involved in some wrong committed by the corporation. The liability of the employee will follow only where the employee has breached a duty that he or she owes to the plaintiff.

§11.220.1 Directors are subject to a number of non-delegable duties that are imposed by statute (*e.g.*, under occupational health and safety legislation). Where injury or death results from a failure to perform that duty, the directors are directly liable, rather than vicariously liable.[656]

§11.221 Where there is a duty of care imposed by law not only upon the corporation (as the party economically concerned in the act of the corporate director, officer or employee), but also upon each person involved in the process, then a personal action lies against the director, officer or employee if he or she is negligent in breach of that personal duty. For instance, there is a duty in law for every operator of dangerous equipment to exercise reasonable care in its operation. That duty is owed not just to the person with whom the corporation that owns that equipment is dealing, but to all persons who may reasonably be foreseen to be at risk of damage if reasonable care is not exercised in connection with its operation. If a director, officer or employee of the corporation operates the equipment without exercising reasonable care, then personal liability will follow by reason of the breach of that personal duty.

---

[655] As to liability for breach of trust, see *Canadian Imperial Bank of Commerce v. Graat*, [1992] O.J. No. 1112, 5 B.L.R. (2d) 271 (Gen. Div.), aff'd [1997] O.J. No. 438, 44 C.B.R. (3d) 161 (C.A.); *Air Canada v. M & L Travel Ltd.*, [1991] O.J. No. 177, 2 O.R. (3d) 184 (C.A.), aff'd [1993] S.C.J. No. 118, [1993] 3 S.C.R. 787.

[656] *Nielsen Estate v. Epton*, [2006] A.J. No. 1573, 23 B.L.R. (4th) 173 (C.A.).

§11.222 It follows that a claim may only be made where it is possible to show that the director, officer, employee or shareholder has himself or herself been guilty of some personal wrong[657] in addition to — although perhaps concurrent and entirely and inseparably integrated with — the wrong committed by the corporation.[658] Absent such a personal wrong on the part of the director, officer, employee or shareholder, there can be no liability.[659]

(3) Misrepresentation

§11.223 The subject of possible director and officer liability for misrepresentation was discussed in detail in Chapter 9. The brief discussion of the subject in this section of the text is intended only to link that earlier discussion with the general principles of director/officer tort liability that are under consideration here.

§11.224 Generally, a director or officer of a corporation will not be personally liable for negligent misrepresentation made while acting on behalf of the corporation.[660] However, he or she can be held personally liable for fraudulent misrepresentation. The difference of approach in these two situations was discussed by the House of Lords in *Standard Chartered Bank v. Pakistan National Shipping Corp. (No. 2).*[661] In that case, a claim for deceit was brought against a managing director of a company that was a beneficiary under a letter of credit. The company presented the bill of lading and other documents to the confirming bank under a letter signed by the managing director that stated that the documents were all those required by the credit. The managing director knew that those statements were false and were being made to obtain payment under the letter of credit. The confirming bank authorized payment even though the documents had been presented late. It sought reimbursement from the issuing bank. Although it was unaware of the false dating of the bill of lading, the issuing bank rejected the documents on account of other discrepancies which the confirming bank had not noticed. On appeal to the House of Lords, it was held that the director was liable for his misstatement even though it was made on behalf of the company. He had made a fraudulent misrepresentation intending the confirming bank to rely upon it and the confirming bank had relied upon it. The fact that, by virtue of the law of agency, the managing director's representation and the knowledge with which he made it would also be attributed to the company did not negate

---

[657] For instance, in *Shillingford v. Dalbridge Group Inc.*, [1996] A.J. No. 1063, 28 B.L.R. (2d) 281 (Q.B.) the directors of a corporation were found personally liable for breach of contract by the corporation where they diverted funds belonging to the corporation from it for their own benefit.

[658] For a case where a director drew personal benefit from breach of trust by a corporation, was personally involved in the sale, and knew that it was in breach of its undertaking, and as a result was held personally liable, see *Ballman v. 600560 Saskatchewan Ltd.*, [1997] S.J. No. 2, 30 B.L.R. (2d) 273 (Q.B.). See also *Re Schuppan (No. 2)*, [1997] B.C.L.C. 256. For a case where a director was held personally liable where he was guilty of misrepresentation see *Island Getaways Inc. v. Destinair Airlines Inc.*, [1996] O.J. No. 4157, 29 B.L.R. (2d) 298 (Gen. Div.).

[659] This point was made clear by Finlayson J.A. in *ScotiaMcLeod Inc. v. Peoples Jewellers Ltd.*, [1995] O.J. No. 3556, 129 D.L.R. (4th) 711 at 720 (C.A.), leave to appeal to S.C.C. refused [1996] S.C.C.A. No. 40.

[660] Note, however, the possibility of statutory liability, as under securities legislation.

[661] [2003] 1 All E.R. 173 (H.L.).

that personal liability, as it did not change his representation and his knowledge. While an agent might assume responsibility on behalf of another without incurring personal liability in respect of a negligent misrepresentation, that reasoning could not apply to fraud.

§11.225 A director of a corporation who individually misrepresents the financial condition of a corporation may well be personally liable to persons injured as a result under the tort of misrepresentation; however, the directors of a corporation are not necessarily personally liable for torts of misrepresentation committed by the corporation where they were not individually responsible for the misrepresentation in question. For instance, in *ScotiaMcLeod Inc. v. Peoples Jewellers Ltd.*[662] two purchasers of debentures issued by Peoples Jewellers under a private placement arrangement sued the firm of underwriters and solicitors who had acted for the purchaser and the corporation at all material times in connection with the issue of the debenture. Third party proceedings were brought against the underwriter directors of the corporation for misrepresentation. A prospectus issued by Peoples in connection with a separate issue of shares rather than the debenture contained the following statement signed by the chief financial officer and chief executive officer of Peoples. It read:

> The foregoing, together with the documents incorporated herein ... constitutes full, true and plain disclosure of all material facts relating to the securities offered by this short form prospectus as required by the securities laws of all of the provinces of Canada. For the purposes of the *Securities Act* (Quebec), this simplified prospectus ... contains no misrepresentation that is likely to affect the value or the market price of the securities to be distributed.

On a preliminary motion, the third party claims against all of the directors were dismissed as disclosing no reasonable cause of action. On appeal, Finlayson J.A. held that sections 130(1) and 58(1) of the *Securities Act* (Ontario) provided no cause of action in relation to the prospectus, as that prospectus did not pertain to the issue of the debentures. However, the claims against the CEO and CFO were allowed to proceed.[663] The claims against the CFO and CEO of the corporation were in "a different position" from the claims against the other directors, because they were the most senior officers of Peoples and it was alleged that they were

> directly and personally involved in the marketing of the debentures and ... in making certain representations personally which were relied upon by the appellants.[664]

The appellants also alleged negligence on the part of the CFO and the CEO.[665]

---

[662] [1995] O.J. No. 3556, 129 D.L.R. (4th) 711 (C.A.), leave to appeal to S.C.C. refused [1996] S.C.C.A. No. 40.
[663] *Ibid.*, at 713.
[664] *Ibid.*, at 724-245.
[665] *Ibid.*, at 725. See also *NBD Bank, Canada v. Dofasco Inc.*, [1997] O.J. No. 1803, 34 B.L.R. (2d) 209 (Gen. Div.), aff'd [1999] O.J. No. 4749, 1 B.L.R. (3d) 1 (C.A.), leave to appeal to S.C.C. refused [2000] S.C.C.A. No. 96.

(4) Intentional Torts

§11.226 In general, it is easier to establish director or officer liability for intentional torts than for non-intentional fault-based torts, but again, personal involvement in the tort is a necessary requirement for liability. A director or officer may be held individually liable for conversion committed on behalf of and for the sole benefit of the corporation where he or she is a direct participant in the act of conversion. There must be proof of active participation in the conversion.[666] The fact that a person is a signatory on the bank account through which a misappropriation was committed is not sufficient to establish liability, if there is no evidence that the person concerned was actually the person who removed funds improperly from that account. The court should not presume wrongdoing where there are other signing officers on the account.[667]

§11.227 Clearly liability will arise where the director or officer commits a tort as part of a scheme for his or her personal benefit. For example, where a person in control of a corporation receives property in trust and either personally breaches the trust or causes the corporation to breach the trust by converting the trust property to the use of the director or officer, liability will most certainly attach. As the officer or director is the controlling force expressly directing that the wrongful thing be done by the company, the personal liability imposed upon the director[668] arises from his or her own act, and is therefore a logical extension of the rule that an agent is always liable for his or her own deliberate acts, even when carried out on behalf of his or her principal.[669] The directors of a corporation may also be personally liable when they encourage the employee of another company to commit a breach of fiduciary duty against that other company. It is no answer in such a case to anyone that in so acting, the directors were seeking to promote the interests of their own corporation.[670]

(5) Claims Against Multiple Directors or Officers

§11.228 Broadly based claims against all directors or senior officers are less likely to be successful than claims that are specifically targeted on individual directors or officers who can be implicated directly in the wrongdoing that has occurred. However, directors are liable for the wrongdoing of their fellow directors where they have a duty of finding out and preventing the type of wrong-

---

[666] *National Acceptance Co. of America v. Pintura Corp.*, 94 Ill. App. 3d 703, 418 N.E.2d 1114 (1981).
[667] *Safeway Insurance Co. v. Daddono and Khano*, 334 Ill. App. 3d 215, 777 N.E.2d 693 (A.C. Ill. 1995).
[668] *Wawanesa Mutual Insurance Co. v. J.A. (Fred) Chalmers & Co.*, [1969] S.J. No. 124, 69 W.W.R. 612, 7 D.L.R. (3d) 283 (Q.B.); *Scott v. Riehl* (1958), 25 W.W.R. 525 (B.C.S.C.). See also *Northern & Central Gas Corp. v. Hillcrest Collieries* (1976), 59 D.L.R. (3d) 533 (Alta. T.D.); *McLaughlin v. Solloway*, [1936] S.C.J. No. 8, [1936] S.C.R. 127, rev'd on other grounds [1937] 4 All E.R. 328 (P.C.).
[669] See Chapter 4.
[670] *ADGA Systems International Ltd. v. Valcom Ltd.*, [1999] O.J. No. 27, 168 D.L.R. (4th) 351 (C.A.), leave to appeal to S.C.C. refused [1999] S.C.C.A. No. 124; *Apotex Fermentation Inc. v. Novopharm Ltd.*, [1998] M.J. No. 297, [1998] 10 W.W.R. 455 (C.A.).

doing in question.[671] *A fortiori* they are liable where they collectively commit a wrong. Deliberate misrepresentation by the board of the financial condition of the corporation will result in liability. In *Re Traders' Trust Co. and Kory*,[672] a director of a trust company which was in serious financial difficulties obtained a sum of money from an investor on the written undertaking of the company that the money would remain on deposit with the company until a suitable mortgage investment was obtained. The money was used to pay certain pressing debts of the company. The transaction was reported and explained to a meeting of directors, by whom it was confirmed. The investor sought to recover her money, charging all the directors with misfeasance and breach of trust. In this action, the court held that all the directors were liable to pay the money to the liquidator for repayment to the investor. They had endeavoured to keep up an appearance of the company's prosperity in order to induce the public to patronize it as a safe medium for investing funds. They were guilty of fraud towards any person thus induced to deal with the company.

(6) Sole Shareholder Corporation

§11.229 In many cases, the principal shareholder of a corporation will also be its sole director and quite possibly its only employee as well. In the case of small corporations of this type, it may seem natural to identify the liability of a corporation for tort with the shareholder-employee-director, so as to fix him or her with that liability. In *Williams v. Natural Life Health Foods Ltd. and Mistlin*,[673] the House of Lords discussed the circumstances that must be present to attach liability in such a case. The underlying dispute in that case arose out of a franchise business. The appellant Mistlin, the managing director of Natural Life, was not the only shareholder, as his wife had a nominal interest in the business. In addition to Mistlin, there were three other employees. In 1987, the respondents Williams and Reid entered into a franchise agreement with Natural Life, relying upon promotional material sent by Natural Life to them. The turnover proved substantially less than that predicted by Natural Life. The franchise traded at a loss over the next 18 months and then ceased trading. The respondents sued, arguing that their losses were attributable to the negligent advice provided by Natural Life. In 1992, Natural Life was itself wound up and in 1993 it was dissolved. In 1992, the respondents joined Mistlin as a defendant in the action, arguing that he was personally responsible for the negligent advice provided by Natural Life. Judgment was given for the respondents at trial, in the amount of £85,000. On appeal to the Court of Appeal, the only issue argued was whether Mistlin was personally liable to the respondents on the basis of an assumption of responsibility. The majority upheld the decision of the trial judge and dismissed the appeal, Hirst L.J. stating:

> ... [I]n order to fix a director with personal liability, it must be shown that he assumed personal responsibility for the negligent misstatement made on behalf of

---

[671] *Re Traders' Trust Co. and Kory* (1915), 26 D.L.R. 41, 9 W.W.R. 538 at 544 (B.C.S.C.), *per* Morrison J.
[672] *Ibid.*
[673] [1998] 1 W.L.R. 830 (H.L.).

the company. In my judgment, having regard to the importance of the status of limited liability, a company director is only to be held personally liable for the company's negligent misstatements if the plaintiffs can establish some special circumstances setting the case apart from the ordinary; and in the case of a director of a one-man company particular vigilance is needed, lest the protection of incorporation should be virtually nullified. But once such special circumstances are established, the fact of incorporation, even in the case of a one-man company, does not preclude the establishment of personal liability. In each case the decision is one of fact and degree.[674]

In a concurring judgment, Wait L.J. stated:

... [W]here representations are made negligently by a company so as to attract tortious liability under the principle of *Hedley Byrne*, the primary liability is that of the corporate representor. In the vast majority of cases it is also the sole liability. The law does, however, recognise a category of case in which a director of the representor will be fixed with personal liability for the negligent misstatement. It is a rare category, and a severely restricted one. If that were not so, representations could set at naught the protection which limited liability is designed to confer on those who incorporate their business activities. The mesh is kept fine by the stringency of the question which the law requires to be asked: do the circumstances, when viewed as a whole, involve an assumption by the director of personal responsibility for the impugned statement?[675]

Thus, even at the Court of Appeal (which upheld judgment for the respondents) there was a clear recognition that the assumption of a personal liability by the director, employee and shareholder of a single-person company is a very narrow exception to the general rule excluding such liability.[676]

§11.230 The House of Lords shared this view as to the narrow scope available for the imposition of personal liability. The main question on the appeal was whether that limited exception had been correctly applied on the facts of the case. In giving the unanimous judgment allowing the appeal, Lord Steyn explained:

What matters is not that the liability of the shareholders of a company is limited but that a company is a separate entity, distinct from its directors, servants or other agents. The trader who incorporates a company to which he transfers his business creates a legal person on whose behalf he may afterwards act as director. For present purposes, his position is the same as if he had sold his business to another individual and agreed to act on his behalf. Thus the issue in this case is not peculiar to companies. Whether the principal is a company or a natural person, someone acting on his behalf may incur personal liability in tort as well as imposing vicarious or attributed liability upon his principal. But in order to establish personal liability under the principle of *Hedley Byrne*, which requires the existence of a special relationship between plaintiff and tortfeasor, it is not sufficient that there should have been a special relationship with the principal. There must have been an as-

---

[674] *Williams v. National Life Health Foods Ltd. and Mistlin*, [1997] B.C.L.R. 121 at 152 (C.A.).
[675] *Ibid.*, at 154.
[676] See also *Trevor Ivory Ltd. v. Anderson*, [1992] 2 N.Z.L.R. 517 at 524 (C.A.), *per* Cooke P.

sumption of responsibility such as to create a special relationship with the director or employee himself.[677]

The Law Lords rejected the notion that the "pivotal role" of Mistlin in the business of the company was sufficient to attach liability to him. Instead, the focus was on whether Mistlin had become involved in the service not as a director, but in a manner which conveyed an intention to assume a personal responsibility towards the prospective franchisees.[678] The facts of the case simply did not support such a finding. The reasoning of Lord Steyn on this point would appear to have broad application:

> Mr. Mistlin owned and controlled the company. The company held itself out as having the expertise to provide reliable advice to the franchisees. The brochure made clear that this expertise was derived from Mr. Mistlin's experience in the operation of the Salisbury shop. In my view these circumstances were insufficient to make Mr. Mistlin personally liable to the respondents. Stripped to the essentials ... the arguments of counsel for the respondents can be considered under two headings. First, it is said that the terms of the brochure, and in particular its description of the role of Mr. Mistlin, are sufficient to amount to an assumption of responsibility by Mr. Mistlin. In his dissenting judgment, Sir Patrick Russell rightly pointed out that in a small one-man company "the managing director will almost inevitably be the one possessed of qualities essential to the functioning of the company". ... By itself this factor does not convey that the managing director is willing to be personally answerable to the customers of the company. Secondly, great emphasis was placed on the fact that it was made clear to the franchisees that Mr. Mistlin's expertise derived from his experience in running the Salisbury shop for his own account. Hirst L.J. summarised the point by saying that "the relevant knowledge and experience was entirely his *qua* Mr. Mistlin and not his *qua* director" ... The point will simply not bear the weight put on it. Postulate a food expert who over ten years gains experience in advising customers on his own account. Then he incorporates his business as a company and he so advises his customers. Surely, it cannot be right to say that in the new situation his earlier experience on his own account is indicative of an assumption of personal responsibility towards his customers. In the present case there were no personal dealings between Mr. Mistlin and the respondents. There were no exchanges or conduct crossing the line which could have conveyed to the respondents that Mr. Mistlin was willing to assume personal responsibility to them. Contrary to the submissions of counsel for the respondents, I am also satisfied that there was not even evidence that the respondents believed that Mr. Mistlin was undertaking personal responsibility to them. Certainly there was nothing in the circumstances to show that the respondents could reasonably have looked to Mr. Mistlin for indemnification of any loss.[679]

§11.231 An important question to resolve is that of how far the decision of the House of Lords may be extended away from the field of negligent misstatement into the wider field of general negligence. A reasonable view would seem to be

---

[677] *Williams v. Natural Life Health Foods Ltd. and Mistlin*, [1998] 1 W.L.R. 830 at 834 (H.L.), *per* Lord Steyn.
[678] See also *Fairline Shipping Corp. v. Adamson*, [1975] Q.B. 180; *Trevor Ivory Ltd. v. Anderson*, [1992] 2 N.Z.L.R. 517 (C.A.), both of these cases being relied upon by Lord Steyn as authority for the proposition in question.
[679] *Williams v. Natural Life Health Foods Ltd. and Mistlin*, [1998] 1 W.L.R. 830 (H.L.), *per* Lord Stein.

that where the duty to exercise reasonable care arises under a contract between a corporation and its customers, a director (or officer or employee) of the corporation can only be affixed with liability if it can be shown that the director concerned has indicated a willingness to assume a personal liability. There is nothing in the above reasoning that would suggest that it is limited only to the negligent misstatement context. On the contrary, the Law Lords expressly stated that the same general principles govern liability for all types of services.[680] Such cases involving a personal assumption of responsibility are likely to be rare, even in the case of one-person companies.[681]

(iii) Breach of Trust

§11.232 A steadily growing number of statutes impose trust obligations of various sorts upon corporations. Moreover, in many cases a corporation will assume a trust responsibility under the terms of an agreement that it may enter. Where the corporation breaches such a trust obligation, the question may arise as to whether the directors or officers of the corporation can be made liable for that breach. In the case of statutory trusts,[682] the question will often be answered by the express terms of the statute itself; where the statute is silent, or where the trust arises outside a statute, it is necessary to determine the liability of officers and directors in accordance with the traditional rules of equitable liability.[683]

§11.233 A person who unwittingly participates in a breach of trust resulting in a conversion of trust funds is not liable to the beneficiary of the trust.[684] The type of knowledge required to affix liability to a stranger to the trust has been described in the following terms.[685] "The knowledge required to hold a stranger

---

[680] See also *London Drugs Ltd. v. Kuehne & Nagel International Ltd.*, [1992] S.C.J. No. 84, [1992] 3 S.C.R. 299, 97 D.L.R. (4th) 261 at 337, *per* Iacobucci J.:

> There is no general rule in Canada to the effect that "an employee" acting in the course of his or her employment and performing the "very essence" of his or her employer's contractual obligations with a customer, does not owe a duty of care, whether one labels it "independent" or otherwise, to the employer's customer. Our law of negligence has long since moved away from a category approach when dealing with duties of care. It is now well established that the question of whether a duty of care arises will depend on the circumstances of each particular case, not on predetermined categories and blanket rules as to who is, and who is not, under a duty to exercise reasonable care.

[681] *ScotiaMcLeod Inc. v. Peoples Jewellers Ltd.*, [1995] O.J. No. 3556, 26 O.R. (3d) 481 at 491 (C.A.), *per* Finlayson J.A., leave to appeal to S.C.C. refused [1996] S.C.C.A. No. 40:

> [O]fficers or employees of limited companies are protected from personal liability unless it can be shown that their actions are themselves tortious or exhibit a separate identity or interest from that of the company so as to make the act or conduct complained of their own.

[682] E.g., in the case of the trusts imposed under Part II of the *Construction Lien Act*, R.S.O. 1990, c. C.30, s. 13, as amended.

[683] *Barnes v. Addy* (1874), L.R. 9 Ch. App. 244 at 251-53, *per* Lord Selborne.

[684] *Austin v. Habitat Development Ltd.*, [1992] N.S.J. No. 315, 94 D.L.R. (4th) 359 at 362 (C.A.), *per* Hallett J.A.

[685] *Selangor United Rubber Estates Ltd. v. Cradock (No. 3)*, [1968] 2 All E.R. 1073 at 1104 (Ch.), *per* Ungoed-Thomas J.

liable as constructive trustee in a dishonest and fraudulent design, is knowledge of circumstances which would indicate to an honest, reasonable man that such a design was being committed or would put him on enquiry, which the stranger failed to make, whether it was being committed." The directors or officers of a company will be liable for breach of trust committed by the corporation if they knowingly participate in the breach, such as a conversion of trust property to an improper use.[686] However, it is not clear whether active participation in the breach of trust is required. Given the statutory duties imposed on directors to manage a company, on public policy grounds, a strong argument can be made for imposing liability at least upon them for knowing, but passive, acquiescence in a breach committed by the corporation.

§11.234 The courts are reluctant to impose liability on a director for breach by the corporation of an implied trust, and generally will do so only in cases where the circumstances clearly warrant such liability.[687]

(iv) Liability in Contract

§11.235 In general, the directors or officers of a corporation do not become personally liable on a contract merely because they sign it on the corporation's behalf. In such a case, it is presumed that they are signing as agents for a disclosed principal (the corporation). This is so even where the signing officer is the directing mind of the corporation.[688] Thus in *Marv-Eon Signs Ltd. v. Vogue Shoppe (1977) Ltd.*,[689] an action against the president of a corporation who had signed a contract was dismissed. In that case, the plaintiff landlord had sent a letter to the defendant president confirming the rental payments payable by a corporate tenant. The defendant president signed the letter following the words approved and accepted by, in his own name. The court held that the president was not personally liable as he only signed the document as president of the corporation.[690]

§11.236 Nevertheless, personal liability will result where the facts indicate that the director or officer intended to assume a personal liability, rather than to sign only as an agent.[691] Such an intention may be implied where the individual concerned receives a direct benefit from the contract — as where food or a communication is provided to the person concerned.[692] It is common, for the directors and officers of small corporations to provide personal guarantees for the debts of

---

[686] *Scott v. Riehl* (1958), 15 D.L.R. (2d) 67 (B.C.S.C.); *Air Canada v. M & L Travel Ltd.*, [1991] O.J. No. 177, 77 D.L.R. (4th) 536 (C.A.), aff'd [1993] S.C.J. No. 118, [1993] 3 S.C.R. 787; *Austin v. Habitat Development Ltd.*, [1992] N.S.J. No. 315, 94 D.L.R. (4th) 359 (C.A.), per Hallett J.A.
[687] See, generally, *Besta International Corp. v. Watercraft Offshore Canada Ltd.*, [1994] B.C.J. No. 2854, 19 B.L.R. (2d) 257 (S.C.).
[688] *Waiser v. Deahy Medical Assessments Inc.* (2006), 14 B.L.R. (4th) 317 (Ont. Sup. Ct.).
[689] [1983] M.J. No. 450, 24 Man. R. (2d) 125 (Co. Ct.).
[690] See also *CIT Financial Ltd. v. 1153461 Ontario Inc.*, [2004] O.J. No. 3308, 47 B.L.R. (3d) 269 (S.C.J.).
[691] *1127905 Ontario Inc. v. Misir*, [2005] O.J. No. 1382, 8 B.L.R. (4th) 56 (S.C.J.), aff'd [2006] O.J. No. 1092, 15 B.L.R. (4th) 1 (C.A.).
[692] *1127905 Ontario Inc. v. Misir* (2006), 15 B.L.R. (4th) 1 (Ont. C.A.).

those corporations. Where the facts support such a finding, a director or officer will not be able to escape liability simply by arguing that the contract might have been signed only as an agent of the corporation. For instance, in *Union Bank of Canada v. Cross*,[693] a promissory note was signed by certain officers of the corporation. Upon default, the bank sued those officers of the company as signatories to the note, claiming that they had assumed a personal liability, and had not signed merely as corporate agents. The court held that both the manner in which the directors signed and the facts of the case showed an intention to assume a personal liability.

(v) Procuring Breach of Contract

§11.237 Since the directors and officers of a corporation are not liable for breach of contract by the corporation in itself, some innovative pleaders have tried to attach liability to them by arguing that they should be liable for procuring breach of contract or other wrongful interference with an economic relationship existing between the corporation and some other person.[694] As a general rule directors or officers of a corporation are not liable in tort for inducing or procuring breach of contract by their employer.[695] However, on usual facts, individual directors may be liable if they induce the board as a whole to breach a contract.[696] A person who is in effect the directing mind of a corporation, and who thereby controls the relevant acts that amount to wrongful conduct on the part of the corporation, may also be liable on this basis.[697] Moreover, if the directors or officers of a company wrongfully and maliciously conspire to induce, or do induce a breach of contract by the company, they will be liable for conspiracy to injure a third party or for acting in furtherance of inflicting injury on a third party rather than in furtherance of the company's business interest.[698] In summary, for liability to apply, special facts must be shown that take a particular case relating to simple breach of contract outside the ordinary realms of contractual default by a corporation.

§11.238 To establish a case for unlawful interference with economic relations, it is necessary to prove that the defendant, with knowledge of the existence of the contract and with the intent to prevent or hinder its performance, and without lawful justification,[699] has either persuaded, induced or procured a party to the contract not to perform his or her obligations under the contract, or has committed

---

[693] (1909), 12 W.L.R. 539 at 544-46, 5 Alta. L.R. 489 (C.A.), rev'g 2 Alta. L.R. 3 (T.D.), *per* Harvey J.
[694] *Einhorn v. Westmount Investments Ltd.* (1970), 73 W.W.R. 161 (Sask. C.A.).
[695] As to the assumption that a corporate officer or director may make when acting as an agent of the corporation, see *CIT Financial Ltd. v. 1153461 Ontario Inc.*, [2004] O.J. No. 3308, 47 B.L.R. (3d) 269 (S.C.J.).
[696] *Schmeichel v. Lane*, [1982] S.J. No. 1017, 28 Sask. R. 311 (Q.B.).
[697] *Outset Media Corp. v. Stewart House Publishing Inc.*, [2002] O.J. No. 5304, 30 B.L.R. (3d) 198 (S.C.J.), rev'd [2003] O.J. No. 2558, 34 B.L.R. (3d) 241 (C.A.).
[698] At least, this conclusion was suggested in *Oceatain Investments Ltd. v. Canadian Commercial Bank*, [1983] A.J. No. 1010, 51 A.R. 364 at 368 (Q.B.).
[699] *Posluns v. Toronto Stock Exchange*, [1964] O.J. No. 792, [1964] 2 O.R. 547 at 598 (H.C.J.), *per* Gale J., aff'd [1965] O.J. No. 1091, [1966] 1 O.R. 285 (C.A.), aff'd [1968] S.C.J. No. 19, [1968] S.C.R. 330.

some act that is wrongful in itself in a design to prevent such performance.[700] The application of the tort in the case of a corporation presents certain problems. In contrast to the normal situation involving two or more individuals, it is mandatory for the directors and officers of a corporation — by reason of their statutory duty to manage the corporation — not only to interfere in but to direct and implement the conduct of its business and affairs. Broadly applied, the torts of unlawful interference with economic relations and inducing breach of contract could render at least some of the directors or officers of a corporation personally liable for every breach of contract that a corporation might commit.[701]

§11.239 In *Kepic v. Tecumseh Road Builders*,[702] the directors of a company entered into a contract with a wrecking company for demolition work. The directors and the principals of the wrecking company were to share the profits resulting from the completion of the contract. The directors of the company terminated the contract with the wrecking company with no share of profits being paid. The wrecking company commenced an action against the two directors for inducing the breach of contract. The evidence established that the directors had caused the corporation to discharge the wrecking company and therefore deprive them of their share of profits. The directors also caused the corporate auditors to present false accounts of project profits both to the company and to the court. The directors thus were acting fraudulently and not in the best interest of the corporation, making the directors accordingly liable in their personal capacities for damages flowing from the breach of contract.

§11.240 In *Phillips v. Montana Educational Association*,[703] the defendants argued that no director or officer would ever make a corporate decision involving the performance of a contract without fear of being sued for the tort of maliciously inducing the corporation to breach a corporate obligation. Consequently, corporations simply could not function if they were to be exposed to individual liability on every occasion when the corporation failed to perform on a contract.

---

[700] *Ed Miller Sales & Rentals Ltd. v. Caterpillar Tractor Co.*, [1994] A.J. No. 210, [1994] 5 W.W.R. 473 at 540 (Q.B.), *per* Berger J., rev'd in part [1996] A.J. No. 722, [1996] 9 W.W.R. 449 (C.A.), leave to appeal to S.C.C. refused [1996] S.C.C.A. No. 511, 215 N.R. 159*n*.

[701] For cases dealing with the liability of directors for inducing breach of contract, see *Imperial Oil Ltd. v. C & G Holdings Ltd.*, [1989] N.J. No. 228, 62 D.L.R. (4th) 261 (C.A.); *Levi v. Chartersoft Canada Inc.*, [1994] M.J. No. 656, [1995] 2 W.W.R. 279 (Q.B.); *Jackson v. Trimac Industries Ltd.*, [1994] A.J. No. 445, 155 A.R. 42 (C.A.); *Lehndorff Canadian Pension Properties Ltd. v. Davis & Co.*, [1987] B.C.J. No. 85, 10 B.C.L.R. (2d) 342 at 348-51 (S.C.), especially the following passage:

> If a director acts within the scope of his authority and with good faith, and if there is any breach of contract, the company is liable as the act of the director is the very act of the company itself ... if the director acts in bad faith and outside the scope of his authority, then he may become personally liable in tort.

See also *Lennard's Carrying Co. v. Asiatic Petroleum Co.*, [1915] A.C. 705 at 713 (H.L.), per Viscount Haldane; *R. v. Electric Contractors Association Ontario*, [1961] O.J. No. 535, [1961] O.R. 265 (C.A.), leave to appeal to S.C.C. refused [1961] S.C.J. ix; *Jim Pattison Developments Ltd. v. Fudex International Inc.*, [1996] A.J. No. 1181, 45 Alta. L.R. (3d) 343 (Q.B. Master); *O'Brien v. Dawson* (1942), 66 C.L.R. 18 at 32 (H.C. Aust.), per Starke. J.

[702] [1985] O.J. No. 410, 29 B.L.R. 85 (H.C.J.), var'd [1987] O.J. No. 890, 23 O.A.C. 72 (C.A.).

[703] 187 Mont. 419, 610 P.2d 154 (Mont. S.C. 1980).

The court concluded that liability usually will turn upon the ultimate purpose or objective that the defendant is seeking to advance. The burden of proving that it is "justified" rests upon the defendant. The defendant may show that the interference is privileged by reason of the interests furthered by his conduct, but the burden rests upon him to do so. The question of privilege must be considered in the light of the means adopted and the relations between the parties. Harrison J. continued:[704]

> To determine whether interference with contractual relations is justified, public policy considerations must be examined. Justification or privilege constitutes the primary defense to an action for interference. ... One public policy consideration is that the officers, directors, employees and agents of a corporation must be shielded from personal liability for acts taken on behalf of the corporation, including the breaching of contracts in furtherance of corporate goals, policies, and business interests. This corporate shield is needed in order to allow corporations to effectively function. A competing public policy consideration is that individual corporate agents, employees, directors and officers should not be allowed to commit torts at will, and then be allowed to hide behind the corporate veil in order to escape accountability for those torts.

§11.241 A person who enters into a contract with a corporation assumes the risk that the corporation will not perform the contract, just as every person who enters into a contract with another person assumes the risk that the other will not perform the contract. If the person who is considering entering into a contract with a corporation is concerned about the prospect of a default by the corporation, then the option is to insist upon a guarantee from the principals of the corporation, or to walk away from the prospective transaction if no such guarantee is forthcoming. It is not appropriate to enter into a contract with what is known to be a limited liability entity, and then to seek to amend the transaction unilaterally (i.e., in an effort to expand the scope of available recovery) by instituting proceedings based upon some trumped up claim of inducing breach of contract. Directors and officers who strip a corporation of its assets so that it cannot perform the contract, are liable because in so doing in effect they are denying the other party of the right of recourse that it has bargained to enjoy. However, in the absence of such wrongdoing or some similar impropriety,[705] a party contracting with a corporation takes the risk that the corporation will default and will not be able to make good any judgment.

§11.242 Nevertheless, personal liability will attach where a director or officer is a directing force in the misconduct of a corporation. The key question in deciding whether personal liability can attach is whether the director is acting in good

---

[704] *Ibid.*, at 425-26 (Mont.).
[705] See, for instance, *Forrester v. Stockstill*, [1992] Tenn. App. LEXIS 42 (C.A.); *Ladd v. Roane Hosiery, Inc.*, 556 S.W.2d 758 (Tenn. S.C. 1977) — supervisor of an employee may be liable for tortious interference with contractual relations between the corporation and that employee, when the supervisor acted outside the scope of his duties to the corporate employer. More generally, when corporate officers or directors act against the interest of the corporation, act for their own pecuniary benefit, or act with the intent to harm the plaintiff in inducing the breach of contract, they can be held liable to the injured party: *Holloway v. Skinner*, 860 S.W.2d 217 (Texas C.A. 1993).

faith within the scope of his or her authority.[706] Where the directors conspire and deliberately do what they know to be improper, there can be no argument that they are acting in good faith.[707] The liability in such cases is not, however, fiduciary based, but arises from general principles of tort law. In *Apple Computer Inc. v. Mackintosh Computers Ltd.*,[708] the plaintiff sued for copyright infringement, relating to the copying of computer programs belonging to the plaintiff and embodied on ROM chips. Judgment was given both against various corporate defendants and against several directors of those various corporations who had knowingly caused or authorized the corporate defendants to infringe the plaintiff's copyright.

§11.243 In deciding whether the directors of a corporation have used their powers for an improper purpose, it is not sufficient to conclude that the directors were not motivated by self-interest.[709] Inquiry must also be made concerning other improper motives. Where the question is one of abuse of powers, the state of mind of those who acted and the motive on which they acted are all important, and a full inquiry is justified to determine whether they were honestly acting in the discharge of their powers in the interests of the company or were acting from some possible motive of personal advantage or for any reason.[710]

§11.244 The response of the courts to the practice of asset stripping illustrates this point. In *McFadden v. 481782 Ontario Ltd.*,[711] certain individuals who were the principal officers, directors and shareholders of a corporation induced the corporation to breach a contract of employment in dismissing an employee without reasonable cause or notice. The officers then stripped the company of funds with the intention of defeating any claim by that employee against the corporation. In an action for wrongful dismissal the court held that the employee should be allowed to succeed against both the corporation and the individuals. In procuring a breach of the employee's contract, the individuals were not acting *bona fide* in the interests of the corporation, but were acting in their own best interests to secure the transfer of the greatest possible amount of the corporation's funds to themselves unhindered by any obligation to the plaintiff. The individual defendants were not acting under a compulsion of duty to the corporation and therefore fell outside the protection usually offered to the servants of the corporation. So too, in *PCM Construction Control Consultants Ltd. v. Heeger*,[712] a claim against directors personally was allowed where they had stripped the corporation of assets in anticipation of a claim against the corporation.

---

[706] *Said v. Butt*, [1920] 3 K.B. 497 at 506, *per* McCardie J.
[707] *De Jetley Marks v. Lord Greenwood*, [1936] 1 All E.R. 863 at 872 (K.B.).
[708] [1986] F.C.J. No. 278, 10 C.P.R. (3d) 1, 28 D.L.R. (4th) 178, additional reasons at [1987] F.C.J. No. 857, 43 D.L.R. (4th) 184 (T.D.), var'd [1987] F.C.J. No. 916, 44 D.L.R. (4th) 74 (C.A.), aff'd [1990] S.C.J. No. 61, [1990] 2 S.C.R. 209.
[709] *Howard Smith Ltd. v. Ampol Petroleum Ltd.*, [1974] A.C. 821 at 834 (P.C.), *per* Lord Wilberforce.
[710] *Hindle v. John Cotton Ltd.* (1919), 56 Sc. L.R. 625 at 630-31 (H.L.), *per* Viscount Findlay.
[711] [1984] O.J. No. 3268, 47 O.R. (2d) 134 (H.C.J.).
[712] [1989] A.J. No. 487, 67 Alta. L.R. (2d) 302, [1989] 5 W.W.R. 598 (Q.B.).

(vi) Conspiracy

§11.245 The range of claims against a corporation for which the directors, officers and employees are also personally liable is not expanded by characterizing a particular claim as a claim for conspiracy,[713] for in the normal case it is not possible to maintain an action for conspiracy against the directors, officers or shareholders controlling a corporation in respect of wrongs committed by the corporation itself.[714] Nevertheless, a claim of conspiracy can be made out where the joint action of the defendant director (officer or employee) of the corporation and the corporation are such that a claim for conspiracy would exist if the corporation were a separate individual. In such a case, the claim for conspiracy cannot be defeated merely by showing that the defendant director was the controlling mind of the corporation, so that in effect he or she was conspiring with himself.[715] To that extent it may be said that the separate personality of the corporation works against the defendant director. However, liability in conspiracy is really no more than an extension of the principle that the directors, officers, employees or shareholders of a corporation will be personally liable where they use a corporate vehicle to commit a tort or other wrongful act that for some reason they are not able to commit personally.[716] In such cases liability attaches because in reality it is the defendant director, officer, employee or shareholder who is committing the wrong. The corporation is merely a tool used to assist the wrongdoing. And it is clear that a corporation may not be established nor its business or affairs conducted or operated for the express or implicit purpose of committing an actionable wrong, and if it is so used, then the persons who stand behind the corporation who are responsible for the wrongdoing will be personally liable.[717]

(vii) Directors Acting Beyond Their Power and Authority

§11.246 The general rule is that unless otherwise provided by the Act under which a corporation is incorporated or by the articles, by-laws or a unanimous shareholder agreement, the board of directors of a corporation is seen to possess the authority to exercise all of the powers of the corporation.[718] However, there

---

[713] *Normart Management Ltd. v. West Hill Redevelopment Co.*, [1998] O.J. No. 391, 37 O.R. (3d) 97 at 102-03 (C.A.), *per* Finlayson J.A.

[714] See, for instance, *Normart Management Ltd. v. West Hill Redevelopment Co.*, [1996] O.J. No. 3655, 140 D.L.R. (4th) 550 (Gen. Div.), aff'd [1998] O.J. No. 391, 37 O.R. (3d) 97 (C.A.). As to the general principles governing liability in conspiracy, see *Canada Cement LaFarge Ltd. v. British Columbia Lightweight Aggregate Ltd.*, [1983] S.C.J. No. 33, 145 D.L.R. (3d) 385 at 398, *per* Estey J.

[715] So, for instance, in *Hall-Chem Inc. v. Vulcan Packaging Inc.*, [1994] O.J. No. 817, 12 B.L.R. (2d) 274 (Gen. Div.), the defendant Belec was the directing and controlling mind of two corporations. On the facts, Spence J. held that he had entered into a conspiracy with those corporations (at 297 B.L.R.).

[716] *B.G. Preeco I (Pacific Coast) Ltd. v. Bon Street Holdings Ltd.*, [1989] B.C.J. No. 1032, 37 B.C.L.R. (2d) 258 (C.A.), *per* Seaton J.A.

[717] *Rylands v. Fletcher* (1868), L.R. 3 H.L. 330 at 476, *per* Buckmaster L.J.; *Performing Right Society Ltd. v. Ciryl Theatrical Syndicate Ltd.*, [1924] 1 K.B. 1 at 14-15 (C.A.), *per* Atkin L.J. See also *Wah Tat Bank Ltd. v. Chan Cheng Kum*, [1975] 2 All E.R. 257 (P.C.).

[718] *Mid-West Collieries, Ltd. v. McEwen*, [1925] S.C.J. No. 11, [1925] S.C.R. 326 at 330, *per* Rinfret J.

are many exceptions to this general rule — a goodly number of which are set out in the Act itself, ranging from amendments to the articles of a corporation, numerous other types of fundamental change, to sale of the business of a corporation and even (in certain cases) the amendment of its by-laws. The nature and scope of these restrictions on directorial authority is considered in detail elsewhere. Here we shall touch on only the shareholders' right to object to directors exceeding their authority.

§11.247 In Chapter 6, we discussed how the doctrine of *ultra vires* has now been abolished insofar as it applies with respect to invalidating acts of the corporation itself. However, it continues to be relevant with respect to the potential liability of directors and officers for corporate acts. In this context, the term *"ultra vires"* encompasses:

- actions and undertakings that were beyond the power and capacity of the corporation itself or

- acts and undertakings that while within the scope of the powers and capacity of a corporation, are inconsistent with its declared objects; and

- acts that while within the power of the corporation, are beyond the power or authority of directors.[719]

To differentiate among these classes of *ultra vires* acts and undertakings, it is convenient to describe those acts and undertakings which are beyond the power or capacity, or outside the objects of a corporation as being *ultra vires* the corporation, while acts *ultra vires* in the secondary sense are *extra vires* the powers and authorities of the directors. Irrespective of how such acts may be described, in order to protect themselves from possible liability to the corporation itself, the directors and the officers of the corporation must keep within any restrictions imposed upon the exercise of powers by the corporation or upon the directors and officers. In this regard, subsection 253(1) of the OBCA[720] provides that:

> 253.(1) Where a corporation or any shareholder, director, officer, employee, agent, auditor, trustee, receiver and manager, receiver, or liquidator of a corporation does not comply with this Act, the regulations, articles, by-laws, or a unanimous shareholder agreement, a complainant or a creditor of the corporation may, despite the imposition of any penalty in respect of such non-compliance and in addition to any other right the complainant or creditor has, apply to the court for an order directing the corporation or any person to comply with, or restraining the corporation or any person from acting in breach of, any provisions thereof, and upon such application the court may so order and make any further order it thinks fit.

In the case of offering corporations, similar standing is granted to the OSC in the case of corporations under the OBCA[721] and to the Director in the case of corpo-

---

[719] *Compagnie de Villas du Cap Gibraltar v. Hughes*, [1884] S.C.J. No. 31, 11 S.C.R. 537, *per* Ritchie C.J.
[720] CBCA, s. 247.
[721] OBCA, s. 253(2); CBCA, s. 154(1).

rations under the CBCA. Under subsection 253(1) it would seem that a restraining order may be obtained with respect to both acts that are *ultra vires* the corporations as well as with respect to acts that are *extra vires* the directors (or officers) of the corporation.

§11.248 Where directors exceed the powers entrusted to them, they are liable for losses that the corporation may suffer, particularly where they do so in an effort to benefit themselves.[722] Directors and officers of a corporation clearly risk personal liability where they willingly permit a corporation to act contrary to regulatory restrictions or in excess of its powers. For instance, in *Walmsley v. Rent Guarantee Co.*,[723] directors of a financial institution authorized the company to receive money on deposit and then discounted certain notes endorsed by it. These transactions were *ultra vires* the company's powers and as such the directors were personally liable to the company for losses arising out of such transaction. In giving his judgment, Proudfoot V.C. stressed that these facts were so clearly beyond the proper purposes of the company that ignorance of the extent of the powers could not be allowed to protect the directors.[724]

§11.249 Subsection 134(2) of the OBCA specifically provides that every director and officer of a corporation shall comply with the Act, the regulations, the articles, the by-laws and any unanimous shareholder resolution, and subsection (3) goes on to provide that no provision in a contract may relieve the director from the duty to comply with the Act or the regulations.[725] Subsections 122(2) and (3) of the CBCA are to a similar effect. In addition to liabilities arising from the contravention of the OBCA or the CBCA, the contravention of general regulatory requirements may also render a director personally liable. Thus it has been held that a grant of financial assistance contrary to a statutory prohibition will render the director liable.[726] Similarly, in *R. v. Kussner*,[727] the directors had made certain loans and cash advances to themselves over a period of years, contrary to section 112 of the *Companies Act*.[728] The court held that the defendants were personally liable for the loans so made as in making them the directors had acted outside the scope of their authority.

§11.250 Furthermore, in the case of the issue of shares for a consideration other than money, subsection 130(1) of the OBCA[729] provides:

> 130.(1) Directors of a corporation who vote for or consent to a resolution authorizing the issue of a share for a consideration other than money contrary to section 23 are jointly and severally liable to the corporation to make good any

---

[722] *Nova Scotia Trust Co. v. Auto Parts Co.*, [1936] 2 D.L.R. 441 (N.S.T.D.).
[723] [1881] O.J. No. 232, 29 Gr. 484 (Ct. Ch.).
[724] *Ibid.*, at 489.
[725] An exception exists to the extent that the duties of a director are assumed under a unanimous shareholder agreement: see OBCA, s. 108(5).
[726] *Hart v. Felsen* (1924), 30 R.L.N.S. 109 (Que.).
[727] [1936] 4 D.L.R. 752 (Ex. Ct.).
[728] R.S.C. 1927, c. 27.
[729] See also s. 118 of the CBCA.

amount by which the consideration received is less than the fair equivalent of the money that the corporation would have received if the share had been issued for money on the date of the resolution.

A director is not liable under subsection 130(1) if he or she proves that he did not know and could not reasonably have known that the share was issued for a consideration less than the fair equivalent of the money that the corporation would have received if the share had been issued for money.[730]

§11.251 The liability under subsection 130(1) of the OBCA is supplemented by further specific liabilities imposed under subsection 130(2):

> 130.(2) Directors of a corporation who vote for or consent to a resolution authorizing,
>
> (a) any financial assistance contrary to section 20;
>
> (b) a purchase, redemption or other acquisition of shares contrary to section 30, 31 or 32;
>
> (c) a commission contrary to section 37;
>
> (d) a payment of a dividend contrary to section 38;
>
> (e) a payment of an indemnity contrary to section 136; or
>
> (f) a payment to a shareholder contrary to section 185 or 248,
>
> are jointly and severally liable to restore to the corporation any amounts so distributed or paid and not otherwise recovered by the corporation.

A director who has satisfied a judgment under section 130 is entitled to contribution from the other directors who are liable under the section in respect of the unlawful act upon which the judgment was founded.[731] Any director liable under subsection (2) may apply to the court for an order compelling a shareholder or other recipient to pay or deliver to the director any money or property that was paid or distributed to the shareholder or other recipient contrary to section 20, 30, 32, 37, 38, 136, 185 or 248. Curiously, no comparable power is given to the court with respect to a claim against a director under subsection 130(1).

§11.252 While the directors and officers must also conform to any unanimous shareholder agreement or restriction in the articles upon the exercise of their powers, in the absence of such a provision, so long as they act within the scope of their management powers, directors are not subject to the wishes of the majority shareholders.[732] Where the directors have acted in what they believe to be the best interests of the corporation, their exercise of power can only be set aside if it can be found that they have truly been serving an improper interest, such as self-interest, or that they so misconstrued their function that it cannot be said

---

[730] OBCA, s. 130(6).

[731] OBCA, s. 130(3). It is curious that subs. (3) requires a judgment, and makes no provision for the payment of a reasonable settlement. *Cf. Negligence Act*, R.S.O. 1990, c. N.1, as amended.

[732] *Automatic Self-Cleansing Filter Syndicate Co. v. Cuninghame*, [1906] 2 Ch. 34; *Salmon v. Quin & Axtens Ltd.*, [1909] 1 Ch. 311, aff'd [1909] A.C. 442 (H.L.).

that they were acting substantially for the purpose of serving the corporation. The largest shareholder, or even a majority of shareholders, of a corporation has no authority to direct the board in their management of the corporation.[733]

§11.253 In general, a court will not interfere with or set aside an exercise of the powers of the directors unless satisfied that the power has been exceeded or abused. The ultimate inquiry is to the good faith of the directors. However, in answering that question, the court will look at the full range of circumstances in a particular case. Moreover, the court will weigh those circumstances, in order to gain a full understanding of the factors motivating the directors, at least to the extent that this can be done by an outside party. In *Howard Smith Ltd. v. Ampol Petroleum Ltd.*, Lord Wilberforce stated:

> But accepting all of this, when a dispute arises whether directors of a company made a particular decision for one purpose or another, or whether, there being more than one purpose, one or another purpose was the substantial or primary purpose, the court, in their Lordship's opinion, is entitled to look at the situation objectively in order to estimate how critical or pressing, or substantial or, *per contra*, insubstantial an alleged requirement may have been. If it finds that a particular requirement, though real, was not urgent or critical, at the relevant time, it may have reason to doubt, or discount the assertions of individuals that they acted solely in order to deal with it, particularly when the action they took was unusual or even extreme.[734]

The court may restrain the exercise of director discretion where the directors are guilty of misconduct. The power of the directors to manage is not a *carte blanche* licence to do as they see fit. If a corporation fails to carry out a statutory duty, an appropriate mandatory order may be obtained requiring the corporation (and necessarily its directors and officers) to perform that duty.[735] If the directors contravene a statutory prohibition or limit, or otherwise exceed their powers, or threaten to do so, they may be restrained by the court.[736] The directors may exceed their authority not only by doing something that they are not entitled to do, but also by refraining from doing something that they are required to do. It is not simply that the directors have a power to manage the corporation. They have the duty to do so, and they may not enter into a contract that prevents them from so doing.[737]

§11.254 The directors must use their powers for the benefit of the company — *i.e.*, for the benefit of its members as a whole. The directors may not use their powers to benefit themselves or a section of the shareholders, or the employees of the company, although a director may take into account the interest of a particular class of shareholders (*e.g.*, the shareholders responsible for his election)

---

[733] See, generally, *Ashburton Oil NL v. Alpha Minerals NL* (1971), 45 A.L.J.R. 162 at 163, per Barwick C.J.
[734] [1974] A.C. 821 at 832 (P.C.).
[735] *Bolton v. County of Wentworth*, [1911] O.J. No. 139, 23 O.L.R. 390 (H.C.J.).
[736] See, generally, *Compagnie de Villas du Cap Gibraltar v. Hughes*, [1884] S.J.C. No. 31, 11 S.C.R. 537.
[737] *Atlas Development Co. v. Calof* (1963), 41 W.W.R. 575 (Man. Q.B.).

provided he or she does not thereby disregard or give less attention to the interests of the shareholders as a whole. In other words, directors need not act with selfless disregard of their own interests, but so long as they act for the collective good of the corporation as a whole, it is not objectionable that they also benefit as a result of the steps that they take.[738]

§11.255 However, where the directors stand to gain from the taking of a particular step they must exercise extreme caution; the most obvious situation in which directors abuse their authority is where they use their position to gain a personal profit. They may not make use of information that comes into their possession in their capacity as directors. They may not usurp an opportunity which properly belongs to the company. Moreover, directors may breach their duties to a company even where they do not make a personal profit. Where a company is controlled by a majority shareholder, the directors elected by that shareholder may not use their power to further the interest of that shareholder to the detriment of the other shareholders.

§11.256 An officer of a corporation is not subject to any general duty to inquire into whether the directors of the corporation have acted within their powers. Consequently, no action will lie against an officer merely because he has carried out instructions of the directors, even though the directors have themselves exceeded their authority.[739] While there is no case law on the point, it seems likely that the officer would be liable, however, where he or she is aware of the fact that the directors have exceeded their authority.

(viii) Corporation Must Exist and Carry on Business

§11.257 The mere fact that a corporate shell exists is not in itself sufficient to protect the directors or officers from personal liability (or for that matter, the shareholders), where the corporation does not in fact carry on business, so that in effect the shareholder(s) or director(s) of the corporation are carrying on business directly on their own account. The limited liability of a corporation flows not from the existence of the corporation itself, but rather from the fact that the corporation (which is in law a separate person) has entered into a contract or otherwise become subject to an obligation that belongs to the corporation. Unless the directors and officers take care to make clear that the obligations are those of the corporation, they risk personal liability.

§11.258 Similarly, liability will attach to the directors and officers where they carry on business in such a way that creditors believe that they are dealing with them personally rather than with a corporation. For instance, in *Trail Tire Service Ltd. v. Scobie*,[740] the officers of the new company failed to advise suppliers that they were contracting on behalf of the new company, and that it would be responsible for goods sold and delivered. The court held that there was an obli-

---

[738] *Hirsche v. Sims*, [1894] A.C. 654 at 660-61 (P.C.), *per* Earl of Eastbourne.
[739] *Cloutier v. Dion*, [1954] Que. Q.B. 595 (C.A.).
[740] *Trail Tire Service Ltd. v. Scobie*, [1976] A.J. No. 343, [1976] 5 W.W.R. 409 (Dist. Ct.).

gation upon a party who intended to rely on the fact of incorporation to claim limited liability protection to give ample notice to suppliers of the change in status, particularly where the new business was carried on in the same premises and the former name was used. There should be no doubt left in the mind of suppliers that what was being done was done as agents and officers of the new corporation. Failure to adequately discharge such a duty resulted in personal liability against the directors.

§11.259 A somewhat different approach was taken in *Olympia & York Developers Ltd. v. Price*[741] — a case that involved an action for moneys owing on the supply of goods. After the supply of goods was made it was discovered that the company had in fact been struck off the register and therefore had no capacity to contract. The supplier of the goods attempted to take action personally against one of the directors of the company for recovery of the moneys owing. In this instance, the court held that the director was not personally liable for the goods supplied as in this instance the director was not aware that the company had been struck off the register.

§11.260 In *Watfield International Enterprises Ltd. v. 655293 Ontario Ltd.*[742] it was held that where a supplier knew that it was dealing with a corporation it is not open to the supplier to argue that the individuals who stood behind a corporation held themselves out as being partners. The requirement in subsection 10(5) of the OBCA that the name of a corporation be set out in all contracts, invoices, orders and the like does not necessarily imply that the directors or shareholders of a corporation will be personally liable under contracts, invoices, orders, *etc.*, that fail to comply with this requirement. In order to impose personal liability, it is necessary for a supplier-plaintiff to show that he or she was misled by reason of the contravention of subsection 10(5).

F. OTHER CRITICAL LIABILITY CONCERNS

(i) Liability for Wages

§11.261 Directors are made personally liable for unpaid wages under a range of different statutory regimes. In Ontario, the key provisions in determining the scope of that liability are:

- section 131 of the OBCA;
- section 119 of the CBCA;
- clause 136(1)(*d*) of the *Bankruptcy and Insolvency Act* (BIA);[743] and
- sections 80 and 81 of the *Employment Standards Act*, 2000

---

[741] [1976] B.C.J. No. 50, [1976] 5 W.W.R. 347 (B.C. Co. Ct.).
[742] [1995] O.J. No. 1146, 21 B.L.R. (2d) 158 (Gen. Div.).
[743] R.S.C. 1985, c. B-3.

These liabilities are entirely statutory[744] for at common law directors were not subject to any liability to the employees of a corporation for wages.[745] The earliest Canadian legislation imposing liability on directors for unpaid wages was section 52 of the *Ontario Joint Stock Companies Letters Patent Act*.[746] It was derived from an 1848 statute of New York state. Employee wage claims are granted a priority against the claims of other unsecured creditors under the *Bankruptcy and Insolvency Act*. In addition, in the recently enacted — but as yet unproclaimed — Bill C-55 amendments to Canadian insolvency law, a super-priority security interest is created in respect of certain claims of this nature.

§11.262 In interpreting director wage liability provisions, three particular areas of concern have arisen. First, does the protection afforded for wages extend to include such employee claims as for reimbursement of expenses, arrears of pension contributions and vacation pay. Second, does that protection extend to claims for severance pay and for damages for wrongful dismissal. Third, to the extent that a claim for wages represents a claim against a director, does that claim enjoy any priority in the event that the director also goes into bankruptcy? There are, of course, important distinctions among each of these classes of claim. Specifically, claims for reimbursement of expenses represent a claim for money actually spent on the employer's behalf. To the extent that vacation pay and pension arrears may be viewed as deferred compensation, the claim can be directly related to some value that has been brought into the business. Vacation pay, however, is a claim of a special kind. It represents deferred compensation for work done, but it is payable in respect of time that will not be worked. Historically, vacation pay entitlements were relatively modest, but now that contractual entitlements to four or five weeks or more of paid vacation a year are anything but uncommon, allowing workers a priority for such claims puts other creditors at substantial risk. The concerns of other creditors are even more pronounced in respect of claims for severance pay or for damages for wrongful dismissal, since such claims do not represent any new value added to the business, but rather only a damage claim for loss of employment.[747]

---

[744] *Kramer v. Humfrey*, [1970] M.J. No. 157, [1971] 1 W.W.R. 607, 17 D.L.R. (3d) 103 (Q.B.).

[745] *Ralph v. Bieberstein*, [1984] O.J. No. 2335, 53 C.B.R. (N.S.) 57 (Prov. Ct.); see also *Darrah v. Wright*, [1914] O.J. No. 696, 7 O.W.N. 233 (H.C.D.); *Young v. Dannecker*, [1926] O.J. No. 479, 30 O.W.N. 394 (H.C.D.).

[746] 1874, S.O. 1874, c. 35.

[747] For more on this question, see: *Re Northland Superior Supply Co. and S.M.W. Local 397* (2005), 81 C.L.A.S. 11; *Kanagaratnam v. Li*, [2005] O.J. No. 771, 9 C.P.C. (6th) 282 (S.C.J.). See also: *Re Rizzo & Rizzo Shoes Ltd.*, [1998] S.C.J. No. 2, 154 D.L.R. (4th) 193. It is argued that severance pay (and similar compensation paid on loss of employment) is a form of deferred compensation payable to an employee in respect of services performed in the past. *Western-National Drug Services and R.W.D.S.U, Local 580* (1978), 20 L.A.C. (2d) 202; *Re Telegram Publishing Co. Ltd. and Marc Zwelling & Gottlob Essig* (1972), 1 L.A.C. (2d) 1. Yet it is difficult to see this as being an accurate description of the nature of the obligation. It is true that in general an employee's entitlement to severance pay increases with the amount of time worked. However, the nature of the payment is very different from holiday pay or pension arrangements, which are truly a form of deferred compensation. When an employee leaves employment, accrued vacation pay is payable as of right. Entitlement to receive that pay does not depend upon whether the employee terminated the employment relationship due to "constructive dismissal" or whether the

(1) The Arguments in Favour of Wage Earner Protection

§11.263 One of the earliest articulations of the policy rationale for imposing on directors was provided by Hall J. in the early years of the last century. He wrote:

> For lack of any other reason it occurs to me that what must have been had in view, was to protect to a limited extent those who were employed by such companies in positions which do not enable them to judge with any special intelligence what is the company's real financial position. The directors have personally this knowledge or should have it, and if, aware of the company's embarrassed affairs, and specially of the danger of a speedy collapse and insolvency, they continue to utilize the services of employees who have no means of securing this knowledge and who give their time and labour upon their sole reliance, often, on the good faith and respectability of the company's directors, it is not inequitable that such directors should be personally liable, within reasonable limits, for arrears of wages, thus given to their service.[748]

Many other arguments have also been advanced in favour of giving wage claims special protection. It is argued that where services are rendered to an insolvent corporation by its employees, all creditors enjoy some benefit of the services so provided. The efforts of employees are necessary to earn the revenue that the corporation will use to pay other claims against the estate. A further ground is that employees represent a particularly vulnerable class of creditor that has a limited ability to spread the risk of loss among other persons with whom the members of that class may do business.

(2) The Counter-arguments

§11.264 While each of these arguments has a certain merit, there are counter-arguments that also cannot easily be dismissed. For instance, if other creditors benefit from the work carried out by employees, it is equally true that those employees benefit from the credit provided by other claimants against the insolvent employer. For instance, trade credit is necessary to provide the raw materials and other inputs required to produce the products and services that a business may sell. In addition, advances made under a bank line of credit will often be used to meet payroll expenses. If the debt owed to a bank has increased by reason of the payment of workers, it is difficult to understand why a further priority of claim *vis-à-vis* the bank should be recognized to the extent that wages remain unpaid. Moreover, if it is true that employees have a limited ability to spread their risk among other customers, it is also true that workers have a unique ability to prompt payment when due, since they may withhold their services until

---

employer wrongfully terminated the relationship. If an employee leaves voluntarily and after giving reasonable notice, he or she is entitled to no severance pay; yet no one would suggest that holiday pay is not payable in such a case. Generally, upon retirement or the expiration of a fixed term employment relationship, no compensation is payable for the severance of the employment relationship, even if the employee rendered sterling service throughout the term of his or her employment. Severance pay is not compensation for what has been done in the past (the precondition for liability under sections 119 CBCA and 131 OBCA). It is compensation for the improper termination of a right to remain in employment.

[748] *Fee v. Turner* (1904), 13 Que. K.B. 435 at 446.

payment is made. However, right or wrong, Hall, J.'s rationale has remained compelling with the courts and the legislatures across the country. So, for instance, in *Re Ginter*, the court would observe:

> The remedy is one to be pursued against directors. The purpose is to make the directors responsible for their actions or inaction. This purpose is satisfied where the directors have the financial resources to meet the obligations imposed upon them. However, in situations such as the cases before me, the directors themselves have made assignments in bankruptcy. They do not have the resources to meet the responsibility imposed by the provincial labour standards legislation. To find a priority as claimed by the Director would be to penalize the other creditors of the bankrupt directors. That is contrary to the scheme of distribution under the B.I.A. Accordingly, the appeal is disallowed.[749]

(3) Review of the Current Schemes

§11.265 The wording of the various statutory provisions imposing liability on directors for wage claims varies slightly, and accordingly the scope of liability under each relevant regime is not necessarily the same.

(a) OBCA AND CBCA WAGE PROTECTION

§11.266 Looking first at liability under the OBCA, subsection 131(1) of that Act imposes a statutory for "all debts" up to the value of six months' wages. Specifically, the provision reads:

> 131.(1) The directors of a corporation are jointly and severally liable to the employees of the corporation for all debts not exceeding six months' wages that become payable while they are directors for services performed for the corporation and for the vacation pay accrued while they are directors for not more than twelve months under the *Employment Standards Act*, and the regulations thereunder, or under any collective agreement made by the corporation.

Although the section contemplates liability for holiday pay, unless there is a collective agreement (which, presumably, must be an agreement of that sort within the meaning of the *Labour Relations Act*) that liability is limited to the statutory (minimum) holiday pay. The scope of this provision was explained in *Proulx v. Sahelian Goldfields Inc.*[750] In that case, the respondents were hired by the corporation ("S") to provide services at its gold mine in West Africa. Their employment contracts entitled them to be reimbursed for reasonable travel and out-of-pocket expenses incurred in connection with their duties. S failed, and it was unable to pay the respondents their salaries, vacation pay and expenses. The respondents sued the directors of S under s. 131(1) of the OBCA claiming that their liability for "all debts not exceeding six months' wages that become due and payable while they are directors for services performed for the corporation" extended to the expenses they incurred on behalf of the corporation in car-

---

[749] [2003] M.J. No. 390, 179 Man. R. (2d) 41 at para. 6 (Q.B. Bkcy), *per* Registrar Lee.
[750] [2001] O.J. No. 3728, 55 O.R. (3d) 775 at paras. 19-20 (C.A.).

rying out their employment contracts. In dismissing the directors' appeal, Borins J.A. commented:

> ... it is clear from the above authorities that ... directors are not liable for all debts owed by a corporation to its employees. Rather, liability will be imposed only where the debts are for "services performed for the corporation". The maximum amount for which a director may be held liable is an amount equivalent to six months' wages payable to each employee.

> ... All that had to be decided was whether the expenses they incurred constituted a debt owed to them for services that they had performed for the corporation. On the uncontested evidence of the employees there is no doubt that the expenses which the employees claimed resulted from the performance of their individual employment contracts with the corporation and were included within the provisions for remuneration contained in the contracts. The expenses constitute a debt of the corporation owing to the employees for services which they had performed for the corporation within the meaning of s. 131(1) of the OBCA which the directors are required to pay.

In contrast, subsection 119(1) of the CBCA provides that:

> 119.(1) Directors of a corporation are jointly and severally ... liable to employees of the corporation for all debts not exceeding six months wages payable to each such employee for services performed for the corporation while they are such directors respectively.

While the CBCA makes no specific reference to vacation pay, such pay is recoverable under that Act.[751] It has been held that the object of the statutory liability for wages is not to impose a penalty upon directors for the purpose of vindicating a public law, but to secure to workers the payment of their wages where payment cannot be obtained from the corporation itself.[752] Thus conceived, the nature of the director's liability has been characterized in the following terms:

> A company director is practically a statutory guarantor of the debt of the company to the extent and under the conditions prescribed by the section. When he accepts office, he, in effect, says to every employee of each of the favoured classes, that if the company does not pay his wages he will do so to the amount and under the circumstances set out in the section.[753]

Liability arises upon the corporation's default, and it is not necessary to show any wrongdoing whatsoever on the part of the director.[754] However, in order to succeed in a claim, the plaintiff must fall squarely within the scope of the statute.

§11.267 In general, the right to claim is limited to employment-related entitlements (including vacation pay), and does not extend to other types of debt owed,

---

[751] *Mills-Hughes v. Raynor*, [1988] O.J. No. 38, 47 D.L.R. (4th) 381 (C.A.); see also *Foriter v. Laurin*, [1962] Que. S.C. 599; see also *Brown v. Shearer*, [1995] M.J. No. 182, 33 C.B.R. (3d) 314 (C.A.).
[752] *MacDonald v. Drake* (1906), 16 Man. R. 220 at 227 (C.A.), *per* Perdue J.A.
[753] *Guenard v. Coe* (1914), 17 D.L.R. 47 (Alta. Q.B.), *per* Stuart J.
[754] *Welch v. Ellis*, [1895] O.J. No. 31, 22 O.A.R. 255 at 262 (C.A.), *per* Maclennan J.A.

no matter how arising.[755] A person may only recover payment under section 119 in his or her capacity as an employee. Older case law tends against holding the directors liable under these provisions in respect of employees claims for damages in respect of wrongful dismissal[756] or statutory severance pay.[757] However, it was held that a claim for severance pay falls within the scope of section 119. In *Barrette v. Crabtree Estate*,[758] L'Heureux-Dube J. interpreted the scope of directors' liability for wages under subsection 119(1) of the CBCA. After noting that "the only benchmark provided by the wording of section 114(1) C.B.C.A. is the performance by the employee of services for the corporation", she held that the directors were not liable for damages for wrongful dismissal, since the damages did not constitute "debts not exceeding six months wages" payable to an employee "for services performed for the corporation while they are such directors respectively".[759] She explained:

> According to the language used by Parliament, the debts must result from "services performed for the corporation". An amount payable in lieu of notice does not flow from services performed for the corporation, but rather from the damage arising from non-performance of a contractual obligation to give sufficient notice.[760]

In *Re Rizzo & Rizzo Shoes Ltd.*,[761] Iacobucci J. concluded that it would be arbitrary and inequitable to deny employees that lost their jobs as a result of the bankruptcy of their employer from claiming pay in lieu of notice while others terminated for some other reason could claim pay in lieu of notice from their bankrupt employer's estate.

§11.268 While the liability imposed under subsections 131(1) of the OBCA and 119(1) of the CBCA is broad, it is tempered by the introduction of certain conditions precedent that must be satisfied in order to establish liability. Thus subsection 131(2) of the OBCA provides:

> 131.(2) A director is liable under subsection (1) only if,
>
> (*a*) the corporation is sued in the action against the director and execution against the corporation is returned unsatisfied in whole or in part, or
>
> (*b*) before or after the action is commenced the corporation goes into liquidation, is ordered to be wound up or makes an authorized assignment under the *Bankruptcy Act* (Canada), or a receiving order under the Act

---

[755] *Coveney v. Glendenning*, [1915] O.J. No. 202, 33 O.L.R. 571, 22 D.L.R. 461 (H.C.D.); *Olson v. Machin* (1912), 23 O.W.R. 531, 8 D.L.R. 188 (Div. Ct.).
[756] *Barrette v. Crabtree Estate*, [1993] S.C.J. No. 37, 101 D.L.R. (4th) 66; *Vopni v. Groenewald*, [1991] O.J. No. 3577, 84 D.L.R. (4th) 366 (Gen. Div.).
[757] *Mills-Hughes v. Raynor*, [1988] O.J. No. 38, 47 D.L.R. (4th) 381 at 385-86 (C.A.), *per* Blair J.A.
[758] [1993] S.C.J. No. 37, [1993] 1 S.C.R. 1027, 101 D.L.R. (4th) 66.
[759] *Ibid.*, at 1050 (S.C.R.). See also: *Mesheau v. Campbell*, [1982] O.J. No. 3567, 39 O.R. (2d) 702 (C.A.); *Mills-Hughes v. Raynor*, [1988] O.J. No. 38, 63 O.R. (2d) 343 (C.A.). Compare, however, *Schwartz v. Scott*, [1985] Q.J. No. 41, 35 A.C.W.S. (2d) 406 (C.A.), dealing with liability under the *Canada Corporations Act,* in which the wording of that Act was held to contemplate possible liability for severance pay owing under a collective agreement.
[760] *Barrette v. Crabtree Estate*, [1993] S.C.J. No. 37, [1993] 1 S.C.R. 1027 at 1048-49 (S.C.R.).
[761] [1998] S.C.J. No. 2, 154 D.L.R. (4th) 193.

is made against it, and, in any such case, the claim for the debts is proved.

Subsection 119(2) of the CBCA is similar. These qualifications aside, the statutory right of employees to recover vacation pay and other arrears of salary from the directors of a corporation is absolute and unfettered by any factors that might affect the liability of a guarantor; nor are there due diligence or dissent defences available to a director, such as those that may be claimed with respect to liability for improperly paid dividends and unremitted tax withholdings.[762]

§11.269 The procedural restrictions imposed under subsections 131(2) of the OBCA and 119(2) of the CBCA must be satisfied in order for a claim to proceed against a director. It is not necessary for directors to notify the employees of a corporation of their resignation or intended resignation in order to avoid their statutory liability for wages.[763] It appears that under the OBCA, an action commenced against a director before an action is instituted against the corporation or the other statutory conditions are satisfied, is a nullity. Paragraph 119(2)(*a*) of the CBCA provides that a director is not liable under subsection (1) unless

> (*a*) the corporation has been sued for the debt within six months after it has become due and execution has been returned unsatisfied in whole or in part ...

This wording differs significantly from the corresponding provision of the OBCA, which requires the director to be sued in the same action as the corporation. Therefore, the CBCA wording leaves open the question of whether it might not be a method of enforcing the judgment against the corporation. Under both of the statutes, the limitation period runs from the date that the director's resignation becomes effective, rather than from the date when the requisite filing is made under the *Corporations Information Act*.[764]

§11.270 The liability of the directors under both the OBCA and the CBCA is secondary in nature. It is the corporation that is and remains primarily liable for the payment of the employees' wage claims. In general, the statutes limit the right to claim against the directors to cases where there is no realistic expectation of payment by the corporation itself. Unless the claim is being made in respect of a bankrupt or dissolved corporation, or a corporation in the process of dissolution, both the OBCA and the CBCA require that execution against the corporation has been returned unsatisfied before any claim may be made against the directors. In *Piroth v. Kalinocha*[765] it was held that the return of a *nulla bona* writ of execution was not proof that the execution was returned unsatisfied in whole or in part, since the *nulla bona* writ referred only to goods.[766] Where exe-

---

[762] *Re Northland Superior Supply Co. and S.M.W. Local 397* (2005), 81 C.L.A.S. 11.
[763] *Bell v. British Columbia (Director of Employment Standards)*, [1996] B.C.J. No. 1372, 41 C.B.R. (3d) 145 (*sub nom. Re Westar Mining Ltd.*) (C.A.).
[764] R.S.O. 1990, c. C.39, as amended; *Laprise v. Julio's Pizza & Spaghetti Parlour*, [1986] O.J. No. 2649, 62 C.B.R. (N.S.). 36 (Prov. Ct.).
[765] [1986] S.J. No. 706, [1986] 2 W.W.R. 88 at 92 (Q.B.), *per* Goldberg J.
[766] See also *Stevens v. Spencer*, [1929] 3 W.W.R. 129, aff'd [1930] 3 D.L.R. 993 (Alta. C.A.).

cution has been issued, the amount recoverable from a director is the amount remaining unsatisfied after execution.[767] Where a director pays a debt under subsection 131(1) that is proved in liquidation and dissolution proceedings, the director is entitled to any preference that the employee would have been entitled to, and where a judgment has been obtained the director is entitled to an assignment of the judgment.[768] A director who has satisfied a claim under section 131 is entitled to contribution from the other directors who were liable for the claim.[769]

§11.271 It appears that the statutory liability will attach to both *de facto* directors and directors *de jure*.[770] The claimant must either be an employee,[771] as that term is understood at common law,[772] or the assignee of an employee.[773] No claim may be made by a person who advances funds to the corporation for the payment of employees.[774] Subsection 119(3) imposes the following special limitation period for claims under the CBCA:

> 119.(3) A director, unless sued for a debt referred to in subsection (1) while a director or within two years after ceasing to be a director, is not liable under this section.

§11.272 It is clear that any action against a director must be commenced within the limitation period allowed.[775] No comparable provision is found in the OBCA. However, section 4 of the *Limitations Act, 2002*[776] sets down the following general limitation period:

> 4. Unless this Act provides otherwise, a proceeding shall not be commenced in respect of a claim after the second anniversary of the day on which the claim was discovered.

---

[767] OBCA, s. 131(3); CBCA, s. 119(4).
[768] OBCA, s. 131(4).
[769] OBCA, s. 131(5). In all probability, this provision merely codifies what would otherwise be a liability in equity to contribute towards money paid under compulsion of law. See, generally *Re Milowski and Director of the Employment Standards Division*, [1985] M.J. No. 165, 37 Man. R. (2d) 248 (C.A.).
[770] *Macdonald v. Drake* (1906), 4 W.L.R. 434, 16 Man. R. 220 at 438 (C.A.), *per* Richards J.A.
[771] *Kornblum v. Dye*, [1986] O.J. No. 2636, 59 C.B.R. (N.S.) 219 (Dist. Ct.). Note, however, that the right to claim is not restricted to manual labourers: *Zavitz v. Brock*, [1974] O.J. No. 1890, 3 O.R. (2d) 583 (C.A.), although such restrictions did at one time apply: see, for instance, *Domanski v. Wilson*, [1935] O.J. No. 248, [1935] O.R. 400 (C.A.). Claims by corporate officers present special problems. There is case law to the effect that a manager of a corporation, whose pay is partly salary and partly commission based on performance is not entitled to claim: *Fahlman v. Independent Northern Laboratories Ltd.*, [1971] S.J. No. 72, [1971] 4 W.W.R. 120 (Q.B.); but *cf. Zavitz v. Brock*, [1974] O.J. No. 1890, 3 O.R. (2d) 583 (C.A.). Nor may a claim be made by an employee who is also a director: *Mulligan v. Lancaster*, [1937] 1 D.L.R. 414 (Alta. C.A.).
[772] *Crew v. Dallas* (1908), 9 W.L.R. 598 (Alta. Dist. Ct.).
[773] *Lee v. Friedman*, [1909] O.J. No. 5, 20 O.L.R. 49 (Div. Ct.), aff'g [1909] O.J. No. 321, 14 O.W.R. 457 (H.C.J.).
[774] *Herman v. Wilson*, [1900] O.J. No. 35, 32 O.R. 60 (H.C.J.).
[775] See, for instance, *George v. Strong*, [1910] O.J. No. 540, 15 O.W.R. 99 (H.C.J.), and see generally, *Davey v. Gibson*, [1930] O.J. No. 122, 11 C.B.R. 341 (C.A.). See also *Leclerc v. Beaulieu* (1924), 63 Que. S.C. 90.
[776] S.O. 2002, c. 24, Sch. B.

An employee wage calim is essentially one for debt. It is unclear whether the time limit begins to run from the time when the debt becomes due, or when there is a default in payment. Section 5(1) of the *Limitations Act, 2002* provides that:

> 5.(1) A claim is discovered on the earlier of,
>
> (a) the day on which the person with the claim first knew,
>
>   (i) that the injury, loss or damage had occurred,
>
>   (ii) that the injury, loss or damage was caused by or contributed to by an act or omission,
>
>   (iii) that the act or omission was that of the person against whom the claim is made, and
>
>   (iv) that, having regard to the nature of the injury, loss or damage, a proceeding would be an appropriate means to seek to remedy it; and
>
> (b) the day on which a reasonable person with the abilities and in the circumstances of the person with the claim first ought to have known of the matters referred to in clause (a).

In addition, subsection 13(1) of that Act provides:

> 13.(1) If a person acknowledges liability in respect of a claim for payment of a liquidated sum ... the act or omission on which the claim is based shall be deemed to have taken place on the day on which the acknowledgment was made.

Generally, subsection 13(1) applies to an acknowledgment of liability in respect of a claim for payment of a liquidated sum even though the person making the acknowledgment refuses or does not promise to pay the sum or the balance of the sum still owing,[777] but the acknowledgment must be in writing and signed to fall within the scope of this provision.[778]

§11.273 The claim of a worker must relate to a period of time during which the director served on the board of directors.[779] Where the directors are sued, they may raise the full range of defences to the wage claim as might have been put by the corporation itself, as well as the defences that are personal to them. The claim against the directors is an original claim; it is not a method of enforcing the judgment obtained against the corporation.[780] Therefore, the directors are not barred from reopening defences abandoned or not raised by the corporation, nor are they estopped from defending the action merely because default judgment has been obtained against the corporation itself.[781]

---

[777] *Limitations Act, 2002*, s. 13(8).
[778] *Limitations Act, 2002*, s. 13(10).
[779] *Vopni v. Groenewald*, [1991] O.J. No. 3577, 10 C.B.R. (3d) 292 at 295 and 298 (Gen. Div.), per McKeown J.
[780] *Derbach v. Shaw*, [1933] 4 D.L.R. 461, [1933] 2 W.W.R. 605 (Man. C.A.); *Feuchter v. Smolek*, [1983] A.J. No. 949, 46 A.R. 58 (Q.B.); but compare *Guenard v. Coe* (1914), 6 W.W.R. 922 (Alta. C.A.).
[781] *Rogers v. Wood* (1912), 22 O.W.R. 48 (H.C.J).

§11.274 A director who pays a debt under section 131 of the OBCA or section 119 of the CBCA is entitled to be subrogated to the rights of the employee who is paid by him.[782] Where a director pays a debt that is provided in liquidation and dissolution or in bankruptcy proceedings, he is entitled to any preference that the employee would have been entitled to, and where a judgment has been obtained, he is entitled to an assignment of the judgment.[783] The director is also entitled to claim contribution from his fellow directors.[784]

(b) EMPLOYMENT STANDARDS

§11.275 In addition to the foregoing, in Ontario Part XX of the *Employment Standards Act, 2000*[785] also imposes liability upon directors for certain unpaid wage claims. Although this legislation obviously applies only with respect to claims by Ontario employees, broadly similar legislation is also in effect in the other provinces of Canada. Looking at the specific terms of the liability imposed, subsection 81(1) provides:

> 81.(1) The directors of an employer are jointly and severally liable for wages as provided in this Part if,
>
> (a) the employer is insolvent, the employee has caused a claim for unpaid wages to be filed with the receiver appointed by a court with respect to the employer or with the employer's trustee in bankruptcy and the claim has not been paid;
>
> (b) an employment standards officer has made an order that the employer is liable for wages, unless the amount set out in the order has been paid or the employer has applied to have it reviewed;
>
> (c) an employment standards officer has made an order that a director is liable for wages, unless the amount set out in the order has been paid or the employer or the director has applied to have it reviewed; or
>
> (d) the Board has issued, amended or affirmed an order under section 119, the order, as issued, amended or affirmed, requires the employer or the directors to pay wages and the amount set out in the order has not been paid.

---

[782] *International Brotherhood of Electrical Workers' Union, Local 2345 v. Callahan*, [1995] O.J. No. 1824, 34 C.B.R. (3d) 18 (*sub nom. Courtnage v. Callahan*) (C.A.), leave to appeal to S.C.C. refused [1996] S.C.C.A. No. 67.

[783] OBCA, s. 131(4); CBCA, s. 119(5).

[784] OBCA, s. 131(5); CBCA, s. 119(6).

[785] S.O. 2000, c. 41. Part XX does not apply with respect to directors of corporations to which Part III of the *Corporations Act* applies or to which the *Co-operative Corporations Act* applies: ESA s. 80(2). In addition, Part XX does not apply with respect to directors, or persons who perform functions similar to those of a director, of a college of a health profession or a group of health professions that is established or continued under an Act of the Legislature: ESA, s. 80(3). Presumably, these exemptions are granted because such directors are not usually remunerated for acting in the capacity of a director. As to the liability of directors for companies incorporated under the corresponding legislation of other jurisdictions than Ontario, see ESA, s. 80(4).

Despite subsection (1), the corporate employer itself remains primarily responsible for an employee's wages but proceedings against the employer do not have to be exhausted before proceedings may be commenced to collect wages from directors under Part XX.[786] The overtime wages that directors are liable for is equal to the greater of the statutory amount of overtime pay to which employees are entitled, and the amount contractually agreed to by the employer and the employee.[787] Liability for interest is also contemplated.[788] However, the liability of the directors is, subject to the following limitation (emphasis added):[789]

> 81.(7) The directors of an employer corporation are jointly and severally liable to the employees of the corporation for all debts *not exceeding six months' wages,* as described in subsection (3), *that become payable while they are directors for services performed for the corporation and for the vacation pay accrued while they are directors for not more than 12 months* under this Act and the regulations made under it or under any collective agreement made by the corporation.

§11.276 In *Morrison v. Fazakas,*[790] Smith J. considered a similar provision of the corresponding Saskatchewan legislation, and concluded that it imposed a cap on a corporate director's liability for outstanding wages, rather than a time limitation for the making of an order.[791]

§11.277 A director who has satisfied a claim for wages is entitled to contribution in relation to the wages from other directors who are liable for the claim.[792] The liability of directors under Part XX cannot be excluded by contract, but the corporation may indemnify the director against that liability and may purchase insurance to protect its directors.[793] For the purposes of Part XX, the term "director" is defined to include a shareholder "who is a party to a unanimous shareholder agreement".[794] However, this expanded definition is qualified by subsection 80(1) of the Act:

> 80.(1) This Part applies with respect to shareholders described in section 79 only to the extent that the directors are relieved, under subsection 108 (5) of the *Business Corporations Act* or subsection 146 (5) of the *Canada Business Corporations Act,* of their liability to pay wages to the employees of the corporation.

---

[786] ESA, s. 81 (2).
[787] ESA, s. 81(6).
[788] ESA, s. 81(8).
[789] ESA, s. 81(7).
[790] [1998] S.J. No. 715, 174 Sask. R. 186, [1998] Sask. D. J. 37 (Q.B.).
[791] More generally, it has been held that this legislation is remedial and therefore should be given a sufficiently fair, large and liberal construction to insure the attainment of its objects: *Helping Hands Agency Ltd. v. British Columbia (Director of Employment Standards),* [1995] B.C.J. No. 2524, 131 D.L.R. (4th) 336 at 340, 15 B.C.L.R. (3d) 27 (C.A.); *Bell v. British Columbia (Director of Employment Standards),* [1996] B.C.J. No. 1372, 136 D.L.R. (4th) 564 (*sub nom. Re Westar Mining Ltd.*) (C.A.). However, because the imposition of personal liability on directors for a corporate obligation constitutes a significant departure from the common law, any provision tending to that effect should be strictly construed: *Jonah v. Quinte Transport (1986) Ltd.,* [1994] O.J. No. 1507, 5 C.C.E.L. (2d) 73 (Gen. Div.).
[792] ESA, s. 81(9).
[793] ESA, s. 82.
[794] ESA, s. 79.

Consequently, it would appear that the expanded definition is intended to apply only where broad managerial powers are reserved to the shareholders, that have some bearing on the payment of employee wages. Indeed, it is difficult to understand why shareholders should be made liable for employee wage claims merely because there is a brief agreement among them providing that by-law amendments and the payment of dividends shall require shareholder approval.

§11.278 Under subsection 81(3) of the Ontario *Employment Standards Act, 2000*, it is specifically provided that the wages for which directors are liable does not include "termination pay and severance pay as they are provided for under this Act or an employment contract and [does not include] amounts that are deemed to be wages under this Act". Generally, this rule is consistent with the approach that evolved in the case law. However, the Act adopts a fairly generous approach with respect to liability for vacation pay.

> 81.(4) The vacation pay that directors are liable for is the greater of the minimum vacation pay provided in Part XI (Vacation With Pay) and the amount contractually agreed to by the employer and the employee.[795]

A similar rule applies with respect to statutory holiday pay:

> 81.(5) The amount of holiday pay that directors are liable for is the greater of the amount payable for holidays at the rate as determined under this Act and the regulations and the amount for the holidays at the rate as contractually agreed to by the employer and the employee.[796]

(c) BANKRUPTCY AND INSOLVENCY

§11.279 The final statute to which reference must be made in the context of director wage liability is the *Bankruptcy and Insolvency Act*. The BIA does not itself impose liability upon directors for unpaid wage claims, but it does govern the priority of wage claims in a bankruptcy proceeding. Specifically, clause 136(1)(d) of the BIA places such claims as the fourth ranking priority claim among unsecured debts:

> wages, salaries, commissions or compensation of any clerk, servant, travelling salesman, labourer or workman for services rendered during the six months immediately preceding the bankruptcy to the extent of two thousand dollars in each case, together with, in the case of a travelling salesman, disbursements properly incurred by that salesman in and about the bankrupt's business, to the extent of an additional one thousand dollars in each case, during the same period, and for the purposes of this paragraph commissions payable when goods are shipped, delivered or paid for, if shipped, delivered or paid for within the six month period, shall be deemed to have been earned therein ...

---

[795] ESA, s. 81(4). *Cf. Bell v. British Columbia (Director of Employment Standards)*, [1996] B.C.J. No. 1372, 136 D.L.R. (4th) 564 (*sub nom. Re Wester Mining Ltd.*) (C.A.).
[796] ESA, s. 81(5).

Wage claims of certain persons closely related to the bankrupt do not enjoy this protection.[797] In particular, section 140 of the BIA provides that no officer or director of the corporation is entitled to a preferred claim in respect of wages, salary, commission or compensation for work done or services rendered to the corporation in any capacity. Thus the claims of directors and officers enjoy only the level of a general and unsecured claim against the corporation. Although there is no express prohibition against a director or officer from obtaining security from the corporation with respect to amounts owing, such a security may be vulnerable to attack as a reviewable transaction.[798]

§11.280 In *Re George*,[799] the court considered the nature of the liability of a corporate director under subsection 63(1) of the Saskatchewan *Labour Standards Act*[800] in respect of unpaid wages owing to a corporation's employees. In that case, George was the sole director of a corporation that operated a grocery store. The corporation permanently closed the grocery store without giving notice to its employees. The employees were not paid severance or holiday pay owing or RSP deductions. George made an assignment into bankruptcy. The employees filed claims under the *Labour Standards Act* for wages and benefits due. The Director of Labour Standards filed a proof of claim with the trustee on behalf of the employees, arguing that they were preferred creditors under clause 136(1)(*d*) of the *Bankruptcy and Insolvency Act*. The claim was disallowed. The Registrar in Bankruptcy held that a corporate director's liability under subsection 63(1) of the *Labour Standards Act* did not constitute a preferred claim under clause 136(1)(*d*) of the *Bankruptcy and Insolvency Act*. The Director of Labour Standards applied to set aside the Registrar's decision. In the Court of Queen's Bench, Klebuc J. held that subsection 63(1) merely makes a director liable for unpaid wages of a corporation's employees. It does not confer any claim to priority in the distribution of a director's assets over his or her other creditors, and to the extent that it purported to do so, it would be in operational conflict with clause 136(1)(*d*) of the BIA, and therefore inoperative to that extent on the basis of the paramountcy of the conflicting Federal legislation.[801]

(d) Bill C-55

§11.281 Canada's bankruptcy and insolvency laws are subject to review every five years. The most recent review led to the enactment of a range of amendments to the law, popularly referred to as Bill C-55. This Act has the full title *An Act to establish the Wage Earner Protection Program Act, to amend the Bankruptcy and Insolvency Act and the Companies' Creditors Arrangement Act, and to make consequential amendments to other Acts.* Bill C-55 was introduced in the House of Commons on June 3, 2005, and was passed by the House of Com-

---

[797] See ss. 137(2), 138, 139 and 140.
[798] BIA, ss. 3, 137(1).
[799] [2002] S.J. No. 190, [2002] Sask. D. J. 1151 (Q.B.).
[800] R.S.S. 1978, c. L-1.
[801] Compare, however: *Re James*, [2000] B.C.J. No. 1529, 18 C.B.R. (4th) 220 (S.C.), rev'd [2002] B.C.J. No. 518, 32 C.B.R. (4th) 250 (C.A.).

mons on November 21, 2005. It was passed by the Senate on November 25, 2005 and subsequently received Royal assent. It was conceded at the time by the then Liberal government that the Bill had been rushed through Parliament, and a commitment was given to defer the coming into force of certain provisions of the new Act "at least until June, 2005," to allow the Standing Senate Committee on Banking, Trade and Commerce (the "Standing Committee") to complete a proper public consultation process. As of the date of writing, portions of the Bill have not yet been proclaimed. With the election of a Conservative minority government some of its more controversial aspects may be changed before they become part of the law.

§11.282 Among the most fundamental aspects of Bill C-55 were the collection of provisions intended to protect workers' claims for unpaid wages and vacation pay as well as unremitted pension contributions in insolvencies. These provisions are not only relevant within the general law of insolvency, but they have important corporate finance implications, and accordingly are of relevance to the subject of this text. In particular, employee claims for unpaid wages and vacation pay will be afforded priority above the claims of secured creditors in bankruptcies, receiverships and restructurings, over the current assets of the employer for such claims up to $2,000. In addition, claims for unremitted pension contributions of employees will rank above the claims of secured creditors in a bankruptcy or receivership.

§11.283 Bill C-55 also creates the long proposed Wage Earners Protection Program (the "WEPP"). It will permit an employee to apply to the Minister for the payment of the amount of wages owing for the six months prior to the date of the bankruptcy or receivership. The maximum amount that the employee will receive is the greater of $3,000 and an amount equal to four times the maximum weekly insurable earnings under the *Employment Insurance Act*, less any applicable deductions under a federal or provincial law. The protection does not apply with respect to severance or termination pay, but it does apply to vacation pay. The government provided the following explanation of WEPP:

> The WEPP will be established under the responsibility of the Minister of Labour and Housing to compensate individuals for amounts earned, but not paid, during the six months preceding the bankruptcy or receivership of their employers under the BIA. The WEPP will help protect workers by providing a guaranteed payment of wages owed up to $3000 should their employer declare bankruptcy. These payments will be subject to income tax and take into consideration other appropriate contributions. The WEPP recognizes that the present insolvency system lacks an effective mechanism to provide prompt and certain payment of unpaid wages and vacation pay in bankruptcy or receivership situations. No longer will workers' claims depend solely upon the asset value of their bankrupt employers' estates. Where a worker's claim is paid by the WEPP, the worker is required to assign their rights under the BIA to the Crown for amounts paid out under the program.

The WEPP will be funded largely through the provision of a super-priority security interest. Instead of recovering individually, unpaid workers will be paid by the Minister, who will then be subrogated as a claimant against the employer.

§11.284 The term "current assets" is defined as unrestricted cash, or any other asset that, in the normal course of operations, is expected to be converted into cash or consumed in the production of income within one year or within the normal operating cycle when it is longer than one year. This claim ranks in priority behind deemed trust claims, unpaid supplier claims, and claims of farmers, fishermen and aquaculturists. Unfortunately, there is a problem in relying on a charge against current assets. The prospect of a proposal or CCAA[802] proceeding also raises the problem of how to finance the company while it is under bankruptcy protection. The assets subject to the special wage claim will likely be used to meet the ongoing expenses of the corporate debtor.

§11.285 Putting WEPP in its proper context, it is largely an old proposal that gets dusted off about every 15 years. It is always resisted strongly by institutional lenders. In a perfectly functioning credit market, there would be two problems with this proposal. First, it would increase the cost of credit, since any subordination of security would mean that secured credit would become more expensive; since unsecured credit is priced relative to secured credit, the cost of unsecured credit will also go up. Workers in contrast have no practical ability to reduce wage costs to reflect their own reduced risk. Second, reduced priority of security means that creditors would more rigorously superintend delinquent accounts, meaning that employers are likely to be shut down earlier than would otherwise be the case.

§11.286 Unfortunately, the credit market is not perfectly functioning for two reasons. First, the proposal provisions of the BIA and the CCAA permit a debtor company to extend employment by a considerable period of time — in principle while it is trying to bring forward a plan of arrangement. Second, the flow of information within the credit market is anything but perfect.

§11.287 Bill C-55 also provides increased protection for defaults in pension contributions — but does not greatly enhance the priority of claims with respect to pension fund deficiencies. It will enact new sections 81.5 and 81.6 of the BIA. Under these provisions, where there are unpaid pension contributions on the date of bankruptcy or the date before the receiver is appointed, the amounts owing with respect thereto will be secured by a charge on all the assets of the debtor. In a bankruptcy, this charge will rank above every other claim, right, charge or security against the bankrupt's assets except the rights under sections 81.1 (unpaid suppliers) and 81.2 (rights of farmers, fishers and aquaculturalists), statutory deemed trust claims under section 67(3) and claims secured under sections 81.3 (unpaid wages). In a receivership, the charge for the unpaid pension contributions only ranks behind claims under sections 81.1 and 81.2 and claims secured under section 81.4 (unpaid wages). Protection is also afforded where a proposal is made under the BIA or relief is sought under the CCAA. Consider-

---

[802] *Companies' Creditors Arrangement Act*, R.S.C. 1985, c. C-36.

able doubts have been raised concerning these super-priority proposals. For instance, the Insolvency Institute has commented:

> IIC is very concerned that the creation of additional statutory charges will make it more difficult and more expensive for Canadian businesses to obtain secured financing. Many significant Canadian businesses depend upon secured financing. Restricting access to that type of funding will hurt the competitiveness of the Canadian economy and hurt employment. Bill C-55 proposes to create charges securing wage and pension contribution arrears that are owing at the outset of an insolvency proceeding. IIC has been advised that on a national basis the aggregate amount of money involved is not large. If, as a social policy matter, it is decided that this issue should be addressed, then it is important to do so in a way that will not be indirectly much more socially expensive.

§11.288 If anything, this comment quite probably understates the case. More so than virtually any other major economy, the Canadian economy is heavily dependent upon the availability of bank financing and other forms of institutional credit. Many of the provisions of Bill C-55 strike at the basic assumptions on which such credit is based. It is almost certain that security-lending ratios will need to be tightened to reflect the changes that will be introduced into law by the Bill. In addition, existing legal agreements and the general terms of which financial commitments are provided will also need to be re-visited. Although the underlying policy objectives of the Bill seem laudable when viewed in isolation, it is far from clear that these goals — even if they are all attained, are worth the probable impact that the Bill will have on credit. Transforming lenders into watchdogs of their borrowers' obligations to third parties may easily prove to have a stifling effect upon entrepreneurial activity. To circumvent these problems, the following results may be imposed upon Canadian capital markets in response to the changes to law inherent in the Bill:

- Requiring entrepreneurs to invest additional "at risk" capital in their businesses. This hampers the development of small business.

- Lenders will be less willing to fund higher-risk ventures. This class of venture includes all high-tech companies.

It follows that any decision to proceed with the wage super-priority proposal is likely to have a potentially detrimental impact on other areas of government concern. This puts the government in the unenviable position of having to decide whether it is more interested in protecting wage earners, helping small business, or the development of new technologies. Governments are not especially good at making these kinds of policy choices.

(ii) Liability for Income Taxes

§11.289 As noted earlier in the chapter, subsection 227.1(1) of the *Income Tax Act*,[803] imposes liability on directors for a variety of different obligations of the corporation under that Act. It provides:

---

[803] R.S.C. 1985, c. 1 (5th Supp.), as amended.

227.1(1) Where a corporation has failed to deduct or withhold an amount as required by subsection 135(3) or 135.17 or section 153 or 215, has failed to remit such an amount or has failed to pay an amount of tax for a taxation year as required under Part VII or VIII, the directors of the corporation at the time the corporation was required to deduct, withhold, remit or pay the amount are jointly and severally or solidarily, liable, together with the corporation, to pay that amount and any interest or penalties relating to it.

Quite clearly subsection 227.1(1) is so broad in scope it would place directors under a severe burden if it were left unqualified, particularly in view of the fact that many directors have only peripheral involvement with the actual day-to-day operation of their corporations.[804] As was discussed earlier, subsection 227.1 is subject to a due diligence defence.[805] In addition to that defence, subsection 227.1(2) goes on to impose certain additional procedural conditions that must be satisfied in order to render a director liable. It reads:

227.1(2) A director is not liable under subsection (1), unless

(a) a certificate for the amount of the corporation's liability referred to in that subsection has been registered in the Federal Court under section 223 and execution for that amount has been returned unsatisfied in whole or in part;

(b) the corporation has commenced liquidation or dissolution proceedings or has been dissolved and a claim for the amount of the corporation's liability referred to in that subsection has been proved within six months after the earlier of the date of the commencement of the proceedings and the date of dissolution; or

(c) the corporation has made an assignment or a bankruptcy order has been made against it under the *Bankruptcy and Insolvency Act* and a claim for the amount of the corporation's liability referred to in that subsection has been proved within six months after the date of the assignment or bankruptcy order.

Thus the liability of a director under subsection 227.1(1) is secondary in nature: it is intended as a back-stop, in cases where the corporation itself is unable to pay.[806] Moreover, no action or proceedings to recover any amount payable by a former director of a corporation may be commenced under subsection 227.1(1) more than two years after he or she ceased to be a director of the corporation concerned.[807]

---

[804] As, for instance, was the case *McCullough v. M.N.R.*, [1989] T.C.J. No. 334, 89 D.T.C. 446 at 448, [1989] C.T.C. 2236; see particularly the reasons of Bonner J. in *McConnachie v. M.N.R.*, [1991] T.C.J. No. 401, as quoted by Dussault T.C.J. in *Nagy v. M.N.R.*, [1991] T.C.J. No. 507, 8 C.B.R. (3d) 267.
[805] Discussed above at §11.4.
[806] In the same vein, s. 227.1(5) provides:

227.1(5) Where execution referred to in paragraph 227.1(2)(a) has issued, the amount recoverable from a director is the amount unsatisfied after execution.

[807] *Income Tax Act*, s. 227.1(4).

§11.290 Where a director is called upon to pay under subsection 227.1 of the *Income Tax Act*, he or she becomes entitled to certain rights relative to other creditors. In particular, subsection 227.1(6) of the Act entitles the director to the benefit of any Crown preference applicable to the debt that the director is called upon to pay:

> 227.1(6) Where a director pays an amount in respect of a corporation's liability referred to in subsection 227.1(1) that is proved in liquidation, dissolution or bankruptcy proceedings, he is entitled to any preference that Her Majesty in right of Canada would have been entitled to had that amount not been so paid and, where a certificate that relates to that amount has been registered, the director is entitled to an assignment of the certificate to the extent of the director's payment, which assignment the Minister is hereby empowered to make.

Where effective control of the corporation is lawfully taken away from the directors (as, for instance, where a receiver and manager is appointed), there is no liability on the directors if the person who takes over control fails to remit the employee deductions. In order to make out a case for personal liability, it is necessary to determine whether the directors had any freedom of choice and control over the corporation.[808] In addition, a director who has satisfied a claim under section 227.1 is entitled to claim contribution from other directors who were liable for the claim.[809] By common law, the director would also be entitled to indemnification from the corporation itself, but given the circumstances in which such a claim is likely to be made against a director, it is doubtful that this right would have any real meaning, beyond the entitlement conferred under subsection 227.1(6).

(iii) Liability for Oppression

§11.291 Directors and officers are potentially liable in their personal capacity under the so-called oppression remedy provided for in sections 248 of the OBCA and 241 of the CBCA. Specifically, a monetary judgment may be entered against a director (or officer or controlling shareholder) of a corporation where that person is responsible for the oppressive conduct forming the basis of the complaint.[810] Although the nature and terms of the oppression remedy are discussed in detail in Chapter 13, in general, liability arises where the power of a director is exercised in a fashion which causes an act or omission of the corporation which effects an oppressive or unfairly prejudicial result, or which unfairly disregards the interest of the complainant, liability may lie against that director or officer.[811] A monetary compensation order will be made against a director whose conduct caused the loss to the complainant even though no order is made against the corporation itself.[812] However, in order to justify an order

---

[808] See, generally, *Robitaille v. Canada*, [1990] F.C.J. No. 1136, [1990] 1 F.C. 310 (T.D.).
[809] *Income Tax Act*, R.S.C. 1985, c. 1 (5th Supp.), s. 227.1(7).
[810] See, for instance, *Gignac, Sutts and Woodall Construction Co. v. Harris*, [1997] O.J. No. 3084, 36 B.L.R. (2d) 210 (Gen. Div.).
[811] *Sidaplex-Plastic Suppliers Inc. v. Elta Group Inc.*, [1995] O.J. No. 4048, 131 D.L.R. (4th) 399 at 407 (Gen. Div.), *per* Blair J., rev'd in part [1998] O.J. No. 2910, 162 D.L.R. (4th) 367 (C.A.).
[812] *Gottlieb v. Adam*, [1994] O.J. No. 2636, 21 O.R. (3d) 248 at 261 (Gen. Div.), *per* Spence J.

against the director, the court must make specific findings of oppressive or unfair conduct on the part of the director. Moreover, a monetary award must also be a suitable remedy for the prejudice, loss or other injury sustained by the complainant.[813] A director of the corporation is not liable for oppression or other grounds for complaint under sections 248 and 241, merely because the corporation for which he or she served treated the complainant in an oppressive or unfair manner, at a time when he or she was a member of the board.

G. THE SPECIAL POSITION OF OUTSIDE DIRECTORS

§11.292 The OBCA and the CBCA draw no real distinction among various categories of directors in terms of their potential liability. The basic statutory requirement for outside directors is imposed under subsection 115(3) of the OBCA, which provides:

> 115.(3) At least one-third of the directors of an offering corporation shall not be officers or employees of the corporation or any of its affiliates.

The CBCA contains a corresponding, but somewhat differently worded, provision in subsection 102(2):

> 102.(2) A corporation shall have one or more directors but a distributing corporation, any of the issued securities of which remain outstanding and are held by more than one person, shall have not fewer than three directors, at least two of whom are not officers or employees of the corporation or its affiliates.

To a very large extent, these limited corporate law requirements have been superseded by more demanding requirements imposed as a matter of securities policy. As discussed in Chapter 9, recent regulatory requirements imposed by the Canadian Securities Administrators (in Ontario under the authority of the *Securities Act*) provide that the majority of the directors of a corporate reporting issuer *should* be independent directors. If a majority of directors are not independent, then Form 58-101F requires the issuer to disclose what "the board of directors does to facilitate its exercise of independent judgment in carrying out its responsibilities".

§11.293 These provisions do not constrain the right of the outside directors to delegate; they have no obligation to involve themselves in the day-to-day management of the corporation, and subject to any statutory restrictions may properly delegate authority to the executive committee of the board and (subject to the general duty of due diligence discussed above) may rely upon that executive committee.[814] Indeed it can be argued that it is not realistic to impose a requirement for outside directors to sit on the board, yet at the same time expect them to have the same degree of intimacy with the business and affairs of the corporation as is possessed by the inside directors. The most recent securities law

---

[813] *Budd v. Gentra*, [1998] O.J. No. 3109, 43 B.L.R. (2d) 27 (C.A.), *per* Doherty J.A.
[814] In particular, members of the audit committee are required to be (or become) financially literate under s. 3.1(4) of National Policy 52-110. See, generally, *Whitehouse v. Carlton Hotel Pty. Ltd.* (1987), 162 C.L.R. 285 (H.C. Aust.).

changes as embodied in National Policy 58-201 have augmented the specific duties of the independent (or outside) directors, so that they now include the following responsibilities:

- The board chair should be independent, and if not there should be an independent "lead director".
- The independent directors should hold regularly scheduled meetings that management do not attend.
- Only independent directors should serve on the nominating committee for directors.
- Only independent directors should serve on the compensation committee (which is to be responsible for determining the compensation of the CEO, other senior officers and board members).

In addition, under National Policy 52-110, with limited exceptions, the members of the audit committee of a reporting issuer must be independent. Despite these requirements, if the outside directors are to remain outside, they cannot be asked to devote as much time or attention to the business and affairs of the corporation as those who are from the inside. If they are so asked, then it is only fair that they be equally compensated, (as noted in Chapter 9, there has been a strong tendency towards significant increases in their remuneration in recent years) but if they are equally compensated, they will become employees of the corporation, and will thereby cease to be outside directors. The question which naturally flows from this reasoning is whether the outside directors of a corporation should therefore be seen as being subject to a lower duty of care than the executive directors of a corporation. Or, to state the proposition another way — the expectations placed on each director respectively must reflect the degree of association that that director has with the corporation, and the role that he or she is expected to play in it.

§11.294 It is clear that different expectations may be placed upon directors who fall into different classifications.[815] For instance, members of the executive committee, which will usually include senior officers of the corporation, may well be exposed to greater liability because of their greater access to information concerning the ongoing business and affairs of the corporation, and because of their ability to withhold information from other members of the board or to control access by other members of the board to relevant information. As noted in Chapter 10, the very wording of the OBCA and CBCA seems to suggest that such considerations should be reflected in fixing the duties of the directors for they specifically relate to the circumstances of the director.

§11.295 Obviously, any discussion on this point must take into account the specific responsibilities and requirements to which independent directors are now

---

[815] See, generally, *Hanson v. Clifford*, [1994] B.C.J. No. 2889, 21 B.L.R. (2d) 108 at 140 (S.C.), *per* Errico J., var'd [1996] B.C.J. No. 2197, 28 B.C.L.R. (3d) 101 (C.A.).

subject. Subject to the proper discharge of the specific responsibilities that are placed on outside directors as such, it can be argued that due to their more limited commitment to the corporation, such directors would naturally seem to be subject to a lesser standard of care than those who come from within the corporation. Outside directors cannot be expected to have the same knowledge of the corporation, its business and affairs as those who are more closely concerned with it. It is unrealistic for them to be expected to monitor the conduct of individual officers of the corporation on a day-to-day basis. Frequently, they will not have the same detailed knowledge of the industry in which it operates, as is possessed by the senior officers of the corporation and its inside directors — all of whom will likely be experts with respect to the industry. Each of these probable situations must to some extent be seen to qualify the liability of the outside directors.

§11.296 Even so, there are clear exceptions on the extent to which such liability will be less than those of other directors. In particular, the liability of members of specialist committees, such as the audit committee, may exceed that of the board of directors in certain circumstances, because of the particular expertise or access to information that members of such committees possess.[816] This possibility reflects the fact that even outside directors are expected to play an important and effective role on the board.[817] They are expected to maintain a separate position independent from the management and to oversee the company's operations and disclosure, particularly where they have notice that the corporation may have serious financial problems. Where they have notice of irregularity, it is appropriate for outside directors to make inquiries and to have discussions in the absence of management where they have a concern about something that management has done.[818]

H. INDEMNIFICATION OF DIRECTORS AND OFFICERS

§11.297 The relationship between general principles of agency and a director's or officer's right to indemnification against liability are inextricably intertwined, and therefore it is worthwhile summarizing briefly the basic right to indemnification to which an agent is entitled when acting on behalf of his or her principal. If A employs B as an agent and instructs B to do a particular task, such as dig a hole at a specified place, there is no question that B will normally be entitled to indemnification against liability should it subsequently be discovered that by digging that hole B was committing an act of trespass. The right of indemnity in such a case arises because B is merely carrying out A's instruction; it would be unconscionable if B were forced to bear a liability where he or she was blameless.[819]

---

[816] *Re Standard Trustco Ltd.* (1992), 6 B.L.R. (2d) 241 at 290-91 (Ont. Sec. Com.).
[817] *Dorchester Finance Co. v. Stebbing*, [1989] B.C.L.C. 498, *per* Foster J.; *Re D'Jan of London Ltd.*, [1994] 1 B.C.L.C. 561 at 563, *per* Hoffman J.
[818] *Re Standard Trustco Ltd.* (1992), 6 B.L.R. (2d) 241 at 292 (Ont. Sec. Com.).
[819] As to the interpretation given express rights of indemnification in the tax context, compare *Adams v. Morgan & Co.*, [1924] 1 K.B. 751; *Re Hollebone's Agreement*, [1959] 2 All E.R. 152; *Perishables Transport Co. v. Spyropoulos (London) Ltd.*, [1964] 2 Lloyd's Rep. 379.

§11.298 However, there is no right of indemnification where the tort is attributable to the manner in which B chooses to perform the assigned task.[820] For instance, if B is instructed to dig a hole on property belonging to A and while so digging that hole throws the dirt onto the property of C so as to commit a trespass against C, then B is not entitled to an indemnity from A. In such a case, B is no longer an innocent person committing a tort as a direct consequence of carrying out A's instruction, but rather is himself or herself the author of that tort. It is not A's instruction that results in the tort, but rather B's manner of carrying out that instruction. By extension, there is no right of indemnification for losses incurred by B in carrying out A's instructions where those losses are attributable to B's own lack of skill in performing the task in question.[821] Moreover, if in such a case A is found vicariously liable for the damages caused by B, then B is subject to an implied obligation to indemnify A — this being a logical consequence of the duty of care that an agent owes to his or her principal in carrying out the principal's instructions.[822]

§11.299 The third type of situation that may arise is where A instructs B to do an act that B knows to be wrongful. A person is always liable for his or her own tortious acts even when carried out on behalf of a principal for whom that person acts as agent.[823] For instance, if A employs B as a bouncer and instructs B to eject C violently from a bar with a use of unreasonable force, B is not entitled to indemnification from A nor is A entitled to indemnification from B. An agent is not bound to carry out an instruction that he or she knows to be unlawful,[824] nor will the agent be exonerated from personal liability if he or she does carry out that instruction. To allow indemnification in favour of A and B would contravene the rule *ex turpi causa non oritur actio*.[825]

§11.300 It is against this background that we come to examine the subject of director indemnification. As noted in Chapter 9, as a matter of law, directors are neither agents of the corporation nor of its shareholders, but as a matter of common sense they are — in that they act on behalf of both the corporation and its shareholders in all practical respects, and it is by reason of so doing that they are

---

[820] *Thacker v. Hardy* (1878), 4 Q.B.D. 685 at 687, *per* Lindley J.
[821] See, generally, *New Zealand Farmers' Co-operative Distributing Co. v. National Mortgage & Agency Co. of New Zealand*, [1961] N.Z.L.R. 999.
[822] *Keppel v. Wheeler*, [1927] 1 K.B. 577 (C.A.); *Hillcrest General Leasing Ltd. v. Guelph Investments Ltd.*, [1970] O.J. No. 1574, 13 D.L.R. (3d) 517 at 522 (C.A.), *per* Grossberg Co. Ct. J., but compare *United Mills Agencies Ltd. v. R.E. Harvey*, [1952] 1 All E.R. 225 (K.B.).
[823] *The Koursk*, [1924] P. 140 at 155; *Weir v. Bell* (1878), 3 Ex. D. 238 at 248 (C.A.).
[824] *Bexwell v. Christie* (1776), 1 Cowp. 395, 98 E.R. 1150 (K.B.).
[825] *Merryweather v. Nixon* (1799), 8 T.R. 186. In the first edition of this text, the question was raised as to the scope of the right of contribution under the *Negligence Act*, R.S.O. 1990, c. N.1. In *Blackwater v. Plint*, [2005] S.C.J. No. 59, [2005] 3 S.C.R. 3 at para. 67, McLachlin C.J.C. stated that: "Fault has been held not to include intentional torts and torts other than negligence." It was also pointed out that in *Bow Valley Husky (Bermuda) Ltd. v. Saint John Shipbuilding Ltd.*, [1997] S.C.J. No. 111, [1997] 3 S.C.R. 1210, the court held that a common law right of contribution between tortfeasors may exist, except for intentional torts or where there was a malicious motivation.

exposed to the risk of liability. The question of the extent to which directors may contract with their corporations for indemnification against potential liability must be approached from several perspectives, including the following: (1) to what extent are the directors or officers of a corporation entitled by law to require the corporation to indemnify them against expense or liability; (2) to what extent may a corporation agree to indemnify its directors and officers; (3) to what extent may the directors and officers require shareholders and each other to indemnify them. The general rule regarding the indemnification of directors in respect of acts done by them that are within the scope of their authority was stated by Turner L.J. in *Re German Mining Co., ex p. Chippendale*:

> ... [A]lthough directors undoubtedly stand in the position of agents and cannot bind their companies beyond the limits of their authority, they also stand in some degree in the position of trustees; and all trustees are entitled to be indemnified against expenses *bona fide* incurred by them in the execution of their trust. There is no inconsistency in this double view of directors. They are agents and cannot bind their companies beyond their powers. They are trustees, and are entitled to be indemnified for expenses incurred by them within the limits of their trust ... No doubt, a company's deed or any other deed may be so framed as to deprive directors or trustees of the right to indemnity, and if the parties think proper to accept directorships or trusts under deeds so framed, they must abide by their consequences; but the right of indemnity is incident to the position of a trustee, and if it is sought to exclude that right, the provisions for that purpose must, as I apprehend, be clearly expressed.[826]

Similar general principles apply in the case of the officers of a corporation; they have a right to recover indemnification in respect of liabilities and expenses incurred while acting in their capacity as agents.[827]

§11.301 The above cases set out the bare minimum of the rights of indemnification to which a corporate director or officer is entitled. These rights of indemnification are restitutionary in nature and as such are subject to the usual restrictions on restitutionary relief. They provide no basis for recovery of indemnification for wrongful and unauthorized acts.

§11.302 As a general rule the law will permit the implied rights of indemnity to which principals and agents are entitled to be modified by agreement between the parties concerned, and will give effect to a promise by A to indemnify the agent B in circumstances where no right of indemnity would otherwise exist. Given the extent of their potential liability, it is understandable that the directors of a corporation will often seek indemnification against liability from either the corporation or its shareholders. In practice, directors and officers often use their effective control over a corporation to arrange contractual indemnity obligations in their favour. Such indemnities will usually provide for full indemnification against all liability, loss or expense. It is also common for directors of any medium or large corporation to seek insurance protection against the risks of liabil-

---

[826] (1853), 4 De G.M. & G. 19 at 52, 43 E.R. 415 (L.JJ.).
[827] *Re Famatina Development Corp.*, [1914] 2 Ch. 271 at 282, *per* Lord Cozens-Hardy M.R.

ity arising from their performance as directors. In recent years, it has been a clear policy evident in corporations, securities and similar legislation to impose personal duties upon the directors and officers of corporations. It would clearly defeat the purposes of this legislation, if directors and officers were able to circumvent in full the liabilities which flow from such legislation by obtaining indemnification from their corporations. Thus the Legislatures have responded by making express provision in corporations legislation to govern the extent to which such relief may be provided. For instance, section 136(1) of the OBCA provides:

> 136.(1) A corporation may indemnify a director or officer of the corporation, a former director or officer of the corporation or a person who acts or acted at the corporation's request as a director or officer of a body corporate of which the corporation is or was a shareholder or creditor, and his or her heirs and legal representatives, against all costs, charges and expenses, including an amount paid to settle an action or satisfy a judgment, reasonably incurred by him or her in respect of any civil, criminal or administrative action or proceeding to which he or she is made a party by reason of being or having been a director or officer of such corporation or body corporate, if,
>
> (a) he or she acted honestly and in good faith with a view to the best interests of the corporation; and
>
> (b) in the case of a criminal or administrative action or proceeding that is enforced by a monetary penalty, he or she had reasonable grounds for believing that his conduct was lawful.

While the subsection 136(1) provision is enabling only, it is doubtful that it would be seen as depriving directors and officers of their common law and equitable rights independent of contract to indemnification in respect of expenses incurred and losses suffered while properly discharging their duties to the corporation. However, it is not appropriate for the majority or control group within a corporation to use corporate funds to defend allegations that they have engaged in misconduct against the corporation. Only if the director or officer is successful is he or she entitled to an indemnity.[828]

§11.303 The corresponding provisions of the CBCA are similar, but as is often the case, differ in detail from those of the CBCA. Section 124 of the CBCA permits a corporation to indemnify "individuals", rather than "persons", who have acted in the capacity of a director or officer. Given the prospect of liability under a unanimous shareholder resolution or sole shareholder declaration, it is not clear why the authority to provide such an indemnity should be limited to "individuals" (a term that is usually equated with natural persons). The CBCA also permits an indemnity to be given to "an individual acting in a similar capacity of another entity", as opposed to the narrower wording of the OBCA, which allows an indemnity for "a person who acts ... as a director or officer of a body corporate of which the corporation is or was a shareholder or creditor". In

---

[828] *Envirodrive v. 836442 Alberta Ltd.*, [2005] A.J. No. 747, 7 B.L.R. (4th) 61 at 93 (Q.B.), per Slatter J.

this respect, it is the OBCA which seems unduly narrow. To give one obvious example: an officer of a corporation may be asked to sit as a representative of the corporation on a credit union that serves the employees of the corporation, even though the corporation may have no shareholder or creditor interest in that credit union. It is difficult to understand why such a person should not be protected by an indemnity from the employer corporation.

§11.304 Subsection 136(1) would appear to limit the availability of such indemnification to those cases where the director or officer is able to meet the two tests set out in clauses (*a*) and (*b*). Under clause (*a*), a right of indemnity can exist only where a director acts honestly and in good faith. Legal couplets of this type always beg such questions as whether it is possible to act honestly but not in good faith, or in good faith but not honestly.[829] These questions are relevant in the case of subsection 136(1), because the ability of a corporation to indemnify a director against liability for criminal liability is clearly a major exception to the general prohibition seen to exist at law against such indemnification. But just how wide is this provision? The lack of any reference to civil liability in clause (*b*) might be taken to suggest that a valid indemnity may be given in respect of conduct that is manifestly and intentionally tortious, but perhaps this is stretching the point, because it is difficult to see how such conduct could be done "honestly and in good faith with a view towards the best interest of the corporation". The extent to which indemnity may be given in respect of criminal liability is also unclear. It is not clear, for instance, whether the requirement that the director or officer must have "reasonable grounds for believing that his conduct was lawful" restricts the availability of indemnification for criminal liability to offences of strict liability. From a public policy perspective, there would certainly be some advantage in giving this provision such an interpretation. While those who are found criminally liable although ignorant of the facts relevant to a crime might be seen to be deserving of indemnification, it is difficult to see why indemnification should be given to those who are possessed of knowledge of those facts. The requirement in clause (*a*) that all acts be done honestly and in good faith is not sufficient to dispose of this question, because a person may know the relevant facts yet simply not know the law; the term "honestly" may refer to the belief of a director (a colour of right), as well as to the lawfulness of the act. In ignorance of the law, a director may act in the genuine hope of furthering the interests of the corporation. It is not clear whether ignorance of law may be sufficiently reasonable to permit recovery under an indemnity. The basis for the common law rule that ignorance of law is not a defence to a criminal charge is that every person is presumed to know the law (or, more realistically, that every person is charged with the duty to determine the law).[830] It is difficult to understand why a less exacting standard should be applied in the corporate sphere than in the criminal courts.[831]

---

[829] See, for instance, *Catalyst Fund General Partner I Inc. v. Hollinger Inc.*, [2006] O.J. No. 2818, 20 B.L.R. (4th) 249 (S.C.).
[830] *Evans v. Bartlam*, [1937] A.C. 473 at 479 (H.L.), *per* Lord Atkin.
[831] Note revised wording to subsection 136(1) enacted by S.O. 2006, c. 34, Sched. B, s. 26 (in force on proclamation).

§11.305 In *R. v. Bata Industries Ltd.*[832] the appellant corporation and two of its director-officers were convicted of pollution-related offences. Under the terms of a probation order, the corporation was prohibited from indemnifying those directors against their fines in respect of those offences. The validity of such a probation order was appealed to the Ontario Court of Appeal.[833] There it was held that the OBCA establishes the circumstances under which a corporation may and must indemnify a director or officer, and by implication also establishes the circumstances under which a corporation cannot indemnify a director or officer. It provides a comprehensive code on the subject of indemnification, which is complemented by statutory provisions which impose liability on a director who votes for indemnification in circumstances other than those permitted by the Act. In order for Bata to be prohibited from indemnifying directors under the terms of its probation order, the prohibition against indemnification must be supported by the OBCA, not the *Provincial Offences Act*.[834] Since the OBCA permits indemnification where the directors act honestly, in good faith, and in the reasonable belief that their conduct was lawful, a ban on indemnification should not be imposed in such circumstances. The court also noted that in any event, a probation order would be an ineffective means of barring indemnification, since the corporation would be entitled to do so once the probation order expired.[835]

§11.306 In terms of the onus of proof, it is an elementary principle of law that people are presumed to act in good faith until it is proven that they have acted otherwise.[836] The onus of proving that a director who is seeking to be indemnified under a contract or indemnification or by-law has not acted in good faith and is therefore disentitled to indemnification lies upon the corporation seeking to avoid the obligation to indemnify, or a person (such as a liquidator or trustee-in-bankruptcy) claiming so on behalf of that corporation.[837] The mere fact that a director has drawn an incidental benefit from a decision that he or she has made is not sufficient to disentitle the director to an indemnity. Provided that the director has acted in good faith and with a view to the best interests of the corporation, an indemnity may still be given. The fact that the director sought legal advice before acting is evidence — although not conclusive evidence — that the director was acting in good faith.[838]

§11.307 Subsection 136(2) of the OBCA deals with the availability of indemnification to a corporate director or officer who is made a party to a proceeding by reason of his position:

---

[832] [1995] O.J. No. 2691, 22 B.L.R. (2d) 135, 127 D.L.R. (4th) 438 (C.A.).
[833] *Ibid.*
[834] R.S.O. 1990, c. P.33, as amended.
[835] *R. v. Bata Industries Ltd.*, [1995] O.J. No. 2691, 22 B.L.R. (2d) 135 at 146 (C.A.), *per* Osborne J.A.
[836] *General Motors Canada Ltd. v. Brunet*, [1977] S.C.J. No. 84, [1977] 2 S.C.R. 537 at 548.
[837] *Blair v. Consolidated Enfield Corp.*, [1995] S.C.J. No. 29, 128 D.L.R. (4th) 73.
[838] *Ibid.*, [1993] O.J. No. 2300, 15 O.R. (3d) 783 (C.A.), aff'd [1995] S.C.J. No. 29, 128 D.L.R. (4th) 73.

136.(2) A corporation may, with the approval of the court, indemnify a person referred to in subsection (1) in respect of an action by or on behalf of the corporation or body corporate to procure a judgment in its favour, to which the person is made a party by reason of being or having been a director or an officer of the corporation or body corporate, against all costs, charges and expenses reasonably incurred by the person in connection with such action if he or she fulfils the conditions set out in clauses (1)(a) and (b).[839]

However, this general provision is then qualified by subsection (3), which provides:

136.(3) Despite anything in this section, a person referred to in subsection (1) is entitled to indemnity from the corporation in respect of all costs, charges and expenses reasonably incurred by the person in connection with the defence of any civil, criminal or administrative action or proceeding to which he or she is made a party by reason of being or having been a director or officer of the corporation or body corporate, if the person seeking indemnity,

(a) was substantially successful on the merits in his or her defence of the action or proceeding; and

(b) fulfils the conditions set out in clauses (1) (a) and (b).

§11.308 Subsection 136(2) of the OBCA deals with derivative actions (*i.e.*, actions brought by or on behalf of the corporation) and is clearly intended to limit the giving of indemnities to corporate officers and directors where such actions are brought. Subsection 136(3) creates an express right of indemnification, independent of contract. It may be seen to codify one part of the common law rights to indemnification of directors and officers, namely the right to recover the costs of an officer or director in defending an action or proceeding that is brought against that person as a result of his being an officer or director. However, there is one aspect of this provision that appears to depart from the common law. In order to claim an indemnity under this provision it is necessary for the defence to be substantially successful on the merits while the director or officer himself must fulfill the conditions set out in clauses 136(1)(a) and (b). This is clearly an unusual requirement, for it means that although a person has acted lawfully, he (or she) is not necessarily entitled to an indemnity from the corporation unless he can also show that he acted honestly and in good faith and with a view to the best interests of the corporation. In addition, the requirement that the defence must be successful on "its merits" raises the question of whether there is an entitlement to indemnity where the director or officer finally disposes of a claim against him on procedural grounds alone. The mere fact that a party to a proceeding wins an action by way of a technical knock-out should not in itself preclude indemnification; there is no reason to believe that the director would not have obtained a full acquittal had the matter proceeded to trial.

§11.309 In addition to section 136, section 130 of the OBCA affords rights of indemnity tied to specific obligations imposed upon the directors personally

---

[839] Note revised wording to come into effect on proclamation of S.O. 2006, c. 34, Sched. B, s. 26. See also new subsection (4.2).

under the Act. Subsection 130(3) expressly permits the recovery of contribution or indemnity where such liability ensues:

> 130.(3) A director who has satisfied a judgment rendered under this section is entitled to contribution from the other directors who voted for or consented to the unlawful act upon which the judgment was founded.

Thus the impropriety or illegality of a director's conduct does not preclude the director from recovering contribution from his or her fellow directors. To eliminate any doubt, subsection (4) makes clear that the right of contribution may be recovered in court:

> 130.(4) A director liable under subsection (2) is entitled to apply to the court for an order compelling a shareholder or other recipient to pay or deliver to the director any money or property that was paid or distributed to the shareholder or other recipient contrary to section 20, 30, 31, 32, 37, 38, 136, 185 or 248.[840]

I. OBCA DIRECTOR AND OFFICER INSURANCE

§11.310 Most corporations of any size purchase directors and officers liability insurance ("D&O") for the benefit of their directors and senior executives. In this section of the chapter, we shall take a general overview of such insurance. In recent years, the cost for such coverage has increased dramatically, while the exclusions for coverage have expanded (in the United States, it is said that between 1996 and 2001, the director and officer insurance industry suffered an increase in exposure of approximately 200 per cent). It is a good idea to consult an insurance broker regarding the insurance needs and requirements of a corporation, before applying for a policy. Therefore, for more detailed information, readers should consult a specialized text on this subject and discuss their specific insurance concerns or requirements with a qualified insurance broker.

§11.311 A D&O policy may be seen as serving to protect the assets of a corporation from being drawn upon, should a director or officer claim under the terms of an indemnification arrangement. Alternatively, such an arrangement may be viewed as protection for the individual directors, officers and employees to which it relates, against claims and litigation expenses arising from their service on behalf of the corporation. D&O coverage is designed to provide coverage for liability with respect to such wrongful acts as breach of the legal duties of care, obedience and loyalty to the organization. Claims such as failing to protect and manage the financial affairs of the organization or wrongful employment practices may also be covered under a D&O policy. The scope of coverage provided under a director and officer insurance policy varies from one insurer to another. In all cases, the scope of the protection afforded is determined by the terms of the policy.[841] Significant variations are often encountered in the nature and

---

[840] Note revised wording to come into effect on proclamation of S.O. 2006, c. 34, Sched. B, s. 26. Note also new subsection (4.1) dealing with derivative proceedings.
[841] *Reid Crowther & Partners Ltd. v. Simcoe & Erie General Insurance Co.*, [1993] S.C.J. No. 10, [1993] 1 S.C.R. 252.

structure of policies offered in the market and consequently in the scope of insurance protection that is afforded against the risks of acting as a director or manager.

(i) Claims Made vs. Occurrence Policies

§11.312 One critical area of concern is the time during which protection is afforded.[842] The first and more traditional approach is occurrence-based. Under such policies, protection is related to the time of the occurrence of the negligent act. If the negligent act giving rise to the damages occurs during the policy period, then the insurer is required to indemnify the insured for any damages arising from it (up to the cap of the policy) regardless of when the actual claim is made. A second approach, known as the claims-made approach, focuses on the time when the claim is made against an insured. Such policies afford protection only if a claim is made during the policy period. However, under such policies the insurer is required to indemnify regardless of when the negligent act giving rise to the claim occurred. A given policy of insurance may use the first or the second approach or a combination of the two approaches.

§11.313 Occurrence-based policies work well where the damage resulting from a particular negligent act is immediately apparent (or becomes apparent shortly thereafter). It is less well-suited where the damage from the negligent act may not be apparent for many years. The "long-tail" nature of the liability in such cases increases the probability that a claim will be made after (and possibly even long after) the policy has expired. Second, the ongoing developments in professional or commercial practice, the applicable standards of professional care, general principles of law and science and technology make it difficult for the insurer to estimate the potential liability arising from claims made many years in the future. Finally, where an insured repeatedly changes insurance companies, a claim made in the future could result in legal battles between insurance companies where the exact timing of the negligence is unknown or where the negligence was of an ongoing nature. These problems increase the difficulty of assessing actuarial risk. As a result, most director and officer policies now tend towards the claims-made side of the spectrum, as do policies covering professional services.

§11.314 On the other hand, claims-made and hybrid policies have their shortcomings. While the premiums for such policies tend to be lower because risk is more susceptible to actuarial estimate, and the period of exposure to claim may be fixed with greater certainty, they also offer more limited coverage. Frequently, such policies provide inadequate coverage for the insured. This is particularly true in the case of a discovery policy, as the insurer is required to indemnify only if the damages are discovered during the policy period. Many claims-made policies exclude from coverage any negligence of which the insured is aware prior to the

---

[842] See, generally, *Jesuit Fathers of Upper Canada v. Guardian Insurance Co. of Canada*, [2006] S.C.J. No. 21, [2006] 1 S.C.R. 744.

coverage period even if no claims have been made. Where the insured changes insurers, the insured may not be protected with respect to claims that relate to acts that occurred at a time when one insurer was providing coverage, if the claim is not made by a third party until a subsequent period. Another potential risk is that an insurer may decline to renew coverage where it learns that there is a serious risk of a claim being made in the near future.

§11.315 To remedy these deficiencies in coverage, a number of new types of coverage have evolved, such as "extended reporting period", "discovery period" and "tail coverage" protection. Insurance of this type will afford protection against claims made for a specified length of time after the expiry of the policy. Another form of expanded coverage is the "notice of circumstance clause". It permits the insured to report during the policy period circumstances that may give rise to future claims. Any claims related to those circumstances made after the expiry of the period are deemed made during the policy period.

(ii) Caps and Policy Limits

§11.316 In general, most such insurance will have a cap on coverage per loss (*e.g.*, $2 million), with a separate annual aggregate cap (*e.g.*, $10 million). It is essential when reviewing a policy to determine whether these caps apply per insured director, or for the corporation as a whole, since the benefit of coverage is clearly limited if the limits are determined on a corporation-wide basis. Usually, each insured director and officer will be subject to a separate deductible (currently ranging from $5,000 to $10,000 retention).

(iii) Scope of Coverage

§11.317 A D&O policy supplements the coverage afforded under a corporation's commercial general liability ("CGL") policy. Usually, a CGL policy will exclude coverage for claims relating to management decisions and activities of the organization; further CGL coverage tends to be limited to death, bodily injury and property damage only.

§11.318 Generally, a D&O policy will provide three types of coverage. First, officers and directors will be covered against defined losses arising from any claim within the scope of the policy during the coverage period. Second, the corporation will be insured for claims made against an officer or director, if and to the extent that the corporation is required or permitted by law to indemnify the officer or director for the alleged wrongful act. Third, the corporation will be directly insured for securities claims that are made directly against the corporation. This last area of coverage has been brought about due to expanded securities litigation in the United States. Until securities coverage was extended often there would be a dispute between the insured and the insurer as to the allocation of responsibility for loss between the corporation and its directors and officers (insurers would argue that damages were attributable to the corporation rather than to individual officers and directors, because the corporation was not itself insured). Securities "entity" coverage avoids this problem. In addition to basic negligence coverage, such policies can also cover claims such as

- discrimination involving employment or potential membership;
- sexual harassment for verbal abuse (usually policies will be written so as to exclude liability for actual physical abuse);
- acts beyond granted authority;
- wrongful termination of contracts and wrongful dismissal of employees;
- failure to comply with relevant statutory obligations;
- libel, slander, or defamation of character.

Since each D&O policy contains its own definitions of what constitutes a covered claim, the actual scope of coverage can vary significantly from one policy to another. Another frequent area of dispute in the past has been to identify the "officers" of the corporation who are protected by the policy. Again, this is an aspect of coverage that is likely to vary from one policy to another.

§11.319 D&O policies are usually written on a "claims-made" basis, which means that a claim is insured only if it is made during the term of the policy. The claim is "made" when the insured officer or director receives it or learns of it. However, it is also typically required that the insured must report the claim to the insurer either within the policy period or within a stipulated number of days of being notified of the claim (often a window of 60 days is allowed following the expiration of the policy to report claims notified during the policy).

§11.320 D&O policies will almost always incorporate broadly worded exclusions on coverage. One of the most important is known as the insured versus insured exclusion. This exclusion was originally intended to prevent the corporation from suing its directors, so as to recover business losses by obtaining recovery under the D&O insurance policy. However, many policies contain broadly worded provisions that exclude coverage for claims against directors and officers asserted even by a trustee-in-bankruptcy. Generally, the insured versus insured exclusion does not apply to shareholder derivative suits, even though the corporation itself will be named as the nominal plaintiff. Nevertheless, it is important to confirm that such coverage is provided with the corporation's insurance broker.

§11.321 D&O policies will invariably exclude coverage for loss connected with claims made against an insured that arise from the director's or officer's own improper personal profit or securing of advantage. Paradoxically, this exclusion will usually not apply, unless a specific finding of culpability is made against the director or officer concerned. Similarly, there will be no coverage for claims arising out of any deliberate criminal act or deliberate fraudulent act by the insured. Generally, where two directors (A, B) are insured under the same policy, and A is guilty of wrongdoing but B is not, B may still obtain indemnification under the policy. However, this is obviously an element of each policy that needs to be specifically confirmed before purchase. Coverage for provincial, state and federal regulatory investigations or enforcement proceedings tends to vary widely by policy, and therefore constitutes a further specific area of each policy that requires careful consideration.

§11.322 Another critical area of concern is whether the D&O policy incorporates a "duty to defend", obliging the insurer to fund the defence of a claim before judgment. Even where this is not the case, it may be possible to arrange an interim funding agreement with the insurer. Under such an arrangement, the insurer and insured each reserve their rights concerning coverage under the policy, but in the meantime the insurer agrees to advance defence costs. The insured is required to undertake to reimburse the insurer if it is ultimately determined that coverage is not available under the policy. Where the defence of directors and officers is left to the insured and their counsel, D&O policies typically provide for cooperation and settlement. While the insurers do not fund the defence of the case, they typically require that cases cannot be settled without their written consent. In addition, insurers may reserve a right to consent to the selection of defence counsel, and the setting of their fees (either of which may prevent the insured from securing representation of his or her own choosing). Finally, D&O policies usually include defence costs within the aggregate limits of coverage. Thus, it is possible (and far from unusual) for the entire policy coverage to be expended on defence costs, leaving little or no funds remaining to satisfy a settlement or judgment.

§11.323 The OBCA does not permit director and officer insurance to cover a person's "failure to act honestly and in good faith with a view to the corporation's best interest". The CBCA does not prohibit insurance covering such liability.[843] The Ministry of Government Services has asked in a discussion paper whether the CBCA should be followed. As there are cases in which it has been held that gross negligence may amount to a breach of fiduciary duty, it is to be hoped that this option is followed.

J. DIRECTOR DISQUALIFICATION

§11.324 In the United Kingdom, a person may be disqualified from serving as a director under the *Company Directors Disqualification Act, 1986*,[844] for periods ranging from two to 15 years. A disqualification order is made by the court. In 2001, the Act was amended to permit a disqualification undertaking, as an administrative equivalent to a disqualification order. Such an undertaking may be given to the Secretary of State. It has the same effect as a disqualification order, but does not require a court order. Disqualification orders (and undertakings) may only be granted where the individual to whom they relate is responsible for such misconduct as:

---

[843] The CBCA provision appears to have been influenced by clause 145(g) of the *Delaware General Corporation Law* (Delaware Code, Title 8, c. 1).

[844] Chapter 46. A comparable remedy is available in Australia under the *Corporations Act, 2001* (Comm.), ss. 206C and 206E.

- continuing to trade to the detriment of creditors at a time when the company was insolvent;
- failure to keep proper accounting records;
- failure to prepare and file accounts or make returns to Companies House;
- failure to submit tax returns or pay over to the Crown tax or other money due; and
- failure to co-operate with the regulatory authorities.[845]

The Act applies not only to a person who has been formally appointed as a director but also to those people who have carried out the functions of a director and to shadow directors. A disqualification order disqualifies a person from:

- acting as a director of a company;
- taking part, directly or indirectly, in the promotion, formation or management of a company;
- being a liquidator or an administrator of a company; and
- being a receiver or manager of a company's property.

The order covers corporations of all types. It is not limited in its effect to reporting issuers for securities law purposes. The court may grant relief from any such order.

§11.325 Neither the OBCA nor the CBCA provides for orders (or undertakings) of this type, although Part XXII of the *Securities Act* does contemplate such an order in the case of a director of an issuer. Invariably, however, proceedings under the *Securities Act* are limited to securities-related misdeeds. It does not provide a comprehensive mechanism for dealing with the wider range of shenanigans often effected through the medium of a private company. The lack of a disqualification procedure in Ontario is a serious oversight, and it is to be hoped that some thought is given to introducing a procedure comparable to that available in the U.K., during the next round of corporate law modernization.

---

[845] As to the principles to be followed in making orders under that Act, see: *Secretary of State for Trade and Industry v. Swan*, [2005] All E.R. (D) 102 (Ch.).

Chapter 12

SHAREHOLDERS AND THEIR RIGHTS

A. INTRODUCTION

§12.1 Both the Ontario *Business Corporations Act*[1] ("OBCA") and the *Canada Business Corporations Act*[2] ("CBCA") contain extensive provisions governing the rights and, in certain cases, liabilities of shareholders. However, neither statute contains an express definition of the term "shareholder". This oversight is unfortunate, because there are several different meanings that may be given to the term. In one sense, the term "shareholder" describes a person who has subscribed for shares of the corporation and to whom such shares have been issued and allotted by the corporation and all required procedural steps have been observed (*e.g.*, approval of the allotment of the shares by the directors, and the registration of the person on the shareholder registry of the corporation)[3] to conclude his or her formal admission as a member of the corporation and registration as such.[4] In addition, there are successor shareholders, such as the personal representatives of deceased or bankrupt shareholders, who have succeeded by law to the interest of a shareholder. Also, shares may be transferred to a third party, and upon his or her name being entered by the corporation in its shareholder registry, that transferee will become subject to the rights and obligations of the original shareholder. Next, there are persons who have subscribed for shares and to whom shares have been allotted, even though some requisite procedure remains to be satisfied, such as the entry of their names into the registers of the corporation or the satisfaction of some other condition.[5] Then there are persons who have subscribed for shares, but to whom shares have not been allotted. Opposite that are also persons who have subscribed for shares but have not yet paid for them.[6] There are those who have never become shareholders in a corporation but who have allowed themselves to be described as such.[7] Next, there are

---

[1] R.S.O. 1990, c. B.16.
[2] R.S.C. 1985, c. C-44.
[3] See, for instance, *Tough Oakes Gold Mines Ltd. v. Foster*, [1917] O.J. No. 221, 39 O.L.R. 144, 34 D.L.R. 748 (H.C.D.).
[4] Once a person becomes a shareholder, he or she remains so despite any subsequent amendment to the articles of the corporation, change in its members or objects, or addition to or subtraction from its powers: *Canada Car & Manufacturing Co. v. Harris*, [1874] O.J. No. 147, 24 U.C.C.P. 380.
[5] See, for instance, *Spitzel v. Chinese Corp.* (1899), 80 L.T. 347, 15 T.L.R. 281 (Ch.).
[6] See, for instance, *Contributories of Home Assurance Co. v. Burton*, [1950] S.C.J. No. 24, [1950] S.C.R. 591.
[7] *Re Acme Products Ltd.* (1932), 14 C.B.R. 40 (Man. C.A.); *Re James Burton*, [1927] 2 Ch. 132 at 141, *per* Romer J.; *cf. Re Pakenham Pork Packing Co.*, [1906] O.J. No. 27, 12 O.L.R. 100 at 113 (C.A.), *per* Moss C.J.O.; see also *Re Port Arthur Wagon Co.*, [1918] S.C.J. No. 50, 57 S.C.R. 388.

persons who have purchased the shares of another person, but who have not yet secured the registration of that transfer in the records of the corporation.[8] Finally, there are persons who have entered into an agreement to purchase shares, or who have otherwise acquired an equitable title to those shares, but to whom the formal transfer of those shares is still to be made.[9] More recently, with the enactment of the *Securities Transfer Act, 2006*, the law has given express recognition to the owners of un-certificated shares. Each of these persons may be a shareholder for some purposes but not for others, and, therefore, may possess the rights, and be subject to the liabilities, of a shareholder *vis-à-vis* some persons and in some circumstances but not in others. Accordingly, in discussing a rule of law relating to a shareholder of a corporation, it is important always to keep in mind precisely the type of shareholder whose rights and obligations are the subject of discussion.[10]

§12.2 Ordinarily, a shareholder of a corporation acquires four basic rights by his or her share ownership: (1) the right to vote on matters to be decided by the shareholders as members of the corporation; (2) the right to participate in the profits of the corporation when distributions of profits are made; (3) the right to participate in the distribution of the assets of the corporation when the corporation is wound up, after the creditors are paid; and (4) the right to transfer his or her shares to some other person.[11] These rights correspond broadly with the rights of a member of a partnership, and no doubt for this reason, very early in the history of corporate law it became common to consider shareholders as being members of the corporation. However, insofar as OBCA and CBCA corporations are concerned, except where otherwise provided by statute, the nature and extent of these membership rights is never absolute, but is subject to definition by the terms of the shares held by the particular shareholder. This point is most evident in the case of shareholder voting rights. Some shares are non-voting, and others carry a vote only with respect to specified matters or in specified circumstances.

§12.3 The law relating to shareholder obligations relates primarily, if not entirely, to the question of the shareholder's liability to the creditors of a corporation. In contrast, the law relating to the rights of a shareholder is to a large extent the law governing disputes between shareholders and the corporation on one hand, and among the shareholders of a corporation on the other. The principal causes of shareholder disputes include:[12] greed and desire for power; misappropriation of

---

[8] See, for instance, *Cooper v. Cayzor Athabasca Mines Ltd.*, [1960] O.J. No. 186, 24 D.L.R. (2d) 544 (C.A.). Until the transfer is registered, the transferor holds the shares as trustee for the transferee: *Hardoon v. Belilios*, [1901] A.C. 118 at 123 (P.C.), *per* Lord Lindley.

[9] See, for instance, *Colonial Bank v. Cady* (1890), 15 App. Cas. 267; *Gaby v. Federal Packaging & Partition Co.*, [1965] O.J. No. 1064, [1965] 1 O.R. 15 (C.A.), aff'd [1966] S.C.J. No. 30, [1966] S.C.R. 527, 57 D.L.R. (2d) 1.

[10] *Kary Investment Corp. v. Tremblay*, [2005] A.J. No. 1030, 8 B.L.R. (4th) 40 at 51 (C.A.), *per* Russell J.A.

[11] See, generally, *Re Central Capital Corp.*, [1996] O.J. No. 359, 132 D.L.R. (4th) 223 at 238 (C.A.), *per* Finlayson J.A.

[12] F. Hodge O'Neal, *Squeeze-Outs of Minority Shareholders: Expulsion or Oppression of Business Associates* (Chicago: Callaghan & Co., 1975), 11 *et seq.*

property by those in control;[13] personality clashes, including marital discord and family quarrels; basic conflict of interest; disagreements over policy;[14] the inactive shareholder;[15] death of the founder or key shareholder, which may lead to dispute either due to disagreement among the heirs,[16] or because the indifference of the heirs causes disagreement with the deceased's former partners;[17] the problem of the aged founder who "hangs on";[18] the drive of superior talent to rise; the autocratic controlling shareholder;[19] disregard of corporate ritual;[20] failure to keep proper books; the obstreperous or uncooperative shareholder;[21] entry of a minority shareholder into a competing business; difficulty of disposing of a minority interest in a corporation; difficulty in valuing an interest in a closely held corporation; under-capitalization of the business; and problems arising out of a change in ownership and control. In many cases, the above problems arise or exacerbate due to a failure to provide measures in the articles or a unanimous shareholder agreement to prevent conflicts or to provide for their resolution. It follows that corporate solicitors should become familiar with the major causes of corporate infighting, and should take care to draft articles and unanimous shareholder agreements in a way that will minimize the risks of dispute and eventual litigation. Solicitors should not allow their clients to convince them that informal arrangements provide an adequate substitute for careful draftsmanship.

B. ON BECOMING A SHAREHOLDER

§12.4 Despite the inherent ambiguity of the term, most basically and strictly defined, a shareholder is a person (1) who has agreed to become a member of a corporation;[22] (2) to whom one or more shares have been issued;[23] and (3) for whom all the required formalities have been completed in connection

---

[13] See, for instance, *Neri v. Finch Hardware (1976) Ltd.*, [1995] O.J. No. 1932, 20 B.L.R. (2d) 216 (Gen. Div.); *Milam v. Cooper Co.*, 258 S.W.2d 953 (Tex. Civ. App. 1953); *Hill v. Bellevue Gardens Inc.*, 190 F. Supp. 760 (D.D.C. 1960), aff'd 297 F.2d 185 (App. D.C. 1961).
[14] See, generally, *Lunn v. B.C.L. Holdings Inc.*, [1996] S.J. No. 814, 30 B.L.R. (2d) 114 (Q.B.).
[15] See, generally, *Arrotta v. Avva Light Corp.*, [1995] A.J. No. 922, 34 Alta. L.R. (3d) 308 (Q.B.), rev'd [1995] A.J. No. 1154, 36 Alta. L.R. (3d) 139 (C.A.).
[16] See, for instance, *Holden v. Construction Machinery Co.*, 202 N.W.2d 348 (Iowa S.C. 1972).
[17] See, for instance, *Coleman v. Coleman*, 191 So.2d 460 (Fla. App. 1966).
[18] See, for instance, *Re Faehndrich Petition*, 151 N.Y.S.2d 261 (1957), aff'd 152 N.Y.S.2d 413, revd 161 N.Y.S.2d 99 (C.A.).
[19] See, for instance, *Holden v. Construction Machinery Co.*, 202 N.W.2d 348 (Iowa S.C. 1972).
[20] See, for instance, *Lycette v. Green River Gorge, Inc.*, 21 Wash.2d 859, 153 P. (2d) 873 (1944).
[21] See, generally, *Intercontinental Precious Metals Inc. v. Cooke*, [1993] B.C.J. No. 1903, 10 B.L.R. (2d) 203 (S.C.).
[22] No one can become a shareholder against his or her will: *Hardoon v. Belilios*, [1901] A.C. 118 (P.C.), *per* Lord Lindley, at 123.
[23] In England, shares are considered issued when the subscriber's name is entered into the share registry, even if no certificate is issued for the shares: *Re Heaton's Steel & Iron Ore Co.* (1876), 4 Ch. D. 140. Section 738(1) of the *U.K. Companies Act, 1985* (U.K.) c. 6, provides that a share is allotted when a person acquires the unconditional right to be entered into the share registry in respect of that share. It is unclear whether this statutory definition is declarative of the common law or a statutory variation of the common law. In Canada, the terms "issue" and "allot" seem to be used interchangeably.

therewith.[24] A person may become a shareholder of a corporation by way of contract with the corporation, or by way of purchase, gift or other acquisition of the share interest of some other person.

§12.5 Less frequently (*e.g.*, upon the death or bankruptcy or amalgamation of a shareholder, or by way of expropriation) a person may succeed to the position of a shareholder by operation of law.[25] Acquisition of shares in this manner is sometimes described as "transmission". Except in the case of amalgamation,[26] the transmission of shares does not make a person a shareholder until such time as the person acquiring the shareholder's interest by such succession has been entered into the share registry.[27] Nevertheless, the person concerned acquires most of the rights associated with the shares.[28] For instance, there is a right to receive any dividend payment or other distribution on the shares concerned. In *Re a Company No 007828 of 1985*,[29] petitioners under section 459 of the U.K. *Companies Act, 1985* relied upon a transaction which, they claimed, gave rise to a constructive trust in their favour. They argued that this amounted to a transmission by operation of law, so bringing them within the scope of subsection 459(2). Harman J. rejected this argument, and said:

> In my view, transmission by operation of law means some act in the law by which the legal estate passes even though there be some further act (such as registration) to be done; and in my view the mere allegation that there arises a constructive trust ... cannot possibly amount to a transmission by operation of law.

§12.6 Like creditors, shareholders are persons interested in a corporation, but in the case of shareholders the interest is one of participatory membership rather than that of debtor and creditor. However, this simple membership-based definition begs numerous questions: what does it mean to be a shareholder; when does a person agree to become a member of a corporation; may a person be a shareholder for some purposes but not others; can a person become a member for a limited purpose; what is the consequence if the parties concerned misunderstand the conditions on which a person agreed to become a member; what steps must be taken to make a person a member of the corporation; does the number of steps that must be so taken differ from one context to another; what is the

---

[24] On this last point, see *National Westminster Bank plc v. Inland Revenue Comm.*, [1995] 1 A.C. 119 (H.L.). In that case, a tax benefit would result if shares were considered to be issued before March 16, 1993. Although the shares had been subscribed for and allotted prior to that date, the shareholders' names were not entered into the company's register of shareholders until April. The majority in the House of Lords concluded that the shares were not issued before the March 16 deadline.

[25] *Miller v. F. Mendel Holdings Ltd.*, [1984] S.J. No. 98, [1984] 2 W.W.R. 683 (Q.B.); *Kary Investment Corp. v. Tremblay*, [2005] A.J. No. 1030, 8 B.L.R. (4th) 40 at 52 (C.A.), *per* Russell J.A.

[26] CBCA, s. 186; OBCA, s. 179.

[27] See, for instance, *Re Bowling & Welby's Contract*, [1895] 1 Ch. 663 at 670 (C.A.), *per* Lindley L.J.

[28] *New Zealand Gold Extraction Co (Newbery-Vautin Process) Ltd. v. Peacock*, [1894] 1 Q.B. 662 (C.A.); *James v. Beuna Ventura Nitrate Grounds Syndicate Ltd.*, [1896] 1 Ch. 456 (C.A.).

[29] (1986), 2 B.C.C. 98,951.

consequence if there is some error made or some other defect in the steps that are actually taken to complete admission to membership?

§12.7 The two most common methods used to become a shareholder are subscription and transfer. In either case, attaining the status of shareholder involves a number of sequential steps. For instance, a subscriber for shares does not normally become a shareholder until his or her subscription is accepted — the acceptance, in most cases, taking the form of an allotment of shares to that person.[30] But allotment is only one method of evidencing acceptance of a subscription.[31] Although the inclusion of the name of a person on the list of shareholders, the issue of a share certificate, the payment of dividends and the sending of notice of shareholders' meetings and participation in such meetings are obviously evidence that the particular person concerned is a shareholder, and may even be sufficient to raise a presumption to that effect, none of these steps by itself is conclusive of that fact.[32] Moreover, in certain cases a person may be released from a subscription for shares (despite acceptance and the allotment of shares to that person) where the subscription contract is void or voidable.

§12.8 Where admission as a shareholder is contingent upon approval by the directors or some other decision-making body within the corporation, a transferee of shares will not normally become a shareholder[33] unless and until that approval is obtained — nor may such approval be compelled by the transferee where the directors act in an honest and genuine belief that it is in the best interests of the corporation to reject the proposed transfer.[34] Still, the bias of the law is towards freedom of share transfer.[35]

§12.9 The fact that a person shown as a shareholder in the records of a corporation does not demand dividends or is inactive in the management and control of the corporation cannot be raised by a corporation as evidence that the person concerned is not truly a shareholder or is not the real owner of the share concerned.[36] This principle is a logical outgrowth of the separation of ownership and

---

[30] See, generally, *Nasmith v. Manning*, [1880] S.C.J. No. 8, 5 S.C.R. 417; see also *Re Standard Fire Insurance Co.*, [1885] O.J. No. 45, 12 O.A.R. 486 (C.A.), aff'd [1886] S.C.J. No. 25, 12 S.C.R. 644.

[31] *Cooper v. Cayzor Athabasca Mines Ltd.*, [1960] O.J. No. 186, 24 D.L.R. (2d) 544 at 550 (C.A.), *per* Laidlaw J.A.; *Nelson Coke & Gas. Co. v. Pellatt*, [1902] O.J. No. 179, 4 O.L.R. 481 at 489 (C.A.), *per* Maclennan J.A.

[32] See, for instance, *Re Universal Banking Corp.* (1867), 3 Ch. App. 40; *Re Essex Provision Co.*, [1925] O.J. No. 543, 27 O.W.N. 503, 5 C.B.R. 549 (S.C. in Bkcy.).

[33] A transfer of a share (like a transfer of any registered security) being incomplete until it is registered: *Société Générale de Paris v. Walker* (1885), 11 App. Cas. 20 (H.L.). As to the effect of transfer without compliance with the terms of a transfer restriction, see *Beechwood Cemetary Co. v. Graham*, [1998] O.J. No. 5311, 41 B.L.R. (2d) 186 (C.A.).

[34] Although obviously these facts may raise serious doubts as to the validity of a purported shareholder's title to shares to a prospective purchaser. See, generally, *Gordon Leaseholds Ltd. v. Metzger*, [1967] O.J. No. 953, [1967] 1 O.R. 580 (H.C.J.), *per* Thompson J.

[35] *Mathers v. Mathers*, [1989] N.S.J. No. 77, 42 B.L.R. 228 at 235 (T.D.), *per* Kelly J., aff'd [1989] N.S.J. No. 164, 90 N.S.R. (2d) 354 (C.A.).

[36] *McWilliams v. Geddes & Moss Undertaking Co.*, 169 So. 894 (C.A. Lo. 1936).

management that results from the use of the corporate form of organization. Whereas directors are obliged to concern themselves in the business and affairs of a coporation, subject to an agreement to the contrary, it is one of the privileges of a shareholder in a corporation to treat an investment in shares as a passive investment, and to say nothing concerning, and not be involved in, the management of its business.

(i) Status of a Shareholder

§12.10 A shareholder of a corporation is not as such a creditor of the corporation.[37] Consequently, a shareholder has no standing (where acting in the capacity of a shareholder) to petition a corporation into bankruptcy[38] or to submit a proof of claim in a bankruptcy proceeding.[39] However, shareholders are entitled to a deferred claim on amounts owed to them in regard to their shares in a winding-up or dissolution, after the payment of all other obligations of the corporation.[40] In addition, a corporation may hold property as a trustee or agent for its shareholders and in this capacity may actually hold shares in itself. The normal presumption is, however, that the corporation holds property for its own use and benefit, and therefore clear evidence of such an agency relationship is required for such a conclusion of agency to be drawn.[41]

§12.11 A shareholder is, by definition, a person with a membership interest in the corporation. The extent of that interest is measured by the stated capital of the shares held by that shareholder, plus (in certain cases) any accrued but unpaid dividends. The amounts paid by creditors for their shares fall into a general common pool known as the stated capital of a corporation. A shareholder has no right to require that a portion of these funds be set aside for one particular series of transactions.[42] The control of all, or practically all, of the shares of a corporation by one person will not make the property of that corporation his or hers, as distinguished from that of the corporation, nor will the business of the corporation become his or her business.[43] Instead, the shareholder's right is limited to a claim against the capital of the corporation; the shareholder has no rights in the assets of the corporation as such.[44] Thus, as a general rule the shareholders of a corporation may not sue in their own names to enforce rights belonging to the corporation, though if individual shareholders have personal interests distinct from the corporation with regard to a particular matter, they may bring an action

---

[37] *Re Patricia Appliance Shops Ltd.*, [1922] O.J. No. 131, 52 O.L.R. 215, 2 C.B.R. 466 (H.C.D.).
[38] *Fan Flame Spark Plug Co. v. Morin* (1925), 64 Que. S.C. 292. A shareholder may, however, seek the liquidation of the corporation where his or her rights as a shareholder are disregarded or may seek relief under the oppression remedy.
[39] *Re Patricia Appliance Shops Ltd.*, [1922] O.J. No. 131, 52 O.L.R. 215, 2 C.B.R. 466 (H.C.D.).
[40] *Embree v. Miller*, [1917] 1 W.W.R. 1200, 33 D.L.R. 331 at 335 (Alta. C.A.), *per* Beck J.
[41] See Chapter 2.
[42] See, generally, *Préfontaine v. Société des arts du Canada* (1909), 11 Que. P.R. 109 (C.S.).
[43] *Lunney v. Welland Securities Ltd.*, [1942] O.J. No. 43, [1942] O.W.N. 262 (H.C.J.).
[44] *Guildford v. Anglo-French Steamship Co.* (1881), 14 N.S.R. 54 (C.A.), aff'd [1883] S.C.J. No. 24, 9 S.C.R. 303.

to protect that interest.[45] A shareholder to whom an unauthorized payment is made or benefit is provided by a corporation must refund that payment or benefit to the corporation.[46]

§12.12 Although a corporation may have different classes of shares to which are attached different rights and conditions,[47] there is a presumption that all shareholders of a corporation are equal.[48] The consideration given by a shareholder to a transferor for the transfer of a share is irrelevant to the shareholder's rights.[49] Even shares obtained as a gift (in the case of a transfer) confer the same rights vis-à-vis the corporation as if the shares had been acquired for full consideration.[50]

(ii) Trustee Shareholders

§12.13 A person may hold the beneficial ownership of shares that he or she holds either for himself (or herself) or for another person.[51] *Prima facie* it is presumed that a person owns and holds property for his or her own beneficial interest. Where spouses are the shareholders of a corporation there is no presumption that the one spouse holds shares in the corporation in trust for the other.[52] Where shares are held in a representative capacity on behalf of another person, the corporation may treat[53] the registered holder of the share as "the person exclusively entitled to vote, to receive notices, to receive any interest, dividend or other payment in respect of the security and otherwise to exercise all the rights and powers of a holder of the security".[54] The registered owner of a share is also the party liable for any obligation of a shareholder in respect of that share. In general, the liability of a trustee is not limited in amount to the trust property.[55]

---

[45] See, generally, *Rigaud-Vaudreuil Gold Fields Co. v. Bolduc* (1915), 25 Que. K.B. 97 (C.A.).
[46] *D'Amore v. McDonald*, [1973] O.J. No. 1860, [1973] 1 O.R. 845 at 865 (H.C.J.), *per* Addy J., aff'd [1973] O.J. No. 2176, 1 O.R. (2d) 370, 40 D.L.R. (3d) 354 (C.A.).
[47] *Andrews v. Gas Meter Co.*, [1897] 1 Ch. 361 (C.A.).
[48] *British & American Trustee & Finance Corp. v. Couper*, [1894] A.C. 399 at 417 (H.L.), *per* Lord Macnaghten.
[49] See, generally, *Oakbank Oil Co. v. Crum* (1882), 8 App. Cas. 65 (H.L.); *Birch v. Cropper* (1889), 14 App. Cas. 525 (H.L.); *Re Anglo-Continental Corp. of Western Australia*, [1898] 1 Ch. 327.
[50] *Miller v. F. Mendel Holdings Ltd.*, [1984] S.J. No. 98, [1984] 2 W.W.R. 683, 26 B.L.R. 85 at 101 (Q.B.), *per* Wimmer J. See also *Re Van-Tel T.V. Ltd.*, [1974] B.C.J. No. 542, 44 D.L.R. (3d) 146 (S.C.); but compare *Jackman v. Jackets Enterprises Ltd.*, [1977] B.C.J. No. 52, 2 B.L.R. 335 at 338 (S.C.), *per* Fulton J.
[51] A distinction exists between a person who holds shares as a secured creditor and a person who holds them as a trustee. A secured creditor holds the shares for his or her own benefit (but limited to the rights of the security interest so conferred): *Daniels v. Noxon* [1889] O.J. No. 47, 17 O.A.R. 206 (C.A.).
[52] *Re Van-Tel T.V. Ltd.*, [1974] B.C.J. No. 542, 44 D.L.R. (3d) 146 (S.C.).
[53] Moreover, the corporation is obliged to do so. For instance, if the shareholder is liable in respect of shares, the corporation may not seek payment from the beneficial shareholder as a contributory: *Re Standard Mutual Fire Insurance Co.*, [1910] O.J. No. 788, 1 O.W.N. 974 (H.C.J.). A person who holds shares on behalf of another person does so not as an agent but as a trustee.
[54] OBCA, s. 67(1); CBCA, s. 51(1). See also *Wilson v. British Columbia Refining Co.*, [1915] B.C.J. No. 56, 8 W.W.R. 838 (C.A.).
[55] *Muir v. City of Glasgow Bank* (1879), 4 App. Cas. 337 (H.L.).

§12.14 Although it is normal for the registered owner of shares to be treated as the holder for all corporate purposes, in certain circumstances the beneficial owner may be entitled to claim the protection of a shareholder. For instance, in *Re Kootenay Valley Fruit Lands Co.*[56] it was held that the beneficiaries of a bare trust had standing to apply for the appointment of an inspector.

§12.15 In recent years, to a steadily increasing extent, securities regulators have introduced measures to secure greater rights for shareholders who chose to hold shares through a broker or other intermediary. In particular the Canadian Securities Administrators document NI 54-10, provide that proxy-related materials must be sent to beneficial owners who hold through proximate intermediaries that are either:

(i) participants in a recognized depository (The Canadian Depository for Securities Limited (CDS)), or

(ii) intermediaries on CDS' intermediary master list.

Section 2.7 of the Instrument requires corporate issuers to send to beneficial owners any proxy-related materials that they are required to send to registered holders. Section 2.9 sets out the procedure for sending materials directly to a non-objecting beneficial owner ("NOBO") and section 2.12 sets out the procedure for sending materials indirectly to beneficial owners. In both instances, the corporation is required to determine the beneficial owners to send materials to by making a request for beneficial ownership information. Section 2.5(1) requires the corporation to seek out beneficial ownership information from proximate intermediaries that are either:

- participants in a recognized depository that hold securities entitling the holder to receive notice of the meeting or to vote at the meeting, or

- intermediaries (or their nominees) on the depository's intermediary master list that are registered holders of securities entitling the holder to receive notice of the meeting or to vote at the meeting.

Non-registered beneficial owners are also entitled to give and revoke voting instructions with respect to their securities.

§12.16 Subject to the foregoing, as a general rule, a corporation is not required to inquire into the existence of, or see to the performance or observance of, any duty that a registered holder of a share or other security owes to any third party beneficiary.[57] Moreover, even where a purchaser "has notice that a security is held for a third person or is registered in the name or endorsed by a fiduciary, the purchaser has no duty to inquire into the rightfulness of the transfer [of a share] and has no notice of an adverse claim" with respect to that share, unless

---

[56] (1911), 18 W.L.R. 145 at 147 (Man. K.B.), *per* Macdonald J.
[57] OBCA, s. 67(4). As to the pre-statutory position, see *Bank of Montreal v. Sweeny* (1887), 12 App. Cas. 617 at 621-22 (P.C.), *per* Lord Halsbury L.C. See also *Elliot v. Hatzic Prairie Ltd.* (1912), 6 D.L.R. 9, 21 W.L.R. 897 (B.C.S.C.), concerning the availability of injunctive relief to prevent a trustee voting shares contrary to the wishes of the beneficiary of the trust.

that purchaser knows what the consideration is to be used for, or that the transaction is for the personal benefit of the fiduciary or is otherwise in breach of the fiduciary's duty.[58]

§12.17 In *Simpson v. Gillespie*[59] a shareholder acquired shares in a company under an agreement that she was not to dispose of any of the shares for 20 years. Despite that agreement, she transferred a single share to her husband and to two solicitors for the sole purpose of enabling them to be present at shareholders' meetings and, if necessary, vote her shares on her behalf. Although the form of transfer used was unconditional, these transfers were subject to the condition that the shares must be returned to her on demand. It was held that such transfers created a trust arrangement and did not violate the agreement not to "dispose" of the shares for the agreed period of 20 years.

§12.18 Although few modern corporations provide in their articles that the directors of a corporation must hold a qualifying share in the corporation, there are a number of older corporations (particularly under the OBCA) that continue to contain such a provision in their articles. The validity of such a requirement is not open to doubt when the provision is found in the articles.[60] Quite often a director's ownership of those shares was nominal only; true ownership belonging to the corporate shareholder by which the director was employed. Where a director holds a share in such a nominee capacity, he or she is an agent only, and the principal is entitled to demand a re-transfer of the share.[61]

(iii) Shareholder by Estoppel (de facto Shareholders)

§12.19 The identification of persons who are shareholders may often be important in settling the contributories of a corporation in a liquidation or bankruptcy — although as a practical matter, the abolition of partly paid shares has greatly reduced the importance of contributories. In such cases, consideration should be given to the possibility that a person may be estopped from denying that he or she is a shareholder.[62] However, the possibility of creating unlimited liability companies in Alberta, Nova Scotia, and perhaps soon Ontario as well, revives the importance of the shareholder by estoppel concept as a practical means of topping up the realizable value of a company, in the event of its liquidation. A shareholder by estoppel is a person who has acted and been treated as a shareholder and has become subject to the liabilities of a shareholder. For instance, in

---

[58] OBCA, s. 70(2); CBCA, s. 61(2).
[59] [1930] O.J. No. 180, 38 O.W.N. 103 (H.C.D.), rev'd on other grounds [1930] O.J. No. 220, 38 O.W.N. 260 (C.A.).
[60] OBCA, s. 118(2) provides:

> 118.(2) Unless the articles otherwise provide, a director of a corporation is not required to hold shares issued by the corporation.

See also CBCA, s. 105(2).
[61] *Molyneux v. Hamm*, [1957] Que. S.C. 108.
[62] *Re Port Arthur Wagon Co.*, [1918] S.C.J. No. 50, 57 S.C.R. 388.

Re Acme Products Ltd.[63] a person applied for shares in a company and those shares were allotted to him. He made a partial payment towards the subscription price and his name was included in the list of shareholders; as a result he attended meetings and was paid (and accepted) a dividend. When the company went into liquidation, he discovered that the directors who had purported to accept his subscription and allot shares to him were not properly qualified. The liquidator sought to include him in the list of contributories, but he resisted, claiming that because the directors were not qualified they had no authority to make him a shareholder. It was held that he was estopped by his conduct from disputing his status as a shareholder. Similarly, in *Gramm Motor Truck Co. of Canada v. Bennett*,[64] a person who subscribed for shares in a company accepted the share certificates issued to him and acted as a director and vice-president of the company for two years. He was held to be estopped from denying that he was a shareholder even though no shares were ever formally allotted to him.[65] A person may also be estopped from denying that he or she is a shareholder where that person has participated with the corporation in a scheme that misrepresents the amount that he or she has invested in its stated capital.[66]

§12.20 The acceptance of a dividend and other forms of participation in the corporation as a shareholder (such as making part payment for shares and attendance at meetings) are, in general, sufficient to estop a person from denying that he or she is a shareholder.[67] In addition, where a person allows a corporation to continue in a mistaken belief that he or she has subscribed for and accepted shares, that acquiescence will give rise to an estoppel against that person.[68] On the other hand, a corporation may not make a person a shareholder against his or her will. Nor may it change the nature of the share subscription that a person has made[69] (such a change being tantamount to a rejection of the subscribers' offer of contract and the making of a counter offer by the corporation). To impute to a person a contract to take shares, ordinarily the usual requirements of a legally binding contract must be established, or something shown that prevents that person from saying that there is no contract.[70] If an alleged shareholder has made an honest mistake, sufficient to give rise to a defence of *non est factum*,[71] he or

---

[63] (1932), 14 C.B.R. 40 (Man. C.A.); see also *Union Bank v. Gourley*, [1917] 1 W.W.R. 935 (Man. C.A.).
[64] [1915] O.J. No. 32, 35 O.L.R. 224 at 231, 26 D.L.R. 557 (C.A.), per Hodgins J.A.
[65] See also *Re Bishop Engraving & Printing Co.* (1887), 4 Man. R. 429 (Q.B.).
[66] *Re Wiarton Beet Sugar Manufacturing Co.*, [1905] O.J. No. 49, 10 O.L.R. 219 (H.C.J.).
[67] *Re Winding-up Act (Canada)* (1914), 7 W.W.R. 562 (Sask. T.D.); *Re Niagara Falls Heating & Supply Co.*, [1910] O.J. No. 581, 1 O.W.N. 439, 15 O.W.R. 326 (H.C.J.).
[68] *Re Ontario Accident Insurance Co.*, [1911] O.J. No. 390, 20 O.W.R. 164 at 167 (H.C.J.), per Middleton J.
[69] *Re Victoria Wood Works Ltd.* (1909), 43 N.S.R. 368 (C.A.).
[70] *Re Packenham Pork Packing Co.*, [1906] O.J. No. 27, 12 O.L.R. 100 (C.A.).
[71] In *Coté v. Stadacona Insurance Co.*, [1881] S.C.J. No. 19, 6 S.C.R. 193, a shareholder subscribed for five shares in a company, but 50 shares were allotted to him. The defendant was an illiterate person and never realized that this had been done. A cheque was issued to him in payment of the dividend to which he was entitled as the holder of 50 shares. It was held that even by accepting that dividend, the shareholder had not been estopped from subsequently denying that he was the shareholder of 50 shares. There was nothing on the face of the cheque to indicate that

she is not estopped from denying liability as a shareholder. Moreover, a person who in good faith acquires shares that are purportedly fully paid is not liable to make good any deficiency should they subsequently prove not to be fully paid.[72]

§12.21 Where a person subscribes for shares in a proposed corporation, but that entity is never incorporated, although the business that was proposed is still conducted in unincorporated form, that person is not liable as a partner in the unincorporated business.[73] The mere subscription by itself does not constitute sufficient involvement in the business to have this effect.[74] This rule reflects the tendency of the common law to view shareholders as investors in a business rather than as participants in it. Each member of a partnership enjoys or exercises an implied agency on behalf of the other members of the partnership.[75] There is no such inherent agency in other investment contexts. A person who has subscribed for shares may be contractually bound to take up and pay for those shares if the corporation accepts the offer which the shareholder has made. Where there is no corporation then the subscription offer is incapable of acceptance, for the person to whom it is made does not exist.

§12.22 In *Long v. Guelph Lumber Co.*[76] the plaintiff subscribed for preference shares in a company and such shares were issued to him. Certain of the preferences conferred under those shares (in particular a redemption provision) were held to be beyond the power of the directors to create. The plaintiff argued that because the shares that were allotted to him were illegal, he was not, in fact, a shareholder. Osler J. rejected this argument, holding that if the creation of preference shares was wholly beyond the power of the directors, the shareholder would have paid his money for something that he did not get. However, in this case, the illegal provisions of the share terms were severable, and therefore it was proper to consider the plaintiff a shareholder.[77]

(iv) Subsidiaries

§12.23 At least in the United States, at common law a corporation could not hold shares in another corporation.[78] The prohibition was relaxed initially with respect to insurance companies — which it was soon appreciated might well

---

it was a dividend paid on 50 rather than five shares. To estop a person, his or her language or conduct must be an act of recognition and confirmation. If the defendant had accepted the dividend cheque knowing that it was a dividend on 50 shares he would have been estopped. But that was simply not the case. Compare *Lake Superior Navigation Co. v. Morrison*, [1872] O.J. No. 101, 22 U.C.C.P. 217 (C.A.).

[72] *Page v. Austin*, [1884] S.C.J. No. 19, 10 S.C.R. 132.
[73] *Sandusky Coal Co. v. Walker*, [1896] O.J. No. 189, 27 O.R. 677 at 681 (C.A.), *per* Boyd. C.
[74] *Sylvester v. McCuaig*, [1878] O.J. No. 237, 28 U.C.C.P. 443.
[75] *Partnerships Act*, R.S.O. 1990, c. P.5, s. 6.
[76] [1880] O.J. No. 242, 31 U.C.C.P. 129.
[77] *Ibid.*, at 138 (U.C.C.P.). Note, however, that in making this ruling, Osler J. seemed particularly impressed with the fact that the plaintiff had continued to act as a shareholder even after he had discovered the problem with the share terms.
[78] *People v. Pullman Co.* (1898), 175 Ill. 125, 64 L.R.A. 366.

wish to invest at least a portion of their asset base in the shares of other corporate entities. Finally, in 1888, New Jersey enacted that:

> Any corporation may purchase, hold, sell, assign, transfer, mortgage, pledge or otherwise dispose of the shares of the capital stock of, or any bond, securities or evidences of indebtedness created by, any other corporation or corporations of this or any other state, and while owner of such stock may exercise all the rights, powers and privileges of ownership, including the right to vote thereon.

Since that time, inter-corporate shareholding has grown to become the predominant form of ownership.

§12.23.1 There is no question that one corporation may be a shareholder in another corporation. The closest form of corporate inter-relationship is that between a parent corporation and its subsidiary. The definition of the term "subsidiary" is found in subsection 1(2) of the OBCA, which provides that:

> 1.(2) For the purposes of this Act, a body corporate shall be deemed to be a subsidiary of another body corporate if, but only if,
>
> (a) it is controlled by,
>
>   (i) that other, or
>
>   (ii) that other and one or more bodies corporate each of which is controlled by that other, or
>
>   (iii) two or more bodies corporate each of which is controlled by that other; or
>
> (b) it is a subsidiary of a body corporate that is that other's subsidiary.

The authority of a corporation to incorporate or acquire a subsidiary and to carry on business through that subsidiary has long been recognized.[79] A subsidiary need not be created under the same Act as the parent corporation, and very often it will be created under the laws of another jurisdiction. Subject to any statutory rule to the contrary, the relationship between a parent corporation and a subsidiary is no different from the relationship existing between any sole shareholder and a corporation.

(v) Inspection of Lists

§12.24 The CBCA confers somewhat broader rights of access to information, particularly in the case of distributing corporations. Subsection 21(1) provides that subject to subsection 21(1.1), the shareholders and creditors of a corporation, their personal representatives and the Director may examine the records described in subsection 20(1) during the usual business hours of the corporation, and may take extracts from those records free of charge. If the corporation is a

---

[79] See, for instance, *Australia, etc. Building Society v. Wells* (1897), 18 N.S.W.L.R. (E.) 61; *Re Financial Corp., Goodson's Claim* (1880), 28 W.R. 760.

distributing corporation, any other person may also do so on payment of a reasonable fee.[80] Subsection 21(1.1) provides:

> 21.(1.1) Any person described in subsection (1) who wishes to examine the securities register of a distributing corporation must first make a request to the corporation or its agent, accompanied by an affidavit referred to in subsection (7). On receipt of the affidavit, the corporation or its agent shall allow the applicant access to the securities register during the corporation's usual business hours, and, on payment of a reasonable fee, provide the applicant with an extract from the securities register.

Subsection 21(3) permits a shareholder, creditor and others to obtain a list of shareholders:

> 21.(3) Shareholders and creditors of a corporation, their personal representatives, the Director and, if the corporation is a distributing corporation, any other person on payment of a reasonable fee and on sending to a corporation or its agent the affidavit referred to in subsection (7), may on application require the corporation or its agent to furnish within ten days after the receipt of the affidavit a list (in this section referred to as the "basic list") made up to a date not more than ten days before the date of receipt of the affidavit setting out the names of the shareholders of the corporation, the number of shares owned by each shareholder and the address of each shareholder as shown on the records of the corporation.

It has been held that the 10-day time period should not be varied by court order simply because the list may in fact be available prior to that time.[81] Subsection 21(4) contemplates the receipt of updated information. It provides:

> 21.(4) A person requiring a corporation to furnish a basic list may, by stating in the affidavit referred to in subsection (3) that they require supplemental lists, require the corporation or its agent on payment of a reasonable fee to furnish supplemental lists setting out any changes from the basic list in the names or addresses of the shareholders and the number of shares owned by each shareholder for each business day following the date the basic list is made up to.

§12.25 It is unclear why subsections (3) and (4) are limited to shareholder lists, since it is conceivable that critical votes may need to be taken among the holders of other types of security (*e.g.*, in the case of a plan of arrangement under the CCAA). Presumably, where a vote is taken among security holders other than shareholders, then an order may be made by the court allowing access to the corresponding list. In any event, the affidavit required in subsections (1.1) and (3) must state:

(*a*) the name and address of the applicant;

(*b*) the name and address for service of the body corporate, if the applicant is a body corporate; and

---

[80] CBCA, s. 21(1).
[81] *Maxx Petroleum Ltd. v. Amercian Eagle Petroleum Ltd.*, [1993] A.J. No. 331, [1993] 6 W.W.R. 476 (C.A.).

(c) that the basic list and any supplemental lists obtained pursuant to subsection (4) or the information contained in the securities register obtained pursuant to subsection (1.1), as the case may be, will not be used except as permitted under subsection (9).[82]

The CBCA restrictions on the use of such information are set out in subsection 21(9):

21.(9) A list of shareholders or information from a securities registered obtained under this section shall not be used by any person except in connection with,

(a) an effort to influence the voting of shareholders of the corporation;

(b) an offer to acquire securities of the corporation; or

(c) any other matter relating to the affairs of the corporation.

C. PRE-EMPTIVE RIGHTS

§12.26 A pre-emptive right is a right in favour of a shareholder of a class or series of shares[83] that entitles the shareholder to take up shares in preference to any new investor. It is in the nature of a right of first refusal. Where such a right applies, a corporation proposing to allot shares of that class or series may not allot them to any person unless it first offers to each existing shareholder respectively (on the same or more favourable terms) a proportion of those shares which is as nearly as practicable equal to the proportion of the shares of the class or series that is held by each shareholder at the time when the offer is made. Rights of this type are usually set out in the articles as one of the terms or conditions attached to the class or series of shares in question. However, it is possible for such a right to be conferred under a unanimous shareholder agreement, or by way of a simple contractual arrangement between the corporation and the shareholder(s) concerned. There are advantages to such an approach. A unanimous shareholder agreement affords a contractual right that (subject to any agreed amending formula) cannot be varied without the consent of all shareholders. In contrast, any right conferred under the articles of a corporation ordinarily may be amended by way of special resolution — a possibility that greatly dilutes the value of any protection afforded under an articles-based pre-emptive right.

§12.27 A pre-emptive right is usually structured so that if the shareholder does not accept them, the corporation is then free to allot the shares offered to that shareholder to any other person. The objective behind the pre-emptive right is to maintain an existing balance of control, while leaving the corporation free to raise such additional capital as it may require from time to time. Although pre-emptive rights are among the most popular of preference terms, their effectiveness as a shareholder protection device ultimately turns upon the liquidity and

---

[82] CBCA, s. 21(7).
[83] Almost always a voting share: see, generally, *Yoakham v. Providence Biltmore Hotel Co.*, 34 F.2d 533 (D.R.I. 1929).

net worth of the shareholders upon whom the right is bestowed; if a shareholder lacks the resources to pick up the shares that are offered, the pre-emptive right affords no protection at all.[84] The OBCA and the CBCA contain no detailed provisions concerning pre-emptive rights, though both permit such rights to be conferred.[85] In contrast, the English *Companies Act, 1985* sets out a number of detailed rules that would serve as an admirable precedent for any solicitor who is asked to draft such provisions.[86]

D. LIMITED LIABILITY

§12.28 The subject of limited liability has already been dealt with in detail elsewhere[87] and will be touched upon here only briefly, in recognition of its overriding importance. In conceptual terms, where one or more persons undertake a course of conduct, including the conduct of business and the arrangement of their affairs, through an artificial entity such as a corporation or partnership, they may do so either on the basis of personal liability or limited liability. Personal liability exists where the members of the artificial entity are individually responsible for the debts, liabilities and obligations of that entity, whether on a joint or several basis, without limit. Under limited liability, the members' liability for the debts, liabilities and obligations of the entity is limited to a specified amount. Both the CBCA and the OBCA provide for limited liability in the case of corporations subject to either of those Acts. More specifically, subsections 92(1) of the OBCA and 45(1) of the CBCA provide that the shareholders of a corporation are not liable as shareholders for any liability, act or default of the corporation except (a) for improper reductions in stated capital, (b) liabilities imposed on the shareholders by operation of law, (c) obligations assumed by them under a unanimous shareholder agreement, and (d) liability for distributions to shareholders on dissolution.[88] In principle, the obligations assumed by a shareholder under (c) are potentially open-ended. Hence it remains essential to be able to decide who, and at what specific point, a person becomes a shareholder within the meaning of the Act.

§12.29 Over and above these specific statutory provisions, the limited liability of shareholders is implicit in the separate personality of the corporation. It is a general principle of common law that except where one person guarantees the obligations of another, the liability for those obligations is limited to the person who incurs them. The only exceptions to this general principle arise under the law relating to agency and vicarious liability (which is in many respects an outgrowth of agency). It is true that the principal of an agent is liable for the debts, defaults and miscarriages incurred by an agent within the scope of his actual,

---

[84] See, for instance, *Bellows v. Porter*, 201 F.2d 429 (8th Cir. 1953), but compare *Gord v. Iowana Farms Milk Co.*, 245 Iowa 1, 60 N.W.2d 820 (1953), where the shareholder was effectively misled about the price of the shares that were to be issued.
[85] OBCA, s. 26; CBCA, s. 28.
[86] (U.K.), c. 6, ss. 89-92.
[87] See Chapter 2.
[88] See, generally, *Skrien v. Waterloo Junction Rail Tours Ltd.*, [1997] O.J. No. 6289, 32 O.R. (3d) 777 (Gen. Div.), aff'd [1998] O.J. No. 3752 (C.A.).

deemed or apparent authority. Yet, in such cases, the obligations for which the principal is liable are not so much those of the agent as those of the principal: in empowering the agent to act on his or her behalf, the principal assumes responsibility for the obligations that the agent thereby incurs. In contrast, the corporation, as a separate person, enjoys its own property and is subject to its own liabilities. Thus, it follows that the shareholders of a corporation are entitled to limited liability. To view a corporation as a mere agent of its shareholders would be to deny the independence that separate personality confers upon it, and would be contrary to the very purpose that separate legal personality from shareholders is intended to achieve — to allow the corporation to acquire property and liabilities in its own right.

E. SHAREHOLDERS AND CORPORATE MANAGEMENT

§12.30 In a sense, the shareholders of a corporation always have ultimate control over a corporation, because they can alter the articles or remove the directors. However, in *Winthrop Investments Ltd. v. Winns Ltd.*, Samuels J.A. reviewed the case law and concluded that in the absence of statutory authority:

> ... they cannot interfere in the conduct of the company's business where management, as here, is vested in the board ... they have no general power to transact the company's business, or to give effective directions about its management. ... "there is no universal rule that shareholders in general meeting may by ordinary resolution bind or represent the company with respect to anything and everything."[89]

§12.31 Similar statements are to be found in the case law across the Commonwealth.[90] Directors were — and essentially still are — required to act independently and were to exercise their discretion in doing what they conceived to be in the best interests of the corporation.[91] To the extent that the shareholders of a corporation sought to prevent the directors from so doing (other than by way of removal at the conclusion of their terms, or as otherwise authorized by statute), the courts would protect them and allow them to continue their management of the corporation. Thus, in *Howard Smith Ltd. v. Ampol Petroleum*, Lord Wilberforce stated:

> The constitution of a limited company normally provides for directors, with powers of management, and shareholders, with defined voting powers having power to appoint the directors, and to take, in general meeting, by majority vote, decisions on matters not reserved for management. ... [It] is established that directors, within their management powers, may take decisions against the wishes of the

---

[89] (1975) 2 N.S.W.L.R. 666 at 683.
[90] See, for instance, *Grundt v. Great Boulder Proprietary Mines Ltd.*, [1948] Ch. 445 at 157 (C.A.), *per* Cohen L.J.; *Charter Oil Co. v. Beaumont* (1967), 65 D.L.R. (2d) 112 at 119-20 (B.C.S.C.); *John Shaw & Sons (Salford) Ltd. v. Shaw*, [1935] 2 K.B. 113 (C.A.); *Macson Development Co. v. Gordon* (1959), 19 D.L.R. (2d) 465 (N.S.S.C.); *Black White & Grey Cabs Ltd. v. Fox*, [1969] N.Z.L.R. 824; but *cf. Salmon v. Quin & Axtens Ltd.*, [1909] 1 Ch. 311, aff'd [1909] A.C. 442 (H.L.).
[91] *McQuade v. Stoneham*, 263 N.Y. 323, 189 N.E. 234 (C.A. 1934), *per* Pound C.J.

majority of shareholders, and indeed the majority of shareholders cannot control them in the exercise of these powers while they remain in office.[92]

Perhaps the most extreme cases along these lines were the decisions of Berger J. of the British Columbia Supreme Court in *Teck Corp. v. Millar*[93] and Barwick C.J. of the High Court of Australia in *Ashburton Oil N.L. v. Alpha Minerals N.L.*[94] In the former case, Berger J. held that the directors could not be prevented by the majority of shareholders in a corporation from issuing additional shares in the corporation unless it was an abuse of their powers as directors. In *Ashburton*, Barwick C.J. stated as a general proposition that:

> Directors who are minded to do something which in their honest view is for the benefit of the company are not to be restrained because a majority shareholder or shareholders holding a majority of shares in the company do not want the directors to act.[95]

§12.32 The precise limits imposed by the common law upon interference by the shareholders in the management of a company were never finally settled, however the following would seem to be a reasonable summary of the law in this regard:

(a) The shareholders could not interfere in any aspect of management assigned by statute to the board.

(b) Unless the articles or memorandum of association of a company otherwise provided, a simple majority of the shareholders could not direct the board with respect to any aspect of day-to-day management.[96]

(c) Where an aspect of day-to-day management was assigned by the articles or memorandum of association to the board, the shareholders could only give directions to the board with respect to the exercise of that aspect of management following a properly authorized amendment of the articles or memorandum, as the case may be.[97] It was unclear whether a provision in the articles or memorandum permitting the shareholders to give directions by way of special resolution would be effective.[98]

---

[92] [1974] A.C. 821 at 837 (P.C.).
[93] [1972] B.C.J. No. 566, 33 D.L.R. (3d) 288 (S.C.).
[94] (1971), 123 C.L.R. 614, 45 A.L.J.R. 162 (H.C. Aust.).
[95] *Ibid.*, at 163 (A.L.J.R.).
[96] As to the ability of the shareholders to give direction to the board under a special resolution, see: *Breckland Group Holdings Ltd. v. London & Suffolk Properties Ltd.*, [1989] B.C.L.C. 100 (Ch.), per Harman J. See also *Alexander Ward & Co. v. Samyang Navigation Co.*, [1975] 1 W.L.R. 673; *Barron v. Potter*, [1914] 1 Ch. 895, dealing with other residual powers of shareholder control.
[97] *Ad hoc* resolutions (even if approved by a two-thirds majority of shareholders) are not usually construed as altering the articles of a company by implication: *Imperial Hydropathic Hotel Co., Blackpool v. Hampson* (1882), 23 Ch. D. 1 (C.A.).
[98] However, see *Re Coachman Tavern (1985) Ltd.*, [1988] 2 N.Z.L.R. 635 at 639, *per* Gallen J., which doubts this possibility. See also: *Queensland Press Ltd. v. Academy Instruments No. 3 Pty. Ltd.*, [1988] 2 Qd. R. 575; *Re Coachman Tavern (1985) Ltd.*, [1988] 2 N.Z.L.R. 635 at 639, *per* Gallen J.

(d) Despite the foregoing, the shareholders of a company have the authority to make decisions with respect to aspects of the management of a company, where the board is prevented from acting with respect to a matter by reason of conflict of interest. For instance, a majority of the shareholders of a corporation may decide on behalf of the corporation not to institute a legal action against the directors of a company for the negligent sale of assets of the company at an improvident price.[99] However, no such decision may be made so as to bind minority shareholders, where the majority of the shareholders voting in favour of not instituting proceedings were guilty of fraud,[100] or even if not so guilty, have personally benefited by reason of the transaction.[101]

The courts never clearly articulated the reason why it was wrong for the directors to take instruction from the shareholders, but several separate reasons may have been the basis for their thinking. One justification for the firm common law position against shareholder interference in day-to-day corporate management[102] is the fact that the directors of a corporation owe fiduciary, statutory and duties of care to the corporation. In contrast, the shareholders of a corporation do not. Second, directors are fiduciaries, whereas shareholders are not. As fiduciaries, directors are subject to the supervision and control of a court, and, perhaps more importantly, are required to maintain a balanced hand among the shareholders. Outsiders have a right to expect that the management of a company will be carried out by people who each have a duty to act in the interests of the company as a whole, rather than by a person or body that is free to act in its own interests.[103] Third, a majority of the directors of a corporation must be resident Canadians, and are therefore more susceptible to control by Canadian law, whereas the shareholders may reside anywhere. Fourth, minority shareholders who invest in a corporation on the understanding that it will be managed by an elected board of directors answerable to all voting shareholders have a right to object where this board is overruled by shareholders over whom they have no control.[104] However, as we will discuss in detail later in the chapter, this overall approach has now been much modified by statute, not least with respect to the possibility of a shareholder proposal or a unanimous shareholder agreement.

§12.33 Nevertheless, the directors' general managerial powers have never been conceived of as being plenipotentiary in nature. While the shareholders were not seen to enjoy a general supervisory power with respect to day-to-day

---

[99] See, for instance, *Pavlides v. Jensen*, [1956] Ch. 565, *per* Dankwerts J.
[100] See, for instance, *Menier v. Hooper's Telegraph Works* (1874), L.R. 9 Ch. App. 350 (C.A.).
[101] *Daniels v. Daniels*, [1978] Ch. 406. However, no action will lie if a majority of independent shareholders (*i.e.*, those not implicated in the impugned act) voted in favour of not proceeding with the action: *Smith v. Croft (No. 2)*, [1988] Ch. 114.
[102] The managerial authority conferred upon directors is usually seen as being limited to the power to carry on the business of the corporation in the ordinary course: *Re Standard Bank of Australia Ltd.* (1898), 24 V.L.R. 304; *Re Galway & Salthill Tramways Co.*, [1918] 1 I.R. 62 (Ireland Ch. D.).
[103] *Massey v. Wales*, [2003] N.S.W.C.A. 212.
[104] *Salmon v. Quin & Axtens Ltd.*, [1909] 1 Ch. 311 at 319-20 (C.A.), *per* Farwell L.J., aff'd [1909] A.C. 442 (H.L.).

management,[105] the directors were first subject to the legal constraints imposed under statute that conferred powers of review or aspects of managerial control in the shareholders.[106] Second, the distribution of managerial authority was subject to any specific allocation made in the articles or memorandum of association of a company[107] — although this possibility would itself be subject to any power conferred by statute upon the directors as such. Moreover, the control of the directors concerning day-to-day management did not extend into areas outside the ordinary course of the corporation's business, such as fundamental changes to the corporate undertaking (*e.g.*, the amendment of the objects of the company, the reorganization of its capital base, or the recasting of its constitution). This authority could only be exercised by the members of the company through the instrument of resolutions of various types adopted at a members' meeting. And it is to the process of such meetings that we shall now turn.

(i) Disclosure of Information

§12.33.1 One of the basic rights of a shareholder is to receive information relating to the corporation in which he or she has invested. As we noted earlier, basic disclosure requirements are imposed under both the OBCA and CBCA. For reporting issuers, the disclosure requirements are greatly expanded and extend to other security-holders as well. For corporations that are reporting issuers for securities law purposes, disclosure is governed by the disclosure standards set down in National Policy 52-101. Under the OBCA and CBCA, the disclosure of information is tied primarily to the annual and general meeting process. Similarly, as we will discuss in detail below, most of the routine disclosure required of reporting issuers is tied (directly or indirectly) to the annual meeting cycle: either information must be provided for the purposes of that meeting, or it must be provided at regular intervals between such meetings.

§12.33.2 In addition to such routine disclosure, reporting issuers are required by law to disclose immediately any "material change" in their business. For changes that an issuer initiates, any such change is considered to occur at the time of the making of the decision to implement it. This may happen even before a corporation's directors approve it, if the management of the corporation is of the opinion that it is probable the directors will do so. A corporation discloses a material change by issuing and filing a press release describing the change. In addition, the corporation must also file a material change report as soon as practicable, and no later than 10 days after the change occurs. Announcements of this nature are expected to be factual and balanced. Unfavourable news must be disclosed just as promptly and completely as any favorable news. The press release should contain enough detail to enable the media and investors to understand the substance and importance of the change to which it relates. Issuers are

---

[105] *Automatic Self-Cleaning Filter Syndicate Co. v. Cuninghame*, [1906] 2 Ch. 34.
[106] See, for instance, *Exeter & Crediton Railway Co. v. Buller* (1846), 5 Ry. & Can. Cas. 211; *Isle of Wight Railway Co. v. Tahourdin* (1883), 25 Ch. D. 320 (C.A.).
[107] *Salmon v. Quin & Axtens Ltd.*, [1909] 1 Ch. 311, aff'd [1909] A.C. 442 (H.L.).

advised to avoid including unnecessary details, exaggerated reports or promotional commentary.[108]

§12.33.3 Specific disclosure requirements applicable to corporate reporting issuers are discussed elsewhere in this text. For instance, later in this chapter, detailed consideration is given to the information circular requirements applicable with respect to the meetings of a corporation. However, the following general principle of uniformity of disclosure (taken from National Policy 52-201,[109] pertaining to disclosure standards) applies with respect to all disclosure that a corporation is obliged to provide.

> It is fundamental that everyone investing in securities have equal access to information that may affect their investment decisions. The Canadian Securities Administrators (the "CSA" or "We") are concerned about the selective disclosure of material corporate information by companies to analysts, institutional investors, investment dealers and other market professionals. Selective disclosure occurs when a company discloses material nonpublic information to one or more individuals or companies and not broadly to the investing public. Selective disclosure can create opportunities for insider trading and also undermines retail investors' confidence in the marketplace as a level playing field.[110]

National Policy 52-201 is intended to provide guidance concerning best disclosure practices, recognizing that the entire subject of disclosure involves "competing business pressures and legislative requirements". The CSA's recommendations as set out in that Policy are not intended to be prescriptive. Instead, it is expected that issuers will need to implement them flexibly and sensibly to fit individual situations.

§12.33.4 In this text, in the interest of brevity, we have focused upon the requirements applicable to non-venture issuers. However, many of the disclosure and other regulatory requirements of securities law do not apply to venture issuers. The policy rationale for the venture issuer definition was to recognize the disproportionate burden of complying with continuous disclosure obligations on smaller issuers.[111] For instance, NI 51-102 distinguishes between venture issuers and issuers that are not venture issuers, and in general imposes less demanding requirements on venture issuers — examples being that venture issuers do not have to file annual information forms and have longer to file their financial statements than issuers that are not venture issuers. The tendency to lessen the regulatory load for those issuers that cannot afford to carry the full burden gives rise to one of the inherent paradoxes — if not perversities — of securities regulation, and indeed much regulation of every kind. It is that very often the heaviest

---

[108] CSA National Policy 52-201, s. 2.1.
[109] The timely disclosure requirements and prohibitions against selective disclosure are substantially similar everywhere in Canada, there are differences among the provinces and territories, so issuers should carefully review with their local counsel the legislation that is applicable to them.
[110] s. 1.1
[111] Currently, there is no specific classification system for debt-only issuers; they are classified, but since most debt-only issuers do not list their debt on any exchanges and so are currently venture issuers.

burden is imposed on those entities that present the least risk, while the lightest is enjoyed by those that give rise to the most. Securities laws do not apply in any real fashion to the small "private company" issuers who comprise the exempt sector of the economy. Yet, historically, it is these types of issuer that give rise to the greatest risk of failure, even when conducted honestly. Among those issuers that are regulated under securities laws, it is the smaller and generally more weakly capitalized entities that are subject to the least burden. In contrast, the well-established, long successful and generally strongly capitalized stock market "listed" entities that comprise the blue chip sector, are the most regulated. Completing the picture, the New York Stock Exchange imposes the tightest regulation on the most established corporations in the world.

(ii) Shareholders' Meetings

§12.34 Both the CBCA and OBCA permit various aspects of the affairs of a corporation to be decided by way of a resolution adopted at a meeting of shareholders. The most common approach to corporate decision making — except in the case of closely held corporations — continues to be by way of shareholder resolution formally submitted to and voted upon at a meeting of the shareholders of the corporation. As we shall discuss in greater detail below the general business of the shareholders must be approved by an ordinary resolution — namely a resolution approved by one-half of the shares being voted plus one[112] (as opposed to one-half of the shareholders entitled to vote). More important shareholder business must be approved by way of special resolution.[113] The term "special resolution" is defined to mean a resolution that is:

(a) submitted to a special meeting of the shareholders of a corporation duly called for the purpose of considering the resolution and passed, with or without amendment, at the meeting by at least two-thirds of the votes cast, or

(b) consented to in writing by each shareholder of the corporation entitled to vote at such a meeting or the shareholder's attorney authorized in writing...[114]

These provisions of the OBCA and CBCA embody a basic principle of the common law of companies dating to at least the 17th century, that a company as a body may act in accordance with the wishes of the majority of its members, so that a decision of a majority of the members of a company is binding upon all of its members.[115] In *Schurek v. Schnelle*,[116] Veit J. said:

> Corporate democracy should prevail: even where there is a dispute amongst shareholders, the shareholders owning the most shares are entitled to run the company while the problems are being worked out.

---

[112] OBCA, s. 97.
[113] Note, however, that these requirements are subject to variation by way of the articles or by-laws, or under a unanimous shareholder agreement. In addition, in certain cases, a vote must be taken by class or series of shares. OBCA, s. 170; CBCA, s. 176.
[114] OBCA, s. 1.
[115] See, generally, *Ritchie v. Vermillion Mining Co.*, [1902] O.J. No. 223, 4 O.L.R. 588 at 594 (C.A.), *per* MacLennan J.A.
[116] [2002] A.J. No. 140 at para. 4 (Alta. Q.B.).

Generally speaking, Canadian courts have been very reluctant to interfere with the democratic, internal workings of the corporation.

§12.35 There must be a strong case to justify a court in interfering with the conduct of a shareholder meeting or other decision making process.[117] The fact that a particular minority shareholder does not like what has been done is no justification in itself for judicial interference. The will of the majority must be duly formulated,[118] legal[119] and properly expressed, of course. It is now settled by statute that the minority within the corporation may not be oppressed or treated unfairly by the majority.[120] The extent of approval required to approve certain specific types of decision may well be specified by statute, or under the articles or by-laws of a corporation, or a unanimous shareholder agreement.[121] Nevertheless, none of these qualifications in the least way disturbs the basic principle of majority rule.[122] However, the term "majority" has a specific meaning within the corporate law sphere distinct from its popular meaning and within the political sphere. It describes neither a majority of members nor even the holders of a majority of shares (for some classes of share may be non-voting), but rather the members who from time to time, or at any time, hold a majority of the votes attached to the shares of the company.[123]

§12.36 Although it is clear that the majority of a company may bind it as a whole, it remains necessary to decide when the majority has made a decision with respect to some matter which it may be called upon to decide.[124] In many early cases, courts sometimes took the view that the members of a company could only decide upon a matter by way of a vote taken at a meeting of members.[125] Such a formalized, almost ritualistic approach to corporate decision making could not long survive the practical requirements of modern business. While the best practice is for formal resolutions to be voted upon and recorded with regard to each matter to be decided by the shareholders, in some (but not all) cases the courts have been willing to accept that real world corporate practice is

---

[117] *Schelew v. Schelew*, [2005] N.B.J. No. 161, 5 B.L.R. (4th) 49 at 58 (Q.B.), *per* Glennie J.
[118] *Re New Cedos Engineering Co.*, [1994] 1 B.C.L.C. 797 (Ch.).
[119] *Towers v. African Tug Co.*, [1904] 1 Ch. 558.
[120] OBCA, s. 248; CBCA, s. 241.
[121] Where a provision of the articles or by-laws limits the powers of the corporation or its members in general meeting, that provision cannot be disregarded even if there is a sufficient majority of the shareholders in support of a particular motion large enough to alter that provision: *Imperial Hydropathic Hotel Co., Blackpool v. Hampson* (1882), 23 Ch. D. 1 (C.A.), *per* Cotton L.J.
[122] *Mozley v. Alston* (1847), 1 Ph. 790.
[123] *Colonist Printing & Publishing Co. v. Dunsmuir*, [1902] S.C.J. No. 64, 32 S.C.R. 679.
[124] *Christopher v. Noxon*, [1883] O.J. No. 273, 4 O.R. 672 at 683-84 (H.C.J.), *per* Proudfoot J.
[125] See, generally, *Re Portugese Consolidated Copper Mines Ltd.* (1889), 42 Ch. D. 160 at 167 (C.A.), *per* Fry L.J.; *Re George Newman & Co.*, [1895] 1 Ch. 674 at 686 (C.A.):

> It was competent to them to waive all formalities as regards notice of meetings, etc., and to resolve themselves into a meeting of shareholders and unanimously pass the resolution in question.

> See also *East v. Bennett Brothers*, [1911] 1 Ch. 163: where there is only one person entitled to vote at a meeting, a decision taken by that person is effective, even in the absence of a meeting.

not always in strict accordance with best practice.[126] Very often over the history of a corporation, many of the shareholders resolutions may be informally adopted at meetings irregularly held, with no concern raised by the shareholders with the respect to the deficiency in procedure. So, for instance, where the directors of a corporation also constitute all of its shareholders, the courts have frequently treated a directors' meeting as being a *de facto* shareholders' meeting.[127] Nevertheless, the mere fact that a majority of the shareholders of a corporation are disposed towards deciding some measure in a particular way is not sufficient to constitute an act of the corporation, even if they set down a record of their disposition in a signed written document.[128] Except in the case of unanimity,[129] a meeting of some kind is required and where there is a dissident minority, the meeting must be duly called and conducted.[130]

§12.37 As discussed in detail below, five basic principles emerge from the case law regarding shareholders' meetings, specifically:

- Except where notice of the meeting is waived,[131] all persons entitled to attend and participate at the meeting must have been notified of the intent to hold the meeting and of the questions to be decided at the meeting,[132] in accordance with applicable law, any unanimous shareholder agreement and the articles and by-laws of the corporation. However, if shareholders attend a meeting despite the absence of proper notice and participate in it (other than to dispute its being held), then they will be bound by any decision taken at the meeting, and they may not subsequently object to the fact that the meeting was held on insufficient notice.[133]

- It is a question of fact whether a meeting has taken place; for a particular assembly to be held to constitute a meeting, there must have been an intention on the part of the persons present to meet for the conduct of business,[134] especially where one of them makes clear that he or she has no intent to meet with the others.

---

[126] *Re Duomatic Ltd.*, [1969] 1 All E.R. 161 (Ch. D.), *per* Buckley J.; *Walton v. Bank of Nova Scotia*, [1965] S.C.J. No. 41, 52 D.L.R. (2d) 506; *Re Express Engineering Works Ltd.*, [1920] 1 Ch. 466 at 471 (C.A.), *per* Warrington L.J.

[127] See, for instance, *Multinational Gas & Petrochemical Co. v. Multinational Gas & Petrochemical Services Ltd.*, [1983] Ch. 258; *Bobbie Pins Ltd. v. Robertson*, [1950] N.Z.L.R. 301; *Re Duomatic Ltd.*, [1969] 1 All E.R. 161 (Ch. D.).

[128] See, generally (with regard to director meetings, but equally applicable to shareholder meetings), *Magnacrete Ltd. v. Douglas-Hill* (1988), 7 A.C.L.R. 117 at 119 (S.A.S.C.), *per* Perry J. — poll taken by separate phone calls to directors not constituting a meeting. See also the rather dubious decision in *Re Associated Color Laboratories Ltd.*, [1970] B.C.J. No. 89, 12 D.L.R. (3d) 338 (S.C.).

[129] See, for instance, *Ho Tung v. Man On Insurance Co. Ltd.*, [1902] A.C. 232 (P.C.); *Re Home Treat Ltd.*, [1991] B.C.L.C. 705 (Ch.); *Baroness Wenlock v. River Dee Co.* (1883), 36 Ch. D. 675 at 681-82 (C.A.), *per* Cotton L.J., aff'd 10 App. Cas. 354 (H.L.).

[130] *Re George Newman & Co.*, [1895] 1 Ch. 674 at 686 (C.A.), *per* Lindley L.J.

[131] OBCA, s. 98; CBCA, s. 136.

[132] OBCA, subss. 96(5) and (6); CBCA, subss. 135(5) and (6).

[133] *Portland & Lancaster Steam Ferry Co. v. Pratt* (1850), 7 N.B.R. 17 (C.A.).

[134] *Barron v. Potter*, [1914] 1 Ch. 895, *per* Warrington J.

- All persons who are entitled to attend and participate at the meeting must be given a fair opportunity to do so.[135]

- A proper debate must be allowed with regard to the question(s) to be decided at the meeting.

- A proper vote must be taken at the meeting on the question(s) to be decided and must be fairly tabulated and recorded.[136]

So, for instance, a shareholder entitled to attend a meeting is entitled to place a proposal before the meeting or move to amend a motion being made by another person, to insist upon a vote being taken upon a motion before the meeting and to express views on any motion to be decided.[137]

§12.38 Shareholders' meetings hold three important roles in the government of a corporation. First, there are certain routine matters with which the shareholders of a corporation must deal on an ongoing basis, including the election of directors and the appointment of auditors. Ordinarily, these matters are dealt with at an annual meeting of the shareholders, though they may also be dealt with at special meetings called during the course of the business year — for instance, where a sufficient number of vacancies occur in the membership of the board of directors to push the number of directors remaining below a quorum, a shareholders' meeting must be held to make up the shortfall. Second, there are certain special measures or steps that a corporation may seek to implement or take (*e.g.*, an amendment to the articles of the corporation) that require the approval of the shareholders. Other than in the case of corporations with only a few shareholders, it is not usually practical to seek such approval except by way of a meeting of the shareholders. Third, both the OBCA and the CBCA permit shareholders to voice their concerns and to give direction to the corporation concerning its management and administration by way of a shareholder proposal submitted to, and approved at, a meeting of the shareholders.

§12.39 There are two kinds of shareholders' meeting: general and special. General meetings of a corporation are regular meetings held periodically at appointed times for the consideration of matters in general. Annual meetings of shareholders are the archetype of general meetings, but a corporation may provide in its by-laws for the holding of more frequent general meetings, if its shareholders are so inclined. In practice, they are rarely so inclined. In the case of small corporations, a preferable alternative is usually to provide for board

---

[135] It is not necessary, however, for all persons to be physically present at the same place: see, generally, *Byng v. London Life Association Ltd.*, [1990] Ch. 170 (C.A.), *per* Browne-Wilkinson V.-C. at 183. Although all persons entitled to attend must be allowed to do so, the effect of allowing persons not entitled to attend to participate in a meeting is unclear, but it can be argued with some force that so doing may invalidate the meeting where the level of interference is so great that it becomes a practical impossibility for the persons entitled to attend and participate to deliberate and make decisions among themselves: see, generally, *Harris v. English Canadian Co.* (1905), 3 W.L.R. 5 (B.C.S.C.).

[136] See, generally, *Dickson v. McMurray*, [1881] O.J. No. 158, 28 Gr. 533 (Ct. Ch.).

[137] *Henderson v. Bank of Australasia* (1890), 45 Ch. D. 330 at 347 (C.A.).

representation for all interested shareholders, thus rendering frequent shareholders' meetings unnecessary; in the case of larger corporations, the cost of holding general meetings is usually sufficient to deter their being held except where they are necessary for some special business. Special meetings are irregularly held meetings that are called to deal with some special or emergency business.[138] The fact that a special meeting must be called to deal with business, does not mean that the proposal to be considered at that meeting must be approved by a special resolution. Unless the relevant Act, or the articles, a unanimous shareholder agreement, or the by-laws of a corporation otherwise provide, an ordinary resolution approved by a majority of the shareholders voting at such a meeting are sufficient. Where the by-laws of a corporation require particular business to be conducted at a particular type of meeting (such as a regular meeting fixed for a specific date) that provision must be respected by the directors, and they are not free to call some other type of meeting to deal with that matter.[139]

(1) When Meetings Required

§12.40 Meetings of the shareholders of a corporation are required in four situations. First, the directors of a corporation are required to call an annual meeting of shareholders not later than 18 months after the corporation comes into existence and, subsequently, not later than 15 months after the holding of the last preceding annual meeting.[140] The requirement that the meeting be called within these time limits means that the meeting must be held within the times so specified; it is not sufficient for the corporation to send out notices of a meeting within that time period, nor is it appropriate for the meeting to commence during the allowed time and then to be adjourned (without considering the business at hand) *sine die* with no intention of reconvening during that time.[141] Second, meetings are also required to consider any matter requiring approval by a resolution or special resolution of shareholders under the Act or the articles of a corporation.[142] Third, the holders of not less than 5 per cent of the issued shares of a corporation that carry the right to vote at a meeting sought to be held may requisition the directors to call a meeting of shareholders for the purposes stated in the requisition.[143] Fourth, a meeting of the shareholders may be requisitioned by the court.[144]

---

[138] *Austin Mining Co. v. Gemmel*, [1886] O.J. No. 249, 10 O.R. 696 (C.A.).
[139] *Portland & Lancaster Steam Ferry Co. v. Pratt* (1850), 7 N.B.R. 17 (C.A.) — although the shareholders themselves may waive the requirement, and will be considered to have done so where they attend and participate in the meeting.
[140] OBCA, s. 94(*a*); CBCA, s. 133. Note, however, the alternative of a unanimous shareholder resolution under s. 104(1) of the OBCA and s. 142 of the CBCA.
[141] *Re Pioneer Savings & Loan Society*, [1928] B.C.J. No. 14, [1928] 1 W.W.R. 361 at 369 (B.C.C.A.), *per* Macdonald J.A.
[142] For instance, any fundamental change to the corporation under Part XIV of the OBCA. Again, there is the alternative of a unanimous shareholder resolution under s. 104(1).
[143] OBCA, s. 105(1); CBCA, s. 143(1). See also *Lobstick Golf & Tennis Club Inc. v. Harris*, [1989] S.J. No. 437, 79 Sask. R. 185 (Q.B.).
[144] OBCA, s. 106(1); CBCA, s. 144(1).

§12.41 At common law, the shareholders of a corporation possessed no authority to requisition a meeting of the shareholders, even where all of the directors of a corporation had resigned.[145] Both the OBCA and the CBCA now confer such a right,[146] though the requisition of a meeting by the shareholders does not affect the ongoing power of the directors to continue with the management of the corporation pending the meeting in question.[147] Shareholders may requisition a special or general meeting as well as an annual meeting.[148] However, the courts have generally required shareholders to comply strictly with the procedural provisions pertaining to the requisition of shareholders' meetings as a condition governing the exercise of their rights.[149]

§12.42 Where one or more shareholders requisition a meeting the requisition must state the business to be transacted at the meeting and must be sent to the registered office of the corporation.[150] Under the CBCA, it is also necessary to send a copy of the requisition to each director as well as to the corporation. Upon receiving that requisition, the directors must call a meeting of shareholders to transact the business stated in the requisition unless:

(a) a record date has been fixed under subsection 95(2) and notice thereof has been given under subsection 95(4);

(b) the directors have called a meeting of shareholders and have given notice thereof under section 96; or

(c) the business of the meeting stated in the requisition includes matters described in clauses 99(5)(b) to (d).[151]

Similar exceptions are provided under subsection 143(3) of the CBCA. Clauses 99(5)(b) to (d) of the OBCA deal with exceptions to the shareholder proposal rights under the Act. If the directors do not call a meeting within 21 days of receiving the requisition (they are obliged to do so) any shareholder who signed the requisition may call the meeting.[152] In such a case, the notice of meeting should set out the authority and the fulfillment of the condition precedent that entitles the shareholder to call the meeting in question, though the failure to do so does not affect the validity of the notice.[153] Where for some reason the first notice sent out by a shareholder is defective it is not necessary for the shareholder to

---

[145] *South Shore Development Ltd. v. Snow*, [1971] N.S.J. No. 172, 4 N.S.R. (2d) 601, 19 D.L.R. (2d) 601 at 608-609 (S.C.T.D.), *per* Jones J.

[146] See, however, *Proprietary Industries Inc. v. eDispatch.com Wireless Data*, [2001] B.C.J. No. 2927, 30 B.L.R. (3d) 87 (S.C.).

[147] *Shield Development Co. v. Snyder*, [1976] B.C.J. No. 51, [1976] 3 W.W.R. 44 (S.C.).

[148] *Airline Industry Revitalization Co. v. Air Canada*, [1999] O.J. No. 3581, 49 B.L.R. (2d) 254 at 264 (S.C.J. — C.L.), *per* Blair J.

[149] See, for instance, *Lobstick Golf & Tennis Club Inc. v. Harris*, [1989] S.J. No. 437, 79 Sask. R. 185 at 191 (Q.B.), *per* Goldenberg J.: "It is clear that the meeting... *can only be* for the purposes of transacting the business stated in the requisition to the directors."

[150] OBCA, s. 105(2); CBCA, s. 143(2).

[151] OBCA, s. 105(3); CBCA, s. 143(3).

[152] OBCA, s. 105(4); CBCA, s. 143(4).

[153] *Dalex Mines Ltd. (N.P.L.) v. Schmidt*, [1973] B.C.J. No. 506, [1973] 5 W.W.R. 357 (S.C.).

initiate a second requisition to send out a valid second notice.[154] The corporation must reimburse the shareholders for the expenses reasonably incurred in requisitioning, calling and holding the meeting, unless the shareholders have not acted in good faith and in the interest of the shareholders of the corporation generally.

§12.43 In addition to the shareholder requisition procedure, it is also possible for the court to requisition the holding of a meeting. Subsection 106(1) of the OBCA provides:

> 106.(1) If for any reason it is impractical to call a meeting of shareholders of a corporation in the manner in which meetings of those shareholders may be called, or to conduct the meeting in the manner prescribed by the by-laws and this Act, or the court thinks fit, the court, on the application of a director or a shareholder entitled to vote at the meeting, may order a meeting to be called, held and conducted in such manner as the court directs ...[155]

Historically (in line with their general policy not to intervene in the internal affairs of a corporation), the courts have exercised this power only in exceptional circumstances — for instance, where there has been no meeting called of the members of a corporation for longer than the maximum period permitted by statute.[156] For the most part, the power of the court has been narrowly construed.[157] Thus, in one line of cases, it has been said that the power is discretionary and should be invoked only where necessary to obviate a practical difficulty in convening a meeting. Under this line of authority, a meeting will not be requisitioned where the difficulty results only from an internal dispute between the management and some shareholders. Courts adopting this approach reason that the court should not take sides in such a dispute.[158] So, for instance, a shareholders' meeting will not be called by the court under subsection 106(1) of the OBCA — nor will the court order the corporation to distribute a shareholder proposal[159] — where the shareholder-applicant seeking the order does so primarily for the purpose of enforcing a personal claim or redressing a personal grievance against the corporation, its directors, officers or security holders. The court's power to order shareholders' meetings will be exercised only where the application for such an order is genuinely related in a significant way to the business or affairs of the corporation.[160]

---

[154] *Gold-Rex Kirkland Mines Ltd. v. Morrow*, [1944] O.J. No. 454, [1944] O.R. 415 at 418 (H.C.J.), *per* Hogg J.

[155] See also CBCA, s. 144(1).

[156] *Nalcap Holdings Inc. v. Kelvin Energy Ltd.*, [1988] Q.J. No. 1921, [1988] R.J.Q. 2768 (S.C.).

[157] See, for instance, *Re British International Finance (Canada) Ltd.*, [1968] O.J. No. 1139, [1968] 2 O.R. 217 at 219 (C.A.), *per* Aylesworth J.A.; see also *Re Morris Funeral Services Ltd.*, [1957] O.J. No. 80, [1957] O.W.N. 161 at 164 (C.A.), *per* Aylesworth J.A.

[158] *Re Morris Funeral Services Ltd.*, [1957] O.J. No. 80, [1957] O.W.N. 161 at 219, 7 D.L.R. (2d) 642 (C.A.), *per* Aylesworth J.A.

[159] *Cappuccitti v. Bank of Montreal*, [1989] O.J. No. 2153, 46 B.L.R. 255 (Ont. H.C.J.).

[160] *Watkin v. Open Window Bakery Ltd.*, [1996] O.J. No. 894, 26 B.L.R. (2d) 301 (Gen. Div. — C.L.), appeal quashed [1996] O.J. No. 1469 (Div. Ct.).

§12.44 Although the preponderance of case law favours a narrow interpretation of the court's authority to intervene under subsection 106(1) of the OBCA, occasionally some courts have taken a more expansive view of their jurisdiction to order shareholders' meetings.[161] Under this second line of cases, it has been suggested that although the court should not intervene in typical internal corporate disputes, the court may act where the internal differences within the corporation have reached the point that the due administration of the corporation has been compromised.[162] Thus in *Canadian Javelin Ltd. v. Boon Strachan Coal Co.*[163] the court requisitioned a meeting where a senior officer of the corporation had been charged with an offence, there was extensive litigation between the two groups disputing control of the corporation, the corporation's financial position had deteriorated to the point that it was precarious, and it was in default under its lending agreements. Similarly, in *Croatian Peasant Party of Ontario, Canada v. Zorkin*,[164] a meeting was called (regarding a non-profit company) in the hope of settling a political dispute among warring factions within the company;[165] the goal behind such an order being not for the court to take over the company,[166] but for the members to be given the opportunity to resolve their differences among themselves. To that end, the court may give directions concerning the manner in which the meeting is to be conducted and may adjust the size of the quorum required for a meeting.[167]

§12.45 The courts are prepared to act, even in ways not expressly authorized by statute, where it is necessary to do so because the normal decision-making process within the corporation has broken down. For instance, in *Re British Union for the Abolition of Vivisection*[168] it was held that the court could order that a meeting of the shareholders would be held with only the executive of the corporation present in person, and with the bulk of the membership participating in the meeting only by postal ballot. In that case, previous efforts to conduct a member meeting had been frustrated by a particularly disruptive minority.

§12.46 In addition to those meetings that are required under the Act, the directors of a corporation may at any time call a special meeting of the shareholders of the corporation.[169] As noted above, special meetings are normally called where it is necessary to obtain shareholder approval for some steps that the corporation proposes to take, such as a fundamental change in the nature of an amendment to the corporation's articles. However, the directors may also take advantage of the special meeting procedure where they consider it advisable to inform the shareholders and seek their input concerning some new direction that

---

[161] See, for instance, *Re El Sombrero Ltd.*, [1958] Ch. 900, *per* Wynn-Parry J.
[162] See, for instance, *Re Routley's Holdings Ltd.*, [1959] O.J. No. 88, [1959] O.W.N. 89 (H.C.J.).
[163] (1976), 69 D.L.R. (3d) 439 (Que. S.C.).
[164] [1981] O.J. No. 3235, 38 O.R. (2d) 659 (H.C.J.).
[165] *Ibid.*, at 665.
[166] The solution in a case of continued deadlock over the control of the corporation is for the corporation to be wound up: *Barsh v. Feldman*, [1986] O.J. No. 164, 54 O.R. (2d) 340 (H.C.J.).
[167] OBCA, s. 106(2).
[168] [1995] 2 B.C.L.C. 1.
[169] OBCA, s. 94(*b*); CBCA, s. 133(2).

the corporation proposes to take in its operations. Even if the directors are not obliged to consult the shareholders concerning a particular measure, there is no reason why they may not consult the shareholders from time to time concerning matters of particular importance.

(2) Quorum for Meeting

§12.47 A quorum is the minimum number of persons required to be in attendance at a meeting for the meeting to be competent to discuss and transact the business for which it was called. The idea of a quorum is that when the specified number of persons is present any business transacted by a decision made at the meeting will be binding upon all members of the corporation (whether or not present) as if every member of the corporation had been in attendance and participated in the meeting.[170] If a particular measure must be approved by a stated percentage of the voting shareholders of the corporation, the question of whether it has been so approved is determined by reference to the number of shares present, and not by reference to the total number of shares.[171] So, for instance, if there are 1000 shares of which 600 are represented at a meeting and 401 vote in favour of a motion, the resolution will be seen to have been approved by a two-thirds majority, even though only slightly more than 40 per cent of shares were actually voted in favour of the resolution. If voting shareholders are present or represented and choose not to vote, their presence may be counted to determine whether there is a quorum, but the number of affirmative votes necessary to attain the required percentage is determined only by reference to the shares actually voting. In other words, abstentions are excluded, and no shows are relevant only for the purpose of determining whether a quorum is present.

§12.48 In contrast, a resolution passed at a meeting at which no quorum is present is void.[172] Somewhat paradoxically, the requirement for a quorum bars a decision even where the number of voters present and supporting a resolution is sufficient to decide the matter. So, for instance, if the quorum of shareholders provided for in the by-laws of the corporation is 67 per cent of all shareholders, but only 50 per cent are actually present and represented, business may not proceed even though the matters to be decided require only a 50 per cent shareholder approval, and even if every one present indicates support for the proposals in question. For this reason, care should be exercised in setting the quorum for meetings, to make sure that it does not permit minorities to control a corporation's destiny, simply by staying home.

§12.49 At common law, the presence or absence of a quorum was determined by the rules of parliamentary procedure.[173] The OBCA and the CBCA now make

---

[170] See, for instance, *Noble v. Cameron*, [1955] O.J. No. 576, [1955] O.R. 608 at 613 (C.A.), *per* Schroeder J.A.; *Famous Players Canadian Corp. v. Hamilton United Theatres Ltd.*, [1944] O.J. No. 444, [1944] O.R. 321 (H.C.J.).

[171] *Ibid., Noble v. Cameron*.

[172] *Re Cambrian Peat, Fuel & Charcoal Co.* (1875), 31 L.T. 773 at 774 (V.C.), *per* Bacon V.-C.

[173] *Lumbers v. Fretz*, [1928] O.J. No. 84, 62 O.L.R. 635 at 650 (H.C.D.), *per* Wright J., aff'd [1928] O.J. No. 111, 63 O.L.R. 190 (C.A.).

express provision regarding the quorum required for the conduct of a shareholders' meeting. Unless the by-laws otherwise provide,[174] the holders of a majority of the shares entitled to vote[175] at a meeting of shareholders constitute a quorum, whether present in person or represented by proxy.[176] Since it is possible for a single person to hold either sufficient shares or sufficient proxies to meet the majority of shares requirement, the common law rule that a single person could not comprise a quorum has now been abrogated.[177]

§12.50 Where it is impossible to obtain a quorum the meeting may not proceed,[178] except by requisition of the court,[179] and any business transacted at a meeting held without such authorization is a nullity.[180] For most corporations, the determination of whether a quorum is present need be made only once for each meeting. Subsection 101(2) of the OBCA provides that unless the by-laws otherwise provide, where a quorum is present at the opening of a meeting of shareholders, the shareholders present may proceed with the business of the meeting even where a sufficient number leave during the course of the meeting to reduce the number present to less than a quorum.[181] Thus, a person who objects to the direction in which a meeting is heading may not prevent it from reaching a conclusion by walking out for the purpose of taking the number present below a quorum. If a quorum is not present at the time appointed for a meeting of the shareholders, or within such reasonable time thereafter as the shareholders present may determine, the shareholders present may adjourn the meeting to a fixed time and place but may not transact other business.[182]

§12.51 It seems ridiculous to speak of a "meeting" of the shareholders of a corporation that has but a single shareholder. Nevertheless, subsection 101(4) of the OBCA provides that if a corporation has only one shareholder or only one holder of any class or series of shares, that shareholder, present in person or by

---

[174] See, for instance, *Cohen-Herrendorf v. Army & Navy Department Store Holdings Ltd.*, [1986] S.J. No. 848, 55 Sask. R. 134 at 145 (Q.B.), *per* Scheibel J.

[175] *Cf.*, *Young v. South African & Australian Exploration and Development Syndicate*, [1896] 2 Ch. 268 at 277, *per* Kekewich J. Under earlier statutes and under some corporate by-laws, the presence of a quorum is determined by the number of shareholders present (rather than the number of shares represented). See, for instance, *Montreal Trust Co. v. Oxford Pipe Line Co.*, [1942] O.J. No. 439, [1942] O.R. 260 (H.C.), aff'd [1942] O.J. No. 439, [1942] O.R. 490 (C.A.).

[176] OBCA, s. 101(1); CBCA, s. 139(1). At common law, there was some doubt whether persons present only by proxy could be counted in determining whether a quorum was present: *Re Cambrian Peat, Fuel & Charcoal Co. Ltd.* (1875), 31 L.T. 773 (V.-C.).

[177] As to the common law rule, see *Sharp v. Dawes* (1876), 2 Q.B.D. 26 at 28-29, *per* Lord Coleridge C.J.; *East v. Bennett Bros.*, [1911] 1 Ch. 163 at 168, *per* Warrington J.; but compare *Moco Management Ltd. v. Llernam Holdings Ltd.*, [1985] B.C.J. No. 2864, 68 B.C.L.R. 128 at 133-34 (S.C.), *per* Catliff L.J.S.C.

[178] *Barsh v. Feldman*, [1986] O.J. No. 164, 54 O.R. (2d) 340 (H.C.J.).

[179] See, for instance, *B. Love Ltd. v. Bulk Steel & Salvage Ltd.*, [1982] O.J. No. 3578, 40 O.R. (2d) 1 (H.C.J.).

[180] *Keyes v. Hope Trading Syndicate*, [1949] O.J. No. 79, [1949] O.W.N. 307 (H.C.J.).

[181] See also CBCA, s. 139(2); *Moco Management Ltd. v. Llernam Holdings Ltd.*, [1985] B.C.J. No. 2864, 68 B.C.L.R. 128 (S.C.).

[182] OBCA, s. 101(3); CBCA, s. 139(3).

proxy, constitutes a meeting.[183] For nearly all purposes, a less costly and more expeditious alternative to the holding of a meeting of shareholders is for the shareholders to adopt a written resolution in lieu of a meeting,[184] at least where there is only a single shareholder or a relatively small number of shareholders. This option however, may not be taken where a written statement is submitted by a director under subsection 123(2)[185] or where representations are submitted by an auditor under subsection 149(6)[186] of the OBCA.[187]

§12.52 In many cases, one shareholder will have such a substantial control over a corporation that the holding of a meeting may seem like a pointless formality. Nevertheless, where a meeting is not held in a situation where it is required under the Act, articles or by-laws, the controlling shareholder cannot simply take the position that whatever was done unlawfully might have been done lawfully if a meeting was called and a vote taken upon a resolution regarding the matter concerned. The minority shareholders are entitled to require that the proper procedures be followed by the corporation.[188] Similarly, they are entitled to express their views and have their votes recorded irrespective of how the majority may be inclined to act. In a highly litigious age, there is a clear benefit to a shareholder in proving that he or she was not involved in conduct forming the basis of an action against the shareholders of a corporation. Moreover, the possibility that the minutes of a shareholders' meeting may come to the attention of a creditor or other concerned person should not be ignored. Such outsiders may benefit from the evidence that a formal vote will provide of disputes within the corporation or of the manner in which its business or affairs are being conducted.

---

[183] See also CBCA, s. 139(4). As for the rule prior to the enactment of this provision, see *Re Primary Distributors Ltd.* (1954), 11 W.W.R. (N.S.) 449 (B.C.S.C.).

[184] Clauses 104(1)(a) and (b) of the OBCA provide:

(a) a resolution in writing signed by all the shareholders or their attorney authorized in writing entitled to vote on that resolution at a meeting of shareholders is as valid as if it had been passed at a meeting of the shareholders; and

(b) a resolution in writing dealing with all matters required by this Act to be dealt with at a meeting of shareholders, and signed by all the shareholders or their attorney authorized in writing entitled to vote at that meeting, satisfies all the requirements of this Act relating to that meeting of shareholders.

A copy of every resolution so adopted must be kept with the minutes of the meetings of shareholders. (s. 104(2)); see also CBCA, s. 142.

[185] Under subsection 123(2), a director who resigns; or who learns that he is to be removed as a director or that another person is to be appointed or elected in his (or her) place upon the expiration of his term of office is entitled to submit to the corporation a written statement giving the reasons for the director's resignation or the reasons why he or she opposes any proposed action or resolution, as the case may be.

[186] Similar rights to those described above are given to the auditor upon his or her resignation or the proposed removal of the auditor or the nomination of a new auditor.

[187] CBCA, ss. 110(2) and 168(5).

[188] See, generally, *Miller v. F. Mendel Holdings Ltd.*, [1984] S.J. No. 98, [1984] 2 W.W.R. 683, 26 B.L.R. 85 at 94 (Sask. Q.B.), *per* Wimmer J.; see also *Smith v. Paringa Mines Ltd.*, [1906] 2 Ch. 193.

(3) Place of Meeting

§12.53 As with the board of directors, the Act envisages the shareholders of a corporation acting as a collective entity, for instance agreeing unanimously on a shareholder agreement or passing a resolution or special resolution at a shareholders' meeting or where unanimously signing a written resolution in lieu of a meeting. Where there is only one shareholder, collective action is notional; but it is nonetheless implicit in subsection 108(3) of the OBCA, which deems any declaration that restricts, in whole or in part, the powers of the directors to manage or supervise the management of the business and affairs of the corporation to be a unanimous shareholder agreement if it is signed by a person who is the beneficial owner of all the issued shares of a corporation.

§12.54 In small corporations, unanimous shareholder resolutions are often a more practical alternative to holding a meeting of the shareholders. In large corporations, a shareholders' meeting is a virtual necessity if the shareholders of a corporation are to act at all. Section 93 of the OBCA provides that, subject to the articles and any unanimous shareholder agreement,[189] a meeting of the shareholders of a corporation shall be held at such place in or outside Ontario as the directors determine, or in the absence of such a determination, at the place where the registered office of the corporation is located.[190] Thus, the Act gives the directors a great degree of control over the fixing of the place for meetings. The corresponding provision of the CBCA is differently worded, but it also confers a substantial authority on the directors:

> 132.(1) Meetings of shareholders of a corporation shall be held at the place within Canada provided in the by-laws, or in the absence of such provision, at the place within Canada that the directors determine.

Despite this provision, a meeting of the shareholders of a CBCA corporation may be held outside Canada, but only if all the shareholders entitled to vote at that meeting so agree. Any shareholder who attends a meeting of shareholders held outside Canada is deemed to have so agreed unless he or she attends for the express purpose of objecting to the transaction of any business on the grounds that the meeting is not lawfully held.[191] It is worth noting the evident implicit assumption in the CBCA that any meeting place in Canada is reasonable. Such a view is doubtful. If all shareholders reside in Windsor, a meeting in Detroit is likely to be far more convenient than a meeting in Toronto, and a meeting in Vancouver is liable to entail substantial travel and accommodation costs.[192] A better approach to the location of meetings than that embodied in section 93 of

---

[189] As to the authority of a court to permit a meeting to be held elsewhere, see: *Re Bradstone Equity Partners Inc.*, [2002] A.J. No. 1306, 31 B.L.R. (3d) 47 (Q.B.) and the cases discussed therein.

[190] If the articles or by-laws require the holding of a meeting within Ontario, and a meeting is actually held outside Ontario, shareholders attending and participating at that meeting will not be permitted to object to its regularity: *Re Lands & Homes of Canada Ltd.*, [1918] 3 W.W.R. 935, 44 D.L.R. 325 at 326-27 (Man. C.A.), *per* Perdue C.J.M.

[191] CBCA, s. 132(2).

[192] See, generally, *T.E.A.P. International Inc. v. Murphy*, [2004] Y.J. No 134, 4 B.L.R. (4th) 320 (S.C.) — meeting ordered to be held in Australia.

the OBCA and section 132 of the CBCA would be to require that all meetings be held within 200 miles of the registered office, unless consent is obtained.

§12.55 The power to fix the place of a meeting provides an obvious opportunity to corporate management to gerrymander the meeting.[193] Consequently, in the case of small corporations, it is common for the by-laws or a unanimous shareholder agreement to require shareholders' meetings to be held in a particular part of the province, to facilitate shareholder participation in such meetings. In larger corporations, such restrictions are less likely to be found in the by-laws, but, as a matter of practice, nearly all corporations conduct shareholders' meetings in a locality having some general nexus with the corporation.

§12.56 The 2001 amendments to the CBCA added the opportunity to hold meetings outside Canada. Subsection 132(2) provides that:

> ... a meeting of shareholders of a corporation may be held at a place outside Canada if the place is specified in the articles or all the shareholders entitled to vote at the meeting agree that the meeting is to be held at that place.

A shareholder who attends a meeting of shareholders held outside Canada is deemed to have agreed to it being held outside Canada except when the shareholder attends the meeting for the express purpose of objecting to the transaction of any business on the grounds that the meeting is not lawfully held.[194] Subsection 132(4) of the CBCA now contemplates shareholder meetings to be held by telephone or other electronic means, albeit subject to possible regulatory control:

> 132.(4) Unless the by-laws otherwise provide, any person entitled to attend a meeting of shareholders may participate in the meeting, in accordance with the regulations, if any, by means of a telephonic, electronic or other communication facility that permits all participants to communicate adequately with each other during the meeting, if the corporation makes available such a communication facility. A person participating in a meeting by such means is deemed for the purposes of this Act to be present at the meeting.

Subject to any regulations that may be adopted for this purpose, the by-laws of a corporation may provide that the directors or the shareholders of a corporation who call a meeting of shareholders may determine whether the meeting shall be held entirely by means of a telephonic, electronic or other communication facility that permits all participants to communicate adequately with each other during the meeting.

(4) Manner of Calling

§12.57 Meetings may be called either by the directors or as a result of a requisition of a meeting by shareholders under section 105 or by the court under

---

[193] See, for instance, *Nash v. Lancegaye Safety Glass (Ireland) Ltd.* (1958), 92 Ir. L.T.R. 11 (H.C.).
[194] CBCA, s. 132(3).

section 106 of the OBCA.[195] Authorization for the calling of a meeting is usually by director resolution, though it is not essential that such a resolution be formally adopted.[196] Many corporate by-laws empower less than the full board of a corporation (*e.g.*, the president of the corporation or the executive committee, and sometimes even as few as two directors) to call a meeting of the shareholders, but the authority for doing so is not clear. Far from authorizing the practice, clause 127(3)(*a*) of the OBCA provides that no managing director or committee of the directors has the authority to "submit to the shareholders any question or matter requiring the approval of the shareholders".[197] The benefit of this restriction is not clear. In the interest of allowing as much flexibility as possible, it is one provision that might be considered for deletion in the next round of statute revision. Where for some reason, the number of directors falls below a quorum (or whatever number may be fixed for the calling of a meeting), the rump remaining may obtain a court order authorizing them to call a meeting of shareholders.[198]

§12.58 Holding an improperly called meeting is irregular, and may be restrained where there is a risk that substantial prejudice may be suffered by the complainant if the meeting is allowed to proceed.[199] To restrain the meeting, the applicant shareholder or director must act quickly.[200] In some cases the courts have shown a particular hostility to the idea of interfering with a meeting, irrespective of whether it was properly called. Very often the remedy of restraint is simply not necessary. If what is proposed to be done at a meeting is lawful, there is no justification for preventing the meeting from taking place; if what is proposed to be done is unlawful, there are more effectual remedies available than enjoining the meeting itself (*e.g.*, to strike down any decision improperly taken).[201] Moreover, it appears that the shareholders may ratify an improperly called meeting.[202]

---

[195] See also CBCA, ss. 143 and 144. As to the authority of the directors to postpone a meeting, see *Oppenheimer & Co. v. United Grain Growers Ltd.*, [1997] M.J. No. 510, 36 B.L.R. (2d) 54 (Q.B.).

[196] *Wood v. Pan-American Investment Ltd.* (1961), 28 D.L.R. (2d) 703 (B.C.S.C.).

[197] Compare CBCA, s. 115(3)(*a*).

[198] See, for instance, *International Baslen Enterprises Ltd. v. Kirwan* [2006] O.J. No. 295, 12 B.L.R. (4th) 169 (C.A.).

[199] There are cases that take the position that a notice is void if it is issued by a person who does not have the authority to issue the notice, so that if the meeting takes place its decisions will be void: See, for instance, *Re Haycraft Gold Reduction & Mining Co.*, [1900] 2 Ch. 230; *Re State of Wyoming Syndicate*, [1901] 2 Ch. 431. A void notice would be of no legal effect whatever. This seems a doubtful proposition. The giving of notice is internal to the corporation, and if there is no objection by the members or other insiders of the corporation, it is difficult to see on what basis an outsider might complain with respect to the invalidity of the notice. This line of argument would suggest that an improperly given notice is at best "voidable". Some support for the overall approach may be found in a second line of cases, in which courts have decided not to invalidate a meeting where the decision would have been the same even if the correct procedure had been followed. See, for instance, *Browne v. La Trinidad* (1887), 37 Ch. D. 1 (C.A.); *Southern Counties Deposit Bank Ltd. v. Rider* (1895), 73 L.T. 374 (C.A.); *Bentley-Stevens v. Jones*, [1974] 1 W.L.R. 638 (Ch.).

[200] *Browne v. La Trinidad* (1887), 37 Ch. D. 1 at 9 (C.A.), *per* Cotton L.J.

[201] *Robinson v. Toronto General Trusts Corp.*, [1921] O.J. No. 600, 19 O.W.N. 477 (C.A.); but compare *Beauchemin v. Beauchemin & Sons Ltd.* (1926), 64 Que. S.C. 300.

[202] *Hooper v. Kerr, Stuart & Co.* (1900), 83 L.T. 729 at 730 (Ch.), *per* Cozens-Hardy J.

(5) Business of Meeting

§12.59 The business that may be transacted at a meeting is limited to that for which proper notice has been given[203] — the requirements concerning such notice is discussed below. Generally, business is transacted at shareholders' meetings by the submission of resolutions (and amendments thereto) to a vote. In a limited range of cases, an actual vote may not be required. The most obvious instance is the election of directors. If the number of persons nominated is the same as, or fewer than, the number of positions for which elections are to be held, there is no need for a vote — all persons nominated (if otherwise qualified) are deemed to be elected.[204]

§12.60 In *Roman Hotels Ltd. v. Desrochers Hotels Ltd.*,[205] the three shareholders of a corporation, whose sole undertaking was the operation of a hotel, agreed in a telephone conversation to sell the hotel. This agreement was followed by the execution of an agreement of purchase and sale by the corporation. In an action for specific performance by the plaintiff purchaser, the defendant corporation argued that the agreement was ineffective because it had not been approved in the manner required by law. It was held that the plaintiff was entitled to damages. Although the statute required the filing of a resolution with the province and the resolution had not been properly passed, a corporate decision to sell the property had been made despite the lack of formality. Therefore, although a formal resolution at a formal meeting is the best evidence of a corporate decision, it is not the only evidence that can be accepted.[206]

(6) Notice of Meeting

§12.61 People who oppose the outcome of a meeting often argue that it was not properly conducted. Given the tendency of dissenting shareholders to dispute not only the decisions that were made at a meeting but also the process by which those decisions were reached, it is not surprising that both the OBCA and the CBCA set out a code of rules to ensure that meetings are conducted fairly. The rules not only protect minority shareholders but also afford majority shareholders some measure of protection from unnecessary litigation. Some of the most important legal controls arise under the rules with respect to notice. Failure to comply with the notice requirements may lead to an order restraining the holding of the

---

[203] *McDougall v. Black Lake Asbestos & Chrome Co.*, [1920] O.J. No. 143, 47 O.L.R. 328 at 332-33 (H.C.D.), *per* Kelly J. See, generally, s. 96(5) of the OBCA which provides:

> 96.(5) All business transacted at a special meeting of shareholders and all business transacted at an annual meeting of shareholders, except consideration of the minutes of an earlier meeting, the financial statements and auditor's report, election of directors and reappointment of the incumbent auditor shall be deemed to be special business.

See also CBCA, s. 135(5).

[204] *Morden Woollen Mills Co. v. Heckles* (1908), 7 W.L.R. 715 at 717 (Man. C.A.), *per* Perdue J.A.
[205] [1976] S.J. No. 415, 69 D.L.R. (3d) 126 at 133-34 (C.A.), *per* Bayda J.A.
[206] See also *Re Express Engineering Works Ltd.*, [1920] 1 Ch. 466. *Farvolden v. Algorithmics Inc.*, [2003] O.J. No. 5003, 42 B.L.R. (3d) 60 at 71-72 (S.C.J.), *per* Sachs J.

meeting.[207] Among the most important of the procedural rules set down in the OBCA and the CBCA are those governing notices of meetings. A notice that is given by a person who does not have the authority to do so may be raised as a ground for voiding any business conducted at the meeting,[208] but the court should not make such an order where the decision would have been the same even if the correct procedure had been followed.[209] In regard to the timing of notice, the legislation seeks first to ensure that the timing of notice is connected to the fixing of the record date, and second to ensure that notice is given neither so long before the meeting that it is forgotten, nor so soon before the meeting that it defeats the shareholder's ability to inform himself or herself of the issues at hand, or to organize with fellow shareholders.

(7) Form of Notice

§12.62 A notice of a shareholders' meeting must be given in writing to every director of the corporation, the auditor and every shareholder entitled to vote at that meeting.[210] There are two basic objectives behind the notice requirement. The first is to enable a shareholder to determine whether a particular matter to be decided at a meeting is of sufficient concern to the shareholder to require his or her attendance.[211] The second is to provide the shareholder with an opportunity to make an informed judgment about that matter.[212] The fundamental requirement with respect to notice is that it must be fair. In other words, a person whose rights may possibly be affected by the adoption of a proposal, or who may be subjected to an obligation by reason of its adoption, must be given a a reasonable opportunity to respond[213] — specifically, whether to participate in the meeting, and how to vote at the meeting. This last objective is supplemented by the provisions of the Act requiring the furnishing of an information circular that sets forth the business to be discussed at the meeting. In the absence of specific statutory or regulatory requirements (including requirements set out in the articles, by-laws or a unanimous shareholder agreement),[214] the general rule is that a notice is sufficient if the essential nature of the business to be transacted is set out; it is not necessary to provide full particulars or details.[215]

---

[207] *T.E.A.P. International Inc. v. Murphy*, [2004] Y.J. No. 129, 3 B.L.R. (4th) 214 (S.C.).
[208] See, for instance, *Re Haycraft Gold Reduction & Mining Co.*, [1900] 2 Ch. 230; *Re State of Wyoming Syndicate*, [1901] 2 Ch. 431.
[209] *Browne v. La Trinidad* (1887), 37 Ch. D. 1 (C.A.); *Southern Counties Deposit Bank Ltd. v. Rider* (1895), 73 L.T. 374 (C.A.); *Bentley-Stevens v. Jones*, [1974] 1 W.L.R. 638.
[210] OBCA, s. 96; CBCA, s. 135.
[211] See, for instance, *Charter Oil Co. v. Beaumont* (1967), 62 W.W.R. 617 (B.C.C.A.); *Jamieson v. Hotel Renfrew (Trustees of)*, [1941] O.J. No. 232, [1941] 4 D.L.R. 470 at 478 (H.C.J.), per Roach J.
[212] *Re N. Slater Co.*, [1947] O.J. No. 23, [1947] 2 D.L.R. 311 at 313-14 (H.C.J.), *per* Lebel J.; *Rudkin v. British Columbia Automobile Assn.*, [1969] B.C.J. No. 39, 70 W.W.R. 649 (S.C.); *Garvie v. Axmith*, [1961] O.J. No. 616, 31 D.L.R. (2d) 65 at 86-87 (H.C.), *per* Spence J.
[213] *City of Calgary v. Northland Properties*, [2003] A.J. No. 970 at para. 27 (Q.B.), *per* Brooker J.
[214] *Lumbers v. Fretz*, [1928] O.J. No. 84, 62 O.L.R. 635 (H.C.D.), aff'd [1928] O.J. No. 111, 63 O.L.R. 190 (C.A.).
[215] *Irvin v. Irvin Porcupine Gold Mines Ltd.*, [1940] O.J. No. 182, [1940] O.W.N. 315 (H.C.J.); see also *Pacific Coast Coal Mines Ltd. v. Arbuthnot* (1917), 36 D.L.R. 564 (J.C.P.C.).

§12.63 The whole purpose of a meeting, as distinguished from the details, must be fairly stated in the notice of meeting. The fairness of the notice is largely determined by whether the information would be misleading and comprehensible to the person to whom it is addressed.[216] However, a slight mistake in the notice, such as calling the meeting a directors' meeting rather than a shareholders' meeting, does not invalidate the notice,[217] provided that it would not mislead a reasonable person in the position of the recipient about the nature of the meeting or the substance of the business to be discussed. The remarks of Young J. are particularly illuminating on the standard which is applied in gauging the validity of a notice:

> In considering the equitable rule one does not adopt the legalistic approach of a 19th Century examiner of titles searching for a base fee nor does one approach the question in what counsel aptly described as a nit-picking way, but one asks what effect will the information provided have on the ordinary shareholder who scans or reads the document quickly, not as a lawyer, but as an ordinary man or woman of commerce or as an ordinary investor. One asks, viewed in such a way, will the information fully and fairly inform and instruct the shareholder about the matter upon which he or she will have to vote.[218]

Although a notice which is misleading with respect to some matter of general concern to the shareholders may invalidate the meeting to which it relates, where the misleading element relates to what is essentially a private dispute between one shareholder and the corporation, the court may disregard that misleading element.[219]

(8) Record Date

§12.64 The persons entitled to receive notice are those persons who are shown as shareholders in the registry of the corporation.[220] The "date of record" for a meeting is essentially the cut-off date for determining the persons who are entitled to receive notice of, and to participate in, a meeting. The need to fix such a date is of particular importance in the case of widely held corporations, where shares may continue trading long after the notice of a meeting has been given; indeed, such trades may continue to occur up to and during the meeting itself. It would be an obvious inconvenience if corporations were not able to fix a particular time at which the list of persons entitled to notice and to participate would be settled for the purposes of an individual meeting. Consequently, both the CBCA and the OBCA contain extensive provisions governing the fixing of the date of record for shareholders' meetings.

---

[216] *McDougall v. Black Lake Asbestos & Chrome Co.*, [1920] O.J. No. 143, 47 O.L.R. 328 at 333 (H.C.D.), *per* Kelly J.
[217] *E.H. McGuire & E.H.J. Forester Ltd. v. Cadzow*, [1932] 3 W.W.R. 337 at 354-55, 26 Alta. L.R. 518 (C.A.), *per* McGillivray J.A.
[218] *Deveraux Holdings Pty. Ltd. v. Pelsart Resources N.L.* (1986), 4 A.C.L.C. 12.
[219] *Cheong v. Noble China Inc.*, [1998] O.J. No. 2388, 34 B.L.R. (2d) 172 (*sub nom. Lei v. Noble China Inc.*) (Gen. Div.).
[220] *Kary Investment Corp. v. Tremblay*, [2005] A.J. No. 1030, 8 B.L.R. (4th) 40 at para. 40 (Alta. C.A.), *per* Russell J.A.

§12.65 Discretion over the fixing of the date of record is, to a large extent, left in the control of the directors. Subsection 95(2) of the OBCA provides that the directors may fix in advance a date to be the record date for determining the shareholders entitled to receive notice of a meeting of the shareholders. The record date so fixed must not be more than 60 nor less than 30 days prior to the date on which the meeting is to be held. If no record date is fixed by the directors, the record date for the determination of the shareholders entitled to receive notice is the close of business on the day immediately preceding the day on which notice is given. Because meetings may be held without notice on consent, it is obviously essential to determine which shareholders are entitled to provide that consent. Thus, the Act provides that if no notice is given, the record date for receiving the notice is the day on which the meeting is held.[221] This rule is in some respects paradoxical. It means that a person who acquires a share after the last date on which notice could have been given is still entitled to object to the failure to be given notice, even though he or she would not have been entitled to notice if the corporation had provided proper notice under the Act.

§12.66 The fixing of the record date for the purpose of voting is somewhat more complicated than the procedure for fixing the record date for notice purposes. Under subsection 100(1) of the OBCA,[222] a corporation is required to prepare an alphabetical list of shareholders entitled to receive notice of a meeting. This list must be arranged in alphabetical order and must show the number of shares held by each shareholder.[223] The list must be prepared not later than 10 days after the record date, where the record date is fixed under subsection 95(2). If no record date has been fixed, then the list must be prepared on the close of business on the day immediately preceding the day on which the notice is given, or where no notice is given, on the day on which the meeting is held. As a general rule, a person named as a shareholder on either such list is entitled to vote the shares shown opposite his or her name at the meeting to which the list relates, except to the extent that:[224]

(*a*) the person has transferred any shares after the record date; and

(*b*) the transferee of those shares,

    (i) produces properly endorsed share certificates, or

    (ii) otherwise establishes that the transferee owns the shares,

and demands, not later than ten days before the meeting, or such shorter period before the meeting as the by-laws of the corporation may provide, that the transferee's name be included in the list before the meeting...[225]

---

[221] OBCA s. 95(3); CBCA, s. 134(3).
[222] See also CBCA, s. 138(1).
[223] Any shareholder of the corporation may examine the list of shareholders during usual business hours at the registered office of the corporation, or at the place where its central securities register is maintained and at the meeting of the shareholders for which the list was prepared: OBCA, s. 100(4); CBCA, s. 138(4).
[224] OBCA, s. 100(2) and (3); CBCA, s. 138(2) and (3).
[225] The by-laws of the corporation may prescribe a shorter period than 10 days.

in which case the transferee is entitled to vote his shares. Any shareholder may examine the list of shareholders during the usual business hours at the registered office of the corporation or at the place where its central securities register is maintained and at the meeting of shareholders for which the list was prepared.[226]

§12.67 If a record date is fixed, notice of that record date must be given no less than seven days before the date so fixed by the following methods:

- by advertisement in a newspaper published or distributed in the place where the corporation has its registered office and in each place in Canada where it has a transfer agent or where a transfer of its shares may be recorded; and

- by written notice to each stock exchange in Canada on which the shares of the corporation are listed for trading.

unless notice of the record date has been waived in writing by every holder of a share of the class or series affected whose name is set out in the securities register at the close of business on the day the directors fix the record date.

§12.68 Subsection 96(2) of the OBCA provides that "a notice of a meeting is not required to be sent to shareholders who were not registered on the records of the corporation or its transfer agent on the record date" — a largely axiomatic proposition. It then states that a failure to receive a notice does not deprive a shareholder of the right to vote at the meeting. A similar exception is provided under subsection 135(2) of the CBCA. Note that a failure to receive is not the same as a failure to give. A corporation may not pick and choose among its shareholders, deciding to which of them it will give notice. Nor is sloppy record-keeping an excuse for a failure to give notice.

§12.69 A shareholder or any other person entitled to attend a meeting of shareholders may, in any manner and at any time, waive notice of a meeting of shareholders, and attendance of any such person at a meeting of shareholders is a waiver of notice of the meeting, except where that person attends a meeting for the express purpose of objecting to the transaction of any business on the grounds that the meeting is not lawfully called.[227]

§12.70 Subsection 134(1) of the CBCA provides that:

>   134.(1) The directors may, within the prescribed period, fix in advance a date as the record date for the purpose of determining shareholders
>
>   (a) entitled to receive payment of a dividend;
>
>   (b) entitled to participate in a liquidation distribution;
>
>   (c) entitled to receive notice of a meeting of shareholders;
>
>   (d) entitled to vote at a meeting of shareholders; or

---

[226] OBCA, s. 100(4).
[227] OBCA, s. 98; CBCA, s. 136.

(e) for any other purpose.

Where a record date is fixed, every holder of a share or a class or series affected whose name is set out in the securities register at the close of business on the day the directors fix the record date, must be given notice of the record date within the prescribed period. However, this provision does not apply where notice of the record date is waived in writing.[228] If no record date is fixed then the following rules apply:

(a) the record date for the determination of shareholders entitled to receive notice of a meeting of shareholders shall be

　(i) at the close of business on the day immediately preceding the day on which the notice is given, or

　(ii) if no notice is given, the day on which the meeting is held; and

(b) the record date for the determination of shareholders for any purpose other than to establish a shareholder's right to receive notice of a meeting or to vote shall be at the close of business on the day on which the directors pass the resolution relating thereto.[229]

(9) Sufficiency (Duration) and Content of Notice

§12.71 The OBCA and CBCA and (in the case of reporting issuers) the *Securities Act*[230] all contain provisions regulating the sufficiency and content of notice of any shareholders' meeting, and with good reason, for unless such matters were regulated, the management group within a corporation could completely rig the outcome of a meeting. The Irish case of *Nash v. Lancegaye Safety Glass (Ireland) Ltd.*[231] provides an interesting and practical demonstration of the various steamroller techniques that management of a corporation may employ in attempting to achieve its object. In that case, some of the shareholders and directors of the company wished to issue a block of shares to the former chair of the company board. It was known that this would be an unpopular move with some of the other shareholders and directors. To ram the measure through, a directors' meeting was called at which the issue of the shares was quickly approved. The court outlined some of the objectionable features of this meeting:

> No agenda or notice of any resolution was sent out beforehand, and in the agenda circulated at the meeting the only heading the matter could be related to was "capital position," which was an item appearing in the agenda and discussed at nearly every meeting. Mr. Nash's plea for adjournment and an opportunity of further consideration was rejected rather summarily.[232]

The management group went on to orchestrate the annual meeting so that it was "deliberately fixed to frustrate as far as possible the wishes and intentions of the

---

[228] CBCA, s. 134(3).
[229] CBCA, s. 134(2).
[230] R.S.O. 1990, c. S.5.
[231] (1958), 92 Ir. L.T.R. 11 at 22 (H.C.).
[232] *Ibid.*

shareholders and to insure the confirmation or re-election of the existing directors". For this purpose, the place of the meeting was moved from Templemore to Dublin, to make it as difficult as possible for the local shareholders to attend.

§12.72 For an offering corporation under the OBCA, notice of the time and place of a shareholders' meeting must be sent no less than 21 days and not more than 50 days before the meeting to each shareholder entitled to vote at the meeting, to each director of the corporation and to the auditor of the corporation. For a corporation that is not an offering corporation, the notice must be sent no less than 10 days and not more than 50 days before the meeting.[233] A deliberate failure to comply with this requirement will lead to the invalidation of the meeting.[234] As noted above, a notice of a meeting is not required to be sent to shareholders who were not registered on the records of the corporation or its transfer agent on the record date,[235] but a failure to receive a notice of a meeting does not deprive a shareholder of the right to vote at the meeting.[236]

§12.73 Subsection 96(3) of the OBCA provides that unless the by-laws of a corporation otherwise provide, where a meeting of shareholders is adjourned for less than 30 days, it is not necessary to give notice of the adjourned meeting except by announcement "at the earliest meeting that is adjourned".[237] The word "earliest" is no grammatical slip — a fact that becomes clear when one contrasts subsection 96(3) with subsection 96(4), which provides that if a meeting is adjourned by one or more adjournments for an aggregate of 30 days or more, notice of the adjourned meeting must be given as was done for the original meeting. Thus, the Act prevents the circumvention of the 30-day restriction by the practice of "creeping adjournments" under which the notice requirement is avoided by never concluding a meeting but merely by adjourning it indefinitely or repeatedly. If a meeting is held on day one, adjourned for 10 days and then for a further 15 days, a single announcement given at the first of these three sessions of the meeting (*i.e.*, on day one — the earliest meeting that is adjourned) is sufficient. If, however, the meeting is adjourned first for 10 days and then for a further 25 days, notice must be given as would be required for an original meeting, because, in that case, the aggregate number of days of adjournment exceeds the 30-day maximum. Such a rule presents little problem where two adjournments are anticipated at the time of the original meeting. It becomes more difficult to apply where the second adjournment is unanticipated.

§12.74 In each of the foregoing cases, "day" means a clear day[238] — both the day on which the notice is given and the day on which the meeting is held are excluded

---

[233] OBCA, s. 96(1); CBCA, s. 135(1).
[234] *Canada Furniture Co. v. Banning*, [1918] 1 W.W.R. 31 at 33, 39 D.L.R. 313 (Man. K.B.), *per* Mathers C.J.K.B.
[235] CBCA, s. 135(2).
[236] OBCA, s. 96(2); CBCA, s. 135(2).
[237] OBCA, s. 96(3); CBCA, s. 135(3).
[238] See *Moco Management Ltd. v. Llernam Holdings Ltd.*, [1985] B.C.J. No. 2864, 68 B.C.L.R. 128 (S.C.).

from the notice period. Consequently, in a calculation of time involving clear days the period of days is deemed to commence the day following the event that began the period and is deemed to terminate at midnight of the last day of the period preceding the day on which the event occurs.[239] This meaning of "day" differs from the meaning under rule 3.01 of the *Rules of Civil Procedure*[240] where the day on which the notice is given is excluded in calculating the number of days of notice given, but the last day is included. If, however, the last day of the period falls on a Sunday or holiday,[241] the period of time terminates on the day next following that is not a holiday or a Sunday.[242]

§12.75 Of at least equal importance to the duration of notice is the required content of notice. Obviously, even an adequate period of notice would afford shareholders little opportunity to make an informed and rational decision if only minimal information was included in the notice. There is a clear overlap between the requirements governing the form of a notice[243] and those governing its content. Under subsection 96(6) of the OBCA, notice of a meeting at which special business is to be transacted must state, or be accompanied by a statement of, the nature of that business. The term "special business" is given a broad definition in subsection 96(5), which provides that all business transacted at a special meeting of shareholders is special business; furthermore, all business transacted at an annual meeting of shareholders except the consideration of the minutes of an earlier meeting, the financial statements, the auditor's report, the election of directors and re-appointment of the incumbent auditor, is also special business.[244] Only the most routine of corporate matters, therefore, fall outside the scope of special business.

---

[239] OBCA, s. 1(1), definition of "day".
[240] R.R.O. 1990, Reg. 194.
[241] The term "holiday" is defined in s. 29 of the *Interpretation Act*, R.S.O. 1990, c. I.11, as follows:

"holiday" includes Sunday, New Year's Day, Good Friday, Easter Monday, Christmas Day, the birthday or the day fixed by proclamation of the Governor General for the celebration of the birthday of the reigning Sovereign, Victoria Day, Dominion Day, Labour Day, Remembrance Day, and any day appointed by proclamation of the Governor General or the Lieutenant Governor as a public holiday or for a general fast or thanksgiving, and when any holiday, except Remembrance Day, falls on a Sunday, the day next following is in lieu thereof a holiday.

[242] Definition of "day" in s. 1(1) of the OBCA. This term is not defined in the CBCA.
[243] See above.
[244] See also CBCA, s. 135(5).

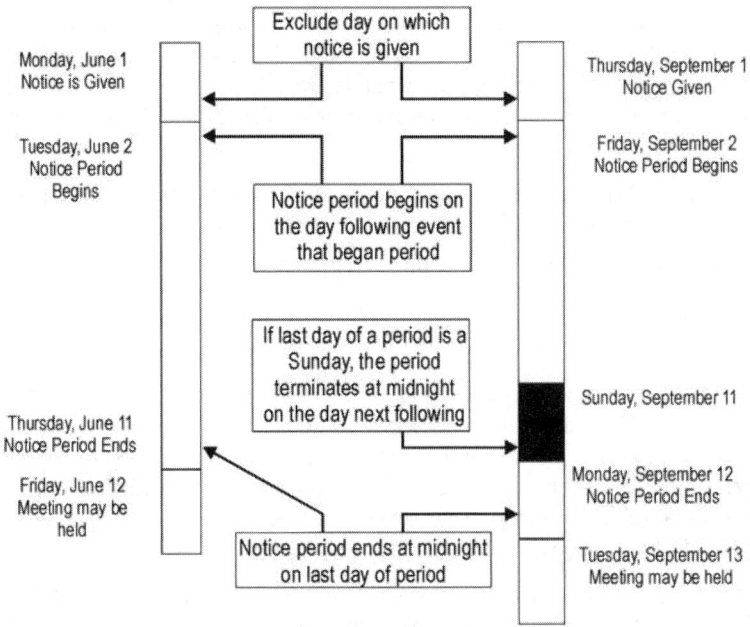

For a non-offering corporation, at least 10 days notice of a shareholder meeting must be given. The "days" must be clear days. If the 10 days notice period ends on a Sunday, the period carries over to the following Monday.

§12.76 The notice must inform the shareholders concerning every subject on which they will be voting,[245] not only so that they may make an informed decision concerning the matter that is to be decided,[246] but also so that the shareholder can decide whether or not it is necessary or advisable to attend the meeting.[247] However, an omission of some otherwise necessary information will

---

[245] *Baillie v. Oriental Telephone & Electric Co.*, [1915] 1 Ch. 503 (C.A.).
[246] *Ibid.*, at 515, *per* Lord Cozens-Hardy M.R.
[247] *Tiessen v. Henderson*, [1899] 1 Ch. 861, *per* Kekewich J.:

> A shareholder may properly and prudently leave matters in which he takes no personal interest to the decision of the majority. But in that case he is content to be bound by the vote of the majority; because he knows the matter about which the majority are to vote

not invalidate a meeting where it is clear that the complainant was aware of that detail despite the deficiency of the notice.[248] Frequently, either the notice or an accompanying information circular will contain a statement of the board's views concerning the issues to be decided. There is nothing improper *per se* in the expression of such opinions. The shareholders are entitled to the advice and counsel of the directors on the matter to be decided.[249] Nevertheless, if the directors take it upon themselves to give notice to current shareholders, they have a duty to advise in good faith and not fraudulently and not to mislead, whether deliberately or carelessly. If they fail to do so, the affected shareholders may have a remedy, including the recovery of what is truly a personal loss sustained by them as a result.[250] Accordingly, the basic or minimum standards that a notice must satisfy are that it must:

- provide a clear and adequate explanation of the nature of the subject matter to be discussed;
- state whether voting or other action is required;
- contain all information necessary to allow the persons entitled to vote to make a properly informed decision;
- contain a recommendation from the directors on the action that the shareholders should take, indicating whether or not the proposal described in the notice or accompanying circulation is, in the opinion of the directors, in the best interests of the shareholders as a whole; where a decision may have adverse effects upon the corporation (*e.g.*, expose it to the risk of lawsuit), these risks should be disclosed.[251]

The directors owe a duty to report conscientiously[252] to the shareholders and to furnish the facts and information necessary for the shareholders to come to a decision on whether to approve or disapprove the motion before them.[253] All information provided must be presented fairly, be reasonably accurate and not misleading in any material respect.[254] The directors must disclose any interest that they have in the matter to be decided by the shareholders of the corporation.[255] Notice of a meeting of shareholders at which special business is to be

---

at the meeting. If he does not know that, he has not a fair chance of determining in his own interest whether he ought to attend the meeting, make further inquiries or leave others to determine the matter for him.

[248] *Re Soft Tracks Enterprises Ltd.*, [2004] B.C.J. No. 364, 43 B.L.R. (3d) 236 (S.C.).
[249] *Campbell v. Australia Mutual Provident Society* (1908), 77 L.J. 117 (P.C.).
[250] *Dawson International plc v. Coats Patons plc*, [1989] B.C.L.C. 223 (Scot.), *per* Lord Cullen.
[251] *Northern Counties Securities Ltd. v. Jackson & Steeple Ltd.*, [1974] 1 W.L.R. 1133.
[252] *Zething v. Kilner*, [1972] 1 W.L.R. 337 at 341, *per* Brightman J.
[253] *Rackham v. Peek Foods Ltd.*, [1990] B.C.L.C. 895 at 899 (Ch.), *per* Templeman J.; *Residues Treatment & Trading Co. v. Southern Resources Ltd.* (1988), 14 A.C.L.R. 375; *TNT Australia Pty Ltd. v. Poseidon Ltd.* (1989), 52 S.A.S.R. 379; *Garvie v. Axmith*, [1961] O.J. No. 616, 31 D.L.R. (2d) 65 (H.C.).
[254] *Garvie v. Axmith*, [1961] O.J. No. 616, 31 D.L.R. (2d) 65 (H.C.).
[255] *Kaye v. Croydon Tramways Co.*, [1898] 1 Ch. 358 (C.A.); *Baillie v. Oriental Telephone & Electric Co.*, [1915] 1 Ch. 503 (C.A.); *Pacific Coast Coal Mines Ltd. v. Arbuthnot*, [1917] A.C. 607 (P.C.), *per* Viscount Haldane.

transacted must state, or be accompanied by a statement of, the nature of that business in sufficient detail to permit the shareholders to form a reasoned judgment thereon and should include the text of any special resolution or by-law that is to be submitted to the meeting.[256] This statement must not be misleading in any material respect.[257]

§12.77 The notice must specify the business to be transacted at a meeting with clearness and accuracy, and a failure to do so may invalidate any step taken regarding that business[258] (unless the shareholders who object to it estop themselves from challenging its validity by participating in the meeting). The notice should present accurate and reasonably complete disclosure of all relevant information; if it is misleading then the meeting may be restrained and any decision reached at it may be invalidated.[259] Where the shareholders go beyond the business that may validly be conducted under the terms of the notice provided for a meeting, that step does not affect the validity of any business conducted at the meeting that fell within the scope of that notice.[260] The notice of meeting must not be overly general or vague (especially if it is deliberately vague),[261] but where the notice of a meeting indicates the subject of a resolution, then adequate notice of the meeting and the resolution to be passed at it has been given, even if an amendment is brought forward that amounts to a substantial departure from the original proposal.[262]

§12.78 Although notice that a particular resolution is to be discussed is sufficient to allow amendments to the relevant resolution to be brought forward, any proposed amendments must not change the basic character of the resolution described in the notice.[263] It is not acceptable for the meeting to deal with business substantially different from that described in the notice.[264] The more unusual the business, the more exact the notice must be.[265] For instance, unequivocal notice must be given of a resolution that will lead to a pecuniary advantage to a

---

[256] OBCA, s. 96(6); CBCA, s. 135(6).
[257] *Charlebois v. Bienvenu*, [1967] O.J. No. 1064, 64 D.L.R. (2d) 683 (H.C.J.), *per* Fraser J., rev'd [1967] O.J. No. 1139, 68 D.L.R. (2d) 578 (C.A.); *Goldex Mines Ltd. v. Revill*, [1974] O.J. No. 2245, 7 O.R. (2d) 216 at 224 (C.A.); but *cf. Babic v. Milinkovic*, [1971] B.C.J. No. 208, 22 D.L.R. (3d) 732 (S.C.), aff'd 25 D.L.R. (3d) 752 (C.A.).
[258] *Zimmerman v. Andrew Motherwell of Canada Ltd. (Trustee of)*, [1923] O.J. No. 48, 54 O.L.R. 342 at 350 (C.A.), *per* Logie J., aff'd [1925] 3 D.L.R. 953 (P.C.); *Baillie v. Oriental Telephone & Electric Co.*, [1915] 1 Ch. 503 (C.A.).
[259] *Chequepoint Securities Ltd. v. Claremont Petroleum N.L.* (1986), 4 A.C.L.C. 711.
[260] *Re Second Standard Royalties Ltd.*, [1930] O.J. No. 45, 66 O.L.R. 288 (H.C.J.).
[261] *Cannon v. Toronto Corn Exchange*, [1879] O.J. No. 218, 27 Gr. 23 (Ct. Ch.), aff'd [1880] O.J. No. 67, 5 O.A.R. 268 (C.A.).
[262] *Betts & Co. v. Macnaghten*, [1910] 1 Ch. 430 at 435-36, *per* Eve J.; but compare *Pacific Coast Coal Mines Ltd. v. Arbuthnot* (1917), 36 D.L.R. 564, [1917] A.C. 607 (P.C.); *Choppington Collieries Ltd. v. Johnson*, [1944] 1 All E.R. 762 (C.A.); *Re Moorgate Mercantile Holdings Ltd.*, [1980] 1 All E.R. 40 (Ch.).
[263] *Re Second Standard Royalties Ltd.*, [1930] O.J. No. 45, 66 O.L.R. 288 at 298-99 (H.C.J.), *per* Orde J.A.
[264] *Re Bridport Old Brewery Co.* (1867), 2 Ch. App. 191 at 194 (L.JJ.), *per* G.L. Turner L.J.
[265] *Irvine v. Union Bank of Australia* (1877), 2 App. Cas. 366 at 375 (P.C.), *per* Sir Barnes Peacock.

director.[266] If a notice is misleading, the court will set aside the meeting, prohibit its being held or restrain any action in consequence to it,[267] unless the same outcome is inevitable even if valid notice is given.[268]

§12.79 There is some case law that suggests that any notice that is given must not only meet the requirements of the law and the terms of any contract but also be reasonable in the circumstances. The American case of *Van Gemert v. Boeing Co.*[269] provides an excellent illustration of a manifestly unreasonable notice. In that case, the Boeing Company called for the redemption of its convertible debentures. The call was announced through newspaper notices and mailings to investors who had registered their debentures, and it was given in strict accordance with the debenture agreement — investors being told of the method by which notice might be given only in a single clause that was buried in a 113-page indenture agreement, copies of which were provided to investors only upon request. The notice of redemption stated that each $100 of principal could be redeemed for $103.25 or converted into two shares of the company. The newspaper notices were published on March 28, 1966 in fine print and buried in a multitude of information and data published about the financial markets.[270] March 29, 1966 was set as the deadline for the exercise of the conversion right. On that date, two common shares of the company were worth $316.25, so it was obviously in the best interests of the debenture holders to exercise the conversion right. When the deadline expired, the holders of debentures having an aggregate face value of $1,544,300 had not answered the call. They received only the redemption price.[271] The notice was held to be inadequate in the circumstances.[272]

§12.80 As noted above, corporate by-laws generally contain a provision to the effect that an accidental failure to provide notice to individual shareholders, or the failure of delivery of any notice given to a particular shareholder, will not invalidate any business otherwise validly transacted at the meeting. Such a provision is clearly ineffective where notice is deliberately withheld from someone entitled to attend the meeting.[273] Taking into account the *Boeing* decision, it seems doubtful that a meeting may properly proceed where it is likely that the majority of persons entitled to notice would not have received it, for instance where the notice was sent by mail and there was a postal strike immediately after the date on which the notice was sent.

---

[266] *Hutton v. West Cork Rwy. Co.* (1883), 23 Ch. D. 654 at 659, *per* Fry J., rev'd on other grounds 23 Ch. D. 662 at 669 (C.A.), *per* Cotton and Bowen L.JJ.
[267] *Kaye v. Croydon Tramways Co.*, [1898] 1 Ch. 358 at 370 (C.A.), *per* Lindley M.R.
[268] *Bentley-Stevens v. Jones*, [1974] 2 All E.R. 653 at 655 (Ch.), *per* Plowman J.A.; see also *Browne v. La Trinidad* (1887), 37 Ch. D. 1 at 17 (C.A.), *per* Lindley L.J.
[269] 520 F.2d 1373 (1975), *cert.* denied 423 U.S. 947 (1975), further proceedings at 590 F.2d 433, aff'd 444 U.S. 472 (1980).
[270] *Ibid.*, at 1379.
[271] Facts taken from *Boeing Co. v. Van Gemert*, 444 U.S. 472 at 474 (1980).
[272] 580 F.2d 1373 at 1383-84 (1980).
[273] *Musselwhite v. C.H. Musselwhite & Son Ltd.*, [1962] Ch. 964.

§12.80.1 The notice requirements of the OBCA and CBCA are heavily supplemented by the requirements imposed under securities laws with respect to information circulars. These are discussed in detail below, in the context of proxy solicitation.[274]

(10) Special Rights of Attendance in the Case of Reporting Issuers

§12.81 At common law, only persons entitled to participate and vote at a meeting were entitled to receive notice of it.[275] The rule may be overridden by statute (as has been done in the case of the auditors of a corporation) and may be overruled by a contrary provision in the articles or by-laws of a corporation.[276] Whether a contractual right to attend and be heard — as in the case of a major creditor of the corporation — is sufficient to overcome the common law presumption is less clear, but it can be argued strongly that any such agreement will be binding where it was approved by the directors of the corporation, given their general authority to govern the business and affairs of the corporation.

§12.82 In effect corporations that are reporting issuers under the *Securities Act* are required to send copies of financial statements to the holders of non-voting shares. Commencing with OSC Policy 1.3, the holders of "Restricted Shares" (as defined in the policy) were granted a right of notice, attendance and participation upon in the case of every such reporting issuer in Ontario. Specifically, section IV of that Policy provided:

> Every reporting issuer shall give notice of shareholders' meetings to holders of Restricted Shares and permit the holders of such shares to attend, in person or by proxy, and to speak at all shareholders' meetings to the extent that a holder of voting securities of that company would be entitled to attend and to speak at shareholders' meetings. For all new issues of Restricted Shares, the constating documents must provide that the holders of such Shares shall be given notice of and be invited to attend meetings of the voting shareholders of the reporting issuer.

Rule 56-501 replaces the former Policy in its entirety. The Rule requires that holders of restricted shares and prospective purchasers of restricted shares be made aware that restricted shares have rights that differ from those attached to an issuer's common shares and that holders of restricted shares receive material sent to holders of common shares. The Rule also removes prospectus exemptions and provides that the Director shall not issue a receipt for a prospectus for a distribution of restricted shares unless shareholder approval, on a majority of the minority basis, was obtained for the distribution or the reorganization that resulted in the creation of the restricted shares. Clause 2.1(7) of the Rule provides that:

---

[274] At §12.142 *seq.*
[275] See, generally, *Re MacKenzie & Co.*, [1916] 2 Ch. 450, *per* Astbury J. Others could, of course, be invited to attend, and could be granted limited privileges of participation (*e.g.*, the privilege of addressing the meeting) if they did attend.
[276] *Royal Mutual Benefit Building Society v. Sharman*, [1963] 1 W.L.R. 581; *Re Compaction Systems Pty. Ltd.*, [1976] 2 N.S.W.L.R. 477.

All documents that a reporting issuer or a CDN issuer sends to the holders of any other class of its equity shares shall also be sent by the issuer at the same time to the holders of its restricted shares.

The Rule does not carry forward the provisions in the Policy that required that constating documents of an issuer provide for holders of non-voting shares to attend and speak at meetings of holders of equity shares. However, the OSC continues to "encourage issuers to provide such rights, either formally in the constating documents or otherwise".[277]

(11) Presiding Officer

§12.83 Except for very small meetings, it is a practical, if not legal, necessity for the meeting to be conducted by a duly appointed presiding officer, or "chair", "chairman" or "chairwoman" as such individuals are popularly, if inexactly, called. As Street J. observed:

> It is an indispensable part of any meeting that a chairman should be appointed and occupy the chair. In the absence of some person (by whatever title he be described) exercising procedural control over a meeting, the meeting is unable to proceed to business. This may perhaps require some qualification if all present are unanimous. And, in a small meeting, procedural control may pass from person to person according to who for the time being is allowed by the acquiescence of those present to have such control. But there must be some person expressly or by acquiescence permitted by those present to put motions to the meeting so as to enable the wish or decision of the meeting to be ascertained.[278]

The OBCA makes only scant provision regarding the actual conduct of shareholders' meetings, and the CBCA provides even less guidance. Clause 97(*c*) of the OBCA provides that, subject to the Act, the articles or by-laws of a corporation or any unanimous shareholder agreement, the president, or in his or her absence, a vice-president who is a director, must chair a meeting of shareholders — this being seen to be an inherent duty and right of the office of president.[279] The president's right to preside applies even to a meeting requisitioned by shareholders, because the right to call or convene a meeting does not confer a right to preside at that meeting.[280] But, if there is no such person present at the meeting within 15 minutes after the time appointed for its holding, the shareholders present must choose a person from their number to chair the meeting.

§12.84 In *National Dwellings Society v. Sykes*, Chitty J. explained the general nature of the duties of the presiding officer, and the limits on his or her powers, in the following terms:

> Unquestionably it is the duty of the chairman, and his function, to preserve order and take care that the proceedings are conducted in a proper manner, and that the

---

[277] Ontario Securities Commission, *Notice of Rule Under the Securities Act, Rule 56-501 Restricted Shares.*
[278] *Colorado Constructions Pty. Ltd. v. Platus*, [1966] 2 N.S.W.R. 598 at 600 (S.C.).
[279] *Freemont Canning Co. v. Wall*, [1941] 3 D.L.R. 96 at 107 (Ont. C.A.), *per* Masten J.A.
[280] *Gray v. Yellowknife Gold Mines Ltd.*, [1946] O.W.N. 938 at 941 (H.C.), *per* Assistant Master Lennox.

sense of the meeting is properly ascertained with regard to any question which is properly before the meeting. But in my opinion, the power which has been contended for is not within the scope of the authority of the chairman — namely to stop the meeting at his own will and pleasure. The meeting is called for the particular purposes of the company. According to the constitution of the company, a certain officer has to preside. He presides with reference to the business which is there to be transacted. In my opinion, he cannot say, after that business has been opened, "I will have no more to do with it; I will not let this meeting proceed; I will stop it; I will declare this meeting dissolved, and I leave the chair." In my opinion, that is not within his power. The meeting by itself ... can resolve to go on with the business for which it has been convened, and appoint a chairman to conduct the business, which the other chairman, forgetful of his duty or violating his duty, has tried to stop because proceedings have taken a turn which he himself does not like.[281]

Thus, the meetings belong to the members and not to the presiding officer. It is the duty of the presiding officer to ensure that the meeting deals with the business with which it is properly charged or that otherwise can be properly brought before it. It is a further duty of the presiding officer to ensure that any other business is ruled out of order. Finally, the duty of the presiding officer is to ensure that the sentiments of the persons assembled are duly recorded. In performing all of these duties, the presiding officer must act in good faith.[282] Where the presiding officer abuses his or her authority, any decision taken at a meeting that is tainted by that misconduct may be set aside by a court, and a new meeting may be ordered (if necessary, under some alternate presiding officer).[283]

§12.85 The courts have taken the general position that there must be a strong case to justify interference with the control of the presiding officer over the conduct of a meeting.[284] In *Cheong v. Noble China Inc.*,[285] Blair J. suggested that a court should interfere only in clear cases involving a substantial risk of harm or patently illegal or abusive conduct. In part, this reluctance to interfere is another reflection of the internal management principle. However, it is also due to the general impracticality of interference in the conduct of a meeting because many steps taken at a meeting are irreversible; for instance, there is usually no practical way to challenge the power of the chair to adjourn a meeting[286] where there is a dispute among the people present on whether the meeting was properly adjourned. Rulings by the presiding officer that are made in good faith and within the scope of his or her authority will be binding upon the shareholders present, even if incorrectly decided, at least where it can be shown that someone may have relied upon such a ruling to his or her detriment. In *Corpique (No. 20) Pty.*

---

[281] [1894] 3 Ch. 159 at 162.
[282] *Johnson v. Hall* (1957), 10 D.L.R. (2d) 243 at 247, 23 W.W.R. 228 (B.C.S.C.), *per* Wilson J.
[283] See, for instance, *Pressello v. Venture Pacific Development Corp.*, [2000] B.C.J. No. 2617, 20 B.L.R. (3d) 96 (S.C.).
[284] See, generally, *Allied Cellular Systems Ltd. v. Bullock*, [1990] B.C.J. No. 1698 (C.A.); *Mercury Partners & Co. v. Cybersurf Corp.*, [2003] A.J. No. 1741, 43 B.L.R. (3d) 37 (Q.B.).
[285] [1996] O.J. No. 2388 (Gen. Div.).
[286] See, generally, *Legion Oils Ltd. v. Barron* (1956), 17 W.W.R. 209 (Alta. S.C.T.D.); *Gray v. Yellowknife Gold Mines Ltd.*, [1946] O.W.N. 938 (H.C.).

Ltd. v. Eastcourt Ltd.[287] the presiding officer at the general meeting of a company closed the meeting after receiving legal advice that the resolutions proposed for the meeting did not satisfy the requirements of the company's articles. After the presiding officer so ruled, he and some of the shareholders left the meeting. Others continued to meet and purported to pass the two resolutions. It was held that although the presiding officer was wrong in stating that the resolutions could not be put to the meeting, it was not open to some of the members to continue the meeting after other members had left in reliance upon the decision of the presiding officer. Moreover, as long as the presiding officer acts in good faith, he or she is not liable to a shareholder for any damages that may be suffered as a result of any ruling that he or she may make, even if it was made in error.[288] Where one presiding officer vacates the chair and another takes his or her place, the second is not bound to accept the rulings of the first.[289]

§12.86 The courts will interfere with the rulings of the presiding officer where the presiding officer has not acted in good faith.[290] The onus lies on the person who disputes the conduct of the presiding officer to establish the existence of bad faith. It is sometimes said that the duty to act in good faith subjects the presiding officer to the high standards of impartiality expected of a quasi-judicial officer. A more appropriate description of the duty is to act honestly and fairly with regard to all individual interests and to act generally toward the best interest of the corporation. Unlike a judge, the presiding officer quite often has an interest in the corporation and, thus, in the business conducted at the meeting, and so he or she is likely to have a personal interest in the matter in issue. Such a personal interest would not be permissible where a person is acting as an adjudicator or a judge.[291] The best practice is for a person not to proceed if he or she has an interest in the matter distinct from the interest of the shareholders generally. Moreover, it is clear that the presiding officer may not act capriciously or arbitrarily[292] (for instance, disregarding a person's rights without reasonable inquiry),[293] or use his or her power to personal advantage.[294] The presiding officer may not act to defeat the purpose for which a meeting was called,[295] but the presiding officer

---

[287] (1989), 7 A.C.L.C. 794.
[288] *Bluechel v. Prefabricated Buildings Ltd.*, [1945] B.C.J. No. 70, [1945] 2 W.W.R. 309 at 317 (C.A.), *per* Macfarlane J.; and see also *Johnson v. Hall* (1957), 10 D.L.R. (2d) 243 at 246-47 (B.C.S.C.), *per* Wilson J.
[289] *Bomac Batten Ltd. v. Pozhke*, [1983] O.J. No. 3176, 43 O.R. (2d) 344 (H.C.J.).
[290] *Re United Canso Oil & Gas Ltd.*, [1980] N.S.J. No. 33, 12 B.L.R. 130 (T.D.).
[291] *Blair v. Consolidated Enfield Corp.*, [1993] O.J. No. 2300, 15 O.R. (3d) 783 at 799 (C.A.), *per* Carthy J.A., aff'd [1995] S.C.J. No. 29, [1995] 4 S.C.R. 5.
[292] *Exco Corp. v. Nova Scotia Savings & Loan Co.*, [1987] N.S.J. No. 56, 35 B.L.R. 149 (T.D.).
[293] *Johnson v. Hall* (1957), 23 W.W.R. 228, 10 D.L.R. (2d) 243 (B.C.S.C.).
[294] *Re Bondi Better Bananas Ltd.*, [1951] O.J. No. 445, 32 C.B.R. 74 at 82 (H.C.J.), *per* Ferguson J., rev'd on other grounds [1951] O.J. No. 510, 32 C.B.R. 171 (C.A.).
[295] *Gray v. Yellowknife Gold Mines Ltd. (No. 1)*, [1946] O.W.N. 938 at 942 (H.C.), *per* Assistant Master Lennox.

must elicit fairly the opinion of the meeting.[296] The presiding officer's other specific duties include the duty:

- to preserve order;
- to ensure that the proceedings are regularly conducted;
- to take care that the sense of the meeting is properly ascertained with regard to any question properly before the meeting; and[297]
- to decide incidental questions arising for decision during the meeting.[298]

§12.87 Although bias or extreme partisanship generally will invalidate rulings made by the presiding officer, it is not sufficient to show that he or she acted where there was a potential conflict of interest.[299] It is necessary to show that an actual conflict has arisen, and a probability that the conflict has influenced the manner in which the meeting was conducted.[300] In deciding how to resolve a particular question that arises for decision at a meeting, he or she is entitled to rely upon the advice of counsel. Where such advice is sought and acted upon in good faith, those facts may be sufficient to defeat any inference of bias.[301]

§12.88 As suggested earlier with respect to deficiency in any notice given with respect to a meeting, when deciding whether to make an order with respect to a meeting, a court should consider whether the party seeking the order has suffered substantial and real prejudice, or will suffer such prejudice if the order is not made.[302] In *John J. Starr (Real Estate) Pty. Ltd. v. Robert R. Andrew (A'Asia) Pty. Ltd.* Young J. stated:

> It is essential in company law that all persons who are entitled to participate in meetings are able to participate in them to the extent which the law allows ... Where the rights of the minority are affected by persistent conduct at the board, so that they are not able fully to participate in meetings, then there is, in my view actual oppression...[303]

§12.89 In *Heil v. T.E.N. Private Cable Systems Ltd.*,[304] the respondent corporation called its annual meeting and set a record date for determining the shareholders entitled to attend and vote. Prior to the record date, the petitioner transferred shares to another person. Because of a cease-trading order issued by the Superintendent of Brokers for the Province of British Columbia, the transfer

---

[296] *Re Lemay Ltd.* (1924), 27 Que. P.R. 1 (H.C.); see also *Second Consolidated Trust Ltd. v. Ceylon Amalgamated Tea & Rubber Estates Ltd.*, [1943] 2 All E.R. 567 at 569 (Ch.), *per* Uthwatt J.
[297] *National Dwellings Society v. Sykes*, [1894] 3 Ch. 159 at 162, *per* Chitty J.
[298] For example, to adjourn the meeting where the question cannot be decided at the meeting: *Byng v. London Life Association Ltd.*, [1990] Ch. 170 (C.A.).
[299] *Consolidated Enfield Corp. v. Blair*, [1995] S.C.J. No. 29, 128 D.L.R. (4th) 73 at 88 (S.C.C.), *per* Iacobucci J.
[300] *Ibid.*, at 87-88.
[301] *Ibid.*, at 91-93.
[302] *NRMA Insurance Group Ltd. v. Spragg*, [2001] N.S.W.S.C. 381, *per* Santow J.
[303] (1991), 6 A.C.S.R. 63 at 71-72 (S.C.N.S.W).
[304] [1993] B.C.J. No. 1171, 11 B.L.R. (2d) 54 at 66 (S.C.), *per* Hutchinson J.; *Byng v. London Life Association Ltd.*, [1990] Ch. 170, 42 B.L.R. 280 (C.A.).

was not recorded by that date, and, indeed, even at the time of the meeting the shares continued to be registered in the name of the petitioner. The presiding officer at the meeting ruled that the transferee was entitled to vote the shares. Because the outcome of the election of directors at that meeting would have been different if the petitioner had been allowed to vote his shares, the petitioner brought a proceeding under section 145 of the CBCA.[305] The British Columbia Supreme Court dismissed the petition and held that the presiding officer correctly exercised his discretion in finding that the transferee, rather than the petitioner, was the person entitled to vote the shares.

§12.90 In widely held companies (particularly cooperatives) the presiding officer will generally take a neutral position on matters raised for discussion, and, if he or she feels strongly about a matter, will relinquish the chair to a more neutral party once that matter arises.[306] Although such neutrality is not necessarily mandatory, it is counsel of perfection and should be encouraged and adopted where possible. Where the presiding officer allows his or her personal feelings or interests to influence the conduct of the meeting, he or she clearly oversteps the bounds of authority. Thus, the presiding officer may not deny a qualified person the right to vote in person or by proxy,[307] for instance, by refusing the registered holder of a share the right to vote and instead recognizing the beneficial owner.[308]

(12) Adjournments

§12.91 Clause 97(*b*) of the OBCA provides that the presiding officer at a meeting may adjourn the meeting from time to time and from place to place. There is no equivalent provision in the CBCA, though such authority may be conferred under the by-laws of a corporation. The OBCA does not require the consent of the meeting to such an adjournment nor is there any suggestion in clause 97(*b*) that the shareholders present may overrule the presiding officer's decision, though any adjournment is subject to such conditions as the meeting decides. No business may be transacted at an adjourned meeting that could not have been transacted at the original meeting.[309] As noted above, the question of whether further notice must be given to the shareholders of the adjourned meeting turns upon the aggregate length of adjournments since the time when the meeting first commenced.

---

[305] Subsection 145 provides that a corporation, shareholder or director may apply to a court to determine any controversy with regard to the election of a director of the corporation. On any such application, the court may make such order as it considers fit, including an order declaring the result of a disputed election or requiring a new election.

[306] *Consolidated Enfield Corp. v. Blair*, [1995] S.C.J. No. 29, 128 D.L.R. (4th) 73 at 90 (S.C.C.), *per* Iacobucci J.

[307] *Re Routley's Holdings Ltd.*, [1959] O.J. No. 283, [1959] O.W.N. 89, aff'd [1960] O.J. No. 415, [1960] O.W.N. 160 (C.A.).

[308] *Tough Oakes Gold Mines Ltd. v. Foster*, [1917] O.J. No. 221, 39 O.L.R. 144 at 157-58 (H.C.D.), *per* Kelly J.; see also *Pender v. Lushington* (1877), 6 Ch. D. 70.

[309] *Christopher v. Noxon*, [1883] O.J. No. 273, 4 O.R. 672 at 686 (H.C.J.), *per* Proudfoot J.

(iii) Voting and the Right to Vote

§12.92 The normal procedure by which the shareholders of a corporation make their decisions is by resolution submitted to a vote of the shareholders at a meeting called for the purpose of considering the resolution. Clause 97(*a*) of the OBCA[310] provides that, subject to the Act, the articles or by-laws of the corporation or any unanimous shareholder agreement,

> ... all questions proposed for the consideration of shareholders shall be determined by the majority of the votes cast and the chair presiding at the meeting shall not have a second or casting vote in case of an equality of votes...

A ballot or other vote must be taken as and when provided in the corporation's articles or by-laws.[311] Subsection 103(1) of the OBCA[312] provides that:

> 103.(1) Unless the by-laws otherwise provide, voting at a meeting of shareholders shall be by show of hands, except where a ballot is demanded by a shareholder or proxyholder entitled to vote at a meeting.

This provision effectively reverses the common law rule, which may be traced back to an old New Zealand case, under which proxies could not be used to demand a poll unless the articles or by-laws so provided.[313] A shareholder or proxy-holder may demand a ballot either before or after any vote by show of hands.[314] The normal rule in Canada is that each share carries one vote,[315] but this rule is frequently modified by the articles of the corporation.

§12.93 The OBCA and the CBCA each envisage several different types of shareholder resolution. An "ordinary resolution" is "a resolution that is submitted to a meeting of the shareholders of a corporation and passed, with or without amendment, at the meeting by at least a majority of the votes cast".[316] The term "special resolution" describes two different types of resolution. The first of these is a resolution "submitted to a special meeting of the shareholders of a corporation duly called for the purpose of considering the resolution and passed, with or without amendment, at the meeting by at least two-thirds of the votes cast" and the second meaning is a resolution "consented to in writing by each shareholder of the corporation entitled to vote at such a meeting or the shareholder's attorney authorized in writing".[317] In general terms, ordinary resolutions are permitted for routine matters, and special resolutions are required for more important matters, such as fundamental changes to the corporate constitution.

---

[310] There is no CBCA equivalent.
[311] *Re Salisbury G.M. Co.* (1894), 15 N.Z.L.R. 232.
[312] CBCA, s. 141.
[313] *McCurdy v. Gorrie* (1913), 32 N.Z.L.R. 769.
[314] OBCA, s. 103(2).
[315] OBCA, s. 102(1); CBCA, s. 140(1).
[316] OBCA, s. 1(1), definition of "ordinary resolution"; CBCA, s. 2(1).
[317] OBCA, s. 1(1), definition of "special resolution". The definition of this term in CBCA, s. 2(1) does not include the second meaning.

§12.94 Unless otherwise provided in the articles of a corporation, each share of a corporation entitles the holder of that share to one vote at a meeting of the shareholders in respect of each vote held.[318] As a general rule, all questions proposed for the consideration of the shareholders are determined by a majority of the votes cast.[319] The system of voting under the OBCA and the CBCA provides not so much for democratic corporate government as for a modified form of plutocratic government; the general rule is that those shareholders who have invested a greater amount in the corporation will be entitled to a greater say over its affairs, and, in so doing, these Acts reject the approach followed in some European jurisdictions, under which a disproportionately large voice is given to small shareholdings.[320] However, the number of votes to which a shareholder is entitled is determined by the number of shares, rather than by the amount invested in the shares of a corporation. Thus, if some of the shares of a particular class or series were issued at an issue price of $5 per share, and others were issued at an issue price of $15 per share, all those shares will still be entitled to the same number of votes, unless the articles otherwise provide.

§12.95 Entitlement to vote on any matter to be decided by the shareholders of a corporation is, primarily, a matter of contract; if the share terms and conditions held by a person provide for a voting right, then the person will be entitled to vote. There is no question that a corporation with more than one class or series of shares may have non-voting shares. However, because subsection 102(1) of the OBCA creates a presumption that every share is entitled to a vote, the articles of a corporation must provide (either expressly or impliedly) that a particular class or series of shares is not entitled to a vote, for the right to a vote to be lost. If the share terms are silent on this question, the presumption of a vote will govern.[321] Moreover, it has been held that the mere fact that issued shares of a corporation are held in escrow does not abrogate the voting rights to which the holders of those shares are entitled.[322] Over and above the contractual voting rights to which shareholders are entitled under the terms and conditions of their shares, both the OBCA and the CBCA provide universal voting rights in favour

---

[318] OBCA, s. 102(1); CBCA, s. 140(1).

[319] OBCA, s. 97(*a*). There is no direct CBCA equivalent, but see the definitions of "ordinary resolution" and "special resolution" in s. 2(1) of that Act — s. 1(1) of the OBCA.

[320] Although it remains open to the shareholders to approve a more democratic (one person-one vote) voting arrangement if they are so inclined: see, for instance *Providence & Worcester Co. v. Baker*, 378 A.2d 121 (Del. S.C. 1977).

[321] It seems doubtful under the OBCA that there is a presumption that the holders of non-voting shares are entitled to receive notice of, and be present at, meetings of shareholders, but see *Miller v. F. Mendel Holdings Ltd.*, [1984] S.J. No. 98, [1984] 2 W.W.R. 683 (Q.B.).

[322] In *Nadeau v. Nadeau & Nadeau Ltd.*, [1972] N.B.J. No. 178, 6 N.B.R. (2d) 512 (Q.B.), some of the plaintiff's shares in the company were placed in escrow with a bank for the purpose of restricting the resale of the shares while there was an outstanding amount due from the corporation. It was held that the escrow agreement in no way abrogated the voting rights that the registered shareholder was entitled to exercise. See also *Sasko-Wainwright Oil & Gas Ltd. v. Old Settlers Oils Ltd.* (1957), 20 W.W.R. 613 (Alta. C.A.).

of all shareholders (whether or not they are otherwise entitled to vote) in the case of very important matters to be considered by the corporation.[323]

§12.96 Although a particular share may entitle its holder to a vote, the question may arise about which holder of that share is entitled to exercise the vote. This question is particularly important where a shareholder has transferred his or her shares to some other person. Subsection 100(2) of the OBCA provides that:

> 100.(2) Where a corporation fixes a record date under subsection 95(2), a person named in the list prepared under clause (1)(*a*) is entitled to vote the shares shown opposite the person's name at the meeting to which the list relates, except to the extent that,[324]
>
> (*a*) the person has transferred any shares after the record date; and
>
> (*b*) the transferee of those shares,
>
> > (i) produces properly endorsed share certificates, or
> >
> > (ii) otherwise establishes that the transferee owns the shares,
> >
> > (iii) and demands, not later than ten days before the meeting, or such shorter period before the meeting as the by-laws of the corporation may provide, that the transferee's name be included in the list before the meeting,
>
> in which case the transferee is entitled to vote those shares at the meeting.

To take advantage of the procedure set out in subsection 100(2) of the OBCA,[325] a new shareholder to whom shares have been transferred must send a formal demand to be included in the list of shareholders entitled to vote.[326]

§12.97 The procedure where no record date has been fixed is similar. Subsection 100(3) of the OBCA provides that in such a case a person named in a list prepared under clause 100(1)(*b*) is entitled to vote the shares opposite his or her name at the meeting to which the list relates, except to the extent that:

> (*a*) the person has transferred any shares after the date on which a list referred to in subclause (1)(*b*)(i) is prepared; and
>
> (*b*) the transferee of those shares,
>
> > (i) produces properly endorsed share certificates, or
> >
> > (ii) otherwise establishes that the transferee owns the shares,
>
> and demands, not later than ten days before the meeting, or such shorter period before the meeting as the by-laws may provide, that the transferee's name be included in the list before the meeting ...[327]

---

[323] These matters are known as "fundamental changes", and the nature of the special voting rights so conferred is discussed in detail in Chapter 14.
[324] Compare CBCA, s. 138(2).
[325] See also CBCA, s. 138(2).
[326] *Re Transwest Energy Inc.* (1997), 47 C.B.R. (3d) 305 (Alta. Q.B.).
[327] Compare CBCA, s. 138(3).

§12.98 National Instrument 54-101 (which replaced the former National Policy 61) requires reporting issuers to distribute audited financial statements to beneficial owners of shares that are registered and held on their behalf in the name of a nominee. Such issuers must also grant voting rights to non-registered beneficial owners in accordance with the proxy procedures set out in the policy. Nevertheless, under the corporations statutes, the right to vote is conferred upon registered shareholders, though both the OBCA and the CBCA require the registered holder of shares beneficially owned by another person to vote those shares in accordance with the instructions of the beneficial owner. In *Verdun v. Toronto-Dominion Bank*,[328] the Supreme Court of Canada considered and rejected a complex argument that various provisions of the *Bank Act*[329] could be interpreted to entitle beneficial owners of shares registered in another person's name to vote personally. It was noted that subsection 93(1) of the *Bank Act*[330] provides that a bank may treat the registered owner of a security as the person exclusively entitled to vote. Given this provision, the court found it impossible to accept the argument that there was a personal voting right conferred on beneficial owners to entitle such an owner to make a shareholder proposal.[331] The same conclusion would likely follow under the OBCA and CBCA. Indeed, not only is a company entitled under subsection 67(1) of the OBCA[332] to look to the registered shareholder as the person exclusively entitled to vote, *etc.*, it is barred from doing otherwise.[333]

§12.99 Even so, there may be exceptional cases in which it is appropriate for the presiding officer to make a ruling in favour of a beneficial owner and against the registered holder, to permit the former to take part in a meeting of shareholders and to vote at that meeting. For instance, in *Heil v. T.E.N. Private Cable Systems Ltd.*[334] the petitioner (a registered shareholder) sought an order under section 145 of the CBCA declaring invalid the election of directors at a meeting of shareholders. The facts were that prior to the record date for the meeting, the petitioner (P) had transferred shares in T.E.N. to one Gene Yamagata (Y), together with the certificate for those shares endorsed for transfer. Owing to a cease trading order against T.E.N. issued by the securities regulator, the transfer agent did not record the transfer prior to the meeting. The Superintendent of Brokers subsequently ruled that the cease trading order was not effective against T.E.N. In accordance with subsection 138(2) of the CBCA, Y demanded to be included in the list of shareholders entitled to vote at the meeting. However, Y took no other steps to compel the registration of the transfer. A dispute ensued at the

---

[328] [1996] S.C.J. No. 50, 28 B.L.R. (2d) 121 at 131-33, *per* Iacobucci J.
[329] S.C. 1991, c. 46.
[330] Which is substantially the same as s. 51(1) of the CBCA.
[331] See also *Greenpeace Foundation of Canada v. Inco* (1984), 25 A.C.W.S. (2d) 149 (Ont. C.A.); *Verdun v. Toronto-Dominion Bank*, [1995] O.J. No. 4288 (C.A.), aff'd [1996] S.C.J. No. 50, [1996] 3 S.C.R. 550.
[332] CBCA, s. 51(1).
[333] *Marshall v. Marshall Boston Iron Mines Ltd.*, [1981] O.J. No. 967, 129 D.L.R. (3d) 378 at 382 (H.C.J.), *per* Callaghan J.; *Tough Oakes Gold Mines Ltd. v. Foster*, [1917] O.J. No. 221, 39 O.L.R. 144 at 157 (S.C.), *per* Kelly J.
[334] [1993] B.C.J. No. 1171, 11 B.L.R. (2d) 54 (S.C.).

meeting as to whether P or Y was entitled to vote the shares concerned. After reviewing the documents and obtaining legal advice, the presiding officer at the meeting ruled that Y was entitled to vote the shares concerned, rather than P, even though P remained the registered shareholder. Y's representative abstained from voting, and as a result five different directors were elected than would have been elected had P been permitted to vote the transferred shares. Hutchinson J. dismissed the petition — thereby upholding the presiding officer's ruling as to voting rights — concluding that to hold otherwise would produce a manifest absurdity.[335] In the *Heil* case, it was implicit in subsection 138(2) of the CBCA that the presiding officer would have the authority to make the ruling that he made. Thus, the general rule that the corporation could not look behind the registered shareholder could not apply.

(1) General Considerations

§12.100 The voting rights attached to securities are partly a matter of contract and partly a matter of law. As discussed in Chapter 14, shareholders of all classes are entitled to vote on some matters by the terms of the OBCA and CBCA — the right to such a vote being in at least some respects a vestigial recognition of the status of shareholders as members of the corporation. The manner of conducting votes among the shareholders will generally be dealt with in the organizational by-law of the corporation. Votes among the holders of debt securities may be provided for by way of contract (*i.e.*, as a term of the securities in question) and are generally considered desirable where the securities in question are expected to be widely held. However, since the holders of debt securities have never been considered members of the corporation, they are not as a general rule bound by provisions of the by-laws. Instead the manner of conducting a vote will be governed by the terms of the instrument under which the securities are issued, as in the case of a trust indenture, or by the terms of the security itself, where there is no such over-arching document with respect to the security concerned.

§12.101 The question of voting marks a further distinction between debt and equity. In the case of equity, there is a presumption in the case of shareholders that a vote may be taken, the results of which will bind all shareholders at least of a class. Indeed, clause 27(*b*) of the *Interpretation Act*[336] provides that in every Act (unless the contrary intention appears) words making any association or number of persons a corporation or body politic and corporate

> vest in a majority of the members of the corporation the power to bind the others by their acts...

In the case of debt, there is no presumption that a vote may be taken among the holders of similar debt interests that will bind all creditors who hold such interests. Debt, in contrast to shareholding, is a matter of contract, and like any contract, a debt obligation may only be amended by the unanimous consent of the

---

[335] *Ibid.*, at 66.
[336] R.S.O 1990, c. I-11.

parties. This presumption will be defeated where the terms of the debt instrument (or some other relevant contract) or a rule of law otherwise provides — but in the absence of any such an agreement among creditors holding even identical debt interests, the majority does not rule.[337]

(2) Voting Trusts and Similar Arrangements

§12.102 Although the majority shareholders of a corporation will not be allowed to exercise their voting control over the corporation to perpetuate a fraud against the minority shareholders,[338] the general rule is that a shareholder may vote his or her shares as he or she pleases, without regard to the wishes, whims, concerns or needs of fellow shareholders.[339] The shareholder is not barred from voting merely because of personal interest.[340] The right to vote is implicit first in the fact that the shareholders are independent investors in a separate juristic person and, therefore, are not partners in the business that the corporation conducts. Consequently, the shareholders of a corporation do not owe each other any duty of good faith. Second, the shareholders of a corporation do not assume a position of trust with regard to each other (indeed, in many cases they are not even aware of each other's identity) and, therefore, ordinarily are not seen to occupy a fiduciary position toward each other. So, for instance, a person who is a director of a corporation is not restricted by his or her status as such when voting as a shareholder. In the ordinary case, the director is not limited in the manner of voting by any principle of fiduciary duty.[341]

§12.103 Despite these general principles, there is no question that particular shareholders may assume contractual or other obligations that restrict their voting freedom. In this regard, subsections 108(1) of the OBCA and 146(1) of the CBCA are particularly clear. These subsections state that a written agreement between two or more shareholders may provide that in exercising voting rights the shares held by them shall be voted as provided in that agreement.[342] In *Waschysyn v. Kildonan Ice and Fuel Co.*,[343] an agreement provided in effect that the shares of a corporation would be voted to confer control over the corporation

---

[337] Except where an arrangement is approved under legislation such as the *Companies' Creditors Arrangement Act*, or in the case of a proposal under the *Bankruptcy and Insolvency Act*, each of which contemplates variation of creditor rights upon a class vote.

[338] See for instance, *Fuller v. Bruce* (1935), 9 M.P.R. 437 (N.S.C.A.), *per* Mellish J., appeal quashed [1936] S.C.J. No. 7, [1936] S.C.R. 124; *Leavens v. Great West Permanent Loan Co.*, [1927] 3 W.W.R. 486 (Man. K.B.); *Regehr v. Ketzakey Silver Mines Ltd.*, [1970] A.J. No. 14, 10 D.L.R. (3d) 171 at 179 (C.A.), *per* McDermid J.A.

[339] *British America Nickel Corp. v. M.J. O'Brien Ltd.*, [1927] A.C. 369 at 371 (P.C.), *per* Viscount Haldane.

[340] *Ritchie v. Vermillion Mining Co.*, [1901] O.J. No. 121, 1 O.L.R. 654 (H.C.J), aff'd [1902] O.J. No. 223, 4 O.L.R. 588 at 595 (C.A.), *per* Maclennan J.A.; *Pender v. Lushington* (1877), 6 Ch. D. 70 at 75-76 (C.A.), *per* Jessell M.R.; see also *Menier v. Hooper's Telegraph Works* (1874), L.R. 9 Ch. 350 at 354 (L.JJ.), *per* Mellish L.J.

[341] *Northern Counties Securities Ltd. v. Jackson & Steeple Ltd.*, [1974] 2 All E.R. 625 (Ch.).

[342] See, for instance, *Field v. Bachynski*, [1976] A.J. No. 353, 1 A.R. 491 (C.A.). The agreement may be enforced by injunction: *Greenwell v. Porter*, [1902] 1 Ch. 530 at 535-36, *per* Swinfen Eady J.; see also *Puddephatt v. Leith*, [1916] 1 Ch. 200.

[343] [1937] 2 D.L.R. 653 at 658 (Man. C.A.).

on a single person. The agreement was upheld. The court took the view that the arrangement was adopted by all the shareholders for the benefit of the company; it, therefore, was wholly a matter of internal management with which the court should not interfere. As a general rule, a shareholder is not restricted in the manner in which he or she votes. A shareholder is not obliged to vote at all, but if he or she chooses to do so, it is perfectly proper for the shareholder to combine with others to obtain the maximum advantage.[344]

§12.104 Historically, one popular method of combining the voting power of individual shareholders has been through the use of a voting trust — a device sometimes employed by the creditors of a corporation as well as by its principal shareholders. In a typical voting trust, the shares of the participants will be deposited with a trustee, who is empowered under the deed of trust to exercise the voting power associated with those shares. Often, a procedure will be set down for determining the wishes of the majority of the participants, with the trustee being obliged to vote in accordance with the wishes that the majority express. Voting trusts remain lawful under the OBCA and the CBCA.[345] Any such agreement or trust will necessarily constrain the voting independence of individual shareholders. In each such case, the restriction upon shareholder independence is not derived from any general principle of fiduciary obligation among shareholders, but rather arises simply on the basis of contract.[346] It is elementary that a trustee may not exercise powers granted in a way that is detrimental to the beneficiary of the trust, nor may one who is trustee for different classes favour one class at the expense of another. Such an exercise of power is in derogation of the trust and will not be upheld, even though the thing done is within the scope of the powers granted to the trustees in general terms.[347] The trustee is, however, free to exercise such discretions conferred upon him or her in accordance with the terms and purpose of the trust.

§12.105 Although a voting agreement has a long term (such as 74 years), its duration is not sufficient to invalidate it.[348] However, voting trust agreements are given a narrow interpretation, both as to their duration,[349] and to their scope.[350] Such an agreement is interpersonal between the shareholders and will not pass with the shares if the member of the trust transfers ownership and, thus, the right to deal with the shares. On the other hand, a party to a voting agreement may not escape his or her obligations by using his or her control over the corporation to change the designation of the shares that he or she holds, or to convert them to a

---

[344] *Ringling Bros.-Barnum & Bailey Combined Shows v. Ringling*, 29 Del. Ch. 610, 53 A.2d 441 (Del. S.C. 1947), *per* Pearson J.
[345] See, for instance, *Milligan v. Bergman*, [1978] B.C.J. No. 42, 7 B.C.L.R. 103 (S.C.).
[346] See, generally, *Ventures West Capital Ltd. v. Bethlehem Copper Corp.*, [1980] A.J. No. 522, 23 A.R. 253 (C.A.).
[347] *Brown v. McLanahan*, 148 F.2d 703 (4th Cir. 1945), *per* Dobie Cir. J.
[348] *Birks v. Birks* (1983), 15 E.T.R. 208 (Que. C.A.), leave to appeal to S.C.C. refused [1983] C.S.C.R. no. 134, 52 N.R. 236.
[349] *Babic v. Milinkovic* (1971), 25 D.L.R. (3d) 752 (B.C.C.A.).
[350] See, for instance, *Re Firstbrook Boxes Ltd.*, [1936] O.J. No. 260, [1936] O.R. 15 at 19 (C.A.), *per* Henderson J.A.

new class. On the contrary, where a new class of shares is substituted for the old class of shares to which the agreement related, the new class of shares will be subject to the voting agreement.[351]

(3) The Role of By-laws as a Governance Device

§12.106 Historically, corporate by-laws have been one of the primary tools used by the shareholders of a corporation to secure a meaningful influence over the conduct of corporate operations. Their importance as a corporate governance device cannot be ignored. The shareholders of a corporation enjoy a statutory right to adopt by-laws, including by-laws that govern the business of the corporation, the conduct of its affairs, and its rights or powers or the rights or powers of its stockholders, directors, officers or employees. This authority is subject to the limitation that the by-laws may not conflict with law or the certificate of incorporation. Traditionally, the by-laws have been the corporate instrument used to set forth the rules by which the board of directors and officers of the corporation conducts its business. There is a general consensus that by-laws that regulate the process by which the board acts are proper.[352] As the articles are the instrument in which the broad and general aspects of a corporate entity's existence and nature are defined, so the by-laws are generally regarded as the proper place for the self-imposed rules and regulations deemed expedient for its convenient functioning to be laid down.[353] In *Frantz Manufacturing Co. v. EAC Industries*,[354] it was held that by-laws could impose severe requirements on the conduct of a board without running afoul of corporate law. The by-law at issue in that case required there to be unanimous attendance and board approval for any board action, and unanimous ratification of any committee action. The Supreme Court found that the by-laws were consistent with the terms of Delaware corporate law. In so ruling, the court noted that the "by-laws of a corporation are presumed to be valid, and the courts will construe the by-laws in a manner consistent with the law rather than strike down the by-laws".

(4) Voting Procedure

§12.107 Subject to the requirements of the OBCA or CBCA, as the case may be, a ballot or other vote must be taken as provided in the corporation's articles or by-laws.[355] As noted above, generally, each share is entitled to a single vote, and (subject to the special resolution requirement) questions are decided on the basis of a simple majority of the votes cast. However, where the articles or a unanimous shareholder agreement require a vote to be decided by a greater number than is required under the Act, the provisions of the articles or the unanimous

---

[351] *Turvey v. Lauder* (1956), 4 D.L.R. (2d) 225 (S.C.C.).
[352] *Hollinger International, Inc. v. Black*, 844 A.2d 1022 (Del. Ch. 2004), *per* Strine V.C., aff'd 872 A.2d 559 (Del. 2005).
[353] *Gow v. Consolidated Coppermines Corp.* (1933), 19 Del. Ch. 172, 165 A. 136 at 140 (Del. Ch.).
[354] (1985), 501 A.2d 401 (Del. S.C.).
[355] *Re Salisbury G.M. Co.* (1894), 15 N.Z.L.R. 232.

shareholder agreement prevail.[356] The presiding officer at the meeting does not have a second or casting vote in the case of an equality of votes — although this general rule is subject to any qualification or special provision set out in the Act, the articles or by-laws of a corporation or any unanimous shareholder agreement.[357] The Act does not specify the effect of a tied vote, but the better view in the event of a tie is that the motion is deemed to be lost (it has failed to obtain the requisite number of votes to pass), and it is quite common for the by-laws of a corporation to make an express provision to this effect.

§12.108 Decisions at a meeting of shareholders are taken by a vote of the shareholders present and entitled to vote at the meeting. It is customary for the presiding officer to ask for the motion to be formally put to a vote and seconded, but (unless the by-laws so provide) the requirement for a seconder would seem to be an unnecessary formalism.[358] Clause 97(*a*) of the OBCA provides that, subject to the Act, the articles or by-laws of a corporation or a unanimous shareholder agreement, "all questions proposed for the consideration of the shareholders shall be determined by the majority of the votes cast and the chair presiding at the meeting shall not have a second or casting vote in case of an equality of votes". Unless the articles otherwise provide, each share of a corporation entitles the holder of that share to one vote at a meeting of shareholders.[359] The presumption is that all voting shares vote together as a single class,[360] though in the case of certain fundamental changes both Acts provide for separate class (and sometimes series) voting.[361]

§12.109 Despite the presumption that each share is entitled to a single vote, the OBCA and the CBCA confer a fair amount of discretion over the number of votes that may be assigned to a share and on the manner in which voting will be conducted. Thus, the shares of one series of a class may carry greater voting rights than the shares of another series of the same class.[362] Similarly, the articles may place a limit on the number of shares that any one shareholder may vote. The voting structure, however, must not permit or encourage fraud. For instance, in *Bowater Canadian Ltd. v. R.L. Crain Inc.*[363] the Court of Appeal considered the validity of a step down vote provision, under which the initial holder of preference shares was entitled to 10 votes per share, but subsequent holders were entitled to only one vote per share. The provision was ruled invalid on the basis that it provided a great opportunity for fraud. However, the step down provision was held severable, and the 10-vote per share provision was allowed to stand, both for initial and for subsequent shareholders.

---

[356] CBCA, s. 6(3); OBCA, s. 5(4).
[357] OBCA, s. 97(*a*).
[358] *Re Horbury Bridge Coal, Iron & Waggon Co.* (1879), 11 Ch. D. 109 at 117 (C.A.), *per* James L.J.
[359] OBCA, s. 102(1); CBCA, s. 140(1).
[360] *Re Second Standard Royalties Ltd.*, [1930] O.J. No. 45, 66 O.L.R. 288 (C.A.).
[361] See Chapter 14.
[362] *Re Union Enterprises Ltd.* (1985), 29 B.L.R. 128 (Dir. Ont. Bus. Corp. Act).
[363] [1987] O.J. No. 1157, 62 O.R. (2d) 752 (C.A.).

§12.110 Except where the by-laws otherwise provide, where two or more persons hold shares jointly, one of those holders present at a meeting of the shareholders may (in the absence of the others) vote the shares. If two or more of those joint owners are present (whether in person or by proxy) they are required to vote as one on the shares jointly held by them.[364] There is no presumption that the first named shareholder is entitled to decide how to vote the shares. The co-owners must agree on how to vote. This rule may present difficulty when the individuals concerned are in disagreement. Because each share carries a separate entitlement to a vote, one option where joint shareholders wish to exercise separate voting rights is for them to divide the votes relating to their jointly held shares between them by giving each a proxy representing a certain number of their total shares. Since any such arrangement will result in the votes cancelling each other out, a simpler alternative is merely to withhold the shares from voting.

§12.111 In the case of shareholders who are natural persons, participation in a meeting requires the personal presence of either the shareholder or a proxy. However, where a company or association is a shareholder of the corporation, the corporation must recognize any individual authorized by a resolution of the directors or governing body of that company or association to represent it at meetings of shareholders of the corporation.[365] Any individual so authorized may exercise all the powers that could be exercised by the company or association that the individual represents if that company were an individual shareholder.[366]

§12.112 Because each shareholder will generally be entitled to one vote per share and because the number of shares held by each shareholder may differ significantly, the apparent support (or lack of support) that a particular proposal enjoys may not be reflected in the division among the shareholders present. Even so, unless the by-laws or articles otherwise provide, voting at a meeting of shareholders is by show of hands,[367] except where a ballot is demanded by a shareholder or a proxy holder[368] entitled to vote at the meeting.[369] In addition, section 87 of the Ontario *Securities Act* provides that:

> 87. The chair at a meeting has the right not to conduct a vote by way of ballot on any matter or group of matters in connection with which the form of proxy has provided a means whereby the person or company whose proxy is solicited may specify how such person or company wishes the securities registered in his, her or its name to be voted unless,
>
> (a) a poll is demanded by any security holder present at the meeting in person or represented thereat by proxy; or

---

[364] OBCA, s. 102(4); CBCA, s. 140(4).
[365] OBCA, s. 102(2). See also *Cohen-Herrendorf v. Army & Navy Department Store Holdings Ltd.*, [1986] S.J. No. 848, 55 Sask. R. 134 (Q.B.).
[366] OBCA, s. 102(3); CBCA, s. 140(3).
[367] Thus, unless the by-laws so provide, it is not appropriate to put the question to a mere voice vote.
[368] *Cf. McCurdy v. Gorrie* (1913), 32 N.Z.L.R. 769.
[369] OBCA, s. 103(1); CBCA, s. 141(1).

(b) proxies requiring that the securities represented thereby be voted against what would otherwise be the decision of the meeting in relation to such matters or group of matters total more than 5 per cent of all the voting rights attached to all the securities entitled to be voted and be represented at the meeting.

A shareholder may demand a ballot either before or after any vote by show of hands.[370] Except where a ballot is demanded, an entry in the minutes of the meeting that the presiding officer declared a motion to be carried is admissible in evidence as proof of that fact, in the absence of evidence to the contrary, without proof of the number or proportion of the votes recorded in favour of, or against, the motion.

§12.113 Unless a separate poll is demanded,[371] it appears that the presiding officer may put two or more motions pertaining to a matter that are before the meeting to a vote on an *en bloc* basis.[372] But such ill-defined voting should not be encouraged, because if one of the resolutions is subsequently ruled invalid, it is not possible to sever the valid resolution and so save it.[373] Except where the motions are tabled or withdrawn, the meeting may not close until a vote is taken on every motion of which the meeting is seized.[374] It is within the authority of the presiding officer to make the initial declaration the results of the vote, but the decision of the presiding officer on the result of a vote is not conclusive,[375] though it must be challenged at the time.[376]

§12.114 A demand for a vote by ballot may be made privately or publicly.[377] Where a vote by ballot is demanded, it must be taken forthwith. The presiding officer chairing a meeting has no authority to disregard a demand for a vote by ballot.[378] If the poll relates to the election of a presiding officer or a motion to adjourn, the count must also be immediate and the result declared before the meeting proceeds to any further business. On all other questions, the count may be made at such time as the presiding officer directs, and, in the meantime, the meeting may proceed to consider any other business — other than business the outcome of which is dependent upon the poll. Until the time that the result of the poll is declared closed and the counting of the ballots begins, any qualified voter may

---

[370] OBCA, s. 103(3). There is no equivalent provision in the CBCA.
[371] *Blair Open Hearth Furnace Co. v. Reigart* (1913), 29 T.L.R. 449; *cf. Patent Word Key Syndicate Ltd. v. Pearse*, [1906] W.N. 164.
[372] *Re R.E. Jones Ltd.* (1933), 50 T.L.R. 31.
[373] *Re Imperial Bank of China, India & Japan* (1866), L.R. 1 Ch. App. 339 at 347; *Thompson v. Herson's Transvaal Estates Ltd.*, [1908] 1 Ch. 765 (C.A.).
[374] *Shaw v. Tati Concessions Ltd.*, [1913] 1 Ch. 292; *Holmes v. Lord Keyes*, [1959] Ch. 199 (C.A.).
[375] *Gold v. Maldaver* (1912), 23 O.W.R. 75 at 77-78, 4 O.W.N. 106, 6 D.L.R. 333 (H.C.), *per* Riddell J.
[376] *Arnot v. United African Lands*, [1901] 1 Ch. 518 (C.A.).
[377] *Re Phoenix Electric Light & Power Co.* (1883), 31 W.R. 398.
[378] *Colonial Assurance Co. v. Smith* (1912), 2 W.W.R. 699 (Man. K.B.); see also *Chen Investments Australia Pty. Ltd. v. Gerrard Corp. of Australia Ltd.* (1988), 6 A.C.L.C. 85. Even where the by-laws provide that a ruling by the presiding officer on the success or failure of a motion is conclusive, the court may disregard the provision where there is fraud or manifest error: *Re Caratal (New) Mines Ltd.*, [1902] 2 Ch. 498.

vote.[379] To prevent the casting of late ballots, therefore, it is advisable for the presiding officer to seek a formal motion declaring the ballot closed. Where the classes vote separately, the better approach is not to declare the outcome of any poll taken among any one class before the other classes have voted. Class voting entitles each class (or series) of shares to an equal say in the outcome of the question to be decided. If a class knows how another class has already voted, the second class to vote may be given a strategic advantage over the first to vote.[380]

§12.115 Counting of ballots is as much a function of the vote as is casting them.[381] The vote must be tabulated in a way that is fair and impartial. In a vote by ballot, it is customary for the presiding officer to appoint objective scrutineers[382] (or, if none are available, then a balanced panel of partisan scrutineers) to conduct the vote and to tabulate the result. They are responsible for distributing ballots, collecting ballots, ascertaining how each ballot was voted, ensuring that only authorized ballots are cast and determining whether any ballot actually cast is invalid, tabulating the final result (including spoiled and unmarked ballots) and reporting the result to the chair. The presiding officer must then announce the result, and the formal division of votes should be recorded in the minutes of the meeting.

§12.116 The Act makes no provision for the holding of secret ballots, and, indeed, the system of weighted voting provided for under subsection 102(1) of the OBCA[383] virtually negates any such possibility. However, there is no obligation on the presiding officer to reveal how any specific shareholder voted on a question and any such revelation would be both unusual and unnecessarily partisan.[384] As noted above, it is presumed under section 97 of the OBCA that a vote will be determined by the majority of votes cast. Spoiled and uncast ballots are excluded in determining whether a particular resolution has been approved or defeated; they are not treated as negative votes.[385] Voters casting spoiled ballots (and also abstentions) may, however, be counted to ascertain the number present, for the purpose of determining whether there was a quorum present sufficient to allow the meeting to deal with the question in issue.

---

[379] *Re Keddy Motor Inns Ltd.*, [1992] N.S.J. No. 98, 13 C.B.R. (3d) 245 at 255 (C.A.), *per* Freeman J.A., quoting J.M. Wainberg, *Company Meetings*, 2nd ed. (Toronto: Canada Law Book, 1969) at 73.
[380] *Ibid.*
[381] *Ibid.*, at 254.
[382] Directors who are also candidates for re-election as directors are disqualified from acting as scrutineers at a meeting to elect directors: *Dickson v. McMurray*, [1881] O.J. No. 158, 28 Gr. 533 (Ct. Ch.).
[383] CBCA, s. 140(1).
[384] See, generally, M. Kaye Kerr and H.W. King, *Procedures for Meetings and Organizations* (Toronto: Carswell, 1986), Chapter 15.
[385] *Shawinigan Lake Recreation Association v. Hansen*, [1988] B.C.J. No. 2718, 42 B.L.R. 104 (S.C.); see also *A.U.P.E. v. University Hospital Board*, [1976] A.J. No. 362, [1976] 4 W.W.R. 494 (T.D.), var'd [1977] A.J. No. 177, [1977] 2 W.W.R. 97 (C.A.). If 100 of 200 possible votes are cast in favour of a resolution, 99 against and 1 spoiled ballot, the resolution is approved: 100 being a majority of the 199 ballots that were not spoiled (although short of an overall majority, if the spoiled ballots were counted).

§12.117 There are numerous provisions of the OBCA that require more than a majority to approve a particular question, namely, all questions that must be decided by a special resolution. The term "special resolution" is defined in subsection 1(1) as follows:

"special resolution" means a resolution that is,

(a) submitted to a special meeting of the shareholders of a corporation duly called for the purpose of considering the resolution and passed, with or without amendment, at the meeting by at least two-thirds of the votes cast, or

(b) consented to in writing by each shareholder of the corporation entitled to vote at such a meeting or the shareholder's attorney authorized in writing.

Because the adoption of a special resolution depends upon the number of votes cast, rather than on registered voters, a person who abstains from voting does not possess a hidden veto. A person who opposes a resolution must vote no, not merely abstain, for silence in essence amounts to consent. A similar rule applies in the case of matters that fall to be decided under the Act by "ordinary resolution", a term that is defined to mean:

... a resolution that is submitted to a meeting of the shareholders of a corporation and passed, with or without amendment, at the meeting by at least a majority of the votes cast.[386]

§12.118 Although a special resolution must be passed at a special meeting, and the notice of any such meeting must include "the text of any special resolution ... to be submitted to the meeting", it is clear from the definition of "special resolution" that the shareholders may also consider any amendment to that resolution, without any requirement for advance notice that such an amendment will be placed before the meeting. Because the purpose of a meeting is, presumably, to elicit discussion and considered thought among the members, it would, obviously, be impractical to restrict the members only to those specific resolutions of which they have received advanced notice.[387] How far may an amendment vary from the original text of the resolution included in the notice before it ceases to be an amendment and becomes an entirely separate resolution? Clearly, there are certain amendments (*e.g.*, modifications to the drafting of a resolution, such as the clarification of ambiguous wording or the inclusion of procedural provisions that are necessary or incidental to the original resolution) that depart neither from the spirit nor the substance of the original resolution and can be seen to be within the statutory concept of an amendment to the resolution.[388] What is less clear, however, is whether a resolution can be so amended that when it is ultimately passed it accomplishes the exact opposite of what was originally proposed.[389] The efficacy of corporate operations would be undermined if the shareholders were not permitted, once an item of business comes before them, to

---

[386] OBCA, s. 1(1).
[387] But see *Re Moorgate Mercantile Holdings Ltd.*, [1980] 1 All E.R. 40.
[388] *Torbock v. Lord Westbury*, [1902] 2 Ch. 871; *Henderson v. Bank of Australasia* (1890), 45 Ch. D. 330; *Betts & Co. v. Macnaghten*, [1910] 1 Ch. 430.
[389] See, generally, *Re Teede & Bishop Ltd.* (1901), 70 L.J. Ch. 409.

consider that item in its fullest scope and to reach a final decision on it. If a particular shareholder knows of the general purpose of a meeting and is interested in that matter,[390] he or she may attend the meeting or give a proxy instructing how his or her shares are to be voted.[391] If a shareholder fails to do so, that shareholder cannot object that the resolution that is ultimately passed differed substantially from that which he or she thought would be passed. On the other hand, it would not be permissible to deal with some entirely new business substantially different from that in the original text of the resolution.

§12.119 The general rule is that matters that result in a restructuring of the constitution of the corporation must be approved by special resolution. For instance, such a resolution is required to amend the articles.[392] Moreover, where the interests of a particular class or series of shares are likely to be especially affected by an amendment to the articles, the holders of those shares are given a statutory right to vote on that amendment whether or not the shares of that class or series carry a voting right.[393] Surprisingly, however, there are a number of relatively important questions that may be resolved by a simple majority vote — e.g., amendments to by-laws — and there are other matters of dubious importance — e.g., the relocation of the registered office of the corporation to another municipality — which, nevertheless, require approval by special resolution.[394] Thus, it would not be correct to surmise that all important matters must be dealt with by special resolution, and less important matters must be decided by majority vote.

§12.120 Clause 97(*a*) of the OBCA indicates that the articles, by-laws or a unanimous shareholder resolution may impose a special requirement on the manner of approving questions are to be decided by the shareholders. Any doubt about this power is eliminated by subsection 5(4) of that Act,[395] which provides

---

[390] See, generally, *Alexander v. Simpson* (1889), 43 Ch. D. 139 at 147 (C.A.), *per* Bowen L.J.; *Re Marra Developments Ltd.* (1976), 1 A.C.L.R. 470 (S.C.N.S.W.); *Young v. South African & Australian Exploration and Development Syndicate*, [1896] 2 Ch. 268.

[391] Management proxy forms are effectively converted to unsolicited shareholder proxies once the names of the proposed management proxy holders are deleted and the names of the shareholder's designees are inserted: *Canadian Express Ltd. v. Blair*, [1989] O.J. No. 1619, 46 B.L.R. 92 (H.C.J.), additional reasons (re costs of proceeding) at [1992] O.J. No. 951, 8 O.R. (3d) 769 (Gen. Div.), appeal quashed [1991] O.J. No. 2176 (Div. Ct.).

[392] OBCA, s. 168(4).

[393] OBCA, s. 170.

[394] OBCA, s. 14(4); CBCA, s. 19(3). It is arguable that the relocation of the registered office may have a substantial effect upon shareholders, because the result of a change in location may be to remove the records generally required to be maintained at the registered office (*e.g.*, the register of shareholders) to a more remote site. However, such an argument ignores the fact that the directors may change the location of those same records by a simple director resolution: OBCA, s. 143(1).

[395] CBCA, s. 6(3).

that, with one limited exception,[396] the articles or a unanimous shareholder resolution may require particular questions to be decided by a greater number of votes than is normally required:

> 5.(4) Subject to subsection (5), if a greater number of votes of directors or shareholders are required by the articles or a unanimous shareholder agreement than are required by this Act to effect any action, the provisions of the articles or of the unanimous shareholder agreement prevail.

Since subsection 5(4) is silent about whether such a requirement for additional approval may be set out in the by-laws it clearly suggests that no such provision may be included. Moreover, subsection 5(4) apparently is limited to the imposition of a requirement for a greater level of approval than that required under the Act. On the basis of the rule of statutory interpretation *expressio unius est exclusio alterius* it would seem the articles may not reduce the required level of approval below the level required by statute.

§12.121 Where the validity of the shares held by particular shareholders is in issue, the court may restrain the holding of a meeting of the corporation at which those shareholders are to vote to maintain the *status quo* pending the resolution of that issue.[397] In *Courchêne v. Cie du parc Viger*,[398] a company illegally increased its stock, and a meeting was held at which both the old and new stockholders participated. At that meeting a resolution was passed under which an option was granted to the secretary-treasurer. Even though it appeared that a majority of those who voted in favour of the resolution were shareholders whose stock was not the subject of the illegal increase, it was held that the resolution was null and void.

(5) Fiduciary Obligations of Shareholders

(a) GENERALLY

§12.122 One of the most hotly debated topics in corporate law during the 1970s and 1980s was whether the shareholders of a corporation owed any fiduciary duty to the corporation or to other shareholders of the corporation. At one time, the courts seemed to be heading in the direction of recognizing widespread fiduciary duties among shareholders. For instance, in *Oliver v. Ruge*[399] a corporation was formed to act as a land developer. Under the articles, the approval of the directors was required for any transfer of shares. Two directors, comprising the

---

[396] This exception is set out in s. 5(5) of the OBCA — s. 6(4) of the CBCA — which reads:

> 5.(5) The articles shall not require a greater number of votes of shareholders to remove a director than the number specified in section 122.

For its part, s. 122 of the Act provides for the removal of directors by ordinary resolution; where the holders of a class or series of shares have an exclusive right to elect a director, then he or she may be removed by an ordinary resolution at a meeting of the holders of that class or series.

[397] *Caufield v. Sunland Biscuit Co.*, [1941] 3 W.W.R. 625 at 629 (Alta. T.D.), *per* O'Connor J.
[398] (1915), 23 D.L.R. 693 (Que. C.A.).
[399] [1989] O.J. No. 2062, 46 B.L.R. 50 at 59 (H.C.J.), *per* Granger J.

majority of the board, decided to sell their shares. By virtue of their votes on the board, the transfer was approved. It was held that this was improper. In the particular circumstances, it was held that a fiduciary duty did exist between the two director shareholders and the third shareholder in the corporation. Despite this earlier case law in support of the proposition,[400] it is now settled in Ontario that even in the case of a small, closely held corporation, the shareholders of the corporation are not fiduciaries in relation to each other — a general fiduciary remedy being rendered unnecessary by the presence of the statutory remedies of the derivative action and the shareholder oppression remedy.[401]

§12.123 A fiduciary obligation may arise, however, when the connection between the parties extends beyond their relationship as shareholders in the same corporation,[402] as for instance, where one shareholder undertakes to advise another in circumstances where there is an element of trust and confidence.[403] The partnership character of a corporate enterprise may give rise to a fiduciary duty between the shareholders.[404] However, this last point must be expressed subject to two important qualifications. First, one reason why entrepreneurs may decide to employ a corporation is because generally there is a lesser duty of care owed between shareholders than partners. If that consideration was taken into account in selecting the form of business vehicle it should not be disregarded should a dispute arise among the principals of a business. Second, the existence of a fiduciary relationship in a commercial contractual setting is the exception rather than the rule.[405] For a fiduciary duty to be seen to exist between two shareholders, it is necessary to show that there is an exceptional relationship of trust and confidence between them, for instance, where one shareholder is a trustee or professional advisor of the other. In the ordinary case, there will be no legally

---

[400] See *Goldex Mines Ltd. v. Revill*, [1974] O.J No. 2245, 7 O.R. (2d) 216 at 224 (C.A), *per* the court.
[401] A shareholder is not a fiduciary of the corporation and is not obliged to account for profits made at the expense of the corporation or its shareholders: See, generally, *William B. Sweet & Associates Ltd. v. Copper Beach Estates Ltd.*, [1993] B.C.J. No. 2375, 86 B.C.L.R. (2d) 19 (C.A.); *Brant Investments Ltd. v. KeepRite Inc.*, [1991] O.J. No. 683, 1 B.L.R. (2d) 225 at 244 (C.A.), *per* McKinlay J.A.; and see also the trial judgment of Anderson J. at [1987] O.J. No. 574, 60 O.R. (2d) 737; and *Trimac Ltd. v. C-I-L Inc.*, [1990] A.J. No. 807, [1990] 1 W.W.R. 133 at 167 (Q.B.), *per* Shannon J.
[402] *Dusik v. Newton*, [1985] B.CJ. No. 18, 62 B.C.L.R. 1 (C.A.); *Bell v. Source Data Control Ltd.*, [1988] O.J. No. 1424, 66 O.R. (2d) 78 at 88 (C.A.), *per* Cory J.A.; *Morton v. Asper*, [1989] M.J. No. 482, 62 Man. R. (2d) 1 (Q.B.); *Lacey v. Stoyles*, [1986] N.J. No. 104, 59 Nfld. & P.E.I.R. 181, 178 A.P.R. 181 (T.D.); *Lavigne v. Robern*, [1984] O.J. No. 3443, 28 B.L.R. 76 (C.A.). See also *Nocton v. Lord Ashburton*, [1914] A.C. 932 at 955, *per* Viscount Haldane L.C.; *Laskin v. Bache & Co.*, [1971] O.J. No. 1804, [1972] 1 O.R. 464 (C.A.).
[403] See, generally, *Agrium Inc. v. Hamilton*, [2005] A.J. No. 83, 2 B.L.R. (4th) 3 at 10 (Q.B.), *per* Hawco J.; see also the dissenting judgment of Wilson J. in *Frame v. Smith*, [1987] S.C.J. No. 49, [1987] 2 S.C.R. 99.
[404] *Tourangeau v. Taillefer*, [2000] O.J. No. 184 (S.C.J.).
[405] J.R.M. Gautreau, "Demystifying the Fiduciary Mystique" (1989) 68 Can. Bar Rev. 1 at 11; see also *Jirna v. Mister Donut of Canada Ltd.*, [1971] O.J. No. 1922, [1972] 1 O.R. 251, 22 D.L.R. (3d) 639 at 646 (C.A.), *per* Brooke J.A., aff'd [1973] S.C.J. No. 129, [1975] 1 S.C.R. 2; *Litwin Const. (1973) Ltd. v. Pan*, [1988] B.C.J. No. 1145, 29 B.C.L.R. (2d) 88 at 105-06 (C.A.), *per curriam*.

recognizable relationship between the shareholders as such; they are merely independent investors in the same enterprise. Even where the circumstances are such that some legal relationship must be seen to exist, the courts are far more likely to view it as being a contractual one rather than a fiduciary one.[406]

§12.124 Within certain limits, each shareholder of a corporation is free to vote his or her shares as he or she pleases. The voting rights attached to a share are part of the proprietary interest conferred by the share,[407] and, accordingly, the voting rights of a particular shareholder are subject to no fiduciary duty either *vis-à-vis* the corporation or any other shareholder.[408] The fact that a shareholder may also be a director does not prevent that shareholder from voting as he or she sees fit when voting at a meeting of shareholders.[409]

§12.125 It is sometimes said that the members of a class entitled to vote must vote in what they perceive to be the interests of that class as a whole, and that similarly the members of a corporation must vote in what they perceive to be the interests of the company as a whole.[410] This limitation on the scope of the voting right, however, does not translate into an obligation to vote altruistically. It is not voting in self-interest which compromises a vote by a shareholder or other security holder. Such a rule would be commercially unrealistic. It can be assumed that every investor will naturally be concerned with his or her interest and will vote in the manner that he or she perceives will best serve that interest. Instead, it is voting out of a self-interest completely unrelated to that holder's status as such that justifies the court in setting aside the vote of a particular holder. An illustration of such misuse of a voting power can be found in the decision of the Nova Scotia Supreme Court in *Re Laserworks Computer Services Inc.*[411] In that case, the appellant company (A) was secretly controlled by a second company (B) that was a client of a lawyer (L). L and an associate purchased a number of unsecured debts owed by an insolvent company (C), that was a competitor of B. A proposal put forward by C to its creditors was defeated when L caused all that purchased debt to be voted against the proposal. It was held that the purpose of the vote was solely to put C out of business, and to benefit B as a competitor. The votes were cast out of a self-interest unrelated to the debt itself and, therefore, without regard to the interests of the unsecured creditors as a class. Cases of this type are very rare.[412]

---

[406] *Green v. Charterhouse Group Canada Ltd.*, [1976] O.J. No. 2114, 12 O.R. (2d) 280 at 311 (C.A.), *per* Arnup J.A.
[407] *Pender v. Lushington* (1877), 6 Ch. D. 70, *per* Jessell M.R.
[408] See, generally, *Stothers v. William Steward (Holdings) Ltd.*, [1994] 2 B.C.L.C. 266 (C.A.).
[409] *Northern Counties Securities Ltd. v. Jackson & Steeple Ltd.*, [1974] 1 W.L.R. 1133 (Ch.), *per* Walton J.
[410] See, for instance, *Allen v. Gold Reefs of West Africa Ltd.*, [1900] 1 Ch. 656 (C.A.), *per* Lindley M.R.
[411] [1997] N.S.J. No. 40, 48 C.B.R. (3d) 8 (T.D.), aff'd [1998] N.S.J. No. 60, 6 C.B.R. (4th) 69 (C.A.).
[412] This exemption is discussed in detail in the next section of the text, at §12.129.

§12.126 The courts also may restrain a shareholder from voting in a particular way (or from causing the corporation to disregard a vote cast in a particular way) where the shareholder concerned intends to vote, or has voted, in a way to escape liability for his or her own wrongdoing,[413] or where the shareholder is acting in a malicious or perverse manner with a view towards the deliberate destruction of the company or the wasting or dissipation of its assets (at least in cases where others might be prejudicially affected by the shareholder so doing).[414] Again, cases falling into these classes are very rare.

§12.127 Subject to these limited exceptions, the voting preferences of shareholders are not subject to judicial review. Normally, there will be no obligation on a shareholder to weigh the views of other persons about what may be in the interests of the corporation at large before he or she decides how to vote. Unless there is an agreement to the contrary, a shareholder has a general right to vote his or her shares as he or she pleases,[415] and he or she may be motivated solely by individual interest.[416] Where there is no limit in the articles of a corporation on the number of shares that a single shareholder may hold, a shareholder may acquire as many shares as he or she wishes. The shareholder may exercise his or her voting power in the election of directors to secure the election of directors whose views agree with his or her own, and the shareholder may support those views where any matter decided or proposed by the directors requires ratification at a meeting of shareholders.[417] Similarly, there is nothing illegal or contrary to public policy in an agreement among shareholders to form a voting block to cause the corporation to pursue a course of policy or to cause the election of certain individuals. The fact that such an agreement may potentially deprive a minority of control or impose some other detriment does not in itself render the agreement illegal.[418]

§12.128 The vote of a shareholder is not to be impugned, even where the shareholder has a personal interest in the subject matter of the vote that is opposed to, or different from, the interests of the corporation or particular shareholders.[419] The basic governing principle of corporate law is that of majority rule. Unless some provision to the contrary is found in the articles, by-laws or a unanimous shareholder agreement, the resolution (or, where required by statute, special resolution) of a majority of the shareholders upon any question that the shareholders of a corporation are competent to vote on is binding upon the minority and, consequently, upon the corporation. Every shareholder has a right to vote upon any such question, even though he or she may have a personal interest in

---

[413] *Cook v. Deeks*, [1916] 1 A.C. 554 (P.C.).
[414] *Standard Chartered Bank v. Walker*, [1992] 1 W.L.R. 561 (Ch.), *per* Vinelott J.
[415] *North-West Transportation v. Beatty* (1887), 12 App. Cas. 589 (P.C.).
[416] *Ritchie v. Vermillion Mining Co.*, [1902] O.J. No. 223, 4 O.L.R. 588 (C.A.); *Pender v. Lushington* (1877), 6 Ch. D. 70.
[417] *North-West Transportation v. Beatty* (1887), 12 App. Cas. 589 (P.C.).
[418] *Ringuet v. Bergeron*, [1960] S.C.J. No. 40, [1960] S.C.R. 672.
[419] *North-West Transportation v. Beatty* (1887), 12 App. Cas. 589 at 593 (P.C.), *per* Sir Richard Baggallay; *Montreal Trust Co. v. Oxford Pipe Line Co.*, [1942] O.J. No. 460, [1942] O.R. 490 at 501 (C.A.), *per* Gillanders J.A.

its outcome or in the subject matter to which it relates that is opposed to, or different from, the general or particular interests of the corporation or its other shareholders. It is sometimes suggested that a shareholder will not be permitted to vote to approve a breach of fiduciary duty for which he or she is liable in some other capacity (*e.g.*, as a director),[420] or to misappropriate property or income of the corporation that rightly should be available for the shareholders generally.[421] Generally, in Ontario, this view is no longer tenable.[422] The shareholder is free to vote as he or she pleases, but that vote may be disregarded if a dissident shareholder seeks to enforce his or her dissent rights under Part XIV of the OBCA.[423]

(b) Voting for the Benefit of the Class

§12.129 Before leaving the subject of shareholder fiduciary duty, it is worthwhile to consider a kindred concept that applies in a limited range of cases. The general rule is that the holder of a security is entitled to vote as he or she pleases with respect to any matter to be decided. So, for instance, in *Pender v. Lushington*, Jessel M.R. stated:

> ... a man may be actuated in giving his vote by interests entirely adverse to the interests of the company as a whole. He may think it more for his particular interest that a certain course may be taken which may be in the opinion of others very adverse to the interests of the company as a whole, but he cannot be restrained from giving his vote in what way he pleases because he is influenced by that motive.[424]

Similarly, in *Carruth v. Imperial Chemical Industries*, Lord Maugham said:

> ... the shareholders' vote is a right of property and *prima faice* may be exercised by a shareholder as he thinks fit in his own interest.[425]

However, it has also been held in numerous cases that where security holders (whether shareholders or bond holders) of a given class of securities are entitled to vote on a matter that will bind all members of that class, they must exercise the voting power for the purpose of benefiting the class as a whole, and not merely for their individual benefit.[426] It is self-evident that the two rules appear

---

[420] *Cook v. Deeks*, [1916] 1 A.C. 554 (P.C.).
[421] See, generally, *Fuller v. Bruce* (1935), 9 M.P.R. 437 (N.S.C.A.), appeal quashed [1936] S.C.R. 124; see also *British America Nickel Corp. v. M.J. O'Brien Ltd.*, [1927] A.C. 369 (P.C.).
[422] *Brant Investments Ltd. v. KeepRite Inc.*, [1991] O.J. No. 683, 1 B.L.R. (2d) 225 at 244 (C.A.).
[423] CBCA, Part XV. Thus s. 249(1) of the OBCA provides that "an action brought or intervened in under [Part XVII] shall not be stayed or dismissed by reason only that it . . . has been or may be approved by the shareholders of the corporation".
[424] (1877), 6 Ch. D. 70 at 75.
[425] [1937] A.C. 707 at 765 (H.L.).
[426] Where the vote to be taken is one among the shareholders of the corporation as a single collective entity, it is said that each shareholder must exercise his or her vote for the benefit of "the company as a whole". Where the vote is to be taken among the holders of a specific class, each member of that class must vote for the benefit of the class. Each of these phrases is highly misleading, insofar as it suggests that the vote of a shareholder (or other security holder) is subject to an analogous duty as that owed by directors to act in the best interest of the corporation. For a discussion of these requirements, see, for instance, *Allen v. Gold Reefs of West Africa Ltd.*, [1900] 1 Ch. 656 (C.A.); *Western Mines Ltd. v. Shield Development Co.*, [1975] B.C.J. No. 53,

to conflict, and their reconciliation has not yet been clearly resolved. It is important to stress that this class interest requirement is not a fiduciary duty. Specifically, it does not entail an obligation to put the interests of another person first. Rather, it limits the terms of reference by which the party entitled to vote may determine his or her own interests. The right to vote is one of the proprietary rights associated with share (and other applicable security) ownership, and thus the general rule is that the holder may exercise a vote in his or her own individual interests even if these are opposed to those of the corporation as a whole.[427] A more accurate formulation of the rule was put forward in *Greenhalgh v. Arderne Cinemas Ltd.*,[428] in which it was stated:

> ... I think that the matter can, in practice, be more accurately and precisely stated by looking at the converse and by saying that a special resolution of this kind would be liable to be impeached if the effect of it were to discriminate between the majority shareholders and the minority shareholders, so as to give to the former an advantage of which the latter were deprived.

§12.130 Very frequently, the real problem that gives rise to a failure by a particular voter to give proper consideration to the best interest of the class is the fact that the classes of voter were poorly conceived, and included different types of security holder whose interests were inconsistent.[429] The requirement to vote in the interest of the class has been applied most frequently in cases where a person has voted shares to validate some improper transaction in which he or she has been engaged.[430] However, in principle another possible situation in which the rule might be applied would be where it was necessary to prevent shareholders and other voters from using their voting control over a corporation to deprive others interested in the corporation, while securing a collateral benefit for themselves.[431] Such a result could arise even where there is no wrongdoing. For instance, where transactions involve two corporations, some persons may hold shares in both of the corporations concerned. Diversity of interest of this nature may prompt them to vote against the interest of one corporation, in order to better the other, since by doing so, they may draw a disproportionate share of whatever is to be divided. The following table relating to a hypothetical transaction in which a gain is to be divided between two corporations (A, B), illustrates the point. Shareholder One is better off to vote in favour of allocating all gains from a proposed transaction to Corporation A, than to vote in favour of Corporation B. In contrast, Shareholder Two (who has no interest in Corporation A), stands to be deprived of everything, if the gain is assigned entirely to Corporation A. Shareholder Three, who has substantial shareholding in both corporations, is

---

65 D.L.R. (3d) 307 (S.C.); *British America Nickel Corp. v. M.J. O'Brien Ltd.*, [1927] A.C. 369 at 371 (P.C.), *per* Viscount Haldane.

[427] *Benson v. Third Canadian General Investment Trust*, [1993] O.J. No. 1491, 14 O.R. (3d) 493 (Gen. Div.), *per* Farley J. quoting *Gower's Principles of Modern Company Law*, 5th ed. (London: Sweet & Maxwell, 1992) at 591 to 593.

[428] [1951] Ch. 286 at 291 (C.A.), *per* Evershed M.R.

[429] See, for instance, *ID Biomedical Corp. v. Glaxo Smith Kline plc* (2006), 14 B.L.R. (4th) 177 (B.C.S.C.).

[430] See, for instance, *Ngurli Ltd. v. Mccann* (1953), 90 C.L.R. 425 at 438-39 (H.C. Aust.).

[431] See, generally, *Re H.R. Harmer Ltd.*, [1959] 1 W.L.R. 62 at 82 (C.A.), *per* Jenkins L.J.

also significantly better off by voting to deprive Corporation B of the benefit. The probable result of any vote would be to deprive Shareholder Two of any share of the gain at all:

	Per cent Interest in Corporation A	Per cent Interest in Corporation B	Value of benefit to be Assigned between two corporations	Gain to Shareholder if Benefit Assigned to A	Gain to Shareholder if Benefit Assigned to B
Shareholder One	5%	4%	$1,000,000	$50,000	$40,000
Shareholder Two	0%	48%	$1,000,000	$0	$480,000
Shareholder Three	60%	47%	$1,000,000	$600,000	$470,000

§12.131 There are three cases that illustrate the application of the class interest rule, to prevent the betterment of the majority at the expense of the minority. In *Re Holders of Investment Trust Ltd.*,[432] the shareholders voted on a proposal to reduce its capital by cancelling its redeemable preference shares and issuing unsecured debt securities to the holders in exchange for those shares. The shares were scheduled for redemption in 10 months. However, the debt securities had terms of 15 to 20 years. The proposal was approved by a majority of the preference shareholders, but it was determined that the majority of those voting in favour of the proposal were also holders of the common shares of the company. After determining that the majority voted in favour of the exchange in order to improve their position as ordinary shareholders, Megarry V.-C. held that the proposal had not been properly approved. More generally, in *Menier v. Hooper's Telegraph Works*[433] the major shareholder in a company:

> The minority of the shareholders say in effect that the majority has divided the assets of the company, more or less, between themselves, to the exclusion of the minority. I think it would be a shocking thing if that could be done, because if so the majority might divide the whole assets of the company, and pass a resolution that everything must be given to them, and that the minority should have nothing to do with it. Assuming the case to be as alleged ... then the majority have put something in their pockets at the expense of the minority. If so, it appears to me that the minority have a right to have their share of benefits ascertained for them in the best way in which the court can do, and given to them.

Similarly, in *Estmanco (Kilner House) Ltd. v. Greater London Council*[434] stated:

> No right of a shareholder to vote in his own selfish interests or to ignore the interests of the company entitles him with impunity to injure his vote-less fellow shareholders by depriving the company of a cause of action or stultifying the purpose for which the company was formed.

---

[432] [1971] 1 W.L.R. 583 (Ch.).
[433] (1874), L.R. 9 Ch. App. 350 at 353 (C.A.).
[434] [1982] 1 W.L.R. 2 (Ch.).

It seems, therefore, that shareholders may not use their voting control in a confiscatory manner, so as to deprive other shareholders of what they are duly entitled to receive or enjoy. The exact manner of applying the class interest rule is unclear, although in principle the oppression remedy would now seem to afford an adequate basis. Where shareholdings are concentrated in the manner indicated in the table, the oppression remedy may afford sufficient protection.[435] In principle, however, the best interests of the class requirement has a hypothetical benefit where the shareholding in the two corporations is dispersed among a large number of shareholders, who are merely voting in their own best financial interest rather than in concert (for instance, if Shareholder Three's shares were divided in the same ratios among 15 different shareholders). Unfortunately, in such cases, the hypothetical benefit of the rule is diluted by the fact that it would be difficult from an evidentiary perspective to inquire into what prompted so many people to vote in a particular way.

(6) Vote by Attorney

§12.132 In many cases, it will prove impossible for a shareholder or other voter to attend a meeting at which a vote is to be taken. In *Harben v. Phillips*[436] Bowen L.J. held that there was no common law right in favour of a member of a corporation to vote by proxy. In England, such a right was not conferred by statute until 1947, although usually the articles of association of widely held companies permitted voting by proxy. In *New South Wales Henry George Foundation v. Booth*,[437] Gzell J. held that there is no common law rule that a shareholder may vote by attorney, and that therefore any authority to do so must be statutory. He further concluded that such an entitlement must be found in statutes in legislation relating to corporations, rather than in statutes of general application, but that the word "proxy" in the *Corporations Act* of New South Wales was sufficiently broad to include an attorney.

(iv) Proxy Solicitation

§12.133 In widely held corporations, it is rarely practical (or sometimes even possible) for the majority shareholders of a corporation to attend shareholders' meetings. For small investors, the cost of attendance may be disproportionate to the amount of the investment held in the corporation. Even where a shareholder has a substantial interest in the corporation, the cost of attendance may be high relative to the importance of the matters to be considered at the meeting. Moreover, as the number of shareholders increases, the potential that a meeting date will conflict with the scheduling commitments of the other members increases exponentially. If shareholders' meetings are to be more than an expensive facade and provide shareholders with a meaningful method of providing input into the government of the corporation, it is necessary to provide some alternative to personal attendance at shareholders' meetings.

---

[435] See also *Clemens v. Clemens Brothers Ltd.*, [1976] 2 All E.R. 268 (Ch.), *per* Foster J.
[436] (1883) 23 Ch. D. 14 at 35-36 (C.A.).
[437] [2002] N.S.W.S.C. 245.

§12.134 Both the OBCA and the CBCA provide such an alternative form of attendance under the proxy provisions of each Act and the provisions of this legislation are supplemented by securities law requirements. A proxy is an authority given by one person to another, which authorizes the person to whom it is given (the "proxy holder") to exercise a voting right or rights of the donor. The nature of the authority conferred by a proxy was described in the following terms by Lang J. in *Patten v. Outerbridge*:

> The proxy is merely the agent of the shareholder, and as between himself and the shareholder is not entitled to vote contrary to the instructions of the shareholder. Proxies are bound by the documents appointing them and the notice convening the meeting. Unless the appointment so authorizes, proxies cannot vote on any business not included in the notice or on any modification or amendment to any business in the notice.[438]

Proxies are only one method of assigning such voting rights; voting trusts and similar requirements are another, but in contrast to a voting trust, in the case of a proxy both legal title and equitable title remain in the donor. In addition, where a shareholder is a company, it must designate a person to represent it at the meeting, since it is obviously incapable of attending the meeting in person. In such a case, subsection 102(2) of the OBCA provides that where a company or association is a shareholder of a corporation, the corporation must recognize any individual authorized by a resolution of the directors or governing body of the company or association to represent the company at meetings of the shareholders.[439] Any individual so designated may exercise on behalf of the company or association that he or she represents, all the powers that the company could exercise if it were an individual shareholder.[440]

§12.135 At common law, a shareholder had no right to attend a meeting of the corporation by proxy unless the articles of the corporation so provided.[441] However, the right to attend a meeting of an OBCA corporation by way of a proxy is now conferred by statute under subsection 110(1) of that Act, which provides:

> 110.(1) Every shareholder entitled to vote at a meeting of shareholders may by means of a proxy appoint a proxyholder or one or more alternate proxyholders, who need not be shareholders, as the shareholder's nominee to attend and act at the meeting in the manner, to the extent and with the authority conferred by the proxy.[442]

Although doubts may be raised about how effective they are as a corporate governance device,[443] proxies are now an established feature of corporate law.

---

[438] [1982] N.J. No. 180, 37 Nfld. & P.E.I.R. 318, 104 A.P.R. 318 at 325 (T.D.).
[439] CBCA, s. 140(2).
[440] OBCA, s. 102(3); CBCA, s. 140(3).
[441] *Harben v. Phillips* (1883), 23 Ch. D. 14 at 35 (C.A.), *per* Bowen L.J.
[442] CBCA, s. 148(1).
[443] In 1940, the United States Temporary National Economic Committee noted with some dismay that many large corporations had fallen under the practical control of their management, who often lacked any significant shareholder interest. The proxy machinery had proved to be of assistance in securing management control, rather than a means of bringing about shareholder control: *Bureaucracy and Trusteeship in Large Corporations* (1940), Monograph 11, at 22-23.

Section 111 of the OBCA[444] imposes a mandatory proxy solicitation requirement which applies to all offering corporations. Subsection 112(1) requires the distribution of an information circular with every solicitation of proxies. Under subsection 253(2), where it appears to the Ontario Securities Commission that any person to whom these provisions apply has failed to comply with, or is contravening, either or both of them, the Commission may apply to the court for an order and the court may make such order as it thinks fit, including:

> (*a*) an order restraining a solicitation, the holding of a meeting or any persons from implementing or acting upon any resolution passed at a meeting to which such non-compliance with or contravention of section 111 or subsection 112(1) relates;
>
> (*b*) an order requiring correction of any form of proxy or information circular and a further solicitation; or
>
> (*c*) an order adjourning the meeting to which such non-compliance with or contravention of section 111 or 112(1) relates.

By including a provision in its articles or by-laws, a corporation cannot exclude the right given to shareholders to attend meetings by proxy. It applies to all corporations whether or not they are offering corporations. However, in the case of an offering corporation, section 111 of the OBCA[445] provides:

> 111. The management of an offering corporation shall, concurrently with or prior to sending notice of a meeting of shareholders, send a form of proxy to each shareholder who is entitled to receive notice of the meeting.

Furthermore, where a person solicits proxies for a proposal that is to be considered by the shareholders, it is also necessary to distribute an information circular for that proposal. Subsection 112(1) of the OBCA provides:

> 112.(1) No person shall solicit proxies in respect of an offering corporation unless,
>
> (*a*) in the case of a solicitation by or on behalf of the management of the corporation, a management information circular in prescribed form, either as an appendix to or as a separate document accompanying the notice of the meeting; or
>
> (*b*) in the case of any other solicitation, a dissident's information circular in prescribed form,
>
> is sent to the auditor of the corporation, to each shareholder whose proxy is solicited and, if clause (*b*) applies, to the corporation.[446]

A proxyholder or an alternate proxyholder has the same rights as the shareholder who appointed him or her to attend and speak at a shareholders' meeting in regard to any matter, to vote by ballot at the meeting and, except where a proxyholder or an alternate proxyholder has conflicting instructions from more than one shareholder, to vote at the meeting in regard to any matter by a show of

---

[444] CBCA, s. 149.
[445] CBCA, s. 149(1).
[446] Compare CBCA, s. 150(1).

hands.[447] A shareholder who attends and participates in a meeting as the proxyholder of another shareholder does not lose the right to object to the regularity of the meeting as long as he or she participates only in the capacity of that other person's proxy.[448]

(1) Proxies Under the OBCA and the CBCA

§12.136 It has been held in England that any written appointment of a person as a proxyholder will suffice, provided that the intention to appoint that person a proxy and the purpose of the appointment are reasonably clear.[449] In contrast, subsection 110(3) of the OBCA provides that every form of proxy must comply with the regulations. The CBCA contains no direct equivalent to this provision, but the CBCA Regulation does prescribe the contents and form of a proxy required to be sent to the Director by subsection 150(2) of the Act.[450] Subsection 27(1) of the OBCA Regulation[451] provides that a form of proxy shall indicate in boldface type the meeting at which it is to be used and whether the proxy is solicited by, or on behalf of, the management of the corporation. The proxy must also provide a designated blank space for the date. If the date is not inserted in the space, the proxy is deemed to be dated on the day on which it is mailed.

§12.137 For an offering corporation, a number of additional requirements apply to the form of proxy.[452] Under subsection 27(2) of the OBCA Regulation, the proxy is required to indicate in boldface type that the shareholder may appoint a proxyholder other than any person designated in the form of proxy, and the form must also contain instruction on the manner in which the shareholder may exercise this right. If the form of proxy shows a person as designated proxyholder, the form must provide some means for the shareholder to designate some other person in the designated proxyholder's place.[453] The form must also provide some means for the shareholder to give voting instructions.[454] Finally, the form of proxy or related information circular must state that the shares represented by the proxy will be voted or withheld from voting in accordance with the instructions of the shareholder on any ballot that may be called for. Notice must also be given that if the shareholder specifies a choice for any matter to be acted upon the shares shall be voted accordingly.[455]

---

[447] OBCA, s. 114(2); CBCA, s. 152(2).
[448] *McKenna v. Spooner Oils Ltd.*, [1934] 1 W.W.R. 255 (Alta. T.D.).
[449] *Isaacs v. Chapman* (1916), 32 T.L.R. 183 (Ch.), aff'd 32 T.L.R. 237 (C.A.).
[450] *Canada Business Corporations Regulations, 2001*, SOR/2001-512, s. 54. Subsection 150(2) of the Act provides:

> 150.(2) A person required to send a management proxy circular or dissident's proxy circular shall send concurrently a copy of it to the Director, together with a statement in prescribed form, the form of proxy any other documents for use in connection with the meeting and, in the case of a management proxy circular, a copy of the notice of meeting.

[451] R.R.O. 1990, Reg. 62.
[452] *Ibid.*, s. 27(9).
[453] *Ibid.*, s. 27(3).
[454] OBCA, s. 27(4), (5) and (6).
[455] *Ibid.*, s. 27(7).

§12.138 Under subsection 148(2) of the CBCA a proxy must be executed by the shareholder or his or her attorney authorized in writing. In contrast, subsection 110(2) of the OBCA provides that a proxy shall be executed by the shareholder or an attorney authorized in writing, or if the shareholder is a company, by an officer or attorney of the company duly authorized for that purpose. The Act gives no guidance on how the officer or attorney is to be duly authorized, but a director resolution giving a general or specific authority to designate proxies would clearly suffice.

§12.139 Subsection 148(3) of the CBCA provides that a proxy is valid only for the meeting for which it is given or any adjournment of that meeting. The OBCA contains no direct equivalent, but instead, subsection 110(2.1) of that Act provides that a proxy ceases to be valid one year from the date of its issue. Thus, it would appear that under the OBCA it is possible to appoint a proxy to attend meetings generally for a period of one year, and under the CBCA it is necessary to appoint proxies to attend specifically designated meetings. Provided the proxy describes the meeting to which it relates with sufficient detail to enable it to be identified, it will be valid, even if the meeting is in some respects misdescribed. For instance, in *Oliver v. Dalgleish*[456] a form of proxy was held valid where the correct date of the meeting was included, but the meeting was described as an annual general meeting rather than an extraordinary meeting of the corporation. More generally stated, an obvious misprint or other palpable mistake on the form of a proxy does not affect the validity of the proxy.

§12.140 The case law was uncertain about whether a person who solicited a proxy was obliged to attend the meeting concerned, or whether a shareholder had a right to compel a proxyholder to vote in accordance with instructions given by the shareholder — although there was some *obiter* that suggested that the proxyholder was under a duty to comply with the directions that he or she was given.[457] Because a proxyholder is an agent of the shareholder, it would seem to be implicit that the proxyholder is under a duty to comply with his or her principal's instructions concerning the manner of voting. Any lingering doubts with regard to this question have been swept away by subsection 114(1) of the OBCA[458] which provides:

> 114.(1) A person who solicits a proxy and is appointed proxyholder shall attend in person or cause an alternate proxyholder to attend the meeting in respect of which the proxy is given and comply with the directions of the shareholder who appointed the person.

---

[456] [1963] 3 All E.R. 330 at 335 (Ch.), *per* Buckley J. As for requirements in the by-laws for attestation of the shareholder's execution of the proxy, see *Harben v. Phillips* (1882), 23 Ch. D. 14 (C.A.).

[457] See, for instance, *Second Consolidated Trust Ltd. v. Ceylon Amalgamated Tea & Rubber Estates Ltd.*, [1943] 2 All E.R. 567 (Ch.), *per* Uthwatt J.; *Oliver v. Dalgleish*, [1963] 3 All E.R. 330 (Ch.), *per* Buckley J.

[458] CBCA, s. 152(1).

The shareholder may, of course, prefer not to give any specific voting instructions, and to leave to the proxyholder the discretion to decide how to vote on a particular matter. Subsection 27(5) of the OBCA Regulation provides:

> 27.(5) A form of proxy may confer authority as to a matter for which a choice is not specified by the shareholder in accordance with subsection (4) if the form of proxy, the management information circular or the dissident's information circular states in bold-face type how the proxyholder will vote the shares in respect of each matter or group of related matters.

In addition, subsection 28(1) of the OBCA Regulation provides:

> 28.(1) Discretionary authority may be conferred by way of a form of proxy in respect of any amendments or variations to matters identified in the notice of meeting or other matters that may properly come before the meeting where,
>
> (a) the person by or on whose behalf the solicitation is made is not aware within a reasonable time before the solicitation that the amendments or other matters are to be presented for action at the meeting; and
>
> (b) the form of proxy, the management information circular or the dissident's information circular states specifically that it confers such discretionary authority.

(2) Proxy Solicitation Under the Securities Act

§12.141 The proxy solicitation provisions of the OBCA and the CBCA are supplemented by the proxy solicitation requirements of the *Securities Act*,[459] the Regulation under the *Securities Act*[460] and the National Policies and OSC Policies adopted under the *Securities Act*. The OBCA provisions apply to any corporation that is an offering corporation within the meaning of that Act. The CBCA provisions apply to corporations that have 50 or fewer shareholders, two or more joint holders being counted as one.[461] The proxy solicitation requirements set down in the *Securities Act*, the Regulation under the *Securities Act* and the National Policies and OSC Policies apply only where the holders of one or more voting securities of a reporting issuer is within Ontario.[462] Moreover, subsection 88(1) of the *Securities Act* provides:

> 88.(1) Where a reporting issuer is complying with the requirements of the laws of the jurisdiction under which it is incorporated, organized or continued and the requirements are substantially similar to the requirements of this Part, the requirements of this Part do not apply.

The OSC is empowered under subsection 88(2) to make exemption orders (subject to such terms and conditions as it considers appropriate) where a requirement of Part XIX of the *Securities Act* (dealing with proxy solicitation) conflicts with the laws of the jurisdiction under which the reporting issuer is incorporated, organized or continued, or if it is otherwise satisfied that such an order should be made.

---

[459] R.S.O. 1990, c. S.5, as amended.
[460] R.R.O. 1990, Reg. 1015, as amended.
[461] CBCA, s. 149(2).
[462] *Securities Act*, s. 85.

§12.142 Part XIX of the *Securities Act* contains a number of specific proxy solicitation requirements that apply to all corporations that are reporting issuers within the meaning of that Act. Section 85 of the *Securities Act* sets down the basic mandatory proxy solicitation requirement applicable to reporting issuers who have holders of their voting securities resident in Ontario. It provides:

> 85. Subject to section 88, if the management of a reporting issuer gives or intends to give to holders of its voting securities notice of a meeting, the management shall, concurrently with or prior to giving the notice to the security holders whose latest address as shown on the books of the reporting issuer is in Ontario, send to each such security holder who is entitled to notice of meeting, at the security holder's latest address as shown on the books of the reporting issuer, a form of proxy for use at the meeting that complies with the regulations.

A management proxy circular must be sent at the same time as the management proxy solicitation and notice of meeting.[463] The *Securities Act*, the Regulations under the *Securities Act* and the National Policies and OSC Policies do not specify which securities are entitled to a vote nor the manner in which notice is to be given — these subjects being left to the articles (or other charter documents) of the issuer, to contract and to the governing corporate legislation. It does, however, set down detailed requirements on the manner in which proxies will be solicited.

§12.143 In addition to the solicitation for proxies, subsection 86(1) of the Act requires reporting issuers to distribute an information circular to the holders of its voting securities:

> 86.(1) Subject to subsection (2) and section 88, no person or company shall solicit proxies from holders of its voting securities whose latest address as shown on the books of the reporting issuer is in Ontario unless,
>
> (*a*) in the case of solicitation by or on behalf of the management of a reporting issuer, an information circular, either as an appendix to or as a separate document accompanying the notice of the meeting, is sent to each such security holder of the reporting issuer whose proxy is solicited at the security holder's latest address as shown on the books of the reporting issuer; or
>
> (*b*) in the case of any other solicitation, the person or company making the solicitation, concurrently with or prior thereto, delivers or sends an information circular to each such security holder whose proxy is solicited.

Thus, an information circular is required both in the case of a management proxy solicitation and a solicitation by other persons.

§12.144 In evaluating the content of an information circular (and other documents provided by a corporation to a shareholder for that matter) the relevant perspective for the purpose of determining the adequacy of disclosure is that of the ordinary businessperson who is likely to receive the circular or other

---

[463] *Pacifica Papers Inc. v. Johnstone*, [2001] B.C.J. No. 1714, 19 B.L.R. (3d) 62 at 66 (C.A.), *per* Finch C.J.B.C.

document.[464] In *SEC v. May*, Clark J. rejected the suggestion that inflammatory language was acceptable.[465] Under subsection 154(1) of the CBCA a restraining order may be obtained where a proxy circular under that Act (whether management or dissident) contains an untrue statement of a material fact or fails to state a material fact or makes a statement that is misleading in the circumstances. No exact equivalent provision appears in the OBCA or the *Securities Act*, but the requirements under those statutes for the content of an information circular would seem to afford a sufficient basis for the grant of a restraining order under section 253 of the OBCA — where the requirements of that Act were in breach — or for the issue of a compliance order or cease trading order under the *Securities Act*,[466] where there was a breach of the requirements of that Act.

(a) SECURITIES LAW REQUIREMENTS

§12.145 The notice of meeting requirements of the OBCA and CBCA are supplemented by the information circular and proxy solicitation requirements imposed under securities law and policy. As discussed above, the notice of meeting required under the OBCA and CBCA specifies the business to be transacted at a meting of the corporation. In contrast, the information circular places that business in its proper context. Normally (*i.e.*, in the case of the annual and general meeting of a corporation), the information circular must be read in conjunction with the disclosure provided by the financial statements, the annual information form, and the MD&A statement. For other meetings, material change reports (Form 51-102F3) and business acquisition reports (Form 51-102F4) may be a relevant source of additional information, to provide further contextual information with respect to the meeting. A form of proxy sent to security-holders of a reporting issuer by a person or company soliciting proxies must indicate in bold-face type whether or not the proxy is solicited by or on behalf of the management of the reporting issuer, provide a specifically designated blank space for dating the form of proxy and specify the meeting in respect of which the proxy is solicited.[467] An information circular sent to security-holders of a reporting issuer or the form of proxy to which the information circular relates must:

(a) indicate in bold-face type that the security-holder has the right to appoint a person or company to represent the security-holder at the meeting other than the person or company if any, designated in the form of proxy; and

(b) contain instructions as to the manner in which the security-holder may exercise the right referred to in paragraph (a).[468]

---

[464] *Dalex Mines Ltd. (N.P.L.) v. Schmidt*, [1973] B.C.J. No. 506, [1973] 5 W.W.R. 357 at 363 (S.C.), *per* Rae J.; *Alexander v. Simpson* (1889), 43 Ch. D. 139 at 147 (C.A.), *per* Bowen L.J.; *Choppington Collieries Ltd. v. Johnson*, [1944] 1 All E.R. 762 at 763 (C.A.), *per* Uthwatt J., aff'd [1944] 1 All E.R. 762 at 764 (C.A.).
[465] 229 F.2d 123 at 124 (2d Cir. 1956).
[466] Sections 127 and 128 respectively.
[467] NI 51-102, s. 9.4(1).
[468] NI 51-102, s. 9.4(2).

§12.146 Where a form of proxy contains a designation of a named person or company as nominee, it must provide an option for the security-holder to designate in the form of proxy some other person or company as the security-holder's nominee.[469] A form of proxy provide an option for the security-holder to specify that the securities registered in the security-holder's name will be voted for or against each matter or group of related matters identified in the form of proxy, in the notice of meeting or in an information circular, other than the appointment of an auditor and the election of directors.[470]

§12.147 A form of proxy may confer discretionary authority, but only if the form of proxy or the information circular states in bold-face type how the securities represented by the proxy will be voted in respect of each matter or group of related matters.[471] The proxy must provide an option for the security-holder to specify that the securities registered in the name of the security-holder must be voted or withheld from voting in respect of the appointment of an auditor or the election of directors.[472] A form of proxy may confer discretionary authority with respect to:

- amendments or variations to matters identified in the notice of meeting; and
- other matters which may properly come before the meeting,[473]

provided that both the following conditions are met:

- the person or company by whom or on whose behalf the solicitation is made is not aware within a reasonable time before the time the solicitation is made that any of those amendments, variations or other matters are to be presented for action at the meeting; and
- a specific statement is made in the information circular or in the form of proxy that the proxy is conferring such discretionary authority.

A form of proxy must not confer authority to vote:

- for the election of any person as a director of a reporting issuer unless a *bona fide* proposed nominee for that election is named in the information circular; or
- at any meeting other than the meeting specified in the notice of meeting or any adjournment of that meeting.[474]

(b) INFORMATION CIRCULAR REQUIREMENTS

§12.148 As noted above, section 186 of the *Securities Act* requires the delivery of an information circular to security-holders, together with the proxy form.

---

[469] NI 51-102, s. 9.4(3).
[470] NI 51-102, s. 9.4(4).
[471] NI 51-102, s. 9(5).
[472] NI 51-102, s. 9(6).
[473] NI 51-102, s. 9.4(8).
[474] NI 51-102, s. 9.4(9).

Until 2005, the relevant securities law rules relating to information circulars were set out in Part IX of the Regulation. Part IX (which included sections 176 to 181)[475] was revoked by O. Reg. 215/05, section 6, at which time securities regulators shifted towards a regulatory scheme based largely on a CSA National Instrument. The current rules governing the content of information circulars are set out in National Instrument 51-102, Companion Policy 51-102CP, and in the instructions provided regarding the preparation of Form 51-102F5, which sets down the content requirements for an information circular. On March 30, 2007, the Canadian Securities Administrators published a number of proposals for reform of their existing requirements governing disclosure. Certain of these proposals relate directly to the information circular requirements.

§12.149 Form 51-102F5 is a template, and it is not necessary to provide all of the information mentioned in the form. Where any item in that Form that is inapplicable, the section may be omitted. Since management proxy solicitation is obligatory, the prescribed content of the form assumes that the information circular will be provided by management. Consequently, as a general rule the same form is followed, whether the information circular is distributed by management or by others. However, in view of the probability that some of the prescribed information may not be known or available to a non-management distributor, the disclosure requirements are relaxed in certain cases. Specifically, information may be omitted where it is not reasonably within the power of the person who is delivering the information circular to obtain, provided that the form contains a statement of the circumstances that render the information unavailable. Information may also be omitted where it is contained in another information circular, notice of meeting or form of proxy sent to the same persons or companies whose proxies were solicited in connection with the same meeting, as long as the person circulating the information circular clearly identifies the particular document containing the information.

§12.150 The following is a very broad brush description of what is required with respect to the information circular (focusing primarily on the requirements applicable to a management information circular). As with regard to other aspects of securities law and policy, readers are cautioned that the applicable requirements change frequently and vary depending on the detail of any given transaction or the circumstances of any given issuer. Accordingly, reference should always be made to current sources of information, and the advice of a securities specialist should be obtained when dealing with an offering corporation.

§12.151 An information circular is intended to provide in plain language relevant information to any decision that is to be made that "readers are able to understand". More specific guidelines are to be found in the plain language principles set out in section 1.5 of Companion Policy 51-102CP. Technical terms may be used, but they must be explained in a clear and concise manner. Where it is practicable and appropriate, information should be presented in

---

[475] The requirements relating to these provisions are discussed in the first edition of this text.

tabular form, and quantitative information should be stated in figures rather than in words. One basic requirement is that an information circular sent to security-holders of a reporting issuer or the form of proxy to which the information circular relates must state that:

> (a) the securities represented by the proxy will be voted or withheld from voting in accordance with the instructions of the security-holder on any ballot that may be called for; and
>
> (b) if the security-holder specifies a choice under subsection 9.4(4) or (6) of NI 51-102 with respect to any matter to be acted upon, the securities will be voted accordingly.[476]

§12.151.1 Assuming that the March 30, 2007, CSA proposals are carried into effect, in general, the following information will be required (the following list is illustrative rather than exhaustive). In particular, the information circular should:

- Identify the person(s) soliciting proxies, along with a statement as to who has borne or will bear, directly or indirectly, the cost of soliciting the proxies.

- Provide a brief description of any material interest, direct or indirect, by way of beneficial ownership of securities or otherwise, of each of the persons or companies in any matter to be acted upon other than the election of directors or the appointment of auditors:

    (a) if the solicitation is made by or on behalf of management of the company, each person who has been a director or executive officer of the company at any time since the beginning of the company's last financial year;

    (b) if the solicitation is made other than by or on behalf of management of the company, each person or company by whom, or on whose behalf, directly or indirectly, the solicitation is made;

    (c) each proposed nominee for election as a director of the company; and

    (d) each associate or affiliate of any of the persons or companies listed in paragraphs (a) to (c).

- Disclose whether to the knowledge of the company's directors or executive officers, any person or company beneficially owns, directly or indirectly, or controls or directs, voting securities carrying 10 per cent or more of the voting rights attached to any class of voting securities of the company, name each person or company and state

    (a) the approximate number of securities beneficially owned, directly or indirectly, or controlled or directed by each such person or company; and

    (b) the percentage of the class of outstanding voting securities of the company represented by the number of voting securities so owned, controlled or directed.

---

[476] NI 51-102, s. 9.4(7).

- Where directors are to be elected at the meeting to which the information circular relates, provide the following information, in tabular form to the extent practicable, for each person proposed to be nominated for election as a director (a "proposed director") and each other person whose term of office as a director will continue after the meeting:

    (a) State the name, province or state, and country of residence, of each director and proposed director.

    (b) State the period or periods during which each director has served as a director and when the term of office for each director and proposed director will expire.

    (c) Identify the members of each committee of the board.

    (d) State the present principal occupation, business or employment of each director and proposed director. Give the name and principal business of any company in which any such employment is carried on. Furnish similar information as to all of the principal occupations, businesses or employments of each proposed director within the five preceding years, unless the proposed director is now a director and was elected to the present term of circular.

    (e) If a director or proposed director has held more than one position in the company, or a parent or subsidiary, state only the first and last position held.

    (f) State the number of securities of each class of voting securities of the company or any of its subsidiaries beneficially owned, directly or indirectly, or controlled or directed by each proposed director.

    (g) If securities carrying 10 per cent or more of the voting rights attached to all voting securities of the company or of any of its subsidiaries are beneficially owned, directly or indirectly, or controlled or directed by any proposed director and the proposed director's associates or affiliates,

        (i) state the number of securities of each class of voting securities beneficially owned, directly or indirectly, or controlled or directed by the associates or affiliates; and

        (ii) name each associate or affiliate whose security holdings are 10 per cent or more.

§12.151.2 Section 7.2 requires a discussion of the background for each proposed director, including disclosure of information relating to any "cease trade or similar order" made with respect to any company for which that individual was acting as a director or executive officer at the time, or within a year of that individual's departure. Information must be similarly disclosed with respect to bankruptcy or insolvency, the denial of any exemption under securities legislation for a period of more than 30 consecutive days, any penalties or sanctions imposed and the grounds on which they were imposed by a court or regulatory body that would likely be considered important to a reasonable security-holder in deciding whether to vote for a proposed director. Where the information circular is being distributed in connection with is an annual general meeting at which the company's directors are to be elected, or at which the company's security-holders will be asked to vote on a matter relating to executive compensation, a completed Form 51-102F6 Statement of Executive Compensation must also be included, and also (where relevant) information relating to outstanding options, warrants and rights included as a form of compensation. Item 10 requires disclosure of a range of information relating to the indebtedness of directors and executive officers. Item 11 requires disclosure of information relating to certain material transactions. Item 13 requires a discussion any management contracts.

§12.151.3 It is only when one reaches item 14, that the information circular finally turns to a discussion of the particulars of matters that are to be acted upon at the meeting to which the information circular relates. Item 14.1 provides that:

- Where action is to be taken on any matter to be submitted to the meeting of security-holders other than the approval of financial statements, briefly describe the substance of the matter, or related groups of matters, except to the extent described under the foregoing items of the information circular, in sufficient detail to enable reasonable security-holders to form a reasoned judgment concerning the matter.

- Without limiting the generality of the foregoing, such matters include alterations of share capital, charter amendments, property acquisitions or dispositions, reverse takeovers, amalgamations, mergers, arrangements or reorganizations and other similar transactions.

Under item 14.2,[477] where the action to be taken is in respect of a significant acquisition as determined under Part 8 of National Instrument 51-102 under which securities of the acquired business are being exchanged for the company's securities, or in respect of a restructuring transaction under which securities are to be changed, exchanged, issued or distributed, it is necessary to include disclosure for:

(a) the company, if the company has not filed all documents required under National Instrument 51-102,

(b) the business being acquired, if the matter is a significant acquisition,

(c) each entity, other than the company, whose securities are being changed, exchanged, issued or distributed, if

 (i) the matter is a restructuring transaction, and

 (ii) the company's current security-holders will have an interest in that entity after the restructuring transaction is completed, and

---

[477] By virtue of item 14.4, section 14.2 does not apply in most cases to an information circular that is sent to holders of voting securities of a reporting issuer soliciting proxies otherwise than on behalf of management of the reporting issuer (a "dissident circular").

(d) each entity that would result from the significant acquisition or restructuring transaction, if the company's security-holders will have an interest in that entity after the significant acquisition or restructuring transaction is completed.

The disclosure provided must be the kind of disclosure prescribed by the form of prospectus (including financial statements), other than a short form prospectus under National Instrument 44-101 *Short Form Prospectus Distributions*, that the entity would be eligible to use for a distribution of securities in the jurisdiction. If the matter is one that is not required to be submitted to a vote of security-holders, it is necessary to provide the reasons for submitting it to security-holders and state what action management intends to take in the event of a negative vote by the security-holders.

§12.151.4 The *Securities Act* does create certain exemptions to the information circular requirement. Specifically, subsection 82(2) of the Act provides that the requirement for the delivery of an information circular imposed under subsection 86(1) does not apply to:

(a) any solicitation, otherwise than by or on behalf of the management of a reporting issuer, where the total number of security holders whose proxies are solicited is not more than fifteen, two or more persons or companies who are the joint registered owners of one or more securities being counted as one security holder;

(a.1) any solicitation, otherwise than by or on behalf of the management of a reporting issuer, in such other circumstances as may be prescribed in the regulations;

(b) any solicitation by a person or company made under section 49; or

(c) any solicitation by a person or company in respect of securities of which he, she or it is the beneficial owner.

The most important of the above exemptions is the *de minimis* exemption set out in clause (a).

§12.151.5 Section 9.3 of NI 51-102 provides that a person required under that Instrument to send an information circular or form of proxy to registered security-holders of a reporting issuer must promptly file a copy of the information circular, form of proxy and all other material required to be sent by the person or company in connection with the meeting to which the information circular or form of proxy relates.

(C) Case Law Regarding Proxy Solicitation

§12.152 In *Re Dairy Corp. of Canada Ltd.*, Middleton J.A. seemed to suggest that any form of proxy that led the hand of a shareholder and that required some positive step by the shareholder to vote contrary to the scheme advanced by the person soliciting the proxy was necessarily bad.[478] A similar view was expressed

---

[478] [1934] O.J. No. 147, [1934] O.R. 436 at 441 (S.C.), *per* Middleton J.A.; *Value Investment Corp. v. Caldwell Gundy Inc.*, [1989] B.C.J. No. 1680, 44 B.L.R. 142 (S.C.).

by Roach J. in *Re National Grocers Co.*[479] But in other cases the courts have taken a less extreme position.[480] Despite these differing views, the case law can be reconciled if it is limited to the general principle that all forms of proxy must be impartial and must not be drafted in such terms as may influence the result of the meeting.

§12.153 It follows that a form of proxy distributed with an information circular must permit shareholders to exercise choice.[481] A corporation may not provide in its by-laws that proxies shall be irrevocable.[482] A shareholder is entitled to appoint whomever the shareholder may wish as proxy.[483] If the shareholder strikes out the name of a management designee on a proxy and appoints a different person, that person has the full authority to vote in his or her discretion on any matter that comes before the meeting. The substitute proxy is not bound to vote for a slate of management designees for directors.[484] Where a shareholder appoints a proxy but then attends the meeting in person, the shareholder may revoke the proxy and participate personally, for the right of personal participation is paramount[485] and the grant of a proxy implicitly reserves the right of revocation.[486]

§12.154 Subsection 110(2) of the OBCA provides that a proxy must be executed in writing. In the documentary context, the verb "to execute" means to complete, to make or to sign.[487] A person's signature normally will take the form of the writing of the person's name or mark or a mark to represent his or her name, at a place sufficient to demonstrate an intention to authenticate the document

---

[479] [1938] O.J. No. 415, [1938] 3 D.L.R. 106 at 112 (H.C.J.).
[480] *Re Langley's Ltd.*, [1938] O.J. No. 414, [1938] 3 D.L.R. 230 at 243 (C.A.); *Garvie v. Axmith*, [1961] O.J. No. 616, [1962] O.R. 65 at 77 (H.C.J.), per Spence J.
[481] *Goldhar v. D'Aragon Mines Ltd.*, [1977] O.J. No. 2153, 15 O.R. (2d) 80 at 82-83 (H.C.J.), per R.E. Holland J.; but compare *Garvie v. Axmith*, [1961] O.J. No. 616, [1962] O.R. 65 (H.C.J.).
[482] *Nadeau v. Nadeau & Nadeau Ltd.*, [1972] N.B.J. No. 178, 6 N.B.R. (2d) 512 (Q.B.).
[483] *Stephenson v. Vokes*, [1896] O.J. No. 191, 27 O.R. 691 at 696 (H.C.J.), per Street J. Prior to the approval of a share transfer, a transferee may be made the proxy of the transferor of the shares in question: *Taylor v. Borger* (1964), 44 D.L.R. (2d) 605 (Alta. C.A.). So may a non-shareholder: *Colonial Assurance Co. v. Smith* (1912), 2 W.W.R. 699 at 703 (Man. K.B.), per Mathers C.J.K.B.
[484] *Canadian Express Ltd. v. Blair*, [1989] O.J. No. 1619, 46 B.L.R. 92 (H.C.J.), appeal quashed [1991] O.J. No. 2176 (Div. Ct.).
[485] But as Roach J. stated in *Re National Grocers Co.*, [1938] O.J. No. 415, [1938] O.R. 106 at 150 (H.C.J.):

> ... it is common knowledge that very often unthinking shareholders more or less automatically sign these forms ... and therefore the vote recorded under such a proxy cannot always be considered as reflecting the considered opinion of the absent shareholder.

[486] *Mercator Enterprises Ltd. v. Harris*, [1978] N.S.J. No. 660, 29 N.S.R. (2d) 691, 45 A.P.R. 691 (C.A.); *Nadeau v. Nadeau & Nadeau Ltd.*, [1972] N.B.J. No. 178, 6 N.B.R. (2d) 512 (Q.B.). But an irrevocable proxy purchased for consideration may be valid: *Milligan v. Bergman*, [1978] B.C.J. No. 42, 7 B.C.L.R. 103 (S.C.).
[487] *Black's Law Dictionary*, 6th ed. (St. Paul: West, 1990).

concerned.[488] In certain cases (*e.g.*, where an administrative or judicial officer is expected to exercise control over the issue of a certain document), a rubber stamp signature affixed to a blank form will not constitute a signature.[489] The purpose of the signature is to give a personal authentication to a document to imply knowledge and approval of its contents. The document is signed where it is marked in a way that provides that level of authentication, and, when such authentication is evident, the manner of marking the document is not particularly relevant. So, once the contents of the document are complete, or where the party executing the document intends to confer an authority on the holder to complete the details, a rubber stamp signature or other facsimile is adequate.[490] In the case of proxies, a liberal interpretation is given to the signature requirement. Thus, it has been held that a printed form of proxy bearing a mechanically produced signature is sufficient to constitute a signed proxy.[491]

§12.155 Chief among the proxy solicitation requirements imposed upon reporting issuers are the obligations with regard to information circulars. Under clause 85(1)(*a*) of the *Securities Act* a prohibition is placed on the solicitation of proxies by any person or company from holders of its voting securities whose latest address, as shown on the books of that person or company, is in Ontario unless in the case of a solicitation by or on behalf of management an information circular is sent by prepaid mail to each security holder of the reporting issuer whose proxy is solicited at his or her address as shown on the books of the reporting issuer. Two obligations are thus imposed upon management: first, to solicit proxies; second, to distribute an information circular. The information circular need not be a separate document: it is sufficient if it is attached as an appendix to the notice of the meeting.

(3) Exemptions From the Securities Act Proxy Requirements

§12.156 Although in general it is necessary for a reporting issuer to comply with both the proxy solicitation and information circular requirements, Part XIX of the *Securities Act* also contemplates certain exceptions from these general requirements. As noted earlier, clause 86(2)(*a*) provides that the information circular requirement does not apply to:

(*a*) any solicitation, otherwise than by or on behalf of the management of a reporting issuer, where the total number of security holders whose proxies are solicited is not more than fifteen, two or more persons or companies who are the joint registered owners of one or more securities being counted as one security holder;

Presumably, the belief is that in any such small solicitation, word of mouth communication will likely take place in support of the solicitation and will be

---

[488] *Canada v. Fredericton Housing Ltd.*, [1973] F.C.J. No. 26, [1973] C.T.C. 160 (T.D.); *Grondin v. Tisi & Turner* (1912), 4 D.L.R. 819 (Que. S.C.).
[489] *R. v. Zwicker*, [1980] N.S.J. No. 387, 5 M.V.R. 283, 53 C.C.C. (2d) 239 (C.A.).
[490] *Goodman v. J. Eban Ltd.*, [1954] 1 Q.B. 550 at 557 (C.A.), *per* Lord Evershed M.R.
[491] *Re United Canso Oil & Gas Ltd.*, [1980] N.S.J. No. 33, 12 B.L.R. 130 at 136-37, 41 N.S.R. (2d) 282 (T.D.), *per* Hallett J.

more effective than compliance with the proxy solicitation provisions. Furthermore, such a limited proxy solicitation may be viewed as a private matter among a limited number of shareholders and, therefore, beyond the scope of concern of securities legislation.

§12.157 A second exemption from the proxy solicitation requirement is given by clause 86(2)(*b*), which provides that no proxy solicitation is required in the case of "any solicitation by a person or company made under section 49" of the *Securities Act*. Section 49 deals with the voting of shares held in the name of a registrant, custodian or the nominee of either where the registrant or custodian, as the case may be, is not the beneficial owner of the shares.[492] The proxy solicitation referred to in clause (*b*) is that which is contemplated under subsections 49(4) and (5) of the *Securities Act*. Subsection 49(4) provides that a registrant or custodian shall vote or give a proxy requiring a nominee to vote any voting securities referred to in subsection 49(1) in accordance with any written voting instructions received from the beneficial owner. Subsection 49(5) requires a registrant or custodian to give to the beneficial owner or to his or her nominee a proxy enabling the beneficial owner or his or her nominee to vote any voting securities referred to in subsection 49(1), if so requested in writing by a beneficial owner.

§12.158 A third exemption from the information circular requirement is set out in clause 86(2)(*c*), which provides that an information circular is not required in the case of,

(*c*) any solicitation by a person or company in respect of securities of which he, she or it is the beneficial owner.

This exemption would apply where the securities are held in the name of a registrant, trustee, agent or similar person, and the beneficial owner solicits proxies from the registered holders of those securities, so that he or she may attend and vote personally at the meeting in question.

§12.159 The exemptions given under subsection 86(2) are limited in scope. Broader exemptions are contemplated under section 88 of the *Securities Act*. In particular, subsection 88(1) of the Act goes on to exempt reporting issuers from compliance with Part XVIII, provided they comply with requirements under the law of their incorporating jurisdiction that are "substantially similar to the requirements" of Part XIX. Moreover, subsection 88(2) of the Act provides:

---

[492] Subsection 49(1) of the *Securities Act* provides:

49.(1) Subject to subsection (4), voting securities of an issuer registered in the name of

(*a*) a registrant or in the name of the registrant's nominee; or

(*b*) a custodian or in the name of the custodian's nominee, where such issuer is a mutual fund that is a reporting issuer,

that are not beneficially owned by the registrant or the custodian, as the case may be, shall not be voted by the registrant or custodian at any meeting of security holders of the issuer.

88.(2) Subject to subsection (1), upon the application of any interested person or company, the Commission may,

(a) if a requirement of this Part conflicts with a requirement of the laws of the jurisdiction under which the reporting issuer is incorporated, organized or continued; or

(b) if otherwise satisfied in the circumstances of the particular case that there is adequate justification for so doing,

make an order on such terms and conditions as the Commission may impose, exempting, in whole or in part, a person or company from the requirements of this Part and of section 81.

(4) Proxy Fights

§12.160 A proxy contest or proxy fight is a struggle for control, almost always within an offering corporation, in which the combatants are the existing management group of directors within the corporation and a non-management group, who are often called the insurgents. The object of each group is to gain control of sufficient proxies to elect a majority of the board of directors and thereby secure control of the corporation.[493] The contest has been likened to a card game in which all the trump cards are held by one side: the management. Management has control over the current list of shareholders and has ready access to it, while the insurgents may be able to obtain it only by going to court. Management also may finance its defence by tapping into the corporation's bank account. Many of the shareholders are likely to be indifferent to the squabble. Many may have a pro-management bias, because it is common for shareholders who are dissatisfied with management performance to sell their shares and, therefore, most of the shareholders who remain will be those who are satisfied with existing management. Given these factors, proxy fights rarely result in victory for the insurgents. The best chance of success for insurgents engaged in a proxy fight will be in a case involving a small- to medium-sized company having a poor earnings history (so the level of dissatisfaction will be high) and a poor secondary market for its shares (so dissatisfied shareholders are trapped within it).

§12.161 Although management will often make use of corporate funds to finance their side of the contest, their right to do so is not unlimited.[494] A distinction has been drawn in some cases between a dispute over control of the board and a dispute over corporate policy. In *Lawyers' Advertising Co. v. Consolidated Railway, Lighting & Refrigeration Co.*[495] the court said that the costs of advertising on behalf of the management faction were not expenses that could properly be met from corporate funds. However, under section 111 of the

---

[493] See, generally, *D'Addario v. Environmental Management Solutions Inc.*, [2005] O.J. No. 3008, 8 B.L.R. (4th) 236 (S.C.J.).
[494] See, generally, *Peel v. London & N.W. Rlwy. Co.*, [1907] 1 Ch. 5 (C.A.); *Advance Bank of Australia Ltd. v. FAI Insurance Australia Ltd.* (1987), 9 N.S.W.L.R. 464 at 487 (C.A.), *per* Kirby P.
[495] 187 N.Y. 395, 80 N.E. 199 at 200 (C.A.).

OBCA[496] the management of an offering corporation is obliged to solicit proxies and under subsection 112(1) it is obliged to distribute a management information circular at the time of so doing.[497] Obviously, the costs of meeting these obligations may be properly charged to the corporation.[498] Moreover, greater freedom to draw on the funds of the corporation exists in the case of policy-related disputes. In *Rosenfeld v. Fairchild Engine & Airplane Corp.*,[499] a shareholder's derivative action was brought demanding reimbursement of amounts paid by the corporation in defraying proxy-related expenses. The action was dismissed. It was held that when the directors act in good faith in a contest over policy, they have the right to incur reasonable and proper expenses for solicitation of proxies and in defence of their corporate policies. They are not obliged to sit idly by, though it is not permissible for them to use corporate funds for personal power, individual gain or private advantage.

(5) Fiduciary Obligations of Proxy Holder

§12.162 A director who holds a proxy on behalf of a shareholder is not acting in the capacity of a director in the exercise of that proxy, and therefore is not required to exercise that proxy in the best interests of the corporation. Instead, a director who accepts appointment as a proxy will have the fiduciary duties of an agent towards the shareholder who made the appointment as principal. If the shareholder directs the proxy/director to vote in a way that the director believes is not in the interests of the corporation, the director will generally, as the member's fiduciary, be obliged to vote in that way.[500]

(v) Vote Withholding

§12.163 One practice that has begun to emerge among widely held corporations (particularly those listed on a stock exchange) is that of allowing shareholders to withhold their vote from the election of individual directors, and even the entire management slate. Such a withholding constitutes an alternative to casting a vote for another candidate — which so often proves an unrealistic option, because there is no such candidate standing. Under a typical vote-withholding system, at each meeting at which directors are subject to an uncontested election, any nominee for director who receives a greater number of votes "withheld" from his or her election than are voted "for" such election will be required to submit a letter of resignation for consideration by the corporation's nominating committee. In its turn, the committee is then required to recommend to the board the action that should be taken with respect to the director concerned. The board is then required to act promptly with respect to that recommendation, and then promptly notify the director concerned of its decision.

---

[496] CBCA, s. 149(1).
[497] CBCA, s. 150(1).
[498] See also OBCA, s. 99(2) and (3) and CBCA, s. 137.
[499] 309 N.Y. 168, 128 N.E. 291 (C.A. 1955).
[500] *Whitlam v. Australian Securities and Investment Commission*, [2003] N.S.W.C.A. 183.

§12.164 The authority for such an arrangement is not entirely clear. It is not provided for in section 119 of the OBCA. However the proposal procedure set out in section 99 and the director removal rights under section 122 of the OBCA[501] may provide a sufficient basis. Where a corporation wishes to afford such a right to its shareholders, it would be advisable to build it either into the by-laws of the corporation or its articles.

(vi) Minutes of Shareholders' Meetings

(1) Generally

§12.165 Every corporation is required to prepare and maintain (either at its registered office or at such other place in Ontario as may be designated by its directors) formal minutes of the meetings and resolutions of its shareholders.[502] The corporation's minutes are not conclusive evidence of what transpired at the meeting, and therefore other evidence may be introduced to establish what actually transpired,[503] even where it is inconsistent with the minutes actually recorded and approved.[504] Simply stated, the parol evidence rule does not apply to corporate minutes.[505]

§12.165.1 Currently, under section 11.3 of NI 51-102, non-venture issuers that conduct a vote by ballot are required to report the number or percentage of votes cast for, against or withheld from the vote. For a vote that is not conducted by ballot (*i.e.*, it is conducted by a show of hands), issuers are required to disclose only a description of the matter voted upon and the outcome of the vote, and not the results of the voting instructions contained in the proxies submitted to the issuer prior to the meeting.

(2) Deficiencies in the Corporate Records and the Practice of Cooperizing

§12.166 Frequently when preparing a legal opinion with respect to the current status of a corporation, it will be determined that there are deficiencies in the record of corporate affairs as set out in the minute book of the corporation. For instance, there may be no evidence that an annual meeting was held in a given year, or the minutes of such a meeting may not record that all business required to be conducted at the meeting did in fact take place. Similarly (in the case of private companies), there may be deficiencies in the documentary record regarding the approval of the transfer of shares from one shareholder to another

---

[501] *Cf.* ss. 109 and 137 of the CBCA.
[502] OBCA, s. 140(1)(*b*); CBCA, s. 20(1)(*b*).
[503] *Classic Hosiery Co. v. Fillis*, [1920] O.J. No. 362, 18 O.W.N. 17 at 18 (H.C.D.), *per* Logie J.; see also *Re Pyle Works*, [1891] 1 Ch. 173 at 184, *per* Stirling J.
[504] *Kerr v. John Mottram Ltd.*, [1940] Ch. 657 at 659, *per* Simonds J. In that case the company's articles of association (generally equivalent to the by-laws of a corporation) provided that the minutes were "conclusive" evidence. In light of that provision, Simonds J. was prepared to allow examination to determine whether the minutes were a good faith record of what had transpired, but he would not permit any further inquiry (at 660).
[505] *Hood v. Eden*, [1905] S.C.J. No. 51, 36 S.C.R. 476 at 487, *per* Sedgewick J.

over the life of the corporation. These deficiencies may be sufficient to raise doubts as to whether the transaction has been duly authorized.

§12.167 The absence of proper minutes for the corporation has an obvious adverse impact upon any effort to confirm whether the required procedures of director and shareholder approval were ever followed with respect to purported acts of the corporation, including the enactment of by-laws and amendments to the articles. If it cannot be shown, for instance, that a by-law was duly enacted, and it also cannot be shown that the by-laws were followed if they were duly enacted, then there is no basis on which to conclude that a transaction has been duly authorized. For instance, without a valid by-law certain in its terms, one cannot conclude whether elections of directors and the admission of new members were carried out correctly. If the records of such elections and admission are also missing, then the entire basis of the corporation as a functioning legal entity could be compromised. In *Re 816682 Ontario Inc.*,[506] Macdonald J. held that where the corporate documents of a corporation are incomplete, backdated, and invalid, and the corporation cannot be proven to have been properly organized, the transactions that it has purported to enter into are of no legal effect. She stated:

> While it may appear trite to observe that incorporation is a privilege, it remains as one of the fundamental tenets of the law of incorporation and the formalities of incorporation must be followed. The irregularities or illegalities are not merely technical in this case. The result is that Messrs. Picano and Oliveira are not, and have never, been directors of the bankrupt. The documents show that they were not incorporators, nor first directors, nor were they issued shares by the first director. They were not elected directors by the shareholders.

§12.168 At least in Ontario, there is a widespread practice among corporate lawyers to remedy minor deficiencies in a corporate record through a process known as "Cooperization", in which *pro forma* documents are created to evidence events that it is assumed must have taken place (*e.g.*, the approval of the transfer of shares, the holding of a meeting to approve a by-law, *etc.*) in light of subsequent documents or transactions.

§12.169 The legal authority for the Cooperization process appears to be little more than the legal maxim *omnia praesemuntur rita esse act* (all acts are presumed to have been done rightly and regularly). There is authority to the effect that compliance with a statutory formality may be presumed after a lengthy lapse in time.[507] The *omnia praesemuntur* rule is essentially a presumption of fact with respect to the regularity of the process followed, that is drawn in the absence of evidence to the contrary. For instance, there is a presumption that persons acting as public officers or in public capacities have been regularly and

---

[506] [1993] O.J. No. 3143 at para. 15, 44 A.C.W.S. (3d) 857 (Gen. Div.).
[507] *Aukland Gas Co. v. Point Chevalier Road Board* (1909), 29 N.Z.L.R. 417; *Clippens Oil Co. v. Edinburgh & District Water Trustees*, [1904] A.C. 64; *Waiakei Ltd. v. Cleave*, [1925] N.Z.L.R. 624.

properly appointed.[508] There is no particular reason, however, to limit the application maxim to public officers. In *Harris v. Knight* Lindley L.J. said:

> The maxim *omnia praesumuntur rite esse acta* is an expression, in a short form, of a reasonable probability, and of the propriety and point of law of acting on such probability. The maxim expresses an inference which may reasonably be drawn when an intention to do some formal act is established; when the evidence is consistent with that intention having been carried into effect in a proper way; but when the actual observance of all due formalities can only be inferred as a matter of probability. The maxim is not warranted where such observance is proved, nor has it any place where such observance is disproved.[509]

§12.170 In *Gibson v. Doeg*,[510] Pollock C.B. also commented on the general scope of the presumption. He stated:

> It is a maxim of the law of England to give effect to everything which appears to have been established for a considerable course of time, and to presume that what has been done was done of right, and not in wrong.

In general terms, the maxim is subject to a number of important qualifications:

- the maxim should be used with care;
- the fact being inferred under the doctrine must be one that is not essential to a party's case, but rather is one that is collateral or related to a procedural question or matter of form;
- the maxim may not be used where such evidence as does exist is inconsistent with regularity.

An unstated assumption which runs throughout the case law is that the maxim should not be invoked where the probability of regularity seems low.

§12.171 Invoking the presumption of regularity seems perfectly sound where there is a minor gap in the record. Where it can be shown that nearly all of the business and affairs of a corporation have been conducted in a regular manner, the regularity of all such matters may seem a reasonable inference even when it cannot be proven with respect to one or two minor matters. However, the presumption becomes progressively less credible as the breadth and number of such gaps increases. When dealing with significant and wide ranging gaps in a corporate history, any effort to "Cooperize" a solution would not amount to filling in details in an otherwise complete corporate history. It would amount to inventing that history.

(vii) Right to Inspect Shareholder Register

§12.172 Subsection 146(1) of the OBCA provides that shareholders and creditors of a corporation, their agents and legal representatives and, where the corporation

---

[508] See *Berryman v. Wise* (1791), 4 T.R. 366.
[509] (1890), 15 P.D. 170 at 179 (C.A.).
[510] (1857), 2 H. & N. 615, 157 E.R. 253 at 623.

is an offering corporation, any other person, upon payment of a reasonable fee and upon sending to the corporation or its transfer agent the statutory declaration referred to in subsection 146(6),[511] may require the corporation or its transfer agent to furnish a basic list setting out the names of the shareholders of the corporation, the number of shares of each class and series owned by each shareholder and the address of each shareholder, all as shown on the records of the corporation.[512] The list must be furnished to the applicant as soon as is practicable and must be as current as practicable.[513] Supplemental lists may also be obtained.[514] In the United States, there has been considerable litigation about whether shareholders have an absolute right (comparable to that of directors) to obtain such a list.[515] As the court noted in *Rogers v. Colvert*, the objective of the provision is to facilitate corporate governance, and this object would be defeated if the right of access was unfuly limited. Under the OBCA and the CBCA, the right to obtain a list is to all intents and purposes absolute as long as the required statutory declaration is provided. Shareholders and creditors of the corporation, their agents and legal representatives may also examine:

- the articles and the by-laws and all amendments thereto, and a copy of any unanimous shareholder agreement known to the directors;

- minutes of meetings and resolutions of shareholders;

- a register of directors in which are set out the names and residence addresses, while directors, including the street and number if any, of all persons who are or have been directors of the corporation with the several dates on which each became or ceased to be a director; and

- all securities registers of the corporation in a form complying with subsection 141(1) of the OBCA.[516]

Any such examination may be conducted during the usual business hours of the corporation, and the person examining the documents may take extracts therefrom,

---

[511] The statutory declaration must state:

    (*a*) the name and address including the street and number, if any, of the applicant and whether the applicant is a shareholder, creditor or any other person referred to in the subsection;

    (*b*) the name and address including the street and number, if any, for service of the body corporate if the applicant is a body corporate; and

    (*c*) that the basic list and supplemental lists shall be used only as permitted under subsection (8).

On a date to be fixed by proclamation, the word "shareholder" in clause (a) will be replaced by "registered holder, beneficial holder". S.O. 2006, c. 34, Sched. B, ss. 28(3) and 42(1).

Clause (*c*) is given a narrow interpretation: *Rogers v. Colvert*, [2004] O.J. No. 3653, 49 B.L.R. (3d) 53 (S.C.J.).

[512] CBCA, s. 21(3).
[513] OBCA, s. 146(2); CBCA, s. 21(3).
[514] OBCA, s. 146(3) (am. 2006, c. 34, Sch. B, s. 28(2) in force Aug. 1/07); CBCA, s. 21(4).
[515] See, for instance, *State, ex rel. Pillsbury v. Honeywell, Inc.*, 291 Minn. 322, 191 N.W.2d 406 (S.C. 1971); *Chas A. Day & Co. v. Booth*, 123 Maine 443, 123 A. 557 (1924); *Sawers v. American Phenolic Corp.*, 404 Ill. 440, 89 N.E.2d 374 (1949).
[516] CBCA, s. 50(1).

free of charge. Where the corporation is an offering corporation, any other person may also inspect those records on payment of a reasonable fee.[517] There is no right given to shareholders or creditors to inspect the accounting or other general business records of the corporation or the minutes or resolutions of directors.

§12.173 Section 147 of the OBCA provides no person may offer for sale, sell or purchase or otherwise traffic in any list of the holders of securities or warrants of a corporation. There is no comparable prohibition under the CBCA.

(viii) Application to Court to Restrain or Set Aside Meeting

§12.174 Where the meeting process is tainted in some way (*e.g.*, a deficiency of notice or a failure to comply properly with proxy requirements) an application may be made: (i) to prevent the meeting taking place, or to delay it; (ii) to prevent a person from voting at the meeting; or (iii) after the meeting is held, to set aside the decision made at the meeting. In deciding whether to restrain the meeting, the court may consider the behaviour of the applicant, the applicant's apparent good faith, the behaviour and apparent good faith of the board or other control group within the corporation, the potential prejudice resulting from any proposed delay, and also the benefit that a delay would afford.[518] Generally, a strong case is required to justify interference with the internal affairs of a corporation.[519] As suggested earlier in the chapter, in deciding whether to make an order with respect to a meeting, a court should consider whether the party seeking the order has suffered or will suffer real and substantial prejudice.[520]

§12.175 It has long been accepted that where a vote taken at a meeting is rigged by trick or artifice the vote is invalid.[521] Whether a court possessed an inherent power to set aside an election of directors on some ground other than the fraudulent nature of the vote was considered by McGillivray J.A. in *Watt v. Commonwealth Petroleum Ltd.*[522] In that case it was found that the annual statement the corporation was required to distribute was not mailed to all shareholders 14 days prior to the meeting as required, and that one of the directors elected at the meeting acted as scrutineer. It was further found that certain votes should not have been recorded. The Alberta Court of Appeal held that the action to set the election aside should be dismissed. The statutory requirements for the mailing of

---

[517] See OBCA, ss. 145(1) and 140(1); CBCA, ss. 21(1) and 20(1). See, generally, *Encana Corp. v. Douglas*, [2005] A.J. No. 1744 (C.A.).
[518] See, generally, *Proprietary Industries Inc. v. eDispatch.com Wireless Data*, [2001] B.C.J. No. 2927, 30 B.L.R. (3d) 87 (S.C.); *Golden Star v. IAM-Gold Corp.*, [2004] O.J. No. 2869, 49 B.L.R. (3d) 36 (S.C.J.).
[519] *Transmountain Pipeline Co. v. Inland Natural Gas*, [1983] B.C.J. No. 1622, 49 B.C.L.R. 126 (C.A.), affg [1983] B.C.J. No. 1720, 43 B.C.L.R. 396 (S.C.).
[520] *NMRA Insurance Group Ltd. v. Spragg*, [2001] N.S.W.S.C. 381, *per* Santow J.
[521] *Toronto Brewing & Malting Co. v. Blake*, [1882] O.J. No. 75, 2 O.R. 175 (H.C.J.); see also *Gething v. Kilner*, [1972] 1 W.L.R. 337 at 341, *per* Brightman J.; *Goldex Mines Ltd. v. Revill*, [1974] O.J. No. 2245, 54 D.L.R. (3d) 672 (C.A.).
[522] [1938] 3 W.W.R. 696 (Alta. C.A.).

the annual statement did not pertain to the election of the directors. The other irregularities were also insufficient to justify setting the election aside.[523]

§12.176 This narrow view must now be considered in light of subsections 107(1) of the OBCA and 145(1) of the CBCA, which permit a corporation, shareholder or director to apply to court to determine any controversy with regard to an election or appointment of a director or auditor of a corporation. Where such an application is made the court may make such order that it thinks fit in the circumstances.[524] Among the various types of order expressly mentioned by the Act in such a case are an order restraining a director or auditor whose election or appointment is challenged from acting pending determination of the dispute.[525] An order may also be made declaring the result of a disputed election or appointment[526] or requiring a new election or appointment and including in the order directions for the management of the business and affairs of the corporation until a new election is held or appointment made.[527] Finally, the court may also make an order determining the voting rights of shareholders and of persons claiming to own its shares.[528]

§12.177 No corresponding provision is found in either Act that expressly allows a court to review decisions made or resolutions adopted at other disputed meetings of a corporation other than with regard to the election of directors. However, it seems probable that a court would be prepared to assume such a power,[529] where there were reasons to believe that unauthorized persons had been allowed to vote or that a shareholders' meeting was otherwise misconducted, at least where the resolution involves fraud or exceeds the powers of the corporation.[530] Moreover, the oppression remedy might also be invoked in such a case.

F. RESOLUTIONS

(i) As an Alternative to Meetings

§12.178 As noted above, in the case of corporations with few shareholders, it is frequently more practical to dispense with shareholders' meetings and to rely instead upon a written resolution signed by all of the shareholders. Also noted

---

[523] *Ibid., per* McGillivray J.A. at 702-03.
[524] OBCA, s. 107(2); CBCA, s. 145(2). See, for instance, *Armstrong v. McGibbon* (1906), 15 Que. K.B. 345 (C.A.), where the court was prepared to declare an election of directors invalid when it was rammed through in short order for the sole purpose of preventing a shareholder who was momentarily out of the room from participating in the election.
[525] OBCA, s. 107(2)(*a*); CBCA, s. 145(2)(*a*).
[526] OBCA, s. 107(2)(*b*); CBCA, s. 145(2)(*b*).
[527] OBCA, s. 107(2)(*c*); CBCA, s. 145(2)(*c*).
[528] OBCA, s. 107(2)(*d*); CBCA, s. 145(2)(*d*).
[529] See, for instance, *Regehr v. Ketzakey Silver Mines Ltd.*, [1970] A.J. No. 14, 10 D.L.R. (3d) 171 (C.A.); *Ho v. Providence Health Care Society*, [2004] B.C.J. No. 2254, 1 B.L.R. (4th) 234 (S.C.).
[530] *Watson v. Barrett*, [1929] B.C.J. No. 102, 41 B.C.R. 478 (S.C.).

above, at common law, a shareholders' resolution approved even by an overwhelming majority of shareholders in the absence of a meeting was not an effective substitute for a meeting.[531] Some cases went so far as to suggest that even a unanimous shareholder resolution would be insufficient.[532] Although the precise reason for such caution was not clearly articulated, one possible rationale for it may have been a concern whether the individual assents of the shareholders given separately would have the effect of binding the company itself.[533]

§12.179 Fortunately, the law in this regard has now been modified and clarified by statute: both the OBCA and the CBCA now provide for written and signed unanimous shareholder resolutions as an alternative to the formal meeting procedures. More specifically, subsection 104(1) of the OBCA provides that

> 104.(1) Except where a written statement is submitted by a director under subsection 123(2), or where representations in writing are submitted by an auditor under subsection 149(6),
>
> (a) a resolution in writing signed by all the shareholders entitled to vote on that resolution at a meeting of shareholders is as valid as if it had been passed at a meeting of the shareholders; and
>
> (b) a resolution dealing with all matters required by this Act to be dealt with at a meeting of shareholders, and signed by all the shareholders or their attorney authorized in writing entitled to vote at that meeting, satisfies all the requirements of this Act relating to that meeting of shareholders.

Subsection 142(1) of the CBCA is to the same effect. A copy of every such resolution must be kept with the minutes of the meetings of shareholders.[534] By implication, any signed shareholder resolution that falls short of the unanimity requirement is insufficient. The practical benefit of a rule to the effect that a resolution signed by the holders of 99 out of 100 shares is ineffective as a substitute for a meeting reflects the general proposition that the minority members of a corporation are entitled to a meeting by law in which they may seek to convince the majority of the error of its ways — distant as the prospect of such success may seem.

§12.180 Despite the general authority to substitute a unanimous written resolution for a resolution adopted at a meeting, there are certain situations in which an actual meeting is required. In particular, written resolutions are not permitted in lieu of a meeting where a director submits a written statement explaining why he or she has resigned or why that director opposes his or her removal from office or the

---

[531] *Re Newman & Co.*, [1895] 1 Ch. 674 (C.A.); *Bartlett v. Bartlett Mines Ltd.*, [1911] O.J. No. 84, 24 O.L.R. 419 (C.A.).

[532] See, for instance, *Re Queen City Plate Glass Co.*, [1910] O.J. No. 235, 1 O.W.N. 863 (H.C.J.); see also *Re Neil M'Leod & Sons Ltd.*, [1967] S.C. 16 at 21 (C.S.), per Clyde L.P.; *Sharp v. Dawes* (1876), 2 Q.B.D. 26 (C.A.), per Mellish L.J.

[533] *Trustees of Gray & Farr Ltd. v. Carlile*, [1931] 3 D.L.R. 785 (Alta. T.D.), aff'd (1931), 13 C.B.R. 229 (Alta. C.A.); *Bartlett v. Bartlett Mines Ltd.*, [1911] O.J. No. 84, 24 O.L.R. 419 (C.A.).

[534] OBCA, s. 104(2); CBCA, s. 145(2).

appointment or election of a person to fill the office of director.[535] The corporation is required to distribute "a copy of the statement to every shareholder entitled to receive notice of meetings of shareholders, unless the statement is included in or attached to a management information circular required by section 112".[536] Moreover, written resolutions are not permitted in lieu of a meeting where the auditor of a corporation seeks to make a written representation concerning the auditor's proposed removal as auditor, the appointment or election of another person to fill the office of auditor or the auditor's resignation.[537] The corporation must forward a copy of that statement with the notice of meeting to every shareholder entitled to receive notice of the meeting.[538] The apparent intent in such a case is to ensure that information is placed before the shareholders before they adopt a proposed resolution or otherwise act collectively.

§12.181 The OBCA[539] now expressly permit a shareholders' meeting to be conducted through the medium of telephones or similar communications technology.[540] In *Re Associated Color Laboratories Ltd.*[541] it was held that a meeting conducted by telephone is not a properly conducted meeting. The court reasoned that it is an essential feature of a meeting that people are together in one place where they can observe each other's demeanour and their reactions to what is said.[542] Although this view has been supported by some academics and other courts,[543] it is difficult to follow the logic of the court's argument, particularly in the case of a corporation whose directors make up the full complement of its shareholders. If the *Associated Color* decision still remains the law, the effect would be that the directors of a corporation who comprise all of its shareholders would be able to meet by telephone as directors, but would have to meet together as individuals if they were to vote as shareholders. Such an arbitrary result is impossible to justify.[544] The modern economy is increasingly global in

---

[535] OBCA, s. 123(2); CBCA, s. 110(2).
[536] OBCA, s. 123(3); CBCA, s. 110(3).
[537] OBCA, s. 149(6); CBCA, s. 168(5).
[538] OBCA, *ibid.*; CBCA, s. 168(6).
[539] Similarly, subsection 132(4) of the CBCA now provides:

> 132.(4) Unless the by-laws otherwise provide, any person entitled to attend a meeting of shareholders may participate in the meeting, in accordance with the regulations, if any, by means of a telephonic, electronic or other communication facility that permits all participants to communicate adequately with each other during the meeting, if the corporation makes available such a communication facility. A person participating in a meeting by such means is deemed for the purposes of this Act to be present at the meeting.

[540] OBCA, s. 94(2).
[541] [1970] B.C.J. No. 89, 12 D.L.R. (3d) 338 (S.C.).
[542] In *Byng v. London Life Association Ltd.*, [1990] Ch. 170 (C.A.), Browne-Wilkinson V.-C. expressed the view that the underlying reason for requiring a corporation to hold meetings is so that its members shall be able to debate among themselves and vote upon matters that are to be decided.
[543] *Higgins v. Nicol* (1971), 18 F.L.R. 343, per Joske J. at 357; *Magnacrete Ltd. v. Douglas-Hill* (1988), 15 A.C.L.R. 325, 48 S.A.S.R. 567.
[544] In *Re GIGA Investments Pty. Ltd.* (1995), 17 A.C.L.R. 472 (F.C. Aust.), it was held that a meeting can be held via telephone or teleconference.

scope. In such an environment, it is not realistic for the courts to cling to outdated notions, such as that of a face-to-face meeting involving protracted debate.

(ii) Discretionary Authority Conferred

§12.182 It is customary for a resolution (whether in the form of a shareholder or a director resolution) to incorporate a provision allowing some discretion to corporate management to approve amendments, deletions, *etc.*, to any contract or other instrument to which the resolution relates. Care must be taken in drafting any such discretion, otherwise the approval apparently obtained by way of that resolution may be declared ineffective.[545] Although the issue does not seem to have yet been decided by the courts, it is reasonable to assume that the courts would give a narrow construction to any such provision. If a proposed amendment departs significantly from what was approved, fresh authorization should be obtained.

G. RIGHT TO RECEIVE AN ACCOUNTING

§12.183 The shareholders of a corporation are entitled to receive an accounting from the directors concerning the manner in which they have conducted the business and affairs of the corporation. The general rule is that such an accounting is provided at least annually, when the annual financial statements are distributed to the shareholders and presented to the annual meeting of the corporation.[546] In recent years, these rights have been reinforced in the case of reporting issuers under securities legislation through the introduction of progressively more onerous continuous disclosure obligations.[547]

§12.184 The statutory rights that a shareholder enjoys to inspect records of the corporation is a right vested in the shareholder personally, to be exercised independently of the consent of a corporation.[548] Where a corporation refuses to permit a shareholder to conduct such an inspection, the shareholder is entitled to obtain a court order requiring the corporation to keep open its securities register for inspection during the usual business hours of the corporation and to permit the shareholder to copy details in those records. The OBCA and CBCA contemplate an unconditional right to carry out an examination of the records of the corporation.[549]

§12.185 A shareholder's right to the information and material included in properly audited financial statements is a clear and mandatory statutory right, with which compliance is prescribed. That right is vested personally in each

---

[545] *Pace Savings and Credit Union v. CU Connection Ltd.*, [2000] O.J. No. 3830, 9 B.L.R. (3d) 266 (S.C.J.).
[546] CBCA, s. 155; OBCA, s. 154(1).
[547] See National Policy 51-102.
[548] See: *Cooper v. The Premier Trust Co.*, [1945] O.J. No. 483, [1945] O.R. 35 (C.A.).
[549] *Klianis v. Poole*, [1992] O.J. No. 1172 (Gen. Div.); *Schelew v. Moncton Family Outfitters, Ltd.*, [2004] N.B.J. No. 329 at para. 24 (Q.B.), *per* Glennie J.

shareholder.[550] A shareholder is not obliged to justify his or her insistence on the corporation complying with its obligation to provide such statements.[551] Moreover, the obligation of the corporation to comply with the disclosure requirements is not contingent upon any shareholder asserting the right to be provided with the information concerned. A shareholder cannot be obliged to pay the cost of providing such disclosure.[552] Lack of the financial resources to pay for an audit is no answer for failing to conduct one.[553] The delivery of unaudited financial statements does not meet the statutory obligation.[554]

H. CONSTRAINING DIRECTOR POWER

§12.186 In most, if not all, industrialized nations, the law relating to business companies has adopted a representative form of government for such companies, under which management is entrusted to an elected board of directors, that — to a greater or lesser degree — is elected by the shareholders of each company voting by the extent of their respective interests in the corporation rather than on a *per capita* basis. Under this representative form of government, the board is entrusted with the right and obligation to manage the business and affairs of the corporation, including the power to set the basic policies of the corporation and to select the officers and other staff who will carry out those policies. The shareholders have little direct say in the running of the corporation.

§12.187 Until the 1970s, there was a steady trend in the evolution of corporate law towards greater restriction upon the ability of the shareholders of a company to control the company that they owned. So great had the restrictions become that in many jurisdictions it was no longer possible for the shareholders of a company to initiate amendments to the by-laws or articles without prior director consent. The limited common law power of the shareholders to control the business and affairs of a company is indicated in the decision of the Nova Scotia Court of Appeal in *Cann v. Eakins*.[555] In that case certain resolutions were adopted at meetings of the shareholders of a company that ordered the purchase of certain property and the issue of bonds of the company to secure the payment of the purchase price and directed the president to execute the necessary documents. After this resolution was passed, the board of directors of the company met and decided by majority vote that it was inexpedient to carry out these resolutions. An interim injunction was sought restraining the president and the company from acting in accordance with the shareholder's resolution. Ritchie J. held that this was a proper case for an injunction preventing the company from carrying out the direction of the majority shareholders.[556]

---

[550] *Cooper v. The Premier Trust Co.*, [1945] O.J. No. 483, [1945] O.R. 35 (C.A.).
[551] *Klianis v. Poole*, [1992] O.J. No. 1172 (Gen. Div.).
[552] *Smith v. ECO Grouting Specialists Ltd.*, [2001] O.J. No. 2784 (S.C.).
[553] *Discovery Enterprises Inc. v. ISE Research Ltd.*, [2002] B.C.J. No. 2642, 29 B.L.R. (3d) 318 (S.C.).
[554] *Labatt Brewing Co. v. Trilon Holdings Inc.*, [1998] O.J. No. 3134, 41 O.R. (3d) 384 (Gen. Div.).
[555] (1891), 23 N.S.R. 475 (C.A.).
[556] *Ibid.*, at 479.

§12.188 As noted earlier in the chapter, in the pre-1975 case law considering the question of shareholder control, the courts saw the directors of the corporation as separate stakeholders in the corporation. They viewed them as exercising a decision making authority not unlike that possessed by members of a Legislature. As a result they imposed upon corporations a judicially conceived separation of powers. The management of a corporation was seen to be divided between the directors and shareholders of the corporation, and the courts consistently prevented efforts by the shareholders of a corporation to intrude upon those powers that were allotted to the directors by law.[557] The classic statement of this principle (which echoes the words of Edmund Burke on the parliamentarians' right and duty to govern without interference from constituents) is to be found in the decision of Buckley L.J. in *Gramophone & Typewriter Ltd. v. Stanley*, where he said:

> The directors are not servants to obey the directions given by the shareholders as individuals; they are not agents appointed by and bound to serve the shareholders as their principals.[558]

Thus, the shareholders might not remove a discretion conferred upon the directors or instruct the directors concerning how a particular power was to be exercised. They could not, for instance, include a provision in the articles or by-laws of a corporation providing that the general management powers of the directors would be subject to directions contained in ordinary[559] or even special[560] resolutions of the shareholders.

§12.189 Despite these considerations, the OBCA and the CBCA have rejected the common law approach towards shareholder management, and the old common law position has now been substantially abrogated by statute in the case of business corporations. It may now be stated with some confidence that Canada — on paper, at least — has one of the most "democratic" corporate law regimes of any of the world's major industrial states (in the sense that it is responsive to shareholders holding a majority of voting shares). Under both the OBCA and the CBCA there are a number of different routes by which the shareholders can exercise control over the conduct of the business and affairs of the corporation, and, indeed, if the shareholders of a corporation are so minded, the unanimous shareholder agreement provisions essentially allow the shareholders of a corporation to reserve to themselves complete control over the corporation's business and affairs.

---

[557] See, for instance, *Grundt v. Great Boulder Proprietary Mines Ltd.*, [1948] Ch. 145 at 157 (C.A.), *per* Cohen L.J.
[558] [1908] 2 K.B. 89 at 105-06 (C.A.).
[559] See, for instance, *John Shaw & Sons (Salford) Ltd. v. Shaw*, [1935] 2 K.B. 113 (C.A.); *Scott v. Scott*, [1943] 1 All E.R. 582.
[560] *Queensland Press Ltd. v. Academy Instruments No. 3 Pty. Ltd.* (1987), 11 A.C.L.R. 419 (Qld. S.C.).

(i) Articles or By-laws

§12.190 The most conventional manner by which the shareholders may exert control is by way of a provision in the articles and, in some cases, the by-laws of a corporation. The prescribed form of articles of incorporation under the OBCA expressly permits a statement in the articles that restricts the business that a corporation may carry on or the powers that the corporation may exercise. Paragraph 6(1)(f) of the CBCA provides that the articles may include restrictions on the business that the corporation may carry on, but makes no reference to restrictions on the exercise of other powers. However, it appears implicit in subsection 16(2) of the CBCA that such restrictions may be imposed. It reads:

> 16.(2) A corporation shall not carry on any business *or exercise any power* that it is restricted by its articles from carrying on or exercising, *nor shall the corporation exercise any of its powers* in a manner contrary to its articles.

(Emphasis added)
The law has always distinguished between "regulation" and "restriction", it being a general principle of administrative law that an authority to regulate does not include an authority to prohibit. However, the power to impose "restrictions" is broader than a mere regulatory power and, accordingly, will include the authority to impose prohibitions in certain cases. Restrictions upon the exercise of powers or the conduct of business might also take the form of a requirement for shareholder approval, and it does not seem unreasonable to extend the shareholder's authority to control over the discontinuation of any particular line of business as well, because any such discontinuation would be no less an exercise of corporate power. Some support for this conclusion can be found in the wording of subsection 17(2) of the OBCA[561] which tracks the wording of subsection 16(2) of the CBCA. In addition, subsection 5(3) permits the articles to include any provisions permitted by the Act or permitted by law to be set out in the by-laws of the corporation. Under subsection 127(1), the power of the directors to delegate their authority may be restricted either by the articles or by-laws. Under subsection 116(1), the power of the directors to make or unmake any by-law may be ousted under the articles, the by-laws or any unanimous shareholder agreement. Under subsection 134(2) of the OBCA, the directors are obliged to comply not only with the Act and regulations but also with the articles, by-laws and any unanimous shareholder agreement.

(ii) Shareholder Proposal

(1) Generally

§12.191 A second method provided under both the OBCA and the CBCA by which the shareholders may assert control over the conduct of a corporation's business or affairs is by a shareholder proposal. In this respect, the current statutory regime departs significantly from the common law position discussed

---

[561] CBCA, s. 16(2).

earlier in the chapter.[562] The procedure governing the making of a shareholder proposal is set out in sections 99 of the OBCA and 137 of the CBCA. The term "proposal" is rather vaguely defined in subsection 99(11) of the OBCA to mean "a matter that a shareholder entitled to vote proposes to raise at a meeting of shareholders".[563] However, some idea of the scope of the term is provided by subsection 169(1) of the OBCA, which provides that a shareholder who is entitled to vote at an annual meeting of shareholders may make a proposal to amend the articles of the corporation in accordance with section 99. Similarly, subsection 116(5) of the OBCA[564] contemplates a shareholder proposal to amend the by-laws of the corporation.[565] Finally, subsection 99(4) of the Act contemplates a proposal to nominate a person to be a director of the corporation.[566] Yet there is some indication in the Act that these specific provisions are little more than illustrative of the type of matter that may be embodied in a proposal. For instance, although the Act does not expressly provide, it would seem to be a logical inference that a proposal may also be made under section 122 to remove a director during his or her term of office.[567]

§12.192 Further support for the conclusion that shareholders are not limited in the subject of a proposal to those matters that are expressly mentioned in the Act can be found in subsection 99(5) of the OBCA,[568] which excludes certain types of subject from being brought forward in a shareholder proposal. More specifically, subsection 99(5) provides that a corporation is not required to circulate a shareholder proposal or any statement made in connection with a proposal in one of four situations, these being where,

> (*a*) the proposal is not submitted to the corporation at least sixty days before the anniversary date of the last annual meeting, if the matter is proposed to be raised at an annual meeting, or at least sixty days before a meeting other than the annual meeting, if the matter is proposed to be raised at a meeting other than the annual meeting;

---

[562] *Automatic Self-Cleansing Filter Syndicate Co. v. Cuninghame*, [1906] 2 Ch. 34.
[563] Compare s. 137(1)(*a*) of the CBCA. On a date to be fixed by regulation, the term "shareholder" in the OBCA provision will be changed to "registered holder, or beneficial holder".
[564] CBCA, s. 103(5).
[565] It reads:
> 116.(5) If a shareholder proposal to make, amend or repeal a by-law is made in accordance with section 99 and is adopted by shareholders at a meeting, the by-law, amendment or repeal is effective from the date of its adoption and requires no further confirmation.

[566] Subsection 99(4) reads:
> 99.(4) A proposal may include nominations for the election of directors if the proposal is signed by one or more holders of shares representing in the aggregate not less than 5 per cent of the shares or 5 per cent of the shares of a class or series of shares of the corporation entitled to vote at the meeting to which the proposal is to be presented, but this subsection does not preclude nominations being made at a meeting of shareholders.

See also CBCA, s. 137(4).
[567] See, for instance, *Goldhar v. D'Aragon Mines Ltd.*, [1977] O.J. No. 2153, 15 O.R. (2d) 80, 75 D.L.R. (3d) 16 (H.C.J.).
[568] CBCA, s. 137(5).

(b) it clearly appears that the proposal is submitted by the shareholder primarily for the purpose of enforcing a personal claim or redressing a personal grievance against the corporation or any of its directors, officers or security holders, or for a purpose that is not related in any significant way to the business or affairs of the corporation;[569]

(c) the corporation, at the shareholder's request, included a proposal in a management information circular relating to a meeting of shareholders held within two years preceding the receipt of the request, and the shareholder failed to present the proposal, in person or by proxy, at the meeting; or

(d) substantially the same proposal was submitted to shareholders in a management information circular or dissident's information circular relating to a meeting of shareholders held within two years preceding the receipt of the shareholder's request and the proposal was defeated.

These exclusions — particularly that contained in clause (b) — would hardly be necessary if the right of shareholders to bring forward a proposal was limited to those matters expressly or implicitly contemplated in one of the other provisions of the Act.[570]

§12.193 Where a corporation receives a notice of a proposal and the corporation solicits proxies (as is mandatory in the case of an offering corporation), the corporation must set out the proposal in its management information circular or attach the proposal to that circular.[571] Furthermore, if so requested by a shareholder giving notice of a proposal, the corporation must include in its management information circular or in an attachment to it a statement by the shareholder of not more than 200 words in support of the proposal, along with the name and address of the shareholder.[572] Corporations that so circulate a proposal are granted a statutory immunity from any liability that might otherwise

---

[569] Compare the wording of the equivalent provision of the CBCA, s. 137(5)(b):

(b) it clearly appears that the primary purpose of the proposal is to enforce a personal claim or redress a personal grievance against the corporation or its directors, officers or security holders;

See, generally, *Medical Committee for Human Rights v. SEC*, 432 F.2d 659 (D.C. Cir. 1970), vacated as moot 404 U.S. 403; *Lovenheim v. Iroquois Brands Ltd.*, 618 F. Supp. 554 (D.D.C. 1985).

[570] On a date to be fixed by proclamation the following revised clauses are added to subsection 99(5) of the OBCA by 2006, c. 34, Sched. B, ss. 14(3), 42(1):

(b) it clearly appears that the primary purpose of the proposal is to enforce a personal claim or redress a personal grievance against the corporation or its directors, officers or security-holders;

(b.1) it clearly appears that the proposal does not relate in a significant way to the business or affairs of the corporation;

(c) not more than two years before the receipt of the proposal, a person failed to present, in person or by proxy, at a meeting of shareholders, a proposal that, at the person's request, had been included in a management information circular relating to the meeting; or

[571] OBCA, s. 99(2); CBCA, s. 137(2).

[572] See, generally, *Clearwater Fine Foods Inc. v. FPI Ltd.*, [2001] N.J. No. 106, 15 B.L.R. (3d) 124 (T.D.).

arise (*e.g.*, in libel) from complying with these provisions. Specifically, subsection 99(6) of the OBCA provides that no corporation or person acting on its behalf incurs any liability for circulating a proposal or statement in compliance with the section.

§12.194 A number of court applications are contemplated under section 99 with regard to proposals. Subsection 99(7) of the OBCA[573] provides that where a corporation refuses to include a proposal in a management information circular, the corporation must notify the shareholder submitting the proposal of its intention to omit the proposal from the management information circular, along with a statement of its reasons for that refusal. This notice must be sent within 10 days after the corporation receives the proposal.[574] Any shareholder aggrieved by a corporation's refusal to circulate a proposal under subsection (7) may then apply to the court[575] for an order to restrain the holding of the meeting to which it is intended to present the proposal. Upon such an application the court may make any further order that it thinks fit.[576] The words "shareholder aggrieved by a corporation's refusal" suggest that the standing to bring such an application is not limited to the shareholder who originally submitted the proposal, but extends to any shareholder who wishes that proposal to be placed before the shareholders for their consideration.

§12.195 Alternatively, an application may also be made to court to restrain the circulation of a proposal. In this regard, subsection 99(9) of the OBCA provides:

> 99.(9) The corporation or any person aggrieved by a proposal may apply to court for an order permitting the corporation to omit the proposal from the management information circular, and the court, if it is satisfied that subsection (5) applies, may make such order as it thinks fit.

Subsection 137(9) of the CBCA is substantially similar, the only differences being cross-references and terminology. While subsection 99(9) is silent on the point, it seems likely that the courts will require an applicant under that subsection to demonstrate a material interest before it will restrain the circulation of a proposal, even though the directors of a corporation are prepared to circulate it. Subsection 99(5) of the OBCA authorizes the corporation not to circulate a proposal in certain circumstances; it does not require the corporation not to do so. If the directors believe that a matter is of sufficient importance that it should be considered by the shareholders of the corporation, it is difficult to see any general basis on which the court may second-guess that decision. The mere fact that there may be some incidental

---

[573] CBCA, s. 137(7).
[574] On a date to be fixed by proclamation, subsection 99(7) will be amended by S.O. 2006, c. 34, Sched. B, s. 14(4) so as to read:

> If a corporation refuses to include a proposal in a management information circular, the corporation shall, within 10 days after receiving the proposal, send notice to the person submitting the proposal of its intention to omit the proposal from the management information circular and send to the person a statement of the reasons for the refusal.

[575] The application must be made on notice to the Director, who is entitled to appear and be heard in person or by counsel: OBCA, s. 99(10).
[576] OBCA, s. 99(8).

cost to the corporation in circulating and considering a proposal can hardly be sufficient to overrule the director's decision. On the other hand, where a person stands to be injured as a result of the circulation of a proposal (for instance, where it is defamatory or demeaning of an individual or group), the court might well consider whether it should restrain that proposal's circulation.

§12.196 Until the 2001 amendments, the CBCA relieves a corporation from the obligation to circulate a shareholder proposal and statement where the proposal is submitted "primarily for the purpose of promoting general economic, political, racial, religious, social and similar causes".[577] In *Varity Corp. v. Jesuit Fathers of Upper Canada*[578] it was held that the specific purpose of terminating the business of a corporation in South Africa was not sufficient to save a proposal when it was clear that the primary purpose of the proposal was to promote the abolition of apartheid. Despite the change in wording, it is at least arguable that a similar result would be reached. The promotion of general economic, political, racial, religious, social and similar causes would not appear to relate significantly to the business or affairs of a corporation.[579]

§12.197 In *Verdun v. Toronto-Dominion Bank*,[580] it was held that only a registered shareholder may submit a proposal. Nevertheless, it is difficult to see why, as a matter of policy, the beneficial owner of shares in a corporation should not be entitled to make a shareholder proposal or to direct the registered holder of the shares to make such a proposal on his or her behalf. In the federal government's 1995 discussion paper on possible amendment of the CBCA, a proposal was made to confer such a right, on the basis that an amendment permitting beneficial shareholders to submit shareholder proposals under section 137 would reflect the current market reality of shareholding as well as increase efforts to improve communication between the corporation and the owners of its shares.

(2) Proposals Under the CBCA

§12.198 The 2001 amendments of the CBCA constrained the availability of the proposal procedure. Specifically, subsection 137(1.1) now provides that to be eligible to submit a proposal, a person

- (*a*) must be, for at least the prescribed period, the registered holder or the beneficial owner of at least the prescribed number of outstanding shares of the corporation; or

- (*b*) must have the support of persons who, in the aggregate, and including or not including the person that submits the proposal, have been, for at least the prescribed period, the registered holders, or the beneficial owners of, at least the prescribed number of outstanding shares of the corporation.

---

[577] CBCA, s. 137(5)(*b*).
[578] [1987] O.J. No. 345, 59 O.R. (2d) 459 (H.C.J.), aff'd [1987] O.J. No. 2680, 60 O.R. (2d) 640 (C.A.).
[579] See also *Rauchman v. Mobil Corp.*, 739 F.2d 205 (6th Cir. 1984); *Lovenheim v. Iroquois Brands Ltd.*, 618 F. Supp. 554 (D.D.C. 1985).
[580] [1996] S.C.J. No. 50, 28 B.L.R. (2d) 121 at 131-33, *per* Iacobucci J.

The obvious purpose behind this provision is to prevent the abuse of the proposal procedure by individuals who hold a nominal interest in the corporation (such as single share). Frequently in the past, proposals have repeatedly been made by members of fringe political, special interest and similar organizations, often with no other purpose in mind than to embarrass the corporation or its management. Subsection (1) recognizes that the purpose of the proposal procedure is to provide a basis for the discussion of measures and other ideas that have a reasonable prospect for adoption. A more focused approach toward proposals is also evident in the newly enacted clause 137(5)(*b*.1), which provides that a corporation may omit the circulation of a proposal where:

> it clearly appears that the proposal does not relate in a significant way to the business and affairs of the corporation.

The apparent goal behind this provision is to eliminate the need to deal with proposals that, while perhaps touching upon matters of some public interest, do not really relate to the corporation or its current business.

§12.199 A more controversial requirement is set out in subsection (1.2), since it entails the disclosure of personal information:

> (1.2) A proposal submitted under paragraph (1)(*a*) must be accompanied by the following information:
>
> > (*a*) the name and address of the person and of the person's supporters, if applicable; and
> >
> > (*b*) the number of shares held or owned by the person and the person's supporters, if applicable, and the date the shares were acquired.

The information provided under subsection (1.2) does not form part of the proposal or of the supporting statement referred to in subsection (3) and is not included for the purposes of the prescribed maximum word limit set out in subsection (3).[581] Given the disclosure required under subsection (1.2), it is difficult to see what function is served by subsection (1.4), which provides:

> (1.4) If requested by the corporation within the prescribed period, a person who submits a proposal must provide proof, within the prescribed period, that the person meets the requirements of subsection (1.1).

One would have thought that the information required under subsection (1.4) would be implicit in the information given under subsection (1.2).

§12.200 Another significant difference between the CBCA and the OBCA relates to the material that the corporation is required to circulate with respect to a proposal. Whereas the OBCA requires the corporation to provide shareholders with the full proposal and an explanation of up to 200 words, subsection 137(3) of the CBCA provides:

> 137.(3) If so requested by the person who submits a proposal, the corporation shall include in the management proxy circular or attach to it a statement in

---

[581] CBCA, s. 137(1.3).

support of the proposal by the person and the name and address of the person. The statement and the proposal must together not exceed the prescribed maximum number of words.

The current maximum number of words is set at 500, which could easily be unreasonably brief, where the proposal is to create (for instance) some form of detailed corporate governance procedure.

(iii) Unanimous Shareholder Agreement

(1) Generally

§12.201 For narrowly held corporations, perhaps the most common method of restraining director managerial authority is by way of a unanimous shareholder agreement ("USA"). As noted above, the common law did not permit the shareholders of a corporation to create a sterilized board of directors.[582] Under the unanimous shareholder agreement provisions of the OBCA and the CBCA, even this now appears to be possible.

§12.202 The term "unanimous shareholder agreement" describes a written agreement among all the shareholders of a corporation, or among all the shareholders and one or more persons who are not shareholders, that restricts, in whole or in part, the powers of the directors to manage or supervise the management of the business and affairs of the corporation.[583] Prior to the enactment of the unanimous shareholder agreement provisions, there was nothing that prevented the shareholders of a corporation from entering into an agreement among themselves on the manner in which they would cause the corporation to conduct its business and affairs.[584] However, while any such agreement would be binding among the shareholders, it would neither bind[585] nor benefit the corporation unless the corporation was a party to it.[586]

§12.203 Moreover, a unanimous shareholder agreement could not remove from the directors of the corporation the powers and discretions vested in them under

---

[582] *Manson v. Curtis* (1918), 223 N.Y. 313 at 323, *per* Collin J.

[583] OBCA, s. 108(2); CBCA, s. 146(1). For corporations that have only one shareholder, s. 108(3) of the OBCA provides:

> 108.(3) Where a person who is the beneficial owner of all the issued shares of a corporation makes a written declaration that restricts in whole or in part the powers of the directors to manage or supervise the management of the business and affairs of the corporation, the declaration shall be deemed to be a unanimous shareholder agreement.

Subsection 146(2) of the CBCA is identical. An amendment to come into effect on proclamation will delete the term "beneficial owner" and replace it with "registered holder". The change reflects the modification of Ontario law made to accommodate uncertificated securities.

[584] But see *Berkinshaw v. Henderson*, [1908] O.J. No. 416, 12 O.W.R. 919 (Div. Ct.), aff'd [1909] O.J. No. 417, 14 O.W.R. 833, 1 O.W.N. 97 at 97 (C.A.), *per* Osler J.A.

[585] *Garvin v. Edmondon*, [1909] O.J. No. 315, 14 O.W.R. 435 (H.C.J.), aff'd [1910] O.J. No. 558, 15 O.W.R. 210 (Div. Ct.); see also *Kelner v. Baxter* (1866), L.R. 2 C.P. 174; *Natal Land & Colonization Co. v. Pauline Colliery & Development Syndicate Ltd.*, [1904] A.C. 120.

[586] See *Barnard v. Duplessis Independent Shoe Machinery Co.* (1907), 31 Que. S.C. 362.

corporate law — though it might qualify the exercise of those powers and discretions in some limited respects. For instance, in *Long Park Inc. v. Trenton-New Brunswick Theaters Co.*[587] all the shareholders of the theatre company entered into an agreement giving one shareholder "full authority and power to supervise and direct the operation and management" of the theatres owned or leased by the company or any of its subsidiaries. The managing-shareholder could not be removed from office, except by arbitrator. The court held that this agreement intruded much too far into the jurisdiction conferred by law on the directors.

§12.204 Both the OBCA and the CBCA now expressly contemplate unanimous shareholder agreements that will affect the manner of corporate governance. Such an agreement may be not merely determinative as to where *de facto* control resides within a corporation, but also as to where *de jure* control resides with respect to those matters to which the agreement pertains.[588] However, the precise status of a unanimous shareholder agreement under the present law is not clear. It is not part of the articles of a corporation and is not filed on public record. For this reason, such an agreement is not generally binding on outsiders to the corporation.[589] However, where an outsider to the corporation (or some other non-party to the unanimous shareholder agreement) has actual knowledge of restrictions imposed under the agreement (or ought to have such knowledge by virtue of his or her relation to the corporation) the outsider or other non-party will be bound by those restrictions.[590]

§12.205 Under the present law, a unanimous shareholder agreement enjoys a status vastly superior to that of a by-law of the corporation or a simple contract. It is binding upon the corporation irrespective of whether it is a party to it. Moreover, it will bind a transferee of shares.[591] Such an agreement may overrule the presumed balance of power between the directors and officers of the corporation,[592] subsection 108(5) of the OBCA providing:

> 108.(5) A shareholder who is a party to a unanimous shareholder agreement has all the rights, powers, duties and liabilities of a director of the corporation, whether arising under this Act or otherwise, to which the agreement relates to the

---

[587] 297 N.Y. 174, 77 N.E.2d 633 (1948).
[588] *Duha Printers (Western) Ltd. v. Canada*, [1998] S.C.J. No. 41, 159 D.L.R. (4th) 457.
[589] *Belleville Driving & Athletic Assn.*, [1914] O.J. No. 15, 31 O.L.R. 79 at 85-86 (C.A.), *per* Meredith C.J.O.
[590] OBCA, s. 19; CBCA, s. 18.
[591] OBCA, s. 108(4); CBCA, s. 146(4). Section 56(3) of the OBCA provides as follows:

> 56.(3) Where a share certificate issued by a corporation ... is, or becomes subject to, ...
>
> (c) a unanimous shareholder agreement ...
>
> the restriction, lien, agreement or endorsement is ineffective against a transferee of the share who has no actual knowledge of it, unless it or a reference to it is noted conspicuously on the share certificate.

[592] See, for instance, *Power v. Vitrak Systems Inc.*, [2006] P.E.I.J. No. 36, 21 B.L.R. (4th) 103 (P.E.I.S.C.).

extent that the agreement restricts the discretion or powers of the directors to manage or supervise the management of the business and affairs of the corporation and the directors are thereby relieved of their duties and liabilities, including any liabilities under section 131, to the same extent.[593]

§12.206 Conceptually, there are two basic types of shareholder agreement: (1) an agreement among any two or more shareholders to which the corporation is not a party, and (2) an agreement between one or more shareholders and the corporation itself. Subsection 108(1) of the OBCA refers to a "written agreement" between two or more shareholders. The use of the word "agreement" rather than "contract" may be significant — it may mean, for instance, that it is unnecessary to establish that the agreement satisfies the requisites of a legally enforceable contract (*e.g.*, consideration), provided that it is drafted in sufficiently specific terms to permit it to be interpreted, applied and enforced.[594]

(2) Status

§12.207 In *Duha Printers (Western) Ltd. v. Canada*[595] Iacobucci J. stated that a USA is "a corporate law hybrid, part contractual and part constitutional in nature". In that case, the Supreme Court concluded that such an agreement is to be treated as one of the constating documents of the corporation along with its articles of incorporation and by-laws. In other words, it forms part of the constitution of the corporation to which it relates. Significantly, both the OBCA[596] and the CBCA[597] provide that compliance orders may be obtained to enforce a USA — the remedy serving in this respect as the corporate law analog of a judgment for specific performance.

---

[593] On a date to be fixed by proclamation, the present text of subsection 108(5) will be repealed and replaced as follows by 2006, c. 34, Sched. B, s. 16 (2):

(5) A shareholder who is a party to a unanimous shareholder agreement has all the rights, powers, duties and liabilities of a director of a corporation, whether arising under this Act or otherwise, including any defences available to the directors, to which the agreement relates to the extent that the agreement restricts the discretion or powers of the directors to manage or supervise the management of the business and affairs of the corporation and the directors are relieved of their duties and liabilities, including any liabilities under section 131, to the same extent.

(5.1) Nothing in this section prevents shareholders from fettering their discretion when exercising the powers of directors under a unanimous shareholder agreement.

With respect to the new subsection (5.1), see: *Alder v. Dobie*, [1999] B.C.J. No. 808, 87 A.C.W.S. (3d) 276 (S.C.); *Ming Minerals Inc. v. Blagdon*, [1998] N.J. No. 87, 78 A.C.W.S. (3d) 492 (S.C.).

[594] *Colborne Capital Corp. v. 542775 Alberta Ltd.*, [1995] A.J. No. 538, 22 B.L.R. (2d) 226 at 285-86 (Q.B.), *per* Virtue J., var'd [1999] A.J. No. 33, 45 B.L.R. (2d) 21 (C.A.). As for the difficulties of interpreting the term "unanimous shareholder agreement" where there is only a single shareholder, a single shareholder of a corporation will not be "deemed" to have entered into a unanimous shareholder agreement: the written declaration procedure set down in the Act must be followed.

[595] [1998] S.C.J. No. 41, [1998] 1 S.C.R. 795 at 829.
[596] OBCA, s. 253.
[597] CBCA, s. 247.

(3) Interpretation

§12.208 The meaning of a USA is determined in accordance with the general rules governing contractual interpretation. The primary rules of contractual interpretation are:

- to construe the document in its entirety; and

- to give the plain literal meaning to the terms that the parties have incorporated into the Agreement, where the terms of the document are unambiguous.

However, the modern approach to the construction of commercial agreements of business people is generally to endeavour to uphold the apparent or evident bargain between the parties. The courts avoid giving such documents a narrow or pedantic approach in favour of a commercially sensible construction, unless some irremediable obscurity or a similar fundamental flaw indicates that there is, in fact, no agreement. It is permissible to have regard to extrinsic evidence of the "factual matrix" or surrounding circumstances in determining the meaning of contractual terms.[598]

(4) Subject Matter

§12.209 Aside from these matters specifically mentioned in section 108 — which other than those contemplated by subsection (5) are surely peripheral to the agreement as a whole — the scope and subject matter of a shareholder agreement is left to the parties' unrestricted discretion. For this reason the specific provisions likely to be found in any such an agreement will be determined by the particular requirements of the parties. In addition, provisions are scattered throughout both the OBCA and CBCA indicating various subjects that may be dealt with in a USA, aside from the general authority to restrict the power of the directors. In particular, a USA may:

- require a greater number of votes to approve a measure than would otherwise be required under the Act;[599]

- place controls on the issue of shares;[600]

- create a pre-emptive right with respect to the issue of new shares;[601]

- vary the procedure for the payment of dividends;[602]

- specify the place where a meeting of shareholders is to be held;[603]

- specify the manner in which a meeting of shareholders is to be conducted;[604]

---

[598] *Hardman Group Ltd. v. Alexander*, [2004] N.S.J. No. 557, 13 B.L.R. (4th) 196 (S.C.). See also, *Patrick Corp. Ltd. v. Toll Holdings Ltd.* (2005), 55 A.C.S.R. 386 (S.C. Vict. Eq.).
[599] OBCA, s. 5(4); CBCA, s. 6(3).
[600] OBCA, s. 23(1); CBCA, s. 25.
[601] OBCA, s. 26.
[602] OBCA, s. 38(1).
[603] OBCA, s. 93(1).
[604] OBCA, s. 97.

- specify a procedure for amending the USA itself;[605]
- vary the procedure for the making of by-laws;[606]
- control the appointment of officers;[607]
- make provision with respect to director, officer and employee remuneration;[608]
- require the disclosure of additional information;[609]
- control borrowing by the corporation; and[610]
- control delegation of authority by the directors.[611]

It is also common for a unanimous shareholder agreement to deal with a wide range of issues that either bind the shareholders themselves, or that create additional rights in their favour. By way of illustration, such agreements may confer a right:

- to require the interest of a shareholder to be bought out upon the occurrence of specified events;[612]
- to representation upon the board of directors;[613]
- to veto any change in the share structure of the corporation;[614]
- to match or better any price offered by another bidder for shares;[615]
- to approve significant transactions;[616] and
- to control security transfer or buyout rights.[617]

Unanimous shareholder agreements may also impose obligations, such as an obligation to contribute funds,[618] either in the event of a loss on corporate operations, or to fund expansion; to vote in a particular way;[619] to disclose information;[620] to devote time[621] or other resources to corporate operations.

---

[605] OBCA, s. 108(6).
[606] OBCA, s. 116(1); CBCA, s. 103.
[607] OBCA, s. 133; CBCA, s. 121.
[608] OBCA, s. 137; CBCA, s. 125.
[609] OBCA, s. 154(1); CBCA, s. 155.
[610] OBCA, s. 184(1); CBCA, s. 189.
[611] OBCA, s. 184(2).
[612] *Kary Investment Corp. v. Tremblay*, [2005] A.J. No. 1030, 141 A.C.W.S. (3d) 954 (C.A.), on appeal from [2004] A.J. No. 612, 131 A.C.W.S. (3d) 1074 (Q.B.).
[613] *Wood v. Wood*, [2004] A.J. No. 1230, 5 B.L.R. (4th) 61 (Q.B.).
[614] *Fiber Connections Inc. v. SVCM Capital Ltd.*, [2005] O.J. No. 3899, 5 B.L.R. (4th) 271 (S.C.J.).
[615] *Linedata Services SA v. Katatakis*, [2005] O.J. No. 813, 2 B.L.R. (4th) 71 (S.C.J.), aff'd [2005] O.J. No. 640, 1 B.L.R. (4th) 168 (C.A.).
[616] *Richardson v. Control Fire Holdings Inc.*, [2002] O.J. No. 1569, 29 B.L.R. (3d) 208 (S.C.J.).
[617] *Trudell partnership Holdings Ltd. v. Retirement Counsel of Canada Inc.*, [2001] O.J. No. 314, 20 B.L.R. (3d) 76 (S.C.J.).
[618] See, generally, *Amneet Holdings Ltd. v. 79548 Manitoba Ltd.*, [2004] M.J. No. 92, 42 B.L.R. (3d) 1 (C.A.).
[619] *Tal v. Lifemark Health Inc.*, [2002] O.J. No. 4208, 29 B.L.R. (3d) 157 (S.C.J. — C.L.).
[620] *McAteer v. Devoncroft Developments Ltd.*, [2001] A.J. No. 1481, 24 B.L.R. (3d) 1 (Q.B.).
[621] *Donnelly v. Steward*, [2001] B.C.J. No. 2072, 18 B.L.R. (3d) 305 (S.C.).

(a) Core (Managerial) Terms

§12.210 By their express terms, the two statutes indicate that a unanimous shareholder agreement may restrict the powers of the directors (*e.g.*, the power over the dismissal of the president of the corporation).[622] Quite clearly, it would be within the scope of the Act to prohibit the directors from taking a particular step, including entering into a particular line of business.[623] Moreover, subsection 108(5)[624] of the OBCA clearly suggests that a unanimous shareholder agreement may transfer the powers normally held by the directors to the shareholders. Less clear is whether the shareholders may enter into a unanimous shareholder agreement to require the directors to take specific action.

§12.211 Since the emphasis in section 108 is placed upon restricting the manner in which the directors manage or supervise the management of the business and affairs of the corporation, it is doubtful that the directors can be granted additional powers under a USA over the corporation, so as to remove the authority that the shareholders are entitled to as a matter of law. Moreover, it is not possible to authorize the directors to issue shares (or pay dividends, *etc.*) in a manner contrary to the requirements of the Act,[625] or to concoct schemes to protect them from removal from office contrary to a statutory authority providing a mechanism for their removal.[626] By extension, it is probable that the USA provisions cannot be used to circumvent or foreclose a shareholder oppression proceeding.

(b) Collateral Matters

§12.212 Since section 108(3) of the OBCA describes a USA solely as being an agreement that restricts "in whole or in part the powers of the directors to manage or supervise the management of the business and affairs of a corporation", the question is sometimes raised as to whether a unanimous agreement may deal with matters outside the management of the corporation. For instance, is it possible to impose some restriction only upon the shareholders with respect to some collateral matter that is sufficient to meet the requirements of the section? Since,

---

[622] See, generally, *Gillespie v. Overs*, [1987] O.J. No. 747, 5 A.C.W.S. (3d) 430 (H.C.J.).

[623] *Zion v. Kurtz*, 50 N.Y.2d 92, 428 N.Y.S.2d 199, 405 N.E.2d 681 (C.A. 1980), *per* Meyer J.

[624] Compare the more narrowly worded corresponding provision in the CBCA, s. 146(5):

> 146.(5) A shareholder who is a party to a unanimous shareholder agreement has all the rights, powers and duties of a director of the corporation to which the agreement relates to the extent that the agreement restricts the powers of the directors to manage the business and affairs of the corporation, and the directors are thereby relieved of their duties and liabilities including any liabilities under section 119, to the same extent.

[625] For instance, at common law a corporation may not enter into a valid contract under which it agrees not to amend its articles or by-laws, despite a statutory authority to do so: *Southern Foundries (1926) Ltd. v. Shirlaw*, [1940] A.C. 701 at 739 (H.L.), *per* Lord Porter; *Allen v. Gold Reefs of West Africa Ltd.*, [1900] 1 Ch. 656 at 671 (C.A.), *per* Lord Lindley M.R. Compare, however: *Welton v. Saffrey*, [1897] A.C. 299 at 331 (H.L.), *per* Lord Davey; *Russell v. Northern Bank Development Corporation Ltd.*, [1992] 1 W.L.R. 588 (H.L.), *per* Lord Jauncey of Tullichettle — no common law prohibition against such an arrangement among the shareholders themselves.

[626] See, for instance, *Bushell v. Faith*, [1969] 2 Ch. 438 at 447-48 (C.A.), *per* Russell L.J.

the purpose behind section 108 was to validate what would otherwise be an unlawful constraint at common law (*i.e.*, the partial or complete sterilization of the directors), it is doubtful that the inclusion of any such collateral provisions would adversely affect the validity of a unanimous shareholder agreement or its status as such. It has always been open to the shareholders to regulate their own relationship.

(5) Formation

(a) EVIDENCE OF APPROVAL

§12.213 As the name suggests, a unanimous shareholder agreement must be signed by all shareholders. A failure by a shareholder to approve such an agreement essentially amounts to a veto — there is no alternative to abstain. The OBCA and the CBCA also impose certain requirements on form. In particular, the agreement must be in writing and must be signed by all shareholders of the corporation. Significantly, neither Act distinguishes in this requirement between the holders of voting and non-voting shares. Failing the unanimity of the shareholders, the shareholders may bind the directors in the management of the business of the corporation by amending the articles of the corporation to impose the desired restriction.[627] Curiously, neither statute specifically permits the articles to restrict the manner in which the affairs[628] of the corporation are conducted, though the ability to impose such a restriction through the articles would appear to be implicit in certain of the sections of the Acts. For instance, subsection 23(1) of the OBCA quite clearly contemplates such a restriction in the articles, because it provides:

> 23.(1) Subject to the articles, the by-laws, any unanimous shareholder agreement and section 26, shares may be issued at such time and to such persons and for such consideration as the directors may determine.

Thus, the general control of the directors over the issue of shares may be constrained by the articles. However, until such time as the statutes are amended or there is a clear judicial pronouncement interpreting their meaning, it will be unclear whether subsection 23(1) is merely an express recognition of the general authority of the shareholders to restrict the conduct of the affairs of a corporation through the articles or is merely an exception to a general rule that the shareholders possess no such discretion. From a policy viewpoint, it is difficult to understand why the articles might contain a restriction upon the power of the directors to manage the business of a corporation but not its affairs. On the contrary, since the affairs of a corporation constitute its dealings with insiders, it would seem more logical to permit rather than prohibit such restrictions.

---

[627] OBCA, s. 5(1); CBCA, s. 6(1)(*f*).
[628] In both the OBCA and the CBCA, the term "affairs" is used to describe (a) internal corporate governance, and (b) dealings between the corporation and its shareholders and other holders of its securities.

(b) NON-SHAREHOLDER PARTIES

§12.214 Subsections 108(2) of the OBCA and 146(1) of the CBCA expressly permit non-shareholders to be additional parties to a unanimous shareholder agreement. Even in the absence of a provision of this sort, it is doubtful that the fact that an agreement includes persons other than shareholders can prejudice its status as a unanimous shareholder agreement. The statutes require all shareholders to be parties. They do not state that only shareholders may be parties. In the absence of a clear indication of a legislative intent to restrict such agreements to shareholders alone, there would seem to be no benefit derived from such a limitation. There could, however, be considerable inconvenience resulting from its introduction, given the obvious need that outsiders may have in certain cases to tie down the manner in which a corporation will be managed.

(c) SUCCESSOR RIGHTS AND OBLIGATIONS

§12.215 Generally, the terms of a USA become attached to the shares to which they pertain, so that they pass with those shares as an incident of property. Section 108(4) of the OBCA provide that a transferee of shares that are subject to a unanimous shareholder agreement shall be deemed to be a party to the agreement. In contrast, subsection 146(3) of the CBCA provides that:

> 146.(3) A purchaser or transferee of shares subject to a unanimous shareholder agreement is deemed to be a party to the agreement.

The apparent intent of the provision is to make each "transferee" a successor party to the USA, enjoying both the rights and obligations of the transferor. It will be noted that subsection 146(3) does not specifically mention a person who acquires shares by transmission of law. Since such a person will usually be a volunteer, or hold the shares under a right of quasi-subrogation, most likely such a person would be construed to be subject to the same rights and obligations.

§12.216 The decision of Blair J. in *Sportscope Television Network Ltd. v. Shaw Communications Inc.*[629] makes clear that considerable care must be taken by a corporation that is subject to a unanimous shareholder agreement, when going through a major reorganization or arrangement. In that case, the original Sportscope corporation amalgamated with another corporation, which then itself amalgamated with a numbered company (1236728 Ontario Inc.) which had been incorporated to form New Sportscope. Prior to this arrangement, a unanimous shareholding agreement was in place that required a high level of shareholder approval for any share disposition. As a result of these transactions, shares were issued to Shaw under a debenture conversion privilege. At one stage of this transaction, one of the shareholders in the original Sportscope ("Clairvest") was released from the USA. The intent of the parties was to enter into a new USA when the transaction was complete. Ultimately, no such contract was ever executed.

---

[629] [1999] O.J. No. 710, 46 B.L.R. (2d) 87, 86 A.C.W.S. (3d) 527 (Gen. Div. — C.L.).

§12.217 Shaw assumed the regulatory risk of CRTC approval, which ultimately was not obtained. The CRTC refused to permit Shaw to take up its shares, which meant that Shaw was required to divest itself of its Sportscope interest. An issue arose over whether Shaw was bound by a 90 per cent shareholder approval requirement imposed under the Sportscope Shareholders' Agreement, and an application was brought to the court by Sportscope for a resolution of that issue. Sportscope argued that Shaw was deemed by subsection 108(4) of the OBCA to be bound by the old USA, which meant that Shaw was not entitled to sell its shares without the shareholder approval required under the USA. Shaw argued that it was not a party to the USA, and that it was not bound by it because:

- the USA was not a unanimous shareholders' agreement, as that term is defined in the OBCA;
- in any event, it is no longer "unanimous", as a result of Clairvest having been released from it before it sold its shares in the first step amalgamation of Amalco One;
- the USA ceased to be applicable upon the second step amalgamation between Amalco One and 1236728 Ontario Inc. to form New Sportscope, as a result of the operation of sections 175 to 177 of the OBCA; and finally,
- Shaw was never a "transferee" of the Sportscope shares and accordingly, subsection 108(4) of the OBCA did not apply.

Blair, J. noted that Shaw had never signed the USA, and therefore had not become a party to it — although he also held that the fact that Shaw had never seen the agreement was of "limited significance". If Shaw were otherwise bound contractually to it, "it would be no answer simply to have ignored it". Shaw knew of the existence of the USA, but did not agree to become bound by it, although Blair J. concluded that Shaw agreed to become bound by a different and new agreement, that ultimately was never executed and delivered. A particular consideration of which the court took note with respect to the old USA, was that Shaw (as a reporting issuer) could not have agreed to be bound by it because of the restrictions that the USA would have imposed on the disposition of its own shares, as a shareholder in Sportscope.

§12.218 When the Debenture conversion closed, the Investment Agreement was not completed. The Purchase Agreement and the Termination Agreement formed part of the corporate transactions through which Shaw acquired the Clairvest interest. The documentation carefully stipulated that the then existing direct and indirect shareholders would continue to be bound by the Sportscope Shareholders' Agreement (except Clairvest, which was released in the process) until a new "made to measure" shareholders' agreement was entered into. However, it was held that this was not sufficient to bind Shaw to the Agreement.

§12.219 Blair J. then turned to the question of whether Shaw was bound by the original USA under section 108 of the OBCA. Although the original USA fit within the statutory definition of a unanimous shareholder agreement, Shaw was not bound by the USA because it was not a transferee of the shares that it held. He explained:

> Shaw received its interest in Sportscope in two fashions. One was by way of the acquisition of shares from treasury as a result of the Convertible Debenture. The other was by way of the "conversion" of its shares in 1236728 Ontario Inc. into shares of New Sportscope upon the amalgamation ... to form New Sportscope. In neither case did Shaw acquire its interest as a "transferee" of shares, as that term is used in the OBCA ...[630]

In reaching this conclusion, Blair J. was guided by the decision of the Divisional Court in *Koch Transport Ltd. v. Class Freight Lines Ltd.*[631] In that case, it was held that a "conversion" of shares in an amalgamation is not a "transfer" of shares. Galligan J. had noted that the word "conversion" has a significant meaning in corporation law,[632] and on this basis he concluded that subsection 9(6) of the *Public Commercial Vehicles Act* — which required a hearing before the Ontario Highway Transport Board when there had been "any issue or transfer of shares" in a corporation that effected a change in the *de facto* control of the corporation — did not apply in circumstances where there had been a "conversion" of shares on an amalgamation. Since Shaw was not a transferee of the first tranche of shares, it fell outside the scope of subsection 108(4) of the OBCA with respect to those shares. A similar line of reasoning was applied with respect to the shares issued out of treasury.

> The same logic applies, in my view, to shares that are acquired by way of "issuance" from treasury. If it is noteworthy — as it was, in *Koch Transport* — that the Legislature had referred to both a "transfer" or an "issue" of shares, but not to a "conversion", it is equally noteworthy when the Legislature refers only to the concept of transfer ("transferee") but not to either "issue" or "conversion". ... Indeed, in subsection 29(6) the Legislature was at pains to indicate that certain defined "transfers" were to be treated in certain cases "as if the transfer were an issue", thus indicating beyond doubt that the Legislature recognizes the difference between the two. In section 27, dealing with conversion privileges, a differentiation between "conversion" and "issue" is maintained, as it is as well in section 35.[633]

§12.220 It is a fair question whether this narrow interpretation will survive the next legislative review. It is worth observing, however, that slight differences in wording in other business corporations statutes may well be sufficient to lead to the conclusion that the *Sportscope* decision should not be followed in respect of statutes other than the OBCA. Section 146(3) of the present CBCA provides that a purchaser and transferee of shares will be bound. It is unclear whether this slight variation in wording would have led to a different result in Sportscope.

---

[630] *Ibid.*, at para. 26 (O.J.).
[631] [1982] O.J. No. 3349, 37 O.R. (2d) 566 (Div. Ct.).
[632] *Ibid.*, at 567.
[633] *Sportscope Television Network Ltd. v. Shaw Communications Inc.*, [1999] O.J. No. 710 at para. 31, 46 B.L.R. (2d) 87 (Gen. Div. — C.L.).

(6) Amendment and Termination

§12.221 In general, the manner of amending a unanimous shareholder agreement is determined in accordance with general principles of contract law, though subsection 108(6) of the OBCA sets out that a shareholder agreement may provide that any amendment of the unanimous shareholder agreement may be effected in the manner specified in the agreement and, in the event that the shareholders who are parties to the unanimous shareholder agreement are unable to agree on or resolve any matter pertaining to the agreement, the agreement may require the matter to be referred to arbitration under such procedures and conditions as are specified in the agreement.

§12.222 A strong argument can be made that the statutes should permit the shareholders of a corporation to set out an amending formula in a USA that is satisfactory to them. If all shareholders agree that the agreement may be amended by a two-thirds majority, or even by a simple majority, there is no apparent public policy rationale that would seem to justify preventing them from doing so. There is, of course, a certain semantic inconsistency in referring to a document as being a "unanimous shareholder agreement", when its actual terms may have been brought about by amendments approved by significantly less than all shareholders, as a result of the application of an amending formula. However, since all shareholders would be required to consent to that formula, at least that degree of unanimity is maintained.

§12.223 Although the question has not been clearly addressed, there is a strong argument that (like any other contract), a unanimous shareholder agreement may lapse or expire by its terms, be cancelled by agreement among the parties, or may be frustrated by supervening events so as to become inoperative. Where such an event occurs, there is nothing for the transferee to succeed to, and accordingly the transferee is neither entitled to rights, nor subject to obligations under the USA.

(7) OBCA Proposed Reforms

§12.224 The Ontario MGS Discussion Paper[634] asks whether the OBCA should provide expressly that where the shareholders of a corporation become subject to the duties and liabilities of the directors, they should also be entitled to raise the defences. While it is probable that a court would read such defences into the statutory imposition of potential liability, there can be little harm in including an express provision entitling shareholders to the same defences as apply to a director.

§12.225 The Discussion Paper also asks whether it should be necessary to provide public notice of the USA.[635] The benefit that such disclosure would yield is far from clear. If the shareholders become potentially liable to third parties by

---

[634] Phase II Business Law Modernization Consultation (Toronto: April 3, 2006) at 4.
[635] Phase II Business Law Modernization Consultation (Toronto: April 3, 2006) at 6.

reason of a USA, generally the effect of such an arrangement is to enhance the rights of third parties, not to reduce them. In many cases, a USA will contain matters that are of no concern to the public (*e.g.*, what salary arrangements will apply, what rights exist to take on work outside the corporation). Third parties are not bound by any restrictions set out in a USA, and really have no legitimate reason to be able to access the terms of private arrangements that may exist among the shareholders of a corporation. It should not be necessary as a matter of law to file a copy of any USA on the public record, or otherwise provide information concerning such an arrangement. If third parties dealing with the corporation feel it necessary to access this information, they may seek to obtain via private contract.

I. THE STA BOOK ENTRY SYSTEM

§12.226 The *Securities Transfer Act, 2006*,[636] (the "STA") was enacted during the final preparation of the manuscript for this text. Similar legislation is expected to be enacted across Canada, given the intensive lobbying in support of this legislation by the investment and finance industry across Canada. The STA creates a regime of law to govern un-certificated securities — these being securities that are not evidenced by a paper security certificate (as has historically been the case), but rather are evidenced by way of an entry in favor of the investor in a securities account.[637] The creation of an un-certificated security regime was crucial to the viability widespread electronic trading in securities.

§12.227 Section 10 of the STA provides that a share or similar equity interest issued by a corporation, business trust or similar entity is a security. Although a full discussion of this Act is beyond the scope of this text, a general understanding of certain key provisions of the STA is relevant to the discussion of the subjects included in this chapter and elsewhere in this text.

§12.228 For the purposes of the Act, shares and other securities are described as "financial assets". The full definition of this term reads:

"financial asset" means, except as otherwise provided in sections 10 to 16,

(a) a security,

(b) an obligation of a person that,

　　(i) is, or is of a type, dealt in or traded on financial markets, or

　　(ii) is recognized in any other market or area in which it is issued or dealt in as a medium for investment,

(c) a share, participation or other interest in a person, or in property or an enterprise of a person, that,

---

[636] S.O. 2006, c. 8.

[637] The term "securities account" is defined to mean "an account to which a financial asset is or may be credited in accordance with an agreement under which the person maintaining the account undertakes to treat the person for whom the account is maintained as entitled to exercise the rights that constitute the financial asset."

(i) is, or is of a type, dealt in or traded on financial markets, or

(ii) is recognized in any other market or area in which it is issued or dealt in as a medium for investment,

(d) any property that is held by a securities intermediary for another person in a securities account if the securities intermediary has expressly agreed with the other person that the property is to be treated as a financial asset under this Act, or

(e) a credit balance in a securities account, unless the securities intermediary has expressly agreed with the person for whom the account is maintained that the credit balance is not to be treated as a financial asset under this Act.

Clearing agencies and their participants are described as "securities intermediaries".[638] The shareholder or other holder of un-certificated security is described as the "entitlement holder".[639]

§12.229 Section 99 of the STA requires a securities intermediary to "take action to obtain a payment or distribution" made by the issuer of a financial asset. In doing so, it must exercise "due care in accordance with reasonable commercial standards to attempt to obtain the payment or distribution". Where a payment or distribution made by an issuer is received by the securities intermediary, it "is obligated to its entitlement holder" for the payment or distribution. Section 100 of the STA deals with the exercise of rights, such as voting rights. It provides that a securities intermediary must exercise rights with respect to a financial asset if directed to do so by an entitlement holder. It satisfies this duty if,

(a) the securities intermediary acts with respect to the duty as agreed to by the entitlement holder and the securities intermediary; or

(b) in the absence of an agreement referred to in clause (a), the securities intermediary either,

(i) places the entitlement holder in a position to exercise the rights directly, or

---

[638] The full definition of "securities intermediary" defines the term to mean:
 (a) a clearing agency, or
 (b) a person, including a broker, bank or trust company, that in the ordinary course of its business maintains securities accounts for others and is acting in that capacity;

[639] The full definition in section 1 of the Act is: " 'entitlement holder' means a person identified in the records of a securities intermediary as the person having a security entitlement against the securities intermediary and includes a person who acquires a security entitlement by virtue of clause 95(1) (b) or (c)." Subsection 95(1) of the STA reads:

Except as otherwise provided in subsections (3) and (4), a person acquires a security entitlement if a securities intermediary,

(a) indicates by book entry that a financial asset has been credited to the person's securities account;

(b) receives a financial asset from the person or acquires a financial asset for the person and, in either case, accepts it for credit to the person's securities account; or

(c) becomes obligated under another statute, law, regulation or rule to credit a financial asset to the person's securities account.

(ii) exercises due care in accordance with reasonable commercial standards to follow the direction of the entitlement holder.

§12.230 Where shares (or other securities) are registered under a book-entry only system, registration of interests in and transfers of the shares can be made only through the book-entry only system of a clearing agency,[640] such as CDS Clearing and Depository Services Inc. ("CDS"). In such a case, the shares must be purchased, transferred and surrendered for retraction or redemption through a participant in the CDS book-entry only system. Beneficial owners of the shares do not have the right to receive physical certificates evidencing their ownership of such shares. However, each investor does receive a customer confirmation of purchase from the CDS Participant from whom shares are purchased in accordance with the practices and procedures of that CDS Participant. No investor is entitled to a certificate or other instrument from the transfer agent for the shares or from CDS itself, to evidence that investor's interest in or ownership of the shares, nor will the investor be shown on the records maintained by CDS, except through an agent who participates in CDS. Shares are also surrendered for conversion or redemption through a participant in the CDS book entry only system. Dividends and other payments are also be to distributed through the CDS system.

§12.231 Recently, Ontario law was amended by the enactment of the *Securities Transfer Act, 2006* ("STA") to provide a regime of law to govern trading and investment in un-certificated securities. Section 14 of the *Executions Act* provides that the interest of an execution debtor in a security or security entitlement may be seized by the sheriff in accordance with sections 47 to 51 of the *Securities Transfer Act, 2006*. Every seizure and sale made by the sheriff shall include all dividends, distributions, interest and other rights to payment in respect of the security, if issued by an issuer incorporated or otherwise organized under Ontario law, or in respect of the security entitlement and, after the seizure becomes effective, the issuer or securities intermediary shall not pay the dividends, distributions or interest or give effect to other rights to payment to or on behalf of anyone except the sheriff or a person who acquires or takes the security or security entitlement from the sheriff.[641]

---

[640] The term "clearing agency" is defined in the Act as follows:

"clearing agency" means a person,

(a) that carries on a business or activity as a clearing agency or clearing house within the meaning of the *Securities Act* or the securities regulatory law of another province or territory in Canada,

(b) that is recognized or otherwise regulated as a clearing agency or clearing house by the Ontario Securities Commission or by a securities regulatory authority of another province or territory in Canada, and

(c) that is a securities and derivatives clearing house for the purposes of section 13.1 of the *Payment Clearing and Settlement Act* (Canada) or whose clearing and settlement system is designated under Part I of that Act.

[641] STA, s. 51(3).

§12.232 By virtue of section 47 of the STA, the general rule is that the ordinary laws governing the civil enforcement of judgments apply to such seizure. In the case of a certificated security, the interest of a judgment debtor in a certificated security normally may be seized only by actual seizure of the security certificate by a sheriff.[642] Ordinarily, in the case of an un-certificated security, seizure may be effected only by a sheriff serving a notice of seizure on the issuer at the issuer's chief executive office. Normally, the interest of a judgment debtor in a security entitlement may be seized only by a sheriff serving a notice of seizure on the securities intermediary with whom the judgment debtor's securities account is maintained.[643] The following exceptions apply to the foregoing general rules:

- A certificated security for which the security certificate has been surrendered to the issuer may be seized by a sheriff serving a notice of seizure on the issuer at the issuer's chief executive office.[644]
- The interest of a judgment debtor in any of the following may be seized by a sheriff serving a notice of seizure on the secured party:
  - A certificated security for which the security certificate is in the possession of a secured party.
  - An un-certificated security registered in the name of a secured party.
  - A security entitlement maintained in the name of a secured party.

§12.233 Subsection 16(1) of the *Executions Act* provides that subject to subsection (4), if the transfer of the seized security is restricted by the terms of the security, a restriction imposed by the issuer or a unanimous shareholder agreement governed by the law of Ontario, the sheriff is bound by the restriction. Subsection 16(4) provides:

> On application by the sheriff or any interested person, if the Superior Court of Justice considers that a restriction on the transfer of the seized security or a person's entitlement to acquire or redeem the seized security was made with intent to defeat, hinder, delay or defraud creditors or others, the court may make any order that that the court considers appropriate regarding the seized security, including an order doing one or more of the following:
>
> 1. Directing the method or terms of sale of the seized security, or the method of realizing the value of the seized security other than through sale.
> 2. Directing the issuer to pay dividends, distributions or interest to the sheriff even though the sheriff is not the registered owner of the security.
> 3. Directing the issuer to register the transfer of the seized security to a person despite a restriction on the transfer of the security described in subsection (2) or the entitlement of another person to acquire or redeem the security described in subsection (3).

---

[642] STA, s. 48(1).
[643] STA, s. 50.
[644] STA, s. 48 (2).

4. Directing that all or part of a unanimous shareholder agreement does not apply to a person who acquires or takes a seized security from the sheriff.

5. Directing that the issuer be dissolved and its proceeds disposed of according to law.

Chapter 13

SHAREHOLDER REMEDIES

A. INTRODUCTION

§13.1 As we have seen, shareholders are entitled to numerous rights under general principles of corporate law — and, to an increasing extent, under securities laws as well. In addition to their rights at law and under statute, shareholders will usually be entitled to a range of contractual rights, under the terms of their shares, and possibly under a unanimous shareholder agreement or other relevant contract. Central to the viability of this complex scheme of rights are effective measures for asserting and defending the rights concerned. It is such mechanisms that form the subject of this Chapter. We will begin this survey by looking at the so-called "oppression" remedy, that has recently emerged as the most important available remedy, both in terms of the scope of protection that is afforded, and by reference to the extent to which it has come to dominate the world of corporate litigation. From there we will proceed to a discussion of shareholder (and other) derivative actions, and then to a number of subsidiary remedies that supplement these two main statutory thrusts.

§13.2 Shareholder litigation and the pursuit of other remedies are almost always directed against corporate management and relate to disputes within the corporation as to the manner in which the corporation should be run. It is self-evident that an overly restrictive approach by the courts towards the pursuit of shareholder remedies will encourage wrongdoing on the part of the control group within a corporation. In economic terms, the effect is to give rise to what are known as management agency costs. However, an overly broad approach towards shareholder remedies results in higher costs of litigation. These include not only the cost of defending the action, but the largely immeasurable cost of diverting management attention away from proper supervision of the ongoing business and affairs of a corporation and the pursuit of business opportunity, towards the defence of the shareholder's claim. From a public policy perspective, it is necessary to properly balance the positive effect of shareholder litigation in reducing management agency cost against the litigation costs. Achieving this balance is necessary to allow the risk of shareholder claims to amount to a significant force in bringing about good corporate governance, while at the same time preventing the actual number of such claims from becoming a drain on the conduct of corporate enterprise. The need to strike this balance, and the consequent need to trade off between two conflicting sources of corporate waste, are often not fully appreciated by the courts.[1] Minority interests within a corporation clearly have rights, and those rights must be properly protected. But all others interested in a corporation also have rights, and their rights must be properly respected by the courts and legislatures as well.

§13.3 Only rarely is the effort to strike a balance a simple matter. In one recent American case dealing with shareholder litigation arising out of a takeover bid, the court commented upon the complexity of the question before it in the following terms:

> These cases present a unique opportunity for our courts to address that balance. They arise at a time when the importance of sound corporate governance to the health of our capital markets is a matter of national concern. The juxtaposition of the class action, the derivative action and a suit by a competing bidder in the setting of one merger transaction, combined with the attorney fees sought by counsel for both class and derivative plaintiffs, sharply focuses the Court's attention on the competing interests and costs. Nowhere is the cost balancing more difficult than in a merger transaction challenged by a third party bidder for the company to be acquired. In those situations, as here, the third party bidder (here, Sun Trust) usually mans the laboring oar in the litigation. In those cases, as here, the goal is not to create a common fund or pool for recovery but to obtain the best offer in an open market for shareholders who are not coerced to sell. While no fund is created, maximization of shareholder value is the goal. The typical case, as here, involves a challenge to deal protection devices that the plaintiffs, including the third party bidder, claim prevent a fair vote on the merger proposal or unfairly restrict competitive bidding. The deal protection devices become more important in a "merger of equals" because the premium to be paid for the acquired company is low. Such deals can frequently attract third-party bidders. They also attract shareholder litigation. Where a subsequent bidder prevails, it is often difficult, if not impossible, to determine how much of the increased offering price was attributable to the litigation as opposed to increased value generated by the market.[2]

B. THE OPPRESSION REMEDY

§13.4 It need hardly be stated that the interests of the various shareholders of a corporation may conflict, particularly where one shareholder or identifiable group of shareholders control the corporation and others are in a minority position. The potential for conflicting interests is even greater between those who have an equity interest in a corporation and the other security holders. Furthermore, because corporate status confers limited liability, there is always a risk that a corporation will be used in such a way that creditors are unacceptably disadvantaged.

---

[1] See, generally, Robert B. Thompson and Randall S. Thomas, "Shareholder Litigation: Reexamining The Balance Between Litigation Agency Costs and Management Agency Costs" (Columbia Center for Law and Economics, Working Paper, December 2002).
[2] *In Re Wachovia Shareholders Litigation, Harbor Finance Partners v. Balloun,* 2003 NCBC 10 at para. 5 (N.C. Sup. Ct.).

§13.5 The problems arising from shareholder disputes are particularly acute in the case of close corporations. A close corporation is one in which the shares of the corporation are held in a few hands (or sometimes by a few families). The shares of such corporations are rarely traded.[3] A common feature of the close corporation is the integration of majority share ownership and the management of the corporation concerned. Generally, there is no ready market for the shares of a closely held corporation, particularly where the shares concerned represent a minority interest in the corporation, which can be frozen out effectively from any say in the running of the company, with the attendant risk that the rights and concerns of the minority will be ignored. In the United States, an extensive body of case law evolved in which a high standard of utmost good faith has been imposed upon the directors and majority shareholders of a closed corporation (to an extent analogous to the duty imposed upon the members of a partnership), with a view towards the protection of the minority shareholders within a close corporation.[4]

§13.6 The Canadian oppression remedy is derived from section 210 of the U.K. *Companies Act, 1948*. Section 210 was enacted following the recommendation set out in the *Report of Cohen Committee on Company Law Amendment*[5] which suggested that courts should be given the power to remedy oppressive conduct by imposing a just and equitable settlement. Until the end of the Second World War, company law within the Commonwealth provided little protection to a shareholder who had been treated unfairly, but lawfully, by the controlling group within the corporation. The guiding principle in corporate decision-making was that of majority rule.[6] Subject to a few limitations, the common law permitted the shareholder to treat his or her right to vote as an incident of the property that the share conferred, and, consequently, each shareholder might exercise his or her votes for his or her own advantage, and was in no way subject to a fiduciary duty to the other shareholders of the corporation.[7] All this began to change with the enactment of the 1948 English *Companies Act*,[8] which included specific statutory relief for shareholders who were subjected to oppression by the control group. Subsection 210(1) of that Act provided:

---

[3] *Galler v. Galler*, 32 Ill.2d 16 at 27, 203 N.E.2d 577 (S.C. Ill. 1964).

[4] See, for instance, *Donahue v. Rodd Electrotype Co. of New England, Inc.*, 367 Mass. 578, 328 N.E.2d 505 (S.J.C. Mass. 1975), per Tauro C.J.; *Wilkes v. Springside Nursing Home, Inc.*, 370 Mass. 842, 353 N.E.2d 657 (S.J.C. 1976); *Bessette v. Bessette*, 385 Mass. 806, 434 N.E. 2d 206 (S.J.C. 1982). As for whether a minority shareholder in a position to block particular corporate action can be in breach of this duty of utmost good faith, see *Smith v. Atlantic Properties Inc.*, 12 Mass. App. Ct. 201, 422 N.E.2d 798 (C.A. 1981). It is doubtful whether a Canadian court would follow this approach: *Brant Investments Ltd. v. KeepRite Inc.*, [1991] O.J. No. 683, 1 B.L.R. (2d) 225 at 244 (C.A.).

[5] 1945, Cmnd. 6659, para. 60.

[6] *Cooper v. Gordon* (1869), L.R. 8 Eq. 249, per Stuart V.C.; *Re Kong Thai Sawmill (Miri) Sdn Bhd*, [1978] 2 M.L.J. 227 at 229 (P.C.), per Lord Wilberforce.

[7] See, generally, *Peter's American Delicacy Co. v. Heath* (1939), 61 C.L.R. 457 (H.C. Aust.); *Rights & Issues Investment Trust Ltd. v. Stylo Shoes Ltd.*, [1965] Ch. 250; *Mills v. Mills* (1938), 60 C.L.R. 150 (H.C. Aust.); *North-West Transportation Co. v. Beatty* (1887), 12 App. Cas. 589 (P.C.).

[8] 11 & 12 Geo. VI, c. 38.

210.(1) Any member of a company who complains that the affairs of the company are being conducted in a manner oppressive to some part of the members (including himself) ... may make an application to the court by petition for an order under this section.

On such an application, the court was vested with the power to make such orders as it thought fit in the circumstances,

210.(2) ... whether for regulating the conduct of the company's affairs in future, or for the purchase of the shares of any members of the company by other members of the company or by the company and, in the case of a purchase by the company, for the reduction accordingly of the company's capital, or otherwise.

While under section 210 as originally drafted, an applicant had to demonstrate that the circumstances were sufficient to justify the issue of an order for the winding-up of the company, the oppression remedy would be granted where in the particular circumstances of the company a winding-up would be unfair. The remedy was expanded in 1964 when unfair prejudice was added as a basis of relief.

§13.7 It took several years before this new remedy secured widespread legislative implementation, but it is now a well-settled feature of Canadian corporate law. The current rule relating to oppression under the Ontario *Business Corporations Act* (OBCA) is now set down in section 248 of that Act,[9] subsection (1) of which provides that a complainant,[10] the Director and, in the case of an offering corporation, the Commission may apply to the court for an order. Subsection 248(2) then continues:

248.(2) Where, upon an application under subsection (1), the court is satisfied that in respect of a corporation or any of its affiliates,

(a) any act or omission of the corporation or any of its affiliates effects or threatens to effect a result;

(b) the business or affairs of the corporation or any of its affiliates are, have been or are threatened to be carried on or conducted in a manner; or

(c) the powers of the directors of the corporation or any of its affiliates are, have been or are threatened to be exercised in a manner,

---

[9] R.S.O. 1990, c. B.16. See also the *Canada Business Corporation Act*, R.S.C. 1985, c. C-44 (CBCA), s. 241.

[10] The term "complainant" is defined in OBCA, s. 245 to mean:

(a) a registered holder or beneficial owner, and a former registered holder or beneficial owner, of a security of a corporation or any of its affiliates;

(b) a director or officer or a former director or officer of a corporation or of any of its affiliates;

(c) any other person who, in the discretion of the court, is a proper person to make an application under this Part.

The meaning of this term is considered in detail later.

that is oppressive or unfairly prejudicial to or that unfairly disregards the interests of any security holder, creditor, director or officer of the corporation, the court may make an order to rectify the matters complained of.

It has been held in Australia — and in all probability it is the law in Canada as well — that the remedy is available in regard to the acts or omissions of anyone taking effective control of a corporation (or its affiliates), whether acting in a *de facto* capacity or with proper lawful authority.[11]

§13.8 As we will discuss in greater detail below, the current statutory relief is available not only for oppression, but also for unfair prejudice to, or unfair disregard of, the interests of a complainant. Despite this apparently separate ground of relief, it is convenient to use the generic term "oppression" as a short form description of all potential grounds of relief for complaint, except in those cases in which it is necessary to distinguish among them for some analytical purpose. Therefore, in the balance of this section, unless the context otherwise requires, the term "oppression" should be taken to include a reference to unfair prejudice or unfair disregard.

(i) Need for the Remedy

§13.9 It is obvious that the interests of the various shareholders of a corporation may conflict, particularly where one shareholder or identifiable group of shareholders control the corporation and others are in a minority position. The potential for conflicting interests is greatest between those who have an equity interest in a corporation and its other security holders. Furthermore, because corporate status confers limited liability, there is always a risk that a corporation will be used in such a way that creditors are unacceptably disadvantaged. The oppression remedy provided for in sections 248 of the OBCA and 241 of the CBCA provide the courts with the power to intervene in the affairs of a corporation at the behest of a complainant where it is necessary to prevent or protect the complainant from, or to stop, oppressive, unfairly prejudicial or similar conduct of the corporation. The remedy affords a lesser and more flexible alternative to an order for the winding-up of the corporation.[12]

§13.10 Little empirical work has been carried out with respect to the utilization of the oppression remedy in Canada. However, in one survey of petitions for relief under the U.K. "unfair prejudice" regime under section 459 of the *Companies Act 1985* — the analog to the OBCA and CBCA oppression remedy — revealed the following profile of claims:

- More than 96 per cent of the cases related to private companies;
- In 22.4 per cent of the cases surveyed, the petitioner was a 50 per cent shareholder;

---

[11] *Re East West Promotions Pty Ltd.* (1986), 10 A.C.L.R. 222.
[12] See, generally, *Re Fish and Game League (Regina)*, [1967] S.J. No. 86, 63 D.L.R. (2d) 47 at 62 (Q.B.), *per* Tucker J.

- In 67 per cent of those cases, exclusion from management was alleged.

In a second recent survey of petitions presented to the Companies Court in England under section 459[13] it was stated that:

- 70.4 per cent of such claims were brought by minority shareholders and 24 per cent by 50 per cent shareholders;
- 96.6 per cent of such claims concerned private companies, with 82 per cent involving companies with 5 shareholders or fewer;
- 64.4 per cent of such claims alleged exclusion from management, well ahead of the proportion for any other particular allegation;
- 52.8 per cent pleaded that a "legitimate expectation" of the petitioner had been broken.[14]

These findings do not seem out of line with the profile indicated in Canadian case law, although the cases that actually result in judgments may well be atypical of the overall profile of such claims.

§13.11 Oppression-type remedies deal with a relatively common problem in the corporate setting which provides the underlying rationale for many different aspects of company law. Specifically, such a remedy is one of several possible responses to the principal-agent problem. Broadly speaking, a principal-agent problem arises whenever one person must entrust the performance of some task in which that person has an economic interest to another person. In the corporate context, the investors in a corporation must entrust the management of the funds that they have invested in the corporation to the directors, officers and others who are in a position to exercise effective control over the operations of the corporation.

§13.12 It is obvious that the interests of the various shareholders of a corporation may conflict, particularly where one shareholder or identifiable group of shareholders control the corporation and another group is in a minority position. There are also potential conflicts between those who hold equity interests in contrast to other interests. In a corporation, management is often entrusted to a few by the many: the few are the agents; the many are the principals.[15] There are significant disparities in the access to information which the potential parties to a contract possess — a situation which is sometimes termed one of "asymmetrical information".

§13.13 The principal-agent problem is not the only consideration militating in favour of oppression-type relief. A further relevant disparity between the real

---

[13] Discussed in detail below.
[14] Law Commission Report No. 246 *Shareholder Remedies* (Cmnd. 3769, TSO 1997), Appendix J, 177–80. This involved an inspection of 233 out of 254 such petitions which had been presented between January 1994 and December 1996.
[15] Note that we are using principal and agent here in their economic sense, rather than their strict legal sense.

world of company investment and the hypothetical world of perfect competition relates to the obvious restrictions on entry and exit for investors in companies. Shares and other securities of a small company are not fungible, and often there is no market for such securities. Indeed, the transfer of securities in such companies will often be restricted. In addition, because the effect of unfairly prejudicial conduct often becomes known on an after-the-fact basis, shareholders who disapprove of the direction in which a company is being taken usually have no practical way of escaping from their investment (by sale or other disposition). Unless they can recover the decline in the value of their investment from those who have caused that decline, they have no effective remedy. Unfortunately, the case law with respect to derivative relief indicates that a much broader remedy is required, if all cases of unfair shareholder prejudice are to be adequately addressed.

§13.14 Neither the principal-agent problem nor the entry-exit problem arises due to deficiencies in the current law. Rather they are inherent in the nature of the corporate relationship, arising in consequence of the separation of ownership from control within a corporation, and also due to the diversity of interests that are represented within a corporation. Where there are economic forces that give rise to a problem, the law cannot eliminate those forces. However, it can provide a suitable remedy and ensure that the remedy is made available at the lowest possible cost, and also impose costs that deter undesirable activities.

§13.15 The jurisdiction of the court to grant relief is one that must be carefully exercised. It requires a balancing of the rights of those who are in control and those who are in a minority position within the corporation. There is no rule preventing a defendant in an oppression case from counterclaiming for oppression.[16] All competing interests within the corporation must be respected and safeguarded by the court, not merely the interests of the complainant.[17] Business decisions that were honestly made will not be second-guessed by the courts or subjected to microscopic examination under the oppression remedy.[18] The court is not justified in granting relief under the oppression provisions merely because the management of a corporation came to a different decision than the judge might have reached in the same circumstances.[19] It is not sufficient for the complainant to show prejudice or disregard of his or her interests. It must also be shown that the prejudice or disregard complained of was unfair:

---

[16] *L & B Electric Ltd. v. Oickle*, [2005] N.S.J. No. 192, 8 B.L.R. (4th) 122 (S.C.), aff'd [2006] N.S.J. No. 119 (C.A.).
[17] *Such v. RW-LB Holdings Ltd.*, [1993] A.J. No. 1033, 11 B.L.R. (2d) 122 (Q.B.) Perhaps the clearest articulation of this balancing requirement may be found in a New Zealand case: *Re H.W. Thomas Ltd.*, [1984] 1 N.Z.L.R. 686, 2 A.C.L.C. 610 (S.C.), *per* Richardson J.
[18] See, for instance, *Wayde v. New South Wales Rugby League* (1985), 3 A.C.L.C. 799 (H.C. Aust.) — court will not review a decision made honestly and reasonably in the interests of promoting the business of the corporation, even if it is harsh to the complainant.
[19] See, generally, *Brant Investments Ltd. v. KeepRite Inc.*, [1987] O.J. No. 574, 37 B.L.R. 65, additional reasons [1987] O.J. No. 2700 (H.C.J.), aff'd [1991] O.J. No. 683 (C.A.).

It is not necessarily unfair for directors in good faith to advance one of the objects of the company to the prejudice of a member where the advancement of the object necessarily entails prejudice to that member or discrimination against him. *Prima facie,* it is for the directors and not for the court to decide whether the furthering of a corporate object which is inimical to a member's interests should prevail over those interests or whether some balance should be struck between them. ... The question of unfairness is one of fact and degree which section 320 requires the court to determine, but not without regard to the view which the directors themselves have formed and not without allowing for any special skill, knowledge and acumen possessed by the directors.[20]

§13.16 The basic intent behind section 248 and its equivalents across Canada was explained by Fulton J. as follows:

[The] scheme is to provide ... the sort of relief formerly provided for [in applications for the winding up of the corporation] without the necessity of proving that the circumstances are such that it would be just and equitable to order a winding-up, but with the power to the court, if it thinks it appropriate, to include within the relief that can then be ordered, an order for winding-up.[21]

Unfortunately, the Act gives no indication as to the type of conduct that is "oppressive or unfairly prejudicial or that unfairly disregards the interests" of potential complainants. Quite likely because of this silence, the section has spawned a considerable amount of case law, through which the courts have attempted to graft some meat onto the bare bones of the legislation. To get a clear understanding of the meaning and scope of the oppression provisions of the OBCA and the CBCA, it is necessary to start with first principles.

(ii) Meaning of Oppression, etc.

§13.17 Where the Legislature creates a new statutory remedy (as it has done in the case of the section 248 oppression remedy), it is a reasonable assumption that the availability of relief under that remedy is not limited to those cases where the complainant is able to demonstrate that he or she has been victimized by some wrong that would have been actionable at his or her instance even if the remedy had never been created. Thus, it would not be an appropriate approach toward section 248 to assume that it was intended to operate only where the complainant could demonstrate that he or she had been the victim of a breach of contract, breach of trust or other fiduciary duty or other actionable wrong at common law or in equity. Had this been the intent, there would have been no need to describe the grounds for relief as being oppression, unfair prejudice or unfair disregard. These new labels suggest an intent to create new grounds of relief.

---

[20] *Wayde v. New South Wales Rugby League* (1985), 3 A.C.L.C. 799 at para. 6 (H.C. Aust.), *per* Brennan J.
[21] *Diligenti v. RWMD Operations Kelowna Ltd.*, [1976] B.C.J. No. 38, 1 B.C.L.R. 36 at 42 (S.C.).

§13.18 The focus of section 248 on the "interests" of the complainant, as opposed to the rights of the complainant, is also significant.[22] Conduct need not be deliberately wrongful in order to sustain a complaint. Attention must be paid not merely to the intentions of the person whose conduct gives rise to the complaint, but also to its effect.[23] The term "interests" has been given a broad interpretation. For instance, in *820099 Ontario Inc. v. Harold E. Ballard Ltd.*,[24] Farley J. equated shareholder interests with the reasonable expectations of a shareholder — expectations which could be said to have been, or which ought to be, considered to be part of the compact made by the shareholders at the time when they invested in the corporation.[25] Aside from cases involving actual fraud[26] or misappropriation of corporate assets,[27] the classic case of prejudice or oppression exists where a corporation conducts its business or affairs to confer a benefit on some of its shareholders that it denies (or that is not available) to its shareholders generally,[28] or seeks to impose excessive costs[29] or risks[30] on one group rather than another. It is oppressive for the majority to misuse their control over the payment of dividends to force a minority shareholder to sell his or her shares.[31]

§13.19 One use that has been made of the oppression remedy is to supplement the range of relief that may be provided where more traditional remedies are inadequate to address the wrong that has been suffered, such as a breach of contract or tort. For instance, oppression relief has been granted[32] where a loss has been sustained resulting from conduct that is "unfair, unscrupulous, offensive to business ethics and principles of fairness, and smacked of unconscionability", in that it amounted to "a classic squeeze out without compensation".[33] Conduct of the control group within a corporation, although not "oppressive" within the strict meaning of the term, "did not meet the minimum standard of 'behaviour

---

[22] *Westfair Foods Ltd. v. Watt*, [1990] A.J. No. 315, 73 Alta. L.R. (2d) 326 at 339 (Q.B.), per Moore C.J.Q.B., aff'd [1991] A.J. No. 321, 79 D.L.R. (4th) 48 (C.A.), leave to appeal to S.C.C. refused 85 D.L.R. (4th) viii.
[23] See, generally, *Sidaplex-Plastic Suppliers, Inc. v. Elta Group Inc.*, [1998] O.J. No. 2910, 162 D.L.R. (4th) 367 (C.A.).
[24] [1991] O.J. No. 266, 3 B.L.R. (2d) 113 at 185 (Gen. Div.), per Farley J., aff'd [1991] O.J. No. 1082 (Div. Ct.).
[25] See also *Ferguson v. Imax Systems Corp.*, [1983] O.J. No. 3156, 43 O.R. (2d) 128 at 137 (C.A.), per Brooke J.A., leave to appeal to S.C.C. refused 2 O.A.C. 158n; *Ebrahimi v. Westbourne Galleries Ltd.*, [1972] 2 All E.R. 492 (H.L.), per Lord Wilberforce.
[26] See, generally, *Re London School of Electronics Ltd.*, [1986] Ch. 211; *Re Cumana Ltd.*, [1986] B.C.L.C. 430 (C.A.); *Belmont Finance Corp. v. Williams Furniture Ltd. (No. 2)*, [1980] 1 All E.R. 393 (C.A.).
[27] *Redekop v. Robco Construction Ltd.*, [1978] B.C.J. No. 46, 5 B.L.R. 58 (S.C.).
[28] See, for instance, *Low v. Ascot Jockey Club*, [1986] B.C.J. No. 3001, 1 B.C.L.R. (2d) 123 (S.C.).
[29] *O'Connor v. Winchester Oil & Gas Inc.*, [1986] B.C.J. No. 3175, 69 B.C.L.R. 330, [1986] 2 W.W.R. 737 (S.C.).
[30] *Westmore v. Old MacDonald's Farms Ltd.*, [1986] B.C.J. No. 3009, 70 B.C.L.R. 332 (S.C.).
[31] *Ferguson v. Imax Systems Corp.*, [1983] O.J. No. 3156, 43 O.R. (2d) 128 (C.A.), leave to appeal to S.C.C. refused 2 O.A.C. 158n.
[32] *Re Jermyn Street Turkish Baths Ltd.*, [1971] 3 All E.R. 184, [1971] 1 W.L.R. 1042 (C.A.).
[33] *Chicago Blower Corp. v. 141209 Canada Ltd.*, [1988] M.J. No. 528, 40 B.L.R. 201 (Q.B.).

and *bona fides*' required of those holding their positions" in the corporation.[34] An example of where the oppression remedy may be employed in order to address a remedial shortcoming in the general corporate law can be seen in the area of takeover bids. As discussed in the context of management buyouts,[35] a takeover bid can involve a breach of fiduciary duty on the part of the bidder. However, even when the bid is made by an outsider, it is possible for a decision by the board with respect to the corporation's response to a proposed takeover to be more influenced by concerns for each director's own best interest, as by what is in the best interest of the corporation itself. Even in cases where directors are at arm's length to the bidder, there is a potential that the directors will find themselves in a conflict of interest. As Weiler J.A. noted in the *Maple Leaf Foods* case:

> A potential conflict of interest arises because as a director of a target company, the senior executive has a duty to act in the best interests of the shareholders, but as a member of senior management the executive retains an interest in continued employment. In actively negotiating with a potential bidder the executive is negotiating with his potential boss or executioner.[36]

This conflict is most evident in the case of senior managers who sit on the board, since they have potentially the most to lose by reason of the takeover bid. On the other hand, completely excluding such management-directors from the negotiation process is unrealistic, since such individuals are almost certain to be the directors who are most familiar with the business. In principle, the availability of the oppression remedy (with the consequent prospect of unwinding the transaction if evidence of abuse can be found) goes a long way to disciplining the takeover process. Where such evidence emerges, the takeover may be attacked either as a form of oppression (*i.e.*, as a cause of some specific injury to the applicant seeking such relief) or by way of derivative proceedings (*i.e.*, for a breach of the directors fiduciary duty to the corporation).

(1) The Distinction Among the Grounds of Relief

§13.20 As mentioned briefly above, although it is common to speak of the oppression remedy, the use of that term is, to some extent, a misnomer because the relief granted under section 248 of the OBCA is not limited to cases of actual oppression; it is sufficient to show that the complainant's interests have been unfairly disregarded or unfairly prejudiced.[37] One's initial inclination might be to doubt whether a meaningful distinction can be drawn among "oppression",

---

[34] *Edwards v. Edwards Dockrill Horwich Inc.*, [2005] N.S.J. No. 451, additional reasons [2006] N.S.J. No. 230 (S.C.).
[35] See Chapter 14, Fundamental Changes.
[36] *Maple Leaf Foods Inc. v. Schneider Corp.*, [1988] O.J. No. 4142, 42 O.R. (3d) 177 at para. 75 (C.A.), reported elsewhere as *Pente Investment Management Ltd. v. Schneider Corp.*
[37] *Brant Investments Ltd. v. KeepRite Inc.*, [1991] O.J. No. 683, 80 D.L.R. (4th) 161 (C.A.), per McKinlay J.A.; *Such v. RW-LB Holdings Ltd.*, [1993] A.J. No. 1033, 11 B.L.R. (2d) 122 at 139 *et seq.* (Q.B.), *per* Mason J.

"unfairly prejudicial" conduct or "unfair disregard".[38] A distinction exists only if it is possible to say that a person is guilty of oppression but not unfair disregard, or of unfair prejudice but not oppression.[39] Unfortunately, it has never been clear exactly how these grounds for relief are intended to interrelate with each other, let alone the more traditional grounds for relief recognized in common law and equity, such as breach of contract[40] or breach of fiduciary duty. It is also unclear how the oppression remedy of section 248 is intended to interrelate with the derivative proceeding remedy under section 246.

§13.21 Even though the courts seem to have made their best efforts to set down general principles to guide the resolution of future disputes, cases decided on the oppression remedy have a definite *ad hoc* quality about them. The case law affords little more than a list of different situations which will (or will not) be considered to amount to oppression or other forms of wrongdoing, and it is impossible to discern any general definition of the types of conduct that will run afoul of the section. A study of the case law concerning the additional criteria of unfair prejudice and unfair disregard reveals that they were intended to expand the range of cases in which relief might be obtained. Section 210 of the 1948 English Act dealt only with conduct that was "oppressive". This term was given a narrow construction by some courts.[41] Unfortunately, if the additional criteria of unfair prejudice and unfair disregard broaden the availability of a remedy, it is difficult to determine how far. Similarly broad wording has been adopted in Australia and New Zealand, and there it has been held that the terms "oppressive, unfairly discriminatory and unfairly prejudicial" are not to be regarded as three distinct alternatives, that are to be considered separately as if in watertight compartments, but, instead, should be read together.[42] Other guidance has been slow in coming and far from definitive in nature.

§13.22 One goal behind the legislation is to ensure the settlement of intra-corporate disputes on equitable principles as opposed to a strict adherence to legal rights;[43] another is to protect the reasonable expectations[44] of shareholders

---

[38] All of the descriptions provided for these terms seem to fall within Viscount Simmonds description of "oppressive conduct", equating it with conduct that was "burdensome, harsh and wrongful": *Scottish Co-operative Wholesale Society v. Meyer*, [1959] A.C. 324 at 342 (H.L.).
[39] In *Bernard v. Montgomery*, [1987] S.J. No. 295, 36 B.L.R. 257 (Q.B.), it was held that to succeed a complainant must demonstrate some oppression, unfair prejudice, or unfair disregard of his or her interests. These were said to be mutually exclusive, but it was only necessary to establish the presence of one of them to obtain relief.
[40] For a case involving a simple breach of contract that was held to amount to oppression, see *Lyall v. 147250 Canada Ltd.*, [1993] B.C.J. No. 874, 84 B.C.L.R. (2d) 234 (C.A.).
[41] See, for instance, *Re Jermyn Steet Turkish Baths Ltd.*, [1971] 3 All E.R. 184, [1971] 1 W.L.R. 1042 (C.A.), *per* Buckley L.J.
[42] *Re H.W. Thomas Ltd.*, [1984] 1 N.Z.L.R. 686, 2 A.C.L.C. 610 (S.C.), *per* Richardson J.; see also *Morgan v. 45 Flyers Avenue Pty Ltd.* (1986), 10 A.C.L.R. 692.
[43] *Keho Holdings Ltd. v. Noble*, [1987] A.J. No. 334, 52 Alta. L.R. (2d) 195 at 201 (C.A.), *per* Haddad J.A.
[44] *Brant Investments Ltd. v. KeepRite Inc.*, [1987] O.J. No. 574, 60 O.R. (2d) 737 at 755 (H.C.J.), *per* Anderson J. However, reasonable shareholder expectations are not a "static matter": *820099*

(and other potential complainants)[45] — a concept that we shall explore in detail later in the chapter. Accordingly, when dealing with a closely held corporation, the court may consider the relation between the shareholders, not simply their legal rights as such. The court may examine the good faith of transactions to determine whether those transactions effect a result that is oppressive or unfairly prejudicial to the complaining shareholder.[46] Recent cases indicate that it is not necessary to show that there is an element of bad faith present to make out a case for relief.[47] However, in *Diligenti v. RWMD Operations Kelowna Ltd.*,[48] the court attempted to define or, at least, describe "unfairly prejudicial" conduct, saying that "the instinctive reaction [is] that what is unjust and inequitable is obviously also unfairly prejudicial". In *Stech v. Davies* the court defined "unfair disregard" as meaning "to unjustly and without cause in the context of Section 234(2), pay no attention, to ignore or treat as of no importance the interests of security holders, creditors, directors or officers of a corporation".[49]

§13.23 In the vast majority of cases where relief has been granted, oppressive conduct has, in fact, been shown[50] — in the sense of an element of lack of probity or fair dealing to a member in the matter of his or her proprietary rights as shareholder.[51] There is no question that deliberately oppressive conduct[52] or other behaviour that is harsh, burdensome or wrongful[53] (such as the majority shareholder managing the corporation for his or her own personal advantage[54] or denying the minority shareholder a right to participate in the profits of the corporation[55]) will provide a basis for relief. So, for instance, relief is almost certain to be available where it can be shown that the intent of the controlling

---

Ontario Inc. v. Harold E. Ballard Ltd., [1991] O.J. No. 266, 3 B.L.R. (2d) 113 at 191 (Gen. Div.), *per* Farley J., aff'd [1991] O.J. No. 1082 (Div. Ct.).

[45] *Naneff v. Con-Crete Holdings Ltd.*, [1993] O.J. No. 1756, 11 B.L.R. (2d) 218 at 246 (Gen. Div. — C.L.), *per* Blair J., var'd [1994] O.J. No. 1811 (Div. Ct.), var'd [1995] O.J. No. 1377 (C.A.); *820099 Ontario Inc. v. Harold E. Ballard Ltd.*, [1991] O.J. No. 266, 3 B.L.R. (2d) 113 at 185 (Gen. Div.), aff'd [1991] O.J. No. 1082 (Div. Ct.).

[46] *Ferguson v. Imax Systems Corp.*, [1983] O.J. No. 3156, 43 O.R. (2d) 128, 150 D.L.R. (3d) 718 at 727 (C.A.) *per* Brooke J.A., leave to appeal to S.C.C. refused 2 O.A.C. 158*n*.

[47] *Naneff v. Con-Crete Holdings Ltd.*, [1993] O.J. No. 1756, 11 B.L.R. (2d) 218 (Gen. Div. — C.L.), var'd [1994] O.J. No. 1811 (Div. Ct.), var'd [1995] O.J. No. 1377 (C.A.).; see also *Safarik v. Ocean Fisheries Ltd.*, [1993] B.C.J. No. 1816, 10 B.L.R. (2d) 246, additional reasons at [1994] B.C.J. No. 2225, 22 C.P.C. (3d) 214 (S.C.), rev'd [1995] B.C.J. No. 1979 (C.A.).

[48] [1976] B.C.J. No. 38, 1 B.C.L.R. 36 at 45-46 (S.C.).

[49] [1987] A.J. No. 618, 53 Alta. L.R. (2d) 373 at 379 (Q.B.).

[50] For a case where oppression was found to have occurred even though the facts did *not* demonstrate bad faith or lack of probity, see *Sidaplex-Plastic Suppliers, Inc. v. Elta Group Inc.*, [1995] O.J. No. 4048, 25 B.L.R. (2d) 179 at 185 (Gen. Div.), *per* Blair J., rev'd in part [1998] O.J. No. 2910, 162 D.L.R. (4th) 367 (C.A.).

[51] *Re National Building Maintenance Ltd.*, [1970] B.C.J. No. 318, [1971] 1 W.W.R. 8 at 60 (S.C.), *per* Aikins J., aff'd [1972] B.C.J. No. 605, [1972] 5 W.W.R. 410 (C.A.).

[52] See, for instance, *Re F. Dalkeith Investments Pty Ltd.* (1985), 3 A.C.L.C. 74.

[53] *Miller v. F. Mendel Holdings Ltd.*, [1984] S.J. No. 98, 26 B.L.R. 85 at 99 (Q.B.), *per* Wimmer J.; see also *Welichka v. Bittner Investments Ltd.*, [1988] A.J. No. 1336, 90 A.R. 224 (Q.B.).

[54] *Naaykens v. Bayes Equipment (Neepawa) Ltd.*, [1988] M.J. No. 566, 56 Man. R. (2d) 272 (Q.B.).

[55] *Metropolitan Commercial Carpet Centre Ltd. v. Donovan*, [1989] N.S.J. No. 254, 42 B.L.R. 306 (S.C.).

group within the corporation was to single out and injure the complainant. In contrast, mere incompetence in management (*i.e.*, unwise, inefficient or careless performance of duties) is not in itself sufficient to give rise to relief.[56]

§13.24 A person's conduct may be oppressive or unfair even where honestly motivated, for it is the result rather than the motive that is material to the question of whether relief is available.[57] In principle, conduct may be oppressive or unfair even where all parties concerned are treated equally.[58] An applicant for relief must show oppression, unfair prejudice or unfair disregard. It is not necessary for him or her to show that he or she has been deliberately singled out for mistreatment, nor to show that the complainant has been victimized by deliberate misconduct. It is sufficient to show that the effect of the act on which the complaint is based has been to prejudice the complainant unfairly. Conduct unfairly disregards the interest of a person where it pays no attention, ignores or treats as of no importance the interests of that person.[59] Relief may be sought to protect the interests of complainants in the widest sense rather than merely their strict legal or equitable rights.[60] Thus, in *Elder v. Elder & Watson Ltd.*, Lord Cooper said:

> The essence of the matter seems to be that the conduct complained of should at the lowest involve a visible departure from the standards of fair dealing and a violation of the conditions of fair play on which every shareholder who entrusts his money to a company is entitled to rely.[61]

It follows that it is not necessary to show fraud or a strict transgression of a legal or equitable right, for if such violations took place they would give rise to relief without need to resort to the section. The policy behind the section is to secure "just and equitable treatment" of minority shareholders[62] and other complainants interested in the corporation who have no control over it. For instance, in *Naaykens v. Bayes Equipment (Neepawa) Ltd.*[63] relief under the section was held to be available not so much because the transaction in question was bad, but because it had been badly put together.

---

[56] *Re Five Minute Car Wash Service Ltd.*, [1966] 1 All E.R. 242 at 247 (Ch.), *per* Buckley J.
[57] *Re H.R. Harmer Ltd.*, [1958] 3 All E.R. 689 (C.A.), *per* Jenkins L.J.
[58] *Re Overton Holdings Pty Ltd.* (1984), 2 A.C.L.C. 777 (S.C. West. Aust.).
[59] *First Edmonton Place Ltd. v. 315888 Alberta Ltd.*, [1988] A.J. No. 511, 60 Alta. L.R. (2d) 122 at 143 (Q.B.), *per* McDonald J.; *Westfair Foods Ltd. v. Watt*, [1990] A.J. No. 315, [1990] 4 W.W.R. 685 at 703-05, 73 Alta. L.R. (2d) 326 (Q.B.), *per* Moore C.J.Q.B., aff'd [1991] A.J. No. 321, 79 Alta. L.R. (2d) 363, leave to appeal to S.C.C. refused 82 Alta. L.R. (2d) lxv.
[60] *Westfair Foods Ltd. v. Watt*, [1990] A.J. No. 315, 73 Alta. L.R. (2d) 326 at 339 (Q.B.), *per* Moore C.J.Q.B., aff'd [1991] A.J. No. 321, 79 Alta. L.R. (2d) 363, leave to appeal to S.C.C. refused 82 Alta. L.R. (2d) lxv; see also *Keho Holdings Ltd. v. Noble*, [1987] A.J. No. 334, 52 Alta. L.R. (2d) 195, 38 D.L.R. (4th) 368 at 373-74 (C.A.), *per* Haddad J.A.
[61] [1952] S.C. 49 at 55.
[62] *Ferguson v. Imax Systems Corp.*, [1983] O.J. No. 3156, 150 D.L.R. (3d) 718 (C.A.), *per* Brooke J.A., leave to appeal to S.C.C. refused (1983), 2 O.A.C. 158*n*.
[63] [1988] M.J. No. 566, 56 Man. R. (2d) 272 (Q.B.). Although not oppressive, the failure to maintain proper financial records may cause unfair prejudice: *Lee v. To*, [1998] S.J. No. 347, [1998] 9 W.W.R. 1 (C.A.).

§13.25 Before leaving this discussion of the grounds for relief, it is worth observing that a consideration of the comparable provision of the U.K. legislation lends some support for the conclusion that there is but a single ground of relief under the OBCA and CBCA. Subsection 459(1) of the U.K. *Companies Act, 1985* provides:

> A member of a company may apply to the court by petition for an order under this Part on the grounds that the company's affairs are being or have been conducted in a manner which is unfairly prejudicial to the interests of its members generally or of some part of its members (including at least himself) or that any actual or proposed act or omission of the company (including an act or omission on its behalf) is or would be so prejudicial.

While the current U.K. legislation affords relief only for unfair prejudice, it can be argued that the scope of the U.K. legislation is essentially the same as in Canada. It is difficult to visualize how unfair disregard can give rise to relief in the absence of prejudice. If the prejudice seems to result from the unfair disregard of interests, then it must surely be an unfair prejudice. By the same token, it is difficult to imagine how "oppression" could exist without unfair prejudice. Thus when reduced to their most basic elements, the three grounds of relief of oppression, unfair prejudice and unfair disregard may ultimately all be equated with the term "unfair prejudice". To date, no Canadian court appears to have considered this question — although it has been noted that the notions of "oppressions", "unfair prejudice" and "unfair disregard" are not exclusive.[64]

(2) Oppression and Majority Rule

§13.26 The primary difficulty that Canadian courts have had in dealing with the oppression remedy is in deciding at which point to draw the line as to the availability of relief. While sections 248 of the OBCA and 241 of the CBCA modify the basic principle of corporate governance that "majority rules" they do not abrogate that rule. In the absence of some injustice, the majority is still free to conduct the corporation as it considers best. Thus, the guiding principle in corporate law matters is still majority rule.[65] Absent a contractual entitlement or a statutory right (usually embedded in a voting right), the majority are not obliged to consult with the minority in the management of the corporation.[66] What is oppressive, prejudicial or disrespectful of interest depends not only upon the conduct in question but also upon the circumstances in which the shareholder became a shareholder. In the absence of an underlying obligation to allow the complainant to participate in management, the exclusion of the complainant as a minority shareholder from the management of the corporation is not in itself

---

[64] See, for instance, *Elliott v. Opticom Technologies Inc.*, [2005] B.C.J. No. 782, 4 B.L.R. (4th) 103 (S.C.).
[65] *Wotherspoon v. Canadian Pacific Ltd.*, [1982] O.J. No. 3148, 35 O.R. (2d) 449 at 485 (C.A.), var'd [1987] S.C.J. No. 40.
[66] See, generally, *de la Giroday v. Giroday Sawmills Ltd.*, [1983] B.C.J. No. 79, 49 B.C.L.R. 378 at 381 (S.C.), *per* Taylor J.

oppressive.[67] In the ordinary case, a person has no right to be a director of a corporation and cannot complain that the majority shareholders have voted to remove him or her as a director. Nevertheless, a court may view this circumstance as part of a pattern of conduct to determine whether the affairs of the corporation are being conducted in a manner that is oppressive or unfair to the plaintiff.[68] In all cases, however, there must be at least some aspect to the transaction that is injurious and wrong.[69]

§13.27 It has frequently been stated that each case of oppression turns upon its own particular facts.[70] As a result, it is difficult to extrapolate general principles of law from the many decisions that have been handed down in the area,[71] because each case is fact specific in at least certain respects.[72] Conduct that is found to be unfairly prejudicial or oppressive in one case may not necessarily be so found in another, even though the factual setting of the two cases is only slightly different.[73] Still, it is worthwhile to summarize some of the decided case law that is indicative of the range of circumstances in which relief may be available. The appropriation of a corporate opportunity can amount to oppression or unfairly prejudicial conduct.[74] It is oppressive for a controlling shareholder to treat the corporation as if it were wholly owned, as, for instance, by causing it to pay repeated and large personal expenses.[75] It is also oppressive for a controlling shareholder or director to orchestrate the business or affairs of a corporation (*e.g.*, by making discretionary or unjustified payments) to frustrate or circumvent his or her obligations under a contract relating to the securities of a corporation.[76] Violations of the *Securities Act*[77] that do not give rise to a civil cause of action under that Act may also be held to constitute oppression to allow relief to be granted under section 248.[78] Defensive tactics employed to defeat a hostile takeover bid may also be oppressive.[79] Nominee directors may be guilty of op-

---

[67] *Keho Holdings Ltd. v. Noble*, [1987] A.J. No. 334, 52 Alta. L.R. (2d) 195 at 202-203, 38 D.L.R. (4th) 368 (C.A.), *per* Haddad J.A.; *Ebrahimi v. Westbourne Galleries Ltd.*, [1973] A.C. 360 at 380 (H.L.), *per* Lord Wilberforce.
[68] *Re H.R. Harmer Ltd.*, [1958] 3 All E.R. 689 (C.A.).
[69] *Scottish Co-operative Wholesale Society v. Meyer*, [1959] A.C. 324 at 363-64 (H.L.), *per* Lord Keith.
[70] *Sidaplex-Plastic Suppliers, Inc. v. Elta Group Inc.*, [1995] O.J. No. 4048, 25 B.L.R. (2d) 179 at 184 (Gen. Div.), *per* Blair J.A., rev'd in part [1998] O.J. No. 2910.
[71] *Themadel Foundation v. Third Canadian General Investment Trust Ltd.*, [1998] O.J. No. 647, 38 O.R. (3d) 749 at 754, 107 O.A.C. 188 (C.A.), *per* Carthy J.A.
[72] *Belman v. Belman*, [1995] O.J. No. 3155, 26 B.L.R. (2d) 52 at 73 (Gen. Div.), *per* Spence J.
[73] *Ferguson v. Imax Systems Corp.*, [1983] O.J. No. 3156, 43 O.R. (2d) 128, 150 D.L.R. (3d) 718 at 727 (C.A.), *per* Brooke J.A.
[74] *Neri v. Finch Hardware (1976) Ltd.*, [1995] O.J. No. 1932, 20 B.L.R. (2d) 216 (Gen. Div.).
[75] *Khayraji v. Safaverdi*, [1996] O.J. No. 3427, 33 B.L.R. (2d) 108 (Gen. Div.).
[76] See, generally, *Ludlow v. McMillan*, [1995] B.C.J. No. 683, 19 B.L.R. (2d) 102 (S.C.).
[77] R.S.O. 1990, c. S.5.
[78] *Themadel Foundation v. Third Canadian General Investment Trust Ltd.*, [1995] O.J. No. 888, 18 B.L.R. (2d) 209 (Gen. Div.), *per* Farley J., rev'd in part [1998] O.J. No. 647, 38 O.R. (3d) 749 (C.A.).
[79] *CW Shareholdings Inc. v. WIC Western International Communications Ltd.*, [1998] O.J. No. 1886, 39 O.R. (3d) 755 (Gen. Div.); but *cf. Armstrong World Industries Inc. v. Arcand*, [1997]

pression where they are caused or required by the shareholder who nominates them to make its interest paramount and to disregard or downplay the interests of other shareholders.[80]

§13.28 The classic case of oppression arises where the complainant has effectively been denied the very benefit he or she sought to obtain when joining the corporation in the capacity of a director, officer, or shareholder, or when investing in it as a security holder. For instance, in *Lunn v. B.C.L. Holdings Inc.*,[81] the parties had formed a company to buy a warehouse to house their separate businesses. The two plaintiffs were brothers who operated one of the businesses. They held 30 shares in the company, the other four shareholders holding 60 shares in total. All five shareholders were appointed as directors of the company, and each agreed that they would contribute to any repairs and improvements to be made to the property. At the time of the purchase of the warehouse, the yard was in a state of sorry repair. The plaintiffs cleared the site of junk, made at least 60 trips to a landfill site requiring a return trip of two and one-half hours, and upgraded the surface of the yard to a superior level. The parties began quarrelling soon after they took possession of the premises. The defendants limited the plaintiffs' access to the yard and threatened to remove the plaintiffs from the company if they did not sell their shares to the defendants at a stipulated price. The plaintiffs refused and they were removed as directors. Efforts were then made by the defendants to evict the plaintiffs and when that failed, to increase the plaintiffs' rent The plaintiffs applied for relief against oppression. In the course of giving judgment in their favour, Dawson J. observed that the oppression remedy is an equitable remedy. It is designed to protect the interests of corporate stakeholders in a variety of circumstances. Accordingly, it is appropriate to take into account the cumulative effect of various individual acts or events.[82]

§13.29 Use of managerial power in a confiscatory manner so as to expropriate the interest of the complainant is another common basis for seeking relief. For instance, the use of the control of a corporation to reduce artificially the percentage ownership of a shareholder can be oppressive.[83] Payment of unreasonable, inflated or unjustified management fees to directors or a controlling shareholder may be considered oppressive,[84] particularly where it has a substantial effect on the income stream flowing to the shareholders from the corporation or upon the solvency of the corporation. More generally, the extraction of significant amounts of money or property from a corporation for the use or benefit of a director or controlling shareholder may be oppressive — if not strictly theft — where the director knows, or reasonably ought to know, that he or she is not

---

O.J. No. 4620, 36 B.L.R. (2d) 171 (Gen. Div. — C.L.), leave to appeal refused [1997] O.J. No. 5427, 36 B.L.R. (2d) 189 (Div. Ct.).
[80] *Deluce Holdings Inc. v. Air Canada*, [1992] O.J. No. 2382, 98 D.L.R. (4th) 509 (Gen. Div.).
[81] [1996] S.J. No. 814, 30 B.L.R. (2d) 114 (Q.B.).
[82] *Ibid.*, at 123 B.L.R.
[83] *Arrotta v. Avva Light Corp.*, [1995] A.J. No. 922, 34 Alta. L.R. (3d) 308 (Q.B.), rev'd [1995] A.J. No. 1154 (C.A.).
[84] *218125 Investments Ltd. v. Patel*, [1995] A.J. No. 1222, 33 Alta. L.R. (3d) 245 (Q.B.).

entitled to that money or property. An attempt to cover up such a payment or to otherwise mislead that the payment was made or its extent is highly indicative that the director or officer concerned knew of the impropriety of the payment.[85] Division of business opportunities away from the corporation may amount to oppression of the shareholders interested in the corporation, as well as a breach of a fiduciary duty owed to the corporation itself.[86] Expulsion of shareholders from a corporation in a manner that ignores uncompensated contributions made by them to the corporation in its formative years may also be oppressive.[87] Where a minority shareholder, who is also a director, uses his or her position as a director of the corporation to deny another shareholder rights that the shareholder is entitled to under the terms of an agreement between the shareholders, that conduct is oppressive, even where the other shareholder concerned is a majority shareholder.[88] A finding of oppression in such a case may entitle the court to grant a wider range of remedies in the circumstances than would be possible in the simple action for breach of contract.

(3) Specific Cases

§13.30 By way of general overview, courts have upheld claims for oppression (including within that term as well as both unfair prejudice and unfair disregard) in the following circumstances:[89]

- a deliberate failure to provide required information, as part of an apparent effort to conduct corporate operations under a veil of secrecy;[90]

- termination of employment without cause;[91]

- pledge of corporate assets to security debt of a controlling shareholder;[92]

- payments made contrary to the corporation's by-laws;[93]

- breach of fiduciary duty (misappropriation of corporate opportunity and entering into competition with the corporation);[94]

---

[85] See, generally, *Calmont Leasing Ltd. v. Kredl*, [1995] A.J. No. 475, 30 Alta. L.R. (3d) 16 at 23, additional reasons [1995] A.J. No. 763 (C.A.).

[86] *400280 Alberta Ltd. v. Franko's Heating & Air Conditioning (1992) Ltd.*, [1995] A.J. No. 121, 26 Alta. L.R. (3d) 421 (Q.B.).

[87] See, generally, *Buckley v. B.C.T.F.*, [1992] B.C.J. No. 2457, 75 B.C.L.R. (2d) 228 (S.C.), var'd on appeal [1994] B.C.J. No. 192, 86 B.C.L.R. (2d) 303, and [1995] B.C.J. No. 2971 (C.A.).

[88] *Gottlieb v. Adam*, [1994] O.J. No. 2636, 16 B.L.R. (2d) 271 at 282-83 (Gen. Div.), *per* Spence J.

[89] As to the application of limitation periods with respect to oppression actions, see: *Hughes v. Bob Tallman Investments Inc.*, [2005] M.J. No. 26, 2 B.L.R. (4th) 200 (C.A.); *Ford Motor Co. of Canada v. Ontario Municipal Employees Retirement Board*, [2004] O.J. No. 191, 41 B.L.R. (3d) 74 (S.C.J.), var'd [2006] O.J. No. 27 (C.A.), leave to appeal to S.C.C. refused [2006] S.C.C.A. No. 77.

[90] *Envirodrive Inc. v. 836442 Alberta Ltd.*, [2005] A.J. No. 747, 7 B.L.R. (4th) 61, additional reasons [2005] A.J. No. 1485 (Q.B.).

[91] *Elliott v. Opticom Technologies Inc.*, [2005] B.C.J. No. 782, 4 B.L.R. (4th) 103 (S.C.); *Beaubien v. Campbell*, [2003] S.J. No. 301, 33 B.L.R. (3d) 33 (Q.B.).

[92] *Cohen v. Jonco Holdings Ltd.*, [2005] M.J. No. 126, 4 B.L.R. (4th) 232 (Man. C.A.).

[93] *Brokx v. Tattoo Technology Inc.*, [2004] B.C.J. No. 2711, 50 B.L.R. (3d) 221 (S.C.).

[94] *Jordan Inc. v. Jordan Engineering Inc.*, [2004] O.J. No. 3260, 48 B.L.R. (3d) 115, additional reasons [2005] O.J. No. 4110 (S.C.J.).

- implementation of a transfer pricing strategy that artificially reduces the profitability of a corporation;[95]
- payment of dividends and management bonuses;[96]
- transfer of property to avoid a claim;[97]
- asset stripping,[98] particularly in the case of a pending claim against a corporation;[99]
- the grant of security interests to non-arm's length parties and the charging of above market rates of interest;[100]
- using technicalities in the articles or by-laws to shut the complainant out of the corporation;[101]
- imposing a discretionary financial loss or burden;[102]
- misappropriation of corporate property, including a corporate opportunity or intellectual asset;[103] and
- using corporate funds to pay personal expenses.[104]

On the other hand, bare allegations of oppression are not sufficient to justify relief. The complainant must make out a strong case for the court to intervene in the corporation's internal affairs,[105] and so the court will not grant relief merely because a minority shareholder objects to the way the business is being run.[106] There must be real evidence of misconduct: mere innuendo based on simple and

---

[95] *Ford Motor Co. of Canada v. Ontario Municipal Employees Retirement Board*, [2004] O.J. No. 191, 41 B.L.R. (3d) 74 (S.C.J.), var'd [2006] O.J. No. 27 (C.A.), leave to appeal refused [2006] S.C.C.A. No. 77.

[96] *Piller Sausages & Delicatessens v. Cobb International Corp.*, [2003] O.J. No. 2647, 35 B.L.R. (3d) 193 (Sup. Ct.), aff'd [2003] O.J. No. 5128, 40 B.L.R. (3d) 88 (C.A.).

[97] *Goldhar v. JM Publications Inc.*, [2000] O.J. No. 843, 13 B.L.R. (3d) 181 (S.C.J.).

[98] *C-L & Associates Inc. v. Airside Equipment Sales Inc.*, [2003] M.J. No. 160, 35 B.L.R. (3d) 124 (Q.B.); *B.J. Kennedy Agency (1984) Ltd. v. Kilgour-Bell Insurance Agencies Ltd.*, [2000] M.J. No. 179 (Q.B.); *ADI Ltd. v. 052987 NB Inc.*, [2000] N.B.J. No. 467, 232 N.B.R. (2d) 47 (C.A.), leave to appeal to S.C.C. refused [2001] S.C.C.A. No. 48.

[99] *Piller Sausages & Delicatessens Ltd. v. Cobb International Corp.*, [2003] O.J. No. 264, 35 B.L.R. (3d) 193 at 196-97 (S.C.J.), aff'd [2003] O.J. No. 5128 (C.A.).

[100] *Levy-Russell Ltd. v. Shieldings Inc.*, [2004] O.J. No. 4291, 48 B.L.R. (3d) 28 at 44 *et seq.* (S.C.J. — C.L.), *per* Cumming J.

[101] *Saarnok-Vuus v. Teng*, [2003] B.C.J. No. 353, 31 B.L.R. (3d) 92 at 108 (S.C.), *per* Ross J.

[102] Discussed, but no such finding made, in *Hillside Investments Ltd. v. Boychuck*, [2001] A.J. No. 1251, 19 B.L.R. (3d) 205, additional reasons [2002] A.J. No. 33 (Q.B.).

[103] *C.I. Covington Fund Inc. v. White*, [2001] O.J. No. 3918, 17 B.L.R. (3d) 277 (Div. Ct.).

[104] *Stethem v. Feher*, [2000] O.J. No. 5015, 11 B.L.R. (3d) 288 (S.C.J.).

[105] *Baniuk v. Carpenter*, [1988] N.B.J. No. 826, 90 N.B.R. (2d) 1 at 42, 228 A.P.R. 1 (Q.B.), *per* Landry J., rev'd in part [1989] N.B.J. No. 519, 104 N.B.R. (2d) 196, 261 A.P.R. 196 (C.A.); *Liu v. Sung*, [1998] B.C.J. No. 1516, 36 B.L.R. (2d) 63 (C.A.).

[106] *Brant Investments Ltd. v. KeepRite Inc.*, [1987] O.J. No. 574, 60 O.R. (2d) 737, additional reasons [1987] O.J. No. 2700 (H.C.J.), *per* Andrews J., aff'd [1991] O.J. No. 683 (C.A.), and see generally, *Keho Holdings Ltd. v. Noble*, [1987] A.J. No. 334, 38 D.L.R. (4th) 368 (C.A.).

readily explicable irregularities are not sufficient to give rise to relief.[107] Moreover, although relief may be available in some circumstances where there is a "threat" of oppressive or prejudicial conduct in the future,[108] unless it is reasonably certain that such future harm will occur, an anticipatory order will not be made.[109] Such an order would be premature; for instance, where there is no more than a possibility that such conduct will occur.[110]

§13.31 More generally, reasonable behaviour on the part of the control group will only rarely be oppression. The courts recognize that corporate managers must make decisions on issues facing the corporation, and that in many cases the practical effect of any decision will be contrary to the interests or wishes of some group or individual concerned in the corporation. A degree of give and take, coupled with reasonable compromise, is inherent in the use of corporate structure and the conduct of collective enterprise. Where a director resigns voluntarily and the corporation offers to place a nominee of his or hers on the board of directors in his or her place, that director cannot claim to have been oppressed.[111] *Bona fide* payments made by a corporation to its directors or shareholders are not oppressive.[112] The failure of a company is not evidence that its business or affairs have been conducted in an oppressive manner.[113] The general rule is that it is not oppressive for a corporation not to declare and pay a dividend on shares where there are sound business reasons for not doing so,[114] but it may be oppressive to refrain from paying dividends on the unusual facts of a particular case.[115] Courts have rejected claims for oppression based upon the following complaints:

- the bare fact that the corporation lacks financial stability;[116]

- the advance of funds by a shareholder acting in good faith to a corporation, and the grant of security for the funds so advanced (the court observed that

---

[107] *Cohen-Herrendorf v. Army & Navy Department Store Holdings*, [1986] S.J. No. 848, 55 Sask. R. 134 (Q.B.).
[108] *Michalak v. Biotech Electronics Ltd.*, [1986] Q.J. No. 1882, 35 B.L.R. 1 at 10-11 (S.C.), *per* Martin J.
[109] *Bank of Montreal v. Dome Petroleum Ltd.*, [1987] A.J. No. 1401, 54 Alta. L.R. (2d) 289 at 299, 67 C.B.R. (N.S.) 296 (Q.B.), *per* Forsyth J.
[110] *Innocan Inc. v. Canadian Pacific Air Lines Ltd.*, [1987] R.J.Q. 2451 (S.C.).
[111] *Three Point Oils Ltd. v. Glencrest Energy Ltd.*, [1997] A.J. No. 451, 55 Alta. L.R. (3d) 140 (C.A.), *per curiam*.
[112] See, generally, *Gainers Inc. v. Pocklington*, [1995] A.J. No. 1128, 35 Alta. L.R. (3d) 348, additional reasons [1996] A.J. No. 126 (Q.B.), rev'd [2000] A.J. No. 1350 (C.A.).
[113] *Novel Energy (North America) Ltd. v. Glowicki*, [1994] A.J. No. 14, 16 Alta. L.R. (3d) 26 (Q.B.).
[114] *N.A. Properties (1994) Ltd. v. D.I.A. Holdings Ltd.*, [1995] A.J. No. 1163, 33 Alta. L.R. (3d) 384 (Q.B.).
[115] See, generally, *Gallelli Estate v. Bill Gallelli Investments Ltd.*, [1994] A.J. No. 117, 16 Alta. L.R. (3d) 417 (Q.B.).
[116] *Shaw v. BCE Inc.*, [2004] O.J. No. 3109, 49 B.L.R. (3d) 1 (C.A.), leave to appeal to S.C.C. refused [2004] S.C.C.A. No. 419 — in this case, the prospectus contained a warning that the investment would be speculative.

public policy in a free market economy suggests this flexibility in the movement and formation of capital);[117]

- a unilateral decision to wind up the corporation, where that decision is not patently unreasonable in the circumstances;[118]

- enforcing forfeiture rights against a shareholder who failed to meet a contractual obligation;[119]

- enforcing the express terms of a security;[120]

- carrying out in good faith the expressed wishes of the majority of shareholders;[121] and

- steps taken in good faith to re-organize a corporation, or restructure management where the corporation has been seriously mismanaged.[122]

(4) Must Be More Than a Dispute

§13.32 Every case of oppression involves a dispute between the complainant and those in control of the corporation concerning some aspect of its operations, but the mere existence of such a dispute is not sufficient to support a claim. A minority shareholder has no right as such to participate in the management of a corporation and cannot claim oppression merely because he or she is not allowed to participate. The insistence by the majority that reasonable conditions be satisfied before a minority shareholder is allowed to participate in the management of a corporation also does not amount to oppression.[123] However, a particular minority shareholder may be entitled to a right of participation in management on the facts of a given case[124] and, where such a right can be shown, the refusal by the corporation to give effect to that right, or its blockage by the controlling shareholders in the corporation may amount to oppression. A "right" of minority participation in corporate management need not be a right in the strictly legal sense of the term; it is sufficient if the impression of such a right of participation constituted a reasonable expectation of a shareholder complainant at the time when he or she first invested in the corporation, made some subsequent investment in it, or refrained from exercising his or her right to remove a prior investment from it.

---

[117] *Levy-Russell Ltd. v. Shieldings Inc.*, [2004] O.J. No. 4291, 48 B.L.R. (3d) 28 at 44 (S.C.J.), *per* Cumming J.

[118] *Bennett v. Riem*, [2004] O.J. No. 4341, 50 B.L.R. (3d) 128, additional reasons [2005] O.J. No. 113 (S.C.J. — C.L.).

[119] *Amneet Holdings Ltd. v. 79548 Manitoba Ltd.*, [2004] M.J. No. 92, 42 B.L.R. (3d) 1 (C.A.).

[120] *6784733 Alberta Ltd. v. Money's Mushrooms Ltd.*, [2003] B.C.J. No. 2475, 40 B.L.R. (3d) 270 (S.C.).

[121] *G & E Vending Ltd. v. 700748 Alberta Ltd.*, [2002] A.J. No. 1208, 30 B.L.R. (3d) 216 (Q.B.).

[122] *Past v. Past*, [2003] B.C.J. No. 1785, 36 B.L.R. (3d) 82 (S.C.); *Krynen v. Bugg*, [2003] O.J. No. 1209, 32 B.L.R. (3d) 61, additional reasons [2003] O.J. No. 2301 (S.C.J.).

[123] *Three Point Oils Ltd. v. Glencrest Energy Ltd.*, [1994] A.J. No. 664, 23 Alta. L.R. (3d) 226 (Q.B.).

[124] *Burnett v. Tsang*, [1985] A.J. No. 604, 37 Alta. L.R. (2d) 154 at 162 (Q.B.), *per* Cawsey J.

§13.33 A dispute among the shareholders of a corporation is not, in and of itself, sufficient to establish that one of the participants has been oppressed by the other, or that one is guilty of acting in bad faith towards the other. Disputes over a business decision made by the corporation are not evidence of oppression.[125] Nor should it be assumed that the complainant is necessarily the innocent party.[126] Ordinarily, there is nothing oppressive in a controlling shareholder exercising rights to which he or she is entitled under a shareholder agreement, provided the terms of that agreement are not in themselves oppressive or would excuse conduct that is oppressive. To the extent that a shareholder agreement represents a consensual arrangement, entered into in good faith with a clear understanding by the parties about its terms, the courts should allow effect to be given to it.[127]

§13.34 Although it is not necessary to show bad faith in an oppression action, the requirement that some oppression or unfair prejudice be shown, or that it be proven that the interests of a director, security holder, creditor or officer of a corporation have been unfairly disregarded, indicates that the act or omission on which the complaint is based must have stepped beyond the normal give and take that is to be expected in the day-to-day conduct of the business and affairs of a corporation. Accordingly, reasonable steps taken by directors, which they believe in good faith to be in the best interests of the corporation and those concerned in it, will not normally be considered to be oppressive or unfairly prejudicial, therefore entitling a complainant to seek relief under section 248 of the OBCA, even where those efforts subsequently prove unsuccessful or futile.[128] Nor is it sufficient to show that the directors or shareholders controlling the corporation have caused the corporation to enter into a business venture or to take some step of which the complainant disapproves,[129] or have not taken some step that the complainant thought necessary or well-advised.[130]

§13.35 While clause 248(2)(*a*) speaks of an act or omission of the corporation or any of its affiliates, clause 248(2)(*b*) speaks of the conduct of the business or affairs of the corporation or its affiliates. Clause 248(2)(*c*) speaks of the exercise of powers by the directors. In the Australian case, *Re Dernacourt Investments Pty Ltd.*,[131] it was held that a refusal by the directors of a company to allow shareholders to inspect the financial records of the company and its subsidiaries could not serve as the basis for relief under the Australian equivalent to section 248. However, under that Act a complaint can be made only in regard to the "conduct" of the affairs of a corporation, and, thus, it was held that inactivity or

---

[125] *Keating v. Bragg*, [1997] N.S.J. No. 248, 34 B.L.R. (2d) 181 (C.A.).
[126] See, generally, *Intercontinental Precious Metals Inc. v. Cooke*, [1993] B.C.J. No. 1903, 10 B.L.R. (2d) 203 at 217 (S.C.), *per* Tysoe J.
[127] See, generally, *Dashney v. McKinlay*, [1996] O.J. No. 2037, 30 B.L.R. (2d) 211 (Gen. Div.).
[128] See, generally, *Liu v. Sung*, [1997] B.C.J. No. 1901, 37 B.C.L.R. (3d) 158 (C.A.).
[129] *Bially v. Churchill Electric & Associates (1987) Ltd.*, [1993] B.C.J. No. 982, 78 B.C.L.R. (2d) 305 (S.C.).
[130] *Schicchi v. Orveas Bay Estates Ltd.*, [1994] B.C.J. No. 2447, 98 B.C.L.R. (2d) 391 (S.C.).
[131] (1990), 8 A.C.L.C. 900 (N.S.W.S.C.).

"negative action" on the part of the directors could constitute conduct only where there is a positive duty at law or in equity to act in a particular way. As there was no such positive duty, relief was not available. It is readily possible that inaction on the part of the directors may give rise to unfair prejudice, for instance, where they forgo a business opportunity available to the corporation so that another corporation in which they are involved may take advantage of it.[132]

§13.36 It has been suggested that the question of fairness or unfairness of a particular act or omission is assessed objectively on the basis of how it would have appeared to a commercial bystander.[133] However, insofar as it is possible to establish subjective unfairness on the part of the directors (or other persons whose conduct is complained of), it is doubtful that their act or omission will be upheld merely because a fairly motivated board might have acted or failed to act in much the same way. In *Pelley v. Pelley*, Wells C.J. stated:

> A court may not have great difficulty in determining whether or not "oppression" exists, in a particular case, because there is a reasonable degree of objectivity involved in making a determination as to whether conduct has been "burdensome, harsh and wrongful". However, making a determination as to whether directors are acting in a manner that is "unfairly prejudicial" to a particular applicant or which, "unfairly disregards [that] applicant's interest as a shareholder" necessarily involves somewhat more subjective considerations. In particular, it will usually involve consideration of the personal circumstances in which the parties developed their business relationship, the expectations of the parties at the time of creation of the corporation and any other considerations necessary in order to identify the full extent of the applicant's interest as a shareholder in that specific case.[134]

(5) When Available

(a) BOTH UNFAIRNESS AND PREJUDICE REQUIRED

§13.37 It is not prejudice as such that gives rise to a claim as unfair prejudice. So, for instance, a creditor has no claim for unfair prejudice merely because the creditor has gone unpaid.[135] Put another way, the existence of prejudice and the unfairness of that prejudice are two different considerations. As Mann J. noted in one recent English case, usually there is not much debate about the prejudice. The dispute will be as to whether it was unfair.[136] The prejudice complained of must be real, rather than merely technical or trivial, and must flow from the conduct said to be unfair.[137] Where dealing with a corporate group, it may be appropriate in some

---

[132] *Re Bright Pine Mills Pty. Ltd.*, [1969] V.R. 1002 (S.C. Vic.).
[133] *Morgan v. 45 Flyers Avenue Pty Ltd.* (1986), 10 A.C.L.R. 692 at 704.
[134] [2003] N.J. No. 13, 221 Nfld. & P.E.I.R. 1 at 18-19 (C.A.), leave to appeal to S.C.C. refused [2003] S.C.C.A. No. 338.
[135] See, for instance, *Olympia & York Developments (Trustee of) v. Olympia & York Realty Corp.*, [2001] O.J. No. 3394, 16 B.L.R. (3d) 74, additional reasons [2001] O.J. No. 5501 (S.C.J. — C.L.), aff'd [2003] O.J. No. 5242 (C.A.).
[136] *Re Metropolis Motorcycles Ltd; Hale v. Waldock*, [2006] EWHC 364 (Ch.) at para. 52.
[137] See *Re BSB Holdings Ltd. (No. 2)*, [1996] 1 B.C.L.C. 155.

circumstances to consider the conduct of the business and affairs of the group as a whole to determine whether such prejudice has occurred.[138]

(b) Misconduct by Party in Control

§13.38 The oppression remedy is available to rectify conduct by directors, or other persons having effective control over the corporation, that amounts to self-dealing at the expense of the corporation or other shareholders.[139] Generally, the oppression remedy is available against the corporation itself and its insiders. Only in very rare cases is such relief available against a stranger to the corporation.[140] Conduct affords a basis for relief under the oppression remedy when:

- it steps outside what the parties might reasonably have contemplated would occur, or that was reasonably likely might occur, in the management of the corporation, its business and affairs, at the time when the complainant was induced to become involved with the corporation, and

- prejudice results to the complainant by reason of that conduct.

§13.39 The oppression remedy is not a tool by which a disgruntled shareholder may secure an amendment of a shareholder agreement to obtain rights that are not provided for in that agreement.[141] It is clearly inappropriate to grant an oppression remedy that grants a shareholder (or other investor) a right that the shareholder sought to obtain by negotiation but was unable to secure. The oppression remedy is not a tool to be used as a lever to aid one side in the contract negotiation process over another.[142] The burden of proof in an oppression application is on the applicant and the respondents in an oppression proceeding are not required to prove that they did not act oppressively.[143]

§13.40 In *Re Saul D. Harrison & Sons plc*,[144] it was held that in deciding what is fair or unfair for the purposes of section 459 of the U.K. *Companies Act, 1985*, it is important to have in mind that the term fairness is being used in the context of a commercial relationship. The articles of association (the U.K. equivalent to the by-laws of an OBCA or CBCA company) set out the contractual terms that govern the relationship of the shareholders with the company and with each other. They determine the powers of the board and the company in general meeting. Everyone who becomes a member of a company is taken to have agreed to

---

[138] See, generally, *Re City Branch Group Ltd., Gross v. Rackind*, [2004] EWCA Civ 815, [2004] 4 All E.R. 735 (C.A. Eng.); *Nicholas v. Soundcraft Electronics Ltd.*, [1993] B.C.L.C. 360 (C.A.).
[139] *C.I. Covington Fund Inc. v. White*, [2000] O.J. No. 4589, 10 C.P.R. (4th) 49 at paras. 21, 40, 41, 43 (S.C.J.), aff'd [2001] O.J. No. 3918, 15 C.P.R. (4th) 144 (Div. Ct.).
[140] *Thomson v. Quality Mechnical Services Inc.*, [2001] O.J. No. 3987, 18 B.L.R. (3d) 99 (S.C.J.); *Imperial Oil Ltd. v. Westlake Fuel Ltd.*, [2001] M.J. No. 337, 16 B.L.R. (3d) 1 (C.A.).
[141] *Rayment Estate v. Rayment & Collins Ltd.*, [2006] O.J. No. 2424, 149 A.C.W.S. (3d) 526 (S.C.J.).
[142] See, generally, *Taylor v. London Guarantee Insurance Co.*, [2000] O.J. No. 1430, 11 B.L.R. (3d) 295 (S.C.J.), cf. *Pantheon Inc. v. Global Pharm Inc.*, [2000] O.J. No. 2532, 9 B.L.R. (3d) 140 (S.C.J.).
[143] *Greenlight Capital Inc. v. Stronach*, [2006] O.J. No. 4353 at para. 18 (S.C.J.), *per* Ground J.
[144] [1995] 1 B.C.L.C. 14 (C.A.).

them. Since keeping promises and honouring agreements is probably the most important element of commercial fairness, the starting point in any case under section 459 will be to ask whether the conduct of which the shareholder complains was in accordance with the articles of association. Similarly, in *O'Neill v. Phillips*,[145] Lord Hoffmann observed that a member of a company will not ordinarily be entitled to complain about unfairness unless there has been some breach of the terms on which he agreed that the affairs of the company should be conducted. However, while any contractual documents and the relevant provisions of the corporate constitution are the starting point for any inquiry into an alleged act of oppression, the inquiry does not end with them. Lord Hoffman added that there will be cases in which equitable considerations will make it unfair for those managing the affairs of the company to rely upon their (or the company's) strict legal rights. The unfairness may consist in using the rules in a manner which equity would regard as contrary to good faith. More recently, in *Hale v. Waldock*,[146] Mann J. noted:

> Not only may conduct be technically unlawful without being unfair: it can also be unfair without being unlawful. In a commercial context this may at first seem surprising. How can it be unfair to act in accordance with what the parties have agreed: as a general rule, it is not. There are cases in which the letter of the articles does not fully reflect the understandings upon which the shareholders are associated.

Similarly, in *Re Wondoflex Textiles Pty Ltd.*,[147] Smith J. (in a winding-up application) contrasted the literal meaning of the articles with the true intentions of the parties:

> Acts which, in law, are a valid exercise of powers conferred by the articles may nevertheless by entirely outside what can fairly be regarded as having been in the contemplation of the parties when they became members of the company; and in such cases the fact that what has been done is not in excess of power will not necessarily be an answer to a claim for winding up. Indeed, it may be said that one purpose of [the just and equitable provision] is to enable the court to relieve a party from this bargain in such cases.

In general, much the same approach is followed in the Canadian case law dealing with the oppression remedy.

(c) APPLICATION OF GENERAL PRINCIPLES OF EQUITY

§13.41 It is often stated that, although statutory in origin, the oppression remedy is fundamentally equitable in nature.[148] The discretion enjoyed by the courts with respect to providing a remedy in a form specifically addressed to the needs of the case is clearly comparable to the discretion historically enjoyed by courts of

---

[145] [1999] 2 All E.R. 961 (H.L.).
[146] [2006] EWHC 364 at para. 52 (Ch.) quoting from *Re Saul D. Harrison & Sons plc*, [1995] 1 B.C.L.C. 14 (C.A.).
[147] [1951] VLR 458 at 467 (Vict. S.C.).
[148] *McEwen v. Goldcorp Inc.*, [2006] O.J. No. 4265 at para. 42 (S.C.J.), *per* Pepall J., aff'd [2006] O.J. No. 4437 (Div. Ct.); but *cf. Seidel v. Kerr*, [2001] A.J. No. 1304, 20 B.L.R. (3d) 66 (Q.B.), aff'd [2003] A.J. No. 1163 (C.A.) — remedy is statutory in nature, not equitable or common law.

equity. The application of other general principles of equity governing the availability of equitable relief is not entirely clear, although there is a considerable body of case law that indicates that at least some similar principles do apply. For instance, an oppression action may be stayed for unreasonable delay.[149] As in the case of other forms of equitable relief, a court may grant a remedy under the oppression remedy with respect to damage that has not yet occurred, if it seems reasonably probable that such damage will occur if the order is not granted.[150]

§13.42 There is no strict requirement that an applicant for relief have clean hands in order to obtain relief under the oppression remedy; nor is it necessary to show that the parties have behaved reasonably.[151] In *Journet v. Superchef Food Industries Ltd.*[152] Gomery J. rejected the argument that the right to institute an oppression proceeding was limited to complainants who could establish their own "perfect probity". He stated:

> Furthermore, the court is not convinced that the clean hands doctrine applies to the recourse provided in s. 234. The statute does not say so or even require that the applicant be in good faith, a requirement when a complainant wishes to commence a derivative action under the C.B.C.A. ... To require perfect probity from an applicant would imply that dishonest or improper management is sanctioned if no spotless complainant may be found to request the Court's intervention. That cannot have been the intention of the drafters of this legislation. Fault on the part of the complainant cannot excuse oppression and unfairness on the part of the corporation or its directors.

Nevertheless, the complainant's conduct is not an irrelevant consideration. The behaviour of the complainant may well be relevant to a determination of whether the steps taken by the management of the corporation were in the best interests of the corporation, or that the control group within the corporation was not acting unfairly in the circumstances. Even where this cannot be shown, it may affect the relief that the court is prepared to grant,[153] or cause the court to exercise its discretion to refuse a remedy.[154] For instance, dismissal from employment or shutting a minority shareholder out from the corporate decision-making process can hardly amount to oppression where management had reasonable grounds to believe at the time when it acted that the complainant was working to subvert the interests of the corporation.[155] In such a case, there is an immediate and necessary relationship between the relief that is sought by the complainant and the complainant's own delinquent behaviour that could easily make it unjust to grant the complainant relief under the oppression remedy.[156]

---

[149] *Hurst v. Societe Nationale de L'Amiante*, [2006] O.J. No. 3998 (S.C.J.).
[150] *Re 3026709 Nova Scotia Ltd.*, [2006] N.S.J. No. 389 at para. 29 (S.C.), *per* Warner J.
[151] See, for example, *Borsook v. Broder*, [1994] O.J. No. 2644, 16 B.L.R. (2d) 265 (Gen. Div.).
[152] [1984] Q.J. No. 15, 29 B.L.R. 206 at 225 (S.C.); see also *Blackmore v. Richardson*, [2005] EWCA Civ 1356 (C.A.).
[153] *Re London School of Electronics Ltd.*, [1985] 3 W.L.R. 474 at 482 (Ch.).
[154] *Re London School of Electronics Ltd.*, [1985] B.C.L.C. 273 at 279 (Ch.), *per* Nourse J.
[155] See, for instance, *Grace v. Biagioli*, [2005] EWCA Civ 1222 (C.A.).
[156] *Greenlight Capital Inc. v. Stronach*, [2006] O.J. No. 4353 (S.C.J.), *per* Ground J.

(iii) Reasonable Expectations of the Complainant

§13.43 Where an extensive body of fact specific case law evolves in relation to a remedy (particularly a statutory remedy), it is common for the courts to seek to reformulate that body of case law by reference to some unifying principle. Such an evolution has occurred with respect to the oppression remedy. The prevailing view in Canadian case law is that the oppression remedy is available where the reasonable expectations of a director, shareholder, security holder, officer, or other complainant have been defeated.[157] In this section, we shall conduct a critical examination of the way in which the concept of reasonable expectations has been employed, with a view towards determining whether it facilitates or merely complicates the law relating to oppression. A subsidiary question is whether the concept can be reformulated on some more specific basis, so as to make the outcome of cases based upon oppression more predictable.

§13.44 Before entering into any critique of the law in this area, it must be conceded that most of the case law in which reasonable expectations have been invoked as the basis of relief have been unexceptionable. While reference has been made to the concept, it has been in a more or less collateral manner. No doubt in most of those cases in which relief was given, it would be fair to say that the defendants had frustrated the reasonable expectations of the complainant. However, it would also be fair to say that they also had behaved in a manner that was unfairly prejudicial or oppressive to the complainant, or had unfairly disregarded the interests of the complainant. In short, the reference to "reasonable expectations" added nothing whatever to the decision that was rendered. For instance, in *Gazit (1997) Inc. v. Centrefund Realty Corp.*[158] it was held that parties dealing with a corporation were entitled to assume that the directors would comply with their obligations (i) to act in the best interests of the shareholders as a whole, and to take active and reasonable steps to maximize shareholder value; (ii) to act honestly and in good faith, with a view to the best interests of the corporation; and (iii) to exercise their reasonable business judgment with the care, diligence and skill of a reasonably prudent person in comparable circumstances, in doing so. It will be noted, of course, that each of these expectations merely reflects a requirement imposed upon the directors under corporate law.

---

[157] See, for instance, *820099 Ontario Inc. v. Harold E. Ballard Ltd.*, [1991] O.J. No. 266, 3 B.L.R. (2d) 113 at 185-87 (Gen. Div.), per Farley J., aff'd [1991] O.J. No. 1082 (Div. Ct.); *Chiaramonte v. World Wide Importing Ltd.*, [1996] O.J. No. 1389, 28 O.R. (3d) 641 (Gen. Div.); *Naneff v. Con-Crete Holdings Ltd.*, [1995] O.J. No. 1377, 23 O.R. (3d) 481 (C.A.); *Pente Investment Management Ltd. v. Schneider Corp.*, [1998] O.J. No. 4142, 42 O.R. (3d) 177 (C.A.) published elsewhere as *Maple Leaf Foods Inc. v. Schneider Corp.*; *Casurina Ltd. Partnership v. Rio Algom Ltd.*, [2004] O.J. No. 177, 181 O.A.C. 19 (C.A.), leave to appeal to S.C.C. refused [2004] S.C.C.A. No. 105; *Sutherland v. Birks*, [2003] O.J. No. 2885, 65 O.R. (3d) 812 (C.A.), leave to appeal to S.C.C. refused [2003] S.C.C.A. No. 424; *Cohen v. Jonco Holdings Ltd.*, [2005] M.J. No. 126, 4 B.L.R. (4th) 232 (C.A.); *American Reserve Energy Corp. v. McDorman*, [2002] N.J. No. 259, 217 Nfld. & P.E.I.R. 7 (C.A.); *LeBlanc v. Corporation v. Eighty-Six Ltd.*, [1997] N.B.J. No. 375, 192 N.B.R. (2d) 321 (C.A.).

[158] [2000] O.J. No. 3070, 8 B.L.R. (3d) 81 at 101 (S.C.J.), per Blair J.

§13.45 Similarly in *SCI Systems, Inc. v. Gornitzki Thompson & Little Co.* the focus was again not so much upon the reasonable expectation of the complainant as upon the evident wrong-doing on the part of the corporate control group.[159] In that case, a corporation was found to have executed a promissory note in favour of a creditor in 1989. The note matured in 1991. A few months prior to that date, the sole shareholder and directors of the corporation had caused it to declare and pay dividends to them, which left the corporation with a negative net worth. They also caused the corporation to reduce certain loans owed to them. In addition, there were a number of transfers between the corporation and affiliated corporations, which reduced the assets available to satisfy the corporation's obligations. The holder of the note sought to recover the amount owing when the note fell due. After obtaining judgment, it brought an application for relief from oppression under section 248 of the OBCA. Epstein J. commented upon the nature of the claim:

> Simply put, SCI has not based its case on bad faith. It has based its case on the *effect* that the various transactions of GTL Co. have had on SCI's interests as a creditor or security holder. Accordingly, in this decision, when I make reference to oppression or oppressive conduct, I mean only in the sense that its effect may have been prejudicial to, or in unfair disregard of, SCI.
>
> It is clear that the dividend payments, the shareholder loan repayments, the corporate reorganizations and other transactions collectively were acts that had the effect of putting SCI in a position where it could not recover the money GTL Co. owed to it; could not realize on its security interest.
>
> However, SCI's finding itself in a position where it could not collect on its judgment is not, in itself, sufficient to establish oppression. The question must still be answered as to whether the circumstances giving rise to this position amount to "unfair" treatment of SCI's interests.[160]

In the course of granting SCI's application for relief, Epstein J. commented upon the duty of the directors to conduct the business of the corporation so that it can perform the obligations into which it has entered:

> I agree that the oppression remedy is designed to protect reasonable expectations. However, one of the most reasonable of all expectations of those dealing with corporations must be that the directors will manage the company in accordance with their legal obligations. Some of these obligations are specifically prescribed by statute. Others are more generally derived from the common law. However, they essentially add up to the same thing: namely, to act honestly and in good faith in the best interests of the corporation and to exercise the diligence expected of a reasonably prudent person.[161]

§13.46 Epstein J. went on to hold that the directors were not free to be selective in the adjustments that they made to the corporation's accounts, when deciding

---

[159] [1997] O.J. No. 2115, 147 D.L.R. (4th) 300 (Gen. Div.), var'd [1998] O.J. No. 2299 (Div. Ct.); see also *Re Astec (BSR) plc*, [1999] B.C.C. 59 (Ch.), per Parker J.; *Re Saul D. Harrison & Sons plc*, [1994] B.C.C. 475 (C.A.).
[160] [1997] O.J. No. 2115, 147 D.L.R. (4th) 300 at 307 (Gen. Div.).
[161] *Ibid.*, at 308.

whether to proceed with the impugned transactions. They could not simply assume that the corporation would be fortunate in the tax treatment that it received.[162] They were required to verify and support the views that they chose to take of the corporation's financial situation and to be reasonable in the assessments that they made.[163] On the evidence before the court, the conduct complained of:

> ... ran contrary to the expectations of SCI as a creditor and security holder. SCI was entitled to expect that the directors would act with appropriate corporate conduct and would particularly not authorize non-arm's length transactions that would have the effect of depriving GTL Co. of its ability to pay the debt when it came due.

However, such behaviour was not merely contrary to the creditor's reasonable expectations. It amounted to an orchestrated effort to effect a breach of contract. At the very least, this would seem to be an actionable wrong in which the control group was directly implicated.

(1) Determination of Reasonable Expectations

§13.47 The identification of the reasonable expectations of the parties is partly a question of law (*i.e.*, what are the complainant's rights), and partly a question of fact (*i.e.*, what were the complainant's reasonable expectations within the context of those rights). In determining the issue of fact, there is no error in principle in looking at prior statements and drawing an inference based on the respective weight of all the individual pieces of evidence. In deciding what is unfair, the history and nature of the corporation, the essential nature of the relationship between the corporation and the complainant, the type of rights affected and general corporate practice are material. Test of unfair prejudice or unfair disregard encompasses the protection of the underlying expectation of a creditor in its arrangement with the corporation, the extent to which the acts complained of were unforeseeable or the creditor could reasonably have protected itself from such acts, and the detriment to the interests of the creditor.[164] The reasonable expectations of a shareholder or other potential complainant are not assessed in the abstract. They must be construed by reference to the context in which the complainant acquired his or her rights, and the context in which the conduct complained of transpired.[165]

§13.48 Simply because a shareholder's interests have been disregarded or his or her legitimate expectations thwarted does not necessarily mean the shareholder is entitled to relief. The interest must have been unfairly disregarded and some

---

[162] *Ibid.*, at 310.
[163] *Ibid.*, at 312.
[164] *First Edmonton Place Ltd. v. 315888 Alberta Ltd.*, [1988] A.J. No. 511, 40 B.L.R. 28 at 67 (Q.B.), *per* Macdonald J.
[165] See, generally, *Canbev Sales & Marketing Inc. v. Natco Trading Corp.*, [1998] O.J. No. 4898, 42 O.R. (3d) 574 (C.A.).

injury thereby ensured.[166] The prejudice suffered to a security holder's interest in having his or her "reasonable expectations" ignored may be unfair, but it need not necessarily be so. A person who invests in a corporation, or who takes up employment with it, may have many expectations, all of which are reasonable, but they are not necessarily the type of expectations that are deserving of protection by law. For instance, there is nothing improper *per se* in a corporation changing established practice and eliminating privileges that were previously allowed to shareholders. Many corporations provide significant shareholders with NHL hockey tickets, pay high fees for attending board meetings, give large annual bonuses, hold board and staff meetings in exotic locales and allow the use of the company plane for personal travel. Each of the perks, may all have been commonplace when an investment was made. On joining the corporation, assurances may easily have been made that such benefits would be provided. By reason of those assurances, the complainant might have had a reasonable expectation that the privileges would continue. However, corporations require the flexibility to adjust pay rates, dividend policy, the range of benefits offered, the availability of shareholder discounts and so forth in light of changing circumstances. If there is no contractual entitlement to provide privileges of this sort, it is difficult to see why an obligation should be imposed to provide the corporation or the majority shareholders purely on the basis of a reasonable expectation. Corporate law does not entitle a complainant to obtain relief merely by showing that a particular benefit or entitlement might reasonably have been provided. The oppression remedy does not afford an opportunity for a complainant to impose his or her individual wishes or unilateral expectations on the corporation or other shareholders.[167] In the *Pente Investment* case,[168] the Court of Appeal stressed that the expectations of shareholders must be reasonable in the circumstances and that the standard for determining reasonable is objective. Relief is not available on the basis of the subjective hopes, projections, speculation or desires of the individual complainant, nor by reference to potential "wish list" items that a reasonable person might desire to occur, but that would lie beyond the realm of what that individual would reasonably expect would occur.[169]

§13.49 In determining the reasonable expectations of a party, it is not sufficient to demonstrate that many other corporations afford their shareholders (or other complainants of a given class) a particular privilege, benefit or entitlement. Moreover, it should not be necessary for the corporation (or its control group) to justify what they have done by reference to the changing circumstances of the corporation. If the majority within a corporation decide to abandon a previous policy of expenditure in order to impose a more spartan regime, it is difficult to see fault in their doing so. Similarly, a corporation may have had a long history

---

[166] *Watergroup Companies Inc. v. Stevens*, [1996] S.J. No. 178, 25 B.L.R. (2d) 148 at 261-62 (Q.B.).
[167] *McEwen v. Goldcorp Inc.*, [2006] O.J. No. 4265 at para. 42 (S.C.J.), *per* Pepall J., aff'd [2006] O.J. No. 4437 (Div. Ct.).
[168] *Pente Investment Management Ltd. v. Schneider Corp.*, [1998] O.J. No. 4142, 42 O.R. (3d) 177 (C.A.), published elsewhere as *Maple Leaf Foods Inc. v. Schneider Corp*.
[169] *Hurst v. Societe Nationale de L'Amiante*, [2006] O.J. No. 3998 at para. 122 (S.C.J.), *per* Spies J.

of generous dividend payments. However, if the control group within the corporation decides to abandon this policy and to re-invest a substantial portion of corporate profit in expansion and research, that decision does not seem oppressive even if it is contrary to what the minority of shareholders hoped and expected would be the case. Such a guarded approach limits the range of cases in which the courts are entitled to intervene and, ultimately, limits the remedies that may be granted. However, there is clear reason for caution when applying so vague a standard as reasonable expectation.[170]

(2) Quasi-Partnership Cases

§13.50 It can be argued that the adoption of a "reasonable expectations" test makes it unnecessary to invoke the aid of partnership concepts when courts attempt to decide whether or not the complainant is entitled to relief. Although many courts have applied a partnership analogy when dealing with oppression cases,[171] this approach is not without difficulty. A corporation is not a partnership; they are mutually exclusive forms of business organization. So, for instance, the shareholders who stand behind a corporation are not in a relationship of quasi-partnership to each other, and they owe each other no fiduciary duty or other duty of utmost good faith. Each is free to pursue his or her own individual interest as each sees fit. Thus a controlling shareholder may choose which of two competing takeover bids to accept, and it is no oppression of minority shareholders if the controlling shareholder elects to accept the lower of the two bids.[172] People may discover to their surprise that a business relationship has unintentionally mutated into a partnership. In contrast, due to the formality of the incorporation process, the selection of a corporate vehicle is always a matter of deliberate choice. The consequences of that choice should not be lightly ignored. There is no reason to believe that the investors who stand behind a corporation intended partnership rules to govern their rights, obligations and remedies, even in cases where there was a close relationship between the parties at the time of incorporation and they entered into the corporation together with a great degree of mutual trust that each reposed in the other. To make out a case of oppression, it is not necessary to show that a breach of a partnership concept has occurred, nor is it sufficient to show that a breach has occurred. In oppression actions, the courts are less concerned with the

---

[170] As Harman J. noted in one English case, the oppression remedy has given rise to considerable litigation and is wide-ranging in scope, allowing

... every sort and kind of conduct which has taken place over an almost unlimited ... period of time in the management of the company's business to be dug up and gone over.

Re Unisoft Group Ltd. (No. 3), [1994] 1 B.C.L.C. 609 (Ch.); see also *Maple Leaf Foods Inc. v. Schneider Corp.*, [1998] O.J. No. 4142, 42 O.R. (3d) 177 (C.A.), published eslewhere as *Pente Investment Management Ltd. v. Schneider Corp.*

[171] See, for instance, *O'Neill v. Phillips*, [1999] B.C.C. 600 (H.L.).

[172] See, generally, *Pente Investment Management Ltd. v. Schneider Corp.*, [1998] O.J. No. 2036, 40 B.L.R. (2d) 244 (Gen. Div.), aff'd [1998] O.J. No. 4142 (C.A.), published elsewhere as *Maple Leaf Foods Inc. v. Schneider Corp.*

question of whether partnership principles have been respected than they are with the underlying reasonable expectations of the parties.[173]

§13.51 The relationship between the "reasonable expectation" and "quasi-partnership" lines of cases was recently considered by the House of Lords in *O'Neill v. Phillips*,[174] — a case which involved a set of facts typical of the partnership analogy cases. The House used this case as an opportunity to clarify the range of circumstances under which relief should be given under section 459 of the *Company Act 1985*, which corresponds to section 248 of the OBCA.[175] Although it is possible to quibble with individual passages of the unanimous judgment delivered by Lord Hoffman, the general thrust of the judgment is highly illuminating, for it clarifies the circumstances in which a complainant may rely upon the existence of a quasi-partnership as a basis for obtaining relief in an oppression action, and also makes clear that quasi-partnership and reasonable expectations are not distinct foundations for relief. Rather, relief may be granted where necessary to give effect to or vindicate the reasonable expectations of the complainant. However, those reasonable expectations must grow out of some personal dealing, relationship or formal or informal understanding between the parties concerned in the corporation, which is such as to bind the conscience of those in control of the corporation, even if not strictly enforceable at law.[176] In such a case, that dealing, relationship or understanding will be binding in equity. One type of instance in which oppression relief is available is where it can be shown that a quasi-partnership relationship exists between the complainant and other principals in the corporation by reason of the manner in which they have dealt with each other, particularly insofar as it has been necessary for the complainant to repose trust in, or otherwise rely upon, the control group.[177] A person is not entitled to complain of unfair, oppressive or similarly improper treatment unless there has been some breach of the terms on which it was understood that the company would be conducted.[178]

§13.52 The facts in the *O'Neill* case were as follows. In 1983, the complainant, A, took employment with Pectel Ltd. — a company which specialized in stripping asbestos from buildings. Pectel was wholly owned by the respondent, B. In January, 1985, A was appointed a director and was given 25 per cent of the outstanding shares of the company. During an informal discussion in May, 1985, B

---

[173] *Safarik v. Ocean Fisheries Ltd.*, [1993] B.C.J. No. 1816, 10 B.L.R. (2d) 246 at 310, *per* Harvey J., additional reasons [1994] B.C.J. No. 2225 (S.C.), rev'd [1995] B.C.J. No. 1979 (C.A.).

[174] [1999] B.C.C. 600 (H.L.). The decision in the Court of Appeal may be found in *Re Pectel Ltd.*, [1998] B.C.C. 405.

[175] Although there is a great deal to interest the Canadian lawyer in the *O'Neill v. Phillips* case, it must be read with a certain degree of caution, as much of what was said in that case was clearly influenced by the narrower scope of s. 459 (compared to its Canadian counterparts), particularly the fact that the English legislation provides relief only to a member of a company.

[176] See also *Re Astec (BSR) plc*, [1999] B.C.C. 59 at 86 (Ch.), *per* Parker J.; *O'Neill v. Phillips*, [1999] B.C.C. 600 at 609 (H.L.). See also *Re Saul D. Harrison & Sons plc*, [1994] B.C.C. 475 at 490 (H.L.), *per* Lord Hoffman.

[177] See also *Re Wondoflex Textiles Pty Ltd.*, [1951] V.L.R. 458 at 467 (Vict. S.C.), *per* Smith J.

[178] *O'Neill v. Phillips*, [1999] B.C.C. 600 at 607 (H.L.).

told A that he hoped that A would be able to take over running the day-to-day operations of Pectel, in exchange for which A would be entitled to 50 per cent of the profits of the company. In December, 1985, this arrangement was put into effect when B retired from the board of the company and A took over as the *de facto* managing director. Over the next few years, the company did very well. A was credited with half the profits of the company (some of which remained in the company as undistributed earnings). In 1989 and 1990, further discussions took place with respect to the possibility of A obtaining 50 per cent ownership of the company, with B indicating his agreement in principle with such a formalization of their existing understanding. The matter was referred by the parties to their professional advisors, but no formal agreement was ever reached.

§13.53 In 1991, the fortunes of the company declined due to a recession in the U.K. economy. In August, B decided that he should resume personal command of the company. He offered A a choice between running the U.K. or German operations of the business, under B's overall supervision. In November, B formally resumed the position of managing director, although at all material times, A continued to be a director of the company. The relationship between A and B deteriorated. At a November meeting, B was critical of the manner in which A had run the company. He announced that A would no longer receive 50 per cent of the profits, but would only be paid his salary and any dividends payable on his 25 per cent shareholding. Following this meeting, A terminated his guarantee of the company's overdraft and arranged to set up a competing business in Germany. A issued a petition under section 459 of the *Company Act, 1985* in January, 1992, complaining that B's conduct had been unfairly prejudicial to A's rights in the company. At first instance, judgment was given for B, but this was reversed on appeal to the Court of Appeal. B took the case to the House of Lords.

§13.54 Essentially A's case came down to two complaints. The first of these was B's termination of the equal profit-sharing arrangement; the second was B's repudiation of an alleged agreement to transfer half-ownership of the business to A. On the facts, Lord Hoffman concluded that there was no ground on which A was entitled to succeed. It was true that A had an expectation that he would become an equal participant in the business. However, Lord Hoffman ruled that such an expectation might serve as a basis for relief under section 459 only where equitable principles would make it unfair for B to exercise his rights under the articles. It was held that the concept of legitimate expectation should not be allowed to lead a life of its own, capable of giving rise to equitable restraints in circumstances to which traditional equitable principles have no application.[179]

§13.55 Numerous obstacles stood in the way of A. First, he was not removed as a director, nor was he removed from participation in the business. He continued to earn his salary as manager of the business in Germany. A's right to receive 50 per cent of the profits was contingent upon his managing the business so that B did not have to be involved on a day-to-day basis. Once B found it necessary to

---

[179] *Ibid.*, at 610.

become reinvolved in the business, that entitlement lapsed. Although discussions had taken place with a view towards A obtaining a 50 per cent interest in the business, no unconditional promise to that effect had ever been made, and no agreement had ever been reached. To impose such an agreement on B:

> ... would not be restraining the exercise of legal rights. It would be imposing upon Mr. Phillips an obligation to which he never agreed. Where, as here, parties enter into negotiations with a view to a transfer of shares on professional advice and subject to a condition that they are not to be bound until a formal document has been executed, I do not think it is possible to say that an obligation has arisen in fairness or equity at an earlier stage.

As his Lordship pointed out, the power of the court to grant relief was not an open-ended authority to rewrite the relationship existing between the parties on such terms as the court might consider appropriate. It was impossible to divorce a discussion of what was fair between the parties from a consideration of the factual context in which the relationship between the parties arose:

> In section 459, Parliament has chosen fairness as the criterion by which the court must decide whether it has jurisdiction to grant relief. It is clear from the legislative history ... that it chose this concept to free the court from technical considerations of legal right and to confer a wide power to do what appeared just and equitable. But this does not mean that the court can do whatever the individual judge happens to think fair. The concept of fairness must be applied judicially and the content which it is given by the courts must be based upon rational principles.
>
> Although fairness is a notion which can be applied to all kinds of activities, its content will depend upon the context in which it is being used. Conduct which is perfectly fair between competing businessmen may not be fair between members of a family. In some sports it may require, at best, observance of the rules, in others ("it's not cricket") it may be unfair in some circumstances to take advantage of them. All is said to be fair in love and war. So the context and background are very important.[180]

(3) Contracting Out of Oppression Protection

§13.56 Although neither the OBCA nor the CBCA is clear on the point, it is doubtful that a person can contract out of the protection afforded under the oppression remedy provisions, at least not where the contract is made before the time when the cause of action for oppression arose.[181] The clear objective of the oppression remedy is to supplement the rights to which minority shareholders and other exposed groups are entitled, to protect them against risks lying outside what they may reasonably have expected at the time when they acquired an interest in

---

[180] *Ibid.*, at 606; *Re J.E. Cade & Son Ltd.*, [1991] B.C.C. 360 at 372, *per* Warner J.: "The court ... has a very wide discretion, but it does not sit under a palm tree."
[181] See, generally, *Neri v. Finch Hardware (1976) Ltd.*, [1995] O.J. No. 1932, 20 B.L.R. (2d) 216 (Gen. Div.). In that case, the court ordered that the controlling shareholders buy up the shares of the complainant, even though the terms of a unanimous shareholder agreement provided that a retiring shareholder had no right to be bought out on leaving the corporation. It was held that the agreement would not apply where the reasons for leaving were oppressive conduct on the part of the controlling shareholders.

the corporation. This apparent legislative purpose would be defeated if the remedy could be ousted by a general contractual prohibition barring its application.

§13.57 Nevertheless, the terms of contracts entered into between persons interested in a corporation are obviously relevant to a determination of the reasonable expectations of the persons concerned. For instance, it has been held that in an oppression case, a court will give consideration to[182] — but if necessary to achieve justice will overrule — the terms of any unanimous shareholder agreement.[183] On the other hand, a breach of the terms of a unanimous shareholder agreement will often be highly indicative of oppression. Insofar as any such agreement may be said to set down the expectations of the parties, it is obviously highly probative.[184] Where the conduct complained of is specifically sanctioned by a contract entered into between the relevant parties, or is of a type that any reasonable person would have seen to be inherent in the type of bargain that the parties have made, then relief under the oppression remedy will not be available. Such conduct cannot be said to be contrary to the parties' reasonable expectations, even though in another case where there is no such contractual understanding the same conduct might well be said to be oppressive.[185] Similarly, the reasonable expectations of a party must take into account the principles of law governing the conduct of business by corporations (particularly the principle of majority rule and the right of the board of directors to manage the corporation as they see fit, albeit subject to their statutory duties to the corporation), and the manner in which private companies generally conduct their business and affairs. Only when conduct goes beyond this description can it be said to justify the grant of a remedy under section 248 or its equivalents under the CBCA and other business corporations legislation. The reasonable expectations of a person interested in a corporation do not exist in the abstract. Thus, the reasonable expectations assumption significantly qualifies the circumstances in which, and the extent to which, the oppression remedy is available.

(4) Summary Regarding Reasonable Expectations

§13.58 It is a fair question whether the frequent reference to reasonable expectations in the case law does much to clarify the law. The term "reasonable expectation" is inherently ambiguous and ultimately is essentially meaningless. Much of the case law invoking "reasonable expectation" merely substitutes that undefined term for oppression and unfair prejudice. The inevitable consequence

---

[182] For instance, courts may refuse to hear an oppression case where a shareholder agreement provides for the arbitration of shareholder disputes. See generally *Seel v. Seel*, [1995] B.C.J. No. 863, 6 B.C.L.R. (3d) 97 (S.C.). See also *Quaglieri v. 374400 Ontario Ltd.*, [1994] O.J. No. 668, 18 O.R. (3d) 616 (Gen. Div.).

[183] *Bury v. Bell Gouinlock Ltd.*, [1984] O.J. No. 2665, 12 D.L.R. (4th) 451 (H.C.), aff'd [1985] O.J. No. 2405, 14 D.L.R. (4th) 488 (Div. Ct.); *Oakley v. McDougall*, [1987] B.C.J. No. 1226, 14 B.C.L.R. (2d) 128 (C.A.).

[184] See, generally, *Fulmer v. Peter D. Fulmer Holdings Inc.*, [1997] O.J. No. 4973, 36 B.L.R. (2d) 257 (Gen. Div.).

[185] See, generally, *Benson v. Third Canadian General Investment Trust Ltd.*, [1993] O.J. No. 1491, 14 O.R. (3d) 493 (Gen. Div.).

is that in attempting to apply the law to the facts of a given case, the court descends into circular reasoning. If it is inclined to give a remedy in the circumstances, it justifies this by saying that the complainant's reasonable expectations were not frustrated. But when the court tries to explain why this is the case, all it can say is that the control group acted in an oppressive or unfairly prejudicial manner. Why was that action unfairly prejudicial? Because it was contrary to the complainant's reasonable expectations.

§13.59 Despite the vague meaning of the term, courts continue to employ it as if merely mentioning it clarified everything. To cite two recent examples: in one recent case, the court stated:

> The purpose of the oppression remedy is to protect the reasonable expectations of the shareholders, which are defined in the context of a particular corporate relationship.[186]

In another it was said

> It appears that the overwhelmingly most significant consideration, and limitation, both in respect to finding entitlement, and the appropriate remedy, is the assessment of whether the act or conduct complained of is consistent with the *reasonable expectations* of the complainant.[187]

There are obvious problems in over-reliance upon the reasonable expectation concept. It is significant to note that neither the OBCA nor the CBCA makes use of the phrase. They provide a remedy that is intended to address a described range of conduct that is "oppressive or unfairly prejudicial to or that unfairly disregards the interests of any security holder". While it is undoubtedly true that very frequently the "interests" and "reasonable expectations" of a person will overlap, it is unwise to place so much emphasis on what the parties reasonably might have expected that the language of the statute comes to be disregarded.

§13.60 There are, in fact, a good many cases in which the courts have indicated a clear unwillingness to stretch the notion of reasonable expectations too far. For instance, in *Clarke v. Rossburger*[188] Paperny J.A. said:

> In determining what expectations deserve protection, this Court favours an approach that considers the relationship between the parties over a restrictive view of their "legal" rights. The complainant's reasonable expectations must be viewed and measured against the backdrop of the entire relationship ...
>
> In assessing reasonableness, the courts are mandated to consider, amongst other things, the history of their relationship, the nature and structure of the company, previous general company practice, and the nature of the rights affected without necessarily considering the intention of the parties whose acts are being impugned.

---

[186] *Cai v. Mo*, [2006] O.J. No. 2215, 19 B.L.R. (4th) 54 at para. 24 (S.C.J.), *per* Mesbur J.
[187] *Re Argo Protective Coatings Inc.*, [2006] N.S.J. No. 389, 248 N.S.R. (2d) 127 at para. 21 (S.C.), *per* Warner J.
[188] [2001] A.J. No. 1168, 293 A.R. 223 at paras. 55-56 (C.A.), leave to appeal to S.C.C. refused [2001] S.C.C.A. No. 570.

In the opinion of the writer, this guarded approach is well warranted. Consideration of what the parties would reasonably expect to occur in the context of a given relationship makes sense when the boundaries of discussion are constrained within realistic limits. In construing the extent to which effect should be given to a particular party's reasonable expectations much guidance can be gained from the law relating to implied terms of contract. For instance:

- Recognition of a particular interest is *necessary* in order to give commercial efficacy to what the parties have actually agreed between them. In particular, reliance upon reasonable expectations makes considerable sense when employing the oppression remedy to prevent a person interested in the corporation from being denied the very rights or benefits that he or she contracted to secure through the devious or otherwise improper manipulation of control over the day-to-day operations of the corporation.

- A party may reasonably expect that statutory and other clearly defined rights will be respected, and that statutory and other clearly defined duties will be performed; similarly, it is a reasonable expectation that where those rights are disregarded improperly or a duty is ignored there will be a remedy against the person in breach at least to the extent that the wrong in question causes a person to suffer a recognizable loss.

- Using reasonable expectations as a tool of construction: For instance, requiring a corporate insider to show that the express term of the arrangement entered into with the complainant clearly contemplate the act in question, where the insider has control over the corporation or some aspect of its activities. Broad rights to act in one's self-interest should not be implied where any such entitlement would be inconsistent with what persons having interests comparable to the complainant would ordinarily expect to be the case.

In contrast, courts should avoid the tendency to use the oppression remedy in an open-ended way, so as to import

- conferring rights and imposing obligations merely because the court concludes that it might have been reasonable for them to be incorporated in the arrangements between the parties;

- denying people the benefit of rights that they have contracted to obtain, or relieving them from obligations or risks that they have agreed to assume;

- drawing inferences that are inconsistent with the wording of the relevant contractual documentation or the communications that have passed between the parties;

- creating new rights, obligations or restrictions that are not necessarily implicit in the rights, obligations or restrictions actually conferred — *i.e.*, by way of logical extension of or inference from those rights, obligations or restrictions that are expressly provided for.

(iv) Reasonable Conduct On the Part of the Control Group

§13.61 In *Ford Motor Co. of Canada v. Ontario Municipal Employees Retirement Board*,[189] the court stated that absent bad faith, or some other improper motive, business judgment that, in hindsight, has proven to be mistaken, misguided or imperfect, will not give rise to liability through the oppression remedy. *A fortiori,* conduct that amounts to a reasonable exercise of business judgment, both by reference to what was known at the time of the conduct in question, and also in light of what has subsequently been learned, will not form the basis for a claim for oppression, even where some alternative approach might also have been reasonably taken.

§13.62 The business decisions that a board of directors or corporate management may be called upon to make concerning the day-to-day operations of a corporation may be influenced by a variety of factors including the income tax laws of different jurisdictions relevant to the transaction, the desire to avoid the need to comply with expensive securities law requirements, and general considerations of commercial efficiency. There is nothing inappropriate in the selection of one available legal structure or commercial arrangement over another, although the consequence of one choice as opposed to another may be to result in detriment to some identifiable shareholder (or other party interested in the corporation). Absent some special factor, it is doubtful whether such routine decision making can lead to a remedy under section 248, even when actual prejudice can be established.[190] A board of directors cannot be expected to carry out an exhaustive inquiry concerning the potential impact of a proposed transaction on each of the shareholders before acting. The failure to do so is not evidence of oppression. What is in the best interests of the corporation may not be in the best interests of particular shareholders.[191]

§13.63 The decision in *Benson v. Third Canadian General Investment Trust Ltd.*,[192] may be cited as support for the conclusion that where shareholders invest in a corporation dominated by a control block they are deemed to have accepted that the controlling shareholder's interest in maximizing value may differ from that of the minority.[193] Therefore, the holders of the control block may ignore, disregard or reject a takeover bid for the corporation as they consider fit, even if to a third party the bid might seem to be a fair and reasonable one in the circumstances. The control block is not to be deprived of its right to retain control of the corporation, merely because,

- the minority shareholders would prefer that they accept the bid; and

- a hypothetical "reasonable person" in the position of the control block would in all probability do so.

---

[189] [2006] O.J. No. 27 (C.A.), leave to appeal to S.C.C. refused [2006] S.C.C.A. No. 77.
[190] See, generally, *Dhanjoon v. Unicity Taxi Ltd.*, [2006] M.J. No. 391, 23 B.L.R. (4th) 207 (Q.B.).
[191] *Re 3026709 Nova Scotia Ltd.*, [2006] N.S.J. No. 389 at para. 19 (S.C.), *per* Warner J.
[192] [1993] O.J. No. 1491, 14 O.R. (3d) 493 at 512 (Gen. Div.).
[193] *Ibid.*, at 499-512.

To conclude otherwise would be to impose a fiduciary duty upon majority shareholders to act for the benefit of the minority shareholders of the corporation, and it is settled that absent very special facts, no such duty exists.[194]

§13.64 A solvent corporation is free to carry on its affairs as it sees fit, subject to its contractual obligations with respect to those debts. Until a debtor is insolvent or has an act of bankruptcy in contemplation, the debtor is free to deal with its property as it wills and it may prefer one creditor over another. A debtor can choose to pay one creditor over another unless it is insolvent or has in its contemplation an event of bankruptcy.[195] It follows that there is no remedy in oppression in such a case.

(v) Standing

(1) Generally

§13.65 The only persons entitled as of right to seek relief under section 248 of the OBCA[196] — and comparable oppression remedies under other business corporations statutes — are persons who fit within the definition of "complainant" under section 245.[197] By virtue of clauses (*a*) and (*b*) of that definition, the following persons are entitled to seek relief against oppression:

- a registered holder or beneficial owner, and a former registered holder or beneficial owner, of a security of a corporation or any of its affiliates;
- a director or an officer or a former director or officer of a corporation or any of its affiliates.

The courts have interpreted these categories broadly.[198]

§13.66 In addition to the standing given to persons who fall within the definition of complainant, the Director and (where the corporation is an offering corporation) the Ontario Securities Commission[199] are also given jurisdiction to apply

---

[194] See, generally, *Brant Investments Ltd. v. KeepRite Inc.*, [1991] O.J. No. 683, 3 O.R. (3d) 289 at 301 (C.A.).

[195] See *Hudson v. Benallack*, [1976] S.C.J. No. 71, [1976] 2 S.C.R. 168 esp. at 175, *per* Dickson J.; *Levy-Russell Ltd. v. Shieldings Inc.*, [2004] O.J. No. 4291 (S.C.J.), *per* Cumming J.

[196] CBCA, s. 241.

[197] CBCA, s. 138. The right to seek an oppression remedy may be assigned by a shareholder to a third party: *Lloyd's Bank Canada v. Canada Life Assurance Co.*, [1990] O.J. No. 953, 21 A.C.W.S. (3d) 98 (H.C.).

[198] See, generally, *Csak v. Aumon*, [1990] O.J. No. 534, 69 D.L.R. (4th) 567 at 571 (H.C.J.), *per* Lane J.; *Mackenzie v. Craig*, [1997] A.J. No. 855, 53 Alta. L.R. (3d) 284 at 293 (Q.B.), *per* Medhurst J., aff'd [1999] A.J. No. 239 (C.A.) but compare *Golden Star Resources Ltd. v. IAM-Gold Corp.*, [2004] O.J. No. 2869, 49 B.L.R. (3d) 36 at 47 (S.C.J.), *per* Hoy J.

[199] *Ontario Securities Commission v. McLaughlin*, [1981] O.J. No. 3193, 35 O.R. (2d) 11 (H.C.J.), var'd [1982] O.J. No. 3431 (Div. Ct.), var'd [1983] O.J. No. 2925 (C.A.). As to when challenges to standing should be raised, see *Levy-Russell Ltd. v. Shieldings Inc.*, [1998] O.J. No. 6471, 42 O.R. (3d) 215 (Gen. Div.).

for an order under section 248.[200] The term "complainant" in section 248 has the same broad meaning as is given to that term in section 245. The OBCA and the CBCA definitions of "complainant" are significantly broader than the corresponding provisions found in the legislation of other provinces. Both Acts expressly identify directors[201] and officers as potential complainants entitled to seek relief from oppression.[202] It has been held that the oppression remedy provisions are remedial legislation[203] and amount to a deliberate departure from the previous judicial policy of non-intervention in the internal management of a corporation.[204] As such, sections 248 and 241 confer a large and sweeping jurisdiction on the court. On the basis of that broad legislative mandate, it has been held that standing is not to be narrowly construed.[205] Protection is not limited to minority shareholders; plurality shareholders (*i.e.*, shareholders holding the largest block of votes) may seek relief under the provisions as well,[206] as may creditors,[207] including Her Majesty.[208] A shareholder does not lose standing where he or she is improperly forced out of the corporation.[209] A majority shareholder may seek relief where effective control over the corporation or some aspect of its operations resides in some other person who has behaved in an oppressive or unfairly prejudicial manner.[210]

§13.67 In addition to shareholders, directors and officers, the statutory definition of "complainant" also includes the registered holders and beneficial owners of securities. The express inclusion of "beneficial owners" within the definition of "complainant" is obviously of great import because it means that such owners enjoy a personal right of action under the section. It is not necessary for them to seek to enforce their rights through an action brought in the name of the registered holder.

---

[200] The Director is included within the CBCA definition of "complainant" for all purposes of Part XX of that Act: CBCA, s. 238.
[201] *Testa v. MacDonnell*, [1986] O.J. No. 1110, 1 A.C.W.S. (3d) 418 (H.C.), *per* Van Camp J.
[202] Compare *Camroux v. Amstrong*, [1990] B.C.J. No. 1027, 47 B.L.R. 302 (S.C.), dealing with standing under the *Company Act*, R.S.B.C. 1979, c. 59, s. 224.
[203] *Moriarity v. Slater*, [1989] O.J. No. 451, 42 B.L.R. 52 at 60 (H.C.J.), *per* White J.
[204] *First Edmonton Place Ltd. v. 315888 Alberta Ltd.*, [1988] A.J. No. 511, 60 Alta. L.R. (2d) 122 (Q.B.), *per* McDonald J.
[205] It is not limited in the protection that it affords to the registered owner of the security: *Csak v. Aumon*, [1990] O.J. No. 534, 69 D.L.R. (4th) 567 at 570 (H.C.J.), *per* Lane J.; *Canadian Opera Co. v. 670800 Ontario Inc.*, [1989] O.J. No. 1307, 69 O.R. (2d) 532, aff'd [1990] O.J. No. 2270, 75 O.R. (2d) 720 (Div. Ct.).
[206] *Gandalman Investments Inc. v. Fogle*, [1985] O.J. No. 2678, 52 O.R. (2d) 614 at 616 (H.C.J.), *per* Callow J.; *Moriarity v. Slater*, [1989] O.J. No. 451, 42 B.L.R. 52 (H.C.); but *cf. Vedova v. Garden House Inn*, [1985] O.J. No. 408, 29 B.L.R. 236 at 236-37 (H.C.), *per* Anderson J.
[207] *Bank of Montreal v. Dome Petroleum Ltd.*, [1987] A.J. No. 1401, 54 Alta. L.R. (2d) 289 (Q.B.).
[208] *R. v. Sands Motor Hotel Ltd.*, [1984] S.J. No. 56, 28 B.L.R. 122 (Q.B.).
[209] *Buckley v. B.C.T.F.*, [1990] B.C.J. No. 491, 44 B.C.L.R. (2d) 31 (S.C.), rev'd [1992] B.C.J. No. 587 (C.A.).
[210] *Shannex Health Care Management Inc. v. Nova Scotia (Attorney General)*, [2005] N.S.J. No. 496 (C.A.); *UPM-Kymmene Corp. v. UPM-Kymmene Miramachi Inc.*, [2004] O.J. No. 636, 42 B.L.R. (3d) 34 (C.A.).

§13.68 Although most oppression claims brought by security owners are brought by shareholders or former shareholders, it is clearly expressed in the section creating the oppression remedy that registered holders and beneficial owners of non-equity securities in the corporation may also seek relief.[211]

(a) DIFFICULTIES OF INTERPRETATION

§13.69 It is fair to say that the statutory definition of "complainant" is far from satisfactory, and its integration into Part XVII of the Act is also unclear. For instance,

- Although shareholders and beneficial owners of securities are entitled to standing as of right, no such standing is conferred upon creditors of the corporation generally.[212] It is difficult to see why a creditor who holds a debt security, such as a promissory note, should be entitled to standing under Part XVII in the OBCA as of right (because a note is a security), whereas other creditors are entitled to such standing only in the discretion of the court.[213]

- Nevertheless, in general the courts are reluctant to convert simple debt actions into oppression proceedings and will not permit this to be done where the creditor's interest in the affairs of the corporation is remote or where the complaints of the creditor have nothing to do with the circumstances giving rise to the debt.[214] Moreover, the courts possess a discretion to prevent an oppression action even by a shareholder (particularly a new shareholder), where it would be abusive to permit such an action to proceed.[215]

---

[211] Creditors who do not hold a security issued by the corporation do not fit in either clause (*a*) or (*b*) of the definition. Nevertheless, the courts have frequently extended standing to such persons: *Sidaplex-Plastic Suppliers, Inc. v. Elta Group Inc.*, [1995] O.J. No. 4048, 131 D.L.R. (4th) 399 (Gen. Div.), var'd [1998] O.J. No. 2910 (C.A.). A person holding an unliquidated or indeterminate claim against the corporation, and even a contingent creditor of a corporation may be permitted to seek relief under the oppression remedy: *AE Realisations (1985) Ltd. v. Time Air Inc.*, [1994] S.J. No. 684, 17 B.L.R. (2d) 203 (Q.B.), aff'd [1995] S.J. No. 273, [1995] 6 W.W.R. 423 (C.A.). However, such persons fall outside of the scope of the definition of complainant in clauses (*a*) and (*b*), and may be allowed to pursue an oppression remedy only where the court in its discretion concludes that they are proper persons to do so.

[212] In contrast to the OBCA and the CBCA, s. 242 of the *Alberta Business Corporations Act*, R.S.A. 2000, c. B-9 (ABCA) expressly confers complainant status on creditors. It has been held that a creditor is a proper complainant for the oppression remedy under that section, where conduct complained of constitutes a fraud on the creditor or frustrates the creditor's reasonable expectations of payment. The conduct complained of need not be unlawful: *Bull HN Information Systems Ltd. v. L.I. Business Solutions Inc.*, [1994] A.J. No. 712, 23 Alta. L.R. (3d) 186 (Q.B.).

[213] Discussed in detail at §13.76 *seq.*

[214] *Royal Trust Corp. of Canada v. Hordo*, [1993] O.J. No. 1560, 10 B.L.R. (2d) 86 at 92 (Gen. Div. — C.L.), per Farley J.; see also *Jacobs Farms Ltd. v. Jacobs*, [1992] O.J. No. 813, unreported April 23, 1992, Doc. No. 92-CQ 17714 (Gen. Div.); *Lee v. International Consort Industries Inc.*, [1992] B.C.J. No. 106, 63 B.C.L.R. (2d) 119 at 127-29 (C.A.); *Quebec Steel Products (Industries) Ltd. v. James United Steel Ltd.*, [1969] O.J. No. 1331, [1969] 2 O.R. 349 at 351-55 (H.C.); *First Edmonton Place Ltd. v. 315888 Alberta Ltd.*, [1988] A.J. No. 511, 40 B.L.R. 28 (Q.B.), rev'd [1989] A.J. No. 1021, 45 B.L.R. 110 at 111-12 (C.A.); *Mohan v. Philmar Lumber (Markham) Ltd.*, [1991] O.J. No. 3451, 50 C.P.C. (2d) 164 at 165-66 (Gen. Div.).

[215] *Royal Trust Corp. of Canada v. Hordo*, [1993] O.J. No. 1560, 10 B.L.R. (2d) 86 at 92-93 (Gen. Div. — C.L.), per Farley J.

- Under section 248(1), a complainant is allowed to seek a remedy by application to court, but it is unclear whether the "security holder, creditor, director or officer of the corporation" who has suffered by reason of oppression, unfair prejudice or unfair disregard must be the same person as the complainant; in other words, may one complainant seek relief for injury to some other complainant? Given the personal nature of the oppression remedy (in constrast to the class action nature of the derivative action), in the normal case the probable answer would be no.

Perhaps most importantly, the scope of the identified categories of complainant are left unclear. Although the definition speaks expressly of "former" and (implicitly) of "present" registered holders, beneficial owners of securities, directors and officers of the corporation or of its affiliates, the reference point in time by which such status is to be ascertained is not made clear.

§13.70 At one time, it was clear that to be entitled to proceed as a complainant under the Act, a person must have qualified for that status at the time of the acts about which that person complains.[216] Under such an interpretation, it would not be possible to buy into an oppression action.[217] In most cases, since the price paid by any such subsequent holder for the security concerned will include an appropriate discount to reflect the misconduct complained of, the subsequent holder cannot claim to have suffered by reason of the oppression. However, recent Ontario case law now suggests that it is sufficient if the complainant is a registered holder or beneficial owner of the security at the time when he or she brings the application.[218] The issue is more one of whether prejudice has in fact been suffered, than one of timing, although timing may of course be highly relevant in deciding whether prejudice has really been suffered.

§13.71 This obscurity of language can lead to uncertainty about who is and who is not entitled to claim relief. For instance, complainant status is expressly conferred upon former directors, former officers, former security holders and former beneficial owners of securities. Obviously, however, "former" complainants have no standing to complain about alleged wrongs done to the corporation or its present directors, shareholders, *etc.* For instance, a person who in the remote and distant past held shares in a corporation could hardly be expected to bring a complaint about some wrong alleged to have been committed only recently; and,

---

[216] *Royal Trust Corp. of Canada v. Hordo*, [1993] O.J. No. 1560, 10 B.L.R. (2d) 86 (Gen. Div. — C.L.); see also *Trillium Computer Resources Inc. v. Taiwan Connection Inc.*, [1992] O.J. No. 2175, 10 O.R. (3d) 249 at 253 (Gen. Div.), leave to appeal to Div. Ct. refused [1992] O.J. No. 4036 (Gen. Div.).
[217] Discussed in detail at §13.73 *seq.*
[218] *Richardson Greenshields of Canada Ltd. v. Kalmacoff*, [1995] O.J. No. 941, 18 B.L.R. (2d) 197 at 204-05 (C.A.), *per* Robins J.A., leave to appeal to S.C.C. refused [1995] S.C.C.A. No. 260. In *Bermuda Cablevision Ltd. v. Colica Trust Co.*, [1997] J.C.J. No. 43, [1998] A.C. 198 (P.C.), it was held that relief could be sought by a person who joined the company at a time when he or she knew that the affairs of the company were being conducted in the manner forming the basis of the complaint.

accordingly, it would seem to be doubtful that the Legislature could have intended to confer standing upon such persons.[219]

§13.72 It can be argued that the logical approach to the question of standing would be to hold that the terms "former" director, *etc.* describe persons who held office, shares or securities at the time when the alleged wrongful conduct occurred, and who have subsequently disposed of them (perhaps in consequence thereof), so, at the time when the application is brought for leave to proceed with a derivative action or to seek an oppression remedy, they have become "former". Such an approach is consistent with the view taken by some courts that the proper persons to bring derivative actions must have a direct financial interest in the wrong the corporation has suffered,[220] and is consistent with the general damage principle applicable to rights of civil action that only persons who have suffered injury by a civil wrong have the standing to sue in regard to that wrong.

(b) Discretionary Claimants

§13.73 In addition to the classes of complainant expressly granted standing under the Act, clause (*c*) of the statutory definition of "complainant" also permits the courts to allow oppression proceedings to be brought by "any other person who, in the discretion of the court, is a proper person to make an application under this Part". In *First Edmonton Place Ltd. v. 315888 Alberta Ltd.*[221] McDonald J. discussed the ramifications of this grant of discretion:

> This is not so much a definition as a grant to the court of a broad power to do justice and equity in the circumstances of a particular case, where a person, who would otherwise not be a "complainant", ought to be permitted to bring an action under either s. 232 or s. 234 to right a wrong done to the corporation which would not otherwise be righted, or to obtain compensation himself or itself where his or its interests have suffered from oppression by the majority controlling the corporation or have been unfairly disregarded ...

Generally, the courts take a fairly liberal approach to the determination of questions of standing to seek relief against oppression — at least in cases in which the conduct complained of is genuinely oppressive or unfairly prejudicial, and normal contractual, trust or proprietary remedies would not afford adequate relief.[222] Significantly, the definition does not provide an express standing as a complainant to the corporation itself. There is case law stating that a corporation may possibly be a proper person to be entitled to seek relief against oppression against a former director or officer, but in order to do so, the circumstances

---

[219] *Jacobs Farms Ltd. v. Jacobs*, [1992] O.J. No. 813, unreported, April 23, 1992, Doc. No. 92-CQ-17714 (Gen. Div.), *per* Blair J.
[220] See, generally, *Re Daon Development Corp.*, [1984] B.C.J. No. 2945, 54 B.C.L.R. 235 at 243 (S.C.); *Chernoff v. Parta Holdings Ltd.*, [1995] B.C.J. No. 1918, 13 B.C.L.R. (3d) 260 (S.C.).
[221] [1988] A.J. No. 511, 60 Alta. L.R. (2d) 122 at 150 (Q.B.), rev'd [1989] A.J. No. 1021 (C.A.).
[222] See, for instance, *347883 Alberta Ltd. v. Producers Pipelines Ltd.*, [1991] S.J. No. 222, [1991] 4 W.W.R. 577 at 602 (C.A.), *per* Sherstobitoff J.A.; *Palmer v. Carling O'Keefe Breweries of Canada Ltd.*, [1989] O.J. No. 32, 41 B.L.R. 128 at 136-37 (Div. Ct.), *per* Southey J.

would have to be unusual.²²³ Ordinarily, it would be more common for the corporation to sue the director or officer either under the OBCA or the CBCA (for a breach of his or her statutory duties to the corporation), or in equity for breach of fiduciary duty. However, as with other types of potential claimant, the oppression remedy may be attractive to the corporation where the relief available under more traditional causes of action is inadequate and more advantageous relief is available under sections 248 of the OBCA or 241 of the CBCA.²²⁴

§13.74 A key hurdle for any potential discretionary complainant to leap is to show that he or she has suffered from the conduct concerned.²²⁵ This hurdle may prove difficult in the case of subsequent holders or owners of securities. Where, however, the oppressive or other misconduct began before a particular subsequent holder acquired the securities and continues afterward, then that holder will fit within the definition of "complainant" because the misconduct in question cannot properly be said to have occurred before the acquisition of the securities, at least in its entirety.²²⁶ In addition, a subsequent holder would most likely be considered to be a proper person to seek relief where the circumstances in which the securities were acquired allowed no opportunity for a discount of the price paid (*e.g.*, where the misconduct was not known to have occurred at that time), or where the securities were acquired by succession, for instance upon the death of the prior holder, or by a secured creditor realizing upon securities under a pledge.²²⁷

(c) TIMING OF A CLAIM (BUYING INTO AN ACTION)

§13.75 Courts have struggled with the question of whether a person is entitled to seek oppression relief where the act giving rise to the claim occurred prior to the time when the person acquired his or her interest in the corporation.²²⁸ A central complication in trying to set down any general rule in this regard is the fact that such a person may acquire his or her rights in a wide range of different circumstances. To give some obvious examples:

---

²²³ See, generally, *Gainers Inc. v. Pocklington*, [1992] A.J. No. 603, 7 B.L.R. (2d) 87 (Q.B.); *Calmont Leasing Ltd. v. Kredl*, [1995] A.J. No. 475, 30 Alta. L.R. (3d) 16, additional reasons at [1995] A.J. No. 763, 32 Alta. L.R. (3d) 345 (C.A.).

²²⁴ See, generally, *Levy-Russell Ltd. v. Shieldings Inc.*, [1998] O.J. No. 3571, 41 O.R. (3d) 54, leave to appeal refused [1988] O.J. No. 6471, 42 O.R. (3d) 215 (Gen. Div.).

²²⁵ See, generally, *Keating v. Bragg*, [1998] N.S.J. No. 248, 34 B.L.R. (2d) 181 (C.A.).

²²⁶ For an instance where a subsequent shareholder was allowed to bring a derivative action as a complainant see *Richardson Greenshields of Canada Ltd. v. Kalmacoff*, [1995] O.J. No. 941, 18 B.L.R. (2d) 197 (C.A.), leave to appeal to S.C.C. refused [1995] S.C.C.A. No. 260 22 B.L.R. (2d) 164.

²²⁷ *Iverson v. Westfair Foods Ltd.*, [1996] A.J. No. 397, 28 B.L.R. (2d) 87 (Q.B.), aff'd [1998] A.J. No. 1145, leave to appeal to S.C.C. refused [1998] S.C.C.A. No. 634.

²²⁸ See, generally, *Ford Motor Co. of Canada v. Ontario Municipal Employees Retirement Board*, [2004] O.J. No. 191, 41 B.L.R. (3d) 74 (S.C.J.), var'd [2006] O.J. No. 27, leave to appeal to S.C.C. refused [2006] S.C.C.A. No. 77; *LSI Logic Corp. of Canada, Inc. v. Logani*, [2001] A.J. 1083 (Q.B.); *Hendin v. Cadillac Fairview Corp.*, [1983] O.J. No. 239 (H.C.); but *cf. PMSM Investments Ltd. v. Bureau*, [1995] O.J. No. 2611, 25 O.R. (3d) 586 at 591 (Gen. Div.), per Farley J.; *Palmer v. Carling O'Keefe Breweries of Canada Ltd.*, [1989] O.J. No. 32, 67 O.R. (2d) 161 (Div. Ct.).

(a) If the complainant purchased an interest in the corporation knowing of the facts that give rise to the claim, then it may be reasonably assumed that the price paid by the complainant reflected those facts. In such a case, the individual concerned suffers no injury that could give rise to a claim. Instead, the proper plaintiff would be the former owner of the securities.

(b) If the complainant did not know the facts, then the price paid would not reflect the act of oppression, and the damage suffered by the potential claimant would be no different from the damage suffered by others who had an interest in the corporation at the time when the acts in question occurred. In such a case, a strong argument can be made for allowing the current holder of the securities to proceed with a claim.

(c) A person may acquire small share holdings so as to achieve a sufficient level of interest in the corporation to justify the cost and inconvenience of proceeding with an oppression action. In such a case, there is merit in granting standing, because otherwise a wrong may go unaddressed. However, in such a case, as a condition of approving the complainant, a court might consider requiring the complainant to pass along any amount recovered to other persons who were injured.

In *HSBC Canada Capital Inc. v. First Mortgage Alberta Fund (V) Inc.*[229] Paperny J. noted that the complainant need not necessarily be the person oppressed, but that there must be a nexus between that person and the complainant. A grey area exists where the complainant has bought into a corporation after the intention to act in the given way that forms the basis of the complaint has become known, but before the actual steps that it entails have been taken.[230] The critical issue in such a case is to be able to show that carrying through with that act was oppressive, in view of the declared intent.[231] Clearly double recovery or recovery in absence of actual damage should not be possible.

(2) Creditors as Complainants

§13.76 The creditors of a corporation necessarily enjoy a contractual relationship with the corporation; they also enjoy greater rights of enforcement against a corporation than that which is possessed by shareholders. Creditors as such are not entitled to standing under the oppression remedy as of right, but they may be given leave of the court to proceed as a discretionary complainant.[232] Creditor, for this purpose, includes a judgment creditor,[233] and also a trustee-in-bankruptcy.[234] It is doubtful, however, whether a person who (at the time when

---

[229] [1999] A.J. No. 614, 72 Alta. L.R. (3d) 356 (Q.B.).

[230] See *Palmer v. Carling O'Keefe Breweries of Canada Ltd.*, [1989] O.J. No. 32, 67 O.R. (2d) 161 (Div. Ct.).

[231] *Ford Motor Co. of Canada v. Ontario Municipal Employees Retirement Board*, [2004] O.J. No. 191, 41 B.L.R. (3d) 74 at 119-21 (S.C.J.), *per* Cumming J.

[232] *Glasvon Great Dane Sales Inc. v. Qureshi*, [2003] O.J. No. 2643, 35 B.L.R. (3d) 217 at 227 (S.C.J.), *per* Hoy J., aff'd [2005] O.J. No. 682 (C.A.).

[233] *C-L & Associates Inc. v. Airside Equipment Sales Inc.*, [2003] M.J. No. 160, 35 B.L.R. (3d) 124 at 130 (Q.B.), *per* Sinclair J.

[234] *Trustee of Dylex Ltd. v. Anderson*, [2003] O.J. No. 833, 32 B.L.R. (3d) 295 at 302-303 (S.C.J.).

the alleged oppressive act occurred) had only a contingent interest in an uncertain claim for unliquidated damages would fall within the definition of a creditor, as such a claim would be too speculative.[235]

§13.77 The general attitude of the courts is that the oppression procedure should not be used by creditors to facilitate the ordinary process of debt collection. In most cases this approach would seem reasonable, for it cannot have been intended that the oppression remedy would be available where a creditor failed to protect himself or herself adequately against the inherent risks of doing business with a corporation. While acts of oppression may entail a breach of contract, or the commission of some tortious or similar wrong, against the complainant, the oppression remedy was not intended to be a substitute for a normal action for breach of contract.[236] There appears to be an implicit attitude in some decided cases that creditors may not seek relief by way of oppression where their only real complaint is that they did not tie down the corporation, its directors and affiliates in a more rigorous loan or security agreement.[237] Where the sole complaint is that of a breach of contract, then a contract action should be pursued. Insofar as the contract deals with a specific matter, it seems only natural to conclude that it sets out exhaustively the underlying intentions, understandings and expectations of the parties.[238] While many — perhaps all — breaches of contract can be characterized as oppressive to the injured party, and while many — perhaps all — forms of tortious injury may be said to be unfairly prejudicial, the legislature clearly cannot have intended for the oppression provisions to serve as a panacea for all manner of legal wrongs, or to make the remedies created under the statute for genuine cases of oppression or unfair prejudice a substitute for the normal legal and equitable remedies that are available to aggrieved parties. Where a simple breach of contract, or comparable legal wrong, has occurred, it is not appropriate for the court to invoke the oppression provisions of the Act merely because the party in breach is a corporation. It is arguable at least that insofar as a corporation remains able to satisfy the obligations owed to a creditor, no oppression proceeding is available, since in such a case the creditor cannot be said to have been unfairly prejudiced. In such a case, the appropriate remedy is an action for breach of contract.

§13.78 However, it does not follow from these observations that a creditor may never be seen to have been oppressed, unfairly prejudiced or unfairly disregarded by the corporation or its control group. On the facts of a given case there may be unusual circumstances sufficient to justify permitting a creditor to seek

---

[235] *Royal Trust Corp. of Canada v. Hordo*, [1993] O.J. No. 1560 at para. 13 (Gen. Div. — C.L.), per Farley, J.; *Devry v. Atwood's Furniture Showrooms Ltd.*, [2000] O.J. No. 4283 at para. 27 (S.C.J. — C.L.), per Swinton J.
[236] *Hurley v. Slate Ventures Inc.*, [1996] N.J. No. 203, 28 B.L.R. (2d) 35 at 64-65 (S.C.), per Osborn J., aff'd [1998] N.J. No. 225, 167 Nfld. & P.E.I.R. 1 (C.A.).
[237] *Ibid.*, at 37; *Heap Noseworthy Ltd. v. Didham*, [1996] N.J. No. 8, 29 B.L.R. (2d) 279 (S.C.).
[238] See, for instance, *Sidaplex-Plastic Suppliers, Inc. v. Elta Group Inc.*, [1995] O.J. No. 4048, 131 D.L.R. (4th) 399 at 405 (Gen. Div.), per R.A. Blair J., rev'd in part [1998] O.J. No. 2910, 162 D.L.R. (4th) 367 (C.A.).

oppression relief.[239] For the oppression remedy to apply, there must be some additional feature to the wrong which has been suffered that makes recourse to the oppression remedies a practical necessity so justice is done for the injured party on the facts of the case.[240] An application for leave of the court to proceed with an oppression claim is not a precondition to the institution of such a proceeding by a creditor, but the application should be made out as early in the proceeding as is reasonably possible.[241]

§13.79 To date, the courts have offered little clear guidance as to when leave will be given to a creditor to proceed with an oppression claim. It is clear from the case law that a creditor must establish on the specific facts of the case that it is appropriate to be granted standing in the exercise of the courts judicial discretion.[242] Generally, the creditor must show not only that it has not been paid, but also that there is some additional element in the facts that establishes unfair prejudice or unfair disregard for its rights. It is also clear that a creditor seeking leave must establish that it is a proper person to bring the proceeding. However, it is not necessary for the creditor to demonstrate that it is the most suitable complainant.[243] No doubt the insolvency of a corporation, without more, is not sufficient to justify a creditor in obtaining relief against the directors of the corporation or its controlling shareholders under the oppression provision. On the other hand, insolvency resulting from the misconduct of those persons would seem to justify relief. The creditors of a corporation may reasonably expect that a corporation will fulfill its contractual commitments. Accordingly, an oppression remedy is available to a creditor where the directors or controlling shareholders misconduct the business or affairs of the corporation, and render it impossible (or exceedingly unlikely) for the corporation to perform its contractual obligations.[244] For instance, in one case an unpaid judgment creditor who had no hope of realizing on its judgment was held to be an appropriate discretionary complainant to seek to recover money allegedly stripped from a corporation by its president, major shareholder and director.[245] In addition, the oppression remedy may be suitable in cases where recovery from the corporation itself is impossible or impractical. In such a case the complainant may pursue an order from the court imposing personal liability upon directors (or shareholders) for the manner in which they have conducted the affairs of the

---

[239] *Trustee of Olympia & York Developments Ltd v. Olympia & York Realty Corp.*, [2001] O.J. No. 3394 (S.C.J.), aff'd [2003] O.J. No. 5242 (C.A.), but compare *Canada (Attorney General) v. Standard Trust Co.*, [1991] O.J. No. 1946 (1991), 5 O.R. (3d) 660 (Gen. Div.)

[240] *Hurley v. Slate Venturers Inc.*, [1996] N.J. No. 203, 28 B.L.R. (2d) 35 at 64-65 (S.C.T.D.), *per* Osborn J.

[241] *First Mortgage Fund (V) Inc. (Receiver and Manager of) v. Boychuk*, [2001] A.J. No. 1071, 96 Alta. L.R. (3d) 306 (Q.B.), var'd [2002] A.J. No. 1025, 8 Alta. L.R. (4th) 212 (C.A.).

[242] *Trillium Computer Resources v. Taiwan Connection Inc.*, [1992] O.J. No. 2175, 10 O.R. (3d) 249 at 252-53 (Gen. Div.), *per* West J.

[243] *HSBC Capital Canada Inc. v. First Mortgage Alberta Fund (V) Inc.*, [1999] A.J. No. 614, 72 Alta. L.R. (3d) 356 (Q.B.), *per* Paperny J.

[244] *SCI Systems, Inc. v. Gornitzki Thompson & Little Co.*, [1997] O.J. No. 2115, 147 D.L.R. (4th) 300 (Gen. Div.), var'd [1998] O.J. No. 2299 (Div. Ct.).

[245] *Prime Computer of Canada Ltd. v. Jeffrey*, [1991] O.J. No. 2317, 6 O.R. (3d) 733 (Gen. Div.).

corporation concerned.[246] The jurisdiction to make such an order appears to supplement the power of the courts to lift the corporate veil.[247]

§13.80 In *Re Sammi Atlas Inc.*,[248] a trade creditors' committee set up to represent the interest of the trade creditors of a corporation was found to be a proper person to bring a derivative proceeding.

(3) Relief Not Limited to Those with a Minority Interest

§13.81 It is common for oppression relief to be sought by a minority shareholder, but the Act does not limit relief to such shareholders.[249] Any security holder may seek relief, irrespective of the extent of his or her ownership. It was noted in the First Edition of this text that on occasion, the courts have granted relief even where the application for relief has been sought by a 50 per cent shareholder of a corporation,[250] or even by a majority shareholder where effective control of the corporation has resided in the hands of some other person. Since that publication the law in this area has been more settled. It may now be stated with confidence that relief for oppression is not limited to those who hold a minority voting interest in the corporation, or who do not have a say in the management of its operations. Although it is unusual for an oppression claim to be brought by the holder of a majority voting interest, the primary concerns are the question of *de facto* control at the time when the alleged oppression occurred, and whether other forms of relief would provide an adequate remedy. If the business and affairs of a corporation have in fact been conducted so as to oppress the holder of the majority interest, there is no reason in principle why that holder may not seek relief.[251] For instance, if the minority somehow seizes control, it is also potentially subject to a claim.[252] Indeed, a claim by the holder of a majority interest may be necessary to unwind a transaction and recover property. Perhaps the most extreme case along these lines was the decision of the Alberta Court of Queen's Bench in *Gainers Inc. v. Pocklington*,[253] in which it was held that the corporation itself could qualify for standing as a complainant in an oppression proceeding. However, where a shareholder has a 50 per cent interest and has adequate alternate remedies, a remedy in oppression will not

---

[246] See, for instance, *Sidaplex-Plastic Suppliers, Inc. v. Elta Group Inc.*, [1995] O.J. No. 4048, 25 B.L.R. (2d) 179 (Gen. Div.) — oppression found where a breach of contract was caused by a director to secure a personal benefit (specifically, to avoid liability on a guarantee) and where it effectively left the creditor with no practical remedy against the corporation, rev'd in part [1998] O.J. No. 2910, 162 D.L.R. (4th) 367 (C.A.).

[247] *Sidaplex-Plastic Suppliers, Inc. v. Elta Group Inc.*, [1995] O.J. No. 4048, 131 D.L.R. 399 at 407 (Gen. Div.), *per* R.A. Blair J., rev'd in part [1998] O.J. No. 2910, 162 D.L.R. (4th) 367 (C.A.).

[248] [1997] O.J. No. 4767, 36 B.L.R. (2d) 318 (Gen. Div.).

[249] For a rare case of what might be described as mutual oppression by two shareholders who each held one-half of the corporation, see *Hobbs v. Dempsey*, [2006] O.J. No. 164, 14 B.L.R. (4th) 65 (S.C.J.).

[250] *Hansen v. Eberle*, [1997] S.J. No. 82, 144 D.L.R. (4th) 422 (C.A.).

[251] See, for instance, *Shannex Health Care Management Inc. v. Nova Scotia (Attorney General)*, [2005] N.S.J. No. 496 (C.A.); *UPM-Kymmene Corp. v. UPM-Kymmene Miramachi Inc.*, [2004] O.J. No. 636, 42 B.L.R. (3d) 34 (C.A.).

[252] *Fiber Connections Inc. v. SVCM Capital Ltd.*, [2005] O.J. No. 3899, 5 B.L.R. (4th) 271 (S.C.J.).

[253] [1992] A.J. No. 603, 7 B.L.R. (2d) 87 (Q.B.).

lie.[254] For instance, relief from oppression was denied to the holder of a 60 per cent share of the corporation where she had made no effort to requisition a shareholders' meeting.[255]

(4) Claims by Former Directors and Officers

(a) GENERALLY

§13.82 In most cases in which a finding of oppression has been made, the complainant has either been ousted as a director or his or her rights as a shareholder have been sterilized. Although it is usual to point to a persistent pattern of conduct as evidence of oppression, even isolated acts can be unfairly prejudicial to minority shareholders (or other potential complainants) and thereby justify a remedy.[256] Although the sterilization of shareholder rights appears to invite a finding of oppression, the removal of a director is less likely to be found oppressive. Findings of oppression are particularly unlikely to be made where (a) the complainant's removal as a director followed a period of discussion and genuine attempts to reach a compromise; and (b) the complainant's rights as a shareholder are still being properly respected. The courts recognize that differences will arise from time to time within a corporate organization on the manner in which its business should be conducted. If no bad faith, lack of probity or malice is shown,[257] but the views of the complainant have simply been rejected by the majority, the complainant will have to live with the wishes of the majority.[258]

(b) OPPRESSION AND WRONGFUL DISMISSAL

§13.83 As discussed in the context of creditor claims, the breach of a contractual right by a corporation is not in and of itself oppressive. Such a breach may, however, be part of an overall pattern of conduct that is oppressive, or may be carried out in such a way as to be oppressive. In other words, a breach of contract is always actionable; but only in a limited range of cases will it give rise to relief under the oppression remedy. It is not enough to show the breach; the plaintiff must establish that the breach amounted to oppression, unfair prejudice or unfair disregard. Unfortunately, this distinction is a difficult one to conceptualize. While it has been mentioned frequently in the context of claims for wrongful dismissal,[259] much of the case law in this area merely demonstrates the complexity of the distinction. For instance, in the *Naneff* case,[260] Blair J. said:

---

[254] *English v. Sylvan Lands Development Corp.*, [2004] A.J. No. 1387, 1 B.L.R. (4th) 163 (Q.B.).
[255] *Coulton v. Slaugher*, [2004] O.J. No. 2999, 49 B.L.R. (3d) 78 (S.C.J.).
[256] *Watergroup Companies Inc. v. Stevens*, [1996] S.J. No. 178, 25 B.L.R. (2d) 248 at 262 (Q.B.).
[257] See, generally, *Diligenti v. RWMD Operations Kelowna Ltd.*, [1976] B.C.J. No. 38, 1 B.C.L.R. 36 (S.C.); *Low v. Ascot Jockey Club Ltd.*, [1986] B.C.J. No. 3001, 1 B.C.L.R. (2d) 123 (S.C.).
[258] *Tkatch v. Heide*, [1996] B.C.J. No. 946, 29 B.L.R. (2d) 266 at 273-74 (S.C.), *per* Hutchinson J., aff'd [1998] B.C.J. No. 2613 (C.A.).
[259] *Mohan v. Philmar Lumber (Markham) Ltd.*, [1991] O.J. No. 3451, 50 C.P.C. (2d) 164 (Gen. Div.); *Daniels v. Fielder*, [1988] O.J. No. 1592, 65 O.R. (2d) 629 (H.C.J.).
[260] *Naneff v. Con-Crete Holdings Ltd.*, [1993] O.J. No. 1756, 11 B.L.R. (2d) 218 at para. 125 (Gen. Div. — C.L.), var'd [1994] O.J. No. 1811 (Div. Ct.), rev'd [1995] O.J. No. 1377 (C.A.).

... a claim for wrongful dismissal is not, in itself, a proper claim to be asserted by way of oppression remedy. Where the dismissal is part of an overall pattern of oppression, and where the complainant's position of employment is closely connected with his or her rights as a shareholder, officer and director of the company, or companies, in question, the dismissal may properly be considered as part of that pattern of conduct, however, in such a case, it seems to me, some form of remedy for the wrongful act may be granted by way of "an order compensating the aggrieved person" ...

In *Flatley v. Algy Corp.*[261] Swinton J. discussed the *Naneff* case and compared it to the facts of the case before her:

> The facts in *Naneff* are quite different from those here. The plaintiff in that action was held to have had an expectation that he would participate in the management and direction of the family group of companies, and he had worked in a senior management position and been an officer and director for a number of years before he was thrown out of the day-to-day operations of the companies.
>
> Here, the evidence does not suggest that Skinulis and Flatley entered into an arrangement in which it was contemplated that Flatley would be integrally involved in the day-to-day management and operation of the business. Her shares were non-voting, and she did not seek to be an officer and director at the time she made her investment. At first, she did not work as an employee at the bar. It was not until sometime in 1997 that she began to work as a bar tender, and even then she took several months off to travel in 1998. She was never an officer and director of the corporation. The fact that she had signing authority at the bank as "secretary" can not elevate her into the kind of corporate management role that was significant in *Naneff*.

Wrongful dismissal is itself a cause of action, and in the ordinary case there is no need to embellish it by adding to it fanciful allegations of corporate oppression, since the common law right of action affords sufficient remedies to provide the plaintiff with full redress. On the other hand, where the person dismissed holds a share or similar interest in the corporation, compensation for wrongful dismissal may not be sufficient to protect that residual interest. For instance, a person who purchased a minority interest in a closely held corporation, as part of the overall arrangement relating to his or her appointment as an officer of the corporation, damages for wrongful dismissal will not redress that purchase. The complainant in such a case still holds the qualifying investment in the corporation, but not the job that induced him or her to make that investment. In such a case, an oppression remedy (*e.g.*, the buying out of the qualifying investment) may be essential to provide for full recovery.

(vi) Special Cases

(1) Claims with Respect to Affiliates

§13.84 The section 248 remedy protects a complainant only in relation to his or her capacity as a director, officer, shareholder, creditor or security holder of the

---

[261] [2000] O.J. No. 3787, 9 B.L.R. (3d) 255 at 260 (S.C.J. — C.L.).

corporation.[262] Thus, section 248 relief is limited to those persons who can show that they have suffered as a result of oppressive conduct, unfair prejudice and the like, insofar as they are persons interested in the corporation. For instance, it has been held that while under section 248(1) of the OBCA the misconduct complained of may involve the corporation *or its affiliates*, the oppression, unfair prejudice, *etc.* that has been caused by reason of that misconduct must affect the interests of a security holder, creditor, director or officer *of the corporation*. If an affiliate of an OBCA or CBCA corporation (such as a subsidiary or parent company of the corporation) is subject to legislation that does not include an oppression type remedy comparable to that provided under section 248, it is not possible for a security holder, creditor, director or officer of that affiliate to seek relief under the OBCA or the CBCA.[263]

(2) Widely Held Corporations

§13.85 The extent to which the "reasonable expectation" approach can be applied where the shares or other securities of which the complainant is the holder are widely held remains a matter of some debate, given the probable diversity of investor interests and intentions in such cases. Although in such cases it may often be highly speculative to attempt to determine what the investor and corporation would have had in mind at the time when the contract was performed beyond that which was specifically set out in the relevant investment contracts, it does not necessarily follow that a reasonable investor would not have made at least some assumptions concerning the future behaviour of the corporation, its directors, officers and other insiders at the time when the investment was made which stand outside the express terms of the stated contractual arrangements. Even where there is an active secondary market for the securities, and an individual security holder intended only to make a brief, transitory investment, it may reasonably be assumed that an investor would expect the directors and officers of a corporation:

- to cause the corporation to use the funds invested for the purpose stated;

- generally to comply with the law and with its articles, by-laws and any unanimous shareholder agreement;

- more specifically, to cause the corporation to comply with relevant securities legislation and with the legislation under which it is incorporated, both in terms of the disclosure of information and otherwise;

- to manage or supervise the management of the corporation, and in so doing,

- to act honestly, in good faith and with a view to the best interests of the corporation; and

---

[262] Authority for this proposition grows out of: *Stone v. Stonehurst Enterprises Ltd.*, [1987] N.B.J. No. 504, 80 N.B.R. (2d) 290 at 305 (Q.B.), *per* Landry J.; *Re H.R. Harmer Ltd.*, [1958] 3 All E.R. 689 at 698 (C.A.), *per* Jenkins L.J.; *Naneff v. Con-Crete Holdings Ltd.*, [1995] O.J. No. 1377, 23 B.L.R. (2d) 286 at 298 (C.A.), *per* Galligan J.A.

[263] *PMSM Investments Ltd. v. Bureau*, [1995] O.J. No. 2611, 24 B.L.R. (2d) 295 (Gen. Div.).

- to exercise the care, diligence and skill that a reasonably prudent person would exercise in comparable circumstances.[264]

§13.86 In *Themadel Foundation v. Third Canadian General Investment Trust Ltd.*[265] the court concluded that the contravention by a corporation of a commitment made in an information circular that it was required to distribute under the *Securities Act* could result in a breach of the reasonable expectations of the shareholders to whom that document was sent. It was held that shareholders are entitled to rely on written and public pronouncements made by the corporations in which they hold shares about what they will do, since it is an offence for such corporations to be other than truthful in public pronouncements.

(3) Oppression and the Family Business

§13.87 A distressingly large percentage of oppression-related cases involve claims relating to the operation of a family business.[266] Frequently in such cases, the relationship existing among the various family parties participating in the business is one of such a high degree of trust and confidence that fiduciary principles are applied across the board. In other cases, however, the parties will each be sophisticated people of substantial experience. It is highly questionable whether fiduciary principles should be applied in such cases.

§13.88 As we noted earlier in the chapter, the oppression remedy supplements other legal and equitable remedies. It is not an alternative to them. In a family business, it may sometimes be possible to couple the protection afforded under the shareholder oppression remedy with the protection offered under the *Family Law Act*[267] and the equitable doctrines of constructive and resulting trust,[268] where one spouse has made a significant contribution to a family business owned or controlled by the other spouse. In most cases, the spouse seeking relief will wish to obtain a cash settlement equivalent to a buyout in respect of his or her notional interest in the business concerned. However, the oppression remedy allows alternative forms of relief. For instance, in *Maloney v. Maloney*[269] it was found that the plaintiff and defendant had lived in a so-called common law relationship from 1966 to 1990. From 1983, they had built up a pet shop business, financed largely with loans taken out by the defendant but secured against the parties' family home. The plaintiff worked in the business on a largely under-remunerated basis, putting in longer hours than the defendant. All funds contributed to the business came from the parties' joint bank account.

---

[264] See, generally, *Palmer v. Carling O'Keefe Breweries of Canada Ltd.*, [1989] O.J. No. 32, 67 O.R. (2d) 161 at 170 (Div. Ct.).
[265] [1995] O.J. No. 888, 18 B.L.R. (2d) 209 at 214-17 (Gen. Div.), *per* Farley J., appeal allowed in part [1998] O.J. No. 647, 38 O.R. (3d) 749, 107 O.A.C. 188 (C.A.).
[266] For perhaps the ultimate case dealing with oppression in connection with a family business, see *Waxman v. Waxman*, [2002] O.J. No. 2528, 25 B.L.R. (3d) 1 (S.C.J.), aff'd [2004] O.J. No. 1765 (C.A.), leave to appeal to S.C.C. refused [2004] S.C.C.A. No. 291.
[267] R.S.O. 1990, c. F.3.
[268] See, for instance, *Re 512760 Ontario Inc.*, [1992] O.J. No. 1057, 91 D.L.R. (4th) 719 (Gen. Div.).
[269] [1993] O.J. No. 2724, 109 D.L.R. (4th) 161 (Gen. Div.).

Prior to their separation, the parties had always treated the business as belonging to them both. Bell J. held that in the circumstance of the case, the plaintiff's efforts in the establishment and maintenance of the business made the making of a monetary award insufficient. An order was made under section 241 of the CBCA allowing the plaintiff to continue as the manager of the business and fixing her salary at $30,000.[270]

§13.89 While some courts have seemed particularly willing to entertain oppression actions in the case of family-run businesses and similar closely held corporations,[271] it cannot be automatically assumed that an oppression remedy applies in the case of every family business. Section 248 protects the interests of a shareholder, creditor, director or officer of a corporation, but only as such. It does not apply to other interests that such a person may have in the corporation or to other claims that the complainant may have against the person who is alleged to be guilty of oppression.[272] Oppression of a person interested in a corporation must be distinguished from mistreatment of that person as a family member.

§13.90 Even where an act of oppression or similar misconduct is found, family business related cases frequently require the courts to take care in fashioning an appropriate remedy. For instance, the court has the power to order the sale of the corporation where oppression has been found. The sale will rectify the oppressive conduct and is directed to the protection of the interest of a shareholder, creditor, director or officer of the corporation as such.[273] Where a sale is ordered, it is common for the complainant and other interested persons both to be entitled to bid for the corporation, the corporation then being transferred to the highest bidder. The interests of the former owners (including the complainant) are then paid out. The advantage of a sale is that it leaves it to the parties (who usually are the persons most sure of its value) to effectively select the price at which the complainant (or, perhaps, the defendant) will be bought out. However, the sale process has little to commend it where the complainant does not possess the funds to participate in the sale process. In such a situation there may be no competitive bid for the property — though in principle, there is no reason why the sale might not be made to an outsider, if that person bid more than the insiders of the corporation. Moreover, a sale may also be rendered inappropriate because of the circumstances in which the oppression occurred or the manner in which the underlying business of the corporation came into being.

---

[270] For another case illustrating the range of remedies available in an oppression action, see *Khayraji v. Safaverdi*, [1996] O.J. No. 3427, 33 B.L.R. (2d) 108 (Gen. Div.).

[271] For instance, in *Eiserman v. Ara Farms Ltd.*, [1988] S.J. No. 344, [1988] 5 W.W.R. 97 at 111-12 (C.A.), *per* Sherstobitoff J.A.

[272] *Stone v. Stonehurst Enterprises Ltd.*, [1987] N.B.J. No. 504, 80 N.B.R. (2d) 290 at 305 (Q.B.), *per* Landry J.; *Re H.R. Harmer Ltd.*, [1958] 3 All E.R. 689 at 698 (C.A.), *per* Jenkins L.J.; *Naneff v. Con-Crete Holdings Ltd.*, [1995] O.J. No. 1377, 23 B.L.R. (2d) 286 at 298 (C.A.), *per* Galligan J.A.

[273] *Footitt v. Gleason*, [1995] O.J. No. 2662, 25 B.L.R. (2d) 190 at 195 (Gen. Div.), *per* Hayley J., aff'd [1998] O.J. No. 945 (C.A.).

§13.91 Accordingly, the sale of the corporation will often be an inappropriate remedy in family business cases. The classic case illustrating this point is the decision of the Ontario Court of Appeal in *Naneff v. Con-Crete Holdings Ltd.*[274] The facts in that case were as follows: as a result of a family disagreement, the oldest son of the founder of a corporate group became estranged from the rest of the family. The argument concerned a personal matter unrelated to the business. Following the break up of the family, the son was removed as an officer from all of the family companies and was ordered to stay off their business premises. The son had worked in the business since 1981, and he had been a shareholder in the business since 1977, when he was given an equity interest in the business under the terms of an estate freeze put into place by his father. The estate freeze left the father in control of the business, and the father remained actively involved in it both before, and throughout the course of, the dispute. In giving judgment, Galligan J.A. discussed the implications of these facts on the ultimate disposition of the appeal:

> ... [I]t is important to keep in mind that this is not a normal commercial operation where partners make contributions and share the equity according to their contributions or where persons invest in a business by the purchase of shares. This is a family business where the dynamics of the relationship between the principals are very different from those between the principals in a normal commercial business. As the courts below have correctly held, the fact that this is a family business cannot oust the provisions of s. 248 of the OBCA. Nevertheless, I am convinced that the fact that this is a family matter must be kept very much in mind when fashioning a remedy under s. 248(3), as it bears directly upon the reasonable expectations of the principals.[275]

Thus, the fact that the business was a family business in no way could be invoked to justify the family (and, in particular, the head of the family) behaving in a tyrannical way toward the complainant. Although the complainant was the child of the person in control of the business (his father), and although the complainant had received his interest in the business as a gift, the father and the other family members involved in the business were still obliged to respect his legal rights. However, the court was not empowered by section 248 to rectify all complaints that the son might have against the father; it was empowered to deal only with the complaints of the son in his capacity as a shareholder, director and officer of the business.[276] Moreover, the family relationship between the parties, the collapse of that relationship, the circumstances in which the son had acquired an interest in the business, the manner in which the business had been built up by his father, all qualified and limited the relief that the court could, in justice, provide, for these circumstances would have circumscribed the reasonable expectations that the son was entitled to hold as a director, officer and shareholder of the business:

> The first consideration is that Alex [the complainant] fully understood that until death or voluntary retirement his father retained ultimate control over the business

---

[274] [1995] O.J. No. 1377, 23 B.L.R. (2d) 286 (C.A.).
[275] *Ibid.*, at 296.
[276] *Ibid.*, at 297.

even to the extent of deciding what dividends would be paid and what would be done with any of those dividends. The second consideration is that this was a family business which had been built by his father. ...

... Alex knew that until his father died or retired he could under no circumstances have any right to have or even share absolute control of the business. Therefore, under no circumstances could Alex's reasonable expectations include the right to control the family business while his father was alive and active. ... while Alex expected that his father would give him an equal share in the control of the business upon his death or retirement, that expectation was based upon his belief that his father would continue to be bountiful to him in the future. ... He must also have known that it would be impossible for him, Mr. Naneff and Boris to work together in the business as a family if the family bonds ceased to exist.[277]

Accordingly, the court held that it was not appropriate for the entire corporation to be put up for sale, as that had the effect of requiring the father to buy his own business back. However, the father was required to buy out his son's shares in the business.

(vii) Oppression Not a Remedy of Last Resort

§13.92 The oppression remedy is not one of last resort; standing to seek relief has been recognized in cases where there was an adequate common law cause of action to protect the complainant, such as breach of contract.[278] However, the remedy is available where a dispute relates to conduct by the corporation and its officers. It is not available where the dispute is between two shareholders as such, and not the corporation — the dispute must relate to the conduct of the corporation itself.[279] Nor is relief available merely because of some dispute between two shareholders outside the corporate context — for instance, in the case of the breakdown of a marriage.[280]

(viii) Procedural Considerations

§13.93 Relief under the oppression remedy provisions may be instituted by notice of application rather than by statement of claim. Where on the hearing of an application for an oppression remedy it is unclear whether oppression or other grounds for relief exist on the facts, the court may direct a trial of that issue.[281] In lieu of the notice of application procedure, the complainant may commence proceedings by statement of claim if he or she so desires.[282] In contrast to relief in

---

[277] *Ibid.*, at 299.
[278] See, for instance, *Canadian Opera Co. v. 670800 Ontario Inc.*, [1989] O.J. No. 1307, 69 O.R. (2d) 532 (H.C.J.), aff'd [1990] O.J. No. 2270, 75 O.R. (2d) 720 (Div. Ct.).
[279] *Bernard v. Montgomery*, [1987] S.J. No. 295, 36 B.L.R. 257 at 261 (Q.B.), per Gerein J.
[280] *Callander v. Eveline Holdings Ltd.*, [1987] M.J. No. 156, 48 Man. R. (2d) 308 (Q.B.).
[281] *Bauscher-Grant Farms Inc. v. Lake Diefenbaker Potato Corp.*, [1988] S.J. No. 344, [1998] 8 W.W.R. 751 (Q.B.).
[282] *Chilian v. Augdome Corp.*, [1991] O.J. No. 414, 2 O.R. (3d) 696 (C.A.); *Muljardi v. O'Brien*, [1990] O.J. No. 1866, 75 O.R. (2d) 270 (Gen. Div.); *Sparling v. Royal Trust Co. Ltd.*, [1983] O.J. No. 265, 21 B.L.R. 97 (H.C.J.), rev'd [1984] O.J. No. 3129, 45 O.R. (2d) 484 (C.A.), aff'd [1986] S.C.J. No. 64, [1986] 2 S.C.R. 537; but *cf. Title Estate v. Harris*, [1990] O.J. No. 452, 72 O.R. (2d) 468 (H.C.J.). There are numerous procedural advantages to proceeding by way of ac-

the nature of a derivative action, it is not necessary to obtain leave of the court before instituting an application under the oppression remedy provisions.[283] However, a motion to contest a person's standing under the oppression remedy provisions may be made under Rule 21 of the *Rules of Civil Procedure*,[284] which governs the determination of issues before trial.[285] The determination made on such an application is one of law rather than one of fact, and, thus, even if on such an application it is held that a person has standing to seek relief as a complainant, it does not mean that the complainant will necessarily be entitled to the relief sought.[286] The complainant will be denied standing only where it is clear that he or she does not fall within the ambit of the provisions so that there is no reasonable cause of action.[287] Where the issues of fact are interwoven with legal issues, it is inappropriate to decide the question of standing on a preliminary motion, and the matter should be left to the trial judge.[288] In dealing with the application, all issues of fact made by the complainant (unless patently ridiculous or incapable of proof) are accepted as proven, and to have the action struck the applicant must show that it is plain, obvious and beyond doubt that the complainant could not succeed.[289] The mere fact that a claim is unique or novel does not militate against the complainant.[290]

§13.94 In cases where the parties (*i.e.*, the complaining shareholder and the controlling shareholder) have agreed to arbitrate disputes relating to the conduct of the corporation, the courts will respect that decision and will require the parties to resort to arbitration rather than to seek their remedy in court.[291] However, a shareholder may go to court to seek relief under the oppression remedy despite the existence of a mandatory arbitration clause in a shareholder agreement, if the oppression complained of is such that it destroys the very underpinning of the arbitration structure.[292] Where such an application to court is made, the applicant

---

tion (*i.e.*, statement of claim), including more detailed pleadings, greater and entrenched rights to discovery, and the availability of default and summary judgment procedures.

[283] Unless the complainant seeks standing under cl. (*c*) of the definition of "complainant" in s. 245 of the OBCA; or cl. (*d*) of the definition of "complainant" in s. 238 of the CBCA.
[284] R.R.O. 1990, Reg. 194.
[285] See, for instance, *Moriarity v. Slater*, [1989] O.J. No. 451, 42 B.L.R. 52 (H.C.J.).
[286] See, for instance, *Ginther v. Rainbow Management Ltd.*, unreported. July 12, 1989, Doc. No. CA010720 (B.C.C.A.).
[287] See, generally, *W.H. Dey Enterprises Ltd. v. Volvo Canada Ltd.*, [1985] O.J. No. 307, 49 C.P.C. 221 at 222 (H.C.J.), *per* Hughes J.
[288] *Wilkes v. Teichmann*, [1985] O.J. No. 77, 50 C.P.C. 151 at 153 (C.A.), *per* Blair J.A.
[289] *Re Welport Investments Ltd.*, [1985] O.J. No. 616, 31 B.L.R. 232 (H.C.J.).
[290] *Air India Flight 182 Disaster Claimants v. Air India*, [1987] O.J. No. 903, 62 O.R. (2d) 130 at 135 (H.C.J.), *per* R.E. Holland J.
[291] *Korogonas v. Andrew*, [1992] A.J. No. 252, 1 Alta. L.R. (3d) 316 at 323 (Q.B.), *per* Veit J.; *Arbitration Act*, S.O. 1991, c. 17, s. 7(1):

> If a party to an arbitration agreement commences a proceeding in respect of a matter to be submitted to arbitration under the agreement, the court in which the proceeding is commenced shall, on the motion of another party to the arbitration agreement, stay the proceeding.

[292] *Deluce Holdings Inc. v. Air Canada*, [1992] O.J. No. 2382, 8 B.L.R. (2d) 294 at 312-13 (Gen. Div. — C.L.), *per* R.A. Blair J.

for relief must establish a strong *prima facie* case on the merits[293] and must convince the court that arbitration would be oppressive or vexatious or an abuse of the process of the court.[294] Accordingly, the commencement of the running of the limitation period may be delayed, where the person responsible for the oppressive conduct has withheld information necessary to allow the potential claimant to discover that a wrong has been committed.

§13.95 In *Deluce Holdings Inc. v. Air Canada*[295] it was found that Air Canada ("A") and Deluce Holdings Inc. ("B") indirectly held 75 per cent and 25 per cent respectively of the shares in Air Ontario. The relationship between A and B was governed by a shareholder agreement under which A had the option to acquire B's shares upon the termination of the services of C, a principal of B, as the vice chair and chief executive officer of Air Ontario. The agreement further provided that all disputes under it were to be resolved by arbitration. In October, 1991, A used its control over the board of B to cause the termination of C's employment. B argued that this was done solely to enable A to acquire complete ownership of Air Ontario. B claimed that A's conduct was oppressive and initiated an action under the oppression remedy provisions set out in section 241 of the CBCA. It also moved for an order staying any arbitration. For its part, A moved under subsection 7(1) of the *Arbitrations Act*[296] for a stay of the oppression action. Blair J. rejected this argument and held that the dispute fell outside the scope of the arbitration provision, concluding that the real subject matter of the dispute, in such circumstances, was not a matter that the parties had agreed to submit to arbitration, but was instead one that struck at the very underpinning of the contractual mechanism itself.[297]

§13.96 Where there are shareholders in a corporation that is the subject of an oppression action, other than the complainant and the controlling shareholder(s), it may be necessary to order that the corporation be represented by separate counsel.[298] In some circumstances, the corporation may be a suitable person to maintain an action for oppression against one of its former directors or officers.[299]

---

[293] *Ibid.*, at 317.
[294] *Ibid.*, at 315.
[295] [1992] O.J. No. 2382, 12 O.R. (3d) 131 (Gen. Div.), *per* R.A. Blair J.
[296] S.O. 1991, c. 17. Note Blair J.'s comments about this Act: [1992] O.J. No. 2382, 12 O.R. (3d) 131 at 148.
[297] *Ibid.*, at 149-50.
[298] *Skrien v. Waterloo Junction Rail Tours*, [1997] O.J. No. 6289, 32 O.R. (3d) 777 at 783-84 (Gen. Div.), *per* Sills J., var'd [1998] O.J. No. 3752 (C.A.); *Alles v. Maurice*, [1992] O.J. No. 331, 9 C.P.C. (3d) 49 (Gen. Div.).
[299] *Gainers Inc. v. Pocklington*, [1992] A.J. No. 603, 7 B.L.R. (2d) 87 (Q.B.), but compare *Canada (Attorney General) v. Standard Trust Co.*, [1991] O.J. No. 1946, 4 B.L.R. (2d) 180 (Gen. Div.), where it was held that a trustee in bankruptcy of a corporation was not a proper person to bring an application for an oppression remedy against a subsidiary company.

(1) Limitation Issues

§13.97 The applicable limitation period for an oppression action is determined by reference to the facts on which the application is grounded and the nature of the relief sought.[300] So, for instance, a complaint based upon tortious conduct will be governed by the limitation period applicable to the tort in question. Similarly, complaints grounded in contractual rights will be subject to the limitation period applicable to contract claims.

(2) Onus of Proof and the Nature of Proof Required

§13.98 In *Robins v. National Trust Co.*,[301] Viscount Dunedin explained the meaning of the phrase onus of proof in the following terms:

> Onus is always on a person who asserts a proposition or fact which is not self-evident. To assert that a man who is alive was born requires no proof. The onus is not on the person making the assertion because it is self-evident that he had been born. But to assert that he was born on a certain date if the date is material, requires proof; the onus is on the person making the assertion. Now, in conducting any inquiry, the determining tribunal, be it judge or jury, will often find that the onus is sometimes on the side of one contending party, sometimes on the side of the other, or, as it is often expressed, that in certain circumstances the onus shifts. But onus as a determining factor of the whole case can only arise if the tribunal finds the evidence pro and con so evenly balanced that it can come to no sure conclusion. Then the onus will determine the matter. But if the tribunal, after hearing and weighing the evidence, comes to a determinate conclusion, the onus has nothing to do with it, and need not be further considered.

These basic principles apply with respect to oppression proceedings. The onus is on the complainant to show that the corporation or those in control of it have been engaging in conduct that is oppressive, unfairly prejudicial or that unfairly disregards the complainant's interest.[302] The onus is also on the complainant to establish the amount of damages that they have suffered (*e.g.*, by proving the undervalue of transactions).[303]

§13.99 The burden of proof concerning unfair prejudice or disregard of interest is less rigorous than the burden of proof where oppression is claimed, because what is at issue is the unfair result rather than a state of mind.[304] The remedy is available only where the complainant is oppressed (or otherwise prejudiced) by

---

[300] *Seidel v. Kerr*, [2003] A.J. No. 1163, 37 B.L.R. (3d) 31 (C.A.).
[301] [1927] A.C. 515, [1927] All E.R. Rep. 73 at para. 5 (P.C.).
[302] *Lindzon v. International Sterling Holdings Inc.*, [1989] B.C.J. No. 1773, 45 B.L.R. 57 (S.C.); *Bosman v. Doric Holdings Ltd.*, [1978] B.C.J. No. 23, 6 B.C.L.R. 189 (S.C.).
[303] See, generally, *Envirodrive Inc. v. 836442 Alberta Ltd.*, [2005] A.J. No. 747, 7 B.L.R. (4th) 61 at 97, *per* Slatter J., additional reasons [2005] A.J. No 1485 (Q.B.).
[304] *Such v. RW-LB Holdings Ltd.*, [1993] A.J. No. 1033, 11 B.L.R. (2d) 122 (Q.B.), *per* Mason J. relying upon *Mason v. Intercity Properties Ltd.*, [1987] O.J. No. 448, 38 D.L.R. (4th) 681 at 685 (C.A.), *per* Blair J.A., leave to appeal to S.C.C. refused 42 D.L.R. (4th) viii, although it is far from clear whether the words quoted are, in fact, sufficient to support the conclusion which Mason J. reached.

the conduct of the corporation or its controller or affiliates.[305] Where the complaint cannot be related back to the corporation or an affiliate, the case is not made out and relief will be refused.[306] Relief will not be ordered as a result of some trivial breach of contract or similar transgression,[307] such as the failure to comply strictly with a notice requirement, nor will it be granted where there is a legitimate dispute between the majority and the minority on the manner in which the corporation should proceed. Management (and the majority shareholders who control them) are entitled to make honest decisions about what is in the corporation's best interests,[308] even if the effect of their decision may be to change the existing balance of power within the corporation.[309] The oppression remedy procedures may not be invoked to allow a disgruntled shareholder to back out of a deal that he or she had earlier approved.[310]

§13.100 It is not sufficient for a complainant to establish that he or she has been prejudiced by some particular thing that was done by the corporation or those in control of it. It is necessary to show *unfair* prejudice. Courts are unlikely to impugn a transaction where the corporation received genuine value.[311] On the other hand, a defendant in an oppression case does not defeat a claim merely by showing that what was done was consistent with the defendant's legal rights. In *Arthur v. Signum Communications Ltd.*,[312] Austin J., summarized a number of factors that a court might consider in deciding whether particular conduct was oppressive. He said:

> Amongst the indicia of conduct which runs afoul of s. 247 are the following:
>
> (i) lack of a valid corporate purpose for the transaction;
>
> (ii) failure on the aprt of the corporation and its controlling shareholders to take reasonable steps to simulate an arm's length transaction;
>
> (iii) lack of good faith on the part of the directors of the corporation;
>
> (iv) discrimination between shareholders with the effect of benefiting the majority shareholder to the exclusion or to the detriment of the minority shareholder;
>
> (v) lack of adequate and appropriate disclosure of material information to the minority shareholders; and
>
> (vi) a plan or design to eliminate the minority shareholder.

---

[305] *Canadian Commercial Bank v. Prudential Steel Ltd.*, [1986] A.J. No. 1142, 49 Alta. L.R. (2d) 58 (Q.B.); *Ruffo v. I.P.C.B.C. Contractors Canada Inc.*, [1983] B.C.J. No. 2536, 33 B.C.L.R. (2d) 74 (S.C.), aff'd [1990] B.C.J. No. 795, 44 B.C.L.R. 293 (C.A.).

[306] See, generally, *Jarman v. Brown*, [1979] B.C.J. No. 1163, 13 B.C.L.R. 152, [1979] 5 W.W.R. 673 (S.C.).

[307] *Dancey v. 229281 Alberta Ltd.*, [1988] A.J. No. 845, 40 B.L.R. 180 at 187 (Q.B.), *per* Roslak J.

[308] *Stone v. Stonehurst Enterprises Ltd.*, [1987] N.B.J. No. 504, 80 N.B.R. (2d) 290, 202 A.P.R. 290 at 309 (Q.B.), *per* Landry J.

[309] *Dicore Resources Ltd. v. Goldstream Resources Ltd.*, [1986] B.C.J. No. 3201, 2 B.C.L.R. (2d) 244 at 246 (S.C.), *per* Spence J.

[310] *Victorov v. Davison*, [1988] O.J. No. 190, 20 C.P.R. (3d) 481 at 515 (H.C.J.), *per* McKeown J.

[311] *Stabile v. Milani Estate*, [2004] O.J. No. 2804, 46 B.L.R. (3d) 294 at 306 (C.A.), *per* Blair J.A., leave to appeal to S.C.C. refused [2004] S.C.C.A. No. 472.

[312] [1991] O.J. No. 86 (Gen. Div.) at 29.

(3) Bars to Action

§13.101 There are a number of cases that deal with bars to oppression relief.[313] For instance, it has been held that the oppression and derivative action remedies will not be permitted to be used by minority shareholders to extort benefits from the majority shareholders or other controlling group in the corporation.[314] Relief is available to a claimant under section 248 of the OBCA or 241 of the CBCA if, and only if, the applicant can establish that he or she has suffered detriment in his or her capacity as a complainant.[315] In the ordinary case, where the corporation abandons the course of action on which the complainant's application is based, no order will be made, for in such a case the abandonment constitutes the remedy.[316]

§13.102 More generally, the oppression remedy is not intended to require (nor to empower) the courts to review every decision made within a corporation. It does not offer a general right of appeal from the internal decision-making process of the corporation.[317] The classic statement to this effect was made by Buckley J. in *Re Five Minute Car Wash Service Ltd.*:

> The mere fact that a member of a company has lost confidence in the manner in which the company's affairs are conducted does not lead to the conclusion that he is oppressed; nor can resentment at being out-voted; nor mere dissatisfaction with or disapproval of the conduct of the company's affairs, whether on grounds relating to policy or to efficiency, however well-founded. Those who are alleged to have acted oppressively must be shown to have acted at least unfairly towards those who claim to have been oppressed.[318]

Although made in regard to the more narrowly drafted 1948 English legislation, this statement, undoubtedly, correctly states a general principle that applies with equal force to the current remedy provided for in the OBCA and the CBCA.

§13.103 The court may refuse a remedy where there has been prolonged delay in bringing an application in regard to oppressive conduct.[319] However, this principle should not be too far extended. Ordinarily, in the case of equitable relief, delay will bar action only where the potential claimant was aware of the facts giving rise to the cause of action and failed to proceed. Because potential claimants will often possess only limited knowledge about what is transpiring in relation to the corporation, its business or affairs, as a practical matter it

---

[313] As to the application of the *Limitation of Actions Act*, R.S.M. 1987, c. L150, to oppression proceedings, see *Jaska v. Jaska*, [1996] M.J. No. 579, 30 B.L.R. (2d) 104 (C.A.). As for whether a complainant may reject a reasonable compromise and insist upon taking the dispute to court, see *Re A Company (No. 00836 of 1995)*, [1996] 2 B.C.L.C. 192 (Ch. D.).

[314] *Mason v. Intercity Properties Ltd.*, [1987] O.J. No. 448, 59 O.R. (2d) 631 (C.A.), leave to appeal to S.C.C. refused 62 O.R. (2d) ix.

[315] *Diligenti v. RWMD Operations Kelowna Ltd.*, [1976] B.C.J. No. 38, 1 B.C.L.R. 36 (S.C.).

[316] *V.F. Erickson Consultants Ltd. v. Ventures West Minerals Ltd.*, [1990] B.C.J. No. 1111 (C.A.).

[317] *Zephyr Holdings Pty Ltd. v. Jack Chia (Australia) Ltd.* (1989), 7 A.C.L.C. 239, *per* Brooking J.; see also *Re H.W. Thomas Ltd.*, [1984] 1 N.Z.L.R. 686, 2 A.C.L.C. 610.

[318] [1966] 1 All E.R. 242 at 246-47, *per* Buckley J.

[319] *Jaska v. Jaska*, [1996] M.J. No. 579, 141 D.L.R. (4th) 385 (C.A.).

may be difficult for them to determine whether they have a realistic chance of a claim, even though they may be dissatisfied in some general way with the manner in which the business or affairs of the corporation are being conducted. Moreover, the voluntary withdrawal of a shareholder from active participation in a corporation does not prevent that shareholder from seeking relief under the oppression remedy, nor does the fact that the shareholders allowed the directors to run the business for a prolonged period of time without demanding that annual meetings be held or financial statements provided. The obligation is upon the directors of a corporation to call annual meetings of shareholders, to carry out their other corporate governance duties and to account for their administration of the corporation, not upon the shareholders to superintend the directors.[320]

(ix) Forms of Relief

(1) The Statutory Regime

§13.104 Sections 248 of the OBCA and 241 of the CBCA provide a statutory means whereby corporate shareholders, directors and other stakeholders may gain redress for corporate conduct which has an oppressive, unfair or unduly prejudicial effect. The sections serve as a judicial brake against abuse of corporate power, particularly, but not exclusively, by those in control of the corporation and permit the court to override the decisions of those who have effective control over the corporation, its business and affairs. If the conduct of the corporation is oppressive, unfairly prejudicial to, or unfairly disregards the interests of the complainant, the court may impose a fit order. The nature and scope of that order is circumscribed by the requirements that the order "rectify the matter complained of". It must address only the aggrieved parties' interests as corporate stakeholders.[321] Relief is not limited to the making of an order against the corporation itself. By providing remedies against individuals, including directors and officers, the OBCA and the CBCA recognize that the rectification of harm done to corporate stakeholders by corporate abuse may necessitate an order against individuals through whom the company acts.[322] A director or officer may be personally liable for a monetary order under sections 248 or 241 if that director or officer is implicated in the wrongful conduct and if in all the circumstances rectification of the harm done by that conduct is appropriately made by an order requiring the director or officer to compensate personally the complainant.

§13.105 Where a corporation unfairly prejudices or disregards the interests of a complainant, the court has a broad discretion under the OBCA and the CBCA to exercise an equitable jurisdiction and determine what is fair.[323] As indicated above, oppressive or prejudicial conduct may take the form of callous indifference

---

[320] See, generally, *Bernhardt v. Main Outboard Centre Ltd.*, [1994] M.J. No. 521, 17 B.L.R. (2d) 219 (Q.B.).
[321] *Naneff v. Con-Crete Holdings Ltd.*, [1995] O.J. No. 1377, 23 O.R. (3d) 481 at 489-90 (C.A.).
[322] *Budd v. Gentra Inc.*, [1998] O.J. No. 3109, 43 B.L.R. (2d) 27 (C.A.).
[323] *Westfair Foods Ltd. v. Watt*, [1990] A.J. No. 315, 48 B.L.R. 43, aff'd [1991] A.J. No. 321, 79 Alta. L.R. (2d) 363, leave to appeal to S.C.C. refused 82 Alta. L.R. (2d) lxv.

as well as an actual desire to injure. A corporation cannot unfairly disregard the interests of the persons who are interested in it.[324] Given the wide range of cases in which relief may be sought, it is self-evident that there is a need for flexibility in the design of the appropriate remedy. The legislation effectively gives the court a broad power to tailor relief to the needs of a particular case.[325] In addition to the specifically enumerated types of relief contemplated in subsection 248(3), the court is given a general power to make any order that it "thinks fit". In *Naneff v. Con-Crete Holdings Ltd.* it was noted that such a broad power leaves little room for an appellate court to second-guess the decision made at first instance.[326] Nevertheless, there are a number of clearly implicit limitations upon the scope of the court's discretion. The oppression provisions of the OBCA and the CBCA are intended to be remedial, not punitive.[327] The job entrusted to the court is to even up the balance within the corporation, not to tip the balance in favour of the complainant and against the party perceived to be in the wrong.[328]

§13.106 Much as there is a great deal of case law indicating when relief will be available, there is extensive case law discussing the nature of the remedies that may be provided. Courts have provided relief along the following lines:

- setting aside security granted to a party in control of the corporation;[329]

- the issue of an order to prevent the corporation from taking up securities tendered in an issuer bid;[330]

- requiring payment of dividends;[331]

- the appointment of a receiver;[332]

- the division of corporate property;[333]

---

[324] *Mazzotta v. Twin Gold Mines Ltd.*, [1987] O.J. No. 837, 37 B.L.R. 218 (H.C.).
[325] There is Australian case law indicating that the share registry of a corporation may be ordered rectified to entitle a particular claimant to seek relief: *Re R.M. Dalley & Co. Pty Ltd.* (1968), 1 A.C.L.R. 489 (S.C. Vic.), *per* Lush J., rev'd on other grounds 43 A.L.J.R. 19 (H.C.).
[326] [1995] O.J. No. 1377, 23 B.L.R. (2d) 286 at 295 (C.A.), *per* Galligan J.A.; *cf.*, however, *Iverson v. Westfair Foods Ltd.*, [1998] A.J. No. 1145, 166 D.L.R. (4th) 448 (C.A.), leave to appeal to S.C.C. refused [1998] S.C.C.A. No. 634.
[327] *Ibid.*, [1995] O.J. No. 1377, 23 B.L.R. (2d) 286 at 301 (C.A.).
[328] *820099 Ontario Inc. v. Harold E. Ballard Ltd.*, [1991] O.J. No. 266, 3 B.L.R. (2d) 113 at 123 (Gen. Div.), aff'd [1991] O.J. No. 1082, 3 B.L.R. (2d) 113 at 197 (Div. Ct.), *per* Farley J.
[329] *Stabile v. Milani Estate*, [2002] O.J. No. 4788, 30 B.L.R. (3d) 69 (S.C.J.), rev'd on other grounds [2004] O.J. No. 2804 (C.A.), leave to appeal to S.C.C. refused [2004] S.C.C.A. No. 472.
[330] *Highfields Capital ILP v. Telesystems International Wireless Inc.*, [2002] O.J. No. 3700, 29 B.L.R. (3d) 249 (S.C.J.).
[331] *827365 Alberta Ltd. v. Alco Gas & Oil Production Equipment Ltd.*, [2001] A.J. No. 342, 14 B.L.R. (3d) 223 at 244 (Q.B.), *per* Murray J.
[332] *Goft v. 1206448 Ontario Ltd.*, [2000] O.J. No. 126, 11 B.L.R. (3d) 131 (S.C.J. — C.L.).
[333] *Etna Foods of Windsor Ltd. v. Caradonna*, [2000] O.J. No. 1732, 6 B.L.R. (3d) 127 (S.C.J.).

- ordering the corporation to pay a complainant a salary, on the condition that the corporation receive services for that salary;[334]
- the issue of an order for the provision of information;[335]
- the issue of order regarding the director election process;[336]
- awarding punitive damages;[337]
- appointing an arm's length receiver-manager in place of a party who was not at arm's length;[338] and
- ordering the repayment of an amount transferred.[339]

From a practice of law perspective, the difficulty with the above case law is in trying to identify unifying rules that may be used to provide guidance to a client.

§13.107 In *Seidel v. Kerr*,[340] Waite J. concluded that the oppression remedy is statutory rather than legal or equitable in nature. Nevertheless, the remedy possesses many features that make it close to an equitable remedy. The grant of the remedy involves the exercise of judicial discretion in much the same way as the grant of equitable relief. Accordingly, cases involving the exercise of equitable discretion should be of assistance in guiding the courts as to when to grant (and withhold) relief. In addition, as in the case of equitable relief, the statutory jurisdiction with respect to oppression allows the court to tailor the remedy to the facts of the case. Again, equitable cases are of guidance as to the extent of jurisdiction, such an authority confers upon the court.

§13.108 The court's exercise of its discretion in the selection of the appropriate remedy must take into account the reasonable expectations of the complainant on the basis of the original arrangements and understandings between the parties.[341] In addition, in tailoring the remedy to the requirements of a particular case, a clear goal for the court is to resolve the problem finally, to as great an extent as possible, rather than to rely upon a remedy that may lead to further disputes in the future. In *Re Enterprise Gold Mines N.L.*[342] Murray J. articulated a minimalist approach towards judicial intervention in the internal affairs of the corporation, stating that any order made by the court should be directed clearly

---

[334] *Pasnak v. Chura*, [1999] B.C.J. No. 2851, 2 B.L.R. (3d) 107 (B.C.S.C.).
[335] *Thomas v. Thomas Health Care Corp.*, [2005] O.J. No. 975, 3 B.L.R. (4th) 104 (S.C.J.), but *cf. Stoody v. Kennedy*, [2005] O.J. No. 1049, 2 B.L.R. (4th) 262 at 268-69 (C.A.), per Gillese J.A., leave to appeal to S.C.C. refused [2005] S.C.C.A. No. 267.
[336] *Holden v. Infolink Technologies Ltd.*, [2004] O.J. No. 4245, 48 B.L.R. (3d) 169 (S.C.J. — C.L.).
[337] *Chiu v. Universal Water Technology Inc.*, [2004] O.J. No. 2209, 45 B.L.R. (3d) 313 (S.C.J.) — in the case of conduct that was blatant, deliberate, malicious and calculated.
[338] *781952 Alberta Ltd. v. 781944 Alberta Ltd.*, [2003] A.J. No. 1485, 40 B.L.R. (3d) 278 (Q.B.) — this was not strictly an oppression case, but similar principles would seem to apply.
[339] *Piller Sausages & Delicatessens Ltd. v. Cobb International Corp.*, [2003] O.J. No. 2647, 35 B.L.R. (3d) 193 (S.C.J.).
[340] [2001] A.J. No. 1304, 20 B.L.R. (3d) 66 (Q.B.), aff'd [2003] A.J. No. 1163 (C.A.).
[341] *Footitt v. Gleason*, [1995] O.J. No. 2662, 25 B.L.R. (2d) 190 at 195 (Gen. Div.), per Hayley J., aff'd [1998] O.J. No. 945 (C.A.).
[342] (1991), 9 A.C.L.C. 168.

to provide a remedy of appropriate character and that the court should approach the matter conservatively, favouring the least meddlesome approach in the affairs of the company that will result in justice to the parties. Similarly, it has been held that the evidence required to support the grant of one remedy need not be sufficient to support the grant of other more intrusive remedies.[343]

§13.109 The oppression and derivative action remedies are not mutually exclusive; both may be pursued for the same wrong. Depending upon the facts of the case, it may be a saving of both time and cost to allow the same complainant to pursue both remedies. Both types of action may be desirable because neither type of action necessarily offers the full range of remedies and relief necessary to correct the damage done to the corporation and the complainant by the alleged wrongful conduct.[344]

(2) Interim Relief

§13.110 The courts may award both interim and final relief.[345] In *Walker v. Walker*[346] (in the context of an application for interim relief) the court observed that:

> The remedies in s. 234 of the [Saskatchewan Business Corporations] Act are exceedingly wide in scope; they are statutory remedies but lie in the discretion of the court.

In *M. v. H.* the court considered the availability of interim relief in detail, and commented upon the broad scope of the remedies that may be awarded in an oppression action, even as interim relief:

> The court is empowered to grant interim relief pursuant to any available remedies. To succeed at the interim stage, the plaintiff must establish a strong *prima facie* case that the corporation or its affairs have been conducted in a manner that is oppressive or unfairly prejudicial to or that unfairly disregards the interests of the applicant as shareholder, creditor, director or officer. ... This threshold test requires some examination of the nature and strength of the plaintiff's case.[347]

In *Watkin v. Open Window Bakery Ltd.*[348] Lederman J. concluded that where it was clear that the plaintiff in an oppression action was entitled to at least some amount, an interim remedy should be provided to the plaintiff:

> The purpose of the broad remedial powers under s. 248(3) of the *OBCA* is to provide a flexible approach to remedies, adaptive to the particular circumstances at hand. A peculiar feature of oppression remedy litigation is that the corporation is usually well-heeled and quite capable of financing costly and lengthy proceedings, whereas the individual shareholder will usually feel the financial pain as proceedings

---

[343] *Re A Company (No. 00314 of 1989)*, [1990] B.C.C. 221 at 227, *per* Mummery J.
[344] *Acapulco Holdings Ltd. v. Jegen*, [1997] A.J. No. 174, 47 Alta. L.R. (3d) 234 (C.A.).
[345] See, generally, *Wark v. Kozicki*, [1999] S.J. No. 794, 10 B.L.R. (3d) 237 (Q.B.).
[346] [1996] S.J. No. 850, 28 B.L.R. (2d) 312 at 315 (Q.B.), *per* Zarzeczny J.
[347] [1993] O.J. No. 2492, 15 O.R. (3d) 721 at 727 (Gen. Div.), *per* Epstein J.
[348] [1996] O.J. No. 894, 26 B.L.R. (2d) 301 at 306 (Gen. Div. — C.L.), appeal quashed [1996] O.J. No. 1469, 28 O.R. (3d) 441 (Div. Ct.).

drag out. If there is entitlement to a value that even the respondent agrees upon, why should there be a prolonged delay in the shareholder receiving that value? Counsel for Open Window put it frankly when he said that the reluctance to make any interim payment arises from the defendant's fear that the payment of such funds would only be used as a war chest by the applicant to continue the litigation. That may be but that suggests that the refusal to pay such funds is merely a method to financially starve the applicant into submission. The point is that there is entitlement to at least a certain minimum amount for which there is no legitimacy in the delay of payment.

§13.111 The most frequently sought interim remedy in an oppression proceeding is an interlocutory injunction to restrain the commission of the alleged oppressive acts, pending the outcome of the proceeding.[349] In general, the same criteria are applied in such proceedings as with respect to a general civil action. The applicable requirements were set down by the Supreme Court of Canada in *RJR-MacDonald v. Canada (Attorney General)*:

> First, a preliminary assessment must be made of the merits of the case to ensure that there is a serious question to be tried. Secondly, it must be determined whether the applicant would suffer irreparable harm if the application were refused. Finally, an assessment must be made as to which of the parties would suffer greater harm from the granting or refusal of the remedy pending a decision on the merits.[350]

§13.112 In the usual civil action, the threshold for the test of a "serious issue" is a low one. If such an approach is adopted, an interlocutory injunction may be issued in an oppression action, despite the oft proclaimed judicial position to the effect that courts should be reluctant to interfere in its internal dealings, particularly with respect to the exercise of business judgment by the board of directors of the corporation,[351] or to upset the expressed wishes of the majority of shareholders. In certain cases, the practical effect of an interlocutory judgment is to effectively grant the claimant a remedy almost as effective as a final judgment. In others, it is to deny the defendants the opportunity to exercise their evident legal rights. At least in some cases, the courts have insisted that a strong case be established, before they have been prepared to issue an interlocutory injunction.[352] In other cases, they have cut back the scope of the requested injunction, limiting it to the extent clearly necessary to protect the claimant's rights pending resolution of the litigation.[353]

§13.113 By virtue of sections 247 of the OBCA and 240 of the CBCA the courts have the jurisdiction to award interim costs in oppression proceedings, but, as yet, no consistent approach has evolved on the conditions that must be satisfied

---

[349] See, for instance, *Nord Resources Corp. v. Nord Pacific Ltd.*, [2003] N.B.J. No. 207, 37 B.L.R. (3d) 115 at 122-23 (Q.B.), per McLellan J.; cf. *O'Hara v. Arkipelago Architecture Inc.*, [2004] O.J. No. 4486, 134 A.C.W.S. (3d) 817 (S.C.J.).

[350] [1994] S.C.J. No. 17, [1994] 1 S.C.R. 311 at 334.

[351] See, for instance, *Corporacion Americana de Equipamientos Urbanos S.L. v. Olifas Marketing Group Inc.*, [2003] O.J. No. 3368, 66 O.R. (3d) 352 (S.C.J.).

[352] See, for instance, *Gazit (1997) Inc. v. Centrefund Realty Corp.*, [2000] O.J. No. 3070, 100 A.C.W.S. (3d) 485 (S.C.J.).

[353] See, e.g., *Galea v. Khosravi*, [2000] O.J. No. 2599, 98 A.C.W.S. (3d) 415 (S.C.J.).

before any order of such costs will be made. It is a general principle of corporate law that a company's money should not be expended on disputes among its shareholders.[354] In general, this principle applies to oppression proceedings, but there may be cases in which on the exceptional facts it should be suspended.[355] One relevant consideration is whether the corporation itself stands to benefit from the proceeding, which might well be the case where the oppression proceeding is inextricably intertwined with a derivative proceeding.[356]

§13.114 It is clear that awards of interim costs are difficult to obtain, and the strong tendency in the case law is that interim costs should not be awarded except in a very unusual case,[357] where there are "exceptional circumstances".[358] However, the circumstances that must be established remain a matter of some debate. The decision of Rosenberg J. in *Wilson v. Conley*[359] may be cited for the proposition that interim costs should be ordered in an oppression proceeding only if three conditions were satisfied:

(1) the applicant is in financial difficulty;

(2) that financial difficulty arose out of the alleged oppression; and

(3) the applicant has made out a *prima facie* case.

In contrast, in *Alles v. Maurice*,[360] Blair J. disagreed with the second of these criteria, and, as for the third, felt that it was necessary for the plaintiff only to show "a case of merit to warrant its pursuit". He continued:

> ... there is nothing in the language of the section, or in the purpose of the statute that would call for an interim cost order of this nature to be placed on the same kind of "extraordinary" pedestal as injunctions.

In *Strilec v. Alpha Pipe Fittings Ltd.*[361] Feldman J. noted that an award of interim costs provides the plaintiff with an extraordinary advantage. In denying such costs in the case before him, he appears to have taken the view that the award of interim costs should be made sparingly.

---

[354] *Re Crossmore Electrical and Civil Engineering Ltd.* (1989), 5 B.C.C. 37, *per* Hoffmann J.

[355] *Jones v. Jones and others; Re Incasep Ltd.*, [2002] EWCA Civ 961 at para. 53, *per* Arden L.J.

[356] As to the distinction between recoverable costs and costs personal to the complainant, see *Weber's Hardware (Huntsville) Ltd. v. Home Hardware Ltd.*, [2006] O.J. No. 4031, 22 B.L.R. (4th) 160 (S.C.J.).

[357] *Discovery Enterprises Inc. v. Ebco Industries Ltd.*, [1999] B.C.J. No. 2849, 50 B.L.R. (2d) 207 (C.A.).

[358] Compare *Alles v. Maurice*, [1992] O.J. No. 297, 5 B.L.R. (2d) 146 (Gen. Div.); *Wilson v. Conley*, [1990] O.J. No. 2283, 1 B.L.R. (2d) 220 (Gen. Div.); *Watkin v. Open Window Bakery Ltd.*, [1996] O.J. No. 884, 26 B.L.R. (2d) 301 (Gen. Div. — C.L.), appeal quashed [1996] O.J. No. 1469, 28 O.R. (3d) 441 (Div. Ct.); *Reay v. Landcorp Ontario Ltd.*, [1993] O.J. No. 883 (Gen. Div.); *Re Hillcrest Housing Ltd.*, [1993] P.E.I.J. No. 80, 20 C.P.C. (3d) 227 (S.C.); *Highfields Capital ILP v. Telesystems International Wireless Inc.*, [2002] O.J. No. 3700, 29 B.L.R. (3d) 249 (S.C.J. — C.L.).

[359] [1990] O.J. No. 2283, 1 B.L.R. (2d) 220 at 222 (Gen. Div.), *per* Rosenberg J.

[360] [1992] O.J. No. 297, 5 B.L.R. (2d) 146 (Gen. Div.).

[361] [1995] O.J. No. 1123, 19 B.L.R. (2d) 316 (Gen. Div.).

§13.115 A court should exercise care when considering the availability of interim relief. An oppression action should not be allowed to become a cause of oppression itself. Consideration should always be given to the impact of any interim injunction or other interim relief on corporation operations, and the corporation's long-term prospects. Where the ultimate remedy that is likely to be given is a monetary one, injunctive relief may well not be merited in the circumstances (although interim relief may be justified where it is aimed at ensuring that sufficient funds will remain in the corporation to satisfy any damage award). The majority should not be denied rights on the basis of a tenuous case. Creditors should not see the strength of the corporation dissipated in order to fund litigation among shareholders whose claims against the corporation are subordinate to those of the creditors concerned.

(3) Final Relief

(a) GENERAL PRINCIPLES GOVERNING RELIEF

§13.116 Where a court concludes that a complainant is the victim of oppression, unfair prejudice or unfair disregard, subsection 248(3) of the OBCA empowers the court to make such order as it considers fit. Perhaps in an effort to provide the judiciary with some notion on the type of orders that may be considered in particular circumstances, subsection 248(3) then goes on to list 14 different types of order that are included within the general order-making power that is conferred upon the court. A similar list is set out in subsection 241(3) of the CBCA, but that statutory list is merely illustrative rather than exhaustive.[362] The statutory list is set out in no particular order and there is little direction given on when each remedy should be employed. The courts have recognized, however, that some of the remedies are more intrusive than others, and they have informally adopted the approach of granting the remedy that is least intrusive but which still stands a reasonable prospect of success.[363]

§13.117 The selection of the appropriate remedy is very much governed by the unique facts of each individual case. Nevertheless, there are some cases that do provide an indication of the considerations that the court should take into account in selecting among the various options open. In *Edwards v. Edwards Dockrill Horwich Inc.*,[364] it was found that three individuals had incorporated an accounting firm. Within 18 months of that incorporation, the plaintiff had been fired and removed as director. He then continued in practice in his own firm and the two individual defendants entered into a new partnership to carry on their accountancy practice. The plaintiff alleged breach of fiduciary duties, oppressive conduct and the tort of intentional interference with economic relations. The

---

[362] *Cairney v. Golden Key Holdings Ltd.*, [1988] B.C.J. No. 184, 40 B.L.R. 289 (S.C.).
[363] See, generally, for instance, *Jackman v. Jackets Enterprises Ltd.*, [1977] B.C.J. No. 52, 2 B.L.R. 335 at 339 (S.C.), per Fulton J.; see also *Algonquin Mercantile Corp. v. Enfield Corp.*, [1990] O.J. No. 1289, 74 O.R. (2d) 457 (H.C.J.).
[364] [2005] N.S.J. No. 451, additional reasons [2006] N.S.J. No. 230 (S.C.).

plaintiff sought an order requiring the control group to purchase the shares. MacAdam J. rejected such an approach, commenting:

> ... I am satisfied the conduct of all parties in these circumstances is not such to warrant one party being ordered to acquire the shares of the other, at any price. All parties conducted themselves in a manner that was designed solely to benefit themselves, without regard to the economic impact on the others. As such they are not entitled to claim the kind of equitable relief that would be required in ordering the purchase of the shares of the one party because of the oppressive or unfair conduct of the other.[365]

§13.118 The most basic of the remedies specifically provided for in section 248 of the OBCA is the injunctive type relief contemplated under clause (3)(*a*), which empowers the court to make an order restraining the conduct giving rise to the complaint.[366] Both interim and permanent injunctions of this nature may be granted.[367] Although the clause does not expressly so state, restraint in this context would seem to include not only the imposition of conditions and procedural safeguards regulating the manner in which that conduct is carried on but also an outright prohibition on its continuation.

§13.119 Several of the clauses in subsection 248(3) contemplate the court taking over varying degrees of control over the ongoing operations of the corporation, its business and affairs. The most basic of these provisions is found in clause (3)(*i*), which empowers the court to make an order requiring a corporation to produce to the court, or to an interested person, financial statements in the form required by section 154 or an accounting in such other form as the court might require.[368] More drastic relief is contemplated in clause (3)(*c*), which empowers the court to make an order to regulate the corporation's affairs by amending the articles or by-laws or creating or amending a unanimous shareholder agreement. Where the court makes an order directing the amendment of the articles or by-laws of a corporation:

- the directors must forthwith file articles of reorganization with the Director, in order to give effect to the amendment; and

- until the court otherwise orders, the corporation is enjoined from making any further amendment to its articles or by-laws without the consent of the court — this last restriction presumably being imposed to prevent the corporation from undoing or circumventing the amendment imposed upon it by the court.[369]

---

[365] *Ibid.*, at para. 167.
[366] CBCA, s. 241(3)(*a*).
[367] *Alexander v. Westeel-Rosco Ltd.*, [1978] O.J. No. 3643, 22 O.R. (2d) 211 (H.C.J.); *Ruskin v. Canada All-News Radio Ltd.*, [1979] O.J. No. 266, 7 B.L.R. 142 (H.C.J.).
[368] See, generally, *Meltzer v. Western Paper Box Co.*, [1977] M.J. No. 213, [1978] 1 W.W.R. 451 (Q.B.); *Burnett v. Tsang*, [1985] A.J. No. 604, 37 Alta. L.R. (2d) 154 (Q.B.); CBCA, s. 241(3)(*i*).
[369] OBCA, s. 248(4); CBCA, s. 241(4).

Significantly, subsection 248(5) of the OBCA[370] provides that a shareholder is not entitled to dissent under section 185 if an amendment to the articles is effected under section 248. This prohibition applies not only to a shareholder-complainant who is seeking relief under the section but also to all other shareholders as well. And this begs the question: how is the court to make sure in a section 248 proceeding that the interests of shareholders other than the complainant are not being unfairly prejudiced. The question is of particular concern where there are persons whose interests in the corporation are unrepresented.

§13.120 Although section 248(3)(c) of the OBCA authorizes the court to "create" a unanimous shareholder agreement, it is not at all clear how the court could impose an "agreement" upon the shareholders without their consent. Similarly, the amendment of an existing agreement — other than the striking out of a provision or prohibiting its application — would also be a power difficult to employ in practice. One's inclination is to conclude that the wording was included so a court would not consider its powers limited; but the very notion of imposing an "agreement" upon someone against his or her wishes seems about as oppressive as nearly any form of shareholder or corporate conduct one can imagine.[371]

§13.121 Section 248(3) also recognizes the possibility that simply making an order prohibiting or restraining the doing of a particular thing, or otherwise regulating the conduct of the affairs of the corporation, may not be sufficient. Thus clause (3)(b) allows the court to appoint a receiver or receiver and manager — a somewhat drastic step which must surely require the court to conclude either that the corporation is out of control[372] or that the present management of the corporation is not suitable at all or will not give effect to any order that the court might give under clauses (a) or (c), or that even if such an order were carried out, it would not be sufficient to rectify the problem concerned.[373] In the case of a CBCA corporation, it is not permissible to bring different applications in different provinces for the appointment of receivers in each.[374] As an alternative to a receivership, the court is also given the power, under clause 248(3)(e) of the OBCA, to appoint new directors "in place of or in addition to all or any of the directors then in office".[375]

§13.122 If such direct intervention also proves, or seems likely to be, insufficient, the court may also consider even more drastic intervention. Clause (3)(m)

---

[370] CBCA, s. 241(5).
[371] See, however, *Daniels v. Fielder*, [1988] O.J. No. 1592, 65 O.R. (2d) 629 (H.C.); *Wiggins v. Savics*, unreported, September 28, 1989, Eberle J. (1989), 19 A.C.W.S. (3d) 14 (Ont. H.C.J.); cf. *Lecce v. Lecce*, [1990] O.J. No. 3032, 72 O.R. (2d) 540 (H.C.J.).
[372] *Inversiones Montforte S.A. v. Javelin International Ltd.* (1982), 17 B.L.R. 230 (Que. S.C.); CBCA, s. 241(3)(b).
[373] *Crédit foncier franco-canadien v. C.S.W. Enterprises Ltd.*, [1986] S.J. No. 782, 54 Sask. R. 97 (Q.B.).
[374] *Wismer v. Javelin International Ltd.*, [1982] O.J. No. 3385, 38 O.R. (2d) 26 at 34 (H.C.J.), per Hughes J.
[375] CBCA, s. 241(3)(e).

allows the court to make an order directing an investigation under Part XIII of the OBCA,[376] and clause (3)(*l*) allows the court to order the wind-up of the corporation.[377] These last two powers, however, are redundant: they add nothing to the power that the court already possesses under section 161(2)(*c*) — in regard to investigations — and section 207(1)(*a*) — in regard to the wind-up of a corporation under court order. The only apparent reason for their inclusion in section 248 as well is to make clear that when an application is made for relief under that section, the court may decide to proceed with it as if the application had been made under section 161 or 207, as the case may be. The courts are reluctant to order the wind-up of a corporation where some other remedy would provide adequate relief and there is a reasonable prospect that this other remedy will be effective if ordered.[378] A wind-up of the corporation should not be offered where there is no evidence of mismanagement and the corporation is operating with a reasonable prospect of success. In such a case more effective remedies are available under the oppression remedy. For instance, an order for the purchase of shares will usually be more appropriate.[379]

§13.123 No doubt, in many cases the complainant's primary goal will be to obtain justice in the form of cold, hard cash. Fortunately for the plaintiff who is so inclined, various clauses in subsection 248(3) authorize the court to provide just that form of relief. Thus, under clause (3)(*f*) the court may order the corporation,[380] or any other person,[381] to purchase securities of a security holder.[382] Such

---

[376] See, generally, *Chung v. Chung* (1984), unreported, August 30, 1984, Gray J., 27 A.C.W.S. (2d) 297 (Ont. H.C.J.); *Michalak v. Biotech Electronics Ltd.*, [1986] Q.J. No. 1882, 35 B.L.R. 1 (S.C.); *PCM Construction Control Consultants Ltd. v. Heeger*, [1989] A.J. No. 487, 67 Alta. L.R. (2d) 302 (Q.B.); CBCA, s. 241(3)(*m*).

[377] See, generally, *LeBlanc v. Corporation Eighty-Six Ltd.*, [1997] N.B.J. No. 375, 37 B.L.R. (2d) 129 (C.A.).

[378] See, for instance, *Triple "L" Construction Ltd. v. Aikens Lake Lodge Ltd.*, [1986] M.J. No. 201, 41 Man. R. (2d) 283 at 292 (Q.B.), *per* Hirschfield J.

[379] *Daniels v. Fielder*, [1988] O.J. No. 1592, 65 O.R. (2d) 629 at 635 (H.C.J.), *per* Eberle J.

[380] See, for instance, *Westfair Foods Ltd. v. Watt*, [1990] A.J. No. 315, 73 Alta. L.R. (2d) 326 at 359 (Q.B.), *per* Moore C.J.Q.B., aff'd [1991] A.J. No. 321 79 Alta. L.R. (2d) 363, leave to appeal to S.C.C. refused 82 Alta. L.R. (2d) lxv.

[381] *Gougen v. Metro Oil Co.*, [1989] N.B.J. No. 136, 42 B.L.R. 30 (C.A.).

[382] See, generally, *Diligenti v. RWMD Operations Kelowna Ltd. (No. 2)* (1977), 4 B.C.L.R. 134 (S.C.); *Jackman v. Jackets Enterprises Ltd.*, [1977] B.C.J. No. 52, 4 B.C.L.R. 358, 2 B.L.R. 335 (S.C.); *Kummen v. Kummen-Shipman Ltd.*, [1983] M.J. No. 110, [1983] 2 W.W.R. 577 (C.A.), leave to appeal to S.C.C. refused 21 Man. R. (2d) 240n; *Bury v. Bell Gouinlock Ltd.* (1984), 48 O.R. (2d) 57 (H.C.J.), aff'd [1985] O.J. No. 2405, 49 O.R. (2d) 91 (Div. Ct.); *Miller v. F. Mendel Holdings Ltd.*, [1984] S.J. No. 298, [1984] 2 W.W.R. 683 (Q.B.); *Journet v. Superchef Food Industries Ltd.*, [1984] Q.J. No. 15, 29 B.L.R. 206 (S.C.); *Burnett v. Tsang*, [1985] A.J. No. 604, 37 Alta. L.R. (2d) 154 (Q.B.); *Abraham v. Inter Wide Investments Ltd. (No. 1)*, [1985] O.J. No. 2595, 51 O.R. (2d) 460 (H.C.J.) var'd [1988] O.J. No. 1880; *Nystad v. Harcrest Apartments Ltd.*, [1986] B.C.J. No. 3145, 3 B.C.L.R. (2d) 39 (S.C.); *Low v. Ascot Jockey Club Ltd.*, [1986] B.C.J. No. 3001, 1 B.C.L.R. (2d) 123 (S.C.); *Stech v. Davies*, [1987] A.J. No. 618, [1987] 5 W.W.R. 563 (Q.B.); *Oakley v. McDougall*, [1987] B.C.J. No. 1226, 37 B.L.R. 47 (C.A.); *Abraham v. Inter Wide Investments Ltd.*, [1988] O.J. No. 1880, 66 O.R. (2d) 684 (H.C.J.); *Eiserman v. Ara Farms Ltd.*, [1988] S.J. No. 344, [1988] 5 W.W.R. 97 (C.A.); *Palmer v. Carling O'Keefe Breweries of Canada Ltd.*, [1989] O.J. No. 32, 67 O.R. (2d) 161 (Div. Ct.).

an order is particularly justified in a long-running case of abuse,[383] or where it is otherwise reasonable to assume that the parties will not be able to work together in the future.[384] Even though the conduct of a minority shareholder justifies his or her exclusion from the corporation, the court may still order the sale and purchase of his or her shares,[385] but in settling the purchase price in such a case, a deduction or discount for the minority interest is justified. In the absence of provocative action by the minority shareholder sufficient to justify his or her exclusion from the corporation, no such deduction or discount should be made.[386]

§13.124 Similarly, clause (3)(g) empowers the court to direct the corporation or any other person to pay a security holder any part of the money paid by the security holder for the security. However, in the case of such orders against the corporation, the court's power is limited by subsection 248(6), which imposes a liquidity and solvency test on payments to a shareholder:

> 248.(6) A corporation shall not make a payment to a shareholder under clause (3)(f) or (g) if there are reasonable grounds for believing that,
>
> > (a) the corporation is or, after the payment, would be unable to pay its liabilities as they become due; or
> >
> > (b) the realizable value of the corporation's assets would thereby be less than the aggregate of its liabilities.[387]

§13.125 The court also possesses the power, under clause (3)(h), to set aside or vary a transaction to which the corporation is a party and compensating the corporation or any other party to the transaction or contract.[388] For instance, in *Metropolitan Commercial Carpet Centre Ltd. v. Donovan*,[389] the corporation was barred from paying management fees provided for in an agreement because those fees were oppressing a minority shareholder of the corporation by denying him a reasonable share of the profits of the corporation.[390] Along the same line, in *Faltakas v. Paskalidis*[391] the repayment of a franchise fee was ordered. Similarly, a transaction that strips a corporation of its assets may be set aside.[392] A related power is conferred under clause (3)(j) to make an order "compensating an aggrieved person".

§13.126 An applicant seeking an order under sections 248 of the OBCA or 241 of the CBCA may seek different types of relief in the alternative, and provided

---

[383] *Sherwood Village Optical Ltd. v. Allied Lumberland Ltd.*, [1989] S.J. No. 140, 74 Sask. R. 172 at 174 (C.A.), *per* Gerwing J.A.
[384] *Baniuk v. Carpenter*, [1988] N.B.J. No. 519, 104 N.B.R. (2d) 196, 261 A.P.R. 196 (C.A.).
[385] *Eiserman v. Ara Farms Ltd.*, [1988] S.J. No. 344, [1988] 5 W.W.R. 97 (C.A.).
[386] *Lajoie v. Lajoie Brothers Contracting Ltd.*, [1989] O.J. No. 920, 45 B.L.R. 113 (H.C.J.).
[387] See also CBCA, s. 241(6).
[388] See, generally, *Re Olympia & York*, [1986] O.J. No. 679 at para. 1, 59 O.R. (2d) 254 (H.C.J.), aff'd [1986] O.J. No. 679 at para. 110 (Div. Ct.).
[389] [1989] N.S.J. No. 254, 42 B.L.R. 306 (T.D.).
[390] See also *Rowe v. National Wholesalers Ltd.*, [1978] N.J. 97, 22 Nfld. & P.E.I.R. 26, 58 A.P.R. 26 (T.D.).
[391] [1983] B.C.J. No. 1773, 45 B.C.L.R. 388, 21 B.L.R. 246 at 253 (S.C.), *per* Wallace J.
[392] *Chicago Blower Corp. v. 141209 Canada Ltd.*, [1988] M.J. No. 528, 40 B.L.R. 201 (Man. Q.B.).

the relief sought is not mutually exclusive, the court may combine two or more types of relief. Thus, it is possible for the court to order that dividends withheld in the past be paid and that shares be purchased back by the corporation.[393]

§13.127 In various cases involving shareholder disputes it has been held that the oppression remedy allows the courts to:

(a) require a wrongdoing majority shareholder to purchase the shares of the complainant;

(b) require the wrongdoing majority shareholder to sell all, or part, of his or her shares to the complainant;[394]

(c) require the corporation to purchase the shares of the complainant; and

(d) transfer all, or some, of the shares of the wrongdoing majority shareholder to the alleged complainant, with no compensation being paid to the majority shareholder for the shares so transferred.

Unfortunately, the case law is not clear about when each of these remedies is appropriate or inappropriate. A review of the findings of fact made in the relevant cases does suggest that:

- a remedy in the form of the sale or transfer of shares (or, presumably, other securities) is appropriate where the wrongful conduct is of an ongoing nature or is liable to continue unless a change is made to the distribution of ownership within the corporation;

- a remedy in the form of the sale or transfer of shares where it is necessary either to remove the complainant or some other person from the corporation to resolve the problem giving rise to the oppression proceeding;

- remedy (a) is appropriate where the wrongdoing majority shareholder,
    - is essential to the viability of the corporation,
    - has the best claim on the merits to the corporation and its business[395] or where the minority shareholder lacks the resources to purchase the majority shareholder's interest or does not wish to do so;[396]

- remedy (b) is the normal remedy where a removal from the corporation of either the complainant or the wrongdoing majority shareholder is considered necessary to remedy the problem giving rise to the proceeding;

- remedy (c) is appropriate where neither the complainant nor any other person is guilty of any real wrongdoing;

---

[393] *Kruger Inc. v. Kruco Inc.*, [1986] R.D.J. 69 (Que. C.A.).
[394] See, for instance, *Re Brenfield Squash Racquets Club Ltd.*, [1996] 2 B.C.L.C. 184 (Ch.).
[395] *Footitt v. Gleason*, [1995] O.J. No. 2662, 25 O.R. (3d) 729 at 736 (Gen. Div.), *per* Haley J., aff'd [1998] O.J. No. 945 (C.A.).
[396] *Wittlin v. Bergman*, [1995] O.J. No. 3095, 25 O.R. (3d) 761 (C.A.).

- remedy (d) should not be used to punish the majority shareholder for wrongdoing, but may be appropriate for restitutionary purposes, where it appears that all or some of the shares held by the majority shareholder were, or ought to have been, held for the benefit of the complainant, and in cases where the complainant and the majority shareholder are spouses, and the business constitutes a family asset;[397]
- generally, but subject to the foregoing considerations, a shareholder guilty of oppressive conduct should not be allowed to take advantage of his or her oppressive conduct to force out a person having an equal right to ownership of the corporation.[398]

§13.128 The selection of the appropriate remedy in an oppression case involves the exercise of a judicial discretion on the part of the trial judge. As a general rule appellate courts are reluctant to interfere with the exercise of such a discretion, and this rule applies with full force in the area of the oppression remedy.[399] In other contexts, it has been said of discretionary authority that:

> The law as to the reversal by a court of appeal of an order made by a judge below in the exercise of his discretion is well-established, and any difficulty that arises is due only to the application of well-settled principles in an individual case. The appellate tribunal is not at liberty merely to substitute its own exercise of discretion for the discretion already exercised by the judge. In other words, appellate authorities ought not to reverse the order merely because they would themselves have exercised the original discretion, had it attached to them, in a different way. But if the appellate tribunal reaches the clear conclusion that there has been a wrongful exercise of discretion in that no weight or no sufficient weight, has been given to relevant considerations, ... then the reversal of the order on appeal may be justified.[400]

And that:

> Assuming the thing done to be within the discretion of the local authority, no Court has power to interfere with the mode in which it has exercised it. Where the Legislature has confided the power to a particular body, with a discretion how it is to be used, it is beyond the power of any Court to contest that discretion.[401]

(b) BUYING OUT OF INTEREST

§13.129 Where the court decides that the appropriate remedy in an oppression case is for one side of a dispute to buy out the interest of the other in the corporation, it is then necessary to decide which side should be obliged (or entitled) to

---

[397] See, generally, *Belman v. Belman*, [1995] O.J. No. 3155, 26 O.R. (3d) 56 (Gen. Div.).
[398] See, generally, *Tilley v. Hails*, [1992] O.J. No. 937, 8 O.R. (3d) 169 (Div. Ct.), aff'd [1992] O.J. No. 4080, 9 O.R. (3d) 255n (C.A.).
[399] See, generally, *Antoniades v. Wong*, [1997] 2 B.C.L.C. 419 (C.A.); *Naneff v. Con-Crete Holdings Ltd.*, [1995] O.J. No. 1377, 23 B.L.R. (2d) 286 at 295 (C.A.), *per* Galligan J.A.
[400] *Friends of the Oldman River Society v. Canada (Minister of Transport)*, [1992] S.C.J. No. 1, [1992] 1 S.C.R. 3 at 76, *per* La Forest J., quoting Simon L.C. in *Charles Osenton Co. v. Johnston*, [1942] A.C. 130 at 138.
[401] *Westminster Corp. v. London and North Western Railway Co.*, [1905] A.C. 426 at 427 (H.L.), *per* Lord Halsbury.

buy out the other. The general rule is that where the equities are evenly balanced, the control party will be expected to buy out the party seeking relief. Such an approach can be justified on the basis that it is the control party that has the superior knowledge of the value of the business. If a shotgun buy/sell arrangement is the court's preferred option, then the control group should be required to make the first offer.[402]

§13.129.1 An alternative approach (of particular utility where each party has an equal share in a business) is to allow each party to quote a price at which it is prepared to buy-out the others. The party offering the highest price "wins" the right to do so at the price that he or she has offered. One advantage of this approach is that it is likely to result in a fair price, and does not require an expensive and often inconclusive professional evaluation. In cases where the parties have an unequal share of the business, much the same approach can be followed, but it is necessary to modify it slightly to accommodate the imbalance in ownership. Essentially, the prices offered must be adjusted to reflect the percentage of ownership that each party would be required to buy-out. A price-per-share to be purchased comparison achieves a fair comparison of the competing offers:

	Number of Shares	Price Offered	Price Per Share
Respondent	276	$175,000	$911.46
Complainant	192	$227,000	$822.46

So, for instance, in the above example, the respondent is clearly offering more on a per share basis for the balance of the corporation, than the complainant is prepared to pay.

§13.130 Where the cause of the complaint (*e.g.*, a conflict of interest problem) is of a continuing nature that would likely give rise to litigation in the future, for instance, where it grows out of the deterioration of the relationship between the parties, or it results from inherent conflict of interest, the court's selection of the appropriate remedy will be influenced by the realization that the underlying problem that gave rise to the oppression proceeding, can be solved only by removing the complainant from the company. In such a case, the usual order is for the complainant to be bought out of the corporation.[403]

§13.131 In an appropriate case, the courts may order a change in the control of the corporation as a remedy against oppression.[404] However, a majority owner should not be forced to sell his or her interests in the business to a complainant where the majority owner is responsible for building up the business, where his

---

[402] *Scott v. Robb*, [2005] S.J. No. 372, 7 B.L.R. (4th) 273 at 274 (Q.B.), *per* Laing J.; *Lee v. Lee*, [2003] B.C.J. No. 1285, 13 B.C.L.R. (4th) 270 (C.A.).
[403] See, generally, *Neri v. Finch Hardware (1976) Ltd.*, [1995] O.J. No. 1932, 20 B.L.R. (2d) 216 at 225-26 (Ont. Gen. Div.).
[404] *Aquino v. First Choice Capital Fund Ltd.*, [1997] S.J. No. 15, 30 B.L.R. (2d) 176 (C.A.).

or her participation in the business is essential to its survival, or where the complainant has no interest in acquiring control or is incapable of doing so.[405] As an alternative to changing the control structure of the corporation, the court may instead augment the cash settlement to which the complainant is entitled to reflect the true extent of his or her contribution to the development of the business of the corporation.[406]

§13.132 In *Richter v. Battle*[407] a shareholder applied to the court for a determination of the effect of an order made under sections 207 and 234 of the Alberta *Business Corporations Act*[408] requiring the respondent to purchase the applicant shareholder's shares in a corporation. The applicant argued that the order requiring the respondents to purchase the applicant's shares within a reasonable time imposed a purchase and payment obligation upon the respondents. The respondents argued that this was not so, but, instead, that the order did no more than establish a procedure by which the applicant's shares could be valued and by which he could be separated permanently through a sale and purchase, which might be made once the valuation was determined. Mackenzie J. rejected the respondent's argument[409] and held that it was not open to the respondents to refuse to proceed with the purchase unless the applicant agreed to certain conditions outside the scope of the court's order. The remedy available to the applicant where the respondents refused to complete the purchase was to order that, upon the applicant providing the court with proof that he had completed a transfer of the shares to the respondent, he would be entitled to a monetary judgment against the respondents, jointly and severally, for the valued price of the shares. The court also ordered that the applicant be indemnified against liability for all personal guarantees given by him in regard to the company's debts and obligations.

(c) VALUATION

§13.133 The determination of an appropriate value to be paid for shares in the corporation can be quite challenging.[410] Problems relating to the valuation of securities are particularly evident in the case of closely held corporations. In *Westfair Foods Ltd. v. Watt*[411] the court suggested that a court should not order the company to buy shares where they could be sold in public securities markets, particularly if the only complaint is one of a lack of confidence. It took the view that the quick, cheap and simple solution in such a case is for the holder of the securities to sell them. Nevertheless, the court went on to order a forced purchase on the facts of the case. Where the articles or a unanimous shareholder

---

[405] *Wittlin v. Bergman*, [1995] O.J. No. 3095, 23 B.L.R. (2d) 182 (C.A.).
[406] *Khayraji v. Safaverdi* (1998), 33 B.L.R. (2d) 108 (Ont. Gen. Div.).
[407] [1995] A.J. No. 1043, 35 Alta. L.R. (3d) 192 (Q.B.).
[408] S.A. 1981, c. B-15.
[409] (1995), 35 Alta. L.R. (3d) 192 at 196-97 (Q.B.).
[410] As for the valuation of shares where a mandatory transfer of shares is ordered under ss. 207 and 248 of the OBCA, see *Belman v. Belman*, [1995] O.J. No. 3155, 26 B.L.R. (2d) 52 (Gen. Div.).
[411] [1991] A.J. No. 321, 115 A.R. 34 at 46 (C.A.), *per* Kerans J.A., leave to appeal to S.C.C. refused [1991] 3 S.C.R. viii.

agreement provide for a method of valuation, the court will pay due regard to that arrangement. However, it is not bound to employ them, and should not do so where there is a serious risk that such an agreed valuation method may lead to further abuse by the control group, or where there are other sound reasons for not doing so.[412]

§13.134 For a publicly traded corporation, the price of the relevant security in the public market has been treated by the courts as highly indicative of its fair value, but it is not conclusive. While there is a certain logic in the foregoing, a number of concerns must be raised. Courts have sometimes argued that the reason for not awarding the public market price is that such markets do not function perfectly.[413] Indeed, on occasion even the stock markets themselves have cautioned against excessive reliance on publicly quoted stock prices. As long ago as 1946, for instance, the London Stock Exchange warned:

> We desire to state authoritatively that Stock Exchange quotations are not related directly to the value of the company's assets, or to the amount of profits, and consequently those quotations no matter what date may be chosen for reference, cannot form a fair and equitable, or rational basis for compensation. ... The quotations ... definitely do not represent a valuation of a company by reference to its assets and its earnings potential. Moreover, any valuation by reference to Stock Exchange quotations must introduce indefeasible anomalies such as between one stock and another of similar standing.[414]

However, it can also be argued that in many cases the market price would be inappropriate even if the market did behave perfectly. Leaving aside the fact that the market price of a security may reflect transient influences on the market as a whole that have no relationship to the corporation, the market price might reflect a discount already applied by sophisticated investors in recognition of the abusive conduct which formed the basis of the action. In such a case the payment of the market price would not remedy the wrong to which the complainant was subjected. Where an order is made for the purchase of the complainant's shares, the price payable should reflect the adverse impact of the oppressive conduct that formed the basis of the complaint, as if this is not done, the complainant will be denied proper compensation. The order for compulsory purchase is a restitutionary mechanism by which the court compensates the minority shareholder for the oppression that he or she has suffered. There must, however, be actual evidence as to its financial consequences sufficient to allow the impact to be identified and assessed.[415]

---

[412] See, generally, the following cases: *Re A Company (No. 04377 of 1986)*, [1987] 1 W.L.R. 102 (Ch.); *Re a Company (No. 06834 of 1988)*, [1989] B.C.L.C. 365 (Ch.); *Re Boswell & Co. (Steels) Ltd.* (1988), 5 B.C.C. 145 (Ch.).
[413] *Re Valuation of Common Stock of Libby, McNeil & Libby*, 406 A.2d 54 at 60 (Me. S.C. 1979), *per* McKusich C.J.
[414] Quoted in I. Campbell, *The Principles and Practices of Business Valuation*.
[415] See, generally, *Shirim v. Fesena*, [2002] NSWSC 10, *per* Davies J. but *cf. Coombs v. Dynasty Pty Ltd.* (1994), 12 A.C.L.C. 915, *per* von Doussa J.

§13.135 *Prima facie*, the appropriate date for valuation is the date of the commencement of the oppressive conduct that forms the basis of the proceeding.[416] The value to be placed upon securities does not involve a question of law, but, rather, a question of fact, and, as such, the value given by the court must be based upon the evidence (expert or otherwise) placed before the court.[417] Proceedings under section 248 are adversarial rather than inquisitorial. Although the court must eventually rule on value, it is the obligation of the parties to provide evidence on value. In *Wittlin v. Bergman*[418] there was no evidence on which the court might make a valuation. The court ordered that the costs of the valuation would be shared by the parties. An order to purchase shares should not be made in an oppression action where the effect of the order would be to breach a contract with a third party, for instance, where it would contravene a provision in a loan agreement, unless the consent of that third party to the order is obtained.[419]

§13.136 Where the value of the shares of a corporation declines between the date of the oppressive conduct complained of and the date of judgment for reasons unrelated to the oppressive conduct, the court should pick the valuation date fairest to all parties on the basis of all facts before the court. The conduct of both the complainant and the person alleged to have been guilty of oppression will be relevant to that determination, including the failure by the complainant to take advantage of remedial steps reasonably afforded to him or her.[420]

(C.1) SOLICITOR AND CLIENT COSTS

§13.137 A finding of oppression on the basis of a breach of fiduciary duty, bad faith or manifestly unfair treatment of the complainant justifies an award of solicitor-and-client costs,[421] because to deny such costs and confine the applicant to party and party costs would be simply to compound the effect of the oppressive conduct.[422] However, in the absence of a specific finding of bad faith or lack of probity, costs on a party-and-party basis are appropriate.[423]

---

[416] See, generally, *Neri v. Finch Hardware (1976) Ltd.*, [1995] O.J. No. 1932, 20 B.L.R. (2d) 216 at 225-26 (Gen. Div.).
[417] *Cyprus Anvil Mining Corp. v. Dickson*, [1986] B.C.J. No. 1204, 8 B.C.L.R. (2d) 145 at 158-59 (C.A.), *per* Lambert J.A.
[418] [1995] O.J. No. 3095, 23 B.L.R. (2d) 182 (C.A.). On the basis of this decision, earlier case law suggesting that the court played an inquisitorial role in fixing the value of shares or securities should now be disregarded.
[419] *Safarik v. Ocean Fisheries Ltd.*, [1995] B.C.J. No. 1979, 22 B.L.R. (2d) 1 (C.A.), additional reasons at [1996] B.C.J. No. 76, 25 B.L.R. (2d) 44.
[420] *Chiaramonte v. World Wide Importing Ltd.*, [1996] O.J. No. 1389, 28 O.R. (3d) 641 (Gen. Div.).
[421] *218125 Investments Ltd. v. Patel*, [1995] A.J. No. 1222, 33 Alta. L.R. (3d) 245 at 268-69 (Q.B.), *per* Rooke J.
[422] *Naneff v. Con-Crete Holdings Ltd.*, [1993] O.J. No. 1756, 11 B.L.R. (2d) 218 at 264 (Gen. Div.), *per* Blair J., var'd [1994] O.J. No. 1811, rev'd in part [1995] O.J. No. 1377, 23 O.R. (3d) 481 (C.A.).
[423] *SCI Systems, Inc. v. Gornitzki Thompson & Little Co.*, [1997] O.J. No. 2571, 36 B.L.R. (2d) 207 (Gen. Div.), var'd [1998] O.J. No. 2299, 110 O.A.C. 160 (Div. Ct.).

(d) Minority Discount

§13.138 The notion of payment of the fair value of shares (or other securities) runs throughout the oppression remedy cases.[424] In fixing the fair value of shares, most courts have applied to the shares a *pro rata* portion of the *en bloc* fair market value[425] of the class of shares to which the shares in question belong,[426] with no discount being applied to reflect the complainant's minority position.[427] Thus, it has been held that where relief is granted under the oppression remedy for oppressive conduct on the part of a majority shareholder and the majority shareholder is required to purchase the shares of a minority shareholder complainant, no minority discount[428] should be applied in valuing the shares to be purchased. Similarly, it has been held that no such discount should be ordered merely because the complainant is shown to be guilty of some inappropriate conduct. Such a discount is acceptable only if the complainant's misconduct was sufficiently grave that he or she deserved to be excluded from the corporation.[429]

§13.139 A minority discount may be applied where it is a minority shareholder who has been guilty of the oppression and the court orders the sale of his or her shares to the oppressed shareholder as the remedy for that oppression and to remove that minority shareholder from the corporation and prevent the recurrence of the oppression.[430] However, a minority discount should not be applied where, on the facts, the minority shareholder had effective control over the

---

[424] In terms of the procedure for fixing value, see *Alldrew Holdings Ltd. v. Nibro Holdings Ltd.*, [1996] O.J. No. 2221, 25 B.L.R. (2d) 302 at 316-17 (C.A.), *per* McKinlay J.A., leave to appeal to S.C.C. refused [1996] S.C.C.A. No. 466.
[425] But see *Nunachiaq v. Chow*, [1993] B.C.J. No. 179, 8 B.L.R. (2d) 109 at 147 (S.C.), aff'd [1994] B.C.J. No. 608 (C.A.).
[426] See, generally, *New Quebec Raglan Mines v. Blok-Anderson*, [1993] O.J. No. 727, 9 B.L.R. (2d) 93 (Gen. Div.), rev'd unreported, June 2, 1997, Doc. No. C15855 (C.A.).
[427] *Brant Investments Ltd. v. KeepRite Inc.*, [1991] O.J. No. 683, 3 O.R. (3d) 289 at 329 (C.A.), *per* McKinley J.A.
[428] Generally, the size of a holding of a block of shares will influence the market value of those shares, so that a holding of 20 per cent of the voting shares of a corporation will not be worth 20 per cent of the *en bloc* value of the corporation. Where a block holding is less than 50 per cent, the market will usually discount that holding to reflect the inability of the minority shareholder to control the corporation, for instance, regarding the payment of dividends on the shares. Where the corporation is private, potential investors will also apply a second discount, known as the illiquidity discount, to reflect the fact that (a) there is no, or only a very limited, secondary market for the shares concerned; and (b) the holder of the shares at any particular time may be unable to compel the directors of the corporation to register a transfer of the shares. See, generally, James Forbes, "Valuation Issues In Shareholder Oppression," in *The Oppression Remedy* (Toronto: LSUC, 1994).
[429] *Safarik v. Ocean Fisheries Ltd.*, [1993] B.C.J. No. 1816, 10 B.L.R. (2d) 246 at 314 (S.C.), *per* Harvey J., additional reasons at [1994] B.C.J. No. 2225, 22 C.P.C. (3d) 214, rev'd [1995] B.C.J. No. 1979, 22 B.L.R. (2d) 1, additional reasons at [1996] B.C.J. No. 76, 25 B.L.R. (2d) 44 (C.A.). *Mason v. Intercity Properties Ltd.*, [1987] O.J. No. 448, 38 D.L.R. (4th) 681 at 698 (C.A.), *per* Blair J.A., leave to appeal to S.C.C. refused 42 D.L.R. (4th) iii — although cl. 248(3)(*j*) of the OBCA does give the courts an express power to order that the complainant be compensated. Contrast, however, *Irvine v. Irvine*, [2006] EWHC 1875 (Ch.) — discount applied in an oppression proceeding.
[430] *Calmont Leasing Ltd. v. Kredl*, [1996] A.J. No. 283, 38 Alta. L.R. (3d) 296 at 303 (Q.B.), *per* Clarke J.

corporation, because, in that case the factual premise for such a discount (*i.e.*, the absence of control) is not present.[431] Because in most cases where oppression occurs, the oppressing shareholder will have at least *de facto* control of the corporation, the number of instances in which a minority discount will be applied to the shares held by that shareholder are likely to be limited.

(e) Premiums

§13.140 Courts are also unwilling to allow the complainant a premium to compensate the shareholder for being forced out of the corporation. Although such premiums have sometimes been allowed where the controlling shareholder has been particularly abusive, the trend in the case law is strongly against such compensation.[432] The rejection of a premium is consistent with the view that the Act does not authorize the courts to punish for oppression.[433]

(f) Removal of a Director

§13.141 On suitable facts, a court may remove a director as a remedy in an oppression proceeding. The removal of a director of a corporation is exceptional and is a remedy rarely granted unless clearly necessary. Such an order requires more than anticipated misconduct, and more than an apprehension of bias.[434] However, where actual conduct rises to level of misconduct that triggers oppression remedy relief, judicial intervention by removing and replacing a director may be warranted in order to rectify or alleviate the oppression.[435] An order may be made where necessary to prevent on-going misconduct that is likely to continue.[436] On occasion, directors have been removed for negligent mismanagement of a serious and continuing nature.[437] Some question must be raised, however, as to whether negligence in itself satisfies the statutory requirements for oppression, unfair prejudice or unfair disregard. In *Wilkinson v. West Coast Capital,* Warren J. indicated that it does not:

> ... it would be a misuse of language to describe an administrator who has managed the company's affairs fairly and impartially and with a proper regard for the interests of all the creditors (and members where necessary), conscientiously endeavoring to

---

[431] *Ibid.,* at 304.
[432] See, for instance, *Brant Investments Ltd. v. KeepRite Inc.,* [1991] O.J. No. 683, 1 B.L.R. 225 at 328 (C.A.), *per* McKinley J.A.
[433] *Naneff v. Con-Crete Holdings Ltd.,* [1995] O.J. No. 1377, 23 B.L.R. (2d) 286 at 301 (C.A.), *per* Galligan J.A.
[434] *Re Stelco Inc.,* [2005] O.J. No. 1171, 75 O.R. (3d) 5 (C.A.) — removal order overturned on appeal as it was based only on an apprehension of bias.
[435] *Catalyst Fund General Partner I Inc. v. Hollinger Inc.,* [2004] O.J. No. 4722, [2004] O.T.C. 1025 (S.C.J.), aff'd [2006] O.J. No. 944, 79 O.R. (3d) 288 (C.A.).
[436] *Brokx v. Tattoo Technology Inc.,* [2004] B.C.J. No. 2711, [2004] BCSC 1723 — director misappropriated corporate funds; *Tsui v. International Capital Corp.,* [1993] S.J. No. 83, 108 Sask. R. 62 (Q.B.) — director's guilty of conflict of interest and deceit; *Aquino v. First Choice Capital Fund Ltd.,* [1996] S.J. No. 184, 143 Sask. R. 81 (Q.B.) — removal of a director to prevent likelihood of future oppression.
[437] See, for instance, *R.S. v. RW-LB Holdings Ltd.,* [1993] A.J. No. 1033, 15 Alta. L.R. (3d) 153 (Q.B.); *Trnkoczy v. Shooting Chrony Inc.,* [1991] O.J. No. 102, 1 B.L.R. (2d) 202 (Gen. Div.).

do his best for them, but who has through oversight or inadvertence fallen below the standards of a reasonably competent insolvency practitioner in the carrying out of some particular transaction, as having managed the affairs of the company in a manner which is unfairly prejudicial to the creditors.[438]

(g) UNWINDING OF TRANSACTIONS, ETC.

§13.142 Both the OBCA and the CBCA permit the court dealing with an oppression proceeding both to unwind oppressive transactions,[439] or to require the consummation of a transaction,[440] where necessary to remedy the oppressive conduct to which the proceeding relates. In *Sparling v. Javelin Internationale Ltee*,[441] the court ordered the cancellation of shares and the removal of a director and an amendment to the articles of association and the by-laws of the corporation to reduce the number of directors to rectify oppressive attempt to maintain control over a corporation.

(h) DAMAGES AND SIMILAR COMPENSATION

§13.143 Clause 248(3)(*j*) of the OBCA empowers a court to make an order "compensating an aggrieved person" within the context of an oppression proceeding. Clause 241(3)(*j*) of the CBCA is to a similar effect. While the courts generally seem to presume that this provision confers the authority to make was is in effect an award of damages,[442] it is not clear from the case law whether the damages that might be awarded are governed by the principles applicable to a remedy for damages in contract or tort, or whether the equitable rules relating to an accounting should apply. This uncertainty would be relevant to such questions as remoteness and the availability of punitive damages. The issue now seems to have been resolved in the course of the judgment of the Ontario Court of Appeal in *Waxman v. Waxman*,[443] in which the court stated:

> Increasingly, courts seek to achieve similar compensation for "similar wrongs", whether the action is framed in contract or tort or as breach of fiduciary duty. Indeed, ... [it] would be odd if a different result followed depending solely on the manner in which one framed an identical claim. What is required is a measure of rationalization.

In giving this decision, the court in *Waxman* quoted the judgment of Finlayson J.A. in *Martin v. Goldfarb*:

> Regardless of the doctrinal underpinning, plaintiffs should not be able to recover higher damage awards merely because their claim is characterized as breach of fiduciary duty, as opposed to breach of contract or tort. The objective of the

---

[438] [2005] EWHC 3009 (Ch.), quoting Millett J. in *Re Charnley Davies Ltd. (No. 2)*, [1990] B.C.L.C. 760 at 783-84.
[439] OBCA, s. 248(3)(*g*), (*h*).
[440] OBCA, s. 248(3)(*d*), (*f*).
[441] [1986] R.J.Q. 1073 (Que. S.C.).
[442] *McEwen v. Goldcorp Inc.*, [2006] O.J. No. 4265 (S.C.J.), aff'd [2006] O.J. No. 4437 (Div. Ct.); *Hurst v. Societe Nationale de L'Amiante*, [2006] O.J. No. 3998 (S.C.J. — C.L.).
[443] (2004), 132 A.C.W.S. (3d) 1046.

expansion of the concept of fiduciary relationship was not to provide plaintiffs with the means to exact higher damages than were already available to them under contract or tort law.[444]

However, the *Waxman* court went on to make clear that a court can consider the principles of remoteness, causation, and intervening act where necessary to reach a just and fair result, and when applying the above principles should take care that in doing so it does not raise any policy concerns.

§13.144 Part XIX.1 of the CBCA deals with the apportionment of an award of damages where damages have been awarded to a plaintiff for a final loss against two or more defendants or a defendant and a third party.[445] However, the Part does not apply to an award of damages to any of the following plaintiffs:

(a) Her Majesty in right of Canada or of a province;

(b) an agent of Her Majesty in right of Canada or of a province or a federal or provincial Crown corporation or government agency, unless a substantial part of its activities involves trading, including making investments in, securities or other financial instruments;

(c) a charitable organization, private foundation or public foundation within the meaning of subsection 149.1(1) of the *Income Tax Act*; or

(d) an unsecured creditor in respect of goods or services that the creditor provided to a corporation.[446]

There is no corresponding Part in the OBCA. The definition of "financial loss" is set out in section 237.1:

> "financial loss" means a financial loss arising out of an error, omission or misstatement in financial information concerning a corporation that is required under this Act or the regulations.

Subsection 237.3(1) adopts a presumption of apportionment based upon degree of responsibility. It provides:

> Subject to this section and sections 237.4 to 237.6, every defendant or third party who has been found responsible for a financial loss is liable to the plaintiff only for the portion of the damages that corresponds to their degree of responsibility for the loss.

This general scheme is subject to exceptions in the case of uncollectable amounts. More specifically, where any part of the damages awarded against a responsible defendant or third party is uncollectable, the court may reallocate that amount to the other responsible defendants or third parties, on the application of the plaintiff. The application must be made within one year after the date that the judgment was made enforceable.[447] The method of reallocation is set out in subsection 237.3(3):

---

[444] (1998), 41 O.R. (3d) 161 at 173 (C.A.).
[445] CBCA, s. 237.2(1).
[446] CBCA, s. 237.2(2).
[447] CBCA s. 237.3(2).

The amount that may be reallocated to each of the other responsible defendants or third parties under subsection (2) is calculated by multiplying the uncollectable amount by the percentage that corresponds to the degree of responsibility of that defendant or third party for the total financial loss.

However, the maximum amount determined under subsection (3), in respect of any responsible defendant or third party, may not be more than 50 per cent of the amount originally awarded against that responsible defendant or third party.[448] Defendants and third parties referred to in subsection 237.2(1) are jointly and severally (or, in Quebec solidarily) liable for the damages awarded to a plaintiff who is an individual or a personal body corporate and who:

(a) had a financial interest in a corporation on the day that an error, omission or misstatement in financial information concerning the corporation occurred, or acquired a financial interest in the period between the day that the error, omission or misstatement occurred and the day, as determined by the court, that it was generally disclosed; and

(b) has established that the value of the plaintiff's total financial interest in the corporation was not more than the prescribed amount at the close of business on the day that the error, omission or misstatement occurred or at the close of business on any day that the plaintiff acquired a financial interest in the period referred to in paragraph (a).[449]

For the purposes of Part XIX.1, "financial interest", with respect to a corporation, includes:

(a) a security;

(b) a title to or an interest in capital, assets, property, profits, earnings or royalties;

(c) an option or other interest in, or a subscription to, a security;

(d) an agreement under which the interest of the purchaser is valued for purposes of conversion or surrender by reference to the value of a proportionate interest in a specified portfolio of assets;

(e) an agreement providing that money received will be repaid or treated as a subscription for shares, units or interests at the option of any person or the corporation;

(f) a profit-sharing agreement or certificate;

(g) a lease, claim or royalty in oil, natural gas or mining, or an interest in the lease, claim or royalty;

(h) an income or annuity contract that is not issued by an insurance company governed by an Act of Parliament or a law of a province;

(i) an investment contract; and

(j) anything that is prescribed to be a financial interest.[450]

---

[448] CBCA, s. 273.3(4).
[449] CBCA, s. 237.5(1).
[450] CBCA, s. 237.1.

Section 237.4 creates a special set of rules with respect to claims based upon fraud (which presumably means civil fraud, as opposed to criminal fraud). It provides that the plaintiff may recover the whole amount of the damages awarded by the court from any defendant or third party who has been held responsible for a financial loss if it was established that the defendant or third party acted fraudulently or dishonestly.[451] However, while there is no available remedy of apportionment, contribution is still contemplated — subsection 237.4(2) providing:

> The defendant or third party referred to in subsection (1) is entitled to claim contribution from any other defendant or third party who is held responsible for the loss.

(i) DISCONTINUANCE AND SETTLEMENT

§13.145 An application made or an action brought or intervened in under Part XVII of the OBCA (which includes the dissent, oppression and compliance order provisions) may not be stayed or dismissed because the alleged breach of a right or duty owed to the corporation or its affiliate has been or may be approved by the shareholders of the company in question, but evidence of such approval may be taken into account by the court in deciding when, or if, to make an order under the Part.[452] Although shareholder ratification does not dispose of the question of whether a derivative action or compliance order application should be allowed to proceed, where a meeting may be called to consider the ratification of the act forming the basis of the action or application, the court may stay the proceeding until such time as the meeting has been held.[453]

§13.146 In recognition of the class action character of many proceedings under Part XVII, subsection 249(2) of the OBCA provides that "an application made or an action brought or intervened in under that Part shall not be stayed, discontinued, settled or dismissed for want of prosecution without the approval of the court". In giving such approval, the court may impose such terms as it thinks fit. If the court determines that the interests of any complainant may be substantially affected by the stay, discontinuance, settlement or dismissal, the court may order any party to the application or action to give notice to the complainant.[454] In deciding whether or not to approve a proposed settlement, the court must be satisfied that the settlement is fair and reasonable to all the shareholders. In considering this question, the court must recognize that settlements are by their very nature compromises, which need not, and usually do not, satisfy every single concern of all affected parties. Acceptable settlements may fall within a broad range of upper and lower limits. Although the court should not act as a rubber stamp, there is a clear public interest in encouraging settlements. Where a

---

[451] CBCA, s. 237.4(1).
[452] OBCA, s. 249(1); CBCA, s. 242(1).
[453] See, for instance, *Grant v. United Kingdom Switchback Railways Co.* (1888), 40 Ch. D. 135.
[454] See also CBCA, s. 242(2).

settlement is proposed by the Director, there is a strong presumption that it is reasonable and fair.[455]

(4) Relief Against Third Parties

§13.147 As mentioned briefly earlier in the chapter, a third party dealing with the corporation that is not an affiliate of the corporation, or concerned in its management, is unlikely to be guilty of conduct that would support an oppression claim.[456] In *Casurina Ltd. Partnership v. Rio Algom Ltd.*,[457] the court considered whether the conduct of a bidder in a takeover bid could support an oppression claim by the security holders of the target corporation. Spence J. found that at the time of the bid, the bidder was not an affiliate of the corporation and concluded:

> ... there are two particular problems with the contention that Billiton has acted with unfair disregard for the interests of the Debentureholders and both of these problems arise from the fact that the conduct in which Billiton has engaged is that of a third party to Rio Algom and does not involve it in dealing with Rio Algom: (i) the difficulty in seeing how the holders could properly be said to have had a reasonable expectation about a third party's actions in buying the shares of Rio Algom, and (ii) the difficulty in seeing how Billiton as a third party buying those shares can be said to be acting unfairly in disregarding the interests of the Debentureholders.

However, a third party may be liable for oppression, where that third party has effective control over corporate decision making, and so was in fact the actual cause of the wrongdoing.[458]

(x) Is the Oppression Remedy a Cure Worse Than the Disease?

§13.148 After more than 30 years in effect, the time has come to take a critical look at the oppression remedy, both with respect to the terms in which it is drafted and the manner in which it has been applied. Despite the efforts of the courts to identify principles guiding the availability of relief, the case law affords little more than a list of different situation that may be considered to amount to oppression or other forms of wrongdoing. In *Abraham v. Inter Wide Investments Ltd.*,[459] Griffiths J. concluded that the oppression remedy should be given "a liberal interpretation". It may fairly be stated that most courts that have considered the application of the remedy have tended towards such an approach. It is said that relief may be sought to protect the interests of complainants in the

---

[455] *Sparling v. Southam Inc.*, [1988] O.J. No. 1745, 41 B.L.R. 22 at 28-29 (H.C.J.), *per* Callaghan A.C.J.H.C.
[456] As to the jurisdiction of the court to make orders with respect to a third party not involved in the alleged oppressive conduct, see: *Re Little Olympian Each-ways Ltd.*, [1994] 2 B.C.L.C. 420 (Ch.).
[457] [2002] O.J. No. 3229 at para. 194 (S.C.J.), aff'd [2004] O.J. No. 177 (C.A.).
[458] *Stern v. Imasco Ltd.*, [1999] O.J. No. 4235, 1 B.L.R. (3d) 198 (S.C.J.).
[459] [1985] O.J. No. 2595, 51 O.R. (2d) 460 at 468-69 (H.C.J.), var'd [1988] O.J. No. 1880 (H.C.J.).

widest sense rather than merely their strict legal or equitable rights.[460] Unfortunately, it is not clear how much wider that "widest sense" may be. Not surprisingly, complainants often have difficulty in deciding whether they are entitled to relief or not. For instance, in *Naaykens v. Bayes Equipment (Neepawa) Ltd.*[461] relief under the section was held to be available not so much because the transaction in question was bad, but because it had been badly put together.

§13.149 Nor are potential defendants in any better position. Conduct which is found to be unfairly prejudicial or oppressive in one case, may not necessarily be so found in another, even though the factual setting of the two cases is only slightly different.[462] Despite the introduction of oppression-type remedies, we are still told that the guiding principle in corporate law matters is still majority rule.[463] The majority are not obliged to consult with the minority in the management of the corporation.[464] In the absence of an underlying obligation to allow the complainant to participate in management, the exclusion of the complainant as a minority shareholder from the management of the corporation is not in itself oppressive.[465] Nevertheless, as noted at the outset of this section of the chapter, exclusion from participation in management remains a principal cause of complaint, as does expulsion of a shareholder from a corporation.[466]

§13.150 Rules of law that lead to voluminous litigation are rarely beneficial to the economy. Where a given rule results in a large number of reported final court decisions, the rule will usually be found to be so vague in its terms and application that it is difficult for lawyers to advise their clients as to what they can and cannot do, and with respect to the availability of relief. In economic terms, vague rules of uncertain application increase transaction costs. At a certain point, the increase in transaction costs resulting from a given rule can be so great that it exceeds any benefit that the intended rule could reasonably be expected to confer. It is a fair question whether the oppression remedy is not a rule of law that falls into this category.

§13.151 In any area of law so closely tied to the health of the national economy as corporate law, there is an obvious benefit in rules of law that are clear in their

---

[460] *Westfair Foods Ltd. v. Watt*, [1990] A.J. No. 315, 73 Alta. L.R. (2d) 326 at 339 (Q.B.), *per* Moore C.J.Q.B., rev'd [1998] A.J. No. 1145 (C.A.), leave to appeal to S.C.C. refused [1998] S.C.C.A. No. 634; see also *Keho Holdings Ltd. v. Noble*, [1987] A.J. No. 334, 52 Alta. L.R. (2d) 195 at 373-74 (C.A.), *per* Haddad J.A.
[461] [1988] M.J. No. 566, 56 Man. R. (2d) 272 (Q.B.).
[462] *Ferguson v. Imax Systems*, [1983] O.J. No. 3156, 43 O.R. (2d) 128, 150 D.L.R. (3d) 718 at 727 (C.A.), *per* Brooke J.A., leave to appeal to S.C.C. refused 2 O.A.C. 158n.
[463] *Wotherspoon v. Canadian Pacific Ltd.*, [1982] O.J. No. 3148, 35 O.R. (2d) 449 at 485 (C.A.), var'd [1987] S.C.J. No. 40.
[464] See, generally, *de la Giroday v. Giroday Sawmills Ltd.*, [1983] B.C.J. No. 79, 49 B.C.L.R. 378 at 381 (S.C.), *per* Taylor J.
[465] *Keho Holdings Ltd. v. Noble*, [1987] A.J. No. 334, 52 Alta. L.R. (2d) 195 at 202-203, 38 D.L.R. (4th) 368 (C.A.), *per* Haddad J.A.; *Ebrahimi v. Westbourne Galleries Ltd.*, [1973] A.C. 360 at 380 (H.L.), *per* Lord Wilberforce.
[466] See, generally, *Buckley v. B.C.T.F.*, [1992] B.C.J. No. 2457, 75 B.C.L.R. (2d) 228 (S.C.), var'd [1994] B.C.J. No. 192, 86 B.C.L.R. (2d) 303 (C.A.).

meaning and predictable in their outcome. In these respects, the current law regarding oppression falls seriously short of the target. In its 1967 *Report on Company Law*, Ontario's Lawrence Committee rejected the adoption of the oppression remedy into Ontario law, concluding that its incorporation as remedy would raise:

> ...as many problems as it lays to rest and, more importantly, is objectionable on the ground that it is a complete dereliction of the established principle of judicial non-interference in the management of companies.[467]

Rarely in history has a prediction of the adverse consequences of adopting a particular legal measure come so close to the mark. Oppression and related claims now dominate the world of corporate law, outnumbering (in the current reported case law) all other types of claim combined.[468] In addition, the case law in the area has an *ad hoc* quality, with judgments in very similar cases leading to different results, due to fine distinctions in fact. In *Themadel Foundation v. Third Canadian General Investment Trust Ltd.*[469] Carthy J. stated:

> The point at which relief [for oppression] is justified and the extent of relief are both so dependent upon the facts of the particular case, that little guidance can be obtained from comparing one case to another ...

§13.152 The less legal guidance that can be gleaned from the case law, the more difficult it is for a lawyer advising a client to be able to give proper advice as to whether a claim is meritorious. In contrast, as the certainty of the law declines, it becomes very easy to predict what will happen with respect to the quantum and the quality of claims. The oppression remedy has become the last port of refuge not just for every crank shareholder who harbours a festering grievance, but for every other disgruntled person who — however so remotely connected with the corporation, and no matter how tenuous the link that may exist to it — believes that some imaginary right has been transgressed. Indeed, as we have seen, the complaint need not even relate to a right — a mere "reasonable expectation" concerning some ill-defined "interest" (whatever that may be) is sufficient according to some strands of the case law.[470]

---

[467] Ontario, *Report on Company Law* (Lawrence Committee (Toronto: Legislative Assembly of Ontario, 1967)) at para. 7.3.12.

[468] In 2001, a seven-year search of the Lexis data base, revealed that out of 699 reported decisions dealing with OBCA corporations, 396 of them (or 56.7 per cent) involved claims for "oppression". A second survey carried out in early 2006 found that out of 343 cases decided in Ontario with respect to OBCA corporations over a four-year period, 187 (or 54.5 per cent) related to oppression claims. One really has to ask whether oppression is this prevalent, or whether the corporate world can sustain such a volume of litigation.

[469] [1998] O.J. No. 647, 38 O.R. (3d) 749 (C.A.).

[470] See, for instance, *Main v. Delcan Group Inc.*, [1999] O.J. No. 1961, 47 B.L.R. (2d) 200 (S.C.J.); *Krynen v. Bugg*, [2003] O.J. No. 1209, 64 O.R. (3d) 393 (S.C.J.); *Westfair Foods Ltd. v. Watt*, [1991] A.J. No. 321, 79 D.L.R. (4th) 48 (C.A.), leave to appeal to S.C.C. refused 85 D.L.R. (4th) viii. In one extreme case, it was held that even a draft agreement could give rise to reasonable expectations: *Gordon Glaves Holdings Ltd. v. Care Corp. of Canada*, [2000] O.J. No. 1989, 48 O.R. (3d) 737 (C.A.), leave to appeal to S.C.C. refused [2000] S.C.C.A. No. 411. Less controversially, so too have securities filings such as prospectuses and information circulars, and even public announcements: *Themadel Foundation v. Third Canadian General Investment Trust Ltd.*, [1998] O.J. No. 647, 38 O.R. (3d) 749 (C.A.); *Deutsche Bank of Canada v. Oxford properties*

§13.153 From a public policy perspective, the key difficulty that courts confront is deciding how broadly to cast the net, so as to allow recovery. The introduction of "unfair prejudice" and "unfair disregard" as grounds for relief has not simply provided protection to possible meritorious claimants. It has made the law less certain, and which has had the result of encouraging a large number of non-meritorious claims. Our discussion of the limited standing of creditors to seek oppression relief provides a suitable springboard for a discussion of another probable limitation on the statutory oppression remedy. While the violation of a legal entitlement of a complainant, or legal requirement applicable to the management of the corporation that adversely affects the complainant, may amount to oppression, it would be unrealistic to conclude that the intent behind section 248 was to create a ubiquitous remedy that would come into play whenever such a violation occurs. Insofar as appropriate alternate remedies are available, there would seem to be no role to be played by an oppression action. Where those more "plain vanilla" remedies fail to afford satisfactory relief, an oppression remedy does not lie.[471]

§13.154 The problem with the oppression remedy

- is not that it does not afford a valuable tool for dealing with serious instances of abuse when they occur, in areas in which contract and fiduciary duty do not,

- but rather that it has proven impossible to deter the institution of frivolous claims or even to provide a clear indication to persons who seek a remedy in good faith, as to what the limits of that remedy are.

This is a very difficult type of legal problem to solve than the problem that the remedy was originally intended to address. Thus far it has been a problem that both the legislative and judicial branches of government have proven unable to resolve.

Group Inc., [1998] O.J. No. 4375, 40 B.L.R. (2d) 302 (Gen. Div. — C.L.); *Gazit (1997) Inc. v. Centrefund Realty Corp.*, [2000] O.J. No. 3070, 8 B.L.R. (3d) 81 (S.C.J.). In *O'Neill v. Phillips*, [1999] 2 All E.R. 961 (H.L.), the House of Lords appears to have moved a significant distance away from this approach. *Per* Lord Hoffmann (at p. 970):

> In *Re Saul D. Harrison & Sons plc*, [1994] B.C.C. 475 (H.L.) I used the term "legitimate expectation" borrowed from public law, as a label for the "correlative right" to which a relationship between company members may give rise in a case when, on equitable principles, it would be regarded as unfair for a majority to exercise a power conferred upon them by the articles to the prejudice of another member. ...
>
> It was probably a mistake to use this term, as it usually is when one introduces a new label to describe a concept which is already sufficiently defined in other terms. In saying that it was "correlative" to the equitable restraint, I meant that it could exist only when equitable principles of the kind I have been describing would make it unfair for a party to exercise rights under the articles. It is a consequence, not a cause, of the equitable restraint. The concept of a legitimate expectation should not be allowed to lead a life of its own, capable of giving rise to equitable restraints in circumstances to which traditional equitable principles have no application.

[471] See, for instance, *Jaska v. Jaska*, 1996 CarswellMan 570 at para. 29.

§13.155 Ultimately, one problem inherent in the corporate setting, and with which oppression remedies must necessarily deal, is that there will frequently be legitimate disputes within a corporation concerning the direction that its business should take and the manner in which its affairs should be conducted. It seems self-evident that the jurisdiction of the court to grant relief is one that must be carefully exercised, for it requires a balancing of the rights of those who are in control and those who are in a minority position within the corporation. All competing interests within the corporation must be respected and safeguarded by the court, not merely the interests of the complainant.[472] Business decisions that were honestly made should not be second-guessed by the courts or subjected to microscopic examination under the oppression remedy.[473] The court is not justified in granting relief under the oppression provisions merely because the management of a corporation came to a different decision than the judge might have reached in the same circumstances.[474] It is not sufficient for the complainant to show prejudice or disregard of his or her interests. It must also be shown that the prejudice or disregard complained of was unfair.[475] Unfortunately, it is very difficult for the courts to draw these kinds of measured distinctions when they are given little in the way of legislative guidance and are instead confronted only with a mass of sometimes inconsistent and in any event fact specific case law.

§13.156 Across the Commonwealth, the experience with respect to oppression type relief has been much the same. In Canada and the U.K., for instance, courts have sought to fill in the gaps in the law by appealing to what Hoffman L.J. describes as the " ... already substantial cast of imaginary characters which the law uses to personify its standards of justice in different situations".[476] In England, it has been suggested that recourse should be made to the "reasonable bystander",[477] in Canada, to the "commercial bystander".[478] The "reasonable expectations" of a

---

[472] *Such v. RW-LB Holdings Ltd.*, [1993] A.J. No. 1033, 11 B.L.R. (2d) 122 (Q.B.) Perhaps the clearest articulation of this balancing requirement may be found in a New Zealand case: *Re H.W. Thomas Ltd.* (1984), 2 A.C.L.C. 610 (N.Z.S.C.), per Richardson J.

[473] See, for instance, *Wayde v. New South Wales Rugby League* (1985), 3 A.C.L.C. 799 (H.C. Aust.) — court will not review a decision made honestly and reasonably in the interests of promoting the business of the corporation, even if harsh to the complainant.

[474] See, generally, *Brant Investments Ltd. v. KeepRite Inc.*, [1987] O.J. No. 574, 37 B.L.R. 65 (H.C.J.), aff'd [1991] O.J. No. 683 (C.A.).

[475] As one court has observed, *Wayde v. New South Wales Rugby League* (1985), 3 A.C.L.C. 799 at para. 6, *per* Brennan J.

> It is not necessarily unfair for directors in good faith to advance one of the objects of the company to the prejudice of a member where the advancement of the object necessarily entails prejudice to that member or discrimination against him. *Prima facie*, it is for the directors and not for the Court to decide whether the furthering of a corporate object which is inimical to a member's interests should prevail over those interests or whether some balance should be struck between them. ... The question of unfairness is one of fact and degree which s. 320 requires the Court to determine, but not without regard to the view which the directors themselves have formed and not without allowing for any special skill, knowledge and acumen possessed by the directors.

[476] *Re Saul D. Harrison & Sons plc*, [1994] B.C.C. 475 at 488 (C.A.).

[477] Per Slade J. in *Re Bovey Hotel Ventures Ltd*, July 31, 1981 (Ch. D.), unreported; it was also propounded by the petitioner's counsel in *Re Saul D Harrison plc*, [1994] B.C.C. 475 at 488.

[478] *Morgan v. 45 Flyers Avenue Pty Ltd.* (1986), 10 A.C.L.R. 692 at 704.

shareholder (in Canada) or its cousin the "legitimate expectations" of a shareholder (in England) are simply the reasonable man de-personified. It is the corollary of this approach that in both jurisdictions conduct may entitle a petitioner to relief even if it is in good faith: it is the result rather than the motive which is material.[479]

§13.157 In both jurisdictions there are criticisms that decided case law has a rather *ad hoc* quality about it making it difficult to predict the outcome in any given case.[480] In the words of Harman J.:

> Petitions under section 459 have become notorious to the judges of this court — and I think also to the Bar — for their length, their unpredictability of management, and the enormous and appalling costs which are incurred upon them particularly by reason of the volume of documents liable to be produced.[481]

The oppression remedy will always require a degree of flexibility, due to variations in the specific nature of each case.[482] The key point to resolve is how much flexibility is required. It is not difficult to identify general categories of behaviour that do and no doubt should give rise to relief. These include: (1) the use of control of a corporation to dilute the proportion of shares held;[483] (2) the diversion of business away from the corporation;[484] (3) the payment of excessive remuneration to directors who are also shareholders and failing to make any or any adequate dividends.[485] However, the courts have been reluctant to permit the remedy to be used to remedy negligence[486] or where a shareholder objects to the

---

[479] *Re H.R. Harmer Ltd.*, [1958] 3 All E.R. 689 (C.A.), *per* Jenkins L.J.

[480] See, for example, Mayson, S.W., French, D. & Ryan, C.L. *Company Law* (London: Blackstone, 1998-99) at 611, and in the first edition of this work, at paras. 9.226 and 9.229.

[481] *Re Unisoft Group Ltd. (No. 3)*, [1994] 1 B.C.L.C. 609 (Ch.) at 611; see also *Maple Leaf Foods Inc. v. Schneider Corp.*, [1998] O.J. No. 4142, 42 O.R. (3d) 177 (C.A.).

[482] *Sidaplex-Plastic Suppliers, Inc. v. Elta Group Inc.* [1995] O.J. No. 4048, 25 B.L.R. (2d) 179 at 184 (Gen. Div.), *per* Blair J., var'd [1998] O.J. No. 2910 (C.A.).

[483] Compare *Re Cumana Ltd.*, [1986] B.C.L.C. 430 (C.A.), *Re a Company (No. 007623 of 1984)*, [1986] B.C.L.C. 362 (Ch. D.) and *Re D.R. Chemicals Ltd.* (1989), 5 B.C.C. 39, with, for example, *Arrotta v. Avva Light Corp.*, [1995] A.J. No. 922, 34 Alta. L.R. (3d) 308 (Q.B.), [rev'd [1995] A.J. No. 1154 (C.A.). To quote Peter Gibson J. in *Re D.R. Chemicals Ltd.* above:

> I cannot conceive of a more blatant case of unfairly prejudicial conduct to a member than the unilateral and secret exercise by a director of the power of allotment so as to increase his own shareholding from 60 per cent to 96 per cent and to reduce the other member's holding thereby from 40 per cent to four per cent.

[484] See also *Re Saul D. Harrison & Sons plc*, [1995] 1 B.C.L.C. 14 (C.A.), but compare *Re London School of Electronics Ltd.*, [1986] Ch. 211, and *Re Cumana Ltd.*, [1986] B.C.L.C. 430 (C.A.), with *400280 Alberta Ltd. v. Franko's Heating & Air Conditioning (1992) Ltd.*, [1995] A.J. No. 121, 26 Alta. L.R. (3d) 421 (Q.B.).

[485] Although initially rejected in England on account of the initial restriction of the remedy to situations where "some part of" the members, and not members "generally" were affected, see *Re a Company, ex p. Glossop*, [1988] 1 W.L.R. 1068, the principle has since been accepted in *Re Sam Weller Ltd.*, [1990] Ch. 682. Compare *218125 Investments Ltd. v. Patel*, [1995] A.J. No. 1222, 33 Alta. L.R. (3d) 245 (Q.B.).

[486] The position in England has been well explained by Warner J. in *Re Elgindata Ltd.*, [1991] B.C.L.C. 959 at 993-94 (Ch. D.) where he said:

> First, there will be cases where there is disagreement ... as to whether a particular managerial decision was, as a matter of commercial judgment, the right one to make, or

way a business is being run.[487] Similarly, the courts in England have decided that trivial matters should not afford relief[488] and those in Canada have found that there must be real evidence of misconduct. Mere innuendo based on simple and readily explicable irregularities is insufficient.[489]

§13.158 Although in Canada the courts have settled upon the concept of "reasonable expectations" as a basis of relief, it is one that affords little guidance to the courts because of its inherent ambiguity. In this area, it is worthwhile to refer to some of the writings of others in the field. Boros, in a comparison of English and Australian company law, has sought to distinguish between "universal" and "personal" expectations. "Universal expectations" are defined as common to all companies and equivalent to external standards of fair dealing.[490] "Personal expectations" are defined as being mutual understandings as to the way in which a corporation is to be run.[491] Goddard has referred to "a diversity of expectations", while distinguishing vital differences between shareholders in the quasi-partnership and the listed company.[492] For convenience of analysis he divides the case law on "personal" expectations into four overlapping categories: (1) participation in management; (2) the right to an investment return; (3) an interest in the status quo; and (4) corporate divorce.[493] Although this is useful there are inconsistencies to which it gives rise which are difficult to resolve, mainly surrounding (3). This is because (3) potentially encapsulates (1) and may conflict with both (2) and (4).

§13.159 A more useful approach to analysis is for expectations to be considered under the following categories: (a) expectations based on actual agreement (whether formal or informal) and (b) expectations based on current notions of commercial fair dealing as generally accepted within the business community. The reason for dropping the label of "personal" expectations is that it adds little

---

as to whether a particular proposal relating to the conduct of the company's business is commercially sound ... there can be no unfairness ... in those in control of the company's affairs taking a different view from theirs on such matters. Secondly, ... a shareholder acquires shares in a company knowing that their value will depend in some measure on the competence of the management. He takes the risk that that management may prove not to be of the highest quality. Short of a breach by a director of his duty of skill and care ... there is prima facie no unfairness to a shareholder in the quality of management turning out to be poor.

But see *Re Macro (Ipswich) Ltd.*, [1994] B.C.C. 781 (Ch. D.).
[487] *Brant Investments Ltd. v. KeepRite Inc.*, [1987] O.J. No. 574, 60 O.R. (2d) 737 (H.C.J.), per Anderson J., aff'd [1991] O.J. No. 683 (C.A.), and see generally, *Keho Holdings Ltd. v. Noble*, [1987] A.J. No. 334, 38 D.L.R. (4th) 368 (C.A.).
[488] See *Re Saul D. Harrison & Sons plc*, [1994] B.C.C. 475 at 489 (C.A.) (trivial or technical infringements of the articles); *Re Unisoft Group Ltd Ltd. (No. 2)*, [1994] B.C.C. 766 (Ch. D.) (harm in a merely emotional sense).
[489] *Cohen-Herrendorf v. Army & Navy Department Store Holdings Ltd.*, [1986] S.J. No. 848, 55 Sask. R. 134 (Q.B.).
[490] E. Boros, *Minority Shareholders Remedies* (Oxford: Oxford University Press, 1995) at 137.
[491] *Ibid.*, at 139.
[492] R. Goddard, "Enforcing the Hypothetical Bargain: Sections 459-461 of the *Companies Act 1985*" [1999] Co. Law 66 at 70.
[493] *Ibid.*, at 76-77.

when the category of expectations is limited to actual agreement. It also tends to imply the existence of an antithesis such as "universal" which is obviously over broad. If it is accepted that the true test is agreement or implicit understanding then the number of parties or their relationship becomes irrelevant. The reasons for establishing a category based on commercial fairness is because this would extend to expectations based on implied or inferred agreement.

§13.160 As noted by Mayson, French and Ryan[494] section 459-type cases are frequently time-consuming and wasteful. One unreported case[495] took up 165 days of court time. In another, costs of £320,000 were incurred in a dispute over £24,600 worth of shares.[496] Nor are such situations unique to England: during the summer of 1998, more than 40 such actions were then pending in the South West judicial region of Ontario, Canada (serving approximately 750,000 people) — which would suggest a total of more than 1000 unfair prejudice cases across Canada at that time. The trial of *Waxman v. Waxman*[497] in the Ontario Superior Court before Sanderson J. involved 165 days of discovery followed by a 200-day trial. There were 4,645 separate documents of which 338 were eventually introduced as exhibits. Some of the exhibits had as many as 400 pages. All of this evidence resulted in a 439-page judgment that awarded $50 million to Morris Waxman against his brother Chester. Thus the practical effect of imprecision has been to open the very floodgates that the courts hoped to close when they adopted the rule in *Foss v. Harbottle*.[498] To an increasing extent in the world of corporate litigation, the courts have been thrust into an apparently bottomless inquiry into the minute details of the day-to-day operations of individual corporation, frequently encompassing every manner of petty grievance and disappointment.

§13.161 As noted above, the law is often called upon to draw a difficult balance between competing desires to provide remedies that are flexible and certain. Few would argue that the law does not need to be certain. People need to be able to determine their rights and obligations, and to govern their behaviour accordingly. There is nothing inherently wrong with the concept of judicial discretion as such. Indeed, it is difficult to see how the law could operate in many types of case other than by conferring a discretion upon the judiciary — particularly where the intent is to create a completely new remedy, as was the case when the oppression remedy was introduced. However, once the relevant issues and range of potential problems were refined through practical experience, it obviously was no longer desirable to offer no clear guidance to the courts as to how discretion ought to be exercised. After 30 years and hundreds of reported cases across the Commonwealth, the legislature should now be able to do better.

---

[494] *Company Law* (London: Blackstone, 1998-99 ed.) 587.
[495] *Re Freudiana Music Co.*, March 24, 1993, *per* Parker J. (unreported).
[496] *Re Elgindata Ltd.*, [1991] B.C.L.C. 959; see also: *Re Macro (Ipswich) Ltd.*, [1994] 2 B.C.L.C. 354 (costs totalling between £1 and £2 million).
[497] [2002] O.J. No. 2528, 25 B.L.R. (3d) 1 (S.C.J.), var'd [2004] O.J. No. 1765 (C.A.), leave to appeal to S.C.C. refused [2004] S.C.C.A. No. 291.
[498] (1843), 2 Hare 461, 67 E.R. 189.

§13.162 Except in very unusual cases, an *ad hoc* system of justice is not satisfactory. No clear case exists for retaining such a regime with respect to oppression. On the contrary, in the contract context and particularly where investment decisions are concerned, it is generally accepted that uniformity and predictability are two essential elements of the law, particularly with respect to commercial matters.[499] Business people and their advisors need to be able to determine the probable outcome of legal disputes without going through the expense and delay of a trial or arbitration. Unless predictability exists, risk cannot be properly weighed and consequently investments cannot properly be priced. Much as great flexibility may once have been essential in the case of the oppression remedy, in order to allow the law to develop, there can be no excuse for uncertainty where the area of law in question has been extensively litigated over a period of 25 years.

§13.163 It is becoming increasingly clear that sections 248 of the OBCA and 241 of the CBCA need to be redrafted to give sufficient guidance to the courts and to parties affected by legislation as to the manner in which the discretion is to be exercised. A range of options are open. The simplest would be to provide a narrowly defined ground for relief, similar to that originally provided under section 210 of the original UK legislation. However, given the experience under that provision, such an approach would need to be very carefully applied. A second option would be to put forward an exhaustive list of facts that the court should consider. In practice, it would be difficult to identify an all-encompassing list of considerations.

§13.164 A third option is to put forward a clear indicative list of grounds for relief, coupled perhaps with an equally indicative list of considerations that should not afford relief. Some discretion might be left to the judiciary to tailor general principles to the facts of particular cases. However, the exercise of that discretion is focused by way of clear principle. Broadly speaking, it is this third option that seems best. Past case law could provide a very useful guide to the legislature in identifying the general considerations that should be taken into account by the courts. The proposed list must be sufficiently detailed and conceptualized so that it provides a clear indication of the types of conduct that give rise to relief. Such a degree of certainty is not possible unless there is a clear overall purpose of the legislation (encompassing both its specific objectives and the theoretical foundation on which it is based). When the oppression remedy was first enacted, flexibility may have been necessary even at the expense of certainty, because of the desire to allow the courts the opportunity to explore the new principles that it enshrined. Today, such flexibility is surely no longer required. The time has come to move back towards a more certain regime.

---

[499] *Maredelanto Compania Naviera S.A. v. Bergbau-Handel Gmbh, The Mihalis Angelos*, [1971] 1 Q.B. 164 at 205 (C.A.), *per* Megaw L.J.

C. INSOLVENCY AND RELATED CONCERNS

(i) General Rules Regarding Claims by a Shareholder

§13.165 Not infrequently, a shareholder will be entitled to a cause of action against the corporation in which he or she owns shares. Ordinarily, any such claim may be enforced by the shareholder as if he or she were a stranger to the corporation. As discussed in Chapter 1, since the decision of the House of Lords in *Salomon v. Salomon*,[500] it has been settled law in common law jurisdictions that the shareholders of a corporation (including an individual who has complete control of the corporation) are not as such liable for the debts or other legal obligations of the corporation. This is known as the principle of limited liability. It is also settled law that a corporation and its shareholder(s) are separate legal persons, and that they may enter into a binding legal contract with each other. Specifically at issue in the *Salomon* case was the question of whether a debenture granted to a controlling shareholder of a company was valid and enforceable by that shareholder against that company, to the detriment (in view of the insolvency of the company). It was held that the debenture was enforceable, even though the effect was that the general creditors of the company would go unpaid.

§13.166 Under Canadian bankruptcy and insolvency law, certain transactions entered into between a corporate insolvent and a person who is not at arm's length to that insolvent may be open to the possibility of successful attack. Generally speaking, however, these transactions are limited in scope, and except where it is possible to come within the clear wording of the provisions in question, the general rule in Canadian corporate insolvency is that the *Salomon* case remains good law. Looking at the relevant provisions in question: Subsection 3(1) of the *Bankruptcy and Insolvency Act* (BIA) provides that:

> For the purposes of this Act, a person who has entered into a transaction with another person otherwise than at arm's length shall be deemed to have entered into a reviewable transaction.[501]

By virtue of section 4 of the Act, the controlling shareholder of a corporation is a related person of the corporation, as is an affiliated (sister) corporation. Subsection 137(1) of the BIA provides that:

---

[500] [1897] A.C. 22 (H.L.). In that case, appellant, Aron Salomon, had transferred his boot cmpany to a joint stock company, taking back shares and a debenture for the value of the business transferred. In accordance with the business transfer arrangement, 100 debentures, with a face value of £100 each, were issued to the appellant. Subsequently, the appellant pledged the debentures as security for an advance of £5000 from Edmund Broderip, and shortly thereafter the original debentures were returned to the company and cancelled; and in lieu thereof, with the consent of the appellant as beneficial owner, fresh debentures to the same amount were issued to Broderip, in order to secure the repayment of the loan to Salomon. After the failure of the joint stock company, Broderip instituted an action in order to enforce his security against the assets of the company. The company then came into liquidation, and the liquidator (appointed at the instance of unsecured creditors of the company) filed a defence in the debenture holder action on behalf of the company, essentially to have the debentures rescinded.

[501] R.S.C. 1985, c. B-3.

A creditor who entered into a reviewable transaction with a debtor *at any time prior* to the bankruptcy of the debtor is not entitled to claim a dividend in respect of a claim arising out of that transaction until all claims of the other creditors have been satisfied unless the transaction was in the opinion of the trustee or of the court a proper transaction.

§13.167 Under subsection 137(1), the remedy of postponement is a legal one, granted as of right, rather than an equitable, discretionary one. Section 137 is not limited to cases where there is conspicuous difference between fair market value and consideration paid for the subject matter of the impugned transaction. There is no time limit on the provision: the reviewable transaction is to be postponed even if entered into at a time when the corporation was perfectly solvent, and even if all of the current creditors of the corporation became creditors after the date on which the reviewable transaction took place.

§13.168 Nevertheless, the wording of subsection 137(1) considerably limits the scope of the protection available. By its terms, the provision applies only with respect to the claiming of a dividend. It does not apply with respect to other methods by which a creditor may obtain payment, as for instance by way of the enforcement of security. The general rule is that secured creditors operate outside the ambit of the *Bankruptcy and Insolvency Act*.

§13.169 Section 100 of the BIA permits certain consummated reviewable transactions (*i.e.* transactions in which the consideration is fully executed by the date of bankruptcy) to be reviewed. Specifically, subsection 100(1) provides:

> Where a bankrupt sold, purchased, leased, hired, supplied or received property or services in a reviewable transaction within the period beginning on the day that is one year before the date of the initial bankruptcy event and ending on the date of the bankruptcy, both dates included, the court may, on the application of the trustee, inquire into whether the bankrupt gave or received, as the case may be, fair market value in consideration for the property or services concerned in the transaction.

Where the court in proceedings under this section finds that the consideration given or received by the bankrupt in the reviewable transaction was *conspicuously greater or less* than the fair market value of the property or services concerned in the transaction, the court may give judgment to the trustee against the other party to the transaction, against any other person being privy to the transaction with the bankrupt or against all those persons for the difference between the actual consideration given or received by the bankrupt and the fair market value, as determined by the court, of the property or services concerned in the transaction.[502] Absent a finding of such a conspicuous difference in value, relief is not available.[503] In *Trustee of Standard Trustco Ltd. v. Standard Trust Co.*,[504] Weiler J. held that, even if the necessary preconditions set out in the subsections

---

[502] BIA, s. 100(2).
[503] *Trustee of Peoples Department Stores Inc. v. Wise*, [2004] S.C.J. No. 64, [2004] 3 S.C.R. 461.
[504] [1995] O.J. No. 3151, 26 O.R. (3d) 1 (C.A.), approved in *Trustee of Peoples Department Stores Inc. v. Wise* [2004] S.C.J. No. 64, [2004] 3 S.C.R. 461.

are present, the exercise of jurisdiction is discretionary and must be guided by equitable principles.

When a contextual approach is adopted it is apparent that although the conditions of the section have been satisfied the court is not obliged to grant judgment. The court has a residual discretion to exercise. The contextual approach indicates that the good faith of the parties, the intention with which the transaction took place, and whether fair value was given and received in the transaction are important considerations as to whether that discretion should be exercised.[505]

§13.170 Related party transactions may also be open to possible attack under section 139 of the *BIA*. It provides:

Where a lender advances money to a borrower engaged or about to engage in trade or business under a contract with the borrower that the lender shall receive a rate of interest varying with the profits or shall receive a share of the profits arising from carrying on the trade or business, and the borrower subsequently becomes bankrupt, the lender of the money is not entitled to recover anything in respect of the loan until the claims of all other creditors of the borrower have been satisfied.

It will be noted that this section is of relatively narrow scope. In order for section 139 to apply, there must be "a contract with the borrower" providing that the lender will "receive a rate of interest varying with the profits or receive a share of the profits". Without such an arrangement, there is no basis on which the section can be applied. This is unfortunate, because as a general rule, the various arrangements under which a shareholder (or other control group within a company) can strip the profits out of a company will be informal in nature, and may not directly relate to the making of a loan at all. Nevertheless, in *Sukloff v. A.H. Rushforth & Co. Estate*,[506] the court gave a broad reading to this provision, and adopted[507] the following statement:

If a person advances money to another not by way of loan but as a contribution to the capital of a business carried on for their joint benefit, the person who has made the advance, even though he is not a partner in the business and has received no share of the profits as such, is debarred from proving in the bankruptcy of the recipient of the money in competition with the creditors of the business.[508]

§13.171 Section 139 is sometimes described as the "silent partner" provision, but this is misleading. The general rule with respect to the liability of a partner in a business — silent or otherwise — is provided for in subsection 10(1) of the *Partnerships Act*,[509] which reads:

Except as provided in subsection (2), every partner in a firm is liable jointly with the other partners for all debts and obligations of the firm incurred while the person is a partner, and after the partner's death the partner's estate is also severally liable in a due course of administration for such debts and obligations so far as

---

[505] *Standard Trust Co.*, *ibid.*, at 23.
[506] [1964] S.C.J. No. 26, [1964] S.C.R. 459.
[507] *Ibid.*, at 467.
[508] Halsbury's Laws of England (3rd ed.), vol. 2 at 495.
[509] R.S.O. 1990, c. P.5.

they remain unsatisfied, but subject to the prior payment of his or her separate debts.

A person who is not a partner is not so liable, even if that person and the insolvent debtor are carrying on an integrated (but separate) commercial operation. So, for instance, in *Lester & Orpen Dennys Ltd. v. Canadian Broadcasting Corp.*,[510] it was held that a joint venturer who is owed money by another as a result of the success of the joint venture is a creditor of rather than an equity holder in the second joint venturer.

§13.172 A person who wishes to invest in a corporation may advance capital to the corporation or for its benefit either as a loan or in the form of equity.[511] In mezzanine financing (*e.g.*, a subordinated debenture), the investment possesses mixed features of both equity and debt. In such cases, the question whether the agreement between the parties creates a relationship of debtor and creditor on the one hand or the acquisition of an equity interest is one of mixed fact and law, but in resolving this question the courts pay considerable attention to the form in which the investment is made.[512] In general, the law will respect both the form of the investment and the terms in which it is structured.[513]

§13.173 A shareholder may also take a security interest against property of a corporation, to secure a debt or other obligation that is owed to the corporation. Historically, the courts have taken the position that such a security will be respected to the same extent as it would be respected were it granted to a person at arm's length to the corporation. The security interest may not, of course, constitute a fraudulent conveyance or preference, and all requirements as to perfection must be satisfied. Provided these steps are taken, however, the security will normally be effective. As Clark J. observed in *Swager v. Couri*:

> What may at first blush appear to constitute the misuse of the corporate form as a device to defraud the unwary, may also, on closer inspection, be revealed to involve more subtle questions of the scope of the concept of 'limited liability' as it applies to investors and managers of closely held corporations; and of the duties and reasonable expectations of persons negotiating arm's-length agreements in the robust environment of daily commercial life.[514]

§13.174 From a policy perspective, doubts are sometimes raised regarding the fairness of permitting shareholders to acquire a security interest, when applied to shareholders who are in a position to control the business and affairs of the

---

[510] [1991] O.J. No. 1399, 6 C.B.R. (3d) 238 (Gen. Div.).
[511] When dealing with thinly capitalized corporations, the courts have not been especially receptive to the argument that shareholder guarantees constitute an alternative to shareholder investment in risk capital — presumably because such guarantees will generally be targeted on a single creditor. See, generally, *State Dep't of Revenue v. Acker*, 636 So.2d 470 (Ala. Civ. App. 1994).
[512] See, for example, *Transport North American Express Inc. v. New Solutions Financial Corp.*, [2001] O.J. No. 1948, 54 O.R. (3d) 144 (S.C.J.), *per* Cullity J., rev'd [2002] O.J. No. 2335 (C.A.), rev'd [2004] S.C.J. No. 9.
[513] See, generally, *Re Central Capital Corp.*, [1996] O.J. No. 359, 27 O.R. (3d) 494, 132 D.L.R. (4th) 223 (C.A.).
[514] 77 Ill. 2d 173, 395 N.E.2d 921 (S.C. Ill. 1979).

corporation. If the approach is applied mechanically, it becomes possible for the shareholders of a corporation to structure a business so that the shareholders are entitled to enjoy whatever profits it may generate, while assuming no (or a very limited) risk of loss should the business fail. Some justification may exist for adopting a mechanical approach in the case of creditors who voluntarily choose to enter into business with a corporation.[515] If they do not know that the corporation is little more than straw, they do at least have the means of determining whether this is the case. If in such circumstances a creditor decides to enter into a contract or other business dealing with the corporation, the creditor may be said to have assumed the risk that the corporation will not be able to honour its obligations. However, there are many classes of potential claimant against a corporation who do not fall in this class. In particular, a corporation may have a number of involuntary creditors. These include:

- various branches of the government, when acting
  - as a taxing authority or insurer;[516]
  - in a quasi fiduciary capacity on behalf of the public generally (as, for instance, for the remedy of a public nuisance or environmental damage); or
  - on behalf of some segment of the public (*e.g.*, claims on behalf of workers); and
- tort victims and victims of breach of trust and similar wrongdoing.

It cannot be said with respect to such "involuntary" claims that the grant of security to the shareholder has been implicitly accepted by the creditor.

(ii) Equity Claims Should Not be Treated as Debt Claims

§13.175 American courts have given fairly extensive consideration to the question of whether a shareholder may claim against a corporation for wrongdoing, so as to elevate what is effectively a claim for the recovery of amounts invested in share capital into a claim for tort (or some other cause) that would allow the shareholder to rank on an equal footing with the general unsecured claims of an insolvent corporation. Not surprisingly, the courts have not been especially receptive to such efforts. In *Re Stirling Homex Corporation*,[517] the court stated that where a debtor company is insolvent, the equities favour its non-shareholder general creditors rather than its shareholders (even if defrauded), since the real party against which the shareholders are seeking relief is the general creditors, whose percentage dividend (*i.e.*, the extent of the realization) will be reduced to the extent that any relief is given to the shareholders. However, the court quoted the following passage from the decision of the court in *Newton National Bank v. Newbegin*:

---

[515] *Swager v. Couri*, 77 Ill. 2d 173, 395 N.E.2d 921 (S.C. Ill. 1979).
[516] A concern that was rejected (in the absence of sanctioning legislation) in one widely cited American case with respect to a claim by a workers' compensation fund: *Johnson v. Bialick State Treasurer, Custodian of Special Compensation Fund*, 294 Minn. 231; 200 N.W.2d 172 (S.C. Minn. 1972).
[517] 579 F.2d 206 at 213 (2d Cir. 1978).

When a corporation becomes bankrupt, the temptation to lay aside the garb of a stockholder, on one pretense or another, and to assume the role of creditor, is very strong, and all attempts of that kind should be viewed with suspicion.[518]

§13.176 In *Re U.S. Financial Incorporated*,[519] the court followed a different approach, suggesting that shareholder claims for fraud should be postponed to the claims of the general creditors, on the grounds that in making an equity investment, the shareholders voluntarily agreed to assume the higher level of risk associated with such an investment. A similar line of reasoning was followed in *Re THC Financial*,[520] where the court concluded that claims of defrauded shareholders must be subordinated to the claims of the general creditors, and noted that the claimant shareholders had bargained for equity-type profits and equity-type risks in purchasing their shares.

(iii) Is Equitable Subordination Part of Canadian Law

§13.177 Having considered the subject of shareholder claims in the event of an insolvency, and also the subject of the oppression remedy, we will now proceed to tie these two areas of the law together, by discussing whether the doctrine of equitable subordination may be incorporated into Canadian insolvency law, under the oppression remedy. The term "equitable subordination" describes a principle of insolvency law under which the courts will exercise an equitable jurisdiction to,

- subordinate a security interest granted to one creditor, or
- postpone the claim of a creditor,

to the claims of some other creditor(s) against an insolvent estate, on the ground that it would be inequitable in the circumstances to give effect to that security interest to the prejudice of those other creditors, or to rank the claim of the creditor whose claim is so subordinated on an equal footing with the claims of those other creditors.

§13.178 In "Equitable Subordination of Claims in Canadian Bankruptcy Law",[521] L.J. Crozier argued that equitable subordination formed (or ought to form) an integral part of Canadian insolvency law. Such suggestions have been raised in a number of cases, but so far with only partial success.[522] In *Canada Deposit Insurance Corp. v. Canadian Commercial Bank*, the Supreme Court of Canada left open the possibility that equitable subordination might form a part of Canadian

---

[518] 74 F. (3rd) 135 at 140 (8th Cir. 1986).
[519] 648 F.2d 515 (9th Cir. 1980).
[520] 679 F.2d 784 (9th Cir. 1982).
[521] (1992), 7 C.B.R. (3d) 40.
[522] See, generally, *Canada Deposit Insurance Corp. v. Canadian Commercial Bank*, [1992] S.C.J. No. 96, [1992] 3 S.C.R. 558; *Olympia & York Development Ltd. v. Royal Trust Co.*, [1993] O.J. No. 1510, 103 D.L.R. (4th) 129 (C.A.); *Bulut v. City of Brampton*, [2000] O.J. No. 1062, 48 O.R. (3d) 108 (C.A.), leave to appeal to S.C.C. refused [2000] S.C.C.A. No. 259; *AEVO Co. v. D & A Macleod Co.*, [1991] O.J. No. 1354, 7 C.B.R. (3d) 33, 4 O.R. (3d) 368 (Gen. Div.); *Pioneer Distributors Ltd. v. Bank of Montreal*, [1995] B.C.J. No. 2093, [1995] 1 W.W.R. 48 (B.C.S.C.).

insolvency law (although it held that there was no basis for awarding this remedy on the facts of that case). The Ontario Court of Appeal did the same in *Olympia & York Development Ltd. v. Royal Trust Co.*[523] In *C.C. Petroleum v. Allen*,[524] O'Driscoll J. applied equitable subordination against a shareholder security interest, where there was evidence of fraud. There are cases in which it has been suggested that security interests may be subordinated in equity to the claims (secured or otherwise) of other creditors where necessary to achieve a just result among the parties.[525] It follows that there is a growing number of Canadian case law in which the availability of equitable subordination or equivalent remedies has been recognized to be available in an insolvency.[526] This case law suggest that equitable subordination is an extraordinary remedy that may be employed in cases where there is some misconduct on the part of the person against whom it is claimed.

§13.179 The limited case law that does exist makes clear that a person seeking equitable subordination as a remedy must demonstrate on "very persuasive" grounds supported by proper evidence that an equity-based rearrangement of priority is essential to prevent an obvious injustice. It is, in other words, exceptional relief. The general rule is that the statutory scheme of distribution in the *Bankruptcy and Insolvency Act* is paramount, and if it is to be interfered with, it should only be in clear cases where it would be demonstrably inequitable to apply that scheme.[527]

§13.180 The first step toward providing a basis on which the concept of equitable subordination might be employed would to provide a firm statement of principle to guide the court as to when relief should be granted. Such a statement must explain the basis upon which such a remedy may be granted, and the principles that limit the extent of relief available. In this section, we will consider the extent to which the remedy of equitable subordination may be available under the oppression provisions of the OBCA and CBCA. The thesis underlying the following analysis is that the principles underlying the oppression remedy are fundamentally the same as those that govern equitable subordination in the United States. Accordingly, an argument can be made that a Canadian court may award such relief under the authority of subsection 248(3) of the OBCA — and equivalent provisions in other jurisdictions — to make any order fit where oppression, unjust prejudice or unfair disregard are shown.

---

[523] *Ibid.* See also *Re Christian Brothers of Ireland*, [2004] O.J. No. 359, 69 O.R. (3d) 507 (S.C.J.).
[524] [2002] O.J. No. 2203, 35 C.B.R. (4th) 22 (S.C.J.), var'd [2003] O.J. No. 3726 (C.A.).
[525] See, for instance, *JP Morgan Chase Bank v. Mystras Maritime Corp.*, [2005] F.C.J. No. 1129, 275 F.T.R. 159 (F.C.), per Morneau, Prothonotary, var'd [2006] F.C.J. No. 503 (F.C.); *Royal Bank of Scotland plc v. The Golden Trinity*, [2004] F.C.J. No. 992.
[526] See, for instance, *Krumm v. McKay*, [2003] A.J. No. 724, [2004] Alta. D.J. 63 (Q.B.); *C.C. Petroleum Ltd. v. Allen*, [2002] O.J. No. 2203, 26 B.L.R. (3d) 47 (S.C.J. — C.L.), [2000] A.J. No. 14; *National Bank of Canada v. Merit Energy Ltd.*, [2001] A.J. No. 918, 28 C.B.R. (4th) 228, (Alta. Q.B.); *Re Blue Range Resource Corp.*, [2000] A.J. No. 14, 15 C.B.R. (4th) 169 (Q.B.).
[527] *National Bank of Canada v. Merit Energy Ltd.*, [2001] Alta. D.J. 1129 (Q.B.), per LoVecchio J. at para. 102.

(1) Origin of Equitable Subordination

§13.181 The present law governing equitable subordination in the United States is founded upon specific statutory authority. In particular, clause 510(c) of the *Bankruptcy Code*[528] provides that a bankruptcy court may, "under principles of equitable subordination, subordinate for purposes of distribution all or part of an allowed claim to all or part of another allowed claim". However, the remedy of equitable subordination evolved first in the case law, and can be traced back in the United States to the decision of the United States Supreme Court in *Pepper v. Litton*.[529] In that case, the Supreme Court held[530] that the mere fact that a shareholder has a claim against the bankrupt company does not mean that the claim must rank on an equal footing with the claims of other creditors. Depending upon the circumstances of the case, the subordination of that claim may be necessitated by principles of equity.

§13.182 The U.S. *Bankruptcy Code* gives little explanation as to how the remedy of equitable subordination is to be applied. However, in *United States v. Noland*,[531] the Supreme Court made clear that in applying section 510, courts should first refer to the body of judge-made law governing equitable subordination as it existed prior to 1978 when the statutory provision was enacted. That body of law may then be brought up to date in light of changing circumstances, as section 510(c) allows the courts "to tweak pre-existing equitable principles and to develop new ones".[532]

§13.183 American case law makes clear that equitable subordination is usually employed to subordinate the claims against a bankrupt estate of claimants who have either directly exercised some degree of control over the affairs of the debtor or dealt directly and improperly with other creditors (*e.g.*, by making misleading statements). In many cases the equitably subordinated creditor will have been a related party to whom the debtor has made payments or transferred property without receiving equivalent value in return.[533] For instance, if a corporate parent is both a creditor of a subsidiary and so dominates the affairs of that entity as to prejudice unfairly its other creditors, a court may grant a payment priority to those other creditors, in order to remedy this inequity. Such re-ordering of priority is known as equitable subordination.[534]

(2) Oppressive Conduct and U.S. Equitable Subordination

§13.184 The emerging trend in American case law relating to equitable subordination is to tie the remedy to abusive conduct. This trend reverses some of the earlier case law dealing with the remedy. At one time, American courts

---

[528] 11 U.S.C.
[529] 308 U.S. 295 (1939).
[530] *Ibid.*, at 305.
[531] 517 U.S. 535 at 539 (1996).
[532] *In Re Merrimac Paper Co.*, [2005] U.S. App. LEXIS 18316 (1st cir.).
[533] *Taylor v. Standard Gas & Electric Co. (Deep Rock)*, 306 U.S. 307 (1939).
[534] *Re Owens Corning* [2005] U.S. App. LEXIS 17150 (3d Cir.)

entertaining a claim for equitable subordination adopted what is sometimes referred to as the "absolute priority" rule, under which the courts take the view the shareholders of a corporation may not receive any of the assets of an insolvent corporation until the corporation's creditors are paid in full. Under this approach, it was not necessary to show that a shareholder engaged in any inequitable conduct before granting the subordination remedy.[535] As recently as in *Re Geneva Steel Co.* the court would say:

> Under [the absolute priority rule], unsecured creditors stand ahead of investors in the receiving line and their claims must be satisfied before any investment loss is compensated.[536]

A number of lower courts adopted the view that a similar categorical "no-fault" subordination should also apply under section 510(c) with respect to claims emanating from share redemption agreements.[537]

§13.185 This absolute priority approach has now largely been rejected. In *Re Merrimac Paper Co.*,[538] Selyla Cir. J. decided that there was no "categorical rule" that claims founded on stock redemption notes are to be automatically subordinated solely on the basis of their intrinsic nature. Instead, a court could consider the grant of relief in the nature of equitable subordination, where a transaction was structured so as "to evade the debt-over-equity paradigm", or where the claim for such relief was otherwise justified "on the totality of the circumstances in the individual case". A totality of circumstances rule allows a court to consider whether oppression and analogous wrongdoing have occurred, and whether that misconduct can be attributed to the shareholders of the corporation. As a general rule, in those recent American cases in which the remedy of equitable subordination has been granted, at least one of the following three conditions has been met:

(1) the defendant has engaged in some type of inequitable conduct;

(2) the misconduct resulted in injury to the creditors of the bankrupt or conferred an unfair advantage on the claimant; and

(3) equitable subordination of the claim would not be inconsistent with the provisions of the bankruptcy statute.[539]

In one of the most widely cited authorities in this field, it was held that "inequitable conduct" for subordination purposes encompasses three general categories of misconduct:

(a) fraud, illegality, and breach of fiduciary duties;

---

[535] See, for instance, *Matthews Bros. v. Pullen*, 268 F. 827 (1st cir. 1920); *Keith v. Kilmer (In re Nat'l Piano Co.)*, 261 F. 733 (1st cir. 1919).
[536] 281 F. (3d) 1173 at 1181 (10th cir. 2002).
[537] See, e.g., *Re Main St. Brewing Co.*, 210 B.R. 662 at 665-66 (Bankr. D. Mass. 1997); *Re New Era Packaging, Inc.*, 186 B.R. 329 at 335-36 (Bankr. D. Mass. 1995).
[538] [2005] U.S. App. LEXIS 18316 (1st cir.)
[539] See *In Re Mobile Steel Co.*, 563 F.2d 692 at 700 (5th cir. 1977); *In Re Multiponics Inc.*, 622 F.2d 709 (5th cir. 1980); *Re Columbus Ave. Realty Trust*, 968 F. (2d) 1332 at 1353 (1st cir. 1992).

(b) under-capitalization; or

(c) the claimant's use of the debtor as a mere instrumentality or alter ego.[540]

Other courts have adopted a more results-oriented approach, holding that the remedy may be granted where,

> ...a fiduciary of the debtor misuses his position to the disadvantage of other creditors; those in which a third party, in effect, controls the debtor to the disadvantage of others; and those in which a third-party defrauds other creditors.[541]

Finally, in *Re Papercraft Corp.*,[542] a claim was made for equitable subordination where an insider of a corporate insolvent purchased certain debt of the insolvent at a substantial discount. Nygaard Cir. J. described the nature of equitable subordination in the following terms by stringing together a number of statements extracted from a series of opinions in other cases. This useful summary read:

> The doctrine of equitable subordination is remedial, and the goal "is to undo or to offset any inequality in the claim position of a creditor that will produce injustice or unfairness to other creditors in terms of the bankruptcy results" ... "to compensate in a manner that will permit a ... remedy to the injury that has been suffered by those [creditors] who will benefit from the subordination"... "The bankruptcy court has the power to sift the circumstances surrounding any claim to see that injustice or unfairness is not done in the administration of the bankrupt estate." The inequitable conduct may arise out of any unfair act by the creditor as long as the conduct affects the bankruptcy results of the other creditors. ... Because equitable subordination is remedial rather than penal, a claim should be equitably subordinated only to the extent necessary to offset the harm suffered by the debtor and its creditors as a result of the inequitable conduct.[543]

(3) Relating Equitable Subordination to Oppression

§13.186 It will be noted that the principles of relief discussed in the foregoing case law resemble closely many of the principles that have guided the courts in Canada in deciding whether or not to grant relief from oppression. As noted above, equitable subordination is a remedy rather than a cause of action. Where oppression, unfair prejudice or unfair disregard of interests can be shown under subsections 248(2) of the OBCA and 241(2) of the CBCA, an order for equitable subordination may be an appropriate form of remedy for the complainant to seek and for the court to grant. More specifically, clauses 248(3)(*h*) of the OBCA and 241(3)(*h*) of the CBCA permit a court in an oppression application to make an order:

> ... varying or setting aside a transaction or contract to which a corporation is a party and compensating the corporation or any other party to the transaction or contract.

---

[540] See *Fabricators, Inc. v. Technical Fabricators, Inc.*, 926 F. (2d) 1458 at 1467 (5th cir. 1991).
[541] *CTS Truss, Inc. v. FDIC*, 868 F.2d 146 at 148-49 (5th cir. 1989).
[542] 323 F.3d 228 (3d cir. 2003).
[543] *Ibid.*

These provisions would appear to confer an express statutory authority for equitable subordination in any case where the requirements of sections 241 and 248 are met.

§13.187 A key question that must be confronted when relying upon sections 241 and 248 as a basis for a claim for equitable subordination is the question of standing. As we have seen, to seek relief under either of these provisions, an applicant must fit within the definition of "complainant". Trustees-in-bankruptcy are not specifically identified as appropriate complainants for oppression relief, nor is the corporation itself a proper claimant. However, there would seem to be abundant good reason to recognize the trustee as the proper person to make an application for such relief in a bankruptcy case. It is axiomatic that the role of the trustee is to protect the creditors of the insolvent estate. To the extent that subordination would augment recovery, a grant of standing would further this purpose. In the U.S. it has been held that the availability of standing to seek equitable subordination depends upon the specific facts of each individual case. Claims for equitable subordination must be evaluated on a case-by-case basis.[544] A similar case-by-case approach governs the grant of standing to a "proper" person in Canadian oppression cases.

(4) When is the Remedy Appropriate?

§13.188 If one concludes that equitable subordination may be granted in an oppression case, the next question to decide is when such a remedy is appropriate. The requirement for oppression, unfair prejudice or unfair disregard makes clear that it is not appropriate to apply subordination to all debt claims made by a shareholder or other corporate insider against a corporation. Even a security interest granted to a shareholder or other controlling stakeholder in a corporation should not necessarily be liable to be set aside or subordinated to the claim of any other person, absent evidence of such misconduct. *Prima facie*, a shareholder may acquire a security interest from a corporation, and any such security interest will be dealt with in accordance with the general law relating to the grant of security interests.

§13.189 One possible ground affording a basis for relief by way of equitable subordination is where there has been unjust enrichment.[545] In *Banque Financiere de la Cite v. Parc (Battersea) Ltd.*,[546] Lord Hoffmann made clear that the remedy of subrogation may be employed to prevent the unjust enrichment of one creditor of an insolvent at the expense of another (provided, of course, that the requirements for unjust enrichment are present). The appropriate questions to be asked in a case concerned with a restitutionary remedy were:

---

[544] *In Re Merrimac Paper Co.*, [2005] U.S. App. LEXIS 18316 (1st. cir.).
[545] *Re Goldin*, [2002] O.T.C. Uned. 122 (Ont. S.C. in Bank.) *per* Sproat, Registrar.
[546] [1999] 1 A.C. 221 (H.L.). A similar list of factors was recently approved by the Supreme Court of Canada in *Garland v. Consumers Gas Co.*, [2004] S.C.J. 21, [2004] 1 S.C.R. 629; see also *Birmingham Midshires Mortgage Services Ltd. v. Sabherwal* (1999), 80 P. & C.R. 256 (C.A.), *per* Walker L.J.

(i) whether the defendant would be enriched at the plaintiff's expense;

(ii) whether such enrichment would be unjust; and

(iii) whether there were nevertheless reasons of policy for denying a remedy.

Point (iii) makes clear that there is no unjust enrichment merely because one person gets a benefit that another does not. Where there has been no misconduct there is no ground for complaint. On the other hand, equitable subordination would be appropriate in instances of fraud,[547] or a gross disregard for statutory restrictions or obligations to which the corporation or its insiders are subject. The remedy should also be available where a business has not been adequately capitalized to provide reasonable protection to creditors: In the case of a grossly undercapitalized business, an argument may be made that any claim by a shareholder for return of a "loan" is in substance a claim for the return of equity and is therefore one that should be subordinate to the claims of unsecured creditors.[548] In *Re Teltronics Servs., Inc.*, the court said:

> The remedy of equitable subordination must remain sufficiently flexible to deal with manifest injustice resulting from the violation of the rules of fair play .... "where ingenuity spawns unprecedented vagaries of unfairness, [bankruptcy courts] should not decline to recognize their marks, nor hesitate to turn the twilight for [offending claimants] into a new dawn for other creditors."[549]

(iv) Insolvent Trading and Oppression

§13.190 In the U.K. and many other common law jurisdictions, the directors of a company risk personal liability if a company continues trading once the company becomes insolvent. [550] Neither Canadian corporate law nor its various insolvency regimes specifically prohibit insolvent trading, nor do they impose any clear liability on directors who persist in trading even when a corporation is

---

[547] *C.C. Petroleum Ltd. v. Allen*, [2002] O.J. No. 2203, 26 B.L.R. (3d) 47 (S.C.J. — C.L.), var'd [2003] O.J. No. 3726 (C.A.), *per* O'Driscoll J.

[548] *Re Blue Range Resource Corp.*, [2000] A.J. No. 14, 15 C.B.R. (4th) 169 (Q.B.). By itself, the under-capitalization of a business has not been held to be sufficient to give rise to a remedy. *Re CTS Truss, Inc.*, 868 F.2d 146 at 148-49 (5th cir. 1989). It has been held that "while undercapitalization may indicate inequitable conduct, undercapitalization is not in itself inequitable conduct". *Re Lifschultz Fast Freight*, 132 F.3d 339 (7th cir. 1997). The court in that case adopted the idea that although low capitalization increases the risk of loss for creditors, in a transparent market with good information flows, prices (and interest rates) will fluctuate accordingly, putting the lender or investor on notice about his risk. However, the court cautioned that "Trickery upsets this logic". In particular, an insider exploitation of secret information or misrepresentation of the borrower's financial health justified equitable subordination. (*Lifschultz* at 346) In *Re Papercraft Corp.*, 323 F.3d 228 (3rd cir. 2003) it was said that:

> Although the pursuit of one's legal rights may not be grounds for equitable subordination, protracted and unjustified litigation tactics that harm the estate by causing it to incur fees may justify subordination.

[549] 29 B.R. 139 at 172 (Bankr. E.D.N.Y. 1983)

[550] See the *Insolvency Act 1986* (U.K.), c. 45, s. 214; *Secretary of State for Trade & Industry v. Taylor*, [1997] 1 W.L.R. 407, *per* Chadwick J.

hopelessly insolvent. In *USF Red Star Inc. v. 1220103 Ontario Ltd.*[551] Hawkins J. went so far as to state:

> I conclude that directors of a company may, with impunity, cause the company to order goods and services which they have no objective reason to believe the company can pay for in the absence of a preference or fraudulent activites which impair the company's ability to meet its obligations.

A strict rule against insolvent trading would be inconsistent with the *Companies' Creditors Arrangement Act*[552] and the proposal provisions of the *Bankruptcy and Insolvency Act*. Nevertheless, one must question whether the law is as clear-cut on this point as Hawkins J. seems to suggest. So long as there remains a faint hope of a company surviving and being able to continue in business, insolvent trading may be acceptable. Even so, continuing to engage in business as if all is well is at least misleading. As hope fades, continuing to place orders and receive supplies takes on a fraudulent character in the same sense as knowingly issuing an NSF cheque. At this point, even if fraud cannot be shown, there would seem to be legitimate reason to complain that the manner in which the corporation is carrying on its business is oppressive to its suppliers, or that it is at least unfairly disregarding and prejudicing their interests.

D. DERIVATIVE ACTIONS

§13.191 Provisions in the articles, by-laws or a unanimous shareholder agreement and shareholder proposals deal with pro-active shareholder involvement in corporate management, usually exercised on a before-the-fact basis. However, in many cases the shareholders will object to the manner in which the corporation's business or affairs are being conducted only after the time when a crucial decision has been made. Both the OBCA and the CBCA provide certain mechanisms for dealing with such after-the-fact objections. Derivative actions are one such mechanism.

§13.192 A derivative action is an action brought in the name or on behalf of a corporation or any of its subsidiaries, or an intervention in an action brought by or against the corporation or its subsidiary, by a shareholder or other complainant, to assert or defend rights to which the corporation or its subsidiary is entitled.[553] A good general description of the nature of such a proceeding was provided in *Santos v. Wood*,[554] in which the court said:

> The "derivative" action is so called because the rights of the plaintiff shareholders derive from the primary corporate right to redress the wrongs against it. ... The

---

[551] [2001] O.J. No. 915 at para. 30, 13 B.L.R. (3d) 295 (S.C.J.).
[552] R.S.C. 1985, c. C-36.
[553] See, generally, *Ozesezginer v. Royal Bank of Canada*, [1990] A.J. No. 24, 102 A.R. 296 (Q.B.); *Creighton Enterprises Ltd. v. Creighton Holdings Ltd.*, [1988] S.J. No. 518, 72 Sask. R. 110 (Q.B.); *Rogers v. Bank of Montreal*, [1985] B.C.J. No. 1120, 64 B.C.L.R. 63 (S.C.), aff'd [1986] B.C.J. No. 1360 (C.A.), leave to appeal to S.C.C. refused 80 N.R. 80*n*.
[554] [2005] Cal. App. Unpub. LEXIS 8996 (C.A. Calif.).

derivative action provides a means for shareholders to assert a claim of misuse of managerial power on behalf of the corporation. However, since such an action 'impinges on the managerial freedom of the directors, the law imposes certain prerequisites to the exercise of this remedy'. ... Thus before undertaking the prosecution of a derivative claim, a shareholder must first make a demand on the corporation's board of directors to consider pursuing the proposed action. ... The demand requirement may only be excused where a shareholder alleges particularized facts, specific to each director, to create a reasonable doubt that a majority of the directors could have properly exercised their independent and disinterested business judgment in responding to the demand.

As we shall see, in broad terms the above general requirements apply under both the OBCA and CBCA.

§13.193 In *Seinfeld v. Coker*,[555] Chandler Ch. discussed the current perception of the role of derivative proceedings in the corporate governance process:

> It is important for shareholders to bring derivative suits because these suits, filed after the alleged wrongdoing, operate as an *ex post* check on corporate behavior. If no incentive existed for shareholders to band together to bring these suits, they would very often not be brought. The reason is simple: for the *group* of shareholders, the benefits exceed the costs; for *individual* shareholders, the costs exceed the benefits in the vast majority of cases. When shareholder plaintiffs bring meritorious lawsuits, they deter improper behavior by similarly situated directors and managers, who want to avoid the expense of being sued and the sometimes larger reputational expense of losing in court.

A derivative action is always a class action brought or conducted in a representative capacity, and it is, therefore, binding upon all of the shareholders, rather than just the complainant.[556] Since the purpose of a derivative proceeding is to recover for any injury to the corporation, any recovery in a derivative proceeding belongs to the corporation. The shareholders may not recover individually in a derivative action.[557] Derivative actions must be distinguished from personal rights of action belonging to a shareholder. In deciding whether a particular cause of action is derivative or personal, the question to resolve is whether the essence of the action is the violation of some right of the corporation or some personal right to which the shareholder is entitled. Either one can produce a loss to the shareholder. The difference is whether the loss is suffered by the shareholder directly or by the reduction in the value of his or her shares. For instance, a claim for wrongful loss of control of a corporation is a personal action rather than a derivative claim, since it arises from a deprivation that the shareholder has suffered personally rather than by virtue of an injury to the corporation.[558] Where a shareholder seeks to recover for an alleged personal wrong, all of the

---

[555] 847 A.2d 330 at para. 7 (Del. Ch. 2000).
[556] *Hoskin v. Price Waterhouse Ltd.*, [1982] O.J. No. 3339, 37 O.R. (2d) 464 at 466 (Div. Ct.), *per* Osborne J.
[557] *In Re Wachovia Shareholders Litigation, Harbor Finance Partners v. Balloun*, [2003] NCBC 10 (N.C. Sup. Ct.).
[558] *Insight Venture Associates III, LLC v. Rampart Securities Inc. (Trustee of)*, [2005] O.J. No. 2505, 5 B.L.R. (4th) 173 (C.A.); *NPV Management Ltd. v. Anthony*, [2003] N.J. No. 194, 36 B.L.R. (3d) 204 (C.A.), leave to appeal to S.C.C. refused [2003] S.C.C.A. No. 436.

requirements of a personal claim must be established to support a private right of action. For instance, in a claim based upon negligence, it is necessary to establish that the shareholder personally was owed a duty of care, as opposed to the corporation,[559] and that foreseeable damage flowed to the shareholder personally as a result of that breach, rather than to the corporation.[560]

§13.194 It is implicit in the separate personality of the corporation that it is the appropriate party (and the only appropriate party) to bring action for wrongs done to it.[561] The shareholders' rights and benefits arising from the business of the corporation or its property are derivative. Except through the corporation, the shareholders have no direct, or even indirect, relation with a person who commits a wrong against the corporation's rights or property.

§13.195 Generally, where the "gravamen", "substance", "real character" or "true basis" of the plaintiff's claim is that the defendant caused a damage or injury to the plaintiff by reason of some wrong committed against the corporation, then the claim will be seen to be derivative in nature.[562] Derivative claims include claims based upon a loss in share value, loss of employment, loss of business opportunity, slander of title, improvident administration, failure to account, additional liability of the plaintiff under a guarantee or indemnity, breach of fiduciary or contractual duty owed to the corporation, and all other claims that may be properly characterized as "consequential" in the sense that they flowed from the damage caused to the corporation, rather than from damages, injury or loss caused to the plaintiff directly.[563] In most cases, when the loss suffered by a shareholder or other stakeholder is merely reflective of a loss suffered by the corporation itself, then the claim is derivative in nature. A decline in the value of a shareholder's shares due to some wrong committed against a corporation is a personal loss to the shareholder in question, but it is nevertheless a derivative claim, because the loss that the individual shareholder(s) suffers, is purely a reflection of the loss suffered by the corporation itself.[564]

§13.196 Where there are several shareholders in a corporation, each of them will suffer a proportionate share of the damage relative to the number of his or her shares, and each will be made whole if the corporation obtains restitution or

---

[559] *Hercules Managements Ltd. v. Ernst & Young*, [1997] S.C.J. No. 51, 146 D.L.R. (4th) 577 at 606 (S.C.C.).

[560] *Pye v. Metro Credit Union Ltd.*, [2005] P.E.I.J. No. 64, 251 Nfld. & P.E.I.R. 305 (S.C.).

[561] See, for instance, *Polar Heating Ltd. v. Banque Nationale de Paris (Canada)*, [1991] A.J. No. 248, 7 C.B.R. (3d) 45 (Q.B.); *Cinapri v. Guettler*, [1997] O.J. No. 1297, 33 B.L.R. (2d) 289 (Gen. Div.).

[562] *Rogers v. Bank of Montreal*, [1985] B.C.J. No. 1120, 64 B.C.L.R. 63 (S.C.), aff'd [1985] B.C.J. No. 1360, 9 B.C.L.R. (2d) 190 (C.A.), *per* Seaton J.A., leave to appeal to S.C.C. refused 80 N.R. 80*n*.

[563] *Alfano v. KPMG Inc.*, [2000] O.J. No. 1634, 17 C.B.R. (4th) 1 (S.C.J.); *Meditrust Healthcare Inc. v. Shoppers Drug Mart*, [2004] O.J. No. 3966 (S.C.J.); *Martin v. Goldfarb*, [1998] O.J. No. 3403, 41 O.R. (3d) 161 (C.A.); *Insight Venture Associates III, LLC v. Trustee of Rampart Securities Inc. (Trustee of)*, [2004] O.J. No. 4781, [2004] O.T.C. 1033 (S.C.J.), rev'd [2005] O.J. No. 2505, 5 B.L.R. (4th) 173 (C.A.).

[564] *Giles v. Rhind*, [2002] 4 All E.R. 977 (C.A.).

compensation from the wrongdoer. Accordingly, as a general rule, it is a sound policy to require a single action to be brought by the corporation rather than to permit separate suits by each shareholder. In logic the result is justified because the only right of the shareholders that has been infringed is a right derived through the corporation. As the shareholder-owners of the corporation have elected to conduct their business in a corporate form, they too (like the outside world) are bound to recognize its independent existence.[565] A derivative claim does not become personal to a shareholder merely by alleging that the shareholder is the victim of a conspiracy,[566] or that the motive behind the wrong to the corporation was malice toward the shareholder personally.[567]

§13.197 Despite the general rule that the shareholders have no right to enforce derivative claims, both the common law, and now the OBCA and CBCA, permit shareholders to enforce a derivative claim on behalf of the corporation in certain cases. In such a derivative proceeding, it is the corporation that is the plaintiff, despite the fact that the complainant who is granted leave to proceed with the claim is, in effect, the litigation guardian of the corporation. In permitting such actions, the law recognizes that a derivative action is a necessary device to protect shareholders against abuses by the corporation, its officers and directors, and is a suitable vehicle to ensure corporate accountability.[568] The derivative nature of the proceeding forestalls the prospect of duplicate proceedings with respect to the same cause of action. A judgment against the corporation in a derivative proceeding settles the subject matter of the dispute, much as any judgment against any other plaintiff makes the cause of the plaintiff's proceeding *res judicata*. The corporation represents the cumulative rights of all those who stand behind it.

> At law ... the corporation itself representing all those rights can alone recover for such injury. Any other rule would admit of as many suits against the wrongdoer as there were stockholders in the corporation.[569]

(i) Common Law Position

§13.198 To understand the present statutory regime relating to derivative proceedings, it is necessary first to grasp the common law rules relating to such proceedings. The rule that the corporation (and it alone) is the proper party to bring actions for wrongs done to the corporation is known as the rule in *Foss v. Harbottle*. The facts in *Foss v. Harbottle*[570] were as follows: the plaintiffs Foss and Turton were the shareholders of a company called the Victoria Park

---

[565] *Green v. Victor Talking Machine Co.*, 24 F.2d 378 at 381(2nd cir. 1928).
[566] *Brown v. Menzies Bay Timber Co.*, [1917] B.C.J. No. 7, [1917] 2 W.W.R. 658 (C.A.); see also *Ward v. Lewis*, [1955] 1 W.L.R. 9 (C.A.), *per* Denning L.J.
[567] *Green v. Victor Talking Machine Co.*, 24 F.2d 378 (2nd cir. 1928); *Ash v. I.B.M.*, 353 F.2d 491 at 494 (3d cir. 1966); *Armstrong v. Frostie*, 453 F.2d 914 (4th cir. 1971).
[568] *Cohen v. Beneficial Industrial Loan Corp.*, 337 U.S. 541 (1949).
[569] *Wells v. Dane*, 101 Me. 67, 63 A. 324 (1905); *E.K. Buck Retail Stores v. Harkert*, 157 Neb. 867, 62 N.W.2d 288 (Neb. S.C.) 1954.
[570] (1843), 2 Hare 461, 67 E.R. 189 (V.C.).

Company, that was formed to buy land for use as a pleasure park. The defendants were the other directors and shareholders of the company. The plaintiffs alleged that the defendants had defrauded the company in various ways. In particular, they complained that certain of the defendants had sold land belonging to them to the company at an exorbitant price. The plaintiffs sued to compel the defendants to make good the losses to the corporation. In dismissing the plaintiff's action, Wigram V.C. held that since the corporation was still in existence and it was still possible to call a general meeting of the company, there was nothing to prevent the company from dealing with the matter.[571] Therefore, the plaintiffs' action was not sustainable.[572]

§13.199 The decision in *Foss v. Harbottle* ultimately became the foundation for an enormous body of case law. As is often true, however, the specific terms of the rule are not especially well articulated in the eponymous case itself. Instead, the classic statement of the rule in *Foss v. Harbottle* may be found in the judgment of Jenkins L.J. in *Edwards v. Halliwell*:

> First, the proper plaintiff in an action in respect of a wrong alleged to be done to a company or association of persons is *prima facie* the company or association of persons itself. Secondly, where the alleged wrong is a transaction which might be made binding on the company or association and on all its members by a simple majority of the members, no individual member of the company is allowed to maintain an action in respect of that matter for the simple reason that, if a mere majority of the members of the company or association is in favour of what has been done, then *cadit quaestio*.[573]

The common law rule in *Foss v. Harbottle* seems to have been motivated by three complementary concerns on the part of the courts, namely:

- the reluctance on the part of the courts to become involved in disputes over business policy;[574]

- a belief on the part of the courts that disputes among the members of a company should be resolved by the members themselves according to the internal decision-making process provided for by statute and by the articles and memorandum of association of the company, to which all had expressly or implicitly agreed;[575]

- a fear of a multiplicity of actions.[576]

---

[571] *Ibid.*, especially at 202-203.
[572] For recent cases in which action was dismissed under the rule in *Foss v. Harbottle*, see *Cinapri v. Guettler*, [1997] O.J. No. 1297, 33 B.L.R. (2d) 289 (Gen. Div.); *Hercules Managements Ltd. v. Ernst & Young*, [1995] M.J. No. 196, 19 B.L.R. (2d) 137 (C.A.), aff'd [1997] S.C.J. No. 51.
[573] [1950] 2 All E.R. 1064 at 1066 (C.A.). See also *Burland v. Earle*, [1902] A.C. 83 at 93 (P.C.), *per* Lord Davey.
[574] *Carlen v. Drury* (1812), 1 Ves. & B. 154 at 158, 35 E.R. 61, *per* Lord Eldon: "This court is not to be required on every occasion to take the management of every playhouse and brewhouse in the Kingdom."
[575] *Mozley v. Alston* (1847), 1 Ph. 790, 41 E.R. 833 (L.C.).
[576] *MacDougall v. Gardiner* (1875), 1 Ch. D. 13 at 25 (C.A.), *per* Mellish L.J.

In England, the rationale for the Rule was reaffirmed and rearticulated by the House of Lords in *Johnson v. Gore Wood & Co.*:

> (1) Where a company suffers loss caused by a breach of duty owed to it, only the company may sue in respect of that loss. No action lies at the suit of a shareholder suing in that capacity and no other to make good a diminution in the value of the shareholder's shareholding where that merely reflects the loss suffered by the company. A claim will not lie by a shareholder to make good a loss which would be made good if the company's assets were replenished through action against the party responsible for the loss, even if the company, acting through its constitutional organs, has declined or failed to make good that loss ... (2) Where a company suffers loss but has no cause of action to sue to recover that loss, the shareholder in the company may sue in respect of it (if the shareholder has a cause of action to do so), even though the loss is a diminution in the value of the shareholding ... (3) Where a company suffers loss caused by breach of duty to it, and a shareholder suffers a loss separate and distinct from that suffered by the company caused by breach of a duty independently owed to the shareholder, each may sue to recover the loss caused to it by breach of the duty owed to it but neither may recover loss caused to the other by breach of the duty owed to that other.[577]

The scope of clause (3) of this passage was explained in *Shaker v. Al-Bedrawi*,[578] where it was held that where a claimant brings an action for an accounting against a director, not as a shareholder but as a beneficiary under a separate trust, and the director is shown to be such a trustee, the reflective loss principle does not preclude the claim even if it can be shown by the defendant that the whole of the claimed profit is reflected in what the company has lost and in which it had a cause of action to recover.[579] The rule applies not only to a corporation but also to all associations of persons such as trade unions and partnerships that carry on business as a collective.[580]

§13.200 Considered in the abstract, the rule in *Foss v. Harbottle* makes perfect sense. If the corporation is the injured party, there would seem to be no reason to permit anyone but the corporation to seek recovery for that wrong. Applying the rule raised a number of practical problems, however, where the directors held a controlling block of shares in the corporation. As Lord Denning M.R. explained:

> The rule is easy enough to apply when the company is defrauded by outsiders. The company itself is the only person who can sue. But suppose it is defrauded by insiders who control its affairs — by directors who hold a majority of shares — who

---

[577] [2001] 1 All E.R. 481, [2002] 2 A.C. 1 at 35-36, *per* Lord Bingham. See also *Gardner v. Parker*, [2004] 1 B.C.L.C. 417 (Ch.).

[578] [2002] E.W.C.A. Civ. 1452.

[579] See also: *Re Lucking's Will Trusts, Renwick v. Lucking*, [1967] 3 All E.R. 726 (Ch.). In that case the majority of shares in a private company were held by the trustees under a will. One of them was also a director of the company. He was aware that the managing director was making substantial withdrawals from the company but failed to intervene. The company was unable to recover. A beneficiary sued the trustees for breach of trust. Cross J. said: "The claim is for breach of trusts alleged to have been committed by both trustees as holders of 70 per cent of the shares in the company, not a claim against Mr. Lucking for breach of his duty to the company as one of its directors."

[580] *Lee v. Block Estates Ltd.*, [1984] B.C.J. No. 2828, [1984] 3 W.W.R. 118 at 140-41 (B.C.S.C.), *per* McEachern C.J.S.C.

can sue for damages. Those directors are the wrongdoers. If a board meeting is held, they will not authorise proceedings to be taken by the company against themselves. Yet the company is the one person who is damnified. It is the one person who could sue. In one way or another some means must be found for the company to sue. Otherwise the law would fail in its purpose. Injustice would be done without redress.[581]

The solution was the derivative proceeding, in which a claim was brought on the corporation's behalf by a stakeholder who had been victimized by the control group. In *Cohen v. Beneficial Industrial Loan Corp.*[582] Jackson J. described the role and evolution of the derivative action, in this widely quoted passage:

Equity came to the relief of the stockholder, who had no standing to bring civil action at law against faithless directors and managers. Equity, however, allowed him to step into the corporation's shoes and to seek in its right the restitution he could not demand in his own. It required him first to demand that the corporation vindicate its own rights, but when, as was usual, those who perpetrated the wrongs also were able to obstruct any remedy, equity would hear and adjudge the corporation's cause through its stockholder with the corporation as a defendant, albeit a rather nominal one. This remedy, born of stockholder helplessness, was long the chief regulator of corporate management and has afforded no small incentive to avoid at least grosser forms of betrayal of stockholders' interests. It is argued, and not without reason, that without it there would be little practical check on such abuses.

Early in the day, however, it was recognized that the benefit of derivative litigation had to be balanced against the risk of the nuisance lawsuit. Thus, did Jackson J. continue:

Unfortunately, the remedy itself provided opportunity for abuse, which was not neglected. Suits sometimes were brought not to redress real wrongs, but to realize upon their nuisance value. They were bought off by secret settlements in which any wrongs to the general body of share owners were compounded by the suing stockholder, who was mollified by payments from corporate assets. These litigations were aptly characterized in professional slang as "strike suits." And it was said that these suits were more commonly brought by small and irresponsible than by large stockholders, because the former put less to risk and a small interest was more often within the capacity and readiness of management to compromise than a large one.

The tension between denial of a right of redress (on the one hand) and the risk of frivolous claims, often in respect of personal grievances (on the other) has remained a problem in derivative proceedings to this day.

§13.201 The scope of possible derivative proceedings against errant directors and officers was explored in *Cook v. Deeks*.[583] In that case, three directors of a corporation obtained a contract in their own names to the exclusion of the corporation, under circumstances that amounted to a breach of fiduciary duty by the directors. However, since they were the holders of three-quarters of the issued

---

[581] *Wallersteiner v. Moir*, [1975] 1 Q.B. 373 at 398 (C.A.).
[582] (1949), 337 U.S. 541 at 548.
[583] [1916] 1 A.C. 554 at 564 (P.C.).

shares, they subsequently secured a resolution at a general meeting of the shareholders, declaring that the corporation had no interest in the contract. The Privy Council held that the benefit of the contract belonged in equity to the corporation, and the directors could not validly use their voting power to vest it in themselves. The rationale for this rule appeared to sit somewhere in the middle ground between the concepts of an *ultra vires* act of the corporation and a fraud upon the minority shareholders.

§13.202 The *Cook v. Deeks* type of derivative actions constituted an exception, albeit a limited one, to the internal management rule set down in *Foss v. Harbottle*[584] and related cases.[585] The courts jealously guarded the equitable remedy afforded under *Cook v. Deeks* and prevented corporations from adopting mechanisms to thwart it. For instance, the courts would not recognize the provision in the articles or by-laws of a corporation to the effect that the corporation might expropriate the shares of any shareholder who instituted or threatened any action, suit or other proceeding against the corporation or its directors, even where that right could be exercised only upon payment of the full market value of the shares of that shareholder.[586] Thus it came to be accepted that at common law (or, to be more precise, in equity) a shareholder might maintain an action for a breach of a duty owed to the corporation in certain cases, namely:

- where the complaint is that the directors or officers have caused or permitted the corporation to act *ultra vires*;[587]

- where the person or persons holding the majority of shares are using those shares to approve a fraud[588] or breach of fiduciary duty[589] committed on the company by themselves or by their associates;

- where the shareholder has been treated in an oppressive or unjust manner to his or her peculiar detriment, or to the detriment of the group of shareholders of which he or she is a member (such a group being determined on the facts of the case);[590] and

- where the complaint is about misconduct by the directors or officers, where the breach involves an infringement of an individual right.

although the normal rule was that the corporation was a necessary party to the action.[591]

---

[584] (1843), 2 Hare 461, 67 E.R. 189; see also *Mozley v. Alston* (1847), 1 Ph. 790, 41 E.R. 833.
[585] A fact noted by Lord Davey, speaking for the Privy Council, in *Burland v. Earle*, [1902] A.C. 83 (P.C.).
[586] *Hope v. International Financial Society* (1876), 4 Ch. D. 327 (C.A.).
[587] *Rose v. British Columbia Refinery Co.*, [1911] B.C.J. No. 31, 18 W.L.R. 299 at 307 (C.A.), per Irving J. (dissenting judgment).
[588] *Burrows v. Becker* (1967), 63 D.L.R. (2d) 100 at 146 (B.C.C.A.), per Tysoe J.A., aff'd [1968] S.C.J. No. 87, [1969] S.C.R. 162.
[589] *Vladi Private Islands Ltd. v. Haase*, [1990] N.S.J. No. 104, 96 N.S.R. (2d) 323, 253 A.P.R. 323 (C.A.).
[590] See, for instance, *Henderson v. Strang* (1920), 60 S.C.R. 201.
[591] *McGauley v. British Columbia*, [1989] B.C.J. No. 1699, 39 B.C.L.R. (2d) 223 (C.A.); *Plummer v. Terra Mining & Exploration Ltd.* (1974), 47 D.L.R. (3d) 268 (B.C.S.C.).

§13.203 Despite the *Cook v. Deeks* line of case law, access at common law to derivative actions was greatly restricted:[592] to bring such an action over the objection of the corporation, the shareholder was required to have exhausted all reasonable means of instituting an action in the name of the company.[593] There was no right to institute such a proceeding unless the acts were manifestly wrong (*e.g.*, fraudulent or *ultra vires*), and even then the right might be lost if the acts complained of had been ratified[594] by a disinterested majority of shareholders[595] — that is a majority of shareholders who were not implicated in the wrongdoing concerned.[596] No mere informality entitled the minority to sue, if the act when done regularly would be within the powers of the company and the intention of the majority of the shareholders is clear.[597] Furthermore, the court possessed no authority to overturn the decision of the disinterested majority[598] — a rule that applied apparently irrespective of the degree of division within the corporation or the magnitude of the loss suffered by the corporation.

(ii) The Statutory Regime

§13.204 When the CBCA came into being in 1975, one of the guiding principles underlying it was to enhance the degree of shareholder control over corporations. The need to expand the availability of derivative relief seems to have been widely accepted. It follows that the equitable rules regarding standing in this area have been supplanted by the derivative (or representative) action provisions of the OBCA and the CBCA,[599] although the common law cases are still useful in providing guidance as to the availability of relief. Both the OBCA and the CBCA contain detailed provisions on such proceedings. They have expanded upon the availability of derivative action relief, compared to its availability in equity,[600] and have introduced more precise procedural and substantive requirements that must be satisfied before such relief will become available. More particularly, subsection 246(1) of the OBCA[601] contemplates the bringing of a derivative action by certain persons having an interest in a corporation to enforce a right, claim or defence to which the corporation is entitled. It provides:

---

[592] *Fisher v. St. John Opera House Co.* (1937), 12 M.P.R. 7, [1937] 4 D.L.R. 337 at 342 (N.B.C.A.), *per* Fairweather J.
[593] *D'Amore v. McDonald*, [1973] O.J. No. 1860, [1973] 1 O.R. 845, 32 D.L.R. 543 (H.C.J.), aff'd [1973] O.J. No. 2176, 40 D.L.R. (3d) 354 (C.A.).
[594] *Prudential Assurance Co. v. Newman Industries (No. 2)*, [1982] Ch. 204 (C.A.).
[595] *Burrows v. Becker*, [1969] S.C.J. No. 87, [1969] S.C.R. 162. Such ratification was not possible in the case of *ultra vires* acts: *Charlebois v. Bienvenu*, [1967] O.J. No. 1064, 64 D.L.R. (2d) 683 at 695 (H.C.J.), *per* Fraser J., rev'd [1968] O.J. No. 217, 68 D.L.R. (2d) 578 (C.A.).
[596] *Brown v. Can-Erin Mines Ltd.*, [1960] O.J. No. 570, [1961] O.R. 9 (H.C.J.).
[597] A fact noted by Lord Davey, speaking for the Privy Council, in *Burland v. Earle*, [1902] A.C. 83 (P.C.).
[598] *Prudential Assurance Co. v. Newman Industries Ltd. (No. 2)*, [1982] Ch. 204 (C.A.).
[599] *Pasnak v. Chura*, [2003] B.C.J. No. 1591, 35 B.L.R. (3d) 71 at 86 (S.C.), *per* Truscott J., var'd [2004] B.C.J. No. 790 (C.A.).
[600] See, generally, *First Edmonton Place Ltd. v. 315888 Alberta Ltd.*, [1988] A.J. No. 511, 60 Alta. L.R. (2d) 122 (Q.B.), rev'd [1989] A.J. No. 1021 (C.A.).
[601] CBCA, s. 239(1).

246.(1) Subject to subsection (2), a complainant may apply to the court for leave to bring an action in the name and on behalf of a corporation or any of its subsidiaries, or intervene in an action to which any such body corporate is a party, for the purpose of prosecuting, defending or discontinuing the action on behalf of the body corporate.

The differences between the common law and statutory derivative action include the following:

- Common law derivative actions could be brought only by shareholders or other members of the company.[602] As discussed in the next paragraph, there is no such limited class of eligible complainant under the OBCA or CBCA.

- It is doubtful whether the common law derivative procedure permitted a complainant to intervene in a proceeding brought by a company.[603] Section 246 (and corresponding provisions in other business corporations legislation) not only authorize the initiation of a proceeding but also the intervention by a complainant in an existing proceeding, either for prosecuting it or for defending it, or to bring about its discontinuation. The possibility of a shareholder intervening to terminate a proceeding was probably included in the provision to round out its scope, where for some reason the corporation is not in a position to proceed with resolving the dispute (*e.g.*, where the corporation cannot fund a possible settlement). However, it is very difficult to imagine a situation in which a complainant should be allowed to interfere in litigation brought in good faith by the corporation in order to terminate the claim against the corporation's wishes. The normal situation in which an order will be made under section 246 of the OBCA[604] occurs when the corporation is not pursuing a claim to which it is entitled with sufficient diligence; and in nearly all cases, the reason for that lethargy is that the claim exists either against the person or persons who have effective control of the corporation or against some person who is not at arm's length to the person in effective control. An order permitting a derivative action should not be made where the corporation has instituted proceedings or authorized institution of proceedings in the matter concerned, and it seems reasonably likely that the corporation will itself diligently pursue the claim.[605]

- Under the statutory rule, the decision of the majority within the corporation is a consideration in deciding whether to permit a derivative proceeding to continue, but it is not determinative.

- Sections 247 of the OBCA and 240 of the CBCA vest the courts with a wider range of procedural controls than existed with respect to common law derivative proceedings. Potentially, this authority could be used by the courts to

---

[602] *Toronto Harbour Commissioners v. Disero*, [1991] O.J. No. 1922, 5 O.R. (3d) 585 (Gen. Div.).
[603] *Crown Trust Co. v. Ontario*, [1988] O.J. No. 225, 64 O.R. (2d) 774 (H.C.J.), per Henry J.: "Here, however, both trust companies are plaintiffs and while they remain so neither Greymac Credit nor Rosenberg have status to sue in their own names for injury done to the plaintiff companies."
[604] CBCA, s. 239.
[605] *Wheeler v. Annesley* (1957), 11 D.L.R. (2d) 573 (B.C.S.C.).

superintend such proceedings, to ensure that litigation costs do not become excessive and that corporate opportunities are not frustrated as a result of the prosecution of a derivative proceeding. However, to date the courts have not used this authority in such a manner, and it is possible that any effort by a trial court to do so might be subject to appellate review, as constituting too much interference in an adversarial proceeding.

§13.205 The statutory derivative action provisions replace the common law rules governing derivative actions, both as to availability of such relief and the procedure to be followed.[606] Derivative proceedings are available only where the applicant for leave fits within the statutory definition of the term "complainant". This term is given a broad definition in section 245 of the OBCA, where it is defined to mean:

(a) a registered holder or beneficial owner, and a former registered holder or beneficial owner, of a security of a corporation or any of its affiliates,

(b) a director or an officer or a former director or officer of a corporation or of any of its affiliates,

(c) any other person who, in the discretion of the court, is a proper person to make an application under this Part.

Thus, the definition is not exhaustive for clause (c) essentially leaves the court a good deal of discretion to permit derivative proceedings. Although the definition is not open-ended,[607] it is no longer necessary that the applicant for relief be a minority shareholder. In *Georbay Developments Inc. v. Smahel*, leave to bring a derivative action was granted to a shareholder owning 50 per cent of the shares of the corporation concerned.[608] Although the holders of securities are expressly mentioned in the definition of "complainant", creditors as such are not. A bare creditor who is not the holder of a security may be given leave to proceed as a complainant.[609] However, the courts are reluctant to convert simple debt actions into derivative claims and will not permit this to be done where the creditor's interest in the affairs of the corporation is remote or where the complaints of the creditor have nothing to do with the circumstances giving rise to the debt.[610]

---

[606] *Pasnak v. Chura*, [2004] B.C.J. No. 790, 45 B.L.R. (3d) 120 (C.A.).
[607] See, generally, *Mackenzie v. Craig*, [1998] A.J. No. 239, 171 D.L.R. (4th) 268 (C.A.).
[608] [1990] O.J. No. 111, 72 O.R. (2d) 200 (H.C.J.); see also *Liu v. Sung*, [1988] B.C.J. No. 988, 39 B.L.R. 236 (S.C.), rev'd [1991] B.C.J. No. 2291, 82 D.L.R. (4th) 283 (C.A.).
[609] Compare *First Edmonton Place Ltd. v. 315888 Alberta Ltd.*, [1988] A.J. No. 511, 60 Alta. L.R. (2d) 122 at 142-43, 156 (Q.B.), per Macdonald J., rev'd on appeal [1989] A.J. No. 1021, 45 B.L.R. 110 at 112 (C.A.), per Stevenson J.A.
[610] *Royal Trust Corp. of Canada v. Hordo*, [1993] O.J. No. 1560, 10 B.L.R. (2d) 86 at 92 (Gen. Div. — C.L.), per Farley J.; see also *Jacobs Farms Ltd. v. Jacobs*, [1992] O.J. No. 813 (QL), unreported, April 23, 1992, Doc. No. 92-CQ-17714 (Gen. Div.); *Lee v. International Consort Industries Inc.*, [1992] B.C.J. No. 106, 63 B.C.L.R. (2d) 119 at 127-29 (C.A.); *Quebec Steel Products (Industries) Ltd. v. James United Steel Ltd.*, [1969] O.J. No. 1331, [1969] 2 O.R. 349 at 351-55 (H.C.J.); *First Edmonton Place Ltd. v. 315888 Alberta Ltd.*, [1988] A.J. No. 511, 40 B.L.R. 28 (Q.B.), rev'd [1989] A.J. No. 1021, 45 B.L.R. 110 at 111-12 (C.A.); *Mohan v. Philmar Lumber (Markham) Ltd.*, [1991] O.J. No. 3451, 50 C.P.C. (2d) 164 at 165-66 (Gen. Div.).

(1) Discretionary Nature of the Remedy

§13.206 A person who fits within the definition of "complainant" does not have a right to bring, prosecute or discontinue a derivative action, but rather may be permitted to do so by the court.[611] To bring any type of derivative action it is necessary to obtain leave of the court;[612] any action instituted without such leave is a nullity[613] (for the complainant has no standing to bring it)[614] and may be struck out and any interlocutory orders made in connection with the action are ineffective.[615] Where no such leave has been obtained but an action is commenced in which personal claims and derivative claims are inextricably intertwined the action will be dismissed.[616] A derivative action may be permitted by a shareholder against a liquidator for the liquidator's maladministration of the corporation during liquidation.[617]

§13.207 The granting of leave is not automatic, but requires the court to exercise a judicial discretion. As is often the case where a judicial discretion must be exercised, it is necessary to balance two conflicting policy objectives that are at least in part contradictory. On the one hand, the practical importance of derivative proceedings in maintaining the integrity of the corporate governance process cannot be overstated and has been repeatedly recognized by the courts. Where the directors of a corporation and its controlling shareholders are acting in concert, derivative proceedings and the related possibility of an oppression will often be the only viable protection afforded by the law to remedy breaches of duty owed to the corporation. As was noted by the court in *Richardson Greenshields of Canada Ltd. v. Kalmacoff*:

> ... [A] derivative action brought by an individual shareholder on behalf of a corporation serves a dual purpose. First, it ensures that a shareholder has a right to recover property or enforce rights for the corporation if the directors refuse to do so. Second, and more important for our present purposes, it helps guarantee some degree of accountability and to ensure that control exists over the board of directors by allowing shareholders the right to bring an action against directors if they have breached their duty to the company.[618]

---

[611] See, for instance, *Archibald v. Sutherland*, [2006] B.C.J. No. 2866, 23 B.L.R. (4th) 188 (S.C.).
[612] *Farnham v. Fingold*, [1973] O.J. No. 1879, [1973] 2 O.R. 132 (C.A.).
[613] However, leave to commence a derivative proceeding may be granted *nunc pro tunc* after the commencement of the proceeding in question: *Vadeko International Inc. v. Philisophe*, [1990] O.J. No. 2010, 1 O.R. (3d) 87 at 93 (Gen. Div.), *per* Potts J.
[614] *Churchill Pulpmill Ltd. v. Manitoba*, [1977] M.J. No. 195, [1977] 3 W.W.R. 581, 24 C.B.R. (N.S.) 116 (Q.B.), rev'd on other grounds [1977] M.J. No. 4, [1977] 6 W.W.R. 109 (C.A.).
[615] *Goldex Mines Ltd. v. Revill*, [1973] O.J. No. 2107, [1973] 3 O.R. 869 (Div. Ct.), aff'd [1974] O.J. No. 2245, 54 D.L.R. (3d) 672 (C.A.). Paradoxically, the courts seem prepared to amend the style of cause where the action is commenced in the complainant's own name but the relief sought is in the nature of derivative relief: *D. & H. Holdings Ltd. v. Trinity Placentia Mall Ltd.*, [1984] N.J. No. 331, 45 Nfld. & P.E.I.R. 172, 132 A.P.R. 172 (S.C.T.D.).
[616] *Hoskin v. Price Waterhouse Ltd.*, [1982] O.J. No. 3339, 37 O.R. (2d) 464 (Div. Ct.).
[617] *Commonwealth Trust Co. v. Canada Deposit Insurance Corp.*, [1990] B.C.J. No. 920, 79 C.B.R. (N.S.) 183 (S.C.).
[618] [1995] O.J. No. 941, 18 B.L.R. (2d) 197 at 205 (C.A.), *per* Robbins J.A., leave to appeal to S.C.C. refused [1995] S.C.C.A. No. 260.

Accordingly, it has been stated frequently that the courts should not confine artificially the availability of derivative relief.

§13.208 Nevertheless, in deciding whether to grant leave, the court must also consider at least equal interest in avoiding undue interference with corporate management that is being conducted in good faith, as well as the need to avoid a multiplicity of actions. As we discussed in Chapter 11, the courts employ the business judgment rule to avoid taking on responsibility for superintending the day-to-day operation of the hundreds of thousands of corporations that are likely to carry on business in any modern economy of significant size. The business judgment rule:

> ... limits judicial review of corporate decision-making when corporate directors make business decisions on an informed basis, in good faith and in the honest belief that the action taken is in the best interests of the company. The business judgment rule shields, to a large extent, the substantive bases for a corporate decision from judicial inquiry. The business judgment rule also ensures that management remains in the hands of the board of directors and protects courts from becoming too deeply implicated in internal corporate matters.[619]

The risk with respect to the derivative action remedy is that unless the courts act carefully when dealing with applications for leave, there is a serious risk that they will end up carrying out the very type of supervisory role that the business judgment rule was intended to avoid. Almost any transaction in which a corporation may engage, and almost any decision made by its board or officers can be challenged on some basis. In a world in which conspiracy theories abound, it is always possible to find some tenuous reason to doubt the propriety of some aspect of corporate management. It is characteristic of the world of commerce that where there is a chance of profit, there is also an inevitable risk of loss. When losses occur, that fact alone is not a sufficient basis on which to suspect wrongdoing. Furthermore, to grant relief too readily would be to defeat the statutory purpose of requiring leave of the court. Corporate law vests directors, not disgruntled shareholders or the courts, with the management of the corporation.

§13.209 In deciding whether to give leave the court may take into account the apparent merit of the claim. A shareholder may not bring a derivative action where he or she has acquiesced in the conduct complained of.[620] It would not seem appropriate for the court to grant leave where the management of the corporation has made a judgment in good faith that it is not in the best interests of the corporation to pursue a particular claim — particularly where that judgment has been made by an independent committee of directors who have conscientiously reviewed the merits of the proposed claim.[621] However, the court must

---

[619] *Harhen v. Brown* (2000), 431 Mass. 838, 845, 730 N.E.2d 859 (2000).
[620] *Fullerton v. Crawford* (1919), 59 S.C.R. 314; *Henderson v. Strang* (1920), 60 S.C.R. 201.
[621] But see, generally, *Zapata Corp. v. Maldonado*, 430 A.2d 779 (S.C. Del. 1981); *Joy v. North*, 692 F.2d 880 (2nd cir. 1982), *certiorari* denied (*sub nom. Citytrust v. Joy*), 460 U.S. 1051 (1983); *Hasan v. Clevetrust Realty Investors*, 729 F.2d 372 (6th cir. 1984); *In Matter of Continental Illinois Securities Litigation*, 732 F.2d 1302 (7th cir. 1984); *cf. Aronson v. Lewis*, 473 A.2d 805 (S.C. Del. 1984).

not decide the merit of the claim before deciding whether to grant such leave.[622] The court should grant leave where the proposed action is in the shareholder's interest unless the action appears likely to be dismissed, or is frivolous, scandalous or vexatious.[623] A person is not barred from bringing a derivative proceeding by reason only of bringing an oppression proceeding in respect of the same matter. The two causes are not mutually exclusive, since each is intended to address a different class of wrong.[624]

§13.210 Leave to institute derivative proceedings will not be given on the basis of a bare allegation of liability. There must be specific allegations of wrongdoing and a disclosure of sufficient evidence that will be relied upon in proof of those allegations to convince the court that the claim has merit.[625] The pleadings must plainly evidence some interest of the corporation that is at stake. The derivative action procedure will not be permitted to operate as:

> some sort of fishing expedition ... in hope that somewhere along the line something will emerge that might assist the corporation in some way ...[626]

Because the institution of legal proceedings can have important cost implications and impose other inconveniences upon a corporation that may complicate the conduct of its business (for instance, by tying up the corporation's officers' time unnecessarily and delaying the taking of necessary measures by management), the courts repeatedly have interpreted this requirement as requiring the complainant to demonstrate that the claim has at least some merit. Put another way, the expected or potential costs of a derivative action are relevant to the question of whether or not a derivative action should be allowed to proceed.[627] However, it is not necessary for the complainant to make out a *prima facie* case before the court will make an order in the complainant's favour. So, for instance, in *Bellman v. Western Approaches Ltd.*, Nemetz C.J.B.C. concluded that it was necessary to establish only an arguable case.[628] As Cashman L.J.S.C. has explained:

> The real question here is whether in the circumstances of this case "it is *prima facie* in the interests of the company that the action be brought." ... It will be noted that the Legislature has said that it is sufficient to show that the action sought is *prima facie* in the interests of the company and does not appear to require that the applicants prove a *prima facie* case. Presumably the authors of that legislation had in mind that a minority shareholder being in a real sense on the outside is often not in a position to obtain the evidence such as that the Crown would be expected to put forward to found a *prima facie* case in a criminal matter. ...

.....

---

[622] *Commonwealth Trust Co. v. Canada Deposit Insurance Corp.*, [1990] B.C.J. No. 920, 79 C.B.R. (N.S.) 183 (S.C.).
[623] *Marc-Jay Investments Inc. v. Levy*, [1974] O.J. No. 2046, 5 O.R. (2d) 235 (H.C.J.).
[624] *Carr v. Cheng*, [2005] B.C.J. No. 664, 3 B.L.R. (4th) 5 (S.C.).
[625] See *Re Jolub Construction Ltd.*, [1993] O.J. No. 2339, 21 C.B.R. (3d) 313 (Gen. Div. in Bankruptcy); *Peddie v. Peddie*, [1996] A.J. No. 994, 38 Alta. L.R. 434 (Q.B.).
[626] *Jerry v. Gillard*, [2005] A.J. No. 104 at para. 37, 3 B.L.R. (4th) 169 at 177 (Q.B.), *per* Weston J.
[627] *Ibid.*, *per* Watson J. at 224.
[628] [1981] B.C.J. No. 1548, 33 B.C.L.R. 45 at 53-54 (C.A.).

This application decides nothing more than whether the applicant has adduced sufficient evidence which on the face of that evidence discloses that it is, so far as can be judged from the first disclosure, in the interests of the company to pursue the action.[629]

Thus, in a derivative action application under section 246 of the OBCA, it is now clear that the court should not attempt to try the case when deciding whether the requirement in clause (c) has been satisfied. Instead, the court should determine whether the proposed action has a reasonable prospect of success or is bound to fail. If it is asserted that the proposed defendants in the derivative action have a defence to the claim, the court must decide whether such a defence is bound to be accepted by the trial judge following the completion of the trial of the derivative action. It is not necessary for the complainant to show that the action will be more likely to succeed than not. However, the court should be satisfied that the potential relief in the proposed action is sufficient to justify the inconvenience to the company of being involved in the action.[630]

§13.211 A shareholder may obtain leave to bring a derivative action even if that shareholder is the only person who will benefit by it should it succeed: all other shareholders being defendants in the action.[631] However, leave to bring a derivative action will not be granted where the dispute is more correctly characterized as a contractual dispute between the applicant shareholder (or other complainant) and some other person, such as another shareholder.[632] Derivative actions are permissible only where the corporation has suffered damages,[633] or has been (or, if the proposed proceeding is for injunctive or similar relief,[634] will be) otherwise prejudiced as a result of the act for which leave is sought[635] — for instance, where a person has usurped a position as a director.[636]

§13.212 In *Breckland Group Holdings Ltd. v. London & Suffolk Properties Ltd.*[637] an action was instituted against A and others in the name of London & Suffolk Properties Ltd. A held 49 per cent of the voting shares of London & Suffolk and was a director. The remaining 51 per cent was held by another director, B. The action in question was instituted on the instructions of B. Under

---

[629] *Re Northwest Forest Products Ltd.*, [1975] B.C.J. No. 975 at paras. 61 and 67, [1975] 4 W.W.R. 724 at 735-36 (B.C.S.C.), *per* Cashman J.
[630] *Primex Investments Ltd. v. Northwest Sports Enterprises Ltd.*, [1995] B.C.J. No. 2262, 13 B.C.L.R. (3d) 300 at 315-16 (S.C.), *per* Tysoe J., var'd [1996] B.C.J. No. 2309, 26 B.C.L.R. (3d) 357 (C.A.), leave to appeal to S.C.C. refused [1997] S.C.C.A. No. 4, 143 W.A.C. 79.
[631] *Anderson v. Wittich*, [1979] O.J. No. 273, 8 B.L.R. 209 (H.C.J.); *Feld v. Glick*, [1975] O.J. No. 2251, 8 O.R. (2d) 7 at 13 (H.C.J.), *per* Morden J.
[632] *Hoffman Products Ltd. v. Karr*, [1989] O.J. No. 2280, 70 O.R. (2d) 789 at 798 (H.C.J.), *per* Chadwick J., leave to appeal refused [1990] O.J. No. 3321, 72 O.R. (2d) 797 (Div. Ct.); *Anderson v. Wittich*, [1979] O.J. No. 273, 8 B.L.R. 209 (H.C.J.).
[633] *Stankovic v. Leighton*, [1988] O.J. No. 615, 28 C.P.C. (2d) 155 (H.C.J.).
[634] *Brown v. Can-Erin Mines Ltd.*, [1961] O.J. No. 570 [1961] O.R. 9 (H.C.J.).
[635] *Johnson v. Meyer*, [1987] S.J. No. 668, 62 Sask. R. 34 at 38 (Q.B.), *per* Barclay J.; *Maxymych v. Kleinstein*, [1985] J.Q. No. 35, 12 C.L.R. 255 (S.C.); *Armstrong v. Gardner*, [1978] O.J. No. 3476, 20 O.R. (2d) 648 (H.C.J.).
[636] *Schiowitz v. I.O.S. Ltd.* (1971), 23 D.L.R. (3d) 102 (N.B.C.A.).
[637] [1989] B.C.L.C. 100.

the terms of a shareholder agreement, various matters required the approval of the two directors who represented London & Suffolk's two major shareholders. The institution of legal proceedings was one of those matters. Harman J. held that this procedural requirement could not be bypassed and that therefore the action was improper. Because provisions of the type encountered in the *Breckland* case are common in unanimous shareholder agreements, it is important to decide whether their effect is to cloak the shareholders who are entitled to withhold their consent to the institution of proceedings with a practical immunity against being sued by the corporation. A strong argument exists that where such a provision applies, the majority shareholders may seek leave to institute a derivative proceeding under the derivative proceeding remedy. On such an application, the court would necessarily have to consider the terms of the shareholder agreement, for these terms would obviously have some bearing upon the question of whether the complainant seeking leave to institute the proceeding was acting in good faith.[638] On the other hand, where there is a legitimate basis of complaint against the director/shareholder who is shielded by the contractual provision, it would clearly appear to be "in the interests of the corporation ... that the action be brought" irrespective of the procedural protection otherwise provided. Since the possibility or actuality of majority shareholder approval does not determine whether leave should be given to proceed with a derivative action,[639] *a fortiori*, the procedural safeguards built into a unanimous shareholder agreement or the articles of a corporation for the protection of a minority shareholder should not be allowed to bar derivative proceedings in a suitable case.

(2) Conditions Precedent to Relief

(a) GENERALLY

§13.213 At one time, it was unclear whether the common law relating to the institution of derivative proceedings remained valid so that it might be invoked as an alternative to the statutory remedy provided for in section 246. Most courts now seem inclined towards the view that the statutory derivative remedy is a complete code pertaining to derivative actions, so that it must be complied with in order for an applicant member to succeed.[640] Before the court grants a complainant leave to proceed, it must be satisfied that the complainant has satisfied the conditions set out in subsection 246(2) of the OBCA, which provides that no action may be brought and no intervention in an action may be made under subsection 246(1) unless the complainant has given 14 days' notice to the directors of the corporation, or its subsidiary, of the complainant's intention to apply to the court under subsection (1) and the court is satisfied that[641]

---

[638] As required by s. 246(2)(*b*) of the OBCA; s. 239(2)(*b*) of the CBCA.
[639] OBCA, s. 249(1); CBCA, s. 242(1).
[640] *LaRoche v. HARS Systems Inc.*, [2001] B.C.J. No. 217, 86 B.C.L.R. (3d) 166 at para. 88 (S.C.), *per* Hood J.
[641] See also CBCA, s. 239(2).

- the directors of the corporation or its subsidiary will not bring, diligently prosecute or defend or discontinue the action;
- the complainant is acting in good faith; and
- it appears to be in the interests of the corporation or its subsidiary that the action be brought, prosecuted, defended or discontinued.[642]

Satisfaction of these conditions is a necessary prerequisite to the bringing of a derivative claim,[643] but their satisfaction is not in itself sufficient to entitle the complainant to leave; even when these conditions have been satisfied, the court must still consider whether it is appropriate to allow the derivative action remedy in the circumstances of the case, taking into account the factors outlined above. Despite the considerable expansion in the availability of relief made by statute, the conditions precedent set out in subsection 246(2) remain similar to those that prevailed in equity.

(b) GOOD FAITH

§13.214 To obtain standing, the complainant must be acting in good faith. Good faith exists where there is a *prima facie* reason to believe that the applicant is acting with proper motives, such as a reasonable belief in its claim. The issue of good faith is ultimately a question of fact to be determined on all of the evidence and the particular circumstances of the case.[644] In *Winfield v. Daniel*[645] it was noted that the derivative action provisions require:

> ... the Court be satisfied that the complainant is acting in good faith. Good faith is said to exist where there is prima facie evidence that the complainant is acting with proper motives such as a reasonable belief in the merits of the claim. Good faith is a question of fact to be determined on the facts of each case. The typical approach by the Courts is not to attempt to define good faith but rather to analyse each set of facts for the existence of bad faith on the part of the applicant. If bad faith is found, then the requirement of good faith has not been met.

There are obvious difficulties in applying this approach. For instance, what would constitute "*prima facie*" evidence of good faith, and how exactly would such evidence be put before the court; is it sufficient for the complainant to make a self-serving declaration to this effect; if so, then what purpose does the requirement serve? A better approach would be to presume good faith, unless those who contest the institution of the derivative proceeding can establish reason to believe that the claim is not being pursued in good faith.

§13.215 Courts have taken different approaches to the demonstration of the requirement that an applicant seeking leave to institute a derivative action

---

[642] *Re Northwest Forest Products Ltd.*, [1975] B.C.J. No. 975, [1975] 4 W.W.R. 724 at 729 (B.C.S.C.), *per* Cashman L.J.S.C.
[643] *8th Street Theatre Co. v. Besenski*, [1981] S.J. No. 1026, 15 Sask. R. 182 at 185 (Q.B.), *per* Batten J.
[644] *L&B Electric Ltd. v. Oickle*, [2006] N.S.J. No. 119, 15 B.L.R. (4th) 195 (C.A.).
[645] [2004] A.J. No. 37, 352 A.R. 82 at para. 16 (Q.B.).

demonstrate that the application is brought in good faith, as required by clause 246(2)(*b*) of the OBCA.[646] In some cases, it has been held that the onus on the petitioner is a substantial one: he or she must show positively that the application is brought in good faith,[647] which suggests that it is not sufficient merely to show that the proposed action appears meritorious. In contrast, other courts have taken the view that where there appears to be an arguable cause, it will normally be presumed that the complainant is proceeding in good faith, unless there is some reason to believe that he or she is using the forum of a derivative action for an improper purpose, for example, to exact some personal advantage from the company or from those connected with its control, or is motivated by a desire to pursue a personal vendetta, by spite, by malice or by some other irrelevant personal concern.[648] As there is a general legal presumption that people act in good faith until it is proven that they have acted otherwise,[649] there would seem to be no reason not to apply such an assumption in the context of a derivative action. If such an approach were taken, the burden would fall upon the defendants to demonstrate the existence of bad faith, where the complainant made out a possibly meritorious case, for instance, by showing that the complainant did not, in fact, believe that the claim had merit[650] or was acting out of personal spite.

(c) Notice of Claim

§13.216 Subsection 246(2) of the OBCA provides that no action may be brought and no intervention in an action may be made, unless the complainant has given 14 days' notice to the directors of the corporation of the complainant's intention to apply to the court for an order permitting the complainant to pursue derivative relief. Subsection 246(3) provides that where the court is satisfied that it is not expedient to give such notice, the court may make such order as it considers fit. Under clause 246(2)(*a*), the court must be satisfied that

> the directors of the corporation or its subsidiary will not bring, diligently prosecute or defend or discontinue the action.

---

[646] *Abraham v. Prosoccer Ltd.*, [1980] O.J. No. 3876, 31 O.R. (2d) 475 (H.C.J.); see also *Vedova v. Garden House Inn Ltd.*, [1985] O.J. No. 408, 29 B.L.R. 236 (H.C.J.); *Solmon v. Elkin*, [1976] O.J. No. 1453, 3 C.P.C. 31 (H.C.J.); *Primex Investments Ltd. v. Northwest Sports Enterprises Ltd.*, [1995] B.C.J. No. 2262, 13 B.C.L.R. (3d) 300 at 311-12 (S.C.), per Tysoe J., var'd [1996] B.C.J. No. 2309, [1997] 2 W.W.R. 129 (C.A.), leave to appeal to S.C.C. refused [1997] S.C.C.A. No. 4; see also *Tremblett v. SCB Fisheries*, [1993] N.J. No. 348, 116 Nfld. & P.E.I.R. 139 at 151 (T.D.).

[647] *Tkatch v. Heide*, [1998] B.C.J. No. 2613, 29 B.L.R. (2d) 266 (S.C.), per Hutchinson J., aff'd [1998] B.C.J. No. 2613 (C.A.).

[648] See, generally, *Primex Investments Ltd. v. Northwest Sports Enterprises Ltd.*, [1995] B.C.J. No. 2262, 13 B.C.L.R. (3d) 300 (S.C.), var'd [1996] B.C.J. No. 2309, [1997] 2 W.W.R. 129 (C.A.), leave to appeal to S.C.C. refused [1997] S.C.C.A. No. 4; *Discovery Enterprises Inc. v. Ebco Industries Ltd.*, [1997] B.C.J. No. 1766, 40 B.C.L.R. (3d) 43 at 59 (S.C.), per Williams J., aff'd [1998] B.C.J. No. 1301, 50 B.C.L.R. (3d) 195 (C.A.), leave to appeal to S.C.C. refused [1998] S.C.C.A. No. 406.

[649] *General Motors of Canada Ltd. v. Brunet*, [1977] S.C.J. No. 84, [1977] 2 S.C.R. 537 at 548.

[650] See, generally, *Intercontinental Precious Metals Inc. v. Cooke*, [1993] B.C.J. No. 1903, 10 B.L.R. (2d) 203 (S.C.).

before it permits the derivative proceeding. Although section 239 of the CBCA contains corresponding provisions, they are differently organized and slightly differently worded. Specifically, subsection 239(2) provides:

> No action may be brought and no intervention in an action may be made under subsection (1) unless the court is satisfied that:
>
> (a) the complainant has given notice to the directors of the corporation or its subsidiary of the complainant's intention to apply to the court under subsection (1) not less than fourteen days before the brining of the application, or as otherwise ordered by the court, if the directors of the corporation or its subsidiary do not bring, diligently prosecute or defend or discontinue the action;
>
> (b) the complainant is acting in good faith; and
>
> (c) it appears to be in the interests of the corporation or its subsidiary that the action be brought, prosecuted, defended or discontinued.

It has been held in one case that the 14-day period provided for in clause (a) need not have expired prior to the seeking of application for leave to commence the action, provided that period has expired by the time the application for leave is heard.[651]

§13.217 The obvious purpose of the requirement for prior notice to the board of the corporation is to give the board an opportunity to decide whether or not to institute a claim in respect of an alleged wrongdoing.[652] From time to time, there are likely to be cases in which giving notice to the board of a pending derivative proceeding will serve no real purpose at all. Subsection 246(3) of the OBCA makes clear that in an appropriate case, a court may relieve altogether from the notice requirement. It provides:

> 246.(3) Where a complainant on application made without notice can establish to the satisfaction of the court that it is not expedient to give notice as required under subsection (2), the court may make such interim order as it thinks fit pending the complainant giving notice as required.

Paragraph 239(2)(a) of the CBCA is less clear, although it does indicate that the period of notice can be reduced.[653] Waiver of notice or the wholesale reduction of notice should be avoided in the absence of compelling circumstances. There are serious policy reasons for insisting upon compliance with the statutory requirements, such as the possibility that there may be valid reasons why the directors of a corporation might not wish to commence an action[654] (*e.g.*, where they have received an opinion of counsel that there is no cause of action, or that

---

[651] *Intercontinental Precious Metals Inc. v. Cooke*, [1993] B.C.J. No. 1903, 10 B.L.R. (2d) 203 at 216 (S.C.), *per* Tysoe J.
[652] As to the jurisdiction to award costs against an unsuccessful applicant for leave, see *Schafer v. International Capital Corp.*, [1997] S.J. No. 374, [1998] 4 W.W.R. 156 (C.A.).
[653] As to orders *nunc pro tunc*, see *Vadeko International Inc. v. Philosophe*, [1990] O.J. No. 2010, 1 O.R. (3d) 87 at 93 (Gen. Div.), *per* Potts J.
[654] *Schelew v. Schelew*, [2004] N.B.J. No. 330, 49 B.L.R. (3d) 68 at 76 (Q.B.), *per* Glennie J.

the costs of an action might outweigh the probable benefit, or that a defendant has no assets and is judgment proof).[655]

§13.218 Furthermore, both the OBCA and CBCA state that leave to proceed may not be given unless the court is satisfied that the directors will not bring or diligently prosecute the claim, *etc.*, it does not necessarily follow that such an order should be made merely because the directors have decided not to bring or prosecute a claim. The court must also be satisfied that it is in the interests of the corporation for a derivative claim to be brought. In assessing that question, the court should not disregard any decision made in good faith and following proper deliberation by the directors. In *Schafer v. International Capital Corp.*,[656] the court discussed the importance of a board of directors' independent decision not to pursue the litigation that is proposed for a derivative action in the following terms.

> The rule is in effect a presumption that if the directors of the corporation make an informed decision that the disadvantages outweigh the advantages of commencing the action, then this is what is in the best interests of the corporation. The decision to commence or not to commence an action is like any other business decision that is ordinarily a matter of internal management to be left to the discretion of the directors absent instruction from the shareholders. Courts seldom interfere with such intra vires discretion unless the directors are guilty of misconduct equivalent to breach of trust, or unless they stand in a dual relation which prevents an unprejudiced exercise of judgment. If there is misconduct or a dual relation then the presumption that the decision of the directors is in the best interests of the corporation will not apply.

In *United Copper Securities Co. v. Amalgamated Copper Co.*,[657] Brandeis J. explained that the prior demand requirement is an extension of the basic principle of corporate law that the directors are entitled to control over the business and affairs of a corporation in accordance with their business judgment. In a number of cases, however, the courts have held that the prior demand requirement will be excused where the circumstances render any such demand futile.[658] Except in that limited band of cases, the shareholder or other complainant must allow the corporation a reasonable time to decide whether to proceed with the action itself,[659] even where a portion of the board of directors are accused of wrongdoing.[660]

---

[655] *Pappas v. Acan Windows Inc.*, [1991] N.J. No. 164, 2 B.L.R. (2d) 180 at 206 (T.D.).
[656] [1996] S.J. No. 770, 153 Sask. R. 241 at para. 25 (Q.B.), aff'd [1997] S.J. No. 374, 152 Sask. R. 273 (C.A.).
[657] 244 U.S. 261 at 263-64 (1917).
[658] See *Winfield v. Daniel*, [2004] A.J. No. 37, 40 B.L.R. (3d) 221 at 225 (Q.B.), *per* Gallant J.; *Zapata Corp. v. Maldonado*, 430 A.2d 779 (Del. S.C. 1981); qualified by *Aronson v. Lewis*, 473 A.2d 805 (Del. S.C. 1984).
[659] *Johnson v. Meyer* (1987), 57 Sask. R. 161 at 166-67 (Q.B.), *per* Grotsky J.
[660] For instances where a derivative action was dismissed due to the complainant's failure to seek to have the corporation pursue the claim, see *Covia Canada Partnership Corp. v. PWA Corp.*, [1993] O.J. No. 1757, 105 D.L.R. (4th) 60 (Gen. Div.), aff'd [1993] O.J. No. 2685, 106 D.L.R. (4th) 608 (C.A.); *Weiller & Williams Ltd. v. Peterson*, [1993] A.J. No. 510, 11 Alta. L.R. (3d) 292 at 298 (Q.B.), *per* Veit J.

§13.219 Many American jurisdictions will take into account whether the decision with respect to the proposed litigation was made by an independent committee of directors who are not implicated in the alleged wrong that forms the basis of the complainant's application for leave. Such committees are generally known as "special litigation committees". Committees of this type may perform a variety of roles in connection with litigation, including the negotiation of a possible settlement or the approval of a settlement offer made to the corporation. Where a committee conducts a proper review of the case, and evaluates the shareholder's allegations and supporting evidence, and prepares a report recommending the termination of the derivative action after an objective and thorough investigation the committee may cause the corporation to file a pretrial motion to dismiss.[661] Independent committees thus provide a corporation with an important tool to rid itself of an unmerited, potentially costly and possibly harmful litigation.[662]

§13.220 To date there has been limited Canadian case law with respect to the role of such committees, and the deference that should be paid to their decisions, but there is at least some indication in that case law that the views of a properly functioning litigation committee will be given a proper weighting[663] in the court's ultimate decision as to whether to grant leave to proceed with the derivative claim.[664] The directors' duty to act in good faith requires that the directors' decisions be disinterested and impartial. The creation of a special committee of independent directors has been accepted by the courts as a mechanism to minimize actual or perceived conflicts of interest in considering transactions that are not at arm's length.[665] Potential derivative claims are clearly one such context.

§13.221 In the American case law, once a duly appointed committee of disinterested directors reasonably determines that it is not in the best interests of the corporation to pursue the claims asserted in the derivative action, that decision is protected by the business judgment rule. The trial court must determine, as a matter of fact, whether the committee members were disinterested and whether they conducted an adequate investigation. If it answers yes to both questions the business judgment rule would seemingly lead it to dismiss the derivative action.[666] The court is required to consider the independence, good faith, and investigative techniques of a special litigation committee. Moreover, courts are less deferential with respect to the deliberations of a special litigation committee than other aspects of the exercise of business judgment, because given their own

---

[661] *Zapata Corp. v. Maldonado*, 430 A. 2d 779 at 788 (Del. S.C. 1981).
[662] See the discussion of this role in *Curtis v. Nevins*, 31 P.3d 146 (S.C. Col. 2001).
[663] *Intercontinental Precious Metals Inc. v. Cooke*, [1993] B.C.J. No. 1903, 10 B.L.R. (2d) 203 at 221 (S.C.), *per* Tysoe J.
[664] See, for instance, *Catalyst Fund General Partner I Inc. v. Hollinger Inc.*, [2004] O.J. No. 3886, 48 B.L.R. (3d) 194 (S.C.J.).
[665] See, generally, *Greenlight Capital Inc. v. Stronach*, [2006] O.J. No. 4353 at para. 119 (S.C.J.), *per* Ground J., quoting *Cairney v. Golden Key Holdings Ltd.*, [1988] B.C.J. No. 184, 40 B.L.R. 289 at 296-98 (S.C.), *per* Houghton L.J.S.C.
[666] *Finley v. Superior Court*, 80 Cal. App. 4th 1152 at 1158 (2000).

legal training and experience, they consider themselves well qualified to review the type of investigation, analysis and exercise of business judgments that such committees are called upon to make.[667]

§13.222 A special litigation committee must consist of persons who are neither directly nor indirectly concerned in the outcome of the proceeding. The conclusion of the special litigation committee must be shown to be the result of a thorough review into the merit of the proceeding. An adequate investigation is evidenced by a "comprehensive and well documented" report.[668] The court will also consider the length and scope of the investigation, the use of experts, whether independent legal advice was obtained, whether the defendant was involved in any way in the process, and the adequacy and reliability of information supplied to the committee.[669]

§13.223 In some American jurisdictions, the special litigation committee is specifically provided for in legislation. In other American jurisdictions, the use of a special litigation committee has grown up in the case law without the underlying base of a specific legislative authority. Where there is a legislative regime, the process for evaluating the decision making process of any such committee will be governed by that statute. However, even in such cases, the reasoning followed in the case law decided in reflection of the statute often deal with a variety of concerns and considerations that would seem to be relevant to a Canadian court in deciding whether to permit a derivative proceeding to continue on the basis that it is in the best interest of the corporation to do so. On the assumption that such reasoning may be persuasive to a Canadian court, the following is a concise survey of the leading American case law with respect to the roles and limitations of special litigation committees.

§13.224 To have credibility, any internal review of the proposed derivative action carried out by the board of the corporation must be insulated from the influence of those who are alleged to have committed the wrong against the corporation, or who are sufficiently connected to them to be under suspicion.[670] A director is independent when he (or she) is in a position to base his decision on the merits of the issue, rather than being governed by extraneous considerations or influences.[671] In the succinct words of one American court:

> At bottom, the question of independence turns on whether a director is, for any substantial reason, incapable of making a decision with only the best interests of the corporation in mind.[672]

---

[667] See the discussion of this role in *Curtis v. Nevins*, 31 P.3d 146 (Col. S.C. 2001).
[668] *Kaplan v. Wyatt*, 484 A.2d 501 at 519-20 (Del. Ch. 1981), aff'd 499 A.2d 1184 (Del. S.C. 1985).
[669] See, for instance, *Drilling v. Berman*, 589 N.W.2d 503 at 509 (Minn. C.A. 1999); *Lewis v. Boyd*, 838 S.W.2d 215 at 224 (Tenn. C.A. 1992).
[670] *Biondi v. Scrushy*, 820 A.2d 1148 at 1156 (Del. Ch. 2003).
[671] *Kaplan v. Wyatt*, 499 A.2d 1184 at 1189 (Del. S.C. 1985).
[672] *Parfi Holding AB v. Mirror Image Internet, Inc.*, 794 A.2d 1211 at 1232 (Del. Ch. 2001), rev'd in part on other grounds 817 A.2d 149 (Del. S.C. 2002), *cert.* denied 123 S. Ct. 2076 (2003).

Both past relationship and existing influence may be sufficient to taint the independence of a committee member. [673]

§13.225 A special litigation committee is not intended to perform the function of a court in superintending the derivative action process, and accordingly the decisions of such a body do not prevent a court from permitting a derivative action to continue. The decision is nevertheless a highly relevant consideration for the court to take into account. Two general approaches have evolved in the United States with respect to the judicial review of the recommendations made by a special litigation approach. The older approach (also called the traditional version or the special litigation committee defence) originated in New York. Under this approach the court is required to determine as a matter of fact whether the committee's members were disinterested and whether they conducted an adequate investigation. If the court answers both questions affirmatively, it must dismiss the derivative action.[674] Under the second approach, which originated in the Delaware formulation, the court carries out an initial analysis similar to that applied under the New York rule, but then adds a second, discretionary step in which the court applies its own business judgment to the committee's conclusion.[675] In other words, the court asks whether the decision made by the committee is one that such a committee might reasonably make in the circumstances.

§13.226 As noted above, under the business judgment rule it is presumed that in making business decisions, the directors of a corporation acted on an informed basis, in good faith and in the honest belief that their actions were in the best interest of the company. A hallmark of the business judgment rule is that a court will not substitute its judgment for that of the board if the latter's decision can be "attributed to any rational business purpose".[676] Considered as an abstract principle, there is no evident reason not to extend similar respect to decisions made with regard to litigation, provided that those decisions appear on the facts to have been properly made.

§13.227 In *Will v. Engerbreston & Co.*,[677] a shareholder derivative action had been dismissed under the business judgment rule after the compensation committee appointed by the board of directors determined that it was in the best interest of the corporation to terminate the lawsuit. This ruling was reversed because the trial court had conducted only a limited review of the issue of the committee's good faith and independence when the defendants moved for summary judgment. The court noted that:

> ... absent a full hearing or trial on these issues [concerning the directors' delegation to a minority committee the authority to terminate the litigation], the derivative plaintiff may lose the one opportunity to contest the decision of the board.

---

[673] See, for instance, *Beam ex rel. Martha Stewart Omnimedia, Inc. v. Stewart*, 845 A.2d 1040 at 1051 (Del. S.C. 2004).
[674] *Auerbach v. Bennett*, 47 N.Y.2d 619, 633, 419 N.Y.S.2d 920, 393 N.E.2d 994 (1979).
[675] *Zapata Corp. v. Maldonado*, 430 A.2d 779 at 787-89 (Del. Sup. Ct. 1981).
[676] *Unocal Corp. v. Mesa Petroleum Co.*, 493 A.2d 946 at 954 (Del. S.C. 1985).
[677] 213 Cal. App. (3d) 1033 (1989).

§13.228 It seems doubtful, however, that the decision by an independent committee of directors not to pursue a proposed claim should be subject to a full trial or hearing, provided that there is credible and convincing evidence before the court hearing the motion (for leave to proceed or to dismiss) to convince the court that the committee has properly performed its responsibilities with respect to evaluation of the potential merit of the claim. In *Zapata Corp. v. Maldonado*,[678] the Delaware Supreme Court stated that a court should apply a procedural standard akin to a summary judgment inquiry when ruling on a special litigation committee's motion to terminate. The evidence in support of the motion should meet the normal burden under the Rules of Practice to satisfy the court that there is no genuine issue as to any material fact, so that the court may dismiss the motion as a matter of law. It has been noted that:

> ... this articulation of a special litigation committee's burden is an odd one, insofar as it applies a procedural standard designed for a particular purpose — the substantive dismissal of a case — with a standard centered on the determination of when a corporate committee's business decision about claims belonging to the corporation should be accepted by the court.[679]

Nevertheless, the approach has a clear attraction to it in terms of maintaining a reasonable control over potentially expensive and disruptive litigation. A ruling with respect to the derivative action should not entail a determination that the claims of the complainant are without merit, but rather whether "the court is satisfied that there is no material factual dispute that the [committee] had a reasonable basis for its decision to seek termination".[680] As the Delaware Court of Chancery noted in *Kaplan v. Wyatt*:

> It is the Special Litigation Committee which is under examination at this first-step stage of the proceedings, and not the merits of the plaintiff's cause of action.[681]

§13.229 The bulk of the case law handed down with respect to special litigations committees has focused on the independence of such committees. In *Biondi v. Scrushy* the court explained that:

> One of the obvious purposes for forming a special litigation committee is to promote confidence in the integrity of corporate decision making by vesting the company's power to respond to accusations of serious misconduct by high officials in an impartial group of independent directors. By forming a committee whose fairness and objectivity cannot be reasonably questioned ... the company can assuage concern among its stockholders and retain, through the SLC, control over any claims belonging to the company itself.[682]

Later in the judgment, the court continued:

---

[678] 430 A.2d 779 at 788-89 (Del. S.C. 1981).
[679] *In Re Oracle Corp. Derivative Litigation*, 824 A.2d 917 at fn. 19 (Del. Ch. 2003), *per* Strine J.
[680] *Ibid.*, at fn. 20.
[681] 484 A.2d 501 at 519 (Del. S.C. 1984), aff'd 499 A.2d 1184 (Del. S.C. 1985).
[682] 820 A.2d 1148 at 1156 (Del. Ch. 2003).

The composition and conduct of a special litigation committee therefore must be such as to instill confidence in the judiciary and, as important, the stockholders of the company that the committee can act with integrity and objectivity.[683]

Similarly, in *Lewis v. Fuqua*[684] the court observed:

> The value of a special litigation committee is coextensive with the extent to which that committee truly exercises business judgment. In order to ensure that special litigation committees do act for the corporation's best interest, a good deal of judicial oversight is necessary in each case. At the same time, however, courts must be careful not to usurp the committee's valuable role in exercising business judgment. At a minimum, a special litigation committee must be independent, unbiased, and act in good faith. Moreover, such a committee must conduct a thorough and careful analysis regarding the plaintiff's derivative suit ... The burden of proving that these procedural requirements have been met must rest, in all fairness, on the party capable of making that proof — the corporation.

§13.230 Tying all of the foregoing together, the critical concerns that a court should address in deciding whether a special litigation committee has reached a proper conclusion with respect to a proposed or pending derivative proceeding include the following:

(a) What, if any, involvement (including indirect influence) did the potential defendants have in the selection of the members of the committee, the choice of its legal advisors or other experts, and the process of inquiry by which the committee arrived at its decision? This is not to say that the potential defendants should be barred from presenting their side of the story. However, it must be clear that there was no serious risk of a gerrymandered process.

(b) Is it reasonably clear that the committee evaluating the proposed claim was independent of those directors or officers of the corporation who might be implicated in the claim if it was to proceed? Not particularly well handled in the American case law with respect to this area of concern is the possibility that personal relationships may influence decision making, as much as financial interest or direct involvement in the wrongful decision.[685] While a casual business relationship may not be a matter of some concern, or even a respectably distant personal relationship, any lengthy, extensive or otherwise close relationship is surely a matter for some concern. Having said that, directors are unlikely to live in isolation from each other, so as to be complete strangers. Even if their contact is limited to board meetings, some personal relationship is likely to emerge. The practical problem is to differentiate close

---

[683] *Ibid.*, at 1166.
[684] 502 A.2d 962 at 967 (Del. Ch. 1985).
[685] *Crescent/Mach I Partners, L.P. v. Turner*, [2000] Del. Ch. LEXIS 145 at para. 11(Del. Ch.), where the court stated that an allegation of a 15-year professional and personal relationship between a CEO and a director does not, in itself, raise a reasonable doubt about the director's independence; *In Re Walt Disney Co. Derivative Litigation.*, 731 A.2d 342 at 354 (Del. Ch. 1998), in which the court downplayed the risk where the "independent committee" was considering whether to sue "their family, friends and business associates". See also *Abrams v. Koether*, 766 F. Supp. 237 at 256 (D.N.J. 1991).

relationships that might influence decision making,[686] from the kind of tenuous casual contact that will occur — and connections that will almost necessarily arise — in the context of any given life in business society.[687]

(c) Is there reason to fear that the committee members might be acting to protect some hidden interest rather than the interest of the corporation and its shareholders? For instance, is there a realistic possibility that the potential defendant could influence the career prospects or business interests of the supposedly independent committee,[688] or benefit some organization in which the committee member has a material concern,[689] or is there evidence that a member of the committee is beholden or under some moral or emotional obligation to the potential defendant? Evidence of this sort would normally be expected to originate with any party contesting the motion to dismiss or refuse leave, since from an epistemological perspective, it is not realistic to impose a burden on a party to prove a negative proposition.

(d) Did the process of evaluation incorporate appropriate measures to prevent potentially implicated directors from influencing the decision with respect to the proposed litigation?

(e) Was the committee sufficiently informed to be in a position to make a reasoned decision?

(f) Was the decision not to proceed with the claim made following a reasonable investigation conducted in apparent good faith?[690]

Critical to the overall process of inquiry is the question of whether a reasonable and objective outside observer would feel confident in the circumstances that the matter had been properly dealt with by the special litigation committee. A *prima facie* conclusion that a reasonable investigation was conducted in good faith would seem merited when an independent committee made up of outside directors receives advice from legal counsel and other experts and reviews the available evidence over a reasonable period of time sufficient to allow the matter to be deliberated properly.[691] The active questioning of experts and discussion of available options, the existence of a proper record of the proceedings in question, are all factors that may be taken into account in deciding whether the conduct of reasonable investigation has occurred. In contrast, where on the balance of the information before the court, there is reason to doubt whether the matter has been properly dealt with by the special litigation committee, the derivative claim should be allowed to proceed.

---

[686] See, for instance, *Harbor Finance Partners v. Huizenga*, 751 A.2d 879 at 889 (Del. Ch. 1999) — CEO's brother-in-law could not impartially consider potential litigation against him; *Mizel v. Connelly*, [1999] Del. Ch. LEXIS 157 at para. 4 (Del. Ch.) — grandson could not impartially consider potential litigation against his grandfather.
[687] *Beam ex rel. Martha Stewart Omnimedia Inc. v. Stewart*, 845 A.2d 1040 (Del. S.C. 2004); *Seibert v. Harper & Row, Publishers, Inc.*, [1984] Del. Ch. LEXIS 523 at para. 3 (Del. Ch.).
[688] *In Re Oracle Corp. Derivative Litigation*, 824 A.2d 917 at fn. 48 (Del. Ch. 2003), *per* Strine J.
[689] See, for instance, *Lewis v. Fuqua*, 502 A.2d 962 at 966-67 (Del. Ch. 1985).
[690] *Robert M. Bass Group Inc. v. Evans*, 552 A.2d 1227 (Del. Ch. 1988).
[691] *Katz v. Chevron Corp.*, 22 Cal. App. 4th 1352 (Cal. C.A. 1994), *per* Benson J.

(3) Derivative Relief Distinguished from Oppression and Other Personal Claims

§13.231 It is important to distinguish between the shareholder's discretionary right to bring derivative proceedings on behalf of the corporation and the unqualified right of a shareholder to initiate proceedings concerning independent causes of action to which the shareholder is entitled personally against the directors. Where the complainant has suffered an injury in his or her individual capacity, he or she has a personal cause of action and, therefore, no leave is required to commence the action.[692] For instance, where the directors undertake to provide advice to shareholders, they have a duty to do so in good faith, but this duty arises under ordinary principles of law rather than any special fiduciary owed to the shareholders as such.[693] A breach of that duty would violate the personal right of the shareholder concerned, even though it relates directly to the corporation.[694] It follows that a shareholder may have a right of personal action even where the directors breach a duty that is owed to the shareholders generally. Similarly, a breach of a duty to the corporation may be coincident with a breach of some separate duty owed to the complainant or some other violation of a personal right enjoyed by the complainant.[695] For instance, the directors have a duty to be honest and not to mislead the shareholders.[696] Depending upon the circumstances, they may also be obliged to disclose material facts to the shareholders.[697] Although these are duties owed to all shareholders, they create personal rights in favour of the shareholders, and therefore it is possible for the shareholders to enforce those rights without resort to the derivative action procedures.

§13.232 As the foregoing suggests, the rights of the corporation are not exhaustive, nor do they exclude the rights of individual members.[698] If the substance of an action is the enforcement of the complainant's personal right, then the derivative action procedure provided for in section 246 is irrelevant. Where the procedure set down in that section has not been followed, it is necessary to decide whether the complainant is seeking to enforce his or her personal right or is seeking redress for the wrong done to the corporation. The distinction between a personal wrong and a wrong to the corporation can be exceedingly fine. It has been held, for instance, that an improper allotment of shares gives rise to a personal wrong against a shareholder of a corporation where the effect of that improper allotment is to dilute the shareholder's interest in the corporation;[699] so also does interference with the right of a shareholder to exercise a proxy voting

---

[692] *Zuckerman v. Zuckerman*, [1980] O.J. No. 859, 3 A.C.W.S. (2d) 168 (H.C.J.).
[693] *Dawson International plc v. Coats Patons Plc.*, [1989] B.C.L.C. 223.
[694] *Re A Company (No. 005136 of 1986)*, [1987] B.C.L.C. 82 at 84, *per* Hoffmann J., but *cf.*, *NPV Management Ltd. v. Anthony*, [2003] N.J. No. 194, 36 B.L.R. (3d) 204 (C.A.), leave to appeal to S.C.C. refused [2003] S.C.C.A. No. 436.
[695] See, for instance, *Pulbrook v. Richmond Consolidated Mining Co.* (1878), 9 Ch. D. 610 (M.R.).
[696] *Gething v. Kilner*, [1972] 1 All E.R. 1166 at 1170 (Ch.), *per* Brightman J.
[697] *Coleman v. Myers*, [1977] 2 N.Z.L.R. 225 (C.A.).
[698] *Re A Company (No. 005136 of 1986)*, [1987] B.C.L.C. 82 at 84, *per* Hoffmann J.
[699] *Residues Treatment & Trading Co. v. Southern Resources Ltd. (No. 4)* (1988), 14 A.C.L.R. 569 (S.C.S.A.).

right.[700] In contrast, in *Lee v. Chou Wen Hsien*,[701] the Privy Council held that the improper removal of a person as a director was a wrong done to the company, rather than to the director. A failure to prepare financial accounts in the form required by the *Companies Act* has also been held to be a wrong to the company rather than a personal wrong to its members.[702] Although a minority shareholder may sue for a fraud committed by the majority against the minority[703] or where the control group within the corporation has misappropriated assets of the corporation for their own benefit at the expense of the minority,[704] an individual shareholder may not sue the directors of a corporation to recover for their negligent administration of the corporation,[705] unless the shareholder has also suffered a personal loss as a result of the negligence within the common law rules governing remoteness of damage.[706] Given the uncertainty of the law in this area, counsel of prudence would be to follow the procedure set down in section 246 of the OBCA whenever a claim might involve a wrong done to the corporation rather than for the complainant who is seeking to institute the proceeding in his or her personal capacity.

§13.233 By extension from the foregoing analysis, it is necessary to distinguish among shareholder oppression, dissent and derivative action rights. The oppression and dissent remedies provided for in the OBCA and the CBCA create personal rights in favour of the shareholder. The mere fact that a shareholder has such a right (for instance, in the case of the right of dissent upon an amalgamation) is not sufficient in itself to justify a derivative action (for in the case of an amalgamation, there is no wrong to the corporation).[707] On the other hand, the fact that derivative relief is available does not in itself mean that there is no personal wrong. Quite often there will be only a fine line between personal rights of action and derivative claims. An important consideration in distinguishing a derivate claim from a personal claim may be the nature of the damage to which the claim relates. For instance, a claim for diminution in the value of shares involves a person financial loss to the shareholder; but it is a derivative claim because that loss is entirely the result of a damage that was done to the corporation.[708] In *Liu v. Sung*,[709] the 10 plaintiffs owned two-thirds of the voting

---

[700] *Pender v. Lushington* (1877), 6 Ch. D. 70.
[701] [1984] 1 W.L.R. 1202 (P.C.).
[702] *Devlin v. Slough Estates Ltd.*, [1983] B.C.L.C. 497, *per* Dillon J.
[703] *Atwool v. Merryweather* (1867), L.R. 5 Eq. 464n (V.C.); *Burland v. Earle*, [1902] A.C. 83 (P.C.); *Estmanco (Kilner House) Ltd. v. Greater London Council*, [1982] 1 W.L.R. 2, [1982] 1 All E.R. 437 (Ch.); but *cf.*, *Prudential Assurance Co. v. Newman Industries Ltd. (No. 2)*, [1982] Ch. 204 (C.A.).
[704] *Menier v. Hooper's Telegraph Works* (1874), 9 Ch. App. 350 (C.A.).
[705] *Pavlides v. Jensen*, [1956] Ch. 565; but *cf.*, *Daniels v. Daniels*, [1978] Ch. 406.
[706] *George Fisher (Great Britain) Ltd. v. Multi Construction Ltd.*, [1995] 1 B.C.L.C. 260 (C.A.); but *cf. Hurley v. BGH Nominees Pty Ltd.* (1982), 6 A.C.L.R. 791; *R.P. Howard Ltd. v. Woodman, Matthews & Co.*, [1983] B.C.L.C. 117.
[707] *Loeb v. Provigo Inc.*, [1978] O.J. No. 3455, 20 O.R. (2d) 497, 4 B.L.R. 272, 88 D.L.R. (3d) 139 (H.C.J.).
[708] See, for instance, *Meditrust Healthcare Inc. v. Shoppers Drug Mart*, [2002] O.J. No. 3891, 28 B.L.R. (3d) 163 (C.A.); *Johnson v. Gore Wood & Co.*, [2001] 1 All E.R. 481 (H.L.); *Rogers v.*

rights and half of all shares of the bankrupt broadcasting company, which was incorporated under the former British Columbia *Company Act*.[710] The plaintiffs sued in their own right and sought leave to commence a derivative action. The defendants included the directors of the company. The plaintiffs alleged a conspiracy among the directors and others to force the bankruptcy of the company, and to bring about the ultimate sale of its assets (including its television licence) to a company owned and controlled by the defendants. The defendants obtained an order in chambers dismissing the plaintiffs' personal action as disclosing no reasonable cause of action. The court refused to permit a derivative action on the grounds that any cause of action to which the corporation was entitled had vested in the trustee in bankruptcy. The British Columbia Court of Appeal allowed the plaintiffs' appeal. Although the personal claims were based largely on the wrongs alleged to be done to the bankrupt company, they were not entirely so based, but included allegations of interference and breach of contract. As for whether the shareholders might seek leave to commence a derivative action where the company was in bankruptcy, Hutcheon J.A. concluded that an order could be made under clause 224(2)(*g*) authorizing the continuation of the proceedings under the name of World View on the terms that they would be responsible for all the expenses and costs of the proceedings.[711]

§13.234 Thus, the fact that the oppression remedy (or some other personal cause of action) is also available to an aggrieved shareholder (and that such proceedings have been instituted) is not determinative of the question of whether leave should be granted to bring a derivative action.[712] The shareholder is not forced to choose between personal and derivative relief.[713] It follows that the commencement of separate personal and derivative claims is not necessarily abusive. A derivative action is one for the redress of a wrong to the corporation itself. A personal action by the shareholder (whether brought solely on his or her own behalf or as a class action on behalf of the other shareholders) is to redress the wrong done to the shareholder(s) as distinct from the corporation. There is, therefore, no duplication in the proceedings.[714]

(4) Procedural Considerations

§13.235 As noted above, strictly speaking, a derivative action is brought for the benefit of the corporation rather than for the complainant. Since the complainant may also wish to pursue an independent but factually related personal remedy against the corporation, its directors or controlling group of shareholders — perhaps for oppression, perhaps for some other cause of action such as breach of

---

Bank of Montreal, [1985] B.C.J. No. 1120, [1985] 5 W.W.R. 193, aff'd [1986] B.C.J. No. 1360, [1987] 2 W.W.R. 364 (C.A.), leave to appeal to S.C.C. refused [1987] 3 W.W.R. lxiii.
[709] [1991] B.C.J. No. 2291, 13 C.B.R. (3d) 285 (C.A.).
[710] R.S.B.C. 1979, c. 59, s. 224(2)(*g*) (rep. S.B.C. 2002, c. 57).
[711] [1991] B.C.J. No. 2291, 13 C.B.R. (3d) 285 at 291 (C.A.).
[712] *Appotive v. Computrex Centres Ltd.*, [1981] B.C.J. No. 1635, 16 B.L.R. 133 (S.C.).
[713] *Pizzo v. Crory*, [1986] N.S.J. No. 40, 71 N.S.R. (2d) 419 at 436-37, 171 A.P.R. 419 (S.C.), *per* Richard J.; *Goldex Mines Ltd. v. Revill*, [1974] O.J. No. 2245, 54 D.L.R. (3d) 672 at 676 (C.A.).
[714] See, generally, *Winchell v. Del Zotto*, [1976] O.J. No. 1410, 1 C.P.C. 338 (H.C.J.).

contract[715] — an obvious question is whether the complainant may use the same counsel for both proceedings. A second question is whether the complainant's desire to pursue both derivative and personal remedies places him or her in a potential or actual conflict of interest. Third, it is possible (though unlikely) that material not properly discoverable in one of the two actions may be discoverable in the other, so that allowing the complainant to pursue both derivative and personal remedies may result in allowing the complainant to take advantage of "improper" discovery.

§13.236 As we have seen, the courts have not been particularly receptive to the argument that these possibilities should require the complainant to elect between personal and derivative relief. The courts have proved similarly unreceptive to procedural based arguments that the simultaneous pursuit of a personal and derivative claim gives rise to a sufficient conflict of interest so as to require the substitution of some new potential complainant in the derivative action, the use of different counsel, or the limitation of rights of discovery. In many cases, the complainant will be the only person entitled to seek relief on both the derivative and the personal claim.[716] In such an extreme case, to bar one remedy or the other because of the alleged "conflict of interest", or to impose broad restrictions on prosecution, would therefore be to bar a final and just resolution to the dispute subsisting among all affected persons which forms the substrata of the two proceedings. Even where there are other potential complainants who might pursue derivative relief, considerations relating to expertise, the costs of litigation, ensuring that the derivative action is pursued by the person most likely to prosecute it as evidenced by demonstrated interest in the allegedly wrongful conduct and the like may outweigh concerns relating to some minor or entirely theoretical conflict of interest. In *Discovery Enterprises Inc. v. Ebco Industries Ltd.*[717] Williams C.J.S. rejected the contention that the same counsel could not act for the complainant in both proceedings.[718] In answer to complaints about impermissible use of information obtained through discovery, the courts have concluded that they are capable of ensuring that the rules relating to discovery are respected by the complainant, and that, therefore, the scope of discovery need not be limited.[719]

§13.237 Hypothetically, it is possible to visualize unusual instances in which a court might wish to restrict simultaneous derivative and personal claims or to impose some procedural restriction on the conduct of the derivative claim in order to protect better the interests of shareholders and other persons concerned

---

[715] Derivative and personal actions are not mutually exclusive provided the complainant was affected in a manner different from, or in addition to, the indirect effect on the value of all shareholders' shares generally arising from the conduct that forms the basis of the derivative proceeding. See, generally, *Furry Creek Timber Corp. v. Laad Ventures Ltd.*, [1992] B.C.J. No. 2298, 75 B.C.L.R. (2d) 246 (S.C.).

[716] See, generally, *Ginther v. Rainbow Management*, [1990] B.C.J. No. 1070 (S.C.), per Maczko J.

[717] [1997] B.C.J. No. 2360, 39 B.C.L.R. (3d) 50 (S.C.), aff'd on appeal [1998] B.C.J. No. 2674, 50 B.L.R. (3d) 207 (C.A.), leave to appeal to S.C.C. refused [1999] S.C.C.A. No. 24.

[718] *Ibid.*, at 61.

[719] *Acapulco Holdings Ltd. v. Jegen*, [1997] A.J. No. 174, [1997] 4 W.W.R. 601 (C.A.).

in the corporation. However, even in such cases, the court should exercise care not to foreclose a valid and possibly necessary avenue of recovery. Where oppression proceedings are pending and a litigant in those proceedings seeks leave to commence a derivative proceeding on behalf of the corporation, the court should consider whether there are any differences (as well as whether there are similarities) in the issues of fact and law that form the basis of the two proceedings, whether there are legitimate procedural or substantive reasons for the commencement of the second (derivative) proceeding, and whether there is any genuine corporate interest that appears to be served in seeing the derivative proceeding continue.[720]

(a) BANKRUPTCY AND DERIVATIVE CLAIMS

§13.238 A complainant may seek leave to bring a derivative action where the corporation is bankrupt.[721] However, it would be unusual for such a proceeding to be allowed.[722] The presumption in a bankruptcy is that the correct party to enforce the rights owed to the bankrupt corporation is the trustee in bankruptcy. As an alternative, however, complainants may also seek relief under section 38 of the *Bankruptcy and Insolvency Act*,[723] subsection (1) of which provides:

> 38.(1) Where a creditor requests the trustee to take any proceeding that in his opinion would be for the benefit of the estate of a bankrupt and the trustee refuses or neglects to take the proceeding, the creditor may obtain from the court an order authorizing him to take the proceeding in his own name and at his own expense and risk, on notice being given the other creditors of the contemplated proceeding, and on such other terms and conditions as the court may direct.

The advantage to a creditor of obtaining an order under section 38 is that any benefit derived from the proceeding taken under subsection (1) belongs to the creditor exclusively to the extent of that creditor's claim, with only the surplus over that amount being payable to the estate of the bankrupt.[724] To bring a proceeding under section 38, the creditor must be able to make out at least a *prima facie* case. However, the court may grant leave to proceed under section 38 without notice to the proposed defendant.[725] Section 38 speaks only of actions by creditors, and therefore there is doubt whether shareholders may proceed under that section.[726] Because the trustee has a right to pre-empt a section 38 proceeding by electing to bring the claim on behalf of the bankrupt, and because the costs of the proceeding are payable by the person who obtains leave under section 38 if the trustee declines this option, there would seem to be no real reason

---

[720] *Jennings v. Bernstein*, [2001] O.J. No. 831, 11 B.L.R. (3d) 259 (S.C.J.).
[721] *Hoskin v. Price Waterhouse Ltd.*, [1982] O.J. No. 3339, 37 O.R. (2d) 464 (Div. Ct.) — although this was doubted in *Gibson v. Manitoba Development Corp.*, [1982] M.J. No. 23, [1982] 5 W.W.R. 168 (C.A.).
[722] See, generally, *Ozesezginer v. Royal Bank of Canada*, [1990] A.J. No. 24, 78 C.B.R. (N.S.) 151 (Q.B.).
[723] R.S.C. 1985, c. B-3.
[724] *Bankruptcy and Insolvency Act*, s. 38(3).
[725] *Re Wagon Stop Inc.*, [1979] O.J. No. 3445, 30 C.B.R. (N.S.) 63 (S.C. in Bkcy.), *per* Registrar Ferron.
[726] *Rickerd v. Weber* (1934), 15 C.B.R. 218 (Alta. T.D.); *cf. Commonwealth Trust Co. v. Canada Deposit Insurance Corp.*, [1990] B.C.J. No. 920, 79 C.B.R. (N.S.) 183 (S.C.).

to prevent shareholders from pursuing section 38 relief if they are inclined to do so. The corporation's right to bring actions on its own behalf may be revived once the trustee in bankruptcy is discharged. For the shareholders or the corporation to bring an action in regard to any pre-bankruptcy wrongs, an order must be obtained from the bankruptcy court under subsection 40(2) of the *Bankruptcy and Insolvency Act* re-vesting in the corporation the right to bring that action.[727] This step must be taken whether the corporation brings the action itself or whether the shareholders of the corporation wish to bring a derivative action.[728]

(b) DOUBLE DERIVATIVE ACTIONS

§13.239 The usual form of a derivative action is the single form derivative action. In a typical proceeding of this sort (the "single derivative action"), a shareholder or other complainant brings a proceeding on behalf of the corporation in which he or she owns shares to enforce some right owed directly to the corporation. In the United States, courts have on occasion discussed what is described as a double derivative action, through which the complainant is allowed to prosecute a cause of action on behalf of a subsidiary that is owned and controlled by a holding company in which he or she is a shareholder. In a single derivative action the shareholder derives the capacity to sue directly from the unexercised capacity of the corporation. In a double derivative suit, the shareholder of a holding company seeks to enforce a right belonging to the subsidiary, and only derivatively to the holding company. This means that the cause of action is a failure by the corporation to pursue what is to it a derivative claim. Thus both the subsidiary and the holding company would have to fail, refuse or be unable to redress the injury to the subsidiary.[729]

§13.240 A holding company is a corporate body with a concentrated ownership of sufficient shares in another company, to control that other company. The holding company exercises control, supervision or influence over the policies and management of that subsidiary and (in most cases) carries on its active business, or at least a distinct portion of that business, through the facilities afforded by the subsidiary.[730] The device is most often employed in complex corporate groups, in which a number of related lines of business carried on by corporations that are technically separate entities are all coordinated from a single control point. In certain cases (particularly where a major multinational corporation is involved), the layers of corporation can be several tiers deep — as is illustrated in the figure below.

---

[727] *Gibson v. Manitoba Development Corp.*, [1982] M.J. No. 23, [1982] 5 W.W.R. 168 (C.A.).
[728] *Ibid.*, at 174 *per* Huband J.A.
[729] *Brown v. Tenney*, 125 Ill. 2d 348, 532 N.E.2d 230 (Ill. S.C. 1988); *Haberman v. Washington Public Power Supply System*, 109 Wash. 2d 107 at 147, 744 P.2d 1032 at 1060 (1987), mod. on other grounds, 110 Wash. 2d 24, 750 P.2d 254 (1988).
[730] *North American Co. v. SEC*, 327 U.S. 686 (1946).

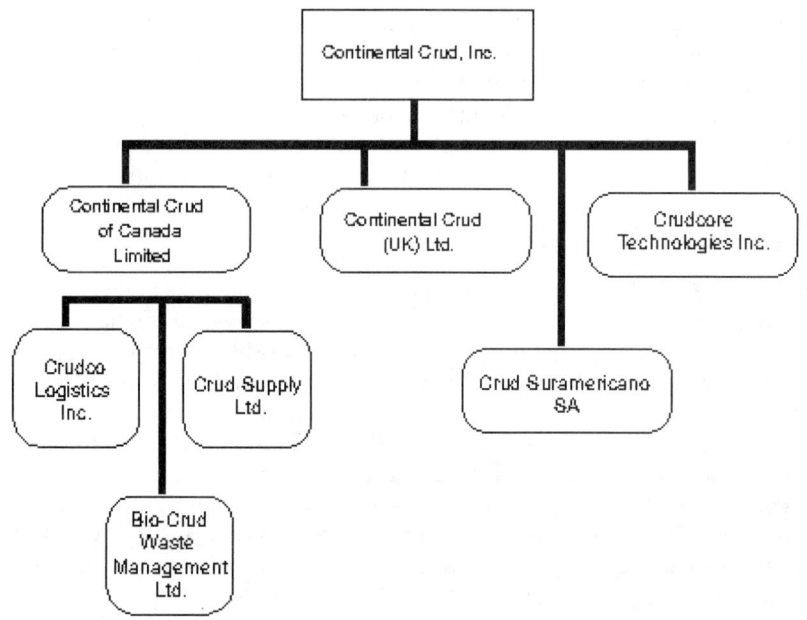

**A Hypothetical Corporate Group
Operated through a Single Holding Company**

In the above illustration of a hypothetical corporate group, only the ultimate holding company, Continental Crud, Inc. may include an actual minority interest. At every other layer, complete control over operations is exercised by the control group within the holding company. From a corporate governance perspective, the use of holding corporations and subsidiaries presents distinct problems, if it is intended to provide effective protection for shareholder and investor rights from misconduct at the hands of those who control the holding corporation. To prevent claims in respect of wrongs committed by the control group against the subsidiaries in such a situation would be to put form over substance, and ignore the very real risk of injury to the minority within the holding company. The façade of the holding company would be used as a transparent shield, against claims being brought in respect of injuries actually impacting upon the minority.

§13.241 In *Brown v. Tenney*,[731] Moran J. explained the function of the double derivative action in the following terms:

> We agree with the plaintiff that this court should not be derailed by convenient corporate formations which do not reflect business realities. It is a well-settled principle that the court will look behind and beneath the corporate veil to view the

---

[731] 125 Ill. 2d 348 (1988).

substance and face of the corporate body, and that it will disregard corporate legal fictions when used as a shield for wrongful acts. ... For beneath the corporate cloak beats the heart of its shareholders.

He continued:

> The double derivative action is a long-standing doctrine of equity jurisprudence, having been woven into the quilt-work of equitable principles covering shareholder-corporate relations over a century ago. ... Although the theory underlying the action has varied ... it has, contrary to defendants' contention, met with nearly universal acceptance. ... This is especially so when, like the case here, a subsidiary controlled or dominated by a holding company is involved. ... It has been said that a shareholder derivative action is nothing more than a suit by a beneficiary of a fiduciary. A double derivative suit is simply an extension of that theory, in that the beneficiary is in turn also a fiduciary. ... [Interlocking] directorates present special problems, and the dealings between the two corporations must be watched with a jaundiced eye.

And finally, with reference to the specific facts of the case, he noted:

> Here, plaintiff contends that the defendants are allegedly the mischief-makers and wrongdoers, directing the subsidiary and its course of events for their own benefit; they control and dictate the policies of the subsidiary at will and without restraint and are not deterred from misconduct, as they also control the holding company. In other words, according to the plaintiff, the subsidiary is accountable to no one since its shareholder, the holding company, is controlled by the wrongdoers. There is no justice in denying relief under these circumstances, and this court may look through the corporate form.

§13.242 In Canada, it appears that double derivative actions were not permissible at common law.[732] However, both subsections 246(1) and 239(1) of the CBCA expressly contemplate the possibility of the double derivative action, since each contemplates claims in respect of subsidiaries. However, such proceedings have proven relatively rare in Canadian corporate litigation, and when brought have usually involved claims by corporate officers in the employment context. As a result, there has been little detailed consideration of the special concerns that arise with respect to such proceedings. It is therefore convenient to consider in some detail the American case law with respect to this type of remedy.

§13.243 In a double derivative action, the injured subsidiary, being the real party in interest, is a necessary party to the action.[733] In addition, since the shareholder or other complainant is enforcing a derivative right belonging to the holding company, the complainant must also name the holding company as a party defendant.[734] Double derivative proceedings are limited to situations where the

---

[732] See, generally, *Crown Trust Co. v. Ontario*, [1988] O.J. No. 225, 64 O.R. (2d) 774 (H.C.J.), *per* Henry J.
[733] *Druckerman v. Harbord* (1940), 174 Misc. 1077, 22 N.Y.S.2d 595 (S.C. 1940).
[734] *Sternberg v. O'Neil*, 532 A.2d 993 at 999 (Del. Ch. 1987).

corporation in which the complainant is directly and immediately concerned holds at least a *de facto* controlling interest in the injured corporation.[735]

(c) BUYING-IN TO A DERIVATIVE PROCEEDING

§13.244 There is no hard and fast rule that a complainant may not "buy in" to a derivative action, by purchasing shares or other securities of the corporation for the sole reason of bringing a derivative action in regard to some wrong committed before the purchase was made. Indeed, since a derivative claim is a claim on behalf of the corporation, the concern with respect to whether the complainant acquired his or her interest in the corporation after the act complained of, or even with knowledge of that act, is of less concern than in an oppression action. However, the right to pursue derivative relief is all the stronger where the complainant has an established relationship with the issuer, and is a person ideally suited to pursue the class-action type proceeding entailed in a derivative action. Thus, in *Richardson Greenshields of Canada Ltd. v. Kalmacoff*[736] Robins J.A. said:

> This case is not at all akin to a strike or bounty action. Although the appellant purchased shares for the purpose of bringing these proceedings, it is by definition a complainant, and stands *vis-à-vis* the company, in the same position as any other person who fits within the definition of "complainant." The issues involved are of a continuing nature, and it seems to me apparent that the appellant is in a better position than most shareholders to pursue the complaint. Indeed, I see no advantage in requiring that the action be brought by another shareholder, as suggested by the judge hearing the application. I think it significant that the appellant has had a long-standing commercial connection with this class of shares and is familiar with the matters in dispute. It acknowledges that it has clients who purchased shares on its recommendation, and, it can be inferred from the shareholders' vote, that it voices the views of a substantial number of the preferred shareholders. Whether it is motivated by altruism, as the motions court judge suggested, or by self-interest, as the respondents suggest, is beside the point. Assuming ... it is the latter, self-interest is hardly a stranger to the security or investment business. Whatever the reason, there are legitimate legal questions raised here that call for judicial resolution. The fact that this shareholder is prepared to assume the costs and undergo the risks of carriage of action ... is no valid reason for concluding that the good faith condition ... has not been satisfied.[737]

Robins J.A. went on to give the following guidance to courts entertaining applications for leave to commence a derivative action:

> In deciding whether leave should be granted, it should be borne in mind that a derivative action brought by an individual shareholder on behalf of a corporation serves a dual purpose. First, it ensures that a shareholder has a right to recover property or enforce rights for the corporation if the directors refuse to do so. Second, and more important for our present purposes, it helps to guarantee some

---

[735] *S. Solomont & Sons Trust, Inc. v. New England Theatres Operating Corp.*, 326 Mass. 99 at 110, 93 N.E.2d 241 at 247 (1950).
[736] [1995] O.J. No. 941, 18 B.L.R. (2d) 197, 123 D.L.R. (4th) 628 (C.A.), leave to appeal to S.C.C. refused [1995] S.C.C.A. No. 260.
[737] *Ibid.*, at 207-208 B.L.R., 637-38 D.L.R.

degree of accountability and to ensure that control exists over the board of directors by allowing shareholders the right to bring an action against directors if they have breached their duty to the company . . .

It should also be borne in mind that s. 339 is drawn in broad terms and, as remedial legislation, should be given a liberal interpretation in favour of the complainant. The court is not called upon at the leave stage to determine questions of credibility or to resolve the issues in dispute, and ought not to try. These are matters for trial. Before granting leave, the court should be satisfied that there is a reasonable basis for the complaint and that the action sought to be instituted is a legitimate or arguable one. The preconditions of s. 339 cannot be considered in isolation. Whether they have been satisfied must be determined in the light of the potential validity of the proposed action.[738]

(d) Jurisdiction of the Court in Derivative Proceedings

§13.245 Section 247 of the OBCA sets out a number of incidental powers that the court possesses in connection with an action brought or intervened in under section 246.[739] It empowers the court to make any order that it thinks fit in such a case, including an order authorizing the complainant or any person to control the conduct of the action. An order of this type would seem to be an essential part of any order permitting the complainant to bring or intervene in an action, for otherwise the control of the action will remain in the corporation, and the status of the complainant will be little more than that of an observer. The court may also make an order giving directions concerning the conduct of the action.

§13.246 In addition to these general powers to make orders concerning the conduct of the action, the court is also vested with the power under section 247 to make orders concerning the financial aspect of the action concerned.[740] Under clause 247(c) the court is empowered to direct that any amount adjudged payable by a defendant in an action shall be paid (in whole or in part) directly to former and present security holders of the corporation instead of to the corporation or its subsidiary.[741] The making of such an order, however, would appear to be subject to the rights of creditors of a corporation among themselves, such as those set out in the *Creditors Relief Act*[742] or the *Bankruptcy and Insolvency Act*,[743] for nothing in section 247 suggests that the court possesses any power to disregard the rights of any stranger to the corporation or to prefer one creditor of the corporation over another.

§13.247 Finally, clause 247(d) of the OBCA empowers the court to make an order requiring the corporation or its subsidiary to pay reasonable legal fees and

---

[738] *Ibid.*, at 205-206 B.L.R., at 635-36 D.L.R. See also *Discovery Enterprises Inc. v. Ebco Industries Ltd.*, [1997] B.C.J. No. 1776, 40 B.C.L.R. (3d) 43, aff'd [1998] B.C.J. No. 1301 50 B.C.L.R. (3d) 195 (C.A.), leave to appeal to S.C.C. refused [1998] No. 406.
[739] CBCA, s. 240.
[740] CBCA, s. 240.
[741] CBCA, s. 240(c).
[742] R.S.O. 1990, c. C.45.
[743] R.S.C. 1985, c. B-3.

other costs reasonably incurred by the complainant in connection with the action.[744] A certain degree of caution might be justified in deciding whether to make indemnification orders. The bringing or prosecution of an action may expose the corporation to potential liability for costs. If a complainant forces the corporation to bring or prosecute that action against its will, it would be unreasonable to indemnify that complainant if the course that he or she advances ultimately proves unsuccessful. But, in fact, the courts have taken a more liberal approach, generally taking the view that assuming that the minority shareholder had reasonable ground for bringing the action — that it was a reasonable and prudent course to take in the interests of the company — he or she should not be liable to pay the costs of the other side, but the corporation itself should be liable because the shareholder was acting for the corporation rather than for himself or herself.[745] The question whether the shareholder would be entitled to indemnity where it is ultimately established at trial that the action was not reasonable or was brought in bad faith remains open, but it is difficult to see why any indemnity should be provided in such a case.

(e) INTERIM RELIEF

§13.248 Subsection 246(4) of the OBCA provides:

> 246.(4) Where a complainant on an application can establish to the satisfaction of the court that an interim order for relief should be made, the court may make such order as it thinks fit.

The authority to make any order that the court considers fit is a broad one,[746] and it clearly encompasses making such orders as are necessary to facilitate the disposition of the application for leave and to prevent the deterioration of the situation during the notice period. Interim relief could also include the right to initiate a proceeding to prevent the expiration of a limitation period. It follows that, despite the general requirement for prior notice to the corporation of the intention to bring an application for leave, in an exceptional case the court has a power to grant interim relief despite a failure to provide the notice required under subsection (2) where the applicant for relief can establish that it is not expedient to give that notice.[747]

§13.249 The power to order costs may be made at any time during the proceeding.[748] It has been held on occasion that interim costs should be awarded in a derivative action only where such an order is financially necessary to ensure that

---

[744] CBCA, s. 240(*d*).
[745] *Wallersteiner v. Moir*, [1975] 1 All E.R. 849 at 858-59 (C.A.), *per* Lord Denning M.R.
[746] OBCA, s. 246(4). There is no directly comparable provision in the CBCA, but see s. 248 of that Act.
[747] OBCA, s. 246(3). There is no directly comparable provision in the CBCA, but see s. 248 of that Act.
[748] *Bruce (Township) v. Thornburn*, [1986] O.J. No. 831, 57 O.R. (2d) 77 (Div. Ct.). As to interim costs, see *LaFontaine v. Drynan*, [1983] O.J. No. 274, 18 A.C.W.S. (2d) 343 (H.C.J.).

the action proceeds,[749] though there is case law on oppression remedy that suggests that interim costs may, perhaps, be awarded in a wider range of cases. What appears clear is that interim costs are an exceptional remedy. They should not normally be awarded in a derivative action where there are doubts about the merit of the proceeding.[750]

§13.250 Simply because the complainant has the financial wherewithal to pay for the action he or she will not be disentitled to indemnification. However, in deciding whether to order indemnification, the court may consider whether the shareholder or other complainant has more to gain from the institution of the derivative action than other shareholders.[751] In principle, shareholders other than those whose misconduct gave rise to the derivative proceeding, who stand to gain little or nothing as a result of the derivative proceeding, should not be obliged to subsidize other shareholders (such as the holders of a special class of shares) who stand to gain everything from it. Where the complainant is the sole potential beneficiary of the derivative proceeding, and there are other innocent shareholders, some care must be taken in crafting any indemnification order.

§13.251 In *Silverman v. Goldman*,[752] the applicant Silverman (one of several debenture holders) proposed to bring a derivative action against the directors of Dominion Trust on behalf of the debenture holders having a first charge on the assets of that trust company. He sought an order under section 247 of the OBCA that the benefits of the proposed action would be restricted to those persons who contributed to the costs of the litigation. Silverman undertook to circulate a notice to all of the debenture holders to allow them to contribute to those costs so that they would be entitled to participate in any proceeds recovered, should they choose to do so. It was held that the motion was premature. No order could be made under section 247 until the court had granted leave to bring or intervene in an action under section 246 (no order having been made under section 246). Moreover, it was doubted by the court whether an order of the type sought could be made:

> ... [T]he type of orders authorized by s. 247 of the OBCA would appear ... to be procedural ... the granting of the order sought would extinguish substantive legal rights of Debenture-holders who do not participate in the funding of the litigation. This seems to me to be the antithesis of a derivative action which is brought in the name of and on behalf of a corporation for wrongs done to the corporation. The benefits of any such action ought to accrue to all of the security holders of the corporation for wrongs done to the corporation, and I see nothing in the statute, which

---

[749] *Intercontinental Precious Metals Inc. v. Cooke*, [1993] B.C.J. No. 1903, 10 B.L.R. (2d) 203 at 224 (S.C.), *per* Tysoe J.; *Johnson v. Meyer*, [1987] S.J. No. 668, 62 Sask. R. 34 at 40 (Q.B.).
[750] *Intercontinental Precious Metals Inc. v. Cooke*, [1993] B.C.J. No. 1903, 10 B.L.R. (2d) 203 at 225 (S.C.), *per* Tysoe J.
[751] *Turner v. Mailhot*, [1985] O.J. No. 2513, 50 O.R. (2d) 561 at 567-68, 28 B.L.R. 222 (H.C.J.), *per* Reid J.
[752] [1995] O.J. No. 1124, 20 B.L.R. (2d) 134 (Gen. Div.).

sets out the procedures for instituting a derivative action, which would authorize an extinguishment of substantive legal rights of security holders . . .[753]

(f) Conflict of Laws

§13.252 In a common law jurisdiction, the law of the place of the incorporation of a company governs the right of a shareholder or other aggrieved person to bring a derivative action. Although for purely domestic purposes, the exceptions to that rule have been regarded as a procedural device, their real nature is not procedural in the conflict of laws context. They confer a right on the shareholders to protect the value of their shares by giving them a right to sue and recover on behalf of the company. Accordingly, where the laws of the foreign incorporating jurisdiction afford no derivative remedy, there is no such right under the laws of any common law jurisdiction.[754] In *LaRoche v. HARS Systems Inc.*[755] Hood J. concluded that the courts of the province of incorporation have no jurisdiction to allow a complainant to intervene and take over a derivative proceeding that has been instituted in another province. Presumably, however, such an application may be made to the court that is seized of the action.

(iii) Ratification of Director Misconduct, etc.

§13.253 Although section 249 of the OBCA[756] indicates that shareholder ratification is no longer a conclusive bar to a derivative action, it remains an important consideration that the court must take into account before deciding whether or not to give leave to proceed with the derivative action. It is an inherent aspect of corporate governance that the majority of the members of a corporation have a right to bind the minority of its members. Moreover, a company may conclude that it is in its interest to condone some improper, irregular or self-interested action on the part of a director or officer.[757] Given these considerations, where there has been some wrongdoing in the administration of the business or affairs of a corporation, or in conduct of one or all of the directors, the shareholders of the corporation may resolve to exonerate the wrong that has been done and to release the directors (or officers) of the corporation from liability.[758]

§13.254 The possibility of such shareholder ratification was outlined succinctly in *Bamford v. Bamford*.[759] There it was said:

> It is trite law ... that if directors do acts, as they do every day, especially in private companies, which, perhaps, because there is no quorum, or because their

---

[753] *Ibid.*, per Ground J. at 137. See, however, s. 38 of the *Bankruptcy and Insolvency Act*, R.S.C. 1985, c. B-3.
[754] *Konamaneni v. Rolls-Royce Industrial Power (India) Ltd.*, [2002] 1 All E.R. 979 (Ch.).
[755] [2001] B.C.J. No. 217, 86 B.C.L.R. (3d) 166 (S.C.).
[756] CBCA, s. 243.
[757] *Imperial Mercantile Credit Association v. Coleman* (1871), 6 Ch. App. 558 at 567, per Lord Hatherley L.C.
[758] See, for instance, *Grant v. United Kingdom Switchback Railways Co.* (1888), 40 Ch. D. 135 (C.A.); *Re Horsley & Weight Ltd.*, [1982] Ch. 442 (C.A.).
[759] [1969] 1 All E.R. 969 (C.A.), per Harman L.J.

appointment was defective, or because sometimes there are no directors properly appointed at all, or because they are actuated by improper motives, they go on doing for years, carrying on the business of the company in a way which, if properly constituted, they should carry it on, and then they find that everything has been, so to speak, wrongly done because it was not done by a proper board, such directors can, by making full and frank disclosure and calling together the general body of the shareholders, obtain absolution and forgiveness of their sins; and provided the acts are not *ultra vires* the company as a whole everything will go on as if it had been done all right from the beginning. I cannot believe that it is not a commonplace of company law. It is done every day. Of course, if the majority of the general meeting will not forgive and approve, then the directors must pay for it.[760]

§13.255 In his classic judgment in *Burland v. Earle*[761] Lord Davey said:

> It is an elementary principle of the law relating to joint stock companies that the court will not interfere with the internal management of companies acting within their powers and in fact has no jurisdiction to do so. Again, it is clear law that in order to redress a wrong done to the company or to recover moneys or damages alleged to be due to the company, the action should prima facie be brought by the company itself. ... It should be added that no mere informality or irregularity which can be remedied by the majority will entitle the minority to sue, if the act when done regularly would be within the powers of the company and the intention of the majority of shareholders is clear.

From this statement it followed (at common law) that if a wrong done against the corporation could be ratified by its members, then an individual member could not sue in regard to it because if it were ratified it would no longer be a wrong, and if it were not ratified, there was no reason for the corporation itself not to proceed with the action in its own name.[762]

§13.256 As the foregoing analysis of derivative actions makes clear, the possibility of shareholder ratification must be taken into account in any case where some type of derivative proceeding is contemplated. Similarly, ratification would also be relevant where a compliance order is sought under section 253 of the OBCA.[763]

§13.257 The possibility of shareholder ratification of wrongful conduct is now dealt with expressly in subsections 249(1) of the OBCA and 242(1) of the CBCA. Subsection 249(1) provides that:

> 249.(1) An application made or an action brought or intervened in under this Part shall not be stayed or dismissed by reason only that it is shown that an alleged breach of a right or duty owed to the corporation or its affiliate has been or may be approved by the shareholders of such corporate body, but evidence of approval by the shareholders may be taken into account by the court in making an order under section 207, 247 or 248.

---

[760] *Ibid.*, at 672; see also *Hogg v. Cramphorn Ltd.*, [1967] Ch. 254.
[761] [1902] A.C. 83 at 93-94 (P.C.).
[762] *Edwards v. Halliwell*, [1950] 2 All E.R. 1064 (C.A.), *per* Jenkins L.J.; *Bagshaw v. Eastern Union Railway Co.* (1849), 7 Hare 114 at 130, 68 E.R. 46, *per* Wigram V.C.
[763] CBCA, s. 247. *MacDougall v. Gardiner*, [1875] Ch. 13 at 25 (C.A.), *per* Mellish L.J.

Surprisingly, the case law decided under section 246 offers little guidance on how the court should exercise its discretion, but on the basis of the old case law and the wording of sections 246 and 248, the following general principles would most likely apply:

- irregularities of procedure not involving a substantive wrong may always be ratified by the shareholders;[764]

- the shareholders of a corporation may ratify a violation of the rules of internal government of the corporation (such as a breach of authority), provided the directors have not contravened a general prohibition to which the corporation itself is subject and no other substantive wrong has occurred;

- ratification by shareholders who are at arm's length of the person alleged to be responsible for a substantive wrong done to the corporation would normally seem to dispose of the matter in regard to whether leave should be given to institute or proceed with a derivative action,[765] — although it is arguable that it is not a conclusive bar to either type of proceeding;[766]

- in all cases, however, the effect of section 248 of the OBCA on the ratification question would seem to be to impose a requirement that any ratification must be fairly obtained and work no unfair prejudice to the complainant and other minority interests;

- ratification of the alleged wrong by shareholders who are also the persons alleged to be responsible for a substantive wrong done to the corporation[767] will have no effect upon a potential or pending derivative proceeding;[768]

- where wrongful conduct has been ratified by a combination of some shareholders who are alleged to be responsible for that wrongful conduct, and by others who are independent of them, the ratification will normally dispose of the question of whether leave should be given to institute or proceed with a derivative action provided that the independent shareholders ratifying the wrongful conduct constitute a (sufficient) majority of the independent shareholders of the corporation to have ratified the conduct;[769]

- the extent of ratification required will depend upon the articles and by-laws of the corporation, and unanimous shareholder agreement and the OBCA or the CBCA, as the case may be (in other words, a simple majority will not always be sufficient);[770]

---

[764] Generally, it is only the shareholders who may ratify, subject to any statutory provision allowing the other directors to do so: *Queensland Mines v. Hudson* (1978), 52 A.L.J.R. 399 (P.C.).
[765] See, for instance, *North-West Transportation Co. v. Beatty* (1887), 12 App. Cas. 589 (P.C.).
[766] OBCA, s. 249(1); CBCA, s. 242(1).
[767] *Menier v. Hooper's Telegraph Works* (1874), L.R. 9 Ch. App. 350 at 353 (C.A.), *per* James L.J.; *Noral v. Parsons*, [1942] O.J. No. 445, [1942] O.R. 358 at 363-64, *per* Masten J.A.; *Prudential Assurance Co. v. Newman Industries Ltd. (No. 2)*, [1982] Ch. 204 (C.A.).
[768] *Menier v. Hooper's Telegraph Works* (1874), L.R. 9 Ch. App. 350 (C.A.).
[769] *Smith v. Croft (No. 2)*, [1988] Ch. 114, *per* Knox J.
[770] *Edwards v. Halliwell*, [1950] 2 All E.R. 1064 (C.A.); *Boschoek Proprietary Co. v. Fuke*, [1906] 1 Ch. 148.

- it is not necessary for there to be formal ratification where it is self-evident that the requisite majority of the independent shareholders oppose the institution of a derivative action;

- ratification by a majority of shareholders can have no effect upon any coincident private wrong done to the individual complainant[771] (*e.g.*, in an oppression action);[772]

- the shareholders of one class (*e.g.*, voting common shares) may not ratify a breach of a duty owed to shareholders of some other class (*e.g.*, the obligation to pay a preference before making distributions to the common shareholders);

- the shareholders of a corporation may not ratify a breach of a duty owed by the directors (or officers) to outsiders of the corporation (*e.g.*, the duty to maintain the capital of the corporation).[773]

§13.258 For ratification to have any effect, the directors (or officers) who seek ratification of their conduct must make a full and frank disclosure of all relevant facts.[774] The degree of detail required depends upon the circumstances of the case. It must be sufficient to allow the shareholders to make an informed judgment.[775] Moreover, the wrong must involve a type of omission, act or other conduct that the majority of the corporation would have had the right to authorize in advance. Thus, the shareholders may not ratify the giving of improper financial assistance,[776] the payment of an excessive commission in connection with the issue of shares,[777] the payment of dividends in contravention of the Act,[778] the improper return of the whole or part of the stated capital to the shareholders contrary to the Act (whether by way of redemption, purchase of shares or other acquisition),[779] or the indemnification of a director where prohibited under section 136 of the OBCA

---

[771] See, generally, *McMillan v. LeRoi Mining Co.*, [1906] 1 Ch. 331; *Re Broadway Motors Holdings Pty, Ltd.* (1986), 11 A.C.L.R. 495.

[772] The directors are not normally under a fiduciary duty to individual members of the corporation: *Percival v. Wright*, [1902] 2 Ch. 421. However, in the particular circumstances of a given case, where they undertake to act on an individual shareholder's behalf, or where there is particular dependence by a shareholder or class of shareholders upon them, or where there are other such justifying considerations, then such a duty may be seen to arise: *Allen v. Hyatt* (1914), 30 T.L.R. 444 (P.C.); *Coleman v. Myers*, [1977] 2 N.Z.L.R. 225, *per* Woodhouse J.; *Re Chez Nico (Restaurants) Ltd.*, [1992] B.C.L.C. 192 at 208, *per* Browne-Wilkinson V.C. An interesting question is whether the fiduciary duty of the director extends to a person who has a direct or indirect interest in the corporation where the director knows or reasonably ought to know that unlawful loss or injury is likely to be caused to that person by the way in which the director causes the business of the corporation to be conducted: see, generally, *Hurley v. BGH Nominees Pty. Ltd.* (1984), 37 S.A.S.R. 499, *per* Walters J.; *Lion Breweries Ltd. v. Scarrott* (1986), 3 N.Z.C.L.C. 100,042; *Re French Protestant Hospital*, [1951] Ch. 567; but *cf. Bath v. Standard Land Co.*, [1911] 1 Ch. 618 (C.A.).

[773] *Kinsela v. Russell Kinsela Pty. Ltd.* (1986), 10 A.C.L.R. 395 at 401 (N.S.W.C.A.), *per* Street C.J.

[774] *Boulting v. Association of Cinematograph, Television & Allied Technicians*, [1963] 2 Q.B. 606 at 636 (C.A.), *per* Upjohn L.J.

[775] *Gray v. New Augarita Porcupine Mines Ltd.*, [1952] 3 D.L.R. 1 at 14 (P.C.).

[776] See OBCA, s. 20; CBCA, s. 44.

[777] OBCA, s. 37; CBCA, s. 41.

[778] See OBCA, s. 38; CBCA, s. 43.

[779] OBCA, ss. 30, 31 and 32; CBCA, ss. 34, 35 and 36.

or 124 of the CBCA, for such wrongdoing is beyond the power of the corporation itself.[780] Similarly, it is not possible for the majority shareholders to ratify a fraud on the minority shareholders, because the majority shareholders have no right to authorize such a fraud;[781] nor may the majority ratify a deliberate and perhaps, even negligent[782] wrongful act to which they are parties or where they otherwise stand *in pari delicto*.[783] Where the shareholders voting in favour of ratification are essentially the same persons who are guilty of the wrong on which the derivative action or oppression remedy application is based their vote may be disregarded[784] (although this may not be so when the complaint relates to a mere procedural irregularity).

E. ORDERS FOR COMPLIANCE

§13.259 There is Australian authority to the effect that a single member of a company has no general personal standing to sue to ensure that the business of the company is conducted in accordance with its articles.[785] However, subsection 253(1) of the OBCA now provides that:

> 253.(1) Where a corporation or any shareholder, director, officer, employee, agent, auditor, trustee, receiver, and manager, receiver, or liquidator of a corporation does not comply with this Act, the regulations, articles, by-laws or a unanimous shareholder agreement, a complainant or a creditor of the corporation may ... apply to the court for an order directing the corporation or any person to comply with, or restraining the corporation or any person from acting in breach of, any provisions thereof...

Comparative relief is provided for in section 247 of the CBCA. Where such an application is made, the court may make such further order as it thinks fit. An application may be made under subsection 253(1) despite the imposition of any penalty for such non-compliance. The right to make such an application is in addition to any other right to which the complainant or creditor may be entitled.

§13.260 One question that remains open is the relationship between the compliance order procedure and the derivative remedy.[786]

---

[780] Directors may, however, seek protection under the procedure set out in OBCA, s. 130; CBCA, s. 118.
[781] See, for instance, *Ngurli Ltd. v. McCann* (1953), 90 C.L.R. 425 (H.C. Aust.).
[782] *Re Horsley & Weight Ltd.*, [1982] Ch. 442 (C.A.), per Cuming-Bruce L.J. and Templeman L.J.
[783] See, for instance, *Gray Eisdell Tims Pty Ltd. v. Combined Auctions Pty Ltd.* (1955), 122 F.L.R. 253.
[784] See, generally, *Ménier v. Hooper's Telegraph Works* (1874), 9 L.R. Ch. App. 350 (C.A.), per James C.J.; *Pavlides v. Jensen*, [1956] 2 All E.R. 518 (Ch.), per Danckwerts J.
[785] *Stanham v. National Trust of Australia (New South Wales)* (1989), 15 A.C.L.R. 87; but *cf. Kraus v. J.G. Lloyd Pty Ltd.*, [1965] V.R. 232.
[786] Compare: *Re Goldhar & Quebec Manitou Mines Ltd.*, [1975] O.J. No. 2454, 61 D.L.R. (3d) 612 (Div. Ct.) and *Caleron Properties Ltd. v. 510207 Alberta Ltd.*, [2001] A.J. No. 1237, [2001, 3 W.W.R. 323 (Q.B.).

F. CURATIVE POWERS OF THE COURTS

§13.261 The oppression remedy is often used in order to set transactions aside. There is little, if any, case law where it has been employed to give effect to a transaction that might otherwise be held to be ineffective. Under section 194 of the *Corporations Law* of New South Wales, courts enjoy a broad power to validate an issue of shares whenever it is just and equitable to do so. While no provision in the OBCA and CBCA directly correspond to section 194, it is arguable that the courts possess the authority to make such an order in an oppression case, as for instance where the parties in control of the corporation are seeking to take advantage of a technical defence to deny the oppressed party a participatory interest in what has proven to be a very successful corporate business. It has been held that the section 194 jurisdiction could be exercised not only where the validation is non-contentious, but also where there is a dispute as to the validity of the issue. That jurisdiction might be exercised when all parties concerned have proceeded for many years on the basis that the share issue was valid.[787] The relevant legislative provision read:

> 194. Where a company has purported to issue or allot shares and:
>
> (*a*) the creation, issue or allotment of those shares is invalid by reason of any provision of this or any other Act or of the memorandum or articles of the company or for any other reason; or
>
> (*b*) the terms of the purported issue or allotment are inconsistent with or are not authorized by any such provision;
>
> the Court may, on application by the company, by a holder or mortgagee of any of those shares or by a creditor of the company and on being satisfied that in all the circumstances it is just and equitable so to do, make an order:
>
> (*c*) validating the purported issue or allotment of those shares; or
>
> (*d*) confirming the terms of the purported issue or allotment of the shares; or both.

G. INVESTIGATION (INSPECTION) ORDERS

§13.262 Under subsection 161(1) of the OBCA, a security holder of a corporation may apply to the court, without notice or upon such notice as the court may require, for an order directing an investigation to be made of the corporation or any of its affiliates.[788] The applicant may be either the legal holder or the beneficial owner of that security.[789] Such an application may also be made by the OSC.[790] The object of the provision is to permit the investigation of the business

---

[787] See, for instance, *Millheim v. Barewa Oil and Mining NL*, [1971] W.A.R. 65; *Kokotovich Constructions Pty Ltd. v. Walling*ton (1995), 17 A.C.S.R. 478 (N.S.W.C.A.).
[788] See also CBCA, s. 229(1). No person may publish anything relating to an application under s. 162 except with the authorization of the court or the written consent of the corporation being investigated: OBCA, s. 162(6). See also CBCA, s. 229(6).
[789] *Re Kootenay Valley Fruit Lands Co.* (1911), 18 W.L.R. 145 (Man. Chbrs.).
[790] OBCA, s. 161(1); CBCA, s. 229(1).

and affairs of a corporation where it is apparent that its books and records are not properly kept or are not accurate, or where there has been some deceit practised against the shareholders.[791] The power of inspection[792] is one vital to the protection of the interests of minority shareholders, but it has been held that it ought to be used sparingly.[793] The remedy is not available where there are other better or equally good methods of obtaining the information that is being sought.[794] It is not intended to be a tool to allow a potential plaintiff to prepare for litigation against the corporation or those concerned in it.[795] The conditions required for an inspection to be ordered were summarized by Southey J. in *Ferguson v. Imax Systems*,[796] where he stated:

> ... [T]he section clearly requires the Court to conclude that it appears that the business or affairs of the corporation have been conducted in a manner that is oppressive or unfairly prejudicial to or that unfairly disregards the interests of the applicant before an investigation may be ordered. It is not enough that there has been a complaint made by a security holder, or that there is some evidence of oppressive conduct. The court must examine the evidence and make a finding that it appears that there has been oppressive conduct. The Court cannot direct that the investigation be made in order to assist the Court in making such finding. The finding must be made before the investigation can be directed.

However, the wording of the section does not require the court to conclude that there has been oppression and so forth, but only that this "appears" to be the case. Thus, if such wrongdoing seems a reasonable inference — *i.e.*, a distinct possibility, more likely than not, rather than a certainty or probability — then the order may be made.

§13.263 Where an application is made for an investigation and it appears to the court that the business of the corporation or any of its affiliates has been carried on with intent to defraud any person,[797] the court may order an investigation to be made of the corporation and any of its affiliates.[798] There must be actual evidence of wrongdoing to justify such an order.[799] The courts also recognize that the inspection process should not be allowed to become overly intrusive, long or costly, or used as a means to overcome solicitor-client privilege, *bona fide* confidentiality

---

[791] *Re Charles J. Wilson Ltd. & Nuform Investments Ltd.*, [1974] O.J. No. 517, [1974] Ont. Corp. Law Guide Rep. 1087 at para. 10,090 (H.C.J.), *per* Weatherston J.

[792] The terms "inspection" and "investigation" are synonymous. Section 162 of the OBCA provides for the appointment of an "inspector" to carry out an "investigation" under s. 161 of the Act. The same wording appears in ss. 229 and 230 of the CBCA.

[793] *Baker v. Paddock Inn Peterborough Ltd.*, [1977] O.J. No. 2247, 16 O.R. (2d) 38 at 40 (H.C.J.), *per* Galligan J.; *Re Town Topics Co.* (1911), 17 W.L.R. 646, 20 Man. R. 574 (K.B.).

[794] *Rosemont Enterprises Ltd. v. Mercury Industrial Inc.*, [2005] B.C.J. No. 2042, 9 B.L.R. (4th) 285 (S.C.).

[795] *Brown v. Maxim Restoration Ltd.*, [1998] O.J. No. 2213, 42 B.L.R. (2d) 243 (Gen. Div.).

[796] [1984] O.J. No. 3275, 44 C.P.C. 17 at 27 (Div. Ct.).

[797] See, for instance, *Baniuk v. Carpenter*, [1986] N.B.J. No. 601, 85 N.B.R. (2d) 372, 217 A.P.R. 372 (Q.B.), and also *Baniuk v. Carpenter (No. 2)*, [1987] N.B.J. No. 1028, 85 N.B.R. (2d) 385, 217 A.P.R. 385 (C.A.).

[798] OBCA, s. 162(2)(*a*); CBCA, s. 229(2)(*a*).

[799] *D'Addario v. Environmental Management Solutions Inc.*, [2005] O.J. No. 3008, 8 B.L.R. (4th) 236 (S.C.J.).

undertakings or the legitimate individual rights of corporate insiders. These concerns must be balanced against the right of the shareholders of a corporation to know what is being done with their money, and to receive information to which they are legally entitled.[800]

§13.264 Where a security holder makes such an application, he or she must give the Director reasonable notice of that application, and similar notice must also be given to the OSC if the corporation is an offering corporation. On receipt of such notice, the Director and, where applicable, the OSC are entitled to appear and be heard in person or by counsel.[801] An applicant under section 161 is not required to give security for costs. Indeed, the costs of an inspection are normally paid by the corporation. It has been held that the court should not depart from this general rule unless it is fair and reasonable for it to do so on the basis of facts in evidence other than those disclosed solely in the report of the inspector.[802]

§13.265 The hearing of an application made without notice under section 161 is closed to the public.[803] Under subsection 164(1) any interested person may apply to the court for an order that a hearing conducted under Part XIII (*i.e.*, either the hearing of the application or a hearing conducted by the inspector) shall be closed to the public. A person whose conduct is being investigated or who is being examined at a hearing conducted by an inspector has a right, however, to be represented by counsel.[804]

§13.266 An inspection may also be ordered where the court is satisfied that the business or affairs of the corporation or any of its affiliates are, or have been, carried on or conducted, or the powers of the directors are, or have been, exercised, in a manner that is oppressive or unfairly prejudicial to, or that unfairly disregards the interests of, a security holder.[805]

§13.267 As with the derivative remedy, there are concerns that the investigation procedure could be abused, so as to provide a cloak for a fishing expedition to determine whether there may be sufficient grounds to institute a civil claim. An order should not be made on bare allegations[806] of bad faith and misconduct based in the main on information and belief, at least where the source of that information is readily available.[807] Furthermore, it has been held that the court

---

[800] See, generally, *Catalyst Fund General Partner I Inc. v. Hollinger Inc.*, [2004] O.J. No. 3886, 48 B.L.R. (3d) 194 at 206 (S.C.J.), *per* Campbell J.
[801] OBCA, s. 162(3); CBCA, s. 229(3). Notice to the OSC is not required under the CBCA.
[802] *Consolidated Enfield Corp. v. Blair*, [1996] O.J. No. 383, 28 O.R. (3d) 714 at 717 (Div. Ct.), *per* Steele J.
[803] OBCA, s. 161(5); CBCA, s. 229(5).
[804] OBCA, s. 164(2); CBCA, s. 232(2).
[805] OBCA, s. 161(2)(*b*); CBCA, s. 229(2)(*b*); see also *Re Town Topics Co.* (1911), 7 W.L.R. 646 at 648, 20 Man. R. 574 (K.B.), *per* Robson J.
[806] *Re Royal Trustco Ltd. (No. 3)*, [1981] O.J. No. 252, 14 B.L.R. 307 (H.C.J.).
[807] *Re H. Flagal (Holdings) Ltd.*, [1965] O.J. No. 1066, [1966] 1 O.R. 33 (H.C.J.).

should not order an investigation to help the applicant make its case. So in *Woodford v. Johnston Equipment (1998) Ltd.*[808] the court stated:

> The court should not make the order sought unless there is sufficient evidence to make a finding of oppressive conduct. In this case, allegations of oppressive conduct have been answered, and, in the face of these answers the court should not, particularly in a motions setting, make findings of such conduct. It is also clear that an investigation should not be ordered to assist the court in making a finding of oppressive conduct.

Nevertheless, in *Re Royal Trustco Ltd. (Nos. 3)*[809] an order for an investigation was made where the impugned conduct was admitted. Similarly, in *Re First Investors Corp.*,[810] Berger J. ordered an investigation that was limited to "facts which otherwise may be inaccessible" other than through the investigative process, and in *Consolidated Enfield Corp. v. Blair*,[811] an investigation was ordered where the court was satisfied that there had been insufficient financial reporting and non-disclosure of related party transactions. Similarly, in *Catalyst Fund General Partner I Inc. v. Hollinger Inc.*,[812] the court ordered an investigation into related party transactions where the respondent failed to explain the purpose, extent or details of a number of such transactions.[813]

§13.268 As the relief provided for is an investigation, it is sufficient to show that there is good reason to believe that the conduct complained of may have occurred.[814] Therefore, the fact that the corporation has unreasonably refused a minority shareholder access to records may justify an order being made.[815] However, an application will be refused where what is sought is not an inquiry into facts, but rather an inquiry into the legal propriety of what has been done.[816]

---

[808] [2001] N.B.J. No. 220, 17 B.L.R. (3d) 42 at para. 33 (Q.B.), quoting from *Brown v. Maxim Restoration Ltd.*, [1998] O.J. No. 2213, 3 C.B.R. (4th) 225 at para. 16 (Gen. Div.).

[809] [1981] O.J. No. 252, 14 B.L.R. 307at para. 18 (H.C.J.):

> ... a court need not be satisfied that the conduct complained of took place, or that such conduct has been proved to have taken place. If such a standard of proof were required, it would make any investigation unnecessary. Having regard to the fact that the relief provided for in the section is an investigation, it seems to me that a court is entitled to make an order for an investigation if it appears on the face of the material submitted to the court that there is good reason to think that the conduct complained of may have taken place.

[810] [1988] A.J. No. 244, 86 A.R. 126 (Q.B.).

[811] [1995] O.J. No. 2593, 10 C.C.L.S. 144 (Gen. Div.), rev'd on another point [1996] O.J. No. 383, 28 O.R. (3d) 714 (Div. Ct.).

[812] [2004] O.J. No. 3644 (S.C.J.).

[813] In *Bentley-Boudreau v. Red Knight Enterprises (1987) Ltd.*, March 8, 2001 S.H. 165510 (unreported) Moir J. stated at 1:

> Respecting an interim remedy of the kind sought [an investigation], I believe a court should determine the question of fitness by first having reference to a threshold similar to the American Cyanamid test on interim injunctions; that is to say, whether the affidavit evidence suggests a case which is not frivolous, but which presents a case serious enough to be heard.

[814] *Re Royal Trustco Ltd. (No. 3)*, [1981] O.J. No. 252, 14 B.L.R. 307 (H.C.J.).

[815] *Re Teperman & Sons Ltd.*, [1984] O.J. No. 536, 29 B.L.R. 1 (H.C.J.).

[816] *Re Automatic Phone Recorder Co.*, [1955] B.C.J. No. 16, 15 W.W.R. 666 (S.C.).

Moreover, the court will not interfere with the management of the corporation merely because some shareholder is disgruntled with the manner in which the business or affairs of the corporation are being managed.[817]

§13.269 The court may also order an investigation where it appears to the court that the corporation or any of its affiliates were formed for a fraudulent or unlawful purpose or is to be dissolved for a fraudulent or unlawful purpose.[818] Finally, the court may order an investigation to be made of a corporation or any of its affiliates where it appears to the court that persons concerned with the formation, business or affairs of the corporation or any of its affiliates have, in connection therewith, acted fraudulently or dishonestly.

§13.270 Where the court orders an investigation under Part XIII of the OBCA, it has the power to make any ancillary order it thinks fit.[819] Subsection 162(1) specifically authorizes a number of different types of such order. For instance, under clause 162(1)(*b*), the court may appoint and fix the remuneration of an inspector, and may make an order replacing an inspector previously appointed. Any such inspector is an officer acting for the court[820] rather than for the corporation or for the person who made the application for the order in question, and any interim report or final report of the investigator is made to the court rather than to the applicant.[821]

§13.271 The functions of an inspector are to investigate and report. In so doing, the inspector must be impartial and the court may refuse to accept his or her report where the inspector is partial, though it is not obliged to do so.[822] In performing the investigation and in making the report, the inspector does not act in a judicial or quasi-judicial capacity[823] and, therefore, is not obliged to comply with the rules of natural justice,[824] but may generally pursue any germane avenue of inquiry, as long as he or she proceeds in a manner that is fair[825] to all parties

---

[817] *Re Sarnia Ranching Co.*, [1915] A.J. No. 21, 8 W.W.R. 697 (S.C.).

[818] OBCA, s. 161(2)(*d*); CBCA, s. 229(2)(*d*).

[819] The court, which appointed the inspector, is seized of the matter. An application may not be made by the corporation for an injunction to bar the inspector from carrying out the investigation: *Johnson Woollen Mills Ltd. v. Southern Canada Power Co.*, [1945] Que. K.B. 134 (C.A.).

[820] *Re Martello & Sons Ltd.*, [1945] O.J. No. 519, [1945] O.R. 453 at 461 (C.A.), *per* McRuer J.A., from which it follows that any person who refuses to produce books to the inspector or to answer questions is liable for contempt.

[821] OBCA, s. 162(1)(*i*); CBCA, s. 230(1)(*i*). Any such report may be sealed by the court: s. 162(1)(*j*); CBCA, s. 230(1)(*j*).

[822] *Ferguson v. Imax Systems Corp.*, [1984] O.J. No. 3275, 44 C.P.C. 17 at 32, 34 (Div. Ct.), *per* Southey J.; *St. John v. Fraser*, [1935] S.C.J. No. 15, [1935] S.C.R. 441.

[823] *Re Pergamon Press Ltd.*, [1971] 1 Ch. 388 at 399 (C.A.), *per* Lord Denning M.R. See also *Re Associated Investors of Canada Ltd.*, [1988] A.J. No. 1045, 64 Alta. L.R. (2d) 107, 71 C.B.R. (N.S.) 299 (Q.B.).

[824] *Canadian Javelin Ltd. v. Sparling*, [1978] F.C.J. No. 136, 4 B.L.R. 284 (T.D.), aff'd 106 D.L.R. (3d) 495 (C.A.), but *cf. Re Pergamon Press Ltd.*, [1970] Ch. 388 (C.A.).

[825] *Grebely v. Seven Mile High Group Inc.*, [1990] B.C.J. No. 1064, 46 B.C.L.R. (2d) 240 (S.C.); *Re Shell Castle Fire Place Ltd.*, [1927] O.J. No. 290, 33 O.W.N. 195 at 196 (H.C.D.), *per* Middleton J.A.

concerned.[826] An inspector does not have the jurisdiction to determine whether a person is criminally or civilly responsible for misconduct. However, the inspector is not limited to making simple findings of fact. The inspector may comment in his or her report upon the findings that he or she has made, and in so doing may characterize the nature of the conduct that he or she has found to have taken place and give his or her opinion on whether it is lawful or unlawful.[827]

§13.272 Given the inspector's limited mandate, it follows that an inspector appointed by the court under section 161 of the OBCA is not intended to operate as a lone ranger. Under subsection 163(2) he or she is authorized to furnish, or exchange information and otherwise cooperate with, any public official in Canada or elsewhere who is authorized to exercise investigatory powers and who is investigating, in regard to the corporation, any allegation of improper conduct that is the same as, or similar to, the conduct giving rise to the inspector's appointment. It has been held that the investigation provisions under provincial corporations law statutes do not entrench upon federal jurisdiction over criminal law, or violate the *Canadian Charter of Rights and Freedoms*.[828]

§13.273 Most of the specific powers conferred upon the court under subsection 162(1) of the OBCA and subsection 230(1) of the CBCA relate to the conduct of the investigation by the investigator. For instance, clause 162(1)(*a*) gives the court the power to order the investigator to investigate (although that direction would surely be implicit in any order appointing an inspector). Clause 162(1)(*d*) allows the court to authorize the inspector to enter any premises in which the court is satisfied that there might be relevant information, and to examine anything and make reasonable copies of any document or record found on the premises. Clause 162(1)(*h*) allows the court to give directions to the inspector or any interested person on any matter arising in the investigation. Despite the general rule that investigation does not contravene the *Charter of Rights*, clause 162(1)(*h*) is essentially a search warrant power, and, accordingly, would seem to be subject to the full range of *Charter* constraints on the grant and exercise of such powers. Under clause 162(1)(*e*) the court may require any person to produce documents or records to the inspector.

§13.274 Under clause 162(1)(*f*) of the OBCA the court is empowered to authorize the inspector to conduct a hearing, administer oaths and examine any person upon oath, and to prescribe rules for the conduct of that hearing.[829] The inspector

---

[826] *Re Associated Investors of Canada Ltd.*, [1988] A.J. No. 1029, 63 Alta. L.R. (2d) 69, 71 C.B.R. (N.S.) 288 (Q.B.), var'd on other grounds [1988] A.J. No. 1105, 54 D.L.R. (4th) 730 (C.A.), leave to appeal to S.C.C. refused 100 N.R. 159*n*.
[827] *Re First Investors Corp.*, [1988] A.J. No. 244, [1988] 4 W.W.R. 22 at 36-37 (Q.B.), *per* Berger J., aff'd [1988] A.J. No. 481, [1988] 5 W.W.R. 65 (Alta. C.A.).
[828] Part I of the *Constitution Act, 1982*, being Schedule B of the *Canada Act 1982* (U.K.), 1982, c. 11. See *Re First Investor Corp.*, [1988] A.J. No. 244, [1988] 4 W.W.R. 22 (Q.B.), aff'd [1988] A.J. No. 481, [1988] 5 W.W.R. 65 (C.A.).
[829] See, for instance, *Catalyst Fund General Partner I Inc. v. Hollinger Inc.*, [2005] O.J. No. 2191, 8 B.L.R. (4th) 95 (S.C.J.), aff'd [2005] O.J. No. 4666, 79 O.R. (3d) 70 (C.A.) dealing, *inter alia*, with the protection of *Charter* rights in such cases.

has the discretion to decide what weight to attach to the evidence that he or she so receives. Where a hearing is authorized, the court may require any person to attend a hearing conducted by the inspector and to give evidence upon oath.[830] The fact that subsection 162(1) specifically provides for the holding of hearings and the attendance of witnesses before such hearings suggests that the inspector has no power to conduct a hearing or to compel the attendance of any person before a hearing that he or she purports to conduct unless so authorized by the court — a conclusion supported by subsection 163(1), which provides that the inspector has the powers set out in the order under which he or she is appointed.

§13.275 In *Virani v. Virani*[831] a receiver-manager was appointed for two Canadian corporations. The receiver-manager was also appointed as inspector of these corporations under section 233 of the British Columbia *Companies Act*.[832] A foreign subsidiary company owned a hotel in a foreign jurisdiction. The receiver-manager moved for an order that a mortgage or lien be created against that hotel as security for its costs. The respondents argued against such an order on the ground that there was no express authority to create a charge over property not belonging to either of the corporations for which the receiver-manager had been appointed. The receiver-manager's motion was allowed. It was held that because the subsidiary was an affiliate of the two corporations, and because subsection 233(3)[833] permitted the court to order at any time by whom costs would be payable, the order that it was seeking was authorized by the Act. The power to grant a charge followed from the power to affix liability on the subsidiary in regard to costs.

H. CONCLUSION

§13.276 In this Chapter, we have discussed the basic package of shareholder remedies that are employed to defend the rights discussed in Chapter 12. The principles discussed in this Chapter apply primarily where the corporation and its management are working (or purporting to be working) within the existing framework of the corporate constitution. Where steps are being taken to recast that constitution on some new basis, a range of additional concerns arise. In this more extreme context, there is a need for a package of remedies specifically

---

[830] As for the standard that must be met to justify an inter-provincial subpoena, see *Re Associated Investors of Canada Ltd.*, [1988] A.J. No. 1349, 61 Alta. L.R. (2d) 360, [1988] 6 W.W.R. 637 (Q.B.). Such subpoena will not be issued unless the attendance of the witness is necessary for the due adjudication of the proceeding and considering the nature and importance of the proceedings, that person's presence is reasonable and essential to the due administration of justice.

[831] [1995] B.C.J. No. 2318, 15 B.C.L.R. (3d) 38 (S.C.).

[832] Repealed March 29, 2004.

[833] The relevant provision read:

> 209(3) The court, before appointing an inspector, may require the applicant to give security for payment of the costs and expenses of the investigation, and, at any time, may set the amount of the costs and expenses, and order by whom and in what proportion they must be paid.

targeted on the unique aspects of a fundamental reorganization of the corporation. It is this subject that forms the basis of the next chapter of this text, as we move to a consideration of the subject of fundamental changes.

Chapter 14

FUNDAMENTAL CHANGES

A. INTRODUCTION

§14.1 Part XIV of the Ontario *Business Corporations Act*[1] ("OBCA") and Part XV of the *Canada Business Corporations Act*[2] ("CBCA") permit a corporation to effect certain fundamental changes to its constitution. Although the term "fundamental change" is used in both statutes, it is not a defined term of art. However, the meaning of this term becomes clear even upon a limited review of the provisions in the two parts in question. In general terms, a fundamental change is an addition, deletion or other change to the articles of a corporation; an amalgamation of the corporation with one or more other corporations; or a continuation of the corporation under another jurisdiction. In practical terms, the effect of such a fundamental change is to alter what would otherwise appear to be the vested proprietary and contractual rights of the shareholders of the corporation concerned.[3]

§14.2 Different procedures and requirements apply to each of these classes of fundamental change. In this chapter, we shall review the rules governing each type of fundamental change.

B. AMENDING THE ARTICLES OF A CORPORATION

§14.3 The most common type of fundamental change to the constitution of a corporation is an amendment to its articles; indeed, most active business corporations experience at least one fundamental change of this type during their lives. When the *Joint Stock Companies Act, 1856* was first enacted in England, it made no provision for the alteration of the memorandum of association which served as the basis for the corporate constitution. It was not until 1862 that a right to amend the corporate charter would be conferred, and even then it was limited to certain specifically authorized types of amendment. Elsewhere in the common law world, the general rule was also that any fundamental change in a company required unanimous consent.[4] Even today in England, subsection 2(7) of the *Companies Act, 1985*[5] provides that:

---

[1] R.S.O. 1990, c. B.16, as amended.
[2] R.S.C. 1985, c. C-44, as amended.
[3] See, generally, *Bove v. Community Hotel Corp. of Newport R.I.*, 105 R.I. 36, 249 A.2d 189 (S.C.R.I. 1969).
[4] See J.E. Calio, "New Appraisals of Old Problems: Reflections on the Delaware Appraisal Proceeding" (1994) 32 Am. Bus. L.J. 1 at 7.
[5] (U.K.), 1985, c. 6.

> 2.(7) A company may not alter the conditions contained in its memorandum except in the cases, in the mode and to the extent, for which express provision is made by this Act.

This notion of a limited right to amend the corporate charter is reflected to a large extent in the refusal of the courts to grant a remedy of rectification, where the corporate is found to have improperly recorded the intentions of the incorporators.[6]

§14.4 Both the OBCA and CBCA adopt a very different approach, permitting almost any change to the constitution of the corporation. Ordinarily, the most radical changes to the constitution of an OBCA or CBCA corporation are effected through an amendment to the articles of the corporation. An amendment of the articles adds to, deletes from or otherwise varies the provisions set out in the existing articles of incorporation — the original articles as amended from time to time. The most common simple type of amendment is probably the creation of a new class of shares. However, as a general principle, every provision of the articles of a corporation may be amended by the shareholders of the corporation in accordance with the procedure set out in the OBCA or the CBCA, as applicable, irrespective of whether it extinguishes or otherwise impairs the rights of certain or all of the shareholders.[7] Thus, subsection 168(1) of the OBCA reads (in part):

> 168.(1) ... a corporation may from time to time amend its articles to add, change or remove any provision that is permitted by this Act to be, or that is, set out in its articles ...[8]

The section then goes on to provide a veritable shopping list detailing the various types of changes that may be made. Although drafted in inclusive language, the list is so extensive that any particular amendment not included in the list must be a very unusual one indeed. The types of amendment expressly described in the list are amendments to:

- change the name of the corporation;

- add, change or remove any restriction upon the business or businesses that the corporation may carry on or upon the powers that the corporation may exercise;

- add, change or remove any maximum number of shares that the corporation is authorized to issue or any maximum consideration for which any shares of the corporation are authorized to be issued;

- create new classes of shares;

- change the designation of all or any of its shares, and add, change or remove any rights, privileges, restrictions and conditions, including rights to accrued dividends, in regard to all or any of its shares, whether issued or unissued;

---

[6] See, for instance, *Scott v. Frank F. Scott (London) Ltd.*, [1940] Ch. 794 (C.A.).
[7] Note, however, that amendment of the existing articles may entitle shareholders who enjoy those rights to relief under the oppression remedy or to exercise a right of dissent.
[8] The wording of the equivalent provision of the CBCA, is slightly different: "... the articles of a corporation may by special resolution be amended to ..." (s. 173(1)).

- change the shares of any class or series, whether issued or unissued, into a different number of shares of the same class or services or into the same or a different number of shares of other classes or series;
- divide a class of shares, whether issued or unissued, into series and fix the number of shares in each series and the rights, privileges, restrictions and conditions thereof;
- authorize the directors to divide any class of unissued shares into series and fix the number of shares in each series and the rights, privileges and restrictions and conditions thereof;
- authorize the directors to change the rights, privileges, restrictions and conditions attached to unissued shares of any series;
- revoke, diminish or enlarge any authority conferred upon the directors to divide any class of unissued shares into series and fix the number of shares in each series and the rights, privileges and restrictions and conditions thereof, or to change the rights, privileges, restrictions and conditions attached to unissued shares of any series;
- subject to section 120 of the Act (which provides for cumulative voting for directors) and section 125 (which provides for change in the number of directors within the minimum and maximum range specified in the articles), increase or decrease the number, or minimum or maximum number, of directors; and
- add, change or remove restrictions on the issue, transfer or ownership of shares of any class or series.

§14.5 The corresponding list set out in subsection 173(1) of the CBCA is worded somewhat differently, using terminology that suggests that it is intended to be exhaustive in its scope rather than inclusive. But, as in the case of the OBCA, the list of permitted amendments in the CBCA is so lengthy and broad that it is not easy to think of a type of amendment that a corporation might seek that would not be permitted under the CBCA.[9] In addition to the amendments permitted under subsection 173(1), subsection 174(1) of the CBCA provides that:

---

[9] The specific types of amendment authorized under s. 173(1) of the CBCA are to:
   (a) change the name of the corporation;
   (b) change the province in which its registered office is situated;
   (c) add, change or remove any restriction on the business or businesses that the corporation may carry on;
   (d) change any maximum number of shares that the corporation is authorized to issue;
   (e) create new classes of shares;
   (f) reduce or increase its stated capital, if its stated capital is set out in the articles;
   (g) change the designation of all or any of its shares, and add, change or remove any rights, privileges, restrictions and conditions, including rights to accrued dividends in regard to all or any of its shares, whether issued or unissued;

174.(1) Subject to sections 176 and 177, a distributing corporation, any of the issued shares of which remain outstanding and are held by more than one person, may by special resolution amend its articles in accordance with the regulations to constrain,

(a) the issue or transfer of shares of any class or series to persons who are not resident Canadians;

(b) the issue or transfer of shares of any class or series to enable the corporation or any of its affiliates or associates to qualify under any prescribed law of Canada or a province,

  (i) to obtain a licence to carry on any business,

  (ii) to become a publisher of a Canadian newspaper or periodical, or

  (iii) to acquire shares of a financial intermediary as defined in the regulations;

(c) the issue, transfer or ownership of shares of any class or series in order to assist the corporation or any of its affiliates or associates to qualify under any prescribed law of Canada or a province to receive licences, permits, grants, payments or other benefits by reason of attaining or maintaining a specified level of Canadian ownership or control;

(d) the issue, transfer or ownership of shares of any class or series in order to assist the corporation to comply with any prescribed law.

(e) the issue, transfer or ownership of shares of any class or series to enable the corporation to be a registered labour-sponsored venture capital corporation under Part X.3 of the *Income Tax Act.*

Although no corresponding provision appears in the OBCA, the broader wording of section 168(1) of that Act would seem to be sufficient to authorize an amendment of the type contemplated in subsection 174(1) of the CBCA.

(h) change the shares of any class or series, whether issued or unissued, into a different number of shares of the same class or series or into the same or a different number of shares of other classes or series;

(i) divide a class of shares, whether issued or unissued, into series and fix the number of shares in each series and the rights, privileges, restrictions and conditions thereof;

(j) authorize the directors to divide any class of unissued shares into series and fix the number of shares in each series and the rights, privileges, restrictions and conditions thereof;

(k) authorize the directors to change the rights, privileges, restrictions and conditions attached to unissued shares of any series;

(l) revoke, diminish or enlarge any authority conferred under (j) and (k);

(m) increase or decrease the number of directors or the minimum or maximum number of directors, subject to sections 107 and 112;

(n) add, change or remove restrictions on the issue, transfer or ownership of shares; or

(o) add, change or remove any other provision that is permitted by this Act to be set out in the articles.

§14.6 Under the OBCA, a special Act corporation may not make an amendment in accordance with the procedure set out in Part XIV, other than to amend the name of the corporation. Thus, the only method by which the articles of an Ontario special Act corporation (*i.e.*, the special Act) can be amended is by way of amending legislation.[10]

§14.7 Subsection 169(1) of the OBCA provides that a proposal to amend the articles may be made by the directors (*i.e.*, by the board collectively) or by any shareholder who is entitled to vote at an annual meeting of the shareholders. Subsection 175(1) of the CBCA is similar, but also allows an individual director to propose an amendment. Where a shareholder seeks to make a proposal to amend the articles, it is necessary for the shareholder to comply with sections 99 of the OBCA or 137 of the CBCA, as the case may be, which sets out the procedures governing shareholder proposals.[11] Whether proposed by the directors or by a shareholder, notice of a meeting of shareholders at which a proposal to amend the articles is to be considered must set out the text of the proposed amendment, and (where applicable) must state that a dissenting shareholder is entitled to be paid the fair value of his or her share under sections 185 of the OBCA or 190 of the CBCA.[12]

(i) Special Voting Rights

§14.8 It is a general principle of corporate law that changes to the fundamental structure or character of the corporation require approval by special resolution. Further, as we shall see, many specific types of change require approval on a class-by-class basis, as well as by the parliamentary majority contemplated in a special resolution. The requirement for such broad-based support can sometimes allow a minority to frustrate the will of the majority. Nevertheless, devices employed by a board of directors to limit or frustrate the right of the shareholders of a corporation to vote with respect to some fundamental change or some other matter that is subject to their direct control over the final decision to be made, are not protected by the business judgment rule. For instance, a board's decision to act to prevent the shareholders from creating a majority of new board positions and filling them cannot be insulated from attack by arguing that it involves some aspect of day-to-day management, even if it incidentally relates to the exercise of the corporation's power over its property, or with respect to its rights or obligations. Properly characterized, it involves the allocation, between shareholders as a class and the board, of effective power with respect to governance of the corporation. Such a struggle between the shareholders and directors can arise only where the directors are purporting to exercise a power conferred upon them. Absent some colour of authority, it is clear that the directors may not

---

[10] On the broader question of the relationship between a special Act of incorporation and a general corporate law statute, see: *Winnipeg Winter Club v. Thorsteinson*, [1997] M.J. No. 289, 119 Man. R. (2d) 300 (Q.B.), leave to appeal to Man. C.A. refused [1997] M.J. No. 409.
[11] Discussed in Chapter 12, Shareholders and Their Rights.
[12] The failure to make that statement, however, does not invalidate any amendment that may be made. Rights of dissent are discussed below at §14.45 *seq.*

interfere with the shareholders. However, there are a range of measures that can be employed in many contexts, such as changes to corporate by-laws. In *Blasius Indus., Inc. v. Atlas Corp.*,[13] the court concluded that such situations required enhanced judicial scrutiny, under which the board of directors "bears the heavy burden of demonstrating a compelling justification for such action". The courts will not allow the wrongful subversion of corporate democracy by manipulation of the corporate machinery or by machinations under the cloak of law. Careful judicial scrutiny will be given a situation in which a right to vote has been effectively frustrated and denied.[14]

§14.9 The general rule is that the shareholders of a corporation vote together as a single decision-making body on any proposed amendment with every voting share being entitled to the same number of votes (*i.e.*, one vote) per share. However, there are many exceptions to this general rule, which have the effect of conferring special voting rights upon certain shareholders of a corporation. Although both the OBCA and CBCA permit votes to be taken by way of a show of hands, where special voting rights apply taking a vote in such a manner is usually misleading. Therefore, even if the procedure is technically legal, in most cases it would be ill-advised.

§14.10 The most elementary type of special voting rights are those that are conferred by the terms of the shares themselves. For instance, in some cases the articles will call for the holders of two or more classes to vote together, but will weight the votes to which each class is entitled. By way of illustration, assume the holders of Class A shares in a given corporation are entitled to two votes per share, while the holders of Class B shares are entitled to only one vote per share. However, weighted voting is by its nature inconsistent with a right to vote separately (if classes vote separately, there is no need to weight the vote to which each is entitled); therefore, where weighted voting is employed all shareholders will normally vote as a single body of shareholders. Weighted voting is often employed to give the shareholders of a particular class an enhanced say in the running of the corporation, but not complete control.[15]

§14.11 In contrast, where the terms of a share specifically provide that the holders of shares of that class or series are entitled to vote separately from the shareholders of the other classes or series of the corporation, effect must be given to that provision. Where such class voting rights apply, the special resolution approving a proposed amendment must be approved by the holders of each class or series entitled to vote separately. A right to vote separately by class obviously increases the degree of control that the holders of each class of shares possess over the corporation, because, for a resolution to be approved, it must be passed by the holders of each class of shares. Such a system of voting is negative; it

---

[13] 564 A.2d 651 at 659-60 (Del. Ch. 1988).
[14] See, generally, *Aronson v. Lewis*, 473 A.2d 805 at 811 (Del. S.C. 1984); *Unocal Corp. v. Mesa Petroleum Co.*, 493 A.2d 946 (Del. S.C. 1985); *MM Companies Inc. v. Liquid Audio Inc.*, 813 A.2d 1118 (Del. S.C. 2003).
[15] See, generally, for instance, *Brown v. McLanahan*, 148 F.2d 703 (4th Cir. 1945).

allows each class a veto, but that same veto necessarily encumbers any effort that the shareholders might make to change the articles of the corporation.

§14.12 In addition to special voting rights conferred under the articles of the corporation, in certain circumstances both the OBCA and the CBCA confer special voting rights on the holders of a class or series of shares which apply irrespective of "whether or not shares of [the] class or series otherwise carry the right to vote".[16] More particularly, subsection 170(1) of the OBCA confers a right to vote upon a shareholder where the effect of a proposed amendment would be to vary the special rights to which the shares of that shareholder are entitled. In such a case the holders of the shares of that class are entitled to vote separately as a class from the holders of other shares of the corporation.[17] Where special class voting rights apply (*i.e.*, whether by the terms of the shares or under the provisions of the OBCA or the CBCA), a special resolution amending the articles of the corporation must be approved by not less than two-thirds of the votes cast by each class of shares entitled to vote on that resolution, including each class whose voting rights arise solely by virtue of subsection 170(1) or its CBCA equivalent, rather than simply two-thirds of the total number of votes cast by all classes.[18]

§14.13 Similar separate voting rights are also conferred on the holders of a series of shares that carries special rights that would be adversely affected by the proposed amendment. The holders of each series of a particular class are entitled to vote separately as a series[19] if that series is affected by an amendment in a different manner from other shares of the same class.[20] On the other hand, there are some important differences between the class and series voting rights. The holders of a class of non-voting shares will be entitled to vote as a single class if the proposed amendment is of a type specified in subsection 170(1), irrespective of whether each series of shares in that class is differently affected. If one or more series in that class is affected in a manner different from other shares of that same class, then the holders of that series will themselves be entitled to vote separately as a series from the other series comprising that class. However, if the

---

[16] OBCA, s. 170(3); CBCA, s. 176(5).
[17] OBCA, s. 170(1); CBCA, s. 176(1).
[18] OBCA, s. 170(4); CBCA, s. 176(6). The following table shows a hypothetical spread of votes taken on a special resolution among three classes of shares, A, B and C:

Class	# of Shares	For	Against	per cent Support
A	500	500	0	100
B	1,000	550	450	55
C	1,000	1,000	0	100
Total	2,500	2,050	450	

The proposal received 2,050 of 2,500 total votes (*i.e.*, 82 per cent). Since two classes voted 100 per cent in favour of the proposal, while one voted 55 per cent in favour, the average percentage support among the three classes was 85 per cent (*i.e.*, 255/300). However, the special resolution would still fail, because support among the Class B shares was less than the required two-thirds.

[19] OBCA, s. 170(1); CBCA, s. 176(1).
[20] OBCA, s. 170(2); CBCA, s. 176(4).

holders of the shares of different series within a class are all affected in a similar way, then there is no right to vote separately by series,[21] though the class voting rights of the entire class of shares remains unaffected. For instance, if there were four series of shares in Class "A" and the proposal was to convert Class A, Series 2 preference shares into common shares, then the Class "A" Series 2 shares would be entitled to vote as a separate series from the other series comprising the Class "A" preference shares, because they are specially affected by the proposal. If, on the other hand, the proposal was to convert all Class "A" preference shares to common shares, then all holders of the Class "A" shares would be entitled to vote as a class, because they are similarly affected by the proposal. Nevertheless, in such a case none of the series would be entitled to vote separately from the others.

§14.14 The specific situations in which special voting rights are conferred under the OBCA are set out in detail in subsection 170(1).[22] In general terms, the various grounds specified are restricted to proposed changes that would have the effect of changing the basic conditions under which the shareholders concerned agreed to invest in the shares of the corporation. Thus, under clause 170(1)(*a*), a class (series) voting right is conferred on a proposal to amend the articles to:

> (*a*) increase or decrease any maximum number of authorized shares of such class or series, or increase any maximum number of authorized shares of a class or series having rights or privileges equal or superior to the shares of such class or series;

It can readily be seen how such changes might work to the disadvantage of the holders of the shares of such a class or series. For instance, a change in the number of authorized shares may lead to a dilution of a dividend entitlement to which the holder(s) of the shares of those classes might otherwise expect to share, or to a reduced degree of control over the board of directors of the corporation, and a decrease in the number of authorized shares might effectively thwart the exercise of a pre-emptive right to which the holder(s) of those shares is entitled. The protection afforded by clause (*a*) is enhanced by clause 170(1)(*h*), which provides a right of class (series) voting in the case of any proposal to:

> (*h*) add, remove or change restrictions on the issue, transfer or ownership of the shares of such class or series.

Obviously, any change of a type contemplated by clause (*h*) may adversely affect the marketability of the affected shares, and thereby completely undermine the basis upon which investments in those shares were made. The effect of such an amendment may also be to change the very nature of the corporation. For instance, if the consent of other shareholders becomes necessary to a transfer of

---

[21] OBCA, s. 170(2); CBCA, s. 176(4).
[22] CBCA, s. 176(1).

shares, the effect of the amendment may be to change the nature of the corporation to that of an incorporated partnership.[23]

§14.15 Clause 170(1)(*b*) of the OBCA[24] provides a further voting right in the case of a proposal to amend the articles of a corporation to:

> (*b*) effect an exchange, reclassification or cancellation of the shares of such class or series;

Such changes might work to the disadvantage of the holders of the shares of such a class or series, if, for instance, Class A shares carry a right to a preferential dividend, while Class B shares carry no such right. In such a case, any reclassification or exchange of the Class A shares for Class B shares would have the effect of depriving the holders of the Class A shares of the preferential dividend which presumably influenced their original investment decision. Clause (*b*) is sufficiently broad to come into play irrespective of whether the proposal is to change the articles to cause Class A shares to be exchanged for Class B shares, or *vice versa*. Thus, the fact that all existing Class A shareholders will continue to hold their preferential shares is not sufficient to take the amendment outside the scope of clause (*b*). To the extent that there is any uncertainty in this regard, clause 170(1)(*g*) confers a class voting right for any proposal to

> (*g*) effect an exchange or create a right of exchange of the shares of another class or series into the shares of such class or series...

§14.16 Subsection 170(1) of the OBCA[25] provides that the special voting rights conferred under clauses (*a*), (*b*) and (*e*) of that subsection do not apply where "the articles otherwise provide". A general exclusion of voting rights (*e.g.*, a statement that the shares of a particular class of shares are non-voting) is not sufficient to take advantage of this exception, because subsection 170(3) of the OBCA[26] provides that the special voting rights under subsection (1) apply whether or not shares of the class otherwise carry a voting right. To defeat the class/series voting right presumption under subsection 170(1), it appears that the corporation must include an express statement in the articles of the corporation that there is no voting right under clause (*a*), (*b*) or (*e*). In the absence of any

---

[23] Note, however, s. 170(5) of the OBCA, which provides:

> 170.(5) Subsection (1) does not apply in respect of a proposal to amend the articles to add a right or privilege for a holder to convert shares of a class or series into shares of another class or series that is subject to restrictions described in clause 42(2)(*d*) but is otherwise equal to the class or series first mentioned.

Compare CBCA, s. 178(2). Clause (*d*) of s. 42(2) of the OBCA relates to restrictions on the issue, transfer or ownership of shares that are necessary

> (*d*) to attain or maintain a specified level of Canadian ownership or control for the purpose of assisting the corporation or any of its affiliates or associates to qualify to receive licences, permits, grants, payments or other benefits under any prescribed Act of Canada or a province or ordinance of a territory.

[24] CBCA, s. 176(1)(*b*).
[25] CBCA, s. 176(1).
[26] CBCA, s. 176(5).

such clear wording, the right to vote would seem to apply on the basis of the general presumption that shares are entitled to vote.[27]

§14.17 Clause 170(1)(c) of the OBCA[28] provides for class or series voting rights where the proposal would amend the articles to add to, remove or change the rights, privileges, restrictions or conditions attached to the shares of such class or series and, without limiting the generality of the foregoing,

(i) remove or change prejudicially rights to accrued dividends or rights to cumulative dividends;

(ii) add, remove or change prejudicially redemption rights or sinking fund provisions;

(iii) reduce or remove a dividend preference or a liquidation preference, or

(vi) add, remove or change prejudicially conversion privileges, options, voting, transfer or pre-emptive rights, or rights to acquire securities of a corporation.

Under clause (c), the special voting right is conferred only where the special rights, privileges, restrictions or conditions attached to the preferred shares are themselves being changed. Clause (c) has no application where shares ranking superior, equal or inferior to those shares are to receive additional rights. Nevertheless, clause 170(1)(d)[29] does confer a class voting right where a proposal would:

(d) add to the rights or privileges of any class or series of shares having rights or privileges equal or superior to the shares of such class or series;

For clause (d) to come into operation, it is not necessary to show that the additional rights or privileges to be conferred on one class of shares (the Class A shares) will have the effect of reducing the rights to which the other class of shares (the Class B shares) are entitled. Therefore, the Class B shares will be entitled to a vote, if the Class A shares receive any additional right or privilege at all. Thus, if the Class A and Class B shares are both non-voting shares, and a proposal is made to confer a voting right upon the Class A shares, then the holders of the Class B shares are entitled to vote as a class on that proposal, even though the giving of that additional right takes nothing away from the Class B shares.

§14.18 In most cases, however, an increase in the rights of one class will necessarily lead to a decrease in the rights of other classes. A proposal to increase the fixed dividend on a preference share would have such an effect. Obviously, any such change will prejudice the holders of inferior shares, because dividends could be paid on the inferior shares only after full payment of the senior shares. Because dividend payment depends on profitability, payment of the enhanced dividend on the superior shares might ultimately prevent or delay the payment of any dividend on the inferior shares. Consequently, it is only reasonable to allow

---

[27] See Chapter 12, Shareholders and Their Rights.
[28] CBCA, s. 176(1)(c).
[29] CBCA, s. 176(1)(d).

a class voting right on a proposal to make such a change. By similar logic, clause 170(1)(*e*) of the OBCA[30] confers class voting rights in the case of a proposal to create a new equal or superior class of shares. However, there is no right for a class vote in the case of the creation of a new series of shares under section 25, which authorizes the creation and issue of distinct series of special shares, each of which series may carry different rights.[31] In order for clause (*e*) to come into play, the new class of shares must be equal or superior to the existing class which claims the benefit of a class voting right. Thus, a proposal to create a new inferior class of shares does not require a class-by-class approval from the holders of the superior shares.

§14.19 In certain cases it may be difficult to settle on a meaning for the terms "equal" or "superior". For instance, if there are two classes of existing shares, and one of those classes (Class B) enjoys no voting right but is entitled to a fixed preferential dividend of $5 as well as a priority on repayment of capital upon dissolution, does a proposal to create a third class of shares (Class C), which is fully participating and enjoys full voting rights create a superior, equal or inferior class of shares? The creation of the Class C shares will take nothing away from the Class B shares; it is clear however, that the holders of the Class C shares will enjoy certain rights that the holders of the Class B shares do not.

§14.20 Clause 170(1)(*f*) of the OBCA[32] deals with the conferring of new rights and privileges on an existing class of shares that is inferior to the shares of another class. Obviously, the rights of a superior class will be diluted if an inferior class is bumped up so that it stands on a par with that superior class. Accordingly, clause (*f*) provides that the shareholders of that other class are entitled to vote separately as a class on a proposal to

> (*f*) make any class or series of shares having rights or privileges inferior to the shares of such class or series equal or superior to the shares of such class or series;

This special voting right does not apply unless the proposed amendment makes the inferior class of shares equal or superior to the class of shares claiming class voting rights. Thus, if the Class A shares carry a right to a fixed first preferential dividend of $5 per share, there would be no right for Class A shares to vote on a proposal to grant the Class B shares of a corporation a fixed second preferential dividend of $3 per share, because the $5 dividend on the Class A shares would still have to be paid before any payment was made of the $3 dividend on the

---

[30] CBCA, s. 176(1)(*e*).

[31] But see below in the case of shares of a reporting issuer under the *Securities Act*, R.S.O. 1990, c. S.5. Moreover, s. 170(6) of the OBCA provides:

> 170.(6) For the purpose of clause (1)(*e*), a new class of shares, the issue, transfer or ownership of which is to be restricted by an amendment to the articles for the purpose of clause 42(2)(*d*) that is otherwise equal to an existing class of shares shall be deemed not to be equal or superior to the existing class of shares.

Section 176(3) of the CBCA has a similar effect.

[32] CBCA, s. 176(1)(*f*).

Class B shares. The Class A shares will not be prejudiced if they carry no right of participation beyond their own fixed dividend. If the Class A shares have a right of participation after their fixed dividend is paid — as is sometimes the case — then the creation of a second fixed preferential dividend will be prejudicial to them, even though that dividend is subordinate to the preferential dividend provided for the Class A shares. The prejudice in such a case pertains not to the preferential dividend of the Class A shares but to the right to participate in residual profits. Any further preferential dividend will reduce the pool of funds from which the holders of the Class A shares might expect to receive participatory dividends. The following table illustrates the point. It shows the dividend requirement for a corporation having two classes of shares (one of which carries a preferential dividend) that proposes to create a third class of shares which will also carry a preferential dividend.

	No. of Shares	Profits	Fixed Dividend	Balance Remaining
Before	10,000 class A	100,000	50,000	50,000
	10,000 class B		---	50,000
After	10,000 class A	100,000	50,000	50,000
	10,000 class B		---	20,000
	10,000 class C		30,000	

Any participatory dividend payable on the Class A shares may only be paid out of the balance remaining after the payment of preferential dividends. As shown above, the second preferential dividend reduces the amount available for such dividends from $50,000 to $20,000, and, as a result, the Class A shareholders will be prejudiced by the creation of the new Class C shares.

§14.21 On the other hand, if the participatory rights of the Class A shares are shared with some other class of shareholder (*e.g.*, the holders of a class of "common shares"), then the Class A shareholders will be no more prejudiced than the holders of that other class by the creation of the new preferential dividend. In such a case, therefore, it would seem that the Class A shareholders and the holders of the common shares would vote as a single group on the proposal. What should be clear from this discussion is that the question of whether a particular class (or series) of shares is specially affected by a proposed amendment is one of fact, and to answer it, it is necessary not only to carefully read the share terms, conditions and restrictions attached to that class (or series) but also to carefully compare and contrast those terms, conditions and restrictions with the corresponding provisions attached to other classes (or series).

§14.22 It is not clear how close a corporation may sail to the wind before it changes inferior shares into equal shares. For instance, if Class A shares carry an exclusive right to elect one director, but the holders of Class B shares have a right to vote with all other shareholders in the election of two other directors, do Class B shares become the equal of Class A shares if the Class B shares are given an exclusive right to elect one of those two directors? An argument can be made both ways. Because the Class B shareholders will now enjoy a right that corresponds to that of the Class A shareholders, the two classes of shares may be said to rank equally. However, the grant of that right in no way prejudices the Class A shareholders. Prior to the amendment they had an exclusive right to elect one director; after that amendment they continue to enjoy that exclusive right. Arguably, the proposal makes the Class A and B shares equal only if it grants the Class B shareholders a right equal to the Class A shareholders to participate or enjoy the benefit. Under this interpretation, as long as the rights remain separate and the giving of the right or privilege in no way prejudices the other class (so that the original right of the other class continues unaffected), there will be no class voting right. On balance, it is this second interpretation that seems preferable, for there is no compelling justification for granting class voting rights where the shareholders of a class are not adversely affected by a proposed amendment. However, as noted above, there are certain instances where class voting rights are conferred by the Act even where no prejudice whatsoever arises from the proposed amendment.

(ii) Extent of Approval Required

§14.23 A special resolution of the shareholders is the minimum required to approve any of the fundamental changes discussed in this chapter. Despite this general rule, both the OBCA and the CBCA provide that where a greater number of votes of shareholders is required by the articles or by a unanimous shareholder agreement than is specified in the Act, the provisions of the articles or agreement prevail.[33] Ordinarily, a special resolution must be approved by at least two-thirds of the votes cast at a meeting of the shareholders, or of each separately voting class (or series) of shareholders, as the case may be, that is called to discuss the resolution in question.[34] It is doubtful whether a corporation may include in its articles a provision that renders the articles incapable of amendment.[35] However, many Canadian corporations have articles requiring any amendment to be approved by all shareholders.

§14.24 The number of persons present at the start of the meeting must constitute a quorum; without such a number being present, the meeting is incapable of transacting any business.[36] It is generally accepted that if there is no quorum present at the scheduled start time, the presiding officer may direct that the start of the meeting will be delayed for a reasonable period to see if additional shareholders (or their proxies) arrive. It may even be argued that there is an obligation to do so. There is an obvious inconvenience in, and cost to, adjourning the

---

[33] OBCA, s. 5(4); CBCA, s. 6(3).
[34] OBCA, s. 1(1), CBCA, s. 2(1), "special resolution".
[35] See, for instance, *Russell v. Northern Bank Development Corporation Ltd.*, [1992] 1 W.L.R. 588 (H.L.).
[36] *Howbeach Coal Co. v. Teague* (1860), 5 H. & N. 151, 157 E.R. 1136 (Q.B.); *Re Cambrian Peat, Fuel & Charcoal Co., De La Mott's & Turner's Cases* (1875), 31 L.T. 773. Indeed, unless a quorum is present, there is no meeting, though the assembled body is considered to be a "meeting" to permit it to be adjourned by the presiding officer: OBCA, s. 101(3); CBCA, s. 139(3); *Byng v. London Life Association Ltd.*, [1989] 1 All E.R. 560.

meeting, particularly where those in attendance have had to travel a considerable distance to attend. Within reason, every effort should be employed to allow the meeting to proceed at its originally scheduled time and place. Any quorum at a meeting must be made up of persons who are entitled to vote.[37] The common law rejected the view that a single person could alone constitute the quorum for the transaction of business at a meeting (for instance, where the proxies of all shareholders were held by that single person).[38] For this reason, it became a widespread practice — still encountered — to spread management proxies among two or more nominees. Subsection 101(1) of the OBCA[39] now deals specifically with the question of single person meetings. It provides:

> 101.(1) Unless the by-laws otherwise provide, the holders of a majority of the shares entitled to vote at a meeting of shareholders, whether present in person or represented by proxy, constitute a quorum.

A single person may thus constitute a quorum, provided he or she holds a sufficient number of shares or proxies. Although the use of the plural word "holders" might be taken to suggest that at least two persons must be present,[40] some confirmation of this conclusion may be derived from the fact that subsection 101(4) of the OBCA[41] provides that if a corporation has only one shareholder (or holder of a class or series of shares) that shareholder being present in person or by proxy constitutes a quorum. It is not normally necessary[42] to obtain approval from two-thirds of all shareholders, including those who are not present or (if present) who do not vote, nor is it actually necessary that a quorum be present at the time when the vote is taken.[43] Thus, once a quorum is reached persons who leave the meeting, who do not attend the meeting, or who do not vote although in attendance, are simply disregarded.[44]

§14.25 The wording of the definition of "special resolution" raises an interesting question concerning the effect of a spoiled ballot. At common law a spoiled ballot is treated as a nullity: it is neither a vote for nor against the matter to which it pertains and is treated for all intents and purposes as if it was never cast. However, the definition of special resolution in the OBCA and the CBCA requires the approval of "at least two-thirds of all votes cast". This wording might be taken to suggest that spoiled ballots (which are nonetheless votes cast) must be taken into account in deciding the number of ballots required to obtain approval. For instance, assume that there are 105 votes cast on a proposal, five of them being spoiled ballots. If spoiled ballots are excluded and there were 67

---

[37] *Henderson v. James Loutitt & Co.* (1894), 21 R. 674.
[38] See, for instance, *Re Sanitary Carbon Co.*, [1877] W.N. 233; *Insomnia (No. 2) Pty. Ltd. v. F.C.T.* (1986), 84 F.L.R. 278.
[39] CBCA, s. 139(1).
[40] Unfortunately, clause 28(j) of the *Interpretation Act*, R.S.O. 1990, c. I.11 provides little guidance with respect to this question.
[41] CBCA, s. 139(4).
[42] Such a requirement may be imposed under the articles or a unanimous shareholder agreement.
[43] See, generally, *Re Hartley Baird Ltd.*, [1955] Ch. 143.
[44] As for deliberate non-attendance to prevent a quorum being present, see *Gearing v. Kelly*, 11 N.Y.2d 201, 227 N.Y.S.2d 897, 182 N.E.2d 391 (C.A. 1962).

votes cast in favour of a proposal and 33 votes against, the resolution would have obtained the requisite consent. If, however, the spoiled ballots are taken into account as votes cast, then the resolution would fail, because the 67 votes in favour of the resolution would not amount to two-thirds of the 105-vote total. There is no particular reason to believe that the people who spoiled their ballot intended to vote against the resolution, any more than there is any reason to believe that they intended to vote in favour of it. For this reason, the preferable approach would be simply to exclude the ballots from consideration: to treat them (since they are spoiled) as uncast votes. Unfortunately, whether such an approach may be taken has not yet been resolved by the courts.

§14.26 A signed resolution may be used as an alternative to a vote at a meeting of the shareholders or a class, to signify the approval of the shareholders concerned. Where a written resolution is proposed in lieu of a vote at a shareholders' meeting, the resolution must be unanimous.[45] In such a case any abstention is the same as a vote against the resolution and has the effect of defeating it.

(iii) Procedure Following Approval of Special Resolution

§14.27 The approval of a proposed amendment by a special resolution of the shareholders authorizes the amendment of the articles, but does not bring it about. For the amendment to be made, it is necessary for the corporation to embody the proposed amendment into articles of amendment and to send that document to the Director.[46] The articles must be submitted in duplicate and signed by a director or an officer of the corporation.[47] Articles of amendment must be in the form prescribed under the OBCA,[48] which resembles the form of original articles of incorporation. The articles of amendment set out the name of the corporation along with its Ontario Corporation Number,[49] the text of the proposed amendment, and include a statement that the amendment was authorized under section 170 of the OBCA. The date on which the special resolution was approved by the shareholders must also be stated.

§14.28 Upon receipt of the articles of amendment, the Director is required to endorse a certificate of amendment on the articles in accordance with section 273 of the OBCA.[50] Specifically, clause 273(1)(*b*) requires the certificate to be endorsed provided the articles are in prescribed form, have been executed in

---

[45] OBCA, s. 1(1), "special resolution"; CBCA, s. 2(1), "special resolution".
[46] OBCA, s. 171(1); CBCA, s. 177(1) — differently worded but to a similar effect.
[47] OBCA, s. 273(1)(*a*); CBCA, s. 262(2).
[48] OBCA Regulations, R.R.O. 1990, Reg. 62, s. 47; *cf.* CBCA Regulations, 2001, SOR/2001-512. SOR/79-316.
[49] All corporations and other companies incorporated under the laws of Ontario are issued an Ontario Corporation Number, as is any Canadian or other extra-provincial corporation or company registered as carrying on business in Ontario under the *Extra-Provincial Corporations Act*, R.S.O. 1990, c. E.27. Corporations under the CBCA are also issued a Canadian corporation number. The prescribed form under the CBCA requires the Canadian corporation number to be stated.
[50] OBCA, s. 172; CBCA, s. 187(4).

duplicate and all prescribed fees have been paid. The endorsement sets out the day, month, and year of the endorsement and also the corporation number. One copy of the endorsed articles is then filed by the Director, and the other is sent to the corporation or its representative. However, the Director is prohibited from endorsing a certificate on the articles if the corporation is in default of a filing requirement under the *Corporations Information Act*[51] or has any unpaid fees or penalties outstanding.[52]

§14.29 Under section 273(2) of the OBCA, as a general rule the certificate endorsed must be dated on the day on which the Director receives the duplicate originals of the articles together with all other required documents executed in accordance with the Act and receives payment of the prescribed fee.[53] It is not possible to backdate the certificate to an earlier date. However, where the person submitting the articles so specifies and the Director agrees, the certificate may be dated on a later date than the date on which the required documents and payment are submitted. Such forward dating may be useful for tax planning purposes. The articles are effective on the date shown on the certificate, even if any action required to be taken by the Director under the Act in regard to the endorsement of the certificate and filing by the Director is taken at a later date.[54]

(iv) Amendments Changing the Name of a Corporation

§14.30 The procedure for changing the name of a corporation resembles the procedure required to obtain approval of the name of a proposed corporation. Where a corporation resolves to change the name of the corporation, the corporation must submit to the Director along with the articles of amendment:

1. An original Ontario biased or weighted computer printed search report for the proposed name from the NUANS automated name search system maintained by the Department of Consumer and Corporate Affairs, Canada, that search being dated not more than 90 days prior to the submission of the articles;

2. Any consent or consent and undertaking required under the Act or the Regulation and, if applicable, in the Form prescribed.[55]

The NUANS name search must confirm that the name is not objectionable. Where the proposed name is in an English form and a French or a combined English and French form, and the English and French names are phonetically dissimilar, a separate computer printed search report must be provided for both the English form and the French form of the name.[56]

---

[51] R.S.O. 1990, c. C-39.
[52] OBCA, s. 274, not yet proclaimed in force.
[53] Compare CBCA, s. 263(3).
[54] OBCA, s. 273(3). There is no corresponding provision in the CBCA.
[55] R.R.O. 1990, Reg. 62, s. 18(1).
[56] R.R.O. 1990, Reg. 62, s. 18(2).

§14.31 Where a corporation that has shares in the hands of the public proposes to decrease its capital, section 19 of the OBCA Regulation, formerly required a name change in certain cases. It provided:

> 19. Where through the filing of articles, other than articles of amalgamation, the capital of a corporation is decreased by the cancellation or consolidation of issued shares and a number of the share certificates of the corporation are in the hands of the public and may not be promptly surrendered, the name of the corporation shall be changed to a different name.

This requirement has now been repealed.[57]

§14.32 A change in the name of a corporation does not create a new corporation, nor (with some statutory exceptions, such as is provided in the *Personal Property Security Act*) does it prejudice any right or obligation of the corporation concerned.[58] Nevertheless, subsection 171(3) of the OBCA prohibits a corporation from changing its name where the corporation is unable to pay its liabilities as they become due or the realizable value of the corporation's assets is less than the aggregate of its liabilities. In such a case, the corporation would be insolvent, and any name change might delay or prejudice the creditors of the corporation in collecting the debts owed to them. There is no comparable provision in the CBCA.

(v) Restated Articles

§14.33 As the life of a corporation continues, it may happen that numerous amendments will be made to the articles of the corporation, for instance, where various classes of shares are created, issued and eventually redeemed and cancelled. Moreover, special provisions that were at one time included in the articles may have been removed or altered by amendment to the articles. Where either or both of these situations prevails, the corporation may consider it expedient to restate the articles in a consolidated form to eliminate ambiguities or otherwise reduce the confusion that may flow from previous amendments to the articles. To assist such an effort, sections 173 of the OBCA and 180 of the CBCA provide a simplified procedure that permits the directors of a corporation to file restated articles of incorporation. Because the purpose of restatement is to consolidate the existing provisions of the articles and delete from formal records all spent and repealed provisions, it is not necessary for such articles to be submitted to the shareholders for approval.

§14.34 The restatement provisions of the OBCA and the CBCA are derived from section 59 of the American *Model Act*. Prior to the introduction of the restatement procedure, there was no procedure under which a corporation could apply for the issue of new charter documents in consolidated form, restating the corporate constitution in comprehensive terms reflecting all previous amendments

---

[57] O. Reg. 400/95, s. 2.
[58] See, generally, *Oshkosh B'Gosh Inc. v. Dan Marbel Inc.*, [1989] B.C.L.C. 507 (C.A.); *Cross v. Aurora Group Ltd.* (1988), 4 N.Z.C.L.C. 64,909.

and other modifications and deleting any spent provisions. The restatement procedure now allows the Director to issue new articles, which do not change the substance of the corporate constitution, but merely consolidate the provisions found in previous articles.[59] The OBCA and the CBCA give no guidance concerning the types of change that are permitted upon restatement. However, some guidance perhaps may be taken from the *Statutes Revision Act*,[60] which empowers the commissioner appointed under that Act to make certain changes to the provincial statutes when they prepare the decennial consolidation and revision. In particular, under that Act the commissioners may:

- omit statutes and provisions that are not of general application or are obsolete;
- alter the numbering and arrangement;
- make changes to the language, including the punctuation, to achieve greater uniformity;
- make any changes necessary to bring out more clearly what is considered to be the Legislature's intention, and to reconcile any apparently inconsistent provisions or to correct clerical, grammatical or typographical errors.

The *Revised Statutes of Ontario* (and Canada) and the decennial statute revision process play such a prominent role in the practice of a solicitor that it seems a natural inference that the Legislature had much the same process in mind when it provided for the restatement procedure set out in the Act.

§14.35 That much said, the restatement procedure is intended as a housekeeping measure and should not be used to circumvent the normal article amendment procedure. This limitation is of particular importance in the case of older corporations created under predecessors to the OBCA, which may still be operating under their original articles of incorporation.[61] Subsection 277(1) of the OBCA provides that any provisions in articles, by-laws or any special resolution of a corporation that was valid immediately before the 29th day of July, 1983 that has not been amended in accordance with the present OBCA is deemed to be amended to the extent necessary to bring the terms of the provisions into conformity with the Act. However, a corporation may not use the restatement procedure to make express amendments to those articles, even if the intent behind the restatement is to bring the express terms of the articles of the corporation into conformity with the Act. Thus subsection 277(3) provides:

> 277.(3) A corporation shall not restate its articles under section 173 unless the articles of the corporation are in conformity with this Act and, where the articles have been deemed to be amended under subsection (1), the corporation has amended the express terms of the provisions in its articles in accordance with subsection (2).

---

[59] Samuel Levine, *The Business Corporations Act: An Analysis* (Toronto: Carswell, 1971) at 289.
[60] S.O. 1989, c. 81, s. 3.
[61] This problem was circumvented under the CBCA by requiring all corporations to go through a formal continuation procedure.

Subsection 277(2) does not provide an alternative procedure for the amendment of non-conforming articles, but merely requires the normal amendment procedure to be followed:

> 277.(2) A corporation may, by articles of amendment, change the express terms of any provision in its articles to which subsection (1) applies to conform to the terms of the provision as deemed to be amended by that subsection.

The only difference between the normal amendment procedure under section 168 and amendment under section 277, is that in the latter case a shareholder is not entitled to a right of dissent under section 185 in regard to any amendment made for the purpose only of bringing the provisions of the articles into conformity with the Act.[62]

§14.36 As always where articles are submitted under the Act, restated articles must be in the prescribed Form under the OBCA Regulation submitted in duplicate and verified by the signature of a director or officer of the corporation.[63] Upon receipt of the restated articles, the Director is required to endorse a restated certificate of incorporation on the articles in accordance with section 273 of the Act.[64] In particular, clause 273(1)(*b*) requires the certificate to be endorsed provided the articles are in prescribed form, have been executed in duplicate and all prescribed fees have been paid. The endorsement sets out the day, month, and year of the endorsement and also the corporation number. One copy of the endorsed articles is then filed by the Director, and the other is sent to the corporation or its representative. However, the Director is prohibited from endorsing a certificate on the articles if the corporation is in default of a filing requirement under the *Corporations Information Act* or has any unpaid fees or penalties outstanding.[65] The restated articles of incorporation supersede the original articles of incorporation and all amendments to them.[66]

(vi) Delegation to Directors

§14.37 It is common for resolutions authorizing amendments to the articles of a corporation to confer a power upon the directors to take consequential steps to carry out the effect of the amendment. Quite frequently, the directors will be delegated the authority to abandon the amendment in cases where the directors consider it necessary, expedient or otherwise in the best interests of the corporation to do so. Subsection 168(3) of the OBCA expressly sanctions this form of delegation. It provides:

> 168.(3) The directors of a corporation may, if so authorized by a special resolution effecting an amendment under this section, revoke the resolution without further approval of the shareholders at any time prior to the endorsement by the Director of a certificate of amendment of articles in respect of such amendment.

---

[62] OBCA, s. 277(4).
[63] OBCA, s. 273.
[64] OBCA, s. 173(3).
[65] OBCA, s. 274, not yet proclaimed in force.
[66] OBCA, s. 173(4).

Subsection 173(2) of the CBCA is to a similar effect, but it leaves open the question whether the power of revocation may be exercised after the amendment is made.[67]

§14.38 It is less clear whether the shareholders may delegate the authority to modify (rather than revoke) an amendment. For instance, if the shareholders approve a change of name from "XYZ" to "ABC", may they empower the directors to substitute another name should the name "ABC" prove unacceptable to the Director — such as changing the application to a similar but acceptable name, like "ABC (Stoney Creek) Inc."? Similarly, it is also unclear whether the shareholders may authorize the directors to defer carrying the amendment into effect until such times as they consider it to be in the best interest of the corporation to proceed with the amendment. Some (albeit limited) support for both of these types of delegation can be found in *Union Fire Insurance Co. v. O'Gara*,[68] where the shareholders of a corporation passed a resolution authorizing the directors of the corporation to arrange for the removal of the head office of the corporation from Ottawa to Toronto. In a subsequent action, certain of the shareholders challenged the validity of such delegation, arguing that the shareholders themselves should have passed a resolution declaring the change in head office. Osler J. rejected the complaint that the resolution was ineffective because it contemplated such delegation.

(vii) Special Powers of Directors to Amend Certain Aspects of the Articles

§14.39 The OBCA expressly provides that where the directors are authorized by the articles to divide any class of unissued shares into series and to determine the designations, rights, privileges, restrictions and conditions of such shares, they may authorize the amendment of the articles to so provide.[69] In such a case it is not necessary for the shareholders to authorize that amendment. There is no corresponding provision in the CBCA, but the power to amend the articles would appear to be inherent under CBCA subsection 27(4), which provides:

> 27.(4) Before the issue of shares of a series authorized under this section, the directors shall send to the Director articles of amendment in prescribed form to designate a series of shares.[70]

§14.40 In addition, both the OBCA and the CBCA confer an express power upon the directors of a corporation to amend the name of a corporation that has a number name. Under the OBCA the directors may change the name to any name

---

[67] Although it is not clear, it may be argued that the resolution is spent once the amendment is made, and that therefore the power of revocation delegated to the directors lapses upon the issue of the certificate of amendment.
[68] [1883] O.J. No. 138, 4 O.R. 359 (H.C.J.).
[69] OBCA, s. 168(2).
[70] See also s. 27(1); compare OBCA, s. 25(4).

that is not a number name.[71] Under the CBCA, the new name must be a verbal name.[72]

C. SALE, LEASE OR EXCHANGE OF CORPORATE PROPERTY

§14.41 Historically, the sale of all, or substantially all, of the assets of a corporation outside the ordinary course of its business required the consent of all of the shareholders, on the basis that, by so doing, the corporation terminated the implied contract among the shareholders that it would pursue the business for which it was formed.[73] Any requirement for unanimous consent puts disgruntled shareholders in a position to demand an excessive price for their cooperation. Both the OBCA and the CBCA now permit the sale of all, or substantially all, of the assets of a business to be made provided majority shareholder approval is obtained. Specifically, under subsections 184(3) of the OBCA and 189(3) of the CBCA, a sale, lease or exchange of all, or substantially all, the property of a corporation other than in the ordinary course of business[74] requires the approval of the shareholders of the corporation. The test of whether sufficient property is being sold to bring it within the scope of these subsections is both qualitative and quantitative.[75] The question to resolve is whether the sale results in a fundamental alteration in the nature of a corporation, for instance, converting it from an operating corporation to a holding corporation.[76] The form of approval required resembles that contemplated in the other fundamental change provisions. The sale, lease or exchange proposal must be submitted to a meeting of the shareholders of the corporation for approval. Prior to the meeting, the shareholders must be sent a notice of meeting which must include or be accompanied by,

(a) a copy or summary of the agreement of sale, lease or exchange; and

(b) a statement that a dissenting shareholder is entitled to be paid the fair value of the shares in accordance with section 185...[77]

However, the failure to include the statement required under clause (4)(b) does not affect the validity of the sale, though it will prevent the clock running against any dissenting shareholder in regard to the assertion of his or her rights of dissent.

---

[71] Section 168(4).
[72] Section 173(3).
[73] See, generally, *Cotton v. Imperial and Foreign Agency & Investment Corp.*, [1892] 3 Ch. 454.
[74] Where the corporation decides to sell its existing business in the ordinary manner but not to purchase replacement inventory, the sale is out of the ordinary course: *85956 Holdings Ltd. v. Fayerman Brothers Ltd.*, [1985] S.J. No. 177, [1985] 2 W.W.R. 647, aff'd [1986] S.J. No. 155, [1986] 2 W.W.R. 754 (C.A.).
[75] *Martin v. F.P. Bourgault Industries Air Seeder Division Ltd.*, [1987] S.J. No. 623, 38 B.L.R. 90 (C.A.); *Lindzon v. International Sterling Holdings Inc.*, [1989] B.C.J. No. 1773, 45 B.L.R. 57 (S.C.).
[76] *Martin v. F.P. Bourgault Industries Air Seeder Division Ltd.*, [1987] S.J. No. 623, 38 B.L.R. 90 (C.A.).
[77] OBCA, s. 184(4); CBCA, s. 189(4).

§14.42 Until recently, section 23 of the Regulations under the OBCA provided that:

> 23. Where shares of a class or series have attached thereto, conditions, restrictions, limitations or prohibitions on the right to vote, the rights, privileges, restrictions and conditions attaching to the class or series of shares shall provide that the holders of that class are entitled to notice of meetings of shareholders called for the purpose of authorizing the dissolution of the corporation or the sale, lease or exchange of all or substantially all the property of the corporation other than in the ordinary course of business of the corporation under subsection 184(3) of the Act.

This provision has now been repealed, although the meaning of the provision obviously is still relevant to any cases pre-dating the time when the repeal took effect.[78] The question whether a sale or other disposition is out of the ordinary course is one of fact. A sale is out of the ordinary course of business when it is a sale with unusual features, given the nature of the business that the corporation has historically conducted, for instance, where the bulk of the inventory of a corporation is to be sold off in a liquidation type process and without a view to its replacement, or where it is otherwise conducted in a manner other than that which a manager might reasonably be expected to conduct in the ongoing, day-to-day business of the corporation.[79]

§14.43 In determining whether a sale involves "substantially all" of the assets of a corporation, the courts apply not only a quantitative test but also a qualitative one.[80] Obviously, the quantitative issue is important and will be determinative where the vast majority of the assets of the corporation are to be sold; the lower the percentage of the assets sold, the less likely it is that the obligation to obtain shareholder approval will apply.[81] In *Cogeco Cable Inc. v. CFCF Inc.*[82] Biron J. (*ad hoc*) concluded that the court should first consider the quantitative effect of the sale — comparing the value of the assets that are to be disposed compared to the total value of the corporation's total assets — before proceeding to the more complicated qualitative considerations. Where the value of the assets transferred exceeds 75 per cent of the total value of the assets, then shareholder approval should be required. Only when the quantitative analysis proves inconclusive should a qualitative analysis be undertaken. In the qualitative analysis, the court is concerned with whether the effect of the transfer will be to destroy effectively the corporate business.[83] The key consideration is whether the effect of the sale will be to transfer substantially the nature of the corporation or its business,[84] or involves the transfer of assets that are integral to the transferor's traditional

---

[78] O. Reg. 190/99, s. 2.
[79] *85956 Holdings Ltd. v. Fayerman Brothers Ltd.*, [1986] S.J. No. 15, 32 B.L.R. 204 (C.A.); *Martin v. F.P. Bourgault Industries Air Seeder Division Ltd.*, [1987] S.J. No. 623, 38 B.L.R. 90 (C.A.); see also *Re Bradford Roofing Industries Property Ltd.*, [1966] 1 N.S.W.R. 674 (S.C.).
[80] See, generally, *Stiles v. Aluminum Product Co.*, 338 Ill. App. 48, 86 N.E.2d 887 (C.A. 1949).
[81] *Olympia & York Enterprises Ltd. v. Hiram Walker Resources Ltd.*, [1986] O.J. No. 679, 59 O.R. (2d) 254 (Div. Ct.).
[82] [1996] Q.J. No. 131, 136 D.L.R. (4th) 243 (C.A.).
[83] *85956 Holdings Ltd. v. Fayerman Brothers. Ltd.*, [1986] S.J. No. 15, 32 B.L.R. 204 (C.A.).
[84] *Good v. Lackawanna Leather Co.*, 233 A.2d 201 at 210 (N.J.S.C. 1967); see also *Campbell v. Vose*, 515 F.2d 256 (10th cir. 1975).

business so that its disposition or transfer strikes at the heart of the transferor's existence or primary corporate purpose.[85] Specific factors to consider include the contribution made by assets to the income of the corporation[86] and whether they are necessary to the corporation's usual/existing operations.[87] Sales to subsidiaries are as much a concern as sales to third parties, as a sale to a subsidiary could be no more than the first step in a two-step liquidation of the corporation's business. The obligation to obtain shareholder approval will also apply where the sale or disposition will have the effect of fundamentally changing or destroying the nature of the corporation's business. In answering this question, the courts look to the relationship between the assets that are to be sold and the corporation's operations as a whole, with a view towards determining whether the assets concerned are so fundamental that they are essential for the ordinary day-to-day business of the corporation.[88]

§14.44 A proposed sale, lease or exchange is approved when the shareholders have approved it by a special resolution of the holders of each class or series entitled to vote on the resolution. If the sale, lease or exchange would affect a particular class or series of shares of the corporation in a manner different from the shares of another class or series of the corporation entitled to vote on the sale, lease or exchange at the meeting referred to in subsection (4), the holders of the differently affected class or series are entitled to vote separately as a class or series on the sale, lease or exchange, whether or not they are otherwise entitled to vote.[89] The shareholder's resolution may authorize the sale, lease or exchange and may fix, or authorize the directors to fix, any of the terms and conditions thereof.[90] The shareholder's resolution may confer upon the directors the discretion to abandon the sale, lease or exchange without further approval of the shareholders, but any such approval is subject to the rights of third parties.[91]

D. RIGHTS OF DISSENT (THE "APPRAISAL" REMEDY)

§14.45 In a good many cases, even granting separate class (or series) voting rights to a proposal will do little to protect dissident minorities within the corporation. The protection afforded to minority shareholders at common law was limited, at least in the absence of contractual entitlement. During the formative period of the company, they were protected by the equitable rules governing promoters and their dealings with the corporation. They were also protected by

---

[85] *Canadian Broadcasting Corp. Pension Plan v. BF Realty Holdings Ltd.*, [2002] O.J. No. 2125, 214 D.L.R. (4th) 121 (C.A.); *Hovsepian v. Westfair Foods Ltd.*, [2003] A.J. No. 1133, 37 B.L.R. (3d) 78 at 112-13 (Q.B.), per Hart J.
[86] *Benson v. Third Canadian General Investment Trust Ltd.*, [1993] O.J. No. 1491, 14 O.R. (3d) 493 at 506 (Gen. Div.), per Farley J.
[87] *GATX Corp. v. Hawker Siddeley Canada Inc.*, [1996] O.J. No. 1462, 27 B.L.R. (2d) 251 at para. 82 (Gen. Div. — C.L.), per Blair J.
[88] *Ibid.*, at 279.
[89] OBCA, s. 184(6); CBCA, s. 189(6).
[90] OBCA, s. 184(5); CBCA, s. 189(5).
[91] OBCA, s. 184(8); CBCA, s. 189(9).

the law governing the fiduciary duty of directors. Minority shareholders were entitled at common law to be present at and participate in shareholder meetings. They were entitled to inspect the corporation's books and records (including its books of account) during its usual hours of business, and to copy information there-from, such as the names of the holders of securities. Fundamental changes in the corporate constitution required their consent. Beyond these limits, except where fraud could be proved, the minority could be almost disregarded by the control group within the corporation. Consistent with this general philosophy of indifference, historically, the common law took the view that disgruntled shareholders must simply live with duly authorized changes (no matter how fundamental) in the corporate constitution[92] or with other steps that radically altered the nature or business of the corporation, even if those changes significantly altered or completely eroded the commercial foundation upon which the minority had originally invested in the shares of the corporation.[93] In recent years, there has been both a legislative and judicial trend away from this approach.[94] One example of this trend towards minority protection can be found in the shareholder dissent rights created under both the OBCA and the CBCA.[95]

§14.46 The aim of the appraisal remedy is to allow the transactions to which it applies to proceed where they are advantageous to the corporation by the majority entitled to vote with respect to them, while assuring that minority shareholders receive a fair value for their shares.[96] The purpose of statutory dissenters' rights is to permit a shareholder to be "cashed out" in the event of a transaction that changes the nature of the business beyond that contemplated by the shareholder. Appraisal rights protect the dissenting minority shareholder against being forced either to remain an investor in an enterprise fundamentally different from that in which he (or she) invested or sacrifice his investment by sale of his shares at less than a fair value.[97]

---

[92] *Peter's American Delicacy Co. v. Heath* (1939), 61 C.L.R. 457 (H.C. Aust.); *Malleson v. National Insurance & Guarantee Corp.*, [1894] 1 Ch. 200.

[93] *Sidebottom v. Kershaw, Leese & Co.*, [1920] 1 Ch. 154; *Shuttleworth v. Cox Bros. & Co. (Maidenhead) Ltd.*, [1927] 2 K.B. 9; *Allen v. Gold Reefs of West Africa Ltd.*, [1900-03] All E.R. Rep. 746 (C.A.), *per* Lord Lindley M.R.

[94] Jerome Frank, "Some Realistic Reflections on Some Aspects of Corporate Reorganization" (1933), 19 Va. L. Rev. 541 at 569.

[95] See, generally, *Smeenk v. Dexleigh Corp.*, [1990] O.J. No. 1500, 72 D.L.R. (4th) 609 at 651, 658-59 (H.C.J.), *per* Henry J., aff'd [1993] O.J. No. 2020, 105 D.L.R. (4th) 193 (C.A.). The dissent concept appears to have originated in the decision of the Supreme Court of Pennsylvania in *Lauman v. Lebanon Valley R.R. Co.*, 30 Pa. 42 (1858), in which it was held that a shareholder who objected to the merger of his company with another company was entitled to treat the merger as a dissolution of the company in which he had invested and to receive the value of his shares upon their surrender.

[96] *Steinberg v. Amplica, Inc.*, 42 Cal.3d 1198 at 1208, 233 Cal. Rptr. 249, 729 P.2d 683 (1986).

[97] *Singhania v. Uttarwar*, 136 Cal. App. 4th 416; 38 Cal. Rptr. 3d 861 at para. 10 (Calif. C.A. 6th Dist. 2006).

(i) Dissent Rights Limited to Registered Holders

§14.47 Sections 185 of the OBCA and 190 of the CBCA provide shareholders with a right of dissent, which, in essence, is the right of a shareholder (a "dissident") who opposes certain proposed amendments to the articles of a corporation to require the corporation to buy him or her out — *i.e.*, to repurchase the dissident's shares at their fair value.[98] The fair value of those shares is determined at the close of business on the day before the resolution was passed. In *Lake & Co. v. Calex Resources Ltd.*,[99] the question arose about the meaning of the Alberta equivalent to subsection 185(5) of the OBCA,[100] which prohibits a partial dissent. This provision reads:

> 184.(4) A dissenting shareholder may only claim under this section with respect to all the shares of a class held by him or on behalf of any one beneficial owner and registered in the name of the dissenting shareholder.

Hunt J.A. concluded that the provision means that dissent rights can be claimed only by a registered shareholder[101] (although on the special facts of the case, beneficial shareholders were held to be entitled to exercise dissent rights, due to the wording of the information circular provided by the corporation).[102]

(ii) Overview of the Dissent Procedure

§14.48 The basic right of dissent under the OBCA is conferred under subsection 185(1).[103] It provides that the holder of a share of any class or series that is entitled to vote on the resolution in regard to the matter concerned, is entitled to dissent where the corporation resolves to:

(*a*) amend its articles under section 168 to add, remove or change restrictions on the issue, transfer or ownership of shares of a class or series of the shares of a corporation;

(*b*) amend its articles under section 168 to add, remove or change any restriction upon the business or businesses that the corporation may carry on or upon the powers that the corporation may exercise;

---

[98] As for the constitutionality of s. 190 of the CBCA, see *Rathie v. Montreal Trust* (1952), 5 W.W.R. (N.S.) 675 at 680 *et seq.* (B.C.S.C.), *per* Coady J., aff'd 6 W.W.R. (N.S.) 652, rev'd [1953] 2 S.C.R. 204. Section 185(31) of the OBCA permits a corporation to apply to the court for an order that the shareholder dissent rights will not apply. No equivalent provision is found in the CBCA. As to the considerations relevant to the making of such an order, see *Re Electrohome Ltd.*, [1998] O.J. No. 1477, 40 B.L.R. (2d) 210 (Gen. Div.).
[99] [1996] A.J. No. 772, 30 B.L.R. (2d) 186 (C.A.).
[100] Section 184(4) of the Alberta *Business Corporations Act*, S.A. 1981, c. B-15.
[101] [1996] A.J. No. 772, 30 B.L.R. (2d) 186 at 194 (C.A.).
[102] See also *Manitoba Securities Commission v. Versatile Cornat Corp.*, [1979] M.J. No. 274, 97 D.L.R. (3d) 45 at 54 (Q.B.), *per* Hewak J.; Note, however, the following considerations voiced in *Tabbi v. Pollution Control Industries*, 508 A.2d 867 at 872-73 (Del. Ch. 1986). See also *Raab v. Villager Industries*, 258 A.2d 888 (Del. Sup. Ct. 1976).
[103] CBCA, s. 190(1).

A further right of dissent arising from the amendment of the articles of a corporation is conferred under subsection 185(2) of the OBCA,[104] which provides:

> 185.(2) If a corporation resolves to amend its articles in a manner referred to in subsection 170(1), a holder of shares of any class or series entitled to vote on the amendment under section 168 or 170 may dissent, except in respect of an amendment referred to in,
>
> (a) clause 170(1)(a), (b) or (e) where the articles provide that the holders of shares of such class or series are not entitled to dissent; or
>
> (b) subsection 170(5) or (6).

As discussed above, subsection 170(1) confers special class and series voting rights in cases where, in general terms, a particular class or series of shares would be adversely affected as a result of the amendment of the articles. More specifically, clause 170(1)(a) confers a class (or series) voting right upon proposals to amend the articles of a corporation to increase or decrease any maximum number of authorized shares of such class or series, or increase any maximum number of authorized shares of a class or series having rights or privileges equal or superior to the shares of such class or series. Clause 170(1)(b) confers a class (or series) voting right upon proposals to amend the articles of a corporation to effect an exchange, reclassification or cancellation of the shares of such class or series. Clause 170(1)(e) confers a class (or series) voting right upon proposals to amend the articles of a corporation to create a new class or series of shares equal or superior to the shares of the class or series claiming to be entitled to class voting right — although this right does not apply to a new series created under section 25 of the Act.[105]

§14.49 Dissent rights are also conferred upon dissident shareholders entitled to vote on a resolution pertaining to three other steps for which shareholder approval must be sought, namely where the corporation resolves to[106]

---

[104] Compare the wording of s. 190(2) of the CBCA:

> 190(2) A holder of shares of any class or series of shares entitled to vote under section 176 may dissent if the corporation resolves to amend its articles in a manner described in that section.

Subsection 190(2.1) of the CBCA specifically provides that the right of dissent in subsection (2) applies even if there is only one class of shares.

[105] Note, however, s. 185(3), which provides:

> 185.(3) A shareholder of a corporation incorporated before the 29th day of July, 1983, is not entitled to dissent under this section in respect of an amendment of the articles of the corporation to the extent that the amendment,
>
> (a) amends the express terms of any provision of the articles of the corporation to conform to the terms of the provision as deemed to be amended by section 277; or
>
> (b) deletes from the articles of the corporation all of the objects of the corporation set out in its articles, provided that the deletion is made by the 29th day of July, 1986.

[106] OBCA, s. 185(1)(c), (d) and (e); CBCA, s. 190(1)(c), (d) and (e).

- amalgamate with another corporation under sections 175 and 176 (*i.e.*, in the case of any amalgamation other than an amalgamation between a corporation and its wholly owned subsidiary or between two wholly owned subsidiaries of the same corporation, which are governed by section 177 of the Act);
- continue under the laws of another jurisdiction under section 181 (note that any right of dissent in a continuation of a company as a corporation under the OBCA and from the laws of another jurisdiction must be found in the laws of that jurisdiction); or
- sell, lease or exchange all, or substantially all, of its property under subsection 184(3).

Because the dissent rights in such cases are essentially the same as those that apply in an amendment of the articles of the corporation, it is convenient to deal with all aspects of dissent at this juncture.

(iii) Nature of the Dissent Right

§14.50 It has long been recognized in the business community that the practical rights of a shareholder in a corporation are limited primarily to the right of exit and the right to voice complaint.[107] For many years, corporate governance measures in Canada and abroad focused primarily upon the provision of information to shareholders and then the process for soliciting proxies from shareholders who are unable to attend meetings. These voice-oriented measures are now supplemented by the increased availability of statutory dissent and appraisal rights, which allow a shareholder to withdraw from membership in a corporation where there is a radical change to the basis on which the shareholder agreed to enter into membership. These rights significantly qualify the majority rule principle of corporate law. Where exercised, the majority still rule, but they must do so on the understanding that they must buy out the dissident shareholder's interest. The nature of the rights conferred upon a dissident shareholder are essentially set down in subsection 185(4) of the OBCA,[108] which provides:

> 185.(4) In addition to any other right that the shareholder may have, but subject to subsection (30), a shareholder who complies with this section is entitled, when the action approved by the resolution from which the shareholder dissents becomes effective, to be paid by the corporation the fair value of the shares held by the shareholder in respect of which the shareholder dissents, determined as of the close of business on the day before the resolution was adopted.

Although consideration must always be given to additional contractual rights to which a particular dissident may be entitled, the "other rights" referred to in subsection (4) are not limited to simple contractual remedies, but include all legal and equitable rights, whether arising by statute, agreement or otherwise. One important "other right" that the dissident may be entitled to raise is the right conferred by the oppression remedy created under sections 248 of the OBCA

---

[107] A. O. Hirschman, *Exit, Voice and Loyalty* (Cambridge, Mass.: Harvard University Press, 1970).
[108] CBCA, s. 190(3).

and 241 of the CBCA.[109] Similarly, a dissident who takes advantage of the right of dissent may still bring an action to challenge the underlying fairness of the transaction.[110] However, standing to seek the winding-up of the corporation is lost once a shareholder invokes his or her dissent rights.[111]

§14.51 The dissident's rights in regard to any particular corporate action are subject to the qualification that the corporation may apply to the court under subsection 185(31),[112] which reads:

> 185.(31) Upon application by a corporation that proposes to take any of the actions referred to in subsection (1) or (2), the court may, if satisfied that the proposed action is not in all the circumstances one that should give rise to the rights arising under subsection (4), by order declare that those rights will not arise upon the taking of the proposed action, and the order may be subject to compliance upon such terms and conditions as the court thinks fit and, if the corporation is an offering corporation, notice of any such application and a copy of any order made by the court upon such application shall be served upon the Commission.

Although the discretion conferred under subsection (31) is clearly broad, it is not clear when that discretion may properly be exercised. There is no indication of the considerations the court should take into account in deciding whether the proposed action is not one that in "all the circumstances ... should give rise" to dissent rights.[113] One possible circumstance in which the court may grant such an order would be where the evidence shows that the shareholders intend to assert their dissent rights not because of some objection to the proposed action, but because of some collateral issue concerning which the shareholders have no right of complaint. For instance, an order under subsection (31) might be possible in the case of a proposal to continue an OBCA corporation under the CBCA, where it is expected that some shareholders will dissent from the proposal because the corporation's return on investment has been poor or because the corporation has failed to pay dividends upon their shares despite having earned sufficient income to do so. The continuation thus provides the investors with an opportunity to abandon ship by invoking the dissent provisions. But even if such facts can be shown, it is not clear why the court should choose to take sides to prevent the dissidents (who may well have been abused in the past) from taking advantage of a fortuitous opportunity to prevent their being abused further in the future.

§14.52 Although the wording of subsection (4) seems to suggest that a particular shareholder may dissent in regard to only part of his or her shareholding, this

---

[109] *Wind Ridge Farms v. Quadra Group Investments*, [1999] S.J. No. 602, 50 B.L.R. (2d) 1 (C.A.); *Alberta (Treasury Branches) v. Seven Way Capital Corp.*, [2000] A.J. No. 801, 8 B.L.R. (3d) 1 (C.A.).
[110] *Brant Investments Ltd. v. KeepRite Inc.*, [1983] O.J. No. 3283, 44 O.R. (2d) 661 at 663-64 (H.C.J.), *per* Callaghan J.
[111] *Alberta (Treasury Branches) v. Seven Way Capital Corp.*, [2000] A.J. No. 801, 8 B.L.R. (3d) 1 at 10 (C.A.), *per* Hunt J.
[112] There is no CBCA equivalent.
[113] See, generally, *689531 B.C. Ltd. v. Anthem Works Ltd.*, [2005] B.C.J. No. 1226, 5 B.L.R. (4th) 289 at 299-307 (S.C.), *per* Davies J.

possibility is excluded, at least in regard to all shares that belong to the same class, by subsection 185(5) of the OBCA,[114] which provides:

> 185.(5) A dissenting shareholder may only claim under this section with respect to all the shares of a class held by the dissenting shareholder on behalf of any one beneficial owner and registered in the name of the dissenting shareholder.

It would seem to follow from subsection (5) that if a shareholder holds 100 Class A shares in trust for X, and a further 200 Class A shares beneficially for himself or herself or in trust for another person, X may instruct the registered holder to dissent in regard to his or her 100 shares without prejudice to the right to dissent in the case of the other 200 shares. Similarly, if X holds 100 Class A shares and 200 Class B shares, X may dissent in regard to the Class B shares while continuing to hold the Class A shares. Although such inconsistent behaviour may seem illogical at first glance, it is important to remember that X's rights (and interests) in regard to each class of shares may be entirely different. It may be in the interest of X, as the holder of Class A shares, for the proposal to pass, while such approval may be against X's interest as the holder of Class B shares.

(iv) Opposition Not the Same as Dissent

§14.53 A dissident does not evidence dissent against a proposed measure merely by voting against it or by executing a proxy that directs that his or her shares should be voted against it.[115] The law recognizes that within every corporation there will be a degree of give and take: each shareholder is likely to support some measures that are put to a shareholder vote, and support others. Subsection 185(1) makes clear that dissent rights are limited to those types of measure that are likely to affect the fundamental basis on which a given shareholder agreed to participate as a member of the corporation. In addition, in order to take advantage of the dissent procedure even with respect to such measures, a prospective dissident shareholder must make clear to the corporation that he or she intends to withdraw from the corporation in the event that it elects to proceed with the measure in question. More specifically, the dissident must comply with the objection procedure set out in subsection 185(6) of the OBCA,[116] which provides:

> 185.(6) A dissenting shareholder shall send to the corporation, at or before any meeting of shareholders at which a resolution referred to in subsection (1) or (2) is to be voted on, a written objection to the resolution, unless the corporation did not give notice to the shareholder of the purpose of the meeting or the shareholder's right to dissent.

§14.54 The requirement for the shareholder to declare his or her intention to dissent prior to the vote being taken can be justified on the basis that the voting

---

[114] CBCA, s. 190(4).
[115] Especially, s. 185(7) of the OBCA provides:
> 185.(7) The execution or exercise of a proxy does not constitute a written objection for the purposes of subsection (6).
[116] CBCA, s. 190(5).

intentions of other shareholders may be influenced by the number of shareholders who indicate an intention to assert the dissent remedy should the proposal be approved. It is mandatory for the shareholder to comply with the time limit imposed on notification to the corporation of his or her dissent, and the courts have no power to grant relief from a failure to comply with that requirement.[117] However, to the extent that there is any ambiguity, the time limits imposed under the OBCA and the CBCA are broadly construed in the shareholder's favour.[118] Moreover, as long as the shareholder complies in substance with the notice requirements applicable under the dissent provisions, the shareholder is entitled to enforce his or her dissent rights.[119] The notice may be given by an agent as well as by the shareholder personally.[120] Although strict compliance is not required, if the dissident does not substantially comply with the requirement for a written objection, the dissident loses his or her dissent rights under section 185.

§14.55 Where the resolution to which the dissident has indicated an intention to dissent is defeated, the dissident has no right to be repaid the fair value of his or her shares. In such a case, there is nothing for the dissident to dissent to, and so the remedy is spent. Similarly, the dissident has no right to be repaid the fair value of his or her shares where (subsequent to the approval of the resolution) the directors revoke a resolution to amend the articles under subsection 168(3), terminate an amalgamation agreement under subsection 176(5) or an application for continuance under subsection 181(5), or abandon a sale, lease or exchange under subsection 184(8).

§14.56 If, on the other hand, the resolution is approved, the onus then falls upon the corporation to notify all dissenting shareholders of this fact. Thus, subsection 185(8) of the OBCA provides:

> 185.(8) The corporation shall, within ten days after the shareholders adopt the resolution, send to each shareholder who has filed the objection referred to in subsection (6) notice that the resolution has been adopted, but such notice is not required to be sent to any shareholder who voted for the resolution or who has withdrawn the objection.[121]

It follows from subsection (8) that where a dissident gives a written objection but subsequently votes in favour of the resolution, the right of dissent is forfeited; similarly, the right of dissent is forfeited if the dissident at any time withdraws that written objection. It is implicit in subsection 185(8) — and also in subsection 185(12) — that the written objection given by the dissident to the corporation prior to the vote is not binding upon the dissident: subsequent to the vote being taken, the dissident may simply elect not to assert his or her right of

---

[117] *Denischuk v. Bonn Energy Corp.*, [1983] S.J. No. 862, 30 Sask. R. 37 at 39 (Q.B.), *per* Estey J.
[118] See, for instance, *Royfor & Co. v. Skye Resources Ltd.*, [1982] O.J. No. 3412, 38 O.R. (2d) 253 (H.C.J.), aff'd [1983] O.J. No. 3302, 40 O.R. (2d) 416 (C.A.).
[119] *Manning v. Harris Steel Group Inc.*, [1985] B.C.J. No. 2015, [1985] 2 W.W.R. 230, 59 B.C.L.R. 1, 28 B.L.R. 240 (C.A.).
[120] *Silber v. Pointer Exploration Corp.*, [1998] A.J. No. 903, [1999] 4 W.W.R. 452 (Q.B.).
[121] CBCA, s. 190(6).

Fundamental Changes **1413**

dissent, and this is done by failing to employ the procedures required after the vote to obtain repayment.

§14.57 The notice sent to each dissident under subsection (8) must set out the rights of the dissident (in sufficient detail and in sufficiently plain language for those rights to be understood)[122] and the procedures to be followed by the dissident to exercise those rights.[123] If the dissident still wishes to enforce his or her dissent rights, then within 20 days after receiving the notice (or, if the dissident does not receive such a notice, within 20 days after learning that the resolution has been adopted),[124] he or she must send to the corporation a written notice containing:

(a) the shareholder's name and address;

(b) the number and class of shares in respect of which the shareholder dissents; and

(c) a demand for the payment of the fair value of such shares.[125]

This, however, is only the first step that the dissident is obliged to take to obtain payment. The dissident must also send to the corporation, or to its transfer agent, the certificates representing the shares in regard to which he or she dissents and must do so not later that the 30th day after the sending of the notice under subsection (10).[126] These procedural requirements are backed up by subsection 185(12),[127] which provides:

185.(12) A dissenting shareholder who fails to comply with subsections (6), (10), and (11) has no right to make a claim under this section.

(v) Procedure for Sole Benefit of Dissidents

§14.58 The dissent procedures contained in the OBCA and CBCA are provided for the entire benefit of the dissident.[128] The corporation may not insist that a shareholder relinquish his or her interest in the corporation merely because the shareholder opposes measures that the majority approve. One question that arises, however, is at what point the corporation may insist that the dissident carry through with a declared intent to invoke his or her dissent rights. This question is answered by subsection 185(14),[129] which states that on sending a

---

[122] *Fitch v. Churchill Corp.*, [1990] A.J. No. 202, 47 B.L.R. 97 (C.A.). *Heil v. ROAM I.T. (Canada) Holdings Inc.*, [2002] A.J. No. 351, 22 B.L.R. (3d) 202 (Q.B.).
[123] OBCA, s. 185(9).
[124] See, for instance, *Jepson v. Canadian Salt Co.*, [1979] A.J. No. 481, [1979] 4 W.W.R. 35, 7 B.L.R. 181 (S.C.).
[125] OBCA, s. 185(10); *Heil v. ROAM I.T. (Canada) Holdings Inc.*, [2002] A.J. No. 351, 22 B.L.R. (3d) 202 (Q.B.).
[126] OBCA, s. 185(11).
[127] CBCA, s. 190(9).
[128] As to the right of the dissident to choose among different types of consideration provided to accepting shareholders, see *Shoom v. Great-West Lifeco Inc.*, [1998] O.J. No. 2220, 40 O.R. (3d) 672 (Gen. Div.), aff'd [1998] O.J. No. 5393, 42 B.L.R. (2d) 40 (C.A.).
[129] CBCA, s. 190(11).

notice under subsection (10), a dissident ceases to have any rights as a shareholder other than the right to be paid the fair value of the shares as determined under section 185.[130] Subsection (14) goes on, however, to provide three exceptions to this general forfeiture of shareholder rights. These exceptions arise where:

(a) the dissenting shareholder withdraws notice before the corporation makes an offer under subsection 185(15);

(b) the corporation fails to make an offer in accordance with subsection 185(15) and the dissenting shareholder withdraws notice; or

(c) the directors revoke a resolution to amend the articles under subsection 168(3), terminate an amalgamation agreement under subsection 176(5) or an application for continuance under subsection 181(5), or abandon a sale, lease or exchange under subsection 184(8).[131]

Thus, even after tendering a notice under subsection 185(10), the dissident retains at least a limited right to change his or her mind. There is old case law (dealing with a right roughly comparable to the dissent provisions under earlier legislation) that suggests that where a dissident participates in, and votes at, a

---

[130] Section 176 of the CBCA provides that on certain fundamental changes, the shareholders of a class must approve the change by special resolution. Thus, as we have seen, a class vote is required where there is a proposal to create a class of shares equal or superior to the shares of another class. Although the CBCA does not deal expressly with the issue, there is case law in British Columbia to the effect that the dissent remedy is not available to shareholders of a corporation with only one class of shares: *McConnell v. NEWCO Financial Corp.*, [1979] B.C.J. No. 612, 8 B.L.R. 180 (S.C.). The facts in that case were somewhat unusual. The case involved an application by minority shareholders for relief against oppression, arising from the approval by the majority shareholders of a "squeeze out" of the minority shareholders of a corporation. The respondent in the case argued that the applicant minority shareholders had no right to bring an oppression application, because they had earlier exercised a dissent right, and under the terms of the dissent remedy of the CBCA, once a shareholder dissents, he or she ceases to have any rights as a shareholder except the right to be paid for his or her shares. The applicants argued that their earlier dissent was invalid, because they could invoke the dissent right only where there was more than one class of shares. Section 190(2) provides:

> 190.(2) A holder of shares of any class or series of shares entitled to vote under section 176 may dissent if the corporation resolves to amend its articles in a manner described in that section.

The court agreed that the corporation had only one class of shares and, therefore, s. 176 did not apply. It allowed the oppression action to proceed. The interpretation given to ss. 176 and 190 in this case is questionable, and it is worth noting that Industry Canada has proposed that this decision be reversed by statutory amendment: *Canada Business Corporations Act, Discussion Paper Proposals for Technical Amendments* (Ottawa: Industry Canada, September, 1995), at 78.

[131] Where one of these three exceptions applies, the dissenting shareholder's rights are reinstated on the date the dissenting shareholder sent the notice referred to in subs. (10) — so there is no hiatus between the time when the notice demanding repayment was sent and the time when the notice withdrawing that demand was sent or received. In addition, the dissenting shareholder is entitled — upon presentation and surrender to the corporation, or to its transfer agent, of any certificate representing the shares that has been endorsed in accordance with subs. (13) — to be issued a new certificate representing the same number of shares as the certificate so presented, without the payment of a fee to the corporation.

meeting of shareholders held after the time when the right of dissent arises, the dissident will be taken to have waived those dissent rights.[132]

§14.59 Once the share certificates are received under subsection (11), the corporation or its transfer agent, as the case may be, must endorse on the share certificate a notice that the holder is a dissident under section 185. It must then return the share certificate to the dissident.[133]

§14.60 The provisions of the OBCA concerning payment to the dissident offer considerably more guidance than that afforded under the corresponding provisions of the CBCA. In general, the shareholder's right to withdraw his or her dissent ends when the corporation makes an offer to purchase the shares of the dissident for their fair value.[134] The procedure for making such an offer is set out in subsection 185(15) of the OBCA. It provides that no later than seven days after the later of (i) the day on which the action approved by the resolution becomes effective, and (ii) the day the corporation received the dissenting shareholder's demand for payment of the fair value of his shares under subsection (10), the corporation is required to send to each dissident who has sent such a demand:

(a) a written offer to pay for the dissenting shareholder's shares in an amount considered by the directors of the corporation to be the fair value thereof, accompanied by a statement showing how the fair value was determined; or

(b) if subsection (30) applies, a notification that it is unable lawfully to pay dissenting shareholders for their shares.

Every offer to pay for shares of the same class or series must be on the same terms.[135] Subsection 185(30) provides that a corporation must not make a payment to a dissident if there are reasonable grounds for believing that:

(a) the corporation is or, after the payment, would be unable to pay its liabilities as they become due; or

(b) the realizable value of the corporation's assets would thereby be less than the aggregate of its liabilities.

These are, of course, the normal solvency tests that must be satisfied in any redemption of share capital.

§14.61 Where subsection 185(30) applies, a dissident has two options: (1) either he or she can withdraw that dissent, in which case the corporation is deemed to consent to the withdrawal and the dissident's full rights as a shareholder are reinstated, or (2) the dissident can retain status as a claimant against the corporation, which entitles the dissident to be paid as soon as the corporation is lawfully able to do so or is in liquidation. It is unclear whether the dissident can institute

---

[132] *Barrow v. Ontario, Simcoe & Huron Rlwy.*, [1853] O.J. No. 91, 11 U.C.Q.B. 124 at 125 (C.A.), *per* Robinson C.J.
[133] OBCA, s. 185(13); CBCA, s. 190(10).
[134] OBCA, s. 185(14)(a); CBCA, s. 190(11)(a).
[135] OBCA, s. 185(16).

liquidation proceedings by reason of the frustration of his or her dissent rights. Neither the CBCA nor the OBCA provides for the winding-up of an insolvent corporation, so in most cases it is doubtful whether such an application may be brought. However, if the corporation is placed into bankruptcy liquidation, the dissident's claim is subordinate to the rights of creditors of the corporation but ranks in priority over that of the corporation's shareholders.[136]

§14.62 The offer made by the corporation under subsection 185(15) may be accepted or rejected by the dissident. The offer is open for acceptance for 30 days after the date on which it was made. At the end of that period, the offer lapses, so it may no longer be accepted by the dissident. At that point, however, first the corporation and then the dissident may insist upon an appraisal of the shares, and, thus, the lapse of the offer does not defeat the dissent rights as such. Where any dissident shareholder seeks an appraisal of the value of his or her shares, the appraisal procedure takes on the nature of a class proceeding: the appraised value binds all other dissidents who have not accepted the corporation's valuation.[137]

(vi) Court Valuation

(1) General Procedure

§14.63 The corporation has the initial right of carriage of the appraisal aspect of the dissent proceeding — the right of a shareholder applying only where the corporation refrains from action.[138] Where the corporation's offer is accepted by a dissident before it lapses, the corporation must pay the dissident the agreed amount within 10 days after the acceptance of the offer.[139] If the corporation fails to make an offer as required, or if the dissident fails to accept an offer, the corporation may apply to the court to fix a fair value for the shares of any dissident[140] within the 50-day period following the taking of the action approved by the resolution.[141] If the corporation makes no offer and fails to apply to the court

---

[136] OBCA, s. 185(29).
[137] *Manning v. Harris Steel Group Inc.*, [1984] B.C.J. No. 2015, 59 B.C.L.R. 1 at 7 (C.A.), *per* Macfarlane J.A.
[138] See, for instance, *Pick v. LSI Logic Corp. of Canada Inc.*, [1995] O.J. No. 4047, 131 D.L.R. (4th) 264 (Gen. Div.).
[139] OBCA, s. 185(17).
[140] As for entitlement to interest on the value so fixed, see *Anderson v. Atlantic Enterprises Ltd.*, [1979] B.C.J. No. 826, 12 C.P.C. 299, 107 D.L.R. (3d) 566 (S.C.).
[141] OBCA, s. 185(18). The application must be made upon notice, as provided in s. 185(22):

> 185.(22) Before making application to the court under subsection (18) or not later than seven days after receiving notice of an application to the court under subsection (19), as the case may be, a corporation shall give notice to each dissenting shareholder who, at the date upon which the notice is given,
>
>> (a) has sent to the corporation the notice referred to in subsection (10); and
>>
>> (b) has not accepted an offer made by the corporation under subsection (15), if such an offer was made,
>
> of the date, place and consequences of the application and of the dissenting shareholder's right to appear and be heard in person or by counsel, and a similar notice shall be given to each dissenting shareholder who, after the date of such first men-

within this 50-day period, the dissident may apply to the court for such a valuation.[142] The application may be made within the 20 days next following the expiration of the 50-day period allowed the corporation, or such further period as the court may allow.[143] A dissident is not required to give security for costs in an application for a court valuation,[144] but if the corporation has failed to comply with subsection (15), then the dissident is entitled to the costs of the application unless the court otherwise orders.[145]

§14.64 Where an application is made for an appraisal, the court is required to fix a fair value for the shares of all dissenting shareholders.[146] The correct approach to take towards valuation varies with the facts of each case.[147] In *Cyprus Anvil Mining Corp. v. Dickson*,[148] Lambert J.A. observed:

> ... the problem of finding fair value of stock ... defies being reduced to a set of rules for selecting a method of valuation, or to a formula or equation which will produce an answer with the illusion of mathematical certainty. Each case must be examined on its own facts, and each presents its own difficulties. Factors which may be critically important in one case may be meaningless in another. Calculations which may be accurate guides for one stock may be entirely flawed when applied to another stock. ... it is a question of judgment.

Appellate courts are very reluctant to interfere with findings of valuation made at the trial level and will usually do so only where the trial court has been guilty of manifest error. This is especially true where the trial judge has relied upon the opinion of one expert in contrast to the conflicting opinion of another.[149] Where there are competing valuations, the court must normally decide which of them is

---

tioned notice and before termination of the proceedings commenced by the application, satisfies the conditions set out in clauses (*a*) and (*b*) within three days after the dissenting shareholder satisfies such conditions.

To avoid possible duplication of proceedings, all dissenting shareholders who satisfy the conditions set out in s. 185(22)(*a*) and (*b*) are deemed to be joined as parties to an application under s. 185(18) or (19) on the later of the date upon which the application is brought and the date upon which they satisfy the conditions, and they are bound by the decision rendered by the court in the proceedings commenced by the application: OBCA, s. 185(23).

[142] In such a case it is possible that an application in regard to a CBCA corporation may be brought in the courts of different provinces. *Manning v. Harris Steel Group Inc.*, [1984] B.C.J. No. 2015, 59 B.C.L.R. 1 at 9 (C.A.), *per* Macfarlane J.A. With respect to *forum conveniens* concerns, see *Persona Communications Inc. v. Mahoney*, [2004] O.J. No. 5180, 50 B.L.R. (3d) 6 at 10 (S.C.J.), *per* Cumming J.

[143] OBCA, s. 185(19).

[144] OBCA, s. 185(20). *Kinexus Holdings Ltd. v. Kineter Pharmaceuticals Inc.*, [2004] B.C.J. No. 2357, 50 B.L.R. (3d) 95 (S.C.).

[145] OBCA, s. 185(21). The court may award costs and interest in a proceeding to value shares under the appraisal remedy: *Nunachiaq Inc. v. Chow*, [1993] B.C.J. No. 3003, 79 B.L.R. (2d) 116 (S.C.), aff'd [1994] B.C.J. No. 608 (C.A.).

[146] OBCA, s. 185(24). The court has a further power to determine whether any other person is a dissenting shareholder who should be joined as a party.

[147] *Silber v. BGR Precious Metals Inc.*, [2000] O.J. No. 101, 2 B.L.R. (3d) 116 (C.A.).

[148] [1986] B.C.J. No. 1204, 8 B.C.L.R. (2d) 145 at 158-59 (C.A.).

[149] *Pocklington Goods Inc. v. Alberta (Provincial Treasurer)*, [2000] A.J. No. 16, 2 B.L.R. (3d) 103 at 105 (Alta. C.A.) *per curiam*.

most realistic.[150] However, a judge is not obliged to accept any expert testimony, provided that he or she has sound reasons for not doing so.[151]

§14.65 An application to appraise (or value) the shares of a dissident is envisaged by the legislation as an expeditious proceeding that ought to be conducted by the party having carriage. Thus, a corporation will not be forced to carry on fair value litigation in several jurisdictions merely because shareholders in different jurisdictions would each prefer the litigation to be carried on where they reside.[152] It seems clearly implicit in the section that resort to court is to be limited to those cases in which it is impossible to arrive at an agreement. In this sense, there is an onus on all parties to be reasonable. It is expected that the corporation will make its best effort to place a fair value on the shares, and the shareholders will accept a reasonable offer. Once the matter reaches court, the procedure to fix the value of shares under the appraisal remedy is an adversarial one.[153] It falls upon the parties to present evidence on the value of the shares. Where one party fails to submit evidence in proof of a particular value, the court may accept the evidence proved by the other party. It is not the duty of the court to conduct an independent inquiry into their value or to appoint its own appraiser to assist in evaluating the expert evidence submitted by the other party.[154]

§14.66 Simply defined, the fair value of shares is the highest price obtainable in an open and unrestricted (*i.e.*, competitive) market between an informed, prudent and willing buyer and a seller acting at arm's length to each other.[155] In fixing the value of shares, the court must determine their value in a real, not an imaginary, market.[156] Valuation is purely a commercial matter. Therefore, in valuing the shares of a corporation, no allowance should be given for their "sentimental value".[157] Nor is there any entitlement to a premium (in a going private

---

[150] *Cha v. 604459 Alberta Ltd.*, [2001] A.J. No. 344, 13 B.L.R. (3d) 301, additional reasons [2001] A.J. No. 1588 (Q.B.).

[151] *Towne Cinema Theaters Ltd. v. The Queen*, [1985] S.C.J. No. 24, [1985] 1 S.C.R. 494 at 517.

[152] See, for instance, *Pick v. LSI Logic Corp. of Canada Inc.*, [1995] O.J. No. 4047, 131 D.L.R. (4th) 264 (Gen. Div.).

[153] *Smeenk v. Dexleigh Corp.*, [1993] O.J. No. 2020, 15 O.R. (3d) 608 at 612-13 (C.A.), *per* McKinlay J.A.

[154] *Smeenk v. Dexleigh Corp.*, [1990] O.J. No. 1500, 72 D.L.R. (4th) 609 at 660 (H.C.J.), *per* Henry J., aff'd [1993] O.J. No. 2020, 15 O.R. (3d) 608 (C.A.).

[155] For a collection of highly useful papers on the subject of valuation, see *Valuing Shares in a Private Company* (Toronto: LSUC, Continuing Education Dept, 1986).

[156] *Cyprus Anvil Mining Corp. v. Dickson*, [1986] B.C.J. No. 1204, 33 D.L.R. (4th) 641 at 656 (C.A.), *per* Lambert J.A. He continued:

> Valuation in a case where the asset has a special enhanced value to only one purchaser was considered in the expropriation cases. ... The special value to the single prospective purchaser through his potential use of the assets should be reflected in the value; but the full value from the realization of the potential use should not be adopted as the value of the asset before acquisition and before realization of that use.

[157] *Fraser Inc. v. Aitken*, [1988] O.J. No. 1962, 41 B.L.R. 87, additional reasons at [1989] O.J. No. 2949, 33 C.P.C. (2d) 46 (H.C.J.).

transaction) because there is a compulsory taking of the shares.[158] The intent behind the legislation is to permit the dissident to walk away from the corporation fully paid in cash for the fair value of the shares.[159]

§14.67 Four methods of valuing shares of a dissident have been adopted from time to time.[160] These are (1) the quoted market price on a stock exchange (also called the market value approach),[161] (2) a valuation based upon the net assets of the corporation at fair market value (the net asset approach),[162] (3) the capitalization of maintainable earnings (also called the earnings or investment value approach),[163] and (4) various combinations of the three previous methods.[164] It should be appreciated that the mere fact that there is a quoted "market" price for shares of a given type, is not conclusive as to their "fair market value". The quoted price approach is objective, but it is prone to fluctuation. Since fluctuations in prices within securities markets may be influenced by factors bearing no relation to the corporation itself (*e.g.*, the assassination or indictment of a prominent political or other public figure, war and civil disturbance, election results, perceptions of trade trends and the direction in which interest rates and security markets are heading and other general conditions within the economy or society as a whole), a strict market value approach may be exceedingly arbitrary. Moreover, the market value method cannot be applied where there is an insufficient market for the shares in question. Some shares listed for trade on a given market will trade far less frequently than others. If a sufficient actual market existed for identical items, in which active trading was occurring, evidence concerning the quoted price might be controlling, and other methods of evidencing

---

[158] *Manning v. Harris Steel Group Inc.*, [1986] B.C.J. No. 816, [1987] 1 W.W.R. 86 (S.C.), aff'd [1989] B.C.J. No. 1988, 63 D.L.R. (4th) 125 (C.A.); but compare *Domglas Inc. v. Jarislowsky Fraser & Co.* (1982), 22 B.L.R. 121 (Que. C.A.).

[159] *Canadian Gas & Energy Fund Ltd. v. Sceptre Resources Ltd.*, [1985] A.J. No. 557, 29 B.L.R. 178 (Q.B.).

[160] *Brant Investments Ltd. v. KeepRite Inc.*, [1987] O.J. No. 574, 37 B.L.R. 65 at 115 (H.C.J.), per Anderson J., aff'd [1991] O.J. No. 683 (C.A.).

[161] *Montgomery v. Shell Canada Ltd.*, [1980] S.J. No. 196, [1980] 5 W.W.R. 543 (Q.B.); *Silber v. BGR Precious Metals Inc.*, [1998] O.J. No. 2931, 41 O.R. (3d) 147 (Gen. Div.), aff'd [2000] O.J. No. 101 (C.A.).

[162] *85956 Holdings Ltd. v. Fayerman Brothers Ltd.*, [1987] S.J. No. 245, 57 Sask. R. 141 (Q.B.).

[163] See, for instance, *Enterprises Payment Solutions Inc. v. Soft Tracks Enterprises Ltd.*, [2005] B.C.J. No. 847, 4 B.L.R. (4th) 129 at 135 (S.C.), *per* Pitfield J.

[164] In the case of valuing an asset, consideration is also given to replacement and reproduction cost of the asset in question. Replacement cost is the estimated cost to construct a building with an equivalent utility to the building being appraised, at current prices, using modern materials, standards, design and layout. Reproduction cost, on the other hand, is the estimated cost to construct an exact replica of the subject property using the same materials, standards, design and layout and embodying all the deficiencies and obsolescence of the subject building. Replacement cost is generally lower and may provide a better indication of current value than reproduction cost because it does not embody obsolescent features which would not be constructed in a new building. However, reproduction cost can be adjusted to account for functional obsolescence through appropriate deductions. Provided that proper deductions for functional obsolescence are made, it is not an error to use reproduction cost in estimating value under the cost approach. *American Express Financial Advisors, Inc. v. County of Carver*, 573 N.W.2d 651 (S.C. Minn. 1998). It is an interesting question whether one of these valuation methodologies might not be more useful where the corporation whose shares are being valued has essentially only one asset.

value could be safely excluded. This would probably be true in most cases involving the valuation of stock which is actively traded on a major stock exchange, where prevailing market conditions are relatively stable. The fair market value at any given time is tied to a hypothetical value that would be fixed in a market of willing buyers and sellers operating from conditions divorced from those of the real world. Such evidence concerning that value as the quoted market price may be more or less persuasive depending upon circumstances such as the activity in the market, the time relationship of transactions, comparableness of items sold, and other factors in that particular market. The impact of actual market conditions on price is open to proper interpretation; attempts to assess that impact may be too speculative for a court to place reliance upon them.[165]

§14.68 Where no suitable actual market exists, total reliance must be placed on other methods of evidencing fair market value. In the absence of any suitable actual price information, estimation of value becomes difficult[166] and the evidentiary problem can become very complex. Each of the foregoing alternative approaches to fixing value has certain strengths and weaknesses and none of the approaches is suitable in all cases. Net asset valuation (break up valuation) tends to produce an undervaluation of the shares, although it does provide an absolute floor that can be used as a back-stop for other valuation methods — because the corporation's assets can always be sold on such a basis. The investment value approach may also lead to undervaluation, particularly in small corporations where the earnings of the corporation may have been influenced by tax planning considerations. Where appropriate, the court may take into account the tax consequences of particular methods of valuation.[167]

§14.69 No one approach to the determination of value can be followed in all cases[168]; instead, the court should select from the various methods available that which is most likely to yield a fair price.[169] In general, the onus is on the corporation to show that the offered price is a fair one.[170] The fair value of the shares is a finding of fact and, on an appeal, is governed by the rules regarding interference with the findings of fact made by a trial judge.[171] The value to which the dissident is entitled is the pre-fundamental change value of his or her shares. Accordingly, the appraised valuation should not reflect the synergies arising

---

[165] See, generally, *Vought v. Republic-Franklin Insurance Co.*, 117 Ohio App. 389, 192 N.E.2d 332 (C.A. Ohio 1962); *cf. Roessler v. Security Savings & Loan Co.*, 147 Ohio St., 480 (1947).
[166] See, for instance, *Edwards v. Edwards Dockrill Horwich Inc.*, [2005] N.S.J. No. 451, 238 N.S.R. (2d) 104, additional reasons [2006] N.S.J. No. 230 (S.C.).
[167] *Abraham v. Inter Wide Investments Ltd.*, [1988] O.J. No. 1880, 66 O.R. (2d) 684 (H.C.J.).
[168] *Silber v. BGR Precious Metals Inc.*, [1998] O.J. No. 2931, 41 O.R. (3d) 147 (Gen. Div.), aff'd [2001] O.J. No. 101 (C.A.).
[169] *Lough v. Canadian Natural Resources Ltd.*, [1983] B.C.J. No. 1748, 45 B.C.L.R. 335 (S.C.); see also *Investissements Mont-Soleil Inc. v. National Drug Ltd.* (1982), 22 B.L.R. 139 (Que. S.C.).
[170] But compare *Neonex International Ltd. v. Kolasa*, [1978] B.C.J. No. 19, [1978] 2 W.W.R. 593, 3 B.L.R. 1 (S.C.). See also *Jefferson v. Omnitron Investments Ltd.*, [1979] B.C.J. No. 843, 18 B.C.L.R. 188 (S.C.); *Robertson v. Canadian Canners Ltd.*, [1978] O.J. No. 882, 4 B.L.R. 290 (H.C.J.).
[171] *LoCicero v. B.A.C.M. Industries Ltd.*, [1988] S.C.J. No. 25, [1988] 1 S.C.R. 399, 82 N.R. 297.

from the transaction to which the shareholders dissent.[172] On the other hand, where the value of the shares of the corporation has declined due to that transaction, the decline should also be disregarded — otherwise the dissident suffers as a result of the very change to which he or she objected.

§14.70 To value the shares of the dissident shareholders, the court may, at its discretion, appoint one or more appraisers to assist it in fixing a fair value for the shares.[173] The person so appointed is not required to hear evidence before placing a value on the shares,[174] though the court may require any party to the proceeding to furnish such evidence.[175] The parties may also tender expert evidence concerning the fair value of the shares. The court may, but is not bound to, act on that expert evidence.[176] Likewise, the court may reject the findings of any referee that it appoints to conduct a valuation.[177] The valuation date included in the reference order is binding on the referee.[178] The valuation made by the court is embodied in a final order that is made against the corporation and in favour of each dissident who is deemed to be a party to the application.[179] The court has the discretion to allow interest to the date of payment.[180]

§14.71 Problems of selecting an appropriate valuation method are anything but the exception. For instance, *Black v. Black*,[181] a family law case, illustrates the widely different results that different valuation methods may provide. The issue in that case was the valuation of the husband's shares in five private companies, which he owned equally with his brother. Four expert witnesses produced five values for the husband's shares, ranging from a low of $8.9 million to a high of $43.9 million. Obviously, in an area where subjective considerations determine results, expert evidence frequently provides little guidance to the court.

§14.72 It has been suggested that the wording of the Act implies that the fair value that the court is required to fix in dissent and appraisal cases is not the same as the fair value that the corporation is required to offer. Subsection 185(15) requires the corporation to offer "the fair value" for the shares, whereas subsection 185(18) requires the court to fix "a fair value".[182] In *Fraser Inc. v.*

---

[172] *Brant Investments Ltd. v. KeepRite Inc.*, [1987] O.J. No. 574, 37 B.L.R. 65 at 113 (H.C.J.), *per* Anderson J., aff'd [1991] O.J. No. 683 (C.A.).
[173] OBCA, s. 185(25). See, for instance, *Wall & Redekop Corp. v. W. & R. Properties Ltd.*, [1975] 1 W.W.R. 621, 50 D.L.R. (3d) 733 at 739 (B.C.S.C.), *per* Macfarlane J.
[174] *VCS Holdings Ltd. v. Helliwell*, [1978] B.C.J. No. 44, [1978] 5 W.W.R. 559 (S.C.).
[175] *Denischuk v. Bonn Energy Corp.*, [1983] S.J. No. 316, 29 Sask. R. 156 at 158 (Q.B.), *per* Batten J.
[176] *Domglas Inc. v. Jarislowsky Fraser & Co.* (1982), 22 B.L.R. 121 (Que. C.A.).
[177] *VCS Holdings Ltd. v. Helliwell*, [1978] B.C.J. No. 44, [1978] 5 W.W.R. 559 at 568 (B.C.S.C.), *per* Ruttan J.
[178] *Mason v. Intercity Properties Ltd.*, [1988] O.J. No. 3113, 66 O.R. (2d) 8 at 10 (H.C.J.), *per* Barr J. aff'd unreported, May 16, 1990, Doc. No. CA 561/88 (C.A.).
[179] OBCA, s. 185(26).
[180] OBCA, s. 185(27).
[181] [1988] O.J. No. 1975, 66 O.R. (2d) 643 (H.C.J.).
[182] The relevant provisions read:

> 185.(15) A corporation shall, not later than seven days after the later of the day on which the action approved by the resolution is effective or the day the corporation re-

Aitken,[183] the court considered whether this difference in wording meant that the court had some form of discretion in fixing the fair value of shares that was not possessed by the corporation, and the court expressed some reservation about exercising such a discretion if, indeed, it exists:

> A right to dissent arises under section 184(1). From subs. (3) arises the express right of a dissenting shareholder to be paid by the corporation "*the* fair value of the shares held by him," and the implied obligation of the corporation to pay "*the* fair value." By subs. (12), the corporation must offer to pay an amount considered by the directors to be "*the* fair value." If a dissenting shareholder fails to accept the offer, then under subs. (15) the Court must fix "*a* fair value." If ... the Court in determining "a fair value" has a discretion, which is denied to the corporation in determining "*the* fair value" for the purposes of its offer, it places the corporation in a potentially difficult position: it may be unable to pay voluntarily an amount which it may ultimately be compelled to pay. If the discretion were not exercised with caution there would be an incentive to every dissenting shareholder to reject the offer made by the corporation and apply to the Court. Given the length and complexity which such proceedings as this have come to assume, and the concomitant burdens cast on the parties and the Courts, there is an element of public policy in assuring that resort be had to the Courts only in cases of necessity.

(Emphasis in original)

It is difficult to accept that so slight a difference in wording could have been intended to confer any discretion on the courts. The conclusion that there is such a discretion built into subsection (18) requires one to assume: first, there are different fair values that may be placed upon shares; second, the corporation is entitled to offer only one of these fair values (although, for some reason, which of these various fair values is not explained); third, the court may order any of them (although how it is intended to differentiate between them, and the factors that should influence its decision on which of them to select, are also not explained); and, fourth, there was some reason behind the Legislature granting a wider valuation power to the courts than that conferred on the parties (although, if there was such a reason, the Legislature left little in the way of a clue as to

---

ceived the notice referred to in subsection (10), send to each dissenting shareholder who has sent such notice,

    (*a*) a written offer to pay for the dissenting shareholder's shares in an amount considered by the directors of the corporation to be the *fair value thereof*, accompanied by a statement showing how the fair value was determined; or

    (*b*) if subsection (30) applies, a notification that it is unable lawfully to pay dissenting shareholders for their shares.

.....

(18) Where a corporation fails to make an offer under subsection (15) or if a dissenting shareholder fails to accept an offer, the corporation may, within fifty days after the action approved by the resolution is effective or within such further period as the court may allow, apply to the court to fix *a fair value* for the shares of any dissenting shareholder.

(Emphasis added)

[183] [1988] O.J. No. 1962, 41 B.L.R. 87 at 109, *per* Anderson J., additional reasons [1989] O.J. No. 2949 (H.C.J.) but contrast *Smeenk v. Dexleigh Corp.*, [1990] O.J. No. 1500, 72 D.L.R. (4) 609 (H.C.J.), aff'd [1993] O.J. No. 2020, 105 D.L.R. (4th) 193 (C.A.).

what that reason might be, or how it might be utilized as a policy guide to the court in applying the discretion allegedly vested in it). These assumptions (and the problems of interpretation that they entail) need only be stated to demonstrate how very unlikely it was that the Legislature intended to confer any kind of discretion upon the court in selecting a fair value for the shares. However, it is even more clear that as a matter of policy it is not desirable for dissident shareholders to seek the assistance of the courts frivolously. Thus, in *Fraser Inc. v. Aitken* Anderson J. continued:

> Recourse to the Court is a necessary safeguard to assure that a corporation acts responsibly and fairly in making its offer of the fair value, but it would be an unfortunate perversion of that safeguard if it came to be assumed by shareholders that application to the Court practically assured a bonus over what was offered. In my view, resort should be had to any discretion which may be found in the section only where the evidence discloses special circumstance will clearly call for its exercise.[184]

§14.73 In *Ford Motor Co. of Canada v. Ontario Municipal Employees Retirement Board*[185] the principal shareholder of the plaintiff corporation sought to take the company private. In 1995, in an offer to the defendant dissenting shareholder, the plaintiff corporation stated that it considered $185 per share to be the fair value of its common shares. No agreement on valuation was reached between the parties, and an action was subsequently commenced to fix the fair value of the shares. The dissident shareholder defendants moved under Rule 20 for a partial summary judgment for $185 per share plus interest to the day of payment, arguing that the value of $185 placed on the shares in the plaintiff's offer was tantamount to an admission of their minimum fair value, and that, accordingly, it was appropriate to give summary judgment for that amount. Farley J. granted the motion for summary judgment (albeit, somewhat reluctantly) holding that where there has been some form of admission of the fair value, it is appropriate to give a partial judgment to that effect. However, it was pointed out by the court that it was open for the court to fix the fair value of the shares at amounts of more or less than the $185. Farley J. expressed concern that the giving of summary judgment would place corporations in an exposed position that would deter them from making reasonable offers to shareholders; they would be reluctant to do so if they were exposed to the risk that dissidents might first reject the offer and then demand partial summary judgment for the amount offered, thus throwing the corporation's offer "back in its face".[186] On appeal to the Court of Appeal it was held that summary judgment was not possible absent an admission that the offer is a minimum value. One way of avoiding this problem might be to state that (like any settlement offer) any offer made by the corporation is made without prejudice to the corporation's right to argue later that the fair value of the shares is, in fact, less than the

---

[184] *Ibid.*, at 109-10. See also *689531 B.C. Ltd. v. Anthem Works Ltd.*, [2005] B.C.J. No. 1226, 5 B.L.R. (4th) 289 (S.C.).

[185] [1996] O.J. No. 4400, 34 B.L.R. (2d) 156 (Gen. Div. — C.L.), rev'd [1997] O.J. No. 4289, 153 D.L.R. (4th) 33 (C.A.).

[186] *Ibid.*, at 164.

amount that the corporation is offering.[187] On the other hand, if on a Rule 20 motion it is clear that there is no dispute between the parties that the minimum value of the shares is at least the amount offered, it is not clear (a) why the dissidents should not be entitled to receive that amount, nor (b) why at trial the court would be prepared to reopen the question of minimum value and receive evidence in regard to that question, when it has already been resolved in a final order of the court. However, if the minimum value is genuinely in dispute, then there would not appear to be any basis for an order under Rule 20.[188]

(2) American Case Law Concerning Valuation

§14.74 There are a large number of American decisions that provide guidance as to the considerations to be taken into account in determining the fair value of the shares upon dissent. A complete survey of this extensive body of case law is not possible in a general corporate law text. However, as many of these cases touch on issues that have not yet been fully resolved in Canada, and have raised perspectives distinct from those considered in Canada, it is worthwhile to provide a quick review of some of the leading cases. As in Canada, American case law has recognized that:

> ... the task of enterprise valuation, even for a finance expert, is fraught with uncertainty. For a lay person, even one who wears judicial robes, it is even more so. No formula exists that can invest with scientific precision a process that is inherently judgmental.[189]

In another leading Delaware case, it was said:

> ... it is one of the conceits of our law that we purport to declare something as elusive as the fair value of an entity on a given date. ... Experience in the adversarial battle of the experts' appraisal process under Delaware law teaches one lesson very clearly: valuation decisions are impossible to make with anything approaching complete confidence. Valuing an entity is a difficult intellectual exercise, especially when business and financial experts are able to organize data in support of wildly divergent valuations for the same entity. For a judge who is not an expert in corporate finance, one can do little more than try to detect gross distortions in the experts' opinions. This effort should, therefore, not be understood, as a matter of intellectual honesty, as resulting in the fair value of a corporation on a given date. [A corporation's]. ... value is not a point on a line, but a range of reasonable values, and the judge's task is to assign one particular value within this range as the most reasonable value ... based on considerations of fairness.[190]

---

[187] It is a fair question whether offers made in connection with the exercise of the appraisal remedy should be privileged as integral to efforts to settle a dispute without resort to litigation. See, generally, *Middelkamp v. Fraser Valley Real Estate Board*, [1992] B.C.J. No. 1947, 71 B.C.L.R. (2d) 276 (C.A.); *Cutts v. Head*, [1984] Ch. 290, [1984] 1 All E.R. 597 (C.A.); but *cf. Mueller Canada Inc. v. State Contractors Inc.*, [1989] O.J. No. 2059, 41 C.P.C. (2d) 291 (H.C.J.).

[188] See, generally, *Royal Bank v. Cadillac Fairview/JMB Properties*, [1995] O.J. No. 472, 21 O.R. (3d) 783 (C.A.); *Irving Ungerman Ltd. v. Galanis*, [1991] O.J. No. 1478, 4 O.R. (3d) 545 (C.A.); *Hotton v. Joyce*, [1990] O.J. No. 1641, 45 C.P.C. (2d) 69 (H.C.J.).

[189] *Prescott Group Small Cap, L.P. v. Coleman Co.*, [2004] Del. Ch. LEXIS 131 (Ct. Ch.).

[190] *Cede & Co. v. Technicolor, Inc.*, [2003] Del. Ch. LEXIS 146.

§14.75 In most cases, the "fair value" of a corporation is its value as a going concern. A merger price resulting from arm's-length negotiations where there are no claims of collusion is a very strong indication of fair value. But in an appraisal action, that merger price must be accompanied by evidence tending to show that it represents the going concern value of the company, rather than just the value of the company to one specific buyer.[191] The valuation may take into account:

- the values given to comparable companies and their assets;[192]
- the discounted value of the cash flow of a business;

Where the appraisal relates to a merger (or similar prospective transaction), the courts tend to prefer valuations based on management projections available as of the date of the merger rather than post-merger adjustments to management projections or the creation of new projections entirely.[193] The rule is not, however, absolute, and management may offer "legitimate reasons" as to why the general practice should be varied on the facts of a given case.[194]

§14.76 Although the appraisal remedy performs a range of minority protection roles (*e.g.*, liquidity to shareholders in the event of self-serving transactions and reorganizations carried out by the majority interest within a corporation), in the United States, much of the current appraisal litigation involves cash-out mergers instituted by a controlling shareholder.[195] In *James Offenbecher v. Baron Services, Inc.*,[196] a company sued one of its minority shareholders to obtain a judicial determination of the fair value of his stock. In March, 1998, the board of directors of the company (which was controlled by its majority shareholders) approved a plan to merge Baron Services into a separate Delaware corporation. The plan included a "cash-out" arrangement under which a cash payment was to be made to any shareholder owning fewer than 150 shares of Baron Services (the defendant Offenbecher owned 130), in lieu of any equity interest in the new merged entity. Such an arrangement effectively provided for the expropriation of the minority shareholder interest. In response to this proposal, Offenbecher demanded payment from the company of the fair value of his 130 shares.

---

[191] *M.P.M. Enterprises, Inc. v. Gilbert*, 731 A.2d 790, 796 (Del. S.C. 1999).

[192] In *Re Radiology Associates, Inc.*, 611 A.2d 485 at 490 (Del. Ch. 1991):

> The utility of the comparable company approach depends on the similarity between the company [being valued] and the companies used for comparison. At some point the differences become so large that the comparable company method becomes meaningless for valuation purposes.

[193] *Cede & Co. v. JRC Acquisition Corp.*, [2004] Del. Ch. LEXIS 12 (Del. Ch.); *In re Emerging Communications, Inc. Shareholders' Litigation*, [2004] Del. Ch. LEXIS 70 (Del. Ch). (Criticizing valuation expert's reliance upon "unsworn, post-merger conversations with management". The court indicated that the valuator should "conduct careful due diligence using the sworn testimony and contemporaneous discovery record").

[194] *Prescott Group Small Cap, L.P. v. Coleman Co.*, [2004] Del. Ch. LEXIS 131 (Ct. Ch.).

[195] B. M. Wertheimer, "The Shareholders' Appraisal Remedy and How Courts Determine Fair Value" (1998), 47 Duke L.J. 613.

[196] [2001] Ala. Civ. App. LEXIS 219 (Ala. Civ. App.).

§14.77 Offenbecher argued that the trial court erred in law by accepting that the valuation of the fair value of individual shares should include a 50 per cent "marketability discount". In reaching this conclusion, the trial court relied heavily upon the testimony of Gary Saliba, the valuation expert retained by Baron Services. Saliba opined that Baron Services stock as of December 31, 1997, was worth $562.47 per share. In doing so, Saliba initially determined a value of $1,124.94 per share, which he called the "marketable value" of the stock, or the value of each share of stock "on a freely traded basis". This value was determined using a discounted annual rate of return of 19.82 per cent. The factors considered in calculating this discount rate included three discounts reflective of the company's small non-public status, namely:

- an "equity risk premium" of 7.5 per cent,
- a "micro- capitalization premium" of 3.5 per cent, and
- a "company-size premium" of 4.35 per cent.

§14.78 Even for a publicly traded company, the current market value of minority ownership interests may be worth considerably less than a *pro rata* portion of the business value of the corporation if it were valued on the assumption of a single, 100 per cent ownership interest. The effect on the *pro rata* value is sometimes described as "the lack of control discount" or "minority discount".[197] In the *Baron Services* case the company argued that a marketability discount was necessary because no adjustments had been made for Baron Services being a private company and for its cost of capital and access to capital and those material factors. In his testimony before the trial court, Saliba had stated:

> If I had not made [the marketability] adjustment, I would have raised my cost of capital numbers and I would have increased the public offering discount and I would have included a liquidity premium.

However, the quantitative significance of the cost of capital factor was not disclosed in the record, nor was the relevance of a "public offering discount" readily apparent from the record, and there was at least a suggestion that the various adjustments overlapped to some extent. In contrast, Offenbecher's valuation expert, Bruce Williams, valued Offenbecher's 130 shares at $215,000, or $1,653.85 per share. Williams's opinion was based upon several different valuation assumptions from those made by Saliba, but the principal reason for the wide gap was Williams's belief that it was not appropriate to apply a marketability discount.

§14.79 The court agreed that a shareholder who sought the protection of the appraisal remedy was not entitled to only the discounted market value of his or her stock as of the date of the challenged transaction. The court noted that minority and marketability discounts create an incentive for oppressive action by

---

[197] *M.G. Bancorporation v. LeBeau*, 737 A.2d 513 at 522-23 and n. 26 (Del. 1999) (affirming Court of Chancery's recognition that the valuation literature, supported determination that "market value of invested capital" approach, which used multiples derived from public market prices, "included a built-in minority discount" and "resulted in a minority valuation").

controlling shareholders, especially in non-public corporations. In particular, permitting such discounts could prompt the control group within a company to take action that would tend to drive down the market value of the stock held by minority shareholders. In addition, a company that squeezes minority shareholders out of a company deprives those shareholders of a valuable right to choose whether and for how long to maintain their investment in the company. The court stated that the compulsion inherent in such transactions, coupled with the corporation's ability to trigger the transaction at a time of its choosing, support a higher measure of "fair value". The court also noted that most of the applicable case law rejects any discounting such as that as was advocated by Baron Services. Murdoch J. continued:

> ... the value of the shares is their value to the corporation. Any rule of law that gave the shareholders less than their proportionate share of the whole firm's fair value would produce a transfer of wealth from the minority shareholders to the shareholders in control. Such a rule would inevitably encourage corporate squeeze-outs. ... [It] seems particularly inappropriate to apply such a [marketability] discount when a shareholder is selling to a person or family that owns all or most of the other shares of the corporation ... while the lack of a market affects the ability to sell minority shares in a company, the market for all of a company's assets or shares or for a controlling interest operates differently and may not be adversely influenced by the fact that the company's shares are not traded.

There was also a suggestion that applying the proposed discount would result in a double benefit to the control group within Baron Services:

> The controlling shareholders are the owners of the new corporation they formed for the purpose of merging Baron Services, and Offenbecher's ownership therein, out of existence. They have achieved that purpose. They will continue to reap the benefit of future earnings of the parties' business enterprise, while Offenbecher has been 'squeezed out'. Such a result, if allowed, will enable the controlling shareholders to accomplish indirectly what Alabama decisions regarding oppression of minority shareholders will not allow them to accomplish directly.

§14.80 In *Lawson Mardon Wheaton, Inc. v. Smith*[198] dissenting shareholders were held to be entitled to receive the full proportionate value of those shares without reference to a 25 per cent marketability discount suggested by the company's valuation expert. The court concluded that the dissenting shareholders' desire for liquidity and their lack of confidence in the corporation's new management were not "extraordinary circumstances" that would justify a departure from the general no-discounting rule.[199]

---

[198] 160 N.J. 383 at 402, 734 A.2d 738 at 749 (1999).
[199] Compare *Rapid-American Corp. v. Harris*, 603 A.2d 796 (Del. Ch. 1992); *ONTI, Inc. v. Integra Bank*, 751 A.2d 904 (Del. Ch. 1999); *Cavalier Oil Corp. v. Harnett*, 564 A.2d 1137 (Del. Ch. 1989); *Perlman v. Permonite Mfg. Co.*, 568 F. Supp. 222 at 231-32 (N.D. Ind. 1983), aff'd 734 F. (2d) 1283 (7th Cir.); *Pioneer Bancorporation, Inc. v. Waters*, 765 P.2d 597 at 599 (Colo. App. 1988); *Atlantic States Construction Inc. v. Beavers*, 169 Ga. App. 584, 314 S.E.2d 245 at 251 (1984); *Stanton v. Republic Bank of S. Chicago*, 144 Ill. 2d 472, 581 N.E.2d 678 at 682, 163 Ill. Dec. 524 (1991); *Independence Tube Corp. v. Levine*, 179 Ill. App. 3d 911, 535 N.E.2d 927 at 931, 129 Ill. Dec. 162 (1988); *Ford v. Courier-Journal Job Printing Co.*, 639 S.W. (2d) 553 at 556 (Ky. App. 1982); *Friedman v. Beway Realty Corp.*, 87 N.Y.2d 161, 661 N.E.2d 972, 638 N.Y.S. 2d 399 at 402-403 (1995); *Matter of Fleischer*, 107 A.D.2d 97, 486 N.Y.S. (2d) 272

§14.81 In *Cavalier Oil Corp. v. Harnett*,[200] the Delaware Supreme Court authorized corporate level discounting but not shareholder level discounting. Under a corporate level approach, a stock discount that affects the entire company may be considered in the appraisal, but a discount that only affects certain shareholders (such as a minority discount does), should not be taken into count. The court found in that case that a shareholder level discount

> ... fail[s] to accord to a minority shareholder the full proportionate value of his shares [which] imposes a penalty for lack of control, and unfairly enriches the majority shareholders ...

It is also inconsistent with the general principle of corporate law that the shareholders of a given class should be treated alike. The court went on to conclude that a dissenting shareholder should receive his or her proportionate share of a company after it has been valued as an entity.[201]

§14.82 In the *Baron Services* case, the majority largely equated a minority discount with a marketability discount (the latter reflecting the discount on the value of shares resulting from the fact that the shares of a private company have a limited market). There are important distinctions between the two:

> A minority discount adjusts for lack of control over the business entity, while a marketability discount adjusts for a lack of liquidity in one's interest in an entity. Even controlling interests in non-public companies may be eligible for marketability discounts, as the field of potential buyers is small, regardless of the size of the interest being sold. ... Some commentators observe that a marketability discount is not a discount at all. Rather, it is a price adjustment reflecting factors typical of close corporations.[202]

In *Balsamides v. Protameen Chemicals, Inc.*, the New Jersey Supreme Court stated that absent extraordinary circumstances, marketability discounts should not be applied in determining the value of a dissenting shareholder's shares. However, the court also suggested that applying a discount at the corporate level might be appropriate.[203]

§14.83 In *Prescott Group Small Cap, L.P. v. Coleman Co.*,[204] an appraisal proceeding related to a going private merger between The Coleman Company, Inc. and Sunbeam Corporation. The transaction was intended to encompass a two-step process, under which Sunbeam would acquire Coleman for a combination of cash and Sunbeam shares yielding a value of $27.50 per Coleman share. In the first or front-end merger (which occurred on March 30, 1998), Sunbeam acquired the existing 79 per cent majority interest in Coleman of MacAndrews & Forbes ("M&F"), in exchange for a package of Sunbeam shares, cash and the

---

(1985); *Columbia Mgmt. Co. v. Wyss*, 94 Or. App. 195 at 204-205, 765 P.2d 207 at 213-14 (1988).
[200] 564 A.2d 1137 at 1145 (Del Ch. 1989).
[201] *Ibid.*, at 1144.
[202] *Balsamides v. Protameen Chemicals, Inc.*, 160 N.J. 352, 734 A.2d 721 at 733, 736 (1999).
[203] See also *ONTI, Inc. v. Integra Bank*, 751 A.2d 904 (Del. Ch. 1999).
[204] [2004] Del. Ch. LEXIS 131 (Ch.).

assumption of debt. The value of this transaction at that time was about $32 per share. Had the second or back-end merger taken place, Coleman's minority stockholders would have received value equivalent to that received by M&F. Unfortunately, not long after the front-end merger took place, it was discovered that the financial statements of Coleman's new majority stockholder, Sunbeam, had fraudulently overstated Sunbeam's earnings and financial condition. As a result, the SEC prevented Sunbeam from completing the back-end merger until January 2000. By that time, the price of Sunbeam's stock (which represented most of the merger consideration originally agreed to in February 1998) had declined dramatically. As a result, the Coleman minority stockholders received consideration worth only $9.31 per share on the January 6, 2000 back-end merger date.

§14.84 The petitioners, who were former minority shareholders of Coleman, commenced the appraisal proceeding on February 22, 2000, claiming that the fair value of Coleman on the merger date was $31.94 per share. The respondent, Coleman, contended that its fair value on the merger date was $5.83 per share, reflecting the insolvency of Sunbeam. The court concluded that the fair value of Coleman on the merger date was $32.35 per share.

§14.85 While much of the decision turned upon the specific and rather unique facts of the case, the following passages are of more general interest. Jacobs J. pointed out that ultimately every valuation process turns upon some notional selling value of the corporation:

> Coleman ... leaps to the conclusion that Delaware case law condemns the use of "sale value". Coleman's argument is misguided and misleading, because it does not distinguish between "sale value: that may be considered as evidence of "fair value" and "sale value" that may not be considered as evidence of "fair value". In point of fact, every major valuation technique uses one or more of these "sale values", but the only "sale value" that Section 262 and the case law proscribe are valuation techniques that improperly include synergistic elements of value and minority and illiquidity discounts.

Jacobs J. also discussed the possibility of a control premium:

> To the extent Dr. Kursh's valuations include a control premium, those valuations are consistent with Delaware law. At the trial, Dr. Kursh stated clearly and explicitly his position and understanding that:
>
> (1) a control premium and minority discount are "flip sides" of the same phenomenon;
>
> (2) "fair value" for purposes of Delaware appraisal proceedings is "control value" (as depicted in Coleman's chart);
>
> (3) "non-control value"; (as depicted in the chart) represents the minority value of the company; that is, the market price of its stock, which reflects a minority discount from "control value;"
>
> (4) "minority" or "non-control" value does not represent "fair value" under Delaware law; and

(5) it is necessary to add a "control premium" to "non-control" value to eliminate the minority discount, and thereby arrive at "control" or "fair" value.

In valuing the Coleman, the court noted that by the proposed Phase II merger date, Coleman had recovered its pre-acquisition value that was squandered during the dishonest administration of Sunbeam and was poised to achieve continued future growth based upon the inherent strength and market position of its product lines. The company should be "viewed as a stand-alone firm" because Coleman was caused to file for bankruptcy in 2001 by the then insolvent Sunbeam, which controlled Coleman. There was no basis on which to conclude that such a development would have occurred if Coleman had not been so controlled. The court continued:

> In this Court's view, the most reliable and persuasive evidence of Coleman's fair value at the time of the March 1998 front-end merger, is the value of the consideration that was negotiated at arm's length, and that Sunbeam actually paid, to acquire the controlling interest in Coleman and to cash out the options held by Messrs. Levin and Perelman. The contractually guaranteed floor price for cashing out the options, it will be recalled, was $27.50 per share. Similarly, the negotiated purchase price for M&F's control block was a package of consideration valued at $27.50 per share. The $27.50 price, however, reflected a 15% marketability "haircut" or discount. Because marketability discounts at the shareholder level are impermissible under Delaware appraisal law, Dr. Kursh "added back" that discount, and arrived at a value of $32.35 per share. I accept that value as the fair value of Coleman in March 1998.

(vii) Costs

§14.86 The ordinary rules of court governing the award of costs do not appear to apply in an appraisal proceeding. For instance, when the *Ford* case came on for adjudication, the court made an award of costs on a substantial indemnity basis. While rejecting the view that such costs should be awarded in all cases, the ruling of Cumming J. on the availability of such costs where a squeeze out of a shareholder interest is the basis for the appraisal of value, are instructive:

> The statutory "squeeze out" afforded to the controlling shareholder by s. 190 of the CBCA is an extraordinary remedy. The minority shareholders are being forced out of the corporation and their property rights expropriated. The corporation is in a very dominant position. From a practical standpoint, it is impossible for virtually any minority shareholder to effectively challenge a corporation's statutory offer because the costs of a court proceeding are prohibitive. It is only the institutional shareholder that can even consider mounting a meaningful challenge. Even if successful in obtaining a higher value, and receiving costs on a partial indemnity basis, the minority shareholder would perhaps suffer a net loss because of the net costs to be absorbed. Most corporations can be comfortable in their view that virtually all minority shareholders will take the statutory offer made rather than fight it with attendant non-reimbursable costs and accompanying opportunity costs in waiting for their money. Indeed, the corporation may discount its offer in the first

instance because of the knowledge of the cost to dissenting shareholders of a challenge.[205]

The above observations may be relevant in the full range of cases in which the appraisal remedy is available.

(viii) Effect of Insolvency on the Dissent and Appraisal Procedure

§14.87 Despite the court's valuation and order, where the corporation is prohibited from paying the dissenting shareholders (because of its insolvency or illiquidity) under subsection 185(30) of the OBCA, the corporation must not pay the dissidents but, instead, must notify them that it is unable lawfully to pay them.[206] Where a dissident receives such a notice, the dissident is allowed 30 days to send a written notice to the corporation either,

- withdrawing his or her notice of dissent, in which case the corporation is deemed to consent to the withdrawal and the dissident's full rights as a shareholder are reinstated; or

- retaining status as a claimant against the corporation, to be paid as soon as the corporation is lawfully able to do so, or, in a liquidation, to be ranked subordinate to the rights of creditors of the corporation but in priority to its shareholders.[207]

The purpose and effect of the 30-day time limit are not clear. The 30-day time limit can only prevent the dissident from asserting one or another of the rights offered to the dissident — it can hardly extinguish the dissident's rights in total. Yet, there is no apparent reason for placing a time limit on the assertion of either right. If the dissident does not withdraw the notice of dissent, the logical presumption would surely be that the dissident continues to assert his or her right to repayment: the dissident has, after all, formally notified the corporation in writing of his or her objection to the proposal, demanded payment of the fair value of his or her shares, and, in all probability, participated in a court proceeding to obtain a valuation of those shares. Surely, by this time, the corporation must have got the message that the dissident wants out. On the one hand, there would seem to be no practical reason for imposing a time limit on the withdrawal of the dissent. If the corporation is insolvent at the time when it notifies the dissident that it cannot lawfully pay the amount owing, that problem is unlikely to be cured within 30 days, if, indeed, it is ever solved at all. On the other hand, a dissident, who during the first few months following the date of the court's order might quite reasonably hope that payment will be made, is more than likely to despair of that belief as time progresses. Once that despair sets in, it is unreasonable for the dissident not to be entitled to resume and exercise his or her rights as a shareholder (such as the right to vote for a change in directors).

---

[205] *Ford Motor Co. of Canada v. Ontario Municipal Employees Retirement Board*, [2005] O.J. No. 1377 at para. 57, 3 B.L.R. (4th) 306 at 316 (S.C.J. — C.L.), aff'd [2006] O.J. No. 990 (C.A.), leave to appeal to S.C.C. refused [2006] S.C.C.A. No. 77.
[206] Compare CBCA, s. 190(24).
[207] OBCA, s. 185(29); CBCA, s. 190(25).

E. AMALGAMATION

§14.88 From time to time it may seem advantageous for two or more companies to combine or merge their separate operations and continue as a single commercial entity. There are four basic techniques that can be employed to accomplish such a merger. First, one company may purchase the other and operate the other as a subsidiary. Second, one company can purchase the assets of the other. Third, both companies can transfer their assets to some newly created entity. Fourth, both companies can join together to form a new corporate entity. Mergers of this last type are called amalgamations, and the defining characteristic of such transactions is the fusion of two or more corporate entities. Every amalgamation involves a merger of two enterprises, but not every merger amounts to an amalgamation.

§14.89 Although it had a vague meaning at common law,[208] the term "amalgamation" is now effectively a term of art under both the OBCA and the CBCA, describing a particular form of corporate change. Under both statutes, amalgamation is the consolidation of two or more corporations (A and B) into a single new corporation. Analogies abound in the world of corporate law, and the one most frequently used in connection with amalgamation is to describe it as being comparable to the conflux of two streams into a single river.[209] Unfortunately, the analogy is a poor one, because every form of merger will essentially have this effect. For instance, where A may purchase the assets of B by issuing shares to B and assuming its liabilities, there is no less of a convergence than in an amalgamation, but both A and B retain their separate identities. Accordingly, it is doubtful whether much purpose is served by such comparisons. A more technically exacting description was provided by Dickson J. in *R. v. Black & Decker Manufacturing Co.*, where he described the procedure and effect of an amalgamation in the following terms:

> The word amalgamation ... is derived from mercantile usage and denotes, one might say, a legal means of achieving an economic end. The juridical nature of an amalgamation need not be determined by juridical criteria alone, to the exclusion of consideration of the purposes of amalgamation. ... The purpose is economic: to build, to consolidate, perhaps to diversify, existing businesses, so that through the union there will be enhanced strength. It is a joining of forces and resources in order to perform better in the economic field. If that be so, it would surely be paradoxical if that process were to involve death by suicide or the mysterious disappearance of those who sought security, strength and, above all, survival in that union. Also, one must recall that the amalgamating companies *physically* continue to exist in the sense that offices, warehouses, factories, corporate records and correspondence are still there, and business goes on. In a physical sense an

---

[208] *Re South African Supply & Cold Storage Co.*, [1904] 2 Ch. 268 at 281-82 (C.A.), per Buckley L.J.; *Ontario (Attorney General) v. Electrical Development Co.*, [1919] O.J. No. 124, 45 O.L.R. 186 (H.C.D.), per Middleton J.; see also *Seaboard Life Insurance Co. v. British Columbia (Attorney General)* (1986), 5 B.C.L.R. (2d) 373 (S.C.); *City of Toronto v. Toronto Electric Light Co.*, [1905] O.J. No. 212, 10 O.L.R. 621 (C.A.).

[209] Donald C. Ross, Chapter 9, "Corporate Changes," *Business Law* (Toronto: Law Society of Upper Canada, 1986-87) at 142.

amalgamating business or company does not disappear although it may become part of a greater enterprise.[210]

(Emphasis in original)
Later, he summarized his views:

> The effect of the statute, on proper construction, is to have the amalgamating companies continue without subtraction in the amalgamated company, with all their strengths and their weaknesses, their perfections and imperfections, and their sins, if sinners they be.[211]

§14.90 Amalgamations are, after amendment to the articles, the second most common type of fundamental change to a corporation. Both the OBCA and the CBCA set out three methods by which corporations may be amalgamated, known respectively as long-form amalgamation, vertical short-form amalgamation and horizontal short-form amalgamation. If the appropriate method is not adopted or if the required steps pertaining to the method selected are not followed, the corporations may be enjoined from proceeding with the amalgamation.[212] The choice among these methods is dictated by the pre-amalgamation relation that exists between the corporations proposing to amalgamate. Long-form amalgamation is the form of amalgamation employed where neither A nor B is the wholly owned subsidiary of the other and both are not wholly owned subsidiaries of the same corporation. Vertical short-form amalgamation is employed where either A or B is the wholly owned subsidiary of the other. Horizontal short-form amalgamation is employed where A and B are each wholly owned subsidiaries of the same corporation.

§14.91 While most amalgamations involve only two corporations, there is no legal barrier against an amalgamation involving three or more corporations. However many corporations may be involved, to amalgamate them, it is necessary to follow strictly the appropriate amalgamation procedure set out in the OBCA or the CBCA, as the case may be. To clearly explain the various rules on corporate amalgamation, we shall refer to hypothetical situations involving two corporations that are to amalgamate (respectively designated Beforeco and Priorco) and the corporation resulting from their amalgamation (designated as "Amalco").

(i) Amalgamating Corporations Must be Governed by Same Law

§14.92 For corporations to amalgamate, it is necessary that they be subject to the same corporations legislation. This requirement is clear from the express wording used in the OBCA and the CBCA, each of which refers to an amalgamation between two or more corporations[213] — the term "corporation" being restricted

---

[210] [1974] S.C.J. No. 56, 43 D.L.R. (3d) 393 at 399.
[211] *Ibid.*, at 400-401.
[212] See, generally, *Ruskin v. Canada All-News Radio Ltd.*, [1979] O.J. No. 266, 7 B.L.R. 142 (H.C.J.).
[213] OBCA, s. 174; CBCA, s. 181.

under each Act to companies that are governed by that statute.[214] Thus, although the OBCA and the CBCA contain very similar amalgamation provisions, it is not possible for a CBCA corporation to amalgamate with an OBCA corporation, even where the one is a wholly owned subsidiary of the other. To amalgamate, one of those corporations must first continue under the same legislation as the other.

§14.93 In contrast, some jurisdictions have recently relaxed their inter-jurisdictional amalgamation procedures. For instance, in British Columbia, section 269 of the *Business Corporations Act* of that province permits a corporation to which it applies to amalgamate with a foreign company and continue under the law of the foreign jurisdiction (thus eliminating the need and expense of first continuing under the laws of a single jurisdiction). It is doubtful whether such legislation can be effective unless a corresponding provision exists in the law of the foreign jurisdiction: a requirement that appears to be appreciated in section 187 of the *Alberta* BCA which provides an analogous procedure for amalgamation with a foreign company as well. However, absent an authorization in the legislation of the other jurisdiction, it is doubtful whether an amalgamation can proceed on such an inter-jurisdictional basis.

§14.94 Until recently, it was not possible for a company such as a cooperative association under the *Canada Cooperative Associations Act*[215] to amalgamate with its wholly owned subsidiary under the CBCA. This particular limitation could create considerable problems should an amalgamation between such corporations be desired, because a cooperative cannot continue under the CBCA (at least not without losing its cooperative status), nor as the law stood, might a business corporation continue under the *Canada Cooperatives Act*. Similar problems existed in amalgamations between CBCA corporations and corporate bodies incorporated under the *Bank Act*,[216] the *Cooperative Credit Associations Act*,[217] the *Insurance Companies Act*[218] and the *Trust and Loan Companies Act*.[219] The only solution was to seek a special Act authorizing the amalgamation in question. In 1994, the CBCA was amended to facilitate such amalgamations.[220] Under subsection 186.1(1),[221] a CBCA corporation is now permitted to amalgamate with one or more corporate bodies incorporated under the *Bank Act*, the *Cooperative Credit Associations Act*, the *Insurance Companies Act* or the *Trust and Loan Companies Act*.[222] Where the long-form amalgamation procedure must be followed, the proposed amalgamation must first be authorized by the

---

[214] OBCA, s. 1(1); CBCA, s. 2(1).
[215] S.C. 1998, c. 1, as amended.
[216] S.C. 1991, c. 46, as amended.
[217] S.C. 1991, c. 48, as amended.
[218] S.C. 1991, c. 47, as amended.
[219] S.C. 1991, c. 45, as amended.
[220] S.C. 1994, c. 24, s. 21.
[221] Proclaimed in force May 30, 1995.
[222] Section 181.1 of the OBCA permits a corporation to continue as a cooperative under the Ontario *Co-operative Corporations Act*, R.S.O. 1990, c. C-35. The two cooperatives may then amalgamate under that Act.

shareholders in accordance with section 183 of the CBCA. In the more likely case of a short-form amalgamation between a parent and subsidiary, subsection 186.1(2) provides:

> 186.1(2) A corporation may not amalgamate with one or more bodies corporate pursuant to the provisions of one of the Acts referred to in subsection (1) respecting short-form amalgamation unless the corporation is first authorized to do so by the directors in accordance with section 184.

The section 186.1 amalgamation route is one way. A CBCA corporation may amalgamate with a corporate body under the *Bank Act*, the *Cooperative Credit Associations Act*, the *Insurance Companies Act* and the *Trust and Loan Companies Act*, so that the amalgamated corporate body continues under one or other of those Acts. It is not possible, however, for a body corporate under the *Bank Act*, the *Cooperative Credit Associations Act*, the *Insurance Companies Act* and the *Trust and Loan Companies Act* to amalgamate with a CBCA corporation and continue under the CBCA.

(ii) Long-Form Amalgamation

§14.95 Long-form amalgamation between two corporations basically involves two steps: (1) the formation of an amalgamation agreement between the corporations that are to amalgamate (Beforeco and Priorco), and (2) the approval of that agreement by the shareholders of each corporation. It is the normal route for amalgamation where the two (or more) amalgamating corporations are at arm's length to each other. In schematic terms, it will typically take the following form:

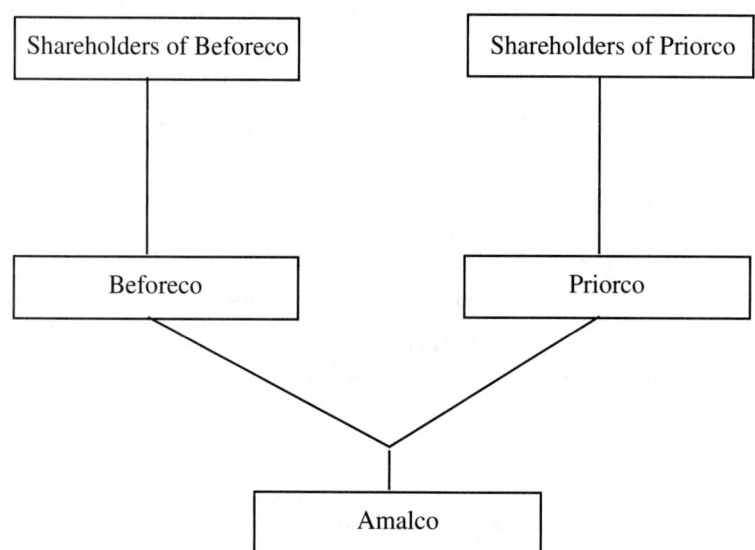

(1) Amalgamation Agreement

§14.96 Section 175 of the OBCA provides that each corporation proposing to amalgamate must enter into an agreement setting out the terms and means of effecting the amalgamation.[223] This agreement must be sufficiently specific to constitute a legally binding contract.[224] Although all amalgamating corporations must be parties to the amalgamation agreement, it is permissible for corporations or other persons that are not parties to merge in the amalgamated corporation to become parties to the agreement. Such additional parties would necessarily be required where, for instance, it is agreed that securities of some other body corporate are to be exchanged for shares of one or other of the amalgamating corporations — a possibility contemplated under clause 175(1)(c) of the OBCA.[225]

§14.97 The amalgamation agreement must, of course, identify the corporations that are parties to the agreement and, in particular, the corporations that are to be amalgamated under the agreement. In addition, the agreement must set out

(a) the provisions that are required to be included in the articles of incorporation under section 5.[226]

Under section 5 of the OBCA, the articles of a corporation must specify the name of the corporation, the municipality or geographic township within Ontario and the address (including the street name and number, if any) where the registered office is to be located, the classes and maximum number of shares of the corporation and the terms, conditions of those shares (including any authorization to issue shares in series) and any restrictions upon them, the number of directors or the minimum and maximum number of directors, the names and addresses of the first directors (of Amalco), a statement of whether the director is a resident of Canada, and any other matter required by the Act to be set out in the articles.[227]

§14.98 The amalgamation agreement must also set out the basis upon which, and manner in which, the holders of the issued shares of Beforeco and Priorco are to receive

- securities of Amalco;
- money; or
- securities of any body corporate other than Amalco.[228]

It is worth noting at this point that until such times as the holders of those securities accept the substitute securities in exchange for the previous obligations

---

[223] CBCA, s. 182.
[224] *Maxwell Taylor's Restaurants Inc. v. Carcasole*, [1990] A.J. No. 187, 72 Alta. L.R. (2d) 376 at 399-400 (Q.B.), *per* Lutz J. — it is necessary to set out the details of the manner in which the amalgamation will be effected; aff'd [1990] A.J. No. 706, [1990] 6 W.W.R. 251 (C.A.).
[225] CBCA, s. 182(1)(c).
[226] OBCA, s. 175(1)(a); CBCA, s. 182(1)(a).
[227] Compare CBCA, s. 6.
[228] OBCA, s. 175(1)(b); CBCA, s. 182(1)(c).

owed to them, all securities of Beforeco and Priorco continue to bind Amalco, for clause 179(*b*) of the OBCA provides that upon the articles of amalgamation becoming effective (*i.e.*, upon the formation of the amalgamated corporation, Amalco)

> (*b*) the amalgamated corporation possesses all the property, rights, privileges and franchises and is subject to all liabilities, including civil, criminal and quasi-criminal, and all contracts, disabilities and debts of each of the amalgamating corporations;

The equivalent provision of the CBCA is differently worded but to a similar effect, paragraphs 186(*b*), (*c*), (*d*) and (*e*) of that Act reading:

> 186. On the date shown in a certificate of amalgamation ...
>
> (*b*) the property of each amalgamating corporation continues to be the property of the amalgamated corporation;
>
> (*c*) the amalgamated corporation continues to be liable for the obligations of each amalgamating corporation;
>
> (*d*) an existing cause of action, claim or liability to prosecution is unaffected;
>
> (*e*) a civil, criminal or administrative action or proceeding pending by or against an amalgamating corporation may be continued to be prosecuted by or against the amalgamated corporation;

§14.99 Generally the shares of the amalgamating corporations A and B are not cancelled, issued or transferred, but are converted into shares of the new corporation, Amalco.[229] In some cases, a straight share-for-share swap may not be practical, given the different values of the shares of the amalgamating corporations. For instance, if there are 10,000 shares in A and the fair market value of the shares of A is $10.75 per share, and there are 5,000 shares in B and the fair market value of the shares of B is $8.33 per share, there is no way of exchanging the shares in A and B for shares in Amalco that will not result in some of the shareholders in A or B (or both, unless the Amalco shares are issued at exactly one of those two values) being issued fractional shares of Amalco. To circumvent this possibility, clause 175(1)(*c*) of the Act further requires that the agreement specify the manner of payment of money instead of the issue of fractional shares of the amalgamated corporation or any other body the securities of which are to be received in the amalgamation.[230]

§14.100 The valuation of the corporations that are amalgamating is often one of the most contentious problems to overcome in the negotiation of an amalgamation agreement. Given current accounting practice, it is unlikely that the book value of assets will reflect their actual value, even if both corporations have adhered scrupulously to the most conservative interpretation of generally accepted accounting principles in the preparation of their financial statements. The use of

---

[229] *Koch Transport Ltd. v. Class Freight Lines Ltd.*, [1982] O.J. No. 3349, 37 O.R. (2d) 566 (Div. Ct.).
[230] CBCA, s. 182(1)(*e*).

historic cost or the book value of capital assets results in the understatement of their value over time. The possibility of exaggerated or understated figures in the financial statements increases, of course, depending upon the extent to which either of the parties has made use of creative accounting techniques. For this reason, it will often be necessary for each amalgamating corporation (or their professional advisors) to review the finances and affairs of the other corporation and to settle upon an agreed value or method of evaluating the assets and liabilities of the corporations. Quite often the valuation cannot be completed by the intended date of amalgamation. In such a case the parties must decide whether to proceed with the amalgamation or to postpone it. Although postponement is the legally prudent course, the same business considerations that prompted amalgamation may discourage such delay.

§14.101 In any such case, the solicitor should caution the client about the risks of proceeding on good faith. Once an amalgamation has been consummated, it is no easy matter to dissolve it; the original corporations cannot be revived under either the OBCA or the CBCA. To provide some protection it is advisable that the assets and business that each brings into the amalgamation be maintained as separate entities pending the conclusion of all valuation. Subject to the *Income Tax Act*,[231] keeping the operations separate will allow the spin-out of assets from the separate successor corporations, if necessary. Such a spin-out can only be done with difficulty once the operations of the amalgamating corporations have been combined. Since tax or other business considerations may necessitate immediate conclusion of amalgamation prior to the completion of the valuation, the agreement should include some provision for maintaining the basic management staff, structure and assets of each amalgamating corporation, pending the final resolution of the valuation issue. At least by some doing, it remains commercially possible to unwind the amalgamation to the extent that the law allows should one party discover that it has been misled by the other. Moreover, where the corporations are closely held, any warranties and covenants on which the estimated valuations of the corporation are based should be backed up by indemnity agreements in favour of the shareholder of the other corporation, should the presumptions on which the agreement is based be found to be false. Finally, even where the securities of a corporation are widely held, consideration should be given to having the proposed shareholders of the amalgamated corporation agree that the money or securities that each will receive on the amalgamation does not necessarily reflect the true value of their respective interests. Thus, if final valuations reveal discrepancies, securities may be transferred or issued, or money may be paid, so that each security holder is, as nearly as possible, restored to the same position that he or she occupied prior to the amalgamation.

§14.102 Where Priorco holds shares in Beforeco (or *vice versa*), the amalgamation agreement must provide for the cancellation of those shares upon the amalgamation becoming effective, without any repayment of capital for those shares. No provision may be made in the agreement for the conversion of those shares

---

[231] R.S.C. 1985, c. 1 (5th Supp.), as amended.

into shares of Amalco.[232] This rule stems from the general policy in the Act that a corporation may not hold shares in itself. Because, upon their amalgamation, Priorco and Beforeco combine into the single corporation, Amalco, the effect of allowing continuation of the shares would be that Amalco would hold shares in Amalco.[233]

§14.103 Clause 175(1)(*d*) of the OBCA requires the amalgamation agreement to specify whether the by-laws of the amalgamated corporation are to be those of one of the amalgamating corporations and the address where a copy of the proposed by-laws may be examined.[234] Thus, it is not necessary for the amalgamation agreement to set out the full text of the by-laws. It is not clear from clause (*d*) whether any proposed by-laws for Amalco must always be made available for inspection, or whether this requirement applies only if by-laws of one of the amalgamating corporations are to be adopted as the by-laws of Amalco. Clause (*d*) is also unclear on whether Amalco is bound to adopt any proposed by-laws specified in the agreement once the articles of amalgamation are issued, or whether the directors and shareholders of Amalco may subsequently approve by-laws in some other form. If the agreement regarding by-laws is binding upon Amalco, a number of subsidiary questions arise: how long must the by-laws in question remain in force and is there any special requirement that must be observed on their amendment or repeal; moreover, who is entitled to enforce this provision of the agreement because the amalgamating corporations. Beforeco and Priorco, effectively cease to exist upon their amalgamation and are entirely subsumed within Amalco.

§14.104 At least in the case of an OBCA corporation, one possible answer to these questions may be found under the OBCA in the approved form of Articles of Amalgamation. Paragraph 12 requires the amalgamation agreement to be attached, as Schedule B, to the articles of amalgamation. Similarly, clause 179(*a*) of the OBCA provides that upon the articles of amalgamation becoming effective (*i.e.*, upon the endorsement of the certificate of amalgamation upon the articles), the amalgamating corporations are amalgamated and continue as one corporation under the terms and conditions prescribed in the amalgamation agreement. The effect of these provisions apparently would make the amalgamation agreement itself part of the articles of the corporation — and therefore make the amalgamation agreement binding upon Amalco, its directors and officers.[235] By being incorporated into the amalgamation agreement, the by-laws come into force as part of the amalgamation process without any further step being required on the part of Amalco to bring them into effect. Consistent with the general principles of contract law on obligations of indefinite duration, the amalgamated corporation would be obliged to maintain those by-laws in force

---

[232] OBCA, s. 175(2); CBCA, s. 182(2).
[233] What is the accounting treatment? Does the former capital investment become contributed surplus?
[234] CBCA, s. 182(1)(*f*).
[235] OBCA, s. 134(2).

for a reasonable time. However, after a reasonable time, the normal by-law amendment procedures set out in section 116 of the OBCA will apply.[236]

§14.105 Finally, under clause 175(1)(e) of the OBCA it is necessary for the amalgamation agreement to set out such other details as may be necessary to perfect the amalgamation and to provide for the subsequent management and operation of the amalgamated corporation. In most straightforward amalgamations, additional provisions are not necessary. Furthermore, because the amalgamation agreement becomes a matter of public record this may encourage the inclusion of such provisions in a side agreement, particularly if they deal with sensitive matters pertaining to Priorco or Beforeco or Amalco (*e.g.*, covenants and warranties concerning financial matters, patent or similar rights, performance covenants, and so forth). For instance, where particular arrangements desired by the prospective shareholders of Amalco can be accomplished through the use of a unanimous shareholder agreement, it may be preferable to employ such an agreement rather than to include the provisions in the amalgamating agreement itself.

(2) Shareholder Approval

§14.106 The OBCA does not specifically require the amalgamation agreement to be approved by the directors of the amalgamating corporations, though in virtually all cases such approval will be an integral step of the amalgamation process. However, the directors of each corporation are required to submit the amalgamation agreement for approval at (separate) meetings of the shareholders of each corporation.[237] Specific notice of the business to be transacted at that meeting must be given to the shareholders. In particular, the notice of the meeting of shareholders must include or be accompanied by:

- a copy or summary of the amalgamation agreement; and
- a statement that a dissenting shareholder is entitled to be paid the fair value of the shares held by him or her in accordance with section 185.[238]

The failure to include a reference to shareholder dissent rights in the notice does not invalidate the amalgamation.[239] Although the Act gives no specific indication

---

[236] The form of articles of amalgamation under the CBCA also requires the amalgamation agreement to be attached to the articles of amalgamation where the amalgamation is effected under s. 183 of the Act. Unfortunately, para. (*a*) of s. 186 of the CBCA provides only that on the date shown in the certificate of amalgamation:

> (*a*) the amalgamation of the amalgamating corporations and their continuance as one corporation become effective;

This wording is narrower than that found in cl. (*a*) of s. 179 of the OBCA:

> (*a*) the amalgamating corporations are amalgamated and continue as one corporation *under the terms and conditions prescribed in the amalgamation agreement*;

(Emphasis added)
[237] OBCA, s. 176(1); CBCA, s. 183(1).
[238] OBCA, s. 176(2); CBCA, s. 183(2).
[239] OBCA, s. 176(2); CBCA, s. 183(2).

about the effect of such a failure, it would seem from section 185 that the lack of any such notice will permit the shareholder to assert dissent rights after amalgamation, even though the shareholder failed to provide a written objection to the proposed amalgamation prior to the amalgamation taking effect.[240]

§14.107 A proposed amalgamation agreement must be approved by a special resolution of the shareholders, approved by the holders of each class or series of shares entitled to vote on the resolution. The agreement is adopted when the shareholders of each corporation have approved the amalgamation. In general, the voting procedure on a proposed amalgamation agreement is essentially the same as for any special resolution requiring shareholder approval. However, under the OBCA the holders of a class or series of shares of an amalgamating corporation are entitled to vote separately as a class or series on an amalgamation (whether or not they are otherwise entitled to vote) if the amalgamation agreement contains a provision that would entitle the holders of each class or series concerned to vote separately as a class or series under section 170.

§14.108 In contrast, the CBCA first provides for class or series voting where the amalgamation agreement contains a provision that would entitle the shareholders of a class or series to vote separately as a class or series if that provision were contained in a proposed amendment to the articles,[241] and second, confers an absolute right to vote in favour of all shareholders in all circumstances. Thus, under the CBCA, the shares of each class or series of an amalgamating corporation have the right to vote on an amalgamation whether or not the shares of a particular class or series otherwise carry the right to vote.[242] Where the amalgamation agreement does not contain a provision that would entitle the holders of a class or series to vote separately as a class, all shares of the corporation will vote as a single class on the resolution, with a single vote being given to the shareholder for each share held.

§14.109 The absolute share voting requirement embodied in the CBCA may be justified on the grounds that the effect of an amalgamation may be to alter fundamentally the basis on which each shareholder agreed to invest in the shares of the corporation. However, while that assumption may be true in some cases, it is not necessarily true in all. Moreover, to the extent that the position of the shareholder may deteriorate by amalgamation, with the consequent assumption of the liabilities of each corporation subsumed in the amalgamation, that risk is no greater than the risk that non-voting shareholders would run if the corporation were to purchase the assets and assume the liabilities of another corporation. Similarly, although an amalgamation may effect a change of management or the ownership of voting shares, the owners of non-voting shares are at risk of such changes outside of the amalgamation context, and in those cases (*e.g.*, a simple sale of shares by a controlling shareholder) they have no right to vote or to

---

[240] OBCA, s. 185(6); CBCA, s. 190(5).
[241] CBCA, s. 183(4).
[242] CBCA, s. 183(3).

dissent from the change in question. If the basic rights of a class (or series) of shares remain unaffected by the amalgamation, there is no rationale for conferring voting rights upon them.

§14.110 Although the amalgamation agreement is adopted when approved by the special resolutions of the shareholders of each amalgamating corporation who are entitled to vote on it, quite often amalgamation agreements will contain a provision empowering the directors of each amalgamating corporation to terminate the agreement, despite the approval of the shareholders, should either board of directors consider it to be in the best interest of their respective corporation to do so. Subsection 176(5) of the OBCA gives legislative sanction to such director override provisions, but where the directors of Beforeco or Priorco wish to terminate the agreement, they may do so only before the endorsement of the certificate of amalgamation on the articles of amalgamation.[243] Moreover, where the directors of a corporation seek to back out of an amalgamation agreement, they must also consider whether in so doing they may expose their corporation to liability for breach of contract.

(3) Shareholder Dissent Rights

§14.111 Under the OBCA, shareholders who are entitled to vote on an amalgamation agreement are entitled to a right of dissent under section 185.[244] Non-voting shares are given a statutory right to vote only where "the amalgamation agreement contains a provision that, if contained in a proposed amendment to the articles, would entitle such holders to vote separately as a class or series under section 170".[245] Thus, there is no general right of dissent in the case of non-voting shares. In contrast, under the CBCA, all shareholders have a right to vote on an amalgamation agreement[246] and, correspondingly, all such shareholders enjoy a right of dissent. As a strategic matter, the broader rights of dissent under the CBCA will often be exploited by disgruntled shareholders of non-voting shares, even in cases where the proposed amalgamation in no way affects their interest. For instance, where a corporation has a class of non-voting shares on which a dividend has not been paid, the holders of those shares may use their right of dissent to bail out of the corporation, even where there is a higher likelihood of a dividend payment should the amalgamation proceed. Because the right of dissent is not contingent upon the shareholder concerned being able to prove prejudice, it is advisable for solicitors to inform clients concerning the possibility that the exercise of dissent rights may be triggered as a result of an amalgamation.

---

[243] CBCA, s. 183(6).
[244] The right appears to be limited to those who are registered shareholders: *Lake & Co. v. Calex Resources Ltd.*, [1996] A.J. No. 772, 42 Alta. L.R. (3d) 309 at para. 29 (C.A.) *per* Hunt J.A.
[245] OBCA, s. 176(3).
[246] CBCA, s. 183(3). See *Lay v. Genevest Inc.*, [2005] A.J. No. 247, 5 B.L.R. (4th) 38 (Q.B.).

(4) Private Company Exemption

§14.112 For Amalco to enjoy the benefit of the private companies exemption under the *Securities Act*,[247] it is necessary for the private company provision to be set out in the articles of amalgamation, otherwise the exemption will be lost even if that provision appeared in the articles of both Beforeco and Priorco. Although two or more corporations may be entitled to the benefit of the private company exemption, it may be that the resulting amalgamated corporation, Amalco, may not qualify — for instance, where the total number of securities holders of both corporations exceeds the limit of 50 imposed on private companies. Clearly, this is a possibility that should be reviewed by counsel during the negotiation of the amalgamation agreement, as the loss of the private company exemption may raise questions concerning the desirability of proceeding with the amalgamation. Where one of the corporations is based in Ontario, a similar concern applies with respect to the closely held issuer exemption, which is provided for in Rule 45-501 in the place of the private company exemption.[248]

(5) Procedure Following Approval of Special Resolution

§14.113 As is the case in regard to the approval of a proposed amendment of the articles of a corporation, the approval of a proposed amalgamation by special resolution of the shareholders of the amalgamating corporations does not effect the amalgamation, but is merely a necessary condition that must be satisfied for the amalgamation to proceed to consummation. For the amalgamation to become effective, articles of amalgamation in prescribed form must be sent to the Director. The contents of the articles of amalgamation are similar to those of articles of incorporation, but certain additional information is required. First, it is necessary to stipulate whether the amalgamation is a short-form amalgamation; if not, it is necessary to state the date(s) on which the special resolution approving the amalgamation agreement was approved by the shareholders of each amalgamating corporation. Second, the name and Ontario corporation numbers of each amalgamating corporation must be stated.[249] Third, in the case of a long-form amalgamation a copy of the agreement must be attached as Schedule B to the articles, and in the case of a short-form amalgamation a copy of the directors' resolution required under section 177 must be attached.

§14.114 Clause 178(2)(*a*) of the OBCA[250] provides that the articles of amalgamation must be attached to a written statement given by a director or an officer of each amalgamating corporation confirming that:

(*a*) there are reasonable grounds for believing that,

---

[247] R.S.O. 1990, c. S.5, as amended.
[248] Discussed in Chapter 7.
[249] The prescribed form under the CBCA requires the disclosure of the Canadian corporation numbers of the amalgamating corporations. The Ontario corporation numbers of those corporations must not be inserted.
[250] CBCA, s. 185(2)(*a*).

(i) each amalgamating corporation is and the amalgamated corporation will be able to pay its liabilities as they become due, and

(ii) the realizable value of the amalgamated corporation's assets will not be less than the aggregate of its liabilities and stated capital of all classes;

Note that clause (*a*) sets out a solvency and liquidity test similar to that found in the sections of the Act dealing with the redemption or other purchase or acquisition of share capital. These tests are consistent with a general goal of the amalgamation procedure, which is to see that no creditor is prejudiced as a result of the amalgamation of two or more corporations. This goal is also clearly evident in clause 178(2)(*b*) of the OBCA,[251] which provides that the director or officer must state:

(*b*) that there are reasonable grounds for believing that,

(i) no creditor will be prejudiced by the amalgamation, or

(ii) adequate notice has been given to all known creditors of the amalgamating corporations;

Subsection 185(2) of the CBCA is similar to subsection 178(2) of the OBCA. Although paragraphs (*a*) and (*b*) clearly require a director or officer to exercise some due diligence before making the statements concerned, neither requires the person making the statement to arrive at a particularly firm conclusion on the facts. That person need conclude only that "there are reasonable grounds for believing", so that any legitimate doubt about the matter in question may be resolved in favour of proceeding with the amalgamation.

§14.115 The OBCA permits creditors to object to a proposed amalgamation through a formal notice procedure,[252] but allows the amalgamation to proceed, unless a genuine case exists for not doing so. Clause 178(2)(*c*) provides that the director or officer must state that:

(*c*) the grounds upon which the objections of all creditors who have notified the corporation that they object to the amalgamation, setting forth with reasonable particularity the grounds for such objections, are either frivolous or vexatious;[253]

The statement must also confirm that the corporations have formally notified the creditors concerned that they reject the legitimacy of their objection to the proposed amalgamation, clause 178(2)(*d*) providing:

(*d*) the corporation has given notice to each person who has, in the manner referred to in clause (*c*), notified the corporation of an objection to the amalgamation, that,

---

[251] CBCA, s. 185(2)(*b*).
[252] Subsection 178(3).
[253] Clause (*b*) of s. 185(2) of the CBCA requires the person providing the declaration to state that "adequate notice has been given to all known creditors of the amalgamating corporations and no creditor objects to the amalgamation otherwise than on grounds that are frivolous or vexatious".

(i) the grounds upon which the person's objection is based are considered to be frivolous or vexatious, and

(ii) a creditor of a corporation who objects to an amalgamation has the status of a complainant under section 248.

Subsection 185(2) of the CBCA contains no equivalent to clause (*d*). Although the wording of subsection 178(2) of the OBCA suggests that the director's or officer's statement is separate from the articles of amendment, this statement has been incorporated into the text of the prescribed form under the OBCA. The articles must, in any event, be signed by authorized directors or officers of each corporation concerned. The combination of these two documents effectively reduces the paper burden imposed in connection with the amalgamation procedure.

§14.116 The requirement for a statement by the director (or officer) that no creditor will be prejudiced by the amalgamation is an alternative to the requirement that notice be given to creditors of the proposed amalgamation. The costs of providing such notice, combined with the transactional problems that may be encountered in dealing with a creditor who unreasonably objects to a proposed amalgamation, are sufficient in most cases to motivate a statement that "no creditor will be prejudiced" by the amalgamation. Unfortunately, the meaning of this phrase is by no means certain. Conservatively interpreted, this phrase would be quite restrictive. Since no two amalgamating corporations can be of exactly the same financial strength, even if both are unquestionably solvent and financially healthy, it would follow that the creditors of the stronger corporation will necessarily be prejudiced as a result of the amalgamation. Such a conservative interpretation seems incorrect for three reasons. First, given the impossibility of Priorco and Beforeco having exactly the same financial strength, the practical consequence of the conservative interpretation would be that directors and officers could never state that no creditor would be prejudiced. It seems highly unlikely that the Legislature would have intended to provide an alternative that could never be taken in practice. Second, the statement is made only in relation to reasonable belief, whereas the conservative interpretation suggests that absolute certainty is required. Third, a creditor is not prejudiced by one of the amalgamating corporations being weaker than the other. Prejudice is not the same as change. A creditor is prejudiced only where the costs of recovery of amounts owed or the general enforcement of obligations is significantly increased, or its ability to recover or its likelihood of timely payment is otherwise materially affected. It would seem that the "prejudice" referred to need not amount to a belief that the amalgamated corporation will be insolvent or illiquid, for these are separate questions that the director or officer is required to address under clause 178(2)(*a*). Indeed, if Priorco is much larger than Beforeco, and Priorco is financially healthy, then the creditors of Priorco might not be prejudiced even if Beforeco were hopelessly insolvent. However, if the creditworthiness of Amalco is significantly inferior to that of its predecessors, Priorco or Beforeco, then the creditors of the corporation that previously enjoyed the higher credit reputation may be said to have been prejudiced as a result of the amalgamation. In all other cases, the director or officer may state that creditors are not prejudiced provided he or she has made reasonable inquiries to determine whether this is the case and those inquiries have brought forward nothing that would cause a reasonable person to believe otherwise.

§14.117 Where the director or officer cannot satisfy himself or herself that "no creditor will be prejudiced by the amalgamation", it is necessary to comply with the notice requirement. The obligation to give notice to creditors under subsection (2) is sufficiently discharged if a written notice is sent to each known creditor (at the creditor's last address known to the corporation) who has a claim against the corporation that exceeds $2,500, and a further notice is published one time in a newspaper published or distributed in the place where the corporation has its registered office. Each of these notices must state that the corporation intended to amalgamate with one or more specified corporations in accordance with the OBCA, unless a creditor of the corporation objects to the amalgamation within 30 days from the date of the notice.[254] It would seem to follow that any creditor who is owed more than $2,500 and who has a legitimate reason to object to the amalgamation may do so, and may block that amalgamation (subject to being repaid). Moreover, if the creditor's objection is not frivolous or vexatious, the creditor may be entitled to seek relief under the oppression remedy,[255] if, for some reason, the amalgamation proceeds despite the raising of a legitimate objection by the creditor.

§14.118 Under earlier legislation, the amalgamation of two or more corporations was conclusive — there was no jurisdiction in any court to set aside or otherwise unwind the amalgamation.[256] Under the CBCA, the court undoubtedly has the power to restrain an amalgamation prior to the time when the certificate of amalgamation is endorsed, but it is doubtful that the court possesses the jurisdiction to unwind the amalgamation after it is consummated (if for no other reason than that there is no procedure in the Act for giving effect to any such order). It is arguable, of course, that the court may issue such an order under section 241 of the CBCA, where oppression can be shown. However, so far no such order ever seems to have been made. Paragraph 213(1)(*c*) of the CBCA empowers the Director under that Act to dissolve a corporation if any certificate under that Act (such as a certificate of amalgamation) has been "procured ... by misrepresentation". But such an order would seem to terminate Amalco rather than revive its predecessors, and therefore the CBCA power falls short of the power given under the OBCA to cancel the certificate of amalgamation. In general, it is difficult to see how a creditor would benefit from an order being made under paragraph 213(1)(*c*).

§14.119 Under the OBCA, the court appears to have no jurisdiction to upset an amalgamation after it takes effect, but the Director does possess such an authority

---

[254] OBCA, s. 178(3); CBCA, s. 185(3).
[255] OBCA, s. 248; CBCA, s. 241.
[256] *Yokohama Enterprises Inc. v. Mascot Enterprises Inc.* (1984), 56 B.C.L.R. 132 (Com. Ap. Trib.); *Norcan Oils Ltd. v. Fogler*, [1964] S.C.J. No. 51, [1965] S.C.R. 36.

under clause 240(1)(*b*), where the corporation or any of its affiliates has been guilty of oppressive conduct within the meaning of section 248.[257] Where a certificate of amalgamation is cancelled, clause 240(1)(*b*) provides that "the matter that became effective upon the issuance of the certificate ceases to be in effect from the date fixed in the order". Thus, the result would appear to be to revive the predecessor corporations. The liability of those corporations for obligations incurred by the amalgamated corporation in the period following the issue of the certificate is not specified.

§14.120 The articles of amalgamation must be submitted in duplicate, in the prescribed form and must be verified by the signature of a director or officer of each amalgamating corporation.[258] Upon receipt of these articles, the Director is required to endorse a certificate of amalgamation on the articles in accordance with section 273 of the Act.[259] In particular, paragraph 273(1)(*b*) requires the certificate to be endorsed provided the articles are in prescribed form, have been executed in duplicate and all prescribed fees have been paid. The endorsement sets out the day, month, and year of the endorsement and also the corporation number. One copy of the endorsed articles is then filed by the Director, and the other is sent to the corporation or its representative. However, the Director is prohibited from endorsing a certificate on the articles if the corporation is in default of a filing requirement under the *Corporations Information Act*[260] or has any unpaid fees or penalties outstanding.[261]

§14.121 The articles of amendment become effective upon their endorsement, at which time the amalgamating corporations are amalgamated and continue as one corporation under the terms and conditions prescribed in the amalgamation agreement.[262] The articles of amalgamation are deemed to be the articles of incorporation of the amalgamated corporation and, except for the purposes of subsection 117(1),[263] the certificate of amalgamation is deemed to be the certificate of incorporation of the amalgamated corporation.[264]

---

[257] OBCA, s. 240(2)(*e*).
[258] OBCA, s. 273.
[259] OBCA, s. 178(4); CBCA, s. 185(4). The director may not refuse an amalgamation or continuation merely because after it takes effect, the corporation will be subject to the laws of another jurisdiction: *Re Canada Business Corporations Act*, [1991] O.J. No. 714, 80 D.L.R. (4th) 619 (C.A.).
[260] R.S.O. 1990, c. C.39, as amended.
[261] OBCA, s. 274(1) (not yet in force).
[262] OBCA, s. 179(*a*). It is not possible to backdate the effective date of the amalgamation, even where the date officially recorded was recorded in error: *Allsco Building Supplies Ltd. v. McAllister*, [1989] N.B.J. No. 507, 44 B.L.R. 201 at 206 (*sub nom. Allsco Building Supplies Ltd. v. New Brunswick (Director, Business Corporations Act))* (Q.B.), *per* Landry J.
[263] The purpose of this exception is to eliminate the requirement for a first directors' meeting (or organizational meeting) in regard to the amalgamated corporation.
[264] OBCA, s. 179(*d*); CBCA, s. 186(*g*).

(iii) Vertical Short-form Amalgamation

§14.122 As noted above, a vertical short-form amalgamation occurs where a parent corporation, A, amalgamates with its subsidiary, B. The simplified procedure in short-form amalgamations reveals that, ultimately, the same shareholder interests remain after the amalgamation as before. A typical short-form amalgamation is illustrated in the following diagram.

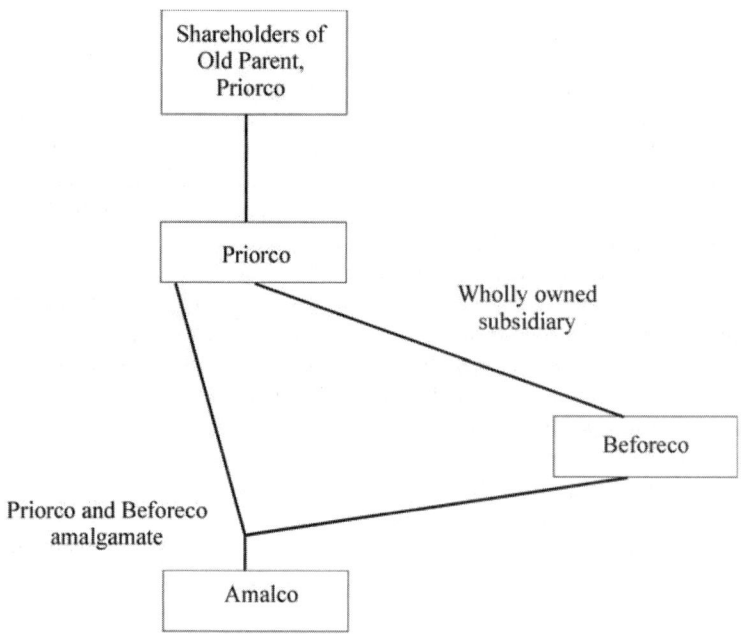

In the preponderant number of cases involving such a process, the new amalgamated corporation Amalco will be essentially indistinguishable from the old parent and will, in all likelihood, continue under the same name as the old parent, with the same articles and by-laws. All that occurs is that the formerly separate corporate status of the old subsidiary will be undone. Because the subsidiary is essentially subsumed into the parent, such a transaction is sometimes described as winding the subsidiary up into the parent. The important differences between a long-form and short-form amalgamation are that in the case of a short-form amalgamation there is no need for an amalgamation agreement, nor is any shareholder approval required for the amalgamation. Because no shareholder approval is required, it follows that there can be no right of dissent in a short-form amalgamation.

§14.123 To take advantage of the vertical short-form procedure, B must be the wholly owned subsidiary of A. If there is a minority interest in the subsidiary, the two corporations may still amalgamate but must follow the long-form amalgamation procedure. Many older corporations will often have nominal shareholders, such as former directors, who may have been required to hold shares in the corporation so that they qualified as directors under earlier legislation. Although such shares are usually beneficially owned by the parent corporation, and, therefore, it is possible to argue that such corporations are "wholly owned" within the meaning of the Act, the safest course is to arrange for the transfer of those shares to the parent corporation prior to proceeding with the amalgamation.

§14.124 If this option is not available (for instance, where the nominal shareholder cannot be traced or refuses to cooperate), it will be necessary to proceed on the basis of beneficial ownership, supported by appropriate statutory declarations to that effect. If beneficial ownership cannot be established, or if there is the smallest outstanding ownership of shares of the subsidiary beneficially owned by some party other than the parent corporation, the vertical short-form amalgamation is not possible. In such cases, it is necessary to proceed by the long-form amalgamation method. Unfortunately, because of the requirement for shareholder approval and the possibility of shareholder dissent, the cost and risk of complying with the long-form procedure may be substantial (particularly where the parent corporation is widely held) and completely overcome the economic benefits that the amalgamation is intended to produce.

§14.125 The procedure for a vertical short-form amalgamation is set out in subsections 177(1) of the OBCA and 184(1) of the CBCA. Essentially, the same procedure applies under both Acts.[265] Subsection 177(1) of the OBCA provides that a holding corporation and one or more of its wholly owned subsidiary corporations may amalgamate and continue as one corporation without complying with sections 175 or 176,[266] provided two conditions are satisfied. The first condition is that the amalgamation must be approved by a resolution of the directors of each amalgamating corporation. The second condition in section 177(1)(*b*) is that these resolutions must each provide that:

---

[265] In 1994, the short-form amalgamation provisions of the CBCA were amended (S.C. 1994, c. 24, s. 20) so that s. 184(1) of the Act now provides that a holding corporation and one or more of its subsidiary corporations may amalgamate and continue as one corporation without complying with ss. 182 and 183 of the CBCA if,

    (*a*) the amalgamation is approved by a resolution of the directors of each amalgamating corporation;

    (*a*.1) all of the issued shares of each amalgamating subsidiary corporation are held by one or more of the other amalgamating corporations; and

    (*b*) the resolutions provide that,

        (i) the shares of each amalgamating subsidiary corporation shall be cancelled without any repayment of capital in respect thereof,

        (ii) except as may be prescribed, the articles of amalgamation shall be the same as the articles of incorporation of the amalgamating holding corporation, and

        (iii) no securities shall be issued by the amalgamated corporation in connection with the amalgamation and the stated capital of the amalgamated corporation shall be the same as the stated capital of the amalgamating holding corporation.

[266] CBCA, ss. 182, 183.

(i) the shares of each amalgamating subsidiary corporation shall be cancelled without any repayment of capital in respect thereof,

(i.1) the by-laws of the amalgamated corporation shall be the same as the by-laws of the amalgamating holding corporation,

(ii) except as may be prescribed, the articles of amalgamation shall be the same as the articles of the amalgamating holding corporation, and

(iii) no securities shall be issued and no assets shall be distributed by the amalgamated corporation in connection with the amalgamation.

Following the adoption of these resolutions, the same administrative procedures must be followed as in a long-form amalgamation (*i.e.*, submission of the articles to the Director, accompanied by a completed director's or officer's statement, the giving of notices to creditors and endorsement of the certificate of amalgamation by the Director) to consummate the amalgamation of the parent corporation and its subsidiary.

(iv) Horizontal Short-form Amalgamation

§14.126 A horizontal short-form amalgamation occurs where two or more corporations (Priorco and Beforeco), each of which is a wholly owned subsidiary of a third corporation (Parentco), amalgamate with each other. The procedure is not available for two corporations that are wholly owned by the same individual. The following diagram illustrates a typical amalgamation of this type.

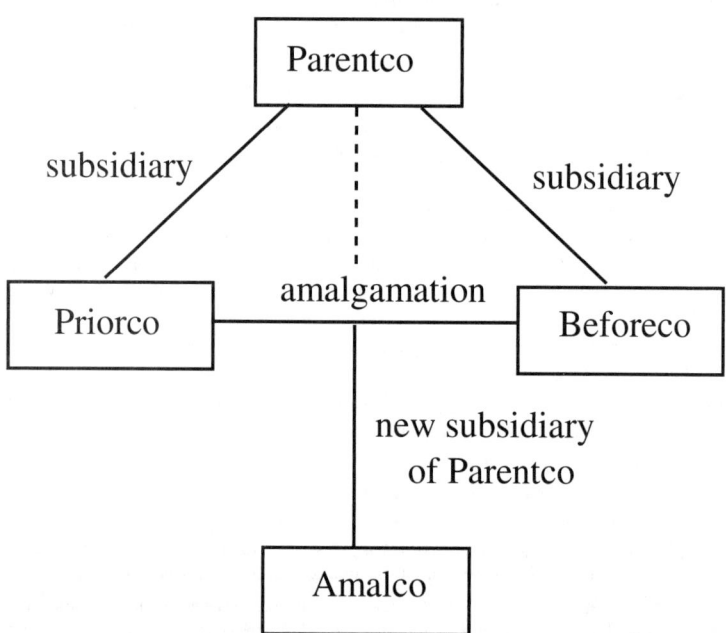

§14.127 The horizontal short-form amalgamation procedure is very similar to that of vertical short-form amalgamation. Under subsection 177(2) of the OBCA,[267] two or more wholly owned subsidiary corporations of the same holding body corporate may amalgamate and continue as one corporation without complying with the amalgamation agreement and shareholder approval provisions, provided two conditions are satisfied.[268] First, as in a vertical short-form amalgamation, the subsidiaries must be wholly owned. Where any subsidiary has a minority shareholder, the corporations may still amalgamate, but they must follow the long-form amalgamation procedure.

§14.128 The second condition is that the shares of all but one of the amalgamating subsidiary corporations must be cancelled without repayment of capital in respect thereof.[269] Although this condition seems similar to the cancellation of share capital in a vertical short-form amalgamation, it is not. In vertical amalgamation, if the share capital of the subsidiary were to be added to that of the parent, the effect would be to double count the amount of capital so added. The capital of the corporation represents the shareholder's at risk investment in the corporation. The investment by a parent in the capital of a subsidiary does not increase the amount that the shareholders of the parent have invested in the parent. In contrast, in horizontal amalgamation the share capital of the two subsidiaries Beforeco and Priorco each represent distinct investments made by the parent corporation in the capital of each of those corporations. If the shares of Priorco were simply to be cancelled upon the amalgamation of Priorco and Beforeco, there would be no recognition given to the investment previously made by the parent in the shares of Priorco. To eliminate this injustice, subclause 177(2)(*b*)(iii) provides:

> (iii) the stated capital of the amalgamating subsidiary corporations whose shares are cancelled shall be added to the stated capital of the amalgamating subsidiary corporation whose shares are not cancelled.

§14.129 The third condition is that, except as may be prescribed, the articles of amalgamation must be the same as the articles of the amalgamating subsidiary corporation whose shares are not cancelled. It is not possible in the course of the amalgamation procedure itself to combine the most desired features of the two sets of articles, or otherwise to make amendments to the articles of the corporations. Any such amendments must be approved in the manner set out in the Act for amending the articles of incorporation. Until recently, it was unclear whether Amalco would inherit the by-laws of its dominant parent, or whether it was necessary to adopt new by-laws. This question has now been resolved. Subclause 177(2)(*b*)(i.1) provides that the by-laws of the amalgamated corporation shall be the same as the by-laws of the amalgamating subsidiary corporation whose shares are not cancelled.

---

[267] CBCA, s. 184(2).
[268] CBCA, s. 184(2).
[269] OBCA, s. 177(2)(*b*)(i).

(v) Two-stream Amalgamation, CBCA Restrictions on

§14.130 Certain federal Acts permit amalgamation with companies to which those Acts apply and corporations under the CBCA. Amalgamations of this type are sometimes referred to as "two-stream" amalgamations, because they involve two (or potentially more) entities that are subject to different streams of corporate regulation. The resulting amalgamated corporation then continues under one of the streams in question. Section 186.1 imposes a number of restrictions that apply with respect to two-stream amalgamations. Specifically, subsection 186.1 provides:

> 186.1 Subject to subsection (2), a corporation may not amalgamate with one or more bodies corporate pursuant to the *Bank Act,* the *Canada Cooperatives Act,* the *Cooperative Credit Associations Act,* the *Insurance Companies Act* or the *Trust and Loan Companies Act* unless the corporation is first authorized to do so by the shareholders in accordance with section 183.

Subsection (2) permits a vertical two-stream short-form amalgamation between one or more subsidiaries and its holding corporation, or a horizontal two-stream short-form amalgamation between two or more subsidiaries of the same holding body corporate, upon director approval alone:

> (2) A corporation may not amalgamate with one or more bodies corporate pursuant to the provisions of one of the Acts referred to in subsection (1) respecting short-form amalgamations unless the corporation is first authorized to do so by the directors in accordance with section 184.

On receipt of a notice satisfactory to the Director under the CBCA that a corporation has amalgamated under one of the Acts referred to in subsection (1), the Director must file the notice and issue a certificate of discontinuance in accordance with section 262.[270] This notice is deemed to be articles that are in the form that the Director fixes,[271] and consequently, section 185 does not apply to a corporation.[272] The CBCA ceases to apply to the corporation on the date shown in the certificate of discontinuance.[273]

(vi) Discretion to Refuse to Approve an Amalgamation

§14.131 The extent to which the Director under the CBCA — and the comparable office holder under the OBCA and other similar legislation — enjoys a discretion in deciding whether to approve a proposed amalgamation was considered by the Ontario Court of Appeal in *Re Canada Business Corporations Act.*[274] The facts in that case were as follows: Varity Corp., a corporation under the CBCA, intended to amalgamate with a second, newly incorporated CBCA corporation. As part of the transaction, the publicly held shares of Varity Corp. would, in effect, be exchanged for equivalent shares in an American corporation ("Varity

---

[270] CBCA, s. 186.1(3).
[271] CBCA, s. 186.1(4).
[272] CBCA, s. 186.1(6).
[273] CBCA, s. 186.1(5).
[274] [1991] O.J. No. 714, 3 O.R. (3d) 336 (C.A.).

U.S."), which was incorporated under the laws of Delaware. The Director, under the CBCA, considered that the transaction amounted to the export of Varity Corp. In anticipation of the amalgamation, the Director applied to the court for directions and for an order that where a corporation incorporated under the CBCA sought to amalgamate with another CBCA corporation under circumstances that would result in the effective export of that corporation, the Director might refuse to accept the articles of amalgamation and to issue a certificate of amalgamation until the CBCA corporation established to the satisfaction of the Director that the proposed amalgamation would not adversely affect creditors or shareholders of the CBCA corporation.[275] It was held that the Director did not possess so broad a discretion.[276]

(vii) Court Approval of Amalgamation

§14.132 Although neither the OBCA nor the CBCA impose such a requirement, in some jurisdictions court approval is required for an amalgamation. For instance, under section 249(1) of the now repealed *British Columbia Company Act*,[277] an amalgamation agreement must be approved by the court before the amalgamation can take effect. No comparable requirement applies under the OBCA or the CBCA. Nevertheless, the considerations raised in the British Columbia case law[278] regarding court approval would appear to be relevant to the question of whether the Director should exercise the apparent discretion vested on him or her under the OBCA or the CBCA in deciding whether or not to refuse an amalgamation by refusing to issue a certificate of amalgamation.[279] Similarly, this case law would also appear to be relevant to applications for relief against oppression, where the remedy sought is an order to enjoin, or otherwise block, a proposed amalgamation. In *Re Denman Street Restaurant Corp.*[280] Koenigsberg J. dealt with a motion by a creditor that a proposed amalgamation not be permitted to proceed. Koenigsberg J. took the view that the key test was whether the amalgamation was fair to the interests of all affected parties. In rejecting the motion not to approve the amalgamation, it was said that the creditor demonstrated prejudice to its position, a prejudice that would not exist but for the amalgamation.[281] Koenigsberg J. relied upon the decision of the Manitoba Court of Appeal in *Triad Oil Holdings Ltd. v. Manitoba*[282] in which the following general statement of principle appears:

> The court is given the broad discretion to approve or not approve an amalgamation agreement having regard to the "rights and interests of all parties". The section does not single out creditors and dissident shareholders for preferred treatment,

---

[275] This being the same standard as that which applies in the case of a continuation of a corporation by virtue of s. 188 of the CBCA.
[276] [1991] O.J. No. 714, 3 O.R. (3d) 336 at 341 (C.A.), *per* Finlayson J.A.
[277] R.S.B.C. 1996, c. 62, as amended.
[278] And consideration raised in cases decided under similar statutes in other provinces.
[279] See, generally, *Re Canada Business Corporations Act*, [1991] O.J. No. 714, 3 O.R. (3d) 336 (C.A.).
[280] [1994] B.C.J. No. 508, 14 B.L.R. (2d) 313 (S.C.).
[281] *Ibid.*, at 315.
[282] (1967), 59 W.W.R. 1 at 9 (Man. C.A.).

though obviously their interests would be given the careful consideration that their position demands. The mere fact that some shareholders dissent or deem their interests adversely affected is not sufficient to preclude the court from approving the amalgamation. It is the function of the court to examine the material and if satisfied that all parties including creditors and dissident shareholders are being fairly dealt with, to approve the agreement.

(viii) Effect of Amalgamation

§14.133 Upon the articles of amalgamation becoming effective, the amalgamating corporations are amalgamated and continue as a single successor corporation under the terms and conditions prescribed in the amalgamation agreement.[283] The term "successor corporation" is not a strict legal term of art. In general terms, it describes a corporation that by merger, amalgamation, or otherwise by operation of law assumes the obligations and burdens and is vested with the rights and privileges of an earlier corporation.[284] The amalgamated corporations do not form a new company; rather, they are subsumed and continue to subsist as a single successor corporation.[285] The amalgamated corporation possesses all the property, rights, privileges and franchises and is subject to all liabilities, including civil, criminal and quasi-criminal, and all contracts, disabilities and debts of each of the amalgamating corporations.[286] However, as the law is clear that a debtor and creditor must be two separate entities, any debt existing between the two predecessor corporations is extinguished upon the merger of the interest and creditor.[287] Although one corporation is not normally liable for debts and other obligations owed by another corporation, this rule does not apply to the corporation fused as a result of the amalgamation *vis-à-vis* the debts and obligations of its predecessors.[288] As one American court has observed in the product liability context:

> A successor corporation, having reaped the benefits of continuing its predecessor's product line, exploiting its accumulated goodwill and enjoying the patronage of its established customers, should be made to bear some of the burdens of continuity, namely, liability for injuries caused by defective products.[289]

Thus, any mortgage or other security agreement entered into by either of the predecessor corporations does not disappear but continues as a security agreement of Amalco,[290] as will any other contract, and Amalco retains the same

---

[283] OBCA, s. 179(*a*).
[284] See, generally, *National Trust Co. v. Mead*, [1990] S.C.J. No. 76, [1990] 2 S.C.R. 410.
[285] *Stanward Corp. v. Denison Mines Ltd.*, [1966] O.J. No. 1020, 57 D.L.R. (2d) 674 at 681 (C.A.), per Kelly J.A., aff'd [1968] S.C.J. No. 23, [1968] S.C.R. 441; *R. v. Black & Decker Manufacturing Co.*, [1974] S.C.J. No. 56, 43 D.L.R. (3d) 393 at 396-97.
[286] OBCA, s. 179(*b*); CBCA, s. 186(*b*), (*c*), (*d*) and (*e*).
[287] *Armstrong v. Shaw*, [1996] O.J. No. 4443, [1996] O.T.C. LEXIS 3917 (Gen. Div.), per Greer J., order varied [1998] O.J. No. 58 (C.A.).
[288] *Ramirez v. Amstead Industries Inc.*, 431 A.2d 811, 86 N.J. 332 (Sup. Ct. 1981).
[289] *Ibid.*, at 817 (A.2d).
[290] *Re Manco Home Systems Ltd.*, [1990] B.C.J. No. 666, 78 C.B.R. (N.S.) 109 (C.A.), also reported as *Gesco Industries Ltd. v. Hongkong Bank of Canada*.

obligations[291] and rights[292] under such agreements as possessed by its predecessors. So, if a bond holder of old corporation A had a right to convert his or her bonds to some other form of security, that right will continue should A amalgamate with B to form Amalco.[293]

§14.134 Following an amalgamation, every conviction against, or a ruling, order or judgment in favour of or against an amalgamating corporation may be enforced against the amalgamated corporation,[294] and the amalgamated corporation (Amalco) is deemed to be the party plaintiff or party defendant, as the case may be, in any civil action commenced by or against either of the amalgamating corporations before the amalgamation became effective.[295] Obviously, the continuation of existing liabilities poses some risk to the shareholders of each of the amalgamating corporations, because they cannot be certain of the extent of the hidden, or otherwise undisclosed, liabilities of the other corporation. In drafting the amalgamation agreement, therefore, it is desirable, when practical, to make sure that adequate representations and indemnities are provided to protect the shareholders of each corporation against the risk of any unknown liability of the other corporation.

§14.135 Where two corporations amalgamate (*e.g.*, A Corp. and B Ltd.) and the name of the amalgamated corporation is the same as one of those corporations (*e.g.*, A Corp.), it is not necessary to register a new financing statement under the *Personal Property Security Act*[296] to maintain the perfection of security interests that were perfected by registration against the corporate name of the old A Corp.[297] However, in regard to (1) security interests perfected by registration against the name of B Ltd., or (2) security interests perfected by registration against the name of A Corp. or B Ltd. where the two corporations amalgamate and continue under a new name (*e.g.*, C Inc.), then it is necessary to comply with section 48(3) of the *Personal Property Security Act*, which provides:

> 48.(3) Where a security interest is perfected by registration and the secured party learns that the name of the debtor has changed, the security interest in the collateral becomes unperfected thirty days after the secured party learns of the change of name and the new name of the debtor unless the secured party registers a financing change statement or takes possession of the collateral within such thirty days.

---

[291] *Stanward Corp. v. Denison Mines Ltd.*, [1966] O.J. No. 1020, [1966] 2 O.R. 585 at 591 (C.A.), per Aylesworth J.A., aff'd [1968] S.C.J. No. 23, [1968] S.C.R. 441.
[292] *Norcen International Ltd. v. Sunco Inc.*, [1988] A.R. No. 919, 91 A.R. 81 at 91 (Q.B.), per McBain J.
[293] *Cayley v. Coburg, Peterborough & Marmora Rlwy. & Mining Co.*, [1868] O.J. No. 225, 14 Gr. 571 (Ch.).
[294] OBCA, s. 179(*c*).
[295] OBCA, s. 179(*e*); see also *C. & J. Enterprises (1971) Ltd. v. Curtis*, [1978] N.B.J. No. 329, 25 N.B.R. (2d) 537, 51 A.P.R. 537 (Q.B.). There is no similar provision in regard to administrative, criminal or quasi-criminal proceedings. The CBCA contains no provision equivalent to s. 179(*c*) of the OBCA.
[296] R.S.O. 1990, c. P.10, as amended.
[297] *Heidelberg Canada Graphic Equipment Ltd. v. Arthur Anderson Inc.*, [1992] O.J. No. 2530, 7 B.L.R. (2d) 236 (Gen. Div.).

A security interest that becomes unperfected by virtue of subsection 48(3) may be re-perfected again by registering a financial change statement at any time during the remainder of the unexpired registration period of the financing statement or any renewal of that statement.[298]

§14.136 There is a surprising absence of case law on the impact of the amalgamation or continuation of a corporate principal or the creditor on the liability of a surety under a guarantee. One reason for this may be that most standard form bank guarantees specifically provide that the amalgamation or continuation of the principal shall not affect the liability of the surety. Where the terms of the guarantee are silent, it is necessary to reason the matter through on the basis of principle and the relevant provisions of the OBCA and CBCA. It is axiomatic that neither amalgamation nor continuation will affect the liability of the surety for advances or other guaranteed obligations that predate the date of amalgamation. The question to resolve is whether such events are sufficient to release the surety from further liability under a continuing guarantee. Although one might initially suspect that the impact of the amalgamation of a corporate creditor with another corporation would be similar to the effect of a change in the membership of a partnership creditor, this does not appear to be the case. On the contrary, it appears that the amalgamation of the creditor with some other corporation does not affect its rights under a guarantee.[299] Section 179(*b*) of the OBCA is particularly clear on this point:

> 179. Upon the articles of amalgamation becoming effective,
>
> .....
>
> (*b*) the amalgamated corporation possesses all the property, rights, privileges and franchises and is subject to all liabilities, including civil, criminal and quasi-criminal, and all contracts, disabilities and debts of each of the amalgamating corporations ...

While the corresponding provisions of the CBCA[300] are not so clear on the point, it seems likely that they would be given a similar interpretation. In contrast, amalgamation of a corporate principal debtor with another corporation might be seen to vary the risk of the surety. Unless that variation is caused by the creditor, however, it is difficult to see why it should affect the liability of the surety for the obligations of the debtor, at least in the case of a *discrete* guarantee relating to a specific transaction.[301] On the other hand, the amalgamation of a corporate principal with another corporation would, on principle, appear to justify the release of a surety from further liability under a *continuing* guarantee. The amalgamation of a corporation constitutes such a fundamental change in the nature and composition of the debtor whose debt is guaranteed that, where such a

---

[298] *Personal Property Security Act*, s. 48(5).
[299] See, for instance, *London, Brighton & South Coast Rlwy. v. Goodwin* (1849), 3 Exch. 320, 154 E.R. 866; *Eastern Union Rlwy. v. Cochrane* (1853), 9 Exch. 197, 156 E.R. 84.
[300] Section 187(7).
[301] *Commcorp Financial Services Inc. v. Mark & Kellog Enterprises Ltd.*, [1995] A.J. No. 816, 33 Alta. L.R. (3d) 177 (Q.B.), *per* Master Funduk.

change takes place, it would seem to be a natural extension of the common law regarding changes in the make-up of a partnership for the surety to be entitled to a release.

§14.137 Where a corporate surety amalgamates with the corporate principal debtor, the liability of the surety under the guarantee merges with the principal debt. In some cases, however, the surety will have provided a security interest in regard to its guarantee that was not available to the creditor in regard to the principal debt itself. In such a case, the security interest charging assets of the surety for the performance of its obligations under the guarantee remains effective as security for the performance of the principal obligation.[302]

§14.138 Continuation is a separate consideration. There are two forms of continuation: continuation under a new jurisdiction and continuation as a new form of corporate entity. The continuation of a corporate creditor or principal in another jurisdiction would not appear to affect the liability of a surety. The continuation of a corporation in another jurisdiction does not affect the nature of a body corporate, but merely changes the regulatory regime to which it is subject. Consequently, it is difficult to see any theoretical basis on which it might be argued that such continuation should affect the liability of a surety, irrespective of whether it is the surety, principal or creditor that is continued in a different jurisdiction. In the case of the continuation of the creditor or surety, clause 180(7)(*a*) of the OBCA makes it clear that such continuation has no effect upon liability:

> 180.(7) When a body corporate is continued ... under this Act,
>
> > (*a*) the corporation possesses all the property, rights, privileges and franchises and is subject to all the liabilities, including civil, criminal and quasi-criminal, and all contracts, disabilities and debts of the body corporate;[303]

§14.139 In the case of continuations that affect the form of a corporate entity (whether effected by private act or otherwise) it is less clear that such continuation will have no effect upon the liability of a surety. These doubts are, perhaps, more justified where there has been a fundamental change in the nature of the body corporate as a result of the continuation. For instance, the continuation of a not-for-profit corporation as a business corporation may be a sufficient change in the character of a principal to justify the release of the surety from further liability. In a case of continuation of this sort, there may be some justification in the release of the surety from liability, because such a continuation would amount to a variation of the risk that the surety had agreed to assume.[304]

---

[302] *Clarke v. Technical Marketing Associates Ltd. Estate*, [1992] O.J. No. 559, 8 O.R. (3d) 734 (Gen. Div. — C.L.).

[303] The corresponding provision of the CBCA is, again, less clear. See s. 187(7).

[304] For one of the few cases dealing with the question of whether creditors and other stakeholders can be prejudiced by a change in the nature of a company, see: *Neato Employment Services v. Australian Securities and Investments Commission*, [2002] A.A.T. 429 (Aust. Admin. App. Trib.).

(ix) Takeover Bids

§14.140 Frequently, amalgamations will be effected within the context of a takeover bid. Although the full mechanics of the takeover bid process are more the province of securities law than corporate law, there is one aspect of such bids that is particularly relevant to the study of corporate law. This critical area of concern relates to the duties of the directors of the takeover target. For this reason, we will give brief consideration to that limited aspect of takeover law in this text.[305]

§14.141 In Ontario, takeover and issuer bids are governed by Part XX of the *Securities Act*. Section 97 of the *Securities Act* sets out a number of restrictions on the consideration payable in respect of a takeover bid. The general rule is set down in subsection 97(1), which provides that:

> 97.(1) Subject to the regulations, where a take-over bid or issuer bid is made, all holders of the same class of securities shall be offered identical consideration.

Subsection 97(2) sets down a general prohibition against collateral benefits:

> 97.(2) If an offeror makes or intends to make a take-over bid or issuer bid, neither the offeror nor any person or company acting jointly or in concert with the offeror shall enter into any collateral agreement, commitment or understanding with any holder or beneficial owner of securities of the offeree issuer that has the effect of providing to the holder or owner a consideration of greater value than that offered to the other holders of the same class of securities.

Subsection 97(3) extends the requirement for uniform treatment to cover the situation where the consideration payable in a bid, is increased during the course of the bid:

> 97.(3) Where a variation in the terms of a take-over bid or issuer bid before the expiry of the bid increases the value of the consideration offered for the securities subject to the bid, the offeror shall pay such increased consideration to each person or company whose securities are taken up pursuant to the bid, whether or not such securities were taken up by the offeror before the variation.

Further regulation regarding such transactions is imposed under Part X of Regulation 1015, the General Regulation[306] under the *Securities Act*. In particular, section 189 of the Regulation provides that:

> (a) A take-over bid circular shall contain the information prescribed in Form 32. [Briefly, this form requires disclosure of the name of the offeror, the name of the offeree issuer, the securities that are subject to the bid, a disclosure of any securities of the offeree issuer currently owed or controlled by the offeror, the trading record during the past six months, any commitments to acquire securities, the terms and conditions of the bid, the method and time of payment, the right to withdraw deposited securities, the arrangements to pay for deposited securities, the trading rights for any securities of the offeree that will be

---

[305] See also the discussion of Rule 61-501 below, particularly as it pertains to issuer bids and insider bids.
[306] R.R.O. 1990, Reg. 1015.

acquired under the takeover bid, any arrangements that exist between the offeror and the directors and officers of the offeree, any material changes in the affairs of the offeree issuer, valuation information, a description of the securities of the offeror or any other issuer that are to be exchanged for the securities of the offeree, a description of the appraisal rights of securities holders, a statement of whether the offer intends to purchase securities in the market that are the subject of the takeover, and certain other information.]

(b) An issuer bid circular shall contain the information prescribed in Form 33. [The information required to be disclosed in this Form includes a description of the securities sought, the time period of the offer, the method of acquisition, the consideration offered, the source of funds, where the bid is for less than all of the securities of the class concerned, a description of participation rights, a discussion of the reasons for the bid, a description of the ownership breakdown of the ownership of securities of the issuer by directors and officers, and also significant shareholders, and persons acting in concert with them, the benefits of the bid to any persons who are listed in those persons, as well as valuation information and current financial statements.]

(c) A directors' circular shall contain the information prescribed in Form 34. [In this Form, disclosure must be made of any directors, officers, *etc.*, who have accepted the bid, the relationship between the offeror and the directors and senior officers of the offeree issuer, any interests of directors and senior officers of the offeree in material contracts of the offeror, the trading records of the directors and officers of the offeree during the preceding six-month period, any recommendation regarding acceptance or rejection of the bid, a disclosure of whether any negotiations are underway in response to the bid.]

§14.142 Depending upon the circumstances of the case, potentially the decision by the board of the target corporation to accept a takeover bid (or management buyout offer) may be attacked either as a form of oppression (*i.e.*, as a cause of some specific injury to the applicant seeking such relief) or by way of derivative proceedings (*i.e.*, for a breach of the directors fiduciary duty to the corporation). Even in cases where the target corporation and all of its directors are both at arm's length to the bidder, there is a potential that the directors will find themselves in a conflict of interest. As Weiler J.A. noted in the *Maple Leaf Foods* case:

> A potential conflict of interest arises because as a director of a target company, the senior executive has a duty, to act in the best interests of the shareholders, but as a member of senior management the executive retains an interest in continued employment. In actively negotiating with a potential bidder the executive is negotiating with his potential boss or executioner.[307]

This conflict is most evident in the case of senior managers who sit on the Board, since they have potentially the most to lose by reason of the takeover bid. On the other hand, completely excluding such management-directors from the negotiation process is unrealistic, since such individuals are almost certain to be the directors who are most familiar with the business.

---

[307] *Maple Leaf Foods Inc. v. Schneider Corp.*, [1998] O.J. No. 4142, 42 O.R. (3d) 177 at para. 75 (C.A.), reported elsewhere as *Pente Investment Management Ltd. v. Schneider Corp.*

§14.143 Ultimately, a take-over bid is no more than a purchase of a corporation. In a hostile take-over, the company is sold by the existing shareholders over the heads of the existing management. In the case of a friendly take-over, management is a willing participant in the sale. In *Revlon, Inc. v. MacAndrews & Forbes Holdings, Inc.* ("*Revlon*"),[308] the Delaware Supreme Court held that once directors decide to sell a corporation, they should do what any fiduciary (such as trustee) should do when selling a trust asset: they should seek to maximize the sales price for the benefit of beneficiaries of the trust. There is a considerable logic in this approach, because the sale of the corporation is really the sale of its business, including the goodwill associated with the name of the business. In terms of the responsibilities of the board, the sale of the business of a corporation is no different from any other transaction in which the corporation is engaged. Their job is to maximize the price that can be obtained.[309] The Delaware Supreme Court reiterated this view in *Paramount Communications, Inc. v. QVC Network, Inc.*:

> In the sale of control context, the directors must focus on one primary objective — to secure the transaction offering the best value reasonably available for the stockholders — and they must exercise their fiduciary duties to further that end.[310]

§14.144 The *Revlon* decision rejected the suggestion in *Unocal Corp. v. Mesa Petroleum Co.*,[311] that where a takeover bid was brought the directors of the target corporation could consider the impact the bid would have on other corporate constituencies, such as employees and communities in which the corporation operated. Under the *Revlon* approach, in the takeover context (or in the context of a decision to put the corporation or its assets up for sale), the directors should only consider those constituencies where and to the extent that doing so is rationally related to some benefit to the shareholders, which in that special context must have a relation to price.[312] In the *Peoples* decision, the Supreme Court of Canada appears to have adopted a fairly similar approach, albeit in a different context, since that case also stressed that the duty of loyalty owed to the corporation meant focusing on the maximization of the value of the corporation.[313]

§14.145 As we have previously noted, the maximization of the value of the corporation can be difficult to accomplish in practice. Very often, efforts to increase the value of equity (common) shares will have a detrimental impact upon the

---

[308] 506 A.2d 173 (1986).
[309] *Robinson v. Pittsburgh Oil Refining Corp.* (1924), 14 Del. Ch. 193 at 126 A. 46 at 49 (Del. Ch. 1924). See also *Trustee of Peoples Department Stores Inc. v. Wise*, [2004] S.C.J. No. 64, [2004] 3 S.C.R. 461.
[310] [1989] Del. Ch. LEXIS 77, [1989] W.L. 79880 (Del. Ch.).
[311] 493 A.2d 946 (Del. 1985).
[312] *Revlon, Inc. v. MacAndrews & Forbes Holdings, Inc.*, 506 A.2d 173 at 176 (1986).
[313] *Trustee of Peoples Department Stores Inc. v. Wise*, [2004] S.C.J. No. 64, [2004] 3 S.C.R. 461, although at para. 42, the court continued: "We accept as an accurate statement of law that in determining whether they are acting with a view to the best interests of the corporation it may be legitimate, given all the circumstances of a given case, for the board of directors to consider, *inter alia*, the interests of shareholders, employees, suppliers, creditors, consumers, governments and the environment." This passage was in reference to the decision of Berger J. in *Teck Corp. v. Millar*, [1972] B.C.J. No. 566, 33 D.L.R. (3d) 288 (S.C.).

market value of existing debt securities. For instance, it is common in the present investment market for take-over bids to be financed as leveraged buyouts ("LBO"). In an LBO the transaction results in a substitution of increased debt for the equity of the pre-takeover business. It is this debt that is used to eliminate the publicly held equity. Often, the post-buyout company will have a debt to asset ratio of 90 per cent or greater. The new debt will be secured against the firm's existing assets. The likely consequence will be a dramatic change in the risk profile of the company's existing outstanding debt, with a consequent down-grading of its market value. In one study of 29 management buy-outs, the authors determined that bondholders lost about three percent of the market value of their bonds where the buy-out was structured on an LBO basis.[314]

§14.145.1 When a tentative deal was struck in April, 2007, for the takeover of the American student-loan firm SLM Corp. (popularly known as Sallie Mae), its shares immediately jumped about 18 per cent when a group of private-equity firms and two major banks for $60 a share, or about $25 billion. However, the jump in share values was offset by a corresponding fall in the market value of debt securities. Corporate bonds of Sallie Mae were sold off even before the deal was announced, after a New York Times report that the company was involved is in takeover talks with private-equity firms, who were planning a leveraged buyout deal that could be worth more than $20 billion. SLM Corp bond spreads widened by 33 basis points (the "spread" represents the distance between the yield on a corporate bond and the yield of a Treasury note of comparable maturity). In effect, the impact of the deal was to down grade corporate grade investments into near junk status. The threat of a down-grade to junk status is anything but hypothetical. When First Data Corp. entered into a leveraged buyout deal, its corporate debt rating was cut five notches by Standard & Poor's down to BB+, which is junk status. In short, debt that is good for the holders of voting shares may not be good for any other stakeholder interest.

§14.145.2 In principle, bond holders can be protected against this risk, by including sufficient restrictive covenants and redemption rights in the terms of their bonds, to allow them to bail out of a transaction, where there is a rapid decline in the value of their investment due to an LBO. The problem is that few existing bonds include terms of this kind. The current market fascination with LBOs as a financing approach is only about a year old. While this type of transaction was popular in the late 1980s, it fell out of favour in the 1990s, only became common again in 2006. Thus, in the present market, LBOs constitute a serious threat to all but a handful of debt investment holders. Needless to say, a similar risk also applies with respect to preferred shares (which usually are non-voting, or carry only restricted voting rights). Indeed, as they are subordinate in priority to the general and unsecured debt of the corporation, preferred shareholders are at even greater risk than are bond holders.

---

[314] Douglas O. Cook, John C. Easterwood, John D. Martin, "Bondholder wealth effects of management buyouts", Financial Management, Leveraged Buyouts Special Issue, Spring, 1992 (Financial Management Association).

§14.146 In subsequent decisions to *Revlon*, Delaware courts have qualified the language of the *Revlon* case to some extent. They have made clear that the courts should not second-guess reasonable, but admittedly debatable, tactical choices that directors may have made in good faith. In particular the Delaware Supreme Court has held that the duty to secure the highest immediately available price does not invariably require a board to conduct an auction process or even a targeted canvass of the market. A board may offer a bidder contractual protection with respect to the bid, so long as its decision to do so was (when granted) reasonably directed to the objective of getting the highest price. However, it was held that a board should support a particular bidder for reasons unrelated to the shareholders' ability to get the best price apparently available.[315]

§14.147 The purpose of the board of directors putting a corporation up for auction is to try to secure the highest value for the shareholders of the target companies for their shares. Despite the foregoing risk to debt and preferred shareholders, the courts have usually taken the view that, in almost all cases, this is an acceptable purpose.[316] However, there are limits to the steps that may be taken to secure higher bids than that put forward by a hostile bidder. For instance, very often in a hostile takeover bid, the board of the target corporation may offer a break fee to another potential bidder to induce it to enter into a competitive auction for the target corporation. A break fee — or "bust-up fee", as such arrangements are also sometimes described — is a payment that will be made to the competitive bidder should its bid fail or be superseded by a better offer. In the ordinary case, the payment is intended to compensate the invited bidder for its time, effort, costs and lost opportunity in putting forward the opposing bid. However, where a break fee is set at an unrealistically high level (*i.e.*, beyond any prospect of the cost to the invited bidder), then it amounts to little more than using corporate assets as bait to lure another party into the arena in order to generate a free-for-all competition. Such fees are effective inducements, and they are common in takeover bid situations and accepted as proper techniques in appropriate circumstances. Where the fee is set at such a high level, it will constitute an improper defensive tactic.[317]

§14.148 In *Paramount Communications, Inc. v. QVC Network, Inc.* Veasey C.J. discussed the role of a court in reviewing the decisions made by the board when selling the corporation:

> ... a court should not ignore the complexity of the directors' task in a sale of control. There are many business and financial considerations implicated in investigating and selecting the best value reasonably available. The board of directors is the corporate decision making body best equipped to make these judgments. Accordingly, a court applying enhanced judicial scrutiny should be deciding whether

---

[315] *Barkan v. Amsted Indus.*, 567 A.2d 1279 at 1286 (Del. S.C. 1989).
[316] *Corona Minerals Corp. v. CSA Management Ltd.*, [1986] O.J. No. 576, 68 O.R. (2d) 425 at 429 (H.C.J.).
[317] See, generally, *Re Everfresh Beverages Inc.*, [1996] O.J. No. 105 (Gen Div. — C.L.); *CW Shareholdings Inc. v. WIC Western International Communications Ltd.*, [1998] O.J. No. 1886, 39 O.R. (3d) 755 (Gen. Div. — C.L.).

the directors make a reasonable decision, not a perfect decision. If a board selected one of several reasonable alternatives, a court should not second guess that choice even though it might have decided otherwise or subsequent events may have cast doubt on the boards' determination. Thus, courts will not substitute their business judgment for that of the directors, but will determine if the directors' decision was, on balance, within a range of reasonableness.[318]

Although in the *Maple Leaf Foods* case,[319] the court stated that "Revlon is not the law in Ontario", this statement (when read in its proper context) means only that there is no firm rule in Ontario that when a corporation is up for sale the directors are under an obligation to conduct some form of auction for the control of the corporation.[320] The court continued:

> An auction is merely one way to prevent the conflicts of interest that may arise when there is a change of control by requiring that directors act in a neutral manner toward a number of bidders. ... [The] obligation of directors when there is a bid for change of control [is] ... an obligation to seek the best value reasonably available to the shareholders in the circumstances. This is a more flexible standard, which recognizes that the particular circumstances are important in determining the best transaction available, and that a board is not limited to considering only the amount of cash or consideration involved, as would be the case with an auction. ... There is no single blueprint that directors must follow.[321]

§14.149 This paragraph resonates with a good deal of economic literature pertaining to bounded rationality: the decision-making process of rational economic actors who are pursuing their own economic best interest. While it is common in economic literature to find references to profit maximization and the maximization of shareholder value, these terms describe theoretical ideals. The limits of time, and the costs of securing information, make it a practical impossibility for any vendor to secure the maximum possible price. As the economist Herbert Simon has explained in considerable detail,[322] rather than being characterized by maximizing or optimizing behaviour, economic actors employ a process of satisfying under conditions of bounded rationality.[323] Within the context of the sale of

---

[318] 637 A.2d 34 at 45 (1994). See also *In Re Toys "R" Us Inc. Shareholder Litigation*, 877 A.2d 975 (Del. Ch. 2005).
[319] *Maple Leaf Foods Inc. v. Schneider Corp.*, [1998] O.J. No. 4142, 42 O.R. (3d) 177 at 91 (C.A.), reported elsewhere as *Pente Investment Management Ltd. v. Schneider Corp.*
[320] A conclusion similar to that reached by the Delaware Superior Court in *Barkan v. Amsted Indus.*, 567 A.2d 1279 (Del. S.C. 1989).
[321] *Maple Leaf Foods Inc. v. Schneider Corp.*, [1998] O.J. No. 4142, 42 O.R. (3d) 177 at para. 92 (C.A.), reported elsewhere as *Pente Investment Management Ltd. v. Schneider Corp.*
[322] See, for instance, H.A. Simon, "Rational Decision Making in Business Organizations" (1979) 69 *American Economic Review* 493 (The 1978 Nobel Memorial Prize in Economics Lecture).
[323] A vendor cannot maximize (or optimize) the price secured for the sale of an asset unless the vendor knows the price that every potential purchaser would be willing to pay for that asset. However, for a number of reasons no vendor can afford to overinvest in the search for a higher price. First, money (like any other thing of utility) has a diminishing marginal value, so that the additional benefit derived from securing a slightly better price may not be justified by the cost (in time and resources) paid to secure that better price. Second, offers are frequently time limited, so that the terms of the offer may itself impose a bound upon the extent to which higher potential bids may be obtained. Third, information is far from costless. Each of these constraints "bounds" the extent to which a person may rationally pursue a higher price.

a business, the vendor will seek to achieve not the maximum value, but rather some satisfactory enhancement upon the level of utility currently generated for the vendor by the asset that will form the subject of the sale, taking into account prevailing market price for the assets (including reasonable efforts to identify alternative bidders) and the anticipated value of the asset to the purchaser. Once the utility of the consideration offered by the purchaser exceeds the present utility of the asset to the vendor — and the price offered reasonably identifiable alternative bidders — by what is perceived by the vendor to be an acceptable margin, the sale will be made. Since even a purchaser acting for his or her own benefit will not seek to acquire the highest possible price, there is no need to subject a board of directors (when acting on behalf of the shareholders) to a more exacting demand.

§14.150 Adopting such an approach, directors confronted with an offer for the sale of control of a corporation are obliged to make an informed judgment and must proceed on a reasonable basis. In resolving this question, a court may inquire whether the directors have exercised reasonable efforts to determine whether the price offered is as good as other potential offers that are likely to be available. In particular, where members of the board have a vested interest in the board's decision with respect to a bid, that decision should be left to an independent committee. Such a committee may take into account such question as whether any other offers have materialized for the corporation over a reasonable period of time, where it is widely known that the control of the corporation is for sale.[324] Provided that the directors have acted honestly and reasonably, the court will not substitute its own business judgment for that of the board.

§14.151 The *Maple Leaf Foods* case also makes clear that the independent directors considering the benefit of a proposed sale of control are entitled to take into account the wishes and intentions of the corporation's existing control group of shareholder, where that person or group has the ability to thwart any takeover bid or other offer for control of a corporation, and has made clear that they are not prepared to consider any offer from a particular bidder, or are only prepared to consider an offer that satisfies specific conditions (not all of which need be price related). More specifically, it now appears to be clear that it is perfectly acceptable for shareholders who effectively have the ability to block any sale, to demand that the sale of control of the corporation take into account considerations beyond the pure dollar value of the offer, including the continuity of employment for employees, the welfare of suppliers and the relationship with customers.

(x) Poison Pills

§14.152 The subject of poison pills and other takeover defences was discussed in Chapter 11. Generally, takeover defences may be employed by the existing

---

[324] *Maple Leaf Foods Inc. v. Schneider Corp.*, [1998] O.J. No. 4142, 42 O.R. (3d) 177 at para. 121 (C.A.), reported elsewhere as *Pente Investment Management Ltd. v. Schneider Corp.*

board and management of the target corporation in a takeover bid, provided that in doing so they act in a manner consistent with their statutory obligation to act in the best interests of the corporation. For reporting issuers, any such arrangement will be subject to National Policy 62-202.[325] Depending upon the manner in which it is structured, a poison pill may require shareholder approval (*e.g.*, if it adds rights to an existing class of shares). In recent years, the shareholders of many publicly traded companies in Canada and elsewhere have rejected such measures. Although they are not necessarily legally invalid, the courts carefully scrutinize such measures when they come before them. In a recent case, it was noted that such devices usually have no other purpose than to give the existing board the leverage to prevent transactions that it does not favour by diluting the buying proponent's interests.[326]

F. GOING PRIVATE TRANSACTIONS

(i) Overview

§14.153 Section 190 of the OBCA creates a number of special rights and obligations that apply in the case of a going private transaction ("GPT"), as defined in that section.[327] A going private transaction has three key elements: First, it will involve a public corporation that has a single shareholder or shareholder group that owns sufficient issued voting shares of the corporation to be in a position to control the corporation. Second, this control is then used to arrange a transaction under which the control group will be treated differently from other shareholders of the same class. Usually, it will be structured so that that they will receive full equity ownership of the corporation as a result of some fundamental change to the corporation (and its issued securities) that forms the centrepiece of the transaction. Third, as a result of the transaction, the shareholding of the other shareholders of the class (the "minority") will in effect be expropriated.

§14.154 GPT transactions may serve a legitimate corporate purpose. The streamlining of ownership through the elimination of "public" shareholders can significantly reduce the costs of capital to a corporation. In particular, the expensive transaction costs associated with public status are eliminated. In addition, the financing premium demanded by equity holders for their subordinate status is eliminated. Management time can be redirected from the burden of securities law compliance towards securing emerging business opportunities for the benefit of the corporation. Where there is little market for the shares of the corporation, a GPT may offer the minority shareholders the opportunity to receive some value for their otherwise illiquid shares. For these reasons, GPT transactions cannot be considered to be inherently unfair, unreasonable or abusive. However,

---

[325] Canadian Securities Administrators, National Policy 62-202, "Take-over Bids — Defensive Tactics", August 4, 1997.
[326] *Hollinger International, Inc. v. Black*, 844 A.2d 1022 (Del. Ch. 2004), *per* Strine V.C.
[327] As to the use of the arrangement procedure for this purpose, see: *Re Sepp's Gourmet Foods Ltd.*, [2002] B.C.J. No. 33, 21 B.L.R. (3d) 291 (S.C.), rev'd [2002] B.C.J. No. 289, 21 B.L.R. (3d) 270 (C.A.).

there can be little question that such transactions can be structured so that they become confiscatory in nature, resulting in the diversion to the control group of value within the corporation that properly belongs to the shareholders as a whole.

§14.155 Legislatures, securities regulators and the courts have each adopted mechanism to balance the risks to the minority against the benefits to the corporation that are presented by GPT transaction. Since GPTs are often carried under a plan of arrangement some element of protection will be built into the process under the requirement for an application to a court to approve the transaction. Under both corporate law and securities regulatory instruments and policies, special minority approval (usually a majority of the minority shareholders) is generally required to obtain court approval. In addition, securities regulators have also imposed valuation and broad disclosure requirements with respect to such transactions. As the following analysis will make clear, the various approaches that have been taken have not always been consistent with each other, and this has led to some considerable confusion as to what is permissible and when.

(ii) The OBCA Regime

§14.156 An OBCA section 190 going-private transaction need not be part of a takeover bid, and it is not necessary that the bidder have the 90 per cent share holding required under sections 188 of the OBCA and 206 of the CBCA. GPTs are also regulated under applicable securities legislation, specifically in Ontario OSC Rule 61-501, which set out specific requirements regarding independent valuations, majority of minority approval and enhanced disclosure. In recent years, it is securities law that has been the most important consideration in this area. The balance between corporate law requirements and those of securities laws is sometimes hard to find, but both must be factored properly into corporate decision making.[328] For instance, a going private transaction may be potentially open to attack as oppressive.[329] In this section, we shall focus attention on the corporate law rules only, and defer for the moment a study of the impact of Rule 61-501.

§14.157 The term "going private transaction" is defined in subsection 190(1) of the OBCA to mean:

>...an amalgamation, arrangement, consolidation or other transaction carried out under the Act by a corporation that would cause the interest of a holder of a participating security of the corporation to be terminated without the consent of the

---

[328] See, generally, *LSI Logic Corp. of Canada Inc. v. Logani*, [2001] A.J. No. 1083, 19 B.L.R. (3d), 101 (Q.B.).

[329] As to the application of a process analogous to a "going private" transaction to a non-offering corporation (*i.e.*, a corporation that is not a reporting issuer for securities purposes) see: *General Accident Assurance Co. of Canada v. Lornex Mining Corp.*, [1988] O.J. No. 2009, 66 O.R. (2d) 783 (H.C.J.).

holder and without the substitution therefor of an interest of equivalent value in a participating security that,

 (*a*) is issued by the corporation, an affiliate of the corporation or a successor body corporate, and

 (*b*) is not limited in the extent of its participation in earnings to any greater extent than the participating security for which it is substituted...

However, the term "going private transaction" specifically excludes:

 (*c*) an acquisition under section 188 [*i.e.*, a takeover or issuer bid, which are subject to alternative requirements],

 (*d*) a redemption of, or other compulsory termination of the interest of the holder in, a security if the security is redeemed or otherwise acquired in accordance with the terms and conditions attaching thereto or under a requirement of the articles relating to the class of securities or of this Act, or

 (*e*) a proceeding under Part XVI of the Act [*i.e.*, the liquidation and dissolution of the corporation].[330]

The term "participating security" is also defined in subsection 190(1). It describes a security issued by a "body corporate" other than a security that is, in all circumstances, limited in the extent of its participation in earnings. The term expressly includes:

 (*a*) a security currently convertible into such a security, and

 (*b*) currently exercisable warrants entitling the holder to acquire such a security or such a convertible security.

§14.158 The various types of going private transaction that may be conceived are limited only by the imagination of legal counsel and financial advisors. The common characteristic of such transactions is that minority shareholders cease to be shareholders in the corporation. For instance, one of the most common types of going private transaction is known as an amalgamation squeeze-out. In such a transaction, a controlling shareholder who owns the majority of the shares of a corporation (A) seeks to oust minority shareholders by amalgamating A with a second corporation (B), that is wholly owned by the shareholder. The first step in the process is for the controlling shareholder to transfer all of his or her shares in A to B. Second, A and B will enter into an amalgamation agreement that provides that B will receive voting shares in Amalco (the amalgamated corporation), but all other shareholders will receive only cash or redeemable shares in Amalco.[331] A second type of common going private transaction is effected by means of an arrangement in which a new class of shares is created, for which all existing shares of the corporation are to be exchanged. The arrangement will also provide that where a person holds insufficient shares to receive a full share,

---

[330] OBCA, s. 190(1).
[331] See for instance, *Carlton Realty Co. v. Maple Leaf Mills Ltd.*, [1978] O.J. No. 3641, 22 O.R. (2d) 198 (H.C.J.); *Alexander v. Westeel-Rosco Ltd.*, [1978] O.J. No. 3643, 22 O.R. (2d) 211 (H.C.J.); *Burdon v. Zellers Ltd.* (1981), 16 B.L.R. 59 (Que. S.C.).

the shareholder will receive cash instead of a fraction of a share. If the exchange ratio is set sufficiently high, only the controlling shareholder will hold sufficient shares to secure one of the new shares under the arrangement. All other shareholders will be paid out instead.[332]

§14.159 While it is generally accepted that going private transactions are not inherently unfair to minority shareholders, a critical concern is whether they adequately compensate minority shareholders for the expropriation of their investment in the corporation, and whether those shareholders have sufficient information upon which to make a decision.[333] A further concern exists where the going private transaction is effectively a bid by the existing control group inside the corporation, since that group will usually enjoy an informational advantage over minority shareholders. Unfairness is unlikely where in the circumstances other potential bidders have had an opportunity to investigate the corporation to decide whether to make competing bids, particularly where the proposed going private transaction is supported by an independent professional valuation (a "fairness opinion"), as to the price offered.

§14.160 Section 190 essentially imposes four obligations in every case where a transaction falls within the scope of the GPT provisions.[334] In light of the potentially confiscatory nature of a GPT, strict compliance with the requirements of the Act is essential.[335] Where the person seeking to expropriate the shares of the dissident shareholders fails to comply with these requirements, the dissidents are not obliged to sell or transfer their shares to that person.[336]

§14.161 The first requirement is an independent valuation. Specifically, subsection 190(2) provides that the corporation must have an independent qualified valuator prepare a written valuation indicating a per security value or range of values for each class of affected securities. The valuation must be prepared and revised as of a date not more than 120 days before the announcement of the going private transaction, with appropriate adjustments being made for subsequent events, other than the going private transaction itself.[337] The valuation must not

---

[332] See, for instance, *Re P.L. Robertson Manufacturing Co.*, [1974] O.J. No. 2237, 7 O.R. (2d) 98 (H.C.J.); *Re Ripley International Ltd.*, [1977] O.J. No. 68, 1 B.L.R. 269 (H.C.J.).

[333] See, generally, "OSC blocks Conrad Black's Going-Private Bid", Canadian Press, March 28 2005, dealing with concerns of this type.

[334] However, s. 190(6) provides:

> 190.(6) Upon an application by an interested person, the Commission may, subject to such terms and conditions as it may impose, exempt any person from any requirement of this section where in its opinion to do so would not be prejudicial to the public interest, and the Commission may publish guidelines as to the manner and circumstances in which it will exercise this discretion.

[335] *Rathie v. Montreal Trust Co.*, [1953] S.C.J. No. 44, [1953] 2 S.C.R. 204 at 210-11, *per* Locke J., at 215 *per* Rand J.; *John Labatt Ltd. v. Lucky Lager Breweries Ltd.* (1959), 29 W.W.R. 323 (B.C.S.C.).

[336] *Waterous v. Koehring-Waterous Ltd.*, [1954] O.J. No. 105, [1954] O.W.N. 445 (H.C.J.), aff'd [1954] O.W.N. 580 (C.A.).

[337] OBCA, s. 190(2)(*a*).

contain a downward adjustment to reflect that the affected securities do not form part of a controlling interest.[338] Moreover, where the consideration to be received by the holders of the affected securities is wholly or partly other than cash or a right to receive cash within 90 days after the approval by security holders of the going private transaction, the valuation must include the valuator's opinion on whether the value of each affected security to be surrendered is equal to, or greater than, the total value of the consideration to be received for the affected securities.

§14.162 The second requirement with which the corporation must comply in a GPT is the distribution of a management information circular to the holders of the affected securities. This document must be sent not less than 40 days prior to the date of a meeting, which must be called by the corporation to consider the going private transaction. The information circular must contain, in addition to any other required information, a summary of the valuation prepared as required by the section and a statement that a holder of an affected security may inspect a copy of the valuation at the registered office of the corporation or may obtain a copy of the valuation upon request and payment of a specified amount sufficient to cover reasonable costs of reproduction and mailing.[339] The information circular must include a statement of the approval of holders of affected securities required to be obtained in accordance with section 190.[340] It must also include a certificate signed by a senior officer or a director of the corporation certifying that he or she (and, to his or her knowledge, the corporation) are unaware of any material fact relevant to the valuation prepared in compliance with subsection (2) that was not disclosed to the valuator.[341] Finally, the information circular must also contain a statement of the class or classes of affected securities and of the number of securities of each class and, if any securities of any such class are not to be taken into account in the vote required by paragraph 3 of subsection 190(4),[342] a statement of the number thereof and why they are not to be taken into account.[343] However, since some of the affected securities may be represented by certificates in unregistered form (*e.g.*, warrants), subsection 190(3) goes on to provide that, in the case of those securities, it is sufficient to make the information circular available to the holders of those securities in the manner provided for in the terms of those securities for sending notice to those holders, or in such other manner as may be prescribed.

§14.163 The third requirement imposed upon OBCA corporations in a GPT is for the holding of a meeting[344] of affected security holders and the conduct of a special vote on the transaction. The voting requirements for that meeting are set

---

[338] OBCA, s. 190(2)(*b*).
[339] OBCA, s. 190(3)(*a*).
[340] OBCA, s. 190(3)(*b*).
[341] OBCA, s. 190(3)(*c*).
[342] Discussed below at §14.163.
[343] OBCA, s. 190(3)(*d*).
[344] OBCA, s. 190(3).

out in subsection 190(4), which provides that the corporation shall not carry out the going private transaction unless, in addition to any other required security holder approval, the transaction is approved by the holders of each class of affected securities by a vote in accordance with the following provisions. First, if the consideration to be received by a holder of an affected security of a particular class is:

   i. payable wholly or partly other than in cash or a right to receive cash within ninety days after the approval of the going private transaction, or
   ii. payable entirely in cash and is less in amount than the per security value or the mid-point of the range of per security values, arrived at by the valuation prepared [by the independent valuator] ...

then the approval must be given by special resolution — in all other cases, the approval may be given by ordinary resolution. Whether a special or ordinary resolution is required, paragraph 3 of subsection (4) imposes a "special majority" or "majority of the minority" test (comparable to that discussed previously in regard to restricted shares) that must be satisfied to determine whether the resolution has the requisite level of approval. This test excludes the holders of certain securities from the voting process. Paragraph 3 states that in determining whether the transaction has been approved by the requisite majority, the votes of:

   i. securities held by affiliates of the corporation,
   ii. securities the beneficial owners of which will, consequent upon the going private transaction, be entitled to a per security consideration greater than that available to the holders of affected securities of the same class,
   iii. securities the beneficial owners of which, alone or in concert with others, effectively control the corporation and who, prior to distribution of the information circular, entered into an understanding that they would support the going private transaction, ... [345]

must be disregarded both in determining the total number of votes cast and in determining the number of votes cast in favour of, or against, the transaction.

§14.164 The rights provided by the section are in addition to any other rights to which the holders of an affected security are entitled.[346] In particular, the holder of an affected security that is a share of any class of a corporation may dissent from a going private transaction upon compliance with the procedures set out in section 185, in which case the holder is entitled to the rights and remedies provided by that section.[347]

§14.165 Subsection 190(6) of the OBCA provides that:

---

[345] See *Re Sepp's Gourmet Foods Ltd.*, [2002] B.C.J. No. 33, 21 B.L.R. (3d) 291 (S.C.), rev'd [2002] B.C.J. No. 289, 21 B.L.R. (3d) 270 (C.A.).
[346] OBCA, s. 190(5).
[347] OBCA, s. 190(7).

190.(6) Upon an application by an interested person, the Commission may, subject to such terms and conditions as it may impose, exempt any person from any requirement of this section where in its opinion to do so would not be prejudicial to the public interest, and the Commission may publish guidelines as to the manner and circumstances in which it will exercise this discretion.

In interpreting and applying subsection (6), the Ontario Security Commission ("OSC") has rejected the proposition that the compulsory acquisition of shares is inherently fair, and in this regard it has followed the lead of the Legislature in providing for such compulsory acquisition. Even though subsection (4) requires a majority of the minority to approve a going private transaction, the Commission has granted exemptions from compliance with section 190 where the majority shareholder holds more than 90 per cent of the shares in the offering corporation.[348] For instance, in *Re Argue Corp.*[349] the OSC granted an exemption where the minority shareholders collectively held less than 2 per cent of each class of shares, and there was an independent opinion on the fairness of the price of the shares. However, the exemption did not release the majority from the obligation of subsection 190(3), which requires that the offeree corporation send a management information circular to the holders of the affected securities, or the requirements of subsection 190(7), which gives the minority dissent rights under section 185 of the Act, thereby allowing a judicial appraisal of fair value. Limited exemptions *may* also be ordered (subject to conditions) where the applicant establishes that the price being offered for the shares or other securities was arrived at through arm's length negotiations between directors and selling shareholders,[350] an independent appraisal,[351] or where the price offered is in excess of the current market price.[352] Exemptions may also be granted where a proposed transaction is only technically within the scope of section 190.[353]

(iii) CBCA Going Private Provisions

§14.166 Section 193 of the CBCA permits a corporation under that Act to carry out a going private transaction. However, if there are any applicable provincial securities laws, a corporation may not carry out a going private transaction unless the corporation complies with those laws. The term "going private" transaction means a going private transaction as defined in the regulations under the CBCA. However, to date no such regulation has been promulgated. Thus, as currently configured, the CBCA borrows provincial law to deal with going private transactions. Specifically, section 193 of the CBCA provides that:

---

[348] *General Accident Assurance Co. of Canada v. Lornex Mining Corp.*, [1988] O.J. No. 2009, 60 O.R. (2d) 783 (H.C.J.).
[349] (1985), 8 O.S.C.R. 4273; see also *Re Superior Acceptance Corp.* (1986), 10 O.S.C.B. 3769.
[350] *Re British Telecommunications plc.* (1985), 8 O.S.C.B. 2073.
[351] *Re Sullivan Resources Ltd. and Sullivan Mines Inc.* (1986), 9 O.S.C.B. 8181; *Re Cadillac Fairview Corp.* (1987), 10 O.S.C.B. 5166.
[352] *Re Highland Queen Sportswear Ltd.* (1986), 9 O.S.C.B. 5196.
[353] *Re Provigo Inc. & Consumers Distributing Co.* (1987), 10 O.S.C.B. 6031.

193. A corporation may carry out a going private transaction. However, if there are any applicable provincial securities laws, a corporation may not carry out a going-private transaction unless the corporation complies with those laws.

In addition to the foregoing, subsection 2(1) of the CBCA defines the term "squeeze-out transaction" in the following terms:

... a transaction by a corporation that is not a distributing corporation that would require an amendment to its articles and would, directly or indirectly, result in the interest of a holder of shares of a class of the corporation being terminated without the consent of the holder, and without substituting an interest of equivalent value in shares issued by the corporation, which shares have equal or greater rights and privileges than the shares of the affected class.

(iv) OSC Rule 61-501 and Going Private Transactions

§14.167 In addition to the requirements set out in the *Securities Act* and Regulation 1015 under that Act, on May 1, 2000, Ontario Securities Commission Rule 61-501 came into effect, in the place of former OSC Policy 9.1.[354] In essence extends certain of the rights applicable to OBCA corporations to other types of issuer that access the Ontario capital market. Rule 61-501 was significantly revised in 2003.[355] It governs both going private transactions ("GPTs"), as well as the broader category of related party transactions ("RPTs"). Section 1.1 of the OSC's Companion Policy states that:

The Commission regards it as essential, in connection with the disclosure, valuation, review and approval processes followed for insider bids, issuer bids, business combinations and related party transactions, that all security holders be treated in a manner that is fair and that is perceived to be fair. In the view of the Commission, issuers and others who benefit from access to the capital markets assume an obligation to treat security holders fairly, and the fulfilment of this obligation is essential to the protection of the public interest in maintaining capital markets that operate efficiently, fairly and with integrity.

§14.168 As noted previously, it is not practical to include within a general text on the law of business corporations a comprehensive discussion of the various rules of securities law that apply to corporations that are reporting issuers. For this reason, the limited purpose of this section is only to provide the reader with a quick synopsis of the various shareholder rights and remedies that securities law affords in regard to a GPT or comparable fundamental changes in a corporate issuer. The goal is to describe the type of transaction to which securities law rights and remedies may apply, so as to put the reader in a position to consider whether such rights and remedies actually do apply within the context of a given

---

[354] While the new Rule has been in effect for several years, the scheme of securities regulation in this area is still widely referred to as Policy 9.1. In part, this may be a consequence of the fact that the OSC frequently exercises its discretion to relieve parties from compliance with Rule 61-501 under section 9.1 of that Rule.

[355] Proposed Multilateral Instrument MI 61-101 was released too late during the course of preparing this chapter to be incorporated into its text. This proposed instrument would revise the securities regime in Ontario and Quebec governing the protection of minority security holders in the case of business combinations, insider bids, issuer bids and related party transactions.

transaction. This section does not include any discussion of the special procedures that must be followed in connection with an affected transaction under the terms of securities regulation. As always with respect to securities law matters discussed in this text, readers are cautioned that such laws are subject to frequent change, and may involve a considerable exercise of discretionary relief from compliance on the part of securities regulators. Therefore, reference to more specialized sources, particularly those that are revised in line with emerging trends in securities law, is advised when dealing with any of the types of transaction contemplated in this section.

(1) Subject Transactions

§14.169 Rule 61-501 does not deal with "going private transactions" as such, but rather with what are termed "business combinations". Briefly, the term "business combination" is defined to mean (emphasis added):

> ... for an issuer, an amalgamation, arrangement, consolidation, amendment to the terms of a class of equity securities or any other transaction of the issuer, as a consequence of which *the interest of a holder of an equity security of the issuer may be terminated without the holder's consent,* regardless of whether the equity security is replaced with another security ...[356]

The change in terminology is partly a matter of semantics, but also partly of substantive consequence. When the business combination nomenclature was first introduced, the OSC explained:

> In Policy 9.1, the term ["going private transaction"] was defined in the traditional manner, essentially covering plans of arrangement or similar transactions in which security holders could receive cash (or non-participating securities) in exchange for their publicly traded securities without their consent. In the Rule (in subsection 1.1(3)), the definition was narrowed in that it applied only if the transaction was "with or involving a related party of the issuer", and the related party was treated differently from other security holders, subject to certain exceptions. The definition was also broadened in that it no longer excluded transactions in which the security holders received participating securities in substitution for their securities of the issuer.[357]

The intent in adopting the new definition was to clarify the scope of Rule 61-501. So the OSC continued in its explanation:

> The changes in the definition that were brought about by the Rule have given rise to some confusion among market participants and their advisers as to the definition's application. One of the reasons for this confusion is that the definition is somewhat counter-intuitive, in that it does not match the normal English meaning of the defined term. As defined in other legislation, including corporate statutes, a "going private transaction" does not entail the substitution of one publicly traded participating security for another. As a result, there have been instances in which issuers have not realized that their transactions were "going private transactions" within the Rule's definition.

---

[356] Numerous exemptions apply with respect to this definition.
[357] "Notice of Proposed Amendments to Rule 61-501", February 28, 2003.

Another area of uncertainty in the definition relates to its introductory words, which refer to involvement of a related party, and paragraph (e) of the definition, which essentially removes a transaction from the definition if the related party is only entitled to receive consideration that is identical to the consideration paid to the other security holders. The Commission's commentary that accompanied the requests for comments preceding the enactment of the Rule made it clear that the intention of the definition was to capture conflict of interest situations, which included transactions that were at arm's length as between the main parties but which entailed unequal treatment or a collateral benefit for a related party to the issuer. The definition was also intended to capture the circumstance where a related party was "taking the issuer private", even if no collateral benefit was being provided. Some users of the Rule have suggested that the definition does not apply to one or both of these types of transactions, although the Commission does not share this interpretation. The definition also does not clearly address its application to non-voting and subordinate voting shares, and to payments for non-participating securities held by related parties. The definition has been revised in the amended Rule (and relocated so that it is together with the rest of the amended Rule's definitions in section 1.1) to clarify these areas.

At least in the view of the OSC, the new definition makes clear that the protection afforded under the Rule applies to security holders in any transaction (other than an exempt transaction) where the holders could receive any combination of cash or securities without their consent, in exchange for their publicly traded securities of the issuer. The regime set down in the Rule applies even where the holders will receive securities of another publicly traded issuer in exchange.[358]

§14.170 Exemptions from the scope of the definition of "business combination" include compulsory acquisitions under an applicable corporations statute, certain transactions with downstream entities, stock consolidations provided that the security-holder elimination effect is nominal, and transactions in which all related parties are treated equally with other security-holders (although a number of conditions must be satisfied to gain the benefit of the latter). As discussed earlier in the chapter, a takeover bid will often be followed by a squeeze-out transaction. The Rule grants a valuation exemption on the second-step squeeze-out transaction, generally permitting the minority shareholders who tender in the first step to count for purposes of the minority approval required in the second step. However, in practice the bidder in the initial takeover bid must state that the bidder intends to acquire the balance to gain the benefit of this exemption.

§14.171 Rule 61-501 imposes different rules with respect to GPTs that are structured as an "insider bid" or an "issuer bid". The Rule also governs valuations and disclosure with respect to "related party transactions" — a much broader term. The Rule sets out lengthy definitions with respect to each of these

---

[358] The Rule also provides for what are known as "downstream transactions". These are exempted from the application of the rules relating to business combinations and related party transactions. A downstream transaction is one that consists of a transaction between an issuer and an entity in which the issuer holds a control block, so long as another related party of the issuer does not also hold a significant position in that entity.

terms. We will defer any study of related party transactions for the moment, but the term "insider bid" is defined to mean a takeover bid made by,

(a) an issuer insider of the offeree issuer,

(b) an associated or affiliated entity of an issuer insider of the offeree issuer,

(c) an associated or affiliated entity of the offeree issuer,

(d) a person or company described in paragraph (a), (b) or (c) at any time within the 12 months preceding the commencement of the bid, or

(e) a joint actor with a person or company referred to in paragraph (a), (b), (c) or (d)...

The 12-month preceding aspect of clause (d) is intended to deter avoidance strategies such as resigning from the target board shortly before launching a bid. The term "issuer insider" is defined to mean, "for an issuer":

(a) a director or senior officer of the issuer,

(b) a director or senior officer of an entity that is itself an issuer insider or subsidiary entity of the issuer; or

(c) a person or company that beneficially owns or exercises control or direction over voting securities of the issuer carrying more than 10 per cent of the voting rights attached to all the outstanding voting securities of the issuer.

In some definitions and elsewhere in the Rule, reference is made to a transaction in which a related party would "directly or indirectly acquire the issuer ... through an amalgamation, arrangement or otherwise, whether alone or with joint actors". This language describes (and is limited to) the acquisition of all of the issuer, rather than the acquisition of a control position. For example, a related party "acquires" an issuer when it acquires all of the securities of the issuer that it does not already own, even if that related party held a control position in the issuer prior to the transaction.[359]

(2) Disclosure Requirements

§14.172 Since our intention in this section is to provide only a broad brush overview of the securities regulatory regime, we shall focus our attention primarily on the rules governing insider bids. Section 98 of the *Securities Act* imposes a general requirement upon the offeror in a takeover bid or issuer bid to deliver, with or as part of the bid, either a takeover bid circular or issuer bid circular, as the case may be. Since an insider bid is merely a particular type of takeover bid, it is subject to this requirement. Subsection 2.2(1) of Rule 61-501 provides that the offeror shall disclose in the disclosure document for an insider bid:

(a) the background to the insider bid;

(b) in accordance with section 6.8, every prior valuation in respect of the offeree issuer

---

[359] Companion Policy 61-501CP, s. 2.10.

(i) that has been made in the 24 months before the date of the insider bid, and

(ii) the existence of which is known, after reasonable inquiry, to the offeror or any director or senior officer of the offeror; and

(c) the formal valuation exemption, if any, on which the offeror is relying under section 2.4 and the facts supporting that reliance.

The term "disclosure document" is used throughout Rule 61-501, but unfortunately has different meanings in different contexts. In the case of a takeover bid or insider bid (and for an issuer bid means an issuer bid circular sent to holders of offeree securities), the term "disclosure document" is defined to mean a takeover bid circular sent to the holders of offeree securities. In the case of a business combination, the term "disclosure document" means an information bid circular sent to holders of offeree securities.

§14.173 In addition to the foregoing disclosure, subsection 2.2(3) requires the board of directors of the offeree issuer to include in the directors' circular for an insider bid:

(a) disclosure, in accordance with section 6.8, of every prior valuation in respect of the offeree issuer not disclosed in the disclosure document for the insider bid

(b) a description of the background to the insider bid to the extent that the background has not been disclosed in the disclosure document for the insider bid;

(c) disclosure of any *bona fide* prior offer that relates to the offeree securities or is otherwise relevant to the insider bid, which offer was received by the issuer during the 24 months before the insider bid was publicly announced, and a description of the offer and the background to the offer; and

(d) a discussion of the review and approval process adopted by the board of directors and the special committee, if any, of the offeree issuer for the insider bid, including a discussion of any materially contrary view or abstention by a director and any material disagreement between the board and the special committee.

§14.174 The OSC takes the position that the directors of an issuer involved in a transaction regulated by the Rule are generally in the best position to assess the formal valuation[360] to be provided to security holders. Accordingly, the OSC takes the view that, in discharging their duty to security holders, the directors should consider the formal valuation and all prior valuations disclosed and discuss them fully in the applicable disclosure document. The Companion Policy to Rule 61-501 makes clear that paragraphs 2.2(3)(d), 3.2(e), 4.2(3)(f), 5.2(1)(e) and 5.3(3)(f) of the Rule require that the disclosure for the applicable transaction include a discussion of the review and approval process adopted by the board of directors and the special committee, if any, of the issuer, including any materially contrary view or abstention by a director and any material disagreement between the board and the special committee. Issuers are expected to provide

---

[360] A "formal valuation" is no more than a valuation prepared in accordance with Part 6 of the Rule.

sufficient information to security holders to enable them to make an informed decision. Accordingly, the directors should disclose their reasonable beliefs as to the desirability or fairness of the proposed transaction and make useful recommendations regarding the transaction. A statement that the directors are unable to make or are not making a recommendation regarding the transaction, without detailed reasons, generally will be viewed as insufficient disclosure. In reaching a conclusion as to the fairness of a transaction, the directors are expected to disclose in reasonable detail the material factors on which are based their beliefs regarding the transaction. Their disclosure should discuss fully the background of deliberations by the directors and any special committee, and any analysis of expert opinions obtained.

§14.175 The Companion Policy further provides that the factors that are important in determining the fairness of a transaction to security holders and the weight to be given to those factors will vary from one specific context to another, in line with the unique circumstances of each case. Normally, the factors considered will include whether the transaction is subject to minority approval, whether the transaction has been reviewed and approved by a special committee and, if there has been a formal valuation, whether the consideration offered is fair in relation to the valuation conclusion arrived at through the application of the valuation methods considered relevant for the subject matter of the formal valuation. A statement that the directors have no reasonable belief as to the desirability or fairness of the transaction or that the transaction is fair in relation to values arrived at through the application of valuation methods considered relevant, without more, generally will be viewed as insufficient disclosure.

§14.176 Under the above provisions, both the offeree and the board of directors of the issuer are required to provide disclosure regarding most prior valuations. The term "prior valuation" (defined in section 1.1) means a valuation or appraisal of an issuer or its securities or material assets (whether or not prepared by an independent valuator), that if disclosed would reasonably be expected to affect the decision of a security holder with respect to the transaction. It follows that — subject to limited exceptions — by virtue of clause (b), valuations and appraisals obtained for purposes entirely unrelated to the proposed transaction may be subject to disclosure. Therefore, a corporation employing an outside professional to prepare a valuation should ensure that the terms of the retainer of the valuator permit the corporation to disclose the valuations provided, where required by applicable securities related regulatory requirements, or where the corporation deemed necessary or advisable.[361] There is a duty to conduct a reasonable inquiry to determine whether there are any prior valuations that must be

---

[361] Note, however, s. 6.10 of the Rule:

> Despite section 196 of the Regulation, a person or company required to disclose a prior valuation under the Rule is not required to obtain or file the valuator's consent to the filing or disclosure of the prior valuation.

disclosed under the Rule. Where none can be identified, the information circular must include a statement to that effect.[362]

§14.177 As the above provisions make clear, a formal valuation report is required to be included in the disclosure material relating to the transaction. In the GPT context, subsection 6.1(1) of Rule 61-501 provides that:

> Every formal valuation required by this Rule for a transaction shall be prepared by a valuator that is independent of all interested parties in the transaction and that has appropriate qualifications.

While the purpose and context of a valuation may require some adjustment in the approach taken toward to valuation, and in its focus, the overall concerns of fairness, materiality, competence and independence remain the same irrespective of the context or purpose of the valuation that is being conducted. The four main concerns in the valuation process are transparency, materiality, competence, and independence. Conclusions should be based upon technical reports and recognized valuation methods. The weight given to each aspect of the valuation should reflect the materiality of the aspect concerned. Those providing the valuation or contributing opinions on which it is based should possess appropriate qualifications as experts and specialists to permit them to draw the conclusions that they have reached.

§14.178 In the GPT and RPT context, the valuation process is an integral element of the fairness opinion, and the overall assessment of the fairness of the transaction. The GPT context is, of course, only one of many in which valuations may be required or encountered in corporate practice. Others include mergers, acquisitions, in connection with the pricing of a public offering of shares, in connection with the audit of certain types of corporate account, as a step in seeking the sale of part of the business of a corporation, to meet stock market listing requirements, in litigation, in connection with securing compensation for expropriation, for income tax or other tax purpose, and in connection with an insurance claim. It is therefore worthwhile to comment briefly upon the expectations that prevail with respect to valuations across these many different contexts and purposes.

§14.179 The implications of transparency may be quickly summarized. Conclusions should be based upon credible and relevant evidence of sufficient weight, including technical reports and recognized valuation methods. Those providing the valuation or contributing opinions on which it is based should possess appropriate qualifications as experts and specialists to permit them to draw the conclusions that they have reached. The valuation should be presented in terms that are comprehensible. Information is material where the inclusion or omission of that information might result in the reader of a valuation report reaching a substantially different conclusion from what that person would reach if the opposite course was taken. Alternatively stated, information is material where it is

---

[362] Rule 61-501, s. 6.8(2).

required to make an informed assessment regarding the subject of the valuation and any proposed transaction concerning it.[363] These two sets of consideration are not entirely synonymous, and yet cannot be completely divorced. The determination of what is material is made on an objective basis: information is material where a reasonable person would consider it to be material, irrespective of what particular individuals may have considered to be the case.

§14.180 The need for independence in a valuator is self-evident. A valuation tainted by self-interest or other biasing influence cannot be relied upon by anyone of sense. The independence of a valuator is largely a matter of fact.[364] A valuator may be seen to be independent where apart from professional fees and disbursements received or to be received in connection with the valuation concerned, the valuator has no pecuniary or other present or contingent beneficial interest in the subject matter of the valuation, nor any interest in the parties concerned with the valuation, of a kind that would create a reasonable apprehension of bias. The following persons are declared not to be independent by subsection 6.1(3) of Rule 61-501:

- an advisor to the interested party in the transaction (but a valuator retained by an issuer to prepare a formal valuation for an issuer bid is not for that reason alone considered to be an adviser to the interested party in respect of the transaction);
- a manager or co-manager of a soliciting dealer group for the transaction;
- depending upon the functions that it is performing, a member of the soliciting dealer group for the transaction;
- the external auditor of the issuer or the interested party, unless the valuator will not be the external auditor of the issuer or the interested party upon completion of the transaction and that fact is publicly disclosed at the time of or prior to the public disclosure of the results of the valuation; or
- the valuator has a material financial interest in the completion of the transaction.

In addition, where the fees to be paid to a valuator depend in whole or in part on an understanding or arrangement that an incentive will be paid based on a certain value being obtained, the valuator is not independent.[365] An issuer or offeror required to obtain a formal valuation for a GPT or other transaction is required to include in the disclosure document for the transaction:[366]

   (a) a statement that the valuator has been determined to be qualified and independent;

---

[363] See s. 2.4 of Companion Policy 43-101CP to National Instrument 43-101.
[364] Rule 61-501, s. 6.1(2).
[365] Rule 61-501, s. 6.1
[366] Rule 61-501, s. 6.2.

(b) a description of any past, present or anticipated relationship between the valuator and the issuer or an interested party that may be relevant to a perception of lack of independence;

(c) a description of the compensation paid or to be paid to the valuator;

(d) a description of any other factors relevant to a perceived lack of independence of the valuator;

(e) the basis for determining that the valuator is qualified; and

(f) the basis for determining that the valuator is independent, despite any perceived lack of independence, having regard to the amount of the compensation and any factors referred to in paragraphs (b) and (d).

§14.181 An issuer that is required to obtain a formal valuation, or the offeree issuer in the case of an insider bid, is expected to cooperate with the valuator to ensure that the requirements of the Rule are satisfied. At the valuator's request, the issuer should promptly furnish the valuator with access to the issuer's management and advisers, and to all material information in the issuer's possession relevant to the formal valuation. The valuator is expected to use that access to perform a comprehensive review and analysis of information on which the formal valuation is based. The valuator should form his or her own independent views concerning the reasonableness of this information, including any forecasts, projections or other measurements of the expected future performance of the enterprise, and of any of the assumptions on which it is based, and adjust the information accordingly.[367]

§14.182 The disclosure in the valuation of the scope of review should include a description of any limitation on the scope of the review and the implications of the limitation on the valuator's conclusion. Scope limitations should not be imposed by the issuer, an interested party[368] or the valuator, but should be limited to those beyond their control that arise solely as a result of unusual circumstances. In addition, it is inappropriate for any interested party to exercise or attempt to exercise any influence over a valuator.[369] National Policy 48 governing "Future-Oriented Financial Information" does not apply to a formal valuation for which financial forecasts and projections are relied on and disclosed.[370]

§14.183 In addition to the disclosure requirements imposed on the offeror in the bid, subsection 99(1) of the *Securities Act* provides that where a takeover bid has

---

[367] Companion Policy 61-501CP, s. 5.1(3).
[368] A lengthy definition is provided in section 1.1 of the rule for the term "interested party", and as with other terms used in the rule, the meaning varies from one type of transaction to another. In the context of a takeover bid, it describes the offeror or any joint actor of the offeror. In the context of an issuer bid, the term describes the issuer and any control block holder of the issuer, or any person or company that would reasonably be expected to be a control block holder of the issuer upon successful completion of the issuer bid. In the business combination context, the term describes certain related parties of the issuer that stand to benefit from the consummation of the transaction.
[369] Companion Policy 61-501, s. 5.1(4).
[370] Companion Policy 61-501CP s. 5.1(7).

been made, a directors' circular must be prepared and delivered by the board of directors of an offeree issuer to every person and company to whom a takeover bid must be delivered under paragraph 1 of section 95, not later than 15 days after the date of the bid. The board of directors of the target corporation must include in that circular either a recommendation to accept or to reject a takeover bid and the reasons for their recommendation, or a statement that they are unable to make or are not making a recommendation and if no recommendation is made, the reasons for not making a recommendation.[371] The Act contemplates the possibility that the board may be divided on the question, by permitting an individual director or officer to recommend acceptance or rejection of a takeover bid if the director or officer delivers with the recommendation a circular prepared in accordance with the regulations.[372]

(3) Information to be Provided in the Valuation

§14.184 Voting is almost universally accepted as the best method for determining whether a proposed measure enjoys consensus support among the disparate stakeholders who comprise the corporation. The utilization of the voting mechanism is based on the assumption that votes, as an expression of the majority opinion, tends to lead to the optimal choice for the group as a whole. Voting, however, can only be effective in formulating where the voters' opinion is based upon an honest appraisal of their best interests. Without adequate disclosure of relevant information, it is self-evident that the voting procedure ceases to pro mote transactional efficiency. As we discussed in Chapter 13, both the OBCA and CBCA contain extensive provisions relating to the solicitation of proxies, and to the provision of information by way of notice and information circular concerning the matters that are to be decided by the shareholders. In addition, Part X of the General Regulation under the *Securities Act*[373] impose specific information circular requirements relevant to takeover and issuer bids.

§14.185 Within the GPT context, section 6.3(1) of Rule 61-501 provides that the issuer or offeror required to obtain a formal valuation must provide a valuation in respect of:

(a) the offeree securities, in the case of an insider bid or issuer bid;

(b) the affected securities, in the case of a business combination;

(c) subject to subsection (2), any non-cash consideration being offered to, or to be received by, the holders of securities referred to in paragraph (a) or (b); and

(d) subject to subsection (2), the non-cash assets involved in a related party transaction.

The terms "offeree security" and "affected security" appear repeatedly in the Rule. "Offeree security" means a security that is subject to a takeover bid or issuer bid. The term "affected security" is defined to mean:

---

[371] *Securities Act*, s. 99(2).
[372] *Securities Act*, s. 99(3).
[373] R.R.O. 1990, Reg. 1015.

(a) for a business combination of an issuer, an equity security of the issuer in which the interest of a holder would be terminated as a consequence of the transaction, and

(b) for a related party transaction of an issuer, an equity security of an issuer.

Subsection 6.3(2) provides that a formal valuation of non-cash consideration or assets referred to in paragraphs (c) or (d) is not required if:

(a) the on-cash consideration or assets are securities of a reporting issuer or are securities of a class for which there is a published market;

(b) the person or company that would otherwise be required to obtain the formal valuation of those securities states in the disclosure document for the transaction that the person or company has no knowledge of any material information concerning the issuer of the securities, or concerning the securities, that has not been generally disclosed;

(c) in the case of an insider bid, issuer bid or business combination

   (i) a liquid market in the class of securities exists,

   (ii) the securities constitute 25 per cent or less of the number of securities of the class that are outstanding immediately before the transaction is completed,

   (iii) the securities are freely tradable at the time the transaction is completed, and

   (iv) the valuator is of the opinion that a valuation of the securities is not required; and

(d) in the case of a related party transaction for the issuer of the securities, the conditions in subparagraphs 4(a) and (b) of section 5.5 are satisfied, regardless of the form of the consideration for the securities.

§14.186 A formal valuation is required to contain the valuator's opinion as to the value or range of values representing the fair market value of the subject matter of the valuation.[374] In most cases, a valuation will yield a range of value, rather than an absolute number.[375] The valuator is required to[376]:

(a) prepare the formal valuation in a diligent and professional manner;

(b) prepare the formal valuation as of an effective date that is not more than 120 days before the earlier of,

   (i) the date that the disclosure document for the transaction is first sent to security holders, if applicable, and

   (ii) the date that the disclosure document is filed;

(c) make appropriate adjustments in the formal valuation for material intervening events of which it is aware between the effective date of the valuation and the earlier of the dates referred in subparagraphs (i) and (ii) of paragraph (b);

---

[374] Rule 61-501, s. 6.4(1).
[375] *Price v. Dept. of Rev.*, 7 O.T.R. 18 at 25 (Ore. Tax Court 1977).
[376] Rule 61-501, s. 6.4(2).

(d) in determining the fair market value of offeree securities or affected securities, not include in the formal valuation a downward adjustment to reflect the liquidity of the securities, the effect of the transaction on the securities or the fact that the securities do not form part of a controlling interest; and

(e) provide sufficient disclosure in the formal valuation to allow the readers to understand the principal judgments and principal underlying reasoning of the valuator so as to form a reasoned judgment of the valuation opinion or conclusion.

The above requirements reflect the fact that a valuation is transparent only where the basis on which the valuation is reached are disclosed, and where other appropriately qualified and experienced valuators with access to the same information would value the property within approximately the same range. Accordingly the material evidence relied upon in the valuation, along with any assumptions and a description of valuation methods should be set out clearly in the valuation report. Where only a summary of a valuation is required, subsection 6.5(1) of Rule 61-501 provides that:

> An issuer or offeror required to provide a summary of a formal valuation shall ensure that the summary provides sufficient detail to allow the readers to understand the principal judgments and principal underlying reasoning of the valuator so as to form a reasoned judgment of the valuation opinion or conclusion.

§14.187 Earlier in the chapter, we discussed the difficulties inherent in the valuation process in our discussion of the appraisal remedy. The requirements for a valuation under Rule 61-501 should be interpreted in light of those inherent difficulties. There is a clear link between the transparency of the valuation and its reasonableness as a matter of professional opinion. A reasonableness test will identify any valuation that is out of step with prevailing valuation standards and norms. The subjective personal belief of an individual valuator, no matter what his or her personal qualifications might be, is not of much assistance to anyone, unless it satisfies this objective standard. Compliance with applicable professional standards of competence and code of ethics and practice established by relevant professional bodies also has clear implications with respect to the transparency of the valuation process.

§14.188 As noted above, in certain situations valuations carried out prior to the GPT must be disclosed, even where prepared without any thought that such a transaction might eventually arise. The disclosure of the *existence* of such a prior valuation should not be confused with an obligation to *distribute* the valuation to all who are notified — although the prospect of eventual widespread distribution is contemplated. A person or company required to disclose a prior valuation must:

(a) disclose sufficient detail to allow the readers to understand the prior valuation and its relevance to the present transaction;

(b) indicate an address where a copy of the prior valuation is available for inspection; and

(c) state that a copy of the prior valuation will be sent to any security holder upon request and without charge, or if the issuer or offeror providing the summary so chooses, for a nominal charge sufficient to cover printing and postage.[377]

The foregoing information must be set out in the document in which the prior valuation is required to be disclosed. A copy of the prior valuation must be filed with the OSC concurrently with the filing of the information circular or other disclosure document.[378] However, the contents of a prior valuation need not be disclosed where the prior valuation is not reasonably obtainable by the person required to disclose it, "irrespective of any obligations of confidentiality".[379] In such a case, it is necessary to include a statement to that effect in the information circular or other document in which disclosure would ordinarily be made.

§14.189 Almost invariably, valuation involves the exercise of professional judgment. A valuator has the responsibility to decide upon which valuation approaches and methods to use. These choices concerning the specific approaches and methods used or rejected, including any assumptions made, must be justified and explained by reference to appropriate criteria upon which a competent professional would rely. Where they may be relevant to the ultimate decisions of the person for report is being prepared, the limitations of each method (and the implications of those methods) should be explained. The parties whose rights may be affected by a valuation are entitled to have the valuator justify the valuation and demonstrate the professional judgment exercised in reaching that valuation. It is widely recognized that the process of estimating a value for property ultimately remains more art than science.[380] In *Knappton Towboat Co. v. Chambers*,[381] the court observed that:

> Men of equal learning and sound judgment may give greater weight to one factor than to another, thus causing variations in the end-result, so that in all assessments latitudes of judgment must be granted an assessing agency.

It is for this reason that the professional basis of the opinion must be indicated. In a complex case reliance upon the mere presentation of a bare number would prevent the parties from defending their right.[382] Proper disclosure of the valuation method and approach allows a valuation to be critiqued and fine-tuned by the court, on the basis of other expert opinion evidence, should the issue of value come to litigation. In one American tax case, the court cited and approved the following statement from the American Institute of Real Estate Appraisers:

> Reconciliation is the part of the valuation process in which the appraiser most directly draws upon his or her experience, expertise, and professional judgment to resolve differences among the value indications derived from the application of the approaches. The appraiser weighs the relative significance, applicability, and

---

[377] Rule 61-501, s. 6.8(1).
[378] Rule 61-501, s. 6.9.
[379] Rule 61-501, s. 6.8(3).
[380] *Benson v. Department of Revenue*, 9 O.T.R. 129 (Ore. Tax Court 1982).
[381] 202 Ore. 618 (1954).
[382] See, generally, *Arizona Dept. of Rev. v. Asarco Inc.*, 189 Ariz. 49, 938 P.2d 98 (C.A. Ariz. 1997) *per* Thompson J.

defensibility of each value indication and relies most heavily on the one that is most appropriate to the purpose of the appraisal. The conclusion drawn in the reconciliation is based on the appropriateness, the accuracy, and the quantity of the evidence in the entire appraisal.[383]

(4) Independent Committee

§14.190 Rule 61-501 recommends the use of a special committee of independent directors in the case of related party transactions, to carry out negotiations with the controlling shareholder or "related parties" and provides that it is essential, in connection with the disclosure, valuation, review and approval processes, that all security holders are treated in a manner that is both fair and perceived to be fair. In addition, as noted above, subsection 2.3(2) of the Rule provides that the valuator who prepares the formal valuation for an insider bid must be selected by an independent committee of directors. Usually in a going private transaction, the independent committee will review the terms and conditions of the proposed transaction and make a recommendation to the board of directors as to the fairness of the transaction to the minority shareholders from a financial and non-financial point of view and oversee the negotiation of the transaction. The Companion Policy to Rule 61-501 states in Part 6 that:

> To safeguard against the potential for an unfair advantage for an interested party as a result of that party's conflict of interest or informational or other advantage in connection with the proposed transaction, it is good practice for negotiations for a transaction involving an interested party to be carried out by or reviewed and reported upon by a special committee of disinterested directors. Following this practice normally would assist in addressing the Commission's interest in maintaining capital markets that operate efficiently, fairly and with integrity. While the Rule only mandates an independent committee in limited circumstances, the Commission is of the view that it generally would be appropriate for issuers involved in a material transaction to which the Rule applies to constitute an independent committee of the board of directors for the transaction. Where a formal valuation is involved, the Commission also would encourage an independent committee to select the valuator, supervise the preparation of the valuation and review the disclosure regarding the valuation.

Under Rule 61-501, in section 2.3(2), the independent committee is also required to supervise the preparation of the formal valuation and use its best efforts to ensure that the formal valuation is completed and provided to the offeror in a timely manner.[384] The independent committee also plays a role with respect to certain exempt collateral benefits.

§14.191 Section 1.1 of the Rule provides that an independent committee must consist *exclusively* of one or more independent directors of the issuer. The requirement for exclusivity indicates that the presence of any one non-independent

---

[383] *Southern Pacific Transportation Co. v. Dept. of Revenue*, 11 O.T.R. 138 (Ore. Tax Court 1989) *per* Byers J.
[384] This last requirement was inserted to prevent the independent committee from dragging its heals so as to defeat the bid merely by delay.

director negates the independence of the entire committee, even where that director makes up only a small minority. The Companion Policy to Rule 61-501, Part 6, provides the following elaboration on this point:

> A special committee should, in the Commission's view, include only directors who are independent from the interested party. While a special committee may invite non-independent board members and other persons possessing specialized knowledge to meet with, provide information to, and carry out instructions from, the committee, in the Commission's view non-independent persons should not be present at or participate in the decision-making deliberations of the special committee.

The requirements that must be satisfied to establish independence are fleshed out in section 7.1 of the Rule. Generally, it is a question of fact whether or not a director of an issuer is independent.[385] However, subsection 7.1(2) goes on to provide that a director of an issuer is not independent in connection with a transaction if he or she,

(a) is an interested party in the transaction;

(b) is currently or has been at any time during the 12 months before the date the transaction is agreed to, an employee, associated entity or issuer insider of an interested party, or of an affiliated entity of an interested party, other than solely in his or her capacity as a director of the issuer;

(c) is currently, or has been at any time during the 12 months before the date the transaction is agreed to, an advisor to an interested party in connection with the transaction, or an employee, associated entity or issuer insider of an adviser to an interested party in connection with the transaction, or of an affiliated entity of such an adviser, other than solely in his or her capacity as a director of the issuer;

(d) has a material interest in an interested party or an affiliated entity of an interested party; or

(e) would reasonably be expected to receive a benefit as a consequence of the transaction that is not also available on a *pro rata* basis to the general body of holders in Canada of offeree securities or affected securities, including, without limitation, the opportunity to obtain a financial interest in an interested party, an affiliated entity of an interested party, the issuer or a successor to the business of the issuer.

§14.192 A management buyout is a "conflict of interest" transaction within the scope of section 132 of the OBCA and section 120 of the CBCA. These provisions require that first the director (or officer) who is making the bid declare his or her interest and obtain board (or shareholder) approval to proceed with the transaction. Over and above this specific disclosure requirement, there are more general transactional requirements that this individual must act honestly and in good faith, and the transaction must be one that is fair and reasonable in the circumstances.

---

[385] Rule 65-501, s. 7.1(1).

§14.193 The application of these standards in the management buyout context has been the subject of a considerable amount of case law in the United States. There it has been held that where the proposed transaction is properly investigated and approved in good faith by a majority of the independent directors, the business judgment rule will normally apply, and the transaction will be valid.[386] However, in *Citron v. E.I. DuPont De Nemours & Co.*,[387] Jacobs V.C. held that the transaction could be set aside where there was "implicit coercion" that the controlling shareholder would retaliate against any negative vote. In *Kahn v. Lynch Communications, Inc.*,[388] the Delaware Supreme Court held that regardless of the procedural protections employed, a merger with a controlling stockholder would always be subject to the fairness standard, even if the transaction was negotiated and approved by a special committee of independent directors; and subject to approval by a majority of the disinterested shares (*i.e.*, those shares not held by the controlling shareholder or its affiliates) — although there was a suggestion that such arrangements might shift the burden of proof from the defendants to the plaintiffs.

§14.194 In *Re Cox Communications Inc.*[389] Strine V.C. placed emphasis on the question of whether the independent directors had the benefit of experienced financial and legal advisors sufficient to overcome the lack of managerial expertise at their disposal. Other concerns included informational asymmetries and the possibility that the outside directors might be more independent in appearance than in substance.

§14.195 In *Weinberger v. UOP, Inc.*,[390] Moore J. held that the concept of fairness has two basic aspects: fair dealing and fair price. The former embraces questions of when a transaction was timed, how it was initiated, structured, negotiated, disclosed to directors and how the directors' approval was obtained. In that case, which dealt with minority shareholders' attack on a cash-at-merger transaction, Moore J. held that the transaction did not meet the requirement for fair dealing, because there were inadequate arm's length negotiations, a lack of material information in the possession of the board and undue haste, including a quickly prepared and superficial fairness opinion supporting the transaction in question. Generally, American courts have cautioned against the adoption of a "fixed or arbitrary standard for the ascertainment of values", in appraisal cases.[391] Instead, courts have encouraged a consideration of every factor that contributes in any degree or has an influence upon the value of shares. In fixing the value of

---

[386] See, for instance, *Puma v. Marriott, Inc.*, 283 A.2d 693 (Del. Ch. 1971) in which an independent board majority approved a transaction with a 46 per cent shareholder. *In re Trans World Airlines, Inc. Shareholders Litigation*, [1988] Del. Ch. LEXIS 139, 1988 W.L. 111271 (Del. Ch.).
[387] 584 A.2d 490 (Del. Ch. 1990).
[388] 638 A.2d 1110 (Del. S.C. 1994).
[389] 879 A.2d 604 (Del. Ch. 2005).
[390] 457 A.2d 701 (Del. S.C. 1983).
[391] *State Dep't of Revenue v. Birmingham Realty Co.*, 255 Ala. 269 at 276, 50 So. 2d 760 at 766 (1951); see also *Blake v. Blake Agency* (1985), 107 A.D.2d 139, 486 N.Y.S.2d 341 at 347.

shares, the court should take into account any techniques or methods which are generally considered acceptable in the financial community.[392]

§14.196 A critical question where an insider bid is made for the corporation is what to do when a disgruntled minority shareholder seeks to derail the process, arguing that an improper review has occurred. In some cases, the prospect of a successful claim may seem very unlikely. In the *Cox Communications* case, Strine V.C. posited the following scenario:

> Imagine, for example, a controlled company on the board of which sat Bill Gates and Warren Buffett. Each owned 5% of the company and had no other business dealings with the controller. The controller announced that it was offering a 25% premium to market to buy the rest of the shares. The controlled company's board meets and appoints Gates and Buffett as a special committee. The board also resolves that it will not agree to a merger unless the special committee recommends it and unless the merger is conditioned on approval by two-thirds of the disinterested stockholders. The special committee hires a top five investment bank and top five law firm and negotiates the price up to a 38% premium. The special committee then votes to approve the deal and the full board accepts their recommendation. The disinterested stockholders vote to approve the deal by a huge margin that satisfies the two-thirds Minority Approval Condition.[393]

Yet even on these facts, it is doubtful whether the claim of the shareholder could be struck out on a motion for summary judgment, and it clearly cannot be struck out on the grounds that the pleadings disclose no cause of action. On the other hand, allowing the claim to proceed, particularly if a preliminary injunction is granted, may derail the prospects of closing the deal, to the detriment of minority shareholders, most of whom have voted to approve the transaction. It is this background that in effect provides the rationale for the appraisal-valuation procedure.[394] Within the take-over context, it affords an additional measure of protection for the minority, short of allowing fractional interests within the minority to undermine a pending take-over that the majority would prefer to approve.

(5) Minority Approval

§14.197 Section 4.5 of Rule 65-101 lays down the general rule that an issuer must not carry out a business combination unless the issuer has obtained minority approval for the business combination in accordance with Part 8 of the Rule. For the purpose of securing such approval, the issuer must call a meeting of

---

[392] *Weinberger v. UOP, Inc.*, 457 A.2d 701 at 713 (Del. S.C. 1983).
[393] *In Re Cox Communications Inc.*, C.A. No. 613-N at 31, 879 A.2d 604 (Del. Ch. 2005).
[394] See above at §14.45 *seq.* To the extent that the appraisal remedy is not a full solution, the following passage of Strine V.C.'s judgment, *ibid.*, at 77, is helpful:

> ... the controller and the directors of the affected company should be able to obtain dismissal of a complaint unless: 1) the plaintiffs plead particularized facts that the special committee was not independent or was not effective because of its own breach of fiduciary duty or wrongdoing by the controller (e.g., fraud on the committee); or 2) the approval of the minority stockholders was tainted by misdisclosure, or actual or structural coercion.

holders of affected securities and send an information circular to those holders.[395] The information circular must include:

(a) the disclosure required by Form 33 of the Regulation, to the extent applicable and with necessary modifications;

(b) the disclosure required by Item 16, "Right of Appraisal and Acquisition", of Form 32 of the Regulation, to the extent applicable, together with a description of rights that may be available to security holders opposed to the transaction;

(c) a description of the background to the business combination;

(d) disclosure in accordance with section 6.8 of every prior valuation in respect of the issuer

  (i) that has been made in the 24 months before the date of the information circular, and

  (ii) the existence of which is known, after reasonable inquiry, to the issuer or to any director or senior officer of the issuer;

(e) disclosure of any bona fide prior offer that relates to the subject matter of or is otherwise relevant to the transaction, which offer was received by the issuer during the 24 months before the business combination was agreed to, and a description of the offer and the background to the offer;

(f) a discussion of the review and approval process adopted by the board of directors and the special committee, if any, of the issuer for the transaction, including a discussion of any materially contrary view or abstention by a director and any material disagreement between the board and the special committee;

(g) disclosure of the formal valuation exemption, if any, on which the issuer is relying under section 4.4 and the facts supporting that reliance; and

(h) disclosure of the number of votes attached to the securities that, to the knowledge of the issuer after reasonable inquiry, will be excluded in determining whether minority approval for the business combination is obtained.[396]

If after sending this information circular, a change occurs that (if disclosed) would reasonably be expected to affect the decision of a holder of affected securities to vote for or against the business combination or to retain or dispose of affected securities, the issuer must promptly provide disclosure of that change.[397] The foregoing requirements apply without limiting the application of any other legal requirements that apply to meetings of security holders and information circulars.[398]

§14.198 Where minority approval is required for a business combination or related party transaction, it must be obtained from the holders of every class of

---

[395] Rule 61-501, s. 4.2(2).
[396] Rule 61-501, s. 4.2(3).
[397] Rule 61-501, s. 4.2(4).
[398] Rule 61-501, s. 4.2(1).

affected securities of the issuer, in each case voting separately as a class.[399] Ordinarily in determining whether minority approval has been secured for a business combination or related party transaction, an issuer must exclude the votes attached to affected securities that, to the knowledge of the issuer or any interested party or their respective directors or senior officers, after reasonable inquiry, are beneficially owned or over which control or direction is exercised by

(a) the issuer;

(b) an interested party;

(c) a related party of an interested party, unless the related party meets that description solely in its capacity as a director or senior officer of one or more entities that are neither interested parties nor issuer insiders of the issuer; or

(d) a joint actor with a person or company referred to in paragraph (b) or (c) in respect of the transaction.[400]

An exception applies in the case of so-called second step business combinations, provided that certain prescribed conditions are met.[401]

§14.199 More specifically, in a second step business combination following an unsolicited takeover bid, section 8.2 of the Rule allows the votes attached to securities acquired under a formal bid to be included as votes in favour of a subsequent business combination in determining whether minority approval has been obtained if certain conditions are met. One of the conditions is that the security holder that tendered the securities in the bid must not receive an advantage in connection with the bid — such as a collateral benefit — that was not available to other security holders. There may be circumstances where this condition could cause difficulty for an offeror who wishes to acquire all of an issuer through a business combination following a bid that was unsolicited by the issuer.

§14.200 Section 4.6 also reserves a discretion in favour of the OSC to grant a discretionary exemption from the minority approval requirement,[402] It also expressly exempts transactions where one or more of the persons who are interested parties beneficially own 90 per cent or more in the aggregate of the outstanding affected securities, provided that the minority are entitled to the benefit of a statutory appraisal remedy or an enforceable right that is substantially equivalent

---

[399] Rule 61-501, s. 8.1(1).
[400] Rule 61-501, s. 8.1(2).
[401] Rule 61-501, s. 8.2.
[402] See, for instance, *In the Matter of Molson Inc.* (Mutual Reliance Review System, August 11, 2004) — exemption granted where it was concluded a "minority vote of each class of shareholders would unduly favor a very small group of shareholders". Section 3.3 of the Companion Policy to the Rule explains that as the purpose of the Rule is to ensure fair treatment of minority security holders, abusive minority tactics in a situation involving a minimal minority position may cause the Director to grant an exemption from the requirement to obtain minority approval. Where an issuer has more than one class of equity securities, an exemption may also be appropriate if the Rule's requirement of separate minority approval for each class could result in unfairness to security holders who are not interested parties, or if the policy objectives of the Rule would be accomplished by the exclusion of an interested party's votes in one or more, but not all, of the separate class votes.

to the appraisal remedy provided for in subsection 185(4) of the OBCA. For example, in order to establish that a benefit received by a tendering security holder is not a collateral benefit under the Rule, the offeror may need the cooperation of an independent committee of the offeree issuer during the bid. This cooperation may not be forthcoming if the bid is unfriendly. In this type of circumstance, the fact that the bid was unsolicited would normally be a factor the Director would take into account in considering whether an exemption should be granted to allow the securities to be voted.[403]

§14.201 Section 4.7 of the Rule also provides the following exemption with respect to OBCA corporations, which in effect brings to GPT requirements applicable to such corporations in line with the general regime administered by the OSC under Rule 61-501 for all reporting issuers in Ontario:

> An issuer that is governed by the OBCA and proposes to carry out a "going private transaction" as defined in subsection 190(1) of the OBCA is exempt from subsections (2), (3) and (4) of section 190 of the OBCA, and is not required to make an application for exemption from those subsections under subsection 190(6) of the OBCA, if
>
> (a) the transaction is not a business combination;
>
> (b) Part 4 does not apply to the transaction by reason of section 4.1; or
>
> (c) the transaction is carried out in compliance with Part 4, and, for this purpose, compliance includes reliance on any applicable exemption from a requirement of Part 4, including a discretionary exemption granted by the Director under section 9.1.

§14.202 The definition of "minority approval" and subsections 4.2(2) and 5.3(2) of the Rule provide that minority approval, if required, must be obtained at a meeting of holders of affected securities. The issuer may be able to demonstrate that holders of a majority of the securities that would be eligible to be voted at a meeting would vote in favour of the transaction under consideration. In such a situation, the Director under the *Securities Act* will consider granting an exemption under section 9.1 of the Rule from the requirement to hold a meeting, conditional on security holders being provided with disclosure similar to that which would be available to them if a meeting were held.[404]

§14.203 Depending upon the circumstances of a transaction, it can be difficult to determine who exactly constitutes part of the outside minority. This problem was illustrated in *Sepp's Gourmet Foods Ltd. v. Janes*,[405] in which the British Columbia Court of Appeal gave a narrow interpretation to the phrase "acting jointly or in concert".

§14.204 The Sepp's case involved a British Columbia incorporated company that was traded on the Toronto Stock Exchange. The Chairman of the company

---

[403] Companion Policy 61-501CP, s. 3.2.
[404] Companion Policy 61-501CP, s. 3.1.
[405] [2002] B.C.J. No. 289 (C.A.), leave to appeal to S.C.C. refused [2002] S.C.J. No. 144.

arranged an "Acquisition Group" of shareholders, who controlled just over 50 per cent of the outstanding shares of the Company, and who agreed to support the GPT. The arrangement provided for the Acquisition Group to transfer their shares to a new private corporation that, in turn, would own Sepp's. The shares of the remaining shareholders (the "Outsiders") would be transferred to Sepp's at 68¢ per share. The Acquisition Group participants signed "lock-up" agreements that required them to vote their shares in favour of the GPT.

§14.205 After this arrangement was put together, the Chairman approached another shareholder ("R") who owned a further 12.4 per cent of the issued shares, to seek his support for the GPT. The shareholder agreed to do so provided that he would receive at least 68¢ per share. Sepp's then sought an *ex parte* interim order from the British Columbia Supreme Court to permit the holding of a shareholders meeting to approve the plan of arrangement. The order provided that the plan would be effective if passed by:

- a majority of not less than three-quarters of the votes cast by the Sepp's shareholders present in person or by proxy at the Meeting and
- a majority of the minority of Sepp's shareholders (i.e. those outside the Acquisition Group).

§14.206 The order excluded from the special minority approval those shareholders who were to the knowledge of Sepp's or any member of the Acquisition Group:

(a) a person acting jointly or in concert with any member of the Acquisition Group in respect of the plan of arrangement,

(b) any person who alone or in combination with others effectively controlled Sepp's and who, prior to receiving the notice of the meeting, had entered into or had agreed to enter into an understanding to support the arrangement.

The specific wording in the order tracked the wording of section 91 of the Ontario *Securities Act* and OSC Rule 61-501. The latter applied because Sepp's was a TSX listed reporting issuer. The wording of the order also tracked the wording of clause 252(8)(*c*) of the British Columbia *Corporation Act* which also applied to Sepp's as a BC company.

§14.207 At the shareholders' meeting, the proposed transaction received the approval of 80.5 per cent of the votes cast by all shareholders, and 64 per cent approval among the votes cast by the special minority. At the fairness hearing in which a final order was sought to confirm the proposed transaction, it was argued by a rival bidder for the company that a number of shareholders who voted in favour of the proposed transaction were wrongly allowed to vote as part of the special minority. In particular, it was argued that R should not have been allowed to vote as part of the special minority.

§14.208 The British Columbia Supreme Court held that even though R had entered into an understanding to support the plan of arrangement, the mere existence of that "lock up" arrangement did not prevent R from being numbered among the special minority. In order to be excluded from the special minority, R would have had to both (a) reached an understanding to support the transaction, and (b) been acting jointly or in concert with the Acquisition Group. The trial court found that, while an understanding with Rosenberg had been reached on how his shares would be voted, since Rosenberg was not otherwise acting jointly or in concert with the Acquisition Group, he was not to be excluded from the special minority. The court concluded that the purpose of lock-up agreements was to allow a board of directors to have some assurance that the transaction will go ahead at the shareholders' meeting and that time and considerable expense would not be wasted. It did not wish to prevent bidders in a GPT transaction from taking advantage of such an option. This conclusion was consistent with the position set out in the OSC's Companion Policy to OSC Rule 61-501.

§14.209 The appeal to the British Columbia Court of Appeal was decided in reference to the part of the interim order derived from the wording of OSC Rule 61-501. Surprisingly, the court disregarded the Companion Policy to Rule 61-501 and based its decision instead solely on the words of the order, focusing on their "grammatical and ordinary sense". It concluded that:

> ... a person who has entered into an agreement with a control group to support a proposed corporate action must be said to be acting jointly or in concert with that group, and indeed that there is not much more one can do than to enter into an agreement to achieve the desired objective, in order to be said to be acting jointly or in concert with its proponents.[406]

Since R had agreed to vote his shares in favour of the proposed transaction, he was excluded from the special minority with the result that the proposed transaction failed to secure the requisite special minority approval.

§14.210 Following this decision, the OSC amended Rule 61-501 to replace the concept of "acting jointly or in concert" with a new definition of "joint actors". The new definition is drafted in terms that are intended to make clear that the existence of a lock-up agreement or support agreement is not determinative of whether a person is or is not a joint actor in a GPT.[407] More specifically, in section 2.2 of the OSC's Companion Policy 61-501CP, the Commission states that:

> The definition of joint actor in the Rule incorporates the interpretation of the term "acting jointly or in concert" in section 91 of the Act, subject to certain qualifications. Among other things, the concept is relevant in determining whether a takeover bid is an insider bid under the Rule and whether securities acquired by an

---

[406] *Ibid.*, at para. 31.
[407] The relevant provision reads:

> "joint actors", when used to describe the relationship among two or more entities, means persons or companies "acting jointly or in concert" as defined in section 91 of the Act, with necessary modifications where the term is used in the context of a transaction that is not a take-over bid or issuer bid, but a security holder is not considered to be a joint actor with an offeror making a formal bid, or with a person or company involved in a business combination or related party transaction, solely because there is an agreement, commitment or understanding that the security holder will tender to the bid or vote in favour of the transaction.

offeror in a formal bid can be included in a minority approval vote regarding a second step business combination under section 8.2 of the Rule. Without limiting the application of the definition, the Commission is of the view that, for a formal bid, an offeror and an insider may be viewed as joint actors if an agreement, commitment or understanding between the offeror and the insider provides that the insider shall not tender to the bid, or provides the insider with an opportunity not offered to all security holders to maintain or acquire a direct or indirect equity interest in the offeror, the issuer or a material asset of the issuer.

(6) Exemptions

§14.211 Exemptions from the valuation requirements are available on a discretionary basis under section 9.1. In addition, certain exemptions apply where neither the offeror nor any joint actor with the offeror has any information concerning the offeree issuer or its securities that has not been generally disclosed, where the consideration per security under the insider bid matches the value per security in certain recent arm's length transactions, or where the insider bid is publicly announced or made in the context of an auction for the corporation.[408]

(7) Proposed National Instrument 62-104

§14.212 In July, 2006, the Canadian Securities Administrators ("CSA") published for comment their proposed National Instrument NI62-104, pertaining to Take-Over Bids and Issuer Bids, together with related Forms and Companion Policy.[409] The proposed instrument is intended to harmonize the takeover bid and issuer bid rules and related requirements across Canada, including in four jurisdictions that have not previously regulated such bids. NI62-104 would also modify the scope of certain previously available exemptions and introduce a number of new codified exemptions in place of frequently granted discretionary exemption orders. At the time of issue, the targeted implementation date is by the end of 2006. Accordingly, in this section, it is assumed that the proposed National Instrument or one very like it will soon come into effect.

§14.213 The general approach of NI62-104 is similar to that of prior rules governing takeover bids and issuer bids. Securities owned by persons acting jointly or in concert with an offeror are included with the offeror's securities when determining whether the takeover bid and early warning thresholds have been triggered, and whether the integration rules apply. Although it is always a question of fact as to whether a person is acting jointly or in concert with the offeror, under NI62-104, certain classes of person will be conclusively deemed to be joint actors with the offeror. These include:

- an offeror's affiliates, and

---

[408] Rule 61-501, s. 2.4.
[409] See also Form 62-104F1 Take-Over Bid Circular, Form 62-104F2 Issuer Bid Circular, Form 62-104F3 Directors' Circular, Form 62-104F4 Director's or Officer's Circular, and Form 62-104F5 Notice of Change or Notice of Variation, together with Companion Policy 62-104CP.

- every person that has entered into an agreement, commitment or understanding with an offeror or its joint actors
- to acquire or offer to acquire the target securities, or
- to exercise, jointly or in concert with the offeror or any of the offeror's joint actors, any voting rights attaching to the target securities.

In addition, a rebuttable presumption will apply in the case of an offeror's associates. Apparently, it was decided that the term "associates" is too broad for the presumption to apply on a conclusive basis in every situation.

§14.214 Under the present regime, neither an offeror nor any person acting jointly or in concert with the offeror may enter into a collateral agreement with any security holder of the target that has the effect of providing the security holder with consideration of greater value than that offered to other security holders.[410] As noted above, the purpose of the present Rule is to ensure fair and equal treatment of all security holders of the class of securities that are the subject of the bid. NI62-104 adopts the definition of collateral benefit in Rule 61-501. However, under the new instrument, a collateral benefit will be permitted where:

- the agreement provides for a payment per security that is identical in amount and form to the entitlement of all other security holders of the same class in Canada, or
- the agreement relates to an enhancement in the security holder's employee benefits as a result of participation in a group plan, other than an incentive plan, for employees of the successor holding a similar position to the security holder, or
- in respect of any other benefit that is received in the security holder's capacity as an employee, director or consultant of the target or an affiliate or of a successor to the business, a number of procedural steps and disclosures are made concerning the agreement, including the requirement that:
    - the benefit is not conferred to increase the value of the consideration paid to the security holder,
    - the conferring of the benefit is not conditional on the security holder's support of the bid,
    - full particulars of the benefit are disclosed in the relevant circular, and
    - either
        - the security holder and its associates hold less than 1 per cent of the equity securities of each class of equity securities, or

---

[410] Both the *Securities Act* and Rule 61-501 contain provisions regarding the provision of identical consideration and prohibiting most collateral benefits. However, under the Rule a variety of exemptions are available under which at least some benefits of this nature may be obtained.

- as determined by an independent committee of directors of the target and disclosed in the circular, in effect, the value of the benefit is less than 5 per cent of the amount that the security holder expects to receive under the terms of the bid in exchange for the security holder's equity securities.

It is unclear whether this approach will ever come into effect: The CSA has indicated that the collateral benefit may be further refined, in line with any developments in the United States — where the subject of collateral benefits is also currently under consideration.

§14.215 NI62-104 will require an offer to file copies of documents related to its bid, including any agreements entered into between the offeror and security holders, directors, or officers of the target, the target itself and any other agreement to which the offeror has access that affects control of the target. This requirement will extend to include so-called lock-up agreements. The filing requirement is intended to increase transparency regarding agreements that affect control of the target. Currently, NI51-102 requires issuers to file such documents where a transaction is subject to a shareholder vote.

G. RELATED PARTY TRANSACTIONS

§14.216 As noted above, Rule 61-501 also imposes valuation, minority voting and disclosure requirements with respect to related party transactions, as defined in that policy. The term "related party" in section 1.1 means with respect to any entity, a person or company that, at the relevant time and after reasonable inquiry, is known by the entity or a director or senior officer of the entity to be:

(a) a control block holder of the entity,

(b) a person or company of which a person or company referred to in paragraph (a) is a control block holder,

(c) a person or company of which the entity is a control block holder,

(d) a person or company, other than a bona fide lender, that beneficially owns or exercises control or direction over voting securities of the entity carrying more than 10 per cent of the voting rights attached to all the outstanding voting securities of the entity,

(e) a director or senior officer of

  (i) the entity, or

  (ii) a person or company described in any other paragraph of this definition,

(f) a person or company that manages or directs, to any substantial degree, the affairs or operations of the entity under an agreement, arrangement or understanding between the person or company and the entity, including the general partner of an entity that is a limited partnership, but excluding a person or company acting under bankruptcy or insolvency law,

(g) a person or company of which persons or companies described in any paragraph of this definition beneficially own, in the aggregate, more than 50 per cent of the securities of any outstanding class of equity securities, or

(h) an affiliated entity of any person or company described in any other paragraph of this definition...

The term "related party transaction" means, with respect to an issuer:

... a transaction between the issuer and a person or company that is a related party of the issuer at the time the transaction is agreed to, whether or not there are also other parties to the transaction, as a consequence of which, either through the transaction itself or together with connected transactions, the issuer directly or indirectly

(a) purchases or acquires an asset from the related party for valuable consideration,

(b) purchases or acquires, as a joint actor with the related party, an asset from a third party if the proportion of the asset acquired by the issuer is less than the proportion of the consideration paid by the issuer,

(c) sells, transfers or disposes of an asset to the related party,

(d) sells, transfers or disposes of, as a joint actor with the related party, an asset to a third party if the proportion of the consideration received by the issuer is less than the proportion of the asset sold, transferred or disposed of by the issuer,

(e) leases property to or from the related party,

(f) acquires the related party, or combines with the related party, through an amalgamation, arrangement or otherwise, whether alone or with joint actors,

(g) issues a security to the related party or subscribes for a security of the related party,

(h) amends the terms of a security of the issuer if the security is beneficially owned, or is one over which control or direction is exercised, by the related party, or agrees to the amendment of the terms of a security of the related party if the security is beneficially owned by the issuer or is one over which the issuer exercises control or direction,

(i) assumes or otherwise becomes subject to a liability of the related party,

(j) borrows money from or lends money to the related party, or enters into a credit facility with the related party,

(k) releases, cancels or forgives a debt or liability owed by the related party,

(l) materially amends the terms of an outstanding debt or liability owed by or to the related party, or the terms of an outstanding credit facility with the related party, or

(m) provides a guarantee or collateral security for a debt or liability of the related party, or materially amends the terms of the guarantee or security...

§14.217 There is no requirement for an RPT to form part of any type of GPT in order for that RPT to fall within the scope of Rule 61-501. However, the related party and business combination aspects of the Rule are not entirely isolated from each other. It is possible for a GPT to contemplate RPTs not simply as intermediate steps in the overall process of acquiring full ownership of the issuer that is the target of the GPT, but as collateral measures carried out at roughly the same time, so as to restructure the business operations of the target. For instance, a related party may buy some of the target's assets that the acquirer in the GPT does not want. The complete series of steps is the "transaction" for the purposes of the application of business combination requirements of the Rule. However, any RPT that is carried out in conjunction with a business combination — but which is not simply one of the procedural steps in implementing the acquisition of the affected securities in the business combination — is also subject to the Rule's requirements for related party transactions.[411]

§14.218 In an RPT, the term "disclosure document" means either an information circular sent to holders of affected securities or (if no such circular is required) another document sent to holders of affected securities in connection with a meeting of the holders of affected securities. If neither such document is required, then it means a material change report filed for the transaction. The term "affected securities" also has a different meaning in the context of a related party transaction than it does with respect to business combinations. It describes any equity security of an issuer.

H. PRIVATE COMPANY SQUEEZE-OUTS

§14.219 Squeeze-out transactions are governed by section 194 of the CBCA. It provides that a corporation may not carry out a squeeze-out transaction unless, the transaction is approved by ordinary resolution of the holders of each class of shares that are affected by the transaction, voting separately, whether or not the shares otherwise carry the right to vote. This voting requirement applies in addition to any approval by holders of shares required by or under this Act or the articles of the corporation. However, the following do not have the right to vote on the resolution:

(a) affiliates of the corporation; and

(b) holders of shares that would, following the squeeze-out transaction, be entitled to consideration of greater value or to superior rights or privileges than those available to other holders of shares of the same class.

No comparable provision has yet been added to the OBCA, although the Ontario Ministry of Government Affairs has raised this question in a discussion paper.

§14.220 Some guidance as to how a court may approach the squeeze out provisions may be found in the decision of the New South Wales Supreme Court in *Winpar Holdings Ltd. v. Goldfields Kalgoorlie Ltd.*[412] In that case, Winpar held approximately .005 per cent of GKL's shares. Other GKL shareholders included the Goldfields Group holding approximately 88 per cent and the QBE Group holding approximately 11 per cent. GKL sought to cancel all GKL shares held by shareholders other than the Goldfields Group for 55¢ per share so that GKL

---

[411] Companion Policy 61-501, s. 2.8(2).
[412] [2000] N.S.W.S.C. 728.

would become wholly owned by the Goldfields Group. Section 256C(2) of the *Corporations Law* provides that for a selective reduction, the reduction must be approved by:

(a) a special resolution passed at a general meeting of the company, with no votes being cast in favour of the resolution by any person who is to receive consideration as part of the reduction or whose liability to pay amounts unpaid on shares is to be reduced, or by their associates; or

(b) a resolution agreed to, at a general meeting, by all ordinary shareholders.

Where the reduction involves the cancellation of shares, the reduction must also be approved by a special resolution passed at a meeting of the shareholders whose shares are to be cancelled. Since GKL's selective reduction did involve the cancellation of shares, two resolutions were necessary: first, a special resolution passed by the Goldfields Group shareholders; and second, a special resolution to be passed by the non-Goldfields Group shareholders. Winpar argued that section 256C(2) required these two resolutions to be passed at separate meetings. Santow J. rejected this argument and noted that it is commonplace to have separate meetings of classes of shareholders without it ever being suggested that the presence of persons who were not entitled to vote invalidated any vote taken among those who were entitled to vote. Santow J. noted that there was no suggestion that the Goldfields Group shareholders attempted to influence the outcome of the second resolution. Santow J. also considered whether general law principles of procedural and substantive fairness applied to a selective reduction of capital. He concluded that the requirements of the relevant New South Wales legislation constituted a "comprehensive, protective code", so that what was fair and reasonable was to be determined by reference to the statute. Santow J. further held that a selective capital reduction could be fair and reasonable even where a single minority shareholder could determine the outcome of the second resolution. On the facts, the interest of QBE was not considered to be so divergent from that of the other members that it should have been treated as a separate class.

I. CONTINUATION

§14.221 The common law did not permit an entity incorporated in one jurisdiction to re-incorporate or re-register so as to become a corporate entity subject to the laws of some other jurisdiction, unless this was permitted both by the laws of the jurisdiction of its domicile and the laws of the jurisdiction under which it wished to so continue.[413] Where it is intended to re-incorporate or re-register a foreign corporate entity in a common law jurisdiction, then the authority to do so must be provided under or by a statute law of that common law jurisdiction. Although it is sometimes suggested that the same rule prevents a foreign partnership from incorporating under the laws of another jurisdiction, this would seem to be true only in the qualified sense that where a partnership is recognized under the laws of its jurisdiction of domicile as being a legal person, it cannot be

---

[413] *Bulkeley v. Schutz* (1871), L.R. 3 P.C. 764; *Bateman v. Service* (1881), 6 App. Cas. 386 (P.C.).

re-constituted under the laws of another jurisdiction except insofar as the laws of the two jurisdictions concerned would permit this to occur. In the case of a foreign partnership that is not a legal person, there is no apparent reason why the same persons who carry on business in partnership in one jurisdiction may not choose to incorporate a similar business in another jurisdiction. In such a case, the partnership and the corporation are legally distinct from each other in the same sense that a corporation and its shareholders are legally distinct from each other.

§14.222 As noted above, neither the OBCA nor the CBCA permits the amalgamation of a corporation under that Act with a company incorporated under the laws of some other jurisdiction, such as the Alberta *Business Corporations Act*.[414] Thus, where an OBCA corporation seeks to amalgamate with a corporation under the Alberta *Business Corporations Act* (or a company under the laws of one of the other provinces), it is necessary for one of them to continue under the same Act as the other, or for them both to continue under the same Act, such as the CBCA. Although the desire to amalgamate is one motivation for making a change, such moves may also be motivated by numerous other considerations, for instance, where the business focus of a corporation has shifted from one jurisdiction to another — a situation that would be likely to occur where the sole shareholder of an Alberta corporation moves to Ontario.

§14.223 The process by which a company operating under one corporate law statute may transfer from that statute to another statute is known as continuation. In nearly all cases, the transfer also involves a transfer from the laws of one jurisdiction (such as Ontario) to another (such as Canada). Both the OBCA and the CBCA contain an administrative procedure by which such a change may be effected. There is a fair degree of similarity between the continuation provisions contained in the OBCA and the CBCA, which is not surprising because in both cases, the continuation provisions were derived from sections 198 and 199 of the former OBCA.[415] Prior to the enactment of these provisions the only method by which a corporation might move from one jurisdiction to another was by way of special Act.[416]

§14.224 Continuation is possible under the OBCA and CBCA provided it is properly approved and provided that such a step will have no untoward effect on the rights of third parties dealing with the corporation.[417] There are two types of continuation: import, such as where a corporation under the Alberta *Business Corporations Act* transfers to the OBCA or the CBCA, as the case may be; and export, such as where a corporation under the OBCA transfers to the Alberta

---

[414] R.S.A. 2000, c. B-9.
[415] In *The Business Corporations Act: An Analysis* (Toronto: Carswell, 1971), at 300, Samuel Levine explains that the continuation regime incorporated into the OBCA was seen to be necessary given the limitations that exist upon the constitutional jurisdiction of Canada and each of the provinces over incorporation.
[416] See, for instance, *The Zurich Life Insurance Company of Canada Act*, S.O. 1971, c. 135.
[417] OBCA, s. 181(9); CBCA, s. 188(1) and (10).

Business Corporations Act. Both the OBCA and the CBCA contain provisions permitting each of these types of transfer. Although the transfer of corporations between Ontario and the laws of other provinces are clearly contemplated in the OBCA, by far the largest number of continuations among corporations active in Ontario are to or from the CBCA.

(i) Importation of Companies

§14.225 The importation of companies to the OBCA is governed by section 180 of the OBCA,[418] which provides:

> 180.(1) A body corporate incorporated under the laws of any jurisdiction other than Ontario may, if it appears to the Director to be thereunto authorized by the laws of the jurisdiction in which it was incorporated, apply to the Director for a certificate of continuance.

Thus, a company may be imported to the OBCA only if it was "incorporated under the laws of any jurisdiction other than Ontario". This wording raises the question whether a corporation originally incorporated in Ontario, then exported to some other jurisdiction, may be repatriated to Ontario. The OBCA does not permit a company that is subject to other Ontario legislation (such as the *Corporations Act*[419] or the *Co-operative Corporations Act*)[420] to continue under section 180. In contrast, section 268 of the CBCA permits companies under Part IV of the *Canada Corporations Act*[421] to transfer to the CBCA, but expressly forbids companies under Part II or Part III of the *Canada Corporations Act* from effecting such a transfer.[422]

§14.226 Section 180 of the OBCA does not set out any of the procedures that must be followed by a company seeking to be imported to the OBCA, to authorize continuation — that matter is left to the laws of the incorporating jurisdiction. The OBCA provisions come into play only after the continuation has been properly authorized under the laws of that jurisdiction — though compliance with those provisions does not relieve the company concerned from completing any other requirements of the incorporating jurisdiction (*e.g.*, necessary filings).

---

[418] CBCA, s. 187.
[419] R.S.O. 1990, c. C.38, as amended.
[420] R.S.O. 1990, c. C.35, as amended.
[421] R.S.C. 1970, c. C-32, as amended.
[422] Note, however, s. 268(6) of the CBCA, which provides:

> 268.(6) The Governor in Council may, by order, require that a body corporate incorporated by or under an Act of Parliament to which Part I or II of the *Canada Corporations Act*... does not apply, apply for a certificate of continuance under section 187 within such period as may be prescribed except for the following:
>
> (*a*) a bank;
>
> (*b*) a company or society to which the *Insurance Companies Act* applies; and
>
> (*c*) a company to which the *Trust and Loan Companies Act* applies.

§14.227 The primary obligation of an importing corporation under the OBCA is to file articles of continuance with the Director. These must be submitted in duplicate and verified by the signature of a director or officer of each amalgamating corporation.[423] Upon receipt of the restated articles, the Director may endorse a certificate of continuance on the articles in accordance with section 273 of the Act.[424] In contrast to many of the other fundamental change provisions, the Director possesses a discretion on whether to endorse the articles, and, if the Director considers it proper, the endorsement may be made on such terms and subject to such limitations and conditions as the Director considers appropriate.[425] Once those terms and conditions are satisfied, the Director must then make the endorsement, provided the articles are in prescribed form, have been executed in duplicate and all prescribed fees have been paid. No such discretion is conferred under subsection 187(4) of the CBCA, which provides only:

> 187.(4) On receipt of articles of continuance, the Director shall issue a certificate of continuance in accordance with section 262.

§14.228 Under the OBCA procedure, the endorsement sets out the day, month, and year of the endorsement and also the corporation number. One copy of the endorsed articles is then filed by the Director, and the other is sent to the corporation or to its representative. The Director then must send a copy of the certificate of continuance to the appropriate official or public body in the jurisdiction in which continuance under the Act was authorized — that is, to the responsible regulatory authority in the jurisdiction of original incorporation. However, the Director is prohibited from endorsing a certificate on the articles if the corporation is in default of a filing requirement under the *Corporations Information Act*,[426] or has any unpaid fees or penalties outstanding.[427] Upon the articles of continuance being endorsed:[428]

- the company becomes a corporation to which the OBCA applies as if it had been incorporated under that Act;

- the articles of continuance are deemed to be the articles of incorporation of the continued corporation; and

- the certificate of continuance is deemed to be the certificate of incorporation of the continued corporation, except for the purposes of subsection 117(1) of the Act, which pertains to the holding of a first directors' meeting.[429]

---

[423] OBCA, s. 273.
[424] OBCA, s. 180(4); CBCA, s. 187(4). See, generally, *Re Canada Business Corporations Act*, [1991] O.J. No. 714, 80 D.L.R. (4th) 619 (C.A.).
[425] OBCA, s. 180(4).
[426] R.S.O. 1990, c. C.39, as amended.
[427] OBCA, s. 274, not yet proclaimed in force.
[428] OBCA, s. 180(5); CBCA, s. 187(5).
[429] There is no such exception under the CBCA.

It follows that it is not necessary for the directors of an imported corporation to hold a first directors (or organizational) meeting.[430]

§14.229 The articles of continuance must effect such amendments to the original or restated articles of incorporation, articles of amalgamation, letters patent, supplementary letters patent, special act or any other instrument by which the importing company was incorporated as are necessary to make the articles of continuance conform to the laws of Ontario. In addition, the articles of continuance may make any other amendments that would be permitted under the OBCA if the corporation were incorporated under the laws of Ontario, provided that at least the same shareholder approval has been obtained for those other amendments as would have been required under the OBCA if the company were incorporated under the laws of Ontario.[431]

§14.230 Where a company is continued as a corporation under the OBCA, the corporation possesses all the property, rights, privileges and franchises and is subject to all the liabilities, including civil, criminal and quasi-criminal liabilities, and all contracts, disabilities and debts that were possessed by the company or to which it was subject.[432] In particular, a conviction against, or ruling, order or judgment in favour of or against the company may be enforced by or against the corporation.[433] Moreover, the corporation is deemed to be the party plaintiff or party defendant, as the case may be, in any civil action commenced by or against the company.[434]

§14.231 In general, a share of a company that was issued before the company was continued under the OBCA is deemed to have been issued in compliance with the OBCA and the provisions of the articles of continuance, irrespective of

---

[430] OBCA, s. 180(5)(c); but *cf.* the wording of CBCA, s. 187(5)(c), which does not include this exception. However, under the CBCA, an exemption from the organizational meeting requirement is granted under s. 104(2). This exemption also applies in the case of an amalgamation.

[431] OBCA, s. 180(3). The CBCA equivalent provision does not require such amendments to obtain the same approval as would be required if the continuing company were a corporation to which the CBCA applies: CBCA, s. 187(2).

[432] OBCA, s. 180(7)(a). The wording of the equivalent provision of the CBCA is sufficiently dissimilar to make clause by clause comparison difficult, but see s. 187(7) of the CBCA, which provides:

> 187.(7) When a body corporate is continued as a corporation under this Act,
>
> (a) the property of the body corporate continues to be the property of the corporation;
>
> (b) the corporation continues to be liable for the obligations of the body corporate;
>
> (c) an existing cause of action, claim or liability to prosecution is unaffected;
>
> (d) a civil, criminal or administrative action or proceeding pending by or against the body corporate may be continued to be prosecuted by or against the corporation; and
>
> (e) a conviction against, ruling, order or judgment in favour of or against the body corporate may be enforced by or against the corporation.

[433] OBCA, s. 180(7)(b); CBCA, s. 187(7).
[434] OBCA, s. 180(7)(c); CBCA, s. 187(7).

whether the share is fully paid and of any designation, rights, privileges, restrictions or conditions set out on or referred to in the certificate representing the share. The continuation under the OBCA does not deprive a holder of an issued share of any right or privilege that the holder claims under, or relieve the holder of any liability in regard to that share.[435] However, these general provisions are subject to subsection 56(3) of the OBCA, which provides that where a share certificate issued by a company prior to its being continued under section 180 is subject to:

(a) a restriction on its transfer other than a restriction referred to in subsection (8);

(b) a lien in favour of the corporation;

(c) a unanimous shareholder agreement; or

(d) an endorsement under subsection 185(13)...

the restriction, lien, agreement or endorsement is ineffective against a transferee of the share who has no actual knowledge of it, unless it, or a reference to it, is noted conspicuously on the share certificate. If the words "private company" or "compagnie fermée" appear on the certificate, those words are deemed to be sufficient notice of the restriction, lien, agreement or endorsement for this purpose.[436]

(ii) Export of Corporations

§14.232 The export of an OBCA corporation to the laws of some other jurisdiction is governed by section 181 of the OBCA. The export of CBCA corporations is governed by section 188 of that Act. In each case, however, it is also necessary to consider the requirements and limitations of the law of the jurisdiction to which the corporation is to be exported.[437] Subsection 181(1) of the OBCA provides:

> 181.(1) Subject to subsection (9), a corporation may, if it is authorized by the shareholders and the Director in accordance with this section, apply to the appropriate official or public body of another jurisdiction requesting that the corporation be continued as if it had been incorporated under the laws of that jurisdiction.

The corresponding provision of the CBCA is similar, but differs in detail. Subsection 188(1) of the CBCA provides:

> 188.(1) Subject to subsection (10), a corporation may apply to the appropriate official or public body of another jurisdiction requesting that the corporation be continued as if it had been incorporated under the laws of that other jurisdiction if the corporation

---

[435] OBCA, s. 180(8); CBCA, s. 187(7).
[436] OBCA, s. 56(4); CBCA, s. 49(10).
[437] As to the process for converting a non-Nova Scotia limited liability corporation into a Nova Scotia unlimited liability company, see: *Re E L Management Incorporated*, [2004] N.S.J. No. 339 (S.C.).

(a) is authorized by the shareholders in accordance with this section to make the application; and

(b) establishes to the satisfaction of the Director that its proposed continuance in the other jurisdiction will not adversely affect creditors or shareholders of the corporation.[438]

Some limitation on the scope of this provision is imposed by virtue of subsection 188(2), which provides that a CBCA corporation to which the *Investment Companies Act* applies may not apply for continuance under subsection 188(1) without the prior consent of the Minister of Finance. Subsection 188(2) further provides:

> 188.(2) A corporation that is authorized by the shareholders in accordance with this section may apply to the appropriate Minister for its continuance under the *Bank Act*, the *Canada Cooperatives Act*, the *Insurance Companies Act*, or the *Trust and Loan Companies Act*.

There is a range of circumstances in which these provisions may come into play. For instance, if the employees of a corporation buy that corporation from its former owner, they may apply to continue the corporation as a worker cooperative. It would also be a suitable route to follow where a corporation in the business of consumer lending wishes to become a bank or trust company, or, perhaps, even a bank.

§14.233 Subsection 181(9) of the OBCA[439] sets out a number of requirements that must be satisfied by the laws of the jurisdiction to which the corporation proposes to export to allow the export to be permitted. It provides:

> 181.(9) A corporation shall not apply under subsection (1) to be continued as a body corporate under the laws of another jurisdiction unless those laws provide in effect that,
>
> (a) the property of the corporation continues to be the property of the body corporate;
>
> (b) the body corporate continues to be liable for the obligations of the corporation;
>
> (c) an existing cause of action, claim or liability to prosecution is unaffected;
>
> (d) a civil, criminal or administrative action or proceeding pending by or against the corporation may be continued to be prosecuted by or against the body corporate; and
>
> (e) a conviction against the corporation may be enforced against the body corporate or a ruling, order or judgment in favour of or against the corporation may be enforced against the body corporate.

---

[438] Enacted by S.C. 1994, c. 24, s. 22(1).
[439] CBCA, s. 188(10).

§14.234 The first step in the export process is to obtain the approval of the shareholders to the change of incorporating jurisdiction.[440] Subsection 181(2) of the OBCA provides that the notice of the meeting of shareholders that is to be held for this purpose must include or be accompanied by a statement that a dissenting shareholder is entitled to be paid the fair value of his or her shares in accordance with section 185.[441] The failure to include such a statement, however, does not invalidate any special resolution authorizing the continuance. In most cases a special resolution of the shareholders authorizing a corporation to continue under the laws of another jurisdiction will contain at least four basic provisions: (1) it will authorize the corporation to apply for a certificate of continuance (or whatever procedure may apply for effecting continuance) as a company under the laws of the intended jurisdiction of export; (2) it will authorize the corporation to apply to the Director under the OBCA to authorize the continuance under the laws of that other jurisdiction; (3) it will authorize such amendments as may be required to bring the corporation's articles into conformity with the laws of that other jurisdiction; and (4) it will authorize the corporation's directors and officers to take all steps that they may consider necessary or advisable to effect the continuance under the laws of that other jurisdiction. Quite often, the resolution will also confer upon the directors of the corporation the discretion to abandon the planned continuance should they consider it to be in the best interests of the corporation to do so. Although this last provision is not essential, it is generally desirable to include it because the advisability of continuance may be affected by some subsequent development (such as a large number of shareholders asserting their rights of dissent). No special voting rights are conferred under section 170 of the OBCA upon the holders of classes or series of shares in regard to a proposal to continue under the laws of another jurisdiction. In contrast, under the CBCA, all shareholders have a right to vote on a proposal to continue under the laws of another jurisdiction, and all shareholders enjoy a right of dissent to the continuation.

§14.235 The second step in the continuation process is to apply to the Director for authorization to proceed with the continuance. This is done by submitting a prescribed application to the Director. In this application, the corporation must disclose whether it is a corporation offering its securities to the public within the meaning of subsection 1(6) of the OBCA, any actions, suits or proceedings that are pending against the corporation and any unsatisfied judgments or orders outstanding against the corporation, the jurisdiction to which the corporation proposes to apply for continuation, and the "necessity" for the continuation. The Director has the discretion to approve the application, but may not authorize continuance unless satisfied that the application is not prohibited under subsection 181(9).[442]

§14.236 The Director's approval of the proposed continuance does not cause the corporation to be continued under the laws of the export jurisdiction. To continue

---

[440] OBCA, s. 181(3)(*a*); compare CBCA, s. 188(5).
[441] CBCA, s. 188(3).
[442] OBCA, s. 181(4).

the corporation, it is necessary to comply with the import provisions of the laws of that jurisdiction. The authorization of the Director for an application for continuance expires six months after the date of the endorsement of the authorization, so the corporation must either have been continued under the laws of the export jurisdiction within that 90-day period or, at the very least, have applied for such a continuation and completed all steps towards continuation that are under its control.[443] The final requirement in connection with an export continuance is that the corporation must file a copy of the instrument of continuance issued to it by the export jurisdiction within 60 days after the issuance of that instrument.[444]

J. ARRANGEMENTS AND REORGANIZATIONS

§14.237 From time to time a corporation may seek to adjust or modify the rights of its shareholders, security holders or creditors of these persons, to compromise the claims or entitlements of these persons against the corporation. Although often motivated by the desperate commercial condition of the corporation, even in less pressing circumstances the corporation may seek to effect such a compromise — for instance, where the capital structure of the corporation is inconvenient, where new capital is required and is obtainable only on the condition that the existing rights of the shareholders are modified or their interest in the corporation is reduced, or where some general compromise is required among the interests of all persons concerned in the corporation. The particular method to be followed depends on the circumstances of the case, and, in particular, with whom the compromise is sought.

(i) Arrangements with Shareholders

§14.238 An arrangement is a plan of corporate reorganization. The arrangement procedure differs from the simpler amendment or amalgamation procedures by introducing the additional requirement for judicial approval of the fundamental change in question. Like many corporate law terms (*e.g.*, debenture) the term "arrangement" is one that lacks any clear and certain legal definition. Etymologically, it is imported from debtor and creditor law where it describes plans for the compromise or composition of debts. Although the term would appear to be more broadly defined in corporate law, the element of compromise has been carried forward into its new context.[445] There is Australian case law to the effect that the term "arrangement" is to be liberally construed. It can embrace any proposal that a reasonable business person *might* carry out *in* good faith in the course of his or her business.[446] The term is clearly sufficient to include a compromise of a claim against or interest in the corporation.[447]

---

[443] OBCA, s. 181(6).
[444] OBCA, s. 181(7).
[445] *Re NFU Development Trust Ltd.*, [1972] 1 W.L.R. 1548, *per* Brightman J.
[446] *Re E D White Ltd.* (1929), 29 S.R. (N.S.W.) 389 at 391, *per* Harvey C.J. See also *Re Inex Pharmaceuticals Corp.*, [2006] B.C.J. No. 1265, 18 B.L.R. (4th) 3 (C.A.).
[447] *Dean-Willcocks v. Soluble Solution Hydroponics Pty Ltd.* (1997), 42 N.S.W.L.R. 209 at 214 *per* Young J.

§14.239 The notion of an arrangement has long been part of Canadian corporate law. Most recently, arrangements have featured in applications for protection by insolvent corporations under the *Companies' Creditors Arrangement Act* ("CCAA"), discussed below, but they are also of use where a corporation plans a complicated fundamental change. The OBCA and CBCA provisions are used primarily in the latter case, for the CCAA sets out its own process for effecting an arrangement.[448]

§14.240 The term "arrangement" is broadly described (as opposed to defined) under section 182 of the OBCA, which indicates that the term includes:

(a) a reorganization of the shares of any class or series of the corporation or of the stated capital of any such class or series,

(b) the addition to or removal from the articles of the corporation of any provision that is permitted by this Act to be, or that is, set out in the articles or the change of any such provision,

(c) an amalgamation of the corporation with another corporation,

(d) an amalgamation of a body corporate with a corporation that results in an amalgamated corporation subject to this Act,[449]

(e) a transfer of all or substantially all of the property of the corporation to another body corporate in exchange for securities, money or other property of the body corporate,

(f) an exchange of securities of the corporation held by security holders for other securities, money or other property of the corporation or securities, money or other property of another body corporate that is not a take-over bid as defined in Part XX of the *Securities Act*...

In *Re Eau Claire Sawmills Ltd.*,[450] it was held that a corporation could not propose the compulsory conversion of preference shares into bonds under the arrangement provisions of the *Companies Act*[451] because such a proposal did not call for a compromise of the rights of the shareholders, but, rather, for a cancellation of their rights as shareholders. However, as clause 182(1)(f) provides for exchanges of securities it would now appear that such a proposal can be carried out under the arrangement provisions. The list of changes falling expressly within the definition also includes:

(g) a liquidation or dissolution of the corporation,

---

[448] *Re Loewen Group Inc.*, [2002] O.J. No. 5640, 22 B.L.R. (3d) 134 at para. 8 (S.C.J. — C.L.). Farley J. also observed:

> Under U.S. bankruptcy law, shareholders having no economic interest to protect have no right to vote on a plan of reorganization. Consistent with that appropriate economic and legal principle, courts in Ontario and Alberta have held that where shareholders similarly have no economic interest to protect, it would defeat the policy objectives of the CCAA to give those shareholders a right to veto a plan of arrangement.

[449] As noted above, such an amalgamation is not contemplated under the legislation.
[450] [1942] 2 W.W.R. 242 (Alta. T.D.).
[451] S.C. 1934, c. 33, ss. 122 and 123.

(h) any other reorganization or scheme involving the business or affairs of the corporation or of any or all of the holders of its securities or of any options or rights to acquire any of its securities that is, at law, an arrangement, and

(i) any combination of the foregoing [*i.e.*, of clauses (a) to (h)].

The arrangement provisions of the Act do not so much empower the corporation to effect changes to its constitution, as restrain the manner in which those changes may be made — most importantly, by requiring the approval of the court. The definition of "arrangement" is inclusive and it has been held that the term should be given a broad interpretation, the only limitation being that an arrangement must not be contrary to any provision of the OBCA or to general corporate law.[452]

§14.241 A similar, but somewhat differently worded, inclusive definition is provided in subsection 192(1) of the CBCA, where the term "arrangement" is said to include:

(a) an amendment to the articles of a corporation;

(b) an amalgamation of two or more corporations;

(c) an amalgamation of a body corporate with a corporation that results in an amalgamated corporation subject to this Act;

(d) a division of the business carried on by a corporation;

(e) a transfer of all or substantially all of the property of a corporation to another body corporate in exchange for property, money or securities of the body corporate;

(f) an exchange of securities of a corporation for property, money or other securities of the corporation or property, money or securities of another body corporate;

(f.1) a going-private transaction or a squeeze-out in relation to a corporation;

(g) a liquidation and dissolution of a corporation; and

(h) any combination of the foregoing.

It will be observed that clause 182(1)(b) of the OBCA includes in the definition of an "arrangement":

(b) the addition to or removal from the articles of the corporation of any provision that is permitted by this Act to be, or that is, set out in the articles or the change of any such provision.

In contrast, paragraph 192(1)(a) of the CBCA provides only that an arrangement includes "an amendment to the articles" of the corporation. Despite the difference in wording, clause (b) of the OBCA and paragraph (a) of the CBCA would

---

[452] *Re West Humber Apartments Ltd.*, [1968] O.J. No. 1296, [1969] 1 O.R. 229 at 232-33 (H.C.J.), *per* Morand J.; see also *Re P.L. Robertson Manufacturing Co.*, [1974] O.J. No. 2237, 7 O.R. (2d) 98 (H.C.J.), where a technical contravention of the Act was allowed; and *Re Ripley International Ltd.*, [1977] O.J. No. 68, 1 B.L.R. 269 (H.C.J.).

appear to have the same effect because there is no apparent amendment to the articles of a corporation that would not be caught within the wording of clause (b), nor is there anything in the wording of paragraph (a) that would appear not to constitute an amendment to the articles of a corporation.

(ii) Shareholder Arrangement Procedure

§14.242 The general intent behind the arrangement provisions of the OBCA and CBCA is to permit flexibility in implementing a complex corporate restructuring, subject to the concern that minority shareholders be treated fairly and that their rights are respected.[453] The procedure for effecting a compromise or arrangement between a corporation and its shareholders involves the submission of a scheme at a meeting of the shareholders. The Act imposes a requirement for separate class voting in a number of circumstances. In any such case, it is not necessarily fatal to hold one meeting of all shareholders and to conduct separate votes among the different classes, but this course is fraught with difficulty and it is preferable for the different classes both to vote and meet separately. The dangers in holding a single joint meeting are, first, it may complicate matters and lead to confusion and, second, it may be impossible to secure a full and frank discussion among the affected parties.[454] However, the meetings may be arranged so that one will follow the others. It has been held that votes by show of hands (at least on the main substantive issue) are improper because they do not reflect the views of shareholders represented by proxy.[455] Where there is apparent overwhelming support for a proposal and no evident opposition to an informal vote, however, it is difficult to see any reason for an absolute requirement of a formal ballot.

§14.243 An OBCA corporation proposing an arrangement must prepare a statement of the arrangement for the approval of the shareholders. The statement must set out in detail what is proposed to be done and the manner in which it is proposed to be done.[456] The information circular must provide sufficient detail to permit shareholders to form a reasoned judgment concerning the matter. The procedure may be invalidated where the statement contains untrue statements of a material fact, or omits to state a material fact in a manner that is misleading. A fact is material if there is a substantial likelihood that a reasonable shareholder would consider it important in deciding how to vote.[457] Given the usual need to move quickly where an arrangement is contemplated, the courts have adopted a reasonably flexible approach towards the content of the information circular that is provided. So in one case Blair J. stated:

---

[453] Re St. Lawrence & Hudson Railway Co., [1998] O.J. No. 3934, 76 O.T.C. 115 (Gen. Div.).
[454] Re Langley's Ltd., [1938] O.J. No. 414, [1938] O.R. 123 at 128 (C.A.), per Middleton J.A.; see also Carruth v. Imperial Chemical Industries Ltd., [1936] Ch. 587 (C.A.), aff'd [1937] A.C. 707 (H.L.).
[455] Re Landley's Ltd., [1938] O.J. No. 414, [1938] O.R. 123 at 129 (C.A.); see also Re Dairy Corp. of Canada Ltd., [1934] O.J. No. 147, [1934] O.R. 436 (C.A.).
[456] OBCA, s. 182(2).
[457] Sparling v. Royal Trust Co., [1984] O.J. No. 3129, 6 D.L.R. (4th) 682 (C.A.), aff'd [1986] S.C.J. No. 64, [1986] 2 S.C.R. 537.

I do not think it is incumbent upon the judge being asked to grant the Interim Order to carry out a detailed examination of the Information Circular, which is to be distributed to the shareholders, for its sufficiency. Unless the Circular is obviously bereft of substance and detail, such considerations are better left to a later occasion where that issue can be determined — either by the Court, or perhaps more appropriately by the Securities Commission (the tribunal with particular expertise in such matters) — with the benefit of the input of those who have concerns. The Court does not "approve" or "authorize" the Circular. The Interim Order simply directs that the Circular prepared by management be distributed to the shareholders. Undoubtedly, if the Information Circular is clearly inadequate, that will be a factor bearing considerable weight at the time of the "fairness hearing" by the Court to determine whether the arrangement will be sanctioned and approved.[458]

Later in that decision, Blair J. also said:

> The question is not whether the Information Circular contains information answering every conceivable query, and follow-up query, that an inquisitive minded shareholder (or shareholder's advisor) can pose. The requirement is that the substance of the pertinent matter be set out "in sufficient detail to permit shareholders to form a reasoned judgment concerning the matter".[459] This standard, it seems to me, is not dissimilar to the frequent declaration that shareholders are entitled to "full, fair and plain disclosure"...[460]

In *Smith v. First Merchant Equities Inc.*,[461] Geatros J. concluded that the alleged misstatements in a circular must be proven before the court should make any order correcting them — this being an issue that would have to be dealt with at a trial, not on the basis of conflicting affidavit evidence. Allegations of minor defects will not be sufficient where the information provided permits shareholders to come to an intelligent conclusion as to whether they should vote in favour of the proposal to be put to the meeting.

§14.244 Where a reorganization or scheme is proposed as an arrangement and involves an amendment of the articles of a corporation or the taking of any other steps that could be made or taken under any other provisions of the OBCA, the procedure provided in section 182 for the approval of the arrangement and not that other procedure applies to that reorganization or scheme.[462] Subject to any order that the court may make on application by the corporation under subsection 182(5), where an arrangement is approved by a special resolution of the shareholders the arrangement is adopted by the shareholders, following which the corporation may apply to the court for an order approving the arrangement.[463] Subsection 182(4) limits special voting class and series rights, except in cases where section 170 applies. It provides:

> 182.(4) The holders of shares of a class or series of shares of a corporation are not entitled to vote separately as a class or series in respect of an arrangement

---

[458] *Re First Marathon Inc.*, [1999] O.J. No. 2805 at para. 11, 102 O.T.C. 194 (S.C.J. — C.L.).
[459] OBCA Regulation 62, s. 30, item 31.
[460] *Ibid.*, para. 17.
[461] [1988] S.J. No. 165, 50 D.L.R. (4th) 369 (Q.B.).
[462] OBCA, s. 182(6).
[463] OBCA, s. 182(4).

unless the statement of the arrangement referred to in subsection (2) contains a provision that, if contained in a proposed amendment to the articles, would entitle such holders to vote separately as a class or series under section 170 and, if the statement of the arrangement contains such a provision, such holders are entitled to vote separately on the arrangement whether or not such shares otherwise carry the right to vote.

Thus, it would appear that irrespective of the special voting rights to which a class or series of shares may be entitled under the articles of the corporation, the shareholders of a class or series are not entitled to vote separately, except where the arrangement is within section 170.

§14.245 Once the shareholders of a corporation have approved an arrangement, the arrangement must be submitted for approval by court order.[464] Court approval is mandatory and such approval is not available merely on a rubber stamp basis. The court must conclude that the proposed arrangement is fair and reasonable in all the circumstances,[465] the onus being on the persons applying for approval to demonstrate that this is the case.[466] Specifically, a court must

- ascertain whether all the statutory requirements have been fulfilled;
- satisfy itself that the arrangement is put forward in good faith;
- consider whether the statutory majority who approved the scheme were acting *bona fide* or were seeking to promote interests adverse to those of the class whom they professed to represent;
- determine whether the arrangement is such as a business person would reasonably approve; and
- determine whether the arrangement is fair and reasonable.

for an arrangement to get court approval. As the above passage indicates, where a corporation applies to the court for the approval of a compromise or arrangement between the corporation and its shareholders, it is the first duty of the court to determine that all statutory conditions have been satisfied.[467] The court must also determine whether anything has been done, or purported to have been done, that is not authorized by the Act. The court must then take a critical look at the scheme and determine whether it is, on balance, fair and reasonable.[468]

---

[464] OBCA, s. 182(3).

[465] It is the arrangement that is at issue in the application, and the process by which it was laid before the shareholders for their approval, that must be fair. It is not appropriate to inquire into past matters relating to the conduct of the corporation: *Samos Investments Inc. v. Pattison*, [2000] B.C.J. No. 1344, 12 B.L.R. (3d) 181 at 207 (B.C.C.A.), *per* Rowles J.A., leave to appeal to S.C.C. refused [2000] S.C.C.A. No. 396.

[466] *Re Ripley International Ltd.*, [1977] O.J. No. 68, 1 B.L.R. 269 (H.C.J.).

[467] *Re St. Lawrence Corp. & Mayer* (1948), 28 C.B.R. 185 (Que. S.C.), proposal rejected on the grounds that insufficient information was provided. See also *Re N. Slater Co.*, [1947] O.J. No. 23, [1947] O.W.N. 226 (H.C.J.).

[468] *Re Dairy Corp. of Canada Ltd.*, [1934] O.J. No. 147, [1934] O.R. 436 at 439 (C.A.), *per* Middleton J.A.; *Re Langley's Ltd.*, [1938] O.J. No. 414, [1938] O.R. 123 at 129 (C.A.), *per* Middleton J.A.; see also *Re Dorman, Long & Co.*, [1934] Ch. 635; *Re Canada Bread Co.*, [1935]

§14.246 The essential test for the court when approving a plan of arrangement is that all statutory requirements have been fulfilled, that the arrangement is put forward in good faith and that the arrangement is fair and reasonable.[469] The first hurdle in obtaining court approval is to demonstrate that all resolutions have been passed by the requisite majority provided in the statute at a properly constituted meeting. Second, the court must be satisfied that nothing has been done, or purported to have been done, that is not authorized by law. Finally (and here the court exercises a discretion), the court must decide whether the scheme of arrangement is one that an intelligent and honest business person, as a member of the class concerned and acting only in his or her interest as a member, might reasonably approve.[470] In exercising that discretion, the job of the court is not to second-guess shareholders who have unanimously approved the arrangement in question. Rather, the court's function is to protect a minority of shareholders who have opposed the adoption of the arrangement.

§14.247 The court will not make substantive changes to a plan at the court approval state merely because a minority creditor or shareholder is dissatisfied with it; moreover, substantive changes require the approval of the majority of the affected interests.[471] In *Re Transwest Energy Inc.*[472] a shareholder meeting was held to approve a proposed arrangement under the Alberta *Business Corporation Act*[473] between two corporations under that Act and the shareholder of one of them. A shareholder that held a large block of shares in one of the subject corporations wished to vote against the plan, but it was denied the opportunity to do so because it had failed to file a formal demand to be registered on the shareholder list within the time allowed under clause 132(*b*) of the Alberta Act. The arrangement was subsequently approved at the meeting. Had the applicant been allowed to vote on the proposed plan, the plan would not have received the required degree of shareholder approval. The applicant brought a motion for an order refusing the arrangement on the grounds that it had been improperly prevented from voting, and that if it had voted the proposal would have been defeated. Forsyth J. refused to grant the motion, explaining that on the facts the court should not exercise its discretion to block the proposed arrangement from proceeding.[474]

§14.248 An application for an interim order for directions related to calling a shareholders meeting is characteristically the first of three steps required to approve an arrangement under the Act. It usually proceeds *ex parte*, due to the administrative burden of notifying all shareholders of the application. The second

---

O.W.N. 429; *Re Brazilian Traction Light & Power Co.*, [1947] O.J. No. 539, [1947] O.R. 791 (H.C.J.).
[469] *Re Trizec Corp.*, [1994] A.J. No. 577, 20 B.L.R. (2d) 202 at 208 (Q.B.).
[470] *Re Dairy Corp. of Canada Ltd.*, [1934] O.J. No. 147, [1934] O.R. 436 (C.A.); *Re Canada Bread Co.*, [1935] O.W.N. 429 (H.C.); *Re Western Canada Flour Mills Ltd.*, [1945] O.J. No. 27, [1945] O.W.N. 152 (H.C.J.).
[471] *Re Trizec Corp.*, [1994] A.J. No. 577, 20 B.L.R. (2d) 202 at 209 (C.A.).
[472] (1997), 32 B.L.R. (2d) 315 (Alta. Q.B.).
[473] S.A. 1981, c. B-15.
[474] *Re Transwest Energy Inc.* (1997), 32 B.L.R. (2d) 315 at 320 (Q.B.).

step is the meeting of the shareholders, where the arrangement is debated. It must be approved by a majority of two-thirds to proceed further. The third step is a further application to the court for a final order approving the arrangement. This is referred to as the fairness hearing, and all interested parties receive notice of it and may appear to contest the final order on the basis of its substantive fairness.[475]

§14.249 In deciding whether to give approval, the court itself must pass upon the merits of the proposed arrangement, taking into account the views of both the majority and the minority. The court must consider whether the scheme was placed fairly and squarely before the shareholders. Although the court is not bound by the outcome of the shareholders' vote, it must not substitute its own view of what is fair and reasonable in the place of the business judgment of the shareholders themselves.[476] The scheme of the legislation is to permit the majority to approve a proposal and thereby bind the minority against their wishes. That power is not to be thwarted by a willful or vocal minority, but then neither is the minority to be oppressed by the majority, particularly where the circumstances of the arrangement or compromise render illusory any right of dissent. The result of the proposal may improve the position of one class of shareholders at the expense of another class, but that is not, in and of itself, sufficient ground for the court to withhold its approval.[477] However, the court must consider whether the proposal results in a proportionate distribution of the burden among all persons within each class or series[478] so that the minority (although opposed) may, at least, feel that the majority are giving up as much proportionately as they are. If the scheme may have the effect of enabling the majority, either directly or through the medium of the directors, to benefit some members of the class at the expense of others, then the scheme must be scrutinized with great care and ought, in most cases, to be rejected.[479]

§14.250 In *Re Canadian Pacific Ltd.*[480] the applicant sought court approval of an arrangement under section 192 of the CBCA. It provided for the transfer of 80 per cent of the shares of a subsidiary to the ordinary shareholders of the parent

---

[475] *Re Pacifica Papers Inc.*, [2001] B.C.J. No. 1484 (S.C.), aff'd [2001] B.C.J. No. 1714 (C.A.).
[476] *Re Western Canada Flour Mills Ltd.*, [1945] O.J. No. 27, [1945] O.W.N. 152 (H.C.J.); *Re United Fuel Investments Ltd.*, [1939] O.W.N. 52; [1939] 1 D.L.R. 779 (S.C.); *Re Hamilton Bridge Co.*, [1939] 4 D.L.R. 803, [1939] O.W.N. 327 (S.C.); *Re National Grocers Co.*, [1938] O.J. No. 415, [1938] O.R. 142 (H.C.J.). Thus, it is doubtful that the court may refuse to sanction a proposal where unanimously approved, though the court may refuse to sanction the proposal (in an appropriate case) even where approved by the vast majority of shareholders: *Re Canada Cotton Ltd.*, [1952] Que. S.C. 276.
[477] Where such a balance is struck, the court may approve the plan even if the explanation of the arrangement provided to the shareholders was not as clear as it should have been: *Re Holdex Group Ltd.*, [1972] O.J. No. 1871, [1972] 3 O.R. 425 (H.C.J.); *Re West Humber Apartments Ltd.*, [1968] O.J. No. 1296, [1969] 1 O.R. 229 (H.C.J.).
[478] See, for instance, *Re Tip Top Canners Ltd.*, [1972] O.J. No. 2040, [1973] 1 O.R. 626 (H.C.J.); but compare *Re National Grocers Co.*, [1938] O.J. No. 415, [1938] O.R. 142 (H.C.J.), where approval was refused where the proposal particularly benefitted the holders of preference shares, and many of the common shares were held by owners of the preference shares.
[479] *Re Second Standard Royalties Ltd.*, [1930] O.J. No. 45, 66 O.L.R. 288 (H.C.J.).
[480] [1990] O.J. No. 864, 73 O.R. (2d) 212 (H.C.J.).

corporation. The preference shareholders were not included in the arrangement. In an earlier hearing it had been determined that the preference shareholders had no right to participate since the arrangement was in essence a dividend and the preference shareholders' right to a dividend was limited to 4 per cent per year. The preference shareholders objected to the arrangement on the grounds that it was of no benefit to the parent company, was prejudicial to the preference shareholders, and would result in the loss of 14 per cent to 16 per cent of the assets of the parent. Further, it would affect the preference shareholders' rights on a liquidation. The parent corporation claimed that there was no prejudice, on the ground that there had been and was no likelihood of future inability to pay the 4 per cent dividends to the preference shareholders and that, as the company had the obligation to run its railway operation in perpetuity, there was no prospect of a liquidation. Austin J. dismissed the application for the approval of the arrangement, concluding that where there is no necessity for the arrangement and where classes of shareholders are treated differently, there is a heavier onus on the applicant. On the facts of the case, Austin J. concluded that there was no benefit to the corporation, and there was prejudice to the preference shareholders, by reason of the decrease of assets. In addition, there was shown to be some potential prejudice by the reduced rights on a liquidation. The duty to operate the railway in perpetuity did not guarantee continuance of the corporation, and the prospect of a winding-up or partial winding-up was not so remote as to be not worth considering. The preference shareholders had shown a real interest in the subject matter, although they had been held not entitled to share in the distribution. In the absence of any necessity for the arrangement, the applicant had failed to meet the heavy onus of showing that the court should grant approval.

§14.251 The CBCA does not specifically provide for a vote on the plan of arrangement.[481] In *Savage v. Amoco Acquisition Co.*[482] the court concluded that it was not essential that the views of shareholders or creditors be canvassed, and that even where they were canvassed, the court might still approve an arrangement that it considered fair despite the opposition of a particular class of creditor or shareholder to the plan (although it was acknowledged that creditor and shareholder approval should be sought and their views considered by the court). The suggestion that such views should only be "considered" seems to understate the case. In *Re Trizec Corp.*[483] the Alberta Court of Queen's Bench imposed an arrangement upon a dissident class of shareholders who had voted by a substantial majority to reject the plan unless certain modifications were made. The court concluded that the class of creditors in question was merely trying to secure a better deal through the court than they had obtained by way of negotiation. Absent evidence of abuse (that might negate any expression of shareholder opinion) or such a miniscule minority interest that it might perhaps be best disregarded in order to do fairness in the broader sense, it would

---

[481] For reporting issuers, see the discussion of going private transactions.
[482] [1988] A.J. No. 330, 59 Alta. L.R. (2d) 260 at 263 (C.A.), *per* Kerans J.A.
[483] [1994] A.J. No. 577, 20 B.L.R. (2d) 202 (Q.B.).

take very strong reasons to disregard the view of those who stand to be most affected by a proposed transaction.

§14.252 By virtue of subsection 182(3) of the OBCA the approval of a planned arrangement by shareholders is a pre-condition to any approval of the arrangement by the court. The approval of a plan of arrangement by creditors is not specifically mentioned (perhaps, since the statutory requirement for solvency was considered to make such approval unnecessary). While there is no procedure set out in the OBCA which provides for an arrangement or compromise with creditors as such, it is readily possible that a plan of arrangement may incidentally affect the interests of creditors. A direct effect upon creditor rights will normally amount to a variation of contract. In order for such a variation to be made, the consent of the affected creditor will be required. However, an incidental effect upon creditor rights may take place outside the four corners of the creditor's contract. This possibility seems to have been considered when the amalgamation provisions of the Act were drafted. Thus subsection 178(2) contemplates creditor intervention to block an amalgamation. However, no similar consideration was incorporated into section 182, at least in the ordinary case.[484]

§14.253 In *Laurentian Bank of Canada v. Princeton Mining Corp.*[485] a mining company (A) owned 100 per cent of the shares of a company, B, and shares in four other companies. Proceedings were commenced to implement a proposed arrangement between the mining company and its shareholders under section 276 of the *Company Act*.[486] Meetings of shareholders were authorized to vote on the arrangement. No notice of the meetings or of the arrangement was given to the mining company's creditors. Under the arrangement, the shareholders of A were to exchange their shares for shares in B, B thereby becoming the sole shareholder of the mining company. Under the terms of a "post arrangement transaction", A was to assign to B its shareholdings in the other four companies in return for shares in B. The shareholders approved the arrangement. A applied for court approval of the arrangement without notice to its creditors, and approval was granted. Subsequently, a creditor applied for an order that the debt owed by A to it to be secured against the assets of B. B objected to the application, arguing that the creditor had no status to bring such an application and that the court, therefore, had no jurisdiction to grant the application. Smith J. held that the creditor had the standing to bring such an application and the court had jurisdiction to hear it and make the order sought. Smith J. concluded that sections 276 and 278 of the BCCA were intended to provide a convenient procedure for effecting compromises and arrangements. They were not intended to allow for the circumvention of the rights of creditors.

---

[484] *Cf.* Subsections 182(5) and (6) and clauses 182(1)(*c*) and (*d*).
[485] [1993] B.C.J. No. 2192, 23 C.B.R. (3d) 106 (S.C.).
[486] R.S.B.C. 1979, c. 59 (am. 2002, c. 57, s. 445(a)).

(iii) Rights of Dissent in a Shareholder Arrangement

§14.254 Because the court exercises a protective role in shareholder arrangement cases, and because it is inherent in an arrangement that the corporation will be in dire circumstances before an arrangement is proposed with shareholders (or other security holders), there is no automatic right of dissent in the case of an arrangement.[487] However, the court does possess authority to permit a shareholder to dissent under section 185 if the arrangement is adopted.[488] Formerly some additional protection of minority interests was contemplated under subsection 182(7), which provided:

> 182.(7) An applicant under this section shall give the Director notice of the application, and the Director is entitled to appear and be heard in person or by counsel.

However, this provision has now been repealed.[489]

§14.255 Under the old OBCA, the court's jurisdiction was limited to the approval of the plan of arrangement. Prior to the adoption of the arrangement by the shareholders, the corporation had no standing to apply to the court to seek directions or a clarification of the rights of various parties to notice or otherwise. This deficiency has been eliminated by subsection 182(5) of the Act[490] which provides:

> 182.(5) The corporation may, at any time, apply to the court for advice and directions in connection with an arrangement or proposed arrangement and the court may make such order as it considers appropriate, including, without limiting the generality of the foregoing,
>
> > (a) an order determining the notice to be given to any interested person or dispensing with notice to any person;
> >
> > (b) an order requiring a corporation to call, hold and conduct an additional meeting of, or to hold a separate vote of, all or any particular group of holders of any securities or warrants of the corporation in such manner as the court directs;
> >
> > (c) an order permitting a shareholder to dissent under section 185 if the arrangement is adopted;
> >
> > (d) an order appointing counsel, at the expense of the corporation, to represent the interests of the shareholders;
> >
> > (e) an order that the arrangement or proposed arrangement shall be deemed not to have been adopted by the shareholders of the corporation unless it has been approved by a specified majority that is greater than two-thirds of the votes cast at a meeting of the holders, or any particular group of holders, of securities or warrants of the corporation; and

---

[487] *Re Systemcorp A.L.G. Ltd.*, [2004] O.J. No. 4798, 50 B.L.R. (3d) 163 (S.C.J.); *Re Riptide Technologies Inc.*, [2003] B.C.J. No. 2431, 38 B.L.R. (3d) 191 (S.C.).
[488] OBCA, s. 182(5)(c); CBCA, s. 192(4)(d).
[489] S.O. 1994, c. 27, s. 71.
[490] CBCA, s. 192(4).

(f) an order approving the arrangement as proposed by the corporation or as amended in any manner the court may direct, subject to compliance with such terms and conditions, if any, as the court thinks fit,

and to the extent that any such order is inconsistent with this section such order shall prevail.

§14.256 A number of observations may be made about section 182(5). First, because clause (f) expressly contemplates the court approving a proposed plan prior to its adoption by shareholders and the subsection then goes on to provide that where the court makes an order to that effect the order shall prevail despite its inconsistency with the section the spectre is raised of a court dispensing with shareholder approval entirely. It is difficult, however, to imagine a situation in which such an order should be made. It is the shareholders, rather than the court, who have money at risk. If shareholders do not approve of the arrangement, it is difficult to think of a basis on which a court may exercise a discretion to override their objection or likely objection. One possible situation in which the court might contemplate making an order dispensing with a vote would be where a sufficient number of shareholders have consented to the proposed order, and none of the other shareholders would be unfairly prejudiced by the proposal, so the holding of an additional meeting would be an unnecessary expense — surely a consideration when the corporation is in financial distress.

§14.257 Standing to bring an application under subsection 182(5) appears to be limited to the corporation.[491] This is surprising, because it would be very unlikely that the corporation would seek to obtain some of the orders contemplated by the section. For instance, it is unclear why the corporation would seek an order that permits a shareholder to dissent under section 185 or that requires a greater majority than two-thirds of the shareholders to approve the arrangement? Presumably, the power to make orders of this sort was included to permit the court to provide disgruntled shareholders with relief, should they appear on an application brought by the corporation. However, the lack of standing in favour of shareholders prior to the corporation bringing such an application is clearly a deficiency in the section.

§14.258 Normally, an order will not be made approving an arrangement until such time as it has been adopted by the shareholders. As noted above, usually approval will occur at a properly called meeting, following appropriate disclosure and notice.[492] Where an order approving the arrangement is made, articles of arrangement in the prescribed form must be sent to the Director. Thus, in the context of the other fundamental change provisions, the arrangement provisions do not contemplate allowing the directors of the corporation any discretion to discontinue with the arrangement once the court's approval has been obtained. There would seem to be no reason, however, why such authority might not be

---

[491] *McEwen v. Goldcorp Inc.*, [2006] O.J. No. 4437, 21 B.L.R. (4th) 306 (Div. Ct.).
[492] As to the requirement for full and fair disclosure, see *Re Bolivar Gold Corp.*, [2006] Y.J. No. 11, 16 B.L.R. (4th) 10 (C.A.).

included in the shareholder resolution, to allow the directors not to seek court approval or to discontinue an application for approval should they conclude that it is in the best interests of the corporation to do so.

(iv) Other Procedural Considerations

§14.259 The articles of arrangement must be submitted in duplicate, in the prescribed form and verified by the signature of a director or officer of each amalgamating corporation.[493] Upon receipt of these articles, the Director is required to endorse a certificate of arrangement on the articles in accordance with section 273 of the Act.[494] Specifically, clause 273(1)(b) requires the certificate to be endorsed provided the articles are in prescribed form, have been executed in duplicate and all prescribed fees have been paid. The endorsement sets out the day, month, and year of the endorsement and also the corporation number. One copy of the endorsed articles is then filed by the Director, and the other is sent to the corporation or to its representative. However, the Director is prohibited from endorsing a certificate on the articles if the corporation is in default of a filing requirement under the *Corporations Information Act*[495] or has any unpaid fees or penalties outstanding.[496] The Act does not specify the effect of articles of arrangement, because the effect that particular articles of arrangement will have will depend upon the character of the arrangement in question.

§14.260 Although the CBCA arrangement provisions are generally similar to those of the OBCA, there are sufficient differences in wording and substance to merit separate consideration of the CBCA provisions. Subsection 192(3) of the CBCA provides that where it is not practicable for a corporation that is not insolvent to effect a fundamental change in the nature of an arrangement under any other provision of the Act, the corporation may apply to a court for an order approving an arrangement proposed by the corporation.[497] In contrast, subsections 182(2) and (3) of the OBCA contemplates shareholder approval of the arrangement as well as court approval.[498] Moreover, under subsection 182(6) of the OBCA the arrangement procedures are the procedures that *must* be followed where a reorganization or scheme proposed as an arrangement involves an amendment of the articles of a corporation or the taking of any other steps that could be made or taken under any other provisions of the Act.

---

[493] OBCA, s. 273.
[494] OBCA, s. 178(4).
[495] R.S.O. 1990, c. C.39.
[496] OBCA, s. 274(1) (not yet in force).
[497] An applicant must give the Director notice of the application and the Director is entitled to appear and be heard in person or by counsel: CBCA, s. 192(5). As to the meaning of "impracticable" see *Imperial Trust Co. v. Canbra Foods Ltd.*, [1987] A.J. No. 156, 78 A.R. 267 (Q.B.); *Re Ultra Petroleum Corp.*, [2000] Y.J. No. 86, 15 B.L.R. (3d) 133 (S.C.): not necessary to show that other procedures are impossible or that the case is one of necessity or that there are dire circumstances. As to the use of the arrangement procedure to effect a squeeze-out of minority interests, see *Re Sepp's Gourmet Foods Ltd.*, [2002] B.C.J. No. 33, 21 B.L.R. (3d) 291 (S.C.), rev'd [2002] B.C.J. No. 289 (C.A.), leave to appeal to S.C.C. refused [2002] S.C.C.A. No. 144.
[498] But *cf.* CBCA, s. 184(4)(c).

§14.261 Where an application for the approval of an arrangement is made under subsection 192(3) of the CBCA, subsection 192(4) of that Act empowers the court to make any interim or final order it thinks fit, including,

(a) an order determining the notice to be given to any interested person or dispensing with notice to any person other than the Director;

(b) an order appointing counsel, at the expense of the corporation, to represent the interests of the shareholders;

(c) an order requiring a corporation to call, hold and conduct a meeting of holders of securities or options or rights to acquire securities in such manner as the court directs;

(d) an order permitting a shareholder to dissent under section 190; and

(e) an order approving an arrangement proposed by the corporation or as amended in any manner the court may direct.

Although such orders are similar to the types of order contemplated under subsection 182(5) of the OBCA, the CBCA permits such orders to be made only ancillary to an application for an order approving an arrangement. In contrast, subsection 182(5) of the OBCA permits an application for such an order to be made at any time, and furthermore empowers the court to give advice and directions in connection with an arrangement or proposed arrangement.

§14.262 Where the court approves a proposed amalgamation, articles of arrangement in prescribed form must be sent to the Director, together with the documents required by sections 19 and 113 of the Act, if applicable.[499] Section 19 of the Act requires the filing of a notice of the registered office or a notice of change of address. Section 113 requires the filing of a notice of a change of directors. Subsection 192(7) of the CBCA provides that on receipt of the articles of arrangement the Director must issue a certificate of amendment in accordance with section 262 of the Act. Interestingly, subsection (7) includes no reference to the other documents that are required to be filed with the articles of arrangement, which suggests that the Director has no authority to withhold the certificate until those documents are received, though such a result seems usual. An arrangement becomes effective on the date shown in the certificate of amendment issued on the filing of the articles of arrangement.[500]

(v) Arrangement as an Alternative to Amendment

§14.263 In *Re Rideau Carleton Raceway Holdings Ltd.*,[501] Galligan J. considered whether the corporation might elect between proceeding by way of amendment to the articles or by the arrangement procedure, where a proposed fundamental change fit within the definition of both an arrangement and an amalgamation. The Director argued that where a proposal amounted to an arrangement, it was

---

[499] CBCA, s. 192(6).
[500] CBCA, s. 192(8).
[501] *Ibid.*, at 91.

not open to the corporation to proceed the simpler amendment route. Galligan J. rejected this argument, saying:

> [The Director] was of the opinion that in this case, it was in the public interest to proceed by way of an arrangement with its requisite judicial investigation of the changes proposed. But how could it be said that the lawful seeking by the appellant of a right granted by statute can in itself, in the absence of lack of statutory authorization, oppressive conduct, bad faith or the like, amount to "sufficient cause" for the setting aside of the results of that quest. ... We think even though the change might have been sought by way of arrangement that this was nevertheless an amendment authorized by section 180. ... It seems to us that if the change was one that might lawfully have been obtained by resort to one or other of the statutory procedures, the right to set aside a certificate for "sufficient cause" could not give to the Director the power to decide in a given case which route the corporation should have followed.[502]

It can be argued that this decision effectively emasculates the protection afforded to the minority interests under the arrangement provisions. As an alternative, the court could have ruled that the amendment procedure is not available where a proposed amendment falls within the scope of an arrangement. Such an interpretation might be more consistent with the probable intent of the Legislature, which must surely have been to require the additional protection of court supervision in cases where the rights of the shareholders are being compromised. Viewed from this perspective, the effect of the decision of the Divisional Court is to allow the corporation to choose between a simple procedure (amendment) and a more burdensome one (arrangement). It would be unusual for a corporation to select arrangement, given the freedom to make that choice. On the other hand, in most cases where the amendment is so far-reaching that it would also amount to an arrangement, the dissent remedy will be available under section 185 of the OBCA to any dissident shareholder. Moreover, the oppression remedy may also be available. Accordingly, it may be argued in reply that irrespective of whether the amendment or arrangement procedure is followed, the minority shareholders will be adequately protected. Viewed in this alternative light, allowing the corporation to choose between amendment and arrangement confers a degree of flexibility upon the management of the corporation that may be advantageous to all parties concerned on the facts of a given case.

(vi) Arrangements with Creditors — the Companies' Creditors Arrangement Act

§14.264 Trust deeds will usually contain provisions under which an arrangement or compromise or other modification of rights between the corporation and the bond holders may be effected by an extraordinary resolution of the bond holders passed at a meeting called for that purpose. In *British America Nickel Corp. v. M. J. O'Brien*, the Privy Council commented that:

---

[502] [1984] O.J. No. 1362, 28 B.L.R. 89 (Div. Ct.).

To give a power to modify the terms on which debentures in a company are secured is not uncommon in practice. The business interests of the company may render such a power expedient, even in the interests of the class of debenture holders as a whole. The provision is usually made in the form of a power, conferred by the instrument constituting the debenture security, upon the majority of the class of holders. It often enables them to modify, by resolution properly passed, the security itself.[503]

Even so, the provisions of a trust deed giving power to a stated majority of bond holders to bind the minority will be strictly construed.[504] Proper notice must be given of any meeting where such a proposal is to be considered, to permit the bond holders both to decide whether to attend that meeting and to make an informed judgment on the merit of the proposal that is to be considered.[505] Where a majority of bond holders are influenced in their voting by any consideration not pertaining to the question of whether the proposed scheme improves the bond holders' security or chances of payment, the court may set aside any amendment that is approved. It is immaterial that the majority of bond holders are influenced by a desire to deal honourably or fairly with shareholders or other creditors, even where the money of those persons has gone to improve the mortgage security and no collateral consideration is received by the majority to induce them to grant that indulgence.[506] A power to modify the terms on which debentures in a corporation are secured must be exercised to benefit the class of bond holders as whole, rather than individual bond holders.[507]

§14.265 Where the trust deed contains no such provision, the only method of modifying the rights of the parties — short of unanimous agreement — will be by way of a proposal under the *Bankruptcy and Insolvency Act*[508] or by an arrangement under the *Companies' Creditors Arrangement Act* (CCAA).[509] Moreover, a corporation that is seeking a major modification to the rights of the bond holders or other creditors will often invoke the protection of either statute, to prevent the trustee, bond holders or other secured creditors from realizing upon the security granted to them, or where the proposal in question relates to, or otherwise affects, the rights of other secured or unsecured creditors.

§14.266 The CCAA and the *Bankruptcy and Insolvency Act* are two distinct statutes prescribing independent remedies. Neither one is supplementary to the

---

[503] [1927] A.C. 369 at 371, [1927] 1 D.L.R. 1121 (P.C.).
[504] *Mercantile Investments & General Trust Co. v. International Co. of Mexico*, [1893] 1 Ch. 484n at 489 (C.A.), *per* Lindley L.J.; *Diehl v. Carritt*, [1907] O.J. No. 45, 15 O.L.R. 202 at 204, *per* Riddell J.
[505] See *Pacific Coast Coal Mines Ltd. v. Arbuthnot*, [1917] A.C. 607, 36 D.L.R. 564 (P.C.); *Re B.C. Portland Cement Co.*, [1916] B.C.J. No. 13, 22 B.C.R. 443 (C.A.).
[506] *M.J. O'Brien Ltd. v. British America Nickel Corp.*, [1925] O.J. No. 81, 57 O.L.R. 536, aff'd [1927] A.C. 369, [1927] D.L.R. 1121 (P.C.).
[507] *Ibid.*
[508] R.S.C. 1985, c. B-3, as amended.
[509] R.S.C. 1985, c. C-36, as amended. As for reconciliation between the OBCA and the federal CCAA reorganization provisions, see *Re Olympia & York Developments Ltd.*, [1993] O.J. No. 900, 102 D.L.R. (4th) 149 at 159-61 (Gen. Div.), *per* R.A. Blair J.

other. Consequently, there are two different procedures available to a debtor for proposing a compromise or arrangement with its creditors.[510] Broadly speaking, the CCAA allows larger corporations that are in serious financial difficulty to carry on their business under court supervision while preserving the *status quo* rights of creditors and other concerned parties, so that the principals of the corporation and its creditors can work out a plan of arrangement or compromise.[511] The *Bankruptcy and Insolvency Act* proposal regime is slightly different in focus. It allows an insolvent debtor the opportunity to put forward a proposed compromise of debts owing for the approval of its creditors, as an alternative to the liquidation procedure normally employed in bankruptcy proceedings. For the most part, smaller corporations will usually make a proposal under that Act, where it is considered advisable to seek a compromise with the creditors of such a corporation.

§14.267 It has been held that a debtor corporation cannot claim the benefit of the CCAA[512] more than once because this would lead to abuse, and, by extension, it can be argued that the same debtor may not seek protection from its creditors under both the CCAA and the *Bankruptcy and Insolvency Act*, though it is possible to transfer from the *Bankruptcy and Insolvency Act* regime to the CCAA regime.

§14.268 The first edition of this text contained a fairly detailed discussion of the CCAA as the law stood at that time. There has been a great deal of new case law since, as well as some amendment of the legislation. The changes that have taken place since the publication of the first edition have resulted in a body of law that is so complex that it can no longer be conveniently discussed within a general work on the law of business corporations. However, by way of broad overview, there are two basic aspects to the CCAA. First, the CCAA grants the court the authority to sanction an alteration of the rights of the creditors of a debtor without the consent of some of them, provided a required level of approval to the proposed change is obtained from the majority of them.[513] It has been said that the right of the majority creditors of a class to bind the minority is an extraordinary one, and that it reflects the willingness of Parliament to deprive some creditors of their contractual rights in the interest of the survival of the economic unit composed of the ailing corporation and its creditors. Fairness is preserved by the requirement for court sanction, but fairness must be understood within the spirit of the statute.[514]

§14.269 The second aspect of the CCAA is the stay procedure that it affords to corporations to which the Act applies. Essentially, the CCAA allows certain

---

[510] *Parisian Cleaners & Laundry Ltd. v. Blondin*, [1939] 4 D.L.R. 791, 66 Que. K.B. 456 (C.A.).
[511] *Siscoe & Savoie v. Royal Bank*, [1994] N.B.J. No. 577, 29 C.B.R. (3d) 1 at 8 (C.A.), *per* Turnbull J.A., leave to appeal to S.C.C. refused [1995] S.C.C.A. No. 62.
[512] *Re Norseman Products Ltd.*, [1949] O.J. No. 346, [1950] O.W.N. 81 (H.C.J.), but see *Re Royal Heaters Ltd.* (1947), 30 C.B.R. 199 (Que. S.C.).
[513] *Re Keddy Motor Inns*, [1992] N.S.J. No. 98, 6 B.L.R. (2d) 116 at 118 (C.A.), *per* Freeman J.A.
[514] *Ibid.*, at 119.

corporations to apply for a stay under the Act[515] to bring forward a compromise or arrangement (a "plan of arrangement") for the approval of its creditors. Although there is no obligation on the court to grant a stay to the debtor corporation, as a matter of practice, the granting of such stays (at least on first application) has become a matter of course.

§14.270 In the past, the scope of stay orders has been a matter of considerable controversy, and it is likely that this will remain so in the future. If it eventually comes into force, Bill C-55 (which amends both the *Bankruptcy and Insolvency Act* and *CCAA*) will confer a number of new powers on a CCAA court (particularly with respect to the provision of interim financing, to fund corporate operations during the stay period) that may well make the overall approach of the legislation even more controversial.

§14.271 Generally, the CCAA stay is available to any company incorporated in Canada, with assets or business activities in Canada, that is not a bank, a railway company, a telegraph company, an insurance company, a trust company or a loan company. The right to seek protection under the Act applies despite any provision to the contrary in a loan or security agreement — though it would not appear to be improper for such an agreement to provide that the seeking of protection under the Act constitutes a breach of its terms.[516] The term "creditor" is broadly defined under the CCAA, and it includes secured and unsecured creditors, including those who have contingent claims or claims for damages.

§14.272 The fundamental purpose of the CCAA is to allow a compromise of debts and other claims as embodied in a plan of arrangement, without obtaining the unanimous consent of all affected parties. It is, therefore, not necessary for all creditors in a class to approve of a proposed plan.[517] However, any plan of arrangement brought forward by a corporation to which the Act applies requires the approval of a majority of creditors of all classes[518] and court approval under section 6 of the Act:

> 6. Where a majority in number representing two-thirds in value of the creditors, or class of creditors, as the case may be, present and voting either in person or by proxy at the meeting or meetings thereof respectively held pursuant to sections 4 and 5, or either of those sections, agree to any compromise or arrangement either as proposed or as altered or modified at the meeting or meetings, the compromise or arrangement may be sanctioned by the court, and if so sanctioned is binding,
>
> > (a) on all creditors or the class of creditors, as the case may be, and on any trustee, for any such class of creditors, whether secured or unsecured, as the case may be, and on the company; and

---

[515] CCAA, ss. 3 and 11.
[516] Such a provision may be useful in settling whether floating charges have crystallized.
[517] *Re Olympia & York Developments Ltd.*, [1993] O.J. No. 545, 12 O.R. (3d) 500 (Gen. Div.).
[518] See, generally, *Re Ursel Investments Ltd.*, [1990] S.J. No. 228, 2 C.B.R. (3d) 260 (Q.B.). The required degree of creditor approval was reduced in 1997 from three-quarters approval to two-thirds approval.

(b) in the case of a company that has made an authorized assignment or against which a bankruptcy order has been made under the *Bankruptcy and Insolvency Act* or is in the course of being wound up under the *Winding-up and Restructuring Act,* on the trustee in bankruptcy or liquidator and contributories of the company.[519]

(vii) Reorganization

§14.273 As discussed briefly above, both the OBCA and the CBCA contain provisions permitting the reorganization of a corporation. Subsection 186(1) of the OBCA provides that the term "reorganization" means:

> ... a court order made under section 248, an order made under the *Bankruptcy and Insolvency Act* (Canada) or an order made under the *Companies' Creditors Arrangement Act* (Canada) approving a proposal.[520]

Where a corporation is subject to a reorganization, its articles may be amended by the order to effect any change that might lawfully be made by an amendment under section 168.[521] The court making the order may also:

(a) authorize the issue of debt obligations of the corporation, whether or not convertible into shares of any class or having attached any rights or options to acquire shares of any class, and fix the terms thereof; and

(b) appoint directors in place of or in addition to all or any of the directors then in office.[522]

After reorganization has been ordered, articles of reorganization in prescribed form must be sent to the Director.[523] Upon receipt of articles of reorganization, the Director is required to endorse those articles with a certificate under section 273, which constitutes the certificate of amendment and the articles are amended accordingly.[524] A shareholder is not entitled to dissent under section 185 where an amendment to the articles is effected under the reorganization provisions.[525]

§14.274 Section 191 of the CBCA is generally similar, although it includes within the scope of the term "reorganization" a court order made under section 241 (*i.e.*, the oppression remedy). Since such a remedy may be granted in

---

[519] See, for instance, *Citibank Canada v. Chase Manhattan Bank of Canada*, [1991] O.J. No. 944, 4 B.L.R. (2d) 147 (Gen. Div.).
[520] This definition of "reorganization" is to be distinguished from "a reorganization of the shares of any class or series of the corporation or of the stated capital of any such class or series", which is an arrangement within the meaning of s. 182(1)(*a*) of the OBCA, and therefore subject to the provisions of that Act pertaining to arrangements. There is no equivalent provision to s. 182(1)(*a*) in the CBCA.
[521] OBCA s. 186(2).
[522] OBCA, s. 186(3).
[523] OBCA, s. 186(4). This section actually reads "After a reorganization has been made" but that wording is not strictly correct since by virtue of s. 273(3), the reorganization is not effective (and therefore is not made) until the certificate of amendment is endorsed upon the articles of reorganization.
[524] OBCA, s. 186(5), but note s. 274.
[525] OBCA, s. 186(6).

respect of a solvent corporation, under the CBCA, reorganizations are not necessarily tied to insolvency. In either case, however, the effect of a reorganization can be to vary unilaterally the terms of a subsisting contract. It is worth observing that the corporate laws of other jurisdictions (in particular the U.K.) gives rise to an even greater risk of such unilateral change.[526]

§14.275 Jurisdiction over the reorganization of the business and affairs of a corporation is within the competence of the jurisdiction under which the corporation is incorporated or continued. In *Canada Southern Railway Co. v. Gebhard*,[527] it was stated:

> ... every person who deals with a foreign corporation impliedly subjects himself to the laws of the foreign government, affecting the powers and obligations of the corporation with which he voluntarily contracts, as the known and established policy of that government authorizes. To all intents and purposes he submits his contract with the corporation to such a policy of the foreign government, and whatever is done by that government in furtherance of that policy which binds those in like situation with himself, who are subjects of the government, in respect to the operation in effect of their contracts with the corporation will necessarily bind him. He is conclusively presumed to have contracted with a view to such laws of that government, because the corporation must of necessity be controlled by them, and it has no power to contract with a view to any other laws with which they are not in entire harmony. It follows, therefore, that anything done at the legal home of the corporation, under the authority of such laws, which discharges it from liability there, discharges it everywhere.

This rule is described in the United States as the internal affairs doctrine, and it is one to which we will return in Chapter 15. In one California case, it was summarized in the following brief terms:[528]

> It is true that the courts in California cannot control the internal affairs of any foreign corporation. Such matters are to be conducted in pursuance of and in compliance with the provisions of the charter of the foreign corporation, and the laws of the country where it was created ...

The home jurisdiction over internal affairs does not depend on the proper law of the contracts relating to the business of the corporation.[529] The reorganization provisions of the OBCA and CBCA differ in scope.

---

[526] See *Re Cavell Insurance Co.*, [2006] O.J. No. 1998 (C.A.).
[527] 109 U.S. 527 at 537-38 (1883).
[528] *Western Air Lines, Inc. v. Sobieski*, 191 Cal. App. 2d 399 at 409 (Calif. C.A. 1961). An exception applies with respect to securities laws, because wherever there is an established capital market, a substantial portion of that marketplace will involve transactions relating to securities issued by foreign corporations. Hence a strict application of the internal affairs doctrine would not be practical. *Friese v. Superior Court of San Diego County*, 134 Cal. App. 4th 693, 36 Cal. Rptr. 3d 558 (Calif. C.A. 1st Div. 2005): "When a corporation sells or encumbers its property, incurs debts or gives securities, it does business, and a statute regulating such transactions does not regulate the internal affairs of the corporation", quoting from *Williams v. Gaylord*, 186 U.S. 157 at 165 (1902).
[529] *Re Cavell Insurance Co.*, [2006] O.J. No. 1998, 269 D.L.R. (4th) 679 (C.A.).

§14.276 Reference should also be made in the case of a reorganization under either the OBCA or the CBCA to section 20 of the CCAA, which provides:

> 20. The provisions of this Act may be applied together with the provisions of any Act of Parliament or of the legislature of any province, that authorizes or makes provision for the sanction of compromises or arrangements between a company and its shareholders or any class of them.

K. CONCLUSION

§14.277 In this chapter, we have surveyed the various rules of corporate and securities law governing the fundamental change process. As we have seen, one critical area of concern with respect to fundamental changes is to provide shareholders protection against the risk that the basis on which they agreed to participate in the corporation will be altered in some significant respect, without their consent. While the regime put into place does not prevent such changes from occurring it is intended to ensure that such changes enjoy broad-based support, and to provide prejudicially affected dissident shareholders with a right of exit.

§14.278 A second general thrust in the law governing fundamental changes is to mitigate against the risk of improper self-dealing. This risk arises from the potential conflict of interest between the shareholders as members of the corporation and those who enjoy effective control over the corporation. Since self-dealing is a complex problem the regime put into place allows considerable flexibility, permitting such transactions to proceed provided that adequate safeguards exist to ensure that they are the product of fair dealing and reflect a fair price. In this examination, we have seen how corporate law incorporates minority protection devices to protect against the worst excesses of majority rule. However, necessary as such mechanisms may be, it is an open question whether the package in place represents the most efficient and coherent approach that might be adopted.

§14.279 The fundamental change provisions of the OBCA and CBCA allow a corporation to grow and evolve over the course of its lifetime. They recognize that in a dynamic economy it may be necessary to reconfigure the corporation repeatedly, to exploit emerging opportunities, and to adjust to changes in the corporation's operating environment. Unfortunately, in the real world, many corporations will fail to adapt properly to the evolving world around them. Those that so fail, are likely to wither. In the next chapter, we will discuss the resulting final stages in corporate life: the process of winding up the corporation and its eventual dissolution.

Chapter 15

WINDING-UP & DISSOLUTION

A. INTRODUCTION

§15.1 The winding-up of a corporation is the process by which the ongoing operations of a corporation are brought to an end, its assets are realized, its liabilities discharged, the persons liable to contribute to any shortfall are identified and collected from and in connection therewith all necessary accountings are made, and disputes concerning it are settled or otherwise resolved. The winding-up process is sometimes called "liquidation",[1] reflecting the fact that the process normally results in the conversion of all assets of the corporation into money, and hence every winding-up is conducted by a corporate operative known as the liquidator. The basic duties of the liquidator are to get in and realize the property of the corporation, to pay its debts and distribute any amount remaining after their payment among its shareholders.

§15.2 In Canada, the United States and the United Kingdom, the law relating to insolvency is essentially statute law. In the United Kingdom, jurisdiction over both incorporation and liquidation lies at the national level of government. In England, therefore, there has tended to be a full integration of corporate and insolvency law. Under English law, insolvent companies have historically been dealt with under the corporate winding-up process. The winding-up of an insolvent company may be commenced either by order of the court or by resolution of the shareholders. In either case, one or more liquidators are appointed to take control of the company's assets. Their duty is to realize the assets, whether on a going concern or a break-up basis. They have investigative powers and may pursue a wide variety of claims, including claims for misfeasance and to set aside prior colourable transactions, against officers and others. They have the further duty to distribute the proceeds of realization among the creditors of the company. Subject to the rights of secured creditors and of the very limited number of classes that are given some statutory priority, the fundamental principle is that the distribution among creditors is on a ratable (sometimes called "*pari passu*" basis). The *Insolvency Rules* lay down procedures for determining the validity and amount of claims by creditors, which in disputed cases will involve determination by the court, although in appropriate cases the court will allow claims to be determined through conventional litigation.[2] The entire process of liquidation and dissolution is an integrated one.

---

[1] The terms "winding-up" and "liquidation" are synonymous.
[2] *Re T&N Ltd*, [2004] All ER (D) 283 at para. 74 (Oct.) (Ch.), per Richards J.

§15.3 In contrast, in Canada, the liquidation of an insolvent corporation is generally a procedure carried out under the *Bankruptcy and Insolvency Act* ("BIA")[3] or (more controversially) the *Companies' Creditors Arrangement Act* ("CCAA").[4] In the United States and Canada, jurisdiction over bankruptcy is a matter of federal jurisdiction. In contrast, most companies are incorporated at the state or provincial level. The degree of integration of corporate and insolvent law is correspondingly limited. Although the procedure for dealing with insolvent companies is fundamentally the same in all three countries, the limited federal jurisdiction over corporate law in North America itself qualifies the extent to which integration is possible. The claims against an insolvent OBCA or CBCA corporation are dealt with in accordance with the BIA. However, the corporate law consequences of the corporation's liquidation must be left for resolution under the OBCA or CBCA, as the case may be. More than occasionally, the process is abandoned when only partly complete.

§15.4 The OBCA and CBCA do not contain a definition of "insolvent". However, since the BIA governs corporations under both of these Acts where such a corporation is "insolvent" within the meaning of the BIA, it is reasonable to conclude that it is the BIA definition of insolvent which governs when the internal winding-up procedures of the OBCA and CBCA cease to apply. Section 2 of the BIA defines the term "insolvent person" to mean

> ... a person who is not bankrupt and who resides, carries on business or has property in Canada, whose liabilities to creditors provable as claims under this Act amount to one thousand dollars, and
>
> (*a*) who is for any reason unable to meet his obligations as they generally become due,
>
> (*b*) who has ceased paying his current obligations in the ordinary course of business as they generally become due, or
>
> (*c*) the aggregate of whose property is not, at a fair valuation, sufficient, or, if disposed of at a fairly conducted sale under legal process, would not be sufficient to enable payment of all his obligations, due and accruing due...

B. GENERAL PRINCIPLES

§15.5 There are several different procedures that may be followed in the liquidation of a corporation. The Ontario *Business Corporations Act*[5] ("OBCA") and the *Canada Business Corporations Act*[6] ("CBCA") allow the shareholders to institute and control the process of liquidation and also provide for liquidation under the control and supervision of the court. There are effectively three methods of liquidation contemplated under both the OBCA and the CBCA. A court liquidation may be instituted by the corporation itself (in which case it has a voluntary character) or by the court on the application of a shareholder, creditor

---

[3] R.S.C. 1985, c. B-3, as amended.
[4] R.S.C. 1985, c. C-36, as amended.
[5] R.S.O. 1990, c. B.16, as amended.
[6] R.S.C. 1985, c. C-44, as amended.

or other person authorized under the legislation (in which case the liquidation is involuntary or compulsory in nature). A liquidation may also begin as a voluntary, shareholder-driven proceeding, but may then be continued under court supervision. But liquidation may also take place completely outside the framework of the OBCA and the CBCA. Where a corporation is insolvent, its business may be liquidated under the provisions of the *Bankruptcy and Insolvency Act*, either by way of assignment into bankruptcy (voluntary) or on petition by a creditor (involuntary). Finally, a corporation may be liquidated informally under contractual arrangement, usually by way of the private appointment of a receiver and manager. Liquidation by receiver is almost always involuntary, but in rare cases may take place on consent. In each of these cases the purpose of the winding-up procedure concerned is essentially the same: it is to provide an expeditious method of resolving any matters or disputes in which the corporation is involved, collecting and liquidating its property and distributing the proceedings derived through that liquidation among the persons entitled thereto.[7] In this chapter, we shall examine only those methods of liquidation that are provided for in the OBCA and CBCA.

§15.6 In addition to discussing the subject of liquidation, this chapter also examines the related procedure of corporate dissolution. After the business and affairs of a corporation are wound up, the corporation may be dissolved. Analogies are generally a poor analytical device, but in certain respects, the dissolution of a corporation may be equated with the death of the corporation.[8] It is the process by which the corporation ceases to exist as a legal entity.

§15.7 The reasons why corporations die differ, but there is no question that the most frequent cause of corporate death is commercial failure. Recent Statistics Canada data show that over two-thirds of micro-sized business firms (*i.e.*, those that have less than five employees) and almost half of small-sized firms (*i.e.*, those that have five to 99 employees) fail within five years of start-up. Nearly 80 per cent of all new firms are gone within 10 years. The most frequently cited cause for these failures is lack of managerial skill. Almost half of the firms in Canada that go bankrupt do so primarily because of their own deficiencies rather than externally generated problems. They do not develop the basic internal strength necessary to survive.

---

[7] *Re J. McCarthy & Sons Co. of Prescott Ltd.*, [1916] O.J. No. 4, 38 O.L.R. 3 at 9 (C.A.); *Re Associated Investors of Canada Ltd.*, [1996] A.J. No. 1062, 29 B.L.R. (2d) 78 at 98 (Q.B.), *per* Cooke J.

[8] Corporations are sometimes described as being perpetual (indeed, one basic attribute ascribed to corporate bodies generally is that they possess perpetual succession and are therefore potentially immortal), but in fact few attain great age. There are probably no more than a dozen business companies in the world that are more than 350 years old. Only a handful of all outstanding corporate charters under the CBCA and the OBCA pertain to corporations more than 100 years old. Quite often corporations are created and pass out of existence within a few months. Thus the typical life expectancy of a corporation (although theoretically perpetual) is usually no greater than that of a human being and may well be considerably less.

§15.8 Similar problems also exist in other countries. In Britain, more than two-thirds of all small businesses fail in the first five years of operation. A basic cause is often the lack of proper financial control. In one recent U.K. study of commercial insolvency (using a sample of 574 companies with assets of more than £10,000 that went into administration during the first six months of 2004), it was found that 74 per cent were at least 12 months late in filing their annual accounts with Companies House — a statutory requirement under British company law. The inability to generate timely financial reports is a clear indication of a lack of financial control and supervision within the corporation.

§15.9 According to a study conducted by the Wharton School of Business, business failure may be generally attributed to inadequate research and development (including with respect to the market for products or services offered); uncontrolled costs; weak marketing strategies; bad timing and competitor activities. A very large percentage of new businesses do not even complete their first year of operation. Studies of businesses that fail during the first year indicate that more than 40 per cent of them fail due to incompetence: a lack of physical, moral or intellectual fitness required to run the business successfully. A further 15 per cent fail because the entrepreneur who sets up the business has little, if any, experience in the product or service offered, while approximately the same percentage fail due to lack of planning or managerial skills — that is little planning or experience of managing a company or employees before going into business.

§15.10 Although the term "lack of management skill" is so broad as to lack any immediate meaning, people who have extensive experience in dealing with failed businesses frequently note a number of common patterns in the way those businesses were conducted. Few businesses fail due to a single cause. The usual experience is for a business to fail because it has repeatedly done the wrong thing. Critical areas of concern include the following:

- poor strategic planning;
- lack of attention to business development, and to the changing environment of the organization;
- poor marketing, including lack of proper market identification or product definition or differentiation;
- poor business planning, including absence of strategic planning, inability to anticipate market trends, *etc.*;
- poor regulatory relations, including franchise relationships;
- poor financial planning and control, including inadequacy of capital, poor tax planning (*e.g.*, lack of understanding of the tax implications of transactions), illiquidity resulting from over-investment in fixed assets or even inventory, lack of control over expenditure, lack of budget supervision;
- poor management of employee relations, including taking the steps necessary to reduce the risk of employee fraud.

Each of these aspects of business failure involves a failure on the part of leadership to position the organization properly, so that vulnerability to risk is reduced and so that the organization is in a position to take advantage of opportunities that present themselves.

§15.11 Although remarkably few businesses survive for even five years, even profitable businesses may endure for only a short period of time. Where a corporation is created for a specified purpose, it will often be terminated once that purpose has been accomplished. In the case of small corporations, quite often the principals in the corporation will sell off the assets of the business and retire. The corporation is then left as an empty shell, which sooner or later lapses into non-existence. In other cases, differences among the principals make the continued operation of a corporation unworkable. In some cases, the disappearance of a corporation may be attributed to a general change in the economic climate of society. For instance, advances in technology and changes in public taste or interest cause entire industries to disappear, together with the corporations that were active in those industries. Even the businesses that do not fail financially may be discontinued because their assets can be more profitably employed by their shareholders. Finally, corporations may be discontinued because of the failure of their owners and management to comply with some regulatory requirement.

(i) Internal Affairs Doctrine

§15.12 In legal terms, corporations die when they are dissolved, rather than when the business that they operate fails, or when they cease to conduct an ongoing business. As noted in Chapters 1 and 4, the creation of a corporation is a sovereign act. The pervasive sovereign authority of the jurisdiction of incorporation over the internal affairs of a corporation was discussed by the United States Supreme Court in *CTS Corp. v. Dynamics Corp. of America*.[9] In that case, it was held that it is "an accepted part of the business landscape in this country for States to create corporations, to prescribe their powers, and to define the rights that are acquired by purchasing their shares". The court also recognized that: "A State has an interest in promoting stable relationships among parties involved in the corporations it charters, as well as in ensuring that investors in such corporations have an effective voice in corporate affairs."[10] The internal affairs doctrine is a long-standing choice of law principle which recognizes that only one state should have the authority to regulate a corporation's internal affairs — the state of incorporation. These principles would seem to be equally applicable in any federal country, in which different states have the authority to create corporations that may ultimately carry on business across the entire nation. The internal affairs doctrine derives from the premise that, in order to prevent corporations from being subjected to inconsistent legal standards, the authority to regulate a corporation's internal affairs should not rest with

---

[9] 481 U.S. 69 at 92 (1987).
[10] *Ibid.*

multiple jurisdictions.[11] It is now well established that only the law of the state of incorporation governs and determines issues relating to a corporation's internal affairs. By providing certainty and predictability, the internal affairs doctrine protects the justified expectations of the parties with interests in the corporation.[12] As will become repeatedly clear in this chapter, the reasoning underlying the internal affairs doctrine has considerable relevance with respect not only to the actual dissolution of corporations, but also with respect to the liquidation of their assets and the reorganization of their affairs.

§15.13 Except where a corporation has been continued under the laws of some other jurisdiction, the exclusive jurisdiction of the jurisdiction of incorporation is an extension of this sovereign control. The dissolution of a corporation is also a sovereign act which can only be carried out by the jurisdiction under which the corporation was created or continued.[13] In *Lazard Bros. & Co. v. Midland Bank Ltd.*, Lord Wright stated with respect to a Russian bank dissolved by decree of the Soviet government:

> ... the creation depends on the act of the foreign state which created them, the annulment of the act of creation by the same power will involve the dissolution and non-existence of the corporation in the eyes of English law. The will of the sovereign authority which created it can also destroy it. English law will recognise the one, as the other, fact. The Industrial Bank was a corporation established by Act of the Tsar; but the governing authority in Russia, as recognised in the English courts, is now and has been since October, 1917, the Soviet state. Soviet law is accordingly the governing law from the same date in virtue of the recognition *de facto* in 1921 and *de jure* in 1924 by this country of the Soviet state as the sovereign power in

---

[11] *Edgar v. MITE Corp.*, 457 U.S. 624 at 645 (1982).
[12] *Vantagepoint Venture Partners 1996 v. Examen, Inc.*, 871 A.2d 1108 (Del. S.C. 2005).
[13] *McCormack v. Carman*, [1919] O.J. No. 560, 17 O.W.N. 241 (C.A.). *Banque Internationale de Commerce de Petrograd v. Goukassow*, [1923] 2 K.B. 682 at 691 (C.A.), *per* Scrutton L.J.:

> ... though the *lex loci contractus* allows a corporation to own land, if the constitution of the corporation forbids it to own land, it cannot do so in spite of the law of the country where the contract was made. But it seems to me that the question here is not as to incidents of contract, or capacity to contract, but existence as a person. A nonexistent person cannot sue. In the case of a natural person, the English courts would decline to entertain an action in his name, and would not be interested in the fact, if it were so, that a foreign country allowed an action in the dead man's name for a year after his death. This would be *lex fori*. So in the case of artificial persons, the existence of such a person depends on the law of the country under whose law it is incorporated, recognised in other countries by international comity, though its incorporation is not in accordance with their law. If the artificial person is destroyed in its country of origin, the country whose law creates it as a person, it appears to me it is destroyed everywhere as a person. I cannot conceive a company, whose existence and attributes arise solely from the law of Russia, continuing to exist when the law of Russia says it is dissolved. With what body and attributes does it survive, and what law constitutes it? It does not comply with the requisites of English companies and is dissolved by the law of Russia. I can understand the French Courts saying: 'This company was validly created by the law of Russia, and we know of and recognize no law which has destroyed it; therefore it still exists.' But the English courts do know and recognise a law which has destroyed it, and, in my opinion, must apply their own *lex fori* to determine what person can or cannot sue in their Courts. In my opinion, therefore, English courts are bound to treat this plaintiff bank as dissolved and incapable of suit in English courts.

Russia. The effect of such recognition is retroactive and dates back to the original establishment of Soviet rule which was in the 1917 October Revolution ...[14]

The shareholders, creditors or members of the corporation have no power among themselves to dissolve the corporation, except with the consent of the sovereign or under the authority of the legislation under which the corporation operates. They may, of course, start the process of dissolution into motion. However, they may complete the dissolution of the corporation only in accordance with the laws governing the process. While the inactivity, insolvency, bankruptcy and the cessation of business of a corporation, and even its winding-up, may afford grounds for its liquidation and dissolution, they do not in themselves result in the dissolution of the corporation so as to put an end to its existence.[15] Subject to any statute, the dissolution of the corporation requires some declaration on the part of the executive branch of government, or the order of a competent court.[16] Moreover, the creation of a corporation vests the rights incident to incorporation in its members and the right of proceeding against the corporation itself in its creditors. Since the executive may not interfere with vested rights except under the authority of law, the sovereign has no inherent power to divest the members and creditors of the corporation of their rights under the corporate charter by fiat alone, but may bring this result about only as provided by law. In Canada, the authority to dissolve a corporation has always involved either some judgment of a court of competent jurisdiction or a lawful administrative order to that effect.[17] This continues to be the approach under both the OBCA and the CBCA.

(ii) The Process of Liquidation and Dissolution

§15.14 In recognition of the fact that there are so many widely different reasons for bringing a corporate existence to an end, the law specifies different methods by which a corporation may be liquidated and dissolved. The availability of each of these methods is determined by whether the initiation of the process is voluntary or involuntary, whether the corporation concerned is solvent or insolvent, whether the corporation has issued shares or not, and whether the corporation has property, liabilities or both. Although there is a certain degree of similarity between the OBCA and the CBCA provisions, there are numerous and important differences in the wording of the respective provisions of each Act, and for this reason it is necessary to consider the approaches taken in each of the two acts separately. We shall begin our review of the law respecting liquidation and dissolution with a consideration of the OBCA provisions.

---

[14] [1933] A.C. 289 at 297 (H.L.). See also *Banque Internationale de Commerce de Petrograd v. Goukassow*, [1923] 2 K.B. 682 at 691 (C.A.), *per* Scrutton L.J.
[15] See, generally, *Hovey v. Whiting*, [1887] S.C.J. No. 21, 14 S.C.R. 515 at 533; *Davey v. Gibson*, [1930] O.J. No. 122, 65 O.L.R. 379 (C.A.); *Kent v. Communauté des Soeurs de Charité de la Providence*, [1903] A.C. 220 (P.C.).
[16] See, generally, *Hardy Lumber Co. v. Pickerel River Improvement Co.*, [1898] 29 S.C.R. 211.
[17] *Mayor of Colchester v. Brooke* (1846), 7 Q.B. 339, 15 L.J.Q.B. 173.

C. VOLUNTARY WIND-UP PROCEDURES UNDER THE OBCA

§15.15 Although a corporation is a separate legal person from its shareholders, it is axiomatic that the purpose of a corporation is to serve the interests of its shareholders. It is they, or their predecessors, who brought the corporation into existence. Similarly, they are entitled at any time to terminate the corporation. Thus subsection 193(1) of the OBCA provides that the shareholders of a corporation may "require the corporation to be wound up voluntarily" by a special resolution to that effect. The requirement for a special resolution is consistent with the general approach of the OBCA and CBCA concerning fundamental changes, but it is inconsistent with that other general principle of corporate law of majority rule.

§15.16 A corporation is wound up where its assets are realized and the proceeds derived from that realization are distributed among the creditors and the shareholders of the corporation in accordance with their respective entitlements.[18] The corporation does not cease to exist by reason only of the wind-up, but in most cases an application will be made to dissolve the corporation once the wind-up is complete. Moreover, the powers of the corporation (and its directors and shareholders) are curtailed once the wind-up commences, so that although the corporation does not lose its status by reason of the commencement of winding-up proceedings, the capacities and powers of the corporation are limited so that they may be exercised only to the extent that those powers and capacities are necessary for the purpose of the winding-up.[19]

§15.17 In order to commence a voluntary liquidation and dissolution of a corporation, it is necessary to comply with the procedures set out in the OBCA or the CBCA, as applicable.[20] Except where a corporation has only a few shareholders, the normal procedure in a voluntary winding-up is to call a special meeting of the members to consider a special resolution[21] to wind up the corporation. Generally, the same rules apply to any such meeting as would apply to any special meeting of the corporation. In particular, specific notice of the proposed resolution must be incorporated into the notice of the meeting given to the shareholders,[22] and there must, of course, be a sufficient number of shares and shareholders represented at the meeting to satisfy the requirements of a quorum (this last requirement can be burdensome where the shareholders remaining in the corporation have little remaining interest in the corporation). The resolution

---

[18] *Re Irma Co-operative Co.* (1924), 5 C.B.R. 367 at 372 (Alta. T.D.), *per* Tweedie J.
[19] *Re Canadian Cereal & Flour Mills Co.*, [1921] O.J. No. 49, 21 C.B.R. 158 at 160 (S.C. in Bank.), *per* Orde J.
[20] *Duncan & Gray Ltd. (Liquidator of) v. Silver Spring Brewery*, [1925] B.C.J. No. 134, [1925] 3 W.W.R. 675 (S.C.).
[21] OBCA, s. 193(1).
[22] See, generally, *Re Essex Centre Manufacturing Co.*, [1890] O.J. No. 1, 19 O.A.R. 125 at 128-29 (C.A.), *per* Osler J.A.

itself must be approved (with or without amendment) by two-thirds of the votes cast at the meeting.

§15.18 As might be imagined, there are several unique aspects of a meeting called to consider the voluntary wind-up of a corporation. A decision to liquidate a corporation is not purely a private matter, since it may affect the rights of outsiders to the corporation. Accordingly, within 10 days of the approval by the shareholders of a resolution to wind up a corporation, it must file with the Director a notice of the intended winding-up, which must be made in the prescribed form. Within 20 days of the approval of the resolution, the corporation must publish that notice in *The Ontario Gazette*. Although a decision to dissolve the corporation will normally be binding on any minority group of shareholders who oppose the motion, where the majority shareholders resolve to liquidate the corporation, the minority may seek to have an investigation of the corporation under Part XIII of the OBCA or Part XIX of the CBCA.[23]

§15.19 Where the shareholders approve a motion to wind up a corporation, they must also appoint one or more persons to be the liquidators of the estate and effects of the corporation. It is the liquidator who has the primary responsibility for winding up the business and affairs of the corporation and distributing its property. As the title of the office suggests, the primary role of the liquidator is to convert the assets of the corporation to cash, to pay off the debts of the corporation, and to distribute the residual property to the shareholders and other persons entitled to share in it.

§15.20 Although the appointment of a liquidator is mandatory under the OBCA, if for some reason the shareholders fail to appoint a liquidator, section 220 of the Act provides that on the application of a shareholder, the court may appoint one or more persons as a liquidator. Until such time as the court makes such an appointment, the estate and effects of the corporation are under the control of the court. Thus it would appear that the resolution to liquidate is valid and binding and the absence of a designated liquidator can be cured by simple motion to the court. Except in a very unusual case, there would seem to be no advantage in delaying the appointment of a liquidator once the wind-up commences. Section 197 of the OBCA provides that a voluntary winding-up commences at the time of the passing of the resolution requiring the winding-up or at such later time as may be specified in that resolution. Section 198 of the Act then provides that from the commencing of the winding-up the corporation must cease to carry on its undertaking, and section 199 imposes a stay on proceedings against the corporation after such commencement. It would appear that these provisions continue to apply irrespective of whether a liquidator is appointed or not.

§15.21 Only a limited analogy can be drawn between the position of a liquidator in a winding-up of a corporation and the position of a trustee in bankruptcy in a

---

[23] *Mexican Light & Power Co. v. Shareholders of Mexican Light & Power Co.*, [1989] O.J. No. 2312, 46 B.L.R. 14 (H.C.J.).

bankruptcy proceeding. In a bankruptcy, the property of the debtor vests in the trustee by operation of law. The trustee has both title as well as control over that property, and ownership is completely divested from the bankrupt. Nothing of this kind takes place in a winding-up. Instead, the corporation retains ownership and control over its property, although the control over the management and disposal of its assets are taken from the directors and placed in the hands of the liquidator.[24] The institution of the winding-up process for the purpose of removing the board does not discharge the members of the board from their existing liability as directors, in respect of acts and omissions prior to the appointment of the liquidator.[25] The liquidator acts as a receiver and manager of the corporation (as well as of its assets) for the purpose of closing up the corporation's business, realizing its assets and making a legal distribution of those assets among the creditors and shareholders of the corporation.[26] The similarity between bankruptcy and winding-up proceedings is that the purpose of both is to get all of the estate of the corporation settled, both the claims for and against the estate, in the simplest and least expensive way, and to distribute the assets in the quickest possible way without incurring needless delay and expense by litigation in other courts.[27]

§15.22 A liquidator appointed by the shareholders under subsection 193(2) of the OBCA is seen to act as the agent of the shareholders — that is, the shareholders generally, rather than any individual shareholder. The shareholders may remove the liquidator by an ordinary resolution passed at a meeting called for that purpose.[28] In general, where the shareholders vote to remove a liquidator, they must appoint a replacement. However, section 194 of the Act provides that the shareholders of the corporation may delegate to a committee of inspectors the power of appointing the liquidator and filling vacancies in appointments.

§15.23 Aside from the power to appoint a replacement liquidator and the power to approve arrangements with creditors, the precise role of the inspectors is vague. In practice, they tend to exercise much the same function as the inspectors in a bankruptcy. Important matters will invariably be referred to the inspectors by the liquidator for their opinion. However, the OBCA itself is very vague as to the nature of their responsibilities.[29] In England, the inspectors of a company have the following powers by statute:

- to fix the remuneration of the liquidator;
- to sanction continuance of the powers of the directors;

---

[24] *Re Farrow's Bank Ltd.*, [1921] 2 Ch. 164 (C.A.), *per* Lord Sterndale M.R.
[25] For a recent case involving a claim by a liquidator against the former board of a company, see: *Liquidator of Iroquois Falls Community Credit Union Ltd. v. Co-Operators General Insurance Co.*, [2006] O.J. No. 3999, 151 A.C.W.S. (3d) 814 (S.C.J.).
[26] *Partington v. Cushing* (1906), 1 E.L.R. 493, 3 N.B. Eq. Rep. 322 (S.C.).
[27] See, generally, *Re Toronto Wood & Shingle Co.* (1894), 30 C.L.T. 353 at 356 (H.C.), *per* the Master in Ordinary.
[28] OBCA, s. 196.
[29] Under subsection 227(2), the inspectors may approve the depository into which money of the corporation is paid.

- to sanction payments to creditors and the compromise of claims;
- to sanction a reconstruction of the company;
- to determine what books and records should be kept by the company, and to approve the disposal of books and records of the corporation;
- to give instructions concerning the interim investment of funds.

At least some of these powers are inconsistent with the Ontario legislation. For instance, subsection 193(2) of the Act empowers the shareholders of a corporation to fix the remuneration of the liquidator, along with the costs, charges and expenses of the winding-up,[30] and therefore it would seem to follow that the inspectors have no control over such remuneration or expenses (although, presumably, the shareholders may vote to delegate this responsibility to the inspectors).[31] Under section 202 of the OBCA, the inspectors may consent to the compromise of a claim against a creditor of the corporation, while under section 203, the inspectors may approve the compromise of a claim with debtors and contributories.

(i) Commencement of Voluntary Winding-up

§15.24 In most cases, a voluntary wind-up will commence at the time when the shareholders resolve to wind up the corporation. However, in some cases it may be advantageous to defer the commencement of the liquidation for tax planning purposes, and therefore section 197 of the OBCA permits the shareholders to provide in their resolution that the wind-up shall not commence until a later time "specified in the resolution". The wording of the section leaves open the question of how specific this later time must be: is it necessary to specify an exact date (*e.g.*, January 31, 1992), or is it sufficient to provide some method by which the date of commencement may be determined? If it is permissible to set only a determinable date (as opposed to a specific date) as the date for the commencement of the wind-up, the next question to resolve is whether any date so selected must be a date that will certainly occur (*e.g.*, the date of the next provincial general election in Ontario), or whether it is permissible to select a date that may, but need not necessarily, occur (*e.g.*, upon the sale of a specific corporate asset). In the latter case, the corporation may then adopt what is in effect a contingent resolution, and if such contingent resolutions are possible, it would seem to follow that the contingency could be specified in such a way that the winding-up would not commence until a date selected by the management or directors of the corporation (*e.g.*, on a date to be specified by the board of directors, in its absolute discretion).

(ii) Effect of Voluntary Winding-up

§15.25 Section 198 of the Act directs that from the time when a voluntary winding-up commences, the corporation must cease to carry on its undertaking

---

[30] See, generally, *Re Amalgamated Syndicates Ltd.*, [1901] 2 Ch. 181.
[31] The court is given the power to review the remuneration fixed by the shareholders, upon the application of any shareholder, the liquidator or a creditor.

except insofar as may be required as beneficial for the winding-up of the corporation. While this direction clearly limits the corporation in the types of business that it may conduct, it may not be so limiting as it might first appear. The words "beneficial for the winding-up" may be variously interpreted to mean facilitating the realization of the assets and liabilities of the corporation, or alternatively anything that would enhance the amount available to shareholders in the winding-up process. Since the Act must operate within the context of commercial reality, it seems likely that the legislature intended the provision to have the wider, latter meaning, rather than the narrow meaning. In many cases, it will be in the best interest of the corporation to maintain its assets as a going concern during the period when they are being realized, so as to increase the amount available to creditors and shareholders. Requiring the corporation to discontinue any line of business or activity that does not relate to the immediate liquidation of the corporate assets would be far too limiting and contrary to the interests of all parties concerned. In *Willis v. Association of Universities of the British Commonwealth*[32] the U.K. Court of Appeal gave a comparable provision in the English legislation a very broad interpretation, holding that the benefit need not even be of a financial nature. Nevertheless, the corporation clearly cannot continue to operate as if no resolution has been passed, and enter into new fields of operation.

§15.26 The debts, obligations and other liabilities for which the corporation is liable are determined as of the commencement of the winding-up.[33] As of that moment, limitation periods cease to run.[34] All claims, vested or contingent, are allowed to prove in the winding-up, to the extent of their value. But "as the tree falls, so must it lie"; so there is no further entitlement to interest after the commencement date, unless there will be a surplus.[35] The appointment of a liquidator serves as notice of dismissal to the employees of the corporation.[36] It does not necessarily terminate their employment immediately, however, as the liquidator may continue to use their services for the purpose of the winding-up. Any employees who are kept on by the liquidator remain employees of the corporation rather than of the liquidator.

§15.27 Section 199 of the OBCA imposes a stay upon proceedings against a corporation that is the subject of a voluntary wind-up. It reads:

> 199. After the commencement of a voluntary winding up,
>
> > (*a*) no action or other proceeding shall be commenced against the corporation; and
> >
> > (*b*) no attachment, sequestration, distress or execution shall be put in force against the estate or effects of the corporation,

---

[32] [1965] 1 Q.B. 140 (C.A.).
[33] *Re General Rolling Stock Co.* (1872), L.R. 7 Ch. App. 646 (C.A.).
[34] *Re Northern Ontario Power Co.* (1953), 33 C.B.R. 260 (Ont. S.C.).
[35] *Re Warrant Finance Co.'s Case* (1869), 4 Ch. App. 643 at 647 (C.A.), *per* Giffard L.J.
[36] *Re General Rolling Stock Co.* (1866), 1 Eq. 346.

except by leave of the court and subject to such terms as the court imposes.

The stay is not absolute. It prohibits the commencement of new proceedings, but allows any proceeding that has been commenced to continue to final judgment. The court may also give leave to proceed with any of the proceedings to which the stay would otherwise apply, although it is far from automatic that it shall do so,[37] and a proceeding commenced without leave of the court is a nullity. It is unclear whether the stay may be lifted on a *nunc pro tunc* basis, although such an approach would have a clear practical value. The Act offers no suggestion as to the meaning of "proceeding". The stay does not affect the validity of any judgment previously rendered against the corporation,[38] or any execution previously levied against the corporation,[39] although on its express terms it prevents any further execution against the corporation except with leave of the court.[40] The stay does not affect proceedings against persons other than the corporation itself.[41] On constitutional grounds, the OBCA could not affect criminal proceedings or proceedings by the Crown in right of Canada.

§15.28 The stay does not affect the right of a secured creditor to proceed with the realization of security. It is unusual in Canada for a liquidator to be appointed with respect to a corporation that is already in receivership under a contract or instrument, since the presence of a receiver will usually (although not necessarily) indicate that the corporation is insolvent. However, there is considerable Australian and English authority concerning the rights of receivers and liquidators in the case of a parallel receivership. In those countries, it has been held that the appointment of a liquidator does not terminate the receivership.[42] So, for instance, a receiver may bring litigation in the name of a corporation in receivership as agent for the security holder in order to enforce a right of the corporation with respect to any of the assets to which the receivership extends,[43] and may continue any such litigation previously commenced.[44]

§15.29 A creditor affected by the stay may apply to the court for leave to institute or continue a proceeding, and the court may give such leave either to a particular creditor or to the creditors or a class of creditors generally. This power is not limited to permitting actual court proceedings, but is sufficiently broad to permit the court to give leave to levy distress.[45] The operating premise of an OBCA or CBCA wind-up is that the corporation that is the subject of the wind-up is solvent. The entire procedure is geared towards paying unsecured creditors

---

[37] See, for instance, *Boland v. Bear Exploration & Radium Ltd.*, [1948] O.J. No. 220, [1949] O.W.N. 503 (H.C.J.), where leave to proceed was denied.
[38] *Imperial Oil Co. v. A.S. McDonald* (1919), 53 N.S.R. 123 at 127 (C.A.), *per* Longley J.
[39] *Re Regina Windmill & Pump Co.* (1909), 10 W.L.R. 65 (Sask. T.D.).
[40] See, generally, *Re Jasper Liquor Co.* (1915), 9 W.W.R. 364 (Alta. C.A.).
[41] *Allen v. Hamilton*, [1910] O.J. No. 742, 1 O.W.N. 659 (H.C.J.).
[42] *Kelaw Pty v. Catco Developments Pty Ltd.* (1989), 7 A.C.L.C. 249 at 252, *per* Brownie J.
[43] *Gough's Garages Ltd. v. Pugsley*, [1930] 1 K.B. 615.
[44] *Bacal Contracting Ltd. v. Modern Engineering (Bristol) Ltd.*, [1980] 2 All E.R. 655.
[45] In *Imperial Canadian Trust Co. v. Potter*, [1917] 2 W.W.R. 128 at 134 (Alta. C.A.), *per* Stuart J., this power was doubted.

in full in an orderly manner. Permitting each of them to pursue remedies independently would greatly compromise the orderly payment mechanism. Following this line of reasoning, leave should be given only in such circumstances as:

- where the failure to grant leave would prejudice some further right to which a particular creditor is entitled (which is the rationale for not extending the stay to secured creditors);
- where the trial of a matter has progressed so far that it would not be practical to resolve it other than by concluding the trial;
- where it is necessary to institute or continue a proceeding in order to determine the extent of a particular creditor's claim; or
- the claim concerned relates to a debt or obligation arising in the course of the liquidation.

(iii) Repayment of Debt of the Corporation

§15.30 A decision by the shareholders of a corporation to liquidate the corporation does not entitle them to depart from the terms of the contracts to which the corporation is subject, merely because those contracts will protract the duration of the wind-up. If the corporation is liable under a term debt, it must continue to honour the term of its obligations. Similarly, it remains obliged to honour the requirements of other contracts which oblige the corporation to perform its obligations over time. In some cases, the most practical option will be for the corporation to buy out its term obligations.

(iv) Arrangements

§15.31 Section 202 of the OBCA provides that with the approval of the inspectors or shareholders, the liquidator may make any compromise or arrangement with a creditor or other person having a claim against the corporation. The claim of the creditor may be disputed, certain or contingent, and may be either future or present, or liquidated or un-liquidated. Similarly, section 194 of the Act permits the shareholders of the corporation to enter into an arrangement with "creditors of the corporation with respect to the powers to be exercised by the liquidator and the manner in which they are to be exercised".

§15.32 Collateral to the power of the liquidator to enter into compromises and arrangements with respect to claims against the corporation, section 203 of the OBCA provides that, with the approval of the inspectors or shareholders, the liquidator may enter into a compromise or arrangement with any contributory, debtor or other person liable to the corporation. The power of the liquidator to enter into a compromise or arrangement with persons liable to the corporation is wider than the power to compromise with persons to whom the corporation is itself liable. More specifically, the liquidator is empowered to take security for the performance of any compromise of a claim of the corporation, but there is no comparable power for the liquidator to give security for the performance of obligations by the corporation.

(v) Sale of Assets for Shares

§15.33 The task of the liquidator is to realize upon the assets and discharge the liabilities of the corporation. For the most part, the performance of this task will require the liquidator to convert the property of the corporation to cash. In some cases, however, it may benefit the corporation to sell its assets for a share consideration, rather than for cash. Thus section 204 of the Act permits the liquidator to accept shares in exchange for assets of the corporation. Where shares are accepted by the liquidator, it is usually with a view toward the distribution of those shares among the shareholders.

§15.34 The power of the liquidator to accept shares may be exercised only where the shareholders give their approval. While the Act suggests that the liquidator may be given a general approval to enter into transactions of this sort, subsection 204(2) of the OBCA provides that:

> 204.(2) A transfer made or arrangement entered into by the liquidator under this section is not binding on the shareholders of the corporation that is being wound up unless the transfer or arrangement is approved in accordance with subsections 184(3), (6) and (7).

It appears, therefore, that every transaction must ultimately be specifically approved by the shareholders in order to be effective. However, the required resolution may be passed either before or concurrently with the resolution approving the wind-up of the corporation or the appointment of the liquidator.[46]

(vi) Account of Voluntary Wind-up

§15.35 The liquidator in a voluntary winding-up is appointed by and is accountable to the shareholders of the corporation.[47] Where a voluntary winding-up continues for more than one year, the liquidator is obliged to call a meeting of the shareholders at the end of the first year and of each succeeding year from the commencement of the winding-up.[48] At that meeting, the liquidator must lay before the shareholders an account showing the liquidator's acts and dealings and the manner in which the winding-up has been conducted during the immediately preceding year.[49] In addition to this mandatory annual meeting, the liquidator may also call other meetings of the shareholders of the corporation for any purpose he or she thinks fit.[50]

---

[46] OBCA, s. 204(3).
[47] As to the potential liability of the liquidator to creditors, see *Pulsford v. Devenish*, [1903] 2 Ch. 625; *Argyll's Ltd. v. Coxeter* (1913), 29 T.L.R. 355 (Ch. D.).
[48] OBCA, s. 201(2).
[49] *Ibid.*
[50] OBCA, s. 201(1).

§15.36 Once the winding-up of the corporation has been completed, the liquidator is required to make a final accounting to the shareholders of the corporation. Subsection 205(1) of the OBCA provides:

> 205.(1) The liquidator shall make up an account showing the manner in which the winding up has been conducted and the property of the corporation disposed of, and thereupon shall call a meeting of the shareholders of the corporation for the purpose of having the account laid before them and hearing any explanation that may be given by the liquidator, and the meeting shall be called in the manner prescribed in the articles or by-laws or, in default thereof, in the manner prescribed by this Act for the calling of meetings of shareholders.

Within 10 days after the holding of this meeting, the liquidator must file a notice in the prescribed form with the Director, stating the date on which the notice was held.[51] In the ordinary course, the corporation will then be dissolved automatically on the expiration of three months after the date of the filing. The liquidator is also required to publish a copy of the notice in *The Ontario Gazette*,[52] but it would appear that a delay or failure on the liquidator's part to so publish the notice will not delay or otherwise affect the liquidation of the corporation.

§15.37 At any time during the three-month period running from the date of the notice required under subsection 205(3) of the OBCA, the liquidator or any other interested person may apply to the court for an order deferring the date on which the dissolution of the corporation is to take effect to a date fixed in the order, and where such an order is made, the corporation will not be dissolved until that later date.[53] The Act expressly requires the court to fix a date on which the extension will expire, and consequently it is not possible for the court to extend (or suspend) the dissolution indefinitely.

§15.38 Subsection 205(5) of the OBCA provides that:

> 205.(5) Despite anything in this Act, the court at any time after the affairs of the corporation have been fully wound up may, upon the application of the liquidator or any other person interested, make an order dissolving it, and it is dissolved on the date fixed in the order.

Since this power may be exercised "despite anything in this Act" it appears that the court may even make such an order before the liquidator delivers an accounting of the winding-up to the shareholders. One possible situation in which a court might be prepared to make such an order would be where the corporation or its shareholders would lose a significant tax or comparable benefit if the corporation is not dissolved by a particular date. In such a case, the benefit to be derived from the shareholders receiving an accounting of the manner in which the winding-up was conducted may be more than offset by the prejudice that they would suffer if the dissolution was delayed to permit such an accounting to be given.

---

[51] OBCA, s. 205(2).
[52] OBCA, s. 205(2)
[53] OBCA, s. 205(4).

D. COURT ORDERED WINDING-UP

§15.39 A corporation may be wound up under court order both voluntarily and involuntarily. The voluntary wind-up of a corporation may be instituted on an application to court or an existing wind-up authorized by the shareholders themselves may be continued under court order at any time after the instigation of a voluntary wind-up. The effect of a court-ordered winding-up, is to place the corporation under the custodianship of a court-appointed liquidator. It must be understood that the role of this officer is not simply to take over the management of the corporation while some dispute or other matter relating to the corporation is decided by the court (as would be the case with the appointment of a court appointed receiver-manager). Instead, it is implicit in the winding-up process that the business and affairs of the corporation are to be liquidated. A court-appointed liquidator has been described as being the statutory representative of the corporation for the purposes of the winding up. In *Liquidator of Coopérants, Mutual Life Insurance Society v. Dubois*,[54] Gonthier J. stated:

> From the perspective of the legal winding-up scheme, therefore, the liquidator is an officer of the court whose function it is to close up the company's business and distribute its assets to its creditors. The liquidator is not a third party in relation to the insolvent company, but is the person designated by the court to act in place of the directors of the company being wound up.

The *Dubois* case involved a mutual life insurance society and the undivided co-owners of two immovables that were the subject of in-division agreements.[55] The question arose as to whether the in-division agreements were valid as against the liquidator. In order to answer this question, the court considered the status of the liquidator. The liquidator was considered to be the person designated by the court to act in place of the directors of the company being wound up. For this reason, the in-division agreements were held to be valid as against the liquidator.

§15.40 A corporation may be wound up involuntarily by court order in a wide range of circumstances. Where there are no outstanding or expected claims against a solvent corporation, nor claims that it seeks to enforce that might involve a counterclaim, and there are no outstanding disputes among the shareholders or others concerned in the corporation, then a voluntary liquidation outside the judicial process can be a cost-saving alternative. In other cases (*e.g.*, where there are disputes even if relatively amiable, or outstanding or expected proceedings) a court-supervised liquidation is the more rational course of action.

(i) Voluntary Wind-up Under Court Order

§15.41 Clause 207(1)(*c*) of the OBCA provides that a corporation may be wound up by order of the court where the shareholders by special resolution

---

[54] [1996] S.C.J. No. 44, [1996] 1 S.C.R. 900, at para. 34.
[55] A form of property ownership-in-common under the law of Quebec that is broadly comparable to a joint tenancy at common law.

authorize an application to be made to the court to wind up the corporation. Subsection 208(1) of the Act further provides that:

> 208.(1) A winding-up order may be made upon the application of the corporation or of a shareholder or, where the corporation is being wound up voluntarily, of the liquidator or of a contributory or of a creditor having a claim of $2,500 or more.

Subsection 208(1) effectively reverses the former law under which it was not possible for the shareholders of a corporation to commence a voluntary liquidation and then seek confirmation of the liquidator's appointment by the court.[56] It follows that subsection 208(1) of the OBCA adds a significant measure of flexibility to the law. The court's jurisdiction to intervene in a voluntary winding-up is clarified by clause 207(1)(*b*)(ii), which provides for the wind-up of the corporation under an order of the court where proceedings have begun to wind it up voluntarily and the court is satisfied that it is in the interest of contributories and creditors that the proceedings should be continued under the supervision of the court. Since the procedure is a voluntary one by the corporation, notice of the application is not necessary.[57]

(ii) Involuntary Winding-up Under Court Order

§15.42 The court may order the compulsory wind-up of a corporation in three general situations: first, where such an order is justified by oppressive or unfairly prejudicial conduct; second, where the corporate purpose of the corporation is spent or frustrated; and third, where it is otherwise just and equitable to do so. The court will not make an order for the wind-up of a corporation where the application is in bad faith or motivated by some collateral purpose.[58] More generally, the courts are reluctant to wind up a solvent corporation on an involuntary basis and will normally do so only where there is a strong case for so doing and there is no other practical option in the circumstances.

---

[56] Section 28 of the *Winding-up and Restructuring Act*, R.S.C. 1985, c. W-11, provides for the appointment of a provisional liquidator in the case of companies to which that Act applies — an office also provided for under the laws of England and Australia. A provisional liquidator's primary duty is to preserve the existing *status quo* with the least possible harm to all concerned so as to enable the court to decide after a proper and final hearing whether or not the company should be wound up: *Re Carapark Industries Pty. Ltd. (in. liq.) & the Companies Act, 1961 (No. 1)*, [1967] 1 N.S.W.R. 337 at 341 (S.C.), *per* Street J. The courts are reluctant to make such appointments: *Deputy Federal Commissioner of Taxation v. Status Constructions Pty. Ltd.* (1988), 12 A.C.L.R. 689; *Re J.N. Taylor Holdings* (1991), 9 A.C.L.C. 1 (S.C.S.A.), *per* Debelle J. There is no authority under the OBCA or CBCA to appoint an "interim liquidator". However, pending the resolution of a winding-up application, the court may appoint an interim receiver, who may act as custodian and manager of the corporation's property: *Re Key Investments Ltd.*, [1974] O.J. No. 2149, 6 O.R. (2d) 144, 20 C.B.R. (N.S.) 93 (Div. Ct.). The office of interim receiver and provisional liquidator are roughly comparable. For cases considering the appointment of a provisional liquidator, see *Re London, Hamburg & Continental Exchange Bank (Emmerson's Case)*, [1866] L.R. 2 Eq. 231; *Re Capital Services Ltd.* (1983), 1 A.C.L.C. 1270; *Re McLennan Holdings Pty. Ltd.* (1983), 1 A.C.L.C. 732; *Re Club Mediterranean Pty. Ltd.* (1975), 11 S.A.S.R. 481 at 484 (S.C.), *per* Bright J.; *Re Roadmakers Pty Ltd.* (1985), 3 A.C.L.C. 591.

[57] OBCA, s. 208(2).

[58] *Re "A" Company*, [1917] 2 W.W.R. 555 at 558, 34 D.L.R. 396 (Man. K.B.), *per* Macdonald J.

§15.43 The application for such a winding-up order may be made on the application of a shareholder, a contributory or a creditor having a claim of $2,500 or more.[59] There is no express authority under the OBCA for two or more creditors each of whom is owed less than $2,500 to combine their claims so as to bring an application. However, as a general principle of statutory interpretation, expressions such as "a creditor" are usually interpreted to include a reference to two or more creditors acting together. It is a matter of discretion to be decided by the judge whether to commence a winding-up where the amount of the debt is disputed.[60] Where the debt is disputed, trial of the issue relating to the alleged debt may be ordered. Any dispute with respect to the debt should be raised at the time of the original hearing of the application.[61] A company may not fight off or delay its liquidation by putting in a spurious defence. Nevertheless, the liquidation procedure is not intended as a substitute for the ordinary judicial mechanisms of debt collection: the institution of an action and execution following judgment.[62] However, it is available to a creditor where the business or affairs of the corporation are in such disarray that the creditor's ability to recover is impaired, particularly if there are many creditors who are at such risk.

§15.44 Four days' notice of the application must be given to the corporation[63] before the making of any such application.[64] Except where the corporation consents to the order,[65] the requirement for prior notice is a condition precedent to the bringing of the application. It must be distinguished from the return of the application before the court. In computing the period of notice given, the day of service is excluded but the return day is included.[66] Any intervening Sunday or holiday is not counted.[67]

§15.45 The application must be supported by formal affidavit evidence,[68] sufficient to establish on the balance of probability that the circumstances exist on which such an order may be made.[69] While the affidavit may include statements

---

[59] OBCA, s. 208(1).
[60] *Brinds Ltd. v. Offshore Oil N.L. (No. 3)* (1985), 10 A.C.L.R. 419 at 424 (P.C.).
[61] *Bateman Television Ltd. (in liq.) v. Coleridge Finance Co.*, [1971] N.Z.L.R. 929 (P.C.).
[62] A court may award costs in a winding-up proceeding. *Rendle v. Stanhope Dairy Farms Ltd.*, [2005] B.C.J. No. 389, 3 B.L.R. (4th) 299 (S.C.). The institution of improper proceedings of this type would be a suitable case for such an award.
[63] Notice to creditors is not generally required, and indeed would not normally be possible: *Re Dominion Shipbuilding & Repair Co.*, [1926] O.J. No. 15, 7 C.B.R. 349 (S.C. Bank.).
[64] OBCA, s. 208(2); but compare *Re I.O.S. Ltd. (No. 2)*, [1973] N.B.J. No. 139, 7 N.B.R. (2d) 336 at 342, 43 D.L.R. (3d) 759 (C.A.), *per* Hughes C.J.N.B.
[65] OBCA, s. 208(2); *Re Consumers' Coal Co.*, [1917] 2 W.W.R. 143 (S.C.); *Re Installations Ltd.* (1914), 5 W.W.R. 1048, 14 D.L.R. 679 (Alta. T.D.).
[66] Rules of Civil Procedure, R.R.O. 1990, Reg. 194, rule 3.01(1)(*a*).
[67] Rules of Civil Procedure, rule 3.01(1)(*b*); see also *J.H. Ashdown Hardware Co. v. Residential Building Co.* (1914), 7 W.W.R. 690 (Man. K.B.).
[68] *Re Commercial Agencies Ltd.*, [1920] O.J. No. 246, 19 O.W.N. 160 (S.C.).
[69] It is not possible to cross-examine officers of the corporation in order to obtain the required evidence: *Re "A" Company*, [1917] 2 W.W.R. 555, 34 D.L.R. 396 (Man. K.B.), unless the court otherwise orders: *Re Baynes Carriage Co.*, [1912] O.J. No. 15, 27 O.L.R. 144 (H.C.J.).

based on information and belief with respect to non-contentious matters,[70] in other respects the substantive allegations must be based upon the personal knowledge of the deponent, rather than the deponent's information and belief.[71] However, although an application or the affidavit supporting it may be deficient, in a suitable case the court will allow leave to amend the affidavit to include some necessary or supportive material inadvertently omitted, provided the amendment does not relate to some new event which has accrued since the date of the application.[72] Amendments will not be permitted where allowing them would prejudice the corporation unfairly.[73]

(1) Oppressive or Prejudicial Conduct

§15.46 The various grounds for the involuntary wind-up of a corporation are not mutually exclusive. Indeed, there tends to be a certain degree of overlap between them,[74] particularly where orders are made on the basis that it is just and equitable to order the wind-up of a corporation in particular circumstances. While the just and equitable basis for such orders (considered in detail below) is the broadest criteria on which an involuntary wind-up may be ordered, clause 207(1)(*a*) of the OBCA also provides a general ground for the making of such an order in cases where the corporation is being conducted in an oppressive or unfairly prejudicial manner. Specifically, clause (*a*) provides that:

> 207.(1) A corporation may be wound up by the court,
>
> > (*a*) where the court is satisfied that in respect of the corporation or any of its affiliates,
> >
> > > (i) any act or omission of the corporation or any of its affiliates effects a result,
> > >
> > > (ii) the business or affairs of the corporation or any of its affiliates are or have been carried on or conducted in a manner, or
> > >
> > > (iii) the powers of the directors of the corporation or any of its affiliates are or have been exercised in a manner,
> >
> > that is oppressive or unfairly prejudicial to or that unfairly disregards the interests of any security holder, creditor, director or officer ...

Clause 207(1)(*a*) continues the long-standing authority of the court in the winding-up of a corporation where the winding-up has been conducted in a manner

---

[70] Provided the source of the information and the fact of the belief are specified in the affidavit: Rules of Civil Procedure, R.R.O. 1990, Reg. 194, rule 39.01(5).

[71] *Re Great West Permanent Loan Co.*, [1927] 2 W.W.R. 15 at 17 (Man. K.B.), *per* Mathers C.J.K.B.; but compare *Re Manitoba Commission Co.* (1912), 2 W.W.R. 276 at 279 (Man. K.B.), *per* Mathers C.J.K.B., aff'd 4 W.W.R. 255 (C.A.). Significantly, the OBCA and the CBCA contain no provision respecting the evidence required to support a winding-up order. See also *Re Sharon Golf & Country Club Ltd.*, [1975] O.J. No. 20, 20 C.B.R. (N.S.) 159 (H.C.J.).

[72] See, generally, *Re Home Bank of Canada*, [1923] O.J. No. 77, 54 O.L.R. 606 at 612 (S.C.), *per* Fisher J.; *Re Canadian General Service Corp. (No. 2)* (1914), 5 W.W.R. 1291 (Man. K.B.).

[73] *Re Manitoba Commission Co.* (1911), 19 W.L.R. 893 (Man. K.B.).

[74] See, for instance, *Re Dominion Steel Corp.*, [1927] 4 D.L.R. 337 (N.S.C.A.).

that was oppressive to a shareholder[75] or creditor, or where the incorporation of the company was obtained through fraud.[76] The court may order the wind-up of a corporation either where an application for such an order is brought under clause 207(1)(*a*) or where an application is made for relief under section 248 of the OBCA.[77] However, even where there has been oppressive conduct in the administration of a corporation, the courts prefer not to order the wind-up of a corporation where there is some suitable alternative,[78] such as requiring the dominant shareholder to buy out the interest of the applicant,[79] or requiring a specific asset to be sold.[80] Essentially, the liquidation remedy is one of last resort.[81]

§15.47 In *Wittlin v. Bergman*[82] it was found that the appellant and respondent, shareholders in a CBCA corporation, were unable to work together. They could not agree on how to remedy the situation. The appellant applied for relief under the section 241 oppression remedy procedure of the CBCA. The trial judge concluded that there was no oppression, but in order to resolve the shareholders' dispute, resorted to the court's jurisdiction to dissolve the corporation on the grounds that it was just and equitable to do so. The trial judge determined that it would be just and equitable for the one side to buy out the other, and ordered the parties to participate in a buy-sell mechanism. The appellants appealed to the Ontario Court of Appeal. There it was held that the trial judge's finding that it was just and equitable for the corporation to be liquidated under subparagraph 214(1)(*b*)(ii) of the CBCA was appropriate. However, it did not follow that he was required to order liquidation as a remedy. Instead, the authority granted to the court under subsection 214(2) to make such order as it considered fit allowed it to tailor the remedy to the particular needs and circumstances of the case. It could, for instance, adopt one of the specifically enumerated remedies provided for in section 241 with respect to oppression, if such a remedy was more in the interest of all parties than the liquidation of the corporation. However, the Ontario Court of Appeal disagreed with the remedy selected by the trial judge, as did the parties:

> In our view, it is not appropriate that either the appellants or the respondents be required to purchase the other's shares. The company will undoubtedly benefit from the absence of the appellants, and the appellants want out. We are of the view that this is a case where it is appropriate to order that the corporation purchase the shares of the appellants pursuant to s. 241(3)(*f*). The purchase should be for cash,

---

[75] See, for instance, *Re National Building Maintenance Ltd.*, [1970] B.C.J. No. 318, [1971] 1 W.W.R. 8 (S.C.); affd *sub nom. National Building Maintenance Ltd. v. Dove*, [1972] B.C.J. No. 605, [1972] 5 W.W.R. 410 (C.A.).
[76] See, generally, *Re Producers Real Estate & Finance Co.*, [1936] V.L.R. 235 (S.C.).
[77] OBCA, s. 207(2), and see s. 248(3)(*l*).
[78] *Stech v. Davies*, [1987] A.J. No. 618, 53 Alta. L.R. (2d) 373, [1987] 5 W.W.R. 563 (Q.B.).
[79] See, for instance, *Kummen v. Kummen-Shipman Ltd.*, [1983] M.J. No. 110, [1983] 2 W.W.R. 577 at 581 (C.A.), *per* Huband J.A., leave to appeal to S.C.C. refused [1983] S.C.C.A. No. 366; *Re Van-Tel T.V. Ltd.* (1974), 44 D.L.R. (3d) 146 (B.C.S.C.).
[80] *Jarman v. Brown*, [1979] B.C.J. No. 1163, 13 B.C.L.R. 152, [1979] 5 W.W.R. 673 (S.C.).
[81] *Condotrust Realty Investments Inc. v. 983177 Ontario Inc.*, [1997] O.J. No. 2454, 35 B.L.R. (2d) 138 (Gen. Div.).
[82] [1995] O.J. No. 3095, 25 O.R. (3d) 761 (C.A.).

unless it is determined by the valuators appointed ... that, after such payment, the corporation would be unable to pay its liabilities as they become due, or the realizable value of the corporation's assets would be less than the aggregate of its liabilities. If it is not possible, for the foregoing reasons, for the corporation to pay the full purchase price of the shares in cash, the portion of the purchase price which cannot be paid in cash shall become a debt of the company, secured by a charge over all of its assets, and ranking only behind all presently existing and validly perfected security over its assets ... with interest at 7 per cent per annum payable annually on the unpaid portion.[83]

To reiterate: winding-up is a remedy of last resort.[84] The court should not order the wind-up of a corporation in an application under section 248 of the Act where such an order has been sought neither by the corporation nor the applicant for relief under that section.[85]

(2) Satisfaction of the Corporate Purpose

§15.48 Subclause 207(1)(*b*)(i) of the OBCA provides that the court may order the winding-up of a corporation where the court is satisfied that an event has occurred which, under the terms of a unanimous shareholder agreement entitles a shareholder to demand the dissolution of the corporation. Although the wording of section 207 indicates that relief is discretionary under this provision, it is difficult to see how an order could be refused in the face of an express agreement to that effect. As a practical matter, in many cases, a shareholder will have such a right to demand dissolution where a corporation has been created for a specific purpose, and that purpose has been accomplished.[86] However, in order for a shareholder to apply for the dissolution of a corporation under subclause (*b*)(i), it is essential that there be a unanimous shareholder agreement which implicitly or explicitly entitles the shareholder to demand dissolution. In the absence of such an agreement it is not sufficient under subclause (*b*)(i) for a shareholder to show only that the limited purpose of the corporation has been satisfied — although that fact may be sufficient to entitle the court to make an order for the dissolution of the corporation on the ground that it is just and equitable to do so.[87]

§15.49 Even where the specific purpose of the corporation is not identified, the winding-up of a corporation may be ordered where such a measure has been agreed between the principals of the corporation, and one of them is refusing to give effect to that agreement.[88] In such a case, the agreement to liquidate essentially defines the point at which the purpose of the corporation has been satisfied.

---

[83] *Ibid.*, at 764.
[84] *Classic Organ Co. v. Artisan Organ Co.*, [1997] O.J. No. 2161, 35 B.L.R. (2d) 285 (Gen. Div.).
[85] *Oakley v. McDougall*, [1987] B.C.J. No. 272, 37 B.L.R. 31, additional reasons [1987] B.C.J. No. 1226, 37 B.L.R. 47 (C.A.).
[86] See, generally, *C.P.H.C. Holding Co. v. Western Pacific Trust Co.* (1973), 36 D.L.R. (3d) 431 (B.C.S.C.).
[87] OBCA, s. 207(1)(*b*)(iv).
[88] See, for instance, *Blattgerste v. Heringa*, [2006] B.C.J. No. 768, 148 A.C.W.S. (3d) 729 (S.C.).

Absent very unusual circumstances, it would normally be inequitable in such a situation to deny the applicant-investor the right to be paid out.

§15.50 In principle, satisfaction of purpose may also be invoked in cases where there is no specific agreement, but it appears just and equitable in the circumstances to wind up the corporation on this basis. In deciding whether to exercise its discretion on this basis, there are no doubt a range of factors for the court to consider. The mere fact that the original purpose for which a corporation was incorporated has been achieved or has ceased to be relevant does not in itself justify a winding-up order.[89] It is far from unusual for corporations to move on to new ventures after completing their original purpose. It has been a long time, for instance, since Wells Fargo operated a stage coach. There is no reason to assume that there was a shared intention among the incorporators or original investors that the corporation would be liquidated as soon as it discontinued its original line of business. Where the shareholders have acquiesced in movement into other fields, any right to seek the winding-up of the corporation by reason of satisfaction of purpose would surely lapse. It is different, however, where the party seeking the liquidation of the corporation made clear at the time of investment, that it was intended for a single purpose only. There would seem to be considerable equity in such a case to grant the order where that purpose has been fulfilled or frustrated, the application for the winding-up of the corporation is brought forthwith, and there is no other reasonable prospect for exit in favour of the person seeking the order.

(3) Frustration of the Corporate Purpose

§15.51 Subclause 207(1)(*b*)(iii) of the OBCA gives at least tacit recognition to the rule of common sense that good money should not be thrown after bad. It provides that the court may order the winding-up of a corporation where the court is satisfied that:

> (iii) the corporation, though it may not be insolvent, cannot by reason of its liabilities continue its business and it is advisable to wind it up...

Thus an order may be made for the wind-up of a corporation where the objects for which it was incorporated have ceased to exist or the corporation has so rearranged its business that it is no longer pursuing the same objects and can no longer do so.[90]

§15.52 This subclause also permits a person to apply for the wind-up of a corporation where the corporation is in a deficit and is eroding its capital base, even though it is not yet insolvent. However, the order may only be made where the

---

[89] See, generally, *Coutu v. San Jose Mines Ltd.*, [2005] B.C.J. No. 675, 3 B.L.R. (4th) 22, at para. 23 (S.C.).

[90] *Dominion Trust Co. v. Boyce*; *Dominion Trust Co., Re*, [1918] B.C.J. No. 32, [1918] 3 W.W.R. 751, aff'd (*sub nom. MacPherson v. Boyce*), [1919] S.C.J. No. 79, 59 S.C.R. 691. See also *Mackenzie v. Craig*, [1997] A.J. No. 855, [1998] 2 W.W.R. 106 (Q.B.), aff'd [1999] A.J. No. 239, 171 D.L.R. (4th) 268 (C.A.).

court is satisfied that the corporation cannot continue in business "by reason of its liabilities" — which it may be argued is sufficiently broad to include considerations of whether the corporation may repay the shareholders their capital, as that obligation is a type of liability, albeit a deferred one. However, the word "liability" would suggest that the clause does not permit the court to order the wind-up of the corporation simply because the corporation is losing money and will likely continue to do so. This is a significant distinction, because views will often differ among shareholders concerning whether a money-losing business should continue. The profitability or loss of a corporation and the prudence or imprudence of its remaining in business are not relevant.[91]

§15.53 The following factors might guide a court in deciding whether to order the winding-up of a corporation under subclause 207(1)(*b*)(iii) of the OBCA where:

- the accrued liabilities of the corporation have entirely dissipated the retained earnings and reserves of the corporation, so that any further losses will erode the issued capital of the corporation;

- there have been a series of losses in successive years and there is no reasonably foreseeable prospect of a reversal;

- any further losses would work to the prejudice of the applicant; and

- continued operations of the business would prejudice a particular class of creditor.

However, the mere fact that one particular shareholder is dissatisfied with the dividend performance of the corporation, but is unable to persuade the majority shareholders to purchase his or her shares, is not generally sufficient grounds for ordering the wind-up of the corporation.[92] Nor will an order be made even where the corporation is operating at a loss and the capital of the corporation has been substantially impaired and cannot be restored within the foreseeable future, provided there is some realistic prospect of recovery.[93]

§15.54 The courts are most likely to make an order under subclause 207(1)(*b*)(iii) of the OBCA where the "substratum" of the business of the corporation has disappeared.[94] To justify the liquidation of the corporation on the substratum criteria it must be shown that the substratum of the business has been withdrawn, so that business within the objects of the corporation has become at least in a practical sense impossible.[95] If some type of business of the same general kind as that originally contemplated may still be carried on, liquidation will

---

[91] *Re European Life Assurance Society* (1869), L.R. 9 Eq. 122 at 131 (V.C.), *per* James V.C.
[92] *Buckner v. Bourbon Farming Co.* (1955), 14 W.W.R. 406 (Sask. Q.B.).
[93] *Re Winnipeg Saddlery Co.* (1934), 16 C.B.R. 57 (Man. K.B.); *Re British Empire Steel Corp.* (1927), 59 N.S.R. 390 (T.D.).
[94] This idea was first explored by Cairns L.J., albeit in very general terms, in *Re Suburban Hotel Co.* (1867), 36 L.J. Ch. 710 at 717-18.
[95] *Galbraith v. Merito Shipping Co.*, [1947] S.C. 446 at 456 (Ct. Sess.), *per* Lord Justice-Clerk Moncreiff.

not be ordered.[96] On the other hand, liquidation may be ordered despite the possibility that the corporation might shift its efforts from the original line of business contemplated, to some entirely new and radically different line of business. If a shareholder has invested money in the shares of a corporation on the understanding that it is going to carry out some particular object, the shareholder cannot be forced against his or her will by the votes of other shareholders or by its directors to continue to invest money on some quite different project or speculation.[97] Whether some new venture is being attempted depends upon the general intention and common understanding among the members of the company at the time when they invested in the corporation, rather than the capacity of the corporation to engage in the new line of business.[98] In *Re Crown Bank*[99] the court looked at a prospectus to determine the original investment intent of the parties.

§15.55 So long as the corporation remains active in its originally intended line of business, the courts will not substitute their own impression as to the likelihood of success of the corporation for that of the majority unless and until it is so clear as to be beyond question that the original purpose of the corporation has been defeated,[100] and will not normally make such an order unless the substratum has been completely extinguished[101] or is no longer workable.[102] The court's willingness to make such an order increases where the corporation is being continued under mysterious and apparently unlawful circumstances.[103]

§15.56 Despite the "substratum" line of cases in *Re Tangier Amalgamated Mining Co.*[104] the court refused to order a wind-up on the basis that it was just and equitable to do so, since it appeared that there would be no assets available for distribution among the shareholders if an order were made, and since the other shareholders had not sought the wind-up of the corporation, from which the court inferred that they did not wish to have it wound up. It is difficult to follow the logic of this thinking, because unless the corporation is wound up it is likely that it will continue to stumble along as an empty shell. There are administrative costs in it doing so, and from the directors' perspective, there is also a risk of continuing liability. Thus liquidation and dissolution have an inherent value themselves, at least from a certain perspective. Nevertheless, the court concluded that a shareholder is not entitled to petition for a winding-up unless he or she can show that the company is sufficiently solvent that shareholders will receive tangible assets if the corporation is wound up. The court's power is

---

[96] See, generally, *Re Kitson & Co.*, [1946] 1 All E.R. 435 (C.A.); *Re Taldua Rubber Co.*, [1946] 2 All E.R. 763 (Ch. D.).
[97] *Re Eastern Telegraph Co.*, [1947] 2 All E.R. 104 at 109 (Ch. D.), per Jenkins J.; *Re Haven Gold Mining Co.* (1882), 20 Ch. D. 151 (C.A.).
[98] *H.A. Stephenson & Son Ltd. v. Gillanders, Arbuthnot & Co.* (1931), 45 C.L.R. 476 at 487-88 (H.C.), per Dixon J.
[99] (1890), 44 Ch. D. 634 at 643.
[100] See, generally, *Re Columbia Gypsum Co.* (1958), 17 D.L.R. (2d) 280 at 285 (B.C.S.C.), per Lord J.
[101] *Re Jury Gold Mine Development Co.*, [1928] O.J. No. 162, 10 C.B.R. 303 (C.A.).
[102] *Re Harris Maxwell Larder Lake Gold Mining Co.*, [1910] O.J. No. 790, 1 O.W.N. 984 (H.C.J.).
[103] See, for instance, *Re Florida Mining Co.*, [1902] B.C.J. No. 23, 9 B.C.R. 108 (C.A.).
[104] (1906), 39 N.S.R. 373 (C.A.).

discretionary,[105] and it is a general principle guiding the exercise of discretionary judicial powers that they should only be exercised where there is a practical benefit in doing so.[106]

(4) Just and Equitable

§15.57 The broadest power of the court to order the winding-up of a corporation is set out in subclause 207(1)(*b*)(iv) of the OBCA, which provides that the court may order a wind-up where it is satisfied[107] that it is just and equitable to do so. It is well established that the application of the just and equitable rule is subject to the normal requirements and limitations applicable to equitable remedies. In particular the person seeking relief must come to court with clean hands.[108] The wording "just and equitable" suggests that there must also be an equitable basis for granting the relief sought, particularly where others interested in the corporation oppose the application for winding-up. However, it is not necessary to demonstrate actual wrongdoing much less malicious intent on the part of the control group within the corporation. In *Re R.J. Jowsey Mining Co.* it was said:

> The "just and equitable" power of the Court connotes a broad discretion which I do not think is limited to required proof of actual wrongdoing. The formula is not one that can be easily translated into any set of principles; rather, it fixes a standard whose application must always be an anxious matter on particular facts.
>
> When is it "just and equitable" for the Court to order a company to be wound up? The remedy is drastic, and hence must be addressed to a serious condition affecting the proper conduct or management of the company's affairs.[109]

In practice, the just and equitable rule is most frequently applied in any one of four situations: where there has been a disappearance of substratum, where there exists the common law oppression of the minority, in situations where, in practical terms, the relationship resembles that of a partnership and lacks the protection of more formal corporate structure, and the deadlock situation where such animosity exists it is impossible to obtain the consensus necessary to manage the corporation.[110]

---

[105] As to appeal from such an exercise of discretion, see *Re P & J Macrae Ltd.*, [1961] 1 W.L.R. 229; *Re J.D. Wain Ltd.*, [1965] 1 W.L.R. 909.

[106] See, generally, *Re Halifax Yacht Co.* (1882), R.E.D. 475 (N.S.T.D.).

[107] "Satisfied" means that the court must be satisfied, in accordance with the normal civil standard on the basis of evidence which is either on agreement or is capable of being discerned by assessment of the existing dispute, that the type of order that is being requested should be granted: *781952 Alberta Ltd. v. 781944 Alberta Ltd.*, [2003] A.J. No. 1485, 347 A.R. 210 (Q.B.), *per* Watson J.

[108] *Baxted v. Warkentin Estate*, [2006] M.J. No. 376, 151 A.C.W.S. (3d) 1077 at para. 24 (Q.B.), *per* McCawley J.

[109] [1969] O.J. No. 1358, 6 D.L.R. (3d) 97 at 100 (C.A.).

[110] *Baxted v. Warkentin Estate*, [2006] M.J. No. 376, 151 A.C.W.S. (3d) 1077 at para. 27 (Q.B.).

§15.58 In *Ebrahimi v. Westbourne Galleries Ltd.*,[111] Lord Wilberforce made the following observations concerning the scope of the authority conferred by the "just and equitable" provision of the English legislation:

> The words are a recognition of the fact that a limited company is more than a mere juridical entity, with a personality in law of its own: that there is room in company law for recognition of the fact that behind it, or amongst it, there are individuals, with rights, expectations and obligations inter se which are not necessarily submerged in the company structure. ... The "just and equitable" provision does not, as the respondents suggest, entitle one party to disregard the obligations he assumes by entering the company, nor the court to dispense him from it. It does, as equity always does, enable the court to subject the exercise of legal rights to equitable considerations; considerations, that is, of a personal character arising between one individual and another, which may make it unjust or inequitable, to insist on legal rights, or to exercise them in a particular way.[112]

Lord Wilberforce then went on to outline one situation in which a winding-up order might be made on the grounds that such an order was just and equitable:

> The superimposition of equitable considerations requires something more, which typically may include one, or probably more, of the following elements: (i) an association formed or continued on the basis of a personal relationship, involving mutual confidence — this element will often be found where a pre-existing partnership has been converted into a limited company; (ii) an agreement or understanding, that all, or some (for there may be "sleeping" members), of the shareholders shall participate in the conduct of the business; (iii) restriction upon the transfer of the members' interest in the company — so that if confidence is lost, or one member is removed from management, he cannot take his stake and go elsewhere.[113]

Orders have been made for the winding-up of the corporation where the controlling interests have effectively shut the applicant out of the corporation and barred him or her from the premises,[114] the termination of employment in an "incorporated partnership";[115] and whether a shareholder is pursuing an adversarial policy towards the corporation.[116] However, in deciding whether to order a winding-up in an oppression case or on just and equitable grounds, a court may consider such matters as the risk of a loss of goodwill, whether a business associated with an individual can be sold, the lower price usually paid in a liquidation and other relevant commercial considerations, as well the respective conduct of the parties and the circumstances of the corporation.[117]

---

[111] [1972] 2 All E.R. 492 (H.L.).
[112] *Ibid.*, at 500.
[113] *Ibid.* See also *Re R.C. Young Insurance Ltd.*, [1955] O.J. No. 575, [1955] O.R. 598 at 601-602 (C.A.), *per* Laidlaw.
[114] *Suleiman v. Saffuri*, [2004] O.J. No. 1721, 48 B.L.R. (3d) 286 (S.C.J.).
[115] *Paley v. Leduc*, [2002] B.C.J. No. 2845, 30 B.L.R. (3d) 243 (S.C.).
[116] *King City Holdings Ltd. v. Preston Springs Gardens Inc.*, [2001] O.J. No. 1464, 14. B.L.R. (3d) 277 (S.C.J.).
[117] See, generally, *Macdonald v. Master Cartage Inc.*, [1999] O.J. No. 2838, 49 B.L.R. (2d) 146 at 152 (S.C.J.) per Farley J., aff'd [2000] O.J. No. 3728, 9 B.L.R. (3d) 270 (Div. Ct.).

§15.59 In *Re Rogers & Agincourt Holdings Ltd.*[118] Lacourcière J.A. cautioned against an overly technical interpretation of the case law on the question of when it is just and equitable to order a winding-up. Each case depends to a large extent on its own facts. The power to order a winding-up of the corporation on just and equitable criteria is a discretionary one and should not be exercised where it is contrary to the interests of the shareholders that the corporation be wound up,[119] nor where the making of an order will not confer an advantage on the applicant that at least balances the disadvantage that will be cast upon others interested in the corporation (creditors as well as shareholders).[120] In deciding whether to make an order on this ground, the court should also take into account the relative contribution made to the corporation by the applicant[121] and those who oppose the application.[122]

(a) THE DEADLOCK CASES

§15.60 The "just and equitable" ground is not limited to cases analogous to the insolvency of the corporation.[123] On the contrary, the courts have relied upon this provision, and its predecessors, in a wide range of cases — one of the most common being where the corporation is deadlocked.[124] The term "deadlock" describes a situation in which the general decision-making process within the corporation has broken down and there is no realistic prospect of it being repaired. While a complete breakdown is clearly satisfactory to justify the grant of a remedy, even a deadlock with respect to a band of critical aspects of decision-making would seem to be sufficient. For instance, in *Kelly v. Condon*[125] the court ordered the wind-up of a company where the plaintiff seeking the order was unable to receive a fair return on his or her investment and the corporation was deadlocked because of the

---

[118] [1976] O.J. No. 2341, 14 O.R. (2d) 489 (C.A.).
[119] *Lefebvre v. Lefebvre Frères Ltée*, [1962] C.C.S. No. 289, 4 C.B.R. (N.S.) 38 (Que. S.C.). In that case, Brossard J. outlined five situations which were required to justify an order:

  (a) there must be no other effective and appropriate remedy but a winding-up;

  (b) there must be two shareholders or groups of shareholders between whom effective control of the corporation is equally divided;

  (c) there must have arisen between the two shareholders or groups a serious and persistent disagreement as to the choice of the directors and officers of the company or as to some important questions respecting its management or functioning;

  (d) a deadlock must have resulted from that disagreement;

  (e) that deadlock must penalize or seriously interfere with the normal operation of the corporation.

[120] *Re Shipway Iron Bell & Wire Manufacturing Co.*, [1926] O.J. No. 132, 58 O.L.R. 585 (C.A.). In that case, the winding-up order was sought by a minority shareholder but was opposed by the majority of the creditors of the corporation.
[121] *Re James Lumbers Co.*, [1925] O.J. No. 143, 58 O.L.R. 100 (H.C.); *Higgins v. Brock & Higgins Insurance Agencies Ltd.*, [1976] O.J. No. 45, 22 C.B.R. (N.S.) 248 (H.C.J.).
[122] *Re Timbers Ltd.*, [1917] 2 W.W.R. 965, 35 D.L.R. 431 (Alta. C.A.).
[123] *Marzitelli v. Verona Construction Ltd.* (1979), 33 C.B.R. (N.S.) 180 (Que. S.C.).
[124] See, for instance, *Scozzafava v. Prosperi*, [2003] A.J. No. 354, 32 B.L.R. (3d) 105 at 168 (Q.B.) *per* Read J.
[125] [1986] N.J. No. 264, 62 Nfld. & P.E.I.R. 196, 190 A.P.R. 196 (T.D.).

equality of its shareholders.[126] In a number of cases, the courts have looked not only for deadlock, but also for some other factor. For instance, in *Nieforth v. Nieforth Bros. Ltd.*, the court took into account both the fact that the controlling shareholder was treating the corporation as his personal business and the fact that the principals in that closely held corporation were unable to agree even on an informal winding-up of the corporation, when ordering a wind-up on the grounds that it was just and equitable.[127] Similarly, in *Zwig v. Schupack*[128] the court looked also at the frustration of the corporate purpose. These cases raise the question as to whether more than deadlock alone is required to justify the winding-up order. On the other hand, if the corporation is truly deadlocked, there would seem to be little practical value in refusing to order the wind-up of the corporation, even if there are no other grounds for doing so.

§15.61 Deadlock does not mean a temporary impasse. The deadlock must be ongoing to justify such an order being made;[129] a single instance or isolated instances of disagreement do not afford sufficient grounds.[130] There must be such a sufficiently serious disagreement that it would not be reasonable to believe that the shareholders will resolve their differences[131] and cooperate in the running of the corporation.[132] In deciding whether to make an order, the court will take into consideration whether it is necessary to act quickly and effectively in order to protect those persons interested in the corporation from the risk of losing a substantial portion of their investment.[133] A corporation may be found to be deadlocked even where the chairman of the corporation possesses a casting vote; such a vote is intended to deal with occasional and infrequent tie votes; it is not intended to be employed on a continuous basis.[134]

§15.62 A wind-up of a corporation will not be ordered, however, merely because a shareholder or creditor is disgruntled with existing management.[135] There is no basis for winding-up a corporation on the ground that it is just and equitable merely because a minority group within the corporation has been outvoted and it is dissatisfied with the result. On the contrary, generally the courts respect

---

[126] See also *Re Alf's Roofing & Contracting Ltd.*, [1985] A.J. No. 871, 61 A.R. 16 (Q.B.).

[127] *Nieforth v. Nieforth Bros. Ltd.*, [1985] N.S.J. No. 254, 69 N.S.R. (2d) 10, 163 A.P.R. 10 (T.D.).

[128] [1985] O.J. No. 616, 31 B.L.R. 232 (H.C.J.), *sub nom. Re Welport Investments Ltd.*

[129] See, for instance, *Re Cappuccitti Potato Co.*, [1972] O.J. No. 536, 17 C.B.R. (N.S.) 213 (H.C.J.).

[130] *Zwig v. Schupack*, [1985] O.J. No. 616 (*sub nom. Re Welport Investments Ltd.*) 31 B.L.R. 232 (H.C.J.).

[131] *Prussin v. Park Distributors Inc.* (1963), 6 C.B.R. (N.S.) 31 (Que. S.C.).

[132] *Dunham v. Apollo Tours Ltd. (No. 2)*, [1978] O.J. No. 3380, 20 O.R. (2d) 9 (H.C.J.); see also *Re Pre-Delco Machine & Tool Ltd.*, [1973] O.J. No. 1997, [1973] 3 O.R. 115 (H.C.J.).

[133] *Re Humberbank Investment & Development Ltd.*, [1972] O.J. No. 3, 17 C.B.R. (N.S.) 220 (H.C.J.).

[134] *Re Citizens Coal & Forwarding Co.*, [1927] 4 D.L.R. 275 (Ont. Co. Ct.); *Dunham v. Apollo Tours Ltd. (No. 2)*, [1978] O.J. No. 3380, 20 O.R. (2d) 9 (H.C.J.).

[135] *B. Love Ltd. v. Bulk Steel & Salvage Ltd.*, [1982] O.J. No. 3469, 38 O.R. (2d) 691, additional reasons [1982] O.J. No. 3578, 40 O.R. (2d) 1 (H.C.J.).

the common sense principle that the business and affairs of a corporation are entitled to be conducted in accordance with the wishes of the majority.[136]

§15.63 The involuntary wind-up of a corporation is a serious step, which will often seriously damage the business conducted by the corporation (so that the majority cannot purchase it in the course of the liquidation), and benefit the corporation's competitors.[137] Therefore, an involuntary wind-up will only be taken by the court where a strong case is made out for so doing.[138] It is a drastic remedy to which resort should be employed only where necessary to address a serious condition in the conduct or management of the corporation's business and affairs.[139] There is a heavy onus placed on the applicant to show that a suitable case exists for making the wind-up order.[140] A winding-up will not be ordered where there are other remedies available which are better suited to the problem[141] or that will be just as effective in dealing with the problem.[142] Unless the wrongs are being conducted systematically or continuously (so that it seems reasonable to conclude that they will continue) it will often be possible to redress past wrongs by ordering an accounting, setting aside a wrongful act, by issuing an injunction to prevent further wrongs in the future, or by employing some combination of these alternative remedies.[143] Moreover, the incompatibility of one shareholder with the others is not in and of itself just and equitable reason for requiring the wind-up of the corporation.[144] There must be something in the way the disgruntled shareholder has been handled which amounts to unfair or inequitable treatment.[145] An order will not be made where the company is well run, simply because the disgruntled shareholder will be locked into his or her investment if the order is not made.[146]

---

[136] *PWA Corp v. Gemini Group Automated Distribution Systems Inc.*, [1993] O.J. No. 1793, 10 B.L.R. (2d) 109 at 142 (C.A.), *per* Griffiths J.A., quoting Callaghan C.J.O.C. at trial [1993] O.J. No. 723, 8 B.L.R. (2d) 221 at 270 (Gen. Div. — C.L.).

[137] *Higgins v. Brock & Higgins Insurance Agencies Ltd.*, [1976] O.J. No. 45, 22 C.B.R. (N.S.) 248 at 250 (H.C.J.), *per* Southey J.

[138] *Crossgrove v. Crossgrove*, [1977] O.J. No. 59, 24 C.B.R. (N.S.) 172 (H.C.J.), *per* Lerner J.

[139] *Re R.J. Jowsey Mining Co.*, [1969] O.J. No. 1358, [1969] 2 O.R. 549 at 552 (C.A.), *per* Laskin J.A., aff'd [1970] S.C.R. 549.

[140] *B. Love Ltd. v. Bulk Steel & Salvage Ltd.*, [1982] O.J. No. 3469, 38 O.R. (2d) 691, additional reasons [1982] O.J. No. 3578, 40 O.R. (2d) 1 (H.C.J.).

[141] *Re National Building Maintenance Ltd.*, [1970] B.C.J. No. 318, [1971] 1 W.W.R. 8; aff'd *sub nom. National Building Maintenance Ltd. v. Dove*, [1972] B.C.J. No. 605, [1972] 5 W.W.R. 410 (C.A); *Shacket v. Universal Factors Corp.*, [1967] C.C.S. No. 33, 10 C.B.R. (N.S.) 166 (Que. S.C.), but compare *Re Humber Valley Broadcasting Co.*, [1978] N.J. No. 161, 19 Nfld. & P.E.I.R. 230 at 233, 50 A.P.R. 230 (T.D.), *per* Mifflin C.J.

[142] *Raicevic v. Nancy G. Dress Corp.* (1969), 15 C.B.R. (N.S.) 149 (Que. S.C.).

[143] *Ibid.*, *per* O'Connor J. at 152.

[144] *Jordan v. McKenzie*, [1980] O.J. No. 3812, 30 O.R. (2d) 705 (H.C.J.).

[145] *Re Humber Valley Broadcasting Co.*, [1978] N.J. No. 161, 19 Nfld. & P.E.I.R. 230, 50 A.P.R. 230 (T.D.).

[146] *Meltzer v. Western Paper Box Co.*, [1978] M.J. No. 213, [1978] 1 W.W.R. 451, 3 B.L.R. 113 at 121 (Q.B.), *per* Hewak J.

(b) Loss of Confidence

§15.64 In the absence of a deadlock,[147] a second situation in which a winding-up order may be made under subclause 207(1)(*b*)(iv) is where there is a justifiable loss of confidence in the way the corporation's business or affairs are being conducted,[148] attributable to tyrannous conduct[149] or a lack of probity, good faith or other improper conduct on the part of those in control of the corporation.[150] For instance, in *Reznick v. Bilecki*[151] the Saskatchewan Court of Appeal ruled that it was just and equitable to order the wind-up of a corporation where the controlling shareholder had disposed of property without the other shareholder's knowledge or consent. Indeed, suspicious transactions often provide the basis for a wind-up order on the grounds that such an order is just and equitable.[152] For instance, where the majority shareholder of a corporation uses it to support a second corporation in which the minority has no interest, the court may order the wind-up of the first corporation on the ground that it is just and equitable to do so.[153] Where there is reason to believe that substantial assets will disappear into unrealizable securities or that investments for the benefit of the majority shareholder will be made if the corporation is not wound up, an order should be made.[154] The misconduct of the dominant shareholder must relate to the corporation itself or to the shareholder applicant;[155] wrongdoing outside the corporate context, even if criminal, will not provide grounds to wind up the corporation where the corporation itself is well run by its staff.[156]

---

[147] Indeed, at one time the courts were reluctant to order a wind-up of a corporation even where there was a deadlock: *Bleau v. Perruquier français Inc.* (1967), 10 C.B.R. (N.S.) 296 (Que. S.C.).

[148] See, for instance, *Re Cravo Equipment Ltd.*, [1982] O.J. No. 318, 44 C.B.R. (N.S.) 208 (H.C.J.), but compare *Re Chetal Enterprises Ltd.*, [1973] S.J. No. 150, (*sub nom. Re Donnelly*), 39 D.L.R. (3d) 116 (Q.B.), where the court held that in order to justify a wind-up, loss of confidence itself arising only from a casual or loose approach to business was not a sufficient ground.

[149] *Re Sovereign Oil Co.*, [1934] B.C.J. No. 104, [1934] 3 W.W.R. 317 at 319 (B.C.S.C.), *per* McDonald J.

[150] At one time it was suggested that the power of the court to order a wind-up due to loss of confidence was limited to actual misconduct: *Re R.C. Young Insurance Ltd.*, [1955] O.R. 598, 35 C.B.R. 72 at 78 (C.A.), *per* Laidlaw J.A.; *Re National Drive-in Theaters Ltd.* (1954), 11 W.W.R. (N.S.) 145 (B.C.S.C.), but this would appear to be overly restrictive. There are numerous cases in which a wind-up has been ordered on the basis of persistent contravention of corporate law requirements (*e.g.*, no shareholder meetings, no provision of proper financial disclosure): see, for instance, *Singh v. Moody Shingles Ltd.*, [1946] B.C.J. No. 133, 28 C.B.R. 86 (C.A.); see also *Re Purvis Fisheries Ltd.*, [1954] M.J. No. 3, 34 C.B.R. 220 (C.A.).

[151] [1986] S.J. No. 120, 49 Sask. R. 232 (C.A.).

[152] See, for instance, *Mammone v. Doralin Investments Ltd.*, [1985] O.J. No. 262, 54 C.B.R. (N.S.) 171 at 175 (H.C.J.), *per* Anderson J. — mortgage granted in suspicious circumstances. Where there is serious evidence of wrongdoing, an interim protective order of some kind may be necessary or advisable. As to the availability of a receivership in lieu of or in addition to a *Mareva* injunction, see: *ASIC v. Burke*, [2000] N.S.W.S.C. 694, *per* Austin J.

[153] *Fedoruk v. Fedoruk Holdings Ltd.*, [1978] M.J. No. 174, [1978] 6 W.W.R. 40 at 43 (Q.B.), *per* Dewar C.J.Q.B.

[154] *Crossgrove v. Crossgrove*, [1977] O.J. No. 59, 24 C.B.R. (N.S.) 172 (H.C.J.).

[155] *Loch v. John Blackwood Ltd.*, [1924] All E.R. Rep. 200 (P.C.), *per* Lord Shaw.

[156] *Re Hillcrest Housing Ltd.*, [1989] P.E.I.J. No. 117, 80 Nfld. & P.E.I.R. 121, 249 A.P.R. 121 (T.D.).

(c) APPLICATION OF THE MAJORITY RULE CONCEPT

§15.65 The courts recognize that the majority of the corporation are entitled to govern it, and indeed must do so.[157] In the absence of fraud or other wrongdoing, the minority must abide by decisions of the majority.[158] Therefore, so long as the majority act within the normal course and do not abuse their control of the corporation, the court will not intervene.[159] The distinction between an acceptable exercise of control and an abuse of control was discussed in *Re Sydney & Whitney Pier Bus Service Ltd.*,[160] where Doull J. held that the fact that the majority shareholders appoint directors who manage the company's affairs is not an oppression or overbearing of the minority unless the majority act illegally or fraudulently or use their voting power to benefit themselves or some of them and in so doing treat the shareholders with inequality. Majority control and a lack of consultation with minority shareholders are not in themselves acts of oppression. The power of the majority to control the affairs of the company is the ordinary rule, indeed the universal rule, unless the constitution of the company declares otherwise as it sometimes does in private companies. Consequently, where there is a dispute between the majority and minority, it is not enough to prove that the minority shareholders have lost confidence in the directors. The reason for losing confidence must be founded upon wrongful actions of those who have control.[161] So strong is this rule that mere lack of confidence *per se* is not a sufficient ground for the court to order the wind-up of a corporation, that it even applies where the applicant shareholder is the largest single shareholder in the corporation. More generally, the courts have taken the view that the involuntary winding-up provisions of the Act are not an alternative for the normal methods of internal corporate government.[162] Where past misconduct by a director destroys shareholder or creditor confidence in a business, the court may look at the business realities of the situation, and consider past and present conduct of the common directors of two corporations in managing the affairs of both corporations in order to assess the propriety of their conduct.[163] Thus in *Re Martello & Sons Ltd.*,[164] McRuer J.A. stated:

> A petitioner is entitled to be protected not only against past misconduct of the management, but against future misconduct. Even though an action might give him some measure of relief for past misconduct, I do not think it would afford adequate relief therefor and certainly it would afford no protection for the future.
>
> ... [There] is a justifiable and well-founded lack of confidence in the conduct and management of the company's affairs resting on the lack of probity in the conduct

---

[157] *Re Harris Maxwell Larder Lake Gold Mining Co.*, [1910] O.J. No. 790, 1 O.W.N. 984 at 986 (H.C.), *per* Middleton J.
[158] *Re Sydney & Whitney Pier Bus Service Ltd.*, [1944] 3 D.L.R. 468 at 471 (N.S.S.C.), *per* Doull J. See also *Gill v. Bhandal*, [1998] B.C.J. No. 2263, 165 D.L.R. (4th) 151 (S.C.).
[159] *Re Dewey & O'Heir Co.*, [1908] O.J. No. 750, 13 O.W.R. 32 at 38 (C.A.), *per* Boyd C.
[160] [1944] 3 D.L.R. 468 (N.S.S.C.).
[161] *Ibid.*, at 472.
[162] *Re Hugh-Pam Porcupine Mines Ltd.*, [1942] O.J. No. 278, 24 C.B.R. 60 (H.C.J.).
[163] *Dunwoody Ltd. v. 358074 Ontario Ltd.*, [1984] O.J. No. 2505, 5 O.A.C. 288 at 291 (Div. Ct.), *per* Hollingworth J.
[164] [1945] O.J. No. 519, [1945] O.R. 453 at 466 (C.A.).

of the business of the company. It is therefore just and equitable that it should be wound up...

(d) So-called "Incorporated Partnerships"

§15.66 The above principles are modified somewhat where the corporation is a private company that may liberally be characterized as an incorporated partnership:

> A shareholder puts his money into a company on certain conditions. The first of them is that the business in which he invests shall be limited to certain definite objects. The second is that it shall be carried on by certain persons elected in a specified way. And the third is that the business shall be conducted in accordance with certain principles of commercial administration defined in the statute, which provide some guarantee of commercial probity and efficiency. If shareholders find that these conditions or some of them are deliberately and consistently violated and set aside by the action of a member and official of the company who wields an overwhelming voting power, and if the result of that is that ... they are deprived of the ordinary facilities which compliance with the Companies Acts would provide them with, then there does arise ... a situation in which it may be just and equitable for the Court to wind-up the company.[165]

Though courts have occasionally objected to the description of incorporated businesses as a partnership on the ground that it is legally inexact,[166] the concept of the "incorporated partnership" is now well-entrenched in the law relating to the wind-up of corporations. The term "partnership" is used in a figurative rather than technical sense, to describe the right of the complainant to participate in the management of the corporation, as well as the level of trust and dependence on which the corporation is founded. The latter gives rise to an implicit obligation of utmost good faith among the principals in the corporation.

§15.67 In cases involving such incorporated partnerships, it is not necessary to show that there has been actual wrongdoing[167] where the applicant has been denied the benefits of membership in the corporation. It is sufficient to show a complete breakdown in the conditions of mutual trust and confidence on which the partnership was based.[168] It is also necessary to show that the majority have departed from the spirit of the partnership arrangement between the shareholders.[169] The onus lies on the applicant to demonstrate that the corporation is essentially a partnership[170] and that he or she has effectively been squeezed out of

---

[165] *Loch v. John Blackwood Ltd.*, [1924] All E.R. Rep. 200 at para. 11, [1924] A.C. 783 at 793-94 (P.C.), *per* Lord Shaw, quoting Lord Clyde P. in *Baird v. Lees*, [1924] S.C. 83 at 92 (Ct. Sess.).
[166] *Ebrahimi v. Westbourne Galleries Ltd.*, [1972] 2 All E.R. 492 (H.L.), *per* Lord Wilberforce.
[167] *Re R.J. Jowsey Mining Co.*, [1969] O.J. No. 1358, [1969] 2 O.R. 549 (C.A.), aff'd [1970] S.C.R. 549.
[168] *B. Love Ltd. v. Bulk Steel & Salvage Ltd.*, [1982] O.J. No. 3469, 38 O.R. (2d) 691, additional reasons at [1982] O.J. No. 3578, 40 O.R. (2d) 1 (H.C.J.).
[169] *Re Wondoflex Textiles Pty. Ltd.*, [1951] V.L.R. 458 at 467 (S.C.), *per* Smith J.; *Classic Organ Co. v. Artisan Organ Co.*, [1997] O.J. No. 2161, 35 B.L.R. (2d) 285 (Gen. Div.).
[170] *Sobrinho v. Oakville Portugese Canadian Club*, [1982] O.J. No. 3354, 37 O.R. (2d) 581 (H.C.J.); *Johnson v. W.S. Johnson & Sons Ltd.*, [1979] A.J. No. 479, 95 D.L.R. (3d) 495 (T.D.);

the corporation.[171] The normal civil standard of proof applies.[172] An order will not be made where there is no partnership character to the corporation in question,[173] so that the dispute in question is more properly characterized as a wrongful dismissal action rather than a corporate law matter.[174]

§15.68 In deciding whether such a partnership arrangement exists, the court inquires into whether the relationship between the principles of the corporation is one of trust and confidence analogous to a partnership. Three particular factors will be taken into account:

- was the corporation formed or continued on the basis of a relationship involving mutual confidence — an element which can often be established by showing that a pre-existing partnership has been continued under a corporate structure;

- whether there was an agreement or understanding among the shareholders (including the applicant, but not necessarily all other shareholders, provided the control group are also parties to it) that the applicant would be entitled to participate in the control of the corporation;

- a restriction on the transfer of the shares of the corporation, as applies where the articles include the normal private company provision generally inserted into the articles to ensure that most share issues enjoy exemption from the prospectus requirements of the *Securities Act*.[175]

The prior relationship between the parties that gave rise to the corporation need not have a commercial character; a lengthy friendship between the parties concerned that led up to the formation of the corporation is sufficient. Consideration may also be given to the extent of the commitment made by the shareholders to the corporation.[176]

§15.69 A company may be wound up on the grounds that it is just and equitable to do so where the corporation fails to satisfy a crucial regulatory test on which its ability to remain in business is contingent, and there is no realistic possibility

---

Re Rogers & Agincourt Holdings Ltd., [1976] O.J. No. 2126, 12 O.R. (2d) 386 (Div. Ct.), aff'd [1976] O.J. No. 2341, 14 O.R. (2d) 489 (C.A.). For an extreme view questioning the extent to which it is necessary to fix the corporation with partnership attributes, see *Re Humber Valley Broadcasting Co.*, [1978] N.J. No. 161, 19 Nfld. & P.E.I.R. 230 at 236-37, 50 A.P.R. 230 (Nfld. T.D.), per Mifflin C.J.

[171] *Rafuse v. Bishop*, [1979] N.S.J. No. 626, 34 N.S.R. (2d) 70 at 82 (T.D.), per Glube J.; *Strickland v. Tricom Associates (1979) Ltd.*, [1982] N.J. No. 161, 38 Nfld. & P.E.I.R. 451, 108 A.P.R. 451 at 469-70 (Nfld. T.D.), per Mahoney J.; *DiRisio v. DeLorenzo*, [1981] O.J. No. 667, 38 C.B.R. (N.S.) 154 (H.C.J.).

[172] *Re Grimm's Foods Ltd.*, [1979] O.J. No. 4264, 25 O.R. (2d) 42 (H.C.J.).

[173] *Re D. & D. Holdings*, [1981] 4 W.W.R. 13 (Alta. Q.B.).

[174] *Graham v. Technequip Ltd.*, [1981] O.J. No. 2948, 32 O.R. (2d) 297, aff'd [1982] O.J. No. 237, 139 D.L.R. (3d) 542 (Div. Ct.). See also *Re British Columbia Aircraft Propeller & Engine Co.* (1968), 63 W.W.R. 80 (B.C.S.C.).

[175] R.S.O. 1990, c. S.5, as amended.

[176] *B. Love Ltd. v. Bulk Steel & Salvage Ltd.*, [1982] O.J. No. 3469, 38 O.R. (2d) 691, additional reasons at [1982] O.J. No. 3578, 40 O.R. (2d) 1 (H.C.J.).

that it will be able to satisfy that test within the foreseeable future. In such a case, it is for all practical purposes impossible for the company to carry on the business for which it was formed.[177]

(iii) Procedure

(1) Generally

§15.70 As noted above, the court may order the wind-up of a corporation upon the application of the corporation itself, or of one of its shareholders or creditors having a claim of $2,500 or more.[178] The standing provided for in the OBCA in respect of the bringing of an application for the winding-up of a corporation is exhaustive.[179] Where a voluntary winding-up has commenced, the court may also intervene in the proceeding on the application of a liquidator or contributory.[180] Winding-up proceedings are intended to be summary even where the court is required to resolve disputes of fact.[181] A person petitioning for the liquidation of a corporation is not required to provide an undertaking in damages as a condition of making such an application.[182]

§15.71 Except where the application is made by the corporation, at least four days' notice must be given to the corporation before the making of the application.[183] By virtue of the definition of "day" in subsection 1(1) of the OBCA, the term "day" means a clear day, so that the period of notice begins on the day following the date on which notice was served and ends at midnight of the last day of the period. The court has no power to relieve an applicant from the requirement for such notice.[184]

§15.72 It is no abuse of process for two shareholders of a corporation (A or B), or any other person having standing, to commence separate, concurrent applications for the wind-up of a corporation. Where A commences an application for the wind-up of the corporation on one ground, and B commences an application for the wind-up of that corporation on some other ground, the two applications will not normally be consolidated, but may be placed on the same trial list so that one application is heard immediately after the other. Consolidation will only

---

[177] *Canada (Attorney General) v. Security Home Mortgage Corp.*, [1996] A.J. No. 1015, 29 B.L.R. (2d) 58 at 69 and 75 (Alta. Q.B.), *per* Fraser J.
[178] OBCA, s. s. 208(1).
[179] *Mann v. Goldstein*, [1968] 1 W.L.R. 1091 at 1094 (Ch. D.).
[180] OBCA, s. 208(1).
[181] *Buckley v. British Columbia Teachers' Federation*, [1992] B.C.J. No. 1329, 70 B.C.L.R. (2d) 210 (S.C.).
[182] *Re Highfield Commodities Ltd.*, [1985] 1 W.L.R. 149.
[183] OBCA, s. 208(2).
[184] As to whether discovery may be ordered in a court supervised winding-up, see *Canada Deposit Insurance Corp. v. Commonwealth Trust Co.*, [1990] B.C.J. No. 2640, 2 C.B.R. (3d) 87 (S.C.); *Madrid Bank Ltd. v. Bayley* (1866), L.R. 2 Q.B. 37.

be ordered where the decision on one application disposes of an essential cause of action in the other.[185]

§15.73 An application for the wind-up of a corporation is brought by way of originating application,[186] and generally speaking should not be included in a statement of claim seeking some other relief.[187] It is up to the applicant for the wind-up order to establish that grounds exist for the making of that order.[188] The application should contain the grounds of the application and only those grounds should be considered, despite the fact that the evidence may suggest that other grounds exist. If no grounds are set out, then the matter ought to be dismissed.[189] However, where there is a dispute concerning any matter before the court, it may direct the trial of an issue to determine whether or not the corporation should be wound up. Where the court makes such an order, it may give directions as to pleadings, cross-examination and production, and may also impose limits on the expenditures that may be made by the corporation.[190] Where the board of the corporation is evenly divided, neither of the groups has the right to appoint counsel to represent the corporation.[191]

§15.74 The courts are adverse to suspending or adjourning a wind-up application as it is obviously disadvantageous to the corporation to have such a proceeding hanging over it indefinitely. Adjournments will be granted if they are essential to the interests of justice, but will not be given where they can be avoided or there is little compelling reason to grant them. The mere possibility (or even certainty) of prejudice to a party in some other proceeding is not in itself sufficient ground for an adjournment or other delay. For instance, an application for the wind-up of a corporation should not be stayed merely because the facts on which that application is based relate to a criminal charge pending against the dominant shareholder.[192] The fact that the winding-up proceedings may result in the disclosure of some facts prejudicial to the defence is not a ground for restraining the wind-up application.[193]

§15.75 Section 209 of the OBCA provides that within the context of an application for the liquidation of a corporation:

> 209. The court may make the order applied for, may dismiss the application with or without costs, may adjourn the hearing conditionally or unconditionally or may make any interim or other order as is considered just, and upon the making of

---

[185] *Re Hillcrest Housing Ltd.*, [1985] P.E.I.J. No. 5, 7 C.P.C. (2d) 60 (S.C.).
[186] See Rules of Civil Procedure, R.R.O. Reg. 194, Rule 14, but compare *Re J.F. Cunningham & Son Ltd.*, [1955] O.J. No. 565, 35 C.B.R. 131 (S.C. Bankruptcy).
[187] *McDougall v. Gamble*, [1942] O.J. No. 133, [1942] O.W.N. 208 (C.A.), although it is now possible to include such a claim for relief as an alternative to other relief under s. 248 of the Act dealing with shareholder oppression: OBCA, s. 248(3)(*l*).
[188] *Re Grimm's Foods Ltd.*, [1979] O.J. No. 4264, 25 O.R. (2d) 42 (H.C.J.).
[189] *Re Michael P. Georgas Ltd.* (1948), 28 C.B.R. 189 at 192 (Ont. H.C.), *per* Urquhart J.
[190] *Re Fopex Discount Ltd.*, [1977] O.J. No. 1106, 25 C.B.R. (N.S.) 180 (H.C.J.).
[191] *Re Rothlish Investments Ltd.* (1953), 8 W.W.R. (N.S.) 334 (Man. Q.B.).
[192] *Rowe v. Brandon Packers Ltd.* (1961), 29 D.L.R. (2d) 246 (Man. C.A.).
[193] *Ibid.*, *per* Miller C.J.M. at 253.

the order may, according to its practice and procedure, refer the proceedings for the winding up to an officer of the court for inquiry and report and may authorize the officer to exercise such powers of the court as are necessary for the reference.

The court may not make an ancillary order in a winding-up proceeding that effectively creates an independent remedy that operates outside the scope of the prospective winding-up order. The power of the court to make an "other order" is qualified by the context in which those words appear.[194]

(2) Conflicts of Law Issues

§15.76 As we have noted, the dissolution of a corporation is within the control of the jurisdiction of the incorporation of a corporate body. The same does not hold true with respect to the winding-up of the business of a corporate body. In *Harbert Distressed Investment Master Fund, Ltd. v. Calpine Canada Energy Finance II ULC*,[195] it was objected, on the basis of the internal affairs doctrine — albeit in the context of an oppression proceeding — that no court other than the courts of the domicile of the corporation should entertain an oppression proceeding. Smith A.C.J.'s observations on this point are equally instructive in the winding-up context:

> In the brief filed by Calpine in relation to this interlocutory application, the Court was referred to a number of cases that indicate that matters relating to the internal affairs or management of a foreign corporation are subject to the law of the corporation's domicile and that the court should not, under its own laws and procedures, purport to affect the status and internal affairs of a foreign corporation. In my view, this line of authority does not prevent the Court from assuming jurisdiction in the circumstances of this case if the real and substantial connection test is satisfied.[196]

The fact that the law of the domicile is the proper law to apply with respect to the internal affairs of a corporation does not lead to the conclusion that the courts of the domicile have exclusive jurisdiction over any proceeding relating to those internal affairs. Two obvious questions arise with respect to the winding-up of an inter-jurisdictional corporate entity. First, in what circumstances will an Ontario court order the winding-up of a corporate entity incorporated outside the province? Second, in what circumstances may a non-Ontario court order the winding-up of the business of an Ontario incorporated corporation?

§15.77 A court-ordered winding-up proceeding will normally proceed within the domicile of the corporation that is being wound up. For an OBCA corporation, that will be before the Ontario Superior Court. Since a given corporation that is the subject of a winding-up proceeding may have assets scattered across several jurisdictions, the question arises as to the extent to which the courts of jurisdictions in which the corporation may carry on business may interfere with the winding-up proceeding, either by taking charge of those assets and liabilities of

---

[194] *Re R.J. Jowsey Mining Co.*, [1969] O.J. No. 1358, 6 D.L.R. (3d) 97 at 100 (C.A.), *per* Laskin J.A., aff'd [1970] S.C.R. 549.
[195] [2005] N.S.J. No. 317, 235 N.S.R. (2d) 297 (S.C.).
[196] *Ibid.*, at para. 90.

the corporation that are situate within their own respective bailiwick, or otherwise. The general rule is that the courts of one jurisdiction will respect the integrity of foreign winding-up proceedings and will not, without compelling reason, take any steps to interfere in that process.[197] In making this point, it must be emphasized that the operating premise for utilization of the OBCA and CBCA winding-up provisions is that the corporation is solvent.

§15.78 Different considerations will necessarily apply where the home jurisdiction has asserted no jurisdiction over a company that has effectively ceased to carry on business — particularly where it is insolvent (has insufficient assets to meet its liabilities) or illiquid (may have sufficient assets to meet its liabilities, but is failing to do so as they generally come due). Generally speaking, there is no rule which prevents the institution of bankruptcy proceedings against a debtor in one jurisdiction merely because such proceedings have already been instituted in another jurisdiction. Commencement of bankruptcy proceedings in two or more jurisdictions may be advantageous for a number of reasons, including to gain access to assets out of reach of the court originally seized of the matter; to set aside transactions that are voidable in one jurisdiction but not another, or to take advantage of a statutory privilege or priority that would not be available to a particular creditor in the debtor's principal place of business. It is the creditors, rather than the bankrupt, who have the right to select the jurisdiction or jurisdictions in which bankruptcy proceedings will be pursued. In common law jurisdictions, the court has a discretion to suspend a bankruptcy proceeding where some other jurisdiction is the more appropriate forum. In order to be effective, however, a bankruptcy proceeding ought to be brought in a jurisdiction in which the debtor has assets and can only be brought in a court which has jurisdiction over the person or assets of the debtor.

§15.79 It appears that a winding-up order may be made within Canada in respect of a company incorporated outside Canada if there are assets of any nature in Canada which the court can administer and the realization of those assets will — or reasonably may — benefit the petitioner or other persons who are interested in the company. In *Re Compania Merabello San Nicholas SA*, Megarry J. said:

> I would accordingly attempt to summarize the essentials of the relevant law relating the existence of jurisdiction to make a winding-up order in normal cases in respect of a foreign company as follows:
>
> (1) There is no need to establish that the company ever had a place of business here;
>
> (2) There is no need to establish that the company ever carried on business here, unless perhaps the petition is based upon the company carrying on or having carried on business.
>
> (3) A proper connection with the jurisdiction must be established by sufficient evidence to show

---

[197] *Banque Indosuez v. Ferromet Resources*, [1993] B.C.L.C. 112 (Ch.); *Pakistan v. Zardari*, [2006] E.W.H.C. 2411, [2006] All E.R. (D) 79 at para. 127 (Q.B.), *per* Collins J.

(a) that the company has some asset or assets within the jurisdiction; and

(b) that there are one or more persons concerned in the proper distribution of assets over whom the jurisdiction is exercised.

(4) It suffices if the assets of the company within the jurisdiction are of any nature; they need not be 'commercial' assets or assets which indicate that the company formerly carried on business here.

(5) The assets need not be assets which will be distributable to creditors by the liquidator in the winding-up; it suffices if by the making of the winding-up order they will be of benefit to a creditor or creditors in some way.

(6) If it is shown that there is no reasonable possibility of benefit accruing to creditors from the making of the winding-up order, the jurisdiction is excluded.[198]

As in the case of a domestic company, the jurisdiction to make an order for the winding-up of a foreign company is discretionary. The international character of such an insolvency introduces a further consideration into the decision by the court as to whether to make such an order: as a general rule, the court will not order the winding-up of an overseas character if the business and affairs of the company can be more satisfactorily dealt with under the laws of its home jurisdiction.

(3) Appointment and Responsibilities of the Liquidator

(a) GENERALLY

§15.80 Where the court orders that a corporation be wound up, the court must appoint a liquidator for the corporation.[199] There may be one or more liquidators. In a court-ordered liquidation, the liquidator is an officer of the court whose function it is to close up the company's business and distribute its assets to its creditors.[200] In *Liquidator of Markham General Insurance Co. v. Bennett*, Cumming J. observed that:

> A liquidator is an officer of the court whose function is to close up the corporation's business and distribute its assets to its creditors. The liquidator acts as a quasi-trustee for creditors and stands in a different position from the corporation. A winding-up order establishes a quasi-trust of which the creditors are the beneficiaries.[201]

The corporation and the liquidator are separate entities and co-exist throughout the winding-up. They are interdependent in their relationship in that one cannot function without the existence of the other, but that does not change the fact that they are separate and distinct. The corporation has a passive existence because it

---

[198] [1972] 3 All E.R. 448, [1973] Ch. 75 at 91.
[199] OBCA, s. 210(1).
[200] *Maranda-Desaulniers v. Peckham*, [1953] C.C.S. No. 423, [1953] Que. Q.B. 163 at 172 (C.A.), *per* Galipault C.J.Q.
[201] [2006] O.J. No. 1989, 81 O.R. (3d) 389 at para. 25 (S.C.J.).

is under the control of the liquidator, but it retains a separate existence. The liquidator has the character of a court-appointed statutory representative on behalf of the corporate entity being wound up. The liquidator's powers and duties arise because of the statutory obligations and by being an officer of the court.[202] However, the liquidator is not a third party in relation to the insolvent company, but is the person designated by the court to act in place of the directors of the company being wound up.[203] A liquidator owes a fiduciary duty to the corporation as a whole, not to individual shareholders.[204] A liquidator may be required to reimburse the corporation where he (or she) fails to discharge his duties properly and a loss results.[205]

§15.81 A person may not act as a court-appointed liquidator where biased or in an actual or potential conflict of interest. However, there must be a basis to infer the existence of a conflict of interest: the potential must be more than a hypothesis.[206]

(b) REPLACEMENT APPOINTMENT

§15.82 If a vacancy occurs in the office of liquidator (whether by death, resignation or other cause), the court may appoint a substitute.[207] The court may fix the remuneration of the liquidator[208] and may also remove a liquidator by order.[209] The Act is silent as to whether the court may remove a liquidator on its own initiative. Since the liquidator is a court officer and the court has control over its officers, it would seem to follow that the court might act on its own initiative. As a matter of practice, however, it is likely that the court would only remove a liquidator where some interested party moves for such an order to be made.

§15.83 Forthwith following appointment, a court-appointed liquidator is required to notify the Director of the appointment, and to publish a notice of that appointment in *The Ontario Gazette*.[210]

(c) DUTY TO REPORT AND APPROVING A LIQUIDATOR'S ACCOUNTS

§15.84 As an officer of the court, a liquidator is obliged to report to the court as to what the liquidator has done with the assets from the time of the appointment to the time of discharge. A report is required because the liquidator is accountable to the court that made the appointment, accountable to all interested parties, and because the liquidator, as a court officer, is required to discharge its duties

---

[202] *Ibid.*, at paras. 30-32.
[203] *Coopérants, Mutual Life Insurance Society (Liquidator of) v. Dubois*, [1996] S.C.J. No. 44, 39 C.B.R. (3d) 253 at 279 (S.C.C.), *per* Gonthier J.
[204] *Re Edelweiss Credit Union and Cobbett*, [1992] B.C.J. No. 1352, 92 D.L.R. (4th) 508 at 514 (C.A.), *per* Locke J.A.
[205] *Canada Deposit Insurance Corp. v. Commonwealth Trust Co.*, [1992] B.C.J. No. 2513, 14 C.B.R. (3d) 251 (S.C.).
[206] *Hughes v. Oakes*, [2005] O.J. No. 2095, 139 A.C.W.S. (3d) 474 (S.C.J.).
[207] OBCA, s. 210(3).
[208] OBCA, s. 210(2).
[209] OBCA, s. 211.
[210] OBCA, s. 210(4).

in a judicial manner. The report should contain a narrative describing what the liquidator did during the winding-up.

§15.85 An important consideration in assessing the accounts will be the number of hours recorded. The size of the estate is not an irrelevant consideration, but even small estates may involve complex issues and serious disagreements within which the liquidator becomes embroiled. However, the time spent by the liquidator on the services rendered must be both fair and reasonable. Courts are reluctant to second-guess liquidators, even if in retrospect it does appear that the matter could have been administered in a far more efficient manner, particularly where the approach taken was constrained by the terms of the order and the parties disputing the liquidator's accounts consented to those terms. A liquidator will not be punished for a decline in value of the corporation's business or assets that results from factors outside his or her control, nor for delays in resolving the business and affairs of the corporation that results from the action or inaction of others.[211]

§15.86 The accounts of a court-appointed liquidator are subject to the approval of the court in the same manner as the accounts of a court-appointed receiver. The report is distinct from the passing of accounts. Generally, a liquidator completes its management and administration of a debtor's assets by passing its accounts. The court can adjust the fees and charges of the liquidator just as it can in the passing of an estate trustee's accounts; the applicable standard of review is whether those fees and charges are fair and reasonable. Where the liquidator's remuneration includes the amount it paid to its solicitor, the debtor (and any other interested party) has the right to have the solicitor's accounts assessed.[212]

§15.87 When a liquidator asks the court to approve its compensation, the onus is on the liquidator to prove that the compensation for which it seeks court approval is fair and reasonable.[213] The accounts should be verified by affidavit, although as a matter of form there is nothing wrong with a liquidator including its claim for compensation in its final report. If included in the report, this does not shield them from proper scrutiny by way of cross-examination. The following is an abbreviated summary of the rules set down in the *Confectionately Yours* case by the Ontario Court of Appeal concerning the passing of accounts:

- The accounts must disclose in detail the name of each person who rendered services, the dates on which the services were rendered, the time expended each day, the rate charged and the total charges for each of the categories of services rendered.[214]

- The accounts should be in a form that can be easily understood by those affected or by the judicial officer who assesses the accounts;

---

[211] See, generally, *Battisti v. Galati*, [2006] O.J. No. 399, 145 A.C.W.S. (3d) 553 (S.C.J.).
[212] *Re Confectionately Yours Inc.*, [2002] O.J. No. 3569, 219 D.L.R. (4th) 72 at para. 35 (C.A.), *per* Borins J.A.
[213] *Ibid.*, at para. 31.
[214] *Hermanns v. Ingle*, [1988] O.J. No. 432, 68 C.B.R. (N.S.) 15 (H.C.J. — Assess. Officer); *Toronto Dominion Bank v. Park Foods Ltd.*, [1986] N.S.J. No. 351, 77 N.S.R. (2d) 202 (S.C.).

- The liquidator's accounts and a solicitor's accounts should be verified by affidavit.

- If there are no objections to the accounts, under Rule 74.18(9) the court may grant a judgment passing the accounts without a hearing. Thus, the practice that requires a court-appointed liquidator to verify its statement of fees and disbursements on the passing of its accounts conforms with the general practice in the assessment of the fees and disbursements of solicitors and trustees.

- The requirement that a liquidator verify by affidavit the remuneration which it claims fulfils two purposes. First, it ensures the veracity of the time spent by the liquidator in carrying out its duties, under the winding-up order, as well as the disbursements incurred by the liquidator. Second, it provides an opportunity to cross-examine the affiant if the debtor or any other interested party objects to the amount claimed by the liquidator for fees and disbursements. In the appropriate case, an objecting party may wish to provide affidavit evidence contesting the remuneration claimed by the liquidator.

- Where the liquidator's disbursements include the fees that it paid its solicitors, similar considerations apply. The solicitors must verify their fees and disbursements by affidavit.

§15.88 As the court noted in that case, a key goal of the requirements for the liquidator to report and to have its accounts approved is to afford the liquidator judicial protection in carrying out its powers and duties, and to satisfy the court that the fees and disbursements were fair and reasonable. A second and no less important purpose is to afford the stakeholders of the corporation the opportunity to question the liquidator's activities and conduct to date. On the passing of accounts, the court has the inherent jurisdiction to review and approve or disapprove of the liquidator's present and past activities even though the order appointing the liquidator is silent as to the court's authority. The approval given is to the extent that the reports accurately summarize the material activities. The approval process does not permit a reopening of any ruling previously made by the court, nor any reconsideration of any authorization previously granted. It is possible, however, to inquire whether or not previous court instructions have been carried out. The court will permit a challenge to any calculation on which the accounts are based and whether the liquidator proceeded without specific authority or exceeded the authority set out in the order. The court may, in addition, consider complaints concerning the alleged negligence of the liquidator and challenges to the liquidator's remuneration. The passing of accounts allows for a detailed analysis of the accounts, the manner and the circumstances in which they were incurred, and the time that the liquidator took to perform its duties. If there are any triable issues, the court can direct a trial of the relevant issues.[215]

§15.89 Historically when approving fees, some courts have fixed remuneration as a percentage of the proceeds of the realization, while others have adopted more of a time-and-disbursements-oriented approach taking into account the

---

[215] F. Bennett, *Bennett on Receiverships*, 2nd ed. (Scarborough, Ont.: Carswell, 1999) at 459-60.

time, trouble and degree of responsibility involved in discharging the liquidator's responsibilities under the court order. At one time, the courts favoured fixing remuneration on a percentage fee basis relative to the amount recovered through the liquidation process. This approach now seems to be falling out of favour, although the amount recovered may well be a relevant concern in capping the total fee payable. In *Prairie Palace Motel Ltd. v. Carlson*,[216] the court rejected a submission that a receiver's fees should be restricted to 5 per cent of the assets realized and stated:

> In any event, the parties to this matter are all aware that the receiver and manager is a firm of chartered accountants of high reputation. In this day and age, if chartered accountants are going to do the work of receiver managers, in order to facilitate the inability of the disputing parties to carry on and preserve the assets of a business, there is no reason why they should not get paid at the going rate they charge all of their clients for the services they render. I reviewed the receiver and manager's account in this matter and the basis upon which it is charged, and I have absolutely no grounds for concluding that it is in any way based on client fees which are not usual for a firm such as Touche Ross Ltd.[217]

The critical concern is to ensure that the fees paid are no more than what is fair and reasonable.

§15.90 In *Federal Business Development Bank v. Belyea*, Stratton J.A. considered the approval of a receiver's accounts and stated:

> There is no fixed rate or settled scale for determining the amount of compensation to be paid a receiver. He is usually allowed either a percentage upon his receipts or a lump sum based upon the time, trouble and degree of responsibility involved. The governing principle appears to be that the compensation allowed a receiver should be measured by the fair and reasonable value of his services and while sufficient fees should be paid to induce competent persons to serve as receivers, receiverships should be administered as economically as reasonably possible. Thus, allowances for services performed must be just, but nevertheless moderate rather than generous.[218]

Discussing the factors to be applied when the court uses a *quantum meruit* basis, Stratton J.A. continued:

> The considerations applicable in determining the reasonable remuneration to be paid to a receiver should, in my opinion, include the nature, extent and value of the assets handled, the complications and difficulties encountered, the degree of assistance provided by the company, its officers or its employees, the time spent, the receiver's knowledge, experience and skill, the diligence and thoroughness displayed, the responsibilities assumed, the results of the receiver's efforts, and the cost of comparable services when performed in a prudent and economical manner.[219]

---

[216] [1980] S.J. No. 320, 35 C.B.R. (N.S.) 312 (Q.B.).
[217] *Ibid.*, at 313-14.
[218] [1983] N.B.J. No. 41, 46 C.B.R. (N.S.) 244 at 246 (N.B.C.A.).
[219] *Ibid.*, at 247. See also *Re West Toronto Stereo Center Ltd.*, [1975] O.J. No. 1623, 19 C.B.R. (N.S.) 306 (S.C. Bankruptcy) dealing with the remuneration of a trustee-in-bankruptcy; *Re Hoskinson*, [1976] O.J. No. 1616, 22 C.B.R. (N.S.) 127 (S.C. Bankruptcy); *Bank of Montreal v. Ni-*

A winding-up should be administered as economically as reasonably possible.[220] However, the fee that is approved should not encourage short-cut procedures or other forms of cutting corners.

(d) SHAREHOLDER MEETINGS

§15.91 In contrast to a voluntary winding-up, there is no overriding duty upon a liquidator in a court-ordered winding-up to report or account to the shareholders of the corporation. The liquidator is an officer of the court, rather than the agent of the shareholders of the corporation. Nevertheless, in many cases it would be inequitable if the winding-up were to proceed without some explanation being given to the shareholders of the steps that were being taken and the progress that had been made. Subsection 215(1) of the Act provides that:

> 215.(1) Where a winding-up order has been made by the court, the court may direct meetings of the shareholders of the corporation to be called, held and conducted in such manner as the court thinks fit for the purpose of ascertaining their wishes, and may appoint a person to act as the chair of any such meeting and to report the result of it to the court.

Section 214 makes no provision as to who may apply for such an order. There can be no doubt that the liquidator would have standing, nor can there be much doubt that any shareholder would have requisite standing, particularly where the shareholder has a significant shareholding. It is less clear whether a contributory may apply for a court-ordered meeting.

(4) Effect of Wind-up Order

§15.92 Unless the court otherwise orders, where the court orders the wind-up of a corporation, the wind-up is deemed to commence at the time of the service of the notice of application on the corporation (where the application is made by someone other than the corporation itself) and at the time of the making of the application, in all other cases.[221] From the time of the commencement of the wind-up by court order, no action or other proceeding may be proceeded with or commenced against the corporation except by leave of the court and subject to such terms as the court imposes.[222] The authority of the directors with respect to the corporation ceases on the appointment of the liquidator.[223]

---

can Trading Co., [1990] B.C.J. No. 340, 78 C.B.R. (N.S.) 85 (C.A.). They have also been applied at the trial level in this province. See, *e.g.*, *MacPherson v. Ritz Management Inc.*, [1992] O.J. No. 506, 32 A.C.W.S. (3d) 241 (Gen. Div.).

[220] See *Federal Business Development Bank v. Belyea*, [1983] N.B.J. No. 41, 46 C.B.R. (N.S.) 244 (C.A.).

[221] OBCA, s. 213.

[222] OBCA, s. 216(*a*).

[223] *In Re Farrow's Bank Ltd.*, [1921] 2 Ch. 164 (C.A.) *per* Lord Sterndale M.R. However, the directors may appeal against the order under which the liquidator is appointed, as the suspension of their authority is a consequence of that order: *Re Diamond Fuel Co.* (1879), 13 Ch. D. 400 (C.A.). The authorities are divided as to whether the directors retain any residual relationship with the corporation. Compare *Madrid Bank Ltd. v. Bayley* (1866), LR. 2 Q.B. 37, *Re Ebsworth & Tidy's Contract* (1889), 42 Ch. D. 23 at 43 (C.A.) *per* Lord Esher, M.R.; *Measures Brothers*

Moreover, no attachment, sequestration, distress or execution may be put in force against the estate or effects of the corporation.[224] A corporation does not cease to exist when it is being wound up. Winding-up requires the corporation to cease carrying on its business, but does not deprive it of its legal existence, its corporate state or status or even the powers it has as a corporation.[225] A liquidator — unlike a trustee-in-bankruptcy — does not acquire title to the property of the company in respect of which he or she is appointed. The corporation remains vested with title, subject to the liquidator's management. The liquidator is not a third party in relation to the corporation, but is an officer of the court (where appointed by the court) or the corporation (where appointed by the membership) who acts in the place of the directors.[226]

§15.93 Section 214 of the OBCA sets out the general rule that proceedings after the order of the court shall be taken in the same manner and with like consequences as provided in a voluntary winding-up, except that all proceedings are subject to the order and discretion of the court. Despite this general rule, section 214 requires that the list of contributories must normally be settled by the court, rather than by the liquidator. This procedural divergence could cause problems where the court-ordered wind-up takes effect during the course of a voluntary wind-up (which is more than possible, given the right of a contributory to apply for a court order winding-up the corporation). For instance, the liquidator may have settled the liability of the contributories in the course of the voluntary wind-up. To circumvent this problem, section 214 recognizes the settlement made by the liquidator, but then goes on to provide that any such settlement "is subject to review by the court".

§15.94 Once a court has intervened in a voluntary winding-up and placed the wind-up under court order, the function of the inspectors is suspended. In such a case, it becomes the duty of the court to supervise the liquidation so as to ensure that all competing interests within the corporation are respected. Thus there is no role left for the inspectors to play.

§15.95 As noted above, once a court-ordered winding-up has commenced, section 216 of the OBCA provides that:

- no action or other proceeding shall be commenced against or proceeded with against the corporation; and

- no attachment, sequestration, distress or execution shall be put in force against the estate or effects of the corporation.

Ltd. v. Measures, [1910] 2 Ch. 248 (C.A.); *Re Country Traders Distributors Ltd.*, [1974] 2 N.S.W.L.R. 135; *Lord Corporation Pty. Ltd. v. Green* (1991), 22 N.S.W.L.R. 532.

[224] OBC, s. 216(*b*).
[225] *Jolicoeur v. Boivin & Cie*, [1951] C.C.S. No. 55, [1951] Que. P.R. 369 at 372 (S.C.).
[226] See, generally, *Coopérants, Mutual Life Insurance Society (Liquidator of) v. Dubois*, [1996] S.C.J. No. 44, 133 D.L.R. (4th) 643.

except with leave of the court and subject to such terms as the court imposes. In *Stewart v. LePage*[227] the following explanation was given for this rule:

> ... Parliament probably thought it necessary in the interest of prudent and economical winding-up that the court charged with that duty should have control not only of the assets and property found in the hands or possession of the company in liquidation, but also of all litigation in which it might be involved.

Nevertheless, the prohibition against commencing or proceeding with an action or enforcement against a corporation being wound up under court supervision is not absolute, for section 216 expressly confers a discretion on the court to grant leave to proceed. Leave to commence proceedings should only be given where there are compelling reasons for doing so or special circumstances The court may consider whether commencing separate proceedings would promote a multiplicity of proceedings; the effect of separate proceedings on the costs of litigation; and which forum is best suited to the interests of all parties.[228] The following factors are also relevant to the decision as to whether to permit an action to be commenced or continued with outside the context of the liquidation proceeding:[229]

- actions in respect of a contingent or unliquidated debt, the proof and valuation of which has that degree of complexity which makes the summary proceedings of the liquidation inappropriate;

- actions between other parties in which the corporation is a necessary party for a complete adjudication of the dispute existing between those other parties;

- actions brought to establish a judgment against the corporation to enable the plaintiff to recover under a contract of insurance or indemnity or under compensatory legislation;

- actions which, at the date of the winding-up, have proceeded to a point where logic dictates that the action be permitted to continue to judgment.

(a) Participation in Distributions

§15.96 As noted above, clause 221(1)(*a*) of the OBCA requires the liquidator to apply the property of the corporation in satisfaction of all its debts, obligations and liabilities and — subject to their prior payment of creditors — to distribute the property ratably among the shareholders according to their rights and interests in the corporation. Section 228 of the OBCA provides that:

> 228. For the purpose of proving claims, sections 23, 24 and 25 of the *Assignments and Preferences Act* apply with necessary modifications, except that where the word "judge" is used therein, the word "court" as used in this Act shall be substituted.

---

[227] [1916] S.C.J. No. 29, 53 S.C.R. 337, *per* Anglin J. at 349.

[228] *Re Associated Investors of Canada Ltd.*, [1996] A.J. No. 1062, 46 Alta. L.R. (3d) 16 at 23 (Q.B.), *per* Cooke J.; *Re Advocate Mines Ltd.*, [1984] O.J. No. 2330, 52 C.B.R. (N.S.) 277 (S.C. Bankruptcy).

[229] *Re Advocate Mines Ltd.*, [1984] O.J. No. 2330, 52 C.B.R. (N.S.) 277 (S.C. Bankruptcy).

Making the necessary modifications, the key relevant rules regarding claims in a winding-up may be summarized as follows:

- It seems to be implicit in section 24 of the *Assignments and Preferences Act* ("APA")[230] that secured creditors may either proceed to realize against their security or may choose to give up their security and participate in the distribution to be made by the liquidator. The procedure for valuing securities, redeeming securities and claiming for deficiencies in security is comparable to the corresponding regime under the *Bankruptcy and Insolvency Act*.

- Any person claiming to be entitled to claim against the corporation must furnish to the liquidator particulars of his or her claim proved by affidavit and such vouchers as the nature of the case admits.[231]

- Claims must be submitted within a reasonable time. Where a person claiming to be entitled to claim against the corporation does not, within a reasonable time after receiving notice of the winding-up of the corporation and of the name and address of the liquidator, furnish to the liquidator a satisfactory proof of claim, the court may order that unless the claim is proved to the satisfaction of the court within the time fixed in that order, the claimant is deemed to be no longer a creditor of the estate and is wholly barred of any right to share in the proceeds thereof.[232]

- If the claim is not so proved within the time so limited or within such further time as the judge by subsequent order allows, it is wholly barred and the liquidator is at liberty to distribute the proceeds of the estate as if no such claim existed, but without prejudice to the liability of the assignor therefor.[233]

- A person whose claim has not accrued due is nevertheless entitled to prove and to vote at meetings of creditors, but in ascertaining the amount of any such claim a deduction for interest shall be made for the time that has to run until the claim becomes due.[234]

§15.97 It follows from the foregoing that the interests of creditors of a corporation become fixed when liquidation occurs, even though before then they may have had only contingent claims against the corporation.[235] The valuation of future and contingent claims is always problematic, since liability to make payment is not necessarily definite nor is the quantum always identifiable. For obvious reasons, it is impossible for the liquidation process to provide for the

---

[230] R.S.O. 1990, c. A.33.
[231] APA, s. 25(1).
[232] APA, s. 25(2).
[233] APA, s. 25(3).
[234] APA, s. 25(5).
[235] As additional support for this conclusion: Subsection 121(1) of the *Bankruptcy and Insolvency Act* provides that: all debts and liabilities, present or future, to which the bankrupt is subject on the day on which the bankrupt becomes bankrupt or to which the bankrupt may become subject before the bankrupt's discharge by reason of any obligation incurred before the day on which the bankrupt becomes bankrupt shall be deemed to be claims provable in proceedings under that Act. There is no reason to believe that the right to recover under the dissolution procedures of the OBCA or CBCA is any more restrictive.

host of unknown claimants who at some point in the future might assert what is at present an unknown interest in the funds that are available for distribution (*e.g.*, with respect to some as yet undiscovered environmental or product liability). Such potential claims are obviously too contingent to be factored into the eventual distribution made by the liquidator. Subsection 238(3) of the OBCA provides some partial protection for unknown creditors. It reads:

> 238.(3) Where a corporation authorizes its dissolution and a creditor is unknown or a creditor's whereabouts is unknown, the corporation may, by agreement with the Public Trustee, pay to the Public Trustee an amount equal to the amount of the debt due to the creditor to be held in trust for the creditor, and such payment shall be deemed to be due provision for the debt for the purposes of clause (1)(*c*).

Analogous protection is afforded under subsection 238(4), where a shareholder or the whereabouts of a shareholder is unknown. Subsection 238(6) provides for payment to the person ultimately entitled, if that person should ever come forward:

> 238.(6) If the amount paid under subsection (3) or the share of the property delivered or conveyed under subsection (4) or its equivalent in cash, as the case may be, is claimed by the person beneficially entitled thereto within ten years after it was so delivered, conveyed or paid, it shall be delivered, conveyed or paid to the person, but, if not so claimed, it vests in the Public Trustee for the use of Ontario, and, if the person beneficially entitled thereto at any time thereafter establishes a right thereto to the satisfaction of the Lieutenant Governor in Council, an amount equal to the amount so vested in the Public Trustee shall be paid to the person.

§15.98 Upon the application of the liquidator or of the inspectors, if any, or of any creditors, the court, after hearing such parties as it directs to be notified or after such steps as the court prescribes have been taken, may by order give its direction in any matter arising in the winding-up.[236] The court may at any time after the commencement of the winding-up summon to appear before the court or liquidator any director, officer or employee of the corporation or any other person known or suspected of having possession of any of the estate or effects of the corporation, or alleged to be indebted to it, or any person whom the court thinks capable of giving information concerning its trade, dealings, estate or effects.[237] In addition, subsection 230(2) provides that:

> 230.(2) Where in the course of the winding up it appears that a person who has taken part in the formation or promotion of the corporation or that a past or present director, officer, employee, liquidator or receiver of the corporation has misapplied or retained in that person's own hands, or become liable or accountable for, property of the corporation, or has committed any misfeasance or breach of trust in relation to it, the court may, on the application of the liquidator or of any creditor, shareholder or contributory, examine the conduct of that person and order that person to restore the property so misapplied or retained, or for which that person has become liable or accountable, or to contribute such sum to the property of the corporation by way of compensation in respect of such misapplication, retention, misfeasance or breach of trust, or both, as the court thinks just.

---

[236] OBCA, s. 229.
[237] OBCA, s. 230(1).

(b) Suing a Liquidator

§15.99 From time to time, those who are dissatisfied with the conduct of a liquidation may seek to pursue a remedy against the liquidator. Court orders appointing a liquidator usually include a provision to the effect that no proceeding may be instituted against the liquidator except with leave of the court that made the appointment. In *Stewart v. LePage*,[238] a trust company was wound up by the B.C. Supreme Court. Certain beneficiaries brought a declaratory proceeding against its liquidator and the company in P.E.I. seeking to have the company declared to be trustee in connection with certain deposits. They also sought the appointment of a new trustee in respect of those deposits. The Supreme Court of Canada ultimately held that the P.E.I. action could not proceed unless leave was first obtained from the B.C. Court. Anglin J. explained:

> No doubt some inconvenience will be involved in such exceptional cases as this where the winding-up of the company is conducted in a province of the Dominion far distant from that in which persons interested as creditors or claimants may reside. But Parliament probably thought it was necessary in the interest of prudent and economical winding-up that the court charged with that duty should have control not only of the assets and property found in the hands or possession of the company in liquidation, but also of all litigation in which it might be involved. The great balance of convenience is probably in favour of such single control though it may work hardship in some few cases.[239]

§15.100 A liquidator is not protected where the claim that is to be brought falls outside the scope of the liquidation.[240] The test can be a difficult one to apply. In *Gillett v. Deloitte & Touche Inc.*[241] a trust company held a second mortgage as bare trustee of a self-directed R.R.S.P. on behalf of the respondent. The appellant (Deloitte & Touche Inc.) was appointed liquidator of the trust company. It thus came into control over that mortgage. The trust company's assets (including the mortgage) were transferred to a bank. The order appointing the appellant prohibited the institution of any legal action against the liquidator without leave of the court. The first mortgagee subsequently commenced foreclosure proceedings against the property and gave written notice to the appellant of the pending foreclosure. The appellant failed to forward the notice of foreclosure to the respondent or to the bank that held the mortgage. The respondent learned of the foreclosure only after the property had been sold. He claimed that if he had been notified of the foreclosure, he would have acted to protect his investment. The respondent sued the lawyer for the first mortgagee alleging that he had breached his duty to give the respondent notice of the foreclosure, and then applied successfully to add the appellant as a defendant. The appellant appealed claiming that leave of the court was required before it might be added as a defendant. The chambers judge had concluded that leave was unnecessary because the issue was an act of alleged negligence by the appellant rather than an act in its official capacity as liquidator.

---

[238] [1916] S.C.J. No. 29, 53 S.C.R. 337.
[239] *Ibid.*, at 349.
[240] *Spivak v. Lee*, [1932] 3 W.W.R. 525 (Man. K.B.).
[241] [2004] N.S.J. No. 47, 236 D.L.R. (4th) 288 (C.A.).

§15.101 The Nova Scotia Court of Appeal dismissed the appeal. Freeman J.A. (giving the judgment of the court) held that the law did not require leave of the Ontario court which had appointed the receiver when the matter fell outside even a generous interpretation of the administration of the winding-up.[242] It was for the chambers judge to determine whether the respondent's negligence claim against the appellant fell outside the liquidation. It was not patently unjust for the respondent to have the right to bring his tort action against the appellant for damages for breach of its duty of care in the civil court. It was noted that the appellant had fulfilled its duty in its capacity as liquidator with respect to the mortgage prior to its receipt of the notice of foreclosure. After transfer to the bank, the asset had been placed beyond the reach of the creditors of the trust company and the liquidator. As a result, so far as that particular asset was concerned, the requirements of the liquidation had been fully discharged. Nothing lingered but the memory. Freeman J.A. continued:

> Mr. Gillett therefore could have no cause of action arising within their liquidation from any act or omission of Deloitte & Touche as liquidator. That is not the basis of his claim. If it were, he would clearly need leave of the Ontario Court. The action he seeks to bring against Deloitte & Touche must therefore have originated from a source entirely outside and distinct from the liquidation. If that is so, then it is not a claim brought under the Winding Up Act, and therefore in my view would not require leave of the Ontario Court. Mr. Gillett says that the source of his claim was Deloitte & Touche's own negligence: it owed him a duty of care, and negligently failed to act on it.[243]

§15.102 The institution of a civil action against an OBCA or CBCA liquidator for negligent or otherwise improper performance or non-performance of the duties to which the liquidator is subject, would seem to be the direct analogue to the institution of a similar claim against a court-appointed receiver or a trustee-in-bankruptcy — and presumably where a prohibition exists against any action without leave, should be subject to similar requirements and restrictions as the institution of such claims. In *Mamone v. Pantzer*,[244] Santow J. discussed the applicable principles governing the requirement that a prospective litigant must obtain leave of the court to sue a court-appointed liquidator: He noted that:

- the court will protect its officers from spurious or vexatious litigation; and
- the court will protect the integrity of the winding-up process to ensure no wrongful interference with that process.[245]

To these ends, a prospective litigant must demonstrate its claim has sufficient merit. The courts will also take into account that liquidators often have to make decisions on the run, so that to expect perfection is unrealistic. Claims against a liquidator should not be permitted where the requirement for the liquidator to pass his or her accounts affords an appropriate opportunity to review the alleged

---

[242] *Ibid.*, at para. 26.
[243] *Ibid.*, at para. 18.
[244] [2001] NSWSC 26.
[245] *Ibid.*, at para. 4.

misconduct of the liquidator. Generally, if the liquidator has done anything which the liquidator ought not to have done, the remedy is to pursue the matter in the accounting.[246]

E. PROVISIONS OF GENERAL APPLICATION RELATING TO LIQUIDATION

(i) Administration of the Corporate Estate

§15.103 So far we have considered only the special rules that apply to voluntary liquidation (in contrast to liquidation under court order). As a general rule, however, the rules and procedures applicable to both classes of wind-up are the same. More specifically, sections 220 to 236 of the OBCA set out a number of rules of general application which apply to both voluntary and court ordered wind-ups. Before looking at those provisions in detail, it is worth noting that the winding-up provisions of the OBCA (and also those of the CBCA and other corporate law statutes, for that matter) are directed toward a number of consistent objectives. These include:[247]

- the equitable treatment of all creditors and other claimants against the corporation;
- the avoidance of preferences;
- the disposition of the assets of the corporation on the most favourable terms, to the betterment of all persons who are interested in the corporation;
- to provide a single procedure and process for marshalling the assets of the corporation and applying them to the payment of its liabilities;
- the avoidance of the flood of claims that might otherwise arise upon the decision to wind up the corporation, as every person with a claim or potential claim against the corporation seeks to make sure that its claim will be properly paid;[248]
- the minimization of the administrative and professional costs associated with resolving all outstanding issues relating to the business and affairs of the corporation (in particular discouraging any race to the courthouse and the institution of numerous lawsuits both by and against the corporation); and

---

[246] *Commonwealth Investors Syndicate Ltd. v. KPMG Inc.*, [2005] B.C.J. No. 18, 7 C.B.R. (5th) 90 at para. 22.

[247] See, generally, *F.D.I.C. as receiver for Buena Vista Bank & Trust Company v. American Casualty Co. of Reading*, 843 P.2d 1285 (S.C. Colo. 1992) — although this decision was with respect to the liquidator of an insolvent bank, much of the discussion is equally applicable in all liquidation contexts.

[248] *Stewart v. LePage*, [1916] S.C.J. No. 29, 53 S.C.R. 337 at para. 62, *per* Brodeur J.: "The object of this legislation is to prevent litigation being carried on by anyone prejudicial to the estate, to prevent the assets being dissipated by law suits, and to have all such matters decided promptly by a summary petition."

- where recovery from contributories is necessary, ensuring the equitable apportionment of losses and minimizing litigation.

The basic duty of the liquidator is set out in clause 221(1)(*a*) of the Act. It requires the liquidator to apply the property of the corporation in satisfaction of all its debts, obligations and liabilities and — subject to their prior payment of creditors — to distribute the property ratably among the shareholders according to their rights and interests in the corporation.

§15.104 The above summary of the principles regarding the administration of the corporate estate is deceptively simplified insofar as it suggests that there will be little controversy with respect to how those principles are to be applied. Often, those who have an interest in the amount realized will complain that a better offer could have obtained for corporate assets, using some other method of sale or disposition than that which the liquidator has employed. In a surprisingly large number of cases, a "late offer" will materialize for corporate assets that appears to better the offer for those assets than the offer accepted by the liquidator. In such cases, the court may be asked to overturn the liquidator's decision.

§15.105 There can be little argument with the general proposition that where the liquidation is proceeding under the supervision of the court, it is the responsibility of the court to see that the above objectives are attained to as great an extent as possible.[249] It is self-evident, however, that as a practical matter, the day-to-day discharge of these responsibilities will be entrusted to the liquidator who (while subject to the overall control of the court) will necessarily exercise a great deal of discretion and decision-making authority. Indeed, clause 221(1)(*a*) and section 223 of the OBCA makes clear that this will be the case.[250] There is considerable case law with respect to the oversight that courts are expected to exercise over trustees-in-bankruptcy and court-appointed receiver-managers with respect to the provident administration of corporate estates. Much of this case law would seem to be directly applicable to court-appointed liquidators.

§15.106 Since the decision in *Crown Trust Co. v. Rosenberg*,[251] it has been accepted that the courts may place reasonable reliance upon the decisions made and recommendations given by such court-appointed officers with respect to the

---

[249] See, for instance, *Re Christian Brothers of Ireland*, [2004] O.J. No. 359, 69 O.R. (3d) 507 at para. 36 (S.C.J.), *per* Blair J.

[250] See, however, subsection 217(1), which provides:

> 217.(1) Where the realization and distribution of the property of a corporation being wound up under an order of the court has proceeded so far that in the opinion of the court it is expedient that the liquidator should be discharged and that the property of the corporation remaining in the liquidator's hands can be better realized and distributed by the court, the court may make an order discharging the liquidator and for payment, delivery and transfer into court, or to such person as the court directs, of such property, and it shall be realized and distributed by or under the direction of the court among the persons entitled thereto in the same way as nearly as may be as if the distribution were being made by the liquidator.

[251] [1986] O.J. No. 2990, 60 O.R. (2d) 87, 39 D.L.R. (4th) 526 (H.C.J.).

sale of assets and other aspects of administration. In many cases, the language suggests a degree of "deference" to the views of the officers concerned, but perhaps a more appropriate description is that of reasonable reliance upon the professional competence and integrity of the officer, in the absence of reason to doubt that such competence and integrity has been exercised.[252] Realistically speaking, any rigorous and ongoing process of micromanagement by the court would essentially defeat the very purpose of appointing an officer such as a liquidator.

§15.107 The liquidator's administration of the corporation's business and affairs, and its dealing with the assets of the corporation should be conducted in a manner that is as transparent as is consistent with the best interests of the corporation and those who are interested in it.[253] Accordingly, the basis for any recommendation should be reasonably clear and capable of explanation. The process followed must be commercially reasonable and fair from the perspective of potential purchasers, creditors and debtors alike. It is equally important from the perspective of preserving public confidence in the liquidation process that the procedure have the appearance of being fair and reasonable.[254] In *Royal Bank of Canada v. Soundair Corp.*[255] the Ontario Court of Appeal approved the summary of the responsibilities of the court with respect to any dispute concerning a proposed sale of corporate assets, as set out in the Crown Trust decision. It stated that the court must:

(a) consider whether the receiver has made a sufficient effort to get the best price and has not acted improvidently;

(b) consider the interests of all parties;

(c) consider the efficacy and integrity of the process by which offers are obtained; and

(d) consider whether there has been unfairness in the working out of the process.

---

[252] *Re Regal Constellation Hotel Ltd.*, [2004] O.J. No. 2744, 71 O.R. (3d) 355 at para. 23 (C.A.), *per* Blair J.A.

Although the courts will carefully scrutinize the procedure followed by a receiver, they rely upon the expertise of their appointed receivers, and are reluctant to second-guess the considered business decisions made by the receiver in arriving at its recommendations. The court will assume that the receiver is acting properly unless the contrary is clearly shown.

[253] See, generally, *Re Wagman*, [2006] O.J. No. 1579, 21 C.B.R. (5th) 144 at para. 10 (S.C.J.), *per* Registrar Nettie.

[254] *Toronto-Dominion Bank v. Crosswinds Golf & Country Club Ltd.*, [2002] O.J. No. 1398, 59 O.R. (3d) 376 (S.C.J.), *per* Wilson J.

[255] [1991] O.J. No. 1137, 4 O.R. (3d) 1 at 42 (C.A.), *per* Galligan J.A.

In *Skyepharma PLC v. Hyal Pharmaceutical Corp.*,[256] Farley J. described the required effort on the part of a receiver (or liquidator) to obtain the best price in the following terms:

> A receiver's duty is not to obtain the best possible price but to do everything reasonably possible in the circumstances with a view to obtaining the best price ... Other offers are irrelevant unless they demonstrate that the price in the proposed sale was so unreasonably low that it shows the receiver as acting improvidently in accepting it. It is the receiver's sale not the sale by the court... The receiver, after a reasonable analysis of the risks, advantages and disadvantages of each offer (or indication of interest if only advanced that far) may accept an unconditional offer rather than risk delay or jeopardize closing due to conditions which are beyond the receiver's control. Furthermore, the receiver is obviously reasonable in preferring any unconditional offer to a conditional offer ...
>
> .....
>
> Provided a receiver has acted reasonably, prudently and not arbitrarily, a court should not sit as in an appeal from a receiver's decision, reviewed in detail every element of the procedure by which the receiver made the decision (so long as that procedure fits with the authorized process specified by the court if a specific order to that affect has been issued). To do so would be futile and duplicative.

In *Re Selkirk*,[257] the court stated that:

> The court will not lightly withhold approval of a sale by the receiver, particularly in a case such as this where the receiver is given rather wide discretionary authority as per the order of Trainor, J. and, of course, where the receiver is an officer of this court. Only in a case where there seems to be some unfairness in the process of the sale or where there are substantially higher offers which would tend to show that the sale was improvident will the court withhold approval. It is important that the court recognize the commercial exigencies that would flow if prospective purchasers are allowed to wait until the sale is in court for approval before submitting their final offer. This is something that must be discouraged.

Certainty, credibility and predictability in this disposition process are required to ensure that good prices can be obtained where a corporation is in liquidation. Prospective purchasers must have confidence that negotiations with liquidators can be relied upon and will be adhered to without undue interference from the court.[258] In practice, it is difficult to challenge the liquidator's recommendation with respect to sale where it follows reasonable advertisement, the property is put on the market for an apparently reasonable period of time, and the offering price was based upon an apparently reliable appraisal prepared by a qualified appraiser.

§15.108 The courts may also place reasonable reliance upon the recommendations made by a liquidator concerning the settlement of claims against the corporation,

---

[256] [1999] O.J. No. 4300, 12 C.B.R. (4th) 87 at paras. 4, 5 and 7 (S.C.J. — C.L.), appeal quashed [2000] O.J. No. 467, 47 O.R. (3d) 234 (C.A.).

[257] [1987] O.J. No. 2006, 64 C.B.R. (N.S.) 14 at 142 (Gen. Div.) *per* McRae J.

[258] *Toronto-Dominion Bank v. Crosswinds Golf & Country Club Ltd.*, [2002] O.J. No. 1398, 59 O.R. (3d) 376 (S.C.J.), *per* Wilson J.

but here the extent of reliance is more qualified and limited in scope than in the case of the sale of the assets of the corporation. The general approach of the courts in this regard was explained in *Re Ravelston Corp.*,[259] in which Farley, J. stated:

> ... it seems to me that there is a subtle distinction to make between reliance on a receiver's commercial expertise concerning a recommended sale and the receiver's expertise in regards to a settlement of a legal dispute (while of course taking into account that such a receiver will have had appropriate legal advice from its own counsel). That distinction is based on the fact that the court is the "expert" in respect of the law and will generally be in a better position to assess the law involved in a situation than it would be as to the commercial aspects of a sale of property. In this regard, one may wish to consider the analogous situation of expert opinions as discussed in *R. v. Mohan*.[260] Thus it seems to me that the court, with the assistance of counsel (both counsel supporting the approval of a settlement and counsel opposing), should conduct an analysis of the strengths and weaknesses of the case, including the general vagaries of litigation plus the benefits of certainty and the avoidance of delay concerning possible appeals, sufficient for the court to conclude that the proposed settlement fell within the range of what was fair and commercially reasonable. The case here involved an all or nothing result if the case went on to a court decision.

However, where the range of claims against a corporation is highly complex, and the liquidator has been specifically entrusted by the court with developing an overall process to treat all claimants who have similar claims reasonably and equally, and the receiver has developed a systematic method for doing so, drawing upon suitable professional expertise and experience, the court may rely upon the liquidator's recommendations.[261]

(ii) Effect of the Liquidation Upon the Directors of the Corporation

§15.109 Clause 221(1)(*c*) of the OBCA provides that upon a winding-up, all the powers of the directors cease upon the appointment of a liquidator, "except in so far as the liquidator may sanction the continuance of such powers". This wording is ambiguous: if the liquidator sanctions the directors to exercise powers, do they exercise those powers as directors or as agents of the liquidator?[262] Whichever view one takes of this question, it is clear that unlike a receivership, in a liquidation (whether voluntary or involuntary) there is no residual power left in the directors as such to commence any proceeding on behalf of the corporation, to petition it into bankruptcy or to seek relief under the *Companies' Creditors Arrangement Act*.[263] However, not all statutes providing for the liquidation of a corporation have such an exhaustive consequence. In particular, the fact that a

---

[259] [2005] O.J. No. 3802, 14 C.B.R. (5th) 207 at para. 3 (S.C.J. — C.L.).
[260] [1994] S.C.J. No. 36, [1994] 2 S.C.R. 9.
[261] See, for instance, *Re Christian Brothers of Ireland*, [2004] O.J. No. 359, 69 O.R. (3d) 507 at para. 39 (S.C.J.), *per* Blair J.
[262] *Re Country Traders Distributors Ltd.*, [1974] 2 N.S.W.L.R. 135 (S.C.), *per* Mahoney J.
[263] R.S.C. 1985, c. C-36, as amended.

corporation is being liquidated under the *Bankruptcy and Insolvency Act* does not destroy the corporate entity or fully restrict its ability to function as a corporation. It continues to exist as a corporation, and to possess certain rights and capacities, such as the power to waive its solicitor-client privilege. The exercise of these residual capacities will usually be complicated by the fact that the corporation will have no officers or directors and so no present means to exercise them, but in such cases a shareholders' meeting may be held for the election of directors.[264]

§15.110 There is an implicit intent in any liquidation proceeding that it be concluded as quickly as the circumstances will allow — ideally with the minimum of expense consistent with prudent administration of the corporation and the closure of its estate. The phrase "as quickly as the circumstances will allow" should not be mistaken to mean that a winding-up should (much less, will) necessarily conclude quickly. Large, complex enterprises can take a very lengthy time to close down, particularly where the business and affairs of the enterprise are in disarray. Since the liquidation of a business is to a very large extent the creditors' last real shot at recovering what is owed to them, in certain cases the final resolution of a corporate estate may need to be deferred until such time as the ultimate damages resulting from a wrong can be estimated with reasonable accuracy.[265] Claims brought by the corporation against others may need to proceed through trial and appeal. The prudent disposition of corporate property may also take time. Each possibility can lead to a lengthy liquidation. In *Commonwealth Investors Syndicate Ltd. v. KPMG Inc.*,[266] counsel for the appellant remarked that the winding-up of that company began when he was in high school. Counsel for the respondent topped that claim by remarking that the proceedings began before he was born.

(iii) Absence of a Liquidator

§15.111 Clause 220(*a*) of the OBCA makes clear that where at any time during the course of either a voluntary or court-ordered winding-up there is no liquidator, the court may appoint a person to act as a liquidator on the application of a shareholder. While this clause makes no reference to an application by anyone other than a shareholder, the power of the court to intervene in a voluntary wind-up under subclause 207(1)(*b*)(ii) and subsections 208(1) and 210(1) would seem to be sufficient authority for the court to appoint a new liquidator on the application of a creditor or contributory. In any event, until such time as a new liquidator is appointed, the estate and effects of the corporation are under the control of the court.[267]

---

[264] *Bre-X Minerals Ltd. (Trustee of) v. Verchere*, [2001] A.J. No. 1264, 293 A.R. 73 (C.A.); *Ciriello v. The Queen*, [2000] T.C.J. No. 829, 21 C.B.R. (4th) 9 at 17; *National Trust Co. v. Ebro Irrigation & Power Co.*, [1954] O.J. No. 545, [1954] 3 D.L.R. 326 (H.C.J.); *Shepherd (Trustee) v. Shepherd*, [1997] O.J. No. 4675, 50 C.B.R. (3d) 115 (Gen. Div. — C.L.).

[265] See, for example, *Re Fund of Funds Ltd.*, [2004] O.J. No. 2580, 2 C.B.R. (5th) 191 (S.C.J.) — claim bar ordered after 30-year liquidation.

[266] [2005] B.C.J. No. 18; 7 C.B.R. (5th) 90 (C.A.).

[267] OBCA, s. 220(*b*).

(iv) Costs of a Liquidator

§15.112 Section 223 of the OBCA provides that the costs, charges and expenses of a winding-up (including the remuneration of the liquidator) are payable out of the property of the corporation in priority to all other claims.[268] The term "property of the corporation" effectively limits this priority in the case of corporate assets subject to a security interest in favour of secured creditors. The liquidator will take the property of the corporation as he or she finds it. If the assets of the corporation are fully encumbered, there will be no equity to which the liquidator may look for remuneration.

(v) Duties and Powers of the Liquidator

§15.113 As an officer of the court, the liquidator is required to maintain an even and impartial hand among all persons whose interests are concerned in the winding up. It is his (or her) duty to the whole body of creditors and shareholders of the corporation, and to the court, to become thoroughly acquainted with the company's affairs, and to suppress or conceal nothing coming to his knowledge in the course of the performance of his office that is material. So far as practical he or she should ascertain the exact truth with respect to matters that the court must decide, and otherwise assist the judge in the performance of his or her duty in this respect.[269] Since the position of a liquidator appears in many respects analogous to that of a trustee-in-bankruptcy, it follows that case law relating to the duties and liabilities of a trustee-in-bankruptcy can provide considerable guidance as to the duties and liabilities of a liquidator. The general nature of the duties of a liquidator were described by Maugham J. in *Re Home & Colonial Insurance Co.* in the following terms:

> The statutory duties cast upon him involve the getting in of the property and applying such property in satisfaction of the liabilities *pari passu*, and subject thereto the distribution of the balance among the members. ... I think there can be no doubt that, in the circumstances of the case, a high standard of care and diligence is required from a liquidator. ... He is, of course paid for his services; he is able to obtain wherever it is expedient the assistance of solicitors and counsel; and, which is a most important consideration, he is entitled, in every case of serious doubt or difficulty in relation to the performance of his statutory duties, to submit the matter to the Court, and to obtain its guidance.[270]

The liquidator must be and appear to be independent and impartial among the creditors and shareholders of the corporation.[271] A person should not be appointed as liquidator where that person's interest and duty may conflict. A person should not be appointed liquidator of a corporation where he or she has an

---

[268] As to the authority of the court to make an order for interim costs in the costs of a liquidation proceeding, see *Re Hillcrest Housing Ltd.*, [1992] P.E.I.J. No. 83, 94 D.L.R. (4th) 165 (C.A.), leave to appeal to S.C.C. refused [1992] S.C.C.A. No. 453.

[269] See, generally, *Commonwealth Investors Syndicate Ltd. v. KPMG Inc.*, [2004] B.C.J. No. 437, 129 A.C.W.S. (3d) 907 at para. 13 (S.C.), *per* Preston J., rev'd on other grounds [2005] B.C.J. No. 18, 7 C.B.R. (5th) 90 (C.A.).

[270] [1930] Ch. 102 at 124-25.

[271] *Re Contract Corporation (Gooch's Case)* (1872), 7 Ch. App. 207 at 211 (H.L.), *per* James L.J.

interest in another company involved in litigation with the corporation.[272] However appointed, the liquidator of a corporation is a fiduciary *vis-à-vis* the corporation and those who are concerned in it.[273] He or she must administer the property of the corporation as a general fund for the benefit of those persons in accordance with their respective rights.[274] The duties of the liquidator are owed to the persons concerned in the corporation generally (whether as creditors, shareholders or contributories), not to any of them individually, no matter how great or small their respective claims may be.[275] As a fiduciary, the liquidator must conduct himself or herself with the utmost propriety in the administration of the corporation and its business affairs, acting always in good faith[276] and for no improper purpose.[277] Where the liquidator is appointed by the court or the liquidation continues under court supervision, the liquidator is also an officer of the court. As a consequence of that office and in addition to the duties the liquidator already owes to the corporation and those interested in it, the liquidator is also subject to duties in favour of the court itself, such as the duty to carry out the instructions of the court, to inform the court fully with respect to all matters relevant to the liquidation that come to his or her notice, to provide such professional or commercial advice to the court as it may require in connection with the liquidation, and to deal on perhaps an even more impartial basis with the persons concerned in the liquidation.

§15.114 The basic duty of the liquidator, no matter how appointed, is to gather in and realize upon the assets of the corporation. The liquidator must do everything possible to augment the disposable assets of the corporation,[278] although the liquidator may compromise a dispute to which the corporation is a party and in connection with settling the dispute may admit liability on behalf of the corporation.[279] In doing so, the liquidator must carry out his or her duties in strict accordance with the governing legislation,[280] and must act in good faith.[281] The liquidator must not be influenced by an improper purpose,[282] fetter his or her discretion,[283] or enter into any conflict of interest.[284] It is clear that a liquidator is expected to possess the skill, competence and knowledge of a

---

[272] *Re Kabat Pty Ltd.* (1985), 3 A.C.L.C. 829.
[273] *Thomas Franklin & Sons Ltd. v. Cameron* (1936), 36 S.R. (N.S.W.) 286.
[274] *Ayerst (Inspector of Taxes) v. C & K (Construction) Ltd.*, [1976] A.C. 167 (H.L.); see also *Canada (Attorney General) v. Confederation Life Insurance Co.*, [1997] O.J. No. 123, 32 O.R. (3d) 102 (C.A.).
[275] *Knowles v. Scott*, [1891] 1 Ch. 717.
[276] *Ibid.*
[277] *Silkstone & Haigh Moor Coal Co. v. Edey*, [1900] 1 Ch. 167.
[278] *Re Tavistock Ironworks Co.* (1871), 24 L.T. 605 at 605 (C.A.), *per* Lord Romilly M.R.
[279] *Re Christian Brothers of Ireland in Canada*, [1998] O.J. No. 823, 38 B.L.R. (2d) 286 (Gen. Div.), vard [2000] O.J. No. 1117, 6 B.L.R. (3d) 151, leave to appeal to S.C.C. refused [2000] S.C.C.A. No. 277.
[280] *Commissioner for Corporate Affairs v. Peter William Harvey*, [1980] V.R. 669 (S.C. Vic.).
[281] *Knowles v. Scott*, [1891] 1 Ch. 717.
[282] *Silkstone & Haigh Moor Coal Co. v. Edey*, [1900] 1 Ch. 167.
[283] *Re Scotch Granite Co.* (1867), 17 L.T. 533 (Ch.).
[284] *Re Gertzenstein Ltd.*, [1937] Ch. 115.

professional business person,[285] and to exercise his or her authority in a diligent manner, acting at all times with reasonable care.[286] The liquidator is under a duty to pay debts of which he or she has notice or knowledge, and to inquire into the business and affairs of the corporation to discover what debts exist.

§15.115 After making such reasonable inquiries and providing the required notice to creditors and others that the corporation is in liquidation, the liquidator is not liable for other debts and other claims that are not discovered. The liquidator is an administrator of the corporation, not its guarantor. In this respect, section 53(1) of the *Trustee Act*[287] applies with the necessary modifications to liquidators.[288] It provides:

> 53. A trustee or assignee acting under the trusts of a deed or assignment for the benefit of creditors generally, or of a particular class or classes of creditors, where the creditors are not designated by name therein, or a personal representative who has given such or the like notices as, in the opinion of the court in which such trustee, assignee or personal representative is sought to be charged, would have been directed to be given by the Superior Court of Justice in an action for the execution of the trusts of such deed or assignment, or in an administration suit for creditors and others to send in to such trustee, assignee or personal representative, their claims against the person for the benefit of whose creditors such deed or assignment is made, or against the estate of the testator or intestate, as the case may be, at the expiration of the time named in the notices, or the last of the notices, for sending in such claims, may distribute the proceeds of the trust estate, or the assets of the testator or intestate, as the case may be, or any part thereof among the persons entitled thereto, having regard to the claims of which the trustee, assignee or representative has then notice, and is not liable for the proceeds of the trust estate, or assets, or any part thereof so distributed to any person of whose claim there was no notice at the time of the distribution.

Essentially section 53 of the *Trustee Act* provides that a liquidator who has given notice comparable to that which a court would require to be given by the liquidator in the case of a court-supervised liquidation to persons having potential claims against the corporation, is not liable for distributing the amount realized through the liquidation of the corporation's assets only among those persons of whose rights the liquidator knew or had received notice as of the time of the distribution, thus a burden lies upon creditors to assert their claims. The liquidator should pay only in respect of legally enforceable obligations of the corporation.[289] In determining whether to admit or reject proof of a debt, a liquidator acts in a quasi-judicial capacity.[290] Claims submitted to the liquidator should not be accepted blindly. When in doubt as to their merit, the liquidator

---

[285] *Chin Keow v. Government of Malaysia*, [1967] 1 W.L.R. 813.
[286] *Re Windsor Steam Coal Co. (1901), Ltd.*, [1929] 1 Ch. 151 at 159 (C.A.), *per* Lord Hanworth M.R.
[287] R.S.O. 1990, c. T.23, as amended.
[288] OBCA, s. 221(2).
[289] *Re Art Reproduction Co.*, [1952] Ch. 89. As to foreign tax liabilities, see *Government of India v. Taylor*, [1955] A.C. 491 at 509 (H.L.), *per* Viscount Simonds.
[290] *Tanning Research Laboratories v. O'Brien* (1990), 1 A.C.S.R. 510 at 514 (H.C. Aust.), *per* Brenna and Dawson JJ.

should seek legal advice, even if those claims are in the form of a judgment.[291] If a creditor disputes the rejection of his or her claim by the liquidator, the creditor should apply to the court for a hearing.[292]

§15.116 The "property" of the corporation that the liquidator is obliged to gather in is not limited to property as understood at common law, but includes any asset or other thing of value whether or not it would ordinarily be recognized as a property right, provided it augments the value of the corporation's estate.[293] The liquidator must then apply that property in satisfaction of all the corporation's debts, obligations and liabilities. After satisfying the claims of the creditors of a corporation with respect to all debts, obligations and liabilities that are owed to them, any property that remains must be distributed ratably among the shareholders of the corporation according to their rights and interests in the corporation.[294] A shareholder who is owed a debt by the corporation (as distinguished from other shareholders who hold only an equity interest in its share capital and surplus) is entitled to claim as a creditor in respect of that debt and to be paid as such. Where the wind-up of a corporation will take a long period of time, the liquidator may make interim dividend payments on the approval of the inspectors. If the liquidator was appointed by the court, he or she should seek court approval of any interim distributions among the creditors or shareholders, as, until the court so orders, there is no authority in the liquidator to pay.[295] The corporation has no right to charge the shareholder seeking the wind-up of a corporation with the costs of the wind-up. Thus the liquidator may not deduct from the amount otherwise payable to a particular shareholder either the costs of the wind-up itself or the costs of holding a special meeting of the shareholders to consider a winding-up motion or some step taken within it.[296]

§15.117 The authority of a court-appointed liquidator stems from the appointment made by the court. All decisions must be made under and within the authority conferred by court order.[297] A court-appointed liquidator may take no

---

[291] *Re Van Laun, ex p. Chatterton*, [1907] 2 K.B. 23 at 31 (C.A.), per Buckley L.J.; *Ayerst (Inspector of Taxes) v. C & K (Construction) Ltd.*, [1976] A.C. 167; *Tanning Research Laboratories v. O'Brien* (1990), 1 A.C.S.R. 510 (H.C. Aust.).

[292] See, generally, *Re Kentwood Construction Ltd.*, [1960] 1 W.L.R. 646; *Re Trepca Mines Ltd.*, [1960] 1 W.L.R. 1273 (C.A.).

[293] See, generally, *Re Toronto Dairies Ltd.* (1952), 32 C.B.R. 180 at 185 (Ont. S.C. in Bank.), per Sr. Master Marriott.

[294] OBCA, ss. 221(1)(*a*) and 238(1)(*d*). However, subs. 238(4) provides:

> 238.(4) Where a corporation authorizes its dissolution and a shareholder is unknown or a shareholder's whereabouts is unknown, it may, by agreement with the Public Trustee, deliver or convey the shareholder's share of the property to the Public Trustee to be held in trust for the shareholder, and such delivery or conveyance shall be deemed to be a distribution to that shareholder of his, her or its rateable share for the purposes of the dissolution.

[295] *Re Fund of Funds Ltd.*, [1986] O.J. No. 497, 59 C.B.R. (N.S.) 310 at 319 (H.C.J.), per Houlden J.A.

[296] *Reader v. Crown Laundry & Dry Cleaning Co.*, [1986] N.J. No. 116, 61 Nfld. & P.E.I.R. 186 at 188-89, 185 A.P.R. 186 (S.C.), per Cameron J.

[297] *Duffy v. Super Centre Development Corp.*, [1967] 1 N.S.W.R. 382 at 383 (S.C.), per Street J.

important or unusual step in the liquidation of the corporation except with the approval and directions of the court, and in obtaining the court's directions and approval the liquidator is bound to assist the court by providing it with as much information as is within his or her possession.[298] However, provided the court-appointed liquidator keeps the court fully informed, acts in good faith and in accordance with the instructions given by the court, the liquidator will enjoy the protection of the court.[299]

§15.118 In carrying out the instructions of the court, the liquidator is expected to use reasonable care. Liquidators who ignore the reasonable complaints of creditors do so at their peril. In *Maelor Jones Investments (Noarlunga) Pty Ltd. v. Heywood Smith*[300] a liquidator was held liable for negligence with respect to the conduct of the sale of certain units. The liquidator had entrusted the sale of the units to an inexperienced real estate agent, who caused all of the units to become vacant and then tried to auction them. The liquidator allowed the situation to continue for eight months despite the protests of creditors and contributories.

§15.119 A high standard of care and diligence is required from a liquidator. By way of protection, the liquidator, wherever necessary or expedient to the liquidation of the corporation or the administration of its affairs, may seek the assistance of solicitors and other professionals, and the reasonable costs and fees thereby incurred are expenses properly chargeable to the estate of the corporation. Moreover, the liquidator is entitled in every case of serious doubt or difficulty in relation to the performance of his statutory duties, to submit the matter to the court to obtain its guidance.[301]

§15.120 It is sometimes said that liquidators are liable for negligence but not for mere errors in judgment, but in recent years the courts have pointed out the fallacious nature of this distinction.[302] A more appropriate distinction lies between decisions and acts on the part of the liquidator that require the exercise of business judgment, or the exercise of discretion based upon some subjective assessment, as opposed to decisions or acts that are mechanical or that should be based upon objective criteria. The courts are less willing to second-guess decisions that called for the exercise of business judgment or the exercise of discretion on the basis of a subjective assessment. However, it is doubtful that a liquidator is entitled to the same extent of protection in respect of errors in judgment as is provided to directors under the business judgment rule. The discretion of a liquidator is necessarily limited by the purpose of the winding-up and the circumstances of the corporation at the time of his or her appointment. The kind of risk that directors might willingly assume when considering the long-term

---

[298] *Re Tavistock Ironworks Co.* (1871), 24 L.T. 605 at 605 (C.A.), *per* Lord Romilly M.R.
[299] *Re Windsor Steam Coal Co., (1901) Ltd.*, [1929] 1 Ch. 151 at 159 and 162-63 (C.A.), *per* Lord Hanworth M.R.
[300] (1989), 7 A.C.L.C. 1232 (S.C.S.A.).
[301] *Re Home & Colonial Insurance Co.*, [1930] 1 Ch. 102 at 125, *per* Maugham J.; see also *Re Windsor Steam Coal Co. (1901) Ltd.*, [1929] 1 Ch. 151 at 162-63 and 165 (C.A.), *per* Lawrence L.J.
[302] *Whitehouse v. Jordan*, [1981] 1 W.L.R. 246 at 263 (H.L.), *per* Lord Fraser of Tulleybelton.

prospects of a corporation that is expected to have an indefinite future clearly cannot be assumed by a liquidator, since such long-term business objects are inconsistent with the purpose of the winding-up. The nature of the office of a liquidator is very much more that of a conservator than a speculator.

§15.121 In deciding which claims to pursue, a liquidator is entitled to base his or her conclusion on reasonable commercial criteria. In *Wilson v. Whitehouse*,[303] the respondents (M and W) were shareholders in a company, in which M held 73.75 per cent of the shares, while W held 25 per cent. The relationship between the respondents broke down, and M put the company into voluntary liquidation. A resolution to wind up was passed at a general meeting and a liquidator, C, was appointed. On C's application, a court order was made which, *inter alia*, sanctioned the appointment of accountants to produce a report as to (a) the remuneration and benefits in kind drawn by M from the company (including payments to persons connected with him) and whether the same were justified and (b) whether there had been any diversion by M of business opportunities to the detriment of the company and the advantage of other companies in which he was interested. The accountants made an interim report in which they stated that they had "identified a number of situations which give rise to possible misfeasance claims ... and a number of possible contractual claims". However, they refused to sign off their report until their fees had been paid. C concluded that the company was unable to pay its debts in full and called a creditors' meeting. It was resolved to place the company in creditors' winding up (the English counterpart to a corporate bankruptcy). The applicant (L) was appointed as liquidator. L wrote to M and W inviting offers for the assignment of the debts and rights of action belonging to the company, and received offers from both of them. He concluded that he should accept the offer from M as it was the most commercially realistic offer for the benefit of the company, but was conscious that to do so would effectively stifle the company's potential claims against M. L sought directions under the *Insolvency Act 1986*, as to whether he might accept M's offer. The judge took the view that the application, although expressed to be for directions should be treated as an application for sanction under section 165(2)(*b*). He adjourned the application for a short time to enable M and W to reconsider their offers in the light of the accountants' report, which had only just been made available to them. Both M and W made further offers. The matter came back before the judge, and he made an order sanctioning the liquidator's decision to accept M's revised offer.

§15.122 W appealed. The two principal issues on the appeal were: (i) whether the compromise with M for which L sought sanction was in the best commercial interests of the company; and (ii) whether, if it was in the best commercial interests of the company, sanction of the compromise should nevertheless be excluded by the public interest in the pursuit of claims against an allegedly wrongdoing director. The appeal was dismissed. The Court of Appeal concluded that the judge had been right to hold that, in relation to the post-liquidation expense creditors,

---

[303] [2006] All E.R. (D) 93 (C.A.)

M's offer was to be preferred on grounds of certainty and finality. He had also been right to take the view that W should not be enabled to pursue M for his own benefit as a pre-liquidation creditor at the expense and risk of the post-liquidation creditors. In the context of the recovery for the benefit of a company's pre-liquidation creditors of funds or commercial opportunities said to have been misappropriated or misdirected by the actions of a director, the relevant question was whether the public interest in the imposition of civil sanctions would lead to the conclusion that litigation to achieve that end should be pursued at the expense and risk of the post-liquidation creditors whose interests would be best served by a compromise with the alleged wrongdoer.

§15.123 A liquidator is expected to obtain professional assistance with respect to matters that are beyond his or her competence. A liquidator is not expected to possess competence in fields outside his or her own area of expertise, and he or she is primarily to be judged by the standards of his or her own discipline. However, the liquidator must exercise common sense and seek qualified assistance where a reasonable person in comparable circumstances would do so.[304] Having obtained such assistance, the liquidator may place reliance on the advice that is provided unless there is some reason to doubt the competence of the professional who gave it.[305]

§15.124 The duty of a liquidator to investigate allegations of past wrongdoing on the part of the directors, officers and other fiduciaries of the corporation is still unsettled. In Australia, there is case law that suggests that such a duty exists. However, in that country the liquidation procedure is used in the case of corporate insolvency in the place of bankruptcy. In *Re Allebart Pty Ltd. and the Companies Act*,[306] Street J. said in the context of an insolvent company:

> A court winding up involves more than a mere realization of the assets and distribution of proceeds. The official liquidator is an officer of the Court, and as such he has public responsibilities to investigate past activities connected with the company, and in appropriate cases, to initiate such further proceedings, civil or criminal, connected therewith as the circumstances may dictate. It is his duty to discover not only breaches of the *Companies Act,* but also conduct falling short of the requisite standards of commercial morality. In every instance the winding up of an insolvent company pursuant to an order of the Court is attended with these obligations resting upon the official liquidator. The due course of such a winding up involves his taking such steps in relation thereto as are necessary to discharge the duties and obligations resting upon him.[307]

The liquidator will usually be the person in the best position to investigate the affairs of the corporation. He or she clearly owes a duty to the shareholders of

---

[304] *Maelor Jones Investments (Noarlunga) Pty Ltd. v. Heywood Smith* (1989), 7 A.C.L.C. 1232 (S.C.S.A.), *per* Olsson J.
[305] *Dunlop v. Woollahra Municipal Council*, [1982] A.C. 158 at 171 (P.C.); evidence of the incompetence of a professional must be clear-cut, in order for liability to attach: *Re Ah Toy* (1986), 4 A.C.L.C. 480 at 495 (S.C.N.T.).
[306] [1971] 1 N.S.W.L.R. 24 (S.C.).
[307] *Ibid.*, at 26-27.

the corporation to maximize the amount available for distribution among them. On these criteria it seems reasonable to conclude that the liquidator should inquire into the past conduct of the corporation where there is reason to doubt that it has been properly conducted, and should proceed with claims to recover amounts improperly taken out of the corporation where facts come to light which suggest that such misappropriation has taken place. It is not just when a corporation is insolvent that misappropriation is a relevant concern. It arises whenever corporate property may have been taken contrary to the scheme of distribution applicable in the circumstances. On the other hand, there would seem to be no justification for a liquidator to squander the assets of a corporation on a fishing trip for evidence on the off-chance that some wrongdoing might have occurred in the corporation's past, where there are no grounds to believe that such wrongdoing has occurred. The liquidator obviously is not entitled to undertake unnecessary inquiries solely for the purpose of inflating the fees payable for his or her services.

§15.125 The liquidator takes the property of the corporation subject to any rights of trust beneficiaries[308] or secured creditors.[309] Among the creditors of the corporation themselves, the relative priority of their claims is determined generally in accordance with the normal rules of debtor and creditor law. The creditors entitled to participate in the assets of the corporation include any person who has a claim for unliquidated damages.[310] Neither the OBCA nor the CBCA requires a valuation by a secured creditor, and therefore such a creditor is not subject to a general duty to value its security interest.[311] But a secured creditor may only claim for a deficiency after its collateral has been valued or realized upon, and any value placed upon particular collateral by the creditor will be conclusive against that creditor should the sale of the collateral by the creditor realize less

---

[308] *Ontario (Securities Commission) v. Xantrex Management Corp.*, [1977] O.J. No. 1213, 25 C.B.R. (N.S.) 272 (H.C.J.).

[309] *Re Saint John River Log Driving Co.*, [1927] 3 D.L.R. 800 (N.B.C.A.) *per* Barry C.J.K.B. Any property sold will be limited to the corporation's equity:

> The creditor cannot by the sale of assets discharge the lien created by the Act in favour of the bondholders, and his having done so does not prejudice their rights. The lien upon the property still persists, and ... it would be neither right nor equitable to apportion amongst the bondholders the proceeds of the property sold, while at the same time [they] retain their right of lien against the very property itself.

However, subsection 25(1) of the *Personal Property Security Act*, R.S.O. 1990, c. P.10 provides:

> 25.(1) Where collateral gives rise to proceeds, the security interest therein,
>
> (a) continues as to the collateral, unless the secured party expressly or impliedly authorized the dealing with the collateral; and
>
> (b) extends to the proceeds.

[310] *G.T. Campbell & Associates Ltd. v. Hugh Carson Co.*, [1979] O.J. No. 4248, 7 B.L.R. 84, 24 O.R. (2d) 758 (C.A.); *Northern Ontario Power Co. v. LaRoche Mines Ltd.*, [1937] O.J. No. 316, [1937] O.R. 824 at 845 (C.A.), *per* Masten J.A., rev'd on other grounds [1938] 3 All E.R. 755 (P.C.). See also *Midland Counties District Bank v. Attwood*, [1905] 1 Ch. 357; *Maritime National Fish Ltd. v. Ocean Trawlers, Ltd.*, [1935] A.C. 524 (P.C.).

[311] *Bank of Ottawa v. Newton*, [1906] 4 W.L.R. 508 at 511 (Alta. C.A.), *per* Howell C.J.A.

than the amount given as the value.[312] A secured creditor may elect to give up his or her security interest and participate as an unsecured creditor.[313] There are two reasons why a secured creditor may wish to forgo the security interest to which it is entitled and claim as a general creditor. First, it is possible for particular collateral to have an increased value when sold as part of the corporation's general undertaking. Second, it is possible that the collateral subject to the security may be worth less than the amount owed a creditor, but the corporation may still be solvent.

§15.126 Since the OBCA liquidation provisions apply only where the corporation is solvent, rules of priority can be of relevance only in determining the order in which claimants are paid. The OBCA grants special priority in a liquidation for wage claims. Specifically, clause 221(1)(*b*) of the OBCA provides that in distributing the property of the corporation, debts due to employees[314] of the corporation for services performed for it due at the commencement of the winding-up or within one month before, not exceeding three months' wages and vacation pay accrued for not more than 12 months are entitled to be paid in priority to the claims of the ordinary creditors.[315] Those employees rank as ordinary creditors for the residue of their claims. Where there is a services contract under which a particular employee is to be employed for a stated period at a defined salary, the employee may claim for the present value of the aggregate sum payable as salary over the unexpired term, subject to adjustment for the risk to health and life and a deduction being made for the liberty to seek alternative employment.[316]

---

[312] *Canadian Bank of Commerce v. Martin*, [1917] B.C.J. No. 75, [1918] 1 W.W.R. 395, 40 D.L.R. 155 (C.A.). Note, however, subsection 64(3) of the *Personal Property Security Act*, R.S.O. 1990, c. P.10:

> 64(3) Unless otherwise agreed in the security agreement, or unless otherwise provided under this or any other Act, the debtor is liable for any deficiency.

[313] The effect of so doing was explained by Barry C.J.K.B. in *Re Saint John River Log Driving Co.*, [1927] 3 D.L.R. 800, 54 N.B.R. 582 at 587 (C.A.).

[314] As to the test of employment, see *Re Western Coal Co.* (1913), 4 W.W.R. 1238, 12 D.L.R. 401 (Alta. T.D.).

[315] This priority does not exist in the case of directors' remuneration: *Re S.E. Walker Co.* (1913), 4 W.W.R. 1288, 12 D.L.R. 769 (Alta. T.D.). *Quaere* the constitutionality of clause 221(1)(*b*), as it can have no application except in an insolvency. However, para. 136(1)(*d*) of the *Bankruptcy and Insolvency Act*, R.S.C. 1985, c. B-3 provides that:

> 136.(1) Subject to the rights of secured creditors, the proceeds realized from the property of a bankrupt shall be applied in priority of payment as follows:
>
> .....
>
> (*d*) wages, salaries, commissions or compensation of any clerk, servant, travelling salesman, labourer or workman for services rendered during the six months immediately preceding the bankruptcy to the extent of two thousand dollars in each case, together with, in the case of a travelling salesman, disbursements properly incurred by that salesman in and about the bankrupt's business, to the extent of an additional one thousand dollars in each case, during the same period, and for the purposes of this paragraph commissions payable when goods are shipped, delivered or paid for, if shipped, delivered or paid for within the six month period, shall be deemed to have been earned therein. ...

[316] *Hawkins v. Allied Truck Co.*, [1919] O.J. No. 360, 16 O.W.N. 381 at 382 (H.C.J.), *per* Sutherland J.

§15.127 The Act confers a number of express powers upon liquidators, and contains several provisions that specify the manner in which particular powers and duties are to be discharged. The appointment of a liquidator terminates the authority of the directors,[317] except as the liquidator may allow. Under the liquidator's general managerial power, he or she may dismiss personnel, including those who act in a managerial capacity.[318] Any such dismissal will be subject to such claims as the employees concerned may have under the *Employment Standards Act*[319] or other applicable legislation and under the common law of wrongful dismissal.

§15.128 A court-appointed liquidator is an officer of the court; a liquidator appointed by the shareholders is not.[320] Whether or not court appointed, the liquidator is a fiduciary for those persons interested in the corporation and therefore is under a duty to act reasonably, prudently and impartially.[321] In particular, the liquidator must assure that reasonable efforts are made to earn such profits as are consistent with the liquidation process. Thus the liquidator may not permit assets of the corporation to sit idle, so that no income is earned upon those assets,[322] although any investments made should be of a suitably liquid nature so that they may be encashed and used for the purposes of the liquidation. The liquidator must discharge the duties of his or her office with reasonable diligence.[323]

§15.129 Clause 223(1)(*a*) of the Act provides that the liquidator may bring or defend any action, suit or prosecution, or other legal proceedings, civil or criminal, in the name and on behalf of the corporation. While liquidators are vested with broad discretion in resolving the debts owed by and due to a corporation, that discretion is not boundless. Such powers are, as with other discretionary authority, limited by "the requirements of rationality, compliance with statute, and prohibition against improper discrimination".[324] Discretion must be exercised in a manner that is neither arbitrary nor improperly discriminatory. Whether appointed by the shareholders or the court, the liquidator is a trustee for the benefit of all persons with claims against the corporation or who are entitled to share in the distribution of any surplus remaining after all claims.[325]

§15.130 The appointment of a liquidator by the court terminates the authority of the directors,[326] and thus the power under clause (*a*) must be seen as exhaustive

---

[317] OBCA, s. 221(1)(*c*).
[318] *Ali Baba Steakhouse Ltd. v. 257593 Restaurant Ltd.*, [1981] O.J. No. 635, 38 C.B.R. (N.S.) 97 (H.C.J.).
[319] S.O. 2000, c. 41, Part XV, as amended.
[320] *Re Great Prairie Investment Co.* (1908), 8 W.L.R. 6 at 7 (Man. K.B.), *per* Mathers J.
[321] *Ali Baba Steakhouse Ltd. v. 257593 Restaurant Ltd.*, [1981] O.J. No. 635, 38 C.B.R. (N.S.) 97 at 99 (H.C.J.), *per* Anderson J.
[322] *Bowman v. Solway*, [1988] O.J. No. 2833, 68 C.B.R. (N.S.) 107 (S.C. Bankruptcy).
[323] *C.P.H.C. Holding Co. v. Western Pacific Trust Co.* (1973), 36 D.L.R. (3d) 431 (B.C.S.C.).
[324] *In re Executive Life Ins. Co.*, 32 Cal. App. 4th 344 at 370 (1995).
[325] *Garamendi v. Golden Eagle Insurance Company*, [2006] Cal. App. Unpub. LEXIS 10043 (Calif. C.A., 1st Dist.)
[326] OBCA, s. 221(1)(*c*).

as far as any action, suit or proceeding brought by the corporation itself. The liquidator is also empowered to carry on the business of the corporation so far as may be required as beneficial for the winding-up of the corporation.[327] The powers conferred in this regard extend to the raising of money upon the security of the property of the corporation.[328] However, any loan so incurred must be borne ratably by the shareholders of the corporation.[329]

§15.131 The OBCA confers all of the powers that are necessary in order to allow the liquidator to gather in and apply the property of the corporation. The provisions in question are drafted in language that allows the liquidator reasonable discretion and the flexibility to enter into arrangements that will maximize proceeds and minimize the costs of realization. Thus clause 223(1)(*c*) provides that the liquidator may sell the property of the corporation by public auction or private sale and receive payment of the purchase price either in cash or otherwise. The power to execute all necessary documentation is conferred under clause 223(1)(*d*). It provides that the liquidator may do all acts and execute all documents in the name and on behalf of the corporation and use the seal of the corporation. Clause 223(1)(*e*) permits the liquidator to draw, accept, make and endorse any bill of exchange or promissory note in the name and on behalf of the corporation. The drawing, accepting, making or endorsing of a bill of exchange or promissory note by the liquidator on behalf of the corporation has the same effect with respect to the liability of the corporation as if that bill or note was drawn, accepted, made or endorsed by or on behalf of the corporation in the course of carrying on its business.[330] The liquidator is also given the general power to do and execute all such other things as are necessary for winding up the business and affairs of the corporation and distributing its property.[331]

(vi) Discharge of the Liquidator

§15.132 A liquidator appointed by the shareholders of a corporation, in the normal course may be removed[332] or replaced by the shareholders. Thus section 195 of the OBCA provides:

> 195. If a vacancy occurs in the office of the liquidator by death, resignation or otherwise, the shareholders may, subject to any arrangement the corporation may have entered into with its creditors upon the appointment of inspectors, fill such vacancy, and a meeting for that purpose may be called by the continuing liquidator, if any, or by any shareholder or contributory, and shall be deemed to have

---

[327] OBCA, s. 223(1)(*b*).
[328] OBCA, s. 223(1)(*f*).
[329] *Re Miller, Court & Manley Ltd. (in Liquidation)*, [1940] B.C.J. No. 83, [1940] 3 W.W.R. 184 (S.C.).
[330] OBCA, s. 223(2).
[331] OBCA, s. 223(3).
[332] In this respect, s. 196 of the OBCA provides:
> 196. The shareholders of a corporation may by ordinary resolution passed at a meeting called for that purpose remove a liquidator appointed under section 193, 194, or 195, and in such case shall appoint a replacement.

been duly held if called in the manner prescribed by the articles or by-laws of the corporation, or, in default thereof, in the manner prescribed by this Act for calling meetings of the shareholders of the corporation.

In contrast, a court-appointed liquidator is an officer of the court and, as such, can only be removed by the court. However the liquidator is appointed, he or she would appear to be free to resign at any time.[333] Generally speaking, the liquidator will continue in office until the business of the corporation has been fully liquidated. In some cases, however, the liquidator of the corporation will reach a stage that the further continuation of the liquidator would impose an undue administrative cost on the corporation. Therefore, section 217(1) of the OBCA provides:

> 217.(1) Where the realization and distribution of the property of a corporation being wound up under an order of the court has proceeded so far that in the opinion of the court it is expedient that the liquidator should be discharged and that the property of the corporation remaining in the liquidator's hands can be better realized and distributed by the court, the court may make an order discharging the liquidator and for payment, delivery and transfer into court, or to such person as the court directs, of such property, and it shall be realized and distributed by or under the direction of the court among the persons entitled thereto in the same way as nearly may be as if the distribution were being made by the liquidator.

Where the court makes an order under subsection 217(1), it may make an ancillary order directing how the documents and records of the corporation and the liquidator are to be disposed of, and may order that they be deposited in court or otherwise dealt with as the court thinks fit.[334]

§15.133 Section 211 of the OBCA provides that the court may by order remove a liquidator appointed by it for cause, and in such a case it is required to appoint a replacement. The court will order the removal of a liquidator where it is in the best interests of the liquidation for such an order to be made. For instance, if there is reason to believe that the liquidator is an unfit person, whether by reason of personal character or from his or her connection with the parties, or from other circumstances in which the liquidator is involved, the court may remove the liquidator from office.[335] The term "unfit" is broadly interpreted in this context. It is not necessary to show that the liquidator is guilty of any personal misconduct.[336] Nor is it necessary to show that the liquidator is "unfit" in any objectively verifiable sense. The position of liquidator is one of confidence and the liquidator may be relieved where he or she has for any reason lost the confidence of a substantial part of the constituency whose interest he or she represents. For instance, in *Re Oxford Building & Investment Co.*[337] Kay J. removed a

---

[333] OBCA, s. 210(3).
[334] OBCA, s. 217(2).
[335] *Re Sir John Moore Gold Mining Co.* (1879), 12 Ch. D. 325 at 331 (C.A.), *per* Jessel M.R.
[336] *Re Adam Eyton Ltd.* (1887), 57 L.J. Ch. 127, 36 Ch. D. 299 (C.A.); see also *Re Rubber & Produce Investment Trust* (1915), 84 L.J. Ch. 534; *Re Federal Bank of Australia Ltd.* (1894), 20 V.L.R. 199.
[337] (1883), 49 L.T. 495 (Ch. D.).

liquidator where all of the creditors and bond holders of a corporation appeared to wish it.

(vii) Rights of Shareholders

§15.134 The two basic rights of the shareholders in a liquidation of a corporation are: (1) to insist upon an accounting by the liquidator of his or her conduct of the liquidation and the property of the corporation disposed of;[338] and (2) after the application of the property of the corporation in satisfaction of all its debts, obligations and other liabilities, to receive a ratable distribution among themselves of the remaining property of the corporation, according to the rights and interests of each shareholder concerned in the corporation. The liquidation of a corporation is a matter in which all shareholders have a common interest, and no one shareholder or group of shareholders may be charged with the costs of the liquidation of the corporation, even where other shareholders or groups of shareholders opposed the liquidation.[339]

§15.135 The right of the shareholders to receive a distribution constitutes a return of share capital rather than a dividend. In the absence of a contrary provision in the articles, the shares of a corporation are presumed to be equal and all are entitled to share equally in the surplus assets remaining after payment of the creditors and the return of stated capital held in respect of each class of shares to the shareholders of those classes.[340] Clearly where a shareholder purchased shares from a prior shareholder, the amount paid at the time of purchase from that prior shareholder is irrelevant to determine the current shareholder's entitlement. However, all holders of the shares of the same class are entitled to receive an equal share of the amount payable to them, irrespective of the amount originally paid to the corporation in respect of the issue of the shares concerned.[341] The following example illustrates the application of this rule:

---

[338] OBCA, s. 205(1).
[339] *Reader v. Crown Laundry & Dry Cleaning Co.*, [1986] N.J. No. 116, 61 Nfld. & P.E.I.R. 186, 185 A.P.R. 186 (T.D.).
[340] *Re Porto Rico Power Co.*; *International Power Co. v. McMaster University*, [1946] S.C.J. No. 4, [1946] S.C.R. 178.
[341] *Superstein v. Albertawest Forest Products Corp. (Liquidators of)* (1966), 58 W.W.R. 147 at 153-54, 59 D.L.R. (2d) 580 (Alta. C.A.), *per* McDermid J.A.

Amount Remaining After Payment of Creditors		$100,000
Class A Shares		
100 shares issued @ $10	$1,000	
500 shares issued @ $20	$10,000	
500 shares issued @ $50	$25,000	
Total Stated Capital Class A		$36,000
Class B Shares		
100 shares issued @ $50	$5,000	
100 shares issued @ $100	$10,000	
Total Stated Capital Class B		$15,000
Total Stated Capital		$51,000
Balance Remaining		$49,000

Each class A share is entitled to receive a ratable share of the $36,000 stated capital of that class. Therefore, each shareholder receives 36,000/1100 or $32.73 per share. Each class B share is entitled to receive a ratable share of the $15,000 stated capital of that class. Therefore, each shareholder receives 15,000/200 or $75 per share. After the repayment of the $51,000 of stated capital, $49,000 of surplus remains. Each class A and class B shareholder is entitled to an equal share of that amount: 49,000/1300 or $37.69 per share.

§15.136 Subject (possibly) to any contrary provision in the terms of the shares concerned, the holders of non-cumulative preferred shares have no right to receive interest or further dividends on the sum payable to them where payment is delayed because of difficulty in realizing upon the assets of the corporation.[342] Any interest earned upon amounts realized pending distribution to the shareholders belongs to those shareholders who are entitled to participate in the residual property of the corporation after repayment of share capital — that is (in most cases), to the holders of the common shares.[343]

§15.137 It may happen that the liquidator may be left with a trifling amount that cannot practically be divided among the shareholders. Subsection 244(1) of the OBCA provides that any property of a corporation that has not been disposed of at the date of its dissolution is immediately forfeited to the Crown in right of Ontario upon that dissolution. In *Re Prairie Fibreboard Ltd.*[344] the question arose as to whether the shareholders of a corporation might resolve to pay such an

---

[342] *Re Fund of Funds Ltd.*, [1986] O.J. No. 497, 59 C.B.R. (N.S.) 310 (Ont. H.C.J.). As to the rights of the holders of shares bearing a cumulative dividend, see *Re Casino Co.*, [1947] 4 D.L.R. 380 (N.S.T.D.).
[343] *Morrow v. Peterborough Water Co.*, [1902] O.J. No. 153, 4 O.L.R. 324 (H.C.J.); see also *Re Fund of Funds Ltd.*, [1986] O.J. No. 497, 59 C.B.R. (N.S.) 310 (H.C.J.).
[344] (1962), 38 W.W.R. 412, 36 D.L.R. (2d) 767 at 771 (Sask. Q.B.), *per* Disberry J.

amount to charity. It was held that there was no right to do so, as there was no power in the Act to pay out property of the corporation to any person other than the creditors or shareholders of the corporation in accordance with their respective entitlements. In the view of the court, the Crown's right of escheat could not be defeated by giving away the surplus to charity.

§15.138 This conclusion is questionable. The Crown, as a volunteer, has no equitable claim on the residue remaining. The surplus belonging in a corporation on its winding-up belongs to the shareholders and is theirs to dispose of as they wish. *Prima facie,* the shareholders are entitled to give away their property, if they wish to do so, and there is no reason why they might not unanimously decide to distribute the entire surplus value of the corporation to charity, rather than participate in a distribution among themselves. Alternatively, individual shareholders might choose, if so inclined, to direct that the payments to which they are entitled be paid instead to some designated person, including a charity. The Crown's escheat rights are no more than a statutory recognition that property must ultimately be owned by someone, and if there is no one with an apparent claim upon property, then it passes to the Crown for the general benefit of the public. Taking into account the general principle of statutory interpretation that legislation conferring a power of expropriation or providing for the confiscation of property is to be given a narrow construction, it is difficult to see why the charitable donation should not have been given effect.

F. CONTRIBUTORIES

§15.139 Throughout most of the Act, attention is focused on two classes of person who are concerned with the business and affairs of a corporation, namely its shareholders and creditors. In Part XVI of the OBCA, attention shifts to contributories. Section 191 of the Act defines the term "contributory" to mean "a person who is liable to contribute to the property of a corporation in the event of the corporation being wound up under this Act".

§15.140 Historically, the primary contributories to a corporation were those shareholders who were liable under the terms of an assessable share or in respect of partially paid shares.[345] Since the present Act provides that shares are non-assessable and that shares may not be issued until they are fully paid, the scope of the definition has been significantly narrowed. The prospect that the Act will soon be amended to provide for unlimited liability corporations renews the relevance of this area of the law. Moreover, there are certain residual classes of shareholder who may still fall within the definition. The list of potential contributories includes persons who have subscribed for shares, but who have not yet paid for them, and persons who have in fact been issued partially paid shares despite the prohibition of such issue under the Act. Most at risk under this aspect of the definition are those persons to whom shares have been issued for an

---

[345] See, for instance, *Tremblay v. Vermette,* [1959] S.C.J. No. 50, [1959] S.C.R. 690 (*sub nom. Tremblay v. Best Wood Manufacturing Co.*).

inadequate non-monetary consideration. The term "contributory" will also include persons who have knowingly received a dividend in contravention of the Act, or who have knowingly received a repayment of share capital in contravention of the Act — on the basis of their willing participation in the misappropriation of corporate property. Arguably, it may include any shareholder to whom corporate property has been improperly distributed, even if the shareholder in question was innocent of any wrongdoing, since that innocence does not enhance the priority of the shareholder's claim if others have a prior claim in respect of the amount so received.[346] The term "contributory" includes any director or officer who is liable to the corporation under section 130 of the Act. The list of contributories would also include those directors and officers of a corporation who are responsible to the corporation for particular acts of misconduct of the corporation.[347] Suffice it to say that in most voluntary wind-ups there will be no contributories. As noted earlier in the text, Ontario is now considering the introduction of unlimited liability companies into the OBCA. The creation of such investment vehicles would greatly increase the importance of the law relating to the determination of contributories.

§15.141 Section 225 of the OBCA provides that the liability of a contributory "creates a debt accruing due from the contributory at the time the contributory's liability commenced, but payable at the time or respective times when calls are made for enforcing such liability". This section must be read together with section 200 of the Act. In effect, section 225 means that once the list of contributories is settled by the liquidator (in the case of a voluntary liquidation) or approved by the court (in the case of a wind-up under court order), a debt is deemed to arise that is owed by the contributory to the corporation.

§15.142 Clause 200(1)(*a*) of the OBCA requires the liquidator to settle the list of contributories. There are two steps in the settlement process. First, the liquidator

---

[346] See OBCA, s. 243(1).
[347] For instance, subsections 130(1) and (2) of the OBCA provide that:

> 130.(1) Directors of a corporation who vote for or consent to a resolution authorizing the issue of a share for a consideration other than money contrary to section 23 are jointly and severally liable to the corporation to make good any amount by which the consideration received is less than the fair equivalent of the money that the corporation would have received if the share had been issued for money on the date of the resolution.
>
> (2) Directors of a corporation who vote for or consent to a resolution authorizing,
>
> (*a*) any financial assistance contrary to section 20;
>
> (*b*) a purchase, redemption or other acquisition of shares contrary to section 30, 31 or 32;
>
> (*c*) a commission contrary to section 37;
>
> (*d*) a payment of a dividend contrary to section 38;
>
> (*e*) a payment of an indemnity contrary to section 136; or
>
> (*f*) a payment to a shareholder contrary to section 185 or 248,
>
> are jointly and severally liable to restore to the corporation any amounts so distributed or paid and not otherwise recovered by the corporation.

See also CBCA, s. 118(1) and (2).

must decide who is liable as a contributory; second, the liquidator must determine the liability of each such person. The "settlement" required under the clause is not a negotiated settlement. Rather, it is a unilateral fixing by the liquidator of liability. Nevertheless, subsection 200(2) provides that once the list has been settled by the liquidator, it becomes, "in the absence of evidence to the contrary, proof of the liability of the persons named therein to be contributories". If a particular contributory disputes liability, he or she may apply to the court to have the list of contributories or the settlement varied. Once the list of contributories is settled by the liquidator, clause 200(1)(b) empowers the liquidator to make a call on the contributories "to pay any sum that the liquidator considers necessary for satisfying the liabilities of the corporation and the costs, charges and expenses of winding up and for adjusting the rights of the contributories among themselves". In so providing, the section is most misleading, because it suggests that there is no limit on the amount that may be called, whereas the liquidator may certainly not call for the payment of more than the amount that is owed by a particular contributory. As noted earlier in the text, Ontario is now considering the introduction of unlimited liability companies into the OBCA. The creation of such investment vehicles would greatly increase the importance of the law relating to the determination of contributories.

§15.143 The debt owed by a contributory to the corporation is in the nature of a demand debt.[348] In a court-supervised liquidation, once the court approves the list of contributories, the liability of the persons named in that list is *res judicata* and may not be disputed by any of them in subsequent proceedings to recover the amount owing,[349] although any such approval would seem to be in accordance with the normal route of appeal from an interlocutory judgment of the court. In contrast, in a shareholder liquidation conducted outside the court, an alleged contributory may dispute the debt he or she is said to owe, although the list settled by the liquidator is assumed to be correct in the absence of evidence to the contrary.[350]

§15.144 If a contributory dies before or after he or she is placed on the list of contributories, his or her personal representative is liable in due course of administration to contribute to the property of the corporation in discharge of the liability of the deceased contributory.[351] The situation is less clear where the administration of the estate of a deceased concludes before the deceased is placed on the list of contributories. Given the fact that the Act makes no provision for a claim against the heirs of a deceased contributory (but instead makes mention only of a claim against the personal representative), it is arguable that if no claim is made before the passing of the accounts of the administrator or executor, the right of the liquidator to claim contribution terminates.

---

[348] OBCA, s. 225.
[349] *Red Deer Mill & Elevator Co. (Liquidators of) v. Hall* (1908), 1 Alta. L.R. 530 at 534 (T.D.), *per* Harvey J.
[350] OBCA, s. 200(2).
[351] OBCA, s. 226.

§15.145 On first reading, the statutory definition of "contributory" might be taken to include any person indebted or otherwise obliged to pay money to the corporation. In fact, it does not. Persons who are indebted to the corporation continue to be liable as debtors, not as contributories. A decision to wind up a corporation does not change either the character of a debt or the terms of its repayment.[352] Demand debts continue to be payable upon demand, and term indebtedness continues to be payable at the contracted time or times. Where a debt owed to the corporation is of a long-term nature, realization on that debt for the purpose of the wind-up may be difficult. Unless the debtor is prepared to accelerate the debt (which is unlikely, if the interest rate is favourable) there may be no practical option other than to discount the debt to another lender who is prepared to buy it. Any such discounting would need to take into account the risk of subsequent contra claims by the account debtor (*e.g.*, breach of warranty) for which there would be no prospect of indemnification. Therefore, in some cases, the discount may be substantial.

§15.146 While the liquidator is obliged to collect debts owing to the corporation, the liquidator is not obliged to employ the call proceeding merely because it is available. Instead, the liquidator may simply sue the contributory on the cause of action which gives rise to the liability of the contributory.[353] The discretion of the liquidator also extends to the timing of the call. Thus clause 200(1)(*b*) of the OBCA provides that the liquidator may make the call "before the liquidator has ascertained the sufficiency of the property of the corporation". The liquidator has no discretion not to make a call where the effect would be to deny a shareholder or creditor the rights to which that person is entitled. As a fiduciary for the corporation and the shareholders and creditors who are interested in it, the liquidator has no right to prefer one group or class of shareholders over another. Thus the liquidator is not permitted to refuse to make a call where the effect of such a refusal would be to give an improper preference to one shareholder over another entitled to equal priority in the repayment of share capital. Moreover, the liquidator cannot refuse to make a call where the corporation has insufficient assets to pay its creditors. The liquidator may, however, agree to compromise a doubtful claim, and possibly even a clear claim if the compromise is intended to economize on the costs of the liquidation or speed the recovery of the amounts owing.[354] In making a call, the liquidator may take into consideration the possi-

---

[352] *Burton v. Contributories of Home Assurance of Canada*, [1950] S.C.J. No. 24, [1950] S.C.R. 591, *per* Rand J.
[353] *Masecar v. McKenzie & Son*, [1924] 2 W.W.R. 521 (Sask. C.A.).
[354] OBCA, s. 203:

> 203. The liquidator may, with the approval referred to in section 202, compromise all debts and liabilities capable of resulting in debts, and all claims, whether present or future, certain or contingent, liquidated or unliquidated, subsisting or supposed to subsist between the corporation and any contributory, alleged contributory or other debtor or person who may be liable to the corporation and all questions in any way relating to or affecting the property of the corporation, or the winding up of the corporation, upon the receipt of such sums payable at such times and generally upon such terms as are agreed, and the liquidator may take any security for the discharge of such debts or liabilities and give a complete discharge in respect thereof.

bility that some of the contributories on whom the call is made may default in the payment of part or the whole of the amount called.[355]

§15.147 Where the wind-up of a corporation is being made voluntarily by the shareholders of a corporation under subsection 193(1) of the OBCA, the liquidator may call on any of the contributories for the time being settled on the list of contributories to the extent of their respective liability to pay any sum that the liquidator considers necessary for satisfying the liabilities of the corporation and the costs, charges and expenses of the winding-up, and also for adjusting the rights of the contributories among themselves.[356] In contrast, in the case of a court-ordered winding-up of a corporation, subsection 215(2) of the OBCA provides:

> 215.(2) Where a winding-up order has been made by the court, the court may require any contributory for the time being settled on the list of contributories, or any director, officer, employee, trustee, banker or agent of the corporation to pay, deliver, convey, surrender or transfer forthwith, or within such time as the court directs, to the liquidator any sum or balance, documents, records, estate or effects that are in his, her or its hands and to which the corporation is apparently entitled.

Section 225 of the OBCA provides that the liability of a contributory creates a debt accruing due from the contributory at the time the contributory's liability commenced, but payable at the time or respective times when calls are made enforcing that liability. Thus limitation periods run from the time when the call is made rather than from the time when the contributory became liable to the corporation.

G. DISSOLUTION

(i) Generally

§15.148 The demise of a corporation is a two-step affair. The winding-up of a corporation brings its business and affairs to an end. The dissolution of a corporation constitutes the termination of the corporation as a legal person. It might naturally be supposed that the dissolution of a corporation would follow automatically following the completion of the winding-up of the business and affairs of the corporation. In fact, this is not the case.[357] Dissolution is a completely separate process. From an administrative perspective, the dissolution of a corporation

---

[355] OBCA, s. 200(3).
[356] OBCA, s. 200(1)(*b*).
[357] Problems of this nature can arise under the BIA, where the trustee-in-bankruptcy is unable to dispose of all of the property of a bankrupt corporation. Mounting concerns with respect to the prospect of environmental liability discourage many buyers from purchasing land that has been used for heavy industrial purposes. Subsection 41(2) of the BIA provides that the court may discharge a trustee with respect to any estate on full administration thereof or, for sufficient cause, before full administration. Where all realizable property of a bankrupt has been disposed of, the trustee may seek discharge: particularly where the remaining property has insufficient value to cover the trustee's expected fees and disbursements. The ordinary rule in such a case would be for any remaining unmarketable property to be returned to the corporate shell, under subsection 40(1), but if the property is heavily burdened with potential environmental liability, it is unlikely that there will be much interest in recovering it.

entails little more than the cancellation of the corporation's charter of incorporation, so that the public franchise under which it has operated as a legally recognized entity is nullified. As we shall see in this section, dissolution may occur voluntarily (*i.e.*, on the application of the corporation) or it may be an involuntary consequence of some default by the corporation in compliance with a specified legal requirement. Involuntary dissolution is particularly problematic because often there are adverse consequences to third parties who have no ability to compel the corporation to comply with its obligations.

§15.149 Although the liquidator may be discharged from office under section 217 of the OBCA prior to the time when the business and affairs of the corporation have been completely wound up, the corporation may not be dissolved until the wind-up is complete. A corporation may be dissolved by statute, but instances in which this has occurred are extremely rare.[358] Instead, most corporations are dissolved following the administrative procedure set out in the OBCA or CBCA, as applicable. The dissolution requires an application to the court (which may be made either by the liquidator or any other interested person).[359] The order will specify the date as of when the corporation is dissolved.[360] Once the order is obtained, the person on whose application it was obtained must file a certified copy of the order with the Director and publish a notice of the order in *The Ontario Gazette*.[361]

§15.150 In general, a corporation cannot be wound up without its consent, except for cause. It might naturally be assumed that as an artificial person a corporation is liable to be cancelled by the very government which created it, where sufficient cause is made out for so doing. And indeed, the OBCA and CBCA each provide for the cancellation of the certificate of incorporation of the corporations subject to those Acts. Such cancellation is the extrajudicial termination of the corporation's existence by government fiat, although there are procedural safeguards built into the cancellation procedures to ensure that such a step is not taken precipitously or otherwise arbitrarily.

§15.151 As a general principle, the will of the sovereign authority that creates a corporation may destroy it,[362] but that principle means only that the power to

---

[358] For a case in which a statutory provision did dissolve a corporation (there the Company of Young Canadians) see *Government Expenditure Restraint Act*, S.C. 1976, c. 3, s. 5

[359] It was held in *Re Kaffarian Steam Mill Co.* (1907), 24 S.C.R. 18 that the length of the life of a corporate entity might be limited by the documents under which it is created. This is an acceptable statement if it is taken to mean that the principals behind a corporation may provide that it will be wound up after a given date, but it is doubtful whether this case remains good law with respect to a CBCA or OBCA corporation in terms of the actual dissolution of the corporation. Also questionable is the decision in *Kepert v. West Australian Pearlers Association* (1926), 38 C.L.R. 507 (H.C. Aust.) to the effect that the life of a corporation may be suspended temporarily. It is undoubtedly possible for the business and affairs of a corporation to be suspended without prejudice to its existence.

[360] OBCA, s. 218(1).

[361] OBCA, s. 218(2).

[362] *Lazard Bros. & Co. v. Midland Bank Ltd.*, [1933] A.C. 289 at 297 (H.L.), *per* Lord Wright. More generally, except where a corporation is continued under the laws of another jurisdiction

unmake a corporation is consistent with corporate law and the corporate personality. At common law the creation of a corporation was a matter of Crown prerogative or legislative fiat; by virtue of the terms of the OBCA and the CBCA, incorporation of a business corporation is now a matter of statutory right, and the creation of such a right necessarily circumscribes any prerogative power that the Crown may possess. But even under the discretionary powers of incorporation recognized at common law, once a corporation had been created, the persons who comprised the corporation might be deprived of corporate status only by due process of law; there was no residual power in the Crown to unmake the corporation without just cause for so doing.[363] Today, the power of cancellation may be exercised only to the extent and in accordance with the procedures and provisions of the OBCA, CBCA or other applicable legislation.[364]

(ii) Cancellation for Cause

§15.152 The cancellation procedure contemplated under the OBCA is set out in subsection 240(1), which provides:

> 240.(1) Where sufficient cause is shown to the Director, despite the imposition of any other penalty in respect thereof and in addition to any rights the Director may have under this or any other Act, the Director may, after having given the corporation an opportunity to be heard, by order, upon such terms and conditions as the Director thinks fit, cancel a certificate of incorporation or any other certificate issued or endorsed under this Act or a predecessor of this Act, and,
>
> (a) in the case of the cancellation of a certificate of incorporation, the corporation is dissolved on the date fixed in the order; and
>
> (b) in the case of the cancellation of any other certificate, the matter that became effective upon the issuance of the certificate ceases to be in effect from the date fixed in the order.

Subsection 240(2) of the OBCA goes on to provide that sufficient cause includes a failure to comply with subsection 115(2) (minimum number of directors) or

---

[363] so as to change its original domicile, only the jurisdiction of incorporation may determine its creation, continuing existence and internal management as well as all other related matters concerning its status including its right to issue and transfer shares, the designation and authority of its directors and the rights of its shareholders. Consequently it follows that proceedings taken in any jurisdiction other than the domicile (whether the corporation operates in that jurisdiction or not) that purport to affect any of the foregoing matters are invalid and it is immaterial whether these proceedings are sanctioned by the laws of the other jurisdiction: *National Trust Co. v. Ebro Irrigation & Power Co.*, [1954] O.J. No. 545, [1954] O.R. 463 (H.C.J.), per Schroeder J.

[363] *R. v. City of London* (1682), Show. 263 at 274, Skin. 310, 90 E.R. 139, 2 Sources of English Constitutional History 581 (K.B.), per Jones J.

[364] The following remarks of Pickup C.J.O. in *Border Cities Press Club v. Ontario (Attorney General)*, [1954] O.J. No. 583, [1955] O.R. 14 at 19 (C.A.) made in reference to the power of the Lieutenant Governor in Council to declare letters patent forfeit would seem to apply with even greater force in the case of the exercise of powers by the Director:

> In exercising the power referred to, the Lieutenant-Governor in Council is not ... exercising a prerogative of the Crown, but a power conferred by statute, and such a statutory power can be validly exercised only by complying with statutory provisions which are, by law, conditions precedent to the exercise of such power.

subsection 118(3) (majority of directors to be resident Canadians), a conviction of the corporation for an offence under the *Criminal Code* (Canada) or an offence as defined in the *Provincial Offences Act*, in circumstances where cancellation of the certificate is in the public interest, or conduct described in subsection 248(2) (oppression).

§15.153 A further power of dissolution is conferred where a corporation fails to comply with filing requirements under the *Corporations Information Act*.[365] In such a case, the Director may give notice by registered mail to the corporation or by publication once in *The Ontario Gazette* that an order dissolving the corporation will be issued unless the corporation complies with the requirements of that Act within 90 days after the notice is given.

§15.154 The power of the Director to cancel a certificate of incorporation for cause is not a prerogative of the Crown, but rather is a statutory power that may only be exercised in accordance with the general law under which it is conferred[366] and in accordance with the *Statutory Powers Procedure Act*.[367] The right of the Director to exercise that power is dependent upon sufficient cause being shown, and there is no right to exercise this power except upon a hearing.[368] The mere fact that grounds exist for cancellation does not in itself affect the corporate status of the corporation concerned; the corporation continues until the Director acts in accordance with the section and actually cancels the certificate.[369] In contrast to earlier legislation,[370] there is no power under the present OBCA empowering the Director to cancel the certificate of incorporation of a corporation merely on the grounds of non-user. So long as the corporation meets the regulatory requirements set out in subsection 240(2), it can be completely inactive and yet remain a valid and subsisting corporation.

§15.155 Subject to any specific statutory provision, it is doubtful that a single act of shareholder or other oppression under subsection 248(2) is sufficient to justify the revocation of the charter. In *A.G. Canada (Attorney General) v. Hel-*

---

[365] R.S.O. 1990, c. 39, as amended.
[366] *Border Cities Press Club v. Ontario (Attorney General)*, [1995] O.J. No. 583, [1955] O.R. 14 (C.A.).
[367] R.S.O. 1990, c. S.22, as amended.
[368] Subsection 3(1) of the *Statutory Powers Procedure Act* provides:

> 3.(1) Subject to subsection (2), this Act applies to a proceeding by a tribunal in the exercise of a statutory power of decision conferred by or under an Act of the Legislature, where the tribunal is required by or under such Act or otherwise by law to hold or to afford to the parties to the proceeding an opportunity for a hearing before making a decision.

See, however, *Re Lubin, Rosen & Associates Ltd.*, [1975] 1 W.L.R. 122 at 128-29 (Ch. D.), *per* Megarry J.; *Canada (Attorney General) v. Continental Trust Co. (No. 2)*, [1985] O.J. No. 2670, 52 O.R. (2d) 525 (H.C.J.), *per* Hollingworth J.

[369] See, generally, *Confederation Land Corp. v. Canadian Pacific Rlwy.*, [1942] 1 W.W.R. 561 (Alta. C.A.).
[370] See, for instance, *Moto-Sway Corp. of America v. Standard Steel Construction Co.*, [1939] O.W.N. 311 (H.C.J.), discussing the *Companies Act*, R.S.O. 1937, c. 251, s. 28.

lenic Colonization Association[371] the court considered the situation in which a corporate charter might be revoked for abusive conduct under the Dominion Companies Act.[372] Farris C.J. commented:

> ... the Dominion Companies Act has taken nothing away from the common law rights to have a charter annulled but has given certain other grounds on which it may be cancelled under the statute.
>
> I therefore find that an action can be maintained to have a charter annulled for abuse or misuser.
>
> ... Isolated cases of abuse or misuse should not be sufficient for a declaration of annulment. The abuse or misuse must be of such a nature as to be offensive to public policy.
>
> ... the abuse or misuse must be of such consecutive acts and the general policy of the association such as would indicate a clear intention that the company or association wished to use the charter as a mere cloak for its improper acts.

The following would seem to constitute grounds sufficiently in the public interest to justify cancellation of a corporate charter: the conduct of an illegal business;[373] misrepresentation in connection with the incorporation of the corporation or the amendment of its articles;[374] persistent *ultra vires* acts;[375] and breach of regulatory requirements, restrictions or prohibitions on the conduct of business.[376]

§15.156 Where the Director is notified by the Minister of Revenue that a corporation is in default in complying with the provisions of the *Corporations Tax Act*,[377] the Director may give notice to the corporation by registered mail, or by publication once in *The Ontario Gazette*, that an order dissolving the corporation will be issued unless the corporation remedies its default within 90 days after the giving of that notice.[378] In the event of a failure to comply with that notice, the Director may cancel the certificate of incorporation by order and where the Director does so the corporation is dissolved on the date fixed in the order.[379] Despite the making of such an order, at any time within the five-year period following the dissolution of the corporation, the Director may revive the corporation[380] on such terms and conditions as the Director sees fit, upon

---

[371] [1946] B.C.J. No. 46, [1946] 3 D.L.R. 840 at 846 (S.C.); see also *Eastern Archipelago Co. v. The Queen* (1853), 23 L.J.Q.B. 82 at 89 (Ex. Ch.), *per* Martin B.; *R. v. City of London* (1691), Skin. 310, 90 E.R. 139 (K.B.).

[372] 1934 (Can.), c. 33.

[373] *Ontario (Attorney General) v. Toronto Junction Recreation Club*, [1904] O.J. No. 97, 8 O.L.R. 440 (H.C.J.).

[374] *Meyers v. Lucknow Elevator Co.*, [1905] O.J. No. 523, 6 O.W.R. 291 (H.C.J.) — a case dealing with revocation of supplementary letters patent, but by extension applicable to the full charter of the corporation.

[375] *Nova Scotia (Attorney General) v. Bergen* (1896), 29 N.S.R. 135 (C.A.).

[376] *Dominion Salvage & Wrecking Co. v. Canada (Attorney General)* (1892), 21 S.C.R. 72.

[377] R.S.O. 1990, c. C.40, as amended.

[378] OBCA, s. 241(1).

[379] OBCA, s. 241(4).

[380] Until the corporation is revived it has no standing to bring an action: see *Dominion Distillery Products Co. v. Canada*, [1937] S.C.J. No. 458, [1938] S.C.R. 458.

the application of any interested person.[381] Where the revival of a corporation is so ordered, the corporation is restored to its legal position, including all property, rights, privileges and franchises, and is subject to all its liabilities, contracts disabilities and debts, as of the date of the dissolution, in the same manner and to the same extent as if it had not been dissolved,[382] although in every case subject to the terms and conditions imposed by the Director and to any rights acquired by any person in the intervening period between dissolution and revival.[383]

(iii) Effect of Dissolution

§15.157 At common law a dissolved corporation could not acquire or exercise rights or property, and could neither sue nor be sued.[384] In *Re Citadel Industries, Inc.*,[385] the court stated:

> At common law, the dissolution of a corporation abruptly ended its existence, thus abating all pending actions by and against it and terminating its capacity thereafter to sue or be sued. Thus, statutory authority is necessary to prolong the life of a corporation past its date of dissolution.

In that case it was held that the statutory survival of certain rights against a dissolved corporation were exhaustive. Hence, a court had no jurisdiction to continue the existence of a corporation except as provided by the statute of incorporation (or some corresponding authority) so as to permit a suit against the corporation that was instituted outside the statutory three-year period following its dissolution.

§15.158 Under modern corporate law, a corporation dissolved for lack of regulatory compliance is not so much a dead company as one that is in a state of suspended animation, since the corporation may be revived with retroactive effect upon its revival. The corporation may sue for a violation of its rights that occurred during the period while it was dissolved, even though it could not have sued for them at the time.[386] Such a dissolution of a corporation is a qualified one only: the contracts that are made in the corporate name are not nullities: they may be validated by the revival of the corporation.[387]

§15.159 In *Litemor Distributors (Ottawa) Ltd. v. W.C. Somers Electric Ltd.*[388] a CBCA corporation incorporated was dissolved in 1993 but, during its dissolution, its business continued nevertheless. Contracts were entered into in the name of the dissolved corporation. On October 20, 2003, Litemor sued the cor-

---

[381] OBCA, s. 241(5).
[382] *Ibid.*
[383] *Ibid.*
[384] *Int'l Pulp Equip. Co. v. St. Regis Kraft Co.*, 54 F. Supp. 745 at 748 (D. Del. 1944).
[385] 423 A.2d 500 at 503 (Del. Ch. 1980).
[386] *Atkinson & Yates Boatbuilders Ltd. v. Hanlon*, [2003] N.J. No. 185, 36 B.L.R. (3d) 44 at 47 (S.C.), *per* Dymond J.
[387] *MacRae v. Broder*, [1998] A.J. No. 1346, 239 A.R. 77 at 90 (Q.B.), *per* Marceau J.
[388] [2004] O.J. No. 4686, 73 O.R. (3d) 228 (S.C.J.).

poration and its principals for the amounts outstanding on 10 separate construction projects that had been entered into during the dissolution of the corporation. On March 25, 2004, the corporation was revived under section 209 of the CBCA. Litemor moved for summary judgment against the corporation and the principals. A key question was whether the principals were personally liable for the corporation's debts that were incurred while the corporation was dissolved. Panet J. concluded that the principals were not liable for any amount owing under the contract by reason of the dissolution of the corporation at the time the contract was entered into and performed, since subsection 209(4) of the CBCA provides that subject to the rights acquired by any person after a corporation's dissolution, a revived corporation is restored to its previous position in law and liable for the obligations that it would have had if it had not been dissolved, whether they arise before its dissolution or after its dissolution and before its revival. The effect of revival was held to be retroactive, and to extend back to the moment of dissolution. Any acts undertaken in the name of the corporation during the dissolution are deemed to have been taken by the corporation itself. It was held that Litemor's right to sue the principals of a dissolved corporation was not a right contemplated by subsection 209(4). Panet J. noted that at the time when the contract was made, Litemor did not know of the dissolution, and therefore did not enter into the contract on the basis of any right to claim against the principals. The liability of the principals was merely a procedural means of enforcing the substance of the right that Litemor thought it was acquiring, if no revival ever occurred.[389]

(iv) Revival and Surviving Rights

§15.160 Subsection 242(1) of the OBCA makes the following provision with respect to the continuation of liabilities and claims against a corporation following its dissolution:

> 242.(1) Despite the dissolution of a corporation under this Act,
>
> (*a*) a civil, criminal or administrative action or proceeding commenced by or against the corporation before its dissolution may be continued as if the corporation had not been dissolved;
>
> (*b*) a civil, criminal or administrative action or proceeding may be brought against the corporation as if the corporation had not been dissolved;
>
> (*c*) any property that would have been available to satisfy any judgment or order if the corporation had not been dissolved remains available for such purpose; and
>
> (*d*) title to land belonging to the corporation immediately before the dissolution remains available to be sold in power of sale proceedings.

It follows that the revocation of a certificate of incorporation does not extinguish the debts or liabilities of the corporation, nor does it release any guarantor from

---

[389] Compare, however, *Dryco Building Supplies Inc. v. Wasylishyn*, [2002] A.J. No. 919, 28 B.L.R. (3d) 109 (Q.B.).

liability in respect thereof.[390] Significantly, clause 242(1)(a) permits the corporation to commence or continue with proceedings to enforce rights owed to the corporation.[391] Where a proceeding is instituted against a dissolved corporation, there is an implicit right in favour of that corporation to institute an appeal, if the proceeding is decided against it.[392]

§15.161 At common law, upon the dissolution of a corporation, the right of an insurer or other person to commence proceedings in the name of a corporation under a right of subrogation lapsed.[393] Clause 242(1)(a) clearly modifies this rule with respect to any subsisting proceeding. If the corporation has been dissolved under section 241 (essentially for non-compliance with the requirements of the *Corporations Tax Act*, the *Securities Act*, or the *Corporations Information Act*) the right to proceed may be reinstated by way of revival. Unfortunately, under the current wording of the OBCA revival (other than by way of private Act) appears to be possible only in a narrow range of cases.[394]

§15.162 As noted above, clause 24(1)(a) permits actions commenced by the corporation prior to dissolution to proceed, and clause 242(1)(b) permits the institution of claims against the corporation after its dissolution. However, there is no express authority for the corporation (or persons acting on its behalf) to institute a proceeding to recover or enforce some right of the corporation after it has been dissolved. The implications of this silence are unsettled where an action is commenced by a corporation while it is subject to an undiscovered dissolution order, and a relevant limitation period expires before the corporation can be revived. In *602533 Ontario Inc. v. Shell Canada Ltd.*[395] it was found that the plaintiff had commenced an action in 1990 for damages for breach of contract and other related causes. Unbeknown to either the plaintiff or defendant, the action was brought after the plaintiff had been ordered, and while it remained, dissolved for non-compliance with the *Corporations Tax Act* (the dissolution had taken effect in 1988). The dissolution of the plaintiff corporation was not noticed by the parties until 1996. When the defendant discovered the dissolution, it served an amended statement of claim to the effect that the plaintiff had no status to commence or continue the action because of its dissolution. Following this amendment, the plaintiff was revived as a corporation under subsection 241(5) of the OBCA. However, the limitation period for the plaintiff's claim had expired prior to the time of its revival. The defendant moved for

---

[390] *Bank of Montreal v. Stephen*, [1989] N.B.J. No. 709, 45 B.L.R. 80 at 89 (Q.B.), per Riordon J., var'd [1990] N.B.J. No. 612 (C.A.) (Stephen) and [1991] N.B.J. No. 328 (C.A.) (Dobbin), leave to appeal to SCC by Dobbin refused [1991] S.C.C.A. No. 246; *Island Recreational Properties Ltd. v. Dyck*, [1998] A.J. No. 625, [1998] 10 W.W.R. 643 (Q.B.).
[391] But see *460354 Ontario Inc. v. M.N.R.*, [1988] T.C.J. No. 939, 88 D.T.C. 1679, [1988] 2 C.T.C. 2338, aff'd [1992] F.C.J. No. 806 (T.D.) in which this right was narrowly construed by Bonner T.C.J.
[392] *460354 Ontario Ltd. v. Canada*, [1992] F.C.J. No. 806, 95 D.L.R. (4th) 351 at 354 (T.D.), per Jerome A.C.J.
[393] See, for instance, *M.H. Smith (Plant Hire) Ltd. v. Mainwaring*, [1986] B.C.L.C. 342 (C.A.)
[394] See OBCA, ss. 241(4) and (5).
[395] [1998] O.J. No. 68, 37 O.R. (3d) 504 (C.A.).

summary judgment, which was granted in its favour. In upholding that judgment on appeal, Moldaver J.A. noted that a subsection 241(5) revival of a corporation takes effect subject to any right acquired by any person after its dissolution. With some reluctance (given the fact that the defendant was fully aware of the claim), he concluded that the expiration of a limitation period constituted a post-dissolution right acquired by the defendant. Since, in Ontario, limitation periods do not extinguish the substantive right underlying a cause of action, but merely impose a procedural bar on the judicial enforcement of that right, it would appear that the post-dissolution "rights" protected by subsection 241(5) encompass procedural defences as well as rights in the strict legal sense.[396] In contrast, in Alberta it has been held that where a corporation is dissolved, and (1) an action is brought in its name before its revival, and (2) the cause of action becomes statute barred during the interval between the initiation of the action and the date of revival, the action is validated by virtue of the revival.[397] Given the wording of subsection 241(5) of the OBCA, the Alberta approach seems more correct: the expiration of the limitation period does not give the defendant a "right" entitling the defendant to a judgment on the merits of the corporation's claim. In contrast, subsection 241(5) would appear to validate the institution of the action at the time when it was commenced.

§15.163 Despite the dissolution of a corporation, each shareholder to whom any property of the corporation has been distributed is liable to any person entitled to claim under section 242 of the OBCA to the extent of the amount received by that shareholder. An action to enforce that liability may be brought within five years after the date of the dissolution of the corporation.[398] The court may order such an action to be brought against the persons who were shareholders as a class, subject to such conditions as the court considers fit. If the plaintiff establishes his or her claim, the court may refer the proceedings to a referee or other officer who may:[399]

- add as a party to the proceedings before him or her each person who was a shareholder found by the plaintiff;

- determine the amount that each person who was a shareholder must contribute towards the satisfaction of the plaintiff's claim; and

- direct payment of the amounts so determined.

---

[396] See also *Profit Sharing Investors of Canada Ltd. v. Coffee Vending Services (Ottawa) Ltd.*, [1983] O.J. No. 3002, 41 O.R. (2d) 470 (H.C.J.); *Ontario Sprinkler Sales Ltd. v. Emco Ltd.*, [1996] O.J. No. 354, 28 O.R. (3d) 155 (Gen. Div.); *Martin v. Perrie*, [1986] S.C.J. No. 1, [1986] 1 S.C.R. 41; but cf. *Modern Livestock Ltd. v. Kansa General Insurance Co.*, [1993] A.J. No. 575, 11 Alta. L.R. (3d) 355 (Q.B.), aff'd [1994] A.J. No. 654, 24 Alta. L.R. (3d) 21 (C.A.).

[397] *Associated Asbestos Services Ltd. v. Canadian Occidental Petroleum Ltd.*, [2004] A.J. No. 39, 43 B.L.R. (3d) 221 (C.A.); cf. *3834761 Manitoba Ltd. v. Optimum Frontier Ins. Co.*, [2003] M.J. No. 196, 34 B.L.R. (3d) 314 (Q.B.).

[398] OBCA, s. 243(1).

[399] OBCA, s. 243(2).

§15.164 Although the question rarely arises, if a corporation is named as a beneficiary in a will but the corporation is dissolved before the will takes effect by reason of the death of the testator, the gift to the corporation lapses.[400]

(v) Dissolution of a Sole Shareholder Corporation (Proposed Reform)

§15.165 The Ontario Ministry of Government Services has published a discussion paper asking whether the executor of the sole shareholder of a corporation should be given the power to authorize and sign articles of dissolution. Presumably, if this option is adopted, an administrator will also be given this right, where acting on behalf of a shareholder who has not left a will or appointed an executor. Currently, only directors or officers of the corporation can sign articles of dissolution if the corporation has commenced business. The idea has a certain merit in terms of simplifying corporate administration (particularly at what is likely to be a difficult time for the person concerned, who very often will be the surviving spouse of the deceased shareholder).

(vi) Property Forfeit to the Crown

§15.166 Subsection 244(1) provides that any property of a corporation that has not been disposed of at the date of its dissolution is immediately upon such dissolution forfeit to and vests in the Crown. This general rule is subject to a number of exceptions with respect to "land" — it is unclear whether the term "land" is used to indicate that the special rules in question are also intended to apply to leasehold interests as well as real property interests. In any event, subsection 244(2) provides that:

> 244.(2) Despite subsection (1), if a judgment is given or an order or decision is made or land is sold in an action, suit or proceeding commenced in accordance with section 242 and the judgment, order, decision or sale affects property belonging to the corporation before the dissolution, unless the plaintiff, applicant or mortgagee has not complied with subsection 242 (3) or (4),
>
> > (a) the property shall be available to satisfy the judgment, order or other decision; and
> >
> > (b) title to the land shall be transferred to a purchaser free of the Crown's interest, in the case of a power of sale proceeding.

Despite subsection (2), if a person commences a power of sale proceeding relating to land before the dissolution of a corporation but the sale of the land is not completed until after the dissolution, the person is not required to serve the notice mentioned in subsection 242(4)[401] and title to the land may be transferred to a

---

[400] *Re Servers of the Blind League*, [1960] 1 W.L.R. 564. The question of gifts to a corporate body arises most frequently with respect to charitable corporations, and in the case of such corporations, the gift may sometimes be saved by application of the *cy-près* doctrine: see *Re Finger's Will Trust*, [1972] Ch. 286.

[401] Subsection 242(3) provides that:

purchaser free of the Crown's interest.[402] A forfeiture of land under subsection (1) or a predecessor of subsection (1) is not effective against a purchaser for value of the land if the forfeiture occurred more than 20 years before the deed or transfer of the purchaser is registered in the proper land registry office.[403]

§15.167 In Ontario, the practice with respect to property forfeited to the Crown under section 244 of the OBCA is to treat such property as being held in trust.[404] Since it is only the "property of the corporation" that is forfeit to the Crown, it would appear that the Crown acquires no more than the corporation's equity interest in the property, so that security interests continue against the property in question unaffected. Property forfeited under section 244 is held and administered by the Public Guardian and Trustee.[405] The trust approach is perfectly sensible in view of the possibility that the corporation may be revived under section 241, and also given the possibility of a claim being made against the former corporation under section 242.[406]

242.(3) A person who commences an action, suit or other proceeding against a corporation after its dissolution, shall serve the writ or other document by which the action, suit or other proceeding was commenced, on the Public Guardian and Trustee in accordance with the rules that apply generally to service on a party to an action, suit or other proceeding.

Since the Ontario rules of court have not provided for the commencement of an action by way of writ of summons since 1984, the wording of this provision is more than a bit anachronistic.

[402] OBCA, s. 244(4).
[403] OBCA, s. 244(3).
[404] *Jolin v. Lart Investments Ltd.*, [1977] O.J. No. 2484, 18 O.R. (2d) 161 at 165 (Dist. Ct.):

The Courts in favour of escheat maintain that there must always be an owner of the legal estate in a fee simple; if the owner corporation is dissolved, and the property is subject to a trust, the estate rests in the Crown as *bona vacatia*, subject to the trusts affecting it.

[405] Thus subsection 1(1) of the *Escheats Act*, R.S.O. 1990, c. E.20, provides:

1.(1) Where any property has become the property of the Crown by reason of the person last seised thereof or entitled thereto having died intestate and without lawful heirs, or has become forfeited for any cause to the Crown, the Public Guardian and Trustee may cause possession thereof to be taken in the name of the Crown, or, if possession is withheld, may cause an action to be brought for the recovery thereof, without an inquisition being first made.

For a specific application of this rule, see, for instance, *Black Estate v. Ontario (Attorney General)*, [1968] O.J. No. 47 (H.C.J.). Subsection 6(1) provides:

6.(1) The Public Guardian and Trustee may transfer, assign or discharge, at such price and on such terms as seem proper, all or part of any interest in real property of which he or she has taken possession under this Act.

[406] See 7 Glanvill, ch. 17 ("*De Ultimis Heredibus*"), 2nd ed. (Oxford: Oxford Univ. Press, 1993):

The ultimate heir of any person is his lord. When, therefore, anyone dies without a certain heir - ... the lords of the fees may ... take and keep those fees in their hands as their escheats, whether such lord is the king or someone else. If anyone later comes and says that he is the right heir, and is allowed by the grace of his lord or by a write of the lord king to pursue his claim, he shall sue and may recover such right as he may have ... However, if no-one appears and claims the inheritance as heir, then it remains perpetually with the lord as an escheat, and so he may dispose of it, as of his own property, at his pleasure ...

§15.167.1 Forfeiture to the Crown is anything but an unmixed blessing. Once the Crown enters into possession of property, it becomes responsible for the performance of legal obligations (and the discharge of liabilities) associated with it.[407] Environmental liabilities are a particular concern, especially where the corporation was formerly engaged in industrial activity. Very often the environmental liability associated with former industrial land will be found to exceed its potential market value, even when rehabilitated. Some protection for the Crown may be offered by subsection 5(5) of the *Proceedings Against the Crown Act*,[408] which provides:

> 5.(5) Where property vests in the Crown independent of the acts or intentions of the Crown, the Crown is not, by virtue of this Act, subject to liability in tort by reason only of the property being so vested; but this subsection does not affect the liability of the Crown under this Act in respect of any period after the Crown, or any servant of the Crown, has in fact taken possession or control of the property.

However, it appears that even the slightest involvement with the property by the Crown, a Crown agent or employee is sufficient to defeat the protection that subsection 5(6) affords.[409]

§15.168 The forfeiture provisions also raise both constitutional and conflicts of law concerns. On its face, provisions such as section 244(1) of the OBCA provide that any property of a corporation that has not been disposed of at the date of its dissolution is immediately upon such dissolution forfeit to and vests in the Crown. It would follow from this wording that all such property, wherever situate, would pass to the Crown in right of Ontario unless by virtue of some principle of law, section 244(1) would be considered inoperative insofar as it would apply to property outside of Ontario.

§15.169 The rules of private international law as they are understood in common law jurisdictions exhibit a strong reluctance to recognize confiscatory legislation. It is unclear whether provisions such as section 244 would be seen to constitute legislation of this sort. Complicating the picture is the unfortunate fact that many of the cases dealing with the dissolution of foreign companies related to corporate entities that were dissolved by state decree in the context of the coming to power of communist governments, with little concern being shown by those governments with respect to the rights of foreign creditors. Working within this context, in England, the courts historically took the view that where a foreign company having assets in England was dissolved by its home jurisdic-

---

See, however, *Mortgage Insurance Co. of Canada v. Innisfil Landfill Corp.*, [1995] O.J. No. 3267, 20 C.E.L.R. (N.S.) 19 (Gen. Div. — C.L.); *Thomson Motors Co. v. British Columbia*, [1993] B.C.J. No. 437 (S.C.); *Metropolitan Toronto Condo. Corp. No. 1000 v. Ontario*, [1997] O.J. No. 283 (Gen. Div.).

[407] See, generally, *SCMLLA Properties Ltd. v. Gesso Properties (BVI) Ltd.*, [1995] B.C.C. 793 (Ch.) with respect to the application of statutory duties to the Crown as owner.

[408] R.S.O. 1990, c. P.27.

[409] See, for instance, *Platts v. Canada*, [1990] F.C.J. No. 648, 35 F.T.R. 262 (T.D.).

tion, the effect was that all English assets vest in the Crown as *bona vacantia*,[410] irrespective of whether the foreign decree purported to vest those assets in the government of that home jurisdiction. So, for instance, in a case concerning the dissolution of a Soviet bank that had assets and liabilities in England, it was said:

> A corporation created and established under a foreign legal system has been allowed by our law to carry on business and to incur debts in this country. Its corporate powers, if not its corporate existence, have been destroyed in its country of origin; many years have elapsed, and no attempt has been made to pay the creditors in this country. Can it be doubted that in such circumstances the court, if it has jurisdiction, ought to make an order which will secure as far as possible the payment of all just claims against the corporation?
>
> .....
>
> I hold that there is jurisdiction to wind up the company under the provisions of the section, whether or not the company has been dissolved or has completely ceased to exist as a company under or by virtue of the laws of the Soviet Government.[411]

Although common law courts frequently have refused to give effect within their jurisdiction to confiscatory legislation enacted in another jurisdiction, even where the legislation in question relates solely to citizens of the enacting jurisdiction,[412] the rule is not, however, an absolute one and is of limited scope.[413]

§15.170 It is also questionable whether it is correct to characterize provisions such as those set out in the OBCA as being truly confiscatory. Given the current trend in the law relating to corporate dissolution to hold assets that escheat to the Crown by virtue of a dissolution order, not for the benefit of the Crown, but rather on a trust basis for those who have legitimate claims against the corporation, there may be some justification for giving effect to the apparent plain wording of the OBCA.

§15.171 An argument is sometimes put forward against doing so, derived from the consensus view in Canadian constitutional law that the provinces have no jurisdiction to enact laws of extraterritorial application.[414] Undoubtedly, there is

---

[410] *Russian & English Bank v. Baring Brothers Ltd.*, [1936] A.C. 405 at 440, *per* Lord Maughan; *Re Azoff-Don Commercial Bank*, [1954] Ch. 315.

[411] *Re Russian Bank for Foreign Trade*, [1933] All E.R. Rep. 754, [1933] Ch. 745 at 764, *per* Maugham J.

[412] See, for instance, *Banco de Vizcaya v. Don Alfonso de Borbon y Austria*, [1935] 1 K.B. 140.

[413] *Luther v. Sagor & Co.*, [1921] 3 K.B. 532 at 559 (C.A.), *per* Strutton L.J.; *Estonian State Cargo & Passenger Steamship Line v. S.S. Elise*, [1948] 4 D.L.R. 247 (Ex. Ct. Can.), rev'd [1949] 2 D.L.R. 641 (S.C.C.).

[414] The Federal government pretends to such a jurisdiction, but insofar as such legislation would affect property in some other jurisdiction, the effectiveness of any such legislation depends upon the extent to which the law of that other jurisdiction are prepared to recognize the validity of any such law. See: *Société Eram Shipping Co. Ltd. v. Compagnie Internationale de Navigation*, [2003] All E.R. 465, *per* Lord Hoffman; and also Lord Millett at para. 80:

> The near universal rule of international law is that sovereignty, both legislative and adjudicative, is territorial, that is to say it may be exercised only in relation to persons and things within the territory of the state concerned or in respect of its own nationals. But in terms of domestic law these limits are self-imposed. A sovereign legislature has

some case law that would support this view. In *Macdonald v. Georgian Bay Lumber*,[415] a British subject (Anson Dodge) who owned lands in Canada, resided and carried on business in partnership with two individuals in the State of New York. In November, 1873, the partnership firm became insolvent, and on February 14, 1874, the firm, executed a deed purporting to "convey, transfer and deliver all their and each of their estate and effects" to one John L. Cadwalader, as trustee for their creditors under the *Bankruptcy Act* of the United States. On September 26, 1874, a writ of execution against Dodge was delivered to the Sheriff of the County of York (Ontario) by the respondents. Subsequently Dodge granted to Cadwalader his lands in Canada. The appellant in the case had succeeded to Cadwalader as trustee, and, as such, filed a Bill in the Court of Chancery to obtain a declaration that the lands specified in the bill were not liable to the writ of execution of the respondents. It was held that a bankruptcy assignment made under the provisions of American bankruptcy legislation, did not transfer immoveable property in Canada. In the course of giving judgment, the Supreme Court stated that:

> ... real estate is exclusively subject to the law of the Government within whose territory it is situate ...

> The universal consent of the tribunals, acting under the common law, both in England and in America, is, in a practical sense, absolutely uniform on the same subject. All the authorities in both countries, so far as they go, recognize the principle in its fullest import, that real estate or immoveable property is exclusively subject to the laws of the Government within whose territory it is situate.[416]

§15.172 In *Duke v. Andler*[417] it was held that a judgment of a court of the State of California on a question of title and ownership of real property situate in British Columbia cannot be recognized as final and be enforced by the courts of that province, in accordance with the general rule that the courts of any country have no jurisdiction to adjudicate on the right and title to lands not situate in such country. However, in that case the court went on to discuss the distinction between judicial decrees which operate *in personam* and those which relate specifically to the property at issue. Legislation with respect to corporate dissolution is clearly legislation *in personam*: it extinguishes the corporation as a legal personality. In other words, any impact of such legislation on land is incidental to its wider purpose of providing for the termination of corporate existence, which is clearly a proper purpose for the corporate laws of an incorporating jurisdiction.

> power under its domestic law to disregard them and a court of "unlimited jurisdiction" (that is to say one which has power to decide the limits of its own jurisdiction) cannot be said to lack power to do so. Where the court observes the limits imposed by international law it may be a matter for debate whether it has no jurisdiction or has a jurisdiction which it refrains from exercising as a matter of principle. But it needs to be appreciated that, whether the court disclaims jurisdiction or merely declines to exercise it, it does so as a matter of principle and not of discretion.

[415] [1878] S.C.J. No. 8, 2 S.C.R. 364.
[416] *Ibid*.
[417] [1932] S.C.J. No. 55, [1932] 4 D.L.R. 529.

§15.173 There is, however, a clear distinction between bankruptcy laws and provisions governing the disposition of property upon the dissolution of a corporation. Debtor creditor laws as they apply to property within a jurisdiction are properly subject matters for legislation by that jurisdiction, since they pertain directly to the rights and obligations of persons who are subject to the laws of that jurisdiction by their presence. In contrast, there is no question that the jurisdiction of incorporation is the only jurisdiction which may dissolve the existence of a corporation. If it has that authority, it must necessarily have the jurisdiction to legislation with respect to the consequences of dissolution. Such legislation is not legislation with respect to land. To the extent that corporation legislation may involve the transfer of title to land, it merely does so as an indirect consequence of dealing with an inherent corporate incident. In *Oppenheimer v. Cattermole*, Lord Templeman said:

> There is undoubtedly a domestic and international rule which prevents one sovereign state from changing title to property so long as that property is situate in another state. If the British government purported to acquire compulsorily the railway lines from London to Newhaven and the railway lines from Dieppe to Paris, the ownership of the railway lines situate in England would vest in the British government but the ownership of the railway lines in France would remain undisturbed. But this territorial limitation on compulsory acquisition is not relevant to the acquisition of shares in a company incorporated in the acquiring state. If the British government compulsorily acquired all the shares in a company incorporated in England which owned a railway line between Dieppe and Paris, the ownership of that railway line would remain vested in the company, subject to any exercise by a French government of power compulsorily to acquire the railway line.[418]

The passing of title to property of a dissolved corporation seems more akin to the incidental change of the indirect ownership of corporate property resulting from the expropriation of shares than it does to legislation that purports to deal directly with property situate in another jurisdiction.

§15.174 As discussed in Chapter 4, recent Supreme Court of Canada decisions have recognized a limited jurisdiction to legislate extra-territorially where necessary to some legitimate provincial purpose. Earlier in the chapter, we made reference to the internal affairs doctrine, and noted that it is, in general, the rule that governs the exercise of legal control over the dissolution of a corporation. In *McDermott, Inc. v. Lewis*,[419] the Delaware Supreme Court noted that application of local internal affairs law of a particular jurisdiction to a corporation created under the laws of some other jurisdiction is "apt to produce inequalities, intolerable confusion, and uncertainty, and intrude into the domain of other states that have a superior claim to regulate the same subject matter". The prospect that the dissolution of a corporation may need to be undone, and its assets restored, so that those with valid claims against the corporation may proceed with enforcement, illustrates why it is imperative that only the law of the state of incorporation

---

[418] [1976] A.C. 249 at 428 (H.L.).
[419] 531 A.2d 206 (1987).

regulate the entirety of the dissolution process, including custodianship of property following the initial dissolution of the corporate entity.

§15.175 In essence, there is no practical distinction between section 244 of the OBCA relating to the disposition of property on dissolution of a corporation, and those provisions of the OBCA that provide for the disposition of property on the amalgamation or continuation of a corporation. In an amalgamation, the property of the predecessor corporations passes to the successor corporation. No one has ever suggested that title to real property located outside the jurisdiction of incorporation will only pass to the successor if there are laws of the jurisdiction in which the property is situate that give local effect to the rules of the jurisdiction of incorporation. Similarly, when an OBCA corporation is continued under legislation of another jurisdiction, the Ontario corporate entity transmutes into a new corporate entity of another jurisdiction. No one has ever suggested that title to real property will only pass to that new corporate entity if the jurisdiction in which the property is situate has legislation that provides to that effect. The only relevant law in such cases is the jurisdiction of incorporation. Passage of property to the successor is an incident of the law relating to jurisdiction and continuation. In much the same way, the disposition of property of a corporation may be properly provided for by its jurisdiction of incorporation.

§15.176 There is also an obvious convenience in having a single rule apply, and a single jurisdiction succeed, to all corporate property wherever it may be sited, particularly since the "dissolution" of a corporation does not extinguish its existence for all purposes (certain claims may continue to be made against it, and the corporation may be revived in certain circumstances). It has been suggested that the law of the site should be applied where the dissolution of the corporation is final, but that the law of the place of incorporation should be applied where the dissolution is final.[420] However, there are very credible reasons for rejecting such a flexible approach. In particular, it would require the courts of the jurisdiction in which the property is situate to make rulings of law on the corporate laws of the jurisdiction of incorporation. Although such rulings must from time to time be made in the conflict of laws setting, for obvious reasons the opportunity to do so is not to be sought out. Since three, four or possibly dozens of jurisdictions might be involved with a given corporation, there is a clear risk that some would arrive at a different interpretation as to the effect of legislation than others. Furthermore, there is no way of telling when a dissolution will become permanent, since any dissolved corporation may be revived by subsequent legislation — and there are numerous examples where this has in fact been done in the past.

§15.177 If proper weight is given to the foregoing considerations, one thus comes to the tentative conclusion that provisions such as subsection 244(1) are capable of vesting extraterritorial property in the government of the jurisdiction

---

[420] *Lloyds Estate v. Roets Estate*, [1965] S.J. No. 147, 54 W.W.R. 543 (Q.B.), *per* MacPherson J., var'd 60 D.L.R. (2d) 559, aff'd [1968] S.C.J. No. 16 (*sub nom. Canada Trust Co. v. Lloyd*).

of incorporation.[421] However, until the matter is dealt with at the senior appellate level, the question is likely one that will remain unsettled for some time.

H. LIQUIDATION AND DISSOLUTION UNDER THE CBCA

§15.178 The general rules governing liquidation and dissolution under the CBCA are set down in Part XVIII of that Act, and in broad terms resemble those set down in Part XVI of the OBCA. However, there are numerous differences in the language and detail of the provisions concerned that are found in each of these statutes.

§15.179 Subsection 208(1) of the CBCA provides that Part XVIII of the Act does not apply to a corporation that is insolvent within the meaning of the *Bankruptcy and Insolvency Act*[422] or that is a bankrupt within the meaning of that Act. While bankruptcy is a matter of status and for the most part readily determinable, insolvency is a question of fact. Thus it may happen that the insolvency of a corporation will not be discovered until after the liquidation and dissolution of the corporation has commenced under Part XVIII of the Act. In such a case, subsection 208(2) of the CBCA provides that any proceedings commenced under Part XVIII to dissolve or to liquidate a corporation shall be stayed[423] if the corporation is at any time found, to be insolvent within the meaning of the *Bankruptcy and Insolvency Act*. Except in such a case, the proceedings under Part XVIII may continue.

(i) Voluntary Liquidation and Dissolution of a Corporation

§15.180 As is the case with OBCA corporations, a CBCA corporation may be dissolved either voluntarily or involuntarily. The procedure governing the voluntary dissolution of a corporation other than under court order is set out in section 211 of the CBCA. Subsection 211(1) provides that the directors may propose, or a shareholder who is entitled to vote at an annual meeting of shareholders may make a proposal in accordance with section 137, for the voluntary liquidation and dissolution of the corporation. Liquidation and dissolution are two separate steps. In liquidation, the property and liabilities of the corporation are converted into cash or monetary debts, with the cash realized through that conversion of property being applied to pay the debts. Once the property and debts of the corporation have been so liquidated, it is then possible to proceed to dissolution.

---

[421] One possible exception would be where the law of the jurisdiction in which the property is situate provides that a foreign government is not to be permitted to own land within its territory. See, for instance, *Khotim v. Mikheev*, 41 N.Y. 2d 845, 362 N.E. 2d 253 (C.A. 1977).

[422] R.S.C. 1985, c. B-3, as amended.

[423] This particular wording raises a number of questions: is the stay automatic, or must the bankruptcy court order a stay; if the latter applies, may the court do so on its own motion or must the motion be brought by a trustee or the creditor or other person who commences the proceeding under the *Bankruptcy and Insolvency Act*, R.S.C. 1985, c. B-3, as amended. If the stay is automatic, what is the consequence if the proceeding under Part XVIII moves ahead in any event?

§15.181 Notice of any meeting of shareholders at which voluntary liquidation and dissolution is to be proposed must set out the terms on which those steps are proposed.[424] The liquidation and dissolution of the corporation must be approved by special resolution of the shareholders, and where there is more than one class of shares, the special resolution must be approved by the holders of each class whether or not they are otherwise entitled to vote.[425] Once the shareholders have approved the proposed liquidation and dissolution, a statement of intent to dissolve must be sent in the prescribed form to the Director.[426]

§15.182 On receipt of a statement of intent to dissolve, the Director is required to issue a certificate of intent to dissolve in accordance with section 262 of the CBCA.[427] Once that certificate is issued, the corporation must cease to carry on business, except to the extent necessary for the liquidation.[428] However, at any time after the issue of a certificate of intent and before the issue of a certificate of dissolution, a certificate of intent to dissolve may be revoked by the corporation sending to the Director a statement of revocation of intent to dissolve. This statement must be provided in the prescribed form and must be approved in the same manner as the original resolution to liquidate and dissolve the corporation.[429]

§15.183 After the issue of a certificate of intent to dissolve, the corporation must take the following steps.[430] First, it must immediately cause a notice of its intent to dissolve to be given to each known creditor of the corporation. Second, it must publish a notice of its intention to dissolve once a week for four consecutive weeks in a newspaper published or distributed in the place where the corporation has its registered office, and it must also take reasonable steps to give notice of that intention in each province in Canada where the corporation was carrying on business at the time that it sent the statement of its intent to dissolve to the Director. Third, the corporation must proceed to collect its property, to dispose of properties that are not to be distributed in kind to its shareholders so as to convert those properties into money, to discharge all of its obligations, and to do all other acts required to liquidate its business. Fourth, after giving the notices required above and adequately providing for the payment or discharge of all of its obligations, the corporation must distribute its remaining property, either in money or in kind, among its shareholders according to their respective rights.

§15.184 Unless the notice of intent has been revoked, once the corporation has complied with the foregoing requirements, the corporation must prepare articles

---

[424] CBCA, s. 211(2).
[425] CBCA, s. 211(3).
[426] CBCA, s. 211(4).
[427] CBCA, s. 211(5).
[428] CBCA, s. 211(6), but the corporation continues in existence until the Director issues a certificate of dissolution.
[429] CBCA, s. 211(10). On receipt of a statement of revocation of intent to dissolve, the Director must issue a certificate of revocation in accordance with s. 262: CBCA, s. 211(11). On the date shown in that certificate the revocation is effective and the corporation may proceed with its business: CBCA, s. 211(12).
[430] CBCA, s. 211(7).

of dissolution in the prescribed form and send them to the Director.[431] On receipt of those articles, the Director must issue a certificate of dissolution in accordance with section 262 of the CBCA.[432] The corporation ceases to exist on the date shown in the certificate of dissolution.[433]

§15.185 At any time during this voluntary liquidation process, the Director or any interested person may apply to the court for an order requiring the liquidation to be continued under the supervision of the court.[434] Where such an application is made, the court may make the order sought and may make any further order that it thinks fit.[435] An applicant seeking an order for court supervision must give the Director notice of that application and the Director is entitled to appear and be heard, either in person or by counsel, on the hearing of that application.[436]

§15.186 The CBCA provisions relating to court intervention in a voluntary liquidation seem considerably more reserved in the extent to which they confer jurisdiction than do the corresponding provisions of the OBCA. An application to a court to supervise a voluntary liquidation and dissolution under subsection 211(8) of the CBCA must state the reasons (verified by affidavit) why the court should intervene and supervise the liquidation and dissolution.[437] However, where it is satisfied that it is appropriate to do so (and, in particular, where the court is satisfied that the corporation is able to pay or adequately provide for the discharge of all its obligations), the court may make an order bringing the liquidation and dissolution under its supervision. If the court makes such an order, the liquidation and dissolution continues thereafter under the supervision of the court.[438] The ancillary order making powers of the court in such a case are the same as in an involuntary liquidation.[439]

(ii) Liquidator

§15.187 In contrast to a winding-up under the OBCA, there appears to be no absolute requirement to have a liquidator in a liquidation and dissolution under the CBCA. Indeed the CBCA includes no express provision permitting the shareholders to appoint a liquidator at the time of commencing a voluntary liquidation and dissolution process. However, under paragraph 217(*b*) of the CBCA the court may appoint a liquidator (with or without security), fix his or her remuneration and replace any liquidator so appointed, where the court is satisfied that the corporation is able to pay or adequately provide for the discharge of all its obligations. Similarly, at the time of making an order for the liquidator of the company or at any time thereafter, the court may appoint any

---

[431] CBCA, s. 211(14).
[432] CBCA, s. 211(15).
[433] CBCA, s. 211(16).
[434] CBCA, s. 211(8).
[435] *Ibid.*
[436] CBCA, s. 211(9).
[437] CBCA, s. 215(1).
[438] CBCA, s. 215(2).
[439] See CBCA, s. 217.

person, including a director, officer or shareholder of the corporation, to be the liquidator of the corporation.[440] Where such an order has been made and the office of liquidator is or becomes vacant, the property of the corporation falls under the control of the court until the office of liquidator is filled.[441]

§15.188 Where the court appoints a liquidator, the powers of the directors and shareholders cease and vest in the liquidator,[442] except as authorized by the court,[443] although the liquidator may delegate any of the powers vested in him or her to the directors or shareholders.[444] The duties of the liquidator are set out in section 221 of the CBCA. The liquidator must give notice of his or her appointment forthwith to the Director and to each claimant and creditor known to the liquidator, and must also publish a notice of appointment in a newspaper published or distributed in the place where the corporation has its registered office[445] requiring any person

(i) indebted to the corporation, to render an account and pay to the liquidator at the time and place specified any amount owing;

(ii) possessing property of the corporation, to deliver it to the liquidator at the time and place specified, and

(iii) having a claim against the corporation, whether liquidated, unliquidated, future or contingent, to present particulars thereof in writing to the liquidator not later than two months after the first publication of the notice ...[446]

The liquidator must also take reasonable steps to give this notice in each province where the corporation carries on business.

§15.189 Under paragraph 221(c), the liquidator is required to take into his or her custody and control the property of the corporation. While section 221 itself makes no provision for the delegation by the liquidator of this responsibility either to the directors (or officers) of the corporation or to its shareholders, such delegation would seem to fall within the scope of paragraph 219(b) of the Act.

§15.190 The liquidator must not commingle corporate property with the liquidator's own property. In particular, the liquidator is obliged to open and maintain a trust account for the moneys of the corporation[447] and must keep accounts of the moneys of the corporation received and paid.[448] A number of other rec-

---

[440] CBCA, s. 220(1).
[441] CBCA, s. 220(2).
[442] *Re Ebsworth & Tidy's Contract* (1889), 42 Ch. D. 23 at 43 (C.A.), per Lord Esher M.R.; *Measures Brothers Ltd. v. Measures*, [1910] 2 Ch. 248 at 256 (C.A.), per Buckley L.J. and per Kennedy L.J. at 257; but cf. *Re Country Traders Distributors Ltd.*, [1974] 2 N.S.W.L.R. 135; *Austral Brick & Co. Pty. Ltd. v. Falgat Constructions Pty. Ltd.* (1990), 2 A.C.S.R. 776; *McAusland v. Deputy Commissioner of Taxation* (1993), 118 A.L.R. 577.
[443] CBCA, s. 219(1)(b).
[444] CBCA, s. 219(2).
[445] This notice must be published at least once a week for two consecutive weeks.
[446] CBCA, s. 221(b).
[447] CBCA, s. 221(d).
[448] CBCA, s. 221(e).

ords-related obligations are also imposed: the liquidator must maintain separate lists of the shareholders, creditors and other persons having claims against the corporation[449] and deliver to the court and to the Director (at least once in every 12-month period after his or her appointment or more often as the court may require) financial statements of the corporation in the form required by section 155 of the Act or in such other form as the liquidator may think proper or as the court may require.

§15.191 In order to carry out his or her duties, the liquidator is vested with certain ancillary powers and shielded by certain immunities. Under section 222 of the CBCA, the liquidator may: retain lawyers, accountants, engineers, appraisers and other professional advisers; bring, defend or take part in any civil, criminal or administrative action or proceeding in the name and on behalf of the corporation; carry on the business of the corporation as required for an orderly liquidation; sell by public auction or private sale any property of the corporation; do all acts and execute any documents in the name and on behalf of the corporation; borrow money on the security of the property of the corporation; settle or compromise any claims by or against the corporation; and do all other things necessary for the liquidation of the corporation and distribution of its property. In addition, where a liquidator has reason to believe that any person has possession or control of, or has concealed, withheld or misappropriated, any property of the corporation, the liquidator may apply to the court for an order requiring that person to appear before the court at the time and place designated by the court in the order and to be examined.[450] In the course of such an examination, the court may order that the person restore, or pay compensation for, any property of the corporation found to have been concealed, withheld or misappropriated.[451]

§15.192 A liquidator is not liable if he or she relies in good faith on financial statements of the corporation represented to the liquidator by an officer of the corporation or in a written report of the auditor of the corporation to reflect fairly the financial condition of the corporation or an opinion, report or a statement of a "person whose profession lends credibility to a statement made by the professional person".[452] It appears likely that this phrase would be seen to include a lawyer, accountant, engineer, appraiser or other professional advisor retained by the liquidator, since these professions were all formerly specifically identified in subsection 222(2).

§15.193 The power of the court to appoint the liquidator is contingent upon the court being satisfied that the corporation is able to pay or adequately provide for the discharge of all of its obligations.[453] Accordingly, where at any time the liquidator determines that the corporation is unable to pay or adequately provide

---

[449] CBCA, s. 221(f).
[450] CBCA, s. 222(3).
[451] CBCA, s. 223(4).
[452] CBCA, s. 222(2).
[453] CBCA, s. 217(b).

for the discharge of its obligations, the liquidator must apply to the court for directions.[454]

§15.194 A liquidator must pay the costs of liquidation out of the property of the corporation and must pay or make adequate provision for all claims against the corporation.[455] In the ordinary case, the claims of the liquidator with respect to these matters are subject to any valid security interest. Within one year after appointment, and after paying or making adequate provision for all claims against the corporation, the liquidator must either apply to the court

    (a) for approval of his final accounts and for an order permitting the liquidator to distribute in money or in kind the remaining property of the corporation to its shareholders according to their respective rights; or

    (b) for an extension of time, setting out the reasons therefor.[456]

If the liquidator fails to make that application, a shareholder of the corporation may apply to the court for an order requiring the liquidator to show cause why a final accounting and distribution should not be made.[457] The liquidator must give notice of his or her intention to make this application to the Director, each inspector appointed under section 217 and any person who provided a security or fidelity bond for the liquidation and must publish a notice in a newspaper published or distributed in the place where the corporation has its registered office or as otherwise directed by the court.[458] Where the court approves the final accounts rendered by the liquidator, the court must make an order directing the Director to issue a certificate of dissolution, directing the custody or disposal of the documents and records of the corporation, and (subject to the obligation to deliver a copy of the order to the Director) discharging the liquidator.[459] After the liquidator's final accounts are approved by the court, the liquidator must distribute any remaining property among the shareholders according to their respective rights.

(iii) Involuntary Dissolution

§15.195 Subsection 212(1) of the CBCA provides that subject to subsections (2) and (3), the Director may

    (a) dissolve a corporation by issuing a certificate of dissolution under this section if the corporation

        (i) has not commenced business within three years after the date shown in its certificate of incorporation,

---

[454] CBCA, s. 221(g).
[455] CBCA, s. 223(1).
[456] CBCA, s. 223(2).
[457] CBCA, s. 223(3).
[458] CBCA, s. 223(4).
[459] CBCA, s. 223(5). The liquidator must forthwith send a certified copy of the order to the Director: CBCA, s. 223(6). On receipt of that copy, the Director must issue a certificate of dissolution: CBCA, s. 223(7). The corporation ceases to exist on the date shown in the certificate of dissolution: CBCA, s. 223(8).

(ii) has not carried on its business for three consecutive years;

(iii) is in default for a period of one year in sending to the Director any fee, notice or document required by this Act, or

(iv) does not have any directors or is in the situation described in subsection 109(4); or

(b) apply to a court for an order dissolving the corporation, in which case section 217 applies.

In addition, under subsection 212(3.1), the Director may dissolve a corporation by issuing a certificate of dissolution if the required fee for the issuance of a certificate of incorporation has not been paid. The Director may not dissolve a corporation under section 212 until the Director has:

(a) given one hundred and twenty days notice of the decision to dissolve the corporation to the corporation and to each director thereof; and

(b) published notice of that decision in a publication generally available to the public.[460]

After the expiration of that period, the corporation ceases to exist on the date shown in the certificate of dissolution.

§15.196 Section 213 sets out a procedure for the dissolution of a corporation for cause by way of court order. Grounds for dissolution under this section are set out in subsection 213(1) which provides:

231.(1) The Director or any interested person may apply to a court for an order dissolving a corporation if the corporation has

(a) failed for two or more consecutive years to comply with the requirements of this Act with respect to the holding of annual meetings of shareholders;

(b) contravened subsection 16(2) or section 21, 157 or 159; or

(c) procured any certificate under this Act by misrepresentation.

An applicant seeking an order under section 213 must give the Director notice of the application, and the Director is entitled to appear and be heard in person or by counsel. Subsection 213(3) indicates that the making of the order is discretionary. Where such an order is made, then subsection 213(4) applies. It provides:

231.(4) On receipt of an order under this section, section 212 or 214, the Director shall

(a) if the order is to dissolve the corporation, issue a certificate of dissolution in the form that the Director fixes; or

(b) if the order is to liquidate and dissolve the corporation under the supervision of the court, issue a certificate of intent to dissolve in the form that

---

[460] CBCA, s. 212(2).

the Director fixes and publish notice of the order in a publication generally available to the public.

The corporation ceases to exist on the date shown in the certificate of dissolution, rather than on the date of the order.[461] The court is given a further power to order dissolution under section 214. It provides that:

> 214. A court may order the liquidation and dissolution of a corporation or any of its affiliated corporations on the application of a shareholder,
>
> (a) if the court is satisfied that in respect of a corporation or any of its affiliates
>
> (i) any act or omission of the corporation or any of its affiliates effects a result,
>
> (ii) the business or affairs of the corporation or any of its affiliates are or have been carried on or conducted in a manner, or
>
> (iii) the powers of the directors of the corporation or any of its affiliates are or have been exercised in a manner
>
> that is oppressive or unfairly prejudicial to or that unfairly disregards the interests of any security holder, creditor, director or officer; or
>
> (b) if the court is satisfied that
>
> (i) a unanimous shareholder agreement entitles a complaining shareholder to demand dissolution of the corporation after the occurrence of a specified event and that event has occurred, or
>
> (ii) it is just and equitable that the corporation should be liquidated and dissolved.

Subsection 214(2) provides that on such an application, a court may make such order under this section or section 241 as it thinks fit.

(iv) Revival Procedure Under the CBCA

§15.197 The 2001 amendments to the CBCA significantly revised the dissolution and revival provisions under that Act. Subsection 209(1) now provides that:

> 209.(1) Where a body corporate is dissolved under this Part or under section 268 of this Act or section 261 of chapter 33 of the Statutes of Canada, 1974-75-76, any interested person may apply to the Director to have the body corporate revived as a corporation under this Act."

Chapter 33 of the Statutes of Canada, 1974-75-76 was the CBCA as originally enacted. The definition of "interested person" is set down in subsection 209(6). It provides that the term includes

(a) a shareholder, a director, an officer, an employee and a creditor of the dissolved corporation;

(b) a person who has a contractual relationship with the dissolved corporation;

---

[461] CBCA, s. 213(5).

(c) a person who, although at the time of dissolution of the corporation was not a person described in paragraph (a), would be such a person if a certificate of revival is issued under this section; and

(d) a trustee in bankruptcy for the dissolved corporation.

Application for revival is effected by sending articles of revival in the form fixed by the Director to the Director. Subsection 209(3) then provides:

> 209.(3) On receipt of articles of revival, the Director shall issue a certificate of revival in accordance with section 262, if
>
> (a) the body corporate has fulfilled all conditions precedent that the Director considers reasonable; and
>
> (b) there is no valid reason for refusing to issue the certificate.

§15.198 Revival is effective on the date shown on the certificate of revival.[462] Subsection 209(4) makes it clear that revival may be made conditional, and also that it does not affect vested rights:

> 209.(4) Subject to any reasonable terms that may be imposed by the Director, to the rights acquired by any person after its dissolution and to any changes to the internal affairs of the corporation after its dissolution, the revived corporation is, in the same manner and to the same extent as if it had not been dissolved,
>
> (a) restored to its previous position in law, including the restoration of any rights and privileges whether arising before its dissolution or after its dissolution and before its revival; and
>
> (b) liable for the obligations that it would have had if it had not been dissolved whether they arise before its dissolution or after its dissolution and before its revival.

Subsection 209(5) provides expressly that any legal action respecting the affairs of a revived corporation taken between the time of its dissolution and its revival is valid and effective.

I. INTERPLAY BETWEEN INSOLVENCY LEGISLATION AND WINDING-UP PROVISIONS

§15.199 The federal *Winding-up and Restructuring Act*[463] does not apply to corporations within the meaning of the OBCA or the CBCA. The CBCA expressly provides that the liquidation provisions of that Act apply only where the corporation is not insolvent. By the same token, the Province of Ontario has no jurisdiction over insolvency, and therefore the winding-up (*i.e.*, liquidation) provisions of the OBCA can apply only where the corporation is solvent,[464] even where the persons interested in an insolvent corporation consent to its being

---

[462] CBCA, s. 209(3.1).
[463] R.S.C. 1985, c. W-11, as amended.
[464] *Re Iron Clay Brick Manufacturing Co.*, [1889] O.J. No. 131, 19 O.R. 113 (Ch.); *Re Tober Enterprises Ltd.* (1980), 109 D.L.R. (3d) 184 (B.C.S.C.).

dealt with and it would be convenient to proceed under that Act.[465] Except in the case of an insolvency, the federal government has no jurisdiction to legislate concerning the winding-up of a provincially incorporated entity.[466] Where a corporation under the OBCA or the CBCA is insolvent, its assets and liabilities must be liquidated in accordance with the *Bankruptcy and Insolvency Act*[467] rather than in accordance with the liquidation provisions of the OBCA or the CBCA. The *Bankruptcy and Insolvency Act* provides a scheme for the orderly realization and distribution of the bankrupt's assets and prevails over other statutes where there is a conflict existing with respect to matters of property and civil rights.[468]

§15.200 Although the federal government has no jurisdiction over the winding-up of provincial companies *per se*,[469] the province may incorporate the procedures set out in the federal *Winding-up and Restructuring Act* to cover the winding-up of solvent corporations.[470] Under the law as it now stands, the *Bankruptcy and Insolvency Act* (which provides for the liquidation of the assets of bankrupt and insolvent debtors) applies to corporations under both the OBCA and the CBCA if the corporation is insolvent. Federal law relating to the winding-up of a corporation does not apply to provincial corporations in circumstances other than insolvency. In particular, although the federal government's jurisdiction over bankruptcy and insolvency is broadly construed to include the whole field of legislation relating to compulsory liquidation and distribution of the assets of insolvent debtors,[471] the mere impairment of capital or a deadlock in management is not sufficient to bring a provincial company within that legislation.[472] There is no standing to commence bankruptcy proceedings solely on the ground that a corporation may be insolvent.

§15.201 From this it follows that unless it can be shown on the civil standard of proof that a particular corporation is insolvent, any proceeding to wind up the corporation should be commenced under the OBCA or the CBCA, as applicable. In the case of an OBCA corporation, if it is subsequently shown that the corporation in question is insolvent, formal bankruptcy proceedings (or a proposal) must then be made under the *Bankruptcy and Insolvency Act*.

---

[465] *Re Tober Enterprises Ltd.*, [1980] B.C.J. No. 1403, 109 D.L.R. (3d) 184 (S.C.).
[466] *Harrison v. Nepisiquit Lumber Co.* (1911), 11 E.L.R. 314, 41 N.B.R. 1 at 27 (C.A.), *per* White J.
[467] R.S.C. 1985, c. B-3, as amended.
[468] *Re Commonwealth Investors Syndicate Ltd.*, [1986] B.C.J. No. 3111, 60 C.B.R. (N.S.) 193 at 195 (B.C.S.C.), *per* Davies J.
[469] *Re Cramp Steel Co.*, [1908] O.J. No. 113, 16 O.L.R. 230 at 231 (H.C.J.), *per* Mabee J.; *Re Empire Timber, Lumber & Tie Co.*, [1920] O.J. No. 34, 1 C.B.R. 370 (H.C.).
[470] R.S.C. 1985, c. W.11, as amended; *Re Waltham Motors Corp. of Canada Ltd.*, [1922] O.J. No. 373, 23 O.W.N. 123 (H.C.).
[471] *Re Colonial Investment Co. of Winnipeg* (1913), 5 W.W.R. 822, 14 D.L.R. 563 (Man. C.A.).
[472] *System Theater Operating Co. v. Pulos*, 33 C.B.R. 235 (Que. C.A.), rev'd [1955] S.C.J. No. 30, [1955] S.C.R. 448.

§15.202 In *Re Jarvis Construction Co.*[473] the British Columbia Supreme Court held that a liquidator in a voluntary liquidation had no power to make an assignment in bankruptcy where he or she discovered the corporation to be insolvent. The opposite conclusion was reached in *Re Western Hemlock Products Ltd.*[474] The latter view seems preferable, since the presumption of a voluntary liquidation is that the corporation is solvent, and where this proves to be incorrect, the voluntary liquidation cannot proceed. Moreover, under clause 223(1)(*a*) of the OBCA, the liquidator is deemed to possess the power to initiate legal proceedings, and bankruptcy is a legal proceeding. From an administrative perspective, allowing the liquidator to proceed with the assignment is likely to prove the quickest and most cost-efficient method of dealing with the problem of an insolvent corporation. In the case of a CBCA corporation, the liquidator is empowered to apply to the court supervising the liquidation of the corporation for directions upon the discovery that the corporation is insolvent.

§15.203 It is clear, however, that the liquidator has the authority to contest any petition in bankruptcy brought against the corporation.[475] On the other hand, although the OBCA and the CBCA impose a stay upon the institution of proceedings against a corporation that is being liquidated under either of those statutes, that stay does not prevent the institution of proceeding[476] under the *Bankruptcy and Insolvency Act* should there be grounds to believe that the corporation is insolvent.[477]

§15.204 The *Bankruptcy and Insolvency Act* itself makes no provision for the dissolution of a corporation, so once an OBCA or a CBCA corporation is dissolved under that Act, it is necessary to dissolve it under the governing corporate statute. Since dissolution involves a matter of corporate status, it is doubtful whether the federal government may enact legislation pertaining to the dissolution of provincially incorporated corporations, or *vice versa*, although it may validly enact legislation (under its jurisdiction over bankruptcy and insolvency) empowering the trustee in bankruptcy of a corporation to apply for the dissolution of the corporation in accordance with provincial law once the corporation has been liquidated. Since the continued existence of near-dead corporations seems to serve little purpose, a provision in the *Bankruptcy and Insolvency Act* requiring a trustee-in-bankruptcy to apply for dissolution as a condition of being discharged as the trustee of a corporation would be a very welcome addition to the law. Presumably, the bankruptcy court could include such a provision in any discharge now, but in the absence of a legislative requirement it is doubtful that

---

[473] [1971] B.C.J. No. 184, 16 C.B.R. (N.S.) 193 (B.C.S.C.).
[474] (1961), 35 W.W.R. 184, 27 D.L.R. (2d) 457 (B.C.S.C.).
[475] *Re Elar Construction Ltd.*, (1961), 3 C.B.R. (N.S.) 249 (Man. Q.B.).
[476] *Re Cadwell's Ltd.*, [1932] O.J. No. 156, 14 C.B.R. 114 at 116 (S.C.), *per* Sedgewick J. But see *Ontario (Milk Control Board) v. Wawanesa Mutual Insurance Co.*, [1949] O.J. No. 46, 29 C.B.R. 262 (H.C.J.). Irrespective of whether or not the stay applies, it is certainly courteous to the court seized of the winding-up proceeding to apply for leave.
[477] See, generally, *Re Ontario Forge & Bolt Co.*, [1894] O.J. No. 151, 25 O.R. 407 (H.C.J.); *Re Fredericton Boom Co.* (1907), 2 E.L.R. 451 (N.B.S.C.).

trustees will take to recommending such a course to a court, when they apply for discharge.

J. CONCLUSION

§15.205 With this review of the law governing the liquidation and dissolution of corporations, this study of the law and practice relating to Canadian business corporations comes to a close. In this text, we have taken a snapshot of how the law and practice relating to Canadian business corporations looked towards the end of 2006. However, no snapshot is able to do the law justice. The law cannot be properly depicted in a single frame. It is a moving picture.

§15.206 The apparent steady evolution of the law is evident, merely by comparing the first edition of this text to the second. In the years since the enactment of the first edition, the CBCA has been extensively revised, and a number of interesting proposals have been made for amendment to the OBCA. Part VI of the OBCA, which formerly governed the investment securities not only of OBCA corporations, but of other corporate entities issuing securities into Ontario, has been replaced by the *Securities Transfer Act, 2006*.[478] The already enormous body of case law in which the various provisions of the OBCA, CBCA and corresponding statutes in other jurisdictions have been construed by the courts has expanded at an unprecedented rate. In face of this steady growth of new law, it is worthwhile to step back for a moment, and see where we stand now in comparison to the overall history of corporate law.

§15.207 More than 162 years have passed since the *Joint Stock Companies Act, 1844* was enacted in England.[479] The world has changed immeasurably over that time. The British Empire — in which the modern notion of the business company came to life — has gone. The German empire has both come and gone. In that same period, France has been a kingdom, an empire and three different kinds of republic. The United States has evolved from a nation of small landowning farmers, still clinging mainly to the Atlantic coast, into a continental industrial and commercial giant that remains without equal. For a time during this period, half the world flirted with the notion of the destruction of capitalism. Today, communism is all but gone. These great changes in the social and political landscape seem small by comparison to the evolution of technology. In 1844, the railway and the steam engine were the state of the art in modern technology. Today, satellite communications and jet aircraft allow commerce to operate on a global scale and scope that our great-grandparents could scarcely imagine. New technologies come and go in less than half a generation. Yet throughout this period, and despite all these upheavals, the business company has gone from strength to strength. Wars and depressions have not diminished its importance.

---

[478] S.O. 2006, c. 8.
[479] 7 & 8 Vic., c. 110.

§15.208 As a form of commercial enterprise the modern business company ranks not first among equals; it stands today as the first, and there are no equals. It is the dominant form of enterprise not only in common law jurisdictions, but even in economies that are at least nominally socialist. Other forms of business enterprise are mere acolytes. In the later part of the 20th Century, favourable tax treatment encouraged the use of limited partnerships. More recently, in Canada, Australia and the United States income trusts enjoyed a momentary popularity — although that popularity is now waning due to a change in tax law. However, both limited partnerships and income trusts made use of an underlying corporate vehicle. The modern world of commerce has evolved as the business company has evolved.

§15.209 The Canadian law and practice of business corporations has long since become independent of the American and English precedents from which it was derived. Yet there remains far more similarity among the corporate laws of the common law world than there are differences. Indeed, to a very great extent, many of the principles worked out in the early years of the business company continue to influence legal thinking with regard to business corporations today. The Rule in *Foss v. Harbottle*,[480] the Rule in *Turquand's Case*,[481] the presumed authority of directors to manage the corporation, and the principles of fiduciary duty all remain relevant to the modern business corporation. An Edwardian jurist who returned to sit in on a modern corporate law proceeding would understand both the issues and the principles being litigated — although he might well see them as leading to a different conclusion than that which would be reached by a judge today. It is a fair question whether the law should have remained so constant. The technological changes of recent years have now made practical a degree of shareholder participation that previously was unthinkable. It is tempting to wonder whether in another century the law then in force would seem as familiar to us, as the present law of today would look to that hypothetical Edwardian jurist.

§15.210 Throughout this period, there have been considerable forces for change. Great scandals inevitably lead to new laws, and in recent years there have been many of these. Most recently, numerous modifications were made to the law to introduce enhanced corporate governance and control measures in reaction to the scandals at Enron, Tyco,[482] Adelphia Business Solutions,[483] WorldCom,[484] and

---

[480] (1843), 2 Hare 461, 67 E.R. 189.
[481] *Royal British Bank v. Turquand*, [1843-60] All E.R. Rep. 435, 6 E. & B 327, 119 E.R. 886 (Ex. Ch.).
[482] The Tyco financial scandal was one of the more complicated scandals of the early years of this Century. In its January 14, 2002 issue, *Business Week Magazine* would name Tyco's CEO L. Dennis Kozlowski as one of the top 25 corporate managers of 2001. On June 17, 2005, a Manhattan jury found Kozlowski, and Tyco's CFO Mark Swartz guilty of stealing more than $150 million from Tyco. During the intervening period there were allegations of insider trading (on January 30, 2002, the New York Times reported that Kozlowski and Tyco CFO Mark Swartz sold more than $100 million of their Tyco stock the previous fiscal year despite public statements that they rarely sold their stock); sales tax evasion (on June 4, 2002, Manhattan District Attorney Robert Morgenthau announced a criminal indictment accusing Kozlowski of conspiring to evade more than $1 million in state and city sales tax on fine art purchases); hidden pay-

elsewhere,[485] that led to a push for reform to enhance the role of the shareholder in the corporation. In addition, corporate operations are now far more regulated than they have been for many decades.

§15.211 It is tempting, in the face of such trends, to assume that the corporate law of 100 years hence will be very different from the corporate laws of today. Such an assumption may well prove wrong. Very often it is found that reactive laws, such as those spawned by Enron and its kin, do not work; or that the cost of compliance with such laws vastly exceeds the benefit that they generate. Similar changes took place following the collapse of Equity Funding Corporation in 1973, the collapse of the U.S. savings and loan industry and many Canadian junior financial institutions in the 1980s, Poly Peck and BCCI in the early 1990s. They did not prove sufficient to prevent Enron, Hollinger and Bre-X. Efforts to enhance the opportunity for direct shareholder involvement have done little to stimulate greater direct shareholder participation. The failure of shareholders to take up this initiative is perhaps not surprising. The corporate democracy reforms introduced in the CBCA in 1975 — such as the possibility of shareholder proposals — have not led to much of a change in actual corporate management practice. Furthermore to an increasing extent, greater attention is now being paid to the financial implications of strict regulatory control.

§15.212 In France there is a saying, *plus ca change, plus c'est la meme chose*. It is for philosophers rather than lawyers to debate whether this saying provides an accurate description of the condition of the human race. If, however, it is accurate, then no doubt in 100 years the law will not be all that different from what we have in place today. History affords good reason to believe that this will be so. In 1844, the law relating to business companies was fundamentally about how to marshal together the finances in the pursuit of greater wealth. So it remains today. During the intervening period, corporate law has evolved steadily as various individuals have sought to appropriate to themselves more than what others considered to be their fair share. The driving energy of individual and collective greed has fueled the evolution of corporate law, as it has also fuelled the spread of capitalism. So long as greed maintains its sway — and there is as yet no sign that its influence has begun to wane — the fundamental issues of corporate law are likely to remain the same.

---

ments of fees and consideration (on December 17, 2002, former Tyco board member Frank Walsh pled guilty to hiding the $20 million in fees relating to a major corporate transaction).

[483] At one time the fifth largest cable company in the United States, Adelphia filed for bankruptcy protection in June 2002 in the aftermath of a financial scandal. It achieved startling growth during the 1980s and 1990s through aggressive acquisition strategies. On March 27, 2002, Adelphia officials disclosed $2.3 billion in previously unrecorded debt incurred through co-borrowings between Adelphia and other entities owned by its controlling Rigas family or the family's private trust, Highland Holdings. Under these loan agreements, the Rigas entities were responsible for repaying the debt, but if they were unable to do so, Adelphia would be liable.

[484] Alleged to have overstated the strength of its financial position by several billions of dollars.

[485] Or, for a non-North American perspective, those at Metallgesellschaft AG, Parmalat, and Simetal-Solo Industries.

INDEX

(all references are to paragraph numbers, fn designates footnote)

A

Abbots, and corporations at common law, 1.8
Accounting
    concepts and limited liability, 3.1
    for share capital, 7.231
Advice of outside experts, etc., 10.119
Affiliated corporations, 3.61
Agency, and directors, 11.300
Agent's right to an indemnity, 11.298
Aggregation principle, 3.28
Alberta unlimited liability companies, 2.89
Alter ego, corporation as, 2.35
Altruism, 11.107, 11.245
Amalgamation
    after special resolution, 14.113
    agreements, 14.96
    corporations governed by same law, 14.92
    court approval of, 14.132
    defined, 14.89
    discretion to refuse to approve, 14.131
    dissent rights, 14.111. *See also* Dissent
    effect of, 14.133
    generally, 14.88
    horizontal short-form, 14.126
    long-form, 14.95
    private company exemption, 14.112
    shareholder approval, 14.106
    two-stream amalgamation, 14.130
    unwinding, 14.101
    vertical short-form, 14.122
Amending the articles
    changing the name of a corporation, 14.30
    delegation to directors, 14.37
    extent of approval required, 14.23
    generally, 14.3
    procedure following approval of special resolution, 14.27
    restated articles, 14.43
    special voting rights, 14.8
American case law, 1.30fn
Annual information form, 10.173
Applying for provincial/federal powers, 4.61
Appraisal remedy. *See* Dissent
Arrangements
    as alternative to amendment, 14.263
    generally, 14.237
    procedural considerations, 14.259
    rights of dissent and, 14.254
    shareholder procedure, 14.241
    with creditors, 14.264

    with shareholders, 14.238
Articles of a corporation (see also amendment)
    generally, 5.42
    not a contract, 5.48
    requirements for, 5.44, 5.46
    restrictions on powers set out in, 6.19
    status of, 5.47
Artificiality of the corporate concept, 2.72
Assignment of debts (or accounts), 8.199
Assignment of specific debts and accounts, 8.204
Assignment of specific securities, 8.213
Assignments and preferences, 8.332
Associates, 3.61
Assumption of office, 9.118
Audit
    change of auditor, 9.189
    clean opinion and qualified opinion, 10.173
    detection of error, 9.173
    dispensing with requirement, 9.188
    duties of an auditor, 9.163
    generally, 9.153
    independence, 9.158
    nature of, 9.154
    place of in the governance process, 9.153
    plan, 9.181
    process, 10.182
    reasonable reliance upon management, 9.169
    standard of care, 9.179
    status of the auditor, 9.162
Audit committee
    and financial statements, 10.89
    and MD&A, 10.88.1
    and Sarbanes-Oxley Act of 2002, 10.154
    generally, 9.190, 10.88
Auditor
    and director negligence, 10.129
    independence, 10.184
    liability, 9.190.1
Authority
    actual, 6.40
    corporate agents, 6.36
    corporate officers, 6.69
    director resolutions as evidence of, 6.92
    evidentiary issues, 6.90
    exceptional cases where outsiders are not protected, 6.82
    generally, 6.35
    implied, 6.46
    indoor management rule, 6.52

Authority — *cont'd*
    ostensible, 6.43
    plenipotentiary, 6.90
    ratification, 6.87
    repudiation for want of, 6.31
Authority to borrow, 8.22
Authorized and issued capital, 7.48

B

Bad faith
    and by-laws, 5.59
    avoiding, 11.45
Bank Act security
    conditions precedent, 8.224
    generally, 214
    loans and advances, 8.223
    nature of section 427 security, 8.218
    permitted borrowers and security, 8.225
    priority of section 426 security, 8.248
    procedure for taking and perfecting section 426 security, 8.246
    procedure for taking section 427 security, 8.220
    section 426 security, 8.238
    section 427 security, 215
Bank of Credit & Commerce, 3.48, 9.34
Best interest of corporation
    and stakeholder theory, 11.67
    and transfer restrictions, 7.222
    generally, 11.111, 11.47, 11.254
    maximization of corporate value, 14.143
    poison pills, 11.50
Best practice, not the legal standard, 11.117
Bill C-45. *See* Criminal liability
Bill C-55, 14.270
Bishops, as corporations sole, 1.8
Board
    and the CEO, 9.57
    requirement for, 9.27
    collegial action, 10.5
    committee structure, 10.87
    confidentiality, 10.15
    control over litigation, 10.35
    decision-making process, 10.1
    first, 9.28
    growing role of, 9.31
    minutes, 10.12
    resolutions in lieu of meetings, 10.111
    role in corporate governance, 9.51
    sterilized, 10.17
    strategic role of, 9.45
    telephone meetings, 10.9
    composition, 9.52
Body corporate, 5.9
Bond and other credit rating, 8.306
Book entry system, 12.226
Book value, 8.21.1
Bounded rationality, 14.149
Bre-X, 9.5fn

Business combination. *See* Going private transactions
Business corporations
    as a species of business enterprise, 1.31, 1.39, 2.1
    generally, 1.23
    special legislation governing, 1.28
Business failure, causes of, 15.7
Business judgment rule, 11.15, 11.35
Business names, 5.81
Business organization, types of, 1.31
Business records protection, 6.128
By-law
    and bad faith, 5.59
    as governance device, 12.1096
    defined, 5.51
    direct election, 9.94
    enactment of, 5.54
    generally, 5.50
    inconsistent with statute, 5.64
    interpretation of, 5.53, 5.60
    judicial review of, 5.61
    purpose, 5.52
    record of, 5.66
    unreasonable or illegal, 5.63, 6.63

C

Cakes and ale case law, 11.94
Canada Revenue Agency record requirements, 6.123
Canadian Public Accountability Board, 10.183
Cancellation of incorporation for cause, 15.152
Capacity and powers of corporations, 6.1
Capital
    alteration of share, 7.51
    fixed and circulating, 7.15
    meaning of, 7.3
    reduction of share, 7.275
    working, 7.14
Capitalization requirements, 5.154
Care
    degree of, 11.35
    extent of, 11.29
    generally, 11.14
Certificate of incorporation, 5.155
Chair. *See also* Presiding officer
Chair and shareholder meetings, 12.83
Charge
    generally, 8.71, 8.82
    terms, 8.96
    property subject to, 8.87
Charity, gifts to, 11.93
Charter of Rights and Freedoms
    corporations and, 4.64
    investigation remedy, 13.272
Chattel mortgage, 8.128
Check-the-box rules, 2.80
Cheque, payment by, 7.165
Chief executive officer, 10.102, 11.37

Chose in action, corporate security as, 7.21
Circulating capital, 7.15
Claims made policies, 11.312
Classes of security, 7.62
Closely held corporation, 6.8
Coattail provisions, 7.66
Coined words, 5.111
Collective responsibility, 10.30
Comity, international, 1.37
Commercial paper, 8.59
Commission on the sale of shares, 7.185
Committee authority, legal restrictions on, 10.95
Common law corporations, 1.7
Common law, corporate criminal liability at, 3.19
Companies Creditors Arrangement Act, 14.264
Comparable circumstances, 11.14
Compensation committee, 10.94
Compliance order, 6.17, 13.259
Concession theory, 1.47
Conditional sale agreement, 8.206
Conduct of business outside the province, 4.21
Confiscatory use of managerial power, 13.29
Conflict of interest
    attendance at meetings, 10.52
    director remuneration, 10.67
    disclosure procedure, 10.47
    effect of non-compliance, 10.54
    fair dealing, 10.57
    fair terms, 10.61
    fiduciary duty, 11.127
    full and fair disclosure, 10.42
    general disclosure statements, 10.43.1
    generally, 10.39
    material contracts and material interests, 10.45
    payments to directors, 10.74
    potential, 11.131
    Sarbanes-Oxley Act of 2002, 101.54
    shareholder access to information, 10.79
    shareholder ratification, 10.76
    single director corporations, 10.44
    statutory requirements for disclosure of, 10.39
Conflicting international corporate behaviour requirements, 10.162
Consequential damages, 7.121
Conspiracy and corporation, 3.52
Constitutional considerations, 4.1
Constraining director power
    generally, 12.186
    under unanimous shareholder agreement, 12.201
Constructive notice, 6.32
Continuation
    export of corporations, 14.232
    generally, 14.38, 14.221
    importation of companies, 14.22

Continuous disclosure, 10.172
Contract (see also pre-incorporation contracts and indoor management rule)
    between shareholder and corporation, 2.13
    breach of, procuring, 11.237
    fettering discretion by way of, 11.200
    "in trust for a body to be incorporated", 5.197
    of the corporation, identification of, 8.25
    re the purchase of shares, 7.281
    unwinding of due to oppression, 13.142
Contributories (see winding-up)
Conversion rights and options, 7.241
Cooperizing, 10.14, 12.166
Core document, 7.137
Corporate concept, 1.1
Corporate constitution, 5.40
Corporate control
    general, 9.1
    nature of directorship, 9.11
    process of, 9.5
Corporate criminal liability
    approaches to, 3.27
    impact of Bill C-45, 3.33
    innocent corporate operative, 3.40
    logic of, 3.41
Corporate domicile, 6.105
Corporate enterprise, types of, 5.5
Corporate entity, identifying the status of, 5.140
Corporate finance
    generally, 7.1
    key concepts, 7.48
Corporate formalities, 2.8fn
Corporate function, 1.1
Corporate governance. *See also* Board, Corporate control and Directors
    creation of a suitable regime, 9.42
    disclosure, 9.140
    executive compensation, 9.54
    practice, 9.33
    role of board, 9.8, 9.51
    TSX best practice, 9.35
Corporate group concept. *See also* Group enterprise doctrine, 2.63
Corporate law, object of, 6.2
Corporate legislative realm, 1.24
Corporate management, generally, 10.10
Corporate name. *See* Names
Corporate opportunity doctrine, 11.165
Corporate records, 6.118
Corporate seal, 5.150, 6.94
Corporate status must be disclosed, 5.206
Corporate theory, 1.39
Corporate undertakings, 6.430
Corporation
    aggregate, 1.9
    as agent, 2.34

Corporation — *cont'd*
    as facade or alter ego, 2.35
    as legal fictions, 1.33, 1.49
    categories of, 1.2
    corporations, distinguishing feature of, 1.32
    creation a sovereign act, 1.47, 1.52
    criminal liability of, 3.17
    declining opportunities, 11.173, 11.187
    different classes of, 1.6
    discrimination against, 4.73
    jurisprudential conceptions of, 1.44
    liability for torts as principal, 3.5, 3.10
    liability of for the acts of its insiders, 3.4
    must exist and carry on business, 11.257
    organization of, 5.165
    power to borrow, 8.23
    sole, 1.7
    types of, 1.31
    with wasting assets, 7.341
Costs of enforcement, 8.90
Covenants, 8.110
Creditors, no duty to as such, 11.74
Criminal liability of corporation, 3.17
Crown
    Agents, 2.119
    Corporation, 4.79, 5.5
    as corporation, 1.8, 1.59
    rights of escheat to, 15.166
Crystallization
    action by some third party, 8.154
    automatic under terms of security agreement, 8.155
    waiver of default, 8.152
Cumulative dividends, 7.321
Cumulative voting, 9.99
Curative powers of the courts, 13.261
Current assets, 11.284
Customer lists, 11.152

D

De facto directors
    generally, 9.109
    liability for wages, 11.271
De facto officer, 6.69
De facto shareholders, 12.19
Deadlock, 15.60
Debenture stock, 8.195
Debentures and bonds, 8.129
Debentures, pledging of, 8.161
Debt
    common types of, 8.52
    distinction between debt and equity, 8.9
    distinguished from other liabilities, 8.3
    financing, 8.1
    foreign currency, 8.62
    nature of, 8.3
Debt and trust, 8.17, 8.60, 8.73, 8.112
Decision making process, 11.24

Defeasance, 8.126
Delaware, corporate laws of, 1.30fn
Delegation of managerial powers, 10.80, 10.95, 10.109
Demand loan, 8.53, 8.147
Depository bills and notes, 8.266fn, 8.275
Derivative action
    and bankruptcy, 13.238
    buying-in to a derivative proceeding, 12.244
    common law position, 13.198
    conditions precedent to relief, 13.21
    conflict of laws, 13.252
    discretionary nature of the remedy, 13.206
    double actions, 13.239
    generally, 13.191
    good faith and, 13.214
    independent committee, 13.219
    interim relief, 13.248
    notice of claim, 13.216
    obtaining leave, 13.207
    procedural considerations, 13.232
    ratification of director misconduct, etc., 13.253
    statutory regime, 13.204
Derivative relief distinguished from oppression & other personal claims, 13.231
Director
    defined, 9.25
    directors and promoters distinguished, 9.26
    disqualification, 11.324
    duty of care, 11.10
    duty of care at common law, 11.13fn
    duty of disclosure, 11.40
    duty of good faith, 11.45
    liability, general, 11.1, 11.5
    liability, specific, 11.3
    meetings, 10.2
    power, constraining, 12.186
    relationship between liability and duty, 11.8
    removal for oppression, 13.141
    statutory liabilities, 11.2
    voting, 10.5, 10.8
Director and officer insurance, 11.310
Director and officer wage claims, 11.279
Director disclosure (see also information circular)
    generally, 9.138, 11.40
    OBCA and CBCA requirements, 9.144
Directors
    acting beyond their power and authority, 11.246
    and corporate torts, 11.203
    and corporations in financial distress, 10.136
    and misrepresentation, 11.223

Directors — *cont'd*
   appointment or election to office, 9.58, 9.92
   approval of share transfer, 12.8
   blind reliance, 10.130
   board evaluation of, 9.88
   breach of trust, 11.232
   claims against multiple, 11.228
   close personal relationships among, 9.91
   conspiracy with corporation, 11.245
   cumulative voting, 9.99
   direct appointment rights, 9.97
   due diligence defense, 10.121
   duty to act honestly and in good faith, 11.44
   effect of liquidation, 10.27, 15.109
   ex officio, 9.59
   excessive generosity, 11.86
   fettering discretion of a future board, 11.58
   general managerial rights of, 10.16
   independent, 9.37, 9.87
   intentional torts, 11.240
   invalid appointment or election, 9.98
   knowledge, skill and experience, 11.28
   liability for civil wrongs of the corporation, 11.207
   liability in contract, 11.235
   managerial powers overview of, 10.20
   minutes of meetings, 10.12
   number of, 9.82
   personal involvement in wrong-doing, 11.218
   power and duty to manage, 10.32
   procuring breach of contract, 11.237
   qualification of, 9.66
   qualifying shareholding, 9.79
   reliance on officers of the corporation, 10.107
   remuneration, 10.67
   resident Canadians, 9.75
   residual powers after receivership, etc., 10.26
   resignation and removal of, 9.120
   separate duty of care, 11.220
   shareholder election, 9.92
   special powers of to amend articles, 14.39
   specific rights and duties, 10.29
Directorship
   nature of, 9.11
   theories of, 9.17
Disclosure
   director's duty of, 11.40
   routine, 10.169
Disclosure of information, 12.33.1
Dissent
   and arrangement, 14.252
   and insolvency, 14.87
   costs, 14.86
   nature of right, 14.50
   opposition not same as, 14.53
   overview of the dissent procedure, 14.48
   procedure, 14.63
   procedure for sole benefit of dissidents, 14.58
   rights limited to registered holders, 14.47
   rights of generally, 14.45
   valuation, American case law concerning, 14.74
   valuation, by court, 14.63
Dissolution
   cancellation for cause, 15.152
   effect of, 15.157
   generally, 15.148
   property forfeit to the Crown, 15.166
   revival and surviving rights, 15.160
   sole shareholder corporation, 15.165
   under CBCA, 15.197
Distributing corporation, 5.13
Distribution of powers, 4.4
Dividend history, 7.300
Dividend record date, 7.330
Dividends
   corporations with wasting assets, 7.341
   covenant against payment, 8.122
   cumulative, 7.321
   director discretion over declaration, 7.298
   entitlement to, 7.327
   form of declaration, 7.303
   generally, 72.95
   and gifts, 7.297
   "guaranteed" payment of, 7.302, 7.325
   liability for improper payment, 7.316, 7.342
   nature of entitlement, 7.297
   preferential, 7.319
   proportionate abatement, 7.324
   restrictions on the declaration and payment, 7.309
   stock, 7.335
   to controlling shareholder/directors, 7.333
Domicile
   of corporation, 6.105
   vs. nationality, 6.108
   vs. residence, 6.110
Dual aspect doctrine, 4.7
Due diligence,
   and Income Tax Act, 11.3
Due diligence, generally, 7.116, 10.121, 11.7, 11.14
Duties of promoters, 5.172
Duty to defend, 11.322

E

Electronic provision of information, 6.129
Electronic securities, 12.226
Employee interests, consideration of, 11.83
Enron, 9.5

Equipment trust certificates, 8.208
Equitable subordination, 13.165, 13.177
Equitable subordination
    is it part of Canadian law, 13.177
    oppressive conduct &, 13.184, 13.186
    origin of, 13.181
    relating to oppression, 13.188
Equity and debt, 7.3
Equity finance, 7.1
Equity follows debt, 13.165, 13.175
Erroneous judgment, 10.22, 11.15
Evolution of incorporation in Ontario, 1.15
Excessive generosity, 11.86
Excluded rights, 6.22
Execution by same person in two capacities, 6.93
Executive compensation, 9.54
Exemptions from the securities act proxy requirements, 12.41
Exit (see also dissent remedy)
Exit, generally, 24.50
Expert opinion, reliance upon, 7.124
Extra-provincial corporations, regulation of, 4.26
Extraterritoriality
    Canadian approach to, 4.20
    generally, 10.166

F

Family business, 13.87
Federal
    companies, provincial regulation of, 4.43
    corporation, nationalization of by provincial government, 4.58
    incorporation power, limitation on, 4.39
    system of government, 4.1
Fettering discretion, 11.58, 11.136, 11.200
Fiction theory, 1.49
Fiduciary duties of directors and officers
    and the individual shareholder, 11.192
    conflict of interest, 11.127
    conflicting duties, 11.130
    corporate opportunity doctrine, 11.165
    duty to inform, 11.199
    extension to officers, 11.118
    flexibility of, 11.196
    generally, 11.115, 11.120
    going into competition with the director's former corporation, 11.151
    Keech v. Sandford rule in, 11.188
    liability to account for profit, 11.177
    maintaining an even hand, 11.203
    material contracts involving a nominating shareholder, 11.146
    misappropriation, 11.164
    nominee directors, 11.135
    non-competing businesses, 11.154
    remoteness, 11.134.1
    restraining freedom of action (fettering discretion), 11.200
    self-dealing, 11.155
    termination of, 11.205
    transaction favorable to corporation, 11.161, 11.171, 11.185.1
    use of knowledge gained during employment, 11.175
Fiduciary duty of proxy holder, 12.162
Fiduciary obligations of shareholders, generally, 12.122
Financial assistance
    conflict of interest, 11.145, 11.131
    generally, 6.25
Financial statements
    and audit committee, 10.89
    distribution of, 10.180
    verification of, 10.186
Fixed capital, 7.15
Fixed charge, 8.115, 8.135
Floating charges
    generally, 8.135
    under the *Personal Property Security Act*, 8.157
Foreclosure, 8.93
Forged document, 6.102
Forgery of a corporate document, 6.69, 6.96
Foss v. Harbottle, Rule in. *See* Derivative action
Fractional share, 7.299
Fraud
    and audit, 9.173, 9.179
    badges of, 8.330
    by a corporate agent, 6.69, 6.96
    generally, 10.116. 2.32, 7.95
Fraudulent conveyance, 8.325
Fraudulent preference, 8.332
Fully paid requirement, 7.152
Fundamental changes
    amending the articles, 14.3
    amalgamation, 14.88
    continuation, 14.38
    generally, 14.1
Future advances, priority of, 8.282
Future oriented financial information, 7.128, 7.137

G

General assignment of book debts (general assignment of accounts), 8.200
General security agreement, 8.205
Gifts
    by corporation, 11.94
    of shares, 7.283
Giving away the farm, 11.86
Going private transactions
    CBCA regime, 14.166
    disclosure requirements, 14.172
    exemptions, 14.211

Going private transactions — *cont'd*
   generally, 14.156
   independent committee, 14.190
   information in valuation, 14.184
   minority approval, 14.197
   OBCA regime, 14.156
   OSC rule, 14.167
   private company squeeze-outs, 14.219
   proposed national instrument, 62-104, 14.212
   related party, 14.216
   subject transactions, 14.168
Governance device, role of by-laws, 12.106
Government owned corporations, 4.79
Group enterprise doctrine. *See also* Corporate group concept, 5.164

H

Hollinger, 9.5fn
Honesty, 10.116. 11.1. 11.123
Honesty and oppression, 13.24
Hudson Bay Company, 1.11
Hypothecation agreement, 8.210

I

Identification theory, 3.29
Incidental benefits, 11.108
Income bonds, 8.196
Income Taxes, 11.289
Incorporated partnerships, 15.58, 15.60
Incorporation
   certificate of, 5.155
   conclusive proof of, 5.159
   direct by statute, 1.57
   effect of, 5.162
   meaning of, 5.1
   methods of, 1.9, 5.2
   procedure for, 5.33
Incorporation of professional practices, 5.15
Indemnification of directors and officers, 11.297
Indemnity, modification of implied rights by contract, 11.302
Independent committee. *See also* Derivative action and Promoters
   business judgment rule and, 13.222
   generally, 13.219
   going private transaction, 14.190
   meaning of independence, 13.222
   review of claim, 13.219
Independent decision making, 11.35
Independent directors, generally, 9.87
Independent directors and promoters, 5.180
Individuals, distinguished from corporations, 2.11
Indoor management rule
   codification of, 6.57
   generally, 6.52
   where outsiders not protected, 6.82

Information circular. *See also* Proxies
   generally, 12.145
   going private transaction, 14.172
Informed and independent decision making, 11.15. 11.26. 11.52
Informed decision, meaning of, 11.19, 11.26
Informed, reasonable and good faith decisions, distinctions among, 11.5
Injunctions
   final, 13.138
   interlocutory, 13.111
Insolvency
   dissent rights, effect upon, 14.87
   equity claims should not be treated as debt claims, 13.175
   general rules regarding claims by a shareholder, 13.165
   insolvent trading, 13.190
   legislation and winding-up, 15.199
   vicinity of, 11.74
Interest
   after default, 8.47
   and bankruptcy, 8.50
   coupons, 8.32
   effect of default and judgment on entitlement, 8.36
   generally, 8.29
   usury and, 8.40
Internal dispute, courts reluctant to take sides, 10.23
Investigation (inspection) orders
   Charter of Rights, 4.69
   Generally, 13.262
Investor immunity and limited liability, 2.21
Issuer bids (see going private transactions)
judicial supervision, problem with exercise of, 11.24
jurisdiction of the court, 13.245
jurisdiction to incorporate, 4.13, 4.62
juristic person, 1.3, 6.1

L

Land, power of corporation to hold, 6.3
Laws of special application, 4.73
Lawyers, and owners of a former corporate client, 2.15
Lease, 8.69, 8.207
Legal advice, providing re incorporation, 5.36
Legality of purpose, 5.17
Legislative grants of power, special, 6.23
Letters patent, incorporation by, 1.56
Lien on shares, 7.344
Lifting the corporate veil. *See* Piercing
Limited liability
   and director liability, 11.1
   as a creation of statute, 1.2
   as a privilege, 2.73
   evolution of, 2.18
   generally, 2.17

Limited liability — *cont'd*
    identifying existence of, 5.140
    limits of, 2.19
Line of credit, 8.55
Liquidation. *See* Winding up
    defined, 14.51
    impact upon corporate directors, 11.91
Liquidator. *See* Winding-up
Lister v. Dunlop, rule in, 8.147
Litigation and corporation, 10.35
Loan and trust corporations, abolition of provincial, 5.5, 5.15, 5.32
Loans, 8.7
Long range interests, and director decision making, 11.99
Loyalty, lesser duty of, 2.125

M

Majority rule
    oppression, 13.149
    and winding-up, 15.65
Management
    corporate responsibility of, 10.105
    impact of foreign law on corporate, 10.138
    separation of, 2.122
Managing director, 10.102
Mareva injunction, 2.40
Market manipulation, 7.148
Material change, 9.205
Material facts, disclosure of, 7.113
Maximization of corporate value, 14.143
Maximization of value, 11.70.1
MD&A
    content of, 10.176
    review by audit committee, 10.88.1
Members, shareholder as, 12.11
Merchant companies, 1.9
Minimal capitalization, 2.37, 5.154
Minutes of director meetings, 10.12
Minutes of shareholders' meetings
    deficiencies in, 12.166
    generally, 12.165
Misappropriation of corporate property, 11.164
Misrepresentation
    and directors, 11.223
    and purchase of shares, 7.90
    common law, 7.93
    disclosure of material facts, 7.113
    generally, 11.223
    liability for in the secondary market, 7.133
    liability for under the securities law, 7.112
Mistake made as to corporate status, 5.199
Mortgage
    distinguished from charges, 8.78
    generally, 8.70, 8.77
Municipal corporations, 5.8

N

Name
    alternate, 5.146
    appeal to Divisional Court, 5.124
    change of, 5.73, 5.147
    corporate, 5.68
    each must be unique, 5.84
    foreign language, 5.137
    general prohibitions and restrictions, 5.125
    general requirements and restrictions, 5.74
    geographic and descriptive, 5.110
    immoral or obscene, 5.125
    language of, 5.135
    maximum length, 5.75
    misleading, 5.78
    number as, 5.139
    objections to, 5.114
    permitted similar, 5.98
    similarity of, 5.38, 5.95
    status indicators, 5.140
    use of other than the legal name, 5.80
    use of personal names, 5.94
    use of under executive and legislative sanction, 5.108
Nationality of corporation, 6.109. *See also* Domicile
Natural person, 6.3
Nature of a corporation, 1.6, 2.1
Negligence, by corporation, liability of directors & officers, 11.220
Negotiable debt securities, 8.263
Nominating and corporate governance committees, 10.92
Nominating shareholder
    contracts with, 11.147
    responsibilities of, 11.47
Nominee directors, 11.135
Non-core document, 7.137
Non-objecting beneficial owners, 12.15
Non-profit corporations, 5.6
Notice, content, 12.75
Notice of shareholder meeting, 12.61
Nova Scotia unlimited liability companies, 2.76
NUANS search, 5.91
Numbered companies, 5.139

O

Occurrence policies, 11.312
Offering corporation, 5.12
Officer
    appointment, 10.114, 9.132
    authority, 6.69
    duty to act honestly and in good faith, 11.44
    generally, 9.129
Ontario corporation number, 5.161

Operations meaning of, 2.57
Oppression
    application of general principles of equity, 13.41
    bars to action, 13.101
    buying out of interest, 13.129
    claims by former directors and officers, 18.82
    claims with respect to affiliates, 13.84
    classic case of, 13.28
    contracting out of, 13.56
    costs, 13.137
    damages and similar compensation, 13.143
    director liability for, 11.29
    directors and, 13.128
    discontinuance and settlement, 13.145
    distinction among the grounds of relief, 13.20
    final relief, 13.116
    forms of relief, 13.104
    general principles governing relief, 13.116
    generally, 13.4
    insolvency and related concerns, 13.165
    insolvent trading, 13.190
    interim relief, 13.110
    is the cure worse than the disease?, 13.138
    limitation issues, 13.97
    majority rule, 13.26
    meaning of oppression, etc., 13.17
    minority discount, 13.138
    misconduct by party in control, 13.38
    must be more than a dispute, 13.32
    need for the remedy, 13.9
    not a remedy of last resort, 13.92
    onus of proof and the nature of proof required, 13.37, 13.98, 13.100
    premiums, 13.140
    procedural considerations, 13.93
    quasi-partnership cases, 13.50
    reasonable conduct on the part of the control group, 13.61
    reasonable expectations, 13.47
    relief against third parties, 13.147
    relief not limited to minority, 13.81
    removal of a director, 13.141
    separate counsel for corporation, 13.96
    special cases, 13.84
    specific cases, 13.30
    stakeholder rights, 11.84
    standing
        buying into an action, 13.75
        generally, 13.65
        creditors as complainants, 13.76
        difficulties of interpretation, 13.69
        discretionary claimants, 13.73
    statutory regime, 13.104
    the family business, 13.87
    timing of a claim, 13.75
    unfairness and prejudice both required, 13.37, 13.100
    unwinding of transactions, etc., 13.142
    valuation, 13.133
    when available, 13.37
    where no, 13.31
    widely held corporations, 13.85
    winding up, 15.48, 15.46
    wrongful dismissal, 13.83
Options, back-dating of, 7.246
Orders for compliance, 13.259
Organization of a corporation, 5.165, 11.257
Outside directors. *See also* Independent directors, 11.292
Ownership, separation of, 2.119

P

Paid up capital, 7.74
Papal corporations, 1.10
Paramountcy, 4.2
Part III corporations, 5.6
Participatory loans, 8.66
Passing-off, 5.85, 5.107
Performance covenants, 8.124
Perpetual debt securities, 8.279
Perpetual existence, 2.123
Person
    meaning of, 5.10, 6.30
    statutory and contractual reference to, 6.30
Personal covenant to pay, 8.89
Personal names, use of, 5.94
Personality, implications of, 2.1, 2.8
Piercing corporate veil
    contract vs. tort, 2.48
    exceptional remedy, 2.72
    fraud, 2.32
    generally, 2.26
    where provided by statute, 2.30
    where the shareholder will benefit, 21.58
Pledge, 8.72, 8.209
Poison pills
    best interests of the corporation, 11.50
    generally, 11.113, 14.151
    types, 11.51
Pope Innocent IV and corporations, 1.4
Powers of sale, 8.93
Pre-emptive rights, 7.251, 12.26
Preferential dividends, 7.319
Preferred shares, 8.318
Pre-incorporation contracts
    adoption of, 5.192
    common law and, 5.186
    excluding liability of promoter, 5.194
    generally, 5.184
    mistakes and, 5.199
    old style contracts, 5.197

Pre-incorporation contracts — *cont'd*
    power of the court to make orders, 5.198
    statutory regime, 5.188
    where rules not applicable, 5.205
Presiding officer at shareholder meetings, 12.83
Price
    generally, 7.150
    payment by cheque, 7.165
    payment by issue of a promissory note, 7.173
    payment by transfer of property, 7.155, 7.166
    payment in services, 7.175
    payment of, 7.161
Professional corporation, 5.18
Professional liability and incorporated practice, 5.25
Professional, meaning of, 10.128
Profits, payment of dividends, 7.299, 7.310
Project financing, 8.317.1
Promoters
    and directors distinguished, 9.26
    duties of, 5.173
    generally, 5.168
    identification of, 5.170
    liability of among themselves, 5.182
    protecting, 5.181
Promotion expenses, 5.183
Proof of claim, 8.302
Proper purpose rule, 11.103
Property, payment for shares in, 7.155, 7.166
Proposal, shareholder
    generally, 12.191
    under the CBCA, 12.198
Provincially incorporated corporations, federal regulation of, 4.42
Proxies and shareholder proposal, 12.193
    fiduciary under the OBCA and the CBCA, 12.136
Proxy
    obligations of holder, 12.162
    fights, 12.160
    solicitation,
        and CSA, 12.145
        generally, 12.122
        under the Securities Act, 12.141
Public Accounting Oversight Board, 10.143
Public and quasi-public corporations, 4.75
Public policy
    by-law contrary to, 5.63
    legality of purpose, 5.17
Public vs. private company, 5.10
Purchase by a corporation of its shares, 7.267

Q

Quasi-criminal liability of corporations, 3.17
Quorum
    generally, 10.6
    of shareholder meeting, 12.47

R

Real property charges and mortgages, 8.77
Realist theory, 1.48
Reasonable expectation
    determination of, 13.47
    generally, 13.43, 13.51, 13.58, 13.85
Receivers and receiver-managers, 8.250
Record date
    for shareholders' meetings, 12.64
    for dividends, 7.330
Records
    and Canada Revenue Agency, 6.123
    of a corporation, 6.118
Redemption of shares, 7.263
Redemption or retraction rights, nature of obligation arising, 8.11
Reduction in share capital
    generally, 7.275
    liability for, 7.278
Registered debt securities, 8.262
Registered office of a corporation, 6.115
Regulatory control, 2.10
Regulatory jurisdiction, 4.41
Related persons, 3.61
Reliance, reasonable, 10.135
Remuneration
    and cakes and ale case law, 11.94
    director, 10.67
Reorganization, 14.273
Repayment of share capital, entitlement to, 7.284
Reporting issuers, special rights of attendance in the case of, 12.81
Repudiation for want of authority, 6.41
Repurchase of shares, 7.269
Residence of corporation, 6.110
Resolutions
    as an alternative to meetings, 12.178
    discretionary authority conferred by, 12.182
    generally, 12.178
    shareholders, 12.178
Restrictions on incorporation, 5.15
Retraction, 7.263
Revolving credit, 8.57
Revolving debt, securing, 8.284
RICO Act, 3.53
Risk and business, 11.13
Role of incorporators, 5.38
Royal charter companies, 1.11, 1.16, 1.22, 1.55
Rule in *Turquand's Case*, 6.53

S

Safeguards, directors' duty to create, 11.38
Sale, lease or exchange of corporate property, 14.41

Salomon case, 2.4
Sarbanes-Oxley Act of 2002
    and audit committees, 10.157
    conflict of interest, 10.154
    generally, 9.36, 10.138
    integrity of financial records, 10.153
    integrity of financial statements, 10.146
    integrity of internal controls, 10.148
    integrity of the audit process, 10.152
    integrity of the disclosure process, 10.151
    oversight of accounting practice, 10.143
    overview of, 10.139
    reporting obligations, 10.138
    special remedies, 10.159
Seal of a corporation, 5.150, 6.94
Secret profit
    generally, 11.178
    promoter and, 5.177
Secured debt, 8.18
Securities convertible to shares, 7.238
Securities disclosure obligations
    annual information form, 9.120
    financial information, 9.192
    generally, 7.141, 9.191
    information circular, 9.204
    management discussion and analysis, 9.199
    timely disclosure, 9.205
Securities law, issue of shares contrary to, 7.55
Securities, regulation of, 4.51
Securities Transfer Act, 7.287, 12.226
Securitization, 8.61
Security agreement
    generally, 8.76
    right to remain in possession, 8.91
Security interest, 8.67
Self-dealing, 11.155
Sentencing of a corporation, 3.51
Separate personality, 1.1, 1.32, 2.1, 2.8, 5.163
Separate taxation, 3.15
Series of securities, 7.63
Sham, corporation as, 2.35
Share certificates, 7.286
Shares. *See also* Equity and shareholders rights
    abolition of par value, 7.68
    as fungible property, 7.288
    classes and series of, 7.60
    classification of, 7.26
    common and preference defined, 7.30
    conditional subscriptions for, 7.86
    creation and issue of, 7.53
    creation of preferences, 7.40
    execution against, 7.23
    generally, 7.16
    held
        by a minor, 7.196
        by aliens, 7.194
        by an intermediary (CBCA). *See also Securities Transfer Act*, 7.193
        in trust, 7.192
        in an unlimited liability corporation, 7.183
    interpretation of terms, 7.47
    issue and proper purpose rule, 11.50, 11.109
    location (situs) of, 7.25
    meaning of, 7.5, 7.17
    misrepresentation and subscriptions, 7.90
    non-assessable, 7.236
    offer and acceptance, 7.79
    popular designations within securities industry, 7.35
    presumption against restriction, 7.221
    presumption of equality, 7.40
    repurchase of, 7.269
    restrictions on issue of, 7.199
    restrictions transfer of shares, 7.199, 7.213, 7.227, 7.293
    self-holding, 7.257
    splits and exchanges, 7.187
    subscription, 7.76
    terms of in articles, 5.46
    trafficking in, 7.255
Shareholder
    and corporate management, 12.30
    basic rights of, 12.2
    by estoppel, 12.19
    defined, 12.1
    disputes, and directors, 11.108
    generally, 13.1
    inspection of lists, 12.24
    limited liability, 12.28
    litigation, 13.2
    no interest in assets of corporation, 2.12
    pre-emptive rights, 12.26
    status of, 12.10
    trustee as, 12.13
Shareholders
    claims against corporation, 13.165
    directors owe no fiduciary duty to, 11.192
    election of directors, 9.92
    fiduciary duty of, 12.122
    frustration of control by directors, 11.112
    new, right to receive notice, 12.68
    on becoming, 12.4
    ratification and conflict of interest, 10.76
    rights to information, 12.33.1
Shareholders' meeting
    adjournments, 12.91
    application to court to restrain or set aside, 12.174
    business of, 12.59
    during winding-up, 15.91
    form of notice, 12.62
    generally, 12.34

Shareholders' meeting — *cont'd*
  improperly called, 12.58
  interference by court, 12.35, 12.43
  manner of calling, 12.57
  minutes of, 12.165
  notice
    content of, 12.71, 12.61
    sufficiency (duration), 12.71
  place of, 12.53
  presiding officer at, 12.83
  quorum for, 12.47
  record date, 12.64
  requisition of, 12.42
  right to inspect, 12.172
  role of, 12.38
  voting and the right to vote at, 12.92
  when required, 12.30
Sinking funds, 7.249
Size of corporations, 1.23
Sole shareholder corporation, 11.229
South Sea Bubble, 1.55fn, 11.12
Sovereign act
  creation of corporation, 1.47, 1.52
  dissolution, 15.12
Special resolution
  amalgamation, 14.06
  amendment of articles, 14.23
  spoiled ballot, 14.25
Speculative ventures, 11.81
Squeeze-outs. *See* Going private transactions
Stakeholder theory, 11.70
Stakeholders, conflicting interests of, 11.44, 11.77
Stated capital account, 7.231
Statute
  direct incorporation by, 1.57, 6.7
  statutory corporation, 5.3
Statute of Monopolies, 1.12, 1.23
Statutory interpretation and corporate law statues, 11.25
Statutory mandate, corporations charged with a, 4.75
Stock dividends, 7.335
Stock exchanges, Canadian, 7.17fn
Stock options, 11.110
Subordinated debt, 8.114
Subordination
  agreements, 8.285
  conditional, 7.86
  for shares, 7.65
  misrepresentation and, 7.90
Subsidiaries, 12.23
Substratum, 15.56
Supervisory board, 11.39.1

T

Take-over bid
  coattail, 7.66
  share issue, 7.57, 7.66
  response of directors, 11.52
  generally, 14.140
  defense strategy, 11.66, 14.151. *See also* Poison pills
Taxi cab cases, 2.51
Term loan, 8.53
Territorial limits of corporate law, 4.18
Three-two corporations, 5.32
Timely disclosure, 7.132
Tort, liability of corporation as principal, 3.10
Tort, liability of directors, officers and others for corporate torts, 3.55
Trade credit, 11.264
Trade custom, 6.50.1
Trade secrets, 11.175
Trade-marks, 5.107
Trafficking in shares, 7.255
Transfer of shares
  director approval of, 12.8
  generally, 7.204
Transmission of interest, 7.227, 12.5
Trust and debt, 8.17, 8.60, 8.73, 8.112
Trust, as security, 8.73
Trust deeds
  conflict of interest, 8.177
  day-to-day administration, 8.167
  fees and expenses of the trustee, 8.191
  generally, 8.163
  interpretation, 8.166
  no action clauses, 8.185
  purpose of, 8.170
  standard of care, 8.176
Trustee
  as shareholder, 12.13
  distinguished from directors, 11.160
TSX, 7.17fn
Turquand's Case Rule in, 6.77

U

Ultra vires
  abolition of, 6.16
  directors authority, 11.246
  doctrine of, 6.10
Unanimous shareholder agreement
  amendment and termination, 12.221
  collateral matters, 12.212
  core (managerial) terms, 12.210
  creation by court, 13.120
  evidence of approva, 12.213
  formation, 12.213
  generally, 12.201
  interpretation, 12.208
  non-shareholder parties, 12.214
  OBCA proposed reforms, 12.224
  Status, 12.207
  subject matter, 12.209
  successor rights and obligations, 12.215
Unclaimed dividends, 7.343
Unfair dealing, 11.6

Unfair disregard. *See* Oppression
Unfair prejudice. *See* Oppression
Unlawful interference with economic relations, 11.238
Unlimited liability companies
    continuation and fundamental changes, 2.112
    director liability, 2.109
    general liability regime, 2.99
    generally, 2.76
    issue of shares for a debt instrument, 2.110
    limitation on the term of shareholder liability, 2.104
    possible Ontario regime, 2.93
    repayment of capital, 2.110
    unlimited status, identification of, 2.94
Unreasonable by-law, 5.63
Unsecured debt, 8.18, 8.21

V

Valuation
    dissent proceedings, 14.63
    going private transaction, 14.187
    methods of, 14.67
    of amalgamating corporations, 14.100
Verification of reports, 10.119
Vicarious liability, 3.4
Vice presidents (growing number of), 6.80fn
Vital part doctrine, 4.50
Voice. *See also* Voting, Unanimous shareholder agreement, Constraining director power
Voice, generally, 14.50
Voting. *See also* Proxies
    and agreement on reasons, 10.5
    by attorney, 12.132
    by ballot, 12.112
    by class, 14.14
    by shareholder, 12.92
    cumulative, 9.99
    for the benefit of the class, 12.129
    general considerations, 12.92, 12.100
    procedure, 12.107
    vote renting, 10.75
    voting trusts and similar arrangements, 12.102
    withholding, 12.163
Vulture funds, 8.313

W

Wage earner protection program, 11.283
Wages
    arguments in favor of wage earner protection, 11.264
    Bankruptcy & Insolvency Act, 11.279
    Bill C-55, 11.281
    counter arguments to wage protection, 11.265
    Employment Standards Act, 11.275
    liability for, 11.261
Waiver, 8.127
Warranties, 8.103
warrants and options, 7.242
Wash trading, 7.142
Wastage of corporate assets, 11.101
Westray, 9.5fn
Widely held corporation, 6.8
Winding up
    "incorporated partnerships" 15.58, 15.66
    absence of a liquidator, 15.111
    account of voluntary, 15.35
    administration of the corporate estate, 15.03
    appointment of liquidator, 15.80
    arrangements, 15.31
    CBCA
        dissolution of a corporation, 15.197
        generally, 15.178
        involuntary, 15.195
        liquidator, 15.187
        revival procedure, 15.197
        voluntary liquidation, 15.180
    commencement of voluntary, 15.24
    conflicts of law issues, 15.76
    contributories, 15.139
    costs of liquidator, 15.112
    court ordered, 15.39
    deadlock cases, 15.60
    defined, 15.1
    duties and powers of liquidator, 15.113
    duty to report and approving a liquidator's accounts, 15.84
    effect of on directors, 15.109
    effect of voluntary, 15.25
    effect of wind-up order, 15.92
    frustration of the corporate purpose, 15.41
    generally, 15.1
    internal affairs doctrine, 15.12
    involuntary under court order, 15.42
    just and equitable, 15.57
    loss of confidence, 15.64
    majority rule, 15.65
    no integrated Canadian law, 15.2
    OBCA procedure, 15.70
    oppressive or prejudicial conduct, 15.46
    participation in distributions, 15.96, 15.134
    principles, 15.3
    process of liquidation and dissolution, 15.14
    provisions of general application, 15.103
    repayment of debt of corporation, 15.30
    replacement liquidator, 15.84
    responsibilities of liquidator, 15.80
    rights of shareholders, 15.134
    sale of assets for shares, 15.33

Winding up — *cont'd*
   satisfaction of the corporate purpose, 15.48
   shareholder meetings, 15.91
   suing a liquidator, 15.99
   voluntary
      under court order, 15.41
      under OBCA, 15.15
   winding-up, discharge of the liquidator, 15.132

Working capital, 7.14